WRITING ABOUT LITERATURE

This five-chapter guide to writing about literature offers guidance about each stage of the writing process, including information about the latest (2009) MLA guidelines for quotation and citation.

P9-DFH-429

CRITICAL APPROACHES

This short guide to important critical approaches briefly explains the tools that professional critics and theorists employ when they write about literature.

The Norton
Introduction to Literature

TENTH EDITION

THE NORTON INTRODUCTION TO *Literature*

TENTH EDITION

ALISON BOOTH
University of Virginia

KELLY J. MAYS
University of Nevada, Las Vegas

W. W. NORTON & COMPANY
New York, London

W. W. Norton & Company has been independent since its founding in 1923, when William Warder and Mary D. Herter Norton first published lectures delivered at the People's Institute, the adult education division of New York City's Cooper Union. The firm soon expanded its program beyond the Institute, publishing books by celebrated academics from America and abroad. By mid-century, the two major pillars of Norton's publishing program–trade books and college texts–were firmly established. In the 1950s, the Norton family transferred control of the company to its employees, and today–with a staff of four hundred and a comparable number of trade, college, and professional titles published each year–W.W. Norton & Company stands as the largest and oldest publishing house owned wholly by its employees.

Editor: Peter Simon
Managing editor, College: Marian Johnson
Developmental editor: Beth Ammerman
Manuscript editor: Mike Fleming
Project editor: Melissa Atkin
Editorial assistant: Conor Sullivan
Production manager: Christine D'Antonio
Photo research: Stephanie Romeo
Permissions clearance: Margaret Gorenstein and Nancy Rodwin
Interior design: Charlotte Staub
Interior art direction: Hope Miller Goodell

Composition: Westchester Book Group
Manufacturing: R. R. Donnelley & Sons

Library of Congress Cataloging-in-Publication Data

The Norton introduction to literature / [edited by] Alison Booth,
Kelly J. Mays.—10th ed.
    p. cm.
  Includes bibliographical references and index.
  ISBN 978-0-393-93426-7 (hardcover)
  1. Literature–Collections.   I. Booth, Alison.   II. Mays, Kelly J.
  PN6014.N67 2010
  808—dc22

                                    2009050457

W.W. Norton & Company, Inc., 500 Fifth Avenue, New York, NY 10110
www.wwnorton.com

W.W. Norton & Company Ltd., Castle House, 75/76 Wells Street, London
W1T 3QT

2 3 4 5 6 7 8 9 0

Brief Contents

Drama

Contents

Fiction

Fiction: Reading, Responding, Writing 12

Understanding the Text 79

Exploring Contexts 490

10 CULTURAL AND HISTORICAL CONTEXTS: WOMEN IN
    TURN-OF-THE-CENTURY AMERICA 602
    KATE CHOPIN, *The Story of an Hour* 607
    CHARLOTTE PERKINS GILMAN, *The Yellow Wallpaper* 608
    SUSAN GLASPELL, *A Jury of Her Peers* 619
    Chronology 633
    CHARLOTTE PERKINS GILMAN, From *Similar Cases* 635
       From *Women and Economics* 636
    BARBARA BOYD, From *Heart and Home Talks: Politics and Milk* 636
    MRS. ARTHUR LYTTELTON, From *Women and Their Work* 637
    RHETA CHILDE DORR, From *What Eight Million Women Want* 638
    THE NEW YORK TIMES, From *Mrs. Delong Acquitted* 638
    THE WASHINGTON POST, From *The Chances of Divorce* 639
    CHARLOTTE PERKINS GILMAN, From *Why I Wrote "The Yellow
       Wallpaper"* 639
    THE WASHINGTON POST, *The Rest Cure* 640
       From *Egotism of the Rest Cure* 640

11 CULTURAL AND HISTORICAL CONTEXTS: THE JAZZ AGE 643
    F. SCOTT FITZGERALD, *Babylon Revisited* 651
       Echoes of the Jazz Age 665
    MALCOLM COWLEY, From *Exile's Return: A Literary Odyssey
       of the 1920s* 667
    ERNEST R. GROVES, From *Social Problems of the Family* 673
    V. F. CALVERTON, From *The Bankruptcy of Marriage* 675

12 CRITICAL CONTEXTS: WILLIAM FAULKNER'S "A ROSE FOR EMILY" 679
    WILLIAM FAULKNER, *A Rose for Emily* 681
    CLEANTH BROOKS JR. AND ROBERT PENN WARREN,
       From *Understanding Fiction* 688
    C. W. M. JOHNSON, *Faulkner's "A Rose for Emily"* 691
    RAY B. WEST JR., *Faulkner's "A Rose for Emily"* 691
    WILLIAM VAN O'CONNOR, From *The State of Faulkner Criticism* 692
    FLOYD C. WATKINS, *The Structure of "A Rose for Emily"* 693
    T. J. STAFFORD, From *Tobe's Significance in "A Rose for Emily"* 694
    JUDITH FETTERLEY, From *A Rose for "A Rose for Emily"* 696
    THOMAS KLEIN, *The Ghostly Voice of Gossip in Faulkner's
       "A Rose for Emily"* 701
    LAWRENCE R. RODGERS, From *"We all said, 'She will kill herself' ": The
       Narrator / Detective in Faulkner's "A Rose for Emily"* 703
    SAMPLE WRITING: ANN WARREN, *The Tragic Plot of
       "A Rose for Emily"* 711

Poetry

Understanding the Text 854

Reading More Poetry   1317

Biographical Sketches: Poets

Drama

Drama: Reading, Responding, Writing

Understanding the Text

Exploring Contexts 1641

Reading More Drama 2092

Biographical Sketches: Playwrights 2265

Writing about Literature 2271

Critical Approaches 2334

Preface for Instructors

Like its predecessors, this Tenth Edition of *The Norton Introduction to Literature* offers in a single volume a complete course in reading literature and writing about it. A teaching anthology focused on the actual tasks, challenges, and questions typically faced by college students and instructors, *The Norton Introduction to Literature* offers practical advice to help students transform their first impressions of literary works into fruitful discussions and meaningful critical essays, and it helps students and instructors together tackle the complex questions at the heart of literary study.

We have revised *The Norton Introduction to Literature* with an eye to providing a book that is as flexible and useful as possible—adaptable to many different teaching styles and individual preferences—and that also conveys the excitement at the heart of literature itself.

FEATURES OF *THE NORTON INTRODUCTION TO LITERATURE*

Although this Tenth Edition contains much that is new or refashioned, the essential features of the text have remained consistent over many editions:

Diverse selections with broad appeal

Because readings are the central component of any literature class, our most important task has been to select a rich array of appealing and challenging literary works. Among the 69 stories, 352 poems, and 18 plays in *The Norton Introduction to Literature*, readers will find selections by well-established and emerging voices alike, representing a broad range of times, places, cultural perspectives, and styles. The readings are excitingly diverse in terms of subject and style as well as authorship and national origin. In selecting and presenting literary texts, our top priorities continue to be quality as well as pedagogical relevance and usefulness. We have integrated the new with the old and the experimental with the canonical, in the conviction that contrast and variety help students recognize and respond to the unique features of any literary work. In this way, we aim to help students and teachers alike approach the unfamiliar by way of the familiar (and vice versa).

Helpful and unobtrusive editorial matter

As always, the instructional material before and after each selection avoids dictating any particular interpretation or response, instead highlighting essential terms and concepts in order to make the literature that follows more accessible to student readers. Questions and writing suggestions help readers apply general concepts to specific readings in order to develop, articulate, refine, and defend their own responses. As in all Norton anthologies, we have annotated the works with a light hand, seeking to be informative but not interpretive.

An introduction to the study of literature

To introduce students to fiction, poetry, and drama is to open up a complex field of study with a long history. The revised Introduction addresses many of the questions that students may have about the nature of literature as well as the practice of literary criticism. By exploring some of the most compelling reasons for reading and studying literature, we clear away much of the mystery about matters of method and approach, and we provide motivated students with a sense of the issues and opportunities that lie ahead as they continue their study of literature. As in earlier editions, we encourage student fascination with particular authors and their careers, introducing featured "Authors on Their Work" along with new single-author chapters.

Helpful guidance for writing about literature

The Tenth Edition integrates opportunities for student writing at each step of the introduction to literature course, highlighting the mastery of skills for students at every level. Freshly reconceived "Reading, Responding, Writing" chapters at the beginning of every genre section offer students concrete advice about how to transform careful reading into productive and insightful writing. We present sample questions to ask of each work or about each element (e.g., "Questions about Character"), provide exercises for answering these questions or for applying new concepts to particular works, and demonstrate how a student's notes on a story or poem may be developed into a response paper or an organized critical argument. New essays bring the total number of examples of student writing to fifteen.

The constructive, step-by-step approach to the writing process is thoroughly demonstrated as well in a special section, "Writing about Literature," which was completely rewritten in the Ninth Edition. As in the chapters introducing concepts and literary selections, the first steps presented in the writing section are simple and straightforward, outlining an essay's basic formal elements—thesis, structure, and so on. Following these steps encourages students to approach the essay both as a distinctive genre with its own elements and as an accessible form of writing with a clear purpose. From here, we walk students through the writing process: how to choose a topic, gather evidence, and develop an argument; the methods of writing a research essay; and the mechanics of effective quotation and responsible citation and documentation. We also include a sample research paper—annotated by the editors to call attention to important features of good student writing. The "Critical Approaches" section provides an overview of contemporary critical theory and its terminology and is useful as an introduction, a refresher, or a preparation for further exploration.

A comprehensive approach to the contexts of literature

The Tenth Edition not only offers expanded resources for interpreting and writing about literature but also extends the perspectives from which students can view particular authors and works. One of the great strengths of *The Norton Introduction to Literature* has been its exploration of the relation between literary texts and a variety of contexts. For several editions, "Author's Work" and "Critical Contexts" chapters have served as mini-casebooks containing a wealth of material for in-depth context-focused reading and writing assignments. In recent editions, we have added "Cultural Contexts" chapters that explore a cultural moment or setting.

In the Tenth Edition, we have added four new context chapters to the mix. In fiction, for example, we now feature two chapters focused on a single author: one on Flannery O'Connor and one on James Joyce's short-story collection *Dubliners*. Both of these chapters are called "The Author's Work," but as the preceding description suggests, the meaning of "work" in each case is different. The chapter on O'Connor takes a wide view of the author's oeuvre and life, so "work" in this case implies "life work." The chapter on *Dubliners* takes a new tack for *The Norton Introduction to Literature*, focusing students' attention on a single book-length "work" by an author. This approach also inspires a chapter in the Poetry section featuring William Blake's *Songs of Innocence and of Experience*, including with color plates of his artwork. While space doesn't allow us to include the entire works by Joyce or Blake, we do hope that students will be inspired by these chapters to seek out and read the full-length works.

Other new "contexts" chapters include a chapter on women's lives in the late nineteenth and early twentieth centuries that features Kate Chopin's "The Story of an Hour," Charlotte Perkins Gilman's "The Yellow Wallpaper," and Susan Glaspell's "A Jury of Her Peers." There is also a new chapter on drama, "Performance as Context," that draws students into the exciting interpretive space between "page" and "stage," introducing the practical side of interpreting drama.

A sensible and teachable organization

We have preserved the accessible format of *The Norton Introduction to Literature*, which has worked well for teachers and students for many editions. Each genre is approached in three logical steps. Fiction, for example, is introduced by "Fiction: Reading, Responding, Writing," which treats the purpose and nature of fiction, the reading experience, and the steps one takes to begin writing about fiction. This is followed by the seven-chapter section called "Understanding the Text," which concentrates on the genre's key elements. The third section, "Exploring Contexts," suggests ways to embrace a work of literature by considering various literary, temporal, and cultural contexts. "Reading More Fiction," the final component in the Fiction section, is a reservoir of additional readings for independent study or a different approach. The Poetry and Drama sections, in turn, follow exactly the same organizational format as Fiction.

The book's arrangement allows movement from narrower to broader frameworks, from simpler to more complex questions and issues, mirroring the way people read—wanting to learn more as they experience more. At the same time, no chapter or section depends on any other, so that individual teachers can pick and choose which chapters or sections to assign and in what order.

NEW TO THE TENTH EDITION

Fifty-three new selections

There are 18 new stories, 33 new poems, and 2 new plays in this edition of *The Norton Introduction to Literature*. You will find new selections from canonical writers such as John Updike, Charlotte Brontë, Italo Calvino, Nathaniel Hawthorne,

Franz Kafka, Flannery O'Connor, James Joyce, Paul Celan, Samuel Taylor Coleridge, T. S. Eliot, William Blake, William Carlos Williams, Robert Frost, Samuel Beckett, and Alfred, Lord Tennyson, as well as from contemporary voices such as Marjane Satrapi, Lara Vapnyar, Alice Randall, Hanif Kureishi, Claudia Emerson, Charles Feldstein, Tony Hoagland, Victoria Redel, Bob Hicok, Afaa Michael Weaver, Joshua Clover, Barbara Hamby, Lynn Powell, Harryette Mullen, Catherine Bowman, Pat Mora, Eavan Boland, Ani di Franco, and Suzan-Lori Parks, among others.

New thematic "albums"

Recognizing that many courses build their reading lists around resonant topics or themes, we have added to this Tenth Edition several topic-oriented clusters of stories or poems. These "albums"—for example, "Encounters across Cultures," "Family," "Romantic Love," among several others—provide students and instructors with ample opportunity to approach their reading (and the course) through a comparison of varied treatments of a common topic, setting, or subgenre.

Deeper representation of select authors

The Norton Introduction to Literature offers a range of opportunities for in-depth study of noted authors. The two new "Author's Work" chapters—one on James Joyce's Dubliners and the other on William Blake's Songs of Innocence and of Experience—join the chapters on Flannery O'Connor and Adrienne Rich in the "Exploring Contexts" sections. In addition, three new "albums" of multiple works by Emily Dickinson, W. B. Yeats, and Pat Mora allow students to explore on their own a larger sampling of each poet's work. Some other chapters, such as the "Cultural and Historical Contexts" chapter that focuses on F. Scott Fitzgerald's "Babylon Revisited" or the "Critical Contexts" chapters in each genre section, which center on William Faulkner's "A Rose for Emily," Sylvia Plath's "Daddy," and Sophocles' "Antigone," encourage students to delve deeper into each author's work after they have sampled the rich and varied tradition of commentary that each author has inspired.

New chapter: "The Longer Work"

A new chapter, "The Longer Work," has been added to the Fiction and Poetry sections of the Tenth Edition. "The Longer Work" chapters encourage students to immerse themselves in longer-form examples of each genre and to bring the skills they've gained in earlier chapters to bear on these meatier works. The new long works—Franz Kafka's novella The Metamorphosis, an action-packed excerpt from Seamus Heaney's translation of Beowulf, T. S. Eliot's "The Love Song of J. Alfred Prufrock," and Samuel Taylor Coleridge's "The Rime of the Ancient Mariner"—join others, such as Herman Melville's "Bartleby, the Scrivener," that are picked up from earlier editions.

Significantly improved writing pedagogy

In the Ninth Edition, The Norton Introduction to Literature featured a completely reconceived and rewritten "Writing about Literature" section. We are pleased that this revision has proved to be popular with instructors and students. With this Tenth Edition, we have turned our attention to the "Reading, Responding, Writing" chapters that open each genre section, revising these chapters to reflect and complement the changes made to "Writing about Literature" in the Ninth Edition. Now more concrete than ever, these chapters focus squarely on the tasks involved in transforming close reading into effective critical writing, from time-tested approaches to literary analysis to close reading and note-taking. In addition, twelve new samples of student writing for different kinds of assignments have been added to the book, bringing the total number of such samples to fifteen. More generally, throughout the Tenth Edition we have thoroughly revised the writing prompts and suggestions.

STUDENT RESOURCES

LitWeb (wwnorton.com/litweb)

This free online companion to *The Norton Introduction to Literature* builds on the reading and writing pedagogy in the text. In addition to quizzes and other review materials, the site offers many tools that help students read and write about literature with skill and understanding. LitWeb's features include:

- In-depth workshops, featuring 50 works from the text, that now complement the "Reading, Responding, Writing" chapters and include two helpful new sections: a "Before You Read" section that prepares the student for the "Reading" and "Re-reading" process, and a "Writing" section that concludes each workshop with practical exercises and writing prompts to reinforce the text's "Writing about Literature" pedagogy.
- Self-grading multiple-choice quizzes on more than 50 of the most widely taught works offer instant feedback that is designed to hone students' close-reading skills.
- The substantial "Writing about Literature" section from *The Norton Introduction to Literature* is included online in its entirety.
- Tutorials on writing research papers and avoiding plagiarism.
- 2009 MLA documentation guidelines.
- Self-grading multiple-choice quizzes on the elements of literature.
- Access to Norton Poets Online (*nortonpoets.com*), which features interviews with more than 60 contemporary poets, dozens of audio recordings of poets reading their work, essays, online poetry workshops, and an e-mail newsletter.

INSTRUCTOR'S RESOURCES

Instructor's Manual

This thorough guide offers in-depth discussions of nearly all the works in the anthology as well as teaching suggestions and tips for the writing-intensive literature course.

Instructor's Resource Disc and Audio CDs

These easy-to-use media resources will enliven lectures and make class preparation easier. The Instructor's Resource Disc includes a selection of images from the text, PowerPoint slides for shaping lectures, and short multimedia slide shows on select themes and contexts, as well as PDF files of the instructor's manual. A two-CD instructor's audio companion includes select poems and stories read by their authors or other readers. All three discs are included in one handy Instructor's Resources folder.

Teaching Poetry: A Handbook of Exercises for Large and Small Classes (Allan J. Gedalof, University of Western Ontario)

This practical handbook offers a wide variety of innovative in-class exercises to enliven classroom discussion of poetry. Each of these flexible teaching exercises includes straightforward, step-by-step guidelines and suggestions for variation.

Blackboard / WebCT coursepack

This free and customizable resource includes lecture PowerPoints; multiple-choice quizzes on the elements of fiction, poetry, and drama; multiple-choice quizzes on selected widely taught individual works of fiction and drama included in the anthology; short-answer questions on selected widely taught poems (with suggested answers in the instructor view); multiple-choice quizzes on the "Writing about Literature" chapters; tutorials on research writing and on avoiding plagiarism; and select short-answer questions from the Instructor's Manual.

Play DVDs

DVDs of most of the plays in the anthology are available to qualified adopters.

To obtain any of these instructional resources, please contact your local Norton representative.

* * *

ACKNOWLEDGMENTS

In all our work on this edition, we have been guided by teachers in other English departments and in our own, by students who have used the textbook and written to us with comments and suggestions, and by students in our own classes. We hope that with such capable help we have been able to offer you a solid and stimulating introduction to the experience of literature.

Our collaboration on this book continually reminds us of why we follow the vocation of teaching literature, which after all is a communal rather than a solitary calling. Our own teachers and students as well as our colleagues have shown us how to join private responses to literature with shared learning and interpretation, both in discussion and in writing.

That spirit of collaboration, high standards, and engagement with varieties of literary experience was instilled in *The Norton Introduction to Literature* by its first editors, and we are grateful to carry on the work begun by the late Carl Bain and

Jerome Beaty. Paul Hunter and Jerry Beaty welcomed us as part of the editorial team and shaped its success, and Paul has continued to be an inspiring collaborator and colleague. We thank him for his continuing presence, not least in the countless effects of his own editing in the present edition and beyond. Among colleagues and teaching assistants who have enhanced the experience of teaching introduction to literature courses, we would like especially to thank Ellen Malenas Ledoux, Jill Rappoport, Chloe Wigston Smith, and Herbert Tucker. The assistance of Jessica Swope, Nick Lolordo, and Anne Stevens made all the difference at key stages in the preparation of this edition.

The Norton Introduction to Literature continues to thrive because teachers and students who use it take the time to provide us with valuable feedback and suggestions for improvement. We thank everyone who does so. This book is as much your making as ours.

For this Tenth Edition, our debt to our critics and friends is immense, and the list of those who offered their advice and critique is especially long. At the beginning of the planning for the Tenth Edition, our friends at Norton solicited the guidance of hundreds of instructors via a Web-hosted survey. The response was impressive, bordering on overwhelming. We thank everyone who either responded to that survey or provided more in-depth written commentary: Margaret Abbott (Fort Peck Community College), Laila Abdalla (Central Washington University), Charles Adams (Whittier College), Mary Adams (Lincoln College Normal), Tanya Agathocleous (Yale University), Marla Ahlgren (Fond du Lac Tribal and Community College), Lynn Alexander (University of Tennessee–Martin), Nancy Allen (Villanova University), Fred Allen (George Fox University), Jennifer Andermatt (Palo Alto College), Eric Anderson (George Mason University), Corey Andrews (Youngstown State University), Kit Andrews (Western Oregon University), Lisa Angelella (University of Iowa), Gwen Argersinger (Mesa Community College at Red Mountain), Karla Armbruster (Webster University), Rebecca Aronson (Northwest Missouri State University), Karen Auvinen (Front Range Community College), Carolyn Ayers (Saint Mary's University of Minnesota), Diana I. Badur (Black Hawk College), Anne Balay (Indiana University Northwest), Dan Baldwin (Scott Community College), Trish Barnes (Skagit Valley College), Helen Bauer (Iona College), Mary Baumhover (Western New Mexico University), Ronald Bayes (St. Andrews College), Randall Beebe (Eastern Illinois University), Roger Berger (Everett Community College), Paul Bergstraesser (University of Wyoming), Chris Beyers (Assumption College), Michael Bibby (Shippensburg University), Linda Bingham (Hawkeye Community College), Clyda Rae Blackburn (Salt Lake Community College), Mark Blackwell (University of Hartford), David Blake (The College of New Jersey), Jill Blaser-Beard (Tennessee Temple University), LaToya Bogard (Mississippi State University), Daniel Boscaljon (University of Iowa), Michele Boyette (University of North Florida), Michael Bozzone (Sacred Heart University), Adam Bradford (University of Iowa), Burton Bradley (Northwest College), Ellen Brand (Broome Community College), Paul Brandt (Kent State University), Mark Bresnan (University of Iowa), Elizabeth Bridgham (Providence College), Nancy Brown (Lourdes College), William Brugger (Brigham Young University–Idaho), Mark Bruhn (Regis University), Neal Bruss (University of Massachusetts–Boston), Laurie Buchanan (Clark State Community College), Martin Buinicki (Valparaiso University), Greg Burgett (Santa Fe Trail High School), Michael Burns (Spokane Community College), Sandra Burr (Northern Michigan University), Jessica Butto

(University of Pittsburgh), Gardner Campbell (University of Mary Washington), Mary Baine Campbell (Brandeis University), Kathleen Carl (John A. Logan College), Wendy Carse Indiana University of Pennsylvania), John Casey (University of Illinois–Chicago), Sean Cavanaugh (Assumption College), Jo Cavins (North Dakota State University), Marlys Cervantes (Cowley College), Rebecca Chalmers (University of Mary), Diane Chambers (Malone College), Javier Chapa (San Jose City College), Darren Chiang-Schultheiss (Fullerton College), Jo Anne Church (University of Great Falls), Michael Clark (Portland State University), Joe Colicchio (Hudson County Community College), Susan Comfort (Indiana University of Pennsylvania), Jim Compton (Muscatine Community College), Cheryl Conover (Carroll College), Beth Cooley (Gonzaga University), Brian Cooney (Gonzaga University), William Corby (Berkshire Community College), Michael Cornelius (Wilson College), Gail Corso (Neumann College), Carol Costello (North Shore Community College), Margaret Cotter-Lynch (Southeastern Oklahoma State University), Laura Cruse (Northwest Iowa Community College), Denise Curry (University of Saint Francis), Carol Bunch Davis (Texas A&M University at Galveston), Glenn Davis (St. Cloud State University), James Davis (University of Northern Iowa), Matthew Davis (University of Wisconsin–Stevens Point), Joanna Davis-McElligatt (University of Iowa), Greg Delanty (St. Michael's College), Tony Demarest (Felician College), Eric d'Evegnee (Brigham Young University–Idaho), Elizabeth DeVore (Nicolet College), Emily Dial-Drier (Rogers State University), Christie Diep (Cypress College), Gerri Dobbins (Gaston College), James Donahue (State University of New York–Potsdam), Kathleen Dorantes (Imperial Valley College), David Dougherty (Loyola College in Maryland), Douglas Dowland (University of Iowa), George Drake (Central Washington University), Geraldine Draper (Fort Peck Community College), Gerald Duchovnay (Texas A&M University–Commerce), Gloria Dumler (Bakersfield College), Karen Dunkley (LDS Business College), Richard DuRocher (St. Olaf College), Cathy Eaton (New Hampshire Technical Institute), Nathan Elliott (University of Notre Dame), Terry Elliott (Western Kentucky University), Marcus Embry (University of Northern Colorado), Scott Emmert (University of Wisconsin Fox Valley), Molly Emmons (Butte College), Kathy Essick (Sandhills Community College), Barbara C. Ewell (Loyola University New Orleans), Alexina Fagan (Virginia Commonwealth University), Tyler Farrell (University of Dubuque), Ruth Feingold (St. Mary's College of Maryland), Charles Feldstein (Florida Community College at Jacksonville), Allison Fernley (Salt Lake Community College), Colin Fewer (Purdue University Calumet), Chuck Fisher (Aims Community College), Jim Fisher (Peninsula College), Judith Fisher (Trinity University), Robert Forman (St. John's University), Ellen Foster (Clarion University–Venango Campus), Allison Francis (Chaminade University of Honolulu), Paula Friedman (Cardinal Stritch University), Bonnie Frunz (Shoreline Community College), Kris Fulkerson (Metropolitan Community College), Paul Fyfe (University of Virginia), Mary Gainer (Indiana University of Pennsylvania), Dane Galloway (Ozarks Technical Community College), Margaret Gardineer (Felician College), Thomas P. Gardner (Southeastern Community College), Michael Geary (Bristol Community College), Deborah Gentry (Middle Tennessee State University), Barb Gerhardt (University of Denver), Peter Gillespie (University of Pittsburgh), Diana Gingo (Richland College), Matthew Giordano (Villa Maria College), Terry Goldmann (St. Mary's University of Minnesota), Janet Gorda (Community College Allegheny County), Rebecca Gorman (Metropolitan State College of Denver), Hugh Grady

(Arcadia University), Ann Green (Saint Joseph's University), Kurt Green (Lake Tahoe Community College), Arlene Greene (Columbia College Chicago), Susan Grine (Sandhills Community College), Rachel Hadas (Rutgers University–Newark), Barry Hall (Eastern Michigan University), Susan Hamilton-Trudell (Scott Community College), David Hanauer (Indiana University of Pennsylvania), Leslie Hannah (Kansas State University), Talbot Hardman (Colorado Mountain College–Roaring Fork Campus), Kenny Harmon (Johnson & Wales University), Amanda Harris (Keuka College), Joan Hartman (William Paterson University), Mary-Anna Harvie (Gwynedd Mercy College), Laura Hayden-Moreland (San Diego State University), Thomas Hayes (Southeastern Community College), Bill Hays (Delta State University), Mark Heberle (University of Hawaii at Manoa), Alan Heineman (University of San Francisco), Rebecca Heintz (Polk Community College), Cathy Henrichs (Pikes Peak Community College), Cara Hersh (University of Portland), Paul Hesselink (Covenant College), Gillian Hettinger (William Paterson University), Scarlett Higgins (University of New Mexico), Eugene Hill (Mount Holyoke College), Joshua Hill (Southeastern University), Theresa Hinchy (Butler Community College), Carol Holly (St. Olaf College), Martha Stoddard Holmes (California State University–San Marcos), Sidney Homan (University of Florida), Thomasita Homan (Benedictine College), Katherine Horn (Framingham State College), George Horneker (Arkansas State University), Carol Howard (Warren Wilson College), Kyra Hudson (Weber State University), Elizabeth Huergo (Montgomery College), Carol Hulse (University of West Florida), Amy Hundley (Merced College), Tom Hunley (Western Kentucky University), Chris Ivic (State University of New York–Potsdam), Joanne Jacobs (Shenandoah University), Mary-Ellen Jacobs (Palo Alto College), Carol Jagielnik (University of Wisconsin Parkside), Zubeda Jalalzai (Rhode Island College), Maryse Jayasuriya (University of Texas at El Paso), Kristin Jensen (University of Virginia), Greg Jewell (Madisonville Community College), Kerry Johnson (Merrimack College), Marcie Johnson (Murray State University), Miranda Johnson-Parries (Old Dominion University), Mary Johnston (Minnesota State University), Ronald Jolliffe (Walla Walla University), Ginger Jones (Louisiana State University–Alexandria), Lillie Jones (Alcorn State University), Rick Jones (South Suburban College), James Kain (Neumann College), Vin Katilius-Boydstun (University of St. Francis), William Kazarian (Hawaii Pacific University), Lawrence Keel (Cypress College), Richard Keller (Emporia State University), Kathleen Kenney (New Hampshire Community Technical College), Lynn Kerr (Baltimore City Community College), Mark Kessler (Washington State Community College), Jenny Kijowski (Queens College), Don King (Montreat College), Noel Kinnamon (Mars Hill College), Jane Kinney (Valdosta State University), Robert Kinsley (Ohio University), Lisa Kirby (North Carolina Wesleyan College), Andrea Krause (Hesston College), David Kuebrich (George Mason University), Tomoko Kuribayashi (University of Wisconsin–Stevens Point), Virginia La Grand (Trinity Christian College), Earle Labor (Centenary College of Louisiana), James Lake (Louisiana State University–Shreveport), Mary Latela (St. Joseph's College of Maine), Dawn Lattin (Idaho State University), Jeanne Laurel (Niagara University), William Lawlor (University of Wisconsin–Stevens Point), Judy Lee (Trinidad State Junior College), Brooke Lenz (Saint Mary's University of Minnesota), Eric Leuschner (Fort Hays State University), Richard Levesque (Fullerton College), Naomi Liebler (Montclair State University), Alan Lindsay (New Hampshire Technical Institute), Mari LoNano (Berkshire Community College), Catherine Loomis

(University of North Carolina–Greensboro), Antonia Losano (Middlebury College), Jennifer Low (Florida Atlantic University), Sarah MacDonald (University of Iowa), Diane Maldonado (Community College Allegheny County South), Pat Mallery (William Paterson University), Charles Malody (Seattle Central College), Michael Malouf (George Mason University), Tony Mancus (Hunter College), Diane Marks (Brooklyn College), Sandra Marshburn (West Virginia State University), Michael Martin (Marygrove College), Lea Masiello (Indiana University Pennsylvania), William Mason (Mid-Continent University), Brian May (Northern Illinois University), John McDonald (University of Portland), Will McDonald (University of Iowa), Susan McDowall (Central Community College), Roberta McFadden (Mount St. Mary's University), David McFarland (Black Hawk College), James McGavran (University of North Carolina–Charlotte), Gayla McGlamery (Loyola College in Maryland), Michael McLane (University of Colorado–Denver), Ellen McQuiston (Thomas College), Stephen Meats (Pittsburg State University), Jolivette Mecenas (University of Hawaii–Manoa), Kathy Mendt (Front Range Community College), Trista Merrill (Finger Lakes Community College), Janet Meyer (Old Dominion University), Christian Michener (Saint Mary's University of Minnesota), Michael Mills (University of Northern Colorado), Joelle Moen Brigham Young University–Idaho), D'Juana Montgomery (Southwestern Assemblies of God University), Robert Morace (Daemen College), Dan Morgan (Scott Community College), Lyle Morgan (Pittsburg State University), Mark Morreale (Marist College), Cleatta Morris (Louisiana State University–Shreveport), Linda Trinh Moser (Missouri State University), Shannon Mrkich (West Chester University of Pennsylvania), Lisa Mueller (Northeast Iowa Community College), Sandra Mulryan (Saint Bonaventure University), Jon Myerov (Middlesex Community College), Nancy Nahra (Champlain College), Sheila Nayar (Greensboro College), Heather Neff (Eastern Michigan University), Nathan Nelson (Evangel University), Miranda Nesler (Vanderbilt University), Ellen Nichols (Middlesex Community College), L. F. Nichols (Loyola College), Matt Nikkari (Ferris State University), Thomas Nowak (Dominican College), Steven Olson (Central Washington University), Keith O'Neill (Dutchess Community College), John Orr (Fullerton College), John Orr (University of Portland), James Papworth (Brigham Young University–Idaho), Jessica Parker (Metro State College), Michael Parker (East Carolina University), Aaron Parrett (University of Great Falls), Abha Patel (Monmouth University), Brenda Paulsen (University of Sioux Falls), Robert Peltier (Trinity College), Rita Perkins (Camden County College), Zina Petersen (Brigham Young University), Thomas Pfister (Idaho State University), Jack Phillips (Delta State University), Philip Phillips (Middle Tennessee State University), James Pipkin (University of Houston), Gordon Pradl (New York University), Daniel Pretto (University of West Florida), Arthur Rankin (Louisiana State University at Alexandria), Ingrid Ranum (Gonzaga University), Angela Rasmussen (Spokane Community College), Keith Ratzlaff (Central College), David Raymond (Northern Maine Community College), Amy Raymond (Idaho State University), Maureen Reddy (Rhode Island College), Janet Reed (Crowder College), Valerie Reimers (Southwestern Oklahoma State University), Marcella Remund (University of South Dakota), Helen Richards (University of West Florida), David Richter (Queens College), Glynis Ridley (University of Louisville), Sharron Riesberg (University of Northern Colorado), Jane Rose (Purdue University North Central), Natania Rosenfeld (Knox College), Ron Ross (Portland Community College), Derek Royal (Texas A&M University–

Commerce), Margaret Rozga (University of Wisconsin Waukesha), Jill Rubinson (University of Maine at Augusta), Randy Russell (Front Range Community College), Deborah Ruth (Owensboro Community & Technical College), Natasha Saje (Westminster College), James Salazar (Temple University), Deborah Sarbin (Clarion University), Stephanie Satie (California State University Northridge), John Saurette (Bristol Community College), Nancy Scannell (Valparaiso University), Peter Schakel (Hope College), Steven Scherwatzky (Merrimack College), Robyn Schiffman (Fairleigh Dickinson University), Rosemary Schlick (Delgado Community College), Desiree Schuler (Johnson & Wales University), Janis Schulte (Colby Community College), George Schwedler (Alpena Community College–Huron Shores Campus), Pam Scott (Pikeville College), David Sebberson (St. Cloud State University), Mary Seel (Broome Community College), David Seelow (Rensselaer Polytechnic Institute), Lynne Shackelford (Furman University), Amie Sharp (Pikes Peak Community College), Kimberly Shepherd (Washtenaw Community College), Ellen Shull (Palo Alto College), Ricco Siasoco (Boston College), Amritjit Singh (Ohio University), Deepa Sitaraman (Shawnee State University), John Sitter (University of Notre Dame), Carolyn Skebe (State University of New York–Albany), Stephen Slimp (University of West Alabama), Christine Smith (Front Range Community College), Mark Smith (Missouri State University), Nora Smith (Montana State University), Phillip Snyder (Brigham Young University), Donald Socha (Central Michigan University), Lisa Spaar (University of Virginia), Daniel Spoth (Vanderbilt University), Ann Spurlock (Mississippi State University), Emily Stauffer (Franklin College), Mary Steible (Southern Illinois University–Edwardsville), Laura Marie Steinert (South Texas College), Michael Stephens (Johnson & Wales University), Steven Stewart (Brigham Young University–Idaho), Brian Stiles (King's College), Karah Stokes (Kentucky State University), Cheryl Stolz (Lake Land College), Pamela Stout (Oklahoma City Community College), Joseph Sullivan (Marietta College), Lynn Sullivan (Trocaire College), Mary Szybist (Lewis & Clark College), Jeff Tate (Northern Oklahoma College), Verena Theile (Gonzaga University), Frieda Thompson (University of Texas–Pan American), Dan Thorpe (College of DuPage), Erik Tsao (Southern Maine Community College), Brenda Tuberville (University of Texas–Tyler), Brian Tucker (Wabash College), Herbert Tucker (University of Virginia), Richard Turner (Indiana University–Purdue University Indianapolis), Chris Twiggs (Florida Community College at Jacksonville), Edward Uehling (Valparaiso University), Harvey Ussach (Bristol Community College), Michael Van Dyke (Cornerstone University), Ryan Van Meter (University of Iowa), Mary Van Ness (Terra Community College), Andrea Van Vorhis (Owens Community College), Barbara Vielma (University of Texas–Pan American), Robin Visel (Furman University), Jennifer Von Ammon (Lansing Community College), Ellen Placey Wadey (Columbia College Chicago), Anne Weed (Keuka College), Sheri Weinstein (Kingsborough Community College), Carol Weir (Hunter College), Lavonne Weller (Spokane Falls Community College), Jeana West (Murray State College), Jeff Wheeler (Long Beach City College), Katharine Whitcomb (Central Washington University), Rebecca Whitten (Mississippi State University), Judith Wigdortz (Monmouth University), Carmaletta Williams (Johnson County Community College), Elizabeth Williams (University of Michigan), Barbara Williamson (Spokane Falls Community College), Lisa M. Wilson (State University of New York–Potsdam), David Wilson-Okamura (East Carolina University), Sallie Wolf (Arapahoe Community College), James Woolley (Lafayette College), Valorie

Worthy (Ohio University), Susan Wright (William Paterson University), Sherida Yoder (Felician College), Chris York (Pine Technical College), Beth Younger (Drake University), Robyn Younkin (Community College of Rhode Island), Dede Yow (Kennesaw State University), Lucy Zimmerman (Glen Oaks Community College), Wanda Zimmerman (Ozarks Technical Community College).

The Norton
Introduction to Literature

TENTH EDITION

Introduction

In the opening chapters of Charles Dickens's novel *Hard Times* (1854), the aptly named Thomas Gradgrind warns the teachers and pupils at his "model" school to avoid using their imaginations. "Teach these boys and girls nothing but Facts. Facts alone are wanted in life," exclaims Mr. Gradgrind. To press his point, Mr. Gradgrind asks "girl number twenty," Sissy Jupe, the daughter of a circus performer, to define a horse. When she cannot, Gradgrind turns to Bitzer, a pale, spiritless boy who "looked as though, if he were cut, he would bleed white." A "model" student of this "model" school, Bitzer gives exactly the kind of definition to satisfy Mr. Gradgrind:

> *Literature is not things but a way to comprehend things.*
> —NORMAN N. HOLLAND

> Quadruped. Graminivorous. Forty teeth, namely, twenty-four grinders, four eye-teeth, and twelve incisive. Sheds coat in spring; in marshy countries, sheds hoofs.

Anyone who has any sense of what a horse is rebels against Bitzer's lifeless picture of that animal and against the "Gradgrind" view of reality. As these first scenes of *Hard Times* lead us to expect, in the course of the novel the fact-grinding Mr. Gradgrind learns that human beings cannot live on facts alone; that it is dangerous to stunt the faculties of imagination and feeling; that, in the words of one of the novel's more lovable characters, "People must be amused." Through the downfall of an exaggerated enemy of the imagination, Dickens reminds us why we like and even *need* to read literature.

What Is Literature?

But what is literature? Before you opened this book, you probably could guess that it would contain the sorts of stories, poems, and plays you have encountered in English classes or in the literature section of a library or bookstore. But why are some written works called *literature* whereas others are not? And who gets to decide? *The American Heritage Dictionary of the English Language* offers a number of definitions for the word *literature*, one of which is "imaginative or creative writing, especially of recognized artistic value." In this book, we adopt a version of that definition by focusing on fictional stories, poems, and plays—the three major kinds (or *genres*) of

> *Writing is not literature unless it gives to the reader a pleasure which arises not only from the things said, but from the way in which they are said.*
> —STOPFORD BROOKE

"imaginative or creative writing" that form the heart of literature as it has been taught in schools and universities for over a century. Many of the works we have chosen to include are already ones "of recognized artistic value" and thus belong to what scholars call the **canon**, a select, if much-debated and ever-evolving, list of the most highly and widely esteemed works. Though quite a few of the literary texts we include are simply too new to have earned that status, they, too, have already drawn praise, and some have even generated controversy.

Certainly it helps to bear in mind what others have thought of a literary work. Yet one of this book's primary goals is to get you to think for yourself, as well as communicate with others, about what "imaginative writing" and "artistic value" are or might be and thus about what counts as literature. What makes a story or poem different from an essay, a newspaper editorial, or a technical manual? For that matter, what makes a published, canonical story like Herman Melville's "Bartleby, the Scrivener" (chapter 7) both like and unlike the sorts of stories we tell each other every day? What about so-called *oral literature*, such as the fables and folktales that circulated by word of mouth for hundreds of years before they were ever written down? Or published works such as comic strips and graphic novels that rely little, if at all, on the written word? Or Harlequin romances, television shows, and the stories you collaborate in making when you play a video game like *Grand Theft Auto*? Likewise, how is Shakespeare's poem "[My mistress's eyes are nothing like the sun]" (chapter 19) both like and unlike a verse you might find in a Hallmark card or even a jingle in a mouthwash commercial?

Today, literature departments offer courses in many of these forms of expression, expanding the realm of literature far beyond the limits of the dictionary definition. An essay, a song lyric, a screenplay, a supermarket romance, a novel by Toni

Morrison or William Faulkner, and a poem by Walt Whitman or Emily Dickinson—each may be read and interpreted in *literary ways* that yield insight and pleasure. What makes the literary way of reading different from pragmatic reading is, as scholar Louise Rosenblatt explains, that it does not focus "on what will remain . . . *after* the reading—the information to be acquired, the logical solution to a problem, the actions to be carried out," but rather on "what happens *during* . . . reading." The difference between pragmatic and literary reading, in other words, resembles the difference between a journey that is only about reaching a destination and one that is just as much about fully experiencing the ride.

In the pages of this book, you will find cartoons, an excerpt from a graphic novel, song lyrics, folktales, and stories and plays that have spawned movies. Through this inclusiveness, we do not intend to suggest that there are no distinctions among these various forms of expression or between a good story, poem, or play and a bad one; rather, we want to get you thinking, talking, and writing both about what the key differences and similarities among these forms are and what makes one work a better example of its genre than another. Sharpening your skills at these peculiarly intensive and responsive sorts of reading and interpretation is a primary purpose of this book and of most literature courses.

Another goal of inclusiveness is simply to remind you that literature doesn't just belong in a textbook or a classroom, even if textbooks and classrooms are essential means for expanding your knowledge of the literary terrain and of the concepts and techniques essential to thoroughly enjoying and understanding a broad range of literary forms. You may or may not be the kind of person who always takes a novel when you go to the beach or secretly writes a poem about your experience when you get back home. You may or may not have taken a literature course (or courses) before. Yet you already have a good deal of literary experience and even expertise, as well as much more to discover about literature. A major aim of this book is to make you more conscious of how and to what end you might use the tools you already possess and to add many new ones to your tool belt.

What Does Literature Do?

One quality that may well differentiate stories, poems, and plays from other kinds of writing is that they help us move beyond and probe beneath abstractions by giving us concrete, vivid particulars. Rather than talking *about* things, they bring them to life for us by *representing* experience, and so they *become* an experience for us—one that engages our emotions, our imagination, and all of our senses, as well as our intellects. As the British poet and critic Matthew Arnold put it more than a century ago, "The interpretations of science do not give us this intimate sense of objects as the interpretations of poetry give it; they appeal to a limited faculty, and not to the whole man. It is not Linnaeus . . . who gives us the true sense of animals, or water, or plants, who seizes their secret for us, who makes us participate in their life; it is Shakespeare . . . Wordsworth . . . Keats."

(Continued on next page)

(Continued)

To test Arnold's theory, compare the *American Heritage Dictionary*'s rather dry definition of *literature* with the following poem, in which John Keats describes his first encounter with a specific literary work—George Chapman's translation of *The Iliad* and *The Odyssey*, two epic poems by the ancient Greek poet Homer.

JOHN KEATS
On First Looking into Chapman's Homer[1]

Much have I traveled in the realms of gold,
And many goodly states and kingdoms seen;
Round many western islands have I been
Which bards in fealty to Apollo[2] hold.
5 Oft of one wide expanse had I been told
That deep-browed Homer ruled as his demesne;
Yet did I never breathe its pure serene[3]
Till I heard Chapman speak out loud and bold:
Then felt I like some watcher of the skies
10 When a new planet swims into his ken;[4]
Or like stout Cortez[5] when with eagle eyes
He stared at the Pacific—and all his men
Looked at each other with a wild surmise—
Silent, upon a peak in Darien.

1816

Keats makes us *see* literature as a "wide expanse" by greatly developing this **metaphor** and complementing it with **similes** likening reading to the sighting of a "new planet" and the first glimpse of an undiscovered ocean. More important, he shows us what literature means and why it matters by allowing us to share with him the subjective experience of reading and the complex sensations it inspires—the dizzying exhilaration of discovery; the sense of power, accomplishment, and pride that comes of achieving something difficult; the wonder we feel in those rare moments when a much-anticipated experience turns out to be even greater than we had imagined it would be.

It isn't the definitions of words alone that bring this experience to life for us as we read Keats's poem, but also their sensual qualities—the way the words look, sound, and even feel in our mouths because of the particular way they are put together on the page. The sensation of excitement—of a racing heart and mind—is reproduced *in* us as we read the poem. For example, notice how the lines in the middle run into each other, but then Keats forces us to slow down at the poem's end—stopped

(Continued on next page)

(Continued)

short by that dash and comma in the poem's final lines, just as Cortez and his men are when they reach the edge of the known world and peer into what lies beyond.

1. George Chapman's were among the most famous Renaissance translations of Homer; he completed his *Iliad* in 1611, his *Odyssey* in 1616. Keats wrote the sonnet after being led to Chapman by a former teacher and reading the *Iliad* all night long.
2. Greek god of poetry and music. *Fealty*: literally, the loyalty owed by a vassal to his feudal lord.
3. Atmosphere.
4. Range of vision; awareness.
5. Actually, Balboa; he first viewed the Pacific from Darien, in Panama.

What Are the Genres of Literature?

The conversation that is literature, as well as the conversation about literature, invites all comers, requiring neither a visa nor a special license of any kind. Yet literary studies, like all disciplines, has developed its own terminology and its own systems of classification. Helping you understand and effectively use both is a major focus of this book; especially important terms appear in bold throughout and are defined in a glossary at the back.

The framework of genre . . . is, when used well, like a comfortable old coat, into which you slip with an anticipatory sigh of comfort.
—NATALIE BENNETT

Some essential literary terms are common, everyday words used in a special way in the conversation about literature. A case in point, perhaps, is the term *literary criticism*, as well as the closely related term *literary critic*. Despite the usual connotations of the word *criticism*, literary criticism is called *criticism* not because it is negative or corrective but rather because those who write criticism ask searching, analytical, "critical" questions about the works they read. Literary criticism is both the process of interpreting and commenting on literature and the result of that process. If you write an essay on the play *Hamlet*, the poetry of John Keats, or the development of the short story in the 1990s, you engage in literary criticism, and by writing the essay, you've become a literary critic.

Similarly, when we classify works of literature, we use terms that may be familiar to you but have specific meanings in a literary context. All academic disciplines have systems of classification, or taxonomies, as well as jargon. Biologists, for example, classify all organisms into a series of ever-smaller, more specific categories: *kingdom, phylum* or *division, class, order, family, genus,* and *species*. Classification and comparison are just as essential in the study of literature. We expect a poem to work in a certain way, for example, when we know from the outset that it *is* a poem and not, say, a factual news report or a short story. And—whether consciously or not—we compare it, as we read, to other poems we've read in the past. If we know, further, that the poem was first published in eighteenth-century Japan, we expect it to work differently from one that appeared in the latest *New*

Yorker. Indeed, we often choose what to read, just as we choose what movie to see, based on the "class" or "order" of book or movie we like or what we are in the mood for that day—horror or comedy, action or science fiction.

As these examples suggest, we generally tend to categorize literary works in two ways: (1) on the basis of contextual factors, especially historical and cultural context—that is, when, by whom, and where it was produced (as in *nineteenth-century* or *Victorian literature*, *the literature of the Harlem Renaissance*, *American literature*, or *African American literature*)—and (2) on the basis of formal textual features. For the latter type of classification, the one we focus on in this book, the key term is **genre**, which simply means, as the *Oxford English Dictionary* tells us, "A particular style or category of works of art; esp. a type of literary work characterized by a particular form, style, or purpose."

Applied rigorously, *genre* refers to the largest categories around which this book is organized—**fiction**, **poetry**, and **drama** (as well as **nonfiction** prose). The word *subgenre* applies to smaller divisions within a genre, and the word *kind* to divisions within a subgenre. *Subgenres* of fiction include the **novel**, the **novella**, and the **short story**. *Kinds* of novels, in turn, include things like the **bildungsroman** or the epistolary novel. Similarly, important subgenres of nonfiction include the essay, as well as **biography** and autobiography; a memoir is a particular kind of autobiography, and so on.

However, the terms of literary criticism are not so fixed or so consistently, rigorously used as biologists' are. You will often see the word *genre* applied both much more narrowly—referring to the novel, for example, or even to a kind of novel such as the epistolary novel or the historical novel.

The way we classify a work depends on which aspects of its form or style we concentrate on, and categories may overlap. When we divide fiction, for example, into the subgenres novel, novella, and short story, we take the length of the works as the salient aspect. (Novels are much longer than short stories.) But other fictional subgenres—detective fiction, **gothic fiction**, **historical fiction**, science fiction, and even **romance**—are based on the types of **plots**, **characters**, **settings**, and so on that are customarily featured in these works. These latter categories may include works from all the other, length-based categories. There are, after all, gothic novels (think Anne Rice), as well as gothic short stories (think Edgar Allan Poe).

A few genres even cut across the boundaries dividing poetry, fiction, drama, and nonfiction. A prime example is **satire**—any literary work (whether poem, play, fiction, or nonfiction) "in which prevailing vices and follies are held up to ridicule" (*Oxford English Dictionary*). Examples of satire include poems such as Alexander Pope's *Dunciad*; plays, movies, and television shows, from Moliere's *Tartuffe* to Stanley Kubrick's *Dr. Strangelove* to *South Park* and *The Colbert Report*; works of fiction like Jonathan Swift's *Gulliver's Travels* and Voltaire's *Candide*; and works of nonfiction such as Swift's "A Modest Proposal" and Ambrose Bierce's *The Devil's Dictionary*. Three other major genres that cross the borders between fiction, poetry, drama, and nonfiction are **parody**, **pastoral**, and **romance**.

Individual works can thus belong simultaneously to multiple generic categories or observe some **conventions** of a genre without being an example of that genre in any simple or straightforward way. *Beowulf* (chapter 20) is an **epic** and, because it's written in verse, a poem. Yet because (like all epics) it narrates a story, it is also a work of fiction in the more general sense of that term. The novels in the *Twilight* series contain elements of romance, fantasy, and even the gothic.

Given this complexity, the system of literary genres can be puzzling, especially to the uninitiated. Used well, however, classification schemes are among the most essential and effective tools we use to understand and enjoy just about everything, including literature.

Why Read Literature?

Because there has never been and never will be absolute, lasting agreement about where exactly the boundaries between one literary genre and another should be drawn or even about what counts as literature at all, it might be more useful from the outset to focus on *why* we look at particular forms of expression.

Literature is the human activity that takes the fullest and most precise account of variousness, possibility, complexity, and difficulty.
—LIONEL TRILLING

Over the ages, people have sometimes dismissed *all* literature or at least certain genres as a luxury, a frivolous pastime, even a sinful indulgence. Plato famously banned poetry from his ideal republic on the grounds that it tells beautiful lies that "feed and water our passions" rather than our reason. Thousands of years later, the influential eighteenth-century philosopher Jeremy Bentham decried the "magic art" of literature as doing a good deal of "mischief" by "stimulating our passions, . . . exciting our prejudices." One of Bentham's contemporaries—a minister—blamed the rise of immorality, irreligion, and especially prostitution on the increasing popularity of that particular brand of literature called the novel.

Today, many Americans express their sense of literature's insignificance by simply not reading it: A 2004 government report entitled *Reading at Risk* indicates that less than half of U.S. adults read imaginative literature, with the sharpest declines occurring among the youngest age groups. Even if they very much enjoy reading on their own, many contemporary U.S. college students nonetheless hesitate to study or major in literature for fear that their degree won't provide them with "marketable" credentials, knowledge, or skills.

Yet the enormous success of Oprah's Book Club is only one of many signs that millions of people continue to find both reading literature and discussing it with others to be enjoyable, meaningful, even essential activities. English thrives as a major at most colleges and universities, almost all of which require undergraduates majoring in other areas to take at least one course in literature. (Perhaps that's why you are reading this book!) Schools of medicine, law, and business are today *more* likely to require their students to take literature courses than they were in past decades, and they continue to welcome literature majors as applicants, as do many corporations. So why do so many people read and study literature, and why do schools encourage and even require students to do so? Even if we know what literature is, what does it *do* for us? What is its value?

There are, of course, as many answers to such questions as there are readers. For centuries, a standard answer has been simply that imaginative literature provides a unique brand of "instruction and delight." John Keats's "On Looking into Chapman's Homer" illustrates some of the many forms such delight can take. Some kinds of imaginative writing offer us the delight of immediate escape, but imaginative writing that is more difficult to read and understand than a Harry Potter or Twilight novel offers escape of a different and potentially more instructive sort, liberating us from the confines of our own time, place, and social milieu, as well as our habitual ways of thinking, feeling, and looking at the world. In this way, a story, poem, or play can satisfy our desire for broader experience—including the sorts of experience we might be unable or unwilling to endure in real life. We can learn what it might be like to grow up on a Canadian fox farm or to clean ashtrays in the Singapore airport. We can travel back into the past, experiencing war from the perspective of a soldier watching his comrade drown in air poisoned by mustard gas or of prisoners suffering in a Nazi labor camp. We can journey into the future or into universes governed by entirely different rules than our own. Perhaps we yearn for such knowledge because we can best come to understand our own identities and outlooks by leaping over the boundaries that separate us from other selves and worlds.

Keats's friend and fellow poet Percy Bysshe Shelley argued that literature increases a person's ability to make such leaps, to "imagine intensely and comprehensively" and "put himself in the place of another and of many othe[r]" people in order "to be greatly good." Shelley meant "good" in a moral sense, reasoning that the ability both to accurately imagine and to truly *feel* the human consequences of our actions is the key to ethical behavior. But universities and professional schools today also define this "good" in distinctly pragmatic ways. In virtually any career you choose, you will need to interact positively and productively with both coworkers and clients, and in today's increasingly globalized world, you will need to learn to deal effectively and empathetically with people vastly different from yourself. At the very least, literature written by people from various backgrounds and depicting various places, times, experiences, and feelings will give you some understanding of how others' lives and worldviews may differ from your own—or how they may be very much the same.

Similarly, our rapidly changing world and economy require intellectual flexibility, adaptability, and ingenuity, making ever more essential the human knowledge, general skills, and habits of mind developed through the study of literature. Literature explores issues and questions relevant in any walk of life. Yet rather than offering us neat or comforting solutions and answers, literature enables us to experience difficult situations and human conundrums in all their complexity and to look at them from various points of view. In so doing, it invites us sometimes to question conventional ways of thinking and sometimes to see its wisdom, even as it helps us imagine altogether new possibilities.

Finally, literature awakens us to the richness and complexity of language—our primary tool for engaging with, understanding, and shaping the world around us. As we read more and more, seeing how different writers use language to help us feel their joy, pain, love, rage, or laughter, we begin to recognize the vast range of possibilities for self-expression. Writing and discussion in turn give us invaluable practice in discovering, expressing, and defending our own nuanced, often contradictory thoughts about both literature and life. The study of literature enhances our command of language and our sensitivity to its effects and meanings in every form or medium, providing interpretation and communication skills especially crucial in our "information age." By learning to appreciate and articulate what the language of a story, poem, a play, or an essay does to us and by considering how it affects others, we also learn much about what we can do with language.

Why Study Literature?

You may already feel the power and pleasure to be gained from a sustained encounter with challenging reading. Then why not simply enjoy it in solitude, on your own free time? Why take a course in literature? Literary study, like all disciplines, has developed its own terminology and its own techniques. Some

Literature is language charged with meaning. . . . Literature is news that stays news.
—EZRA POUND

knowledge and understanding of both can greatly enhance our personal appreciation of literature and our conversations with others about it. Literature also has a context and a history, and learning something about them can make all the difference in the amount and kind of pleasure and insight you derive from literature. By reading and discussing different genres of literature, as well as works from dramatically different times and places, you may well come to appreciate and even love works that you might never have discovered or chosen to read on your own or that you might have disliked or misunderstood if you did.

Most important, writing about works of literature and discussing them with your teachers and other students will give you practice in analyzing literature in greater depth and in considering alternative views of both the works themselves and the situations and problems the works explore. A clear understanding of the aims and designs of a story, poem, or play never falls like a bolt from the blue. Instead, it emerges from a process that involves trying to put into words *how* and *why* this work had such an effect on you and, just as important, responding to what others say or write about it. Literature itself is essentially a vast, ongoing, ever-evolving conversation in which we most fully participate when we enter into actual conversation with others.

As you engage in this conversation, you will notice that interpretation is always variable, always open to discussion. A great diversity of interpretations might suggest that the discussion is pointless. On the contrary, that's when the discussion gets most interesting. Because there is no single, straight, paved road to an understanding of a literary text, you can explore a variety of blazed trails and less-traveled paths. In sharing your own interpretations, tested against your peers' responses and guided by your instructor's or other critics' expertise, you will hone your skills at both interpretation and communication. After the intricate and interactive process of interpretation, you will find that the work has changed when you read it again. What we do with literature alters what it does to us.

READING, RESPONDING, WRITING

Fiction

Fiction: Reading, Responding, Writing

Stories are a part of daily life in every culture. Stories are what we tell when we return from vacation or survive an accident or illness. They help us make sense of growing up or growing old, of a hurricane or a war, of the country and world we live in. In conversations, a story may be invited by the listener ("What did you do last night?") or initiated by the teller ("Guess what I saw when I was driving home!"). We assume such stories are true, or at least that they are meant to describe an experience honestly. Of course, many of the stories we encounter daily, from jokes to online games to television sitcoms to novels and films, are intended to be **fiction**—that is, stories or narratives about imaginary persons and events. Every story, however, whether a news story, sworn testimony, idle gossip, or a fairy tale, is always a version of events told from a particular (or several) perspectives, and it may be incomplete, biased, misinformed, or just plain made up. As we listen to others' stories, we keep alert to the details, which make the stories rich and entertaining. But we also need to spend considerable time and energy making sure that we accurately interpret what we hear: We ask ourselves who is telling the story, why the story is being told, and whether we have all the information we need to understand it fully.

Even newspaper articles, which are supposed to tell true stories—the facts of what actually happened—may be open to such interpretation. Take as an example the following article, which appeared in the *New York Times* on January 1, 1920.

ACCUSED WIFE KILLS HER ALLEGED LOVER

Cumberland (Md.) Woman Becomes Desperate When Her Husband Orders Her from Home.

Special to The New York Times.

CUMBERLAND, Md., Dec. 31.—Accused by her husband of unfaithfulness, Mrs. Kate Uhl, aged 25, this morning stabbed to death Bryan Pownall, who she alleged was the cause of the estrangement with her husband, Mervin Uhl.

Mrs. Uhl, who is the mother of three children, deniès her husband's charge of misconduct with Pownall, asserting that the latter forced his attentions on her by main physical strength against her will.

The stabbing this morning came as a dramatic sequel to the woman's dilemma after she had been ordered to leave her home. Mrs. Uhl summoned Pownall after her husband had gone to work this morning, and according to her story begged him to tell her husband that she, Mrs. Uhl, was not to blame. This Pownall refused to do, but again tried to make love to her, Mrs. Uhl said. When Pownall sought to kiss her Mrs. Uhl seized a thin-bladed butcher knife and stabbed the man to the heart, she admitted.

The report's appearance in a reliable newspaper; its identification of date, location, and other information; and the legalistic adjectives "accused" and "alleged" suggest that it strives to be accurate and objective. But given the distance between us and the events described here, it's also easy to imagine this chain of events being recounted as a play, murder mystery, Hollywood film, or televised trial. In other words, this news story is still fundamentally a *story*. Note that certain points of view are better represented than others and certain details are highlighted, as might be the case in a novel or short story. The news item is based almost entirely on what Kate Uhl asserts, and even the subtitle, "Woman Becomes Desperate," plays up the "dramatic sequel to the woman's dilemma." We don't know what Mervin Uhl said when he allegedly accused his wife and turned her out of the house, and Bryan Pownall, the murdered man, never had a chance to defend himself. Presumably, the article reports accurately the husband's accusation of adultery and the wife's accusation of rape, but we have no way of knowing whose accusations are true. Further reading in court records about this incident and in newspapers from that time might reveal more of what happened, as far as anyone was able to find out.

Our everyday interpretation of the stories we hear from various sources—including other people, television, newspapers, advertisements, and countless others—has much in common with the interpretation of stories such as those in this anthology. In fact, you'll probably discover that the processes of reading, responding to, and writing about stories are already familiar to you on some level. Most readers already know, for instance, that they should pay close attention to seemingly trivial details; they should ask questions and find out more about any matters of fact that seem mysterious, odd, or unclear. Most readers are well aware that words can have several meanings and that there are alternative ways to tell a story. How would someone else have told the story? What are the storyteller's perspective and motives? What is the context of the tale—for instance, when is it supposed to have taken place and what was the occasion of telling it? These and other questions from our experience of everyday storytelling are equally relevant in reading fiction. Similarly, we can usually tell in reading a story or hearing it whether it is supposed to make us laugh, shock us, or provoke some other response.

TELLING STORIES: INTERPRETATION

Everyone has a unique story to tell. In fact, many stories are about this difference or divergence among people's interpretations of reality. A number of the stories in this chapter explore issues of storytelling and interpretation.

Consider a well-known tale, "The Blind Men and the Elephant," a Buddhist story over two thousand years old. Like other stories that have been transmitted orally, this one exists in many versions. Here's one way of telling it:

The Elephant in the Village of the Blind

Once there was a village high in the mountains in which everyone was born blind. One day a traveler arrived from far away with many fine things to sell and many tales to tell. The villagers asked, "How did you travel so far and so high carrying so much?" The traveler said, "On my elephant." "What is an elephant?"

the villagers asked, having never even heard of such an animal in their remote mountain village. "See for yourself," the traveler replied.

The elders of the village were a little afraid of the strange-smelling creature that took up so much space in the middle of the village square. They could hear it breathing and munching on hay, and feel its slow, swaying movements disturbing the air around them. First one elder reached out and felt its flapping ear. "An elephant is soft but tough, and flexible, like a leather fan." Another grasped its back leg. "An elephant is a rough, hairy pillar." An old woman took hold of a tusk and gasped, "An elephant is a cool, smooth staff." A young girl seized the tail and declared, "An elephant is a fringed rope." A boy took hold of the trunk and announced, "An elephant is a water pipe." Soon others were stroking its sides, which were furrowed like a dry plowed field, and others determined that its head was an overturned washing tub attached to the water pipe.

At first each villager argued with the others on the definition of the elephant, as the traveler watched in silence. Two elders were about to come to blows about a fan that could not possibly be a pillar. Meanwhile the elephant patiently enjoyed the investigations as the cries of curiosity and angry debate mixed in the afternoon sun. Soon someone suggested that a list could be made of all the parts: the elephant had four pillars, one tub, two fans, a water pipe, and two staffs, and was covered in tough, hairy leather or dried mud. Four young mothers, sitting on a bench and comparing impressions, realized that the elephant was in fact an enormous, gentle ox with a stretched nose. The traveler agreed, adding only that it was also a powerful draft horse and that if they bought some of his wares for a good price he would be sure to come that way again in the new year.

. . .

The different versions of such a tale, like the different descriptions of the elephant, alter the meaning that is understood. Changing any aspect of the story will inevitably change how it works and what it means to the listener or reader. For example, most versions of this story feature not an entire village of blind people (as this version does), but a small group of blind men who claim to be wiser than their sighted neighbors. These blind men quarrel endlessly because none of them can see; none can put together all the evidence of all their senses or all the elephant's various parts to create a whole. Such traditional versions of the story criticize people who are too proud of what they think they know; these versions imply that sighted people would know better what an elephant is. However, other versions of the tale, like the one above, are set in an imaginary "country" of the blind. This setting changes the emphasis of the story from the errors of a few blind wise men to the value and the insufficiency of *any* one person's perspective. For though it's clear that the various members of the community in this version will never agree entirely on one interpretation of (or story about) the elephant, they do not let themselves get bogged down in endless dispute. Instead they compare and combine their various stories and "readings" in order to form a more satisfying, holistic understanding of the wonder in their midst. Similarly, listening to others' different interpretations of stories, based on their different perspectives, can enhance your experience of a work of literature and your skill in responding to new works.

Just as stories vary depending on who is telling them, their meaning varies depending on who is responding to them. In the elephant story, the villagers pay attention to what the tail or the ear feels like, and then they draw on comparisons to what they already know. But ultimately, the individual interpretations of the elephant depend on what previous experiences each villager brings to bear (of pillars, water pipes, oxen, and dried mud, for example), and also on where (quite literally) he or she stands in relation to the elephant. In the same way, readers participate in re-creating a story as they interpret it. When you read a story for the first time, your response will be informed by other stories you have heard and read as well as your expectations for this kind of story. To grapple with what is new in any story, start by observing one part at a time and gradually trying to understand how those parts work together to form a whole. As you make sense of each new piece of the picture, you adjust your expectations about what is yet to come. When you have read and grasped it as fully as possible, you may share your interpretation with other readers, discussing different ways of seeing the story. Finally, you might express your reflective understanding in writing—in a sense, telling *your* story about the work.

Questions about the Elements of Fiction

- Expectations: What do you expect?
  - from the title? from the first sentence or paragraph?
  - after the first events or interactions of characters?
  - as the conflict is resolved?
- What happens in the story? (See chapter 1.)
  - Do the characters or the situation change from the beginning to the end?
  - Can you summarize the **plot**? Is it a recognizable kind or **genre** of story?
- How is the story narrated? (See chapter 2.)
  - Is the narrator identified as a character?
  - Is it narrated in the past or present tense?
  - Is it narrated in the first, second, or third person?
  - Do you know what every character is thinking, or only some characters, or none?
- Who are the **characters**? (See chapter 3.)
  - Who is the **protagonist**(s) (hero, heroine)?
  - Who is the **antagonist**(s) (villain, opponent, obstacle)?
  - Who are the other characters? What is their role in the story?
  - Do your expectations change with those of the characters, or do you know more or less than each of the characters?
- What is the **setting** of the story? (See chapter 4.)
  - What is the time of the story? Is it contemporary or set in the past?
  - Where does it take place? Is it in the United States or another country, or in a specific town or region?
  - Does the story move from one setting to another? Does it move in one direction only or back and forth in time and place?
- What do you notice about how the story is written?
  - What is the **style** of the prose? Are the sentences and the vocabulary simple or complex?
  - Are there any **images** or **figures of speech**? (See chapter 5.)
  - What is the **tone** or mood? Does the reader feel sad, amused, worried, curious?
- What does the story mean? Can you express its **theme** or themes? (See chapter 6.)
  - Answers to these big questions may be found in many instances in your answers to the previous questions. The story's meaning or theme depends on all its features.

READING AND RESPONDING TO FICTION

When imaginary events are acted out onstage or onscreen, our experience of those events is that of being a witness to them. In contrast, prose narrative fiction, whether oral or written, is relayed to us by someone. Reading it is more like hearing what happened after the fact than witnessing it before our very eyes. The teller, or **narrator**, of fiction addresses a listener or reader, often referred to as the audience. How much or how little we know about the characters and what they say or do depends on what a narrator tells us.

You should read a story attentively, just as you would listen attentively to someone telling a story out loud. This means limiting distractions and interruptions; you should take a break from social networking and obtrusive music. Literary prose, as well as poetry, works with the sounds as well as meanings of words, just as film works with music and sound as well as images and dramatic action. Be prepared to mark up the text and to make notes.

The following short short story is a contemporary work. As in "The Elephant in the Village of the Blind," this narrator gives us a minimal amount of information, merely observing the characters' different perceptions and interpretations of things they see during a cross-country car trip. As you read the story, pay attention to your expectations, drawing on your personal experience as well as such clues as the title; the characters' opinions, behavior, and speech; specifics of setting (time and place); and any repetitions or changes. When and how does the story begin to challenge and change your initial expectations? You can use the questions given below to guide your reading of any story and help you focus on some of the important features.

LINDA BREWER

20/20

By the time they reached Indiana, Bill realized that Ruthie, his driving companion, was incapable of theoretical debate. She drove okay, she went halves on gas, etc., but she refused to argue. She didn't seem to know how. Bill was used to East Coast women who disputed everything he said, every step of the way. Ruthie stuck to simple observation, like "Look, cows." He chalked it up to the fact that she was from rural Ohio and thrilled to death to be anywhere else.

She didn't mind driving into the setting sun. The third evening out, Bill rested his eyes while she cruised along making the occasional announcement.

"Indian paintbrush. A golden eagle."

Miles later he frowned. There was no Indian paintbrush, that he knew of, near Chicago.

5   The next evening, driving, Ruthie said, "I never thought I'd see a Bigfoot in real life." Bill turned and looked at the side of the road streaming innocently out behind them. Two red spots winked back—reflectors nailed to a tree stump.

"Ruthie, I'll drive," he said. She stopped the car and they changed places in the light of the evening star.

"I'm so glad I got to come with you," Ruthie said. Her eyes were big, blue, and capable of seeing wonderful sights. A white buffalo near Fargo. A UFO above

Twin Falls. A handsome genius in the person of Bill himself. This last vision came to her in Spokane and Bill decided to let it ride.

• • •

SAMPLE WRITING: ANNOTATION AND NOTES

Now re-read the story, along with the brief annotations one reader made in the margins, based on the questions in the box on page 15. The reader then expanded these annotations into longer, more detailed notes.

20/20

Like "20/20 hind-sight" or perfect vision? Also like the way Bill and Ruthie go 50/50 on the trip, and see things in two different ways.

By the time they reached Indiana, Bill realized that Ruthie, his driving companion, was incapable of theoretical debate. She drove okay, she went halves on gas, etc., but she refused to argue. She didn't seem to know how. Bill was used to East Coast women who disputed everything he said, every step of the way. Ruthie stuck to simple observation, like "Look, cows." He chalked it up to the fact that she was from rural Ohio and thrilled to death to be anywhere else.

Bill's doubts about Ruthie. Is he reliable? Does she "refuse" or not "know how" to argue? What's her view of him?

Bill's keeping score; maybe Ruthie's nicer, or has better eye-sight. She notices things.

She didn't mind driving into the setting sun. The third evening out, Bill rested his eyes while she cruised along making the occasional announcement.

"Indian paintbrush. A golden eagle."

Miles later he frowned. There was no Indian paintbrush, that he knew of, near Chicago.

Repetition, like a folk tale: 2nd sun-set drive, 3rd time she speaks. Not much dialogue in story.

The next evening, driving, Ruthie said, "I never thought I'd see a Bigfoot in real life." Bill turned and looked at the side of the road streaming innocently out behind them. Two red spots winked back—reflectors nailed to a tree stump.

Bill's only speech. Turning point: Bill sees something he doesn't already know.

"Ruthie, I'll drive," he said. She stopped the car and they changed places in the light of the evening star.

Repetition, like a joke, in 3 things Ruthie sees.

Story begins and ends in the middle of things: "By the time," "let it ride."

"I'm so glad I got to come with you," Ruthie said. Her eyes were big, blue, and capable of seeing wonderful sights. A white buffalo near Fargo. A UFO above Twin Falls. A handsome genius in the person of Bill himself. This last vision came to her in Spokane and Bill decided to let it ride.

Initial Impressions

Plot: begins in the middle of action, on a journey. *Narration*: past tense, third person. *Character*: Bill is the focal character, and he and Ruthie have been driving for a while. *Setting*: Indiana is a middling, unromantic place.

Paragraph 1

Narration and Character: Bill's judgments of Ruthie show that he prides himself on arguing about abstract ideas; that he thinks Ruthie must be stupid; that they didn't know each other well and aren't suited for a long trip together. Bill is from the unfriendly East Coast; Ruthie, from easy-going, dull "rural Ohio." *Style*: The casual language—"okay" and "etc."—sounds like Bill's voice, but he's not the narrator. The vague "etc." hints that Bill isn't really curious about her. The observation of cows sounds funny, childlike, even stupid. But why does he have to "chalk it up" or keep score?

Paragraph 2

Plot and Character: This is the first specific time given in the story, the "third evening": Ruthie surprises the reader and Bill with more than dull "observation."

Paragraph 4

Style, Character, Setting, and Tone: Dozing in the speeding car, Bill is too late to check out what she says. He frowns (he doesn't argue) because the plant and the bird can't be seen in the Midwest. Brewer uses a series of place names to indicate the route of the car. There's humor in Ruthie's habit of pointing out bizarre sights.

Paragraph 5

Character and Setting: Bigfoot is a legendary monster living in Western forests. Is Ruthie's imagination getting the better of Bill's logic? "Innocently" personifies the road, and the reflectors on the stump wink like the monster; Bill is finally looking (though in hindsight). The scenery seems to be playing a joke on him.

Paragraph 6

Plot and Character: Here the characters change places. He wants to drive (is she hallucinating?), but it's as if she has won. The narration (which has been relying on Bill's voice and perspective) for the first time notices a romantic detail of scenery that Ruthie doesn't point out (the evening star).

Paragraph 7

Character and Theme: Bill begins to see Ruthie and what she is capable of. What they see *is* the journey these characters take toward falling in love, in the West where things become unreal. *Style*: The long "o" sounds and images in "A white buffalo near Fargo. A UFO above Twin Falls" (along with the words Ohio, Chicago, and Spokane) give a feeling for the wildness (notice the Indian place names). The outcome of the story is that they *go far* to Fargo, see double and fall in love at Twin Falls—see and imagine wonderful things in each other. They end up with perfectly matched vision.

These notes could be organized and expanded into a response paper on the story. Some of your insights might even form the basis for a longer essay on one of the elements of the story.

You may approach any kind of narrative with the same kinds of questions that have been applied to "20/20." Try it on the following chapter of Marjane Satrapi's *Persepolis*. This bestselling graphic novel, or graphic memoir, originally written in French and now a successful film, relates Satrapi's own experience as a girl in Iran through her artwork and words. *Persepolis* begins with a portrait of ten-year-old Satrapi, wearing a black veil, in 1980. The Islamic leaders of Iran had recently imposed religious law, including mandatory head coverings for schoolgirls. On September 22, 1980, Iraq invaded Iran, beginning a conflict that lasted until 1988, greatly affecting Satrapi's childhood in Tehran (once known as Persepolis). The Iran-Iraq War was a precursor of the Persian Gulf War of 1990–91 and the ongoing Iraq War or Second Gulf War that began in 2003.

This excerpt resembles an illustrated short story, though it is understood to be closely based on actual events. How do the images and designs of the panels on each page contribute to expectations, narration (here, telling and showing), characterization, plot, setting, style, and themes? Read (and view) with these questions in mind and a pencil in hand. Annotating or taking notes will guide you to a more reflective response.

THE SHABBAT

TO KEEP US FROM FORGETTING THAT WE WERE AT WAR, IRAQ OPTED FOR A NEW STRATEGY...

I HEARD THEY'RE GOING TO USE BALLISTIC MISSILES AGAINST US.

WHAT ARE YOU SAYING? WE'RE NOT AT WAR WITH THE SOVIET UNION. I DON'T BELIEVE THE IRAQIS HAVE WEAPONS LIKE THAT.

FROM THE IRAQI BORDER TO TEHRAN IT'S THOUSANDS OF MILES. MISSILES THAT CAN GO THAT FAR COST A FORTUNE!

WELL, THAT'S WHAT THE RUMORS SAY!

WE IRANIANS ARE OLYMPIC CHAMPIONS WHEN IT COMES TO GOSSIP.

SHE'S RIGHT. WE LOVE TO EXAGGERATE.

YOU SEEM TO HAVE THE OPPOSITE SYMPTOM.

WHY DO YOU SAY THAT?

EVEN WHEN YOU SEE SOMETHING WITH YOUR OWN EYES, YOU NEED CONFIRMATION FROM THE BBC.

MY NATURAL OPTIMISM JUST LEADS ME TO BE SKEPTICAL.

Shabbat: Sabbath (Hebrew).

MOM'S PESSIMISM SOON WON OUT OVER DAD'S OPTIMISM. IT TURNED OUT THAT THE IRAQIS DID HAVE MISSILES. THEY WERE CALLED "SCUDS" AND TEHRAN BECAME THEIR TARGET.

WHEN THE SIRENS WENT ON, IT MEANT WE HAD THREE MINUTES TO KNOW IF THE END HAD COME.

WE'RE NOT GOING TO THE BASEMENT?

IT WOULDN'T MAKE ANY DIFFERENCE!!

CONSIDERING THE DAMAGE THEY DO, WHETHER WE'RE IN THE BASEMENT OR ON THE ROOF, IT'S THE SAME THING.

THE THREE MINUTES SEEMED LIKE THREE DAYS. FOR THE FIRST TIME, I REALIZED JUST HOW MUCH DANGER WE WERE IN.

BOOM!!

I DON'T WANT TO DIE!

YOU WON'T DEAR. I PROMISE YOU!

NOW THAT TEHRAN WAS UNDER ATTACK, MANY FLED. THE CITY WAS DESERTED. AS FOR US, WE STAYED. NOT JUST OUT OF FATALISM. IF THERE WAS TO BE A FUTURE, IN MY PARENTS' EYES, THAT FUTURE WAS LINKED TO MY FRENCH EDUCATION. AND TEHRAN WAS THE ONLY PLACE I COULD GET IT.

SOME PEOPLE, MORE CIRCUMSPECT, TOOK SHELTER IN THE BASEMENTS OF BIG HOTELS, WELL-KNOWN FOR THEIR SAFETY. APPARENTLY, THEIR REINFORCED CONCRETE STRUCTURES WERE BOMBPROOF.

ONE EXAMPLE WAS OUR NEIGHBORS, THE BABA-LEVYS. THEY WERE AMONG THE FEW JEWISH FAMILIES THAT HAD STAYED AFTER THE REVOLUTION. MR. BABA-LEVY SAID THEIR ANCESTORS HAD COME THREE THOUSAND YEARS AGO, AND IRAN WAS THEIR HOME.

...THEIR DAUGHTER NEDA WAS A QUIET GIRL WHO DIDN'T PLAY MUCH, BUT WE WOULD TALK ABOUT ROMANCE FROM TIME TO TIME.

...ONE DAY A BLOND PRINCE WITH BLUE EYES WILL COME AND TAKE ME TO HIS CASTLE...

OH YEAH! ME TOO!

SO LIFE WENT ON...

The Shah: The shah, or king, of Iran was deposed in 1979, the beginning of what was soon known as the Islamic Revolution under the leadership of Ayatollah Ruholla Khomeini (1900–89). An Ayatollah is a high-ranking cleric in the Shia branch of Islam, of which most Iranians are adherents.

FASTER! PLEASE HURRY...

A CROWD HAD GATHERED IN FRONT OF MY STREET! THE BOMB HAD HIT MY STREET!

MA'AM, WHICH BUILDING WAS HIT?

APPARENTLY, IT EXPLODED AT THE END OF THE STREET.

MY BUILDING AND THE BABA-LEVY'S WERE AT THE END OF THE STREET.

LET ME THROUGH.

ONE CHANCE IN TWO THAT IT WAS OUR BUILDING.

PLEASE, LET ME THROUGH.

YOU CAN'T GO BEYOND THIS POINT!

...I LIVE HERE...

AND HE LET ME THROUGH.

I DIDN'T WANT TO LOOK UP. I LOOKED AT MY TREMBLING LEGS. I COULDN'T GO FORWARD, LIKE IN A NIGHTMARE.

LET THEM BE ALIVE. LET THEM BE ALIVE. LET THEM...

MARJI

MARJI!

MOM!

YOU'RE ALL RIGHT? DAD'S ALL RIGHT? GRANDMA'S ALL RIGHT?

EVERYONE'S OK. I WAS THE ONLY ONE HOME.

OH, MOM.

...

WHERE DID IT HIT?

THE BABA-LEVY'S HOUSE.

AT LEAST THEY WEREN'T HOME!

...

MOM, THEY WEREN'T, RIGHT?

WELL, I DON'T KNOW. IT'S SATURDAY, YOU KNOW.

I KNOW IT'S SATURDAY. SO?

SATURDAY IS THE JEWISH SABBATH. WHEREVER THEY ARE, JEWS ARE SUPPOSED TO GO HOME.

...YOU THINK THAT...?

IT'S TRUE THAT THEY WEREN'T VERY OBSERVANT. I THINK YOU'RE RIGHT. THEY MUST HAVE STAYED AT THE HILTON.

YOU KNOW THE TAPE I PUT ON THE WINDOWS? IT WORKED PERFECTLY. ALL THE WINDOWS ARE BROKEN, BUT THERE'S NOT A PIECE OF BROKEN GLASS IN THE HOUSE!

I COULD TELL THAT MY MOTHER WAS TRYING TO CHANGE THE SUBJECT.

WHEN WE WALKED PAST THE BABA-LEVY'S HOUSE, WHICH WAS COMPLETELY DESTROYED, I COULD FEEL THAT SHE WAS DISCREETLY PULLING ME AWAY. SOMETHING TOLD ME THAT THE BABA-LEVYS HAD BEEN AT HOME. SOMETHING CAUGHT MY ATTENTION.

I SAW A TURQUOISE BRACELET. IT WAS NEDA'S. HER AUNT HAD GIVEN IT TO HER FOR HER FOURTEENTH BIRTHDAY...

THE BRACELET WAS STILL ATTACHED TO... I DON'T KNOW WHAT...

NO SCREAM IN THE WORLD COULD HAVE RELIEVED MY SUFFERING AND MY ANGER.

WRITING ABOUT FICTION

During your first reading of any story, you may want to read without stopping to address each of the questions on page 15. After you have read the whole piece once, re-read it carefully, using the questions as a guide. It's always interesting to compare your initial reactions with your later ones. In fact, a paper may focus on comparing the expectations of readers (and characters) at the beginning of a story and at the end. Responses to fiction may come in unpredictable order, so feel free to address the questions as they arise. Looking at how the story is told and what happens to which characters may lead to observations on expectations or setting. Consideration of setting and style can help explain the personalities, actions, mood, and effect of the story, which can lead to well-informed ideas about the meaning of the whole. But any one of the questions, pursued further, can serve as the focus of more formal writing.

Below are some examples of written responses to Raymond Carver's short story "Cathedral." First, read the story and make notes on any features that you find interesting, important, or confusing. Then look at the notes and response paper by Wesley Rupton and the essay by Bethany Qualls, which show two different ways of writing about "Cathedral."

RAYMOND CARVER

Cathedral

This blind man, an old friend of my wife's, he was on his way to spend the night. His wife had died. So he was visiting the dead wife's relatives in Connecticut. He called my wife from his in-laws'. Arrangements were made. He would come by train, a five-hour trip, and my wife would meet him at the station. She hadn't seen him since she worked for him one summer in Seattle ten years ago. But she and the blind man had kept in touch. They made tapes and mailed them back and forth. I wasn't enthusiastic about his visit. He was no one I knew. And his being blind bothered me. My idea of blindness came from the movies. In the movies, the blind moved slowly and never laughed. Sometimes they were led by seeing-eye dogs. A blind man in my house was not something I looked forward to.

That summer in Seattle she had needed a job. She didn't have any money. The man she was going to marry at the end of the summer was in officers' training school. He didn't have any money, either. But she was in love with the guy, and he was in love with her, etc. She'd seen something in the paper: HELP WANTED—*Reading to Blind Man,* and a telephone number. She phoned and went over, was hired on the spot. She'd worked with this blind man all summer. She read stuff to him, case studies, reports, that sort of thing. She helped him organize his little office in the county social-service department. They'd become good friends, my wife and the blind man. How do I know these things? She told me. And she told me something else. On her last day in the office, the blind man asked if he could touch her face. She agreed to this. She told me he touched his fingers to every part of her face, her nose—even her neck! She never forgot it. She even tried to write a poem about it. She was always trying to write a poem. She wrote a poem or two every year, usually after something really important had happened to her.

When we first started going out together, she showed me the poem. In the poem, she recalled his fingers and the way they had moved around over her face. In the poem, she talked about what she had felt at the time, about what went through her mind when the blind man touched her nose and lips. I can remember I didn't think much of the poem. Of course, I didn't tell her that. Maybe I just don't understand poetry. I admit it's not the first thing I reach for when I pick up something to read.

Anyway, this man who'd first enjoyed her favors, the officer-to-be, he'd been her childhood sweetheart. So okay. I'm saying that at the end of the summer she let the blind man run his hands over her face, said goodbye to him, married her childhood etc., who was now a commissioned officer, and she moved away from Seattle. But they'd kept in touch, she and the blind man. She made the first contact after a year or so. She called him up one night from an Air Force base in Alabama. She wanted to talk. They talked. He asked her to send him a tape and tell him about her life. She did this. She sent the tape. On the tape, she told the blind man about her husband and about their life together in the military. She told the blind man she loved her husband but she didn't like it where they lived and she didn't like it that he was a part of the military-industrial thing. She told the blind man she'd written a poem and he was in it. She told him that she was writing a poem about what it was like to be an Air Force officer's wife. The poem wasn't finished yet. She was still writing it. The blind man made a tape. He sent her the tape. She made a tape. This went on for years. My wife's officer was posted to one base and then another. She sent tapes from Moody AFB, McGuire, McConnell, and finally Travis, near Sacramento, where one night she got to feeling lonely and cut off from people she kept losing in that moving-around life. She got to feeling she couldn't go it another step. She went in and swallowed all the pills and capsules in the medicine chest and washed them down with a bottle of gin. Then she got into a hot bath and passed out.

But instead of dying, she got sick. She threw up. Her officer—why should he have a name? he was the childhood sweetheart, and what more does he want?— came home from somewhere, found her, and called the ambulance. In time, she put it all on a tape and sent the tape to the blind man. Over the years, she put all kinds of stuff on tapes and sent the tapes off lickety-split. Next to writing a poem every year, I think it was her chief means of recreation. On one tape, she told the blind man she'd decided to live away from her officer for a time. On another tape, she told him about her divorce. She and I began going out, and of course she told her blind man about it. She told him everything, or so it seemed to me. Once she asked me if I'd like to hear the latest tape from the blind man. This was a year ago. I was on the tape, she said. So I said okay, I'd listen to it. I got us drinks and we settled down in the living room. We made ready to listen. First she inserted the tape into the player and adjusted a couple of dials. Then she pushed a lever. The tape squeaked and someone began to talk in this loud voice. She lowered the volume. After a few minutes of harmless chitchat, I heard my own name in the mouth of this stranger, this blind man I didn't even know! And then this: "From all you've said about him, I can only conclude—" But we were interrupted, a knock at the door, something, and we didn't ever get back to the tape. Maybe it was just as well. I'd heard all I wanted to.

5

Now this same blind man was coming to sleep in my house.

"Maybe I could take him bowling," I said to my wife. She was at the draining board doing scalloped potatoes. She put down the knife she was using and turned around.

"If you love me," she said, "you can do this for me. If you don't love me, okay. But if you had a friend, any friend, and the friend came to visit, I'd make him feel comfortable." She wiped her hands with the dish towel.

"I don't have any blind friends," I said.

10   "You don't have *any* friends," she said. "Period. Besides," she said, "goddamn it, his wife's just died! Don't you understand that? The man's lost his wife!"

I didn't answer. She'd told me a little about the blind man's wife. Her name was Beulah. Beulah! That's a name for a colored woman.

"Was his wife a Negro?" I asked.

"Are you crazy?" my wife said. "Have you just flipped or something?" She picked up a potato. I saw it hit the floor, then roll under the stove. "What's wrong with you?" she said. "Are you drunk?"

"I'm just asking," I said.

15   Right then my wife filled me in with more detail than I cared to know. I made a drink and sat at the kitchen table to listen. Pieces of the story began to fall into place.

Beulah had gone to work for the blind man the summer after my wife had stopped working for him. Pretty soon Beulah and the blind man had themselves a church wedding. It was a little wedding—who'd want to go to such a wedding in the first place?—just the two of them, plus the minister and the minister's wife. But it was a church wedding just the same. It was what Beulah had wanted, he'd said. But even then Beulah must have been carrying the cancer in her glands. After they had been inseparable for eight years—my wife's word, *inseparable*—Beulah's health went into a rapid decline. She died in a Seattle hospital room, the blind man sitting beside the bed and holding on to her hand. They'd married, lived and worked together, slept together—had sex, sure—and then the blind man had to bury her. All this without his having ever seen what the goddamned woman looked like. It was beyond my understanding. Hearing this, I felt sorry for the blind man for a little bit. And then I found myself thinking what a pitiful life this woman must have led. Imagine a woman who could never see herself as she was seen in the eyes of her loved one. A woman who could go on day after day and never receive the smallest compliment from her beloved. A woman whose husband could never read the expression on her face, be it misery or something better. Someone who could wear makeup or not—what difference to him? She could, if she wanted, wear green eye-shadow around one eye, a straight pin in her nostril, yellow slacks and purple shoes, no matter. And then to slip off into death, the blind man's hand on her hand, his blind eyes streaming tears—I'm imagining now—her last thought maybe this: that he never even knew what she looked like, and she on an express to the grave. Robert was left with a small insurance policy and half of a twenty-peso Mexican coin. The other half of the coin went into the box with her. Pathetic.

So when the time rolled around, my wife went to the depot to pick him up. With nothing to do but wait—sure, I blamed him for that—I was having a drink and watching the TV when I heard the car pull into the drive. I got up from the sofa with my drink and went to the window to have a look.

I saw my wife laughing as she parked the car. I saw her get out of the car and shut the door. She was still wearing a smile. Just amazing. She went around to the other side of the car to where the blind man was already starting to get out. This blind man, feature this, he was wearing a full beard! A beard on a blind man! Too much, I say. The blind man reached into the back seat and dragged out a suitcase. My wife took his arm, shut the car door, and, talking all the way, moved him down the drive and then up the steps to the front porch. I turned off the TV. I finished my drink, rinsed the glass, dried my hands. Then I went to the door.

My wife said, "I want you to meet Robert. Robert, this is my husband. I've told you all about him." She was beaming. She had this blind man by his coat sleeve.

The blind man let go of his suitcase and up came his hand.

20

I took it. He squeezed hard, held my hand, and then he let it go.

"I feel like we've already met," he boomed.

"Likewise," I said. I didn't know what else to say. Then I said, "Welcome. I've heard a lot about you." We began to move then, a little group, from the porch into the living room, my wife guiding him by the arm. The blind man was carrying his suitcase in his other hand. My wife said things like, "To your left here, Robert. That's right. Now watch it, there's a chair. That's it. Sit down right here. This is the sofa. We just bought this sofa two weeks ago."

I started to say something about the old sofa. I'd liked that old sofa. But I didn't say anything. Then I wanted to say something else, small-talk, about the scenic ride along the Hudson. How going *to* New York, you should sit on the right-hand side of the train, and coming *from* New York, the left-hand side.

"Did you have a good train ride?" I said. "Which side of the train did you sit on, by the way?"

25

"What a question, which side!" my wife said. "What's it matter which side?" she said.

"I just asked," I said.

"Right side," the blind man said. "I hadn't been on a train in nearly forty years. Not since I was a kid. With my folks. That's been a long time. I'd nearly forgotten the sensation. I have winter in my beard now," he said. "So I've been told, anyway. Do I look distinguished, my dear?" the blind man said to my wife.

"You look distinguished, Robert," she said. "Robert," she said. "Robert, it's just so good to see you."

My wife finally took her eyes off the blind man and looked at me. I had the feeling she didn't like what she saw. I shrugged.

30

I've never met, or personally known, anyone who was blind. This blind man was late forties, a heavy-set, balding man with stooped shoulders, as if he carried a great weight there. He wore brown slacks, brown shoes, a light-brown shirt, a tie, a sports coat. Spiffy. He also had this full beard. But he didn't use a cane and he didn't wear dark glasses. I'd always thought dark glasses were a must for the blind. Fact was, I wished he had a pair. At first glance, his eyes looked like anyone else's eyes. But if you looked close, there was something different about them. Too much white in the iris, for one thing, and the pupils seemed to move around in the sockets without his knowing it or being able to stop it. Creepy. As I stared at his face, I saw the left pupil turn in toward his nose while the other made an effort to keep in one place. But it was only an effort, for that eye was on the roam without his knowing it or wanting it to be.

I said, "Let me get you a drink. What's your pleasure? We have a little of everything. It's one of our pastimes."

"Bub, I'm a Scotch man myself," he said fast enough in this big voice.

"Right," I said. Bub! "Sure you are. I knew it."

35 He let his fingers touch his suitcase, which was sitting alongside the sofa. He was taking his bearings. I didn't blame him for that.

"I'll move that up to your room," my wife said.

"No, that's fine," the blind man said loudly. "It can go up when I go up."

"A little water with the Scotch?" I said.

"Very little," he said.

40 "I knew it," I said.

He said, "Just a tad. The Irish actor, Barry Fitzgerald? I'm like that fellow. When I drink water, Fitzgerald said, I drink water. When I drink whiskey, I drink whiskey." My wife laughed. The blind man brought his hand up under his beard. He lifted his beard slowly and let it drop.

I did the drinks, three big glasses of Scotch with a splash of water in each. Then we made ourselves comfortable and talked about Robert's travels. First the long flight from the West Coast to Connecticut, we covered that. Then from Connecticut up here by train. We had another drink concerning that leg of the trip.

I remembered having read somewhere that the blind didn't smoke because, as speculation had it, they couldn't see the smoke they exhaled. I thought I knew that much and that much only about blind people. But this blind man smoked his cigarette down to the nubbin and then lit another one. This blind man filled his ashtray and my wife emptied it.

When we sat down at the table for dinner, we had another drink. My wife heaped Robert's plate with cube steak, scalloped potatoes, green beans. I buttered him up two slices of bread. I said, "Here's bread and butter for you." I swallowed some of my drink. "Now let us pray," I said, and the blind man lowered his head. My wife looked at me, her mouth agape. "Pray the phone won't ring and the food doesn't get cold," I said.

45 We dug in. We ate everything there was to eat on the table. We ate like there was no tomorrow. We didn't talk. We ate. We scarfed. We grazed that table. We were into serious eating. The blind man had right away located his foods, he knew just where everything was on his plate. I watched with admiration as he used his knife and fork on the meat. He'd cut two pieces of meat, fork the meat into his mouth, and then go all out for the scalloped potatoes, the beans next, and then he'd tear off a hunk of buttered bread and eat that. He'd follow this up with a big drink of milk. It didn't seem to bother him to use his fingers once in a while, either.

We finished everything, including half a strawberry pie. For a few moments, we sat as if stunned. Sweat beaded on our faces. Finally, we got up from the table and left the dirty plates. We didn't look back. We took ourselves into the living room and sank into our places again. Robert and my wife sat on the sofa. I took the big chair. We had us two or three more drinks while they talked about the major things that had come to pass for them in the past ten years. For the most part, I just listened. Now and then I joined in. I didn't want him to think I'd left the room, and I didn't want her to think I was feeling left out. They talked of things that had happened to them—to them!—these past ten years. I waited in vain to hear my name on my wife's sweet lips: "And then my dear husband came into my life"—something like that. But I heard nothing of the sort. More talk of Robert. Robert had done a little of everything, it seemed, a regular blind jack-of-all-trades. But most recently he and his wife had had an Amway distributorship, from which, I gathered, they'd earned their living, such as it was. The blind man was also a ham radio operator. He talked in his loud voice about conversations he'd had with fellow operators in Guam, in the Philippines, in Alaska, and even in Tahiti. He said he'd have a lot of friends there if he ever wanted to go visit those places. From time to time, he'd turn his blind face toward me, put his hand under his beard, ask me something. How long had I been in my present position? (Three years.) Did I like my work? (I didn't.) Was I going to stay with it? (What were the options?) Finally, when I thought he was beginning to run down, I got up and turned on the TV.

My wife looked at me with irritation. She was heading toward a boil. Then she looked at the blind man and said, "Robert, do you have a TV?"

The blind man said, "My dear, I have two TVs. I have a color set and a black-and-white thing, an old relic. It's funny, but if I turn the TV on, and I'm always turning it on, I turn on the color set. It's funny, don't you think?"

I didn't know what to say to that. I had absolutely nothing to say to that. No opinion. So I watched the news program and tried to listen to what the announcer was saying.

"This is a color TV," the blind man said. "Don't ask me how, but I can tell."   50

"We traded up a while ago," I said.

The blind man had another taste of his drink. He lifted his beard, sniffed it, and let it fall. He leaned forward on the sofa. He positioned his ashtray on the coffee table, then put the lighter to his cigarette. He leaned back on the sofa and crossed his legs at the ankles.

My wife covered her mouth, and then she yawned. She stretched. She said, "I think I'll go upstairs and put on my robe. I think I'll change into something else. Robert, you make yourself comfortable," she said.

"I'm comfortable," the blind man said.

"I want you to feel comfortable in this house," she said.   55

"I am comfortable," the blind man said.

After she'd left the room, he and I listened to the weather report and then to the sports roundup. By that time, she'd been gone so long I didn't know if she was going to come back. I thought she might have gone to bed. I wished she'd come back downstairs. I didn't want to be left alone with a blind man. I asked him if he wanted another drink, and he said sure. Then I asked if he wanted to smoke some dope with me. I said I'd just rolled a number. I hadn't, but I planned to do so in about two shakes.

"I'll try some with you," he said.

"Damn right," I said. "That's the stuff."

I got our drinks and sat down on the sofa with him. Then I rolled us two fat   60
numbers. I lit one and passed it. I brought it to his fingers. He took it and inhaled.

"Hold it as long as you can," I said. I could tell he didn't know the first thing.

My wife came back downstairs wearing her pink robe and her pink slippers.

"What do I smell?" she said.

"We thought we'd have us some cannabis," I said.

My wife gave me a savage look. Then she looked at the blind man and said,   65
"Robert, I didn't know you smoked."

He said, "I do now, my dear. There's a first time for everything. But I don't feel anything yet."

"This stuff is pretty mellow," I said. "This stuff is mild. It's dope you can rea- son with," I said. "It doesn't mess you up."

"Not much it doesn't, bub," he said, and laughed.

My wife sat on the sofa between the blind man and me. I passed her the num- ber. She took it and toked and then passed it back to me. "Which way is this going?" she said. Then she said, "I shouldn't be smoking this. I can hardly keep my eyes open as it is. That dinner did me in. I shouldn't have eaten so much."

70   "It was the strawberry pie," the blind man said. "That's what did it," he said, and he laughed his big laugh. Then he shook his head.

"There's more strawberry pie," I said.

"Do you want some more, Robert?" my wife said.

"Maybe in a little while," he said.

We gave our attention to the TV. My wife yawned again. She said, "Your bed is made up when you feel like going to bed, Robert. I know you must have had a long day. When you're ready to go to bed, say so." She pulled his arm. "Robert?"

75   He came to and said, "I've had a real nice time. This beats tapes, doesn't it?"

I said, "Coming at you," and I put the number between his fingers. He inhaled, held the smoke, and then let it go. It was like he'd been doing it since he was nine years old.

"Thanks, bub," he said. "But I think this is all for me. I think I'm beginning to feel it," he said. He held the burning roach out for my wife.

"Same here," she said. "Ditto. Me, too." She took the roach and passed it to me. "I may just sit here for a while between you two guys with my eyes closed. But don't let me bother you, okay? Either one of you. If it bothers you, say so. Otherwise, I may just sit here with my eyes closed until you're ready to go to bed," she said. "Your bed's made up, Robert, when you're ready. It's right next to our room at the top of the stairs. We'll show you up when you're ready. You wake me up now, you guys, if I fall asleep." She said that and then she closed her eyes and went to sleep.

The news program ended. I got up and changed the channel. I sat back down on the sofa. I wished my wife hadn't pooped out. Her head lay across the back of the sofa, her mouth open. She'd turned so that her robe had slipped away from her legs, exposing a juicy thigh. I reached to draw her robe back over her, and it was then that I glanced at the blind man. What the hell! I flipped the robe open again.

80   "You say when you want some strawberry pie," I said.

"I will," he said.

I said, "Are you tired? Do you want me to take you up to your bed? Are you ready to hit the hay?"

"Not yet," he said. "No, I'll stay up with you, bub. If that's all right. I'll stay up until you're ready to turn in. We haven't had a chance to talk. Know what I mean? I feel like me and her monopolized the evening." He lifted his beard and he let it fall. He picked up his cigarettes and his lighter.

"That's all right," I said. Then I said, "I'm glad for the company."

85   And I guess I was. Every night I smoked dope and stayed up as long as I could before I fell asleep. My wife and I hardly ever went to bed at the same time. When I did go to sleep, I had these dreams. Sometimes I'd wake up from one of them, my heart going crazy.

Something about the church and the Middle Ages was on the TV. Not your run-of-the-mill TV fare. I wanted to watch something else. I turned to the other channels. But there was nothing on them, either. So I turned back to the first channel and apologized.

"Bub, it's all right," the blind man said. "It's fine with me. Whatever you want to watch is okay. I'm always learning something. Learning never ends. It won't hurt me to learn something tonight. I got ears," he said.

We didn't say anything for a time. He was leaning forward with his head turned at me, his right ear aimed in the direction of the set. Very disconcerting. Now and then his eyelids drooped and then they snapped open again. Now and then he put his fingers into his beard and tugged, like he was thinking about something he was hearing on the television.

On the screen, a group of men wearing cowls was being set upon and tormented by men dressed in skeleton costumes and men dressed as devils. The men dressed as devils wore devil masks, horns, and long tails. This pageant was part of a procession. The Englishman who was narrating the thing said it took place in Spain once a year. I tried to explain to the blind man what was happening.

"Skeletons," he said. "I know about skeletons," he said, and he nodded.

The TV showed this one cathedral. Then there was a long, slow look at another one. Finally, the picture switched to the famous one in Paris, with its flying buttresses and its spires reaching up to the clouds. The camera pulled away to show the whole of the cathedral rising above the skyline.

There were times when the Englishman who was telling the thing would shut up, would simply let the camera move around over the cathedrals. Or else the camera would tour the countryside, men in fields walking behind oxen. I waited as long as I could. Then I felt I had to say something. I said, "They're showing the outside of this cathedral now. Gargoyles. Little statues carved to look like monsters. Now I guess they're in Italy. Yeah, they're in Italy. There's paintings on the walls of this one church."

"Are those fresco paintings, bub?" he asked, and he sipped from his drink.

I reached for my glass. But it was empty. I tried to remember what I could remember. "You're asking me are those frescoes?" I said. "That's a good question. I don't know."

The camera moved to a cathedral outside Lisbon. The differences in the Portuguese cathedral compared with the French and Italian were not that great. But they were there. Mostly the interior stuff. Then something occurred to me, and I said, "Something has occurred to me. Do you have any idea what a cathedral is? What they look like, that is? Do you follow me? If somebody says cathedral to you, do you have any notion what they're talking about? Do you know the difference between that and a Baptist church, say?"

He let the smoke dribble from his mouth. "I know they took hundreds of workers fifty or a hundred years to build," he said. "I just heard the man say that, of course. I know generations of the same families worked on a cathedral. I heard him say that, too. The men who began their life's work on them, they never lived to see the completion of their work. In that wise, bub, they're no different from the rest of us, right?" He laughed. Then his eyelids drooped again. His head nodded. He seemed to be snoozing. Maybe he was imagining himself in Portugal. The TV was showing another cathedral now. This one was in Germany. The Englishman's voice droned on. "Cathedrals," the blind man said. He sat up and rolled his head back and forth. "If you want the truth, bub, that's about all I know. What I just said. What I heard him say. But maybe you could describe one to me? I wish you'd do it. I'd like that. If you want to know, I really don't have a good idea."

90

95

I stared hard at the shot of the cathedral on the TV. How could I even begin to describe it? But say my life depended on it. Say my life was being threatened by an insane guy who said I had to do it or else.

I stared some more at the cathedral before the picture flipped off into the countryside. There was no use. I turned to the blind man and said, "To begin with, they're very tall." I was looking around the room for clues. "They reach way up. Up and up. Toward the sky. They're so big, some of them, they have to have these supports. To help hold them up, so to speak. These supports are called buttresses. They remind me of viaducts, for some reason. But maybe you don't know viaducts, either? Sometimes the cathedrals have devils and such carved into the front. Sometimes lords and ladies. Don't ask me why this is," I said.

He was nodding. The whole upper part of his body seemed to be moving back and forth.

100   "I'm not doing so good, am I?" I said.

He stopped nodding and leaned forward on the edge of the sofa. As he listened to me, he was running his fingers through his beard. I wasn't getting through to him, I could see that. But he waited for me to go on just the same. He nodded, like he was trying to encourage me. I tried to think what else to say. "They're really big," I said. "They're massive. They're built of stone. Marble, too, sometimes. In those olden days, when they built cathedrals, men wanted to be close to God. In those olden days, God was an important part of everyone's life. You could tell this from their cathedral-building. I'm sorry," I said, "but it looks like that's the best I can do for you. I'm just no good at it."

"That's all right, bub," the blind man said. "Hey, listen. I hope you don't mind my asking you. Can I ask you something? Let me ask you a simple question, yes or no. I'm just curious and there's no offense. You're my host. But let me ask if you are in any way religious? You don't mind my asking?"

I shook my head. He couldn't see that, though. A wink is the same as a nod to a blind man. "I guess I don't believe in it. In anything. Sometimes it's hard. You know what I'm saying?"

"Sure, I do," he said.

105   "Right," I said.

The Englishman was still holding forth. My wife sighed in her sleep. She drew a long breath and went on with her sleeping.

"You'll have to forgive me," I said. "But I can't tell you what a cathedral looks like. It just isn't in me to do it. I can't do any more than I've done."

The blind man sat very still, his head down, as he listened to me.

I said, "The truth is, cathedrals don't mean anything special to me. Nothing. Cathedrals. They're something to look at on late-night TV. That's all they are."

110   It was then that the blind man cleared his throat. He brought something up. He took a handkerchief from his back pocket. Then he said, "I get it, bub. It's okay. It happens. Don't worry about it," he said. "Hey, listen to me. Will you do me a favor? I got an idea. Why don't you find us some heavy paper? And a pen. We'll do something. We'll draw one together. Get us a pen and some heavy paper. Go on, bub, get the stuff," he said.

So I went upstairs. My legs felt like they didn't have any strength in them. They felt like they did after I'd done some running. In my wife's room, I looked around. I found some ballpoints in a little basket on her table. And then I tried to think where to look for the kind of paper he was talking about.

Downstairs, in the kitchen, I found a shopping bag with onion skins in the bottom of the bag. I emptied the bag and shook it. I brought it into the living room and sat down with it near his legs. I moved some things, smoothed the wrinkles from the bag, spread it out on the coffee table.

The blind man got down from the sofa and sat next to me on the carpet.

He ran his fingers over the paper. He went up and down the sides of the paper. The edges, even the edges. He fingered the corners.

"All right," he said. "All right, let's do her."

He found my hand, the hand with the pen. He closed his hand over my hand. "Go ahead, bub, draw," he said. "Draw. You'll see. I'll follow along with you. It'll be okay. Just begin now like I'm telling you. You'll see. Draw," the blind man said.

So I began. First I drew a box that looked like a house. It could have been the house I lived in. Then I put a roof on it. At either end of the roof, I drew spires. Crazy.

"Swell," he said. "Terrific. You're doing fine," he said. "Never thought anything like this could happen in your lifetime, did you, bub? Well, it's a strange life, we all know that. Go on now. Keep it up."

I put in windows with arches. I drew flying buttresses. I hung great doors. I couldn't stop. The TV station went off the air. I put down the pen and closed and opened my fingers. The blind man felt around over the paper. He moved the tips of his fingers over the paper, all over what I had drawn, and he nodded.

"Doing fine," the blind man said.

I took up the pen again, and he found my hand. I kept at it. I'm no artist. But I kept drawing just the same.

My wife opened up her eyes and gazed at us. She sat up on the sofa, her robe hanging open. She said, "What are you doing? Tell me, I want to know."

I didn't answer her.

The blind man said, "We're drawing a cathedral. Me and him are working on it. Press hard," he said to me. "That's right. That's good," he said. "Sure. You got it, bub. I can tell. You didn't think you could. But you can, can't you? You're cooking with gas now. You know what I'm saying? We're going to really have us something here in a minute. How's the old arm?" he said. "Put some people in there now. What's a cathedral without people?"

My wife said, "What's going on? Robert, what are you doing? What's going on?"

"It's all right," he said to her. "Close your eyes now," the blind man said to me.

I did it. I closed them just like he said.

"Are they closed?" he said. "Don't fudge."

"They're closed," I said.

"Keep them that way," he said. He said, "Don't stop now. Draw."

So we kept on with it. His fingers rode my fingers as my hand went over the paper. It was like nothing else in my life up to now.

Then he said, "I think that's it. I think you got it," he said. "Take a look. What do you think?"

But I had my eyes closed. I thought I'd keep them that way for a little longer. I thought it was something I ought to do.

"Well?" he said. "Are you looking?"

My eyes were still closed. I was in my house. I knew that. But I didn't feel like I was inside anything.

"It's really something," I said.

1983

SAMPLE WRITING: NOTES AND RESPONSE PAPER

Wesley Rupton wrote the notes below in response to the questions on page 15. As you read these notes, compare them to the notes you took as you read "Cathedral." Do Rupton's notes reveal anything to you that you didn't notice while reading the story? Did you notice anything he did not, or do you disagree with any of his interpretations?

Notes on Raymond Carver's "Cathedral"

What do you expect?
- Title: The first words are "this blind man," and those words keep being repeated. Why not call it "The Blind Man" or "The Blind Man's Visit"?
- The threatening things the husband says made me expect that he would attack the blind man. I thought the wife might leave her husband for the blind man, who has been nicer to her.
- When they talk about going up to bed, and the wife goes to "get comfortable" and then falls asleep, I thought there was a hint about sex.

What happens in the story?
- Not that much. It is a story about one evening in which a husband and wife and their guest drink, have dinner, talk, and then watch TV.
- These people have probably drunk two bottles of hard liquor (how many drinks?) before, during, and after a meal. And then they smoke marijuana.
- In the final scene, the two men try to describe and draw cathedrals that are on the TV show. Why cathedrals? Though it connects with the title.
- The husband seems to have a different attitude at the end: He likes Robert and seems excited about the experience "like nothing else in my life up to now."

How is the story narrated?
- It's told in first person and past tense. The husband is the narrator. We never get inside another character's thoughts. He seems to be telling someone about the incident, first saying the blind man was coming, and then filling in the background about his wife and the blind man, and then telling what happens after the guest arrives.
- The narrator describes people and scenes and summarizes the past; there is dialogue.
- It doesn't have episodes or chapters, but there are two gaps on the page, before paragraph 57 and before paragraph 88. Maybe time passes here.

Who are the characters?

- Three main characters: husband, wife, and blind man (the blind man's own wife has just died, and the wife divorced her first husband). I don't think we ever know the husband's or wife's names. The blind man, Robert, calls him "Bub," like "buddy." They seem to be white, middle-class Americans. The wife is lonely and looking for meaning. The blind man seems sensitive, and he cares about the poetry and tapes.
- The husband is sort of acting out, though mostly in his own mind. Asking "Was his wife a Negro?" sounds like he wants to make fun of black or blind people. His wife asks, "Are you drunk?" and says that he has no friends; I thought he's an unhappy man who gets drunk and acts "crazy" a lot and that she doesn't really expect him to be that nice.
- It sounds like these people have plenty of food and things, but aren't very happy. They all sound smart, but the narrator is ignorant and he has no religion. All three characters have some bad or nervous habits (alcohol, cigarettes, drugs; insomnia; suicide attempt; divorce).

What is the setting and time of the story?

- Mostly in the house the evening the blind man arrives. But after the intro there's a kind of flashback to the summer in Seattle ten years ago (par. 2). The story about the visit starts again in paragraph 6, and then the wife tells the husband more about the blind man's marriage—another flashback in paragraph 16. In paragraph 17, "the time rolled around" to the story's main event. After that, it's chronological.
- We don't know the name of the town, but it seems to be on the U.S. East Coast (five hours by train from Connecticut [par. 1]). It can't be too long ago or too recent either: They mention trains, audio tapes, color TV, no Internet. No one seems worried about food or health the way they might be today.
- I noticed that travel came up in the story. Part of what drives the wife crazy about her first husband is moving around to different military bases (par. 4). In paragraph 46, Robert tells us about his contact with ham radio operators in places he would like to visit (Guam, Alaska). The TV show takes Robert and the narrator on a tour of France, Italy, and Portugal.

What do you notice about how the story is written?

- The narrator is irritating. He repeats words a lot. He uses stereotypes. He seems to be informally talking to someone, as if he can't get over it. But then he sometimes uses exaggerated or bored-sounding phrases, "this man who'd first enjoyed her favors," "So okay. I'm saying . . . married her childhood etc." (par. 4). His style is almost funny.
- Things he repeats: Paragraphs 2 and 3: "She told me" (3 times), "he could touch her face . . . he touched his fingers to every part of her face . . ." (and later "touched her nose" and "they'd kept in touch"). "She even tried to write a poem . . . always trying to write a poem" (and 4 more times "poem"). The words "talk," "tape," "told" are also repeated.

> **What does the story mean? Can you express its theme or themes?**
> - The way the narrator learns to get along with the blind man must be important. The narrator is disgusted by blind people at first, and at the end he closes his eyes on purpose.
> - I think it makes a difference that the two men imagine and try to draw a cathedral, not a flower or an airplane. It's something made by human beings, and it's religious. As they mention, the builders of cathedrals don't live to see them finished, but the buildings last for centuries. It's not like the narrator is saved or becomes a great guy, but he gets past whatever he's afraid of at night and he seems inspired for a little while. I don't know why the wife has to be left out of this, but probably the husband couldn't open up if he was worrying about how close she is to Robert.

Now read the following brief paper responding to Raymond Carver's "Cathedral." A response paper may use a less formal organization and style than a longer, more analytical essay, but it should not just be a summary or complete description of the work. Indeed, a response paper could be a step on the way to a longer essay. You need not form a single thesis or argument, but you should try to develop your ideas and feelings about the story through your writing. The point is to get your thoughts in writing without worrying too much about form and style.

Almost everything in the following response paper comes directly from the notes, but notice how the writer has combined observations, adding a few direct quotations or details from the text to support claims about the effects and meaning of the story. Also notice that the writer cites the details from the text by referring to paragraph numbers. Some teachers may ask students to cite the text with page numbers.

Wesley Rupton
Professor Suarez
English 170

Response Paper on Raymond Carver's "Cathedral"

Not much happens in Raymond Carver's short story "Cathedral," and at first I wondered what it was about and why it was called "Cathedral." The narrator, the unnamed husband, seems to be telling someone about the evening that Robert, a blind friend of his wife, came to stay at their house, not long after Robert's own wife has died. After the narrator fills us in about his wife's first marriage and her relationship with the blind man, he describes what the three characters do that evening: they drink a lot of alcohol, eat a huge dinner that leaves them "stunned" (par. 46), smoke marijuana, and after the wife falls asleep the two men watch TV. A show about cathedrals leads the husband to try to describe what a cathedral looks like, and then the men try to draw one together. The husband seems to have a different attitude at the end: he likes Robert and seems excited about an experience "like nothing else in my life up to now" (par. 131).

The husband's way of telling the story is definitely important. He is sort of funny, but also irritating. As he makes jokes about stereotypes, you start to dislike or distrust him. When he hears about Robert's wife, Beulah, he asks, "Was his wife a Negro?" (par. 12) just because her name sounds like a black woman's name to him. In three paragraphs, he flashes back to the time ten years ago when his wife was the blind man's assistant and the blind man

> asked if he could touch her face. . . . She told me he touched his fingers to every part of her face. . . . She even tried to write a poem about it. . . . In the poem, she recalled his fingers . . . over her face. In the poem, she talked about what she had felt . . . when the blind man touched her nose and lips. (pars. 2, 3)

The narrator seems to be going over and over the same creepy idea of a man feeling his wife's face. It seems to disgust him that his wife and the blind man communicated or expressed themselves, perhaps because he seems incapable of doing so. When his wife asks, "Are you drunk?" and says that he has no friends, I got a feeling that the husband is an unhappy man who gets drunk and acts "crazy" a lot and that his wife doesn't really expect him to be very nice (pars. 8-13). He's going to make fun of their guest (asking a blind man to go bowling). The husband is sort of acting out, though he's mostly rude in his own mind.

There's nothing heroic or dramatic or even unusual about these people (except that one is blind). The events take place in a house somewhere in an American suburb and not too long ago. Other than the quantity of alcohol and drugs they consume, these people don't do anything unusual, though the blind man seems strange to the narrator. The ordinary setting and plot make the idea of something as grand and old as a European cathedral come as a surprise at the end of the story. I wondered if part of the point is that they desperately want to get out of a trap they're in. I noticed that travel came up in the story. Part of what drove the wife crazy with her first husband was moving around to different military bases (par. 4). In paragraph 46, Robert tells us about his contact with ham radio operators in places he would like to visit (Guam, Alaska). The TV show takes Robert and the narrator on a tour of France, Italy, and Portugal.

The way the narrator changes from disliking the blind man to getting along with him must be important to the meaning of the story. After the wife goes up to "get comfortable," suggesting that they might go to bed, the story focuses on the two men. Later she falls asleep on the sofa between them, and the narrator decides not to cover up her leg where her robe has fallen open, as if he has stopped being jealous. At this point the narrator decides he is "glad for the company" of his guest (par. 84). The cooperation between the two men is the turning point. The narrator is disgusted by blind people at first, and at the end he closes his eyes on purpose. The two men try to imagine something and build something together, and Robert is coaching the narrator. Robert says, "let's do her," and then says, "*you're* doing fine" (pars. 115, 118, emphasis added). I think it makes a difference that they imagine and draw a cathedral, not a flower or a cow or an airplane. It's something made by human beings, and it's religious. I don't think the men are converted to believing in God at the end, but this narrow-minded guy gets past whatever he's afraid of at night and finds some sort of inspiring feeling. I don't know why the wife has to be left out, but probably the husband couldn't open up if he was worrying about how close she is to Robert.

The ideas of communicating or being in touch and travel seem connected to me. I think that the husband tries to tell this story about the cathedral the way his wife tried to write a poem. The narrator has had an exciting experience that gets him in touch with something beyond his small house. After drawing the cathedral, the narrator says that he "didn't feel like I was inside anything" (par. 135). Though I still didn't like the narrator, I felt more sympathy, and I thought the story showed that even this hostile person could open up.

SAMPLE WRITING: FIRST-DRAFT ANALYSIS

Bethany Qualls wrote the following first draft of a paper analyzing character and narration in Carver's "Cathedral." Read this paper as you would one of your peers' papers, looking for opportunities for the writer to improve her presentation. Is the language consistently appropriate for academic writing? Does the essay maintain its focus? Does it demonstrate a steady progression of well-supported arguments toward a strong, well-earned conclusion? Is there any redundant or otherwise unnecessary material? Are there ideas that need to be developed further?

Bethany Qualls

Professor Netherton

English 301

A Narrator's Blindness in Raymond Carver's "Cathedral"

A reader in search of an exciting plot will be pretty disappointed by Raymond Carver's "Cathedral" because the truth is nothing much happens. A suburban husband and wife receive a visit from her former boss, who is blind. After the wife falls asleep, the two men watch a TV program about cathedrals and eventually try to draw one. Along the way the three characters down a few cocktails and smoke a little pot. But that's about as far as the action goes. Instead of focusing on plot, then, the story really asks us to focus on the characters, especially the husband who narrates the story. Through his words even more than his actions the narrator unwittingly shows us why nothing much happens to him by continually demonstrating his utter inability to connect with others or to understand himself.

The narrator's isolation is most evident in the distanced way he introduces his own story and the people in it. He does not name the other characters or himself, referring to them only by using labels such as "this blind man," "his wife," "my wife" (par. 1; all page references are to the class text, *The Norton Introduction to Literature*, 10th ed.) and "the man [my wife] was going to marry" (par. 2). Even after the narrator's wife starts referring to their visitor as "Robert," the narrator keeps calling him "the blind man." These labels distance him from the other characters and also leave readers with very little connection to them.

At least three times the narrator himself notices that this habit of not naming or really acknowledging people is significant. Referring to his wife's "officer," he asks, "why should he have a name? he was the childhood sweetheart, and what more does he want?" (par. 5). Moments later he describes how freaked out he was when he listened to a tape the blind man had sent his wife and "heard [his] own name in the mouth of this . . . blind man . . . [he] didn't even know!" (par. 5). Yet once the blind man arrives and begins to talk with the wife, the narrator finds himself "wait[ing] in vain to hear [his] name on [his] wife's sweet lips" and disappointed to hear "nothing of the sort" (par. 46). Simply using someone's name suggests a kind of intimacy that the narrator avoids and yet secretly yearns for.

Also reinforcing the narrator's isolation and dissatisfaction with it are the awkward euphemisms and clichés he uses, which emphasize how disconnected he is from his own feelings and how uncomfortable he is with other people's. Referring to his wife's first husband, the narrator says it was he "who'd first enjoyed her favors" (par. 4), an antiquated expression even in 1983, the year the story was published. Such language reinforces our sense that the narrator is unable to speak in language that is meaningful or heartfelt, especially when he actually tries to talk about emotions. He describes his wife's feelings for her first husband, for example, by using generic language and then just trailing off entirely: "she was in love with the guy, and he was in love with her, etc." (par. 2). When he refers to the blind man and his wife as "inseparable," he points out that this is, in fact, his "wife's word," not one that he's come up with (par. 16). And even when he admits that he would like to hear his wife talk about him (par. 46), he speaks in language that seems to come from books or movies rather than the heart.

Once the visit actually begins, the narrator's interactions and conversations with the other characters are even more awkward. His discomfort with the very idea of the visit is obvious to his wife and to the reader. As he says in his usual deadpan manner, "I wasn't enthusiastic about his visit" (par. 1). During the visit he sits silent when his wife and Robert are talking and then answers Robert's questions about his life and feelings with the shortest possible phrases: "How long had I been in my present position? (Three years.) Did I like my work? (I didn't.)" (par. 46). Finally, he tries to escape even that much involvement by simply turning on the TV and tuning Robert out.

Despite Robert's best attempt to make a connection with the narrator, the narrator resorts to a label again, saying that he "didn't want to be left alone with a blind man" (par. 57). Robert, merely "a blind man," remains a category, not a person, and the narrator can initially relate to Robert only by invoking the stereotypes about that category that he has learned "from the movies" (par. 1). He confides to the reader that he believes that blind people always wear dark glasses, that they never smoke (par. 43), and that a beard on a blind man is "too much" (par. 18). It follows that the narrator is amazed about the connection his wife and Robert have because he is unable to see Robert as a person like any other. "Who'd want to go to such a wedding in the first place?" (par. 16) he asks rhetorically about Robert's wedding to his wife, Beulah.

Misconceptions continue as the narrator assumes Beulah would "never receive the smallest compliment from her beloved" since the compliments he is thinking about are physical ones (par. 16). Interestingly, when faced with a name that is specific (Beulah), the narrator immediately assumes that he knows what the person with that name must be like ("a colored woman," par. 11), even though she is not in the room or known to him. Words fail or mislead the narrator in both directions, as he's using them and as he hears them.

There is hope for the narrator at the end as he gains some empathy and forges a bond with Robert over the drawing of a cathedral. That process seems to begin when the narrator admits to himself, the reader, and Robert that he is "glad for the [Robert's] company" (par. 84) and, for the first time, comes close to disclosing the literally nightmarish loneliness of his life. It culminates in a moment of physical and emotional intimacy that the narrator admits is "like nothing else in my life up to now" (par. 131)—a moment in which discomfort with the very idea of blindness gives way to an attempt to actually experience blindness from the inside. Because the narrator has used words to distance himself from the world, it seems fitting that all this happens when the narrator *stops* using words. They have a tendency to blind him.

However, even at the very end it isn't clear just whether or how the narrator has really changed. He does not completely interact with Robert but has to be prodded into action by him. By choosing to keep his eyes closed, he not only temporarily experiences blindness but also shuts out the rest of the world, since he "didn't feel like [he] was inside anything" (par. 135). Perhaps most important, he remains unable to describe his experience meaningfully, making it difficult for readers to decide whether or not he has really changed. For example, he says, "It was like nothing else in my life up to now" (par. 131), but he doesn't explain why this is true. Is it because he is doing something for someone else? Because he is thinking about the world from another's perspective? Because he feels connected to Robert? Because he is drawing a picture while probably drunk and high? There is no way of knowing.

It's possible that not feeling "inside anything" (par. 135) could be a feeling of freedom from his own habits of guardedness and insensitivity, his emotional "blindness." But even with this final hope for connection, for the majority of the story the narrator is a closed, judgmental man who isolates himself and cannot connect with others. The narrator's view of the world is one filled with misconceptions that the visit from Robert starts to slowly change, yet it is not clear what those changes are, how far they will go, or whether they will last.

KEY CONCEPTS: FICTION

As you read, respond to, and write about fiction, some key terms and concepts may be useful in comparing or distinguishing different kinds of stories you read. Stories may be oral rather than written down, and they may be of different lengths. They may be based on true stories or completely invented. They may be written in verse rather than prose, or they may be created in media other than the printed page. While reading and writing, you should always have a good college-level dictionary on hand so that you can look up any unfamiliar terms. In the era of the Internet it's especially easy to learn more about any word or concept—and it can help you enrich the ideas in your papers. Another excellent resource is the *Oxford English Dictionary*, available in the reference section of most academic libraries, which reveals the wide range of meanings words have had over time. Words in English always have a long story to tell because over the centuries so many languages have contributed to our current vocabulary. It's not uncommon for meanings to overlap or even reverse themselves.

Generally speaking, a *story* is a short account of an incident or series of incidents, whether actual or invented. The word is often used to refer to an entertaining tale of imaginary people and events, but it is also used in phrases like "the *story* of my life"—suggesting a true account. The term **narrative** is especially useful as a general concept for the substance rather than the form of what is told about persons and their actions. A story or a tale is usually short, whereas a narrative may be of any length from a sentence to a series of novels and beyond.

Narratives in Daily Life

Narrative plays an important role in our lives beyond the telling of fictional stories. Consider the following:

- Today, sociologists and historians may collect *personal narratives* to present an account of society and everyday life in a certain time or place.
- Since the 1990s, the practice of *narrative medicine* has spread as an improved technique of diagnosis and treatment from the patient's point of view.
- There is a movement to encourage *mediation* rather than litigation in divorce cases. A mediator may collaborate with the couple in arriving at a shared perspective on the divorce; in a sense, they try to agree on the story of their marriage and how it ended.
- Some countries have attempted to recover from the trauma of genocidal ethnic conflict through *official hearings of testimony* by victims as well as defendants. South Africa's Truth and Reconciliation Commission is an example of this use of stories.

We tend to think of stories in their written form, but many of the stories that we now regard as among the world's greatest, such as Homer's *Iliad* and the Old

English epic *Beowulf*, were sung or recited by generations of storytellers before being written down. Just as rumors change shape as they circulate, oral stories tend to be more fluid than printed stories. Traditionally oral **tales** such as fairy tales or folktales may endure for a very long time yet take different forms in various countries and eras. And it's often difficult or impossible to trace such a story back to a single "author" or creator. In a sense, then, an oral story is the creation of a whole community or communities, just as oral storytelling tends to be a more communal event than reading.

Certain recognizable signals set a story or tale apart from common speech and encourage us to pay a different kind of attention. Children know that a story is beginning when they hear or read "Once upon a time . . . ," and traditional oral storytellers have formal ways to set up a tale, such as *Su-num-twee* ("listen to me"), as Spokane storytellers say. "And they lived happily ever after," or simply "The End," may similarly indicate when the story is over. Such conventions have been adapted since the invention of printing and the spread of literacy.

Notice to Little Children

Final page of *More English Fairy Tales*, ed. Joseph Jacobs. Jacobs published volumes of popular tales that had been collected over several centuries from oral storytellers in the British countryside.

FICTION AND NONFICTION

The word *fiction* comes from the Latin root *fingere*, to fashion or form. The earliest definitions concern the act of making something artificial to imitate something else. In the past two centuries, *fiction* has become more narrowly defined as "prose narrative about imaginary people and events," the main meaning of the word as we use it in this anthology.

Genres of Prose Fiction by Length

A **novel** is a work of prose fiction of about 40,000 words or more. The form arose in the seventeenth and early eighteenth centuries as prose romances and adventure tales began to adopt techniques of history and travel narrative as well as memoir, letters, and biography.

A **novella** is a work of prose fiction of about 17,000 to 40,000 words. The novella form was especially favored between about 1850 and 1950, largely because it can be more tightly controlled and concentrated than a long novel while focusing on the inner workings of a character.

A **short story** is broadly defined as anywhere between 1,000 and 20,000 words. One expectation of a short story is that it may be read in a single sitting. The modern short story developed in the mid-nineteenth century, in part because of the growing popularity of magazines.

A **short short story**, sometimes called "flash fiction" or "micro-fiction," is generally not much longer than 1,000 words and sometimes much shorter. There have always been very short fictions, including parables and fables, but this genre as we follow it today is an invention cultivated in recent decades.

In contrast with fiction, **nonfiction** usually refers to *factual* prose narrative. Some major nonfiction genres are history, biography, and autobiography. In film, documentaries and "biopics," or biographical feature films, similarly attempt to represent real people, places, and events. The boundary between fiction and nonfiction is often blurred today, as it was centuries ago. So-called true crime novels such as Truman Capote's *In Cold Blood* and novelized biographies such as Colm Tóibín's *The Master*, about the life of the novelist Henry James, use the techniques of fiction writing to narrate actual events. Graphic novels, with a format derived from comic books, have become an increasingly popular medium for memoirs. (Two examples are Art Spiegelman's *Maus* and Marjane Satrapi's *Persepolis*.) Some Hollywood movies and TV shows dramatize real people in everyday situations or contexts, or real events such as the assassination of President John F. Kennedy. In contrast, **historical fiction**, developed by Sir Walter Scott around 1815, refers to prose narratives that present history in imaginative ways. Such works of prose narrative fiction adhere closely to the facts of history and actual lives, just as many "true" life stories are more or less fictionalized.

· · ·

The fiction chapters in this volume present a collection of prose works—mostly short stories—almost all of which were printed within the author's lifetime. Even as you read the short prose fiction in this book, bear in mind the many ways we encounter stories or narrative in everyday life, and consider the almost limitless variety of forms that fiction may take.

The fiction chapters in this volume present a collection of prose works—mostly
short stories—about what it means to be human in this world. In a lifetime, Even
as you read this . . .

Telling Stories: An Album

Is it human nature or human culture? Is it hardwired in our brains, or inspired by our need to live with others in a community? Whatever the cause, people tell stories in every known society. Professional and amateur storytellers, as well as scholars in the humanities and sciences, have been paying more attention to the phenomenon of stories or narrative in recent decades. Online forums and organizations around the world are dedicated to a revival of oral storytelling, rather like the twentieth-century revival of folk music. (Examples of groups with annual festivals, publications, and directories are the National Storytelling Network and Britain's Society for Storytelling.) Educators, religious leaders, therapists, and organizers of programs for the young or the needy have turned to various publications and programs for guidance on how the techniques of storytelling might benefit their clients.

Yet stories are part of our everyday lives, and everyone has stories to tell. You may have listened to Chicago Public Radio's *This American Life*, a weekly radio program of stories based on real life and now also an Emmy Award–winning television series on Showtime. Perhaps you have heard the life stories broadcast every week on National Public Radio's *Morning Edition* in conjunction with the StoryCorps project, which allows ordinary Americans to record their own interviews with friends or family (often in a traveling "studio" van) and have their recordings archived in the Library of Congress. Most likely you are familiar with blogs, Facebook, MySpace, YouTube videos, and other means of producing or sharing some version of yourself, some aspect of your experience or your life.

Even as countless people discover more ways to tell and broadcast their own true stories, the art of short fiction is thriving. Such stories about imaginary people and events—sometimes called "non-actual" stories—may be closely based on the lives of real people or on episodes in the author's own life. Yet because they are acknowledged to be fiction, no one objects if the story is shaped and enhanced for specific effects.

Authors of short fiction have often reflected on the irresistible appeal of stories by making storytelling part of the plot or action *within* their fiction. We gather here three stories that do just that—Sherman Alexie's "Flight Patterns," Grace Paley's "A Conversation with My Father," and Lara Vapnyar's "Puffed Rice and Meatballs." All three stories might be called *frame narratives*: The main stories contain (and thus "frame") another story or stories told by characters. Within the fictional frame, the listeners expect to be told the truth, but at the same time they may not really want to hear or believe it. The tellers are influenced by what they think their listeners want to hear, and they try to capture the listener by being funny or sensational, or to startle or move the listener with a harsh lesson. In each case, touches of humor belie the traumatic story being told.

Though Alexie, Paley, and Vapnyar come from widely different backgrounds, they have much in common nonetheless. Each of these authors has found rich material in his or her personal experience of cultural difference—Alexie as a Native American (or Indian, as he prefers to be called), Paley as the daughter of Jewish immigrants from Ukraine, and Vapnyar as a child of the former Soviet Union who has lived her adult life in the United States. They draw on a venerable literary tradition of realistic short stories that depict small incidents of everyday life, a tradition embodied by the work of the Russian writer Anton Chekhov, alluded to in Paley's story. Yet at the same time all three of these writers draw on, and show pride in, their own particular cultural and literary experience and traditions—Spokane storytelling customs, humorous Yiddish folktales about the wise fools and eccentrics in Eastern European *shtetls* (Jewish villages and ghettos), the resilience of Russians under Communism. They explore the comedy of our sometimes awkward attempts to tell stories, the sadness of our failures to communicate, and the trauma that stories and humor can help us endure and understand, as well as deny.

SHERMAN ALEXIE

Flight Patterns

At 5:05 A.M., Patsy Cline fell loudly to pieces on William's clock radio.[1] He hit the snooze button, silencing lonesome Patsy, and dozed for fifteen more minutes before Donna Fargo bragged about being the happiest girl in the whole USA. William wondered what had ever happened to Donna Fargo, whose birth name was the infinitely more interesting Yvonne Vaughn, and wondered *why* he knew Donna Fargo's birth name. Ah, he was the bemused and slightly embarrassed owner of a twenty-first-century American mind.[1] His intellect was a big comfy couch stuffed with sacred and profane trivia. He knew the names of all nine of Elizabeth Taylor's husbands and could quote from memory the entire Declaration of Independence. William knew Donna Fargo's birth name because he *wanted* to know her birth name. He wanted to know all of the great big and tiny little American details. He didn't want to choose between Ernie Hemingway and the Spokane tribal elders, between Mia Hamm and Crazy Horse, between *The Heart Is a Lonely Hunter* and Chief Dan George. William wanted all of it. Hunger was his crime. As for dear Miss Fargo, William figured she probably played the Indian casino circuit along with the Righteous Brothers, Smokey Robinson, Eddie Money, Pat Benatar, RATT, REO Speedwagon, and dozens of other formerly famous rock- and country-music stars. Many of the Indian casino acts were bad, and most of the rest were pure nostalgic entertainment, but a small number made beautiful and timeless music. William knew the genius Merle Haggard played thirty or forty Indian casinos every year, so long live Haggard and long live tribal economic sovereignty. Who cares about fishing and hunting rights? Who cares about uranium mines and nuclear-waste-dump sites on sacred land? Who cares about the recovery of tribal languages? Give me Freddy Fender singing "Before the Next Teardrop Falls" in English and Spanish to 206 Spokane Indians, William thought, and I will be a happy man.

But William wasn't happy this morning. He'd slept poorly—he always slept poorly—and wondered again if his insomnia was a physical or a mental condition. His doctor had offered him sleeping-pill prescriptions, but William declined for philosophical reasons. He was an Indian who didn't smoke or drink or eat processed sugar. He lifted weights three days a week, ran every day, and competed in four triathlons a year. A two-mile swim, a 150-mile bike ride, and a full mara-

---

1. Reference to country music singer Patsy Cline's recording of "I Fall to Pieces" (1961). *Donna Fargo:* American singer (b. 1949) best known for her recording of "Happiest Girl in the Whole U.S.A." (1972).
2. The story contains many references to American popular culture of the post–World War II era.

thon. A triathlon was a religious quest. If Saint Francis were still around, he'd be a triathlete. Another exaggeration! Theological hyperbole! Rabid self-justification! Diagnostically speaking, William was an obsessive-compulsive workaholic who was afraid of pills. So he suffered sleepless nights and constant daytime fatigue.

This morning, awake and not awake, William turned down the radio, changing Yvonne Vaughn's celebratory anthem into whispered blues, and rolled off the couch onto his hands and knees. His back and legs were sore because he'd slept on the living room couch so the alarm wouldn't disturb his wife and daughter upstairs. Still on his hands and knees, William stretched his spine, using the twelve basic exercises he'd learned from Dr. Adams, that master practitioner of white middle-class chiropractic voodoo. This was all part of William's regular morning ceremony. Other people find God in ornate ritual, but William called out to Geronimo, Jesus Christ, Saint Therese, Buddha, Allah, Billie Holiday, Simon Ortiz, Abe Lincoln, Bessie Smith, Howard Hughes, Leslie Marmon Silko, Joan of Arc and Joan of Collins, John Woo, Wilma Mankiller, and Karl and Groucho Marx while he pumped out fifty push-ups and fifty abdominal crunches. William wasn't particularly religious; he was generally religious. Finished with his morning calisthenics, William showered in the basement, suffering the water that was always too cold down there, and threaded his long black hair into two tight braids— the indigenous businessman's tonsorial special—and dressed in his best travel suit, a navy three-button pinstripe he'd ordered online. He'd worried about the fit, but his tailor was a magician and had only mildly chastised William for such an impulsive purchase. After knotting his blue paisley tie, purchased in person and on sale, William walked upstairs in bare feet and kissed his wife, Marie, good-bye.

"Cancel your flight," she said. "And come back to bed."

"You're supposed to be asleep," he said.   5

She was a small and dark woman who seemed to be smaller and darker at that time of the morning. Her long black hair had once again defeated its braids, but she didn't care. She sometimes went two or three days without brushing it. William was obsessive about his mane, tying and retying his ponytail, knotting and reknotting his braids, experimenting with this shampoo and that conditioner. He greased down his cowlicks (inherited from a cowlicked father and grandfather) with shiny pomade, but Marie's hair was always unkempt, wild, and renegade. William's hair hung around the fort, but Marie's rode on the warpath! She constantly pulled stray strands out of her mouth. William loved her for it. During sex, they spent as much time readjusting her hair as they did readjusting positions. Such were the erotic dangers of loving a Spokane Indian woman.

"Take off your clothes and get in bed," Marie pleaded now.

"I can't do that," William said. "They're counting on me."

"Oh, the plane will be filled with salesmen. Let some other salesman sell what you're selling."

"Your breath stinks."   10

"So do my feet, my pits, and my butt, but you still love me. Come back to bed, and I'll make it worth your while."

William kissed Marie, reached beneath her pajama top, and squeezed her breasts. He thought about reaching inside her pajama bottoms. She wrapped her arms and legs around him and tried to wrestle him into bed. Oh, God, he wanted to climb into bed and make love. He wanted to fornicate, to sex, to breed, to screw, to make the beast with two backs. *Oh, sweetheart, be my little synonym!* He wanted her to be both subject and object. Perhaps it was wrong (and unavoidable) to objectify female strangers, but shouldn't every husband seek to objectify his wife at least once a day? William loved and respected his wife, and delighted in her intelligence, humor, and kindness, but he also loved to watch her lovely ass when she walked, and stare down the front of her loose shirts when she leaned over, and grab her breasts at wildly inappropriate times—during dinner parties and piano recitals and uncontrolled intersections, for instance. He constantly made passes at her, not necessarily expecting to be successful, but to remind her he still desired her and was excited by the thought of her. She was his passive and active.

"Come on," she said. "If you stay home, I'll make you Scooby."

He laughed at the inside joke, created one night while he tried to give her sexual directions and was so aroused that he sounded exactly like Scooby-Doo.

15   "Stay home, stay home, stay home," she chanted and wrapped herself tighter around him. He was supporting all of her weight, holding her two feet off the bed.

"I'm not strong enough to do this," he said.

"Baby, baby, I'll make you strong," she sang, and it sounded like she was writing a Top 40 hit in the Brill Building, circa 1962. How could he leave a woman who sang like that? He hated to leave, but he loved his work. He was a man, and men needed to work. More sexism! More masculine tunnel vision! More need for gender-sensitivity workshops! He pulled away from her, dropping her back onto the bed, and stepped away.

"Willy Loman," she said, "you must pay attention to me."[3]

"I love you," he said, but she'd already fallen back to sleep—a narcoleptic gift William envied—and he wondered if she would dream about a man who never left her, about some unemployed agoraphobic Indian warrior who liked to cook and wash dishes.

20   William tiptoed into his daughter's bedroom, expecting to hear her light snore, but she was awake and sitting up in bed, and looked so magical and androgynous with her huge brown eyes and crew-cut hair. She'd wanted to completely shave her head: *I don't want long hair, I don't want short hair, I don't want hair at all, and I don't want to be a girl or a boy, I want to be a yellow and orange leaf some little kid picks up and pastes in his scrapbook.*

"Daddy," she said.

"Grace," he said. "You should be asleep. You have school today."

"I know," she said. "But I wanted to see you before you left."

"Okay," said William as he kissed her forehead, nose, and chin. "You've seen me. Now go back to sleep. I love you and I'm going to miss you."

25   She fiercely hugged him.

"Oh," he said. "You're such a lovely, lovely girl."

Preternaturally serious, she took his face in her eyes and studied his eyes. Morally examined by a kindergartner!

"Daddy," she said. "Go be silly for those people far away."

She cried as William left her room. Already quite sure he was only an adequate husband, he wondered, as he often did, if he was a bad father. During these mornings, he felt generic and violent, like some caveman leaving the fire to hunt animals in the cold and dark. Maybe his hands were smooth and clean, but they felt bloody.

Downstairs, he put on his socks and shoes and overcoat and listened for his daughter's crying, but she was quiet, having inherited her mother's gift for instant sleep. She had probably fallen back into one of her odd little dreams. While he was gone, she often drew pictures of those dreams, coloring the sky green and the grass blue—everything backward and wrong—and had once sketched a man in a suit crashing an airplane into the bright yellow sun. Ah, the rage, fear, and loneliness of a five-year-old, simple and true! She'd been especially afraid since September 11 of the previous year and constantly quizzed William about what he would do if terrorists hijacked his plane.

"I'd tell them I was your father," he'd said to her before he left for his last business trip. "And they'd stop being bad."

"You're lying," she'd said. "I'm not supposed to listen to liars. If you lie to me, I can't love you."

He couldn't argue with her logic. Maybe she was the most logical person on the planet. Maybe she should be illegally elected president of the United States.

William understood her fear of flying and of his flight. He was afraid of flying, too, but not of terrorists. After the horrible violence of September 11, he figured hijacking was no longer a useful weapon in the terrorist arsenal. These days, a terrorist armed with a box cutter would be torn to pieces by all of the coach-class passengers and fed to the first-class upgrades. However, no matter how much he tried to laugh his fear away, William always scanned the airports and airplanes for little brown guys who reeked of fundamentalism. That meant William was equally afraid of Osama bin Laden and Jerry Falwell wearing the last vestiges of a summer tan. William himself was a little brown guy, so the other travelers were always sniffing around him, but he smelled only of Dove soap, Mennen deodorant, and sarcasm. Still, he understood why people were afraid of him, a brown-skinned man with dark hair and eyes. If Norwegian terrorists had exploded the World Trade Center, then blue-eyed blondes would be viewed with more suspicion. Or so he hoped.

Locking the front door behind him, William stepped away from his house, carried his garment bag and briefcase onto the front porch, and waited for his taxi to arrive. It was a cold and foggy October morning. William could smell the saltwater of Elliott Bay and the freshwater of Lake Washington. Surrounded by gray water and gray fog and gray skies and gray mountains and a gray sun, he'd lived with his family in Seattle for three years and loved it. He couldn't imagine living anywhere else, with any other wife or child, in any other time.

William was tired and happy and romantic and exaggerating the size of his familial devotion so he could justify his departure, so he could survive his departure. He did sometimes think about other women and other possible lives with them. He wondered how his life would have been different if he'd married a white woman and fathered half-white children who grew up to complain and brag about their biracial identities: *Oh, the only box they have for me is Other! I'm not going to check any box! I'm not the Other! I am Tiger Woods!* But William most often fantasized about being single and free to travel as often as he wished—maybe two million miles a year—and how much he'd enjoy the benefits of being a platinum frequent flier. Maybe he'd have one-night stands with a long series of traveling saleswomen, all of them thousands of miles away from husbands and children who kept looking up "feminism" in the dictionary. William knew that was yet another sexist thought. In this capitalistic and democratic culture, talented women should also enjoy the freedom to emotionally and physically abandon their families. After all, talented and educated men have been doing it for generations. Let freedom ring!

Marie had left her job as a corporate accountant to be a full-time mother to Grace. William loved his wife for making the decision, and he tried to do his share of the housework, but he suspected he was an old-fashioned bastard who wanted his wife to stay at home and wait, wait, wait for him.

Marie was always waiting for William to call, to come home, to leave messages saying he was getting on the plane, getting off the plane, checking in to the hotel, going to sleep, waking up, heading for the meeting, catching an earlier or later flight home. He spent one third of his life trying to sleep in uncomfortable beds and one third of his life trying to stay awake in airports. He traveled with thousands of other capitalistic foot soldiers, mostly men but increasing numbers of women, and stayed in the same Ramadas, Holiday Inns, and Radissons. He ate the same room-service meals and ran the same exercise-room treadmills and watched the same pay-per-view porn and stared out the windows at the same strange and lonely cityscapes. Sure, he was an enrolled member of the Spokane Indian tribe, but he was also a fully recognized member of the notebook-computer tribe and the security-checkpoint tribe and the rental-car tribe and the hotel-shuttle-bus tribe and the cell-phone-roaming-charge tribe.

William traveled so often, the Seattle-based flight attendants knew him by first name.

40   At five minutes to six, the Orange Top taxi pulled into the driveway. The driver, a short and thin black man, stepped out of the cab and waved. William rushed down the stairs and across the pavement. He wanted to get away from the house before he changed his mind about leaving.

"Is that everything, sir?" asked the taxi driver, his accent a colonial cocktail of American English, formal British, and French sibilants added to a base of what must have been North African.

"Yes, it is, sir," said William, self-consciously trying to erase any class differences between them. In Spain the previous summer, an elderly porter had cursed at William when he insisted on carrying his own bags into the hotel. "Perhaps there is something wrong with the caste system, sir," the hotel concierge had explained to William. "But all of us, we want to do our jobs, and we want to do them well."

William didn't want to insult anybody; he wanted the world to be a fair and decent place. At least that was what he wanted to want. More than anything, he wanted to stay home with his fair and decent family. He supposed he wanted the world to be fairer and more decent to his family. We are special, he thought, though he suspected they were just one more family on this block of neighbors, in this city of neighbors, in this country of neighbors, in a world of neighbors. He looked back at his house, at the windows behind which slept his beloved wife and daughter. When he traveled, he had nightmares about strangers breaking into the house and killing and raping Marie and Grace. In other nightmares, he arrived home in time to save his family by beating the intruders and chasing them away. During longer business trips, William's nightmares became more violent as the days and nights passed. If he was gone over a week, he dreamed about mutilating the rapists and eating them alive while his wife and daughter cheered for him.

"Let me take your bags, sir," said the taxi driver.

"What?" asked William, momentarily confused.

"Your bags, sir."

William handed him the briefcase but held on to the heavier garment bag. A stupid compromise, thought William, but it's too late to change it now. God, I'm supposed to be some electric aboriginal warrior, but I'm really a wimpy liberal pacifist. *Dear Lord, how much longer should I mourn the death of Jerry Garcia?*

The taxi driver tried to take the garment bag from William.

"I've got this one," said William, then added, "I've got it, sir."

The taxi driver hesitated, shrugged, opened the trunk, and set the briefcase inside. William laid the garment bag next to his briefcase. The taxi driver shut the trunk and walked around to open William's door.

"No, sir," said William as he awkwardly stepped in front of the taxi driver, opened the door, and took a seat. "I've got it."

"I'm sorry, sir," said the taxi driver and hurried around to the driver's seat. This strange American was making him uncomfortable, and he wanted to get behind the wheel and drive. Driving comforted him.

"To the airport, sir?" asked the taxi driver as he started the meter.

"Yes," said William. "United Airlines."

"Very good, sir."

In silence, they drove along Martin Luther King Jr. Way, the bisector of an African American neighborhood that was rapidly gentrifying. William and his family were Native American gentry! They were the very first Indian family to ever move into a neighborhood and bring up the property values! That was one of William's favorite jokes, self-deprecating and politely racist. White folks could laugh at a joke like that and not feel guilty. But how guilty could white people feel in Seattle? Seattle might be the only city in the country where white people lived comfortably on a street named after Martin Luther King, Jr.

No matter where he lived, William always felt uncomfortable, so he enjoyed other people's discomfort. These days, in the airports, he loved to watch white people enduring random security checks. It was a perverse thrill, to be sure, but William couldn't help himself. He knew those white folks wanted to scream and rage: *Do I look like a terrorist?* And he knew the security officers, most often low-paid brown folks, wanted to scream back: *Define terror, you Anglo bastard!* William figured he'd been pulled over for pat-down searches about 75 percent of the time. Random, my ass! But that was okay! William might have wanted to irritate other people, but he didn't want to scare them. He wanted his fellow travelers to know exactly who and what he was: *I am a Native American and therefore have ten thousand more reasons to terrorize the U.S. than any of those Taliban jerk-offs, but I have chosen instead to become a civic American citizen, so all of you white folks should be celebrating my kindness and moral decency and awesome ability to forgive!* Maybe William should have worn beaded vests when he traveled. Maybe he should have brought a hand drum and sang "Way, ya, way, ya, hey." Maybe he should have thrown casino chips into the crowd.

The taxi driver turned west on Cherry, drove twenty blocks into downtown, took the entrance ramp onto I-5, and headed south for the airport. The freeway was moderately busy for that time of morning.

"Where are you going, sir?" asked the taxi driver.

60   "I've got business in Chicago," William said. He didn't really want to talk. He needed to meditate in silence. He needed to put his fear of flying inside an imaginary safe deposit box and lock it away. We all have our ceremonies, thought William, our personal narratives. He'd always needed to meditate in the taxi on the way to the airport. Immediately upon arrival at the departure gate, he'd listen to a tape he'd made of rock stars who died in plane crashes. Buddy Holly, Otis Redding, Stevie Ray, "Oh Donna," "Chantilly Lace," "(Sittin' on) The Dock of the Bay." William figured God would never kill a man who listened to such a morbid collection of music. Too easy a target, and plus, God could never justify killing a planeful of innocents to punish one minor sinner.

    "What do you do, sir?" asked the taxi driver.

    "You know, I'm not sure," said William and laughed. It was true. He worked for a think tank and sold ideas about how to improve other ideas. Two years ago, his company had made a few hundred thousand dollars by designing and selling the idea of a better shopping cart. The CGI prototype was amazing. It looked like a mobile walk-in closet. But it had yet to be manufactured and probably never would be.

    "You wear a good suit," said the taxi driver, not sure why William was laughing. "You must be a businessman, no? You must make lots of money."

    "I do okay."

65   "Your house is big and beautiful."

    "Yes, I suppose it is."

    "You are a family man, yes?"

    "I have a wife and daughter."

    "Are they beautiful?"

70   William was pleasantly surprised to be asked such a question. "Yes," he said. "Their names are Marie and Grace. They're very beautiful. I love them very much."

    "You must miss them when you travel."

    "I miss them so much I go crazy," said William. "I start thinking I'm going to disappear, you know, just vanish, if I'm not home. Sometimes I worry their love is the only thing that makes me human, you know? I think if they stopped loving me, I might burn up, spontaneously combust, and turn into little pieces of oxygen and hydrogen and carbon. Do you know what I'm saying?"

    "Yes sir, I understand love can be so large."

    William wondered why he was being honest and poetic with a taxi driver. There is emotional safety in anonymity, he thought.

75   "I have a wife and three sons," said the driver. "But they live in Ethiopia with my mother and father. I have not seen any of them for many years."

    For the first time, William looked closely at the driver. He was clear-eyed and handsome, strong of shoulder and arm, maybe fifty years old, maybe older. A thick scar ran from his right ear down his neck and beneath his collar. A black man with a violent history; William thought and immediately reprimanded himself for racially profiling the driver: *Excuse me, sir, but I pulled you over because your scar doesn't belong in this neighborhood.*

    "I still think of my children as children," the driver said. "But they are men now. Taller and stronger than me. They are older now than I was when I last saw them."

    William did the math and wondered how this driver could function with such fatherly pain. "I bet you can't wait to go home and see them again," he said, following the official handbook of the frightened American male: *When confronted with the mysterious, you can defend yourself by speaking in obvious generalities.*

"I cannot go home," said the taxi driver, "and I fear I will never see them again."

William didn't want to be having this conversation. He wondered if his silence 80 would silence the taxi driver. But it was too late for that.

"What are you?" the driver asked.

"What do you mean?"

"I mean, you are not white, your skin, it is dark like mine."

"Not as dark as yours."

"No," said the driver and laughed. "Not so dark, but too dark to be white. 85 What are you? Are you Jewish?"

Because they were so often Muslim, taxi drivers all over the world had often asked William if he was Jewish. William was always being confused for something else. He was ambiguously ethnic, living somewhere in the darker section of the Great American Crayola Box, but he was more beige than brown, more mauve than sienna.

"Why do you want to know if I'm Jewish?" William asked.

"Oh, I'm sorry, sir, if I offended you. I am not anti-Semitic. I love all of my brothers and sisters. Jews, Catholics, Buddhists, even the atheists, I love them all. Like you Americans sing, 'Joy to the world and Jeremiah Bullfrog!'"

The taxi driver laughed again, and William laughed with him.

"I'm Indian," William said. 90

"From India?"

"No, not jewel-on-the-forehead Indian," said William. "I'm a bows-and-arrows Indian."

"Oh, you mean ten little, nine little, eight little Indians?"

"Yeah, sort of," said William. "I'm that kind of Indian, but much smarter. I'm a Spokane Indian. We're salmon people."

"In England, they call you Red Indians." 95

"You've been to England?"

"Yes, I studied physics at Oxford."

"Wow," said William, wondering if this man was a liar.

"You are surprised by this, I imagine. Perhaps you think I'm a liar?"

William covered his mouth with one hand. He smiled this way when he was 100 embarrassed.

"Aha, you do think I'm lying. You ask yourself questions about me. How could a physicist drive a taxi? Well, in the United States, I am a cabdriver, but in Ethiopia, I was a jet-fighter pilot."

By coincidence or magic, or as a coincidence that could willfully be interpreted as magic, they drove past Boeing Field at that exact moment.

"Ah, you see," said the taxi driver, "I can fly any of those planes. The prop planes, the jet planes, even the very large passenger planes. I can also fly the experimental ones that don't fly. But I could make them fly because I am the best pilot in the world. Do you believe me?"

"I don't know," said William, very doubtful of this man but fascinated as well. If he was a liar, then he was a magnificent liar.

On both sides of the freeway, blue-collared men and women drove trucks and 105 forklifts, unloaded trains, trucks, and ships, built computers, televisions, and airplanes. Seattle was a city of industry, of hard work, of calluses on the palms of hands. So many men and women working so hard. William worried that his job—his selling of the purely theoretical—wasn't a real job at all. He didn't build anything. He couldn't walk into department and grocery stores and buy what he'd created, manufactured, and shipped. William's life was measured by imaginary numbers: the binary code of computer languages, the amount of money in his bank accounts, the interest rate on his mortgage, and the rise and fall of the stock market. He invested much of his money in socially responsible funds. Imagine that! Imagine choosing to trust your money with companies that supposedly made their millions through ethical means. Imagine the breathtaking privilege of such a choice. All right, so maybe this was an old story for white men. For most of American history, who else but a white man could endure the existential crisis of economic success? But this story was original and aboriginal for William. For thousands of years, Spokane Indians had lived subsistence lives, using every last part of the salmon and deer because they'd die without every last part, but William only ordered salmon from menus and saw deer on television. Maybe he romanticized the primal—for thousands of years, Indians also died of ear infections—but William wanted his comfortable and safe life to contain more *wilderness*.

"Sir, forgive me for saying this," the taxi driver said, "but you do not look like the Red Indians I have seen before."

"I know," William said. "People usually think I'm a longhaired Mexican."

"What do you say to them when they think such a thing?"

"No habla español. Indio de Norteamericanos."

110 "People think I'm black American. They always want to hip-hop rap to me. 'Are you East Coast or West Coast?' they ask me, and I tell them I am Ivory Coast."

"How have things been since September eleventh?"

"Ah, a good question, sir. It's been interesting. Because people think I'm black, they don't see me as a terrorist, only as a crackhead addict on welfare. So I am a victim of only one misguided idea about who I am."

"We're all trapped by other people's ideas, aren't we?"

"I suppose that is true, sir. How has it been for you?"

115 "It's all backward," William said. "A few days after it happened, I was walking out of my gym downtown, and this big phallic pickup pulled up in front of me in the crosswalk. Yeah, this big truck with big phallic tires and a big phallic flagpole and a big phallic flag flying, and the big phallic symbol inside leaned out of his window and yelled at me, 'Go back to your own country!'"

"Oh, that is sad and funny," the taxi driver said.

"Yeah," William said. "And it wasn't so much a hate crime as it was a crime of irony, right? And I was laughing so hard, the truck was halfway down the block before I could get breath enough to yell back, 'You first!'"

William and the taxi driver laughed and laughed together. Two dark men laughing at dark jokes.

"I had to fly on the first day you could fly," William said. "And I was flying into Baltimore, you know, and D.C. and Baltimore are pretty much the same damn town, so it was like flying into Ground Zero, you know?"

120 "It must have been terrifying."

"It was, it was. I was sitting in the plane here in Seattle, getting ready to take off, and I started looking around for suspicious brown guys. I was scared of little brown guys. So was everybody else. We were all afraid of the same things. I started looking around for big white guys because I figured they'd be undercover cops, right?"

"Imagine wanting to be surrounded by white cops!"

"Exactly! I didn't want to see some pacifist, vegan, whole-wheat, free-range, organic, progressive, gray-ponytail, communist, liberal, draft-dodging, NPR-listening wimp! What are they going to do if somebody tries to hijack the plane? Throw a Birkenstock at him? Offer him some pot?"

"Marijuana might actually stop the violence everywhere in the world," the taxi driver said.

"You're right," William said. "But on that plane, I was hoping for about 125 twenty-five NRA-loving, gun-nut, serial-killing, psychopathic, Ollie North, Norman Schwarzkopf, right-wing, Agent Orange, post-traumatic-stress-disorder, CIA, FBI, automatic-weapon, smart-bomb, laser-sighting bastards!"

"You wouldn't want to invite them for dinner," the taxi driver said. "But you want them to protect your children, am I correct?"

"Yes, but it doesn't make sense. None of it makes sense. It's all contradictions."

"The contradictions are the story, yes?"

"Yes."

"I have a story about contradictions," said the taxi driver. "Because you are a 130 Red Indian, I think you will understand my pain."

"*Su-num-twee*," said William.

"What is that? What did you say?"

"*Su-num-twee*. It's Spokane. My language."

"What does it mean?"

"Listen to me." 135

"Ah, yes, that's good. *Su-num-twee, su-num-twee*. So, what is your name?"

"William."

The taxi driver sat high and straight in his seat, like he was going to say something important. "William, my name is Fekadu. I am Oromo and Muslim, and I come from Addis Ababa in Ethiopia, and I want you to *su-num-twee*."

There was nothing more important than a person's name and the names of his clan, tribe, city, religion, and country. By the social rules of his tribe, William should have reciprocated and officially identified himself. He should have been polite and generous. He was expected to live by so many rules, he sometimes felt like he was living inside an indigenous version of an Edith Wharton[3] novel.

"Mr. William," asked Fekadu, "do you want to hear my story? Do you want to 140 *su-num-twee*?"

"Yes, I do, sure, yes, please," said William. He was lying. He was twenty minutes away from the airport and so close to departure.

"I was not born into an important family," said Fekadu. "But my father worked for an important family. And this important family worked for the family of Emperor Haile Selassie.[4] He was a great and good and kind and terrible man, and he loved his country and killed many of his people. Have you heard of him?"

"No, I'm sorry, I haven't."

---

4. American novelist (1862–1937) known for her sophisticated depictions of upper-class mores.

5. Haile Selassie (1892–1975), emperor of Ethiopia from 1930 to 1936 and again from 1941 to 1974, when he was overthrown in a violent military coup.

"He was magical. Ruled our country for forty-three years. Imagine that! We Ethiopians are strong. White people have never conquered us. We won every war we fought against white people. For all of our history, our emperors have been strong, and Selassie was the strongest. There has never been a man capable of such love and destruction."

145   "You fought against him?"

Fekadu breathed in so deeply that William recognized it as a religious moment, as the first act of a ceremony, and with the second act, an exhalation, the ceremony truly began.

"No," Fekadu said. "I was a smart child. A genius. A prodigy. It was Selassie who sent me to Oxford. And there I studied physics and learned the math and art of flight. I came back home and flew jets for Selassie's army."

"Did you fly in wars?" William asked.

"Ask me what you really want to ask me, William. You want to know if I was a killer, no?"

150   William had a vision of his wife and daughter huddling terrified in their Seattle basement while military jets screamed overhead. It happened every August when the U.S. Navy Blue Angels came to entertain the masses with their aerial acrobatics.

"Do you want to know if I was a killer?" asked Fekadu. "Ask me if I was a killer."

William wanted to know the terrible answer without asking the terrible question.

"Will you not ask me what I am?" asked Fekadu.

"I can't."

155   "I dropped bombs on my own people."

In the sky above them, William counted four, five, six jets flying in holding patterns while awaiting permission to land.

"For three years, I killed my own people," said Fekadu. "And then, on the third of June in 1974, I could not do it anymore. I kissed my wife and sons goodbye that morning, and I kissed my mother and father, and I lied to them and told them I would be back that evening. They had no idea where I was going. But I went to the base, got into my plane, and flew away."

"You defected?" William asked. How could a man steal a fighter plane? Was that possible? And if possible, how much courage would it take to commit such a crime? William was quite sure he could never be that courageous.

"Yes, I defected," said Fekadu. "I flew my plane to France and was almost shot down when I violated their airspace, but they let me land, and they arrested me, and soon enough, they gave me asylum. I came to Seattle five years ago, and I think I will live here the rest of my days."

160   Fekadu took the next exit. They were two minutes away from the airport. William was surprised to discover that he didn't want this journey to end so soon. He wondered if he should invite Fekadu for coffee and a sandwich, for a slice of pie, for brotherhood. William wanted to hear more of this man's stories and learn from them, whether they were true or not. Perhaps it didn't matter if any one man's stories were true. Fekadu's autobiography might have been completely fabricated, but William was convinced that somewhere in the world, somewhere in Africa or the United States, a man, a jet pilot, wanted to fly away from the war he was supposed to fight. There must be hundreds, maybe thousands, of such men, and how many were courageous enough to fly away? If Fekadu wasn't describ-

ing his own true pain and loneliness, then he might have been accidentally describing the pain of a real and lonely man.

"What about your family?" asked William, because he didn't know what else to ask and because he was thinking of his wife and daughter. "Weren't they in danger? Wouldn't Selassie want to hurt them?"

"I could only pray Selassie would leave them be. He had always been good to me, but he saw me as impulsive, so I hoped he would know my family had nothing to do with my flight. I was a coward for staying and a coward for leaving. But none of it mattered, because Selassie was overthrown a few weeks after I defected."

"A coup?"

"Yes, the Derg⁵ deposed him, and they slaughtered all of their enemies and their enemies' families. They suffocated Selassie with a pillow the next year. And now I could never return to Ethiopia because Selassie's people would always want to kill me for my betrayal and the Derg would always want to kill me for being Selassie's soldier. Every night and day, I worry that any of them might harm my family. I want to go there and defend them. I want to bring them here. They can sleep on my floor! But even now, after democracy has almost come to Ethiopia, I cannot go back. There is too much history and pain, and I am too afraid."

"How long has it been since you've talked to your family?"   165

"We write letters to each other, and sometimes we receive them. They sent me photos once, but they never arrived for me to see. And for two days, I waited by the telephone because they were going to call, but it never rang."

Fekadu pulled the taxi to a slow stop at the airport curb. "We are here, sir," he said. "United Airlines."

William didn't know how this ceremony was supposed to end. He felt small and powerless against the collected history. "What am I supposed to do now?" he asked.

"Sir, you must pay me thirty-eight dollars for this ride," said Fekadu and laughed. "Plus a very good tip."

"How much is good?"   170

"You see, sometimes I send cash to my family. I wrap it up and try to hide it inside the envelope. I know it gets stolen, but I hope some of it gets through to my family. I hope they buy themselves gifts from me. I hope."

"You pray for this?"

"Yes, William, I pray for this. And I pray for your safety on your trip, and I pray for the safety of your wife and daughter while you are gone."

"Pop the trunk, I'll get my own bags," said William as he gave sixty dollars to Fekadu, exited the taxi, took his luggage out of the trunk, and slammed it shut. Then William walked over to the passenger-side window, leaned in, and studied Fekadu's face and the terrible scar on his neck.

"Where did you get that?" William asked.   175

Fekadu ran a finger along the old wound. "Ah," he said. "You must think I got this flying in a war. But no, I got this in a taxicab wreck. William, I am a much better jet pilot than a car driver."

Fekadu laughed loudly and joyously. William wondered how this poor man could be capable of such happiness, however temporary it was.

6. The brutal military junta that overthrew Haile Selassie in 1974 and ruled Ethiopia until the Derg ("Committee") was itself toppled in 1991.

"Your stories," said William. "I want to believe you."

"Then believe me," said Fekadu.

180   Unsure, afraid, William stepped back.

"Good-bye, William American," Fekadu said and drove away.

Standing at curbside, William couldn't breathe well. He wondered if he was dying. Of course he was dying, a flawed mortal dying day by day, but he felt like he might fall over from a heart attack or stroke right there on the sidewalk. He left his bags and ran inside the terminal. Let a luggage porter think his bags were dangerous! Let a security guard x-ray the bags and find mysterious shapes! Let a bomb-squad cowboy explode the bags as precaution! Let an airport manager shut down the airport and search every possible traveler! Let the FAA president order every airplane to land! Let the American skies be empty of everything with wings! Let the birds stop flying! Let the very air go still and cold! William didn't care. He ran through the terminal, searching for an available pay phone, a landline, something true and connected to the ground, and he finally found one and dropped two quarters into the slot and dialed his home number, and it rang and rang and rang and rang, and William worried that his wife and daughter were harmed, were lying dead on the floor, but then Marie answered.

"Hello, William," she said.

"I'm here," he said.

2003

QUESTIONS

1. William tells himself a variety of stories to cope with his feelings. How do these stories relate to his dialogue with the taxi driver and the stories the driver tells?
2. The taxi driver asks William, "The contradictions are the story, yes?" What might this indicate about Sherman Alexie's conception of the reality behind a good story?
3. At the end of "Flight Patterns," does William fully believe Fekadu's story? Does it matter to William whether or not Fekadu's story is factual?

Authors on Their Work: SHERMAN ALEXIE (b. 1966)

From "All Rage and Heart" (2008)*

"[Alexie's] siblings, with whom he was raised on the Spokane Indian reservation in the east of Washington state, are surprised people find him funny, he says. 'I was always the depressed guy in the basement. But I've borrowed their sense of humour and made it darker and more deadly—a weapon of self-defence. Being funny you win hearts quicker; people laughing are more apt to listen.'

(Continued on next page)

(Continued)

"Alexie's maternal grandmother was a 'traditional storyteller, and my dad was an alcoholic liar who loved books: genre stuff—westerns, mysteries, true crime, conspiracy theory. I loved my dad, so his obsessions became mine.'

"He went to Washington State University in Pullman, where . . . a teacher gave him a poetry anthology that included Leslie Silko, James Welch, Adrian Louis, and Joy Harjo. 'It was the first time I'd seen anything creative by an Indian,' he says. 'Everything else was archaic, loincloth literature. But they combined the day-to-day desperation of being Indian with the magic of being alive, in poems about powwows, broken-down cars, the food we eat, basketball. It was a revelation.'"

* Maya Jaggi, "All Rage and Heart," *The Guardian*. 3 May 2008. Web. 4 August 2008.

GRACE PALEY

A Conversation with My Father

My father is eighty-six years old and in bed. His heart, that bloody motor, is equally old and will not do certain jobs any more. It still floods his head with brainy light. But it won't let his legs carry the weight of his body around the house. Despite my metaphors, this muscle failure is not due to his old heart, he says, but to a potassium shortage. Sitting on one pillow, leaning on three, he offers last-minute advice and makes a request.

"I would like you to write a simple story just once more," he says, "the kind de Maupassant wrote, or Chekhov, the kind you used to write. Just recognizable people and then write down what happened to them next."

I say, "Yes, why not? That's possible." I want to please him, though I don't remember writing that way. I *would* like to try to tell such a story, if he means the kind that begins: "There was a woman . . ." followed by plot, the absolute line between two points which I've always despised. Not for literary reasons, but because it takes all hope away. Everyone, real or invented, deserves the open destiny of life.

Finally I thought of a story that had been happening for a couple of years right across the street. I wrote it down, then read it aloud. "Pa," I said, "how about this? Do you mean something like this?"

> Once in my time there was a woman and she had a son. They lived nicely, in a small apartment in Manhattan. This boy at about fifteen became a junkie, which is not unusual in our neighborhood. In order to maintain her close friendship with him, she became a junkie too. She said it was part of the youth culture, with which she felt very much at home. After a while, for a number of reasons, the boy gave it all up and left the city and his mother in disgust. Hopeless and alone, she grieved. We all visit her.

5

"O.K., Pa, that's it," I said, "an unadorned and miserable tale."

"But that's not what I mean," my father said. "You misunderstood me on purpose. You know there's a lot more to it. You know that. You left everything out. Turgenev[1] wouldn't do that. Chekhov wouldn't do that. There are in fact Russian writers you never heard of, you don't have an inkling of, as good as anyone, who can write a plain ordinary story, who would not leave out what you have left out. I object not to facts but to people sitting in trees talking senselessly, voices from who knows where . . ."

"Forget that one, Pa, what have I left out now? In this one?"

"Her looks, for instance."

10 "Oh. Quite handsome, I think. Yes."

"Her hair?"

"Dark, with heavy braids, as though she were a girl or a foreigner."

"What were her parents like, her stock? That she became such a person. It's interesting, you know."

"From out of town. Professional people. The first to be divorced in their county. How's that? Enough?" I asked.

15 "With you, it's all a joke," he said. "What about the boy's father. Why didn't you mention him? Who was he? Or was the boy born out of wedlock?"

"Yes," I said. "He was born out of wedlock."

"For Godsakes, doesn't anyone in your stories get married? Doesn't anyone have the time to run down to City Hall before they jump into bed?"

"No," I said. "In real life, yes. But in my stories, no."

"Why do you answer me like that?"

20 "Oh, Pa, this is a simple story about a smart woman who came to N.Y.C. full of interest love trust excitement very up to date, and about her son, what a hard time she had in this world. Married or not, it's of small consequence."

"It is of great consequence," he said.

"O.K.," I said.

"O.K. O.K. yourself," he said, "but listen. I believe you that she's good-looking, but I don't think she was so smart."

"That's true," I said. "Actually that's the trouble with stories. People start out fantastic. You think they're extraordinary, but it turns out as the work goes along, they're just average with a good education. Sometimes the other way around, the person's a kind of dumb innocent, but he outwits you and you can't even think of an ending good enough."

25 "What do you do then?" he asked. He had been a doctor for a couple of decades and then an artist for a couple of decades and he's still interested in details, craft, technique.

"Well, you just have to let the story lie around till some agreement can be reached between you and the stubborn hero."

"Aren't you talking silly, now?" he asked. "Start again," he said. "It so happens I'm not going out this evening. Tell the story again. See what you can do this time."

"O.K.," I said. "But it's not a five-minute job." Second attempt:

1. Ivan Sergeyevich Turgenev (1818–83); his best-known novel, *Fathers and Sons*, deals with the conflict between generations.

Once, across the street from us, there was a fine handsome woman, our neighbor. She had a son whom she loved because she'd known him since birth (in helpless chubby infancy, and in the wrestling, hugging ages, seven to ten, as well as earlier and later). This boy, when he fell into the fist of adolescence, became a junkie. He was not a hopeless one. He was in fact hopeful, an ideologue and successful converter. With his busy brilliance, he wrote persuasive articles for his high-school newspaper. Seeking a wider audience, using important connections, he drummed into Lower Manhattan newsstand distribution a periodical called *Oh! Golden Horse!*[2]

In order to keep him from feeling guilty (because guilt is the stony heart of   30
nine tenths of all clinically diagnosed cancers in America today, she said), and because she had always believed in giving bad habits room at home where one could keep an eye on them, she too became a junkie. Her kitchen was famous for a while—a center for intellectual addicts who knew what they were doing. A few felt artistic like Coleridge[3] and others were scientific and revolutionary like Leary.[4] Although she was often high herself, certain good mothering reflexes remained, and she saw to it that there was lots of orange juice around and honey and milk and vitamin pills. However, she never cooked anything but chili, and that no more than once a week. She explained, when we talked to her, seriously, with neighborly concern, that it was her part in the youth culture and she would rather be with the young, it was an honor, than with her own generation.

One week, while nodding through an Antonioni[5] film, this boy was severely jabbed by the elbow of a stern and proselytizing girl, sitting beside him. She offered immediate apricots and nuts for his sugar level, spoke to him sharply, and took him home.

She had heard of him and his work and she herself published, edited, and wrote a competitive journal called *Man Does Live By Bread Alone*. In the organic heat of her continuous presence he could not help but become interested once more in his muscles, his arteries, and nerve connections. In fact he began to love them, treasure them, praise them with funny little songs in *Man Does Live* . . .

> *the fingers of my flesh transcend*
> *my transcendental soul*
> *the tightness in my shoulders end*
> *my teeth have made me whole*

To the mouth of his head (that glory of will and determination) he brought hard apples, nuts, wheat germ, and soybean oil. He said to his old friends, From now on, I guess I'll keep my wits about me. I'm going on the natch. He said he was about to begin a spiritual deep-breathing journey. How about you too, Mom? he asked kindly.

His conversion was so radiant, splendid, that neighborhood kids his age began to say that he had never been a real addict at all, only a journalist along for the smell of the story. The mother tried several times to give up what had become without her son and his friends a lonely habit. This effort only

2. *Horse* is slang for heroin.
3. Samuel Taylor Coleridge (1772–1834), English Romantic poet, claimed that his poem "Kubla Khan" recorded what he remembered of a dream stimulated by opium.
4. Timothy Leary (1920–96), American psychologist, promoted the use of psychedelic drugs.
5. Michelangelo Antonioni (b. 1912), Italian film director (*Blow-Up*, *Zabriskie Point*). *Nodding*: a slang term referring to the narcotic effect of heroin.

brought it to supportable levels. The boy and his girl took their electronic mimeograph and moved to the bushy edge of another borough. They were very strict. They said they would not see her again until she had been off drugs for sixty days.

At home alone in the evening, weeping, the mother read and reread the seven issues of *Oh! Golden Horse!* They seemed to her as truthful as ever. We often crossed the street to visit and console. But if we mentioned any of our children who were at college or in the hospital or dropouts at home, she would cry out, My baby! My baby! and burst into terrible, face-scarring, time-consuming tears. The End.

First my father was silent, then he said, "Number One: You have a nice sense of humor. Number Two: I see you can't tell a plain story. So don't waste time." Then he said sadly, "Number Three: I suppose that means she was alone, she was left like that, his mother. Alone. Probably sick?"

I said, "Yes."

"Poor woman. Poor girl, to be born in a time of fools, to live among fools. The end. The end. You were right to put that down. The end."

I didn't want to argue, but I had to say, "Well, it is not necessarily the end, Pa."

"Yes," he said, "what a tragedy. The end of a person."

"No, Pa," I begged him. "It doesn't have to be. She's only about forty. She could be a hundred different things in this world as time goes on. A teacher or a social worker. An ex-junkie! Sometimes it's better than having a master's in education."

"Jokes," he said. "As a writer that's your main trouble. You don't want to recognize it. Tragedy! Plain tragedy! Historical tragedy! No hope. The end."

"Oh, Pa," I said. "She could change."

"In your own life, too, you have to look it in the face." He took a couple of nitroglycerin.[6] "Turn to five," he said, pointing to the dial on the oxygen tank. He inserted the tubes into his nostrils and breathed deep. He closed his eyes and said, "No."

I had promised the family to always let him have the last word when arguing, but in this case I had a different responsibility. That woman lives across the street. She's my knowledge and my invention. I'm sorry for her. I'm not going to leave her there in that house crying. (Actually neither would Life, which unlike me has no pity.)

Therefore: She did change. Of course her son never came home again. But right now, she's the receptionist in a storefront community clinic in the East Village. Most of the customers are young people, some old friends. The head doctor said to her, "If we only had three people in this clinic with your experiences . . ."

"The doctor said that?" My father took the oxygen tubes out of his nostrils and said, "Jokes. Jokes again."

"No, Pa, it could really happen that way, it's a funny world nowadays."

"No," he said. "Truth first. She will slide back. A person must have character. She does not."

"No, Pa," I said. "That's it. She's got a job. Forget it. She's in that storefront working."

6. Medicine for certain heart conditions.

"How long will it be?" he asked. "Tragedy! You too. When will you look it in the face?"

1974

QUESTIONS

1. What different ideas about stories and storytelling do the narrator and her father seem to have in "A Conversation with My Father"? What might account for their different attitudes?
2. In what ways is the narrator's second version of her story an improvement over the first? Why does her father still reject the story?
3. Why does the narrator's father object so strongly to the jokes in the stories, even though he compliments her "nice sense of humor"? Are jokes out of place in a story about someone facing death?

Authors on Their Work: GRACE PALEY (1922–2007)

From "Lit Chat: Grace Paley" (1995)*

Grace Paley, poet and educator as well as story writer, grew up in the Bronx in New York City speaking Russian, Yiddish, and English. "I'm not writing a history of famous people," Paley once said. "I am interested in a history of everyday life."

In a 1995 interview for the online magazine *Salon*, Paley described her beginnings as a poet who wrote as much as possible in the style of W. H. Auden:

"I look at all those poems now, and I see I didn't yet realize that you have two ears. One ear is that literary ear, and it's a good old ear. It's with us when we write in the tradition of English writing, or Western writing that includes Proust and Flaubert, and German writers and so on, and also Joyce.

"But there was also something else that I had but I didn't know it. I only knew it in my own speech, and that is the ear of the language of home, and the language of your street and your own people.

"When I started writing stories, I had a kind of a breakthrough. I had enough poetry from this ear, and I suddenly broke into the language that I then continued to write with. That was an important hour in my life. It was a sudden thing. I was sick and had a few weeks off, so I had the time to listen. I was able to use both ears suddenly."

* "Lit Chat: Grace Paley," *Salon*. 1995. Web. 25 March 2009.

LARA VAPNYAR

Puffed Rice and Meatballs

Once, in a hazy, postcoital silence, Katya's lover came back from a shower, dropped the towel to the floor, climbed into the bed, and said, "Tell me about your childhood. Tell me about the horrors of Communism."

Katya sat hugging her knees so that her body resembled a triangle with her head as an apex. She had put on her bra and panties—she hated nakedness, how it turned into something sadly irrelevant after sex.

The request startled her. What exactly were the horrors of Communism? Katya's childhood coincided with the stagnation period. People weren't killed or put in prisons as easily as before, there was plenty of space in mental hospitals, and as for the freedoms of speech, residence, and such—what did little Katya need them for? Was it horrible to have to wear a red tie, or stand in a two-hour line to see Lenin's body in his tomb, or stand in an even longer line to buy toilet paper? Katya didn't think so. It was rather funny, even nostalgic now.

So then why would a man with whom she'd gone on only a few dates and exchanged a few embraces be interested in something as intimate as her childhood?

5   She stared at her lover suspiciously.

He had propped up his head with his elbow. His expression was of calm anticipation. He didn't want to know her better. The man was simply asking for some entertainment—for an easy, amusing, and preferably sexy story about the exotic world to which his lover belonged. Katya's shoulders relaxed.

After some mental probing she picked a story. She wasn't sure if it had anything to do with Communism, but she thought that with a few effective details she would be able to make the narrative exotic enough. She put her right cheek on her knee and turned to her lover.

"Do you want to hear about my first sexual encounter?"

"Gladly!"

10   "When I was little, I attended a daylong preschool, like most city kids. We were on a very strict schedule similar to a prison, or a labor camp. Every day, at 1 PM, we had a nap. Our teacher—I remember only that she had red ears and a long, lumpy nose—put us in two lines and led us to the bedroom, a gloomy semi-dark room, where blinds were drawn at all times, where the beds stood in tight rows, a girl's bed alternating with a boy's."

"I see," Katya's lover noted with enthusiasm. "So you were sandwiched between two boys."

"Not exactly. Between a boy and a wall, because my bed was the last in a row."

"We stripped to our underwear—boys and girls had identical white underpants and undershirts—climbed into the beds, pulled the blankets to our chins, and turned to the right side. We weren't allowed to sleep on our backs or left side. As soon as we all were in bed the teacher said: 'I'm going now, but if I hear even a squeak from you, I'm coming back and I'm coming back with the thing!' Nobody knew what 'the thing' was, and nobody wanted to find out.

"'And if you go to the bathroom, it better be an emergency!' she added before leaving for the dining room.

"I couldn't sleep on my right side. I just lay there scared and bored, facing the back of the boy next to me, staring at his blanket's pattern through the rectangular slit in the blanket cover.

"Delicious sounds coming from the dining room distracted me even more. I listened to the plates' clatter and the persistent scraping of a serving spoon against a pot's bottom. I knew that in a few minutes the teacher would open the entrance door and let in her sons, twin boys, nine years of age. She would seat them at our tables and feed them the food left over from our lunch. I saw them once, when I pleaded an emergency and ran through the dining room to the bathroom. Their plates were piled up with shrunken meatballs and pale mounds of mashed potatoes. Their knees were bent awkwardly under our kid-size table. Their ears moved along with their jaws.

"I tossed in bed and thought about meatballs, which during the nap time always seemed awfully tempting, even though I'd repeatedly refused them during lunch. 'Want to be hungry—fine,' the teacher had said, hastily taking away my plate. 'This school is no place for picky eaters.'"

Katya's lover listened with a warm and amused expression, tinted with slight shadows of impatience. She didn't know why she mentioned the teacher's boys at all. She'd better hurry up and get to the sex part.

"'Hey, are you asleep?'" she continued. "A thin voice from the next bed interrupted my meatballs fantasies. The voice belonged to a chunky, blue-eyed boy named Vova. He had turned to me and lay blinking with his white eyelashes.

"'Can't you see that my eyes are open?' I asked.

"'Shh,' he pointed in the dining room's direction. The white eyelashes blinked some more. 'I'll show you my *peesya* if you show me yours.'

"I didn't have any problems with that.

"We moved our blankets aside and pulled down our underpants. We craned our necks. We stared.

"'Mine's better,' Vova said at last.

"I agreed. His was better. His looked like something you could play with.

"'It's so pretty and small,' I said.

That was the only time when I didn't lie about a man's size, Katya wanted to add, but then changed her mind.

"'What do you do with it?'

"'Not much really,' he shrugged, tucking his *peesya* into his underpants. 'I pee with it, I pull on it sometimes. Not much.'

"'Not much?' I frowned. Such a pretty, fun toy. I would have known what to do with it! For one thing I would've dressed it in all the clothes from my tiny dolls collection. I would've tried little hats, socks, and dresses on it. Then I would've tried to feed it and put it into bed."

"Classic case of penis envy," Katya's lover said, laughing. He was playing with her bra straps.

"Oh, no, not at all. I didn't feel envy. It was rather a feeling of waste that such a promising thing wasn't properly used.

"Anyway, I was excited, and I couldn't wait to go home and tell my mother. In fact, I didn't wait. I told her on the way from school. I stopped in the middle of the dry summer sidewalk, let go of my mother's hand, and said, 'Mom, you wouldn't believe what I saw today!'

"Several hours of yelling, sobbing, and hysterical phone confessions to her friends followed. Then there was a lecture. My mother led me into a room that we shared—my little bed stood perpendicular to her big one—sat me on a little chair in the corner, and walked to the middle of the room, her arms folded on her chest and her brows furrowed. I think I might have spurted a giggle, because I remember my mother suddenly yelling: 'It's not funny. It's a very serious matter.'

35   "The lecture wasn't long. I remember sitting patiently through the whole of it, and I couldn't have possibly done that if the lecture lasted more than twenty minutes. At one point, my mother broke into sobs at midsentence and ran to lock herself in the bathroom."

"Oh, my god. It could've left you scarred for life."

Katya stopped. Her lover looked mildly horrified. He'd even freed his fingers from under the straps of her bra.

It would've been a bad idea to mention that she then banged on the bathroom door, yelling "Mommy, please, please forgive me!" It would've been even worse to add that she dropped to her knees and tried to calm her mother by whispering through the slit under the door. The last thing Katya needed was to show her scars.

She continued in a lighter tone.

40   "After my mother had gone, I decided to go on with the lecture. Probably wanted to try on the role of an authority figure. I gathered all my dolls—some I had to pull from under the beds and bookcases—and sat them on little chairs from my toy furniture set. It was a peculiar group with the dolls ranging from one inch to three feet high, a few with missing body parts. 'Listen to me,' I said, looming above them with my arms folded on my chest. 'Listen hard, you bunch of stupid, irresponsible dolls. And don't you giggle! Never ever show your little *peesya* to anyone. First of all, good dolls don't do that. Second of all, you can go to prison for that.'"

Katya paused before a punch line.

"And guess what? They never did."

The punch line worked. Katya's lover lifted his hands back to her bra straps, and he even laughed.

"But you did. You did! You weren't as obedient as your dolls."

45   "No, I wasn't," Katya agreed, and helped him to unhook her bra.

The story was a success. It was certainly better than watching the news broadcast, as they had the last time. "You were great," he had said, pulling on his socks afterward, but she hadn't been sure whether he referred to their lovemaking or her ability to patiently watch the news.

It wasn't until much later, when Katya returned to her Brooklyn apartment, that the story started to bother her. It felt like the onset of a toothache—a vague gnawing sensation that would grow into real pain at any moment. Katya brewed some bitter, dark tea right in the mug and opened a jar of walnut jam, which having cost her a ridiculous $5.99 still didn't taste like home. It was too sugary—wrong, just like her story. The very lightness of her carefully dispensed jokes made her shiver with disgust now. "It's not funny!" she wanted to scream like her mother, whom she'd just betrayed for a strange man's entertainment.

Katya became awash in shame, for herself, for her mother, but most of all for the teacher's hungry boys who had to eat leftovers at the kids' tables.

At the bottom of her mug sat a little pile of tea leaves. Years ago, Katya attempted to read the leaves with her best friend, Vera. They sat leaning over their mugs, the tip of Katya's yellow braid touching the table. "I don't see anything," Vera complained. "I see a shape," Katya said. "A shape of what? A man?" Katya shrugged. "A shape of something."

Katya peered into the pile and tried to determine whether she would ever   50 meet a man who would understand her pity and her shame, to whom she could tell her real stories, the ones that mattered, the ones that haunted her, without dressing them up to his taste.

* * *

There were two things I craved as a child—imported clothes and imported junk food in crunchy bags, she would have started her real story. One day I came close to having the one and the other.

It happened soon after I turned thirteen. I remember the year exactly, because it was the year I developed breasts, and it was also the year my Aunt Marusya returned from West Germany and brought me a bunch of hip German clothes. "Here. Ransack it!" she said, handing me a tightly packed plastic bag.

I ran to my room and shook the bag's contents right onto the floor. The clothes made an impressive pile. I wanted to dive in and swim in that colorful sea of fabric. Instead I sat in the middle of the pile and ran the material through my fingers—I felt like somebody who'd opened a treasure box. I stretched stockings, I stroked fuzzy sweaters, I played with shiny metallic belts. I even kissed one nylon blouse I particularly liked. Then I hurried to try them on, afraid that if I waited, they might disappear. I pulled the pieces on, one by one, admiring my reflection in the shiny glass doors of the bookcase. The clothes, even obscured by the reflected book covers, looked divine, even more than divine—they looked just like the ones in the dog-eared J.C. Penney catalogue I'd once seen at my best friend Vera's place.

The last piece in the pile was a modest beige sweater with funny shoulder straps. Why would somebody sew shoulder straps to a sweater, I'd thought when I saw it first. And why bother spending precious currency when you could buy a simple thing like that here. But I was wrong, I was very wrong. And I saw it as soon as I tried the sweater on. The pale, unimpressive piece of fabric could perform miracles. I didn't know whether it was because of the shoulder straps or some other tailor's trick, but it made me appear as if I had breasts! I couldn't believe my eyes. For several months I'd been staring into a bathroom mirror hoping to discover much-desired swellings on my chest. I kneaded and pinched myself, but no matter how hard I tried, it didn't work. My chest was as flat and as hard as my grandmother's washing board. Drink more milk, my happier, breasts-equipped girlfriends advised. I did. I drank about six to eight glasses a day, fighting the spasms of nausea. It didn't work.

And now here they were. Two soft little knobs pushing against the beige fab-   55 ric. They were my very real breasts. They were beautiful. The girl who blinked at me from the bookcase's glass surface was beautiful. She was not just pretty or cute, as people mistakenly called her. She was strikingly, undeniably beautiful. Apparently, the beauty had always been there, but buried under the wrong clothes.

I had to show it to the world.

I dialed Vera's number and asked her to meet me by the playground.

I threw on a new miniskirt and new tights and ran to the door past my parents, who were getting drunk on foreign liquor and Aunt Marusya's stories of foreign life.

Clomping with my shoes on the steps of the littered staircase, I suddenly thought of my newfound beauty as a burden. Being beautiful couldn't be easy. It could be troublesome, and even embarrassing. People would stare at me now; I would produce some reaction in the outside world, make some change. And I would have to react back. But how? What exactly was a beautiful person supposed to do? What was I supposed to do when boys stared at me and at my breasts, which I was certain they would? I had a surge of titillating panic as I opened the entrance door and stopped, blinded by the orange rays of the setting sun.

60   I'd just keep my eyes down, I decided. I'd let them stare, but I'd keep my eyes down.

Vera presented a bigger problem. Would it be possible to stay friends? Vera, with her flat, square face and thick waist, wasn't even pretty, let alone beautiful, and about 80 percent of our conversations had consisted of berating the stupid and boy-crazy pretty girls. Yet, she'd been my best friend for years and I didn't want to lose her.

She loped toward me now, swinging a canvas bag in one hand and waving a wad of money with the other. Was she ungraceful! I slouched and messed up my hair, trying to make my beauty a little less obvious.

But when Vera drew near, I saw that my worries had been in vain. Her nose and forehead were covered with sweat, her eyes bulged with excitement—she clearly was oblivious to everything in the world, including the sudden beauty of her friend.

"The puffed . . . puffed, the puffed rice," she panted. "They are selling puffed rice in the little store." She clutched my sleeve and tried to catch a breath. "American puffed rice in crunchy bags! A friend of my mother's hairdresser told us. We have to run because the line is getting bigger every second."

65   "But I don't have any money!"

"I'll lend you some."

And we loped in the store's direction together.

We were two hundred fifty-sixth and two hundred fifty-seventh in the line. The reason we knew it was they had scribbled the numbers in blue ink right on our palms. I had to keep my marked hand outslung, so the number wouldn't rub off accidentally, as happened to a woman who stood ahead of us. She kept showing her sweaty palm to everybody and asking if they could still read her number, when there wasn't anything but a faded blue stain. I was sure they would turn her away at the counter. The subjects of clothes, boys, and beauty lost their importance somehow, or maybe it was just hard to think of such nonsense while guarding your marked hand.

The line moved slowly. Everybody shifted from one foot to the other waiting to take a step forward. They let in people in batches of ten or twelve—as many as could fit into the narrow strip of the store.

70   I bit on my ponytail. Vera rolled and unrolled the ruble bills in her hand. We were too tired to talk, as were other people. All eyes focused on the exit door, where the happy ones squeezed by with armfuls of crunchy, silver-and-yellow bags. The people looked shabby and crumpled, but the bags shone winningly in the orange rays.

"Let's buy two each," Vera suggested when the line advanced to the hundreds. I nodded. She smoothed the crumpled ruble bills in her hand. There were five of them, enough to buy ten bags of puffed rice or two bags and a round can of instant coffee in the big store next door, as Vera's mother had suggested. I thought what a good friend Vera was. Another person would've just taken all the money, without sharing it with me. I asked myself if I would've done the same thing for Vera. I wasn't sure.

"Let's buy six," Vera said, when we advanced to the store doors. I nodded.

She reached with her hand and touched a bag of puffed rice in somebody's arms. It crunched just as I'd expected.

"You know what, let's buy ten," Vera decided.

I nodded.

My feet hurt and my lips were parched. But instead of craving for a drink, I craved dry and salty puffed rice.

We stood just a few people away from the doors now. They'd let us in with the next batch! It would take just a little bit longer before I could feel the crunchy surface of a bag, before I could rip it open, before I could let the golden avalanche pour into my hands. I licked a trickle of saliva off the corner of my mouth.

Then a saleswoman appeared in the doorway.

"Seven o'clock. The store is closed," she said.

For a few moments nobody moved. Nobody made a sound. People just stood gazing at the woman intently, as if she spoke a foreign language and they were struggling to interpret her words. Then the crowd erupted. The feeble, polite pleas grew into demands, then into curses, then into angry, unintelligible murmur.

The woman listened with a tired and annoyed expression. She shook her head and pulled on the door. She wore a white apron and a white hat above thin dark hair gathered in a loose bun. She had a smooth round birthmark on the right side of her chin. I had never hated anybody as much as I hated her. My hands clenched into fists. I prepared to punch her in the face. Even though I had never done that before, I knew exactly what it would be like. I heard the swishing sound of my striking arm and her scream. I saw the thin skin of her cheeks breaking under my knuckles. I saw her blood. I saw her sink to the floor. Then I realized it was somebody else who punched her.

Almost immediately I felt a strong shove in the back and found myself swimming inside the store. I was squeezed between other bodies and I was going in. I was going in! In! We were storming the store. Just like the crowd that stormed the Tsar's palace in all the Revolution movies. Only now I was more than the audience—I was a part of the crowd.

There was a drunken determination on people's faces. We crashed through the entrance, and the last thing I saw on the outside was Vera, who had been pushed away.

"Vera!" I yelled half-heartedly, because in my toxic excitement I didn't really care whether she'd make it or not.

Soon I found myself pushed to the very back of the store, next to the cracked plywood door that led to the storage area. I was squeezed in among twenty or thirty people filling the tiny space between the entrance and the back door. There wasn't any puffed rice around, but I was sure they had more in the storage.

"Bring it out, you bitch! We won't leave," piercing voices screamed behind me. I wiggled to turn away from the door and see what was happening.

The saleswoman had scrambled onto her knees and stood by the entrance holding her cheek. Her face flinched with a cold hatred.

"Ivan, Vasyok!" she called to somebody in a tired voice. "Where the hell are you? Call the police!"

People kept pushing. An old man to my left shoved me between my ribs with his elbow, somebody hit me in the stomach, somebody stepped on my foot, the light hair of a woman in front of me stuck to my sweaty nose.

90 The excitement had faded. All I wanted was to get out. I looked for the slightest opening between people's bodies, where I could sneak through. There wasn't any.

Then a man appeared, either Vasyok or Ivan. He pushed through the plywood door and stopped right behind me. I managed to turn my head sideways to look at him. He wasn't tall but rather broad and heavy, like my grandmother's commode. He smiled.

"Why are you standing there like an idiot?" the saleswoman screamed. "Do something! Call the police!"

Vasyok or Ivan snorted.

"Why police? No need for police." He rolled up his sleeves and smiled again. His arms were red and perfectly round with pale hairs scattered among scars and tattoos.

95 He drew some air in and huffed into my neck. His breath was hot and garlicky-wet.

I screamed.

"No need for police," Vasyok repeated in the same calm and cheerful tone.

And then he lifted me off the ground. It was the first thing that I noticed, the sensation of being in the air, of losing control. His hands were on my chest, right where I'd felt the precious little knobs just a couple hours earlier. His index fingers crushed my nipples to the bone, while his thumbs pressed into my back ribs, an inch away from my shoulder blades. Half crazy with fear and pain, I kicked with my knees, which was exactly what he needed. He used me as a battering ram, crashing me into the crowd to push people out of the store.

I don't remember how long it took him to clear the room. I don't remember at which point my feet met the ground, and whether I fell or not. It is strange, but I don't even remember if Vera was waiting for me at the store doors or if I had to walk home alone. I don't remember whether I walked or ran.

100 I do remember that after changing into my pajamas that night, I took the new sweater, folded it several times, and shoved it into the garbage pail between an empty sour cream container and long strings of potato peel. And I do remember thinking that I wasn't beautiful and never would be.

Later, when I lay in bed trying to fall asleep, I heard the rumble of a refuse chute—my mother was taking the garbage out. I pressed my face into the pillow and sobbed, suddenly regretting that I'd thrown the sweater out.

Katya peered into her mug again. The tea leaves looked like a bunch of dead flies. They didn't show the face of a man, nor did they give any hint of his name. If they knew something, they certainly kept it secret. Katya put the mug away and went to brush her teeth.

2004

QUESTIONS

1. The heroine of "Puffed Rice and Meatballs," Katya, tells two stories, one in dialogue with her lover and one as a first-person story imbedded in the main story without surrounding quotation marks. What differences do you notice between the two stories? What similarities? Why is it easier to tell one story than the other?

2. What is the significance of the title, "Puffed Rice and Meatballs"? Can you suggest an alternative title? This short story (2004) was reprinted in Vapnyar's collection *Broccoli and Other Tales of Food and Love* (2008), each story involving desires for a kind of food and a sexual relationship. Does this context change your response to the title? Compare the foods in the two stories Katya tells. How does the specific food relate to the incident in each framed story?

3. What clues does the narrator give us about Katya's feelings and attitudes as an adult? What do Katya's stories reveal about her as a child? What lasting effects do you think the incidents had on Katya, based on details in the framing story as well as the internal stories?

Authors on Their Work: LARA VAPNYAR (b. 1971)

From *The O. Henry Prize Stories 2006**

Russian-born, Vapnyar emigrated to the United States in 1994, knowing little English. She began publishing fiction in English in 2002. She writes,

"I have always felt compelled by the theme of sexual awakening in a country as bizarre as Soviet Russia. The comical was then blended with the tragic, and we never knew if a certain episode would with time turn into an amusing memory or a long-lasting trauma.

"'Puffed Rice and Meatballs' is based on two real episodes. Both made a deep impression on me, yet for some reason I kept telling the first episode to many different people under different circumstances and in very different forms, while the second episode stayed buried in my memory. I often wondered why people choose to share certain episodes, and try to suppress the others. I think this wondering made me write 'Puffed Rice and Meatballs.'"

**The O. Henry Prize Stories 2006*, ed. Laura Furman (New York: Anchor, 2006).

SUGGESTIONS FOR WRITING

1. Citing examples from one or more of the stories in this album, write an essay discussing the effects of storytelling on the actions, attitudes, or relationships of the characters.

2. A joke can be ruined if you tell the punchline first. Some stories, however, can begin at the end or interrupt the action to fill in the past. Choose one of the stories in this album and look carefully at the order in which events are told. Notice any points that seem out of chronological order or not set in the "present" of the story, and note whether any long periods of time are skipped or summarized. Would another arrangement work just as well? Write an essay in which you show how time and the order of telling are arranged in this story, and explain why this is an effective way to provide what readers or characters need to know at each stage.

3. Some stories are very specific about when and where they take place, and some allude to history, culture, or social issues. Others are more sparing in details and may seem magical or abstract, or as if they could take place anywhere at any time. Write an essay discussing the significance of setting, historical context, or other references in two of these stories, comparing the ways that the presence or absence of such details contributes to each story's effects.

4. Write a first-person account of "A Conversation with My [Relative]" in which you try to get along with that relative although you are confronting an issue that you disagree about. Or write a first-person account of a time you met someone you expected to dislike, but instead that person changed your mind or your attitude in some way. Your account may be true or fictitious, and the narrator or speaker may be you or a fictional person. Whether imagined or accurate to your experience, the story should provide details of personality and situation that seem realistic, as if it actually happened.

5. Retell all or part of any story in this anthology in an entirely different way. For example, you might recast "The Elephant in the Village of the Blind" as a newspaper story or retell the after-dinner events of "Cathedral" through the voice of the blind man.

6. Sherman Alexie published "Flight Patterns" in a collection called *Ten Little Indians* (2003), ten stories concerning educated Native American or interracial protagonists in the Pacific Northwest. Find a copy of this collection in your library or a bookstore, and read two or more of the other stories. What qualities do the stories have in common? Are the main characters similar to each other or different? Who tells stories *within* these stories? Does reading more of his work change or confirm your views of Sherman Alexie as a writer of stories? Does it make the business traveler William, in "Flight Patterns," seem more like the author or less? Write an essay comparing two stories from *Ten Little Indians*, focusing on the main characters' relationship to storytelling.

7. The setting and the occasion for telling a story make a difference in the tone and substance of the story. Write an essay closely examining the changing stories told within either "A Conversation with My Father" or "Puffed Rice and Meatballs." How does the context of each story-within-a-story shape what is revealed? Consider, for example, the person to whom the story is told, why the story is told, and how the story is told.

Understanding the Text

1 PLOT

At its most basic, every story is an attempt to answer the question, *What happened?* In some cases, this question is easy to answer. J. R. R. Tolkien's *The Lord of the Rings* trilogy (1954–55) is full of battles, chases, and other heart-stopping dramatic action; Mark Twain's *Adventures of Huckleberry Finn* (1884) relates Huck and Jim's adventures as they travel down the Mississippi River. Yet if we ask what happens in other works of fiction, our initial answer might well be, "Not much." In one of the most memorable and pivotal scenes in Henry James's masterly novel *The Portrait of a Lady* (1881), for example, a woman enters a room, sees a man sitting down and a woman standing up, and beats a hasty retreat. Not terribly exciting stuff, it would seem. Yet this event ends up radically transforming the lives of just about everyone in the novel. "On very tiny pivots do human lives turn" would thus seem to be one common message—or **theme**—of fiction.

All fiction, regardless of its subject matter, should make us ask, *What will happen next?* and *How will all this turn out?* And responsive readers of fiction will often pause to answer those questions, trying to articulate just what their expectations are and how the story has shaped them. But great fiction and responsive readers are often just as interested in questions about *why* things happen and about *how* the characters' lives are affected as a result. These *how* and *why* questions are likely to be answered very differently by different readers of the very same fictional work; as a result, such questions will often generate powerful essays, whereas mainly factual questions about what happens in the work usually won't.

PLOT VERSUS ACTION, SEQUENCE, AND SUBPLOT

The term **plot** is sometimes used to refer to the events recounted in a fictional work. But in this book we instead use the term **action** in this way, reserving the term *plot* for the way the author sequences and paces the events so as to shape our response and interpretation.

The difference between action and plot resembles the difference between ancient chronicles that merely list the events of a king's reign in chronological order and more modern histories that make a meaningful sequence out of those events. As the British novelist and critic E. M. Forster put it, "The king died and then the queen died" is not a plot, for it has not been "tampered with." "The queen died after the king died" describes the same events, but the order in which they are reported has been changed. The reader of the first sentence focuses on the king first, the reader of the second on the queen. The second sentence, moreover, subtly encourages us to speculate about *why* things happened, not just *what* happened and *when*: Did the queen die *because* her husband did? If so, was her death the result of her grief? Or was she murdered by a rival who saw the king's death as the perfect opportunity to get rid of her, too? Though our two sentences describe the same action, each has quite a different focus, emphasis, effect, and meaning thanks to its *sequencing*—the precise order in which events are related.

Like chronicles, many fictional works do relate events in chronological order, starting with the earliest and ending with the latest. Folktales, for example, have this sort of plot. But fiction writers have other choices; events need not be recounted in the particular order in which they happened. Quite often, then, a writer will choose to mix things up, perhaps opening a story with the most recent event and then moving backward to show us all that led up to it. Still other stories begin somewhere in the middle of the action or, to use the Latin term, *in medias res* (literally, "in the middle of things"). In such plots, events that occurred before the story's opening are sometimes presented in **flashbacks**. Conversely, a story might jump forward in time to recount a later **episode** or event in a **flashforward**. **Foreshadowing** occurs when an author merely gives subtle clues or hints about what will happen later in the story.

Though we often talk about the plot of a fictional work, however, keep in mind that some works, especially longer ones, have two or more. A plot that receives significantly less time and attention than another is called a **subplot**.

PACE

In life, we sometimes have little choice about how long a particular event lasts. If you want a driver's license, you may have to spend a boring hour or two at the motor vehicle office. And much as you might prefer to relax and enjoy your lunch, occasionally you have to scarf it down in the ten minutes it takes you to drive to campus.

One of the pleasures of turning experiences into a story, however, is that doing so gives a writer more power over them. In addition to choosing the order in which to recount events, the writer can also decide how much time and attention to devote to each. *Pacing*, or the duration of particular episodes—especially relative to each other and to the time they would have taken in real life—is a vital tool of storytellers and another important factor to consider in analyzing plots. In all fiction, pace as much as sequence determines focus and emphasis, effect and meaning. And though it can be very helpful to differentiate between "fast-paced" and "slow-paced" fiction, all effective stories contain both faster and slower bits. When an author slows down to home in on a particular moment and scene, often introduced by a phrase such as "Later that evening . . ." or "the day before Maggie fell down . . . ," we call this a **discriminated occasion**. For example, the first paragraph of Linda Brewer's "20/20" (in "Fiction: Reading, Responding, Writing") quickly and generally refers to events that occur over three days. Then Brewer suddenly slows down, pinpointing an incident that takes place on "The third evening out. . . ." That episode consumes four paragraphs of the story, even though the action described in those paragraphs accounts for only a few minutes of Bill and Ruthie's time. Next the story devotes two more paragraphs to an incident that occurs "The next evening. . . ." In the last paragraph, Brewer speeds up again, telling us about the series of "wonderful sights" Ruthie sees between Indiana and Spokane, Washington.

CONFLICTS

Whatever their sequence and pace, all plots hinge on at least one **conflict**—some sort of struggle—and its resolution. Conflicts may be *external* or *internal*. External conflicts arise between a character and something or someone outside themselves. Adventure stories and films often present this sort of conflict in its purest form, keeping us poised on the edge of our seats as James Bond struggles to outwit and outfight an arch-villain intent on world domination or destruction. Yet external conflicts can also be much subtler, pitting an individual against nature or fate, against a social force such as racism or poverty, or against another person or group of people with a different way of looking at things (as in "20/20"). The cartoon below presents an external conflict of the latter type and one you may well see quite differently than the cartoonist does.

Internal conflicts occur when a character struggles to reconcile two competing desires, needs, or duties, or two parts or aspects of himself: His head, for instance, might tell him to do one thing, his heart another. Often, a conflict is simultaneously external and internal, as in the following brief folktale, in which a woman seems to struggle simultaneously with nature, with mortality, with God, and with her desire to hold onto someone she loves versus her need to let go.

JACOB AND WILHELM GRIMM

The Shroud

There was once a mother who had a little boy of seven years old, who was so handsome and lovable that no one could look at him without liking him, and she herself worshipped him above everything in the world. Now it so happened that he suddenly became ill, and God took him to himself; and for this the mother could not be comforted, and wept both day and night. But soon afterwards, when the child had been buried, it appeared by night in the places where it had sat and played during its life, and if the mother wept, it wept also, and, when morning came, it disappeared. As, however, the mother would not stop crying, it came one night, in the little white shroud in which it had been laid in its coffin, and with its wreath of flowers round its head, and stood on the bed at her feet, and said, "Oh, mother, do stop crying, or I shall never fall asleep in my coffin, for my shroud will not dry because of all thy tears which fall upon it." The mother was afraid when she heard that, and wept no more. The next night the child came again, and held a little light in its hand, and said, "Look, mother, my shroud is nearly dry, and I can rest in my grave." Then the mother gave her sorrow into God's keeping, and bore it quietly and patiently, and the child came no more, but slept in its little bed beneath the earth.

• • •

THE FIVE PARTS OF PLOT

Even compact and simple plots, like that of "The Shroud," have the same five parts or phases as lengthy and complex plots: (1) exposition, (2) rising action, (3) climax or turning point, (4) falling action, and (5) conclusion or resolution. The following diagram, known as Freytag's pyramid after the nineteenth-century German scholar Gustav Freytag, maps out a typical plot structure:

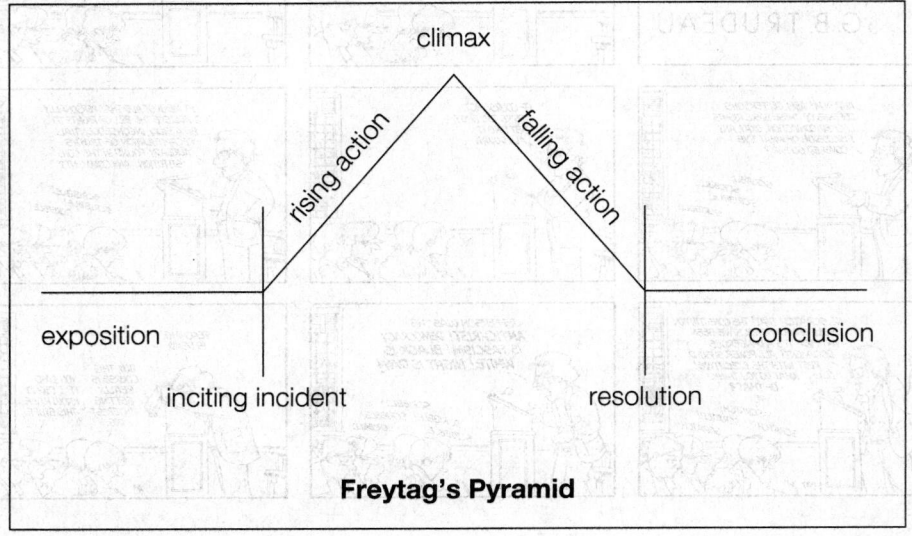

Freytag's Pyramid

EXPOSITION

The first part of the plot, called the **exposition**, introduces the characters, their situations, and, usually, a time and place, giving us all the basic information we need to understand what is to come. In longer works of fiction, exposition may go on for paragraphs or even pages, and some exposition may well be deferred until later phases of the plot. But in our examples, the exposition is all up-front and brief: Trudeau's first panel shows us a teacher (or at least his words), a group of students, and a classroom; the Grimms' first sentence introduces a mother, her young son, and the powerful love she feels for him.

Exposition usually reveals some source or seed of potential conflict in the initial situation, of which the characters may be as yet unaware. In Trudeau's cartoon, the contrast between the talkative teacher, who expects "independent thought" from those in his class, and the silent, scribbling students suggests a conflict in the making. So, too, does the Grimms' statement that the mother "worshipped" her boy "above everything" else in a world in which nothing and no one lasts forever.

RISING ACTION

By suggesting a conflict, exposition may blend into the second phase of the plot, the **rising action**, which begins with an **inciting incident** or *destabilizing event*—that is, some action that destabilizes the initial situation and incites open conflict, as does the death of the little boy in the second sentence of the folktale. Typically, what keeps the action rising is a **complication**, an event that introduces a new conflict or intensifies an existing one. This happens in the third sentence of "The Shroud," when the mother begins to see her little boy every night, although he is dead and buried.

CLIMAX OR TURNING POINT

The plot's **climax** or **turning point** is the moment of greatest emotional intensity. (Notice the way boldface lettering appears and exclamation points replace question marks in the second-to-last panel of the *Doonesbury* strip.) The climax is also the moment when the outcome of the plot and the fate of the characters are decided. (A climax thus tends to be a literally *pivotal* incident that "turns things around," or involves, in Aristotle's words, "the change from one state of things . . . to its opposite.") "The Shroud" reaches its climax when the mother stops crying after her little boy tells her that her grief is what keeps him from sleeping and that peaceful sleep is what he craves.

Here, as in many plots, the turning point involves a discovery or new insight or even an **epiphany,** a sudden revelation of truth inspired by a seemingly trivial event. As a result, turning points often involve internal or psychological events, even if they are prompted by, and lead to, external action. In "The Shroud," for instance, the mother's new insight results in different behavior: She "wept no more."

Sometimes, though, critics differentiate between the story's climax and the **crisis** that precedes and precipitates it. In "The Shroud," for example, these critics would describe the crisis as the moment when the son confronts the mother with information that implicitly requires her to make a choice, the climax as the moment when she makes it. This distinction might be especially helpful when you grapple with longer works of fiction in which much more time and action intervenes between the crisis and the climax.

FALLING ACTION

The **falling action** brings a release of emotional tension and moves us toward the resolution of the conflict or conflicts. This release occurs in "The Shroud" when the boy speaks for the second and last time, assuring his mother that her more peaceful demeanor is giving him peace as well.

In some works of fiction, resolution is achieved through an utterly unexpected twist, as in "Meanwhile, unknown to our hero, the Marines were just on the other side of the hill," or "Susan rolled over in bed and realized the whole thing had been just a dream." Such a device is sometimes called a **deus ex machina**. (This Latin term literally means "god out of a machine" and derives from the ancient theatrical practice of using a machine to lower onto the stage a god who solves the problems of the human characters.)

CONCLUSION

Finally, just as a plot begins with a situation that is later destabilized, so its **conclusion** presents us with a new and at least somewhat stable situation—one that gives a sense of closure because the conflict or conflicts have been resolved, if only temporarily and not necessarily in the way we or the characters had hoped. In "The Shroud," that resolution comes in the last sentence, in which the mother bears her grief "quietly and patiently" and the child quietly sleeps his last sleep. The final *Doonesbury* panel presents us with a situation that is essentially the reverse of the one with which the strip begins—with the teacher silently slumped over his podium, his students suddenly talking to each other instead of scribbling down his words. Many plots instead end with a situation that outwardly looks almost identical to the one with which they began. But thanks to all that has happened between the story's beginning and its end, the final "steady state" at which the characters arrive can never be exactly the same as the one in which they started. A key question to ask at the end of a work of fiction is precisely why, as well as how, things are different.

Some fictional works may also include a final section called an **epilogue**, which ties up loose ends left dangling in the conclusion proper, updates us on what has happened to the characters since their conflicts were resolved, and/or provides some sort of commentary on the story's larger significance. (An epilogue is thus a little like this paragraph, which comes after we have concluded our discussion of the five phases of plot but still feel that there are one or two more terms to deal with.)

A NOTE ON *DÉNOUEMENT*

In discussions of plot, you will very often encounter the French word **dénouement** (literally, "untying," as of a knot). In this anthology, however, we generally try to avoid using *dénouement* because it can be, and often is, used in three different, potentially contradictory ways—as a synonym for *falling action*; as a synonym for *conclusion* or *resolution*; and even as a label for a certain kind of epilogue.

Plot Summary: An Example and an Exercise

Although any good **plot summary** should be a relatively brief recounting (or *synopsis*) of what happens in a work of fiction, it need not necessarily tell what happens in the same order that the work itself does. As a result, many a plot summary is in fact more like an action summary in the sense that we define the terms *action* and *plot* in this book. But unless you have a good reason for reordering events, it is generally a good idea to follow the plot. The following plot summary of Raymond Carver's "Cathedral" does just that:

> The narrator is annoyed to learn that his wife's old friend Robert, a blind man who once employed her as a reader, is coming to visit the couple. The wife has corresponded with her friend for years via cassette tapes, describing the details of her early marriage, divorce, and remarriage to her husband, the narrator. Uncomfortable with the prospect of having a blind person in his home, the narrator is surprised by Robert's appearance and behavior: his booming voice and full beard are not what he expected, and he eats, drinks, and smokes marijuana with relish. After dinner the three watch television. After the narrator's wife has fallen asleep, a program about cathedrals begins. The narrator asks Robert if he knows what cathedrals look like or represent, and Robert, admitting that he does not, asks the narrator to draw one. With Robert's hand lying on top of his own, the narrator traces roofs, spires, arches, and even people. Eventually Robert instructs the narrator to close his eyes and continue drawing. The narrator reports that this experience was like nothing else in my life up to now. (From "Raymond Carver: 'Cathedral,'" *Characters in Twentieth Century Literature*, Book Two [Gale Research, 1995])

Now try this yourself: Choose any of the stories in this anthology and write a one-paragraph plot summary. Then, in a paragraph or two, reflect on your choices about which details to include, which to omit, and how to order them (especially if you've deviated from the plot). What does your summary imply about the story's focus, meaning, and significance? Now repeat the exercise, summarizing the story in a different way and then reflecting on the significance and effect of the changes you've made.

Alternatively, try the same exercise with a friend who has also read the story: Each of you should write your own summary; then exchange them and (separately or together) write a few paragraphs comparing your summaries and reflecting on the significance of the similarities and differences.

COMMON PLOT TYPES

If most plots are essentially variations on the same five-part pattern, some plots have even more features in common. As you think back over the fiction you have read and the movies you have seen (not to mention the video games you have played), you might be surprised to discover just how many of their plots involve a quest—a character or characters' journey to find something or someone that seems, at least at first, of tremendous material or spiritual value. Traditionally, that requires a literal journey, the challenge being not only to find and acquire the object but also to return home with it. Such quests occur often in folktales and are a **convention** of chivalric romance and epic, in which the questing heroes are often men of high rank sent on their quests by someone with even greater power—a god, a wizard, a prophet, a king. And many works of modern fiction— from James Joyce's "Araby" (chapter 9) to Tolkien's *Lord of the Rings* to William Gibson's science-fiction classic *Neuromancer* (1984)—depend for their full effect on our knowledge of the conventions of traditional quest plots.

Many fictional works both ancient and modern also (or instead) follow patterns derived from the two most important and ancient forms (or subgenres) of drama— **tragedy** and **comedy**. Tragic plots, on the one hand, trace a downward movement centering on a character's fall from fortune into misfortune and isolation; they end unhappily, often with death. Comedic plots, on the other hand, tend to end happily, often with marriage or some other act of social integration and celebration.

• • •

The fact that many plots are ultimately tragic or comedic is one of the many tendencies of fictional plot explored in the final story in this chapter, Margaret Atwood's "Happy Endings." For this story is an example of **metafiction**—a deliberately nonrealistic work that playfully draws attention to its own status as a work of fiction in order to help us think about how fiction works.

As you read Atwood's story, or the three more conventionally realistic stories in this chapter, or any other work of fiction, think about what sets each one apart when it comes to plot; how each uses variations on common plot conventions; how each generates, fulfills, and often frustrates our expectations about the action to come; and how each uses sequence, pace, and other techniques to endow action with both emotional charge and meaning. When it comes to action and plot, every good story holds its own surprises and offers a unique answer to the nagging question *What happened?*

Questions about Plot

1. Read the first few paragraphs and then stop. What potential for conflict do you see here? What do you expect to happen in the rest of the story?
2. What is the inciting incident or destabilizing event? How and why does this event destabilize the initial situation?

(Continued on next page)

(Continued)

3. How would you describe the conflict that ultimately develops? To what extent is it external, internal, or both? What, if any, complications or secondary conflicts arise?
4. Where, when, how, and why does the story defy your expectations about what will happen next? What in this story—and in your experience of other stories—created these expectations?
5. What is the climax or turning point? Why and how so?
6. How is the conflict resolved? How and why might this resolution fulfill or defy your expectations? How and why is the situation at the end of the story different from what it was at the beginning?
7. Looking back at the story as a whole, what seems especially significant and effective about its plot, especially in terms of the sequence and pace of the action?
8. Does this plot follow any common plot pattern? Is there, for example, a quest of any kind? Or does this plot follow a tragic or comedic pattern?

GUY DE MAUPASSANT

The Jewelry[1]

Having met the girl one evening, at the house of the office-superintendent, M. Lantin became enveloped in love as in a net.

She was the daughter of a country-tutor, who had been dead for several years. Afterward she had come to Paris with her mother, who made regular visits to several bourgeois families of the neighborhood, in hopes of being able to get her daughter married. They were poor and respectable, quiet and gentle. The young girl seemed to be the very ideal of that pure good woman to whom every young man dreams of entrusting his future. Her modest beauty had a charm of angelic shyness; and the slight smile that always dwelt about her lips seemed a reflection of her heart.

Everybody sang her praises; all who knew her kept saying: "The man who gets her will be lucky. No one could find a nicer girl than that."

M. Lantin, who was then chief clerk in the office of the Minister of the Interior, with a salary of 3,500 francs a year,[2] demanded her hand, and married her.

He was unutterably happy with her. She ruled his home with an economy so 5 adroit that they really seemed to live in luxury. It would be impossible to conceive of any attentions, tendernesses, playful caresses which she did not lavish upon her husband; and such was the charm of her person that, six years after he married her, he loved her even more than he did the first day.

There were only two points upon which he ever found fault with her—her love of the theater, and her passion for false jewelry.

1. Translated by Lafcadio Hearn.
2. Midlevel bureaucratic wage, perhaps about $30,000 to $40,000 today.

Her lady-friends (she was acquainted with the wives of several small office holders) were always bringing her tickets for the theaters; whenever there was a performance that made a sensation, she always had her *loge* secured, even for first performances; and she would drag her husband with her to all these entertainments, which used to tire him horribly after his day's work. So at last he begged her to go to the theater with some lady-acquaintances who would consent to see her home afterward. She refused for quite a while—thinking it would not look very well to go out thus unaccompanied by her husband. But finally she yielded, just to please him; and he felt infinitely grateful to her therefore.

Now this passion for the theater at last evoked in her the desire of dress. It was true that her toilette remained simple, always in good taste, but modest; and her sweet grace, her irresistible grace, ever smiling and shy, seemed to take fresh charm from the simplicity of her robes. But she got into the habit of suspending in her pretty ears two big cut pebbles, fashioned in imitation of diamonds; and she wore necklaces of false pearls, bracelets of false gold, and haircombs studded with paste-imitations of precious stones.

Her husband, who felt shocked by this love of tinsel and show, would often say—"My dear, when one has not the means to afford real jewelry, one should appear adorned with one's natural beauty and grace only—and these gifts are the rarest of jewels."

10   But she would smile sweetly and answer: "What does it matter? I like those things—that is my little whim. I know you are right; but one can't make oneself over again. I've always loved jewelry so much!"

And then she would roll the pearls of the necklaces between her fingers, and make the facets of the cut crystals flash in the light, repeating: "Now look at them—see how well the work is done. You would swear it was real jewelry."

He would then smile in his turn, and declare to her: "You have the tastes of a regular Gypsy."

Sometimes, in the evening, when they were having a chat by the fire, she would rise and fetch the morocco box in which she kept her "stock" (as M. Lantin called it)—would put it on the tea-table, and begin to examine the false jewelry with passionate delight, as if she experienced some secret and mysterious sensations of pleasure in their contemplation; and she would insist on putting one of the necklaces round her husband's neck, and laugh till she couldn't laugh any more, crying out: "Oh! how funny you look!" Then she would rush into his arms, and kiss him furiously.

One winter's night, after she had been to the Opera, she came home chilled through, and trembling. Next day she had a bad cough. Eight days after that, she died of pneumonia.

15   Lantin was very nearly following her into the tomb. His despair was so frightful that in one single month his hair turned white. He wept from morning till night, feeling his heart torn by inexpressible suffering—ever haunted by the memory of her, by the smile, by the voice, by all the charm of the dead woman.

Time did not assuage his grief. Often during office hours his fellow-clerks went off to a corner to chat about this or that topic of the day—his cheeks might have been seen to swell up all of a sudden, his nose wrinkle, his eyes fill with water—he would pull a frightful face, and begin to sob.

He had kept his dead companion's room just in the order she had left it, and he used to lock himself up in it every evening to think about her—all the furniture, and even all her dresses, remained in the same place they had been on the last day of her life.

But life became hard for him. His salary, which, in his wife's hands, had amply sufficed for all household needs, now proved scarcely sufficient to supply his own few wants. And he asked himself in astonishment how she had managed always to furnish him with excellent wines and with delicate eating which he could not now afford at all with his scanty means.

He got a little into debt, like men obliged to live by their wits. At last one morning that he happened to find himself without a cent in his pocket, and a whole week to wait before he could draw his monthly salary, he thought of selling something; and almost immediately it occurred to him to sell his wife's "stock"—for he had always borne a secret grudge against the flash-jewelry that used to annoy him so much in former days. The mere sight of it, day after day, somewhat spoiled the sad pleasure of thinking of his darling.

He tried a long time to make a choice among the heap of trinkets she had left 20 behind her—for up to the very last day of her life she had kept obstinately buying them, bringing home some new thing almost every night—and finally he resolved to take the big pearl necklace which she used to like the best of all, and which he thought ought certainly to be worth six or eight francs, as it was really very nicely mounted for an imitation necklace.

He put it in his pocket, and walked toward the office, following the boulevards, and looking for some jewelry-store on the way, where he could enter with confidence.

Finally he saw a place and went in; feeling a little ashamed of thus exposing his misery, and of trying to sell such a trifling object.

"Sir," he said to the jeweler, "please tell me what this is worth."

The jeweler took the necklace, examined it, weighed it, took up a magnifying glass, called his clerk, talked to him in whispers, put down the necklace on the counter, and drew back a little bit to judge of its effect at a distance.

M. Lantin, feeling very much embarrassed by all these ceremonies, opened 25 his mouth and began to declare—"Oh! I know it can't be worth much" . . . when the jeweler interrupted him saying:

"Well, sir, that is worth between twelve and fifteen thousand francs; but I cannot buy it unless you can let me know exactly how you came by it."

The widower's eyes opened enormously, and he stood gaping—unable to understand. Then after a while he stammered out: "You said? . . . Are you sure?" The jeweler, misconstruing the cause of this astonishment, replied in a dry tone—"Go elsewhere if you like, and see if you can get any more for it. The very most I would give for it is fifteen thousand. Come back and see me again, if you can't do better."

M. Lantin, feeling perfectly idiotic, took his necklace and departed; obeying a confused desire to find himself alone and to get a chance to think.

But the moment he found himself in the street again, he began to laugh, and he muttered to himself: "The fool!—oh! what a fool; If I had only taken him at his word. Well, well!—a jeweler who can't tell paste from real jewelry!"

And he entered another jewelry-store, at the corner of the Rue de la Paix. The 30 moment the jeweler set eyes on the necklace, he examined—"Hello! I know that necklace well—it was sold here!"

M. Lantin, very nervous, asked:

"What's it worth?"

"Sir, I sold it for twenty-five thousand francs. I am willing to buy it back again for eighteen thousand—if you can prove to me satisfactorily, according to legal prescriptions, how you came into possession of it."—This time, M. Lantin was simply paralyzed with astonishment. He said: "Well ... but please look at it again, sir. I always thought until now that it was ... was false."

The jeweler said:

35   "Will you give me your name, sir?"

"Certainly. My name is Lantin; I am employed at the office of the Minister of the Interior. I live at No. 16, Rue des Martyrs."

The merchant opened the register, looked, and said: "Yes; this necklace was sent to the address of Madame Lantin, 16 Rue des Martyrs, on July 20th, 1876."

And the two men looked into each other's eyes—the clerk wild with surprise; the jeweler suspecting he had a thief before him.

The jeweler resumed:

40   "Will you be kind enough to leave this article here for twenty-four hours only—I'll give you a receipt."

M. Lantin stuttered: "Yes—ah! certainly." And he went out folding up the receipt, which he put in his pocket.

Then he crossed the street, went the wrong way, found out his mistake, returned by way of the Tuileries, crossed the Seine, found out he had taken the wrong road again, and went back to the Champs-Élysées without being able to get one clear idea into his head. He tried to reason, to understand. His wife could never have bought so valuable an object as that. Certainly not. But then, it must have been a present! .... A present from whom? What for?

He stopped and stood stock-still in the middle of the avenue.

A horrible suspicion swept across his mind.... She? ... But then all those other pieces of jewelry must have been presents also! ... Then it seemed to him that the ground was heaving under his feet; that a tree, right in front of him, was falling toward him; he thrust out his arms instinctively, and fell senseless.

45   He recovered his consciousness again in a drug-store to which some bystanders had carried him. He had them lead him home, and he locked himself into his room.

Until nightfall he cried without stopping, biting his handkerchief to keep himself from screaming out. Then, completely worn out with grief and fatigue, he went to bed, and slept a leaden sleep.

A ray of sunshine awakened him, and he rose and dressed himself slowly to go to the office. It was hard to have to work after such a shock. Then he reflected that he might be able to excuse himself to the superintendent, and he wrote to him. Then he remembered he would have to go back to the jeweler's; and shame made his face purple. He remained thinking a long time. Still he could not leave the necklace there; he put on his coat and went out.

It was a fine day; the sky extended all blue over the city, and seemed to make it smile. Strollers were walking aimlessly about, with their hands in their pockets.

Lantin thought as he watched them passing: "How lucky the men are who have fortunes! With money a man can even shake off grief—you can go where you please—travel—amuse yourself! Oh! if I were only rich!"

50   He suddenly discovered he was hungry—not having eaten anything since the evening before. But his pockets were empty; and he remembered the necklace.

Eighteen thousand francs! Eighteen thousand francs!—that was a sum—that was!

He made his way to the Rue de la Paix and began to walk backward and forward on the sidewalk in front of the store. Eighteen thousand francs! Twenty times he started to go in; but shame always kept him back.

Still he was hungry—very hungry—and had not a cent. He made one brusque resolve, and crossed the street almost at a run, so as not to let himself have time to think over the matter; and he rushed into the jeweler's.

As soon as he saw him, the merchant hurried forward, and offered him a chair with smiling politeness. Even the clerks came forward to stare at Lantin, with gaiety in their eyes and smiles about their lips.

The jeweler said: "Sir, I made inquiries; and if you are still so disposed, I am ready to pay you down the price I offered you."

The clerk stammered: "Why, yes—sir, certainly."   55

The jeweler took from a drawer eighteen big bills,[3] counted them, and held them out to Lantin, who signed a little receipt, and thrust the money feverishly into his pocket.

Then, as he was on the point of leaving, he turned to the ever-smiling merchant, and said, lowering his eyes: "I have some—I have some other jewelry, which came to me in the same—from the same inheritance. Would you purchase them also from me?"

The merchant bowed, and answered: "Why, certainly, sir—certainly. . . ." One of the clerks rushed out to laugh at his ease; another kept blowing his nose as hard as he could.

Lantin, impassive, flushed and serious, said: "I will bring them to you."

And he hired a cab to get the jewelry.   60

When he returned to the store, an hour later, he had not yet breakfasted. They examined the jewelry—piece by piece—putting a value on each. Nearly all had been purchased from that very house.

Lantin, now, disputed estimates made, got angry, insisted on seeing the books, and talked louder and louder the higher the estimates grew.

The big diamond earrings were worth 20,000 francs; the bracelets, 35,000; the brooches, rings and medallions, 16,000; a set of emeralds and sapphires, 14,000; solitaire, suspended to a gold neckchain, 40,000; the total value being estimated at 196,000 francs.

The merchant observed with mischievous good nature: "The person who owned these must have put all her savings into jewelry."

Lantin answered with gravity: "Perhaps that is as good a way of saving money   65
as any other." And he went off, after having agreed with the merchant that an expert should make a counter-estimate for him the next day.

When he found himself in the street again, he looked at the Column Vendôme[4] with the desire to climb it, as if it were a May pole. He felt jolly enough to play leapfrog over the Emperor's head—up there in the blue sky.

He breakfasted at Voisin's[5] restaurant, and ordered wine at 20 francs a bottle.

3. French paper money varies in size; the larger the bill, the larger the denomination.
4. Famous column with a statue of the emperor Napoleon at the top.
5. Like the Café Anglais below, a well-known and high-priced restaurant.

Then he hired a cab and drove out to the Bois.[6] He looked at the carriages passing with a sort of contempt, and a wild desire to yell out to the passers-by: "I am rich, too—I am! I have 200,000 francs!"

The recollection of the office suddenly came back to him. He drove there, walked right into the superintendent's private room, and said: "Sir, I come to give you my resignation. I have just come into a fortune of *three* hundred thousand francs." Then he shook hands all round with his fellow-clerks; and told them all about his plans for a new career. Then he went to dinner at the Café Anglais.

70   Finding himself seated at the same table with a man who seemed to him quite genteel, he could not resist the itching desire to tell him, with a certain air of coquetry, that he had just inherited a fortune of *four* hundred thousand francs.

For the first time in his life he went to the theater without feeling bored by the performance; and he passed the night in revelry and debauch.

Six months after he married again. His second wife was the most upright of spouses, but had a terrible temper. She made his life very miserable.

1883

QUESTIONS

1. What parts of "The Jewelry" correspond to the five traditional phases of plot: exposition, rising action, turning point or climax, falling action, and conclusion?
2. Once the secret of Madame Lantin's jewelry is revealed, what details from earlier in the story take on a different significance?
3. How and why might the story's end—especially its last paragraph—defy expectations? How does it once again change your interpretation of earlier events and of Lantin's first marriage?

JAMES BALDWIN

Sonny's Blues

I read about it in the paper, in the subway, on my way to work. I read it, and I couldn't believe it, and I read it again. Then perhaps I just stared at it, at the newsprint spelling out his name, spelling out the story. I stared at it in the swinging lights of the subway car, and in the faces and bodies of the people, and in my own face, trapped in the darkness which roared outside.

It was not to be believed and I kept telling myself that, as I walked from the subway station to the high school. And at the same time I couldn't doubt it. I was scared, scared for Sonny. He became real to me again. A great block of ice got settled in my belly and kept melting there slowly all day long, while I taught my classes algebra. It was a special kind of ice. It kept melting, sending trickles of ice water all up and down my veins, but it never got less. Sometimes it hardened and seemed to expand until I felt my guts were going to come spilling out or that I was going to choke or scream. This would always be at a

6. Large Parisian park where the rich took their outings.

moment when I was remembering some specific thing Sonny had once said or done.

When he was about as old as the boys in my classes his face had been bright and open, there was a lot of copper in it; and he'd had wonderfully direct brown eyes, and great gentleness and privacy. I wondered what he looked like now. He had been picked up, the evening before, in a raid on an apartment downtown, for peddling and using heroin.

I couldn't believe it: but what I mean by that is that I couldn't find any room for it anywhere inside me. I had kept it outside me for a long time. I hadn't wanted to know. I had had suspicions, but I didn't name them, I kept putting them away. I told myself that Sonny was wild, but he wasn't crazy. And he'd always been a good boy, he hadn't ever turned hard or evil or disrespectful, the way kids can, so quick, so quick, especially in Harlem. I didn't want to believe that I'd ever see my brother going down, coming to nothing, all that light in his face gone out, in the condition I'd already seen so many others. Yet it had happened and here I was, talking about algebra to a lot of boys who might, every one of them for all I knew, be popping off needles every time they went to the head.[1] Maybe it did more for them than algebra could.

I was sure that the first time Sonny had ever had horse,[2] he couldn't have been much older than these boys were now. These boys, now, were living as we'd been living then, they were growing up with a rush and their heads bumped abruptly against the low ceiling of their actual possibilities. They were filled with rage. All they really knew were two darknesses, the darkness of their lives, which was now closing in on them, and the darkness of the movies, which had blinded them to that other darkness, and in which they now, vindictively, dreamed, at once more together than they were at any other time, and more alone.

When the last bell rang, the last class ended, I let out my breath. It seemed I'd been holding it for all that time. My clothes were wet—I may have looked as though I'd been sitting in a steam bath, all dressed up, all afternoon. I sat alone in the classroom a long time. I listened to the boys outside, downstairs, shouting and cursing and laughing. Their laughter struck me for perhaps the first time. It was not the joyous laughter which—God knows why—one associates with children. It was mocking and insular, its intent was to denigrate. It was disenchanted, and in this, also, lay the authority of their curses. Perhaps I was listening to them because I was thinking about my brother and in them I heard my brother. And myself.

One boy was whistling a tune, at once very complicated and very simple, it seemed to be pouring out of him as though he were a bird, and it sounded very cool and moving through all that harsh, bright air, only just holding its own through all those other sounds.

I stood up and walked over to the window and looked down into the courtyard. It was the beginning of the spring and the sap was rising in the boys. A teacher passed through them every now and again, quickly, as though he or she couldn't wait to get out of that courtyard, to get those boys out of their sight and off their minds. I started collecting my stuff. I thought I'd better get home and talk to Isabel.

5

1. Lavatory. 2. Heroin.

The courtyard was almost deserted by the time I got downstairs. I saw this boy standing in the shadow of a doorway, looking just like Sonny. I almost called his name. Then I saw that it wasn't Sonny, but somebody we used to know, a boy from around our block. He'd been Sonny's friend. He'd never been mine, having been too young for me, and, anyway, I'd never liked him. And now, even though he was a grown-up man, he still hung around that block, still spent hours on the street corners, was always high and raggy. I used to run into him from time to time and he'd often work around to asking me for a quarter or fifty cents. He always had some real good excuse, too, and I always gave it to him. I don't know why.

10   But now, abruptly, I hated him. I couldn't stand the way he looked at me, partly like a dog, partly like a cunning child. I wanted to ask him what the hell he was doing in the school courtyard.

He sort of shuffled over to me, and he said, "I see you got the papers. So you already know about it."

"You mean about Sonny? Yes, I already know about it. How come they didn't get you?"

He grinned. It made him repulsive and it also brought to mind what he'd looked like as a kid. "I wasn't there. I stay away from them people."

"Good for you." I offered him a cigarette and I watched him through the smoke. "You come all the way down here just to tell me about Sonny?"

15   "That's right." He was sort of shaking his head and his eyes looked strange, as though they were about to cross. The bright sun deadened his damp dark brown skin and it made his eyes look yellow and showed up the dirt in his kinked hair. He smelled funky. I moved a little away from him and I said, "Well, thanks. But I already know about it and I got to get home."

"I'll walk you a little ways," he said. We started walking. There were a couple of kids still loitering in the courtyard and one of them said goodnight to me and looked strangely at the boy beside me.

"What're you going to do?" he asked me. "I mean, about Sonny?"

"Look. I haven't seen Sonny for over a year, I'm not sure I'm going to do anything. Anyway, what the hell *can* I do?"

"That's right," he said quickly, "ain't nothing you can do. Can't much help old Sonny no more, I guess."

20   It was what I was thinking and so it seemed to me he had no right to say it.

"I'm surprised at Sonny, though," he went on—he had a funny way of talking, he looked straight ahead as though he were talking to himself—"I thought Sonny was a smart boy, I thought he was too smart to get hung."

"I guess he thought so too," I said sharply, "and that's how he got hung. And how about you? You're pretty goddamn smart, I bet."

Then he looked directly at me, just for a minute. "I ain't smart," he said. "If I was smart, I'd have reached for a pistol a long time ago."

"Look. Don't tell *me* your sad story, if it was up to me, I'd give you one." Then I felt guilty—guilty, probably, for never having supposed that the poor bastard *had* a story of his own, much less a sad one, and I asked, quickly, "What's going to happen to him now?"

25   He didn't answer this. He was off by himself some place.

"Funny thing," he said, and from his tone we might have been discussing the quickest way to get to Brooklyn, "when I saw the papers this morning, the first thing I asked myself was if I had anything to do with it. I felt sort of responsible."

I began to listen more carefully. The subway station was on the corner, just before us, and I stopped. He stopped, too. We were in front of a bar and he ducked slightly, peering in, but whoever he was looking for didn't seem to be there. The juke box was blasting away with something black and bouncy and I half watched the barmaid as she danced her way from the juke box to her place behind the bar. And I watched her face as she laughingly responded to something someone said to her, still keeping time to the music. When she smiled one saw the little girl, one sensed the doomed, still-struggling woman beneath the battered face of the semi-whore.

"I never *give* Sonny nothing," the boy said finally, "but a long time ago I come to school high and Sonny asked me how it felt." He paused, I couldn't bear to watch him, I watched the barmaid, and I listened to the music which seemed to be causing the pavement to shake. "I told him it felt great." The music stopped, the barmaid paused and watched the juke box until the music began again. "It did."

All this was carrying me some place I didn't want to go. I certainly didn't want to know how it felt. It filled everything, the people, the houses, the music, the dark, quicksilver barmaid, with menace; and this menace was their reality.

"What's going to happen to him now?" I asked again.   30

"They'll send him away some place and they'll try to cure him." He shook his head. "Maybe he'll even think he's kicked the habit. Then they'll let him loose"—he gestured, throwing his cigarette into the gutter. "That's all."

"What do you mean, that's *all*?"

But I knew what he meant.

"I *mean,* that's *all*." He turned his head and looked at me, pulling down the corners of his mouth. "Don't you know what I mean?" he asked, softly.

"How the hell *would* I know what you mean?" I almost whispered it, I don't   35
know why.

"That's right," he said to the air, "how would *he* know what I mean?" He turned toward me again, patient and calm, and yet I somehow felt him shaking, shaking as though he were going to fall apart. I felt that ice in my guts again, the dread I'd felt all afternoon; and again I watched the barmaid, moving about the bar, washing glasses, and singing. "Listen. They'll let him out and then it'll just start all over again. That's what I mean."

"You mean—they'll let him out. And then he'll just start working his way back in again. You mean he'll never kick the habit. Is that what you mean?"

"That's right," he said, cheerfully. "*You* see what I mean."

"Tell me," I said at last, "why does he want to die? He must want to die, he's killing himself, why does he want to die?"

He looked at me in surprise. He licked his lips. "He don't want to die. He wants   40
to live. Don't nobody want to die, ever."

Then I wanted to ask him—too many things. He could not have answered, or if he had, I could not have borne the answers. I started walking. "Well, I guess it's none of my business."

"It's going to be rough on old Sonny," he said. We reached the subway station. "This is your station?" he asked. I nodded. I took one step down. "Damn!" he said, suddenly. I looked up at him. He grinned again. "Damn it if I didn't leave all my money home. You ain't got a dollar on you, have you? Just for a couple of days, is all."

All at once something inside gave and threatened to come pouring out of me. I didn't hate him any more. I felt that in another moment I'd start crying like a child.

"Sure," I said. "Don't sweat." I looked in my wallet and didn't have a dollar, I only had a five. "Here," I said. "That hold you?"

45   He didn't look at it—he didn't want to look at it. A terrible, closed look came over his face, as though he were keeping the number on the bill a secret from him and me. "Thanks," he said, and now he was dying to see me go. "Don't worry about Sonny. Maybe I'll write him or something."

"Sure," I said. "You do that. So long."

"Be seeing you," he said. I went on down the steps.

And I didn't write Sonny or send him anything for a long time. When I finally did, it was just after my little girl died, and he wrote me back a letter which made me feel like a bastard.

Here's what he said:

50   Dear brother,

   You don't know how much I needed to hear from you. I wanted to write you many a time but I dug how much I must have hurt you and so I didn't write. But now I feel like a man who's been trying to climb up out of some deep, real deep and funky hole and just saw the sun up there, outside. I got to get outside.

   I can't tell you much about how I got here. I mean I don't know how to tell you. I guess I was afraid of something or I was trying to escape from something and you know I have never been very strong in the head (smile). I'm glad Mama and Daddy are dead and can't see what's happened to their son and I swear if I'd known what I was doing I would never have hurt you so, you and a lot of other fine people who were nice to me and who believed in me.

   I don't want you to think it had anything to do with me being a musician. It's more than that. Or maybe less than that. I can't get anything straight in my head down here and I try not to think about what's going to happen to me when I get outside again. Sometime I think I'm going to flip and *never* get outside and sometime I think I'll come straight back. I tell you one thing, though, I'd rather blow my brains out than go through this again. But that's what they all say, so they tell me. If I tell you when I'm coming to New York and if you could meet me, I sure would appreciate it. Give my love to Isabel and the kids and I was sure sorry to hear about little Gracie. I wish I could be like Mama and say the Lord's will be done, but I don't know it seems to me that trouble is the one thing that never does get stopped and I don't know what good it does to blame it on the Lord. But maybe it does some good if you believe it.

Your brother,
Sonny

Then I kept in constant touch with him and I sent him whatever I could and I went to meet him when he came back to New York. When I saw him many things I thought I had forgotten came flooding back to me. This was because I had begun, finally, to wonder about Sonny, about the life that Sonny lived inside. This life, whatever it was, had made him older and thinner and it had deepened the distant stillness in which he had always moved. He looked very unlike my baby brother. Yet, when he smiled, when we shook hands, the baby brother I'd never known looked out from the depths of his private life, like an animal waiting to be coaxed into the light.

"How you been keeping?" he asked me.

"All right. And you?"

"Just fine." He was smiling all over his face. "It's good to see you again." 55

"It's good to see you."

The seven years' difference in our ages lay between us like a chasm: I wondered if these years would ever operate between us as a bridge. I was remembering, and it made it hard to catch my breath, that I had been there when he was born; and I had heard the first words he had ever spoken. When he started to walk, he walked from our mother straight to me. I caught him just before he fell when he took the first steps he ever took in this world.

"How's Isabel?"

"Just fine. She's dying to see you."

"And the boys?" 60

"They're fine, too. They're anxious to see their uncle."

"Oh, come on. You know they don't remember me."

"Are you kidding? Of course they remember you."

He grinned again. We got into a taxi. We had a lot to say to each other, far too 65 much to know how to begin.

As the taxi began to move, I asked, "You still want to go to India?"

He laughed. "You still remember that. Hell, no. This place is Indian enough for me."

"It used to belong to them," I said.

And he laughed again. "They damn sure knew what they were doing when they got rid of it."

Years ago, when he was around fourteen, he'd been all hipped on the idea of 70 going to India. He read books about people sitting on rocks, naked, in all kinds of weather, but mostly bad, naturally, and walking barefoot through hot coals and arriving at wisdom. I used to say that it sounded to me as though they were getting away from wisdom as fast as they could. I think he sort of looked down on me for that.

"Do you mind," he asked, "if we have the driver drive alongside the park? On the west side—I haven't seen the city in so long."

"Of course not," I said. I was afraid that I might sound as though I were humoring him, but I hoped he wouldn't take it that way.

So we drove along, between the green of the park and the stony, lifeless elegance of hotels and apartment buildings, toward the vivid, killing streets of our childhood. These streets hadn't changed, though housing projects jutted up out of them now like rocks in the middle of a boiling sea. Most of the houses in which we had grown up had vanished, as had the stores from which we had stolen, the basements in which we had first tried sex, the rooftops from which we had hurled tin cans and bricks. But houses exactly like the houses of our past yet dominated the landscape, boys exactly like the boys we once had been found themselves smothering in these houses, came down into the streets for light and air and found themselves encircled by disaster. Some escaped the trap, most didn't. Those who got out always left something of themselves behind, as some animals amputate a leg and leave it in the trap. It might be said, perhaps, that I had escaped, after all, I was a school teacher; or that Sonny had, he hadn't lived in Harlem for years. Yet, as the cab moved uptown through streets which seemed, with a rush, to darken with dark people, and as I covertly studied Sonny's face, it came to me that what we both were seeking through our separate cab windows was that part of ourselves which had been left behind. It's always at the hour of trouble and confrontation that the missing member aches.

We hit 110th Street and started rolling up Lenox Avenue. And I'd known this avenue all my life, but it seemed to me again, as it had seemed on the day I'd first heard about Sonny's trouble, filled with a hidden menace which was its very breath of life.

75   "We almost there," said Sonny.

"Almost." We were both too nervous to say anything more.

We live in a housing project. It hasn't been up long. A few days after it was up it seemed uninhabitably new, now, of course, it's already rundown. It looks like a parody of the good, clean, faceless life—God knows the people who live in it do their best to make it a parody. The beat-looking grass lying around isn't enough to make their lives green, the hedges will never hold out the streets, and they know it. The big windows fool no one, they aren't big enough to make space out of no space. They don't bother with the windows, they watch the TV screen instead. The playground is most popular with the children who don't play at jacks, or skip rope, or roller skate, or swing, and they can be found in it after dark. We moved in partly because it's not too far from where I teach, and partly for the kids; but it's really just like the houses in which Sonny and I grew up. The same things happen, they'll have the same things to remember. The moment Sonny and I started into the house I had the feeling that I was simply bringing him back into the danger he had almost died trying to escape.

Sonny has never been talkative. So I don't know why I was sure he'd be dying to talk to me when supper was over the first night. Everything went fine, the oldest boy remembered him, and the youngest boy liked him, and Sonny had remembered to bring something for each of them; and Isabel, who is really much nicer than I am, more open and giving, had gone to a lot of trouble about dinner and was genuinely glad to see him. And she's always been able to tease Sonny in a way that I haven't. It was nice to see her face so vivid again and to hear her laugh and watch her make Sonny laugh. She wasn't, or, anyway, she didn't seem to be, at all uneasy or embarrassed. She chatted as though there were no subject which had to be avoided and she got Sonny past his first, faint stiffness. And thank God she was there, for I was filled with that icy dread again. Everything I did seemed awkward to me, and everything I said sounded freighted with hidden meaning. I was trying to remember everything I'd heard about dope addiction and I couldn't help watching Sonny for signs. I wasn't doing it out of malice. I was trying to find out something about my brother. I was dying to hear him tell me he was safe.

"Safe!" my father grunted, whenever Mama suggested trying to move to a neighborhood which might be safer for children. "Safe, hell! Ain't no place safe for kids, nor nobody."

He always went on like this, but he wasn't, ever, really as bad as he sounded, 80 not even on weekends, when he got drunk. As a matter of fact, he was always on the lookout for "something a little better," but he died before he found it. He died suddenly, during a drunken weekend in the middle of the war, when Sonny was fifteen. He and Sonny hadn't ever got on too well. And this was partly because Sonny was the apple of his father's eye. It was because he loved Sonny so much and was frightened for him, that he was always fighting with him. It doesn't do any good to fight with Sonny. Sonny just moves back, inside himself, where he can't be reached. But the principal reason that they never hit it off is that they were so much alike. Daddy was big and rough and loud-talking, just the opposite of Sonny, but they both had—that same privacy.

Mama tried to tell me something about this, just after Daddy died. I was home on leave from the army.

This was the last time I ever saw my mother alive. Just the same, this picture gets all mixed up in my mind with pictures I had of her when she was younger. The way I always see her is the way she used to be on a Sunday afternoon, say, when the old folks were talking after the big Sunday dinner. I always see her wearing pale blue. She'd be sitting on the sofa. And my father would be sitting in the easy chair, not far from her. And the living room would be full of church folks and relatives. There they sit, in chairs all around the living room, and the night is creeping up outside, but nobody knows it yet. You can see the darkness growing against the windowpanes and you hear the street noises every now and again, or maybe the jangling beat of a tambourine from one of the churches close by, but it's real quiet in the room. For a moment nobody's talking, but every face looks darkening, like the sky outside. And my mother rocks a little from the waist, and my father's eyes are closed. Everyone is looking at something a child can't see. For a minute they've forgotten the children. Maybe a kid is lying on the rug, half asleep. Maybe somebody's got a kid in his lap and is absent-mindedly stroking the kid's head. Maybe there's a kid, quiet and big-eyed, curled up in a big chair in the corner. The silence, the darkness coming, and the darkness in the faces frighten the child obscurely. He hopes that the hand which strokes his forehead will never stop—will never die. He hopes that there will never come a time when the old folks won't be sitting around the living room, talking about where they've come from, and what they've seen, and what's happened to them and their kinfolk.

But something deep and watchful in the child knows that this is bound to end, is already ending. In a moment someone will get up and turn on the light. Then the old folks will remember the children and they won't talk any more that day. And when light fills the room, the child is filled with darkness. He knows that every time this happens he's moved just a little closer to that darkness outside. The darkness outside is what the old folks have been talking about. It's what they've come from. It's what they endure. The child knows that they won't talk any more because if he knows too much about what's happened to *them,* he'll know too much too soon, about what's going to happen to *him.*

The last time I talked to my mother, I remember I was restless. I wanted to get out and see Isabel. We weren't married then and we had a lot to straighten out between us.

There Mama sat, in black, by the window. She was humming an old church 85 song, *Lord, you brought me from a long ways off.* Sonny was out somewhere. Mama kept watching the streets.

"I don't know," she said, "if I'll ever see you again, after you go off from here. But I hope you'll remember the things I tried to teach you."

"Don't talk like that," I said, and smiled. "You'll be here a long time yet."

She smiled, too, but she said nothing. She was quiet for a long time. And I said, "Mama, don't you worry about nothing. I'll be writing all the time, and you be getting the checks. . . ."

"I want to talk to you about your brother," she said, suddenly. "If anything happens to me he ain't going to have nobody to look out for him."

90   "Mama," I said, "ain't nothing going to happen to you *or* Sonny. Sonny's all right. He's a good boy and he's got good sense."

"It ain't a question of his being a good boy," Mama said, "nor of his having good sense. It ain't only the bad ones, nor yet the dumb ones that gets sucked under." She stopped, looking at me. "Your Daddy once had a brother," she said, and she smiled in a way that made me feel she was in pain. "You didn't never know that, did you?"

"No," I said, "I never knew that," and I watched her face.

"Oh, yes," she said, "your Daddy had a brother." She looked out of the window again. "I know you never saw your Daddy cry. But *I* did—many a time, through all these years."

I asked her, "What happened to his brother? How come nobody's ever talked about him?"

95   This was the first time I ever saw my mother look old.

"His brother got killed," she said, "when he was just a little younger than you are now. I knew him. He was a fine boy. He was maybe a little full of the devil, but he didn't mean nobody no harm."

Then she stopped and the room was silent, exactly as it had sometimes been on those Sunday afternoons. Mama kept looking out into the streets.

"He used to have a job in the mill," she said, "and, like all young folks, he just liked to perform on Saturday nights. Saturday nights, him and your father would drift around to different places, go to dances and things like that, or just sit around with people they knew, and your father's brother would sing, he had a fine voice, and play along with himself on his guitar. Well, this particular Saturday night, him and your father was coming home from some place, and they were both a little drunk and there was a moon that night, it was bright like day. Your father's brother was feeling kind of good, and he was whistling to himself, and he had his guitar slung over his shoulder. They was coming down a hill and beneath them was a road that turned off from the highway. Well, your father's brother, being always kind of frisky, decided to run down this hill, and he did, with that guitar banging and clanging behind him, and he ran across the road, and he was making water behind a tree. And your father was sort of amused at him and he was still coming down the hill, kind of slow. Then he heard a car motor and that same minute his brother stepped from behind the tree, into the road, in the moonlight. And he started to cross the road. And your father started to run down the hill, he says he don't know why. This car was full of white men. They was all drunk, and when they seen your father's brother they let out a great whoop and holler and they aimed the car straight at him. They was having fun, they just wanted to scare him, the way they do sometimes, you know. But they was drunk. And I guess the boy, being drunk, too, and scared, kind of lost his head. By the time he jumped it was too late. Your father says he heard his brother scream when the car rolled over him, and he heard the wood of that guitar when it give, and he heard them strings go flying, and he heard them white men shouting, and the car kept on a-going and it ain't stopped till this day. And, time your father got down the hill, his brother weren't nothing but blood and pulp."

Tears were gleaming on my mother's face. There wasn't anything I could say.

"He never mentioned it," she said, "because I never let him mention it before you children. Your Daddy was like a crazy man that night and for many a night thereafter. He says he never in his life seen anything as dark as that road after the lights of that car had gone away. Weren't nothing, weren't nobody on that road, just your Daddy and his brother and that busted guitar. Oh, yes. Your Daddy never did really get right again. Till the day he died he weren't sure but that every white man he saw was the man that killed his brother." 100

She stopped and took out her handkerchief and dried her eyes and looked at me.

"I ain't telling you all this," she said, "to make you scared or bitter or to make you hate nobody. I'm telling you this because you got a brother. And the world ain't changed."

I guess I didn't want to believe this. I guess she saw this in my face. She turned away from me, toward the window again, searching those streets.

"But I praise my Redeemer," she said at last, "that He called your Daddy home before me. I ain't saying it to throw no flowers at myself, but, I declare, it keeps me from feeling too cast down to know I helped your father get safely through this world. Your father always acted like he was the roughest, strongest man on earth. And everybody took him to be like that. But if he hadn't had me there—to see his tears!"

She was crying again. Still, I couldn't move. I said, "Lord, Lord, Mama, I didn't know it was like that." 105

"Oh, honey," she said, "there's a lot that you don't know. But you are going to find out." She stood up from the window and came over to me. "You got to hold on to your brother," she said, "and don't let him fall, no matter what it looks like is happening to him and no matter how evil you gets with him. You going to be evil with him many a time. But don't you forget what I told you, you hear?"

"I won't forget," I said. "Don't you worry, I won't forget. I won't let nothing happen to Sonny."

My mother smiled as though she was amused at something she saw in my face. Then, "You may not be able to stop nothing from happening. But you got to let him know you's *there*."

Two days later I was married, and then I was gone. And I had a lot of things on my mind and I pretty well forgot my promise to Mama until I got shipped home on a special furlough for her funeral.

And, after the funeral, with just Sonny and me alone in the empty kitchen, I tried to find out something about him. 110

"What do you want to do?" I asked him.

"I'm going to be a musician," he said.

For he had graduated, in the time I had been away, from dancing to the juke box to finding out who was playing what, and what they were doing with it, and he had bought himself a set of drums.

"You mean, you want to be a drummer?" I somehow had the feeling that being a drummer might be all right for other people but not for my brother Sonny.

115 "I don't think," he said, looking at me very gravely, "that I'll ever be a good drummer. But I think I can play a piano."

I frowned. I'd never played the role of the oldest brother quite so seriously before, had scarcely ever, in fact, *asked* Sonny a damn thing. I sensed myself in the presence of something I didn't really know how to handle, didn't understand. So I made my frown a little deeper as I asked: "What kind of musician do you want to be?"

He grinned. "How many kinds do you think there are?"

"Be *serious*," I said.

He laughed, throwing his head back, and then looked at me. "I *am* serious."

120 "Well, then, for Christ's sake, stop kidding around and answer a serious question. I mean, do you want to be a concert pianist, you want to play classical music and all that, or—or what?" Long before I finished he was laughing again. "For Christ's *sake*, Sonny!"

He sobered, but with difficulty. "I'm sorry. But you sound so—*scared!*" and he was off again.

"Well, you may think it's funny now, baby, but it's not going to be so funny when you have to make your living at it, let me tell you *that*." I was furious because I knew he was laughing at me and I didn't know why.

"No," he said, very sober now, and afraid, perhaps, that he'd hurt me, "I don't want to be a classical pianist. That isn't what interests me. I mean"—he paused, looking hard at me, as though his eyes would help me to understand, and then gestured helplessly, as though perhaps his hand would help—"I mean, I'll have a lot of studying to do, and I'll have to study *everything*, but, I mean, I want to play *with*—jazz musicians." He stopped. "I want to play jazz," he said.

Well, the word had never before sounded as heavy, as real, as it sounded that afternoon in Sonny's mouth. I just looked at him and I was probably frowning a real frown by this time. I simply couldn't see why on earth he'd want to spend his time hanging around nightclubs, clowning around on bandstands, while people pushed each other around a dance floor. It seemed—beneath him, somehow. I had never thought about it before, had never been forced to, but I suppose I had always put jazz musicians in a class with what Daddy called "good-time people."

125 "Are you *serious*?"

"Hell, *yes*, I'm serious."

He looked more helpless than ever, and annoyed, and deeply hurt.

I suggested, helpfully: "You mean—like Louis Armstrong?"[3]

His face closed as though I'd struck him. "No. I'm not talking about none of that old-time, down-home crap."

130 "Well, look, Sonny, I'm sorry, don't get mad. I just don't altogether get it, that's all. Name somebody—you know, a jazz musician you admire."

"Bird."

"Who?"

***

3. New Orleans-born trumpeter and singer (1901–71); by the 1950s, his music would have seemed old-fashioned to a jazz afficionado.

"Bird! Charlie Parker![4] Don't they teach you nothing in the goddamn army?"

I lit a cigarette. I was surprised and then a little amused to discover that I was trembling. "I've been out of touch," I said. "You'll have to be patient with me. Now. Who's this Parker character?"

"He's just one of the greatest jazz musicians alive," said Sonny, sullenly, his hands in his pockets, his back to me. "Maybe *the* greatest," he added, bitterly, "that's probably why *you* never heard of him."   135

"All right," I said, "I'm ignorant. I'm sorry. I'll go out and buy all the cat's records right away, all right?"

"It don't," said Sonny, with dignity, "make any difference to me. I don't care what you listen to. Don't do me no favors."

I was beginning to realize that I'd never seen him so upset before. With another part of my mind I was thinking that this would probably turn out to be one of those things kids go through and that I shouldn't make it seem important by pushing it too hard. Still, I didn't think it would do any harm to ask: "Doesn't all this take a lot of time? Can you make a living at it?"

He turned back to me and half leaned, half sat, on the kitchen table. "Everything takes time," he said, "and—well, yes, sure, I can make a living at it. But what I don't seem to be able to make you understand is that it's the only thing I want to do."

"Well, Sonny," I said gently, "you know people can't always do exactly what they *want* to do—"   140

"*No,* I don't know that," said Sonny, surprising me. "I think people *ought* to do what they want to do, what else are they alive for?"

"You getting to be a big boy," I said desperately, "it's time you started thinking about your future."

"I'm thinking about my future," said Sonny, grimly. "I think about it all the time."

I gave up. I decided, if he didn't change his mind, that we could always talk about it later. "In the meantime," I said, "you got to finish school." We had already decided that he'd have to move in with Isabel and her folks. I knew this wasn't the ideal arrangement because Isabel's folks are inclined to be dicty[5] and they hadn't especially wanted Isabel to marry me. But I didn't know what else to do. "And we have to get you fixed up at Isabel's."

There was a long silence. He moved from the kitchen table to the window.   145
"That's a terrible idea. You know it yourself."

"Do you have a *better* idea?"

He just walked up and down the kitchen for a minute. He was as tall as I was. He had started to shave. I suddenly had the feeling that I didn't know him at all.

He stopped at the kitchen table and picked up my cigarettes. Looking at me with a kind of mocking, amused defiance, he put one between his lips. "You mind?"

4. Charlie ("Bird") Parker (1920–55), brilliant saxophonist and jazz innovator; working in New York in the mid-1940s, he developed, with Dizzy Gillespie and others, the style of jazz called "bebop." He was a narcotics addict.
5. Snobbish, bossy.

"You smoking already?"

150 He lit the cigarette and nodded, watching me through the smoke. "I just wanted to see if I'd have the courage to smoke in front of you." He grinned and blew a great cloud of smoke to the ceiling. "It was easy." He looked at my face. "Come on, now. I bet you was smoking at my age, tell the truth."

I didn't say anything but the truth was on my face, and he laughed. But now there was something very strained in his laugh. "Sure. And I bet that ain't all you was doing."

He was frightening me a little. "Cut the crap," I said. "We already decided that you was going to go and live at Isabel's. Now what's got into you all of a sudden?"

"*You* decided it," he pointed out. "*I* didn't decide nothing." He stopped in front of me, leaning against the stove, arms loosely folded. "Look, brother. I don't want to stay in Harlem no more, I really don't." He was very earnest. He looked at me, then over toward the kitchen window. There was something in his eyes I'd never seen before, some thoughtfulness, some worry all his own. He rubbed the muscle of one arm. "It's time I was getting out of here."

"Where do you want to *go*, Sonny?"

155 "I want to join the army. Or the navy, I don't care. If I say I'm old enough, they'll believe me."

Then I got mad. It was because I was so scared. "You must be crazy. You god-damn fool, what the hell do you want to go and join the *army* for?"

"I just told you. To get out of Harlem."

"Sonny, you haven't even finished *school*. And if you really want to be a musician, how do you expect to study if you're in the *army*?"

He looked at me, trapped, and in anguish. "There's ways. I might be able to work out some kind of deal. Anyway, I'll have the G.I. Bill when I come out."

160 "*If* you come out." We stared at each other. "Sonny, please. Be reasonable. I know the setup is far from perfect. But we got to do the best we can."

"I ain't learning nothing in school," he said. "Even when I go." He turned away from me and opened the window and threw his cigarette out into the narrow alley. I watched his back. "At least, I ain't learning nothing you'd want me to learn." He slammed the window so hard I thought the glass would fly out, and turned back to me. "And I'm sick of the stink of these garbage cans!"

"Sonny," I said, "I know how you feel. But if you don't finish school now, you're going to be sorry later that you didn't." I grabbed him by the shoulders. "And you only got another year. It ain't so bad. And I'll come back and I swear I'll help you do *whatever* you want to do. Just try to put up with it till I come back. Will you please do that? For me?"

He didn't answer and he wouldn't look at me.

"Sonny. You hear me?"

165 He pulled away. "I hear you. But you never hear anything *I* say."

I didn't know what to say to that. He looked out of the window and then back at me. "OK," he said, and sighed. "I'll try."

Then I said, trying to cheer him up a little, "They got a piano at Isabel's. You can practice on it."

And as a matter of fact, it did cheer him up for a minute. "That's right," he said to himself. "I forgot that." His face relaxed a little. But the worry, the thoughtfulness, played on it still, the way shadows play on a face which is staring into the fire.

But I thought I'd never hear the end of that piano. At first, Isabel would write me, saying how nice it was that Sonny was so serious about his music and how, as soon as he came in from school, or wherever he had been when he was supposed to be at school, he went straight to that piano and stayed there until suppertime. And, after supper, he went back to that piano and stayed there until everybody went to bed. He was at the piano all day Saturday and all day Sunday. Then he bought a record player and started playing records. He'd play one record over and over again, all day long sometimes, and he'd improvise along with it on the piano. Or he'd play one section of the record, one chord, one change, one progression, then he'd do it on the piano. Then back to the record. Then back to the piano.

Well, I really don't know how they stood it. Isabel finally confessed that it 170 wasn't like living with a person at all, it was like living with sound. And the sound didn't make any sense to her, didn't make any sense to any of them—naturally. They began, in a way, to be afflicted by this presence that was living in their home. It was as though Sonny were some sort of god, or monster. He moved in an atmosphere which wasn't like theirs at all. They fed him and he ate, he washed himself, he walked in and out of their door; he certainly wasn't nasty or unpleasant or rude, Sonny isn't any of those things; but it was as though he were all wrapped up in some cloud, some fire, some vision all his own; and there wasn't any way to reach him.

At the same time, he wasn't really a man yet, he was still a child, and they had to watch out for him in all kinds of ways. They certainly couldn't throw him out. Neither did they dare to make a great scene about that piano because even they dimly sensed, as I sensed, from so many thousands of miles away, that Sonny was at that piano playing for his life.

But he hadn't been going to school. One day a letter came from the school board and Isabel's mother got it—there had, apparently, been other letters but Sonny had torn them up. This day, when Sonny came in, Isabel's mother showed him the letter and asked where he'd been spending his time. And she finally got it out of him that he'd been down in Greenwich Village, with musicians and other characters, in a white girl's apartment. And this scared her and she started to scream at him and what came up, once she began—though she denies it to this day—was what sacrifices they were making to give Sonny a decent home and how little he appreciated it.

Sonny didn't play the piano that day. By evening, Isabel's mother had calmed down but then there was the old man to deal with, and Isabel herself. Isabel says she did her best to be calm but she broke down and started crying. She says she just watched Sonny's face. She could tell, by watching him, what was happening with him. And what was happening was that they penetrated his cloud, they had reached him. Even if their fingers had been a thousand times more gentle than human fingers ever are, he could hardly help feeling that they had stripped him naked and were spitting on that nakedness. For he also had to see that his presence, that music, which was life or death to him, had been torture for them and that they had endured it, not at all for his sake, but only for mine. And Sonny couldn't take that. He can take it a little better today than he could then but he's still not very good at it and, frankly, I don't know anybody who is.

The silence of the next few days must have been louder than the sound of all the music ever played since time began. One morning, before she went to work,

Isabel was in his room for something and she suddenly realized that all of his records were gone. And she knew for certain that he was gone. And he was. He went as far as the navy would carry him. He finally sent me a postcard from some place in Greece and that was the first I knew that Sonny was still alive. I didn't see him any more until we were both back in New York and the war had long been over.

175 He was a man by then, of course, but I wasn't willing to see it. He came by the house from time to time, but we fought almost every time we met. I didn't like the way he carried himself, loose and dreamlike all the time, and I didn't like his friends, and his music seemed to be merely an excuse for the life he led. It sounded just that weird and disordered.

Then we had a fight, a pretty awful fight, and I didn't see him for months. By and by I looked him up, where he was living, in a furnished room in the Village, and I tried to make it up. But there were lots of other people in the room and Sonny just lay on his bed, and he wouldn't come downstairs with me, and he treated these other people as though they were his family and I weren't. So I got mad and then he got mad, and then I told him that he might just as well be dead as live the way he was living. Then he stood up and he told me not to worry about him any more in life, that he *was* dead as far as I was concerned. Then he pushed me to the door and the other people looked on as though nothing were happening, and he slammed the door behind me. I stood in the hallway, staring at the door. I heard somebody laugh in the room and then the tears came to my eyes. I started down the steps, whistling to keep from crying, I kept whistling to myself, *You going to need me, baby, one of these cold, rainy days.*

I read about Sonny's trouble in the spring. Little Grace died in the fall. She was a beautiful little girl. But she only lived a little over two years. She died of polio and she suffered. She had a slight fever for a couple of days, but it didn't seem like anything and we just kept her in bed. And we would certainly have called the doctor, but the fever dropped, she seemed to be all right. So we thought it had just been a cold. Then, one day, she was up, playing, Isabel was in the kitchen fixing lunch for the two boys when they'd come in from school, and she heard Grace fall down in the living room. When you have a lot of children you don't always start running when one of them falls, unless they start screaming or something. And, this time, Gracie was quiet. Yet, Isabel says that when she heard that *thump* and then that silence, something happened to her to make her afraid. And she ran to the living room and there was little Grace on the floor, all twisted up, and the reason she hadn't screamed was that she couldn't get her breath. And when she did scream, it was the worst sound, Isabel says, that she'd ever heard in all her life, and she still hears it sometimes in her dreams. Isabel will sometimes wake me up with a low, moaning, strangling sound and I have to be quick to awaken her and hold her to me and where Isabel is weeping against me seems a mortal wound.

I think I may have written Sonny the very day that little Grace was buried. I was sitting in the living room in the dark, by myself, and I suddenly thought of Sonny. My trouble made his real.

One Saturday afternoon, when Sonny had been living with us, or anyway, been in our house, for nearly two weeks, I found myself wandering aimlessly about the living room, drinking from a can of beer, and trying to work up courage to search Sonny's room. He was out, he was usually out whenever I was home, and Isabel had taken the children to see their grandparents. Suddenly I was standing still in front of the living room window, watching Seventh Avenue. The idea of searching Sonny's room made me still. I scarcely dared to admit to myself what I'd be searching for. I didn't know what I'd do if I found it. Or if I didn't.

On the sidewalk across from me, near the entrance to a barbecue joint, some people were holding an old-fashioned revival meeting. The barbecue cook, wearing a dirty white apron, his conked[6] hair reddish and metallic in the pale sun, and a cigarette between his lips, stood in the doorway, watching them. Kids and older people paused in their errands and stood there, along with some older men and a couple of very tough-looking women who watched everything that happened on the avenue, as though they owned it, or were maybe owned by it. Well, they were watching this, too. The revival was being carried on by three sisters in black, and a brother. All they had were their voices and their Bibles and a tambourine. The brother was testifying[7] and while he testified two of the sisters stood together, seeming to say, amen, and the third sister walked around with the tambourine outstretched and a couple of people dropped coins into it. Then the brother's testimony ended and the sister who had been taking up the collection dumped the coins into her palm and transferred them to the pocket of her long black robe. Then she raised both hands, striking the tambourine against the air, and then against one hand, and she started to sing. And the two other sisters and the brother joined in.

It was strange, suddenly, to watch, though I had been seeing these meetings all my life. So, of course, had everybody else down there. Yet, they paused and watched and listened and I stood still at the window. " *'Tis the old ship of Zion,*" they sang, and the sister with the tambourine kept a steady, jangling beat, *"it has rescued many a thousand!"* Not a soul under the sound of their voices was hearing this song for the first time, not one of them had been rescued. Nor had they seen much in the way of rescue work being done around them. Neither did they especially believe in the holiness of the three sisters and the brother, they knew too much about them, knew where they lived, and how. The woman with the tambourine, whose voice dominated the air, whose face was bright with joy, was divided by very little from the woman who stood watching her, a cigarette between her heavy, chapped lips, her hair a cuckoo's nest, her face scarred and swollen from many beatings, and her black eyes glittering like coal. Perhaps they both knew this, which was why, when, as rarely, they addressed each other, they addressed each other as Sister. As the singing filled the air the watching, listening faces underwent a change, the eyes focusing on something within; the music seemed to soothe a poison out of them; and time seemed, nearly, to fall away from the sullen, belligerent, battered faces, as though they were fleeing back to their first condition, while dreaming of their last. The barbecue cook half shook his head and smiled, and dropped his cigarette and disappeared into his joint. A man fumbled in his pockets for change and stood holding it in his hand impatiently, as though he had just remembered a pressing appointment further up the avenue. He looked furious. Then I saw Sonny, standing on the edge of the crowd. He was carrying a wide, flat notebook with a green cover, and it made him look, from where I was standing, almost like a schoolboy. The coppery sun brought out

6. Processed: straightened and greased.   7. Publicly professing belief.

the copper in his skin, he was very faintly smiling, standing very still. Then the singing stopped, the tambourine turned into a collection plate again. The furious man dropped in his coins and vanished, so did a couple of the women, and Sonny dropped some change in the plate, looking directly at the woman with a little smile. He started across the avenue, toward the house. He has a slow, loping walk, something like the way Harlem hipsters walk, only he's imposed on this his own half-beat. I had never really noticed it before.

I stayed at the window, both relieved and apprehensive. As Sonny disappeared from my sight, they began singing again. And they were still singing when his key turned in the lock.

"Hey," he said.

"Hey, yourself. You want some beer?"

185 "No. Well, maybe." But he came up to the window and stood beside me, looking out. "What a warm voice," he said.

They were singing *If I could only hear my mother pray again!*

"Yes," I said, "and she can sure beat that tambourine."

"But what a terrible song," he said, and laughed. He dropped his notebook on the sofa and disappeared into the kitchen. "Where's Isabel and the kids?"

"I think they went to see their grandparents. You hungry?"

190 "No." He came back into the living room with his can of beer. "You want to come some place with me tonight?"

I sensed, I don't know how, that I couldn't possibly say no. "Sure. Where?"

He sat down on the sofa and picked up his notebook and started leafing through it. "I'm going to sit in with some fellows in a joint in the Village."

"You mean, you're going to play, tonight?"

"That's right." He took a swallow of his beer and moved back to the window. He gave me a sidelong look. "If you can stand it."

195 "I'll try," I said.

He smiled to himself and we both watched as the meeting across the way broke up. The three sisters and the brother, heads bowed, were singing *God be with you till we meet again.* The faces around them were very quiet. Then the song ended. The small crowd dispersed. We watched the three women and the lone man walk slowly up the avenue.

"When she was singing before," said Sonny, abruptly, "her voice reminded me for a minute of what heroin feels like sometimes—when it's in your veins. It makes you feel sort of warm and cool at the same time. And distant. And—and sure." He sipped his beer, very deliberately not looking at me. I watched his face. "It makes you feel—in control. Sometimes you've got to have that feeling."

"Do you?" I sat down slowly in the easy chair.

"Sometimes." He went to the sofa and picked up his notebook again. "Some people do."

200 "In order," I asked, "to play?" And my voice was very ugly, full of contempt and anger.

"Well"—he looked at me with great, troubled eyes, as though, in fact, he hoped his eyes would tell me things he could never otherwise say—"they *think* so. And *if* they think so—!"

"And what do *you* think?" I asked.

He sat on the sofa and put his can of beer on the floor. "I don't know," he said, and I couldn't be sure if he were answering my question or pursuing his thoughts.

His face didn't tell me. "It's not so much to *play*. It's to *stand* it, to be able to make it at all. On any level." He frowned and smiled: "In order to keep from shaking to pieces."

"But these friends of yours," I said, "they seem to shake themselves to pieces pretty goddamn fast."

"Maybe." He played with the notebook. And something told me that I should curb my tongue, that Sonny was doing his best to talk, that I should listen. "But of course you only know the ones that've gone to pieces. Some don't—or at least they haven't *yet* and that's just about all *any* of us can say." He paused. "And then there are some who just live, really, in hell, and they know it and they see what's happening and they go right on. I don't know." He sighed, dropped the notebook, folded his arms. "Some guys, you can tell from the way they play, they on something *all* the time. And you can see that, well, it makes something real for them. But of course," he picked up his beer from the floor and sipped it and put the can down again, "they *want* to, too, you've got to see that. Even some of them that say they don't—*some*, not all."

"And what about you?" I asked—I couldn't help it. "What about you? Do *you* want to?"

He stood up and walked to the window and I remained silent for a long time. Then he sighed. "Me," he said. Then: "While I was downstairs before, on my way here, listening to that woman sing, it struck me all of a sudden how much suffering she must have had to go through—to sing like that. It's *repulsive* to think you have to suffer that much."

I said: "But there's no way not to suffer—is there, Sonny?"

"I believe not," he said and smiled, "but that's never stopped anyone from trying." He looked at me. "Has it?" I realized, with this mocking look, that there stood between us, forever, beyond the power of time or forgiveness, the fact that I had held silence—so long!—when he had needed human speech to help him. He turned back to the window. "No, there's no way not to suffer. But you try all kinds of ways to keep from drowning in it, to keep on top of it, and to make it seem—well, like *you*. Like you did something, all right, and now you're suffering for it. You know?" I said nothing. "Well you know," he said, impatiently, "why *do* people suffer? Maybe it's better to do something to give it a reason, *any* reason."

"But we just agreed," I said, "that there's no way not to suffer. Isn't it better, then, just to—take it?"

"But nobody just takes it," Sonny cried, "that's what I'm telling you! *Everybody* tries not to. You're just hung up on the *way* some people try—it's not *your* way!"

The hair on my face began to itch, my face felt wet. "That's not true," I said, "that's not true. I don't give a damn what other people do, I don't even care how they suffer. I just care how *you* suffer." And he looked at me. "Please believe me," I said, "I don't want to see you—die—trying not to suffer."

"I won't," he said flatly, "die trying not to suffer. At least, not any faster than anybody else."

"But there's no need," I said, trying to laugh, "is there? in killing yourself."

I wanted to say more, but I couldn't. I wanted to talk about will power and how life could be—well, beautiful. I wanted to say that it was all within; but was it? or, rather, wasn't that exactly the trouble? And I wanted to promise that I would never fail him again. But it would all have sounded—empty words and lies.

So I made the promise to myself and prayed that I would keep it.

"It's terrible sometimes, inside," he said, "that's what's the trouble. You walk these streets, black and funky and cold, and there's not really a living ass to talk to, and there's nothing shaking, and there's no way of getting it out—that storm inside. You can't talk it and you can't make love with it, and when you finally try to get with it and play it, you realize *nobody's* listening. So *you've* got to listen. You got to find a way to listen."

And then he walked away from the window and sat on the sofa again, as though all the wind had suddenly been knocked out of him. "Sometimes you'll do *anything* to play, even cut your mother's throat." He laughed and looked at me. "Or your brother's." Then he sobered. "Or your own." Then: "Don't worry. I'm all right now and I think I'll *be* all right. But I can't forget—where I've been. I don't mean just the physical place I've been, I mean where I've *been*. And *what* I've been."

"What have you been, Sonny?" I asked.

220   He smiled—but sat sideways on the sofa, his elbow resting on the back, his fingers playing with his mouth and chin, not looking at me. "I've been something I didn't recognize, didn't know I could be. Didn't know anybody could be." He stopped, looking inward, looking helplessly young, looking old. "I'm not talking about it now because I feel *guilty* or anything like that—maybe it would be better if I did, I don't know. Anyway, I can't really talk about it. Not to you, not to anybody," and now he turned and faced me. "Sometimes, you know, and it was actually when I was most *out* of the world, I felt that I was in it, that I was *with* it, really, and I could play or I didn't really have to *play*, it just came out of me, it was there. And I don't know how I played, thinking about it now, but I know I did awful things, those times, sometimes, to people. Or it wasn't that I *did* anything to them—it was that they weren't real." He picked up the beer can; it was empty; he rolled it between his palms: "And other times—well, I needed a fix, I needed to find a place to lean, I needed to clear a space to *listen*—and I couldn't find it, and I—went crazy, I did terrible things to *me*, I was terrible *for* me." He began pressing the beer can between his hands, I watched the metal begin to give. It glittered, as he played with it like a knife, and I was afraid he would cut himself, but I said nothing. "Oh well. I can never tell you. I was all by myself at the bottom of something, stinking and sweating and crying and shaking, and I smelled it, you know? *my* stink, and I thought I'd die if I couldn't get away from it and yet, all the same, I knew that everything I was doing was just locking me in with it. And I didn't know," he paused, still flattening the beer can, "I didn't know, I still *don't* know, something kept telling me that maybe it was good to smell your own stink, but I didn't think that *that* was what I'd been trying to do—and—who can stand it?" and he abruptly dropped the ruined beer can, looking at me with a small, still smile, and then rose, walking to the window as though it were the lodestone rock. I watched his face, he watched the avenue. "I couldn't tell you when Mama died—but the reason I wanted to leave Harlem so bad was to get away from drugs. And then, when I ran away, that's what I was running from—really. When I came back, nothing had changed, *I* hadn't changed, I was just—older." And he stopped, drumming with his fingers on the windowpane. The sun had vanished, soon darkness would fall. I watched his face. "It can come again," he said, almost as though speaking to himself. Then he turned to me. "It can come again," he repeated. "I just want you to know that."

"All right," I said, at last. "So it can come again. All right."

He smiled, but the smile was sorrowful. "I had to try to tell you," he said.

"Yes," I said. "I understand that."

"You're my brother," he said, looking straight at me, and not smiling at all.

"Yes," I repeated, "yes. I understand that."

He turned back to the window, looking out. "All that hatred down there," he said, "all that hatred and misery and love. It's a wonder it doesn't blow the avenue apart."

We went to the only nightclub on a short, dark street, downtown. We squeezed through the narrow, chattering, jampacked bar to the entrance of the big room, where the bandstand was. And we stood there for a moment, for the lights were very dim in this room and we couldn't see. Then, "Hello, boy," said the voice and an enormous black man, much older than Sonny or myself, erupted out of all that atmospheric lighting and put an arm around Sonny's shoulder. "I been sitting right here," he said, "waiting for you."

He had a big voice, too, and heads in the darkness turned toward us.

Sonny grinned and pulled a little away, and said, "Creole, this is my brother. I told you about him."

Creole shook my hand. "I'm glad to meet you, son," he said, and it was clear that he was glad to meet me *there,* for Sonny's sake. And he smiled, "You got a real musician in *your* family," and he took his arm from Sonny's shoulder and slapped him, lightly, affectionately, with the back of his hand.

"Well. Now I've heard it all," said a voice behind us. This was another musician, and a friend of Sonny's, a coal-black, cheerful-looking man, built close to the ground. He immediately began confiding to me, at the top of his lungs, the most terrible things about Sonny, his teeth gleaming like a lighthouse and his laugh coming up out of him like the beginning of an earthquake. And it turned out that everyone at the bar knew Sonny, or almost everyone; some were musicians, working there, or nearby, or not working, some were simply hangers-on, and some were there to hear Sonny play. I was introduced to all of them and they were all very polite to me. Yet, it was clear that, for them, I was only Sonny's brother. Here, I was in Sonny's world. Or, rather: his kingdom. Here, it was not even a question that his veins bore royal blood.

They were going to play soon and Creole installed me, by myself, at a table in a dark corner. Then I watched them, Creole, and the little black man, and Sonny, and the others, while they horsed around, standing just below the bandstand. The light from the bandstand spilled just a little short of them and, watching them laughing and gesturing and moving about, I had the feeling that they, nevertheless, were being most careful not to step into that circle of light too suddenly; that if they moved into the light too suddenly, without thinking, they would perish in flame. Then, while I watched, one of them, the small black man, moved into the light and crossed the bandstand and started fooling around with his drums. Then—being funny and being, also, extremely ceremonious—Creole took Sonny by the arm and led him to the piano. A woman's voice called Sonny's name and a few hands started clapping. And Sonny, also being funny and being ceremonious, and so touched, I think, that he could have cried, but neither hiding it nor showing it, riding it like a man, grinned, and put both hands to his heart and bowed from the waist.

Creole then went to the bass fiddle and a lean, very bright-skinned brown man jumped up on the bandstand and picked up his horn. So there they were, and the atmosphere on the bandstand and in the room began to change and tighten. Someone stepped up to the microphone and announced them. Then there were all kinds of murmurs. Some people at the bar shushed others. The waitress ran around, frantically getting in the last orders, guys and chicks got closer to each other, and the lights on the bandstand, on the quartet, turned to a kind of indigo. Then they all looked different there. Creole looked about him for the last time, as though he were making certain that all his chickens were in the coop, and then he—jumped and struck the fiddle. And there they were.

All I know about music is that not many people ever really hear it. And even then, on the rare occasions when something opens within, and the music enters, what we mainly hear, or hear corroborated, are personal, private, vanishing evocations. But the man who creates the music is hearing something else, is dealing with the roar rising from the void and imposing order on it as it hits the air. What is evoked in him, then, is of another order, more terrible because it has no words, and triumphant, too, for that same reason. And his triumph, when he triumphs, is ours. I just watched Sonny's face. His face was troubled, he was working hard, but he wasn't with it. And I had the feeling that, in a way, everyone on the bandstand was waiting for him, both waiting for him and pushing him along. But as I began to watch Creole, I realized that it was Creole who held them all back. He had them on a short rein. Up there, keeping the beat with his whole body, wailing on the fiddle, with his eyes half closed, he was listening to everything, but he was listening to Sonny. He was having a dialogue with Sonny. He wanted Sonny to leave the shoreline and strike out for the deep water. He was Sonny's witness that deep water and drowning were not the same thing—he had been there, and he knew. And he wanted Sonny to know. He was waiting for Sonny to do the things on the keys which would let Creole know that Sonny was in the water.

235   And, while Creole listened, Sonny moved, deep within, exactly like someone in torment. I had never before thought of how awful the relationship must be between the musician and his instrument. He has to fill it, this instrument, with the breath of life, his own. He has to make it do what he wants it to do. And a piano is just a piano. It's made out of so much wood and wires and little hammers and big ones, and ivory. While there's only so much you can do with it, the only way to find this out is to try; to try and make it do everything.

And Sonny hadn't been near a piano for over a year. And he wasn't on much better terms with his life, not the life that stretched before him now. He and the piano stammered, started one way, got scared, stopped; started another way, panicked, marked time, started again; then seemed to have found a direction, panicked again, got stuck. And the face I saw on Sonny I'd never seen before. Everything had been burned out of it, and, at the same time, things usually hidden were being burned in, by the fire and fury of the battle which was occurring in him up there.

Yet, watching Creole's face as they neared the end of the first set, I had the feeling that something had happened, something I hadn't heard. Then they finished, there was scattered applause, and then, without an instant's warning, Creole started into something else, it was almost sardonic, it was *Am I Blue*.[8] And, as

8. A favorite jazz standard, brilliantly recorded by Billie Holiday.

JAMES BALDWIN Sonny's Blues 113

though he commanded, Sonny began to play. Something began to happen. And Creole let out the reins. The dry, low, black man said something awful on the drums, Creole answered, and the drums talked back. Then the horn insisted, sweet and high, slightly detached perhaps, and Creole listened, commenting now and then, dry, and driving, beautiful and calm and old. Then they all came together again, and Sonny was part of the family again. I could tell this from his face. He seemed to have found, right there beneath his fingers, a damn brand-new piano. It seemed that he couldn't get over it. Then, for a while, just being happy with Sonny, they seemed to be agreeing with him that brand-new pianos certainly were a gas.

Then Creole stepped forward to remind them that what they were playing was the blues. He hit something in all of them, he hit something in me, myself, and the music tightened and deepened, apprehension began to beat the air. Creole began to tell us what the blues were all about. They were not about anything very new. He and his boys up there were keeping it new, at the risk of ruin, destruction, madness, and death, in order to find new ways to make us listen. For, while the tale of how we suffer, and how we are delighted, and how we may triumph is never new, it always must be heard. There isn't any other tale to tell, it's the only light we've got in all this darkness.

And this tale, according to that face, that body, those strong hands on those strings, has another aspect in every country, and a new depth in every generation. Listen, Creole seemed to be saying, listen. Now these are Sonny's blues. He made the little black man on the drums know it, and the bright, brown man on the horn. Creole wasn't trying any longer to get Sonny in the water. He was wishing him Godspeed. Then he stepped back, very slowly, filling the air with the immense suggestion that Sonny speak for himself.

Then they all gathered around Sonny and Sonny played. Every now and again 240 one of them seemed to say, amen. Sonny's fingers filled the air with life, his life. But that life contained so many others. And Sonny went all the way back, he really began with the spare, flat statement of the opening phrase of the song. Then he began to make it his. It was very beautiful because it wasn't hurried and it was no longer a lament. I seemed to hear with what burning he had made it his, and what burning we had yet to make it ours, how we could cease lamenting. Freedom lurked around us and I understood, at last, that he could help us to be free if we would listen, that he would never be free until we did. Yet, there was no battle in his face now, I heard what he had gone through, and would continue to go through until he came to rest in earth. He had made it his: that long line, of which we knew only Mama and Daddy. And he was giving it back, as everything must be given back, so that, passing through death, it can live forever. I saw my mother's face again, and felt, for the first time, how the stones of the road she had walked on must have bruised her feet. I saw the moonlit road where my father's brother died. And it brought something else back to me, and carried me past it, I saw my little girl again and felt Isabel's tears again, and I felt my own tears begin to rise. And I was yet aware that this was only a moment, that the world waited outside, as hungry as a tiger, and that trouble stretched above us, longer than the sky.

Then it was over. Creole and Sonny let out their breath, both soaking wet, and grinning. There was a lot of applause and some of it was real. In the dark, the girl came by and I asked her to take drinks to the bandstand. There was a long pause, while they talked up there in the indigo light and after awhile I saw the girl put a Scotch and milk on top of the piano for Sonny. He didn't seem to notice it, but just before they started playing again, he sipped from it and looked toward me, and nodded. Then he put it back on top of the piano. For me, then, as they began to play again, it glowed and shook above my brother's head like the very cup of trembling.[9]

1957

QUESTIONS

1. "Sonny's Blues" begins *in medias res*. What does Baldwin achieve by beginning the story as he does? How does the order in which events are related later in the story affect your experience of reading it and interpreting its meaning?

2. What external conflict(s) is (or are) depicted in the story? What internal conflict(s)? How are they resolved?

3. James Baldwin famously avowed that "It is only in his music . . . that the Negro in America has been able to tell his story," and music of various kinds features promi-nently in "Sonny's Blues." Note all the times when music is mentioned, as well as all the varieties of music. What story seems to be told both *through* and *about* music in "Sonny's Blues"?

EDITH WHARTON

Roman Fever[1]

I

From the table at which they had been lunching two American ladies of ripe but well-cared-for middle age moved across the lofty terrace of the Roman restau-rant and, leaning on its parapet, looked first at each other, and then down on the outspread glories of the Palatine[2] and the Forum,[3] with the same expression of vague but benevolent approval.

As they leaned there a girlish voice echoed up gaily from the stairs leading to the court below. "Well, come along, then," it cried, not to them but to an invisible companion, "and let's leave the young things to their knitting"; and a voice as fresh laughed back: "Oh, look here, Babs, not actually *knitting*—" "Well, I mean figuratively," rejoined the first. "After all, we haven't left our poor par-ents much else to do . . ." and at that point the turn of the stairs engulfed the dialogue.

9. See Isaiah 51.17, 22–23: "Awake, awake, stand up, O Jerusalem, which hast drunk at the hand of the Lord the cup of his fury; thou hast drunken the dregs of the cup of trembling, and wrung them out. . . . Behold, I have taken out of thine hand the cup of trembling, even the dregs of the cup of my fury; thou shalt no more drink it again: But I will put it into the hand of them that afflict thee. . . ."
1. Type of malaria once thought to be caused by the alternating hot and cool temperatures of the Roman climate. Anglo-American tourists traditionally feared exposure to it at certain times and seasons.
2. One of the seven hills on which the oldest part of Rome was built.
3. Central plaza of ancient Rome.

The two ladies looked at each other again, this time with a tinge of smiling embarrassment, and the smaller and paler one shook her head and colored slightly.

"Barbara!" she murmured, sending an unheard rebuke after the mocking voice in the stairway.

The other lady, who was fuller, and higher in color, with a small determined   5
nose supported by vigorous black eyebrows, gave a good-humored laugh. "That's what our daughters think of us!"

Her companion replied by a deprecating gesture. "Not of us individually. We must remember that. It's just the collective modern idea of Mothers. And you see—" Half guiltily she drew from her handsomely mounted black hand-bag a twist of crimson silk run through by two fine knitting needles. "One never knows," she murmured. "The new system has certainly given us a good deal of time to kill; and sometimes I get tired just looking—even at this." Her gesture was now addressed to the stupendous scene at their feet.

The dark lady laughed again, and they both relapsed upon the view, contemplating it in silence, with a sort of diffused serenity which might have been borrowed from the spring effulgence of the Roman skies. The luncheon-hour was long past, and the two had their end of the vast terrace to themselves. At its opposite extremity a few groups, detained by a lingering look at the outspread city, were gathering up guide-books and fumbling for tips. The last of them scattered, and the two ladies were alone on the air-washed height.

"Well, I don't see why we shouldn't just stay here," said Mrs. Slade, the lady of the high color and energetic brows. Two derelict basket-chairs stood near, and she pushed them into the angle of the parapet, and settled herself in one, her gaze upon the Palatine. "After all, it's still the most beautiful view in the world."

"It always will be, to me," assented her friend Mrs. Ansley, with so slight a stress on the "me" that Mrs. Slade, though she noticed it, wondered if it were not merely accidental, like the random underlinings of old-fashioned letter-writers.

"Grace Ansley was always old-fashioned," she thought; and added aloud,   10
with a retrospective smile: "It's a view we've both been familiar with for a good many years. When we first met here we were younger than our girls are now. You remember?"

"Oh, yes, I remember," murmured Mrs. Ansley, with the same undefinable stress—"There's that head-waiter wondering," she interpolated. She was evidently far less sure than her companion of herself and of her rights in the world.

"I'll cure him of wondering," said Mrs. Slade, stretching her hand toward a bag as discreetly opulent-looking as Mrs. Ansley's. Signing to the head-waiter, she explained that she and her friend were old lovers of Rome, and would like to spend the end of the afternoon looking down on the view—that is, if it did not disturb the service? The headwaiter, bowing over her gratuity, assured her that the ladies were most welcome, and would be still more so if they would condescend to remain for dinner. A full moon night, they would remember . . .

Mrs. Slade's black brows drew together, as though references to the moon were out-of-place and even unwelcome. But she smiled away her frown as the headwaiter retreated. "Well, why not? We might do worse. There's no knowing, I suppose, when the girls will be back. Do you even know back from *where*? I don't!"

Mrs. Ansley again colored slightly. "I think those young Italian aviators we met at the Embassy invited them to fly to Tarquinia[4] for tea. I suppose they'll want to wait and fly back by moonlight."

15   "Moonlight—moonlight! What a part it still plays. Do you suppose they're as sentimental as we were?"

"I've come to the conclusion that I don't in the least know what they are," said Mrs. Ansley. "And perhaps we didn't know much more about each other."

"No; perhaps we didn't."

Her friend gave her a shy glance. "I never should have supposed you were sentimental, Alida."

"Well, perhaps I wasn't." Mrs. Slade drew her lids together in retrospect; and for a few moments the two ladies, who had been intimate since childhood, reflected how little they knew each other. Each one, of course, had a label ready to attach to the other's name; Mrs. Delphin Slade, for instance, would have told herself, or any one who asked her, that Mrs. Horace Ansley, twenty-five years ago, had been exquisitely lovely—no, you wouldn't believe it, would you? . . . though, of course, still charming, distinguished . . . Well, as a girl she had been exquisite; far more beautiful than her daughter Barbara, though certainly Babs, according to the new standards at any rate, was more effective—had more *edge,* as they say. Funny where she got it, with those two nullities as parents. Yes; Horace Ansley was—well, just the duplicate of his wife. Museum specimens of old New York. Good-looking, irreproachable, exemplary. Mrs. Slade and Mrs. Ansley had lived opposite each other—actually as well as figuratively—for years. When the drawing-room curtains in No. 20 East 73rd Street were renewed, No. 23, across the way, was always aware of it. And of all the movings, buyings, travels, anniversaries, illnesses—the tame chronicle of an estimable pair. Little of it escaped Mrs. Slade. But she had grown bored with it by the time her husband made his big *coup* in Wall Street, and when they bought in upper Park Avenue had already begun to think: "I'd rather live opposite a speak-easy[5] for a change; at least one might see it raided." The idea of seeing Grace raided was so amusing that (before the move) she launched it at a woman's lunch. It made a hit, and went the rounds—she sometimes wondered if it had crossed the street, and reached Mrs. Ansley. She hoped not, but didn't much mind. Those were the days when respectability was at a discount, and it did the irreproachable no harm to laugh at them a little.

20   A few years later, and not many months apart, both ladies lost their husbands. There was an appropriate exchange of wreaths and condolences, and a brief renewal of intimacy in the half-shadow of their mourning; and now, after another interval, they had run across each other in Rome, at the same hotel, each of them the modest appendage of a salient daughter. The similarity of their lot had again drawn them together, lending itself to mild jokes, and the mutual confession that, if in old days it must have been tiring to "keep up" with daughters, it was now, at times, a little dull not to.

No doubt, Mrs. Slade reflected, she felt her unemployment more than poor Grace ever would. It was a big drop from being the wife of Delphin Slade to being his widow. She had always regarded herself (with a certain conjugal pride)

---

4. Now Corneto, Italy, an ancient Etruscan city, 90 km from Rome, the site of well-preserved underground tombs with vivid wall paintings.

5. Illegal tavern during the period of Prohibition (1919–31) in the United States.

as his equal in social gifts, as contributing her full share to the making of the exceptional couple they were: but the difference after his death was irremediable. As the wife of the famous corporation lawyer, always with an international case or two on hand, every day brought its exciting and unexpected obligation: the impromptu entertaining of eminent colleagues from abroad, the hurried dashes on legal business to London, Paris or Rome, where the entertaining was so handsomely reciprocated; the amusement of hearing in her wake: "What, that handsome woman with the good clothes and the eyes is Mrs. Slade—*the* Slade's wife? Really? Generally the wives of celebrities are such frumps."

Yes; being *the* Slade's widow was a dullish business after that. In living up to such a husband all her faculties had been engaged; now she had only her daughter to live up to, for the son who seemed to have inherited his father's gifts had died suddenly in boyhood. She had fought through that agony because her husband was there, to be helped and to help; now, after the father's death, the thought of the boy had become unbearable. There was nothing left but to mother her daughter; and dear Jenny was such a perfect daughter that she needed no excessive mothering. "Now with Babs Ansley I don't know that I *should* be so quiet," Mrs. Slade sometimes half-enviously reflected; but Jenny, who was younger than her brilliant friend, was that rare accident, an extremely pretty girl who somehow made youth and prettiness seem as safe as their absence. It was all perplexing— and to Mrs. Slade a little boring. She wished that Jenny would fall in love—with the wrong man, even; that she might have to be watched, outmanoeuvred, rescued. And instead, it was Jenny who watched her mother, kept her out of draughts, made sure that she had taken her tonic . . .

Mrs. Ansley was much less articulate than her friend, and her mental portrait of Mrs. Slade was slighter, and drawn with fainter touches. "Alida Slade's awfully brilliant; but not as brilliant as she thinks," would have summed it up; though she would have added, for the enlightenment of strangers, that Mrs. Slade had been an extremely dashing girl; much more so than her daughter, who was pretty, of course, and clever in a way, but had none of her mother's—well, "vividness," someone had once called it. Mrs. Ansley would take up current words like this, and cite them in quotation marks, as unheard-of audacities. No; Jenny was not like her mother. Sometimes Mrs. Ansley thought Alida Slade was disappointed; on the whole she had had a sad life. Full of failures and mistakes; Mrs. Ansley had always been rather sorry for her . . .

So these two ladies visualized each other, each through the wrong end of her little telescope.

II

For a long time they continued to sit side by side without speaking. It seemed as though, to both, there was a relief in laying down their somewhat futile activities in the presence of the vast Memento Mori[6] which faced them. Mrs. Slade sat quite still, her eyes fixed on the golden slope of the Palace of the Caesars,[7] and after a while Mrs. Ansley ceased to fidget with her bag, and she too sank into meditation. Like many intimate friends, the two ladies had never before had occasion to be silent together, and Mrs. Ansley was slightly embarrassed by what

25

6. Reminder of human mortality; literally, "Remember that you must die" (Latin).
7. The palace of the Roman emperors is on the Palatine hill.

seemed, after so many years, a new stage in their intimacy, and one with which she did not yet know how to deal.

Suddenly the air was full of that deep clangor of bells which periodically covers Rome with a roof of silver. Mrs. Slade glanced at her wrist-watch. "Five o'clock already," she said, as though surprised.

Mrs. Ansley suggested interrogatively: "There's bridge at the Embassy at five." For a long time Mrs. Slade did not answer. She appeared to be lost in contemplation, and Mrs. Ansley thought the remark had escaped her. But after a while she said, as if speaking out of a dream: "Bridge, did you say? Not unless you want to . . . But I don't think I will, you know."

"Oh, no," Mrs. Ansley hastened to assure her. "I don't care to at all. It's so lovely here; and so full of old memories, as you say." She settled herself in her chair, and almost furtively drew forth her knitting. Mrs. Slade took sideway note of this activity, but her own beautifully cared-for hands remained motionless on her knee.

"I was just thinking," she said slowly, "what different things Rome stands for to each generation of travellers. To our grandmothers, Roman fever; to our mothers, sentimental dangers—how we used to be guarded!—to our daughters, no more dangers than the middle of Main Street. They don't know it—but how much they're missing!"

30   The long golden light was beginning to pale, and Mrs. Ansley lifted her knitting a little closer to her eyes. "Yes; how we were guarded!"

"I always used to think," Mrs. Slade continued, "that our mothers had a much more difficult job than our grandmothers. When Roman fever stalked the streets it must have been comparatively easy to gather in the girls at the danger hour; but when you and I were young, with such beauty calling us, and the spice of disobedience thrown in, and no worse risk than catching cold during the cool hour after sunset, the mothers used to be put to it to keep us in—didn't they?"

She turned again toward Mrs. Ansley, but the latter had reached a delicate point in her knitting. "One, two, three—slip two; yes, they must have been," she assented, without looking up.

Mrs. Slade's eyes rested on her with a deepened attention. "She can knit—in the face of *this*! How like her . . ."

Mrs. Slade leaned back, brooding, her eyes ranging from the ruins which faced her to the long green hollow of the Forum, the fading glow of the church fronts beyond it, and the outlying immensity of the Colosseum.[8] Suddenly she thought: "It's all very well to say that our girls have done away with sentiment and moonlight. But if Babs Ansley isn't out to catch that young aviator—the one who's a Marchese—then I don't know anything. And Jenny has no chance beside her. I know that too. I wonder if that's why Grace Ansley likes the two girls to go everywhere together? My poor Jenny as a foil—I" Mrs. Slade gave a hardly audible laugh, and at the sound Mrs. Ansley dropped her knitting.

35   "Yes—?"

"I—oh, nothing. I was only thinking how your Babs carries everything before her. That Campolieri boy is one of the best matches in Rome. Don't look so innocent, my dear—you know he is. And I was wondering, ever so respectfully, you understand . . . wondering how two such exemplary characters as you and

8. Great Roman amphitheater built in the first century C.E., site of lavish spectacles that included wild animals and mortal combat.

Horace had managed to produce anything quite so dynamic." Mrs. Slade laughed again, with a touch of asperity.

Mrs. Ansley's hands lay inert across her needles. She looked straight out at the great accumulated wreckage of passion and splendor at her feet. But her small profile was almost expressionless. At length she said: "I think you overrate Babs, my dear."

Mrs. Slade's tone grew easier. "No; I don't. I appreciate her. And perhaps envy you. Oh, my girl's perfect; if I were a chronic invalid I'd—well, I think I'd rather be in Jenny's hands. There must be times . . . but there! I always wanted a brilliant daughter . . . and never quite understood why I got an angel instead."

Mrs. Ansley echoed her laugh in a faint murmur. "Babs is an angel too."

"Of course—of course! But she's got rainbow wings. Well, they're wandering   40
by the sea with their young men; and here we sit . . . and it all brings back the past a little too acutely."

Mrs. Ansley had resumed her knitting. One might almost have imagined (if one had known her less well, Mrs. Slade reflected) that, for her also, too many memories rose from the lengthening shadows of those august ruins. But no; she was simply absorbed in her work. What was there for her to worry about? She knew that Babs would almost certainly come back engaged to the extremely eligible Campolieri. "And she'll sell the New York house, and settle down near them in Rome, and never be in their way . . . she's much too tactful. But she'll have an excellent cook, and just the right people in for bridge and cocktails . . . and a perfectly peaceful old age among her grandchildren."

Mrs. Slade broke off this prophetic flight with a recoil of self-disgust. There was no one of whom she had less right to think unkindly than of Grace Ansley. Would she never cure herself of envying her? Perhaps she had begun too long ago.

She stood up and leaned against the parapet, filling her troubled eyes with the tranquillizing magic of the hour. But instead of tranquillizing her the sight seemed to increase her exasperation. Her gaze turned toward the Colosseum. Already its golden flank was drowned in purple shadow, and above it the sky curved crystal clear, without light or color. It was the moment when afternoon and evening hang balanced in mid-heaven.

Mrs. Slade turned back and laid her hand on her friend's arm. The gesture was so abrupt that Mrs. Ansley looked up, startled.

"The sun's set. You're not afraid, my dear?"   45

"Afraid—?"

"Of Roman fever or pneumonia? I remember how ill you were that winter. As a girl you had a very delicate throat, hadn't you?"

"Oh, we're all right up here. Down below, in the Forum, it does get deathly cold, all of a sudden . . . but not here."

"Ah, of course you know because you had to be so careful." Mrs. Slade turned back to the parapet. She thought: "I must make one more effort not to hate her." Aloud she said. "Whenever I look at the Forum from up here, I remember that story about a great-aunt of yours, wasn't she? A dreadfully wicked great-aunt?"

"Oh, yes; Great-aunt Harriet. The one who was supposed to have sent her   50
young sister out to the Forum after sunset to gather a nightblooming flower for her album. All our great-aunts and grandmothers used to have albums of dried flowers."

Mrs. Slade nodded. "But she really sent her because they were in love with the same man—"

"Well, that was the family tradition. They said Aunt Harriet confessed it years afterward. At any rate, the poor little sister caught the fever and died. Mother used to frighten us with the story when we were children."

"And you frightened *me* with it, that winter when you and I were here as girls. The winter I was engaged to Delphin."

Mrs. Ansley gave a faint laugh. "Oh, did I? Really frightened you? I don't believe you're easily frightened."

55 "Not often; but I was then. I was easily frightened because I was too happy. I wonder if you know what that means?"

"I—yes . . ." Mrs. Ansley faltered.

"Well, I suppose that was why the story of your wicked aunt made such an impression on me. And I thought: 'There's no more Roman fever, but the Forum is deathly cold after sunset—especially after a hot day. And the Colosseum's even colder and damper.'"

"The Colosseum—?"

"Yes. It wasn't easy to get in, after the gates were locked for the night. Far from easy. Still, in those days it could be managed; it *was* managed, often. Lovers met there who couldn't meet elsewhere. You knew that?"

60 "I—I daresay. I don't remember."

"You don't remember? You don't remember going to visit some ruins or other one evening, just after dark, and catching a bad chill? You were supposed to have gone to see the moon rise. People always said that expedition was what caused your illness."

There was a moment's silence; then Mrs. Ansley rejoined: "Did they? It was all so long ago."

"Yes. And you got well again—so it didn't matter. But I suppose it struck your friends—the reason given for your illness, I mean—because everybody knew you were so prudent on account of your throat, and your mother took such care of you . . . You *had* been out late sight-seeing, hadn't you, that night?"

"Perhaps I had. The most prudent girls aren't always prudent. What made you think of it now?"

65 Mrs. Slade seemed to have no answer ready. But after a moment she broke out: "Because I simply can't bear it any longer—!"

Mrs. Ansley lifted her head quickly. Her eyes were wide and very pale. "Can't bear what?"

"Why—your not knowing that I've always known why you went."

"Why I went—?"

"Yes. You think I'm bluffing, don't you? Well, you went to meet the man I was engaged to—and I can repeat every word of the letter that took you there."

70 While Mrs. Slade spoke Mrs. Ansley had risen unsteadily to her feet. Her bag, her knitting and gloves, slid in a panic-stricken heap to the ground. She looked at Mrs. Slade as though she were looking at a ghost.

"No, no—don't," she faltered out.

"Why not? Listen, if you don't believe me. 'My one darling, things can't go on like this. I must see you alone. Come to the Colosseum immediately after dark tomorrow. There will be somebody to let you in. No one whom you need fear will suspect'—but perhaps you've forgotten what the letter said?"

Mrs. Ansley met the challenge with an unexpected composure. Steadying herself against the chair she looked at her friend, and replied: "No; I know it by heart too."

"And the signature? 'Only *your* D.S.' Was that it? I'm right, am I? That was the letter that took you out that evening after dark?"

Mrs. Ansley was still looking at her. It seemed to Mrs. Slade that a slow strug- 75 gle was going on behind the voluntarily controlled mask of her small quiet face. "I shouldn't have thought she had herself so well in hand," Mrs. Slade reflected, almost resentfully. But at this moment Mrs. Ansley spoke. "I don't know how you knew. I burnt that letter at once."

"Yes; you would, naturally—you're so prudent!" The sneer was open now. "And if you burnt the letter you're wondering how on earth I know what was in it. That's it, isn't it?"

Mrs. Slade waited, but Mrs. Ansley did not speak.

"Well, my dear, I know what was in that letter because I wrote it!"

"You wrote it?"

"Yes." 80

The two women stood for a minute staring at each other in the last golden light. Then Mrs. Ansley dropped back into her chair. "Oh," she murmured, and covered her face with her hands.

Mrs. Slade waited nervously for another word or movement. None came, and at length she broke out. "I horrify you."

Mrs. Ansley's hands dropped to her knee. The face they uncovered was streaked with tears. "I wasn't thinking of you. I was thinking—it was the only letter I ever had from him!"

"And I wrote it. Yes; I wrote it! But I was the girl he was engaged to. Did you happen to remember that?"

Mrs. Ansley's head drooped again. "I'm not trying to excuse myself . . . I 85 remembered . . ."

"And still you went?"

"Still I went."

Mrs. Slade stood looking down on the small bowed figure at her side. The flame of her wrath had already sunk, and she wondered why she had ever thought there would be any satisfaction in inflicting so purposeless a wound on her friend. But she had to justify herself.

"You do understand? I'd found out—and I hated you, hated you. I knew you were in love with Delphin—and I was afraid; afraid of you, of your quiet ways, your sweetness . . . your . . . well, I wanted you out of the way, that's all. Just for a few weeks; just till I was sure of him. So in a blind fury I wrote that letter . . . I don't know why I'm telling you now."

"I suppose," said Mrs. Ansley slowly, "it's because you've always gone on hat- 90 ing me."

"Perhaps. Or because I wanted to get the whole thing off my mind." She paused. "I'm glad you destroyed the letter. Of course I never thought you'd die."

Mrs. Ansley relapsed into silence, and Mrs. Slade, leaning above her, was conscious of a strange sense of isolation, of being cut off from the warm current of human communion. "You think me a monster!"

"I don't know . . . It was the only letter I had, and you say he didn't write it?"

"Ah, how you care for him, still!"

95   "I cared for that memory," said Mrs. Ansley.

Mrs. Slade continued to look down on her. She seemed physically reduced by the blow—as if, when she got up, the wind might scatter her like a puff of dust. Mrs. Slade's jealousy suddenly leapt up again at the sight. All these years the woman had been living on that letter. How she must have loved him, to treasure the mere memory of its ashes! The letter of the man her friend was engaged to. Wasn't it she who was the monster?

"You tried your best to get him away from me, didn't you? But you failed; and I kept him. That's all."

"Yes. That's all."

"I wish now I hadn't told you. I'd no idea you'd feel about it as you do; I thought you'd be amused. It all happened so long ago, as you say; and you must do me the justice to remember that I had no reason to think you'd ever taken it seriously. How could I, when you were married to Horace Ansley two months afterward? As soon as you could get out of bed your mother rushed you off to Florence and married you. People were rather surprised—they wondered at its being done so quickly; but I thought I knew. I had an idea you did it out of *pique*—to be able to say you'd got ahead of Delphin and me. Girls have such silly reasons for doing the most serious things. And your marrying so soon convinced me that you'd never really cared."

100   "Yes. I suppose it would," Mrs. Ansley assented.

The clear heaven overhead was emptied of all its gold. Dusk spread over it, abruptly darkening the Seven Hills. Here and there lights began to twinkle through the foliage at their feet. Steps were coming and going on the deserted terrace—waiters looking out of the doorway at the head of the stairs, then reappearing with trays and napkins and flasks of wine. Tables were moved, chairs straightened. A feeble string of electric lights flickered out. Some vases of faded flowers were carried away, and brought back replenished. A stout lady in a dustcoat suddenly appeared, asking in broken Italian if any one had seen the elastic band which held together her tattered Baedeker.[9] She poked with her stick under the table at which she had lunched, the waiters assisting.

The corner where Mrs. Slade and Mrs. Ansley sat was still shadowy and deserted. For a long time neither of them spoke. At length Mrs. Slade began again: "I suppose I did it as a sort of joke—"

"A joke?"

"Well, girls are ferocious sometimes, you know. Girls in love especially. And I remember laughing to myself all that evening at the idea that you were waiting around there in the dark, dodging out of sight, listening for every sound, trying to get in—. Of course I was upset when I heard you were so ill afterward."

105   Mrs. Ansley had not moved for a long time. But now she turned slowly toward her companion. "But I didn't wait. He'd arranged everything. He was there. We were let in at once," she said.

Mrs. Slade sprang up from her leaning position. "Delphin there? They let you in?—Ah, now you're lying!" she burst out with violence.

Mrs. Ansley's voice grew clearer, and full of surprise. "But of course he was there. Naturally he came—"

"Came? How did he know he'd find you there? You must be raving!"

---

9. Any one of the very popular tourist guidebooks published by German-publisher Karl Baedeker (founded 1827).

Mrs. Ansley hesitated, as though reflecting. "But I answered the letter. I told him I'd be there. So he came."

Mrs. Slade flung her hands up to her face. "Oh, God—you answered! I never 110 thought of your answering . . ."

"It's odd you never thought of it, if you wrote the letter."

"Yes. I was blind with rage."

Mrs. Ansley rose, and drew her fur scarf about her. "It is cold here. We'd better go . . . I'm sorry for you," she said, as she clasped the fur about her throat.

The unexpected words sent a pang through Mrs. Slade. "Yes; we'd better go." She gathered up her bag and cloak. "I don't know why you should be sorry for me," she muttered.

Mrs. Ansley stood looking away from her toward the dusky secret mass of the 115 Colosseum. "Well—because I didn't have to wait that night."

Mrs. Slade gave an unquiet laugh. "Yes; I was beaten there. But I oughtn't to begrudge it to you, I suppose. At the end of all these years. After all, I had everything; I had him for twenty-five years. And you had nothing but that one letter that he didn't write."

Mrs. Ansley was again silent. At length she turned toward the door of the terrace. She took a step, and turned back, facing her companion.

"I had Barbara," she said, and began to move ahead of Mrs. Slade toward the stairway.

1936

QUESTIONS

1. What are the first hints of submerged conflict between Mrs. Slade and Mrs. Ansley? What details in part 1 bring out the differences in their personalities and their lives? How has their relationship changed in the end, and how do the last six paragraphs of the story show the change?
2. Discuss how dramatic irony plays out in "Roman Fever." What is the full story that neither Mrs. Slade nor Mrs. Ansley knows? What prompts the two ladies to reveal what they know to each other?
3. In part 2, Mrs. Slade remembers how earlier generations tried to protect their daughters in Rome. What are the similarities and differences between the older women's memories and the daughters' current experiences of courtship in Italy?

MARGARET ATWOOD

Happy Endings

John and Mary meet.
What happens next?
If you want a happy ending, try A.

A. John and Mary fall in love and get married. They both have worthwhile and remunerative jobs which they find stimulating and challenging. They buy a charming house. Real estate values go up. Eventually, when they can afford live-in help, they have two children, to whom they are devoted. The children turn out well. John and Mary have a stimulating and challenging sex life and worthwhile friends. They go on fun vacations together. They retire. They both have hobbies which they find stimulating and challenging. Eventually they die. This is the end of the story.

5 B. Mary falls in love with John but John doesn't fall in love with Mary. He merely uses her body for selfish pleasure and ego gratification of a tepid kind. He comes to her apartment twice a week and she cooks him dinner, you'll notice that he doesn't even consider her worth the price of a dinner out, and after he's eaten the dinner he fucks her and after that he falls asleep, while she does the dishes so he won't think she's untidy, having all those dirty dishes lying around, and puts on fresh lipstick so she'll look good when he wakes up, but when he wakes up he doesn't even notice, he puts on his socks and his shorts and his pants and his shirt and his tie and his shoes, the reverse order from the one in which he took them off. He doesn't take off Mary's clothes, she takes them off herself, she acts as if she's dying for it every time, not because she likes sex exactly, she doesn't, but she wants John to think she does because if they do it often enough surely he'll get used to her, he'll come to depend on her and they will get married, but John goes out the door with hardly so much as a good-night and three days later he turns up at six o'clock and they do the whole thing over again.

Mary gets run-down. Crying is bad for your face, everyone knows that and so does Mary but she can't stop. People at work notice. Her friends tell her John is a rat, a pig, a dog, he isn't good enough for her, but she can't believe it. Inside John, she thinks, is another John, who is much nicer. This other John will emerge like a butterfly from a cocoon, a Jack from a box, a pit from a prune, if the first John is only squeezed enough.

One evening John complains about the food. He has never complained about the food before. Mary is hurt.

Her friends tell her they've seen him in a restaurant with another woman, whose name is Madge. It's not even Madge that finally gets to Mary: it's the restaurant. John has never taken Mary to a restaurant. Mary collects all the sleeping pills and aspirins she can find, and takes them and a half a bottle of sherry. You can see what kind of a woman she is by the fact that it's not even whiskey. She leaves a note for John. She hopes he'll discover her and get her to the hospital in time and repent and then they can get married, but this fails to happen and she dies.

John marries Madge and everything continues as in A.

10 C. John, who is an older man, falls in love with Mary, and Mary, who is only twenty-two, feels sorry for him because he's worried about his hair falling out. She sleeps with him even though she's not in love with him. She met him at work. She's in love with someone called James, who is twenty-two also and not yet ready to settle down.

John on the contrary settled down long ago: this is what is bothering him. John has a steady, respectable job and is getting ahead in his field, but Mary isn't impressed by him, she's impressed by James, who has a motorcycle and a fabulous record collection. But James is often away on his motorcycle, being free. Freedom isn't the same for girls, so in the meantime Mary spends Thursday evenings with John. Thursdays are the only days John can get away.

John is married to a woman called Madge and they have two children, a charming house which they bought just before the real estate values went up, and hobbies which they find stimulating and challenging, when they have the time. John tells Mary how important she is to him, but of course he can't leave his wife because a commitment is a commitment. He goes on about this more than is necessary and Mary finds it boring, but older men can keep it up longer so on the whole she has a fairly good time.

One day James breezes in on his motorcycle with some top-grade California hybrid and James and Mary get higher than you'd believe possible and they climb into bed. Everything becomes very underwater, but along comes John, who has a key to Mary's apartment. He finds them stoned and entwined. He's hardly in any position to be jealous, considering Madge, but nevertheless he's overcome with despair. Finally he's middle-aged, in two years he'll be bald as an egg and he can't stand it. He purchases a handgun, saying he needs it for target practice—this is the thin part of the plot, but it can be dealt with later—and shoots the two of them and himself.

Madge, after a suitable period of mourning, marries an understanding man called Fred and everything continues as in A, but under different names.

D. Fred and Madge have no problems. They get along exceptionally well and are good at working out any little difficulties that may arise. But their charming house is by the seashore and one day a giant tidal wave approaches. Real estate values go down. The rest of the story is about what caused the tidal wave and how they escape from it. They do, though thousands drown, but Fred and Madge are virtuous and lucky. Finally on high ground they clasp each other, wet and dripping and grateful, and continue as in A.

E. Yes, but Fred has a bad heart. The rest of the story is about how kind and understanding they both are until Fred dies. Then Madge devotes herself to charity work until the end of A. If you like, it can be "Madge," "cancer," "guilty and confused," and "bird watching."

F. If you think this is all too bourgeois, make John a revolutionary and Mary a counterespionage agent and see how far that gets you. Remember, this is Canada. You'll still end up with A, though in between you may get a lustful brawling saga of passionate involvement, a chronicle of our times, sort of.

You'll have to face it, the endings are the same however you slice it. Don't be deluded by any other endings, they're all fake, either deliberately fake, with malicious intent to deceive, or just motivated by excessive optimism if not by downright sentimentality.

The only authentic ending is the one provided here:
John and Mary die. John and Mary die. John and Mary die.
So much for endings. Beginnings are always more fun. True connoisseurs, however, are known to favor the stretch in between, since it's the hardest to do anything with.

That's about all that can be said for plots, which anyway are just one thing after another, a what and a what and a what.

Now try How and Why.

1983

QUESTIONS

1. In Margaret Atwood's "Happy Endings," why is A so unsatisfying as a story, even though its conclusion ("Eventually they die. This is the end of the story.") is, as Atwood says, the "only authentic ending"?
2. Has the narrator of "Happy Endings" indeed said "about all that can be said for plots" by the end of the story? Are plots no more than "a what and a what and a what"? What else are plots besides a sequence of events?
3. Compare "Happy Endings" with "A Conversation with My Father"; what significant similarities and differences do you see between these two "stories about stories"?

SUGGESTIONS FOR WRITING

1. Write an essay comparing the way any two of the stories in this chapter handle the traditional elements of plot: exposition, rising action, climax, falling action, conclusion. Consider especially how plot elements contribute to the overall artistic effect.
2. Many stories depict events out of chronological order. For example, "Sonny's Blues" makes liberal use of flashbacks. Select any story from this anthology, and write an essay discussing the significance of sequence.
3. Reread "Roman Fever" and record the instances when the story prompts you to form expectations that may or may not be borne out by the events to follow. Write an essay in which you analyze the way Wharton has rearranged the chronology of events in order to build suspense and stimulate reader engagement with the text.
4. Write an essay that explores the central conflict in any one of the stories in this chapter. What is the nature of the conflict? When, where, and how does it develop or become more complicated as the story unfolds? How is it resolved at the end of the story? Why and how is that resolution satisfying?
5. Using Margaret Atwood's "Happy Endings" as a model, write a short story in which the reader is prompted to make choices that can produce a variety of results.

Initiation Stories: An Album

It may be true that most people's lives mainly consist of the "middle"—a long, stable passage of adult years—instead of the promising start, the turning point or crisis, the eventual catastrophe or triumph. Nevertheless, a great deal of fiction (as well as movies, television, and other media) focuses on the more momentous changes that we associate with youth. This album features a common kind of short fiction, the **initiation story**, also known as the coming-of-age story—the story of what happens as we define ourselves and set our own course toward the future. And short fiction focused on a brief, momentous occasion is a form well suited to telling this sort of story.

Across cultures, social groups have various initiation rites to mark the *coming of age* of their youths—from "sweet sixteen" parties, bar and bat mitzvahs, debutante balls, and the *quinceañera*, to the laws that permit twenty-one-year-olds to inherit property and buy alcohol. These social concepts and practices may be prominent in stories that explore the transformation from childhood to adulthood, but such fiction doesn't have to include an obvious scene of initiation like a fraternity hazing or a birthday party.

Initiation stories usually have common characteristics related to the "plot" of growing up. They always feature at least one young person, a child, an adolescent, or a young adult, who undergoes some sort of transformation. This character learns a significant truth about the world, society, people, or himself or herself. The nature of this knowledge differs widely in such stories, as does the character's response, but the plot of the story must culminate in a change of status or awareness that is more adult. The protagonist may struggle to find a place in society, but more often the challenge is to adjust his or her ideals to actual circumstances. Initiation stories may zoom in on such moments as when a child loses the protection of adults, a teenager sees a fellow creature die, or a young person faced with rejection or disappointment is suddenly made aware of a separate, lonely identity and an unknown future. Sometimes newfound freedom can lead to a joyful, if frightening, sense of possibility. In other stories, the response of the young protagonist may be disbelief, denial, or retreat from the truth. Often the reader can only guess how the character will adapt to the hard-won, still-confusing knowledge gained in the experience.

Naturally there are countless such stories to tell, from the tragic to the euphoric and everything in between. Innumerable novels, films, and television shows—*The Catcher in the Rye, Ferris Bueller's Day Off, Happy Days*, to name a few—center on the trials and adventures of teens, often with pain, whimsy, humor, embarrassment, nostalgia, sympathy, and insight. Here we offer a variety of initiation stories—Max Apple's "Stepdaughters," Toni Cade Bambara's "Gorilla, My Love," Alice Munro's "Boys and Girls," and John Updike's "A&P"—that have some common features as well as some very different visions of initiation. Which characters undergo initiation in each of these stories? What general or specific social conditions is each character initiated into, and how does each respond? Is there something about the passage of time and growing up that is both necessary and cruel? Can you recognize common elements in this selection of stories? In your own experience?

MAX APPLE

Stepdaughters

My wife sits beside me on our new leather couch. *Strength* is between us. "Who would have ever thought of this," Helen says. "I worried about boys, not about male hormones."

Our family life had been serene and moving toward joyful until Stephanie began shot-putting. Her eight-pound steel ball is now hammering all three of us. Stephanie is training for the state meet; Helen is fighting for her daughter's female body, and perhaps her soul. I am stepfather number three trying to stay on the sidelines.

If the battle over shot-putting was not destroying us, maybe I could laugh at it the way I now laugh at my fear of Harold. Two years ago, when I married Helen, I thought Harold, the real father, dead since Stephanie was three, would be the major obstacle in our new little family.

Steph kept a Harold shrine in her room: his glasses, some of his books, a few tapes of him reading stories to her, his college yearbooks, and a very thin family album started only a month or two before his death. Presiding over these scraps of her father's life Stephanie had hanging beside her bed a wall-size silkscreen of Harold's face.

The first time I saw that gigantic idolized father in her room I realized how 5
impossible stepfathering would be.

I was timid and sentimental. For weeks I dreaded going near Stephanie's room. I even thought of suggesting that we move but I knew she could just roll Harold up and carry him anywhere we might go. Then, one day, in the early stages of getting used to a teenager in my life, I noticed what I thought was a second Harold, a more ragged, menacing version of father on the wall opposite him.

"You like him?" Steph asked.

I didn't know how to answer.

"I'm not sure I do," she said, "but he was on sale for $7.98, so it was no big deal. Most of the Steps are crazy about him."

The Steps are the Stepdaughters, a club Stephanie founded. He is Mick 10
Jagger.[1]

I burst out laughing and hugged my stepdaughter. A few weeks later I noticed that Steph had made an awkward twine pulley to raise and lower the image of her father. On nice days the sun streams in beneath Harold's eyebrows to illuminate Mick Jagger scowling across the room.

After that, I bought Stephanie a wall hanging, too, of a group called Genesis.[2] I told her I hoped it would signify a beginning for the three of us.

She told me I was corny but she liked it. I started taking Stephanie places, too. I tried to take her to some event at least a couple of times a month.

"Al and Jerome ignored her," Helen told me, "and she doesn't even remember Harold."

---

1. World-famous lead singer (b. 1943) of the Rolling Stones, a rock group formed in London in 1962.
2. English rock group formed in 1967 whose founding members have included Phil Collins and Peter Gabriel. The name of the band, like that of the first book of the Bible, means "beginning."

15   Steph was thirteen then, the only daughter I would ever have. I took her to the ballet during the season, to the movies lots of times, and once to a track meet. Helen blames me for it.

"It's not the track meet alone," she says. "Secretly you condone the shot-putting, secretly you're on her side."

"I'm neutral."

"Nobody's neutral."

"It could be a lot worse."

20   "What could be worse?" She tosses *Strength* onto my lap.

"Go ahead, imagine her in this magazine next year surrounded by East German brutes."

"Helen, she's only fifteen, she's not going to be an Olympic athlete."

"Of course she will be," Helen says. "Look what she did with Stepdaughters, look at her grades, look at what that slimy coach told us."

Reluctantly, I had gone with Helen to threaten Coach Larry Zalenka. Helen wanted Stephanie off the team. Period. The coach, though only about thirty, was not a bit intimidated by Helen.

25   "Mrs. Harrison," he said, "if Steph was a man and in a popular sport she could turn pro at eighteen and become a millionaire. That's how good she is. She breathes shot-putting. You can't discourage something that strong."

"I can," Helen said, "and I will."

So far Helen has not succeeded in discouraging shot-putting, but it has become the only issue in our family. Helen had never heard of the event until last year. Even when Stephanie started carrying the big ball around the house as she chatted with us or helped set the table one-handed, Helen thought carrying the ball was some sort of exercise from *Jane Fonda's Workout Book*.[3]

"I don't understand what you mean by throwing it," she told Stephanie. "You mean, you just throw it and that's all there is to it, no running around the bases or putting it through a basket, just throwing it anywhere?"

Stephanie tried to explain the complexity of the throw. She compared it to weight lifting, which took only a few seconds but was the most demanding of all sports.

30   "But what pleasure is there for you in practicing the same thing over and over, and what difference does it make if you throw it a few inches more or a few inches less?"

"I can't explain it, Mom, it just makes me feel better than anything else ever has."

At first, Helen considered the shot a heavy but harmless toy, like a Hula-Hoop or a yo-yo. She didn't begin to see how serious it was until Stephanie's new neck muscles began to be plainly visible.

Steph has never been petite. At school, her nickname since seventh grade has been Hulk. When Helen objected to the name Steph defended it.

"I'm five eight and I weigh one hundred fifty-five pounds," Stephanie said. "I'm not the kind of girl who is going to be called Cutie Pie. Anyway, I like being strong. I don't see why I should be ashamed of it."

---

3. Best-selling exercise book released by the actress Jane Fonda (b. 1937) as part of a series of videos and guides that inspired the aerobics boom in the 1980s.

In spite of her size Stephanie had not seemed exceptionally strong until she began her serious training about six months ago. 35

Now, Steph is fifteen, so is her neck. It surprises you sliding out from under her thin delicate face, as thin and delicate as Helen's own face. The neck is an introduction to Stephanie's powerful shoulders and upper arms, which descend into thin wrists and long symmetrical fingers. It almost looks as if there are two Stephanies, one a somewhat delicate girl, the other a bulky Steph placed on top but not quite filling in all the open spaces.

Helen knew something was happening to Steph. She suggested that Stephanie grow her hair longer or stop wearing turtleneck blouses. Then, one morning on the *Today* show Helen watched a report on drug use by female athletes. Steph had already gone to school.

Helen drove to St. James Academy in her housecoat and had Stephanie summoned from homeroom. They sat in Helen's car in front of the school. Helen accused her daughter of taking male hormones.

"I knew it as soon as I saw the report on TV. I knew something had changed you and now I understand." Helen wept against the steering column.

Stephanie denied it. 40

"I do weights and dynamic tension, that's all, just Nautilus. Mom, I'm not crazy, I wouldn't take drugs like that. I don't even smoke grass. You can ask Jackie or any of the Steps if you don't believe me."

Helen does not believe her, though there is no evidence against Stephanie, only her body. She is getting stronger right before our eyes. Of course, she works at it during all her waking hours. At night the shot lies on the pillow beside her.

She does dynamic tension, pitting muscle groups against each other, while she studies.

"Do you do it in school, too?" Helen asks.

"Yes, nobody can tell most of the time and it doesn't get in the way. I don't do it in Chem lab or when I'm giving an oral report or something like that, just when I'm sitting quietly reading or listening." 45

Steph was doing dynamic tension at the dinner table, too, until Helen banned it, but since the *Today* report Helen has declared total war on shot-putting. Stephanie is standing up for her right to be big and strong and throw the steel ball as far as she can.

They are both strong-minded women. When I was dating Helen I admired the way mother and daughter worked together starting the Stepdaughters. Stephanie lobbied parents and teachers as if she were a thirteen-year-old union organizer. She and Jackie prepared a membership pamphlet and designed a T-shirt logo.

Several parents called Helen to complain about a club of stepdaughters discussing intimate family details without any adult supervision. Helen defended her daughter then as wholly as she now attacks Stephanie's shot-putting.

"All the girls were just sitting around and complaining," Steph told me. "Jackie's mother and father have each been married twice and her father's second wife has four stepchildren of her own. Once, in the line at the supermarket, all three girls ahead of her were Jackie's stepsisters and she hardly knew them. She said she would need a computer just to keep track of who was talking to who. One day we were complaining about how stupid all the school clubs were—who wants to be in Latin Club or Future Teachers, so I thought, 'What about a stepdaughters club?' When I told Mom she said it could become the Alcoholics Anonymous of the new century."

50　　One of the first things I ever did with Steph was to drive her to a Stepdaughters meeting. The girls meet at the public library on Friday night. Wisely, they realized the necessity for a public meeting place. A house, anybody's house, would put them at the mercy of family life. I decided to wait for her in the car across the street.

　　I noticed that after the meeting the girls loitered on the tall steps of the library. Teenage boys in their parents' cars circled the library as if waiting for the sudden onset of moral dehydration.

　　"They're a drag," Stephanie told me later. "One of the things we talk about in Stepdaughters is that there is no Mr. Right and there's no perfect therapist either."

　　Jackie, whom I met that night, told me she thought Steph would become a senator or at least go around the country making speeches and establishing Stepdaughters franchises like Weight Watchers and Speedreaders all over the country.

　　Helen had equally ambitious hopes for her daughter's future.

55　　"Of course," she said, "I want her to be happy. I told her that and I told the coach and the psychiatrist the same thing."

　　"'Let her assert herself,' that silly psychiatrist said, 'let her do what she chooses.'

　　"I reminded him that one of his colleagues told Mr. and Mrs. Hinckley the same thing a few weeks before their son went out to shoot President Reagan."[4]

　　"That's not exactly right," I told her.

　　"It's close enough. All I'm trying to tell you is the simple fact that there is no professional I can turn to in this crisis. For almost anything else you can think of there is a hot line or a UN agency or a readathon. All the miserable have company and sympathy. I have to sit alone and watch my daughter, my beautiful Stephanie, do dynamic tension to her neck and arms. Every morning while she chews her toast I look to see if the facial hair has started to grow."

60　　I try to put my arms around Helen but she resists comfort. She has always looked facts in the face. She survived her husband's early death and then two bad marriages. On her way to becoming a successful executive, she started as a young widow selling Avon products door to door.

　　When I told Helen I wanted to marry her she asked for some time to think about it. Two days later she gave me a computer printout based on Prudential Insurance Company statistics that predicted the likelihood of everything from breast cancer to senility in her person during the next twenty-five years.

　　"I'm forty-one," she said, "I can't treat getting married as a honeymoon. You should know what you're getting into."

　　"Maybe I should give you my computer breakdown too."

　　"I have it." Out of her purse she produced the melancholy table of my projected decline. "This tells us more about love than music and moonlight do. This is what's coming for both of us—alone or together is the question."

65　　After reading the insurance projections, I asked for a few days, then I decided—together. The tables were for death and disease, they left out love, health, and

4. On March 30, 1981, John Warnock Hinckley Jr. shot and wounded U.S. President Ronald Reagan.

happiness, the things you seek in life. I told her the tables had nothing to do with marriage.

"I know," she said, "I've just learned to look at the bleakness first."

For two years Helen, Steph, and I were oblivious of statistical disaster. We were in love with one another and with our little unit, a functioning family, so new to each of us. Now an eight-pound steel ball seemed as dangerous as another woman, a runaway, or financial ruin, the less exotic tragedies of other families.

"You can't blame puberty," Helen said. "I wish it was something that simple, that physical." She looked at me in all sincerity.

"Would you break her wrist or dislocate it or something?" Finally Helen started to cry. For two months form alone carried the day; finally Helen had reached the end of her good manners.

In order to understand her objection to shot-putting, you have to understand the kind of woman Helen is. In almost every way she is as open-minded and straightforward as she can be. When we met she told me she was lonesome and sensual and intelligent. She said she had no patience for fools. She described herself accurately. When depression awakened her at 4 AM, she told me, she arose to read from the novels of Balzac.[5] Helen rarely looks backward. 70

After Jerome, her second bad marriage, she went to a behavioral psychologist. From him she learned that she was not able to profit from the study of her past.

I told her that a year from now the shot-putting might seem no big deal.

"A year from now," she said, "I could be dead and Bin Laden[6] could be ruling the world. I'm only interested in today."

From the start of our romance I admired her unrelenting honesty. She said that she was skeptical about love but admitted great needs and great pleasures as they arose.

"You love me because I'm a beautiful woman," she said. "I'm not speaking of vanity, you know that: I'm telling you that you love me because I am a woman, because I'm not what you are. Every woman, no matter how weak, no matter how abused, understands her importance in the world because she is a woman. Men don't have that feeling. They don't need it, they have everything else. 75

"No matter how ridiculous it seems, beauty and femininity are necessities. When I was an Avon lady I would spend hours with ugly women, disfigured women. They took me into their homes. We drank coffee and talked about Pan-Cake makeup and eye shadow and blush and fragrance. A few of my ten-dollar products made all the difference to them. I was never ashamed of being an Avon lady. I think their work is more important than IBM.[7]

"There are women who lose their femininity. Then they have nothing because they're not men either, and they're not children, though they often act as if they are. I'm seeing that happen to Steph right before my eyes. Just while she is blossoming in puberty, she is dewomanizing herself. I would rather have her be a

5. Honoré de Balzac (1799–1850), renowned French writer, author of many long, realistic novels collected as a series called *La Comédie humaine* (The Human Comedy).
6. Osama bin Laden, born in 1957 in Saudi Arabia, leader of the Islamist terrorist organization Al Qaeda, which is notorious for its attacks on the World Trade Center in New York City and the Pentagon in Washington, DC, on September 11, 2001.
7. International Business Machines Corporation, an information technology company.

Moonie[8] or a cocaine addict, you can recover from those things. If she loses the core of being a woman, then she'll end up playing touch football and drinking beer in some trailer park in New Mexico—or worse."

Stephanie is unmoved by this argument.

"You just want me to have ruddy cheeks," she says, "and giggle when boys call and worry about my periods. I don't have to do any of those things. That's an act, what girls are supposed to be like. You should know better, you helped me start Stepdaughters, you should want me to tell you my true feelings."

80   "Stephanie, my love, you know I want you to tell me your true feelings."

"My truest feeling is that I want to throw the shot as far as possible, maybe sixty feet."

Helen has removed all drugs from the house; there are no aspirins, no antihistamines, no cold tablets. She also allows Stephanie no seconds at dinner. In fact, she is cooking such small portions that all three of us leave the table hungry. Still, Stephanie's neck thrives, her shoulders grow like breasts. She has also switched her everyday shoes from penny loafers to gray climbing shoes in order to strengthen her ankles for her gliding technique.

When Stephanie and I are alone she does talk to me about her passion.

"It's not just strength," she tells me, "it's mostly the feel of it, the rhythm. Some people think it's shoulder and wrist—not true, anybody can get shoulders and wrists. It's the neck that's crucial."

85   She asks me very matter-of-factly if I'm going to divorce Helen because of the shot-putting dispute.

"That's between your mother and you. Why should that lead to a divorce between Helen and me?"

"Well, it can't be much fun for you hanging around the two of us always at each other."

Like Helen, she has a knack for the bleak truth.

"You can just pack up whenever you want. You don't have to put up with us. You must know by now that this is not going to stop. After the state meet I start training for the regionals and then I'm going for all the Olympic trials. Coach says you peak at about eighteen. I'm going to give it everything I've got for the next three years and you can bet that Mom's going to fight me every inch. Life around this house is not going to be a picnic."

90   She holds an imaginary ball against her neck, turns her back to me, and begins to practice her glide technique. She leans backward on her right leg, points her left leg at the fireplace, and takes one powerful hop across the white carpet. When she lets go, her hips lead, then her arm, her head, and her neck snap up in a strong united motion.

As I watch Stephanie constantly repeating her approach and throwing motion, I think of her girlfriends, that hypnotic clan of stepdaughters: Ellen, with her belt made of lacquered Xerox copies of alimony checks; Carol, who tells all adults she just wants to be left alone—forever; Harriet, who talks constantly of wanting to take long silent horseback rides through fields of wildflowers. I think

---

8. Mocking nickname for members of the Unification Church, founded in Korea in 1954 and led by the Reverend Sun Myung Moon (b. 1920).

of these pale followers of my shot-putting Stephanie, these youngsters who have shriveled into the dimensions that loneliness allows them.

Not Stephanie. With her eyes closed and the imaginary ball pressed against her neck she is in the trance of hope. Her father is a window shade, her previous stepfathers long gone, her mother destined to misunderstand the beauty of Stephanie's strength. As Stephanie rocks on her back leg, eyes closed, lips pressed tight, I see that shot-putting is as solemn as prayer. She has a lot to throw away, this stepdaughter of mine; in eight-pound chunks she might be able to manage it, maybe all the way to the Olympics.

When she opens her eyes I am standing across the room imitating her stance. Stephanie laughs.

"At least take off your tie," she says. "Nobody shot-puts in a tie."

Even before I begin my arm feels sore. My legs are fifty—I remember the insur- 95 ance company table. I feel the cholesterol, the blood pressure, the statistical saga of a tired body that must gear itself up each day for a 150-pound throw against the darkness. Yet, I feel as filled with hope and prayer as she is.

Steph and I point our left feet at one another like swordsmen in a Douglas Fairbanks movie.[9]

"On three," she says. And we begin.

2007

QUESTIONS

1. What details of popular culture are mentioned in "Stepdaughters"? How do magazines, television programs, movies, music, athletics, or other influences and sources of information shape the way each member of the family behaves?
2. The narrator is "stepfather number three." How does he make an effort to be initiated into the family of Helen and Stephanie? Who changes the most in the story?
3. In the Stepdaughters club, the girls decide that they can't expect much from boyfriends or adults. Helen insists that getting married is no honeymoon and shows the narrator statistics about life expectancy. Are these views cynical, pessimistic, or realistic? Does anything in the story support hope and optimism for the teenagers or for the adults?

TONI CADE BAMBARA

Gorilla, My Love

That was the year Hunca Bubba changed his name. Not a change up, but a change back, since Jefferson Winston Vale was the name in the first place. Which was news to me cause he'd been my Hunca Bubba my whole lifetime, since I couldn't manage Uncle to save my life. So far as I was concerned it was a change completely to somethin soundin very geographical weatherlike to me, like somethin you'd find in a almanac. Or somethin you'd run across when you sittin in the navigator seat with a wet thumb on the map crinkly in your lap, watchin the roads and signs so when Granddaddy Vale say "Which way, Scout," you got sense enough to say take the next exit or take a left or whatever it is. Not that Scout's my name. Just the name Granddaddy call whoever sittin in the navigator seat.

9. American movie star (1883–1939) known especially for silent-film roles as Zorro and Robin Hood.

Which is usually me cause I don't feature sittin in the back with the pecans. Now, you figure pecans all right to be sittin with. If you thinks so, that's your business. But they dusty sometime and make you cough. And they got a way of slidin around and dippin down sudden, like maybe a rat in the buckets. So if you scary like me, you sleep with the lights on and blame it on Baby Jason and, so as not to waste good electric, you study the maps. And that's how come I'm in the navigator seat most times and get to be called Scout.

So Hunca Bubba in the back with the pecans and Baby Jason, and he in love. And we got to hear all this stuff about this woman he in love with and all. Which really ain't enough to keep the mind alive, though Baby Jason got no better sense than to give his undivided attention and keep grabbin at the photograph which is just a picture of some skinny woman in a countrified dress with her hand shot up to her face like she shame fore cameras. But there's a movie house in the background which I ax about. Cause I am a movie freak from way back, even though it do get me in trouble sometime.

Like when me and Big Brood and Baby Jason was on our own last Easter and couldn't go to the Dorset cause we'd seen all the Three Stooges they was. And the RKO Hamilton was closed readying up for the Easter Pageant that night. And the West End, the Regun and the Sunset was too far, less we had grownups with us which we didn't. So we walk up Amsterdam Avenue to the Washington and *Gorilla, My Love* playin, they say, which suit me just fine, though the "my love" part kinda drag Big Brood some. As for Baby Jason, shoot, like Granddaddy say, he'd follow me into the fiery furnace if I say come on. So we go in and get three bags of Havmore potato chips which not only are the best potato chips but the best bags for blowin up and bustin real loud so the matron come trottin down the aisle with her chunky self, flashin that flashlight dead in your eye so you can give her some lip, and if she answer back and you already finish seein the show anyway, why then you just turn the place out. Which I love to do, no lie. With Baby Jason kickin at the seat in front, egging me on, and Big Brood mumblin bout what fiercesome things we goin do. Which means me. Like when the big boys come up on us talkin bout Lemme a nickel. It's me that hide the money. Or when the bad boys in the park take Big Brood's Spaudeen[1] way from him. It's me that jump on they back and fight awhile. And it's me that turns out the show if the matron get too salty.

So the movie come on and right away it's this churchy music and clearly not about no gorilla. Bout Jesus. And I am ready to kill, not cause I got anything gainst Jesus. Just that when you fixed to watch a gorilla picture you don't wanna get messed around with Sunday School stuff. So I am mad. Besides, we see this raggedy old brown film *King of Kings*[2] every year and enough's enough. Grownups figure they can treat you just anyhow. Which burns me up. There I am, my feet up and my Havmore potato chips really salty and crispy and two jawbreakers in my lap and the money safe in my shoe from the big boys, and there comes this Jesus stuff. So we all go wild. Yellin, booin, stompin and carryin on. Really to wake the man in the booth up there who musta went to sleep and put on the wrong reels. But no, cause he holler down to shut up and then he turn the sound up so we really gotta holler like crazy to even hear ourselves good. And the matron ropes

---

1. Probably refers to "Spaldeen," the small pink rubber ball made by the Spalding company and used for stickball.

2. Although there is a 1961 version, this probably refers to the silent movie made in the 1920s.

off the children section and flashes her light all over the place and we yell some more and some kids slip under the rope and run up and down the aisle just to show it take more than some dusty ole velvet rope to tie us down. And I'm flingin the kid in front of me's popcorn. And Baby Jason kickin seats. And it's really somethin. Then here come the big and bad matron, the one they let out in case of emergency. And she totin that flashlight like she gonna use it on somebody. This here the colored matron Brandy and her friends call Thunderbuns. She do not play. She do not smile. So we shut up and watch the simple ass picture.

Which is not so simple as it is stupid. Cause I realized that just about anybody 5
in my family is better than this god they always talkin about. My daddy wouldn't stand for nobody treatin any of us that way. My mama specially. And I can just see it now, Big Brood up there on the cross talkin bout Forgive them Daddy cause they don't know what they doin. And my Mama say Get on down from there you big fool, whatcha think this is, playtime? And my Daddy yellin to Granddaddy to get him a ladder cause Big Brood actin the fool, his mother side of the family showin up. And my mama and her sister Daisy jumpin on them Romans beatin them with they pocketbooks. And Hunca Bubba tellin them folks on they knees they better get out the way and go get some help or they goin to get trampled on. And Granddaddy Vale sayin Leave the boy alone, if that's what he wants to do with his life we ain't got nothin to say about it. Then Aunt Daisy givin him a taste of that pocketbook, fussin bout what a damn fool old man Granddaddy is. Then everybody jumpin in his chest like the time Uncle Clayton went in the army and come back with only one leg and Granddaddy say somethin stupid about that's life. And by this time Big Brood off the cross and in the park playin handball or skully[3] or somethin. And the family in the kitchen throwin dishes at each other, screamin bout if you hadn't done this I wouldn't had to do that. And me in the parlor trying to do my arithmetic yellin Shut it off.

Which is what I was yellin all by myself which make me a sittin target for Thunderbuns. But when I yell We want our money back, that gets everybody in chorus. And the movie windin up with this heavenly cloud music and the smart-ass up there in his hole in the wall turns up the sound again to drown us out. Then there comes Bugs Bunny which we already seen so we know we been had. No gorilla my nuthin. And Big Brood say Awwww sheeet, we goin to see the manager and get our money back. And I know from this we business. So I brush the potato chips out of my hair which is where Baby Jason like to put em, and I march myself up the aisle to deal with the manager who is a crook in the first place for lyin out there sayin *Gorilla, My Love* playin. And I never did like the man cause he oily and pasty at the same time like the bad guy in the serial, the one that got a hideout behind a push-button bookcase and play "Moonlight Sonata"[4] with gloves on. I knock on the door and I am furious. And I am alone, too. Cause Big Brood suddenly got to go so bad even though my mama told us bout goin in them nasty bathrooms. And I hear him sigh like he disgusted when he get to the door and see only a little kid there. And now I'm really furious cause I get so tired grownups messin over kids cause they little and can't take em to court. What is it, he say to me like I lost my mittens or wet myself or am somebody's

---

3. Basketball game that tests shooting skill and can be played alone or as a contest between two people.
4. Popular name for Beethoven's *Piano Sonata in C Sharp Minor*, Opus 27, No. 2. The "bad guy" who plays this piece is the Phantom of the Opera.

retarded child. When in reality I am the smartest kid P.S. 186 ever had in its whole lifetime and you can ax anybody. Even them teachers that don't like me cause I won't sing them Southern songs or back off when they tell me my questions are out of order. And cause my Mama come up there in a minute when them teachers start playin the dozens[5] behind colored folks. She stalks in with her hat pulled down bad and that Persian lamb coat draped back over one hip on account of she got her fist planted there so she can talk that talk which gets us all hypnotized, and teacher be comin undone cause she know this could be her job and her behind cause Mama got pull with the Board and bad by her own self anyhow.

So I kick the door open wider and just walk right by him and sit down and tell the man about himself and that I want my money back and that goes for Baby Jason and Big Brood too. And he still trying to shuffle me out the door even though I'm sittin which shows him for the fool he is. Just like them teachers do fore they realize Mama like a stone on that spot and ain't backin up. So he ain't gettin up off the money. So I was forced to leave, takin the matches from under his ashtray, and set a fire under the candy stand, which closed the raggedy ole Washington down for a week. My Daddy had the suspect it was me cause Big Brood got a big mouth. But I explained right quick what the whole thing was about and I figured it was even-steven. Cause if you say Gorilla, My Love, you supposed to mean it. Just like when you say you goin to give me a party on my birthday, you gotta mean it. And if you say me and Baby Jason can go South pecan haulin with Granddaddy Vale, you better not be comin up with no stuff about the weather look uncertain or did you mop the bathroom or any other trickified business. I mean even gangsters in the movies say My word is my bond. So don't nobody get away with nothin far as I'm concerned. So Daddy put his belt back on. Cause that's the way I was raised. Like my Mama say in one of them situations when I won't back down, Okay Badbird, you right. Your point is well-taken. Not that Badbird my name, just what she say when she tired arguin and know I'm right. And Aunt Jo, who is the hardest head in the family and worse even than Aunt Daisy, she say, You absolutely right Miss Muffin, which also ain't my real name but the name she gave me one time when I got some medicine shot in my behind and wouldn't get up off her pillows for nothin. And even Grand-daddy Vale—who got no memory to speak of, so sometime you can just plain lie to him, if you want to be like that—he say, Well if that's what I said, then that's it. But this name business was different they said. It wasn't like Hunca Bubba had gone back on his word or anything. Just that he was thinkin bout gettin married and was usin his real name now. Which ain't the way I saw it at all.

So there I am in the navigator seat. And I turned to him and just plain ole ax him. I mean I come right on out with it. No sense goin all around that barn the old folks talk about. And like my mama say, Hazel—which is my real name and what she remembers to call me when she bein serious—when you got somethin on your mind, speak up and let the chips fall where they may. And if anybody don't like it, tell em to come see your mama. And Daddy look up from the paper and say, You hear your Mama good, Hazel. And tell em to come see me first. Like that. That's how I was raised.

So I turn clear round in the navigator seat and say, "Look here, Hunca Bubba or Jefferson Windsong Vale or whatever your name is, you gonna marry this girl?"

5. Ritualized game or contest in which two participants exchange artfully stylized insults.

"Sure am," he say, all grins.

And I say, "Member that time you was baby-sittin me when we lived at four-o-nine and there was this big snow and Mama and Daddy got held up in the country so you had to stay for two days?"

And he say, "Sure do."

"Well. You remember how you told me I was the cutest thing that ever walked the earth?"

"Oh, you were real cute when you were little," he say, which is supposed to be funny. I am not laughin.

"Well. You remember what you said?"

And Granddaddy Vale squintin over the wheel and axin Which way, Scout. But Scout is busy and don't care if we all get lost for days.

"Watcha mean, Peaches?"

"My name is Hazel. And what I mean is you said you were going to marry *me* when I grew up. You were going to wait. That's what I mean, my dear Uncle Jefferson." And he don't say nuthin. Just look at me real strange like he never saw me before in life. Like he lost in some weird town in the middle of night and lookin for directions and there's no one to ask. Like it was me that messed up the maps and turned the road posts round. "Well, you said it, didn't you?" And Baby Jason lookin back and forth like we playin ping-pong. Only I ain't playin. I'm hurtin and I can hear that I am screamin. And Granddaddy Vale mumblin how we never gonna get to where we goin if I don't turn around and take my navigator job serious.

"Well, for cryin out loud, Hazel, you just a little girl. And I was just teasin."

"'And I was just teasin,'" I say back just how he said it so he can hear what a terrible thing it is. Then I don't say nuthin. And he don't say nuthin. And Baby Jason don't say nuthin nohow. Then Granddaddy Vale speak up. "Look here, Precious, it was Hunca Bubba what told you them things. This here, Jefferson Winston Vale." And Hunca Bubba say, "That's right. That was somebody else. I'm a new somebody."

"You a lyin dawg," I say, when I meant to say treacherous dog, but just couldn't get hold of the word. It slipped away from me. And I'm crying and crumplin down in the seat and just don't care. And Granddaddy say to hush and steps on the gas. And I'm losin my bearins and don't even know where to look on the map cause I can't see for cryin. And Baby Jason cryin too. Cause he is my blood brother and understands that we must stick together or be forever lost, what with grown-ups playin change-up and turnin you round every which way so bad. And don't even say they sorry.

1971

QUESTIONS

1. What details in the story reveal that Hazel, the narrator, is still a young girl? In what ways does she seem aware beyond her years and circumstances? How does Toni Cade Bambara establish Hazel's age, sex, ethnicity, and personality?
2. Some characters in this story, including Hazel, have multiple names. How do these names contribute to the initiation or coming-of-age plot of the story? Which changes or realizations are related to names or identities, and which are unrelated?
3. How and why does Hazel's view of adults change over the course of the story? What truth does she seem to learn?

ALICE MUNRO

Boys and Girls

My father was a fox farmer. That is, he raised silver foxes, in pens; and in the fall and early winter, when their fur was prime, he killed them and skinned them and sold their pelts to the Hudson's Bay Company or the Montreal Fur Traders. These companies supplied us with heroic calendars to hang, one on each side of the kitchen door. Against a background of cold blue sky and black pine forests and treacherous northern rivers, plumed adventurers planted the flags of England or of France; magnificent savages bent their backs to the portage.

For several weeks before Christmas, my father worked after supper in the cellar of our house. The cellar was white-washed, and lit by a hundred-watt bulb over the worktable. My brother Laird and I sat on the top step and watched. My father removed the pelt inside-out from the body of the fox, which looked surprisingly small, mean and rat-like, deprived of its arrogant weight of fur. The naked, slippery bodies were collected in a sack and buried at the dump. One time the hired man, Henry Bailey, had taken a swipe at me with this sack, saying, "Christmas present!" My mother thought that was not funny. In fact she disliked the whole pelting operation—that was what the killing, skinning, and preparation of the furs was called—and wished it did not have to take place in the house. There was the smell. After the pelt had been stretched inside-out on a long board my father scraped away delicately, removing the little clotted webs of blood vessels, the bubbles of fat; the smell of blood and animal fat, with the strong primitive odour of the fox itself, penetrated all parts of the house. I found it reassuringly seasonal, like the smell of oranges and pine needles.

Henry Bailey suffered from bronchial troubles. He would cough and cough until his narrow face turned scarlet, and his light blue, derisive eyes filled up with tears; then he took the lid off the stove, and, standing well back, shot out a great clot of phlegm—hsss—straight into the heart of the flames. We admired him for this performance and for his ability to make his stomach growl at will, and for his laughter, which was full of high whistlings and gurglings and involved the whole faulty machinery of his chest. It was sometimes hard to tell what he was laughing at, and always possible that it might be us.

After we had been sent to bed we could still smell fox and still hear Henry's laugh, but these things, reminders of the warm, safe, brightly lit downstairs world, seemed lost and diminished, floating on the stale cold air upstairs. We were afraid at night in the winter. We were not afraid of *outside* though this was the time of year when snowdrifts curled around our house like sleeping whales and the wind harassed us all night, coming up from the buried fields, the frozen swamp, with its old bugbear chorus of threats and misery. We were afraid of *inside*, the room where we slept. At this time the upstairs of our house was not finished. A brick chimney went up one wall. In the middle of the floor was a square hole, with a wooden railing around it; that was where the stairs came up. On the other side of the stairwell were the things that nobody had any use for any more—a soldiery roll of linoleum, standing on end, a wicker baby carriage, a fern basket, china jugs and basins with cracks in them, a picture of the Battle of Balaclava,[1] very sad to look at. I had told

1. Indecisive Crimean War battle fought on October 25, 1854, famous for the Charge of the Light Brigade (see pp. 1006–1007).

Laird, as soon as he was old enough to understand such things, that bats and skeletons lived over there; whenever a man escaped from the county jail, twenty miles
away, I imagined that he had somehow let himself in the window and was hiding
behind the linoleum. But we had rules to keep us safe. When the light was on, we
were safe as long as we did not step off the square of worn carpet which defined
our bedroom-space; when the light was off no place was safe but the beds themselves. I had to turn out the light kneeling on the end of my bed, and stretching as
far as I could to reach the cord.

In the dark we lay on our beds, our narrow life rafts, and fixed our eyes on the   5
faint light coming up the stairwell, and sang songs. Laird sang "Jingle Bells,"
which he would sing any time, whether it was Christmas or not, and I sang
"Danny Boy." I loved the sound of my own voice, frail and supplicating, rising in
the dark. We could make out the tall frosted shapes of the windows now, gloomy
and white. When I came to the part, *When I am dead, as dead I well may be*—a fit of
shivering caused not by the cold sheets but by pleasurable emotion almost
silenced me. *You'll kneel and say, an Ave there above me*—What was an Ave? Every
day I forgot to find out.

Laird went straight from singing to sleep. I could hear his long, satisfied, bubbly breaths. Now for the time that remained to me, the most perfectly private
and perhaps the best time of the whole day, I arranged myself tightly under the
covers and went on with one of the stories I was telling myself from night to
night. These stories were about myself, when I had grown a little older; they took
place in a world that was recognizably mine, yet one that presented opportunities for courage, boldness and self-sacrifice, as mine never did. I rescued people
from a bombed building (it discouraged me that the real war had gone on so far
away from Jubilee). I shot two rabid wolves who were menacing the schoolyard
(the teachers cowered terrified at my back). I rode a fine horse spiritedly down
the main street of Jubilee, acknowledging the townspeople's gratitude for some
yet-to-be-worked-out piece of heroism (nobody ever rode a horse there, except
King Billy in the Orangemen's Day[2] parade). There was always riding and shooting in these stories, though I had only been on a horse twice—bareback because
we did not own a saddle—and the second time I had slid right around and
dropped under the horse's feet; it had stepped placidly over me. I really was
learning to shoot, but I could not hit anything yet, not even tin cans on fence
posts.

Alive, the foxes inhabited a world my father made for them. It was surrounded
by a high guard fence, like a medieval town, with a gate that was padlocked at
night. Along the streets of this town were ranged large, sturdy pens. Each of
them had a real door that a man could go through, a wooden ramp along the
wire, for the foxes to run up and down on, and a kennel—something like a
clothes chest with airholes—where they slept and stayed in winter and had their
young. There were feeding and watering dishes attached to the wire in such a
way that they could be emptied and cleaned from the outside. The dishes were
made of old tin cans, and the ramps and kennels of odds and ends of old lumber. Everything was tidy and ingenious; my father was tirelessly inventive and

2. The Orange Society is an Irish Protestant group named after William of Orange, who, as King William
III of England, defeated the Catholic James II. The society sponsors an annual procession on July 12 to
commemorate the victory of William III at the Battle of the Boyne (1690).

his favourite book in the world was *Robinson Crusoe*.[3] He had fitted a tin drum on a wheelbarrow, for bringing water down to the pens. This was my job in summer, when the foxes had to have water twice a day. Between nine and ten o'clock in the morning, and again after supper, I filled the drum at the pump and trundled it down through the barnyard to the pens, where I parked it, and filled my watering can and went along the streets. Laird came too, with his little cream and green gardening can, filled too full and knocking against his legs and slopping water on his canvas shoes. I had the real watering can, my father's, though I could only carry it three-quarters full.

The foxes all had names, which were printed on a tin plate and hung beside their doors. They were not named when they were born, but when they survived the first year's pelting and were added to the breeding stock. Those my father had named were called names like Prince, Bob, Wally and Betty. Those I had named were called Star or Turk, or Maureen or Diana. Laird named one Maud after a hired girl we had when he was little, one Harold after a boy at school, and one Mexico, he did not say why.

Naming them did not make pets out of them, or anything like it. Nobody but my father ever went into the pens, and he had twice had blood-poisoning from bites. When I was bringing them their water they prowled up and down on the paths they had made inside their pens, barking seldom—they saved that for night-time, when they might get up a chorus of community frenzy—but always watching me, their eyes burning, clear gold, in their pointed, malevolent faces. They were beautiful for their delicate legs and heavy, aristocratic tails and the bright fur sprinkled on dark down their backs—which gave them their name—but especially for their faces, drawn exquisitely sharp in pure hostility, and their golden eyes.

10 Besides carrying water I helped my father when he cut the long grass, and the lamb's quarter and flowering money-musk, that grew between the pens. He cut with the scythe and I raked into piles. Then he took a pitchfork and threw fresh-cut grass all over the top of the pens, to keep the foxes cooler and shade their coats, which were browned by too much sun. My father did not talk to me unless it was about the job we were doing. In this he was quite different from my mother, who, if she was feeling cheerful, would tell me all sorts of things—the name of a dog she had had when she was a little girl, the names of boys she had gone out with later on when she was grown up, and what certain dresses of hers had looked like—she could not imagine now what had become of them. What-ever thoughts and stories my father had were private, and I was shy of him and would never ask him questions. Nevertheless I worked willingly under his eyes, and with a feeling of pride. One time a feed salesman came down into the pens to talk to him and my father said, "Like to have you meet my new hired man." I turned away and raked furiously, red in the face with pleasure.

"Could of fooled me," said the salesman. "I thought it was only a girl."

After the grass was cut, it seemed suddenly much later in the year. I walked on stubble in the earlier evening, aware of the reddening skies, the entering silences, of fall. When I wheeled the tank out of the gate and put the padlock on, it was almost dark. One night at this time I saw my mother and father standing talk-ing on the little rise of ground we called the gangway, in front of the barn. My

3. Novel (1719) by Daniel Defoe about a man shipwrecked on a desert island; it goes into great detail about the ingenious contraptions he fashions from simple materials.

father had just come from the meathouse; he had his stiff bloody apron on, and a pail of cut-up meat in his hand.

It was an odd thing to see my mother down at the barn. She did not often come out of the house unless it was to do something—hang out the wash or dig potatoes in the garden. She looked out of place, with her bare lumpy legs, not touched by the sun, her apron still on and damp across the stomach from the supper dishes. Her hair was tied up in a kerchief, wisps of it falling out. She would tie her hair up like this in the morning, saying she did not have time to do it properly, and it would stay tied up all day. It was true, too; she really did not have time. These days our back porch was piled with baskets of peaches and grapes and pears, bought in town, and onions and tomatoes and cucumbers grown at home, all waiting to be made into jelly and jam and preserves, pickles and chili sauce. In the kitchen there was a fire in the stove all day, jars clinked in boiling water, sometimes a cheesecloth bag was strung on a pole between two chairs, straining blue-black grape pulp for jelly. I was given jobs to do and I would sit at the table peeling peaches that had been soaked in the hot water, or cutting up onions, my eyes smarting and streaming. As soon as I was done I ran out of the house, trying to get out of earshot before my mother thought of what she wanted me to do next. I hated the hot dark kitchen in summer, the green blinds and the flypapers, the same old oilcloth table and wavy mirror and bumpy linoleum. My mother was too tired and preoccupied to talk to me, she had no heart to tell about the Normal School Graduation Dance; sweat trickled over her face and she was always counting under her breath, pointing at jars, dumping cups of sugar. It seemed to me that work in the house was endless, dreary and peculiarly depressing; work done out of doors, and in my father's service, was ritualistically important.

I wheeled the tank up to the barn, where it was kept, and I heard my mother saying, "Wait till Laird gets a little bigger, then you'll have a real help."

What my father said I did not hear. I was pleased by the way he stood listening, politely as he would to a salesman or a stranger, but with an air of wanting to get on with his real work. I felt my mother had no business down here and I wanted him to feel the same way. What did she mean about Laird? He was no help to anybody. Where was he now? Swinging himself sick on the swing, going around in circles, or trying to catch caterpillars. He never once stayed with me till I was finished.

"And then I can use her more in the house," I heard my mother say. She had a dead-quiet, regretful way of talking about me that always made me uneasy. "I just get my back turned and she runs off. It's not like I had a girl in the family at all."

I went and sat on a feed bag in the corner of the barn, not wanting to appear when this conversation was going on. My mother, I felt, was not to be trusted. She was kinder than my father and more easily fooled, but you could not depend on her, and the real reasons for the things she said and did were not to be known. She loved me, and she sat up late at night making a dress of the difficult style I wanted, for me to wear when school started, but she was also my enemy. She was always plotting. She was plotting now to get me to stay in the house more, although she knew I hated it (*because* she knew I hated it) and keep me from working for my father. It seemed to me she would do this simply out of perversity, and to try her power. It did not occur to me that she could be lonely, or jealous. No grown-up could be; they were too fortunate. I sat and kicked my heels monotonously against a feedbag, raising dust, and did not come out till she was gone.

15

At any rate, I did not expect my father to pay any attention to what she said. Who could imagine Laird doing my work—Laird remembering the padlock and cleaning out the watering-dishes with a leaf on the end of a stick, or even wheeling the tank without it tumbling over? It showed how little my mother knew about the way things really were.

I have forgotten to say what the foxes were fed. My father's bloody apron reminded me. They were fed horsemeat. At this time most farmers still kept horses, and when a horse got too old to work, or broke a leg or got down and would not get up, as they sometimes did, the owner would call my father, and he and Henry went out to the farm in the truck. Usually they shot and butchered the horse there, paying the farmer from five to twelve dollars. If they had already too much meat on hand, they would bring the horse back alive, and keep it for a few days or weeks in our stable, until the meat was needed. After the war the farmers were buying tractors and gradually getting rid of horses altogether, so it sometimes happened that we got a good healthy horse, that there was just no use for any more. If this happened in the winter we might keep the horse in our stable till spring, for we had plenty of hay and if there was a lot of snow—and the plow did not always get our road cleared—it was convenient to be able to go to town with a horse and cutter.[4]

20   The winter I was eleven years old we had two horses in the stable. We did not know what names they had had before, so we called them Mack and Flora. Mack was an old black workhorse, sooty and indifferent. Flora was a sorrel mare, a driver. We took them both out in the cutter. Mack was slow and easy to handle. Flora was given to fits of violent alarm, veering at cars and even at other horses, but we loved her speed and high-stepping, her general air of gallantry and abandon. On Saturdays we went down to the stable and as soon as we opened the door on its cosy, animal-smelling darkness Flora threw up her head, rolled her eyes, whinnied despairingly and pulled herself through a crisis of nerves on the spot. It was not safe to go into her stall; she would kick.

This winter also I began to hear a great deal more on the theme my mother had sounded when she had been talking in front of the barn. I no longer felt safe. It seemed that in the minds of the people around me there was a steady undercurrent of thought, not to be deflected, on this one subject. The word *girl* had formerly seemed to me innocent and unburdened, like the world *child*; now it appeared that it was no such thing. A girl was not, as I had supposed, simply what I was; it was what I had to become. It was a definition, always touched with emphasis, with reproach and disappointment. Also it was a joke on me. Once Laird and I were fighting, and for the first time ever I had to use all my strength against him; even so, he caught and pinned my arm for a moment, really hurting me. Henry saw this, and laughed, saying, "Oh, that there Laird's gonna show you, one of these days!" Laird was getting a lot bigger. But I was getting bigger too.

My grandmother came to stay with us for a few weeks and I heard other things. "Girls don't slam doors like that." "Girls keep their knees together when they sit down." And worse still, when I asked some questions, "That's none of girls' business." I continued to slam the doors and sit as awkwardly as possible, thinking that by such measures I kept myself free.

When spring came, the horses were let out in the barnyard. Mack stood against the barn wall trying to scratch his neck and haunches, but Flora trotted

4. Small, light sleigh.

up and down and reared at the fences, clattering her hooves against the rails. Snow drifts dwindled quickly, revealing the hard grey and brown earth, the familiar rise and fall of the ground, plain and bare after the fantastic landscape of winter. There was a great feeling of opening-out, of release. We just wore rubbers now, over our shoes; our feet felt ridiculously light. One Saturday we went out to the stable and found all the doors open, letting in the unaccustomed sunlight and fresh air. Henry was there, just idling around looking at his collection of calendars which were tacked up behind the stalls in a part of the stable my mother had probably never seen.

"Come to say goodbye to your old friend Mack?" Henry said. "Here, you give him a taste of oats." He poured some oats into Laird's cupped hands and Laird went to feed Mack. Mack's teeth were in bad shape. He ate very slowly, patiently shifting the oats around in his mouth, trying to find a stump of a molar to grind it on. "Poor old Mack," said Henry mournfully. "When a horse's teeth's gone, he's gone. That's about the way."

"Are you going to shoot him today?" I said. Mack and Flora had been in the stable so long I had almost forgotten they were going to be shot.   25

Henry didn't answer me. Instead he started to sing in a high, trembly, mocking-sorrowful voice, *Oh, there's no more work, for poor Uncle Ned, he's gone where the good darkies go.*[5] Mack's thick, blackish tongue worked diligently at Laird's hand. I went out before the song was ended and sat down on the gangway.

I had never seen them shoot a horse, but I knew where it was done. Last summer Laird and I had come upon a horse's entrails before they were buried. We had thought it was a big black snake, coiled up in the sun. That was around in the field that ran up beside the barn. I thought that if we went inside the barn, and found a wide crack or knothole to look through we would be able to see them do it. It was not something I wanted to see; just the same, if a thing really happened, it was better to see it, and know.

My father came down from the house, carrying the gun.

"What are you doing here?" he said.

"Nothing."   30

"Go on up and play around the house."

He sent Laird out of the stable. I said to Laird, "Do you want to see them shoot Mack?" and without waiting for an answer led him around to the front door of the barn, opened it carefully, and went in. "Be quiet or they'll hear us," I said. We could hear Henry and my father talking in the stable, then the heavy, shuffling steps of Mack being backed out of his stall.

In the loft it was cold and dark. Thin, crisscrossed beams of sunlight fell through the cracks. The hay was low. It was a rolling country, hills and hollows, slipping under our feet. About four feet up was a beam going around the walls. We piled hay up in one corner and I boosted Laird up and hoisted myself. The beam was not very wide; we crept along it with our hands flat on the barn walls. There were plenty of knotholes, and I found one that gave me the view I wanted— a corner of the barnyard, the gate, part of the field. Laird did not have a knothole and began to complain.

I showed him a widened crack between two boards. "Be quiet and wait. If they hear you you'll get us in trouble."

5. Lines from the Stephen Foster song "Old Uncle Ned."

35   My father came in sight carrying the gun. Henry was leading Mack by the halter. He dropped it and took out his cigarette papers and tobacco; he rolled cigarettes for my father and himself. While this was going on Mack nosed around in the old, dead grass along the fence. Then my father opened the gate and they took Mack through. Henry led Mack way from the path to a patch of ground and they talked together, not loud enough for us to hear. Mack again began searching for a mouthful of fresh grass, which was not to be found. My father walked away in a straight line, and stopped short at a distance which seemed to suit him. Henry was walking away from Mack too, but sideways, still negligently holding on to the halter. My father raised the gun and Mack looked up as if he had noticed something and my father shot him.

Mack did not collapse at once but swayed, lurched sideways and fell, first on his side; then he rolled over on his back and, amazingly, kicked his legs for a few seconds in the air. At this Henry laughed, as if Mack had done a trick for him. Laird, who had drawn a long, groaning breath of surprise when the shot was fired, said out loud, "He's not dead." And it seemed to me it might be true. But his legs stopped, he rolled on his side again, his muscles quivered and sank. The two men walked over and looked at him in a businesslike way; they bent down and examined his forehead where the bullet had gone in, and now I saw his blood on the brown grass.

"Now they just skin him and cut him up," I said. "Let's go." My legs were a little shaky and I jumped gratefully down into the hay. "Now you've seen how they shoot a horse," I said in a congratulatory way, as if I had seen it many times before. "Let's see if any barn cat's had kittens in the hay." Laird jumped. He seemed young and obedient again. Suddenly I remembered how, when he was little, I had brought him into the barn and told him to climb the ladder to the top beam. That was in the spring, too, when the hay was low. I had done it out of a need for excitement, a desire for something to happen so that I could tell about it. He was wearing a little bulky brown and white checked coat, made down from one of mine. He went all the way up, just as I told him, and sat down on the top beam with the hay far below him on one side, and the barn floor and some old machinery on the other. Then I ran screaming to my father, "Laird's up on the top beam!" My father came, my mother came, my father went up the ladder talking very quietly and brought Laird down under his arm, at which my mother leaned against the ladder and began to cry. They said to me, "Why weren't you watching him?" but nobody ever knew the truth. Laird did not know enough to tell. But whenever I saw the brown and white checked coat hanging in the closet, or at the bottom of the rag bag, which was where it ended up, I felt a weight in my stomach, the sadness of unexorcized guilt.

I looked at Laird who did not even remember this, and I did not like the look on this thin, winter-pale face. His expression was not frightened or upset, but remote, concentrating. "Listen," I said, in an unusually bright and friendly voice, "you aren't going to tell, are you?"

"No," he said absently.

40   "Promise."

"Promise," he said. I grabbed the hand behind his back to make sure he was not crossing his fingers. Even so, he might have a nightmare; it might come out that way. I decided I had better work hard to get all thoughts of what he had seen out of his mind—which, it seemed to me, could not hold very many things at a time. I got some money I had saved and that afternoon we went into Jubilee and saw a show, with Judy Canova,[6] at which we both laughed a great deal. After that I thought it would be all right.

Two weeks later I knew they were going to shoot Flora. I knew from the night before, when I heard my mother ask if the hay was holding out all right, and my father said, "Well, after to-morrow there'll just be the cow, and we should be able to put her out to grass in another week." So I knew it was Flora's turn in the morning.

This time I didn't think of watching it. That was something to see just one time. I had not thought about it very often since, but sometimes when I was busy, working at school, or standing in front of the mirror combing my hair and wondering if I would be pretty when I grew up, the whole scene would flash into my mind: I would see the easy, practised way my father raised the gun, and hear Henry laughing when Mack kicked his legs in the air. I did not have any great feeling of horror and opposition, such as a city child might have had; I was too used to seeing the death of animals as a necessity by which we lived. Yet I felt a little ashamed, and there was a new wariness, a sense of holding-off, in my attitude to my father and his work.

It was a fine day, and we were going around the yard picking up tree branches that had been torn off in winter storms. This was something we had been told to do, and also we wanted to use them to make a teepee. We heard Flora whinny, and then my father's voice and Henry's shouting, and we ran down to the barnyard to see what was going on.

The stable door was open. Henry had just brought Flora out, and she had   45
broken away from him. She was running free in the barnyard, from one end to the other. We climbed up on the fence. It was exciting to see her running, whinnying, going up on her hind legs, prancing and threatening like a horse in a Western movie, an unbroken ranch horse, though she was just an old driver, an old sorrel mare. My father and Henry ran after her and tried to grab the dangling halter. They tried to work her into a corner, and they had almost succeeded when she made a run between them, wild-eyed, and disappeared around the corner of the barn. We heard the rails clatter down as she got over the fence, and Henry yelled, "She's into the field now!"

That meant she was in the long L-shaped field that ran up by the house. If she got around the center, heading towards the lane, the gate was open; the truck had been driven into the field this morning. My father shouted to me, because I was on the other side of the fence, nearest the lane, "Go shut the gate!"

I could run very fast. I ran across the garden, past the tree where our swing was hung, and jumped across a ditch into the lane. There was the open gate. She had not got out, I could not see her up on the road; she must have run to the other end of the field. The gate was heavy. I lifted it out of the gravel and carried it across the roadway. I had it half-way across when she came in sight, galloping straight towards me. There was just time to get the chain on. Laird came scrambling through the ditch to help me.

Instead of shutting the gate, I opened it as wide as I could. I did not make any decision to do this, it was just what I did. Flora never slowed down; she galloped straight past me, and Laird jumped up and down, yelling, "Shut it, shut it!" even

---

6. American comedian (1913–83) best known for her yodeling in hillbilly movies of the 1940s.

after it was too late. My father and Henry appeared in the field a moment too late to see what I had done. They only saw Flora heading for the township road. They would think I had not got there in time.

They did not waste any time asking about it. They went back to the barn and got the gun and the knives they used, and put these in the truck; then they turned the truck around and came bouncing up the field toward us. Laird called to them, "Let me go too, let me go too!" and Henry stopped the truck and they took him in. I shut the gate after they were all gone.

50   I supposed Laird would tell. I wondered what would happen to me. I had never disobeyed my father before, and I could not understand why I had done it. Flora would not really get away. They would catch up with her in the truck. Or if they did not catch her this morning somebody would see her and telephone us this afternoon or tomorrow. There was no wild country here for her to run to, only farms. What was more, my father had paid for her, we needed the meat to feed the foxes, we needed the foxes to make our living. All I had done was make more work for my father who worked hard enough already. And when my father found out about it he was not going to trust me any more, he would know that I was not entirely on his side. I was on Flora's side, and that made me no use to anybody, not even to her. Just the same, I did not regret it; when she came running at me and I held the gate open, that was the only thing I could do.

I went back to the house, and my mother said, "What's all the commotion?" I told her that Flora had kicked down the fence and got away. "Your poor father," she said, "now he'll have to go chasing over the countryside. Well, there isn't any use planning dinner before one." She put up the ironing board. I wanted to tell her, but thought better of it and went upstairs and sat on my bed.

Lately I had been trying to make my part of the room fancy, spreading the bed with old lace curtains, and fixing myself a dressing-table with some leftovers of cretonne for a skirt. I planned to put up some kind of barricade between my bed and Laird's, to keep my section separate from his. In the sunlight, the lace curtains were just dusty rags. We did not sing at night any more. One night when I was singing Laird said, "You sound silly," and I went right on but the next night I did not start. There was not so much need to anyway, we were no longer afraid. We knew it was just old furniture over there, old jumble and confusion. We did not keep to the rules. I still stayed awake after Laird was asleep and told myself stories, but even in these stories something different was happening, mysterious alterations took place. A story might start off in the old way, with a spectacular danger, a fire or wild animals, and for a while I might rescue people; then things would change around, and instead, somebody would be rescuing me. It might be a boy from our class at school, or even Mr. Campbell, our teacher, who tickled girls under the arms. And at this point the story concerned itself at great length with what I looked like—how long my hair was, and what kind of dress I had on; by the time I had these details worked out the real excitement of the story was lost.

It was later than one o'clock when the truck came back. The tarpaulin was over the back, which meant there was meat in it. My mother had to heat dinner up all over again. Henry and my father had changed from their bloody overalls into ordinary working overalls in the barn, and they washed their arms and necks and faces at the sink, and splashed water on their hair and combed it. Laird lifted his arm to show off a streak of blood. "We shot old Flora," he said, "and cut her up in fifty pieces."

"Well I don't want to hear about it," my mother said. "And don't come to my table like that."

My father made him go and wash the blood off.

We sat down and my father said grace and Henry pasted his chewing-gum on the end of his fork, the way he always did; when he took it off he would have us admire the pattern. We began to pass the bowls of steaming, overcooked vegetables. Laird looked across the table at me and said proudly, distinctly, "Anyway it was her fault Flora got away."

"What?" my father said.

"She could of shut the gate and she didn't. She just open' it up and Flora run out."

"Is that right?" my father said.

Everybody at the table was looking at me. I nodded, swallowing food with great difficulty. To my shame, tears flooded my eyes.

My father made a curt sound of disgust. "What did you do that for?"

I did not answer. I put down my fork and waited to be sent from the table, still not looking up.

But this did not happen. For some time nobody said anything, then Laird said matter-of-factly, "She's crying."

"Never mind," my father said. He spoke with resignation, even good humour, the words which absolved and dismissed me for good. "She's only a girl," he said.

I didn't protest that, even in my heart. Maybe it was true.

1968

QUESTIONS

1. There is only one girl character (the narrator) and one boy character (the narrator's younger brother) in "Boys and Girls." Why do you think Alice Munro uses plural words in the title?
2. Find the two occurrences of the phrase "only a girl." Why and how does the meaning of the phrase change in each case?
3. Why does the narrator choose not to shut the gate on Flora? What role does this act play in her initiation?

JOHN UPDIKE

A & P[1]

In walks these three girls in nothing but bathing suits. I'm in the third checkout slot, with my back to the door, so I don't see them until they're over by the bread. The one that caught my eye first was the one in the plaid green two-piece. She was a chunky kid, with a good tan and a sweet broad soft-looking can with those two crescents of white just under it, where the sun never seems to hit, at the top

---

1. The Great Atlantic and Pacific Tea Company, so named in 1869, became by the 1930s the leading national chain of supermarkets. The A&P Corporation today has more than 400 stores under various names.

of the backs of her legs. I stood there with my hand on a box of HiHo crackers trying to remember if I rang it up or not. I ring it up again and the customer starts giving me hell. She's one of these cash-register-watchers, a witch about fifty with rouge on her cheekbones and no eyebrows, and I know it made her day to trip me up. She'd been watching cash registers for fifty years and probably never seen a mistake before.

By the time I got her feathers smoothed and her goodies into a bag—she gives me a little snort in passing, if she'd been born at the right time they would have burned her over in Salem[2]—by the time I get her on her way the girls had circled around the bread and were coming back, without a pushcart, back my way along the counters, in the aisle between the checkouts and the Special bins. They didn't even have shoes on. There was this chunky one, with the two-piece—it was bright green and the seams on the bra were still sharp and her belly was still pretty pale so I guessed she just got it (the suit)—there was this one, with one of those chubby berry-faces, the lips all bunched together under her nose, this one, and a tall one, with black hair that hadn't quite frizzed right, and one of these sunburns right across under the eyes, and a chin that was too long—you know, the kind of girl other girls think is very "striking" and "attractive" but never quite makes it, as they very well know, which is why they like her so much—and then the third one, that wasn't quite so tall. She was the queen. She kind of led them, the other two peeking around and making their shoulders round. She didn't look around, not this queen, she just walked straight on slowly, on these long white prima-donna legs. She came down a little hard on her heels, as if she didn't walk in her bare feet that much, putting down her heels and then letting the weight move along to her toes as if she was testing the floor with every step, putting a little deliberate extra action into it. You never know for sure how girls' minds work (do you really think it's a mind in there or just a little buzz like a bee in a glass jar?) but you got the idea she had talked the other two into coming in here with her, and now she was showing them how to do it, walk slow and hold yourself straight.

She had on a kind of dirty-pink—beige maybe, I don't know—bathing suit with a little nubble all over it and, what got me, the straps were down. They were off her shoulders looped loose around the cool tops of her arms, and I guess as a result the suit had slipped a little on her, so all around the top of the cloth there was this shining rim. If it hadn't been there you wouldn't have known there could have been anything whiter than those shoulders. With the straps pushed off, there was nothing between the top of the suit and the top of her head except just *her*, this clean bare plane of the top of her chest down from the shoulder bones like a dented sheet of metal tilted in the light. I mean, it was more than pretty.

She had sort of oaky hair that the sun and salt had bleached, done up in a bun that was unravelling, and a kind of prim face. Walking into the A & P with your straps down, I suppose it's the only kind of face you *can* have. She held her head so high her neck, coming up out of those white shoulders, looked kind of stretched, but I didn't mind. The longer her neck was, the more of her there was.

5   She must have felt in the corner of her eye me and over my shoulder Stokesie in the second slot watching, but she didn't tip. Not this queen. She kept her eyes moving across the racks, and stopped, and turned so slow it made my stomach

2. The store is located not far from Salem, Massachusetts, where in 1692 nineteen women and men were hanged after being convicted of witchcraft.

rub the inside of my apron, and buzzed to the other two, who kind of huddled against her for relief, and then they all three of them went up the cat-and-dog-food-breakfast-cereal-macaroni-rice-raisins-seasonings-spreads-spaghetti-soft-drinks-crackers-and-cookies aisle. From the third slot I look straight up this aisle to the meat counter, and I watched them all the way. The fat one with the tan sort of fumbled with the cookies, but on second thought she put the package back. The sheep pushing their carts down the aisle—the girls were walking against the usual traffic (not that we have one-way signs or anything)—were pretty hilarious. You could see them, when Queenie's white shoulders dawned on them, kind of jerk, or hop, or hiccup, but their eyes snapped back to their own baskets and on they pushed. I bet you could set off dynamite in an A & P and the people would by and large keep reaching and checking oatmeal off their lists and muttering "Let me see, there was a third thing, began with A, asparagus, no, ah, yes, applesauce!" or whatever it is they do mutter. But there was no doubt, this jiggled them. A few houseslaves in pin curlers even looked around after pushing their carts past to make sure what they had seen was correct.

You know, it's one thing to have a girl in a bathing suit down on the beach, where what with the glare nobody can look at each other much anyway, and another thing in the cool of the A & P, under the fluorescent lights, against all those stacked packages, with her feet paddling along naked over our checkerboard green-and-cream rubber-tile floor.

"Oh Daddy," Stokesie said beside me. "I feel so faint."

"Darling," I said. "Hold me tight." Stokesie's married, with two babies chalked up on his fuselage already, but as far as I can tell that's the only difference. He's twenty-two, and I was nineteen this April.

"Is it done?" he asks, the responsible married man finding his voice. I forgot to say he thinks he's going to be manager some sunny day, maybe in 1990 when it's called the Great Alexandrov and Petrooshki Tea Company or something.

What he meant was, our town is five miles from a beach, with a big summer colony out on the Point, but we're right in the middle of town, and the women generally put on a shirt or shorts or something before they get out of the car into the street. And anyway these are usually women with six children and varicose veins mapping their legs and nobody, including them, could care less. As I say, we're right in the middle of town, and if you stand at our front doors you can see two banks and the Congregational church and the newspaper store and three real-estate offices and about twenty-seven old freeloaders tearing up Central Street because the sewer broke again. It's not as if we're on the Cape; we're north of Boston and there's people in this town haven't seen the ocean for twenty years.

The girls had reached the meat counter and were asking McMahon something. He pointed, they pointed, and they shuffled out of sight behind a pyramid of Diet Delight peaches. All that was left for us to see was old McMahon patting his mouth and looking after them sizing up their joints. Poor kids, I began to feel sorry for them, they couldn't help it.

• • •

Now here comes the sad part of the story, at least my family says it's sad, but I don't think it's so sad myself. The store's pretty empty, it being Thursday afternoon, so there was nothing much to do except lean on the register and wait for the girls to show up again. The whole store was like a pinball machine and I didn't know which tunnel they'd come out of. After a while they come around out of the far aisle, around the light bulbs, records at discount of the Caribbean Six or Tony Martin Sings[3] or some such gunk you wonder they waste the wax on, sixpacks of candy bars, and plastic toys done up in cellophane that fall apart when a kid looks at them anyway. Around they come, Queenie still leading the way, and holding a little gray jar in her hand. Slots Three through Seven are unmanned and I could see her wondering between Stokes and me, but Stokesie with his usual luck draws an old party in baggy gray pants who stumbles up with four giant cans of pineapple juice (what do these bums *do* with all that pineapple juice? I've often asked myself) so the girls come to me. Queenie puts down the jar and I take it into my fingers icy cold. Kingfish Fancy Herring Snacks in Pure Sour Cream: 49¢. Now her hands are empty, not a ring or a bracelet, bare as God made them, and I wonder where the money's coming from. Still with that prim look she lifts a folded dollar bill out of the hollow at the center of her nubbled pink top. The jar went heavy in my hand. Really, I thought that was so cute.

Then everybody's luck begins to run out. Lengel comes in from haggling with a truck full of cabbages on the lot and is about to scuttle into that door marked MANAGER behind which he hides all day when the girls touch his eye. Lengel's pretty dreary, teaches Sunday school and the rest, but he doesn't miss that much. He comes over and says, "Girls, this isn't the beach."

Queenie blushes, though maybe it's just a brush of sunburn I was noticing for the first time, now that she was so close. "My mother asked me to pick up a jar of herring snacks." Her voice kind of startled me, the way voices do when you see the people first, coming out so flat and dumb yet kind of tony, too, the way it ticked over "pick up" and "snacks." All of a sudden I slid right down her voice into her living room. Her father and the other men were standing around in ice-cream coats and bow ties and the women were in sandals picking up herring snacks on toothpicks off a big glass plate and they were all holding drinks the color of water with olives and sprigs of mint in them. When my parents have somebody over they get lemonade and if it's a real racy affair Schlitz in tall glasses with "They'll Do It Every Time" cartoons stencilled on.[4]

15   "That's all right," Lengel said. "But this isn't the beach." His repeating this struck me as funny, as if it had just occurred to him, and he had been thinking all these years the A & P was a great big dune and he was the head lifeguard. He didn't like my smiling—as I say he doesn't miss much—but he concentrates on giving the girls that sad Sunday-school-superintendent stare.

Queenie's blush is no sunburn now, and the plump one in plaid, that I liked better from the back—a really sweet can—pipes up, "We weren't doing any shopping. We just came in for the one thing."

"That makes no difference," Lengel tells her, and I could see from the way his eyes went that he hadn't noticed she was wearing a two-piece before. "We want you decently dressed when you come in here."

"We *are* decent," Queenie says suddenly, her lower lip pushing, getting sore now that she remembers her place, a place from which the crowd that runs the A & P must look pretty crummy. Fancy Herring Snacks flashed in her very blue eyes.

3. Typical titles of record albums at the time of the story (1962). Tony Martin (b. 1913), a popular singer and actor, was featured on radio and television in the 1940s and 1950s.
4. Schlitz is an inexpensive brand of beer. The cheap glasses are decorated with a popular saying derived from a syndicated series of single-panel cartoons printed between 1929–2008.

"Girls, I don't want to argue with you. After this come in here with your shoulders covered. It's our policy." He turns his back. That's policy for you. Policy is what the kingpins want. What the others want is juvenile delinquency.

All this while, the customers had been showing up with their carts but, you 20 know, sheep, seeing a scene, they had all bunched up on Stokesie, who shook open a paper bag as gently as peeling a peach, not wanting to miss a word. I could feel in the silence everybody getting nervous, most of all Lengel, who asks me, "Sammy, have you rung up their purchase?"

I thought and said "No" but it wasn't about that I was thinking. I go through the punches, 4, 9, GROC, TOT—it's more complicated than you think, and after you do it often enough, it begins to make a little song, that you hear words to, in my case "Hello (*bing*) there, you (*gung*) hap-py pee-pul (*splat*)!"—the *splat* being the drawer flying out. I uncrease the bill, tenderly as you may imagine, it just having come from between the two smoothest scoops of vanilla I had ever known were there, and pass a half and a penny into her narrow pink palm, and nestle the herrings in a bag and twist its neck and hand it over, all the time thinking.

The girls, and who'd blame them, are in a hurry to get out, so I say "I quit" to Lengel quick enough for them to hear, hoping they'll stop and watch me, their unsuspected hero. They keep right on going, into the electric eye; the door flies open and they flicker across the lot to their car, Queenie and Plaid and Big Tall Goony-Goony (not that as raw material she was so bad), leaving me with Lengel and a kink in his eyebrow.

"Did you say something, Sammy?"

"I said I quit."

"I thought you did." 25

"You didn't have to embarrass them."

"It was they who were embarrassing us."

I started to say something that came out "Fiddle-de-doo." It's a saying of my grandmother's, and I know she would have been pleased.

"I don't think you know what you're saying," Lengel said.

"I know you don't," I said. "But I do." I pull the bow at the back of my apron 30 and start shrugging it off my shoulders. A couple customers that had been heading for my slot begin to knock against each other, like scared pigs in a chute.

Lengel sighs and begins to look very patient and old and gray. He's been a friend of my parents for years. "Sammy, you don't want to do this to your Mom and Dad," he tells me. It's true, I don't. But it seems to me that once you begin a gesture it's fatal not to go through with it. I fold the apron, "Sammy" stitched in red on the pocket, and put it on the counter, and drop the bow tie on top of it. The bow tie is theirs, if you've ever wondered. "You'll feel this for the rest of your life," Lengel says, and I know that's true, too, but remembering how he made that pretty girl blush makes me so scrunchy inside I punch the No Sale tab and the machine whirs "pee-pul" and the drawer splats out. One advantage to this scene taking place in summer, I can follow this up with a clean exit, there's no fumbling around getting your coat and galoshes, I just saunter into the electric eye in my white shirt that my mother ironed the night before, and the door heaves itself open, and outside the sunshine is skating around on the asphalt.

I look around for my girls, but they're gone, of course. There wasn't anybody but some young married screaming with her children about some candy they didn't get by the door of a powder-blue Falcon station wagon. Looking back in the big windows, over the bags of peat moss and aluminum lawn furniture stacked on the pavement, I could see Lengel in my place in the slot, checking the sheep through. His face was dark gray and his back stiff, as if he'd just had an injection of iron, and my stomach kind of fell as I felt how hard the world was going to be to me hereafter.

1962

QUESTIONS

1. The narrator of "A & P" announces the turning point or climax of the action, "the sad part of the story," adding, "then everyone's luck begins to run out." Is the climax of the story as significant as this sounds? Does the tone of Sammy's telling of the story match the events?
2. This brief incident at the grocery store involves both younger and older females and males, married or not. Compare and contrast the male employees and female customers of different ages and status. How does Sammy's view of these people suggest the theme of growing up, or predict the options in life of the various people?
3. Sammy is familiar with every detail of the store and describes it for the reader. How does the setting of the story shape the initiation and its meaning? How do details about the merchandise or space reveal Sammy's character and the interaction of the various other characters?

Authors on Their Work: JOHN UPDIKE (1932–2009)

From *"An Interview with John Updike"* (1995)*

"There is always some ambiguity or some room for various responses to a story. But I certainly see him [Sammy] as a typical, well-intentioned American male trying to find his way in the society and full of good impulses. I think that he quit his job on a good impulse. . . . A kind of feminist protest, in a way, is what he does here. Who knows what his adult life will bring, but I think for the moment he's a boy who's tried to reach out of his immediate environment toward something bigger and better."

*"An Interview with John Updike," conducted by Donald M. Murray, directed by Bruce Schwartz (1995), posted by Murray, *Spike*. 2001. Web. 10 April 2009.

SUGGESTIONS FOR WRITING

1. Initiation stories often concern a choice to abandon or join a family, group, or community. Write an essay in which you examine the choices made by one or more of the main characters in "Stepdaughters." How do such choices shape the plot of the

story or the changes characters go through? In what ways are the decisions to join a team or club in conflict with decisions about relationships?

2. A child, teenager, or adult will have different perspectives on the same situations, and initiation stories often dramatically reveal such differences in the way characters and narrators respond. The stories in this album all use first-person narrators, whether still speaking as the young person who recently experienced a change or as an older person looking back on youth or witnessing someone else change. Write an essay on the way the young or grown-up narrator affects your understanding of the "initiation" in one of the stories in this album.

3. How is space designated at the farm and in the house in "Boys and Girls"? Write an essay examining how the uses and restrictions of different spaces might indicate stages of growing up or initiation into the proper roles for adult women and men.

4. Write an essay that identifies and explores the significance of a group of related words or images that recurs in one of the stories in this album.

5. Traditional cultures like that of the Masai people of East Africa have highly ritualized methods of inducting young people into adulthood. Might developed Western societies also be said to have ritual forms of initiation? Drawing evidence from at least two stories in this album, write an essay exploring how young people in modern Western societies are initiated into adulthood.

6. Choose a story from any other chapter of this book and write an essay explaining why it should be considered an initiation story.

7. Using any story in this album as a model, write a first-person narrative of an actual or fictional initiation into adulthood.

2 NARRATION AND POINT OF VIEW

When we read fiction, our sense of who is telling us the story is as important as discovering what happens to the characters. Unlike drama, in which events are acted out in front of an audience, fiction is always mediated or represented to us by someone else, a **narrator**. Often a reader is very aware of the **voice** of a narrator telling the story, as if the words are being spoken aloud. Commonly, stories also reveal a distinct angle of vision or perspective from which the characters, events, and other aspects are viewed. Just as the verbal quality of narration is called the voice, the visual angle is called the **focus**. Focus acts much as a camera does, choosing the direction of our gaze, the proportions and framework in which we see things. Both voice and focus are generally considered together in the term **point of view**. To understand how a story is narrated, you need to recognize both voice and focus. These in turn shape what we know and care about as the plot unfolds, and they make us feel close to or distant from certain characters.

A story is said to be from a character's point of view, or a character is said to be a focal or focalizing character, if for the most part the action centers on that character, as if we see with that character's eyes or we watch that character closely. But the effects of narration certainly involve more than attaching a video camera to a character's head or tracking wherever the character moves. What about the spoken and unspoken words? In some stories, the narrator is a character, and we may feel as if we are overhearing his or her thoughts, whereas in other stories the narrator takes a very distant or critical view of the characters. At times a narrator seems more like a disembodied, unidentified voice. Prose fiction has many ways to convey speech and thought, so it is important to consider voice as well as focus when we try to understand the narration of a story.

Besides focus and voice, point of view encompasses more general matters of value. A story's narrator may explicitly endorse or subtly support whatever a certain character values, knows, or seeks, even when the character is absent or silent or unaware. Other narrators may treat characters and their interests with far more detachment. At the same time, the **style** and **tone** of the narrator's voice—from echoing the characters' feelings to mocking their pretentious speech or thoughts to stating their actions in formal diction—may convey clues that a character or a narrator's perspective is limited. Such discrepancies or gaps between vision and voice, intentions and understandings, or expectations and outcomes generate **irony**. For instance, Sister, the narrator of Eudora Welty's "Why I Live at the P.O.," is unaware that her resentful tone and spiteful behavior undermine both her dignity and her story, which she thinks is a justified complaint and self-defense. Sometimes, too, the point of view shifts, as in Flannery O'Connor's "Good Country People," challenging the reader's bias toward any one character. Or the style of narration may even change dramatically from one section to another. Bram Stoker's novel *Dracula* (1897), for example, is variously narrated through characters' journals, letters, reports, and newspaper articles.

Questions about Narration and Point of View

1. Does the narrator speak in the first, second, or third person?
2. Is the story narrated in the past or present tense? Does the verb tense affect your reading of it in any way?
3. Does the narrator use a distinctive vocabulary, style, and tone, or is the language more standard and neutral?
4. Is the narrator identified as a character, and if so, how much does he or she participate in the action?
5. Does the narrator ever seem to speak to the reader directly (addressing "you") or explicitly state opinions or values?
6. Do you know what every character is thinking, or only some characters, or none?
7. Does the narrative voice or focus shift during the story or remain consistent?
8. Do the narrator, the characters, and the reader all perceive matters in the same way, or are there differences in levels of understanding?

The point of view varies according to the narrator's position in the story and the grammatical person (for example, first or third) the narrative voice assumes. These elements determine who is telling the story, whom it is about, and what information the reader has access to.

A *third-person narrator* tells an unidentified listener or reader what happened, referring to all characters using the pronouns *he*, *she*, or *they*. Third-person narration is virtually always external, meaning that the narrator is not a character in and does not participate in the action of the story. Even so, different types of third-person narration—omniscient, limited, and objective—provide the reader with various amounts of information about the characters.

An *omniscient* or *unlimited narrator* has access to the thoughts, perceptions, or experiences of more than one character (often of several), though such narrators usually focus selectively on a few important characters. A *limited narrator* is an external, third-person narrator who tells the story from a distinct point of view, usually that of a single character, revealing that character's thoughts and relating the action from his or her perspective. This focal character is also known as a **central consciousness**. Sometimes, a limited narrator will reveal the thoughts and feelings of a small number of the characters in order to enhance the story told about the central consciousness. Jane Austen's novel *Emma* includes a few episodes from Mr. Knightley's point of view to show what he thinks about Emma Woodhouse, the focal character, and her relationships. Finally, an *objective narrator* does not explicitly report the characters' thoughts and feelings but may obliquely suggest them through the characters' speech and actions. For example, Ernest Hemingway's "Hills Like White Elephants" consists mostly of dialogue interspersed with minimal action and description.

Instead of using third-person narration, an author might choose to tell a story from the point of view of a *first-person narrator*. Most common is first-person singular narration, where the narrator uses the pronoun *I*. The narrator may be a major or minor character within the story and therefore is an *internal narrator*. Notice that the first-person narrator may be telling a story mainly about someone else or about his or her own experience. Sometimes the first-person narrator addresses an **auditor**, a listener within the fiction whose possible reaction is part of the story. Edgar Allan Poe's "The Cask of Amontillado" begins, "The thousand injuries of Fortunato I had borne as best I could. . . . I vowed revenge. You, who so well know the nature of my soul. . . ." Poe's story is controlled by Montresor's point of view: both what he perceived during his act of revenge and what he says about it years later. We never know what the victim, Fortunato, is thinking, nor do we know how the auditor (an unidentified friend) feels about Montresor's character and deeds. We have only Montresor's perspective and voice, but that doesn't stop us from taking a very different view of what happens than Montresor intends for us to have. Such incompatibility between what someone intends to communicate and what auditors understand is one form of irony, as we have noted.

One kind of narrator that is especially effective at producing irony is the *unreliable narrator*. First-person narrators may unintentionally reveal their flaws as they try to impress. Or narrators may make claims that other characters or the audience know to be false or distorted. Some fictions are narrated by villains (Montresor surely counts), insane people, fools, liars, or hypocrites. When we resist a narrator's point of view and judge his or her flaws or misperceptions, we call that narrator unreliable. This does not mean you should dismiss everything such a narrator says, but that you should be on the alert for ironies.

Less common is the first-person plural, where the narrator uses the pronoun *we*. The plural may be used effectively to express a shared perspective of a community. William Faulkner's "A Rose for Emily" is narrated by an unidentified resident of the town. The vision, voice, and tone of the narration suggest that the townspeople all act and speak together. Novels that are about a close-knit community may be narrated primarily in first-person plural. Elizabeth Gaskell's classic short novel *Cranford* (1853) is a good example. The narrator is a young woman who visits a community of genteel widows and spinsters in the English village of Cranford and describes their customs. At one point, a visitor arrives, Lady Glenmire, and all of Cranford society is in awe of her aristocratic rank and title. At an evening party, "We were all very silent at first. We were thinking what we could talk about, that should be high enough to interest My Lady. There had been a rise in the price of sugar, which, as preserving-time was near, was a piece of intelligence to all our housekeeping hearts, and would have been the natural topic if Lady Glenmire had not been by. But we were not sure if the Peerage ate preserves," that is, whether aristocrats like Lord Glenmire ate fruit jam. The high price of sugar doesn't seem "high enough" in another sense for a high-ranked guest to talk about.

The narrator of Cranford does refer to herself as "I" and sometimes addresses the reader as "you." The narrative perspective and voice is rather similar in Kazuo Ishiguro's *Never Let Me Go* (2005), a novel that also portrays an isolated group that follows regulated customs. At a boarding school, a student, Polly, suddenly questions one of the rules: "*We* all went silent. Miss Lucy [the teacher] didn't often get cross, but when she did, *you* certainly knew about it, and we thought for a second Polly was for it [would be punished]. But then we saw Miss Lucy wasn't angry, just deep in thought. *I* remember feeling furious at Polly for so stupidly breaking the unwritten rule, but at the same time, being terribly excited about what answer Miss Lucy might give" (emphasis added). Ishiguro's narrator, like Gaskell's, resorts to different narrative perspectives and voices to represent the experience of a community.

Like narrators who refer to themselves as "we" throughout a work of fiction, *second-person narrators* who consistently speak to *you* are unusual. This technique has the effect of turning the reader into a character in the story. Jay McInerney, for example, in his novel *Bright Lights, Big City* (1984) employed the second-person voice, creating an effect similar to conversational anecdotes. Lorrie Moore's "How" and Jamaica Kincaid's "Girl" experiment in different ways with second-person narration, addressing the central consciousness, or protagonist, as "you" and using imperative verbs: "Begin by meeting him" (in "How"); "Wash the white clothes on Monday" (in "Girl"). Moore occasionally uses the future tense ("He will laugh at your jokes"), and Kincaid alternates direct commands with indirect instructions ("This is how you sew on a button").

Along with the grammatical "person," the verb tense used has an effect on the narration of a story. Since narrative is so wrapped up in memory, most stories rely on the past tense. In contemporary fiction, however, the present tense is also frequently used. The present tense can lend an impression of immediacy, of frequent repetition, or of a dreamlike or magical state that isn't subject to the passage of time. An author might also use the present tense to create a conversational tone. Rarely, for a strange prophetic outlook, a narrator may even use the future tense, predicting what *will* happen.

NARRATOR VERSUS IMPLIED AUTHOR

As you discover how a story is being narrated, by whom, and from what point of view, how should you respond to the shifting points of view, tones of voice, and hints of critical distance or irony toward characters? Who is really shaping the story, and how do you know what is intended? Readers may answer the question "Who is telling this story?" with the name of the author. It is more accurate and practical, however, to distinguish between the narrator who presents the story and the flesh-and-blood author who wrote it, even when the two are hard to tell apart. If you are writing an essay about a short story, you do not need to research the biography of the author or find letters or interviews in which the author comments on the writing process or the intended themes of the work. This sort of biographical information may enrich your study of the story (it can be a good critical approach), but it is not *necessary* to an understanding of the text. And yet if you only consider the narrator when you interpret a story, you may find it difficult to account for the effects of distance and irony that come from a narrator's or a character's limitations. Many critics rely on the concept of the *implied author*, not to be confused with either the flesh-and-blood person who wrote the work or the narrator who relates the words to us. Most of the time, when we ask questions about the "author" of a work, we are asking about its implied author, the perspective and intended values that govern the whole work, including the narrator.

Why not ignore the idea of the narrator or the implied author? What's wrong with writing an essay about *Great Expectations* (1860–1861) in which you refer only to the author, Charles Dickens? After all, his name is on the title page, and we know that Pip's coming-of-age story has some autobiographical aspects. Yet from the first sentence of the novel it is clear that someone besides Charles Dickens is telling his life story: Pip, the first-person narrator. "My father's family name being Pirrip, and my Christian name Philip, my infant tongue could make of both names nothing longer or more explicit than Pip. So, I called myself Pip, and came to be called Pip." The reader sympathizes with Pip, the focal character-narrator, as an abused child, but he is also flawed and makes mistakes, as Pip himself realizes when he has grown up and tells the story of his own life. The reader understands Pip's errors through the subtle guidance of the implied author who created the narrator and shaped the plot and other characters. How useful or accurate would it be to attribute Pip's character and experience to the real Charles Dickens? The facts of the flesh-and-blood author's life and his actual personality differ widely from the novel's character, which in turn may differ from what Charles Dickens himself consciously intended. Hence the value of referring to a narrator and an implied author of a work of fiction. In critical essays, these concepts help us make an effort to discover what even the most detailed biography might never pin down: Who in fact was Charles Dickens and what did he actually intend in *Great Expectations*?

Reading a story, we know that it consists of words on a page, but we imagine the narrator speaking to us, giving shape, focus, and voice to a particular history. At the same time, we recognize that the reader should not take the narrator's words as absolute truth, but rather as effects shaped by an implied author. The concept of the implied author helps keep the particulars of the real author's (naturally imperfect) personality and life out of the picture. But it also reminds us to distinguish between the act of writing the work and the imaginary utterance of "telling" the story: The narrator is *neither* the real nor the implied author.

• • •

Because our responses to a work of fiction are largely guided by the designs and values implied in a certain way of telling the story, questions about narration and point of view can often lead to good essay topics. You might start by considering any other choices the implied author might have made and how these would change your reading of the story. As you read the stories in this chapter, imagine different voices and visions, different narrative techniques, in order to assess the effectiveness of the particular types of narration and point of view. How would the impact of "The Cask of Amontillado" change if an omniscient third-person narrator took turns to show us what Fortunato as well as Montresor was thinking and feeling? Which character in "Hills Like White Elephants" might make the best first-person narrator of the incident, and how would that affect the reader's response? Could you imagine either "How" or "Girl" rewritten as a single scene or plot with a third-person external narrator? What would be lost in removing the repetitions of actions that "you" might or must perform? Can you show the reader of your essay how the specific narration and point of view of a story contribute to its significant effects?

EDGAR ALLAN POE

The Cask of Amontillado

The thousand injuries of Fortunato I had borne as I best could, but when he ventured upon insult I vowed revenge. You, who so well know the nature of my soul, will not suppose, however, that I gave utterance to a threat. *At length* I would be avenged; this was a point definitively settled—but the very definitiveness with which it was resolved precluded the idea of risk. I must not only punish but punish with impunity. A wrong is unredressed when retribution overtakes its redresser. It is equally unredressed when the avenger fails to make himself felt as such to him who has done the wrong.

It must be understood that neither by word nor deed had I given Fortunato cause to doubt my good will. I continued, as was my wont, to smile in his face, and he did not perceive that my smile *now* was at the thought of his immolation.

He had a weak point—this Fortunato—although in other regards he was a man to be respected and even feared. He prided himself upon his connoisseurship in wine. Few Italians have the true virtuoso spirit. For the most part their enthusiasm is adopted to suit the time and opportunity, to practice imposture upon the British and Austrian *millionaires.* In painting and gemmary, Fortunato, like his countrymen, was a quack, but in the matter of old wines he was sincere. In this respect I did not differ from him materially;—I was skilful in the Italian vintages myself, and bought largely whenever I could.

It was about dusk, one evening during the supreme madness of the carnival season, that I encountered my friend. He accosted me with excessive warmth, for he had been drinking much. The man wore motley. He had on a tight-fitting parti-striped dress,[1] and his head was surmounted by the conical cap and bells. I was so pleased to see him that I should never have done wringing his hand.

I said to him—"My dear Fortunato, you are luckily met. How remarkably well 5 you are looking to-day. But I have received a pipe[2] of what passes for Amontillado, and I have my doubts."

"How?" said he. "Amontillado? A pipe? Impossible! And in the middle of the carnival!"

"I have my doubts," I replied; "and I was silly enough to pay the full Amontillado price without consulting you in the matter. You were not to be found, and I was fearful of losing a bargain."

"Amontillado!"

"I have my doubts."

"Amontillado!"

"And I must satisfy them." 10

"Amontillado!"

"As you are engaged, I am on my way to Luchresi. If any one has a critical turn it is he. He will tell me——"

"Luchresi cannot tell Amontillado from Sherry."

"And yet some fools will have it that his taste is a match for your own." 15

"Come, let us go."

1. Fortunato wears a jester's costume (i.e., motley), not a woman's dress.   2. Large cask.

"Whither?"

"To your vaults."

"My friend, no; I will not impose upon your good nature. I perceive you have an engagement. Luchresi——"

20   "I have no engagement;—come."

"My friend, no. It is not the engagement, but the severe cold with which I perceive you are afflicted. The vaults are insufferably damp. They are encrusted with nitre."

"Let us go, nevertheless. The cold is merely nothing. Amontillado! You have been imposed upon. And as for Luchresi, he cannot distinguish Sherry from Amontillado."

Thus speaking, Fortunato possessed himself of my arm; and putting on a mask of black silk and drawing a *roquelaire*³ closely about my person, I suffered him to hurry me to my palazzo.

There were no attendants at home; they had absconded to make merry in honour of the time. I had told them that I should not return until the morning, and had given them explicit orders not to stir from the house. These orders were sufficient, I well knew, to insure their immediate disappearance, one and all, as soon as my back was turned.

25   I took from their sconces two flambeaux,⁴ and giving one to Fortunato, bowed him through several suites of rooms to the archway that led into the vaults. I passed down a long and winding staircase, requesting him to be cautious as he followed. We came at length to the foot of the descent, and stood together upon the damp ground of the catacombs of the Montresors.

The gait of my friend was unsteady, and the bells upon his cap jingled as he strode.

"The pipe," said he.

"It is farther on," said I; "but observe the white web-work which gleams from these cavern walls."

He turned towards me, and looked into my eyes with two filmy orbs that distilled the rheum of intoxication.

30   "Nitre⁵?" he asked, at length.

"Nitre," I replied. "How long have you had that cough?"

"Ugh! ugh! ugh!—ugh! ugh! ugh!—ugh! ugh! ugh!—ugh! ugh! ugh!—ugh! ugh! ugh!"

My poor friend found it impossible to reply for many minutes.

"It is nothing," he said, at last.

35   "Come," I said, with decision, "we will go back; your health is precious. You are rich, respected, admired, beloved; you are happy, as once I was. You are a man to be missed. For me it is no matter. We will go back; you will be ill, and I cannot be responsible. Besides, there is Luchresi——"

"Enough," he said; "the cough is a mere nothing; it will not kill me. I shall not die of a cough."

---

3. Man's heavy, knee-length cloak.   4. That is, two torches from their wall brackets.
5. Potassium nitrate (saltpeter), a white mineral often found on the walls of damp caves and used in gunpowder.

"True—true," I replied; "and, indeed, I had no intention of alarming you unneccessarily—but you should use all proper caution. A draught of this Medoc[6] will defend us from the damps."

Here I knocked off the neck of a bottle which I drew from a long row of its fellows that lay upon the mould.

"Drink," I said, presenting him the wine.

He raised it to his lips with a leer. He paused and nodded to me familiarly, 40 while his bells jingled.

"I drink," he said, "to the buried that repose around us."

"And I to your long life."

He again took my arm, and we proceeded.

"These vaults," he said, "are extensive."

"The Montresors," I replied, "were a great and numerous family." 45

"I forget your arms."

"A huge human foot d'or,[7] in a field azure; the foot crushes a serpent rampant whose fangs are imbedded in the heel."

"And the motto?"

"Nemo me impune lacessit."[8]

"Good!" he said. 50

The wine sparkled in his eyes and the bells jingled. My own fancy grew warm with the Medoc. We had passed through long walls of piled skeletons, with casks and puncheons[9] intermingling, into the inmost recesses of the catacombs. I paused again, and this time I made bold to seize Fortunato by an arm above the elbow.

"The nitre!" I said; "see, it increases. It hangs like moss upon the vaults. We are below the river's bed. The drops of moisture trickle among the bones. Come, we will go back ere it is too late. Your cough——"

"It is nothing," he said; "let us go on. But first, another draught of the Medoc."

I broke and reached him a flaçon of De Grâve. He emptied it at a breath. His eyes flashed with a fierce light. He laughed and threw the bottle upwards with a gesticulation I did not understand.

I looked at him in surprise. He repeated the movement—a grotesque one. 55

"You do not comprehend?" he said.

"Not I," I replied.

"Then you are not of the brotherhood."

"How?"

"You are not of the masons."[1]

"Yes, yes," I said; "yes, yes." 60

"You? Impossible! A mason?"

"A mason," I replied.

"A sign," he said, "a sign."

"It is this," I answered producing from beneath the folds of my *roquelaire* a 65 trowel.

6. Like De Grâve (below), a French wine.   7. Of gold.   8. No one provokes me with impunity.
9. Large casks.
1. Masons or Freemasons, an international secret society condemned by the Catholic Church. Montresor means by mason one who builds with stone, brick, etc.

"You jest," he exclaimed, recoiling a few paces. "But let us proceed to the Amontillado."

"Be it so," I said, replacing the tool beneath the cloak and again offering him my arm. He leaned upon it heavily. We continued our route in search of the Amontillado. We passed through a range of low arches, descended, passed on, and descending again, arrived at a deep crypt, in which the foulness of the air caused our flambeaux rather to glow than flame.

At the most remote end of the crypt there appeared another less spacious. Its walls had been lined with human remains, piled to the vault overhead, in the fashion of the great catacombs of Paris. Three sides of this interior crypt were still ornamented in this manner. From the fourth side the bones had been thrown down, and lay promiscuously upon the earth, forming at one point a mound of some size. Within the wall thus exposed by the displacing of the bones, we perceived a still interior crypt or recess, in depth about four feet, in width three, in height six or seven. It seemed to have been constructed for no especial use within itself, but formed merely the interval between two of the colossal supports of the roof of the catacombs, and was backed by one of their circumscribing walls of solid granite.

It was in vain that Fortunato, uplifting his dull torch, endeavoured to pry into the depth of the recess. Its termination the feeble light did not enable us to see.

70   "Proceed," I said; "herein is the Amontillado. As for Luchresi——"

"He is an ignoramus," interrupted my friend, as he stepped unsteadily forward, while I followed immediately at his heels. In an instant he had reached the extremity of the niche, and finding his progress arrested by the rock, stood stupidly bewildered. A moment more and I had fettered him to the granite. In its surface were two iron staples, distant from each other about two feet, horizontally. From one of these depended a short chain, from the other a padlock. Throwing the links about his waist, it was but the work of a few seconds to secure it. He was too much astounded to resist. Withdrawing the key I stepped back from the recess.

"Pass your hand," I said, "over the wall; you cannot help feeling the nitre. Indeed, it is *very* damp. Once more let me *implore* you to return. No? Then I must positively leave you. But I will first render you all the little attentions in my power."

"The Amontillado!" ejaculated my friend, not yet recovered from his astonishment.

"True," I replied; "the Amontillado."

75   As I said these words I busied myself among the pile of bones of which I have before spoken. Throwing them aside, I soon uncovered a quantity of building stone and mortar. With these materials and with the aid of my trowel, I began vigorously to wall up the entrance of the niche.

I had scarcely laid the first tier of the masonry when I discovered that the intoxication of Fortunato had in great measure worn off. The earliest indication I had of this was a low moaning cry from the depth of the recess. It was *not* the cry of a drunken man. There was then a long and obstinate silence. I laid the second tier, and the third, and the fourth; and then I heard the furious vibration of the chain. The noise lasted for several minutes, during which, that I might hearken to it with the more satisfaction, I ceased my labours and sat down upon the bones. When at last the clanking subsided, I resumed the trowel, and finished without interruption the fifth, the sixth, and the seventh tier. The wall was now nearly upon a level with my breast. I again paused, and holding the flambeaux over the mason-work, threw a few feeble rays upon the figure within.

A succession of loud and shrill screams, bursting suddenly from the throat of the chained form, seemed to thrust me violently back. For a brief moment I hesitated, I trembled. Unsheathing my rapier, I began to grope with it about the recess; but the thought of an instant reassured me. I placed my hand upon the solid fabric of the catacombs and felt satisfied. I reapproached the wall. I replied to the yells of him who clamoured. I re-echoed, I aided, I surpassed them in volume and in strength. I did this, and the clamourer grew still.

It was now midnight, and my task was drawing to a close. I had completed the eighth, the ninth and the tenth tier. I had finished a portion of the last and the eleventh; there remained but a single stone to be fitted and plastered in. I struggled with its weight; I placed it partially in its destined position. But now there came from out the niche a low laugh that erected the hairs upon my head. It was succeeded by a sad voice, which I had difficulty in recognizing as that of the noble Fortunato. The voice said—

"Ha! ha! ha!—he! he! he!—a very good joke, indeed—an excellent jest. We will have many a rich laugh about it at the palazzo—he! he! he!—over our wine—he! he! he!"

"The Amontillado!" I said. 80

"He! he! he!—he! he! he!—yes, the Amontillado. But is it not getting late? Will not they be awaiting us at the palazzo—the Lady Fortunato and the rest? Let us be gone."

"Yes," I said, "let us be gone."

"For the love of God, Montresor!"

"Yes," I said, "for the love of God!"

But to these words I hearkened in vain for a reply. I grew impatient. I called aloud— 85
"Fortunato!"

No answer. I called again—
"Fortunato!"

No answer still. I thrust a torch through the remaining aperture and let it fall within. There came forth in return only a jingling of the bells. My heart grew sick; it was the dampness of the catacombs that made it so. I hastened to make an end of my labour. I forced the last stone into its position; I plastered it up. Against the new masonry I re-erected the old rampart of bones. For the half of a century no mortal has disturbed them. *In pace requiescat!*[2]

1846

QUESTIONS

1. What can the reader infer about Montresor's social position and character from hints in the text? What evidence does the text provide that Montresor is an unreliable narrator?
2. Who is the auditor, the "You," addressed in the first paragraph of "The Cask of Amontillado"? When is the story being told? Why is it being told? How does your knowledge of the auditor and the occasion influence the effect the story has on you?
3. What devices does Poe use to create and heighten the suspense in the story? Is the outcome ever in doubt?

2. May he rest in peace!

ERNEST HEMINGWAY

Hills Like White Elephants

The hills across the valley of the Ebro[1] were long and white. On this side there was no shade and no trees and the station was between two lines of rails in the sun. Close against the side of the station there was the warm shadow of the building and a curtain, made of strings of bamboo beads, hung across the open door into the bar, to keep out flies. The American and the girl with him sat at a table in the shade, outside the building. It was very hot and the express from Barcelona would come in forty minutes. It stopped at this junction for two minutes and went on to Madrid.

"What should we drink?" the girl asked. She had taken off her hat and put it on the table.

"It's pretty hot," the man said.

"Let's drink beer."

5   "Dos cervezas," the man said into the curtain.

"Big ones?" a woman asked from the doorway.

"Yes. Two big ones."

The woman brought two glasses of beer and two felt pads. She put the felt pads and the beer glasses on the table and looked at the man and the girl. The girl was looking off at the line of hills. They were white in the sun and the country was brown and dry.

"They look like white elephants," she said.

10   "I've never seen one," the man drank his beer.

"No, you wouldn't have."

"I might have," the man said. "Just because you say I wouldn't have doesn't prove anything."

The girl looked at the bead curtain. "They've painted something on it," she said. "What does it say?"

"Anis del Toro. It's a drink."

15   "Could we try it?"

The man called "Listen" through the curtain. The woman came out from the bar.

"Four reales."[2]

"We want two Anis del Toro."

"With water?"

20   "Do you want it with water?"

"I don't know," the girl said. "Is it good with water?"

"It's all right."

"You want them with water?" asked the woman.

"Yes, with water."

25   "It tastes like licorice," the girl said and put the glass down.

"That's the way with everything."

"Yes," said the girl. "Everything tastes of licorice. Especially all the things you've waited so long for, like absinthe."

"Oh, cut it out."

---

1. River in northern Spain.   2. Spanish coins.

"You started it," the girl said. "I was being amused. I was having a fine time."

"Well, let's try and have a fine time."

"All right. I was trying. I said the mountains looked like white elephants. Wasn't that bright?"

"That was bright."

"I wanted to try this new drink. That's all we do, isn't it—look at things and try new drinks?"

"I guess so."

The girl looked across at the hills.

"They're lovely hills," she said. "They don't really look like white elephants. I just meant the coloring of their skin through the trees."

"Should we have another drink?"

"All right."

The warm wind blew the bead curtain against the table.

"The beer's nice and cool," the man said.

"It's lovely," the girl said.

"It's really an awfully simple operation, Jig," the man said. "It's not really an operation at all."

The girl looked at the ground the table legs rested on.

"I know you wouldn't mind it, Jig. It's really not anything. It's just to let the air in."

The girl did not say anything.

"I'll go with you and I'll stay with you all the time. They just let the air in and then it's all perfectly natural."

"Then what will we do afterward?"

"We'll be fine afterward. Just like we were before."

"What makes you think so?"

"That's the only thing that bothers us. It's the only thing that's made us unhappy."

The girl looked at the bead curtain, put her hand out and took hold of two of the strings of beads.

"And you think then we'll be all right and be happy."

"I know we will. You don't have to be afraid. I've known lots of people that have done it."

"So have I," said the girl. "And afterward they were all so happy."

"Well," the man said, "if you don't want to you don't have to. I wouldn't have you do it if you didn't want to. But I know it's perfectly simple."

"And you really want to?"

"I think it's the best thing to do. But I don't want you to do it if you don't really want to."

"And if I do it you'll be happy and things will be like they were and you'll love me?"

"I love you now. You know I love you."

"I know. But if I do it, then it will be nice again if I say things are like white elephants, and you'll like it?"

"I'll love it. I love it now but I just can't think about it. You know how I get when I worry."

"If I do it you won't ever worry?"

"I won't worry about that because it's perfectly simple."

"Then I'll do it. Because I don't care about me."

65   "What do you mean?"

"I don't care about me."

"Well, I care about you."

"Oh, yes. But I don't care about me. And I'll do it and then everything will be fine."

"I don't want you to do it if you feel that way."

70   The girl stood up and walked to the end of the station. Across, on the other side, were fields of grain and trees along the banks of the Ebro. Far away, beyond the river, were mountains. The shadow of a cloud moved across the field of grain and she saw the river through the trees.

"And we could have all this," she said. "And we could have everything and every day we make it more impossible."

"What did you say?"

"I said we could have everything."

"We can have everything."

75   "No, we can't."

"We can have the whole world."

"No, we can't."

"We can go everywhere."

"No, we can't. It isn't ours anymore."

80   "It's ours."

"No, it isn't. And once they take it away, you never get it back."

"But they haven't taken it away."

"We'll wait and see."

"Come on back in the shade," he said. "You mustn't feel that way."

85   "I don't feel any way," the girl said. "I just know things."

"I don't want you to do anything that you don't want to do—"

"Nor that isn't good for me," she said. "I know. Could we have another beer?"

"All right. But you've got to realize—"

"I realize," the girl said. "Can't we maybe stop talking?"

90   They sat down at the table and the girl looked across at the hills on the dry side of the valley and the man looked at her and at the table.

"You've got to realize," he said, "that I don't want you to do it if you don't want to. I'm perfectly willing to go through with it if it means anything to you."

"Doesn't it mean anything to you? We could get along."

"Of course it does. But I don't want anybody but you. I don't want any one else. And I know it's perfectly simple."

"Yes, you know it's perfectly simple."

95   "It's all right for you to say that, but I do know it."

"Would you do something for me now?"

"I'd do anything for you."

"Would you please please please please please please please stop talking?"

He did not say anything but looked at the bags against the wall of the station. There were labels on them from all the hotels where they had spent nights.

100   "But I don't want you to," he said, "I don't care anything about it."

"I'll scream," the girl said.

The woman came out through the curtains with two glasses of beer and put them down on the damp felt pads. "The train comes in five minutes," she said.

"What did she say?" asked the girl.

"That the train is coming in five minutes."

The girl smiled brightly at the woman, to thank her.   105

"I'd better take the bags over to the other side of the station," the man said. She smiled at him.

"All right. Then come back and we'll finish the beer."

He picked up the two heavy bags and carried them around the station to the other tracks. He looked up the tracks but could not see the train. Coming back, he walked through the barroom, where people waiting for the train were drinking. He drank an Anis at the bar and looked at the people. They were all waiting reasonably for the train. He went out through the bead curtain. She was sitting at the table and smiled at him.

"Do you feel better?" he asked.

"I feel fine," she said. "There's nothing wrong with me. I feel fine."   110

1927

QUESTIONS

1. Find the first indication in "Hills Like White Elephants" that the two main characters are not getting along. What is the first clue about the exact nature of their conflict? Why are they going to Madrid? Why do the characters (and the author) refrain from speaking about it explicitly?
2. Point of view includes what characters see. Notice each use of the word "look." What does each person in the story look at, and what does each person seem to understand or feel? Is there anything in the story that none of these people would be able to see or know? How do the different kinds of observation add to the effect of the story?
3. Research the phrase "white elephant." What is the significance of this phrase in the story's title?

LORRIE MOORE

How

So all things limp together for the only possible. —BECKETT, *Murphy*[1]

Begin by meeting him in a class, in a bar, at a rummage sale. Maybe he teaches sixth grade. Manages a hardware store. Foreman at a carton factory. He will be a good dancer. He will have perfectly cut hair. He will laugh at your jokes.

A week, a month, a year. Feel discovered, comforted, needed, loved, and start sometimes, somehow, to feel bored. When sad or confused, walk uptown to the movies. Buy popcorn. These things come and go. A week, a month, a year.

1. Samuel Beckett (1906–89), Nobel Prize–winning Irish novelist and playwright who lived in France, perhaps best known today for his play *Waiting for Godot*. This epigraph, from his 1938 novel *Murphy*, is representative of Beckett's absurdist vision and verbal experimentation.

Make attempts at a less restrictive arrangement. Watch them sputter and deflate like balloons. He will ask you to move in. Do so hesitantly, with ambivalence. Clarify: rents are high, nothing long-range, love and all that, hon, but it's footloose. Lay out the rules with much elocution. Stress openness, nonexclusivity. Make room in his closet, but don't rearrange the furniture.

And yet from time to time you will gaze at his face or his hands and want nothing but him. You will feel passing waves of dependency, devotion, and sentimentality. A week, a month, a year, and he has become your family. Let's say your real mother is a witch. Your father a warlock. Your brothers twin hunchbacks of Notre Dame. They all live in a cave together somewhere.

5   His name means savior. He rolls into your arms like Ozzie and Harriet, the whole Nelson genealogy. He is living rooms and turkey and mantels and Vicks, a nip at the collarbone and you do a slow syrup sink into those arms like a hearth, into those living rooms, well hello Mary Lou.[2]

Say you work in an office but you have bigger plans. He wants to go with you. He wants to be what it is that you want to be. Say you're an aspiring architect. Playwright. Painter. He shows you his sketches. They are awful. What do you think?

Put on some jazz. Take off your clothes. Carefully. It is a craft. He will lie on the floor naked, watching, his arms crossed behind his head. Shirt: brush on snare, steady. Skirt: the desultory talk of piano keys, rocking slow, rambling. Dance together in the dark though it is only afternoon.

Go to a wedding. His relatives. Everyone will compare weight losses and gains. Maiden cousins will be said to have fattened embarrassingly. His mother will be a bookkeeper or a dental hygienist. She will introduce you as his *girl*. Try not to protest. They will have heard a lot about you. Uncles will take him aside and query, What is keeping you, boy? Uncomfortable, everywhere, women in stiff blue taffeta will eye you pitifully, then look quickly away. Everyone will polka. Someone will flash a fifty to dance with the bride and she will hike up her gown and flash back: freshly shaven legs, a wide rolled-out-barrel of a grin. Feel spared. Thought you two'd be doing this by now, you will hear again. Smile. Shrug. Shuffle back for more potato salad.

It hits you more insistently. A restlessness. A virus of discontent. When you pass other men in the street, smile and stare them straight in the eye, straight in the belt buckle.

10   Somehow—in a restaurant or a store—meet an actor. From Vassar or Yale. He can quote Coriolanus's mother.[3] This will seem good. Sleep with him once and

---

2. Popular song by Ricky Nelson includes the refrain "So hello Mary Lou / Goodbye heart." Ozzie and Harriet were the lead characters in a popular family TV show of the 1950s starring Nelson, his parents, and his brother.

3. *Coriolanus* is a violent, disturbing tragedy by William Shakespeare; it is rarely produced today.

ride home at 5 a.m. crying in a taxicab. Or: don't sleep with him. Kiss him good night at Union Square and run for your life.

Back at home, days later, feel cranky and tired. Sit on the couch and tell him he's stupid. That you bet he doesn't know who Coriolanus is. That since you moved in you've noticed he rarely reads. He will give you a hurt, hungry-to-learn look, with his James Cagney[4] eyes. He will try to kiss you. Turn your head. Feel suffocated.

When he climbs onto the covers, naked and hot for you, unleash your irritation in short staccato blasts. Show him your book. Your aspirin. Your clock on the table reading 12:45. He will flop back over to his side of the bed, exasperated. Maybe he'll say something like: Christ, what's wrong? Maybe he won't. If he spends too long in the bathroom, don't ask questions.

The touchiest point will always be this: he craves a family, a neat nest of human bowls; he wants to have your children. On the street he pats their heads. In the supermarket they gather around him by the produce. They form a tight little cluster of cheeks and smiles and hopes. They look like grapes. It will all be for you, baby; reel, sway backward into the frozen foods. An unwitting sigh will escape from your lips like gas. He will begin to talk about a movie camera and children's encyclopedias, picking up size-one shoes in department stores and marveling in one high, amazed whistle. Avoid shopping together.

He will have a nephew named Bradley Bob. Or perhaps a niece named Emily who is always dressed in pink and smells of milk and powder and dirty diapers, although she is already three. At visits she will prance and squeal. She will grab his left leg like a tree trunk and not let go. She will call him nunko. He will know tricks: pulling dimes from her nose, quarters from her ears. She will shriek with glee, flapping her hands in front of her. Leg released, he will pick her up, carry her around like a prize. He is the best nunko in town.

Think about leaving. About packing a bag and slithering off, out the door. 15
    But it is hot out there. And dry. And he can look somehow good to you, like Robert Goulet in a bathing suit.
    No, it wouldn't be in summer.[5]

Escape into books. When he asks what you're reading, hold it up without comment. The next day look across to the brown chair and you will see him reading it too. A copy from the library that morning. He has seven days. He will look over the top and wink, saying: Beat you.

He will seem to be listening to the classical music station, glancing quickly at you for approval.

4. Early Hollywood movie star (1899–1986), more tough guy than romantic lead.
5. Robert Goulet starred as Lancelot in the 1960s musical *Camelot*; the lyrics for one of his character's songs included "If ever I would leave you, / How could it be in summer . . . or winter or fall?"

20   At the theater he will chomp Necco wafers loudly and complain about the head in front of him.

He will ask you what *supercilious* means.

He will ask you who Coriolanus is.

He might want to know where Sardinia is located.

What's a *croissant*?

25   Begin to plot your getaway. Envision possibilities for civility. These are only possibilities.

A week, a month, a year: Tell him you've changed. You no longer like the same music, eat the same food. You dress differently. The two of you are incongruous together. When he tells you that he is changing too, that he loves your records, your teas, your falafel, your shoes, tell him: See, that's the problem. Endeavor to baffle.

Pace around in the kitchen and say that you are unhappy.

But I love you, he will say in his soft, bewildered way, stirring the spaghetti sauce but not you, staring into the pan as if waiting for something, a magic fish, to rise from it and say: That is always enough, why is that not always enough?

You will forget whoever it was that said never trust a thought that doesn't come while walking. But clutch at it. Apartments can shrink inward like drying ponds. You will gasp. Say: I am going for a walk. When he follows you to the door, buzzing at your side like a fly by a bleeding woman, add: *alone*. He will look surprised and hurt and you will hate him. Slam the door, out, down, hurry, it will be colder than you thought, but not far away will be a bar, smoky and dark and sticky with spilled sours. The bartender will be named Rusty or Max and he will know you. A flashy jukebox will blare Jimmy Webb.[6] A balding, purple-shirted man to your left will try to get your attention, mouthing, singing drunkenly. Someone to your right will sniffle to the music. Blink into your drink. Hide behind your hair. Sweet green icing will be flowing down.[7] Flowing, baby, like the Mississippi.

30   Next: there are medical unpleasantries. Kidneys. He will pee blood. Say you can't believe it. When he shows you later, it will be dark, the color of meat drippings. A huge invisible fist will torpedo through your gut, your face, your pounding heart.

This is no time to leave.

6. Jimmy Webb (b. 1946), American songwriter who won many Grammys in the later 1960s for such hits as "By the Time I Get to Phoenix," "Wichita Lineman," "Up, Up and Away," and "MacArthur Park."
7. Webb's "MacArthur Park" includes the lines "MacArthur Park is melting in the dark, / All the sweet green icing flowing down."

There will be doctor's appointments, various opinions. There is nothing conclusive, just an endless series of tests. He will have jarred urine specimens in the refrigerator among the eggs and peanut butter. Some will be in salad dressing bottles. They will be different colors: some green, some purple, some brown. Ask which is the real salad dressing. He will point it out and smile helplessly. Smile back. He will begin to laugh and so will you. Collapse. Roll. Roar together on the floor until you cannot laugh anymore. Bury your face in the crook of his neck. There will be nothing else in the world you can do. That night lie next to each other, silent, stiff, silvery-white in bed. Lie like sewing needles.

Continue to doctor-hop. Await the reports. Look at your watch. If ever you would leave him. Look at your calendar. It wouldn't be in autumn.

There is never anything conclusive, just an endless series of tests.

Once a week you will feel in love with him again. Massage his lower back 35 when it is aching. Lay your cheek against him, feeling, listening for his kidneys. Stay like that all night, never quite falling asleep, never quite wanting to.

The thought will occur to you that you are waiting for him to die.

You will meet another actor. Or maybe it's the same one. Begin to have an affair. Begin to lie. Have dinner with him and his Modigliani-necked mother.[8] She will smoke cigars, play with the fondue, discuss the fallacy of feminine maternal instinct. Afterward, you will all get high.

There is never anything conclusive, just an endless series of tests.

And could you leave him tripping merrily through the snow?

You will fantasize about a funeral. At that you could cry. It would be a study in 40 post-romantic excess, something vaguely Wagnerian.[9] You would be comforted by his lugubrious sisters and his dental hygienist mom. The four of you in the cemetery would throw yourselves at his grave's edge, heaving and sobbing like old Israeli women. You, in particular, would shout, bare your wrists, shake them at the sky, foam at the mouth. There would be no shame, no dignity. You would fly immediately to Acapulco and lounge drunk and malodorous in the casinos until three.

After dinners with the actor: creep home. Your stomach will get fluttery, your steps smaller as you approach the door. Neighbors will be playing music you recall from your childhood—an opera about a pretty lady who was bad and cut a man's hair in his sleep.[1] You recall, recall your grandfather playing it with a sort

8. Amedeo Modigliani (1884–1920), Italian painter famous for nudes with elongated features.
9. Richard Wagner (1813–83), German composer of massive, stormy operas.
1. Delilah cut the Old Testament hero Samson's hair while he slept, as depicted in the opera *Samson et Dalila,* by Camille Saint-Saëns (1835–1921), first performed in 1877; *Ray pawned off my ten dresses:* an English-speaking child's hearing of *Samson et Dalila's* original French lyric, *réponds à ma tendresse!* ("respond to my affection!"), as sung by Dalila ("Dolly-la").

of wrath, his visage laminated with Old Testament righteousness, the violins warming, the scenario unfolding now as you stand outside the door. Ray pawned off my ten dresses: it cascades like a waterfall. Dolly-la, Dolly-la: it is the wail, the next to the last good solo of a doomed man.

Tiptoe. It won't matter. He will be sitting up in bed looking empty. Kiss him, cajole him. Make love to him like never before. At four in the morning you will still be awake, staring at the ceiling. You will horrify yourself.

Thoughts of leaving will move in, bivouac throughout the living room; they will have eyes like rodents and peer out at you from under the sofa, in the dark, from under the sink, luminous glass beads positioned in twos. The houseplants will appear to have chosen sides. Some will thrust stems at you like angry limbs. They will seem to caw like crows. Others will simply sag.

When you go out, leave him with a sinkful of dirty dishes. He will slowly dry them with paper towels, his skin scalded red beneath the wet, flattened hair of his forearms. You will be tempted to tell him to leave them, or to use the terry-cloth in the drawer. But you won't. You will put on your coat and hurry away.

45   When you return, the bathroom light will be on. You will see blouses of yours that he has washed by hand. They will hang in perfect half-inches, dripping, scolding from the shower curtain rod. They will be buttoned with his Cagney eyes, faintly hooded, the twinkle sad and dulled.

Slip quietly under the covers; hold his sleeping hand.

There is never anything conclusive.

At work you will be lachrymose and distracted. You will shamble through the hall like a legume with feet. People will notice.

Nightmares have seasons like hurricanes. Be prepared. You will dream that someone with a violin case is trailing you through the city. Little children come at you with grins and grenades. You may bolt awake with a spasm, reach for him, and find he is not there, but lost in his own sleep, somnambulant, is roaming through the apartment like an old man, babbling gibberish, bumping into tables and lamps, a blanket he has torn from the bed wrapped clumsily around him, toga-style. Get up. Go to him. Touch him. At first he will look at you, wide-eyed, and not see. Put your arms around his waist. He will wake and gasp and cry into your hair. In a minute he will know where he is.

50   Dream about rainbows, about escapes, about wizards. Your past will fly by you, event by event, like Dorothy's tornadoed neighborhood, past the blown-out window.[2] Airborne. One by one. Wave hello, good-bye. Practice.

2. In the film *The Wizard of Oz*, Dorothy dreams of a place "somewhere over the rainbow," and her home is struck by a tornado.

Begin to call in sick. Make sure it is after he has already left for work. Sit in a rocking chair. Stare around at the apartment. It will be mid-morning and flooded in a hush of sunlight. You rarely see it like this. It will seem strangely deserted, premonitory. There will be apricots shrunk to buttons on the window-sill. A fly will bang stupidly against the panes. The bed will lie open, revealed, like something festering, the wrinkles in the sheets marking time, marking territory like the capillaries of a map. Rock. Hush. Breathe.

On the night you finally tell him, take him out to dinner. Translate the entrees for him. When you are home, lying in bed together, tell him that you are going to leave. He will look panicked, but not surprised. Perhaps he will say, Look, I don't care who else you're seeing or anything: what is your reason?

Do not attempt to bandy words. Tell him you do not love him anymore. It will make him cry, rivulets wending their way into his ears. You will start to feel sick. He will say something like: Well, you lose some, you lose some. You are supposed to laugh. Exhale. Blow your nose. Flick off the light. Have a sense of humor, he will whisper into the black. Have a heart.

Make him breakfast. He will want to know where you will go. Reply: To the actor. Or: To the hunchbacks. He will not eat your breakfast. He will glare at it, stir it around the plate with a fork, and then hurl it against the wall.

When you walk up Third Avenue toward the IRT,[3] do it quickly. You will have 55
a full bag. People will seem to know what you have done, where you are going. They will have his eyes, the same pair, passed along on the street from face to face, like secrets, like glasses at the opera.

This is how you are.
Rushing downstairs into the steamy burn of the subway.
Unable to look a panhandler in the pan.

You will never see him again. Or perhaps you will be sitting in Central Park one April eating your lunch and he will trundle by on roller skates. You will greet him with a wave and a mouth full of sandwich. He will nod, but he will not stop.

There will be an endless series of tests.   60

A week, a month, a year. The sadness will die like an old dog. You will feel nothing but indifference. The logy whine of a cowboy harmonica, plaintive, weary, it will fade into the hills slow as slow Hank Williams.[4] One of those endings.

1985

3. One of the lines of the New York City subway system.
4. (Hiram) Hank Williams (1923–53), pioneer of American country music, had many hits in his short, hard life, including "Lovesick Blues" (1949) and "Your Cheatin' Heart" (1953).

QUESTIONS

1. Elaborate on the title. "How" to *what?* Why do you think Lorrie Moore has adapted the mode of an instructional guide to the purpose of storytelling?
2. Who is the narrator, and who is the audience ("you") addressed by the story?
3. From the first paragraph onward, "How" offers alternative "facts" or circumstances as if it is up to you to choose. Which, if any, aspects of character, action, setting, or circumstances are fixed or certain? For instance, could the story be set in a rural village in the 1920s? Could the main characters be in their sixties?

JAMAICA KINCAID

Girl

Wash the white clothes on Monday and put them on the stone heap; wash the color clothes on Tuesday and put them on the clothesline to dry; don't walk bare-head in the hot sun; cook pumpkin fritters in very hot sweet oil; soak your little cloths right after you take them off; when buying cotton to make yourself a nice blouse, be sure that it doesn't have gum on it, because that way it won't hold up well after a wash; soak salt fish overnight before you cook it; is it true that you sing benna[1] in Sunday school?; always eat your food in such a way that it won't turn someone else's stomach; on Sundays try to walk like a lady and not like the slut you are so bent on becoming; don't sing benna in Sunday school; you mustn't speak to wharf-rat boys, not even to give directions; don't eat fruits on the street—flies will follow you; *but I don't sing benna on Sundays at all and never in Sunday school;* this is how to sew on a button; this is how to make a buttonhole for the button you have just sewed on; this is how to hem a dress when you see the hem coming down and so to prevent yourself from looking like the slut I know you are so bent on becoming; this is how you iron your father's khaki shirt so that it doesn't have a crease; this is how you iron your father's khaki pants so that they don't have a crease; this is how you grow okra—far from the house, because okra tree harbors red ants; when you are growing dasheen, make sure it gets plenty of water or else it makes your throat itch when you are eating it; this is how you sweep a corner; this is how you sweep a whole house; this is how you sweep a yard; this is how you smile to someone you don't like too much; this is how you smile to someone you don't like at all; this is how you smile to someone you like completely; this is how you set a table for tea; this is how you set a table for dinner; this is how you set a table for dinner with an important guest; this is how you set a table for lunch; this is how you set a table for breakfast; this is how to behave in the presence of men who don't know you very well, and this way they won't recognize immediately the slut I have warned you against becoming; be sure to wash every day, even if it is with your own spit; don't squat down to play marbles—you are not a boy, you know; don't pick people's flowers—you might catch something; don't throw stones at blackbirds, because it might not be a blackbird at all; this is how to make a bread pudding; this is how to make doukona[2] this is how to make pepper pot; this is how to make a good medicine for a cold; this is how to make a good

1. Caribbean folk-music style.
2. Spicy pudding, often made from plantain and wrapped in a plantain or banana leaf.

medicine to throw away a child before it even becomes a child; this is how to catch a fish; this is how to throw back a fish you don't like, and that way something bad won't fall on you; this is how to bully a man; this is how a man bullies you; this is how to love a man, and if this doesn't work there are other ways, and if they don't work don't feel too bad about giving up; this is how to spit up in the air if you feel like it, and this is how to move quick so that it doesn't fall on you; this is how to make ends meet; always squeeze bread to make sure it's fresh; *but what if the baker won't let me feel the bread?;* you mean to say that after all you are really going to be the kind of woman who the baker won't let near the bread?

1983

QUESTIONS

1. Describe the focus or focalization in "Girl." Do we see what one person sees, or observe one person in particular? Describe the voice of the narrator in "Girl." Who is the "you"? How do the focus and voice contribute to the reader's response to the story?
2. Look closely at the indications of time in the story. What actions take place at certain times? Does any event or action happen only once? Is there a plot in "Girl"? If so, how would you summarize it?
3. The instructions in "Girl" have different qualities, as if they come from different people or have different purposes. Why are two phrases in italics? Can you pick out the phrases that are more positive from the girl's point of view? Are there some that seem humorous or ironic?

SUGGESTIONS FOR WRITING

1. Write a parody of "The Cask of Amontillado" set in modern times, perhaps on a college campus ("A Barrel of Bud"?).
2. Both Hemingway's "Hills Like White Elephants" and Moore's "How" offer a detached perspective on relationships between men and women at the time the stories were published. Each story is narrated in a specific style and tone, whether removed or close to what a character sees, thinks, or says. Both stories rely on repetition of some ordinary phrases (e.g., "you've got to realize"; "a week, a month, a year"). Write an essay on either story, or a comparison of both stories, in which you show how the voice (style and tone) of the narration and the point of view help convey the text's perspective on contemporary sexual relationships.
3. In "How," the man that the narrator lives with "craves a family" and plays well with children. Notice other details of his domestic behavior. "You" is referred to as a woman, but does she do some things that are usually thought of as masculine? Write an essay discussing the ways that the story works against expectations about women's and men's roles in relationships.
4. Compare the second-person voice and imperatives in "How" with the choices offered to the reader in Atwood's "Happy Endings" (chapter 1). What activities or responses are expected of "you," as reader or auditor in each story? Write an essay commenting on the author/reader relationship suggested in these two stories.
5. Write your own short story, "Boy," modeled on Jamaica Kincaid's "Girl," or write your own version of "Girl." Use either your own point of view or that of an unwelcome advisor.

6. Carry a notebook or tape recorder for a day or two, and note any stories you tell or hear, such as in daydreams, in conversation, on the phone, through e-mail or instant messaging. Consider what makes stories. Your transcripts may be short and may consist of memories, observations about your own character or those of people around you, plans, or predictions about the future. Choose two of your notes and modify them into plot summaries (no more than a paragraph each), using the first or the third person, the present or the past tense. Add a note about whether a full version of each story should give the inner thoughts of one or more characters, and why.

3 CHARACTER

Robert Buss, *Dickens' Dream* (1870)

In the unfinished watercolor *Dickens' Dream*, the nineteenth-century writer peacefully dozes while above and around him float ghostly images of the hundreds of characters that people his novels and, apparently, his dreams. This image captures the undeniable fact that characters loom large in the experience of fiction, for both its writers and its readers. Speaking for the former, Elie Wiesel describes a novelist like himself as practically possessed by characters who "force the writer to tell their stories" because "they want to get out." As readers of fiction, we care about *what* happens and *how* mainly because it happens *to* someone. Indeed, without a "someone," it is unlikely that anything would happen at all.

It is also often a "someone," or the *who* of a story, that sticks with us long after we have forgotten the details of what, where, and how. In this way, characters sometimes seem to take on a life of their own, to float free of the texts where we first encounter them, and even to haunt us. You may know almost nothing about

Charles Dickens, but you probably have a vivid sense of his characters Ebenezer Scrooge and Tiny Tim from *A Christmas Carol*.

A **character** is any personage in a literary work who acts, appears, or is referred to as playing a part. Though *personage* usually means a human being, it doesn't have to. Whole genres or subgenres of fiction are distinguished, in part, by the specific kinds of nonhuman characters they conventionally feature, whether alien species and intelligent machines (as in science fiction), animals (as in fables), or elves and monsters (as in traditional fairy tales and modern fantasy). All characters must have at least some human qualities, however, such as the ability to think, to feel pain, or to fall in love.

Evidence to Consider in Analyzing a Character: A Checklist

- the character's name
- the character's physical appearance
- objects and places associated with the character
- the character's actions
- the character's thoughts and speech, including
  - content (what he or she thinks or says)
  - timing (when he or she thinks or says it)
  - phrasing (how he or she thinks or says it)
- other characters' thoughts about the character
- other characters' comments to and about the character
- the narrator's comments about the character

HEROES AND VILLAINS VERSUS PROTAGONISTS AND ANTAGONISTS

A common term for the character with the leading male role is **hero**, the "good guy," who opposes the **villain**, or "bad guy." The leading female character is the **heroine**. Heroes and heroines are usually larger than life, stronger or better than most human beings, sometimes almost godlike. They are characters that a text encourages us to admire and even to emulate, so that the words *hero* and *heroine* can also be applied to especially admirable characters who do not play leading roles.

In most modern fiction, however, the leading character is much more ordinary, not so clearly or simply a "good guy." For that reason, it is usually more appropriate to use the older and more neutral terms *protagonist* and *antagonist* for the leading character and his or her opponent. These terms do not imply either the presence or the absence of outstanding virtue or vice. The claim that a particular character either is or is not heroic might well make a good thesis for an essay, whereas the claim that he is or is not the protagonist generally won't. You might argue, for instance, that Montresor (in Poe's "The Cask of Amontillado," chapter 2) or Ebenezer Scrooge (in Dickens's *A Christmas Carol*) is a hero, but most readers would agree that each is his story's protagonist. Like most rules, however, this one admits of exceptions. Some stories do leave open to debate the question of which character most deserves to be called the *protagonist*. In "Sonny's Blues," for example, Sonny and his brother are equally central. Controversial in a different way is a particular type of protagonist known as an **antihero**. Found mainly in fiction written since around 1850, an antihero, as the name implies, possesses traits that make him or her the opposite of a traditional hero. An antihero may be difficult to like or admire. One early and influential example of an antihero is the narrator-protagonist of Fyodor Dostoevsky's 1864 Russian-language novella *Notes from the Underground*—a man utterly paralyzed by his own hypersensitivity. More familiar and recent examples are Homer and Bart Simpson. Yet it would be a mistake to see the quality of a work of fiction as dependent on whether we find its characters likable or admirable, just as it would be wrong to assume that an author's outlook or values are the same as those of the protagonist. Often, the characters we initially find least likable or admirable may ultimately move and teach us the most.

MAJOR VERSUS MINOR CHARACTERS

The *major* or *main characters* are those we see more of over time; we learn more about them, and we think of them as more complex and, frequently, as more "realistic" than the *minor characters*, the figures who fill out the story. These major characters can grow and change too, sometimes defying our expectations.

Yet even though minor characters are less prominent and may seem less complex, they are ultimately just as indispensable to a story as major characters. Minor characters often play a key role in shaping our interpretations of, and attitudes toward, the major characters, and also in precipitating the changes that major characters undergo. For example, a minor character might function as a **foil**—a character that helps by way of contrast to reveal the unique qualities of another (especially main) character.

Questions about minor characters can lead to good essay topics precisely because such characters' significance to a story is not immediately apparent. Rather, we often have to probe the details of the story to formulate a persuasive interpretation of their roles.

FLAT VERSUS ROUND AND STATIC VERSUS DYNAMIC CHARACTERS

Characters that act from varied, often conflicting motives, impulses, and desires, and who seem to have psychological complexity are said to be *round characters*; they can "surprise convincingly," as one critic puts it. Simple, one-dimensional characters that behave and speak in predictable or repetitive (if sometimes odd) ways are called *flat*. Sometimes, characters seem round to us because our impression of them evolves as a story unfolds. Other times, the characters themselves—not just our impression of them—change as a result of events that occur in the story. A character that changes is *dynamic*; one that doesn't is *static*. Roundness and dynamism tend to go together. But the two qualities are distinct, and one does not require the other: Not all round characters are dynamic, not all dynamic characters are round. Terms like *flat* and *round* or *dynamic* and *static* are useful so long as we do not let them harden into value judgments.

Because flat characters are less complex than round ones, it is easy to assume they are artistically inferior; however, we need only to think of the characters of Charles Dickens, almost all of whom are flat, to realize that this is not always the case. A truly original flat character with only one or two very distinctive traits or behavioral or verbal tics will often prove more memorable than a round one. Unrealistic as such characters might seem, in real life you probably know at least one or two people who can always be counted on to say or do pretty much the same thing every time you see them. Exaggeration can provide insight, as well as humor. Dickens's large gallery of lovable flat characters includes a middle-aged man who constantly pulls himself up by his own hair and an old one who must continually be "fluffed up" by others because he tends to slide right out of his chair. *South Park*'s Kenny is little more than a hooded orange snowsuit and a habit of dying in ever more outrageous ways only to come back to life over and over again.

Flat characters who represent a familiar, frequently recurring type—the dumb blonde, the mad scientist, the inept sidekick, the plain yet ever-sympathetic best friend—are called *stock characters* because they seem to be pulled out of a stock-room of familiar, prefabricated figures. Characters that recur in the myths and literature of many different ages and cultures are instead called **archetypes**, though this term also applies to recurring elements other than characters (such as actions or symbols). One archetypal character is the trickster figure that appears in the guise of Brer Rabbit in the Uncle Remus stories, the spider Anansi in certain African and Afro-Caribbean folktales, the coyote in Native American folklore, and, perhaps, Bugs Bunny.

READING CHARACTER IN FICTION AND LIFE

On the one hand, we get to know characters in a work of fiction and try to understand them, much as we do people in real life. We observe what they own and wear, what they look like and where they live, how they carry themselves and what expressions flit across their faces, how they behave in various situations, what they say and how they say it, what they do or don't say, what others say about them, and how others act in their presence. Drawing on all that evidence and on our own past experience of both literature and life, we try to deduce characters' motives and desires, their values and beliefs, their strengths and weaknesses—in short, to figure out what makes them tick and how they might react if circumstances changed. In our daily lives, being able to "read" other people in this way is a vital set of skills, one that we may well hone by reading fiction. The skills of observation and interpretation, the enlarged experience and capacity for empathy, that we develop in reading fiction can help us better navigate our real world.

On the other hand, however, fictional characters are not real people; they are imaginary personages crafted by authors. Fiction offers us a more orderly and expansive world than the one we inhabit every day—one in which every person and every gesture and even every word is a meaningful part of a coherent, purposeful design—one in which our responses to people are guided by a narrator and, ultimately, an author; one in which we can sometimes crawl inside other people's heads and know their thoughts; one in which we can get to know murderers and ministers, monsters and miracle workers—the sorts of people (or personages) we might be afraid, unwilling, or simply unable to meet or spend time with in real life.

In other words, fictional characters are the products not of nature, chance, or God, but of careful, deliberate **characterization**—the art and technique of representing fictional personages. In analyzing character, we thus need to consider not only who a character is and what precisely are his or her most important traits, motivations, and values, but also precisely how the text shapes our interpretation of, and degree of sympathy or admiration for, the character; what function the character serves in the story; and what the character might represent.

This last issue is important because all characters, no matter how individualized and idiosyncratic, ultimately become meaningful to us only if they represent something beyond the story, something bigger than themselves—a type of person, a particular set of values or way of looking at the world, a human tendency, a demographic group. When you set out to write about a character, consider how the story would be different without the character and what the author says or shows us through the character.

Direct and Indirect Characterization: An Example and an Exercise

The following conversation appears in the pages of a well-known nineteenth-century novel. Even without being familiar with this novel, you should be able to discern a great deal about the two characters that converse in this scene simply by carefully attending to what each says and how each says it. As you will see, one of the things that differentiates the two speakers is that they hold conflicting views of "character" itself:

"In what order you keep these rooms, Mrs Fairfax!" said I. "No dust, no canvas coverings: except that the air feels chilly, one would think they were inhabited daily."

"Why, Miss Eyre, though Mr Rochester's visits here are rare, they are always sudden and unexpected; and as I observed that it put him out to find everything swathed up, and to have a bustle of arrangement on his arrival, I thought it best to keep the rooms in readiness."

"Is Mr Rochester an exacting, fastidious sort of man?"

"Not particularly so; but he has a gentleman's tastes and habits, and he expects to have things managed in conformity to them."

"Do you like him? Is he generally liked?"

"O yes; the family have always been respected here. Almost all the land in this neighbourhood, as far as you can see, has belonged to the Rochesters time out of mind."

"Well, but leaving his land out of the question, do you like him? Is he liked for himself?"

"I have no cause to do otherwise than like him; and I believe he is considered a just and liberal landlord by his tenants: but he has never lived much amongst them."

(Continued on next page)

(Continued)

"But has he no peculiarities? What, in short, is his character?"

"Oh! his character is unimpeachable, I suppose. He is rather peculiar, perhaps: he has travelled a great deal, and seen a great deal of the world, I should think. I daresay he is clever: but I never had much conversation with him."

"In what way is he peculiar?"

"I don't know—it is not easy to describe—nothing striking, but you feel it when he speaks to you: you cannot be always sure whether he is in jest or earnest, whether he is pleased or the contrary; you don't thoroughly understand him, in short—at least, I don't: but it is of no consequence, he is a very good master."

- What facts about the two speakers can you glean from this conversation? What do you infer about their individual outlooks, personalities, and values?
- What different definitions of the word *character* emerge here? How would you describe each speaker's view of what matters most in the assessment of character?

This scene—from Charlotte Brontë's *Jane Eyre* (1847)—demonstrates the first of the two major methods of presenting character—*indirect characterization* or showing (as opposed to *direct characterization* or telling). In this passage Brontë simply *shows* us what Jane (the narrator) and Mrs. Fairfax say and invites the reader to infer from their words who each character is (including the absent Mr. Rochester), how each looks at the world, and what each cares about.

Sometimes, however, authors present characters more directly, having narrators *tell* us what makes a character tick and what we are to think of him or her. Charlotte Brontë engages in both direct and indirect characterization in the paragraph of *Jane Eyre* that immediately follows the passage above. Here, Jane tells the reader precisely what she thinks this conversation reveals about Mrs. Fairfax, even as she reveals more about herself in the process:

This was all the account I got from Mrs Fairfax of her employer and mine. There are people who seem to have no notion of sketching a character, or observing and describing salient points, either in persons or things: the good lady evidently belonged to this class; my queries puzzled, but did not draw her out. Mr Rochester was Mr Rochester in her eyes; a gentleman, a landed proprietor—nothing more: she inquired and searched no further, and evidently wondered at my wish to gain a more definite notion of his identity.

- How does Jane's interpretation of Mrs. Fairfax compare to yours?
- How and why might this paragraph corroborate or complicate your view of Jane?

CHARACTERS, CONVENTIONS, AND BELIEFS

Just as fiction and the characters that inhabit it operate by somewhat different rules than do the real world and real people, so the rules that govern particular fictional worlds and their characters differ from one another. As the critic James Wood argues,

> our hunger for the particular depth or reality level of a character is tutored by each writer, and adapts to the internal conventions of each book. This is how we can read W. G. Sebald one day and Virginia Woolf or Philip Roth the next, and not demand that each resemble the other. . . . [Works of fiction] tend to fail not when the characters are not vivid or "deep" enough, but when the [work] in question has failed to teach us how to adapt to its conventions, has failed to manage a specific hunger for its own characters, its own reality level.

Works of fiction in various subgenres differ widely in how they handle characterization. Were a folktale, for example, to depict more than a few, mainly flat, archetypal characters, to make us privy to its characters' thoughts, or to offer up detailed descriptions of their physiques and wardrobes, it would cease to be a folktale and cease to yield up the particular sorts of pleasures and insights that only a folktale can. By the same token, readers of a folktale miss out on its pleasures and insights if they expect the wrong things of its characters and modes of characterization.

But even within the same fictional subgenre, the treatment of character varies over time and across cultures. Such variations sometimes reflect profound differences in the way people understand human nature. Individuals and cultures hold conflicting views of what produces personality, whether innate factors such as genes, environmental factors such as upbringing, supernatural forces, unconscious impulses or drives, or a combination of some or all of these. Views differ as well as to whether character is simply an unchanging given or something that can change through experience, conversion, or an act of will. Some works of fiction tackle such issues head on. But many others—especially from cultures or eras different from our own—may raise these questions for us simply because their modes of characterization imply an understanding of the self different from the one we take for granted.

We can thus learn a lot about our own values, prejudices, and beliefs by reading a wide array of fiction. Similarly, we learn from encountering a wide array of fictional characters, including those whose values, beliefs, and ways of life are vastly different from our own.

• • •

The four stories in this chapter—William Faulkner's "Barn Burning," Toni Morrison's "Recitatif," Ha Jin's "In Broad Daylight," and Toby Litt's "The Monster"—differ widely in terms of the number and types of characters they depict and the techniques they use to depict them. In their pages, you will meet a range of diverse individuals—some complex and compelling, some utterly ordinary—struggling to make sense of the people around them just as you work to make sense of them and, through them, yourself.

Questions about Character

1. Who is the protagonist, or might there be more than one? Why and how so? Which other characters, if any, are main or major characters? Which are minor characters?
2. What are the protagonist's most distinctive traits, and what is most distinctive about his or her outlook and values? What motivates the character? What is it about the character that creates internal and/or external conflict?
3. Which textual details and moments reveal most about this character? Which are most surprising or might complicate your interpretation of this character? How is your view of the character affected by what you *don't* know about him or her?
4. What are the roles of other characters? Which, if any, functions as an antagonist? Which, if any, serves as a foil? Why and how so? How would the story as a whole (not just its action or plot) be different if any of these characters disappeared? What points might the author be raising or illustrating through each character?
5. Which of the characters, or which aspects of the characters, does the text encourage us to sympathize with or to admire? to view negatively? Why and how so?
6. Does your view of any character change over the course of the story, or do any of the characters themselves change because of the events in the story? If so, when, how, and why?
7. Does characterization tend to be indirect or direct in the story? What kinds of information do and don't we get about the characters, and how does the story tend to give us that information?

WILLIAM FAULKNER

Barn Burning

The store in which the Justice of the Peace's court was sitting smelled of cheese. The boy, crouched on his nail keg at the back of the crowded room, knew he smelled cheese, and more: from where he sat he could see the ranked shelves close-packed with the solid, squat, dynamic shapes of tin cans whose labels his stomach read, not from the lettering which meant nothing to his mind but from the scarlet devils and the silver curve of fish—this, the cheese which he knew he smelled and the hermetic meat which his intestines believed he smelled coming in intermittent gusts momentary and brief between the other constant one, the smell and sense just a little of fear because mostly of despair and grief, the old fierce pull of blood. He could not see the table where the Justice sat and before which his father and his father's enemy (*our enemy* he thought in that despair; *ourn! mine and hisn both! He's my father!*) stood, but he could hear them, the two of them that is, because his father had said no word yet:

"But what proof have you, Mr. Harris?"

"I told you. The hog got into my corn. I caught it up and sent it back to him. He had no fence that would hold it. I told him so, warned him. The next time I put the hog in my pen. When he came to get it I gave him enough wire to patch up his pen. The next time I put the hog up and kept it. I rode down to his house and saw the wire I gave him still rolled on to the spool in his yard. I told him he could have the hog when he paid me a dollar pound fee. That evening a nigger came with the dollar and got the hog. He was a strange nigger. He said, 'He say to tell you wood and hay kin burn.' I said, 'What?' 'That whut he say to tell you,' the nigger said. 'Wood and hay kin burn.' That night my barn burned. I got the stock out but I lost the barn."

"Where is the nigger? Have you got him?"

"He was a strange nigger, I tell you. I don't know what became of him." 5

"But that's not proof. Don't you see that's not proof?"

"Get that boy up here. He knows." For a moment the boy thought too that the man meant his older brother until Harris said, "Not him. The little one. The boy," and, crouching, small for his age, small and wiry like his father, in patched and faded jeans even too small for him, with straight, uncombed, brown hair and eyes gray and wild as storm scud, he saw the men between himself and the table part and become a lane of grim faces, at the end of which he saw the Justice, a shabby, collarless, graying man in spectacles, beckoning him. He felt no floor under his bare feet; he seemed to walk beneath the palpable weight of the grim turning faces. His father, stiff in his black Sunday coat donned not for the trial but for the moving, did not even look at him. *He aims for me to lie,* he thought, again with that frantic grief and despair. *And I will have to do hit.*

"What's your name, boy?" the Justice said.

"Colonel Sartoris Snopes," the boy whispered.

"Hey?" the Justice said. "Talk louder. Colonel Sartoris? I reckon anybody 10 named for Colonel Sartoris in this country can't help but tell the truth, can they?" The boy said nothing. *Enemy! Enemy!* he thought; for a moment he could not even see, could not see that the Justice's face was kindly nor discern that his voice was troubled when he spoke to the man named Harris: "Do you want me to question this boy?" But he could hear, and during those subsequent long seconds while there was absolutely no sound in the crowded little room save that of quiet and intent breathing it was as if he had swung outward at the end of a grape vine, over a ravine, and at the top of the swing had been caught in a prolonged instant of mesmerized gravity, weightless in time.

"No!" Harris said violently, explosively. "Damnation! Send him out of here!" Now time, the fluid world, rushed beneath him again, the voices coming to him again through the smell of cheese and sealed meat, the fear and despair and the old grief of blood:

"This case is closed. I can't find against you, Snopes, but I can give you advice. Leave this country and don't come back to it."

His father spoke for the first time, his voice cold and harsh, level, without emphasis: "I aim to. I don't figure to stay in a country among people who . . ." he said something unprintable and vile, addressed to no one.

"That'll do," the Justice said. "Take your wagon and get out of this country before dark. Case dismissed."

His father turned, and he followed the stiff black coat, the wiry figure walk- 15 ing a little stiffly from where a Confederate provost's man's[1] musket ball had

1. Military policeman's.

taken him in the heel on a stolen horse thirty years ago, followed the two backs now, since his older brother had appeared from somewhere in the crowd, no taller than the father but thicker, chewing tobacco steadily, between the two lines of grim-faced men and out of the store and across the worn gallery and down the sagging steps and among the dogs and half-grown boys in the mild May dust, where as he passed a voice hissed:

"Barn burner!"

Again he could not see, whirling; there was a face in a red haze, moonlike, bigger than the full moon, the owner of it half again his size, he leaping in the red haze toward the face, feeling no blow, feeling no shock when his head struck the earth, scrabbling up and leaping again, feeling no blow this time either and tasting no blood, scrabbling up to see the other boy in full flight and himself already leaping into pursuit as his father's hand jerked him back, the harsh, cold voice speaking above him: "Go get in the wagon."

It stood in a grove of locusts and mulberries across the road. His two hulking sisters in their Sunday dresses and his mother and her sister in calico and sunbonnets were already in it, sitting on and among the sorry residue of the dozen and more movings which even the boy could remember—the battered stove, the broken beds and chairs, the clock inlaid with mother-of-pearl, which would not run, stopped at some fourteen minutes past two o'clock of a dead and forgotten day and time, which had been his mother's dowry. She was crying, though when she saw him she drew her sleeve across her face and began to descend from the wagon. "Get back," the father said.

"He's hurt. I got to get some water and wash his . . ."

20   "Get back in the wagon," his father said. He got in too, over the tail-gate. His father mounted to the seat where the older brother already sat and struck the gaunt mules two savage blows with the peeled willow, but without heat. It was not even sadistic; it was exactly that same quality which in later years would cause his descendants to overrun the engine before putting a motor car into motion, striking and reining back in the same movement. The wagon went on, the store with its quiet crowd of grimly watching men dropped behind; a curve in the road hid it. *Forever* he thought. *Maybe he's done satisfied now, now that he has* . . . stopping himself, not to say it aloud even to himself. His mother's hand touched his shoulder.

"Does hit hurt?" she said.

"Naw," he said. "Hit don't hurt. Lemme be."

"Can't you wipe some of the blood off before hit dries?"

"I'll wash to-night," he said. "Lemme be, I tell you."

25   The wagon went on. He did not know where they were going. None of them ever did or ever asked, because it was always somewhere, always a house of sorts waiting for them a day or two days or even three days away. Likely his father had already arranged to make a crop on another farm before he . . . Again he had to stop himself. He (the father) always did. There was something about his wolf-like independence and even courage when the advantage was at least neutral which impressed strangers, as if they got from his latent ravening ferocity not so much a sense of dependability as a feeling that his ferocious conviction in the rightness of his own actions would be of advantage to all whose interest lay with his.

That night they camped, in a grove of oaks and beeches where a spring ran. The nights were still cool and they had a fire against it, of a rail lifted from a nearby fence and cut into lengths—a small fire, neat, niggard almost, a shrewd fire; such fires were his father's habit and custom always, even in freezing weather. Older, the boy might have remarked this and wondered why not a big one; why should not a man who had not only seen the waste and extravagance of war, but who had in his blood an inherent voracious prodigality with material not his own, have burned everything in sight? Then he might have gone a step farther and thought that that was the reason: that niggard blaze was the living fruit of nights passed during those four years in the woods hiding from all men, blue or gray,[2] with his strings of horses (captured horses, he called them). And older still, he might have divined the true reason: that the element of fire spoke to some deep mainspring of his father's being, as the element of steel or of powder spoke to other men, as the one weapon for the preservation of integrity, else breath were not worth the breathing, and hence to be regarded with respect and used with discretion.

But he did not think this now and he had seen those same niggard blazes all his life. He merely ate his supper beside it and was already half asleep over his iron plate when his father called him, and once more he followed the stiff back, the stiff and ruthless limp, up the slope and on to the starlit road where, turning, he could see his father against the stars but without face or depth—a shape black, flat, and bloodless as though cut from tin in the iron folds of the frockcoat which had not been made for him, the voice harsh like tin and without heat like tin:

"You were fixing to tell them. You would have told him." He didn't answer. His father struck him with the flat of his hand on the side of the head, hard but without heat, exactly as he had struck the two mules at the store, exactly as he would strike either of them with any stick in order to kill a horse fly, his voice still without heat or anger: "You're getting to be a man. You got to learn. You got to learn to stick to your own blood or you ain't going to have any blood to stick to you. Do you think either of them, any man there this morning, would? Don't you know all they wanted was a chance to get at me because they knew I had them beat? Eh?" Later, twenty years later, he was to tell himself, "If I had said they wanted only truth, justice, he would have hit me again." But now he said nothing. He was not crying. He just stood there. "Answer me," his father said.

"Yes," he whispered. His father turned.

"Get on to bed. We'll be there tomorrow." 30

Tomorrow they were there. In the early afternoon the wagon stopped before a paintless two-room house identical almost with the dozen others it had stopped before even in the boy's ten years, and again, as on the other dozen occasions, his mother and aunt got down and began to unload the wagon, although his two sisters and his father and brother had not moved.

"Likely hit ain't fitten for hawgs," one of the sisters said.

"Nevertheless, fit it will and you'll hog it and like it," his father said. "Get out of them chairs and help your Ma unload."

The two sisters got down, big, bovine, in a flutter of cheap ribbons; one of them drew from the jumbled wagon bed a battered lantern, the other a worn broom. His father handed the reins to the older son and began to climb stiffly over the wheel. "When they get unloaded, take the team to the barn and feed them." Then he said, and at first the boy thought he was still speaking to his brother: "Come with me."

2. The colors of Union and Confederate Civil War (1861–65) uniforms, respectively.

35   "Me?" he said.

"Yes," his father said. "You."

"Abner," his mother said. His father paused and looked back—the harsh level stare beneath the shaggy, graying, irascible brows.

"I reckon I'll have a word with the man that aims to begin to-morrow owning me body and soul for the next eight months."

They went back up the road. A week ago—or before last night, that is—he would have asked where they were going, but not now. His father had struck him before last night but never before had he paused afterward to explain why; it was as if the blow and the following calm, outrageous voice still rang, repercussed, divulging nothing to him save the terrible handicap of being young, the light weight of his few years, just heavy enough to prevent his soaring free of the world as it seemed to be ordered but not heavy enough to keep him footed solid in it, to resist it and try to change the course of its events.

40   Presently he could see the grove of oaks and cedars and the other flowering trees and shrubs, where the house would be, though not the house yet. They walked beside a fence massed with honeysuckle and Cherokee roses and came to a gate swinging open between two brick pillars, and now, beyond a sweep of drive, he saw the house for the first time and at that instant he forgot his father and the terror and despair both, and even when he remembered his father again (who had not stopped) the terror and despair did not return. Because, for all the twelve movings, they had sojourned until now in a poor country, a land of small farms and fields and houses, and he had never seen a house like this before. *Hit's big as a courthouse* he thought quietly, with a surge of peace and joy whose reason he could not have thought into words, being too young for that: *They are safe from him. People whose lives are a part of this peace and dignity are beyond his touch, he no more to them than a buzzing wasp: capable of stinging for a little moment but that's all; the spell of this peace and dignity rendering even the barns and stable and cribs which belong to it impervious to the puny flames he might contrive* . . . this, the peace and joy, ebbing for an instant as he looked again at the stiff black back, the stiff and implacable limp of the figure which was not dwarfed by the house, for the reason that it had never looked big anywhere and which now, against the serene columned back-drop, had more than ever that impervious quality of something cut ruthlessly from tin, depthless, as though, sidewise to the sun, it would cast no shadow. Watching him, the boy remarked the absolutely undeviating course which his father held and saw the stiff foot come squarely down in a pile of fresh drop-pings where a horse had stood in the drive and which his father could have avoided by a simple change of stride. But it ebbed only for a moment, though he could not have thought this into words either, walking on in the spell of the house, which he could even want but without envy, without sorrow, certainly never with that ravening and jealous rage which unknown to him walked in the ironlike black coat before him: *Maybe he will feel it too. Maybe it will even change him now from what maybe he couldn't help but be.*

They crossed the portico. Now he could hear his father's stiff foot as it came down on the boards with clocklike finality, a sound out of all proportion to the displacement of the body it bore and which was not dwarfed either by the white door before it, as though it had attained to a sort of vicious and ravening mini-mum not to be dwarfed by anything—the flat, wide, black hat, the formal coat of broadcloth which had once been black but which had now that friction-glazed greenish cast of the bodies of old house flies, the lifted sleeve which was too large, the lifted hand like a curled claw. The door opened so promptly that the boy knew the Negro must have been watching them all the time, an old man with neat grizzled hair, in a linen jacket, who stood barring the door with his body, saying, "Wipe yo foots, white man, fo you come in here. Major ain't home nohow."

"Get out of my way, nigger," his father said, without heat too, flinging the door back and the Negro also and entering, his hat still on his head. And now the boy saw the prints of the stiff foot on the doorjamb and saw them appear on the pale rug behind the machinelike deliberation of the foot which seemed to bear (or transmit) twice the weight which the body compassed. The Negro was shouting "Miss Lula! Miss Lula!" somewhere behind them, then the boy, deluged as though by a warm wave by a suave turn of carpeted stair and a pendant glitter of chandeliers and a mute gleam of gold frames, heard the swift feet and saw her too, a lady—perhaps he had never seen her like before either—in a gray, smooth gown with lace at the throat and an apron tied at the waist and the sleeves turned back, wiping cake or biscuit dough from her hands with a towel as she came up the hall, looking not at his father at all but at the tracks on the blond rug with an expression of incredulous amazement.

"I tried," the Negro cried. "I tole him to . . ."

"Will you please go away?" she said in a shaking voice. "Major de Spain is not at home. Will you please go away?"

His father had not spoken again. He did not speak again. He did not even look at her. He just stood stiff in the center of the rug, in his hat, the shaggy iron-gray brows twitching slightly above the pebble-colored eyes as he appeared to examine the house with brief deliberation. Then with the same deliberation he turned; the boy watched him pivot on the good leg and saw the stiff foot drag round the arc of the turning, leaving a final long and fading smear. His father never looked at it, he never once looked down at the rug. The Negro held the door. It closed behind them, upon the hysteric and indistinguishable woman-wail. His father stopped at the top of the steps and scraped his boot clean on the edge of it. At the gate he stopped again. He stood for a moment, planted stiffly on the stiff foot, looking back at the house. "Pretty and white, ain't it?" he said. "That's sweat. Nigger sweat. Maybe it ain't white enough yet to suit him. Maybe he wants to mix some white sweat with it." 45

Two hours later the boy was chopping wood behind the house within which his mother and aunt and the two sisters (the mother and aunt, not the two girls, he knew that; even at this distance and muffled by walls the flat loud voices of the two girls emanated an incorrigible idle inertia) were setting up the stove to prepare a meal, when he heard the hooves and saw the linen-clad man on a fine sorrel mare, whom he recognized even before he saw the rolled rug in front of the Negro youth following on a fat bay carriage horse—a suffused, angry face vanishing, still at full gallop, beyond the corner of the house where his father and brother were sitting in the two tilted chairs; and a moment later, almost before he could have put the axe down, he heard the hooves again and watched the sorrel mare go back out of the yard, already galloping again. Then his father began to shout one of the sisters' names, who presently emerged backward from the kitchen door dragging the rolled rug along the ground by one end while the other sister walked behind it.

"If you ain't going to tote, go on and set up the wash pot," the first said.

"You, Sarty!" the second shouted. "Set up the wash pot!" His father appeared at the door, framed against that shabbiness, as he had been against that other bland perfection, impervious to either, the mother's anxious face at his shoulder.

"Go on," the father said. "Pick it up." The two sisters stooped, broad, lethargic; stooping, they presented an incredible expanse of pale cloth and a flutter of tawdry ribbons.

50   "If I thought enough of a rug to have to git hit all the way from France I wouldn't keep hit where folks coming in would have to tromp on hit," the first said. They raised the rug.

"Abner," the mother said. "Let me do it."

"You go back and git dinner," his father said. "I'll tend to this."

From the woodpile through the rest of the afternoon the boy watched them, the rug spread flat in the dust beside the bubbling wash-pot, the two sisters stooping over it with that profound and lethargic reluctance, while the father stood over them in turn, implacable and grim, driving them though never raising his voice again. He could smell the harsh homemade lye they were using; he saw his mother come to the door once and look toward them with an expression not anxious now but very like despair; he saw his father turn, and he fell to with the axe and saw from the corner of his eye his father raise from the ground a flattish fragment of field stone and examine it and return to the pot, and this time his mother actually spoke: "Abner. Abner. Please don't. Please, Abner."

Then he was done too. It was dusk; the whippoorwills had already begun. He could smell coffee from the room where they would presently eat the cold food remaining from the mid-afternoon meal, though when he entered the house he realized they were having coffee again probably because there was a fire on the hearth, before which the rug now lay spread over the backs of the two chairs. The tracks of his father's foot were gone. Where they had been were now long, water-cloudy scoriations resembling the sporadic course of a Lilliputian mowing machine.

55   It still hung there while they ate the cold food and then went to bed, scattered without order or claim up and down the two rooms, his mother in one bed, where his father would later lie, the older brother in the other, himself, the aunt, and the two sisters on pallets on the floor. But his father was not in bed yet. The last thing the boy remembered was the depthless, harsh silhouette of the hat and coat bending over the rug and it seemed to him that he had not even closed his eyes when the silhouette was standing over him, the fire almost dead behind it, the stiff foot prodding him awake. "Catch up the mule," his father said.

When he returned with the mule his father was standing in the black door, the rolled rug over his shoulder. "Ain't you going to ride?" he said.

"No. Give me your foot."

He bent his knee into his father's hand, the wiry, surprising power flowed smoothly, rising, he rising with it, on to the mule's bare back (they had owned a saddle once; the boy could remember it though not when or where) and with the same effortlessness his father swung the rug up in front of him. Now in the starlight they retraced the afternoon's path, up the dusty road rife with honeysuckle, through the gate and up the black tunnel of the drive to the lightless house, where he sat on the mule and felt the rough warp of the rug drag across his thighs and vanish.

"Don't you want me to help?" he whispered. His father did not answer and now he heard again that stiff foot striking the hollow portico with that wooden and clocklike deliberation, that outrageous overstatement of the weight it carried. The rug, hunched, not flung (the boy could tell that even in the darkness) from his father's shoulder struck the angle of wall and floor with a sound unbelievably loud, thunderous, then the foot again, unhurried and enormous; a light came on in the house and the boy sat, tense, breathing steadily and quietly and just a little fast, though the foot itself did not increase its beat at all, descending the steps now; now the boy could see him.

"Don't you want to ride now?" he whispered. "We kin both ride now," the light 60 within the house altering now, flaring up and sinking. *He's coming down the stairs now,* he thought. He had already ridden the mule up beside the horse block; presently his father was up behind him and he doubled the reins over and slashed the mule across the neck, but before the animal could begin to trot the hard, thin arm came round him, the hard, knotted hand jerking the mule back to a walk.

In the first red rays of the sun they were in the lot, putting plow gear on the mules. This time the sorrel mare was in the lot before he heard it at all, the rider collarless and even bareheaded, trembling, speaking in a shaking voice as the woman in the house had done, his father merely looking up once before stooping again to the hame he was buckling, so that the man on the mare spoke to his stooping back:

"You must realize you have ruined that rug. Wasn't there anybody here, any of your women . . ." he ceased, shaking, the boy watching him, the older brother leaning now in the stable door, chewing, blinking slowly and steadily at nothing apparently. "It cost a hundred dollars. But you never had a hundred dollars. You never will. So I'm going to charge you twenty bushels of corn against your crop. I'll add it in your contract and when you come to the commissary you can sign it. That won't keep Mrs. de Spain quiet but maybe it will teach you to wipe your feet off before you enter her house again."

Then he was gone. The boy looked at his father, who still had not spoken or even looked up again, who was now adjusting the logger-head in the hame.

"Pap," he said. His father looked at him—the inscrutable face, the shaggy brows beneath which the gray eyes glinted coldly. Suddenly the boy went toward him, fast, stopping as suddenly. "You done the best you could!" he cried. "If he wanted hit done different why didn't he wait and tell you how? He won't git no twenty bushels! He won't git none! We'll gether hit and hide hit! I kin watch . . ."

"Did you put the cutter back in that straight stock like I told you?" 65

"No, sir," he said.

"Then go do it."

That was Wednesday. During the rest of that week he worked steadily, at what was within his scope and some which was beyond it, with an industry that did not need to be driven nor even commanded twice; he had this from his mother, with the difference that some at least of what he did he liked to do, such as splitting wood with the half-size axe which his mother and aunt had earned, or saved money somehow, to present him with at Christmas. In company with the two older women (and on one afternoon, even one of the sisters), he built pens for the shoat and the cow which were a part of his father's contract with the landlord, and one afternoon, his father being absent, gone somewhere on one of the mules, he went to the field.

They were running a middle buster[3] now, his brother holding the plow straight while he handled the reins, and walking beside the straining mule, the rich black soil shearing cool and damp against his bare ankles, he thought *Maybe this is the end of it. Maybe even that twenty bushels that seems hard to have to pay for just a rug will be a cheap price for him to stop forever and always from being what he used to be;* thinking, dreaming now, so that his brother had to speak sharply to him to mind the mule: *Maybe he even won't collect the twenty bushels. Maybe it will all add up and balance and vanish—corn, rug, fire; the terror and grief, the being pulled two ways like between two teams of horses—gone, done with for ever and ever.*

70   Then it was Saturday; he looked up from beneath the mule he was harnessing and saw his father in the black coat and hat. "Not that," his father said. "The wagon gear." And then, two hours later, sitting in the wagon bed behind his father and brother on the seat, the wagon accomplished a final curve, and he saw the weathered paintless store with its tattered tobacco- and patent-medicine posters and the tethered wagons and saddle animals below the gallery. He mounted the gnawed steps behind his father and brother, and there again was the lane of quiet, watching faces for the three of them to walk through. He saw the man in spectacles sitting at the plank table and he did not need to be told this was a Justice of the Peace; he sent one glare of fierce, exultant, partisan defiance at the man in collar and cravat now, whom he had seen but twice before in his life, and that on a galloping horse, who now wore on his face an expression not of rage but of amazed unbelief which the boy could not have known was at the incredible circumstance of being sued by one of his own tenants, and came and stood against his father and cried at the Justice: "He ain't done it! He ain't burnt . . ."

"Go back to the wagon," his father said.

"Burnt?" the Justice said. "Do I understand this rug was burned too?"

"Does anybody here claim it was?" his father said. "Go back to the wagon." But he did not, he merely retreated to the rear of the room, crowded as that other had been, but not to sit down this time, instead, to stand pressing among the motionless bodies, listening to the voices:

"And you claim twenty bushels of corn is too high for the damage you did to the rug?"

75   "He brought the rug to me and said he wanted the tracks washed out of it. I washed the tracks out and took the rug back to him."

"But you didn't carry the rug back to him in the same condition it was in before you made the tracks on it."

His father did not answer, and now for perhaps half a minute there was no sound at all save that of breathing, the faint, steady suspiration of complete and intent listening.

"You decline to answer that, Mr. Snopes?" Again his father did not answer. "I'm going to find against you, Mr. Snopes. I'm going to find that you were responsible for the injury to Major de Spain's rug and hold you liable for it. But twenty bushels of corn seems a little high for a man in your circumstances to have to pay. Major de Spain claims it cost a hundred dollars. October corn will be worth about fifty cents. I figure that if Major de Spain can stand a ninety-five dollar loss on something he paid cash for, you can stand a five-dollar loss you haven't earned yet. I hold you in damages to Major de Spain to the amount of

---

3. Double moldboard plow that throws a ridge of earth both ways.

ten bushels of corn over and above your contract with him, to be paid to him out of your crop at gathering time. Court adjourned."

It had taken no time hardly, the morning was but half begun. He thought they would return home and perhaps back to the field, since they were late, far behind all other farmers. But instead his father passed on behind the wagon, merely indicating with his hand for the older brother to follow with it, and crossed the road toward the blacksmith shop opposite, pressing on after his father, overtaking him, speaking, whispering up at the harsh, calm face beneath the weathered hat: "He won't git no ten bushels neither. He won't git one. We'll . . ." until his father glanced for an instant down at him, the face absolutely calm, the grizzled eyebrows tangled above the cold eyes, the voice almost pleasant, almost gentle:

"You think so? Well, we'll wait till October anyway." 80

The matter of the wagon—the setting of a spoke or two and the tightening of the tires—did not take long either, the business of the tires accomplished by driving the wagon into the spring branch behind the shop and letting it stand there, the mules nuzzling into the water from time to time, and the boy on the seat with the idle reins, looking up the slope and through the sooty tunnel of the shed where the slow hammer rang and where his father sat on an upended cypress bolt, easily, either talking or listening, still sitting there when the boy brought the dripping wagon up out of the branch and halted it before the door.

"Take them on to the shade and hitch," his father said. He did so and returned. His father and the smith and a third man squatting on his heels inside the door were talking, about crops and animals; the boy, squatting too in the ammoniac dust and hoof-parings and scales of rust, heard his father tell a long and unhurried story out of the time before the birth of the older brother even when he had been a professional horsetrader. And then his father came up beside him where he stood before a tattered last year's circus poster on the other side of the store, gazing rapt and quiet at the scarlet horses, the incredible poisings and convolutions of tulle and tights and the painted leers of comedians, and said, "It's time to eat."

But not at home. Squatting beside his brother against the front wall, he watched his father emerge from the store and produce from a paper sack a segment of cheese and divide it carefully and deliberately into three with his pocket knife and produce crackers from the same sack. They all three squatted on the gallery and ate, slowly, without talking; then in the store again, they drank from a tin dipper tepid water smelling of the cedar bucket and of living beech trees. And still they did not go home. It was a horse lot this time, a tall rail fence upon and along which men stood and sat and out of which one by one horses were led, to be walked and trotted and then cantered back and forth along the road while the slow swapping and buying went on and the sun began to slant westward, they—the three of them—watching and listening, the older brother with his muddy eyes and his steady, inevitable tobacco, the father commenting now and then on certain of the animals, to no one in particular.

It was after sundown when they reached home. They ate supper by lamplight, then, sitting on the doorstep, the boy watched the night fully accomplish, listening to the whippoorwills and the frogs, when he heard his mother's voice: "Abner! No! No! Oh, God. Oh, God. Abner!" and he rose, whirled, and saw the altered light through the door where a candle stub now burned in a bottle neck on the table and his father, still in the hat and coat, at once formal and burlesque as though dressed carefully for some shabby and ceremonial violence, emptying the reservoir of the lamp back into the five-gallon kerosene can from which it had been filled, while the mother tugged at his arm until he shifted the lamp to the other hand and flung her back, not savagely or viciously, just hard, into the wall, her hands flung out against the wall for balance, her mouth open and in her face the same quality of hopeless despair as had been in her voice. Then his father saw him standing in the door.

85   "Go to the barn and get that can of oil we were oiling the wagon with," he said. The boy did not move. Then he could speak.

"What . . ." he cried. "What are you . . ."

"Go get that oil," his father said. "Go."

Then he was moving, running, outside the house, toward the stable: this the old habit, the old blood which he had not been permitted to choose for himself, which had been bequeathed him willy nilly and which had run for so long (and who knew where, battening on what of outrage and savagery and lust) before it came to him. *I could keep on,* he thought. *I could run on and on and never look back, never need to see his face again. Only I can't. I can't,* the rusted can in his hand now, the liquid sploshing in it as he ran back to the house and into it, into the sound of his mother's weeping in the next room, and handed the can to his father.

"Ain't you going to even send a nigger?" he cried. "At least you sent a nigger before!"

90   This time his father didn't strike him. The hand came even faster than the blow had, the same hand which had set the can on the table with almost excruciating care flashing from the can toward him too quick for him to follow it, gripping him by the back of his shirt and on to tiptoe before he had seen it quit the can, the face stooping at him in breathless and frozen ferocity, the cold, dead voice speaking over him to the older brother, who leaned against the table, chewing with that steady, curious, sidewise motion of cows:

"Empty the can into the big one and go on. I'll catch up with you."

"Better tie him up to the bedpost," the brother said.

"Do like I told you," the father said. Then the boy was moving, his bunched shirt and the hard, bony hand between his shoulder-blades, his toes just touching the floor, across the room and into the other one, past the sisters sitting with spread heavy thighs in the two chairs over the cold hearth, and to where his mother and aunt sat side by side on the bed, the aunt's arms about his mother's shoulders.

"Hold him," the father said. The aunt made a startled movement. "Not you," the father said. "Lennie. Take hold of him. I want to see you do it." His mother took him by the wrist. "You'll hold him better than that. If he gets loose don't you know what he is going to do? He will go up yonder." He jerked his head toward the road. "Maybe I'd better tie him."

95   "I'll hold him," his mother whispered.

"See you do then." Then his father was gone, the stiff foot heavy and measured upon the boards, ceasing at last.

Then he began to struggle. His mother caught him in both arms, he jerking and wrenching at them. He would be stronger in the end, he knew that. But he had no time to wait for it. "Lemme go!" he cried. "I don't want to have to hit you!"

"Let him go!" the aunt said. "If he don't go, before God, I am going up there myself!"

"Don't you see I can't?" his mother cried. "Sarty! Sarty! No! No! Help me, Lizzie!"

Then he was free. His aunt grasped at him but it was too late. He whirled, running, his mother stumbled forward on to her knees behind him, crying to the nearer sister: "Catch him, Net! Catch him!" But that was too late too, the sister (the sisters were twins, born at the same time, yet either of them now gave the impression of being, encompassing as much living meat and volume and weight as any other two of the family) not yet having begun to rise from the chair, her head, face, alone merely turned, presenting to him in the flying instant an astonishing expanse of young female features untroubled by any surprise even, wearing only an expression of bovine interest. Then he was out of the room, out of the house, in the mild dust of the starlit road and the heavy rifeness of honeysuckle, the pale ribbon unspooling with terrific slowness under his running feet, reaching the gate at last and turning in, running, his heart and lungs drumming, on up the drive toward the lighted house, the lighted door. He did not knock, he burst in, sobbing for breath, incapable for the moment of speech; he saw the astonished face of the Negro in the linen jacket without knowing when the Negro had appeared.

"De Spain!" he cried, panted. "Where's . . ." then he saw the white man too emerging from a white door down the hall. "Barn!" he cried. "Barn!"

"What?" the white man said. "Barn?"

"Yes!" the boy cried. "Barn!"

"Catch him!" the white man shouted.

But it was too late this time too. The Negro grasped his shirt, but the entire sleeve, rotten with washing, carried away, and he was out that door too and in the drive again, and had actually never ceased to run even while he was screaming into the white man's face.

Behind him the white man was shouting, "My horse! Fetch my horse!" and he thought for an instant of cutting across the park and climbing the fence into the road, but he did not know the park nor how high the vine-massed fence might be and he dared not risk it. So he ran on down the drive, blood and breath roaring; presently he was in the road again though he could not see it. He could not hear either: the galloping mare was almost upon him before he heard her, and even then he held his course, as if the very urgency of his wild grief and need must in a moment more find his wings, waiting until the ultimate instant to hurl himself aside and into the weed-choked roadside ditch as the horse thundered past and on, for an instant in furious silhouette against the stars, the tranquil early summer night sky which, even before the shape of the horse and rider vanished, stained abruptly and violently upward: a long, swirling roar incredible and soundless, blotting the stars, and he springing up and into the road again, running again, knowing it was too late yet still running even after he heard the shot and, an instant later, two shots, pausing now without knowing he had ceased to run, crying "Pap! Pap!", running again before he knew he had begun to run, stumbling, tripping over something and scrabbling up again without ceasing to run, looking backward over his shoulder at the glare as he got up, running on among the invisible trees, panting, sobbing, "Father! Father!"

At midnight he was sitting on the crest of a hill. He did not know it was mid-night and he did not know how far he had come. But there was no glare behind him now and he sat now, his back toward what he had called home for four days anyhow, his face toward the dark woods which he would enter when breath was strong again, small, shaking steadily in the chill darkness, hugging himself into the remainder of his thin, rotten shirt, the grief and despair now no longer ter-ror and fear but just grief and despair. *Father. My father,* he thought. "He was brave!" he cried suddenly, aloud but not loud, no more than a whisper: "He was! He was in the war! He was in Colonel Sartoris' cav'ry!" not knowing that his father had gone to that war a private in the fine old European sense, wearing no uniform, admitting the authority of and giving fidelity to no man or army or flag, going to war as Malbrouck[4] himself did: for booty—it meant nothing and less than nothing to him if it were enemy booty or his own.

The slow constellations wheeled on. It would be dawn and then sun-up after a while and he would be hungry. But that would be to-morrow and now he was only cold, and walking would cure that. His breathing was easier now and he decided to get up and go on, and then he found that he had been asleep because he knew it was almost dawn, the night almost over. He could tell that from the whippoorwills. They were everywhere now among the dark trees below him, con-stant and inflectioned and ceaseless, so that, as the instant for giving over to the day birds drew nearer and nearer, there was no interval at all between them. He got up. He was a little stiff, but walking would cure that too as it would the cold, and soon there would be the sun. He went on down the hill, toward the dark woods within which the liquid silver voices of the birds called unceasing—the rapid and urgent beating of the urgent and quiring heart of the late spring night. He did not look back.

1939

QUESTIONS

1. At one point in "Barn Burning," Sarty thinks that *"maybe"* his father *"couldn't help but be"* what he is (par. 40). What *is* Abner Snopes? What desires, motives, values, and views—especially of justice—seem to drive and explain him? What does the story imply about how and why he has become the man he is? What might be admi-rable, as well as abhorrent, about him? How does the narrative point of view shape your understanding of, and attitude toward, Abner?

2. How is Sarty characterized? How is this characterization affected by the multiple flashforwards in the story and by the way Sarty's thoughts are presented? Does Sarty change over the course of the story? How and why does he change or not change?

3. What do each of the minor characters contribute to the story, especially Sarty's mother, sisters, and older brother?

---

4. John Churchill, the first duke of Marlborough (1650–1722), an English general whose name became distorted as Malbrough and Malbrouch in English and French popular songs celebrating his exploits.

TONI MORRISON

Recitatif [1]

My mother danced all night and Roberta's was sick. That's why we were taken to St. Bonny's. People want to put their arms around you when you tell them you were in a shelter, but it really wasn't bad. No big long room with one hundred beds like Bellevue.[2] There were four to a room, and when Roberta and me came, there was a shortage of state kids, so we were the only ones assigned to 406 and could go from bed to bed if we wanted to. And we wanted to, too. We changed beds every night and for the whole four months we were there we never picked one out as our own permanent bed.

It didn't start out that way. The minute I walked in and the Big Bozo introduced us, I got sick to my stomach. It was one thing to be taken out of your own bed early in the morning—it was something else to be stuck in a strange place with a girl from a whole other race. And Mary, that's my mother, she was right. Every now and then she would stop dancing long enough to tell me something important and one of the things she said was that they never washed their hair and they smelled funny. Roberta sure did. Smell funny, I mean. So when the Big Bozo (nobody ever called her Mrs. Itkin, just like nobody ever said St. Bonaventure)—when she said, "Twyla, this is Roberta. Roberta, this is Twyla. Make each other welcome." I said, "My mother won't like you putting me in here."

"Good," said Bozo. "Maybe then she'll come and take you home."

How's that for mean? If Roberta had laughed I would have killed her, but she didn't. She just walked over to the window and stood with her back to us.

"Turn around," said the Bozo. "Don't be rude. Now Twyla. Roberta. When 5 you hear a loud buzzer, that's the call for dinner. Come down to the first floor. Any fights and no movie." And then, just to make sure we knew what we would be missing, *"The Wizard of Oz."*

Roberta must have thought I meant that my mother would be mad about my being put in the shelter. Not about rooming with her, because as soon as Bozo left she came over to me and said, "Is your mother sick too?"

"No," I said. "She just likes to dance all night."

"Oh," she nodded her head and I liked the way she understood things so fast. So for the moment it didn't matter that we looked like salt and pepper standing there and that's what the other kids called us sometimes. We were eight years old and got F's all the time. Me because I couldn't remember what I read or what the teacher said. And Roberta because she couldn't read at all and didn't even listen to the teacher. She wasn't good at anything except jacks, at which she was a killer: pow scoop pow scoop pow scoop.

We didn't like each other all that much at first, but nobody else wanted to play with us because we weren't real orphans with beautiful dead parents in the sky. We were dumped. Even the New York City Puerto Ricans and the upstate Indians ignored us. All kinds of kids were in there, black ones, white ones, even two Koreans. The food was good, though. At least I thought so. Roberta hated it

---

1. In classical music such as opera, a vocal passage that is sung in a speechlike manner.
2. Large New York City hospital best known for its psychiatric wards.

and left whole pieces of things on her plate: Spam, Salisbury steak—even jello with fruit cocktail in it, and she didn't care if I ate what she wouldn't. Mary's idea of supper was popcorn and a can of Yoo-Hoo. Hot mashed potatoes and two weenies was like Thanksgiving for me.

10   It really wasn't bad, St. Bonny's. The big girls on the second floor pushed us around now and then. But that was all. They wore lipstick and eyebrow pencil and wobbled their knees while they watched TV. Fifteen, sixteen, even, some of them were. They were put-out girls, scared runaways most of them. Poor little girls who fought their uncles off but looked tough to us, and mean. God did they look mean. The staff tried to keep them separate from the younger children, but sometimes they caught us watching them in the orchard where they played radios and danced with each other. They'd light out after us and pull our hair or twist our arms. We were scared of them, Roberta and me, but neither of us wanted the other one to know it. So we got a good list of dirty names we could shout back when we ran from them through the orchard. I used to dream a lot and almost always the orchard was there. Two acres, four maybe, of these little apple trees. Hundreds of them. Empty and crooked like beggar women when I first came to St. Bonny's but fat with flowers when I left. I don't know why I dreamt about that orchard so much. Nothing really happened there. Nothing all that important, I mean. Just the big girls dancing and playing the radio. Roberta and me watching. Maggie fell down there once. The kitchen woman with legs like parentheses. And the big girls laughed at her. We should have helped her up, I know, but we were scared of those girls with lipstick and eyebrow pencil. Maggie couldn't talk. The kids said she had her tongue cut out, but I think she was just born that way: mute. She was old and sandy-colored and she worked in the kitchen. I don't know if she was nice or not. I just remember her legs like parentheses and how she rocked when she walked. She worked from early in the morning till two o'clock, and if she was late, if she had too much cleaning and didn't get out till two-fifteen or so, she'd cut through the orchard so she wouldn't miss her bus and have to wait another hour. She wore this really stupid little hat—a kid's hat with ear flaps—and she wasn't much taller than we were. A really awful little hat. Even for a mute, it was dumb—dressing like a kid and never saying anything at all.

"But what about if somebody tries to kill her?" I used to wonder about that. "Or what if she wants to cry? Can she cry?"

"Sure," Roberta said. "But just tears. No sounds come out."

"She can't scream?"

"Nope. Nothing."

15   "Can she hear?"

"I guess."

"Let's call her," I said. And we did.

"Dummy! Dummy!" She never turned her head.

"Bow legs! Bow legs!" Nothing. She just rocked on, the chin straps of her baby-boy hat swaying from side to side. I think we were wrong. I think she could hear and didn't let on. And it shames me even now to think there was somebody in there after all who heard us call her those names and couldn't tell on us.

20   We got along all right, Roberta and me. Changed beds every night, got F's in civics and communication skills and gym. The Bozo was disappointed in us, she said. Out of 130 of us state cases, 90 were under twelve. Almost all were real orphans

with beautiful dead parents in the sky. We were the only ones dumped and the only ones with F's in three classes including gym. So we got along—what with her leaving whole pieces of things on her plate and being nice about not asking questions.

I think it was the day before Maggie fell down that we found out our mothers were coming to visit us on the same Sunday. We had been at the shelter twenty-eight days (Roberta twenty-eight and a half) and this was their first visit with us. Our mothers would come at ten o'clock in time for chapel, then lunch with us in the teachers' lounge. I thought if my dancing mother met her sick mother it might be good for her. And Roberta thought her sick mother would get a big bang out of a dancing one. We got excited about it and curled each other's hair. After breakfast we sat on the bed watching the road from the window. Roberta's socks were still wet. She washed them the night before and put them on the radiator to dry. They hadn't, but she put them on anyway because their tops were so pretty—scalloped in pink. Each of us had a purple construction-paper basket that we had made in craft class. Mine had a yellow crayon rabbit on it. Roberta's had eggs with wiggly lines of color. Inside were cellophane grass and just the jelly beans because I'd eaten the two marshmallow eggs they gave us. The Big Bozo came herself to get us. Smiling she told us we looked very nice and to come downstairs. We were so surprised by the smile we'd never seen before, neither of us moved.

"Don't you want to see your mommies?"

I stood up first and spilled the jelly beans all over the floor. Bozo's smile disappeared while we scrambled to get the candy up off the floor and put it back in the grass.

She escorted us downstairs to the first floor, where the other girls were lining up to file into the chapel. A bunch of grown-ups stood to one side. Viewers mostly. The old biddies who wanted servants and the fags who wanted company looking for children they might want to adopt. Once in a while a grandmother. Almost never anybody young or anybody whose face wouldn't scare you in the night. Because if any of the real orphans had young relatives they wouldn't be real orphans. I saw Mary right away. She had on those green slacks I hated and hated even more now because didn't she know we were going to chapel? And that fur jacket with the pocket linings so ripped she had to pull to get her hands out of them. But her face was pretty—like always, and she smiled and waved like she was the little girl looking for her mother—not me.

I walked slowly, trying not to drop the jelly beans and hoping the paper handle would hold. I had to use my last Chiclet because by the time I finished cutting everything out, all the Elmer's was gone. I am left-handed and the scissors never worked for me. It didn't matter, though; I might just as well have chewed the gum. Mary dropped to her knees and grabbed me, mashing the basket, the jelly beans, and the grass into her ratty fur jacket.

"Twyla, baby. Twyla, baby!"

I could have killed her. Already I heard the big girls in the orchard the next time saying, "Twyyyyyla, baby!" But I couldn't stay mad at Mary while she was smiling and hugging me and smelling of Lady Esther dusting powder. I wanted to stay buried in her fur all day.

To tell the truth I forgot about Roberta. Mary and I got in line for the traipse into chapel and I was feeling proud because she looked so beautiful even in those ugly green slacks that made her behind stick out. A pretty mother on earth is better than a beautiful dead one in the sky even if she did leave you all alone to go dancing.

I felt a tap on my shoulder, turned, and saw Roberta smiling. I smiled back, but not too much lest somebody think this visit was the biggest thing that ever happened in my life. Then Roberta said, "Mother, I want you to meet my roommate, Twyla. And that's Twyla's mother."

30   I looked up it seemed for miles. She was big. Bigger than any man and on her chest was the biggest cross I'd ever seen. I swear it was six inches long each way. And in the crook of her arm was the biggest Bible ever made.

Mary, simple-minded as ever, grinned and tried to yank her hand out of the pocket with the raggedy lining—to shake hands, I guess. Roberta's mother looked down at me and then looked down at Mary too. She didn't say anything, just grabbed Roberta with her Bible-free hand and stepped out of line, walking quickly to the rear of it. Mary was still grinning because she's not too swift when it comes to what's really going on. Then this light bulb goes off in her head and she says "That bitch!" really loud and us almost in the chapel now. Organ music whining; the Bonny Angels singing sweetly. Everybody in the world turned around to look. And Mary would have kept it up—kept calling names if I hadn't squeezed her hand as hard as I could. That helped a little, but she still twitched and crossed and uncrossed her legs all through service. Even groaned a couple of times. Why did I think she would come there and act right? Slacks. No hat like the grandmothers and viewers, and groaning all the while. When we stood for hymns she kept her mouth shut. Wouldn't even look at the words on the page. She actually reached in her purse for a mirror to check her lipstick. All I could think of was that she really needed to be killed. The sermon lasted a year, and I knew the real orphans were looking smug again.

We were supposed to have lunch in the teachers' lounge, but Mary didn't bring anything, so we picked fur and cellophane grass off the mashed jelly beans and ate them. I could have killed her. I sneaked a look at Roberta. Her mother had brought chicken legs and ham sandwiches and oranges and a whole box of chocolate-covered grahams. Roberta drank milk from a thermos while her mother read the Bible to her.

Things are not right. The wrong food is always with the wrong people. Maybe that's why I got into waitress work later—to match up the right people with the right food. Roberta just let those chicken legs sit there, but she did bring a stack of grahams up to me later when the visit was over. I think she was sorry that her mother would not shake my mother's hand. And I liked that and I liked the fact that she didn't say a word about Mary groaning all the way through the service and not bringing any lunch.

Roberta left in May when the apple trees were heavy and white. On her last day we went to the orchard to watch the big girls smoke and dance by the radio. It didn't matter that they said, "Twyyyyyla, baby." We sat on the ground and breathed. Lady Esther. Apple blossoms. I still go soft when I smell one or the other. Roberta was going home. The big cross and the big Bible was coming to get her and she seemed sort of glad and sort of not. I thought I would die in that room of four beds without her and I knew Bozo had plans to move some other dumped kid in there with me. Roberta promised to write every day, which was really sweet of her because she couldn't read a lick so how could she write anybody. I would have drawn pictures and sent them to her but she never gave me her address. Little by little she faded. Her wet socks with the pink scalloped tops and her big serious-looking eyes—that's all I could catch when I tried to bring her to mind.

I was working behind the counter at the Howard Johnson's on the Thruway just before the Kingston exit. Not a bad job. Kind of a long ride from Newburgh,[3] but okay once I got there. Mine was the second night shift—eleven to seven. Very light until a Greyhound checked in for breakfast around six-thirty. At that hour the sun was all the way clear of the hills behind the restaurant. The place looked better at night—more like shelter—but I loved it when the sun broke in, even if it did show all the cracks in the vinyl and the speckled floor looked dirty no matter what the mop boy did.

It was August and a bus crowd was just unloading. They would stand around a long while: going to the john, and looking at gifts and junk-for-sale machines, reluctant to sit down so soon. Even to eat. I was trying to fill the coffee pots and get them all situated on the electric burners when I saw her. She was sitting in a booth smoking a cigarette with two guys smothered in head and facial hair. Her own hair was so big and wild I could hardly see her face. But the eyes. I would know them anywhere. She had on a powder-blue halter and shorts outfit and earrings the size of bracelets. Talk about lipstick and eyebrow pencil. She made the big girls look like nuns. I couldn't get off the counter until seven o'clock, but I kept watching the booth in case they got up to leave before that. My replacement was on time for a change, so I counted and stacked my receipts as fast as I could and signed off. I walked over to the booth, smiling and wondering if she would remember me. Or even if she wanted to remember me. Maybe she didn't want to be reminded of St. Bonny's or to have anybody know she was ever there. I know I never talked about it to anybody.

I put my hands in my apron pockets and leaned against the back of the booth facing them.

"Roberta? Roberta Fisk?"

She looked up. "Yeah?"

"Twyla."

She squinted for a second and then said, "Wow."

"Remember me?"

"Sure. Hey. Wow."

"It's been a while," I said, and gave a smile to the two hairy guys.

"Yeah. Wow. You work here?"

"Yeah," I said. "I live in Newburgh."

"Newburgh? No kidding?" She laughed then a private laugh that included the guys but only the guys, and they laughed with her. What could I do but laugh too and wonder why I was standing there with my knees showing out from under that uniform. Without looking I could see the blue and white triangle on my head, my hair shapeless in a net, my ankles thick in white oxfords. Nothing could have been less sheer than my stockings. There was this silence that came down right after I laughed. A silence it was her turn to fill up. With introductions, maybe, to her boyfriends or an invitation to sit down and have a Coke. Instead she lit a cigarette off the one she'd just finished and said, "We're on our way to the Coast. He's got an appointment with Hendrix." She gestured casually toward the boy next to her.

"Hendrix? Fantastic," I said. "Really fantastic. What's she doing now?"

---

3. City on the Hudson River north of New York City.

Roberta coughed on her cigarette and the two guys rolled their eyes up at the ceiling.

50   "Hendrix. Jimi Hendrix, asshole. He's only the biggest—Oh, wow. Forget it."

I was dismissed without anyone saying goodbye, so I thought I would do it for her.

"How's your mother?" I asked. Her grin cracked her whole face. She swallowed. "Fine," she said. "How's yours?"

"Pretty as a picture," I said and turned away. The backs of my knees were damp. Howard Johnson's really was a dump in the sunlight.

James is as comfortable as a house slipper. He liked my cooking and I liked his big loud family. They have lived in Newburgh all of their lives and talk about it the way people do who have always known a home. His grandmother is a porch swing older than his father and when they talk about streets and avenues and buildings they call them names they no longer have. They still call the A & P[4] Rico's because it stands on property once a mom and pop store owned by Mr. Rico. And they call the new community college Town Hall because it once was. My mother-in-law puts up jelly and cucumbers and buys butter wrapped in cloth from a dairy. James and his father talk about fishing and baseball and I can see them all together on the Hudson in a raggedy skiff. Half the population of Newburgh is on welfare now, but to my husband's family it was still some upstate paradise of a time long past. A time of ice houses and vegetable wagons, coal furnaces and children weeding gardens. When our son was born my mother-in-law gave me the crib blanket that had been hers.

55   But the town they remembered had changed. Something quick was in the air. Magnificent old houses, so ruined they had become shelter for squatters and rent risks, were bought and renovated. Smart IBM[5] people moved out of their suburbs back into the city and put shutters up and herb gardens in their backyards. A brochure came in the mail announcing the opening of a Food Emporium. Gourmet food it said—and listed items the rich IBM crowd would want. It was located in a new mall at the edge of town and I drove out to shop there one day—just to see. It was late in June. After the tulips were gone and the Queen Elizabeth roses were open everywhere. I trailed my cart along the aisle tossing in smoked oysters and Robert's sauce and things I knew would sit in my cupboard for years. Only when I found some Klondike ice cream bars did I feel less guilty about spending James's fireman's salary so foolishly. My father-in-law ate them with the same gusto little Joseph did.

Waiting in the check-out line I heard a voice say, "Twyla!"

The classical music piped over the aisles had affected me and the woman leaning toward me was dressed to kill. Diamonds on her hand, a smart white summer dress. "I'm Mrs. Benson," I said.

"Ho. Ho. The Big Bozo," she sang.

For a split second I didn't know what she was talking about. She had a bunch of asparagus and two cartons of fancy water.

60   "Roberta!"

---

4. Supermarket, part of a chain originally known as The Great Atlantic and Pacific Tea Company.
5. The International Business Machine Corporation, which had its executive headquarters in Poughkeepsie, New York.

"Right."

"For heaven's sake. Roberta."

"You look great," she said.

"So do you. Where are you? Here? In Newburgh?"

"Yes. Over in Annandale." 65

I was opening my mouth to say more when the cashier called my attention to her empty counter.

"Meet you outside." Roberta pointed her finger and went into the express line.

I placed the groceries and kept myself from glancing around to check Roberta's progress. I remembered Howard Johnson's and looking for a chance to speak only to be greeted with a stingy "wow." But she was waiting for me and her huge hair was sleek now, smooth around a small, nicely shaped head. Shoes, dress, everything lovely and summery and rich. I was dying to know what happened to her, how she got from Jimi Hendrix to Annandale, a neighborhood full of doctors and IBM executives. Easy, I thought. Everything is so easy for them. They think they own the world.

"How long," I asked her. "How long have you been here?"

"A year. I got married to a man who lives here. And you, you're married too, 70 right? Benson, you said."

"Yeah. James Benson."

"And is he nice?"

"Oh, is he nice?"

"Well, is he?" Roberta's eyes were steady as though she really meant the question and wanted an answer.

"He's wonderful, Roberta. Wonderful." 75

"So you're happy."

"Very."

"That's good," she said and nodded her head. "I always hoped you'd be happy. Any kids? I know you have kids."

"One. A boy. How about you?"

"Four." 80

"Four?"

She laughed. "Step kids. He's a widower."

"Oh."

"Got a minute? Let's have a coffee."

I thought about the Klondikes melting and the inconvenience of going all the 85 way to my car and putting the bags in the trunk. Served me right for buying all that stuff I didn't need. Roberta was ahead of me.

"Put them in my car. It's right here."

And then I saw the dark blue limousine.

"You married a Chinaman?"

"No," she laughed. "He's the driver."

"Oh, my. If the Big Bozo could see you now." 90

We both giggled. Really giggled. Suddenly, in just a pulse beat, twenty years disappeared and all of it came rushing back. The big girls (whom we called gar girls—Roberta's misheard word for the evil stone faces described in a civics class) there dancing in the orchard, the ploppy mashed potatoes, the double weenies, the Spam with pineapple. We went into the coffee shop holding on to one another and I tried to think why we were glad to see each other this time and not before. Once, twelve years ago, we passed like strangers. A black girl and a white girl meeting in a Howard Johnson's on the road and having nothing to say. One in a blue and white triangle waitress hat—the other on her way to see Hendrix. Now we were behaving like sisters separated for much too long. Those four short months were nothing in time. Maybe it was the thing itself. Just being there, together. Two little girls who knew what nobody else in the world knew—how not to ask questions. How to believe what had to be believed. There was politeness in that reluctance and generosity as well. Is your mother sick too? No, she dances all night. Oh—and an understanding nod.

We sat in a booth by the window and fell into recollection like veterans.

"Did you ever learn to read?"

"Watch." She picked up the menu. "Special of the day. Cream of corn soup. Entrées. Two dots and a wriggly line. Quiche. Chef salad, scallops . . ."

95   I was laughing and applauding when the waitress came up.

"Remember the Easter baskets?"

"And how we tried to *introduce* them?"

"Your mother with that cross like two telephone poles."

"And yours with those tight slacks."

100   We laughed so loudly heads turned and made the laughter harder to suppress.

"What happened to the Jimi Hendrix date?"

Roberta made a blow-out sound with her lips.

"When he died I thought about you."

"Oh, you heard about him finally?"

105   "Finally. Come on, I was a small-town country waitress."

"And I was a small-town country dropout. God, were we wild. I still don't know how I got out of there alive."

"But you did."

"I did. I really did. Now I'm Mrs. Kenneth Norton."

"Sounds like a mouthful."

110   "It is."

"Servants and all?"

Roberta held up two fingers.

"Ow! What does he do?"

"Computers and stuff. What do I know?"

115   "I don't remember a hell of a lot from those days, but Lord, St. Bonny's is as clear as daylight. Remember Maggie? The day she fell down and those gar girls laughed at her?"

Roberta looked up from her salad and stared at me. "Maggie didn't fall," she said.

"Yes, she did. You remember."

"No, Twyla. They knocked her down. Those girls pushed her down and tore her clothes. In the orchard."

"I don't—that's not what happened."

120   "Sure it is. In the orchard. Remember how scared we were?"

"Wait a minute. I don't remember any of that."

"And Bozo was fired."

"You're crazy. She was there when I left. You left before me."

"I went back. You weren't there when they fired Bozo."

"What?"　125

"Twice. Once for a year when I was about ten, another for two months when I was fourteen. That's when I ran away."

"You ran away from St. Bonny's?"

"I had to. What do you want? Me dancing in that orchard?"

"Are you sure about Maggie?"

"Of course I'm sure. You've blocked it, Twyla. It happened. Those girls had　130 behavior problems, you know."

"Didn't they, though. But why can't I remember the Maggie thing?"

"Believe me. It happened. And we were there."

"Who did you room with when you went back?" I asked her as if I would know her. The Maggie thing was troubling me.

"Creeps. They tickled themselves in the night."

My ears were itching and I wanted to go home suddenly. This was all very well　135 but she couldn't just comb her hair, wash her face and pretend everything was hunky-dory. After the Howard Johnson's snub. And no apology. Nothing.

"Were you on dope or what that time at Howard Johnson's?" I tried to make my voice sound friendlier than I felt.

"Maybe, a little. I never did drugs much. Why?"

"I don't know; you acted sort of like you didn't want to know me then."

"Oh, Twyla, you know how it was in those days: black—white. You know how everything was."

But I didn't know. I thought it was just the opposite. Busloads of blacks and　140 whites came into Howard Johnson's together. They roamed together then: students, musicians, lovers, protesters. You got to see everything at Howard Johnson's and blacks were very friendly with whites in those days. But sitting there with nothing on my plate but two hard tomato wedges wondering about the melting Klondikes it seemed childish remembering the slight. We went to her car, and with the help of the driver, got my stuff into my station wagon.

"We'll keep in touch this time," she said.

"Sure," I said. "Sure. Give me a call."

"I will," she said, and then just as I was sliding behind the wheel, she leaned into the window. "By the way. Your mother. Did she ever stop dancing?"

I shook my head. "No. Never."

Roberta nodded.　145

"And yours? Did she ever get well?"

She smiled a tiny sad smile. "No. She never did. Look, call me, okay?"

"Okay," I said, but I knew I wouldn't. Roberta had messed up my past somehow with that business about Maggie. I wouldn't forget a thing like that. Would I?

Strife came to us that fall. At least that's what the paper called it. Strife. Racial strife. The word made me think of a bird—a big shrieking bird out of 1,000,000,000 B.C. Flapping its wings and cawing. Its eye with no lid always bearing down on you. All day it screeched and at night it slept on the rooftops. It woke you in the morning and from the *Today* show to the eleven o'clock news it kept you an awful company. I couldn't figure it out from one day to the next. I knew I was supposed to feel something strong, but I didn't know what, and James wasn't any help. Joseph was on the list of kids to be transferred from the junior high school to another one at some far-out-of-the-way place and I thought it was a good thing until I heard it was a bad thing. I mean I didn't know. All the schools seemed dumps to me, and the fact that one was nicer looking didn't hold much weight. But the papers were full of it and then the kids began to get jumpy. In August, mind you. Schools weren't even open yet. I thought Joseph might be frightened to go over there, but he didn't seem scared so I forgot about it, until I found myself driving along Hudson Street out there by the school they were trying to integrate and saw a line of women marching. And who do you suppose was in line, big as life, holding a sign in front of her bigger than her mother's cross? MOTHERS HAVE RIGHTS TOO! it said.

150   I drove on, and then changed my mind. I circled the block, slowed down, and honked my horn.

Roberta looked over and when she saw me she waved. I didn't wave back, but I didn't move either. She handed her sign to another woman and came over to where I was parked.

"Hi."

"What are you doing?"

"Picketing. What's it look like?"

155   "What for?"

"What do you mean. 'What for?' They want to take my kids and send them out of the neighborhood. They don't want to go."

"So what if they go to another school? My boy's being bussed too, and I don't mind. Why should you?"

"It's not about us, Twyla. Me and you. It's about our kids."

"What's more *us* than that?"

160   "Well, it is a free country."

"Not yet, but it will be."

"What the hell does that mean? I'm not doing anything to you."

"You really think that?"

"I know it."

165   "I wonder what made me think you were different."

"I wonder what made me think you were different."

"Look at them," I said. "Just look. Who do they think they are? Swarming all over the place like they own it. And now they think they can decide where my child goes to school. Look at them, Roberta. They're Bozos."

Roberta turned around and looked at the women. Almost all of them were standing still now, waiting. Some were even edging toward us. Roberta looked at me out of some refrigerator behind her eyes. "No, they're not. They're just mothers."

"And what am I? Swiss cheese?"

170   "I used to curl your hair."

"I hated your hands in my hair."

The women were moving. Our faces looked mean to them of course and they looked as though they could not wait to throw themselves in front of a police car, or better yet, into my car and drag me away by my ankles. Now they surrounded my car and gently, gently began to rock it. I swayed back and forth like a sideways yo-yo. Automatically I reached for Roberta, like the old days in the orchard when they saw us watching them and we had to get out of there, and if one of us fell the other pulled her up and if one of us was caught the other stayed to kick and scratch, and neither would leave the other behind. My arm shot out of the car window but no receiving hand was there. Roberta was looking at me sway from side to side in the car and her face was still. My purse slid from the car seat down under the dashboard. The four policemen who had been drinking Tab in their car finally got the message and strolled over, forcing their way through the women. Quietly, firmly they spoke. "Okay, ladies. Back in line or off the streets."

Some of them went away willingly; others had to be urged away from the car doors and the hood. Roberta didn't move. She was looking steadily at me. I was fumbling to turn on the ignition, which wouldn't catch because the gearshift was still in drive. The seats of the car were a mess because the swaying had thrown my grocery coupons all over it and my purse was sprawled on the floor.

"Maybe I am different now, Twyla. But you're not. You're the same little state kid who kicked a poor old black lady when she was down on the ground. You kicked a black lady and you have the nerve to call me a bigot."

The coupons were everywhere and the guts of my purse were bunched under 175 the dashboard. What was she saying? Black? Maggie wasn't black.

"She wasn't black," I said.

"Like hell she wasn't, and you kicked her. We both did. You kicked a black lady who couldn't even scream."

"Liar!"

"You're the liar! Why don't you just go on home and leave us alone, huh?"

She turned away and I skidded away from the curb. 180

The next morning I went into the garage and cut the side out of the carton our portable TV had come in. It wasn't nearly big enough, but after a while I had a decent sign: red spray-painted letters on a white background—AND SO DO CHIL-DREN ****. I meant just to go down to the school and tack it up somewhere so those cows on the picket line across the street could see it, but when I got there, some ten or so others had already assembled—protesting the cows across the street. Police permits and everything. I got in line and we strutted in time on our side while Roberta's group strutted on theirs. That first day we were all digni-fied, pretending the other side didn't exist. The second day there was name call-ing and finger gestures. But that was about all. People changed signs from time to time, but Roberta never did and neither did I. Actually my sign didn't make sense without Roberta's. "And so do children what?" one of the women on my side asked me. Have rights, I said, as though it was obvious.

Roberta didn't acknowledge my presence in any way and I got to thinking maybe she didn't know I was there. I began to pace myself in the line, jostling people one minute and lagging behind the next, so Roberta and I could reach the end of our respective lines at the same time and there would be a moment in our turn when we would face each other. Still, I couldn't tell whether she saw me and knew my sign was for her. The next day I went early before we were sched-uled to assemble. I waited until she got there before I exposed my new creation. As soon as she hoisted her MOTHERS HAVE RIGHTS TOO I began to wave my new one, which said, HOW WOULD YOU KNOW? I know she saw that one, but I had gotten addicted now. My signs got crazier each day, and the women on my side decided that I was a kook. They couldn't make heads or tails out of my brilliant scream-ing posters.

I brought a painted sign in queenly red with huge black letters that said, IS YOUR MOTHER WELL? Roberta took her lunch break and didn't come back for the rest of the day or any day after. Two days later I stopped going too and couldn't have been missed because nobody understood my signs anyway.

It was a nasty six weeks. Classes were suspended and Joseph didn't go to anybody's school until October. The children—everybody's children—soon got bored with that extended vacation they thought was going to be so great. They looked at TV until their eyes flattened. I spent a couple of mornings tutoring my son, as the other mothers said we should. Twice I opened a text from last year that he had never turned in. Twice he yawned in my face. Other mothers organized living room sessions so the kids would keep up. None of the kids could concentrate so they drifted back to *The Price Is Right*[6] and *The Brady Bunch*. When the school finally opened there were fights once or twice and some sirens roared through the streets every once in a while. There were a lot of photographers from Albany. And just when ABC was about to send up a news crew, the kids settled down like nothing in the world had happened. Joseph hung my HOW WOULD YOU KNOW? sign in his bedroom. I don't know what became of AND SO DO CHILDREN ****. I think my father-in-law cleaned some fish on it. He was always puttering around in our garage. Each of his five children lived in Newburgh and he acted as though he had five extra homes.

185   I couldn't help looking for Roberta when Joseph graduated from high school, but I didn't see her. It didn't trouble me much what she had said to me in the car. I mean the kicking part. I know I didn't do that, I couldn't do that. But I was puzzled by her telling me Maggie was black. When I thought about it I actually couldn't be certain. She wasn't pitch-black, I knew, or I would have remembered that. What I remember was the kiddie hat, and the semicircle legs. I tried to reassure myself about the race thing for a long time until it dawned on me that the truth was already there, and Roberta knew it. I didn't kick her; I didn't join in with the gar girls and kick that lady, but I sure did want to. We watched and never tried to help her and never called for help. Maggie was my dancing mother. Deaf, I thought, and dumb. Nobody inside. Nobody who would hear you if you cried in the night. Nobody who could tell you anything important that you could use. Rocking, dancing, swaying as she walked. And when the gar girls pushed her down, and started roughhousing, I knew she wouldn't scream, couldn't—just like me—and I was glad about that.

We decided not to have a tree, because Christmas would be at my mother-in-law's house, so why have a tree at both places? Joseph was at SUNY New Paltz and we had to economize, we said. But at the last minute, I changed my mind. Nothing could be that bad. So I rushed around town looking for a tree, something small but wide. By the time I found a place, it was snowing and very late. I dawdled like it was the most important purchase in the world and the tree man was fed up with me. Finally I chose one and had it tied onto the trunk of the car. I drove away slowly because the sand trucks were not out yet and the streets could be murder at the beginning of a snowfall. Downtown the streets were wide and rather empty except for a cluster of people coming out of the Newburgh Hotel. The one hotel in town that wasn't built out of cardboard and Plexiglas. A party, probably. The men huddled in the snow were dressed in tails and the women had on furs. Shiny things glittered from underneath their coats. It made me tired to look at them. Tired, tired, tired. On the next corner was a small diner with loops and loops of paper bells in the window. I stopped the car and went in. Just for a

6. Television game show popular in the 1970s. *The Brady Bunch:* television sitcom popular in the 1970s.

cup of coffee and twenty minutes of peace before I went home and tried to finish everything before Christmas Eve.

"Twyla?"

There she was. In a silvery evening gown and dark fur coat. A man and another woman were with her, the man fumbling for change to put in the cigarette machine. The woman was humming and tapping on the counter with her fingernails. They all looked a little bit drunk.

"Well. It's you."

"How are you?"

190

I shrugged. "Pretty good. Frazzled. Christmas and all."

"Regular?" called the woman from the counter.

"Fine," Roberta called back and then, "Wait for me in the car."

She slipped into the booth beside me. "I have to tell you something, Twyla. I made up my mind if I ever saw you again, I'd tell you."

"I'd just as soon not hear anything, Roberta. It doesn't matter now, anyway." 195

"No," she said. "Not about that."

"Don't be long," said the woman. She carried two regulars to go and the man peeled his cigarette pack as they left.

"It's about St. Bonny's and Maggie."

"Oh, please."

"Listen to me. I really did think she was black. I didn't make that up. I really 200 thought so. But now I can't be sure. I just remember her as old, so old. And because she couldn't talk—well, you know, I thought she was crazy. She'd been brought up in an institution like my mother was and like I thought I would be too. And you were right. We didn't kick her. It was the gar girls. Only them. But, well, I wanted to. I really wanted them to hurt her. I said we did it, too. You and me, but that's not true. And I don't want you to carry that around. It was just that I wanted to do it so bad that day—wanting to is doing it."

Her eyes were watery from the drinks she'd had, I guess. I know it's that way with me. One glass of wine and I start bawling over the littlest thing.

"We were kids, Roberta."

"Yeah. Yeah. I know, just kids."

"Eight."

"Eight."

"And lonely."

205

"Scared, too."

She wiped her cheeks with the heel of her hand and smiled. "Well, that's all I wanted to say."

I nodded and couldn't think of any way to fill the silence that went from the diner past the paper bells on out into the snow. It was heavy now. I thought I'd better wait for the sand trucks before starting home.

"Thanks, Roberta."

210

"Sure."

"Did I tell you? My mother, she never did stop dancing."

"Yes. You told me. And mine, she never got well." Roberta lifted her hands from the tabletop and covered her face with her palms. When she took them away she really was crying. "Oh shit, Twyla. Shit, shit, shit. What the hell happened to Maggie?"

1983

QUESTIONS

1. At the end of "Recitatif," how does Twyla's and Roberta's exploration of the "truth" of what they had seen at St. Bonny's many years earlier affect your sense of the "truth" of later episodes in the story? Is either Twyla or Roberta more reliable than the other?

2. At what point in the story do you first begin to make assumptions about the race and class of the two main characters, Twyla and Roberta? Why? Do you change your mind later in the story? When and why so—or not? What is the significance of Morrison's choice both to withhold information about the characters' race and class and to have Twyla narrate the story?

3. How does the relationship between Twyla and Roberta evolve over the course of the story?

Authors on Their Work: TONI MORRISON

From "*Toni Morrison: The Art of Fiction CXXXIV*" (1993)*

MORRISON: [William] Faulkner in *Absalom, Absalom!* spends the entire book tracing race, and you can't find it. No one can see it, even the character who *is* black can't see it. . . . Do you know how hard it is to withhold that kind of information but hinting, pointing all of the time? And then to reveal it in order to say that it is *not* the point anyway? It is technically just astonishing. As a reader you have been forced to hunt for a drop of black blood that means everything and nothing. The insanity of racism.

• • •

MORRISON: . . . I wrote a story entitled "Recitatif," in which there are two little girls in an orphanage, one white and one black. But the reader doesn't know which is white and which is black. I use class codes, but no racial codes.

INTERVIEWER: Is this meant to confuse the reader?

MORRISON: Well, yes. But to provoke and enlighten. I did that as a lark. What was exciting was to be forced as a writer not to be lazy and rely on obvious codes. Soon as I say, "Black woman . . ." I can rest on or provoke predictable responses, but if I leave it out then I have to talk about her in a complicated way—as a person.

*Elisa Shappell, with Claudia Brodsky Lacour, "Toni Morrison: The Art of Fiction CXXXIV." *Paris Review* 128 (Fall 1993): 82–125.

HA JIN

In Broad Daylight

While I was eating corn cake and jellyfish at lunch, our gate was thrown open and Bare Hips hopped in. His large wooden pistol was stuck partly inside the waist of his blue shorts. "White Cat," he called me by my nickname, "hurry, let's go. They caught Old Whore at her home. They're going to take her through the streets this afternoon."

"Really?" I put down my bowl, which was almost empty, and rushed to the inner room for my undershirt and sandals. "I'll be back in a second."

"Bare Hips, did you say they'll parade Mu Ying today?" I heard Grandma ask in her husky voice.

"Yes, all the kids on our street have left for her house. I came to tell White Cat." He paused. "Hey, White Cat, hurry up!"

"Coming," I cried out, still looking for my sandals.   5

"Good, good!" Grandma said to Bare Hips, while flapping at flies with her large palm-leaf fan. "They should burn the bitch on Heaven Lamp like they did in the old days."

"Come, let's go," Bare Hips said to me the moment I was back. He turned to the door; I picked up my wooden scimitar and followed him.

"Put on your shoes, dear." Grandma stretched out her fan to stop me.

"No time for that, Grandma. I've got to be quick, or I'll miss something and won't be able to tell you the whole story when I get back."

We dashed into the street while Grandma was shouting behind us. "Come   10 back. Take the rubber shoes with you."

We charged toward Mu Ying's home on Eternal Way, waving our weapons above our heads. Grandma was crippled and never came out of our small yard. That was why I had to tell her about what was going on outside. But she knew Mu Ying well, just as all the old women in our town knew Mu well and hated her. Whenever they heard that she had a man in her home again, these women would say, "This time they ought to burn Old Whore on Heaven Lamp."

What they referred to was the old way of punishing an adulteress. Though they had lived in New China for almost two decades, some ancient notions still stuck in their heads. Grandma told me about many of the executions in the old days that she had seen with her own eyes. Officials used to have the criminals of adultery executed in two different ways. They beheaded the man. He was tied to a stake on the platform at the marketplace. At the first blare of horns, a masked headsman ascended the platform holding a broad ax before his chest; at the second blare of horns, the headsman approached the criminal and raised the ax over his head; at the third blare of horns, the head was lopped off and fell to the ground. If the man's family members were waiting beneath the platform, his head would be picked up to be buried together with his body; if no family member was nearby, dogs would carry the head away and chase each other around until they ate up the flesh and returned for the body.

Unlike the man, the woman involved was executed on Heaven Lamp. She was hung naked upside down above a wood fire whose flames could barely touch her scalp. And two men flogged her away with whips made of bulls' penises. Meanwhile she screamed for help and the whole town could hear her. Since the fire merely scorched her head, it took at least half a day for her to stop shrieking and a day and a night to die completely. People used to believe that the way of punishment was justified by Heaven, so the fire was called Heaven Lamp. But that was an old custom; nobody believed they would burn Mu Ying in that way.

Mu's home, a small granite house with cement tiles built a year before, was next to East Wind Inn on the northern side of Eternal Way. When we entered that street, Bare Hips and I couldn't help looking around tremulously, because that area was the territory of the children living there. Two of the fiercest boys, who would kill without having second thoughts, ruled that part of our town. Whenever a boy from another street wandered into Eternal Way, they'd capture him and beat him up. Of course we did the same thing; if we caught one of them in our territory, we'd at least confiscate whatever he had with him: grasshopper cages, slingshots, bottle caps, marbles, cartridge cases, and so on. We would also make him call every one of us "Father" or "Grandfather." But today hundreds of children and grown-ups were pouring into Eternal Way; two dozen urchins on that street surely couldn't hold their ground. Besides, they had already adopted a truce, since they were more eager to see the Red Guards[1] drag Mu Ying out of her den.

15   When we arrived, Mu was being brought out through a large crowd at the front gate. Inside her yard there were three rows of colorful washing hung on iron wires, and there was also a grape trellis. Seven or eight children were in there, plucking off grapes and eating them. Two Red Guards held Mu Ying by the arms, and the other Red Guards, about twenty of them, followed behind. They were all from Dalian City and wore home-made army uniforms. God knew how they came to know that there was a bad woman in our town. Though people hated Mu and called her names, no one would rough her up. Those Red Guards were strangers, so they wouldn't mind doing it.

Surprisingly, Mu looked rather calm; she neither protested nor said a word. The two Red Guards let go of her arms, and she followed them quietly into West Street. We all moved with them. Some children ran several paces ahead to look back at her.

Mu wore a sky-blue dress, which made her different from the other women who always wore jackets and pants suitable for honest work. In fact, even we small boys could tell that she was really handsome, perhaps the best looking woman of her age in our town. Though in her fifties, she didn't have a single gray hair; she was a little plump, but because of her long legs and arms she appeared rather queenly. While most of the women had sallow faces, hers looked white and healthy like fresh milk.

Skipping in front of the crowd, Bare Hips turned around and cried out at her, "Shameless Old Whore!"

She glanced at him, her round eyes flashing; the purple wart beside her left nostril grew darker. Grandma had assured me that Mu's wart was not a beauty-wart but a tear-wart. This meant that her life would be soaked in tears.

20   We knew where we were going, to White Mansion, which was our classroom building, the only two-storied house in the town. As we came to the end of West Street, a short man ran out from a street corner, panting for breath and holding a sickle. He was Meng Su, Mu Ying's husband, who sold bean jelly in summer

---

1. National student organization sponsored by Mao Zedong as an instrument to start and develop the Great Proletarian Cultural Revolution (1966–76).

and sugar-coated haws in winter at the marketplace. He paused in front of the large crowd, as though having forgotten why he had rushed over. He turned his head around to look back; there was nobody behind him. After a short moment he moved close, rather carefully.

"Please let her go," he begged the Red Guards. "Comrade Red Guards, it's all my fault. Please let her go." He put the sickle under his arm and held his hands together before his chest.

"Get out of the way!" commanded a tall young man, who must have been the leader.

"Please don't take her away. It's my fault. I haven't disciplined her well. Please give her a chance to be a new person. I promise, she won't do it again."

The crowd stopped to circle about. "What's your class status?" a square-faced young woman asked in a sharp voice.

"Poor peasant," Meng replied, his small eyes tearful and his cupped ears twitching a little. "Please let her go, sister. Have mercy on us! I'm kneeling down to you if you let her go." Before he was able to fall on his knees, two young men held him back. Tears were rolling down his dark fleshy cheeks, and his gray head began waving about. The sickle was taken away from him.

"Shut up," the tall leader yelled and slapped him across the face. "She's a snake. We traveled a hundred and fifty *li*[2] to come here to wipe out poisonous snakes and worms. If you don't stop interfering, we'll parade you with her together. Do you want to join her?"

Silence. Meng covered his face with his large hands as though feeling dizzy.

A man in the crowd said aloud, "If you can share the bed with her, why can't you share the street?"

Many of the grown-ups laughed. "Take him, take him too!" someone told the Red Guards. Meng looked scared, sobbing quietly.

His wife stared at him without saying a word. Her teeth were clenched; a faint smile passed the corners of her mouth. Meng seemed to wince under her stare. The two Red Guards let his arms go, and he stepped aside, watching his wife and the crowd move toward the school.

Of Meng Su people in our town had different opinions. Some said he was a born cuckold who didn't mind his wife's sleeping with any man as long as she could bring money home. Some believed he was a good-tempered man who had stayed with his wife mainly for their children's sake; they forgot that the three children had grown up long before and were working in big cities far away. Some thought he didn't leave his wife because he had no choice—no woman would marry such a dwarf. Grandma, for some reason, seemed to respect Meng. She told me that Mu Ying had once been raped by a group of Russian soldiers under Northern Bridge and was left on the river bank afterwards. That night her husband sneaked there and carried her back. He looked after her for a whole winter till she recovered. "Old Whore doesn't deserve that good-hearted man," Grandma would say. "She's heartless and knows only how to sell her thighs."

We entered the school's playground where about two hundred people had already gathered. "Hey, White Cat and Bare Hips," Big Shrimp called us, waving his claws. Many boys from our street were there too. We went to join them.

2. Approximately 50 miles.

The Red Guards took Mu to the front entrance of the building. Two tables had been placed between the stone lions that crouched on each side of the entrance. On one of the tables stood a tall paper hat with the big black characters on its side: "Down with Old Bitch!"

A young man in glasses raised his bony hand and started to address us, "Folks, we've gathered here today to denounce Mu Ying, who is a demon in this town."

35 "Down with Bourgeois Demons!" a slim woman Red Guard shouted. We raised our fists and repeated the slogan.

"Down with Old Bitch Mu Ying," a middle-aged man cried out with both hands in the air. He was an active revolutionary in our commune. Again we shouted, in louder voices.

The nearsighted man went on, "First, Mu Ying must confess her crime. We must see her attitude toward her own crime. Then we'll make the punishment fit both her crime and her attitude. All right, folks?"

"Right," some voices replied from the crowd.

"Mu Ying," he turned to the criminal, "you must confess everything. It's up to you now."

40 She was forced to stand on a bench. Staying below the steps, we had to raise our heads to see her face.

The questioning began. "Why do you seduce men and paralyze their revolutionary will with your bourgeois poison?" the tall leader asked in a solemn voice.

"I've never invited any man to my home, have I?" she said rather calmly. Her husband was standing at the front of the crowd, listening to her without showing any emotion, as though having lost his mind.

"Then why did they go to your house and not to others' houses?"

"They wanted to sleep with me," she replied.

45 "Shameless!" Several women hissed in the crowd.

"A true whore!"

"Scratch her!"

"Rip apart her filthy mouth!"

"Sisters," she spoke aloud. "All right, it was wrong to sleep with them. But you all know what it feels like when you want a man, don't you? Don't you once in a while have that feeling in your bones?" Contemptuously, she looked at the few withered middle-aged women standing in the front row, then closed her eyes. "Oh, you want that real man to have you in his arms and let him touch every part of your body. For that man alone you want to blossom into a woman, a real woman—"

50 "Take this, you Fox Spirit!" A stout young fellow struck her on the side with a fist like a sledgehammer. The heavy blow silenced her at once. She held her sides with both hands, gasping for breath.

"You're wrong, Mu Ying," Bare Hips's mother spoke from the front of the crowd, her forefinger pointing upward at Mu. "You have your own man, who doesn't lack an arm or a leg. It's wrong to have others' men and more wrong to pocket their money."

"I have my own man?" Mu glanced at her husband and smirked. She straightened up and said, "My man is nothing. He is no good, I mean in bed. He always comes before I feel anything."

All the adults burst out laughing. "What's that? What's so funny?" Big Shrimp asked Bare Hips.

"You didn't get it?" Bare Hips said impatiently. "You don't know anything about what happens between a man and a woman. It means that whenever she doesn't want him to come close to her he comes. Bad timing."

"It doesn't sound like that," I said.   55

Before we could argue, a large bottle of ink smashed on Mu's head and knocked her off the bench. Prone on the cement terrace, she broke into swearing and blubbering. "Oh, damn your ancestors! Whoever hit me will be childless!" Her left hand was rubbing her head. "Oh Lord of Heaven, they treat their grandma like this!"

"Serves you right!"

"A cheap weasel."

"Even a knife on her throat can't stop her."

"A pig is born to eat slop!"   60

When they put her back up on the bench, she became another person—her shoulders covered with black stains, and a red line trickling down her left temple. The scorching sun was blazing down on her as though all the black parts on her body were about to burn up. Still moaning, she turned her eyes to the spot where her husband had been standing a few minutes before. But he was no longer there.

"Down with Old Whore!" a farmer shouted in the crowd. We all followed him in one voice. She began trembling slightly.

The tall leader said to us, "In order to get rid of her counterrevolutionary airs, first, we're going to cut her hair." With a wave of his hand, he summoned the Red Guards behind him. Four men moved forward and held her down. The square-faced woman raised a large pair of scissors and thrust them into the mass of the dark hair.

"Don't, don't, please. Help, help! I'll do whatever you want me to—"

"Cut!" someone yelled.   65

"Shave her head bald!"

The woman Red Guard applied the scissors skillfully. After four or five strokes, Mu's head looked like the tail of a molting hen. She started blubbering again, her nose running and her teeth chattering.

A breeze came and swept away the fluffy curls from the terrace and scattered them on the sandy ground. It was so hot that some people took out fans, waving them continuously. The crowd stank of sweat.

Wooooo, wooooo, woo, woo. That was the train coming from Sand County at 3:30. It was a freight train, whose young drivers would toot the steam horn whenever they saw a young woman in a field beneath the track.

The questioning continued. "How many men have you slept with these years?"   70
the nearsighted man asked.

"Three."

"She's lying," a woman in the crowd cried out.

"I told the truth, sister." She wiped off the tears from her cheeks with the back of her hand.

"Who are they?" the young man asked again. "Tell us more about them."

"An officer from the Little Dragon Mountain, and—"   75

"How many times did he come to your house?"

"I can't remember. Probably twenty."

"What's his name?"

"I don't know. He told me he was a big officer."

80   "Did you take money from him?"

"Yes."

"How much for each time?"

"Twenty *yuan*."[3]

"How much altogether?"

85   "Probably five hundred."

"Comrades and Revolutionary Masses," the young man turned to us, "how shall we handle this parasite that sucked blood out of a revolutionary officer?"

"Quarter her with four horses!" an old woman yelled.

"Burn her on Heaven Lamp!"

"Poop on her face!" a small fat girl shouted, her hand raised like a tiny pistol with the thumb cocked up and the forefinger aimed at Mu. Some grown-ups snickered.

90   Then a pair of old cloth-shoes, a symbol for a promiscuous woman, were passed to the front. The slim young woman took the shoes and tied them together with the laces. She climbed on a table and was about to hang the shoes around Mu's neck. Mu elbowed the woman aside and knocked the shoes to the ground. The stout young fellow picked up the shoes, and jumped twice to slap her on the cheeks with the soles. "You're so stubborn. Do you want to change yourself or not?" he asked.

"Yes, I do," she replied meekly and dared not stir a bit. Meanwhile the shoes were being hung around her neck.

"Now she looks like a real whore," a woman commented.

"Sing us a tune, Sis," a farmer demanded.

"Comrades," the man in glasses resumed, "let us continue the denunciation." He turned to Mu and asked, "Who are the other men?"

95   "A farmer from Apple Village."

"How many times with him?"

"Once."

"Liar!"

"She's lying!"

100   "Give her one on the mouth!"

The young man raised his hands to calm the crowd down and questioned her again, "How much did you take from him?"

"Eighty *yuan*."

"One night?"

"Yes."

105   "Tell us more about it. How can you make us believe you?"

"That old fellow came to town to sell piglets. He sold a whole litter for eighty, and I got the money."

"Why did you charge him more than the officer?"

"No, I didn't. He did it four times in one night."

Some people were smiling and whispering to each other. A woman said that old man must have been a widower or never married.

110   "What's his name?" the young man went on.

---

3. Chinese currency; today, a yuan is worth about 15 cents U.S.

"No idea."

"Was he rich or poor?"

"Poor."

"Comrades," the young man addressed us, "here we have a poor peasant who worked with his sow for a whole year and got only a litter of piglets. That money is the salt and oil money for his family, but this snake swallowed the money with one gulp. What shall we do with her?"

"Kill her!"   115

"Break her skull!"

"Beat the piss out of her!"

A few farmers began to move forward to the steps, waving their fists or rubbing their hands.

"Hold," a woman Red Guard with a huge Chairman Mao badge on her chest spoke in a commanding voice. "The Great Leader has instructed us: 'For our struggle we need words but not force.' Comrades, we can easily wipe her out with words. Force doesn't solve ideological problems." What she said restrained those enraged farmers, who remained in the crowd.

Wooo, woo, wooo, wooooooooooooo, an engine screamed in the south. It was strange, 120
because the drivers of the four o'clock train were a bunch of old men who seldom blew the horn.

"Who is the third man?" the nearsighted man continued to question Mu.

"A Red Guard."

The crowd broke into laughter. Some women asked the Red Guards to give her another bottle of ink. "Mu Ying, you're responsible for your own words," the young man said in a serious voice.

"I told you the truth."

"What's his name?"   125

"I don't know. He led the propaganda team that passed here last month."

"How many times did you sleep with him?"

"Once."

"How much did you make out of him?"

"None. That stingy dog wouldn't pay a cent. He said he was the worker who 130
should be paid."

"So you were outsmarted by him?"

Some men in the crowd guffawed. Mu wiped her nose with her thumb, and at once she wore a thick mustache. "I taught him a lesson, though," she said.

"How?"

"I tweaked his ears, gave him a bleeding nose, and kicked him out. I told him never come back."

People began talking to each other. Some said that she was a strong woman 135
who knew what was hers. Some said the Red Guard was no good; if you got something you had to pay for it. A few women declared that the rascal deserved such a treatment.

"Dear Revolutionary Masses," the tall leader started to speak. "We all have heard the crime Mu Ying committed. She lured one of our officers and one of our poor peasants into the evil water, and she beat a Red Guard black and blue. Shall we let her go home without punishment or shall we teach her an unforgettable lesson so that she won't do it again?"

"Teach her a lesson!" some voices cried out in unison.

"Then we're going to parade her through the streets."

Two Red Guards pulled Mu off the bench, and another picked up the tall hat. "Brothers and sisters," she begged, "please let me off just for once. Don't, don't! I promise I'll correct my fault. I'll be a new person. Help! Oh, help!"

140 It was no use resisting; within seconds the huge hat was firmly planted on her head. They also hung a big placard between the cloth-shoes lying against her chest. The words on the placard read:

> I am a Broken Shoe
> My Crime Deserves Death

They put a gong in her hands and ordered her to strike it when she announced the words written on the inner side of the gong.

My pals and I followed the crowd, feeling rather tired. Boys from East Street were wilder; they threw stones at Mu's back. One stone struck the back of her head and blood dropped on her neck. But they were stopped immediately by the Red Guards, because a stone missed Mu and hit a man on the shoulder. Old people, who couldn't follow us, were standing on chairs and windowsills with pipes and towels in their hands. We were going to parade her through every street. It would take several hours to finish the whole thing, as the procession would stop for a short while at every street corner.

Bong, Mu struck the gong and declared, "I am an evil monster."

"Louder!"

Dong, bong—"I have stolen men. I stink for a thousand years."

145 When we were coming out of the marketplace, Cross Eyes emerged from a narrow lane. He grasped my wrist and Bare Hips's arm and said, "Someone is dead at the train station. Come, let's go there and have a look." The word "dead" at once roused us. We, half a dozen boys, set out running to the train station.

The dead man was Meng Su. A crowd had gathered at the railroad a hundred meters east of the station house. A few men were examining the rail that was stained with blood and studded with bits of flesh. One man paced along the darker part of the rail and announced that the train had dragged Meng at least twenty meters.

Beneath the track, Meng's headless body lay in a ditch. One of his feet was missing, and the whitish shinbone stuck out several inches long. There were so many openings on his body that he looked like a large piece of fresh meat on the counter in the butcher's. Beyond him, ten paces away, a big straw hat remained on the ground. We were told that his head was under the hat.

Bare Hips and I went down the slope to have a glimpse at the head. Other boys dared not take a peep. We two looked at each other, asking with our eyes who should raise the straw hat. I held out my wooden scimitar and lifted the rim of the hat a little with the sword. A swarm of bluebottles charged out, droning like provoked wasps. We bent over to peek at the head. Two long teeth pierced through the upper lip. An eyeball was missing. The gray hair was no longer perceivable, as it was covered with mud and dirt. The open mouth filled with purplish mucus. A tiny lizard skipped, sliding away into the grass.

"Oh!" Bare Hips began vomiting. Sorghum gruel mixed with bits of string beans splashed on a yellowish boulder. "Leave it alone, White Cat."

150 We lingered at the station, listening to different versions of the accident. Some people said that Meng had gotten drunk and dropped asleep on the track.

Some said he hadn't slept at all but laughed hysterically walking in the middle of the track toward the coming train. Some said he had not drunk a drop, as he had spoken with tears in his eyes to a few persons he had run into on his way to the station. In any case, he was dead, torn to pieces.

That evening when I was coming home, I heard Mu Ying groaning in the smoky twilight. "Take me home. Oh, help me. Who can help me? Where are you? Why don't you come and carry me home?"

She was lying at the bus stop, alone.

1993

QUESTIONS

1. Which, if any, character seems to be the protagonist of "In Broad Daylight"? Or might its protagonist be the townspeople collectively or even New China as a whole?
2. At one point in the story, the narrator tells us about the "different opinions" of Meng Su held by the townspeople (par. 31). What different opinions about both Meng Su and his wife, Mu Ying, are expressed and enacted by the other characters in the story? Why do the townspeople and the Red Guard seem to behave as they do toward the couple?
3. What do you think happened to Meng Su, and why? What is the effect of Ha Jin's choice not to tell us? What is the significance of Ha Jin's choice to end the story with two very brief paragraphs about Mu Ying?

TOBY LITT

The Monster

The monster didn't know what it was—what kind of monster or even, now and again, whether a monster at all. It had lived for what felt like a long time without mirrors, which didn't exist, or puddles, which it instinctively avoided. There were other monsters in creation, or the monster assumed they were other monsters (it did not philosophize on the nature of monstrosity—all could be monsters, without a norm from which to deviate), and, had it asked them, these other monsters would probably have described it to itself, using the few words and concepts available to them: monster, creation, sun, tree, fruit, merd,[1] good, bad, up and down. But the monster was for some reason averse to this, just as it was averse to puddles, and had only learnt of the practice by overhearing one monster being described by another. The sentence it overheard was: 'Monster up up good fruit, down down bad merd.' And so the monster had always found out most about itself by touch. There were two soft floppy growths upon each side of its head, and its long curved back felt rough at the bottom, like the skin of a fruit. The monster couldn't see its own feet because its belly, which was huge, got in the way. Every time the monster explored itself, though, its hands (it definitely had hands) seemed to encounter something different. With no written language, it was impossible for the monster to record these changes or the supposed status quo which had preceded them. For example, the monster had a vague sense that,

1. Dung.

sometime in the distant past, it had either been smaller or had walked upon four legs rather than two. It didn't have a very good memory, but it was disturbed by the thought that once upon a time it had had to look up at things which now it looked down at, yes, and it had had to stretch on tiptoes to reach things which were now at eye level. Most of these things observed and grabbed were fruit, fruit on trees, and of course trees grew, too—as the monster rediscovered countless times. But not everything in creation grew at the same rate, as the monster had rediscovered more rarely. The monster tended to conclude that one of the best explanations for its sense of bigness was that it was growing faster than the rest of creation. Also, the memory of walking upon all fours could be deceptive: if the monster wanted to, it could still do this—just as, when tired, it would lower itself down until its back was flat on the ground. Because of the size of its belly, the monster could lie in no other position but this. Again because of the belly, the monster had only an intimation of what sex it was—and this it gained socially, from the kinds of monster which most commonly approached it with what seemed to be sexual intent, meaning an intent to sexually describe. 'Up up good fruit down down good good sun creation fruit.' Our monster, however, was not interested in pleasure or reproduction—it was put off the latter by its doubt as to its own nature, the former by its misery. At night, it slept—under the stars, there were many stars in creation, and its dreams were frequently of absolute certainty of being. I am this thing. This thing is me. Waking, the fact of waking and the quality of it, was invariably a disappointment. Despite its morning rage, the monster was almost always gentle with the world of creation. It had never killed anything, and if it had harmed anything, that harm had been done accidentally (except, that is, harm the monster had done to itself). It knew of the quality of good and constantly aspired towards it. And it was this sense, rather than a visual image of beauty or handsomeness, that the monster thought of as its true parentage. Someone had taught the monster not to be unnecessarily cruel, and that was mother, someone had warned it never to be unwarrantedly proud, and that was father. Whatever kinds of creation they had been, the monster's memory had finally failed any longer to remember them. Perhaps this was because the monster had lived so many days and nights. Among all the things it monstrously lacked, an accurate sense of time was the most disturbing. It knew there were days and, halfway through the days, it believed there were nights. Just after waking, it knew that the time of dreaming had passed in a different way to the time it was now in; just before sleeping, it felt joy: something was about to change and for the better. One definite experience was pain. When our monster hit its head against a tree, by accident or at full force, it knew for certain it had done it. The sharp stab at first and the dull ache afterwards helped it locate parts of its body in relation to one another. The monster wondered whether this behaviour, being cruel to itself and proud of its badness, was bad behaviour. For periods, the monster gave it up—but then it came to an indistinguished lump of time, usually during the middle of the day, and its desire for certain knowledge grew into an unbearable anguish. If the monster could have been content with the pain of anguish rather than the pain of pain, perhaps it could have been content in all areas of its life—though this thought was beyond it. The monster wandered around the areas of creation it knew best, aware that certain features were identities: trees were always different or the plural was a lie; in other words, there was only a single tree which was sometimes close to, sometimes far away from, where the monster had slept, or there were multiple trees but placed so far apart that they were not visible, one to the other, and by the time the monster had walked far enough away from one tree to find another, it had forgotten the memorized features of the first, and so was able to make a comparison. On the tree or trees were fruit, which were tastily colourful—the monster reached in the morning to touch their brightness, then found itself with half of one in its mouth. Eating had been reinvented, yet again—and the monster knew it was something that had happened before. It knew this because the action felt, like mother, both comfortable and comforting; the sensation of chewing seemed repetitive and, thus, repeated from before. This was probably, apart from the moments just after a headbash, when our monster came closest to happiness. Excretion, too, unexpectedly occurred. But, being a business of the unseen nether regions, beneath the belly, the monster wasn't all that involved with it. Just as the fruits were bright, off the ground, and attractive, so the merds were dull, underfoot, and repellent. Whether by instinct or not, the monster only deposited them at some little distance from the tree or the nearest tree. And when the slight straining was done, which took care of itself, the monster would walk away—usually without looking. Again, because of the belly, if the monster did become curious about its merds, it couldn't examine them from close up—not from above, anyway. The monster could have lain down and rolled towards the dull round smelly objects, but, before it ever did this, a feeling overcame it that nothing dull and smelly was worth the effort of rolling towards. Round objects, the monster had no objection to—and in the case of fruit was actively attracted towards. In hope, sometimes, the monster thought of its belly as a big round fruit. But just as often, in despair, the belly's roundness was that of a merd. It, the belly, was where merds came from, after all—though the monster was capable of forgetting this. The trees were also possessed of leaves. If these taught the monster any lesson, it was one of uselessness—and use. By mistake, the monster sometimes ate some leaf along with the fruit. It wasn't a bad taste, not proud or cruel like a monster could be, but it was useless. The monster spat them out, away from the tree, towards the merds. When the leaves became useful was when the sun overhead became too hot. This was when the cool beside the tree-trunk was the only good place. Several monsters would gather. 'Down tree down sun good.' The leaves were also useful when it rained and made puddles. Then, they stopped the monster becoming too cold. One day, the monster set off to—but no, there was to be no quest for true identity, no storing up of fruit for the long journey into the away-from-this-tree self. No. One day, one day of *that* sort, would never come. One day, instead, would continue to be one day—one day very like the day before and almost indistinguishable from the day after. The monster had no story, unless being a monster is story enough.

2007

QUESTIONS

1. Early in "The Monster," the narrator points out that "all could be monsters, without a norm from which to deviate." What might this mean? In what ways can and can't the monster himself seem to establish "norms" and "deviations" from norms, or to differentiate one thing or time from another? How does this shape his character and experience? How does it shape our experience of him?

2. What might you learn about what it means to be human by spending time with Litt's monster?
3. The very end of "The Monster" makes clear that it is, in part, a story about stories and fictional characters. What might it suggest about what makes both a story and a fictional character effective? What does it suggest about the relationship between character and plot? How is or isn't "being a monster . . . story enough"? Why or why not?

SUGGESTIONS FOR WRITING

1. Choose any story in this anthology in which a character changes because of the events that occur in the story. Write an essay exploring exactly how, when, and why the character changes.
2. Choose any story in this chapter and write an essay analyzing its handling of character and methods of characterization. Do the story's characters tend to be more flat or round, static or dynamic, highly individualized or nearly indistinguishable? Is indirect or direct characterization more important? How important is each type of evidence listed on the checklist that appears on page 180 in this chapter? Why and how is this treatment of character appropriate to the story?
3. Imagine that you are a lawyer with the job of defending Abner Snopes. He is undoubtedly guilty of the crime of burning Major de Spain's barn, but how might you persuade the court that he deserves leniency? Write a paper in which you lay out your argument to a jury, making sure both to support your claims with facts from the story and to anticipate the portrayal of Abner Snopes's character and behavior that the prosecution will likely put forward.
4. Write an essay comparing how the adult lives and personalities of the two central characters in "Recitatif" are shaped by their experience in the orphanage. Why and how is this experience so traumatic? How does each character understand and cope with this experience over time? In these terms, how are Twyla and Roberta both similar and different, and what role does Maggie play in their efforts to come to terms with their past?
5. Both Maggie in "Recitatif" and Mu Ying in "In Broad Daylight" might be described as *scapegoat* figures (an archetype)—a person or group of people whom a community harshly punishes, casts out, or even kills in the hope of coming together as a stronger, more united, and purer community. Write an essay exploring the validity of this claim. Why are Maggie and Mu Ying singled out? What do the other characters in each story consciously or unconsciously hope to gain by treating Maggie and Mu Ying as they do? What might these stories suggest about those whom we tend to treat as scapegoats, and why?
6. Write a few paragraphs that, like "The Monster," vividly describe a type of character whose interior life we rarely see depicted in fiction—your dog, a parakeet, a vacuum cleaner that suddenly becomes sentient. Try to give your own reader a vivid sense of what it would be like to be this character.

4 SETTING

If plot and action are the way fictional works answer the question *What happened?* and characters are the *who*, **setting** is the *where* and *when*. All action in fiction, as in the real world, takes place in a context or setting—a time and place and a social environment or milieu.

TEMPORAL AND PHYSICAL, GENERAL AND PARTICULAR SETTING

The **time**—a work's *temporal setting* or *plot time*—can be roughly the same as that in which the work was written (its *author time*); or it can be much later, as in most science fiction; or much earlier, as in most **historical fiction**. Especially in short stories, which tend not to cover as much time or space as novels do, time may be very restricted, involving only a few hours or even minutes. Yet even in short stories, the action may span years or even decades.

Similarly, the place—a work's *geographical* or *physical setting*—might be limited to a single locale, or it might encompass several disparate ones. Those places might be common and ordinary, unique and extraordinary, or fantastic and even impossible according to the laws of our world (as in modern **fantasy** or **magic realism**).

Even when a story's action takes place in different times and places, we still sometimes refer to its *setting* (singular). By this, we indicate what we might call the entire story's *general setting*—the year(s) and the region, country, or even world in which the story unfolds and which often provides a historical and cultural context for the action. The general setting of Margaret Mitchell's historical novel *Gone with the Wind* (1936), for instance, is the Civil War–era South. But this work, like many, has many *particular settings*; it opens, for instance, on an April morning on the porch of a north Georgia mansion called Tara, where Scarlett O'Hara flirts with two beaus and ignores their talk of a possible war to come. To fully appreciate the nature and role of setting, we thus need to consider the specific time of day and year as well as the specific locales in which the action unfolds.

Sometimes stories merely offer hints about setting; others describe setting in great sensory detail. Especially in the latter case, we might be tempted to skim through what seems like mere "scenery" or "background information" to find out what happens next or how things turn out. But in good fiction, setting always functions as an integral part of the whole.

FUNCTIONS OF SETTING

Fiction often relies on setting to establish mood, situation, and character. The first sentence of Edgar Allan Poe's short story "The Fall of the House of Usher," for example, quickly sets the tone:

> During the whole of a dull, dark, and soundless day in the autumn of the year, when the clouds hung oppressively low in the heavens, I had been passing alone, on horseback, through a singularly dreary tract of country; and at length found myself, as the shades of the evening drew on, within view of the melancholy House of Usher.

This sentence aims to instill in the reader the same fear, "melancholy," and "sense of insufferable gloom" the narrator feels. With it, Poe prepares the reader emotionally, as well as mentally, for the sad and eerie tale that is about to unfold. He also generates suspense and certain expectations about just what might happen, as well as empathy with the narrator-protagonist.

Here, as in other fiction, specific details prove crucial to setting's emotional effect and meaning precisely because, as Poe's narrator himself observes,

> there *are* combinations of very simple natural objects which have the power of thus affecting us. . . . A mere different arrangement of the particulars of the scene, of the details of the picture, would be sufficient to modify, or perhaps to annihilate its capacity for sorrowful impression.

In addition to creating such emotional impressions, setting can reveal or even shape a character's personality, outlook, and values; it can occasionally be an actor in the plot; and it often prompts characters' actions. (Who might you become and what might you do if you lived in the isolated, gloomy House of Usher?) To gloss over descriptions of setting would thus mean not only missing much of the pleasure fiction affords, but also potentially misreading its meanings. Setting is one of the many ways we learn about characters and the chief means by which characters and plots take on a larger historical, social, or even universal significance.

VAGUE AND VIVID SETTINGS

Not all stories, of course, rely so heavily on setting as Poe's does. In some individual works and in some subgenres, the general time, place, or both may be so vague as to seem, at first glance, unimportant. Many folktales and fairy tales take place in **archetypal** settings: "A long time ago," in "the forest" or "a village" or "a cottage," "in a land far, far away." By offering little, if any, specific information about their settings—neither locating the "forest" or "village" or faraway land in a place we can find on a map or a time we can locate on a calendar or clock, nor describing it in any detail—these works implicitly urge us to see the conflicts and aspects of human experience they depict (death, grief, a mother's relationship to her child, the danger and incomprehensibility of the unknown) as timeless and universal. Here, the very lack of attention to setting paradoxically turns out to be all-important.

At the opposite extreme are works and genres of fiction in which setting generates the conflicts, defines the characters, and gives the story purpose and meaning—so much so that there would be little, if any, story left if all the details about setting were removed or the characters and plot somehow transported to a different time, place, and social milieu. Without their settings, what would remain of historical novels like *Gone with the Wind* or Nathaniel Hawthorne's *The Scarlet Letter* (1850)? A more extreme example is Italo Calvino's fantasy novel *Invisible Cities* (1972), which consists almost entirely of a series of descriptions of impossible, yet often hauntingly beautiful places like the following one.

ITALO CALVINO

From *Invisible Cities*

What makes Argia different from other cities is that it has earth instead of air. The streets are completely filled with dirt, clay packs the rooms to the ceiling, on every stair another stairway is set in negative, over the roofs of the houses hang layers of rocky terrain like skies with clouds. We do not know if the inhabitants can move about the city, widening the worm tunnels and the crevices where roots twist: the dampness destroys people's bodies and they have scant strength; everyone is better off remaining still, prone; anyway, it is dark.

From up here, nothing of Argia can be seen; some say, "It's down below there," and we can only believe them. The place is deserted. At night, putting your ear to the ground, you can sometimes hear a door slam.

. . .

Most fiction, of course, occupies a middle ground between the extremes of Calvino's novel or historical fiction (with their highly particularized settings) versus folklore (with its generic, archetypal setting). Though all fiction may ultimately deal with some types of people, aspects of human experience, and conflicts that can crop up in some form or fashion anywhere or at any time, much fiction also draws our attention to the way people, their experience, and their conflicts are twisted into a particular "form and fashion" by specific contexts.

Analyzing Descriptions of Setting: An Example and an Exercise

The novel *Gone with the Wind*, like the movie, opens on the front porch of Tara, where a carefree Scarlett O'Hara flirts with the Tarleton twins and studiously ignores the first rumors of war. Then, the narrator pulls back to show us, with great detail, both the time of year and the landscape in which that particular place is situated. After you read the following description, write a paragraph or two that draws on details from the passage to explain the feelings and impressions it conjures up, the functions it might serve at the beginning of the novel, and the way it achieves its effects. How, for example, might this description **foreshadow** and even help explain subsequent events? Why else might the novel need all this detail?

Spring had come early that year, with warm quick rains and sudden frothing of pink peach blossoms and dogwood dappling with white stars the dark river swamp and far-off hills. Already the plowing was nearly finished, and the bloody glory of the sunset colored the fresh-cut furrows of red Georgia clay to even redder hues. The moist hungry earth, waiting upturned for the cotton seeds, showed pinkish on the sandy tops of furrows, vermilion and scarlet and maroon where shadows lay along the sides

(Continued on next page)

(Continued)

of the trenches. The whitewashed brick plantation house seemed an island set in a wild red sea, a sea of spiraling, curving, crescent billows petrified suddenly at the moment when the pink-tipped waves were breaking into surf. For here were no long, straight furrows, such as could be seen in the yellow clay fields of the flat middle Georgia country or in the lush black earth of the coastal plantations. The rolling foothill country of north Georgia was plowed in a million curves to keep the rich earth from washing down into the river bottoms.

It was a savagely red land, blood-colored after rains, brick dust in droughts, the best cotton land in the world. It was a pleasant land of white houses, peaceful plowed fields and sluggish yellow rivers, but a land of contrasts, of bright sun glare and densest shade. The plantation clearings and miles of cotton fields smiled up to a warm sun, placid, complacent. At their edges rose the virgin forests, dark and cool even in the hottest noons, mysterious, a little sinister, the soughing pines seem to wait with an age-old patience, to threaten with soft sighs: "Be careful! Be careful! We had you once. We can take you back again."

This early scene from the novel *Gone with the Wind* (1939) takens place on the porch of a mansion in Georgia, just before the start of the Civil War.

TRADITIONAL EXPECTATIONS OF TIME AND PLACE

The effects and meanings evoked by setting depend on our traditional associations with, and often unconscious assumptions about, particular times, places, and even such factors as weather conditions—autumn, evening, a deserted country road, a house grand enough to have a name, a sky full of low and lowering clouds (to refer back to the Poe example).

Traditional associations derive, in part, from literature and myth, and some are culturally specific. (To someone unfamiliar with the Old Testament, an apple orchard would simply be an apple orchard, without any suggestion of evil or sin. Likewise, to someone who knows little about the Civil War, a big white house in the middle of a cotton field might seem like nothing more than a very beautiful place full of lucky, wealthy, happy people.) These associations also come from our learning, our experience, our own specific social and historical context, and even our primal instincts and physical condition as human beings. Almost all of us are more vulnerable in the dark and in inclement weather. And people do behave differently and expect different things to happen in different times and places—on a Saturday versus a Sunday versus a Monday, during spring break versus mid-semester or mid-week, at a posh beach resort we are just visiting versus the grocery store in our own neighborhood, and so on.

Often, however, authors draw on such associations precisely in order to reverse and question them. John Updike has said that he was initially inspired to write "A & P" (in "Initiation Stories") because a suburban grocery store seemed just the sort of mundane place no reader would expect either heroism or a story to take place. ("Why don't you ever read a story set in an A & P?" he reportedly asked his wife.) By reversing expectations in this way, stories not only deepen their emotional effect but also encourage us to rethink our assumptions about particular times and places and the people who inhabit them.

Connecting Setting, Point of View, and Character: An Example and an Exercise

For the purpose of analysis, we distinguish setting from other elements such as character, plot, point of view, and language. Perhaps paradoxically, we need to do so precisely in order to understand how these elements work together. The following passage from Alice Randall's controversial novel *The Wind Done Gone* (2002), for example, paints a dramatically different picture of the antebellum South than do earlier novels and films like *Gone with the Wind*, in part because it looks at that time and place from a very different point of view.

After you read the passage, write a paragraph or two about how its effect and meaning are shaped by point of view and **figurative language** or **imagery**. What might the passage tell us about Randall's narrator?

(Continued on next page)

(Continued)

How does the passage encourage us to rethink traditional views of the antebellum South?

Alternatively, compare this passage to the one from Mitchell's *Gone with the Wind* in this chapter's first "Example and Exercise," focusing on how each passage differently depicts the same time and place and how each passage's effect and meaning derive from its point of view and from its distinctive use of somewhat similar language and images.

Mammy worked from can't-see in the morning to can't-see at night, in that great whitewashed wide-columned house surrounded by curvy fur-rowed fields. The mud, the dirt, was so red, when you looked at the cotton blooming in a field it brought to mind a sleeping gown after childbirth—all soft white cotton and blood.

If it was mine to be able to paint pictures, if I possessed the gift of painting, I would paint a cotton gown balled up and thrown into a corner waiting to be washed, and I would call it "Georgia."

• • •

Setting is key to each of the three stories gathered in this chapter—Anton Chekhov's "The Lady with the Dog," Katherine Anne Porter's "Flowering Judas," and Amy Tan's "A Pair of Tickets"—as well as the three stories in the "Suburbia" album that follows the chapter. The settings in these stories range from the U.S. to the U.K., Mexico, Soviet Russia, and China; from the late-nineteenth century to the late-twentieth; from neat suburban houses to messy urban hotel rooms; from coastal resorts to crowded, cosmopolitan cities. The stories take place in just about every season and all kinds of weather, but regardless of the specific setting each paints a revealing portrait of a time and place. Just as our own memories of important experiences include complex impressions of when and where they occurred—the weather, the shape of the room, the music that was playing, even the fashions or the events in the news back then—so stories rely on setting to evoke emotion and generate meaning.

Questions about Setting

General Setting

1. What is the general temporal and geographical setting of this work of fiction? How do you know?
2. How important does the general setting seem to be? In what ways is it important? What about the plot and characters would remain the same if they were magically transported to a different setting? What wouldn't? For example, how does the setting

(Continued on next page)

(Continued)

- create or shape conflict?
- affect characters' personalities, outlooks, and actions?
- shape our impressions of who the characters are and what they represent?
- establish mood?

Particular Settings

3. Does all the action occur in one time and place, or in more than one? If the latter, what are those times and places?
4. What patterns do you notice regarding where and when things happen? Which characters are associated with each setting? How do different characters relate to the same setting? When, how, and why do characters move from one setting to another? Are there significant deviations from these patterns?
5. Are particular settings described in detail, or merely sketched? If the former, what seems significant about the details? How might they establish mood, reveal character, and affect individual characters and the characters' interactions with one another?

ANTON CHEKHOV

The Lady with the Dog[1]

I

It was said that a new person had appeared on the sea-front: a lady with a little dog. Dmitri Dmitritch Gurov, who had by then been a fortnight at Yalta,[2] and so was fairly at home there, had begun to take an interest in new arrivals. Sitting in Verney's pavilion, he saw, walking on the sea-front, a fair-haired young lady of medium height, wearing a *béret*; a white Pomeranian dog was running behind her.

And afterwards he met her in the public gardens and in the square several times a day. She was walking alone, always wearing the same *béret*, and always with the same white dog; no one knew who she was, and every one called her simply "the lady with the dog."

"If she is here alone without a husband or friends, it wouldn't be amiss to make her acquaintance," Gurov reflected.

He was under forty, but he had a daughter already twelve years old, and two sons at school. He had been married young, when he was a student in his second year, and by now his wife seemed half as old again as he. She was a tall, erect woman with dark eyebrows, staid and dignified, and, as she said of herself, intellectual. She read a great deal, used phonetic spelling, called her husband, not Dmitri, but Dimitri, and he secretly considered her unintelligent, narrow, inelegant, was afraid of her, and did not like to be at home. He had begun being unfaithful to her long ago—had been unfaithful to her often, and, probably on

1. Translated by Constance Garnett.   2. Russian city on the Black Sea; a resort.

that account, almost always spoke ill of women, and when they were talked about in his presence, used to call them "the lower race."

5   It seemed to him that he had been so schooled by bitter experience that he might call them what he liked, and yet he could not get on for two days together without "the lower race." In the society of men he was bored and not himself, with them he was cold and uncommunicative; but when he was in the company of women he felt free, and knew what to say to them and how to behave; and he was at ease with them even when he was silent. In his appearance, in his character, in his whole nature, there was something attractive and elusive which allured women and disposed them in his favour; he knew that, and some force seemed to draw him, too, to them.

Experience often repeated, truly bitter experience, had taught him long ago that with decent people, especially Moscow people—always slow to move and irresolute—every intimacy, which at first so agreeably diversifies life and appears a light and charming adventure, inevitably grows into a regular problem of extreme intricacy, and in the long run the situation becomes unbearable. But at every fresh meeting with an interesting woman this experience seemed to slip out of his memory, and he was eager for life, and everything seemed simple and amusing.

One evening he was dining in the gardens, and the lady in the *béret* came up slowly to take the next table. Her expression, her gait, her dress, and the way she did her hair told him that she was a lady, that she was married, that she was in Yalta for the first time and alone, and that she was dull there. . . . The stories told of the immorality in such places as Yalta are to a great extent untrue; he despised them, and knew that such stories were for the most part made up by persons who would themselves have been glad to sin if they had been able; but when the lady sat down at the next table three paces from him, he remembered these tales of easy conquests, of trips to the mountains, and the tempting thought of a swift, fleeting love affair, a romance with an unknown woman, whose name he did not know, suddenly took possession of him.

He beckoned coaxingly to the Pomeranian, and when the dog came up to him he shook his finger at it. The Pomeranian growled: Gurov shook his finger at it again.

The lady looked at him and at once dropped her eyes.

10   "He doesn't bite," she said, and blushed.

"May I give him a bone?" he asked; and when she nodded he asked courteously, "Have you been long in Yalta?"

"Five days."

"And I have already dragged out a fortnight here."

There was a brief silence.

15   "Time goes fast, and yet it is so dull here!" she said, not looking at him.

"That's only the fashion to say it is dull here. A provincial will live in Belyov or Zhidra and not be dull, and when he comes here it's 'Oh, the dulness! Oh, the dust!' One would think he came from Grenada."[3]

She laughed. Then both continued eating in silence, like strangers, but after dinner they walked side by side; and there sprang up between them the light jesting conversation of people who are free and satisfied, to whom it does not matter where they go or what they talk about. They walked and talked of the strange light on the sea: the water was of a soft warm lilac hue, and there was a golden

3. Romantic city in southern Spain.

streak from the moon upon it. They talked of how sultry it was after a hot day. Gurov told her that he came from Moscow, that he had taken his degree in Arts, but had a post in a bank; that he had trained as an opera-singer, but had given it up, that he owned two houses in Moscow.... And from her he learnt that she had grown up in Petersburg, but had lived in S—since her marriage two years before, that she was staying another month in Yalta, and that her husband, who needed a holiday too, might perhaps come and fetch her. She was not sure whether her husband had a post in a Crown Department or under the Provincial Council[4]—and was amused by her own ignorance. And Gurov learnt, too, that she was called Anna Sergeyevna.

Afterwards he thought about her in his room at the hotel—thought she would certainly meet him next day; it would be sure to happen. As he got into bed he thought how lately she had been a girl at school, doing lessons like his own daughter; he recalled the diffidence, the angularity, that was still manifest in her laugh and her manner of talking with a stranger. This must have been the first time in her life she had been alone in surroundings in which she was followed, looked at, and spoken to merely from a secret motive which she could hardly fail to guess. He recalled her slender, delicate neck, her lovely grey eyes.

"There's something pathetic about her, anyway," he thought, and fell asleep.

II

A week had passed since they had made acquaintance. It was a holiday. It was sultry indoors, while in the street the wind whirled the dust round and round, and blew people's hats off. It was a thirsty day, and Gurov often went into the pavilion, and pressed Anna Sergeyevna to have syrup and water or an ice. One did not know what to do with oneself.

In the evening when the wind had dropped a little, they went out on the groyne to see the steamer come in. There were a great many people walking about the harbour; they had gathered to welcome some one, bringing bouquets. And two peculiarities of a well-dressed Yalta crowd were very conspicuous: the elderly ladies were dressed like young ones, and there were great numbers of generals.

Owing to the roughness of the sea, the steamer arrived late, after the sun had set, and it was a long time turning about before it reached the groyne. Anna Sergeyevna looked through her lorgnette at the steamer and the passengers as though looking for acquaintances, and when she turned to Gurov her eyes were shining. She talked a great deal and asked disconnected questions, forgetting next moment what she had asked; then she dropped her lorgnette in the crush.

The festive crowd began to disperse; it was too dark to see people's faces. The wind had completely dropped, but Gurov and Anna Sergeyevna still stood as though waiting to see some one else come from the steamer. Anna Sergeyevna was silent now, and sniffed the flowers without looking at Gurov.

"The weather is better this evening," he said. "Where shall we go now? Shall we drive somewhere?"

She made no answer.

Then he looked at her intently, and all at once put his arm round her and kissed her on the lips, and breathed in the moisture and the fragrance of the flowers; and he immediately looked round him, anxiously wondering whether any one had seen them.

4. That is, a post in a national department, appointed by the czar, or a post in an elective local council.

"Let us go to your hotel," he said softly. And both walked quickly.

The room was close and smelt of the scent she had bought at the Japanese shop. Gurov looked at her and thought: "What different people one meets in the world!" From the past he preserved memories of careless, good-natured women, who loved cheerfully and were grateful to him for the happiness he gave them, however brief it might be; and of women like his wife who loved without any genuine feeling, with superfluous phrases, affectedly, hysterically, with an expression that suggested that it was not love nor passion, but something more significant; and of two or three others, very beautiful, cold women, on whose faces he had caught a glimpse of a rapacious expression—an obstinate desire to snatch from life more than it could give, and these were capricious, unreflecting, domineering, unintelligent women not in their first youth, and when Gurov grew cold to them their beauty excited his hatred, and the lace on their linen seemed to him like scales.

But in this case there was still the diffidence, the angularity of inexperienced youth, an awkward feeling; and there was a sense of consternation as though some one had suddenly knocked at the door. The attitude of Anna Sergeyevna—"the lady with the dog"—to what had happened was somehow peculiar, very grave, as though it were her fall—so it seemed, and it was strange and inappropriate. Her face dropped and faded, and on both sides of it her long hair hung down mournfully; she mused in a dejected attitude like "the woman who was a sinner" in an old-fashioned picture.

30   "It's wrong," she said. "You will be the first to despise me now."

There was a water-melon on the table. Gurov cut himself a slice and began eating it without haste. There followed at least half an hour of silence.

Anna Sergeyevna was touching; there was about her the purity of a good, simple woman who had seen little of life. The solitary candle burning on the table threw a faint light on her face, yet it was clear that she was very unhappy.

"How could I despise you?" asked Gurov. "You don't know what you are saying."

"God forgive me," she said, and her eyes filled with tears. "It's awful."

35   "You seem to feel you need to be forgiven."

"Forgiven? No. I am a bad, low woman; I despise myself and don't attempt to justify myself. It's not my husband but myself I have deceived. And not only just now; I have been deceiving myself for a long time. My husband may be a good, honest man, but he is a flunkey! I don't know what he does there, what his work is, but I know he is a flunkey! I was twenty when I was married to him. I have been tormented by curiosity; I wanted something better. 'There must be a different sort of life,' I said to myself. I wanted to live! To live, to live! . . . I was fired by curiosity . . . you don't understand it, but, I swear to God, I could not control myself; something happened to me: I could not be restrained. I told my husband I was ill, and came here. . . . And here I have been walking about as though I were dazed, like a mad creature; . . . and now I have become a vulgar, contemptible woman whom any one may despise."

Gurov felt bored already, listening to her. He was irritated by the naïve tone, by this remorse, so unexpected and inopportune; but for the tears in her eyes, he might have thought she was jesting or playing a part.

"I don't understand," he said softly. "What is it you want?"

She hid her face on his breast and pressed close to him.

"Believe me, believe me, I beseech you . . ." she said. "I love a pure, honest life, 40
and sin is loathsome to me. I don't know what I am doing. Simple people say: 'The
Evil One has beguiled me.' And I may say of myself now that the Evil One has
beguiled me."

"Hush, hush! . . ." he muttered.

He looked at her fixed, scared eyes, kissed her, talked softly and affectionately, and by degrees she was comforted, and her gaiety returned; they both
began laughing.

Afterwards when they went out there was not a soul on the sea-front. The
town with its cypresses had quite a deathlike air, but the sea still broke noisily
on the shore; a single barge was rocking on the waves, and a lantern was blinking sleepily on it.

They found a cab and drove to Oreanda.

"I found out your surname in the hall just now: it was written on the board— 45
Von Diderits," said Gurov. "Is your husband a German?"

"No; I believe his grandfather was a German, but he is an Orthodox Russian
himself."

At Oreanda they sat on a seat not far from the church, looked down at the sea,
and were silent. Yalta was hardly visible through the morning mist; white clouds
stood motionless on the mountain-tops. The leaves did not stir on the trees,
grasshoppers chirruped, and the monotonous hollow sound of the sea rising up
from below, spoke of the peace, of the eternal sleep awaiting us. So it must have
sounded when there was no Yalta, no Oreanda here; so it sounds now, and it will
sound as indifferently and monotonously when we are all no more. And in this
constancy, in this complete indifference to the life and death of each of us, there
lies hid, perhaps, a pledge of our eternal salvation, of the unceasing movement
of life upon earth, of unceasing progress towards perfection. Sitting beside a
young woman who in the dawn seemed so lovely, soothed and spellbound in
these magical surroundings—the sea, mountains, clouds, the open sky—Gurov
thought how in reality everything is beautiful in this world when one reflects:
everything except what we think or do ourselves when we forget our human dignity and the higher aims of our existence.

A man walked up to them—probably a keeper—looked at them and walked
away. And this detail seemed mysterious and beautiful, too. They saw a steamer
come from Theodosia, with its lights out in the glow of dawn.

"There is dew on the grass," said Anna Sergeyevna, after a silence.

"Yes. It's time to go home."   50

They went back to the town.

Then they met every day at twelve o'clock on the sea-front, lunched and dined
together, went for walks, admired the sea. She complained that she slept badly,
that her heart throbbed violently; asked the same questions, troubled now by
jealousy and now by the fear that he did not respect her sufficiently. And often in
the square or gardens, when there was no one near them, he suddenly drew her
to him and kissed her passionately. Complete idleness, these kisses in broad daylight while he looked round in dread of some one's seeing them, the heat, the
smell of the sea, and the continual passing to and fro before him of idle, well-
dressed, well-fed people, made a new man of him; he told Anna Sergeyevna how
beautiful she was, how fascinating. He was impatiently passionate, he would not
move a step away from her, while she was often pensive and continually urged

him to confess that he did not respect her, did not love her in the least, and thought of her as nothing but a common woman. Rather late almost every evening they drove somewhere out of town, to Oreanda or to the waterfall; and the expedition was always a success, the scenery invariably impressed them as grand and beautiful.

They were expecting her husband to come, but a letter came from him, saying that there was something wrong with his eyes, and he entreated his wife to come home as quickly as possible. Anna Sergeyevna made haste to go.

"It's a good thing I am going away," she said to Gurov. "It's the finger of destiny!"

55 She went by coach and he went with her. They were driving the whole day. When she had got into a compartment of the express, and when the second bell had rung, she said:

"Let me look at you once more . . . look at you once again. That's right."

She did not shed tears, but was so sad that she seemed ill, and her face was quivering.

"I shall remember you . . . think of you," she said. "God be with you; be happy. Don't remember evil against me. We are parting forever—it must be so, for we ought never to have met. Well, God be with you."

The train moved off rapidly, its lights soon vanished from sight, and a minute later there was no sound of it, as though everything had conspired together to end as quickly as possible that sweet delirium, that madness. Left alone on the platform, and gazing into the dark distance, Gurov listened to the chirrup of the grasshoppers and the hum of the telegraph wires, feeling as though he had only just waked up. And he thought, musing, that there had been another episode or adventure in his life, and it, too, was at an end, and nothing was left of it but a memory. . . . He was moved, sad, and conscious of a slight remorse. This young woman whom he would never meet again had not been happy with him; he was genuinely warm and affectionate with her, but yet in his manner, his tone, and his caresses there had been a shade of light irony, the coarse condescension of a happy man who was, besides, almost twice her age. All the time she had called him kind, exceptional, lofty; obviously he had seemed to her different from what he really was, so he had unintentionally deceived her. . . .

60 Here at the station was already a scent of autumn; it was a cold evening.

"It's time for me to go north," thought Gurov as he left the platform. "High time!"

III

At home in Moscow everything was in its winter routine; the stoves were heated, and in the morning it was still dark when the children were having breakfast and getting ready for school, and the nurse would light the lamp for a short time. The frosts had begun already. When the first snow has fallen, on the first day of sledge-driving it is pleasant to see the white earth, the white roofs, to draw soft, delicious breath, and the season brings back the days of one's youth. The old limes and birches, white with hoar-frost, have a good-natured expression; they are nearer to one's heart than cypresses and palms, and near them one doesn't want to be thinking of the sea and the mountains.

Gurov was Moscow born; he arrived in Moscow on a fine frosty day, and when he put on his fur coat and warm gloves, and walked along Petrovka, and when on Saturday evening he heard the ringing of the bells, his recent trip and the places he had seen lost all charm for him. Little by little he became absorbed in Moscow life, greedily read three newspapers a day, and declared he did not read the Moscow papers on principle! He already felt a longing to go to restaurants, clubs, dinner-parties, anniversary celebrations, and he felt flattered at entertaining distinguished lawyers and artists, and at playing cards with a professor at the doctors' club. He could already eat a whole plateful of salt fish and cabbage. . . .

In another month, he fancied, the image of Anna Sergeyevna would be shrouded in a mist in his memory, and only from time to time would visit him in his dreams with a touching smile as others did. But more than a month passed, real winter had come, and everything was still clear in his memory as though he had parted with Anna Sergeyevna only the day before. And his memories glowed more and more vividly. When in the evening stillness he heard from his study the voices of his children, preparing their lessons, or when he listened to a song or the organ at the restaurant, or the storm howled in the chimney, suddenly everything would rise up in his memory: what had happened on the groyne, and the early morning with the mist on the mountains, and the steamer coming from Theodosia, and the kisses. He would pace a long time about his room, remembering it all and smiling; then his memories passed into dreams, and in his fancy the past was mingled with what was to come. Anna Sergeyevna did not visit him in dreams, but followed him about everywhere like a shadow and haunted him. When he shut his eyes he saw her as though she were living before him, and she seemed to him lovelier, younger, tenderer than she was; and he imagined himself finer than he had been in Yalta. In the evenings she peeped out at him from the bookcase, from the fireplace, from the corner—he heard her breathing, the caressing rustle of her dress. In the street he watched the women, looking for some one like her.

He was tormented by an intense desire to confide his memories to some one. 65 But in his home it was impossible to talk of his love, and he had no one outside; he could not talk to his tenants nor to any one at the bank. And what had he to talk of? Had he been in love, then? Had there been anything beautiful, poetical, or edifying or simply interesting in his relations with Anna Sergeyevna? And there was nothing for him but to talk vaguely of love, of woman, and no one guessed what it meant; only his wife twitched her black eyebrows, and said: "The part of a lady-killer does not suit you at all, Dimitri."

One evening, coming out of the doctors' club with an official with whom he had been playing cards, he could not resist saying:

"If only you knew what a fascinating woman I made the acquaintance of in Yalta!"

The official got into his sledge and was driving away, but turned suddenly and shouted:

"Dmitri Dmitritch!"

"What?"

"You were right this evening: the sturgeon was a bit too strong!" 70

These words, so ordinary, for some reason moved Gurov to indignation, and struck him as degrading and unclean. What savage manners, what people! What senseless nights, what uninteresting, uneventful days! The rage for card-playing, the gluttony, the drunkenness, the continual talk always about the same thing. Useless pursuits and conversations always about the same things absorb the better part of one's time, the better part of one's strength, and in the end there is left a life grovelling and curtailed, worthless and trivial, and there is no escaping or getting away from it—just as though one were in a madhouse or a prison.

Gurov did not sleep all night, and was filled with indignation. And he had a headache all next day. And the next night he slept badly; he sat up in bed, thinking, or paced up and down his room. He was sick of his children, sick of the bank; he had no desire to go anywhere or to talk of anything.

In the holidays in December he prepared for a journey, and told his wife he was going to Petersburg to do something in the interests of a young friend—and he set off for S—. What for? He did not very well know himself. He wanted to see Anna Sergeyevna and to talk with her—to arrange a meeting, if possible.

75   He reached S—in the morning, and took the best room at the hotel, in which the floor was covered with grey army cloth, and on the table was an inkstand, grey with dust and adorned with a figure on horseback, with its hat in its hand and its head broken off. The hotel porter gave him the necessary information; Von Diderits lived in a house of his own in Old Gontcharny Street—it was not far from the hotel: he was rich and lived in good style, and had his own horses; every one in the town knew him. The porter pronounced the name "Dridirits."

Gurov went without haste to Old Gontcharny Street and found the house. Just opposite the house stretched a long grey fence adorned with nails.

"One would run away from a fence like that," thought Gurov, looking from the fence to the windows of the house and back again.

He considered: to-day was a holiday, and the husband would probably be at home. And in any case it would be tactless to go into the house and upset her. If he were to send her a note it might fall into her husband's hands, and then it might ruin everything. The best thing was to trust to chance. And he kept walking up and down the street by the fence, waiting for the chance. He saw a beggar go in at the gate and dogs fly at him; then an hour later he heard a piano, and the sounds were faint and indistinct. Probably it was Anna Sergeyevna playing. The front door suddenly opened, and an old woman came out, followed by the familiar white Pomeranian. Gurov was on the point of calling to the dog, but his heart began beating violently, and in his excitement he could not remember the dog's name.

He walked up and down, and loathed the grey fence more and more, and by now he thought irritably that Anna Sergeyevna had forgotten him, and was perhaps already amusing herself with some one else, and that that was very natural in a young woman who had nothing to look at from morning till night but that confounded fence. He went back to his hotel room and sat for a long while on the sofa, not knowing what to do, then he had dinner and a long nap.

80   "How stupid and worrying it is!" he thought when he woke and looked at the dark windows: it was already evening. "Here I've had a good sleep for some reason. What shall I do in the night?"

He sat on the bed, which was covered by a cheap grey blanket, such as one sees in hospitals, and he taunted himself in his vexation:

"So much for the lady with the dog . . . so much for the adventure. . . . You're in a nice fix. . . ."

That morning at the station a poster in large letters had caught his eye. "The Geisha"[5] was to be performed for the first time. He thought of this and went to the theatre.

"It's quite possible she may go to the first performance," he thought.

5. Operetta by Sidney Jones (1861–1946) that toured eastern Europe in 1898–99.

The theatre was full. As in all provincial theatres, there was a fog above the 85 chandelier, the gallery was noisy and restless; in the front row the local dandies were standing up before the beginning of the performance, with their hands behind them; in the Governor's box the Governor's daughter, wearing a boa, was sitting in the front seat, while the Governor himself lurked modestly behind the curtain with only his hands visible; the orchestra was a long time tuning up; the stage curtain swayed. All the time the audience were coming in and taking their seats Gurov looked at them eagerly.

Anna Sergeyevna, too, came in. She sat down in the third row, and when Gurov looked at her his heart contracted, and he understood clearly that for him there was in the whole world no creature so near, so precious, and so important to him; she, this little woman, in no way remarkable, lost in a provincial crowd, with a vulgar lorgnette in her hand, filled his whole life now, was his sorrow and his joy, the one happiness that he now desired for himself, and to the sounds of the inferior orchestra, of the wretched provincial violins, he thought how lovely she was. He thought and dreamed.

A young man with small side-whiskers, tall and stooping, came in with Anna Sergeyevna and sat down beside her; he bent his head at every step and seemed to be continually bowing. Most likely this was the husband whom at Yalta, in a rush of bitter feeling, she had called a flunkey. And there really was in his long figure, his side-whiskers, and the small bald patch on his head, something of the flunkey's obsequiousness; his smile was sugary, and in his buttonhole there was some badge of distinction like the number on a waiter.

During the first interval the husband went away to smoke; she remained alone in her stall. Gurov, who was sitting in the stalls, too, went up to her and said in a trembling voice, with a forced smile:

"Good-evening."

She glanced at him and turned pale, then glanced again with horror, unable to 90 believe her eyes, and tightly gripped the fan and the lorgnette in her hands, evidently struggling with herself not to faint. Both were silent. She was sitting, he was standing, frightened by her confusion and not venturing to sit down beside her. The violins and the flute began tuning up. He felt suddenly frightened; it seemed as though all the people in the boxes were looking at them. She got up and went quickly to the door; he followed her, and both walked senselessly along passages, and up and down stairs, and figures in legal, scholastic, and civil service uniforms, all wearing badges, flitted before their eyes. They caught glimpses of ladies, of fur coats hanging on pegs; the draughts blew on them, bringing a smell of stale tobacco. And Gurov, whose heart was beating violently, thought:

"Oh, heavens! Why are these people here and this orchestra! . . ."

And at that instant he recalled how when he had seen Anna Sergeyevna off at the station he had thought that everything was over and they would never meet again. But how far they were still from the end!

On the narrow, gloomy staircase over which was written "To the Amphitheatre," she stopped.

"How you have frightened me!" she said, breathing hard, still pale and overwhelmed. "Oh, how you have frightened me! I am half dead. Why have you come? Why?"

"But do understand, Anna, do understand . . ." he said hastily in a low voice. 95 "I entreat you to understand. . . ."

She looked at him with dread, with entreaty, with love; she looked at him intently, to keep his features more distinctly in her memory.

"I am so unhappy," she went on, not heeding him. "I have thought of nothing but you all the time; I live only in the thought of you. And I wanted to forget, to forget you; but why, oh, why, have you come?"

On the landing above them two schoolboys were smoking and looking down, but that was nothing to Gurov; he drew Anna Sergeyevna to him, and began kissing her face, her cheeks, and her hands.

"What are you doing, what are you doing!" she cried in horror, pushing him away. "We are mad. Go away to-day; go away at once. . . . I beseech you by all that is sacred, I implore you. . . . There are people coming this way!"

100   Some one was coming up the stairs.

"You must go away," Anna Sergeyevna went on in a whisper. "Do you hear, Dmitri Dmitritch? I will come and see you in Moscow. I have never been happy; I am miserable now, and I never, never shall be happy, never! Don't make me suffer still more! I swear I'll come to Moscow. But now let us part. My precious, good, dear one, we must part!"

She pressed his hand and began rapidly going downstairs, looking round at him, and from her eyes he could see that she really was unhappy. Gurov stood for a little while, listened, then, when all sound had died away, he found his coat and left the theatre.

IV

And Anna Sergeyevna began coming to see him in Moscow. Once in two or three months she left S—, telling her husband that she was going to consult a doctor about an internal complaint—and her husband believed her, and did not believe her. In Moscow she stayed at the Slaviansky Bazaar hotel, and at once sent a man in a red cap to Gurov. Gurov went to see her, and no one in Moscow knew of it.

Once he was going to see her in this way on a winter morning (the messenger had come the evening before when he was out). With him walked his daughter, whom he wanted to take to school: it was on the way. Snow was falling in big wet flakes.

105   "It's three degrees above freezing-point, and yet it is snowing," said Gurov to his daughter. "The thaw is only on the surface of the earth; there is quite a different temperature at a greater height in the atmosphere."

"And why are there no thunderstorms in the winter, father?"

He explained that, too. He talked, thinking all the while that he was going to see *her*, and no living soul knew of it, and probably never would know. He had two lives: one, open, seen and known by all who cared to know, full of relative truth and of relative falsehood, exactly like the lives of his friends and acquaintances; and another life running its course in secret. And through some strange, perhaps accidental, conjunction of circumstances, everything that was essential, of interest and of value to him, everything in which he was sincere and did not deceive himself, everything that made the kernel of his life, was hidden from other people; and all that was false in him, the sheath in which he hid himself to conceal the truth—such, for instance, as his work in the bank, his discussions at the club, his "lower race," his presence with his wife at anniversary festivities—all that was open. And he judged of others by himself, not believing in what he saw, and always believing that every man had his real, most interesting life under the cover of secrecy and under the cover of night. All personal life rested on secrecy, and possibly it was partly on that account that civilised man was so nervously anxious that personal privacy should be respected.

After leaving his daughter at school, Gurov went on to the Slaviansky Bazaar. He took off his fur coat below, went upstairs, and softly knocked at the door. Anna Sergeyevna, wearing his favourite grey dress, exhausted by the journey and the suspense, had been expecting him since the evening before. She was pale; she looked at him, and did not smile, and he had hardly come in when she fell on his breast. Their kiss was slow and prolonged, as though they had not met for two years.

"Well, how are you getting on there?" he asked. "What news?"

"Wait; I'll tell you directly. . . . I can't talk." 110

She could not speak; she was crying. She turned away from him, and pressed her handkerchief to her eyes.

"Let her have her cry out. I'll sit down and wait," he thought, and he sat down in an arm-chair.

Then he rang and asked for tea to be brought him, and while he drank his tea she remained standing at the window with her back to him. She was crying from emotion, from the miserable consciousness that their life was so hard for them; they could only meet in secret, hiding themselves from people, like thieves! Was not their life shattered?

"Come, do stop!" he said.

It was evident to him that this love of theirs would not soon be over, that he 115 could not see the end of it. Anna Sergeyevna grew more and more attached to him. She adored him, and it was unthinkable to say to her that it was bound to have an end some day; besides, she would not have believed it!

He went up to her and took her by the shoulders to say something affectionate and cheering, and at that moment he saw himself in the looking-glass.

His hair was already beginning to turn grey. And it seemed strange to him that he had grown so much older, so much plainer during the last few years. The shoulders on which his hands rested were warm and quivering. He felt compassion for this life, still so warm and lovely, but probably already not far from beginning to fade and wither like his own. Why did she love him so much? He always seemed to women different from what he was, and they loved in him not himself, but the man created by their imagination, whom they had been eagerly seeking all their lives; and afterwards, when they noticed their mistake, they loved him all the same. And not one of them had been happy with him. Time passed, he had made their acquaintance, got on with them, parted, but he had never once loved; it was anything you like, but not love.

And only now when his head was grey he had fallen properly, really in love— for the first time in his life.

Anna Sergeyevna and he loved each other like people very close and akin, like husband and wife, like tender friends; it seemed to them that fate itself had meant them for one another, and they could not understand why he had a wife and she a husband; and it was as though they were a pair of birds of passage, caught and forced to live in different cages. They forgave each other for what they were ashamed of in their past, they forgave everything in the present, and felt that this love of theirs had changed them both.

In moments of depression in the past he had comforted himself with any 120 arguments that came into his mind, but now he no longer cared for arguments; he felt profound compassion, he wanted to be sincere and tender. . . .

"Don't cry, my darling," he said. "You've had your cry; that's enough. . . . Let us talk now, let us think of some plan."

Then they spent a long while taking counsel together, talked of how to avoid the necessity for secrecy, for deception, for living in different towns and not seeing each other for long at a time. How could they be free from this intolerable bondage?

"How? How?" he asked, clutching his head. "How?"

And it seemed as though in a little while the solution would be found, and then a new and splendid life would begin; and it was clear to both of them that they had still a long, long road before them, and that the most complicated and difficult part of it was only just beginning.

1899

QUESTIONS

1. When Gurov and Anna take their first walk together, they discuss "the strange light of the sea: the water was of a soft warm lilac hue, and there was a golden streak from the moon upon it." Why do you think Chekhov waits until this moment to provide descriptive details of the story's setting in Yalta?
2. How do the weather and season described in each section relate to the action in that section?
3. What is Gurov's attitude toward his affair with Anna at the outset? What is Anna's attitude? What are some indications that both Gurov and Anna are unprepared for the relationship that develops between them?

KATHERINE ANNE PORTER

Flowering Judas

Braggioni sits heaped upon the edge of a straight-backed chair much too small for him, and sings to Laura in a furry, mournful voice. Laura has begun to find reasons for avoiding her own house until the latest possible moment, for Braggioni is there almost every night. No matter how late she is, he will be sitting there with a surly, waiting expression, pulling at his kinky yellow hair, thumbing the strings of his guitar, snarling a tune under his breath. Lupe the Indian maid meets Laura at the door, and says with a flicker of a glance towards the upper room, "He waits."

Laura wishes to lie down, she is tired of her hairpins and the feel of her long tight sleeves, but she says to him, "Have you a new song for me this evening?" If he says yes, she asks him to sing it. If he says no, she remembers his favorite one, and asks him to sing it again. Lupe brings her a cup of chocolate and a plate of rice, and Laura eats at the small table under the lamp, first inviting Braggioni, whose answer is always the same: "I have eaten, and besides, chocolate thickens the voice."

Laura says, "Sing, then," and Braggioni heaves himself into song. He scratches the guitar familiarly as though it were a pet animal, and sings passionately off key, taking the high notes in a prolonged painful squeal. Laura, who haunts the markets listening to the ballad singers, and stops every day to hear the blind boy playing his reed-flute in Sixteenth of September Street,[1] listens to Braggioni with pitiless courtesy, because she dares not smile at his miserable performance. Nobody dares to smile at him. Braggioni is cruel to everyone, with a kind of specialized insolence, but he is so vain of his talents, and so sensitive to slights, it would require a cruelty and vanity greater than his own to lay a finger on the vast cureless wound of his self-esteem. It would require courage, too, for it is dangerous to offend him, and nobody has this courage.

Braggioni loves himself with such tenderness and amplitude and eternal charity that his followers—for he is a leader of men, a skilled revolutionist, and his skin had been punctured in honorable warfare—warm themselves in the reflected glow, and say to each other: "He has a real nobility, a love of humanity raised above mere personal affections." The excess of this self-love has flowed out, inconveniently for her, over Laura, who, with so many others, owes her comfortable situation and her salary to him. When he is in a very good humor, he tells her, "I am tempted to forgive you for being a *gringa*. *Gringita!*"[2] and Laura, burning, imagines herself leaning forward suddenly, and with a sound backhanded slap wiping the suety smile from his face. If he notices her eyes at these moments he gives no sign.

She knows what Braggioni would offer her, and she must resist tenaciously without appearing to resist, and if she could avoid it she would not admit even to herself the slow drift of his intention. During these long evenings which have spoiled a long month for her, she sits in her deep chair with an open book on her knees, resting her eyes on the consoling rigidity of the printed page when the sight and sound of Braggioni singing threaten to identify themselves with all her remembered afflictions and to add their weight to her uneasy premonitions of the future. The gluttonous bulk of Braggioni has become a symbol of her many disillusions, for a revolutionist should be lean, animated by heroic faith, a vessel of abstract virtues. This is nonsense, she knows it now and is ashamed of it. Revolution must have leaders, and leadership is a career for energetic men. She is, her comrades tell her, full of romantic error, for what she defines as cynicism in them is merely "a developed sense of reality." She is almost too willing to say, "I am wrong, I suppose I don't really understand the principles," and afterward she makes a secret truce with herself, determined not to surrender her will to such expedient logic. But she cannot help feeling that she has been betrayed irreparably by the disunion between her way of living and her feeling of what life should be, and at times she is almost contented to rest in this sense of grievance as a private store of consolation. Sometimes she wishes to run away, but she stays. Now she longs to fly out of this room, down the narrow stairs, and into the street where the houses lean together like conspirators under a single mottled lamp, and leave Braggioni singing to himself.

Instead she looks at Braggioni, frankly and clearly, like a good child who understands the rules of behavior. Her knees cling together under sound blue serge, and her round white collar is not purposely nun-like. She wears the uniform of an idea, and has renounced vanities. She was born Roman Catholic, and in spite of her fear of being seen by someone who might make a scandal of it, she slips now and again into some crumbling little church, kneels on the chilly

1. Street in Morelia, a city in central Mexico.
2. Diminutive of *gringa*: non-Mexican woman, used pejoratively.

stone, and says a Hail Mary on the gold rosary she bought in Tehuantepec. It is no good and she ends by examining the altar with its tinsel flowers and ragged brocades, and feels tender about the battered doll-shape of some male saint whose white, lace-trimmed drawers hang limply around his ankles below the hieratic dignity of his velvet robe. She has encased herself in a set of principles derived from her early training, leaving no detail of gesture or of personal taste untouched, and for this reason she will not wear lace made on machines. This is her private heresy, for in her special group the machine is sacred, and will be the salvation of the workers. She loves fine lace, and there is a tiny edge of fluted cobweb on this collar, which is one of twenty precisely alike, folded in blue tissue paper in the upper drawer of her clothes chest.

Braggioni catches her glance solidly as if he had been waiting for it, leans forward, balancing his paunch between his spread knees, and sings with tremendous emphasis, weighing his words. He has, the song relates, no father and no mother, nor even a friend to console him; lonely as a wave of the sea he comes and goes, lonely as a wave. His mouth opens round and yearns sideways, his balloon cheeks grow oily with the labor of song. He bulges marvelously in his expensive garments. Over his lavender collar, crushed upon a purple necktie, held by a diamond hoop: over his ammunition belt of tooled leather worked in silver, buckled cruelly around his gasping middle: over the tops of his glossy yellow shoes Braggioni swells with ominous ripeness, his mauve silk hose stretched taut, his ankles bound with the stout leather thongs of his shoes.

When he stretches his eyelids at Laura she notes again that his eyes are the true tawny yellow cat's eyes. He is rich, not in money, he tells her, but in power, and this power brings with it the blameless ownership of things, and the right to indulge his love of small luxuries. "I have a taste for the elegant refinements," he said once, flourishing a yellow silk handkerchief before her nose. "Smell that? It is Jockey Club, imported from New York." Nonetheless he is wounded by life. He will say so presently. "It is true everything turns to dust in the hand, to gall on the tongue." He sighs and his leather belt creaks like a saddle girth. "I am disappointed in everything as it comes. Everything." He shakes his head. "You, poor thing, you will be disappointed too. You are born for it. We are more alike than you realize in some things. Wait and see. Some day you will remember what I have told you, you will know that Braggioni was your friend."

Laura feels a slow chill, a purely physical sense of danger, a warning in her blood that violence, mutilation, a shocking death, wait for her with lessening patience. She has translated this fear into something homely, immediate, and sometimes hesitates before crossing the street. "My personal fate is nothing, except as the testimony of a mental attitude," she reminds herself, quoting from some forgotten philosophic primer, and is sensible enough to add, "Anyhow, I shall not be killed by an automobile if I can help it."

10   "It may be true I am as corrupt, in another way, as Braggioni," she thinks in spite of herself, "as callous, as incomplete," and if this is so, any kind of death seems preferable. Still she sits quietly, she does not run. Where could she go? Uninvited she has promised herself to this place; she can no longer imagine herself as living in another country, and there is no pleasure in remembering her life before she came here.

Precisely what is the nature of this devotion, its true motives, and what are its obligations? Laura cannot say. She spends part of her days in Xochimilco, near by, teaching Indian children to say in English, "The cat is on the mat." When she appears in the classroom they crowd about her with smiles on their wise, inno-cent, clay-colored faces, crying "Good morning, my titcher!" in immaculate voices, and they make of her desk a fresh garden of flowers every day.

During her leisure she goes to union meetings and listens to busy important voices quarreling over tactics, methods, internal politics. She visits the prisoners of her own political faith in their cells, where they entertain themselves with counting cockroaches, repenting of their indiscretions, composing their memoirs, writing out manifestoes and plans for their comrades who are still walking about free, hands in pockets, sniffing fresh air. Laura brings them food and cigarettes and a little money, and she brings messages disguised in equivocal phrases from the men outside who dare not set foot in the prison for fear of disappearing into the cells kept empty for them. If the prisoners confuse night and day, and complain, "Dear little Laura, time doesn't pass in this infernal hole, and I won't know when it is time to sleep unless I have a reminder," she brings them their favorite narcotics, and says in a tone that does not wound them with pity, "Tonight will really be night for you," and though her Spanish amuses them, they find her comforting, useful. If they lose patience and all faith, and curse the slowness of their friends in coming to their rescue with money and influence, they trust her not to repeat everything, and if she inquires, "Where do you think we can find money, or influence?" they are certain to answer, "Well, there is Braggioni, why doesn't he do something?"

She smuggles letters from headquarters to men hiding from firing squads in back streets in mildewed houses, where they sit in tumbled beds and talk bit-terly as if all Mexico were at their heels, when Laura knows positively they might appear at the band concert in the Alameda on Sunday morning, and no one would notice them. But Braggioni says, "Let them sweat a little. The next time they may be careful. It is very restful to have them out of the way for a while." She is not afraid to knock on any door in any street after midnight, and enter in the dark-ness, and say to one of these men who is really in danger: "They will be looking for you—seriously—tomorrow morning after six. Here is some money from Vicente. Go to Vera Cruz and wait."

She borrows money from the Roumanian agitator to give to his bitter enemy the Polish agitator. The favor of Braggioni is their disputed territory, and Brag-gioni holds the balance nicely, for he can use them both. The Polish agitator talks love to her over café tables, hoping to exploit what he believes is her secret sentimental preference for him, and he gives her misinformation which he begs her to repeat as the solemn truth to certain persons. The Roumanian is more adroit. He is generous with his money in all good causes, and lies to her with an air of ingenuous candor, as if he were her good friend and confidant. She never repeats anything they may say. Braggioni never asks questions. He has other ways to discover all that he wishes to know about them.

Nobody touches her, but all praise her gray eyes, and the soft, round under lip which promises gayety, yet is always grave, nearly always firmly closed: and they cannot understand why she is in Mexico. She walks back and forth on her errands, with puzzled eyebrows, carrying her little folder of drawings and music and school papers. No dancer dances more beautifully than Laura walks, and she inspires some amusing, unexpected ardors, which cause little gossip, because nothing comes of them. A young captain who had been a soldier in Zapata's[3] army

3. Emiliano Zapata (1879–1919), Mexican peasant-revolutionary general.

attempted, during a horseback ride near Cuernavaca, to express his desire for her with the noble simplicity befitting a rude folk-hero: but gently, because he was gentle. This gentleness was his defeat, for when he alighted, and removed her foot from the stirrup, and essayed to draw her down into his arms, her horse, ordinarily a tame one, shied fiercely, reared and plunged away. The young hero's horse careered blindly after his stable-mate, and the hero did not return to the hotel until rather late that evening. At breakfast he came to her table in full charro[4] dress, gray buckskin jacket and trousers with strings of silver buttons down the leg, and he was in a humorous, careless mood. "May I sit with you?" and "You are a wonderful rider. I was terrified that you might be thrown and dragged. I should never have forgiven myself. But I cannot admire you enough for your riding!"

"I learned to ride in Arizona," said Laura.

"If you will ride with me again this morning, I promise you a horse that will not shy with you," he said. But Laura remembered that she must return to Mexico City at noon.

Next morning the children made a celebration and spent their playtime writing on the blackboard, "We lov ar ticher," and with tinted chalks they drew wreaths of flowers around the words. The young hero wrote her a letter: "I am a very foolish, wasteful, impulsive man. I should have first said I love you, and then you would not have run away. But you shall see me again." Laura thought, "I must send him a box of colored crayons," but she was trying to forgive herself for having spurred her horse at the wrong moment.

A brown, shock-haired youth came and stood in her patio one night and sang like a lost soul for two hours, but Laura could think of nothing to do about it. The moonlight spread a wash of gauzy silver over the clear spaces of the garden, and the shadows were cobalt blue. The scarlet blossoms of the Judas tree were dull purple, and the names of the colors repeated themselves automatically in her mind, while she watched not the boy, but his shadow, fallen like a dark garment across the fountain rim, trailing in the water. Lupe came silently and whispered expert counsel in her ear: "If you will throw him one little flower, he will sing another song or two and go away." Laura threw the flower, and he sang a last song and went away with the flower tucked in the band of his hat. Lupe said, "He is one of the organizers of the Typographers Union, and before that he sold corridos[5] in the Merced market, and before that, he came from Guanajuato, where I was born. I would not trust any man, but I trust least those from Guanajuato."

20   She did not tell Laura that he would be back again the next night, and the next, nor that he would follow her at a certain fixed distance around the Merced market, through the Zócalo, up Francisco I. Madero Avenue, and so along the Paseo de la Reforma to that Chapultepec Park, and into the Philosopher's Footpath, still with that flower withering in his hat, and an indivisible attention in his eyes.

Now Laura is accustomed to him, it means nothing except that he is nineteen years old and is observing a convention with all propriety, as though it were founded on a law of nature, which in the end it might well prove to be. He is beginning to write poems which he prints on a wooden press, and he leaves them stuck like handbills in her door. She is pleasantly disturbed by the abstract, unhurried watchfulness of his black eyes which will in time turn easily towards another object. She tells herself that throwing the flower was a mistake, for she is

---

4. Costume worn by peasant horsemen of special status.   5. Popular ballads.

twenty-two years old and knows better; but she refuses to regret it, and persuades herself that her negation of all external events as they occur is a sign that she is gradually perfecting herself in the stoicism she strives to cultivate against that disaster she fears, though she cannot name it.

She is not at home in the world. Every day she teaches children who remain strangers to her, though she loves their tender round hands and their charming opportunist savagery. She knocks at unfamiliar doors not knowing whether a friend or a stranger shall answer, and even if a known face emerges from the sour gloom of that unknown interior, still it is the face of a stranger. No matter what this stranger says to her, nor what her message to him, the very cells of her flesh reject knowledge and kinship in one monotonous word. No. No. No. She draws her strength from this one holy talismanic word which does not suffer her to be led into evil. Denying everything, she may walk anywhere in safety, she looks at everything without amazement.

No, repeats this firm unchanging voice of her blood; and she looks at Braggioni without amazement. He is a great man, he wishes to impress this simple girl who covers her great round breasts with thick dark cloth, and who hides long, invaluably beautiful legs under a heavy skirt. She is almost thin except for the incomprehensible fullness of her breasts, like a nursing mother's, and Braggioni, who considers himself a judge of women, speculates again on the puzzle of her notorious virginity, and takes the liberty of speech which she permits without a sign of modesty, indeed, without any sort of sign, which is disconcerting.

"You think you are so cold, *gringita!* Wait and see. You will surprise yourself some day! May I be there to advise you!" He stretches his eyelids at her, and his ill-humored cat's eyes waver in a separate glance for the two points of light marking the opposite ends of a smoothly drawn path between the swollen curve of her breasts. He is not put off by that blue serge, nor by her resolutely fixed gaze. There is all the time in the world. His cheeks are bellying with the wind of song. "O girl with the dark eyes," he sings, and reconsiders. "But yours are not dark. I can change all that. O girl with the green eyes, you have stolen my heart away!" then his mind wanders to the song, and Laura feels the weight of his attention being shifted elsewhere. Singing thus, he seems harmless, he is quite harmless, there is nothing to do but sit patiently and say "No," when the moment comes. She draws a full breath, and her mind wanders also, but not far. She dares not wander too far.

Not for nothing has Braggioni taken pains to be a good revolutionist and a 25 professional lover of humanity. He will never die of it. He has the malice, the cleverness, the wickedness, the sharpness of wit, the hardness of heart, stipulated for loving the world profitably. *He will never die of it.* He will live to see himself kicked out from his feeding trough by other hungry world-saviors. Traditionally he must sing in spite of his life which drives him to bloodshed, he tells Laura, for his father was a Tuscany[6] peasant who drifted to Yucatan and married a Maya woman: a woman of race, an aristocrat. They gave him the love and knowledge of music, thus: and under the rip of his thumbnail, the strings of the instrument complain like exposed nerves.

Once he was called Delgadito by all the girls and married women who ran after him; he was so scrawny all his bones showed under his thin cotton clothing, and he could squeeze his emptiness to the very backbone with his two hands. He

6. Region in northern Italy.

was a poet and the revolution was only a dream then; too many women loved him and sapped away his youth, and he could never find enough to eat anywhere, anywhere! Now he is a leader of men, crafty men who whisper in his ear, hungry men who wait for hours outside his office for a word with him, emaciated men with wild faces who waylay him at the street gate with a timid, "Comrade, let me tell you . . ." and they blow the foul breath from their empty stomachs in his face.

He is always sympathetic. He gives them handfuls of small coins from his own pocket, he promises them work, there will be demonstrations, they must join the unions and attend the meetings, above all they must be on the watch for spies. They are closer to him than his own brothers, without them he can do nothing—until tomorrow, comrade!

Until tomorrow. "They are stupid, they are lazy, they are treacherous, they would cut my throat for nothing," he says to Laura. He has good food and abundant drink, he hires an automobile and drives in the Paseo on Sunday morning, and enjoys plenty of sleep in a soft bed beside a wife who dares not disturb him; and he sits pampering his bones in easy billows of fat, singing to Laura, who knows and thinks these things about him. When he was fifteen, he tried to drown himself because he loved a girl, his first love, and she laughed at him. "A thousand women have paid for that," and his tight little mouth turns down at the corners. Now he perfumes his hair with Jockey Club, and confides to Laura: "One woman is really as good as another for me, in the dark. I prefer them all."

His wife organizes unions among the girls in the cigarette factories, and walks in picket lines, and even speaks at meetings in the evening. But she cannot be brought to acknowledge the benefits of true liberty. "I tell her I must have my freedom, net. She does not understand my point of view." Laura has heard this many times. Braggioni scratches the guitar and meditates. "She is an instinctively virtuous woman, pure gold, no doubt of that. If she were not, I should lock her up, and she knows it."

30   His wife, who works so hard for the good of the factory girls, employs part of her leisure lying on the floor weeping because there are so many women in the world, and only one husband for her, and she never knows where nor when to look for him. He told her: "Unless you can learn to cry when I am not here, I must go away for good." That day he went away and took a room at the Hotel Madrid.

It is this month of separation for the sake of higher principles that has been spoiled not only for Mrs. Braggioni, whose sense of reality is beyond criticism, but for Laura, who feels herself bogged in a nightmare. Tonight Laura envies Mrs. Braggioni, who is alone, and free to weep as much as she pleases about a concrete wrong. Laura has just come from a visit to the prison, and she is waiting for tomorrow with a bitter anxiety as if tomorrow may not come, but time may be caught immovably in this hour, with herself transfixed, Braggioni singing on forever, and Eugenio's body not yet discovered by the guard.

Braggioni says: "Are you going to sleep?" Almost before she can shake her head, he begins telling her about the May-day disturbances coming on in Morelia, for the Catholics hold a festival in honor of the Blessed Virgin, and the Socialists celebrate their martyrs on that day. "There will be two independent processions, starting from either end of town, and they will march until they meet, and the rest depends . . ." He asks her to oil and load his pistols. Standing up, he unbuckles his ammunition belt, and spreads it laden across her knees. Laura sits with the shells slipping through the cleaning cloth dipped in oil, and he says again he cannot understand why she works so hard for the revolutionary idea unless she loves some man who is in it. "Are you not in love with someone?" "No," says Laura. "And no one is in love with you?" "No." "Then it is your own fault. No woman need go begging. Why, what is the matter with you? The legless beggar woman in the Alameda has a perfectly faithful lover. Did you know that?"

Laura peers down the pistol barrel and says nothing, but a long, slow faintness rises and subsides in her; Braggioni curves his swollen fingers around the throat of the guitar and softly smothers the music out of it, and when she hears him again he seems to have forgotten her, and is speaking in the hypnotic voice he uses when talking in small rooms to a listening, close-gathered crowd. Some day this world, now seemingly so composed and eternal, to the edges of every sea shall be merely a tangle of gaping trenches, of crashing walls and broken bodies. Everything must be torn from its accustomed place where it has rotted for centuries, hurled skyward and distributed, cast down again clean as rain, without separate identity. Nothing shall survive that the stiffened hands of poverty have created for the rich and no one shall be left alive except the elect spirits destined to procreate a new world cleansed of cruelty and injustice, ruled by benevolent anarchy: "Pistols are good, I love them, cannon are even better, but in the end I pin my faith to good dynamite," he concludes, and strokes the pistol lying in her hands. "Once I dreamed of destroying this city, in case it offered resistance to General Ortíz, but it fell into his hands like an overripe pear."

He is made restless by his own words, rises and stands waiting. Laura holds up the belt to him: "Put that on, and go kill somebody in Morelia, and you will be happier," she says softly. The presence of death in the room makes her bold. "Today, I found Eugenio going into a stupor. He refused to allow me to call the prison doctor. He had taken all the tablets I brought him yesterday. He said he took them because he was bored."

"He is a fool, and his death is his own business," says Braggioni, fastening his belt carefully.   35

"I told him if he had waited only a little while longer, you would have got him set free," says Laura. "He said he did not want to wait."

"He is a fool and we are well rid of him," says Braggioni, reaching for his hat.

He goes away. Laura knows his mood has changed, she will not see him any more for a while. He will send word when he needs her to go on errands into strange streets, to speak to the strange faces that will appear, like clay masks with the power of human speech, to mutter their thanks to Braggioni for his help. Now she is free, and she thinks, I must run while there is time. But she does not go.

Braggioni enters his own house where for a month his wife has spent many hours every night weeping and tangling her hair upon her pillow. She is weeping now, and she weeps more at the sight of him, the cause of all her sorrows. He looks about the room. Nothing is changed, the smells are good and familiar, he is well acquainted with the woman who comes toward him with no reproach except grief on her face. He says to her tenderly: "You are so good, please don't cry any more, you dear good creature." She says, "Are you tired, my angel? Sit here and I will wash your feet." She brings a bowl of water, and kneeling, unlaces his shoes, and when from her knees she raises her sad eyes under her blackened lids, he is sorry for everything, and bursts into tears. "Ah, yes, I am hungry, I am tired, let us eat something together," he says, between sobs. His wife leans her head on his arm and says, "Forgive me!" and this time he is refreshed by the solemn, endless rain of her tears.

40   Laura takes off her serge dress and puts on a white linen nightgown and goes to bed. She turns her head a little to one side, and lying still, reminds herself that it is time to sleep. Numbers tick in her brain like little clocks, soundless doors close of themselves around her. If you would sleep, you must not remember anything, the children will say tomorrow, good morning, my teacher, the poor prisoners who come every day bringing flowers to their jailor. 1-2-3-4-5—it is monstrous to confuse love with revolution, night with day, life with death—ah, Eugenio!

The tolling of the midnight bell is a signal, but what does it mean? Get up, Laura, and follow me: come out of your sleep, out of your bed, out of this strange house. What are you doing in this house? Without a word, without fear she rose and reached for Eugenio's hand, but he eluded her with a sharp, sly smile and drifted away. This is not all, you shall see—Murderer, he said, follow me, I will show you a new country, but it is far away and we must hurry. No, said Laura, not unless you take my hand, no; and she clung first to the stair rail, and then to the topmost branch of the Judas tree that bent down slowly and set her upon the earth, and then to the rocky ledge of a cliff, and then to the jagged wave of a sea that was not water but a desert of crumbling stone. Where are you taking me, she asked in wonder but without fear. To death, and it is a long way off, and we must hurry, said Eugenio. No, said Laura, not unless you take my hand. Then eat these flowers, poor prisoner, said Eugenio in a voice of pity, take and eat: and from the Judas tree he stripped the warm bleeding flowers, and held them to her lips. She saw that his hand was fleshless, a cluster of small white petrified branches, and his eye sockets were without light, but she ate the flowers greedily for they satisfied both hunger and thirst. Murderer! said Eugenio, and Cannibal! This is my body and my blood. Laura cried No! and at the sound of her own voice, she awoke trembling, and was afraid to sleep again.

1929, 1930

QUESTIONS

1. The main events in "Flowering Judas" take place on a single evening and mostly in a single room. What is the effect and significance of that temporal and spatial restriction? How, for example, does the setting affect Laura? How does it reflect or reveal her character? Why does she simply "si[t] quietly" (par. 10)? What does Porter gain when she deviates from this pattern by taking us inside Braggioni's house near the end of the story?

2. The general setting of "Flowering Judas" is Mexico just after the Mexican revolution of 1910–20. What attracts Laura to Mexico? to the Leftist movement? What keeps her both in Mexico and involved in the movement? What is her relationship to each? To what extent is all this a result and reflection of her personality, outlook, and values? of the place or other people?

3. When and how are the Judas tree and its flowers mentioned and described in the story? What is their significance to the story?

AMY TAN

A Pair of Tickets

The minute our train leaves the Hong Kong border and enters Shenzhen, China, I feel different. I can feel the skin on my forehead tingling, my blood rushing through a new course, my bones aching with a familiar old pain. And I think, My mother was right. I am becoming Chinese.

"Cannot be helped," my mother said when I was fifteen and had vigorously denied that I had any Chinese whatsoever below my skin. I was a sophomore at Galileo High in San Francisco, and all my Caucasian friends agreed: I was about as Chinese as they were. But my mother had studied at a famous nursing school in Shanghai, and she said she knew all about genetics. So there was no doubt in her mind, whether I agreed or not: Once you are born Chinese, you cannot help but feel and think Chinese.

"Someday you will see," said my mother. "It's in your blood, waiting to be let go."

And when she said this, I saw myself transforming like a werewolf, a mutant tag of DNA suddenly triggered, replicating itself insidiously into a *syndrome,* a cluster of telltale Chinese behaviors, all those things my mother did to embarrass me—haggling with store owners, pecking her mouth with a toothpick in public, being color-blind to the fact that lemon yellow and pale pink are not good combinations for winter clothes.

But today I realize I've never really known what it means to be Chinese. I am 5 thirty-six years old. My mother is dead and I am on a train, carrying with me her dreams of coming home. I am going to China.

We are going to Guangzhou, my seventy-two-year-old father, Canning Woo, and I, where we will visit his aunt, whom he has not seen since he was ten years old. And I don't know whether it's the prospect of seeing his aunt or if it's because he's back in China, but now he looks like he's a young boy, so innocent and happy I want to button his sweater and pat his head. We are sitting across from each other, separated by a little table with two cold cups of tea. For the first time I can ever remember, my father has tears in his eyes, and all he is seeing out the train window is a sectioned field of yellow, green, and brown, a narrow canal flanking the tracks, low rising hills, and three people in blue jackets riding an ox-driven cart on this early October morning. And I can't help myself. I also have misty eyes, as if I had seen this a long, long time ago, and had almost forgotten.

In less than three hours, we will be in Guangzhou, which my guidebook tells me is how one properly refers to Canton these days. It seems all the cities I have heard of, except Shanghai, have changed their spellings. I think they are saying China has changed in other ways as well. Chungking is Chongqing. And Kweilin is Guilin. I have looked these names up, because after we see my father's aunt in Guangzhou, we will catch a plane to Shanghai, where I will meet my two half-sisters for the first time.

They are my mother's twin daughters from her first marriage, little babies she was forced to abandon on a road as she was fleeing Kweilin for Chungking in 1944. That was all my mother had told me about these daughters, so they had remained babies in my mind, all these years, sitting on the side of a road, listening to bombs whistling in the distance while sucking their patient red thumbs.

And it was only this year that someone found them and wrote with this joyful news. A letter came from Shanghai, addressed to my mother. When I first heard about this, that they were alive, I imagined my identical sisters transforming from little babies into six-year-old girls. In my mind, they were seated next to each other at a table, taking turns with the fountain pen. One would write a neat row of characters: *Dearest Mama. We are alive.* She would brush back her wispy bangs and hand the other sister the pen, and she would write: *Come get us. Please hurry.*

10   Of course they could not know that my mother had died three months before, suddenly, when a blood vessel in her brain burst. One minute she was talking to my father, complaining about the tenants upstairs, scheming how to evict them under the pretense that relatives from China were moving in. The next minute she was holding her head, her eyes squeezed shut, groping for the sofa, and then crumpling softly to the floor with fluttering hands.

So my father had been the first one to open the letter, a long letter it turned out. And they did call her Mama. They said they always revered her as their true mother. They kept a framed picture of her. They told her about their life, from the time my mother last saw them on the road leaving Kweilin to when they were finally found.

And the letter had broken my father's heart so much—these daughters calling my mother from another life he never knew—that he gave the letter to my mother's old friend Auntie Lindo and asked her to write back and tell my sisters, in the gentlest way possible, that my mother was dead.

But instead Auntie Lindo took the letter to the Joy Luck Club and discussed with Auntie Ying and Auntie An-mei what should be done, because they had known for many years about my mother's search for her twin daughters, her endless hope. Auntie Lindo and the others cried over this double tragedy, of losing my mother three months before, and now again. And so they couldn't help but think of some miracle, some possible way of reviving her from the dead, so my mother could fulfill her dream.

So this is what they wrote to my sisters in Shanghai: "Dearest Daughters, I too have never forgotten you in my memory or in my heart. I never gave up hope that we would see each other again in a joyous reunion. I am only sorry it has been too long. I want to tell you everything about my life since I last saw you. I want to tell you this when our family comes to see you in China. . . ." They signed it with my mother's name.

15   It wasn't until all this had been done that they first told me about my sisters, the letter they received, the one they wrote back.

"They'll think she's coming, then," I murmured. And I had imagined my sisters now being ten or eleven, jumping up and down, holding hands, their pigtails bouncing, excited that their mother—*their* mother—was coming, whereas my mother was dead.

"How can you say she is not coming in a letter?" said Auntie Lindo. "She is their mother. She is your mother. You must be the one to tell them. All these years, they have been dreaming of her." And I thought she was right.

But then I started dreaming, too, of my mother and my sisters and how it would be if I arrived in Shanghai. All these years, while they waited to be found, I had lived with my mother and then had lost her. I imagined seeing my sisters at the airport. They would be standing on their tiptoes, looking anxiously, scanning from one dark head to another as we got off the plane. And I would recognize them instantly, their faces with the identical worried look.

"*Jyejye, Jyejye*. Sister, Sister. We are here," I saw myself saying in my poor version of Chinese.

"Where is Mama?" they would say, and look around, still smiling, two flushed and eager faces. "Is she hiding?" And this would have been like my mother, to stand behind just a bit, to tease a little and make people's patience pull a little on their hearts. I would shake my head and tell my sisters she was not hiding.

"Oh, that must be Mama, no?" one of my sisters would whisper excitedly, pointing to another small woman completely engulfed in a tower of presents. And that, too, would have been like my mother, to bring mountains of gifts, food, and toys for children—all bought on sale—shunning thanks, saying the gifts were nothing, and later turning the labels over to show my sisters, "Calvin Klein, 100% wool."

I imagined myself starting to say, "Sisters, I am sorry, I have come alone . . ." and before I could tell them—they could see it in my face—they were wailing, pulling their hair, their lips twisted in pain, as they ran away from me. And then I saw myself getting back on the plane and coming home.

After I had dreamed this scene many times—watching their despair turn from horror into anger—I begged Auntie Lindo to write another letter. And at first she refused.

"How can I say she is dead? I cannot write this," said Auntie Lindo with a stubborn look.

"But it's cruel to have them believe she's coming on the plane," I said. "When they see it's just me, they'll hate me."

"Hate you? Cannot be." She was scowling. "You are their own sister, their only family."

"You don't understand," I protested.

"What I don't understand?" she said.

And I whispered, "They'll think I'm responsible, that she died because I didn't appreciate her."

And Auntie Lindo looked satisfied and sad at the same time, as if this were true and I had finally realized it. She sat down for an hour, and when she stood up she handed me a two-page letter. She had tears in her eyes. I realized that the very thing I had feared, she had done. So even if she had written the news of my mother's death in English, I wouldn't have had the heart to read it.

"Thank you," I whispered.

The landscape has become gray, filled with low flat cement buildings, old factories, and then tracks and more tracks filled with trains like ours passing by in the opposite direction. I see platforms crowded with people wearing drab Western clothes, with spots of bright colors: little children wearing pink and yellow, red and peach. And there are soldiers in olive green and red, and old ladies in gray tops and pants that stop mid-calf. We are in Guangzhou.

Before the train even comes to a stop, people are bringing down their belongings from above their seats. For a moment there is a dangerous shower of heavy suitcases laden with gifts to relatives, half-broken boxes wrapped in miles of string to keep the contents from spilling out, plastic bags filled with yarn and vegetables and packages of dried mushrooms, and camera cases. And then we are caught in a stream of people rushing, shoving, pushing us along, until we find ourselves in one of a dozen lines waiting to go through customs. I feel as if I were getting on a number 30 Stockton bus in San Francisco. I am in China, I remind myself. And somehow the crowds don't bother me. It feels right. I start pushing too.

I take out the declaration forms and my passport. "Woo," it says at the top, and below that, "June May," who was born in "California, U.S.A.," in 1951. I wonder if the customs people will question whether I'm the same person as in the passport photo. In this picture, my chin-length hair is swept back and artfully styled. I am wearing false eyelashes, eye shadow, and lip liner. My cheeks are hollowed out by bronze blusher. But I had not expected the heat in October. And now my hair hangs limp with the humidity. I wear no makeup; in Hong Kong my mascara had melted into dark circles and everything else had felt like layers of grease. So today my face is plain, unadorned except for a thin mist of shiny sweat on my forehead and nose.

35   Even without makeup, I could never pass for true Chinese. I stand five-foot-six, and my head pokes above the crowd so that I am eye level only with other tourists. My mother once told me my height came from my grandfather, who was a northerner, and may have even had some Mongol blood. "This is what your grandmother once told me," explained my mother. "But now it is too late to ask her. They are all dead, your grandparents, your uncles, and their wives and children, all killed in the war, when a bomb fell on our house. So many generations in one instant."

She had said this so matter-of-factly that I thought she had long since gotten over any grief she had. And then I wondered how she knew they were all dead.

"Maybe they left the house before the bomb fell," I suggested.

"No," said my mother. "Our whole family is gone. It is just you and I."

"But how do you know? Some of them could have escaped."

40   "Cannot be," said my mother, this time almost angrily. And then her frown was washed over by a puzzled blank look, and she began to talk as if she were trying to remember where she had misplaced something. "I went back to that house. I kept looking up to where the house used to be. And it wasn't a house, just the sky. And below, underneath my feet, were four stories of burnt bricks and wood, all the life of our house. Then off to the side I saw things blown into the yard, nothing valuable. There was a bed someone used to sleep in, really just a metal frame twisted up at one corner. And a book, I don't know what kind, because every page had turned black. And I saw a teacup which was unbroken but filled with ashes. And then I found my doll, with her hands and legs broken, her hair burned off. . . . When I was a little girl, I had cried for that doll, seeing it all alone in the store window, and my mother had bought it for me. It was an American doll with yellow hair. It could turn its legs and arms. The eyes moved up and down. And when I married and left my family home, I gave the doll to my youngest niece, because she was like me. She cried if that doll was not with her always. Do you see? If she was in the house with that doll, her parents were there, and so everybody was there, waiting together, because that's how our family was."

The woman in the customs booth stares at my documents, then glances at me briefly, and with two quick movements stamps everything and sternly nods me along. And soon my father and I find ourselves in a large area filled with thousands of people and suitcases. I feel lost and my father looks helpless.

"Excuse me," I say to a man who looks like an American. "Can you tell me where I can get a taxi?" He mumbles something that sounds Swedish or Dutch.

"Syau Yen! Syau Yen!" I hear a piercing voice shout from behind me. An old woman in a yellow knit beret is holding up a pink plastic bag filled with wrapped trinkets. I guess she is trying to sell us something. But my father is staring down at this tiny sparrow of a woman, squinting into her eyes. And then his eyes widen, his face opens up and he smiles like a pleased little boy.

"Aiyi! Aiyi!"—Auntie Auntie!—he says softly.

"Syau Yen!" coos my great-aunt. I think it's funny she has just called my father "Little Wild Goose." It must be his baby milk name, the name used to discourage ghosts from stealing children. 45

They clasp each other's hands—they do not hug—and hold on like this, taking turns saying, "Look at you! You are so old. Look how old you've become!" They are both crying openly, laughing at the same time, and I bite my lip, trying not to cry. I'm afraid to feel their joy. Because I am thinking how different our arrival in Shanghai will be tomorrow, how awkward it will feel.

Now Aiyi beams and points to a Polaroid picture of my father. My father had wisely sent pictures when he wrote and said we were coming. See how smart she was, she seems to intone as she compares the picture to my father. In the letter, my father had said we would call her from the hotel once we arrived, so this is a surprise, that they've come to meet us. I wonder if my sisters will be at the airport.

It is only then that I remember the camera. I had meant to take a picture of my father and his aunt the moment they met. It's not too late.

"Here, stand together over here," I say, holding up the Polaroid. The camera flashes and I hand them the snapshot. Aiyi and my father still stand close together, each of them holding a corner of the picture, watching as their images begin to form. They are almost reverentially quiet. Aiyi is only five years older than my father, which makes her around seventy-seven. But she looks ancient, shrunken, a mummified relic. Her thin hair is pure white, her teeth are brown with decay. So much for stories of Chinese women looking young forever, I think to myself.

Now Aiyi is crooning to me: *"Jandale."* So big already. She looks up at me, at my full height, and then peers into her pink plastic bag—her gifts to us, I have figured out—as if she is wondering what she will give to me, now that I am so old and big. And then she grabs my elbow with her sharp pincerlike grasp and turns me around. A man and a woman in their fifties are shaking hands with my father, everybody smiling and saying, "Ah! Ah!" They are Aiyi's oldest son and his wife, and standing next to them are four other people, around my age, and a little girl who's around ten. The introductions go by so fast, all I know is that one of them is Aiyi's grandson, with his wife, and the other is her granddaughter, with her husband. And the little girl is Lili, Aiyi's great-granddaughter. 50

Aiyi and my father speak the Mandarin dialect from their childhood, but the rest of the family speaks only the Cantonese of their village. I understand only Mandarin but can't speak it that well. So Aiyi and my father gossip unrestrained in Mandarin, exchanging news about people from their old village. And they stop only occasionally to talk to the rest of us, sometimes in Cantonese, sometimes in English.

"Oh, it is as I suspected," says my father, turning to me. "He died last summer." And I already understood this. I just don't know who this person, Li Gong, is. I feel as if I were in the United Nations and the translators had run amok.

"Hello," I say to the little girl. "My name is Jing-mei." But the little girl squirms to look away, causing her parents to laugh with embarrassment. I try to think of Cantonese words I can say to her, stuff I learned from friends in Chinatown, but all I can think of are swear words, terms for bodily functions, and short phrases like "tastes good," "tastes like garbage," and "she's really ugly." And then I have another plan: I hold up the Polaroid camera, beckoning Lili with my finger. She immediately jumps forward, places one hand on her hip in the manner of a fashion model, juts out her chest, and flashes me a toothy smile. As soon as I take the picture she is standing next to me, jumping and giggling every few seconds as she watches herself appear on the greenish film.

By the time we hail taxis for the ride to the hotel, Lili is holding tight onto my hand, pulling me along.

55 In the taxi, Aiyi talks nonstop, so I have no chance to ask her about the different sights we are passing by.

"You wrote and said you would come only for one day," says Aiyi to my father in an agitated tone. "One day! How can you see your family in one day! Toishan is many hours' drive from Guangzhou. And this idea to call us when you arrive. This is nonsense. We have no telephone."

My heart races a little. I wonder if Auntie Lindo told my sisters we would call from the hotel in Shanghai?

Aiyi continues to scold my father. "I was so beside myself, ask my son, almost turned heaven and earth upside down trying to think of a way! So we decided the best was for us to take the bus from Toishan and come into Guangzhou— meet you right from the start."

And now I am holding my breath as the taxi driver dodges between trucks and buses, honking his horn constantly. We seem to be on some sort of long freeway overpass, like a bridge above the city. I can see row after row of apartments, each floor cluttered with laundry hanging out to dry on the balcony. We pass a public bus, with people jammed in so tight their faces are nearly wedged against the window. Then I see the skyline of what must be downtown Guangzhou. From a distance, it looks like a major American city, with highrises and construction going on everywhere. As we slow down in the more congested part of the city, I see scores of little shops, dark inside, lined with counters and shelves. And then there is a building, its front laced with scaffolding made of bamboo poles held together with plastic strips. Men and women are standing on narrow platforms, scraping the sides, working without safety straps or helmets. Oh, would OSHA[1] have a field day here, I think.

60 Aiyi's shrill voice rises up again: "So it is a shame you can't see our village, our house. My sons have been quite successful, selling our vegetables in the free market. We had enough these last few years to build a big house, three stories, all of new brick, big enough for our whole family and then some. And every year, the money is even better. You Americans aren't the only ones who know how to get rich!"

The taxi stops and I assume we've arrived, but then I peer out at what looks like a grander version of the Hyatt Regency. "This is communist China?" I wonder out loud. And then I shake my head toward my father. "This must be the wrong hotel." I quickly pull out our itinerary, travel tickets, and reservations. I had explicitly instructed my travel agent to choose something inexpensive, in

1. The Occupational Safety and Health Administration, a division of the U.S. Department of Labor.

the thirty-to-forty-dollar range. I'm sure of this. And there it says on our itinerary: Garden Hotel, Huanshi Dong Lu. Well, our travel agent had better be prepared to eat the extra, that's all I have to say.

The hotel is magnificent. A bellboy complete with uniform and sharp-creased cap jumps forward and begins to carry our bags into the lobby. Inside, the hotel looks like an orgy of shopping arcades and restaurants all encased in granite and glass. And rather than be impressed, I am worried about the expense, as well as the appearance it must give Aiyi, that we rich Americans cannot be without our luxuries even for one night.

But when I step up to the reservation desk, ready to haggle over this booking mistake, it is confirmed. Our rooms are prepaid, thirty-four dollars each. I feel sheepish, and Aiyi and the others seem delighted by our temporary surroundings. Lili is looking wide-eyed at an arcade filled with video games.

Our whole family crowds into one elevator, and the bellboy waves, saying he will meet us on the eighteenth floor. As soon as the elevator door shuts, everybody becomes very quiet, and when the door finally opens again, everybody talks at once in what sounds like relieved voices. I have the feeling Aiyi and the others have never been on such a long elevator ride.

Our rooms are next to each other and are identical. The rugs, drapes, bed- 65 spreads are all in shades of taupe. There's a color television with remote-control panels built into the lamp table between the two twin beds. The bathroom has marble walls and floors. I find a built-in wet bar with a small refrigerator stocked with Heineken beer, Coke Classic, and Seven-Up, mini-bottles of Johnnie Walker Red, Bacardi rum, and Smirnoff vodka, and packets of M & M's, honey-roasted cashews, and Cadbury chocolate bars. And again I say out loud, "This is communist China?"

My father comes into my room. "They decided we should just stay here and visit," he says, shrugging his shoulders. "They say, Less trouble that way. More time to talk."

"What about dinner?" I ask. I have been envisioning my first real Chinese feast for many days already, a big banquet with one of those soups steaming out of a carved winter melon, chicken wrapped in clay, Peking duck, the works.

My father walks over and picks up a room service book next to a *Travel & Leisure* magazine. He flips through the pages quickly and then points to the menu. "This is what they want," says my father.

So it's decided. We are going to dine tonight in our rooms, with our family, sharing hamburgers, french fries, and apple pie à la mode.

Aiyi and her family are browsing the shops while we clean up. After a hot ride on 70 the train, I'm eager for a shower and cooler clothes.

The hotel has provided little packets of shampoo which, upon opening, I discover is the consistency and color of hoisin sauce.[2] This is more like it, I think. This is China. And I rub some in my damp hair.

Standing in the shower, I realize this is the first time I've been by myself in what seems like days. But instead of feeling relieved, I feel forlorn. I think about what my mother said, about activating my genes and becoming Chinese. And I wonder what she meant.

---

2. Sweet brownish-red sauce made from soybeans, sugar, water, spices, garlic, and chili.

Right after my mother died, I asked myself a lot of things, things that couldn't be answered, to force myself to grieve more. It seemed as if I wanted to sustain my grief, to assure myself that I had cared deeply enough.

But now I ask the questions mostly because I want to know the answers. What was that pork stuff she used to make that had the texture of sawdust? What were the names of the uncles who died in Shanghai? What had she dreamt all these years about her other daughters? All the times when she got mad at me, was she really thinking about them? Did she wish I were they? Did she regret that I wasn't?

---

75 At one o'clock in the morning, I awake to tapping sounds on the window. I must have dozed off and now I feel my body uncramping itself. I'm sitting on the floor, leaning against one of the twin beds. Lili is lying next to me. The others are asleep, too, sprawled out on the beds and floor. Aiyi is seated at a little table, looking very sleepy. And my father is staring out the window, tapping his fingers on the glass. The last time I listened my father was telling Aiyi about his life since he last saw her. How he had gone to Yenching University, later got a post with a newspaper in Chungking, met my mother there, a young widow. How they later fled together to Shanghai to try to find my mother's family house, but there was nothing there. And then they traveled eventually to Canton and then to Hong Kong, then Haiphong and finally to San Francisco. . . .

"Suyuan didn't tell me she was trying all these years to find her daughters," he is now saying in a quiet voice. "Naturally, I did not discuss her daughters with her. I thought she was ashamed she had left them behind."

"Where did she leave them?" asks Aiyi. "How were they found?"

I am wide awake now. Although I have heard parts of this story from my mother's friends.

"It happened when the Japanese took over Kweilin," says my father.

80 "Japanese in Kweilin?" says Aiyi. "That was never the case. Couldn't be. The Japanese never came to Kweilin."

"Yes, that is what the newspapers reported. I know this because I was working for the news bureau at the time. The Kuomintang[3] often told us what we could say and could not say. But we knew the Japanese had come into Kwangsi Province. We had sources who told us how they had captured the Wuchang-Canton railway. How they were coming overland, making very fast progress, marching toward the provincial capital."

Aiyi looks astonished. "If people did not know this, how could Suyuan know the Japanese were coming?"

"An officer of the Kuomintang secretly warned her," explains my father. "Suyuan's husband also was an officer and everybody knew that officers and their families would be the first to be killed. So she gathered a few possessions and, in the middle of the night, she picked up her daughters and fled on foot. The babies were not even one year old."

"How could she give up those babies!" sighs Aiyi. "Twin girls. We have never had such luck in our family." And then she yawns again.

---

3. National People's Party, led by Generalissimo Chiang Kai-shek (1887–1975), which fought successfully against the Japanese occupation before being defeated militarily in 1949 by the Chinese Communist Party, led by Mao Zedong (1893–1976).

"What were they named?" she asks. I listen carefully. I had been planning on using just the familiar "Sister" to address them both. But now I want to know how to pronounce their names.

"They have their father's surname, Wang," says my father. "And their given names are Chwun Yu and Chwun Hwa."

"What do the names mean?" I ask.

"Ah." My father draws imaginary characters on the window. "One means 'Spring Rain,' the other 'Spring Flower,'" he explains in English, "because they born in the spring, and of course rain come before flower, same order these girls are born. Your mother like a poet, don't you think?"

I nod my head. I see Aiyi nod her head forward, too. But it falls forward and stays there. She is breathing deeply, noisily. She is asleep.

"And what does Ma's name mean?" I whisper.

"'Suyuan,'" he says, writing more invisible characters on the glass. "The way she write it in Chinese, it mean 'Long-Cherished Wish.' Quite a fancy name, not so ordinary like flower name. See this first character, it mean something like 'For-ever Never Forgotten.' But there is another way to write 'Suyuan.' Sound exactly the same, but the meaning is opposite." His finger creates the brushstrokes of another character. "The first part look the same: 'Never Forgotten.' But the last part add to first part make the whole word mean 'Long-Held Grudge.' Your mother get angry with me, I tell her her name should be Grudge."

My father is looking at me, moist-eyed. "See, I pretty clever, too, hah?"

I nod, wishing I could find some way to comfort him. "And what about my name," I ask, "what does 'Jing-mei' mean?"

"Your name also special," he says. I wonder if any name in Chinese is not something special. "'Jing' like excellent *jing*. Not just good, it's something pure, essential, the best quality. *Jing* is good leftover stuff when you take impurities out of something like gold, or rice, or salt. So what is left—just pure essence. And 'Mei,' this is common *mei*, as in *meimei*, 'younger sister.'"

I think about this. My mother's long-cherished wish. Me, the younger sister who was supposed to be the essence of the others. I feed myself with the old grief, wondering how disappointed my mother must have been. Tiny Aiyi stirs suddenly, her head rolls and then falls back, her mouth opens as if to answer my question. She grunts in her sleep, tucking her body more closely into the chair.

"So why did she abandon those babies on the road?" I need to know, because now I feel abandoned too.

"Long time I wondered this myself," says my father. "But then I read that letter from her daughters in Shanghai now, and I talk to Auntie Lindo, all the others. And then I knew. No shame in what she done. None."

"What happened?"

"Your mother running away—" begins my father.

"No, tell me in Chinese," I interrupt. "Really, I can understand."

He begins to talk, still standing at the window, looking into the night.

After fleeing Kweilin, your mother walked for several days trying to find a main road. Her thought was to catch a ride on a truck or wagon, to catch enough rides until she reached Chungking, where her husband was stationed.

She had sewn money and jewelry into the lining of her dress, enough, she thought, to barter rides all the way. If I am lucky, she thought, I will not have to trade the heavy gold bracelet and jade ring. These were things from her mother, your grandmother.

By the third day, she had traded nothing. The roads were filled with people, everybody running and begging for rides from passing trucks. The trucks rushed by, afraid to stop. So your mother found no rides, only the start of dysentery pains in her stomach.

105   Her shoulders ached from the two babies swinging from scarf slings. Blisters grew on the palms from holding two leather suitcases. And then the blisters burst and began to bleed. After a while, she left the suitcases behind, keeping only the food and a few clothes. And later she also dropped the bags of wheat flour and rice and kept walking like this for many miles, singing songs to her little girls, until she was delirious with pain and fever.

Finally, there was not one more step left in her body. She didn't have the strength to carry those babies any farther. She slumped to the ground. She knew she would die of her sickness, or perhaps from thirst, from starvation, or from the Japanese, who she was sure were marching right behind her.

She took the babies out of the slings and sat them on the side of the road, then lay down next to them. You babies are so good, she said, so quiet. They smiled back, reaching their chubby hands for her, wanting to be picked up again. And then she knew she could not bear to watch her babies die with her.

She saw a family with three young children in a cart going by. "Take my babies, I beg you," she cried to them. But they stared back with empty eyes and never stopped.

She saw another person pass and called out again. This time a man turned around, and he had such a terrible expression—your mother said it looked like death itself—she shivered and looked away.

110   When the road grew quiet, she tore open the lining of her dress, and stuffed jewelry under the shirt of one baby and money under the other. She reached into her pocket and drew out the photos of her family, the picture of her father and mother, the picture of herself and her husband on their wedding day. And she wrote on the back of each the names of the babies and this same message: "Please care for these babies with the money and valuables provided. When it is safe to come, if you bring them to Shanghai, 9 Weichang Lu, the Li family will be glad to give you a generous reward. Li Suyuan and Wang Fuchi."

And then she touched each baby's cheek and told her not to cry. She would go down the road to find them some food and would be back. And without looking back, she walked down the road, stumbling and crying, thinking only of this one last hope, that her daughters would be found by a kindhearted person who would care for them. She would not allow herself to imagine anything else.

She did not remember how far she walked, which direction she went, when she fainted, or how she was found. When she awoke, she was in the back of a bouncing truck with several other sick people, all moaning. And she began to scream, thinking she was now on a journey to Buddhist hell. But the face of an American missionary lady bent over her and smiled, talking to her in a soothing language she did not understand. And yet she could somehow understand. She had been saved for no good reason, and it was now too late to go back and save her babies.

When she arrived in Chungking, she learned her husband had died two weeks before. She told me later she laughed when the officers told her this news, she was so delirious with madness and disease. To come so far, to lose so much and to find nothing.

I met her in a hospital. She was lying on a cot, hardly able to move, her dysentery had drained her so thin. I had come in for my foot, my missing toe, which was cut off by a piece of falling rubble. She was talking to herself, mumbling.

"Look at these clothes," she said, and I saw she had on a rather unusual dress 115 for wartime. It was silk satin, quite dirty, but there was no doubt it was a beautiful dress.

"Look at this face," she said, and I saw her dusty face and hollow cheeks, her eyes shining black. "Do you see my foolish hope?"

"I thought I had lost everything, except these two things," she murmured. "And I wondered which I would lose next. Clothes or hope? Hope or clothes?"

"But now, see here, look what is happening," she said, laughing, as if all her prayers had been answered. And she was pulling hair out of her head as easily as one lifts new wheat from wet soil.

It was an old peasant woman who found them. "How could I resist?" the peasant woman later told your sisters when they were older. They were still sitting obediently near where your mother had left them, looking like little fairy queens waiting for their sedan to arrive.

The woman, Mei Ching, and her husband, Mei Han, lived in a stone cave. 120 There were thousands of hidden caves like that in and around Kweilin so secret that the people remained hidden even after the war ended. The Meis would come out of their cave every few days and forage for food supplies left on the road, and sometimes they would see something that they both agreed was a tragedy to leave behind. So one day they took back to their cave a delicately painted set of rice bowls, another day a little footstool with a velvet cushion and two new wedding blankets. And once, it was your sisters.

They were pious people, Muslims, who believed the twin babies were a sign of double luck, and they were sure of this when, later in the evening, they discovered how valuable the babies were. She and her husband had never seen rings and bracelets like those. And while they admired the pictures, knowing the babies came from a good family, neither of them could read or write. It was not until many months later that Mei Ching found someone who could read the writing on the back. By then, she loved these baby girls like her own.

In 1952 Mei Han, the husband, died. The twins were already eight years old, and Mei Ching now decided it was time to find your sisters' true family.

She showed the girls the picture of their mother and told them they had been born into a great family and she would take them back to see their true mother and grandparents. Mei Ching told them about the reward, but she swore she would refuse it. She loved these girls so much, she only wanted them to have what they were entitled to—a better life, a fine house, educated ways. Maybe the family would let her stay on as the girls' amah.[4] Yes, she was certain they would insist.

Of course, when she found the place at 9 Weichang Lu, in the old French Concession, it was something completely different. It was the site of a factory building, recently constructed, and none of the workers knew what had become of the family whose house had burned down on that spot.

4. Maidservant or nurse.

125   Mei Ching could not have known, of course, that your mother and I, her new husband, had already returned to that same place in 1945 in hopes of finding both her family and her daughters.

Your mother and I stayed in China until 1947. We went to many different cities—back to Kweilin, to Changsha, as far south as Kunming. She was always looking out of one corner of her eye for twin babies, then little girls. Later we went to Hong Kong, and when we finally left in 1949 for the United States, I think she was even looking for them on the boat. But when we arrived, she no longer talked about them. I thought, At last, they have died in her heart.

When letters could be openly exchanged between China and the United States, she wrote immediately to old friends in Shanghai and Kweilin. I did not know she did this. Auntie Lindo told me. But of course, by then, all the street names had changed. Some people had died, others had moved away. So it took many years to find a contact. And when she did find an old schoolmate's address and wrote asking her to look for her daughters, her friend wrote back and said this was impossible, like looking for a needle on the bottom of the ocean. How did she know her daughters were in Shanghai and not somewhere else in China? The friend, of course, did not ask, How do you know your daughters are still alive?

So her schoolmate did not look. Finding babies lost during the war was a matter of foolish imagination, and she had no time for that.

But every year, your mother wrote to different people. And this last year, I think she got a big idea in her head, to go to China and find them herself. I remember she told me, "Canning, we should go, before it is too late, before we are too old." And I told her we were already too old, it was already too late.

130   I just thought she wanted to be a tourist! I didn't know she wanted to go and look for her daughters. So when I said it was too late, that must have put a terrible thought in her head that her daughters might be dead. And I think this possibility grew bigger and bigger in her head, until it killed her.

Maybe it was your mother's dead spirit who guided her Shanghai schoolmate to find her daughters. Because after your mother died, the schoolmate saw your sisters, by chance, while shopping for shoes at the Number One Department Store on Nanjing Dong Road. She said it was like a dream, seeing these two women who looked so much alike, moving down the stairs together. There was something about their facial expressions that reminded the schoolmate of your mother.

She quickly walked over to them and called their names, which of course, they did not recognize at first, because Mei Ching had changed their names. But your mother's friend was so sure, she persisted. "Are you not Wang Chwun Yu and Wang Chwun Hwa?" she asked them. And then these double-image women became very excited, because they remembered the names written on the back of an old photo, a photo of a young man and woman they still honored, as their much-loved first parents, who had died and become spirit ghosts still roaming the earth looking for them.

At the airport, I am exhausted. I could not sleep last night. Aiyi had followed me into my room at three in the morning, and she instantly fell asleep on one of the twin beds, snoring with the might of a lumberjack. I lay awake thinking about my mother's story, realizing how much I have never known about her, grieving that my sisters and I had both lost her.

And now at the airport, after shaking hands with everybody, waving good-bye, I think about all the different ways we leave people in this world. Cheerily waving good-bye to some at airports, knowing we'll never see each other again. Leaving others on the side of the road, hoping that we will. Finding my mother in my father's story and saying good-bye before I have a chance to know her better.

Aiyi smiles at me as we wait for our gate to be called. She is so old. I put one arm around her and one arm around Lili. They are the same size, it seems. And then it's time. As we wave good-bye one more time and enter the waiting area, I get the sense I am going from one funeral to another. In my hand I'm clutching a pair of tickets to Shanghai. In two hours we'll be there. 135

The plane takes off. I close my eyes. How can I describe to them in my broken Chinese about our mother's life? Where should I begin?

"Wake up, we're here," says my father. And I awake with my heart pounding in my throat. I look out the window and we're already on the runway. It's gray outside.

And now I'm walking down the steps of the plane, onto the tarmac and toward the building. If only, I think, if only my mother had lived long enough to be the one walking toward them. I am so nervous I cannot even feel my feet. I am just moving somehow.

Somebody shouts, "She's arrived!" And then I see her. Her short hair. Her small body. And that same look on her face. She has the back of her hand pressed hard against her mouth. She is crying as though she had gone through a terrible ordeal and were happy it is over.

And I know it's not my mother, yet it is the same look she had when I was five and had disappeared all afternoon, for such a long time, that she was convinced I was dead. And when I miraculously appeared, sleepy-eyed, crawling from underneath my bed, she wept and laughed, biting the back of her hand to make sure it was true. 140

And now I see her again, two of her, waving, and in one hand there is a photo, the Polaroid I sent them. As soon as I get beyond the gate, we run toward each other, all three of us embracing, all hesitations and expectations forgotten.

"Mama, Mama," we all murmur, as if she is among us.

My sisters look at me, proudly. *"Meimei jandale,"* says one sister proudly to the other. "Little Sister has grown up." I look at their faces again and I see no trace of my mother in them. Yet they still look familiar. And now I also see what part of me is Chinese. It is so obvious. It is my family. It is in our blood. After all these years, it can finally be let go.

My sisters and I stand, arms around each other, laughing and wiping the tears from each other's eyes. The flash of the Polaroid goes off and my father hands me the snapshot. My sisters and I watch quietly together, eager to see what develops.

The gray-green surface changes to the bright colors of our three images, sharpening and deepening all at once. And although we don't speak, I know we all see it: Together we look like our mother. Her same eyes, her same mouth, open in surprise to see, at last, her long-cherished wish. 145

1989

QUESTIONS

1. Why is the opening scene of "A Pair of Tickets"—the train journey from Hong Kong to Guangzhou—an appropriate setting for June May's remark that she is "becoming Chinese"?
2. When June May arrives in Guangzhou, what are some details that seem familiar to her, and what are some that seem exotic? Why is she so preoccupied with comparing China to America?
3. June May says that "she could never pass for true Chinese," yet by the end of the story she has discovered "the part of me that is Chinese." How does the meaning of "Chinese" evolve throughout the story?

SUGGESTIONS FOR WRITING

1. Write an essay in which you compare the use of setting in any two stories in this book. You might compare the re-creation of two similar settings, such as landscapes far from home, foreign cities, or stifling suburbs; or you might contrast the treatment of different kinds of settings. Be sure to consider not only the authors' descriptive techniques but also the way the authors use setting to shape plot, point of view, and character.
2. In "A Pair of Tickets," Amy Tan provides detailed descriptions of June May's journeys to Guangzhou and Shanghai. In his account of his wife's escape from Kweilin, June May's father says little about the landscape. Write an essay in which you compare the two very different storytelling techniques used in this story.
3. In at least two of the stories in this chapter, a place encountered for the first time by a traveler is described with great vividness: the city of Guangzhou in "A Pair of Tickets" and the city of Yalta in "The Lady with the Dog." Citing examples from these stories, write an essay in which you discuss the effect of new surroundings on our perceptions, emotions, and memories.
4. Choose any story in this chapter and write an essay that explores how the story both draws on and also encourages us to rethink our ideas about a particular place and time and social milieu, perhaps (but not necessarily) by showing us characters who themselves either come to see a setting differently or refuse to do so.
5. Write a fifth section for "The Lady with the Dog."
6. Write a story in which a newcomer brings a fresh perspective to a familiar setting.

SAMPLE WRITING

In the following essay, student writer Steven Matview explores the role of setting in Anton Chekhov's "The Lady with the Dog." His essay could well have been written in response to the second of the "Suggestions for Writing" in this chapter. Read the essay responsively and critically, taking time to consider the details Steven chooses to highlight and the way he interprets them. Does he manage to build a convincing and thorough argument about the role of setting in "The Lady with the Dog"? What other details from the story might deserve a place in this argument? In particular, notice how Steven concentrates on temporal setting (the seasons) while commenting only briefly on spatial setting and on the interconnections between time and space in the story. If Steven were your classmate, what three things would you suggest he most needs to do in order to improve the essay in revision?

Steven Matview
Professor Anne Stevens
English 298
12 March 2008

The Importance of Good Setting: How Setting Reflects Emotions in Anton Chekhov's "The Lady with the Dog"

Setting is important to Chekhov's "The Lady with the Dog." But wait, isn't setting important to all stories? Not necessarily. In many stories, like Hemingway's "Hills like White Elephants," the plot could be happening anywhere, and it would not matter. But in "The Lady with the Dog" the setting plays an important role in the story, in particular to Dmitri, who is the main character and who experiences the most growth throughout. He goes from being a man at 40 who is full of youthful energy and thinks he has been loved by many women to an old man who realizes that he is just experiencing love for the first time. During the course of the narrative, the setting Chekhov maps out shows the progression of Dmitri's affair with Anna Sergeyevna, Dmitri's state of mind, and the changes that Dmitri undergoes. The setting in this story is just as important as any character. In fact, I would argue that the setting is the single most important component of the story.

Dmitri's relationship with the lady with the dog has its ups and downs, which are reflected in the seasons and the descriptions of weather. Anna, the lady with the dog, makes this apparent when she says, "The weather is better this evening" (184). Their lives are better when they are together in the summer. This is the time Dmitri and Anna meet and start their courtship. Both are married, and both have spent so much time forcing themselves to love their partners that they do not recognize real love when they feel it. Dmitri initially only wants a fling and doesn't even learn or use Anna's name, referring to her only as "the lady with the dog." There isn't any stress yet, and the two can be just happy with things the way they are. They go on dates and spend time together in Anna's hotel room. Dmitri starts to think of her as "Anna Sergeyevna—'the lady with the dog'" (par. 29), showing a shift within the relationship. He shows he's started to think of this as more of a relationship by using her full name but doesn't completely switch, as he adds in that epithet "lady with the dog." He is trying to resist because he is still married. Dmitri feels young and alive and thinks back to all the women he has made happy in his life.

Another aspect of the setting are the places described in the story, which relate to things the characters feel or know on a subconscious level. At the start of the story, Dmitri is staying at a seaside resort in Yalta. We know that a resort is an impersonal place, where someone can reinvent themselves or get away from the things they don't like about home. Dmitri reinvents his idea about what love is while getting away from a wife he does not care for. Dmitri meets Anna for the first time "in the public gardens" (par. 2). A garden is a place of growth, reflecting the soon-to-be growth of their relationship, as well as the growth Dmitri will experience as a person. They then go on a date, and we become privy to a metaphor describing Dmitri's marriage and how things will go with Anna: "Owing to the roughness of the sea, the steamer arrived late, after the sun had set, and it was a long time turning about before it reached the groyne" (par. 22). The steamer is Dmitri, the sea is his life, and the groyne, a device designed to disrupt the flow of water, is Anna. It took Dmitri longer to find true love, and he has gone through a rough time in a boring marriage, and now there is someone to break that up. This is when Dmitri starts to feel love for Anna, though he does not realize it is love because it is so different from what he has known in the past.

Things change as soon as the next season approaches. The first challenges that arise in the courtship of Dmitri and Anna come when the season begins to change from summer to autumn. Dmitri mentions here that "it's a cold evening" (par. 60), the first time cold is mentioned in the present (before it was only used to describe the unhappy places Anna and Dmitri were escaping from) and a stark contrast to Anna's comment about the weather earlier in the story. Things are starting to get worse for the relationship. Word gets to Anna that she must travel back to her home to be with her husband, who has fallen ill. Dmitri finds that he does not want to let Anna go, that the fling he wanted has turned into something much more. Dmitri thinks that he was "warm and affectionate with [Anna]" (par. 59), terms associated with summer weather. But, with autumn approaching, Dmitri decides that they were not really in love. This is because the feeling he has does not resemble the forced love he has always experienced with his wife and mistresses, but it is brought up as the object of his "warm feelings" leaves and is replaced with the "cold night."

Change of place goes hand in hand with a change of seasons and weather here. And we are told shortly before Anna leaves that "Yalta was hardly visible through the morning mist; white clouds stood motionless on mountain-tops" (par. 47). The mist covering Yalta is like the uncertainty that lies in their future as the summer is winding down. Neither can see clearly what will come from their summer tryst when the time comes to separate. White is a color that is often associated with purity, and Dmitri is experiencing a pure, true kind of love for the first time, but he also has obstacles to overcome that are represented by the mountains.

Dmtri thinks he will get over Anna quickly now that she's gone, but winter brings him even more hardships. The most difficult time the couple face comes in the season of winter. Winter is a cold season often affiliated with sadness and the absence of hope. We find out that "the frosts had begun already" (par. 62), meaning the bad times have already started, and we join Dmitri after he's already been back in Moscow for a short time. In Moscow Dmitri has not stopped thinking of Anna Sergeyevna, who is only referred to by her full name now. Referring to her as "Anna Sergeyevna" instead of "the lady with the dog" is a subtle way of letting us know that Dmitri is thinking of her as more than a fling that has gone by, as we saw earlier that he only called her "the lady with the dog" when he didn't have feelings for her. They are separated by cities and by circumstance, and it seems the relationship might be over. In winter all the plants die, and Dmitri and Anna, whose relationship first blossomed in a garden, seem to have a dead relationship. We find out that "more than a month has past" and that "real winter has come" (186), real winter representing the increasing feelings of separation anxiety Dmitri is suffering from.

We get more visual descriptions in Moscow and Anna's unnamed city relating to the characters' thoughts. After Anna leaves and Dmitri returns to his home in Moscow, we find out that he wants to escape to "restaurants, clubs, dinner-parties, [and] anniversary celebrations" (par. 63), showing us that Dmitri is feeling repressed at home compared to the freedom he had at the resort. After confiding in a local his problems, Dmitri thinks, "there is no escaping or getting away from it— just as though one were in a madhouse or a prison" (par. 72). A madhouse and a prison are two places that no one wants to be. Both places are where you are kept from loved ones. But they are also places you are put in when you have done something wrong, a hint that Dmitri feels he's made mistakes in the past, done his time, and now wants to be free to be with Anna.

Dmitri then decides to go to Anna's city, which is left unnamed in the story. This reflects that it is really Dmitri's journey. Dmitri has a hard time reaching Anna at first, as she is tucked away in the house she shares with her husband.

When Dmitri finally does confront Anna she does not initially seem happy to see him. Dmitri confronts Anna at a performance of the play *The Geisha*. The opera and the opera house it is performed in have many qualities that suggest Dmitri's emotional state. The opera house is described as having "a thick fog above the chandelier," and its "gallery was noisy and restless" (par. 85). Dmitri has lots of noisy thoughts in his head as he approaches Anna with uncertainty. As Dmitri approaches Anna the musicians begin tuning their instruments. They are getting ready for the big performance, as Dmitri is getting ready to renew his relationship with Anna. Anna at first appears to be unhappy and takes Dmitri down a path of winding corridors and then up and down a "narrow, gloomy staircase" (par. 93). The outlook seems gloomy for Dmitri, but she does agree to see him again and proceeds to profess her love for him.

At the end of winter, with spring fast approaching, things between Dmitri and Anna begin to show slight improvement over early winter. The weather is described as being "three degrees above freezing-point, and yet it is snowing" (par. 105). Things are getting better for Dmitri, who knows now that Anna loves him and wants to be with him, but it's not all great yet as both are still married and forced to keep their relationship a secret. The open-air setting of the gardens that their relationship started in is replaced by a hotel room, giving the final scene a claustrophobic feel as Anna wonders how they can be together. At the end of the story the couple is still trying to find a way to make their relationship work when we are told, "it seemed as though in a little while the solution would be found" (par. 124). Winter is ending, and spring, a season of growth, new beginnings, and love, is on the horizon. From this we might deduce that the couple will make it, at least into the spring.

But will they? The fact that the story ends with the couple in a "gray area" is fitting because gray, a color associated with ambiguity (shades of gray compared to a black-and-white situation; a "gray area"), in fact appears often in the story. Dmitri is in a situation that involves a lot of moral ambiguity. During the course of the narrative he ends up in love with a married woman while he himself is also married. They begin existing in this gray area where we as readers begin to wonder if what they are doing is really wrong, since they are committing adultery. Anna's eyes are gray, reminding us that Dmitri is entering into a moral gray area whenever he is engaging in this relationship. When Dmitri goes to find Anna and resume their relationship in her home town, he stays at a hotel room whose "floor was covered with grey army cloth" (par. 75) and where there is gray dust and a gray blanket. He enters another gray area when he wants to do what his heart says is right by reuniting with Anna, but doing so is committing more adultery.

But I feel that the recurring gray colors also imply something besides ambiguity—the sadness and lack of excitement that Dmitri has always had in his life thanks to his unhappy marriage and that he might, paradoxically, have come to expect or even need. We can see this when he refers to his hotel in Anna's city as "the best room at the hotel" (par. 75), but filled with items of gray, or when Anna is "wearing his favourite grey dress" (par. 108). The hotel room and Anna are both things that are great or that he adores, but they have that tinge of sadness, represented by the gray, that he needs.

Looking back over the story, we as readers can come to our own conclusions about whether or not Dmitri and Anna stay together. From looking at the progression of the weather we see that in the summer things are good, in fall bad situations arise, winter is the worst time, and the dawn of spring shows slight hope. Following this progression, I believe that when spring finally hits they will be able to come up with a plan to stay a couple. Dmitri and Anna would be happy. We would see Dmitri and Anna figuring out a way to make their relationship public and no longer to be confined to enclosed hiding places. The real question then would be whether the gray would fade out of Dmitri's life after he finds a happiness with Anna that will last past the following summer or whether the cycle is just doomed to repeat itself, as summer eventually turns into winter and the brightest of colors and emotions fade into gray.

Suburbia: An Album

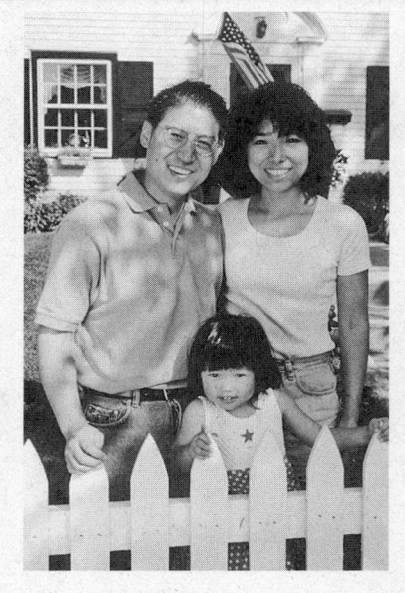

Comparing texts that share the same or similar settings is one way to better appreciate how each handles setting, what view of a time and place each affords, and how their views compare with conventional ones. To help you make such comparisons, this album gathers three stories set in similar places but different times, ranging from just after World War II (which ended in 1945) to the 1980s. To say that these stories share a geographical setting may at first seem odd, however, since the action of John Cheever's "The Country Husband" takes place near New York City, Hanif Kureishi's "Long Ago Yesterday" near London, and Michael Chabon's "The Lost World" outside Boston. The common denominator is that all these locales are *near* rather than *in* a city—these stories' shared setting is suburbia.

Little boxes on the hillside,
Little boxes made of ticky tacky
Little boxes on the hillside,
Little boxes all the same
—MALVINA REYNOLDS

Merriam-Webster's Online Dictionary defines a *suburb* as "an outlying part of a city or town" or "a smaller community adjacent to or within commuting distance of a city." But no dictionary definition can capture the complex connotations of *suburbia* or its central role in modern life, literature, and popular culture. If you try to conjure it in your mind's eye, what you are likely to picture are not just particular sorts of buildings and streets arranged in a particular way, but also particular sorts of people in a particular kind of family living a particular sort of life. That picture likely derives from your experience not only of actual suburbs but also of the countless television programs and movies set in this milieu—from *Father Knows Best* (1954–63) and *The Brady Bunch* (1969–74), to *The Sopranos* (1999–2007), *Desperate Housewives* (2004–present), and *Weeds* (2005–present); from *The Stepford Wives* (1975), *Back to the Future* (1985), and *Blue Velvet* (1986), to *Pleasantville* (1998), *American Beauty* (1999), *Little Children* (2006), and *Disturbia* (2007). The fictions we watch, as well as those we read, help shape our view of places and times.

Especially in the United States, suburbia has, since at least the 1940s, been an idea and an ideal as much as a place. Yet that ideal has always been, and remains, a contested and evolving one. Is suburbia a place of "wide lawns and narrow minds," as Ernest Hemingway purportedly said of the affluent Chicago-area neighborhood in which he grew up? Is it a place of "ticky tacky" houses and people who all both look and think "all the same" as the *Weeds* theme song would have it? Or is it a "paradise" so complete that "a family can live a full and happy life and never leave," as a character claims in the 1961 comedy *Bachelor in Paradise*? Or might suburbia be something else entirely? How do each of the three stories that follow implicitly answer such questions? What might they imply about how suburbia and our views of it have and haven't evolved over time? How might their views compare to, and perhaps complicate, your own?

JOHN CHEEVER

The Country Husband

To begin at the beginning, the airplane from Minneapolis in which Francis Weed was traveling East ran into heavy weather. The sky had been a hazy blue, with the clouds below the plane lying so close together that nothing could be seen of the earth. The mist began to form outside the windows, and they flew into a white cloud of such density that it reflected the exhaust fires. The color of the cloud darkened to gray, and the plane began to rock. Francis had been in heavy weather before, but he had never been shaken up so much. The man in the seat beside him pulled a flask out of his pocket and took a drink. Francis smiled at his neighbor, but the man looked away; he wasn't sharing his pain killer with anyone. The plane began to drop and flounder wildly. A child was crying. The air in the cabin was overheated and stale, and Francis' left foot went to sleep. He read a little from a paper book that he had bought at the airport, but the violence of the storm divided his attention. It was black outside the ports. The exhaust fires blazed and shed sparks in the dark, and, inside, the shaded lights, the stuffiness, and the window curtains gave the cabin an atmosphere of intense and misplaced domesticity. Then the light flickered and went out. "You know what I've always wanted to do?" the man beside Francis said suddenly. "I've always wanted to buy a farm in New Hampshire and raise beef cattle." The stewardess announced that they were going to make an emergency landing. All but the children saw in their minds the spreading wings of the Angel of Death. The pilot could be heard singing faintly, "I've got sixpence, jolly, jolly sixpence. I've got sixpence to last me all my life . . ."[1] There was no other sound.

The loud groaning of the hydraulic valves swallowed up the pilot's song, and there was a shrieking high in the air, like automobile brakes, and the plane hit flat on its belly in a cornfield and shook them so violently that an old man up forward howled, "Me kidneys! Me kidneys!" The stewardess flung open the door, and someone opened an emergency door at the back, letting in the sweet noise of their continuing mortality—the idle splash and smell of a heavy rain. Anxious for their lives, they filed out of the doors and scattered over the cornfield in all directions, praying that the thread would hold. It did. Nothing happened. When it was clear that the plane would not burn or explode, the crew and the stewardess gathered the passengers together and led them to the shelter of a barn. They were not far from Philadelphia, and in a little while a string of taxis took them into the city. "It's just like the Marne,"[2] someone said, but there was surprisingly little relaxation of that suspiciousness with which many Americans regard their fellow travelers.

In Philadelphia, Francis Weed got a train to New York. At the end of that journey, he crossed the city and caught just as it was about to pull out the commuting train that he took five nights a week to his home in Shady Hill.

He sat with Trace Bearden. "You know, I was in that plane that just crashed outside Philadelphia," he said. "We came down in a field. . . ." He had traveled faster than the newspapers or the rain, and the weather in New York was sunny and mild. It was a day in late September, as fragrant and shapely as an apple. Trace listened to the story, but how could he get excited? Francis had no powers that would let him re-create a brush with death—particularly in the atmosphere of a commuting train, journeying through a sunny countryside where already, in the slum gardens, there were signs of harvest. Trace picked up his newspaper,

1. Song popular with Allied troops in World War II.
2. On September 8, 1914, over one thousand Paris taxicabs were requisitioned to move troops to the Marne River to halt the encircling Germans.

and Francis was left alone with his thoughts. He said good night to Trace on the platform at Shady Hill and drove in his secondhand Volkswagen up to the Blenhollow neighborhood, where he lived.

The Weeds' Dutch Colonial house was larger than it appeared to be from the driveway. The living room was spacious and divided like Gaul,[3] into three parts. Around an ell to the left as one entered from the vestibule was the long table, laid for six, with candles and a bowl of fruit in the center. The sounds and smells that came from the open kitchen door were appetizing, for Julia Weed was a good cook. The largest part of the living room centered on a fireplace. On the right were some bookshelves and a piano. The room was polished and tranquil, and from the windows that opened to the west there was some late-summer sunlight, brilliant and as clear as water. Nothing here was neglected; nothing had not been burnished. It was not the kind of household where, after prying open a stuck cigarette box, you would find an old shirt button and a tarnished nickel. The hearth was swept, the roses on the piano were reflected in the polish of the broad top, and there was an album of Schubert waltzes on the rack. Louisa Weed, a pretty girl of nine, was looking out the western windows. Her young brother Henry was standing beside her. Her still younger brother, Toby, was studying the figures of some tonsured monks drinking beer on the polished brass of the woodbox. Francis, taking off his hat and putting down his paper, was not consciously pleased with the scene; he was not that reflective. It was his element, his creation, and he returned to it with that sense of lightness and strength with which any creature returns to his home. "Hi, everybody," he said. "The plane from Minneapolis. . . ."

Nine times out of ten, Francis would be greeted with affection, but tonight the children are absorbed in their own antagonisms. Francis had not finished his sentence about the plane crash before Henry plants a kick in Louisa's behind. Louisa swings around, saying, *"Damn you!"* Francis makes the mistake of scolding Louisa for bad language before he punishes Henry. Now Louisa turns on her father and accuses him of favoritism. Henry is always right; she is persecuted and lonely; her lot is hopeless. Francis turns to his son, but the son has justification for the kick—she hit him first; she hit him on the ear, which is dangerous. Louisa agrees with this passionately. She hit him on the ear, and she *meant* to hit him on the ear, because he messed up her china collection. Henry says that this is a lie. Little Toby turns away from the woodbox to throw in some evidence for Louisa. Henry claps his hand over little Toby's mouth. Francis separates the two boys but accidentally pushes Toby into the woodbox. Toby begins to cry. Louisa is already crying. Just then, Julia Weed comes into that part of the room where the table is laid. She is a pretty, intelligent woman, and the white in her hair is premature. She does not seem to notice the fracas. "Hello, darling," she says serenely to Francis. "Wash your hands, everyone. Dinner is ready." She strikes a match and lights the six candles in this vale of tears.[4]

This simple announcement, like the war cries of the Scottish chieftains, only refreshes the ferocity of the combatants. Louisa gives Henry a blow on the

---

3. Ancient France (Gaul) is so described by Julius Caesar in *The Gallic War*.
4. Common figurative reference to earthly life (vale is valley); allusion to Bible: "Blessed is the man whose help is from thee: in his heart he hath disposed to ascend by steps, in the vale of tears, in the place which he hath set" (Psalms 83.6–7).

shoulder. Henry, although he seldom cries, has pitched nine innings and is tired. He bursts into tears. Little Toby discovers a splinter in his hand and begins to howl. Francis says loudly that he has been in a plane crash and that he is tired. Julia appears again from the kitchen and, still ignoring the chaos, asks Francis to go upstairs and tell Helen that everything is ready. Francis is happy to go; it is like getting back to headquarters company.[5] He is planning to tell his oldest daughter about the airplane crash, but Helen is lying on her bed reading a *True Romance* magazine, and the first thing Francis does is to take the magazine from her hand and remind Helen that he has forbidden her to buy it. She did not buy it, Helen replies. It was given to her by her best friend, Bessie Black. Everybody reads *True Romance*. Bessie Black's father reads *True Romance*. There isn't a girl in Helen's class who doesn't read *True Romance*. Francis expresses his detestation of the magazine and then tells her that dinner is ready—although from the sounds downstairs it doesn't seem so. Helen follows him down the stairs. Julia has seated herself in the candlelight and spread a napkin over her lap. Neither Louisa nor Henry has come to the table. Little Toby is still howling, lying face down on the floor. Francis speaks to him gently: "Daddy was in a plane crash this afternoon, Toby. Don't you want to hear about it?" Toby goes on crying. "If you don't come to the table now, Toby," Francis says, "I'll have to send you to bed without any supper." The little boy rises, gives him a cutting look, flies up the stairs to his bedroom, and slams the door. "Oh, dear," Julia says, and starts to go after him. Francis says that she will spoil him. Julia says that Toby is ten pounds underweight and has to be encouraged to eat. Winter is coming, and he will spend the cold months in bed unless he has his dinner. Julia goes upstairs. Francis sits down at the table with Helen. Helen is suffering from the dismal feeling of having read too intently on a fine day, and she gives her father and the room a jaded look. She doesn't understand about the plane crash, because there wasn't a drop of rain in Shady Hill.

Julia returns with Toby, and they all sit down and are served. "Do I have to look at that big, fat slob?" Henry says, of Louisa. Everybody but Toby enters into this skirmish, and it rages up and down the table for five minutes. Toward the end, Henry puts his napkin over his head and, trying to eat that way, spills spinach all over his shirt. Francis asks Julia if the children couldn't have their dinner earlier. Julia's guns are loaded for this. She can't cook two dinners and lay two tables. She paints with lightning strokes that panorama of drudgery in which her youth, her beauty, and her wit have been lost. Francis says that he must be understood; he was nearly killed in an airplane crash, and he doesn't like to come home every night to a battlefield. Now Julia is deeply concerned. Her voice trembles. He doesn't come home every night to a battlefield. The accusation is stupid and mean. Everything was tranquil until he arrived. She stops speaking, puts down her knife and fork, and looks into her plate as if it is a gulf. She begins to cry. "Poor Mummy!" Toby says, and when Julia gets up from the table, drying her tears with a napkin, Toby goes to her side. "Poor Mummy," he says. "Poor Mummy!" And they climb the stairs together. The other children drift away from the battlefield, and Francis goes into the back garden for a cigarette and some air.

It was a pleasant garden, with walks and flower beds and places to sit. The sunset had nearly burned out, but there was still plenty of light. Put into a thought-

---

5. That is, like escaping from combat to relative safety behind the lines.

ful mood by the crash and the battle, Francis listened to the evening sounds of Shady Hill. "Varmints! Rascals!" old Mr. Nixon shouted to the squirrels in his bird-feeding station. "Avaunt and quit my sight!" A door slammed. Someone was cutting grass. Then Donald Goslin, who lived at the corner, began to play the "Moonlight Sonata."[6] He did this nearly every night. He threw the tempo out the window and played it *rubato*[7] from beginning to end, like an outpouring of tearful petulance, lonesomeness, and self-pity—of everything it was Beethoven's greatness not to know. The music rang up and down the street beneath the trees like an appeal for love, for tenderness, aimed at some lovely housemaid—some fresh-faced, homesick girl from Galway, looking at old snapshots in her third-floor room. "Here, Jupiter, here, Jupiter," Francis called to the Mercers' retriever. Jupiter crashed through the tomato vines with the remains of a felt hat in his mouth.

Jupiter was an anomaly. His retrieving instincts and his high spirits were out of place in Shady Hill. He was as black as coal, with a long, alert, intelligent, rakehell face. His eyes gleamed with mischief, and he held his head high. It was the fierce, heavily collared dog's head that appears in heraldry, in tapestry, and that used to appear on umbrella handles and walking sticks. Jupiter went where he pleased, ransacking wastebaskets, clotheslines, garbage pails, and shoe bags. He broke up garden parties and tennis matches, and got mixed up in the processional at Christ Church on Sunday, barking at the men in red dresses.[8] He crashed through old Mr. Nixon's rose garden two or three times a day, cutting a wide swath through the Condesa de Sastagos,[9] and as soon as Donald Goslin lighted his barbecue fire on Thursday nights, Jupiter would get the scent. Nothing the Goslins did could drive him away. Sticks and stones and rude commands only moved him to the edge of the terrace, where he remained, with his gallant and heraldic muzzle, waiting for Donald Goslin to turn his back and reach for the salt. Then he would spring onto the terrace, lift the steak lightly off the fire, and run away with the Goslins' dinner. Jupiter's days were numbered. The Wrightsons' German gardener or the Farquarsons' cook would soon poison him. Even old Mr. Nixon might put some arsenic in the garbage that Jupiter loved. "Here, Jupiter, Jupiter!" Francis called, but the dog pranced off, shaking the hat in his white teeth. Looking at the windows of his house, Francis saw that Julia had come down and was blowing out the candles.

Julia and Francis Weed went out a great deal. Julia was well liked and gregarious, and her love of parties sprang from a most natural dread of chaos and loneliness. She went through the morning mail with real anxiety, looking for invitations, and she usually found some, but she was insatiable, and if she had gone out seven nights a week, it would not have cured her of a reflective look—the look of someone who hears distant music—for she would always suppose that there was a more brilliant party somewhere else. Francis limited her to two week-night parties, putting a flexible interpretation on Friday, and rode through the weekend like a dory in a gale. The day after the airplane crash, the Weeds were to have dinner with the Farquarsons.

---

6. Beethoven's *Sonata Quasi una Fantasia* (1802), a famous and frequently sentimentalized piano composition.

7. With intentional deviations from strict tempo.   8. Probably the choir.

9. Uncommon yellow and red roses, difficult to grow.

Francis got home late from town, and Julia got the sitter while he dressed, and then hurried him out of the house. The party was small and pleasant, and Francis settled down to enjoy himself. A new maid passed the drinks. Her hair was dark, and her face was round and pale and seemed familiar to Francis. He had not developed his memory as a sentimental faculty. Wood smoke, lilac, and other such perfumes did not stir him, and his memory was something like his appendix—a vestigial repository. It was not his limitation at all to be unable to escape the past; it was perhaps his limitation that he had escaped it so successfully. He might have seen the maid at other parties, he might have seen her taking a walk on Sunday afternoons, but in either case he would not be searching his memory now. Her face was, in a wonderful way, a moon face—Norman or Irish—but it was not beautiful enough to account for his feeling that he had seen her before, in circumstances that he ought to be able to remember. He asked Nellie Farquarson who she was. Nellie said that the maid had come through an agency, and that her home was Trénon, in Normandy—a small place with a church and a restaurant that Nellie had once visited. While Nellie talked on about her travels abroad, Francis realized where he had seen the woman before. It had been at the end of the war. He had left a replacement depot with some other men and taken a three-day pass in Trénon. On their second day, they had walked out to a crossroads to see the public chastisement of a young woman who had lived with the German commandant during the Occupation.

It was a cool morning in the fall. The sky was overcast, and poured down onto the dirt crossroads a very discouraging light. They were on high land and could see how like one another the shapes of the clouds and the hills were as they stretched off toward the sea. The prisoner arrived sitting on a three-legged stool in a farm cart. She stood by the cart while the Mayor read the accusation and the sentence. Her head was bent and her face was set in that empty half smile behind which the whipped soul is suspended. When the Mayor was finished, she undid her hair and let it fall across her back. A little man with a gray mustache cut off her hair with shears and dropped it on the ground. Then, with a bowl of soapy water and a straight razor, he shaved her skull clean. A woman approached and began to undo the fastenings of her clothes, but the prisoner pushed her aside and undressed herself. When she pulled her chemise over her head and threw it on the ground, she was naked. The women jeered; the men were still. There was no change in the falseness or the plaintiveness of the prisoner's smile. The cold wind made her white skin rough and hardened the nipples of her breasts. The jeering ended gradually, put down by the recognition of their common humanity. One woman spat on her, but some inviolable grandeur in her nakedness lasted through the ordeal. When the crowd was quiet, she turned—she had begun to cry—and, with nothing on but a pair of worn black shoes and stockings, walked down the dirt road alone away from the village. The round white face had aged a little, but there was no question but that the maid who passed his cocktails and later served Francis his dinner was the woman who had been punished at the crossroads.

The war seemed now so distant and that world where the cost of partisanship had been death or torture so long ago. Francis had lost track of the men who had been with him in Vésey. He could not count on Julia's discretion. He could not tell anyone. And if he had told the story now, at the dinner table, it would have been a social as well as a human error. The people in the Farquar-sons' living room seemed united in their tacit claim that there had been no past, no war—that there was no danger or trouble in the world. In the recorded history of human arrangements, this extraordinary meeting would have fallen into place, but the atmosphere of Shady Hill made the memory unseemly and impolite. The prisoner withdrew after passing the coffee, but the encounter left Francis feeling languid; it had opened his memory and his senses, and left them dilated. Julia went into the house. Francis stayed in the car to take the sitter home.

Expecting to see Mrs. Henlein, the old lady who usually stayed with the chil- 15 dren, he was surprised when a young girl opened the door and came out onto the lighted stoop. She stayed in the light to count her textbooks. She was frowning and beautiful. Now, the world is full of beautiful young girls, but Francis saw here the difference between beauty and perfection. All those endearing flaws, moles, birthmarks, and healed wounds were missing, and he experienced in his consciousness that moment when music breaks glass, and felt a pang of recogni-tion as strange, deep and wonderful as anything in his life. It hung from her frown, from an impalpable darkness in her face—a look that impressed him as a direct appeal for love. When she had counted her books, she came down the steps and opened the car door. In the light, he saw that her cheeks were wet. She got in and shut the door.

"You're new," Francis said.

"Yes. Mrs. Henlein is sick. I'm Anne Murchison."

"Did the children give you any trouble?"

"Oh, no, no." She turned and smiled at him unhappily in the dim dashboard light. Her light hair caught on the collar of her jacket, and she shook her head to set it loose.

"You've been crying." 20

"Yes."

"I hope it was nothing that happened in our house."

"No, no, it was nothing that happened in your house." Her voice was bleak. "It's no secret. Everybody in the village knows. Daddy's an alcoholic, and he just called me from some saloon and gave me a piece of his mind. He thinks I'm immoral. He called just before Mrs. Weed came back."

"I'm sorry."

"Oh, *Lord!*" She gasped and began to cry. She turned toward Francis, and he 25 took her in his arms and let her cry on his shoulder. She shook in his embrace, and this movement accentuated his sense of the fineness of her flesh and bone. The layers of their clothing felt thin, and when her shuddering began to dimin-ish, it was so much like a paroxysm of love that Francis lost his head and pulled her roughly against him. She drew away. "I live on Belleview Avenue," she said. "You go down Lansing Street to the railroad bridge."

"All right." He started the car.

"You turn left at that traffic light. . . . Now you turn right here and go straight on toward the tracks."

The road Francis took brought him out of his own neighborhood, across the tracks, and toward the river, to a street where the near-poor lived, in houses whose peaked gables and trimmings of wooden lace conveyed the purest feelings of pride and romance, although the houses themselves could not have offered much privacy or comfort, they were all so small. The street was dark, and, stirred by the grace and beauty of the troubled girl, he seemed, in turning into it, to have come into the deepest part of some submerged memory. In the distance, he saw a porch light burning. It was the only one, and she said that the house with the light was where she lived. When he stopped the car, he could see beyond the porch light into a dimly lighted hallway with an old-fashioned clothes tree. "Well, here we are," he said, conscious that a young man would have said something different.

She did not move her hands from the books, where they were folded, and she turned and faced him. There were tears of lust in his eyes. Determinedly—not sadly—he opened the door on his side and walked around to open hers. He took her free hand, letting his fingers in between hers, climbed at her side the two concrete steps, and went up a narrow walk through a front garden where dahlias, marigolds, and roses—things that had withstood the light frosts—still bloomed, and made a bittersweet smell in the night air. At the steps, she freed her hand and then turned and kissed him swiftly. Then she crossed the porch and shut the door. The porch light went out, then the light in the hall. A second later, a light went on upstairs at the side of the house, shining into a tree that was still covered with leaves. It took her only a few minutes to undress and get into bed, and then the house was dark.

30   Julia was asleep when Francis got home. He opened a second window and got into bed to shut his eyes on that night, but as soon as they were shut—as soon as he had dropped off to sleep—the girl entered his mind, moving with perfect freedom through its shut doors and filling chamber after chamber with her light, her perfume, and the music of her voice. He was crossing the Atlantic with her on the old *Mauretania*[1] and, later, living with her in Paris. When he woke from his dream, he got up and smoked a cigarette at the open window. Getting back into bed, he cast around in his mind for something he desired to do that would injure no one, and he thought of skiing. Up through the dimness in his mind rose the image of a mountain deep in snow. It was late in the day. Wherever his eyes looked, he saw broad and heartening things. Over his shoulder, there was a snow-filled valley, rising into wooded hills where the trees dimmed the whiteness like a sparse coat of hair. The cold deadened all sound but the loud, iron clanking of the lift machinery. The light on the trails was blue, and it was harder than it had been a minute or two earlier to pick the turns, harder to judge—now that the snow was all deep blue—the crust, the ice, the bare spots, and the deep piles of dry powder. Down the mountain he swung, matching his speed against the contours of a slope that had been formed in the first ice age, seeking with ardor some simplicity of feeling and circumstance. Night fell then, and he drank a Martini with some old friend in a dirty country bar.

In the morning, Francis' snow-covered mountain was gone, and he was left with his vivid memories of Paris and the *Mauretania*. He had been bitten gravely. He washed his body, shaved his jaws, drank his coffee, and missed the seventy-thirty-one. The train pulled out just as he brought his car to the station, and the longing he felt for the coaches as they drew stubbornly away from him reminded him of the humors of love. He waited for the eight-two, on what was now an

1. The original *Mauretania* (1907–35), sister ship of the *Lusitania,* which was sunk by the Germans in 1915, was the most famous transatlantic liner of its day.

empty platform. It was a clear morning; the morning seemed thrown like a gleaming bridge of light over his mixed affairs. His spirits were feverish and high. The image of the girl seemed to put him into a relationship to the world that was mysterious and enthralling. Cars were beginning to fill up the parking lot, and he noticed that those that had driven down from the high land above Shady Hill were white with hoarfrost. This first clear sign of autumn thrilled him. An express train—a night train from Buffalo or Albany—came down the tracks between the platforms, and he saw that the roofs of the foremost cars were covered with a skin of ice. Struck by the miraculous physicalness of everything, he smiled at the passengers in the dining car, who could be seen eating eggs and wiping their mouths with napkins as they traveled. The sleeping-car compartments, with their soiled bed linen, trailed through the fresh morning like a string of rooming-house windows. Then he saw an extraordinary thing; at one of the bedroom windows sat an unclothed woman of exceptional beauty, combing her golden hair. She passed like an apparition through Shady Hill, combing and combing her hair, and Francis followed her with his eyes until she was out of sight. Then old Mrs. Wrightson joined him on the platform and began to talk.

"Well, I guess you must be surprised to see me here the third morning in a row," she said, "but because of my window curtains I'm becoming a regular commuter. The curtains I bought on Monday I returned on Tuesday, and the curtains I bought Tuesday I'm returning today. On Monday, I got exactly what I wanted—it's a wool tapestry with roses and birds—but when I got them home, I found they were the wrong length. Well, I exchanged them yesterday, and when I got them home, I found they were still the wrong length. Now I'm praying to high heaven that the decorator will have them in the right length, because you know my house, you *know* my living-room windows, and you can imagine what a problem they present. I don't know what to do with them."

"I know what to do with them," Francis said.

"What?"

"Paint them black on the inside, and shut up."   35

There was a gasp from Mrs. Wrightson, and Francis looked down at her to be sure that she knew he meant to be rude. She turned and walked away from him, so damaged in spirit that she limped. A wonderful feeling enveloped him, as if light were being shaken about him, and he thought again of Venus combing and combing her hair as she drifted through the Bronx. The realization of how many years had passed since he had enjoyed being deliberately impolite sobered him. Among his friends and neighbors, there were brilliant and gifted people— he saw that—but many of them, also, were bores and fools, and he had made the mistake of listening to them all with equal attention. He had confused a lack of discrimination with Christian love, and the confusion seemed general and destructive. He was grateful to the girl for this bracing sensation of independence. Birds were singing—cardinals and the last of the robins. The sky shone like enamel. Even the smell of ink from his morning paper honed his appetite for life, and the world that was spread out around him was plainly a paradise.

If Francis had believed in some hierarchy of love—in spirits armed with hunting bows, in the capriciousness of Venus and Eros[2]—or even in magical potions,

___

2. Roman name for the goddess of love (Greek: *Aphrodite*) and Greek name for her son (Roman: *Cupid*).

philters, and stews, in scapulae and quarters of the moon,[3] it might have explained his susceptibility and his feverish high spirits. The autumnal loves of middle age are well publicized, and he guessed that he was face to face with one of these, but there was not a trace of autumn in what he felt. He wanted to sport in the green woods, scratch where he itched, and drink from the same cup.

His secretary, Miss Rainey, was late that morning—she went to a psychiatrist three mornings a week—and when she came in, Francis wondered what advice a psychiatrist would have for him. But the girl promised to bring back into his life something like the sound of music. The realization that this music might lead him straight to a trial for statutory rape at the country courthouse collapsed his happiness. The photograph of his four children laughing into the camera on the beach at Gay Head reproached him. On the letterhead of his firm there was a drawing of the Laocoön,[4] and the figure of the priest and his sons in the coils of the snake appeared to him to have the deepest meaning.

He had lunch with Pinky Trabert. At a conversational level, the mores of his friends were robust and elastic, but he knew that the moral card house would come down on them all—on Julia and the children as well—if he got caught taking advantage of a baby-sitter. Looking back over the recent history of Shady Hill for some precedent, he found there was none. There was no turpitude; there had not been a divorce since he lived there; there had not even been a breath of scandal. Things seemed arranged with more propriety even than in the Kingdom of Heaven. After leaving Pinky, Francis went to a jeweler's and bought the girl a bracelet. How happy this clandestine purchase made him, how stuffy and comical the jeweler's clerks seemed, how sweet the women who passed at his back smelled! On Fifth Avenue, passing Atlas with his shoulders bent under the weight of the world,[5] Francis thought of the strenuousness of containing his physicalness within the patterns he had chosen.

40   He did not know when he would see the girl next. He had the bracelet in his inside pocket when he got home. Opening the door of his house, he found her in the hall. Her back was to him, and she turned when she heard the door close. Her smile was open and loving. Her perfection stunned him like a fine day—a day after a thunderstorm. He seized her and covered her lips with his, and she struggled but she did not have to struggle for long, because just then little Gertrude Flannery appeared from somewhere and said, "Oh, Mr. Weed. . . ."

Gertrude was a stray. She had been born with a taste for exploration, and she did not have it in her to center her life with her affectionate parents. People who did not know the Flannerys concluded from Gertrude's behavior that she was the child of a bitterly divided family, where drunken quarrels were the rule. This was not true. The fact that little Gertrude's clothing was ragged and thin was her own triumph over her mother's struggle to dress her warmly and neatly. Garrulous, skinny, and unwashed, she drifted from house to house around the Blenhollow neighborhood, forming and breaking alliances based on an attach-

3. Love-inducing and predictive magic. *Scapulae:* small Roman Catholic icons that hang from a ribbon worn around the shoulders.
4. Famous Greek statue, now in the Vatican museum; the "meaning" for Weed seems to reside in the physical struggle, not in the legend (in which the priest and his sons were punished for warning the Trojans about the wooden horse).
5. In Greek legend the Titan Atlas supported the heavens on his shoulders, but he has come to be depicted as bearing the globe; the statue is at Rockefeller Center.

ment to babies, animals, children her own age, adolescents, and sometimes adults. Opening your front door in the morning, you would find Gertrude sitting on your stoop. Going into the bathroom to shave, you would find Gertrude using the toilet. Looking into your son's crib, you would find it empty, and, looking further, you would find that Gertrude had pushed him in his baby carriage into the next village. She was helpful, pervasive, honest, hungry, and loyal. She never went home of her own choice. When the time to go arrived, she was indifferent to all its signs. "Go home, Gertrude," people could be heard saying in one house or another, night after night. "Go home, Gertrude. It's time for you to go home now, Gertrude." "You had better go home and get your supper, Gertrude." "I told you to go home twenty minutes ago, Gertrude." "Your mother will be worrying about you, Gertrude." "Go home, Gertrude, go home."

There are times when the lines around the human eye seem like shelves of eroded stone and when the staring eye itself strikes us with such a wilderness of animal feeling that we are at a loss. The look Francis gave the little girl was ugly and queer, and it frightened her. He reached into his pockets—his hands were shaking—and took out a quarter. "Go home, Gertrude, go home, and don't tell anyone, Gertrude. Don't—" He choked and ran into the living room as Julia called down to him from upstairs to hurry and dress.

The thought that he would drive Anne Murchison home later that night ran like a golden thread through the events of the party that Francis and Julia went to, and he laughed uproariously at dull jokes, dried a tear when Mabel Mercer told him about the death of her kitten, and stretched, yawned, sighed, and grunted like any other man with a rendezvous at the back of his mind. The bracelet was in his pocket. As he sat talking, the smell of grass was in his nose, and he was wondering where he would park the car. Nobody lived in the old Parker mansion, and the driveway was used as a lovers' lane. Townsend Street was a dead end, and he could park there, beyond the last house. The old lane that used to connect Elm Street to the riverbanks was overgrown, but he had walked there with his children, and he could drive his car deep enough into the brushwoods to be concealed.

The Weeds were the last to leave the party, and their host and hostess spoke of their own married happiness while they all four stood in the hallway saying good night. "She's my girl," their host said, squeezing his wife. "She's my blue sky. After sixteen years, I still bite her shoulders. She makes me feel like Hannibal crossing the Alps."[6]

The Weeds drove home in silence. Francis brought the car up the driveway and sat still, with the motor running. "You can put the car in the garage," Julia said as she got out. "I told the Murchison girl she could leave at eleven. Someone drove her home." She shut the door, and Francis sat in the dark. He would be spared nothing then, it seemed, that a fool was not spared: ravening lewdness, jealousy, this hurt to his feelings that put tears in his eyes, even scorn—for he could see clearly the image he now presented, his arms spread over the steering wheel and his head buried in them for love. 45

Francis had been a dedicated Boy Scout when he was young, and, remembering the precepts of his youth, he left his office early the next afternoon and played

---

6. The Carthaginian general (274–183 B.C.E.) attacked the Romans from the rear by crossing the Alps, considered impregnable, with the use of elephants.

some round-robin squash, but, with his body toned up by exercise and a shower, he realized that he might better have stayed at his desk. It was a frosty night when he got home. The air smelled sharply of change. When he stepped into the house, he sensed an unusual stir. The children were in their best clothes, and when Julia came down, she was wearing a lavender dress and her diamond sunburst. She explained the stir: Mr. Hubber was coming at seven to take their photograph for the Christmas card. She had put out Francis' blue suit and a tie with some color in it, because the picture was going to be in color this year. Julia was lighthearted at the thought of being photographed for Christmas. It was the kind of ceremony she enjoyed.

Francis went upstairs to change his clothes. He was tired from the day's work and tired with longing, and sitting on the edge of the bed had the effect of deepening his weariness. He thought of Anne Murchison, and the physical need to express himself, instead of being restrained by the pink lamps of Julia's dressing table, engulfed him. He went to Julia's desk, took a piece of writing paper, and began to write on it. "Dear Anne, I love you, I love you, I love you...." No one would see the letter, and he used no restraint. He used phrases like "heavenly bliss," and "love nest." He salivated, sighed, and trembled. When Julia called him to come down, the abyss between his fantasy and the practical world opened so wide that he felt it affected the muscles of his heart.

Julia and the children were on the stoop, and the photographer and his assistant had set up a double battery of floodlights to show the family and the architectural beauty of the entrance to their house. People who had come home on a late train slowed their cars to see the Weeds being photographed for their Christmas card. A few waved and called to the family. It took half an hour of smiling and wetting their lips before Mr. Hubber was satisfied. The heat of the lights made an unfresh smell in the frosty air, and when they were turned off, they lingered on the retina of Francis' eyes.

Later that night, while Francis and Julia were drinking their coffee in the living room, the doorbell rang. Julia answered the door and let in Clayton Thomas. He had come to pay for some theatre tickets that she had given his mother some time ago, and that Helen Thomas had scrupulously insisted on paying for, though Julia had asked her not to. Julia invited him in to have a cup of coffee. "I won't have any coffee," Clayton said, "but I will come in for a minute." He followed her into the living room, said good evening to Francis, and sat awkwardly in a chair.

50   Clayton's father had been killed in the war, and the young man's fatherlessness surrounded him like an element. This may have been conspicuous in Shady Hill because the Thomases were the only family that lacked a piece; all the other marriages were intact and productive. Clayton was in his second or third year of college, and he and his mother lived alone in a large house, which she hoped to sell. Clayton had once made some trouble. Years ago, he had stolen some money and run away; he had got to California before they caught up with him. He was tall and homely, wore horn-rimmed glasses, and spoke in a deep voice.

"When do you go back to college, Clayton?" Francis asked.

"I'm not going back," Clayton said. "Mother doesn't have the money, and there's no sense in all this pretense. I'm going to get a job, and if we sell the house, we'll take an apartment in New York."

"Won't you miss Shady Hill?" Julia asked.

"No," Clayton said. "I don't like it."

"Why not?" Francis asked. 55

"Well, there's a lot here I don't approve of," Clayton said gravely. "Things like the club dances. Last Saturday night, I looked in toward the end and saw Mr. Granner trying to put Mrs. Minot into the trophy case. They were both drunk. I disapprove of so much drinking."

"It was Saturday night," Francis said.

"And all the dovecotes are phony," Clayton said. "And the way people clutter up their lives. I've thought about it a lot, and what seems to me to be really wrong with Shady Hill is that it doesn't have any future. So much energy is spent in perpetuating the place—in keeping out undesirables, and so forth—that the only idea of the future anyone has is just more and more commuting trains and more parties. I don't think that's healthy. I think people ought to be able to dream big dreams about the future. I think people ought to be able to dream great dreams."

"It's too bad you couldn't continue with college," Julia said.

"I want to go to divinity school," Clayton said. 60

"What's your church?" Francis asked.

"Unitarian, Theosophist, Transcendentalist, Humanist,"[7] Clayton said.

"Wasn't Emerson a transcendentalist?" Julia asked.

"I mean the English transcendentalists," Clayton said. "All the American transcendentalists were goops."

"What kind of job do you expect to get?" Francis asked. 65

"Well, I'd like to work for a publisher," Clayton said, "but everyone tells me there's nothing doing. But it's the kind of thing I'm interested in. I'm writing a long verse play about good and evil. Uncle Charlie might get me into a bank, and that would be good for me. I need the discipline. I have a long way to go in forming my character. I have some terrible habits. I talk too much. I think I ought to take vows of silence. I ought to try not to speak for a week, and discipline myself. I've thought of making a retreat at one of the Episcopalian monasteries, but I don't like Trinitarianism."

"Do you have any girl friends?" Francis asked.

"I'm engaged to be married," Clayton said. "Of course, I'm not old enough or rich enough to have my engagement observed or respected or anything, but I bought a simulated emerald for Anne Murchison with the money I made cutting lawns this summer. We're going to be married as soon as she finishes school."

Francis recoiled at the mention of the girl's name. Then a dingy light seemed to emanate from his spirit, showing everything—Julia, the boy, the chairs—in their true colorlessness. It was like a bitter turn of the weather.

"We're going to have a large family," Clayton said. "Her father's a terrible 70 rummy, and I've had my hard times, and we want to have lots of children. Oh, she's wonderful, Mr. and Mrs. Weed, and we have so much in common. We like all the same things. We sent out the same Christmas card last year without planning it, and we both have an allergy to tomatoes, and our eyebrows grow together in the middle. Well, goodnight."

---

7. All are deviations from orthodox Christianity and tend to be more human- than God-oriented; the American transcendentalists (see below) tended to change the emphasis from the study of thought to belief in "intuition." Unitarians reject Trinitarianism—the doctrine that God exists simultaneously in three beings: the Father, Son (Jesus), and Holy Ghost.

Julia went to the door with him. When she returned, Francis said that Clayton was lazy, irresponsible, affected, and smelly. Julia said that Francis seemed to be getting intolerant; the Thomas boy was young and should be given a chance. Julia had noticed other cases where Francis had been short-tempered. "Mrs. Wrightson has asked everyone in Shady Hill to her anniversary party but us," she said.

"I'm sorry, Julia."

"Do you know why they didn't ask us?"

"Why?"

75 "Because you insulted Mrs. Wrightson."

"Then you know about it?"

"June Masterson told me. She was standing behind you."

Julia walked in front of the sofa with a small step that expressed, Francis knew, a feeling of anger.

"I did insult Mrs. Wrightson, Julia, and I meant to. I've never liked her parties, and I'm glad she's dropped us."

80 "What about Helen?"

"How does Helen come into this?"

"Mrs. Wrightson's the one who decides who goes to the assemblies."

"You mean she can keep Helen from going to the dances?"

"Yes."

85 "I hadn't thought of that."

"Oh. I knew you hadn't thought of it," Julia cried, thrusting hiltdeep into this chink of his armor. "And it makes me furious to see this kind of stupid thoughtlessness wreck everyone's happiness."

"I don't think I've wrecked anyone's happiness."

"Mrs. Wrightson runs Shady Hill and has run it for the last forty years. I don't know what makes you think that in a community like this you can indulge every impulse you have to be insulting, vulgar, and offensive."

"I have very good manners," Francis said, trying to give the evening a turn toward the light.

90 "Damn you, Francis Weed!" Julia cried, and the spit of her words struck him in the face. "I've worked hard for the social position we enjoy in this place, and I won't stand by and see you wreck it. You must have understood when you settled here that you couldn't expect to live like a bear in a cave."

"I've got to express my likes and dislikes."

"You can conceal your dislikes. You don't have to meet everything head on, like a child. Unless you're anxious to be a social leper. It's no accident that we get asked out a great deal! It's no accident that Helen has so many friends. How would you like to spend your Saturday nights at the movies? How would you like to spend your Sunday raking up dead leaves? How would you like it if your daughter spent the assembly nights sitting at her window, listening to the music from the club? How would you like it—" He did something then that was, after all, not so unaccountable, since her words seemed to raise up between them a wall so deadening that he gagged. He struck her full in the face. She staggered and then, a moment later, seemed composed. She went up the stairs to their room. She didn't slam the door. When Francis followed, a few minutes later, he found her packing a suitcase.

"Julia, I'm very sorry."

"It doesn't matter," she said. She was crying.

"Where do you think you're going?"   95
"I don't know. I just looked at a timetable. There's an eleven-sixteen into New York. I'll take that."
"You can't go, Julia."
"I can't stay. I know that."
"I'm sorry about Mrs. Wrightson, Julia, and I'm—"
"It doesn't matter about Mrs. Wrightson. That isn't the trouble."   100
"What is the trouble?"
"You don't love me."
"I do love you, Julia."
"No, you don't."
"Julia, I do love you, and I would like to be as we were—sweet and bawdy and   105
dark—but now there are so many people."
"You hate me."
"I don't hate you, Julia."
"You have no idea of how much you hate me. I think it's subconscious. You don't realize the cruel things you've done."
"What cruel things, Julia?"
"The cruel acts your subconscious drives you to in order to express your   110
hatred of me."
"What, Julia?"
"I've never complained."
"Tell me."
"You don't know what you're doing."
"Tell me."   115
"Your clothes."
"What do you mean?"
"I mean the way you leave your dirty clothes around in order to express your subconscious hatred of me."
"I don't understand."
"I mean your dirty socks and your dirty pajamas and your dirty underwear   120
and your dirty shirts!" She rose from kneeling by the suitcase and faced him, her eyes blazing and her voice ringing with emotion. "I'm talking about the fact that you've never learned to hang up anything. You just leave your clothes all over the floor where they drop, in order to humiliate me. You do it on purpose!" She fell on the bed, sobbing.
"Julia, darling!" he said, but when she felt his hand on her shoulder she got up.
"Leave me alone," she said. "I have to go." She brushed past him to the closet and came back with a dress. "I'm not taking any of the things you've given me," she said. "I'm leaving my pearls and the fur jacket."
"Oh, Julia!" Her figure, so helpless in its self-deceptions, bent over the suitcase made him nearly sick with pity. She did not understand how desolate her life would be without him. She didn't understand the hours that working women have to keep. She didn't understand that most of her friendships existed within the framework of their marriage, and that without this she would find herself alone. She didn't understand about travel, about hotels, about money. "Julia, I can't let you go! What you don't understand, Julia, is that you've come to be dependent on me."
She tossed her head back and covered her face with her hands. "Did you say that *I* was dependent on *you*?" she asked. "Is that what you said? And who is it that tells you what time to get up in the morning and when to go to bed at night?

Who is it that prepares your meals and picks up your dirty clothes and invites your friends to dinner? If it weren't for me, your neckties would be greasy and your clothing would be full of moth holes. You were alone when I met you, Francis Weed, and you'll be alone when I leave. When Mother asked you for a list to send out invitations to our wedding, how many names did you have to give her? Fourteen!"

125   "Cleveland wasn't my home, Julia."

"And how many of your friends came to the church? Two!"

"Cleveland wasn't my home, Julia."

"Since I'm not taking the fur jacket," she said quietly, "you'd better put it back into storage. There's an insurance policy on the pearls that comes due in January. The name of the laundry and maid's telephone number—all those things are in my desk. I hope you won't drink too much, Francis. I hope that nothing bad will happen to you. If you do get into serious trouble, you can call me."

"Oh, my darling, I can't let you go!" Francis said. "I can't let you go, Julia!" He took her in his arms.

130   "I guess I'd better stay and take care of you for a little while longer," she said.

Riding to work in the morning, Francis saw the girl walk down the aisle of the coach. He was surprised; he hadn't realized that the school she went to was in the city, but she was carrying books, she seemed to be going to school. His surprise delayed his reaction, but then he got up clumsily and stepped into the aisle. Several people had come between them, but he could see her ahead of him, waiting for someone to open the car door, and then, as the train swerved, putting out her hand to support herself as she crossed the platform into the next car. He followed her through that car and halfway through another before calling her name— "Anne! Anne!"—but she didn't turn. He followed her into still another car, and she sat down in an aisle seat. Coming up to her, all his feelings warm and bent in her direction, he put his hand on the back of her seat—even this touch warmed him— and leaning down to speak to her, he saw that it was not Anne. It was an older woman wearing glasses. He went on deliberately into another car, his face red with embarrassment and the much deeper feeling of having his good sense challenged; for if he couldn't tell one person from another, what evidence was there that his life with Julia and the children had as much reality as his dreams of iniquity in Paris or the litter, the grass smell, and the cave-shaped trees in Lovers' Lane.

Late that afternoon, Julia called to remind Francis that they were going out for dinner. A few minutes later, Trace Bearden called. "Look, fellar," Trace said. "I'm calling for Mrs. Thomas. You know? Clayton, that boy of hers, doesn't seem able to get a job, and I wondered if you could help. If you'd call Charlie Bell—I know he's indebted to you—and say a good word for the kid, I think Charlie would—"

"Trace, I hate to say this," Francis said, "but I don't feel that I can do anything for that boy. The kid's worthless. I know it's a harsh thing to say, but it's a fact. Any kindness done for him would backfire in everybody's face. He's just a worthless kid, Trace, and there's nothing else to be done about it. Even if we got him a job, he wouldn't be able to keep it for a week. I know that to be a fact. It's an awful thing, Trace, and I know it is, but instead of recommending that kid, I'd feel obligated to warn people against him—people who knew his father and would naturally want to step in and do something. I'd feel obliged to warn them. He's a thief. . . ."

The moment this conversation was finished, Miss Rainey came in and stood by his desk. "I'm not going to be able to work for you any more, Mr. Weed," she said. "I can stay until the seventeenth if you need me, but I've been offered a whirlwind of a job, and I'd like to leave as soon as possible."

She went out, leaving him to face alone the wickedness of what he had done 135 to the Thomas boy. His children in their photograph laughed and laughed, glazed with all the bright colors of summer, and he remembered that they had met a bagpiper on the beach that day and he had paid the piper a dollar to play them a battle song of the Black Watch.[8] The girl would be at the house when he got home. He would spend another evening among his kind neighbors, picking and choosing dead-end streets, cart tracks, and the driveways of abandoned houses. There was nothing to mitigate his feeling—nothing that laughter or a game of softball with the children would change—and, thinking back over the plane crash, the Farquarsons' new maid, and Anne Murchison's difficulties with her drunken father, he wondered how he could have avoided arriving at just where he was. He was in trouble. He had been lost once in his life, coming back from a trout stream in the north woods, and he had now the same bleak realization that no amount of cheerfulness or hopefulness or valor or perseverance could help him find, in the gathering dark, the path that he'd lost. He smelled the forest. The feeling of bleakness was intolerable, and he saw clearly that he had reached the point where he would have to make a choice.

He could go to a psychiatrist, like Miss Rainey; he could go to church and confess his lusts; he could go to a Danish-massage parlor[9] in the West Seventies that had been recommended by a salesman; he could rape the girl or trust that he would somehow be prevented from doing this; or he could get drunk. It was his life, his boat, and, like every other man, he was made to be the father of thousands, and what harm could there be in a tryst that would make them both feel more kindly toward the world? This was the wrong train of thought, and he came back to the first, the psychiatrist. He had the telephone number of Miss Rainey's doctor, and he called and asked for an immediate appointment. He was insistent with the doctor's secretary—it was his manner in business—and when she said that the doctor's schedule was full for the next few weeks, Francis demanded an appointment that day and was told to come at five.

The psychiatrist's office was in a building that was used mostly by doctors and dentists, and the hallways were filled with the candy smell of mouthwash and memories of pain. Francis' character had been formed upon a series of private resolves—resolves about cleanliness, about going off the high diving board or repeating any other feat that challenged his courage, about punctuality, honesty, and virtue. To abdicate the perfect loneliness in which he had made his most vital decisions shattered his concept of character and left him now in a condition that felt like shock. He was stupefied. The scene for his *miserere mei Deus*[1] was, like the waiting room of so many doctors' offices, a crude token gesture toward the sweets of domestic bliss: a place arranged with antiques, coffee tables, potted plants, and etchings of snow-covered bridges and geese in flight, although there were no children, no marriage bed, no stove, even, in this travesty of a house, where no one had ever spent the night and where the curtained windows looked straight onto a dark air shaft. Francis gave his name and address to

---

8. Originally a British Highland regiment that became a line regiment and distinguished itself in battle.
9. Sometimes fronts for houses of prostitution.
1. "Have mercy upon me, O God"; first words of Psalm 51.

a secretary and then saw, at the side of the room, a policeman moving toward him. "Hold it, hold it," the policeman said. "Don't move. Keep your hands where they are."

"I think it's all right, Officer," the secretary began. "I think it will be—"

"Let's make sure," the policeman said, and he began to slap Francis' clothes, looking for what—pistols, knives, an icepick? Finding nothing, he went off and the secretary began a nervous apology: "When you called on the telephone, Mr. Weed, you seemed very excited, and one of the doctor's patients has been threatening his life, and we have to be careful. If you want to go in now?" Francis pushed open a door connected to an electrical chime, and in the doctor's lair sat down heavily, blew his nose into a handkerchief, searched in his pockets for cigarettes, for matches, for something, and said hoarsely, with tears in his eyes, "I'm in love, Dr. Herzog."

140   It is a week or ten days later in Shady Hill. The seven-fourteen has come and gone, and here and there dinner is finished and the dishes are in the dish-washing machine. The village hangs, morally and economically, from a thread; but it hangs by its thread in the evening light. Donald Goslin has begun to worry the "Moonlight Sonata" again. *Marcato ma sempre pianissimo!*[2] He seems to be wringing out a wet bath towel, but the housemaid does not heed him. She is writing a letter to Arthur Godfrey.[3] In the cellar of his house, Francis Weed is building a coffee table. Dr. Herzog recommends woodwork as a therapy, and Francis finds some true consolation in the simple arithmetic involved and in the holy smell of new wood. Francis is happy. Upstairs, little Toby is crying, because he is tired. He puts off his cowboy hat, gloves, and fringed jacket, unbuckles the belt studded with gold and rubies, the silver bullets and holsters, slips off his suspenders, his checked shirt, and Levi's, and sits on the edge of his bed to pull off his high boots. Leaving this equipment in a heap, he goes to the closet and takes his space suit off a nail. It is a struggle for him to get into the long tights, but he succeeds. He loops the magic cape over his shoulders and, climbing onto the footboard of his bed, he spreads his arms and flies the short distance to the floor, landing with a thump that is audible to everyone in the house but himself.

"Go home, Gertrude, go home," Mrs. Masterson says. "I told you to go home an hour ago, Gertrude. It's way past your suppertime, and your mother will be worried. Go home!" A door on the Babcocks' terrace flies open, and out comes Mrs. Babcock without any clothes on, pursued by a naked husband. (Their children are away at boarding school, and their terrace is screened by a hedge.) Over the terrace they go and in at the kitchen door, as passionate and handsome a nymph and satyr as you will find on any wall in Venice. Cutting the last of the roses in her garden, Julia hears old Mr. Nixon shouting at the squirrels in his bird-feeding station. "Rapscallions! Varmints! Avaunt and quit my sight!" A miserable cat wanders into the garden, sunk in spiritual and physical discomfort. Tied to its head is a small straw hat—a doll's hat—and it is securely buttoned into a doll's dress, from the skirts of which protrudes its long, hairy tail. As it walks, it shakes its feet, as if it had fallen into water.

"Here, pussy, pussy, pussy!" Julia calls.

2. Stressed but always very softly.
3. At the time of the story, host of a daytime radio program especially popular with housewives.

"Here, pussy, here, poor pussy!" But the cat gives her a skeptical look and stumbles away in its skirts. The last to come is Jupiter. He prances through the tomato vines, holding in his generous mouth the remains of an evening slipper. Then it is dark; it is a night where kings in golden suits ride elephants over the mountains.[4]

1958

QUESTIONS

1. Francis Weed commutes by train "five nights a week to his home in Shady Hill," but "The Country Husband" begins on the night his plane makes an emergency landing and he nearly doesn't make it home. How does this interruption of routine help to prepare for the rest of the story? Why is it significant that everyone else acts as if nothing unusual has happened?
2. Francis "had not developed his memory as a sentimental faculty." Why is memory important in this story? What kinds of memories do people try to ignore and what kinds of memories actually do surface in the story?
3. How is the suburb of Shady Hill characterized, and what role does it play in the story? How is Francis Weed's experience shaped by time as well as place? For example, in what ways is Shady Hill a kind of place that still exists, and in what ways might it seem different from a modern suburb?

HANIF KUREISHI

Long Ago Yesterday

One evening just after my fiftieth birthday, I pushed against the door of a pub not far from my childhood home. My father, on the way back from his office in London, was inside, standing at the bar. He didn't recognize me, but I was delighted, almost ecstatic, to see the old man again, particularly as he'd been dead for ten years, and my mother for five.

"Good evening," I said, standing next to him. "Nice to see you."

"Good evening," he replied.

"This place never changes," I said.

"We like it this way," he said.   5

I ordered a drink; I needed one.

I noticed the date on a discarded newspaper and calculated that Dad was just a little older than me, nearly fifty-one. We were as close to equals—or contemporaries—as we'd ever be.

He was talking to a man sitting on a stool next to him, and the barmaid was laughing extravagantly with them both. I knew Dad better than anyone, or thought I did, and I was tempted to embrace him or at least kiss his hands, as I used to. I refrained, but watched him looking comfortable at the bar beside the

4. Reference to Hannibal; see note 6, p. 281, above. Also, see Sinclair Lewis, *Main Street* (1920), in which the protagonist finds the small town of Gopher Prairie stifling and leaves with her son for Washington, DC, where, she tells him, "We're going to find elephants with golden howdahs from which peep young maharanees with necklaces of rubies. . . ."

man I now realized was the father of a school friend of mine. Neither of them seemed to mind when I joined in.

Like a lot of people, I have some of my best friendships with the dead. I dream frequently about both of my parents and the house where I grew up, undistinguished though it was. Of course, I never imagined that Dad and I might meet up like this, for a conversation.

Lately I had been feeling unusually foreign to myself. My fiftieth hit me like a tragedy, with a sense of wasted purpose and many wrong moves made. I could hardly complain: I was a theatre and film producer, with houses in London, New York, and Brazil. But complain I did. I had become keenly aware of various mental problems that enervated but did not ruin me.

I ran into Dad on a Monday. Over the weekend I'd been staying with some friends in the country who had a fine house and pretty acquaintances, good paintings to look at, and an excellent cook. The Iraq war, which had just started, had been on TV continuously. About twenty of us, old and young men, lay on deep sofas drinking champagne and giggling until the prospect of thousands of bombs smashing into donkey carts, human flesh, and primitive shacks had depressed everyone in the house. We were aware that disgust was general in the country and that Tony Blair,[1] once our hope after years in opposition, had become the most tarnished and loathed leader since Anthony Eden.[2] We were living in a time of lies, deceit, and alienation. This was heavy, and our lives seemed uncomfortably trivial in comparison.

Just after lunch, I had left my friend's house, and the taxi got me as far as the railway station when I realized I'd left behind a bent paper clip I'd been fiddling with. It was in my friend's library, where I'd been reading about mesmerism[3] in the work of Maupassant, as well as Dickens's experiments with hypnotism, which had got him into a lot of trouble with the wife of a friend. The taxi took me back, and I hurried into the room to retrieve the paper clip, but the cleaner[4] had just finished. Did I want to examine the contents of the vacuum? my hosts asked. They were making faces at one another. Yet I had begun to see myself as heroic in terms of what I'd achieved in spite of my obsessions. This was a line my therapist used. Luckily, I would be seeing the good doctor the next day.

Despite my devastation over the paper clip, I returned to the station and got on the train. I had come down by car, so it was only now I realized that the route of the train meant we would stop at the suburban railway station nearest to my childhood home. As we drew into the platform, I found myself straining to see things I recognized, even familiar faces, though I had left the area some thirty years before. But it was raining hard and almost impossible to make anything out. Then, just as the train was about to pull away, I grabbed my bag and got off, walking out into the street with no idea what I would do.

Near the station there had been a small record shop, a bookshop, and a place to buy jeans, along with several pubs that I'd been taken to as a young man by a local bed-sit[5] aesthete, the first person I came out to. Of course, he knew straight away.

1. British Labor Party politician and Prime Minister from 1997 to 2007.
2. British Prime Minister (1955–57) forced to resign in the wake of his controversial decision to send British troops into Egypt to retake control of the Suez Canal.
3. Early and controversial form of hypnosis.   4. Janitor.
5. Rented room in someone else's house or apartment.

His hero was Jean Cocteau.[6] We'd discuss French literature and Wilde and Pop,[7] before taking our speed pills and applying our makeup in the station toilet and getting the train into the city. Along with another white friend who dressed as Jimi Hendrix, we saw all the plays and shows. Eventually I got a job in a West End[8] box office. This led to work as a stagehand, usher, dresser—even a director— before I found my "vocation" as a producer.

Now I asked my father his name and what he did. I knew how to work Dad, of course. Soon he was more interested in me than in the other man. Yet my fear didn't diminish: didn't we look similar? I wasn't sure. My clothes, as well as my sparkly new teeth, were more expensive than his, and I was heavier and taller, about a third bigger all over—I have always worked out. But my hair was going gray; I don't dye it. Dad's hair was still mostly black.

An accountant all his life, my father had worked in the same office for fifteen years. He was telling me that he had two sons: Dennis, who was in the Air Force, and me—Billy. A few months ago I'd gone away to university, where, apparently, I was doing well. My all-female production of "Waiting for Godot"[9]—"a bloody depressing play," according to Dad—had been admired. I wanted to say, "But I didn't direct it, Dad, I only produced it."

I had introduced myself to Dad as Peter, the name I sometimes adopted, along with quite a developed alternative character, during anonymous sexual encounters. Not that I needed a persona: Father would ask me where I was from and what I did, but whenever I began to answer he'd interrupt with a stream of advice and opinions.

My father said he wanted to sit down because his sciatica was playing up, and I joined him at a table. Eying the barmaid, Dad said, "She's lovely, isn't she?"

"Lovely hair," I said. "Unfortunately, none of her clothes fit."

"Who's interested in her clothes?"

This was an aspect of my father I'd never seen; perhaps it was a departure for him. I'd never known him to go to the pub after work; he came straight home. And once Dennis had left I was able to secure Father's evenings for myself. Every day I'd wait for him at the bus stop, ready to take his briefcase. In the house I'd make him a cup of tea while he changed.

Now the barmaid came over to remove our glasses and empty the ashtrays. As she leaned across the table, Dad put his hand behind her knee and slid it all the way up her skirt to her arse, which he caressed, squeezed, and held until she reeled away and stared at him in disbelief, shouting that she hated the pub and the men in it, and would he get out before she called the landlord and he flung him out personally?

The landlord did indeed rush over. He snatched away Dad's glass, raising his fist as Dad hurried to the door, forgetting his briefcase. I'd never known Dad to

6. French poet, playwright, artist, and film director (1889–1963), a leading member of the surrealist movement, which explored and celebrated the realm of dreams and the unconscious.

7. Visual art movement of the 1950s and 1960s that emphasized the themes and techniques of popular culture such as advertising and comic books.

8. Area of central London known for its shops, theaters, and museums.

9. 1952 play by Samuel Beckett in which two tramps bicker and banter as they await the arrival of the mysterious Godot; an influential example of absurdist drama, it depicts the human condition as absurd and meaningless.

go to work without his briefcase, and I'd never known him to leave it anywhere. As my brother and I used to say, his attaché case was always attached to him. Outside, where Dad was brushing himself down, I handed it back to him.

"Thank you," he said. "Shouldn't have done that. But once, just once, I had to. Suppose it's the last time I touch anyone!" He asked, "Which way are you going?"

25 "I'll walk with you a bit," I said. "My bag isn't heavy. I'm passing through. I need to get a train into London, but there's no hurry."

He said, "Why don't you come and have a drink at my house?"

My parents lived according to a strict regime, mathematical in its exactitude. Why, now, was he inviting a stranger to his house? I had always been his only friend; our involvement had kept us both busy.

"Are you sure?"

"Yes," he said. "Come."

30 Noise and night and rain streaming everywhere: you couldn't see farther than your hand. But we both knew the way, Dad moving slowly, his mouth hanging open to catch more air. He seemed happy enough, perhaps with what he'd done in the pub, or maybe my company cheered him up.

Yet when we turned the corner into the neat familiar road, a road that had, to my surprise, remained exactly where it was all the time I hadn't been there, I felt wrapped in coldness. In my recent dreams—fading as they were like frescoes in the light—the suburban street had been darkly dismal under the yellow shadows of the streetlights, and filled with white flowers and a suffocating, deathly odor, like being buried in roses. But how could I falter now? Once inside the house, Dad threw open the door to the living room. I blinked; there she was, Mother, knitting in her huge chair with her feet up, an open box of chocolates on the small table beside her, her fingers rustling for treasure in the crinkly paper.

Dad left me while he changed into his pajamas and dressing gown. The fact that he had a visitor, a stranger, didn't deter him from his routine, outside of which there were no maps.

I stood in my usual position, just behind Mother's chair. Here, where I wouldn't impede her enjoyment with noise, complaints, or the sight of my face, I explained that Dad and I had met in the pub and he'd invited me back for a drink.

Mother said, "I don't think we've got any drink, unless there's something left over from last Christmas. Drink doesn't go bad, does it?"

35 "It doesn't go bad."

"Now shut up," she said. "I'm watching this. D'you watch the soaps?"

"Not much."

Maybe the ominous whiteness of my dreams had been stimulated by the whiteness of the things Mother had been knitting and crocheting—headrests, gloves, cushion covers; there wasn't a piece of furniture in the house without a knitted thing on it. Even as a grown man, I couldn't buy a pair of gloves without thinking I should be wearing Mother's.

In the kitchen, I made a cup of tea for myself and Dad. Mum had left my father's dinner in the oven: sausages, mash,[1] and peas, all dry as lime by now, and presented on a large cracked plate, with space between each item. Mum had asked me if I wanted anything, but how would I have been able to eat anything here?

1. That is, mashed potatoes.

As I waited for the kettle to boil, I washed up the dishes at the sink over- 40
looking the garden. Then I carried Father's tea and dinner into his study, formerly the family dining room. With one hand I made a gap for the plate at the
table, which was piled high with library books.

After I'd finished my homework, Dad always liked me to go through the radio
schedules, marking programs I might record for him. If I was lucky, he would
read to me, or talk about the lives of the artists he was absorbed with—these were
his companions. Their lives were exemplary, but only a fool would try to emulate
them. Meanwhile I would slip my hand inside his pajama top and tickle his back,
or I'd scratch his head or rub his arms until his eyes rolled in appreciation.

Now in his bedwear, sitting down to eat, Dad told me he was embarked on a
"five-year reading plan." He was working on "War and Peace."[2] Next it would be
"Remembrance of Things Past," then "Middlemarch," all of Dickens, Homer,
Chaucer, and so on. He kept a separate notebook for each author he read.

"This methodical way," he pointed out, "you get to know everything in literature. You will never run out of interest, of course, because then there is music,
painting, in fact the whole of human history. . . ."

His talk reminded me of the time I won the school essay prize for a tract on
time-wasting. The piece was not about how to fritter away one's time profitlessly,
which might have made it a useful and lively work, but about how much can be
achieved by filling every moment with activity! Dad was my ideal. He would read
even in the bath, and as he reclined there my job was to wash his feet, back, and
hair with soap and a flannel.[3] When he was done, I'd be waiting with a warm,
open towel.

I interrupted him, "You certainly wanted to know that woman this evening." 45
"What? How quiet it is! Shall we hear some music?"

He was right. Neither the city nor the country was quiet like the suburbs, the
silence of people holding their breath.

Dad was holding up a record he had borrowed from the library. "You will
know this, but not well enough, I guarantee you."

Beethoven's Fifth was an odd choice of background music, but how could I
sneer? Without his enthusiasm, my life would never have been filled with music.
Mother had been a church pianist, and she'd taken us to the ballet, usually "The
Nutcracker," or the Bolshoi[4] when they visited London. Mum and Dad sometimes went ballroom dancing; I loved it when they dressed up. Out of such minute inspirations I have found meaning sufficient for a life.

Dad said, "Do you think I'll be able to go in that pub again?" 50
"If you apologize."

"Better leave it a few weeks. I don't know what overcame me. That woman's
not a Jewess, is she?"

"I don't know."

"Usually she's happy to hear about my aches and pains, and who else is, at our
age?"

2. Novel (1865–69) by Leo Tolstoy; like Marcel Proust's *Remembrance of Things Past* (1913–27) and George
Eliot's *Middlemarch* (1871–72), it is both very long and widely considered a classic.
3. British term for washcloth.
4. Moscow's Bolshoi ("Grand") Theater is home to renowned opera and ballet companies that tour
internationally.

55   "Where d'you ache?"

"It's the walk to and from the station—sometimes I just can't make it. I have to stop and lean against something."

I said, "I've been learning massage."

"Ah." He put his feet in my lap. I squeezed his feet, ankles, and calves; he wasn't looking at me now. He said, "Your hands are strong. You're not a plumber, are you?"

"I've told you what I do. I have the theatre, and now I'm helping to set up a teaching foundation, a studio for the young."

60   He whispered, "Are you homosexual?"

"I am, yes. Never seen a cock I didn't like. You?"

"Queer? It would have shown up by now, wouldn't it? But I've never done much about my female interests."

"You've never been unfaithful?"

"I've always liked women."

65   I asked, "Do they like you?"

"The local secretaries are friendly. Not that you can do anything. I can't afford a 'professional.'"

"How often do you go to the pub?"

"I've started popping in after work. My Billy has gone."

"For good?"

70   "After university he'll come running back to me, I can assure you of that. Around this time of night, I'd always be talking to him. There's a lot you can put in a kid, without his knowing it. My wife doesn't have a word to say to me. She doesn't like to do anything for me, either."

"Sexually?"

"She might look large to you, but in the flesh she is even larger, and she crushes me like a gnat in bed. I can honestly say we haven't had it off for eighteen years."

"Since Billy was born?"

He said, letting me caress him, "She never had much enthusiasm for it. Now she is indifferent . . . frozen . . . almost dead."

75   I said, "People are more scared of their own passion than of anything else. But it's a grim deprivation she's made you endure."

He nodded. "You dirty homos have a good time, I bet, looking at one another in toilets and that—"

"People like to think so. But I've lived alone for five years."

He said, "I am hoping she will die before me, then I might have a chance. . . . We ordinary types carry on in these hateful situations for the single reason of the children, and you'll never have that."

"You're right."

80   He indicated photographs of me and my brother. "Without those babies, there is nothing for me. It is ridiculous to try to live for yourself alone."

"Don't I know it? Unless one can find others to live for."

"I hope you do!" he said. "But it can never be the same as your own."

If the mortification of fidelity imperils love, there's always the consolation of children. I had been Dad's girl, his servant, his worshipper; my faith had kept him alive. It was a cult of personality he had set up, with my brother and me as his mirrors.

Now Mother opened the door—not so wide that she could see us, or us her—and announced that she was going to bed.

"Good night," I called. 85

Dad was right about kids. But what could I do about it? I had bought an old factory at my own expense and had converted it into a theatre studio, a place where young people could work with established artists. I spent so much time in this building that I had moved my office there. It was where I would head when I left here, to sit in the café, seeing who would turn up and what they wanted from me, if anything. I was gradually divesting myself, as I aged, of all I'd accumulated. One of Father's favorite works was Tolstoy's "How Much Land Does a Man Need?"[5]

I said, "With or without children, you are still a man. There are things you want that children cannot provide."

He said, "We all, in this street, are devoted to hobbies."

"The women, too?"

"They sew, or whatever. There's never an idle moment. My son has written a 90 beautiful essay on the use of time."

He sipped his tea; the Beethoven, which was on repeat, boomed away. He seemed content to let me work on his legs. Since he didn't want me to stop, I asked him to lie on the floor. With characteristic eagerness, he removed his dressing gown and then his pajama top; I massaged every part of him, murmuring "Dad, Dad" under my breath. When at last he stood up, I was ready with his warm dressing gown, which I had placed on the radiator.

It was late, but not too late to leave. It was never too late to leave the suburbs, but Dad invited me to stay. I agreed, though it hadn't occurred to me that he would suggest I sleep in my old room, in my bed.

He accompanied me upstairs and in I went, stepping over record sleeves, magazines, clothes, books. My piano I was most glad to see. I can still play a little, but my passion was writing the songs that were scrawled in notebooks on top of the piano. Not that I would be able to look at them. When I began to work in the theatre, I didn't show my songs to anyone, and eventually I came to believe they were a waste of time.

Standing there shivering, I had to tell myself the truth: my secret wasn't that I hadn't propagated but that I'd wanted to be an artist, not just a producer. If I chose, I could blame my parents for this: they had seen themselves as spectators, in the background of life. But I was the one who'd lacked the guts—to fail, to succeed, to engage with the whole undignified, insane attempt at originality. I had only ever been a handmaiden, first to Dad and then to others—the artists I'd supported—and how could I have imagined that that would be sufficient?

My bed was narrow. Through the thin ceiling, I could hear my father snoring; 95 I knew whenever he turned over in bed. It was true that I had never heard them making love. Somehow, between them, they had transformed the notion of physical love into a ridiculous idea. Why would people want to do something so awkward with their limbs?

5. 1886 short story about a man whose greed for land leads him to forfeit everything, including his own life; the story ends with his burial in a six-foot grave, which thus turns out to be all the land that a man truly needs.

I couldn't hear Mother. She didn't snore, but she could sigh for England. I got up and went to the top of the stairs. By the kitchen light I could see her in her dressing gown, stockings around her ankles, trudging along the hall and into each room, wringing her hands as she went, muttering back to the ghosts clamoring within her skull.

She stood still to scratch and tear at her exploded arms. During the day, she kept them covered because of her "eczema." Now I watched while flakes of skin fell onto the carpet, as though she were converting herself into dust. She dispersed the shreds of her body with her delicately pointed dancer's foot.

As a child—even as a young man—I would never have approached Mother in this state. She had always made it clear that the uproar and demands of two boys were too much for her. Naturally, she couldn't wish for us to die, so she died herself, inside.

One time, my therapist asked whether Dad and I were able to be silent together. More relevant, I should have said, was whether Mother and I could be together without my chattering on about whatever occurred to me, in order to distract her from herself. Now I made up my mind and walked down the stairs, watching her all the while. She was like difficult music, and you wouldn't want to get too close. But, as with such music, I wouldn't advise trying to make it out—you have to sit with it, wait for it to address you.

100   I was standing beside her, and with her head down she looked at me sideways. "I'll make you some tea," I said, and she even nodded.

Before, during one of her nighttime wanderings, she had found me masturbating in front of some late-night TV program. It must have been some boy group, or Bowie.[6] I know what you are," she said. She was not disapproving. She was just a lost ally.

I made a cup of lemon tea and gave it to her. As she stood sipping it, I took up a position beside her, my head bent also, attempting to see—as she appeared to vibrate with inner electricity—what she saw and felt. It was clear that there was no chance of my ever being able to cure her. I could only become less afraid of her madness.

In his bed, Father was still snoring. He wouldn't have liked me to be with her. He had taken her sons for himself, charmed them away, and he wasn't a sharer.

105   She was almost through with the tea and getting impatient. Wandering, muttering, scratching: she had important work to do and time was passing. I couldn't detain her anymore.

I slept in her chair in the front room.

When I got up, my parents were having breakfast. My father was back in his suit, and my mother was in the uniform she wore to work in the supermarket. I dressed rapidly in order to join Dad as he walked to the station. It had stopped raining.

I asked him about his day, but couldn't stop thinking about mine. I was living, as my therapist enjoyed reminding me, under the aegis of the clock. I wanted to go to the studio and talk; I wanted to eat well and make love well, go to a show and then dance, and make love again. I could not be the same as them.

At the station in London, Father and I parted. I said I'd always look out for him when I was in the area, but couldn't be sure when I'd be coming his way again.

6. Rock star David Bowie (b. 1947), known in the 1970s for his glamorously androgynous stage persona "Ziggy Stardust."

QUESTIONS

1. By the end of the story, what would you say are the "various mental problems that enervated but did not ruin" this story's narrator-protagonist (par. 10)? What do you think he learns over the course of the story, especially about himself and his parents?
2. As the title of the story implies, its narrator-protagonist essentially travels back in time to a "long ago yesterday"—an earlier time both in his personal history and in that of his country and the world. How are these two historical moments characterized? What might the story imply about the similarities and differences between "yesterday" and "today"?
3. What might the narrator mean when he says, "It was never too late to leave the suburbs" (par. 92)? How are the suburbs and the city characterized and contrasted in the story? What is the significance of the contrast? How much does the story's effect and meaning depend upon the fact that it is set in a *British* suburb?

MICHAEL CHABON

The Lost World

One summer night not long after he turned sixteen, Nathan Shapiro drank four tall cans of Old English 800 and very soon found himself sitting in the front seat of a huge, banana-colored Ford LTD, with his friends Buster, Felix, and Tiger Montaine. They had swallowed the malt liquor while bathing in Buster French's hot tub (the Frenches were from Los Angeles) and, as a result, were driving around boiled, steaming drunk, and in various stages of undress. Buster and Felix E. still had on their scant Speedo bathing suits, Tiger Montaine wore only a black mesh tank top and one sanitary sock, and Nathan, through some combination of glee and desperation, was naked from head to toe.

Two weeks before this, his mother, in a modest and homemade little ceremony, had married a man named Ed, a kindly, balding geologist from Idaho whom she had been dating for six months. And then just this evening, an hour before Nathan went over to Buster French's house, Dr. Shapiro had telephoned jubilantly from Boston to announce the first pregnancy of his wife, Anne. Ricky, Nathan's brother, had been living in Boston for a year now, and he went on and on over the phone about the little bubble of life that had blossomed in the vial of Anne's home pregnancy test, which Ricky had taken to his room and placed between his soccer trophy and a photograph of his mother and father and Nathan standing in the wind at Nag's Head.[1]

All of these developments, though he did his best to welcome them, had left Nathan somewhat more than normally confused. He liked his new stepfather, who had been to Antarctica and Peru and Novaya Zemlya[2] and returned with all sorts of hair-raising tales and queer stones; in his own way he was genuinely as excited as Ricky by the prospect of a new baby; and he was old enough to regard these changes as the inevitable outward expansion, as of an empire or a galaxy, of what once had been his family. He was happy for his parents in their new lives, the way he had always been happy for them, all along, as step by step they had dismantled their marriage; and so he was looking for a reason, an excuse to feel

1. Beach town on North Carolina's Outer Banks.   2. Russian islands in the Arctic Ocean.

so unmoored, at once so angry and nostalgic; and alcohol seemed to be doing the job. He had no idea of where he and his friends were going, and it was not until they had been lurching aimlessly along the empty, fragrant streets of Huxley for what seemed like hours that he understood that they were headed—as Buster French put it—to the crib of Chaya Feldman.

Buster, driving Mrs. French's car, made this declaration just as the drink, the deep velour seats, and the sweet smell of lawns flowing in through the open windows had begun to lull Nathan to sleep, and at the mention of Chaya's name Nathan sat bolt upright. Buster then called Chaya a "skeezer," which meant, as far as Nathan had been able to determine, that she was certain to permit them—all four of them—those dark liberties of which he was still very much ignorant, a notion which filled him only with wonder, and with solicitude for Chaya, whom he had known since he was six years old. She was a quiet girl, with a serious brown face and tangled hair, and her parents dressed her like a doll. He remembered her as someone who was always coming upon orphaned puppies and sparrow chicks with broken wings, in meadows and along roads where anyone else would have found nothing at all, and then trying imperfectly and with an eyedropper full of milk or sugar water to nurse them back to health. Her chief social art—until recently, at least—had been that, upon request, she could draw you an extremely realistic picture of an eyeball, with a sparkle on the iris, and fathomless pupils, and the finest tracery of veins.

5   They had never really been friends, but from time to time Nathan still thought about one distant afternoon when he and Chaya had somehow ended up playing together, in the fields behind the Huxley Interfaith Plexus. In the tall grass and the weeds they had played a game of Chaya's own invention, called Planet of the Birds. Nathan had been an intergalactic castaway trying to survive in a windy, grassy world, and Chaya's hair had tossed like a crest of feathers as she sang to him in a variety of cries. Chaya even claimed that when she grew up she was going to write a book set on this imaginary planet, whose name, she said, was Jadis;[3] in the dust she scratched a map of its oceans and aeries. As with all of those blissful Sunday afternoons he had ever passed with some child with whom he never played again—every childhood has a dozen or so—his memory of this vanished afternoon was luminous and clear. In the three years since his liberation from Hebrew school he had seen Chaya twice, from a distance, coming out of a movie with her parents and her sister, Mara. Now Nathan was suddenly afraid for her, and he was afraid, for the first time ever, of the raucous bodies of his friends.

"Hey, Buster," said Felix E. Scott, leaning forward so that for an instant his thigh lay smooth and cool against Nathan's, "what you going to do to Chaya Feldman?"

"Don't tell me you don't already know, Felix E.," said Buster, heaving the LTD into a small cul-de-sac which Nathan recognized, from some long-ago car pool, as Chaya's street.

"Cut the engine," suggested Tiger Montaine, who excelled in stealthy behavior. He ran his battered little Fiat on siphoned gasoline, filched cigarettes from the supermarket, and had for several months, with Nathan's shocked connivance, been replacing Mrs. Shapiro's codeine pills with extra-strength Tylenol, one at a

3. French word meaning "in times past, formerly."

time. "Don't be waking up that mean Israelite daddy." Chaya's father, Moshe, an oncologist, had been born and raised in Israel, and was, in fact, the most humorless and stern of the one hundred and five fathers Nathan had known in his life. He had a dense black beard and crazy eyebrows, and it was widely half-believed that he kept an Uzi submachine gun, from his days in the army of Israel, hidden under his bed.

Buster turned off the ignition and the car began to glide silently toward Chaya's house. The sudden calm cast a pall over the party and no one spoke; perhaps they were only being careful. Nathan pictured Chaya, asleep, her legs tangled under a light summer blanket; a skeezer! Then, because the ignition had been cut, the steering wheel locked, automatically, and before Buster could do anything they had hopped up over the curb, and came to a stop halfway across somebody's front lawn.

"We're there," said Buster, and everyone laughed. "Now who's going to go 10 knocking on that skeezer's window?"

"I'll go," said Nathan. "I know her."

All of the other boys turned to regard him. Although Nathan felt fairly confident that his friends held him in a certain esteem—his naked presence among them was testimony to that—he had never distinguished himself for his daring, and in fact generally had to be persuaded even to perform minor feats such as dancing with Twanda Woods, or wearing his sneakers without any laces, an affectation which drove his mother out of her mind. And all of the boys knew, for Nathan had been unable, despite himself, to conceal it, that he had never made love to a girl. Emboldened by the malt liquor, he reached out and pushed Felix E. and Tiger in their faces, so that they fell backward into each other.

"I went to Hebrew school with her," he explained.

Perhaps it was only their shock at this uncharacteristic display of fearlessness, but as Nathan stepped out of the car, he noticed a strange look in the eyes of his friends. It was a kind of blank, blinking puzzlement, as though the game had gone awry. Nathan wondered if the whole thing was a lie, if Chaya was not a skeezer at all, and the boys were all of them virgins, and none of them knew what fate awaited him as he began to make his way, naked, barefoot as a child, across the soft grass. He glanced toward the car, toward the three shadowy heads now drawn together in what looked like anxious parley, and almost turned back.

The next moment, however, he felt an entirely new kind of drunkenness; the 15 air was warm against his skin, his lips, his forearms, and—incredibly—moonlight fell upon his penis. He wished that it were a mile to Chaya's house, and not a few short steps, so that he might walk this way a little longer, like a fairy on a moonlit heath. Just this summer—just this month—his body had begun to grow lean, and he strode across the grass with the jangling gait of a young man, delighting in the purpose of his legs. He came to the Feldmans' driveway and zigzagged quickly around to the left side of the house, where he was confronted with a gated, wooden fence. He stopped and contemplated the latticed gate. His breath came quickly now and there was sweat in his eyebrows; a drop spattered against his cheek. Just when he felt the water on his face he saw, through the spaces in the lattice, that a swimming pool, long and unusually narrow, lay beyond. It was not a pool for a pleasure swim; it was a lap pool, no wider than a pair of racing freestylers. Nathan remembered hearing that Dr. Feldman required himself and his family to swim a mile every day.

Pretending for the moment that he was tricksy Tiger Montaine, Nathan held his breath, eased up the steel latch, and slowly let open the gate, without a sound. He walked to the railroad ties that formed the near end of the lap pool and curled his toes over their edge. Thus perched he stood a moment, looking at the reflected moon on the black water and trying to force the tumult in his stomach to abate. He was so nervous that he forgot why he was nervous, and simply hovered at the edge of Chaya's swimming pool, shaking. What was he doing here? Where were his clothes?

He crouched and then slipped, like a deer fleeing a forest fire, into the cool water. He swam across the pool with a light and leisurely stroke. The exercise of his arms and heart in the cold water cleared his thoughts, and left him with a pleasant chlorine sting in his eyes, and when he arrived at the far side of the lap pool, he felt a greater trust in himself and in the general benevolence of a Tuesday night in July. He pulled himself from the pool and tiptoed around to the back of the Feldmans' house. There were some bedsheets, striped pillow-cases, and a pair of bath towels hanging from a revolving clothesline in the backyard, and he considered taking a towel and tying it around his waist. But he felt, obscurely, that there was some advantage in his nakedness, an almost magical advantage that Tiger Montaine, for example, would never have sur-rendered, and he went over to the windows of the daylight basement in which Chaya had always had her room and stood a moment, with his hands on his wet hips, looking into the dark windows, preparing to wake her. The pool water streamed down his chest to his thighs, raising goosebumps along his legs and arms as Nathan drummed lightly on the glass, attempting a sort of suave seductive rhythm that came out, inexorably, as shave-and-a-hair-cut, two-bits.

· · ·

A light snapped on inside. Someone sat up in the bed—in Chaya's bed—and this someone did not appear to be Chaya. She was too tall, and her hair was fuller and darker, and through the armhole of her sheer short nightgown he saw the startling contour of a woman's heavy breast. He turned and began to hightail it out of the backyard, but the door opened almost immediately, and he turned sheepishly back.

"Is, uh, Chaya here?" he said, in a tone which he hoped would make him sound too stupid to be doing something illicit.

"Nathan? Nathan Shapiro?"

20   "Chaya?"

"What are you doing here? Where are your clothes?"

The light spilling out around her reduced her to a silhouette and he could not tell if she looked angry or merely puzzled. Her voice was a cracked whisper and sounded rather plaintive in the dark, as though she were also afraid of getting into some kind of trouble.

"I swam in your pool," Nathan offered, uncertain if this would explain every-thing adequately.

25   "Well, you'd better get out of here. My dad is sleeping and he hasn't been well."

"Okay," said Nathan. "Good-bye. You got so big, Chaya." He was staring.

"Puberty," she said. "Ever hear of it?" She stepped back into the light of her room and smiled a sort of frowny smile she had always had, and then Nathan felt that he recognized her.

"Chaya, I feel so weird," he said. At the sight of her familiar, serious face he was all at once on the verge of tears.

"Well. Okay, come inside. You have to be quiet."

"Okay."

Nathan followed Chaya into her room, which had the drop ceiling and damp-carpet odor of a basement. On one paneled wall there was a print of *The Starry Night* and an El Al[4] poster with a picture of the Old City of Jerusalem; on the other wall was a painting that Chaya herself must have made, a picture of a palm tree full of bright parrots under a double sun, and Nathan remembered the day he had spent on the Planet Jadis. Beside the painting was an old mounted deer's head, with a split ear, wearing sunglasses and a purple beret. On the table beside her bed was a squat jug lamp with a green shade, a package of Kool cigarettes, and a book by Erica Jong[5] that Nathan had twice been admonished against reading by his grandfather. The circle of light from the lamp seemed to fall almost entirely on the bed, and Nathan averted his eyes, so intimate was the sight of the exposed white sheets and the deep declivity in the pillow. The imprint of her sleeping head, the whole idea of Chaya asleep, struck him as terribly poignant, and he could not look. He heard the creak of the bedsprings and the rustle of sheets as she climbed back into bed.

"I mean you're not ugly, or anything, Nathan," said Chaya, "but put something on, okay?"

"I'm naked!" said Nathan. He looked down at himself, and knew that he was naked. And he saw, as through Chaya's eyes, that in assuming some of its manly proportions and features, his penis had also begun to take on a concomitant forlorn and humorous aspect, sort of like the Jeep in Popeye cartoons;[6] and he made an apron of his hands and forearms. This did nothing to conceal, however, the whiteness of his thighs, or the soft, sad divot of hair around his left—but not yet his right—nipple.

"There's a towel on the chair."

"I'd better go," said Nathan. He turned and began to walk out the door, attempting now to cover his probably ridiculous-looking rear end.

"It's okay, go ahead, put it on, Nathan," said Chaya.

"They brought me," he said, turning again and crab-walking over to the chair beside Chaya's desk. "The guys. Tiger and Buster and Felix E." Hurriedly he wrapped the towel around his waist and tucked in one end, in the fashion that his grandmother had always referred to, for some reason, as Turkish. It was a scratchy white towel that had been stolen, to judge from the illegible Hebrew lettering that was woven like a pattern into one side, from some hotel in Israel. The lopsided situation of his chest hair remained a keen embarrassment, and the towel was so skimpy that the knot at his hip just barely held.

"Are they out there?"

"Yeah. They sent me in. They said—"

"Your hair is all wet." She folded her hands over her stomach, on the pleat of the bedclothes, and stared at him. She seemed all in all only mildly surprised to

30

35

40

---

4. The national airline of Israel. *Starry Night*: well-known painting by Dutch artist Vincent van Gogh (1853–90).

5. American novelist (b. 1942) best known for her erotically charged first novel, *Fear of Flying* (1973).

6. Mysterious doglike animal with little ears, a long red nose, and a large stomach, as well as magical abilities.

see Nathan, as though he were visiting her in a dream. Her face had grown wider, her cheekbones more pronounced, since the last time he had seen her, and with her tawny skin and her thick eyebrows and that big, wild hair Nathan thought she looked beautiful and a little scary. He sat down and hugged himself. His teeth were chattering.

"Okay, now I better go." He stood up again.

"Wait," said Chaya. She patted the sheets and indicated that he sit beside her. He came to sit gingerly at her feet, keeping hold with one hand of the tenuous Turkish knot.

"Nathan Shapiro," she said, shaking her head.

"Chaya Feldman."

45   "Mrs. Falutnick's class."

"Kvit chewink your gum in fronta da r-radio," said Nathan, repeating a favorite inscrutable admonishment of Mrs. Falutnick's in an accent he had not mimicked for six or seven years. Chaya laughed, but Nathan only snorted once through his nose. It had been so long since the days of Mrs. Falutnick's class! He saw himself sitting in a flecked plastic chair at the back of the droning classroom in the Huxley Interfaith Plexus, defacing with moustaches and monkey's fur the grave photographs of Emma Lazarus and Abraham Cahan[7] in his copy of *Adventures in American Jewry*, furtively folding all ten inches of a stick of grape Big Buddy into his mouth when Mrs. Falutnick turned her enormous back on the class, and at this he was unaccountably saddened, and he sighed, startling Chaya out of her dream.

"I heard your parents got a divorce," she said. She looked down, and her long hair splashed her folded hands.

"Yeah," said Nathan, hugging himself again. The shiver that this word produced in him never lasted more than a second or two.

"Why did they?"

"I don't know," Nathan said.

50   "You don't?"

He thought about it for a few seconds, then shook his head. "I mean they told me, but I forget what they said."

"It's complicated," Chaya offered, helpfully. "People change."

"I think that was part of it," Nathan said, but he didn't believe that there was really any explanation at all.

55   "Does your dad still live around here?"

"He moved to Boston."

"That's cool," said Chaya. She lifted the curtain of hair from her face and smiled another crooked smile. "I wish my dad would move to Boston."

Nathan said automatically, "No, you don't." He had hitherto managed to forget about the fearsome doctor and he glanced over his shoulder. In the far corner of the room he noticed three large plastic suitcases and a guitar case, neatly lined up as for an imminent departure.

"Where are you going?" he said, gesturing toward the luggage.

60   "Jerusalem," said Chaya. "Tomorrow. Today, I guess. Later this morning."

"With your family? Or all alone?"

7. Abraham Cahan (1860–1951), American novelist known for chronicling the Jewish-American immigrant experience; Emma Lazarus (1849–87), American poet best known for her sonnet "The New Colossus," written for the dedication of the Statue of Liberty.

"All alone."

"Are you ever coming back?"

"Of course I am, you," she said. "My father thinks I've gotten—he just wants me to learn to be an Israeli."

"Oh," said Nathan. He was not certain what this entailed, but he suddenly 65 pictured Chaya operating a crane on the bristling lip of a giant construction site in the desert, lowering a turbine generator or a sheaf of I-beams down into the void, the dust of the Negev[8] blowing around her like a long scarf.

"Did they tell you I put out?" said Chaya. "Those guys?"

"Kind of," said Nathan, taken aback, before it occurred to him that this was admitting he had come here for sex, when in fact he had come—why had he come? "It was more like a dare, I guess," he said. "They sort of more or less dared me to come."

"None of them's ever sat on my bed the way you are," said Chaya.

Nathan wondered for a moment exactly what she meant by this, and then, in the next moment, leaned toward her and kissed her lips. This was done only on an off chance and he did not expect that she would take such forceful hold of his body. Startled, without a clue of what he ought to do next, he put one hand on the nape of her neck, the other at the small of her back, and then he lay very still in her arms. He could feel the bones of her hips pressing against him, like a pair of fists, and his lips and somehow his breathing became entangled in her hair. The laundered smell of her bedclothes was overpowering and sweet.

"Are you a virgin, Nathan?" she said, her mouth very close to his. 70

He considered his reply much longer than he needed to, trying to phrase it as ambiguously as he could. "In a manner of speaking," he said at last, blushing in self-congratulation at the urbanity of this reply.

Her grip upon him relaxed, and she drew back slowly and then fell back against her pillow, looking calm again. He had the feeling that she had been hoping for some reply totally other than the one he had given. Then Chaya sighed, in a bored, theatrical way that to Nathan's ears sounded very grown up, and he was afraid, at last, that she really might have become a skeezer, that it really was possible to lose track of someone so completely that they turned into someone else without your knowing about it.

"Can you still draw eyeballs?" he said.

"Eyeballs?" she said, her face blank. "Sure, I can."

"Chaya! Mara!" called Dr. Feldman from somewhere in the house. His voice 75 resounded like an axe-blow. "That's enough!"

They both started, and stared a moment at one another as children or as lovers caught.

"Can I tell you something, Nathan?" she said. "When I get to Israel I'm *not* coming back."

"You have to come back," he said, taking her hand.

"Chaya!" thundered Dr. Feldman from very far away. "Go to sleep."

"I'll write you," said Chaya. "Give me your address." 80

"Sixty-four twenty-three Les Adieux[9] Circle. Is he going to come down here?"

"No," she said. "He thinks you're my little sister. I'll never remember that address. Let me write it down."

8. Desert in southern Israel.   9. Literally, "The Good-byes" (French).

"Oh, that's all right," said Nathan, getting up. "You don't need to write me a letter."

"No, wait. Hold on."

85   She climbed out of bed again, grinning, and went to a blue wooden desk, under the stairs that led up to the first floor of the house. Nathan watched the play of her nightgown across her little behind as she bent over to open a drawer, and then scrabbled around in it, looking for a pen. She found a sheet of pink stationery and began to scratch across it with a Smurf pencil.

"Chaya, I'd better go," said Nathan. He headed for the door.

"Wait!" said Chaya. She was writing furiously now, in a pointed, ribbony script almost like cursive Hebrew, and he waited, one hand on the knob, for her to finish, and hoped that Dr. Feldman would not call out again. When she put down her pen she took a red, white, and blue airmail envelope from another drawer, folded the slip of pink paper in half, slid it into the envelope, and ran her tongue along the flap. Then she bent over the desk again and, brushing her hair from the face of the envelope, wrote out what Nathan knew even from a distance to be his name and address.

"There, I wrote you a letter from Jerusalem," she said, turning toward him. "Don't read it until tomorrow."

"Okay," said Nathan. "Good-bye." He hugged her awkwardly, afraid that he might get an erection, and then eased open the basement door. "Have fun in Jerusalem."

90   "But I'm already there," she said, continuing in this teasing and mysterious vein. She put a hand on each of his shoulders and kissed him on the cheek. Nathan took the letter from her, a little uncertainly. Probably it was just a bunch of scribble, or an apology for not wanting to have sex with him.

"I know what you're doing!" said Dr. Feldman, with that weird Yisraeli accent of his, and Nathan went out naked into the night. He was not quite so drunk anymore, and this time the trip around the house, past the swimming pool, did not seem especially fine or ominous. The dog next door to the Feldmans' caught wind of Nathan and began to rail at him, and he ran the rest of the way, all the while trying to determine if Dr. Feldman and his Uzi were in pursuit. As he was running across the Feldmans' yard and into the neighbors', the white towel finally slipped from his waist and fell away, nearly tripping him; he left it to Chaya to explain how it got there, and went naked the rest of the way.

He came around to his side of the car and hesitated with a hand on the door. They were asleep, all three of them, Felix E. and Tiger slumped in opposite corners of the backseat, Buster stretched out across the front seat of the car. The radio played very softly and threw green light across Buster's thighs. They were snoring with the lustiness of children, and Nathan felt a surge of pity for them and wished that they might just keep on sleeping. When he got into the car, he knew, his friends would want to know what, or rather how much, Chaya had given him; and when he showed them the letter, they would want to read what she had written. He was afraid that its contents might somehow embarrass him, and now he looked for somewhere to conceal it.

At first he considered retrieving the discarded towel, but he was afraid to go back, and anyway, if he wrapped the letter in the towel it would make a pretty suspicious bundle. Then he looked around at the lawn on which they were parked, to see if it held any place in which he could hide the letter, but there was only the silver expanse of lawn, an entire neighborhood of grass and flat moon-light. Under the front windows of the neighbors' house stood one small row of bushes, and he tried poking the envelope deep into this, but you could see it from a mile away, reflecting the light of the moon like a shard of mirror glass, and he retrieved it and looked around again.

Just when he was about to give up and try to hide the letter somewhere in the Frenches' car itself, under a mat, or even in the glove compartment, he spotted a bird feeder, about twenty feet away, hanging from the low branch of a young maple tree. It was shaped like a small transparent house, with a peaked plastic roof and glass walls, about half-filled with birdseed. Nathan unhooked it from its wire and turned it over, his hands shaking with fear and with the aptness of his plan. He pulled off the plastic base of the bird feeder and laid the letter within, burying it amid the smooth and rattling seeds. When he returned the little house to its hook, the letter was nearly invisible, and he trotted back, with a certain air of coolness, to the big yellow LTD.

His friends clambered upright when Nathan climbed back into the car; they 95 were sober and embarrassed, and slapped Nathan constantly on the side of his head. They demanded to know what had happened to Nathan in Chaya's room, and as they drove slowly home he made up a story, filled with sophisticated orgasms, and accurate anatomical impressions, and some bits of sexual dialog in half-remembered Hebrew. The other boys seemed on the whole to believe him, although they were surprised, and blamed malt liquor and hormonal agitation, when halfway through the tale Nathan suddenly burst into tears—then stopped, and resumed his lying account.

The next night Nathan sneaked out of the house after his mother and Ed had gone to sleep. He rode half an hour on his bicycle, through the darkness, to retrieve the letter from Jerusalem. There was no moon, and black shapes seemed to dart and loom across his path. He pulled up in front of the Feldmans' house and contemplated it for a moment, straddling the hard bar of his bike. There was no sign of the towel he had dropped. He hated it that Chaya was not there in her house anymore, that she could so quickly be gone. He had a great curios-ity to read what she had written him, but when he crept across to open up the little bird feeder, past the two long scars in the lawn from the wheels of the LTD, he found there was nothing inside it anymore but birdseed. The hairs on the back of his neck stood on end, and he whirled, half expecting to see Chaya, with the letter in her hand, laughing at him from behind the curtain in the low side window of her bedroom. He looked around on the grass, in the row of low shrubs, in the branches of the maple, but the letter was nowhere to be found, and after a few more minutes of baffled searching he got back on his bicycle and pedaled home. As he lay in bed that night he tried to imagine what she might have set down in her letter, what professions of love, what unhappiness, what nonsense, what shame, what news of the planet of her childhood. Then he fell asleep.

• • •

One Saturday a few weeks afterward, Nathan and his stepfather were in the kitchen, trying to work their way out of an incipient argument about whether or not tuna salad ought to be made with chopped gherkins, the way Ed's grand-mother had always made it. The dispute was merely the latest and perhaps the most trivial in what was becoming a disheartening routine for Nathan and Ed, and this particular volley of intransigent politeness had just begun to make Nathan's stomach hurt—without inclining him to capitulate—when Mrs. Shapiro-Knipper entered the kitchen, carrying the Saturday mail.

"Two things," she said, handing Nathan two envelopes, one of them tricolor and heartstopping.

"I'm going to put pickles," said Ed. "You'll see. It's an acquired taste."

100 This time, though everything Ed liked to eat, from raw oysters to pizza with pineapple and ham, seemed to be an acquired taste, Nathan let it pass. He rose from the kitchen table and carried the two letters out into the hallway and down to his bedroom. The second, in a plain business envelope, was evidently from his father, who had never before sent a letter to Nathan, and Nathan sat on his bed for a long time without opening them, just thinking about mailmen, and sealed envelopes, and the mysteries of the post.

He supposed that the neighbor had found Chaya's letter hidden in the bird feeder before Nathan could retrieve it, and had finally gotten around to affixing a stamp to it and sending it along. Since, in the past weeks, Nathan had decided that he was in love with Chaya, and had been busy erecting all the necessary buttresses and towers and fluttering pennants in his imagination, the surprise arrival of her letter, which he had presumed lost, was a delicious addition to the structure, and he delayed as long as he could stand before finally tearing open the envelope.

DEAR NATHAN,

Sometimes it is very hot here. I have a thousand boyfriends.
It is scary if a gun goes off in the night.

You made me laugh a lot of times in class I remember.

105 "Take it easy."

Love,
CHAYA

He was sharply disappointed. He hated the fact that he had made her laugh, for one; and it angered him, unreasonably, he knew, that all of the other things— and there were so few of them—she had written were hypothetical, as insubstantial as her Planet of the Birds, or as his parents' marriage, or as the baby that was growing in his stepmother's belly. He stuffed the bogus letter back into the envelope and tore it to pieces.

He was still feeling bad when at last he brought himself to open the letter from his father. It was a brief, barely legible note, on a sheet of legal paper. After some facetious chitchat about the Red Sox and Ricky's karate lessons, Nathan's father had written, "Your mother tells me that you have made some new friends and she is a little worried because you're going around with your shoes untied. Tie your shoelaces. Don't be angry with us, Nate. I know that everything seems different now but you have to get used to it. I will always love you as much as I will love any new Shapiros that come along."

110 "Nathan?" his mother called to him through the door of his room. "Come on and eat."

"I hate it with gherkins," said Nathan, but his heart had gone out of the argument, and he stood up to join his mother and Ed for lunch. Hastily he dried his eyes, and scrambled to gather up the letter from his father and the scraps of Chaya's letter that were scattered across his bed. It was as he laid them carefully in the Roi-Tan cigar box in which he kept his most important papers that he noticed the strange and beautiful postage stamp in the torn corner of the airmail envelope, and the postmark, printed in an alien script.

1990

QUESTIONS

1. What has Nathan lost in the process of growing up? How might your answer change over the course of "The Lost World"?
2. What are the key symbolic details included in the description of Nathan's journey to Chaya's bedroom?
3. How do place and time (physical and temporal setting) shape Nathan's experience and its meaning for us? How does this story implicitly characterize modern suburbia?

SUGGESTIONS FOR WRITING

1. Though only one of these stories (Michael Chabon's "The Lost World") is a straightforward initiation story, one might say that the protagonists of all three learn something from their experiences. Write an essay in which you compare how and why any two of these protagonists change and what they seem to learn over the course of the story.
2. Family and especially the relationship between, and roles of, husbands and wives and parents and children are a major focus of all these stories. Compare the ways the family and these particular roles and relationships are depicted in at least two of these stories. What might they imply about both our ideal of family life and the reality? In these terms, how and why is the suburban setting important?
3. Write an essay exploring the ways in which suburbia is characterized in these three stories, as well as, perhaps, Bobbie Mason's "Shiloh" (in "Reading More Fiction"). What do the stories individually and collectively suggest about what is unique about suburbia and the life people live there? Which aspects of suburban life are portrayed positively and which negatively? In these terms, what difference does it make that the stories were written, and are set, in different times? in different countries or in different regions of the United States?

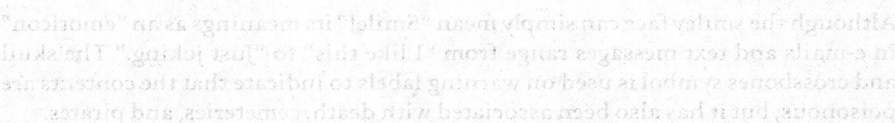

5 SYMBOL AND FIGURATIVE LANGUAGE

A symbol is something that stands for or represents something else. Sometimes a symbol resembles or closely relates to what it represents, but often the association is arbitrary or subtle. Even so, through common usage, many symbols are instantly understood by almost everyone in a particular group. Although we rarely think of them as such, the letters of the English alphabet are themselves symbols, representing different sounds. We simply learn to recognize them, however, without thinking about whether there is any resemblance between what the symbols look like and what they represent. In other languages, one character may stand for an object or concept, such as the Chinese characters for "fire." Yet some symbols do help us by resembling what they stand for, such as the symbol for a fire alarm.

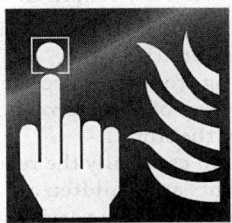

Similarly, abstractions may be represented by symbols that resemble things that are associated with them:

Although the smiley face can simply mean "Smile!" its meanings as an "emoticon" in e-mails and text messages range from "I like this" to "Just joking." The skull and crossbones symbol is used on warning labels to indicate that the contents are poisonous, but it has also been associated with death, cemeteries, and pirates.

Other symbols are more arbitrary, having no literal connection with what they represent. Octagons and the color red have little to do with stopping a car, but most Americans, even if they are too young to drive, understand what a stop sign means. Such symbols, though not based on resemblances, elicit an unconscious and reflexive response from us. The meaning of a symbol is not always so concrete and practical, however. The U.S. national flag is an arbitrary symbol, having no direct resemblance to what it represents, but most people recognize its primary significance; the "stars and stripes" undoubtedly stands for the United States. Nevertheless, the flag differs from a traffic sign in the sense that people respond on various levels to the many meanings associated with that vast country.

LITERARY SYMBOLISM

A **symbol** in a work of literature compares or puts together two things that are in some ways dissimilar. But literary symbolism rarely comes down to a simple equation of one thing to another. Unlike an arbitrary symbol such as a letter or traffic sign, a symbol in literature usually carries richer and various meanings, as does a flag or a religious image. And because of its significance, a symbol usually appears or is hinted at numerous times throughout the work. In reading litera-ture, it may be challenging to recognize symbols, and readers may have good reasons to disagree about their interpretation, since literary works often incorpo-rate symbolism for which there is no single "correct" interpretation. No one would say that reading a short story should be like a treasure hunt for some shiny symbol that clearly reveals all the hidden meanings; the complexity remains and requires further exploration even when we have recognized a symbol's signifi-cance at some level. A literary symbol may be understood as an extended figure of speech that rewards further interpretation.

A symbol usually conveys an abstraction or cluster of abstractions, from the ideal to the imperceptible or the irrational, in a more concrete form. Some sym-bols have been in use by many people for a long time (in which case it is known as a *traditional symbol*); a white dove, for example, is a traditional symbol of peace and love. A rose can be a symbol of godly love, of romantic desire, of female beauty, of mortality (because the flower wilts), or of hidden cruelty (because it has thorns). The snake has traditionally been a symbol of evil, but in Rudyard Kipling's *The Jungle Book*, the python Ka, while frightening, is on the side of law and order. A few symbolic character types, plots, objects, or settings—for example, the trickster, the quest, the garden—have become so pervasive and have recurred in so many cul-tures that they are considered **archetypes** (literary elements that recur in cultural and cross-cultural myth). Fire, water, a flower, or a tree can all be considered arche-types because numerous cultures use them symbolically, often within their sys-tem of religion or myth. Literary symbolism frequently borrows from the symbols and archetypes associated with religion or myth.

A common literary form, especially in works written by and for religious believ-ers, is the **allegory,** which may be regarded as an "extended" symbol or series of symbols that encompasses a whole work. In an allegory, concrete things and abstract concepts may be associated with each other across a narrative with at least two distinct levels of meaning. Because allegories set up series of correspondences, they usually help the reader translate these correspondences through the use of names that readily function as labels, often with obvious moral implications. In

The Pilgrim's Progress, probably the most famous prose allegory in English, the central character is named Christian; he was born in the City of Destruction and sets out for the Celestial City, passes through the Slough of Despond and Vanity Fair, meets men named Pliable and Obstinate, and so on. The point of an allegory is not to make us hunt for disguised meanings, so it is no defect if an allegory's intended meaning is clear. Instead, the purpose is to let us enjoy an invented world where everything is especially meaningful and everything corresponds to something else according to a moral or otherwise "correct" plan.

When an entire story is allegorical or symbolic, it is sometimes called a **myth**. *Myth* originally referred to a story of communal origin that provided an explanation or religious interpretation of humanity, nature, the universe, or the relations among them. Sometimes we apply the term *myth* to stories associated with religions we do not believe in, and sometimes to literature that seeks to express experiences or truths that transcend any one location, culture, or time.

FIGURES OF SPEECH

Figures of speech, or **figurative language**, are similar to symbols in that they supplement or replace literal meaning, often by creating imaginative connections between our ideas and our senses. Sometimes referred to as *tropes* (literally, "turnings"), figures of speech could be described as *bending* the usual meaning of language and *shaping* our response to a work. Whether or not they have anything to do with spatial forms or "figures," or whether they rely on vision, such tropes contribute to what are called the **images** or **imagery** of a story. Many figures of speech are known by the Latin or Greek names used in classical Greek and Roman *rhetoric*, the art and science of speech and persuasion.

Just as you can enjoy gymnastics or diving events during the Olympics without knowing the names of the specific twists and turns, you can enjoy the figurative language in a story without identifying each figure of speech. Yet for the purposes of interpreting and writing about literature, it is important to learn some basic terms and distinctions. The box below defines some of the most frequently encountered figures of speech.

Key Figures of Speech

allegory   an extended association, often sustained in every element (character, plot, setting, etc.) and throughout an entire work, between two levels of meaning, usually literal and abstract. In *Animal Farm* (1945), for example, George Orwell uses an uprising of barnyard animals as an allegory for the Bolshevik revolution in Russia.

allusion   a reference, usually brief, to another text or some person or entity external to the work. Examples may range from a direct quotation of the Bible to the mention of a famous name.

irony   a meaning or outcome contrary to what is expected; in *verbal irony*, the text says one thing and means the reverse. When the intended meaning

(Continued on next page)

(Continued)

is harshly critical or mocking, it is called *sarcasm*. Sister in "Why I Live at the P.O." ("Reading More Fiction") unintentionally creates verbal irony in recalling how Stella-Rondo stole Mr. Whitaker from her: "Told him I was one-sided. Bigger on one side than the other, which is a deliberate, calculated falsehood: I'm the same." "One-sided" in this quarrel means having breasts of different sizes, but Sister doesn't realize that she truly is biased or one-sided as a personality. She tells her own calculated false-hoods. An example of sarcasm occurs when the girl in "Hills Like White Elephants" (chapter 2) agrees that many people have had the operation, "And afterward they were all so happy." She means the opposite, bitterly mocking her companion's promise that they will be happy.

metaphor   a representation of one thing as if it were something else, with-out a verbal signal such as *like* or *as*. "She was the queen," Sammy tells us in John Updike's story "A & P" (chapter 1)—not *like* a queen, but simply "the queen." Sammy calls her this to express her high status, beauty, and leadership among the girls.

metonymy   using the name of one thing to refer to another thing associ-ated with it. The common phrase *red tape* is a metonymy for excessive paperwork and procedure that slows down an official transaction, based on the fact that papers used to be tied up with red tape.

oxymoron   a combination of contradictory or opposite ideas, qualities, or entities, as in wise fool.

personification   sometimes called *anthropomorphism*, attributing human qualities to objects or animals. In "The Open Boat" (chapter 6), Stephen Crane personifies the birds who "sat comfortably in groups" and looked at the men with "unblinking scrutiny." He pushes personification to comic extreme in the shipwrecked men's thoughts: "If this old ninny-woman, Fate, cannot do better than this . . . she is an old hen who knows not her intention." Here, "hen" is a metaphor for a silly woman, who in turn personifies the idea of destiny or fate.

simile   a representation of one thing as if it were something else, with an explicit verbal signal such as *like* or *as*. A. S. Byatt's story "The Thing in the Forest" begins by describing the forlorn and slightly grotesque child evac-uees in World War II England with the help of several similes: They wear gloves "like a scarecrow" and march "like a disorderly dwarf regiment."

symbol   a person, place, object, or image that represents more than its lit-eral meaning. A symbol is more than a passing comparison (such as a simile); instead, as in allegory, its meaning usually relates to most details and themes of the work. Unlike allegory, a symbol usually associates more than two entities or ideas and may be obscure or ambiguous in its mean-ing. Short stories (or poems) may refer to their central symbolic figure in the title, as in "Cathedral" ("Fiction: Reading, Responding, Writing") or "The Thing in the Forest."

synecdoche   a form of metonymy (or name substitution) in which the part represents the whole (a *sail* refers to a ship).

INTERPRETING SYMBOLISM AND FIGURATIVE LANGUAGE

The context of an entire story or poem or play can guide you in deciding how far to push your own "translation" of a figure of speech or whether a metaphor has the deeper significance of a symbol. It is best to read the entire story and note all of the figures of speech or imagery before you examine one as a symbol. Often, a symbol is a focal point in a story, a single object or situation that draws the attention of one or more characters.

In Edwidge Danticat's "A Wall of Fire Rising," for example, the hot-air balloon takes on a central and multilayered significance, though there is no longstanding tradition of symbolic meaning for hot-air balloons. Although the story appears to be a matter-of-fact picture of a poor family in Haiti, the climactic action focuses on the father's desire to fly in the balloon, which in turn relates to the title's allusion to a line in a revolutionary speech. Thus the balloon flight, as an effort to rise in every sense, becomes symbolic—but a symbol of what, exactly? The fact that we cannot say with certainty what the balloon flight "means" does not diminish but rather increases its symbolic power. In Nathaniel Hawthorne's "The Birth-Mark," Aylmer explicitly calls Georgiana's one defect "the symbol of his wife's liability to sin, sorrow, decay, and death." The symbolism, allegory, and moral of Hawthorne's story are traditional and accessible. Yet the story remains ambiguous and complex because of its distinctive combination of literal and figurative elements and meanings.

Effective symbols and figurative language cannot be extracted from the story in which they serve, but they can leave a lasting image of what the story is about. With guidance and practice, identifying and interpreting literary symbolism and other figurative language will begin to feel almost as familiar to you as reading the letter symbols on a page, though the meanings may be subtle, ambiguous, and far-reaching rather than straightforward.

Responding to Symbolism: Some Guidelines

1. Read the story carefully, noting any details that seem to have exceptional significance such as names, repeated actions or statements, recurring references to objects, peculiar places, allusions, or other figures of speech.

2. Using your list of such possibly symbolic details, look back through the story to find the passages that feature these details. Are any of the passages connected to each other in a pattern? Do any of these interconnected details suggest themes of the story?

3. Note any symbols or images that you recognize from mythology, religion, or any other literature, art, or popular culture. Look again at the way the story presents such material. What are the signals that the fire is more than a fire, the tree is more than a tree, the ring is more than a ring? If the story invents its own symbol, find any words in the story that show how the characters see something meaningful in the birthmark, monster, hot-air balloon, or coin.

(Continued on next page)

(Continued)

4. Once you have found a symbol—an aspect of the story that is a figure of speech, trope, image, or connection between literal and nonliteral; is extended beyond a few sentences; is more complicated than an allegory's one-to-one translation; and may be interpreted in multiple ways—review every aspect of the story, on the literal level, that relates to this symbol.

5. As you write about the symbol or symbolism in a story, consider your claims about its meaning. Try not to narrow down the possible meanings of either the symbol or the story, but at the same time don't make too grand claims for their ability to reveal the meaning of life. When in doubt, refer back to the story and its literal level of characterization, plot, and setting.

6. Remember to cite specific passages that will help your reader understand the symbol's significance. Your reader may suspect that you are reading too much into it, so this evidence will help you both explain your interpretation and persuade your reader that it is reasonable.

NATHANIEL HAWTHORNE

The Birth-Mark

In the latter part of the last century[1] there lived a man of science, an eminent proficient in every branch of natural philosophy,[2] who not long before our story opens had made experience of a spiritual affinity more attractive than any chemical one. He had left his laboratory to the care of an assistant, cleared his fine countenance from the furnace-smoke, washed the stain of acids from his fingers, and persuaded a beautiful woman to become his wife. In those days, when the comparatively recent discovery of electricity and other kindred mysteries of Nature seemed to open paths into the region of miracle, it was not unusual for the love of science to rival the love of woman in its depth and absorbing energy. The higher intellect, the imagination, the spirit, and even the heart might all find their congenial aliment in pursuits which, as some of their ardent votaries believed, would ascend from one step of powerful intelligence to another, until the philosopher should lay his hand on the secret of creative force and perhaps make new worlds for himself. We know not whether Aylmer possessed this degree of faith in man's ultimate control over nature. He had devoted himself, however, too unreservedly to scientific studies ever to be weakened from them by any second passion. His love for his young wife might prove the stronger of the two; but it could only be by intertwining itself with his love of science and uniting the strength of the latter to his own.

Such a union accordingly took place, and was attended with truly remarkable consequences and a deeply impressive moral. One day, very soon after their marriage, Aylmer sat gazing at his wife with a trouble in his countenance that grew stronger until he spoke.

1. That is, the eighteenth century; this story was first published in 1843.
2. The body of knowledge we now call science.

"Georgiana," said he, "has it never occurred to you that the mark upon your cheek might be removed?"

"No, indeed," said she, smiling; but, perceiving the seriousness of his manner, she blushed deeply. "To tell you the truth, it has been so often called a charm, that I was simple enough to imagine it might be so."

5   "Ah, upon another face perhaps it might," replied her husband; "but never on yours. No, dearest Georgiana, you came so nearly perfect from the hand of Nature, that this slightest possible defect, which we hesitate whether to term a defect or a beauty, shocks me, as being the visible mark of earthly imperfection."

"Shocks you, my husband!" cried Georgiana, deeply hurt; at first reddening with momentary anger, but then bursting into tears. "Then why did you take me from my mother's side? You cannot love what shocks you!"

To explain this conversation, it must be mentioned that in the center of Georgiana's left cheek there was a singular mark, deeply interwoven, as it were, with the texture and substance of her face. In the usual state of her complexion—a healthy though delicate bloom—the mark wore a tint of deeper crimson, which imperfectly defined its shape amid the surrounding rosiness. When she blushed it gradually became more indistinct, and finally vanished amid the triumphant rush of blood that bathed the whole cheek with its brilliant glow. But if any shifting motion caused her to turn pale there was the mark again, a crimson stain upon the snow, in what Aylmer sometimes deemed an almost fearful distinctness. Its shape bore not a little similarity to the human hand, though of the smallest pygmy size. Georgiana's lovers were wont to say that some fairy at her birth-hour had laid her tiny hand upon the infant's cheek, and left this impress there in token of the magic endowments that were to give her such sway over all hearts. Many a desperate swain would have risked life for the privilege of pressing his lips to the mysterious hand. It must not be concealed, however, that the impression wrought by this fairy sign-manual varied exceedingly according to the difference of temperament in the beholders. Some fastidious persons—but they were exclusively of her own sex—affirmed that the bloody hand, as they chose to call it, quite destroyed the effect of Georgiana's beauty and rendered her countenance even hideous. But it would be as reasonable to say that one of those small blue stains which sometimes occur in the purest statuary marble would convert the Eve of Powers[3] to a monster. Masculine observers, if the birth-mark did not heighten their admiration, contented themselves with wishing it away, that the world might possess one living specimen of ideal loveliness without the semblance of a flaw. After his marriage—for he thought little or nothing of the matter before—Aylmer discovered that this was the case with himself.

Had she been less beautiful—if Envy's self could have found aught else to sneer at—he might have felt his affection heightened by the prettiness of this mimic hand, now vaguely portrayed, now lost, now stealing forth again and glimmering to and fro with every pulse of emotion that throbbed within her heart; but, seeing her otherwise so perfect, he found this one defect grow more and more intolerable with every moment of their united lives. It was the fatal flaw of humanity which Nature, in one shape or another, stamps ineffaceably on all her productions, either to imply that they are temporary and finite, or that their perfection

---

3. Hiram Powers (1805–73), American sculptor and friend of Hawthorne, produced noted marble statues, including *Eve Tempted* and *Eve Disconsolate*.

must be wrought by toil and pain. The crimson hand expressed the ineludible gripe in which mortality clutches the highest and purest of earthly mould, degrading them into kindred with the lowest, and even with the very brutes, like whom their visible frames return to dust. In this manner, selecting it as the symbol of his wife's liability to sin, sorrow, decay, and death, Aylmer's somber imagination was not long in rendering the birthmark a frightful object, causing him more trouble and horror than ever Georgiana's beauty, whether of soul or sense, had given him delight.

At all the seasons which should have been their happiest he invariably, and without intending it, nay, in spite of a purpose to the contrary, reverted to this one disastrous topic. Trifling as it at first appeared, it so connected itself with innumerable trains of thought and modes of feeling that it became the central point of all. With the morning twilight Aylmer opened his eyes upon his wife's face and recognized the symbol of imperfection; and when they sat together at the evening hearth his eyes wandered stealthily to her cheek, and beheld, flickering with the blaze of the wood-fire, the spectral hand that wrote mortality where he would fain[4] have worshipped. Georgiana soon learned to shudder at his gaze. It needed but a glance with the peculiar expression that his face often wore to change the roses of her cheek into a death-like paleness, amid which the crimson hand was brought strongly out, like a bas relief of ruby on the whitest marble.

Late one night, when the lights were growing dim so as hardly to betray the stain on the poor wife's cheek, she herself, for the first time, voluntarily took up the subject.

"Do you remember, my dear Aylmer," said she, with a feeble attempt at a smile, "have you any recollection, of a dream last night about this odious hand?"

"None! none whatever!" replied Aylmer, starting; but then he added, in a dry, cold tone, affected for the sake of concealing the real depth of his emotion, "I might well dream of it; for, before I fell asleep, it had taken a pretty firm hold of my fancy."

"And you did dream of it?" continued Georgiana, hastily; for she dreaded lest a gush of tears should interrupt what she had to say. "A terrible dream! I wonder that you can forget it. Is it possible to forget this one expression?—'It is in her heart now; we must have it out!' Reflect, my husband; for by all means I would have you recall that dream."

The mind is in a sad state when Sleep, the all-involving, cannot confine her specters within the dim region of her sway, but suffers them to break forth, affrighting this actual life with secrets that perchance belong to a deeper one. Aylmer now remembered his dream. He had fancied himself with his servant Aminadab attempting an operation for the removal of the birth-mark; but the deeper went the knife, the deeper sank the hand, until at length its tiny grasp appeared to have caught hold of Georgiana's heart; whence, however, her husband was inexorably resolved to cut or wrench it away.

When the dream had shaped itself perfectly in his memory, Aylmer sat in his wife's presence with a guilty feeling. Truth often finds its way to the mind close muffled in robes of sleep, and then speaks with uncompromising directness of matters in regard to which we practice an unconscious self-deception during our waking moments. Until now he had not been aware of the tyrannizing influence

4. Eagerly, preferably.

acquired by one idea over his mind, and of the lengths which he might find in his heart to go for the sake of giving himself peace.

"Aylmer," resumed Georgiana, solemnly, "I know not what may be the cost to both of us to rid me of this fatal birth-mark. Perhaps its removal may cause cureless deformity; or it may be the stain goes as deep as life itself. Again: do we know that there is a possibility, on any terms, of unclasping the firm gripe of this little hand which was laid upon me before I came into the world?"

"Dearest Georgiana, I have spent much thought upon the subject," hastily interrupted Aylmer. "I am convinced of the perfect practicability of its removal."

"If there be the remotest possibility of it," continued Georgiana, "let the attempt be made, at whatever risk. Danger is nothing to me; for life, while this hateful mark makes me the object of your horror and disgust—life is a burden which I would fling down with joy. Either remove this dreadful hand, or take my wretched life! You have deep science. All the world bears witness of it. You have achieved great wonders. Cannot you remove this little, little mark, which I cover with the tips of two small fingers? Is this beyond your power, for the sake of your own peace, and to save your poor wife from madness?"

20   "Noblest, dearest, tenderest wife," cried Aylmer, rapturously, "doubt not my power. I have already given this matter the deepest thought—thought which might almost have enlightened me to create a being less perfect than yourself. Georgiana, you have led me deeper than ever into the heart of science. I feel myself fully competent to render this dear cheek as faultless as its fellow; and then, most beloved, what will be my triumph when I shall have corrected what Nature left imperfect in her fairest work! Even Pygmalion,[5] when his sculptured woman assumed life, felt not greater ecstasy than mine will be."

"It is resolved, then," said Georgiana, faintly smiling. "And, Aylmer, spare me not, though you should find the birth-mark take refuge in my heart at last."

Her husband tenderly kissed her cheek—her right cheek—not that which bore the impress of the crimson hand.

The next day Aylmer apprised his wife of a plan that he had formed whereby he might have opportunity for the intense thought and constant watchfulness which the proposed operation would require; while Georgiana, likewise, would enjoy the perfect repose essential to its success. They were to seclude themselves in the extensive apartments occupied by Aylmer as a laboratory, and where, during his toilsome youth, he had made discoveries in the elemental powers of Nature that had roused the admiration of all the learned societies in Europe. Seated calmly in this laboratory, the pale philosopher had investigated the secrets of the highest cloud-region and of the profoundest mines; he had satisfied himself of the causes that kindled and kept alive the fires of the volcano; and had explained the mystery of fountains, and how it is that they gush forth, some so bright and pure, and others with such rich medicinal virtues, from the dark bosom of the earth. Here, too, at an earlier period, he had studied the wonders of the human frame, and attempted to fathom the very process by which Nature assimilates all her precious influences from earth and air, and from the spiritual world, to create and foster man, her masterpiece. The latter pursuit, however, Aylmer had long laid aside in unwilling recognition of the truth—against which

5. Pygmalion was a legendary artist of Cyprus who fell in love with the statue he made of a beautiful woman; in Ovid's *Metamorphoses,* she comes to life.

all seekers sooner or later stumble—that our great creative Mother, while she amuses us with apparently working in the broadest sunshine, is yet severely careful to keep her own secrets, and, in spite of her pretended openness, shows us nothing but results. She permits us, indeed, to mar, but seldom to mend, and, like a jealous patentee, on no account to make. Now, however, Aylmer resumed these half-forgotten investigations; not, of course, with such hopes or wishes as first suggested them; but because they involved much physiological truth and lay in the path of his proposed scheme for the treatment of Georgiana.

As he led her over the threshold of the laboratory Georgiana was cold and tremulous. Aylmer looked cheerfully into her face, with intent to reassure her, but was so startled with the intense glow of the birth-mark upon the whiteness of her cheek that he could not restrain a strong convulsive shudder. His wife fainted.

"Aminadab! Aminadab!" shouted Aylmer, stamping violently on the floor. 25

Forthwith there issued from an inner apartment a man of low stature, but bulky frame, with shaggy hair hanging about his visage, which was grimed with the vapors of the furnace. This personage had been Aylmer's underworker during his whole scientific career, and was admirably fitted for that office by his great mechanical readiness, and the skill with which, while incapable of comprehending a single principle, he executed all the details of his master's experiments. With his vast strength, his shaggy hair, his smoky aspect, and the indescribable earthiness that incrusted him, he seemed to represent man's physical nature; while Aylmer's slender figure, and pale, intellectual face, were no less apt a type of the spiritual element.

"Throw open the door of the boudoir, Aminadab," said Aylmer, "and burn a pastil."[6]

"Yes, master," answered Aminadab, looking intently at the lifeless form of Georgiana; and then he muttered to himself. "If she were my wife, I'd never part with that birth-mark."

When Georgiana recovered consciousness she found herself breathing an atmosphere of penetrating fragrance, the gentle potency of which had recalled her from her death-like faintness. The scene around her looked like enchantment. Aylmer had converted those smoky, dingy, somber rooms, where he had spent his brightest years in recondite pursuits, into a series of beautiful apartments not unfit to be the secluded abode of a lovely woman. The walls were hung with gorgeous curtains, which imparted the combination of grandeur and grace that no other species of adornment can achieve; and, as they fell from the ceiling to the floor, their rich and ponderous folds, concealing all angles and straight lines, appeared to shut in the scene from infinite space. For aught Georgiana knew, it might be a pavilion among the clouds. And Aylmer, excluding the sunshine, which would have interfered with his chemical processes, had supplied its place with perfumed lamps, emitting flames of various hue, but all uniting in a soft, impurpled radiance. He now knelt by his wife's side, watching her earnestly, but without alarm; for he was confident in his science, and felt that he could draw a magic circle round her within which no evil might intrude.

"Where am I? Ah, I remember," said Georgiana, faintly; and she placed her 30 hand over her cheek to hide the terrible mark from her husband's eyes.

6. Pastille, a lozenge or tablet of medicinal incense.

"Fear not, dearest!" exclaimed he. "Do not shrink from me! Believe me, Georgiana, I even rejoice in this single imperfection, since it will be such a rapture to remove it."

"O, spare me!" sadly replied his wife. "Pray do not look at it again. I never can forget that convulsive shudder."

In order to soothe Georgiana, and, as it were, to release her mind from the burden of actual things, Aylmer now put in practice some of the light and playful secrets which science had taught him among its profounder lore. Airy figures, absolutely bodiless ideas, and forms of unsubstantial beauty came and danced before her, imprinting their momentary footsteps on beams of light. Though she had some indistinct idea of the method of these optical phenomena, still the illusion was almost perfect enough to warrant the belief that her husband possessed say over the spiritual world. Then again, when she felt a wish to look forth from her seclusion, immediately, as if her thoughts were answered, the procession of external existence flitted across a screen. The scenery and the figures of actual life were perfectly represented but with that bewitching yet indescribable difference which always makes a picture, an image, or a shadow so much more attractive than the original. When wearied of this, Aylmer bade her cast her eyes upon a vessel containing a quantity of earth. She did so, with little interest at first; but was soon startled to perceive the germ of a plant shooting upward from the soil. Then came the slender stalk; the leaves gradually unfolded themselves; and amid them was a perfect and lovely flower.

"It is magical!" cried Georgiana. "I dare not touch it."

35   "Nay, pluck it," answered Aylmer— "pluck it, and inhale its brief perfume while you may. The flower will wither in a few moments and leave nothing save its brown seed vessels; but thence may be perpetuated a race as ephemeral as itself."

But Georgiana had no sooner touched the flower than the whole plant suffered a blight, its leaves turning coal-black as if by the agency of fire.

"There was too powerful a stimulus," said Aylmer, thoughtfully.

To make up for this abortive experiment, he proposed to take her portrait by a scientific process of his own invention. It was to be affected by rays of light striking upon a polished plate of metal. Georgiana assented; but, on looking at the result, was affrighted to find the features of the portrait blurred and indefinable; while the minute figure of a hand appeared where the cheek should have been. Aylmer snatched the metallic plate and threw it into a jar of corrosive acid.

Soon, however, he forgot these mortifying failures. In the intervals of study and chemical experiment he came to her flushed and exhausted, but seemed invigorated by her presence, and spoke in glowing language of the resources of his art. He gave a history of the long dynasty of the alchemists, who spent so many ages in quest of the universal solvent by which the golden principle might be elicited from all things vile and base.[7] Aylmer appeared to believe that, by the plainest scientific logic, it was altogether within the limits of possibility to discover this long-sought medium. "But," he added, "a philosopher who should go deep enough to acquire the power would attain too lofty a wisdom to stoop to the exercise of it." Not less singular were his opinions in regard to the elixir

---

7. Before the advent of modern chemistry, alchemists studied the properties of matter in a search for spiritual essences and the secret of transforming base metals into gold.

vitae.[8] He more than intimated that it was at his option to concoct a liquid that should prolong life for years, perhaps interminably; but that it would produce a discord in Nature which all the world, and chiefly the quaffer of the immortal nostrum, would find cause to curse.

"Aylmer, are you in earnest?" asked Georgiana, looking at him with amazement 40 and fear. "It is terrible to possess such power, or even to dream of possessing it."

"O, do not tremble, my love," said her husband. "I would not wrong either you or myself by working such inharmonious effects upon our lives; but I would have you consider how trifling, in comparison, is the skill requisite to remove this little hand."

At the mention of the birth-mark, Georgiana, as usual, shrank as if a red-hot iron had touched her cheek.

Again Aylmer applied himself to his labors. She could hear his voice in the distant furnace-room giving directions to Aminadab, whose harsh, uncouth, misshapen tones were audible in response, more like the grunt or growl of a brute than human speech. After hours of absence, Aylmer reappeared and proposed that she should now examine his cabinet of chemical products and natural treasures of the earth. Among the former he showed her a small vial, in which, he remarked, was contained a gentle yet most powerful fragrance, capable of impregnating all the breezes that blow across a kingdom. They were of inestimable value, the contents of that little vial; and, as he said so, he threw some of the perfume into the air and filled the room with piercing and invigorating delight.

"And what is this?" asked Georgiana, pointing to a small crystal globe containing a gold-colored liquid. "It is so beautiful to the eye that I could imagine it the elixir of life."

"In one sense it is," replied Aylmer; "or rather, the elixir of immortality. It is 45 the most precious poison that ever was concocted in this world. By its aid I could apportion the lifetime of any mortal at whom you might point your finger. The strength of the dose would determine whether he were to linger out years, or drop dead in the midst of a breath. No king on his guarded throne could keep his life if I, in my private station, should deem that the welfare of millions justified me in depriving him of it."

"Why do you keep such a terrific drug?" inquired Georgiana, in horror.

"Do not mistrust me, dearest," said her husband, smiling; "its virtuous potency is yet greater than its harmful one. But see! here is a powerful cosmetic. With a few drops of this in a vase of water, freckles may be washed away as easily as the hands are cleansed. A stronger infusion would take the blood out of the cheek, and leave the rosiest beauty a pale ghost."

"Is it with this lotion that you intend to bathe my cheek?" asked Georgiana, anxiously.

"O no," hastily replied her husband; "this is merely superficial. Your case demands a remedy that shall go deeper."

In his interviews with Georgiana, Aylmer generally made minute inquiries as 50 to her sensations, and whether the confinement of the rooms and the temperature of the atmosphere agreed with her. These questions had such a particular drift that Georgiana began to conjecture that she was already subjected to certain physical influences, either breathed in with the fragrant air or taken with

8. Literally, the drink or potion of life (Latin), imagined to give immortality.

her food. She fancied likewise, but it might be altogether fancy, that there was a stirring up of her system—a strange, indefinite sensation creeping through her veins, and tingling, half painfully, half pleasurably, at her heart. Still, whenever she dared to look into the mirror, there she beheld herself pale as a white rose and with the crimson birth-mark stamped upon her cheek. Not even Aylmer now hated it so much as she.

To dispel the tedium of the hours which her husband found it necessary to devote to the processes of combination and analysis, Georgiana turned over the volumes of his scientific library. In many dark old tomes she met with chapters full of romance and poetry. They were the works of the philosophers of the Middle Ages, such as Albertus Magnus, Cornelius Agrippa, Paracelsus, and the famous friar who created the prophetic Brazen Head.[9] All these antique natural- ists stood in advance of their centuries, yet were imbued with some of their cre- dulity, and therefore were believed, and perhaps imagined themselves to have acquired from the investigation of Nature a power above Nature, and from phys- ics a away over the spiritual world. Hardly less curious and imaginative were the early volumes of the Transactions of the Royal Society,[1] in which the members, knowing little of the limits of natural possibility, were continually recording wonders or proposing methods whereby wonders might be wrought.

But, to Georgiana, the most engrossing volume was a large folio from her hus- band's own hand, in which he had recorded every experiment of his scientific career, its original aim, the methods adopted for its development, and its final suc- cess or failure, with the circumstances to which either event was attributable. The book, in truth was both the history and emblem of his ardent, ambitious, imagi- native, yet practical and laborious life. He handled physical details as if there were nothing beyond them; yet spiritualized them all, and redeemed himself from materialism by his strong and eager aspiration towards the infinite. In his grasp the veriest clod of earth assumed a soul. Georgiana, as she read, reverenced Aylmer and loved him more profoundly than ever, but with a less entire dependence on his judgment than heretofore. Much as he had accomplished, she could not but observe that his most splendid successes were almost invariably failures, if com- pared with the ideal at which he aimed. His brightest diamonds were the merest pebbles, and felt to be so by himself, in comparison with the inestimable gems which lay hidden beyond his reach. The volume, rich with achievements that had won renown for its author, was yet as melancholy a record as ever mortal hand had penned. It was the sad confession and continual exemplification of the shortcom- ings of the composite man, the spirit burdened with clay and working in matter, and of the despair that assails the higher nature at finding itself so miserably thwarted by the earthly part. Perhaps every man of genius, in whatever sphere, might recognize the image of his own experience in Aylmer's journal.

So deeply did these reflections affect Georgiana that she laid her face upon the open volume and burst into tears. In this situation she was found by her husband.

9. The Brazen Head, a brass bust of a man, was supposed to be able to answer any question; the "famous friar" is Roger Bacon (c. 1214–94), an English natural philosopher, as scientists were then called. Albertus Magnus (1193/1206–80), Agrippa (1496–1535), and Paracelsus (1493–1541) were all European experi- menters reputed to have near-magical powers in alchemy or astrology.

1. *The Philosophical Transactions of the Royal Society* is the oldest scientific journal in English, published since 1665.

"It is dangerous to read in a sorcerer's books," said he with a smile, though his countenance was uneasy and displeased. "Georgiana, there are pages in that volume which I can scarcely glance over and keep my senses. Take heed lest it prove as detrimental to you."

"It has made me worship you more than ever," said she.   55

"Ah, wait for this one success," rejoined he, "then worship me if you will. I shall deem myself hardly unworthy of it. But come, I have sought you for the luxury of your voice. Sing to me, dearest."

So she poured out the liquid music of her voice to quench the thirst of his spirit. He then took his leave with a boyish exuberance of gayety, assuring her that her seclusion would endure but a little longer, and that the result was already certain. Scarcely had he departed when Georgiana felt irresistibly impelled to follow him. She had forgotten to inform Aylmer of a symptom which for two or three hours past had begun to excite her attention. It was a sensation in the fatal birth-mark, not painful, but which induced a restlessness throughout her system. Hastening after her husband, she intruded for the first time into the laboratory.

The first thing that struck her eye was the furnace, that hot and feverish worker, with the intense glow of its fire, which by the quantities of soot clustered above it seemed to have been burning for ages. There was a distilling-apparatus in full operation. Around the room were retorts, tubes, cylinders, crucibles, and other apparatus of chemical research. An electrical machine stood ready for immediate use. The atmosphere felt oppressively close, and was tainted with gaseous odors which had been tormented forth by the processes of science. The severe and homely simplicity of the apartment, with its naked walls and brick pavement, looked strange, accustomed as Georgiana had become to the fantastic elegance of her boudoir. But what chiefly, indeed almost solely, drew her attention, was the aspect of Aylmer himself.

He was pale as death, anxious and absorbed, and hung over the furnace as if it depended upon his utmost watchfulness whether the liquid which it was distilling should be the draught of immortal happiness or misery. How different from the sanguine and joyous mien that he had assumed for Georgiana's encouragement!

"Carefully now, Aminadab; carefully, thou human machine; carefully, thou   60
man of clay," muttered Aylmer, more to himself than his assistant. "Now, if there be a thought too much or too little, it is all over."

"Ho! ho!" mumbled Aminadab. "Look, master! look!"

Aylmer raised his eyes hastily, and at first reddened, then grew paler than ever, on beholding Georgiana. He rushed towards her and seized her arm with a gripe that left the print of his fingers upon it.

"Why do you come hither? Have you no trust in your husband?" cried he, impetuously. "Would you throw the blight of that fatal birth-mark over my labors? It is not well done. Go, prying woman! go!"

"Nay, Aylmer," said Georgiana with the firmness of which she possessed no stinted endowment, "it is not you that have a right to complain. You mistrust your wife; you have concealed the anxiety with which you watch the development of this experiment. Think not so unworthily of me, my husband. Tell me all the risk we run, and fear not that I shall shrink; for my share in it is far less than your own."

65   "No, no, Georgiana!" said Aylmer, impatiently; "it must not be."

"I submit," replied she, calmly. "And, Aylmer, I shall quaff whatever draught you bring me; but it will be on the same principle that would induce me to take a dose of poison if offered by your hand."

"My noble wife," said Aylmer, deeply moved, "I knew not the height and depth of your nature until now. Nothing shall be concealed. Know, then, that this crimson hand, superficial as it seems, has clutched its grasp into your being with a strength of which I had no previous conception. I have already administered agents powerful enough to do aught except to change your entire physical system. Only one thing remains to be tried. If that fail us we are ruined."

"Why did you hesitate to tell me this?" asked she.

"Because, Georgiana," said Aylmer, in a low voice, "there is danger."

70   "Danger? There is but one danger—that this horrible stigma shall be left upon my cheek!" cried Georgiana. "Remove it, remove it, whatever be the cost, or we shall both go mad!"

"Heaven knows your words are too true," said Aylmer, sadly. "And now, dearest, return to your boudoir. In a little while all will be tested."

He conducted her back and took leave of her with a solemn tenderness which spoke far more than his words how much was now at stake. After his departure Georgiana became rapt in musings. She considered the character of Aylmer, and did it completer justice than at any previous moment. Her heart exulted, while it trembled, at his honorable love—so pure and lofty that it would accept nothing less than perfection, nor miserably make itself contented with an earthlier nature than he had dreamed of. She felt how much more precious was such a sentiment than that meaner kind which would have borne with the imperfection for her sake, and have been guilty of treason to holy love by degrading its perfect idea to the level of the actual; and with her whole spirit she prayed that, for a single moment, she might satisfy his highest and deepest conception. Longer than one moment she well knew it could not be; for his spirit was ever on the march, ever ascending, and each instant required something that was beyond the scope of the instant before.

The sound of her husband's footsteps aroused her. He bore a crystal goblet containing a liquor colorless as water, but bright enough to be the draught of immortality. Aylmer was pale; but it seemed rather the consequence of a highly wrought state of mind and tension of spirit than of fear or doubt.

"The concoction of the draught has been perfect," said he, in answer to Georgiana's look. "Unless all my science have deceived me, it cannot fail."

75   "Save on your account, my dearest Aylmer," observed his wife, "I might wish to put off this birth-mark of mortality by relinquishing mortality itself in preference to any other mode. Life is but a sad possession to those who have attained precisely the degree of moral advancement at which I stand. Were I weaker and blinder, it might be happiness. Were I stronger, it might be endured hopefully. But, being what I find myself, methinks I am of all mortals the most fit to die."

"You are fit for heaven without tasting death!" replied her husband. "But why do we speak of dying? The draught cannot fail. Behold its effect upon this plant."

On the window-seat there stood a geranium diseased with yellow blotches, which had overspread all its leaves. Aylmer poured a small quantity of the liquid upon the soil in which it grew. In a little time, when the roots of the plant had taken up the moisture, the unsightly blotches began to be extinguished in a living verdure.

"There needed no proof," said Georgiana, quietly. "Give me the goblet. I joyfully stake all upon your word."

"Drink, then, thou lofty creature!" exclaimed Aylmer, with fervid admiration. "There is no taint of imperfection on thy spirit. Thy sensible frame, too, shall soon be all perfect."

She quaffed the liquid and returned the goblet to his hand.

"It is grateful," said she, with a placid smile. "Methinks it is like water from a heavenly fountain; for it contains I know not what of unobtrusive fragrance and deliciousness. It allays a feverish thirst that had parched me for many days. Now, dearest, let me sleep. My earthly senses are closing over my spirit like the leaves around the heart of a rose at sunset."

She spoke the last words with a gentle reluctance, as if it required almost more energy than she could command to pronounce the faint and lingering syllables. Scarcely had they loitered through her lips ere she was lost in slumber. Aylmer sat by her side, watching her aspect with the emotions proper to a man, the whole value of whose existence was involved in the process now to be tested. Mingled with this mood, however, was the philosophic investigation characteristic of the man of science. Not the minutest symptom escaped him. A heightened flush of the cheek, a slight irregularity of breath, a quiver of the eyelid, a hardly perceptible tremor through the frame—such were the details which, as the moments passed, he wrote down in his folio volume. Intense thought had set its stamp upon every previous page of that volume; but the thoughts of years were all concentrated upon the last.

While thus employed, he failed not to gaze often at the fatal hand, and not without a shudder. Yet once, by a strange and unaccountable impulse, he pressed it with his lips. His spirit recoiled, however, in the very act; and Georgiana, out of the midst of her deep sleep, moved uneasily and murmured, as if in remonstrance. Again Aylmer resumed his watch. Nor was it without avail. The crimson hand, which at first had been strongly visible upon the marble paleness of Georgiana's cheek, now grew more faintly outlined. She remained not less pale than ever; but the birth-mark, with every breath that came and went, lost somewhat of its former distinctness. Its presence had been awful; its departure was more awful still. Watch the stain of the rainbow fading out of the sky, and you will know how that mysterious symbol passed away.

"By Heaven! it is wellnigh gone!" said Aylmer to himself, in almost irrepressible ecstasy. "I can scarcely trace it now. Success! success! And now it is like the faintest rose-color. The lightest flush of blood across her cheek would overcome it. But she is so pale!"

He drew aside the window-curtain and suffered the light of natural day to fall into the room and rest upon her cheek. At the same time he heard a gross, hoarse chuckle, which he had long known as his servant Aminadab's expression of delight.

"Ah, clod! ah, earthly mass!" cried Aylmer, laughing in a sort of fenzy, "you have served me well! Matter and spirit—earth and heaven—have both done their part in this! Laugh, thing of the senses! You have earned the right to laugh."

These exclamations broke Georgiana's sleep. She slowly unclosed her eyes and gazed into the mirror which her husband had arranged for that purpose. A faint smile fitted over her lips when she recognized how barely perceptible was now that crimson hand which had once blazed forth with such disastrous brilliancy as to scare away all their happiness. But then her eyes sought Aylmer's face with a trouble and anxiety that he could by no means account for.

"My poor Aylmer!" murmured she.

"Poor? Nay, richest, happiest, most favored!" exclaimed he. "My peerless bride, it is successful! You are perfect!"

90   "My poor Aylmer," she repeated, with a more than human tenderness, "you have aimed loftily; you have done nobly. Do not repent that, with so high and pure a feeling, you have rejected the best the earth could offer. Aylmer, dearest Aylmer, I am dying!"

Alas! it was too true! The fatal hand had grappled with the mystery of life, and was the bond by which an angelic spirit kept itself in union with a mortal frame. As the last crimson tint of the birth-mark—that sole token of human imperfection—faded from her cheek, the parting breath of the now perfect woman passed into the atmosphere, and her soul, lingering a moment near her husband, took its heavenward flight. Then a hoarse, chuckling laugh was heard again! Thus ever does the gross fatality of earth exult in its invariable triumph over the immortal essence which, in this dim sphere of half-development, demands the completeness of a higher state. Yet, had Aylmer reached a profounder wisdom, he need not thus have flung away the happiness which would have woven his mortal life of the self-same texture with the celestial. The momentary circumstance was too strong for him; he failed to look beyond the shadowy scope of time, and, living once for all in eternity, to find the perfect future in the present.

1843

QUESTIONS

1. What difference would it make if the mark on Georgiana's cheek were shaped like a fish, a heart, or an irregular oval? Why (and when) does the mark appear redder or more visible or fainter? If the birthmark is explicitly a "symbol of imperfection" (par. 9), what *kinds* of imperfection does it represent?

2. Aylmer says to his wife, "Even Pygmalion, when his sculptured woman assumed life, felt not greater ecstasy than mine will be" (par. 19). How does this literary allusion to the myth of Pygmalion enhance the meaning of "The Birth-Mark"? Is this allusion ironic, given what happens to Alymer's project to make his wife perfect?

3. Look closely at the setting of the story, from the laboratory to the boudoir. Note the similes, metaphors, and other figures of speech that help characterize these places. How do these different patterns of imagery contribute to the symbolism of the story? to an allegorical reading of the story?

A. S. BYATT

The Thing in the Forest

There were once two little girls who saw, or believed they saw, a thing in a forest. The two little girls were evacuees, who had been sent away from the city by train with a large number of other children.[1] They all had their names attached to their coats with safety pins, and they carried little bags or satchels, and the regulation gas mask. They wore knitted scarves and bonnets or caps, and many had knitted gloves attached to long tapes that ran along their sleeves, inside their coats, and over their shoulders and out, so that they could leave their ten woollen fingers dangling, like a spare pair of hands, like a scarecrow. They all had bare legs and scuffed shoes and wrinkled socks. Most had wounds on their knees in varying stages of freshness and scabbiness. They were at the age when children fall often and their knees were unprotected. With their suitcases, some of which were almost too big to carry, and their other impedimenta, a doll, a toy car, a comic, they were like a disorderly dwarf regiment, stomping along the platform.

The two little girls had not met before, and made friends on the train. They shared a square of chocolate, and took alternate bites at an apple. Their names were Penny and Primrose. Penny was thin and dark and taller, possibly older, than Primrose, who was plump and blond and curly. Primrose had bitten nails, and a velvet collar on her dressy green coat. Penny had a bloodless transparent paleness, a touch of blue in her fine lips. Neither of them knew where they were going, nor how long the journey might take. They did not even know why they were going, since neither of their mothers had quite known how to explain the danger to them. How do you say to your child, I am sending you away, because enemy bombs may fall out of the sky, but I myself am staying here, in what I believe may be daily danger of burning, being buried alive, gas, and ultimately perhaps a gray army rolling in on tanks over the suburbs? So the mothers (who did not resemble each other at all) behaved alike, and explained nothing—it was easier. Their daughters, they knew, were little girls, who would not be able to understand or imagine.

The girls discussed whether it was a sort of holiday or a sort of punishment, or a bit of both. Both had the idea that these were all perhaps not very good children, possibly being sent away for that reason. They were pleased to be able to define each other as "nice." They would stick together, they agreed.

The train crawled sluggishly farther and farther away from the city and their homes. It was not a clean train—the upholstery of their carriage had the dank smell of unwashed trousers, and the gusts of hot steam rolling backward past their windows were full of specks of flimsy ash, and sharp grit, and occasionally fiery sparks that pricked face and fingers like hot needles if you opened the window. It was very noisy, too, whenever it picked up a little speed. The window-panes were both grimy and misted up. The train stopped frequently, and when it stopped they used their gloves to wipe rounds, through which they peered out at flooded fields, furrowed hillsides, and tiny stations whose names were carefully blacked out, whose platforms were empty of life.

The children did not know that the namelessness was meant to baffle or 5 delude an invading army. They felt—they did not think it out, but somewhere inside them the idea sprouted—that the erasure was because of them, because they were not meant to know where they were going or, like Hansel and Gretel, to find the way back. They did not speak to each other of this anxiety, but began the

1. The story takes place during the Blitz—that is, during the period (1940–41) when British cities were frequently bombed by German warplanes. Many children were evacuated from cities to safer locations in the countryside.

kind of conversation children have about things they really dislike, things that upset, or disgust, or frighten them. Semolina pudding with its grainy texture, mushy peas, fat on roast meat. Having your head held roughly back over the basin to have your hair washed, with cold water running down inside your liberty bodice. Gangs in playgrounds. They felt the pressure of all the other alien children in all the other carriages as a potential gang. They shared another square of chocolate, and licked their fingers, and looked out at a great white goose flapping its wings beside an inky pond.

The sky grew dark gray and in the end the train halted. The children got out, and lined up in a crocodile,[2] and were led to a mud-colored bus. Penny and Primrose managed to get a seat together, although it was over the wheel, and both of them began to feel sick as the bus bumped along snaking country lanes, under whipping branches, with torn strips of thin cloud streaming across a full moon.

They were billeted in a mansion commandeered from its owner. The children were told they were there temporarily, until families were found to take them. Penny and Primrose held hands, and said to each other that it would be wizard if they could go to the same family, because at least they would have each other. They didn't say anything to the rather tired-looking ladies who were ordering them about, because, with the cunning of little children, they knew that requests were most often counterproductive—adults liked saying no. They imagined possible families into which they might be thrust. They did not discuss what they imagined, as these pictures, like the black station signs, were too frightening, and words might make some horror solid, in some magical way. Penny, who was a reading child, imagined Victorian dark pillars of severity, like Jane Eyre's Mr. Brocklehurst, or David Copperfield's Mr. Murdstone. Primrose imagined—she didn't know why—a fat woman with a white cap and round red arms who smiled nicely but made the children wear sacking aprons and scrub the steps and the stove. "It's like we were orphans," she said to Penny. "But we're not." Penny said, "If we manage to stick together. . . ."

The great house had a double flight of imposing stairs to its front door, and carved griffins and unicorns on its balustrade. There was no lighting, because of the blackout. All the windows were shuttered. The children trudged up the staircase in their crocodile, and were given supper (Irish stew and rice pudding with a dollop of blood-red jam) before going to bed in long makeshift dormitories, where once servants had slept. They had camp beds (military issue) and gray shoddy blankets. Penny and Primrose got beds together but couldn't get a corner. They queued[3] to brush their teeth in a tiny washroom, and both suffered (again without speaking) suffocating anxiety about what would happen if they wanted to pee in the middle of the night. They also suffered from a fear that in the dark the other children would start laughing and rushing and teasing, and turn themselves into a gang. But that did not happen. Everyone was tired and anxious and orphaned. An uneasy silence, a drift of perturbed sleep, came over them all. The only sounds—from all parts of the great dormitory, it seemed—were suppressed snuffles and sobs, from faces pressed into thin pillows.

2. Group of people lined up two by two.   3. Lined up.

When daylight came, things seemed, as they mostly do, brighter and better. The children were given breakfast in a large vaulted room, at trestle tables, porridge made with water, and a dab of the red jam, heavy cups of strong tea. Then they were told they could go out and play until lunchtime. Children in those days—wherever they came from—were not closely watched, were allowed to come and go freely, and those evacuated children were not herded into any kind of holding pen or transit camp. They were told they should be back for lunch at twelve-thirty, by which time those in charge hoped to have sorted out their provisional future lives. It was not known how they would know when it was twelve-thirty, but it was expected that—despite the fact that few of them had wristwatches—they would know how to keep an eye on the time. It was what they were used to.

Penny and Primrose went out together, in their respectable coats and laced 10 shoes, onto the terrace. The terrace appeared to them to be vast. It was covered with a fine layer of damp gravel, stained here and there bright green, or invaded by mosses. Beyond it was a stone balustrade, with a staircase leading down to a lawn. Across the lawn was a sculpted yew hedge. In the middle of the hedge was a wicket gate, and beyond the gate were trees. A forest, the little girls said to themselves.

"Let's go into the forest," said Penny, as though the sentence were required of her.

Primrose hesitated. Most of the other children were running up and down the terrace. Some boys were kicking a ball on the grass.

"O.K.," said Primrose. "We needn't go far."

"No. I've never been in a forest."

"Nor me." 15

"We ought to look at it, while we've got the opportunity," said Penny.

There was a very small child—one of the smallest—whose name, she told everyone, was Alys. With a "y," she told those who could spell, and those who couldn't, which surely included herself. She was barely out of nappies.[4] She was quite extraordinarily pretty, pink and white, with large pale-blue eyes, and sparse little golden curls all over her head and neck, through which her pink skin could be seen. Nobody seemed to be in charge of her, no elder brother or sister. She had not quite managed to wash the tearstains from her dimpled cheeks.

She had made several attempts to attach herself to Penny and Primrose. They did not want her. They were excited about meeting and liking each other. She said now, "I'm coming, too, into the forest."

"No, you aren't," said Primrose.

"You are too little, you must stay here," said Penny. 20

"You'll get lost," said Primrose.

"You won't get lost. I'll come with you," said the little creature, with an engaging smile, made for loving parents and grandparents.

"We don't want you, you see," said Primrose.

"It's for your own good," said Penny.

Alys went on smiling hopefully, the smile becoming more of a mask. 25

"It will be all right," said Alys.

"Run," said Primrose.

4. Diapers.

They ran; they ran down the steps and across the lawn, and through the gate, into the forest. They didn't look back. They were long-legged little girls. The trees were silent round them, holding out their branches to the sun.

Primrose touched the warm skin of the nearest saplings, taking off her gloves to feel the cracks and knots. Penny looked into the thick of the forest. There was undergrowth—a mat of brambles and bracken. There were no obvious paths. Dark and light came and went, inviting and mysterious, as the wind pushed clouds across the face of the sun.

30 "We have to be careful not to get lost," she said. "In stories, people make marks on tree trunks, or unroll a thread, or leave a trail of white pebbles—to find their way back."

"We needn't go out of sight of the gate," said Primrose. "We could just explore a little bit."

They set off, very slowly. They went on tiptoe, making their own narrow passages through the undergrowth, which sometimes came as high as their thin shoulders. They were urban, and unaccustomed to silence. Then they began to hear small sounds. The chatter and repeated lilt and alarm of invisible birds, high up, further in. Rustling in dry leaves. Slitherings, dry coughs, sharp cracks. They went on, pointing out to each other creepers draped with glistening berries, crimson, black, and emerald, little crops of toadstools, some scarlet, some ghostly pale, some a dead-flesh purple, some like tiny parasols—and some like pieces of meat protruding from tree trunks. They met blackberries, but didn't pick them, in case in this place they were dangerous or deceptive. They admired from a safe distance the stiff upright fruiting rods of the lords-and-ladies,[5] packed with fat red berries.

Did they hear it first or smell it? Both sound and scent were at first infinitesimal and dispersed. They gave the strange impression of moving in—in waves—from the whole perimeter of the forest. Both increased very slowly in intensity, and both were mixed, a sound and a smell fabricated of many disparate sounds and smells. A crunching, a crackling, a crushing, a heavy thumping, combining with threshing and thrashing, and added to that a gulping, heaving, boiling, bursting, steaming sound, full of bubbles and farts, piffs and explosions, swallowings and wallowings. The smell was worse, and more aggressive, than the sound. It was a liquid smell of putrefaction, the smell of maggoty things at the bottom of untended dustbins, blocked drains, mixed with the smell of bad eggs, and of rotten carpets and ancient polluted bedding. The ordinary forest smells and sounds were extinguished. The two little girls looked at each other, and took each other's hand. Speechlessly and instinctively, they crouched down behind a fallen tree trunk, and trembled, as the thing came into view.

Its head appeared to form, or first become visible in the distance, between the trees. Its face—which was triangular—appeared like a rubbery or fleshy mask over a shapeless sprouting bulb of a head, like a monstrous turnip. Its color was the color of flayed flesh, pitted with wormholes, and its expression was neither wrath nor greed but pure misery. Its most defined feature was a vast mouth, pulled down and down at the corners, tight with a kind of pain. Its lips were thin, and raised, like welts from whip-strokes. It had blind, opaque white eyes, fringed with

5. Wild arum, a flowering perennial common to southern Britain.

fleshy lashes and brows like the feelers of sea anemones. Its face was close to the ground and moved toward the children between its forearms, which were squat, thick, powerful, and akimbo, like a cross between a washer-woman's and a primeval dragon's. The flesh on these forearms was glistening and mottled.

The rest of its very large body appeared to be glued together, like still wet papier-mâché, or the carapace of stones and straws and twigs worn by caddis flies underwater. It had a tubular shape, as a turd has a tubular shape, a provisional amalgam. It was made of rank meat, and decaying vegetation, but it also trailed veils and prostheses of man-made materials, bits of wire netting, foul dishcloths, wire-wool full of pan scrubbings, rusty nuts and bolts. It had feeble stubs and stumps of very slender legs, growing out of it at all angles, wavering and rippling like the suckered feet of a caterpillar or the squirming fringe of a centipede. On and on it came, bending and crushing whatever lay in its path, including bushes, though not substantial trees, which it wound between, awkwardly. The little girls observed, with horrified fascination, that when it met a sharp stone, or a narrow tree trunk, it allowed itself to be sliced through, flowed sluggishly round in two or three smaller worms, convulsed, and reunited. Its progress was apparently very painful, for it moaned and whined among its other burblings and belchings. They thought it could not see, or certainly could not see clearly. It and its stench passed within a few feet of their tree trunk, humping along, leaving behind it a trail of bloody slime and dead foliage.

Its end was flat and blunt, almost transparent, like some earthworms.

When it had gone, Penny and Primrose, kneeling on the moss and dead leaves, put their arms about each other, and hugged each other, shaking with dry sobs. Then they stood up, still silent, and stared together, hand in hand, at the trail of obliteration and destruction, which wound out of the forest and into it again. They went back, hand in hand, without looking behind them, afraid that the wicket gate, the lawn, the stone steps, the balustrade, the terrace, and the great house would be transmogrified, or simply not there. But the boys were still playing football on the lawn, a group of girls were skipping and singing shrilly on the gravel. They let go each other's hand, and went back in.

They did not speak to each other again.

The next day, they were separated and placed with strange families. Their stay in these families—Primrose was in a dairy farm, Penny was in a parsonage—did not in fact last very long, though then the time seemed slow motion and endless. Later, Primrose remembered the sound of milk spurting in the pail, and Penny remembered the empty corsets of the Vicar's wife, hanging bony on the line. They remembered dandelion clocks, but you can remember those from anywhere, any time. They remembered the thing they had seen in the forest, on the contrary, in the way you remember those very few dreams—almost all nightmares—that have the quality of life itself. (Though what are dreams if not life itself?) They remembered too solid flesh, too precise a stink, a rattle and a soughing that thrilled the nerves and the cartilage of their growing ears. In the memory, as in such a dream, they felt, I cannot get out, this is a real thing in a real place.

They returned from evacuation, like many evacuees, so early that they then lived through wartime in the city, bombardment, blitz, unearthly light and roaring, changed landscapes, holes in their world where the newly dead had been. Both lost their fathers. Primrose's father was in the Army, and was killed, very late in the war, on a crowded troop carrier sunk in the Far East. Penny's father, a much older man, was in the Auxiliary Fire Service, and died in a sheet of flame in the East India Docks on the Thames, pumping evaporating water from a puny coil of hose. They found it hard, after the war, to remember these different men. The claspers of memory could not grip the drowned and the burned. Primrose saw an inane grin under a khaki cap, because her mother had a snapshot. Penny thought she remembered her father, already gray-headed, brushing ash off his boots and trouser cuffs as he put on his tin hat to go out. She thought she remembered a quaver of fear in his tired face, and the muscles composing themselves into resolution. It was not much what either of them remembered.

After the war, their fates were still similar and dissimilar. Penny's widowed mother embraced grief, closed her face and her curtains. Primrose's mother married one of the many admirers she had had before the ship went down, gave birth to another five children, and developed varicose veins and a smoker's cough. She dyed her blond hair with peroxide when it faded. Both Primrose and Penny were only children who now, because of the war, lived in amputated or unreal families. Penny was a good student and in due course went to university, where she chose to study developmental psychology. Primrose had little education. She was always being kept off school to look after the others. She, too, dyed her blond curls with peroxide when they turned mousy and faded. She got fat as Penny got thin. Neither of them married. Penny became a child psychologist, working with the abused, the displaced, the disturbed. Primrose did this and that. She was a barmaid. She worked in a shop. She went to help at various church crèches and Salvation Army gatherings, and discovered she had a talent for storytelling. She became Aunty Primrose, with her own repertoire. She was employed to tell tales to kindergartens and entertain at children's parties. She was much in demand at Halloween, and had her own circle of bright-colored plastic chairs in a local shopping mall, where she kept an eye on the children of burdened women, keeping them safe, offering them just a frisson of fear and terror, which made them wriggle with pleasure.

The house in the country aged differently. During this period of time—while the little girls became women—it was handed over to the nation, which turned it into a living museum. Guided tours took place in it, at regulated times. During these tours, the ballroom and intimate drawing rooms were fenced off with crimson twisted ropes on little brass one-eyed pedestals. The bored and the curious peered in at four-poster beds and pink silk fauteuils,[6] at silver-framed photographs of wartime royalty, and crackling crazing[7] Renaissance and Enlightenment portraits. In the room where the evacuees had eaten their rationed meals, the history of the house was displayed, on posters, in glass cases, with helpful notices and opened copies of old diaries and records. There was no mention of the evacuees, whose presence appeared to have been too brief to have left any trace.

The two women met in this room on an autumn day in 1984. They had come with a group, walking in a chattering crocodile behind a guide. They prowled around the room, each alone with herself, in opposite directions, each without acknowledging the other's presence. Their mothers had died that spring, within a week of each other, though this coincidence was unknown to them. It had

---

6. Armchairs.   7. Sealed with varnish that, with age, has cracked in patterns.

made both of them think of taking a holiday, and both had chosen that part of the world. Penny was wearing a charcoal trouser suit and a black velvet hat. Primrose wore a floral knit long jacket over a shell-pink cashmere sweater, over a rustling long skirt with an elastic waist, in a mustard-colored tapestry print. Her hips and bosom were bulky. Both of them, at the same moment, leaned over an image in a medieval-looking illustrated book. Primrose thought it was a very old book. Penny assumed it was nineteenth-century mock-medieval. It showed a knight, on foot, in a forest, lifting his sword to slay something. The knight shone on the rounded slope of the page, in the light, which caught the gilding on his helmet and sword belt. It was not possible to see what was being slain. This was because, both in the tangled vegetation of the image and in the way the book was displayed in the case, the enemy, or victim, was in shadows.

Neither of them could read the ancient (or pseudo-ancient) black letter of the text beside the illustration. There was a typed description, under the book. They had to lean forward to read it, and to see what was worming its way into, or out of, the deep spine of the book, and that was how each came to see the other's face, close up, in the glass, which was both transparent and reflective. Their transparent reflected faces lost detail—cracked lipstick, pouches, fine lines of wrinkles—and looked both younger and grayer, less substantial. And that is how they came to recognize each other, as they might not have done, plump face to bony face. They breathed each other's names—Penny, Primrose—and their breath misted the glass, obscuring the knight and his opponent. I could have died, I could have wet my knickers, said Penny and Primrose afterward to each other, and both experienced this still moment as pure, dangerous shock. They read the caption, which was about the Loathly Worm, which, tradition held, had infested the countryside and had been killed more than once by scions of that house—Sir Lionel, Sir Boris, Sir Guillem. The Worm, the typewriter had tapped out, was an English worm, not a European dragon, and, like most such worms, was wingless. In some sightings it was reported as having vestigial legs, hands, or feet. In others it was limbless. It had, in monstrous form, the capacity of common or garden worms to sprout new heads or trunks if it was divided, so that two worms, or more, replaced one. This was why it had been killed so often, yet reappeared. It had been reported travelling with a slithering pack of young ones, but these may have been only revitalized segments.

Being English, they thought of tea. There was a tearoom in the great house, in 45 a converted stable at the back. There they stood silently side by side, clutching floral plastic trays spread with briar roses, and purchased scones, superior raspberry jam in tiny jam jars, little plastic tubs of clotted cream. "You couldn't get cream or real jam in the war," said Primrose as they found a corner table. She said wartime rationing had made her permanently greedy, and thin Penny agreed it had—clotted cream was still a treat.

They watched each other warily, offering bland snippets of autobiography in politely hushed voices. Primrose thought Penny looked gaunt, and Penny thought Primrose looked raddled.[8] They established the skein of coincidences—dead fathers, unmarried status, child-caring professions, recently dead mothers. Circling like beaters,[9] they approached the covert thing in the forest. They discussed the great house, politely. Primrose admired the quality of the carpets. Penny said it was nice to see the old pictures back on the wall. Primrose said, Funny really,

8. Frazzled.   9. Hunters who beat the bushes to drive out game.

that there was all that history, but no sign that they, the children, that was, had ever been there. Funny, said Penny, that they should meet each other next to that book, with that picture. "Creepy," said Primrose in a light, light cobweb voice, not looking at Penny. "We saw that thing. When we went in the forest."

"Yes, we did," said Penny. "We saw it."

"Did you ever wonder," asked Primrose, "if we really saw it?"

"Never for a moment," said Penny. "That is, I don't know what it was, but I've always been quite sure we saw it."

50 "Does it change—do you remember all of it?"

"It was a horrible thing, and yes, I remember all of it, there isn't a bit of it I can manage to forget. Though I forget all sorts of things," said Penny, in a thin voice, a vanishing voice.

"And have you ever told anyone of it, spoken of it?" asked Primrose more urgently, leaning forward.

"No," said Penny. She had not. She said, "Who would believe it?"

"That's what I thought," said Primrose. "I didn't speak. But it stuck in my mind like a tapeworm in your gut. I think it did me no good."

55 "It did me no good either," said Penny. "No good at all. I've thought about it," she said to the aging woman opposite, whose face quivered under her dyed goldilocks. "I think, I think there are things that are real—more real than we are—but mostly we don't cross their paths, or they don't cross ours. Maybe at very bad times we get into their world, or notice what they are doing in ours."

Primrose nodded energetically. She looked as though sharing was solace, and Penny, to whom it was not solace, grimaced with pain.

"Sometimes I think that thing finished me off," Penny said to Primrose, a child's voice rising in a woman's gullet, arousing a little girl's scared smile, which wasn't a smile on Primrose's face.

Primrose said, "It did finish her off, that little one, didn't it? She got into its path, didn't she? And when it had gone by—she wasn't anywhere," said Primrose. "That was how it was?"

"Nobody ever asked where she was or looked for her," said Penny.

60 "I wondered if we'd made her up," said Primrose. "But I didn't, we didn't."

"Her name was Alys."

"With a 'y.'"

There had been a mess, a disgusting mess, they remembered, but no particular sign of anything that might have been, or been part of, or belonged to, a persistent little girl called Alys.

Primrose shrugged voluptuously, let out a gale of a sigh, and rearranged her flesh in her clothes.

65 "Well, we know we're not mad, anyway," she said. "We've got into a mystery, but we didn't make it up. It wasn't a delusion. So it was good we met, because now we needn't be afraid we're mad, need we—we can get on with things, so to speak?"

They arranged to have dinner together the following evening. They were staying in different bed-and-breakfasts and neither of them thought of exchanging addresses. They agreed on a restaurant in the market square of the local town—Seraphina's Hot Pot—and a time, seven-thirty. They did not even discuss spending the next day together. Primrose went on a local bus tour. Penny took a long solitary walk. The weather was gray, spitting fine rain. Both arrived at their lodgings with headaches, and both made tea with the tea bags and kettle provided in their rooms. They sat on their beds. Penny's had a quilt with blowsy cabbage roses. Primrose's had a black-and-white checked gingham duvet. They turned on their televisions, watched the same game show, listened to the inordinate jolly laughter.

Seven-thirty came and went, and neither woman moved. Both, indistinctly, imagined the other waiting at a table, watching a door open and shut. Neither moved. What could they have said, they asked themselves, but only perfunctorily.

The next day, Penny thought about the wood, put on her walking shoes, and set off obliquely in the opposite direction. Primrose sat over her breakfast, which was English and ample. The wood, the real and imagined wood—both before and after she had entered it with Penny—had always been simultaneously a source of attraction and of discomfort, shading into terror. Without speaking to herself a sentence in her head—"I shall go there"—Primrose decided. And she went straight there, full of warm food, arriving as the morning brightened with the first busload of tourists, and giving them the slip, to take the path they had once taken, across the lawn and through the wicket gate.

The wood was much the same, but denser and more inviting in its new green-ness. Primrose's body decided to set off in a rather different direction from the one the little girls had taken. New bracken was uncoiling with snaky force. Yes-terday's rain still glittered on limp new hazel leaves and threads of gossamer. Small feathered throats above her whistled and trilled with enchanting territo-rial aggression and male self-assertion, which were to Primrose simply the cho-rus. She found a mossy bank, with posies of primroses, which she recognized and took vaguely as a good sign, a personal sign. She was better at flowers than birds, because there had been Flower Fairies in the school bookshelves when she was little, with the flowers painted accurately, accompanied by truly pretty human creatures, all children, clothed in the blues and golds, russets and purples of the flowers and fruits. Here she saw and recognized them, windflower and bryony, self-heal and dead nettle, and had—despite where she was—a lovely lapping sense of invisible, just invisible life swarming in the leaves and along the twigs.

She stopped. She did not like the sound of her own toiling breath. She was not very fit. She saw, then, a whisking in the bracken, a twirl of fur, thin and flaming, quivering on a tree trunk. She saw a squirrel, a red squirrel, watching her from a bough. She had to sit down, as she remembered her mother. She sat on a hum-mock of grass, rather heavily. She remembered them all, Nutkin and Moldywarp, Brock and Sleepy Dormouse, Natty Newt and Ferdy Frog. Her mother hadn't told stories and hadn't opened gates into imaginary worlds. But she had been good with her fingers. Every Christmas during the war, when toys, and indeed materi-als, were not to be had, Primrose had woken to find in her stocking a new stuffed creature, made from fur fabric, with button eyes and horny claws. There had been an artistry to them. The stuffed squirrel was the essence of squirrel, the fox was watchful, the newt was slithery. They did not wear anthropomorphic jackets or caps, which made it easier to invest them with imaginary natures. She believed in Father Christmas, and the discovery that her mother had made the toys, the van-ishing of magic, had been a breathtaking blow. She could not be grateful for the skill and the imagination, so uncharacteristic of her flirtatious mother. The creatures continued to accumulate. A spider, a Bambi. She told herself stories at night about a girlwoman, an enchantress in a fairy wood, loved and protected by

70

an army of wise and gentle animals. She slept banked in by stuffed creatures, as the house in the blitz was banked in by inadequate sandbags.

Primrose registered the red squirrel as disappointing—stringier and more ratlike than its plump gray city cousins. But she knew it was special, and when it took off from branch to branch, flicking its extended tail like a sail, gripping with its tiny hands, she set out to follow it. It would take her to the center, she thought. It could easily have leaped out of sight, she thought, but it didn't. She pushed through brambles into denser, greener shadows. Juices stained her skirts and skin. She began to tell herself a story about staunch Primrose, not giving up, making her way to "the center." Her childhood stories had all been in the third person. "She was not afraid." "She faced up to the wild beasts. They cowered." She laddered her tights and muddied her shoes and breathed heavier. The squirrel stopped to clean its face. She crushed bluebells and saw the sinister hoods of arum lilies.

She had no idea how far she had come, but she decided that the clearing where she found herself was the center. The squirrel had stopped, and was running up and down a single tree. There was a mossy mound that could have had a thronelike aspect, if you were being imaginative. So she sat on it. "She came to the center and sat on the mossy chair."

Now what?

She had not forgotten what they had seen, the blank miserable face, the powerful claws, the raggle-taggle train of accumulated decay. She had come neither to look for it nor to confront it, but she had come because it was there. She had known all her life that she, Primrose, had really been in a magic forest. She knew that the forest was the source of terror. She had never frightened the littluns she entertained, with tales of lost children in forests. She frightened them with slimy things that came up the plughole, or swarmed out of the U-bend in the lavatory, and were dispatched by bravery and magic. But the woods in her tales bred glamour. They were places where you used words like "spangles" and "sequins" for real dewdrops on real dock leaves. Primrose knew that glamour and the thing they had seen, brilliance and the ashen stink, came from the same place. She made both things safe for the littluns by restricting them to pantomime flats and sweet illustrations. She didn't look at what she knew, better not, but she did know she knew, she recognized confusedly.

75   Now what?

She sat on the moss, and a voice in her head said, "I want to go home." And she heard herself give a bitter, entirely grownup little laugh, for what was home? What did she know about home?

Where she lived was above a Chinese takeaway. She had a dangerous cupboard-corner she cooked in, a bed, a clothes-rail, an armchair deformed by generations of bottoms. She thought of this place in faded browns and beiges, seen through drifting coils of Chinese cooking steam, scented with stewing pork and a bubbling chicken broth. Home was not real, as all the sturdy twigs and roots in the wood were real. The stuffed animals were piled on the bed and the carpet, their fur rubbed, their pristine stare gone from their scratched eyes. She thought about what one thought was real, sitting there on the moss throne at the center. When Mum had come in, snivelling, to say Dad was dead, Primrose herself had been preoccupied with whether pudding would be tapioca or semolina, whether there would be jam, and, subsequently, how ugly Mum's dripping nose was, how she looked as though she were putting it on.[1] She remembered the semolina and the rather nasty blackberry jam, the taste and the texture, to this day. So was that real, was that home?

She had later invented a picture of a cloudy aquamarine sea under a gold sun, in which a huge fountain of white curling water rose from a foundering ship. It was very beautiful but not real. She could not remember Dad. She could remember the Thing in the Forest, and she could remember Alys. The fact that the mossy tump had lovely colors—crimson and emerald—didn't mean she didn't remember the Thing. She remembered what Penny had said about "things that are more real than we are." She had met one. Here at the center, the spout of water was more real than the semolina, because she was where such things reign. The word she found was "reign." She had understood something, and did not know what she had understood. She wanted badly to go home, and she wanted never to move. The light was lovely in the leaves. The squirrel flirted its tail and suddenly set off again, springing into the branches. The woman lumbered to her feet and licked the bramble scratches on the back of her hands.

Penny walked very steadily, keeping to hedgerows and field-edge paths. She remembered the Thing. She remembered it clearly and daily. But she walked away, noticing and not noticing that her path was deflected by field forms and the lay of the land into a snaking sickle shape. As the day wore on, she settled into her stride and lifted her eyes. When she saw the wood on the horizon, she knew it was the wood, although she was seeing it from an unfamiliar aspect, from where it appeared to be perched on a conical hillock, ridged as though it had been grasped and squeezed by coils of strength. It was almost dusk. She mounted the slope, and went in over a suddenly discovered stile.[2]

Once inside, she moved cautiously. She stood stock-still, and snuffed the air   80
for the remembered rottenness: she listened to the sounds of the trees and the creatures. She smelled rottenness, but it was normal rottenness, leaves and stems mulching back into earth. She heard sounds. Not birdsong, for it was too late in the day, but the odd raucous warning croak. She heard her own heartbeat in the thickening brown air.

It was no use looking for familiar tree trunks or tussocks. They had had a lifetime, her lifetime, to alter out of recognition.

She began to think she discerned dark tunnels in the undergrowth, where something might have rolled and slid. Mashed seedlings, broken twigs and fronds, none of it very recent. There were things caught in the thorns, flimsy colorless shreds of damp wool or fur. She peered down the tunnels and noted where the scrapings hung thickest. She forced herself to go into the dark, stooping, occasionally crawling on hands and knees. The silence was heavy. She found threadworms of knitting wool, unravelled dishcloth cotton, clinging newsprint. She found odd sausage-shaped tubes of membrane, containing fragments of hair and bone and other inanimate stuffs. They were like monstrous owl pellets, or the gut-shaped hairballs vomited by cats. Penny went forward, putting aside briars and tough stems with careful fingers. It had been here, but how long ago?

Quite suddenly, she came out at a place she remembered. The clearing was larger, the tree trunks were thicker, but the great log behind which they had

1. Pretending.   2. Set of steps for climbing over a fence or hedge.

hidden still lay there. The place was almost the ghost of a camp. The trees round about were hung with pennants and streamers, like the scorched, hacked, threadbare banners in the chapel of the great house, with their brown stains of earth or blood. It had been here, it had never gone away.

Penny moved slowly and dreamily round, looking for things. She found a mock-tortoiseshell hairslide, and a shoe button with a metal shank. She found a bird skeleton, quite fresh, bashed flat. She found ambivalent shards and several teeth, of varying sizes and shapes. She found—spread around, half hidden by roots, stained green but glinting white—a collection of small bones, finger bones, tiny toes, a rib, and finally what might be a brainpan and brow. She thought of putting them in her knapsack, and then thought she could not. She was not an anatomist. The tiny bones might have been badger or fox.

85   She sat down, with her back against the fallen trunk. She thought, Now I am watching myself as you do in a safe dream, but then, when I saw it, it was one of those dreams where you are inside and cannot get out. Except that it wasn't a dream.

It was the encounter with the Thing that had led her to deal professionally in dreams. Something that resembled unreality had lumbered into reality, and she had seen it. She had been the reading child, but after the sight of the Thing she had not been able to inhabit the customary and charming unreality of books. She had become good at studying what could not be seen. She took an interest in the dead, who inhabited real history. She was drawn to the invisible forces that moved in molecules and caused them to coagulate or dissipate. She had become a psychotherapist "to be useful." That was not quite accurate. The corner of the blanket that covered the unthinkable had been turned back enough for her to catch sight of it. She was in its world. It was not by accident that she had come to specialize in severely autistic children, children who twittered, or banged, or stared, who sat damp and absent on Penny's official lap and told her no dreams. The world they knew was a real world. Often Penny thought it was the real world, from which even their desperate parents were at least partly shielded. Somebody had to occupy themselves with the hopeless. Penny felt she could.

All the leaves of the forest began slowly to quaver and then to clatter. Far away, there was the sound of something heavy, and sluggish, stirring. Penny sat very still and expectant. She heard the old blind rumble, she sniffed the old stink. It came from no direction; it was all around; as though the Thing encompassed the wood, or as though it travelled in multiple fragments, as it was described in the old text. It was dark now. What was visible had no distinct color, only shades of ink and elephant.

Now, thought Penny, and just as suddenly as it had begun the turmoil ceased. It was as though the Thing had turned away; she could feel the tremble of the wood recede and become still. Quite rapidly, over the treetops, a huge disk of white gold mounted and hung. Penny remembered her father, standing in the cold light of the full moon, and saying wryly that the bombers would not come tonight, they were safe under a cloudless full moon. He had vanished in an oven of red-yellow roaring, Penny had guessed, or been told, or imagined. Her mother had sent her away before allowing the fireman to speak, who had come with the news. She had been a creep-mouse on stairs and in cubbyholes, trying to overhear what was being imparted. Her mother didn't, or couldn't, want her company. She caught odd phrases of talk—"nothing really to identify," "absolutely no doubt." He had been a tired, gentle man with ash in his trouser turnups. There had been a funeral. Penny remembered thinking there was nothing, or next to nothing, in the coffin his fellow-firemen shouldered. It went up so lightly. It was so easy to set down on the crematorium slab.

They had been living behind the blackout anyway, but her mother went on living behind drawn curtains long after the war was over.

The moon had released the wood, it seemed. Penny stood up and brushed leaf mold off her clothes. She had been ready for it, and it had not come. She felt disappointed. But she accepted her release and found her way back to the fields and her village along liquid trails of moonlight.

90

The two women took the same train back to the city, but did not encounter each other until they got out. The passengers scurried and shuffled toward the exit, mostly heads down. Both women remembered how they had set out in the wartime dark, with their twig legs and gas masks. Both raised their heads as they neared the barrier, not in hope of being met, for they would not be, but automatically, to calculate where to go and what to do. They saw each other's faces in the cavernous gloom, two pale, recognizable rounds, far enough apart for speech, and even greetings, to be awkward. In the dimness, they were reduced to similarity— dark eyeholes, set mouth. For a moment or two, they stood and simply stared. On that first occasion the station vault had been full of curling steam, and the air gritty with ash. Now the blunt-nosed sleek diesel they had left was blue and gold under a layer of grime. They saw each other through the black imagined veil that grief or pain or despair hangs over the visible world. Each saw the other's face and thought of the unforgettable misery of the face they had seen in the forest. Each thought that the other was the witness, who made the thing certainly real, who prevented her from slipping into the comfort of believing she had imagined it or made it up. So they stared at each other, blankly, without acknowledgment, then picked up their baggage, and turned away into the crowd.

Penny found that the black veil had somehow become part of her vision. She thought constantly about faces, her father's, her mother's, Primrose's face, the hopeful little girl, the woman staring up at her from the glass case, staring at her conspiratorially over the clotted cream. The blond infant Alys, an ingratiating sweet smile. The half-human face of the Thing. She tried to remember that face completely, and suffered over the detail of the dreadful droop of its mouth, the exact inanity of its blind squinnying.[3] Present faces were blank disks, shadowed moons. Her patients came and went. She was increasingly unable to distinguish one from another. The face of the Thing hung in her brain, jealously soliciting her attention, distracting her from dailiness. She had gone back to its place, and had not seen it. She needed to see it. Why she needed it was because it was more real than she was. She would go and face it. What else was there, she asked herself, and answered herself, nothing.

So she made her way back, sitting alone in the train as the fields streaked past, drowsing through a century-long night under the cabbage quilt in the B. and B. This time, she went in the old way, from the house, through the garden gate; she found the old trail quickly, her sharp eye picked up the trace of its detritus, and soon enough she was back in the clearing, where her cairn of tiny bones

3. Squinting.

by the tree trunk was undisturbed. She gave a little sigh, dropped to her knees, and then sat with her back to the rotting wood and silently called the Thing. Almost immediately, she sensed its perturbation, saw the trouble in the branches, heard the lumbering, smelled its ancient smell. It was a grayish, unremarkable day. She closed her eyes briefly as the noise and movement grew stronger. When it came, she would look it in the face, she would see what it was. She clasped her hands loosely in her lap. Her nerves relaxed. Her blood slowed. She was ready.

Primrose was in the shopping mall, putting out her circle of rainbow-colored plastic chairs. She creaked as she bent over them. It was pouring with rain outside, but the mall was enclosed like a crystal palace in a casing of glass. The floor under the rainbow chairs was gleaming dappled marble. They were in front of a dimpling fountain, with lights shining up through the greenish water, making golden rings round the polished pebbles and wishing coins that lay there. The little children collected round her: their mothers kissed them goodbye, told them to be good and quiet and listen to the nice lady. They had little transparent plastic cups of shining orange juice, and each had a biscuit in silver foil. They were all colors—black skin, brown skin, pink skin, freckled skin, pink jacket, yellow jacket, purple hood, scarlet hood. Some grinned and some whimpered, some wriggled, some were still. Primrose sat on the edge of the fountain. She had decided what to do. She smiled her best, most comfortable smile, and adjusted her golden locks. Listen to me, she told them, and I'll tell you something amazing, a story that's never been told before.

95   There were once two little girls who saw, or believed they saw, a thing in a forest. . . .

                                                                                      2000

QUESTIONS

1. Traditional fairy tales often rely on symbolic objects, actions, settings, or characters. How is "The Thing in the Forest" like a fairy tale in this respect? How is it different? Are there figures of speech in this story that you would argue are not symbolic?

2. Is the "loathly worm" supernatural, imaginary, or real? Notice the description of its appearances. Can you identify different *kinds* of literal or physical traits that people see in it? Can you identify three or more concepts, feelings, or historical conditions that it might represent? Is it personified? Does it resemble other monsters in literature, art, or media?

3. Are "Penny" and "Primrose" allegorical names? How do the differences between the characters add to the symbolic meaning of the Thing? How do their different actions in the story help reveal the meanings of that symbolism?

EDWIDGE DANTICAT

A Wall of Fire Rising

"Listen to what happened today," Guy said as he barged through the rattling door of his tiny shack.

His wife, Lili, was squatting in the middle of their one-room home, spreading cornmeal mush on banana leaves for their supper.

"Listen to what happened to *me* today!" Guy's seven-year-old son—Little Guy—dashed from a corner and grabbed his father's hand. The boy dropped his composition notebook as he leaped to his father, nearly stepping into the corn mush and herring that his mother had set out in a trio of half gourds on the clay floor.

"Our boy is in a play." Lili quickly robbed Little Guy of the honor of telling his father the news.

"A play?" Guy affectionately stroked the boy's hair.   5

The boy had such tiny corkscrew curls that no amount of brushing could ever make them all look like a single entity. The other boys at the Lycée Jean-Jacques[1] called him "pepper head" because each separate kinky strand was coiled into a tight tiny ball that looked like small peppercorns.

"When is this play?" Guy asked both the boy and his wife. "Are we going to have to buy new clothes for this?"

Lili got up from the floor and inclined her face towards her husband's in order to receive her nightly peck on the cheek.

"What role do you have in the play?" Guy asked, slowly rubbing the tip of his nails across the boy's scalp. His fingers made a soft grating noise with each invisible circle drawn around the perimeters of the boy's head. Guy's fingers finally landed inside the boy's ears, forcing the boy to giggle until he almost gave himself the hiccups.

"Tell me, what is your part in the play?" Guy asked again, pulling his fingers   10
away from his son's ear.

"I am Boukman," the boy huffed out, as though there was some laughter caught in his throat.

"Show Papy your lines," Lili told the boy as she arranged the three open gourds on a piece of plywood raised like a table on two bricks, in the middle of the room. "My love, Boukman is the hero of the play."

The boy went back to the corner where he had been studying and pulled out a thick book carefully covered in brown paper.

"You're going to spend a lifetime learning those." Guy took the book from the boy's hand and flipped through the pages quickly. He had to strain his eyes to see the words by the light of an old kerosene lamp, which that night—like all others—flickered as though it was burning its very last wick.

"All these words seem so long and heavy," Guy said. "You think you can do   15
this, son?"

"He has one very good speech," Lili said. "Page forty, remember, son?"

---

1. Haiti is French-speaking; Little Guy attends a *lycée* (school) named after Jean-Jacques Dessalines (1758–1806), the founder of independent Haiti. A former slave, Dessalines was declared emperor Jacques I in 1804.

The boy took back the book from his father. His face was crimped in an of-course-I-remember look as he searched for page forty.

"Bouk-man," Guy struggled with the letters of the slave revolutionary's name as he looked over his son's shoulders. "I see some very hard words here, son."

"He already knows his speech," Lili told her husband.

20   "Does he now?" asked Guy.

"We've been at it all afternoon," Lili said. "Why don't you go on and recite that speech for your father?"

The boy tipped his head towards the rusting tin on the roof as he prepared to recite his lines.

Lili wiped her hands on an old apron tied around her waist and stopped to listen.

"Remember what you are," Lili said, "a great rebel leader. Remember, it is the revolution."

25   "Do we want him to be all of that?" Guy asked.

"He is Boukman," Lili said. "What is the only thing on your mind now, Boukman?"

"Supper," Guy whispered, enviously eyeing the food cooling off in the middle of the room. He and the boy looked at each other and began to snicker.

"Tell us the other thing that is on your mind," Lili said, joining in their laughter.

"Freedom!" shouted the boy, as he quickly slipped into his role.

30   "Louder!" urged Lili.

"Freedom is on my mind!" yelled the boy.

"Why don't you start, son?" said Guy. "If you don't, we'll never get to that other thing that we have on our minds."

The boy closed his eyes and took a deep breath. At first, his lips parted but nothing came out. Lili pushed her head forward as though she were holding her breath. Then like the last burst of lightning out of clearing sky, the boy began.

"A wall of fire is rising and in the ashes, I see the bones of my people. Not only those people whose dark hollow faces I see daily in the fields, but all those souls who have gone ahead to haunt my dreams. At night I relive once more the last caresses from the hand of a loving father, a valiant love, a beloved friend."[2]

35   It was obvious that this was a speech written by a European man, who gave to the slave revolutionary Boukman the kind of European phrasing that might have sent the real Boukman turning in his grave. However, the speech made Lili and Guy stand on the tips of their toes from great pride. As their applause thundered in the small space of their shack that night, they felt as though for a moment they had been given the rare pleasure of hearing the voice of one of the forefathers of Haitian independence in the forced baritone of their only child. The experience left them both with a strange feeling that they could not explain. It left the hair on the back of their necks standing on end. It left them feeling much more love than they ever knew that they could add to their feeling for their son.

"Bravo," Lili cheered, pressing her son into the folds of her apron. "Long live Boukman and long live my boy."

2. On the night of August 22, 1791, slaves led by a slave foreman named Boukman (who was secretly a voodoo high priest) built a "wall of fire" that destroyed many plantations in the north of the French colony of Saint-Domingue, marking the beginning of a mass slave revolt that would lead, fourteen years later, to the establishment of independent Haiti.

"Long live our supper," Guy said, quickly batting his eyelashes to keep tears from rolling down his face.

The boy kept his eyes on his book as they ate their supper that night. Usually Guy and Lili would not have allowed that, but this was a special occasion. They watched proudly as the boy muttered his lines between swallows of cornmeal.

The boy was still mumbling the same words as the three of them used the last of the rainwater trapped in old gasoline containers and sugarcane pulp from the nearby sugarcane mill to scrub the gourds that they had eaten from.

When things were really bad for the family, they boiled clean sugarcane pulp 40
to make what Lili called her special sweet water tea. It was supposed to suppress gas and kill the vermin in the stomach that made poor children hungry. That and a pinch of salt under the tongue could usually quench hunger until Guy found a day's work or Lili could manage to buy spices on credit and then peddle them for a profit at the marketplace.

That night, anyway, things were good. Everyone had eaten enough to put all their hunger vermin to sleep.

The boy was sitting in front of the shack on an old plastic bucket turned upside down, straining his eyes to find the words on the page. Sometimes when there was no kerosene for the lamp, the boy would have to go sit by the side of the road and study under the street lamps with the rest of the neighborhood children. Tonight, at least, they had a bit of their own light.

Guy bent down by a small clump of old mushrooms near the boy's feet, trying to get a better look at the plant. He emptied the last drops of rainwater from a gasoline container on the mushroom, wetting the bulging toes sticking out of his sons' sandals, which were already coming apart around his endlessly growing feet.

Guy tried to pluck some of the mushrooms, which were being pushed into the dust as though they wanted to grow beneath the ground as roots. He took one of the mushrooms in his hand, running his smallest finger over the round bulb. He clipped the stem and buried the top in a thick strand of his wife's hair.

The mushroom looked like a dried insect in Lili's hair. 45

"It sure makes you look special," Guy said, teasing her.

"Thank you so much," Lili said, tapping her husband's arm. "It's nice to know that I deserve these much more than roses."

Taking his wife's hand, Guy said, "Let's go to the sugar mill."

"Can I study my lines there?" the boy asked.

"You know them well enough already," Guy said. 50

"I need many repetitions," the boy said.

Their feet sounded as though they were playing a wet wind instrument as they slipped in and out of the puddles between the shacks in the shantytown. Near the sugar mill was a large television screen in an iron grill cage that the government had installed so that the shantytown dwellers could watch the state-sponsored news at eight o'clock every night. After the news, a gendarme[3] would come and turn off the television set, taking home the key. On most nights, the people stayed at the site long after this gendarme had gone and told stories to one another beneath the big blank screen. They made bonfires with dried sticks, corn husks, and paper, cursing the authorities under their breath.

3. Policeman or guard (French).

There was a crowd already gathering for the nightly news event. The sugar mill workers sat in the front row in chairs or on old buckets.

Lili and Guy passed the group, clinging to their son so that in his childhood naïveté he wouldn't accidentally glance at the wrong person and be called an insolent child. They didn't like the ambiance of the nightly news watch. They spared themselves trouble by going instead to the sugar mill, where in the past year they had discovered their own wonder.

55   Everyone knew that the family who owned the sugar mill were eccentric "Arabs," Haitians of Lebanese or Palestinian descent whose family had been in the country for generations. The Assad family had a son who, it seems, was into all manner of odd things, the most recent of which was a hot-air balloon, which he had brought to Haiti from America and occasionally flew over the shantytown skies.

As they approached the fence surrounding the field where the large wicker basket and deflated balloon rested on the ground, Guy let go of the hands of both his wife and the boy.

Lili walked on slowly with her son. For the last few weeks, she had been feeling as though Guy was lost to her each time he reached this point, twelve feet away from the balloon. As Guy pushed his hand through the barbed wire, she could tell from the look on his face that he was thinking of sitting inside the square basket while the smooth rainbow surface of the balloon itself floated above his head. During the day, when the field was open, Guy would walk up to the basket, staring at it with the same kind of longing that most men display when they admire very pretty girls.

Lili and the boy stood watching from a distance as Guy tried to push his hand deeper, beyond the chain link fence that separated him from the balloon. He reached into his pants pocket and pulled out a small pocketknife, sharpening the edges on the metal surface of the fence. When his wife and child moved closer, he put the knife back in his pocket, letting his fingers slide across his son's tightly coiled curls.

"I wager you I can make this thing fly," Guy said.

60   "Why do you think you can do that?" Lili asked.

"I know it," Guy replied.

He followed her as she circled the sugar mill, leading to their favorite spot under a watch light. Little Guy lagged faithfully behind them. From this distance, the hot-air balloon looked like an odd spaceship.

Lili stretched her body out in the knee-high grass in the field. Guy reached over and tried to touch her between her legs.

"You're not one to worry, Lili," he said. "You're not afraid of the frogs, lizards, or snakes that could be hiding in this grass?"

65   "I am here with my husband," she said. "You are here to protect me if anything happens."

Guy reached into his shirt pocket and pulled out a lighter and a crumpled piece of paper. He lit the paper until it burned to an ashy film. The burning paper floated in the night breeze for a while, landing in fragments on the grass.

"Did you see that, Lili?" Guy asked with a flame in his eyes brighter than the lighter's. "Did you see how the paper floated when it was burned? This is how that balloon flies."

"What did you mean by saying that you could make it fly?" Lili asked.

"You already know all my secrets," Guy said as the boy came charging towards them.

"Papa, could you play *Lago* with me?" the boy asked.   70

Lili lay peacefully on the grass as her son and husband played hide-and-seek. Guy kept hiding and his son kept finding him as each time Guy made it easier for the boy.

"We rest now." Guy was becoming breathless.

The stars were circling the peaks of the mountains, dipping into the cane fields belonging to the sugar mill. As Guy caught his breath, the boy raced around the fence, running as fast as he could to purposely make himself dizzy.

"Listen to what happened today," Guy whispered softly in Lili's ear.

"I heard you say that when you walked in the house tonight," Lili said. "With   75 the boy's play, I forgot to ask you."

The boy sneaked up behind them, his face lit up, though his brain was spinning. He wrapped his arms around both their necks.

"We will go back home soon," Lili said.

"Can I recite my lines?" asked the boy.

"We have heard them," Guy said. "Don't tire your lips."

The boy mumbled something under his breath. Guy grabbed his ear and twirled   80 it until it was a tiny ball in his hand. The boy's face contorted with agony as Guy made him kneel in the deep grass in punishment.

Lili looked tortured as she watched the boy squirming in the grass, obviously terrified of the crickets, lizards, and small snakes that might be there.

"Perhaps we should take him home to bed," she said.

"He will never learn," Guy said, "if I say one thing and you say another."

Guy got up and angrily started walking home. Lili walked over, took her son's hand, and raised him from his knees.

"You know you must not mumble," she said.   85

"I was saying my lines," the boy said.

"Next time say them loud," Lili said, "so he knows what is coming out of your mouth."

That night Lili could hear her son muttering his lines as he tucked himself in his corner of the room and drifted off to sleep. The boy still had the book with his monologue in it clasped under his arm as he slept.

Guy stayed outside in front of the shack as Lili undressed for bed. She loosened the ribbon that held the old light blue cotton skirt around her waist and let it drop past her knees. She grabbed half a lemon that she kept in the corner by the folded mat that she and Guy unrolled to sleep on every night. Lili let her blouse drop to the floor as she smoothed the lemon over her ashen legs.

Guy came in just at that moment and saw her bare chest by the light of the   90 smaller castor oil lamp that they used for the later hours of the night. Her skin had coarsened a bit over the years, he thought. Her breasts now drooped from having nursed their son for two years after he was born. It was now easier for him to imagine their son's lips around those breasts than to imagine his anywhere near them.

He turned his face away as she fumbled for her nightgown. He helped her open the mat, tucking the blanket edges underneath.

Fully clothed, Guy dropped onto the mat next to her. He laid his head on her chest, rubbing the spiky edges of his hair against her nipples.

"What was it that happened today?" Lili asked, running her fingers along Guy's hairline, an angular hairline, almost like a triangle, in the middle of his forehead. She nearly didn't marry him because it was said that people with angular hairlines often have very troubled lives.

"I got a few hours' work for tomorrow at the sugar mill," Guy said. "That's what happened today."

95   "It was such a long time coming," Lili said.

It was almost six months since the last time Guy had gotten work there. The jobs at the sugar mill were few and far between. The people who had them never left, or when they did they would pass the job on to another family member who was already waiting on line.

Guy did not seem overjoyed about the one day's work.

"I wish I had paid more attention when you came in with the news," Lili said. "I was just so happy about the boy."

"I was born in the shadow of that sugar mill," Guy said. "Probably the first thing my mother gave me to drink as a baby was some sweet water tea from the pulp of the sugarcane. If anyone deserves to work there, I should."

100   "What will you be doing for your day's work?"

"Would you really like to know?"

"There is never any shame in honest work," she said.

"They want me to scrub the latrines."

"It's honest work," Lili said, trying to console him.

105   "I am still number seventy-eight on the permanent hire list," he said. "I was thinking of putting the boy on the list now, so maybe by the time he becomes a man he can be up for a job."

Lili's body jerked forward, rising straight up in the air. Guy's head dropped with a loud thump onto the mat.

"I don't want him on that list," she said. "For a young boy to be on any list like that might influence his destiny. I don't want him on the list."

"Look at me," Guy said. "If my father had worked there, if he had me on the list, don't you think I would be working?"

"If you have any regard for me," she said, "you will not put him on the list."

110   She groped for her husband's chest in the dark and laid her head on it. She could hear his heart beating loudly as though it were pumping double, triple its normal rate.

"You won't put the boy on any lists, will you?" she implored.

"Please, Lili, no more about the boy. He will not go on the list."

"Thank you."

"Tonight I was looking at that balloon in the yard behind the sugar mill," he said. "I have been watching it real close."

115   "I know."

"I have seen the man who owns it," he said. "I've seen him get in it and put it in the sky and go up there like it was some kind of kite and he was the kite master. I see the men who run after it trying to figure out where it will land. Once I was there and I was one of those men who were running and I actually guessed correctly. I picked a spot in the sugarcane fields. I picked the spot from a distance and it actually landed there."

"Let me say something to you, Guy—"

"Pretend that this is the time of miracles and we believed in them. I watched the owner for a long time, and I think I can fly that balloon. The first time I saw him do it, it looked like a miracle, but the more and more I saw it, the more ordinary it became."

"You're probably intelligent enough to do it," she said.

"I am intelligent enough to do it. You're right to say that I can." 120

"Don't you think about hurting yourself?"

"Think like this. Can't you see yourself up there? Up in the clouds somewhere like some kind of bird?"

"If God wanted people to fly, he would have given us wings on our backs."

"You're right, Lili, you're right. But look what he gave us instead. He gave us reasons to want to fly. He gave us the air, the birds, our son."

"I don't understand you," she said. 125

"Our son, your son, you do not want him cleaning latrines."

"He can do other things."

"Me too. I can do other things too."

A loud scream came from the corner where the boy was sleeping. Lili and Guy rushed to him and tried to wake him. The boy was trembling when he opened his eyes.

"What is the matter?" Guy asked. 130

"I cannot remember my lines," the boy said.

Lili tried to string together what she could remember of her son's lines. The words slowly came back to the boy. By the time he fell back to sleep, it was almost dawn.

The light was slowly coming up behind the trees. Lili could hear the whispers of the market women, their hisses and swearing as their sandals dug into the sharp-edged rocks on the road.

She turned her back to her husband as she slipped out of her nightgown, quickly putting on her day clothes.

"Imagine this," Guy said from the mat on the floor. "I have never really seen 135 your entire body in broad daylight."

Lili shut the door behind her, making her way out to the yard. The empty gasoline containers rested easily on her head as she walked a few miles to the public water fountains. It was harder to keep them steady when the containers were full. The water splashed all over her blouse and rippled down her back.

The sky was blue as it was most mornings, a dark indigo-shaded turquoise that would get lighter when the sun was fully risen.

Guy and the boy were standing in the yard waiting for her when she got back.

"You did not get much sleep, my handsome boy," she said, running her wet fingers over the boy's face.

"He'll be late for school if we do not go right now," Guy said. "I want to drop 140 him off before I start work."

"Do we remember our lines this morning?" Lili asked, tucking the boy's shirt down deep into his short pants.

"We just recited them," Guy said. "Even I know them now."

Lili watched them walk down the footpath, her eyes following them until they disappeared.

As soon as they were out of sight, she poured the water she had fetched into a large calabash, letting it stand beside the house.

She went back into the room and slipped into a dry blouse. It was never too 145 early to start looking around, to scrape together that night's meal.

"Listen to what happened again today," Lili said when Guy walked through the door that afternoon.

Guy blotted his face with a dust rag as he prepared to hear the news. After the day he'd had at the factory, he wanted to sit under a tree and have a leisurely smoke, but he did not want to set a bad example for his son by indulging his very small pleasures.

"You tell him, son," Lili urged the boy, who was quietly sitting in a corner, reading.

"I've got more lines," the boy announced, springing up to his feet. "Papy, do you want to hear them?"

150   "They are giving him more things to say in the play," Lili explained, "because he did such a good job memorizing so fast."

"My compliments, son. Do you have your new lines memorized too?" Guy asked.

"Why don't you recite your new lines for your father?" Lili said.

The boy walked to the middle of the room and prepared to recite. He cleared his throat, raising his eyes towards the ceiling.

"*There is so much sadness in the faces of my people. I have called on their gods, now I call on our gods. I call on our young. I call on our old. I call on our mighty and the weak. I call on everyone and anyone so that we shall all let out one piercing cry that we may either live freely or we should die.*"

155   "I see your new lines have as much drama as the old ones," Guy said. He wiped a tear away, walked over to the chair, and took the boy in his arms. He pressed the boy's body against his chest before lowering him to the ground.

"Your new lines are wonderful, son. They're every bit as affecting as the old." He tapped the boy's shoulder and walked out of the house.

"What's the matter with Papy?" the boy asked as the door slammed shut behind Guy.

"His heart hurts," Lili said.

After supper, Lili took her son to the field where she knew her husband would be. While the boy ran around, she found her husband sitting in his favorite spot behind the sugar mill.

160   "Nothing, Lili," he said. "Ask me nothing about this day that I have had."

She sat down on the grass next to him, for once feeling the sharp edges of the grass blades against her ankles.

"You're really good with that boy," he said, drawing circles with his smallest finger on her elbow. "You will make a performer of him. I know you will. You can see the best in that whole situation. It's because you have those stars in your eyes. That's the first thing I noticed about you when I met you. It was your eyes, Lili, so dark and deep. They drew me like danger draws a fool."

He turned over on the grass so that he was staring directly at the moon up in the sky. She could tell that he was also watching the hot-air balloon behind the sugar mill fence out of the corner of his eye.

"Sometimes I know you want to believe in me," he said. "I know you're wishing things for me. You want me to work at the mill. You want me to get a pretty house for us. I know you want these things too, but mostly you want me to feel like a man. That's why you're not one to worry about, Lili. I know you can take things as they come."

"I don't like it when you talk this way," she said. 165

"Listen to this, Lili. I want to tell you a secret. Sometimes, I just want to take that big balloon and ride it up in the air. I'd like to sail off somewhere and keep floating until I got to a really nice place with a nice plot of land where I could be something new. I'd build my own house, keep my own garden. Just *be* something new."

"I want you to stay away from there."

"I know you don't think I should take it. That can't keep me from wanting."

"You could be injured. Do you ever think about that?"

"Don't you ever want to be something new?" 170

"I don't like it," she said.

"Please don't get angry with me," he said, his voice straining almost like the boy's.

"If you were to take that balloon and fly away, would you take me and the boy?"

"First you don't want me to take it and now you want to go?"

"I just want to know that when you dream, me and the boy, we're always in 175
your dreams."

He leaned his head on her shoulders and drifted off to sleep. Her back ached as she sat there with his face pressed against her collar bone. He drooled and the saliva dripped down to her breasts, soaking her frayed polyester bra. She listened to the crickets while watching her son play, muttering his lines to himself as he went in a circle around the field. The moon was glowing above their heads. Winking at them, as Guy liked to say, on its way to brighter shores.

Opening his eyes, Guy asked her, "How do you think a man is judged after he's gone?"

How did he expect her to answer something like that?

"People don't eat riches," she said. "They eat what it can buy."

"What does that mean, Lili? Don't talk to me in parables. Talk to me honestly." 180

"A man is judged by his deeds," she said. "The boy never goes to bed hungry. For as long as he's been with us, he's always been fed."

Just as if he had heard himself mentioned, the boy came dashing from the other side of the field, crashing in a heap on top of his parents.

"My new lines," he said. "I have forgotten my new lines."

"Is this how you will be the day of this play, son?" Guy asked. "When people give you big responsibilities, you have to try to live up to them."

The boy had relearned his new lines by the time they went to bed. 185

That night, Guy watched his wife very closely as she undressed for bed.

"I would like to be the one to rub that piece of lemon on your knees tonight," he said.

She handed him the half lemon, then raised her skirt above her knees.

Her body began to tremble as he rubbed his fingers over her skin.

"You know that question I asked you before," he said, "how a man is remem- 190
bered after he's gone? I know the answer now. I know because I remember my father, who was a very poor struggling man all his life. I remember him as a man that I would never want to be."

Lili got up with the break of dawn the next day. The light came up quickly above the trees. Lili greeted some of the market women as they walked together to the public water fountain.

On her way back, the sun had already melted a few gray clouds. She found the boy standing alone in the yard with a terrified expression on his face, the old withered mushrooms uprooted at his feet. He ran up to meet her, nearly knocking her off balance.

"What happened?" she asked. "Have you forgotten your lines?"

The boy was breathing so heavily that his lips could not form a single word.

195 "What is it?" Lili asked, almost shaking him with anxiety.

"It's Papa," he said finally, raising a stiff finger in the air.

The boy covered his face as his mother looked up at the sky. A rainbow-colored balloon was floating aimlessly above their heads.

"It's Papa," the boy said. "He is in it."

She wanted to look down at her son and tell him that it wasn't his father, but she immediately recognized the spindly arms, in a bright flowered shirt that she had made, gripping the cables.

200 From the field behind the sugar mill a group of workers were watching the balloon floating in the air. Many were clapping and cheering, calling out Guy's name. A few of the women were waving their head rags at the sky, shouting, "Go! Beautiful, go!"

Lili edged her way to the front of the crowd. Everyone was waiting, watching the balloon drift higher up into the clouds.

"He seems to be right over our heads," said the factory foreman, a short slender mulatto with large buckteeth.

Just then, Lili noticed young Assad, his thick black hair sticking to the beads of sweat on his forehead. His face had the crumpled expression of disrupted sleep.

"He's further away than he seems," said young Assad. "I still don't understand. How did he get up there? You need a whole crew to fly these things."

205 "I don't know," the foreman said. "One of my workers just came in saying there was a man flying above the factory."

"But how the hell did he start it?" Young Assad was perplexed.

"He just did it," the foreman said.

"Look, he's trying to get out!" someone hollered.

A chorus of screams broke out among the workers.

210 The boy was looking up, trying to see if his father was really trying to jump out of the balloon. Guy was climbing over the side of the basket. Lili pressed her son's face into her skirt.

Within seconds, Guy was in the air hurtling down towards the crowd. Lili held her breath as she watched him fall. He crashed not far from where Lili and the boy were standing, his blood immediately soaking the landing spot.

The balloon kept floating free, drifting on its way to brighter shores. Young Assad rushed towards the body. He dropped to his knees and checked the wrist for a pulse, then dropped the arm back to the ground.

"It's over!" The foreman ordered the workers back to work.

Lili tried to keep her son's head pressed against her skirt as she moved closer to the body. The boy yanked himself away and raced to the edge of the field where his father's body was lying on the grass. He reached the body as young Assad still knelt examining the corpse. Lili rushed after him.

215 "He is mine," she said to young Assad. "He is my family. He belongs to me."

Young Assad got up and raised his head to search the sky for his aimless balloon, trying to guess where it would land. He took one last glance at Guy's bloody corpse, then raced to his car and sped away.

The foreman and another worker carried a cot and blanket from the factory.

Little Guy was breathing quickly as he looked at his father's body on the ground. While the foreman draped a sheet over Guy's corpse, his son began to recite the lines from his play.

"A wall of fire is rising and in the ashes, I see the bones of my people. Not only those people whose dark hollow faces I see daily in the fields, but all those souls who have gone ahead to haunt my dreams. At night I relive once more the last caresses from the hand of a loving father, a valiant love, a beloved friend."

"Let me look at him one last time," Lili said, pulling back the sheet.   220

She leaned in very close to get a better look at Guy's face. There was little left of that countenance that she had loved so much. Those lips that curled when he was teasing her. That large flat nose that felt like a feather when rubbed against hers. And those eyes, those night-colored eyes. Though clouded with blood, Guy's eyes were still bulging open. Lili was searching for some kind of sign—a blink, a smile, a wink—something that would remind her of the man that she had married.

"His eyes aren't closed," the foreman said to Lili. "Do you want to close them, or should I?"

The boy continued reciting his lines, his voice rising to a man's grieving roar. He kept his eyes closed, his fists balled at his side as he continued with his newest lines.

"There is so much sadness in the faces of my people. I have called on their gods, now I call on our gods. I call on our young. I call on our old. I call on our mighty and the weak. I call on everyone and anyone so that we shall all let out one piercing cry that we may either live freely or we should die."

"Do you want to close the eyes?" the foreman repeated impatiently.   225

"No, leave them open," Lili said. "My husband, he likes to look at the sky."

1991

QUESTIONS

1. What do you think the hot-air balloon symbolizes to Assad, its owner? to Guy? to Edwidge Danticat?
2. The title of the story alludes to a speech that Little Guy must memorize for a school play about Haiti's history. The lines of the speech are rich in figurative language, including metaphors: "A wall of fire is rising and in the ashes I see the bones of my people" (par. 34). How do the title's allusion and other aspects of the story confirm that the speech's image of *"a wall of fire"* is symbolic?
3. What do you think happens at the end of "A Wall of Fire Rising"? Is Guy's plunge to the earth a deliberate suicide or an accident? What are some symbolic interpretations of both possibilities?

———————————

SUGGESTIONS FOR WRITING

1. Choose any story in this chapter, read it thoroughly, and follow the guidelines for responding to symbolism on pages 312–313. Write an essay in which you explore the

various meanings of the story's major symbol and the way these emerge over the course of the story.

2. In "The Birth-Mark," Aylmer the scientist is portrayed as "spiritual" and "intellectual," in contrast with his crudely physical laboratory assistant, Aminadab (par. 25). Write an essay in which you argue that the allegory of Aylmer's terrible experiment on his wife refers not only to a man's desire for immortal beauty but also to his desire for control of everything physical, including the laborer.

3. Write an essay in which you compare and contrast the way symbolism works in "The Birth-Mark" and "A Wall of Fire Rising." For example, what is the effect and significance of both the magical atmosphere of Hawthorne's story and the way its characters explicitly refer to particular objects as symbols? How might symbolism work differently in Danticat's story because of its realistic, contemporary setting and plot and the fact that its characters don't explicitly refer to anything as a symbol?

4. To what extent are characters aware of the symbolism in a story? Do characters accept the symbolism as objective and real, even if what happens seems magical or impossible? Write an essay focused on characters' different ways of responding to or believing in a symbol or symbolism in one or two stories. For instance, in "The Thing in the Forest" Primrose says "We've got into a mystery, but we didn't make it up." What else in the story confirms that their memories are more than illusion? How do the two women respond differently after they meet again? You might raise similar questions concerning "The Birth-Mark" and compare and contrast the characters' awareness and response to the respective symbols in Byatt's and Hawthorne's stories.

5. Write a parody of any of the stories in this chapter. See if you can make the symbolism deliberately heavy-handed and obvious, or perhaps obscure and puzzling.

6 THEME

At some point, a responsive reader of any story or novel will inevitably ask, *Why does it all matter? What does it all mean? What's the point?* When we ask what a text means, we are inquiring, at least in part, about its **theme**—a general idea or insight conveyed by the work in its entirety. Theme is certainly not the only way fiction matters nor the only thing we take away from our experience of reading it. Nor is theme fiction's *point* in the sense of its sole "objective" or "purpose." Yet theme is a fictional work's *point* in the sense of its "essential meaning" (or meanings). And our experience of any work isn't complete unless we grapple with the question of its theme.

On rare occasions, we might not have to grapple hard or look far: A very few texts, such as **fables** and certain fairy tales and folktales, explicitly state their themes. To succeed, however, even these works must ultimately "earn" their themes, bringing a raw statement to life through their characters, plot, setting, symbols, and narration. The following fable, by Aesop, succinctly makes its point through a brief dialogue.

AESOP
The Two Crabs

ONE fine day two crabs came out from their home to take a stroll on the sand. "Child," said the mother, "you are walking very ungracefully. You should accustom yourself to walking straight forward without twisting from side to side."

"Pray, mother," said the young one, "do but set the example yourself, and I will follow you."

"EXAMPLE IS THE BEST PRECEPT."

. . .

In most works, however, all the elements work together to imply an unstated theme that usually requires re-reading to decipher. Even the most careful and responsive readers will likely disagree about just what the theme is or how best to state it. And each statement of a given theme will imply a slightly different view of what matters most and why.

THEME(S): SINGULAR OR PLURAL?

In practice, readers disagree about the precise meaning of the term *theme*. One source of disagreement hinges on the question of whether any single work of fiction can convey more than one theme. On one side of the debate are those who use the word *theme* to refer only to the central or main idea of a work. On the other are those who use the term, as we generally do in this book, to refer to any idea a work conveys. While the former readers tend to talk about *the* theme, the latter instead refer to *a* theme in order to stress that each theme is only one of many. Regardless of whether we call all of the ideas expressed in a work *themes* or instead refer to some of them as *subthemes,* the essential points on which all agree are that a single literary work often expresses multiple ideas, and that at least one of those ideas is likely to be more central or overarching and inclusive than others. "The Two Crabs" demonstrates that even the most simple and straightforward of stories can have more than one theme. This fable's main, stated theme, "Example is the best precept," emerges only because the little crab "back-talks" to its mother, implicitly suggesting another theme: that children are sometimes wiser than their parents or even that we sometimes learn by questioning, rather than blindly following, authority. The fact that crabs naturally "twist from side to side"—that no crab *can* walk straight—certainly adds **irony** to the fable, but might it also imply yet another theme?

BE SPECIFIC: THEME AS IDEA VERSUS TOPIC OR SUBJECT

Often, you will see the term *theme* used very loosely to refer to a topic or subject captured in a noun phrase—"the wisdom of youth," "loss of innocence," "the dangers of perfectionism"—or even a single noun—"loss," "youth," "grief," or "prejudice." Identifying such topics—especially those specific enough to require a noun phrase rather than a simple noun—can be a useful first step on the way to figuring out a particular story's themes and also to grouping stories together for the purpose of comparison.

For now, though, we urge you to consider this merely a first step on the path to interpreting a story. The truth is, we haven't yet said anything very insightful, revealing, or debatable about the meaning of an individual story until we articulate the idea it expresses *about* a topic such as love, prejudice, or grief. To state a theme in this much more restricted and helpful sense you will need at least one complete sentence. Note, however, that a complete sentence is still not necessarily a statement of theme. For example, an online student essay begins with the less than scintillating sentence, "In Nathaniel Hawthorne's 'The Birthmark' the reader finds several themes—guilt, evil, love and alienation." One reason this sentence is both unexciting and unhelpful is that—despite its specific list of topics—we could in fact substitute for "The Birth-Mark" almost any other story in this book. (Try it yourself.) Notice how much more interesting things get, however, when we instead articulate the story's particular insight about just one of these very general topics: "Nathaniel Hawthorne's 'The Birth-Mark' shows us that we too often destroy the very thing we love by trying to turn the good into the perfect."

DON'T BE TOO SPECIFIC: THEME AS *GENERAL* IDEA

Though a theme is specific in the sense that it is a complete idea or statement rather than a topic, it is nonetheless a *general* idea rather than one that describes the characters, plot, or settings unique to one story. Theme is a general insight illustrated *through* these elements rather than an insight *about* any of them. Look again at the statement above—"Nathaniel Hawthorne's 'The Birth-Mark' shows us that we too often destroy the very thing we love by trying to turn the good into the perfect." Now compare this statement with one such as this: "In Nathaniel Hawthorne's 'The Birth-Mark,' the scientist Aylmer kills his wife because he can't tolerate imperfection." Though both statements are valid, only the first of them is truly a statement of theme—of what the story shows us about love through Aylmer rather than what it suggests about Aylmer himself.

THEME VERSUS MORAL

In some cases, a theme may take the form of a **moral**—a rule of conduct or maxim for living. But most themes are instead general observations and insights about how humans actually *do* behave, or about how life, the world, or some particular corner of it actually *is*, rather than moral imperatives about how people *should* behave or how life *should* ideally be. As one contemporary critic puts it, a responsive reader should thus "ask not *What does this story teach?* but *What does this story reveal?*" By the same token, we're usually on safer and more fertile ground if we phrase a theme as a statement rather than a command. Hawthorne's "The Birth-Mark," for example, certainly demonstrates the dangers of arrogantly seeking a perfection that isn't natural or human. As a result, we might well be tempted to reduce its theme to a moral such as "Accept imperfection," "Avoid arrogance," or "Don't mess with Mother Nature." None of these statements is wholly inappropriate to the story. Yet each of them seems to underestimate the story's complexity and especially its implicit emphasis on all that humanity gains, as well as loses, in the search for perfection. As a result, a better statement of the story's theme might be "Paradoxically, both our drive for perfection and our inevitable imperfection together make us human."

. . .

As you decipher and discuss the themes of the four powerful stories that follow—Stephen Crane's "The Open Boat," Gabriel García Márquez's "A Very Old Man with Enormous Wings," Louise Erdrich's "Love Medicine," and Yasunara Kawabata's "The Grasshopper and the Bell Cricket"—keep in mind that to identify a theme is not to "close the case" but rather to begin a more searching investigation of the details that make each story vivid and unique. Theme is an abstraction from the story; the story and its details do not disappear or lose significance once distilled into theme, nor could you reconstruct a story merely from a statement of its theme. Indeed, theme and story are fused, inseparable. Often difficult to put into words, themes are the common ground that helps you recognize and care about a story, and relate it to your own life—even though it seems to be about lives and experiences very different from your own.

Tips for Identifying Themes

Because theme emerges from a work in its entirety and from all the other elements working together, there is no "one-size-fits-all" method for identifying theme. Here, however, are some things to look for and consider as you read and re-read the work.

(Continued on next page)

(Continued)

TIP	EXAMPLE
1. Pay attention to the title. A title will seldom spell out in full a work's main theme, but some titles do suggest a central topic or topics or a clue to theme. Probe the rest of the story to see what, if any, insights about that topic it ultimately seems to offer.	What might Bharati Mukherjee's "The Management of Grief" suggest about whether and how grief can be "managed"?
2. List any recurring phrases and words, especially those for abstract concepts (love, honor). Certain concrete terms (especially if noted in the title) may likewise provide clues; objects of value or potency might attract significant attention in the text (an heirloom, a weapon, a tree in a garden). Then probe the story to see how and where else it might implicitly deal with that concept or entity and what, if any, conclusions the story proposes.	Versions of the word *blind* occur six times in the relatively short first paragraph of Raymond Carver's "Cathedral," and the word recurs throughout the story. What different kinds of blindness does the story depict? What truth or insight about blindness might it ultimately offer?
3. Identify any statements that the characters or narrator(s) make about a general concept, issue, or topic such as human nature, the natural world, and so on. Look, too, for statements that potentially have a general meaning or application beyond the story, even if they refer to a specific situation. Then consider whether and how the story as a whole corroborates, overturns, or complicates any one such view or statement.	In A. S. Byatt's "The Thing in the Forest," one of the two protagonists observes, "I think there are things that are real—more real than we are—but mostly we don't cross their paths, or they don't cross ours. Maybe at very bad times we get into their world, or notice what they are doing in ours" (par. 55). How does the rest of the story both flesh out what these "things" might be and either corroborate or complicate Penny's generalization about them?
4. If a character changes over the course of the story, articulate the truth or insight that he or she seems to discover. Then consider whether and how the story as a whole corroborates or complicates that insight.	The end of "The Thing in the Forest" implies that one of its protagonists has come to believe that even the most fantastic stories have an important function in real life. What is that function? Does the story as a whole confirm her conclusions?
5. Identify a conflict depicted in the work and state it in general terms or turn it into a general question, leaving out any reference to specific characters, situations, and so on. Then think about the insight or theme that might be implied by the way the conflict is resolved.	Through Sarty, William Faulkner's "Barn Burning" (chapter 3) raises the question of how we should reconcile loyalty to our family with our own individual sense of right and wrong. In the end, the story implies that following our own moral code can sometimes be the more painful, as well as the more noble, option.

STEPHEN CRANE

The Open Boat

A Tale Intended to Be after the Fact:[1] Being the Experience
of Four Men from the Sunk Steamer Commodore

I

None of them knew the color of the sky. Their eyes glanced level and were fastened upon the waves that swept toward them. These waves were of the hue of slate, save for the tops, which were of foaming white, and all of the men knew the colors of the sea. The horizon narrowed and widened, and dipped and rose, and at all times its edge was jagged with waves that seemed thrust up in points like rocks.

Many a man ought to have a bathtub larger than the boat which here rode upon the sea. These waves were most wrongfully and barbarously abrupt and tall, and each froth-top was a problem in small-boat navigation.

The cook squatted in the bottom, and looked with both eyes at the six inches of gunwale which separated him from the ocean. His sleeves were rolled over his fat forearms, and the two flaps of his unbuttoned vest dangled as he bent to bail out the boat. Often he said, "Gawd! that was a narrow clip." As he remarked it he invariably gazed eastward over the broken sea.

The oiler, steering with one of the two oars in the boat, sometimes raised himself suddenly to keep clear of water that swirled in over the stern. It was a thin little oar, and it seemed often ready to snap.

The correspondent, pulling at the other oar, watched the waves and wondered 5 why he was there.

The injured captain, lying in the bow, was at this time buried in that profound dejection and indifference which comes, temporarily at least, to even the bravest and most enduring when, willy-nilly, the firm fails, the army loses, the ship goes down. The mind of the master of a vessel is rooted deep in the timbers of her, though he command for a day or a decade; and this captain had on him the stern impression of a scene in the grays of dawn of seven turned faces, and later a stump of a topmast with a white ball on it, that slashed to and fro at the waves, went low and lower, and down. Thereafter there was something strange in his voice. Although steady, it was deep with mourning, and of a quality beyond oration or tears.

"Keep'er a little more south, Billie," said he.

"A little more south, sir," said the oiler in the stern.

A seat in his boat was not unlike a seat upon a bucking broncho, and by the same token a broncho is not much smaller. The craft pranced and reared and plunged like an animal. As each wave came, and she rose for it, she seemed like a horse making at a fence outrageously high. The manner of her scramble over these walls of water is a mystic thing, and, moreover, at the top of them were ordinarily these problems in white water, the foam racing down from the summit of each wave requiring a new leap, and a leap from the air. Then, after scornfully bumping a crest, she would slide and race and splash down a long incline, and arrive bobbing and nodding in front of the next menace.

1. Crane had an experience very like the one here re-created in fiction. His autobiographical account of his adventure at sea was published in the *New York Press* on January 7, 1897.

10   A singular disadvantage of the sea lies in the fact that after successfully sur-
mounting one wave you discover that there is another behind it just as important
and just as nervously anxious to do something effective in the way of swamping
boats. In a ten-foot dinghy one can get an idea of the resources of the sea in the
line of waves that is not probable to the average experience, which is never at sea
in a dinghy. As each slaty wall of water approached, it shut all else from the view
of the men in the boat, and it was not difficult to imagine that this particular
wave was the final outburst of the ocean, the last effort of the grim water. There
was a terrible grace in the move of the waves, and they came in silence, save for the
snarling of the crests.
        In the wan light the faces of the men must have been gray. Their eyes must
have glinted in strange ways as they gazed steadily astern. Viewed from a balcony, the whole thing would, doubtless, have been weirdly picturesque. But the
men in the boat had no time to see it, and if they had had leisure, there were
other things to occupy their minds. The sun swung steadily up the sky, and they
knew it was broad day because the color of the sea changed from slate to emerald-
green streaked with amber lights, and the foam was like tumbling snow. The
process of the breaking day was unknown to them. They were aware only of this
effect upon the color of the waves that rolled toward them.
        In disjointed sentences the cook and the correspondent argued as to the dif-
ference between a life-saving station and a house of refuge. The cook had said:
"There's a house of refuge just north of the Mosquito Inlet Light, and as soon as
they see us they'll come off in their boat and pick us up."
        "As soon as who see us?" said the correspondent.
        "The crew," said the cook.
15   "Houses of refuge don't have crews," said the correspondent. "As I understand
them, they are only places where clothes and grub are stored for the benefit of
shipwrecked people. They don't carry crews."
        "Oh, yes, they do," said the cook.
        "No, they don't," said the correspondent.
        "Well, we're not there yet, anyhow," said the oiler, in the stern.
        "Well," said the cook, "perhaps it's not a house of refuge that I'm thinking of
as being near Mosquito Inlet Light; perhaps it's a life-saving station."
20   "We're not there yet," said the oiler in the stern.

        II

As the boat bounced from the top of each wave the wind tore through the hair of
the hatless men, and as the craft plopped her stern down again the spray slashed
past them. The crest of each of these waves was a hill, from the top of which the
men surveyed for a moment a broad tumultuous expanse, shining and wind-
riven. It was probably splendid, it was probably glorious, this play of the free sea,
wild with lights of emerald and white and amber.
        "Bully good thing it's an on-shore wind," said the cook. "If not, where would
we be? Wouldn't have a show."
        "That's right," said the correspondent.
        The busy oiler nodded his assent.
25   Then the captain, in the bow, chuckled in a way that expressed humor, contempt, tragedy, all in one. "Do you think we've got much of a show now, boys?"
said he.

Whereupon the three were silent, save for a trifle of hemming and hawing. To express any particular optimism at this time they felt to be childish and stupid, but they all doubtless possessed this sense of the situation in their minds. A young man thinks doggedly at such times. On the other hand, the ethics of their condition was decidedly against any open suggestion of hopelessness. So they were silent.

"Oh, well," said the captain, soothing his children, "we'll get ashore all right."

But there was that in his tone which made them think; so the oiler quoth, "Yes! if this wind holds."

The cook was bailing. "Yes! if we don't catch hell in the surf."

Canton-flannel[2] gulls flew near and far. Sometimes they sat down on the sea, near patches of brown seaweed that rolled over the waves with a movement like carpets on a line in a gale. The birds sat comfortably in groups, and they were envied by some in the dinghy, for the wrath of the sea was no more to them than it was to a covey of prairie chickens a thousand miles inland. Often they came very close and stared at the men with black bead-like eyes. At these times they were uncanny and sinister in their unblinking scrutiny, and the men hooted angrily at them, telling them to be gone. One came, and evidently decided to alight on the top of the captain's head. The bird flew parallel to the boat and did not circle, but made short sidelong jumps in the air in chicken fashion. His black eyes were wistfully fixed upon the captain's head. "Ugly brute," said the oiler to the bird. "You look as if you were made with a jackknife." The cook and the correspondent swore darkly at the creature. The captain naturally wished to knock it away with the end of the heavy painter,[3] but he did not dare do it, because anything resembling an emphatic gesture would have capsized this freighted boat; and so, with his open hand, the captain gently and carefully waved the gull away. After it had been discouraged from the pursuit the captain breathed easier on account of his hair, and others breathed easier because the bird struck their minds at this time as being somehow gruesome and ominous.

In the meantime the oiler and the correspondent rowed; and also they rowed. They sat together in the same seat, and each rowed an oar. Then the oiler took both oars; then the correspondent took both oars, then the oiler; then the correspondent. They rowed and they rowed. The very ticklish part of the business was when the time came for the reclining one in the stern to take his turn at the oars. By the very last star of truth, it is easier to steal eggs from under a hen than it was to change seats in the dinghy. First the man in the stern slid his hand along the thwart and moved with care, as if he were of Sèvres.[4] Then the man in the rowing-seat slid his hand along the other thwart. It was all done with the most extraordinary care. As the two sidled past each other, the whole party kept watchful eyes on the coming wave, and the captain cried: "Look out, now! Steady, there!"

The brown mats of seaweed that appeared from time to time were like islands, bits of earth. They were travelling, apparently, neither one way nor the other. They were, to all intents, stationary. They informed the men in the boat that it was making progress slowly toward the land.

The captain, rearing cautiously in the bow after the dinghy soared on a great swell, said that he had seen the lighthouse at Mosquito Inlet. Presently the

2. Plain-weave cotton fabric.   3. Mooring rope attached to the bow of a boat.
4. Type of fine china.

cook remarked that he had seen it. The correspondent was at the oars then, and for some reason he too wished to look at the lighthouse; but his back was toward the far shore, and the waves were important, and for some time he could not seize an opportunity to turn his head. But at last there came a wave more gentle than the others, and when at the crest of it he swiftly scoured the western horizon.

"See it?" said the captain.

35   "No," said the correspondent, slowly; "I didn't see anything."

"Look again," said the captain. He pointed. "It's exactly in that direction."

At the top of another wave the correspondent did as he was bid, and this time his eyes chanced on a small, still thing on the edge of the swaying horizon. It was precisely like the point of a pin. It took an anxious eye to find a lighthouse so tiny.

"Think we'll make it, Captain?"

"If this wind holds and the boat don't swamp, we can't do much else," said the captain.

40   The little boat, lifted by each towering sea and splashed viciously by the crests, made progress that in the absence of seaweed was not apparent to those in her. She seemed just a wee thing wallowing, miraculously top up, at the mercy of five oceans. Occasionally a great spread of water, like white flames, swarmed into her.

"Bail her, cook," said the captain, serenely.

"All right, Captain," said the cheerful cook.

III

It would be difficult to describe the subtle brotherhood of men that was here established on the seas. No one said that it was so. No one mentioned it. But it dwelt in the boat, and each man felt it warm him. They were a captain, an oiler, a cook, and a correspondent, and they were friends—friends in a more curiously iron-bound degree than may be common. The hurt captain, lying against the water jar in the bow, spoke always in a low voice and calmly; but he could never command a more ready and swiftly obedient crew than the motley three of the dinghy. It was more than a mere recognition of what was best for the common safety. There was surely in it a quality that was personal and heart-felt. And after this devotion to the commander of the boat, there was this comradeship, that the correspondent, for instance, who had been taught to be cynical of men, knew even at the time was the best experience of his life. But no one said that it was so. No one mentioned it.

"I wish we had a sail," remarked the captain. "We might try my overcoat on the end of an oar, and give you two boys a chance to rest." So the cook and the correspondent held the mast and spread wide the overcoat; the oiler steered; and the little boat made good way with her new rig. Sometimes the oiler had to scull sharply to keep a sea from breaking into the boat, but otherwise sailing was a success.

45   Meanwhile the lighthouse had been growing slowly larger. It had now almost assumed color, and appeared like a little gray shadow on the sky. The man at the oars could not be prevented from turning his head rather often to try for a glimpse of this little gray shadow.

At last, from the top of each wave, the men in the tossing boat could see land. Even as the lighthouse was an upright shadow on the sky, this land seemed but a long black shadow on the sea. It certainly was thinner than paper. "We must be about opposite New Smyrna,"[5] said the cook, who had coasted this shore often in schooners. "Captain, by the way, I believe they abandoned that life-saving station there about a year ago."

"Did they?" said the captain.

The wind slowly died away. The cook and the correspondent were not now obliged to slave in order to hold high the oar. But the waves continued their old impetuous swooping at the dinghy, and the little craft, no longer underway, struggled woundily over them. The oiler or the correspondent took the oars again.

Shipwrecks are *apropos* of nothing. If men could only train for them and have them occur when the men had reached pink condition, there would be less drowning at sea. Of the four in the dinghy none had slept any time worth mentioning for two days and two nights previous to embarking in the dinghy, and in the excitement of clambering about the deck of a foundering ship they had also forgotten to eat heartily.

For these reasons, and for others, neither the oiler nor the correspondent was 50 fond of rowing at this time. The correspondent wondered ingenuously how in the name of all that was sane could there be people who thought it amusing to row a boat. It was not an amusement; it was a diabolical punishment, and even a genius of mental aberrations could never conclude that it was anything but a horror to the muscles and a crime against the back. He mentioned to the boat in general how the amusement of rowing struck him, and the weary-faced oiler smiled in full sympathy. Previously to the foundering, by the way, the oiler had worked a double watch in the engine-room of the ship.

"Take her easy, now, boys," said the captain. "Don't spend yourselves. If we have to run a surf you'll need all your strength, because we'll sure have to swim for it. Take your time."

Slowly the land arose from the sea. From a black line it became a line of black and a line of white—trees and sand. Finally the captain said that he could make out a house on the shore. "That's the house of refuge, sure," said the cook. "They'll see us before long, and come out after us."

The distant lighthouse reared high. "The keeper ought to be able to make us out now, if he's looking through a glass," said the captain. "He'll notify the life-saving people."

"None of those other boats could have got ashore to give word of the wreck," said the oiler, in a low voice, "else the life-boat would be out hunting us."

Slowly and beautifully the land loomed out of the sea. The wind came again. 55 It had veered from the northeast to the southeast. Finally a new sound struck the ears of the men in the boat. It was the low thunder of the surf on the shore. "We'll never be able to make the lighthouse now," said the captain. "Swing her head a little more north, Billie."

"A little more north, sir," said the oiler.

Whereupon the little boat turned her nose once more down the wind, and all but the oarsman watched the shore grow. Under the influence of this expansion doubt and direful apprehension were leaving the minds of the men. The management of the boat was still most absorbing, but it could not prevent a quiet cheerfulness. In an hour, perhaps, they would be ashore.

---

5. Town on the Florida coast.

Their backbones had become thoroughly used to balancing in the boat, and they now rode this wild colt of a dinghy like circus men. The correspondent thought that he had been drenched to the skin, but happening to feel in the top pocket of his coat, he found therein eight cigars. Four of them were soaked with sea-water; four were perfectly scatheless. After a search, somebody produced three dry matches; and thereupon the four waifs rode impudently in their little boat and, with an assurance of an impending rescue shining in their eyes, puffed at the big cigars, and judged well and ill of all men. Everybody took a drink of water.

IV

"Cook," remarked the captain, "there don't seem to be any signs of life about your house of refuge."

60 "No," replied the cook. "Funny they don't see us!"

A broad stretch of lowly coast lay before the eyes of the men. It was of low dunes topped with dark vegetation. The roar of the surf was plain, and sometimes they could see the white lip of a wave as it spun up the beach. A tiny house was blocked out black upon the sky. Southward, the slim lighthouse lifted its little gray length.

Tide, wind, and waves were swinging the dinghy northward. "Funny they don't see us," said the men.

The surf's roar was here dulled, but its tone was nevertheless thunderous and mighty. As the boat swam over the great rollers the men sat listening to this roar. "We'll swamp sure," said everybody.

It is fair to say here that there was not a life-saving station within twenty miles in either direction; but the men did not know this fact, and in consequence they made dark and opprobrious remarks concerning the eyesight of the nation's life-savers. Four scowling men sat in the dinghy and surpassed records in the invention of epithets.

65 "Funny they don't see us."

The light-heartedness of a former time had completely faded. To their sharpened minds it was easy to conjure pictures of all kinds of incompetency and blindness and, indeed, cowardice. There was the shore of the populous land, and it was bitter and bitter to them that from it came no sign.

"Well," said the captain, ultimately, "I suppose we'll have to make a try for ourselves. If we stay out here too long, we'll none of us have strength left to swim after the boat swamps."

And so the oiler, who was at the oars, turned the boat straight for the shore. There was a sudden tightening of muscles. There was some thinking.

"If we don't all get ashore," said the captain—"if we don't all get ashore, I suppose you fellows know where to send news of my finish?"

70 They then briefly exchanged some addresses and admonitions. As for the reflections of the men, there was a great deal of rage in them. Perchance they might be formulated thus: "If I am going to be drowned—if I am going to be drowned—if I am going to be drowned, why, in the name of the seven mad gods who rule the sea, was I allowed to come thus far and contemplate sand and trees? Was I brought here merely to have my nose dragged away as I was about to nibble the sacred cheese of life? It is preposterous. If this old ninny-woman, Fate, cannot do better than this, she should be deprived of the management of men's fortunes. She is an old hen who knows not her intention. If she has decided to

drown me, why did she not do it in the beginning and save me all this trouble? The whole affair is absurd. . . . But no; she cannot mean to drown me. She dare not drown me. She cannot drown me. Not after all this work." Afterward the man might have had an impulse to shake his fist at the clouds. "Just you drown me, now, and then hear what I call you!"

The billows that came at this time were more formidable. They seemed always just about to break and roll over the little boat in a turmoil of foam. There was a preparatory and long growl in the speech of them. No mind unused to the sea would have concluded that the dinghy could ascend these sheer heights in time. The shore was still afar. The oiler was a wily surfman. "Boys," he said, swiftly, "she won't live three minutes more, and we're too far out to swim. Shall I take her to sea again, Captain?"

"Yes; go ahead!" said the captain.

This oiler, by a series of quick miracles and fast and steady oarsmanship, turned the boat in the middle of the surf and took her safely to sea again.

There was a considerable silence as the boat bumped over the furrowed sea to deeper water. Then somebody in gloom spoke: "Well, anyhow, they must have seen us from the shore by now."

The gulls went in slanting flight up the wind toward the gray, desolate east. 75 A squall, marked by dingy clouds and clouds brick-red, like smoke from a burning building, appeared from the southeast.

"What do you think of those life-saving people? Ain't they peaches?"

"Funny they haven't seen us."

"Maybe they think we're out here for sport! Maybe they think we're fishin'. Maybe they think we're damned fools."

It was a long afternoon. A changed tide tried to force them southward, but wind and wave said northward. Far ahead, where coast-line, sea, and sky formed their mighty angle, there were little dots which seemed to indicate a city on the shore.

"St. Augustine." 80

The captain shook his head. "Too near Mosquito Inlet."

And the oiler rowed, and then the correspondent rowed; then the oiler moved. It was a weary business. The human back can become the seat of more aches and pains than are registered in books for the composite anatomy of a regiment. It is a limited area, but it can become the theatre of innumerable muscular conflicts, tangles, wrenches, knots, and other comforts.

"Did you ever like to row, Billie?" asked the correspondent.

"No," said the oiler. "Hang it."

When one exchanged the rowing-seat for a place in the bottom of the boat, he 85 suffered a bodily depression that caused him to be careless of everything save an obligation to wiggle one finger. There was cold sea-water swashing to and fro in the boat, and he lay in it. His head, pillowed on a thwart, was within an inch of the swirl of a wave-crest, and sometimes a particularly obstreperous sea came inboard and drenched him once more. But these matters did not annoy him. It is almost certain that if the boat had capsized he would have tumbled comfortably out upon the ocean as if he felt sure that it was a great soft mattress.

"Look! There's a man on the shore!"

"There? See 'im? See 'im?"

"Yes, sure! He's walking along."

"Now he's stopped. Look! He's facing us!"

90 "He's waving at us!"

"So he is! By thunder!"

"Ah, now we're all right! Now we're all right! There'll be a boat out here for us in half an hour."

"He's going on. He's running. He's going up to that house there."

The remote beach seemed lower than the sea, and it required a searching glance to discern the little black figure. The captain saw a floating stick, and they rowed to it. A bath towel was by some weird chance in the boat, and, tying this on the stick, the captain waved it. The oarsman did not dare turn his head, so he was obliged to ask questions.

95 "What's he doing now?"

"He's standing still again. He's looking, I think. . . . There he goes again— toward the house. . . . Now he's stopped again."

"Is he waving at us?"

"No, not now; he was, though."

"Look! There comes another man!"

100 "He's running."

"Look at him go, would you!"

"Why, he's on a bicycle. Now he's met the other man. They're both waving at us. Look!"

"There comes something up the beach."

"What the devil is that thing?"

105 "Why, it looks like a boat."

"Why, certainly, it's a boat."

"No; it's on wheels."

"Yes, so it is. Well, that must be the life-boat. They drag them along shore on a wagon."

"That's the life-boat, sure."

110 "No, by God, it's—it's an omnibus."

"I tell you it's a life-boat."

"It is not! It's an omnibus. I can see it plain. See? One of these big hotel omnibuses."

"By thunder, you're right. It's an omnibus, sure as fate. What do you suppose they are doing with an omnibus? Maybe they are going around collecting the life-crew, hey?"

"That's it, likely. Look! There's a fellow waving a little black flag. He's standing on the steps of the omnibus. There comes those other two fellows. Now they're all talking together. Look at the fellow with the flag. Maybe he ain't waving it!"

115 "That ain't a flag, is it? That's his coat. Why, certainly, that's his coat."

"So it is: it's his coat. He's taken it off and is waving it around his head. But would you look at him swing it!"

"Oh, say, there isn't any life-saving station there. That's just a winter-resort."

"What's that idiot with the coat mean? What's he signaling, anyhow?"

"It looks as if he were trying to tell us to go north. There must be a life-saving station up there."

120 "No; he thinks we're fishing. Just giving us a merry hand. See? Ah, there, Willie!"

"Well, I wish I could make something out of those signals. What do you suppose he means?"

"He don't mean anything; he's just playing."

"Well, if he'd just signal us to try the surf again, or to go to sea and wait, or go north, or go south, or go to hell, there would be some reason in it. But look at him! He just stands there and keeps his coat revolving like a wheel. The ass!"

"There come more people."

"Now there's quite a mob. Look! Isn't that a boat?" 125

"Where? Oh, I see where you mean. No, that's no boat."

"That fellow is still waving his coat."

"He must think we like to see him to do that. Why don't he quit? It don't mean anything."

"I don't know. I think he is trying to make us go north. It must be that there's a life-saving station there somewhere."

"Say, he ain't tired yet. Look at 'im wave!" 130

"Wonder how long he can keep that up. He's been revolving his coat ever since he caught sight of us. He's an idiot. Why aren't they getting men to bring a boat out? A fishing boat—one of those big yawls—could come out here all right. Why don't he do something?"

"Oh, it's all right now."

"They'll have a boat out here for us in less than no time, now that they've seen us."

A faint yellow tone came into the sky over the low land. The shadows on the sea slowly deepened. The wind bore coldness with it, and the men began to shiver.

"Holy smoke!" said one, allowing his voice to express his impious mood, "if 135 we keep on monkeying out here! If we've got to flounder out here all night!"

"Oh, we'll never have to stay here all night! Don't you worry. They've seen us now, and it won't be long before they'll come chasing out after us."

The shore grew dusky. The man waving a coat blended gradually into this gloom, and it swallowed in the same manner the omnibus and the group of people. The spray, when it dashed uproariously over the side, made the voyagers shrink and swear like men who were being branded.

"I'd like to catch the chump who waved the coat. I feel like socking him one, just for luck."

"Why? What did he do?"

"Oh, nothing, but then he seemed so damned cheerful." 140

In the meantime the oiler rowed, and then the correspondent rowed, and then the oiler rowed. Gray-faced and bowed forward, they mechanically, turn by turn, plied the leaden oars. The form of the lighthouse had vanished from the southern horizon, but finally a pale star appeared, just lifting from the sea. The streaked saffron in the west passed before the all-merging darkness, and the sea to the east was black. The land had vanished, and was expressed only by the low and drear thunder of the surf.

"If I am going to be drowned—if I am going to be drowned—if I am going to be drowned, why, in the name of the seven mad gods who rule the sea, was I allowed to come thus far and contemplate sand and trees? Was I brought here merely to have my nose dragged away as I was about to nibble the sacred cheese of life?"

The patient captain, drooped over the water-jar, was sometimes obliged to speak to the oarsman.

"Keep her head up! Keep her head up!"

"Keep her head up, sir." The voices were weary and low. 145

This was surely a quiet evening. All save the oarsman lay heavily and listlessly in the boat's bottom. As for him, his eyes were just capable of noting the tall black waves that swept forward in a most sinister silence, save for an occasional subdued growl of a crest.

The cook's head was on a thwart, and he looked without interest at the water under his nose. He was deep in other scenes. Finally he spoke. "Billie," he murmured, dreamfully, "what kind of pie do you like best?"

V

"Pie!" said the oiler and the correspondent, agitatedly. "Don't talk about those things, blast you!"

"Well," said the cook, "I was just thinking about ham sandwiches, and——"

150   A night on the sea in an open boat is a long night. As darkness settled finally, the shine of the light, lifting from the sea in the south, changed to full gold. On the northern horizon a new light appeared, a small bluish gleam on the edge of the waters. These two lights were the furniture of the world. Otherwise there was nothing but waves.

Two men huddled in the stern, and distances were so magnificent in the dinghy that the rower was enabled to keep his feet partly warm by thrusting them under his companions. Their legs indeed extended far under the rowing-seat until they touched the feet of the captain forward. Sometimes, despite the efforts of the tired oarsman, a wave came piling into the boat, an icy wave of the night, and the chilling water soaked them anew. They would twist their bodies for a moment and groan, and sleep the dead sleep once more, while the water in the boat gurgled about them as the craft rocked.

The plan of the oiler and the correspondent was for one to row until he lost the ability, and then arouse the other from his sea-water couch in the bottom of the boat.

The oiler plied the oars until his head drooped forward and the overpowering sleep blinded him; and he rowed yet afterward. Then he touched a man in the bottom of the boat, and called his name. "Will you spell me for a little while?" he said meekly.

"Sure, Billie," said the correspondent, awaking and dragging himself to a sitting position. They exchanged places carefully, and the oiler, cuddling down in the sea-water at the cook's side, seemed to go to sleep instantly.

155   The particular violence of the sea had ceased. The waves came without snarling. The obligation of the man at the oars was to keep the boat headed so that the tilt of the rollers would not capsize her, and to preserve her from filling when the crests rushed past. The black waves were silent and hard to be seen in the darkness. Often one was almost upon the boat before the oarsman was aware.

In a low voice the correspondent addressed the captain. He was not sure that the captain was awake, although this iron man seemed to be always awake. "Captain, shall I keep her making for that light north, sir?"

The same steady voice answered him. "Yes. Keep it about two points off the port bow."

The cook had tied a life-belt around himself in order to get even the warmth which this clumsy cork contrivance could donate, and he seemed almost stove-like when a rower, whose teeth invariably chattered wildly as soon as he ceased his labor, dropped down to sleep.

The correspondent, as he rowed, looked down at the two men sleeping underfoot. The cook's arm was around the oiler's shoulders, and, with their fragmentary clothing and haggard faces, they were the babes of the sea—a grotesque rendering of the old babes in the wood.

Later he must have grown stupid at his work, for suddenly there was a growling of water, and a crest came with a roar and a swash into the boat, and it was a wonder that it did not set the cook afloat in his life-belt. The cook continued to sleep, but the oiler sat up, blinking his eyes and shaking with the new cold.

"Oh, I'm awful sorry, Billie," said the correspondent, contritely.

"That's all right, old boy," said the oiler, and lay down again and was asleep.

Presently it seemed that even the captain dozed, and the correspondent thought that he was the one man afloat on all the ocean. The wind had a voice as it came over the waves, and it was sadder than the end.

There was a long, loud swishing astern of the boat, and a gleaming trail of phosphorescence, like blue flame, was furrowed on the black waters. It might have been made by a monstrous knife.

Then there came a stillness, while the correspondent breathed with open mouth and looked at the sea.

Suddenly there was another swish and another long flash of bluish light, and this time it was alongside the boat, and might almost have been reached with an oar. The correspondent saw an enormous fin speed like a shadow through the water, hurling the crystalline spray and leaving the long glowing trail.

The correspondent looked over his shoulder at the captain. His face was hidden, and he seemed to be asleep. He looked at the babes of the sea. They certainly were asleep. So, being bereft of sympathy, he leaned a little way to one side and swore softly into the sea.

But the thing did not then leave the vicinity of the boat. Ahead or astern, on one side or the other, at intervals long or short, fled the long sparkling streak, and there was to be heard the *whirroo* of the dark fin. The speed and power of the thing was greatly to be admired. It cut the water like a gigantic and keen projectile.

The presence of this biding thing did not affect the man with the same horror that it would if he had been a picnicker. He simply looked at the sea dully and swore in an undertone.

Nevertheless, it is true that he did not wish to be alone with the thing. He wished one of his companions to awake by chance and keep him company with it. But the captain hung motionless over the water-jar and the oiler and the cook in the bottom of the boat were plunged in slumber.

VI

"If I am going to be drowned—if I am going to be drowned—if I am going to be drowned, why, in the name of the seven mad gods who rule the sea, was I allowed to come thus far and contemplate sand and trees?"

During this dismal night, it may be remarked that a man would conclude that it was really the intention of the seven mad gods to drown him, despite the abominable injustice of it. For it was certainly an abominable injustice to drown a man who had worked so hard, so hard. The man felt it would be a crime most unnatural. Other people had drowned at sea since galleys swarmed with painted sails, but still——

When it occurs to a man that nature does not regard him as important, and that she feels she would not maim the universe by disposing of him, he at first wishes to throw bricks at the temple, and he hates deeply the fact that there are no bricks and no temples. Any visible expression of nature would surely be pelleted with his jeers.

Then, if there be no tangible thing to hoot, he feels, perhaps, the desire to confront a personification and indulge in pleas, bowed to one knee, and with hands supplicant, saying, "Yes, but I love myself."

175   A high cold star on a winter's night is the word he feels that she says to him. Thereafter he knows the pathos of his situation.

The men in the dinghy had not discussed these matters, but each had, no doubt, reflected upon them in silence and according to his mind. There was seldom any expression upon their faces save the general one of complete weariness. Speech was devoted to the business of the boat.

To chime the notes of his emotions, a verse mysteriously entered the correspondent's head. He had even forgotten that he had forgotten this verse, but it suddenly was in his mind.

> A soldier of the Legion lay dying in Algiers;
> There was lack of woman's nursing, there was dearth of woman's tears;
> But a comrade stood beside him, and he took the comrade's hand,
> And he said, "I never more shall see my own, my native land."[6]

In his childhood the correspondent had been made acquainted with the fact that a soldier of the Legion lay dying in Algiers, but he had never regarded it as important. Myriads of his schoolfellows had informed him of the soldier's plight, but the dinning had naturally ended by making him perfectly indifferent. He had never considered it his affair that a soldier of the Legion lay dying in Algiers, nor had it appeared to him as a matter for sorrow. It was less to him than the breaking of a pencil's point.

Now, however, it quaintly came to him as a human, living thing. It was no longer merely a picture of a few throes in the breast of a poet, meanwhile drinking tea and warming his feet at the grate; it was an actuality—stern, mournful, and fine.

The correspondent plainly saw the soldier. He lay on the sand with his feet out straight and still. While his pale left hand was upon his chest in an attempt to thwart the going of his life, the blood came between his fingers. In the far Algerian distance, a city of low square forms was set against a sky that was faint with the last sunset hues. The correspondent, plying the oars and dreaming of the slow and slower movements of the lips of the soldier, was moved by a profound and perfectly impersonal comprehension. He was sorry for the soldier of the Legion who lay dying in Algiers.

180   The thing which had followed the boat and waited had evidently grown bored at the delay. There was no longer to be heard the slash of the cutwater, and there was no longer the flame of the long trail. The light in the north still glimmered, but it was apparently no nearer to the boat. Sometimes the boom of the surf rang in the correspondent's ears, and he turned the craft seaward then and rowed harder. Southward, some one had evidently built a watch-fire on the beach. It was too low and too far to be seen, but it made a shimmering, roseate

6. From "Bingen on the Rhine," by Caroline Norton (1808–77).

reflection upon the bluff in back of it, and this could be discerned from the boat. The wind came stronger, and sometimes a wave suddenly raged out like a mountain-cat, and there was to be seen the sheen and sparkle of a broken crest.

The captain, in the bow, moved on his water-jar and sat erect. "Pretty long night," he observed to the correspondent. He looked at the shore. "Those life-saving people take their time."

"Did you see that shark playing around?"

"Yes, I saw him. He was a big fellow, all right."

"Wish I had known you were awake."

Later the correspondent spoke into the bottom of the boat. "Billie!" There was a slow and gradual disentanglement. "Billie, will you spell me?"   185

"Sure," said the oiler.

As soon as the correspondent touched the cold, comfortable seawater in the bottom of the boat and had huddled close to the cook's life-belt he was deep in sleep, despite the fact that his teeth played all the popular airs. This sleep was so good to him that it was but a moment before he heard a voice call his name in a tone that demonstrated the last stages of exhaustion. "Will you spell me?"

"Sure, Billie."

The light in the north had mysteriously vanished, but the correspondent took his course from the wide-awake captain.

Later in the night they took the boat farther out to sea, and the captain   190
directed the cook to take one oar at the stern and keep the boat facing the seas. He was to call out if he should hear the thunder of the surf. This plan enabled the oiler and the correspondent to get respite together. "We'll give those boys a chance to get into shape again," said the captain. They curled down and, after a few pre-liminary chatterings and trembles, slept once more the dead sleep. Neither knew they had bequeathed to the cook the company of another shark, or perhaps the same shark.

As the boat caroused on the waves, spray occasionally bumped over the side and gave them a fresh soaking, but this had no power to break their repose. The ominous slash of the wind and the water affected them as it would have affected mummies.

"Boys," said the cook, with the notes of every reluctance in his voice, "she's drifted in pretty close. I guess one of you had better take her to sea again." The correspondent, aroused, heard the crash of the toppled crests.

As he was rowing, the captain gave him some whiskey-and-water, and this steadied the chills out of him. "If I ever get ashore and anybody shows me even a photograph of an oar——"

At last there was a short conversation.

"Billie! . . . Billie, will you spell me?"   195

"Sure," said the oiler.

VII

When the correspondent again opened his eyes, the sea and the sky were each of the gray hue of the dawning. Later, carmine and gold was painted upon the waters. The morning appeared finally, in its splendor, with a sky of pure blue, and the sunlight flamed on the tips of the waves.

On the distant dunes were set many little black cottages, and a tall white windmill reared above them. No man, nor dog, nor bicycle appeared on the beach. The cottages might have formed a deserted village.

The voyagers scanned the shore. A conference was held in the boat. "Well," said the captain, "if no help is coming, we might better try a run through the surf right away. If we stay out here much longer we will be too weak to do anything for ourselves at all." The others silently acquiesced in this reasoning. The boat was headed for the beach. The correspondent wondered if none ever ascended the tall wind-tower,[7] and if then they never looked seaward. This tower was a giant, standing with its back to the plight of the ants. It represented in a degree, to the correspondent, the serenity of nature amid the struggles of the individual—nature in the wind, and nature in the vision of men. She did not seem cruel to him then, nor beneficent, nor treacherous, nor wise. But she was indifferent, flatly indifferent. It is, perhaps, plausible that a man in this situation, impressed with the unconcern of the universe, should see the innumerable flaws of his life, and have them taste wickedly in his mind, and wish for another chance. A distinction between right and wrong seems absurdly clear to him, then, in this new ignorance of the grave-edge, and he understands that if he were given another opportunity he would mend his conduct and his words, and be better and brighter during an introduction or at a tea.

200   "Now, boys," said the captain, "she is going to swamp sure. All we can do is to work her in as far as possible, and then when she swamps, pile out and scramble for the beach. Keep cool now, and don't jump until she swamps sure."

The oiler took the oars. Over his shoulders he scanned the surf. "Captain," he said, "I think I'd better bring her about and keep her head-on to the seas and back her in."

"All right, Billie," said the captain. "Back her in." The oiler swung the boat then, and, seated in the stern, the cook and the correspondent were obliged to look over their shoulders to contemplate the lonely and indifferent shore.

The monstrous inshore rollers heaved the boat high until the men were again enabled to see the white sheets of water scudding up the slanted beach. "We won't get in very close," said the captain. Each time a man could wrest his attention from the rollers, he turned his glance toward the shore, and in the expression of the eyes during this contemplation there was a singular quality. The correspondent, observing the others, knew that they were not afraid, but the full meaning of their glances was shrouded.

As for himself, he was too tired to grapple fundamentally with the fact. He tried to coerce his mind into thinking of it, but the mind was dominated at this time by the muscles, and the muscles said they did not care. It merely occurred to him that if he should drown it would be a shame.

205   There were no hurried words, no pallor, no plain agitation. The men simply looked at the shore. "Now, remember to get well clear of the boat when you jump," said the captain.

Seaward the crest of a roller suddenly fell with a thunderous crash, and the long white comber came roaring down upon the boat.

"Steady now," said the captain. The men were silent. They turned their eyes from the shore to the comber and waited. The boat slid up the incline, leaped at the furious top, bounced over it, and swung down the long back of the wave. Some water had been shipped, and the cook bailed it out.

But the next crest crashed also. The tumbling, boiling flood of white water caught the boat and whirled it almost perpendicular. Water swarmed in from all

7. Watchtower for observing weather.

sides. The correspondent had his hands on the gunwale at this time, and when the water entered at that place he swiftly withdrew his fingers, as if he objected to wetting them.

The little boat, drunken with this weight of water, reeled and snuggled deeper into the sea.

"Bail her out, cook! Bail her out!" said the captain. 210

"All right, Captain," said the cook.

"Now, boys, the next one will do for us sure," said the oiler. "Mind to jump clear of the boat."

The third wave moved forward, huge, furious, implacable. It fairly swallowed the dinghy, and almost simultaneously the men tumbled into the sea. A piece of life-belt had lain in the bottom of the boat, and as the correspondent went overboard he held this to his chest with his left hand.

The January water was icy, and reflected immediately that it was colder than he had expected to find it off the coast of Florida. This appeared to his dazed mind as a fact important enough to be noted at the time. The coldness of the water was sad; it was tragic. This fact was somehow mixed and confused with his opinion of his own situation, so that it seemed almost a proper reason for tears. The water was cold.

When he came to the surface he was conscious of little but the noisy water. 215 Afterward he saw his companions in the sea. The oiler was ahead in the race. He was swimming strongly and rapidly. Off to the correspondent's left, the cook's great white and corked back bulged out of the water, and in the rear the captain was hanging with his one good hand to the keel of the overturned dinghy.

There is a certain immovable quality to a shore, and the correspondent wondered at it amid the confusion of the sea.

It seemed also very attractive; but the correspondent knew that it was a long journey, and he paddled leisurely. The piece of life-preserver lay under him, and sometimes he whirled down the incline of a wave as if he were on a hand-sled.

But finally he arrived at a place in the sea where travel was beset with difficulty. He did not pause swimming to inquire what manner of current had caught him, but there his progress ceased. The shore was set before him like a bit of scenery on a stage, and he looked at it and understood with his eyes each detail of it.

As the cook passed, much farther to the left, the captain was calling to him, "Turn over on your back, cook! Turn over on your back and use the oar."

"All right, sir." The cook turned on his back, and, paddling with an oar, went 220 ahead as if he were a canoe.

Presently the boat also passed to the left of the correspondent, with the captain clinging with one hand to the keel. He would have appeared like a man raising himself to look over a board fence if it were not for the extraordinary gymnastics of the boat. The correspondent marvelled that the captain could still hold to it.

They passed on nearer to shore—the oiler, the cook, the captain—and following them went the water-jar, bouncing gaily over the seas.

The correspondent remained in the grip of this strange new enemy, a current. The shore, with its white slope of sand and its green bluff topped with little silent cottages, was spread like a picture before him. It was very near to him then, but he was impressed as one who, in a gallery, looks at a scene from Brittany or Algiers.

He thought: "I am going to drown? Can it be possible? Can it be possible? Can it be possible?" Perhaps an individual must consider his own death to be the final phenomenon of nature.

225   But later a wave perhaps whirled him out of this small deadly current, for he found suddenly that he could again make progress toward the shore. Later still he was aware that the captain, clinging with one hand to the keel of the dinghy, had his face turned away from the shore and toward him, and was calling his name. "Come to the boat! Come to the boat!"

In his struggle to reach the captain and the boat, he reflected that when one gets properly wearied drowning must really be a comfortable arrangement—a cessation of hostilities accompanied by a large degree of relief; and he was glad of it, for the main thing in his mind for some moments had been horror of the temporary agony; he did not wish to be hurt.

Presently he saw a man running along the shore. He was undressing with most remarkable speed. Coat, trousers, shirt, everything flew magically off him.

"Come to the boat!" called the captain.

"All right, Captain." As the correspondent paddled, he saw the captain let himself down to bottom and leave the boat. Then the correspondent performed his one little marvel of the voyage. A large wave caught him and flung him with ease and supreme speed completely over the boat and far beyond it. It struck him even then as an event in gymnastics and a true miracle of the sea. An overturned boat in the surf is not a plaything to a swimming man.

230   The correspondent arrived in water that reached only to his waist, but his condition did not enable him to stand for more than a moment. Each wave knocked him into a heap, and the undertow pulled at him.

Then he saw the man who had been running and undressing, and undressing and running, come bounding into the water. He dragged ashore the cook, and then waded toward the captain; but the captain waved him away and sent him to the correspondent. He was naked—naked as a tree in winter; but a halo was about his head, and he shone like a saint. He gave a strong pull, and a long drag, and a bully heave at the correspondent's hand. The correspondent, schooled in the minor formulae, said, "Thanks, old man." But suddenly the man cried, "What's that?" He pointed a swift finger. The correspondent said, "Go."

In the shallows, face downward, lay the oiler. His forehead touched sand that was periodically, between each wave, clear of the sea.

The correspondent did not know all that transpired afterward. When he achieved safe ground he fell, striking the sand with each particular part of his body. It was as if he had dropped from a roof, but the thud was grateful to him.

It seems that instantly the beach was populated with men with blankets, clothes, and flasks, and women with coffee-pots and all the remedies sacred to their minds. The welcome of the land to the men from the sea was warm and generous; but a still and dripping shape was carried slowly up the beach, and the land's welcome for it could only be the different and sinister hospitality of the grave.

235   When it came night, the white waves paced to and fro in the moonlight, and the wind brought the sound of the great sea's voice to the men on the shore, and they felt that they could then be interpreters.

1898

QUESTIONS

1. When do you become aware that your view of events in "The Open Boat" is limited to things seen and heard by the four men in the boat? In what specific ways is that important to the story's effect? Where does the story's perspective "expand" to include larger reflections and generalizations? How are they justified by the narrative point of view?

2. Examine paragraphs 3–6; then differentiate the four men as fully as you can. What distinguishing features help you keep them straight as the narrative proceeds? What facts are provided later about each of the men? In which of the men do you become most interested as the story develops?

3. Which, if any, of the following seem like apt statements of the story's theme, and why? Which, if any, seems most central?

   a. All human beings are ultimately the same in that we are all equally powerless against nature.
   b. As the novelist George Eliot once said, "Character is destiny."
   c. In the face of disaster, people tend to become selfless, forgetting their differences and bonding together.
   d. Our individual fates are ultimately determined by forces beyond our control.
   e. We can never know the full truth; all we have is our own limited individual perspective.
   f. Pride is man's downfall.

GABRIEL GARCÍA MÁRQUEZ

A Very Old Man with Enormous Wings[1]

A Tale for Children

On the third day of rain they had killed so many crabs inside the house that Pelayo had to cross his drenched courtyard and throw them into the sea, because the newborn child had a temperature all night and they thought it was due to the stench. The world had been sad since Tuesday. Sea and sky were a single ashgray thing and the sands of the beach, which on March nights glimmered like powdered light, had become a stew of mud and rotten shellfish. The light was so weak at noon that when Pelayo was coming back to the house after throwing away the crabs, it was hard for him to see what it was that was moving and groaning in the rear of the courtyard. He had to go very close to see that it was an old man, a very old man, lying face down in the mud, who, in spite of his tremendous efforts, couldn't get up, impeded by his enormous wings.

Frightened by that nightmare, Pelayo ran to get Elisenda, his wife, who was putting compresses on the sick child, and he took her to the rear of the courtyard. They both looked at the fallen body with mute stupor. He was dressed like a ragpicker.[2] There were only a few faded hairs left on his bald skull and very few teeth in his mouth, and his pitiful condition of a drenched great-grandfather had taken away any sense of grandeur he might have had. His huge buzzard wings, dirty and half-plucked, were forever entangled in the mud. They looked at him so long and

1. Translated by Gregory Rabassa.   2. Someone who earns a living by collecting rags and other refuse.

so closely that Pelayo and Elisenda very soon overcame their surprise and in the end found him familiar. Then they dared speak to him, and he answered in an incomprehensible dialect with a strong sailor's voice. That was how they skipped over the inconvenience of the wings and quite intelligently concluded that he was a lonely castaway from some foreign ship wrecked by the storm. And yet, they called in a neighbor woman who knew everything about life and death to see him, and all she needed was one look to show them their mistake.

"He's an angel," she told them. "He must have been coming for the child, but the poor fellow is so old that the rain knocked him down."

On the following day everyone knew that a flesh-and-blood angel was held captive in Pelayo's house. Against the judgment of the wise neighbor woman, for whom angels in those times were the fugitive survivors of a celestial conspiracy, they did not have the heart to club him to death. Pelayo watched over him all afternoon from the kitchen, armed with his bailiff's[3] club, and before going to bed he dragged him out of the mud and locked him up with the hens in the wire chicken coop. In the middle of the night, when the rain stopped, Pelayo and Elisenda were still killing crabs. A short time afterward the child woke up without a fever and with a desire to eat. Then they felt magnanimous and decided to put the angel on a raft with fresh water and provisions for three days and leave him to his fate on the high seas. But when they went out into the courtyard with the first light of dawn, they found the whole neighborhood in front of the chicken coop having fun with the angel, without the slightest reverence, tossing him things to eat through the openings in the wire as if he weren't a supernatural creature but a circus animal.

5   Father Gonzaga arrived before seven o'clock, alarmed at the strange news. By that time onlookers less frivolous than those at dawn had already arrived and they were making all kinds of conjectures concerning the captive's future. The simplest among them thought that he should be named mayor of the world. Others of sterner mind felt that he should be promoted to the rank of five-star general in order to win all wars. Some visionaries hoped that he could be put to stud in order to implant on earth a race of winged wise men who could take charge of the universe. But Father Gonzaga, before becoming a priest, had been a robust woodcutter. Standing by the wire, he reviewed his catechism in an instant and asked them to open the door so that he could take a close look at that pitiful man who looked more like a huge decrepit hen among the fascinated chickens. He was lying in a corner drying his open wings in the sunlight among the fruit peels and breakfast leftovers that the early risers had thrown him. Alien to the impertinences of the world, he only lifted his antiquarian eyes and murmured something in his dialect when Father Gonzaga went into the chicken coop and said good morning to him in Latin. The parish priest had his first suspicion of an imposter when he saw that he did not understand the language of God or know how to greet His ministers. Then he noticed that seen close up he was much too human: he had an unbearable smell of the outdoors, the back side of his wings was strewn with parasites and his main feathers had been mistreated by terrestrial winds, and nothing about him measured up to the proud dignity of angels. Then he came out of the chicken coop and in a brief sermon warned the curious against the risks of being ingenuous. He reminded them that the devil had the bad habit

3. Local government official, usually one employed to make arrests and serve warrants.

of making use of carnival tricks in order to confuse the unwary. He argued that if wings were not the essential element in determining the difference between a hawk and an airplane, they were even less so in the recognition of angels. Nevertheless, he promised to write a letter to his bishop so that the latter would write to his primate[4] so that the latter would write to the Supreme Pontiff in order to get the final verdict from the highest courts.

His prudence fell on sterile hearts. The news of the captive angel spread with such rapidity that after a few hours the courtyard had the bustle of a marketplace and they had to call in troops with fixed bayonets to disperse the mob that was about to knock the house down. Elisenda, her spine all twisted from sweeping up so much marketplace trash, then got the idea of fencing in the yard and charging five cents admission to see the angel.

The curious came from far away. A traveling carnival arrived with a flying acrobat who buzzed over the crowd several times, but no one paid any attention to him because his wings were not those of an angel but, rather, those of a sidereal[5] bat. The most unfortunate invalids on earth came in search of health: a poor woman who since childhood had been counting her heartbeats and had run out of numbers; a Portuguese man who couldn't sleep because the noise of the stars disturbed him; a sleepwalker who got up at night to undo the things he had done while awake; and many others with less serious ailments. In the midst of that shipwreck disorder that made the earth tremble, Pelayo and Elisenda were happy with fatigue, for in less than a week they had crammed their rooms with money and the line of pilgrims waiting their turn to enter still reached beyond the horizon.

The angel was the only one who took no part in his own act. He spent his time trying to get comfortable in his borrowed nest, befuddled by the hellish heat of the oil lamps and sacramental candles that had been placed along the wire. At first they tried to make him eat some mothballs, which, according to the wisdom of the wise neighbor woman, were the food prescribed for angels. But he turned them down, just as he turned down the papal lunches[6] that the penitents brought him, and they never found out whether it was because he was an angel or because he was an old man that in the end he ate nothing but eggplant mush. His only supernatural virtue seemed to be patience. Especially during the first days, when the hens pecked at him, searching for the stellar parasites that proliferated in his wings, and the cripples pulled out feathers to touch their defective parts with, and even the most merciful threw stones at him, trying to get him to rise so they could see him standing. The only time they succeeded in arousing him was when they burned his side with an iron for branding steers, for he had been motionless for so many hours that they thought he was dead. He awoke with a start, ranting in his hermetic language and with tears in his eyes, and he flapped his wings a couple of times, which brought on a whirlwind of chicken dung and lunar dust and a gale of panic that did not seem to be of this world. Although many thought that his reaction had been one not of rage but of pain, from then on they were careful not to annoy him, because the majority understood that his passivity was not that of a hero taking his ease but that of a cataclysm in repose.

4. Highest bishop of a given state.   5. Of, or relating to, the stars.
6. Expensive, elaborately prepared meals.

Father Gonzaga held back the crowd's frivolity with formulas of maidservant inspiration while awaiting the arrival of a final judgment on the nature of the captive. But the mail from Rome showed no sense of urgency. They spent their time finding out if the prisoner had a navel, if his dialect had any connection with Aramaic, how many times he could fit on the head of a pin, or whether he wasn't just a Norwegian with wings. Those meager letters might have come and gone until the end of time if a providential event had not put an end to the priest's tribulations.

10   It so happened that during those days, among so many other carnival attractions, there arrived in town the traveling show of the woman who had been changed into a spider for having disobeyed her parents. The admission to see her was not only less than the admission to see the angel, but people were permitted to ask her all manner of questions about her absurd state and to examine her up and down so that no one would ever doubt the truth of her horror. She was a frightful tarantula the size of a ram and with the head of a sad maiden. What was most heart-rending, however, was not her outlandish shape but the sincere affliction with which she recounted the details of her misfortune. While still practically a child she had sneaked out of her parents' house to go to a dance, and while she was coming back through the woods after having danced all night without permission, a fearful thunderclap rent the sky in two and through the crack came the lightning bolt of brimstone that changed her into a spider. Her only nourishment came from the meatballs that charitable souls chose to toss into her mouth. A spectacle like that, full of so much human truth and with such a fearful lesson, was bound to defeat without even trying that of a haughty angel who scarcely deigned to look at mortals. Besides, the few miracles attributed to the angel showed a certain mental disorder, like the blind man who didn't recover his sight but grew three new teeth, or the paralytic who didn't get to walk but almost won the lottery, and the leper whose sores sprouted sunflowers. Those consolation miracles, which were more like mocking fun, had already ruined the angel's reputation when the woman who had been changed into a spider finally crushed him completely. That was how Father Gonzaga was cured forever of his insomnia and Pelayo's courtyard went back to being as empty as during the time it had rained for three days and crabs walked through the bedrooms.

The owners of the house had no reason to lament. With the money they saved they built a two-story mansion with balconies and gardens and high netting so that crabs wouldn't get in during the winter, and with iron bars on the windows so that angels wouldn't get in. Pelayo also set up a rabbit warren close to town and gave up his job as bailiff for good, and Elisenda bought some satin pumps with high heels and many dresses of iridescent silk, the kind worn on Sunday by the most desirable women in those times. The chicken coop was the only thing that didn't receive any attention. If they washed it down with creolin[7] and burned tears of myrrh inside it every so often, it was not in homage to the angel but to drive away the dungheap stench that still hung everywhere like a ghost and was turning the new house into an old one. At first, when the child learned to walk, they were careful that he not get too close to the chicken coop. But then they began to lose their fears and got used to the smell, and before the child got his second teeth he'd gone inside the chicken coop to play, where the wires were fall-

---

7. Disinfectant.

ing apart. The angel was no less standoffish with him than with other mortals, but he tolerated the most ingenious infamies with the patience of a dog who had no illusions. They both came down with chicken pox at the same time. The doctor who took care of the child couldn't resist the temptation to listen to the angel's heart, and he found so much whistling in the heart and so many sounds in his kidneys that it seemed impossible for him to be alive. What surprised him most, however, was the logic of his wings. They seemed so natural on that completely human organism that he couldn't understand why other men didn't have them too.

When the child began school it had been some time since the sun and rain had caused the collapse of the chicken coop. The angel went dragging himself about here and there like a stray dying man. They would drive him out of the bedroom with a broom and a moment later find him in the kitchen. He seemed to be in so many places at the same time that they grew to think that he'd been duplicated, that he was reproducing himself all through the house, and the exasperated and unhinged Elisenda shouted that it was awful living in that hell full of angels. He could scarcely eat and his antiquarian eyes had also become so foggy that he went about bumping into posts. All he had left were the bare cannulae of his last feathers. Pelayo threw a blanket over him and extended him the charity of letting him sleep in the shed, and only then did they notice that he had a temperature at night, and was delirious with the tongue twisters of an old Norwegian. That was one of the few times they became alarmed, for they thought he was going to die and not even the wise neighbor woman had been able to tell them what to do with dead angels.

And yet he not only survived his worst winter, but seemed improved with the first sunny days. He remained motionless for several days in the farthest corner of the courtyard, where no one would see him, and at the beginning of December some large, stiff feathers began to grow on his wings, the feathers of a scarecrow, which looked more like another misfortune of decrepitude. But he must have known the reason for those changes, for he was quite careful that no one should notice them, that no one should hear the sea chanteys that he sometimes sang under the stars. One morning Elisenda was cutting some bunches of onions for lunch when a wind that seemed to come from the high seas blew into the kitchen. Then she went to the window and caught the angel in his first attempts at flight. They were so clumsy that his fingernails opened a furrow in the vegetable patch and he was on the point of knocking the shed down with the ungainly flapping that slipped on the light and couldn't get a grip on the air. But he did manage to gain altitude. Elisenda let out a sigh of relief, for herself and for him, when she saw him pass over the last houses, holding himself up in some way with the risky flapping of a senile vulture. She kept watching him even when she was through cutting the onions and she kept on watching until it was no longer possible for her to see him, because then he was no longer an annoyance in her life but an imaginary dot on the horizon of the sea.

1968

QUESTIONS

1. The subtitle of this story is "A Tale for Children." Why and how does this seem like an apt description? an inapt or ironic one?

2. How do the various characters interpret the winged man? How do they arrive at their interpretations? What might their interpretations reveal about them? about people and/or the process of interpretation in general?
3. Why do so many people at first come to see the winged man and later stop doing so? Why is Elisenda so relieved when he finally flies away? What insights into human behavior might be revealed here?

LOUISE ERDRICH

Love Medicine

I never really done much with my life, I suppose. I never had a television. Grandma Kashpaw had one inside her apartment at the Senior Citizens, so I used to go there and watch my favorite shows. For a while she used to call me the biggest waste on the reservation and hark back to how she saved me from my own mother, who wanted to tie me in a potato sack and throw me in a slough. Sure, I was grateful to Grandma Kashpaw for saving me like that, for raising me, but gratitude gets old. After a while, stale. I had to stop thanking her. One day I told her I had paid her back in full by staying at her beck and call. I'd do anything for Grandma. She knew that. Besides, I took care of Grandpa like nobody else could, on account of what a handful he'd gotten to be.

But that was nothing. I know the tricks of mind and body inside out without ever having trained for it, because I got the touch. It's a thing you got to be born with. I got secrets in my hands that nobody ever knew to ask. Take Grandma Kashpaw with her tired veins all knotted up in her legs like clumps of blue snails. I take my fingers and I snap them on the knots. The medicine flows out of me. The touch. I run my fingers up the maps of those rivers of veins or I knock very gentle above their hearts or I make a circling motion on their stomachs, and it helps them. They feel much better. Some women pay me five dollars.

I couldn't do the touch for Grandpa, though. He was a hard nut. You know, some people fall right through the hole in their lives. It's invisible, but they come to it after time, never knowing where. There is this woman here, Lulu Lamartine, who always had a thing for Grandpa. She loved him since she was a girl and always said he was a genius. Now she says that his mind got so full it exploded.

How can I doubt that? I know the feeling when your mental power builds up too far. I always used to say that's why the Indians got drunk. Even statistically we're the smartest people on the earth. Anyhow with Grandpa I couldn't hardly believe it, because all my youth he stood out as a hero to me. When he started getting toward second childhood he went through different moods. He would stand in the woods and cry at the top of his shirt. It scared me, scared everyone, Grandma worst of all.

5   Yet he was so smart—do you believe it?—that he *knew* he was getting foolish.

He said so. He told me that December I failed school and come back on the train to Hoopdance. I didn't have nowhere else to go. He picked me up there and he said it straight out: "I'm getting into my second childhood." And then he said something else I still remember: "I been chosen for it. I couldn't say no." So I figure that a man so smart all his life—tribal chairman and the star of movies and even pictured in the statehouse and on cans of snuff—would know what he's doing by saying yes. I think he was called to second childhood like anybody else gets a call for the priesthood or the army or whatever. So I really did not listen too hard when the doctor said this was some kind of disease old people got eating too much sugar. You just can't tell me that a man who went to Washington and gave them bureaucrats what for could lose his mind from eating too much Milky Way. No, he put second childhood on himself.

Behind those songs he sings out in the middle of Mass, and back of those stories that everybody knows by heart, Grandpa is thinking hard about life. I know the feeling. Sometimes I'll throw up a smokescreen to think behind. I'll hitch up to Winnipeg and play the Space Invaders[1] for six hours, but all the time there and back I will be thinking some fairly deep thoughts that surprise even me, and I'm used to it. As for him, if it was just the thoughts there wouldn't be no problem. Smokescreen is what irritates the social structure, see, and Grandpa has done things that just distract people to the point they want to throw him in the cookie jar where they keep the mentally insane. He's far from that, I know for sure, but even Grandma had trouble keeping her patience once he started sneaking off to Lamartine's place. He's not supposed to have his candy, and Lulu feeds it to him. That's *one* of the reasons why he goes.

Grandma tried to get me to put the touch on Grandpa soon after he began stepping out. I didn't want to, but before Grandma started telling me again what a bad state my bare behind was in when she first took me home, I thought I should at least pretend.

I put my hands on either side of Grandpa's head. You wouldn't look at him and say he was crazy. He's a fine figure of a man, as Lamartine would say, with all his hair and half his teeth, a beak like a hawk, and cheeks like the blades of a hatchet. They put his picture on all the tourist guides to North Dakota and even copied his face for artistic paintings. I guess you could call him a monument all of himself. He started grinning when I put my hands on his templates, and I knew right then he knew how come I touched him. I knew the smokescreen was going to fall.

And I was right: just for a moment it fell.

"Let's pitch whoopee," he said across my shoulder to Grandma.

They don't use that expression much around here anymore, but for damn sure it must have meant something. It got her goat right quick.

She threw my hands off his head herself and stood in front of him, overmatching him pound for pound, and taller too, for she had a growth spurt in middle age while he had shrunk, so now the length and breadth of her surpassed him. She glared and spoke her piece into his face about how he was off at all hours tomcatting and chasing Lamartine again and making a damn old fool of himself.

"And you got no more whoopee to pitch anymore anyhow!" she yelled at last, surprising me so my jaw just dropped, for us kids all had pretended for so long that those rustling sounds we heard from their side of the room at night never happened. She sure had pretended it, up till now, anyway. I saw that tears were in her eyes. And that's when I saw how much grief and love she felt for him. And it gave me a real shock to the system. You see I thought love got easier over the years so it didn't hurt so bad when it hurt, or feel so good when it felt good. I thought it smoothed out and old people hardly noticed it. I thought it curled up and died, I guess. Now I saw it rear up like a whip and lash.

10

1. Extremely popular and influential 1980s arcade video game.

15   She loved him. She was jealous. She mourned him like the dead.

And he just smiled into the air, trapped in the seams of his mind.

So I didn't know what to do. I was in a laundry then. They was like parents to me, the way they had took me home and reared me. I could see her point for wanting to get him back the way he was so at least she could argue with him, sleep with him, not be shamed out by Lamartine. She'd always love him. That hit me like a ton of bricks. For one whole day I felt this odd feeling that cramped my hands. When you have the touch, that's where longing gets you. I never loved like that. It made me feel all inspired to see them fight, and I wanted to go out and find a woman who I would love until one of us died or went crazy. But I'm not like that really. From time to time I heal a person all up good inside, however when it comes to the long shot I doubt that I got staying power.

And you need that, staying power, going out to love somebody. I knew this quality was not going to jump on me with no effort. So I turned my thoughts back to Grandma and Grandpa. I felt her side of it with my hands and my tangled guts, and I felt his side of it within the stretch of my mentality. He had gone out to lunch one day and never came back. He was fishing in the middle of Matchimanito. And there was big thoughts on his line, and he kept throwing them back for even bigger ones that would explain to him, say, the meaning of how we got here and why we have to leave so soon. All in all, I could not see myself treating Grandpa with the touch, bringing him back, when the real part of him had chose to be off thinking somewhere. It was only the rest of him that stayed around causing trouble, after all, and we could handle most of it without any problem.

Besides, it was hard to argue with his reasons for doing some things. Take Holy Mass. I used to go there just every so often, when I got frustrated mostly, because even though I know the Higher Power dwells everyplace, there's something very calming about the cool greenish inside of our mission. Or so I thought, anyway. Grandpa was the one who stripped off my delusions in this matter, for it was he who busted right through what Father calls the sacred serenity of the place.

20   We filed in that time. Me and Grandpa. We sat down in our pews. Then the rosary got started up pre-Mass and that's when Grandpa filled up his chest and opened his mouth and belted out them words.

HAIL MARIE FULL OF GRACE.

He had a powerful set of lungs.

And he kept on like that. He did not let up. He hollered and he yelled them prayers, and I guess people was used to him by now, because they only muttered theirs and did not quit and gawk like I did. I was getting red-faced, I admit. I give him the elbow once or twice, but that wasn't nothing to him. He kept on. He shrieked to heaven and he pleaded like a movie actor and he pounded his chest like Tarzan in the Lord I Am Not Worthies. I thought he might hurt himself. Then after a while I guess I got used to it, and that's when I wondered: how come?

So afterwards I out and asked him. "How come? How come you yelled?"

25   "God don't hear me otherwise," said Grandpa Kashpaw.

I sweat. I broke right into a little cold sweat at my hairline because I knew this was perfectly right and for years not one damn other person had noticed it. God's been going deaf. Since the Old Testament, God's been deafening up on us. I read, see. Besides the dictionary, which I'm constantly in use of, I had this Bible once. I read it. I found there was discrepancies between then and now. It struck me. Here God used to raineth bread from clouds, smite the Phillipines, sling fire down on red-light districts where people got stabbed. He even appeared in person every once in a while. God used to pay attention, is what I'm saying.

Now there's your God in the Old Testament and there is Chippewa Gods as well. Indian Gods, good and bad, like tricky Nanabozho or the water monster, Missepeshu, who lives over in Matchimanito. That water monster was the last God I ever heard to appear. It had a weakness for young girls and grabbed one of the Pillagers off her rowboat. She got to shore all right, but only after this monster had its way with her. She's an old lady now. Old Lady Pillager. She still doesn't like to see her family fish that lake.

Our Gods aren't perfect, is what I'm saying, but at least they come around. They'll do a favor if you ask them right. You don't have to yell. But you do have to know, like I said, how to ask in the right way. That makes problems, because to ask proper was an art that was lost to the Chippewas once the Catholics gained ground. Even now, I have to wonder if Higher Power turned it back, if we got to yell, or if we just don't speak its language.

I looked around me. How else could I explain what all I had seen in my short life—King smashing his fist in things, Gordie drinking himself down to the Bismarck hospitals, or Aunt June left by a white man to wander off in the snow. How else to explain the times my touch don't work, and farther back, to the oldtime Indians who was swept away in the outright germ warfare and dirty-dog killing of the whites. In those times, us Indians was so much kindlier than now.

We took them in. 30

Oh yes, I'm bitter as an old cutworm just thinking of how they done to us and doing still.

So Grandpa Kashpaw just opened my eyes a little there. Was there any sense relying on a God whose ears was stopped? Just like the government? I says then, right off, maybe we got nothing but ourselves. And that's not much, just personally speaking. I know I don't got the cold hard potatoes it takes to understand everything. Still, there's things I'd like to do. For instance, I'd like to help some people like my Grandpa and Grandma Kashpaw get back some happiness within the tail ends of their lives.

I told you once before I couldn't see my way clear to putting the direct touch on Grandpa's mind, and I kept my moral there, but something soon happened to make me think a little bit of mental adjustment wouldn't do him and the rest of us no harm.

It was after we saw him one afternoon in the sunshine courtyard of the Senior Citizens with Lulu Lamartine. Grandpa used to like to dig there. He had his little dandelion fork out, and he was prying up them dandelions right and left while Lamartine watched him.

"He's scratching up the dirt, all right," said Grandma, watching Lamartine 35 watch Grandpa out the window.

Now Lamartine was about half the considerable size of Grandma, but you would never think of sizes anyway. They were different in an even more noticeable way. It was the difference between a house fixed up with paint and picky fence, and a house left to weather away into the soft earth, is what I'm saying. Lamartine was jacked up, latticed, shuttered, and vinyl sided, while Grandma sagged and bulged on her slipped foundations and let her hair go the silver gray of rain-dried lumber. Right now, she eyed the Lamartine's pert flowery dress with such a look it despaired me. I knew what this could lead to with Grandma.

Alternating tongue storms and rock-hard silences was hard on a man, even one who didn't notice, like Grandpa. So I went fetching him.

But he was gone when I popped through the little screen door that led out on the courtyard. There was nobody out there either, to point which way they went. Just the dandelion fork quibbling upright in the ground. That gave me an idea. I snookered over to the Lamartine's door and I listened in first, then knocked. But nobody. So I went walking through the lounges and around the card tables. Still nobody. Finally it was my touch that led me to the laundry room. I cracked the door. I went in. There they were. And he was really loving her up good, boy, and she was going hell for leather. Sheets was flapping on the lines above, and wash-cloths, pillowcases, shirts was also flying through the air, for they was trying to clear out a place for themselves in a high-heaped but shallow laundry cart. The washers and dryers was all on, chock-full of quarters, shaking and moaning. I couldn't hear what Grandpa and the Lamartine was billing and cooing, and they couldn't hear me.

I didn't know what to do, so I went inside and shut the door.

The Lamartine wore a big curly light-brown wig. Looked like one of them squeaky little white-people dogs. Poodles they call them. Anyway, that wig is what saved us from the worse. For I could hardly shout and tell them I was in there, no more could I try and grab him. I was trapped where I was. There was nothing I could really do but hold the door shut. I was scared of somebody else upsetting in and really getting an eyeful. Turned out though, in the heat of the clinch, as I was trying to avert my eyes you see, the Lamartine's curly wig jumped off her head. And if you ever been in the midst of something and had a big change like that occur in the someone, you can't help know how it devastates your basic urges. Not only that, but her wig was almost with a life of its own. Grandpa's eyes were bugging at the change already, and swear to God if the thing didn't rear up and pop him in the face like it was going to start something. He scrambled up, Grandpa did, and the Lamartine jumped up after him all addled looking. They just stared at each other, huffing and puffing, with quizzical expression. The surprise seemed to drive all sense completely out of Grandpa's mind.

40   "The letter was what started the fire," he said. "I never would have done it."

"What letter?" said the Lamartine. She was stiff-necked now, and elegant, even bald, like some alien queen. I gave her back the wig. The Lamartine replaced it on her head, and whenever I saw her after that, I couldn't help thinking of her bald, with special powers, as if from another planet.

"That was a close call," I said to Grandpa after she had left.

But I think he had already forgot the incident. He just stood there all quiet and thoughtful. You really wouldn't think he was crazy. He looked like he was just about to say something important, explaining himself. He said something, all right, but it didn't have nothing to do with anything that made sense.

He wondered where the heck he put his dandelion fork. That's when I decided about the mental adjustment.

45 Now what was mostly our problem was not so much that he was not all there, but that what was there of him often hankered after Lamartine. If we could put a stop to that, I thought, we might be getting someplace. But here, see, my touch was of no use. For what could I snap my fingers at to make him faithful to Grandma? Like the quality of staying power, this faithfulness was invisible. I

know it's something that you got to acquire, but I never known where from. Maybe there's no rhyme or reason to it, like my getting the touch, and then again maybe it's a kind of magic.

It was Grandma Kashpaw who thought of it in the end. She knows things. Although she will not admit she has a scrap of Indian blood in her, there's no doubt in my mind she's got some Chippewa. How else would you explain the way she'll be sitting there, in front of her TV story, rocking in her armchair and suddenly she turns on me, her brown eyes hard as lake-bed flint.

"Lipsha Morrissey," she'll say, "you went out last night and got drunk."

How did she know that? I'll hardly remember it myself. Then she'll say she just had a feeling or ache in the scar of her hand or a creak in her shoulder. She is constantly being told things by little aggravations in her joints or by her household appliances. One time she told Gordie never to ride with a crazy Lamartine boy. She had seen something in the polished-up tin of her bread toaster. So he didn't. Sure enough, the time came we heard how Lyman and Henry went out of control in their car, ending up in the river. Lyman swam to the top, but Henry never made it.

Thanks to Grandma's toaster, Gordie was probably spared.

Someplace in the blood Grandma Kashpaw knows things. She also remem- 50 bers things, I found. She keeps things filed away. She's got a memory like them video games that don't forget your score. One reason she remembers so many details about the trouble I gave her in early life is so she can flash back her total when she needs to.

Like now. Take the love medicine. I don't know where she remembered that from. It came tumbling from her mind like an asteroid off the corner of the screen.[2]

Of course she starts out by mentioning the time I had this accident in church and did she leave me there with wet overhalls? No she didn't. And ain't I glad? Yes I am. Now what you want now, Grandma?

But when she mentions them love medicines, I feel my back prickle at the danger. These love medicines is something of an old Chippewa specialty. No other tribe has got them down so well. But love medicines is not for the layman to handle. You don't just go out and get one without paying for it. Before you get one, even, you should go through one hell of a lot of mental condensation. You got to think it over. Choose the right one. You could really mess up your life grinding up the wrong little thing.

So anyhow, I said to Grandma I'd give this love medicine some thought. I knew the best thing was to go ask a specialist like Old Lady Pillager, who lives up in a tangle of bush and never shows herself. But the truth is I was afraid of her, like everyone else. She was known for putting the twisted mouth on people, seizing up their hearts. Old Lady Pillager was serious business, and I have always thought it best to steer clear of that whenever I could. That's why I took the powers in my own hands. That's why I did what I could.

I put my whole mentality to it, nothing held back. After a while I started to 55 remember things I'd heard gossiped over.

I heard of this person once who carried a charm of seeds that looked like baby pearls. They was attracted to a metal knife, which made them powerful. But I didn't know where them seeds grew. Another love charm I heard about I couldn't

---

2. Allusion to *Asteroids*, another popular 1980s video arcade game.

go along with, because how was I suppose to catch frogs in the act, which it required. Them little creatures is slippery and fast. And then the powerfullest of all, the most extreme, involved nail clips and such. I wasn't anywhere near asking Grandma to provide me all the little body bits that this last love recipe called for. I went walking around for days just trying to think up something that would work.

Well I got it. If it hadn't been the early fall of the year, I never would have got it. But I was sitting underneath a tree one day down near the school just watching people's feet go by when something tells me, look up! Look up! So I look up, and I see two honkers, Canada geese, the kind with little masks on their faces, a bird what mates for life. I see them flying right over my head naturally preparing to land in some slough on the reservation, which they certainly won't get off of alive.

It hits me, anyway. Them geese, they mate for life. And I think to myself, just what if I went out and got a pair? And just what if I fed some part—say the goose heart—of the female to Grandma and Grandpa ate the other heart? Wouldn't that work? Maybe it's all invisible, and then maybe again it's magic. Love is a stony road. We know that for sure. If it's true that the higher feelings of devotion get lodged in the heart like people say, then we'd be home free. If not, eating goose heart couldn't harm nobody anyway. I thought it was worth my effort, and Grandma Kashpaw thought so, too. She had always known a good idea when she heard one. She borrowed me Grandpa's gun.

So I went out to this particular slough, maybe the exact same slough I never got thrown in by my mother, thanks to Grandma Kashpaw, and I hunched down in a good comfortable pile of rushes. I got my gun loaded up. I ate a few of these soft baloney sandwiches Grandma made me for lunch. And then I waited. The cattails blown back and forth above my head. Them stringy blue herons was spearing up their prey. The thing I know how to do best in this world, the thing I been training for all my life, is to wait. Sitting there and sitting there was no hardship on me. I got to thinking about some funny things that happened. There was this one time that Lulu Lamartine's little blue tweety bird, a paraclete, I guess you'd call it, flown up inside her dress and got lost within there. I recalled her running out into the hallway trying to yell something, shaking. She was doing a right good jig there, cutting the rug for sure, and the thing is it *never* flown out. To this day people speculate where it went. They fear she might perhaps of crushed it in her corsets. It sure hasn't ever yet been seen alive. I thought of funny things for a while, but then I used them up, and strange things that happened started weaseling their way into my mind.

60   I got to thinking quite naturally of the Lamartine's cousin named Wrist-watch. I never knew what his real name was. They called him Wristwatch because he got his father's broken wristwatch as a young boy when his father passed on. Never in his whole life did Wristwatch take his father's watch off. He didn't care if it worked, although after a while he got sensitive when people asked what time it was, teasing him. He often put it to his ear like he was listening to the tick. But it was broken for good and forever, people said so, at least that's what they thought.

Well I saw Wristwatch smoking in his pickup one afternoon and by nine that evening he was dead.

He died sitting at the Lamartine's table, too. As she told it, Wristwatch had just eaten himself a good-size dinner and she said would he take seconds on the hot dish when he fell over to the floor. They turnt him over. He was gone. But here's the strange thing: when the Senior Citizen's orderly took the pulse he noticed that the wristwatch Wristwatch wore was now working. The moment he died the wristwatch started keeping perfect time. They buried him with the watch still ticking on his arm.

I got to thinking. What if some gravediggers dug up Wristwatch's casket in two hundred years and that watch was still going? I thought what question they would ask and it was this: Whose hand wound it?

I started shaking like a piece of grass at just the thought.

Not to get off the subject or nothing. I was still hunkered in the slough. It was passing late into the afternoon and still no honkers had touched down. Now I don't need to tell you that the waiting did not get to me, it was the chill. The rushes was very soft, but damp. I was getting cold and debating to leave, when they landed. Two geese swimming here and there as big as life, looking deep into each other's little pinhole eyes. Just the ones I was looking for. So I lifted Grandpa's gun to my shoulder and I aimed perfectly, and *blam! Blam!* I delivered two accurate shots. But the thing is, them shots missed. I couldn't hardly believe it. Whether it was that the stock had warped or the barrel got bent someways, I don't quite know, but anyway them geese flown off into the dim sky, and Lipsha Morrissey was left there in the rushes with evening fallen and his two cold hands empty. He had before him just the prospect of another day of bone-cracking chill in them rushes, and the thought of it got him depressed.

Now it isn't my style, in no way, to get depressed.

So I said to myself, Lipsha Morrissey, you're a happy S.O.B. who could be covered up with weeds by now down at the bottom of this slough, but instead you're alive to tell the tale. You might have problems in life, but you still got the touch. You got the power, Lipsha Morrissey. Can't argue that. So put your mind to it and figure out how not to be depressed.

I took my advice. I put my mind to it. But I never saw at the time how my thoughts led me astray toward a tragic outcome none could have known. I ignored all the danger, all the limits, for I was tired of sitting in the slough and my feet were numb. My face was aching. I was chilled, so I played with fire. I told myself love medicine was simple. I told myself the old superstitions was just that— strange beliefs. I told myself to take the ten dollars Mary MacDonald had paid me for putting the touch on her arthritis joint, and the other five I hadn't spent yet from winning bingo last Thursday. I told myself to go down to the Red Owl store.

And here is what I did that made the medicine backfire. I took an evil shortcut. I looked at birds that was dead and froze.

All right. So now I guess you will say, "Slap a malpractice suit on Lipsha Morrissey."

I heard of those suits. I used to think it was a color clothing quack doctors had to wear so you could tell them from the good ones. Now I know better that it's law.

As I walked back from the Red Owl with the rock-hard, heavy turkeys, I argued to myself about malpractice. I thought of faith. I thought to myself that faith could be called belief against the odds and whether or not there's any proof. How does that sound? I thought how we might have to yell to be heard by Higher Power, but that's not saying it's not *there*. And that is faith for you. It's belief even when the goods don't deliver. Higher Power makes promises we all know they can't back up, but anybody ever go and slap an old malpractice suit on God? Or the U.S. government? No they don't. Faith might be stupid, but it gets us through. So what I'm heading at is this. I finally convinced myself that the real actual power to the love medicine was not the goose heart itself but the faith in the cure.

I didn't believe it, I knew it was wrong, but by then I had waded so far into my lie I was stuck there. And then I went one step further.

The next day, I cleaned the hearts away from the paper packages of gizzards inside the turkeys. Then I wrapped them hearts with a clean hankie and brung them both to get blessed up at the mission. I wanted to get official blessings from the priest, but when Father answered the door to the rectory, wiping his hands on a little towel, I could tell he was a busy man.

75   "Booshoo,[3] Father," I said. "I got a slight request to make of you this afternoon."

"What is it?" he said.

"Would you bless this package?" I held out the hankie with the hearts tied inside it.

He looked at the package, questioning it.

"It's turkey hearts," I honestly had to reply.

80   A look of annoyance crossed his face.

"Why don't you bring this matter over to Sister Martin," he said. "I have duties."

And so, although the blessing wouldn't be as powerful, I went over to the Sisters with the package.

I rung the bell, and they brought Sister Martin to the door. I had her as a music teacher, but I was always so shy then. I never talked out loud. Now, I had grown taller than Sister Martin. Looking down, I saw that she was not feeling up to snuff. Brown circles hung under her eyes.

"What's the matter?" she said, not noticing who I was.

85   "Remember me, Sister?"

She squinted up at me.

"Oh yes," she said after a moment. "I'm sorry, you're the youngest of the Kashpaws. Gordie's brother."

Her face warmed up.

"Lipsha," I said, "that's my name."

90   "Well, Lipsha," she said, smiling broad at me now, "what can I do for you?"

They always said she was the kindest-hearted of the Sisters up the hill, and she was. She brought me back into their own kitchen and made me take a big yellow wedge of cake and a glass of milk.

"Now tell me," she said, nodding at my package. "What have you got wrapped up so carefully in those handkerchiefs?"

Like before, I answered honestly.

"Ah," said Sister Martin. "Turkey hearts." She waited.

95   "I hoped you could bless them."

She waited some more, smiling with her eyes. Kindhearted though she was, I began to sweat. A person could not pull the wool down over Sister Martin. I stumbled through my mind for an explanation, quick, that wouldn't scare her off.

3. That is, *Bonjour,* French for "good day" or "hello."

"They're a present," I said, "for Saint Kateri's[4] statue."

"She's not a saint yet."

"I know," I stuttered on. "In the hopes they will crown her."

"Lipsha," she said, "I never heard of such a thing." 100

So I told her. "Well the truth is," I said, "it's a kind of medicine."

"For what?"

"Love."

"Oh Lipsha," she said after a moment, "you don't need any medicine. I'm sure any girl would like you exactly the way you are."

I just sat there. I felt miserable, caught in my pack of lies. 105

"Tell you what," she said, seeing how bad I felt, "my blessing won't make any difference anyway. But there is something you can do."

I looked up at her, hopeless.

"Just be yourself."

I looked down at my plate. I knew I wasn't much to brag about right then, and I shortly became even less. For as I walked out the door I stuck my fingers in the cup of holy water that was sacred from their touches. I put my fingers in and blessed the hearts, quick, with my own hand.

I went back to Grandma and sat down in her little kitchen at the Senior Citi- 110 zens. I unwrapped them hearts on the table, and her hard agate eyes went soft. She said she wasn't even going to cook those hearts up but eat them raw so their power would go down strong as possible.

I couldn't hardly watch when she munched hers. Now that's true love. I was worried about how she would get Grandpa to eat his, but she told me she'd think of something and don't worry. So I did not. I was supposed to hide off in her bedroom while she put dinner on a plate for Grandpa and fixed up the heart so he'd eat it. I caught a glint of the plate she was making for him. She put that heart smack on a piece of lettuce like in a restaurant and then attached to it a little heap of boiled peas.

He sat down. I was listening in the next room.

She said, "Why don't you have some mash potato?" So he had some mash potato. Then she gave him a little piece of boiled meat. He ate that. Then she said, "Why you didn't never touch your salad yet. See that heart? I'm feeding you it because the doctor said your blood needs building up."

I couldn't help it, at that point I peeked through a crack in the door.

I saw Grandpa picking at that heart on his plate with a certain look. He didn't 115 look appetized at all, is what I'm saying. I doubted our plan was going to work. Grandma was getting worried, too. She told him one more time, loudly, that he had to eat that heart.

"Swallow it down," she said. "You'll hardly notice it."

He just looked at her straight on. The way he looked at her made me think I was going to see the smokescreen drop a second time, and sure enough it happened.

"What you want me to eat this for so bad?" he asked her uncannily.

4. Kateri Kekakwitha (1656–80), "Lily of the Mohawk," born in what is now upstate New York to a Mohawk father and an Algonquin mother who was a devout Christian. Following the deaths of her parents, Kateri moved to a Jesuit mission near Montreal to spend the rest of her short life in prayer and chastity. Miracles were attributed to her after her death; she was beatified in 1980 and canonized in 1991.

386 CH. 6 / THEME

Now Grandma knew the jig was up. She knew that he knew she was working medicine. He put his fork down. He rolled the heart around his saucer plate.

120   "I don't want to eat this," he said to Grandma. "It don't look good."

"Why it's fresh grade-A," she told him. "One hundred percent."

He didn't ask percent what, but his eyes took on an even more warier look.

"Just go on and try it," she said, taking the salt shaker up in her hand. She was getting annoyed. "Not tasty enough? You want me to salt it for you?" She waved the shaker over his plate.

"All right, skinny white girl!" She had got Grandpa mad. Oopsy-daisy, he popped the heart into his mouth. I was about to yawn loudly and come out of the bedroom. I was about ready for this crash of wills to be over, when I saw he was still up to his old tricks. First he rolled it into one side of his cheek. "Mmmmm," he said. Then he rolled it into the other side of his cheek. "Mmmmmmm," again. Then he stuck his tongue out with the heart on it and put it back, and there was no time to react. He had pulled Grandma's leg once too far. Her goat was got. She was so mad she hopped up quick as a wink and slugged him between the shoulderblades to make him swallow.

125   Only thing is, he choked.

He choked real bad. A person can choke to death. You ever sit down at a restaurant table and up above you there is a list of instructions what to do if something slides down the wrong pipe? It sure makes you chew slow, that's for damn sure. When Grandpa fell off his chair better believe me that little graphic illustrated poster fled into my mind. I jumped out the bedroom. I done everything within my power that I could do to unlodge what was choking him. I squeezed underneath his rib cage. I socked him in the back. I was desperate. But here's the factor of decision: he wasn't choking on the heart alone. There was more to it than that. It was other things that choked him as well. It didn't seem like he wanted to struggle or fight. Death came and tapped his chest, so he went just like that. I'm sorry all through my body at what I done to him with that heart, and there's those who will say Lipsha Morrissey is just excusing himself off the hook by giving song and dance about how Grandpa gave up.

Maybe I can't admit what I did. My touch had gone worthless, that is true. But here is what I seen while he lay in my arms.

You hear a person's life will flash before their eyes when they're in danger. It was him in danger, not me, but it was *his* life come over me. I saw him dying, and it was like someone pulled the shade down in a room. His eyes clouded over and squeezed shut, but just before that I looked in. He was still fishing in the middle of Matchimanito. Big thoughts was on his line and he had half a case of beer in the boat. He waved at me, grinned, and then the bobber went under.

Grandma had gone out of the room crying for help. I bunched my force up in my hands and I held him. I was so wound up I couldn't even breathe. All the moments he had spent with me, all the times he had hoisted me on his shoulders or pointed into the leaves was concentrated in that moment. Time was flashing back and forth like a pinball machine. Lights blinked and balls hopped and rubber bands chirped, until suddenly I realized the last ball had gone down the drain and there was nothing. I felt his force leaving him, flowing out of Grandpa never to return. I felt his mind weakening. The bobber going under in the lake. And I felt the touch retreat back into the darkness inside my body, from where it came.

130   One time, long ago, both of us were fishing together. We caught a big old snapper what started towing us around like it was a motor. "This here fishline is

pretty damn good," Grandpa said. "Let's keep this turtle on and see where he takes us." So we rode along behind that turtle, watching as from time to time it surfaced. The thing was just about the size of a washtub. It took us all around the lake twice, and as it was traveling, Grandpa said something as a joke. "Lipsha," he said, "we are glad your mother didn't want you because we was always looking for a boy like you who would tow us around the lake."

"I ain't no snapper. Snappers is so stupid they stay alive when their head's chopped off," I said.

"That ain't stupidity," said Grandpa. "Their brain's just in their heart, like yours is."

When I looked up, I knew the fuse had blown between my heart and my mind and that a terrible understanding was to be given.

Grandma got back into the room and I saw her stumble. And then she went down too. It was like a house you can't hardly believe has stood so long, through years of record weather, suddenly goes down in the worst yet. It makes sense, is what I'm saying, but you still can't hardly believe it. You think a person you know has got through death and illness and being broke and living on commodity rice will get through anything. Then they fold and you see how fragile were the stones that underpinned them. You see how instantly the ground can shift you thought was solid. You see the stop signs and the yellow dividing markers of roads you traveled and all the instructions you had played according to vanish. You see how all the everyday things you counted on was just a dream you had been having by which you run your whole life. She had been over me, like a sheer overhang of rock dividing Lipsha Morrissey from outer space. And now she went underneath. It was as though the banks gave way on the shores of Matchimanito, and where Grandpa's passing was just the bobber swallowed under by his biggest thought, her fall was the house and the rock under it sliding after, sending half the lake splashing up to the clouds.

Where there was nothing.

135

You play them games never knowing what you see. When I fell into the dream alongside of both of them I saw that the dominions I had defended myself from anciently was but delusions of the screen. Blips of light. And I was scot-free now, whistling through space.

I don't know how I come back. I don't know from where. They was slapping my face when I arrived back at Senior Citizens and they was oxygenating her. I saw her chest move, almost unwilling. She sighed the way she would when somebody bothered her in the middle of a row of beads she was counting. I think it irritated her to no end that they brought her back. I knew from the way she looked after they took the mask off, she was not going to forgive them disturbing her restful peace. Nor was she forgiving Lipsha Morrissey. She had been stepping out onto the road of death, she told the children later at the funeral. I asked was there any stop signs or dividing markers on that road, but she clamped her lips in a vise the way she always done when she was mad.

Which didn't bother me. I knew when things had cleared out she wouldn't have no choice. I was not going to speculate where the blame was put for Grandpa's death. We was in it together. She had slugged him between the shoulders. My touch had failed him, never to return.

All the blood children and the took-ins, like me, came home from Minneapolis and Chicago, where they had relocated years ago. They stayed with friends on the reservation or with Aurelia or slept on Grandma's floor. They were struck down with grief and bereavement to be sure, every one of them. At the funeral I sat down in the back of the church with Albertine. She had gotten all skinny and ragged haired from cramming all her years of study into two or three. She had decided that to be a nurse was not enough for her so she was going to be a doctor. But the way she was straining her mind didn't look too hopeful. Her eyes were bloodshot from driving and crying. She took my hand. From the back we watched all the children and the mourners as they hunched over their prayers, their hands stuffed full of Kleenex. It was someplace in that long sad service that my vision shifted. I began to see things different, more clear. The family kneeling down turned to rocks in a field. It struck me how strong and reliable grief was, and death. Until the end of time, death would be our rock.

140   So I had perspective on it all, for death gives you that. All the Kashpaw children had done various things to me in their lives—shared their folks with me, loaned me cash, beat me up in secret—and I decided, because of death, then and there I'd call it quits. If I ever saw King again, I'd shake his hand. Forgiving somebody else made the whole thing easier to bear.

Everybody saw Grandpa off into the next world. And then the Kashpaws had to get back to their jobs, which was numerous and impressive. I had a few beers with them and I went back to Grandma, who had sort of got lost in the shuffle of everybody being sad about Grandpa and glad to see one another.

Zelda had sat beside her the whole time and was sitting with her now. I wanted to talk to Grandma, say how sorry I was, that it wasn't her fault, but only mine. I would have, but Zelda gave me one of her looks of strict warning as if to say, "I'll take care of Grandma. Don't horn in on the women."

If only Zelda knew, I thought, the sad realities would change her. But of course I couldn't tell the dark truth.

It was evening, late. Grandma's light was on underneath a crack in the door. About a week had passed since we buried Grandpa. I knocked first but there wasn't no answer, so I went right in. The door was unlocked. She was there but she didn't notice me at first. Her hands were tied up in her rosary, and her gaze was fully absorbed in the easy chair opposite her, the one that had always been Grandpa's favorite. I stood there, staring with her, at the little green nubs in the cloth and plastic armrest covers and the sad little hair-tonic stain he had made on the white doily where he laid his head. For the life of me I couldn't figure what she was staring at. Thin space. Then she turned.

145   "He ain't gone yet," she said.

Remember that chill I luckily didn't get from waiting in the slough? I got it now. I felt it start from the very center of me, where fear hides, waiting to attack. It spiraled outward so that in minutes my fingers and teeth were shaking and clattering. I knew she told the truth. She seen Grandpa. Whether or not he had been there is not the point. She had *seen* him, and that meant anybody else could see him, too. Not only that but, as is usually the case with these here ghosts, he had a certain uneasy reason to come back. And of course Grandma Kashpaw had scanned it out.

I sat down. We sat together on the couch watching his chair out of the corner of our eyes. She had found him sitting in his chair when she walked in the door.

"It's the love medicine, my Lipsha," she said. "It was stronger than we thought. He came back even after death to claim me to his side."

I was afraid. "We shouldn't have tampered with it," I said. She agreed. For a while we sat still. I don't know what she thought, but my head felt screwed on backward. I couldn't accurately consider the situation, so I told Grandma to go to bed. I would sleep on the couch keeping my eye on Grandpa's chair. Maybe he would come back and maybe he wouldn't. I guess I feared the one as much as the other, but I got to thinking, see, as I lay there in darkness, that perhaps even through my terrible mistakes some good might come. If Grandpa did come back, I thought he'd return in his right mind. I could talk with him. I could tell him it was all my fault for playing with power I did not understand. Maybe he'd forgive me and rest in peace. I hoped this. I calmed myself and waited for him all night.

He fooled me though. He knew what I was waiting for, and it wasn't what he was looking to hear. Come dawn I heard a blood-splitting cry from the bedroom and I rushed in there. Grandma turnt the lights on. She was sitting on the edge of the bed and her face looked harsh, pinched-up, gray. 150

"He was here," she said. "He came and laid down next to me in bed. And he touched me."

Her heart broke down. She cried. His touch was so cold. She laid back in bed after a while, as it was morning, and I went to the couch. As I lay there, falling asleep, I suddenly felt Grandpa's presence and the barrier between us like a swollen river. I felt how I had wronged him. How awful was the place where I had sent him. Behind the wall of death, he'd watched the living eat and cry and get drunk. He was lonesome, but I understood he meant no harm.

"Go back," I said to the dark, afraid and yet full of pity. "You got to be with your own kind now," I said. I felt him retreating, like a sigh, growing less. I felt his spirit as it shrunk back through the walls, the blinds, the brick courtyard of Senior Citizens. "Look up Aunt June," I whispered as he left.

I slept late the next morning, a good hard sleep allowing the sun to rise and warm the earth. It was past noon when I awoke. There is nothing, to my mind, like a long sleep to make those hard decisions that you neglect under stress of wakefulness. Soon as I woke up that morning, I saw exactly what I'd say to Grandma. I had gotten humble in the past week, not just losing the touch but getting jolted into the understanding that would prey on me from here on out. Your life feels different on you, once you greet death and understand your heart's position. You wear your life like a garment from the mission bundle sale ever after—lightly because you realize you never paid nothing for it, cherishing because you know you won't ever come by such a bargain again. Also you have the feeling someone wore it before you and someone will after. I can't explain that, not yet, but I'm putting my mind to it.

"Grandma," I said, "I got to be honest about the love medicine." 155

She listened. I knew from then on she would be listening to me the way I had listened to her before. I told her about the turkey hearts and how I had them blessed. I told her what I used as love medicine was purely a fake, and then I said to her what my understanding brought me.

"Love medicine ain't what brings him back to you, Grandma. No, it's something else. He loved you over time and distance, but he went off so quick he never got the chance to tell you how he loves you, how he doesn't blame you, how he understands. It's true feeling, not no magic. No supermarket heart could have brung him back."

She looked at me. She was seeing the years and days I had no way of knowing, and she didn't believe me. I could tell this. Yet a look came on her face. It was like the look of mothers drinking sweetness from their children's eyes. It was tenderness.

"Lipsha," she said, "you was always my favorite."

160   She took the beads off the bedpost, where she kept them to say at night, and she told me to put out my hand. When I did this, she shut the beads inside of my fist and held them there a long minute, tight, so my hand hurt. I almost cried when she did this. I don't really know why. Tears shot up behind my eyelids, and yet it was nothing. I didn't understand, except her hand was so strong, squeezing mine.

The earth was full of life and there were dandelions growing out the window, thick as thieves, already seeded, fat as big yellow plungers. She let my hand go. I got up. "I'll go out and dig a few dandelions," I told her.

Outside, the sun was hot and heavy as a hand on my back. I felt it flow down my arms, out my fingers, arrowing through the ends of the fork into the earth. With every root I prized up there was return, as if I was kin to its secret lesson. The touch got stronger as I worked through the grassy afternoon. Uncurling from me like a seed out of the blackness where I was lost, the touch spread. The spiked leaves full of bitter mother's milk. A buried root. A nuisance people dig up and throw in the sun to wither. A globe of frail seeds that's indestructible.

1982

QUESTIONS

1. How, if at all, do you think Lipsha changes over the course of the story? What might he learn by the end? What might the story show us through him?
2. What different meanings does the phrase *love medicine* take on over the course of the story? How might you use the phrase to state the story's theme?
3. Lipsha tells the stories of Lulu's "tweety bird" that disappeared up her dress and of Wristwatch, whose broken watch started keeping time after its owner dropped dead. He then says, "Not to get off the subject or nothing" (par. 65). Are these stories off the subject? How do they arouse expectations? How do they function in the plot? What do they tell you of Lipsha's character? of the nature of the people on the reservation? Are they related to the theme? If so, how?

YASUNARI KAWABATA

The Grasshopper and the Bell Cricket[1]

Walking along the tile-roofed wall of the university, I turned aside and approached the upper school. Behind the white board fence of the school playground, from a dusky clump of bushes under the black cherry trees, an insect's voice could be

1. Translated by Lane Dunlop.

heard. Walking more slowly and listening to that voice, and furthermore reluctant to part with it, I turned right so as not to leave the playground behind. When I turned to the left, the fence gave way to an embankment planted with orange trees. At the corner, I exclaimed with surprise. My eyes gleaming at what they saw up ahead, I hurried forward with short steps.

At the base of the embankment was a bobbing cluster of beautiful varicolored lanterns, such as one might see at a festival in a remote country village. Without going any farther, I knew that it was a group of children on an insect chase among the bushes of the embankment. There were about twenty lanterns. Not only were there crimson, pink, indigo, green, purple, and yellow lanterns, but one lantern glowed with five colors at once. There were even some little red store-bought lanterns. But most of the lanterns were beautiful square ones which the children had made themselves with love and care. The bobbing lanterns, the coming together of children on this lonely slope—surely it was a scene from a fairy tale?

One of the neighborhood children had heard an insect sing on this slope one night. Buying a red lantern, he had come back the next night to find the insect. The night after that, there was another child. This new child could not buy a lantern. Cutting out the back and front of a small carton and papering it, he placed a candle on the bottom and fastened a string to the top. The number of children grew to five, and then to seven. They learned how to color the paper that they stretched over the windows of the cutout cartons, and to draw pictures on it. Then these wise child-artists, cutting out round, three-cornered, and lozenge leaf shapes in the cartons, coloring each little window a different color, with circles and diamonds, red and green, made a single and whole decorative pattern. The child with the red lantern discarded it as a tasteless object that could be bought at a store. The child who had made his own lantern threw it away because the design was too simple. The pattern of light that one had had in hand the night before was unsatisfying the morning after. Each day, with cardboard, paper, brush, scissors, penknife, and glue, the children made new lanterns out of their hearts and minds. Look at my lantern! Be the most unusually beautiful! And each night, they had gone out on their insect hunts. These were the twenty children and their beautiful lanterns that I now saw before me.

Wide-eyed, I loitered near them. Not only did the square lanterns have old-fashioned patterns and flower shapes, but the names of the children who had made them were cut out in squared letters of the syllabary. Different from the painted-over red lanterns, others (made of thick cutout cardboard) had their designs drawn onto the paper windows, so that the candle's light seemed to emanate from the form and color of the design itself. The lanterns brought out the shadows of the bushes like dark light. The children crouched eagerly on the slope wherever they heard an insect's voice.

"Does anyone want a grasshopper?" A boy, who had been peering into a bush ₅ about thirty feet away from the other children, suddenly straightened up and shouted.

"Yes! Give it to me!" Six or seven children came running up. Crowding behind the boy who had found the grasshopper, they peered into the bush. Brushing away their outstretched hands and spreading out his arms, the boy stood as if guarding the bush where the insect was. Waving the lantern in his right hand, he called again to the other children.

"Does anyone want a grasshopper? A grasshopper!"

"I do! I do!" Four or five more children came running up. It seemed you could not catch a more precious insect than a grasshopper. The boy called out a third time.

"Doesn't anyone want a grasshopper?"

10   Two or three more children came over.

"Yes. I want it."

It was a girl, who just now had come up behind the boy who'd discovered the insect. Lightly turning his body, the boy gracefully bent forward. Shifting the lantern to his left hand, he reached his right hand into the bush.

"It's a grasshopper."

"Yes. I'd like to have it."

15   The boy quickly stood up. As if to say "Here!" he thrust out his fist that held the insect at the girl. She, slipping her left wrist under the string of her lantern, enclosed the boy's fist with both hands. The boy quietly opened his fist. The insect was transferred to between the girl's thumb and index finger.

"Oh! It's not a grasshopper. It's a bell cricket." The girl's eyes shone as she looked at the small brown insect.

"It's a bell cricket! It's a bell cricket!" The children echoed in an envious chorus.

"It's a bell cricket. It's a bell cricket."

Glancing with her bright intelligent eyes at the boy who had given her the cricket, the girl opened the little insect cage hanging at her side and released the cricket in it.

20   "It's a bell cricket."

"Oh, it's a bell cricket," the boy who'd captured it muttered. Holding up the insect cage close to his eyes, he looked inside it. By the light of his beautiful many colored lantern, also held up at eye level, he glanced at the girl's face.

Oh, I thought. I felt slightly jealous of the boy, and sheepish. How silly of me not to have understood his actions until now! Then I caught my breath in surprise. Look! It was something on the girl's breast which neither the boy who had given her the cricket, nor she who had accepted it, nor the children who were looking at them noticed.

In the faint greenish light that fell on the girl's breast, wasn't the name "Fujio" clearly discernible? The boy's lantern, which he held up alongside the girl's insect cage, inscribed his name, cut out in the green papered aperture, onto her white cotton kimono. The girl's lantern, which dangled loosely from her wrist, did not project its pattern so clearly, but still one could make out, in a trembling patch of red on the boy's waist, the name "Kiyoko." This chance interplay of red and green—if it was chance or play—neither Fujio nor Kiyoko knew about.

Even if they remembered forever that Fujio had given her the cricket and that Kiyoko had accepted it, not even in dreams would Fujio ever know that his name had been written in green on Kiyoko's breast or that Kiyoko's name had been inscribed in red on his waist, nor would Kiyoko ever know that Fujio's name had been inscribed in green on her breast or that her own name had been written in red on Fujio's waist.

25   Fujio! Even when you have become a young man, laugh with pleasure at a girl's delight when, told that it's a grasshopper, she is given a bell cricket; laugh with affection at a girl's chagrin when, told that it's a bell cricket, she is given a grasshopper.

Even if you have the wit to look by yourself in a bush away from the other children, there are not many bell crickets in the world. Probably you will find a girl like a grasshopper whom you think is a bell cricket.

And finally, to your clouded, wounded heart, even a true bell cricket will seem like a grasshopper. Should that day come, when it seems to you that the world is only full of grasshoppers, I will think it a pity that you have no way to remember tonight's play of light, when your name was written in green by your beautiful lantern on a girl's breast.

1988

QUESTIONS

1. Who might the narrator of this story be? What clues are provided in the story?
2. What might the grasshopper and the bell cricket each come to symbolize in the story?
3. Might the final three paragraphs of this story come close to stating its theme(s)? How would you state the theme(s)?

SUGGESTIONS FOR WRITING

1. Choose any story in this chapter and write an essay exploring how character, point of view, setting, symbolism, or any recurring word or phrase contributes to the development of theme. Be sure to state that theme in a sentence.
2. Sometimes the theme in a work of literature can be expressed as a strong, clear statement: "A always follows from B," or "An X can never be a Y." More often, though, especially in modern literature, authors offer subtler, often ambiguous themes that deliberately undermine our faith in simple absolutes: "A doesn't necessarily always follow B," or "There are times when an X can be a Y." Write an essay in which you argue that one of the four stories in this chapter has an "always" or "never" kind of theme, and contrast it to the more indeterminate theme in one of the other three stories.
3. Write an essay exploring how theme is developed through the juxtaposition of realistic detail and fantastic elements in "A Very Old Man with Enormous Wings," especially (but not exclusively) in the description of the winged man himself.
4. Though the main theme of "Love Medicine" may well be a universal one (an insight that applies to all or most people), its major characters are all Native Americans living on a reservation. Write an essay exploring how the story characterizes contemporary Native American life and how this characterization shapes the story's theme, perhaps giving the story a culturally and historically specific, as well as universal, resonance and relevance.
5. Write an essay comparing the way Stephen Crane's "The Open Boat" and Nathaniel Hawthorne's "The Birth-Mark" portray the relationship between human beings and nature. What is similar and different about the nature-related themes of the two stories?
6. Write two versions of a poem or short story. In the first version, be explicit, even obvious, about your theme. In the second, employ any strategies you wish for veiling the theme as much as possible. Then write a brief essay discussing which version is more successful, and why.

Encounters across Cultures: An Album

Today, when you take a course in English literature, some of the writers and works you study are likely to be *not* English per se but from other parts of the English-speaking world. For centuries now, literary traditions have been developing in places that were once colonies of the British Empire. Particularly in the last half century, various writers have won international reputations writing about the clash of languages, cultures, and values not only within former colonies but also within immigrant communities in North America and Europe. The educated newcomer may feel out of place both at home and in the adopted country. Magical or spiritual beliefs may continue with surprising and even devastating force in spite of new technologies and cosmopolitan perspectives. The outsider's assimilation—or failure to assimilate—may be among the oldest of stories, and the conflict between cultures is certainly a widespread theme, from Exodus in the Bible and Homer's *The Iliad* to Shakespeare's *Romeo and Juliet* to more recent novels such as Salman Rushdie's *The Satanic Verses* or Zadie Smith's *White Teeth*. A fiction writer may develop the details of setting and everyday life as well as the private perceptions of characters, conveying the subtleties of interaction among different peoples and cultures.

This album features stories of encounters across cultures within a postcolonial context. The three stories emphasize cultural and social differences while pondering estrangement or loss within families. Each story exposes the gaps between ancient traditions and modern institutions, between group identification and individual fulfillment. In Bharati Mukherjee's "The Management of Grief," Jhumpa Lahiri's "Interpreter of Maladies," and William Saidi's "The Nightmare," these gaps determine the experience of outsiders and insiders alike. Misunderstandings across great cultural divides—and the self-deceiving stories people tell—are themes in each of these stories. Yet even with their interrelated themes, these stories differ widely in substance, form, and effect.

How much does character depend on culture and environment? Will the children of immigrants who are born and grow up in North America lose any common ground with those who remember traditional life on another continent? Why do some newcomers quickly take on every feature of modern living while others cling to traditional ways? How does someone who can speak both languages—both literally and figuratively—decide where his or her loyalties lie? Do these stories take sides between the cultures or values, the new ways and the old? Do they depict adopting a new home as an empowering act of self-definition, of self-liberation? Or do they suggest that there can be deadly or deadening consequences in losing touch with family roots and ancient mysteries?

BHARATI MUKHERJEE

The Management of Grief

A woman I don't know is boiling tea the Indian way in my kitchen. There are a lot of women I don't know in my kitchen, whispering, and moving tactfully. They open doors, rummage through the pantry, and try not to ask me where things are kept. They remind me of when my sons were small, on Mother's Day or when Vikram and I were tired, and they would make big, sloppy omelets. I would lie in bed pretending I didn't hear them.

Dr. Sharma, the treasurer of the Indo-Canada Society, pulls me into the hallway. He wants to know if I am worried about money. His wife, who has just come up from the basement with a tray of empty cups and glasses, scolds him. "Don't bother Mrs. Bhave with mundane details." She looks so monstrously pregnant her baby must be days overdue. I tell her she shouldn't be carrying heavy things. "Shaila," she says, smiling, "this is the fifth." Then she grabs a teenager by his shirttails. He slips his Walkman off his head. He has to be one of her four children, they have the same domed and dented foreheads. "What's the official word now?" she demands. The boy slips the headphones back on. "They're acting evasive, Ma. They're saying it could be an accident or a terrorist bomb."

All morning, the boys have been muttering, Sikh Bomb, Sikh Bomb. The men, not using the word, bow their heads in agreement. Mrs. Sharma touches her forehead at such a word. At least they've stopped talking about space debris and Russian lasers.

Two radios are going in the dining room. They are tuned to different stations. Someone must have brought the radios down from my boys' bedrooms. I haven't gone into their rooms since Kusum came running across the front lawn in her bathrobe. She looked so funny, I was laughing when I opened the door.

5   The big TV in the den is being whizzed through American networks and cable channels.

"Damn!" some man swears bitterly. "How can these preachers carry on like nothing's happened?" I want to tell him we're not that important. You look at the audience, and at the preacher in his blue robe with his beautiful white hair, the potted palm trees under a blue sky, and you know they care about nothing.

The phone rings and rings. Dr. Sharma's taken charge. "We're with her," he keeps saying. "Yes, yes, the doctor has given calming pills. Yes, yes, pills are having necessary effect." I wonder if pills alone explain this calm. Not peace, just a deadening quiet. I was always controlled, but never repressed. Sound can reach me, but my body is tensed, ready to scream. I hear their voices all around me. I hear my boys and Vikram cry, "Mommy, Shaila!" and their screams insulate me, like headphones.

The woman boiling water tells her story again and again. "I got the news first. My cousin called from Halifax before six A.M., can you imagine? He'd gotten up for prayers and his son was studying for medical exams and he heard on a rock channel that something had happened to a plane. They said first it had disappeared from the radar, like a giant eraser just reached out. His father called me, so I said to him, what do you mean, 'something bad'? You mean a hijacking? And he said, *behn,*[1] there is no confirmation of anything yet, but check with your neighbors because a lot of them must be on that plane. So I called poor Kusum straightaway. I knew Kusum's husband and daughter were booked to go yesterday."

Kusum lives across the street from me. She and Satish had moved in less than a month ago. They said they needed a bigger place. All these people, the Sharmas and friends from the Indo-Canada Society had been there for the housewarming. Satish and Kusum made homemade tandoori on their big gas grill and even the

---

1. Sister.

white neighbors piled their plates high with that luridly red, charred, juicy chicken. Their younger daughter had danced, and even our boys had broken away from the Stanley Cup telecast to put in a reluctant appearance. Everyone took pictures for their albums and for the community newspapers—another of our families had made it big in Toronto—and now I wonder how many of those happy faces are gone. "Why does God give us so much if all along He intends to take it away?" Kusum asks me.

I nod. We sit on carpeted stairs, holding hands like children. "I never once told 10 him that I loved him," I say. I was too much the well brought up woman. I was so well brought up I never felt comfortable calling my husband by his first name.

"It's all right," Kusum says. "He knew. My husband knew. They felt it. Modern young girls have to say it because what they feel is fake."

Kusum's daughter, Pam, runs in with an overnight case. Pam's in her McDonald's uniform. "Mummy! You have to get dressed!" Panic makes her cranky. "A reporter's on his way here."

"Why?"

"You want to talk to him in your bathrobe?" She starts to brush her mother's long hair. She's the daughter who's always in trouble. She dates Canadian boys and hangs out in the mall, shopping for tight sweaters. The younger one, the goody-goody one according to Pam, the one with a voice so sweet that when she sang *bhajans*[2] for Ethiopian relief even a frugal man like my husband wrote out a hundred dollar check, *she* was on that plane. *She* was going to spend July and August with grandparents because Pam wouldn't go. Pam said she'd rather waitress at McDonald's. "If it's a choice between Bombay and Wonderland, I'm picking Wonderland," she'd said.

"Leave me alone," Kusum yells. "You know what I want to do? If I didn't have 15 to look after you now, I'd hang myself."

Pam's young face goes blotchy with pain. "Thanks," she says, "don't let me stop you."

"Hush," pregnant Mrs. Sharma scolds Pam. "Leave your mother alone. Mr. Sharma will tackle the reporters and fill out the forms. He'll say what has to be said."

Pam stands her ground. "You think I don't know what Mummy's thinking? *Why her?* that's what. That's sick! Mummy wishes my little sister were alive and I were dead."

Kusum's hand in mine is trembly hot. We continue to sit on the stairs.

She calls before she arrives, wondering if there's anything I need. Her name is 20 Judith Templeton and she's an appointee of the provincial government. "Multiculturalism?" I ask, and she says, "partially," but that her mandate is bigger. "I've been told you knew many of the people on the flight," she says. "Perhaps if you'd agree to help us reach the others . . . ?"

She gives me time at least to put on tea water and pick up the mess in the front room. I have a few *samosas*[3] from Kusum's housewarming that I could fry up, but then I think, why prolong this visit?

Judith Templeton is much younger than she sounded. She wears a blue suit with a white blouse and a polka dot tie. Her blond hair is cut short, her only

2. Hymns.   3. Fried turnovers filled with finely chopped meat or vegetables.

jewelry is pearl drop earrings. Her briefcase is new and expensive looking, a gleaming cordovan leather. She sits with it across her lap. When she looks out the front windows onto the street, her contact lenses seem to float in front of her light blue eyes.

"What sort of help do you want from me?" I ask. She has refused the tea, out of politeness, but I insist, along with some slightly stale biscuits.[4]

"I have no experience," she admits. "That is, I have an MSW and I've worked in liaison with accident victims, but I mean I have no experience with a tragedy of this scale—"

25   "Who could?" I ask.

"—and with the complications of culture, language, and customs. Someone mentioned that Mrs. Bhave is a pillar—because you've taken it more calmly."

At this, perhaps, I frown, for she reaches forward, almost to take my hand. "I hope you understand my meaning, Mrs. Bhave. There are hundreds of people in Metro directly affected, like you, and some of them speak no English. There are some widows who've never handled money or gone on a bus, and there are old parents who still haven't eaten or gone outside their bedrooms. Some houses and apartments have been looted. Some wives are still hysterical. Some husbands are in shock and profound depression. We want to help, but our hands are tied in so many ways. We have to distribute money to some people, and there are legal documents—these things can be done. We have interpreters, but we don't always have the human touch, or maybe the right human touch. We don't want to make mistakes, Mrs. Bhave, and that's why we'd like to ask you to help us."

"More mistakes, you mean," I say.

"Police matters are not in my hands," she answers.

30   "Nothing I can do will make any difference," I say. "We must all grieve in our own way."

"But you are coping very well. All the people said, Mrs. Bhave is the strongest person of all. Perhaps if the others could see you, talk with you, it would help them."

"By the standards of the people you call hysterical, I am behaving very oddly and very badly, Miss Templeton." I want to say to her, *I wish I could scream, starve, walk into Lake Ontario, jump from a bridge.* "They would not see me as a model. I do not see myself as a model."

I am a freak. No one who has ever known me would think of me reacting this way. This terrible calm will not go away.

She asks me if she may call again, after I get back from a long trip that we all must make. "Of course," I say. "Feel free to call, anytime."

35   Four days later, I find Kusum squatting on a rock overlooking a bay in Ireland. It isn't a big rock, but it juts sharply out over water. This is as close as we'll ever get to them. June breezes balloon out her sari and unpin her knee-length hair. She has the bewildered look of a sea creature whom the tides have stranded.

It's been one hundred hours since Kusum came stumbling and screaming across my lawn. Waiting around the hospital, we've heard many stories. The police, the diplomats, they tell us things thinking that we're strong, that knowledge is helpful to the grieving, and maybe it is. Some, I know, prefer ignorance,

4. Cookies.

or their own versions. The plane broke into two, they say. Unconsciousness was instantaneous. No one suffered. My boys must have just finished their breakfasts. They loved eating on planes, they loved the smallness of plates, knives, and forks. Last year they saved the airline salt and pepper shakers. Half an hour more and they would have made it to Heathrow.

Kusum says that we can't escape our fate. She says that all those people—our husbands, my boys, her girl with the nightingale voice, all those Hindus, Christians, Sikhs, Muslims, Parsis, and atheists on that plane—were fated to die together off this beautiful bay. She learned this from a swami in Toronto.

I have my Valium.

Six of us "relatives"—two widows and four widowers—choose to spend the day today by the waters instead of sitting in a hospital room and scanning photographs of the dead. That's what they call us now: relatives. I've looked through twenty-seven photos in two days. They're very kind to us, the Irish are very understanding. Sometimes understanding means freeing a tourist bus for this trip to the bay, so we can pretend to spy our loved ones through the glassiness of waves or in sunspeckled cloud shapes.

I could die here, too, and be content. 40

"What is that, out there?" She's standing and flapping her hands and for a moment I see a head shape bobbing in the waves. She's standing in the water, I, on the boulder. The tide is low, and a round, black, headsized rock has just risen from the waves. She returns, her sari end dripping and ruined and her face is a twisted remnant of hope, the way mine was a hundred hours ago, still laughing but inwardly knowing that nothing but the ultimate tragedy could bring two women together at six o'clock on a Sunday morning. I watch her face sag into blankness.

"That water felt warm, Shaila," she says at length.

"You can't," I say. "We have to wait for our turn to come."

I haven't eaten in four days, haven't brushed my teeth.

"I know," she says. "I tell myself I have no right to grieve. They are in a better 45 place than we are. My swami says I should be thrilled for them. My swami says depression is a sign of our selfishness."

Maybe I'm selfish. Selfishly I break away from Kusum and run, sandals slapping against stones, to the water's edge. What if my boys aren't lying pinned under the debris? What if they aren't stuck a mile below that innocent blue chop? What if, given the strong currents. . . .

Now I've ruined my sari, one of my best. Kusum has joined me, knee-deep in water that feels to me like a swimming pool. I could settle in the water, and my husband would take my hand and the boys would slap water in my face just to see me scream.

"Do you remember what good swimmers my boys were, Kusum?"

"I saw the medals," she says.

One of the widowers, Dr. Ranganathan from Montreal, walks out to us, 50 carrying his shoes in one hand. He's an electrical engineer. Someone at the hotel mentioned his work is famous around the world, something about the place where physics and electricity come together. He has lost a huge family, something indescribable. "With some luck," Dr. Ranganathan suggests to me, "a good swimmer could make it safely to some island. It is quite possible that there may be many, many microscopic islets scattered around."

"You're not just saying that?" I tell Dr. Ranganathan about Vinod, my elder son. Last year he took diving as well.

"It's a parent's duty to hope," he says. "It is foolish to rule out possibilities that have not been tested. I myself have not surrendered hope."

Kusum is sobbing once again. "Dear lady," he says, laying his free hand on her arm, and she calms down.

"Vinod is how old?" he asks me. He's very careful, as we all are. *Is,* not was.

55   "Fourteen. Yesterday he was fourteen. His father and uncle were going to take him down to the Taj and give him a big birthday party. I couldn't go with them because I couldn't get two weeks off from my stupid job in June." I process bills for a travel agent. June is a big travel month.

Dr. Ranganathan whips the pockets of his suit jacket inside out. Squashed roses, in darkening shades of pink, float on the water. He tore the roses off creepers in somebody's garden. He didn't ask anyone if he could pluck the roses, but now there's been an article about it in the local papers. When you see an Indian person, it says, please give him or her flowers.

"A strong youth of fourteen," he says, "can very likely pull to safety a younger one."

My sons, though four years apart, were very close. Vinod wouldn't let Mithun drown. *Electrical engineering,* I think, foolishly perhaps: this man knows important secrets of the universe, things closed to me. Relief spins me lightheaded. No wonder my boys' photographs haven't turned up in the gallery of photos of the recovered dead. "Such pretty roses," I say.

"My wife loved pink roses. Every Friday I had to bring a bunch home. I used to say, why? After twenty-odd years of marriage you're still needing proof positive of my love?" He has identified his wife and three of his children. Then others from Montreal, the lucky ones, intact families with no survivors. He chuckles as he wades back to shore. Then he swings around to ask me a question. "Mrs. Bhave, you are wanting to throw in some roses for your loved ones? I have two big ones left."

60   But I have other things to float: Vinod's pocket calculator; a half-painted model B-52 for my Mithun. They'd want them on their island. And for my husband? For him I let fall into the calm, glassy waters a poem I wrote in the hospital yesterday. Finally he'll know my feelings for him.

"Don't tumble, the rocks are slippery," Dr. Ranganathan cautions. He holds out a hand for me to grab.

Then it's time to get back on the bus, time to rush back to our waiting posts on hospital benches.

Kusum is one of the lucky ones. The lucky ones flew here, identified in multiplicate their loved ones, then will fly to India with the bodies for proper ceremonies. Satish is one of the few males who surfaced. The photos of faces we saw on the walls in an office at Heathrow and here in the hospital are mostly of women. Women have more body fat, a nun said to me matter-of-factly. They float better. Today I was stopped by a young sailor on the street. He had loaded bodies, he'd gone into the water when—he checks my face for signs of strength—when the sharks were first spotted. I don't blush, and he breaks down. "It's all right," I say. "Thank you." I had heard about the sharks from Dr. Ranganathan. In his orderly mind, science brings understanding, it holds no terror. It is the shark's duty. For every deer there is a hunter, for every fish a fisherman.

The Irish are not shy; they rush to me and give me hugs and some are crying. 65
I cannot imagine reactions like that on the streets of Toronto. Just strangers, and
I am touched. Some carry flowers with them and give them to any Indian they see.

After lunch, a policeman I have gotten to know quite well catches hold of me.
He says he thinks he has a match for Vinod. I explain what a good swimmer
Vinod is.

"You want me with you when you look at photos?" Dr. Ranganathan walks
ahead of me into the picture gallery. In these matters, he is a scientist, and I am
grateful. It is a new perspective. "They have performed miracles," he says. "We are
indebted to them."

The first day or two the policemen showed us relatives only one picture at a
time; now they're in a hurry, they're eager to lay out the possibles, and even the
probables.

The face on the photo is of a boy much like Vinod; the same intelligent eyes,
the same thick brows dipping into a V. But this boy's features, even his cheeks,
are puffier, wider, mushier.

"No." My gaze is pulled by other pictures. There are five other boys who look 70
like Vinod.

The nun assigned to console me rubs the first picture with a fingertip. "When
they've been in the water for a while, love, they look a little heavier." The bones
under the skin are broken, they said on the first day—try to adjust your memories. It's important.

"It's not him. I'm his mother. I'd know."

"I know this one!" Dr. Ranganathan cries out suddenly from the back of the
gallery. "And this one!" I think he senses that I don't want to find my boys. "They
are the Kutty brothers. They were also from Montreal." I don't mean to be crying. On the contrary, I am ecstatic. My suitcase in the hotel is packed heavy with
dry clothes for my boys.

The policeman starts to cry. "I am so sorry, I am so sorry, ma'am. I really
thought we had a match."

With the nun ahead of us and the policeman behind, we, the unlucky ones 75
without our children's bodies, file out of the makeshift gallery.

From Ireland most of us go on to India. Kusum and I take the same direct flight
to Bombay, so I can help her clear customs quickly. But we have to argue with a
man in uniform. He has large boils on his face. The boils swell and glow with
sweat as we argue with him. He wants Kusum to wait in line and he refuses to
take authority because his boss is on a tea break. But Kusum won't let her coffins out of sight, and I shan't desert her though I know that my parents, elderly
and diabetic, must be waiting in a stuffy car in a scorching lot.

"You bastard!" I scream at the man with the popping boils. Other passengers
press closer. "You think we're smuggling contraband in those coffins!"

Once upon a time we were well brought up women; we were dutiful wives who
kept our heads veiled, our voices shy and sweet.

In India, I become, once again, an only child of rich, ailing parents. Old friends
of the family come to pay their respects. Some are Sikh, and inwardly, involuntarily, I cringe. My parents are progressive people; they do not blame communities for a few individuals.

80   In Canada it is a different story now.

"Stay longer," my mother pleads. "Canada is a cold place. Why would you want to be all by yourself?" I stay.

Three months pass. Then another.

"Vikram wouldn't have wanted you to give up things!" they protest. They call my husband by the name he was born with. In Toronto he'd changed to Vik so the men he worked with at his office would find his name as easy as Rod or Chris. "You know, the dead aren't cut off from us!"

My grandmother, the spoiled daughter of a rich *zamindar*,[5] shaved her head with rusty razor blades when she was widowed at sixteen. My grandfather died of childhood diabetes when he was nineteen, and she saw herself as the harbinger of bad luck. My mother grew up without parents, raised indifferently by an uncle, while her true mother slept in a hut behind the main estate house and took her food with the servants. She grew up a rationalist. My parents abhor mindless mortification.

85   The zamindar's daughter kept stubborn faith in Vedic rituals; my parents rebelled. I am trapped between two modes of knowledge. At thirty-six, I am too old to start over and too young to give up. Like my husband's spirit, I flutter between worlds.

Courting aphasia, we travel. We travel with our phalanx of servants and poor relatives. To hill stations and to beach resorts. We play contract bridge in dusty gymkhana clubs. We ride stubby ponies up crumbly mountain trails. At tea dances, we let ourselves be twirled twice round the ballroom. We hit the holy spots we hadn't made time for before. In Varanasi, Kalighat, Rishikesh, Hardwar, astrologers and palmists seek me out and for a fee offer me cosmic consolations.

Already the widowers among us are being shown new bride candidates. They cannot resist the call of custom, the authority of their parents and older brothers. They must marry; it is the duty of a man to look after a wife. The new wives will be young widows with children, destitute but of good family. They will make loving wives, but the men will shun them. I've had calls from the men over crackling Indian telephone lines. "Save me," they say, these substantial, educated, successful men of forty. "My parents are arranging a marriage for me." In a month they will have buried one family and returned to Canada with a new bride and partial family.

I am comparatively lucky. No one here thinks of arranging a husband for an unlucky widow.

Then, on the third day of the sixth month into this odyssey, in an abandoned temple in a tiny Himalayan village, as I make my offering of flowers and sweetmeats to the god of a tribe of animists, my husband descends to me. He is squatting next to a scrawny *sadhu*[6] in moth-eaten robes. Vikram wears the vanilla suit he wore the last time I hugged him. The *sadhu* tosses petals on a butter-fed flame, reciting Sanskrit mantras and sweeps his face of flies. My husband takes my hands in his.

90   *You're beautiful,* he starts. Then, *What are you doing here?*

Shall I stay? I ask. He only smiles, but already the image is fading. *You must finish alone what we started together.* No seaweed wreathes his mouth. He speaks too

5. Landowner.   6. Hindu holy man.

fast just as he used to when we were an envied family in our pink split-level. He is gone.

In the windowless altar room, smoky with joss sticks and clarified butter lamps, a sweaty hand gropes for my blouse. I do not shriek. The *sadhu* arranges his robe. The lamps hiss and sputter out.

When we come out of the temple, my mother says, "Did you feel something weird in there?"

My mother has no patience with ghosts, prophetic dreams, holy men, and cults.

"No," I lie. "Nothing." 95

But she knows that she's lost me. She knows that in days I shall be leaving.

Kusum's put her house up for sale. She wants to live in an ashram in Hardwar. Moving to Hardwar was her swami's idea. Her swami runs two ashrams, the one in Hardwar and another here in Toronto.

"Don't run away," I tell her.

"I'm not running away," she says. "I'm pursuing inner peace. You think you or that Ranganathan fellow are better off?"

Pam's left for California. She wants to do some modelling, she says. She says 100 when she comes into her share of the insurance money she'll open a yoga-cum-aerobics studio in Hollywood. She sends me postcards so naughty I daren't leave them on the coffee table. Her mother has withdrawn from her and the world.

The rest of us don't lose touch, that's the point. Talk is all we have, says Dr. Ranganathan, who has also resisted his relatives and returned to Montreal and to his job, alone. He says, whom better to talk with than other relatives? We've been melted down and recast as a new tribe.

He calls me twice a week from Montreal. Every Wednesday night and every Saturday afternoon. He is changing jobs, going to Ottawa. But Ottawa is over a hundred miles away, and he is forced to drive two hundred and twenty miles a day. He can't bring himself to sell his house. The house is a temple, he says; the king-sized bed in the master bedroom is a shrine. He sleeps on a folding cot. A devotee.

There are still some hysterical relatives. Judith Templeton's list of those needing help and those who've "accepted" is in nearly perfect balance. Acceptance means you speak of your family in the past tense and you make active plans for moving ahead with your life. There are courses at Seneca and Ryerson[7] we could be taking. Her gleaming leather briefcase is full of college catalogues and lists of cultural societies that need our help. She has done impressive work, I tell her.

"In the textbooks on grief management," she replies—I am her confidante, I realize, one of the few whose grief has not sprung bizarre obsessions—"there are stages to pass through: rejection, depression, acceptance, reconstruction." She has compiled a chart and finds that six months after the tragedy, none of us still reject reality, but only a handful are reconstructing. "Depressed Acceptance" is the plateau we've reached. Remarriage is a major step in reconstruction (though she's a little surprised, even shocked, over *how* quickly some of the men have

7. Seneca College of Applied Arts and Technology, in Willowdale; Ryerson Polytechnical Institute, Toronto.

taken on new families). Selling one's house and changing jobs and cities is healthy.

105   How do I tell Judith Templeton that my family surrounds me, and that like creatures in epics, they've changed shapes? She sees me as calm and accepting but worries that I have no job, no career. My closest friends are worse off than I. I cannot tell her my days, even my nights, are thrilling.

She asks me to help with families she can't reach at all. An elderly couple in Agincourt whose sons were killed just weeks after they had brought their parents over from a village in Punjab. From their names, I know they are Sikh. Judith Templeton and a translator have visited them twice with offers of money for air fare to Ireland, with bank forms, power-of-attorney forms, but they have refused to sign, or to leave their tiny apartment. Their sons' money is frozen in the bank. Their sons' investment apartments have been trashed by tenants, the furnishings sold off. The parents fear that anything they sign or any money they receive will end the company's or the country's obligations to them. They fear they are selling their sons for two airline tickets to a place they've never seen.

The high-rise apartment is a tower of Indians and West Indians, with a sprinkling of Orientals. The nearest bus stop kiosk is lined with women in saris. Boys practice cricket in the parking lot. Inside the building, even I wince a bit from the ferocity of onion fumes, the distinctive and immediate Indianness of frying *ghee,* but Judith Templeton maintains a steady flow of information. These poor old people are in imminent danger of losing their place and all their services.

I say to her, "They are Sikh. They will not open up to a Hindu woman." And what I want to add is, as much as I try not to, I stiffen now at the sight of beards and turbans. I remember a time when we all trusted each other in this new country, it was only the new country we worried about.

The two rooms are dark and stuffy. The lights are off, and an oil lamp sputters on the coffee table. The bent old lady has let us in, and her husband is wrapping a white turban over his oiled, hip-length hair. She immediately goes to the kitchen, and I hear the most familiar sound of an Indian home, tap water hitting and filling a teapot.

110   They have not paid their utility bills, out of fear and the inability to write a check. The telephone is gone; electricity and gas and water are soon to follow. They have told Judith their sons will provide. They are good boys, and they have always earned and looked after their parents.

We converse a bit in Hindi. They do not ask about the crash and I wonder if I should bring it up. If they think I am here merely as a translator, then they may feel insulted. There are thousands of Punjabi-speakers, Sikhs, in Toronto to do a better job. And so I say to the old lady, "I too have lost my sons, and my husband, in the crash."

Her eyes immediately fill with tears. The man mutters a few words which sound like a blessing. "God provides and God takes away," he says.

I want to say, but only men destroy and give back nothing. "My boys and my husband are not coming back," I say. "We have to understand that."

Now the old woman responds. "But who is to say? Man alone does not decide these things." To this her husband adds his agreement.

115   Judith asks about the bank papers, the release forms. With a stroke of the pen, they will have a provincial trustee to pay their bills, invest their money, send them a monthly pension.

"Do you know this woman?" I ask them.

The man raises his hand from the table, turns it over and seems to regard each finger separately before he answers. "This young lady is always coming here, we make tea for her and she leaves papers for us to sign." His eyes scan a pile of papers in the corner of the room. "Soon we will be out of tea, then will she go away?"

The old lady adds, "I have asked my neighbors and no one else gets *angrezi*[8] visitors. What have we done?"

"It's her job," I try to explain. "The government is worried. Soon you will have no place to stay, no lights, no gas, no water."

"Government will get its money. Tell her not to worry, we are honorable people." 120

I try to explain the government wishes to give money, not take. He raises his hand. "Let them take," he says. "We are accustomed to that. That is no problem."

"We are strong people," says the wife. "Tell her that."

"Who needs all this machinery?" demands the husband. "It is unhealthy, the bright lights, the cold air on a hot day, the cold food, the four gas rings. God will provide, not government."

"When our boys return," the mother says. Her husband sucks his teeth. "Enough talk," he says.

Judith breaks in. "Have you convinced them?" The snaps on her cordovan 125 briefcase go off like firecrackers in that quiet apartment. She lays the sheaf of legal papers on the coffee table. "If they can't write their names, an X will do— I've told them that."

Now the old lady has shuffled to the kitchen and soon emerges with a pot of tea and two cups. "I think my bladder will go first on a job like this," Judith says to me, smiling. "If only there was some way of reaching them. Please thank her for the tea. Tell her she's very kind."

I nod in Judith's direction and tell them in Hindi, "She thanks you for the tea. She thinks you are being very hospitable but she doesn't have the slightest idea what it means."

I want to say, humor her. I want to say, my boys and my husband are with me too, more than ever. I look in the old man's eyes and I can read his stubborn, peasant's message: *I have protected this woman as best I can. She is the only person I have left. Give to me or take from me what you will, but I will not sign for it. I will not pretend that I accept.*

In the car, Judith says, "You see what I'm up against? I'm sure they're lovely people, but their stubbornness and ignorance are driving me crazy. They think signing a paper is signing their sons' death warrants, don't they?"

I am looking out the window. I want to say, *In our culture, it is a parent's duty to* 130 *hope.*

"Now Shaila, this next woman is a real mess. She cries day and night, and she refuses all medical help. We may have to—"

"—Let me out at the subway," I say.

"I beg your pardon?" I can feel those blue eyes staring at me.

It would not be like her to disobey. She merely disapproves, and slows at a corner to let me out. Her voice is plaintive. "Is there anything I said? Anything I did?"

8. English, Anglo.

135   I could answer her suddenly in a dozen ways, but I choose not to. "Shaila? Let's talk about it," I hear, then slam the door.

A wife and mother begins her new life in a new country, and that life is cut short. Yet her husband tells her: Complete what we have started. We, who stayed out of politics and came halfway around the world to avoid religious and political feuding have been the first in the New World to die from it. I no longer know what we started, nor how to complete it. I write letters to the editors of local papers and to members of Parliament. Now at least they admit it was a bomb. One MP answers back, with sympathy, but with a challenge. You want to make a difference? Work on a campaign. Work on mine. Politicize the Indian voter.

My husband's old lawyer helps me set up a trust. Vikram was a saver and a careful investor. He had saved the boys' boarding school and college fees. I sell the pink house at four times what we paid for it and take a small apartment downtown. I am looking for a charity to support.

We are deep in the Toronto winter, gray skies, icy pavements. I stay indoors, watching television. I have tried to assess my situation, how best to live my life, to complete what we began so many years ago. Kusum has written me from Hardwar that her life is now serene. She has seen Satish and has heard her daughter sing again. Kusum was on a pilgrimage, passing through a village when she heard a young girl's voice, singing one of her daughter's favorite *bhajans*. She followed the music through the squalor of a Himalayan village, to a hut where a young girl, an exact replica of her daughter, was fanning coals under the kitchen fire. When she appeared, the girl cried out, "Ma!" and ran away. What did I think of that?

I think I can only envy her.

140   Pam didn't make it to California, but writes me from Vancouver. She works in a department store, giving make-up hints to Indian and Oriental girls. Dr. Ranganathan has given up his commute, given up his house and job, and accepted an academic position in Texas where no one knows his story and he has vowed not to tell it. He calls me now once a week.

I wait, I listen, and I pray, but Vikram has not returned to me. The voices and the shapes and the nights filled with visions ended abruptly several weeks ago.

I take it as a sign.

One rare, beautiful, sunny day last week, returning from a small errand on Yonge Street, I was walking through the park from the subway to my apartment. I live equidistant from the Ontario Houses of Parliament and the University of Toronto. The day was not cold, but something in the bare trees caught my attention. I looked up from the gravel, into the branches and the clear blue sky beyond. I thought I heard the rustling of larger forms, and I waited a moment for voices. Nothing.

"What?" I asked.

145   Then as I stood in the path looking north to Queen's Park and west to the university, I heard the voices of my family one last time. *Your time has come,* they said. *Go, be brave.*

I do not know where this voyage I have begun will end. I do not know which direction I will take. I dropped the package on a park bench and started walking.

                                                                          1988

QUESTIONS

1. What words and images in the opening paragraphs of "The Management of Grief" provide the reader with clues to the story's underlying themes of cultural dislocation and the mixing of cultures?
2. Throughout the story Bharati Mukherjee pays close attention to the significance of words and the ways that words express, or fail to express, emotional truths. Find some examples of words and phrases that the narrator and other characters notice as having special significance. Can you think of words in one culture that defy translation into the language of another?
3. What is the thematic significance of this story's central event, a plane disaster? How does the story's narrator, Mrs. Bhave, view the Irish people at the crash site, who give flowers and hug the surviving relatives? What is the significance of her comment, "I cannot imagine reactions like that on the streets of Toronto" (par. 65)?

JHUMPA LAHIRI

Interpreter of Maladies

At the tea stall Mr. and Mrs. Das bickered about who should take Tina to the toilet. Eventually Mrs. Das relented when Mr. Das pointed out that he had given the girl her bath the night before. In the rearview mirror Mr. Kapasi watched as Mrs. Das emerged slowly from his bulky white Ambassador, dragging her shaved, largely bare legs across the back seat. She did not hold the little girl's hand as they walked to the rest room.

They were on their way to see the Sun Temple at Konarak.[1] It was a dry, bright Saturday, the mid-July heat tempered by a steady ocean breeze, ideal weather for sightseeing. Ordinarily Mr. Kapasi would not have stopped so soon along the way, but less than five minutes after he'd picked up the family that morning in front of Hotel Sandy Villa, the little girl had complained. The first thing Mr. Kapasi had noticed when he saw Mr. and Mrs. Das, standing with their children under the portico of the hotel, was that they were very young, perhaps not even thirty. In addition to Tina they had two boys, Ronny and Bobby, who appeared very close in age and had teeth covered in a network of flashing silver wires. The family looked Indian but dressed as foreigners did, the children in stiff, brightly colored clothing and caps with translucent visors. Mr. Kapasi was accustomed to foreign tourists; he was assigned to them regularly because he could speak English. Yesterday he had driven an elderly couple from Scotland, both with spotted faces and fluffy white hair so thin it exposed their sunburnt scalps. In comparison, the tanned, youthful faces of Mr. and Mrs. Das were all the more striking. When he'd introduced himself, Mr. Kapasi had pressed his palms together in greeting, but Mr. Das squeezed hands like an American so that Mr. Kapasi felt it in his elbow. Mrs. Das, for her part, had flexed one side of her mouth, smiling dutifully at Mr. Kapasi, without displaying any interest in him.

---

1. In paragraphs 91–98, the story provides an accurate history and description of the Sun Temple at Konark (or Konarak), still a pilgrimage as well as tourist site near the east coast in the Orissa region of India. According to legend, the temple was built because Samba, son of Lord Krishna, was cured of leprosy by Surya, the sun god.

As they waited at the tea stall, Ronny, who looked like the older of the two boys, clambered suddenly out of the back seat, intrigued by a goat tied to a stake in the ground.

"Don't touch it," Mr. Das said. He glanced up from his paperback tour book, which said "INDIA" in yellow letters and looked as if it had been published abroad. His voice, somehow tentative and a little shrill, sounded as though it had not yet settled into maturity.

5   "I want to give it a piece of gum," the boy called back as he trotted ahead.

Mr. Das stepped out of the car and stretched his legs by squatting briefly to the ground. A clean-shaven man, he looked exactly like a magnified version of Ronny. He had a sapphire blue visor, and was dressed in shorts, sneakers, and a T-shirt. The camera slung around his neck, with an impressive telephoto lens and numerous buttons and markings, was the only complicated thing he wore. He frowned, watching as Ronny rushed toward the goat, but appeared to have no intention of intervening. "Bobby, make sure that your brother doesn't do anything stupid."

"I don't feel like it," Bobby said, not moving. He was sitting in the front seat beside Mr. Kapasi, studying a picture of the elephant god taped to the glove compartment.

"No need to worry," Mr. Kapasi said. "They are quite tame." Mr. Kapasi was forty-six years old, with receding hair that had gone completely silver, but his butterscotch complexion and his unlined brow, which he treated in spare moments to dabs of lotus-oil balm, made it easy to imagine what he must have looked like at an earlier age. He wore gray trousers and a matching jacket-style shirt, tapered at the waist, with short sleeves and a large pointed collar, made of a thin but durable synthetic material. He had specified both the cut and the fabric to his tailor—it was his preferred uniform for giving tours because it did not get crushed during his long hours behind the wheel. Through the windshield he watched as Ronny circled around the goat, touched it quickly on its side, then trotted back to the car.

"You left India as a child?" Mr. Kapasi asked when Mr. Das had settled once again into the passenger seat.

10   "Oh, Mina and I were both born in America," Mr. Das announced with an air of sudden confidence. "Born and raised. Our parents live here now, in Assansol.[2] They retired. We visit them every couple years." He turned to watch as the little girl ran toward the car, the wide purple bows of her sundress flopping on her narrow brown shoulders. She was holding to her chest a doll with yellow hair that looked as if it had been chopped, as a punitive measure, with a pair of dull scissors. "This is Tina's first trip to India, isn't it, Tina?"

"I don't have to go to the bathroom anymore," Tina announced.

"Where's Mina?" Mr. Das asked.

Mr. Kapasi found it strange that Mr. Das should refer to his wife by her first name when speaking to the little girl. Tina pointed to where Mrs. Das was purchasing something from one of the shirtless men who worked at the tea stall. Mr. Kapasi heard one of the shirtless men sing a phrase from a popular Hindi love song as Mrs. Das walked back to the car, but she did not appear to understand

---

2. Or Asonsol, a city in northeastern India, not far from Calcutta and about three hundred miles from Puri, the coastal city in Orissa that the Das family is visiting. Puri is both a tourist resort and a Hindu holy city, said to be dominated by the forces of both the gods and humanity.

the words of the song, for she did not express irritation, or embarrassment, or react in any other way to the man's declarations.

He observed her. She wore a red-and-white-checkered skirt that stopped above her knees, slip-on shoes with a square wooden heel, and a close-fitting blouse styled like a man's undershirt. The blouse was decorated at chest-level with a calico appliqué in the shape of a strawberry. She was a short woman, with small hands like paws, her frosty pink fingernails painted to match her lips, and was slightly plump in her figure. Her hair, shorn only a little longer than her husband's, was parted far to one side. She was wearing large dark brown sunglasses with a pinkish tint to them, and carried a big straw bag, almost as big as her torso, shaped like a bowl, with a water bottle poking out of it. She walked slowly, carrying some puffed rice tossed with peanuts and chili peppers in a large packet made from newspapers. Mr. Kapasi turned to Mr. Das.

"Where in America do you live?"   15

"New Brunswick, New Jersey."

"Next to New York?"

"Exactly. I teach middle school there."

"What subject?"

"Science. In fact, every year I take my students on a trip to the Museum of   20
Natural History in New York City. In a way we have a lot in common, you could say, you and I. How long have you been a tour guide, Mr. Kapasi?"

"Five years."

Mrs. Das reached the car. "How long's the trip?" she asked, shutting the door.

"About two and a half hours," Mr. Kapasi replied.

At this Mrs. Das gave an impatient sigh, as if she had been traveling her whole life without pause. She fanned herself with a folded Bombay film magazine written in English.

"I thought that the Sun Temple is only eighteen miles north of Puri," Mr. Das   25
said, tapping on the tour book.

"The roads to Konarak are poor. Actually it is a distance of fifty-two miles," Mr. Kapasi explained.

Mr. Das nodded, readjusting the camera strap where it had begun to chafe the back of his neck.

Before starting the ignition, Mr. Kapasi reached back to make sure the crank-like locks on the inside of each of the back doors were secured. As soon as the car began to move the little girl began to play with the lock on her side, clicking it with some effort forward and backward, but Mrs. Das said nothing to stop her. She sat a bit slouched at one end of the back seat, not offering her puffed rice to anyone. Ronny and Tina sat on either side of her, both snapping bright green gum.

"Look," Bobby said as the car began to gather speed. He pointed with his finger to the tall trees that lined the road. "Look."

"Monkeys!" Ronny shrieked. "Wow!"   30

They were seated in groups along the branches, with shining black faces, silver bodies, horizontal eyebrows, and crested heads. Their long gray tails dangled like a series of ropes among the leaves. A few scratched themselves with black leathery hands, or swung their feet, staring as the car passed.

"We call them the hanuman," Mr. Kapasi said. "They are quite common in the area."

As soon as he spoke, one of the monkeys leaped into the middle of the road, causing Mr. Kapasi to brake suddenly. Another bounced onto the hood of the car, then sprang away. Mr. Kapasi beeped his horn. The children began to get excited, sucking in their breath and covering their faces partly with their hands. They had never seen monkeys outside of a zoo, Mr. Das explained. He asked Mr. Kapasi to stop the car so that he could take a picture.

While Mr. Das adjusted his telephoto lens, Mrs. Das reached into her straw bag and pulled out a bottle of colorless nail polish, which she proceeded to stroke on the tip of her index finger.

35   The little girl stuck out a hand. "Mine too. Mommy, do mine too."

"Leave me alone," Mrs. Das said, blowing on her nail and turning her body slightly. "You're making me mess up."

The little girl occupied herself by buttoning and unbuttoning a pinafore on the doll's plastic body.

"All set," Mr. Das said, replacing the lens cap.

The car rattled considerably as it raced along the dusty road, causing them all to pop up from their seats every now and then, but Mrs. Das continued to polish her nails. Mr. Kapasi eased up on the accelerator, hoping to produce a smoother ride. When he reached for the gearshift the boy in front accommodated him by swinging his hairless knees out of the way. Mr. Kapasi noted that this boy was slightly paler than the other children. "Daddy, why is the driver sitting on the wrong side in this car, too?" the boy asked.

40   "They all do that here, dummy," Ronny said.

"Don't call your brother a dummy," Mr. Das said. He turned to Mr. Kapasi. "In America, you know . . . it confuses them."

"Oh yes, I am well aware," Mr. Kapasi said. As delicately as he could, he shifted gears again, accelerating as they approached a hill in the road. "I see it on *Dallas*, the steering wheels are on the left-hand side."

"What's *Dallas*?" Tina asked, banging her now naked doll on the seat behind Mr. Kapasi.

"It went off the air," Mr. Das explained. "It's a television show."[3]

45   They were all like siblings, Mr. Kapasi thought as they passed a row of date trees. Mr. and Mrs. Das behaved like an older brother and sister, not parents. It seemed that they were in charge of the children only for the day; it was hard to believe they were regularly responsible for anything other than themselves. Mr. Das tapped on his lens cap, and his tour book, dragging his thumbnail occasionally across the pages so that they made a scraping sound. Mrs. Das continued to polish her nails. She had still not removed her sunglasses. Every now and then Tina renewed her plea that she wanted her nails done, too, and so at one point Mrs. Das flicked a drop of polish on the little girl's finger before depositing the bottle back inside her straw bag.

"Isn't this an air-conditioned car?" she asked, still blowing on her hand. The window on Tina's side was broken and could not be rolled down.

"Quit complaining," Mr. Das said. "It isn't so hot."

"I told you to get a car with air-conditioning," Mrs. Das continued. "Why do you do this, Raj, just to save a few stupid rupees. What are you saving us, fifty cents?"

3. Reruns of this American television show (1978–91) featuring the rich, dysfunctional Ewing family of Dallas continue worldwide.

Their accents sounded just like the ones Mr. Kapasi heard on American television programs, though not like the ones on *Dallas*.

"Doesn't it get tiresome, Mr. Kapasi, showing people the same thing every 50 day?" Mr. Das asked, rolling down his own window all the way. "Hey, do you mind stopping the car. I just want to get a shot of this guy."

Mr. Kapasi pulled over to the side of the road as Mr. Das took a picture of a barefoot man, his head wrapped in a dirty turban, seated on top of a cart of grain sacks pulled by a pair of bullocks. Both the man and the bullocks were emaciated. In the back seat Mrs. Das gazed out another window, at the sky, where nearly transparent clouds passed quickly in front of one another.

"I look forward to it, actually," Mr. Kapasi said as they continued on their way. "The Sun Temple is one of my favorite places. In that way it is a reward for me. I give tours on Fridays and Saturdays only. I have another job during the week."

"Oh? Where?" Mr. Das asked.

"I work in a doctor's office."

"You're a doctor?" 55

"I am not a doctor. I work with one. As an interpreter."

"What does a doctor need an interpreter for?"

"He has a number of Gujarati patients. My father was Gujarati, but many people do not speak Gujarati in this area,[4] including the doctor. And so the doctor asked me to work in his office, interpreting what the patients say."

"Interesting. I've never heard of anything like that," Mr. Das said.

Mr. Kapasi shrugged. "It is a job like any other." 60

"But so romantic," Mrs. Das said dreamily, breaking her extended silence. She lifted her pinkish brown sunglasses and arranged them on top of her head like a tiara. For the first time, her eyes met Mr. Kapasi's in the rearview mirror: pale, a bit small, their gaze fixed but drowsy.

Mr. Das craned to look at her. "What's so romantic about it?"

"I don't know. Something." She shrugged, knitting her brows together for an instant. "Would you like a piece of gum, Mr. Kapasi?" she asked brightly. She reached into her straw bag and handed him a small square wrapped in green-and-white-striped paper. As soon as Mr. Kapasi put the gum in his mouth a thick sweet liquid burst onto his tongue.

"Tell us more about your job, Mr. Kapasi," Mrs. Das said.

"What would you like to know, madame?" 65

"I don't know," she shrugged, munching on some puffed rice and licking the mustard oil from the corners of her mouth. "Tell us a typical situation." She settled back in her seat, her head tilted in a patch of sun, and closed her eyes. "I want to picture what happens."

"Very well. The other day a man came in with a pain in his throat."

"Did he smoke cigarettes?"

"No. It was very curious. He complained that he felt as if there were long pieces of straw stuck in his throat. When I told the doctor he was able to prescribe the proper medication."

"That's so neat." 70

---

4. Gujarat is a northwestern region of India, on the Arabian Sea. Mr. Kapasi speaks several of India's disparate regional languages—those of Bengal and Orissa, near where he lives, and Gujarati, from the opposite coast—along with the more widespread Hindi and English.

"Yes," Mr. Kapasi agreed after some hesitation.

"So these patients are totally dependent on you," Mrs. Das said. She spoke slowly, as if she were thinking aloud. "In a way, more dependent on you than the doctor."

"How do you mean? How could it be?"

"Well, for example, you could tell the doctor that the pain felt like a burning, not straw. The patient would never know what you had told the doctor, and the doctor wouldn't know that you had told the wrong thing. It's a big responsibility."

75   "Yes, a big responsibility you have there, Mr. Kapasi," Mr. Das agreed.

Mr. Kapasi had never thought of his job in such complimentary terms. To him it was a thankless occupation. He found nothing noble in interpreting people's maladies, assiduously translating the symptoms of so many swollen bones, countless cramps of bellies and bowels, spots on people's palms that changed color, shape, or size. The doctor, nearly half his age, had an affinity for bell-bottom trousers and made humorless jokes about the Congress party.[5] Together they worked in a stale little infirmary where Mr. Kapasi's smartly tailored clothes clung to him in the heat, in spite of the blackened blades of a ceiling fan churning over their heads.

The job was a sign of his failings. In his youth he'd been a devoted scholar of foreign languages, the owner of an impressive collection of dictionaries. He had dreamed of being an interpreter for diplomats and dignitaries, resolving conflicts between people and nations, settling disputes of which he alone could understand both sides. He was a self-educated man. In a series of notebooks, in the evenings before his parents settled his marriage, he had listed the common etymologies of words, and at one point in his life he was confident that he could converse, if given the opportunity, in English, French, Russian, Portuguese, and Italian, not to mention Hindi, Bengali, Orissi, and Gujarati. Now only a handful of European phrases remained in his memory, scattered words for things like saucers and chairs. English was the only non-Indian language he spoke fluently anymore. Mr. Kapasi knew it was not a remarkable talent. Sometimes he feared that his children knew better English than he did, just from watching television. Still, it came in handy for the tours.

He had taken the job as an interpreter after his first son, at the age of seven, contracted typhoid—that was how he had first made the acquaintance of the doctor. At the time Mr. Kapasi had been teaching English in a grammar school, and he bartered his skills as an interpreter to pay the increasingly exorbitant medical bills. In the end the boy had died one evening in his mother's arms, his limbs burning with fever, but then there was the funeral to pay for, and the other children who were born soon enough, and the newer, bigger house, and the good schools and tutors, and the fine shoes and the television, and the countless other ways he tried to console his wife and to keep her from crying in her sleep, and so when the doctor offered to pay him twice as much as he earned at the grammar school, he accepted. Mr. Kapasi knew that his wife had little regard for his career as an interpreter. He knew it reminded her of the son she'd lost, and that she resented the other lives he helped, in his own small way, to save. If ever she

---

5. The Indian National Congress party, founded in 1885, led the movement for independence from Britain (gained in 1947) through the successive leadership of Mohandas Gandhi and Jawaharlal Nehru. The party divided and subdivided, but a faction once led by Indira Gandhi dominated through the 1980s and much of the 1990s, despite being constantly accused of corruption and of using violent tactics.

referred to his position, she used the phrase "doctor's assistant," as if the process of interpretation were equal to taking someone's temperature, or changing a bedpan. She never asked him about the patients who came to the doctor's office, or said that his job was a big responsibility.

For this reason it flattered Mr. Kapasi that Mrs. Das was so intrigued by his job. Unlike his wife, she had reminded him of its intellectual challenges. She had also used the word "romantic." She did not behave in a romantic way toward her husband, and yet she had used the word to describe him. He wondered if Mr. and Mrs. Das were a bad match, just as he and his wife were. Perhaps they, too, had little in common apart from three children and a decade of their lives. The signs he recognized from his own marriage were there—the bickering, the indifference, the protracted silences. Her sudden interest in him, an interest she did not express in either her husband or her children, was mildly intoxicating. When Mr. Kapasi thought once again about how she had said "romantic," the feeling of intoxication grew.

He began to check his reflection in the rearview mirror as he drove, feeling 80 grateful that he had chosen the gray suit that morning and not the brown one, which tended to sag a little in the knees. From time to time he glanced through the mirror at Mrs. Das. In addition to glancing at her face he glanced at the strawberry between her breasts, and the golden brown hollow in her throat. He decided to tell Mrs. Das about another patient, and another: the young woman who had complained of a sensation of raindrops in her spine, the gentleman whose birthmark had begun to sprout hairs. Mrs. Das listened attentively, stroking her hair with a small plastic brush that resembled an oval bed of nails, asking more questions, for yet another example. The children were quiet, intent on spotting more monkeys in the trees, and Mr. Das was absorbed by his tour book, so it seemed like a private conversation between Mr. Kapasi and Mrs. Das. In this manner the next half hour passed, and when they stopped for lunch at a roadside restaurant that sold fritters and omelette sandwiches, usually something Mr. Kapasi looked forward to on his tours so that he could sit in peace and enjoy some hot tea, he was disappointed. As the Das family settled together under a magenta umbrella fringed with white and orange tassels, and placed their orders with one of the waiters who marched about in tricornered caps, Mr. Kapasi reluctantly headed toward a neighboring table.

"Mr. Kapasi, wait. There's room here," Mrs. Das called out. She gathered Tina onto her lap, insisting that he accompany them. And so, together, they had bottled mango juice and sandwiches and plates of onions and potatoes deep-fried in graham-flour batter. After finishing two omelette sandwiches Mr. Das took more pictures of the group as they ate.

"How much longer?" he asked Mr. Kapasi as he paused to load a new roll of film in the camera.

"About half an hour more."

By now the children had gotten up from the table to look at more monkeys perched in a nearby tree, so there was a considerable space between Mrs. Das and Mr. Kapasi. Mr. Das placed the camera to his face and squeezed one eye shut, his tongue exposed at one corner of his mouth. "This looks funny. Mina, you need to lean in closer to Mr. Kapasi."

She did. He could smell a scent on her skin, like a mixture of whiskey and 85 rosewater. He worried suddenly that she could smell his perspiration, which he knew had collected beneath the synthetic material of his shirt. He polished off his mango juice in one gulp and smoothed his silver hair with his hands. A bit of the juice dripped onto his chin. He wondered if Mrs. Das had noticed.

She had not. "What's your address, Mr. Kapasi?" she inquired, fishing for something inside her straw bag.

"You would like my address?"

"So we can send you copies," she said. "Of the pictures." She handed him a scrap of paper which she had hastily ripped from a page of her film magazine. The blank portion was limited, for the narrow strip was crowded by lines of text and a tiny picture of a hero and heroine embracing under a eucalyptus tree.

The paper curled as Mr. Kapasi wrote his address in clear, careful letters. She would write to him, asking about his days interpreting at the doctor's office, and he would respond eloquently, choosing only the most entertaining anecdotes, ones that would make her laugh out loud as she read them in her house in New Jersey. In time she would reveal the disappointment of her marriage, and he his. In this way their friendship would grow, and flourish. He would possess a picture of the two of them, eating fried onions under a magenta umbrella, which he would keep, he decided, safely tucked between the pages of his Russian grammar. As his mind raced, Mr. Kapasi experienced a mild and pleasant shock. It was similar to a feeling he used to experience long ago when, after months of translating with the aid of a dictionary, he would finally read a passage from a French novel, or an Italian sonnet, and understand the words, one after another, unencumbered by his own efforts. In those moments Mr. Kapasi used to believe that all was right with the world, that all struggles were rewarded, that all of life's mistakes made sense in the end. The promise that he would hear from Mrs. Das now filled him with the same belief.

90   When he finished writing his address Mr. Kapasi handed her the paper, but as soon as he did so he worried that he had either misspelled his name, or accidentally reversed the numbers of his postal code. He dreaded the possibility of a lost letter, the photograph never reaching him, hovering somewhere in Orissa, close but ultimately unattainable. He thought of asking for the slip of paper again, just to make sure he had written his address accurately, but Mrs. Das had already dropped it into the jumble of her bag.

They reached Konarak at two-thirty. The temple, made of sandstone, was a massive pyramid-like structure in the shape of a chariot. It was dedicated to the great master of life, the sun, which struck three sides of the edifice as it made its journey each day across the sky. Twenty-four giant wheels were carved on the north and south sides of the plinth. The whole thing was drawn by a team of seven horses, speeding as if through the heavens. As they approached, Mr. Kapasi explained that the temple had been built between A.D. 1243 and 1255, with the efforts of twelve hundred artisans, by the great ruler of the Ganga dynasty, King Narasimhadeva the First, to commemorate his victory against the Muslim army.

"It says the temple occupies about a hundred and seventy acres of land," Mr. Das said, reading from his book.

"It's like a desert," Ronny said, his eyes wandering across the sand that stretched on all sides beyond the temple.

"The Chandrabhaga River once flowed one mile north of here. It is dry now," Mr. Kapasi said, turning off the engine.

They got out and walked toward the temple, posing first for pictures by the 95
pair of lions that flanked the steps. Mr. Kapasi led them next to one of the
wheels of the chariot, higher than any human being, nine feet in diameter.

"'The wheels are supposed to symbolize the wheel of life,'" Mr. Das read.
"'They depict the cycle of creation, preservation, and achievement of realization.'
Cool." He turned the page of his book. "'Each wheel is divided into eight thick
and thin spokes, dividing the day into eight equal parts. The rims are carved with
designs of birds and animals, whereas the medallions in the spokes are carved
with women in luxurious poses, largely erotic in nature.'"

What he referred to were the countless friezes of entwined naked bodies,
making love in various positions, women clinging to the necks of men, their
knees wrapped eternally around their lovers' thighs. In addition to these were
assorted scenes from daily life, of hunting and trading, of deer being killed with
bows and arrows and marching warriors holding swords in their hands.

It was no longer possible to enter the temple, for it had filled with rubble years
ago, but they admired the exterior, as did all the tourists Mr. Kapasi brought
there, slowly strolling along each of its sides. Mr. Das trailed behind, taking pictures. The children ran ahead, pointing to figures of naked people, intrigued in
particular by the Nagamithunas, the half-human, half-serpentine couples who
were said, Mr. Kapasi told them, to live in the deepest waters of the sea. Mr.
Kapasi was pleased that they liked the temple, pleased especially that it appealed
to Mrs. Das. She stopped every three or four paces, staring silently at the carved
lovers, and the processions of elephants, and the topless female musicians beating on two-sided drums.

Though Mr. Kapasi had been to the temple countless times, it occurred to
him, as he, too, gazed at the topless women, that he had never seen his own wife
fully naked. Even when they had made love she kept the panels of her blouse
hooked together, the string of her petticoat knotted around her waist. He had
never admired the backs of his wife's legs the way he now admired those of Mrs.
Das, walking as if for his benefit alone. He had, of course, seen plenty of bare
limbs before, belonging to the American and European ladies who took his
tours. But Mrs. Das was different. Unlike the other women, who had an interest
only in the temple, and kept their noses buried in a guidebook, on their eyes
behind the lens of a camera, Mrs. Das had taken an interest in him.

Mr. Kapasi was anxious to be alone with her, to continue their private conversa- 100
tion, yet he felt nervous to walk at her side. She was lost behind her sunglasses,
ignoring her husband's requests that she pose for another picture, walking past
her children as if they were strangers. Worried that he might disturb her, Mr.
Kapasi walked ahead, to admire, as he always did, the three life-sized bronze avatars of Surya, the sun god, each emerging from its own niche on the temple facade
to greet the sun at dawn, noon, and evening. They wore elaborate headdresses,
their languid, elongated eyes closed, their bare chests draped with carved chains
and amulets. Hibiscus petals, offerings from previous visitors, were strewn at their
gray-green feet. The last statue, on the northern wall of the temple, was Mr. Kapasi's
favorite. This Surya had a tired expression, weary after a hard day of work, sitting
astride a horse with folded legs. Even his horse's eyes were drowsy. Around his
body were smaller sculptures of women in pairs, their hips thrust to one side.

"Who's that?" Mrs. Das asked. He was startled to see that she was standing
beside him.

"He is the Astachala-Surya," Mr. Kapasi said. "The setting sun."

"So in a couple of hours the sun will set right here?" She slipped a foot out of one of her square-heeled shoes, rubbed her toes on the back of her other leg.

"That is correct."

105 She raised her sunglasses for a moment, then put them back on again. "Neat."

Mr. Kapasi was not certain exactly what the word suggested, but he had a feeling it was a favorable response. He hoped that Mrs. Das had understood Surya's beauty, his power. Perhaps they would discuss it further in their letters. He would explain things to her, things about India, and she would explain things to him about America. In its own way this correspondence would fulfill his dream, of serving as an interpreter between nations. He looked at her straw bag, delighted that his address lay nestled among its contents. When he pictured her so many thousands of miles away he plummeted, so much so that he had an overwhelming urge to wrap his arms around her, to freeze with her, even for an instant, in an embrace witnessed by his favorite Surya. But Mrs. Das had already started walking.

"When do you return to America?" he asked, trying to sound placid.

"In ten days."

He calculated: A week to settle in, a week to develop the pictures, a few days to compose her letter, two weeks to get to India by air. According to his schedule, allowing room for delays, he would hear from Mrs. Das in approximately six weeks' time.

110 The family was silent as Mr. Kapasi drove them back, a little past four-thirty, to Hotel Sandy Villa. The children had bought miniature granite versions of the chariot's wheels at a souvenir stand, and they turned them round in their hands. Mr. Das continued to read his book. Mrs. Das untangled Tina's hair with her brush and divided it into two little ponytails.

Mr. Kapasi was beginning to dread the thought of dropping them off. He was not prepared to begin his six-week wait to hear from Mrs. Das. As he stole glances at her in the rearview mirror, wrapping elastic bands around Tina's hair, he wondered how he might make the tour last a little longer. Ordinarily he sped back to Puri using a shortcut, eager to return home, scrub his feet and hands with sandalwood soap, and enjoy the evening newspaper and a cup of tea that his wife would serve him in silence. The thought of that silence, something to which he'd long been resigned, now oppressed him. It was then that he suggested visiting the hills at Udayagiri and Khandagiri, where a number of monastic dwellings were hewn out of the ground, facing one another across a defile. It was some miles away, but well worth seeing, Mr. Kapasi told them.

"Oh yeah, there's something mentioned about it in this book," Mr. Das said. "Built by a Jain king or something."[6]

"Shall we go then?" Mr. Kapasi asked. He paused at a turn in the road. "It's to the left."

Mr. Das turned to look at Mrs. Das. Both of them shrugged.

115 "Left, left," the children chanted.

6. This site is not a major tourist attraction; "giri" means mountain. Jainism, one of the several main religions of India, is an atheist sect that emerged from Hinduism around 580 B.C.E., at about the same time as Buddhism.

Mr. Kapasi turned the wheel, almost delirious with relief. He did not know what he would do or say to Mrs. Das once they arrived at the hills. Perhaps he would tell her what a pleasing smile she had. Perhaps he would compliment her strawberry shirt, which he found irresistibly becoming. Perhaps, when Mr. Das was busy taking a picture, he would take her hand.

He did not have to worry. When they got to the hills, divided by a steep path thick with trees, Mrs. Das refused to get out of the car. All along the path, dozens of monkeys were seated on stones, as well as on the branches of the trees. Their hind legs were stretched out in front and raised to shoulder level, their arms resting on their knees.

"My legs are tired," she said, sinking low in her seat. "I'll stay here."

"Why did you have to wear those stupid shoes?" Mr. Das said. "You won't be in the pictures."

"Pretend I'm there." 120

"But we could use one of these pictures for our Christmas card this year. We didn't get one of all five of us at the Sun Temple. Mr. Kapasi could take it."

"I'm not coming. Anyway, those monkeys give me the creeps."

"But they're harmless," Mr. Das said. He turned to Mr. Kapasi. "Aren't they?"

"They are more hungry than dangerous," Mr. Kapasi said. "Do not provoke them with food, and they will not bother you."

Mr. Das headed up the defile with the children, the boys at his side, the little 125 girl on his shoulders. Mr. Kapasi watched as they crossed paths with a Japanese man and woman, the only other tourists there, who paused for a final photograph, then stepped into a nearby car and drove away. As the car disappeared out of view some of the monkeys called out, emitting soft whooping sounds, and then walked on their flat black hands and feet up the path. At one point a group of them formed a little ring around Mr. Das and the children. Tina screamed in delight. Ronny ran in circles around his father. Bobby bent down and picked up a fat stick on the ground. When he extended it, one of the monkeys approached him and snatched it, then briefly beat the ground.

"I'll join them," Mr. Kapasi said, unlocking the door on his side. "There is much to explain about the caves."

"No. Stay a minute," Mrs. Das said. She got out of the back seat and slipped in beside Mr. Kapasi. "Raj has his dumb book anyway." Together, through the windshield, Mrs. Das and Mr. Kapasi watched as Bobby and the monkey passed the stick back and forth between them.

"A brave little boy," Mr. Kapasi commented.

"It's not so surprising," Mrs. Das said.

"No?" 130

"He's not his."

"I beg your pardon?"

"Raj's. He's not Raj's son."

Mr. Kapasi felt a prickle on his skin. He reached into his shirt pocket for the small tin of lotus-oil balm he carried with him at all times, and applied it to three spots on his forehead. He knew that Mrs. Das was watching him, but he did not turn to face her. Instead he watched as the figures of Mr. Das and the children grew smaller, climbing up the steep path, pausing every now and then for a picture, surrounded by a growing number of monkeys.

"Are you surprised?" The way she put it made him choose his words with care. 135

"It's not the type of thing one assumes," Mr. Kapasi replied slowly. He put the tin of lotus-oil balm back in his pocket.

"No, of course not. And no one knows, of course. No one at all. I've kept it a secret for eight whole years." She looked at Mr. Kapasi, tilting her chin as if to gain a fresh perspective. "But now I've told you."

Mr. Kapasi nodded. He felt suddenly parched, and his forehead was warm and slightly numb from the balm. He considered asking Mrs. Das for a sip of water, then decided against it.

"We met when we were very young," she said. She reached into her straw bag in search of something, then pulled out a packet of puffed rice. "Want some?"

140 "No, thank you."

She put a fistful in her mouth, sank into the seat a little, and looked away from Mr. Kapasi, out the window on her side of the car. "We married when we were still in college. We were in high school when he proposed. We went to the same college, of course. Back then we couldn't stand the thought of being separated, not for a day, not for a minute. Our parents were best friends who lived in the same town. My entire life I saw him every weekend, either at our house or theirs. We were sent upstairs to play together while our parents joked about our marriage. Imagine! They never caught us at anything, though in a way I think it was all more or less a setup. The things we did those Friday and Saturday nights, while our parents sat downstairs drinking tea . . . I could tell you stories, Mr. Kapasi."

As a result of spending all her time in college with Raj, she continued, she did not make many close friends. There was no one to confide in about him at the end of a difficult day, or to share a passing thought or a worry. Her parents now lived on the other side of the world, but she had never been very close to them, anyway. After marrying so young she was overwhelmed by it all, having a child so quickly, and nursing, and warming up bottles of milk and testing their temperature against her wrist while Raj was at work, dressed in sweaters and corduroy pants, teaching his students about rocks and dinosaurs. Raj never looked cross or harried, or plump as she had become after the first baby.

Always tired, she declined invitations from her one or two college girlfriends, to have lunch or shop in Manhattan. Eventually the friends stopped calling her, so that she was left at home all day with the baby, surrounded by toys that made her trip when she walked or wince when she sat, always cross and tired. Only occasionally did they go out after Ronny was born, and even more rarely did they entertain. Raj didn't mind; he looked forward to coming home from teaching and watching television and bouncing Ronny on his knee. She had been outraged when Raj told her that a Punjabi friend,[7] someone whom she had once met but did not remember, would be staying with them for a week for some job interviews in the New Brunswick area.

Bobby was conceived in the afternoon, on a sofa littered with rubber teething toys, after the friend learned that a London pharmaceutical company had hired him, while Ronny cried to be freed from his playpen. She made no protest when the friend touched the small of her back as she was about to make a pot of coffee, then pulled her against his crisp navy suit. He made love to her swiftly, in silence, with an expertise she had never known, without the meaningful expressions and smiles Raj always insisted on afterward. The next day Raj drove the friend to

7. Person from the Punjab, a northern region of India, near Pakistan.

JFK.[8] He was married now, to a Punjabi girl, and they lived in London still, and every year they exchanged Christmas cards with Raj and Mina, each couple tucking photos of their families into the envelopes. He did not know that he was Bobby's father. He never would.

"I beg your pardon, Mrs. Das, but why have you told me this information?" 145 Mr. Kapasi asked when she had finally finished speaking, and had turned to face him once again.

"For God's sake, stop calling me Mrs. Das. I'm twenty-eight. You probably have children my age."

"Not quite." It disturbed Mr. Kapasi to learn that she thought of him as a parent. The feeling he had had toward her, that had made him check his reflection in the rearview mirror as they drove, evaporated a little.

"I told you because of your talents." She put the packet of puffed rice back into her bag without folding over the top.

"I don't understand," Mr. Kapasi said.

"Don't you see? For eight years I haven't been able to express this to anybody, 150 not to friends, certainly not to Raj. He doesn't even suspect it. He thinks I'm still in love with him. Well, don't you have anything to say?"

"About what?"

"About what I've just told you. About my secret, and about how terrible it makes me feel. I feel terrible looking at my children, and at Raj, always terrible. I have terrible urges, Mr. Kapasi, to throw things away. One day I had the urge to throw everything I own out of the window, the television, the children, everything. Don't you think it's unhealthy?"

He was silent.

"Mr. Kapasi, don't you have anything to say? I thought that was your job."

"My job is to give tours, Mrs. Das." 155

"Not that. Your other job. As an interpreter."

"But we do not face a language barrier. What need is there for an interpreter?"

"That's not what I mean. I would never have told you otherwise. Don't you realize what it means for me to tell you?"

"What does it mean?"

"It means that I'm tired of feeling so terrible all the time. Eight years, Mr. 160 Kapasi, I've been in pain eight years. I was hoping you could help me feel better, say the right thing. Suggest some kind of remedy."

He looked at her, in her red plaid skirt and strawberry T-shirt, a woman not yet thirty, who loved neither her husband nor her children, who had already fallen out of love with life. Her confession depressed him, depressed him all the more when he thought of Mr. Das at the top of the path, Tina clinging to his shoulders, taking pictures of ancient monastic cells cut into the hills to show his students in America, unsuspecting and unaware that one of his sons was not his own. Mr. Kapasi felt insulted that Mrs. Das should ask him to interpret her common, trivial little secret. She did not resemble the patients in the doctor's office, those who came glassy-eyed and desperate, unable to sleep or breathe or urinate with ease, unable, above all, to give words to their pains. Still, Mr. Kapasi believed it was his duty to assist Mrs. Das. Perhaps he ought to tell her to confess the truth to Mr. Das. He would explain that honesty was the best policy. Honesty, surely, would

8. John F. Kennedy International Airport, in New York City.

help her feel better, as she'd put it. Perhaps he would offer to preside over the discussion, as a mediator. He decided to begin with the most obvious question, to get to the heart of the matter, and so he asked, "Is it really pain you feel, Mrs. Das, or is it guilt?"

She turned to him and glared, mustard oil thick on her frosty pink lips. She opened her mouth to say something, but as she glared at Mr. Kapasi some certain knowledge seemed to pass before her eyes, and she stopped. It crushed him; he knew at that moment that he was not even important enough to be properly insulted. She opened the car door and began walking up the path, wobbling a little on her square wooden heels, reaching into her straw bag to eat handfuls of puffed rice. It fell through her fingers, leaving a zigzagging trail, causing a monkey to leap down from a tree and devour the little white grains. In search of more, the monkey began to follow Mrs. Das. Others joined him, so that she was soon being followed by about half a dozen of them, their velvety tails dragging behind.

Mr. Kapasi stepped out of the car. He wanted to holler, to alert her in some way, but he worried that if she knew they were behind her, she would grow nervous. Perhaps she would lose her balance. Perhaps they would pull at her bag or her hair. He began to jog up the path, taking a fallen branch in his hand to scare away the monkeys. Mrs. Das continued walking, oblivious, trailing grains of puffed rice. Near the top of the incline, before a group of cells fronted by a row of squat stone pillars, Mr. Das was kneeling on the ground, focusing the lens of his camera. The children stood under the arcade, now hiding, now emerging from view.

"Wait for me," Mrs. Das called out. "I'm coming."

165   Tina jumped up and down. "Here comes Mommy!"

"Great," Mr. Das said without looking up. "Just in time. We'll get Mr. Kapasi to take a picture of the five of us."

Mr. Kapasi quickened his pace, waving his branch so that the monkeys scampered away, distracted, in another direction.

"Where's Bobby?" Mrs. Das asked when she stopped.

Mr. Das looked up from the camera. "I don't know. Ronny, where's Bobby?"

170   Ronny shrugged. "I thought he was right here."

"Where is he?" Mrs. Das repeated sharply. "What's wrong with all of you?"

They began calling his name, wandering up and down the path a bit. Because they were calling, they did not initially hear the boy's screams. When they found him, a little farther down the path under a tree, he was surrounded by a group of monkeys, over a dozen of them, pulling at his T-shirt with their long black fingers. The puffed rice Mrs. Das had spilled was scattered at his feet, raked over by the monkeys' hands. The boy was silent, his body frozen, swift tears running down his startled face. His bare legs were dusty and red with welts from where one of the monkeys struck him repeatedly with the stick he had given to it earlier.

"Daddy, the monkey's hurting Bobby," Tina said.

Mr. Das wiped his palms on the front of his shorts. In his nervousness he accidentally pressed the shutter on his camera; the whirring noise of the advancing film excited the monkeys, and the one with the stick began to beat Bobby more intently. "What are we supposed to do? What if they start attacking?"

175   "Mr. Kapasi," Mrs. Das shrieked, noticing him standing to one side. "Do something, for God's sake, do something!"

Mr. Kapasi took his branch and shooed them away, hissing at the ones that remained, stomping his feet to scare them. The animals retreated slowly, with a measured gait, obedient but unintimidated. Mr. Kapasi gathered Bobby in his arms and brought him back to where his parents and siblings were standing. As he carried him he was tempted to whisper a secret into the boy's ear. But Bobby was stunned, and shivering with fright, his legs bleeding slightly where the stick had broken the skin. When Mr. Kapasi delivered him to his parents, Mr. Das brushed some dirt off the boy's T-shirt and put the visor on him the right way. Mrs. Das reached into her straw bag to find a bandage which she taped over the cut on his knee. Ronny offered his brother a fresh piece of gum. "He's fine. Just a little scared, right, Bobby?" Mr. Das said, patting the top of his head.

"God, let's get out of here," Mrs. Das said. She folded her arms across the strawberry on her chest. "This place gives me the creeps."

"Yeah. Back to the hotel, definitely," Mr. Das agreed.

"Poor Bobby," Mrs. Das said. "Come here a second. Let Mommy fix your hair." Again she reached into her straw bag, this time for her hairbrush, and began to run it around the edges of the translucent visor. When she whipped out the hairbrush, the slip of paper with Mr. Kapasi's address on it fluttered away in the wind. No one but Mr. Kapasi noticed. He watched as it rose, carried higher and higher by the breeze, into the trees where the monkeys now sat, solemnly observing the scene below. Mr. Kapasi observed it too, knowing that this was the picture of the Das family he would preserve forever in his mind.

1999

QUESTIONS

1. For centuries philosophers have argued whether "nature" or "nurture" is the main shaping principal in our lives. In "Interpreter of Maladies," what details make the Indian-American Das family seem more "naturally" Indian or more "nurtured" by their American upbringing?
2. How might his encounter with the Das family alter Mr. Kapasi's sense of what it means to be Indian? Why is it important that this encounter has as its background a visit to ancient Indian religious shrines?
3. What is the thematic significance of the secret that Mrs. Das reveals to Mr. Kapasi? What is its relationship to the rest of the story and aspects of human behavior that transcend culture and upbringing?

WILLIAM SAIDI

The Nightmare

This time he had to contend with seven frenzied, weird and indomitable witch-doctors. Their myriad feathers, multi-coloured and multi-evil to his eyes, fluttered in the slight breeze as they danced around him. Occasionally they pointed their bony, sweaty fingers at him, all the time chanting some eerie incantations which seemed to increase in volume with the breeze.

It was a macabre scene, which in other circumstances the sophisticated Mr Benjamin Chadiza would have carelessly attributed to his rather flamboyant imagination.

But this scene was real. His presence there in the middle of these emaciated skeletal creatures was indisputable. Even his cynical nature could not cast off the nauseating feeling that these people, if such indeed they were, were real and that the danger they collectively constituted to his life was just as real.

The seven came towards him, the eerie music and the breeze swelling in volume. Their fingers were no longer bony; they were stubby, short, nail-broken, sweat-drenched monstrosities which seemed to have evil powers of their own.

5   Suddenly, only one of the fingers stood out, as if the others were out of focus. That one finger came nearer . . . nearer . . . until it was pointing straight at his face. He was incapable of motion. His whole being was focused on that finger. It held a mystic power over him. He felt that he could have done anything it commanded him to do. But it did not command him to do anything. It merely touched his nose, ever so slightly. But the effect was fantastic.

Chadiza felt his soul leap out of his body through his mouth and his body go limp, like an emptied sack of potatoes. Death. So this was death. When you stood on a high peak and looked at your own body from a distance. You saw it as if it were near, as if you were using powerful binoculars to look at it. But you knew one thing, that you could never return to it. It had been a strong body, he mused irrelevantly. Now it was no more. Without its life-giving motor, it was nothing.

He found himself crying for his body, crying for his spirit to return to it. When it did not, he cried some more.

"Ben! Ben! Ben!"

He heard the familiar voice from far away. He was breathing very heavily, like a man who had witnessed a great tragedy for the first time in his life and did not believe that he could live to tell about it.

10   "Ben! Ben! Ben!"

The familiar voice again. Whose was it? Where was he? With a sinking feeling, he realised he was still crying out aloud for his spirit to return to his body. He cried like a small child, monotonously and without any particular desire to be heard.

He stopped crying abruptly but his mouth remained open as if he would resume crying at any moment. The desire subsided and he heaved a sigh. He opened his eyes and looked into the eyes of his wife.

He gave a shrill scream of terror, remembering the macabre faces of the seven witchdoctors. His wife put her arms around him and soothed him with her warmth, pressing her breasts to his chest and whispering comfort close to his ear. At last he was quiet, breathing steadily but still afraid of opening his eyes.

"I have never known you to have such wild nightmares. In fact, I have never known you to have any nightmares at all," Maria said when they were seated at the breakfast table. Her husband looked fresh and infused with a new strength that she found rather disconcerting.

15   He was normally a very energetic man; it had taken a man of his singular energies to change the school from what it had been before he arrived here. But this morning he seemed all too powerful for her.

"There is always a first time, I understand. A man can live up to fifty without having a single nightmare and then bang! he finds himself panting in the night like a six-year-old. It is nothing that I should worry about, if I were you. The fact that I do not recollect quite what it was all about does not make it any more sinister, as far as I am concerned. It was just a bad dream."

A bad dream? Maria did not think so. Not taken in conjunction with what she knew. She thought he was making a great effort to minimise the significance of the experience—for her sake. But he must realise what it means. He must. She cried out to him in her heart.

The little village was about twenty-five miles from Lusaka.[1] You could not call it entirely rural or primitive, because a bus stopped there once a week to deliver the school mail. But even though it was close to modern civilisation it retained the aura of mysticism which had pervaded it even before the days of the trousered white man.

Benjamin Chadiza had been born in Chipata, then Fort Jameson.[2] He was a dedicated nationalist and the fact that this little village in the Central Province was not his birthplace did not detract from the formidable fact that it was part of the country in which he lived and which he loved. He was a teacher with exceptional talents. The head of his department in the Ministry of Education, back in Lusaka, had been enthusiastic about his new posting.

"The people are apathetic to the educational advances we are trying to make 20 in this country. They pay their school fees but in most cases a school cannot run entirely on its school fees. It needs the spiritual support of those whose children it is intended to benefit. They do not give us their spiritual support. No. They are practically indifferent to every effort we have made to teach their children.

"Mind you, the children attend school. But that in itself is not enough for success. The children have no idea whatsoever what they stand to gain by availing themselves of this opportunity. Their parents have, by their indifference, given them the idea that they can do without this education. And that is dangerous. You cannot teach a child anything if that attitude prevails. I hope you will remedy the situation."

Chadiza's presence had changed the situation, probably remedied it. It had changed the situation so much that it had changed his and Maria's lives.

The witchdoctor had had nothing to do with it. His had been a personal and entirely materialistic war against Chadiza. The fact that Chadiza had accepted the challenge rather dubiously had not made it seem any more patriotic in the eyes of the villagers. The villagers were indifferent to the feud between teacher and witchdoctor. They did not particularly like the witchdoctor but it cannot be said that they loved Chadiza either. They feared the witchdoctor but they had no sympathy for Chadiza.

The witchdoctor was an old man of about seventy-five. His body was withered and he suffered perennially from all the afflictions of senility. But it never seemed to daunt his spirit. He was everywhere in the village, invincible and imperturbable. He moved among the villagers during the day, spoke to few and was spoken to by none. During the night he prowled the village like an unpaid sentry. He had delegated to himself the duties of overseeing the lives of the villagers. He watched over them, but there were those who looked at his philanthropic nocturnal vigils with great scepticism. They thought he was naturally up to no good. Witchdoctors' reputations throughout the country were not respected by anyone.

1. Capital city of Zambia in southern Africa.
2. The town of Fort Jameson, in eastern Zambia near the border with Malawi, was renamed Chipata after Zambia became independent in 1964.

25   Chadiza understood that the villagers had accepted the witchdoctor as something to be feared but something they could do absolutely nothing about. He was there, omnipresent and almost omnipotent, and nobody questioned his presence. Several people had died, according to stories Chadiza had heard. It was not just by coincidence that these men and women had, at one time, crossed verbal swords with the witchdoctor. That they had died under the most unusual circumstances also made it difficult for Chadiza to believe that Nature had actually taken her course.

Chadiza was at first indifferent to the witchdoctor and his alleged powers. He had settled down to do his job, changing the attitude of the villagers towards the school. He did not wish to disappoint the head of his department in Lusaka. He had never disappointed his masters before. That was why they had sent him to Oxford to take a special diploma in teaching. He was now back with enthusiasm and dedicated to the noble cause for which his profession stood.

He was friendly with the villagers. Maria, who set out to do so, found the womenfolk of the village prepared to accept her as one of them. Slowly, the village's attitude towards the school changed until now, five years later, every child in school was proud to be there. Every parent whose child was at the school was also proud of it.

It was long after the villagers had accepted the school as something beneficial to them and their children that the vendetta between Chadiza and the witchdoctor developed in earnest. Chadiza had, of course, foreseen that his presence would not be taken for granted by the witchdoctor. You could not expect a man who had held the position of a minor king to accept relegation to second place without any disapproval. But the disapproval, like everything else about the old man's trade, was subtle.

It became apparent one very dark night, so dark you could not imagine that at times the black sky was illumined by a million stars. Chadiza and Maria were asleep in their house. It was a modern house by the village standards. It was the only house built of burnt bricks. And it had proper windows. The interior was even more surprising to the villagers. The furniture was highly polished and the floor was covered with an expensive carpet on which the villagers treaded with awe whenever they visited the house.

30   Maria was loved by practically every woman in the village. She taught some of them the things she had learnt while at Chipembi Girls' School near Lusaka. They were eager to learn from her and soon she was running a small domestic science class for them.

Maria slept peacefully, her head nestling comfortably in the crook of her husband's arm. Then she stirred slightly and made a childish sound in her sleep. Chadiza was fast asleep.

Then Maria woke up. She left the bed carefully and made for the door without bumping into any of the bedroom furniture.

There stood the witchdoctor, his aging face wreathed in humourless wrinkles. He stood there immobile and apparently not startled by Maria's sudden appearance. He looked at her with yellow eyes that reflected nothing whatever of the emotions running through his withered body.

It was only after he had turned and walked away, without any change of expression on the old face, that the scream suddenly tore out of Maria's heart and blasted the dark silence of the village.

Chadiza was out of bed and standing beside her before she had finished ₃₅ screaming. He rushed after the receding figure of the old man, but did not catch him up. The old man did not seem to have been in a hurry to get away, but Chadiza lost sight of him in the darkness. He returned to find Maria now surrounded by a group of concerned and jabbering village women.

Chadiza let his anger lie low for three days before he went to the witchdoctor's small hut on the outskirts of the village, 'to warn him off,' as he put it to Maria. On that day two people visited the witchdoctor's hut, each at different occasions and for entirely different reasons. The first was Chadiza himself. The second was his wife, Maria.

Chadiza visited the lonely hut one dark starless night. As he strolled to it, the anger he had suppressed during the past three days surged to the surface. He clenched his fists. He made a great effort to steel himself against the seemingly insurmountable desire to smash the old man's face at first sight. The consequences could either be disastrous or downright ridiculous. The witchdoctor could cripple him; that would be tragic. Then again the witchdoctor could make him the laughingstock of the village—a young man hitting a defenceless old man.

There was no door on the witchdoctor's hut. It was dark inside, although Chadiza saw later that an old candle cast lame light in the hut.

"Come in, my son," the strong, faintly sneering voice said from somewhere near the flickering light of the candle. For a moment, a small chill ran down Chadiza's spine. My son? Chadiza wondered. Why "my son"?

That voice! It seemed to drip with evil, with multiple innuendoes of wicked ₄₀ intentions. But he could not allow such ridiculous superstitious nonsense to influence him. Here he was, a twentieth-century educated and intelligent African who had no ties with the forgotten past of his people's dark ages. What could the witchdoctor do to him? What, indeed, could anybody—the witchdoctor or anybody else in the village, except God—do to him that he could not do to them?

Chadiza thought there was nothing. So he stepped into the little dark hut, sensing as he did that it would be very difficult to see the old man in the restricted light. He also sensed, rather than saw, the paraphernalia of the man's trade. They hung from the soot-blackened grass roof, like their master's guardians. They swayed slightly, although the night was still and windless. Chadiza had vague ideas about the wares of the witchdoctor in his beloved country. But he had never come face to face with them. Now he consoled himself with the thought that in the doubtful light he was not going to see them at close quarters.

The whole interview was a "shambles," as far as Chadiza was concerned. Instead of being the aggressor that he had intended to be, he ended up cowering before the vitriolic abuse the old man poured out at him from his old toothless mouth.

"You are not one of us. You do not understand. You are educated. You think you know better. You despise me. You think I cannot harm you. You think I am just a spent old man playing a game that has long become obsolete."

The witchdoctor's voice rose. "I am not! I tell you, I am not! I can do things to you that your white people cannot do to you. I am an old man. That is true. But I am only old in my body. Not in my mind. I still have the power bestowed upon me by my forefathers, the powers that have made these people in the village fear me, respect me. And you come here and think you can lower their respect for me. I am telling you here and now that before you leave this village—whether before or after I have joined my distinguished ancestors—you will learn a few things."

45   He paused. Chadiza could not see him. He himself had not said a word. After that outburst, he had no wish to say anything either. All he wanted to do was to leave the hut.

The old man said, his voice softening imperceptibly: "You would not know about this, but do you know what it feels to be disowned by your own daughter because of the powers bestowed on you by your forefathers? Never mind, it is something you will not understand. You think you are too educated. But I am telling you. . . ."

Chadiza could not laugh at the threats. He had intended to take them lightly. But as he walked back to his own house he found it increasingly difficult to do so. And what about the daughter who disowned her father? He was not supposed to understand that. He did not understand it.

The intense feeling with which the old man had infused his voice during the one-sided interview had gone right to his heart. The old man was not to be dismissed perfunctorily like a medical charlatan. There was nothing Bacchanalian[3] about him, or about his hut, for that matter. The village did take him seriously. Maybe Chadiza should start taking him seriously too.

But his wife refused to let it worry him. "It cannot be that serious. That old man is just a ranting old weasel with nothing useful to do around here."

50   Maria said this before she herself went to visit the old man. She thought she would come to no harm. She did not come to any harm at all. But when she left the old man she wished he had cast a spell on her.

She held the secret from her husband, much against her will. She held it until the witchdoctor, unable to use his wares to postpone an appointment with his own Armageddon,[4] died.

For five years she lived with it. And for five years, her husband lived quite happily, with thoughts of the vendetta with the old man carefully shelved into the back of his mind. Occasionally, however, a shadow crossed his mind as he remembered the hate with which the old man had spoken to him. And he was convinced that the reference to the daughter who disowned her father had had nothing whatsoever to do with him.

It was, however, just five years after the witchdoctor's death that Chadiza began to have bad dreams. On the day of his first nightmare, Chadiza was unfortunate. He was unfortunate because only his wife knew that he had cried and ranted in his sleep. He had no recollection of the experience whatsoever. It pained Maria to see him so happy, so unaware of the ordeal he was going through. She was disturbed because she knew something that he did not know about the deceased old man. She suggested they leave the village.

"What? Leave all this? All these things we have done for the villagers? You must be out of your mind. Back to the maddening confusion of the town? No. I am afraid I must disagree with you. We shall remain here until we die."

55   They died. Both of them. They died in a raging inferno which the villagers, watching helplessly from a distance, knew to have been their peaceful and well-furnished house.

"If only they had known. At least, if only he had known. . . ."

3. Wildly festive, unrestrained.
4. Site in Israel of a final decisive battle between God and Satan, as foretold in the Book of Revelation.

"But how could he? She obviously never told him. Never told him that she was the witchdoctor's granddaughter. You cannot blame her, probably, for she loved her husband. She feared to lose him."

They chatted on about the tragedy. They—the whole village—had known. They had known that Maria had been watched by the old man on the first day she arrived at the village. The old man had boasted quite publicly that his granddaughter—the child of a daughter who had forsaken him because of his sorcery—was going to live among them.

"But he swore he would do her in because his daughter forsook him. And now he has done it. Poor girl. She was such a beautiful and kind woman. And that husband of hers! Such a wonderful man."

The villagers walked slowly away from the charred debris.   60

"I wonder if she told him that she was born right here in this village," said one villager.

"Oh, I do not think so. They would have left right after they arrived here," another countered.

The smoke rose high in the early morning sky. It faded into nothingness as if signing an epitaph on the lives of the occupants of the house from which it originated.

1985

QUESTIONS

1. The story begins with Chadiza's nightmare, which his wife cannot dismiss as an ordinary bad dream because she knows something. Retrace the sequence of events in the story: What does Maria know at the time that her husband begins to have nightmares? Why is Maria more likely than her husband to believe that the nightmare is a sign?

2. William Saidi himself was born in 1937 in Zimbabwe (then called Rhodesia, under British rule) and worked there as a journalist. Zambia, the setting of "The Nightmare," was Saidi's adopted country until he returned to Zimbabwe in 1980. How does the author's own experience affect your understanding of the theme of cross-cultural encounter in the story?

3. Look closely at the way Benjamin Chadiza's views and goals are described. What difference does it make that he was not born in the village or province, and that he was educated at Oxford? What difference does it make that he was born in another province of Zambia and is a nationalist with the best intentions for the Zambian people? Is this an encounter of two cultures or two aspects of one culture?

SUGGESTIONS FOR WRITING

1. "Interpreter of Maladies" is the title story of a collection by Jhumpa Lahiri, who is also the author of the novel *The Namesake* (now adapted as a film) and other works that are largely set in the United States. Consult several biographical sources on Lahiri (including reviews and interviews online). Write an essay about the setting of "Interpreter of Maladies" in present-day India in light of Lahiri's and her characters' backgrounds. How does setting contribute to theme in this story?

2. Choose one of the stories in this album and examine closely how it is narrated as well as how the characters adapt to or resist adapting to a new environment. Write

an essay discussing how narration, point of view, and characterization enhance the theme. Is the protagonist traditional or modern, an insider or an outsider? Will the difference eventually be resolved?

3. William Saidi, who was educated in English and often writes in English as a journalist, also translates his own work. Discuss the significance of translation (of concepts as well as words) in any story in this collection. When does a failure to understand words determine plot as well as theme? What is the significance of any words that remain untranslated? How does the fact of translation become thematic in its own right?

4. The narrator of "The Management of Grief" describes being "trapped between two modes of knowledge." Write an essay examining the *sources* of knowledge in the story as well as the ways the different people respond to knowledge or information. Are these responses more a matter of individual personality or of cultural "modes of knowledge"?

7 THE LONGER WORK

In terms of all the elements—plot, narration and point of view, character, setting, symbol, and theme—longer works of fiction are built out of the same components as shorter works and invite similar interpretive strategies. So what are the differences? Definitions of the short story and novel—and in between them, the novella—tend to focus wholly on length. Most critics today define a **short story** as a work of prose fiction up to approximately 15,000–20,000 words, a **novella** as one of about 15,000–50,000 words, and a **novel** as one of at least 40,000 words (these approximate and overlapping lengths indicate that individual works may be placed in different genre categories by different critics). Yet the size of fiction matters in part because size affects fiction's substance and scope as well as how we read and experience it. Shorter fiction, not unlike lyric poetry, depends on compression and implication (*showing* versus *telling*), whereas longer fiction permits extended development and greater detail. One modern critic, Mark Shorer, describes shorter fiction, especially the modern short story, as an "art of moral revelation," longer fiction, especially the novel, as an "art of moral evolution." Champions of the novella have praised its combination of the "revelation" or intensity of the short story with the "evolution" or extension of the novel.

Perhaps the most important differences between short and long fiction have to do with the way we read them. Edgar Allan Poe, one of the first and best writers of the modern short story, attributed the "unity of effort or impression" in "the brief tale" to the fact that it may be read "at one sitting." Yet as Thomas A. Gullason insists, the spare economy of a story and its reliance on implying rather than fully explaining or developing its elements means that we *need* to read a story more than once: "like the diamond, the short story throws off glints of meanings" only captured through careful reading and re-reading. The reading of longer works of fiction, in contrast, tends to be a prolonged and often interrupted process. We may be likely to read most novels only once, over several days or weeks. Our attention to them may be just as concentrated, and their implications may be just as brilliant as those of short fiction, but the scope and effects are on a different scale.

How can you apply your reading skills to novellas like the two in this chapter, Herman Melville's *Bartleby, the Scrivener* and Franz Kafka's *The Metamorphosis*? It helps to review some of the history and the characteristics of longer fiction—not only the familiar elements but also the conventions of the genre and its modes of representing human experience. Some of the literary context offered in this chapter concerns concepts such as comedy, tragedy, and realism that are relevant to many forms and genres of literature, not just fiction, but these concepts help put the special achievements of these novellas in perspective.

A BRIEF HISTORY OF THE NOVEL

Before the eighteenth century, longer fiction would usually take the form of **epic** or **romance**, whether in verse or prose. Shorter narratives, referred to in Spanish as *novelas*, or in Italian as *novellas*, usually ranged less widely in space and time, and presented more-common characters in less magical or supernatural circumstances than found in epic or romance. Forerunners of the modern novel, such as Boccaccio's *Decameron*, were interconnected prose *novellas* (what we would call tales or stories) with contemporary setting and characters of middling or low rank. Miguel de Cervantes's *Don Quixote* (Spain, 1605, 1615) is often identified as the first novel, though both the tales that are told by characters within *Don Quixote* and the work as a whole were referred to in Spanish as *novelas*. The protagonist is an elderly gentleman who ignores the realities of his contemporary surroundings to embark on madly idealistic quests, believing he is a knight-errant like the protagonists of the countless romances he has read. Thus *Don Quixote* is sometimes called a "mock romance" or "anti-romance."

As longer prose narratives began to be published in book form, they drew on the resources of other kinds of literature, particularly those that purported to offer a true picture of the world abroad as well as familiar social life at home, including journalism, histories, travels, biography, and letters. (Tellingly, the word *novel* also means "new" and is related to the word *news*.) The earliest novels in English were influenced by Italian, Spanish, and French models of prose romance, epic, novellas, and travel memoirs. Many early novels were *epistolary*, as if reprinting a series of letters (or *epistles*) written by real people in contemporary society. In addition to drawing on the models of nonfiction prose, novels adapted the plot structures of drama. Novels often followed the conventions of **comedy** (with its happy ending in success or marriage), rather than **tragedy** (with its ultimate destruction of a noble or admirable protagonist), though some novellas and novels since the mid-nineteenth century follow the five-act structure of tragic drama. One of the popular comedic forms of fiction has been the **bildungsroman**—from the German terms for "shaping" or "portrait" and novel—modeled on Johan Wolfgang von Goethe's *Wilhelm Meister's Apprenticeship* (1795–1796). In a bildungsroman—an "education" or "development" novel—the protagonist overcomes adversity to attain social standing, vocation, and marriage; classics in English include Charlotte Brontë's *Jane Eyre* (1847) and Charles Dickens's *David Copperfield* (1850).

A prevalent mode for novels since the mid-nineteenth century has been **realism**. Realist fiction of any length has certain characteristics:

1. settings correspond in detail with historical or contemporary time and space, with facts and conditions known;
2. the main characters are complex, individualized, and often working class or middle class; and
3. the plot is explicable and probable—the sorts of things that could happen to ordinary people in the real world.

Yet the supernatural and imaginative aspects of romance, epic, and folktales retain their influence, and novels, novellas, and stories often gain effects by bending some of the rules of the reader's realm of possibility. By the 1790s, **gothic** novels were widely popular, with their special effects of horror and terror. More-recent novelists have continued to exploit the more uncanny or imaginative possibilities of gothic and romance genres, along with **fantasy** and science fiction. Thus today, in fiction of various lengths as in film and television, we still encounter the different aims of representing everyday experience versus traveling into the past, the future, or imaginary or exotic societies and worlds.

In the United States today, the novel is so popular and ubiquitous that the words *novel* and *book* sometimes seem to be taken as synonyms. The label *graphic novel* is routinely used as a blanket term for any book-length "comic," whether it is nonfiction or a collection of shorter pieces. And despite its name, Oprah's Book Club has over the years featured far more novels than any other kind of book.

THE NOVELLA

If the novel is a relatively new genre that has absorbed the traits of many other genres and has come to dominate literature today, the novella (in the English meaning of the term) is newer still, and less common. Mid-length fiction (between 15,000 and 50,000 words) came into favor around 1880 and afterward, as novels began to be published in one volume and shorter fiction became more popular in mass-circulation magazines. Modern fiction writers like Henry James (1843–1916) and Joseph Conrad (1857–1924) favored the scale of the novella as right for their intended effects: It combines the focus on significant detail and the controlled structure of the short story with room to develop complex characters, more than one setting, and more complex plots.

A novella may:

- have a more complex **plot** than a short story (and even a **subplot**), involving more discriminated occasions and episodes;
- feature more **characters** and give more of them an individualized, dynamic treatment—that is, it may have more round characters than a short story;
- cover more time and space, having more numerous and more thoroughly described **settings** than a short story; and
- include more description, summary, or commentary on characters, circumstances, or **themes** than a short story, which usually must dramatize one main event.

A novella has scope to give readers a sense of a **central consciousness**'s isolation or alienation, as in James Joyce's *The Dead* (chapter 9). Instead of limiting itself to one main character or the events of one evening, a novella can describe weeks or months in which a group of people are tested in their response to an outsider or in which an unusual or artistic personality pushes the limits of what is socially acceptable. A novella allows for a transformation of outlook from beginning to end, but with the momentum of a play, opera, or ballet rather than the episodic journey of a novel.

Often the outcome of a modern novella is bleak. In fact, a remarkable number of classic novellas are tragedies. Henry James's *Daisy Miller* (1878), Kate Chopin's

The Awakening (1899), and Nella Larsen's *Quicksand* (1928) are all realist novellas that are also tragedies in which society proves too strong for an exceptional woman. But some novellas end without dooming the main character, and the novella's length gives writers sufficient space to vary the mood of even the most somber piece by including humorous scenes or curious observations.

• • •

In responding to longer fiction, as always when interpreting a literary work, you should ask what effect the form, including the length, has on the meaning. As you read the two novellas in this chapter, ask yourself: What would have to be eliminated to convert these novellas into short stories? What could be added to *Bartleby, the Scrivener* or *The Metamorphosis* to lengthen them into novels? What precisely might be improved, marred, or lost by either shrinking or expanding each narrative? For example, how does length affect characterization in Melville's or Kafka's work? How does the portrayal of everyday, modern life and people affect our response to the extraordinary action in these novellas? What aspects of the characterization or plot cannot be explained by the standards of fact and reality that we— and some characters in the novellas—live by? Are these novellas tragedies?

HERMAN MELVILLE

Bartleby, the Scrivener

A Story of Wall Street

I am a rather elderly man. The nature of my avocations for the last thirty years has brought me into more than ordinary contact with what would seem an interesting and somewhat singular set of men, of whom as yet nothing that I know of has ever been written:—I mean the law-copyists or scriveners. I have known very many of them, professionally and privately, and if I pleased, could relate divers histories, at which good-natured gentlemen might smile, and sentimental souls might weep. But I waive the biographies of all other scriveners for a few passages in the life of Bartleby, who was a scrivener the strangest I ever saw or heard of. While of other law-copyists I might write the complete life, of Bartleby nothing of that sort can be done. I believe that no materials exist for a full and satisfactory biography of this man. It is an irreparable loss to literature. Bartleby was one of those beings of whom nothing is ascertainable, except from the original sources, and in his case those are very small. What my own astonished eyes saw of Bartleby, *that* is all I know of him, except, indeed, one vague report which will appear in the sequel.[1]

Ere introducing the scrivener, as he first appeared to me, it is fit I make some mention of myself, my *employées,* my business, my chambers, and general surroundings; because some such description is indispensable to an adequate understanding of the chief character about to be presented.

Imprimis:[2] I am a man who, from his youth upwards, has been filled with a profound conviction that the easiest way of life is the best. Hence, though I

1. That is, in the following story.   2. In the first place.

belong to a profession proverbially energetic and nervous, even to turbulence, at times, yet nothing of that sort have I ever suffered to invade my peace. I am one of those unambitious lawyers who never addresses a jury, or in any way draws down public applause; but in the cool tranquillity of a snug retreat, do a snug business among rich men's bonds and mortgages and title-deeds. All who know me, consider me an eminently *safe* man. The late John Jacob Astor,[3] a personage little given to poetic enthusiasm, had no hesitation in pronouncing my first grand point to be prudence; my next, method. I do not speak it in vanity, but simply record the fact, that I was not unemployed in my profession by the late John Jacob Astor; a name which, I admit, I love to repeat, for it hath a rounded and orbicular sound to it, and rings like unto bullion. I will freely add that I was not insensible to the late John Jacob Astor's good opinion.

Some time prior to the period at which this little history begins, my avocations had been largely increased. The good old office, now extinct in the State of New York, of a Master in Chancery[4] had been conferred upon me. It was not a very arduous office, but very pleasantly remunerative. I seldom lose my temper; much more seldom indulge in dangerous indignation at wrongs and outrages; but I must be permitted to be rash here and declare, that I consider the sudden and violent abrogation of the office of Master in Chancery, by the new Constitution, as a—premature act; inasmuch as I had counted upon a life-lease of the profits, whereas I only received those of a few short years. But this is by the way.

My chambers were up stairs at No. —— Wall Street. At one end they looked upon the white wall of the interior of a spacious skylight shaft, penetrating the building from top to bottom. This view might have been considered rather tame than otherwise, deficient in what landscape painters call "life." But if so, the view from the other end of my chambers offered, at least, a contrast, if nothing more. In that direction my windows commanded an unobstructed view of a lofty brick wall, black by age and everlasting shade; which wall required no spyglass to bring out its lurking beauties, but for the benefit of all near-sighted spectators, was pushed up to within ten feet of my window panes. Owing to the great height of the surrounding buildings, and my chambers being on the second floor, the interval between this wall and mine not a little resembled a huge square cistern.

At the period just preceding the advent of Bartleby, I had two persons as copyists in my employment, and a promising lad as an office-boy. First, Turkey; second, Nippers, third, Ginger Nut. These may seem names the like of which are not usually found in the Directory.[5] In truth they were nicknames, mutually conferred upon each other by my three clerks, and were deemed expressive of their respective persons or characters. Turkey was a short, pursy[6] Englishman of about my own age, that is, somewhere not far from sixty. In the morning, one might say, his face was of a fine florid hue, but after twelve o'clock, meridian—his dinner hour—it blazed like a grate full of Christmas coals; and continued blazing—but, as it were, with a gradual wane—till 6 o'clock, P.M. or thereabouts, after which I saw no more of the proprietor of the face, which gaining its meridian with the sun, seemed to

3. New York fur merchant and landowner (1763–1848) who died the richest man in the United States.

4. A court of chancery can temper the law, applying "dictates of conscience" or "the principles of natural justice"; the office of Master was abolished in 1847.

5. Post Office Directory.   6. Fat, short-winded.

set with it, to rise, culminate, and decline the following day, with the like regularity and undiminished glory. There are many singular coincidences I have known
in the course of my life, not the least among which was the fact, that exactly when
Turkey displayed his fullest beams from his red and radiant countenance, just
then, too, at that critical moment, began the daily period when I considered his
business capacities as seriously disturbed for the remainder of the twenty-four
hours. Not that he was absolutely idle, or averse to business then; far from it. The
difficulty was, he was apt to be altogether too energetic. There was a strange,
inflamed, flurried, flighty recklessness of activity about him. He would be incau-
tious in dipping his pen into his inkstand. All his blots upon my documents were
dropped there after twelve o'clock, meridian. Indeed, not only would he be reckless and sadly given to making blots in the afternoon, but some days he went further, and was rather noisy. At such times, too, his face flamed with augmented
blazonry, as if cannel coal had been heaped on anthracite.[7] He made an unpleasant racket with his chair; spilled his sand-box; in mending his pens, impatiently
split them all to pieces, and threw them on the floor in a sudden passion; stood up
and leaned over his table, boxing his papers about in a most indecorous manner,
very sad to behold in an elderly man like him. Nevertheless, as he was in many
ways a most valuable person to me, and all the time before twelve o'clock, meridian, was the quickest, steadiest creature too, accomplishing a great deal of work in
a style not easy to be matched—for these reasons, I was willing to overlook his
eccentricities, though indeed, occasionally, I remonstrated with him. I did this
very gently, however, because, though the civilest, nay, the blandest and most rever-
ential of men in the morning, yet in the afternoon he was disposed, upon provocation, to be slightly rash with his tongue, in fact, insolent. Now, valuing his morning
services as I did, and resolved not to lose them; yet, at the same time made uncomfortable by his inflamed ways after twelve o'clock; and being a man of peace,
unwilling by my admonitions to call forth unseemly retorts from him; I took
upon me, one Saturday noon (he was always worse on Saturdays), to hint to him,
very kindly, that perhaps now that he was growing old, it might be well to abridge
his labors; in short, he need not come to my chambers after twelve o'clock, but,
dinner over, had best go home to his lodgings and rest himself till tea-time. But
no; he insisted upon his afternoon devotions. His countenance became intolerably
fervid, as he oratorically assured me—gesticulating with a long ruler at the other
end of the room—that if his services in the morning were useful, how indispensable, then, in the afternoon?

"With submission, sir," said Turkey on this occasion, "I consider myself your
right-hand man. In the morning I but marshal and deploy my columns; but in
the afternoon I put myself at their head, and gallantly charge the foe, thus!"—
and he made a violent thrust with the ruler.

"But the blots, Turkey," intimated I.

"True,—but, with submission, sir, behold these hairs! I am getting old. Surely,
sir, a blot or two of a warm afternoon is not to be severely urged against gray
hairs. Old age—even if it blot the page—is honorable. With submission, sir, we
both are getting old."

10   This appeal to my fellow-feeling was hardly to be resisted. At all events, I saw
that go he would not. So I made up my mind to let him stay, resolving, neverthe-

---

7. Fast, bright-burning coal heaped on slow-burning, barely glowing coal.

less, to see to it, that during the afternoon he had to do with my less important papers.

Nippers, the second on my list, was a whiskered, sallow, and, upon the whole, rather piratical-looking young man of about five and twenty. I always deemed him the victim of two evil powers—ambition and indigestion. The ambition was evinced by a certain impatience of the duties of a mere copyist, an unwarrantable usurpation of strictly professional affairs, such as the original drawing up of legal documents. The indigestion seemed betokened in an occasional nervous testiness and grinning irritability, causing the teeth to audibly grind together over mistakes committed in copying; unnecessary maledictions, hissed, rather than spoken, in the heat of business; and especially by a continual discontent with the height of the table where he worked. Though of a very ingenious mechanical turn, Nippers could never get this table to suit him. He put chips under it, blocks of various sorts, bits of pasteboard, and at last went so far as to attempt an exquisite adjustment by final pieces of folded blotting-paper. But no invention would answer. If, for the sake of easing his back, he brought the table lid at a sharp angle well up towards his chin, and wrote there like a man using the steep roof of a Dutch house for his desk:—then he declared that it stopped the circulation in his arms. If now he lowered the table to his waistbands, and stooped over it in writing, then there was a sore aching in his back. In short, the truth of the matter was, Nippers knew not what he wanted. Or, if he wanted any thing, it was to be rid of a scrivener's table altogether. Among the manifestations of his diseased ambition was a fondness he had for receiving visits from certain ambiguous-looking fellows in seedy coats, whom he called his clients. Indeed I was aware that not only was he, at times, considerable of a ward-politician, but he occasionally did a little business at the Justices' courts, and was not unknown on the steps of the Tombs.[8] I have good reason to believe, however, that one individual who called upon him at my chambers, and who, with a grand air, he insisted was his client, was no other than a dun,[9] and the alleged title-deed, a bill. But with all his failings, and the annoyances he caused me, Nippers, like his compatriot Turkey, was a very useful man to me; wrote a neat, swift hand; and, when he chose, was not deficient in a gentlemanly sort of deportment. Added to this, he always dressed in a gentlemanly sort of way: and so, incidentally, reflected credit upon my chambers. Whereas with respect to Turkey, I had much ado to keep him from being a reproach to me. His clothes were apt to look oily and smell of eating-houses. He wore his pantaloons very loose and baggy in summer. His coats were execrable; his hat not to be handled. But while the hat was a thing of indifference to me, inasmuch as his natural civility and deference, as a dependent Englishman, always led him to doff it the moment he entered the room, yet his coat was another matter. Concerning his coats, I reasoned with him; but with no effect. The truth was, I suppose, that a man with so small an income, could not afford to sport such a lustrous face and a lustrous coat at one and the same time. As Nippers once observed, Turkey's money went chiefly for red ink. One winter day I presented Turkey with a highly-respectable looking coat of my own, a padded gray coat, of a most comfortable warmth, and which buttoned straight up from the knee to the neck. I thought Turkey would appreciate the favor, and abate his rashness and obstreperousness of afternoons. But no. I verily believe that buttoning himself

8. Prison in New York City.   9. Bill collector.

up in so downy and blanket-like a coat had a pernicious effect upon him; upon the same principle that too much oats are bad for horses. In fact, precisely as a rash, restive horse is said to feel his oats, so Turkey felt his coat. It made him insolent. He was a man whom prosperity harmed.

Though concerning the self-indulgent habits of Turkey I had my own private surmises, yet touching Nippers I was well persuaded that whatever might be his faults in other respects, he was, at least, a temperate young man. But indeed, nature herself seemed to have been his vintner,[1] and at his birth charged him so thoroughly with an irritable, brandy-like disposition, that all subsequent potations were needless. When I consider how, amid the stillness of my chambers, Nippers would sometimes impatiently rise from his seat, and stooping over his table, spread his arms wide apart, seize the whole desk, and move it, and jerk it, with a grim, grinding motion on the floor, as if the table were a perverse voluntary agent, intent on thwarting and vexing him; I plainly perceive that for Nippers, brandy and water were altogether superfluous.

It was fortunate for me that, owing to its peculiar cause—indigestion—the irritability and consequent nervousness of Nippers, were mainly observable in the morning, while in the afternoon he was comparatively mild. So that Turkey's paroxysms only coming on about twelve o'clock, I never had to do with their eccentricities at one time. Their fits relieved each other like guards. When Nippers' was on, Turkey's was off; and *vice versa*. This was a good natural arrangement under the circumstances.

Ginger Nut, the third on my list, was a lad some twelve years old. His father was a carman,[2] ambitious of seeing his son on the bench instead of a cart, before he died. So he sent him to my office as student at law, errand boy, and cleaner and sweeper, at the rate of one dollar a week. He had a little desk to himself, but he did not use it much. Upon inspection, the drawer exhibited a great array of the shells of various sorts of nuts. Indeed, to this quick-witted youth the whole noble science of the law was contained in a nutshell. Not the least among the employments of Ginger Nut, as well as one which he discharged with the most alacrity, was his duty as cake and apple purveyor for Turkey and Nippers. Copying law papers being proverbially a dry, husky sort of business, my two scriveners were fain to moisten their mouths very often with Spitzenbergs[3] to be had at the numerous stalls nigh the Custom House and Post Office. Also, they sent Ginger Nut very frequently for that peculiar cake—small, flat, round, and very spicy—after which he had been named by them. Of a cold morning when business was but dull, Turkey would gobble up scores of these cakes, as if they were mere wafers—indeed they sell them at the rate of six or eight for a penny—the scrape of his pen blending with the crunching of the crisp particles in his mouth. Of all the fiery afternoon blunders and flurried rashnesses of Turkey, was his once moistening a ginger-cake between his lips, and clapping it on to a mortgage for a seal. I came within an ace of dismissing him then. But he mollified me by making an oriental bow, and saying—"With submission, sir, it was generous of me to find you in[4] stationery on my own account."

---

1. Wine seller.   2. Driver of wagon or cart that hauls goods.   3. Red-and-yellow American apple.
4. Supply you with.

Now my original business—that of a conveyancer and title hunter,[5] and 15 drawer-up of recondite documents of all sorts—was considerably increased by receiving the master's office. There was now great work for scriveners. Not only must I push the clerks already with me, but I must have additional help. In answer to my advertisement, a motionless young man one morning stood upon my office threshold, the door being open, for it was summer. I can see that figure now—pallidly neat, pitiably respectable, incurably forlorn! It was Bartleby.

After a few words touching his qualifications, I engaged him, glad to have among my corps of copyists a man of so singularly sedate an aspect, which I thought might operate beneficially upon the flighty temper of Turkey, and the fiery one of Nippers.

I should have stated before that ground glass folding-doors divided my premises into two parts, one of which was occupied by my scriveners, the other by myself. According to my humor I threw open these doors, or closed them. I resolved to assign Bartleby a corner by the folding-doors, but on my side of them, so as to have this quiet man within easy call, in case any trifling thing was to be done. I placed his desk close up to a small side-window in that part of the room, a window which originally had afforded a lateral view of certain grimy backyards and bricks, but which, owing to subsequent erections, commanded at present no view at all, though it gave some light. Within three feet of the panes was a wall, and the light came down from far above, between two lofty buildings, as from a very small opening in a dome. Still further to a satisfactory arrangement, I procured a high green folding screen, which might entirely isolate Bartleby from my sight, though not remove him from my voice. And thus, in a manner, privacy and society were conjoined.

At first Bartleby did an extraordinary quantity of writing. As if long famishing for something to copy, he seemed to gorge himself on my documents. There was no pause for digestion. He ran a day and night line, copying by sunlight and by candlelight. I should have been quite delighted with his application, had he been cheerfully industrious. But he wrote on silently, palely, mechanically.

It is, of course, an indispensable part of a scrivener's business to verify the accuracy of his copy, word by word. Where there are two or more scriveners in an office, they assist each other in this examination, one reading from the copy, the other holding the original. It is a very dull, wearisome, and lethargic affair. I can readily imagine that to some sanguine temperaments it would be altogether intolerable. For example, I cannot credit that the mettlesome poet Byron would have contentedly sat down with Bartleby to examine a law document of, say, five hundred pages, closely written in a crimpy hand.

Now and then, in the haste of business, it had been my habit to assist in com- 20 paring some brief document myself, calling Turkey or Nippers for this purpose. One object I had in placing Bartleby so handy to me behind the screen, was to avail myself of his services on such trivial occasions. It was on the third day, I think, of his being with me, and before any necessity had arisen for having his own writing examined, that, being much hurried to complete a small affair I had in hand, I abruptly called to Bartleby. In my haste and natural expectancy of instant compliance, I sat with my head bent over the original on my desk, and

5. Lawyer who draws up deeds for transferring property, and one who searches out legal control of title deeds.

my right hand sideways, and somewhat nervously extended with the copy, so that immediately upon emerging from his retreat, Bartleby might snatch it and proceed to business without the least delay.

In this very attitude did I sit when I called to him, rapidly stating what it was I wanted him to do—namely, to examine a small paper with me. Imagine my surprise, nay, my consternation, when without moving from his privacy, Bartleby, in a singularly mild, firm voice, replied, "I would prefer not to."

I sat awhile in perfect silence, rallying my stunned faculties. Immediately it occurred to me that my ears had deceived me, or Bartleby had entirely misunderstood my meaning. I repeated my request in the clearest tone I could assume. But in quite as clear a one came the previous reply, "I would prefer not to."

"Prefer not to," echoed I, rising in high excitement, and crossing the room with a stride. "What do you mean? Are you moon-struck?[6] I want you to help me compare this sheet here—take it," and I thrust it towards him.

"I would prefer not to," said he.

25   I looked at him steadfastly. His face was leanly composed; his gray eye dimly calm. Not a wrinkle of agitation rippled him. Had there been the least uneasiness, anger, impatience or impertinence in his manner; in other words, had there been anything ordinarily human about him, doubtless I should have violently dismissed him from the premises. But as it was, I should have as soon thought of turning my pale plaster-of-paris bust of Cicero[7] out-of-doors. I stood gazing at him awhile, as he went on with his own writing, and then reseated myself at my desk. This is very strange, thought I. What had one best do? But my business hurried me. I concluded to forget the matter for the present, reserving it for my future leisure. So calling Nippers from the other room, the paper was speedily examined.

A few days after this, Bartleby concluded four lengthy documents, being quadruplicates of a week's testimony taken before me in my High Court of Chancery. It became necessary to examine them. It was an important suit, and great accuracy was imperative. Having all things arranged I called Turkey, Nippers and Ginger Nut from the next room, meaning to place the four copies in the hands of my four clerks, while I should read from the original. Accordingly Turkey, Nippers and Ginger Nut had taken their seats in a row, each with his document in hand, when I called to Bartleby to join this interesting group.

"Bartleby! quick, I am waiting."

I heard a slow scrape of his chair legs on the uncarpeted floor, and soon he appeared standing at the entrance of his hermitage.

"What is wanted?" said he mildly.

30   "The copies, the copies," said I hurriedly. "We are going to examine them. There"—and I held towards him the fourth quadruplicate.

"I would prefer not to," he said, and gently disappeared behind the screen.

For a few moments I was turned into a pillar of salt,[8] standing at the head of my seated column of clerks. Recovering myself, I advanced towards the screen, and demanded the reason for such extraordinary conduct.

6. Crazy.

7. Marcus Tullius Cicero (106–43 B.C.E.), pro-republican Roman statesman, barrister, writer, and orator.

8. Struck dumb; in Genesis 19.26, Lot's wife, defying God's command, "looked back from behind him, and she became a pillar of salt."

"*Why* do you refuse?"

"I would prefer not to."

With any other man I should have flown outright into a dreadful passion, 35 scorned all further words, and thrust him ignominiously from my presence. But there was something about Bartleby that not only strangely disarmed me, but in a wonderful manner touched and disconcerted me. I began to reason with him.

"These are your own copies we are about to examine. It is labor saving to you, because one examination will answer for your four papers. It is common usage. Every copyist is bound to help examine his copy. Is it not so? Will you not speak? Answer!"

"I prefer not to," he replied in a flute-like tone. It seemed to me that while I had been addressing him, he carefully revolved every statement that I made; fully comprehended the meaning; could not gainsay the irresistible conclusion; but, at the same time, some paramount consideration prevailed with him to reply as he did.

"You are decided, then, not to comply with my request—a request made according to common usage and common sense?"

He briefly gave me to understand that on that point my judgment was sound. Yes: his decision was irreversible.

It is not seldom the case that when a man is browbeaten in some unprece- 40 dented and violently unreasonable way, he begins to stagger in his own plainest faith. He begins, as it were, vaguely to surmise that, wonderful as it may be, all the justice and all the reason is on the other side. Accordingly, if any disinterested persons are present, he turns to them for some reinforcement for his own faltering mind.

"Turkey," said I, "what do you think of this? Am I not right?"

"With submission, sir," said Turkey, with his blandest tone, "I think that you are."

"Nippers," said I, "what do *you* think of it?"

"I think I should kick him out of the office."

(The reader of nice perceptions will here perceive that, it being morning, Tur- 45 key's answer is couched in polite and tranquil terms, but Nippers replies in illtempered ones. Or, to repeat a previous sentence, Nippers's ugly mood was on duty, and Turkey's off.)

"Ginger Nut," said I, willing to enlist the smallest suffrage[9] in my behalf, "what do *you* think of it?"

"I think, sir, he's a little *luny*," replied Ginger Nut, with a grin.

"You hear what they say," said I, turning towards the screen, "come forth and do your duty."

But he vouchsafed no reply. I pondered a moment in sore perplexity. But once more business hurried me. I determined again to postpone the consideration of this dilemma to my future leisure. With a little trouble we made out to examine the papers without Bartleby, though at every page or two, Turkey deferentially dropped his opinion that this proceeding was quite out of the common; while Nippers, twitching in his chair with a dyspeptic nervousness, ground out between his set teeth occasional hissing maledictions against the stubborn oaf behind the screen. And for his (Nippers's) part, this was the first and the last time he would do another man's business without pay.

9. Favorable vote.

50   Meanwhile Bartleby sat in his hermitage, oblivious to everything but his own peculiar business there.

    Some days passed, the scrivener being employed upon another lengthy work. His late remarkable conduct led me to regard his ways narrowly. I observed that he never went to dinner; indeed that he never went anywhere. As yet I had never of my personal knowledge known him to be outside of my office. He was a perpetual sentry in the corner. At about eleven o'clock though, in the morning, I noticed that Ginger Nut would advance toward the opening in Bartleby's screen, as if silently beckoned thither by a gesture invisible to me where I sat. The boy would then leave the office jingling a few pence, and reappear with a handful of ginger-nuts which he delivered in the hermitage, receiving two of the cakes for his trouble.

    He lives, then, on ginger-nuts, thought I; never eats a dinner, properly speaking; he must be a vegetarian then; but no; he never eats even vegetables, he eats nothing but ginger-nuts. My mind then ran on in reveries concerning the probable effects upon the human constitution of living entirely on ginger-nuts. Ginger-nuts are so called because they contain ginger as one of their peculiar constituents, and the final flavoring one. Now what was ginger? A hot, spicy thing. Was Bartleby hot and spicy? Not at all. Ginger, then, had no effect upon Bartleby. Probably he preferred it should have none.

    Nothing so aggravates an earnest person as a passive resistance. If the individual so resisted be of a not inhumane temper, and the resisting one perfectly harmless in his passivity; then, in the better moods of the former, he will endeavor charitably to construe to his imagination what proves impossible to be solved by his judgment. Even so, for the most part, I regarded Bartleby and his ways. Poor fellow! thought I, he means no mischief; it is plain he intends no insolence; his aspect sufficiently evinces that his eccentricities are involuntary. He is useful to me. I can get along with him. If I turn him away, the chances are he will fall in with some less indulgent employer, and then he will be rudely treated, and perhaps driven forth miserably to starve. Yes. Here I can cheaply purchase a delicious self-approval. To befriend Bartleby; to humor him in his strange wilfulness, will cost me little or nothing, while I lay up in my soul what will eventually prove a sweet morsel for my conscience. But this mood was not invariable with me. The passiveness of Bartleby sometimes irritated me. I felt strangely goaded on to encounter him in new opposition, to elicit some angry spark from him answerable to my own. But indeed I might as well have essayed to strike fire with my knuckles against a bit of Windsor soap.[1] But one afternoon the evil impulse in me mastered me, and the following little scene ensued:

    "Bartleby," said I, "when those papers are all copied, I will compare them with you."

55   "I would prefer not to."

    "How? Surely you do not mean to persist in that mulish vagary?"

    No answer.

    I threw open the folding-doors near by, and turning upon Turkey and Nippers, exclaimed in an excited manner—

    "He says, a second time, he won't examine his papers. What do you think of it, Turkey?"

---

1. Scented soap, usually brown.

It was afternoon, be it remembered. Turkey sat glowing like a brass boiler, his 60
bald head steaming, his hands reeling among his blotted papers.

"Think of it?" roared Turkey; "I think I'll just step behind his screen, and
black his eyes for him!"

So saying, Turkey rose to his feet and threw his arms into a pugilistic position. He was hurrying away to make good his promise, when I detained him,
alarmed at the effect of incautiously rousing Turkey's combativeness after
dinner.

"Sit down, Turkey," said I, "and hear what Nippers has to say. What do you
think of it, Nippers? Would I not be justified in immediately dismissing
Bartleby?"

"Excuse me, that is for you to decide, sir. I think his conduct quite unusual,
and indeed unjust, as regards Turkey and myself. But it may only be a passing
whim."

"Ah," exclaimed I, "you have strangely changed your mind then—you speak 65
very gently of him now."

"All beer," cried Turkey; "gentleness is effects of beer—Nippers and I dined
together today. You see how gentle *I* am, sir. Shall I go and black his eyes?"

"You refer to Bartleby, I suppose. No, not today, Turkey," I replied; "pray, put
up your fists."

I closed the doors, and again advanced towards Bartleby. I felt additional
incentives tempting me to my fate. I burned to be rebelled against again. I
remembered that Bartleby never left the office.

"Bartleby," said I, "Ginger Nut is away; just step round to the Post Office,
won't you? (it was but a three minutes' walk,) and see if there is anything for
me."

"I would prefer not to." 70

"You *will* not?"

"I *prefer* not."

I staggered to my desk, and sat there in a deep study. My blind inveteracy
returned. Was there any other thing in which I could procure myself to be ignominiously repulsed by this lean, penniless wight?—my hired clerk? What added
thing is there, perfectly reasonable, that he will be sure to refuse to do?

"Bartleby!"

No answer. 75

"Bartleby," in a louder tone.

No answer.

"Bartleby," I roared.

Like a very ghost, agreeably to the laws of magical invocation, at the third
summons, he appeared at the entrance of his hermitage.

"Go to the next room, and tell Nippers to come to me." 80

"I prefer not to," he respectfully and slowly said, and mildly disappeared.

"Very good, Bartleby," said I, in a quiet sort of serenely severe self-possessed
tone, intimating the unalterable purpose of some terrible retribution very close at
hand. At the moment I half intended something of the kind. But upon the whole,
as it was drawing towards my dinner-hour, I thought it best to put on my hat and
walk home for the day, suffering much from perplexity and distress of mind.

Shall I acknowledge it? The conclusion of this whole business was, that it soon
became a fixed fact of my chambers, that a pale young scrivener, by the name of

Bartleby, had a desk there; that he copied for me at the usual rate of four cents a folio (one hundred words); but he was permanently exempt from examining the work done by him, that duty being transferred to Turkey and Nippers, one of compliment doubtless to their superior acuteness; moreover, said Bartleby was never on any account to be dispatched on the most trivial errand of any sort; and that even if entreated to take upon him such a matter, it was generally understood that he would prefer not to—in other words, that he would refuse point-blank.

As days passed on, I became considerably reconciled to Bartleby. His steadiness, his freedom from all dissipation, his incessant industry (except when he chose to throw himself into a standing revery behind his screen), his great stillness, his unalterableness of demeanor under all circumstances, made him a valuable acquisition. One prime thing was this,—*he was always there*;—first in the morning, continually through the day, and the last at night. I had a singular confidence in his honesty. I felt my most precious papers perfectly safe in his hands. Sometimes to be sure I could not, for the very soul of me, avoid falling into sudden spasmodic passions with him. For it was exceeding difficult to bear in mind all the time those strange peculiarities, privileges, and unheard of exemptions, forming the tacit stipulations on Bartleby's part under which he remained in my office. Now and then, in the eagerness of dispatching pressing business, I would inadvertently summon Bartleby, in a short, rapid tone, to put his finger, say, on the incipient tie of a bit of red tape with which I was about compressing some papers. Of course, from behind the screen the usual answer, "I prefer not to," was sure to come; and then, how could a human creature with the common infirmities of our nature, refrain from bitterly exclaiming upon such perverseness—such unreasonableness? However, every added repulse of this sort which I received only tended to lessen the probability of my repeating the inadvertence.

85　　Here it must be said, that according to the custom of most legal gentlemen occupying chambers in densely-populated law buildings, there were several keys to my door. One was kept by a woman residing in the attic, which person weekly scrubbed and daily swept and dusted my apartments. Another was kept by Turkey for convenience sake. The third I sometimes carried in my own pocket. The fourth I knew not who had.

Now, one Sunday morning I happened to go to Trinity Church, to hear a celebrated preacher, and finding myself rather early on the ground, I thought I would walk round to my chambers for a while. Luckily I had my key with me; but upon applying it to the lock, I found it resisted by something inserted from the inside. Quite surprised, I called out; when to my consternation a key was turned from within; and thrusting his lean visage at me, and holding the door ajar, the apparition of Bartleby appeared, in his shirt sleeves, and otherwise in a strangely tattered dishabille, saying quietly that he was sorry, but he was deeply engaged just then, and—preferred not admitting me at present. In a brief word or two, he moreover added, that perhaps I had better walk round the block two or three times, and by that time he would probably have concluded his affairs.

Now, the utterly unsurmised appearance of Bartleby, tenanting my law-chambers of a Sunday morning, with his cadaverously gentlemanly *nonchalance*, yet withal firm and self-possessed, had such a strange effect upon me, that incontinently I slunk away from my own door, and did as desired. But not without sundry twinges of impotent rebellion against the mild effrontery of this unaccountable scrivener. Indeed, it was his wonderful mildness, chiefly, which not only disarmed me, but unmanned me, as it were. For I consider that one, for the time, is sort of unmanned when he tranquilly permits his hired clerk to dictate to him, and order him away from his own premises. Furthermore, I was full of uneasiness as to what Bartleby could possibly be doing in my office in his shirt sleeves, and in an otherwise dismantled condition of a Sunday morning. Was anything amiss going on? Nay, that was out of the question. It was not to be thought of for a moment that Bartleby was an immoral person. But what could he be doing there?—copying? Nay again, whatever might be his eccentricities, Bartleby was an eminently decorous person. He would be the last man to sit down to his desk in any state approaching to nudity. Besides, it was Sunday; and there was something about Bartleby that forbade the supposition that he would by any secular occupation violate the proprieties of the day.

Nevertheless, my mind was not pacified; and full of a restless curiosity, at last I returned to the door. Without hindrance I inserted my key, opened it, and entered. Bartleby was not to be seen. I looked round anxiously, peeped behind his screen; but it was very plain that he was gone. Upon more closely examining the place, I surmised that for an indefinite period Bartleby must have ate, dressed, and slept in my office, and that too without plate, mirror, or bed. The cushioned seat of a ricketty old sofa in one corner bore the faint impress of a lean, reclining form. Rolled away under his desk, I found a blanket under the empty grate, a blacking box[2] and brush; on a chair, a tin basin, with soap and a ragged towel; in a newspaper a few crumbs of ginger-nuts and a morsel of cheese. Yes, thought I, it is evident enough that Bartleby has been making his home here, keeping bachelor's hall all by himself. Immediately then the thought came sweeping across me, What miserable friendlessness and loneliness are here revealed! His poverty is great; but his solitude, how horrible! Think of it. Of a Sunday, Wall Street is deserted as Petra;[3] and every night of every day it is an emptiness. This building too, which of weekdays hums with industry and life, at nightfall echoes with sheer vacancy, and all through Sunday is forlorn. And here Bartleby makes his home; sole spectator of a solitude which he has seen all populous—a sort of innocent and transformed Marius brooding among the ruins of Carthage![4]

For the first time in my life a feeling of overpowering stinging melancholy seized me. Before, I had never experienced aught but a not-unpleasing sadness. The bond of a common humanity now drew me irresistibly to gloom. A fraternal melancholy! For both I and Bartleby were sons of Adam. I remembered the bright silks and sparkling faces I had seen that day, in gala trim, swan-like sailing down the Mississippi of Broadway; and I contrasted them with the pallid copyist, and thought to myself, Ah, happiness courts the light, so we deem the world is gay; but misery hides aloof, so we deem that misery there is none. These

---

2. Box of black shoe polish.   3. Once a flourishing Middle Eastern trade center, long in ruins.
4. Gaius (or Caius) Marius (157–86 B.C.E.), Roman consul and general, expelled from Rome in 88 B.C.E. by Sulla; when an officer of Sextilius, the governor, forbade him to land in Africa, Marius replied, "Go tell him that you have seen Caius Marius sitting in exile among the ruins of Carthage," applying the example of the fortune of that city to the change of his own condition. The image was so common that a few years after "Bartleby," Dickens apologizes for using it: "like that lumbering Marius among the ruins of Carthage, who has sat heavy on a thousand millions of similes" ("The Calais Night-Mail," in *The Uncommercial Traveler*).

sad fancyings—chimeras, doubtless, of a sick and silly brain—led on to other and
more special thoughts, concerning the eccentricities of Bartleby. Presentiments
of strange discoveries hovered round me. The scrivener's pale form appeared to
me laid out, among uncaring strangers, in its shivering winding sheet.

90　　Suddenly I was attracted by Bartleby's closed desk, the key in open sight left
in the lock.

I mean no mischief, seek the gratification of no heartless curiosity, thought I;
besides, the desk is mine, and its contents too, so I will make bold to look within.
Everything was methodically arranged, the papers smoothly placed. The pigeon-
holes were deep, and removing the files of documents, I groped into their recesses.
Presently I felt something there, and dragged it out. It was an old bandanna
handkerchief, heavy and knotted. I opened it, and saw it was a savings' bank.

I now recalled all the quiet mysteries which I had noted in the man. I remembered that he never spoke but to answer; that though at intervals he had considerable time to himself, yet I had never seen him reading—no, not even a newspaper;
that for long periods he would stand looking out, at his pale window behind the
screen, upon the dead brick wall; I was quite sure he never visited any refectory or
eating house; while his pale face clearly indicated that he never drank beer like
Turkey, or tea and coffee even, like other men; that he never went anywhere in
particular that I could learn; never went out for a walk, unless indeed that was
the case at present; that he had declined telling who he was, or whence he came, or
whether he had any relatives in the world; that though so thin and pale, he never
complained of ill health. And more than all, I remembered a certain unconscious
air of pallid—how shall I call it?—of pallid haughtiness, say, or rather an austere
reserve about him, which had positively awed me into my tame compliance with
his eccentricities, when I had feared to ask him to do the slightest incidental thing
for me, even though I might know, from his long-continued motionlessness, that
behind his screen he must be standing in one of those dead-wall reveries of his.

Revolving all these things, and coupling them with the recently discovered fact
that he made my office his constant abiding place and home, and not forgetful of
his morbid moodiness; revolving all these things, a prudential feeling began to
steal over me. My first emotions had been those of pure melancholy and sincerest
pity; but just in proportion as the forlornness of Bartleby grew and grew to my
imagination, did that same melancholy merge into fear, that pity into repulsion.
So true it is, and so terrible too, that up to a certain point the thought or sight of
misery enlists our best affections; but, in certain special cases, beyond that point
it does not. They err who would assert that invariably this is owing to the inherent selfishness of the human heart. It rather proceeds from a certain hopelessness
of remedying excessive and organic ill. To a sensitive being, pity is not seldom
pain. And when at last it is perceived that such pity cannot lead to effectual succor, common sense bids the soul be rid of it. What I saw that morning persuaded
me that the scrivener was the victim of innate and incurable disorder. I might
give alms to his body; but his body did not pain him; it was his soul that suffered,
and his soul I could not reach.

I did not accomplish the purpose of going to Trinity Church that morning.
Somehow, the things I had seen disqualified me for the time from churchgoing. I
walked homeward, thinking what I would do with Bartleby. Finally, I resolved
upon this;—I would put certain calm questions to him the next morning, touching his history, &c., and if he declined to answer them openly and unreservedly

(and I supposed he would prefer not), then to give him a twenty-dollar bill over and above whatever I might owe him, and tell him his services were no longer required; but that if in any other way I could assist him, I would be happy to do so, especially if he desired to return to his native place, wherever that might be, I would willingly help to defray the expenses. Moreover, if, after reaching home, he found himself at any time in want of aid, a letter from him would be sure of a reply.

The next morning came.   95

"Bartleby," said I, gently calling to him behind his screen.

No reply.

"Bartleby," said I, in a still gentler tone, "come here; I am not going to ask you to do anything you would prefer not to do—I simply wish to speak to you."

Upon this he noiselessly slid into view.

"Will you tell me, Bartleby, where you were born?"   100

"I would prefer not to."

"Will you tell me *anything* about yourself?"

"I would prefer not to."

"But what reasonable objection can you have to speak to me? I feel friendly towards you."

He did not look at me while I spoke, but kept his glance fixed upon my bust of 105 Cicero, which as I then sat, was directly behind me, some six inches above my head.

"What is your answer, Bartleby?" said I, after waiting a considerable time for a reply, during which his countenance remained immovable, only there was the faintest conceivable tremor of the white attenuated mouth.

"At present I prefer to give no answer," he said, and retired into his hermitage.

It was rather weak in me I confess, but his manner on this occasion nettled me. Not only did there seem to lurk in it a certain calm disdain, but his perverseness seemed ungrateful, considering the undeniable good usage and indulgence he had received from me.

Again I sat ruminating what I should do. Mortified as I was at his behavior, and resolved as I had been to dismiss him when I entered my office, nevertheless I strangely felt something superstitious knocking at my heart, and forbidding me to carry out my purpose, and denouncing me for a villain if I dared to breathe one bitter word against this forlornest of mankind. At last, familiarly drawing my chair behind his screen, I sat down and said: "Bartleby, never mind then about revealing your history; but let me entreat you, as a friend, to comply as far as may be with the usages of this office. Say now you will help to examine papers tomorrow or next day: in short, say now that in a day or two you will begin to be a little reasonable:—say so, Bartleby."

"At present I would prefer not to be a little reasonable," was his mildly cadav- 110 erous reply.

Just then the folding-doors opened, and Nippers approached. He seemed suffering from an unusually bad night's rest, induced by severer indigestion than common. He overheard those final words of Bartleby.

"*Prefer not*, eh?" gritted Nippers—"I'd *prefer* him, if I were you, sir," addressing me—"I'd *prefer* him; I'd give him preferences, the stubborn mule! What is it, sir, pray, that he *prefers* not to do now?"

Bartleby moved not a limb.

"Mr. Nippers," said I, "I'd prefer that you would withdraw for the present."

115   Somehow, of late I had got into the way of involuntarily using this word "prefer" upon all sorts of not exactly suitable occasions. And I trembled to think that my contact with the scrivener had already and seriously affected me in a mental way. And what further and deeper aberration might it not yet produce? This apprehension had not been without efficacy in determining me to summary means.

     As Nippers, looking very sour and sulky, was departing, Turkey blandly and deferentially approached.

     "With submission, sir," said he, "yesterday I was thinking about Bartleby here, and I think that if he would but prefer to take a quart of good ale every day, it would do much towards mending him and enabling him to assist in examining his papers."

     "So you have got the word too," said I, slightly excited.

     "With submission, what word, sir?" asked Turkey, respectfully crowding himself into the contracted space behind the screen, and by so doing making me jostle the scrivener. "What word, sir?"

120   "I would prefer to be left alone here," said Bartleby, as if offended at being mobbed in his privacy.

     "*That's* the word, Turkey," said I—"*that's* it."

     "Oh, *prefer*? oh yes—queer word. I never use it myself. But, sir, as I was saying, if he would but prefer—"

     "Turkey," interrupted I, "you will please withdraw."

     "Oh certainly, sir, if you prefer that I should."

125   As he opened the folding-door to retire, Nippers at his desk caught a glimpse of me, and asked whether I would prefer to have a certain paper copied on blue paper or white. He did not in the least roguishly accent the word *prefer*. It was plain that it involuntarily rolled from his tongue. I thought to myself, surely I must get rid of a demented man, who already has in some degree turned the tongues, if not the heads of myself and clerks. But I thought it prudent not to break the dismission at once.

     The next day I noticed that Bartleby did nothing but stand at his window in his dead-wall revery. Upon asking him why he did not write, he said that he had decided upon doing no more writing.

     "Why, how now? what next?" exclaimed I, "do no more writing?"

     "No more."

     "And what is the reason?"

130   "Do you not see the reason for yourself," he indifferently replied.

     I looked steadfastly at him, and perceived that his eyes looked dull and glazed. Instantly it occurred to me, that his unexampled diligence in copying by his dim window for the first few weeks of his stay with me might have temporarily impaired his vision.

     I was touched. I said something in condolence with him. I hinted that of course he did wisely in abstaining from writing for a while; and urged him to embrace that opportunity of taking wholesome exercise in the open air. This, however, he did not do. A few days after this, my other clerks being absent, and being in a great hurry to dispatch certain letters by the mail, I thought that, having nothing else earthly to do, Bartleby would surely be less inflexible than usual, and carry these letters to the post office. But he blankly declined. So, much to my inconvenience, I went myself.

Still added days went by. Whether Bartleby's eyes improved or not, I could not say. To all appearance, I thought they did. But when I asked him if they did, he vouchsafed no answer. At all events, he would do no copying. At last, in reply to my urgings, he informed me that he had permanently given up copying.

"What!" exclaimed I; "suppose your eyes should get entirely well—better than ever before—would you not copy then?"

"I have given up copying," he answered, and slid aside. 135

He remained, as ever, a fixture in my chamber. Nay—if that were possible—he became still more of a fixture than before. What was to be done? He would do nothing in the office: why should he stay there? In plain fact, he had now become a millstone[5] to me, not only useless as a necklace, but afflictive to bear. Yet I was sorry for him. I speak less than truth when I say that, on his own account, he occasioned me uneasiness. If he would but have named a single relative or friend, I would instantly have written, and urged their taking the poor fellow away to some convenient retreat. But he seemed alone, absolutely alone in the universe. A bit of wreck in the mid-Atlantic. At length, necessities connected with my business tyrannized over all other considerations. Decently as I could, I told Bartleby that in six days' time he must unconditionally leave the office. I warned him to take measures, in the interval, for procuring some other abode. I offered to assist him in this endeavor, if he himself would but take the first step towards a removal. "And when you finally quit me, Bartleby," added I, "I shall see that you go not away entirely unprovided. Six days from this hour, remember."

At the expiration of that period, I peeped behind the screen, and lo! Bartleby was there.

I buttoned up my coat, balanced myself; advanced slowly towards him, touched his shoulder, and said, "The time has come; you must quit this place; I am sorry for you; here is money; but you must go."

"I would prefer not," he replied, with his back still towards me.

"You *must*." 140

He remained silent.

Now I had an unbounded confidence in this man's common honesty. He had frequently restored to me sixpences and shillings[6] carelessly dropped upon the floor, for I am apt to be very reckless in such shirt-button affairs. The proceeding then which followed will not be deemed extraordinary.

"Bartleby," said I, "I owe you twelve dollars on account; here are thirty-two; the odd twenty are yours.—Will you take it?" and I handed the bills towards him.

But he made no motion.

"I will leave them here then," putting them under a weight on the table. Then 145 taking my hat and cane and going to the door I tranquilly turned and added—"After you have removed your things from these offices, Bartleby, you will of course lock the door—since everyone is now gone for the day but you—and if you please, slip your key underneath the mat, so that I may have it in the morning. I shall not see you again; so good-bye to you. If hereafter in your new place of

---

5. Heavy stone for grinding grain. See Matthew 18.6: "But whoso shall offend one of these little ones which believe in me, it were better for him that a millstone were hanged about his neck, and that he were drowned in the depth of the sea."   6. Coins.

abode I can be of any service to you, do not fail to advise me by letter. Good-bye, Bartleby, and fare you well."

But he answered not a word; like the last column of some ruined temple, he remained standing mute and solitary in the middle of the otherwise deserted room.

As I walked home in a pensive mood, my vanity got the better of my pity. I could not but highly plume myself on my masterly management in getting rid of Bartleby. Masterly I call it, and such it must appear to any dispassionate thinker. The beauty of my procedure seemed to consist in its perfect quietness. There was no vulgar bullying, no bravado of any sort, no choleric hectoring, and striding to and fro across the apartment, jerking out vehement commands for Bartleby to bundle himself off with his beggarly traps.[7] Nothing of the kind. Without loudly bidding Bartleby depart—as an inferior genius might have done—I *assumed* the ground that depart he must; and upon that assumption built all I had to say. The more I thought over my procedure, the more I was charmed with it. Nevertheless, next morning, upon awakening, I had my doubts,—I had somehow slept off the fumes of vanity. One of the coolest and wisest hours a man has is just after he awakes in the morning. My procedure seemed as sagacious as ever,—but only in theory. How it would prove in practice—there was the rub. It was truly a beautiful thought to have assumed Bartleby's departure; but, after all, that assumption was simply my own, and none of Bartleby's. The great point was, not whether I had assumed that he would quit me, but whether he would prefer so to do. He was more a man of preferences than assumptions.

After breakfast, I walked downtown, arguing the probabilities *pro* and *con*. One moment I thought it would prove a miserable failure, and Bartleby would be found all alive at my office as usual; the next moment it seemed certain that I should see his chair empty. And so I kept veering about. At the corner of Broadway and Canal Street, I saw quite an excited group of people standing in earnest conversation.

"I'll take odds he doesn't," said a voice as I passed.

150   "Doesn't go?—done!" said I, "put up your money."

I was instinctively putting my hand in my pocket to produce my own, when I remembered that this was an election day. The words I had overheard bore no reference to Bartleby, but to the success or non-success of some candidate for the mayoralty. In my intent frame of mind, I had, as it were, imagined that all Broadway shared in my excitement, and were debating the same question with me. I passed on, very thankful that the uproar of the street screened my momentary absent-mindedness.

As I had intended, I was earlier than usual at my office door. I stood listening for a moment. All was still. He must be gone. I tried the knob. The door was locked. Yes, my procedure had worked to a charm; he indeed must be vanished. Yet a certain melancholy mixed with this: I was almost sorry for my brilliant success. I was fumbling under the door mat for the key, which Bartleby was to have left there for me, when accidentally my knee knocked against a panel, producing a summoning sound, and in response a voice came to me from within—"Not yet; I am occupied."

It was Bartleby.

---

7. Personal belongings, luggage.

I was thunderstruck. For an instant I stood like the man who, pipe in mouth, was killed one cloudless afternoon long ago in Virginia, by summer lightning; at his own warm open window he was killed, and remained leaning out there upon the dreamy afternoon, till some one touched him, when he fell.

"Not gone!" I murmured at last. But again obeying that wondrous ascendancy which the inscrutable scrivener had over me, and from which ascendency, for all my chafing, I could not completely escape, I slowly went downstairs and out into the street, and while walking round the block, considered what I should next do in this unheard-of perplexity. Turn the man out by an actual thrusting I could not; to drive him away by calling him hard names would not do; calling in the police was an unpleasant idea; and yet, permit him to enjoy his cadaverous triumph over me,—this too I could not think of. What was to be done? or, if nothing could be done, was there anything further that I could *assume* in the matter? Yes, as before I had prospectively assumed that Bartleby would depart, so now I might retrospectively assume that departed he was. In the legitimate carrying out of this assumption, I might enter my office in a great hurry, and pretending not to see Bartleby at all, walk straight against him as if he were air. Such a proceeding would in a singular degree have the appearance of a home-thrust.[8] It was hardly possible that Bartleby could withstand such an application of the doctrine of assumptions. But upon second thoughts the success of the plan seemed rather dubious. I resolved to argue the matter over with him again.

"Bartleby," said I, entering the office, with a quietly severe expression, "I am seriously displeased. I am pained, Bartleby. I had thought better of you. I had imagined you of such a gentlemanly organization, that in any delicate dilemma a slight hint would suffice—in short, an assumption. But it appears I am deceived. Why," I added, unaffectedly starting, "you have not even touched that money yet," pointing to it, just where I had left it the evening previous.

He answered nothing.

"Will you, or will you not, quit me?" I now demanded in a sudden passion, advancing close to him.

"I would prefer *not* to quit you," he replied, gently emphasizing the *not*.

"What earthly right have you to stay here? Do you pay any rent? Do you pay my taxes? Or is this property yours?"

He answered nothing.

"Are you ready to go on and write now? Are your eyes recovered? Could you copy a small paper for me this morning? or help examine a few lines? or step round to the post office? In a word, will you do anything at all, to give a coloring to your refusal to depart the premises?"

He silently retired into his hermitage.

I was now in such a state of nervous resentment that I thought it but prudent to check myself at present from further demonstrations. Bartleby and I were alone. I remembered the tragedy of the unfortunate Adams and the still more unfortunate Colt in the solitary office of the latter;[9] and how poor Colt, being dreadfully incensed by Adams, and imprudently permitting himself to get wildly excited, was at unawares hurried into his fatal act—an act which certainly no

8. In fencing, a successful thrust to the opponent's body.
9. In 1841, John C. Colt, brother of the famous gunmaker, unintentionally killed Samuel Adams, a printer, when he hit him on the head during a fight.

man could possibly deplore more than the actor himself. Often it had occurred to me in my ponderings upon the subject, that had that altercation taken place in the public street, or at a private residence, it would not have terminated as it did. It was the circumstance of being alone in a solitary office, up stairs, of a building entirely unhallowed by humanizing domestic associations—an uncarpeted office, doubtless, of a dusty, haggard sort of appearance;—this it must have been, which greatly helped to enhance the irritable desperation of the hapless Colt.

165   But when this old Adam[1] of resentment rose in me and tempted me concerning Bartleby, I grappled him and threw him. How? Why, simply by recalling the divine injunction: "A new commandment[2] give I unto you, that ye love one another." Yes, this it was that saved me. Aside from higher considerations, charity often operates as a vastly wise and prudent principle—a great safeguard to its possessor. Men have committed murder for jealousy's sake, and anger's sake, and hatred's sake, and selfishness' sake, and spiritual pride's sake; but no man that ever I heard of, ever committed a diabolical murder for sweet charity's sake. Mere self-interest, then, if no better motive can be enlisted, should, especially with high-tempered men, prompt all beings to charity and philanthropy. At any rate, upon the occasion in question, I strove to drown my exasperated feelings towards the scrivener by benevolently construing his conduct. Poor fellow, poor fellow! thought I, he don't mean anything; and besides, he has seen hard times, and ought to be indulged.

I endeavored also immediately to occupy myself, and at the same time to comfort my despondency. I tried to fancy that in the course of the morning, at such time as might prove agreeable to him, Bartleby, of his own free accord, would emerge from his hermitage, and take up some decided line of march in the direction of the door. But no. Half-past twelve o'clock came; Turkey began to glow in the face, overturn his inkstand, and become generally obstreperous; Nippers abated down into quietude and courtesy; Ginger Nut munched his noon apple; and Bartleby remained standing at his window in one of his profoundest dead-wall reveries. Will it be credited? Ought I to acknowledge it? That afternoon I left the office without saying one further word to him.

Some days now passed, during which, at leisure intervals I looked a little into "Edwards on the Will," and "Priestley on Necessity."[3] Under the circumstances, those books induced a salutary feeling. Gradually I slid into the persuasion that these troubles of mine touching the scrivener, had been all predestinated from eternity, and Bartleby was billeted upon me for some mysterious purpose of an all-wise Providence, which it was not for a mere mortal like me to fathom. Yes, Bartleby, stay there behind your screen, thought I; I shall persecute you no more; you are harmless and noiseless as any of these old chairs; in short, I never feel so

1. Sinful element in human nature; see, e.g., "Invocation of Blessing on the Child" in the *Book of Common Prayer:* "Grant that the old Adam in this child may be so buried, that the new man may be raised up in him." Christ is sometimes called the "new Adam."
2. In John 13.34, where, however, the phrasing is "I give unto . . ."
3. Jonathan Edwards (1703–58), New England Calvinist theologian and revivalist, in *The Freedom of the Will* (1754) argued that human beings are not in fact free, for though they choose according to the way they see things, that way is predetermined (by biography, environment, and character), and they act out of personality rather than by will. Joseph Priestley (1733–1804), dissenting preacher, scientist, grammarian, and philosopher, argued in *The Doctrine of Philosophical Necessity* (1777) that free will is theologically objectionable, metaphysically incomprehensible, and morally undesirable.

private as when I know you are here. At least I see it, I feel it; I penetrate to the predestinated purpose of my life. I am content. Others may have loftier parts to enact; but my mission in this world, Bartleby, is to furnish you with office-room for such period as you may see fit to remain.

I believe that this wise and blessed frame of mind would have continued with me, had it not been for the unsolicited and uncharitable remarks obtruded upon me by my professional friends who visited the rooms. But thus it often is, that the constant friction of illiberal minds wears out at last the best resolves of the more generous. Though to be sure, when I reflected upon it, it was not strange that people entering my office should be struck by the peculiar aspect of the unaccountable Bartleby, and so be tempted to throw out some sinister observations concerning him. Sometimes an attorney having business with me, and calling at my office, and finding no one but the scrivener there, would undertake to obtain some sort of precise information from him touching my whereabouts; but without heeding his idle talk, Bartleby would remain standing immovable in the middle of the room. So after contemplating him in that position for a time, the attorney would depart, no wiser than he came.

Also, when a Reference[4] was going on, and the room full of lawyers and witnesses and business was driving fast; some deeply occupied legal gentleman present, seeing Bartleby wholly unemployed, would request him to run round to his (the legal gentleman's) office and fetch some papers for him. Thereupon, Bartleby would tranquilly decline, and yet remain idle as before. Then the lawyer would give a great stare, and turn to me. And what could I say? At last I was made aware that all through the circle of my professional acquaintance, a whisper of wonder was running round, having reference to the strange creature I kept at my office. This worried me very much. And as the idea came upon me of his possibly turning out a long-lived man, and keep occupying my chambers, and denying my authority; and perplexing my visitors; and scandalizing my professional reputation; and casting a general gloom over the premises; keeping soul and body together to the last upon his savings (for doubtless he spent but half a dime a day), and in the end perhaps outlive me, and claim possession of my office by right of his perpetual occupancy: as all these dark anticipations crowded upon me more and more, and my friends continually intruded their relentless remarks upon the apparition in my room; a great change was wrought in me. I resolved to gather all my faculties together, and forever rid me of this intolerable incubus.[5]

Ere revolving any complicated project, however, adapted to this end, I first sim- 170 ply suggested to Bartleby the propriety of his permanent departure. In a calm and serious tone, I commended the idea to his careful and mature consideration. But having taken three days to meditate upon it, he apprised me that his original determination remained the same; in short, that he still preferred to abide with me.

What shall I do? I now said to myself, buttoning up my coat to the last button. What shall I do? what ought I to do? what does conscience say I *should* do with this man, or rather ghost. Rid myself of him, I must; go, he shall. But how? You will not thrust him, the poor, pale, passive mortal,—you will not thrust such a helpless creature out of your door? you will not dishonor yourself by such cruelty? No, I will not, I cannot do that. Rather would I let him live and die here, and then mason up his remains in the wall. What then will you do? For all your

4. Consultation or committee meeting.   5. Evil spirit.

coaxing, he will not budge. Bribes he leaves under your own paperweight on your table; in short, it is quite plain that he prefers to cling to you.

Then something severe, something unusual must be done. What! surely you will not have him collared by a constable, and commit his innocent pallor to the common jail? And upon what ground could you procure such a thing to be done?—a vagrant, is he? What! he a vagrant, a wanderer, who refuses to budge? It is because he will *not* be a vagrant, then, that you seek to count him *as* a vagrant. That is too absurd. No visible means of support: there I have him. Wrong again: for indubitably he *does* support himself, and that is the only unanswerable proof that any man can show of his possessing the means so to do. No more then. Since he will not quit me, I must quit him. I will change my offices; I will move elsewhere; and give him fair notice, that if I find him on my new premises I will then proceed against him as a common trespasser.

Acting accordingly, next day I thus addressed him: "I find these chambers too far from the City Hall; the air is unwholesome. In a word, I propose to remove my offices next week, and shall no longer require your services. I tell you this now, in order that you may seek another place."

He made no reply, and nothing more was said.

175   On the appointed day I engaged carts and men, proceeded to my chambers, and having but little furniture, everything was removed in a few hours. Throughout, the scrivener remained standing behind the screen, which I directed to be removed the last thing. It was withdrawn; and being folded up like a huge folio, left him the motionless occupant of a naked room. I stood in the entry watching him a moment, while something from within me upbraided me.

I re-entered, with my hand in my pocket—and—and my heart in my mouth.

"Good-bye, Bartleby; I am going—good-bye, and God some way bless you; and take that," slipping something in his hand. But it dropped upon the floor, and then,—strange to say—I tore myself from him whom I had so longed to be rid of.

Established in my new quarters, for a day or two I kept the door locked, and started at every footfall in the passages. When I returned to my rooms after any little absence, I would pause at the threshold for an instant, and attentively listen, ere applying my key. But these fears were needless. Bartleby never came nigh me.

I thought all was going well, when a perturbed-looking stranger visited me, inquiring whether I was the person who had recently occupied rooms at No.—— Wall Street.

180   Full of forebodings, I replied that I was.

"Then sir," said the stranger, who proved a lawyer, "you are responsible for the man you left there. He refuses to do any copying; he refuses to do anything; he says he prefers not to; and he refuses to quit the premises."

"I am very sorry, sir," said I, with assumed tranquillity, but an inward tremor, "but, really, the man you allude to is nothing to me—he is no relation or apprentice of mine, that you should hold me responsible for him."

"In mercy's name, who is he?"

"I certainly cannot inform you. I know nothing about him. Formerly I employed him as a copyist; but he has done nothing for me now for some time past."

185   "I shall settle him then,—good morning, sir."

Several days passed, and I heard nothing more; and though I often felt a charitable prompting to call at the place and see poor Bartleby, yet a certain squeamishness of I know not what withheld me.

All is over with him, by this time, thought I at last, when through another week no further intelligence reached me. But coming to my room the day after, I found several persons waiting at my door in a high state of nervous excitement.

"That's the man—here he comes," cried the foremost one, whom I recognized as the lawyer who had previously called upon me alone.

"You must take him away, sir, at once," cried a portly person among them, advancing upon me, and whom I knew to be the landlord of No. —— Wall Street. "These gentlemen, my tenants, cannot stand it any longer; Mr. B——" pointing to the lawyer, "has turned him out of his room, and he now persists in haunting the building generally, sitting upon the banisters of the stairs by day, and sleeping in the entry by night. Everybody is concerned; clients are leaving the offices; some fears are entertained of a mob; something you must do, and that without delay."

Aghast at this torrent, I fell back before it, and would fain have locked myself 190 in my new quarters. In vain I persisted that Bartleby was nothing to me—no more than to anyone else. In vain:—I was the last person known to have anything to do with him, and they held me to the terrible account. Fearful then of being exposed in the papers (as one person present obscurely threatened) I considered the matter, and at length said, that if the lawyer would give me a confidential interview with the scrivener, in his (the lawyer's) own room, I would that afternoon strive my best to rid them of the nuisance they complained of.

Going upstairs to my old haunt, there was Bartleby silently sitting upon the banister at the landing.

"What are you doing here, Bartleby?" said I.

"Sitting upon the banister," he mildly replied.

I motioned him into the lawyer's room, who then left us.

"Bartleby," said I, "are you aware that you are the cause of great tribulation to 195 me, by persisting in occupying the entry after being dismissed from the office?" No answer.

"Now one of two things must take place. Either you must do something, or something must be done to you. Now what sort of business would you like to engage in? Would you like to re-engage in copying for someone?"

"No; I would prefer not to make any change."

"Would you like a clerkship in a drygoods store?"

"There is too much confinement about that. No, I would not like a clerkship; 200 but I am not particular."

"Too much confinement," I cried, "why you keep yourself confined all the time!"

"I would prefer not to take a clerkship," he rejoined, as if to settle that little item at once.

"How would a bartender's business suit you? There is no trying of the eyesight in that."

"I would not like it at all; though, as I said before, I am not particular."

His unwonted wordiness inspirited me. I returned to the charge. 205

"Well then, would you like to travel through the country collecting bills for the merchants? That would improve your health."

"No, I would prefer to be doing something else."

"How then would going as a companion to Europe, to entertain some young gentleman with your conversation,—how would that suit you?"

"Not at all. It does not strike me that there is anything definite about that. I like to be stationary. But I am not particular."

210　　"Stationary you shall be then," I cried, now losing all patience, and for the first time in all my exasperating connection with him fairly flying into a passion. "If you do not go away from these premises before night, I shall feel bound—indeed I *am* bound—to—to—to quit the premises myself!" I rather absurdly concluded, knowing not with what possible threat to try to frighten his immobility into compliance. Despairing of all further efforts, I was precipitately leaving him, when a final thought occurred to me—one which had not been wholly unindulged before.

　　"Bartleby," said I, in the kindest tone I could assume under such exciting circumstances, "will you go home with me now—not to my office, but my dwelling—and remain there till we can conclude upon some convenient arrangement for you at our leisure? Come, let us start now, right away."

　　"No: at present I would prefer not to make any change at all."

　　I answered nothing; but effectually dodging everyone by the suddenness and rapidity of my flight, rushed from the building, ran up Wall Street toward Broadway, and jumping into the first omnibus was soon removed from pursuit. As soon as tranquillity returned I distinctly perceived that I had now done all that I possibly could, both in respect to the demands of the landlord and his tenants, and with regard to my own desire and sense of duty, to benefit Bartleby, and shield him from rude persecution. I now strove to be entirely carefree and quiescent; and my conscience justified me in the attempt; though indeed it was not so successful as I could have wished. So fearful was I of being again hunted out by the incensed landlord and his exasperated tenants, that, surrendering my business to Nippers, for a few days I drove about the upper part of the town and through the suburbs, in my rockaway;[6] crossed over to Jersey City and Hoboken, and paid fugitive visits to Manhattanville and Astoria. In fact I almost lived in my rockaway for the time.

　　When again I entered my office, lo, a note from the landlord lay upon the desk. I opened it with trembling hands. It informed me that the writer had sent to the police, and had Bartleby removed to the Tombs as a vagrant. Moreover, since I knew more about him than anyone else, he wished me to appear at that place, and make a suitable statement of the facts. These tidings had a conflicting effect upon me. At first I was indignant; but at last almost approved. The landlord's energetic, summary disposition had led him to adopt a procedure which I do not think I would have decided upon myself; and yet as a last resort, under such peculiar circumstances, it seemed the only plan.

215　　As I afterwards learned, the poor scrivener, when told that he must be conducted to the Tombs, offered not the slightest obstacle, but in his pale unmoving way, silently acquiesced.

　　Some of the compassionate and curious bystanders joined the party; and headed by one of the constables arm in arm with Bartleby, the silent procession filed its way through all the noise, and heat, and joy of the roaring thoroughfares at noon.

　　The same day I received the note I went to the Tombs, or to speak more properly, the Halls of Justice. Seeking the right officer, I stated the purpose of my call, and was informed that the individual I described was indeed within. I then assured the functionary that Bartleby was a perfectly honest man, and greatly to be compassionated, however unaccountably eccentric. I narrated all I knew, and

6. Light, four-wheeled carriage.

closed by suggesting the idea of letting him remain in as indulgent confinement as possible till something less harsh might be done—though indeed I hardly knew what. At all events, if nothing else could be decided upon, the alms-house must receive him. I then begged to have an interview.

Being under no disgraceful charge, and quite serene and harmless in all his ways, they had permitted him freely to wander about the prison, and especially in the inclosed grass-platted yards thereof. And so I found him there, standing all alone in the quietest of the yards, his face towards a high wall, while all around, from the narrow slits of the jail windows, I thought I saw peering out upon him the eyes of murderers and thieves.

"Bartleby!"

"I know you," he said, without looking round,—"and I want nothing to say to 220 you."

"It was not I that brought you here, Bartleby," said I, keenly pained at his implied suspicion. "And to you, this should not be so vile a place. Nothing reproachful attaches to you by being here. And see, it is not so sad a place as one might think. Look, there is the sky, and here is the grass."

"I know where I am," he replied, but would say nothing more, and so I left him.

As I entered the corridor again, a broad meat-like man, in an apron, accosted me, and jerking his thumb over his shoulder said—"Is that your friend?"

"Yes."

"Does he want to starve? If he does, let him live on the prison fare, that's all." 225

"Who are you?" asked I, not knowing what to make of such an unofficially-speaking person in such a place.

"I am the grub-man. Such gentlemen as have friends here, hire me to provide them with something good to eat."

"Is this so?" said I, turning to the turnkey.

He said it was.

"Well then," said I, slipping some silver into the grub-man's hands (for so they 230 called him). "I want you to give particular attention to my friend there; let him have the best dinner you can get. And you must be as polite to him as possible."

"Introduce me, will you?" said the grub-man, looking at me with an expression which seemed to say he was all impatience for an opportunity to give a specimen of his breeding.

Thinking it would prove of benefit to the scrivener, I acquiesced; and asking the grub-man his name, went up with him to Bartleby.

"Bartleby, this is Mr. Cutlets; you will find him very useful to you."

"Your sarvant, sir, your sarvant," said the grub-man, making a low salutation behind his apron. "Hope you find it pleasant here, sir;—spacious grounds—cool apartments, sir—hope you'll stay with us some time—try to make it agreeable. May Mrs. Cutlets and I have the pleasure of your company to dinner, sir, in Mrs. Cutlets' private room?"

"I prefer not to dine today," said Bartleby, turning away. "It would disagree 235 with me; I am unused to dinners." So saying he slowly moved to the other side of the inclosure, and took up a position fronting the dead-wall.

"How's this?" said the grub-man, addressing me with a stare of astonishment. "He's odd, ain't he?"

"I think he is a little deranged," said I, sadly.

"Deranged? deranged is it? Well now, upon my word, I thought that friend of yourn was a gentleman forger; they are always pale and genteel-like, them forgers. I can't help pity 'em—can't help it, sir. Did you know Monroe Edwards?"[7] he added touchingly, and paused. Then laying his hand pityingly on my shoulder, sighed, "he died of consumption at Sing Sing. So you weren't acquainted with Monroe?"

"No, I was never socially acquainted with any forgers. But I cannot stop longer. Look to my friend yonder. You will not lose by it. I will see you again."

240 Some few days after this, I again obtained admission to the Tombs, and went through the corridors in quest of Bartleby; but without finding him.

"I saw him coming from his cell not long ago," said a turnkey, "may be he's gone to loiter in the yards."

So I went in that direction.

"Are you looking for the silent man?" said another turnkey passing me. "Yonder he lies—sleeping in the yard there. 'Tis not twenty minutes since I saw him lie down."

The yard was entirely quiet. It was not accessible to the common prisoners. The surrounding walls, of amazing thickness, kept off all sounds behind them. The Egyptian character of the masonry weighed upon me with its gloom. But a soft imprisoned turf grew under foot. The heart of the eternal pyramids, it seemed, wherein, by some strange magic, through the clefts, grass seed, dropped by birds, had sprung.

245 Strangely huddled at the base of the wall, his knees drawn up, and lying on his side, his head touching the cold stones, I saw the wasted Bartleby. But nothing stirred. I paused; then went close up to him; stooped over, and saw that his dim eyes were open; otherwise he seemed profoundly sleeping. Something prompted me to touch him. I felt his hand, when a tingling shiver ran up my arm and down my spine to my feet.

The round face of the grub-man peered upon me now. "His dinner is ready. Won't he dine today, either? Or does he live without dining?"

"Lives without dining," said I, and closed the eyes.

"Eh!—He's asleep, ain't he?"

"With kings and counsellors,"[8] murmured I.

250 There would seem little need for proceeding further in this history. Imagination will readily supply the meager recital of poor Bartleby's interment. But ere parting with the reader, let me say, that if this little narrative has sufficiently interested him, to awaken curiosity as to who Bartleby was, and what manner of life he led prior to the present narrator's making his acquaintance, I can only reply, that in such curiosity I fully share, but am wholly unable to gratify it. Yet here I hardly know whether I should divulge one little item of rumor, which came to my ear a few months after the scrivener's decease. Upon what basis it rested, I could never ascertain; and hence, how true it is I cannot now tell. But inasmuch as this vague report has not been without a certain strange suggestive interest to me, however sad, it may prove the same with some others; and so I will

---

7. Famously flamboyant swindler and forger (1808–47) who died in Sing Sing prison, north of New York City.

8. I.e., dead. See Job 3.13–14: "then had I been at rest, With kings and counsellors of the earth, which built desolate places for themselves."

briefly mention it. The report was this: that Bartleby had been a subordinate clerk in the Dead Letter Office at Washington, from which he had been suddenly removed by a change in the administration. When I think over this rumor, I cannot adequately express the emotions which seize me. Dead letters! does it not sound like dead men? Conceive a man by nature and misfortune prone to a pallid hopelessness, can any business seem more fitted to heighten it than that of continually handling these dead letters, and assorting them for the flames? For by the cartload they are annually burned. Sometimes from out the folded paper the pale clerk takes a ring:—the finger it was meant for, perhaps, molders in the grave; a banknote sent in swiftest charity:—he whom it would relieve, nor eats nor hungers any more; pardon for those who died despairing; hope for those who died unhoping; good tidings for those who died stifled by unrelieved calamities. On errands of life, these letters speed to death.

Ah Bartleby! Ah humanity!

1853

QUESTIONS

1. By the end of "Bartleby, the Scrivener," what does the reader know for certain about Bartleby? Why do you think Melville provides so little explicit information about this character?
2. The narrator tells us that his clerks' nicknames are "expressive of their respective persons or characters," but he explains only Turkey's nickname in this regard. How would you explain the appropriateness of Nipper's nickname? of Ginger Nut's?
3. One of the few words Bartleby utters is *prefer,* and the other characters find themselves using this "queer word." What can we learn about Bartleby and the others by the ways in which they use the word *prefer?*

FRANZ KAFKA

The Metamorphosis[1]

I

When Gregor Samsa awoke one morning from troubled dreams, he found himself changed into a monstrous cockroach in his bed. He lay on his tough, armoured back, and, raising his head a little, managed to see—sectioned off by little crescent-shaped ridges into segments—the expanse of his arched, brown belly, atop which the coverlet perched, forever on the point of slipping off entirely. His numerous legs, pathetically frail by contrast to the rest of him, waved feebly before his eyes.

"What's the matter with me?" he thought. It was no dream. There, quietly between the four familiar walls, was his room, a normal human room, if always a little on the small side. Over the table, on which an array of cloth samples was spread out—Samsa was a travelling salesman—hung the picture he had only recently clipped from a magazine, and set in an attractive gilt frame. It was a picture of a lady in a fur

1. Translated from the original German by Michael Hofmann.

hat and stole,[2] sitting bolt upright, holding in the direction of the onlooker a heavy fur muff into which she had thrust the whole of her forearm.

From there, Gregor's gaze directed itself towards the window, and the drab weather outside—raindrops could be heard plinking against the tin window-ledges—made him quite melancholy. "What if I went back to sleep for a while, and forgot about all this nonsense?" he thought, but that proved quite impossible, because he was accustomed to sleeping on his right side, and in his present state he was unable to find that position. However vigorously he flung himself to his right, he kept rocking on to his back. He must have tried it a hundred times, closing his eyes so as not to have to watch his wriggling legs, and only stopped when he felt a slight ache in his side which he didn't recall having felt before.

"Oh, my Lord!" he thought. "If only I didn't have to follow such an exhausting profession! On the road, day in, day out. The work is so much more strenuous than it would be in head office, and then there's the additional ordeal of travelling, worries about train connections, the irregular, bad meals, new people all the time, no continuity, no affection. Devil take it!" He felt a light itch at the top of his belly; slid a little closer to the bedpost, so as to be able to raise his head a little more effectively; found the itchy place, which was covered with a sprinkling of white dots the significance of which he was unable to interpret; assayed the place with one of his legs, but hurriedly withdrew it, because the touch caused him to shudder involuntarily.

5   He slid back to his previous position. "All this getting up early," he thought, "is bound to take its effect. A man needs proper bed rest. There are some other travelling salesmen I could mention who live like harem women. Sometimes, for instance, when I return to the *pension*[3] in the course of the morning, to make a note of that morning's orders, some of those gents are just sitting down to breakfast. I'd like to see what happened if I tried that out with my director some time; it would be the order of the boot[4] just like that. That said, it might be just the thing for me. If I didn't have to exercise restraint for the sake of my parents, then I would have quit a long time ago; I would have gone up to the director and told him exactly what I thought of him. He would have fallen off his desk in surprise! That's a peculiar way he has of sitting anyway, up on his desk, and talking down to his staff from on high, making them step up to him very close because he's so hard of hearing. Well, I haven't quite given up hope; once I've got the money together to pay back what my parents owe him—it may take me another five or six years—then I'll do it, no question. Then we'll have the parting of the ways. But for the time being, I'd better look sharp, because my train leaves at five."

And he looked across at the alarm clock, ticking away on the bedside table. "Great heavenly Father!" he thought. It was half past six, and the clock hands were moving smoothly forward—in fact it was after half past, it was more like a quarter to seven. Had the alarm not gone off? He could see from the bed that it had been quite correctly set for four o'clock; it must have gone off. But how was it possible to sleep calmly through its ringing, which caused even the furniture to shake? Well, his sleep hadn't exactly been calm, but maybe it had been all the more profound. What to do now? The next train left at seven; to catch it meant hurrying like a madman, and his samples weren't yet packed, and he himself

2. Garment to cover the shoulders.   3. Small hotel or boarding house (French).
4. That is, he would be fired.

didn't feel exactly agile or vigorous. And even if he caught that train, he would still get a carpeting from the director, because the office boy would be on the platform at five o'clock, and would certainly have reported long since that Gregor hadn't been on the train. That boy was a real piece of work, so utterly beholden to the director, without any backbone or nous.[5] Then what if he called in sick? That would be rather embarrassing and a little suspicious too, because in the course of the past five years, Gregor hadn't once been ill. The director was bound to retaliate by calling in the company doctor, would upbraid the parents for their idle son, and refute all objections by referring to the doctor, for whom there were only perfectly healthy but workshy patients. And who could say he was wrong, in this instance anyway? Aside from a continuing feeling of sleepiness that was quite unreasonable after such a long sleep, Gregor felt perfectly well, and even felt the stirrings of a healthy appetite.

As he was hurriedly thinking this, still no nearer to getting out of bed—the alarm clock was just striking a quarter to seven—there was a cautious knock on the door behind him. "Gregor," came the call—it was his mother—"it's a quarter to seven. Shouldn't you ought to be gone by now?" The mild voice. Gregor was dismayed when he heard his own in response. It was still without doubt his own voice from before, but with a little admixture of an irrepressible squeaking that left the words only briefly recognizable at the first instant of their sounding, only to set about them afterwards so destructively that one couldn't be at all sure what one had heard. Gregor had wanted to offer a full explanation of everything but, in these circumstances, kept himself to: "All right, thank you, Mother, I'm getting up!" The wooden door must have muted the change in Gregor's voice, because his mother seemed content with his reply, and shuffled away. But the brief exchange had alerted other members of the family to the surprising fact that Gregor was still at home, and already there was his father, knocking on the door at the side of the room, feebly, but with his fist. "Gregor, Gregor?" he shouted, "what's the matter?" And after a little while, he came again, in a lower octave: "Gregor! Gregor!" On the door on the other side of the room, meanwhile, he heard his sister lamenting softly: "Oh, Gregor? Are you not well? Can I bring you anything?" To both sides equally Gregor replied, "Just coming," and tried by careful enunciation and long pauses between the words to take any unusual quality from his voice. His father soon returned to his breakfast, but his sister whispered: "Gregor, please, will you open the door." Gregor entertained no thought of doing so; instead he gave silent thanks for the precaution, picked up on his travels, of locking every door at night, even at home.

His immediate intention was to get up calmly and leisurely, to get dressed and, above all, to have breakfast before deciding what to do next, because he was quite convinced he wouldn't arrive at any sensible conclusions as long as he remained in bed. There were many times, he remembered, when he had lain in bed with a sense of some dim pain somewhere in his body, perhaps from lying awkwardly, which then turned out, as he got up, to be mere imagining, and he looked forward to his present fanciful state gradually falling from him. He had not the least doubt that the alteration in his voice was just the first sign of a head-cold, always an occupational malady with travelling salesmen.

5. Common sense.

Casting off the blanket proved to be straightforward indeed; all he needed to do was to inflate himself a little, and it fell off by itself. But further tasks were more problematical, not least because of his great breadth. He would have needed arms and hands with which to get up; instead of which all he had were those numerous little legs, forever in varied movement, and evidently not under his control. If he wanted to bend one of them, then it was certain that that was the one that was next fully extended; and once he finally succeeded in performing whatever task he had set himself with that leg, then all its neglected fellows would be in a turmoil of painful agitation. "Whatever I do, I mustn't loaf around in bed," Gregor said to himself.

10   At first he thought he would get out of bed bottom half first, but this bottom half of himself, which he had yet to see, and as to whose specifications he was perfectly ignorant, turned out to be not very manoeuvrable; progress was slow; and when at last, almost in fury, he pushed down with all his strength, he misjudged the direction, and collided with the lower bedpost, the burning pain he felt teaching him that this lower end of himself might well be, for the moment, the most sensitive to pain.

He therefore tried to lever his top half out of bed first, and cautiously turned his head towards the edge of the bed. This was easily done, and, in spite of its breadth and bulk, the rest of his body slowly followed the direction of the head. But, now craning his neck in empty space well away from the bed, he was afraid to move any further, because if he were to fall in that position, it would take a miracle if he didn't injure his head. And he mustn't lose consciousness at any price; it were better then to stay in bed.

But as he sighed and lay there at the end of his endeavours, and once again beheld his legs struggling, if anything, harder than before, and saw no possibility of bringing any order or calm to their randomness, he told himself once more that he couldn't possibly stay in bed and that the most sensible solution was to try anything that offered even the smallest chance of getting free of his bed. At the same time, he didn't forget to remind himself periodically that clarity and calm were better than counsels of despair. At such moments, he levelled his gaze as sharply as possible at the window, but unfortunately there was little solace or encouragement to be drawn from the sight of the morning fog, which was thick enough to obscure even the opposite side of the street. "Seven o'clock already," he said to himself as his alarm clock struck another quarter, "seven o'clock already, and still such dense fog." And he lay there for a while longer, panting gently, as though perhaps expecting that silence would restore the natural order of things.

But then he said to himself: "By quarter past seven, I must certainly have got out of bed completely. In any case, somebody will have come from work by then to ask after me, because the business opens before seven o'clock." And he set about rhythmically rocking his body clear of the bed. If he dropped out of bed in that way, then he would try to raise his head sharply at the last moment, so that it remained uninjured. His back seemed to be tough; a fall on to the carpet would surely not do it any harm. What most concerned him was the prospect of the loud crash he would surely cause, which would presumably provoke anxiety, if not consternation, behind all the doors. But that was a risk he had to take.

As Gregor was already half-clear of the bed—this latest method felt more like play than serious exertion, requiring him only to rock himself from side to side— he thought how simple everything would be if he had some help. Two strong people—he thought of his father and the servant-girl—would easily suffice; they needed only to push their arms under his curved back, peel him out of bed, bend down under his weight, and then just pay attention while they flipped him over on to the floor, where his legs would hopefully come into their own. But then, even if the doors hadn't been locked, could he have really contemplated calling for help? Even in his extremity, he couldn't repress a smile at the thought.

He had already reached the point where his rocking was almost enough to send him off balance, and he would soon have to make up his mind once and for all what he was going to do, because it was ten past seven—when the doorbell rang. "It must be someone from work," he said to himself and went almost rigid, while his little legs, if anything, increased their agitation. For a moment there was silence. "They won't open the door," Gregor said to himself, from within some mad hope. But then of course, as always, the servant-girl walked with firm stride to the door and opened it. Gregor needed only to hear the first word from the visitor to know that it was the chief clerk in person. Why only was Gregor condemned to work for a company where the smallest lapse was greeted with the gravest suspicion? Were all the employees without exception scoundrels, were there really no loyal and dependable individuals among them, who, if once a couple of morning hours were not exploited for work, were driven so demented by pangs of conscience that they were unable to get out of bed? Was it really not enough to send a trainee to inquire—if inquiries were necessary at all—and did the chief clerk need to come in person, thereby demonstrating to the whole blameless family that the investigation of Gregor's delinquency could only be entrusted to the seniority and trained intelligence of a chief clerk? And more on account of the excitement that came over Gregor with these reflections, than as the result of any proper decision on his part, he powerfully swung himself right out of bed. There was a loud impact, though not a crash as such. The fall was somewhat muffled by the carpet; moreover, his back was suppler than Gregor had expected, and therefore the result was a dull thump that did not draw such immediate attention to itself. Only he had been a little careless of his head, and had bumped it; frantic with rage and pain, he turned and rubbed it against the carpet.

"Something's fallen down in there," said the chief clerk in the hallway on the left. Gregor tried to imagine whether the chief clerk had ever experienced something similar to what had happened to himself today; surely it was within the bounds of possibility. But as if in blunt reply to this question, the chief clerk now took a few decisive steps next door, his patent-leather boots creaking. From the room on the right, his sister now whispered to Gregor: "Gregor, the chief clerk's here." "I know," Gregor replied to himself; but he didn't dare say it sufficiently loudly for his sister to hear him.

"Gregor," his father now said from the left-hand room, "the chief clerk has come, and wants to know why you weren't on the early train. We don't know what to tell him. He wants a word with you too. So kindly open the door. I'm sure he'll turn a blind eye to the untidiness in your room." "Good morning, Mr Samsa," called the cheery voice of the chief clerk. "He's not feeling well," Gregor's mother interjected to the chief clerk, while his father was still talking by the door, "he's not feeling well, believe me, Chief Clerk. How otherwise could Gregor miss his train! You know that boy has nothing but work in his head! It almost worries me that he never goes out on his evenings off; he's been in the city now for the past week, but he's spent every evening at home. He sits at the table quietly reading the newspaper, or studying the railway timetable. His only hobby is a little occasional woodwork. In the past two or three evenings, he's carved a little picture-frame; I think you'll be surprised by the workmanship; he's got it up on the wall in his room; you'll see it the instant Gregor opens the door. You've no idea how happy I am to see you, Chief Clerk; by ourselves we would never have been able to induce Gregor to open the door, he's so obstinate; and I'm sure he's not feeling well, even though he told us he was fine." "I'm just coming," Gregor said slowly and deliberately, not stirring, so as not to miss a single word of the conversation outside. "I'm sure you're right, madam," said the chief clerk, "I only hope it's nothing serious. Though again I have to say that—unhappily or otherwise—we businesspeople often find ourselves in the position of having to set aside some minor ailment, in the greater interest of our work." "So can we admit the chief clerk now?" asked his impatient father, knocking on the door again. "No," said Gregor. In the left-hand room there was now an awkward silence, while on the right his sister began to sob.

Why didn't his sister go and join the others? She had presumably only just got up, and hadn't started getting dressed yet. And then why was she crying? Because he wouldn't get up and admit the chief clerk, because he was in danger of losing his job, and because the director would then pursue his parents with the old claims? Surely those anxieties were still premature at this stage. Gregor was still here, and wasn't thinking at all about leaving the family. For now he was sprawled on the carpet, and no one who was aware of his condition could have seriously expected that he would allow the chief clerk into his room. But this minor breach of courtesy, for which he could easily find an explanation later, hardly constituted reason enough for Gregor to be sent packing. Gregor thought it was much more sensible for them to leave him alone now, rather than bother him with tears and appeals. It was just the uncertainly that afflicted the others and accounted for their behaviour.

"Mr Samsa," the chief clerk now called out loudly, "what's the matter? You've barricaded yourself into your room, you give us one-word answers, you cause your parents grave and needless anxiety and—this just by the by—you're neglecting your official duties in a quite unconscionable way. I am talking to you on behalf of your parents and the director, and I now ask you in all seriousness for a prompt and full explanation. I must say, I'm astonished, I'm astonished. I had taken you for a quiet and sensible individual, but you seem set on indulging a bizarre array of moods. This morning the director suggested a possible reason for your missing your train—it was to do with the authority to collect payments recently entrusted to you—but I practically gave him my word of honour that that couldn't be the explanation. Now, though, in view of your baffling obstinacy, I'm losing all inclination to speak up on your behalf. And your position is hardly the most secure. I had originally come with the intention of telling you as much in confidence, but as you seem to see fit to waste my time, I really don't know why your parents shouldn't get to hear about it as well. Your performances of late have been extremely unsatisfactory; it's admittedly not the time of year for the best results, we freely concede that; but a time of year for no sales, that doesn't exist in our calendars, Mr Samsa, and it mustn't exist."

20   "But Chief Clerk," Gregor exclaimed, in his excitement forgetting everything else, "I'll let you in right away. A light indisposition, a fit of giddiness, have prevented me from getting up. I'm still lying in bed. But I feel almost restored. I'm even now getting out of bed. Just one moment's patience! It seems I'm not as much improved as I'd hoped. But I feel better just the same. How is it something like this can befall a person! Only last night I felt fine, my parents will confirm it

to you, or rather, last night I had a little inkling already of what lay ahead. It probably showed in my appearance somewhere. Why did I not think to inform work! It's just that one always imagines that one will get over an illness without having to take time off. Chief Clerk, sir! Spare my parents! All those complaints you bring against me, they're all of them groundless; it's the first I've heard of any of them. Perhaps you haven't yet perused the last batch of orders I sent in. By the way, I mean to set out on the eight o'clock train—the couple of hours rest have done me the world of good. Chief Clerk, don't detain yourself any longer; I'll be at work myself presently. Kindly be so good as to let them know, and pass on my regards to the director!"

While Gregor blurted all this out, almost unaware of what he was saying, he had moved fairly effortlessly—no doubt aided by the practice he had had in bed—up to the bedside table, and now attempted to haul himself into an upright position against it. He truly had it in mind to open the door, to show himself and to speak to the chief clerk; he was eager to learn what the others, who were all clamouring for him, would say when they got to see him. If they were shocked, then Gregor would have no more responsibility, and could relax. Whereas if they took it all calmly, then he wouldn't have any cause for agitation either, and if he hurried, he might still get to the station by eight o'clock. To begin with he could get no purchase on the smooth bedside table, but at last he gave himself one more swing, and stood there upright; he barely noticed the pain in his lower belly, though it did burn badly. Then he let himself drop against the back of a nearby chair, whose edges he clasped with some of his legs. With that he had attained mastery over himself, and was silent, because now he could listen to the chief clerk.

"Did you understand a single word of that?" the chief clerk asked Gregor's parents, "you don't suppose he's pulling our legs, do you?" "In the name of God," his mother cried, her voice already choked with tears, "perhaps he's gravely ill, and we're tormenting him. Grete! Grete!" she called out. "Mother?" his sister called back from the opposite side. They were communicating with one another through Gregor's room. "Go to the doctor right away. Gregor's ill. Hurry and fetch the doctor. Were you able to hear him just now?" "That was the voice of an animal," said the chief clerk, strikingly much more quietly than his mother and her screaming. "Anna! Anna!" his father shouted through the hallway, in the direction of the kitchen, and clapped his hands, "get the locksmith right away!" And already two girls in rustling skirts were hurrying through the hallway—however had his sister managed to dress so quickly?—and out through the front door. There wasn't the bang of it closing either; probably they had left it open, as happens at times when a great misfortune has taken place.

Meanwhile, Gregor had become much calmer. It appeared his words were no longer comprehensible, though to his own hearing they seemed clear enough, clearer than before, perhaps because his ear had become attuned to the sound. But the family already had the sense of all not being well with him, and were ready to come to his assistance. The clarity and resolve with which the first instructions had been issued did him good. He felt himself back within the human ambit, and from both parties, doctor and locksmith, without treating them really in any way as distinct one from the other, he hoped for magnificent and surprising feats. In order to strengthen his voice for the decisive conversations that surely lay ahead, he cleared his throat a few times, as quietly as possible, as it appeared that even this sound was something other than a human cough, and he no longer trusted himself to tell the difference. Next door, things had become very quiet. Perhaps his parents were sitting at the table holding whispered consultations with the chief clerk, or perhaps they were all pressing their ears to the door, and listening.

Gregor slowly pushed himself across to the door with the chair, there let go of it and dropped against the door, holding himself in an upright position against it—the pads on his little legs secreted some sort of sticky substance—and there rested a moment from his exertions. And then he set himself with his mouth to turn the key in the lock. Unfortunately, it appeared that he had no teeth as such—what was he going to grip the key with?—but luckily his jaws were very powerful; with their help, he got the key to move, and he didn't stop to consider that he was certainly damaging himself in some way, because a brown liquid came out of his mouth, ran over the key, and dribbled on to the floor. "Listen," the chief clerk was saying next door, "he's turning the key." This was a great encouragement for Gregor; but they all of them should have called out to him, his father and mother too: "Go, Gregor," they should have shouted, "keep at it, work at the lock!" And with the idea that they were all following his efforts with tense concentration, he bit fast on to the key with all the strength he possessed, to the point when he was ready to black out. The more the key moved in the door, the more he danced around the lock; now he was holding himself upright with just his mouth, and, depending on the position, he either hung from the key, or was pressing against it with the full weight of his body. The light click of the snapping lock brought Gregor round, as from a spell of unconsciousness. Sighing with relief, he said to himself: "Well, I didn't need the locksmith after all," and he rested his head on the door handle to open the door fully.

25   As he had had to open the door in this way, it was already fairly ajar while he himself was still out of sight. He first had to twist round one half of the door, and very cautiously at that, if he wasn't to fall flat on his back just at the point of making his entry into the room. He was still taken up with the difficult manoeuvre, and didn't have time to think about anything else, when he heard the chief clerk emit a sharp "Oh!"—it actually sounded like the rushing wind—and then he saw him as well, standing nearest to the door, his hand pressed against his open mouth, and slowly retreating, as if being pushed back by an invisible but irresistible force. Gregor's mother—in spite of the chief clerk's arrival, she was standing there with her hair loose, though now it was standing up stiffly in the air—first looked at his father with folded hands, then took two steps towards Gregor and collapsed in the midst of her skirts spreading out around her, her face irretrievably sunk against her bosom. His father clenched his fist with a pugnacious expression, as if ready to push Gregor back into his room, then looked uncertainly round the living room, covered his eyes with his hands and cried, his mighty chest shaking with sobs.

Now Gregor didn't even set foot in the room, but leaned against the inside of the fixed half of the door, so that only half his body could be seen, and the head with which he was peering across at the others cocked on its side a little. It was much brighter now; a little section of the endless grey-black frontage of the building opposite—it was a hospital—could clearly be seen, with its rhythmically recurring windows; it was still raining, but now only in single large drops, individually fashioned and flung to the ground. The breakfast things were out on the table in profusion, because for his father breakfast was the most important meal of the day, which he liked to draw out for hours over the perusal of several newspapers. Just opposite, on the facing wall, was a photograph of Gregor from his period in the army, as a lieutenant, his hand on his sabre, smiling confidently, the posture and uniform demanding respect. The door to the hallway was open, and as the front door was open too one could see out to the landing, and the top of the flight of stairs down.

"Now," said Gregor, in the knowledge that he was the only one present to have maintained his equanimity, "I'm just going to get dressed, pack up my samples, and then I'll set off. Do you want to let me set out, do you? You see, Chief Clerk, you see, I'm not stubborn, I like my work; the travel is arduous, but I couldn't live without it. Where are you off to, Chief Clerk? To work? Is that right? Will you accurately report everything you've seen here? It is possible to be momentarily unfit for work, but that is precisely the time to remind oneself of one's former achievements, and to reflect that, once the present obstacle has been surmounted, one's future work will be all the more diligent and focused. As you know all too well, I am under a very great obligation to the director. In addition, I have responsibilities for my parents and my sister. I am in a jam, but I will work my way out of it. Only don't make it any harder for me than it is already! Give me your backing at head office! I know the travelling salesman is not held in the highest regard there. People imagine he earns a packet, and has a nice life on top of it. These and similar assumptions remain unexamined. But you, Chief Clerk, you have a greater understanding of the circumstances than the rest of the staff, you even, if I may say this to you in confidence, have an understanding superior to that of the director himself, who, as an entrepreneur, is perhaps too easily swayed against an employee. You are also very well aware that the travelling salesman, spending, as he does, the best part of the year away from head office, may all too easily fall victim to tittle-tattle, to mischance, and to baseless allegations, against which he has no way of defending himself—mostly even does not get to hear of—and when he returns exhausted from his travels, it is to find himself confronted directly by practical consequences of whose causes he is ignorant. Chief Clerk, don't leave without showing me by a word or two of your own that you at least partly agree with me!"

But the chief clerk had turned his back on Gregor the moment he had begun speaking, and only stared back at him with mouth agape, over his trembling shoulder. All the while Gregor was speaking, he wasn't still for a moment, but, without taking his eyes off Gregor, moved towards the door, but terribly gradually, as though in breach of some secret injunction not to leave the room. Already he was in the hallway, and to judge by the sudden movement with which he snatched his foot back out of the living room for the last time, one might have supposed he had burned his sole. Once in the hallway, he extended his right hand fervently in the direction of the stairs, as though some supernatural salvation there awaited him.

Gregor understood that he must on no account allow the chief clerk to leave in his present frame of mind, not if he wasn't to risk damage to his place in the company. His parents didn't seem to grasp this issue with the same clarity; over the course of many years, they had acquired the conviction that in this business Gregor had a job for life and, besides, they were so consumed by their anxieties of the present moment, that they had lost any premonitory sense they might have had. Gregor, though, had his. The chief clerk had to be stopped, calmed, convinced, and finally won over; the future of Gregor and his family depended on that! If only his sister were back already! There was a shrewd person; she had begun to cry even as Gregor was still lying calmly on his back. And no doubt the chief clerk, notorious skirt-chaser that he was, would have allowed himself to be influenced by her; she would have closed the front door, and in the hallway talked him out of his panic. But his sister wasn't there. Gregor would have to act on his own behalf. Without stopping to think that he didn't understand his given loco-motive powers, without even thinking that this latest speech of his had possibly— no, probably—not been understood either, he left the shelter of the half-door and pushed through the opening, making for the chief clerk, who was laughably hold-ing on to the balustrade on the landing with both hands. But straightaway, look-ing for a grip, Gregor dropped with a short cry on to his many little legs. No sooner had this happened, than for the first time that morning he felt a sense of physical well-being; the little legs had solid ground under them; they obeyed perfectly, as he noticed to his satisfaction, even seeking to carry him where he wanted to go; and he was on the point of believing a final improvement in his condition was immi-nent. But at that very moment, while he was still swaying from his initial impetus, not far from his mother and just in front of her on the ground, she, who had seemed so utterly immersed in herself, suddenly leaped into the air, arms wide, fingers spread, and screamed: "Help, oh please God, help me!" inclined her head as though for a better view of Gregor, but then, quite at variance with that, ran sense-lessly away from him; she forgot the breakfast table was behind her; on reaching it, she hurriedly, in her distractedness, sat down on it, seeming oblivious to the fact that coffee was gushing all over the carpet from the large upset coffee pot.

30 "Mother, mother," Gregor said softly, looking up at her. For the moment, he forgot all about the chief clerk; on the other hand, he couldn't help but move his jaws several times at the sight of the flowing coffee. At that his mother screamed again and fled from the table into the arms of Gregor's father who was rushing towards her. But now Gregor had no time for his parents; the chief clerk was already on the stairs; his chin on the balustrade, he stared behind him one last time. Gregor moved sharply to be sure of catching him up; the chief clerk must have sensed something, because he took the last few steps at a single bound and disappeared. "Oof!" he managed to cry, the sound echoing through the stairwell. Regrettably, the consequence of the chief clerk's flight was finally to turn the senses of his father, who to that point had remained relatively calm, because, instead of himself taking off after the man, or at least not getting in the way of Gregor as he attempted to do just that, he seized in his right hand the chief clerk's cane, which he had left behind on a chair along with his hat and coat, with his left grabbed a large newspaper from the table, and, by stamping his feet, and brandishing stick and newspaper, attempted to drive Gregor back into his room. No pleas on Gregor's part were any use, no pleas were even understood. However imploringly he might turn his head, his father only stamped harder with his feet. Meanwhile, in spite of the cool temperature, his mother had thrown open a win-dow on the other side of the room and, leaning out of it, plunged her face in her hands. A powerful draught was created between the stairwell and the street out-side, the window curtains flew up, the newspapers rustled on the table, some individual pages fluttered across the floor. His father was moving forward impla-cably, emitting hissing sounds like a savage. Gregor had no practice in moving backwards, and he was moving, it had to be said, extremely slowly. If he had been able to turn round, he would have been back in his room in little or no time, but he was afraid lest the delay incurred in turning around would make his father

impatient, and at any moment the stick in his father's hand threatened to strike him a fatal blow to the back of the head. Finally, Gregor had no alternative, because he noticed to his consternation that in his reversing he was unable to keep to a given course; and so, with continual fearful sidelong looks to his father, he started as quickly as possible, but in effect only very slowly, to turn round. It was possible that his father was aware of his good intentions, because he didn't obstruct him, but even directed the turning manoeuvre from a distance with gestures from his cane. If only there hadn't been those unbearable hissing sounds issuing from his father! They caused Gregor to lose all orientation. He had turned almost completely round, when, distracted by the hissing, he lost his way, and moved a little in the wrong direction. Then, when he found himself with his head successfully in the doorway, it became apparent that his body was too wide to slip through it. To his father, in his present frame of mind, it didn't remotely occur to open the other wing of the door, and so make enough space for Gregor. He was, rather, obsessed with the notion of getting Gregor back in his room post-haste. He could not possibly have countenanced the cumbersome preparations Gregor would have required to get up and perhaps so get around the door. Rather, as though there were no hindrance at all, he drove Gregor forward with even greater din; the sound to Gregor's ears was not that of one father alone; now it was really no laughing matter, and Gregor drove himself—happen what might—against the door. One side of his body was canted up, he found himself lifted at an angle in the doorway, his flank was rubbed raw, and some ugly stains appeared on the white door. Before long he was caught fast and could not have moved any more unaided, his little legs on one side were trembling in mid-air while those on the other found themselves painfully pressed against the ground—when from behind his father now gave him a truly liberating kick, and he was thrown, bleeding profusely, far into his room. The door was battered shut with the cane, and then at last there was quiet.

II

Not until dusk did Gregor awake from his heavy, almost comatose sleep. Probably he would have awoken around that time anyway, even if he hadn't been roused, because he felt sufficiently rested and restored. Still, it seemed to him as though a hurried footfall and a cautious shutting of the door to the hallway had awoken him. The pale gleam of the electric street-lighting outside showed on the ceiling and on the upper parts of the furniture, but down on the floor, where Gregor lay, it was dark. Slowly he rose and, groping clumsily with his feelers, whose function he only now began to understand, he made for the door, to see what had happened there. His whole left side was one long, unpleasantly stretched scab, and he was positively limping on his two rows of legs. One of his little legs had been badly hurt in the course of the morning's incidents—it was a wonder that it was only one—and it dragged after the rest inertly.

Not until he reached the door did he realize what had tempted him there; it was the smell of food. There stood a dish full of sweetened milk, with little slices of white bread floating in it. He felt like laughing for joy, because he was even hungrier now than he had been that morning, and straightaway he dunked his head into the milk past his eyes. But before long he withdrew it again in disappointment; it wasn't just that he found eating difficult on account of his damaged left flank—it seemed he could only eat if the whole of his body, panting, participated—more that he disliked the taste of milk, which otherwise was a favourite drink, and which his sister had certainly put out for him for that reason. In fact, he pulled his head away from the dish almost with revulsion, and crawled back into the middle of the room.

In the living room the gas-jet had been lit, as Gregor saw by looking through the crack in the door, but whereas usually at this time his father would be reading aloud to Gregor's mother or sometimes to his sister from the afternoon edition of the newspaper, there was now silence. Well, it was possible that this reading aloud, of which his sister had written and spoken to him many times, had been discontinued of late. But it was equally quiet to either side, even though it was hardly possible that there was no one home. 'What a quiet life the family used to lead,' Gregor said to himself, and, staring into the blackness, he felt considerable pride that he had made such a life possible for his parents and his sister, and in such a lovely flat. But what if all peace, all prosperity, all contentment, were to come to a sudden and terrible end? So as not to fall into such thoughts, Gregor thought he would take some exercise instead, and he crawled back and forth in the room.

Once in the course of the long evening one of the side-doors was opened a crack, and once the other, and then hurriedly closed again; someone seemed to feel a desire to step inside, but then again had too many cavils about so doing. Gregor took up position right against the living-room door, resolved to bring in the reluctant visitor in some way if he could, or, if nothing more, at least discover his identity; but then the door wasn't opened again, and Gregor waited in vain. Previously, when the doors were locked, everyone had tried to come in and see him, but now that he had opened one door himself, and the others had apparently been opened in the course of the day, no visitors came, and the keys were all on the outside too.

35 The light in the living room was left on far into the night, and that made it easy to verify that his parents and his sister had stayed up till then, because, as he could very well hear, that was when the three of them left on tiptoed feet. Now it was certain that no one would come in to Gregor's room until morning; so he had a long time ahead of him to reflect undisturbed on how he could reorder his life. But the empty high-ceilinged room where he was forced to lie flat on the floor disquieted him, without him being able to find a reason for his disquiet, because after all this was the room he had lived in these past five years—and with a half unconscious turn, and not without a little shame, he hurried under the sofa, where, even though his back was pressed down a little, and he was unable to raise his head, he straightaway felt very much at home, and only lamented the fact that his body was too broad to be entirely concealed under the sofa.

He stayed there all night, either half asleep, albeit woken by hunger at regular intervals, or kept half awake by anxieties and unclear hopes, which all seemed to lead to the point that he would comport himself quietly for the moment, and by patience and the utmost consideration for the family make the inconveniences he was putting them through in his present state a little bearable for them.

Early the next morning, while it was almost still night, Gregor had an opportunity to put his resolutions to the test, because the door from the hallway opened, and his sister, almost completely dressed, looked in on him with some agitation. It took her a while to find him, but when she spotted him under the sofa—my God, he had to be somewhere, he couldn't have flown off into space—she was so terrified that in an uncontrollable revulsion she slammed the door shut.

But then, as if sorry for her behaviour, she straightaway opened the door again, and tiptoed in, as if calling on a grave invalid, or even a stranger. Gregor had pushed his head forward to the edge of the sofa, and observed her. Would she notice that he had left his milk, and then not by any means because he wasn't hungry, and would she bring in some different food that would suit him better? If she failed to do so of her own accord, then he preferred to die rather than tell her, even though he did feel an incredible urge to shoot out from under the sofa, hurl himself at his sister's feet, and ask her for some nice titbit to eat. But his sister was promptly startled by the sight of the full dish, from which only a little milk had been spilled round the edges. She picked it up right away, not with her bare hands but with a rag, and carried it out. Gregor was dying to see what she would bring him instead, and he entertained all sorts of conjectures on the subject. But never would he have been able to guess what in the goodness of her heart his sister did. She brought him, evidently to get a sense of his likes and dislikes, a whole array of things, all spread out on an old newspaper. There were some half-rotten vegetables; bones left over from dinner with a little congealed white sauce; a handful of raisins and almonds; a cheese that a couple of days ago Gregor had declared to be unfit for human consumption; a piece of dry bread, a piece of bread and butter, and a piece of bread and butter sprinkled with salt. In addition she set down a dish that was probably to be given over to Gregor's personal use, into which she had poured some water. Then, out of sheer delicacy, knowing that Gregor wouldn't be able to eat in front of her, she hurriedly left the room, even turning the key, just as a sign to Gregor that he could settle down and take his time over everything. Gregor's legs trembled as he addressed his meal. His wounds too must have completely healed over, for he didn't feel any hindrance, he was astonished to realize, and remembered how a little more than a month ago he had cut his finger with a knife, and only the day before yesterday the place still had hurt. "I wonder if I have less sensitivity now?" he thought, as he sucked avidly on the cheese, which of all the proffered foodstuffs had most spontaneously and powerfully attracted him. Then, in rapid succession, and with eyes watering with satisfaction, he ate up the cheese, the vegetables and the sauce; the fresh foods, on the other hand, were not to his liking—he couldn't even bear the smell of them, and dragged such things as he wanted to eat a little way away from them. He was long done with everything, and was just lounging lazily where he had eaten, when his sister, to signal that he was to withdraw, slowly turned the key in the lock. That immediately stung him out of his drowsiness, and he dashed back under the sofa. But it cost him a great effort to remain there, even for the short time his sister was in the room, because his big meal had filled out his belly, and he was scarcely able to breathe in his little space. Amidst little fits of panic suffocation, he watched with slightly bulging eyes, as his sister, all unawares, swept everything together with a broom—not only the leftovers, but also those elements of food that Gregor hadn't touched, as though they too were now not good for anything—and as she hastily tipped everything into a bucket, on which she set a wooden lid, whereupon she carried everything back out. No sooner had she turned her back than Gregor came out from under the sofa, stretched and puffed himself up.

This was how Gregor was now fed every day, once in the morning, while his parents and the maid were still asleep, and a second time after lunch, when his parents had their little lie-down, and his sister sent the maid out on some errand or other. For sure, none of them wanted Gregor to starve, but maybe they didn't want to confront in so much material detail the idea of him eating anything. Perhaps also his sister wanted to spare them a little grief, because certainly they were suffering enough as it was.

With what excuses the doctor and locksmith were got rid of on that first morning was something Gregor never learned, because as he was not able to make himself understood, it didn't occur to anyone, not even his sister, that he could understand others, and so, when his sister was in his room, he had to content himself with hearing her occasional sighs and appeals to various saints. Only later, once she had got adjusted to everything a little—of course there could be no question of becoming fully used to it—Gregor sometimes caught a well-intentioned remark, or one that was capable of being interpreted as such. "He had a good appetite today," she said, when Gregor had dealt with his food in determined fashion, whereas, in the opposite case, which came to be the rule, she would sometimes say, almost sorrowfully: "Oh, it's hardly been touched today."

40   While Gregor was not given any news directly he was sometimes able to glean developments from the adjoining rooms, and whenever he heard anyone speaking, he would rush to the door in question, and press his whole body against it. Especially in the early days, there was no conversation that did not somehow, in some oblique way, deal with him. For two days, at each meal, there were debates as to how one ought to behave; and in between meals, the same subject was also discussed, because there were always at least two members of the household at home, probably as no one wanted to be alone at home, and couldn't in any case wholly leave it. On the very first day the cook had begged on her knees—it was unclear what and how much she knew about what had happened—to be let go right away, and when she took her leave a quarter of an hour later, she said thank-you for her dismissal, as if it was the greatest kindness she had experienced here, and, without anyone demanding it of her, gave the most solemn oath never to betray the least thing to anyone.

Now his sister had to do the cooking in harness with his mother; admittedly, it didn't create much extra work for her, because no one ate anything. Gregor kept hearing them vainly exhorting one another to eat, and receiving no reply, other than: "Thank you, I've enough," or words to that effect. Perhaps they didn't drink anything either. Often, his sister asked his father whether he would like a beer, and offered to fetch it herself, and when her father made no reply, she said, to get over his hesitation, that she could equally well send the janitor woman out for it, but in the end his father said a loud "No," and there was an end of the matter.

Already in the course of that first day his father set out the fortunes and prospects of the family to his mother and sister. From time to time, he got up from the table and produced some certificate or savings book from his little home safe, which he had managed to rescue from the collapse of his business five years ago. One could hear him opening the complicated lock, and shutting it again after taking out the desired item. These explanations from his father constituted the first good news that had reached Gregor's ears since his incarceration. He had been of the view that the winding-up of the business had left his father with nothing—at any rate his father had never said anything to the contrary, and Gregor hadn't questioned him either. At the time Gregor had bent all his endeavours to helping the family to get over the commercial catastrophe, which had plunged them all into complete despair, as quickly as possible. And so he had begun working with an especial zeal and almost overnight had moved from being a little junior clerk to a travelling salesman, who of course had earning power of an entirely different order, and whose successes in the form of percentages were instantly turned into money, which could be laid out on the table of the surprised and delighted family. They had been good times, and they had never returned, at least not in that magnificence, even though Gregor went on to earn so much money that he was able to bear, and indeed bore, the expenses of the whole family. They had just become used to it, both the family and Gregor; they gratefully took receipt of his money, which he willingly handed over, but there was no longer any particular warmth about it. Only his sister had remained close to Gregor, and it was his secret project to send her, who unlike himself loved music and played the violin with great feeling, to the conservatory next year, without regard to the great expense that was surely involved, and that needed to be earned, most probably in some other fashion. In the course of Gregor's brief stays in the city, the conservatory often came up in conversations with his sister, but always as a beautiful dream, not conceivably to be realized, and their parents disliked even such innocent references; but Gregor thought about it quite purposefully, and meant to make a formal announcement about it at Christmas.

Such—in his present predicament—perfectly useless thoughts crowded his head, while he stuck to the door in an upright position, listening. Sometimes, from a general fatigue, he was unable to listen, and carelessly let his head drop against the door, before holding it upright again, because even the little noise he had made had been heard next door, and had caused them all to fall silent. "Wonder what he's doing now," said his father after a while, evidently turning towards the door, and only then was the interrupted conversation gradually resumed.

Because his father tended to repeat himself in his statements—partly because he had long disregarded these matters, and partly because Gregor's mother often didn't understand when they were first put to her—Gregor now had plenty of occasion to hear that, in spite of the calamity, an admittedly small nest egg had survived from the old days, and had grown a little over the intervening years through the compounding of interest. In addition to this, the money that Gregor had brought home every month—he kept back no more than a couple of guilder for himself—had not been used up completely, and had accrued to another small lump sum. Behind his door, Gregor nodded enthusiastically, delighted by this unexpected caution and prudence. The surplus funds might have been used to pay down his father's debt to the director, thereby bringing closer the day when he might quit this job, but now it seemed to him better done the way his father had done it.

Of course, the money was nowhere near enough for the family to live off the 45 interest, say; it might be enough to feed them all for a year or two, at most, but no more. Really it was a sum that mustn't be touched, that ought to be set aside for an emergency; money for day-to-day living expenses needed to be earned. His father was a healthy, but now elderly man, who hadn't worked for five years now, and who surely shouldn't expect too much of himself; in those five years, which were the first holidays of a strenuous and broadly unsuccessful life, he had put on a lot of fat, and had slowed down considerably. And was his old mother to go out and earn money, who suffered from asthma, to whom merely going from one end of the flat to the other was a strain, and who spent every other day on the sofa struggling for breath in front of the open window? Or was his sister to make money, still a child with her seventeen years, and who so deserved to be left in the manner of her life heretofore, which had consisted of wearing pretty frocks, sleeping in late, helping out at the pub, taking part in a few modest celebrations and, above all, playing the violin? Whenever the conversation turned to the necessity of earning money, Gregor would let go of the door, and throw himself on to the cool leather sofa beside it, because he was burning with sorrow and shame.

Often he would lie there all night, not sleeping a wink, and just scraping against the leather for hours. Nor did he shun the great effort of pushing a chair over to the window, creeping up to the window-sill, and, propped against the armchair, leaning in the window, clearly in some vague recollection of the liberation he had once used to feel, gazing out of the window. For it was true to say that with each passing day his view of distant things grew fuzzier; the hospital across the road, whose ubiquitous aspect he had once cursed, he now no longer even saw, and if he hadn't known for a fact that he lived in the leafy, but perfectly urban Charlottenstrasse,[6] he might have thought that his window gave on to a wasteland where grey sky merged indistinguishably with grey earth. His alert sister needed only to spot that the armchair had been moved across to the window once or twice, before she took to pushing the chair over there herself after tidying Gregor's room, and even leaving the inner window ajar.

Had Gregor been able to speak to his sister and to thank her for everything she had to do for him, he would have found it a little easier to submit to her ministrations; but, as it was, he suffered from them. His sister, for her part, clearly sought to blur the embarrassment of the whole thing, and the more time passed, the better able she was to do so, but Gregor was also able to see through everything more acutely. Even her entry was terrible for him. No sooner had she stepped into his room, than without even troubling to shut the door behind her—however much care she usually took to save anyone passing the sight of Gregor's room—she darted over to the window and flung it open with febrile hands, almost as if she were suffocating, and then, quite regardless of how cold it might be outside, she stood by the window for a while, taking deep breaths. She subjected Gregor to her scurrying and her din twice daily; for the duration of her presence, he trembled under the sofa, even though he knew full well that she would have been only too glad to spare him the awkwardness, had it been possible for her to remain in the same room as her brother with the window closed.

On one occasion—it must have been a month or so after Gregor's metamorphosis, and there was surely no more cause for his sister to get agitated about Gregor's appearance—she came in a little earlier than usual and saw Gregor staring out of the window, immobile, almost as though set up on purpose to give her a fright. Gregor would not have been surprised if she had stopped in her tracks, seeing as he impeded her from going over and opening the window, but not only did she not come in, she leaped back and locked the door; a stranger might have supposed that Gregor had been lying in wait for her, to bite her. Naturally, Gregor straightaway went and hid under the sofa, but he had to wait till noon for his sister to reappear, and then she seemed more agitated than usual. From that he understood that the sight of him was still unbearable to her and would continue to be unbearable to her, and that she probably had to control herself so as not to run away at the sight of that little portion of his body that peeped out from under the sofa. One day, in a bid to save her from that as well, he moved the tablecloth

6. Charlotte Street (German).

on to the sofa—the labour took him four hours—and arranged it in such a way that he was completely covered, and that his sister, even if she bent down, would be unable to see him. If this covering hadn't been required in her eyes, she could easily have removed it, because it was surely clear enough that it was no fun for Gregor to screen himself from sight so completely, but she left the cloth in situ,[7] and once Gregor even thought he caught a grateful look from her, as he moved the cloth ever so slightly with his head to see how his sister was reacting to the new arrangement.

During the first fortnight, his parents would not be induced to come in and visit him, and he often heard their professions of respect for what his sister was now doing, whereas previously they had frequently been annoyed with her for being a somewhat useless girl. Now, though, both of them, father and mother, often stood outside Gregor's room while his sister was cleaning up inside, and no sooner had she come out than she had to tell them in precise detail how things looked in the room, what Gregor had eaten, how he had behaved this time, and whether there wasn't some sign of an improvement in his condition. His mother, by the way, quite soon wanted to visit Gregor herself, but his father and sister kept her from doing so with their common-sense arguments, to which Gregor listened attentively, and which met with his wholehearted approval. Later on, it took force to hold her back, and when she cried, "Let me see Gregor, after all he is my unhappy son! Won't you understand that I have to see him?" then Gregor thought it might after all be a good thing if his mother saw him, not every day of course, but perhaps as often as once a week; she did have a much better grasp of everything than his sister, who, for all her pluck, was still a child, and ultimately had perhaps taken on such a difficult task purely out of childish high spirits.

Before very long, Gregor's desire to see his mother was granted. Gregor didn't 50 care to sit in the window in the daytime out of regard for his parents, nor was he able to crawl around very much on the few square yards of floor; even at night he was scarcely able to lie quietly, his food soon stopped affording him the least pleasure, and so, to divert himself, he got into the habit of crawling all over the walls and ceiling. He was particularly given to hanging off the ceiling; it felt very different from lying on the floor; he could breathe more easily; a gentle thrumming vibration went through his body; and in the almost blissful distraction Gregor felt up there, it could even happen that to his own surprise he let himself go, and smacked down on the floor. Of course his physical mastery of his body was of a different order from what it had been previously, and so now he didn't hurt himself, even after a fall from a considerable height. His sister observed the new amusement Gregor had found for himself—as he crept here and there he couldn't avoid leaving some traces of his adhesive secretion—and she got it into her head to maximize the amount of crawling Gregor could do, by removing those pieces of furniture that got in his way, in particular the wardrobe and the desk. But it was not possible for her to do so unaided; she didn't dare ask her father for help; the maid would certainly not have helped, because while this girl of about sixteen had bravely stayed on after the cook's departure, she had also asked in return that she might keep the kitchen locked, and only have to open it when particularly required to do so; so Gregor's sister had no alternative but to ask her mother on an occasion when her father was away. Gregor's mother duly came along with cries of joy and

7. In place (Latin).

excitement, only to lapse into silence outside Gregor's door. First, his sister checked to see that everything in the room was tidy; only then did she allow her mother to step inside. In a very great rush, Gregor had pulled the tablecloth down lower, with more pleats, and the whole thing really had the appearance of a cloth draped casually over the sofa. He also refrained from peeping out from underneath it; he declined to try to see his mother on this first visit, he was just happy she had come. "It's all right, you won't see him," said his sister, who was evidently taking her mother by the hand. Now Gregor heard the two weak women shifting the heavy old wardrobe from its place, and how his sister always did the bulk of the work, ignoring the warnings of his mother, who kept fearing she might overstrain herself. It took a very long time. It was probably after fifteen minutes of toil that his mother said it would be better to leave the wardrobe where it was, because firstly it was too heavy, they would never manage to get it moved before father's return, and by leaving it in the middle of the room they would only succeed in leaving an irritating obstruction for Gregor, and secondly it was by no means certain that they were doing Gregor a favour by removing that piece of furniture anyway. She rather thought the opposite; the sight of the empty stretch of wall clutched at her heart; and why shouldn't Gregor have a similar sensation too, seeing as he was long accustomed to his bedroom furniture, and was therefore bound to feel abandoned in the empty room. "And isn't it the case as well," his mother concluded very quietly—indeed she was barely talking above a whisper throughout, as though to prevent Gregor, whose whereabouts she didn't know, from even hearing the sound of her voice, seeing as she felt certain that he wasn't capable of understanding her words anyway—"isn't it the case as well, that by taking away his furniture, we would be showing him we were abandoning all hope of an improvement in his condition, and leaving him utterly to his own devices? I think it would be best if we try to leave the room in exactly the condition it was before, so that, if Gregor is returned to us, he will find everything unaltered, and will thereby be able to forget the intervening period almost as if it hadn't happened."

As he listened to these words of his mother, Gregor understood that the want of any direct human address, in combination with his monotonous life at the heart of the family over the past couple of months, must have confused his understanding, because otherwise he would not have been able to account for the fact that he seriously wanted to have his room emptied out. Was it really his wish to have his cosy room, comfortably furnished with old heirlooms, transformed into a sort of cave, merely so that he would be able to crawl around in it freely, without hindrance in any direction—even at the expense of rapidly and utterly forgetting his human past? He was near enough to forgetting it now, and only the voice of his mother, which he hadn't heard for a long time, had reawakened the memory in him. Nothing was to be taken out; everything was to stay as it was; the positive influence of the furniture on his condition was indispensable; and if the furniture prevented him from crawling around without rhyme or reason, then that was no drawback either, but a great advantage.

But his sister was unfortunately of a different mind; she had become accustomed, not without some justification either, to cast herself in the role of a sort of expert when Gregor's affairs were discussed with her parents, and so her mother's urgings now had the effect on his sister of causing her to insist on the removal not merely of the wardrobe and the desk, which was all she had originally proposed, but of all the furniture, with the sole exception of the indispensable sofa. It wasn't merely childish stubbornness and a surge of unexpected and hard-won self-confidence that prompted her to take this view; she had observed that Gregor needed a lot of space for his crawling, and in the course of it, so far as she had seen, made no use whatever of the furniture. Perhaps the natural enthusiasm of a girl of her age played a certain role too, a quality that seeks its own satisfaction in any matter, and this now caused Grete to present Gregor's situation in even starker terms, so that she might do even more for him than she had thus far. For it was unthinkable that anyone else would dare to set foot in a room where Gregor all alone made free with the bare walls.

And so she refused to abandon her resolution in the face of the arguments of her mother, who seemed to have been overwhelmed by uncertainty in this room, and who, falling silent, to the best of her ability helped his sister to remove the wardrobe from the room. Well, Gregor could do without the wardrobe if need be, but the writing-desk had to stay. And no sooner had the two women left with the wardrobe, against which they pressed themselves groaning with effort, than Gregor thrust his head out from under the sofa, to see how best, with due care and respect, he might intervene on his own behalf. It was unfortunate that it was his mother who came back in first, while Grete was still clasping the wardrobe in the next-door room, hefting it this way and that, without of course being able to budge it from the spot. His mother was not accustomed to the sight of Gregor, it could have made her ill, and so Gregor reversed hurriedly to the far end of the sofa, but was unable to prevent the cloth from swaying slightly. That was enough to catch his mother's attention. She paused, stood still for a moment, and then went back to Grete.

Even though Gregor kept telling himself there was nothing particular going on, just a few sticks of furniture being moved around, he soon had to admit to himself that the to-ing and fro-ing of the two women, their little exhortations to one another, the scraping of the furniture on the floor, did have the effect on him of a great turmoil nourished on all sides, and he was compelled to admit that, however he drew in his head and his legs and pressed his belly to the floor, he would be unable to tolerate much more of it. They were clearing his room out; taking away everything that was dear to him; they had already taken the wardrobe that contained his jigsaw and his other tools; now they were prising away the desk that seemed to have taken root in the floor, where he had done his homework at trade school, at secondary, even at elementary school—he really had no more time to consider the good intentions of the two women, whose existence he had practically forgotten, because they were now so exhausted they were doing their work in near silence, all that could be heard of them being their heavy footfalls.

And so he erupted forth—the women were just resting on the desk next door, to 55 catch their breath—and four times changed his direction for he really didn't know what he should rescue first, when he saw the picture of the fur-clad woman all the more prominent now, because the wall on which it hung had now been cleared, crawled hurriedly up to it and pressed himself against the glass, which stuck to him and imparted a pleasant coolness to his hot belly. At least no one would now take away this picture, which Gregor now completely covered. He turned his head in the direction of the living-room door, to see the women as they returned.

They hadn't taken much of a break, and here they came again; Grete had laid her arm around her mother, and was practically carrying her. "Well, what shall we take next?" Grete said, looking around. Then her eyes encountered those of Gregor, up on the wall. She kept her calm, probably only on account of the presence of her mother, inclined her face towards her, to keep her from looking around, and said, with a voice admittedly trembling and uncontrolled: "Oh, let's just go back to the living room for a moment, shall we?" Grete's purpose was clear enough to Gregor; she wanted to get her mother to safety, and then chase him off the wall. Well, just let her try! He would perch on his picture, and never surrender it. He would rather fly in Grete's face.

But Grete's words served only to disquiet her mother, who stepped to one side, spotted the giant brown stain on the flowered wallpaper, and, before she had time to understand what she saw, she cried in a hoarse, screaming voice, "Oh my God, oh my God!" and with arms outspread, as though abandoning everything she had, fell across the sofa, and didn't stir. "Ooh, Gregor!" cried his sister, brandishing her fist and glowering at him. Since his metamorphosis, they were the first words she had directly addressed to him. She ran next door to find some smelling-salts to rouse her mother from her faint; Gregor wanted to help too—he could always go back and rescue the picture later on—but he was stuck fast to the glass, and had to break free of it by force; then he trotted next door as though he could give his sister some advice, as in earlier times; was forced to stand around idly behind her while she examined various different flasks; and gave her such a shock, finally, when she spun round, that a bottle crashed to the ground and broke. One splinter cut Gregor in the face, the fumes of some harshly corrosive medicine causing him to choke; Grete ended up by grabbing as many little flasks as she could hold, and ran with them to her mother; she slammed the door shut with her foot. Gregor was now shut off from his mother, who, through his fault, was possibly close to death; there was nothing he could do but wait; and assailed by reproach and dread, he began to crawl. He crawled over everything, the walls, the furniture, the ceiling, and finally in his despair, with the whole room already spinning round him, he dropped on to the middle of the dining table.

Some time passed, Gregor lay there dully, there was silence all round, perhaps it was a good sign. Then the bell rang. The maid, of course, was locked away in her kitchen, and so Grete had to go to the door. His father was back. "What happened?" were his first words; Grete's appearance must have given everything away. She answered in muffled tones; clearly she must be pressing her face to her father's chest: "Mother had a faint, but she's feeling better now. Gregor's got loose." "I knew it," said his father. "Wasn't I always telling you, but you women never listen." Gregor understood that his father must have put the worst possible construction on Grete's all too brief account, and supposed that Gregor had perpetrated some act of violence. Therefore Gregor must try to mollify his father, because for an explanation there was neither time nor means. And so he fled to the door of his room, and pressed himself against it, so that his father, on stepping in from the hallway, might see right away that Gregor had every intention of going back promptly into his room, and there was no necessity to use force, he had only to open the door for him, and he would disappear through it right away.

But his father wasn't in the mood to observe such details; "Ah!" he roared, the moment he entered, in a tone equally enraged and delighted. Gregor withdrew his head from the door, and turned to look at his father. He really hadn't imagined him the way he was; admittedly, he had been distracted of late by the novel sensation of crawling, and had neglected to pay attention to goings-on in the rest of the flat, as he had previously, and so really he should have been prepared to come upon some alterations. But really, really, was that still his father? The same man who had lain feebly buried in bed, when Gregor had set out formerly on a business trip; who had welcomed him back at night, in his nightshirt and rocking-chair; not even properly able to get to his feet any more, but merely raising both arms in token of his pleasure; and who on his infrequent walks on one or two Sundays per year, and on the most solemn holidays, walked between Gregor and his wife slowly enough anyway, but still slower than them, bundled into his old overcoat, feeling his way forward with his carefully jabbing stick, and each time he wanted to speak, stopping to gather his listeners about him? And now here he was fairly erect; wearing a smart blue uniform with gold buttons, like the doorman of a bank; over the stiff collar of his coat, the bulge of a powerful double-chin; under the bushy eyebrows an alert and vigorous expression in his black eyes; his habitually unkempt white hair now briskly parted and combed into a shining tidy arrangement. He threw his cap, which had on it a gold monogram, presumably that of the bank, across the whole room in an arc on to the sofa, and, hands in his pockets, with the skirts of his long coat trailing behind him, he walked up to Gregor with an expression of grim resolve. He probably didn't know himself what he would do next; but even so, he raised his feet to an uncommon height, and Gregor was startled by the enormous size of his bootsoles. But he didn't allow himself the leisure to stop and remark on it; he had understood from the first day of his new life that his father thought the only policy to adopt was one of the utmost severity towards him. And so he scurried along in front of his father, pausing when he stopped, and hurrying on the moment he made another movement. In this way, they circled the room several times, without anything decisive taking place, yes, even without the whole process having the appearance of a chase, because of its slow tempo. It was for that reason too that Gregor remained on the floor for the time being, because he was afraid that if he took to the walls or ceiling, his father might interpret that as a sign of particular wickedness on his part. Admittedly, Gregor had to tell himself he couldn't keep up even this slow pace for very long, because in the time his father took a single step, he needed to perform a whole multiplicity of movements. He was already beginning to get out of breath—even in earlier times his lungs hadn't been altogether reliable. As he teetered along, barely keeping his eyes open, in order to concentrate all his resources on his movement—in his dull-wittedness not even thinking of any other form of salvation beyond merely keeping going; and had almost forgotten that the walls were available to him, albeit obstructed by carefully carved items of furniture, full of spikes and obstructions—something whizzed past him, something had been hurled at him, something now rolling around on the floor in front of him. It was an apple; straightaway it was followed by another; Gregor in terror was rooted to the spot; there was no sense in keeping moving, not if his father had decided to have recourse to artillery. He had filled his pockets from the fruit bowl on the sideboard, and was hurling one apple after another, barely pausing to take aim. These little red apples rolled around on the floor as though electrified, often caroming into one another. A feebly tossed apple brushed against Gregor's back, only to bounce off it harmlessly. One thrown a moment later, however, seemed to pierce it; Gregor tried to drag himself away, as though the bewildering and scarcely credible pain might pass if he changed position; but he felt as though nailed to the spot, and in complete disorientation, he stretched out. With one last look he saw how the door to his room was flung open, and his mother ran out in front of his howling sister, in her chemise—his sister must have undressed her to make it easier for her to breathe after her fainting fit—how his mother ran towards his father, and as she ran her loosened skirts successively slipped to the floor, and how, stumbling over them she threw herself at his father, and embracing him, in complete union with him—but now Gregor's eyesight was failing him—with her hands clasping the back of his head, begged him to spare Gregor's life.

III

60   The grave wound to Gregor, from whose effects he suffered for over a month—as no one dared to remove the apple, it remained embedded in his flesh, as a visible memento—seemed to have reminded even his father that in spite of his current sorry and loathsome form, Gregor remained a member of the family, and must not be treated like an enemy, but as someone whom—all revulsion to the contrary—family duty compelled one to choke down, and who must be tolerated, simply tolerated.

Even if Gregor had lost his mobility, and presumably for good, so that now like an old invalid he took an age to cross his room—there could be no more question of crawling up out of the horizontal—this deterioration of his condition acquired a compensation, perfectly adequate in his view, in the fact that each evening now, the door to the living room, which he kept under sharp observation for an hour or two before it happened, was opened, so that, lying in his darkened room, invisible from the living room, he was permitted to see the family at their lit-up table, and, with universal sanction, as it were, though now in a completely different way than before, to listen to them talk together.

Admittedly, these were not now the lively conversations of earlier times, which Gregor had once called to mind with some avidity as he lay down exhausted in the damp sheets of some poky hotel room. Generally, things were very quiet. His father fell asleep in his armchair not long after supper was over; his mother and sister enjoined one another to be quiet; his mother, sitting well forward under the lamp, sewed fine linen for some haberdashery; his sister, who had taken a job as salesgirl, studied stenography and French in the evenings, in the hope of perhaps one day getting a better job. Sometimes his father would wake up, and as though unaware that he had been asleep, would say to his mother: 'Oh, you've been sewing all this time!' and promptly fall asleep again, while mother and sister exchanged tired smiles.

With an odd stubbornness, his father now refused to take off his uniform coat when he was at home; and while his dressing-gown hung uselessly on its hook, his fully dressed father dozed in his chair, as though ready at all times to be of service, waiting, even here, for the voice of his superior. As a result, the uniform, which even to begin with had not been new, in spite of all the precautions of mother and sister, rapidly lost its cleanliness, and Gregor often spent whole evenings staring at this comprehensively stained suit, with its invariably gleaming gold buttons, in which the old man slept so calmly and uncomfortably.

As soon as the clock struck ten, his mother would softly wake his father, and talk him into going to bed, because he couldn't sleep properly where he was, and proper sleep was precisely what he needed, given that he had to be back on duty at six in the morning. But with the obstinacy that characterized him ever since he had become a commissionaire, he would always insist on staying at table longer, even though he quite regularly fell asleep there, and it was only with the greatest difficulty that he was then persuaded to exchange his chair for bed. However Gregor's mother and sister pleaded and remonstrated with him, he would slowly shake his head for a whole quarter of an hour at a time, keep his eyes shut, and refuse to get up. Gregor's mother would tug at his sleeve, whisper blandishments in his ear, his sister would leave her work to support her mother, but all in vain. His father would only slump deeper into his chair. Only when the women took him under the arms did he open his eyes, look alternately at them both, and then usually say: "What sort of life is this? What sort of peace and dignity in my old days?" And propped up by the women, he would cumbersomely get to his feet, as though he was a great weight on himself, let them conduct him as far as the door, then gesture to them, and go on himself, while Gregor's mother hurriedly threw down her sewing, and his sister her pen, to run behind him and continue to be of assistance.

Who in this exhausted and overworked family had the time to pay any more 65 attention to Gregor than was absolutely necessary? The household seemed to shrink; the maid was now allowed to leave after all; a vast bony charwoman with a great mane of white hair came in the morning and evening to do the brunt of the work; everything else had to be done by mother, in addition to her copious needlework. Things even came to such a pass that various family jewels, in which mother and sister had once on special occasions decked themselves, were sold off, as Gregor learned one evening, from a general discussion of the prices that had been achieved. The bitterest complaint, however, concerned the impossibility of leaving this now far too large apartment, as there was no conceivable way of moving Gregor. Gregor understood perfectly well that it wasn't any regard for him that stood in the way of a move, because all it would have taken was a suitably sized shipping crate, with a few holes drilled in it for him to breathe through; no, what principally kept the family from moving to another flat was their complete and utter despair—the thought that they in all the circle of relatives and acquaintances had been singled out for such a calamity. The things the world requires of poor people, they performed to the utmost, his father running out to get breakfast for the little bank officials, his mother hurling herself at the personal linen of strangers, his sister trotting back and forth behind the desk, doing the bidding of the customers, but that was as far as the strength of the family reached. The wound in Gregor's back would start to play up again, when mother and sister came back, having taken his father to bed, and neglected their work to sit pressed together, almost cheek to cheek; when his mother pointed to Gregor's room and said, "Will you shut the door now, Grete"; and when Gregor found himself once more in the dark, while next door the women were mingling their tears, or perhaps sitting staring dry-eyed at the table.

Gregor spent his days and nights almost without sleeping. Sometimes he thought that the next time they opened the door he would take the business of the family in hand, just exactly as he had done before; after a long time the director figured in his thoughts again, and the chief clerk, the junior clerk and the trainees, the dim-witted factotum, a couple of friends he had in other companies, a chambermaid in a hotel out in the provinces somewhere, a sweet, fleeting memory, a cashier in a hat shop whom he had courted assiduously, but far too slowly—all these appeared to him, together with others he never knew or had already forgotten, but instead of helping him and his family, they were all inaccessible to him, and he was glad when they went away again. And then he wasn't in the mood to worry about the family, but instead was filled with rage at how they neglected him, and even though he couldn't imagine anything for which he had an appetite, he made schemes as to how to inveigle himself into the pantry, to take there what was rightfully his, even if he didn't feel the least bit hungry now. No longer bothering to think what might please Gregor, his sister before going to work in the morning and afternoon now hurriedly shoved some food or other into Gregor's room with her foot, and in the evening reached in with the broom to hook it back out again, indifferent as to whether it had been only tasted or even—as most regularly happened—had remained quite untouched. The tidying of the room, which she now did always in the evening, really could not have been done more cursorily. The walls were streaked with grime, and here and there lay little tangled balls of dust and filth. At first, Gregor liked to take up position, for her coming, in the worst affected corners, as if to reproach her for their condition. But he could probably have stayed there for weeks without his sister doing anything better; after all, she could see the dirt as clearly as he could, she had simply taken it into her head to ignore it. And at the same time, with a completely new pernicketiness that seemed to have come over her, as it had indeed the whole family, she jealously guarded her monopoly on the tidying of Gregor's room. On one occasion, his mother had subjected Gregor's room to a great cleaning, involving several buckets full of water—the humidity was upsetting to Gregor, who lay miserably and motionlessly stretched out on the sofa—but his mother didn't get away with it either. Because no sooner had his sister noticed the change in Gregor's room that evening than, mortally offended, she ran into the sitting room, and ignoring her mother's imploringly raised hands, burst into a crying fit that her parents—her father had of course been shaken from his slumbers in his armchair—witnessed first with helpless surprise, and then they too were touched by it; his father on the one side blaming Gregor's mother for not leaving the cleaning of the room to his sister; while on the other yelling at the sister that she would never be allowed to clean Gregor's room again; while the mother tried to drag the father, who was quite beside himself with excitement, into the bedroom; his sister, shaken with sobs, pummelled at the table with her little fists; and Gregor hissed loudly in impotent fury that no one thought to shut the door, and save him from such a noise and spectacle.

But even if his sister, exhausted by office work, no longer had it in her to care for Gregor as she had done earlier, that still didn't mean that his mother had to take a hand to save Gregor from being utterly neglected. Because now there was the old charwoman. This old widow, who with her strong frame had survived everything that life had had to throw at her, was evidently quite undismayed by Gregor. It wasn't that she was nosy, but she had by chance once opened the door to Gregor's room, and at the sight of Gregor, who, caught out, started to scurry hither and thither, even though no one was chasing him, merely stood there with her hands folded and watched in astonishment. Since then, she let no morning or evening slip without opening the door a crack and looking in on Gregor. To begin with, she called to him as well, in terms she probably thought were friendly, such things as: "Come here, you old dung-beetle!" or "Will you take a look at that old dung-beetle!" Gregor of course didn't reply, but ignored the fact that the door had been opened, and stayed just exactly where he was. If only this old charwoman, instead of being allowed to stand and gawp at him whenever she felt like it, had been instructed to clean his room every day! Early one morning—a heavy rain battered against the windowpanes, a sign already, perhaps, of the approaching spring—Gregor felt such irritation when the charwoman came along with her words that, albeit slowly and ponderously, he made as if to attack her. The charwoman, far from being frightened, seized a chair that was standing near the door, and as she stood there with mouth agape it was clear that she would only close it when she had brought the chair crashing down on Gregor's back. "So is that as far as it goes then?" she asked, as Gregor turned away, and she calmly put the chair back in a corner.

Gregor was now eating almost nothing at all. Only sometimes, happening to pass the food that had been put out for him, he would desultorily take a morsel in his mouth, and keep it there for hours, before usually spitting it out again. At first he thought it was grief about the condition of his room that was keeping him from eating, but in fact the alterations to his room were the things he came to terms with most easily. They had started pushing things into his room that would otherwise have been in the way, and there were now a good many such items, since one room in the flat had been let out to a trio of bachelors. These serious-looking gentlemen—all three wore full beards, as Gregor happened to see once, peering through a crack in the door—were insistent on hygiene, not just where their own room was concerned, but throughout the flat where they were now tenants, and therefore most especially in the kitchen. Useless or dirty junk was something for which they had no tolerance. Besides, they had largely brought their own furnishings with them. For that reason, many things had now become superfluous that couldn't be sold, and that one didn't want to simply throw away either. All these things came into Gregor's room. And also the ashcan and the rubbish-bin from the kitchen. Anything that seemed even temporarily surplus to requirements was simply slung into Gregor's room by the charwoman, who was always in a tearing rush; it was fortunate that Gregor rarely saw more than the hand and the object in question, whatever it was. It might be that the charwoman had it in mind to reclaim the things at some future time, or to go in and get them all out one day, but what happened was that they simply lay where they had been thrown, unless Gregor, crawling about among the junk, happened to displace some of it, at first perforce, because there was simply no more room in which to move, but later on with increasing pleasure, even though, after such peregrinations he would find himself heartsore and weary to death, and wouldn't move for many hours.

Since the tenants sometimes took their supper at home in the shared living room, the door to it remained closed on some evenings, but Gregor hardly missed the opening of the door. After all, there were enough evenings when it had been open, and he had not profited from it, but, instead, without the family noticing at all, had merely lain still in the darkest corner of his room. On one occasion, however, the charwoman had left the door to the living room slightly ajar, and it remained ajar, even when the tenants walked in that evening, and the lights were turned on. They took their places at the table, where previously father, mother and Gregor had sat, unfurled their napkins and took up their eating irons. Straightaway his mother appeared in the doorway carrying a dish of meat, and hard behind her came his sister with a bowl heaped with potatoes. The food steamed mightily. The tenants inclined themselves to the dishes in front of them, as though to examine them before eating, and the one who was sitting at the head of the table, and who seemed to have some authority over the other two flanking him, cut into a piece of meat in the dish, as though to check whether it was sufficiently done, and didn't have to be sent back to the kitchen. He seemed content with what he found, and mother and sister, who had been watching in some trepidation, broke into relieved smiles.

70   The family were taking their meal in the kitchen. Even so, before going in there, the father came in and with a single reverence, cap in hand, walked once round the table. All the tenants got up and muttered something into their beards. Once they were on their own again, they ate in near silence. It struck Gregor that out of all the various sounds one could hear, it was that of their grinding teeth that stood out, as though to demonstrate to Gregor that teeth were needed to eat with, and the best toothless gums were no use. "But I do have an appetite," Gregor said to himself earnestly, "only not for those things. The way those tenants fill their boots, while I'm left to starve!"

On that same evening—Gregor couldn't recall having heard the violin once in all this time—it sounded from the kitchen. The tenants had finished their supper, the one in the middle had produced a newspaper, and given the other two a page apiece, and now they were leaning back, reading and smoking. When the violin sounded, they pricked up their ears, got up and tiptoed to the door of the hallway where they stayed pressed together. They must have been heard from the kitchen, because father called: "Do the gentlemen have any objection to the music? It can be stopped right away." "On the contrary," said the middle gentleman, "mightn't the young lady like to come in to us and play here, where it's more cosy and convenient?" "Only too happy to oblige," called the father, as if he were the violin player. The gentlemen withdrew to their dining room and waited. Before long up stepped the father with the music stand, the mother with the score, and the sister with the violin. Calmly the sister set everything up in readiness; the parents, who had never let rooms before, and therefore overdid politeness towards the tenants, didn't even dare to sit in their own chairs; Gregor's father leaned in the doorway, his right hand pushed between two buttons of his closed coat; Gregor's mother was offered a seat by one of the gentlemen, and, not presuming to move, remained sitting just where the gentleman had put her, off in a corner.

The sister began to play; father and mother, each on their respective side, attentively followed the movements of her hands. Gregor, drawn by the music, had slowly inched forward, and his head was already in the living room. He was no longer particularly surprised at his lack of discretion, where previously this discretion had been his entire pride. Even though now he would have had additional cause to remain hidden, because as a result of the dust that lay everywhere in his room, and flew up at the merest movement, he himself was covered with dust; on his back and along his sides he dragged around an assortment of threads, hairs and bits of food; his indifference to everything was far too great for him to lie down on his back, as he had done several times a day before, and rub himself clean on the carpet. And, in spite of his condition, he felt no shame at moving out on to the pristine floor of the living room.

Admittedly, no one paid him any regard. The family was completely absorbed by the violin playing; the tenants, on the other hand, hands in pockets, had initially taken up position far too close behind the music stand, so that they all could see the music, which must surely be annoying to his sister, but before long, heads lowered in half-loud conversation, they retreated to the window, where they remained, nervously observed by the father. It really did look all to evident

that they were disappointed in their expectation of hearing some fine or entertaining playing, were fed up with the whole performance, and only suffered
themselves to be disturbed out of politeness. The way they all blew their cigar
smoke upwards from their noses and mouths indicated in particular a great
nervousness on their part. And yet his sister was playing so beautifully. Her face
was inclined to the side, and sadly and searchingly her eyes followed the columns of notes. Gregor crept a little closer and held his head close to the ground,
so as to be prepared to meet her gaze. Could he be an animal, to be so moved by
music? It was as though he sensed a way to the unknown sustenance he longed
for. He was determined to go right up to his sister, to pluck at her skirt, and so
let her know she was to come into his room with her violin, because no one
rewarded music here as much as he wanted to reward it. He would not let her out
of his room, at least not as long as he lived; for the first time his frightening form
would come in useful for him; he would appear at all doors to his room at once,
and hiss in the faces of attackers; but his sister wasn't to be forced, she was to
remain with him of her own free will; she was to sit by his side on the sofa, and
he would tell her he was resolved to send her to the conservatory, and that, if the
calamity hadn't struck, he would have told everyone so last Christmas—was
Christmas past? surely it was—without brooking any objections. After this declaration, his sister would burst into tears of emotion, and Gregor would draw
himself up to her oxter[8] and kiss her on the throat, which, since she'd started
going to the office, she wore exposed, without a ribbon or collar.

"Mr Samsa!" cried the middle of the gentlemen, and not bothering to say
another word, pointed with his index finger at the slowly advancing Gregor. The
violin stopped, the middle gentleman first smiled, shaking his head, at his two
friends, and then looked at Gregor once more. His father seemed to think it his
first priority, even before driving Gregor away, to calm the tenants, though they
were not at all agitated, and in fact seemed to find Gregor more entertaining
than they had the violin playing. He hurried over to them, and with outspread
arms tried simultaneously to push them back into their room, and with his
body to block their sight of Gregor. At this point, they seemed to lose their temper. It wasn't easy to tell whether it was the father's behaviour or the understanding now dawning on them that they had been living next door to someone like
Gregor. They called on the father for explanations, they too started waving their
arms around, plucked nervously at their beards, and were slow to retreat into
their room. In the meantime, Gregor's sister had overcome the confusion that
had befallen her after the sudden interruption in her playing, had, after holding
her violin and bow in her slackly hanging hands a while and continuing to read
the score as if still playing suddenly got a grip on herself, deposited the instrument in the lap of her mother who was still sitting on her chair struggling for
breath, and ran into the next room, which the tenants, yielding now to pressure
from her father, were finally more rapidly nearing. Gregor could see how, under
the practised hands of his sister, the blankets and pillows on the beds flew up in
the air and were plumped and pulled straight. Even before the gentlemen had
reached their room, she was finished with making the beds, and had slipped
out. Father seemed once more so much in the grip of his stubbornness that he
quite forgot himself towards the tenants. He merely pushed and pushed, till the

8. Arm (Scottish).

middle gentleman stamped thunderously on the floor, and so brought him to a stop. "I hereby declare," he said, raising his hand and with his glare taking in also mother and sister, "that as a result of the vile conditions prevailing in this flat and in this family"—here, he spat emphatically on the floor—"I am giving notice with immediate effect. I of course will not pay one cent for the days I have lived here, in fact I will think very carefully whether or not to proceed with—believe me—very easily substantiated claims against you." He stopped and looked straight ahead of him, as though waiting for something else. And in fact his two friends chimed in with the words: "We too are giving in our notice, with immediate effect." Thereupon he seized the doorknob, and slammed the door with a mighty crash.

75   Gregor's father, with shaking hands, tottered to his chair, and slumped down into it; it looked as though he were settling to his regular evening snooze, but the powerful nodding of his somehow disconnected head showed that he was very far from sleeping. All this time, Gregor lay just exactly where he had been when the tenants espied him. Disappointment at the failure of his plan, perhaps also a slight faintness from his long fasting kept him from being able to move. With a certain fixed dread he awaited the calamity about to fall upon his head. Even the violin failed to startle him, when it slipped through the trembling fingers of his mother, and with a jangling echo fell to the floor.

"Dear parents," said his sister, and brought her hand down on the table top to obtain silence, "things cannot go on like this. You might not be able to see it, but I do. I don't want to speak the name of my brother within the hearing of that monster, and so I will merely say: we have to try to get rid of it. We did as much as humanly possible to try and look after it and tolerate it. I don't think anyone can reproach us for any measure we have taken or failed to take."

"She's right, a thousand times right," his father muttered to himself. His mother, who—with an expression of derangement in her eyes—was still experiencing difficulty breathing, started coughing softly into her cupped hand.

His sister ran over to her mother, and held her by the head. The sister's words seemed to have prompted some more precise form of thought in the father's mind, and he sat up and was toying with his doorman's cap among the plates, which still hadn't been cleared after the tenants' meal, from time to time shooting a look at the silent Gregor.

"We must try and get rid of it," the sister now said, to her father alone, as her mother was caught up in her coughing and could hear nothing else, "otherwise it'll be the death of you. I can see it coming. If we have to work as hard as we are all at present doing, it's not possible to stand this permanent torture at home as well. I can't do it any more either." And she burst into such a flood of tears that they flowed down on to her mother's face, from which she wiped them away, with mechanical movements of her hand.

80   "My child," said her father compassionately and with striking comprehension, "but what shall we do?"

Grete merely shrugged her shoulders as a sign of the uncertainty into which—in striking contrast to her previous conviction—she had now fallen in her weeping.

"If only he understood us," said the father, with rising intonation; the sister, still weeping, waved her hand violently to indicate that such a thing was out of the question.

"If only he understood us," the father repeated, by closing his eyes accepting the sister's conviction of the impossibility of it, "then we might come to some sort of settlement with him. But as it is . . ."

"We must get rid of it," cried the sister again, "that's the only thing for it, Father. You just have to put from your mind any thought that it's Gregor. Our continuing to think that it was, for such a long time, therein lies the source of our misfortune. But how can it be Gregor? If it was Gregor, he would long ago have seen that it's impossible for human beings to live together with an animal like that, and he would have left of his own free will. That would have meant I didn't have a brother, but we at least could go on with our lives, and honour his memory. But as it is, this animal hounds us, drives away the tenants, evidently wants to take over the whole flat, and throw us out on to the street. Look, Father," she suddenly broke into a scream, "he's coming again!" And in an access of terror wholly incomprehensible to Gregor, his sister even quit her mother, actually pushing herself away from her chair, as though she would rather sacrifice her mother than remain anywhere near Gregor, and dashed behind her father, who, purely on the basis of her agitation, got to his feet and half-raised his arms to shield the sister.

Meanwhile, Gregor of course didn't have the least intention of frightening anyone, and certainly not his sister. He had merely begun to turn around, to make his way back to his room, which was a somewhat laborious and eye-catching process, as, in consequence of his debility he needed his head to help with such difficult manoeuvres, raising it many times and bashing it against the floor. He stopped and looked around. His good intentions seemed to have been acknowledged; it had just been a momentary fright he had given them. Now they all looked at him sadly and silently. There lay his mother in her armchair, with her legs stretched out and pressed together, her eyes almost falling shut with fatigue; his father and sister were sitting side by side, his sister having placed her hand on her father's neck.

"Well, maybe they'll let me turn around now," thought Gregor, and recommenced the manoeuvre. He was unable to suppress the odd grunt of effort, and needed to take periodic rests as well. But nobody interfered with him, and he was allowed to get on with it by himself. Once he had finished his turn, he straightaway set off wandering back. He was struck by the great distance that seemed to separate him from his room, and was unable to understand how, in his enfeebled condition, he had just a little while ago covered the same distance, almost without noticing. Intent on making the most rapid progress he could, he barely noticed that no word, no exclamation from his family distracted him. Only when he was in the doorway did he turn his head, not all the way, as his neck felt a little stiff, but even so he was able to see that behind him nothing had changed, only that his sister had got up. His last look lingered upon his mother, who was fast asleep.

No sooner was he in his room than the door was pushed shut behind him, and locked and bolted. The sudden noise so alarmed Gregor that his little legs gave way beneath him. It was his sister who had been in such a hurry. She had been already standing on tiptoe, waiting, and had then light-footedly leaped forward. Gregor hadn't even heard her until she cried "At last!" as she turned the key in the lock.

"What now?" wondered Gregor, and looked around in the dark. He soon made the discovery that he could no longer move. It came as no surprise to him; if anything, it seemed inexplicable that he had been able to get as far as he had on his frail little legs. Otherwise, he felt as well as could be expected. He did have pains all over his body, but he felt they were gradually abating, and would finally cease altogether. The rotten apple in his back and the inflammation all round it, which was entirely coated with a soft dust, he barely felt anymore. He thought back on his family with devotion and love. His conviction that he needed to disappear was, if anything, still firmer than his sister's. He remained in this condition of empty and peaceful reflection until the church clock struck three a.m. The last thing he saw was the sky gradually lightening outside his window. Then his head involuntarily dropped, and his final breath passed feebly from his nostrils.

When the charwoman came early in the morning—so powerful was she, and in such a hurry, that, even though she had repeatedly been asked not to, she slammed all the doors so hard that sleep was impossible after her coming—she at first found nothing out of the ordinary when she paid her customary brief call on Gregor. She thought he was lying there immobile on purpose, and was playing at being offended; in her opinion, he was capable of all sorts of understanding. Because she happened to be holding the long broom, she tried to tickle Gregor away from the doorway. When that bore no fruit, she grew irritable, and jabbed Gregor with the broom, and only when she had moved him from the spot without any resistance on his part did she take notice. When she understood what the situation was, her eyes went large and round, she gave a half-involuntary whistle, didn't stay longer, but tore open the door of the bedroom and loudly called into the darkness: "Have a look, it's gone and perished; it's lying there, and it's perished!"

90   The Samsas sat up in bed, and had trouble overcoming their shock at the charwoman's appearance in their room, before even beginning to register the import of what she was saying. But then Mr and Mrs Samsa hurriedly climbed out of bed, each on his or her respective side, Mr Samsa flinging a blanket over his shoulders, Mrs Samsa coming along just in her nightdress; and so they stepped into Gregor's room. By now the door from the living room had been opened as well, where Grete had slept ever since the tenants had come; she was fully dressed, as if she hadn't slept at all, and her pale face seemed to confirm that. "Dead?" said Mrs Samsa, and looked questioningly up at the charwoman, even though she was in a position to check it all herself, and in fact could have seen it without needing to check. "I should say so," said the charwoman and, by way of proof, with her broom pushed Gregor's body across the floor a ways. Mrs Samsa moved as though to restrain the broom, but did not do so. "Ah," said Mr Samsa, "now we can give thanks to God." He crossed himself, and the three women followed his example. Grete, not taking her eye off the body, said: "Look how thin he had become. He stopped eating such a long time ago. I brought food in and took it out, and it was always untouched." Indeed, Gregor's body was utterly flat and desiccated—only so apparent now that he was no longer up on his little legs, and there was nothing else to distract the eye.

"Come in with us a bit, Grete," said Mrs Samsa with a melancholy smile, and, not without turning back to look at the corpse, Grete followed her parents into the bedroom. The charwoman shut the door and opened the window as far as it would go. In spite of the early hour, there was already something sultry in the morning air. It was, after all, the end of March.

The three tenants emerged from their room and looked around for their breakfast in outrage; they had been forgotten about. "Where's our breakfast?" the middle gentleman sulkily asked the charwoman. She replied by setting her finger to her lips, and then quickly and silently beckoning the gentlemen into Gregor's room. They followed and with their hands in the pockets of their somewhat shiny little jackets stood around Gregor's body in the bright sunny room.

The door from the bedroom opened, and Mr Samsa appeared in his uniform, with his wife on one arm and his daughter on the other. All were a little teary; from time to time Grete pressed her face against her father's arm.

"Leave my house at once!" said Mr Samsa, and pointed to the door, without relinquishing the women. "How do you mean?" said the middle gentleman, with a little consternation, and smiled a saccharine smile. The other two kept their hands behind their backs and rubbed them together incessantly, as if in the happy expectation of a great scene, which was sure to end well for them. "I mean just exactly what I said," replied Mr Samsa, and with his two companions, walked straight towards the tenant. To begin with the tenant stood his ground, and looked at the floor, as if the things in his head were recombining in some new arrangement. "Well, I suppose we'd better go then," he said, and looked up at Mr Samsa, as if he required authority for this novel humility. Mr Samsa merely nodded curtly at him with wide eyes. Thereupon the gentleman did indeed swing into the hallway with long strides; his two friends had been listening for a little while, their hands laid to rest, and now skipped after him, as if afraid Mr Samsa might get to the hallway before them, and cut them off from their leader. In the hallway all three took their hats off the hatstand, pulled their canes out of the umbrella holder, bowed silently, and left the flat. Informed by what turned out to be a wholly unjustified suspicion, Mr Samsa and his womenfolk stepped out on to the landing; leaning against the balustrade, they watched the three gentlemen proceeding slowly but evenly down the long flight of stairs, disappearing on each level into a certain twist of the stairwell and emerging a couple of seconds later; the further they descended, the less interest the Samsa family took in their progress, and when a butcher's apprentice passed them and eventually climbed up much higher with his tray on his head, Mr Samsa and the women left the balustrade altogether, and all turned back, with relief, into their flat.

They decided to use the day to rest and to go for a walk; not only had they 95 earned a break from work, but they stood in dire need of one. And so they all sat down at the table, and wrote three separate letters of apology—Mr Samsa to the board of his bank, Mrs Samsa to her haberdasher, and Grete to her manager. While they were so engaged, the charwoman came in to say she was leaving, because her morning's tasks were done. The three writers at first merely nodded without looking up, and only when the charwoman made no move to leave did they look up in some irritation. "Well?" asked Mr Samsa. The charwoman stood smiling in the doorway, as though she had some wonderful surprise to tell the family about, but would only do so if asked expressly about it. The almost vertical ostrich feather in her hat, which had annoyed Mr Samsa the whole time she had been working for them, teetered in every direction. "So what is it you want?" asked Mrs Samsa, who was the person most likely to command respect from the charwoman. "Well," replied the charwoman, and her happy laughter kept her from speaking, "well, just to say, you don't have to worry about how to get rid of the thing next door. I'll take care of it." Mrs Samsa and Grete inclined their heads over their letters, as if to go on writing; Mr Samsa, who noticed that the woman was about to embark on a more detailed description of everything, put up a hand to cut her off. Being thus debarred from speaking, she remembered the great rush she was in, and, evidently piqued, called out, "Well, so long everyone," spun round and left the apartment with a terrible slamming of doors.

"I'm letting her go this evening," said Mr Samsa, but got no reply from wife or daughter, because the reference to the charwoman seemed to have disturbed their concentration, no sooner than it had returned. The two women rose, went over to the window, and stayed there, holding one another in an embrace. Mr Samsa turned towards them in his chair, and watched them in silence for a while. Then he called: "Well now, come over here. Leave that old business. And pay a little attention to me." The women came straightaway, caressed him, and finished their letters.

Then the three of them all together left the flat, which was something they hadn't done for months, and took the tram to the park at the edge of the city. The carriage in which they sat was flooded with warm sunshine. Sitting back comfortably in their seats, they discussed the prospects for the future; it turned out that on closer inspection these were not at all bad, because the work of all of them, which they had yet to talk about properly, was proceeding in a very encouraging way, particularly in regard to future prospects. The greatest alleviation of the situation must be produced by moving house; they would take a smaller, cheaper, but also better situated and more practical apartment than their present one, which Gregor had found for them. While they were talking in these terms, almost at one and the same time Mr and Mrs Samsa noticed their increasingly lively daughter, the way that of late, in spite of the trouble that had made her cheeks pale, she had bloomed into an attractive and well-built girl. Falling silent, and communicating almost unconsciously through glances, they thought it was about time to find a suitable husband for her. And it felt like a confirmation of their new dreams and their fond intentions when, as they reached their destination, their daughter was the first to get up, and stretched her nubile young body.

1915

QUESTIONS

1. What characteristics of *The Metamorphosis* are specific to its being a novella? What would likely be sacrificed in the narrative had Kafka opted for the short story form, particularly in terms of plot and character development? Would the meaning have been different? How so?
2. How does Kafka use Gregor's metamorphosis into an insect as a metaphor? What does he seem to be suggesting about the human condition by using this particular image?
3. What are the practical implications of Gregor's transformation for the Samsa family? What negative effects does it have on the family? What positive effects?
4. What is the significance of Gregor's loss of appetite for food over the course of the novella? What does he become more "hungry" for, and how do his actions prior to his death signify this growing need?
5. How are alienation and isolation—prevailing themes of modernist fiction—exemplified in *The Metamorphosis*? In what ways does Gregor's room become symbolic of his alienation? How does the treatment of the room by others both illustrate and exacerbate Gregor's isolation?

6. How does time work in the story? How is it symbolized? Does your understanding of the passing of time change throughout the sections of the novella?

SUGGESTIONS FOR WRITING

1. Write an essay analyzing the character of Bartleby the scrivener. Is Bartleby a flat or a fully rounded character? Does his character change or remain static? Is he best understood as a realistic character or as a type or representative of an idea? How do the narrator and the focused time and action of this novella affect the characterization of Bartleby?

2. A short story about Bartleby would be simpler and more comic because the situation is so incongruous: an employee who refuses to work. In a shorter story, both Bartleby and the narrator might be flat characters like the other office workers, Turkey, Nippers, and Ginger Nut. Write an essay in which you argue that the novella allows room for the narrator's gradual change of perspective on Bartleby, noting comments and responses that add complexity or roundness to the employer as well as Bartleby, for instance, "Poor fellow! thought I, he means no mischief. . . . I can get along without him."

3. Though Gregor Samsa's bodily transformation into a "monstrous insect" is *the* prevailing metamorphosis in the novella, other changes also occur, both for Gregor and his family. Write an essay in which you follow the transformations in the novella, supporting the thesis that a short novel or novella is the appropriate scope for such alterations in more than one character over a certain period of time. Could the full effect have been achieved in a short story? What would be diminished in a longer novel?

4. Write an essay in which you trace the development of Gregor's consciousness in the story. How does he first react to his transformation? What are his initial preoccupations in Section I? How does his attitude toward his condition develop, and how are his preoccupations different by the novella's conclusion?

5. Of the various relationships explored in the story, the one between Gregor and his sister, Grete, stands out as particularly complex. Write an essay in which you evaluate the dynamics of this relationship, especially the role reversals and emotional shifts that take place, using evidence from the text. Do these characters genuinely care about each other? How do they show their care or lack thereof? How does this relationship highlight the themes of the narrative as a whole? How does the scope of a novella allow Kafka to reveal changing attitudes in more than one character while maintaining focus on one problem?

6. Although *The Metamorphosis* and *Bartleby, the Scrivener* are realist novellas in many respects, they both depend on a central character's improbable difference from the rest of society around him. Write an essay in which you compare and contrast the alienation or isolation of Gregor Samsa and Bartleby in their respective narratives. Be sure to take into account the narration and point of view. Kafka's novella uses a third-person external narrator and focuses largely on the thoughts and perceptions of Gregor Samsa, whereas Melville's novella is narrated by an observer of Bartleby who never knows what the scrivener is thinking.

Exploring Contexts

8   THE AUTHOR'S WORK: FLANNERY O'CONNOR

As soon as we read more than one work by an author, we begin to recognize similar qualities in the works, as if we are getting to know a personality. Each story, poem, or play is part of the author's entire body of work, or **oeuvre**, across his or her career. Though the voice and vision may vary from work to work, there will be continuities across the oeuvre. But the concerns and assumptions that permeate an author's oeuvre do more than relate the individual works to one another; they also serve as the author's trademark. We read each new work by the same author with certain expectations about setting, characterization, style, tone, and the other elements of literary writing.

Unless a work of literature is anonymous or ancient, it is relatively easy to find out about the person who wrote it. In this book we provide short biographies of writers, and numerous sources in libraries and online can add detail and complexity to your first impressions of an author. Curiosity about a writer may lead you not only to biographies, but also to everything else the author wrote, including essays, letters, diaries, and memoirs—anything that promises insight into the experience, the worldview, and the process that went into the work.

In this chapter we will look closely at the work of the American fiction writer Flannery O'Connor (1925–1964), focusing on three stories: the title stories of both her first collection, *A Good Man Is Hard to Find* (1955), and her last, *Everything That Rises Must Converge* (published posthumously in 1965), as well as "Good Country People," which appeared in the first collection. O'Connor's career was short, hampered by her struggles with lupus, but her accomplishments were considerable: She died at thirty-nine, having published some thirty-one stories and two novels, as well as numerous essays and reviews.

O'Connor's settings are most often in the American South, rural or urban, and her characters most often Southerners, white or black. Consequently, her subject is often

Flannery O'Connor

what she called "the race business." O'Connor had a keen eye for realistic detail and for the truth that lies beneath the surface of language and self-image. Her means of uncovering this truth was often violence that shocks the reader and, often, the characters themselves. Though O'Connor was a deeply religious and serious writer, her stories are replete with irony and wit and are sometimes downright funny. Indeed, as you will see, she was not above mixing comedy and horror or using comic pratfalls to achieve serious (even tragic) ends. As with many other powerful writers, it is not difficult to recognize a story by Flannery O'Connor.

In the rest of this chapter, we first offer general guidance on biographical approaches to authors and their works, with some examples. Then we discuss more fully some terms and concepts that you have encountered in earlier chapters, but that are especially useful in studies of several works by the same author: the distinctions among types of narration as well as matters of tone, style, and imagery. To round out the picture of Flannery O'Connor and to provide suitable material for a critical essay, the chapter also offers passages from O'Connor's essays and letters and samples of biographical criticism.

BIOGRAPHICAL APPROACHES TO LITERATURE

An author's set of works always relates in some way to his or her life, though not necessarily as direct copies of experience. A biographical approach not only brings us closer to the person behind the work but also gives us a stronger sense of where the work originates. Even a few biographical references about the author can help guide our expectations about the work and place its themes in perspective.

It is always a good idea to find out when and where an author lived and wrote before you write about any work, just as you would notice the setting (the time and place) within the work. Any essay on a work of literature may include carefully cited information or evidence about the author's life, career, and views. For example, it may be useful to know that Franz Kafka (1883–1924) was a well-educated Jewish civil servant who wrote in German while living in Prague and Vienna. His novella *The Metamorphosis*, then, should not be read as if it were written yesterday in a suburb of Los Angeles. And it *may* be read, in part, as a response to the mixture of assimilation and exile that many Eastern European Jews experienced at that time.

Be aware, however, that the biographical approach has some limitations and drawbacks. In a short essay on one or more works by a single author, it is usually better to focus on the works themselves. But even if you are writing a longer paper, knowing a great deal about the author's life and personality or about the author's stated intentions can bias you for or against the author's work regardless of its merits, or lead to irrelevant or reductive interpretations. On the one hand, learning negative details about an author's life—that he or she held abhorrent political views, was addicted to alcohol or drugs, or abused spouses and friends—may adversely color the way you feel about the work. On the other hand, some readers may view their favorite writers as heroes, glamorizing their failings and confusing their interest in a personality with their response to the text.

More important, you should always be careful not to misread the fictional work as factual autobiography or to explain features of the work as direct results of some biographical cause. Such cause-and-effect biographical critiques ignore other explanations and limit your interpretation of the work. Finally, when you read essays, reviews, and criticism in which writers reflect on their own work, it is tempting to take such comments as the final word about the work. But anyone who has ever tried to write knows that the result can have unintended effects on other people. Literary writing opens itself up to multiple interpretations, and any evidence of a writer's conscious intentions shouldn't close down the interpretive process.

It is possible to avoid these pitfalls and take a moderate approach to biographical criticism, however. After all, the text didn't pop into existence in a vacuum; a real human being in a historical time and place did write it. Knowing more about the context in which a work was created—including the circumstances and vision of the author who created it—can lead you to a deeper understanding and appreciation of the work.

A Biographical Approach to Ernest Hemingway's "Hills Like White Elephants"

Ernest Hemingway finished writing "Hills Like White Elephants" during his honeymoon with his second wife, Pauline Pfeiffer, and published it in 1927 in a collection entitled *Men without Women*. Hemingway prided himself on a modernist style of only hinting at emotions, and until recently this story has inspired little biographical criticism. Of course the story has been associated with Hemingway's subject matter and themes as well as his experience as an American writer living abroad between the two World Wars. The story's setting in Spain and the characterization of two disillusioned American travelers who drink a lot seem generally true to Hemingway's own experience and outlook. For sixty years or so, the story has been read as a bleak, even painful episode in which the man persuades the pregnant American woman to get an abortion. Only in the 1990s did some critics propose a very different reading of the ending of the story, in light of some biographical information.

Hemingway's early work was more autobiographical, portraying his own stand-in, Nick Adams, in stories set in his boyhood home of Michigan. But "Hills Like White Elephants" seems to have little in it that is directly autobiographical. Nevertheless, literary scholar Hilary K. Justice has proposed a biographical key to "Hills Like White Elephants" that makes a dramatic difference in how we interpret the outcome for the two main characters. As noted, the story was written during Hemingway's second honeymoon. Justice calls attention to the fact that Hemingway wrote a dedication on the manuscript of the story: "Ms [manuscript] for Pauline—Well, well, well." * Why would he give this manuscript to his new wife, a Catholic who had been reluctant to marry a divorced man and who would be opposed to abortion according to the teaching of her religion? There is no evidence that any of Hemingway's four wives ever had an abortion. There *is* evidence in the manuscript, however, that Hemingway changed his mind about the way the story ends: The manuscript he dedicated to Pauline contains a handwritten alteration in wording that suggests that the man in the story changes his mind about pressuring Jig to have an abortion and that Jig wins the argument. This change is reflected in the published version of the story. Instead of a dialogue in which the man

(Continued on next page)

(Continued)

convinces the woman to have the "perfectly simple" operation in Madrid, it is a dialogue in which the two eventually agree to take a train going in the other direction. Just as the girl smiles at the end of the story, Pauline Hemingway might have accepted the revised manuscript as an appropriate wedding gift, a sign that things were "well." Justice thus considered the biographical context of Hemingway's relationship with his Catholic wife, in conjunction with a close reading of details in the published story and the manuscript, in order to revise the accepted reading of the story.

* Quoted in Hilary K. Justice, "'Well, Well, Well': Cross-Gendered Autobiography and the Manuscript of 'Hills Like White Elephants,'" *The Hemingway Review* 18 (1998): 17–32.

THE AUTHOR OF FICTION: IMPLIED AUTHOR OR NARRATOR

Chapter 2 introduced key concepts about narrators that will help you in reading Flannery O'Connor's stories. "A Good Man Is Hard to Find," "Good Country People," and "Everything That Rises Must Converge," like the rest of O'Connor's stories, are narrated in the third person. Yet these narrators are not the same in every story. In the first and last of the stories gathered here, a central focalizing character (the grandmother in "A Good Man," Julian in "Everything That Rises") functions much like a first-person unreliable narrator, misperceiving situations and characters around them. In "Good Country People," with limited omniscient narration, O'Connor offers us more than one character's point of view. But these third-person narrators are not characters in the story; nor are they the voice of Flannery O'Connor.

In the three stories in this chapter, each narrator adopts a slightly different position toward the focal character. Immediately this difference in narration indicates that Flannery O'Connor, who wrote all of the stories, is *not* the fictional teller or narrator of them, and the narrators didn't actually write or speak the words we read. Did the real Flannery O'Connor share the voice and perspective of any of her narrators? We will never know. What did the real O'Connor hope to teach her readers? We have only a few of her statements to go on; the actual author is inaccessible to us. These gaps in what a reader can access or know have led to the concept of the *implied author*. This concept helps us avoid reading the story as the writer's direct personal communication, allows for the variety of stories by one writer, and reminds us not only that the narrator of a story is *not* the author of it but also that we aren't talking about the flesh-and-blood person who wrote other works as well. When writing your critical essays, be sure to identify the narrator (as a character or not) and to distinguish the narrator from the author.

THE AUTHOR OF FICTION: STYLE AND TONE

Exploring multiple works by the same author immediately gives you a broader view of the way that author writes. Each author has certain tendencies of **style**, which includes **figures of speech** and **imagery**. O'Connor's attention to physical detail is especially witty. Take, for instance, the extended **metaphor** that opens "Good Country People," comparing Mrs. Freeman's facial expressions to gears of a "heavy truck": "Besides the neutral expression that she wore when she was alone, Mrs. Freeman had two others, forward and reverse." This unusual image gives us a more vivid sense of Mrs. Freeman's character than a straightforward description would. A **simile** is more explicit, using *like* or *as* to show comparison. In "A Good Man Is Hard to Find," Red Sam's "stomach hung over [his trousers] like a sack of meal swaying under his shirt"; in "Good Country People," the Bible salesman looks at Hulga "as if a fantastical animal at the zoo had put its paw through the bars and given him a loving poke."

Imagery can refer to any sensory detail indicated in a work—patterns of smell, sound, and touch as well as sight—and it need not be an explicit figure of speech. Descriptions of setting, clothing, or other details serve as imagery reflective of the state of characters. For example, in "A Good Man Is Hard to Find," the descriptions of clothing ("tan and white shoes and no socks" [par. 74]) contribute to imagery without using figures of speech, whereas the woods surrounding the family, though described simply as "tall and dark and deep," become symbolic wild spaces. In the realistic urban world of "Everything That Rises Must Converge," O'Connor carefully manages the imagery through such telling physical details as the mother's "folding fan, black with a Japanese scene on it" (par. 48), her cheap attempt at elegance.

A writer's style also includes **diction** or word choice—whether *formal* or *informal* (think *implement* versus *tool*, or *coiffure* versus *hairdo*), whether ornate, standard, colloquial, dialect, or slang. The diction of many of the stories in this book is somewhat informal, particularly those narrated in the first person. An author may highlight the regional or dialect differences of a narrator's language, just as Flannery O'Connor filters the everyday Southern speech patterns of her characters through an articulate, perceptive narrator with correct diction.

In O'Connor's fiction, such distinctions between the diction and syntax of the characters and of the narrator contribute to the **tone** of her work, or the attitude of the implied author and the narrator toward the characters and events, an element somewhat analogous to tone of voice. When what is being said and how it is said (tone) are in harmony, it is difficult to separate one from the other; when there seems to be a discrepancy, we have a number of terms to describe the difference. If the language seems exaggerated, we call it **overstatement**, or *hyperbole*. Sometimes it will be the narrator, sometimes a character, who uses language so intensive or exaggerated that we must read it at a discount, as it were, and judge the speaker's accuracy or honesty in the process. When Julian's mother, in "Everything That Rises Must Converge," says, "I've always had a great respect for my colored friends. . . . I'd do anything in the world for them" (par. 32), we know she protests too much, that she is indulging in hyperbole, and we see the racism lurking beneath her language. The opposite of overstatement is **understatement**, or **litotes**.

O'Connor's work is also characterized by **irony**. When a word or expression carries not only its literal meaning but a different meaning for the speaker as well, we have an example of *verbal irony*. For example, the phrase "good country people" accumulates ironies when Hulga, who has groaned at the idea, uses it herself. There are also nonverbal forms of irony, the most common of which is *situational irony*, which occurs when a character holds a position or has an expectation that is reversed or fulfilled in an unexpected way. Hulga's plan to seduce the Bible salesman leads to an ironic reversal of the situation, bringing a number of surprises for her and the reader.

A form of situational irony known as *dramatic irony* occurs when a gap opens between what a character believes or expects and what the reader or audience knows. This gap may be revealed when a character says something that has unintended alternative meanings to a better-informed listener, or that later becomes true in an unintended way. Dramatic irony also may be sustained throughout an entire work by an unreliable first-person narrator, who perceives or tries to "spin" his or her circumstances in a distorted way. In "A Good Man Is Hard to Find," the grandmother's careful attention to her dress, she believes, ensures respect: "In case of an accident, anyone seeing her dead on the highway would know at once that she was a lady" (par. 12). She takes this seriously, though most readers find it ludicrous or pathetic; hence it is an example of dramatic irony. At the same time, her remark unknowingly foretells the outcome of the story, a form of situational irony. Such ironic statements and outcomes occur throughout O'Connor's stories. Rather than demeaning her characters, O'Connor's ironic treatment testifies to her keen observation of the common limits of human awareness, and the way people tend to rationalize and misconstrue their situations and their own characters.

The distinctive Southern voices of the dialogue in an O'Connor story and the vivid setting and imagery add much to our sense of this author's style. But even more, we know an O'Connor story by the dryly humorous distance her narrators maintain from all characters, the often violent harm characters do to one another, the belated revelation that destroys a character's pride in knowing more than others—the commandment, in a sense, to awaken before we meet eternal damnation.

FLANNERY O'CONNOR

A Good Man Is Hard to Find

The grandmother didn't want to go to Florida. She wanted to visit some of her connections in east Tennessee and she was seizing at every chance to change Bailey's mind. Bailey was the son she lived with, her only boy. He was sitting on the edge of his chair at the table, bent over the orange sports section of the *Journal*. "Now look here, Bailey," she said, "see here, read this," and she stood with one hand on her thin hip and the other rattling the newspaper at his bald head. "Here this fellow that calls himself The Misfit is aloose from the Federal Pen and headed toward Florida and you read here what it says he did to these people. Just you read it. I wouldn't take my children in any direction with a criminal like that aloose in it. I couldn't answer to my conscience if I did."

Bailey didn't look up from his reading so she wheeled around then and faced the children's mother, a young woman in slacks, whose face was as broad and innocent as a cabbage and was tied around with a green head-kerchief that had two points on the top like a rabbit's ears. She was sitting on the sofa, feeding the baby his apricots out of a jar. "The children have been to Florida before," the old lady said. "You all ought to take them somewhere else for a change so they would see different parts of the world and be broad. They never have been to east Tennessee."

The children's mother didn't seem to hear her but the eight-year-old boy, John Wesley, a stocky child with glasses, said, "If you don't want to go to Florida, why dontcha stay at home?" He and the little girl, June Star, were reading the funny papers on the floor.

"She wouldn't stay at home to be queen for a day," June Star said without raising her yellow head.

5   "Yes and what would you do if this fellow, The Misfit, caught you?" the grandmother asked.

"I'd smack his face," John Wesley said.

"She wouldn't stay at home for a million bucks," June Star said. "Afraid she'd miss something. She has to go everywhere we go."

"All right, Miss," the grandmother said. "Just remember that the next time you want me to curl your hair."

June Star said her hair was naturally curly.

10   The next morning the grandmother was the first one in the car, ready to go. She had her big black valise that looked like the head of a hippopotamus in one corner, and underneath it she was hiding a basket with Pitty Sing,[1] the cat, in it. She didn't intend for the cat to be left alone in the house for three days because he would miss her too much and she was afraid he might brush against one of the gas burners and accidentally asphyxiate himself. Her son, Bailey, didn't like to arrive at a motel with a cat.

She sat in the middle of the back seat with John Wesley and June Star on either side of her. Bailey and the children's mother and the baby sat in front and they left Atlanta at eight forty-five with the mileage on the car at 55890. The grandmother wrote this down because she thought it would be interesting to say how many miles they had been when they got back. It took them twenty minutes to reach the outskirts of the city.

The old lady settled herself comfortably, removing her white cotton gloves and putting them up with her purse on the shelf in front of the back window. The children's mother still had on slacks and still had her head tied up in a green kerchief, but the grandmother had on a navy blue straw sailor hat with a bunch of white violets on the brim and a navy blue dress with a small white dot in the print. Her collars and cuffs were white organdy trimmed with lace and at her neckline she had pinned a purple spray of cloth violets containing a sachet. In case of an accident, anyone seeing her dead on the highway would know at once that she was a lady.

She said she thought it was going to be a good day for driving, neither too hot nor too cold, and she cautioned Bailey that the speed limit was fifty-five miles an hour and that the patrolmen hid themselves behind billboards and small clumps of trees and sped out after you before you had a chance to slow down. She pointed out interesting details of the scenery: Stone Mountain; the blue granite that in some places came up to both sides of the highway; the brilliant red clay banks slightly streaked with purple; and the various crops that made rows of green lace-work on the ground. The trees were full of silver-white sunlight and the meanest of them sparkled. The children were reading comic magazines and their mother had gone back to sleep.

1. Named after Pitti-Sing, one of the "three little maids from school" in Gilbert and Sullivan's operetta *The Mikado* (1885).

"Let's go through Georgia fast so we won't have to look at it much," John Wesley said.

"If I were a little boy," said the grandmother, "I wouldn't talk about my native state that way. Tennessee has the mountains and Georgia has the hills." 15

"Tennessee is just a hillbilly dumping ground," John Wesley said, "and Georgia is a lousy state too."

"You said it," June Star said.

"In my time," said the grandmother, folding her thin veined fingers, "children were more respectful of their native states and their parents and everything else. People did right then. Oh look at the cute little pickaninny!" she said and pointed to a Negro child standing in the door of a shack. "Wouldn't that make a picture, now?" she asked and they all turned and looked at the little Negro out of the back window. He waved.

"He didn't have any britches on," June Star said.

"He probably didn't have any," the grandmother explained. "Little niggers in 20 the country don't have things like we do. If I could paint, I'd paint that picture," she said.

The children exchanged comic books.

The grandmother offered to hold the baby and the children's mother passed him over the front seat to her. She set him on her knee and bounced him and told him about the things they were passing. She rolled her eyes and screwed up her mouth and stuck her leathery thin face into his smooth bland one. Occasionally he gave her a faraway smile. They passed a large cotton field with five or six graves fenced in the middle of it, like a small island. "Look at the graveyard!" the grandmother said, pointing it out. "That was the old family burying ground. That belonged to the plantation."

"Where's the plantation?" John Wesley asked.

"Gone with the Wind,"[2] said the grandmother. "Ha. Ha."

When the children finished all the comic books they had brought, they 25 opened the lunch and ate it. The grandmother ate a peanut butter sandwich and an olive and would not let the children throw the box and the paper napkins out the window. When there was nothing else to do they played a game by choosing a cloud and making the other two guess what shape it suggested. John Wesley took one the shape of a cow and June Star guessed a cow and John Wesley said, no, an automobile, and June Star said he didn't play fair, and they began to slap each other over the grandmother.

The grandmother said she would tell them a story if they would keep quiet. When she told a story, she rolled her eyes and waved her head and was very dramatic. She said once when she was a maiden lady she had been courted by a Mr. Edgar Atkins Teagarden from Jasper, Georgia. She said he was a very good-looking man and a gentleman and that he brought her a watermelon every Saturday afternoon with his initials cut in it, E. A. T. Well, one Saturday, she said, Mr. Teagarden brought the watermelon and there was nobody at home and he left it on the front porch and returned in his buggy to Jasper, but she never got the watermelon, she said, because a nigger boy ate it when he saw the initials,

2. Title of an immensely popular novel, published in 1936, by Margaret Mitchell (1900–49); the novel depicts a large, prosperous Southern plantation, Tara, that is destroyed by Northern troops in the American Civil War.

E. A. T.! This story tickled John Wesley's funny bone and he giggled and giggled but June Star didn't think it was any good. She said she wouldn't marry a man that just brought her a watermelon on Saturday. The grandmother said she would have done well to marry Mr. Teagarden because he was a gentleman and had bought Coca-Cola stock when it first came out and that he had died only a few years ago, a very wealthy man.

They stopped at The Tower for barbecued sandwiches. The Tower was a part stucco and part wood filling station and dance hall set in a clearing outside of Timothy. A fat man named Red Sammy Butts ran it and there were signs stuck here and there on the building and for miles up and down the highway saying, TRY RED SAMMY'S FAMOUS BARBECUE. NONE LIKE FAMOUS RED SAMMY'S! RED SAM! THE FAT BOY WITH THE HAPPY LAUGH! A VETERAN! RED SAMMY'S YOUR MAN!

Red Sammy was lying on the bare ground outside The Tower with his head under a truck while a gray monkey about a foot high, chained to a small chinaberry tree, chattered nearby. The monkey sprang back into the tree and got on the highest limb as soon as he saw the children jump out of the car and run toward him.

Inside, The Tower was a long dark room with a counter at one end and tables at the other and dancing space in the middle. They all sat down at a board table next to the nickelodeon[3] and Red Sam's wife, a tall burnt-brown woman with hair and eyes lighter than her skin, came and took their order. The children's mother put a dime in the machine and played "The Tennessee Waltz," and the grandmother said that tune always made her want to dance. She asked Bailey if he would like to dance but he only glared at her. He didn't have a naturally sunny disposition like she did and trips made him nervous. The grandmother's brown eyes were very bright. She swayed her head from side to side and pretended she was dancing in her chair. June Star said play something she could tap to so the children's mother put in another dime and played a fast number and June Star stepped out onto the dance floor and did her tap routine.

30   "Ain't she cute?" Red Sam's wife said, leaning over the counter. "Would you like to come be my little girl?"

"No I certainly wouldn't," June Star said. "I wouldn't live in a broken-down place like this for a million bucks!" and she ran back to the table.

"Ain't she cute?" the woman repeated, stretching her mouth politely.

"Aren't you ashamed?" hissed the grandmother.

Red Sam came in and told his wife to quit lounging on the counter and hurry up with these people's order. His khaki trousers reached just to his hip bones and his stomach hung over them like a sack of meal swaying under his shirt. He came over and sat down at a table nearby and let out a combination sigh and yodel. "You can't win," he said. "You can't win," and he wiped his sweating red face off with a gray handkerchief. "These days you don't know who to trust," he said. "Ain't that the truth?"

35   "People are certainly not nice like they used to be," said the grandmother.

"Two fellers come in here last week," Red Sammy said, "driving a Chrysler. It was a old beat-up car but it was a good one and these boys looked all right to me. Said they worked at the mill and you know I let them fellers charge the gas they bought? Now why did I do that?"

3. Jukebox.

"Because you're a good man!" the grandmother said at once.

"Yes'm, I suppose so," Red Sam said as if he were struck with this answer.

His wife brought the orders, carrying the five plates all at once without a tray, two in each hand and one balanced on her arm. "It isn't a soul in this green world of God's that you can trust," she said. "And I don't count nobody out of that, not nobody," she repeated, looking at Red Sammy.

"Did you read about that criminal, The Misfit, that's escaped?" asked the grandmother. 40

"I wouldn't be a bit surprised if he didn't attact this place right here," said the woman. "If he hears about it being here, I wouldn't be none surprised to see him. If he hears it's two cent in the cash register, I wouldn't be a tall surprised if he . . ."

"That'll do," Red Sam said. "Go bring these people their Co'-Colas," and the woman went off to get the rest of the order.

"A good man is hard to find," Red Sammy said. "Everything is getting terrible. I remember the day you could go off and leave your screen door unlatched. Not no more."

He and the grandmother discussed better times. The old lady said that in her opinion Europe was entirely to blame for the way things were now. She said the way Europe acted you would think we were made of money and Red Sam said it was no use talking about it, she was exactly right. The children ran outside into the white sunlight and looked at the monkey in the lacy chinaberry tree. He was busy catching fleas on himself and biting each one carefully between his teeth as if it were a delicacy.

They drove off again into the hot afternoon. The grandmother took cat naps 45 and woke up every few minutes with her own snoring. Outside of Toombsboro she woke up and recalled an old plantation that she had visited in this neighborhood once when she was a young lady. She said the house had six white columns across the front and that there was an avenue of oaks leading up to it and two little wooden trellis arbors on either side in front where you sat down with your suitor after a stroll in the garden. She recalled exactly which road to turn off to get to it. She knew that Bailey would not be willing to lose any time looking at an old house, but the more she talked about it, the more she wanted to see it once again and find out if the little twin arbors were still standing. "There was a secret panel in this house," she said craftily, not telling the truth but wishing that she were, "and the story went that all the family silver was hidden in it when Sherman came through but it was never found . . ."

"Hey!" John Wesley said. "Let's go see it! We'll find it! We'll poke all the woodwork and find it! Who lives there? Where do you turn off at? Hey Pop, can't we turn off there?"

"We never have seen a house with a secret panel!" June Star shrieked. "Let's go to the house with the secret panel! Hey Pop, can't we go see the house with the secret panel!"

"It's not far from here, I know," the grandmother said. "It wouldn't take over twenty minutes."

Bailey was looking straight ahead. His jaw was as rigid as a horseshoe. "No," he said.

The children began to yell and scream that they wanted to see the house with 50 the secret panel. John Wesley kicked the back of the front seat and June Star hung over her mother's shoulder and whined desperately into her ear that they never had any fun even on their vacation, that they could never do what THEY wanted to do. The baby began to scream and John Wesley kicked the back of the seat so hard that his father could feel the blows in his kidney.

"All right!" he shouted and drew the car to a stop at the side of the road. "Will you all shut up? Will you all just shut up for one second? If you don't shut up, we won't go anywhere."

"It would be very educational for them," the grandmother murmured.

"All right," Bailey said, "but get this: this is the only time we're going to stop for anything like this. This is the one and only time."

"The dirt road that you have to turn down is about a mile back," the grandmother directed. "I marked it when we passed."

55 "A dirt road," Bailey groaned.

After they had turned around and were headed toward the dirt road, the grandmother recalled other points about the house, the beautiful glass over the front doorway and the candle-lamp in the hall. John Wesley said that the secret panel was probably in the fireplace.

"You can't go inside this house," Bailey said. "You don't know who lives there."

"While you all talk to the people in front, I'll run around behind and get in a window," John Wesley suggested.

"We'll all stay in the car," his mother said.

60 They turned onto the dirt road and the car raced roughly along in a swirl of pink dust. The grandmother recalled the times when there were no paved roads and thirty miles was a day's journey. The dirt road was hilly and there were sudden washes in it and sharp curves on dangerous embankments. All at once they would be on a hill, looking down over the blue tops of trees for miles around, then the next minute, they would be in a red depression with the dust-coated trees looking down on them.

"This place had better turn up in a minute," Bailey said, "or I'm going to turn around."

The road looked as if no one had traveled on it in months.

"It's not much farther," the grandmother said and just as she said it, a horrible thought came to her. The thought was so embarrassing that she turned red in the face and her eyes dilated and her feet jumped up, upsetting her valise in the corner. The instant the valise moved, the newspaper top she had over the basket under it rose with a snarl and Pitty Sing, the cat, sprang onto Bailey's shoulder.

The children were thrown to the floor and their mother, clutching the baby, out the door onto the ground; the old lady was thrown into the front seat. The car turned over once and landed right-side-up in a gulch off the side of the road. Bailey remained in the driver's seat with the cat—gray-striped with a broad white face and an orange nose—clinging to his neck like a caterpillar.

65 As soon as the children saw they could move their arms and legs, they scrambled out of the car, shouting, "We've had an ACCIDENT!" The grandmother was curled up under the dashboard, hoping she was injured so that Bailey's wrath would not come down on her all at once. The horrible thought she had had before the accident was that the house she had remembered so vividly was not in Georgia but in Tennessee.

Bailey removed the cat from his neck with both hands and flung it out the window against the side of a pine tree. Then he got out of the car and started looking for the children's mother. She was sitting against the side of the red gutted ditch, holding the screaming baby, but she only had a cut down her face and a broken shoulder. "We've had an ACCIDENT!" the children screamed in a frenzy of delight.

"But nobody's killed," June Star said with disappointment as the grandmother limped out of the car, her hat still pinned to her head but the broken front brim standing up at a jaunty angle and the violet spray hanging off the side. They all sat down in the ditch, except the children, to recover from the shock. They were all shaking.

"Maybe a car will come along," said the children's mother hoarsely.

"I believe I have injured an organ," said the grandmother, pressing her side, but no one answered her. Bailey's teeth were clattering. He had on a yellow sport shirt with bright blue parrots designed in it and his face was as yellow as the shirt. The grandmother decided that she would not mention that the house was in Tennessee.

The road was about ten feet above and they could see only the tops of the 70 trees on the other side of it. Behind the ditch they were sitting in there were more woods, tall and dark and deep. In a few minutes they saw a car some distance away on top of a hill, coming slowly as if the occupants were watching them. The grandmother stood up and waved both arms dramatically to attract their attention. The car continued to come on slowly, disappeared around a bend and appeared again, moving even slower, on top of the hill they had gone over. It was a big black battered hearselike automobile. There were three men in it.

It came to a stop just over them and for some minutes, the driver looked down with a steady expressionless gaze to where they were sitting, and didn't speak. Then he turned his head and muttered something to the other two and they got out. One was a fat boy in black trousers and a red sweat shirt with a silver stallion embossed on the front of it. He moved around on the right side of them and stood staring, his mouth partly open in a kind of loose grin. The other had on khaki pants and a blue striped coat and a gray hat pulled down very low, hiding most of his face. He came around slowly on the left side. Neither spoke.

The driver got out of the car and stood by the side of it, looking down at them. He was an older man than the other two. His hair was just beginning to gray and he wore silver-rimmed spectacles that gave him a scholarly look. He had a long creased face and didn't have on any shirt or undershirt. He had on blue jeans that were too tight for him and was holding a black hat and a gun. The two boys also had guns.

"We've had an ACCIDENT!" the children screamed.

The grandmother had the peculiar feeling that the bespectacled man was someone she knew. His face was as familiar to her as if she had known him all her life but she could not recall who he was. He moved away from the car and began to come down the embankment, placing his feet carefully so that he wouldn't slip. He had on tan and white shoes and no socks, and his ankles were red and thin. "Good afternoon," he said. "I see you all had you a little spill."

"We turned over twice!" said the grandmother. 75

"Oncet," he corrected. "We seen it happen. Try their car and see will it run, Hiram," he said quietly to the boy with the gray hat.

"What you got that gun for?" John Wesley asked. "Whatcha gonna do with that gun?"

"Lady," the man said to the children's mother, "would you mind calling them children to sit down by you? Children make me nervous. I want all you all to sit down right together there where you're at."

"What are you telling US what to do for?" June Star asked.

80 Behind them the line of woods gaped like a dark open mouth. "Come here," said their mother.

"Look here now," Bailey began suddenly, "we're in a predicament! We're in . . ."

The grandmother shrieked. She scrambled to her feet and stood staring. "You're The Misfit!" she said. "I recognized you at once!"

"Yes'm," the man said, smiling slightly as if he were pleased in spite of himself to be known, "but it would have been better for all of you, lady, if you hadn't of reckernized me."

Bailey turned his head sharply and said something to his mother that shocked even the children. The old lady began to cry and The Misfit reddened.

85 "Lady," he said, "don't you get upset. Sometimes a man says things he don't mean. I don't reckon he meant to talk to you thataway."

"You wouldn't shoot a lady, would you?" the grandmother said and removed a clean handkerchief from her cuff and began to slap at her eyes with it.

The Misfit pointed the toe of his shoe into the ground and made a little hole and then covered it up again. "I would hate to have to," he said.

"Listen," the grandmother almost screamed, "I know you're a good man. You don't look a bit like you have common blood. I know you must come from nice people!"

"Yes mam," he said, "finest people in the world." When he smiled he showed a row of strong white teeth. "God never made a finer woman than my mother and my daddy's heart was pure gold," he said. The boy with the red sweat shirt had come around behind them and was standing with his gun at his hip. The Misfit squatted down on the ground. "Watch them children, Bobby Lee," he said. "You know they make me nervous." He looked at the six of them huddled together in front of him and he seemed to be embarrassed as if he couldn't think of anything to say. "Ain't a cloud in the sky," he remarked, looking up at it. "Don't see no sun but don't see no cloud neither."

90 "Yes, it's a beautiful day," said the grandmother. "Listen," she said, "you shouldn't call yourself The Misfit because I know you're a good man at heart. I can just look at you and tell."

"Hush!" Bailey yelled. "Hush! Everybody shut up and let me handle this!" He was squatting in the position of a runner about to sprint forward but he didn't move.

"I pre-chate that, lady," The Misfit said and drew a little circle in the ground with the butt of his gun.

"It'll take a half a hour to fix this here car," Hiram called, looking over the raised hood of it.

"Well, first you and Bobby Lee get him and that little boy to step over yonder with you," The Misfit said, pointing to Bailey and John Wesley. "The boys want to ast you something," he said to Bailey. "Would you mind stepping back in them woods there with them?"

95 "Listen," Bailey began, "we're in a terrible predicament! Nobody realizes what this is," and his voice cracked. His eyes were as blue and intense as the parrots in his shirt and he remained perfectly still.

The grandmother reached up to adjust her hat brim as if she were going to the woods with him but it came off in her hand. She stood staring at it and after a second she let it fall on the ground. Hiram pulled Bailey up by the arm as if he were assisting an old man. John Wesley caught hold of his father's hand and Bobby Lee followed. They went off toward the woods and just as they reached the dark edge, Bailey turned and supporting himself against a gray naked pine trunk, he shouted, "I'll be back in a minute, Mamma, wait on me!"

"Come back this instant!" his mother shrilled but they all disappeared into the woods.

"Bailey Boy!" the grandmother called in a tragic voice but she found she was looking at The Misfit squatting on the ground in front of her. "I just know you're a good man," she said desperately. "You're not a bit common!"

"Nome, I ain't a good man," The Misfit said after a second as if he had considered her statement carefully, "but I ain't the worst in the world neither. My daddy said I was a different breed of dog from my brothers and sisters. 'You know,' Daddy said, 'it's some that can live their whole life out without asking about it and it's others has to know why it is, and this boy is one of the latters. He's going to be into everything!'" He put on his black hat and looked up suddenly and then away deep into the woods as if he were embarrassed again. "I'm sorry I don't have on a shirt before you ladies," he said, hunching his shoulders slightly. "We buried our clothes that we had on when we escaped and we're just making do until we can get better. We borrowed these from some folks we met," he explained.

"That's perfectly all right," the grandmother said. "Maybe Bailey has an extra 100 shirt in his suitcase."

"I'll look and see terrectly," The Misfit said.

"Where are they taking him?" the children's mother screamed.

"Daddy was a card himself," The Misfit said. "You couldn't put anything over on him. He never got in trouble with the Authorities though. Just had the knack of handling them."

"You could be honest too if you'd only try," said the grandmother. "Think how wonderful it would be to settle down and live a comfortable life and not have to think about somebody chasing you all the time."

The Misfit kept scratching in the ground with the butt of his gun as if he were 105 thinking about it. "Yes'm, somebody is always after you," he murmured.

The grandmother noticed how thin his shoulder blades were just behind his hat because she was standing up looking down on him. "Do you ever pray?" she asked.

He shook his head. All she saw was the black hat wiggle between his shoulder blades. "Nome," he said.

There was a pistol shot from the woods, followed closely by another. Then silence. The old lady's head jerked around. She could hear the wind move through the tree tops like a long satisfied insuck of breath. "Bailey Boy!" she called.

"I was a gospel singer for a while," The Misfit said. "I been most everything. Been in the arm service, both land and sea, at home and abroad, been twict married, been an undertaker, been with the railroads, plowed Mother Earth, been in a tornado, seen a man burnt alive oncet," and looked up at the children's mother and the little girl who were sitting close together, their faces white and their eyes glassy; "I even seen a woman flogged," he said.

"Pray, pray," the grandmother began, "pray, pray. . . ." 110

"I never was a bad boy that I remember of," The Misfit said in an almost dreamy voice, "but somewheres along the line I done something wrong and got sent to the penitentiary. I was buried alive," and he looked up and held her attention to him by a steady stare.

"That's when you should have started to pray," she said. "What did you do to get sent to the penitentiary that first time?"

"Turn to the right, it was a wall," The Misfit said, looking up again at the cloudless sky. "Turn to the left, it was a wall. Look up it was a ceiling, look down it was a floor. I forgot what I done, lady. I set there and set there, trying to remember what it was I done and I ain't recalled it to this day. Oncet in a while, I would think it was coming to me, but it never come."

"Maybe they put you in by mistake," the old lady said vaguely.

115   "Nome," he said. "It wasn't no mistake. They had the papers on me."

"You must have stolen something," she said.

The Misfit sneered slightly. "Nobody had nothing I wanted," he said. "It was a head-doctor at the penitentiary said what I had done was kill my daddy but I known that for a lie. My daddy died in nineteen ought nineteen of the epidemic flu and I never had a thing to do with it. He was buried in the Mount Hopewell Baptist churchyard and you can go there and see for yourself."

"If you would pray," the old lady said, "Jesus would help you."

"That's right," The Misfit said.

120   "Well then, why don't you pray?" she asked trembling with delight suddenly.

"I don't want no hep," he said. "I'm doing all right by myself."

Bobby Lee and Hiram came ambling back from the woods. Bobby Lee was dragging a yellow shirt with bright blue parrots in it.

"Thow me that shirt, Bobby Lee," The Misfit said. The shirt came flying at him and landed on his shoulder and he put it on. The grandmother couldn't name what the shirt reminded her of. "No, lady," The Misfit said while he was buttoning it up, "I found out the crime don't matter. You can do one thing or you can do another, kill a man or take a tire off his car, because sooner or later you're going to forget what it was you done and just be punished for it."

The children's mother had begun to make heaving noises as if she couldn't get her breath. "Lady," he asked, "would you and that little girl like to step off yonder with Bobby Lee and Hiram and join your husband?"

125   "Yes, thank you," the mother said faintly. Her left arm dangled helplessly and she was holding the baby, who had gone to sleep, in the other. "Hep that lady up, Hiram," The Misfit said as she struggled to climb out of the ditch, "and Bobby Lee, you hold onto that little girl's hand."

"I don't want to hold hands with him," June Star said. "He reminds me of a pig."

The fat boy blushed and laughed and caught her by the arm and pulled her off into the woods after Hiram and her mother.

Alone with The Misfit, the grandmother found that she had lost her voice. There was not a cloud in the sky nor any sun. There was nothing around her but woods. She wanted to tell him that he must pray. She opened and closed her mouth several times before anything came out. Finally she found herself saying, "Jesus, Jesus," meaning, Jesus will help you, but the way she was saying it, it sounded as if she might be cursing.

"Yes'm," The Misfit said as if he agreed. "Jesus thown everything off balance. It was the same case with Him as with me except He hadn't committed any crime and they could prove I had committed one because they had the papers on me. Of course," he said, "they never shown me my papers. That's why I sign myself now. I said long ago, you get you a signature and sign everything you do and keep a copy of it. Then you'll know what you done and you can hold up the crime to the punishment and see do they match and in the end you'll have something to prove you ain't been treated right. I call myself The Misfit," he said, "because I can't make what all I done wrong fit what all I gone through in punishment."

There was a piercing scream from the woods, followed closely by a pistol report. "Does it seem right to you, lady, that one is punished a heap and another ain't punished at all?" 130

"Jesus!" the old lady cried. "You've got good blood! I know you wouldn't shoot a lady! I know you come from nice people! Pray! Jesus, you ought not to shoot a lady. I'll give you all the money I've got!"

"Lady," The Misfit said, looking beyond her far into the woods, "there never was a body that give the undertaker a tip."

There were two more pistol reports and the grandmother raised her head like a parched old turkey hen crying for water and called, "Bailey Boy, Bailey Boy!" as if her heart would break.

"Jesus was the only One that ever raised the dead." The Misfit continued, "and He shouldn't have done it. He thown everything off balance. If He did what He said, then it's nothing for you to do but thow away everything and follow Him, and if He didn't, then it's nothing for you to do but enjoy the few minutes you got left the best way you can—by killing somebody or burning down his house or doing some other meanness to him. No pleasure but meanness," he said and his voice had become almost a snarl.

"Maybe He didn't raise the dead," the old lady mumbled, not knowing what she was saying and feeling so dizzy that she sank down in the ditch with her legs twisted under her. 135

"I wasn't there so I can't say He didn't," The Misfit said. "I wisht I had of been there," he said, hitting the ground with his fist. "It ain't right I wasn't there because if I had of been there I would of known. Listen lady," he said in a high voice, "if I had of been there I would of known and I wouldn't be like I am now." His voice seemed about to crack and the grandmother's head cleared for an instant. She saw the man's face twisted close to her own as if he were going to cry and she murmured, "Why you're one of my babies. You're one of my own children!" She reached out and touched him on the shoulder. The Misfit sprang back as if a snake had bitten him and shot her three times through the chest. Then he put his gun down on the ground and took off his glasses and began to clean them.

Hiram and Bobby Lee returned from the woods and stood over the ditch, looking down at the grandmother who half sat and half lay in a puddle of blood with her legs crossed under her like a child's and her face smiling up at the cloudless sky.

Without his glasses, The Misfit's eyes were red-rimmed and pale and defenseless-looking. "Take her off and thow her where you thown the others," he said, picking up the cat that was rubbing itself against his leg.

"She was a talker, wasn't she?" Bobby Lee said, sliding down the ditch with a yodel.

"She would of been a good woman," The Misfit said, "if it had been somebody there to shoot her every minute of her life." 140

"Some fun!" Bobby Lee said.

"Shut up, Bobby Lee," The Misfit said. "It's no real pleasure in life."

1953

FLANNERY O'CONNOR

Good Country People

Besides the neutral expression that she wore when she was alone, Mrs. Freeman had two others, forward and reverse, that she used for all her human dealings. Her forward expression was steady and driving like the advance of a heavy truck. Her eyes never swerved to left or right but turned as the story turned as if they followed a yellow line down the center of it. She seldom used the other expression because it was not often necessary for her to retract a statement, but when she did, her face came to a complete stop, there was an almost imperceptible movement of her black eyes, during which they seemed to be receding, and then the observer would see that Mrs. Freeman, though she might stand there as real as several grain sacks thrown on top of each other, was no longer there in spirit. As for getting anything across to her when this was the case, Mrs. Hopewell had given it up. She might talk her head off. Mrs. Freeman could never be brought to admit herself wrong on any point. She would stand there and if she could be brought to say anything, it was something like, "Well, I wouldn't of said it was and I wouldn't of said it wasn't," or letting her gaze range over the top kitchen shelf where there was an assortment of dusty bottles, she might remark, "I see you ain't ate many of them figs you put up last summer."

They carried on their most important business in the kitchen at breakfast. Every morning Mrs. Hopewell got up at seven o'clock and lit her gas heater and Joy's. Joy was her daughter, a large blonde girl who had an artificial leg. Mrs. Hopewell thought of her as a child though she was thirty-two years old and highly educated. Joy would get up while her mother was eating and lumber into the bathroom and slam the door, and before long, Mrs. Freeman would arrive at the back door. Joy would hear her mother call, "Come on in," and then they would talk for a while in low voices that were indistinguishable in the bathroom. By the time Joy came in, they had usually finished the weather report and were on one or the other of Mrs. Freeman's daughters, Glynese or Carramae, Joy called them Glycerin and Caramel. Glynese, a redhead, was eighteen and had many admirers; Carramae, a blonde, was only fifteen but already married and pregnant. She could not keep anything on her stomach. Every morning Mrs. Freeman told Mrs. Hopewell how many times she had vomited since the last report.

Mrs. Hopewell liked to tell people that Glynese and Carramae were two of the finest girls she knew and that Mrs. Freeman was a *lady* and that she was never ashamed to take her anywhere or introduce her to anybody they might meet. Then she would tell how she had happened to hire the Freemans in the first place and how they were a godsend to her and how she had had them four years. The reason for her keeping them so long was that they were not trash. They were good country people. She had telephoned the man whose name they had given as a reference and he had told her that Mr. Freeman was a good farmer but that his wife was the nosiest woman ever to walk the earth. "She's got to be into everything," the man said. "If she don't get there before the dust settles, you can bet she's dead, that's all. She'll want to know all your business. I can stand him real good," he had said, "but me nor my wife neither could have stood that woman one more minute on this place." That had put Mrs. Hopewell off for a few days.

She had hired them in the end because there were no other applicants but she had made up her mind beforehand exactly how she would handle the woman. Since she was the type who had to be into everything, then, Mrs. Hopewell had decided, she would not only let her be into everything, she would *see to it* that she was into everything—she would give her the responsibility of everything, she would put her in charge. Mrs. Hopewell had no bad qualities of her own but she was able to use other people's in such a constructive way that she never felt the lack. She had hired the Freemans and she had kept them four years.

Nothing is perfect. This was one of Mrs. Hopewell's favorite sayings. Another 5 was: that is life! And still another, the most important, was: well, other people have their opinions too. She would make these statements, usually at the table, in a tone of gentle insistence as if no one held them but her, and the large hulking Joy, whose constant outrage had obliterated every expression from her face, would stare just a little to the side of her, her eyes icy blue, with the look of someone who has achieved blindness by an act of will and means to keep it.

When Mrs. Hopewell said to Mrs. Freeman that life was like that, Mrs. Freeman would say, "I always said so myself." Nothing had been arrived at by anyone that had not first been arrived at by her. She was quicker than Mr. Freeman. When Mrs. Hopewell said to her after they had been on the place a while, "You know, you're the wheel behind the wheel," and winked, Mrs. Freeman had said, "I know it. I've always been quick. It's some that are quicker than others."

"Everybody is different," Mrs. Hopewell said.

"Yes, most people is," Mrs. Freeman said.

"It takes all kinds to make the world."

"I always said it did myself." 10

The girl was used to this kind of dialogue for breakfast and more of it for dinner; sometimes they had it for supper too. When they had no guest they ate in the kitchen because that was easier. Mrs. Freeman always managed to arrive at some point during the meal and to watch them finish it. She would stand in the doorway if it were summer but in the winter she would stand with one elbow on top of the refrigerator and look down on them, or she would stand by the gas heater, lifting the back of her skirt slightly. Occasionally she would stand against the wall and roll her head from side to side. At no time was she in any hurry to leave. All this was very trying on Mrs. Hopewell but she was a woman of great patience. She realized that nothing is perfect and that in the Freemans she had good country people and that if, in this day and age, you get good country people, you had better hang onto them.

She had had plenty of experience with trash. Before the Freemans she had averaged one tenant family a year. The wives of these farmers were not the kind you would want to be around you for very long. Mrs. Hopewell, who had divorced her husband long ago, needed someone to walk over the fields with her; and when Joy had to be impressed for these services, her remarks were usually so ugly and her face so glum that Mrs. Hopewell would say, "If you can't come pleasantly, I don't want you at all," to which the girl, standing square and rigid-shouldered with her neck thrust slightly forward, would reply, "If you want me, here I am— LIKE I AM."

Mrs. Hopewell excused this attitude because of the leg (which had been shot off in a hunting accident when Joy was ten). It was hard for Mrs. Hopewell to realize that her child was thirty-two now and that for more than twenty years she had had only one leg. She thought of her still as a child because it tore her heart to think instead of the poor stout girl in her thirties who had never danced a step or had any *normal* good times. Her name was really Joy but as soon as she was twenty-one and away from home, she had had it legally changed. Mrs. Hopewell was certain that she had thought and thought until she had hit upon the ugliest name in any language. Then she had gone and had the beautiful name, Joy, changed without telling her mother until after she had done it. Her legal name was Hulga.

When Mrs. Hopewell thought the name, Hulga, she thought of the broad blank hull of a battleship. She would not use it. She continued to call her Joy to which the girl responded but in a purely mechanical way.

15   Hulga had learned to tolerate Mrs. Freeman who saved her from taking walks with her mother. Even Glynese and Carramae were useful when they occupied attention that might otherwise have been directed at her. At first she had thought she could not stand Mrs. Freeman for she had found that it was not possible to be rude to her. Mrs. Freeman would take on strange resentments and for days together she would be sullen but the source of her displeasure was always obscure; a direct attack, a positive leer, blatant ugliness to her face—these never touched her. And without warning one day, she began calling her Hulga.

She did not call her that in front of Mrs. Hopewell who would have been incensed but when she and the girl happened to be out of the house together, she would say something and add the name Hulga to the end of it, and the big spectacled Joy-Hulga would scowl and redden as if her privacy had been intruded upon. She considered the name her personal affair. She had arrived at it first purely on the basis of its ugly sound and then the full genius of its fitness had struck her. She had a vision of the name working like the ugly sweating Vulcan who stayed in the furnace and to whom, presumably, the goddess had to come when called. She saw it as the name of her highest creative act. One of her major triumphs was that her mother had not been able to turn her dust into Joy, but the greater one was that she had been able to turn it herself into Hulga. However, Mrs. Freeman's relish for using the name only irritated her. It was as if Mrs. Freeman's beady steel-pointed eyes had penetrated far enough behind her face to reach some secret fact. Something about her seemed to fascinate Mrs. Freeman and then one day Hulga realized that it was the artificial leg. Mrs. Freeman had a special fondness for the details of secret infections, hidden deformities, assaults upon children. Of diseases, she preferred the lingering or incurable. Hulga had heard Mrs. Hopewell give her the details of the hunting accident, how the leg had been literally blasted off, how she had never lost consciousness. Mrs. Freeman could listen to it any time as if it had happened an hour ago.

When Hulga stumped into the kitchen in the morning (she could walk without making the awful noise but she made it—Mrs. Hopewell was certain—because it was ugly-sounding), she glanced at them and did not speak. Mrs. Hopewell would be in her red kimono with her hair tied around her head in rags. She would be sitting at the table, finishing her breakfast and Mrs. Freeman would be hanging by her elbow outward from the refrigerator, looking down at the table. Hulga always put her eggs on the stove to boil and then stood over them with her arms folded, and Mrs. Hopewell would look at her—a kind of indirect gaze divided between her and Mrs. Freeman—and would think that if she would only keep herself up a little, she wouldn't be so bad looking. There was nothing wrong with her face that a pleasant expression wouldn't help. Mrs. Hopewell said that people who looked on the bright side of things would be beautiful even if they were not.

Whenever she looked at Joy this way, she could not help but feel that it would have been better if the child had not taken the Ph.D. It had certainly not brought her out any and now that she had it, there was no more excuse for her to go to school again. Mrs. Hopewell thought it was nice for girls to go to school to have a good time but Joy had "gone through." Anyhow, she would not have been strong enough to go again. The doctors had told Mrs. Hopewell that with the best of care, Joy might see forty-five. She had a weak heart. Joy had made it plain that if it had not been for this condition, she would be far from these red hills[1] and good country people. She would be in a university lecturing to people who knew what she was talking about. And Mrs. Hopewell could very well picture her there, looking like a scarecrow and lecturing to more of the same. Here she went about all day in a six-year-old skirt and a yellow sweat shirt with a faded cowboy on a horse embossed on it. She thought this was funny; Mrs. Hopewell thought it was idiotic and showed simply that she was still a child. She was brilliant but she didn't have a grain of sense. It seemed to Mrs. Hopewell that every year she grew less like other people and more like herself—bloated, rude, and squint-eyed. And she said such strange things! To her own mother she had said—without warning, without excuse, standing up in the middle of a meal with her face purple and her mouth half full—"Woman! do you ever look inside? Do you ever look inside and see what you are *not*? God!" she had cried sinking down again and staring at her plate, "Malebranche[2] was right: we are not our own light. We are not our own light!" Mrs. Hopewell had no idea to this day what brought that on. She had only made the remark, hoping Joy would take it in, that a smile never hurt anyone.

The girl had taken the Ph.D. in philosophy and this left Mrs. Hopewell at a complete loss. You could say, "My daughter is a nurse," or "My daughter is a schoolteacher," or even, "My daughter is a chemical engineer." You could not say, "My daughter is a philosopher." That was something that had ended with the Greeks and Romans. All day Joy sat on her neck in a deep chair, reading. Sometimes she went for walks but she didn't like dogs or cats or birds or flowers or nature or nice young men. She looked at nice young men as if she could smell their stupidity.

One day Mrs. Hopewell had picked up one of the books the girl had just put 20 down and opening it at random, she read, "Science, on the other hand, has to assert its soberness and seriousness afresh and declare that it is concerned solely

1. Like many of O'Connor's stories, this one is set in rural Georgia, in a hilly landscape of red soil similar to the surroundings of O'Connor's mother's farm, Andalusia, near Milledgeville, Georgia.
2. Nicolas Malebranche (1638–1715), renowned philosopher and author of *The Search after Truth*, expressing his skepticism about the human capacity to know one's own mind or the world except through God. Here, Hulga rephrases Malebranche's quotation from St. Augustine to the effect that we are not our own "light."

with what-is. Nothing—how can it be for science anything but a horror and a phantasm? If science is right, then one thing stands firm: science wishes to know nothing of nothing. Such is after all the strictly scientific approach to Nothing. We know it by wishing to know nothing of Nothing."[3] These words had been underlined with a blue pencil and they worked on Mrs. Hopewell like some evil incantation in gibberish. She shut the book quickly and went out of the room as if she were having a chill.

This morning when the girl came in, Mrs. Freeman was on Carramae. "She thrown up four times after supper," she said, "and was up twict in the night after three o'clock. Yesterday she didn't do nothing but ramble in the bureau drawer. All she did. Stand up there and see what she could run up on."

"She's got to eat," Mrs. Hopewell muttered, sipping her coffee, while she watched Joy's back at the stove. She was wondering what the child had said to the Bible salesman. She could not imagine what kind of a conversation she could possibly have had with him.

He was a tall gaunt hatless youth who had called yesterday to sell them a Bible. He had appeared at the door, carrying a large black suitcase that weighted him so heavily on one side that he had to brace himself against the door facing. He seemed on the point of collapse but he said in a cheerful voice, "Good morning, Mrs. Cedars!" and set the suitcase down on the mat. He was not a bad-looking young man though he had on a bright blue suit and yellow socks that were not pulled up far enough. He had prominent face bones and a streak of sticky-looking brown hair falling across his forehead.

"I'm Mrs. Hopewell," she said.

25   "Oh!" he said, pretending to look puzzled but with his eyes sparkling, "I saw it said 'The Cedars' on the mailbox so I thought you was Mrs. Cedars!" and he burst out in a pleasant laugh. He picked up the satchel and under cover of a pant, he fell forward into her hall. It was rather as if the suitcase had moved first, jerking him after it. "Mrs. Hopewell!" he said and grabbed her hand. "I hope you are well!" and he laughed again and then all at once his face sobered completely. He paused and gave her a straight earnest look and said, "Lady, I've come to speak of serious things."

"Well, come in," she muttered, none too pleased because her dinner was almost ready. He came into the parlor and sat down on the edge of a straight chair and put the suitcase between his feet and glanced around the room as if he were sizing her up by it. Her silver gleamed on the two sideboards; she decided he had never been in a room as elegant as this.

"Mrs. Hopewell," he began, using her name in a way that sounded almost intimate, "I know you believe in Chrustian service."

"Well yes," she murmured.

"I know," he said and paused, looking very wise with his head cocked on one side, "that you're a good woman. Friends have told me."

30   Mrs. Hopewell never liked to be taken for a fool. "What are you selling?" she asked.

"Bibles," the young man said and his eye raced around the room before he added, "I see you have no family Bible in your parlor, I see that is the one lack you got!"

3. Passage from German philosopher Martin Heidegger's (1889–1976) inaugural lecture (1929) at the University of Freiburg, "What Is Metaphysics?"

Mrs. Hopewell could not say, "My daughter is an atheist and won't let me keep the Bible in the parlor." She said, stiffening slightly, "I keep my Bible by my bedside." This was not the truth. It was in the attic somewhere.

"Lady," he said, "the word of God ought to be in the parlor."

"Well, I think that's a matter of taste," she began. "I think. . . ."

"Lady," he said, "for a Chrustian, the word of God ought to be in every room 35 in the house besides in his heart. I know you're a Chrustian because I can see it in every line of your face."

She stood up and said, "Well, young man, I don't want to buy a Bible and I smell my dinner burning."

He didn't get up. He began to twist his hands and looking down at them, he said softly, "Well lady, I'll tell you the truth—not many people want to buy one nowadays and besides, I know I'm real simple. I don't know how to say a thing but to say it. I'm just a country boy." He glanced up into her unfriendly face. "People like you don't like to fool with country people like me!"

"Why!" she cried, "good country people are the salt of the earth! Besides, we all have different ways of doing, it takes all kinds to make the world go 'round. That's life!"

"You said a mouthful," he said.

"Why, I think there aren't enough good country people in the world!" she 40 said, stirred. "I think that's what's wrong with it!"

His face had brightened. "I didn't inraduce myself," he said. "I'm Manley Pointer from out in the country around Willohobie, not even from a place, just from near a place."

"You wait a minute," she said. "I have to see about my dinner." She went out to the kitchen and found Joy standing near the door where she had been listening.

"Get rid of the salt of the earth," she said, "and let's eat."

Mrs. Hopewell gave her a pained look and turned the heat down under the vegetables. "*I* can't be rude to anybody," she murmured and went back into the parlor.

He had opened the suitcase and was sitting with a Bible on each knee. 45

"You might as well put those up," she told him. "I don't want one."

"I appreciate your honesty," he said. "You don't see any more real honest people unless you go way out in the country."

"I know," she said, "real genuine folks!" Through the crack in the door she heard a groan.

"I guess a lot of boys come telling you they're working their way through college," he said, "but I'm not going to tell you that. Somehow," he said, "I don't want to go to college. I want to devote my life to Chrustian service. See," he said, lowering his voice, "I got this heart condition. I may not live long. When you know it's something wrong with you and you may not live long, well then, lady . . ." He paused, with his mouth open, and stared at her.

He and Joy had the same condition! She knew that her eyes were filling 50 with tears but she collected herself quickly and murmured, "Won't you stay for dinner? We'd love to have you!" and was sorry the instant she heard herself say it.

"Yes mam," he said in an abashed voice, "I would sher love to do that!"

Joy had given him one look on being introduced to him and then throughout the meal had not glanced at him again. He had addressed several remarks to her, which she had pretended not to hear. Mrs. Hopewell could not understand deliberate rudeness, although she lived with it, and she felt she had always to overflow with hospitality to make up for Joy's lack of courtesy. She urged him to talk about himself and he did. He said he was the seventh child of twelve and that his father had been crushed under a tree when he himself was eight year old. He had been crushed very badly, in fact, almost cut in two and was practically not recognizable. His mother had got along the best she could by hard working and she had always seen that her children went to Sunday School and that they read the Bible every evening. He was now nineteen year old and he had been selling Bibles for four months. In that time he had sold seventy-seven Bibles and had the promise of two more sales. He wanted to become a missionary because he thought that was the way you could do most for people. "He who losest his life shall find it," he said simply and he was so sincere, so genuine and earnest that Mrs. Hopewell would not for the world have smiled. He prevented his peas from sliding onto the table by blocking them with a piece of bread which he later cleaned his plate with. She could see Joy observing sidewise how he handled his knife and fork and she saw too that every few minutes, the boy would dart a keen appraising glance at the girl as if he were trying to attract her attention.

After dinner Joy cleared the dishes off the table and disappeared and Mrs. Hopewell was left to talk with him. He told her again about his childhood and his father's accident and about various things that had happened to him. Every five minutes or so she would stifle a yawn. He sat for two hours until finally she told him she must go because she had an appointment in town. He packed his Bibles and thanked her and prepared to leave, but in the doorway he stopped and wrung her hand and said that not on any of his trips had he met a lady as nice as her and he asked if he could come again. She had said she would always be happy to see him.

Joy had been standing in the road, apparently looking at something in the distance, when he came down the steps toward her, bent to the side with his heavy valise. He stopped where she was standing and confronted her directly. Mrs. Hopewell could not hear what he said but she trembled to think what Joy would say to him. She could see that after a minute Joy said something and that then the boy began to speak again, making an excited gesture with his free hand. After a minute Joy said something else at which the boy began to speak once more. Then to her amazement, Mrs. Hopewell saw the two of them walk off together, toward the gate. Joy had walked all the way to the gate with him and Mrs. Hopewell could not imagine what they had said to each other, and she had not yet dared to ask.

55   Mrs. Freeman was insisting upon her attention. She had moved from the refrigerator to the heater so that Mrs. Hopewell had to turn and face her in order to seem to be listening. "Glynese gone out with Harvey Hill again last night," she said. "She had this sty."

"Hill," Mrs. Hopewell said absently, "is that the one who works in the garage?"

"Nome,[4] he's the one that goes to chiropracter school," Mrs. Freeman said. "She had this sty. Been had it two days. So she says when he brought her in the other night he says, 'Lemme get rid of that sty for you,' and she says, 'How?' and he says, 'You just lay yourself down acrost the seat of that car and I'll show you.'

---

4. Contraction of "No, ma'am."

So she done it and he popped her neck. Kept on a-popping it several times until she made him quit. This morning," Mrs. Freeman said, "she ain't got no sty. She ain't got no traces of a sty."

"I never heard of that before," Mrs. Hopewell said.

"He ast her to marry him before the Ordinary,"[5] Mrs. Freeman went on, "and she told him she wasn't going to be married in no *office*."

"Well, Glynese is a fine girl," Mrs. Hopewell said. "Glynese and Carramae are both fine girls."

"Carramae said when her and Lyman was married Lyman said it sure felt sacred to him. She said he said he wouldn't take five hundred dollars for being married by a preacher."

"How much would he take?" the girl asked from the stove.

"He said he wouldn't take five hundred dollars," Mrs. Freeman repeated.

"Well we all have work to do," Mrs. Hopewell said.

"Lyman said it just felt more sacred to him," Mrs. Freeman said. "The doctor wants Carramae to eat prunes. Says instead of medicine. Says them cramps is coming from pressure. You know where I think it is?"

"She'll be better in a few weeks," Mrs. Hopewell said.

"In the tube,"[6] Mrs. Freeman said. "Else she wouldn't be as sick as she is."

Hulga had cracked her two eggs into a saucer and was bringing them to the table along with a cup of coffee that she had filled too full. She sat down carefully and began to eat, meaning to keep Mrs. Freeman there by questions if for any reason she showed an inclination to leave. She could perceive her mother's eye on her. The first round-about question would be about the Bible salesman and she did not wish to bring it on. "How did he pop her neck?" she asked.

Mrs. Freeman went into a description of how he had popped her neck. She said he owned a '55 Mercury but that Glynese said she would rather marry a man with only a '36 Plymouth who would be married by a preacher. The girl asked what if he had a '32 Plymouth and Mrs. Freeman said what Glynese had said was a '36 Plymouth.

Mrs. Hopewell said there were not many girls with Glynese's common sense. She said what she admired in those girls was their common sense. She said that reminded her that they had had a nice visitor yesterday, a young man selling Bibles. "Lord," she said, "he bored me to death but he was so sincere and genuine I couldn't be rude to him. He was just good country people, you know," she said, "—just the salt of the earth."

"I seen him walk up," Mrs. Freeman said, "and then later—I seen him walk off," and Hulga could feel the slight shift in her voice, the slight insinuation, that he had not walked off alone, had he? Her face remained expressionless but the color rose into her neck and she seemed to swallow it down with the next spoonful of egg. Mrs. Freeman was looking at her as if they had a secret together.

"Well, it takes all kinds of people to make the world go 'round," Mrs. Hopewell said. "It's very good we aren't all alike."

"Some people are more alike than others," Mrs. Freeman said.

5. That is, a legal official, in the local county courthouse.
6. That is, an ectopic or tubal pregnancy outside the uterus, a life-threatening condition for both mother and baby.

Hulga got up and stumped, with about twice the noise that was necessary, into her room and locked the door. She was to meet the Bible salesman at ten o'clock at the gate. She had thought about it half the night. She had started thinking of it as a great joke and then she had begun to see profound implications in it. She had lain in bed imagining dialogues for them that were insane on the surface but that reached below to depths that no Bible salesman would be aware of. Their conversation yesterday had been of this kind.

75 He had stopped in front of her and had simply stood there. His face was bony and sweaty and bright, with a little pointed nose in the center of it, and his look was different from what it had been at the dinner table. He was gazing at her with open curiosity, with fascination, like a child watching a new fantastic animal at the zoo, and he was breathing as if he had run a great distance to reach her. His gaze seemed somehow familiar but she could not think where she had been regarded with it before. For almost a minute he didn't say anything. Then on what seemed an insuck of breath, he whispered, "You ever ate a chicken that was two days old?"

The girl looked at him stonily. He might have just put this question up for consideration at the meeting of a philosophical association. "Yes," she presently replied as if she had considered it from all angles.

"It must have been mighty small!" he said triumphantly and shook all over with little nervous giggles, getting very red in the face, and subsiding finally into his gaze of complete admiration, while the girl's expression remained exactly the same.

"How old are you?" he asked softly.

She waited some time before she answered. Then in a flat voice she said, "Seventeen."

80 His smiles came in succession like waves breaking on the surface of a little lake. "I see you got a wooden leg," he said. "I think you're brave. I think you're real sweet."

The girl stood blank and solid and silent.

"Walk to the gate with me," he said. "You're a brave sweet little thing and I liked you the minute I seen you walk in the door."

Hulga began to move forward.

"What's your name?" he asked, smiling down on the top of her head.

85 "Hulga," she said.

"Hulga," he murmured, "Hulga. Hulga. I never heard of anybody name Hulga before. You're shy, aren't you, Hulga?" he asked.

She nodded, watching his large red hand on the handle of the giant valise.

"I like girls that wear glasses," he said. "I think a lot. I'm not like these people that a serious thought don't ever enter their heads. It's because I may die."

"I may die too," she said suddenly and looked up at him. His eyes were very small and brown, glittering feverishly.

90 "Listen," he said, "don't you think some people was meant to meet on account of what all they got in common and all? Like they both think serious thoughts and all?" He shifted the valise to his other hand so that the hand nearest her was free. He caught hold of her elbow and shook it a little. "I don't work on Saturday," he said. "I like to walk in the woods and see what Mother Nature is wearing. O'er the hills and far away. Pic-nics and things. Couldn't we go on a pic-nic tomorrow? Say yes, Hulga," he said and gave her a dying look as if he felt

his insides about to drop out of him. He had even seemed to sway slightly toward her.

During the night she had imagined that she seduced him. She imagined that the two of them walked on the place until they came to the storage barn beyond the two back fields and there, she imagined, that things came to such a pass that she very easily seduced him and that then, of course, she had to reckon with his remorse. True genius can get an idea across even to an inferior mind. She imagined that she took his remorse in hand and changed it into a deeper understanding of life. She took all his shame away and turned it into something useful.

She set off for the gate at exactly ten o'clock, escaping without drawing Mrs. Hopewell's attention. She didn't take anything to eat, forgetting that food is usually taken on a picnic. She wore a pair of slacks and a dirty white shirt, and as an afterthought, she had put some Vapex[7] on the collar of it since she did not own any perfume. When she reached the gate no one was there.

She looked up and down the empty highway and had the furious feeling that she had been tricked, that he had only meant to make her walk to the gate after the idea of him. Then suddenly he stood up, very tall, from behind a bush on the opposite embankment. Smiling, he lifted his hat which was new and wide-brimmed. He had not worn it yesterday and she wondered if he had bought it for the occasion. It was toast-colored with a red and white band around it and was slightly too large for him. He stepped from behind the bush still carrying the black valise. He had on the same suit and the same yellow socks sucked down in his shoes from walking. He crossed the highway and said, "I knew you'd come!"

The girl wondered acidly how he had known this. She pointed to the valise and asked, "Why did you bring your Bibles?"

He took her elbow, smiling down on her as if he could not stop. "You can 95 never tell when you'll need the word of God, Hulga," he said. She had a moment in which she doubted that this was actually happening and then they began to climb the embankment. They went down into the pasture toward the woods. The boy walked lightly by her side, bouncing on his toes. The valise did not seem to be heavy today; he even swung it. They crossed half the pasture without saying anything and then, putting his hand easily on the small of her back, he asked softly, "Where does your wooden leg join on?"

She turned an ugly red and glared at him and for an instant the boy looked abashed. "I didn't mean you no harm," he said. "I only meant you're so brave and all. I guess God takes care of you."

"No," she said, looking forward and walking fast, "I don't even believe in God."

At this he stopped and whistled. "No!" he exclaimed as if he were too astonished to say anything else.

She walked on and in a second he was bouncing at her side, fanning with his hat. "That's very unusual for a girl," he remarked, watching her out of the corner of his eye. When they reached the edge of the wood, he put his hand on her back again and drew her against him without a word and kissed her heavily.

The kiss, which had more pressure than feeling behind it, produced that 100 extra surge of adrenaline in the girl that enables one to carry a packed trunk out

7. Brand of nasal decongestant.

of a burning house, but in her, the power went at once to the brain. Even before he released her, her mind, clear and detached and ironic anyway, was regarding him from a great distance, with amusement but with pity. She had never been kissed before and she was pleased to discover that it was an unexceptional experience and all a matter of the mind's control. Some people might enjoy drain water if they were told it was vodka. When the boy, looking expectant but uncertain, pushed her gently away, she turned and walked on, saying nothing as if such business, for her, were common enough.

He came along panting at her side, trying to help her when he saw a root that she might trip over. He caught and held back the long swaying blades of thorn vine until she had passed beyond them. She led the way and he came breathing heavily behind her. Then they came out on a sunlit hillside, sloping softly into another one a little smaller. Beyond, they could see the rusted top of the old barn where the extra hay was stored.

The hill was sprinkled with small pink weeds. "Then you ain't saved?" he asked suddenly, stopping.

The girl smiled. It was the first time she had smiled at him at all. "In my economy," she said, "I'm saved and you are damned but I told you I didn't believe in God."

Nothing seemed to destroy the boy's look of admiration. He gazed at her now as if the fantastic animal at the zoo had put its paw through the bars and given him a loving poke. She thought he looked as if he wanted to kiss her again and she walked on before he had the chance.

105   "Ain't there somewheres we can sit down sometime?" he murmured, his voice softening toward the end of the sentence.

"In that barn," she said.

They made for it rapidly as if it might slide away like a train. It was a large two-story barn, cool and dark inside. The boy pointed up the ladder that led into the loft and said, "It's too bad we can't go up there."

"Why can't we?" she asked.

"Yer leg," he said reverently.

110   The girl gave him a contemptuous look and putting both hands on the ladder, she climbed it while he stood below, apparently awestruck. She pulled herself expertly through the opening and then looked down at him and said, "Well, come on if you're coming," and he began to climb the ladder, awkwardly bringing the suitcase with him.

"We won't need the Bible," she observed.

"You never can tell," he said, panting. After he had got into the loft, he was a few seconds catching his breath. She had sat down in a pile of straw. A wide sheath of sunlight, filled with dust particles, slanted over her. She lay back against a bale, her face turned away, looking out the front opening of the barn where hay was thrown from a wagon into the loft. The two pink-speckled hillsides lay back against a dark ridge of woods. The sky was cloudless and cold blue. The boy dropped down by her side and put one arm under her and the other over her and began methodically kissing her face, making little noises like a fish. He did not remove his hat but it was pushed far enough back not to interfere. When her glasses got in his way, he took them off of her and slipped them into his pocket.

The girl at first did not return any of the kisses but presently she began to and after she had put several on his cheek, she reached his lips and remained there, kissing him again and again as if she were trying to draw all the breath out of him. His breath was clear and sweet like a child's and the kisses were sticky like a child's. He mumbled about loving her and about knowing when he first seen her that he loved her, but the mumbling was like the sleepy fretting of a child being put to sleep by his mother. Her mind, throughout this, never stopped or lost itself for a second to her feelings. "You ain't said you loved me none," he whispered finally, pulling back from her. "You got to say that."

She looked away from him off into the hollow sky and then down at a black ridge and then down farther into what appeared to be two green swelling lakes. She didn't realize he had taken her glasses but this landscape could not seem exceptional to her for she seldom paid any close attention to her surroundings.

"You got to say it," he repeated. "You got to say you love me."   115

She was always careful how she committed herself. "In a sense," she began, "if you use the word loosely, you might say that. But it's not a word I use. I don't have illusions. I'm one of those people who see *through* to nothing."

The boy was frowning. "You got to say it. I said it and you got to say it," he said.

The girl looked at him almost tenderly. "You poor baby," she murmured. "It's just as well you don't understand," and she pulled him by the neck, face-down, against her. "We are all damned," she said, "but some of us have taken off our blindfolds and see that there's nothing to see. It's a kind of salvation."

The boy's astonished eyes looked blankly through the ends of her hair. "Okay," he almost whined, "but do you love me or don'tcher?"

"Yes," she said and added, "in a sense. But I must tell you something. There   120 mustn't be anything dishonest between us." She lifted his head and looked him in the eye. "I am thirty years old," she said. "I have a number of degrees."

The boy's look was irritated but dogged. "I don't care," he said. "I don't care a thing about what all you done. I just want to know if you love me or don'tcher?" and he caught her to him and wildly planted her face with kisses until she said, "Yes, yes."

"Okay then," he said, letting her go. "Prove it."

She smiled, looking dreamily out on the shifty landscape. She had seduced him without even making up her mind to try. "How?" she asked, feeling that he should be delayed a little.

He leaned over and put his lips to her ear. "Show me where your wooden leg joins on," he whispered.

The girl uttered a sharp little cry and her face instantly drained of color. The   125 obscenity of the suggestion was not what shocked her. As a child she had some-times been subject to feelings of shame but education had removed the last traces of that as a good surgeon scrapes for cancer; she would no more have felt it over what he was asking than she would have believed in his Bible. But she was as sensitive about the artificial leg as a peacock about his tail. No one ever touched it but her. She took care of it as someone else would his soul, in private and almost with her own eyes turned away. "No," she said.

"I known it," he muttered, sitting up. "You're just playing me for a sucker."

"Oh no no!" she cried. "It joins on at the knee. Only at the knee. Why do you want to see it?"

The boy gave her a long penetrating look. "Because," he said, "it's what makes you different. You ain't like anybody else."

She sat staring at him. There was nothing about her face or her round freezing-blue eyes to indicate that this had moved her; but she felt as if her heart had stopped and left her mind to pump her blood. She decided that for the first time in her life she was face to face with real innocence. This boy, with an instinct that came from beyond wisdom, had touched the truth about her. When after a minute, she said in a hoarse high voice, "All right," it was like surrendering to him completely. It was like losing her own life and finding it again, miraculously, in his.

130   Very gently he began to roll the slack leg up. The artificial limb, in a white sock and brown flat shoe, was bound in a heavy material like canvas and ended in an ugly jointure where it was attached to the stump. The boy's face and his voice were entirely reverent as he uncovered it and said, "Now show me how to take it off and on."

She took it off for him and put it back on again and then he took it off himself, handling it as tenderly as if it were a real one. "See!" he said with a delighted child's face. "Now I can do it myself!"

"Put it back on," she said. She was thinking that she would run away with him and that every night he would take the leg off and every morning put it back on again. "Put it back on," she said.

"Not yet," he murmured, setting it on its foot out of her reach. "Leave it off for a while. You got me instead."

She gave a little cry of alarm but he pushed her down and began to kiss her again. Without the leg she felt entirely dependent on him. Her brain seemed to have stopped thinking altogether and to be about some other function that it was not very good at. Different expressions raced back and forth over her face. Every now and then the boy, his eyes like two steel spikes, would glance behind him where the leg stood. Finally she pushed him off and said, "Put it back on me now."

135   "Wait," he said. He leaned the other way and pulled the valise toward him and opened it. It had a pale blue spotted lining and there were only two Bibles in it. He took one of these out and opened the cover of it. It was hollow and contained a pocket flask of whiskey, a pack of cards, and a small blue box with printing on it. He laid these out in front of her one at a time in an evenly-spaced row, like one presenting offerings at the shrine of a goddess. He put the blue box in her hand. THIS PRODUCT TO BE USED ONLY FOR THE PREVENTION OF DISEASE, she read, and dropped it. The boy was unscrewing the top of the flask. He stopped and pointed, with a smile, to the deck of cards. It was not an ordinary deck but one with an obscene picture on the back of each card. "Take a swig," he said, offering her the bottle first. He held it in front of her, but like one mesmerized, she did not move.

Her voice when she spoke had an almost pleading sound. "Aren't you," she murmured, "aren't you just good country people?"

The boy cocked his head. He looked as if he were just beginning to understand that she might be trying to insult him. "Yeah," he said, curling his lip slightly, "but it ain't held me back none. I'm as good as you any day in the week."

"Give me my leg," she said.

He pushed it farther away with his foot. "Come on now, let's begin to have us a good time," he said coaxingly. "We ain't got to know one another good yet."

"Give me my leg!" she screamed and tried to lunge for it but he pushed her 140 down easily.

"What's the matter with you all of a sudden?" he asked, frowning as he screwed the top on the flask and put it quickly back inside the Bible. "You just a while ago said you didn't believe in nothing. I thought you was some girl!"

Her face was almost purple. "You're a Christian!" she hissed. "You're a fine Christian! You're just like them all—say one thing and do another. You're a perfect Christian, you're . . ."

The boy's mouth was set angrily. "I hope you don't think," he said in a lofty indignant tone, "that I believe in that crap! I may sell Bibles but I know which end is up and I wasn't born yesterday and I know where I'm going!"

"Give me my leg!" she screeched. He jumped up so quickly that she barely saw him sweep the cards and the blue box into the Bible and throw the Bible into the valise. She saw him grab the leg and then she saw it for an instant slanted forlornly across the inside of the suitcase with a Bible at either side of its opposite ends. He slammed the lid shut and snatched up the valise and swung it down the hole and then stepped through himself.

When all of him had passed but his head, he turned and regarded her with a 145 look that no longer had any admiration in it. "I've gotten a lot of interesting things," he said. "One time I got a woman's glass eye this way. And you needn't to think you'll catch me because Pointer ain't really my name. I use a different name at every house I call at and don't stay nowhere long. And I'll tell you another thing, Hulga," he said, using the name as if he didn't think much of it, "you ain't so smart. I been believing in nothing ever since I was born!" and then the toast-colored hat disappeared down the hole and the girl was left, sitting on the straw in the dusty sunlight. When she turned her churning face toward the opening, she saw his blue figure struggling successfully over the green speckled lake.

Mrs. Hopewell and Mrs. Freeman, who were in the back pasture, digging up onions, saw him emerge a little later from the woods and head across the meadow toward the highway. "Why, that looks like that nice dull young man that tried to sell me a Bible yesterday," Mrs. Hopewell said, squinting. "He must have been selling them to the Negroes back in there. He was so simple," she said, "but I guess the world would be better off if we were all that simple."

Mrs. Freeman's gaze drove forward and just touched him before he disappeared under the hill. Then she returned her attention to the evil-smelling onion shoot she was lifting from the ground. "Some can't be that simple," she said. "I know I never could."

1955

FLANNERY O'CONNOR

Everything That Rises Must Converge

Her doctor had told Julian's mother that she must lose twenty pounds on account of her blood pressure, so on Wednesday nights Julian had to take her downtown on the bus for a reducing class at the Y. The reducing class was designed for working girls over fifty, who weighed from 165 to 200 pounds. His mother was one of the slimmer ones, but she said ladies did not tell their age or weight. She would not ride the buses by herself at night since they had been integrated, and because the reducing class was one of her few pleasures, necessary for her health, and *free*, she said Julian could at least put himself out to take her, considering all she did for him. Julian did not like to consider all she did for him, but every Wednesday night he braced himself and took her.

She was almost ready to go, standing before the hall mirror, putting on her hat, while he, his hands behind him, appeared pinned to the door frame, waiting like Saint Sebastian for the arrows to begin piercing him.[1] The hat was new and had cost her seven dollars and a half. She kept saying, "Maybe I shouldn't have paid that for it. No, I shouldn't have. I'll take it off and return it tomorrow. I shouldn't have bought it."

Julian raised his eyes to heaven. "Yes, you should have bought it," he said. "Put it on and let's go." It was a hideous hat. A purple velvet flap came down on one side of it and stood up on the other; the rest of it was green and looked like a cushion with the stuffing out. He decided it was less comical than jaunty and pathetic. Everything that gave her pleasure was small and depressed him.

She lifted the hat one more time and set it down slowly on top of her head. Two wings of gray hair protruded on either side of her florid face, but her eyes, sky-blue, were as innocent and untouched by experience as they must have been when she was ten. Were it not that she was a widow who had struggled fiercely to feed and clothe and put him through school and who was supporting him still, "until he got on his feet," she might have been a little girl that he had to take to town.

5   "It's all right, it's all right," he said. "Let's go." He opened the door himself and started down the walk to get her going. The sky was a dying violet and the houses stood out darkly against it, bulbous liver-colored monstrosities of a uniform ugliness though no two were alike. Since this had been a fashionable neighborhood forty years ago, his mother persisted in thinking they did well to have an apartment in it. Each house had a narrow collar of dirt around it in which sat, usually, a grubby child. Julian walked with his hands in his pockets, his head down and thrust forward and his eyes glazed with the determination to make himself completely numb during the time he would be sacrificed to her pleasure.

The door closed and he turned to find the dumpy figure, surmounted by the atrocious hat, coming toward him. "Well," she said, "you only live once and paying a little more for it, I at least won't meet myself coming and going."

"Some day I'll start making money," Julian said gloomily—he knew he never would—"and you can have one of those jokes whenever you take the fit." But first they would move. He visualized a place where the nearest neighbors would be three miles away on either side.

"I think you're doing fine," she said, drawing on her gloves. "You've only been out of school a year. Rome wasn't built in a day."

She was one of the few members of the Y reducing class who arrived in hat and gloves and who had a son who had been to college. "It takes time," she said, "and the world is in such a mess. This hat looked better on me than any of the others, though when she brought it out I said, 'Take that thing back. I wouldn't have it on my head,' and she said, 'Now wait till you see it on,' and when she put

---

1. Discovered to be a Christian, Sebastian, Roman commander in Milan, was tied to a tree, shot with arrows, and left for dead. (He recovered, but when he reasserted his faith he was clubbed to death.)

it on me, I said, 'We-ull,' and she said, 'If you ask me, that hat does something for you and you do something for the hat, and besides,' she said, 'with that hat, you won't meet yourself coming and going.'"

Julian thought he could have stood his lot better if she had been selfish, if she had been an old hag who drank and screamed at him. He walked along, saturated in depression, as if in the midst of his martyrdom he had lost his faith. Catching sight of his long, hopeless, irritated face, she stopped suddenly with a grief-stricken look, and pulled back on his arm. "Wait on me," she said. "I'm going back to the house and take this thing off and tomorrow I'm going to return it. I was out of my head. I can pay the gas bill with that seven-fifty."

He caught her arm in a vicious grip. "You are not going to take it back," he said. "I like it."

"Well," she said, "I don't think I ought . . ."

"Shut up and enjoy it," he muttered, more depressed than ever.

"With the world in the mess it's in," she said, "it's a wonder we can enjoy anything. I tell you, the bottom rail is on the top."

Julian sighed.

"Of course," she said, "if you know who you are, you can go anywhere." She said this every time he took her to the reducing class. "Most of them in it are not our kind of people," she said, "but I can be gracious to anybody. I know who I am."

"They don't give a damn for your graciousness," Julian said savagely. "Knowing who you are is good for one generation only. You haven't the foggiest idea where you stand now or who you are."

She stopped and allowed her eyes to flash at him. "I most certainly do know who I am," she said, "and if you don't know who you are, I'm ashamed of you."

"Oh hell," Julian said.

"Your great-grandfather was a former governor of this state," she said. "Your grandfather was a prosperous land-owner. Your grandmother was a Godhigh."

"Will you look around you," he said tensely, "and see where you are now?" and he swept his arm jerkily out to indicate the neighborhood, which the growing darkness at least made less dingy.

"You remain what you are," she said. "Your great-grandfather had a plantation and two hundred slaves."

"There are no more slaves," he said irritably.

"They were better off when they were," she said. He groaned to see that she was off on that topic. She rolled onto it every few days like a train on an open track. He knew every stop, every junction, every swamp along the way, and knew the exact point at which her conclusion would roll majestically into the station: "It's ridiculous. It's simply not realistic. They should rise, yes, but on their own side of the fence."

"Let's skip it," Julian said.

"The ones I feel sorry for," she said, "are the ones that are half white. They're tragic."

"Will you skip it?"

"Suppose we were half white. We would certainly have mixed feelings."

"I have mixed feelings now," he groaned.

"Well let's talk about something pleasant," she said. "I remember going to Grandpa's when I was a little girl. Then the house had double stairways that went up to what was really the second floor—all the cooking was done on the first. I used to like to stay down in the kitchen on account of the way the walls smelled. I would sit with my nose pressed against the plaster and take deep breaths. Actually the place belonged to the Godhighs but your grandfather Chestny paid the mortgage and saved it for them. They were in reduced circumstances," she said, "but reduced or not, they never forgot who they were."

"Doubtless that decayed mansion reminded them," Julian muttered. He never spoke of it without contempt or thought of it without longing. He had seen it once when he was a child before it had been sold. The double stairways had rotted and been torn down. Negroes were living in it. But it remained in his mind as his mother had known it. It appeared in his dreams regularly. He would stand on the wide porch, listening to the rustle of oak leaves, then wander through the high-ceilinged hall into the parlor that opened onto it and gaze at the worn rugs and faded draperies. It occurred to him that it was he, not she, who could have appreciated it. He preferred its threadbare elegance to anything he could name and it was because of it that all the neighborhoods they had lived in had been a torment to him—whereas she had hardly known the difference. She called her insensitivity "being adjustable."

"And I remember the old darky who was my nurse, Caroline. There was no better person in the world. I've always had a great respect for my colored friends," she said. "I'd do anything in the world for them and they'd . . ."

"Will you for God's sake get off that subject?" Julian said. When he got on a bus by himself, he made it a point to sit down beside a Negro, in reparation as it were for his mother's sins.

"You're mighty touchy tonight," she said. "Do you feel all right?"

35 "Yes I feel all right," he said. "Now lay off."

She pursed her lips. "Well, you certainly are in a vile humor," she observed. "I just won't speak to you at all."

They had reached the bus stop. There was no bus in sight and Julian, his hands still jammed in his pockets and his head thrust forward, scowled down the empty street. The frustration of having to wait on the bus as well as ride on it began to creep up his neck like a hot hand. The presence of his mother was borne in upon him as she gave a pained sigh. He looked at her bleakly. She was holding herself very erect under the preposterous hat, wearing it like a banner of her imaginary dignity. There was in him an evil urge to break her spirit. He suddenly unloosened his tie and pulled it off and put it in his pocket.

She stiffened. "Why must you look like *that* when you take me to town?" she said. "Why must you deliberately embarrass me?"

"If you'll never learn where you are," he said, "you can at least learn where I am."

40 "You look like a—thug," she said.

"Then I must be one," he murmured.

"I'll just go home," she said. "I will not bother you. If you can't do a little thing like that for me . . ."

Rolling his eyes upward, he put his tie back on. "Restored to my class," he muttered. He thrust his face toward her and hissed, "True culture is in the mind, the *mind*," he said, and tapped his head, "the mind."

"It's in the heart," she said, "and in how you do things and how you do things is because of who you *are*."

45 "Nobody in the damn bus cares who you are."

"I care who I am," she said icily.

The lighted bus appeared on top of the next hill and as it approached, they moved out into the street to meet it. He put his hand under her elbow and hoisted her up on the creaking step. She entered with a little smile, as if she were going into a drawing room where everyone had been waiting for her. While he put in the tokens, she sat down on one of the broad front seats for three which faced the aisle. A thin woman with protruding teeth and long yellow hair was sitting on the end of it. His mother moved up beside her and left room for Julian beside herself. He sat down and looked at the floor across the aisle where a pair of thin feet in red and white canvas sandals were planted.

His mother immediately began a general conversation meant to attract anyone who felt like talking. "Can it get any hotter?" she said and removed from her purse a folding fan, black with a Japanese scene on it, which she began to flutter before her.

"I reckon it might could," the woman with the protruding teeth said, "but I know for a fact my apartment couldn't get no hotter."

"It must get the afternoon sun," his mother said. She sat forward and looked up and down the bus. It was half filled. Everybody was white. "I see we have the bus to ourselves," she said. Julian cringed. 50

"For a change," said the woman across the aisle, the owner of the red and white canvas sandals. "I come on one the other day and they were thick as fleas—up front and all through."

"The world is in a mess everywhere," his mother said. "I don't know how we've let it get in this fix."

"What gets my goat is all those boys from good families stealing automobile tires," the woman with the protruding teeth said. "I told my boy, I said you may not be rich but you been raised right and if I ever catch you in any such mess, they can send you on to the reformatory. Be exactly where you belong."

"Training tells," his mother said. "Is your boy in high school?"

"Ninth grade," the woman said. 55

"My son just finished college last year. He wants to write but he's selling typewriters until he gets started," his mother said.

The woman leaned forward and peered at Julian. He threw her such a malevolent look that she subsided against the seat. On the floor across the aisle there was an abandoned newspaper. He got up and got it and opened it out in front of him. His mother discreetly continued the conversation in a lower tone but the woman across the aisle said in a loud voice, "Well that's nice. Selling typewriters is close to writing. He can go right from one to the other."

"I tell him," his mother said, "that Rome wasn't built in a day."

Behind the newspaper Julian was withdrawing into the inner compartment of his mind where he spent most of his time. This was a kind of mental bubble in which he established himself when he could not bear to be a part of what was going on around him. From it he could see out and judge but in it he was safe from any kind of penetration from without. It was the only place where he felt free of the general idiocy of his fellows. His mother had never entered it but from it he could see her with absolute clarity.

The old lady was clever enough and he thought that if she had started from any of the right premises, more might have been expected of her. She lived according to the laws of her own fantasy world, outside of which he had never 60 seen her set foot. The law of it was to sacrifice herself for him after she had first created the necessity to do so by making a mess of things. If he had permitted her sacrifices, it was only because her lack of foresight had made them necessary. All of her life had been a struggle to act like a Chestny without the Chestny goods, and to give him everything she thought a Chestny ought to have; but since, said she, it was fun to struggle, why complain? And when you had won, as she had won, what fun to look back on the hard times! He could not forgive her that she had enjoyed the struggle and that she thought *she* had won.

What she meant when she said she had won was that she had brought him up successfully and had sent him to college and that he had turned out so well—good looking (her teeth had gone unfilled so that his could be straightened), intelligent (he realized he was too intelligent to be a success), and with a future ahead of him (there was of course no future ahead of him). She excused his gloominess on the grounds that he was still growing up and his radical ideas on his lack of practical experience. She said he didn't yet know a thing about "life," that he hadn't even entered the real world—when already he was as disenchanted with it as a man of fifty.

The further irony of all this was that in spite of her, he had turned out so well. In spite of going to only a third-rate college, he had, on his own initiative, come out with a first-rate education; in spite of growing up dominated by a small mind, he had ended up with a large one; in spite of all her foolish views, he was free of prejudice and unafraid to face facts. Most miraculous of all, instead of being blinded by love for her as she was for him, he had cut himself emotionally free of her and could see her with complete objectivity. He was not dominated by his mother.

The bus stopped with a sudden jerk and shook him from his meditation. A woman from the back lurched forward with little steps and barely escaped falling in his newspaper as she righted herself. She got off and a large Negro got on. Julian kept his paper lowered to watch. It gave him a certain satisfaction to see injustice in daily operation. It confirmed his view that with a few exceptions there was no one worth knowing within a radius of three hundred miles. The Negro was well dressed and carried a briefcase. He looked around and then sat down on the other end of the seat where the woman with the red and white canvas sandals was sitting. He immediately unfolded a newspaper and obscured himself behind it. Julian's mother's elbow at once prodded insistently into his ribs. "Now you see why I won't ride on these buses by myself," she whispered.

The woman with the red and white canvas sandals had risen at the same time the Negro sat down and had gone further back in the bus and taken the seat of the woman who had got off. His mother leaned forward and cast her an approving look.

65   Julian rose, crossed the aisle, and sat down in the place of the woman with the canvas sandals. From this position, he looked serenely across at his mother. Her face had turned an angry red. He stared at her, making his eyes the eyes of a stranger. He felt his tension suddenly lift as if he had openly declared war on her.

He would have liked to get in conversation with the Negro and to talk with him about art or politics or any subject that would be above the comprehension of those around them, but the man remained entrenched behind his paper. He was either ignoring the change of seating or had never noticed it. There was no way for Julian to convey his sympathy.

His mother kept her eyes fixed reproachfully on his face. The woman with the protruding teeth was looking at him avidly as if he were a type of monster new to her.

"Do you have a light?" he asked the Negro.

Without looking away from his paper, the man reached in his pocket and handed him a packet of matches.

"Thanks," Julian said. For a moment he held the matches foolishly. A NO SMOKING sign looked down upon him from over the door. This alone would not have deterred him; he had no cigarettes. He had quit smoking some months before because he could not afford it. "Sorry," he muttered and handed back the matches. The Negro lowered the paper and gave him an annoyed look. He took the matches and raised the paper again.

His mother continued to gaze at him but she did not take advantage of his momentary discomfort. Her eyes retained their battered look. Her face seemed to be unnaturally red, as if her blood pressure had risen. Julian allowed no glimmer of sympathy to show on his face. Having got the advantage, he wanted desperately to keep it and carry it through. He would have liked to teach her a lesson that would last her a while, but there seemed no way to continue the point. The Negro refused to come out from behind his paper.

Julian folded his arms and looked stolidly before him, facing her but as if he did not see her, as if he had ceased to recognize her existence. He visualized a scene in which, the bus having reached their stop, he would remain in his seat and when she said, "Aren't you going to get off?" he would look at her as a stranger who had rashly addressed him. The corner they got off on was usually deserted, but it was well lighted and it would not hurt her to walk by herself the four blocks to the Y. He decided to wait until the time came and then decide whether or not he would let her get off by herself. He would have to be at the Y at ten to bring her back, but he could leave her wondering if he was going to show up. There was no reason for her to think she could always depend on him.

He retired again into the high-ceilinged room sparsely settled with large pieces of antique furniture. His soul expanded momentarily but then he became aware of his mother across from him and the vision shriveled. He studied her coldly. Her feet in little pumps dangled like a child's and did not quite reach the floor. She was training on him an exaggerated look of reproach. He felt completely detached from her. At that moment he could with pleasure have slapped her as he would have slapped a particularly obnoxious child in his charge.

He began to imagine various unlikely ways by which he could teach her a lesson. He might make friends with some distinguished Negro professor or lawyer and bring him home to spend the evening. He would be entirely justified but her blood pressure would rise to 300. He could not push her to the extent of making her have a stroke, and moreover, he had never been successful at making any Negro friends. He had tried to strike up an acquaintance on the bus with some of the better types, with ones that looked like professors or ministers or lawyers. One morning he had sat down next to a distinguished-looking dark brown man who had answered his questions with a sonorous solemnity but who had turned out to be an undertaker. Another day he had sat down beside a cigar-smoking Negro with a diamond ring on his finger, but after a few stilted pleasantries, the Negro had rung the buzzer and risen, slipping two lottery tickets into Julian's hand as he climbed over him to leave.

75   He imagined his mother lying desperately ill and his being able to secure only a Negro doctor for her. He toyed with that idea for a few minutes and then dropped it for a momentary vision of himself participating as a sympathizer in a sit-in demonstration. This was possible but he did not linger with it. Instead, he approached the ultimate horror. He brought home a beautiful suspiciously Negroid woman. Prepare yourself, he said. There is nothing you can do about it. This is the woman I've chosen. She's intelligent, dignified, even good, and she's suffered and she hasn't thought it *fun*. Now persecute us, go ahead and persecute us. Drive her out of here, but remember, you're driving me too. His eyes were narrowed and through the indignation he had generated, he saw his mother across the aisle, purple-faced, shrunken to the dwarf-like proportions of her moral nature, sitting like a mummy beneath the ridiculous banner of her hat.

He was tilted out of his fantasy again as the bus stopped. The door opened with a sucking hiss and out of the dark a large, gaily dressed, sullen-looking colored woman got on with a little boy. The child, who might have been four, had on a short plaid suit and a Tyrolean hat with a blue feather in it. Julian hoped that he would sit down beside him and that the woman would push in beside his mother. He could think of no better arrangement.

As she waited for her tokens, the woman was surveying the seating possibilities—he hoped with the idea of sitting where she was least wanted. There was something familiar-looking about her but Julian could not place what it was. She was a giant of a woman. Her face was set not only to meet opposition but to seek it out. The downward tilt of her large lower lip was like a warning sign: DON'T TAMPER WITH ME. Her bulging figure was encased in a green crepe dress and her feet overflowed in red shoes. She had on a hideous hat. A purple velvet flap came down on one side of it and stood up on the other; the rest of it was green and looked like a cushion with the stuffing out. She carried a mammoth red pocketbook that bulged throughout as if it were stuffed with rocks.

To Julian's disappointment, the little boy climbed up on the empty seat beside his mother. His mother lumped all children, black and white, into the common category, "cute," and she thought little Negroes were on the whole cuter than little white children. She smiled at the little boy as he climbed on the seat.

Meanwhile the woman was bearing down upon the empty seat beside Julian. To his annoyance, she squeezed herself into it. He saw his mother's face change as the woman settled herself next to him and he realized with satisfaction that this was more objectionable to her than it was to him. Her face seemed almost gray and there was a look of dull recognition in her eyes, as if suddenly she had sickened at some awful confrontation. Julian saw that it was because she and the woman had, in a sense, swapped sons. Though his mother would not realize the symbolic significance of this, she would feel it. His amusement showed plainly on his face.

80   The woman next to him muttered something unintelligible to herself. He was conscious of a kind of bristling next to him, a muted growling like that of an angry cat. He could not see anything but the red pocketbook upright on the bulging green thighs. He visualized the woman as she had stood waiting for her tokens—the ponderous figure, rising from the red shoes upward over the solid hips, the mammoth bosom, the haughty face, to the green and purple hat.

His eyes widened.

The vision of the two hats, identical, broke upon him with the radiance of a brilliant sunrise. His face was suddenly lit with joy. He could not believe that

Fate had thrust upon his mother such a lesson. He gave a loud chuckle so that she would look at him and see that he saw. She turned her eyes on him slowly. The blue in them seemed to have turned a bruised purple. For a moment he had an uncomfortable sense of her innocence, but it lasted only a second before principle rescued him. Justice entitled him to laugh. His grin hardened until it said to her as plainly as if he were saying aloud: Your punishment exactly fits your pettiness. This should teach you a permanent lesson.

Her eyes shifted to the woman. She seemed unable to bear looking at him and to find the woman preferable. He became conscious again of the bristling presence at his side. The woman was rumbling like a volcano about to become active. His mother's mouth began to twitch slightly at one corner. With a sinking heart, he saw incipient signs of recovery on her face and realized that this was going to strike her suddenly as funny and was going to be no lesson at all. She kept her eyes on the woman and an amused smile came over her face as if the woman were a monkey that had stolen her hat. The little Negro was looking up at her with large fascinated eyes. He had been trying to attract her attention for some time.

"Carver!" the woman said suddenly. "Come heah!"

When he saw that the spotlight was on him at last, Carver drew his feet up 85 and turned himself toward Julian's mother and giggled.

"Carver!" the woman said. "You heah me? Come heah!"

Carver slid down from the seat but remained squatting with his back against the base of it, his head turned slyly around toward Julian's mother, who was smiling at him. The woman reached a hand across the aisle and snatched him to her. He righted himself and hung backwards on her knees, grinning at Julian's mother. "Isn't he cute?" Julian's mother said to the woman with the protruding teeth.

"I reckon he is," the woman said without conviction.

The Negress yanked him upright but he eased out of her grip and shot across the aisle and scrambled, giggling wildly, onto the seat beside his love.

"I think he likes me," Julian's mother said, and smiled at the woman. It was 90 the smile she used when she was being particularly gracious to an inferior. Julian saw everything was lost. The lesson had rolled off her like rain on a roof.

The woman stood up and yanked the little boy off the seat as if she were snatching him from contagion. Julian could feel the rage in her at having no weapon like his mother's smile. She gave the child a sharp slap across his leg. He howled once and then thrust his head into her stomach and kicked his feet against her shins. "Behave," she said vehemently.

The bus stopped and the Negro who had been reading the newspaper got off. The woman moved over and set the little boy down with a thump between herself and Julian. She held him firmly by the knee. In a moment he put his hands in front of his face and peeped at Julian's mother through his fingers.

"I see yoooooooo!" she said and put her hand in front of her face and peeped at him.

The woman slapped his hand down. "Quit yo' foolishness," she said, "before I knock the living Jesus out of you!"

Julian was thankful that the next stop was theirs. He reached up and pulled 95 the cord. The woman reached up and pulled it at the same time. Oh my God, he thought. He had the terrible intuition that when they got off the bus together, his mother would open her purse and give the little boy a nickel. The gesture would be as natural to her as breathing. The bus stopped and the woman got up and lunged to the front, dragging the child, who wished to stay on, after her. Julian and his mother got up and followed. As they neared the door, Julian tried to relieve her of her pocketbook.

"No," she murmured, "I want to give the little boy a nickel."

"No!" Julian hissed. "No!"

She smiled down at the child and opened her bag. The bus door opened and the woman picked him up by the arm and descended with him, hanging at her hip. Once in the street she set him down and shook him.

Julian's mother had to close her purse while she got down the bus step but as soon as her feet were on the ground, she opened it again and began to rummage inside. "I can't find but a penny," she whispered, "but it looks like a new one."

100   "Don't do it!" Julian said fiercely between his teeth. There was a streetlight on the corner and she hurried to get under it so that she could better see into her pocketbook. The woman was heading off rapidly down the street with the child still hanging backward on her hand.

"Oh little boy!" Julian's mother called and took a few quick steps and caught up with them just beyond the lamppost. "Here's a bright new penny for you," and she held out the coin, which shone bronze in the dim light.

The huge woman turned and for a moment stood, her shoulders lifted and her face frozen with frustrated rage, and stared at Julian's mother. Then all at once she seemed to explode like a piece of machinery that had been given one ounce of pressure too much. Julian saw the black fist swing out with the red pocketbook. He shut his eyes and cringed as he heard the woman shout, "He don't take nobody's pennies!" When he opened his eyes, the woman was disappearing down the street with the little boy staring wide-eyed over her shoulder. Julian's mother was sitting on the sidewalk.

"I told you not to do that," Julian said angrily. "I told you not to do that!"

He stood over her for a minute, gritting his teeth. Her legs were stretched out in front of her and her hat was on her lap. He squatted down and looked her in the face. It was totally expressionless. "You got exactly what you deserved," he said. "Now get up."

105   He picked up her pocketbook and put what had fallen out back in it. He picked the hat up off her lap. The penny caught his eye on the sidewalk and he picked that up and let it drop before her eyes into the purse. Then he stood up and leaned over and held his hands out to pull her up. She remained immobile. He sighed. Rising above them on either side were black apartment buildings, marked with irregular rectangles of light. At the end of the block a man came out of a door and walked off in the opposite direction. "All right," he said, "suppose somebody happens by and wants to know why you're sitting on the sidewalk?"

She took the hand and, breathing hard, pulled heavily up on it and then stood for a moment, swaying slightly as if the spots of light in the darkness were circling around her. Her eyes, shadowed and confused, finally settled on his face. He did not try to conceal his irritation. "I hope this teaches you a lesson," he said. She leaned forward and her eyes raked his face. She seemed trying to determine his identity. Then, as if she found nothing familiar about him, she started off with a headlong movement in the wrong direction.

"Aren't you going on to the Y?" he asked.

"Home," she muttered.

"Well, are we walking?"

For answer she kept going. Julian followed along, h
saw no reason to let the lesson she had had go withou
explanation of its meaning. She might as well be made t
happened to her. "Don't think that was just an uppity N
"That was the whole colored race which will no longer tak
pennies. That was your black double. She can wear the sar
be sure," he added gratuitously (because he thought it wa
better on her than it did on you. What all this means," he sa
world is gone. The old manners are obsolete and your graciou
a damn." He thought bitterly of the house that had been lost fo.
who you think you are," he said.

She continued to plow ahead, paying no attention to him. He.
undone on one side. She dropped her pocketbook and took no not
and picked it up and handed it to her but she did not take it.

"You needn't act as if the world had come to an end," he said,
hasn't. From now on you've got to live in a new world and face a few
a change. Buck up," he said, "it won't kill you."

She was breathing fast.

"Let's wait on the bus," he said.

"Home," she said thickly.

"I hate to see you behave like this," he said. "Just like a child. I should be
expect more of you." He decided to stop where he was and make her stop an
for a bus. "I'm not going any farther," he said stopping. "We're going on the l

She continued to go on as if she had not heard him. He took a few steps
caught her arm and stopped her. He looked into her face and caught his breath.
was looking into a face he had never seen before. "Tell Grandpa to come get me
she said.

He stared, stricken.

"Tell Caroline to come get me," she said.

Stunned, he let her go and she lurched forward again, walking as if one leg
were shorter than the other. A tide of darkness seemed to be sweeping her from
him. "Mother!" he cried. "Darling, sweetheart, wait!" Crumpling, she fell to the
pavement. He dashed forward and fell at her side, crying, "Mamma, Mamma!"
He turned her over. Her face was fiercely distorted. One eye, large and staring,
moved slightly to the left as if it had become unmoored. The other remained
fixed on him, raked his face again, found nothing and closed.

"Wait here, wait here!" he cried and jumped up and began to run for help
toward a cluster of lights he saw in the distance ahead of him. "Help, help!" he
shouted, but his voice was thin, scarcely a thread of sound. The lights drifted
farther away the faster he ran and his feet moved numbly as if they carried him
nowhere. The tide of darkness seemed to sweep him back to her, postponing
from moment to moment his entry into the world of guilt and sorrow.

1961

Y O'CONNOR

sages from Essays and Letters

m "The Fiction Writer and His Country" (1957)

/]hen I look at stories I have written I find that they are, for the most part,
t people who are poor, who are afflicted in both mind and body, who have
—or at best a distorted—sense of spiritual purpose, and whose actions do
apparently give the reader a great assurance of the joy of life.
et how is this? For I am no disbeliever in spiritual purpose and no vague
iever. I see from the standpoint of Christian orthodoxy. This means that for
the meaning of life is centered in our Redemption by Christ and what I see in
e world I see in its relation to that.

ome may blame preoccupation with the grotesque on the fact that here we have
Southern writer and that this is just the type of imagination that Southern life
fosters. . . . I find it hard to believe that what is observable behavior in one section can be entirely without parallel in another. At least, of late, Southern writers have had the opportunity of pointing out that none of us invented Elvis
Presley and that that youth is himself probably less an occasion for concern
than his popularity, which is not restricted to the Southern part of the country.

When you can assume that your audience holds the same beliefs you do, you
can relax a little and use more normal means of talking to it; when you have to
assume that it does not, then you have to make your vision apparent by shock—to
the hard of hearing you shout, and for the almost-blind you draw large and startling figures.

From "The Nature and Aim of Fiction"[1] *(posthumously published
in 1972)*

. . . The beginning of human knowledge is through the senses, and the fiction
writer begins where human perception begins. He appeals through the senses,
and you cannot appeal to the senses with abstractions. . . . [F]iction is so very
much an incarnational art.

Now the word *symbol* scares a good many people off, just as the word *art* does.
They seem to feel that a symbol is some mysterious thing put in arbitrarily by
the writer to frighten the common reader. . . . They seem to think that it is a way
of saying something that you aren't actually saying, and so . . . they approach it
as if it were a problem in algebra. Find *x*. And when they do find or think they
find this abstraction, *x*, then they go off with an elaborate sense of satisfaction
and the notion that they have "understood" the story. . . .

I think for the fiction writer himself, symbols are something he uses simply
as a matter of course. You might say that these are details that, while having
their essential place in the literal level of the story, operate in depth as well as on
the surface, increasing the story in every direction.

---

1. These selections and those that follow (from "Writing Short Stories") are composites, edited from
O'Connor manuscripts by Sally and Robert Fitzgerald and published in *Mystery and Manners*.

O'Connor alongside self-portrait with peacock

From "Writing Short Stories" (posthumously published in 1972)

Nothing essential to the main experience can be left out of a short story. All the action has to be satisfactorily accounted for in terms of motivation, and there has to be a beginning, a middle, and an end, though not necessarily in that order. . . .

People talk about the theme of a story as if the theme were like the string that a sack of chicken feed is tied with. They think that if you can pick out the theme, the way you pick the right thread in the chicken-feed sack, you can rip the story open and feed the chickens. But this is not the way meaning works in fiction.

When you can state the theme of a story, when you can separate it from the story itself, then you can be sure the story is not a very good one. The meaning of a story has to be embodied in it, has to be made concrete in it. A story is a way to say something that can't be said any other way, and it takes every word in the story to say what the meaning is. You tell a story because a statement would be inadequate.

An idiom characterizes a society, and when you ignore the idiom, you are very likely ignoring the whole social fabric that could make a meaningful character. You can't cut characters off from their society and say much about them as individuals. You can't say anything meaningful about the mystery of a personality unless you put that personality in a believable and significant social context.

From "On Her Own Work" (posthumously published in 1972)

In most English classes the short story has become a kind of literary specimen to be dissected. Every time a story of mine appears in a Freshman anthology, I have a vision of it, with its little organs laid open, like a frog in a bottle.

I realize that a certain amount of this what-is-the-significance has to go on. . . .

I often ask myself what makes a story work, and what makes it hold up as a story, and I have decided that it is probably some action, some gesture of a character that is unlike any other in the story, one which indicates where the real heart of the story lies. This would have to be an action or a gesture which was both totally right and totally unexpected; it would have to be one that was both in character and beyond character; it would have to suggest both the world and eternity. The action or gesture I'm talking about would have to be on the anagogical level, that is, the level which has to do with the Divine life and our participation in it. It would be a gesture that transcended any neat allegory that might have been intended or any pat moral categories a reader could make. It would be a gesture which somehow made contact with mystery.

. . . [I]n my own stories I have found that violence is strangely capable of returning my characters to reality and preparing them to accept their moment of grace. . . .

We hear many complaints about the prevalence of violence in modern fiction, and it is always assumed that this violence is a bad thing and meant to be an end in itself. With the serious writer, violence is never an end in itself. It is the extreme situation that best reveals what we are essentially. . . .

From "Novelist and Believer" (written 1963; posthumously published in 1972)

. . . Great fiction . . . is not simply an imitation of feeling. The good novelist not only finds a symbol for feeling, he finds a symbol and a way of lodging it which tells the intelligent reader whether this feeling is adequate or inadequate, whether it is moral or immoral, whether it is good or evil. And his theology, even in its most remote reaches, will have a direct bearing on this.

. . . The artist penetrates the concrete world in order to find at its depths the image of its source, the image of ultimate reality. This in no way hinders his perception of evil but rather sharpens it, for only when the natural world is seen as good does evil become intelligible as a destructive force and a necessary result of our freedom.

From the Letters

To a Professor of English, 28 March 1961

The meaning of a story should go on expanding for the reader the more he thinks about it, but meaning cannot be captured in an interpretation. If teachers are in the habit of approaching a story as if it were a research problem for which any answer is believable so long as it is not obvious, then I think students will never learn to enjoy fiction. Too much interpretation is certainly worse than too little, and where feeling for a story is absent, theory will not supply it.

To Louise and Tom Gossett, 10 April 1961

I have just read a review of my book [*The Violent Bear It Away*], long and damming [*sic*], which says it don't give us hope and courage and that all novels should give us hope and courage. I think if the novel is to give us virtue the selection of hope and courage is rather arbitrary—why not charity, peace, patience, joy, benignity, long-suffering and fear of the Lord? Or faith? The fact of the matter is that the modern mind opposes courage to faith. It also demands that the novel provide us with gifts that only religion can give. I don't think the novel can offend against the truth, but I think its truths are more particular than general. But this is a large subject and I ain't no aesthetician.

To Roslyn Barnes, 17 June 1961

Can you tell me if the statement: "everything that rises must converge" is a true proposition in physics? I can easily see its moral, historical and evolutionary significance, but I want to know if it is also a correct physical statement.

To John Hawkes, 28 November 1961

You haven't convinced me that I write with the Devil's will or belong in the romantic tradition and I'm prepared to argue some more with you on this if I can remember where we left off at. I think the reason we can't agree on this is because there is a difference in our two devils. My Devil has a name, a history and a definite plan. His name is Lucifer, he's a fallen angel, his sin is pride, and his aim is the destruction of the Divine plan. Now I judge that your Devil is co-equal to God, not his creature: that pride is his virtue not his sin; and that his aim is not to destroy the Divine plan because there isn't any Divine plan to destroy. My Devil is objective and yours is subjective. You say one becomes "evil" when one leaves the herd. I say that depends entirely on what the herd is doing.

To "A," 9 December 1961

Some friends of mine in Texas wrote me that a friend of theirs went into a bookstore looking for a paperback copy of *A Good Man*. The clerk said, "We don't have that one but we have another by that author, called *The Bear That Ran Away With It*." I foresee the trouble I am going to have with "Everything That Rises Must Converge"—"Every Rabbit That Rises Is a Sage."

To Marion Montgomery, 16 June 1963

I never wrote and thanked you for innerducing me at Georgia or for the copy of *The Sermon of Introduction*, but I liked them. They made up for my present lack of popularity with the *Atlanta Journal-Constitution* book page, that alert sheet of Sunday criticism. Did you ever see their mention of "Everything That Rises Must Converge"? Unsigned. I suspect somebody from Atlanta U. did it.

To "A," 1 September 1963

The topical is poison. I got away with it in "Everything That Rises" but only because I say a plague on everybody's house as far as the race business goes.

MARY GORDON
From *"Flannery's Kiss"*[1]

I have been asked to speak at an academic conference devoted to Flannery O'Connor. It is taking place in her home town, Milledgeville, Georgia. I arrive in the middle of a session. One of the speakers is a young Jesuit. He talks about some letters of Flannery O'Connor's that were not included in Sally Fitzgerald's collection. They were written in 1955, to a young Danish man who was a book salesman for her publisher, Harcourt Brace. The Jesuit reads the letters. They are girlish. If there are not triple exclamation points, there should be. She tells the Dane how much she enjoys his company. "If you were here we could talk for about a million years," she says. The Jesuit tracks the Dane down in Denmark. He is now an old man, but he remembers the encounter with Flannery vividly. He tells the Jesuit that he enjoyed Flannery's companionship very much and that one day when he'd taken her for a drive in the country, it occurs to him that

1. From *Michigan Quarterly Review* 43 (Summer 2004): 328–49.

she is a woman, and that she would like him to kiss her. When he does kiss her, the experience horrifies him. He says that Flannery did not know how to kiss. Whereas when he had kissed other women they had offered him soft lips, Flannery presented him with teeth. He remembered that she was chronically ill and he felt like he was kissing a skull. Worried that she was in love with him, he returned quite soon to Denmark. Six months later, he wrote her that he was engaged to be married. Flannery sat down upon receiving the letter and within a matter of days completed her story, "Good Country People," which is about a Bible salesman who is a fetishist of prosthetic devices and who steals a girl's wooden leg when she thinks she is seducing him. Flannery sends the story to the Dane and tells him not to think it's about him, even though the fetishist, whose name is Manley Pointer, is a Bible salesman and the Dane is a book salesman.

In a letter to a friend, Flannery says that the character she most identifies with is the girl whose wooden leg is stolen.

• • •

Flannery O'Connor represents two images of the artist, both of which suggest that the way I have lived my life means I cannot be a real artist. The Catholic and the Romantic, both insisting on the inferiority of human connectedness, the superiority of artistic isolation. Among the least acceptable of human connections for the artist: the connection to one's children. When Faulkner's daughter complained that he didn't pay attention to her, he replied, "Whoever heard of Shakespeare's daughter?" Even Virginia Woolf only spoke of Shakespeare's sister. Until very recently, no important woman writer has had children. I am the mother of a daughter and a son.

For a variety of reasons then, Flannery has for many years caused me to feel unworthy. She has for many years caused me to feel ashamed. And in revenge, the words come to me unbidden, "No one would say I don't know how to kiss."

• • •

Miraculously, Flannery got herself out of Milledgeville, a town that was once the state capital of Georgia, a town noted for its prison and its mental hospital, a town of fewer than ten thousand people not any of whom, perhaps, really understood her, to the Writers' Workshop at the University of Iowa. Having graduated from Iowa, she went to the writers' colony Yaddo, in Saratoga Springs, briefly to New York, and then to live with Sally and Robert Fitzgerald in their house in Connecticut. But then she became ill; she was diagnosed with lupus, the disease that had killed her father. She resigned herself to the life of an invalid. She resigned herself to being taken care of by her mother.

Andalusia, which is pronounced AnduLOOZia, not AndaluTHEEa, is a dairy farm on a gently sloping tract of land. The line of trees which finds its way into so many of O'Connor's stories is visible from the front porch, screened in, with many rockers, looking as if they belonged more properly on the front porch of a small hotel. Just inside the front door, your eye falls on a velvet rope, cordoning something off. It is Flannery's bedroom. I ask the curator if I can go behind the velvet ropes and he says no.

I have rarely seen a more uncomfortable room. Her bed is single, dark wooden, monastic. The desk is near the bed, so she could get to it easily in the days when walking was difficult for her. The bedspread and the drapes are a heavy ungiving blue. There is a black and white picture of the Sacred Heart, books in bookcases, some knickknacks on the mantle which I cannot see from the doorway across which the velvet rope stretches. Propped against the wall are Flannery's crutches, cruel-looking steel devices with semicircles where her arms might rest. The most famous picture of Flannery O'Connor catches her standing on the porch, leaning on her crutches. One of her peacocks stands beside her, a little to her left, on a lower porch step.

. . .

If Flannery had not been ill, would she have traveled? Met new people, had experiences that would have changed the quality of her work? She says in one of her letters: "I have never been anywhere but sick. In a sense sickness is a place, more instructive than a long trip to Europe, and it's always a place where there's no company. . . . The surface hereabouts has always been very flat. I come from a family where the only emotion respectable to show is irritation. In some this tendency produces hives, in others literature, in me both."[2]

If she had traveled, if she had met new people, if she had been able to give and receive more affection (which she gives and receives in her letters, written from the house that she never leaves), would her work have changed?

Do we want that work changed?

. . .

She would deny that her stories are loveless. She would say that the love of God scalds, it does not comfort. Let us take her on her own terms. In her stories there is very little comfort. But there is also very little kindness from the author to her characters. And after reading her for a while, I become impatient at the partialness of her vision. At what is left out. Love. I can see the mocking spelling she might use for the word love. She might spell it *looove*. Or *lurv*.

. . .

O'Connor does not allow her characters to feel the pain of loss. They are denied the experience of grieving. I have often wondered if people are more comfortable with violence than with grief: violence is sharp, clear, bounded; grief can be eternal; it percolates and permutates. Its path is gradual and slow. It's the kind of thing that, as an artist, O'Connor can't do. . . . Her stories, as she says, are romances, in the tradition of Hawthorne. She is interested in the climactic moment, not in the consequences of the climax. She is interested in redemption, but not in forgiveness. Consider the vast tonal difference in the two words: *redemption* and *forgiveness*. Consider the differences in temperature. . . . In Catholic sacramentology, sins can only be forgiven in the sacrament if the sinner asks forgiveness. As we all go on sinning, we must constantly be forgiven. Indeed reforgiven. Redemption took place once in history; forgiveness must be relived. . . .

. . .

In trying to understand my feelings about Flannery O'Connor, the best I can say is that I often do not like Flannery O'Connor, but I can't get over loving her. The woman and the work. I go back and back to her. The reason for that is something she would despise. I am drawn not only to Flannery O'Connor the writer, but to Flannery O'Connor the woman. The woman who lived the life I refused and was grateful not to have to live. But who lived it with purity and gallantry. With singleness of heart. With bravery and good humor. She is the good Catholic I can never be. And yet she made me feel there was a place for me, or for the likes of me.

2. All citations from Flannery O'Connor's letters are from *Flannery O'Connor: The Habit of Being: Letters Selected and with an Introduction by Sally Fitzgerald* (NY: Farrar, Straus, Giroux, 1979). [Author's note]

ANN E. REUMAN

From *"Revolting Fictions: Flannery O'Connor's Letter to Her Mother"*[1]

The parallels between Kafka's portrait of his father and O'Connor's depiction of her mother are striking.[2] In her letters, O'Connor sketches the portrait of Regina Cline O'Connor, who, though slight in build, possessed a commanding presence. Proud of her patrician family and immensely self-assured, Regina was more Cline than O'Connor, conscious of lineage, propriety, and appearance. . . . With proud reverence for the past, she hosted at the Cline House visitors who made the annual garden club pilgrimage to notable, historic homes in the community. When walking through the town center, she would be recognized for her social prominence before her daughter would be remembered for her nationally acclaimed literature. And, as manager of her house and affairs, she expected unquestioning observance of her rules, with gratitude for her generosity. . . . Attentive to appearances, Mrs. O'Connor checked extensions of herself—her house, her daughter—as she checked herself. She displayed the Cline family portraits in her parlor, proud of their visible claim to an honorable heritage; . . . she tried to show her daughter to advantage, spotlighting her public awards and curtaining her less glamorous habits. Writing to the Fitzgeralds about her recent receipt of the Kenyon Fellowship awarded on the basis of her work on *Wise Blood* (her first novel, dedicated to her mother), O'Connor comments, "My mamma [sic] is getting a big bang out of notifying all the kin who didn't like the book that the Rockerfeller [sic] Foundation, etc. etc.—this very casual like on the back of Christmas cards. Money talks, she says, and the name Rockerfeller don't hurt a bit" (*Habit* 49). And in a later note regarding a television play of one of her stories, she remarks, "My mother has been collecting congratulations . . . all week like eggs in a basket" (207).

Yet, while she praised what was already publicly acclaimed, O'Connor's mother worked just as hard to repress the socially unacceptable in her daughter's writing and behavior, urging O'Connor not to publish near the reading populace of Millidgeville a story which she found objectionable from the local standpoint; clearly expressing her disapproval of Flannery's tendency to "make a spectacle" of herself by wearing adolescent clothes into her thirties; and tersely reminding her daughter that her language was a reflection on herself. As O'Connor reports in one of her letters in a seemingly offhand way, her mother once said, "You talk just like a nigger and someday you are going to be away from home and do it and people are going to wonder WHERE YOU CAME FROM" (148; O'Connor's emphasis).

Clearly, under the surface of controlled and witty letters in which Mrs. O'Connor appears to be as Sally Fitzgerald sees her, "relished and admired, joked with and about, altogether clearly loved" (Fitzgerald x) by her daughter, O'Connor hints at a darker and more complicated portrait. . . . Punctuating her letters with refrains of "You can't get ahead of mother" and "My parent is back at large,"

---

1. From *Papers on Language and Literature: A Journal for Scholars and Critics of Language and Literature* 29.2 (1993): 197–214.
2. This essay begins by comparing a letter written by a character in an O'Connor story, "The Enduring Chill," to the 45-page letter that Franz Kafka wrote to his father, accusing him of blighting his life and keeping him as a dependent child.

O'Connor hints at a domineering, invasive, and aloof mother whose presence "never contribute[d] to [O'Connor's] articulateness" (195).

O'Connor's self-portrait is equally complex. Like Kafka, she used distortion to great effect in her work, though unlike the intensely introspective European writer whose tone was embittered, anguished, and tragic, O'Connor most often in her letters refers to herself comically and with an outside observer's eye.... Frequently in reference to the proofs she received of photographs to be pasted on jacket backs, she caricatured herself as being "all teeth and spectacles" (454), looking alternately "like a refugee from deep thought" (33) or like she "had just bitten [her] grandmother and this was one of [her] few pleasures" (31). In an unpublished fragment, O'Connor captioned her look, identifying herself as "a pigeon-toed only-child with a receding chin and a you-leave-me-alone-or-I'll-bite-you complex" (Getz 9)....

Having left Milledgeville to become a writer "on her own," O'Connor earned her Master of Fine Arts degree from the State University of Iowa and went on to work at Yaddo, a writer's colony in Saratoga Springs, New York. The following year, after a brief stay in New York City, O'Connor joined the Fitzgeralds on their Connecticut farm, where, given the choice, she wanted to live and carry on her writing. O'Connor's recurrent bouts with lupus, however, redirected her course, first sending her back to Milledgeville for medical tests and ultimately returning her to her mother's home. Like Kafka, who spent much of his adult life in his parents' house, O'Connor found little escape from her mother's presence while living under the same roof. Bottled up by Southern codes of silence and Catholic respect for elders, and aggravated by dependence on her mother without hope of change in her status, O'Connor's adolescent resentment carried into adulthood, building in intensity and exploding into her fiction.

Clearly there is a change in tone, characterization, and focus in O'Connor's stories written after 1951 when she was forced to live with her mother and move to Andalusia. In her earlier works, O'Connor deals primarily with Georgia folks, often displaced by a move to the city, usually struggling against personal fears to assert themselves or gain affection.... In each of these stories, though the character has a fearful glimpse of his or her vulnerability and impotence, the action is minimal, the tone is subdued, and the focus is primarily on an individual protagonist. The shift from passive and personal experience to explosive interaction, from humility and withdrawal to angry and violent revelation, from timid attempts to win love to fierce refusal of it, marks an abrupt redirection in O'Connor's writing after her return home, as if to dramatize her mother's crippling influence on her life.

• • •

Like the literal-minded mother in "The Enduring Chill" who wishes her son would go out and do work—real work, not writing—and who urges him to write something good like *Gone With the Wind*, Mrs. O'Connor, an inveterate subscriber to *Reader's Digest*, does not seem to appreciate her daughter's brand of writing. O'Connor's confession to a fellow writer tells much:

> The other day [my mother] asked me why I didn't try to write something that people liked instead of the kind of thing I do write. Do you think, she said, that you are really using the talent God gave you when you don't write something that a lot, a LOT, of people like? This always leaves me shaking and speechless, raises my blood pressure 140 degrees, etc. All I can ever say is, if you have to ask, you'll never know. (*Habit* 326)

... O'Connor may have written her stories for her mother, hiding the "letter to her parent" in her text, eager to have her mother find her private revelation yet protecting her from public embarrassment. As O'Connor suggested in several letters, her mother was her primary and most trying reader, preferring O'Connor's painting (which she felt she could understand) to her writing, and constantly falling asleep on her books. . . .

Where relative passivity and emotional suicide fail to register with her mother, O'Connor lodges her discontent in more violent, boldly stroked stories, filled with troops of Flannerys and Reginas in a wild assortment of shapes, sizes, ages, and sexes, but always quite recognizable versions of the original pair. In "The Comforts of Home" and "Everything That Rises Must Converge," effeminate sons bristle against overpowering mothers. . . .

• • •

In "Everything That Rises Must Converge," Julian Chestny, a thirty-year-old unappreciated writer, strikes out indirectly at his mother's ignorance, bigotry, and oppressive expectation of gratitude. In the portrait of the mother, O'Connor once again draws from material in her own life. . . .

Unable either to communicate with his mother or break the tie that binds him, Julian—much like O'Connor in her fiction—retreats into his fantasy world:

> This was a kind of mental bubble in which he established himself when he could not bear to be a part of what was going on around him. . . . His mother had never entered it but from it he could see her with absolute clarity. (411)

Stating in one of her letters her annoyance with her mother's repeated "assault" on her bedroom, which she periodically would invade and clean, installing revolting curtains and changing her rug—an experience which O'Connor tellingly claimed made her feel "like she was being sawed in two without ether" (*Habit* 158–59)—O'Connor suggests that her "fiction," expressive of herself and unviolated by her mother's penchant for "tidiness," is the only "room" which she can preserve intact. . . .

• • •

The recurrence in O'Connor's later fiction of these intolerable parents and murderous children struggling for articulation and dominance suggests an intense and urgent need expressible only in violent action—and in fiction. In one letter, O'Connor herself remarks, "Most of the violences carried to their logical conclusions in the stories manage to be warded off in fact here [at the dairy farm]—*though most of them exist in potentiality*" (198; emphasis added). . . .

That O'Connor saw herself in her fiction is clear. As she wrote to one correspondent, "My heroine already is, and is Hulga . . . a projection of myself into this kind of tragic comic action" (106). In "Good Country People," thirty-two-year-old Joy Hopewell, who in an act of self-appropriation changed her name to Hulga on the basis of its ugly sound, is a crippled Ph.D. who uses intellectualism to defend her wooden soul. Her mother, like many of O'Connor's characters, is a self-satisfied, platitudinous woman who "had no bad qualities of her own but . . . was able to use other people's in such a constructive way that she never felt the lack" (272).

. . . In its portrayal of a world without love, "Good Country People" touches the core of O'Connor's own life. As she wrote in an early letter, "Everything funny I have written is more terrible than it is funny, or only funny because it is terrible, or only terrible because it is funny" (*Habit* 105).

As "Good Country People" and other stories written after 1951 suggest, O'Connor's sense of entrapment, impotence, and frustration in the face of her mother's willful blindness and infuriating dominance precipitated a fierce and boiling rage which precluded any chance of sustained and unconflicted love.... Hinting at the ultimate irresolution of her "adolescent" conflict, O'Connor, like Kafka, leaves the key in her fiction for her parent to discover the "letter" hidden in its depths.

WORKS CITED

Fitzgerald, Sally. Introduction. In O'Connor, *The Habit of Being.*

Getz, Lorine. *Flannery O'Connor: Her Life, Library and Book Reviews.* New York: The Edwin Mellen Press, 1980.

Hendin, Josephine. *The World of Flannery O'Connor.* Bloomington: Indiana UP, 1970.

Kafka, Franz. *Letter to His Father.* New York: Schocken, 1966.

O'Connor, Flannery. *Complete Stories.* New York: Farrar, Straus & Giroux, 1981.

——. *The Habit of Being: Letters.* Ed. Sally Fitzgerald. New York: Farrar, Straus & Giroux, 1979.

——. *Mystery and Manners: Occasional Prose.* Ed. Sally and Robert Fitzgerald. New York: Farrar, Straus & Giroux, 1969.

EILEEN POLLACK

From *Flannery O'Connor and the New Criticism* (2007)[1]

... To writers who teach to earn their living, Flannery O'Connor has long represented the benefits that accrue to writers who refuse to teach (or, in O'Connor's case, are prevented from doing so by illness). Her continued exposure to irritating Southern matrons and Jesus-haunted back-woods preachers kept her fiction gritty and eccentric in ways that might have been impossible if she had remained in the academy.

However, ... studying for two years at Iowa was enough to influence O'Connor's fiction for the rest of her life. Although legend would have it that she arrived in Iowa City fully formed as a writer,[2] then sat quietly in the back of her workshops except for the "occasional amused and shy smile at something absurd" (as Robert Giroux tells us in his introduction to the collected stories) (viii), ... the New Critical approach O'Connor absorbed from studying with Robert Penn Warren and reading the textbook/anthology he authored with Cleanth Brooks is evident in everything she ever published. ...[3]

1. From *American Literary History* 19 (2007): 546–56.
2. O'Connor graduated with an M.A. degree from the prestigious Iowa Writers' Workshop at the University of Iowa in 1947.
3. Novelist Robert Penn Warren (1905–89) and critic Cleanth Brooks (1906–94) collaborated on an influential series of essays and textbooks that helped lay the foundations for what came to be known as the New Criticism, a school of thought that urged the importance of "close reading" and rejected the use of biography and secondary sources in literary studies.

For O'Connor, the advice that she write what she know took the form of setting her stories in rural Georgia and centering each story on the thematic question of what it might take to get a sinner to recognize the central mysteries of Christianity. Her problem as an artist was how to write about such a theme for an audience composed largely of nonbelievers. Preaching or moralizing about her characters' sins would have been not only inartistic but ineffective. The advice that she show rather than tell was particularly well suited to her thematic concerns as a Christian because it would allow her to bring alive for her readers the spiritual struggles of characters unlike themselves, creating on the page the power of unfamiliar sacraments such as baptism and/or the operation of grace in the material world.[4]

In addition, she believed that the divine (the thematic, the expository, that which must be told) is immanent in the concrete details of the material world (that which can be shown). Just as the spirit is made flesh in the Word, just as God assumed the body of a man and suffered as humans suffered, so too the grand themes of Christianity can be embodied in the physical particulars of a flawed character's very human struggles against the devil. The fiction writer, O'Connor tells us in "The Teaching of Literature," "is concerned with mystery that is lived. He's concerned with ultimate mystery as we find it embodied in the concrete world of sense experience" (*Mystery* 125).

In the same way, O'Connor's obsessive use of the effaced third-person narrator was a choice that came not from her time at Iowa or a mindless adherence to some stricture laid down by Brooks and Warren but rather from the demands imposed by the Southern setting of her work, her thematic concerns as a believing Christian, and her friendship with the novelist Caroline Gordon.[5] . . . It is clear from O'Connor's letters that she sent nearly everything she ever wrote to Gordon for editing and that Gordon scolded her every time she lapsed from strict adherence to this limited third-person point of view.[6]

. . . O'Connor could not use first-person narrators because those narrators would have spoken in a thick rural Southern dialect that few readers would have understood or had the patience to decipher, just as Engel[7] could not understand O'Connor's speech when she showed up in his office to try to worm her way into his workshop. . . . O'Connor chose to rely on narrators who spoke standard English, allowing her characters to speak dialect only in limited and easily digestible doses in dialogue.

• • •

O'Connor endowed her narrators with perfect diction in accordance with Gordon's dictum that allowing the narrator to slip into dialect lowers the tone of a story and saps it of the tension that might otherwise have accrued from the subtle conflict between the cultures represented by the two ways of speaking. . . .

We have seen, then, that O'Connor chose to show rather than tell and used limited third-person narrators because this style and this technique suited her

---

4. See O'Connor, *Mystery*, 162. [Pollack's note]
5. American novelist Caroline Ferguson Gordon (1895–1981); like O'Connor, she was best known for her short stories and her Roman Catholicism.
6. See O'Connor, *Habit*, 69, 95, 157, 260, 295. [Pollack's note]
7. American writer Paul Engel (1908–91), O'Connor's teacher at the Iowa Writers' Workshop.

particular needs as a Southerner and a Christian rather than because she was slavishly adhering to some New Critical creed she picked up at Iowa. . . .

As she wrote in a letter to Betty Hester ("A") in September 1955, "I understand that something of oneself gets through and often something that one is not conscious of. Also to have sympathy for any character, you have to put a good deal of yourself into him." . . . [The artist must] make sure that those elements of the author's personality "that don't bear on the subject at hand are excluded. . . . Everything has to be subordinated to a whole which is not you" (*Habit* 105).

WORKS CITED

O'Connor, Flannery. *The Complete Stories*. New York: Farrar, Straus, Giroux, 1973.

O'Connor, Flannery. In Fitzgerald, Sally, ed., *The Habit of Being: Letters of Flannery O'Connor*. New York: Farrar, Straus, Giroux, 1979.

O'Connor, Flannery. In Sally Fitzgerald and Robert Fitzgerald, eds., *Mystery and Manners*. New York: Farrar, Straus, Giroux, 1970.

SUGGESTIONS FOR WRITING

1. Flannery O'Connor wrote that "the beginning of human knowledge is through the senses, and the fiction writer begins where human perception begins." Citing examples from the O'Connor stories and the nonfiction passages in this chapter, write an essay exploring O'Connor's use of imagery, including figurative language (metaphor, simile, symbol) and references to vision or other senses. Are the senses trustworthy? How does the physical world portrayed through this imagery affect other elements of the story or stories (characterization, plot, theme, etc.)?

2. Flannery O'Connor wrote that "in my own stories I have found that violence is strangely capable of returning my characters to reality and preparing them to accept their moment of grace" and that violence "is the extreme situation that best reveals what we are essentially." Discuss the three stories by O'Connor in this chapter in light of these statements about violence. What "moments of grace" do you see? Can you assess what O'Connor considers the essence of humanity ("what we are")?

3. Jean W. Cash's biography, *Flannery O'Connor: A Life,* provides details about O'Connor's experience at Georgia State College for Women in the 1940s, when she was planning to be a cartoonist and contributed cartoons as well as writings to the school's publications. Write an essay in which you use this biographical information as an insight into one or more of O'Connor's stories. For instance, identify two or three scenes in a story and analyze their effect as primarily physical comedy or visual effect similar to that in cartoons.

4. Write an essay interpreting some aspect of one of O'Connor's stories in light of information about O'Connor's life. Be sure to cite Flannery O'Connor's own words from her letters and essays excerpted in this chapter, from the critical essays, or from other sources. What does the biographical context help explain? What qualities or aspects of the story does your biographical approach *not* account for?

5. Choose two of the stories in this chapter and write an essay comparing and contrasting the way they are narrated (see the excerpt from Pollack's essay above). Pay close attention to passages in which the narrator relates the voice, vision, thoughts, or perspective of a focal character. How does the treatment of each character contribute to tone, irony, or other effects of the story?

6. After making your own list of what all three stories in this chapter have in common, write a short story in the Flannery O'Connor manner. Are you able to make it

a little humorous without being too absurd? Violent or shocking without being too cruel? Unsettling but not disgusting? Is your story at all autobiographical?

7. Read "A Biographical Approach to Ernest Hemingway's 'Hills Like White Elephants'" (see pp. 492–93). Read two or three short biographies or biographical articles about Hemingway. Write an essay on "Hills Like White Elephants" in which you use close reading of details of setting, dialogue, action, imagery, and narration, taking a biographical approach.

8. Choose a favorite writer in this book and investigate his or her life (your choice should be someone about whom biographical evidence is available). Read carefully one story, poem, or play by this writer, and write an essay in which you argue either that the life would be a misleading key to the author's work or that the work would be a misleading key to understanding the author's life.

9

THE AUTHOR'S WORK: JAMES JOYCE'S *DUBLINERS*

Today, a good short story, like a popular song, will likely appear in four different forms over time:

- The story appears in a periodical, whether a general-interest, large-circulation venue like *Atlantic Monthly* or the *San Francisco Chronicle*, or a smaller, more specialized one such as filmmaker Francis Ford Coppola's *Zoetrope: All Story*. (Similarly, a song—let's take Radiohead's "Lucky" as an example—might be released as a single.)
- The story becomes part of a short-story collection—a book that collects multiple, often related stories by the same author (just as a song will turn up on an album, as "Lucky" did on Radiohead's 1997 *OK Computer*). Alternatively, the story might be transformed into a chapter in a novel.
- With a little luck, the story might be chosen for inclusion in an anthology of works by many authors, whether a textbook like the one you are reading right now or a book such as *Best American Short Stories of 2009*. (The musical equivalent would be a compilation album such as *Help: A Charity Project for the Children of Bosnia* [1995] or *Six Feet Under: Everything Ends, Vol. 2* [2005], both of which included "Lucky.")
- Finally, often years later, the story might make its way into the author's "collected" or "selected" works. (The musical parallel would be a greatest hits or remix album such as Radiohead's 2008 *The Best of Radiohead*—again including "Lucky.")

This is not the place to pursue all the ways that music reaches its audience today, though the analogy between story and song is thought-provoking. The same recording of a song on the radio, in a random mix or playlist, or in a crowded room will get different levels of your attention and may move you in different ways. Similarly, a short story changes when it appears in different formats or venues. Sometimes the change is literal if the author decides to revise the story at one of these stages, just as a singer or band might do a remix, live, or acoustic version of a song. But even if a writer or publisher doesn't alter a word or move a comma, the story changes nonetheless simply because each of these different publishing contexts subtly alters the work's effect on its audience. Whether you are reading a story or listening to a song, then, it's worth paying attention to how its effects and meanings are shaped and reshaped by the different contexts in which you and other audiences encounter it.

For example, long before Annie Proulx's short story "Brokeback Mountain" was turned into a major motion picture featuring two Hollywood heartthrobs, it first appeared in *The New Yorker*, a magazine aimed at affluent, well-educated, mainly urban readers. In *The New Yorker*, Proulx's story was broken up by a poem by Marie Howe and cartoons depicting businessmen swilling martinis and precocious children using words like *juvenilia*; it was sandwiched between articles on the writer Truman Capote and the PBS cooking-show host Julia Child, as well as ads for Salvador Dali prints, Steinway pianos, goose-down robes, and exclusive vacation destinations ("RENT YOUR OWN IRISH CASTLE"). In such a context, the story's gritty Western setting, its sheep-tending protagonists, their hard-scrabble, often violent way of life, and their rural speech stand out as strange and exotic, if not crude. Such factors may well have been more jarring to *New Yorker* readers than the evolving relationship between the main characters that has since become the most controversial aspect of "Brokeback Mountain."

Yet if you pick up Proulx's *Close Range: Wyoming Stories* and read it from back to front, you encounter "Brokeback Mountain" only after making your way through ten other stories that depict the same general geographical and social environment. Here, Jack and Ennis suddenly seem right at home amid a cast of characters consisting of what one reviewer dubs "hardpan ranchers, battered cowpokes and bull riders, bar girls and bar brawlers" whose "lives are a futile uphill struggle" to "wres[t] a living out of a land as poor as it is beautiful." Because reading all these stories makes this milieu more familiar, the collection gives readers both a clearer picture of Jack and Ennis as individuals (rather than types living in a remote land) and a deeper understanding of all that the word *it* might mean when Ennis says, "If you can't fix it, you got to stand it."

THE SHORT-STORY SEQUENCE OR CYCLE

All works written by a single author have something in common, as the stories by Flannery O'Connor in chapter 8 demonstrate. But the stories a writer publishes together in a single collection usually have even more in common, becoming interrelated parts of a larger work sometimes labeled a *short-story* **sequence** or *cycle*. At the very least, the stories in such a collection are usually written during roughly the same period of an author's life and thus provide a window into one phase in the author's biography and career.

At the opposite extreme, a short-story cycle might closely resemble a novel, its stories all depicting the same characters and general setting, the action of one story taking up where the last leaves off. For example, Armistead Maupin's story collection *Tales of the City* (1978) traces the intertwined lives and careers of an intriguing and diverse group of characters who all live in the same fictional San Francisco apartment building; it was turned into a television miniseries in 1993. Like *Close Range*, however, most modern short-story collections fall somewhere in between these two extremes: Their stories feature similar characters, settings, situations, plots, conflicts, imagery, and other stylistic features, without being overtly related to each other. The reader is invited to trace connections and make comparisons. Each of the stories works fine on its own and is thus a complete, self-contained "work" in its own right. But the stories also work together to form a single, larger work that is somehow more than the sum of its parts.

As a result, some authors feel that any one story in a sequence or cycle can never be all that it was meant to be unless it is read in the context of the whole. Such a cycle "suffers from being broken up or crowded in with other books," in the words of short-story writer Frank O'Connor, because cycles "should be read by themselves, as unities." We could liken the experience of reading one part of a carefully constructed story collection to downloading only one or two music tracks from a CD or listening to the tracks in a different order than the artist intended, practices that famed Clash guitarist Mick Jones compares to "buying the *Mona Lisa* and only buying the eyeball because that was the bit you liked. . . . It's not going to ultimately be the complete experience that [the artist] had in mind." Jhumpa Lahiri, author of the short-story cycle *The Interpreter of Maladies* (the title story of which appears here, in "Encounters across Cultures"), uses a different metaphor:

> [Readers] think of [short-story collections] as a chocolate box, an assorted thing. You present it, and readers can say, I like that one, that was my favorite, I like the orange cream. Whereas with a novel I think they regard it more as a thing of substance, an entrée, if you will; they don't pick it apart in terms of the mashed potato part of it and the peas and the meat part, it's all this thing in concert.

All things considered, Lahiri's gustatory metaphor is probably more apt than Mick Jones's more extreme one. Reading a single short story from a collection usually does much less violence to the work than cutting out the eyeball of Leonardo's famous painting. But both Jones and Lahiri have a point: A story does work and signify differently when we read it in isolation or in the context of stories by various authors than it does when we read it in the context of the collection or cycle of which it is a part. And the order in which stories appear in a cycle or collection also affects the way we read and respond to them.

JAMES JOYCE'S *DUBLINERS*

At the risk of presenting you with the eyeball from the *Mona Lisa*, this chapter invites you to sample three stories from one of the most famous and influential short-story collections in the English language. First begun in 1904, when its author was only 22, and completed in 1907, James Joyce's *Dubliners* wasn't published in its entirety until ten years later, largely because of publishers' concerns about potential lawsuits. Yet from the beginning it was conceived by Joyce not just as a coherent collection but also and specifically as a very deliberately ordered "series" or sequence of what he called "epiclets" (that is, mini-**epics**).

As the book's title makes clear, the most obvious element that unifies its stories is their setting—

James Joyce at age 22 (1904)

New Irish Books
Ready or to appear shortly

DUBLINERS. By J. Joyce. Crown 8vo, cloth. 3s. 6d. net (*24th Nov.*)

A book of studies of Dublin life, which, although detached, is by no means a mere collection of sketches, but has a very distinct unity. Never before has this side of Dublin life been presented in quite so real a manner. The author's style at once removes the book from the category of ordinary fiction and makes it the piece of literature that will no doubt win the same recognition from discerning critics as did his book of poems published a few years ago, of which Mr. Arthur Symons wrote: " . . . so singularly good, so fine and delicate, and yet so full of music and suggestion, that I can hardly choose among them . . . to do such tiny evanescent things . . . is to evoke, not only roses in mid-winter, but the very dew on the roses. Sometimes we are reminded of Elizabethan, more often of Jacobean lyrics."

MAUNSEL & CO., LIMITED
96 Middle Abbey Street, Dublin.

Advertisement for an edition of *Dubliners* that never appeared.

Dublin, Ireland, in the late nineteenth and early twentieth century the hometown Joyce permanently left behind while writing the book. But the title and the stories focus on the people as much as the place—Dublin*ers*, not just Dublin. And Joyce himself insisted in his letters that the book's fifteen stories fell into four groups, each corresponding to a particular aspect or phase of Dubliners' lives—childhood, adolescence, mature life, and public life.

The three stories we include here represent three of those four groups and phases. The **initiation story** "Araby" is the third story in *Dubliners* and the last of its three stories of childhood. It is immediately followed—both in this chapter and in *Dubliners*—by "Eveline," the first of three stories of adolescence. "The Dead" is the final story of both the entire collection and its stories of public life, as well as the last short story Joyce ever wrote. In fact, however, "The Dead" is not short, especially in comparison with the fourteen stories that precede it, and its length has ensured that it is sometimes classed as a **novella** rather than a short story. Joyce's main pursuit in the years after he completed *Dubliners* was the writing of novels—*A Portrait of the Artist as a Young Man* (1916), *Ulysses* (1922), and *Finnegans Wake* (1939).

A wealth of useful material about *Dubliners* and about Joyce's life and career appears at the end of this chapter, including a timeline of major events both in Joyce's life and in what Joyce called the very "curious history" of his only short-story collection; excerpts from Joyce's early essays and from "Gas from a Burner," a farcical poem Joyce wrote from the point of view of the printer and publisher who initially agreed, but later refused, to bring out the book; and parts of three essays by Joyce scholars, each of whom offers his own, slightly different interpretation of the relations among the *Dubliners* stories and of the book's overall style and themes. These essays also demonstrate both the kinds of questions a responsive reader may pose when reading a story in the context of an entire collection and the way such questions can be used to build an effective essay.

Questions about Short-Story Collections

1. What is the overall **tone** of these stories? Does it change across the stories—and if so, how? How might the order of the stories affect the overall tone of the collection?

2. How would you describe the stories' **protagonists**? What characteristics do the protagonists share? In these terms, do you see any development across the stories?

3. How would you describe the other **characters** whom the protagonists encounter? Are there similar types, or characters who perform similar functions (as **foils** or **antagonists**, for example)? Again, is there a pattern of development here? For instance, do certain types of characters appear in early stories, but not in later ones?

4. What problems and **conflicts** do the protagonists typically face? How are the conflicts resolved? In both the nature of the conflicts and their resolution, do you see any development across the stories, and what is the effect and significance of their order?

5. What similarities do you see in the stories' **action** and **plots**? What typically happens in these stories? How do they tend to begin and end? Are there similarities in the way events are ordered? (For example, do the stories begin *in medias res* or make use of **flashbacks**?)

6. How would you characterize the **setting** of these stories? How detailed is the description of setting, and what is its significance and role in the stories?

7. What patterns do you see in the **narration** of these stories? Does the narrative strategy or **point of view** change or evolve across the stories? If so, how?

8. Do the stories make use of **symbols**? Are there recurring symbols?

9. What are the most distinctive features of the **style** of these stories and the language used in them (diction, syntax, and so on)? Do the same or similar **images** recur in the various stories?

10. Thinking of the stories as a unit, what is or are its major **theme(s)**? How does each story contribute to the articulation of the theme(s)? In these terms, what is the effect and significance of the order of the stories?

Araby

North Richmond Street, being blind,[1] was a quiet street except at the hour when the Christian Brothers' School set the boys free. An uninhabited house of two storeys stood at the blind end, detached from its neighbours in a square ground. The other houses of the street, conscious of decent lives within them, gazed at one another with brown imperturbable faces.

The former tenant of our house, a priest, had died in the back drawing-room. Air, musty from having been long enclosed, hung in all the rooms, and the waste

---

1. That is, a dead-end street.

room behind the kitchen was littered with old useless papers. Among these I found a few paper-covered books, the pages of which were curled and damp: *The Abbot*, by Walter Scott, *The Devout Communicant* and *The Memoirs of Vidocq*.[2] I liked the last best because its leaves were yellow. The wild garden behind the house contained a central apple-tree and a few straggling bushes under one of which I found the late tenant's rusty bicycle-pump. He had been a very charitable priest; in his will he had left all his money to institutions and the furniture of his house to his sister.

When the short days of winter came dusk fell before we had well eaten our dinners. When we met in the street the houses had grown sombre. The space of sky above us was the colour of ever-changing violet and towards it the lamps of the street lifted their feeble lanterns. The cold air stung us and we played till our bodies glowed. Our shouts echoed in the silent street. The career of our play brought us through the dark muddy lanes behind the houses where we ran the gantlet of the rough tribes from the cottages, to the back doors of the dark dripping gardens where odours arose from the ashpits,[3] to the dark odorous stables where a coachman smoothed and combed the horse or shook music from the buckled harness. When we returned to the street light from the kitchen windows had filled the areas. If my uncle was seen turning the corner we hid in the shadow until we had seen him safely housed. Or if Mangan's sister came out on the doorstep to call her brother in to his tea we watched her from our shadow peer up and down the street. We waited to see whether she would remain or go in and, if she remained, we left our shadow and walked up to Mangan's steps resignedly. She was waiting for us, her figure defined by the light from the half-opened door. Her brother always teased her before he obeyed and I stood by the railings looking at her. Her dress swung as she moved her body and the soft rope of her hair tossed from side to side.

Every morning I lay on the floor in the front parlour watching her door. The blind was pulled down to within an inch of the sash so that I could not be seen. When she came out on the doorstep my heart leaped. I ran to the hall, seized my books and followed her. I kept her brown figure always in my eye and, when we came near the point at which our ways diverged, I quickened my pace and passed her. This happened morning after morning. I had never spoken to her, except for a few casual words, and yet her name was like a summons to all my foolish blood.

5   Her image accompanied me even in places the most hostile to romance. On Saturday evenings when my aunt went marketing I had to go to carry some of the parcels. We walked through the flaring streets, jostled by drunken men and bargaining women, amid the curses of labourers, the shrill litanies of shop-boys who stood on guard by the barrels of pigs' cheeks, the nasal chanting of street-singers, who sang a *come-all-you* about O'Donovan Rossa,[4] or a ballad about the troubles in our native land. These noises converged in a single sensation of life for me: I

2. The "memoirs" were probably *not* written by François Vidocq (1775–1857), a French criminal who became chief of detectives and who died poor and disgraced for his part in a crime that he solved; the 1820 novel by Sir Walter Scott (1771–1834) is a romance about the Catholic Mary, Queen of Scots (1542–87), who was beheaded; *The Devout Communicant: or Pious Meditations and Aspirations for the Three Days Before and Three Days after Receiving the Holy Eucharist* (1813) is a Catholic religious tract.
3. Where fireplace ashes and other household refuse were dumped.
4. Jeremiah O'Donovan (1831–1915) was a militant Irish nationalist who fought on despite terms in prison and banishment. *Come-all-you*: a song, of which there were many, that began "Come, all you Irishmen."

imagined that I bore my chalice safely through a throng of foes. Her name sprang to my lips at moments in strange prayers and praises which I myself did not understand. My eyes were often full of tears (I could not tell why) and at times a flood from my heart seemed to pour itself out into my bosom. I thought little of the future. I did not know whether I would ever speak to her or not or, if I spoke to her, how I could tell her of my confused adoration. But my body was like a harp and her words and gestures were like fingers running upon the wires.

One evening I went into the back drawing-room in which the priest had died. It was a dark rainy evening and there was no sound in the house. Through one of the broken panes I heard the rain impinge upon the earth, the fine incessant needles of water playing in the sodden beds. Some distant

lamp or lighted window gleamed below me. I was thankful that I could see so little. All my senses seemed to desire to veil themselves and, feeling that I was about to slip from them, I pressed the palms of my hands together until they trembled, murmuring: *O love! O love!* many times.

At last she spoke to me. When she addressed the first words to me I was so confused that I did not know what to answer. She asked me was I going to *Araby*.[5] I forget whether I answered yes or no. It would be a splendid bazaar, she said; she would love to go.

—And why can't you? I asked.

While she spoke she turned a silver bracelet round and round her wrist. She could not go, she said, because there would be a retreat[6] that week in her convent. Her brother and two other boys were fighting for their caps and I was alone at the railings. She held one of the spikes, bowing her head towards me. The light from the lamp opposite our door caught the white curve of her neck, lit up her hair that rested there and, falling, lit up the hand upon the railing. It fell over one side of her dress and caught the white border of a petticoat, just visible as she stood at ease.

—It's well for you, she said.

—If I go, I said, I will bring you something.

What innumerable follies laid waste my waking and sleeping thoughts after that evening! I wished to annihilate the tedious intervening days. I chafed

10

---

5. A charity bazaar billed as a "Grand Oriental Fete," Dublin, May 1894.
6. A period of withdrawal dedicated to prayer and religious study.

against the work of school. At night in my bedroom and by day in the classroom her image came between me and the page I strove to read. The syllables of the word *Araby* were called to me through the silence in which my soul luxuriated and cast an Eastern enchantment over me. I asked for leave to go to the bazaar on Saturday night. My aunt was surprised and hoped it was not some Freemason[7] affair. I answered few questions in class. I watched my master's face pass from amiability to sternness; he hoped I was not beginning to idle. I could not call my wandering thoughts together. I had hardly any patience with the serious work of life which, now that it stood between me and my desire, seemed to me child's play, ugly monotonous child's play.

On Saturday morning I reminded my uncle that I wished to go to the bazaar in the evening. He was fussing at the hall-stand, looking for the hat-brush, and answered me curtly:

—Yes, boy, I know.

15   As he was in the hall I could not go into the front parlour and lie at the window. I left the house in bad humour and walked slowly towards the school. The air was pitilessly raw and already my heart misgave me.

When I came home to dinner my uncle had not yet been home. Still it was early. I sat staring at the clock for some time and, when its ticking began to irritate me, I left the room. I mounted the staircase and gained the upper part of the house. The high cold empty gloomy rooms liberated me and I went from room to room singing. From the front window I saw my companions playing below in the street. Their cries reached me weakened and indistinct and, leaning my forehead against the cool glass, I looked over at the dark house where she lived. I may have stood there for an hour, seeing nothing but the brown-clad figure cast by my imagination, touched discreetly by the lamplight at the curved neck, at the hand upon the railings and at the border below the dress.

When I came downstairs again I found Mrs Mercer sitting at the fire. She was an old garrulous woman, a pawnbroker's widow, who collected used stamps for some pious purpose. I had to endure the gossip of the tea-table. The meal was prolonged beyond an hour and still my uncle did not come. Mrs Mercer stood up to go: she was sorry she couldn't wait any longer, but it was after eight o'clock and she did not like to be out late, as the night air was bad for her. When she had gone I began to walk up and down the room, clenching my fists. My aunt said:

—I'm afraid you may put off your bazaar for this night of Our Lord.

At nine o'clock I heard my uncle's latchkey in the halldoor. I heard him talking to himself and heard the hallstand rocking when it had received the weight of his overcoat. I could interpret these signs. When he was midway through his dinner I asked him to give me the money to go to the bazaar. He had forgotten.

20   —The people are in bed and after their first sleep now, he said.

I did not smile. My aunt said to him energetically:

—Can't you give him the money and let him go? You've kept him late enough as it is.

My uncle said he was very sorry he had forgotten. He said he believed in the old saying: *All work and no play makes Jack a dull boy.* He asked me where I was going and, when I had told him a second time he asked me did I know *The Arab's*

---

7. Freemasons—members of an influential, secretive, and highly ritualistic fraternal organization—were considered enemies of the Catholics.

Farewell to his Steed.[8] When I left the kitchen he was about to recite the opening lines of the piece to my aunt.

I held a florin[9] tightly in my hand as I strode down Buckingham Street towards the station. The sight of the streets thronged with buyers and glaring with gas recalled to me the purpose of my journey. I took my seat in a third-class carriage of a deserted train. After an intolerable delay the train moved out of the station slowly. It crept onward among ruinous houses and over the twinkling river. At Westland Row Station a crowd of people pressed to the carriage doors; but the porters moved them back, saying that it was a special train for the bazaar. I remained alone in the bare carriage. In a few minutes the train drew up beside an improvised wooden platform. I passed out on to the road and saw by the lighted dial of a clock that it was ten minutes to ten. In front of me was a large building which displayed the magical name.

I could not find any sixpenny entrance and, fearing that the bazaar would be 25 closed, I passed in quickly through a turnstile, handing a shilling to a weary-looking man. I found myself in a big hall girdled at half its height by a gallery. Nearly all the stalls were closed and the greater part of the hall was in darkness. I recognized a silence like that which pervades a church after a service. I walked into the centre of the bazaar timidly. A few people were gathered about the stalls which were still open. Before a curtain, over which the words *Café Chantant*[1] were written in coloured lamps, two men were counting money on a salver. I listened to the fall of the coins.

Remembering with difficulty why I had come I went over to one of the stalls and examined porcelain vases and flowered tea-sets. At the door of the stall a young lady was talking and laughing with two young gentlemen. I remarked their English accents and listened vaguely to their conversation.

—O, I never said such a thing!

—O, but you did!

—O, but I didn't!

—Didn't she say that? 30

—Yes. I heard her.

—O, there's a . . . fib!

Observing me the young lady came over and asked me did I wish to buy anything. The tone of her voice was not encouraging; she seemed to have spoken to me out of a sense of duty. I looked humbly at the great jars that stood like eastern guards at either side of the dark entrance to the stall and murmured:

—No, thank you.

The young lady changed the position of one of the vases and went back to the 35 two young men. They began to talk of the same subject. Once or twice the young lady glanced at me over her shoulder.

I lingered before her stall, though I knew my stay was useless, to make my interest in her wares seem the more real. Then I turned away slowly and walked down the middle of the bazaar. I allowed the two pennies to fall against the sixpence in my pocket. I heard a voice call from one end of the gallery that the light was out. The upper part of the hall was now completely dark.

8. Or *The Arab's Farewell to His Horse,* a sentimental nineteenth-century poem by Caroline Norton. The speaker has sold the horse.

9. A two-shilling piece; thus four times the "sixpenny entrance" fee.   1. Café with music (French).

Gazing up into the darkness I saw myself as a creature driven and derided by vanity; and my eyes burned with anguish and anger.

1914

Eveline

She sat at the window watching the evening invade the avenue. Her head was leaned against the window curtains and in her nostrils was the odour of dusty cretonne.[2] She was tired.

Few people passed. The man out of the last house passed on his way home; she heard his footsteps clacking along the concrete pavement and afterwards crunching on the cinder path before the new red houses. One time there used to be a field there in which they used to play every evening with other people's children. Then a man from Belfast bought the field and built houses in it—not like their little brown houses but bright brick houses with shining roofs. The children of the avenue used to play together in that field—the Devines, the Waters, the Dunns, little Keogh the cripple, she and her brothers and sisters. Ernest, however, never played: he was too grown up. Her father used often to hunt them in out of the field with his blackthorn stick; but usually little Keogh used to keep *nix*[3] and call out when he saw her father coming. Still they seemed to have been rather happy then. Her father was not so bad then; and besides, her mother was alive. That was a long time ago; she and her brothers and sisters were all grown up; her mother was dead. Tizzie Dunn was dead, too, and the Waters had gone back to England. Everything changes. Now she was going to go away like the others, to leave her home.

Home! She looked round the room, reviewing all its familiar objects which she had dusted once a week for so many years, wondering where on earth all the dust came from. Perhaps she would never see again those familiar objects from which she had never dreamed of being divided. And yet during all those years she had never found out the name of the priest whose yellowing photograph hung on the wall above the broken harmonium[4] beside the coloured print of the promises made to Blessed Margaret Mary Alacoque.[5] He had been a school friend of her father. Whenever he showed the photograph to a visitor her father used to pass it with a casual word:

—He is in Melbourne[6] now.

5   She had consented to go away, to leave her home. Was that wise? She tried to weigh each side of the question. In her home anyway she had shelter and food; she had those whom she had known all her life about her. Of course she had to

2. Heavy fabric for upholstery and drapery.   3. That is, keep watch.
4. Musical instrument similar to an organ.
5. French nun (1647–90) officially declared "blessed" by the Catholic Church in 1864 and canonized as a saint in 1920. A series of divine visitations that began in her childhood revealed to her Jesus's twelve promises to the faithful, including (1) *I will give them all the graces necessary for their state of life*, (2) *I will establish peace in their families or homes*, and (3) *I will console them in all their troubles*.
6. City in Australia, a British colony and, like the United States, a frequent destination of nineteenth-century Irish immigrants.

work hard both in the house and at business. What would they say of her in the Stores when they found out that she had run away with a fellow? Say she was a fool, perhaps; and her place would be filled up by advertisement. Miss Gavan would be glad. She had always had an edge[7] on her, especially whenever there were people listening.

—Miss Hill, don't you see these ladies are waiting?

—Look lively, Miss Hill, please.

She would not cry many tears at leaving the Stores.

But in her new home, in a distant unknown country, it would not be like that. Then she would be married—she, Eveline. People would treat her with respect then. She would not be treated as her mother had been. Even now, though she was over nineteen, she sometimes felt herself in danger of her father's violence. She knew it was that that had given her the palpitations. When they were growing up he had never gone for her, like he used to go for Harry and Ernest, because she was a girl; but latterly he had begun to threaten her and say what he would do to her only for her dead mother's sake. And now she had nobody to protect her. Ernest was dead and Harry, who was in the church decorating business, was nearly always down somewhere in the country. Besides, the invariable squabble for money on Saturday nights had begun to weary her unspeakably. She always gave her entire wages—seven shillings—and Harry always sent up what he could but the trouble was to get any money from her father. He said she used to squander the money, that she had no head,[8] that he wasn't going to give her his hard-earned money to throw about the streets, and much more, for he was usually fairly bad of a Saturday night. In the end he would give her the money and ask her had she any intention of buying Sunday's dinner. Then she had to rush out as quickly as she could and do her marketing, holding her black leather purse tightly in her hand as she elbowed her way through the crowds and returning home late under her load of provisions. She had hard work to keep the house together and to see that the two young children who had been left to her charge went to school regularly and got their meals regularly. It was hard work—a hard life—but now that she was about to leave it she did not find it a wholly undesirable life.

She was about to explore another life with Frank. Frank was very kind, manly, open-hearted. She was to go away with him by the night-boat to be his wife and to live with him in Buenos Ayres[9] where he had a home waiting for her. How well she remembered the first time she had seen him; he was lodging in a house on the main road where she used to visit. It seemed a few weeks ago. He was standing at the gate, his peaked cap pushed back on his head and his hair tumbled forward over a face of bronze. Then they had come to know each other. He used to meet her outside the Stores every evening and see her home. He took her to see *The Bohemian Girl*[1] and she felt elated as she sat in an unaccustomed part of the theatre with him. He was awfully fond of music and sang a little. People knew

10

7. That is, a hard, sarcastic manner.
8. That is, no common sense or intelligence, especially regarding business matters.
9. Or Buenos Aires, capital and largest city of Argentina, in South America; its Spanish name literally means "good air."
1. 1843 opera by Dubliner Michael Balfe (1808–70) in which a young noblewoman, kidnapped by gypsies, falls in love with a nobleman who has taken refuge with the gypsies, and—after being restored to her father and home—decides to leave home once again to marry her lover.

Dublin docks, ca. 1890

that they were courting and, when he sang about the lass that loves a sailor,[2] she always felt pleasantly confused. He used to call her Poppens out of fun. First of all it had been an excitement for her to have a fellow and then she had begun to like him. He had tales of distant countries. He had started as a deck boy at a pound a month on a ship of the Allan Line going out to Canada. He told her the names of the ships he had been on and the names of the different services. He had sailed through the Straits of Magellan[3] and he told her stories of the terrible Patagonians.[4] He had fallen on his feet in Buenos Ayres, he said, and had come over to the old country just for a holiday. Of course, her father had found out the affair and had forbidden her to have anything to say to him.

—I know these sailor chaps, he said.

One day he had quarrelled with Frank and after that she had to meet her lover secretly.

The evening deepened in the avenue. The white of two letters in her lap grew indistinct. One was to Harry; the other was to her father. Ernest had been her favourite but she liked Harry too. Her father was becoming old lately, she noticed; he would miss her. Sometimes he could be very nice. Not long before, when she had been laid up for a day, he had read her out a ghost story and made toast for her at the fire. Another day, when their mother was alive, they had all gone for a picnic to the Hill of Howth.[5] She remembered her father putting on her mother's bonnet to make the children laugh.

Her time was running out but she continued to sit by the window, leaning her head against the window curtain, inhaling the odour of dusty cretonne. Down

2. Popular song by Charles Dibdin (1745–1814) about drunken sailors' toasts to their wives and sweethearts. "The Lass That Loved a Sailor" is also the subtitle of *H.M.S. Pinafore,* a well-known 1878 comic operetta by W. S. Gilbert and Arthur Sullivan.
3. Sea passage in South America through which ships can pass between the Atlantic and Pacific oceans.
4. Name given by Ferdinand Magellan (1480–1521) and other early explorers to the supposedly fearsome giants native to southernmost South America.
5. The Howth peninsula is just northeast of Dublin; the hill overlooking its harbor is a popular picnic spot.

far in the avenue she could hear a street organ[6] playing. She knew the air. Strange that it should come that very night to remind her of the promise to her mother, her promise to keep the home together as long as she could. She remembered the last night of her mother's illness; she was again in the close dark room at the other side of the hall and outside she heard a melancholy air of Italy. The organ-player had been ordered to go away and given sixpence. She remembered her father strutting back into the sickroom saying:

—Damned Italians! coming over here!

As she mused the pitiful vision of her mother's life laid its spell on the very quick of her being—that life of commonplace sacrifices closing in final craziness. She trembled as she heard again her mother's voice saying constantly with foolish insistence:

—Derevaun Seraun! Derevaun Seraun![7]

She stood up in a sudden impulse of terror. Escape! She must escape! Frank would save her. He would give her life, perhaps love, too. But she wanted to live. Why should she be unhappy? She had a right to happiness. Frank would take her in his arms, fold her in his arms. He would save her.

• • •

She stood among the swaying crowd in the station at the North Wall.[8] He held her hand and she knew that he was speaking to her, saying something about the passage over and over again. The station was full of soldiers[9] with brown baggages. Through the wide doors of the sheds she caught a glimpse of the black mass of the boat, lying in beside the quay wall, with illumined portholes. She answered nothing. She felt her cheek pale and cold and, out of a maze of distress, she prayed to God to direct her, to show her what was her duty. The boat blew a long mournful whistle into the mist. If she went, to-morrow she would be on the sea with Frank, steaming towards Buenos Ayres. Their passage had been booked. Could she still draw back after all he had done for her? Her distress awoke a nausea in her body and she kept moving her lips in silent fervent prayer.

A bell clanged upon her heart. She felt him seize her hand:

—Come!

All the seas of the world tumbled about her heart. He was drawing her into them: he would drown her. She gripped with both hands at the iron railing.

—Come!

No! No! No! It was impossible. Her hands clutched the iron in frenzy. Amid the seas she sent a cry of anguish!

—Eveline! Evvy!

He rushed beyond the barrier and called to her to follow. He was shouted at to go on but he still called to her. She set her white face to him, passive, like a helpless animal. Her eyes gave him no sign of love or farewell or recognition.

1914

---

6. Portable harmonium usually played by professional street musicians, many of whom were Italian immigrants.
7. The meaning of this phrase is unknown, though scholars speculate that the words are either pure nonsense or a garbled version of Gaelic phrases meaning "The end of pleasure is pain" or "The end of song is derangement."   8. Embarkation point for Dublin emigrants.
9. Probably English soldiers stationed in Ireland.

The Dead

Lily, the caretaker's daughter, was literally run off her feet. Hardly had she brought one gentleman into the little pantry behind the office on the ground floor and helped him off with his overcoat than the wheezy hall-door bell clanged again and she had to scamper along the bare hallway to let in another guest. It was well for her she had not to attend to the ladies also. But Miss Kate and Miss Julia had thought of that and had converted the bathroom upstairs into a ladies' dressing-room. Miss Kate and Miss Julia were there, gossiping and laughing and fussing, walking after each other to the head of the stairs, peering down over the banisters and calling down to Lily to ask her who had come.

It was always a great affair, the Misses Morkan's annual dance. Everybody who knew them came to it, members of the family, old friends of the family, the members of Julia's choir, any of Kate's pupils that were grown up enough and even some of Mary Jane's pupils too. Never once had it fallen flat. For years and years it had gone off in splendid style as long as anyone could remember; ever since Kate and Julia, after the death of their brother Pat, had left the house in Stoney Batter and taken Mary Jane, their only niece, to live with them in the dark gaunt house on Usher's Island, the upper part of which they had rented from Mr Fulham, the corn-factor[1] on the ground floor. That was a good thirty years ago if it was a day. Mary Jane, who was then a little girl in short clothes, was now the main prop of the household for she had the organ in Haddington Road. She had been through the Academy[2] and gave a pupils' concert every year in the upper room of the Antient Concert Rooms. Many of her pupils belonged to better-class families on the Kingstown and Dalkey line. Old as they were, her aunts also did their share. Julia, though she was quite grey, was still the leading soprano in Adam and Eve's,[3] and Kate, being too feeble to go about much, gave music lessons to beginners on the old square piano in the back room. Lily, the caretaker's daughter, did housemaid's work for them. Though their life was modest they believed in eating well; the best of everything: diamond-bone sirloins, three-shilling tea[4] and the best bottled stout. But Lily seldom made a mistake in the orders so that she got on well with her three mistresses. They were fussy, that was all. But the only thing they would not stand was back answers.

Of course they had good reason to be fussy on such a night. And then it was long after ten o'clock and yet there was no sign of Gabriel and his wife. Besides they were dreadfully afraid that Freddy Malins might turn up screwed.[5] They would not wish for worlds that any of Mary Jane's pupils should see him under the influence; and when he was like that it was sometimes very hard to manage him. Freddy Malins always came late but they wondered what could be keeping Gabriel: and that was what brought them every two minutes to the banisters to ask Lily had Gabriel or Freddy come.

1. Someone who buys and sells grain. *Usher's Island*: Dublin neighborhood, beside the River Liffey.
2. The Royal Academy of Music (founded 1848), Ireland's most important and prestigious music school. *Haddington Road*: Mary Jane is the organist at St. Mary's Roman Catholic Church on Haddington Road.
3. Nickname of the Franciscan Church of St. Francis of Assisi near Usher's Island.
4. That is, especially expensive tea and cuts of beef.   5. Drunk.

—O, Mr Conroy, said Lily to Gabriel when she opened the door for him, Miss Kate and Miss Julia thought you were never coming. Good-night, Mrs Conroy.

—I'll engage they did, said Gabriel, but they forget that my wife here takes 5 three mortal hours to dress herself.

He stood on the mat, scraping the snow from his goloshes, while Lily led his wife to the foot of the stairs and called out:

—Miss Kate, here's Mrs Conroy.

Kate and Julia came toddling down the dark stairs at once. Both of them kissed Gabriel's wife, said she must be perished alive and asked was Gabriel with her.

—Here I am as right as the mail, Aunt Kate! Go on up. I'll follow, called out Gabriel from the dark.

He continued scraping his feet vigorously while the three women went upstairs, 10 laughing, to the ladies' dressing-room. A light fringe of snow lay like a cape on the shoulders of his overcoat and like toecaps on the toes of his goloshes; and, as the buttons of his overcoat slipped with a squeaking noise through the snow-stiffened frieze, a cold fragrant air from out-of-doors escaped from crevices and folds.

—Is it snowing again, Mr Conroy? asked Lily.

She had preceded him into the pantry to help him off with his overcoat. Gabriel smiled at the three syllables she had given his surname and glanced at her. She was a slim, growing girl, pale in complexion and with hay-coloured hair. The gas in the pantry made her look still paler. Gabriel had known her when she was a child and used to sit on the lowest step nursing a rag doll.

—Yes, Lily, he answered, and I think we're in for a night of it.

He looked up at the pantry ceiling, which was shaking with the stamping and shuffling of feet on the floor above, listened for a moment to the piano and then glanced at the girl, who was folding his overcoat carefully at the end of a shelf.

—Tell me, Lily, he said in a friendly tone, do you still go to school? 15

—O no, sir, she answered. I'm done schooling this year and more.

—O, then, said Gabriel gaily, I suppose we'll be going to your wedding one of these fine days with your young man, eh?

The girl glanced back at him over her shoulder and said with great bitterness:

—The men that is now is only all palaver[6] and what they can get out of you.

Gabriel coloured as if he felt he had made a mistake and, without looking at 20 her, kicked off his goloshes and flicked actively with his muffler at his patent-leather shoes.

He was a stout tallish young man. The high colour of his cheeks pushed upwards even to his forehead where it scattered itself in a few formless patches of pale red; and on his hairless face there scintillated restlessly the polished lenses and the bright gilt rims of the glasses which screened his delicate and restless eyes. His glossy black hair was parted in the middle and brushed in a long curve behind his ears where it curled slightly beneath the groove left by his hat.

When he had flicked lustre into his shoes he stood up and pulled his waist-coat down more tightly on his plump body. Then he took a coin rapidly from his pocket.

—O Lily, he said, thrusting it into her hands, it's Christmas-time, isn't it? Just . . . here's a little. . . .

He walked rapidly towards the door.

—O no, sir! cried the girl, following him. Really, sir, I wouldn't take it. 25

6. Flattery, empty talk.

—Christmas-time! Christmas-time! said Gabriel, almost trotting to the stairs and waving his hand to her in deprecation.

The girl, seeing that he had gained the stairs, called out after him:

—Well, thank you, sir.

He waited outside the drawing-room door until the waltz should finish, listening to the skirts that swept against it and to the shuffling of feet. He was still discomposed by the girl's bitter and sudden retort. It had cast a gloom over him which he tried to dispel by arranging his cuffs and the bows of his tie. Then he took from his waistcoat pocket a little paper and glanced at the headings he had made for his speech. He was undecided about the lines from Robert Browning for he feared they would be above the heads of his hearers. Some quotation that they could recognise from Shakespeare or from the Melodies[7] would be better. The indelicate clacking of the men's heels and the shuffling of their soles reminded him that their grade of culture differed from his. He would only make himself ridiculous by quoting poetry to them which they could not understand. They would think that he was airing his superior education. He would fail with them just as he had failed with the girl in the pantry. He had taken up a wrong tone. His whole speech was a mistake from first to last, an utter failure.

30   Just then his aunts and his wife came out of the ladies' dressing-room. His aunts were two small plainly dressed old women. Aunt Julia was an inch or so the taller. Her hair, drawn low over the tops of her ears, was grey; and grey also, with darker shadows, was her large flaccid face. Though she was stout in build and stood erect her slow eyes and parted lips gave her the appearance of a woman who did not know where she was or where she was going. Aunt Kate was more vivacious. Her face, healthier than her sister's, was all puckers and creases, like a shrivelled red apple, and her hair, braided in the same old-fashioned way, had not lost its ripe nut colour.

They both kissed Gabriel frankly. He was their favourite nephew, the son of their dead elder sister, Ellen, who had married T. J. Conroy of the Port and Docks.[8]

—Gretta tells me you're not going to take a cab back to Monkstown to-night, Gabriel, said Aunt Kate.

—No, said Gabriel, turning to his wife, we had quite enough of that last year, hadn't we? Don't you remember, Aunt Kate, what a cold Gretta got out of it? Cab windows rattling all the way, and the east wind blowing in after we passed Merrion. Very jolly it was. Gretta caught a dreadful cold.

Aunt Kate frowned severely and nodded her head at every word.

35   —Quite right, Gabriel, quite right, she said. You can't be too careful.

—But as for Gretta there, said Gabriel, she'd walk home in the snow if she were let.

Mrs Conroy laughed.

—Don't mind him, Aunt Kate, she said. He's really an awful bother, what with green shades for Tom's eyes at night and making him do the dumb-bells, and forcing Eva to eat the stirabout.[9] The poor child! And she simply hates the sight of it! . . . O, but you'll never guess what he makes me wear now!

7. *Irish Melodies* (1807–35), an extremely popular collection of poems by Dublin-born writer Thomas Moore (1779–1852). *Robert Browning*: English poet (1812–89) best known for his dramatic monologues.

8. The Dublin Port and Docks Board was the very powerful group that regulated shipping activities, managed harbor facilities, and collected customs duties.   9. Oatmeal or cornmeal porridge.

She broke out into a peal of laughter and glanced at her husband, whose admiring and happy eyes had been wandering from her dress to her face and hair. The two aunts laughed heartily too, for Gabriel's solicitude was a standing joke with them.

—Goloshes! said Mrs Conroy. That's the latest. Whenever it's wet underfoot 40 I must put on my goloshes. To-night even he wanted me to put them on, but I wouldn't. The next thing he'll buy me will be a diving suit.

Gabriel laughed nervously and patted his tie reassuringly while Aunt Kate nearly doubled herself, so heartily did she enjoy the joke. The smile soon faded from Aunt Julia's face and her mirthless eyes were directed towards her nephew's face. After a pause she asked:

—And what are goloshes, Gabriel?

—Goloshes, Julia! exclaimed her sister. Goodness me, don't you know what goloshes are? You wear them over your . . . over your boots, Gretta, isn't it?

—Yes, said Mrs Conroy. Guttapercha things.[1] We both have a pair now. Gabriel says everyone wears them on the continent.

—O, on the continent, murmured Aunt Julia, nodding her head slowly. 45

Gabriel knitted his brows and said, as if he were slightly angered:

—It's nothing very wonderful but Gretta thinks it very funny because she says the word reminds her of Christy Minstrels.[2]

—But tell me, Gabriel, said Aunt Kate, with brisk tact. Of course, you've seen about the room. Gretta was saying . . .

—O, the room is all right, replied Gabriel. I've taken one in the Gresham.

—To be sure, said Aunt Kate, by far the best thing to do. And the children, 50 Gretta, you're not anxious about them?

—O, for one night, said Mrs Conroy. Besides, Bessie will look after them.

—To be sure, said Aunt Kate again. What a comfort it is to have a girl like that, one you can depend on! There's that Lily, I'm sure I don't know what has come over her lately. She's not the girl she was at all.

Gabriel was about to ask his aunt some questions on this point but she broke off suddenly to gaze after her sister who had wandered down the stairs and was craning her neck over the banisters.

—Now, I ask you, she said, almost testily, where is Julia going? Julia! Julia! Where are you going?

Julia, who had gone halfway down one flight, came back and announced 55 blandly:

—Here's Freddy.

At the same moment a clapping of hands and a final flourish of the pianist told that the waltz had ended. The drawing-room door was opened from within and some couples came out. Aunt Kate drew Gabriel aside hurriedly and whispered into his ear:

—Slip down, Gabriel, like a good fellow and see if he's all right, and don't let him up if he's screwed. I'm sure he's screwed. I'm sure he is.

1. Tough plastic substance resembling rubber.
2. New York–based theatrical company founded by Edward Christy in the 1840s, which pioneered the blackface minstrel shows that became wildly popular in the mid- to late nineteenth century. These music and comedy shows featured white performers in dark makeup playing stereotypical African American characters. The word *goloshes* may remind Greta of the Christy Minstrels because it sounds like *gollywog*, a doll with exaggerated black features that first appeared in 1895.

Gabriel went to the stairs and listened over the banisters. He could hear two persons talking in the pantry. Then he recognised Freddy Malins' laugh. He went down the stairs noisily.

60 —It's such a relief, said Aunt Kate to Mrs Conroy, that Gabriel is here. I always feel easier in my mind when he's here. . . . Julia, there's Miss Daly and Miss Power will take some refreshment. Thanks for your beautiful waltz, Miss Daly. It made lovely time.

A tall wizen-faced man, with a stiff grizzled moustache and swarthy skin, who was passing out with his partner said:

—And may we have some refreshment, too, Miss Morkan?

—Julia, said Aunt Kate summarily, and here's Mr Browne and Miss Furlong. Take them in, Julia, with Miss Daly and Miss Power.

—I'm the man for the ladies, said Mr Browne, pursing his lips until his moustache bristled and smiling in all his wrinkles. You know, Miss Morkan, the reason they are so fond of me is—

65 He did not finish his sentence, but, seeing that Aunt Kate was out of earshot, at once led the three young ladies into the back room. The middle of the room was occupied by two square tables placed end to end, and on these Aunt Julia and the caretaker were straightening and smoothing a large cloth. On the sideboard were arrayed dishes and plates, and glasses and bundles of knives and forks and spoons. The top of the closed square piano served also as a sideboard for viands and sweets. At a smaller sideboard in one corner two young men were standing, drinking hop-bitters.[3]

Mr Browne led his charges thither and invited them all, in jest, to some ladies' punch, hot, strong and sweet. As they said they never took anything strong he opened three bottles of lemonade for them. Then he asked one of the young men to move aside, and, taking hold of the decanter, filled out for himself a goodly measure of whisky. The young men eyed him respectfully while he took a trial sip.

—God help me, he said, smiling, it's the doctor's orders.

His wizened face broke into a broader smile, and the three young ladies laughed in musical echo to his pleasantry, swaying their bodies to and fro, with nervous jerks of their shoulders. The boldest said:

—O, now, Mr Browne, I'm sure the doctor never ordered anything of the kind.

70 Mr Browne took another sip of his whisky and said, with sidling mimicry:

—Well, you see, I'm like the famous Mrs Cassidy, who is reported to have said: *Now, Mary Grimes, if I don't take it, make me take it, for I feel I want it.*

His hot face had leaned forward a little too confidentially and he had assumed a very low Dublin accent so that the young ladies, with one instinct, received his speech in silence. Miss Furlong, who was one of Mary Jane's pupils, asked Miss Daly what was the name of the pretty waltz she had played; and Mr Browne, seeing that he was ignored, turned promptly to the two young men who were more appreciative.

A red-faced young woman, dressed in pansy,[4] came into the room, excitedly clapping her hands and crying:

—Quadrilles! Quadrilles![5]

---

3. Nonalcoholic drink. 4. That is, a dress the color of a pansy—bluish-purple or violet.
5. Elaborate square dance of French origin composed of five different sections or "figures" performed by four couples.

Close on her heels came Aunt Kate, crying: 75

—Two gentlemen and three ladies, Mary Jane!

—O, here's Mr Bergin and Mr Kerrigan, said Mary Jane. Mr Kerrigan, will you take Miss Power? Miss Furlong, may I get you a partner, Mr Bergin. O, that'll just do now.

—Three ladies, Mary Jane, said Aunt Kate.

The two young gentlemen asked the ladies if they might have the pleasure, and Mary Jane turned to Miss Daly.

—O, Miss Daly, you're really awfully good, after playing for the last two dances,   80
but really we're so short of ladies to-night.

—I don't mind in the least, Miss Morkan.

—But I've a nice partner for you, Mr Bartell D'Arcy, the tenor. I'll get him to sing later on. All Dublin is raving about him.

—Lovely voice, lovely voice! said Aunt Kate.

As the piano had twice begun the prelude to the first figure Mary Jane led her recruits quickly from the room. They had hardly gone when Aunt Julia wandered slowly into the room, looking behind her at something.

—What is the matter, Julia? asked Aunt Kate anxiously. Who is it?   85

Julia, who was carrying in a column of table-napkins, turned to her sister and said, simply, as if the question had surprised her:

—It's only Freddy, Kate, and Gabriel with him.

In fact right behind her Gabriel could be seen piloting Freddy Malins across the landing. The latter, a young man of about forty, was of Gabriel's size and build, with very round shoulders. His face was fleshy and pallid, touched with colour only at the thick hanging lobes of his ears and at the wide wings of his nose. He had coarse features, a blunt nose, a convex and receding brow, tumid and protruded lips. His heavy-lidded eyes and the disorder of his scanty hair made him look sleepy. He was laughing heartily in a high key at a story which he had been telling Gabriel on the stairs and at the same time rubbing the knuckles of his left fist backwards and forwards into his left eye.

—Good-evening, Freddy, said Aunt Julia.

Freddy Malins bade the Misses Morkan good-evening in what seemed an off-   90
hand fashion by reason of the habitual catch in his voice and then, seeing that Mr Browne was grinning at him from the sideboard, crossed the room on rather shaky legs and began to repeat in an undertone the story he had just told to Gabriel.

—He's not so bad, is he? said Aunt Kate to Gabriel.

Gabriel's brows were dark but he raised them quickly and answered:

—O no, hardly noticeable.

—Now, isn't he a terrible fellow! she said. And his poor mother made him take the pledge[6] on New Year's Eve. But come on, Gabriel, into the drawing-room.

Before leaving the room with Gabriel she signaled to Mr Browne by frowning   95
and shaking her forefinger in warning to and fro. Mr Browne nodded in answer and, when she had gone, said to Freddy Malins:

—Now, then, Teddy, I'm going to fill you out a good glass of lemonade just to buck you up.

Freddy Malins, who was nearing the climax of his story, waved the offer aside impatiently but Mr Browne, having first called Freddy Malins' attention to a

---

6. Temperance or teetotal pledge, an oath not to drink alcohol.

disarray in his dress, filled out and handed him a full glass of lemonade. Freddy Malins' left hand accepted the glass mechanically, his right hand being engaged in the mechanical readjustment of his dress. Mr Browne, whose face was once more wrinkling with mirth, poured out for himself a glass of whisky while Freddy Malins exploded, before he had well reached the climax of his story, in a kink of high-pitched bronchitic laughter and, setting down his untasted and overflowing glass, began to rub the knuckles of his left fist backwards and forwards into his left eye, repeating words of his last phrase as well as his fit of laughter would allow him.

· · ·

Gabriel could not listen while Mary Jane was playing her Academy piece, full of runs and difficult passages, to the hushed drawing-room. He liked music but the piece she was playing had no melody for him and he doubted whether it had any melody for the other listeners, though they had begged Mary Jane to play something. Four young men, who had come from the refreshment-room to stand in the doorway at the sound of the piano, had gone away quietly in couples after a few minutes. The only persons who seemed to follow the music were Mary Jane herself, her hands racing along the key-board or lifted from it at the pauses like those of a priestess in momentary imprecation, and Aunt Kate standing at her elbow to turn the page.

Gabriel's eyes, irritated by the floor, which glittered with beeswax under the heavy chandelier, wandered to the wall above the piano. A picture of the balcony scene in *Romeo and Juliet*[7] hung there and beside it was a picture of the two murdered princes in the Tower[8] which Aunt Julia had worked in red, blue and brown wools when she was a girl. Probably in the school they had gone to as girls that kind of work had been taught, for one year his mother had worked for him as a birthday present a waistcoat of purple tabinet,[9] with little foxes' heads upon it, lined with brown satin and having round mulberry buttons. It was strange that his mother had had no musical talent though Aunt Kate used to call her the brains carrier of the Morkan family. Both she and Julia had always seemed a little proud of their serious and matronly sister. Her photograph stood before the pierglass.[1] She held an open book on her knees and was pointing out something in it to Constantine who, dressed in a man-o'-war suit,[2] lay at her feet. It was she who had chosen the names for her sons for she was very sensible of the dignity of family life. Thanks to her, Constantine was now senior curate[3] in Balbriggan and, thanks to her, Gabriel himself had taken his degree in the Royal University. A shadow passed over his face as he remembered her sullen opposition to his marriage. Some slighting phrases she had used still rankled in his memory; she had once spoken of Gretta as being country cute[4] and that was not true of

---

7. Famous scene of Shakespeare's tragedy (2.2) in which Romeo declares his love to Juliet as she stands on the balcony above him.

8. In 1483, the two very young sons of King Edward IV of England died while imprisoned in the Tower of London, their deaths purportedly ordered by their uncle, who became King Richard III the same year.

9. Damask-like poplin fabric.

1. Large high mirror, especially one designed to be hung between two windows.

2. That is, a sailor suit—a child's outfit designed to look like the uniform worn by a sailor serving on the type of ship known as a man-of-war.   3. Clergyman in charge of a parish or church district.

4. Beginning of a pejorative idiomatic expression that ends "and city clever"; *cute* in this context is an abbreviation of *acute*.

Gretta at all. It was Gretta who had nursed her during all her last long illness in their house at Monkstown.

He knew that Mary Jane must be near the end of her piece for she was playing again the opening melody with runs of scales after every bar and while he waited for the end the resentment died down in his heart. The piece ended with a trill of octaves in the treble and a final deep octave in the bass. Great applause greeted Mary Jane as, blushing and rolling up her music nervously, she escaped from the room. The most vigorous clapping came from the four young men in the door-way who had gone away to the refreshment-room at the beginning of the piece but had come back when the piano had stopped.

Lancers[5] were arranged. Gabriel found himself partnered with Miss Ivors. She was a frank-mannered talkative young lady, with a freckled face and promi-nent brown eyes. She did not wear a low-cut bodice and the large brooch which was fixed in the front of her collar bore on it an Irish device.

When they had taken their places she said abruptly:

—I have a crow to pluck with you.

—With me? said Gabriel.

She nodded her head gravely.

—What is it? asked Gabriel, smiling at her solemn manner.

—Who is G. C.? answered Miss Ivors, turning her eyes upon him.

Gabriel coloured and was about to knit his brows, as if he did not under-stand, when she said bluntly:

—O, innocent Amy! I have found out that you write for *The Daily Express*. Now, aren't you ashamed of yourself?

—Why should I be ashamed of myself? asked Gabriel, blinking his eyes and trying to smile.

—Well, I'm ashamed of you, said Miss Ivors frankly. To say you'd write for a rag like that. I didn't think you were a West Briton.[6]

A look of perplexity appeared on Gabriel's face. It was true that he wrote a literary column every Wednesday in *The Daily Express*, for which he was paid fifteen shillings. But that did not make him a West Briton surely. The books he received for review were almost more welcome than the paltry cheque. He loved to feel the covers and turn over the pages of newly printed books. Nearly every day when his teaching in the college was ended he used to wander down the quays to the second-hand booksellers, to Hickey's on Bachelor's Walk, to Webb's or Massey's on Aston's Quay, or to O'Clohissey's in the by-street. He did not know how to meet her charge. He wanted to say that literature was above politics. But they were friends of many years' standing and their careers had been parallel, first at the University and then as teachers: he could not risk a grandiose phrase with her. He continued blinking his eyes and trying to smile and murmured lamely that he saw nothing political in writing reviews of books.

When their turn to cross had come he was still perplexed and inattentive. Miss Ivors promptly took his hand in a warm grasp and said in a soft friendly tone:

—Of course, I was only joking. Come, we cross now.

5. Popular form of quadrille that could be danced by more than four couples.
6. Irishman so loyal to Britain that he considers Ireland to be merely Britain's westernmost province.

When they were together again she spoke of the University question[7] and Gabriel felt more at ease. A friend of hers had shown her his review of Browning's poems. That was how she had found out the secret: but she liked the review immensely. Then she said suddenly:

—O, Mr Conroy, will you come for an excursion to the Aran Isles[8] this summer? We're going to stay there a whole month. It will be splendid out in the Atlantic. You ought to come. Mr Clancy is coming, and Mr Kilkelly and Kathleen Kearney. It would be splendid for Gretta too if she'd come. She's from Connacht,[9] isn't she?

—Her people are, said Gabriel shortly.

—But you will come, won't you? said Miss Ivors, laying her warm hand eagerly on his arm.

—The fact is, said Gabriel, I have already arranged to go—

120 —Go where? asked Miss Ivors.

—Well, you know, every year I go for a cycling tour with some fellows and so—

—But where? asked Miss Ivors.

—Well, we usually go to France or Belgium or perhaps Germany, said Gabriel awkwardly.

—And why do you go to France and Belgium, said Miss Ivors, instead of visiting your own land?

125 —Well, said Gabriel, it's partly to keep in touch with the languages and partly for a change.

—And haven't you your own language to keep in touch with—Irish? Asked Miss Ivors.

—Well, said Gabriel, if it comes to that, you know, Irish is not my language.

Their neighbours had turned to listen to the cross-examination. Gabriel glanced right and left nervously and tried to keep his good humour under the ordeal which was making a blush invade his forehead.

—And haven't you your own land to visit, continued Miss Ivors, that you know nothing of, your own people, and your own country?

130 —O, to tell you the truth, retorted Gabriel suddenly, I'm sick of my own country, sick of it!

—Why? Asked Miss Ivors.

Gabriel did not answer for his retort had heated him.

—Why? repeated Miss Ivors.

They had to go visiting together and, as he had not answered her, Miss Ivors said warmly:

135 —Of course, you've no answer.

Gabriel tried to cover his agitation by taking part in the dance with great energy. He avoided her eyes for he had seen a sour expression on her face. But when they met in the long chain he was surprised to feel his hand firmly pressed. She looked at him from under her brows for a moment quizzically until he smiled.

---

7. Controversy over the organization and character of Irish higher education, primarily regarding both the role of Catholicism and Protestantism and the possible admission of women.

8. Islands off Galway on the west coast of Ireland whose largely Gaelic-speaking inhabitants continued to live in what many in the late nineteenth century regarded as traditional, hence "true" Irish fashion; the islands were made famous by Irish Revivalist J. M. Synge's play *Riders to the Sea* (1901) and his nonfictional *Aran Islands* (1907).   9. Ireland's westernmost province; it includes both the county and city of Galway.

Then, just as the chain was about to start again, she stood on tiptoe and whispered into his ear:

—West Briton!

When the lancers were over Gabriel went away to a remote corner of the room where Freddy Malins' mother was sitting. She was a stout feeble old woman with white hair. Her voice had a catch in it like her son's and she stuttered slightly. She had been told that Freddy had come and that he was nearly all right. Gabriel asked her whether she had had a good crossing. She lived with her married daughter in Glasgow and came to Dublin on a visit once a year. She answered placidly that she had had a beautiful crossing and that the captain had been most attentive to her. She spoke also of the beautiful house her daughter kept in Glasgow, and of all the nice friends they had there. While her tongue rambled on Gabriel tried to banish from his mind all memory of the unpleasant incident with Miss Ivors. Of course the girl or woman, or whatever she was, was an enthusiast but there was a time for all things. Perhaps he ought not to have answered her like that. But she had no right to call him a West Briton before people, even in joke. She had tried to make him ridiculous before people, heckling him and staring at him with her rabbit's eyes.

He saw his wife making her way towards him through the waltzing couples. When she reached him she said into his ear:

—Gabriel, Aunt Kate wants to know won't you carve the goose as usual. Miss 140 Daly will carve the ham and I'll do the pudding.

—All right, said Gabriel.

—She's sending in the younger ones first as soon as this waltz is over so that we'll have the table to ourselves.

—Were you dancing? Asked Gabriel.

—Of course I was. Didn't you see me? What words had you with Molly Ivors?

—No words. Why? Did she say so? 145

—Something like that. I'm trying to get that Mr D'Arcy to sing. He's full of conceit, I think.

—There were no words, said Gabriel moodily, only she wanted me to go for a trip to the west of Ireland and I said I wouldn't.

His wife clasped her hands excitedly and gave a little jump.

—O, do go, Gabriel, she cried. I'd love to see Galway again.

—You can go if you like, said Gabriel coldly. 150

She looked at him for a moment, then turned to Mrs Malins and said:

—There's a nice husband for you, Mrs Malins.

While she was threading her way back across the room Mrs Malins, without adverting to the interruption, went on to tell Gabriel what beautiful places there were in Scotland and beautiful scenery. Her son-in-law brought them every year to the lakes and they used to go fishing. Her son-in-law was a splendid fisher. One day he caught a fish, a beautiful big big fish, and the man in the hotel boiled it for their dinner.

Gabriel hardly heard what she said. Now that supper was coming near he began to think again about his speech and about the quotation. When he saw Freddy Malins coming across the room to visit his mother Gabriel left the chair free for him and retired into the embrasure of the window. The room had already cleared and from the back room came the clatter of plates and knives. Those who still remained in the drawing-room seemed tired of dancing and were conversing quietly in little groups. Gabriel's warm trembling fingers tapped the cold pane of the window. How cool it must be outside! How pleasant it would be to walk out alone, first along by the river and then through the park! The snow would be lying on the branches of the trees and forming a bright cap on the top of the Wellington Monument.[1] How much more pleasant it would be there than at the supper-table!

155   He ran over the headings of his speech: Irish hospitality, sad memories, the Three Graces, Paris,[2] the quotation from Browning. He repeated to himself a phrase he had written in his review: *One feels that one is listening to a thought-tormented music.* Miss Ivors had praised the review. Was she sincere? Had she really any life of her own behind all her propagandism? There had never been any ill-feeling between them until that night. It unnerved him to think that she would be at the supper-table, looking up at him while he spoke with her critical quizzing eyes. Perhaps she would not be sorry to see him fail in his speech. An idea came into his mind and gave him courage. He would say, alluding to Aunt Kate and Aunt Julia: *Ladies and Gentlemen, the generation which is now on the wane among us may have had its faults but for my part I think it had certain qualities of hospitality, of humour, of humanity, which the new and very serious and hypereducated generation that is growing up around us seems to me to lack.* Very good: that was one for Miss Ivors. What did he care that his aunts were only two ignorant old women?

A murmur in the room attracted his attention. Mr Browne was advancing from the door, gallantly escorting Aunt Julia, who leaned upon his arm, smiling and hanging her head. An irregular musketry of applause escorted her also as far as the piano and then, as Mary Jane seated herself on the stool, and Aunt Julia, no longer smiling, half turned so as to pitch her voice fairly into the room, gradually ceased. Gabriel recognised the prelude. It was that of an old song of Aunt Julia's—*Arrayed for the Bridal.*[3] Her voice, strong and clear in tone, attacked with great spirit the runs which embellish the air and though she sang very rapidly she did not miss even the smallest of the grace notes. To follow the voice, without looking at the singer's face, was to feel and share the excitement of swift and secure flight. Gabriel applauded loudly with all the others at the close of the song and loud applause was borne in from the invisible supper-table. It sounded so genuine that a little colour struggled into Aunt Julia's face as she bent to replace in the music-stand the old leather-bound song-book that had her initials on the cover. Freddy Malins, who had listened with his head perched sideways to hear her better, was still applauding when everyone else had ceased and talking animatedly to his mother who nodded her head gravely and slowly in acquiescence. At last, when he

---

1. Monument in Dublin's Phoenix Park (just to the west of Usher Island) commemorating the achievements of Dublin-born Arthur Wellesley (1769–1852), Duke of Wellington, the Anglo-Irish Protestant and political conservative who defeated Napoleon at Waterloo (1816) and later served as British prime minister (1828–30).

2. Trojan prince of Greek literature and myth who, asked to judge a beauty contest between the three principal Greek goddesses, chooses Aphrodite, who bribes or rewards him with Helen, the human world's most beautiful woman. Because Helen is already married to the King of Sparta, however, her elopement with Paris ultimately causes the war with the Greeks that destroys Troy. *Three Graces*: Aglaia, Thalia, and Euphrosyne, the three goddesses of Greek mythology who personified and bestowed beauty, charm, and grace.

3. Song by George Linley based on an aria in Italian composer Vincenzo Bellini's *I Puritani di Scozia* ("The Puritans of Scotland," 1835), an opera based, in turn, on Scottish writer Sir Walter Scott's novel *Old Mortality* (1816). In the opera, set during the English Civil War, a Puritan father wishes to marry his daughter to another Puritan despite her love for a Royalist; she ultimately wins her father's consent to marry her true love.

could clap no more, he stood up suddenly and hurried across the room to Aunt Julia whose hand he seized and held in both his hands, shaking it when words failed him or the catch in his voice proved too much for him.

—I was just telling my mother, he said, I never heard you sing so well, never. No, I never heard your voice so good as it is to-night. Now! Would you believe that now? That's the truth. Upon my word and honour that's the truth. I never heard your voice sound so fresh and so . . . so clear and fresh, never.

Aunt Julia smiled broadly and murmured something about compliments as she released her hand from his grasp. Mr Browne extended his open hand towards her and said to those who were near him in the manner of a showman introducing a prodigy to an audience:

—Miss Julia Morkan, my latest discovery!

He was laughing very heartily at this himself when Freddy Malins turned to 160 him and said:

—Well, Browne, if you're serious you might make a worse discovery. All I can say is I never heard her sing half so well as long as I am coming here. And that's the honest truth.

—Neither did I, said Mr Browne. I think her voice has greatly improved.

Aunt Julia shrugged her shoulders and said with meek pride:

—Thirty years ago I hadn't a bad voice as voices go.

—I often told Julia, said Aunt Kate emphatically, that she was simply thrown 165 away in that choir. But she never would be said[4] by me.

She turned as if to appeal to the good sense of the others against a refractory child while Aunt Julia gazed in front of her, a vague smile of reminiscence play-ing on her face.

—No, continued Aunt Kate, she wouldn't be said or led by anyone, slaving there in that choir night and day, night and day. Six o'clock on Christmas morn-ing! And all for what?

—Well, isn't it for the honour of God, Aunt Kate? asked Mary Jane, twisting round on the piano-stool and smiling.

Aunt Kate turned fiercely on her niece and said:

—I know all about the honour of God, Mary Jane, but I think it's not at all 170 honourable for the pope to turn out the women out of the choirs that have slaved there all their lives and put little whipper-snappers of boys over their heads.[5] I suppose it is for the good of the Church if the pope does it. But it's not just, Mary Jane, and it's not right.

She had worked herself into a passion and would have continued in defence of her sister for it was a sore subject with her but Mary Jane, seeing that all the dancers had come back, intervened pacifically:

—Now, Aunt Kate, you're giving scandal to Mr Browne who is of the other persuasion.[6]

Aunt Kate turned to Mr Browne, who was grinning at this allusion to his religion, and said hastily:

---

4. That is, advised or gainsaid.
5. In 1903, Pope Pius X ordered that women should not be allowed to sing in church choirs because cho-risters (like priests) perform "a real liturgical office," which women are "incapable of exercising." Their place was to be taken by boys.   6. That is, a Protestant.

—O, I don't question the pope's being right. I'm only a stupid old woman and I wouldn't presume to do such a thing. But there's such a thing as common everyday politeness and gratitude. And if I were in Julia's place I'd tell that Father Healy straight up to his face . . .

175 —And besides, Aunt Kate, said Mary Jane, we really are all hungry and when we are hungry we are all very quarrelsome.

—And when we are thirsty we are also quarrelsome, added Mr Browne.

—So that we had better go to supper, said Mary Jane, and finish the discussion afterwards.

On the landing outside the drawing-room Gabriel found his wife and Mary Jane trying to persuade Miss Ivors to stay for supper. But Miss Ivors, who had put on her hat and was buttoning her cloak, would not stay. She did not feel in the least hungry and she had already overstayed her time.

—But only for ten minutes, Molly, said Mrs Conroy. That won't delay you.

180 —To take a pick itself,[7] said Mary Jane, after all your dancing.

—I really couldn't, said Miss Ivors.

—I am afraid you didn't enjoy yourself at all, said Mary Jane hopelessly.

—Ever so much, I assure you, said Miss Ivors, but you really must let me run off now.

—But how can you get home? asked Mrs Conroy.

185 —O, it's only two steps up the quay.

Gabriel hesitated a moment and said:

—If you will allow me, Miss Ivors, I'll see you home if you really are obliged to go.

But Miss Ivors broke away from them.

—I won't hear of it, she cried. For goodness sake go in to your suppers and don't mind me. I'm quite well able to take care of myself.

190 —Well, you're the comical girl, Molly, said Mrs Conroy frankly.

—*Beannacht libh,*[8] cried Miss Ivors, with a laugh, as she ran down the staircase.

Mary Jane gazed after her, a moody puzzled expression on her face, while Mrs Conroy leaned over the banisters to listen for the hall-door. Gabriel asked himself was he the cause of her abrupt departure. But she did not seem to be in ill humour: she had gone away laughing. He stared blankly down the staircase.

At that moment Aunt Kate came toddling out of the supper-room, almost wringing her hands in despair.

—Where is Gabriel? she cried. Where on earth is Gabriel? There's everyone waiting in there, stage to let, and nobody to carve the goose!

195 —Here I am, Aunt Kate! cried Gabriel, with sudden animation, ready to carve a flock of geese, if necessary.

A fat brown goose lay at one end of the table and at the other end, on a bed of creased paper strewn with sprigs of parsley, lay a great ham, stripped of its outer skin and peppered over with crust crumbs, a neat paper frill round its shin and beside this was a round of spiced beef. Between these rival ends ran parallel lines of side-dishes: two little minsters of jelly, red and yellow; a shallow dish full of blocks of blancmange[9] and red jam, a large green leaf-shaped dish with a stalk-shaped handle, on which lay bunches of purple raisins and peeled almonds, a

---

7. Bite (of food). 8. Gaelic farewell; literally, "Blessing to ye" or "My blessings go with you."
9. White gelatin dessert or pudding made with milk and cornstarch or gelatin and flavored with almonds, vanilla, rum, or brandy.

companion dish on which lay a solid rectangle of Smyrna figs, a dish of custard topped with grated nutmeg, a small bowl full of chocolates and sweets wrapped in gold and silver papers and a glass vase in which stood some tall celery stalks. In the centre of the table there stood, as sentries to a fruit-stand which upheld a pyramid of oranges and American apples, two squat old-fashioned decanters of cut glass, one containing port and the other dark sherry. On the closed square piano a pudding in a huge yellow dish lay in waiting and behind it were three squads of bottles of stout and ale and minerals,[1] drawn up according to the colours of their uniforms, the first two black, with brown and red labels, the third and smallest squad white, with transverse green sashes.

Gabriel took his seat boldly at the head of the table and, having looked to the edge of the carver, plunged his fork firmly into the goose. He felt quite at ease now for he was an expert carver and liked nothing better than to find himself at the head of a well-laden table.

—Miss Furlong, what shall I send you? he asked. A wing or a slice of the breast?

—Just a small slice of the breast.

—Miss Higgins, what for you?

—O, anything at all, Mr Conroy.   200

While Gabriel and Miss Daly exchanged plates of goose and plates of ham and spiced beef Lily went from guest to guest with a dish of hot floury potatoes wrapped in a white napkin. This was Mary Jane's idea and she had also suggested apple sauce for the goose but Aunt Kate had said that plain roast goose without apple sauce had always been good enough for her and she hoped she might never eat worse. Mary Jane waited on her pupils and saw that they got the best slices and Aunt Kate and Aunt Julia opened and carried across from the piano bottles of stout and ale for the gentlemen and bottles of minerals for the ladies. There was a great deal of confusion and laughter and noise, the noise of orders and counter-orders, of knives and forks, of corks and glass-stoppers. Gabriel began to carve second helpings as soon as he had finished the first round without serving himself. Everyone protested loudly so that he compromised by taking a long draught of stout for he had found the carving hot work. Mary Jane settled down quietly to her supper but Aunt Kate and Aunt Julia were still toddling round the table, walking on each other's heels, getting in each other's way and giving each other unheeded orders. Mr Browne begged of them to sit down and eat their suppers and so did Gabriel but they said there was time enough so that, at last, Freddy Malins stood up and, capturing Aunt Kate, plumped her down on her chair amid general laughter.

When everyone had been well served Gabriel said, smiling:

—Now, if anyone wants a little more of what vulgar people call stuffing[2] let him or her speak.

A chorus of voices invited him to begin his own supper and Lily came forward   205
with three potatoes which she had reserved for him.

—Very well, said Gabriel amiably, as he took another preparatory draught, kindly forget my existence, ladies and gentlemen, for a few minutes.

He set to his supper and took no part in the conversation with which the table covered Lily's removal of the plates. The subject of talk was the opera company which was then at the Theatre Royal. Mr Bartell D'Arcy, the tenor, a dark-complexioned young man with a smart moustache, praised very highly the

1. That is, mineral water.   2. *Forcemeat* would be the more genteel term.

leading contralto of the company but Miss Furlong thought she had a rather vulgar style of production. Freddy Malins said there was a negro chieftain singing in the second part of the Gaiety pantomime who had one of the finest tenor voices he had ever heard.

—Have you heard him? he asked Mr Bartell D'Arcy across the table.

—No, answered Mr Bartell D'Arcy carelessly.

210 —Because, Freddy Malins explained, now I'd be curious to hear your opinion of him. I think he has a grand voice.

—It takes Teddy to find out the really good things, said Mr Browne familiarly to the table.

—And why couldn't he have a voice too? asked Freddy Malins sharply. Is it because he's only a black?

Nobody answered this question and Mary Jane led the table back to the legitimate opera. One of her pupils had given her a pass for *Mignon*.[3] Of course it was very fine, she said, but it made her think of poor Georgina Burns.[4] Mr Browne could go back farther still, to the old Italian companies that used to come to Dublin—Tietjens, Ilma de Murzka, Campanini, the great Trebelli, Giuglini, Ravelli, Aramburo.[5] Those were the days, he said, when there was something like singing to be heard in Dublin. He told too of how the top gallery of the old Royal used to be packed night after night, of how one night an Italian tenor had sung five encores to *Let Me Like a Soldier Fall*,[6] introducing a high C every time, and of how the gallery boys would sometimes in their enthusiasm unyoke the horses from the carriage of some great *prima donna* and pull her themselves through the streets to her hotel. Why did they never play the grand old operas now, he asked, *Dinorah*,[7] *Lucrezia Borgia*? Because they could not get the voices to sing them: that was why.

—O, well, said Mr Bartell D'Arcy, I presume there are as good singers to-day as there were then.

215 —Where are they? asked Mr Browne defiantly.

—In London, Paris, Milan, said Mr Bartell D'Arcy warmly. I suppose Caruso,[8] for example, is quite as good, if not better than any of the men you have mentioned.

3. 1886 opera by French composer Ambroise Thomas (1811–96); its heroine is a girl abducted by Gypsies and ultimately revealed to be of noble birth—but only after being tortured by unrequited love, nearly dying in a building set on fire by the madman who loves her, learning that her own mother died of grief after her disappearance, and finally winning the hand of her true love.

4. Celebrated soprano who debuted in Dublin in the 1878 Theatre Royal production of *The Bohemian Girl* and also appeared in *Mignon*. The Irish baritone to whom she was married apparently died suddenly only months before the Morkans' fictional party.

5. Many of the singers listed here met tragic ends: Ill with cancer, Therese Titjiens collapsed onstage at the end of her final London performance; Ilma di Murska died in poverty after losing her voice, her death inspiring her daughter's suicide; Campanini, too, lost his voice, while Giuglini died shortly after his release from a London mental asylum.

6. Aria sung by the hero of William Vincent Wallace's 1845 opera *Maritana*, after he learns that by marrying the title character he will be allowed to die nobly, "like a soldier," by firing squad rather than by hanging.

7. 1859 opera by Giacomo Meyerbeer in which a peasant girl's marriage to a goatherd is frustrated by natural disasters (a thunderbolt destroys her father's house), supernatural forces (after her fiancé leaves in search of a cursed treasure), and her own madness; *Lucrezia Borgia*: 1833 opera by Gaetano Donizetti about an infamous fifteenth-century Venetian noblewoman; it culminates with Borgia dying of grief after learning that her son is among the six men she has just poisoned.

8. Italian tenor Enrico Caruso (1873–1921) was perhaps the most famous singer of the early twentieth century.

—Maybe so, said Mr Browne. But I may tell you I doubt it strongly.

—O, I'd give anything to hear Caruso sing, said Mary Jane.

—For me, said Aunt Kate, who had been picking a bone, there was only one tenor. To please me, I mean. But I suppose none of you ever heard of him.

—Who was he, Miss Morkan? asked Mr Bartell D'Arcy politely.

—His name, said Aunt Kate, was Parkinson.[9] I heard him when he was in his prime and I think he had then the purest tenor voice that was ever put into a man's throat.

—Strange, said Mr Bartell D'Arcy. I never even heard of him.

—Yes, yes, Miss Morkan is right, said Mr Browne. I remember hearing of old Parkinson but he's too far back for me.

—A beautiful pure sweet mellow English tenor, said Aunt Kate with enthusiasm.

Gabriel having finished, the huge pudding was transferred to the table. The clatter of forks and spoons began again. Gabriel's wife served out spoonfuls of the pudding and passed the plates down the table. Midway down they were held up by Mary Jane, who replenished them with raspberry or orange jelly or with blancmange and jam. The pudding was of Aunt Julia's making and she received praises for it from all quarters. She herself said that it was not quite brown enough.

—Well, I hope, Miss Morkan, said Mr Browne, that I'm brown enough for you because, you know, I'm all brown.

All the gentlemen, except Gabriel, ate some of the pudding out of compliment to Aunt Julia. As Gabriel never ate sweets the celery had been left for him. Freddy Malins also took a stalk of celery and ate it with his pudding. He had been told that celery was a capital thing for the blood and he was just then under doctor's care. Mrs Malins, who had been silent all through the supper, said that her son was going down to Mount Melleray[1] in a week or so. The table then spoke of Mount Melleray, how bracing the air was down there, how hospitable the monks were and how they never asked for a penny-piece from their guests.

—And do you mean to say, asked Mr Browne incredulously, that a chap can go down there and put up there as if it were a hotel and live on the fat of the land and then come away without paying a farthing?

—O, most people give some donation to the monastery when they leave, said Mary Jane.

—I wish we had an institution like that in our Church, said Mr Browne candidly.

He was astonished to hear that the monks never spoke, got up at two in the morning and slept in their coffins. He asked what they did it for.

—That's the rule of the order,[2] said Aunt Kate firmly.

—Yes, but why? asked Mr Browne.

Aunt Kate repeated that it was the rule, that was all. Mr Browne still seemed not to understand. Freddy Malins explained to him, as best he could, that the monks were trying to make up for the sins committed by all the sinners in the

---

9. Perhaps an English-born organist who had a relatively brief career as a singer with a well-known Dublin opera company before becoming a theatrical manager.

1. Cistercian Abbey in southeastern Ireland founded in the 1830s, a refuge for alcoholics in need of rest, cure, and spiritual renewal.

2. Though the rules of the Cistercian monks do not require sleeping in coffins, they are rigorous, mandating a vow of silence and a day that begins with prayers at 2 A.M.

outside world. The explanation was not very clear for Mr Browne grinned and said:

235   —I like that idea very much but wouldn't a comfortable spring bed do them as well as a coffin?

—The coffin, said Mary Jane, is to remind them of their last end.

As the subject had grown lugubrious it was buried in a silence of the table during which Mrs Malins could be heard saying to her neighbour in an indistinct undertone:

—They are very good men, the monks, very pious men.

The raisins and almonds and figs and apples and oranges and chocolates and sweets were now passed about the table and Aunt Julia invited all the guests to have either port or sherry. At first Mr Bartell D'Arcy refused to take either but one of his neighbours nudged him and whispered something to him upon which he allowed his glass to be filled. Gradually as the last glasses were being filled the conversation ceased. A pause followed, broken only by the noise of the wine and by unsettlings of chairs. The Misses Morkan, all three, looked down at the tablecloth. Someone coughed once or twice and then a few gentlemen patted the table gently as a signal for silence. The silence came and Gabriel pushed back his chair and stood up.

240   The patting at once grew louder in encouragement and then ceased altogether. Gabriel leaned his ten trembling fingers on the tablecloth and smiled nervously at the company. Meeting a row of upturned faces he raised his eyes to the chandelier. The piano was playing a waltz tune and he could hear the skirts sweeping against the drawing-room door. People, perhaps, were standing in the snow on the quay outside, gazing up at the lighted windows and listening to the waltz music. The air was pure there. In the distance lay the park where the trees were weighted with snow. The Wellington Monument wore a gleaming cap of snow that flashed westward over the white field of Fifteen Acres.

He began:

—Ladies and Gentlemen.

—It has fallen to my lot this evening, as in years past, to perform a very pleasing task but a task for which I am afraid my poor powers as a speaker are all too inadequate.

—No, no! said Mr Browne.

245   —But, however that may be, I can only ask you to-night to take the will for the deed and to lend me your attention for a few moments while I endeavour to express to you in words what my feelings are on this occasion.

—Ladies and Gentlemen. It is not the first time that we have gathered together under this hospitable roof, around this hospitable board. It is not the first time that we have been the recipients—or perhaps, I had better say, the victims—of the hospitality of certain good ladies.

He made a circle in the air with his arm and paused. Everyone laughed or smiled at Aunt Kate and Aunt Julia and Mary Jane who all turned crimson with pleasure. Gabriel went on more boldly:

—I feel more strongly with every recurring year that our country has no tradition which does it so much honour and which it should guard so jealously as that of its hospitality. It is a tradition that is unique as far as my experience goes (and I have visited not a few places abroad) among the modern nations. Some would say, perhaps, that with us it is rather a failing than anything to be boasted of. But granted even that, it is, to my mind, a princely failing, and one that I trust will long be cultivated among us. Of one thing, at least, I am sure. As long as this one roof shelters the good ladies aforesaid—and I wish from my heart it may do so for many and many a long year to come—the tradition of genuine warm-hearted courteous Irish hospitality, which our forefathers have handed down to us and which we in turn must hand down to our descendants, is still alive among us.

A hearty murmur of assent ran round the table. It shot through Gabriel's mind that Miss Ivors was not there and that she had gone away discourteously: and he said with confidence in himself:

—Ladies and Gentlemen. 250

—A new generation is growing up in our midst, a generation actuated by new ideas and new principles. It is serious and enthusiastic for these new ideas and its enthusiasm, even when it is misdirected, is, I believe, in the main sincere. But we are living in a sceptical and, if I may use the phrase, a thought-tormented age: and sometimes I fear that this new generation, educated or hypereducated as it is, will lack those qualities of humanity, of hospitality, of kindly humour which belonged to an older day. Listening to-night to the names of all those great singers of the past it seemed to me, I must confess, that we were living in a less spacious age. Those days might, without exaggeration, be called spacious days: and if they are gone beyond recall let us hope, at least, that in gatherings such as this we shall still speak of them with pride and affection, still cherish in our hearts the memory of those dead and gone great ones whose fame the world will not willingly let die.[3]

—Hear, hear! said Mr Browne loudly.

—But yet, continued Gabriel, his voice falling into a softer inflection, there are always in gatherings such as this sadder thoughts that will recur to our minds: thoughts of the past, of youth, of changes, of absent faces that we miss here to-night. Our path through life is strewn with many such sad memories: and were we to brood upon them always we could not find the heart to go on bravely with our work among the living. We have all of us living duties and living affections which claim, and rightly claim, our strenuous endeavours.

—Therefore, I will not linger on the past. I will not let any gloomy moralising intrude upon us here to-night. Here we are gathered together for a brief moment from the bustle and rush of our everyday routine. We are met here as friends, in the spirit of good-fellowship, as colleagues, also to a certain extent, in the true spirit of *camaraderie*, and as the guests of—what shall I call them?—the Three Graces of the Dublin musical world.

The table burst into applause and laughter at this sally. Aunt Julia vainly 255 asked each of her neighbours in turn to tell her what Gabriel had said.

—He says we are the Three Graces, Aunt Julia, said Mary Jane.

Aunt Julia did not understand but she looked up, smiling, at Gabriel, who continued in the same vein:

—Ladies and Gentlemen.

—I will not attempt to play to-night the part that Paris played on another occasion. I will not attempt to choose between them. The task would be an invidious one and one beyond my poor powers. For when I view them in turn, whether it be our chief hostess herself, whose good heart, whose too good heart,

3. In *The Reason of Church Government Urg'd against Prelaty* (1641), John Milton expresses the hope that he "might perhaps leave something so written to after times as they should not willingly let it die."

has become a byword with all who know her, or her sister, who seems to be gifted with perennial youth and whose singing must have been a surprise and a revelation to us all to-night, or, last but not least, when I consider our youngest hostess, talented, cheerful, hard-working and the best of nieces, I confess, Ladies and Gentlemen, that I do not know to which of them I should award the prize.

260   Gabriel glanced down at his aunts and, seeing the large smile on Aunt Julia's face and the tears which had risen to Aunt Kate's eyes, hastened to his close. He raised his glass of port gallantly, while every member of the company fingered a glass expectantly, and said loudly:

—Let us toast them all three together. Let us drink to their health, wealth, long life, happiness and prosperity and may they long continue to hold the proud and self-won position which they hold in their profession and the position of honour and affection which they hold in our hearts.

All the guests stood up, glass in hand, and, turning towards the three seated ladies, sang in unison, with Mr Browne as leader:

> *For they are jolly gay fellows,*
> *For they are jolly gay fellows,*
> *For they are jolly gay fellows,*
> *Which nobody can deny.*

Aunt Kate was making frank use of her handkerchief and even Aunt Julia seemed moved. Freddy Malins beat time with his pudding-fork and the singers turned towards one another, as if in melodious conference, while they sang, with emphasis:

> *Unless he tells a lie,*
> *Unless he tells a lie.*

Then, turning once more towards their hostesses, they sang:

> *For they are jolly gay fellows,*
> *For they are jolly gay fellows,*
> *For they are jolly gay fellows,*
> *Which nobody can deny.*

265   The acclamation which followed was taken up beyond the door of the supper-room by many of the other guests and renewed time after time, Freddy Malins acting as officer with his fork on high.

· · ·

The piercing morning air came into the hall where they were standing so that Aunt Kate said:

—Close the door, somebody. Mrs Malins will get her death of cold.

—Browne is out there, Aunt Kate, said Mary Jane.

—Browne is everywhere, said Aunt Kate, lowering her voice.

270   Mary Jane laughed at her tone.

—Really, she said archly, he is very attentive.

—He has been laid on here like the gas, said Aunt Kate in the same tone, all during the Christmas.

She laughed herself this time good-humouredly and then added quickly:

—But tell him to come in, Mary Jane, and close the door. I hope to goodness he didn't hear me.

At that moment the hall-door was opened and Mr Browne came in from the 275
doorstep, laughing as if his heart would break. He was dressed in a long green
overcoat with mock astrakhan[4] cuffs and collar and wore on his head an oval
fur cap. He pointed down the snow-covered quay from where the sound of shrill
prolonged whistling was borne in.

—Teddy will have all the cabs in Dublin out, he said.

Gabriel advanced from the little pantry behind the office, struggling into his
overcoat and, looking round the hall, said:

—Gretta not down yet?

—She's getting on her things, Gabriel, said Aunt Kate.

—Who's playing up there? asked Gabriel. 280

—Nobody. They're all gone.

—O no, Aunt Kate, said Mary Jane. Bartell D'Arcy and Miss O'Callaghan aren't
gone yet.

—Someone is strumming at the piano, anyhow, said Gabriel.

Mary Jane glanced at Gabriel and Mr Browne and said with a shiver:

—It makes me feel cold to look at you two gentlemen muffled up like that. I 285
wouldn't like to face your journey home at this hour.

—I'd like nothing better this minute, said Mr Browne stoutly, than a rattling
fine walk in the country or a fast drive with a good spanking goer between the
shafts.

—We used to have a very good horse and trap at home, said Aunt Julia sadly.

—The never-to-be-forgotten Johnny, said Mary Jane, laughing.

Aunt Kate and Gabriel laughed too.

—Why, what was wonderful about Johnny? asked Mr Browne. 290

—The late lamented Patrick Morkan, our grandfather, that is, explained Gabriel,
commonly known in his later years as the old gentleman, was a glue-boiler.[5]

—O, now, Gabriel, said Aunt Kate, laughing, he had a starch mill.

—Well, glue or starch, said Gabriel, the old gentleman had a horse by the
name of Johnny. And Johnny used to work in the old gentleman's mill, walking
round and round in order to drive the mill. That was all very well; but now
comes the tragic part about Johnny. One fine day the old gentleman thought
he'd like to drive out with the quality[6] to a military review in the park.

—The Lord have mercy on his soul, said Aunt Kate compassionately.

—Amen, said Gabriel. So the old gentleman, as I said, harnessed Johnny and 295
put on his very best tall hat and his very best stock collar and drove out in grand
style from his ancestral mansion somewhere near Back Lane, I think.

Everyone laughed, even Mrs Malins, at Gabriel's manner and Aunt Kate said:

—O now, Gabriel, he didn't live in Back Lane, really. Only the mill was there.

—Out from the mansion of his forefathers, continued Gabriel, he drove with
Johnny. And everything went on beautifully until Johnny came in sight of King
Billy's[7] statue: and whether he fell in love with the horse King Billy sits on or

---

4. Expensive fabric made from the wool of newborn lambs from the Russian city of Astrakhan.
5. Glue was made by boiling the hides and hooves of animals, especially old horses.
6. That is, the upper classes.
7. 1701 equestrian statue, which stands outside the Irish Parliament and commemorates King William
III or William of Orange; Parliament chose to put William on the British throne because he was Protestant, and he went on to vanquish Ireland's last kings at the Battle of the Boyne in 1690, which effectively
turned Ireland into a British colony.

whether he thought he was back again in the mill, anyhow he began to walk round the statue.

Gabriel paced in a circle round the hall in his goloshes amid the laughter of the others.

300 —Round and round he went, said Gabriel, and the old gentleman, who was a very pompous old gentleman, was highly indignant. *Go on, sir! What do you mean, sir? Johnny! Johnny! Most extraordinary conduct! Can't understand the horse!*

The peals of laughter which followed Gabriel's imitation of the incident were interrupted by a resounding knock at the hall-door. Mary Jane ran to open it and let in Freddy Malins. Freddy Malins, with his hat well back on his head and his shoulders humped with cold, was puffing and steaming after his exertions.

—I could only get one cab, he said.

—O, we'll find another along the quay, said Gabriel.

—Yes, said Aunt Kate. Better not keep Mrs Malins standing in the draught.

305 Mrs Malins was helped down the front steps by her son and Mr Browne and, after many manœuvres, hoisted into the cab. Freddy Malins clambered in after her and spent a long time settling her on the seat, Mr Browne helping him with advice. At last she was settled comfortably and Freddy Malins invited Mr Browne into the cab. There was a good deal of confused talk, and then Mr Browne got into the cab. The cabman settled his rug over his knees, and bent down for the address. The confusion grew greater and the cabman was directed differently by Freddy Malins and Mr Browne, each of whom had his head out through a window of the cab. The difficulty was to know where to drop Mr Browne along the route and Aunt Kate, Aunt Julia and Mary Jane helped the discussion from the door-step with cross-directions and contradictions and abundance of laughter. As for Freddy Malins he was speechless with laughter. He popped his head in and out of the window every moment, to the great danger of his hat, and told his mother how the discussion was progressing till at last Mr Browne shouted to the bewildered cabman above the din of everybody's laughter:

—Do you know Trinity College?[8]

—Yes, sir, said the cabman.

—Well, drive bang up against Trinity College gates, said Mr Browne, and then we'll tell you where to go. You understand now?

310 —Yes, sir, said the cabman.

—Make like a bird for Trinity College.

—Right, sir, cried the cabman.

The horse was whipped up and the cab rattled off along the quay amid a chorus of laughter and adieus.

Gabriel had not gone to the door with the others. He was in a dark part of the hall gazing up the staircase. A woman was standing near the top of the first flight, in the shadow also. He could not see her face but he could see the terracotta and salmonpink panels of her skirt which the shadow made appear black and white. It was his wife. She was leaning on the banisters, listening to something. Gabriel was surprised at her stillness and strained his ear to listen also. But he could hear little save the noise of laughter and dispute on the front steps, a few chords struck on the piano and a few notes of a man's voice singing.

8. Ireland's oldest and most prestigious university, founded by Queen Elizabeth I in 1592.

He stood still in the gloom of the hall, trying to catch the air that the voice was   315
singing and gazing up at his wife. There was grace and mystery in her attitude as
if she were a symbol of something. He asked himself what is a woman standing on
the stairs in the shadow, listening to distant music, a symbol of. If he were a
painter he would paint her in that attitude. Her blue felt hat would show off the
bronze of her hair against the darkness and the dark panels of her skirt would
show off the light ones. *Distant Music* he would call the picture if he were a painter.

The hall-door was closed; and Aunt Kate, Aunt Julia and Mary Jane came
down the hall, still laughing.

—Well, isn't Freddy terrible? said Mary Jane. He's really terrible.

Gabriel said nothing but pointed up the stairs towards where his wife was
standing. Now that the hall-door was closed the voice and the piano could be
heard more clearly. Gabriel held up his hand for them to be silent. The song
seemed to be in the old Irish tonality and the singer seemed uncertain both of his
words and of his voice. The voice, made plaintive by distance and by the singer's
hoarseness, faintly illuminated the cadence of the air with words expressing grief:

> *O, the rain falls on my heavy locks*
> *And the dew wets my skin,*
> *My babe lies cold . . .*[9]

—O, exclaimed Mary Jane. It's Bartell D'Arcy singing and he wouldn't sing all
the night. O, I'll get him to sing a song before he goes.

—O do, Mary Jane, said Aunt Kate.   320

Mary Jane brushed past the others and ran to the staircase but before she
reached it the singing stopped and the piano was closed abruptly.

—O, what a pity! she cried. Is he coming down, Gretta?

Gabriel heard his wife answer yes and saw her come down towards them. A
few steps behind her were Mr Bartell D'Arcy and Miss O'Callaghan.

—O, Mr D'Arcy, cried Mary Jane, it's downright mean of you to break off like
that when we were all in raptures listening to you.

—I have been at him all the evening, said Miss O'Callaghan, and Mrs Conroy   325
too and he told us he had a dreadful cold and couldn't sing.

—O, Mr D'Arcy, said Aunt Kate, now that was a great fib to tell.

—Can't you see that I'm as hoarse as a crow? said Mr D'Arcy roughly.

He went into the pantry hastily and put on his overcoat. The others, taken
aback by his rude speech, could find nothing to say. Aunt Kate wrinkled her
brows and made signs to the others to drop the subject. Mr D'Arcy stood swath-
ing his neck carefully and frowning.

—It's the weather, said Aunt Julia, after a pause.

—Yes, everybody has colds, said Aunt Kate readily, everybody.   330

—They say, said Mary Jane, we haven't had snow like it for thirty years; and I
read this morning in the newspapers that the snow is general all over Ireland.

—I love the look of snow, said Aunt Julia sadly.

—So do I, said Miss O'Callaghan. I think Christmas is never really Christmas
unless we have the snow on the ground.

9. Tragic old Irish ballad often called *The Lass of Aughrim* (after a small village in County Galway) about a
peasant girl either seduced and abandoned by her noble lover (in some versions) or separated from him by
the machinations of his mother (in other versions).

—But poor Mr D'Arcy doesn't like the snow, said Aunt Kate, smiling.

335   Mr D'Arcy came from the pantry, fully swathed and buttoned, and in a repentant tone told them the history of his cold. Everyone gave him advice and said it was a great pity and urged him to be very careful of his throat in the night air. Gabriel watched his wife who did not join in the conversation. She was standing right under the dusty fanlight and the flame of the gas lit up the rich bronze of her hair which he had seen her drying at the fire a few days before. She was in the same attitude and seemed unaware of the talk about her. At last she turned towards them and Gabriel saw that there was colour on her cheeks and that her eyes were shining. A sudden tide of joy went leaping out of his heart.

—Mr D'Arcy, she said, what is the name of that song you were singing?

—It's called *The Lass of Aughrim*, said Mr D'Arcy, but I couldn't remember it properly. Why? Do you know it?

—*The Lass of Aughrim*, she repeated. I couldn't think of the name.

—It's a very nice air, said Mary Jane. I'm sorry you were not in voice to-night.

340   —Now, Mary Jane, said Aunt Kate, don't annoy Mr D'Arcy. I won't have him annoyed.

Seeing that all were ready to start she shepherded them to the door where good-night was said:

—Well, good-night, Aunt Kate, and thanks for the pleasant evening.

—Good-night, Gabriel. Good-night, Gretta!

—Good-night, Aunt Kate, and thanks ever so much. Good-night, Aunt Julia.

345   —O, good-night, Gretta, I didn't see you.

—Good-night, Mr D'Arcy. Good-night, Miss O'Callaghan.

—Good-night, Miss Morkan.

—Good-night, again.

—Good-night, all. Safe home.

350   —Good-night. Good-night.

The morning was still dark. A dull yellow light brooded over the houses and the river; and the sky seemed to be descending. It was slushy underfoot; and only streaks and patches of snow lay on the roofs, on the parapets of the quay and on the area railings. The lamps were still burning redly in the murky air and, across the river, the palace of the Four Courts stood out menacingly against the heavy sky.

She was walking on before him with Mr Bartell D'Arcy, her shoes in a brown parcel tucked under one arm and her hands holding her skirt up from the slush. She had no longer any grace of attitude but Gabriel's eyes were still bright with happiness. The blood went bounding along his veins; and the thoughts went rioting through his brain, proud, joyful, tender, valorous.

She was walking on before him so lightly and so erect that he longed to run after her noiselessly, catch her by the shoulders and say something foolish and affectionate into her ear. She seemed to him so frail that he longed to defend her against something and then to be alone with her. Moments of their secret life together burst like stars upon his memory. A heliotrope[1] envelope was lying beside his breakfast-cup and he was caressing it with his hand. Birds were twittering in the ivy and the sunny web of the curtain was shimmering along the floor: he could not eat for happiness. They were standing on the crowded platform and he was placing a ticket inside the warm palm of her glove. He was standing with her in

1. Shade of purple.

the cold, looking in through a grated window at a man making bottles in a roaring furnace. It was very cold. Her face, fragrant in the cold air, was quite close to his; and suddenly she called out to the man at the furnace:

—Is the fire hot, sir?

But the man could not hear her with the noise of the furnace. It was just as well. He might have answered rudely.

A wave of yet more tender joy escaped from his heart and went coursing in warm flood along his arteries. Like the tender fires of stars moments of their life together, that no one knew of or would ever know of, broke upon and illumined his memory. He longed to recall to her those moments, to make her forget the years of their dull existence together and remember only their moments of ecstasy. For the years, he felt, had not quenched his soul or hers. Their children, his writing, her household cares had not quenched all their souls' tender fire. In one letter that he had written to her then he had said: *Why is it that words like these seem to me so dull and cold? Is it because there is no word tender enough to be your name?* 355

Like distant music these words that he had written years before were borne towards him from the past. He longed to be alone with her. When the others had gone away, when he and she were in their room in the hotel, then they would be alone together. He would call her softly:

—Gretta!

Perhaps she would not hear at once: she would be undressing. Then something in his voice would strike her. She would turn and look at him. . . .

At the corner of Winetavern Street they met a cab. He was glad of its rattling noise as it saved him from conversation. She was looking out of the window and seemed tired. The others spoke only a few words, pointing out some building or street. The horse galloped along wearily under the murky morning sky, dragging his old rattling box after his heels, and Gabriel was again in a cab with her, galloping to catch the boat, galloping to their honeymoon.

As the cab drove across O'Connell Bridge Miss O'Callaghan said: 360

—They say you never cross O'Connell Bridge without seeing a white horse.

—I see a white man this time, said Gabriel.

—Where? asked Mr Bartell D'Arcy.

Gabriel pointed to the statue,[2] on which lay patches of snow. Then he nodded familiarly to it and waved his hand.

—Good-night, Dan, he said gaily. 365

When the cab drew up before the hotel Gabriel jumped out and, in spite of Mr Bartell D'Arcy's protest, paid the driver. He gave the man a shilling over his fare. The man saluted and said:

—A prosperous New Year to you, sir.

—The same to you, said Gabriel cordially.

She leaned for a moment on his arm in getting out of the cab and while standing at the curbstone, bidding the others good-night. She leaned lightly on his arm, as lightly as when she had danced with him a few hours before. He had felt proud and happy then, happy that she was his, proud of her grace and wifely

---

2. 1882 monument commemorating Irish politician Daniel O'Connell (1775–1847), after whom the most important bridge over the river Liffey (built in 1880) is also named. An early champion of Irish self-rule, O'Connell is widely known as "The Liberator" because of his key role in overturning laws prohibiting Catholics from serving in the British Parliament.

O'Connell Bridge, Dublin, ca. 1880

carriage. But now, after the kindling again of so many memories, the first touch of her body, musical and strange and perfumed, sent through him a keen pang of lust. Under cover of her silence he pressed her arm closely to his side; and, as they stood at the hotel door, he felt that they had escaped from their lives and duties, escaped from home and friends and run away together with wild and radiant hearts to a new adventure.

370   An old man was dozing in a great hooded chair in the hall. He lit a candle in the office and went before them to the stairs. They followed him in silence, their feet falling in soft thuds on the thickly carpeted stairs. She mounted the stairs behind the porter, her head bowed in the ascent, her frail shoulders curved as with a burden, her skirt girt tightly about her. He could have flung his arms about her hips and held her still for his arms were trembling with desire to seize her and only the stress of his nails against the palms of his hands held the wild impulse of his body in check. The porter halted on the stairs to settle his guttering candle. They halted too on the steps below him. In the silence Gabriel could hear the falling of the molten wax into the tray and the thumping of his own heart against his ribs.

    The porter led them along a corridor and opened a door. Then he set his unstable candle down on a toilet-table and asked at what hour they were to be called in the morning.

    —Eight, said Gabriel.

    The porter pointed to the tap of the electric-light and began a muttered apology but Gabriel cut him short.

375   —We don't want any light. We have light enough from the street. And I say, he added, pointing to the candle, you might remove that handsome article, like a good man.

The porter took up his candle again, but slowly for he was surprised by such a novel idea. Then he mumbled good-night and went out. Gabriel shot the lock to.

A ghostly light from the street lamp lay in a long shaft from one window to the door. Gabriel threw his overcoat and hat on a couch and crossed the room towards the window. He looked down into the street in order that his emotion might calm a little. Then he turned and leaned against a chest of drawers with his back to the light. She had taken off her hat and cloak and was standing before a large swinging mirror, unhooking her waist. Gabriel paused for a few moments, watching her, and then said:

—Gretta!

She turned away from the mirror slowly and walked along the shaft of light towards him. Her face looked so serious and weary that the words would not pass Gabriel's lips. No, it was not the moment yet.

—You looked tired, he said.   380

—I am a little, she answered.

—You don't feel ill or weak?

—No, tired: that's all.

She went on to the window and stood there, looking out. Gabriel waited again and then, fearing that diffidence was about to conquer him, he said abruptly:

—By the way, Gretta!   385

—What is it?

—You know that poor fellow Malins? he said quickly.

—Yes. What about him?

—Well, poor fellow, he's a decent sort of chap after all, continued Gabriel in a false voice. He gave me back that sovereign[3] I lent him and I didn't expect it really. It's a pity he wouldn't keep away from that Browne, because he's not a bad fellow at heart.

He was trembling now with annoyance. Why did she seem so abstracted? He   390
did not know how he could begin. Was she annoyed, too, about something? If she would only turn to him or come to him of her own accord! To take her as she was would be brutal. No, he must see some ardour in her eyes first. He longed to be master of her strange mood.

—When did you lend him the pound? she asked, after a pause.

Gabriel strove to restrain himself from breaking out into brutal language about the sottish Malins and his pound. He longed to cry to her from his soul, to crush her body against his, to overmaster her. But he said:

—O, at Christmas, when he opened that little Christmas-card shop in Henry Street.

He was in such a fever of rage and desire that he did not hear her come from the window. She stood before him for an instant, looking at him strangely. Then, suddenly raising herself on tiptoe and resting her hands lightly on his shoulders, she kissed him.

—You are a very generous person, Gabriel, she said.   395

Gabriel, trembling with delight at her sudden kiss and at the quaintness of her phrase, put his hands on her hair and began smoothing it back, scarcely touching it with his fingers. The washing had made it fine and brilliant. His heart was brimming over with happiness. Just when he was wishing for it she had come to him of her own accord. Perhaps her thoughts had been running with his. Perhaps

---

3. Gold coin worth one pound or 20 shillings.

she had felt the impetuous desire that was in him and then the yielding mood had come upon her. Now that she had fallen to him so easily he wondered why he had been so diffident.

He stood, holding her head between his hands. Then, slipping one arm swiftly about her body and drawing her towards him, he said softly:

—Gretta dear, what are you thinking about?

She did not answer nor yield wholly to his arm. He said again, softly:

—Tell me what it is, Gretta. I think I know what is the matter. Do I know?

She did not answer at once. Then she said in an outburst of tears:

—O, I am thinking about that song, *The Lass of Aughrim*.

She broke loose from him and ran to the bed and, throwing her arms across the bed-rail, hid her face. Gabriel stood stock-still for a moment in astonishment and then followed her. As he passed in the way of the cheval-glass[4] he caught sight of himself in full length, his broad, well-filled shirt-front, the face whose expression always puzzled him when he saw it in a mirror and his glimmering gilt-rimmed eyeglasses. He halted a few paces from her and said:

—What about the song? Why does that make you cry?

She raised her head from her arms and dried her eyes with the back of her hand like a child. A kinder note than he had intended went into his voice.

—Why, Gretta? he asked.

—I am thinking about a person long ago who used to sing that song.

—And who was the person long ago? asked Gabriel, smiling.

—It was a person I used to know in Galway when I was living with my grandmother, she said.

The smile passed away from Gabriel's face. A dull anger began to gather again at the back of his mind and the dull fires of his lust began to glow angrily in his veins.

—Someone you were in love with? he asked ironically.

—It was a young boy I used to know, she answered, named Michael Furey. He used to sing that song, *The Lass of Aughrim*. He was very delicate.

Gabriel was silent. He did not wish her to think that he was interested in this delicate boy.

—I can see him so plainly, she said after a moment. Such eyes as he had: big dark eyes! And such an expression in them—an expression!

—O then, you were in love with him? said Gabriel.

—I used to go out walking with him, she said, when I was in Galway.

A thought flew across Gabriel's mind.

—Perhaps that was why you wanted to go to Galway with that Ivors girl? he said coldly.

She looked at him and asked in surprise:

—What for?

Her eyes made Gabriel feel awkward. He shrugged his shoulders and said:

—How do I know? To see him perhaps.

She looked away from him along the shaft of light towards the window in silence.

—He is dead, she said at length. He died when he was only seventeen. Isn't it a terrible thing to die so young as that?

—What was he? asked Gabriel, still ironically.

---

4. Full-length, frame-mounted, adjustable mirror.

—He was in the gasworks,[5] she said.

Gabriel felt humiliated by the failure of his irony and by the evocation of this figure from the dead, a boy in the gasworks. While he had been full of memories of their secret life together, full of tenderness and joy and desire, she had been comparing him in her mind with another. A shameful consciousness of his own person assailed him. He saw himself as a ludicrous figure, acting as a pennyboy[6] for his aunts, a nervous well-meaning sentimentalist, orating to vulgarians and idealising his own clownish lusts, the pitiable fatuous fellow he had caught a glimpse of in the mirror. Instinctively he turned his back more to the light lest she might see the shame that burned upon his forehead.

He tried to keep up his tone of cold interrogation but his voice when he spoke was humble and indifferent.

—I suppose you were in love with this Michael Furey, Gretta, he said.

—I was great with him at that time, she said.   430

Her voice was veiled and sad. Gabriel, feeling now how vain it would be to try to lead her whither he had purposed, caressed one of her hands and said, also sadly:

—And what did he die of so young, Gretta? Consumption,[7] was it?

—I think he died for me, she answered.

A vague terror seized Gabriel at this answer as if, at that hour when he had hoped to triumph, some impalpable and vindictive being was coming against him, gathering forces against him in its vague world. But he shook himself free of it with an effort of reason and continued to caress her hand. He did not question her again for he felt that she would tell him of herself. Her hand was warm and moist: it did not respond to his touch but he continued to caress it just as he had caressed her first letter to him that spring morning.

—It was in the winter, she said, about the beginning of the winter when I was   435
going to leave my grandmother's and come up here to the convent. And he was ill at the time in his lodgings in Galway and wouldn't be let out and his people in Oughterard were written to. He was in decline, they said, or something like that. I never knew rightly.

She paused for a moment and sighed.

—Poor fellow, she said. He was very fond of me and he was such a gentle boy. We used to go out together, walking, you know, Gabriel, like the way they do in the country. He was going to study singing only for his health. He had a very good voice, poor Michael Furey.

—Well; and then? asked Gabriel.

—And then when it came to the time for me to leave Galway and come up to the convent he was much worse and I wouldn't be let see him so I wrote a letter saying I was going up to Dublin and would be back in the summer and hoping he would be better then.

She paused for a moment to get her voice under control and then went on: 440

—Then the night before I left I was in my grandmother's house in Nuns' Island,[8] packing up, and I heard gravel thrown up against the window. The window was so wet I couldn't see so I ran downstairs as I was and slipped out the back into the garden and there was the poor fellow at the end of the garden, shivering.

---

5. Factory where gas for heating was manufactured from coal.
6. Cheap entertainer or someone who performs small tasks and errands for very little money.
7. Tuberculosis, a lung disease.
8. Semi-island in the river that runs through the city of Galway, somewhat like Dublin's Usher Island.

—And did you not tell him to go back? asked Gabriel.

—I implored of him to go home at once and told him he would get his death in the rain. But he said he did not want to live. I can see his eyes as well as well! He was standing at the end of the wall where there was a tree.

—And did he go home? asked Gabriel.

445 —Yes, he went home. And when I was only a week in the convent he died and he was buried in Oughterard where his people came from. O, the day I heard that, that he was dead!

She stopped, choking with sobs, and, overcome by emotion, flung herself face downward on the bed, sobbing in the quilt. Gabriel held her hand for a moment longer, irresolutely, and then, shy of intruding on her grief, let it fall gently and walked quietly to the window.

She was fast asleep.

Gabriel, leaning on his elbow, looked for a few moments unresentfully on her tangled hair and half-open mouth, listening to her deep-drawn breath. So she had had that romance in her life: a man had died for her sake. It hardly pained him now to think how poor a part he, her husband, had played in her life. He watched her while she slept as though he and she had never lived together as man and wife. His curious eyes rested long upon her face and on her hair: and, as he thought of what she must have been then, in that time of her first girlish beauty, a strange friendly pity for her entered his soul. He did not like to say even to himself that her face was no longer beautiful but he knew that it was no longer the face for which Michael Furey had braved death.

Perhaps she had not told him all the story. His eyes moved to the chair over which she had thrown some of her clothes. A petticoat string dangled to the floor. One boot stood upright, its limp upper fallen down: the fellow of it lay upon its side. He wondered at his riot of emotions of an hour before. From what had it proceeded? From his aunt's supper, from his own foolish speech, from the wine and dancing, the merrymaking when saying good-night in the hall, the pleasure of the walk along the river in the snow. Poor Aunt Julia! She, too, would soon be a shade with the shade of Patrick Morkan and his horse. He had caught that haggard look upon her face for a moment when she was singing *Arrayed for the Bridal*. Soon, perhaps, he would be sitting in that same drawing-room, dressed in black, his silk hat on his knees. The blinds would be drawn down and Aunt Kate would be sitting beside him, crying and blowing her nose and telling him how Julia had died. He would cast about in his mind for some words that might console her, and would find only lame and useless ones. Yes, yes: that would happen very soon.

450 The air of the room chilled his shoulders. He stretched himself cautiously along under the sheets and lay down beside his wife. One by one they were all becoming shades. Better pass boldly into that other world, in the full glory of some passion, than fade and wither dismally with age. He thought of how she who lay beside him had locked in her heart for so many years that image of her lover's eyes when he had told her that he did not wish to live.

Generous tears filled Gabriel's eyes. He had never felt like that himself towards any woman but he knew that such a feeling must be love. The tears gathered more thickly in his eyes and in the partial darkness he imagined he saw the form of a young man standing under a dripping tree. Other forms were near. His soul had approached that region where dwell the vast hosts of the dead. He was conscious of, but could not apprehend, their wayward and flickering existence. His own identity was fading out into a grey impalpable world: the solid world itself which these dead had one time reared and lived in was dissolving and dwindling.

A few light taps upon the pane made him turn to the window. It had begun to snow again. He watched sleepily the flakes, silver and dark, falling obliquely against the lamplight. The time had come for him to set out on his journey westward. Yes, the newspapers were right: snow was general all over Ireland. It was falling on every part of the dark central plain, on the treeless hills, falling softly upon the Bog of Allen and, farther westward, softly falling into the dark mutinous Shannon[9] waves. It was falling, too, upon every part of the lonely churchyard on the hill where Michael Furey lay buried. It lay thickly drifted on the crooked crosses and headstones, on the spears of the little gate, on the barren thorns. His soul swooned slowly as he heard the snow falling faintly through the universe and faintly falling, like the descent of their last end, upon all the living and the dead.

1914

James Joyce and Dubliners: *A Chronology*

1882	February 2	James Augustine Aloysius Joyce is born in a suburb of Dublin, Ireland, first of the ten surviving children of John and Mary Joyce, a pianist. (In *Stephen Hero*, Joyce will describe the father of his fictional alter ego, Stephen Daedalus, as "a medical student, an oarsman, a tenor, an amateur actor, a shouting politician, a small landlord, a small investor, a drinker, a good fellow, a storyteller, somebody's secretary, something in a distillery, a taxgatherer, a bankrupt.")
1888		Joyce enters Clongowes Wood College, a Jesuit boarding school just outside Dublin.
1891	October	The death of beloved but disgraced Irish politician Charles Stewart Parnell inspires Joyce's earliest known literary effort, a poem entitled "Et Tu, Healy" ("And you, Healy," an allusion to Julius Caesar's last words to his assassins).
1892		John Joyce is granted a small pension when his position as tax collector is abolished; he will have only occasional employment for the rest of his life.
1893		Joyce enters Belvedere College, a Jesuit day school in Dublin.
1899		Joyce enters University College, Dublin, another Jesuit institution.
1900	January	Joyce presents "Drama and Life," an essay written partly in defense of the controversial Norwegian playwright Henrik Ibsen, to the college Literary and Historical Society.
	April	Joyce's review of Ibsen's latest play appears in the prestigious London-based *Fortnightly Review*. Joyce begins a series of prose poems he calls *Epiphanies*.

9. The River Shannon is the informal boundary separating the West of Ireland (including Galway) from the rest of the country.

1902	October	Joyce graduates and begins to introduce himself to Ireland's most important writers, including poet W. B. Yeats.
	December	Joyce moves to Paris, ostensibly to begin medical studies.
1903	April	Joyce returns to Dublin because of his mother's illness; she dies in August. In an August 1904 letter to his future wife, Joyce will avow that his "mind rejects the whole present social order and Christianity—home, the recognised virtues." "How could I like the idea of home?" he asks, explaining that when he saw his mother in her coffin, he "cursed the system which had made her a victim."
1904	January	Joyce writes an essay entitled "A Portrait of the Artist." After its rejection by a magazine, Joyce begins turning it into the autobiographical novel *Stephen Hero*.
	July	The editor of *The Irish Homestead* magazine invites Joyce to submit a short story that is "simple, rural?, livemaking?" and won't "shock the readers." In response, Joyce writes "The Sisters." Around the same time, Joyce writes to a former college classmate that he is "writing a series of epicleti," titling it *Dubliners* "to betray the soul of that hemiplagia or paralysis which many consider a city."
	August	"The Sisters" appears in *The Irish Homestead* under the pseudonym "Stephen Daedalus."
	September	"Eveline" appears in *The Irish Homestead*. In a letter, Joyce avows that "There is no life" in Ireland, "no naturalness or honesty. People live together in the same houses all their lives and at the end they are as far apart as ever."
	October	Joyce leaves for Europe with Nora Barnacle, a hotel employee whom he had met four months earlier. Unable to find work in Zurich, Switzerland, the unmarried couple settles in Pola, Austro-Hungary (now Croatia), where Joyce teaches English at the Berlitz school.
	December	*The Irish Homestead* publishes a third Joyce story, and Joyce informs a correspondent that all three stories are part of "a series of [ten] epiclets" (mini-epics) called *Dubliners*.
1905	March	Berlitz transfers Joyce to Trieste, Austro-Hungary (now Italy).
	July	Nora gives birth to a son.
	October	Joyce persuades his favorite brother, Stanislaus, to join them in Trieste.
		Meanwhile, though *The Irish Homestead* rejects a fourth story, Joyce completes a total of ten by the time he writes to English publisher William Heinemann (in September) offering him "a collection of twelve short stories" called *Dubliners*. When Heinemann declines, Joyce sends the manuscript to English publisher Grant Richards (in November). After a contract is signed, more stories are submitted, and the first pages are printed, the book's printer and publisher discover what they believe to be legally actionable material, initiating months of wrangling with Joyce and some changes to

the manuscript. (For excerpts from Joyce's correspondence with Richards, see Patrick McCarthy's introduction to *Rejoycing: New Readings of* Dubliners, later in this chapter.)

1906	July	Joyce moves his family to Rome, Italy, where he works as a bank clerk and writes two more *Dubliners* stories.
	September	Grant Richards decides not to publish *Dubliners*.
1907	March	Joyce moves his family back to Trieste, where he works as a private tutor.
	May	*Chamber Music*, a collection of poems, appears; meanwhile, *Dubliners* is rejected by another English publisher.

After the birth of a daughter in July and while recovering from rheumatic fever, Joyce writes the fifteenth and final *Dubliners* story, "The Dead," and turns to his reconceived and retitled novel *A Portrait of the Artist as a Young Man*.

1908		Seven more English publishers reject *Dubliners*. In part because of his father's straitened circumstances, Joyce persuades one of his sisters to join his family in Trieste.
1909	August	Joyce visits Dublin, secures a contract with Maunsel and Company for publication of *Dubliners*, and convinces a second sister to move to Trieste.
1910		A fearful Maunsel indefinitely postpones publication of *Dubliners*.
1912	July	Joyce makes what will turn out to be his very last visit to Dublin and secures a proof of *Dubliners*, which Maunsel now definitely refuses to publish. Joyce writes the satirical poem "Gas from a Burner."

By year's end, at least five other publishers reject *Dubliners*.

1914	January	Grant Richards agrees to publish *Dubliners*.
	February	Thanks to American poet Ezra Pound, *Portrait* begins to appear serially in the London-based *Egoist* magazine.
	15 June	*Dubliners* appears (almost ten years after publication of "The Sisters"); Joyce begins work on the novel *Ulysses* and a play, *Exiles*.
1915		After the outbreak of World War I and the internment of Stanislaus (in January), Joyce moves his family to Zurich, Switzerland (a neutral country). On the recommendation of Pound and Yeats, Joyce receives a small grant from Britain's Royal Literary Fund and, later, the British Society of Authors.
1916		*A Portrait of the Artist* appears in volume form in New York, followed by the first U.S. edition of *Dubliners*. In August, the British government awards Joyce a Civil List grant.
1917		*Portrait* is published in volume form in London by one of Joyce's patrons. Attacked by glaucoma, Joyce has the first of eleven eye surgeries and begins to receive monetary gifts from various sympathetic patrons.

1918	March	The American *Little Review* begins to serialize *Ulysses*.
	May	*Exiles* is published in England and the United States.
1919		*Exiles* is staged for the first time in Munich, Germany; *The Egoist* begins to serialize *Ulysses*.
1920		At Pound's urging, Joyce moves his family to Paris, France.
	October	The New York Society for the Suppression of Vice lodges a complaint of obscenity against the *Little Review* because of *Ulysses*.
1921		The *Ulysses* obscenity trial begins in the United States, ultimately resulting in a guilty verdict and ending its serialization.
1922	February	*Ulysses* is published by Joyce supporters in Paris and London.
1923		Joyce begins work on the novel *Finnegans Wake*, fragments of which will begin to appear in periodicals in April 1924.
1931	July	Concerned about the future of his adult children and first grandchild, Joyce marries Nora Barnacle in London.
	December	Joyce's 82-year-old father dies.
1932		Joyce's daughter, Lucia, experiences the first of many mental breakdowns; she will later be institutionalized.
1933		A U.S. judge rules that *Ulysses* is not pornographic, paving the way for an American edition.
1934		The first complete U.S. edition of *Ulysses* appears, and Joyce makes his first visit to the United States.
1939		*Finnegans Wake* is published in England and the United States.
1940		The outbreak of World War II and the occupation of Paris by German troops force Joyce to move his family back to Zurich, Switzerland.
1941	January	Joyce dies in Zurich following surgery for a perforated ulcer.

JAMES JOYCE

Passages from the Early Writings

From *Drama and Life* (1900)

Life indeed nowadays is often a sad bore. Many feel . . . that they have been born too late in a world too old, and their wanhope[1] and nerveless unheroism point on ever sternly to a last nothing, a vast futility and meanwhile—a bearing of fardels.[2] Epic savagery is rendered impossible by vigilant policing, chivalry has been killed by the fashion oracles of the boulevards. There is no clank of mail, no halo about gallantry, no hat-sweeping, no roystering! The traditions of

1. Hopelessness, despair.   2. Bundles or burdens.

Dublin street scence, ca. 1890s

romance are upheld only in Bohemia.[3] Still I think out of the dreary sameness of existence, a measure of dramatic life may be drawn. Even the most commonplace, the deadest among the living, may play a part in a great drama. It is a sinful foolishness to sigh back for the good old times, to feed the hunger of us with the cold stones they afford. Life we must accept as we see it before our eyes, men and women as we meet them in the real world, not as we apprehend them in the world of faery. The great human comedy in which each has a share, gives limitless scope to the true artist, to-day as yesterday and as in years gone by.

From Ireland, Island of Saints and Sages (1907)

... The Irish nation's [present-day] insistence on developing its own culture by itself[1] is not so much the demand of a young nation that wants to make good in the European concert as the demand of a very old nation to renew under new forms the glories of a past civilization.

· · ·

Ireland prides itself on being faithful body and soul to its national tradition as well as to the Holy See. The majority of the Irish consider fidelity to these two traditions their cardinal article of faith.

· · ·

... When the Irishman is found outside of Ireland in another environment, he very often becomes a respected man. The economic and intellectual conditions that prevail in his own country do not permit the development of individuality. The soul of the country is weakened by centuries of useless struggle and broken treaties, and individual initiative is paralysed by the influence and admonitions of the church, while its body is manacled by the police, the tax office, and the garrison. No one who has any self-respect stays in Ireland, but flees afar as though from a country that has undergone the visitation of an angered Jove.[2]

· · ·

... If Ireland has been able to give all this practical talent to the service of others, it means that there must be something inimical, unpropitious, and despotic in

---

3. Imaginary place inhabited by artists and writers who pursue an unconventional lifestyle, named for the literal Bohemia, a former kingdom of the Czech Republic.

1. Joyce here alludes to the Irish Revival, a movement to revive traditional Irish culture and language (Gaelic); the Revival was closely associated with, but distinct from, the movement to make Ireland politically independent of Britain.

The Old World and the New.

An 1854 cartoon

its own present condition, since her sons cannot give their efforts to their own native land.

Because, even today, the flight of the wild geese continues. Every year, Ireland, decimated as she already is, loses 60,000 of her sons. From 1850 to the present day, more than 5,000,000 emigrants have left for America, and every post brings to Ireland their inviting letters to friends and relatives at home. The old men, the corrupt, the children, and the poor stay at home, where the double yoke wears another groove in the tamed neck; and around the death bed where the poor, anaemic, almost lifeless body lies in agony, the rulers give orders and the priests administer last rites.

Is this country destined to resume its ancient position as the Hellas[3] of the north some day? Is the Celtic mind . . . destined to enrich the civil conscience with new discoveries and new insights in the future? Or must the Celtic world, . . . driven by stronger nations to the edge of the continent, to the outermost islands of Europe, finally be cast into the ocean after a struggle of centuries?

. . .

. . . I confess that I do not see what good it does to fulminate against the English tyranny while the Roman tyranny occupies the palace of the soul.

I do not see the purpose of the bitter invectives against the English despoiler, the disdain for the vast Anglo-Saxon civilization, even though it is almost entirely a materialistic civilization, nor the empty boasts that the art of miniature in the ancient Irish books, such as the *Book of Kells* . . . ,[4] which date back to a time when England was an uncivilized country, is almost as old as the Chinese, and that Ireland made and exported to Europe its own fabrics for several generations before the first Fleming arrived in London to teach the English how to make bread. If an appeal to the past in this manner were valid, the

2. Ruler of the gods in Greek mythology.   3. Greece.
4. Illuminated manuscript (c. 800 C.E.) regarded as a masterwork of Western calligraphy and as one of Ireland's greatest national treasures.

fellahin[5] of Cairo would have all the right in the world to disdain to act as porters for English tourists. Ancient Ireland is dead just as ancient Egypt is dead. Its death chant has been sung, and on its gravestone has been placed the seal.

From Gas from a Burner (1912)[1]

Ladies and gents, you are here assembled
To hear why earth and heaven trembled
Because of the black and sinister arts
Of an Irish writer in foreign parts.[2]
5   He sent me a book ten years ago.
I read it a hundred times or so,
Backwards and forwards, down and up,
Through both ends of a telescope.
I printed it all to the very last word
10 But by the mercy of the Lord
The darkness of my mind was rent
And I saw the writer's foul intent.
But I owe a duty to Ireland:
I hold her honour in my hand,
15 This lovely land that always sent
Her writers and artists to banishment
And in a spirit of Irish fun
Betrayed her own leaders, one by one.
        . . .
O Ireland my first and only love
20 Where Christ and Caesar are hand and glove!
O lovely land where the shamrock grows!
(Allow me, ladies, to blow my nose)
To show you for strictures I don't care a button
I printed the poems of Mountainy Mutton[3]
25 And a play he wrote (you've read it I'm sure)
Where they talk of "bastard," "bugger" and "whore"[4]
        . . .
I printed folklore from North and South
By Gregory of the Golden Mouth:[5]
I printed poets, sad, silly and solemn:
30 I printed Patrick What-do-you-Colm:[6]
        . . .
But I draw the line at that bloody fellow,

---

5. Arab peasants or agricultural laborers.
1. The speaker of Joyce's poem is a fictional amalgam of the head of the Dublin publishing company Maunsel and Company and its printer, who first agreed and later refused to print and publish *Dubliners*.
2. At this time, Joyce lived in Trieste, Austria.
3. Joseph Campbell (1879–1944); his collection of poems, *The Mountainy Singer*, was published by Maunsel in 1909.   4. Campbell's play *Judgment*, published by Maunsel in 1912.
5. Dramatist and folklorist Lady Augusta Gregory (1852–1932), a major figure in the Irish Literary Revival; Maunsel published her *Kiltartan History Book* and *The Kiltartan Wonder Book* (1909, 1910).
6. Padraic Colum (1881–1972), a poet associated with the Irish Revival.

That was over here dressed in Austrian yellow,
Spouting Italian by the hour
To O'Leary Curtis[7] and John Wyse Power
35 And writing of Dublin, dirty and dear,
In a manner no blackamoor printer could bear.
Shite and onions! Do you think I'll print
The name of the Wellington Monument,
Sydney Parade and Sandymount tram,
40 Downes's cakeshop and Williams's jam?[8]
I'm damned if I do—I'm damned to blazes!
Talk about *Irish Names of Places*![9]
It's a wonder to me, upon my soul,
He forgot to mention Curly's Hole.[1]
45 No, ladies, my press shall have no share in
So gross a libel on Stepmother Erin.
   . . .
Who was it said: Resist not evil?[2]
I'll burn that book, so help me devil.
I'll sing a psalm as I watch it burn
50 And the ashes I'll keep in a one-handled urn.
I'll penance do with farts and groans
Kneeling upon my marrowbones.
This very next Lent I will unbare
My penitent buttocks to the air
55 And sobbing beside my printing press
My awful sin I will confess.
My Irish foreman from Bannockburn[3]
Shall dip his right hand in the urn
And sign crisscross with reverent thumb
60 *Memento homo*[4] upon my bum.

7. Dublin journalist, as was John Wyse Power (1859–1926); Power was also a member of the Irish Republican Brotherhood and a founder of the still-extant Gaelic Athletic Association for the Preservation and Cultivation of National Pastimes.
8. One objection to publishing *Dubliners* was the fear that the volume's many references to specific, actual Dublin places and businesses (like the ones listed here) would inspire lawsuits.
9. *The Origin and History of Irish Names and Places* (1869), by Patrick Joyce (no relation).
1. Dublin-area bathing and fishing spot.
2. Jesus says these words in the Sermon on the Mount: "But I say unto you, that ye resist not evil: but whosoever shall smite thee on thy right cheek, turn to him the other also" (Matthew 5:39).
3. Village in Scotland.
4. "Memento, homo, quia pulvis es, et in pulverem reverteris" ("Remember, human, that you are dust, and to dust you will return"); words, adapted from Genesis 3:19, that begin the prayer spoken on Ash Wednesday by priests as they mark the sign of the cross on congregants' foreheads with ashes.

PATRICK A. McCARTHY

From *Rejoycing: New Readings of* Dubliners*

James Joyce began *Dubliners* in 1904 as a short story sequence for . . . [the] agricultural journal *The Irish Homestead,* which published versions of "The Sisters," "Eveline," and "After the Race" before complaints from readers offended by the stories' caustic treatment of Irish life led [the editor] to suspend publication of the stories. By then, however, Joyce was already planning to recast his series of discrete narratives into a book of stories linked by their common concern with Catholic middle-class life in Dublin as well as by various overlapping themes, images, and situations. *Dubliners* was published in 1914, after numerous delays and complicated negotiations with the English publisher Grant Richards (who canceled a 1906 contract but issued a new one eight years later and finally brought out the volume) and with the Dublin firm of Maunsel and Company, whose printer raised objections to the stories both because of their alleged obscenity and because he feared lawsuits by people and businesses named in them.[1] When it was published the book attracted none of the legal actions feared by Joyce's publishers and printers; on the other hand, it received mixed reviews, and its sales were meager, as Joyce noted in a letter to Richards in which he expressed regret that "neither you nor I have gained anything" from the book's publication (*D* 292; *Letters* 2:340–41). For Joyce, the lack of royalties was less disappointing than the fact that the book had done little to stimulate interest in his new projects or to establish him as a major author.

The publication of *Dubliners* thus proved anticlimactic, an event easily overshadowed by the appearance of *A Portrait of the Artist as a Young Man* (serialized in *The Egoist,* 1914–15; first book publication, December 1916) and, far more spectacularly, by the 1922 publication of *Ulysses,* after which Joyce was widely recognized as a central modernist writer—indeed, as one of the most important avant-garde artists of his time. In retrospect, however, 1914 stands out as an important year in the history of the modernist short story and modern fiction in general. Several reasons for the importance of *Dubliners* are suggested by Joyce's own description of his aims and methods in a May 1906 letter to Grant Richards:

> My intention was to write a chapter of the moral history of my country and
> I chose Dublin for the scene because that city seemed to me the centre of paralysis. I have tried to present it to the indifferent public under four of its aspects:
> childhood, adolescence, maturity and public life. The stories are arranged in
> this order. I have written it for the most part in a style of scrupulous meanness
> and with the conviction that he is a very bold man who dares to alter in the

*From the introduction to *New Readings of* Dubliners, ed. Rosa M. Bollettieri Bosinelli and Harold F. Mosher Jr. (Lexington: UP of Kentucky, 1998), pp. 1–9. Copyright 1998 by The University Press of Kentucky. All notes are McCarthy's; some of his works cited have been omitted.

1. For more detailed accounts of the composition of *Dubliners* (hereafter cited with page numbers as *D*) and the disputes involved in its publication, see Morris Beja 32–39; Richard Ellmann 207–11, 219–22, 231–32, 267, 290–91, 310–11, 313–15, 323–24, 328–38, 348–54; Michael Groden 78–84; Florence L. Walzl 160–64; and "The Evidence of the Letters" (*D* 257–93). See especially "A Curious History" (*D* 289–92). Joyce satirized Maunsel and Company and the Dublin printer John Falconer in his 1912 broadside "Gas from a Burner" (*Critical Writings* 242–45).

presentment, still more to deform, whatever he has seen and heard. [*D* 269; *Letters* 2:134]

Here, in capsule form, are Joyce's defenses of the collection on the bases of its subject matter (a critique of Dublin society as "the centre of paralysis"), its comprehensive organization, its "style of scrupulous meanness," and above all its realism and adherence to the truth. Setting himself against "the indifferent public," Joyce implies that by portraying the "paralysis" at the heart of Dublin's public life he will force readers out of their apathy. A similar note appears in a letter to Richards written seven weeks later, in which Joyce argues that "the odour of ashpits and old weeds and offal" emanating from his stories is a necessary part of his depiction of the city and grandly declares that Richard's failure to publish *Dubliners* would "retard the course of civilisation in Ireland by preventing the Irish people from having one good book to look at themselves in [his] nicely polished looking-glass" (*D* 286; *Letters* 1:63–64).

As a contribution to the art of the short story, *Dubliners* is noteworthy for several reasons. Its sparse yet economical style, its use of suggestive details that at times seem to have a symbolic meaning, its refusal of any sort of neat conclusion have all influenced the shape of the modern short story.[2] Equally important is the fact that *Dubliners* is a coherent collection of related stories, a sort of novel with a collective rather than an individual protagonist. A few earlier collections had included stories with common locations, themes, and images . . . but *Dubliners* is the most fully realized, and most influential, volume of the kind. Apart from the first few stories that Joyce wrote, all of the *Dubliners* narratives were composed with book publication in mind, and the stories often take on different meanings when read within the context of the collection than they do in isolation. Sometimes the connections between stories are made by small touches, as when Eveline's "holding her black leather purse tightly in her hand as she elbowed her way through the crowds" (*D* 38) ironically undercuts the more romantic version of this image in "Araby," where, as he makes his way through a similar crowd, the narrator imagines himself bearing a "chalice" rather than a purse (*D* 31). Some of the book's forms of repetition are obvious enough—the conclusions of several stories involve darkness, tears, or both . . . —while others are more subtle, but they all contribute to the economy of *Dubliners*.

As an example of a significant recurrent element in Joyce's portrayal of Dublin we might cite the emphasis on absence. The theme is introduced on the first page of "The Sisters," whose narrator associates the key word *paralysis* with two other words whose contexts he specifies: "*gnomon* in the Euclid and . . . *simony* in the Catechism" (*D* 9). These three italicized words connect Joyce's themes of passivity (*paralysis*), corruption (*simony*), and absence (*gnomon*).[3] . . . Absence, for Joyce, is a

---

2. The most thorough examination of Joyce's relationship to earlier short story writers remains that of Marvin Magalaner and Richard M. Kain.

3. "Simony," so called after the example of Simon Magus (see Acts 8:18–19), refers to attempts to buy or sell pardons or other spiritual things; "gnomon," as the term is used in Euclidean geometry, denotes the irregular geometrical figure created by removing a parallelogram from one of the corners of a larger parallelogram. Other meanings of the *gnomon* image have been explored in Joyce criticism, most recently (and interestingly) by David Weir in *Joyce's Art of Mediation* and by Fritz Senn in the essay ["Gnomon Inverted"] printed in this volume. For discussions of Joyce's "gnomonics" in terms related to those I have touched on here, see Bernard Benstock's chapter 2 and Phillip F. Herring's argument that the gnomon image "suggests that certain kinds of absence are typical of the whole of Dublin at a significant *time* in its history. . . . In effect, a *gnomon* may be a key synecdoche of absence, part of a political rhetoric of silence within a larger framework of language" (4).

kind of presence, exerting pressure on what remains, as we see from the examples of dead people who continue to influence the living: Eveline Hill's mother in "Eveline," . . . Michael Furey in "The Dead." Characters who are alive but absent . . . play their own parts in the stories, as do any number of missing items. . . .

Joyce's original plan for a series of ten stories had been expanded to twelve by the time he sent the manuscript to Richards at the end of 1905, with two more— "Two Gallants" and "A Little Cloud"—following in 1906. Had the book been published as it then stood, a collection of fourteen stories beginning with "The Sisters" and ending with "Grace," it would have been very different from the book we now have: opening with a story of a priest whom the boy associates with simony and concluding with another whose treatment of God as an accountant implies a related corruption of the spiritual realm by materialism, *Dubliners* would have been a more insistently ironical portrayal of Dublin's "paralysis," focusing on the characters' inability to escape or improve their stagnant lives. The addition of "The Dead" in 1907 not only gave the book a very different—a more ambiguous as well as a more symbolic and more stylistically powerful— conclusion; it also balanced Joyce's criticism of Dublin with a display of its hospitality. In other ways as well, the scope of the collection was enlarged by "The Dead," which has a far broader vision of the human condition than any other story in *Dubliners.* That scope is especially evident in the final apocalyptic vision of "all the living and the dead," which is strikingly unlike the abrupt, minimalist conclusions of the earlier stories.

While "The Dead" may be read in isolation, some of its effects are lost if we do not recognize that it was the only story Joyce wrote with the rest of the collection in mind, a fact that led Joyce to incorporate into the story many coda-like echoes of other *Dubliners* stories. . . . While recapitulating themes, images, situations, and verbal motifs from earlier *Dubliners* stories, however, "The Dead" also serves as a turning point in Joyce's fiction, for it is the story whose mundane materials are most fully transformed, even redeemed, by their incorporation within its grand human vision.

Just as the stories of *Dubliners* may be read in isolation or as part of the collection, the book may be read by itself or as an integral part of Joyce's major work, which, apart from *Dubliners,* consists primarily of *A Portrait of the Artist as a Young Man* (1916), *Ulysses* (1922), and *Finnegans Wake* (1939). Each book could be regarded as the unique product of a phase in Joyce's career, an experiment in literary form that he never repeated: *Dubliners,* a realistic collection of short stories, was followed by *A Portrait,* an impressionistic novel, based on Joyce's early life, that describes the growth of an artist's imagination; by *Ulysses,* a stylistic and narrational tour de force filled with innumerable allusions and based in part on an analogy between the epic world of *Odyssey* and the modern Dublin traversed by a humane advertising canvasser; and by *Finnegans Wake,* a fantastic dream vision narrated in an obscure but often hilarious punning language. Thus the pattern of Joyce's career is one of incessant internalization, moving from realism toward a concern with the mind and the language through which the mind attempts to come to terms with the world and with itself. At the same time, *Dubliners* gives us fine examples of several important recurrent features of Joyce's work, including its intricate craftsmanship, its careful attention to all aspects of style, its concern with the relationship between individual characters and the cultural and historical environment in which they live, and its exploration of the relationship between art and politics. . . .

WORKS CITED

Beja, Morris. *James Joyce: A Literary Life*. Columbus: Ohio State Univ. Press, 1992.

Benstock, Bernard. *Narrative Con/Texts in* Dubliners. Urbana: Univ. of Illinois Press, 1994.

Ellmann, Richard. *James Joyce*. Rev. ed. New York: Oxford Univ. Press, 1982.

Groden, Michael. "A Textual and Publishing History." In *A Companion to Joyce Studies,* ed. Zack Bowen and James F. Carens, 71–128. Westport, Conn.: Greenwood, 1984.

Herring, Phillip F. *Joyce's Uncertainty Principle*. Princeton, N.J.: Princeton Univ. Press, 1987.

Joyce, James. *The Critical Writings of James Joyce*. Ed. Ellsworth Mason and Richard Ellmann. New York: Viking, 1964.

——. Dubliners: *Text, Criticism, and Notes*. Ed. Robert Scholes and A. Walton Litz. New York: Viking, 1969.

——. *Letters of James Joyce*. Ed. Stuart Gilbert and Richard Ellmann. 3 vols. New York: Viking, 1966.

Magalaner, Marvin, and Richard M. Kain. *Joyce: The Man, the Work, the Reputation*. New York: New York Univ. Press, 1956.

Walzl, Florence L. "*Dubliners*." In *A Companion to Joyce Studies,* ed. Zack Bowen and James F. Carens, 157–228. Westport, Conn.: Greenwood, 1984.

Weir, David. *Joyce's Art of Mediation*. Ann Arbor: Univ. of Michigan Press, 1996.

ROBERT SCHOLES

From *Counterparts**

[The *Dubliners* story called] "Counterparts" offers us, in its title and in its plan, a major clue to the whole structure of *Dubliners*—to the almost musical fabric of themes and variations on the people of Dublin which Joyce has so carefully arranged for us. The title of this story suggests both the harmonious balance of counterpointed musical parts and the anonymous interchangeability of cogs in a great machine. In the story itself, Mr. Alleyne bullies [his clerk,] the shiftless Farrington and Farrington bullies [his son,] the hapless Tom. But Farrington and Mr. Alleyne are counterparts as abusers of authority. . . . The "Gallant" Corley with his slavey's coin in his palm is connected by a thread of counterpointed irony to Lily, the caretaker's bitter daughter (in "The Dead"), with Gabriel Conroy's clumsily bestowed but well-meant coin clutched in her hand. . . . The connection of the coins enriches our perspective on these events and other similar ones with many shades of thought and feeling beyond simple irony. Connections like these, multiplied many times over, are the principal means by which Joyce has blended his separate stories into an imposing portrait of a society and a whole race of people. Not just details, but details alive with echoes and resonances, make these Dubliners vibrate with significance for us.

Farrington himself, waiting for a tram with twopence in his pocket after his evening of frustration, reminds us of the boy in "Araby," with eightpence in *his* pocket and a fourpenny train ride home ahead of him: both are "driven and derided" by similar but separate vanities, even as they are frustrated financially. The finances of "Counterparts"—so carefully accounted for—remind us of the astonishing role petty cash plays in so many of these stories. The pettiness of Dublin life as Joyce presents it here is in part a response to the pressures of financial distress on a pretentious gentility. . . .

The financial stagnation which contributes to the musty odor Joyce felt he had achieved in *Dubliners* has *its* counterpart in the city's spiritual paralysis. The paralyzed priest of "The Sisters" is a counterpart to the Blessed Margaret Mary Alacoque—the paralytic saint who presides over Eveline Hill's failure of nerve and loss of faith in her beloved at the North Wall. . . . A puritanical religion of senseless rigidity insists upon a destructive chastity for these Dubliners, and it often combines neatly with powerful financial pressures to add to their worldly torments. . . .

In a letter to his wife, Joyce once explained that he, like other Irish writers, was trying "to create a conscience" for his race. This phrase, which he also gave to his character Stephen Daedalus at the end of *Portrait*, has much to do with *Dubliners*. Why, we must ask, should a people need to have a conscience created for them—especially a people so conspicuously religious as the Irish? Joyce felt—and his letters support the evidence of the works themselves—that it was precisely their religious orthodoxy, combined with other sorts of "belatedness," that made the Irish so conscienceless. They had turned over the moral responsibility for their lives to their confessors and religious leaders. Thus their ability to react sensitively to moral problems, to make ethical discriminations—to use their consciences—had atrophied. In *Dubliners* he offered his countrymen his own counterpart to St. Ignatius's *Spiritual Exercises*. The evaluation of motive and responsibility in these stories—the histories of "painful" cases for the most part—must inevitably lead the reader beyond any easy orthodoxy. These delicately imagined case histories encourage us to exercise our spirits, develop our consciences. They lead us inevitably toward the view that morality is a matter of individual responses to particular situations rather than an automatic invocation of religious or ethical rules of thumb. And though Joyce's own race—the Irish—was first in his mind, he was certainly addressing all of us. Nothing is easier than to slip into the habit of invoking formulae instead of making judgments. New orthodoxies always arise to replace the old. . . . But Joyce's painful cases always bring us back to individuality. In entering the world of *Dubliners* we all acknowledge our Irishness. As Martin Cunningham [a character in "Grace"] so complacently puts it, "we're a nice collection of scoundrels, one and all." But what *we* must see—precisely what Mr. Cunningham does not—is that it is our moral complacency that *makes* us scoundrels. Because the spiritual life is an art and not a science, because it is rich and subtle beyond all orthodox formulae, only art can begin to do it justice.

Joyce's art has the necessary delicacy. Not only does Joyce develop a formidable structure of interconnections, making of his separate cases a portrait of a city; he also presents each of these cases with an exquisite control of tone. Inviting us to judge and evaluate, he guides our responses without coercing them; he allows us freedom of response but suggests an order in which some responses are more valuable than others.

. . .

By . . . subtle guidance Joyce makes us aware of the quality of Dublin life. . . . In the early story "Araby" the boy hears his uncle come home: "I heard him talking to himself and heard the hallstand rocking when it had received the weight of his overcoat. I could interpret these signs." The uncle had been drinking, but we are not told so directly. Like the boy himself we must "interpret these signs." This is Joyce's way in story after story. We must interpret for ourselves, but the signs are meaningful, making some interpretations better than others. In the work of interpretation, sifting and weighing details, listening carefully for the various tones of irony and pathos, we develop and refine our consciences.

Joyce's way . . . is to give us much food for interpretation and put the work of interpretation squarely upon us. He gives us the maximum of conscience-creating labor by inviting us to participate with him in the creative process. To become the ideal reader of *Dubliners* each of us must accept this complicity. Between the mind of the reader and the mind of the artist these stories can flower fully and achieve their richest shape. The opportunity—and the challenge—offered us is that of becoming, in our own small way, Joyce's counterparts.

DAVID G. WRIGHT

From *Interactive Stories in* Dubliners*

In "The Boarding House" Bob Doran, fearing that his affair with Polly will become known, reflects that "Dublin is such a small city: everyone knows everyone else's business" (*Dubliners* 66). Most readers probably skip past this comment cheerfully enough, finding it commonplace; yet it seems on reflection quite false as an account of the community depicted in *Dubliners*. It's often striking how *little* the characters know of each other's business.

The tone and meaning of *Dubliners* owe much to the gap between what the characters know and what we know (or can discover). This discrepancy in turn depends on the hermetic confinement of the major characters to a single story each. . . .

. . . [But] the individual stories in *Dubliners* do furnish contexts for each other.

In discussing "The Dead" in letters Joyce said that in the earlier stories he had slighted certain positive aspects of Dublin: "I have not [so far] reproduced its . . . hospitality" (*Letters* 2: 166). The new story might, he implies, attempt to redress the balance. The last line in "Grace"—the line that immediately precedes "The Dead"—is "I will set right my accounts" (*Dubliners* 174), and the new story might seem to be Joyce's own attempt to "set right [his] accounts." This redressing nevertheless appears much more equivocal in the text than Joyce's letters imply: Gabriel's speech in praise of hospitality is itself an ambivalent performance at best (serving as a parody of Joyce's own letters on the subject of Irish hospitality,

* From *Studies in Short Fiction* 32 (1995): 285–93. Copyright 1995 by Newberry College. Some of Wright's works cited have been omitted.

but also incorporating an inhospitable swipe at Molly Ivors); and the story abounds in depictions of social awkwardness and uncertainty....

Joyce's attempt to "redress the balance" of *Dubliners* by adding "The Dead" hinged partly on his increasing fondness for self-parody. Whereas in the earlier stories he had mostly "rewritten" and probed the discourses of his fellow Dubliners, from "The Dead" onward the primary targets of such investigative rewriting became his own earlier texts. In part, then, "The Dead" operates as a kind of parody of the earlier stories in the collection.

"The Dead" ... restates surreptitiously several propositions first introduced in "Araby." That earlier title reflects a yearning for exotic eastern things rather than for authentic Irish experience, something of which Gabriel will also be accused; and the boy who narrates "Araby," like Gabriel, makes a journey eastward, to a scene of disillusionment, in the course of the story. Both stories depict their protagonists in a series of encounters with women, encounters which produce sometimes bitter self-knowledge. As Gabriel learns to see himself as "a ludicrous figure," so the boy in "Araby" comes to see himself as "a creature driven and derided by vanity" (*Dubliners* 35). The links between the two stories are further reinforced by insistently repeated imagery of money, horses, darkness, and winter. We could interpret this association in various ways, but in any case, it discloses implications to us which are concealed from the characters within the stories.

While we could no doubt find clear allusions in "The Dead" to all fourteen of the earlier stories, the links with the very first story, "The Sisters," are especially numerous....

The primary reason for all these associations is to tie the ending of *Dubliners* closely to the beginning. That tends to shape the whole collection into the circular configuration that, throughout the individual stories, has served as a symbol for Dublin paralysis and entrapment. The more associations with "The Sisters" we find in "The Dead," the more we're likely to feel that the last story assesses Dublin paralysis from a new angle but doesn't, finally, achieve a way out of it; rather, it sends us back to the beginning....

WORKS CITED

Joyce, James. Dubliners: *Text, Criticism, and Notes*. Ed. Robert Scholes and A. Walton Litz. New York: Viking, 1969.
———. *Letters of James Joyce*. Vol. 1, corrected ed., ed. Stuart Gilbert. New York: Viking, 1965. Vol. 2 and 3, ed. Richard Ellmann. New York: Viking, 1966.

SUGGESTIONS FOR WRITING

1. First, read "Araby" and write a brief response paper outlining what you see as its two or three most memorable and important elements or aspects. Next, read the story again after reading the stories in the "Initiation Stories" album; then write another brief response paper describing two new things in or about Joyce's story that this reading experience has helped you to see for the first time or in a different way. (That is, how is your interpretation of "Araby" different when you read it in the context of other initiation stories?) Finally, read "Eveline" and "The Dead" and

then reread "Araby" one more time; in a final response paper, describe how reading these three stories together has changed your impression and interpretation of "Araby." (That is, how is your interpretation of "Araby" different when you read it in the context of other *Dubliners* stories?)

2. In his letters, Joyce identified "paralysis" as the central problem explored in *Dubliners*. Write an essay outlining the various kinds of paralysis that plague the characters in at least two of the stories in this chapter, perhaps drawing on some of the other materials included here, as well as the stories themselves. In these terms, what are the most important similarities and differences among characters and stories? What might the stories individually and collectively suggest about why Dubliners suffer from this paralysis and whether it might be overcome and how? In these terms, what is the effect or significance of the order of the stories?

3. Literary critic Berni Benstock argues that "Every time-revered percept of the [middle classes] is carefully dismantled in *Dubliners*: that they are hard-working, honest, religious, temperate, and secure." Drawing on evidence from all three stories in this chapter, write an essay exploring the validity of Benstock's claim. In other words, how and to what extent do some or all of these stories suggest that middle-class Dubliners aren't in fact as "hard-working, honest, religious, temperate, and [or] secure" as they might seem, even to themselves? Or identify any other arguable claim made in the essays by Joyce scholars excerpted in this chapter and write an essay exploring the claim's validity.

4. Benstock also argues that gender plays a vital role in determining the different social and economic fates of the characters in *Dubliners*. Write an essay exploring this or any way that gender matters in these stories. For example, what role do girls and women play in the two stories in which the focal characters and protagonists are male? By instead giving us a female protagonist and point of view, how might "Eveline" give us a different perspective on the kind of situations, relationships, and issues explored in the other stories?

5. Drawing on the James Joyce and *Dubliners* chronology in this chapter and on the excerpts from Joyce's early writings, write an essay that explores how at least one Joyce story expresses any of the strong personal feelings or ideas that Joyce articulates in his other writings.

6. Research the history of Joyce's life and career up to the completion of *Dubliners*. Then write an essay exploring how any two stories from the sequence allow Joyce to reflect critically on, or even perhaps come to terms with, what he called—in an August 1904 letter to his future wife—"the actual difficulties of [his own] life."

7. Use online resources to identify any story in this anthology that also appears in a short-story collection to which you have access. Read or reread the story and record your impressions. Then read at least two other stories in the collection and reread the story you started with. In a short essay, explain how and why your impression and interpretation of the story changed after the second reading.

8. Write a short story that depicts an encounter between characters from at least two of the Joyce stories in this chapter. (For instance, what might happen if Eveline met the protagonist of "Araby" on her way home from the docks, or if Eveline took a job as maid at the hotel where Gabriel and Gretta Conroy spend the night at the end of "The Dead"? Alternatively, if you imagine that Gabriel Conroy is the grown-up version of the narrator-protagonist of "Araby," what might have happened to him in between to explain how and why he becomes the man he does?)

Cultural and Historical Contexts

Over the past two hundred years, the meaning of the word *culture* has broadened considerably, from "cultivation" (as in *agriculture*) to "the arts or familiarity with the arts" (*high culture, a cultured person*) to "a whole way of life" (*American culture, African American culture*). The fact that we still use the one word for both "the arts" and "a whole way of life" implies a close, even fundamental relationship between the two. The double implications of "culture" suggest that works of art both reflect and help shape the way we live, and also that art in a particular time and place takes the form it does because of the larger cultural context—what the nineteenth-century writer William Hazlitt called "the spirit of the age." In other words, authors, like the rest of us, live in particular times and places, and authorial visions, however unique, are inevitably shaped by cultural and historical context. Our understanding of a particular text or of an author's entire body of work often is enhanced if we learn more about that context.

This is not to say if we texts and authors *merely* reflect their cultural moment. Although authors—their personalities, viewpoints, concerns, and values—are shaped by the times and places in which they live, they often choose to write because they want to comment on, and maybe even change, the way their contemporaries think, feel, and behave. Literature can and sometimes does shape, as well as reflect, history. Testifying to the powerful effect that literature can exercise, one member of the generation born just after World War I noted that Ernest Hemingway's "impact upon us was tremendous. . . . We could follow him, ape his manner"; "we began unconsciously to . . . impose on everything we did and felt the particular emotions [his fiction] aroused in us."

But what happens to either the individual or the "universal" aspects of a literary work as we focus on its relationship to its cultural and historical context? At its best, the process is one of addition rather than subtraction. Reading a text in light of its cultural and historical context simply gives us a different but complementary perspective to that of reading the text on its own terms. Indeed, what makes the study of literature both exciting and enriching is its multilayered, multidimensional quality: the way that Flannery O'Connor's "Everything That Rises Must Converge," for example, simultaneously embodies its author's unique vision of the association between violence and enlightenment, explores the universal problem of generational conflict, and evaluates the dramatic cultural transformations that shook the American South in particular during the 1960s. The point, then, of reading with an eye toward cultural and historical context is not to foreclose other ways of reading but rather to enrich our experience of the text and, through it, our sense of what is both common to and different about human experience across ages and cultures.

10 CULTURAL AND HISTORICAL CONTEXTS: WOMEN IN TURN-OF-THE-CENTURY AMERICA

The period between about 1890 and 1920, often referred to as "the turn of the century" or the Progressive Era, saw transformations in many aspects of society in the United States. The nation's rapid industrialization and urbanization, in changing the way people worked and lived, also brought about a number of economic, political, and social reforms to respond to these changes. The Progressive Era saw attempts to regulate corporations and improve working conditions through the creation of new government agencies and the passage of labor laws. In the social sphere, reformers sought advances in education, sanitation, and health care. Many of these efforts, perhaps most notably the women's suffrage and temperance movements, were spearheaded by middle-class women, trying to improve their own circumstances and those of women in all socioeconomic classes.

Works of literature written by American women during this period provide valuable insights into the predicaments of married middle-class white women in Progressive-Era America. This chapter examines three classics in the context of women's roles at the turn of the century: Charlotte Perkins Gilman's "The Yellow Wallpaper" (1892), Kate Chopin's "The Story of an Hour" (1894), and Susan Glaspell's "A Jury of Her Peers" (1917, based on her 1916 play *Trifles*; see "Drama: Reading Responding Writing"). Without directly commenting on historic developments, these realistic stories about married women in domestic settings reflect the changing national outlook at the turn of the twentieth century. The chapter includes a selective chronology (from the first Women's Rights Convention in 1848 and the birth of Kate Chopin in 1850 to the death of Susan Glaspell in 1948) and a sample of contemporary documents on topics related to these stories. The list of sources and the writing suggestions point out several possible avenues for interpreting and writing about these stories. But first, we introduce some of the issues women faced at the time: work inside and outside the home; marriage law, domestic violence, and divorce; and the medical treatment of women—all matters that came under scrutiny through the advocacy of Charlotte Perkins Gilman and other women leaders at the time.

WOMEN AT THE TURN OF THE CENTURY: AN OVERVIEW

A close look at the three stories in this chapter calls attention to conditions of domestic life for married women at the turn of the century. Why do Mrs. Mallard in "The Story of an Hour" and the woman who narrates "The Yellow Wallpaper"

Susan Glaspell at typewriter (Berg Collection, New York Public Library)

feel confined, even to the point of madness, in their marriages to loving and prosperous men? Why would Mrs. Wright in *Trifles* be exhausted and enraged to the point of violence? It helps to consider the conditions and opportunities of women's lives. In these decades from 1890 to 1920, it was still the norm for a married white woman to serve as full-time manager of the home and any servants in it: By 1920, only 6.5 percent of married white women worked outside the home. In contrast, married African American women, who in the post–Civil War South had long been forced to work for minimal pay in the fields or as laundresses or cooks in white households, continued to seek paid work after migrating to Northern cities. There were some regional differences: In 1920, for example, 25.5 percent of black married women in Detroit worked for wages, but 46.4 percent in New York did. Among single women of all races, half worked as paid employees at this time.

Work in the home, for wives or servants, could also be very hard, however. For decades after the Civil War, women of all classes produced most of their households' clothing and food and were kept busy tending wood or coal fires, making candles, or tending oil or gas lamps. Water had to be pumped, carried, and heated over fires, and laundry took more than a day's hard labor. It was rare, even among poorer families, for a house to be run without at least part-time hired help. In "A Jury of Her Peers," Mrs. Wright apparently does all the housework herself.

A kind of record of Mrs. Wright's life appears in one result of her labors, the quilt. Mrs. Hale and Mrs. Peters notice that Mrs. Wright was preparing pieces for a quilt in a "log cabin pattern," a popular traditional design that may reflect pioneer women's experience creating homes. Strips of printed fabric in different colors are "stacked" like logs built around a central square, which may be red like a fireplace or heating stove. These varied strips of cloth are usually sewn onto a cloth backing and then the whole is knotted instead of quilted (quilting adds decorative stitching through all layers of a patchwork quilt). Quilt designs were sometimes used to communicate messages among slaves or to record family histories. Today folklorists and historians collect, document, and interpret heirloom quilts as evidence of women's history, even as a form of chronicle or memoir by women in different regions and ethnic traditions. Mrs. Hale and Mrs. Peters are experts on quilting and seem to decode a message in Mrs. Wright's handiwork. The log-cabin design reflects her lonely farmhouse life, and the decision to knot it may indicate how little time she has free from her farmhouse labors as well as her lack of companions for a quilting bee. Finally, Mrs. Wright's uneven stitches reveal that she was angry and upset. In a subtle way, the knotting may also suggest the rope used to strangle the man who strangled the bird.

Toward the end of the nineteenth century, a series of inventions reduced domestic chores, and so domestic service declined. After the 1850s, sewing machines gradually became affordable not only for manufacturers but also for individuals, and the invention of the Mason jar in 1857 enabled families to preserve their home-grown fruits and vegetables for the winter. In 1931, the National Association of Real Estate Boards looked back at changes in the home: A newspaper article, "Home Necessities Once Were Luxury," quotes the association's finding that since the 1870s, "The electric light and the development of the array of electrical appliances did the work of the modern housewife," while bathtubs, once rare, newsworthy luxuries, were now installed in many homes (*New York Times* January 18, 1931).

Some Innovations in Travel and Communication

- **Train**—first available for passengers in the 1820s, widely used in the United States by the 1890s.
- **Automobile**—mass produced by 1908, though horse-drawn carts and carriages remained in use in many areas through the 1930s.
- **Telegraph**—first developed in the 1830s; transatlantic in 1866; improved in the 1870s; wireless by the 1890s.
- **Telephone**—Alexander Graham Bell's first patent was granted in 1876; hand-crank telephones reached Iowa farms by 1900, with households sharing "party" lines.
- **Typewriter**—available in less expensive models for more businesses from the 1870s onward; women began to work as "typewriters."

A new convenience or labor-saving device, from the automobile to electricity to the telephone, could free a housewife from hours of work and make possible other occupations or become the means to stay in touch with friends, to develop artistic talents, or to experience the world. The changes spread slowly, however, and were more common in urban areas and well-to-do homes than on farms or in working-class tenements. And social expectations for upper-class women might have kept many of them idle and dependent on servants.

Middle-class women's usefulness as household producers declined before opportunities for education and meaningful careers opened up. Medicine and law became organized, standardized professions at the turn of the century, for example, but both of these highly paid fields excluded women (and many men). At the same time, medical treatments and legal procedures that responded to any of the dysfunctions of married life directly and indirectly increased men's domination of women. The "rest cure," psychoanalysis, and other medical practices developed by professional men became common ways to treat women suffering from the illnesses and depressions that may have resulted in part from their feelings of purposelessness and inactivity. A woman might find her desire to pursue a career diagnosed as an illness; her acts of self-determination or resistance might be prohibited, punished, or judged to be insane.

The isolation of a married woman in her own house, whether the idle wife of a wealthy man or the poor, hard-working wife of a farmer, might often be experienced as restrictive and oppressive. Even the wife of a caring and generous husband might envision widowhood or divorce as an escape. However, well into the twentieth century, divorce was expensive and difficult and usually resulted in a clouded reputation for the woman (as it did for the divorced Charlotte Stetson before she married Gilman). Not until 1900 were some women able to sue successfully for divorce on the grounds of the husband's "mental cruelty"; previously, they would have needed to prove that he was violent or had committed adultery.

WOMEN WRITERS IN A CHANGING WORLD

In the United States and Europe, women's roles were slowly changing, however, thanks to the efforts of reform groups. Both Gilman and Glaspell participated in such efforts, on behalf of women and others, through their work with Heterodoxy, a group in New York that advocated women's civil rights and suffrage. Gilman, in testimony before Congress on January 28, 1896, argued for extending the vote to women:

> It will improve the race by improving the women. . . . You can not have as good a citizen, as good a class of people, where half the people are no part of the Government. . . . For unnumbered thousands of years women have suffered from repression. . . . And to debar any part of the race from its development is to carry along with society a dead weight, a part of the organism which is not living. . . . To give suffrage to this half of the race will develop it as it never has been developed before.[1]

Gilman and Glaspell both lived to see women gain the vote in the United States in 1920.

The new technologies and consumer goods that improved the standard of living for most Americans opened other roles for women besides maintaining the home. Especially after 1870, women began to gain access to higher education and to demand more opportunities for respected careers beyond teaching, writing, or

---

1. Charlotte Perkins Gilman, testimony before Congress of the National American Woman Suffrage Association Committee on the Judiciary in Washington, DC, January 28, 1896. Originally published in *In This Our World* (Boston: Small, Maynard & Company Publishing, 1893), pp. 95–100.

the arts. By the beginning of the twentieth century, some women pursued careers in nursing, social work, libraries, fashion, and business, though usually they were employed in lower-paid positions, as clerical or support staff rather than as managers. Writing had long been a way to earn a living for some educated women, but the spread of newspapers and mass-market magazines from the 1890s onward provided openings for a new kind of worker, the woman journalist.

Chopin, Gilman, and Glaspell, needing to earn a living, found opportunities to publish in the newspapers and magazines. A surprising range of fiction and poetry as well as sensational reporting appeared in these media, aimed at a range of audiences. Susan Glaspell began her journalism career after college, as a reporter in Iowa, and covered a scandalous murder case similar to the one in her story "A Jury of Her Peers." She contributed to what was called "yellow" journalism, a term invented in 1897 for popular illustrated news printed on cheap wood-pulp paper that yellowed with age—a phenomenon alluded to in Gilman's story "The Yellow Wallpaper," according to Sari Edelstein. These writers' careers and writings, including the works featured here, reflect both the expanding prospects and continuing limitations on women's lives in this transitional period.

Remington typewriter advertisement, 1919

KATE CHOPIN

The Story of an Hour

Knowing that Mrs. Mallard was afflicted with a heart trouble, great care was taken to break to her as gently as possible the news of her husband's death.

It was her sister Josephine who told her, in broken sentences; veiled hints that revealed in half concealing. Her husband's friend Richards was there, too, near her. It was he who had been in the newspaper office when intelligence of the railroad disaster was received, with Brently Mallard's name leading the list of "killed." He had only taken the time to assure himself of its truth by a second telegram, and had hastened to forestall any less careful, less tender friend in bearing the sad message.

She did not hear the story as many women have heard the same, with a paralyzed inability to accept its significance. She wept at once, with sudden, wild abandonment, in her sister's arms. When the storm of grief had spent itself she went away to her room alone. She would have no one follow her.

There stood, facing the open window, a comfortable, roomy armchair. Into this she sank, pressed down by a physical exhaustion that haunted her body and seemed to reach into her soul.

She could see in the open square before her house the tops of trees that were 5 all aquiver with the new spring life. The delicious breath of rain was in the air. In the street below a peddler was crying his wares. The notes of a distant song which some one was singing reached her faintly, and countless sparrows were twittering in the eaves.

There were patches of blue sky showing here and there through the clouds that had met and piled one above the other in the west facing her window.

She sat with her head thrown back upon the cushion of the chair, quite motionless, except when a sob came up into her throat and shook her, as a child who has cried itself to sleep continues to sob in its dreams.

She was young, with a fair, calm face, whose lines bespoke repression and even a certain strength. But now there was a dull stare in her eyes, whose gaze was fixed away off yonder on one of those patches of blue sky. It was not a glance of reflection, but rather indicated a suspension of intelligent thought.

There was something coming to her and she was waiting for it, fearfully. What was it? She did not know; it was too subtle and elusive to name. But she felt it, creeping out of the sky, reaching toward her through the sounds, the scents, the color that filled the air.

Now her bosom rose and fell tumultuously. She was beginning to recognize 10 this thing that was approaching to possess her, and she was striving to beat it back with her will—as powerless as her two white slender hands would have been.

When she abandoned herself a little whispered word escaped her slightly parted lips. She said it over and over under her breath: "free, free, free!" The vacant stare and the look of terror that had followed it went from her eyes. They stayed keen and bright. Her pulses beat fast, and the coursing blood warmed and relaxed every inch of her body.

She did not stop to ask if it were or were not a monstrous joy that held her. A clear and exalted perception enabled her to dismiss the suggestion as trivial.

She knew that she would weep again when she saw the kind, tender hands folded in death; the face that had never looked save with love upon her, fixed and gray and dead. But she saw beyond that bitter moment a long procession of years to come that would belong to her absolutely. And she opened and spread her arms out to them in welcome.

There would be no one to live for her during those coming years; she would live for herself. There would be no powerful will bending hers in that blind persistence with which men and women believe they have a right to impose a private will upon a fellow-creature. A kind intention or a cruel intention made the act seem no less a crime as she looked upon it in that brief moment of illumination.

15   And yet she had loved him—sometimes. Often she had not. What did it matter! What could love, the unsolved mystery, count for in face of this possession of self-assertion which she suddenly recognized as the strongest impulse of her being!

"Free! Body and soul free!" she kept whispering.

Josephine was kneeling before the closed door with her lips to the keyhole, imploring for admission. "Louise, open the door! I beg; open the door—you will make yourself ill. What are you doing, Louise? For heaven's sake open the door."

"Go away. I am not making myself ill." No; she was drinking in a very elixir of life through that open window.

Her fancy was running riot along those days ahead of her. Spring days, and summer days, and all sorts of days that would be her own. She breathed a quick prayer that life might be long. It was only yesterday she had thought with a shudder that life might be long.

20   She arose at length and opened the door to her sister's importunities. There was a feverish triumph in her eyes, and she carried herself unwittingly like a goddess of Victory. She clasped her sister's waist, and together they descended the stairs. Richards stood waiting for them at the bottom.

Some one was opening the front door with a latchkey. It was Brently Mallard who entered, a little travel-stained, composedly carrying his grip-sack and umbrella. He had been far from the scene of accident, and did not even know there had been one. He stood amazed at Josephine's piercing cry; at Richards' quick motion to screen him from the view of his wife.

But Richards was too late.

When the doctors came they said she had died of heart disease—of joy that kills.

1894

CHARLOTTE PERKINS GILMAN

The Yellow Wallpaper

It is very seldom that mere ordinary people like John and myself secure ancestral halls for the summer.

A colonial mansion, a hereditary estate, I would say a haunted house, and reach the height of romantic felicity—but that would be asking too much of fate!

Still I will proudly declare that there is something queer about it.

Else, why should it be let so cheaply? And why have stood so long untenanted?

John laughs at me, of course, but one expects that in marriage.   5

John is practical in the extreme. He has no patience with faith, an intense horror of superstition, and he scoffs openly at any talk of things not to be felt and seen and put down in figures.

John is a physician, and *perhaps*—(I would not say it to a living soul, of course, but this is dead paper and a great relief to my mind—) *perhaps* that is one reason I do not get well faster.

You see he does not believe I am sick!

And what can one do?

If a physician of high standing, and one's own husband, assures friends and   10 relatives that there is really nothing the matter with one but temporary nervous depression—a slight hysterical tendency—what is one to do?

My brother is also a physician, and also of high standing, and he says the same thing.

So I take phosphates or phosphites—whichever it is, and tonics, and journeys, and air, and exercise, and am absolutely forbidden to "work" until I am well again.

Personally, I disagree with their ideas.

Personally, I believe that congenial work, with excitement and change, would do me good.

But what is one to do?   15

I did write for a while in spite of them; but it *does* exhaust me a good deal—having to be so sly about it, or else meet with heavy opposition.

I sometimes fancy that in my condition if I had less opposition and more society and stimulus—but John says the very worst thing I can do is to think about my condition, and I confess it always makes me feel bad.

So I will let it alone and talk about the house.

The most beautiful place! It is quite alone, standing well back from the road, quite three miles from the village. It makes me think of English places that you read about, for there are hedges and walls and gates that lock, and lots of separate little houses for the gardeners and people.

There is a *delicious* garden! I never saw such a garden—large and shady, full of   20 box-bordered paths, and lined with long grape-covered arbors with seats under them.

There were greenhouses, too, but they are all broken now.

There was some legal trouble, I believe, something about the heirs and co-heirs; anyhow, the place has been empty for years.

That spoils my ghostliness, I am afraid, but I don't care—there is something strange about the house—I can feel it.

I even said so to John one moonlight evening, but he said what I felt was a *draught,* and shut the window.

I get unreasonably angry with John sometimes. I'm sure I never used to be so   25 sensitive. I think it is due to this nervous condition.

But John says if I feel so, I shall neglect proper self-control; so I take pains to control myself—before him, at least, and that makes me very tired.

I don't like our room a bit. I wanted one downstairs that opened on the piazza and had roses all over the window, and such pretty old-fashioned chintz hangings! but John would not hear of it.

He said there was only one window and not room for two beds, and no near room for him if he took another.

He is very careful and loving, and hardly lets me stir without special direction.
30 I have a schedule prescription for each hour in the day; he takes all care from me, and so I feel basely ungrateful not to value it more.

He said we came here solely on my account, that I was to have perfect rest and all the air I could get. "Your exercise depends on your strength, my dear," said he, "and your food somewhat on your appetite; but air you can absorb all the time." So we took the nursery at the top of the house.

It is a big, airy room, the whole floor nearly, with windows that look all ways, and air and sunshine galore. It was nursery first and then playroom and gymnasium, I should judge; for the windows are barred for little children, and there are rings and things in the walls.

The paint and paper look as if a boys' school had used it. It is stripped off—the paper—in great patches all around the head of my bed, about as far as I can reach, and in a great place on the other side of the room low down. I never saw a worse paper in my life.

One of those sprawling flamboyant patterns committing every artistic sin.
35 It is dull enough to confuse the eye in following, pronounced enough to constantly irritate and provoke study, and when you follow the lame uncertain curves for a little distance they suddenly commit suicide—plunge off at outrageous angles, destroy themselves in unheard of contradictions.

The color is repellant, almost revolting; a smouldering unclean yellow, strangely faded by the slow-turning sunlight.

It is a dull yet lurid orange in some places, a sickly sulphur tint in others.

No wonder the children hated it! I should hate it myself if I had to live in this room long.

There comes John, and I must put this away,—he hates to have me write a word.

40 We have been here two weeks, and I haven't felt like writing before, since that first day.

I am sitting by the window now, up in this atrocious nursery, and there is nothing to hinder my writing as much as I please, save lack of strength.

John is away all day, and even some nights when his cases are serious.

I am glad my case is not serious!

But these nervous troubles are dreadfully depressing.

45 John does not know how much I really suffer. He knows there is no *reason* to suffer, and that satisfies him.

Of course it is only nervousness. It does weigh on me so not to do my duty in any way!

I mean to be such a help to John, such a real rest and comfort, and here I am a comparative burden already!

Nobody would believe what an effort it is to do what little I am able,—to dress and entertain, and order things.

It is fortunate Mary is so good with the baby. Such a dear baby!

50 And yet I *cannot* be with him, it makes me so nervous.

I suppose John never was nervous in his life. He laughs at me so about this wallpaper!

At first he meant to repaper the room, but afterwards he said that I was letting it get the better of me, and that nothing was worse for a nervous patient than to give way to such fancies.

He said that after the wallpaper was changed it would be the heavy bedstead, and then the barred windows, and then that gate at the head of the stairs, and so on.

"You know the place is doing you good," he said, "and really, dear, I don't care to renovate the house just for a three months' rental."

"Then do let us go downstairs," I said, "there are such pretty rooms there." 55

Then he took me in his arms and called me a blessed little goose, and said he would go down cellar, if I wished, and have it whitewashed into the bargain.

But he is right enough about the beds and windows and things.

It is an airy and comfortable room as any one need wish, and, of course, I would not be so silly as to make him uncomfortable just for a whim.

I'm really getting quite fond of the big room, all but that horrid paper.

Out of one window I can see the garden, those mysterious deep-shaded arbors, 60 the riotous old-fashioned flowers, and bushes and gnarly trees.

Out of another I get a lovely view of the bay and a little private wharf belonging to the estate. There is a beautiful shaded lane that runs down there from the house. I always fancy I see people walking in these numerous paths and arbors, but John has cautioned me not to give way to fancy in the least. He says that with my imaginative power and habit of story-making, a nervous weakness like mine is sure to lead to all manner of excited fancies, and that I ought to use my will and good sense to check the tendency. So I try.

I think sometimes that if I were only well enough to write a little it would relieve the press of ideas and rest me.

But I find I get pretty tired when I try.

It is so discouraging not to have any advice and companionship about my work. When I get really well, John says we will ask Cousin Henry and Julia down for a long visit; but he says he would as soon put fireworks in my pillow-case as to let me have those stimulating people about now.

I wish I could get well faster. 65

But I must not think about that. This paper looks to me as if it *knew* what a vicious influence it had!

There is a recurrent spot where the pattern lolls like a broken neck and two bulbous eyes stare at you upside down.

I get positively angry with the impertinence of it and the everlastingness. Up and down and sideways they crawl, and those absurd, unblinking eyes are everywhere. There is one place where two breadths didn't match, and the eyes go all up and down the line, one a little higher than the other.

I never saw so much expression in an inanimate thing before, and we all know how much expression they have! I used to lie awake as a child and get more entertainment and terror out of blank walls and plain furniture than most children could find in a toy-store.

I remember what a kindly wink the knobs of our big, old bureau used to have, 70 and there was one chair that always seemed like a strong friend.

I used to feel that if any of the other things looked too fierce I could always hop into that chair and be safe.

The furniture in this room is no worse than inharmonious, however, for we had to bring it all from downstairs. I suppose when this was used as a playroom they had to take the nursery things out, and no wonder! I never saw such ravages as the children have made here.

The wallpaper, as I said before, is torn off in spots, and it sticketh closer than a brother—they must have had perseverance as well as hatred.

Then the floor is scratched and gouged and splintered, the plaster itself is dug out here and there, and this great heavy bed which is all we found in the room, looks as if it had been through the wars.

75 But I don't mind it a bit—only the paper.

There comes John's sister. Such a dear girl as she is, and so careful of me! I must not let her find me writing.

She is a perfect and enthusiastic housekeeper, and hopes for no better profession. I verily believe she thinks it is the writing which made me sick!

But I can write when she is out, and see her a long way off from these windows.

There is one that commands the road, a lovely shaded winding road, and one that just looks off over the country. A lovely country, too, full of great elms and velvet meadows.

80 This wallpaper has a kind of sub-pattern in a different shade, a particularly irritating one, for you can only see it in certain lights, and not clearly then.

But in the places where it isn't faded and where the sun is just so—I can see a strange, provoking, formless sort of figure, that seems to skulk about behind that silly and conspicuous front design.

There's sister on the stairs!

Well, the Fourth of July is over! The people are all gone and I am tired out. John thought it might do me good to see a little company, so we just had mother and Nellie and the children down for a week.

Of course I didn't do a thing. Jennie sees to everything now.

85 But it tired me all the same.

John says if I don't pick up faster he shall send me to Weir Mitchell[1] in the fall.

But I don't want to go there at all. I had a friend who was in his hands once, and she says he is just like John and my brother, only more so!

Besides, it is such an undertaking to go so far.

I don't feel as if it was worth while to turn my hand over for anything, and I'm getting dreadfully fretful and querulous.

90 I cry at nothing, and cry most of the time.

Of course I don't when John is here, or anybody else, but when I am alone.

And I am alone a good deal just now. John is kept in town very often by serious cases, and Jennie is good and lets me alone when I want her to.

So I walk a little in the garden or down that lovely lane, sit on the porch under the roses, and lie down up here a good deal.

I'm getting really fond of the room in spite of the wallpaper. Perhaps *because* of the wallpaper.

95 It dwells in my mind so!

I lie here on this great immovable bed—it is nailed down, I believe—and follow that pattern about by the hour. It is as good as gymnastics, I assure you. I start, we'll say, at the bottom, down in the corner over there where it has not been touched, and I determine for the thousandth time that I *will* follow that pointless pattern to some sort of conclusion.

1. Silas Weir Mitchell (1829–1914), American physician, novelist, and specialist in nerve disorders, popularized the rest cure.

I know a little of the principle of design, and I know this thing was not arranged on any laws of radiation, or alternation, or repetition, or symmetry, or anything else that I ever heard of.

It is repeated, of course, by the breadths, but not otherwise.

Looked at in one way each breadth stands alone, the bloated curves and flourishes—a kind of "debased Romanesque" with *delirium tremens*—go waddling up and down in isolated columns of fatuity.

But, on the other hand, they connect diagonally, and the sprawling outlines run off in great slanting waves of optic horror, like a lot of wallowing seaweeds in full chase.

The whole thing goes horizontally, too, at least it seems so, and I exhaust myself in trying to distinguish the order of its going in that direction.

They have used a horizontal breadth for a frieze, and that adds wonderfully to the confusion.

There is one end of the room where it is almost intact, and there, when the crosslights fade and the low sun shines directly upon it, I can almost fancy radiation after all,—the interminable grotesque seem to form around a common center and rush off in headlong plunges of equal distraction.

It makes me tired to follow it. I will take a nap I guess.

I don't know why I should write this.

I don't want to.

I don't feel able.

And I know John would think it absurd. But I *must* say what I feel and think in some way—it is such a relief!

But the effort is getting to be greater than the relief.

Half the time now I am awfully lazy, and lie down ever so much.

John says I mustn't lose my strength, and has me take cod liver oil and lots of tonics and things, to say nothing of ale and wine and rare meat.

Dear John! He loves me very dearly, and hates to have me sick. I tried to have a real earnest reasonable talk with him the other day, and tell him how I wish he would let me go and make a visit to Cousin Henry and Julia.

But he said I wasn't able to go, nor able to stand it after I got there; and I did not make out a very good case for myself, for I was crying before I had finished.

It is getting to be a great effort for me to think straight. Just this nervous weakness I suppose.

And dear John gathered me up in his arms, and just carried me upstairs and laid me on the bed, and sat by me and read to me till it tired my head.

He said I was his darling and his comfort and all he had, and that I must take care of myself for his sake, and keep well.

He says no one but myself can help me out of it, that I must use my will and self-control and not let any silly fancies run away with me.

There's one comfort, the baby is well and happy, and does not have to occupy this nursery with the horrid wallpaper.

If we had not used it, that blessed child would have! What a fortunate escape! Why, I wouldn't have a child of mine, an impressionable little thing, live in such a room for worlds.

I never thought of it before, but it is lucky that John kept me here after all, I can stand it so much easier than a baby, you see.

Of course I never mention it to them any more—I am too wise,—but I keep watch of it all the same.

There are things in that paper that nobody knows but me, or ever will.

Behind that outside pattern the dim shapes get clearer every day.

It is always the same shape, only very numerous.

125 And it is like a woman stooping down and creeping about behind that pattern. I don't like it a bit. I wonder—I begin to think—I wish John would take me away from here!

It is so hard to talk with John about my case, because he is so wise, and because he loves me so.

But I tried it last night.

It was moonlight. The moon shines in all around just as the sun does.

I hate to see it sometimes, it creeps so slowly, and always comes in by one window or another.

130 John was asleep and I hated to waken him, so I kept still and watched the moonlight on that undulating wallpaper till I felt creepy.

The faint figure behind seemed to shake the pattern, just as if she wanted to get out.

I got up softly and went to feel and see if the paper *did* move, and when I came back John was awake.

"What is it, little girl?" he said. "Don't go walking about like that—you'll get cold."

I thought it was a good time to talk, so I told him that I really was not gaining here, and that I wished he would take me away.

135 "Why, darling!" said he, "our lease will be up in three weeks, and I can't see how to leave before.

"The repairs are not done at home, and I cannot possibly leave town just now. Of course if you were in any danger, I could and would, but you really are better, dear, whether you can see it or not. I am a doctor, dear, and I know. You are gaining flesh and color, your appetite is better, I feel really much easier about you."

"I don't weigh a bit more," said I, "nor as much; and my appetite may be better in the evening when you are here, but it is worse in the morning when you are away!"

"Bless her little heart!" said he with a big hug, "she shall be as sick as she pleases! But now let's improve the shining hours by going to sleep, and talk about it in the morning!"

"And you won't go away?" I asked gloomily.

140 "Why, how can I, dear? It is only three weeks more and then we will take a nice little trip of a few days while Jennie is getting the house ready. Really dear you are better!"

"Better in body perhaps—" I began, and stopped short, for he sat up straight and looked at me with such a stern, reproachful look that I could not say another word.

"My darling," said he, "I beg of you, for my sake and for our child's sake, as well as for your own, that you will never for one instant let that idea enter your mind! There is nothing so dangerous, so fascinating, to a temperament like yours. It is a false and foolish fancy. Can you not trust me as a physician when I tell you so?"

So of course I said no more on that score, and we went to sleep before long. He thought I was asleep first, but I wasn't, and lay there for hours trying to decide whether that front pattern and the back pattern really did move together or separately.

On a pattern like this, by daylight, there is a lack of sequence, a defiance of law, that is a constant irritant to a normal mind.

The color is hideous enough, and unreliable enough, and infuriating enough, but the pattern is torturing. 145

You think you have mastered it, but just as you get well underway in following, it turns a back-somersault and there you are. It slaps you in the face, knocks you down, and tramples upon you. It is like a bad dream.

The outside pattern is a florid arabesque, reminding one of a fungus. If you can imagine a toadstool in joints, an interminable string of toadstools, budding and sprouting in endless convolutions—why, that is something like it.

That is, sometimes!

There is one marked peculiarity about this paper, a thing nobody seems to notice but myself, and that is that it changes as the light changes.

When the sun shoots in through the east window—I always watch for that first long, straight ray—it changes so quickly that I never can quite believe it. 150

That is why I watch it always.

By moonlight—the moon shines in all night when there is a moon—I wouldn't know it was the same paper.

At night in any kind of light, in twilight, candlelight, lamplight, and worst of all by moonlight, it becomes bars! The outside pattern I mean, and the woman behind it is as plain as can be.

I didn't realize for a long time what the thing was that showed behind, that dim sub-pattern, but now I am quite sure it is a woman.

By daylight she is subdued, quiet. I fancy it is the pattern that keeps her so still. It is so puzzling. It keeps me quiet by the hour. 155

I lie down ever so much now. John says it is good for me, and to sleep all I can.

Indeed he started the habit by making me lie down for an hour after each meal.

It is a very bad habit I am convinced, for you see I don't sleep.

And that cultivates deceit, for I don't tell them I'm awake—O no!

The fact is I am getting a little afraid of John. 160

He seems very queer sometimes, and even Jennie has an inexplicable look.

It strikes me occasionally, just as a scientific hypothesis,—that perhaps it is the paper!

I have watched John when he did not know I was looking, and come into the room suddenly on the most innocent excuses, and I've caught him several times *looking at the paper!* And Jennie too. I caught Jennie with her hand on it once.

She didn't know I was in the room, and when I asked her in a quiet, a very quiet voice, with the most restrained manner possible, what she was doing with the paper—she turned around as if she had been caught stealing, and looked quite angry—asked me why I should frighten her so!

Then she said that the paper stained everything it touched, that she had found yellow smooches on all my clothes and John's, and she wished we would be more careful! 165

Did not that sound innocent? But I know she was studying that pattern, and I am determined that nobody shall find it out but myself!

Life is very much more exciting now than it used to be. You see I have something more to expect, to look forward to, to watch. I really do eat better, and am more quiet than I was.

John is so pleased to see me improve! He laughed a little the other day, and said I seemed to be flourishing in spite of my wallpaper.

I turned it off with a laugh. I had no intention of telling him it was *because* of the wallpaper—he would make fun of me. He might even want to take me away.

170   I don't want to leave now until I have found it out. There is a week more, and I think that will be enough.

I'm feeling ever so much better! I don't sleep much at night, for it is so interesting to watch developments; but I sleep a good deal in the daytime.

In the daytime it is tiresome and perplexing.

There are always new shoots on the fungus, and new shades of yellow all over it. I cannot keep count of them, though I have tried conscientiously.

It is the strangest yellow, that wallpaper! It makes me think of all the yellow things I ever saw—not beautiful ones like buttercups, but old foul, bad yellow things.

175   But there is something else about that paper—the smell! I noticed it the moment we came into the room, but with so much air and sun it was not bad. Now we have had a week of fog and rain, and whether the windows are open or not, the smell is here.

It creeps all over the house.

I find it hovering in the dining-room, skulking in the parlor, hiding in the hall, lying in wait for me on the stairs.

It gets into my hair.

Even when I go to ride, if I turn my head suddenly and surprise it—there is that smell!

180   Such a peculiar odor, too! I have spent hours in trying to analyze it, to find what it smelled like.

It is not bad—at first, and very gentle, but quite the subtlest, most enduring odor I ever met.

In this damp weather it is awful, I wake up in the night and find it hanging over me.

It used to disturb me at first. I thought seriously of burning the house—to reach the smell.

But now I am used to it. The only thing I can think of that it is like is the *color* of the paper! A yellow smell.

185   There is a very funny mark on this wall, low down, near the mopboard. A streak that runs round the room. It goes behind every piece of furniture, except the bed, a long, straight, even *smooch,* as if it had been rubbed over and over.

I wonder how it was done and who did it, and what they did it for. Round and round and round—round and round and round—it makes me dizzy!

I really have discovered something at last.

Through watching so much at night, when it changes so, I have finally found out.

The front pattern *does* move—and no wonder! The woman behind shakes it!

190   Sometimes I think there are a great many women behind, and sometimes only one, and she crawls around fast, and her crawling shakes it all over.

Then in the very bright spots she keeps still, and in the very shady spots she just takes hold of the bars and shakes them hard.

And she is all the time trying to climb through. But nobody could climb through that pattern—it strangles so; I think that is why it has so many heads.

They get through, and then the pattern strangles them off and turns them upside down, and makes their eyes white!

If those heads were covered or taken off it would not be half so bad.

I think that woman gets out in the daytime!

And I'll tell you why—privately—I've seen her!

I can see her out of every one of my windows!

It is the same woman, I know, for she is always creeping, and most women do not creep by daylight.

I see her in that long shaded lane, creeping up and down. I see her in those dark grape arbors, creeping all around the garden.

I see her on that long road under the trees, creeping along, and when a carriage comes she hides under the blackberry vines.

I don't blame her a bit. It must be very humiliating to be caught creeping by daylight!

I always lock the door when I creep by daylight. I can't do it at night, for I know John would suspect something at once.

And John is so queer now, that I don't want to irritate him. I wish he would take another room! Besides, I don't want anybody to get that woman out at night but myself.

I often wonder if I could see her out of all the windows at once.

But, turn as fast as I can, I can only see out of one at one time.

And though I always see her, she *may* be able to creep faster than I can turn!

I have watched her sometimes away off in the open country, creeping as fast as a cloud shadow in a high wind.

If only that top pattern could be gotten off from the under one! I mean to try it, little by little.

I have found out another funny thing, but I shan't tell it this time! It does not do to trust people too much.

There are only two more days to get this paper off, and I believe John is beginning to notice. I don't like the look in his eyes.

And I heard him ask Jennie a lot of professional questions about me. She had a very good report to give.

She said I slept a good deal in the daytime.

John knows I don't sleep very well at night, for all I'm so quiet!

He asked me all sorts of questions, too, and pretended to be very loving and kind.

As if I couldn't see through him!

Still, I don't wonder he acts so, sleeping under this paper for three months.

It only interests me, but I feel sure John and Jennie are secretly affected by it.

Hurrah! This is the last day, but it is enough. John is to stay in town over night, and won't be out until this evening.

Jennie wanted to sleep with me—the sly thing! but I told her I should undoubtedly rest better for a night all alone.

220   That was clever, for really I wasn't alone a bit! As soon as it was moonlight and that poor thing began to crawl and shake the pattern, I got up and ran to help her.

I pulled and she shook, I shook and she pulled, and before morning we had peeled off yards of that paper.

A strip about as high as my head and half around the room.

And then when the sun came and that awful pattern began to laugh at me, I declared I would finish it to-day!

We go away to-morrow, and they are moving all my furniture down again to leave things as they were before.

225   Jennie looked at the wall in amazement, but I told her merrily that I did it out of pure spite at the vicious thing.

She laughed and said she wouldn't mind doing it herself, but I must not get tired.

How she betrayed herself that time!

But I am here, and no person touches this paper but me,—not *alive*!

She tried to get me out of the room—it was too patent! But I said it was so quiet and empty and clean now that I believed I would lie down again and sleep all I could; and not to wake me even for dinner—I would call when I woke.

230   So now she is gone, and the servants are gone, and the things are gone, and there is nothing left but that great bedstead nailed down, with the canvas mattress we found on it.

We shall sleep downstairs to-night, and take the boat home to-morrow.

I quite enjoy the room, now it is bare again.

How those children did tear about here!

This bedstead is fairly gnawed!

235   But I must get to work.

I have locked the door and thrown the key down into the front path.

I don't want to go out, and I don't want to have anybody come in, till John comes.

I want to astonish him.

I've got a rope up here that even Jennie did not find. If that woman does get out, and tries to get away, I can tie her!

240   But I forgot I could not reach far without anything to stand on!

This bed will *not* move!

I tried to lift and push it until I was lame, and then I got so angry I bit off a little piece at one corner—but it hurt my teeth.

Then I peeled off all the paper I could reach standing on the floor. It sticks horribly and the pattern just enjoys it! All those strangled heads and bulbous eyes and waddling fungus growths just shriek with derision!

I am getting angry enough to do something desperate. To jump out of the window would be admirable exercise, but the bars are too strong even to try.

245   Besides I wouldn't do it. Of course not. I know well enough that a step like that is improper and might be misconstrued.

I don't like to *look* out of the windows even—there are so many of those creeping women, and they creep so fast.

I wonder if they all come out of that wallpaper as I did?

But I am securely fastened now by my well-hidden rope—you don't get *me* out in the road there!

I suppose I shall have to get back behind the pattern when it comes night, and that is hard!

It is so pleasant to be out in this great room and creep around as I please! 250

I don't want to go outside. I won't, even if Jennie asks me to.

For outside you have to creep on the ground, and everything is green instead of yellow.

But here I can creep smoothly on the floor, and my shoulder just fits in that long smooch around the wall, so I cannot lose my way.

Why there's John at the door!

It is no use, young man, you can't open it! 255

How he does call and pound!

Now he's crying for an axe.

It would be a shame to break down that beautiful door!

"John dear!" said I in the gentlest voice, "the key is down by the front steps, under a plantain leaf!"

That silenced him for a few moments. 260

Then he said—very quietly indeed, "Open the door, my darling!"

"I can't," said I. "The key is down by the front door under a plantain leaf!"

And then I said it again, several times, very gently and slowly, and said it so often that he had to go and see, and he got it of course, and came in. He stopped short by the door.

"What is the matter?" he cried. "For God's sake, what are you doing!"

I kept on creeping just the same, but I looked at him over my shoulder. 265

"I've got out at last," said I, "in spite of you and Jane. And I've pulled off most of the paper, so you can't put me back!"

Now why should that man have fainted? But he did, and right across my path by the wall, so that I had to creep over him every time!

1892

SUSAN GLASPELL

A Jury of Her Peers

When Martha Hale opened the storm door and got a cut of the north wind, she ran back for her big woolen scarf. As she hurriedly wound that round her head her eye made a scandalized sweep of her kitchen. It was no ordinary thing that called her away—it was probably farther from ordinary than anything that had ever happened in Dickson County. But what her eye took in was that her kitchen was in no shape for leaving: her bread all ready for mixing, half the flour sifted and half unsifted.

She hated to see things half done; but she had been at that when the team from town stopped to get Mr. Hale, and then the sheriff came running in to say his wife wished Mrs. Hale would come too—adding, with a grin, that he guessed she was getting scary and wanted another woman along. So she had dropped everything right where it was.

"Martha!" now came her husband's impatient voice. "Don't keep folks waiting out here in the cold."

She again opened the storm door, and this time joined the three men and the one woman waiting for her in the big two-seated buggy.

5   After she had the robes tucked around her she took another look at the woman who sat beside her on the back seat. She had met Mrs. Peters the year before at the county fair, and the thing she remembered about her was that she didn't seem like a sheriff's wife. She was small and thin and didn't have a strong voice. Mrs. Gorman, sheriff's wife before Gorman went out and Peters came in, had a voice that somehow seemed to be backing up the law with every word. But if Mrs. Peters didn't look like a sheriff's wife, Peters made it up in looking like a sheriff. He was to a dot the kind of man who could get himself elected sheriff—a heavy man with a big voice, who was particularly genial with the law-abiding, as if to make it plain that he knew the difference between criminals and noncriminals. And right there it came into Mrs. Hale's mind, with a stab, that this man who was so pleasant and lively with all of them was going to the Wrights' now as a sheriff.

"The country's not very pleasant this time of year," Mrs. Peters at last ventured, as if she felt they ought to be talking as well as the men.

Mrs. Hale scarcely finished her reply, for they had gone up a little hill and could see the Wright place now, and seeing it did not make her feel like talking. It looked very lonesome this cold March morning. It had always been a lonesome-looking place. It was down in a hollow, and the poplar trees around it were lonesome-looking trees. The men were looking at it and talking about what had happened. The county attorney was bending to one side of the buggy, and kept looking steadily at the place as they drew up to it.

"I'm glad you came with me," Mrs. Peters said nervously, as the two women were about to follow the men in through the kitchen door.

Even after she had her foot on the doorstep, her hand on the knob, Martha Hale had a moment of feeling she could not cross that threshold. And the reason it seemed she couldn't cross it now was simply because she hadn't crossed it before. Time and time again it had been in her mind. "I ought to go over and see Minnie Foster"—she still thought of her as Minnie Foster, though for twenty years she had been Mrs. Wright. And then there was always something to do and Minnie Foster would go from her mind. But *now* she could come.

10   The men went over to the stove. The women stood close together by the door. Young Henderson, the county attorney, turned around and said, "Come up to the fire, ladies."

Mrs. Peters took a step forward, then stopped. "I'm not—cold," she said.

And so the two women stood by the door, at first not even so much as looking around the kitchen.

The men talked for a minute about what a good thing it was the sheriff had sent his deputy out that morning to make a fire for them, and then Sheriff Peters stepped back from the stove, unbuttoned his outer coat, and leaned his hands on the kitchen table in a way that seemed to mark the beginning of official business. "Now, Mr. Hale," he said in a sort of semi-official voice, "before we move things about, you tell Mr. Henderson just what it was you saw when you came here yesterday morning."

The county attorney was looking around the kitchen.

15   "By the way," he said, "has anything been moved?" He turned to the sheriff. "Are things just as you left them yesterday?"

Peters looked from cupboard to sink; from that to a small worn rocker a little to one side of the kitchen table.

"It's just the same."

"Somebody should have been left here yesterday," said the county attorney.

"Oh—yesterday," returned the sheriff, with a little gesture as of yesterday having been more than he could bear to think of. "When I had to send Frank to Morris Center for that man who went crazy—let me tell you, I had my hands full *yesterday*. I knew you could get back from Omaha by today, George, and as long as I went over everything here myself—"

"Well, Mr. Hale," said the county attorney, in a way of letting what was past 20 and gone go, "tell just what happened when you came here yesterday morning."

Mrs. Hale, still leaning against the door, had that sinking feeling of the mother whose child is about to speak a piece. Lewis often wandered along and got things mixed up in a story. She hoped he would tell this straight and plain, and not say unnecessary things that would just make things harder for Minnie Foster. He didn't begin at once, and she noticed that he looked queer—as if standing in that kitchen and having to tell what he had seen there yesterday morning made him almost sick.

"Yes, Mr. Hale?" the county attorney reminded.

"Harry and I had started to town with a load of potatoes," Mrs. Hale's husband began.

Harry was Mrs. Hale's oldest boy. He wasn't with them now, for the very good reason that those potatoes never got to town yesterday and he was taking them this morning, so he hadn't been home when the sheriff stopped to say he wanted Mr. Hale to come over to the Wright place and tell the county attorney his story there, where he could point it all out. With all Mrs. Hale's other emotions came the fear that maybe Harry wasn't dressed warm enough—they hadn't any of them realized how that north wind did bite.

"We come along this road," Hale was going on, with a motion of his hand to 25 the road over which they had just come, "and as we got in sight of the house I says to Harry, 'I'm goin' to see if I can't get John Wright to take a telephone.' You see," he explained to Henderson, "unless I can get somebody to go in with me they won't come out this branch road except for a price *I* can't pay. I'd spoke to Wright about it once before; but he put me off, saying folks talked too much anyway, and all he asked was peace and quiet—guess you know about how much he talked himself. But I thought maybe if I went to the house and talked about it before his wife, and said all the womenfolks liked the telephones, and that in this lonesome stretch of road it would be a good thing—well, I said to Harry that that was what I was going to say—though I said at the same time that I didn't know as what his wife wanted made much difference to John—"

Now, there he was!—saying things he didn't need to say. Mrs. Hale tried to catch her husband's eye, but fortunately the county attorney interrupted with:

"Let's talk about that a little later, Mr. Hale. I do want to talk about that, but I'm anxious now to get along to just what happened when you got here."

When he began this time, it was very deliberately and carefully:

"I didn't see or hear anything. I knocked at the door. And still it was all quiet inside. I knew they must be up—it was past eight o'clock. So I knocked again, louder, and I thought I heard somebody say 'Come in.' I wasn't sure—I'm not sure yet. But I opened the door—this door," jerking a hand toward the door by which the two women stood, "and there, in that rocker"—pointing to it—"sat Mrs. Wright."

Everyone in the kitchen looked at the rocker. It came into Mrs. Hale's mind 30 that the rocker didn't look in the least like Minnie Foster—the Minnie Foster of twenty years before. It was a dingy red, with wooden rungs up the back, and the middle rung was gone, and the chair sagged to one side.

"How did she—look?" the county attorney was inquiring.

"Well," said Hale, "she looked—queer."

"How do you mean—queer?"

As he asked it he took out a notebook and pencil. Mrs. Hale did not like the sight of that pencil. She kept her eye fixed on her husband, as if to keep him from saying unnecessary things that would go into that notebook and make trouble.

35   Hale did speak guardedly, as if the pencil had affected him too.

"Well, as if she didn't know what she was going to do next. And kind of—done up."

"How did she seem to feel about your coming?"

"Why, I don't think she minded—one way or other. She didn't pay much attention. I said, 'Ho' do, Mrs. Wright? It's cold, ain't it!' And she said, 'Is it?'—and went on pleatin' at her apron.

"Well, I was surprised. She didn't ask me to come up to the stove, or to sit down, but just set there, not even lookin' at me. And so I said: 'I want to see John.'

40   "And then she—laughed. I guess you would call it a laugh.

"I thought of Harry and the team outside, so I said, a little sharp, 'Can I see John?' 'No,' says she—kind of dull like. 'Ain't he home?' says I. Then she looked at me. 'Yes,' says she, 'he's home.' 'Then why can't I see him?' I asked her, out of patience with her now. ''Cause he's dead,' says she, just as quiet and dull—and fell to pleatin' her apron. 'Dead?' says I, like you do when you can't take in what you've heard.

"She just nodded her head, not getting a bit excited, but rockin' back and forth.

"'Why—where is he?'" says I, not knowing *what* to say.

"She just pointed upstairs—like this"—pointing to the room above.

45   "I got up, with the idea of going up there myself. By this time I—didn't know what to do. I walked from there to here; then I says: 'Why, what did he die of?'

"'He died of a rope around his neck,' says she; and just went on pleatin' at her apron."

Hale stopped speaking, and stood staring at the rocker, as if he were still seeing the woman who had sat there the morning before. Nobody spoke; it was as if everyone were seeing the woman who had sat there the morning before.

"And what did you do then?" the county attorney at last broke the silence.

"I went out and called Harry. I thought I might—need help. I got Harry in, and we went upstairs." His voice fell almost to a whisper. "There he was—lying over the—"

50   "I think I'd rather have you go into that upstairs," the county attorney interrupted, "where you can point it all out. Just go on now with the rest of the story."

"Well, my first thought was to get that rope off. It looked—"

He stopped, his face twitching.

"But Harry, he went up to him, and he said, 'No, he's dead all right, and we'd better not touch anything.' So we went downstairs.

"She was still sitting the same way. 'Has anybody been notified?' I asked. 'No,' says she, unconcerned.

55   "'Who did this, Mrs. Wright?' said Harry. He said it business-like, and she stopped pleatin' at her apron. 'I don't know,' she says. 'You don't *know?*' says

Harry. 'Weren't you sleepin' in the bed with him?' 'Yes,' says she, 'but I was on the inside.' 'Somebody slipped a rope round his neck and strangled him, and you didn't wake up?' says Harry. 'I didn't wake up,' she said after him.

"We may have looked as if we didn't see how that could be, for after a minute she said, 'I sleep sound.'

"Harry was going to ask her more questions, but I said maybe that weren't our business; maybe we ought to let her tell her story first to the coroner or the sheriff. So Harry went fast as he could over to High Road—the Rivers' place, where there's a telephone."

"And what did she do when she knew you had gone for the coroner?" The attorney got his pencil in his hand all ready for writing.

"She moved from that chair to this one over here"—Hale pointed to a small chair in the corner—"and just sat there with her hands held together and looking down. I got a feeling that I ought to make some conversation, so I said I had come in to see if John wanted to put in a telephone; and at that she started to laugh, and then she stopped and looked at me—scared."

At the sound of a moving pencil the man who was telling the story looked up. 60

"I dunno—maybe it wasn't scared," he hastened; "I wouldn't like to say it was. Soon Harry got back, and then Dr. Lloyd came, and you, Mr. Peters, and so I guess that's all I know that you don't."

He said that last with relief, and moved a little, as if relaxing. Everyone moved a little. The county attorney walked toward the stair door.

"I guess we'll go upstairs first—then out to the barn and around there."

He paused and looked around the kitchen.

"You're convinced there was nothing important here?" he asked the sheriff. 65
"Nothing that would—point to any motive?"

The sheriff too looked all around, as if to reconvince himself.

"Nothing here but kitchen things," he said, with a little laugh for the insignificance of kitchen things.

The county attorney was looking at the cupboard—a peculiar, ungainly structure, half closet and half cupboard, the upper part of it being built in the wall, and the lower part just the old-fashioned kitchen cupboard. As if its queerness attracted him, he got a chair and opened the upper part and looked in. After a moment he drew his hand away sticky.

"Here's a nice mess," he said resentfully.

The two women had drawn nearer, and now the sheriff's wife spoke. 70

"Oh—her fruit," she said, looking to Mrs. Hale for sympathetic understanding. She turned back to the county attorney and explained: "She worried about that when it turned so cold last night. She said the fire would go out and her jars might burst."

Mrs. Peters' husband broke into a laugh.

"Well, can you beat the women! Held for murder, and worrying about her preserves!"

The young attorney set his lips.

"I guess before we're through with her she may have something more serious 75
than preserves to worry about."

"Oh, well," said Mrs. Hale's husband, with good-natured superiority, "women are used to worrying over trifles."

The two women moved a little closer together. Neither of them spoke. The county attorney seemed suddenly to remember his manners—and think of his future.

"And yet," said he, with the gallantry of a young politician, "for all their worries, what would we do without the ladies?"

The women did not speak, did not unbend. He went to the sink and began washing his hands. He turned to wipe them on the roller towel—whirled it for a cleaner place.

80 "Dirty towels! Not much of a housekeeper, would you say, ladies?"

He kicked his foot against some dirty pans under the sink.

"There's a great deal of work to be done on a farm," said Mrs. Hale stiffly.

"To be sure. And yet"—with a little bow to her—"I know there are some Dickson County farmhouses that do not have such roller towels." He gave it a pull to expose its full length again.

"Those towels get dirty awful quick. Men's hands aren't always as clean as they might be."

85 "Ah, loyal to your sex, I see," he laughed. He stopped and gave her a keen look. "But you and Mrs. Wright were neighbors. I suppose you were friends, too."

Martha Hale shook her head.

"I've seen little enough of her of late years. I've not been in this house—it's more than a year."

"And why was that? You didn't like her?"

"I liked her well enough," she replied with spirit. "Farmers' wives have their hands full, Mr. Henderson. And then"—She looked around the kitchen.

90 "Yes?" he encouraged.

"It never seemed a very cheerful place," said she, more to herself than to him.

"No," he agreed; "I don't think anyone would call it cheerful. I shouldn't say she had the homemaking instinct."

"Well, I don't know as Wright had, either," she muttered.

"You mean they didn't get on very well?" he was quick to ask.

95 "No; I don't mean anything," she answered, with decision. As she turned a little away from him, she added: "But I don't think a place would be any the cheerfuler for John Wright's bein' in it."

"I'd like to talk to you about that a little later, Mrs. Hale," he said. "I'm anxious to get the lay of things upstairs now."

He moved toward the stair door, followed by the two men.

"I suppose anything Mrs. Peters does'll be all right?" the sheriff inquired. "She was to take in some clothes for her, you know—and a few little things. We left in such a hurry yesterday."

The county attorney looked at the two women whom they were leaving alone there among the kitchen things.

100 "Yes—Mrs. Peters," he said, his glance resting on the woman who was not Mrs. Peters, the big farmer woman who stood behind the sheriff's wife. "Of course Mrs. Peters is one of us," he said, in a manner of entrusting responsibility. "And keep your eye out, Mrs. Peters, for anything that might be of use. No telling; you women might come upon a clue to the motive—and that's the thing we need."

Mr. Hale rubbed his face after the fashion of a showman getting ready for a pleasantry.

"But would the women know a clue if they did come upon it?" he said; and, having delivered himself of this, he followed the others through the stair door.

The women stood motionless and silent, listening to the footsteps, first upon the stairs, then in the room above them.

Then, as if releasing herself from something strange, Mrs. Hale began to arrange the dirty pans under the sink, which the county attorney's disdainful push of the foot had deranged.

"I'd hate to have men comin' into my kitchen," she said testily—"snoopin' round and criticizin'." 105

"Of course it's no more than their duty," said the sheriff's wife, in her manner of timid acquiescence.

"Duty's all right," replied Mrs. Hale bluffly; "but I guess that deputy sheriff that come out to make the fire might have got a little of this on." She gave the roller towel a pull. "Wish I'd thought of that sooner! Seems mean to talk about her for not having things slicked up, when she had to come away in such a hurry."

She looked around the kitchen. Certainly it was not "slicked up." Her eye was held by a bucket of sugar on a low shelf. The cover was off the wooden bucket, and beside it was a paper bag—half full.

Mrs. Hale moved toward it.

"She was putting this in there," she said to herself—slowly. 110

She thought of the flour in her kitchen at home—half sifted, half not sifted. She had been interrupted and had left things half done. What had interrupted Minnie Foster? Why had that work been left half done? She made a move as if to finish it,—unfinished things always bothered her,—and then she glanced around and saw that Mrs. Peters was watching her—and she didn't want Mrs. Peters to get that feeling she had got of work begun and then—for some reason—not finished.

"It's a shame about her fruit," she said, and walked toward the cupboard that the county attorney had opened, and got on the chair, murmuring: "I wonder if it's all gone."

It was a sorry enough looking sight, but "Here's one that's all right," she said at last. She held it toward the light. "This is cherries, too." She looked again. "I declare I believe that's the only one."

With a sigh, she got down from the chair, went to the sink, and wiped off the bottle.

"She'll feel awful bad, after all her hard work in the hot weather. I remember 115
the afternoon I put up my cherries last summer."

She set the bottle on the table, and, with another sigh, started to sit down in the rocker. But she did not sit down. Something kept her from sitting down in that chair. She straightened—stepped back, and, half turned away, stood looking at it, seeing the woman who sat there "pleatin' at her apron."

The thin voice of the sheriff's wife broke in upon her: "I must be getting those things from the front room closet." She opened the door into the other room, started in, stepped back. "You coming with me, Mrs. Hale?" she asked nervously. "You—you could help me get them."

They were soon back—the stark coldness of that shut-up room was not a thing to linger in.

"My!" said Mrs. Peters, dropping the things on the table and hurrying to the stove.

Mrs. Hale stood examining the clothes the woman who was being detained 120
in town had said she wanted.

"Wright was close!" she exclaimed, holding up a shabby black skirt that bore the marks of much making over. "I think maybe that's why she kept so much to herself. I s'pose she felt she couldn't do her part; and then, you don't enjoy things when you feel shabby. She used to wear pretty clothes and be lively—when she was Minnie Foster, one of the town girls, singing in the choir. But that—oh, that was twenty years ago."

With a carefulness in which there was something tender, she folded the shabby clothes and piled them at one corner of the table. She looked at Mrs. Peters, and there was something in the other woman's look that irritated her.

"She don't care," she said to herself. "Much difference it makes to her whether Minnie Foster had pretty clothes when she was a girl."

Then she looked again, and she wasn't so sure; in fact, she hadn't at any time been perfectly sure about Mrs. Peters. She had that shrinking manner, and yet her eyes looked as if they could see a long way into things.

125   "This all you was to take in?" asked Mrs. Hale.

"No," said the sheriff's wife; "she said she wanted an apron. Funny thing to want," she ventured in her nervous little way, "for there's not much to get you dirty in jail, goodness knows. But I suppose just to make her feel more natural. If you're used to wearing an apron—. She said they were in the bottom drawer of this cupboard. Yes—here they are. And then her little shawl that always hung on the stair door."

She took the small gray shawl from behind the door leading upstairs, and stood a minute looking at it.

Suddenly Mrs. Hale took a quick step toward the other woman.

"Mrs. Peters!"

130   "Yes, Mrs. Hale?"

"Do you think she—did it?"

A frightened look blurred the other things in Mrs. Peters' eyes.

"Oh, I don't know," she said, in a voice that seemed to shrink away from the subject.

"Well, I don't think she did," affirmed Mrs. Hale stoutly. "Asking for an apron, and her little shawl. Worryin' about her fruit."

135   "Mr. Peters says—" Footsteps were heard in the room above; she stopped, looked up, then went on in a lowered voice: "Mr. Peters says—it looks bad for her. Mr. Henderson is awful sarcastic in a speech, and he's going to make fun of her saying she didn't—wake up."

For a moment Mrs. Hale had no answer. Then, "Well, I guess John Wright didn't wake up—when they was slippin' that rope under his neck," she muttered.

"No, it's *strange*," breathed Mrs. Peters. "They think it was such a—funny way to kill a man."

She began to laugh; at sound of the laugh, abruptly stopped.

"That's just what Mr. Hale said," said Mrs. Hale, in a resolutely natural voice. "There was a gun in the house. He says that's what he can't understand."

140   "Mr. Henderson said, coming out, that what was needed for the case was a motive. Something to show anger—or sudden feeling."

"Well, I don't see any signs of anger around here," said Mrs. Hale. "I don't—"

She stopped. It was as if her mind tripped on something. Her eye was caught by a dish towel in the middle of the kitchen table. Slowly she moved toward the table. One half of it was wiped clean, the other half messy. Her eyes made a slow, almost unwilling turn to the bucket of sugar and the half empty bag beside it. Things begun—and not finished.

After a moment she stepped back, and said, in that manner of releasing herself:

"Wonder how they're finding things upstairs? I hope she had it a little more red-up up there. You know,"—she paused, and feeling gathered,—"it seems kind of *sneaking*; locking her up in town and coming out here to get her own house to turn against her!"

"But, Mrs. Hale," said the sheriff's wife, "the law is the law."   145

"I s'pose 'tis," answered Mrs. Hale shortly.

She turned to the stove, saying something about that fire not being much to brag of. She worked with it a minute, and when she straightened up she said aggressively:

"The law is the law—and a bad stove is a bad stove. How'd you like to cook on this?"—pointing with the poker to the broken lining. She opened the oven door and started to express her opinion of the oven; but she was swept into her own thoughts, thinking of what it would mean, year after year, to have that stove to wrestle with. The thought of Minnie Foster trying to bake in that oven—and the thought of her never going over to see Minnie Foster—.

She was startled by hearing Mrs. Peters say: "A person gets discouraged—and loses heart."

The sheriff's wife had looked from the stove to the sink—to the pail of water   150
which had been carried in from outside. The two women stood there silent, above them the footsteps of the men who were looking for evidence against the woman who had worked in that kitchen. That look of seeing into things, of seeing through a thing to something else, was in the eyes of the sheriff's wife now. When Mrs. Hale next spoke to her, it was gently:

"Better loosen up your things, Mrs. Peters. We'll not feel them when we go out."

Mrs. Peters went to the back of the room to hang up the fur tippet she was wearing. A moment later she exclaimed, "Why, she was piecing a quilt," and held up a large sewing basket piled high with quilt pieces.

Mrs. Hale spread some of the blocks on the table.

"It's log-cabin pattern," she said, putting several of them together. "Pretty, isn't it?"

They were so engaged with the quilt that they did not hear the footsteps on   155
the stairs. Just as the stair door opened Mrs. Hale was saying:

"Do you suppose she was going to quilt it or just knot it?"

The sheriff threw up his hands.

"They wonder whether she was going to quilt it or just knot it!"

There was a laugh for the ways of women, a warming of hands over the stove, and then the county attorney said briskly:

"Well, let's go right out to the barn and get that cleared up."   160

"I don't see as there's anything so strange," Mrs. Hale said resentfully, after the outside door had closed on the three men—"our taking up our time with little things while we're waiting for them to get the evidence. I don't see as it's anything to laugh about."

"Of course they've got awful important things on their minds," said the sheriff's wife apologetically.

They returned to an inspection of the blocks for the quilt. Mrs. Hale was looking at the fine, even sewing, and preoccupied with thoughts of the woman who had done that sewing, when she heard the sheriff's wife say, in a queer tone:

"Why, look at this one."

165   She turned to take the block held out to her.

"The sewing," said Mrs. Peters, in a troubled way. "All the rest of them have been so nice and even—but—this one. Why, it looks as if she didn't know what she was about!"

Their eyes met—something flashed to life, passed between them; then, as if with an effort, they seemed to pull away from each other. A moment Mrs. Hale sat there, her hands folded over that sewing which was so unlike all the rest of the sewing. Then she had pulled a knot and drawn the threads.

"Oh, what are you doing, Mrs. Hale?" asked the sheriff's wife, startled.

"Just pulling out a stitch or two that's not sewed very good," said Mrs. Hale mildly.

170   "I don't think we ought to touch things," Mrs. Peters said, a little helplessly.

"I'd just finish up this end," answered Mrs. Hale, still in that mild, matter-of-fact fashion.

She threaded a needle and started to replace bad sewing with good. For a little while she sewed in silence. Then, in that thin, timid voice, she heard:

"Mrs. Hale!"

"Yes, Mrs. Peters?"

175   "What do you suppose she was so—nervous about?"

"Oh, *I* don't know," said Mrs. Hale, as if dismissing a thing not important enough to spend much time on. "I don't know as she was—nervous. I sew awful queer sometimes when I'm just tired."

She cut a thread, and out of the corner of her eye looked up at Mrs. Peters. The small, lean face of the sheriff's wife seemed to have tightened up. Her eyes had that look of peering into something. But the next moment she moved, and said in her thin, indecisive way:

"Well, I must get those clothes wrapped. They may be through sooner than we think. I wonder where I could find a piece of paper—and string."

"In that cupboard, maybe," suggested Mrs. Hale, after a glance around.

180   One piece of the crazy sewing remained unripped. Mrs. Peters' back turned, Martha Hale now scrutinized that piece, compared it with the dainty, accurate sewing of the other blocks. The difference was startling. Holding this block made her feel queer, as if the distracted thoughts of the woman who had perhaps turned to it to try and quiet herself were communicating themselves to her.

Mrs. Peters' voice roused her.

"Here's a birdcage," she said. "Did she have a bird, Mrs. Hale?"

"Why, I don't know whether she did or not." She turned to look at the cage Mrs. Peters was holding up. "I've not been here in so long." She sighed. "There was a man round last year selling canaries cheap—but I don't know as she took one. Maybe she did. She used to sing real pretty herself."

Mrs. Peters looked around the kitchen.

185   "Seems kind of funny to think of a bird here." She half laughed—an attempt to put up a barrier. "But she must have had one—or why would she have a cage? I wonder what happened to it."

"I suppose maybe the cat got it," suggested Mrs. Hale, resuming her sewing.

"No; she didn't have a cat. She's got that feeling some people have about cats—being afraid of them. When they brought her to our house yesterday, my cat got in the room, and she was real upset and asked me to take it out."

"My sister Bessie was like that," laughed Mrs. Hale.

The sheriff's wife did not reply. The silence made Mrs. Hale turn round. Mrs. Peters was examining the birdcage.

"Look at this door," she said slowly. "It's broke. One hinge has been pulled apart." 190

Mrs. Hale came nearer.

"Looks as if someone must have been—rough with it."

Again their eyes met—startled, questioning, apprehensive. For a moment neither spoke nor stirred. Then Mrs. Hale, turning away, said brusquely:

"If they're going to find any evidence, I wish they'd be about it. I don't like this place."

"But I'm awful glad you came with me, Mrs. Hale." Mrs. Peters put the birdcage 195 on the table and sat down. "It would be lonesome for me—sitting here alone."

"Yes, it would, wouldn't it?" agreed Mrs. Hale, a certain determined naturalness in her voice. She picked up the sewing, but now it dropped in her lap, and she murmured in a different voice: "But I tell you what I *do* wish, Mrs. Peters. I wish I had come over sometimes when she was here. I wish—I had."

"But of course you were awful busy, Mrs. Hale. Your house—and your children."

"I could've come," retorted Mrs. Hale shortly. "I stayed away because it weren't cheerful—and that's why I ought to have come. I"—she looked around—"I've never liked this place. Maybe because it's down in a hollow and you don't see the road. I don't know what it is, but it's a lonesome place, and always was. I wish I had come over to see Minnie Foster sometimes. I can see now—" She did not put it into words.

"Well, you mustn't reproach yourself," counseled Mrs. Peters. "Somehow, we just don't see how it is with other folks till—something comes up."

"Not having children makes less work," mused Mrs. Hale, after a silence, "but 200 it makes a quiet house—and Wright out to work all day—and no company when he did come in. Did you know John Wright, Mrs. Peters?"

"Not to know him. I've seen him in town. They say he was a good man."

"Yes—good," conceded John Wright's neighbor grimly. "He didn't drink, and kept his word as well as most, I guess, and paid his debts. But he was a hard man, Mrs. Peters. Just to pass the time of day with him—." She stopped, shivered a little. "Like a raw wind that gets to the bone." Her eye fell upon the cage on the table before her, and she added, almost bitterly: "I should think she would've wanted a bird!"

Suddenly she leaned forward, looking intently at the cage. "But what do you s'pose went wrong with it?"

"I don't know," returned Mrs. Peters; "unless it got sick and died."

But after she said it she reached over and swung the broken door. Both women 205 watched it as if somehow held by it.

"You didn't know—her?" Mrs. Hale asked, a gentler note in her voice.

"Not till they brought her yesterday," said the sheriff's wife.

"She—come to think of it, she was kind of like a bird herself. Real sweet and pretty, but kind of timid and—fluttery. How—she—did—change."

That held her for a long time. Finally, as if struck with a happy thought and relieved to get back to everyday things, she exclaimed:

"Tell you what, Mrs. Peters, why don't you take the quilt in with you? It might 210 take up her mind."

"Why, I think that's a real nice idea, Mrs. Hale," agreed the sheriff's wife, as if she too were glad to come into the atmosphere of a simple kindness. "There couldn't possibly be any objection to that, could there? Now, just what will I take? I wonder if her patches are in here—and her things."

They turned to the sewing basket.

"Here's some red," said Mrs. Hale, bringing out a roll of cloth. Underneath that was a box. "Here, maybe her scissors are in here—and her things." She held it up. "What a pretty box! I'll warrant that was something she had a long time ago—when she was a girl."

She held it in her hand a moment; then, with a little sigh, opened it.

215   Instantly her hand went to her nose.

"Why—!"

Mrs. Peters drew nearer—then turned away.

"There's something wrapped up in this piece of silk," faltered Mrs. Hale.

"This isn't her scissors," said Mrs. Peters in a shrinking voice.

220   Her hand not steady, Mrs. Hale raised the piece of silk. "Oh, Mrs. Peters!" she cried. "It's—"

Mrs. Peters bent closer.

"It's the bird," she whispered.

"But, Mrs. Peters!" cried Mrs. Hale. "*Look* at it! Its neck—look at its neck! It's all—other side *to*."

She held the box away from her.

225   The sheriff's wife again bent closer.

"Somebody wrung its neck," said she, in a voice that was slow and deep.

And then again the eyes of the two women met—this time clung together in a look of dawning comprehension, of growing horror. Mrs. Peters looked from the dead bird to the broken door of the cage. Again their eyes met. And just then there was a sound at the outside door.

Mrs. Hale slipped the box under the quilt pieces in the basket, and sank into the chair before it. Mrs. Peters stood holding to the table. The county attorney and the sheriff came in from outside.

"Well, ladies," said the county attorney, as one turning from serious things to little pleasantries, "have you decided whether she was going to quilt it or knot it?"

230   "We think," began the sheriff's wife in a flurried voice, "that she was going to—knot it."

He was too preoccupied to notice the change that came in her voice on that last.

"Well, that's very interesting, I'm sure," he said tolerantly. He caught sight of the birdcage. "Has the bird flown?"

"We think the cat got it," said Mrs. Hale in a voice curiously even.

He was walking up and down, as if thinking something out.

235   "Is there a cat?" he asked absently.

Mrs. Hale shot a look up at the sheriff's wife.

"Well, not *now*," said Mrs. Peters. "They're superstitious, you know; they leave." She sank into her chair.

The county attorney did not heed her. "No sign at all of anyone having come in from the outside," he said to Peters, in the manner of continuing an interrupted conversation. "Their own rope. Now let's go upstairs again and go over it, piece by piece. It would have to have been someone who knew just the—"

240   The stair door closed behind them and their voices were lost.

The two women sat motionless, not looking at each other, but as if peering into something and at the same time holding back. When they spoke now it was as if they were afraid of what they were saying, but as if they could not help saying it.

"She liked the bird," said Martha Hale, low and slowly. "She was going to bury it in that pretty box."

"When I was a girl," said Mrs. Peters, under her breath, "my kitten—there was a boy took a hatchet, and before my eyes—before I could get there—" She covered her face an instant. "If they hadn't held me back I would have"—she caught herself, looked upstairs where footsteps were heard, and finished weakly—"hurt him."

Then they sat without speaking or moving.

"I wonder how it would seem," Mrs. Hale at last began, as if feeling her way over strange ground—"never to have had any children around?" Her eyes made a slow sweep of the kitchen, as if seeing what that kitchen had meant through all the years. "No, Wright wouldn't like the bird," she said after that—"a thing that sang. She used to sing. He killed that too." Her voice tightened. 245

Mrs. Peters moved uneasily.

"Of course we don't know who killed the bird."

"I knew John Wright," was Mrs. Hale's answer.

"It was an awful thing was done in this house that night, Mrs. Hale," said the sheriff's wife. "Killing a man while he slept—slipping a thing round his neck that choked the life out of him."

Mrs. Hale's hand went out to the birdcage. 250

"His neck. Choked the life out of him."

"We don't *know* who killed him," whispered Mrs. Peters wildly. "We don't *know*."

Mrs. Hale had not moved. "If there had been years and years of—nothing, then a bird to sing to you, it would be awful—still—after the bird was still."

It was as if something within her not herself had spoken, and it found in Mrs. Peters something she did not know as herself.

"I know what stillness is," she said, in a queer, monotonous voice. "When we homesteaded in Dakota, and my first baby died—after he was two years old—and me with no other then—" 255

Mrs. Hale stirred.

"How soon do you suppose they'll be through looking for evidence?"

"I know what stillness is," repeated Mrs. Peters, in just that same way. Then she too pulled back. "The law has got to punish crime, Mrs. Hale," she said in her tight little way.

"I wish you'd seen Minnie Foster," was the answer, "when she wore a white dress with blue ribbons, and stood up there in the choir and sang."

The picture of that girl, the fact that she had lived neighbor to that girl for twenty years, and had let her die for lack of life, was suddenly more than she could bear. 260

"Oh, I *wish* I'd come over here once in a while!" she cried. "That was a crime! That was a crime! Who's going to punish that?"

"We mustn't take on," said Mrs. Peters, with a frightened look toward the stairs.

"I might 'a' *known* she needed help! I tell you, it's *queer,* Mrs. Peters. We live close together, and we live far apart. We all go through the same things—it's all just a different kind of the same thing! If it weren't—why do you and I *understand?* Why do we *know*—what we know this minute?"

She dashed her hand across her eyes. Then, seeing the jar of fruit on the table, she reached for it and choked out:

265   "If I was you I wouldn't *tell* her her fruit was gone! Tell her it *ain't*. Tell her it's all right—all of it. Here—take this in to prove it to her! She—she may never know whether it was broke or not."

She turned away.

Mrs. Peters reached out for the bottle of fruit as if she were glad to take it—as if touching a familiar thing, having something to do, could keep her from something else. She got up, looked about for something to wrap the fruit in, took a petticoat from the pile of clothes she had brought from the front room, and nervously started winding that round the bottle.

"My!" she began, in a high, false voice, "it's a good thing the men couldn't hear us! Getting all stirred up over a little thing like a—dead canary." She hurried over that. "As if that could have anything to do with—with—My, wouldn't they *laugh?*"

Footsteps were heard on the stairs.

270   "Maybe they would," muttered Mrs. Hale—"maybe they wouldn't."

"No, Peters," said the county attorney incisively; "it's all perfectly clear, except the reason for doing it. But you know juries when it comes to women. If there was some definite thing—something to show. Something to make a story about. A thing that would connect up with this clumsy way of doing it."

In a covert way Mrs. Hale looked at Mrs. Peters. Mrs. Peters was looking at her. Quickly they looked away from each other. The outer door opened and Mr. Hale came in.

"I've got the team round now," he said. "Pretty cold out there."

"I'm going to stay here awhile by myself," the county attorney suddenly announced. "You can send Frank out for me, can't you?" he asked the sheriff. "I want to go over everything. I'm not satisfied we can't do better."

275   Again, for one brief moment, the two women's eyes found one another.

The sheriff came up to the table.

"Did you want to see what Mrs. Peters was going to take in?"

The county attorney picked up the apron. He laughed.

"Oh, I guess they're not very dangerous things the ladies have picked out."

280   Mrs. Hale's hand was on the sewing basket in which the box was concealed. She felt that she ought to take her hand off the basket. She did not seem able to. He picked up one of the quilt blocks which she had piled on to cover the box. Her eyes felt like fire. She had a feeling that if he took up the basket she would snatch it from him.

But he did not take it up. With another little laugh, he turned away, saying:

"No; Mrs. Peters doesn't need supervising. For that matter, a sheriff's wife is married to the law. Ever think of it that way, Mrs. Peters?"

Mrs. Peters was standing beside the table. Mrs. Hale shot a look up at her; but she could not see her face. Mrs. Peters had turned away. When she spoke, her voice was muffled.

"Not—just that way," she said.

285   "Married to the law!" chuckled Mrs. Peters' husband. He moved toward the door into the front room, and said to the county attorney:

"I just want you to come in here a minute, George. We ought to take a look at these windows."

"Oh—windows," said the county attorney scoffingly.

"We'll be right out, Mr. Hale," said the sheriff to the farmer, who was still waiting by the door.

Hale went to look after the horses. The sheriff followed the county attorney into the other room. Again—for one moment—the two women were alone in that kitchen.

Martha Hale sprang up, her hands tight together, looking at that other woman, 290 with whom it rested. At first she could not see her eyes, for the sheriff's wife had not turned back, since she turned away at that suggestion of being married to the law. But now Mrs. Hale made her turn back. Her eyes made her turn back. Slowly, unwillingly, Mrs. Peters turned her head until her eyes met the eyes of the other woman. There was a moment when they held each other in a steady, burning look in which there was no evasion nor flinching. Then Martha Hale's eyes pointed the way to the basket in which was hidden the thing that would make certain the conviction of the other woman—that woman who was not there and yet who had been there with them all through the hour.

For a moment Mrs. Peters did not move. And then she did it. With a rush forward, she threw back the quilt pieces, got the box, tried to put it in her handbag. It was too big. Desperately she opened it, started to take the bird out. But there she broke—she could not touch the bird. She stood helpless, foolish.

There was the sound of a knob turning in the inner door. Martha Hale snatched the box from the sheriff's wife, and got it in the pocket of her big coat just as the sheriff and the county attorney came back into the kitchen.

"Well, Henry," said the county attorney facetiously, "at least we found out that she was not going to quilt it. She was going to—what is it you call it, ladies?"

Mrs. Hale's hand was against the pocket of her coat.

"We call it—knot it, Mr. Henderson."   295

1917

Chronology

1888	Charlotte Perkins Stetson separates from her husband and moves with daughter and mother to California.
1890	Wyoming becomes the first of several western states to grant women the vote; National American Woman Suffrage Association formed.
1892	Charlotte Perkins Stetson publishes "The Yellow Wall-Paper" in *New England Magazine*.
1894	Kate Chopin publishes "The Story of an Hour" in *Vogue*.
1898	Charlotte Perkins publishes *Women and Economics*; divorces Stetson.
1899	Chopin publishes *The Awakening*.
1900	Charlotte Perkins marries Charles Houghton Gilman.
	Planned collection of Kate Chopin's stories, *A Vocation and a Voice*, to include "The Story of an Hour"; publisher may have backed off because of controversy over *The Awakening*.
	Susan Glaspell reports on the Hossack murder for the *Des Moines Daily News*: 26 stories by April 11, 1901.
	By now, every state has passed legislation granting married women some control over their property and earnings.
1903	Height of suffragette agitation in Britain (1903–1914). Gilman addresses International Congress of Women in Berlin.
1904	Kate Chopin dies.
1909	Gilman begins producing her own magazine, *The Forerunner*.
1910	Glaspell co-founds Heterodoxy, a group of feminist socialists in New York, including Charlotte Perkins Gilman; it lasts through 1920.
1913	Susan Glaspell marries George Cram Cook.
1914–1918	World War I
1915	Glaspell and Cook form the Provincetown Players in a theater in an abandoned wharf in Provincetown, Massachusetts.
1916	Glaspell's play *Trifles* first performed at Wharf Theatre.
1917	Russian Revolution. Glaspell's "A Jury of Her Peers" published in *Everyweek*.
1920	Nineteenth Amendment to Constitution: women get the vote.
1929	Stock Market Crash
1930	Glaspell's full-length play *Alison's House* wins the Pulitzer Prize.
1935	Charlotte Perkins Gilman, with incurable breast cancer, commits suicide.
1939–1945	World War II
1948	Susan Glaspell dies in Provincetown, Massachusetts.

CHARLOTTE PERKINS GILMAN

From *Similar Cases* (1893)*

There was once a Neolithic Man,
An enterprising wight,
Who made his chopping implements
Unusually bright.
5 Unusually clever he,
Unusually brave,
And he drew delightful Mammoths
On the borders of his cave.
To his Neolithic neighbors,
10 Who were startled and surprised,
Said he, "My friends, in course of time,
We shall be civilized!
We are going to live in cities!
We are going to fight in wars!
15 We are going to eat three times a day
Without the natural cause!
We are going to turn life upside down
About a thing called gold!
We are going to want the earth, and take
20 As much as we can hold!
We are going to wear great piles of stuff
Outside our proper skins!
We are going to have diseases!
And Accomplishments!! And Sins!!!"

25 Then they all rose up in fury
Against their boastful friend,
For prehistoric patience
Cometh quickly to an end.
Said one, "This is chimerical!
30 Utopian! Absurd!"
Said another, "What a stupid life!
Too dull, upon my word!"
Cried all, "Before such things can come,
You idiotic child,
35 You must alter Human Nature!"

---

* Originally published in *In This Our World* (Boston: Small, Maynard & Company Publishing, 1893), 95-100. Like many at the turn of the century, Charlotte Perkins Stetson, later Gilman, applied Darwin's theory of evolution to society. She advocated *eugenics*—literally "good breeding" or racial improvement—through restricting the reproduction of those considered to be mentally or physically deficient. She believed that traditional domestic relations were retarding human progress. This eugenicist poem spread throughout the newspapers in the country in 1893 and made "Mrs. Stetson" famous. In the first stanzas, an advanced "Eohippus" (evolutionary ancestor of the horse) predicts that he will evolve into a horse, only to be laughed to scorn by other primitive creatures, and later an ape foretells that he will be a man, encountering similar mockery from his inferior contemporaries. The concluding stanzas of the poem appear here.

And they all sat back and smiled.
Thought they, "An answer to that last
It will be hard to find!"
It was a clinching argument
40   To the Neolithic Mind!

CHARLOTTE PERKINS GILMAN

From *Women and Economics: A Study of the Economic Relation between Men and Women as a Factor in Social Evolution* (1898)

In the human species the condition [of women's economic dependence on men] is permanent and general, though there are exceptions, and though the present century is witnessing the beginnings of a great change in this respect. . . .

To many this view will not seem clear at first; and the case of working peasant women or females of savage tribes, and the general household industry of women, will be instanced against it. Some careful and honest discrimination is needed to make plain to ourselves the essential facts of the relation, even in these cases. The horse, in his free natural condition, is economically independent. He gets his living by his own exertions, irrespective of any other creature. The horse, in his present condition of slavery, is economically dependent. He gets his living at the hands of his master; and his exertions, though strenuous, bear no direct relation to his living. In fact, the horses who are the best fed and cared for and the horses who are the hardest worked are quite different animals. The horse works, it is true; but what he gets to eat depends on the power and will of his master. His living comes through another. He is economically dependent. So with the hard-worked savage or peasant women. Their labor is the property of another: they work under another will; and what they receive depends not on their labor, but on the power and will of another. They are economically dependent. This is true of the human female both individually and collectively.

BARBARA BOYD

From *Heart and Home Talks: Politics and Milk* (1911)*

Politics are no longer outside the home. They are very apt to be inside the baby, as Charlotte Perkins Gilman cleverly remarks. And being inside the baby, they certainly become a matter of woman's concerns.

The sphere of politics has changed within the last 50 years. And the sphere of woman's work has changed. Consequently, they are overlapping each other. . . .

* *The Washington Post* (September 11, 1911).

Politics, in their workings out, have entered the home. Women, in their new fields of labor, have entered domains affected by politics. As a result, women, both in the home and out of it, must take into consideration politics as a factor in their lives.

... The condition of the milk supplied to all large cities comes under the thumb of politics. Whether it is up to certain healthful requirements or not depends almost altogether upon the laws upon the subject, and upon the inspectors. And both these depend upon politics.

But not only the milk that enters the home and goes inside the baby, but many other things affecting the health of the family depend today upon politics. And so the woman in the home is affected by politics. . . .

In the field of labor, politics enter with equal importance into her life. The conditions under which she works, the hours of labor, wages even, can all be affected by the ballot box. And she needs to have a voice in saying what all these shall be, if justice is to be done her.

So no longer can women say that politics have nothing to do with her.

MRS. ARTHUR LYTTELTON

From *Women and Their Work* (1901)*

... At present the supply [of servants] is unequal to the demand. This is due to several causes. First, to the fact that many occupations are now open to women which were formerly closed, and that therefore a girl has a choice. . . . Then there is the large increase in the number of families who keep servants, for while the larger households have in many cases diminished their establishments, many people who formerly kept no servant now keep one, and those who kept one keep two or more, and consequently the mistresses of the middle class now do less work in the household than was formerly the case. Lastly, there is the fact that in spite of the great rise in the wages of domestic servants, service is looked down upon by the girls of the poorer classes. . . . The "business young lady" and the factory girl consider themselves as higher in the social scale than the parlourmaid or the cook.

... Some . . . think that by a system of co-operative kitchens and other laboursaving appliances, we may almost succeed in doing without servants altogether. But probably the best remedy of all would be to raise the whole profession of domestic service. . . . And . . . we must begin at the top, and convince women of the upper and middle classes that it is their part to learn to manage households. . . . The discomfort and misery and ill-health caused by badly-managed households is incalculable, while, on the other hand, a woman who can manage a household properly . . . is fitted for every sort of work outside the home. The administrative gifts, when properly trained, are just those which prove most useful in many kinds of philanthropic and social work.

* Lyttelton's reference to cooperative kitchens would have been recognized as an idea promoted by Charlotte Perkins Gilman in her magazine, *Forerunner*, and in Gilman's internationally influential book, *Women and Economics* (1898).

RHETA CHILDE DORR

From *What Eight Million Women Want* (1910)*

Men, ardently, eternally, interested in Woman—one woman at a time—are almost never even faintly interested in women. Strangely, deliberately ignorant of women, they argue that their ignorance is justified by an innate unknowableness of the sex.

I am persuaded that the time is at hand when this sentimental, half contemptuous attitude of half the population towards the other half will have to be abandoned. ...

The Census of 1900 reported nearly six million women in the United States engaged in wage earning outside their homes. Between 1890 and 1900 the number of women in industry increased faster than the number of men in industry. ... Nine million women who have forsaken the traditions of the hearth and are competing with men in the world of paid labor, means that women are rapidly passing from the domestic control of their fathers and their husbands. Surely this is the most important economic fact in the world to-day.

Within the past twenty years no less than nine hundred and fifty-four thousand divorces have been granted in the United States. Two thirds of these divorces were granted to aggrieved wives. In spite ... of tradition and ... social ostracism ... more than six hundred thousand women, in the short space of twenty years, repudiated the burden of uncongenial marriage. Without any doubt this is the most important social fact we have had to face since the slavery question was settled.

... In half a dozen countries women are already completely enfranchised. In England the opposition is seeking terms of surrender. In the United States the stoutest enemy of the movement acknowledges that woman suffrage is ultimately inevitable. ... Does any one question that this is the most important political fact the modern world has ever faced?

THE NEW YORK TIMES

From *Mrs. Delong Acquitted. She Killed Her Husband, but the Jury Has Set Her Free* (December 1, 1892)*

Binghamton, N.Y., Nov. 30

... In October, 1891, Mrs. Delong found her husband with a woman of low character. She remonstrated and a quarrel ensued, which led up to the shooting

---

* A journalist from Nebraska, Dorr was a follower of Gilman; she praises Gilman's *Women and Economics* in this book.

* *New York Times* (December 1, 1892). On December 2, 1900, in Indianola, Iowa, someone killed farmer John Hossack with an axe as he was sleeping in bed beside his wife. Susan Glaspell's reporting and public opinion were largely against Mrs. Hossack, and the first trial ended in a guilty verdict; a retrial ended without a verdict. (Sixteen years after the Hossack murder, Glaspell adapted the case into a play and story, written from a more sympathetic perspective.) Yet at the turn of the century, public opinion about such cases frequently sided with the wife of an abusive husband, as this newspaper account of an earlier muder trial suggests. A husband's history of adultery, cruelty, and violence could lead a jury to acquit the wife rather than convict and punish her for the murder.

of her husband. The plea put in by the defense was insanity and self-defense. The evidence was at times quite contradictory, but the story of wrongs and abuse which the defendant had suffered at the hands of her husband . . . evidently satisfied the jury that Mrs. Delong acted in self-defense. . . .

The scene in the courtroom when the verdict was announced was one of great excitement. . . . The room was filled with cheers and hurrahs, the clapping of hands, and the stamping of feet. The defendant raised her hands and implored God's blessing upon the jury.

THE WASHINGTON POST

From *The Chances of Divorce* (November 28, 1909)

If you are married or about to be married, the Government's latest statistics showing the probability of divorce may be of interest. . . . Your chances of divorce are about one in fifteen, so the odds are fairly long that if you are already married or later do marry, death, and not the Divorce Court, will sever your bonds.

Wives who seek freedom will be interested to know that 66.6 per cent of all decrees have been granted to wives, and that alimony has been also allowed in two cases out of every twenty-two.

Divorce is most frequent in the fourth and fifth years of married life. Actors and showmen are the most frequently divorced classes. Commercial travelers come next on the list of guilty. Agricultural laborers are the prize winners for matrimonial constancy. Clergymen are next desirable.

About one third of those divorced remarry, and divorcees enjoy an advantage over widows in this respect, due, as the unfeeling Government ungallantly remarks, to the fact that those who get rid of their husbands by law are usually younger than those who leave his removal to Providence.

CHARLOTTE PERKINS GILMAN

From *Why I Wrote "The Yellow Wall-paper"* (1913)*

For many years I suffered from a severe and continuous nervous breakdown tending to melancholia—and beyond. During about the third year of this trouble I went, in devout faith and some faint stir of hope, to a noted specialist in nervous diseases, the best known in the country. This wise man put me to bed and applied the rest cure, to which a still good physique responded so promptly that he concluded that there was nothing much the matter with me, and sent me home with solemn advice to "live as domestic a life as possible," to "have but two

* Published in Gilman's magazine *The Forerunner* (October 1913). Gilman suffered postpartum depression after the birth of her daughter. In 1886 she sought treatment by S. Weir Mitchell. Gilman repeatedly affirmed that the horrors she described in "The Yellow Wall-paper" had persuaded Weir Mitchell to abandon the "rest cure" treatment, and biographers have tended to repeat this assertion though there is no evidence that it was true.

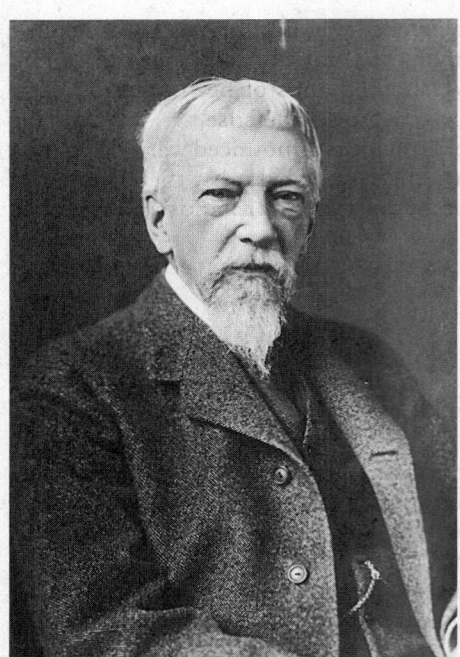

Silas Weir Mitchell, 1829–1914

hours' intelligent life a day," and "never to touch pen, brush or pencil again as long as I lived."

THE WASHINGTON POST

The Rest Cure (August 4, 1902)

What makes people tired is not over-work, but overconcentration, over-niceness in clinging to one settled rule till the nerves rebel.

What is most needed for recreation is relaxation. In carrying burdens, either mental or physical, there is nothing like "changing hands" often.

Recreation need not always consist of social diversion—of going to the theater or the show. One must vary his routine, if nothing more than to change his position while at work.

Routine kills more Americans than anything else. It brings about depression, despondency, and nervous breakdowns.

These general principles and their application constitute what the doctors call "the rest cure." There's nothing like keeping out of the ruts.

THE WASHINGTON POST

From Egotism of the Rest Cure (September 10, 1905)

Many a smart dame spends August at a rest cure, but the woman who would enjoy such a holiday is to be pitied, for the essential point about a rest cure is the egotism of the patient's attitude to herself and those about her. It is significant that this type of holiday is one very rarely advised in the case of a man or in the case of a real worker.

SOURCES FOR FURTHER READING

Ben-Zvi, Linda. "'Murder, She Wrote': The Genesis of Susan Glaspell's *Trifles*." *Susan Glaspell: Essays on Her Theater and Fiction*. Ed. Linda Ben-Zvi. Ann Arbor: U Michigan P, 1995. 19–48. Print.

Bose, Christine E. *Women in 1900*. Philadelphia: Temple U P, 2001. Print.

Edelstein, Sari. "Charlotte Perkins Gilman and the Yellow Newspaper." *Legacy* 24.1 (2007): 72–92. Print.

Griswold, Robert L. "Law, Sex, Cruelty, and Divorce in Victorian America, 1840–1900." In Hawes and Nybakken, *Family and Society,* 145–72. Print.

Hard, William. *The Women of To-Morrow.* New York: Baker & Taylor, 1911. Print.

Hawes, Joseph M., and Elizabeth I. Nybakken. *Family and Society in American History.* Urbana, IL: University of Illinois Press, 2001. Print.

Hedges, Elaine. "Small Things Reconsidered: 'A Jury of Her Peers.'" *Susan Glaspell: Essays on Her Theater and Fiction.* Ed. Linda Ben-Zvi. Ann Arbor: U Michigan P, 1995. 49–69. Print.

Karpinski, Joanne B., ed. *Critical Essays on Charlotte Perkins Gilman.* New York: G. K. Hall, 1992. Print.

Koloski, Bernard. *Kate Chopin: A Study of the Short Fiction.* New York: Twayne, 1996. Print.

Kleinberg, S. J. *Women in the United States, 1830-1945.* London: Macmillan, 1999. Print.

Leach, William R. *True Love and Perfect Union: The Feminist Reform of Sex and Society.* New York: Basic Books, 1980. Print.

Llewellyn, K. N. "Behind the Law of Divorce: I." *Columbia Law Review* 32: 8 (Dec. 1932): 1281–1308. Print.

Roosevelt, Eleanor [Mrs. Franklin D.]. *It's Up to the Women.* New York: Stokes, 1933. Print.

Smith-Rosenberg, Carroll. *Disorderly Conduct: Visions of Gender in Victorian America.* New York: Knopf, 1985. Print.

SUGGESTIONS FOR WRITING

1. In "The Story of an Hour" Louise Mallard receives at home the false report—relayed in two telegrams to a newspaper office and then through her sister—of her husband's death in a railroad accident. Other than these particulars of transportation and communication, the story's simple setting and action might belong to an earlier period. Looking closely at details of the story, write an essay that examines its relation to the historical context of 1894, when it was published. In what respects does the story reflect changes or continuities in family life? Could the same events have happened without the modern means of travel and communication? What role do time or history play in this short incident?

2. The narrator of "The Yellow Wallpaper" writes, "congenial work . . . would do me good. But what is one to do?" Notice places in the story where the patient's views or wishes are contradicted, or where she is able to do something to change how she is treated. Write an essay bringing a historical perspective to this story's representation of women's work or ability to act, or "do." The essay might include reference to S. Weir Mitchell's rest cure or other treatments of women's illness in 1880–1920.

3. In "A Jury of Her Peers," Mrs. Peters is "married to the law" (in the form of her husband the sheriff), whereas Mrs. Hale is married to the farmer who first discovered the murder. In what ways, including dress, speech and manners, action, and attitude, are the two visiting women alike or different? In what ways do they identify with or distance themselves from the absent wife, Mrs. Wright? How do the men and women take sides separately or together? Is the idea that the murder was provoked a sign of the story's realistic portrayal of marriage around 1900? Write an essay focusing on turn-of-the-century marriage, the law, and alliances as well as differences between men and women ("peers") in this story.

4. "The Story of an Hour," "A Jury of Her Peers," and "The Yellow Wallpaper" all take place inside a house, and almost entirely within one room of that house. Entering

through a door or gazing out a window may play a significant part in the action. Write an essay in which you focus on domestic space and women's confinement in this period of American society, comparing at least two of these stories.

5. At the end of each of these stories, a husband or wife has collapsed or is dead—a marriage has ended. Write an essay in which you discuss one or more of these three stories as an indirect commentary on turn-of-the-century views of marriage and divorce.

6. In 1911, William Hard wrote a book called *The Women of To-Morrow*, with an illustration on the cover of an old-fashioned spindle beside a contemporary telephone. Hard describes and advocates the new trade schools and vocational colleges for girls and women so that they could earn a living. In trade schools girls learn "such occupations as sample-mounting and candle-shade-making . . . , photograph-retouching and costume-sketching, to be milliners, to be dressmakers, to be operators of electric-power sewing-machines" (50–51). He argues that the historic New England household was already a "trade school," and he lists a humorous "curriculum" that included "courses" in gardening, medicinal herbs, pickling and preserves, salting and smoking meat; making beer, butter, cheese, soap, brooms, and candles; and of course cooking and cleaning. Examine the details of the women's housekeeping in "A Jury of Her Peers" and *Trifles*, the play by Susan Glaspell, both in the physical setting of the farm kitchen and in the characters' conversations or thoughts. Write an essay on women's work at the turn of the twentieth century as reflected in Glaspell's story and play.

7. Charlotte Perkins Gilman and Barbara Boyd acknowledged that many women were opposed to the idea of changing traditional feminine roles and did not want the vote. Examine sources on the history of the women's movement in the United States—for instance, by consulting the National Women's History Project (http://www.nwhp.org/resourcecenter/index.php and http://www.legacy98.org/) or printed sources. Write an essay on the ways that women such as the sisters in "The Story of an Hour" or "The Yellow Wallpaper" or the more timid Mrs. Peters in "A Jury of Her Peers" might resist or slow down what Chopin, Gilman, or Glaspell considered to be progress for women. Choose one or two stories and focus on a specific issue such as the idea that women are naturally domestic and subordinate to husbands.

8. For a biographical and historical approach to one of these stories, consult the biography about Chopin, Gilman, or Glaspell in this volume; the entry on this author on Wikipedia; and the entries on her in the online or print *Dictionary of National Biography*, the online *Literature Resource Center, Literature Online,* or other resources available on the Web or in your library. Compare at least three versions of the author's life to confirm some of the general facts. Write an essay that interprets the story by this author ("The Story of an Hour," "The Yellow Wallpaper," or "A Jury of Her Peers") in relation both to her life and career and to the changes in turn-of-the-century roles and conditions for women as outlined in this chapter.

11 CULTURAL AND HISTORICAL CONTEXTS: THE JAZZ AGE

F. Scott Fitzgerald and his story "Babylon Revisited" provide a rich opportunity to explore the complex interaction among author, text, and context. The name *Fitzgerald* has become almost synonymous with the spirit of 1920s and 1930s America. As literary critic and editor Malcolm Cowley puts it in his autobiographical *Exile's Return: A Literary Odyssey of the 1920s* (excerpted below), Fitzgerald's "novels and stories are in some ways the best record of the whole period."

Born in 1896, F. Scott Fitzgerald was in his twenties as America entered the 1920s. After attending Princeton, serving in the army during the final days of World War I, and working briefly in a New York advertising agency, Fitzgerald published his first novel, *This Side of Paradise*, in 1920. On the strength of the eighteen-thousand-dollar advance he received for the novel, Fitzgerald married Zelda Sayre, and soon they had a daughter. After moving between New York City, St. Paul, and Long Island in the early years of their marriage, the Fitzgeralds then lived mainly in Europe between 1924 and 1931, pursuing a nomadic, expensive, bohemian lifestyle saturated in alcohol. Having spent nearly 113 thousand dollars in four years and finding himself five thousand dollars in debt, Fitzgerald sought to supplement the income derived from his novels (*The Beautiful and the Damned* [1922], *The Great Gatsby* [1925]) by writing short stories for American newspapers and magazines. The beginning of the end of this way of life came in 1930, when Zelda had the first of a series of nervous breakdowns. Thus in December 1930, Zelda was in a Swiss sanatorium, nine-year-old daughter Scottie was installed in a Paris apartment with a French nanny, and Fitzgerald was shuttling back and forth between Paris and Switzerland, writing short stories (including "Babylon Revisited") to keep the family afloat financially, and fending off the efforts of Zelda's disapproving sister to assume custody of Scottie. The situation of the families at the center of "Babylon Revisited" thus closely parallels that of the Fitzgeralds, who were by this time being forced to "pay" in various ways for the life they lived in the 1920s. The summer before writing "Babylon Revisited," Fitzgerald—sounding like the story's protagonist, Charlie Wales—reminisced about that life in a letter to Zelda: "You were going crazy and calling it genius—I was going to ruin and calling it anything that came to hand. And I think everyone far enough away to see us outside of our glib presentation of ourselves guessed at your almost meglomaniacal [*sic*] selfishness and my insane indulgence in drink. Toward the end nothing mattered." Zelda responded, "You were literally eternally drunk."

As "Babylon Revisited" continually reminds us, Charlie Wales's situation is by no means unique, and neither was the Fitzgeralds': Their experience was, as one literary critic insists, "a distillation of the social history of the age." Instead of

The Fitzgeralds celebrate Christmas, early 1920s

one age, however, there are in fact two ages depicted in "Babylon Revisited." Written and set in a newly sober, subdued 1930, the story nonetheless "revisits" the previous decade, a decade variously referred to (then and now) as the "Roaring Twenties," the "Jazz Age," and the "Age of Excess." Like Charlie Wales, Fitzgerald is thus seeking to understand the past from the point of view of the present, to trace effects back to their causes.

THE JAZZ AGE AND THE GREAT CRASH

The mood of "Babylan Revisited" is characteristic of the early 1930s, expressing itself in semiautobiographical works like Fitzgerald's own "Echoes of the Jazz Age" (November 1931; excerpted below) and Cowley's *Exile's Return* (1934), as well as in historical studies such as Frederick Lewis Allen's *Only Yesterday: An Informal History of the Nineteen-Twenties* (1931). For these writers, what separated "today" from "yesterday" was the Great Crash of October 1929, which preceded the writing of "Babylon Revisited" by only fourteen months. As Fitzgerald wrote in "Echoes," the crash represented the "spectacular death" of the Jazz Age, this cataclysmic event ensuring that the previous decade gained a peculiar kind of distinctness in the American psyche.

The story of what happened in October 1929 can be told in part through numbers: On "Black Thursday," October 24, 1929, thirteen million shares of stock were traded in New York; five days later, on Tuesday, October 29, the number of shares sold mounted to over sixteen million, setting a record that would stand for decades. More important, on that horrible Tuesday alone, stock values fell a total of fourteen billion dollars. The results were countless individual bankruptcies and a general collapse of the national economy that eventually culminated in what we now call the Great Depression. By April 1930, the government esti-

Life magazine covers the Jazz Age

mated that three million people were unemployed in the United States. By January 1931 (one month before the publication of "Babylon Revisited"), the official number was six million; unofficial (and probably more accurate) estimates hovered around eight million. Though many insisted in 1930 that the situation was temporary, conditions in fact worsened in the coming years: By 1932, the value of U.S. stocks had fallen by 89 percent; approximately nine million savings accounts had been wiped out; eighty-six thousand businesses had failed; and even the lucky few who were employed had seen their wages drop by around 60 percent.

Such numbers serve as vivid testimony to the economic effects of the crash. But what they can't capture nearly so well are its emotional, psychological, and cultural effects. As Frederick Allen reminded his readers in 1930,

> Prosperity is more than an economic condition; it is a state of mind. The Big Bull Market had been more than the climax of a business cycle; it had been the climax of a cycle in American mass thinking and mass emotion. There was hardly a man or woman in the country whose attitude toward life had not been affected by it in some degree and was not now affected by the sudden and brutal shattering of hope. With the Big Bull Market gone and prosperity going, Americans were soon to find themselves living in an altered world which called for new adjustments, new ideas, new habits of thought, and a new order of values. The psychological climate was changing; the ever-shifting currents of American life were turning into new channels.

The Postwar Decade had come to its close. An era had ended. Fitzgerald insisted that what died in the fall of 1929 was "the utter confidence which was [the age's] essential prop."

Looking back across that great divide in time, Fitzgerald described the 1920s as "the most expensive orgy in history." He was far from alone in suggesting that 1929 represented the inevitable reaping of what was sown in the previous decade, yet he was also in good company when he mixed condemnation with nostalgia: "after two years the Jazz Age seems as far away as the days before the War. It was borrowed time anyhow—the whole upper tenth of a nation living with the insouciance of grand ducs and the casualness of chorus girls. But moralizing is easy now and it was pleasant to be in one's twenties in such a certain and unworried time."

When Fitzgerald refers to the "upper tenth," he isn't exaggerating: One historian estimates that on the eve of the crash in 1929, the sixty thousand families "at the top of the economic pyramid controlled as much wealth as the twenty-five million families at the bottom"—people like those employed in the North Carolina textile industry, for example, who earned eighteen dollars for a seventy-hour workweek if they were men, half that if they were women. Yet one reason the 1929 crash was so devastating was that during the 1920s the stock market became the province not just of the millionaire few but also of countless middle- and working-class Americans, who could buy stocks "on margin" by putting down just 10 percent of the purchase price. The *New York Times* reported in March 1929, "Playing the Stock market has become a major American pastime."

CONSUMERISM AND TRAVEL

Ordinary Americans had been drawn into the stock market in part by the desire to participate in a flourishing consumer culture that floated on credit. As one historian remarks, "Going into debt for consumer purchases, a practice condemned

Wall Street on the day of the Great Crash

in previous more frugal eras as the last refuge of the spendthrift incompetent, came to be honored," by economist and layperson alike, "as a way to raise the standard of living and stave off depression." Such unprecedented consumerism was inspired not only by "utter confidence" but also by the aggressive advertising industry, which occasionally employed writers like Fitzgerald and Cowley. American businesses spent unprecedented amounts of money on advertising in the 1920s—about one and a half billion dollars in 1927, 50 percent more than in 1921. The brash consumerism that resulted is perhaps best illustrated by the rise in automobile sales. Once a luxury item far beyond the reach and the aspirations of average people, the automobile became by the mid-1920s something for which they clamored and which, thanks to economy of scale and the installment plan, they were able to get. Whereas a total of two and a half million automobiles plied U.S. roads in 1915, that number had climbed to eight million by 1920, and to an astonishing seventeen million five years later. In one year (1920–21), the Ford Motor Company alone sold 1,250,000 cars.

For many, the vast increase in the ownership and use of automobiles reflected not only an unprecedented, culture-wide dedication to conspicuous consumption but also a new kind of restlessness and rootlessness. In a textbook on the family published in 1927 (excerpted below), Boston University sociologist Ernest R. Groves remarks upon a rather curious phenomenon—"a new type of gypsy," the "automobile migrants":

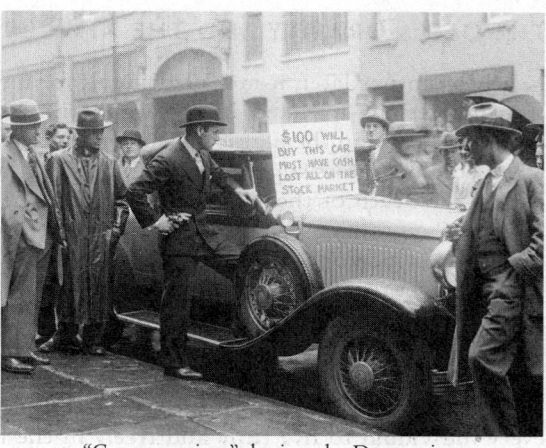

"Consumerism" during the Depression

> Some travel in expensive cars, splendidly equipped, because they enjoy the life better than conventional travel, while others take to the car because only so have they hope of satisfying their wanderlust. . . .
>
> There are all sorts of motives behind the wanderer: restlessness, response to advertising, the lure of the romance of the West and South, expectations of a new start in life, the desire to improve or find health, craving for frontier experience, longing to be rid of conventional habits of life, and pure love of automobile travel.

These "automobile migrants" had their upscale counterparts in the thousands of Americans, like Charlie Wales and writers such as Fitzgerald, Hemingway, and Cowley, for whom frequent travel to and across Europe, and particularly France, became almost a requirement in the 1920s.

For sociologists and educators like Groves, the peripatetic lifestyles of these expatriates would likely have been as serious a concern as that of the "automobile migrants" because both undermined the foundations of the traditional (or, in Groves's words, "normal") family:

> A real home requires permanent settlement. This is well illustrated by the family life of the gypsy, which, even when strongly knit together, has been necessarily meagre. A wandering family cannot establish the community contacts that form part of the substance of a normal home. . . .
>
> It has become the conviction of social workers familiar with this type of wanderers, that the problem they present is with us permanently. If so, we have a new but serious family instability. Many of the migrants have children who, as they travel from place to place with their parents, are denied not only proper schooling but normal family experience. . . . It is not to be expected that such individuals upon maturity will find it easy to settle down and maintain normal home life. They are no more likely to take root than the tramp. The children of these auto parties are frequently exploited and suffer not only along lines of health and education but at times also morally.

THE OLD MORALITY AND THE NEW

Nearly a century later, it may be difficult for us to grasp the dramatic cultural transformations reflected in the wanderings of expatriates and automobile enthusiasts and in the manic consumerism of the 1920s. What was involved, as many commentators suggested at the time, was a profound shift in outlook and ethics: the death of the "old morality" and the birth of the "new." The "old," "Puritan" morality—seen by many then as hopelessly outmoded, repressive, and especially damaging to women—emphasized self-control, self-sacrifice, and faithful adherence to rules and traditions. In its place, the new morality instead championed self-expression and even self-indulgence, encouraging men and women alike to flout any rule, law, or tradition that might infringe upon their individual liberty. Whereas the old morality taught one to keep an eye on the future in order to ensure one's self and the country a better tomorrow, the new ethos encouraged every individual to live fully and freely in the here and now, leaving both the country and the future to take care of themselves.

The conflict between these two moralities reached its climax in the struggle over the prohibition of alcohol. Fittingly enough, the moral crisis of the 1920s took the form of a confrontation over consumers' rights. Prohibition, which became law when the Eighteenth Amendment to the United States Constitution was ratified in 1919 and put into effect in January 1920, can be seen as a kind of last-ditch effort to enforce the old morality, though its proponents included feminist and other "progressive" groups. The conflict between old and new moralities was also one between rural "heartland" America and the urban "Babylon" America, as suggested by the fact that Congressional representatives for urban areas were by and large anti-Prohibitionists and that pro-Prohibition forces insisted that their fight was against "great city domination," "the rock upon which past civilizations have been wrecked." Cities, though they might be the centers of fashion and culture, were also regarded by traditionalist or provincial observers as harboring mobs of immigrants and other industrial poor who seemed to spawn children, disease, disorderly conduct, and even political rebellion. In one of countless books published on the alcohol question both before and during Prohibition, *King Alcohol Dethroned* (1917), "Dry" advocate Ferdinand Cowle Iglehart, D.D., uses language that connects Christianity and the Prohibition campaign, "the most important moral event in the history of mankind":

> The thirst of the soul which alcohol pretends to satisfy is that for stimulation, illumination, and inspiration. This is a God-given appetite which He intended should be satisfied by truth, righteousness, love, by himself, the embodiment of these attributes. . . . To satisfy this appetite the father of lies, in the person of King Alcohol, offers himself as a substitute instead of God as the inspiration, the life, the joy of the soul. What a failure, what a fraud, what a tragedy is the substitute, and how long-continued and widespread has been his diabolical deception!

Iglehart is quite sure that God's ways are also the ways of business and industry: "Society," he writes, "is putting up a fierce fight against booze" not just because God wants it, but "on account of the inefficiency that it causes in every department of industry."

Illegal beer being poured away during Prohibition

Though the fight against the devil, alcohol, and industrial inefficiency was ostensibly won with the passage of the Eighteenth Amendment, that triumph was a hollow one at best. Among other things, as Cowley argued, the coming of Prohibition merely "surrounded the new customs with illicit glamour"—it was, in short, the best advertisement of all. Rather than taking their spirits in a respectable public bar as they might have done before Prohibition, for example, New Yorkers in 1929 could sip "King Alcohol" in any of the thirty-two thousand speakeasies that the Police Commissioner estimated were operating in the city; and whereas in 1918 they had probably sipped nothing stronger than beer or wine, by 1929 they were almost certainly indulging in hard liquor. In addition to the obvious allure of defying the law, customers of the speakeasy typically enjoyed two other disreputable, if not illegal, pleasures: listening to a jazz band and engaging in what some called "pelvic dancing." Prohibition also helped turn organized crime into a major, efficient, and profitable, if violent, machine with close links to "legitimate" industry: Al Capone's Chicago-based organization alone made an estimated one hundred million dollars per year during Prohibition, while major industrialists and their trade-union antagonists fought each other with the help or interference of mobsters.

THE GENERATION GAP AND THE FAMILY

In the early 1920s the conflict between old and new moralities that led to open battle between Treasury agents, rumrunners, and speakeasy clientele was often described in generational terms. For the new morality was associated with "flaming youth," the generation that Gertrude Stein labeled "lost" and that Fitzgerald described in *This Side of Paradise* as "a new generation dedicated more than the last to the fear of poverty and the worship of success; grown up to find all Gods dead, all wars fought, all faiths in man shaken." Not surprisingly, *This Side of Paradise* was often cited by Fitzgerald's contemporaries as a guidebook to "the new morality," as well as a manifesto for what a 1925 book called *The Revolt of Modern Youth*. That revolt was only partly a reaction to the national repression and denial symbolized by a federal prohibition of alcohol. Fitzgerald and many of his contemporaries agreed that World War I also exercised a decisive, if complex and multifaceted, influence.

Although the "new morality" was initially associated with bohemian circles and with those who came of age during and just after the war, it soon transformed all sectors of American society. For many, especially experts in the relatively new fields of psychology and sociology, the effects of the new morality, and especially of the dramatic changes in women's roles associated with it, were felt most profoundly in the area of family life. Ernest R. Groves's *Social Problems of the Family* and V. F. Calverton's *The Bankruptcy of Marriage* (both excerpted below) were merely two of the countless books and articles published in the 1920s about what another book labeled "the Marriage Crisis." Fitzgerald's fictional Wales family seems to have broken up in large part because of the death of Helen, Charlie's wife, and widowers like Charlie get some attention in *Social Problems of the Family*. Yet what inspired most commentary was the fact that more American families than ever before were being broken up by divorce: From 1916 to 1922, the number of divorces in the United States increased 33 percent. Perhaps more important, the shape of intact middle-class American families and the very concept of marriage were profoundly changing—whether for good (as Calverton has it) or for ill (as Groves argues).

. . .

As these different assessments of the American family in the 1920s may remind us, the spirit of the Jazz Age, like the spirit of any age, is as much about debate as about consensus, as much about divisions among various groups as about an underlying unity of experience or outlook. Indeed, the work of the African American writers associated with the 1920s Harlem Renaissance—including Countee Cullen, Langston Hughes, and Claude McKay (all of whom are represented in this book)—reflects a very different experience than does that of white Americans such as Fitzgerald, Cowley, and Edna St. Vincent Millay. And however close in spirit Millay's poetry might be to Fitzgerald's fiction, one can't help but wonder how she, as a "new woman" writer, might have depicted her own "Babylon." Like "American culture" itself, any cultural moment or context is a tapestry woven out of many diverse threads.

At the end of this chapter, you will find excerpts from texts published in the 1920s and 1930s that will give you a fuller sense of the events, feelings, moods, concerns, and viewpoints that make up the cultural and historical context of "Babylon Revisited." They should help you better understand both Fitzgerald's era and his story's complex and ambiguous commentary on it.

F. SCOTT FITZGERALD

Babylon Revisited

I

"And where's Mr. Campbell?" Charlie asked.

"Gone to Switzerland. Mr. Campbell's a pretty sick man, Mr. Wales."

"I'm sorry to hear that. And George Hardt?" Charlie inquired.

"Back in America, gone to work."

"And where is the Snow Bird?"   5

"He was in here last week. Anyway, his friend, Mr. Schaeffer, is in Paris."

Two familiar names from the long list of a year and a half ago. Charlie scribbled an address in his notebook and tore out the page.

"If you see Mr. Schaeffer, give him this," he said. "It's my brother-in-law's address. I haven't settled on a hotel yet."

He was not really disappointed to find Paris was so empty. But the stillness in the Ritz bar was strange and portentous. It was not an American bar any more—he felt polite in it, and not as if he owned it. It had gone back into France. He felt the stillness from the moment he got out of the taxi and saw the doorman, usually in a frenzy of activity at this hour, gossiping with a *chasseur*[1] by the servants' entrance.

Passing through the corridor, he heard only a single, bored voice in the once-   10
clamorous women's room. When he turned into the bar he travelled the twenty feet of green carpet with his eyes fixed straight ahead by old habit; and then, with his foot firmly on the rail, he turned and surveyed the room, encountering only a single pair of eyes that fluttered up from a newspaper in the corner. Charlie asked for the head barman, Paul, who in the latter days of the bull market had come to work in his own custom-built car—disembarking, however, with due nicety at the nearest corner. But Paul was at his country house today and Alix giving him information.

"No, no more," Charlie said, "I'm going slow these days."

Alix congratulated him: "You were going pretty strong a couple of years ago."

"I'll stick to it all right," Charlie assured him. "I've stuck to it for over a year and a half now."

"How do you find conditions in America?"

"I haven't been to America for months. I'm in business in Prague, represent-   15
ing a couple of concerns there. They don't know about me down there."

Alix smiled.

"Remember the night of George Hardt's bachelor dinner here?" said Charlie. "By the way, what's become of Claude Fessenden?"

Alix lowered his voice confidentially: "He's in Paris, but he doesn't come here any more. Paul doesn't allow it. He ran up a bill of thirty thousand francs, charging all his drinks and his lunches, and usually his dinner, for more than a year. And when Paul finally told him he had to pay, he gave him a bad check."

Alix shook his head sadly.

"I don't understand it, such a dandy fellow. Now he's all bloated up—" He   20
made a plump apple of his hands.

1. Bellhop.

Charlie watched a group of strident queens installing themselves in a corner.

"Nothing affects them," he thought. "Stocks rise and fall, people loaf or work, but they go on forever." The place oppressed him. He called for the dice and shook with Alix for the drink.

"Here for long, Mr. Wales?"

"I'm here for four or five days to see my little girl."

25   "Oh-h! You have a little girl?"

Outside, the fire-red, gas-blue, ghost-green signs shone smokily through the tranquil rain. It was late afternoon and the streets were in movement; the *bistros* gleamed. At the corner of the Boulevard des Capucines he took a taxi. The Place de la Concorde moved by in pink majesty; they crossed the logical Seine, and Charlie felt the sudden provincial quality of the Left Bank.[2]

Charlie directed his taxi to the Avenue de l'Opera, which was out of his way. But he wanted to see the blue hour spread over the magnificent façade, and imagine that the cab horns, playing endlessly the first few bars of *La Plus que Lent,* were the trumpets of the Second Empire.[3] They were closing the iron grill in front of Brentano's Book-store, and people were already at dinner behind the trim little bourgeois hedge of Duval's. He had never eaten at a really cheap restaurant in Paris. Five-course dinner, four francs fifty, eighteen cents, wine included. For some odd reason he wished that he had.

As they rolled on to the Left Bank and he felt its sudden provincialism, he thought, "I spoiled this city for myself. I didn't realize it, but the days came along one after another, and then two years were gone, and everything was gone, and I was gone."

He was thirty-five, and good to look at. The Irish mobility of his face was sobered by a deep wrinkle between his eyes. As he rang his brother-in-law's bell in the Rue Palatine, the wrinkle deepened till it pulled down his brows; he felt a cramping sensation in his belly. From behind the maid who opened the door darted a lovely little girl of nine who shrieked "Daddy!" and flew up, struggling like a fish, into his arms. She pulled his head around by one ear and set her cheek against his.

30   "My old pie," he said.

"Oh, daddy, daddy, daddy, daddy, dads, dads, dads!"

She drew them into the salon, where the family waited, a boy and girl his daughter's age, his sister-in-law and her husband. He greeted Marion with his voice pitched carefully to avoid either feigned enthusiasm or dislike, but her response was more frankly tepid, though she minimized her expression of unalterable distrust by directing her regard toward his child. The two men clasped hands in a friendly way and Lincoln Peters rested his for a moment on Charlie's shoulder.

The room was warm and comfortably American. The three children moved intimately about, playing through the yellow oblongs that led to other rooms; the cheer of six o'clock spoke in the eager smacks of the fire and the sounds of

2. The Seine River flows westward through Paris, cutting the city into two sections—the elegant Right Bank (to the north) and the more bohemian Left Bank (to the south). Located on the Right Bank along the Seine, the Place de la Concorde (literally, "place of the peace") is the largest plaza in Paris.
3. Elected president of the Second French Republic after the Revolution of 1848, Louis-Napoléon Bonaparte (1808–73), nephew of France's first emperor, Napoléon Bonaparte, founded the Second Empire by declaring himself Emperor Napoléon III in 1852; he was ousted by republicans in 1871. *La plus que Lent* (literally, "more than slow"): piano work composed in 1910 by French composer Claude Debussy (1862–1918).

French activity in the kitchen. But Charlie did not relax; his heart sat up rigidly in his body and he drew confidence from his daughter, who from time to time came close to him, holding in her arms the doll he had brought.

"Really extremely well," he declared in answer to Lincoln's question. "There's a lot of business there that isn't moving at all, but we're doing even better than ever. In fact, damn well. I'm bringing my sister over from America next month to keep house for me. My income last year was bigger than it was when I had money. You see, the Czechs—"

His boasting was for a specific purpose; but after a moment, seeing a faint 35 restiveness in Lincoln's eye, he changed the subject:

"Those are fine children of yours, well brought up, good manners."

"We think Honoria's a great little girl too."

Marion Peters came back from the kitchen. She was a tall woman with worried eyes, who had once possessed a fresh American loveliness. Charlie had never been sensitive to it and was always surprised when people spoke of how pretty she had been. From the first there had been an instinctive antipathy between them.

"Well, how do you find Honoria?" she asked.

"Wonderful. I was astonished how much she's grown in ten months. All the 40 children are looking well."

"We haven't had a doctor for a year. How do you like being back in Paris?"

"It seems very funny to see so few Americans around."

"I'm delighted," Marion said vehemently. "Now at least you can go into a store without their assuming you're a millionaire. We've suffered like everybody, but on the whole it's a good deal pleasanter."

"But it was nice while it lasted," Charlie said. "We were a sort of royalty, almost infallible, with a sort of magic around us. In the bar this afternoon"—he stumbled, seeing his mistake—"there wasn't a man I knew."

She looked at him keenly. "I should think you'd have had enough of bars." 45

"I only stayed a minute. I take one drink every afternoon, and no more."

"Don't you want a cocktail before dinner?" Lincoln asked.

"I take only one drink every afternoon, and I've had that."

"I hope you keep to it," said Marion.

Her dislike was evident in the coldness with which she spoke, but Charlie 50 only smiled; he had larger plans. Her very aggressiveness gave him an advantage, and he knew enough to wait. He wanted them to initiate the discussion of what they knew had brought him to Paris.

At dinner he couldn't decide whether Honoria was most like him or her mother. Fortunate if she didn't combine the traits of both that had brought them to disaster. A great wave of protectiveness went over him. He thought he knew what to do for her. He believed in character; he wanted to jump back a whole generation and trust in character again as the eternally valuable element. Everything wore out.

He left soon after dinner, but not to go home. He was curious to see Paris by night with clearer and more judicious eyes than those of other days. He bought a *strapontin* for the Casino and watched Josephine Baker[4] go through her chocolate arabesques.

4. African American jazz singer and dancer (1906–75) who starred in the Broadway show *Chocolate Dandies*; in 1924 she became one of France's most popular entertainers in the 1920s and 1930s, creating a sensation with her *danse sauvage* ("wild dance") and revealing costumes. *Strapontin:* foldaway seat.

After an hour he left and strolled toward Montmartre,[5] up the Rue Pigalle into the Place Blanche. The rain had stopped and there were a few people in evening clothes disembarking from taxis in front of cabarets, and *cocottes*[6] prowling singly or in pairs, and many Negroes. He passed a lighted door from which issued music, and stopped with the sense of familiarity; it was Bricktop's, where he had parted with so many hours and so much money. A few doors farther on he found another ancient rendezvous and incautiously put his head inside. Immediately an eager orchestra burst into sound, a pair of professional dancers leaped to their feet and a maître d'hôtel swooped toward him, crying, "Crowd just arriving, sir!" But he withdrew quickly.

"You have to be damn drunk," he thought.

55   Zelli's was closed, the bleak and sinister cheap hotels surrounding it were dark; up in the Rue Blanche there was more light and a local, colloquial French crowd. The Poet's Cave had disappeared, but the two great mouths of the Café of Heaven and the Café of Hell[7] still yawned—even devoured, as he watched, the meager contents of a tourist bus—a German, a Japanese, and an American couple who glanced at him with frightened eyes.

So much for the effort and ingenuity of Montmartre. All the catering to vice and waste was on an utterly childish scale, and he suddenly realized the meaning of the word "dissipate"—to dissipate into thin air; to make nothing out of something. In the little hours of the night every move from place to place was an enormous human jump, an increase of paying for the privilege of slower and slower motion.

He remembered thousand-franc notes given to an orchestra for playing a single number, hundred-franc notes tossed to a doorman for calling a cab.

But it hadn't been given for nothing.

It had been given, even the most wildly squandered sum, as an offering to destiny that he might not remember the things most worth remembering, the things that now he would always remember—his child taken from his control, his wife escaped to a grave in Vermont.

60   In the glare of a *brasserie*[8] a woman spoke to him. He bought her some eggs and coffee, and then, eluding her encouraging stare, gave her a twenty-franc note and took a taxi to his hotel.

II

He woke upon a fine fall day—football weather. The depression of yesterday was gone and he liked the people on the streets. At noon he sat opposite Honoria at Le Grand Vatel, the only restaurant he could think of not reminiscent of champagne dinners and long luncheons that began at two and ended in a blurred and vague twilight.

"Now, how about vegetables? Oughtn't you to have some vegetables?"

"Well, yes."

"Here's *épinards* and *chou-fleur* and carrots and *haricots*."[9]

---

5. Hilltop neighborhood in north-central Paris long associated with artists and intellectuals.
6. Prostitutes.
7. A 1907 guidebook labels the cafés of Montmarte "eccentric, fantastic," and "morbid," and describes "cabarets of Heaven, Hell, and Death, where the waiters are dressed respectively as angels, devils, undertakers."
8. Restaurant, especially one that sells beer.   9. Spinach and cauliflower and carrots and beans.

"I'd like *chou-fleur*." 65

"Wouldn't you like to have two vegetables?"

"I usually only have one at lunch."

The waiter was pretending to be inordinately fond of children. *"Qu'elle est mignonne la petite? Elle parle exactement comme une Française."*[1]

"How about dessert? Shall we wait and see?"

The waiter disappeared. Honoria looked at her father expectantly. 70

"What are we going to do?"

"First, we're going to that toy store in the Rue Saint-Honoré and buy you anything you like. And then we're going to the vaudeville at the Empire."

She hesitated. "I like it about the vaudeville, but not the toy store."

"Why not?"

"Well, you brought me this doll." She had it with her. "And I've got lots of 75 things. And we're not rich any more, are we?"

"We never were. But today you are to have anything you want."

"All right," she agreed resignedly.

When there had been her mother and a French nurse he had been inclined to be strict; now he extended himself, reached out for a new tolerance; he must be both parents to her and not shut any of her out of communication.

"I want to get to know you," he said gravely. "First let me introduce myself. My name is Charles J. Wales, of Prague."

"Oh, daddy!" her voice cracked with laughter. 80

"And who are you, please?" he persisted, and she accepted a rôle immediately: "Honoria Wales, Rue Palatine, Paris."

"Married or single?"

"No, not married. Single."

He indicated the doll. "But I see you have a child, madame."

Unwilling to disinherit it, she took it to her heart and thought quickly: "Yes, 85 I've been married, but I'm not married now. My husband is dead."

He went on quickly, "And the child's name?"

"Simone. That's after my best friend at school."

"I'm very pleased that you're doing so well at school."

"I'm third this month," she boasted. "Elsie"—that was her cousin—"is only about eighteenth, and Richard is about at the bottom."

"You like Richard and Elsie, don't you?" 90

"Oh, yes. I like Richard quite well and I like her all right."

Cautiously and casually he asked: "And Aunt Marion and Uncle Lincoln—which do you like best?"

"Oh, Uncle Lincoln, I guess."

He was increasingly aware of her presence. As they came in, a murmur of ". . . adorable" followed them, and now the people at the next table bent all their silences upon her, staring as if she were something no more conscious than a flower.

"Why don't I live with you?" she asked suddenly. "Because mamma's dead?" 95

"You must stay here and learn more French. It would have been hard for daddy to take care of you so well."

"I don't really need much taking care of any more. I do everything for myself."

---

1. Isn't she a cute little girl? She speaks exactly like a French girl.

Going out of the restaurant, a man and a woman unexpectedly hailed him.

"Well, the old Wales!"

100 "Hello there, Lorraine. . . . Dunc."

Sudden ghosts out of the past: Duncan Schaeffer, a friend from college. Lorraine Quarrles, a lovely, pale blonde of thirty; one of a crowd who had helped them make months into days in the lavish times of three years ago.

"My husband couldn't come this year," she said, in answer to his question. "We're poor as hell. So he gave me two hundred a month and told me I could do my worst on that. . . . This your little girl?"

"What about coming back and sitting down?" Duncan asked.

"Can't do it." He was glad for an excuse. As always, he felt Lorraine's passionate, provocative attraction, but his own rhythm was different now.

105 "Well, how about dinner?" she asked.

"I'm not free. Give me your address and let me call you."

"Charlie, I believe you're sober," she said judicially. "I honestly believe he's sober, Dunc. Pinch him and see if he's sober."

Charlie indicated Honoria with his head. They both laughed.

"What's your address?" said Duncan sceptically.

110 He hesitated, unwilling to give the name of his hotel.

"I'm not settled yet. I'd better call you. We're going to see the vaudeville at the Empire."

"There! That's what I want to do," Lorraine said. "I want to see some clowns and acrobats and jugglers. That's just what we'll do, Dunc."

"We've got to do an errand first," said Charlie. "Perhaps we'll see you there."

"All right, you snob. . . . Good-by, beautiful little girl."

115 "Good-by."

Honoria bobbed politely.

Somehow, an unwelcome encounter. They liked him because he was functioning, because he was serious; they wanted to see him, because he was stronger than they were now, because they wanted to draw a certain sustenance from his strength.

At the Empire, Honoria proudly refused to sit upon her father's folded coat. She was already an individual with a code of her own, and Charlie was more and more absorbed by the desire of putting a little of himself into her before she crystallized utterly. It was hopeless to try to know her in so short a time.

Between the acts they came upon Duncan and Lorraine in the lobby where the band was playing.

120 "Have a drink?"

"All right, but not up at the bar. We'll take a table."

"The perfect father."

Listening abstractedly to Lorraine, Charlie watched Honoria's eyes leave their table, and he followed them wistfully about the room, wondering what they saw. He met her glance and she smiled.

"I liked that lemonade," she said.

125 What had she said? What had he expected? Going home in a taxi afterward, he pulled her over until her head rested against his chest.

"Darling, do you ever think about your mother?"

"Yes, sometimes," she answered vaguely.

"I don't want you to forget her. Have you got a picture of her?"

"Yes, I think so. Anyhow, Aunt Marion has. Why don't you want me to forget her?"

"She loved you very much." 130

"I loved her too."

They were silent for a moment.

"Daddy, I want to come and live with you," she said suddenly.

His heart leaped; he had wanted it to come like this.

"Aren't you perfectly happy?" 135

"Yes, but I love you better than anybody. And you love me better than anybody, don't you, now that mummy's dead?"

"Of course I do. But you won't always like me best, honey. You'll grow up and meet somebody your own age and go marry him and forget you ever had a daddy."

"Yes, that's true," she agreed tranquilly.

He didn't go in. He was coming back at nine o'clock and he wanted to keep himself fresh and new for the thing he must say then.

"When you're safe inside, just show yourself in that window." 140

"All right. Good-by, dads, dads, dads, dads."

He waited in the dark street until she appeared, all warm and glowing, in the window above and kissed her fingers out into the night.

III

They were waiting. Marion sat behind the coffee service in a dignified black dinner dress that just faintly suggested mourning. Lincoln was walking up and down with the animation of one who had already been talking. They were as anxious as he was to get into the question. He opened it almost immediately:

"I suppose you know what I want to see you about—why I really came to Paris."

Marion played with the black stars on her necklace and frowned. 145

"I'm awfully anxious to have a home," he continued. "And I'm awfully anxious to have Honoria in it. I appreciate your taking in Honoria for her mother's sake, but things have changed now"—he hesitated and then continued more forcibly—"changed radically with me, and I want to ask you to reconsider the matter. It would be silly for me to deny that about three years ago I was acting badly—"

Marion looked up at him with hard eyes.

"—but all that's over. As I told you, I haven't had more than a drink a day for over a year, and I take that drink deliberately, so that the idea of alcohol won't get too big in my imagination. You see the idea?"

"No," said Marion succinctly.

"It's a sort of stunt I set myself. It keeps the matter in proportion." 150

"I get you," said Lincoln. "You don't want to admit it's got any attraction for you."

"Something like that. Sometimes I forget and don't take it. But I try to take it. Anyhow, I couldn't afford to drink in my position. The people I represent are more than satisfied with what I've done, and I'm bringing my sister over from Burlington to keep house for me, and I want awfully to have Honoria too. You know that even when her mother and I weren't getting along well we never let anything that happened touch Honoria. I know she's fond of me and I know I'm able to take care of her and—well, there you are. How do you feel about it?"

He knew that now he would have to take a beating. It would last an hour or two hours, and it would be difficult, but if he modulated his inevitable resentment to the chastened attitude of the reformed sinner, he might win his point in the end.

Keep your temper, he told himself. You don't want to be justified. You want Honoria.

155 Lincoln spoke first: "We've been talking it over ever since we got your letter last month. We're happy to have Honoria here. She's a dear little thing, and we're glad to be able to help her, but of course that isn't the question—"

Marion interrupted suddenly. "How long are you going to stay sober, Charlie?" she asked.

"Permanently, I hope."

"How can anybody count on that?"

"You know I never did drink heavily until I gave up business and came over here with nothing to do. Then Helen and I began to run around with—"

160 "Please leave Helen out of it. I can't bear to hear you talk about her like that."

He stared at her grimly; he had never been certain how fond of each other the sisters were in life.

"My drinking only lasted about a year and a half—from the time we came over until I—collapsed."

"It was time enough."

"It was time enough," he agreed.

165 "My duty is entirely to Helen," she said. "I try to think what she would have wanted me to do. Frankly, from the night you did that terrible thing you haven't really existed for me. I can't help that. She was my sister."

"Yes."

"When she was dying she asked me to look out for Honoria. If you hadn't been in a sanitarium then, it might have helped matters."

He had no answer.

"I'll never in my life be able to forget the morning when Helen knocked at my door, soaked to the skin and shivering, and said you'd locked her out."

170 Charlie gripped the sides of the chair. This was more difficult than he expected; he wanted to launch out into a long expostulation and explanation, but he only said: "The night I locked her out—" and she interrupted, "I don't feel up to going over that again."

After a moment's silence Lincoln said: "We're getting off the subject. You want Marion to set aside her legal guardianship and give you Honoria. I think the main point for her is whether she has confidence in you or not."

"I don't blame Marion," Charlie said slowly, "but I think she can have entire confidence in me. I had a good record up to three years ago. Of course, it's within human possibilities I might go wrong any time. But if we wait much longer I'll lose Honoria's childhood and my chance for a home." He shook his head, "I'll simply lose her, don't you see?"

"Yes, I see," said Lincoln.

"Why didn't you think of all this before?" Marion asked.

175 "I suppose I did, from time to time, but Helen and I were getting along badly. When I consented to the guardianship, I was flat on my back in a sanitarium and the market had cleaned me out. I knew I'd acted badly, and I thought if it would bring any peace to Helen, I'd agree to anything. But now it's different. I'm functioning, I'm behaving damn well, so far as—"

"Please don't swear at me," Marion said.

He looked at her, startled. With each remark the force of her dislike became more and more apparent. She had built up all her fear of life into one wall and faced it toward him. This trivial reproof was possibly the result of some trouble with the cook several hours before. Charlie became increasingly alarmed at leaving Honoria in this atmosphere of hostility against himself; sooner or later it would come out, in a word here, a shake of the head there, and some of that distrust would be irrevocably implanted in Honoria. But he pulled his temper down out of his face and shut it up inside him; he had won a point, for Lincoln realized the absurdity of Marion's remark and asked her lightly since when she had objected to the word "damn."

"Another thing," Charlie said: "I'm able to give her certain advantages now. I'm going to take a French governess to Prague with me. I've got a lease on a new apartment—"

He stopped, realizing that he was blundering. They couldn't be expected to accept with equanimity the fact that his income was again twice as large as their own.

"I suppose you can give her more luxuries than we can," said Marion. "When you were throwing away money we were living along watching every ten francs. . . . I suppose you'll start doing it again." 180

"Oh, no," he said. "I've learned. I worked hard for ten years, you know—until I got lucky in the market, like so many people. Terribly lucky. It didn't seem any use working any more, so I quit. It won't happen again."

There was a long silence. All of them felt their nerves straining, and for the first time in a year Charlie wanted a drink. He was sure now that Lincoln Peters wanted him to have his child.

Marion shuddered suddenly; part of her saw that Charlie's feet were planted on the earth now, and her own maternal feeling recognized the naturalness of his desire; but she had lived for a long time with a prejudice—a prejudice founded on a curious disbelief in her sister's happiness, and which, in the shock of one terrible night, had turned to hatred for him. It had all happened at a point in her life where the discouragement of ill health and adverse circumstances made it necessary for her to believe in tangible villainy and a tangible villain.

"I can't help what I think!" she cried out suddenly. "How much you were responsible for Helen's death, I don't know. It's something you'll have to square with your own conscience."

An electric current of agony surged through him; for a moment he was almost on his feet, an unuttered sound echoing in his throat. He hung on to himself for a moment, another moment. 185

"Hold on there," said Lincoln uncomfortably. "I never thought you were responsible for that."

"Helen died of heart trouble," Charlie said dully.

"Yes, heart trouble." Marion spoke as if the phrase had another meaning for her.

Then, in the flatness that followed her outburst, she saw him plainly and she knew he had somehow arrived at control over the situation. Glancing at her husband, she found no help from him, and as abruptly as if it were a matter of no importance, she threw up the sponge.

"Do what you like!" she cried, springing up from her chair. "She's your child. I'm not the person to stand in your way. I think if it were my child I'd rather see 190 her—" She managed to check herself. "You two decide it. I can't stand this. I'm sick. I'm going to bed."

She hurried from the room; after a moment Lincoln said:

"This has been a hard day for her. You know how strongly she feels—" His voice was almost apologetic: "When a woman gets an idea in her head."

"Of course."

"It's going to be all right. I think she sees now that you—can provide for the child, and so we can't very well stand in your way or Honoria's way."

195   "Thank you, Lincoln."

"I'd better go along and see how she is."

"I'm going."

He was still trembling when he reached the street, but a walk down the Rue Bonaparte to the quais set him up, and as he crossed the Seine, fresh and new by the quai lamps, he felt exultant. But back in his room he couldn't sleep. The image of Helen haunted him. Helen whom he had loved so until they had senselessly begun to abuse each other's love, tear it into shreds. On that terrible February night that Marion remembered so vividly, a slow quarrel had gone on for hours. There was a scene at the Florida, and then he attempted to take her home, and then she kissed young Webb at a table; after that there was what she had hysterically said. When he arrived home alone he turned the key in the lock in wild anger. How could he know she would arrive an hour later alone, that there would be a snowstorm in which she wandered about in slippers, too confused to find a taxi? Then the aftermath, her escaping pneumonia by a miracle, and all the attendant horror. They were "reconciled," but that was the beginning of the end, and Marion, who had seen with her own eyes and who imagined it to be one of many scenes from her sister's martyrdom, never forgot.

Going over it again brought Helen nearer, and in the white, soft light that steals upon half sleep near morning he found himself talking to her again. She said that he was perfectly right about Honoria and that she wanted Honoria to be with him. She said she was glad he was being good and doing better. She said a lot of other things—very friendly things—but she was in a swing in a white dress, and swinging faster and faster all the time, so that at the end he could not hear clearly all that she said.

IV

200   He woke up feeling happy. The door of the world was open again. He made plans, vistas, futures for Honoria and himself, but suddenly he grew sad, remembering all the plans he and Helen had made. She had not planned to die. The present was the thing—work to do and someone to love. But not to love too much, for he knew the injury that a father can do to a daughter or a mother to a son by attaching them too closely: afterward, out in the world, the child would seek in the marriage partner the same blind tenderness and, failing probably to find it, turn against love and life.

It was another bright, crisp day. He called Lincoln Peters at the bank where he worked and asked if he could count on taking Honoria when he left for Prague. Lincoln agreed that there was no reason for delay. One thing—the legal guardianship. Marion wanted to retain that a while longer. She was upset by the whole matter, and it would oil things if she felt that the situation was still in her control for another year. Charlie agreed, wanting only the tangible, visible child.

Then the question of a governess. Charlie sat in a gloomy agency and talked to a cross Béarnaise and to a buxom Breton[2] peasant, neither of whom he could have endured. There were others whom he would see tomorrow.

He lunched with Lincoln Peters at Griffons, trying to keep down his exultation.

"There's nothing quite like your own child," Lincoln said. "But you understand how Marion feels too."

"She's forgotten how hard I worked for seven years there," Charlie said. "She   205
just remembers one night."

"There's another thing." Lincoln hesitated. "While you and Helen were tearing around Europe throwing money away, we were just getting along. I didn't touch any of the prosperity because I never got ahead enough to carry anything but my insurance. I think Marion felt there was some kind of injustice in it—you not even working toward the end, and getting richer and richer."

"It went just as quick as it came," said Charlie.

"Yes, a lot of it stayed in the hands of *chasseurs* and saxophone players and maîtres d'hôtel—well, the big party's over now. I just said that to explain Marion's feeling about those crazy years. If you drop in about six o'clock tonight before Marion's too tired, we'll settle the details on the spot."

Back at his hotel, Charlie found a *pneumatique*[3] that had been redirected from the Ritz bar where Charlie had left his address for the purpose of finding a certain man.

> Dear Charlie: You were so strange when we saw you the other day that I won-   210
> dered if I did something to offend you. If so, I'm not conscious of it. In fact,
> I have thought about you too much for the last year, and it's always been in the
> back of my mind that I might see you if I came over here. We *did* have such good
> times that crazy spring, like the night you and I stole the butcher's tricycle, and
> the time we tried to call on the president and you had the old derby rim and the
> wire cane. Everybody seems so old lately, but I don't feel old a bit. Couldn't we
> get together some time today for old time's sake? I've got a vile hang-over for
> the moment, but will be feeling better this afternoon and will look for you
> about five in the sweat-shop at the Ritz.
>
> Always devotedly,
> Lorraine.

His first feeling was one of awe that he had actually, in his mature years, stolen a tricycle and pedalled Lorraine all over the Étoile[4] between the small hours and dawn. In retrospect it was a nightmare. Locking out Helen didn't fit in with any other act of his life, but the tricycle incident did—it was one of many. How many weeks or months of dissipation to arrive at that condition of utter irresponsibility?

He tried to picture how Lorraine had appeared to him then—very attractive; Helen was unhappy about it, though she said nothing. Yesterday, in the restaurant, Lorraine had seemed trite, blurred, worn away. He emphatically did not

---

2. Native or inhabitant of Brittany, in northwestern France; *Béarnaise*: native or inhabitant of Béarn, in southwestern France.   3. Message or letter sent by pneumatic tube.
4. Intersection at the northwestern end of the Champs-Élysées, where twelve streets join to form a "star" (or *étoile*).

want to see her, and he was glad Alix had not given away his hotel address. It was a relief to think, instead, of Honoria, to think of Sundays spent with her and of saying good morning to her and of knowing she was there in his house at night, drawing her breath in the darkness.

At five he took a taxi and bought presents for all the Peters—a piquant cloth doll, a box of Roman soldiers, flowers for Marion, big linen handkerchiefs for Lincoln.

He saw, when he arrived in the apartment, that Marion had accepted the inevitable. She greeted him now as though he were a recalcitrant member of the family, rather than a menacing outsider. Honoria had been told she was going; Charlie was glad to see that her tact made her conceal her excessive happiness. Only on his lap did she whisper her delight and the question "When?" before she slipped away with the other children.

215   He and Marion were alone for a minute in the room, and on an impulse he spoke out boldly:

"Family quarrels are bitter things. They don't go according to any rules. They're not like aches or wounds; they're more like splits in the skin that won't heal because there's not enough material. I wish you and I could be on better terms."

"Some things are hard to forget," she answered. "It's a question of confidence." There was no answer to this and presently she asked, "When do you propose to take her?"

"As soon as I can get a governess. I hoped the day after tomorrow."

"That's impossible. I've got to get her things in shape. Not before Saturday."

220   He yielded. Coming back into the room, Lincoln offered him a drink.

"I'll take my daily whisky," he said.

It was warm here, it was a home, people together by a fire. The children felt very safe and important; the mother and father were serious, watchful. They had things to do for the children more important than his visit here. A spoonful of medicine was, after all, more important than the strained relations between Marion and himself. They were not dull people, but they were very much in the grip of life and circumstances. He wondered if he couldn't do something to get Lincoln out of his rut at the bank.

A long peal at the door-bell; the *bonne à tout faire*[5] passed through and went down the corridor. The door opened upon another long ring, and then voices, and the three in the salon looked up expectantly; Lincoln moved to bring the corridor within his range of vision, and Marion rose. Then the maid came back along the corridor, closely followed by the voices, which developed under the light into Duncan Schaeffer and Lorraine Quarrles.

They were gay, they were hilarious, they were roaring with laughter. For a moment Charlie was astounded, unable to understand how they ferreted out the Peters' address.

225   "Ah-h-h!" Duncan wagged his finger roguishly at Charlie. "Ah-h-h!"

They both slid down another cascade of laughter. Anxious and at a loss, Charlie shook hands with them quickly and presented them to Lincoln and Marion. Marion nodded, scarcely speaking. She had drawn back a step toward the fire; her little girl stood beside her, and Marion put an arm about her shoulder.

---

5. Maid of all work.

With growing annoyance at the intrusion, Charlie waited for them to explain themselves. After some concentration Duncan said:

"We came to invite you out to dinner. Lorraine and I insist that all this shishi, cagy business 'bout your address got to stop."

Charlie came closer to them, as if to force them backward down the corridor.

"Sorry, but I can't. Tell me where you'll be and I'll phone you in half an 230 hour."

This made no impression. Lorraine sat down suddenly on the side of a chair, and focussing her eyes on Richard, cried, "Oh, what a nice little boy! Come here, little boy." Richard glanced at his mother, but did not move. With a perceptible shrug of her shoulders, Lorraine turned back to Charlie:

"Come and dine. Sure your cousins won' mine. See you so sel'om. Or solemn."

"I can't," said Charlie sharply. "You two have dinner and I'll phone you."

Her voice became suddenly unpleasant. "All right, we'll go. But I remember once when you hammered on my door at four A.M. I was enough of a good sport to give you a drink. Come on, Dunc."

Still in slow motion, with blurred, angry faces, with uncertain feet, they retired 235 along the corridor.

"Good night," Charlie said.

"Good night!" responded Lorraine emphatically.

When he went back into the salon Marion had not moved, only now her son was standing in the circle of her other arm. Lincoln was still swinging Honoria back and forth like a pendulum from side to side.

"What an outrage!" Charlie broke out. "What an absolute outrage!"

Neither of them answered. Charlie dropped into an armchair, picked up his 240 drink, set it down again and said:

"People I haven't seen for two years having the colossal nerve—"

He broke off. Marion had made the sound "Oh!" in one swift, furious breath, turned her body from him with a jerk and left the room.

Lincoln set down Honoria carefully.

"You children go in and start your soup," he said, and when they obeyed, he said to Charlie:

"Marion's not well and she can't stand shocks. That kind of people make her 245 really physically sick."

"I didn't tell them to come here. They wormed your name out of somebody. They deliberately—"

"Well, it's too bad. It doesn't help matters. Excuse me a minute."

Left alone, Charlie sat tense in his chair. In the next room he could hear the children eating, talking in monosyllables, already oblivious to the scene between their elders. He heard a murmur of conversation from a farther room and then the ticking bell of a telephone receiver picked up, and in a panic he moved to the other side of the room and out of earshot.

In a minute Lincoln came back. "Look here, Charlie. I think we'd better call off dinner for tonight. Marion's in bad shape."

"Is she angry with me?" 250

"Sort of," he said, almost roughly. "She's not strong and—"

"You mean she's changed her mind about Honoria?"

"She's pretty bitter right now. I don't know. You phone me at the bank tomorrow."

"I wish you'd explain to her I never dreamed these people would come here. I'm just as sore as you are."

255 "I couldn't explain anything to her now."

Charlie got up. He took his coat and hat and started down the corridor. Then he opened the door of the dining room and said in a strange voice, "Good night, children."

Honoria rose and ran around the table to hug him.

"Good night, sweetheart," he said vaguely, and then trying to make his voice more tender, trying to conciliate something, "Good night, dear children."

V

Charlie went directly to the Ritz bar with the furious idea of finding Lorraine and Duncan, but they were not there, and he realized that in any case there was nothing he could do. He had not touched his drink at the Peters', and now he ordered a whisky-and-soda. Paul came over to say hello.

260 "It's a great change," he said sadly. "We do about half the business we did. So many fellows I hear about back in the States lost everything, maybe not in the first crash, but then in the second. Your friend George Hardt lost every cent, I hear. Are you back in the States?"

"No, I'm in business in Prague."

"I heard that you lost a lot in the crash."

"I did," and he added grimly, "but I lost everything I wanted in the boom."

"Selling short."[6]

265 "Something like that."

Again the memory of those days swept over him like a nightmare—the people they had met travelling; then people who couldn't add a row of figures or speak a coherent sentence. The little man Helen had consented to dance with at the ship's party, who had insulted her ten feet from the table; the women and girls carried screaming with drink or drugs out of public places—

—The men who locked their wives out in the snow, because the snow of twenty-nine wasn't real snow. If you didn't want it to be snow, you just paid some money.

He went to the phone and called the Peters' apartment; Lincoln answered.

"I called up because this thing is on my mind. Has Marion said anything definite?"

270 "Marion's sick," Lincoln answered shortly. "I know this thing isn't altogether your fault, but I can't have her go to pieces about it. I'm afraid we'll have to let it slide for six months; I can't take the chance of working her up to this state again."

"I see."

"I'm sorry, Charlie."

He went back to his table. His whisky glass was empty, but he shook his head when Alix looked at it questioningly. There wasn't much he could do now except send Honoria some things; he would send her a lot of things tomorrow. He thought rather angrily that this was just money—he had given so many people money. . . .

"No, no more," he said to another waiter. "What do I owe you?"

---

6. Selling securities, particularly in anticipation of falling prices, that the seller does not actually possess at the time of sale.

He would come back some day; they couldn't make him pay forever. But he   275
wanted his child, and nothing was much good now, beside that fact. He wasn't
young anymore, with a lot of nice thoughts and dreams to have by himself. He
was absolutely sure Helen wouldn't have wanted him to be so alone.

1931

F. SCOTT FITZGERALD

Echoes of the Jazz Age (November 1931)

It is too soon to write about the Jazz Age with perspective. . . . It is as dead as were
the Yellow Nineties in 1902. Yet the present writer already looks back to it with
nostalgia. It bore him up, flattered him and gave him more money than he had
dreamed of, simply for telling people that he felt as they did, that something had
to be done with all the nervous energy stored up and unexpended in the War.

The ten-year period that, as if reluctant to die outmoded in its bed, leaped to
a spectacular death in October, 1929, began about the time of the May Day riots
in 1919.[1] When the police rode down the demobilized country boys gaping at
the orators in Madison Square, it was the sort of measure bound to alienate the
more intelligent young men from the prevailing order. . . . If goose-livered business men had this effect on the government, then maybe we had gone to war for
J. P. Morgan's loans after all.[2] But, because we were tired of Great Causes, there
was no more than a short outbreak of moral indignation. . . . The events of 1919
left us cynical rather than revolutionary. . . . It was characteristic of the Jazz Age
that it had no interest in politics at all.

It was an age of miracles, it was an age of art, it was an age of excess, and it was
an age of satire. . . .

The first social revelation created a sensation out of all proportion to its novelty. As far back as 1915 the unchaperoned young people of the smaller cities had
discovered the mobile privacy of that automobile given to young Bill at sixteen to
make him "self-reliant." At first petting was a desperate adventure even under
such favorable conditions, but presently confidences were exchanged and the old
commandment broke down. As early as 1917 there were references to such sweet
and casual dalliance in any number[3] of the *Yale Record* or the *Princeton Tiger.*

But petting in its more audacious manifestations was confined to the wealth-
ier classes—among other young people the old standard prevailed until after the

1. On May Day (May 1), 1919, during a period of heated public controversy over Communists, radicals
and unionists organized rallies, mass meetings, and parades throughout the U.S.; riots ensued in several
cities, including Boston, Detroit, Cleveland, and New York. Fitzgerald's short story "May Day" focuses
partly on these events.
2. John Pierpont Morgan (1867–1943), the most important American financier of his day and head of the
banking firm founded by his father, brought together over two thousand American banks to float a total
of more than one and a half billion dollars in Allied bonds during World War I.
3. Issue (as of a periodical).

War, and a kiss meant that a proposal was expected. . . . Only in 1920 did the veil finally fall—the Jazz Age was in flower.

. . . By 1923 their elders, tired of watching the carnival with ill-concealed envy, had discovered that young liquor will take the place of young blood, and with a whoop the orgy began. . . .

A whole race going hedonistic, deciding on pleasure. The precocious intimacies of the younger generation would have come about with or without prohibition. . . . But the general decision to be amused that began with the cocktail parties of 1921 had more complicated origins.

The word jazz in its progress toward respectability has meant first sex, then dancing, then music. It is associated with a state of nervous stimulation, not unlike that of big cities behind the lines of a war. . . .

. . . Society, even in small cities, now dined in separate chambers, and the sober table learned about the gay table only from hearsay. There were very few people left at the sober table. . . .

The gay elements of society had divided into two main streams, one flowing toward Palm Beach and Deauville,[4] and the other, much smaller, toward the summer Riviera. One could get away with more on the summer Riviera, and whatever happened seemed to have something to do with art. From 1926 to 1929, the great years of the Cap d'Antibes, this corner of France was dominated by a group quite distinct from that American society which is dominated by Europeans. Pretty much of anything went at Antibes. . . .

. . . I remember a fellow expatriate opening a letter from a mutual friend of ours, urging him to come home and be revitalized by the hardy, bracing qualities of the native soil. It was a strong letter and it affected us both deeply, until we noticed that it was headed from a nerve sanitarium in Pennsylvania.

By this time contemporaries of mine had begun to disappear into the dark maw of violence. A classmate killed his wife and himself on Long Island, another tumbled "accidently" from a skyscraper in Philadelphia, another purposely from a skyscraper in New York. One was killed in a speak-easy in Chicago; another was beaten to death in a speak-easy in New York and crawled home to the Princeton Club to die; still another had his skull crushed by a maniac's axe in an insane asylum where he was confined. . . . [T]hese things happened not during the depression but during the boom.

. . . Americans were wandering ever more widely. . . . And by 1928 Paris had grown suffocating. With each new shipment of Americans spewed up by the boom the quality fell off, until toward the end there was something sinister about the crazy boatloads. . . . [I]t was evident that money and power were falling into the hands of people in comparison with whom the leader of a village Soviet would be a gold-mine of judgment and culture. There were citizens travelling in luxury in 1928 and 1929 who, in the distortion of their new condition,

4. Fashionable resort town in northern France, located on the English Channel. *Palm Beach:* resort town in Florida that became a popular destination in the 1920s.

had the human value of Pekinese, bivalves, cretins, goats. . . . But in those days life was like the race in *Alice in Wonderland*, there was a prize for every one. . . . Somebody had blundered and the most expensive orgy in history was over.

It ended two years ago, because the utter confidence which was its essential prop received an enormous jolt, and it didn't take long for the flimsy structure to settle earthward. And after two years the Jazz Age seems as far away as the days before the War. It was borrowed time anyhow—the whole upper tenth of a nation living with the insouciance of grand ducs and the casualness of chorus girls. But moralizing is easy now and it was pleasant to be in one's twenties in such a certain and unworried time. Even when you were broke you didn't worry about money, because it was in such profusion around you. . . .

Now once more the belt is tight and we summon the proper expression of horror as we look back at our wasted youth. Sometimes, though, there is a ghostly rumble among the drums, an asthmatic whisper in the trombones that swings me back into the early twenties when we drank wood alcohol and every day in every way grew better and better, . . . and it seemed only a question of a few years before the older people would step aside and let the world be run by those who saw things as they were—and it all seems rosy and romantic to us who were young then, because we will never feel quite so intensely about our surroundings any more.

MALCOLM COWLEY

From *Exile's Return: A Literary Odyssey of the 1920s* (1934)

It often seems to me that our years in school and after school, in college and later in the army, might be regarded as a long process of deracination. Looking backward, I feel that our whole training was involuntarily directed toward destroying whatever roots we had in the soil, toward eradicating our local and regional peculiarities, toward making us homeless citizens of the world.

In school, unless we happened to be Southerners, we were divested of any local pride. We studied Ancient History and American History, but not, in my own case, the history of western Pennsylvania. We learned by name the rivers of Siberia—Obi, Yenisei, Lena, Amur—but not the Ohio with its navigable tributaries, or why most of them had ceased to be navigated, or why Pittsburgh was built at its forks. We had high-school courses in Latin, German, Chemistry, good courses all of them, and a class in Civics where we learned to list the amendments to the Constitution and name the members of the Supreme Court; but we never learned how Presidents were really chosen or how a law was put through Congress. If one of us had later come into contact with the practical side of government—that is, if he wished to get a street paved, an assessment reduced, a friend out of trouble with the police or a relative appointed to office—well, fortunately the ward boss[1] wouldn't take much time to set him straight.

---

1. The vote gatherer and dispenser of patronage for his ward (small division of a city for representative, electoral, or administrative purposes). Seen as bases for corrupt political machines, wards diminished in stature after the early twentieth century.

Of the English texts we studied, I can remember only one, "The Legend of Sleepy Hollow,"[2] that gave us any idea that an American valley could be as effectively clothed in romance as Ivanhoe's castle or the London of Henry Esmond.[3] It seemed to us that America was beneath the level of great fiction; it seemed that literature in general, and art and learning, were things existing at an infinite distance from our daily lives. For those of us who read independently, this impression became even stronger: the only authors to admire were foreign authors. We came to feel that wisdom was an attribute of Greece and art of the Renaissance, that glamour belonged only to Paris or Vienna and that glory was confined to the dim past. If we tried, notwithstanding, to write about more immediate subjects, we were forced to use a language not properly our own. A definite effort was being made to destroy all trace of local idiom or pronunciation and have us speak "correctly"—that is, in a standardized Amerenglish as colorless as Esperanto.[4] Some of our instructors had themselves acquired this public-school dialect only by dint of practice, and now set forth its rules with an iron pedantry, as if they were teaching a dead language.

In college the process of deracination went on remorselessly. We were not being prepared for citizenship in a town, a state or a nation; we were not being trained for an industry or profession essential to the common life; instead we were being exhorted to enter that international republic of learning whose traditions are those of Athens, Florence, Paris, Berlin and Oxford. . . .

. . . School and college had uprooted us in spirit; now[5] we were physically uprooted, hundreds of us, millions, plucked from our own soil as if by a clamshell bucket and dumped, scattered among strange people. All our roots were dead now, even the Anglo-Saxon tradition of our literary ancestors, even the habits of slow thrift that characterized our social class. We were fed, lodged, clothed by strangers, commanded by strangers, infected with the poison of irresponsibility—the poison of travel, too, for we had learned that problems could be left behind us merely by moving elsewhere—and the poison of danger, excitement, that made our old life seem intolerable. Then, as suddenly as it began for us, the war ended.

When we first heard of the Armistice we felt a sense of relief too deep to express, and we all got drunk. We had come through, we were still alive, and nobody at all would be killed tomorrow. The composite fatherland for which we had fought and in which some of us still believed—France, Italy, the Allies, our English homeland, democracy, the self-determination of small nations—had triumphed. We danced in the streets, embraced old women and pretty girls, swore blood brotherhood with soldiers in little bars, drank with our elbows locked in theirs, reeled through the streets with bottles of champagne, fell asleep somewhere. On the next day, after we got over our hangovers, we didn't know what to do, so we got drunk. But slowly, as the days went by, the intoxication passed, and the tears of joy: it appeared that our composite fatherland

---

2. Washington Irving's short story (1819–20), set in a Dutch enclave on the Hudson River in New York State.

3. The protagonist of William Makepeace Thackeray's novel *The History of Henry Esmond, Esquire* (1852), which takes place partly amidst London society. *Ivanhoe's castle*: a setting in Sir Walter Scott's historical romance *Ivanhoe* (1819), which concerns the life of Sir Wilfred of Ivanhoe, a fictional Saxon knight.

4. An artificial international language based on common elements of the principal European languages.

5. During World War I.

was dissolving into quarreling statesmen and oil and steel magnates. Our own nation had passed the Prohibition Amendment as if to publish a bill of separation between itself and ourselves; it wasn't our country any longer. Nevertheless we returned to it: there was nowhere else to go. We returned to New York, appropriately—to the homeland of the uprooted, where everyone you met came from another town and tried to forget it; where nobody seemed to have parents, or a past more distant than last night's swell party, or a future beyond the swell party this evening and the disillusioned book he would write tomorrow.

Greenwich Village was not only a place, a mood, a way of life: like all bohemias, it was also a doctrine. Since the days of Gautier and Murger,[6] this doctrine had remained the same in spirit, but it had changed in several details. By 1920, it had become a system of ideas that could roughly be summarized as follows:

1. The idea of salvation by the child.—Each of us at birth has special potentialities which are slowly crushed and destroyed by a standardized society and mechanical methods of teaching. If a new educational system can be introduced, one by which children are encouraged to develop their own personalities, to blossom freely like flowers, then the world will be saved by this new, free generation.

2. The idea of self-expression.—Each man's, each woman's, purpose in life is to express himself, to realize his full individuality through creative work and beautiful living in beautiful surroundings.

3. The idea of paganism.—The body is a temple in which there is nothing unclean, a shrine to be adorned for the ritual of love.

4. The idea of living for the moment.—It is stupid to pile up treasures that we can enjoy only in old age, when we have lost the capacity for enjoyment. Better to seize the moment as it comes, to dwell in it intensely, even at the cost of future suffering. Better to live extravagantly, gather June rosebuds, "burn my candle at both ends. . . . It gives a lovely light."[7]

5. The idea of liberty.—Every law, convention or rule of art that prevents self-expression or the full enjoyment of the moment should be shattered and abolished. Puritanism is the great enemy. The crusade against puritanism is the only crusade with which free individuals are justified in allying themselves.

6. The idea of female equality.—Women should be the economic and moral equals of men. They should have the same pay, the same working conditions, the same opportunity for drinking, smoking, taking or dismissing lovers.

7. The idea of psychological adjustment.—We are unhappy because we are maladjusted, and maladjusted because we are repressed. If our individual repressions can be removed—by confessing them to a Freudian psychologist—then we can adjust ourselves to any situation, and be happy in it. (But Freudianism is only one method of adjustment. What is wrong with us may be our glands, and by a slight operation,

6. Théophile Gautier (1811–72) and Louis-Henri Murger (1822–61), French writers known for celebrating art for art's sake and depicting bohemian life, respectively.
7. Slight misquotation of "First Fig" (1920) by American poet Edna St. Vincent Millay (1892–1950). The full poem reads: "My candle burns at both ends; / It will not last the night; / But ah, my foes, and oh, my friends— / It gives a lovely light!"

or merely by taking a daily dose of thyroid, we may alter our whole personalities. Again, we may adjust ourselves by some such psychophysical discipline as was taught by Gurdjieff.[8] The implication of all these methods is the same—that the environment itself need not be altered. That explains why most radicals who became converted to psychoanalysis or glands or Gurdjieff gradually abandoned their political radicalism.)

8. The idea of changing place—"They do things better in Europe." England and Germany have the wisdom of old cultures; the Latin peoples have admirably preserved their pagan heritage. By expatriating himself, by living in Paris, Capri or the South of France, the artist can break the puritan shackles, drink, live freely and be wholly creative.

All these, from the standpoint of the business-Christian ethic then represented by the *Saturday Evening Post*, were corrupt ideas. This older ethic is familiar to most people, but one feature of it has not been sufficiently emphasized. Substantially, it was a *production* ethic. The great virtues it taught were industry, foresight, thrift and personal initiative. The workman should be industrious in order to produce more for his employer; he should look ahead to the future; he should save money in order to become a capitalist himself; then he should exercise personal initiative and found new factories where other workmen would toil industriously, and save, and become capitalists in their turn.

During the process many people would suffer privations: most workers would live meagerly and wrack their bodies with labor; even the employers would deny themselves luxuries that they could easily purchase, choosing instead to put back the money into their business; but after all, our bodies were not to be pampered; they were temporary dwelling places, and we should be rewarded in Heaven for our self-denial. On earth, our duty was to accumulate more wealth and produce more goods, the ultimate use of which was no subject for worry. They would somehow be absorbed, by new markets opened in the West, or overseas in new countries, or by the increased purchasing power of workmen who had saved and bettered their position.

That was the ethic of a young capitalism, and it worked admirably, so long as the territory and population of the country were expanding faster than its industrial plant. But after the war the situation changed. Our industries had grown enormously to satisfy a demand that suddenly ceased. To keep the factory wheels turning, a new domestic market had to be created. Industry and thrift were no longer adequate. There must be a new ethic that encouraged people to buy, a *consumption* ethic.

It happened that many of the Greenwich Village ideas proved useful in the altered situation. Thus, *self-expression* and *paganism* encouraged a demand for all sorts of products—modern furniture, beach pajamas, cosmetics, colored bathrooms with toilet paper to match. *Living for the moment* meant buying an automobile, radio or house, using it now and paying for it tomorrow. *Female equality* was capable of doubling the consumption of products—cigarettes, for example—that

8. George Ivanovitch Gurdjieff (1872–1945), Armenian spiritualist and philosopher, founded a quasi-religious movement that involved dialogue, exercise, and dance. Gurdjieff's Institute for the Harmonious Development of Man, centered in Russia and then France, furthered its influence through performances in U.S. cities during 1924.

had formerly been used by men alone. Even *changing place* would help to stimulate business in the country from which the artist was being expatriated. The exiles of art were also trade missionaries: involuntarily they increased the foreign demand for fountain pens, silk stockings, grapefruit and portable typewriters. They drew after them an invading army of tourists, thus swelling the profits of steamship lines and travel agencies. Everything fitted into the business picture.

•

I don't mean to say that Greenwich Village was the source of the revolution in morals that affected all our lives in the decade after the war, and neither do I mean that big business deliberately plotted to render the nation extravagant, pleasure worshiping and reckless of tomorrow.

The new moral standards arose from conditions that had nothing to do with the Village. They were, as a matter of fact, not really new. Always, even in the great age of the Puritans, there had been currents of licentiousness that were favored by the immoderate American climate and held in check only by hellfire preaching and the hardships of settling a new country. Old Boston, Providence, rural Connecticut, all had their underworlds. The reason puritanism became so strong in America was perhaps that it had to be strong in order to checkmate its enemies. But it was already weakening as the country grew richer in the twenty years before the war; and the war itself was the puritan crisis and defeat.

All standards were relaxed in the stormy-sultry wartime atmosphere. It wasn't only the boys of my age, those serving in the army, who were transformed by events: their sisters and younger brothers were affected in a different fashion. With their fathers away, perhaps, and their mothers making bandages or tea-dancing[9] with lonely officers, it was possible for boys and girls to do what they pleased. For the first time they could go to dances unchaperoned, drive the family car and park it by the roadside while they made love, and come home after midnight, a little tipsy, with nobody to reproach them in the hallway. They took advantage of these stolen liberties—indeed, one might say that the revolution in morals began as a middle-class children's revolt.

But everything conspired to further it. Prohibition came and surrounded the new customs with illicit glamour; prosperity made it possible to practice them; Freudian psychology provided a philosophical justification and made it unfashionable to be repressed; still later the sex magazines and the movies, even the pulpit, would advertise a revolution that had taken place silently and triumphed without a struggle. In all this Greenwich Village had no part. The revolution would have occurred if the Village had never existed, but—the point is important—it would not have followed the same course. The Village, older in revolt, gave form to the movement, created its fashions, and supplied the writers and illustrators who would render them popular. As for American business, though it laid no plots in advance, it was quick enough to use the situation, to exploit the new markets for cigarettes and cosmetics, and to realize that, in advertising pages and movie palaces, sex appeal was now the surest appeal.

The Greenwich Village standards, with the help of business, had spread through the country. Young women east and west had bobbed their hair, let it

9. Dancing and socializing that follows or is accompanied by afternoon tea.

grow and bobbed it again; they had passed through the period when corsets were checked in the cloakroom at dances and the period when corsets were not worn. They were not very self-conscious when they talked about taking a lover; and the conversations ran from mother fixations to birth control while they smoked cigarettes between the courses of luncheons eaten in black-and-orange tea shops[1] just like those in the Village. People of forty had been affected by the younger generation: they spent too much money, drank too much gin, made love to one another's wives and talked about their neuroses. Houses were furnished to look like studios. Stenographers went on parties, following the example of the boss and his girl friend and her husband. The "party," conceived as a gathering together of men and women to drink gin cocktails, flirt, dance to the phonograph or radio and gossip about their absent friends, had in fact become one of the most popular American institutions; nobody stopped to think how short its history had been in this country. It developed out of the "orgies" celebrated by the French 1830 Romantics,[2] but it was introduced into this country by Greenwich Villagers—before being adopted by salesmen from Kokomo and the younger country-club set in Kansas City.

Wherever one turned the Greenwich Village ideas were making their way: even the *Saturday Evening Post*[3] was feeling their influence. Long before Repeal, it began to wobble on Prohibition. It allowed drinking, petting and unfaithfulness to be mentioned in the stories it published; its illustrations showed women smoking. Its advertising columns admitted one after another of the strictly pagan products—cosmetics, toilet tissues, cigarettes—yet still it continued to thunder against Greenwich Village and bohemian immorality. It even nourished the illusion that its long campaign had been successful. On more than one occasion it announced that the Village was dead and buried: "The sad truth is," it said in the autumn of 1931, "that the Village was a flop." Perhaps it was true that the Village was moribund—of that we can't be sure, for creeds and ways of life among artists are hard to kill. If, however, the Village was really dying, it was dying of success. It was dying because it became so popular that too many people insisted on living there. It was dying because women smoked cigarettes on the streets of the Bronx, drank gin cocktails in Omaha and had perfectly swell parties in Seattle and Middletown—in other words, because American business and the whole of middle-class America had been going Greenwich Village.

Ever since 1920 there had been no break in the movement toward France. Artists and writers, art photographers, art salesmen, dancers, movie actors, Guggenheim

1. Shops serving "exotic" black teas such as English Breakfast, Earl Grey, Darjeeling, Assam, Lapsang Souchong, and Orange Pekoe. (Orange refers to the royal Dutch house of Orange and not the color of the tea.)

2. Prompted by an antiroyalist revolution in July 1830 that yielded the "citizen-king" Louis-Philippe's eighteen-year July Monarchy, French romantic writers led by the poet, novelist, and playwright Victor Hugo (1802–55) began a vigorous and long-standing literary battle against neoclassicists. They viewed the artist as a noble outlaw at war with society, free in both choice and treatment of a subject, dedicated to passionate love.

3. Popular weekly magazine best known for its mainstream content and for many cover illustrations by artist Norman Rockwell (1894–1978). Fitzgerald's "Babylon Revisited" appeared in the *Post* in 1931.

fellows,[4] divorcées dabbling in sculpture, unhappy ex-débutantes wondering whether a literary career wouldn't take the place of marriage—a whole world of people with and without talent but sharing the same ideals happily deserted the homeland. Each year some of them returned while others crowded into their places: the migration continued at a swifter rate. But after the middle of the decade the motives behind it underwent an imperceptible but real change in emphasis. The earlier exiles had been driven abroad by a hatred of American dullness and puritanism, yet primarily they had traveled *in search of* something— leisure, freedom, knowledge, some quality that was offered by an older culture. Their successors felt the same desires, but felt them a little less strongly. Instead of being drawn ahead, they were propelled from behind, pushed eastward by the need for *getting away from* something. They were not so much exiles as refugees.

ERNEST R. GROVES

From *Social Problems of the Family* (1927)

[The family] does more than minister to the physical needs of children; it serves society by its effect upon the various members of the family who live together within the home, and particularly by its influence upon the personality of the growing child.

Thus the family has become of primary importance as an effective socializing agency. It is chiefly through the family that culture is transmitted from generation to generation. . . . From parent to child the fundamentals of culture, traditions, . . . social habits descend, and in this manner the continuity of social life is assured.

. . . [M]odern civilization is stimulating the increase of divorce. A large number of modern men and women express in all sorts of ways a tendency toward social instability as a result of rapid changes in modes of living. The pulsations of life move swiftly, thoughts are discarded, conventions superseded, thrilling experiences not previously dreamed of are provided, former habits loosened, and the formation of new habits accelerated by the momentum of present-day civilization. Marriage is one of the most delicate and sensitive of human relationships, and it would be strange indeed if it did not reflect the general unrest of our times. . . .

A careful investigation recently made regarding divorces granted in Suffolk County (about 90 per cent. of which is the city of Boston) from January, 1900, through December, 1921, shows the effect of the World War upon the increase of divorces within that county. A remarkable increase of divorces appears for the years 1919, 1920 and 1921. . . . The essential cause of this phenomenal increase . . .

4. Professionals (in the natural sciences, the social sciences, the humanities, and the creative arts) who receive fellowships from the John Simon Guggenheim Memorial Foundation.

was the disrupting influence of the World War; this great conflict was both an expression of the general restlessness which is the bitter fruit of contemporary civilization, and, itself, a source of social discontent. All parts of life felt its upheaval. Nowhere was its effect more clearly registered in disturbing and uprooting influences than in the family.

. . . . War snatches from home the breadwinner, affords opportunity through the absence of fathers for children to drift into delinquency, gives to countless husbands who finally return home restlessness and wanderlust; it brings to both men and women temptations that lead them to deviate from former moral standards, it stimulates and brings to expression neurotic tendencies that might not have developed to the point of hurting the family had there not been the stress of war. . . . [War] stimulates fatalistic attitudes toward life which lessen the sense of family responsibility. . . . During the war when the minds of the people are concentrated on the conflict and the general excitement makes sane thinking difficult, the havoc suffered by the family is not keenly felt, but once the war is over its effects appear. . . .

·

No greater tragedy can come to a family than the death of the father or mother, for added to the grief at the parting of the life of the parent beloved, there is in the case of children a broken family of the most serious kind.

Although the surviving parent may double his efforts in his endeavor to make good the loss suffered by the children, in spite of all he or she does, the family circle is at once stripped of its normal atmosphere and the home functions as a broken instrument. There is general agreement that the family that has lost its mother encounters greater trials than if it is the father who has died, for hers is the larger contribution. The father who is left to care for little children because of the death of the mother faces a very difficult problem and one increasingly hard to solve. A generation ago, an unmarried relative offered the commonest and best solution and in cases where there were none to be called upon a housekeeper could usually be had. The new economic opportunities for women have greatly changed this situation; relatives are far less likely to feel it their duty to assume a task that all recognize to be a severe test of character, and efficient housekeepers, at least for men with moderate incomes, are even more scarce than sacrificing relatives.

It is not at all surprising that we find children who have lost their mothers or fathers by death, and who have not been given satisfactory home life by the successful re-marriage of their remaining parent, so often drifting toward some sort of delinquency; their unsuccessful social adjustment bears tribute to the social values of the normal family and reveals in a striking way the misfortunes that must come to children whose family life is mutilated by death.

·

Many homes whose mothers are employed outside have conditions resembling those in the homes where death has removed the mother.

V. F. CALVERTON

From *The Bankruptcy of Marriage* (1928)

Pirouetting to the rhythm of the tango, ravaged by the contortions of the Charleston, or, cigarette in hand, shimmeying to the music of the masses, the New Woman and the New Morality have made their theatric debut upon the modern scene. At nights, in the large cities, life spins itself into melodrama. The mad dance of youth, intoxicated with the swell of its new freedom, has encircled the western world. . . . The wild, Corybantian[1] antics of the flapper,[2] flinging herself, in this delirium of escape, night after night upon the edge of nervous ecstasy, are no longer peculiar to our nation. . . .

Jazz has become an accepted institution. . . . It expresses the spirit of the age. Youth has steeped itself in its intoxications. Repressions have been released, and in the abandonments of modern life, exhibitionism has changed from a vice into a virtue.

In the flapper we find a vivid symbol of this change. This new girl, with all her emptiness of ideas and effusiveness of emotions, is a revolutionary outgrowth on the feminine scene. . . . Her speech, her dress, her gesture are outspoken evidences of the nature of her insurrection. . . .

In this whirling race of Change, all restraints and restrictions have been sacrificed. The inhibitions once indispensable to feminine virtue have become riddled with scorn. The old sanctity of marriage has been ridiculed by sallies of wit and satire fired at it from every side. Sexual excitements and ecstasies have become experiences to crave and not to constrain. The flapper is consumed by them. . . . The old conventions that separated the sexes have been shattered. The old waltz has surrendered to the new jazz. . . .

The old family has decayed. The old home has been replaced by the movie, the club, the dance-hall. Home has become a place to dine and die. . . .

. . . This new girl, this modern flapper, with her lack of respect for the ideals of her predecessors; and this new masculine youth, with his disregard for the old responsibilities, his disdain for marriage, and contempt for virtue—both were born in the fury of their revolt, in the days of the World War and those that have immediately followed.

The jazz age was born in its tornado of intensity from the vortices of the World War and its aftermath. . . .

The World War not only annihilated the flower of European youth, but it left its deeper effects on the youth that remained. . . .

Youth was disillusioned of purpose and aspiration.

. . . The psychosis of the last fling predominated. The imminence of death drove men to the last extremities of desire. Nothing mattered! . . .

1. Like the wild music and dancing associated with the rites of the Corybantes—attendants and priests of Cybele, an ancient Asiatic goddess of nature.
2. Common term for the young women of the 1920s who flouted traditional social norms of dress and behavior.

The modern dance was an inevitable outgrowth of this war-madness. Modern youth responded to the wild call. What mattered? To live, to live intensely, to live furiously, to seize from life its every thrill. Such became the new motivation.

In Paris, after the war, they danced. . . . They wanted an escape that was active, dynamic, electrical. . . . The spirit of tranquillity was alien to the trend of the age.

Every year, every month, the dance takes new forms, assumes new disguises. Each form is more futile than the other. Each change is more sexual. Only the thin division of clothes and the wild cry of the victrola or violin distinguishes the dance from the pageantry of an ancient saturnalia—or the abandonment of the first act in a brothel.

Youth in its revolt has not only turned against the old traditions, but in its search for the new it is dissipating its energies in extravagance and excess. . . .

This World War, then, shot into shreds the old ideals, the old morals, the old customs. . . .

The Age of Innocence is dead.

The question—how did we get this way—is . . . one of very intricate and compli-cated character. The World War, after all, was in itself but a sharp climax in the career of modern industrial civilization. . . . Industrialism brought with it the factory-system of production with mass-economics as its main manifesta-tion; it drew women into industry, destroyed the unity of the home, and brought the family to a rapid ruin. It brought a new social class into power, the bourgeoisie[3]. . . .

One of the important factors that has undermined th[e] old ethics has been the great change that has taken place in the attitude of the bourgeoisie. . . . its ethics, under the influence of new conditions, has lost its former asceticism and rigor. . . . The bourgeoisie was originally a working class. It did not have a leisure-class attitude. In fact it condemned a leisure-class attitude. Today this has altered. The bourgeoisie who now represent our plutocracy constitute a leisure class. Prosperity has brought us to the billionaire epoch. . . . With the centralization of capital, the acceleration of production, and the achievement of absentee-ownership of industry, combined with the inheritance of wealth which frees the larger part of the younger members of this group also from the necessity of toil, a leisure class was an inevitable result. The bourgeois mores, the old morality that is, was never made for a leisure-class ethic. It was an ethic that grew out of hard and trying struggle, an ethic in which asceticism was a virtue and diversion a sin. But a leisure class cannot live upon asceticism, nor exist without diversion. . . . The old morals had to crack and crumble. And so they have.

3. The middle class.

The release of the new morals is closely connected with the fading of the old conception of marriage. Monogamous marriage is based upon the idea of a life-time relationship between one man and one woman. This is the religious as well as the social idea. . . .

. . . If we say that marriage has decayed, we do not mean that people do not still marry, or that they will not marry in the future. In speaking of the bankruptcy of marriage we mean the bankruptcy of modern marriage and the moral founda-tions upon which it has been constructed. Even under a state of "free love," people may marry, but their marriages may signify nothing more binding than ephem-eral affections and alliances of a fortnight. . . . This theory of free contract is all that the modern revolutionist or free-lover desires. But this attitude is a viola-tion, in fact is the very antithesis, of the *binding-contract* upon which modern mar-riage has been founded. It is marriage as we know it, therefore, the marriage of modern monogamy, of the binding-contract variety, our system of marriage, in other words, that has broken down, and today is bankrupt.

In 1887 there was one divorce to every 17.3 marriages; in 1924 there was one divorce to every 6.9 marriages.

Over two divorces . . . were granted to wives for every one that was granted to husbands [between 1887 and 1906], which signifies . . . an attitude on the part of woman that is distantly removed from that of her Victorian predecessors. . . . Women then were not to "take arms against a sea of trouble,"[4] but to accept it with resignation. Such response was supposed to be part of the innate nobility of her nature. Today woman is in a state of protest and revolt. . . .

. . . There should be nothing bewildering or strangely novel in this recent revolu-tion in ethics. Scores of such revolutions have occurred in the past, . . . express-ing each in turn fundamental alterations in social and economic structure. With the candor in which sex is now beginning to be treated, there should again be no cause for astonishment. It is merely a return to an older attitude which was far more clean than the one which we have known.

While in the past we have known the costs of repression, it is the future which will introduce to us the costs of freedom. If freedom as a theory is perfect, and as an aspiration is ideal, it is foolish of us, however, to imagine that in practice it will be accompanied by a complete absence of discord. There will still be indi-vidual dilemmas, individual difficulties, and individual disasters. . . .

. . . The present direction of sex attitudes . . . holds forth hope as a rich incen-tive. The escape from the old ethics can only be viewed as an advance.

In order to progress we must hazard new seas. . . . Until the new ways have been tried and tested, and the rapids conquered in the crossing, movement in this direction and that will be uncertain and insecure. These are the dangers that accompany exploration. . . .

4. *Hamlet* 3.1.59: "Or to take arms against a sea of troubles" (from Hamlet's famous "To be or not to be" soliloquy).

SUGGESTIONS FOR WRITING

1. Write an essay that examines one aspect of the lifestyle of Americans in Paris as portrayed in F. Scott Fitzgerald's "Babylon Revisited" and that same aspect of the history of the age (the 1920s and 1930s) as documented in the short pieces, by Fitzgerald and others, that accompany the story in this chapter. For example, consider how the economic crash affected the getting and the spending of money. Or compare the different models of family or social life depicted and recalled in the story with the writings that discuss social changes in this era. If there are parallels between Charlie Wales's fictional life and the actual trends and events of that time, does the story clearly take sides for or against old-fashioned ways, the "Roaring Twenties" of excess, or the effort to recover in the early 1930s?

2. In "Babylon Revisited" much is implied about the changing roles of women in modern society. Citing specific passages from Fitzgerald's story as well as from the excerpts by Ernest R. Groves and V. F. Calverton, write an essay discussing the way that "Babylon Revisited" depicts girls and women. What conflicts do you see in the story between characters with different notions of proper female roles?

3. Research the life of F. Scott Fitzgerald and write an essay examining the parallels between the author and his character Charlie Wales in "Babylon Revisited." How are they similar and how are they different, and why do you think Fitzgerald used the medium of fiction in the way he did? Be sure to cite Fitzgerald's *Echoes of the Jazz Age,* excerpted in this chapter.

4. Write an essay in which you connect a theme, action or event, or character in Fitzgerald's story with one or more of the eight revolutionary new values expressed in Malcolm Cowley's *Exile's Return.* How does the story show the limitations or inconsistencies of these new values? For instance, did the Americans in Paris really seek "a change of place," or did they just occupy parts of Paris and make them American? Is Charlie going to correct his own "psychological adjustment," or is he suffering from something wrong with his culture? Address such questions with reference to the biographical and historical information about Fitzgerald and the period provided here or elsewhere.

5. What is the equivalent in our own time of the stock-market crash of 1929? Is it the events of September 11, 2001? the collapse of the "Internet bubble" in 2000–2001 or the "mortgage crisis" of 2008? Write a short story in which the lives of your characters reflect the social, economic, and moral upheavals of the present day. You might employ Fitzgerald's method of looking back at one era, however recent, from the standpoint of drastically altered circumstances.

Actual statements from Faulkner interviews, however, scarcely identify him as a feminist. Two such quotations appear, for example, in The Paris Review Interviews Writers at Work, First Series (Baltimore: Penguin, 1958). The first of these Sayre claims that "the perfect milieu for the artist to work in" is brothel; "the house is quiet in the mornings—the best time to write—the work is easy, and the pay ade-quate, the life offers him" have cordial life he wants; "gives him a certain" and. The whole passage and "all the human to" bloom upon "" and "to social" intercourse for — —" success is feminine and like a would" — "" "" "" "" "" "" "" "" "" override you. So the way to treat her is to show her the back of your hand" (132).

This is not at discount Fetterley's feminist reading of the story, but only to.

We have already seen that, although stories may be read as if they stand alone, they are enriched by being situated in authorial, literary, or cultural and histori-cal contexts. Once a work has earned a place in the canon of literature, it has already become surrounded by a critical context—readers who write about the work and others who engage those readers or critics in dialogue about that work. To write critically about a work of literature is to engage not only the text but also those who have written about the text. It is often advisable, however, to read and reread the story several times until you have come to terms with it—that is, settled in your own mind what you think about the story and how you interpret it. Then you may go to other critics—"secondary sources"—to expand or corroborate or reconsider your reading of the story. Sometimes when you read criticism before you have made up your own mind, *all* the critics seem "right" (and the most recently read seem the "most clearly right"), and your own responses can be dulled or deflected. On the other hand, when you have settled on your own responses to the story, you can read critics and pick up *additional* information or insights that can enhance rather than erase your own response and judgment. Reading criticism will not rob you of, or substitute for, your individual response. Rather, in addition to being informative in various ways, it may provide you with the means to con-vince someone else to share your opinion of the work.

The story that stands here in the middle of critical discussion is William Faulkner's popular, classic, and controversial tale "A Rose for Emily." It is followed by several published analyses of the story and a student essay. There are hundreds of critical essays and commentaries on "A Rose for Emily" published as far away as Costa Rica and Turkey, and in languages as varied as German and Japanese. It is virtually impossible, then, to fully "report" the history of the critical discussion of this fascinating story. The critical pieces reprinted here are not necessarily the best (and not necessarily not the best), nor do they fully represent the spectrum of com-ment and argument about the story. But they do suggest some of the approaches that have been applied to the story, as well as some aspects of the story that have often been singled out for analysis.

One piece, Judith Fetterley's "A Rose for 'A Rose for Emily,'" is adapted from her book *The Resisting Reader: A Feminist Approach to American Fiction*. It suggests that what Emily has done seems grotesque primarily because she is a woman—indeed, a lady—in a society with restrictive standards for what a lady might prop-erly do. Faulkner, Fetterley says, sees Emily as "a woman victimized and betrayed by the system of sexual politics, who nevertheless has discovered, within the structures that victimize her, sources of power for herself." Faulkner himself has implied this, she says, alluding to (but not quoting) occasional comments of his.

Actual statements from Faulkner interviews, however, scarcely identify him as a feminist. Two such quotations appear, for example, in *The Paris Review Interviews: Writers at Work*, first series (Baltimore: Penguin, 1958). The first of these wryly claims that "the perfect milieu for the artist to work in" is a brothel. The house is quiet in the mornings—the best time to write—the work is easy, and the pay adequate; the job offers him whatever social life he wants, "gives him a certain standing in his society," and "all the inmates of the house are female and would defer to him and call him 'sir'" (124). The second statement is even more provocative: "Success is feminine and like a woman; if you cringe before her, she will override you. So the way to treat her is to show her the back of your hand" (125).

This is not to discount Fetterley's feminist reading of the story, but only to make you wary of trusting what an author says about his or her own work—we should trust the tale, not the teller. After all, evidence in Faulkner's stories, letters, and life can support the view that he was a stereotypical Mississippi white racist or, conversely, that he empathized with African Americans and deplored racism. And over the years critics have noted that Faulkner made contradictory statements about "A Rose for Emily" itself. We naturally and properly read stories as if they are communications from another human mind and experience that we are trying to understand. All readings must begin with this intention. But even our friends sometimes tell us things about themselves, their attitudes and actions, that they do not know they are revealing; sometimes they claim intentions or accomplishments that we know not to be "true" or that contradict claims they have made earlier. We must be alert to the possibility that even authors cannot always distinguish between what they mean and what they have said, and we should treat an author's remarks about his or her own work much as we would those of other very knowledgeable, yet not omniscient, critics.

When a work has engaged a number of critics, and especially when something in the work is difficult or controversial, subsequent commentaries need to acknowledge the previous readings and, by contradicting or modifying their conclusions with new evidence or more persuasive argument, articulate a motive for still another essay on the oft-debated topic. (On motive, see "Writing about Literature," 33.3.1 and 35.1.1.)

A NOTE ON DOCUMENTATION

Alert readers will notice that these commentaries use different forms of documentation. Fetterley's book was published in 1978. It cites its references in endnotes such as "See *Faulkner in the University: Class Conferences at the University of Virginia 1957–1958*, edited by Frederick L. Gwynn and Joseph L. Blotner (Charlottesville: University Press of Virginia, 1959), 87–88; *Faulkner at Nagano*, edited by Robert A. Jeliffe (Tokyo: Kenkyusha, 1956), 71." It does not include a bibliography or a list of works cited. The essay by Lawrence R. Rodgers published in 1992 does give such a list and interpolates the references with the page number(s) in the text parenthetically—for example, "(Going 53)," "(Wilson 56)." The suggested standard form for literary essays and books is set by the Modern Language Association; between the publication of the earlier and the later essays, the MLA changed the form it recommended. Not everyone uses the newer form. But it is not only for that reason that the older form has been left here in the older essays: Whenever you do literary research in books and articles from earlier decades, you will run into this earlier form, so it is just as well to be familiar with it. Note that while this documentation is standard for *literary* commentary, critical and scholarly works in other disciplines—psychology, chemistry, and so forth—use other forms. (For more on documentation, see "Writing about Literature," chapter 36.)

WILLIAM FAULKNER

A Rose for Emily

I

When Miss Emily Grierson died, our whole town went to her funeral: the men through a sort of respectful affection for a fallen monument, the women mostly out of curiosity to see the inside of her house, which no one save an old man-servant—a combined gardener and cook—had seen in at least ten years.

It was a big, squarish frame house that had once been white, decorated with cupolas and spires and scrolled balconies in the heavily lightsome style of the seventies,[1] set on what had once been our most select street. But garages and cotton gins had encroached and obliterated even the august names of that neighborhood; only Miss Emily's house was left, lifting its stubborn and coquettish decay above the cotton wagons and the gasoline pumps—an eyesore among eyesores. And now Miss Emily had gone to join the representatives of those august names where they lay in the cedar-bemused cemetery among the ranked and anonymous graves of Union and Confederate soldiers who fell at the battle of Jefferson.

Alive, Miss Emily had been a tradition, a duty, and a care; a sort of hereditary obligation upon the town, dating from that day in 1894 when Colonel Sartoris, the mayor—he who fathered the edict that no Negro woman should appear on the streets without an apron—remitted her taxes, the dispensation dating from the death of her father on into perpetuity. Not that Miss Emily would have accepted charity. Colonel Sartoris invented an involved tale to the effect that Miss Emily's father had loaned money to the town, which the town, as a matter of business, preferred this way of repaying. Only a man of Colonel Sartoris' generation and thought could have invented it, and only a woman could have believed it.

When the next generation, with its more modern ideas, became mayors and aldermen, this arrangement created some little dissatisfaction. On the first of the year they mailed her a tax notice. February came, and there was no reply. They wrote her a formal letter, asking her to call at the sheriff's office at her convenience. A week later the mayor wrote her himself, offering to call or to send his car for her, and received in reply a note on paper of an archaic shape, in a thin, flowing calligraphy in faded ink, to the effect that she no longer went out at all. The tax notice was also enclosed, without comment.

They called a special meeting of the Board of Aldermen. A deputation waited upon her, knocked at the door through which no visitor had passed since she

5

---

1. The 1870s, the decade following the Civil War between the "Union and Confederate soldiers" mentioned at the end of the paragraph.

ceased giving china-painting lessons eight or ten years earlier. They were admitted by the old Negro into a dim hall from which a stairway mounted into still
more shadow. It smelled of dust and disuse—a close, dank smell. The Negro
led them into the parlor. It was furnished in heavy, leather-covered furniture.
When the Negro opened the blinds of one window, a faint dust rose sluggishly
about their thighs, spinning with slow motes in the single sun-ray. On a tarnished
gilt easel before the fireplace stood a crayon portrait of Miss Emily's father.

They rose when she entered—a small, fat woman in black, with a thin gold
chain descending to her waist and vanishing into her belt, leaning on an ebony
cane with a tarnished gold head. Her skeleton was small and spare; perhaps that
was why what would have been merely plumpness in another was obesity in her.
She looked bloated, like a body long submerged in motionless water, and of that
pallid hue. Her eyes, lost in the fatty ridges of her face, looked like two small pieces
of coal pressed into a lump of dough as they moved from one face to another while
the visitors stated their errand.

She did not ask them to sit. She just stood in the door and listened quietly
until the spokesman came to a stumbling halt. Then they could hear the invisible watch ticking at the end of the gold chain.

Her voice was dry and cold. "I have no taxes in Jefferson. Colonel Sartoris
explained it to me. Perhaps one of you can gain access to the city records and
satisfy yourselves."

"But we have. We are the city authorities, Miss Emily. Didn't you get a notice
from the sheriff, signed by him?"

10   "I received a paper, yes," Miss Emily said. "Perhaps he considers himself the
sheriff. . . . I have no taxes in Jefferson."

"But there is nothing on the books to show that, you see. We must go by the—"

"See Colonel Sartoris. I have no taxes in Jefferson."

"But, Miss Emily—"

"See Colonel Sartoris." (Colonel Sartoris had been dead almost ten years.) "I have
no taxes in Jefferson. Tobe!" The Negro appeared. "Show these gentlemen out."

II

15   So she vanquished them, horse and foot, just as she had vanquished their fathers
thirty years before about the smell. That was two years after her father's death
and a short time after her sweetheart—the one we believed would marry her—
had deserted her. After her father's death she went out very little; after her sweetheart went away, people hardly saw her at all. A few of the ladies had the temerity
to call, but were not received, and the only sign of life about the place was the
Negro man—a young man then—going in and out with a market basket.

"Just as if a man—any man—could keep a kitchen properly," the ladies said; so
they were not surprised when the smell developed. It was another link between
the gross, teeming world and the high and mighty Griersons.

A neighbor, a woman, complained to the mayor, Judge Stevens, eighty years old.

"But what will you have me do about it, madam?" he said.

"Why, send her word to stop it," the woman said. "Isn't there a law?"

20   "I'm sure that won't be necessary," Judge Stevens said. "It's probably just a
snake or a rat that nigger of hers killed in the yard. I'll speak to him about it."

The next day he received two more complaints, one from a man who came in
diffident deprecation. "We really must do something about it, Judge. I'd be the

last one in the world to bother Miss Emily, but we've got to do something." That night the Board of Aldermen met—three gray-beards and one younger man, a member of the rising generation.

"It's simple enough," he said. "Send her word to have her place cleaned up. Give her a certain time to do it in, and if she don't . . ."

"Dammit, sir," Judge Stevens said, "will you accuse a lady to her face of smelling bad?"

So the next night, after midnight, four men crossed Miss Emily's lawn and slunk about the house like burglars, sniffing along the base of the brickwork and at the cellar openings while one of them performed a regular sowing motion with his hand out of a sack slung from his shoulder. They broke open the cellar door and sprinkled lime there, and in all the outbuildings. As they recrossed the lawn, a window that had been dark was lighted and Miss Emily sat in it, the light behind her, and her upright torso motionless as that of an idol. They crept quietly across the lawn and into the shadow of the locusts that lined the street. After a week or two the smell went away.

That was when people had begun to feel really sorry for her. People in our 25 town, remembering how old lady Wyatt, her great-aunt, had gone completely crazy at last, believed that the Griersons held themselves a little too high for what they really were. None of the young men were quite good enough for Miss Emily and such. We had long thought of them as a tableau; Miss Emily a slender figure in white in the background, her father a spraddled silhouette in the foreground, his back to her and clutching a horsewhip, the two of them framed by the back-flung front door. So when she got to be thirty and was still single, we were not pleased exactly, but vindicated; even with insanity in the family she wouldn't have turned down all of her chances if they had really materialized.

When her father died, it got about that the house was all that was left to her; and in a way, people were glad. At last they could pity Miss Emily. Being left alone, and a pauper, she had become humanized. Now she too would know the old thrill and the old despair of a penny more or less.

The day after his death all the ladies prepared to call at the house and offer condolence and aid, as is our custom. Miss Emily met them at the door, dressed as usual and with no trace of grief on her face. She told them that her father was not dead. She did that for three days, with the ministers calling on her, and the doctors, trying to persuade her to let them dispose of the body. Just as they were about to resort to law and force, she broke down, and they buried her father quickly.

We did not say she was crazy then. We believed she had to do that. We remembered all the young men her father had driven away, and we knew that with nothing left, she would have to cling to that which had robbed her, as people will.

III

She was sick for a long time. When we saw her again, her hair was cut short, making her look like a girl, with a vague resemblance to those angels in colored church windows—sort of tragic and serene.

The town had just let the contracts for paving the sidewalks, and in the sum- 30 mer after her father's death they began to work. The construction company came with niggers and mules and machinery, and a foreman named Homer

Barron, a Yankee—a big, dark, ready man, with a big voice and eyes lighter than his face. The little boys would follow in groups to hear him cuss the niggers, and the niggers singing in time to the rise and fall of picks. Pretty soon he knew everybody in town. Whenever you heard a lot of laughing anywhere about the square, Homer Barron would be in the center of the group. Presently we began to see him and Miss Emily on Sunday afternoons driving in the yellow-wheeled buggy and the matched team of bays from the livery stable.

At first we were glad that Miss Emily would have an interest, because the ladies all said, "Of course a Grierson would not think seriously of a Northerner, a day laborer." But there were still others, older people, who said that even grief could not cause a real lady to forget *noblesse oblige*—without calling it *noblesse oblige*.[2] They just said, "Poor Emily. Her kinsfolk should come to her." She had some kin in Alabama; but years ago her father had fallen out with them over the estate of old lady Wyatt, the crazy woman, and there was no communication between the two families. They had not even been represented at the funeral.

And as soon as the old people said, "Poor Emily," the whispering began. "Do you suppose it's really so?" they said to one another. "Of course it is. What else could . . ." This behind their hands; rustling of craned silk and satin behind jalousies[3] closed upon the sun of Sunday afternoon as the thin, swift clop-clop-clop of the matched team passed: "Poor Emily."

She carried her head high enough—even when we believed that she was fallen. It was as if she demanded more than ever the recognition of her dignity as the last Grierson; as if it had wanted that touch of earthiness to reaffirm her imperviousness. Like when she bought the rat poison, the arsenic. That was over a year after they had begun to say "Poor Emily," and while the two female cousins were visiting her.

"I want some poison," she said to the druggist. She was over thirty then, still a slight woman, though thinner than usual, with cold, haughty black eyes in a face the flesh of which was strained across the temples and about the eyesockets as you imagine a lighthouse-keeper's face ought to look. "I want some poison," she said.

35 "Yes, Miss Emily. What kind? For rats and such? I'd recom—"

"I want the best you have. I don't care what kind."

The druggist named several. "They'll kill anything up to an elephant. But what you want is—"

"Arsenic," Miss Emily said. "Is that a good one?"

"Is . . . arsenic? Yes ma'am. But what you want—"

40 "I want arsenic."

The druggist looked down at her. She looked back at him, erect, her face like a strained flag. "Why, of course," the druggist said. "If that's what you want. But the law requires you to tell what you are going to use it for."

Miss Emily just stared at him, her head tilted back in order to look him eye for eye, until he looked away and went and got the arsenic and wrapped it up. The Negro delivery boy brought her the package; the druggist didn't come back. When she opened the package at home there was written on the box, under the skull and bones: "For rats."

2. The obligation, coming with noble or upper-class birth, to behave with honor and generosity toward those less privileged.   3. Window blinds made of adjustable horizontal slats.

IV

So the next day we all said, "She will kill herself"; and we said it would be the best thing. When she had first begun to be seen with Homer Barron, we had said, "She will marry him." Then we said, "She will persuade him yet," because Homer himself had remarked—he liked men, and it was known that he drank with the younger men in the Elk's Club—that he was not a marrying man. Later we said, "Poor Emily," behind the jalousies as they passed on Sunday afternoon in the glittering buggy, Miss Emily with her head high and Homer Barron with his hat cocked and a cigar in his teeth, reins and whip in a yellow glove.

Then some of the ladies began to say that it was a disgrace to the town and a bad example to the young people. The men did not want to interfere, but at last the ladies forced the Baptist minister—Miss Emily's people were Episcopal—to call upon her. He would never divulge what happened during that interview, but he refused to go back again. The next Sunday they again drove about the streets, and the following day the minister's wife wrote to Miss Emily's relations in Alabama.

So she had blood-kin under her roof again and we sat back to watch develop- 45 ments. At first nothing happened. Then we were sure that they were to be married. We learned that Miss Emily had been to the jeweler's and ordered a man's toilet set in silver, with the letters H. B. on each piece. Two days later we learned that she had bought a complete outfit of men's clothing, including a nightshirt, and we said, "They are married." We were really glad. We were glad because the two female cousins were even more Grierson than Miss Emily had ever been.

So we were not surprised when Homer Barron—the streets had been finished some time since—was gone. We were a little disappointed that there was not a public blowing-off, but we believed that he had gone on to prepare for Miss Emily's coming, or to give her a chance to get rid of the cousins. (By that time it was a cabal, and we were all Miss Emily's allies to help circumvent the cousins.) Sure enough, after another week they departed. And, as we had expected all along, within three days Homer Barron was back in town. A neighbor saw the Negro man admit him at the kitchen door at dusk one evening.

And that was the last we saw of Homer Barron. And of Miss Emily for some time. The Negro man went in and out with the market basket, but the front door remained closed. Now and then we would see her at a window for a moment, as the men did that night when they sprinkled the lime, but for almost six months she did not appear on the streets. Then we knew that this was to be expected too; as if that quality of her father which had thwarted her woman's life so many times had been too virulent and too furious to die.

When we next saw Miss Emily, she had grown fat and her hair was turning gray. During the next few years it grew grayer and grayer until it attained an even pepper-and-salt iron-gray, when it ceased turning. Up to the day of her death at seventy-four it was still that vigorous iron-gray, like the hair of an active man.

From that time on her front door remained closed, save for a period of six or seven years, when she was about forty, during which she gave lessons in china-painting. She fitted up a studio in one of the downstairs rooms, where the daughters and grand-daughters of Colonel Sartoris' contemporaries were sent to her with the same regularity and in the same spirit that they were sent on Sundays with a twenty-five cent piece for the collection plate. Meanwhile her taxes had been remitted.

50   Then the newer generation became the backbone and the spirit of the town, and the painting pupils grew up and fell away and did not send their children to her with boxes of color and tedious brushes and pictures cut from the ladies' magazines. The front door closed upon the last one and remained closed for good. When the town got free postal delivery Miss Emily alone refused to let them fasten the metal numbers above her door and attach a mailbox to it. She would not listen to them.

    Daily, monthly, yearly we watched the Negro grow grayer and more stooped, going in and out with the market basket. Each December we sent her a tax notice, which would be returned by the post office a week later, unclaimed. Now and then we would see her in one of the downstairs windows—she had evidently shut up the top floor of the house—like the carven torso of an idol in a niche, looking or not looking at us, we could never tell which. Thus she passed from generation to generation—dear, inescapable, impervious, tranquil, and perverse.

    And so she died. Fell ill in the house filled with dust and shadows, with only a doddering Negro man to wait on her. We did not even know she was sick; we had long since given up trying to get any information from the Negro. He talked to no one, probably not even to her, for his voice had grown harsh and rusty, as if from disuse.

    She died in one of the downstairs rooms, in a heavy walnut bed with a curtain, her gray head propped on a pillow yellow and moldy with age and lack of sunlight.

V

The Negro met the first of the ladies at the front door and let them in, with their hushed, sibilant voices and their quick, curious glances, and then he disappeared. He walked right through the house and out the back and was not seen again.

55   The two female cousins came at once. They held the funeral on the second day, with the town coming to look at Miss Emily beneath a mass of bought flowers, with the crayon face of her father musing profoundly above the bier and the ladies sibilant and macabre; and the very old men—some in their brushed Confederate uniforms—on the porch and the lawn, talking of Miss Emily as if she had been a contemporary of theirs, believing that they had danced with her and courted her perhaps, confusing time with its mathematical progression, as the old do, to whom all the past is not a diminishing road, but, instead, a huge meadow which no winter ever quite touches, divided from them now by the narrow bottleneck of the most recent decade of years.

    Already we knew that there was one room in that region above stairs which no one had seen in forty years, and which would have to be forced. They waited until Miss Emily was decently in the ground before they opened it.

    The violence of breaking down the door seemed to fill this room with pervading dust. A thin, acrid pall as of the tomb seemed to lie everywhere upon this room decked and furnished as for a bridal: upon the valance curtains of faded rose color, upon the rose-shaded lights, upon the dressing table, upon the delicate array of crystal and the man's toilet things backed with tarnished silver, silver so tarnished that the monogram was obscured. Among them lay a collar and tie, as if they had just been removed, which, lifted, left upon the surface a pale crescent in the dust. Upon a chair hung the suit, carefully folded; beneath it the two mute shoes and the discarded socks.

The man himself lay in the bed.

For a long while we just stood there, looking down at the profound and fleshless grin. The body had apparently once lain in the attitude of an embrace, but now the long sleep that outlasts love, that conquers even the grimace of love, had cuckolded him. What was left of him, rotted beneath what was left of the nightshirt, had become inextricable from the bed in which he lay; and upon him and upon the pillow beside him lay that even coating of the patient and biding dust.

Then we noticed that in the second pillow was the indentation of a head. One   60 of us lifted something from it, and leaning forward, that faint and invisible dust dry and acrid in the nostrils, we saw a long strand of iron-gray hair.

1931

Authors on Their Work: WILLIAM FAULKNER

From *Faulkner in the University* (1959)[*]

[FAULKNER:] The conflict was in Miss Emily.... She had been trained that you do not take a lover. You marry, you don't take a lover. She had broken all the laws of her tradition, her background, and she had finally broken the law of God too, which says you do not take human life. And she knew she was doing wrong, and that's why her own life was wrecked. Instead of murdering one lover, and then to go on and take another and when she used him up to murder him, she was expiating her crime.

[QUESTIONER:] ... Do you think it's fair to feel pity for her, because in a way she made her adjustment, and it seems to have wound up in a happy sort of a way—certainly tragic, but maybe it suited her just fine.

[FAULKNER:] Yes, it may have, but then I don't think that one should withhold pity simply because the subject of the pity.... is pleased and satisfied.... It's not the state of the individual, it's man in conflict with his heart, or with his fellows, or with his environment—that's what deserves the pity.

* * *

[QUESTIONER:] I was wondering, one of your short stories, "A Rose for Emily," what ever inspired you to write this story ...?

[FAULKNER:] That to me was another sad and tragic manifestation of man's condition in which he dreams and hopes, in which he is in conflict with

[*]*Faulkner in the University: Class Conferences at the University of Virginia, 1957–1958,* ed. Frederick L. Gwynn and Joseph L. Blotner (New York: Vintage, 1959), pp. 58–9, 184–5.

(Continued on next page)

(Continued)

himself or with his environment or with others. In this case there was the young girl with a young girl's normal aspirations to find love and then a husband and a family, who was brow-beaten and kept down by her father, a selfish man who didn't want her to leave home because he wanted a housekeeper, and it was a natural instinct of . . . —you can't repress it—you can mash it down but it comes up somewhere else and very likely in a tragic form, and that was simply another manifestation of man's injustice to man, of the poor tragic human being struggling with its own heart, with others, with its environment, for the simple things which all human beings want.

. . .

From *Faulkner at Nagano* (1956)**

[FAULKNER:] I feel sorry for Emily's tragedy; her tragedy was, she was an only child, an only daughter. At the time when she could have found a husband, could have had a life of her own, there was probably some one, her father, who said, "No, you must stay here and take care of me." And then when she found a man, she had had no experience in people. She picked out probably a bad one, who was about to desert her. And when she lost him she could see that for her that was the end of life, there was nothing left, except to grow older, alone, solitary; she had had something and she wanted to keep it, which is bad—to go to any length to keep something; but I pity Emily. I don't know whether I would have liked her or not, I might have been afraid of her. Not of her but of anyone who had suffered, had been warped, as her life had probably been warped by a selfish father.

. . .

[The title] was an allegorical title; the meaning was, here was a woman who had had a tragedy, an irrevocable tragedy and nothing could be done about it, and I pitied her and this was a salute . . . to a woman you would hand a rose. . . .

** *Faulkner at Nagano*, ed. Robert Jeliffe (Tokyo: Kenyusha, 1956), pp. 70–1.

CLEANTH BROOKS JR. AND ROBERT PENN WARREN

From *Understanding Fiction**

This story, like Poe's "The Fall of the House of Usher," is a story of horror. In both stories we have a decaying mansion in which the protaganist, shut away from the world, grows into something monstrous. . . . What is found in the upstairs room [at the story's end] gives perhaps a sense of more penetrating and gruesome horror than ever Poe has achieved.

*Brooks, Cleanth, Jr., and Robert Penn Warren. *Understanding Fiction*. (New York: Appleton-Century-Crofts, 1943).

It has been indicated that, in the case of Poe, the sense of horror has been conjured up for its own sake. Is this true of Faulkner's story? ... In other words, does the horror contribute to the theme of Faulkner's story? Is the horror meaningful?

In order to answer this question, we shall have to examine rather carefully some of the items earlier in the story. In the first place, why does Miss Emily commit her monstrous act? Is she supplied with a proper motivation ... ? Faulkner has been rather careful to prepare for his *dénouement*. ... Miss Emily, it becomes obvious fairly early in the story, is one of those persons for whom the distinction between reality and illusion has blurred out. For example, she refuses to admit that she owes any taxes. When the mayor protests, she does not recognize him as mayor. Instead, she refers the committee to Colonel Sartoris, who, as the reader is told, has been dead for nearly ten years. ... Most specific preparation of all, when her father dies, she denies to the townspeople for three days that he is dead. ...

Miss Emily is obviously a pathological case. The narrator indicates plainly enough that people felt that she was crazy. All of this explanation prepares us for what Miss Emily does in order to hold her lover—the dead lover is in one sense still alive for her—the realms of reality and appearance merge. But ... if Faulkner is merely interested in relating a case history of abnormal psychology, the story lacks meaning and justification as a story. ... If the story is to be justified, there must be what may be called a moral significance, a meaning in moral terms—not merely psychological terms. ...

Suppose we approach the motivation again in these terms: what is Miss Emily like? What are the mainsprings of her character? What causes the distinction between illusion and reality to blur out for her? She is obviously a woman of tremendous firmness of will. In the matter of the taxes, crazed though she is, she is never at a loss. She is utterly composed. She dominates the rather frightened committee of officers who see her. In the matter of her purchase of the poison, she completely overawes the clerk. She makes no pretenses. She refuses to tell him what she wants the poison for. And yet this firmness of will and this iron pride have not kept her from being thwarted and hurt. Her father has run off the young men who came to call upon her. ...

... [H]er pride is connected with her contempt for public opinion. This comes to the fore, of course, when she rides around about the town with the foreman whom everybody believes is beneath her. And it is her proud refusal to admit an external set of codes, or conventions, or other wills which contradict her own will, which makes her capable at the end of keeping her lover from going away. Confronted with his jilting her, she tries to override not only his will and the opinion of other people, but the laws of death and decay themselves.

But this, still, hardly gives the meaning of the story. For in all that has been said thus far, we are still merely accounting for a psychological aberration—we are still merely dealing with a case history in abnormal psychology. In order to make a case for the story as "meaningful," we shall have to tie Miss Emily's thoughts and actions back into the normal life of the community, and establish some sort of relationship between them. And just here one pervasive element in the narration suggests a clue. The story is told by one of the townspeople. And in it, as a constant factor, is the reference to what the community thought of Miss Emily. Continually through the story it is what "we" said, and then what "we" did, and what seemed true to "us," and so on. The narrator puts the matter even more sharply still. He says, in the course of the story, that to the community Miss

Emily seemed "dear, inescapable, impervious, tranquil, and perverse." Each of the adjectives is important and meaningful. In a sense, Miss Emily because of her very isolation and perversity belongs to the whole community. She is even something treasured by it. Ironically, because of Emily's perversion of an aristocratic . . . contempt for "what people say," her life is public, even communal. And various phrases used by the narrator underline this view of her position. For example, her face looks "as you imagine a lighthouse-keeper's face ought to look," like the face of a person who lives in the kind of isolation imposed on a lighthouse-keeper, who looks out into the blackness and whose light serves a public function. Or, again, after her father's death, . . . and when she appears after the illness, she has "a vague resemblance to those angels in colored church windows—sort of tragic and serene." . . . the author is trying to suggest a kind of calm and dignity which is super-mundane, unearthly, or "over-earthly," such as an angel might possess.

Miss Emily, then, is a combination of idol and scapegoat for the community. On the one hand, the community feels admiration for Miss Emily—she represents something in the past of the community which the community is proud of. . . . On the other hand, her queerness, the fact that she cannot compete with them in their ordinary life, the fact that she is hopelessly out of touch with the modern world—all of these things make them feel superior to her, and also to that past which she represents. It is, then, Miss Emily's complete detachment which gives her actions their special meaning for the community.

Miss Emily, since she is the conscious aristocrat, since she is consciously "better" than other people . . . can, at the same time, be worse than other people. . . . She is worse than other people, but at the same time, as the narrator implies, she remains somehow admirable. This raises a fundamental question: why is this true?

. . . She never cringes, she never begs for sympathy, she refuses to shrink into an amiable old maid, she never accepts the community's ordinary judgments or values. This independence of spirit and pride can, and does in her case, twist the individual into a sort of monster, but, at the same time, this refusal to accept the herd values carries with it a dignity and courage. The community senses this, as we gather from the fact that the community carries out the decencies of the funeral before breaking in the door of the upper room. There is, as it were, a kind of secret understanding that she has won her right of privacy. . . . Her funeral is something of a state occasion, with "the very old men—some in their brushed Confederate uniforms—on the porch and the lawn, talking of Miss Emily as if she had been a contemporary of theirs, believing that they had danced with her and courted her perhaps . . ." In other words, the community accepts her into its honored history. . . . The *community*, we are told earlier, had wanted to pity Miss Emily when she had lost her money, just as they had wanted to commiserate over her when they believed that she had actually become a fallen woman, but she had triumphed over their pity and commiseration and condemnation, just as she had triumphed over all their other attitudes.

. . . Her madness is simply a development of her pride and her refusal to submit to ordinary standards of behavior. So, because of this fact, her "madness" is meaningful after all. It involves issues which in themselves are really important and have to do with the world of conscious moral choice. Second, the community interprets her "madness" as meaningful. They admire her, even if they are disappointed by her refusals to let herself be pitied, and the narrator, who is a spokesman for the community, recognizes the last grim revelation as an instance of her having carried her own values to their ultimate conclusion. . . .

It has been suggested by many critics that tragedy implies a hero who is completely himself, who insists on meeting the world on his own terms, who wants something so intensely, or lives so intensely, that he cannot accept any compromise. . . . Certainly, Miss Emily's pride, isolation, and independence remind one of factors in the character of the typical tragic hero. And . . . just as the horror of her deed lies outside the ordinary life of the community, so the magnificence of her independence lies outside their ordinary virtues.

C. W. M. JOHNSON

Faulkner's "A Rose for Emily"*

The analysis of this story by Brooks and Warren in *Understanding Fiction* stops short of grasping the key to Emily's character. For her, they state, "the distinction between reality and illusion has blurred out"; and they cite her "proud refusal to admit an external set of codes." There they let the matter rest. But we can tackle the problem of Miss Emily's motivation more effectively if we say at once that the trouble with her is her obstinate refusal to submit to, or even to concede, the inevitability of change.

Hence her refusal to pay taxes. A procedure has been established and must be allowed to continue. Hence the dust in her house, which no other woman of her standing would have permitted. Hence the murder of Homer Barron (and her tolerance of his rotting corpse); he was slipping out of her life. She acts out of character only in allowing her father to be buried. Social pressure had been too great, but she learned from that incident the necessity for concealment. The story is a success story—of success in maintaining an untenable position.

It is in the sense that she resists change that Miss Emily is "impervious," and that the twice-used metaphor of the idol is justified. The theme of the story can be stated: "If one resists change, he must love and live with death," and in this theme it is difficult not to see an implied criticism of the South.

RAY B. WEST JR.

Faulkner's "A Rose for Emily"*

I agree with the major statements made by Mr. C. W. M. Johnson in his note on Faulkner's "A Rose For Emily" (Exp., May, 1948, VI, 45), especially his comment concerning the inadequate reading given the story by Brooks and Warren. However, it seems to me that there are inadequacies also in Mr. Johnson's final position. Miss Emily's resistance to change is, as Mr. Johnson states, certainly untenable; but he overlooks the important fact that she did not always resist. Faulkner implies that there was once a time when Emily would have participated in the normal activities of her age and would have been acceptable to the young

*From *Explicator* 6 (May 1948).
*From *Explicator* 7 (1948/9).

men except for her father. Then she was not a "monument" but "a slender figure in white." She does not resist change completely (she *does* allow her father to be buried) until she has known two separate betrayals, the first by her father (traditional decorum), the second by Homer Barron (modern indecorum).

The subject of the story is man's relation to Time. Emily becomes monstrous (like her house) when she resists the passage of time, and the story is a tragedy, as Brooks and Warren state. It is the story of Emily's passage from the normal time-world to a world in which she denies Time, even to the point of ignoring (Homer Barron's) Death. Faulkner's theme is suggested as a paradox in the two conflicting views of Time which he presents: (1) Time as a huge meadow which no winter ever quite touches, (2) Time as a mechanical progression in which the past is a diminishing road. Both views imply social criticism, but not of the South alone. The first suggests the South (Emily, the Griersons, the old Confederate soldiers), the second the North (Homer Barron and the "modern" younger generation). It was unnatural—even monstrous—for Emily to deny death. Death is the final sign of the passage of time, and Emily pretends that it, like the sheriff's tax bill, does not exist. (Was it vain of Colonel Sartoris to give his word that Emily would *never* be taxed? He too was resisting Time and Change.) Likewise, it proved fatal for Homer Barron to deny the traditional obligations of social decorum (past-time) and to act as though all time were present-time.

Here is depicted the dilemma of our age, not of the South alone nor of the North alone; it is the fictional portrayal of this conflict which is enacted in Emily's rose-tinted room abovestairs. If one must have a statement of theme, I would propose: "One must neither resist nor wholly accept change, for to do either is to live as though one were never to die; i. e., to live *with* Death without knowing it." Ironically, and significantly, Emily's resistance is better than Homer Barron's, for, while it is no more effective in the long run, it is certainly more "heroic". To paraphrase Mr. Johnson: here it is difficult not to see an implied criticism of the North.

WILLIAM VAN O'CONNOR

From *The State of Faulkner Criticism**

... Stressing or rather over-stressing historical and sociological, or regional, aspects of Faulkner's fiction, even when the mythic qualities are acknowledged, leads to distorting the more basic intention of many, perhaps most, of the stories—to reading them somehow as documents in a legendary history of the South. (I am not of course trying to say that one can ignore these aspects. They are inevitably and powerfully interwoven with the themes; they may have brought some of the themes sharply to his consciousness; and certainly the regional characteristics modify and qualify the ways in which the themes are developed.) Perhaps a review of Ray West's account of "A Rose for Emily" will indicate the dangers in the "historical" emphasis. West reads the story as a conflict between the values of the Old South and the new order, business-like, pragmatic, self-

*From *The Sewanee Review* 60.1 (Winter 1952): 180–85.

centered. But it can't be read in these terms because the Old South and the new order are merely a part of the flavor and tone of the story, *not* the poles of conflict. The theme is that a denial of normal emotions invites retreat into a marginal world, into fantasy. The severity of Miss Emily's father was the cause of her frustrations and her retreat. The past becomes a part of her fantasies, just as the present does. It is incidental that her relationship to the Old South makes her a part of the town's nostalgia; it was the nostalgia, not her being a "lady," which caused her to be treated reverently by the town's board when she refused to acknowledge her taxes; presumably even ladies paid their taxes in the Old South. If the conflict is between the two orders it seems curious indeed that Miss Emily would choose Homer Barron, Yankee, amoral, and without loyalty, as her beloved. And her murder of the new order, Homer Barron, is the reverse of what actually happened, the destruction of the old order by the new. The story is simple enough when read as an account of Miss Emily's becoming mad as a consequence of her frustrations, the denial to her of normal emotional relations. That the Old South, which as a physical presence (in its houses, memories, and so on) lingers in the new order and in doing so seems unreal, has its parallel, obviously, in Miss Emily, who was most strangely detached from reality. But this is a parallel only—it is not the dramatic pull or struggle that composes the action.

FLOYD C. WATKINS

The Structure of "A Rose for Emily"*

If analyses in periodicals and inclusion in anthologies are a dependable criterion for a short story, William Faulkner's "A Rose for Emily" is not only his best story, but also one of the best written by any modern American writer. Most of these treatments have especially noted the conflicts in the story between the past and the present, the South and the North, the old and the new, the traditional and the traditionless, and the gentility and the middle-lower class.

Faulkner's structural problem in "A Rose for Emily" demanded that he treat all of Miss Emily's life and her increasing withdrawal from the community and that by extreme selection he give a unity, a focus to these conflicts. Thus he divided the story into five parts and based them on incidents of isolation and intrusion. These divisions have a perfect symmetry. . . . The contrast between Emily and the townspeople and between her home and its surroundings is carried out by the invasions of her home by the adherents of the new order in the town. Each visit by her antagonists is a movement in the overall plot, a contributing element to the excellent suspense in the story, and a crisis in its own particular division of the story.

In youth Emily is not wholly separated from her somewhat sympathetic environment. In later life, however, she withdraws more and more until her own death again exposes her to the townspeople. In part one there is one invasion: after several notifications, the Board of Aldermen enter her home in a futile effort to collect her taxes. The second part describes two forced entrances into her isolation, both of them caused by a death. Four men cover her lawn with

*From *Modern Language Notes* 69.7 (Nov. 1954): 508–10.

lime and break open her cellar door to sprinkle lime there, hoping to stop a terrible odor—though they are not aware that it is caused by the rotting corpse of her poisoned lover; the burial of her dead father, the purpose of the second intrusion, is accomplished only after three days of persuasion.

The inviolability of Miss Emily's isolation is maintained in the central division, part three, in which no outsider enters her home. Her triumph is further revealed in this part when she buys the arsenic without telling what she plans to use it for. Like the second part, the fourth contains two forced entrances. The Baptist minister calls upon Miss Emily to chide her for the disgrace to the town caused by her affair with the Yankee Homer Barron; and a letter from the rebuked minister's wife causes the second intrusion, a visit from her relations in Alabama. The symmetricalness of the story is rounded out in the fifth part when the horde comes to bury a corpse, a Miss Emily no longer able to defy them.

. . . Faulkner has made the form a perfect vehicle for the content. At the center of the story is the indomitableness of the decadent Southern aristocrat, and the enclosing parts reveal the invasion of the aristocracy by the changing order.

T. J. STAFFORD

From *Tobe's Significance in "A Rose for Emily"*[*]

. . . A search for the motivation of Emily Grierson's murder of Homer Barron usually begins with an effort to understand Miss Emily herself. Until she is understood, everything remains an enigma. In trying to solve the puzzle, Brooks and Warren conclude that her behavior reflects a pride and independence of spirit which are highly regarded by Faulkner.[1] Such a view, however, fails to account for the disparity between the admirable qualities motivating the action and the ignominy of the act. To view Miss Emily in this way is to come to the story with a presupposition about what Faulkner is doing and not to look at the story as it actually operates, for the fact remains that Miss Emily's relation with Homer is an abnormal, degenerate, and meaningless human association which is unworthy of the pride it took to attain it.

In a work of art, one cannot always isolate the part he wishes to understand, for other parts may offer a necessary perspective. In this case, Faulkner's purpose becomes more clear by seeing Miss Emily in contrast to her Negro servant. While Emily occupies the foreground and provides the primary movement (a movement toward decay), the servant hovers in the background and offers a countermovement of purposeful activity. Although only ten separate references are made to the Negro, each is strategically placed and richly suggestive of his contrast with Miss Emily.

Faulkner gives a rather full impression of the servant's activities. He does the gardening, marketing, and cooking, all of which sustain Miss Emily physically.

---

[*]From *Modern Fiction Studies* 14 (Winter 1968–9): 451–53. The note is Stafford's.
1. This story, one of Faulkner's most popular, has received many interpretations, but no one has approached it, at least in print, as it is here explicated. Brooks and Warren (*Understanding Fiction*, New York, 1959) are cited as an example of the type of readings it has had.

He conducts the townsmen in and shows them out when she is finished with them, and later he admits Homer at the kitchen door. He is, as protector of Miss Emily, thought of as having killed a snake or a rat. He thus engages in purposeful and altruistic action. Miss Emily, by contrast, gives an impression of immobility, "motionless as that of an idol," an image which Faulkner reiterates. In only one section (III) is Emily able to perform action, courting Homer Barron, riding about town, and buying arsenic. Ironically, it is the only section in which the Negro does not appear, and Emily's one set of deeds, performed without the servant's being present in the story, results in violence and destruction.

The servant offers Miss Emily the means for contact with humanity in two ways. On the one hand, his errands furnish a link between her deteriorating world and human society, while on the other hand, he is in himself a whole and healthy human (a fact established by his ability to perform and to remain in contact with the world). But his provision for an access to the human heart for Miss Emily also contrasts with her condition. First, his sallies forth to the marketplace, his meeting the world that comes to her door (and turning it away only at her command), and his final liberation into the world after her death, all stand in juxtaposition to her isolation and alienation. Second, although he is himself a human, she does not even talk with him, for, as the narrator says, his voice "had grown harsh and rusty, as if from disuse."

The Negro servant's importance actually lies beyond the story's end. Faulkner suggests this meaning through the choice of name, "Tobe," emphasized by avoiding the usual spelling of "Toby" and clearly implying that he is "to be," that once he is liberated from the foul atmosphere of Miss Emily's alienation and paralysis his fulfillment will be. The ending reinforces this suggestion, for, while exposing Miss Emily's inability to engage in meaningful human associations, it frees Tobe from her decayed sphere into a world that is to be. . . .

Tobe . . . has thus been more than a servant to Miss Emily's physical needs. While serving as cook and gardener, he has demonstrated the possibility of meaningful action; while meeting the world for her, he has provided her with the means for contact with it. But she has been unable to avail herself of his humanity. . . .

While it may be true, as Brooks and Warren say, that Emily reveals pride and independence of spirit, qualities which Faulkner greatly valued, it is even more clear that in Miss Emily they do not lead to a richer life but are perverted into destruction and decay. Thus, Faulkner here qualifies his feelings about pride, demonstrating that it is insufficient in itself and that other qualities are needed to humanize it. These qualities are shown through Tobe who reveals humility, patience, endurance, courage, and pity. A clearer picture of Miss Emily's true nature is therefore given by her sharp contrast with Tobe's wholeness. Toward the end, a feeling of release is associated with Tobe as he disappears into the future and the narrator turns to lead the reader into the room of dust, death, and decay which Emily Grierson has created.

JUDITH FETTERLEY

A Rose for "A Rose for Emily"*

Justifying Faulkner's use of the grotesque has been a major concern of critics who have written on the story ["A Rose for Emily"]. If, however, one approaches "A Rose for Emily" from a feminist perspective, one notices that the grotesque aspects of the story are a result of its violation of the expectations generated by the conventions of sexual politics. The ending shocks us not simply by its hint of necrophilia; more shocking is the fact that it is a woman who provides the hint. It is one thing for Poe to spend his nights in the tomb of Annabel Lee and another thing for Miss Emily Grierson to deposit a strand of iron-gray hair on the pillow beside the rotted corpse of Homer Barron. Further, we do not expect to discover that a woman has murdered a man. . . . To reverse [the] "natural" pattern inevitably produces the grotesque.

Faulkner, however, is not interested in invoking the kind of grotesque which is the consequence of reversing the clichés of sexism for the sake of a cheap thrill. . . . Rather, Faulkner invokes the grotesque in order to illuminate and define the true nature of the conventions on which it depends. "A Rose for Emily" is a story not of a conflict between the South and the North or between the old order and the new; it is a story of the patriarchy North and South, new and old, and of the sexual conflict within it. As Faulkner himself has implied,[1] it is a story of a woman victimized and betrayed by the system of sexual politics, who nevertheless has discovered, within the structures that victimize her, sources of power for herself. . . . Faulkner's story is an analysis of how men's attitudes toward women turn back upon themselves; it is a demonstration of the thesis that it is impossible to oppress without in turn being oppressed, it is impossible to kill without creating the conditions for your own murder. "A Rose for Emily" is the story of a *lady* and of her revenge for that grotesque identity.

"When Miss Emily Grierson died, our whole town went to her funeral." The public and communal nature of Emily's funeral, a festival that brings the town together, clarifying its social relationships and revitalizing its sense of the past, indicates her central role in Jefferson. Alive, Emily is town property and the subject of shared speculation; dead, she is town history and the subject of legend. It is her value as a symbol, however obscure and however ambivalent, of something that is of central significance to the identity of Jefferson and to the meaning of its history that compels the narrator to assume a communal voice to tell her story. For Emily . . . is a man-made object, a cultural artifact, and what she is reflects and defines the culture that has produced her.

The history the narrator relates to us reveals Jefferson's continuous emotional involvement with Emily. Indeed, though she shuts herself up in a house which she rarely leaves and which no one enters, her furious isolation is in direct pro-

---

*From *The Resisting Reader: A Feminist Approach to American Fiction*, by Judith Fetterley (Bloomington and London: Indiana UP, 1978). Copyright 1978 by Judith Fetterley. Reprinted by permission. All notes are Fetterley's.

1. See *Faulkner in the University: Class Conferences at the University of Virginia 1957–1958*, edited by Frederick L. Gwynn and Joseph I. Blotner (Charlottesville: University Press of Virginia, 1959), 87–88; *Faulkner at Nagamo*, edited by Robert A. Jeliffe (Tokyo: Kenkyusha, 1956), 71.

portion to the town's obsession with her: . . . she is the object of incessant attention; her every act is immediately consumed by the town for gossip and seized on
to justify their interference in her affairs. Her private life becomes a public document that the town folk feel free to interpret at will, and they are alternately
curious, jealous, spiteful, pitying, partisan, proud, disapproving, admiring, and
vindicated. Her funeral is not simply a communal ceremony; it is also the climax
of their invasion of her private life and the logical extension of their voyeuristic
attitude toward her. Despite the narrator's demurral, getting inside Emily's house
is the all-consuming desire of the town's population, both male and female . . . :
"Already we knew that there was one room in that region above stairs which no
one had seen in forty years, and which would have to be forced. They waited until
Miss Emily was decently in the ground before they opened it."

In a context in which the overtones of violation and invasion are so palpable,
the word "decently" has that ironic ring which gives the game away. When the
men finally do break down the door, they find that Emily has satisfied their pruri-
ence with a vengeance and in doing so has created for them a mirror image of
themselves. The true nature of Emily's relation to Jefferson is contained in the
analogies between what those who break open that room see in it and what has
brought them there to see it. The perverse, violent, and grotesque aspects of the
sight of Homer Barron's rotted corpse in a room decked out for a bridal and now
faded and covered in dust reflects back to them the perverseness of their own prurient interest in Emily, the violence implicit in their continued invasions of her
life, and the grotesqueness of the symbolic artifact they have made of her—their
monument, their idol, their lady. Thus, the figure that Jefferson places at the center of its legendary history does indeed contain the clue to the meaning of that
history—a history which began long before Emily's funeral and long before Homer
Barron's disappearance or appearance and long before Colonel Sartoris' fathering
of edicts and remittances. It is recorded in that emblem which lies at the heart of
the town's memory and at the heart of patriarchal culture: "We had long thought
of them as a tableau, Miss Emily a slender figure in white in the background, her
father a spraddled silhouette in the foreground, his back to her and clutching a
horsewhip, the two of them framed by the back-flung front door."

The importance of Emily's father in shaping the quality of her life is insistent
throughout the story. Even in her death the force of his presence is felt; above her
dead body sits "the crayon face of her father musing profoundly," symbolic of the
degree to which he has dominated and shadowed her life, "as if that quality of
her father which had thwarted her woman's life so many times had been too virulent and too furious to die." The violence of this consuming relationship is made
explicit in the imagery of the tableau. Although the violence is apparently directed
outward—the upraised horsewhip against the would-be suitor—the real object of
it is the woman-daughter, forced into the background. . . . [Emily's] . . . spatial
confinement [is] . . . a metaphor for her psychic confinement: her identity is determined by the constructs of her father's mind, and she can no more escape from
his creation of her as "a slender figure in white" than she can escape his house.

What is true for Emily in relation to her father is equally true for her in relation
to Jefferson: her status as a lady is a cage from which she cannot escape. To them
she is always *Miss* Emily; she is never referred to and never thought of as otherwise.
In omitting her title from his, Faulkner emphasizes the point that the real violence done to Emily is in making her a "Miss"; the omission is one of his roses for

her. Because she is *Miss* Emily *Grierson*, Emily's father dresses her in white, places her in the background, and drives away her suitors. Because she is Miss Emily Grierson, the town invests her with that communal significance which makes her the object of their obsession and the subject of their incessant scrutiny. And because she is a lady, the town is able to impose a particular code of behavior on her ("But there were still others, older people, who said that even grief could not cause a real lady to forget *noblesse oblige*") and to see in her failure to live up to that code an excuse for interfering in her life. As a lady, Emily is venerated, but veneration results in the more telling emotions of envy and spite: "It was another link between the gross, teeming world and the high and mighty Griersons"; "People . . . believed that the Griersons held themselves a little too high for what they really were." The violence implicit in the desire to see the monument fall and reveal itself for clay suggests the violence inherent in the original impulse to venerate.

The violence behind veneration is emphasized through another telling emblem in the story. Emily's position as a hereditary obligation upon the town dates from "that day in 1894 when Colonel Sartoris, the mayor—he who fathered the edict that no Negro woman should appear on the streets without an apron on—remitted her taxes, the dispensation dating from the death of her father on into perpetuity." The conjunction of these two actions in the same syntactic unit is crucial, for it insists on their essential similarity. It indicates that the impulse to exempt is analogous to the desire to restrict, and that what appears to be a kindness or an act of veneration is in fact an insult. Sartoris' remission of Emily's taxes is a public declaration of the fact that a lady is not considered to be, and hence not allowed or enabled to be, economically independent (consider, in this connection, Emily's lessons in china painting; they are a latter-day version of Sartoris' "charity" and a brilliant image of Emily's economic uselessness). His act is a public statement of the fact that a lady, if she is to survive, must have either husband or father, and that, because Emily has neither, the town must assume responsibility for her. . . . Indeed, the use of the word "fathered" in describing Sartoris' behavior as mayor underlines the fact that his chivalric attitude toward Emily is simply a subtler and more dishonest version of her father's horsewhip.

The narrator is the last of the patriarchs who take upon themselves the burden of defining Emily's life, and his violence toward her is the most subtle of all. His tone of incantatory reminiscence and nostalgic veneration seems free of the taint of horsewhip and edict. Yet a thoroughgoing contempt for the "ladies" who spy and pry and gossip out of their petty jealousy and curiosity is one of the clearest strands in the narrator's consciousness. Emily is exempted from the general indictment because she is a *real* lady—that is, eccentric, slightly crazy, obsolete, a "stubborn and coquettish decay," absurd but indulged; "dear, inescapable, impervious, tranquil, and perverse"; indeed, anything and everything but human.

Not only does "A Rose for Emily" expose the violence done to a woman by making her a lady; it also explores the particular form of power the victim gains from this position and can use on those who enact this violence. . . . One of the most striking aspects of the story is the disparity between Miss Emily Grierson and the Emily to whom Faulkner gives his rose in ironic imitation of the chivalric behavior the story exposes. The form of Faulkner's title establishes a camaraderie between author and protagonist and signals that a distinction must be made between the story Faulkner is telling and the story the narrator is telling. This distinction is of major importance because it suggests, of course, that the narrator, looking through a patriarchal lens, does not see Emily at all but rather a figment of his own imagination created in conjunction with the cumulative imagination of the town:. . . nobody sees *Emily*. And because nobody sees *her*, she can literally get away with murder. Emily is characterized by her ability to understand and utilize the power that accrues to her from the fact that men do not see her but rather their concept of her: "'I have no taxes in Jefferson. Colonel Sartoris explained it to me. . . . Tobe! . . . Show these gentlemen out." Relying on the conventional assumptions about ladies who are expected to be neither reasonable nor in touch with reality, Emily presents an impregnable front that vanquishes the men "horse and foot, just as she had vanquished their fathers thirty years before." In spite of their "modern" ideas, this new generation, when faced with Miss Emily, are as much bound by the code of gentlemanly behavior as their fathers were ("They rose when she entered"). This code gives Emily a power that renders the gentlemen unable to function in a situation in which a lady neither sits down herself nor asks them to. They are brought to a "stumbling halt" and can do nothing when confronted with her refusal to engage in rational discourse. Their only recourse in the face of such eccentricity is to engage in behavior unbecoming to gentlemen, and Emily can count on their continuing to see themselves as gentlemen and her as a lady and on their returning a verdict of helpless noninterference.

It is in relation to Emily's disposal of Homer Barron, however, that Faulkner demonstrates most clearly the power of conventional assumptions about the nature of ladies to blind the town to what is going on and to allow Emily to murder with impunity. When Emily buys the poison, it never occurs to anyone that she intends to use it on Homer, so strong is the presumption that ladies when jilted commit suicide, not murder. And when her house begins to smell, the women blame it on the eccentricity of having a man servant rather than a woman, "as if a man—any man—could keep a kitchen properly." And when they hint that her eccentricity may have shaded over into madness, "remembering how old lady Wyatt, her great aunt, had gone completely crazy at last." The presumption of madness, that preeminently female response to bereavement, can be used to explain away much in the behavior of ladies whose activities seem a bit odd.

But even more pointed is what happens when the men try not to explain but to do something about the smell: "'Dammit, sir,' Judge Stevens said, 'will you accuse a lady to her face of smelling bad?'" But if a lady cannot be told that she smells, then the cause of the smell cannot be discovered and so her crime is "perfect." Clearly, the assumptions behind the Judge's outraged retort go beyond the myth that ladies are out of touch with reality. His outburst insists that it is the responsibility of gentlemen to make them so. Ladies must not be confronted with facts; they must be shielded from all that is unpleasant. Thus Colonel Sartoris remits Emily's taxes with a palpably absurd story, designed to protect her from an awareness of her poverty and her dependence on charity, and to protect him from having to confront her with it. And thus Judge Stevens will not confront Emily with the fact that her house stinks, though she is living in it and can hardly be unaware of the odor. Committed as they are to the myth that ladies and bad smells cannot coexist, these gentlemen insulate themselves from reality. And by defining a lady as a subhuman and hence sublegal entity, they have created a situation their laws can't touch. They have made it possible for Emily to be extra-legal: "'Why, of course,' the druggist said, 'If that's what you want.

But the law requires you to tell what you are going to use it for.' Miss Emily just stared at him, her head tilted back in order to look him eye for eye, until he looked away and went and got the arsenic and wrapped it up." And, finally, they have created a situation in which they become the criminals: "So the next night, after midnight, four men crossed Miss Emily's lawn and slunk about the house like burglars." Above them, "her upright torso motionless as that of an idol," sits Emily, observing them act out their charade of chivalry. As they leave, she confronts them with the reality they are trying to protect her from: she turns on the light so that they may see her watching them. One can only wonder at the fact, and regret, that she didn't call the sheriff and have them arrested for trespassing.

Not only is "A Rose for Emily" a supreme analysis of what men do to women by making them ladies; it is also an exposure of how this act in turn defines and recoils upon men. This is the significance of the dynamic that Faulkner establishes between Emily and Jefferson. And it is equally the point of the dynamic implied between the tableau of Emily and her father and the tableau which greets the men who break down the door of that room in the region above the stairs. When the would-be "suitors" finally get into her father's house, they discover the consequences of his oppression of her, for the violence contained in the rotted corpse of Homer Barron is the mirror image of the violence represented in the tableau, the back-flung front door flung back with a vengeance. Having been consumed by her father, Emily in turn feeds off Homer Barron, becoming, after his death, suspiciously fat. Or, to put it another way, it is as if, after her father's death, she has reversed his act of incorporating her by incorporating and becoming him, metamorphosed from the slender figure in white to the obese figure in black whose hair is "a vigorous iron-gray, like the hair of an active man." She has taken into herself the violence in him which thwarted her and has reenacted it upon Homer Barron.

That final encounter, however, is not simply an image of the reciprocity of violence. Its power of definition also derives from its grotesqueness, which makes finally explicit the grotesqueness that has been latent in the description of Emily throughout the story: "Her skeleton was small and spare; perhaps that was why what would have been merely plumpness in another was obesity in her. She looked bloated, like a body long submerged in motionless water, and of that pallid hue. Her eyes, lost in the fatty ridges of her face, looked like two small pieces of coal pressed into a lump of dough." The impact of this description depends on the contrast it establishes between Emily's reality as a fat, bloated figure in black and the conventional image of a lady—expectations that are fostered in the town by its emblematic memory of Emily as a slender figure in white and in us by the narrator's tone of romantic invocation and by the passage itself. Were she not expected to look so different, were her skeleton not small and spare, Emily would not be so grotesque. Thus, the focus is on the grotesqueness that results when stereotypes are imposed upon reality. And the implication of this focus is that the real grotesque is the stereotype itself. If Emily is both lady and grotesque, then the syllogism must be completed thus: the idea of a lady is grotesque. So Emily is metaphor and mirror for the town of Jefferson; and when, at the end, the town folk finally discover who and what she is, they have in fact encountered who and what they are. . . . The efforts to read "A Rose for Emily" as a parable of the relations between North and South, or as a conflict between an old order and a new, or as a story about the human relation to Time, don't work because the attempt to make Emily representative of such concepts stumbles over the fact that woman's condition is not the "human" condition.[2] To understand Emily's experience requires a primary awareness of the fact that she is a woman.

But, more important, Faulkner provides us with an image of retaliation. [Emily] does not simply acquiesce; she prefers to murder rather than to die. In this respect she is a welcome change from the image of woman as willing victim that fills the pages of our literature. . . . Nevertheless, Emily's action is still reaction. "A Rose for Emily" exposes the poverty of a situation in which turnabout is the only possibility and in which one's acts are neither self-generated nor self-determined but are simply a response to and a reflection of forces outside oneself. Though Emily may be proud, strong, and indomitable, her murder of Homer Barron is finally an indication of the severely limited nature of the power women can wrest from the system that oppresses them. . . . Emily's act . . . is possible only because it can be kept secret; and it can be kept secret only at the cost of exploiting her image as a lady. . . .

Patriarchal culture is based to a considerable extent on the argument that men and women are made for each other and on the conviction that "masculinity" and "feminity" are the natural reflection of that divinely ordained complement. Yet, if one reads . . . "A Rose for Emily" as [an] analys[i]s of the consequences of a massive differentiation of everything according to sex, one sees that in reality a sexist culture is one in which men and women are not simply incompatible but murderously so. . . . Emily murders Homer Barron because she must at any cost get a man. The [gap] . . . between cultural myth and cultural reality . . . suggest[s] that in this disparity is the ultimate grotesque.

THOMAS KLEIN

*The Ghostly Voice of Gossip in Faulkner's "A Rose for Emily"**

William Faulkner's famous story "A Rose for Emily" concludes with this line: "We saw a long strand of iron-gray hair." Its effect derives especially from two features: the story's complex chronology and the unusual voice of the narrator. In this article, I will explore that voice and suggest a possible model for it.

From the beginning of the story, we notice several curious things about this voice. First, the narrator studiously avoids identifying his or her own sex: "Our whole town went, [. . .] the men through a respectful affection [. . .] the women mostly out of curiosity to see the inside of her house" (167). Similarly, the narrator avoids signaling allegiance to a particular generation. . . .

Things would be simple if, from the opening, the narrator simply reported what he or she observed people doing. Certainly, this happens at points, for instance when the narrator remarks, "When [. . .] it got about that the house was all that

---

2. For a sense of some of the difficulties involved in reading the story in these terms, I refer the reader to the collection of criticism edited by M. Thomas Inge, *A Rose for Emily* (Columbus, Ohio: Merrill, 1970).
*From *Explicator* 65.4 (Summer 2007): 229–32.

was left to her, [. . .] people were glad" (173). The narrator might reasonably profess knowledge of what had "got about." . . . Sometimes we even learn the source: "Homer Barron was back in town. A neighbor saw the Negro man admit him at the kitchen door" (178). . . .

But what do we make of those moments when the narrator purports to speak for the town, but logic tells us that he or she cannot be doing so? For, whereas it is easy to imagine someone reporting a group consensus such as "[a]t first we were glad that Miss Emily would have an interest" (174) . . . , it is harder to imagine when we read, "We had long thought of them as a tableau" (172). Can a group of people think of something "as a tableau"? Likewise, a group could hardly have produced this line of thinking: "We did not say she was crazy then. We believed she had to do that. We remembered all the young men her father had driven away, and we knew [. . .] she would have to cling to that which had robbed her" (173).

We may conclude that, at such moments, the narrator is using the corporate "we" but indicating what he or she, as an individual, thought or did. This works up to a point. The difficulty is that so much of what the story claims "we said" or "we learned" reflects the incoherence (and cruelty) of group thought. Perhaps the best example is found in section 3, which begins, "So the next day we all said, 'She will kill herself'; and we said it would be the best thing" (176). Say what? The statement's harshness is tempered only by the difficulty of placing it in the temporal movement of the narrative. For immediately following this statement, the story shifts backward: "When she had first begun to be seen with Homer Barron, we had said, 'She will marry him.' Then we said, 'She will persuade him yet.'" The two cousins are called into town, and "we learned that Miss Emily had been to the jeweler's [. . .] and we said, 'They are married'" (177). The comment that follows, "We were glad," seems sympathetic, but then we read, "We were glad because the two cousins were even more Grierson than Miss Emily had ever been." Finally, further on we read, "By that time it was a cabal, and we were all Miss Emily's allies to help circumvent the cousins" (178). The idea that it would be "best" that Emily take her own life has been forgotten in the general babble of contradictory and self-interested conclusions, which derive apparently from the town's conversation with itself.

Even more curious are those instances where a third-person account is later revised into the first person. In section 3, we read, "As soon as the old people said, 'Poor Emily,' the whispering began. 'Do you suppose it's really so?' they said to one another. [. . .] This behind their hands; rustling of craned silk and satin behind jalousies" (175). Here, the narrator takes an ironic, almost writerly view of the townspeople. But in section 4, the narrator relocates himself or herself among them: "Later *we* said, 'Poor Emily' behind the jalousies" (177; emphasis added). Similarly, we may be surprised to find that although originally it was "the next generation" of aldermen who mailed the tax notices, the narrator later reports, "Each December *we* sent her a tax notice" (180; emphasis added). It is as if all points of view were being given over to this creeping "we," hedging Emily's story round with susurrating voices. . . .

Where did Faulkner get this voice? I would like to suggest that he was thinking of, and wanted readers to recall, the gossipy, first-person style of society columnists, especially that found in the "The Talk of the Town" section of the *New Yorker*. "A Rose" was first published in April 1930 (Inge 1). The column appeared with the 1925 debut of the magazine, and its special style was developed by writers such as E. B. White and James Thurber. Lillian Ross explains that "Harold Ross, the magazine's founding editor, [. . .] wanted the department to sound like 'our' voice, the voice of the magazine." In those early days, readers of the magazine might encounter such sentences as "In these particular twilights, we don't know any place in the world we'd rather not be than in the country, russet and golden and beautiful though we know perfectly well it is" ("Talk," 6 Oct. 1928) or "[a]t the earliest possible moment we intend to drop what we are doing and go out of our way to make his acquaintance" ("Talk," 3 Dec. 1927). Did Faulkner know the *New Yorker*? It seems likely; later, in fall 1931, he visited New York and was the topic of a "Talk" article (28 Nov. 1931).

Faulkner described "A Rose for Emily" as "a ghost story" (Gwynn and Blotner 26). So who is the ghost? Assuming Faulkner was not just using a generic classification, there are several candidates: obviously Miss Emily, "the carven torso of an idol in a niche" (180); the disappeared Homer Barron; the wraithlike Tobe. But the voice of the town is the most ghostlike: pervasive, shape-shifting, haunting. No wonder Miss Emily stayed indoors.

WORKS CITED

Faulkner, William. "A Rose for Emily." *These Thirteen: Stories by William Faulkner.* New York: Cape, 1931. 167–82.

Gwynn, Frederick L., and Joseph Blotner, eds. *Faulkner in the University: Class Conferences at the University of Virginia, 1957–1958.* 1959. New York: Random House, 1965.

Inge, M. Thomas, ed. *William Faulkner: A Rose for Emily.* Merrill Literary Casebook Ser. Columbus: Merrill, 1970.

Ross, Lillian. Interview with Susan Morrison. *New Yorker Online Only.* 7 May 2001. <www.newyorker.com/online/content/articles/010514on_onlineonly01>.

"The Talk of the Town." *The Complete New Yorker.* DVD. New York: Bondi Digital, 2005.

LAWRENCE R. RODGERS

From *"We all said, 'She will kill herself'"*: The Narrator / Detective in William Faulkner's *"A Rose for Emily"**

William Faulkner's most famous short story, "A Rose for Emily," is a classic expression of American gothicism. Rich in interpretive possibility and long a critical favorite, this 1929 story is a dark parable of the decline of southern sensibility. Its impact relies on a slow accretion of atmospheric detail, with each new

*From *Clues: A Journal of Detection* 16 (1995): 117–29. Some of Rodgers's notes and works cited have been omitted.

detail further illuminating the many mysteries surrounding the life of confederate matriarch Emily Grierson. The story also may be read within the framework of a related popular genre, the classical detective story, whose American origins are traced to Edgar Allan Poe. It is commonly known that Faulkner learned much about genre-writing from his fellow southerner. He capitalized on Poe's legacy in novels such as *Intruder in the Dust* (1948) and *Knight's Gambit* (1949) as well as in "An Error in Chemistry," his 1946 short story published in *Ellery Queen's Mystery Magazine*. Faulkner's ability to expand and rework the devices of the detective story in these later works makes him a worthy successor to Poe.[1] But it is in the earlier, less straightforward story of detection, "A Rose for Emily," that Faulkner's lifelong interest in shaping his fiction around the theme of detection can be observed in its nascent form, and the important presence of the detective figure throughout his fiction can begin to be more fully appreciated. . . .

In his well-known discussion of detective story conventions in *Adventure, Mystery and Romance*, John Cawelti provides a useful, simple litmus test for establishing whether a text follows the classical detective formula. In his scheme, there are three conditions that must be met: 1) the story must have a mystery that needs solving; 2) there must be concealed facts that a detective has to explore; and 3) these facts must become clear in the end (132). "A Rose for Emily" easily satisfies these conditions. Homer Barron, a laborer from the North, comes to work in the tightly knit community of Jefferson, Mississippi. After he is seen in the company of Emily, the eccentric daughter of one of Jefferson's finest families, Homer's courtship fuels town gossip. Various loosely related details soon mount up to suggest something is seriously amiss. Homer mysteriously disappears, reappears and then disappears again not long after Miss Emily purchases rat poison. A foul smell emanates from her old home, causing some men from the town to sneak into her yard to sprinkle it with lime. Emily herself goes through profound physical changes, growing fat and grey-headed. Finally, after her death, Homer's disappearance is solved in what Irving Howe has wryly noted makes for a hair-raising conclusion (265). Miss Emily, aware of the town's penchant for judgment, ruled by the codes of etiquette of a once-proud lineage, and unable to fathom the changing conditions of the new South, has indeed poisoned Homer and retreated (with his corpse) into the recesses of her attic, where, liberated from prying eyes, she has been allowed to carry on her illicit love affair in post-mortem privacy. The evidence betraying her necrophilia is a single strand of iron-grey hair lying on a head-shaped indentation next to the corpse, which, much like the values that Emily tried to uphold by removing her affairs from public view, has become a grotesque, rotted perversion of its former self.

In light of all the praise given over to the originality, ambiguity, technical merit, and skillful manipulation of discontinuous, fragmentary narrative time in "A Rose for Emily," it is, within these considerations, an interestingly conventional detective tale. Its pattern of action is ordered around the basic elements of the popular genre: a southern setting circumscribing an eerie, decaying mansion; a curious disappearance; portents of a murder, in this case a poisoning; an unlikely, peculiar suspect, and a mysterious locked room whose assortment of clues turns up a corpse, a murderer and, finally, a solution to a macabre but oddly

---

1. For discussions of Faulkner's debt to Poe, see especially Cawelti, 134; Irwin; and Stronks, 11.

plausible crime. What appears to be missing here is the detective, the detached figure whose analytic insight allows him (or, more rarely, her) to solve the crime and thus restore rationality and a sense of order to a world of uncertainty.

However, on examination, we find that Faulkner (who made a career of stretching the boundaries of convention, literary and otherwise, to suit his own needs) provides a kind of detective, but with an inventive twist. Cawelti notes that a detective story need not contain a professional crime solver like a Maigret, a Dupin or a Holmes as long as some character "performs the role of successful inquirer" (132).

In "A Rose for Emily" the unnamed narrator that pieces together the fragmented decline of the Grierson lineage plays just such a role. More originally, this narrator/detective is also an unknowing driving force behind Emily's crime. Speaking in the "we" voice, the narrator, an overwhelming presence throughout the narrative, embodies the town's shared sentiments toward Emily. Having spent years not only observing but also commenting and rendering judgment upon the woman described as "a tradition, a duty, and a care,"[2] this *vox populi* is so persistent in assuming its natural right to intrude on Emily's life, that she—obsessively mindful of the need to honor the town's, and her father's, rigid code of genteel behavior—chooses murder rather than a public flouting of the town's values. The dramatic distance on display here provides an ironic layer to the narrative. As the observers of the conflict between the teller-of-tale's desire to solve the curious mysteries that surround Emily's life—indeed, his complicity in shaping them—and his undetective-like detachment from her crimes, readers occupy the tantalizing position of having insight into unraveling the mystery which the narrator lacks.

A classical detective story, quite simply, begins with an unsolved crime and moves toward its solution. Introduced into a world of ambiguity, mystery, and multiple possibilities, the reader is steadily made aware of key details that eventually allow a series of events to be placed into a comprehendable order. In "A Rose for Emily" the air of mystery commences with the first sentence: "When Miss Emily Grierson died, our whole town went to her funeral: the men through a sort of respectful affection for a fallen monument, the women mostly out of curiosity to see the inside of her house, which no one save an old manservant . . . had seen in at least ten years" (119). Playing off the detective convention of entering a locked room and delaying the revelation of its contents until the story's conclusion, this teasing beginning invites the reader to participate in unraveling the mysteries that have led up to Emily's funeral. However, making order out of Emily's life is a complicated matter, since the narrator recalls the details through a non-linear filter.

Cloaking an additional layer of mystery on Emily's story, the narrator's disjointed, associational recollection of details has led readers and critics to become the surrogate detectives of Faulkner's world. They have tried to "unscramble" the chronology and thus "solve" the structural ambiguities of the story by reconstructing Faulkner's calendar.[3] With evidence sparse and at times contradictory,

---

2. All subsequent quotes from the primary text are from *Collected Stories of William Faulkner*, 119–30, and will be cited internally by page number.

3. In the Merrill Literary Casebook series for "A Rose for Emily," editor M. Thomas Inge reprints four articles that posit slightly different time-lines, all of which focus on the story's chronology: see 34, 50–53, 83, 84–86, 90–92.

these attempts, relying on close reading, conjecture, and extra-textual evidence, have yielded several slightly different time-lines. Although these time-lines claim to be pedagogically useful in allowing students to grasp "the elusive, illusive quality of time that lies at the heart of the story" (Going 53), their more immediate appeal is as a kind of armchair detective's game. They offer the challenge of taking the story's one exact reference to time (the remitting of Colonel Sartoris, taxes "in 1894") and combining it with the two dozen or so more approximate references to come up with a set of dates corresponding to the major events of Emily's life. Since the temporal world of Faulkner's Yoknapatawpha County remains relatively consistent (if inexact) throughout his entire corpus, other texts besides "A Rose for Emily," like his 1929 novel *Sartoris*, also help provide clues. Thus the more familiar the detective-critic becomes with the entire Faulkner corpus, the more equipped he or she is to place the events of Emily's life in the context of Yoknapatawpha County's overall pattern of myth.

But beyond offering superficial clarification about the plot, an exact chronology hardly seems to matter. As is invariably the case with Faulkner, appreciating the text's brilliance only begins with comprehending the plot, however ordered. Reduced to its basic situation, "A Rose for Emily" is fairly standard melodrama, probably loosely based on a conflation of actual odd events that occurred around Oxford in the 1920s (cf. Cullen and Watkins 70–71). Faulkner's plots can be brilliantly imagined, but what infuses this particular story with its force is the *manner* in which the plot is related to us by the purportedly innocuous observer of Emily's life. In other words, Faulkner conceives of "A Rose for Emily" quite cunningly by bending the traditional presentation of the detective. The narrative's overwhelming presence is the narrator himself, speaking as a representative voice of Jefferson (or, in using the "we" pronoun throughout, perhaps even as the collective voice of the town). In culling the data of Emily's life, the narrator/detective's favored posture is, in the classic mode of the genre, one of surveillance and, less classically, one of judgment. From the initial sentence, the narrator demands not just to retell the events of Emily's life, but to relish the manner in which the town intrudes upon them. Town members try to collect her taxes, insist on burying her father, attempt to rid her house of its odor, force the Baptist minister and her Alabama relatives into her home, and, after her death, eagerly break into her mysterious upstairs room.

Fully in keeping with the town's invasive aesthetic of observation, the narrator/detective's willingness to pass judgment on all he witnesses so completely overturns the illusion of objectivity that he speaks, if you will, not as the detached soloist of a Greek chorus, but as a prime participant in the tragic drama he relates. The ways of interpreting Emily's decision to murder Homer are numerous, as the many critical pieces on the story bear out. For simple clarification, they can be summarized along two lines. One group finds the murder growing out of Emily's demented attempt to forestall the inevitable passage of time—toward her abandonment by Homer, toward her own death, and toward the steady encroachment of the North and the New South on something loosely defined as the "tradition" of the Old South. Another view sees the murder in more psychological terms. It grows out of Emily's complex relationship to her father, who, by elevating her above all of the eligible men of Jefferson, insured that to yield to what one commentator called the "normal emotions" associated with desire, his daughter had to "retreat into a marginal world, into fantasy" (O'Connor 184).

These lines of interpretation complement more than critique each other, and 10
collectively they offer an interesting range of views on the story. Together, they
de-emphasize the element of detection, viewing the murder and its solution not
as the central action but as manifestations of the principal element, the decline
of the Grierson lineage and all it represents. Recognizing the way in which the
story makes use of the detective genre, however, adds another interpretive layer
to the story by making the narrator—or more precisely, the collective sensibility
the narrator represents—a central player in the pattern of action. Detective stories typically place less emphasis on the crime, the criminal, and the victim than
on the detective. Detectives such as Dupin, Holmes, Poirot, Sergeant Cuff, Dr.
Gideon Fell, and Nero Wolfe may be detached from the society they observe but
they still rest at the center of the author's narrative world. Faulkner bends his
narrator/detective in some obvious ways away from these more traditional
examples. Strictly speaking, his detective is no nearer Poe's Dupin than Emily is
a re-creation of Minister D, the master criminal of "The Purloined Letter." But
the narrative is an ongoing investigation of Emily's life and the narrator is the
principal detective in this investigation.

Much of the story's action is centered around the combination of Emily's
desire to remain isolated and the narrator and his fellow townsfolk's refusal to
honor that desire. Consider, among many examples, the language of intrusion
and judgment implied in the following passages.

They were not surprised when the smell developed.

That was when people had begun to feel really sorry for her. People in our
town . . . believed that the Griersons held themselves a little too high for what
they really were.

So when she got to be thirty and was still single, we were not pleased exactly,
but vindicated.

When her father died, it got about that the house was all that was left to her;
and in a way, people were glad. At last they could pity Miss Emily.

We did not say she was crazy then. We believed she had to do that.

As soon as the old people said, "Poor Emily," the whispering began.

She carried her head high enough—even when we believed that she was fallen.

And finally, the story's most startling and significant statement made shortly
after Emily purchases rat poison: "So the next day we all said, 'she will kill herself'; and *we said it would be the best thing*" (my emphasis, 121–26). The town, it is
evident, has made Emily its obsession, with every detail of her life subject to discussion, speculation and assessment. Without means by which to carry on her
affair in public (and a noticeably diminishing lack of interest on Homer's part,
since he "liked men" and was not ready to settle down), Emily insures her isolation in a cunningly ironic and comic verbal reversal on the town's recommendation of suicide; she herself kills Homer Barron, and from the town's point of
view, it was the best thing.

"The detective novel features two expulsions of 'bad' or socially unfit characters: the victim and the murderer" (Grella 49). In the context of the genre, as
George Grella describes it, Homer is a classic victim because he is guilty of an

unpardonable crime against the community. He was born in the North, which in the world of Jefferson, Mississippi, since the days of the Civil War, has been a capital offense. After he disappears, no more attention is paid to him ("that was the last we saw of Homer Barron" [127]). The town's purported lack of interest can be formally explained as a crafty plotting device of Faulkner's to draw suspicion away from the existence of the murder (which is further obscured by the temporal shifts in the narrative). To this end, the narrator casually mentions Homer for the first time in the story as the "sweetheart" who "deserted" Emily. But it is also significant that as a northerner—as well as a common day-laborer— Homer represents the kind of unwelcomed resident and ineligible mate the town wants to repel if it is to preserve its traditional arrangements. His very proximity to Emily is, according to Jefferson's ladies, "a disgrace to the town and a bad example to the young people" (126). Homer is, to echo Grella's apt phrase, "an exceptionally murderable man" (49)—a victim whose disappearance invites a conspiracy of silence.

The very failure of the narrator and the town to "solve" the crime until the murderer herself has died indicates much about the true nature of the society in which the murder occurred. If we assume that the narrator/detective and other townsfolk know about the crime (although the textual evidence for this can only be ambiguously inferred), we also realize that for the town to reveal Emily's crime and indicate what it will do in response is far more complicated than silently ignoring the entire matter. For the people of Jefferson, the illusion of *noblesse oblige* is to be preserved at all costs, whether it means remitting Emily's taxes, inviting her Alabama kinfolk to come to Jefferson and regulate her embarrassing courtship, or ignoring a murder by passing off the foul smell emanating from her house shortly after Homer's disappearance as "probably just a snake or a rat."

. . . The statement can be read several ways. It emphasizes Emily's status as a Poe-like "least-likely" criminal, a misfit so unsuited for the role of murderer that the town's leading citizen does not suspect her. In this light, the Judge's pronouncement is not a red herring, but its opposite, a statement that has the effect of allowing a very real clue to be introduced before allowing a purportedly disinterested observer to shift the narrative's emphasis away from the crime. However, it can also be suggested that, given the facts at hand (e.g., Emily's resistance to allowing her father to be buried and Stevens' reluctance to accuse a "lady" of smelling bad), Stevens' statement is not the naive observation of a casual onlooker but a conveniently calculating means on his part of preserving order, glossing over the rather obvious fact that a well-known citizen has a murder victim rotting inside her house. Where the reader stands in relation to the very tangible clue of the smell depends on his or her willingness to accept the judge's explanation at face value. Like the best detective writers, Faulkner is able to offer pieces of information about the crime, thus putting the careful reader on equal footing with characters in the story, but to do so in such a way as to delay the obvious solution until more substantial proof of the murder comes forth.

15   That proof comes in the story's final three paragraphs, beginning with the one-sentence paragraph: "The man himself lay in the bed." The crime is both confirmed and solved; the detective pattern is compressed into one climactic scene, which inventively re-imagines a version of Poe's "locked room" mystery, "The Murders in the Rue Morgue." In the classic locked-room story, Dupin

unravels the story behind a mother and daughter's murder, which has occurred in an apartment where all the windows and doors are sealed from the inside. In Faulkner's version, a victim's body is similarly discovered inside a mysterious upstairs room, whose door has to be broken down to gain admittance. But since the killer's identity and the mechanism of the murder are readily apparent, the narrator's puzzle is not solved simply by answering "who done it" and "how she done it." The narrator has the more challenging goal of comprehending the gruesome spectacle in the context of the town's obsession with Emily's entire life. This is accomplished with the minuscule clue of a single strand of hair, a temporarily "hidden object" that once detected sets Emily's disturbed mind state into stark relief and provides the town with just the kind of hindsight evidence it needs to justify all of the attention it paid to her over the years.

Finally, in a single sentence, Faulkner skillfully brings the mystery to a close and leaves the reader to reflect upon the narrator/detective's involvement in Emily's deranged decision to murder Homer Barron. As an inventive precursor to Faulkner's own later detective characters, this narrator is an example of how the author, rather than simply mimicking other detective stories, re-worked the classical devices of detection to suit his own ends. "A Rose for Emily" is a notable example of Faulkner's talent for taking the raw materials of his surroundings and working them into original forms—whether this meant drawing from his literary antecedents, re-configuring actual events, or delving into his own considerable imagination. John T. Irwin, in his discussion of *Knight's Gambit*, sets Faulkner next to Poe as a "worthy successor" and a "formidable competitor to the [detective] genre's originator" (173). When viewed as a detective story, "A Rose for Emily" helps buttress this claim and thereby furthers our appreciation of Faulkner's lifelong interest in laying out and then solving the many curious mysteries of what he famously termed his "own little postage stamp of native soil" (qtd. in Minter 76).

WORKS CITED

Cawelti, John G. *Adventure, Mystery, and Romance: Formula Stories as Art and Popular Culture*. Chicago: U of Chicago P, 1976.

Cullen, John B., and Floyd C. Watkins, *Old Times in the Faulkner Country*. Chapel Hill: U of North Carolina P, 1961.

Faulkner, William. *Collected Stories of William Faulkner*. New York: Vintage, 1977.

Going, William T. "Chronology in Teaching 'A Rose for Emily.'" *A Rose for Emily*. Ed. M. Thomas Inge. Columbus: Merrill, 1970. 50–53.

Grella, George. "Murder and Manners: The Formal Detective Novel." *Dimensions of Detective Fiction*. Ed. Larry N. Landrum, Pat Browne, and Ray B. Browne. Bowling Green, OH: Bowling Green State U Popular P, 1976. 37–57.

Inge, M. Thomas, ed. *A Rose for Emily*. Columbus: Merrill, 1970.

Irwin, John T. "*Knight's Gambit*: Poe, Faulkner, and the Tradition of the Detective Story." *Faulkner and the Short Story*. Ed. Evans Harrington and Ann J. Abadie. Jackson: U of Mississippi P, 1992. 149–73.

Karl, Frederick R. *William Faulkner: An American Writer*. New York: Weidenfeld and Nicolson, 1989.

Minter, David. *William Faulkner: His Life and Work*. Baltimore: Johns Hopkins UP, 1980.

O'Connor, William. "The State of Faulkner Criticism." *Sewanee Review* 60 (1952): 184.

Stronks, James. "A Poe Source for Faulkner? 'To Helen' and 'A Rose for Emily.'" *Poe Newsletter* I (Apr. 1968): 11.

SUGGESTIONS FOR WRITING

1. William Faulkner's "A Rose for Emily" shares its southern setting with several other stories in this book: one by Eudora Welty ("Why I Live at the P.O." in "Reading More Fiction") and three by Flannery O'Connor ("A Good Man Is Hard to Find," "The Lame Shall Enter First," and "Everything That Rises Must Converge" in chapter 8). What makes each of these stories distinctively "southern"? Does "southern" mean the same thing to each of these authors? Write an essay in which you compare and contrast the southern setting of "A Rose for Emily" with the setting of at least one of these other stories.

2. What information can a reader detect, or infer, about the narrator of "A Rose for Emily"? What sort of person or persons could be telling the story (young, old, male, female, black, white, a southern local or a northern visitor)? Does the narrator share all the values of the townspeople, or express any mixed feelings about their views or behavior? Does Faulkner (or the implied author of the story) share all the narrator's attitudes, or does the story place the narrator at a certain ironic distance from author and reader? Write an essay in which you characterize the authority and limitations of the narrator in relation to the society of Jefferson and to the implied author of the story.

3. In his essay "We all said, 'She will kill herself,'" Lawrence R. Rodgers argues that "A Rose for Emily" is, in fact, essentially a detective story. Do you agree? Does it really matter whether or not "A Rose for Emily" is a certain "kind" of fiction? Write an essay in which you either agree or disagree with Rodgers's approach to the story and the significance of that approach.

4. In "The State of Faulkner Criticism," William Van O'Connor argues that critics err when they suggest that the central conflict in Faulkner's story is between North and South or between New South and Old. Write an essay in which you both summarize the various ways in which the critical works in this chapter describe the story's central conflict and make your own argument about what the story's central conflict and theme ultimately are. Is one or the other of these critics right about the conflict and theme, or might there be an entirely different way to understand the story?

5. Judith Fetterley urges a feminist reading of Faulkner's story in her essay "A Rose for 'A Rose for Emily.'" Do you find her arguments persuasive? Write an essay comparing Fetterley's take on "A Rose for Emily" with that of other critics who do not consider the social subordination of women or the gender of characters or the narrator to be crucial to the meaning of this story.

6. Both Floyd C. Watkins's and T. J. Stafford's essays on "A Rose for Emily" stand out because each focuses on an aspect or element of Faulkner's story ignored by other critics—plot structure in Watkins's essay and the minor character Tobe in Stafford's. Write an essay that explains and explores the significance of any other aspect or element of the story that you feel has not received adequate attention from critics.

7. In this chapter you have seen how a single work of literature (Faulkner's "A Rose for Emily") can generate a broad range of critical responses. Taken together, these texts represent a kind of ongoing conversation between a "primary text" and "secondary texts," and among these "secondary texts" themselves. Using secondary texts available to you at a library and on the Internet, write an essay in which you join in the critical "conversation" about any of the stories you have read in this book. Be sure to follow the standard scholarly procedures for citing and documenting your sources.

SAMPLE WRITING

In the following essay, student writer Ann Warren draws on published criticism to develop her own argument about both the significance of plotting and structure in "A Rose for Emily" and its similarities to William Shakespeare's *Hamlet* (chapter 28). Her essay was an inventive response to an assignment that asked students to analyze one of four short stories by drawing on at least five secondary sources. Like many writers, Ann reports that she discovered what she wanted to say about the story only when she began to write about it. And in hindsight, both she and her instructor agree that her essay might be stronger if it focused from the beginning more on the *Hamlet* comparison and developed it further. Some matters of style and organization could also be much improved. Even in its current form, however, the essay holds together quite well, provides interesting and original insights into Faulkner's story, and does an especially good job of synthesizing sources and of summarizing and quoting from primary and secondary sources.

Ann Warren
ENG 3011: The Short Story
Mr. Jeffreys
3 November 2008

The Tragic Plot of "A Rose for Emily"

In "The Structure of 'A Rose for Emily,'" Floyd C. Watkins says that "If analyses in periodicals and inclusion in anthologies are a dependable criterion for a short story," then this Faulkner story is "not only his best story, but also one of the best written by any modern American writer" (46). The amount of attention the story has gotten does not seem surprising. It's definitely the only story I've ever read about someone who sleeps with the dead body of a man she poisoned! A lot of criticism on the story focuses on figuring out why Emily did it, how we should feel about her and what she did, and what we're supposed to take away from the story. In terms of how we should feel about her, there are two opposite points of view. On one side, Cleanth Brooks and Robert Penn Warren declare she's a tragic hero, and her "refusal to accept the herd values carries with it a dignity and courage" that are admirable (28). On the other side, T. J. Stafford says that Miss Emily's actions are simply "abnormal, degenerate, and meaningless" and "unworthy of . . . pride" (87).

As far as I know, only Floyd Watkins has paid attention to how the plot is structured. His article shows it is important that Faulkner "divided the story into five parts and based them on incidents of isolation and intrusion" (46). Because the one part that doesn't include incidents like this is the middle one (III), it helps give the story "a perfect symmetry" and shows "the indomitableness of the decadent Southern aristocrat" (46, 47). While I think Watkins's argument is good, I also think he and other writers have missed something about the five-part structure and the third part that I think shows that Miss Emily is a tragic hero. Specifically, she's like Hamlet.

As Watkins says, parts I, II, IV, and V of the story show how "adherents of the new order in the town" invade her house (46). In part I, Miss Emily dies, and the neighbors come to the funeral and to look in her house. Then we hear about how earlier the "deputation" from the Board of Aldermen of a younger "generation" came to tell her she had to pay taxes that an earlier generation (specifically, Colonel Sartoris) had told her she never had to pay (10). Section II also has two invasions. Four men from the Board of Aldermen spread lime to try to get rid of the smell at Miss Emily's house. Then, after Miss Emily's father's death (which is actually earlier in time), people from the town come in to "offer condolence and aid" and then "to persuade her to let them dispose of the body" (12). As Watkins writes, part IV "contains two forced entrances" by a minister and then Miss Emily's relatives, who are trying to make her break up with Homer Barron (46). Then in part V everyone comes to Miss Emily's house for the funeral and then to force open the room upstairs that no one except her has been in for forty years.

Part III is different. Watkins says, "The inviolability of Miss Emily's isolation is maintained in the central division, part three, in which no outsider enters her home. Her triumph is further revealed in this part when she buys the arsenic without telling what she plans to use it for" (47). But there's more to it than that. It's not just that no one "enters her home"; it's that she *leaves it for the first time in the story!* In fact, we hear about her leaving it twice just like people invade her home twice in other sections. First Homer Barron arrives in town, and the neighbors "began to see him and Miss Emily on Sunday afternoons driving in the yellow-wheeled buggy" (12). Then she buys the poison to kill Homer, and we know she goes to the drugstore to do that because the narrator says, "she opened the package *at home*" later (13; emphasis added).

At first, I thought that this was the only section where we see Miss Emily go out, but then I noticed that in the next section the narrator says she "had been to the jeweler's" and "bought a complete outfit of men's clothing" (14). Still, Part III is the real turning point because it's the only time where she has the chance for love and a real life of her own (the first time or reason she leaves the house) and where she reacts to losing that chance by buying rat poison to kill Homer with.

Before and after this, the story is more about everybody else doing things to Emily, even in a way trying to kill her or at least to kill her chance of having any kind of real life of her own, if only by judging and talking about her all the time. Even the moments when she seems strong are more about her not doing or saying things, saying "no" to other people, and just holing up in her house and not letting people in, just like her father started all this by not letting in the young men she might have married. As the narrator says it in part II, she "vanquished" (11) the tax deputation in part I just by the fact that "She did not ask them to sit" and "just stood in the door and listened quietly" (10). In part II, she just "sat . . . motionless as . . . an idol" inside her house while the "four men slunk about the house like burglars" (11). Then when her father dies she won't let people in and just "told them that her father was not dead" for three days before "she broke down" (12). In Part IV, she "did not appear on the streets" and "closed" the door of her house "for good" after opening it up for Homer and then some painting students (because she needed the money) (15). In Part V, again, she's dead (like in the first part) and can't do anything.

But she still surprises and even "vanquishes" them in this last part—because of the active thing she did in Part III by going out of the house to buy the poison. In that section she takes things into her own hands. Having gone out with Homer, it's like if she can't keep going out with him (literally!), she'll make sure he can't go out either. It's after that (in time and in the story) that she stops going out almost at all, but at least she has made sure that she is not the only one buried in that "tomb" of a house from then on (16). The thing she does might be "abnormal" and "degenerate." I'm not saying it was right, but it doesn't seem "meaningless" either (Stafford 87). It's like she is literally backed into a corner. She doesn't have any money, just that house, which is what she retreats to and takes Homer home with her. Part III is the turning point where Emily takes the action that decides what happens at the end.

How Faulkner mixes up the chronology to divide the story into five parts makes the plot and story even more perfect (and difficult to explain!). In addition to everything else, this makes the story like a tragedy like *Hamlet,* which also has five acts and the turning point in the third. Other plays besides *Hamlet* have five acts, and their turning points also might come in the third act, but there are other connections to *Hamlet*. First, what happens in Act 3 of *Hamlet* is that Hamlet kills Polonius when he hides behind a curtain to spy on Hamlet and his mother. Hamlet doesn't mean to kill Polonius (he thinks it's the king hiding), but he does mean to kill someone like Miss Emily apparently gets ready to do in the third part of her story.

Also, Hamlet calls Polonius "a rat" after he kills him (III.4.26), which Polonius is. He may not be a little brown furry animal, but he is "a sneaky, contemptible person" and "an informer" (*Webster's New World College Dictionary* 4th ed.). In "A Rose for Emily," Homer is also "a sneaky, contemptible person," though not exactly "an informer," for seeing what Miss Emily's life is like and taking her out of it (literally!) and then just dumping her. (Also, he sneaks into her house at night, which seems to be when he dies, even though it's not the main character he's hiding from like in *Hamlet*.) Homer is also called a "rat," but indirectly because of the way his murder is mistaken for a rat's three times: Judge Stevens says that the smell at the house is "probably just a snake or a rat" that the servant "killed in the yard" when it's really Homer that was killed in the house by Miss Emily (11), and when Miss Emily goes to the druggist for poison, he says to her it's "For rats" and then writes it on the box she sees when she gets home (13).

Noticing these details made me see deeper similarities in the characters and conflicts of Emily and Hamlet. Both spend a lot of time not doing much very active, both are being watched by other people, and both are seen by those people as crazy and maybe they even plan to be seen as crazy (at least Hamlet). What's more important is that both of them become murderers, if not crazy, because they were haunted by their fathers. In *Hamlet*, there is an actual ghost. "A Rose for Emily" has a symbolic or psychological ghost. Her father is like a ghost in the story because his death is mentioned so many times:[1] "the death of her father" (9), "her father's death" (11, 12), "her father died" (12). He is like a ghost in her actual house because "On a tarnished gilt easel before the fireplace stood a crayon portrait of Miss Emily's father" (9). This portrait is first shown in the first section (like the ghost appears in the first act of *Hamlet*). And the story is also organized so that all the other quotations about Emily's father's death above are in the first three sections, and the last two sections don't say anything about her father until in the last one where she's dead and "the crayon face of her father mus[es] profoundly above the bier" (15). The picture being in the first and last sections is another kind of "symmetry," and it might be more evidence that the third part is a turning point and that in a way Homer's ghost replaces her father's once she's killed him.

Maybe she even kills Homer because of her father. The narrator, author, and critics strongly blame him. The narrator says, "her father had driven away" "all the young men" and "robbed her" (12) and "thwarted her woman's life so many times" and was "too virulent and too furious to die" (14). Faulkner said so when someone asked him why he wrote the story:

> In this case there was the young girl with a young girl's normal aspirations to find love and then a husband and a family, who was brow-beaten and kept down by her father, a selfish man who didn't want her to leave home because he wanted a housekeeper, and it was a natural instinct . . . —you can't repress it—you can mash it down but it comes up somewhere else and very likely in a tragic form, and that was simply another manifestation of man's injustice to man. . . . ("Comments" 22).

---

1. In his recent article, Thomas Klein backs me up when he says that Faulkner "described 'A Rose for Emily'" as a 'ghost story,'" but the only "candidates" for the ghost position that he mentions are Miss Emily, Homer, Tobe, and the "pervasive, shape-shifting, haunting" "voice of the town" that narrates the story (231).

Ray B. West, Jr. says, "She does not resist change completely . . . until she has known two separate betrayals, the first by her father (traditional decorum)" (36). William Van O'Connor writes, "The severity of Miss Emily's father was the cause of her frustrations and her retreat" (45). Irving Malin argues, "Emily's attachment to the will of the father—it is said that he had driven all the young men away—has stunted her growth" (48).

These writers don't associate Miss Emily and Hamlet. But I think all this still supports the view that Miss Emily is like a tragic hero and especially like Hamlet. The two characters or the two stories are obviously not exactly alike, and Faulkner didn't necessarily mean the comparison. But Hamlet is the most famous tragic hero, and I do think that Faulkner meant to portray Miss Emily as a tragic hero, someone we pity even if we don't like her (he says he might not have) or even if she is sort of perversely happy. Faulkner even says above that her "normal aspirations to find love" come out in "a *tragic* form" because of how she's made to "mash them down." The plot is one thing Faulkner uses to make the story and Miss Emily tragic.

WORKS CITED

Brooks, Cleanth, and Robert Penn Warren. "An Interpretation of 'A Rose for Emily.'" *Understanding Fiction.* 2nd ed. New York: Appleton-Century Crofts, 1959. Rpt. in Inge 25–29.

Faulkner, William. "Comments on 'A Rose for Emily.'" *Faulkner in the University: Class Conferences at the University of Virginia 1957–1958.* Charlottesville: University Press of Virginia, 1959. Rpt. in Inge 20–22.

———. "A Rose for Emily." *Collected Stories of William Faulkner.* New York: Random House, 1950. 119–130. Rpt. in Inge 9–16.

Inge, M. Thomas, ed. *William Faulkner: A Rose for Emily.* The Merrill Literary Casebook Series. Ed. Edward P. J. Corbett. Columbus, Ohio: Charles E. Merrill, 1970.

Klein, Thomas. "The Ghostly Voice of Gossip in Faulkner's 'A Rose for Emily.'" *Explicator* 65.4 (Summer 2007): 229–32.

Malin, Irving. "Miss Emily's Perversion." *William Faulkner: An Interpretation.* Stanford: Stanford UP, 1957. 37–38. Rpt. in Inge 48–49.

O'Connor, William Van. "History in 'A Rose for Emily.'" *Sewanee Review* 60 (1952): 182–184. Rpt. in Inge 44–45.

Shakespeare, William. *Hamlet.* New York: Washington Square Press, 1992.

Stafford, T. J. "Tobe's Significance in 'A Rose for Emily.'" *Modern Fiction Studies* 14 (Winter 1968–69): 451–453. Rpt. in Inge 87–89.

Watkins, Floyd C. "The Structure of 'A Rose for Emily.'" *Modern Language Notes* 69 (Nov. 1954): 508–510. Rpt. in Inge 46–47.

West, Jr., Ray B. "Faulkner's 'A Rose for Emily.'" *Explicator* 7 (Oct. 1948): item 8. Rpt. in Inge 36–37.

Reading More Fiction

MARGARET ATWOOD

Scarlet Ibis

Some years ago now, Christine went with Don to Trinidad. They took Lilian, their youngest child, who was four then. The others, who were in school, stayed with their grandmother.

Christine and Don sat beside the hotel pool in the damp heat, drinking rum punch and eating strange-tasting hamburgers. Lilian wanted to be in the pool all the time—she could already swim a little—but Christine didn't think it was a good idea, because of the sun. Christine rubbed sun block on her nose, and on the noses of Lilian and Don. She felt that her legs were too white and that people were looking at her and finding her faintly ridiculous, because of her pinky-white skin and the large hat she wore. More than likely, the young black waiters who brought the rum punch and the hamburgers, who walked easily through the sun without paying any attention to it, who joked among themselves but were solemn when they set down the glasses and plates, had put her in a category; one that included fat, although she was not fat exactly. She suggested to Don that perhaps he was tipping too much. Don said he felt tired.

"You felt tired before," Christine said. "That's why we came, remember? So you could get some rest."

Don took afternoon naps, sprawled on his back on one of the twin beds in the room—Lilian had a fold-out cot—his mouth slightly open, the skin of his face pushed by gravity back down towards his ears, so that he looked tauter, thinner, and more aquiline in this position than he did when awake. Deader, thought Christine, taking a closer look. People lying on their backs in coffins usually—in her limited experience—seemed to have lost weight. This image, of Don encoffined, was one that had been drifting through her mind too often for comfort lately.

5   It was hopeless expecting Lilian to have an afternoon nap too, so Christine took her down to the pool or tried to keep her quiet by drawing with her, using Magic Markers. At that age Lilian drew nothing but women or girls, wearing very fancy dresses, full-skirted, with a lot of decoration. They were always smiling, with red, curvy mouths, and had abnormally long thick eyelashes. They did not stand on any ground—Lilian was not yet putting the ground into her pictures—but floated on the page as if it were a pond they were spread out on, arms out-stretched, feet at the opposite sides of their skirts, their elaborate hair billowing around their heads. Sometimes Lilian put in some birds or the sun, which gave these women the appearance of giant airborne balloons, as if the wind had caught them under their skirts and carried them off, light as feathers, away from everything. Yet, if she were asked, Lilian would say these women were walking.

After a few days of all this, when they ought to have adjusted to the heat, Christine felt they should get out of the hotel and do something. She did not want to go shopping by herself, although Don suggested it; she felt that nothing she tried on helped her look any better, or, to be more precise, that it didn't much matter how she looked. She tried to think of some other distraction, mostly for the sake of Don. Don was not noticeably more rested, although he had a sunburn—which, instead of giving him a glow of health, made him seem angry—and he'd started drumming his fingers on tabletops again. He said he was having trouble sleeping: bad dreams, which he could not remember. Also the air-conditioning was clogging up his nose. He had been under a lot of pressure lately, he said.

Christine didn't need to be told. She could feel the pressure he was under, like a clenched mass of something, tissue, congealed blood, at the back of her own head. She thought of Don as being encased in a sort of metal carapace, like the shell of a crab, that was slowly tightening on him, on all parts of him at once, so that something was sure to burst, like a thumb closed slowly in a car door. The metal skin was his entire body, and Christine didn't know how to unlock it for him and let him out. She felt as if all her ministrations—the cold washcloths for his headaches, the trips to the drugstore for this or that bottle of pills, the hours of tiptoeing around, intercepting the phone, keeping Lilian quiet, above all the mere act of witnessing him, which was so draining—were noticed by him hardly at all: moths beating on the outside of a lit window, behind which someone important was thinking about something of major significance that had nothing to do with moths. This vacation, for instance, had been her idea, but Don was only getting redder and redder.

Unfortunately, it was not carnival season. There were restaurants, but Lilian hated sitting still in them, and one thing Don did not need was more food and especially more drink. Christine wished Don had a sport, but considering the way he was, he would probably overdo it and break something.

"I had an uncle who took up hooking rugs," she'd said to him one evening after dinner. "When he retired. He got them in kits. He said he found it very restful." The aunt that went with that uncle used to say, "I said for better or for worse, but I never said for lunch."

"Oh, for God's sake, Christine," was all Don had to say to that. He'd never thought much of her relatives. His view was that Christine was still on the raw side of being raw material. Christine did not look forward to the time, twenty years away at least, when he would be home all day, pacing, drumming his fingers, wanting whatever it was that she could never identify and never provide.

In the morning, while the other two were beginning breakfast, Christine went bravely to the hotel's reception desk. There was a thin, elegant brown girl behind it, in lime green, Rasta beads, and *Vogue* make-up, coiled like spaghetti around the phone. Christine, feeling hot and porous, asked if there was any material on things to do. The girl, sliding her eyes over and past Christine as if she were a minor architectural feature, selected and fanned an assortment of brochures, continuing to laugh lightly into the phone.

Christine took the brochures into the ladies' room to preview them. Not the beach, she decided, because of the sun. Not the boutiques, not the night clubs, not the memories of Old Spain.

She examined her face, added lipstick to her lips, which were getting thin and pinched together. She really needed to do something about herself, before it was too late. She made her way back to the breakfast table. Lilian was saying that the pancakes weren't the same as the ones at home. Don said she had to eat them because she had ordered them, and if she was old enough to order for herself she was old enough to know that they cost money and couldn't be wasted like that. Christine wondered silently if it was a bad pattern, making a child eat everything on her plate, whether she liked the food or not: perhaps Lilian would become fat, later on.

Don was having bacon and eggs. Christine had asked Don to order yoghurt and fresh fruit for her, but there was nothing at her place.

15   "They didn't have it," Don said.

"Did you order anything else?" said Christine, who was now hungry.

"How was I supposed to know what you want?" said Don.

"We're going to see the Scarlet Ibis," Christine announced brightly to Lilian. She would ask them to bring back the menu, so she could order.

"What?" said Don. Christine handed him the brochure, which showed some red birds with long curved bills sitting in a tree; there was another picture of one close up, in profile, one demented-looking eye staring out from its red feathers like a target.

20   "They're very rare," said Christine, looking around for a waiter. "It's a preservation."

"You mean a preserve," said Don, reading the brochure. "In a swamp? Probably crawling with mosquitoes."

"I don't want to go," said Lilian, pushing scraps of a pancake around in a pool of watery syrup. This was her other complaint, that it wasn't the right kind of syrup.

"Imitation maple flavouring," Don said, reading the label.

"You don't even know what it is," said Christine. "We'll take some fly dope. Anyway, they wouldn't let tourists go there if there were that many mosquitoes. It's a *mangrove*[1] swamp; that isn't the same as our kind."

25   "I'm going to get a paper," said Don. He stood up and walked away. His legs, coming out of the bottoms of his Bermuda shorts, were still very white, with an overglaze of pink down the backs. His body, once muscular, was losing tone, sliding down towards his waist and buttocks. He was beginning to slope. From the back, he had the lax, demoralized look of a man who has been confined in an institution, though from the front he was brisk enough.

Watching him go, Christine felt the sickness in the pit of her stomach that was becoming familiar to her these days. Maybe the pressure he was under was her. Maybe she was a weight. Maybe he wanted her to lift up, blow away somewhere, like a kite, the children hanging on behind her in a long string. She didn't know when she had first noticed this feeling; probably after it had been there some time, like a knocking on the front door when you're asleep. There had been a shifting of forces, unseen, unheard, underground, the sliding against each other of giant stones; some tremendous damage had occurred between them, but who could tell when?

"Eat your pancakes," she said to Lilian, "or your father will be annoyed." He would be annoyed anyway: she annoyed him. Even when they made love, which was not frequently any more, it was perfunctory, as if he were listening for something else, a phone call, a footfall. He was like a man scratching himself. She was like his hand.

Christine had a scenario she ran through often, the way she used to run through scenarios of courtship, back in high school: flirtation, pursuit, joyful

1. Tropical trees that grow in shallow coastal waters.

acquiescence. This was an adult scenario, however. One evening she would say to Don as he was getting up from the table after dinner, "Stay there." He would be so surprised by her tone of voice that he would stay.

"I just want you to sit there and look at me," she would say.

He would not say, "For God's sake, Christine." He would know this was serious.   30

"I'm not asking much from you," she would say, lying.

"What's going on?" he would say.

"I want you to see what I really look like," she would say. "I'm tired of being invisible." Maybe he would, maybe he wouldn't. Maybe he would say he was coming on with a headache. Maybe she would find herself walking on nothing, because maybe there was nothing there. So far she hadn't even come close to beginning, to giving the initial command: "Stay," as if he were a trained dog. But that was what she wanted him to do, wasn't it? "Come back" was more like it. He hadn't always been under pressure.

Once Lilian was old enough, Christine thought, she could go back to work full time. She could brush up her typing and shorthand, find something. That would be good for her; she wouldn't concentrate so much on Don, she would have a reason to look better, she would either find new scenarios or act out the one that was preoccupying her. Maybe she was making things up, about Don. It might be a form of laziness.

• • •

Christine's preparations for the afternoon were careful. She bought some mos-   35
quito repellant at a drugstore, and a chocolate bar. She took two scarves, one for herself, one for Lilian, in case it was sunny. The big hat would blow off, she thought, as they were going to be in a boat. After a short argument with one of the waiters, who said she could only have drinks by the glass, she succeeded in buying three cans of Pepsi, not chilled. All these things she packed into her bag; Lilian's bag, actually, which was striped in orange and yellow and blue and had a picture of Mickey Mouse on it. They'd used it for the toys Lilian brought with her on the plane.

After lunch they took a taxi, first through the hot streets of the town, where the sidewalks were too narrow or nonexistent and the people crowded onto the road and there was a lot of honking, then out through the cane fields, the road becoming bumpier, the driver increasing speed. He drove with the car radio on, the left-hand window open, and his elbow out, a pink jockey cap tipped back on his head. Christine had shown him the brochure and asked him if he knew where the swamp was; he'd grinned at her and said everybody knew. He said he could take them, but it was too far to go out and back so he would wait there for them. Christine knew it meant extra money, but did not argue.

They passed a man riding a donkey, and two cows wandering around by the roadside, anchored by ropes around their necks which were tied to dragging stones. Christine pointed these out to Lilian. The little houses among the tall cane were made of cement blocks, painted light green or pink or light blue; they were built up on open-work foundations, almost as if they were on stilts. The women who sat on the steps turned their heads, unsmiling, to watch their taxi as it went by.

Lilian asked Christine if she had any gum. Christine didn't. Lilian began chewing on her nails, which she'd taken up since Don had been under pressure. Christine told her to stop. Then Lilian said she wanted to go for a swim. Don looked out the window. "How long did you say?" he asked. It was a reproach, not a question.

Christine hadn't said how long because she didn't know; she didn't know because she'd forgotten to ask. Finally they turned off the main road onto a smaller, muddier one, and parked beside some other cars in a rutted space that had once been part of a field.

40   "I meet you here," said the driver. He got out of the car, stretched, turned up the car radio. There were other drivers hanging around, some of them in cars, others sitting on the ground drinking from a bottle they were passing around, one asleep.

Christine took Lilian's hand. She didn't want to appear stupid by having to ask where they were supposed to go next. She didn't see anything that looked like a ticket office.

"It must be that shack," Don said, so they walked towards it, a long shed with a tin roof; on the other side of it was a steep bank and the beginning of the water. There were wooden steps leading down to a wharf, which was the same brown as the water itself. Several boats were tied up to it, all of similar design: long and thin, almost like barges, with rows of bench-like seats. Each boat had a small outboard motor at the back. The names painted on the boats looked East Indian.

Christine took the scarves out of her bag and tied one on her own head and one on Lilian's. Although it was beginning to cloud over, the sun was still very bright, and she knew about rays coming through overcast, especially in the tropics. She put sun block on their noses, and thought that the chocolate bar had been a silly idea. Soon it would be a brown puddle at the bottom of her bag, which luckily was waterproof. Don paced behind them as Christine knelt.

An odd smell was coming up from the water: a swamp smell, but with something else mixed in. Christine wondered about sewage disposal. She was glad she'd made Lilian go to the bathroom before they'd left.

45   There didn't seem to be anyone in charge, anyone to buy the tickets from, although there were several people beside the shed, waiting, probably: two plumpish, middle-aged men in T-shirts and baseball caps turned around backwards, an athletic couple in shorts with outside pockets, who were loaded down with cameras and binoculars, a trim woman in a tailored pink summer suit that must have been far too hot. There was another woman off to the side, a somewhat large woman in a floral print dress. She'd spread a Mexican-looking shawl on the weedy grass near the shed and was sitting down on it, drinking a pint carton of orange juice through a straw. The others looked wilted and dispirited, but not this woman. For her, waiting seemed to be an activity, not something imposed: she gazed around her, at the bank, the brown water, the line of sullen mangrove trees beyond, as if she were enjoying every minute.

This woman seemed the easiest to approach, so Christine went over to her. "Are we in the right place?" she said. "For the birds."

The woman smiled at her and said they were. She had a broad face, with high, almost Slavic cheekbones and round red cheeks like those of an old-fashioned wooden doll, except that they were not painted on. Her taffy-coloured hair was done in waves and rolls, and reminded Christine of the pictures on the Toni home-permanent boxes of several decades before.

"We will leave soon," said the woman. "Have you seen these birds before? They come back only at sunset. The rest of the time they are away, fishing." She smiled again, and Christine thought to herself that it was a pity she hadn't had bands put on to even out her teeth when she was young.

This was the woman's second visit to the Scarlet Ibis preserve, she told Christine. The first was three years ago, when she stopped over here on her way to South America with her husband and children. This time her husband and children had stayed back at the hotel: they hadn't seen a swimming pool for such a long time. She and her husband were Mennonite missionaries, she said. She herself didn't seem embarrassed by this, but Christine blushed a little. She had been raised Anglican, but the only vestige of that was the kind of Christmas cards she favoured: prints of mediaeval or Renaissance old masters. Religious people of any serious kind made her nervous: they were like men in raincoats who might or might not be flashers. You would be going along with them in the ordinary way, and then there could be a swift movement and you would look down to find the coat wide open and nothing on under it but some pant legs held up by rubber bands. This had happened to Christine in a train station once.

"How many children do you have?" she said, to change the subject. Mennonite would explain the wide hips: they liked women who could have a lot of children.

The woman's crooked-toothed smile did not falter. "Four," she said, "but one of them is dead."

"Oh," said Christine. It wasn't clear whether the four included the one dead, or whether that was extra. She knew better than to say, "That's too bad." Such a comment was sure to produce something about the will of God, and she didn't want to deal with that. She looked to make sure Lilian was still there, over by Don. Much of the time Lilian was a given, but there were moments at which she was threatened, unknown to herself, with sudden disappearance. "That's my little girl, over there," Christine said, feeling immediately that this was a callous comment; but the woman continued to smile, in a way that Christine now found eerie.

A small brown man in a Hawaiian-patterned shirt came around from behind the shed and went quickly down the steps to the wharf. He climbed into one of the boats and lowered the outboard motor into the water.

"Now maybe we'll get some action," Don said. He had come up behind her, but he was talking more to himself than to her. Christine sometimes wondered whether he talked in the same way when she wasn't there at all.

A second man, East Indian, like the first, and also in a hula-dancer shirt, was standing at the top of the steps, and they understood they were to go over. He took their money and gave each of them a business card in return; on one side of it was a coloured picture of an ibis, on the other a name and a phone number. They went single file down the steps and the first man handed them into the boat. When they were all seated—Don, Christine, Lilian, and the pink-suited woman in a crowded row, the two baseball-cap men in front of them, the Mennonite woman and the couple with the cameras at the very front—the second man cast off and hopped lightly into the bow. After a few tries the first man got the motor started, and they putt-putted slowly towards an opening in the trees, leaving a wispy trail of smoke behind them.

It was cloudier now, and not so hot. Christine talked with the pink-suited woman, who had blonde hair elegantly done up in a French roll. She was from Vienna, she said; her husband was here on business. This was the first time she had been on this side of the Atlantic Ocean. The beaches were beautiful, much finer than those of the Mediterranean. Christine complimented her on her good English, and the woman smiled and told her what a beautiful little girl she had, and Christine said Lilian would get conceited, a word that the woman had not yet added to her vocabulary. Lilian was quiet; she had caught sight of the woman's bracelet, which was silver and lavishly engraved. The woman showed it to her. Christine began to enjoy herself, despite the fact that the two men in front of her were talking too loudly. They were drinking beer, from cans they'd brought with them in a paper bag. She opened a Pepsi and shared some with Lilian. Don didn't want any.

They were in a channel now; she looked at the trees on either side, which were all the same, dark-leaved, rising up out of the water, on masses of spindly roots. She didn't know how long they'd been going.

It began to rain, not a downpour but heavily enough, large cold drops. The Viennese woman said, "It's raining," her eyes open in a parody of surprise, holding out her hand and looking up at the sky like someone in a child's picture book. This was for the benefit of Lilian. "We will get wet," she said. She took a white embroidered handkerchief out of her purse and spread it on the top of her head. Lilian was enchanted with the handkerchief and asked Christine if she could have one, too. Don said they should have known, since it always rained in the afternoons here.

The men in baseball caps hunched their shoulders, and one of them said to the Indian in the bow, "Hey, we're getting wet!"

60   The Indian's timid but closed expression did not change; with apparent reluctance he pulled a rolled-up sheet of plastic out from somewhere under the front seat and handed it to the men. They spent some time unrolling it and getting it straightened out, and then everyone helped to hold the plastic overhead like a roof, while the boat glided on at its unvarying pace, through the mangroves and the steam or mist that was now rising around them.

"Isn't this an adventure?" Christine said, aiming it at Lilian. Lilian was biting her nails. The rain pattered down. Don said he wished he'd brought a paper. The men in baseball caps began to sing, sounding oddly like boys at a summer camp who had gone to sleep one day and awakened thirty years later, unaware of the sinister changes that had taken place in them, the growth and recession of hair and flesh, the exchange of their once-clear voices for the murky ones that were now singing off-key, out of time:

> "They say that in the army,
> the girls are rather fine,
> They promise Betty Grable,[2]
> they give you Frankenstein . . ."

They had not yet run out of beer. One of them finished a can and tossed it overboard, and it bobbed beside the boat for a moment before falling behind, a bright red dot in the borderless expanse of dull green and dull grey. Christine felt virtuous: she'd put her Pepsi can carefully into her bag, for disposal later.

Then the rain stopped, and after some debate about whether it was going to start again or not, the two baseball-cap men began to roll up the plastic sheet. While they were doing this there was a jarring thud. The boat rocked violently, and the one man who was standing up almost pitched overboard, then sat down with a jerk.

"What the hell?" he said.

2. American movie star and pinup girl of the 1940s (1916–73).

The Indian at the back reversed the motor.

"We hit something," said the Viennese woman. She clasped her hands, another 65 classic gesture.

"Obviously," Don said in an undertone. Christine smiled at Lilian, who was looking anxious. The boat started forward again.

"Probably a mangrove root," said the man with the cameras, turning half round. "They grow out under the water." He was the kind who would know.

"Or an alligator," said one of the men in baseball caps. The other man laughed.

"He's joking, darling," Christine said to Lilian.

"But we are sinking," said the Viennese woman, pointing with one out- 70 stretched hand, one dramatic finger.

Then they all saw what they had not noticed before. There was a hole in the boat, near the front, right above the platform of loose boards that served as a floor. It was the size of a small fist. Whatever they'd hit had punched right through the wood, as if it were cardboard. Water was pouring through.

"This tub must be completely rotten," Don muttered, directly to Christine this time. This was a role she was sometimes given when they were among people Don didn't know: the listener. "They get like that in the tropics."

"Hey," said one of the men in baseball caps. "You up front. There's a hole in the goddamned boat."

The Indian glanced over his shoulder at the hole. He shrugged, looked away, began fishing in the breast pocket of his sports shirt for a cigarette.

"Hey. Turn this thing around," said the man with the camera. 75

"Couldn't we get it fixed, and then start again?" said Christine, intending to conciliate. She glanced at the Mennonite woman, hoping for support, but the woman's broad flowered back was towards her.

"If we go back," the Indian said patiently—he could understand English after all—"you miss the birds. It will be too dark."

"Yeah, but if we go forward we sink."

"You will not sink," said the Indian. He had found a cigarette, already half-smoked, and was lighting it.

"He's done it before," said the largest baseball cap. "Every week he gets a hole 80 in the goddamned boat. Nothing to it."

The brown water continued to come in. The boat went forward.

"Right," Don said, loudly, to everyone this time. "He thinks if we don't see the birds, we won't pay him."

That made sense to Christine. For the Indians, it was a lot of money. They probably couldn't afford the gas if they lost the fares. "If you go back, we'll pay you anyway," she called to the Indian. Ordinarily she would have made this suggestion to Don, but she was getting frightened.

Either the Indian didn't hear her or he didn't trust them, or it wasn't his idea of a fair bargain. He didn't smile or reply.

For a few minutes they all sat there, waiting for the problem to be solved. The 85 trees went past. Finally Don said, "We'd better bail. At this rate we'll be in serious trouble in about half an hour."

"I should not have come," said the Viennese woman, in a tone of tragic despair.

"What with?" said the man with the cameras. The men in baseball caps had turned to look at Don, as if he were worthy of attention.

"Mummy, are we going to sink?" said Lilian.

"Of course not, darling," said Christine. "Daddy won't let us."

90   "Anything there is," said the largest baseball-cap man. He poured the rest of his beer over the side. "You got a jackknife?" he said.

Don didn't, but the man with the cameras did. They watched while he cut the top out of the can, knelt down, moved a loose platform board so he could get at the water, scooped, dumped brown water over the side. Then the other men started taking the tops off their own beer cans, including the full ones, which they emptied out. Christine produced the Pepsi can from her bag. The Mennonite woman had her pint juice carton.

"No mosquitoes, at any rate," Don said, almost cheerfully.

They'd lost a lot of time, and the water was almost up to the floor platform. It seemed to Christine that the boat was becoming heavier, moving more slowly through the water, that the water itself was thicker. They could not empty much water at a time with such small containers, but maybe, with so many of them doing it, it would work.

"This really *is* an adventure," she said to Lilian, who was white-faced and forlorn. "Isn't this fun?"

95   The Viennese woman was not bailing; she had no container. She was making visible efforts to calm herself. She had taken out a tangerine, which she was peeling, over the embroidered handkerchief which she'd spread out on her lap. Now she produced a beautiful little pen-knife with a mother-of-pearl handle. To Lilian she said, "You are hungry? Look, I will cut in pieces, one piece for you, then one for me, *ja*?" The knife was not really needed, of course. It was to distract Lilian, and Christine was grateful.

There was an audible rhythm in the boat: scrape, dump; scrape, dump. The men in baseball caps, rowdy earlier, were not at all drunk now. Don appeared to be enjoying himself, for the first time on the trip.

But despite their efforts, the level of the water was rising.

"This is ridiculous," Christine said to Don. She stopped bailing with her Pepsi can. She was discouraged and also frightened. She told herself that the Indians wouldn't keep going if they thought there was any real danger, but she wasn't convinced. Maybe they didn't care if everybody drowned; maybe they thought it was Karma. Through the hole the brown water poured, with a steady flow, like a cut vein. It was up to the level of the loose floor boards now.

Then the Mennonite woman stood up. Balancing herself, she removed her shoes, placing them carefully side by side under the seat. Christine had once watched a man do this in a subway station; he'd put the shoes under the bench where she was sitting, and a few minutes later had thrown himself in front of the oncoming train. The two shoes had remained on the neat yellow-tiled floor, like bones on a plate after a meal. It flashed through Christine's head that maybe the woman had become unhinged and was going to leap overboard; this was plausible, because of the dead child. The woman's perpetual smile was a fraud then, as Christine's would have been in her place.

100   But the woman did not jump over the side of the boat. Instead she bent over and moved the platform boards. Then she turned around and lowered her large flowered rump onto the hole. Her face was towards Christine now; she continued to smile, gazing over the side of the boat at the mangroves and their monotonous roots and leaves as if they were the most interesting scenery she had seen in a long time. The water was above her ankles; her skirt was wet. Did she look a

little smug, a little clever or self-consciously heroic? Possibly, thought Christine, though from that round face it was hard to tell.

"Hey," said one of the men in baseball caps, "now you're cooking with gas!" The Indian in the bow looked at the woman; his white teeth appeared briefly.

The others continued to bail, and after a moment Christine began to scoop and pour with the Pepsi can again. Despite herself, the woman impressed her. The water probably wasn't that cold but it was certainly filthy, and who could tell what might be on the other side of the hole? Were they far enough south for piranhas? Yet there was the Mennonite woman plugging the hole with her bottom, serene as a brooding hen, and no doubt unaware of the fact that she was more than a little ridiculous. Christine could imagine the kinds of remarks the men in baseball caps would make about the woman afterwards. "Saved by a big butt." "Hey, never knew it had more than one use." "Finger in the dike had nothing on her." That was the part that would have stopped Christine from doing such a thing, even if she'd managed to think of it.

Now they reached the long aisle of mangroves and emerged into the open; they were in a central space, like a lake, with the dark mangroves walling it around. There was a chicken-wire fence strung across it, to keep any boats from going too close to the Scarlet Ibis' roosting area: that was what the sign said, nailed to a post that was sticking at an angle out of the water. The Indian cut the motor and they drifted towards the fence; the other Indian caught hold of the fence, held on, and the boat stopped, rocking a little. Apart from the ripples they'd caused, the water was dead flat calm; the trees doubled in it appeared black, and the sun, which was just above the western rim of the real trees, was a red disk in the hazy grey sky. The light coming from it was orangy-red and tinted the water. For a few minutes nothing happened. The man with the cameras looked at his watch. Lilian was restless, squirming on the seat. She wanted to draw; she wanted to swim in the pool. If Christine had known the whole thing would take so long she wouldn't have brought her.

"They coming," said the Indian in the bow.

"Birds ahoy," said one of the men in baseball caps, and pointed, and then 105 there were the birds all right, flying through the reddish light, right on cue, first singly, then in flocks of four or five, so bright, so fluorescent that they were like painted flames. They settled into the trees, screaming hoarsely. It was only the screams that revealed them as real birds.

The others had their binoculars up. Even the Viennese woman had a little pair of opera glasses. "Would you look at that," said one of the men. "Wish I'd brought my movie camera."

Don and Christine were without technology. So was the Mennonite woman. "You could watch them forever," she said, to nobody in particular. Christine, afraid that she would go on to say something embarrassing, pretended not to hear her. *Forever* was loaded.

She took Lilian's hand. "See those red birds?" she said. "You might never see one of those again in your entire life." But she knew that for Lilian these birds were no more special than anything else. She was too young for them. She said, "Oh," which was what she would have said if they had been pterodactyls or angels with wings as red as blood. Magicians, Christine knew from Lilian's last birthday party, were a failure with small children, who didn't see any reason why rabbits shouldn't come out of hats.

Don took hold of Christine's hand, a thing he had not done for some time; but Christine, watching the birds, noticed this only afterwards. She felt she was looking at a picture, of exotic flowers or of red fruit growing on trees, evenly spaced, like the fruit in the gardens of mediaeval paintings, solid, clear-edged, in primary colours. On the other side of the fence was another world, not real but at the same time more real than the one on this side, the men and women in their flimsy clothes and aging bodies, the decrepit boat. Her own body seemed fragile and empty, like blown glass.

110   The Mennonite woman had her face turned up to the sunset; her body was cut off at the neck by shadow, so that her head appeared to be floating in the air. For the first time she looked sad; but when she felt Christine watching her she smiled again, as if to reassure her, her face luminous and pink and round as a plum. Christine felt the two hands holding her own, mooring her, one on either side.

Weight returned to her body. The light was fading, the air chillier. Soon they would have to return in the increasing darkness, in a boat so rotten a misplaced foot would go through it. The water would be black, not brown; it would be full of roots.

"Shouldn't we go back?" she said to Don.

Lilian said, "Mummy, I'm hungry," and Christine remembered the chocolate bar and rummaged in her bag. It was down at the bottom, limp as a slab of bacon but not liquid. She brought it out and peeled off the silver paper, and gave a square to Lilian and one to Don, and ate one herself. The light was pink and dark at the same time, and it was difficult to see what she was doing.

When she told about this later, after they were safely home, Christine put in the swamp and the awful boat, and the men singing and the suspicious smell of the water. She put in Don's irritability, but only on days when he wasn't particularly irritable. (By then, there was less pressure; these things went in phases, Christine decided. She was glad she had never said anything, forced any issues.) She put in how good Lilian had been even though she hadn't wanted to go. She put in the hole in the boat, her own panic, which she made amusing, and the ridiculous bailing with the cans, and the Indians' indifference to their fate. She put in the Mennonite woman sitting on the hole like a big fat hen, making this funny, but admiring also, since the woman's solution to the problem had been so simple and obvious that no one else had thought of it. She left out the dead child.

115   She put in the rather hilarious trip back to the wharf, with the Indian standing up in the bow, beaming his heavy-duty flashlight at the endless, boring mangroves, and the two men in the baseball caps getting into a mickey[3] and singing dirty songs.

She ended with the birds, which were worth every minute of it, she said. She presented them as a form of entertainment, like the Grand Canyon: something that really ought to be seen, if you liked birds, and if you should happen to be in that part of the world.

1983

3. Drunken argument

ANN BEATTIE

Janus

The bowl was perfect. Perhaps it was not what you'd select if you faced a shelf of bowls, and not the sort of thing that would inevitably attract a lot of attention at a crafts fair, yet it had real presence. It was as predictably admired as a mutt who has no reason to suspect he might be funny. Just such a dog, in fact, was often brought out (and in) along with the bowl.

Andrea was a real estate agent, and when she thought that some prospective buyers might be dog lovers, she would drop off her dog at the same time she placed the bowl in the house that was up for sale. She would put a dish of water in the kitchen for Mondo, take his squeaking plastic frog out of her purse and drop it on the floor. He would pounce delightedly, just as he did every day at home, batting around his favorite toy. The bowl usually sat on a coffee table, though recently she had displayed it on top of a pine blanket chest and on a lacquered table. It was once placed on a cherry table beneath a Bonnard[1] still life, where it held its own.

Everyone who has purchased a house or who has wanted to sell a house must be familiar with some of the tricks used to convince a buyer that the house is quite special: a fire in the fireplace in early evening; jonquils in a pitcher on the kitchen counter, where no one ordinarily has space to put flowers; perhaps the slight aroma of spring, made by a single drop of scent vaporizing from a lamp bulb.

The wonderful thing about the bowl, Andrea thought, was that it was both subtle and noticeable—a paradox of a bowl. Its glaze was the color of cream and seemed to glow no matter what light it was placed in. There were a few bits of color in it—tiny geometric flashes—and some of these were tinged with flecks of silver. They were as mysterious as cells seen under a microscope; it was difficult not to study them, because they shimmered, flashing for a split second, and then resumed their shape. Something about the colors and their random placement suggested motion. People who liked country furniture always commented on the bowl, but then it turned out that people who felt comfortable with Biedermeier[2] loved it just as much. But the bowl was not at all ostentatious, or even so noticeable that anyone would suspect that it had been put in place deliberately. They might notice the height of the ceiling on first entering a room, and only when their eye moved down from that, or away from the refraction of sunlight on a pale wall, would they see the bowl. Then they would go immediately to it and comment. Yet they always faltered when they tried to say something. Perhaps it was because they were in the house for a serious reason, not to notice some object.

Once, Andrea got a call from a woman who had not put in an offer on a house she had shown her. That bowl, she said—would it be possible to find out where the owners had bought that beautiful bowl? Andrea pretended that she did not know what the woman was referring to. A bowl, somewhere in the house? Oh, on a table under the window. Yes, she would ask, of course. She let a couple of days pass, then called back to say that the bowl had been a present and the people did not know where it had been purchased.

When the bowl was not being taken from house to house, it sat on Andrea's coffee table at home. She didn't keep it carefully wrapped (although she transported it that way, in a box); she kept it on the table, because she liked to see it. It was large enough so that it didn't seem fragile, or particularly vulnerable if anyone sideswiped the table or Mondo blundered into it at play. She had asked her husband to please not drop his house key in it. It was meant to be empty.

When her husband first noticed the bowl, he had peered into it and smiled briefly. He always urged her to buy things she liked. In recent years, both of them had acquired many things to make up for all the lean years when they were graduate students, but now that they had been comfortable for quite a while, the pleasure of new possessions dwindled. Her husband had pronounced the bowl "pretty," and he had turned away without picking it up to examine it. He had no more interest in the bowl than she had in his new Leica.[3]

She was sure that the bowl brought her luck. Bids were often put in on houses where she had displayed the bowl. Sometimes the owners, who were always asked to be away or to step outside when the house was being shown, didn't even know that the bowl had been in their house. Once—she could not imagine how—she left it behind, and then she was so afraid that something might have happened to it that she rushed back to the house and sighed with relief when the woman owner opened the door. The bowl, Andrea explained—she had purchased a bowl and set it on the chest for safekeeping while she toured the house with the prospective buyers, and she . . . She felt like rushing past the frowning woman and seizing her bowl. The owner stepped aside, and it was only when Andrea ran to the chest that the lady glanced at her a little strangely. In the few seconds before Andrea picked up the bowl, she realized that the owner must have just seen that it had been perfectly placed, that the sunlight struck the bluer part of it. Her pitcher had been moved to the far side of the chest, and the bowl predominated. All the way home, Andrea wondered how she could have left the bowl behind. It was like leaving a friend at an outing—just walking off. Sometimes there were stories in the paper about families forgetting a child somewhere and driving to the next city. Andrea had only gone a mile down the road before she remembered.

In time, she dreamed of the bowl. Twice, in a waking dream—early in the morning, between sleep and a last nap before rising—she had a clear vision of it. It came into sharp focus and startled her for a moment—the same bowl she looked at every day.

10   She had a very profitable year selling real estate. Word spread, and she had more clients than she felt comfortable with. She had the foolish thought that if only the bowl were an animate object she could thank it. There were times when she wanted to talk to her husband about the bowl. He was a stockbroker, and sometimes told people that he was fortunate to be married to a woman who had such a fine aesthetic sense and yet could also function in the real world. They were a lot alike, really—they had agreed on that. They were both quiet people—reflective, slow to make value judgments, but almost intractable once they had come to a

3. An expensive German camera.

conclusion. They both liked details, but while ironies attracted her, he was more impatient and dismissive when matters became many sided or unclear. But they both knew this; it was the kind of thing they could talk about when they were alone in the car together, coming home from a party or after a weekend with friends. But she never talked to him about the bowl. When they were at dinner, exchanging their news of the day, or while they lay in bed at night listening to the stereo and murmuring sleepy disconnections, she was often tempted to come right out and say that she thought that the bowl in the living room, the cream-colored bowl, was responsible for her success. But she didn't say it. She couldn't begin to explain it. Sometimes in the morning, she would look at him and feel guilty that she had such a constant secret.

Could it be that she had some deeper connection with the bowl—a relationship of some kind? She corrected her thinking: how could she imagine such a thing, when she was a human being and it was a bowl? It was ridiculous. Just think of how people lived together and loved each other . . . But was that always so clear, always a relationship? She was confused by these thoughts, but they remained in her mind. There was something within her now, something real, that she never talked about.

The bowl was a mystery, even to her. It was frustrating, because her involvement with the bowl contained a steady sense of unrequited good fortune; it would have been easier to respond if some sort of demand were made in return. But that only happened in fairy tales. The bowl was just a bowl. She did not believe that for one second. What she believed was that it was something she loved.

In the past, she had sometimes talked to her husband about a new property she was about to buy or sell—confiding some clever strategy she had devised to persuade owners who seemed ready to sell. Now she stopped doing that, for all her strategies involved the bowl. She became more deliberate with the bowl, and more possessive. She put it in houses only when no one was there, and removed it when she left the house. Instead of just moving a pitcher or a dish, she would remove all the other objects from a table. She had to force herself to handle them carefully, because she didn't really care about them. She just wanted them out of sight.

She wondered how the situation would end. As with a lover, there was no exact scenario of how matters would come to a close. Anxiety became the operative force. It would be irrelevant if the lover rushed into someone else's arms, or wrote her a note and departed to another city. The horror was the possibility of the disappearance. That was what mattered.

She would get up at night and look at the bowl. It never occurred to her that 15 she might break it. She washed and dried it without anxiety, and she moved it often, from coffee table to mahogany corner table or wherever, without fearing an accident. It was clear that she would not be the one who would do anything to the bowl. The bowl was only handled by her, set safely on one surface or another; it was not very likely that anyone would break it. A bowl was a poor conductor of electricity: it would not be hit by lightning. Yet the idea of damage persisted. She did not think beyond that—to what her life would be without the bowl. She only continued to fear that some accident would happen. Why not, in a world where people set plants where they did not belong, so that visitors touring a house would be fooled into thinking that dark corners got sunlight—a world full of tricks?

She had first seen the bowl several years earlier, at a crafts fair she had visited half in secret, with her lover. He had urged her to buy the bowl. She didn't *need* any more things, she told him. But she had been drawn to the bowl, and they had lingered near it. Then she went on to the next booth, and he came up behind her, tapping the rim against her shoulder as she ran her fingers over a wood carving. "You're still insisting that I buy that?" she said. "No," he said. "I bought it for you." He had bought her other things before this—things she liked more, at first—the child's ebony-and-turquoise ring that fitted her little finger; the wooden box, long and thin, beautifully dovetailed, that she used to hold paper clips; the soft gray sweater with a pouch pocket. It was his idea that when he could not be there to hold her hand she could hold her own—clasp her hands inside the lone pocket that stretched across the front. But in time she became more attached to the bowl than to any of his other presents. She tried to talk herself out of it. She owned other things that were more striking or valuable. It wasn't an object whose beauty jumped out at you; a lot of people must have passed it by before the two of them saw it that day.

Her lover had said that she was always too slow to know what she really loved. Why continue with her life the way it was? Why be two-faced, he asked her. He had made the first move toward her. When she would not decide in his favor, would not change her life and come to him, he asked her what made her think she could have it both ways. And then he made the last move and left. It was a decision meant to break her will, to shatter her intransigent ideas about honoring previous commitments.

Time passed. Alone in the living room at night, she often looked at the bowl sitting on the table, still and safe, unilluminated. In its way, it was perfect: the world cut in half, deep and smoothly empty. Near the rim, even in dim light, the eye moved toward one small flash of blue, a vanishing point on the horizon.

1986

AMBROSE BIERCE

An Occurrence at Owl Creek Bridge

I

A man stood upon a railroad bridge in Northern Alabama, looking down into the swift waters twenty feet below. The man's hands were behind his back, the wrists bound with a cord. A rope loosely encircled his neck. It was attached to a stout cross-timber above his head, and the slack fell to the level of his knees. Some loose boards laid upon the sleepers supporting the metals of the railway supplied a footing for him and his executioners—two private soldiers of the Federal army, directed by a sergeant, who in civil life may have been a deputy sheriff. At a short remove upon the same temporary platform was an officer in the uniform of his rank, armed. He was a captain. A sentinel at each end of the bridge stood with his rifle in the position known as "support," that is to say, vertical in front of the left shoulder, the hammer resting on the forearm thrown straight across the chest—a formal and unnatural position, enforcing an erect carriage of the body. It did not appear to be the duty of these two men to know what was occurring at the centre of the bridge; they merely blockaded the two ends of the foot plank which traversed it.

Beyond one of the sentinels nobody was in sight; the railroad ran straight away into a forest for a hundred yards, then, curving, was lost to view. Doubtless there was an outpost further along. The other bank of the stream was open ground—a gentle acclivity crowned with a stockade of vertical tree trunks, loopholed for rifles, with a single embrasure through which protruded the muzzle of a brass cannon commanding the bridge. Midway of the slope between bridge and fort were the spectators—a single company of infantry in line, at "parade rest," the butts of the rifles on the ground, the barrels inclining slightly backward against the right shoulder, the hands crossed upon the stock. A lieutenant stood at the right of the line, the point of his sword upon the ground, his left hand resting upon his right. Excepting the group of four at the centre of the bridge not a man moved. The company faced the bridge, staring stonily, motionless. The sentinels, facing the banks of the stream, might have been statues to adorn the bridge. The captain stood with folded arms, silent, observing the work of his subordinates but making no sign. Death is a dignitary who, when he comes announced, is to be received with formal manifestations of respect, even by those most familiar with him. In the code of military etiquette silence and fixity are forms of deference.

The man who was engaged in being hanged was apparently about thirty-five years of age. He was a civilian, if one might judge from his dress, which was that of a planter. His features were good—a straight nose, firm mouth, broad forehead, from which his long, dark hair was combed straight back, falling behind his ears to the collar of his well-fitting frock coat. He wore a moustache and pointed beard, but no whiskers; his eyes were large and dark grey and had a kindly expression which one would hardly have expected in one whose neck was in the hemp. Evidently this was no vulgar assassin. The liberal military code makes provision for hanging many kinds of people, and gentlemen are not excluded.

The preparations being complete, the two private soldiers stepped aside and each drew away the plank upon which he had been standing. The sergeant turned to the captain, saluted and placed himself immediately behind that officer, who in turn moved apart one pace. These movements left the condemned man and the sergeant standing on the two ends of the same plank, which spanned three of the cross-ties of the bridge. The end upon which the civilian stood almost, but not quite, reached a fourth. This plank had been held in place by the weight of the captain; it was now held by that of the sergeant. At a signal from the former, the latter would step aside, the plank would tilt and the condemned man go down between two ties. The arrangement commended itself to his judgment as simple and effective. His face had not been covered nor his eyes bandaged. He looked a moment at his "unsteadfast footing," then let his gaze wander to the swirling water of the stream racing madly beneath his feet. A piece of dancing driftwood caught his attention and his eyes followed it down the current. How slowly it appeared to move! What a sluggish stream!

He closed his eyes in order to fix his last thoughts upon his wife and children. 5 The water, touched to gold by the early sun, the brooding mists under the banks at some distance down the stream, the fort, the soldiers, the piece of drift—all had distracted him. And now he became conscious of a new disturbance. Striking through the thought of his dear ones was a sound which he could neither ignore nor understand, a sharp, distinct, metallic percussion like the stroke of a black-smith's hammer upon the anvil; it had the same ringing quality. He wondered what it was, and whether immeasurably distant or near by—it seemed both. Its recurrence was regular, but as slow as the tolling of a death knell. He awaited each stroke with impatience and—he knew not why—apprehension. The inter-vals of silence grew progressively longer, the delays became maddening. With their greater infrequency the sounds increased in strength and sharpness. They hurt his ear like the thrust of a knife; he feared he would shriek. What he heard was the ticking of his watch.

He unclosed his eyes and saw again the water below him. "If I could free my hands," he thought, "I might throw off the noose and spring into the stream. By diving I could evade the bullets, and, swimming vigorously, reach the bank, take to the woods, and get away home. My home, thank God, is as yet outside their lines; my wife and little ones are still beyond the invader's farthest advance."

As these thoughts, which have here to be set down in words, were flashed into the doomed man's brain rather than evolved from it, the captain nodded to the sergeant. The sergeant stepped aside.

II

Peyton Farquhar was a well-to-do planter, of an old and highly-respected Ala-bama family. Being a slave owner, and, like other slave owners, a politician, he was naturally an original secessionist and ardently devoted to the Southern cause. Circumstances of an imperious nature which it is unnecessary to relate here, had prevented him from taking service with the gallant army which had fought the disastrous campaigns ending with the fall of Corinth,[1] and he chafed under the inglorious restraint, longing for the release of his energies, the larger life of the soldier, the opportunity for distinction. That opportunity, he felt, would come, as it comes to all in war time. Meanwhile he did what he could. No service was too humble for him to perform in aid of the South, no adventure too perilous for him to undertake if consistent with the character of a civilian who was at heart a soldier, and who in good faith and without too much qualifica-tion assented to at least a part of the frankly villainous dictum that all is fair in love and war.

One evening while Farquhar and his wife were sitting on a rustic bench near the entrance to his grounds, a grey-clad soldier rode up to the gate and asked for a drink of water. Mrs. Farquhar was only too happy to serve him with her own white hands. While she was gone to fetch the water, her husband approached the dusty horseman and inquired eagerly for news from the front.

10   "The Yanks are repairing the railroads," said the man, "and are getting ready for another advance. They have reached the Owl Creek bridge, put it in order, and built a stockade on the other bank. The commandant has issued an order, which is posted everywhere, declaring that any civilian caught interfering with the railroad, its bridges, tunnels, or trains, will be summarily hanged. I saw the order."

"How far is it to the Owl Creek bridge?" Farquhar asked.

"About thirty miles."

"Is there no force on this side the creek?"

---

1. Corinth, Mississippi, captured by General Ulysses S. Grant in April 1862.

"Only a picket post half a mile out, on the railroad, and a single sentinel at this end of the bridge."

"Suppose a man—a civilian and student of hanging—should elude the picket 15 post and perhaps get the better of the sentinel," said Farquhar, smiling, "what could he accomplish?"

The soldier reflected. "I was there a month ago," he replied. "I observed that the flood of last winter had lodged a great quantity of driftwood against the wooden pier at this end of the bridge. It is now dry and would burn like tow."

The lady had now brought the water, which the soldier drank. He thanked her ceremoniously, bowed to her husband, and rode away. An hour later, after nightfall, he repassed the plantation, going northward in the direction from which he had come. He was a Federal scout.

III

As Peyton Farquhar fell straight downward through the bridge, he lost consciousness and was as one already dead. From this state he was awakened—ages later, it seemed to him—by the pain of a sharp pressure upon his throat, followed by a sense of suffocation. Keen, poignant agonies seemed to shoot from his neck downward through every fibre of his body and limbs. These pains appeared to flash along well-defined lines of ramification, and to beat with an inconceivably rapid periodicity. They seemed like streams of pulsating fire heating him to an intolerable temperature. As to his head, he was conscious of nothing but a feeling of fullness—of congestion. These sensations were unaccompanied by thought. The intellectual part of his nature was already effaced; he had power only to feel, and feeling was torment. He was conscious of motion. Encompassed in a luminous cloud, of which he was now merely the fiery heart, without material substance, he swung through unthinkable arcs of oscillation, like a vast pendulum. Then all at once, with terrible suddenness, the light about him shot upward with the noise of a loud plash; a frightful roaring was in his ears, and all was cold and dark. The power of thought was restored; he knew that the rope had broken and he had fallen into the stream. There was no additional strangulation; the noose about his neck was already suffocating him, and kept the water from his lungs. To die of hanging at the bottom of a river!—the idea seemed to him ludicrous. He opened his eyes in the blackness and saw above him a gleam of light, but how distant, how inaccessible! He was still sinking, for the light became fainter and fainter until it was a mere glimmer. Then it began to grow and brighten, and he knew that he was rising toward the surface—knew it with reluctance, for he was now very comfortable. "To be hanged and drowned," he thought, "that is not so bad; but I do not wish to be shot. No; I will not be shot; that is not fair."

He was not conscious of an effort, but a sharp pain in his wrist apprised him that he was trying to free his hands. He gave the struggle his attention, as an idler might observe the feat of a juggler, without interest in the outcome. What splendid effort!—what magnificent, what superhuman strength! Ah, that was a fine endeavour! Bravo! The cord fell away; his arms parted and floated upward, the hands dimly seen on each side in the growing light. He watched them with a new interest as first one and then the other pounced upon the noose at his neck. They tore it away and thrust it fiercely aside, its undulations resembling those of a water-snake. "Put it back, put it back!" He thought he shouted these words to his hands, for the undoing of the noose had been succeeded by the direst pang which he had yet experienced. His neck ached horribly; his brain was on fire; his heart, which had been fluttering faintly, gave a great leap, trying to force itself out at his mouth. His whole body was racked and wrenched with an insupportable anguish! But his disobedient hands gave no heed to the command. They beat the water vigorously with quick, downward strokes, forcing him to the surface. He felt his head emerge; his eyes were blinded by the sunlight; his chest expanded convulsively, and with a supreme and crowning agony his lungs engulfed a great draught of air, which instantly he expelled in a shriek!

20   He was now in full possession of his physical senses. They were, indeed, preternaturally keen and alert. Something in the awful disturbance of his organic system had so exalted and refined them that they made record of things never before perceived. He felt the ripples upon his face and heard their separate sounds as they struck. He looked at the forest on the bank of the stream, saw the individual trees, the leaves and the veining of each leaf—the very insects upon them, the locusts, the brilliant-bodied flies, the grey spiders stretching their webs from twig to twig. He noted the prismatic colors in all the dewdrops upon a million blades of grass. The humming of the gnats that danced above the eddies of the stream, the beating of the dragon flies' wings, the strokes of the water spiders' legs, like oars which had lifted their boat—all these made audible music. A fish slid along beneath his eyes and he heard the rush of its body parting the water.

He had come to the surface facing down the stream; in a moment the visible world seemed to wheel slowly round, himself the pivotal point, and he saw the bridge, the fort, the soldiers upon the bridge, the captain, the sergeant, the two privates, his executioners. They were in silhouette against the blue sky. They shouted and gesticulated, pointing at him; the captain had drawn his pistol, but did not fire; the others were unarmed. Their movements were grotesque and horrible, their forms gigantic.

Suddenly he heard a sharp report and something struck the water smartly within a few inches of his head, spattering his face with spray. He heard a second report, and saw one of the sentinels with his rifle at his shoulder, a light cloud of blue smoke rising from the muzzle. The man in the water saw the eye of the man on the bridge gazing into his own through the sights of the rifle. He observed that it was a grey eye, and remembered having read that grey eyes were keenest and that all famous marksmen had them. Nevertheless, this one had missed.

A counter swirl had caught Farquhar and turned him half round; he was again looking into the forest on the bank opposite the fort. The sound of a clear, high voice in a monotonous singsong now rang out behind him and came across the water with a distinctness that pierced and subdued all other sounds, even the beating of the ripples in his ears. Although no soldier, he had frequented camps enough to know the dread significance of that deliberate, drawling, aspirated chant; the lieutenant on shore was taking a part in the morning's work. How coldly and pitilessly—with what an even, calm intonation, presaging and enforcing tranquillity in the men—with what accurately-measured intervals fell those cruel words:

"Attention, company. . . . Shoulder arms. . . . Ready. . . . Aim. . . . Fire."

25   Farquhar dived—dived as deeply as he could. The water roared in his ears like the voice of Niagara, yet he heard the dulled thunder of the volley, and rising again toward the surface, met shining bits of metal, singularly flattened, oscil-

lating slowly downward. Some of them touched him on the face and hands, then fell away, continuing their descent. One lodged between his collar and neck; it was uncomfortably warm, and he snatched it out.

As he rose to the surface, gasping for breath, he saw that he had been a long time under water; he was perceptibly farther down stream—nearer to safety. The soldiers had almost finished reloading; the metal ramrods flashed all at once in the sunshine as they were drawn from the barrels, turned in the air, and thrust into their sockets. The two sentinels fired again, independently and ineffectually.

The hunted man saw all this over his shoulder; he was now swimming vigorously with the current. His brain was as energetic as his arms and legs; he thought with the rapidity of lightning.

"The officer," he reasoned, "will not make that martinet's error a second time. It is as easy to dodge a volley as a single shot. He has probably already given the command to fire at will. God help me, I cannot dodge them all!"

An appalling plash within two yards of him, followed by a loud rushing sound, *diminuendo,* which seemed to travel back through the air to the fort and died in an explosion which stirred the very river to its deeps! A rising sheet of water, which curved over him, fell down upon him, blinded him, strangled him! The cannon had taken a hand in the game. As he shook his head free from the commotion of the smitten water, he heard the deflected shot humming through the air ahead, and in an instant it was cracking and smashing the branches in the forest beyond.

"They will not do that again," he thought; "the next time they will use a charge 30 of grape. I must keep my eye upon the gun; the smoke will apprise me—the report arrives too late; it lags behind the missile. It is a good gun."

Suddenly he felt himself whirled round and round—spinning like a top. The water, the banks, the forest, the now distant bridge, fort and men—all were commingled and blurred. Objects were represented by their colors only; circular horizontal streaks of color—that was all he saw. He had been caught in a vortex and was being whirled on with a velocity of advance and gyration which made him giddy and sick. In a few moments he was flung upon the gravel at the foot of the left bank of the stream—the southern bank—and behind a projecting point which concealed him from his enemies. The sudden arrest of his motion, the abrasion of one of his hands on the gravel, restored him and he wept with delight. He dug his fingers into the sand, threw it over himself in handfuls and audibly blessed it. It looked like gold, like diamonds, rubies, emeralds; he could think of nothing beautiful which it did not resemble. The trees upon the bank were giant garden plants; he noted a definite order in their arrangement, inhaled the fragrance of their blooms. A strange, roseate light shone through the spaces among their trunks, and the wind made in their branches the music of æolian harps. He had no wish to perfect his escape, was content to remain in that enchanting spot until retaken.

A whizz and rattle of grapeshot among the branches high above his head roused him from his dream. The baffled cannoneer had fired him a random farewell. He sprang to his feet, rushed up the sloping bank, and plunged into the forest.

All that day he travelled, laying his course by the rounding sun. The forest seemed interminable; nowhere did he discover a break in it, not even a woodman's road. He had not known that he lived in so wild a region. There was something uncanny in the revelation.

By nightfall he was fatigued, footsore, famishing. The thought of his wife and children urged him on. At last he found a road which led him in what he knew to be the right direction. It was as wide and straight as a city street, yet it seemed untravelled. No fields bordered it, no dwelling anywhere. Not so much as the barking of a dog suggested human habitation. The black bodies of the great trees formed a straight wall on both sides, terminating on the horizon in a point, like a diagram in a lesson in perspective. Overhead, as he looked up through this rift in the wood, shone great golden stars looking unfamiliar and grouped in strange constellations. He was sure they were arranged in some order which had a secret and malign significance. The wood on either side was full of singular noises, among which— once, twice, and again—he distinctly heard whispers in an unknown tongue.

35   His neck was in pain, and, lifting his hand to it, he found it horribly swollen. He knew that it had a circle of black where the rope had bruised it. His eyes felt congested; he could no longer close them. His tongue was swollen with thirst; he relieved its fever by thrusting it forward from between his teeth into the cool air. How softly the turf had carpeted the untravelled avenue! He could no longer feel the roadway beneath his feet!

Doubtless, despite his suffering, he fell asleep while walking, for now he sees another scene—perhaps he has merely recovered from a delirium. He stands at the gate of his own home. All is as he left it, and all bright and beautiful in the morning sunshine. He must have travelled the entire night. As he pushes open the gate and passes up the wide white walk, he sees a flutter of female garments; his wife, looking fresh and cool and sweet, steps down from the verandah to meet him. At the bottom of the steps she stands waiting, with a smile of ineffable joy, an attitude of matchless grace and dignity. Ah, how beautiful she is! He springs forward with extended arms. As he is about to clasp her, he feels a stunning blow upon the back of the neck; a blinding white light blazes all about him, with a sound like the shock of a cannon—then all is darkness and silence!

Peyton Farquhar was dead; his body, with a broken neck, swung gently from side to side beneath the timbers of the Owl Creek bridge.

1891

JORGE LUIS BORGES
The Garden of Forking Paths[1]

On page 22 of Liddell Hart's *History of World War I* you will read that an attack against the Serre-Montauban line by thirteen British divisions (supported by 1,400 artillery pieces), planned for the 24th of July, 1916, had to be postponed until the morning of the 29th. The torrential rains, Captain Liddell Hart comments, caused this delay, an insignificant one, to be sure.

The following statement, dictated, reread and signed by Dr. Yu Tsun, former professor of English at the *Hochschule* at Tsingtao,[2] throws an unsuspected light over the whole affair. The first two pages of the document are missing.

1. Translated by Donald A. Yates.
2. Major port in east China on the Yellow Sea controlled and developed by Germany in the early 1900s. *Hochschule:* university (German).

"... and I hung up the receiver. Immediately afterwards, I recognized the voice that had answered in German. It was that of Captain Richard Madden. Madden's presence in Viktor Runeberg's apartment meant the end of our anxieties and—but this seemed, *or should have seemed,* very secondary to me—also the end of our lives. It meant that Runeberg had been arrested or murdered.[3] Before the sun set on that day, I would encounter the same fate. Madden was implacable. Or rather, he was obliged to be so. An Irishman at the service of England, a man accused of laxity and perhaps of treason, how could he fail to seize and be thankful for such a miraculous opportunity: the discovery, capture, maybe even the death of two agents of the German Reich? I went up to my room; absurdly I locked the door and threw myself on my back on the narrow iron cot. Through the window I saw the familiar roofs and the cloud-shaded six o'clock sun. It seemed incredible to me that that day without premonitions or symbols should be the one of my inexorable death. In spite of my dead father, in spite of having been a child in a symmetrical garden of Hai Feng, was I—now—going to die? Then I reflected that everything happens to a man precisely, precisely *now.* Centuries of centuries and only in the present do things happen; countless men in the air, on the face of the earth and the sea, and all that really is happening is happening to me.... The almost intolerable recollection of Madden's horselike face banished these wanderings. In the midst of my hatred and terror (it means nothing to me now to speak of terror, now that I have mocked Richard Madden, now that my throat yearns for the noose) it occurred to me that that tumultuous and doubtless happy warrior did not suspect that I possessed the Secret. The name of the exact location of the new British artillery park on the River Ancre. A bird streaked across the gray sky and blindly I translated it into an airplane and that airplane into many (against the French sky) annihilating the artillery station with vertical bombs. If only my mouth, before a bullet shattered it, could cry out that secret name so it could be heard in Germany ... My human voice was very weak. How might I make it carry to the ear of the Chief? To the ear of that sick and hateful man who knew nothing of Runeberg and me save that we were in Staffordshire[4] and who was waiting in vain for our report in his arid office in Berlin, endlessly examining newspapers ... I said out loud: *I must flee.* I sat up noiselessly, in a useless perfection of silence, as if Madden were already lying in wait for me. Something—perhaps the mere vain ostentation of proving my resources were nil—made me look through my pockets. I found what I knew I would find. The American watch, the nickel chain and the square coin, the key ring with the incriminating useless keys to Runeberg's apartment, the notebook, a letter which I resolved to destroy immediately (and which I did not destroy), a crown, two shillings and a few pence, the red and blue pencil, the handkerchief, the revolver with one bullet. Absurdly, I took it in my hand and weighed it in order to inspire courage within myself. Vaguely I thought that a pistol report can be heard at a great distance. In ten minutes my plan was perfected. The telephone book listed the name of the only person capable of transmitting the message; he lived in a suburb of Fenton, less than a half hour's train ride away.

3. A hypothesis both hateful and odd. The Prussian spy Hans Rabener, alias Viktor Runeberg, attacked with drawn automatic the bearer of the warrant for his arrest, Captain Richard Madden. The latter, in self-defense, inflicted the wound which brought about Runeberg's death. (Editor's note.) [This note is by Borges as "Editor."]   4. County in west-central England.

I am a cowardly man. I say it now, now that I have carried to its end a plan whose perilous nature no one can deny. I know its execution was terrible. I didn't do it for Germany, no. I care nothing for a barbarous country which imposed upon me the abjection of being a spy. Besides, I know of a man from England—a modest man—who for me is no less great than Goethe.[5] I talked with him for scarcely an hour, but during that hour he was Goethe.... I did it because I sensed that the Chief somehow feared people of my race—for the innumerable ancestors who merge within me. I wanted to prove to him that a yellow man could save his armies. Besides, I had to flee from Captain Madden. His hands and his voice could call at my door at any moment. I dressed silently, bade farewell to myself in the mirror, went downstairs, scrutinized the peaceful street and went out. The station was not far from my home, but I judged it wise to take a cab. I argued that in this way I ran less risk of being recognized; the fact is that in the deserted street I felt myself visible and vulnerable, infinitely so. I remember that I told the cab driver to stop a short distance before the main entrance. I got out with voluntary, almost painful slowness; I was going to the village of Ashgrove but I bought a ticket for a more distant station. The train left within a very few minutes, at eight-fifty. I hurried; the next one would leave at nine-thirty. There was hardly a soul on the platform. I went through the coaches; I remember a few farmers, a woman dressed in mourning, a young boy who was reading with fervor the *Annals* of Tacitus,[6] a wounded and happy soldier. The coaches jerked forward at last. A man whom I recognized ran in vain to the end of the platform. It was Captain Richard Madden. Shattered, trembling, I shrank into the far corner of the seat, away from the dreaded window.

5   From this broken state I passed into an almost abject felicity. I told myself that the duel had already begun and that I had won the first encounter by frustrating, even if for forty minutes, even if by a stroke of fate, the attack of my adversary. I argued that this slightest of victories foreshadowed a total victory. I argued (no less fallaciously) that my cowardly felicity proved that I was a man capable of carrying out the adventure successfully. From this weakness I took strength that did not abandon me. I foresee that man will resign himself each day to more atrocious undertakings; soon there will be no one but warriors and brigands; I give them this counsel: *The author of an atrocious undertaking ought to imagine that he has already accomplished it, ought to impose upon himself a future as irrevocable as the past.* Thus I proceeded as my eyes of a man already dead registered the elapsing of that day, which was perhaps the last, and the diffusion of the night. The train ran gently along, amid ash trees. It stopped, almost in the middle of the fields. No one announced the name of the station. "Ashgrove?" I asked a few lads on the platform. "Ashgrove," they replied. I got off.

A lamp enlightened the platform but the faces of the boys were in shadow. One questioned me, "Are you going to Dr. Stephen Albert's house?" Without waiting for my answer, another said, "The house is a long way from here, but you won't get lost if you take this road to the left and at every crossroads turn again to your left." I tossed them a coin (my last), descended a few stone steps and started down the solitary road. It went downhill, slowly. It was of elemental earth; overhead the branches were tangled; the low, full moon seemed to accompany me.

5. Johann Wolfgang von Goethe (1749–1832), German poet and dramatist, author of *Faust*.
6. Cornelius Tacitus (c. 55–c. 117 C.E.), Roman historian.

For an instant, I thought that Richard Madden in some way had penetrated my desperate plan. Very quickly, I understood that that was impossible. The instructions to turn always to the left reminded me that such was the common procedure for discovering the central point of certain labyrinths. I have some understanding of labyrinths: not for nothing am I the great grandson of that Ts'ui Pên who was governor of Yunnan and who renounced worldly power in order to write a novel that might be even more populous than the *Hung Lu Meng*[7] and to construct a labyrinth in which all men would become lost. Thirteen years he dedicated to these heterogeneous tasks, but the hand of a stranger murdered him—and his novel was incoherent and no one found the labyrinth. Beneath English trees I meditated on that lost maze: I imagined it inviolate and perfect at the secret crest of a mountain; I imagined it erased by rice fields or beneath the water; I imagined it infinite, no longer composed of octagonal kiosks and returning paths, but of rivers and provinces and kingdoms . . . I thought of a labyrinth of labyrinths, of one sinuous spreading labyrinth that would encompass the past and the future and in some way involve the stars. Absorbed in these illusory images, I forgot my destiny of one pursued. I felt myself to be, for an unknown period of time, an abstract perceiver of the world. The vague, living countryside, the moon, the remains of the day worked on me, as well as the slope of the road which eliminated any possibility of weariness. The afternoon was intimate, infinite. The road descended and forked among the now confused meadows. A high-pitched, almost syllabic music approached and receded in the shifting of the wind, dimmed by leaves and distance. I thought that a man can be an enemy of other men, of the moments of other men, but not of a country: not of fireflies, words, gardens, streams of water, sunsets. Thus I arrived before a tall, rusty gate. Between the iron bars I made out a poplar grove and a pavilion. I understood suddenly two things, the first trivial, the second almost unbelievable: the music came from the pavilion, and the music was Chinese. For precisely that reason I had openly accepted it without paying it any heed. I do not remember whether there was a bell or whether I knocked with my hand. The sparkling of the music continued.

From the rear of the house within a lantern approached: a lantern that the trees sometimes striped and sometimes eclipsed, a paper lantern that had the form of a drum and the color of the moon. A tall man bore it. I didn't see his face for the light blinded me. He opened the door and said slowly, in my own language: "I see that the pious Hsi P'êng persists in correcting my solitude. You no doubt wish to see the garden?"

I recognized the name of one of our consuls and I replied, disconcerted, "The garden?"

"The garden of forking paths."

10

Something stirred in my memory and I uttered with incomprehensible certainty, "The garden of my ancestor Ts'ui Pên."

"Your ancestor? Your illustrious ancestor? Come in."

The damp path zigzagged like those of my childhood. We came to a library of Eastern and Western books. I recognized bound in yellow silk several volumes of the Lost Encyclopedia, edited by the Third Emperor of the Luminous Dynasty

---

7. *The Story of the Stone* (1791), a panoramic Chinese novel that features more than 430 characters.

but never printed.[8] The record on the phonograph revolved next to a bronze phoenix. I also recall a *famille rose* vase and another, many centuries older, of that shade of blue which our craftsmen copied from the potters of Persia. . . .

Stephen Albert observed me with a smile. He was, as I have said, very tall, sharp-featured, with gray eyes and a gray beard. He told me that he had been a missionary in Tientsin "before aspiring to become a Sinologist."[9]

15   We sat down—I on a long, low divan, he with his back to the window and a tall circular clock. I calculated that my pursuer, Richard Madden, could not arrive for at least an hour. My irrevocable determination could wait.

"An astounding fate, that of Ts'ui Pên," Stephen Albert said. "Governor of his native province, learned in astronomy, in astrology and in the tireless interpretation of the canonical books, chess player, famous poet and calligrapher—he abandoned all this in order to compose a book and a maze. He renounced the pleasures of both tyranny and justice, of his populous couch, of his banquets and even of erudition—all to close himself up for thirteen years in the Pavilion of the Limpid Solitude. When he died, his heirs found nothing save chaotic manuscripts. His family, as you may be aware, wished to condemn them to the fire; but his executor—a Taoist or Buddhist monk—insisted on their publication."

"We descendants of Ts'ui Pên," I replied, "continue to curse that monk. Their publication was senseless. The book is an indeterminate heap of contradictory drafts. I examined it once: in the third chapter the hero dies, in the fourth he is alive. As for the other undertaking of Ts'ui Pên, his labyrinth. . . ."

"Here is Ts'ui Pên's labyrinth," he said, indicating a tall lacquered desk.

"An ivory labyrinth!" I exclaimed. "A minimum labyrinth."

20   "A labyrinth of symbols," he corrected. "An invisible labyrinth of time. To me, a barbarous Englishman, has been entrusted the revelation of this diaphanous mystery. After more than a hundred years, the details are irretrievable; but it is not hard to conjecture what happened. Ts'ui Pên must have said once: *I am withdrawing to write a book*. And another time: *I am withdrawing to construct a labyrinth*. Every one imagined two works; to no one did it occur that the book and the maze were one and the same thing. The Pavilion of the Limpid Solitude stood in the center of a garden that was perhaps intricate; that circumstance could have suggested to the heirs a physical labyrinth. Ts'ui Pên died; no one in the vast territories that were his came upon the labyrinth; the confusion of the novel suggested to me that *it* was the maze. Two circumstances gave me the correct solution of the problem. One: the curious legend that Ts'ui Pên had planned to create a labyrinth which would be strictly infinite. The other: a fragment of a letter I discovered."

Albert rose. He turned his back on me for a moment; he opened a drawer of the black and gold desk. He faced me and in his hands he held a sheet of paper that had once been crimson, but was now pink and tenuous and cross-sectioned. The fame of Ts'ui Pên as a calligrapher had been justly won. I read, uncomprehendingly and with fervor, these words written with a minute brush by a man of my blood: *I leave to the various futures (not to all) my garden of forking paths*. Wordlessly, I returned the sheet. Albert continued:

---

8. A massive encyclopedia commissioned in the early 1400s by the Yung-lo emperor of the Ming dynasty. One copy of the 11,095 manuscript volumes was made in the mid-1500s; the original was destroyed; and only 370 volumes of the copy survive today.   9. One who studies China and the Chinese.

"Before unearthing this letter, I had questioned myself about the ways in which a book can be infinite. I could think of nothing other than a cyclic volume, a circular one. A book whose last page was identical with the first, a book which had the possibility of continuing indefinitely. I remembered too that night which is at the middle of the Thousand and One Nights[1] when Scheherazade (through a magical oversight of the copyist) begins to relate word for word the story of the Thousand and One Nights, establishing the risk of coming once again to the night when she must repeat it, and thus on to infinity. I imagined as well a Platonic, hereditary work, transmitted from father to son, in which each new individual adds a chapter or corrects with pious care the pages of his elders. These conjectures diverted me; but none seemed to correspond, not even remotely, to the contradictory chapters of Ts'ui Pên. In the midst of this perplexity, I received from Oxford the manuscript you have examined. I lingered, naturally, on the sentence: *I leave to the various futures (not to all) my garden of forking paths.* Almost instantly, I understood: 'The garden of forking paths' was the chaotic novel; the phrase 'the various futures (not to all)' suggested to me the forking in time, not in space. A broad rereading of the work confirmed the theory. In all fictional works, each time a man is confronted with several alternatives, he chooses one and eliminates the others; in the fiction of Ts'ui Pên, he chooses—simultaneously—all of them. *He creates,* in this way, diverse futures, diverse times which themselves also proliferate and fork. Here, then, is the explanation of the novel's contradictions. Fang, let us say, has a secret; a stranger calls at his door; Fang resolves to kill him. Naturally, there are several possible outcomes: Fang can kill the intruder, the intruder can kill Fang, they both can escape, they both can die, and so forth. In the work of Ts'ui Pên, all possible outcomes occur; each one is the point of departure for other forkings. Sometimes, the paths of this labyrinth converge: for example, you arrive at this house, but in one of the possible pasts you are my enemy, in another, my friend. If you will resign yourself to my incurable pronunciation, we shall read a few pages."

His face, within the vivid circle of the lamplight, was unquestionably that of an old man, but with something unalterable about it, even immortal. He read with slow precision two versions of the same epic chapter. In the first, an army marches to a battle across a lonely mountain; the horror of the rocks and shadows makes the men undervalue their lives and they gain an easy victory. In the second, the same army traverses a palace where a great festival is taking place; the resplendent battle seems to them a continuation of the celebration and they win the victory. I listened with proper veneration to these ancient narratives, perhaps less admirable in themselves than the fact that they had been created by my blood and were being restored to me by a man of a remote empire, in the course of a desperate adventure, on a Western isle. I remember the last words, repeated in each version like a secret commandment: *Thus fought the heroes, tranquil their admirable hearts, violent their swords, resigned to kill and to die.*

From that moment on, I felt about me and within my dark body an invisible, intangible swarming. Not the swarming of the divergent, parallel and finally coalescent armies, but a more inaccessible, more intimate agitation that they in some manner prefigured. Stephen Albert continued:

---

1. Also known as the *Arabian Nights*, a thousand and one tales told by Scheherazade to her husband, the Persian king Shahryar, to trick him into postponing her execution.

25   "I don't believe that your illustrious ancestor played idly with these variations. I don't consider it credible that he would sacrifice thirteen years to the infinite execution of a rhetorical experiment. In your country, the novel is a subsidiary form of literature; in Ts'ui Pên's time it was a despicable form. Ts'ui Pên was a brilliant novelist, but he was also a man of letters who doubtless did not consider himself a mere novelist. The testimony of his contemporaries proclaims—and his life fully confirms—his metaphysical and mystical interests. Philosophic controversy usurps a good part of the novel. I know that of all problems, none disturbed him so greatly nor worked upon him so much as the abysmal problem of time. Now then, the latter is the only problem that does not figure in the pages of the *Garden*. He does not even use the word that signifies *time*. How do you explain this voluntary omission?"

I proposed several solutions—all unsatisfactory. We discussed them. Finally, Stephen Albert said to me:

"In a riddle whose answer is chess, what is the only prohibited word?"

I thought a moment and replied, "The word *chess*."

"Precisely," said Albert. "*The Garden of Forking Paths* is an enormous riddle, or parable, whose theme is time; this recondite cause prohibits its mention. To omit a word always, to resort to inept metaphors and obvious periphrases, is perhaps the most emphatic way of stressing it. That is the tortuous method preferred, in each of the meanderings of his indefatigable novel, by the oblique Ts'ui Pên. I have compared hundreds of manuscripts, I have corrected the errors that the negligence of the copyists has introduced, I have guessed the plan of this chaos, I have re-established—I believe I have re-established—the primordial organization, I have translated the entire work: it is clear to me that not once does he employ the word 'time.' The explanation is obvious: *The Garden of Forking Paths* is an incomplete, but not false, image of the universe as Ts'ui Pên conceived it. In contrast to Newton and Schopenhauer,[2] your ancestor did not believe in a uniform, absolute time. He believed in an infinite series of times, in a growing, dizzying net of divergent, convergent and parallel times. This network of times which approached one another, forked, broke off, or were unaware of one another for centuries, embraces *all* possibilities of time. We do not exist in the majority of these times; in some you exist, and not I; in others I, and not you; in others, both of us. In the present one, which a favorable fate has granted me, you have arrived at my house; in another, while crossing the garden, you found me dead; in still another, I utter these same words, but I am a mistake, a ghost."

30   "In every one," I pronounced, not without a tremble to my voice, "I am grateful to you and revere you for your re-creation of the garden of Ts'ui Pên."

"Not in all," he murmured with a smile. "Time forks perpetually toward innumerable futures. In one of them I am your enemy."

Once again I felt the swarming sensation of which I have spoken. It seemed to me that the humid garden that surrounded the house was infinitely saturated with invisible persons. Those persons were Albert and I, secret, busy and multiform in other dimensions of time. I raised my eyes and the tenuous nightmare dissolved. In the yellow and black garden there was only one man; but this man

---

2. Arthur Schopenhauer (1788–1860), German philosopher; Sir Isaac Newton (1642–1727), English mathematician and physicist.

was as strong as a statue . . . this man was approaching along the path and he was Captain Richard Madden.

"The future already exists," I replied, "but I am your friend. Could I see the letter again?"

Albert rose. Standing tall, he opened the drawer of the tall desk; for the moment his back was to me. I had readied the revolver. I fired with extreme caution. Albert fell uncomplainingly, immediately. I swear his death was instantaneous—a lightning stroke.

The rest is unreal, insignificant. Madden broke in, arrested me. I have been 35 condemned to the gallows. I have won out abominably; I have communicated to Berlin the secret name of the city they must attack. They bombed it yesterday; I read it in the same papers that offered to England the mystery of the learned Sinologist Stephen Albert who was murdered by a stranger, one Yu Tsun. The Chief had deciphered this mystery. He knew my problem was to indicate (through the uproar of the war) the city called Albert, and that I had found no other means to do so than to kill a man of that name. He does not know (no one can know) my innumerable contrition and weariness.

For Victoria Ocampo

1941

RALPH ELLISON

King of the Bingo Game

The woman in front of him was eating roasted peanuts that smelled so good that he could barely contain his hunger. He could not even sleep and wished they'd hurry and begin the bingo game. There, on his right, two fellows were drinking wine out of a bottle wrapped in a paper bag, and he could hear soft gurgling in the dark. His stomach gave a low, gnawing growl. "If this was down South," he thought, "all I'd have to do is lean over and say, 'Lady, gimme a few of those peanuts, please ma'am,' and she'd pass me the bag and never think nothing of it." Or he could ask the fellows for a drink in the same way. Folks down South stuck together that way; they didn't even have to know you. But up here it was different. Ask somebody for something, and they'd think you were crazy. Well, I ain't crazy. I'm just broke, 'cause I got no birth certificate to get a job, and Laura 'bout to die 'cause we got no money for a doctor. But I ain't crazy. And yet a pinpoint of doubt was focused in his mind as he glanced toward the screen and saw the hero stealthily entering a dark room and sending the beam of a flashlight along a wall of bookcases. This is where he finds the trapdoor, he remembered. The man would pass abruptly through the wall and find the girl tied to a bed, her legs and arms spread wide, and her clothing torn to rags. He laughed softly to himself. He had seen the picture three times, and this was one of the best scenes.

On his right the fellow whispered wide-eyed to his companion, "Man, look ayonder!"

"Damn!"

"Wouldn't I like to have her tied up like that . . ."

5   "Hey! That fool's letting her loose!"

"Aw, man, he loves her."

"Love or no love!"

The man moved impatiently beside him, and he tried to involve himself in the scene. But Laura was on his mind. Tiring quickly of watching the picture he looked back to where the white beam filtered from the projection room above the balcony. It started small and grew large, specks of dust dancing in its whiteness as it reached the screen. It was strange how the beam always landed right on the screen and didn't mess up and fall somewhere else. But they had it all fixed. Everything was fixed. Now suppose when they showed that girl with her dress torn the girl started taking off the rest of her clothes, and when the guy came in he didn't untie her but kept her there and went to taking off his own clothes? *That* would be something to see. If a picture got out of hand like that those guys up there would go nuts. Yeah, and there'd be so many folks in here you couldn't find a seat for nine months! A strange sensation played over his skin. He shuddered. Yesterday he'd seen a bedbug on a woman's neck as they walked out into the bright street. But exploring his thigh through a hole in his pocket he found only goose pimples and old scars.

The bottle gurgled again. He closed his eyes. Now a dreamy music was accompanying the film and train whistles were sounding in the distance, and he was a boy again walking along a railroad trestle down South, and seeing the train coming, and running back as fast as he could go, and hearing the whistle blowing, and getting off the trestle to solid ground just in time, with the earth trembling beneath his feet, and feeling relieved as he ran down the cinder-strewn embankment onto the highway, and looking back and seeing with terror that the train had left the track and was following him right down the middle of the street, and all the white people laughing as he ran screaming. . . .

10   "Wake up there, buddy! What the hell do you mean hollering like that? Can't you see we trying to enjoy this here picture?"

He stared at the man with gratitude.

"I'm sorry, old man," he said. "I musta been dreaming."

"Well, here, have a drink. And don't be making no noise like that, damn!"

His hands trembled as he tilted his head. It was not wine, but whiskey. Cold rye whiskey. He took a deep swoller, decided it was better not to take another, and handed the bottle back to its owner.

15   "Thanks, old man," he said.

Now he felt the cold whiskey breaking a warm path straight through the middle of him, growing hotter and sharper as it moved. He had not eaten all day, and it made him light-headed. The smell of the peanuts stabbed him like a knife, and he got up and found a seat in the middle aisle. But no sooner did he sit than he saw a row of intense-faced young girls, and got up again, thinking, "You chicks musta been Lindy-hopping[1] somewhere." He found a seat several rows ahead as the lights came on, and he saw the screen disappear behind a heavy red and gold curtain; then the curtain rising, and the man with the microphone and a uniformed attendant coming on the stage.

He felt for his bingo cards, smiling. The guy at the door wouldn't like it if he knew about his having *five* cards. Well, not everyone played the bingo game; and

1. Dancing.

even with five cards he didn't have much of a chance. For Laura, though, he had to have faith. He studied the cards, each with its different numerals, punching the free center hole in each and spreading them neatly across his lap; and when the lights faded he sat slouched in his seat so that he could look from his cards to the bingo wheel with but a quick shifting of his eyes.

Ahead, at the end of the darkness, the man with the microphone was pressing a button attached to a long cord and spinning the bingo wheel and calling out the number each time the wheel came to rest. And each time the voice rang out his finger raced over the cards for the number. With five cards he had to move fast. He became nervous; there were too many cards, and the man went too fast with his grating voice. Perhaps he should just select one and throw the others away. But he was afraid. He became warm. Wonder how much Laura's doctor would cost? Damn that, watch the cards! And with despair he heard the man call three in a row which he missed on all five cards. This way he'd never win. . . .

When he saw the row of holes punched across the third card, he sat paralyzed and heard the man call three more numbers before he stumbled forward, screaming,

"Bingo! Bingo!"   20

"Let that fool up there," someone called.

"Get up there, man!"

He stumbled down the aisle and up the steps to the stage into a light so sharp and bright that for a moment it blinded him, and he felt that he had moved into the spell of some strange, mysterious power. Yet it was as familiar as the sun, and he knew it was the perfectly familiar bingo.

The man with the microphone was saying something to the audience as he held out his card. A cold light flashed from the man's finger as the card left his hand. His knees trembled. The man stepped closer, checking the card against the numbers chalked on the board. Suppose he had made a mistake? The pomade on the man's hair made him feel faint, and he backed away. But the man was checking the card over the microphone now, and he had to stay. He stood tense, listening.

"Under the O, forty-four," the man chanted. "Under the I, seven. Under the G, 25
three. Under the B, ninety-six. Under the N, thirteen!"

His breath came easier as the man smiled at the audience.

"Yes sir, ladies and gentlemen, he's one of the chosen people!"

The audience rippled with laughter and applause.

"Step right up to the front of the stage."

He moved slowly forward, wishing that the light was not so bright.   30

"To win tonight's jackpot of $36.90 the wheel must stop between the double zero, understand?"

He nodded, knowing the ritual from the many days and nights he had watched the winners march across the stage to press the button that controlled the spinning wheel and receive the prizes. And now he followed the instructions as though he'd crossed the slippery stage a million prize-winning times.

The man was making some kind of joke, and he nodded vacantly. So tense had he become that he felt a sudden desire to cry and shook it away. He felt vaguely that his whole life was determined by the bingo wheel; not only that which would happen now that he was at last before it, but all that had gone before, since his birth, and his mother's birth and the birth of his father. It had always been there, even though he had not been aware of it, handing out the unlucky cards and numbers of his days. The feeling persisted, and he started quickly away. I better get down from here before I make a fool of myself, he thought.

"Here, boy," the man called. "You haven't started yet."

35   Someone laughed as he went hesitantly back.

"Are you all reet?"

He grinned at the man's jive talk, but no words would come, and he knew it was not a convincing grin. For suddenly he knew that he stood on the slippery brink of some terrible embarrassment.

"Where are you from, boy?" the man asked.

"Down South."

40   "He's from down South, ladies and gentlemen," the man said. "Where from? Speak right into the mike."

"Rocky Mont," he said. "Rock' Mont, North Car'lina."

"So you decided to come down off that mountain to the U.S.," the man laughed. He felt that the man was making a fool of him, but then something cold was placed in his hand, and the lights were no longer behind him.

Standing before the wheel he felt alone, but that was somehow right, and he remembered his plan. He would give the wheel a short quick twirl. Just a touch of the button. He had watched it many times, and always it came close to double zero when it was short and quick. He steeled himself; the fear had left, and he felt a profound sense of promise, as though he were about to be repaid for all the things he'd suffered all his life. Trembling, he pressed the button. There was a whirl of lights, and in a second he realized with finality that though he wanted to, he could not stop. It was as though he held a high-powered line in his naked hand. His nerves tightened. As the wheel increased its speed it seemed to draw him more and more into its power, as though it held his fate; and with it came a deep need to submit, to whirl, to lose himself in its swirl of color. He could not stop it now. So let it be.

The button rested snugly in his palm where the man had placed it. And now he became aware of the man beside him, advising him through the microphone, while behind the shadowy audience hummed with noisy voices. He shifted his feet. There was still that feeling of helplessness within him, making part of him desire to turn back, even now that the jackpot was right in his hand. He squeezed the button until his fist ached. Then, like the sudden shriek of a subway whistle, a doubt tore through his head. Suppose he did not spin the wheel long enough? What could he do, and how could he tell? And then he knew, even as he wondered, that as long as he pressed the button, he could control the jackpot. He and only he could determine whether or not it was to be his. Not even the man with the microphone could do anything about it now. He felt drunk. Then, as though he had come down from a high hill into a valley of people, he heard the audience yelling.

45   "Come down from there, you jerk!"

"Let somebody else have a chance. . . ."

"Ole Jack thinks he done found the end of the rainbow. . . ."

The last voice was not unfriendly, and he turned and smiled dreamily into the yelling mouths. Then he turned his back squarely on them.

"Don't take too long, boy," a voice said.

He nodded. They were yelling behind him. Those folks did not understand 50
what had happened to him. They had been playing the bingo game day in and
night out for years, trying to win rent money or hamburger change. But not one
of those wise guys had discovered this wonderful thing. He watched the wheel
whirling past the numbers and experienced a burst of exaltation: This is God!
This is the really truly God! He said it aloud, "This is God!"

He said it with such absolute conviction that he feared he would fall fainting
into the footlights. But the crowd yelled so loud that they could not hear. These
fools, he thought. I'm here trying to tell them the most wonderful secret in the
world, and they're yelling like they gone crazy. A hand fell upon his shoulder.

"You'll have to make a choice now, boy. You've taken too long."

He brushed the hand violently away.

"Leave me alone, man. I know what I'm doing!"

The man looked surprised and held on to the microphone for support. And 55
because he did not wish to hurt the man's feelings he smiled, realizing with a
sudden pang that there was no way of explaining to the man just why he had to
stand there pressing the button forever.

"Come here," he called tiredly.

The man approached, rolling the heavy microphone across the stage.

"Anybody can play this bingo game, right?" he said.

"Sure, but . . ."

He smiled, feeling inclined to be patient with this slick looking white man 60
with his blue shirt and his sharp gabardine suit.

"That's what I thought," he said. "Anybody can win the jackpot as long as
they get the lucky number, right?"

"That's the rule, but after all . . ."

"That's what I thought," he said. "And the big prize goes to the man who knows
how to win it?"

The man nodded speechlessly.

"Well then, go on over there and watch me win like I want to. I ain't going to 65
hurt nobody," he said, "and I'll show you how to win. I mean to show the whole
world how it's got to be done."

And because he understood, he smiled again to let the man know that he held
nothing against him for being white and impatient. Then he refused to see the
man any longer and stood pressing the button, the voices of the crowd reaching
him like sounds in distant streets. Let them yell. All the Negroes down there were
just ashamed because he was black like them. He smiled inwardly, knowing how it
was. Most of the time he was ashamed of what Negroes did himself. Well, let them
be ashamed for something this time. Like him. He was like a long thin black wire
that was being stretched and wound upon the bingo wheel; wound until he wanted
to scream; wound, but this time himself controlling the winding and the sadness
and the shame, and because he did, Laura would be all right. Suddenly the lights
flickered. He staggered backwards. Had something gone wrong? All this noise.
Didn't they know that although he controlled the wheel, it also controlled him,
and unless he pressed the button forever and forever and ever it would stop, leaving him high and dry, dry and high on this hard high slippery hill and Laura
dead? There was only one chance; he had to do whatever the wheel demanded.
And gripping the button in despair, he discovered with surprise that it imparted a
nervous energy. His spine tingled. He felt a certain power.

Now he faced the raging crowd with defiance, its screams penetrating his ear-drums like trumpets shrieking from a juke-box. The vague faces glowing in the bingo lights gave him a sense of himself that he had never known before. He was running the show, by God! They had to react to him, for he was their luck. This is *me*, he thought. Let the bastards yell. Then someone was laughing inside him, and he realized that somehow he had forgotten his own name. It was a sad, lost feeling to lose your name, and a crazy thing to do. That name had been given him by the white man who had owned his grandfather a long lost time ago down South. But maybe those wise guys knew his name.

"Who am I?" he screamed.

"Hurry up and bingo, you jerk!"

70 They didn't know either, he thought sadly. They didn't even know their own names, they were all poor nameless bastards. Well, he didn't need that old name; he was reborn. For as long as he pressed the button he was The-man-who-pressed-the-button-who-held-the-prize-who-was-the-King-of-Bingo. That was the way it was, and he'd have to press the button even if nobody understood, even though Laura did not understand.

"Live!" he shouted.

The audience quieted like the dying of a huge fan.

"Live, Laura, baby. I got holt of it now, sugar. Live!"

He screamed it, tears streaming down his face. "I got nobody but YOU!"

75 The screams tore from his very guts. He felt as though the rush of blood to his head would burst out in baseball seams of small red droplets, like a head beaten by police clubs. Bending over he saw a trickle of blood splashing the toe of his shoe. With his free hand he searched his head. It was his nose. God, sup-pose something has gone wrong? He felt that the whole audience had somehow entered him and was stamping its feet in his stomach and he was unable to throw them out. They wanted the prize, that was it. They wanted the secret for themselves. But they'd never get it; he would keep the bingo wheel whirling for-ever, and Laura would be safe in the wheel. But would she? It had to be, because if she were not safe the wheel would cease to turn; it could not go on. He had to get away, *vomit* all, and his mind formed an image of himself running with Laura in his arms down the tracks of the subway just ahead of an A train, run-ning desperately *vomit* with people screaming for him to come out but knowing no way of leaving the tracks because to stop would bring the train crushing down upon him and to attempt to leave across the other tracks would mean to run into a hot third rail as high as his waist which threw blue sparks that blinded his eyes until he could hardly see.

He heard singing and the audience was clapping its hands.

Shoot the liquor to him, Jim, boy!
Clap-clap-clap
Well a-calla the cop
He's blowing his top!
Shoot the liquor to him, Jim, boy!

Bitter anger grew within him at the singing. They think I'm crazy. Well let 'em laugh. I'll do what I got to do.

He was standing in an attitude of intense listening when he saw that they were watching something on the stage behind him. He felt weak. But when he turned he saw no one. If only his thumb did not ache so. Now they were applauding. And for a moment he thought that the wheel had stopped. But that was impossible, his thumb still pressed the button. Then he saw them. Two men in uniform beckoned from the end of the stage. They were coming toward him, walking in step, slowly, like a tap-dance team returning for a third encore. But their shoulders shot forward, and he backed away, looking wildly about. There was nothing to fight them with. He had only the long black cord which led to a plug somewhere back stage, and he couldn't use that because it operated the bingo wheel. He backed slowly, fixing the men with his eyes as his lips stretched over his teeth in a tight, fixed grin; moved toward the end of the stage and realizing that he couldn't go much further, for suddenly the cord became taut and he couldn't afford to break the cord. But he had to do something. The audience was howling. Suddenly he stopped dead, seeing the men halt, their legs lifted as in an interrupted step of a slow-motion dance. There was nothing to do but run in the other direction and he dashed forward, slipping and sliding. The men fell back, surprised. He struck out violently going past.

"Grab him!"

He ran, but all too quickly the cord tightened, resistingly, and he turned and   80
ran back again. This time he slipped them, and discovered by running in a circle before the wheel he could keep the cord from tightening. But this way he had to flail his arms to keep the men away. Why couldn't they leave a man alone? He ran, circling.

"Ring down the curtain," someone yelled. But they couldn't do that. If they did the wheel flashing from the projection room would be cut off. But they had him before he could tell them so, trying to pry open his fist, and he was wrestling and trying to bring his knees into the fight and holding on to the button, for it was his life. And now he was down, seeing a foot coming down, crushing his wrist cruelly, down, as he saw the wheel whirling serenely above.

"I can't give it up," he screamed. Then quietly, in a confidential tone, "Boys, I really can't give it up."

It landed hard against his head. And in the blank moment they had it away from him, completely now. He fought them trying to pull him up from the stage as he watched the wheel spin slowly to a stop. Without surprise he saw it rest at double-zero.

"You see," he pointed bitterly.

"Sure, boy, sure, it's O.K.," one of the men said smiling.   85

And seeing the man bow his head to someone he could not see, he felt very, very happy; he would receive what all the winners received.

But as he warmed in the justice of the man's tight smile he did not see the man's slow wink, nor see the bow-legged man behind him step clear of the swiftly descending curtain and set himself for a blow. He only felt the dull pain exploding in his skull, and he knew even as it slipped out of him that his luck had run out on the stage.

1944

D. H. LAWRENCE

The Rocking-Horse Winner

There was a woman who was beautiful, who started with all the advantages, yet she had no luck. She married for love, and the love turned to dust. She had bonny children, yet she felt they had been thrust upon her, and she could not love them. They looked at her coldly, as if they were finding fault with her. And hurriedly she felt she must cover up some fault in herself. Yet what it was that she must cover up she never knew. Nevertheless, when her children were present, she always felt the centre of her heart go hard. This troubled her, and in her manner she was all the more gentle and anxious for her children, as if she loved them very much. Only she herself knew that at the centre of her heart was a hard little place that could not feel love, no, not for anybody. Everybody else said of her: "She is such a good mother. She adores her children." Only she herself, and her children themselves, knew it was not so. They read it in each other's eyes.

There were a boy and two little girls. They lived in a pleasant house, with a garden, and they had discreet servants, and felt themselves superior to anyone in the neighbourhood.

Although they lived in style, they felt always an anxiety in the house. There was never enough money. The mother had a small income, and the father had a small income, but not nearly enough for the social position which they had to keep up. The father went in to town to some office. But though he had good prospects, these prospects never materialized. There was always the grinding sense of the shortage of money, though the style was always kept up.

At last the mother said: "I will see if *I* can't make something." But she did not know where to begin. She racked her brains, and tried this thing and the other, but could not find anything successful. The failure made deep lines come into her face. Her children were growing up, they would have to go to school. There must be more money, there must be more money. The father, who was always very handsome and expensive in his tastes, seemed as if he never *would* be able to do anything worth doing. And the mother, who had a great belief in herself, did not succeed any better, and her tastes were just as expensive.

5   And so the house came to be haunted by the unspoken phrase: *There must be more money! There must be more money!* The children could hear it all the time, though nobody said it aloud. They heard it at Christmas, when the expensive and splendid toys filled the nursery. Behind the shining modern rocking-horse, behind the smart doll's-house, a voice would start whispering: "There *must* be more money! There *must* be more money!" And the children would stop playing, to listen for a moment. They would look into each other's eyes, to see if they had all heard. And each one saw in the eyes of the other two that they too had heard. "There *must* be more money! There *must* be more money!"

It came whispering from the springs of the still-swaying rocking-horse, and even the horse, bending his wooden, champing head, heard it. The big doll, sitting so pink and smirking in her new pram,[1] could hear it quite plainly, and seemed to be smirking all the more self-consciously because of it. The foolish puppy, too, that took the place of the teddy-bear, he was looking so extraordinarily foolish for

1. Baby carriage.

no other reason but that he heard the secret whisper all over the house: "There *must* be more money!"

Yet nobody ever said it aloud. The whisper was everywhere, and therefore no one spoke it. Just as no one ever says: "We are breathing!" in spite of the fact that breath is coming and going all the time.

"Mother," said the boy Paul one day, "why don't we keep a car of our own? Why do we always use uncle's, or else a taxi?"

"Because we're the poor members of the family," said the mother.

"But why *are* we, mother?" 10

"Well—I suppose," she said slowly and bitterly, "it's because your father has no luck."

The boy was silent for some time.

"Is luck money, mother?" he asked rather timidly.

"No, Paul. Not quite. It's what causes you to have money."

"Oh!" said Paul vaguely. "I thought when Uncle Oscar said *filthy lucker,* it 15 meant money."

"*Filthy lucre* does mean money," said the mother. "But it's lucre, not luck."

"Oh!" said the boy. "Then what *is* luck, mother?"

"It's what causes you to have money. If you're lucky you have money. That's why it's better to be born lucky than rich. If you're rich, you may lose your money. But if you're lucky, you will always get more money."

"Oh! Will you? And is father not lucky?"

"Very unlucky, I should say," she said bitterly. 20

The boy watched her with unsure eyes.

"Why?" he asked.

"I don't know. Nobody ever knows why one person is lucky and another unlucky."

"Don't they? Nobody at all? Does *nobody* know?"

"Perhaps God. But He never tells." 25

"He ought to, then. And aren't you lucky either, mother?"

"I can't be, if I married an unlucky husband."

"But by yourself, aren't you?"

"I used to think I was, before I married. Now I think I am very unlucky indeed."

"Why?" 30

"Well—never mind! Perhaps I'm not really," she said.

The child looked at her, to see if she meant it. But he saw, by the lines of her mouth, that she was only trying to hide something from him.

"Well, anyhow," he said stoutly, "I'm a lucky person."

"Why?" said his mother, with a sudden laugh.

He stared at her. He didn't even know why he had said it. 35

"God told me," he asserted, brazening it out.

"I hope He did, dear!" she said, again with a laugh, but rather bitter.

"He did, mother!"

"Excellent!" said the mother, using one of her husband's exclamations.

The boy saw she did not believe him; or, rather, that she paid no attention to 40 his assertion. This angered him somewhat, and made him want to compel her attention.

He went off by himself, vaguely, in a childish way, seeking for the clue to "luck." Absorbed, taking no heed of other people, he went about with a sort of stealth, seeking inwardly for luck. He wanted luck, he wanted it, he wanted it. When the two girls were playing dolls in the nursery, he would sit on his big rocking-horse, charging madly into space, with a frenzy that made the little girls peer at him uneasily. Wildly the horse careered, the waving dark hair of the boy tossed, his eyes had a strange glare in them. The little girls dared not speak to him.

When he had ridden to the end of his mad little journey, he climbed down and stood in front of his rocking-horse, staring fixedly into its lowered face. Its red mouth was slightly open, its big eye was wide and glassy-bright.

"Now!" he would silently command the snorting steed. "Now, take me to where there is luck! Now take me!"

And he would slash the horse on the neck with the little whip he had asked Uncle Oscar for. He *knew* the horse could take him to where there was luck, if only he forced it. So he would mount again, and start on his furious ride, hoping at last to get there. He knew he could get there.

45   "You'll break your horse, Paul!" said the nurse.

"He's always riding like that! I wish he'd leave off!" said his elder sister Joan.

But he only glared down on them in silence. Nurse gave him up. She could make nothing of him. Anyhow he was growing beyond her.

One day his mother and his Uncle Oscar came in when he was on one of his furious rides. He did not speak to them.

"Hallo, you young jockey! Riding a winner?" said his uncle.

50   "Aren't you growing too big for a rocking-horse? You're not a very little boy any longer, you know," said his mother.

But Paul only gave a blue glare from his big, rather close-set eyes. He would speak to nobody when he was in full tilt. His mother watched him with an anxious expression on her face.

At last he suddenly stopped forcing his horse into the mechanical gallop, and slid down.

"Well, I got there!" he announced fiercely, his blue eyes still flaring, and his sturdy long legs straddling apart.

"Where did you get to?" asked his mother.

55   "Where I wanted to go," he flared back at her.

"That's right, son!" said Uncle Oscar. "Don't you stop till you get there. What's the horse's name?"

"He doesn't have a name," said the boy.

"Gets on without all right?" asked the uncle.

"Well, he has different names. He was called Sansovino last week."

60   "Sansovino, eh? Won the Ascot.[2] How did you know his name?"

"He always talks about horse-races with Bassett," said Joan.

The uncle was delighted to find that his small nephew was posted with all the racing news. Bassett, the young gardener, who had been wounded in the left foot in the war[3] and had got his present job through Oscar Cresswell, whose batman[4]

2. A race run at a course of that name in Berkshire. Other races mentioned in the story are Lincolnshire Handicap, then run at Lincoln Downs; the St. Leger Stakes, run at Doncaster; the Grand National Steeplechase, run at Aintree, the most famous steeplechase in the world; the famous Derby, a mile-and-a-half race for three-year-olds run at Epsom Downs.   3. World War I, 1914–18.   4. British officer's orderly.

he had been, was a perfect blade of the "turf."[5] He lived in the racing events, and the small boy lived with him.

Oscar Cresswell got it all from Bassett.

"Master Paul comes and asks me, so I can't do more than tell him, sir," said Bassett, his face terribly serious, as if he were speaking of religious matters.

"And does he ever put anything on a horse he fancies?" 65

"Well—I don't want to give him away—he's a young sport, a fine sport, sir. Would you mind asking him himself? He sort of takes a pleasure in it, and perhaps he'd feel I was giving him away, sir, if you don't mind."

Bassett was serious as a church.

The uncle went back to his nephew and took him off for a ride in the car.

"Say, Paul, old man, do you ever put anything on a horse?" the uncle asked.

The boy watched the handsome man closely. 70

"Why, do you think I oughtn't to?" he parried.

"Not a bit of it! I thought perhaps you might give me a tip for the Lincoln."

The car sped on into the country, going down to Uncle Oscar's place in Hampshire.

"Honour bright?" said the nephew.

"Honour bright, son!" said the uncle. 75

"Well, then, Daffodil."

"Daffodil! I doubt it, sonny. What about Mirza?"

"I only know the winner," said the boy. "That's Daffodil."

"Daffodil, eh?"

There was a pause. Daffodil was an obscure horse comparatively. 80

"Uncle!"

"Yes, son?"

"You won't let it go any further, will you? I promised Bassett."

"Bassett be damned, old man! What's he got to do with it?"

"We're partners. We've been partners from the first. Uncle, he lent me my first 85 five shillings, which I lost. I promised him, honour bright, it was only between me and him; only you gave me that ten-shilling note I started winning with, so I thought you were lucky. You won't let it go any further, will you?"

The boy gazed at his uncle from those big, hot, blue eyes, set rather close together. The uncle stirred and laughed uneasily.

"Right you are, son! I'll keep your tip private. Daffodil, eh? How much are you putting on him?"

"All except twenty pounds," said the boy. "I keep that in reserve."

The uncle thought it a good joke.

"You keep twenty pounds in reserve, do you, you young romancer? What are 90 you betting, then?"

"I'm betting three hundred," said the boy, gravely. "But it's between you and me, Uncle Oscar! Honour bright?"

The uncle burst into a roar of laughter.

"It's between you and me all right, you young Nat Gould,"[6] he said, laughing. "But where's your three hundred?"

"Bassett keeps it for me. We're partners."

---

5. That is, a dashing young horseplayer.
6. Nathaniel Gould (1857–1919), novelist and journalist who wrote about horse racing.

95   "You are, are you! And what is Bassett putting on Daffodil?"

"He won't go quite as high as I do, I expect. Perhaps he'll go a hundred and fifty."

"What, pennies?" laughed the uncle.

"Pounds," said the child, with a surprised look at his uncle. "Bassett keeps a bigger reserve than I do."

Between wonder and amusement Uncle Oscar was silent. He pursued the matter no further, but he determined to take his nephew with him to the Lincoln races.

100   "Now, son," he said, "I'm putting twenty on Mirza, and I'll put five for you on any horse you fancy. What's your pick?"

"Daffodil, uncle."

"No, not the fiver on Daffodil!"

"I should if it was my own fiver," said the child.

"Good! Good! Right you are! A fiver for me and a fiver for you on Daffodil."

105   The child had never been to a race-meeting before, and his eyes were blue fire. He pursed his mouth tight, and watched. A Frenchman just in front had put his money on Lancelot. Wild with excitement, he flayed his arms up and down, yelling *"Lancelot! Lancelot!"* in his French accent.

Daffodil came in first, Lancelot second, Mirza third. The child, flushed and with eyes blazing, was curiously serene. His uncle brought him four five-pound notes, four to one.

"What am I to do with these?" he cried, waving them before the boy's eyes.

"I suppose we'll talk to Bassett," said the boy. "I expect I have fifteen hundred now; and twenty in reserve; and this twenty."

His uncle studied him for some moments.

110   "Look here, son!" he said. "You're not serious about Bassett and that fifteen hundred, are you?"

"Yes, I am. But it's between you and me, uncle. Honour bright!"

"Honour bright all right, son! But I must talk to Bassett."

"If you'd like to be a partner, uncle, with Bassett and me, we could all be partners. Only, you'd have to promise, honour bright, uncle, not to let it go beyond us three. Bassett and I are lucky, and you must be lucky, because it was your ten shillings I started winning with. . . ."

Uncle Oscar took both Bassett and Paul into Richmond Park for an afternoon, and there they talked.

115   "It's like this, you see, sir," Bassett said. "Master Paul would get me talking about racing events, spinning yarns, you know, sir. And he was always keen on knowing if I'd made or if I'd lost. It's about a year since, now, that I put five shillings on Blush of Dawn for him—and we lost. Then the luck turned, with the ten shillings he had from you, that we put on Singhalese. And since that time, it's been pretty steady, all things considering. What do you say, Master Paul?"

"We're all right when we're sure," said Paul. "It's when we're not quite sure that we go down."

"Oh, but we're careful then," said Bassett.

"But when are you *sure?*" smiled Uncle Oscar.

"It's Master Paul, sir," said Bassett, in a secret, religious voice. "It's as if he had it from heaven. Like Daffodil, now, for the Lincoln. That was as sure as eggs."

120   "Did you put anything on Daffodil?" asked Oscar Cresswell.

"Yes, sir. I made my bit."

"And my nephew?"

Bassett was obstinately silent, looking at Paul.

"I made twelve hundred, didn't I, Bassett? I told uncle I was putting three hundred on Daffodil."

"That's right," said Bassett, nodding.

"But where's the money?" asked the uncle.

"I keep it safe locked up, sir. Master Paul he can have it any minute he likes to ask for it."

"What, fifteen hundred pounds?"

"And twenty! And *forty*, that is, with the twenty he made on the course."

"It's amazing!" said the uncle.

"If Master Paul offers you to be partners, sir, I would, if I were you; if you'll excuse me," said Bassett.

Oscar Cresswell thought about it.

"I'll see the money," he said.

They drove home again, and sure enough, Bassett came round to the garden-house with fifteen hundred pounds in notes. The twenty pounds reserve was left with Joe Glee, in the Turf Commission deposit.

"You see, it's all right, uncle, when I'm *sure!* Then we go strong, for all we're worth. Don't we, Bassett?"

"We do that, Master Paul"

"And when are you sure?" said the uncle, laughing.

"Oh, well, sometimes I'm *absolutely* sure, like about Daffodil," said the boy; "and sometimes I have an idea; and sometimes I haven't even an idea, have I, Bassett? Then we're careful, because we mostly go down."

"You do, do you! And when you're sure, like about Daffodil, what makes you sure, sonny?"

"Oh, well, I don't know," said the boy uneasily. "I'm sure, you know, uncle; that's all."

"It's as if he had it from heaven, sir," Bassett reiterated.

"I should say so!" said the uncle.

But he became a partner. And when the Leger was coming on, Paul was "sure" about Lively Spark, which was a quite inconsiderable horse. The boy insisted on putting a thousand on the horse, Bassett went for five hundred, and Oscar Cresswell two hundred. Lively Spark came in first, and the betting had been ten to one against him. Paul had made ten thousand.

"You see," he said, "I was absolutely sure of him."

Even Oscar Cresswell had cleared two thousand.

"Look here, son," he said, "this sort of thing makes me nervous."

"It needn't, uncle! Perhaps I shan't be sure again for a long time."

"But what are you going to do with your money?" asked the uncle.

"Of course," said the boy, "I started it for mother. She said she had no luck, because father is unlucky, so I thought if *I* was lucky, it might stop whispering."

"What might stop whispering?"

"Our house. I *hate* our house for whispering."

"What does it whisper?"

"Why—why"—the boy fidgeted—"why, I don't know. But it's always short of money, you know, uncle."

"I know it, son, I know it."

155 "You know people send mother writs, don't you, uncle?"

"I'm afraid I do," said the uncle.

"And then the house whispers, like people laughing at you behind your back. It's awful, that is! I thought if I was lucky . . ."

"You might stop it," added the uncle.

The boy watched him with big blue eyes, that had an uncanny cold fire in them, and he said never a word.

160 "Well, then!" said the uncle. "What are we doing?"

"I shouldn't like mother to know I was lucky," said the boy.

"Why not, son?"

"She'd stop me."

"I don't think she would."

165 "Oh!"—and the boy writhed in an odd way—"I *don't* want her to know, uncle."

"All right, son! We'll manage it without her knowing."

They managed it very easily. Paul, at the other's suggestion, handed over five thousand pounds to his uncle, who deposited it with the family lawyer, who was then to inform Paul's mother that a relative had put five thousand pounds into his hands, which sum was to be paid out a thousand pounds at a time, on the mother's birthday, for the next five years.

"So she'll have a birthday present of a thousand pounds for five successive years," said Uncle Oscar. "I hope it won't make it all the harder for her later."

Paul's mother had her birthday in November. The house had been "whispering" worse than ever lately, and, even in spite of his luck, Paul could not bear up against it. He was very anxious to see the effect of the birthday letter, telling his mother about the thousand pounds.

170 When there were no visitors, Paul now took his meals with his parents, as he was beyond the nursery control. His mother went into town nearly every day. She had discovered that she had an odd knack of sketching furs and dress materials, so she worked secretly in the studio of a friend who was the chief "artist" for the leading drapers. She drew the figures of ladies in furs and ladies in silk and sequins for the newspaper advertisements. This young woman artist earned several thousand pounds a year, but Paul's mother only made several hundreds, and she was again dissatisfied. She so wanted to be first in something, and she did not succeed, even in making sketches for drapery advertisements.

She was down to breakfast on the morning of her birthday. Paul watched her face as she read her letters. He knew the lawyer's letter. As his mother read it, her face hardened and became more expressionless. Then a cold, determined look came on her mouth. She hid the letter under the pile of others, and said not a word about it.

"Didn't you have anything nice in the post for your birthday, mother?" said Paul.

"Quite moderately nice," she said, her voice cold and absent.

She went away to town without saying more.

175 But in the afternoon Uncle Oscar appeared. He said Paul's mother had had a long interview with the lawyer, asking if the whole five thousand could not be advanced at once, as she was in debt.

"What do you think, uncle?" said the boy.

"I leave it to you, son."

"Oh, let her have it, then! We can get some more with the other," said the boy.

"A bird in the hand is worth two in the bush, laddie!" said Uncle Oscar.

"But I'm sure to *know* for the Grand National; or the Lincolnshire; or else the Derby. I'm sure to know for *one* of them," said Paul.

So Uncle Oscar signed the agreement, and Paul's mother touched the whole five thousand. Then something very curious happened. The voices in the house suddenly went mad, like a chorus of frogs on a spring evening. There were certain new furnishings, and Paul had a tutor. He was *really* going to Eton, his father's school, in the following autumn. There were flowers in the winter, and a blossoming of the luxury Paul's mother had been used to. And yet the voices in the house, behind the sprays of mimosa and almond blossom, and from under the piles of iridescent cushions, simply trilled and screamed in a sort of ecstasy: "There *must* be more money! Oh-h-h; there *must* be more money Oh, now, now-w! Now-w-w—there *must* be more money!—more than ever! More than ever!"

It frightened Paul terribly. He studied away at his Latin and Greek with his tutors. But his intense hours were spent with Bassett. The Grand National had gone by: he had not "known," and had lost a hundred pounds. Summer was at hand. He was in agony for the Lincoln. But even for the Lincoln he didn't "know," and he lost fifty pounds. He became wild-eyed and strange, as if something were going to explode in him.

"Let it alone, son! Don't you bother about it!" urged Uncle Oscar. But it was as if the boy couldn't really hear what his uncle was saying.

"I've got to know for the Derby! I've got to know for the Derby!" the child reiterated, his big blue eyes blazing with a sort of madness.

His mother noticed how overwrought he was.

"You'd better go to the seaside. Wouldn't you like to go now to the seaside, instead of waiting? I think you'd better," she said, looking down at him anxiously, her heart curiously heavy because of him.

But the child lifted his uncanny blue eyes.

"I couldn't possibly go before the Derby, mother!" he said. "I couldn't possibly!"

"Why not?" she said, her voice becoming heavy when she was opposed. "Why not? You can still go from the seaside to see the Derby with your Uncle Oscar, if that's what you wish. No need for you to wait here. Besides, I think you care too much about these races. It's a bad sign. My family has been a gambling family, and you won't know till you grow up how much damage it has done. But it has done damage. I shall have to send Bassett away, and ask Uncle Oscar not to talk racing to you, unless you promise to be reasonable about it; go away to the seaside and forget it. You're all nerves!"

"I'll do what you like, mother, so long as you don't send me away till after the Derby," the boy said.

"Send you away from where? Just from this house?"

"Yes," he said, gazing at her.

"Why, you curious child, what makes you care about this house so much, suddenly? I never knew you loved it."

He gazed at her without speaking. He had a secret within a secret, something he had not divulged, even to Bassett or to his Uncle Oscar.

But his mother, after standing undecided and a little bit sullen for some moments, said:

"Very well, then! Don't go to the seaside till after the Derby, if you don't wish it. But promise me you won't let your nerves go to pieces. Promise you won't think so much about horse-racing and events, as you call them!"

"Oh, no," said the boy casually. "I won't think much about them, mother. You needn't worry. I wouldn't worry, mother, if I were you."

"If you were me and I were you," said his mother, "I wonder what we *should* do!"

"But you know you needn't worry, mother, don't you?" the boy repeated.

200   "I should be awfully glad to know it," she said wearily.

"Oh, well, you *can,* you know. I mean, you *ought* to know you needn't worry," he insisted.

"Ought I? Then I'll see about it," she said.

Paul's secret of secrets was his wooden horse, that which had no name. Since he was emancipated from a nurse and a nursery-governess, he had had his rocking-horse removed to his own bedroom at the top of the house.

"Surely, you're too big for a rocking-horse!" his mother had remonstrated.

205   "Well, you see, mother, till I can have a *real* horse, I like to have *some* sort of animal about," had been his quaint answer.

"Do you feel he keeps you company?" she laughed.

"Oh, yes! He's very good, he always keeps me company, when I'm there," said Paul.

So the horse, rather shabby, stood in an arrested prance in the boy's bedroom.

The Derby was drawing near, and the boy grew more and more tense. He hardly heard what was spoken to him, he was very frail, and his eyes were really uncanny. His mother had sudden strange seizures of uneasiness about him. Sometimes, for half-an-hour, she would feel a sudden anxiety about him that was almost anguish. She wanted to rush to him at once, and know he was safe.

210   Two nights before the Derby, she was at a big party in town, when one of her rushes of anxiety about her boy, her first-born, gripped her heart till she could hardly speak. She fought with the feeling, might and main, for she believed in common-sense. But it was too strong. She had to leave the dance and go downstairs to telephone to the country. The children's nursery-governess was terribly surprised and startled at being rung up in the night.

"Are the children all right, Miss Wilmot?"

"Oh, yes, they are quite all right."

"Master Paul? Is he all right?"

"He went to bed as right as a trivet. Shall I run up and look at him?"

215   "No," said Paul's mother reluctantly. "No! Don't trouble. It's all right. Don't sit up. We shall be home fairly soon." She did not want her son's privacy intruded upon.

"Very good," said the governess.

It was about one o'clock when Paul's mother and father drove up to their house. All was still. Paul's mother went to her room and slipped off her white fur cloak. She had told her maid not to wait up for her. She heard her husband downstairs, mixing a whisky-and-soda.

And then, because of the strange anxiety at her heart, she stole upstairs to her son's room. Noiselessly she went along the upper corridor. Was there a faint noise? What was it?

She stood, with arrested muscles, outside his door, listening. There was a strange, heavy, and yet not loud noise. Her heart stood still. It was a soundless noise, yet rushing and powerful. Something huge, in violent, hushed motion. What was it? What in God's name was it? She ought to know. She felt that she knew the noise. She knew what it was.

Yet she could not place it. She couldn't say what it was. And on and on it went, 220 like a madness.

Softly, frozen with anxiety and fear, she turned the door-handle.

The room was dark. Yet in the space near the window, she heard and saw something plunging to and fro. She gazed in fear and amazement.

Then suddenly she switched on the light, and saw her son, in his green pyjamas, madly surging on the rocking-horse. The blaze of light suddenly lit him up, as he urged the wooden horse, and lit her up, as she stood, blonde, in her dress of pale green and crystal, in the doorway.

"Paul!" she cried. "Whatever are you doing?"

"It's Malabar!" he screamed, in a powerful, strange voice. "It's Malabar!" 225

His eyes blazed at her for one strange and senseless second, as he ceased urging his wooden horse. Then he fell with a crash to the ground, and she, all her tormented motherhood flooding upon her, rushed to gather him up.

But he was unconscious, and unconscious he remained, with some brain-fever. He talked and tossed, and his mother sat stonily by his side.

"Malabar! It's Malabar! Bassett, Bassett, I *know*! It's Malabar!"

So the child cried, trying to get up and urge the rocking-horse that gave him his inspiration.

"What does he mean by Malabar?" asked the heart-frozen mother. 230

"I don't know," said the father stonily.

"What does he mean by Malabar?" she asked her brother Oscar.

"It's one of the horses running for the Derby," was the answer.

And, in spite of himself, Oscar Cresswell spoke to Bassett, and himself put a thousand on Malabar: at fourteen to one.

The third day of the illness was critical: they were waiting for a change. The 235 boy, with his rather long, curly hair, was tossing ceaselessly on the pillow. He neither slept nor regained consciousness, and his eyes were like blue stones. His mother sat, feeling her heart had gone, turned actually into a stone.

In the evening, Oscar Cresswell did not come, but Bassett sent a message, saying could he come up for one moment, just one moment? Paul's mother was very angry at the intrusion, but on second thought she agreed. The boy was the same. Perhaps Bassett might bring him to consciousness.

The gardener, a shortish fellow with a little brown moustache, and sharp little brown eyes, tip-toed into the room, touched his imaginary cap to Paul's mother, and stole to the bedside, staring with glittering, smallish eyes, at the tossing, dying child.

"Master Paul!" he whispered. "Master Paul! Malabar came in first all right, a clean win. I did as you told me. You've made over seventy thousand pounds, you have; you've got over eighty thousand. Malabar came in all right, Master Paul."

"Malabar! Malabar! Did I say Malabar, mother? Did I say Malabar? Do you think I'm lucky, mother? I knew Malabar, didn't I? Over eighty thousand pounds! I call that lucky, don't you, mother? Over eighty thousand pounds! I knew, didn't I know I knew! Malabar came in all right. If I ride my horse till I'm sure, then I tell you, Bassett, you can go as high as you like. Did you go for all you were worth, Bassett?"

240   "I went a thousand on it, Master Paul."

"I never told you, mother, that if I can ride my horse, and *get there,* then I'm absolutely sure—oh absolutely! Mother, did I ever tell you? I *am* lucky!"

"No, you never did," said the mother.

But the boy died in the night.

And even as he lay dead, his mother heard her brother's voice saying to her: "My God, Hester, you're eighty-odd thousand to the good, and a poor devil of a son to the bad. But, poor devil, poor devil, he's best gone out of a life where he rides his rocking-horse to find a winner."

1932

BOBBIE ANN MASON

Shiloh

Leroy Moffitt's wife, Norma Jean, is working on her pectorals. She lifts three-pound dumbbells to warm up, then progresses to a twenty-pound barbell. Standing with her legs apart, she reminds Leroy of Wonder Woman.

"I'd give anything if I could just get these muscles to where they're real hard," says Norma Jean. "Feel this arm. It's not as hard as the other one."

"That's cause you're right-handed," says Leroy, dodging as she swings the barbell in an arc.

"Do you think so?"

5   "Sure."

Leroy is a truckdriver. He injured his leg in a highway accident four months ago, and his physical therapy, which involves weights and a pulley, prompted Norma Jean to try building herself up. Now she is attending a body-building class. Leroy has been collecting temporary disability since his tractor-trailer jack-knifed in Missouri, badly twisting his left leg in its socket. He has a steel pin in his hip. He will probably not be able to drive his rig again. It sits in the backyard, like a gigantic bird that has flown home to roost. Leroy has been home in Kentucky for three months, and his leg is almost healed, but the accident frightened him and he does not want to drive any more long hauls. He is not sure what to do next. In the meantime, he makes things from craft kits. He started by building a miniature log cabin from notched Popsicle sticks. He varnished it and placed it on the TV set, where it remains. It reminds him of a rustic Nativity scene. Then he tried string art (sailing ships on black velvet), a macramé owl kit, a snap-together B-17 Flying Fortress,[1] and a lamp made out of a model truck, with a light fixture screwed in the top of the cab. At first the kits were diversions, something to kill time, but now he is thinking about building a full-scale log house from a kit. It would be considerably cheaper than building a regular house, and besides, Leroy has grown to appreciate how things are put together. He has begun to realize that in all the years he was on the road he never took time to examine anything. He was always flying past scenery.

1. American World War II bomber.

"They won't let you build a log cabin in any of the new subdivisions," Norma Jean tells him.

"They will if I tell them it's for you," he says, teasing her. Ever since they were married, he has promised Norma Jean he would build her a new home one day. They have always rented, and the house they live in is small and nondescript. It does not even feel like a home, Leroy realizes now.

Norma Jean works at the Rexall drugstore, and she has acquired an amazing amount of information about cosmetics. When she explains to Leroy the three stages of complexion care, involving creams, toners, and moisturizers, he thinks happily of other petroleum products—axle grease, diesel fuel. This is a connection between him and Norma Jean. Since he has been home, he has felt unusually tender about his wife and guilty over his long absences. But he can't tell what she feels about him. Norma Jean has never complained about his traveling; she has never made hurt remarks, like calling his truck a "widow-maker." He is reasonably certain she has been faithful to him, but he wishes she would celebrate his permanent homecoming more happily. Norma Jean is often startled to find Leroy at home, and he thinks she seems a little disappointed about it. Perhaps he reminds her too much of the early days of their marriage, before he went on the road. They had a child who died as an infant, years ago. They never speak about their memories of Randy, which have almost faded, but now that Leroy is home all the time, they sometimes feel awkward around each other, and Leroy wonders if one of them should mention the child. He has the feeling that they are waking up out of a dream together—that they must create a new marriage, start afresh. They are lucky they are still married. Leroy has read that for most people losing a child destroys the marriage—or else he heard this on *Donahue*. He can't always remember where he learns things anymore.

At Christmas, Leroy bought an electric organ for Norma Jean. She used to play the piano when she was in high school. "It don't leave you," she told him once. "It's like riding a bicycle."

The new instrument had so many keys and buttons that she was bewildered by it at first. She touched the keys tentatively, pushed some buttons, then pecked out "Chopsticks." It came out in an amplified fox-trot rhythm, with marimba sounds.

"It's an orchestra!" she cried.

The organ had a pecan-look finish and eighteen preset chords, with optional flute, violin, trumpet, clarinet, and banjo accompaniments. Norma Jean mastered the organ almost immediately. At first she played Christmas songs. Then she bought *The Sixties Songbook* and learned every tune in it, adding variations to each with the rows of brightly colored buttons.

"I didn't like these old songs back then," she said. "But I have this crazy feeling I missed something."

"You didn't miss a thing," said Leroy.

Leroy likes to lie on the couch and smoke a joint and listen to Norma Jean play "Can't Take My Eyes Off You" and "I'll Be Back."[2] He is back again. After fifteen years on the road, he is finally settling down with the woman he loves. She is still pretty. Her skin is flawless. Her frosted curls resemble pencil trimmings.

2. Hit songs of the 1960s.

Now that Leroy has come home to stay, he notices how much the town has changed. Subdivisions are spreading across western Kentucky like an oil slick. The sign at the edge of town says "Pop: 11,500"—only seven hundred more than it said twenty years before. Leroy can't figure out who is living in all the new houses. The farmers who used to gather around the courthouse square on Saturday afternoons to play checkers and spit tobacco juice have gone. It has been years since Leroy has thought about the farmers, and they have disappeared without his noticing.

Leroy meets a kid named Stevie Hamilton in the parking lot at the new shopping center. While they pretend to be strangers meeting over a stalled car, Stevie tosses an ounce of marijuana under the front seat of Leroy's car. Stevie is wearing orange jogging shoes and a T-shirt that says CHATTAHOOCHEE SUPER-RAT. His father is a prominent doctor who lives in one of the expensive subdivisions in a new white-columned brick house that looks like a funeral parlor. In the phone book under his name there is a separate number, with the listing "Teenagers."

"Where do you get this stuff?" asks Leroy. "From your pappy!"

20   "That's for me to know and you to find out," Stevie says. He is slit-eyed and skinny.

"What else you got?"

"What you interested in?"

"Nothing special. Just wondered."

Leroy used to take speed on the road. Now he has to go slowly. He needs to be mellow. He leans back against the car and says, "I'm aiming to build me a log house, soon as I get time. My wife, though, I don't think she likes the idea."

25   "Well, let me know when you want me again," Stevie says. He has a cigarette in his cupped palm, as though sheltering it from the wind. He takes a long drag, then stomps it on the asphalt and slouches away.

Stevie's father was two years ahead of Leroy in high school. Leroy is thirty-four. He married Norma Jean when they were both eighteen, and their child Randy was born a few months later, but he died at the age of four months and three days. He would be about Stevie's age now. Norma Jean and Leroy were at the drive-in, watching a double feature (*Dr. Strangelove* and *Lover Come Back*),[3] and the baby was sleeping in the back seat. When the first movie ended, the baby was dead. It was the sudden infant death syndrome. Leroy remembers handing Randy to a nurse at the emergency room, as though he were offering her a large doll as a present. A dead baby feels like a sack of flour. "It just happens sometimes," said the doctor, in what Leroy always recalls as a nonchalant tone. Leroy can hardly remember the child anymore, but he still sees vividly a scene from *Dr. Strangelove* in which the President of the United States was talking in a folksy voice on the hot line to the Soviet premier about the bomber accidentally headed toward Russia. He was in the War Room, and the world map was lit up. Leroy remembers Norma Jean catatonically beside him in the hospital and himself thinking: Who is this strange girl? He had forgotten who she was. Now scientists are saying that crib death is caused by a virus. Nobody knows anything, Leroy thinks. The answers are always changing.

---

3. A 1963 satire on nuclear war and a 1961 Rock Hudson-Doris Day romantic comedy satirizing the advertising business, respectively.

When Leroy gets home from the shopping center, Norma Jean's mother, Mabel Beasley, is there. Until this year, Leroy has not realized how much time she spends with Norma Jean. When she visits, she inspects the closets and then the plants, informing Norma Jean when a plant is droopy or yellow. Mabel calls the plants "flowers," although there are never any blooms. She always notices if Norma Jean's laundry is piling up. Mabel is a short, overweight woman whose tight, brown-dyed curls look more like a wig than the actual wig she sometimes wears. Today she has brought Norma Jean an off-white dust ruffle she made for the bed; Mabel works in a custom-upholstery shop.

"This is the tenth one I made this year," Mabel says. "I got started and couldn't stop."

"It's real pretty," says Norma Jean.

"Now we can hide things under the bed," says Leroy, who gets along with his 30 mother-in-law primarily by joking with her. Mabel has never really forgiven him for disgracing her by getting Norma Jean pregnant. When the baby died, she said that fate was mocking her.

"What's that thing?" Mabel says to Leroy in a loud voice, pointing to a tangle of yarn on a piece of canvas.

Leroy holds it up for Mabel to see. "It's my needlepoint," he explains. "This is a *Star Trek* pillow cover."

"That's what a woman would do," says Mabel. "Great day in the morning!"

"All the big football players on TV do it," he says.

"Why, Leroy, you're always trying to fool me. I don't believe you for one min- 35 ute. You don't know what to do with yourself—that's the whole trouble. Sewing!"

"I'm aiming to build us a log house," says Leroy. "Soon as my plans come."

"Like *heck* you are," says Norma Jean. She takes Leroy's needlepoint and shoves it into a drawer. "You have to find a job first. Nobody can afford to build now anyway."

Mabel straightens her girdle and says, "I still think before you get tied down y'all ought to take a little run to Shiloh."

"One of these days, Mama," Norma Jean says impatiently.

Mabel is talking about Shiloh, Tennessee. For the past few years, she has been 40 urging Leroy and Norma Jean to visit the Civil War battleground there.[4] Mabel went there on her honeymoon—the only real trip she ever took. Her husband died of a perforated ulcer when Norma Jean was ten, but Mabel, who was accepted into the United Daughters of the Confederacy in 1975, is still preoccupied with going back to Shiloh.

"I've been to kingdom come and back in that truck out yonder," Leroy says to Mabel, "but we never yet set foot in that battleground. Ain't that something? How did I miss it?"

"It's not even that far," Mabel says.

After Mabel leaves, Norma Jean reads to Leroy from a list she has made. "Thing you could do," she announces. "You could get a job as a guard at Union

---

4. Where, in April 1862, more than twenty-three thousand troops of the North and South, one-quarter of those who fought there, died. This was the first real indication of how bitter and bloody the war was to be. When Union reinforcements arrived, General Ulysses S. Grant drove the Confederate forces, which had gained an initial victory by a surprise attack, back to their base in Corinth, Mississippi.

Carbide, where they'd let you set on a stool. You could get on at the lumberyard. You could do a little carpenter work, if you want to build so bad. You could—"

"I can't do something where I'd have to stand up all day."

45   "You ought to try standing up all day behind a cosmetics counter. It's amazing that I have strong feet, coming from two parents that never had strong feet at all." At the moment Norma Jean is holding on to the kitchen counter, raising her knees one at a time as she talks. She is wearing two-pound ankle weights.

"Don't worry," says Leroy. "I'll do something."

"You could truck calves to slaughter for somebody. You wouldn't have to drive any big old truck for that."

"I'm going to build you this house," says Leroy. "I want to make you a real home."

"I don't want to live in any log cabin."

50   "It's not a cabin. It's a house."

"I don't care. It looks like a cabin."

"You and me together could lift those logs. It's just like lifting weights."

Norma Jean doesn't answer. Under her breath, she is counting. Now she is marching through the kitchen. She is doing goose steps.

Before his accident, when Leroy came home he used to stay in the house with Norma Jean, watching TV in bed and playing cards. She would cook fried chicken, picnic ham, chocolate pie—all his favorites. Now he is home alone much of the time. In the mornings, Norma Jean disappears, leaving a cooling place in the bed. She eats a cereal called Body Buddies, and she leaves the bowl on the table, with soggy tan balls floating in a milk puddle. He sees things about Norma Jean that he never realized before. When she chops onions, she stares off into a corner, as if she can't bear to look. She puts on her house slippers almost precisely at nine o'clock every evening and nudges her jogging shoes under the couch. She saves bread heels for the birds. Leroy watches the birds at the feeder. He notices the peculiar way goldfinches fly past the window. They close their wings, then fall, then spread their wings to catch and lift themselves. He wonders if they close their eyes when they fall. Norma Jean closes her eyes when they are in bed. She wants the lights turned out. Even then, he is sure she closes her eyes.

55   He goes for long drives around town. He tends to drive a car rather carelessly. Power steering and an automatic shift make a car feel so small and inconsequential that his body is hardly involved in the driving process. His injured leg stretches out comfortably. Once or twice he has almost hit something, but even the prospect of an accident seems minor in a car. He cruises the new subdivisions, feeling like a criminal rehearsing for a robbery. Norma Jean is probably right about a log house being inappropriate here in the new subdivisions. All the houses look grand and complicated. They depress him.

One day when Leroy comes home from a drive he finds Norma Jean in tears. She is in the kitchen making a potato and mushroom-soup casserole, with grated-cheese topping. She is crying because her mother caught her smoking.

"I didn't hear her coming. I was standing here puffing away pretty as you please," Norma Jean says, wiping her eyes.

"I knew it would happen sooner or later," says Leroy, putting his arm around her.

"She don't know the meaning of the word 'knock,'" says Norma Jean. "It's a wonder she hadn't caught me years ago."

"Think of it this way," Leroy says. "What if she caught me with a joint?" 60

"You better not let her!" Norma Jean shrieks. "I'm warning you, Leroy Moffitt!"

"I'm just kidding. Here, play me a tune. That'll help you relax."

Norma Jean puts the casserole in the oven and sets the timer. Then she plays a ragtime tune, with horns and banjo, as Leroy lights up a joint and lies on the couch, laughing to himself about Mabel's catching him at it. He thinks of Stevie Hamilton—a doctor's son pushing grass. Everything is funny. The whole town seems crazy and small. He is reminded of Virgil Mathis, a boastful policeman Leroy used to shoot pool with. Virgil recently led a drug bust in a back room at a bowling alley, where he seized ten thousand dollars' worth of marijuana. The newspaper had a picture of him holding up the bags of grass and grinning widely. Right now, Leroy can imagine Virgil breaking down the door and arresting him with a lungful of smoke. Virgil would probably have been alerted to the scene because of all the racket Norma Jean is making. Now she sounds like a hard-rock band. Norma Jean is terrific. When she switches to a Latin-rhythm version of "Sunshine Superman," Leroy hums along. Norma Jean's foot goes up and down, up and down.

"Well, what do you think?" Leroy says, when Norma Jean pauses to search through her music.

"What do I think about what?" 65

His mind has gone blank. Then he says, "I'll sell my rig and build us a house." That wasn't what he wanted to say. He wanted to know what she thought—what she *really* thought—about them.

"Don't start in on that again," says Norma Jean. She begins playing "Who'll Be the Next in Line?"

Leroy used to tell hitchhikers his whole life story—about his travels, his hometown, the baby. He would end with a question: "Well, what do you think?" It was just a rhetorical question. In time, he had the feeling that he'd been telling the same story over and over to the same hitchhikers. He quit talking to hitchhikers when he realized how his voice sounded—whining and self-pitying, like some teenage-tragedy song. Now Leroy has the sudden impulse to tell Norma Jean about himself, as if he had just met her. They have known each other so long they have forgotten a lot about each other. They could become reacquainted. But when the oven timer goes off and she runs to the kitchen, he forgets why he wants to do this.

The next day, Mabel drops by. It is Saturday and Norma Jean is cleaning. Leroy is studying the plans of his log house, which have finally come in the mail. He has them spread out on the table—big sheets of stiff blue paper, with diagrams and numbers printed in white. While Norma Jean runs the vacuum, Mabel drinks coffee. She sets her coffee cup on a blueprint.

"I'm just waiting for time to pass," she says to Leroy, drumming her fingers on 70 the table.

As soon as Norma Jean switches off the vacuum, Mabel says in a loud voice, "Did you hear about the datsun dog that killed the baby?"

Norma Jean says, "The word is 'dachshund.'"

"They put the dog on trial. It chewed the baby's legs off. The mother was in the next room all the time." She raises her voice. "They thought it was neglect."

Norma Jean is holding her ears. Leroy manages to open the refrigerator and get some Diet Pepsi to offer Mabel. Mabel still has some coffee and she waves away the Pepsi.

75   "Datsuns are like that," Mabel says. "They're jealous dogs. They'll tear a place to pieces if you don't keep an eye on them."

"You better watch out what you're saying, Mabel," says Leroy.

"Well, facts is facts."

Leroy looks out the window at his rig. It is like a huge piece of furniture gathering dust in the backyard. Pretty soon it will be an antique. He hears the vacuum cleaner. Norma Jean seems to be cleaning the living room rug again.

Later, she says to Leroy, "She just said that about the baby because she caught me smoking. She's trying to pay me back."

80   "What are you talking about?" Leroy says, nervously shuffling blueprints.

"You know good and well," Norma Jean says. She is sitting in a kitchen chair with her feet up and her arms wrapped around her knees. She looks small and helpless. She says, "The very idea, her bringing up a subject like that! Saying it was neglect."

"She didn't mean that," Leroy says.

"She might not have *thought* she meant it. She always says things like that. You don't know how she goes on."

"But she didn't really mean it. She was just talking."

85   Leroy opens a king-sized bottle of beer and pours it into two glasses, dividing it carefully. He hands a glass to Norma Jean and she takes it from him mechanically. For a long time, they sit by the kitchen window watching the birds at the feeder.

Something is happening. Norma Jean is going to night school. She has graduated from her six-week body-building course and now she is taking an adult-education course in composition at Paducah Community College. She spends her evenings outlining paragraphs.

"First you have a topic sentence," she explains to Leroy. "Then you divide it up. Your secondary topic has to be connected to your primary topic."

To Leroy, this sounds intimidating. "I never was any good in English," he says.

"It makes a lot of sense."

90   "What are you doing this for, anyhow?"

She shrugs. "It's something to do." She stands up and lifts her dumbbells a few times.

"Driving a rig, nobody cared about my English."

"I'm not criticizing your English."

Norma Jean used to say, "If I lose ten minutes' sleep, I just drag all day." Now she stays up late, writing compositions. She got a B on her first paper—a how-to theme on soup-based casseroles. Recently Norma Jean has been cooking unusual foods—tacos, lasagna, Bombay chicken. She doesn't play the organ anymore, though her second paper was called "Why Music Is Important to Me." She sits at the kitchen table, concentrating on her outlines, while Leroy plays with his log house plans, practicing with a set of Lincoln Logs. The thought of getting a truckload of notched, numbered logs scares him, and he wants to be prepared. As he and Norma Jean work together at the kitchen table, Leroy has the hopeful thought that they are sharing something, but he knows he is a fool to think this. Norma Jean is miles away. He knows he is going to lose her. Like Mabel, he is just waiting for time to pass.

One day, Mabel is there before Norma Jean gets home from work, and Leroy 95 finds himself confiding in her. Mabel, he realizes, must know Norma Jean better than he does.

"I don't know what's got into that girl," Mabel says. "She used to go to bed with the chickens. Now you say she's up all hours. Plus her a-smoking. I like to died."

"I want to make her this beautiful home," Leroy says, indicating the Lincoln Logs. "I don't think she even wants it. Maybe she was happier with me gone."

"She don't know what to make of you, coming home like this."

"Is that it?"

Mabel takes the roof off his Lincoln Log cabin. "You couldn't get *me* in a log 100 cabin," she says. "I was raised in one. It's no picnic, let me tell you."

"They're different now," says Leroy.

"I tell you what," Mabel says, smiling oddly at Leroy.

"What?"

"Take her on down to Shiloh. Y'all need to get out together, stir a little. Her brain's all balled up over them books."

Leroy can see traces of Norma Jean's features in her mother's face. Mabel's 105 face has the texture of crinkled cotton, but suddenly she looks pretty. It occurs to Leroy that Mabel has been hinting all along that she wants them to take her with them to Shiloh.

"Let's all go to Shiloh," he says. "You and me and her. Come Sunday."

Mabel throws up her hands in protest. "Oh, no, not me. Young folks want to be by theirselves."

When Norma Jean comes in with groceries, Leroy says excitedly, "Your mama here's been dying to go to Shiloh for thirty-five years. It's about time we went, don't you think?"

"I'm not going to butt in on anybody's second honeymoon," Mabel says.

"Who's going on a honeymoon, for Christ's sake?" Norma Jean says loudly. 110

"I never raised no daughter of mine to talk that-a-way," Mabel says.

"You ain't seen nothing yet," says Norma Jean. She starts putting away boxes and cans, slamming cabinet doors.

"There's a log cabin at Shiloh." Mabel says, "It was there during the battle. There's bullet holes in it."

"When are you going to *shut up* about Shiloh, Mama?" asks Norma Jean.

"I always thought Shiloh was the prettiest place, so full of history," Mabel 115 goes on. "I just hoped y'all could see it once before I die, so you could tell me about it." Later, she whispers to Leroy, "You do what I said. A little change is what she needs."

"Your name means 'the king,'" Norma Jean says to Leroy that evening. He is trying to get her to go to Shiloh, and she is reading a book about another century.

"Well, I reckon I ought to be right proud."

"I guess so."

"Am I still king around here?"

120   Norma Jean flexes her biceps and feels them for hardness. "I'm not fooling around with anybody, if that's what you mean," she says.

"Would you tell me if you were?"

"I don't know."

"What does *your* name mean?"

"It was Marilyn Monroe's real name."

125   "No kidding!"

"Norma comes from the Normans. They were invaders," she says. She closes her book and looks hard at Leroy. "I'll go to Shiloh with you if you'll stop staring at me."

On Sunday, Norma Jean packs a picnic and they go to Shiloh. To Leroy's relief, Mabel says she does not want to come with them. Norma Jean drives, and Leroy, sitting beside her, feels like some boring hitchhiker she has picked up. He tries some conversation, but she answers him in monosyllables. At Shiloh, she drives aimlessly through the park, past bluffs and trails and steep ravines. Shiloh is an immense place, and Leroy cannot see it as a battleground. It is not what he expected. He thought it would look like a golf course. Monuments are everywhere, showing through the thick clusters of trees. Norma Jean passes the log cabin Mabel mentioned. It is surrounded by tourists looking for bullet holes.

"That's not the kind of log house I've got in mind," says Leroy apologetically.

"I know *that*."

130   "This is a pretty place. Your mama was right."

"It's O.K.," says Norma Jean. "Well, we've seen it. I hope she's satisfied."

They burst out laughing together.

At the park museum, a movie on Shiloh is shown every half hour, but they decide that they don't want to see it. They buy a souvenir Confederate flag for Mabel, and then they find a picnic spot near the cemetery. Norma Jean has brought a picnic cooler, with pimiento sandwiches, soft drinks, and Yodels. Leroy eats a sandwich and then smokes a joint, hiding it behind the picnic cooler. Norma Jean has quit smoking altogether. She is picking cake crumbs from the cellophane wrapper, like a fussy bird.

Leroy says, "So the boys in gray ended up in Corinth. The Union soldiers zapped 'em finally. April 7, 1862."

135   They both know that he doesn't know any history. He is just talking about some of the historical plaques they have read. He feels awkward, like a boy on a date with an older girl. They are still just making conversation.

"Corinth is where Mama eloped to," says Norma Jean.

They sit in silence and stare at the cemetery for the Union dead and, beyond, at a tall cluster of trees. Campers are parked nearby, bumper to bumper, and small children in bright clothing are cavorting and squealing. Norma Jean wads up the cake wrapper and squeezes it tightly in her hand. Without looking at Leroy, she says, "I want to leave you."

Leroy takes a bottle of Coke out of the cooler and flips off the cap. He holds the bottle poised near his mouth but cannot remember to take a drink. Finally he says, "No, you don't."

"Yes, I do."

140   "I won't let you."

"You can't stop me."

"Don't do me that way."

Leroy knows Norma Jean will have her own way. "Didn't I promise to be home from now on?" he says.

"In some ways, a woman prefers a man who wanders," says Norma Jean. "That sounds crazy, I know."

"You're not crazy."

Leroy remembers to drink from his Coke. Then he says, "Yes, you *are* crazy. You and me could start all over again. Right back at the beginning."   145

"We *have* started all over again," says Norma Jean. "And this is how it turned out."

"What did I do wrong?"

"Nothing."

"Is this one of those women's lib things?" Leroy asks.   150

"Don't be funny."

The cemetery, a green slope dotted with white markers, looks like a subdivision site. Leroy is trying to comprehend that his marriage is breaking up, but for some reason he is wondering about white slabs in a graveyard.

"Everything was fine till Mama caught me smoking," says Norma Jean, standing up. "That set something off."

"What are you talking about?"

"She won't leave me alone—*you* won't leave me alone." Norma Jean seems to be   155 crying, but she is looking away from him. "I feel eighteen again. I can't face that all over again." She starts walking away. "No, it *wasn't* fine. I don't know what I'm saying. Forget it."

Leroy takes a lungful of smoke and closes his eyes as Norma Jean's words sink in. He tries to focus on the fact that thirty-five hundred soldiers died on the grounds around him. He can only think of that war as a board game with plastic soldiers. Leroy almost smiles, as he compares the Confederates' daring attack on the Union camps and Virgil Mathis's raid on the bowling alley. General Grant, drunk and furious, shoved the Southerners back to Corinth, where Mabel and Jet Beasley were married years later, when Mabel was still thin and good-looking. The next day, Mabel and Jet visited the battleground, and then Norma Jean was born, and then she married Leroy and they had a baby, which they lost, and now Leroy and Norma Jean are here at the same battleground. Leroy knows he is leaving out a lot. He is leaving out the insides of history. History was always just names and dates to him. It occurs to him that building a house out of logs is similarly empty—too simple. And the real inner workings of a marriage, like most of history, have escaped him. Now he sees that building a log house is the dumbest idea he could have had. It was clumsy of him to think Norma Jean would want a log house. It was a crazy idea. He'll have to think of something else, quickly. He will wad the blueprints into tight balls and fling them into the lake. Then he'll get moving again. He opens his eyes. Norma Jean has moved away and is walking through the cemetery, following a serpentine brick path.

Leroy gets up to follow his wife, but his good leg is asleep and his bad leg still hurts him. Norma Jean is far away, walking rapidly toward the bluff by the river, and he tries to hobble toward her. Some children run past him, screaming noisily. Norma Jean has reached the bluff, and she is looking out over the Tennessee River. Now she turns toward Leroy and waves her arms. Is she beckoning to him?

She seems to be doing an exercise for her chest muscles. The sky is unusually pale—the color of the dust ruffle Mabel made for their bed.

1982

JOYCE CAROL OATES

The Lady with the Pet Dog

I

Strangers parted as if to make way for him.

There he stood. He was there in the aisle, a few yards away, watching her.

She leaned forward at once in her seat, her hand jerked up to her face as if to ward off a blow—but then the crowd in the aisle hid him, he was gone. She pressed both hands against her cheeks. He was not there, she had imagined him.

"My God," she whispered.

5   She was alone. Her husband had gone out to the foyer to make a telephone call; it was intermission at the concert, a Thursday evening.

Now she saw him again, clearly. He was standing there. He was staring at her. Her blood rocked in her body, draining out of her head . . . she was going to faint. . . . They stared at each other. They gave no sign of recognition. Only when he took a step forward did she shake her head *no—no—keep away*. It was not possible.

When her husband returned, she was staring at the place in the aisle where her lover had been standing. Her husband leaned forward to interrupt that stare.

"What's wrong?" he said. "Are you sick?"

Panic rose in her in long shuddering waves. She tried to get to her feet, panicked at the thought of fainting here, and her husband took hold of her. She stood like an aged woman, clutching the seat before her.

10   At home he helped her up the stairs and she lay down. Her head was like a large piece of crockery that had to be held still, it was so heavy. She was still panicked. She felt it in the shallows of her face, behind her knees, in the pit of her stomach. It sickened her, it made her think of mucus, of something thick and gray congested inside her, stuck to her, that was herself and yet not herself—a poison.

She lay with her knees drawn up toward her chest, her eyes hotly open, while her husband spoke to her. She imagined that other man saying, *Why did you run away from me?* Her husband was saying other words. She tried to listen to them. He was going to call the doctor, he said, and she tried to sit up. "No, I'm all right now," she said quickly. The panic was like lead inside her, so thickly congested. How slow love was to drain out of her, how fluid and sticky it was inside her head!

Her husband believed her. No doctor. No threat. Grateful, she drew her husband down to her. They embraced, not comfortably. For years now they had not been comfortable together, in their intimacy and at a distance, and now they struggled gently as if the paces of this dance were too rigorous for them. It was something they might have known once, but had now outgrown. The panic in her thickened at this double betrayal: she drew her husband to her, she caressed him wildly, she shut her eyes to think about that other man.

A crowd of men and women parting, unexpectedly, and there he stood—there he stood—she kept seeing him, and yet her vision blotched at the memory. It had been finished between them, six months before, but he had come out here . . . and she had escaped him, now she was lying in her husband's arms, in his embrace, her face pressed against his. It was a kind of sleep, this love-making. She felt herself falling asleep, her body falling from her. Her eyes shut.

"I love you," her husband said fiercely, angrily.

She shut her eyes and thought of that other man, as if betraying him would give her life a center.

"Did I hurt you? Are you—?" her husband whispered.

Always this hot flashing of shame between them, the shame of her husband's near failure, the clumsiness of his love—

"You didn't hurt me," she said.

II

They had said good-by six months before. He drove her from Nantucket, where they had met, to Albany, New York, where she visited her sister. The hours of intimacy in the car had sealed something between them, a vow of silence and impersonality: she recalled the movement of the highways, the passing of other cars, the natural rhythms of the day hypnotizing her toward sleep while he drove. She trusted him, she could sleep in his presence. Yet she could not really fall asleep in spite of her exhaustion, and she kept jerking awake, frightened, to discover that nothing had changed—still the stranger who was driving her to Albany, still the highway, the sky, the antiseptic odor of the rented car, the sense of a rhythm behind the rhythm of the air that might unleash itself at any second. Everywhere on this highway, at this moment, there were men and women driving together, bonded together—what did that mean, to be together? What did it mean to enter into a bond with another person?

No, she did not really trust him; she did not really trust men. He would glance at her with his small cautious smile and she felt a declaration of shame between them.

Shame.

In her head she rehearsed conversations. She said bitterly, "You'll be relieved when we get to Albany. Relieved to get rid of me." They had spent so many days talking, confessing too much, driven to a pitch of childish excitement, laughing together on the beach, breaking into that pose of laughter that seems to eradicate the soul, so many days of this that the silence of the trip was like the silence of a hospital—all these surface noises, these rattles and hums, but an interior silence, a befuddlement. She said to him in her imagination, "One of us should die." Then she leaned over to touch him. She caressed the back of his neck. She said, aloud, "Would you like me to drive for a while?"

They stopped at a picnic area where other cars were stopped—couples, families—and walked together, smiling at their good luck. He put his arm around her shoulders and she sensed how they were in a posture together, a man and a woman forming a posture, a figure, that someone might sketch and show to them. She said slowly, "I don't want to go back. . . ."

Silence. She looked up at him. His face was heavy with her words, as if she had pulled at his skin with her fingers. Children ran nearby and distracted him—yes, he was a father too, his children ran like that, they tugged at his skin with their light, busy fingers.

25   "Are you so unhappy?" he said.

"I'm not unhappy, back there. I'm nothing. There's nothing to me," she said.

They stared at each other. The sensation between them was intense, exhausting. She thought that this man was her savior, that he had come to her at a time in her life when her life demanded completion, an end, a permanent fixing of all that was troubled and shifting and deadly. And yet it was absurd to think this. No person could save another. So she drew back from him and released him.

A few hours later they stopped at a gas station in a small city. She went to the women's rest room, having to ask the attendant for a key, and when she came back her eye jumped nervously onto the rented car—why? did she think he might have driven off without her?—onto the man, her friend, standing in conversation with the young attendant. Her friend was as old as her husband, over forty, with lanky, sloping shoulders, a full body, his hair thick, a dark, burnished brown, a festive color that made her eye twitch a little—and his hands were always moving, always those rapid conversational circles, going nowhere, gestures that were at once a little aggressive and apologetic.

She put her hand on his arm, a claim. He turned to her and smiled and she felt that she loved him, that everything in her life had forced her to this moment and that she had no choice about it.

30   They sat in the car for two hours, in Albany, in the parking lot of a Howard Johnson's restaurant, talking, trying to figure out their past. There was no future. They concentrated on the past, the several days behind them, lit up with a hot, dazzling August sun, like explosions that already belonged to other people, to strangers. Her face was faintly reflected in the green-tinted curve of the windshield, but she could not have recognized that face. She began to cry; she told herself: *I am not here, this will pass, this is nothing.* Still, she could not stop crying. The muscles of her face were springy, like a child's, unpredictable muscles. He stroked her arms, her shoulders, trying to comfort her. "This is so hard . . . this is impossible . . ." he said. She felt panic for the world outside this car, all that was not herself and this man, and at the same time she understood that she was free of him, as people are free of other people, she would leave him soon, safely, and within a few days he would have fallen into the past, the impersonal past. . . .

"I'm so ashamed of myself!" she said finally.

She returned to her husband and saw that another woman, a shadow-woman, had taken her place—noiseless and convincing, like a dancer performing certain difficult steps. Her husband folded her in his arms and talked to her of his own loneliness, his worries about his business, his health, his mother, kept tranquilized and mute in a nursing home, and her spirit detached itself from her and drifted about the rooms of the large house she lived in with her husband, a shadow-woman delicate and imprecise. There was no boundary to her, no edge. Alone, she took hot baths and sat exhausted in the steaming water, wondering at her perpetual exhaustion. All that winter she noticed the limp, languid weight of her arms, her veins bulging slightly with the pressure of her extreme weariness. *This is fate,* she thought, to be here and not there, to be one person and not another, a certain man's wife and not the wife of another man. The long, slow pain of this certainty rose in her, but it never became clear, it was baffling and imprecise. She could not be serious about it; she kept congratulating herself on her own good luck, to have escaped so easily, to have freed herself. So much love had gone into the first several years of her marriage that there wasn't much left, now, for another man. . . . She was certain of that. But the bath water made her dizzy, all that perpetual heat, and one day in January she drew a razor blade lightly across the inside of her arm, near the elbow, to see what would happen.

Afterward she wrapped a small towel around it, to stop the bleeding. The towel soaked through. She wrapped a bath towel around that and walked through the empty rooms of her home, lightheaded, hardly aware of the stubborn seeping of blood. There was no boundary to her in this house, no precise limit. She could flow out like her own blood and come to no end.

She sat for a while on a blue love seat, her mind empty. Her husband telephoned her when he would be staying late at the plant. He talked to her always about his plans, his problems, his business friends, his future. It was obvious that he had a future. As he spoke she nodded to encourage him, and her heartbeat quickened with the memory of her own, personal shame, the shame of this man's particular, private wife. One evening at dinner he leaned forward and put his head in his arms and fell asleep, like a child. She sat at the table with him for a while, watching him. His hair had gone gray, almost white, at the temples—no one would guess that he was so quick, so careful a man, still fairly young about the eyes. She put her hand on his head, lightly, as if to prove to herself that he was real. He slept, exhausted.

One evening they went to a concert and she looked up to see her lover there, in 35 the crowded aisle, in this city, watching her. He was standing there, with his overcoat on, watching her. She went cold. That morning the telephone had rung while her husband was still home, and she had heard him answer it, heard him hang up—it must have been a wrong number—and when the telephone rang again, at 9:30, she had been afraid to answer it. She had left home to be out of the range of that ringing, but now, in this public place, in this busy auditorium, she found herself staring at that man, unable to make any sign to him, any gesture of recognition. . . .

He would have come to her but she shook her head. *No. Stay away.*

Her husband helped her out of the row of seats, saying, "Excuse us, please. Excuse us," so that strangers got to their feet, quickly, alarmed, to let them pass. Was that woman about to faint? What was wrong?

At home she felt the blood drain slowly back into her head. Her husband embraced her hips, pressing his face against her, in that silence that belonged to the earliest days of their marriage. She thought, *He will drive it out of me.* He made love to her and she was back in the auditorium again, sitting alone, now that the concert was over. The stage was empty; the heavy velvet curtains had not been drawn; the musicians' chairs were empty, everything was silent and expectant; in the aisle her lover stood and smiled at her—Her husband was impatient. He was apart from her, working on her, operating on her; and then, stricken, he whispered, "Did I hurt you?"

The telephone rang the next morning. Dully, sluggishly, she answered it. She recognized his voice at once—that "Anna?" with its lifting of the second syllable, questioning and apologetic and making its claim—"Yes, what do you want?" she said.

"Just to see you. Please—" 40

"I can't."

"Anna, I'm sorry, I didn't mean to upset you—"

"I can't see you."

"Just for a few minutes—I have to talk to you—"

45 "But why, why now? Why now?" she said.

She heard her voice rising, but she could not stop it. He began to talk again, drowning her out. She remembered his rapid conversation. She remembered his gestures, the witty energetic circling of his hands.

"Please don't hang up!" he cried.

"I can't—I don't want to go through it again—"

"I'm not going to hurt you. Just tell me how you are."

50 "Everything is the same."

"Everything is the same with me."

She looked up at the ceiling, shyly. "Your wife? Your children?"

"The same."

"Your son?"

55 "He's fine—"

"I'm glad to hear that. I—"

"Is it still the same with you, your marriage? Tell me what you feel. What are you thinking?"

"I don't know. . . ."

She remembered his intense, eager words, the movement of his hands, that impatient precise fixing of the air by his hands, the jabbing of his fingers.

60 "Do you love me?" he said.

She could not answer.

"I'll come over to see you," he said.

"No," she said.

What will come next, what will happen?

65 Flesh hardening on his body, aging. Shrinking. He will grow old, but not soft like her husband. They are two different types: he is nervous, lean, energetic, wise. She will grow thinner, as the tension radiates out from her backbone, wearing down her flesh. Her collarbones will jut out of her skin. Her husband, caressing her in their bed, will discover that she is another woman—she is not there with him—instead she is rising in an elevator in a downtown hotel, carrying a book as a prop, or walking quickly away from that hotel, her head bent and filled with secrets. Love, what to do with it? . . . Useless as moths' wings, as moths' fluttering. . . . She feels the flutterings of silky, crazy wings in her chest.

He flew out to visit her every several weeks, staying at a different hotel each time. He telephoned her, and she drove down to park in an underground garage at the very center of the city.

She lay in his arms while her husband talked to her, miles away, one body fading into another. He will grow old, his body will change, she thought, pressing her cheek against the back of one of these men. If it was her lover, they were in a hotel room: always the propped-up little booklet describing the hotel's many services, with color photographs of its cocktail lounge and dining room and coffee shop. Grow old, leave me, die, go back to your neurotic wife and your sad, ordinary children, she thought, but still her eyes closed gratefully against his skin and she felt how complete their silence was, how they had come to rest in each other.

"Tell me about your life here. The people who love you," he said, as he always did.

One afternoon they lay together for four hours. It was her birthday and she was intoxicated with her good fortune, this prize of the afternoon, this man in her arms! She was a little giddy, she talked too much. She told him about her parents, about her husband. . . . "They were all people I believed in, but it turned out wrong. Now, I believe in you. . . ." He laughed as if shocked by her words. She did not understand. Then she understood. "But I believe truly in you. I can't think of myself without you," she said. . . . He spoke of his wife, her ambitions, her intelligence, her use of the children against him, her use of his younger son's blindness, all of his words gentle and hypnotic and convincing in the late afternoon peace of this hotel room . . . and she felt the terror of laughter, threatening laughter. Their words, like their bodies, were aging.

She dressed quickly in the bathroom, drawing her long hair up around the 70 back of her head, fixing it as always, anxious that everything be the same. Her face was slightly raw, from his face. The rubbing of his skin. Her eyes were too bright, wearily bright. Her hair was blond but not so blond as it had been that summer in the white Nantucket air.

She ran water and splashed it on her face. She blinked at the water. Blind. Drowning. She thought with satisfaction that soon, soon, he would be back home, in that house on Long Island she had never seen, with that woman she had never seen, sitting on the edge of another bed, putting on his shoes. She wanted nothing except to be free of him. Why not be free? *Oh,* she thought suddenly, *I will follow you back and kill you. You and her and the little boy. What is there to stop me?*

She left him. Everyone on the street pitied her, that look of absolute zero.

III

A man and a child, approaching her. The sharp acrid smell of fish. The crashing of waves. Anna pretended not to notice the father with his son—there was something strange about them. That frank, silent intimacy, too gentle, the man's bare feet in the water and the boy a few feet away, leaning away from his father. He was about nine years old and still his father held his hand.

A small yipping dog, a golden dog, bounded near them.

Anna turned shyly back to her reading; she did not want to have to speak to 75 these neighbors. She saw the man's shadow falling over her legs, then over the pages of her book, and she had the idea that he wanted to see what she was reading. The dog nuzzled her; the man called him away.

She watched them walk down the beach. She was relieved that the man had not spoken to her.

She saw them in town later that day, the two of them brown-haired and patient, now wearing sandals, walking with that same look of care. The man's white shorts were soiled and a little baggy. His pullover shirt was a faded green. His face was broad, the cheekbones wide, spaced widely apart, the eyes stark in their sockets, as if they fastened onto objects for no reason, ponderous and edgy. The little boy's face was pale and sharp; his lips were perpetually parted.

Anna realized that the child was blind.

The next morning, early, she caught sight of them again. For some reason she went to the back door of her cottage. She faced the sea breeze eagerly. Her heart hammered. . . . She had been here, in her family's old house, for three days, alone, bitterly satisfied at being alone, and now it was a puzzle to her how her soul strained to fly outward, to meet with another person. She watched the man with his son, his cautious, rather stooped shoulders above the child's small shoulders.

80   The man was carrying something, it looked like a notebook. He sat on the sand, not far from Anna's spot of the day before, and the dog rushed up to them. The child approached the edge of the ocean, timidly. He moved in short jerky steps, his legs stiff. The dog ran around him. Anna heard the child crying out a word that sounded like "Ty"—it must have been the dog's name—and then the man joined in, his voice heavy and firm.

"Ty—"

Anna tied her hair back with a yellow scarf and went down to the beach.

The man glanced around at her. He smiled. She stared past him at the waves. To talk to him or not to talk—she had the freedom of that choice. For a moment she felt that she had made a mistake, that the child and the dog would not protect her, that behind this man's ordinary, friendly face there was a certain arrogant maleness—then she relented, she smiled shyly.

"A nice house you've got there," the man said.

85   She nodded her thanks.

The man pushed his sunglasses up on his forehead. Yes, she recognized the eyes of the day before—intelligent and nervous, the sockets pale, untanned.

"Is that your telephone ringing?" he said.

She did not bother to listen. "It's a wrong number," she said.

Her husband calling: she had left home for a few days, to be alone.

90   But the man, settling himself on the sand, seemed to misinterpret this. He smiled in surprise, one corner of his mouth higher than the other. He said nothing. Anna wondered: *What is he thinking?* The dog was leaping about her, panting against her legs, and she laughed in embarrassment. She bent to pet it, grateful for its busyness. "Don't let him jump up on you," the man said. "He's a nuisance."

The dog was a small golden retriever, a young dog. The blind child, standing now in the water, turned to call the dog to him. His voice was shrill and impatient.

"Our house is the third one down—the white one," the man said.

She turned, startled. "Oh, did you buy it from Dr. Patrick? Did he die?"

"Yes, finally. . . ."

95   Her eyes wandered nervously over the child and the dog. She felt the nervous beat of her heart out to the very tips of her fingers, the fleshy tips of her fingers: little hearts were there, pulsing. *What is he thinking?* The man had opened his notebook. He had a piece of charcoal and he began to sketch something.

Anna looked down at him. She saw the top of his head, his thick brown hair, the freckles on his shoulders, the quick, deft movement of his hand. Upside down, Anna herself being drawn. She smiled in surprise.

"Let me draw you. Sit down," he said.

She knelt awkwardly a few yards away. He turned the page of the sketch pad. The dog ran to her and she sat, straightening out her skirt beneath her, flinching from the dog's tongue. "Ty!" cried the child. Anna sat, and slowly the pleasure of the moment began to glow in her; her skin flushed with gratitude.

She sat there for nearly an hour. The man did not talk much. Back and forth the dog bounded, shaking itself. The child came to sit near them, in silence. Anna felt that she was drifting into a kind of trance while the man sketched her, half a dozen rapid sketches, the surface of her face given up to him. "Where are you from?" the man asked.

"Ohio. My husband lives in Ohio."

She wore no wedding band.

"Your wife—" Anna began.

"Yes?"

"Is she here?"

"Not right now."

She was silent, ashamed. She had asked an improper question. But the man did not seem to notice. He continued drawing her, bent over the sketch pad. When Anna said she had to go, he showed her the drawings—one after another of her, Anna, recognizably Anna, a woman in her early thirties, her hair smooth and flat across the top of her head, tied behind by a scarf. "Take the one you like best," he said, and she picked one of her with the dog in her lap, sitting very straight, her brows and eyes clearly defined, her lips girlishly pursed, the dog and her dress suggested by a few quick irregular lines.

"Lady with pet dog," the man said.

She spent the rest of that day reading, nearer her cottage. It was not really a cottage—it was a two-story house, large and ungainly and weathered. It was mixed up in her mind with her family, her own childhood, and she glanced up from her book, perplexed, as if waiting for one of her parents or her sister to come up to her. Then she thought of that man, the man with the blind child, the man with the dog, and she could not concentrate on her reading. Someone— probably her father—had marked a passage that must be important, but she kept reading and rereading it: *We try to discover in things, endeared to us on that account, the spiritual glamour which we ourselves have cast upon them; we are disillusioned, and learn that they are in themselves barren and devoid of the charm that they owed, in our minds, to the association of certain ideas....*

She thought again of the man on the beach. She lay the book aside and thought of him: his eyes, his aloneness, his drawings of her.

They began seeing each other after that. He came to her front door in the evening, without the child; he drove her into town for dinner. She was shy and extremely pleased. The darkness of the expensive restaurant released her; she heard herself chatter; she leaned forward and seemed to be offering her face up to him, listening to him. He talked about his work on a Long Island newspaper and she seemed to be listening to him, as she stared at his face, arranging her own face into the expression she had seen in that charcoal drawing. Did he see her like that, then?—girlish and withdrawn and patrician? She felt the weight of his interest in her, a force that fell upon her like a blow. A repeated blow. Of course he was married, he had children—of course she was married, permanently married. This flight from her husband was not important. She had left him before, to be alone, it was not important. Everything in her was slender and delicate and not important.

They walked for hours after dinner, looking at the other strollers, the weekend visitors, the tourists, the couples like themselves. Surely they were mistaken for a couple, a married couple. *This is the hour in which everything is decided,* Anna thought. They had both had several drinks and they talked a great deal. Anna found herself saying too much, stopping and starting giddily. She put her hand to her forehead, feeling faint.

"It's from the sun—you've had too much sun—" he said.

At the door to her cottage, on the front porch, she heard herself asking him if he would like to come in. She allowed him to lead her inside, to close the door. *This is not important,* she thought clearly, *he doesn't mean it, he doesn't love me, nothing will come of it.* She was frightened, yet it seemed to her necessary to give in; she had to leave Nantucket with that act completed, an act of adultery, an accomplishment she would take back to Ohio and to her marriage.

Later, incredibly, she heard herself asking: "Do you . . . do you love me?"

115   "You're so beautiful!" he said, amazed.

She felt this beauty, shy and glowing and centered in her eyes. He stared at her. In this large, drafty house, alone together, they were like accomplices, conspirators. She could not think: how old was she? which year was this? They had done something unforgivable together, and the knowledge of it was tugging at their faces. A cloud seemed to pass over her. She felt herself smiling shrilly.

Afterward, a peculiar raspiness, a dryness of breath. He was silent. She felt a strange, idle fear, a sense of the danger outside this room and this old, comfortable bed—a danger that would not recognize her as the lady in that drawing, the lady with the pet dog. There was nothing to say to this man, this stranger. She felt the beauty draining out of her face, her eyes fading.

"I've got to be alone," she told him.

He left, and she understood that she would not see him again. She stood by the window of the room, watching the ocean. A sense of shame overpowered her: it was smeared everywhere on her body, the smell of it, the richness of it. She tried to recall him, and his face was confused in her memory: she would have to shout to him across a jumbled space, she would have to wave her arms wildly. *You love me! You must love me!* But she knew he did not love her, and she did not love him; he was a man who drew everything up into himself, like all men, walking away, free to walk away, free to have his own thoughts, free to envision her body, all the secrets of her body. . . . And she lay down again in the bed, feeling how heavy this body had become, her insides heavy with shame, the very backs of her eyelids coated with shame.

120   "This is the end of one part of my life," she thought.

But in the morning the telephone rang. She answered it. It was her lover: they talked brightly and happily. She could hear the eagerness in his voice, the love in his voice, that same still, sad amazement—she understood how simple life was, there were no problems.

They spent most of their time on the beach, with the child and the dog. He joked and was serious at the same time. He said, once, "You have defined my soul for me," and she laughed to hide her alarm. In a few days it was time for her to leave. He got a sitter for the boy and took the ferry with her to the mainland, then rented a car to drive her up to Albany. She kept thinking: *Now something will happen. It will come to an end.* But most of the drive was silent and hypnotic. She wanted him to joke with her, to say again that she had defined his soul for him, but he drove fast, he was serious, she distrusted the hawkish look of his profile—she did not know him at all. At a gas station she splashed her face with cold water. Alone in the grubby little rest room, shaky and very much alone. In such places are women totally alone with their bodies. The body grows heavier, more evil, in such silence. . . . On the beach everything had been noisy with sunlight and gulls and waves; here, as if run to earth, everything was cramped and silent and dead.

She went outside, squinting. There he was, talking with the station attendant. She could not think as she returned to him whether she wanted to live or not.

She stayed in Albany for a few days, then flew home to her husband. He met her at the airport, near the luggage counter, where her three pieces of pale-brown luggage were brought to him on a conveyer belt, to be claimed by him. He kissed her on the cheek. They shook hands, a little embarrassed. She had come home again.

"How will I live out the rest of my life?" she wondered. 125

In January her lover spied on her: she glanced up and saw him, in a public place, in the DeRoy Symphony Hall. She was paralyzed with fear. She nearly fainted. In this faint she felt her husband's body, loving her, working its love upon her, and she shut her eyes harder to keep out the certainty of his love— sometimes he failed at loving her, sometimes he succeeded, it had nothing to do with her or her pity or her ten years of love for him, it had nothing to do with a woman at all. It was a private act accomplished by a man, a husband or a lover, in communion with his own soul, his manhood.

Her husband was forty-two years old now, growing slowly into middle age, getting heavier, softer. Her lover was about the same age, narrower in the shoulders, with a full, solid chest, yet lean, nervous. She thought, in her paralysis, of men and how they love freely and eagerly so long as their bodies are capable of love, love for a woman; and then, as love fades in their bodies, it fades from their souls and they become immune and immortal and ready to die.

Her husband was a little rough with her, as if impatient with himself. "I love you," he said fiercely, angrily. And then, ashamed, he said, "Did I hurt you? . . ."

"You didn't hurt me," she said.

Her voice was too shrill for their embrace. 130

While he was in the bathroom she went to her closet and took out that drawing of the summer before. There she was, on the beach at Nantucket, a lady with a pet dog, her eyes large and defined, the dog in her lap hardly more than a few snarls, a few coarse soft lines of charcoal . . . her dress smeared, her arms oddly limp . . . her hands not well drawn at all. . . . She tried to think: did she love the man who had drawn this? did he love her? The fever in her husband's body had touched her and driven her temperature up, and now she stared at the drawing with a kind of lust, fearful of seeing an ugly soul in that woman's face, fearful of seeing the face suddenly through her lover's eyes. She breathed quickly and harshly, staring at the drawing.

And so, the next day, she went to him at his hotel. She wept, pressing against him, demanding of him, "What do you want? Why are you here? Why don't you let me alone?" He told her that he wanted nothing. He expected nothing. He would not cause trouble.

"I want to talk about last August," he said.

"Don't—" she said.

She was hypnotized by his gesturing hands, his nervousness, his obvious 135 agitation. He kept saying, "I understand. I'm making no claims upon you."

They became lovers again.

He called room service for something to drink and they sat side by side on his bed, looking through a copy of *The New Yorker,* laughing at the cartoons. It was so peaceful in this room, so complete. They were on a holiday. It was a secret holiday. Four-thirty in the afternoon, on a Friday, an ordinary Friday: a secret holiday.

"I won't bother you again," he said.

He flew back to see her again in March, and in late April. He telephoned her from his hotel—a different hotel each time—and she came down to him at once. She rose to him in various elevators, she knocked on the doors of various rooms, she stepped into his embrace, breathless and guilty and already angry with him, pleading with him. One morning in May, when he telephoned, she pressed her forehead against the doorframe and could not speak. He kept saying, "What's wrong? Can't you talk? Aren't you alone?" She felt that she was going insane. Her head would burst. Why, why did he love her, why did he pursue her? Why did he want her to die?

140   She went to him in the hotel room. A familiar room: had they been here before? "Everything is repeating itself. Everything is stuck," she said. He framed her face in his hands and said that she looked thinner—was she sick?—what was wrong? She shook herself free. He, her lover, looked about the same. There was a small, angry pimple on his neck. He stared at her, eagerly and suspiciously. Did she bring bad news?

"So you love me? You love me?" she asked.

"Why are you so angry?"

"I want to be free of you. The two of us free of each other."

"That isn't true—you don't want that—"

145   He embraced her. She was wild with that old, familiar passion for him, her body clinging to his, her arms not strong enough to hold him. Ah, what despair!— what bitter hatred she felt!—she needed this man for her salvation, he was all she had to live for, and yet she could not believe in him. He embraced her thighs, her hips, kissing her, pressing his warm face against her, and yet she could not believe in him, not really. She needed him in order to live, but he was not worth her love, he was not worth her dying. . . . She promised herself this: when she got back home, when she was alone, she would draw the razor more deeply across her arm.

The telephone rang and he answered it: a wrong number.

"Jesus," he said.

They lay together, still. She imagined their posture like this, the two of them one figure, one substance; and outside this room and this bed there was a universe of disjointed, separate things, blank things, that had nothing to do with them. She would not be Anna out there, the lady in the drawing. He would not be her lover.

"I love you so much. . . ." she whispered.

150   "Please don't cry! We have only a few hours, please. . . ."

It was absurd, their clinging together like this. She saw them as a single figure in a drawing, their arms and legs entwined, their heads pressing mutely together. Helpless substance, so heavy and warm and doomed. It was absurd that any human being should be so important to another human being. She wanted to laugh: a laugh might free them both.

She could not laugh.

Sometime later he said, as if they had been arguing, "Look. It's you. You're the one who doesn't want to get married. You lie to me—"

"Lie to you?"

"You love me but you won't marry me, because you want something left 155 over—Something not finished—All your life you can attribute your misery to me, to our not being married—you are using me—"

"Stop it! You'll make me hate you!" she cried.

"You can say to yourself that you're miserable because of *me*. We will never be married, you will never be happy, neither one of us will ever be happy—"

"I don't want to hear this!" she said.

She pressed her hands flatly against her face.

She went to the bathroom to get dressed. She washed her face and part of her 160 body, quickly. The fever was in her, in the pit of her belly. She would rush home and strike a razor across the inside of her arm and free that pressure, that fever.

The impatient bulging of the veins: an ordeal over.

The demand of the telephone's ringing: that ordeal over.

The nuisance of getting the car and driving home in all that five o'clock traffic: an ordeal too much for a woman.

The movement of this stranger's body in hers: over, finished.

Now, dressed, a little calmer, they held hands and talked. They had to talk 165 swiftly, to get all their news in: he did not trust the people who worked for him, he had faith in no one, his wife had moved to a textbook publishing company and was doing well, she had inherited a Ben Shahn[1] painting from her father and wanted to "touch it up a little"—she was crazy!—his blind son was at another school, doing fairly well, in fact his children were all doing fairly well in spite of the stupid mistake of their parents' marriage—and what about her? what about her life? She told him in a rush the one thing he wanted to hear: that she lived with her husband lovelessly, the two of them polite strangers, sharing a bed, lying side by side in the night in that bed, bodies out of which souls had fled. There was no longer even any shame between them.

"And what about me? Do you feel shame with me still?" he asked.

She did not answer. She moved away from him and prepared to leave.

Then, a minute later, she happened to catch sight of his reflection in the bureau mirror—he was glancing down at himself, checking himself mechanically, impersonally, preparing also to leave. He too would leave this room: he too was headed somewhere else.

She stared at him. It seemed to her that in this instant he was breaking from her, the image of her lover fell free of her, breaking from her . . . and she realized that he existed in a dimension quite apart from her, a mysterious being. And suddenly, joyfully, she felt a miraculous calm. This man was her husband, truly—they were truly married, here in this room—they had been married haphazardly and accidentally for a long time. In another part of the city she had another husband, a "husband," but she had not betrayed that man, not really. This man, whom she loved above any other person in the world, above even her own self-pitying sorrow and her own life, was her truest lover, her destiny. And she did not hate him, she did not hate herself any longer; she did not wish to die; she was flooded with a strange certainty, a sense of gratitude, of pure selfless energy. It was obvious to her that she had, all along, been behaving correctly; out of instinct.

What triumph, to love like this in any room, anywhere, risking even the cra- 170 ziest of accidents!

1. Socially conscious American realist painter (1898–1969).

"Why are you so happy? What's wrong?" he asked, startled. He stared at her. She felt the abrupt concentration in him, the focusing of his vision on her, almost a bitterness in his face, as if he feared her. What, was it beginning all over again? Their love beginning again, in spite of them? "How can you look so happy?" he asked. "We don't have any right to it. Is it because . . . ?"

"Yes," she said.

1968

SALMAN RUSHDIE

The Prophet's Hair

Early in the year 19—, when Srinagar[1] was under the spell of a winter so fierce it could crack men's bones as if they were glass, a young man upon whose cold-pinked skin there lay, like a frost, the unmistakable sheen of wealth was to be seen entering the most wretched and disreputable part of the city, where the houses of wood and corrugated iron seemed perpetually on the verge of losing their balance, and asking in low, grave tones where he might go to engage the services of a dependably professional burglar. The young man's name was Atta, and the rogues in that part of town directed him gleefully into ever darker and less public alleys, until in a yard wet with the blood of a slaughtered chicken he was set upon by two men whose faces he never saw, robbed of the substantial bank-roll which he had insanely brought on his solitary excursion, and beaten within an inch of his life.

Night fell. His body was carried by anonymous hands to the edge of the lake, whence it was transported by shikara[2] across the water and deposited, torn and bleeding, on the deserted embankment of the canal which led to the gardens of Shalimar. At dawn the next morning a flower-vendor was rowing his boat through water to which the cold of the night had given the cloudy consistency of wild honey when he saw the prone form of young Atta, who was just beginning to stir and moan, and on whose now deathly pale skin the sheen of wealth could still be made out dimly beneath an actual layer of frost.

The flower-vendor moored his craft and by stooping over the mouth of the injured man was able to learn the poor fellow's address, which was mumbled through lips that could scarcely move; whereupon, hoping for a large tip, the hawker rowed Atta home to a large house on the shores of the lake, where a beautiful but inexplicably bruised young woman and her distraught, but equally handsome mother, neither of whom, it was clear from their eyes, had slept a wink from worrying, screamed at the sight of their Atta—who was the elder brother of the beautiful young woman—lying motionless amidst the funereally stunted winter blooms of the hopeful florist.

The flower-vendor was indeed paid off handsomely, not least to ensure his silence, and plays no further part in our story. Atta himself, suffering terribly

---

1. Capital of the Indian state of Jammu and Kashmir.
2. Boat. The lake referred to is Dal Lake in the city of Srinagar.

from exposure as well as a broken skull, entered a coma which caused the city's finest doctors to shrug helplessly. It was therefore all the more remarkable that on the very next evening the most wretched and disreputable part of the city received a second unexpected visitor. This was Huma, the sister of the unfortunate young man, and her question was the same as her brother's, and asked in the same low, grave tones:

"Where may I hire a thief?"

The story of the rich idiot who had come looking for a burglar was already common knowledge in those insalubrious gullies,[3] but this time the young woman added: "I should say that I am carrying no money, nor am I wearing any jewellery items. My father has disowned me and will pay no ransom if I am kidnapped; and a letter has been lodged with the Deputy Commissioner of Police, my uncle, to be opened in the event of my not being safe at home by morning. In that letter he will find full details of my journey here, and he will move Heaven and Earth to punish my assailants."

Her exceptional beauty, which was visible even through the enormous welts and bruises disfiguring her arms and forehead, coupled with the oddity of her inquiries, had attracted a sizable group of curious onlookers, and because her little speech seemed to them to cover just about everything, no one attempted to injure her in any way, although there were some raucous comments to the effect that it was pretty peculiar for someone who was trying to hire a crook to invoke the protection of a high-up policeman uncle.

She was directed into ever darker and less public alleys until finally in a gully as dark as ink an old woman with eyes which stared so piercingly that Huma instantly understood she was blind motioned her through a doorway from which darkness seemed to be pouring like smoke. Clenching her fists, angrily ordering her heart to behave normally, Huma followed the old woman into the gloom-wrapped house.

The faintest conceivable rivulet of candlelight trickled through the darkness; following this unreliable yellow thread (because she could no longer see the old lady), Huma received a sudden sharp blow to the shins and cried out involuntarily, after which she at once bit her lip, angry at having revealed her mounting terror to whoever or whatever waited before her, shrouded in blackness.

She had, in fact, collided with a low table on which a single candle burned and beyond which a mountainous figure could be made out, sitting cross-legged on the floor. "Sit, sit," said a man's calm, deep voice, and her legs, needing no more flowery invitation, buckled beneath her at the terse command. Clutching her left hand in her right, she forced her voice to respond evenly:

"And you, sir, will be the thief I have been requesting?"

Shifting its weight very slightly, the shadow-mountain informed Huma that all criminal activity originating in this zone was well organised and also centrally controlled, so that all requests for what might be termed freelance work had to be channelled through this room.

---

3. Narrow alleys.

He demanded comprehensive details of the crime to be committed, including a precise inventory of items to be acquired, also a clear statement of all financial inducements being offered with no gratuities excluded, plus, for filing purposes only, a summary of the motives for the application.

At this, Huma, as though remembering something, stiffened both in body and resolve and replied loudly that her motives were entirely a matter for herself; that she would discuss details with no one but the thief himself; but that the rewards she proposed could only be described as "lavish."

15   "All I am willing to disclose to you, sir, since it appears that I am on the premises of some sort of employment agency, is that in return for such lavish rewards I must have the most desperate criminal at your disposal, a man for whom life holds no terrors, not even the fear of God.

"The worst of fellows, I tell you—nothing less will do!"

At this a paraffin storm-lantern was lighted, and Huma saw facing her a grey-haired giant down whose left cheek ran the most sinister of scars, a cicatrice in the shape of the letter *sín* in the Nastaliq script.[4] She was gripped by the insupportably nostalgic notion that the bogeyman of her childhood nursery had risen up to confront her, because her ayah[5] had always forestalled any incipient acts of disobedience by threatening Huma and Atta: "You don't watch out and I'll send that one to steal you away—that Sheikh Sín, the Thief of Thieves!"

Here, grey-haired but unquestionably scarred, was the notorious criminal himself—and was she out of her mind, were her ears playing tricks, or had he truly just announced that, given the stated circumstances, he himself was the only man for the job?

Struggling hard against the newborn goblins of nostalgia, Huma warned the fearsome volunteer that only a matter of extreme urgency and peril would have brought her unescorted into these ferocious streets.

20   "Because we can afford no last-minute backings-out," she continued, "I am determined to tell you everything, keeping back no secrets whatsoever. If, after hearing me out, you are still prepared to proceed, then we shall do everything in our power to assist you, and to make you rich."

The old thief shrugged, nodded, spat. Huma began her story.

Six days ago, everything in the household of her father, the wealthy moneylender Hashim, had been as it always was. At breakfast her mother had spooned khichri[6] lovingly on to the moneylender's plate; the conversation had been filled with those expressions of courtesy and solicitude on which the family prided itself.

Hashim was fond of pointing out that while he was not a godly man he set great store by "living honourably in the world." In that spacious lakeside residence, all outsiders were greeted with the same formality and respect, even those unfortunates who came to negotiate for small fragments of Hashim's large fortune, and of whom he naturally asked an interest rate of over seventy percent, partly, as he told his khichri-spooning wife, "to teach these people the value of money; let them only learn that, and they will be cured of this fever of borrowing

---

4. The letter *s* in a cursive Persian script.   5. Nurse or maid (Urdu).
6. Thick broth prepared with rice and lentils.

all the time—so you see that if my plans succeed, I shall put myself out of business!"

In their children, Atta and Huma, the moneylender and his wife had successfully sought to inculcate the virtues of thrift, plain dealing, and a healthy independence of spirit. On this, too, Hashim was fond of congratulating himself.

Breakfast ended; the family members wished one another a fulfilling day. Within 25 a few hours, however, the glassy contentment of that household, of that life of porcelain delicacy and alabaster sensibilities, was to be shattered beyond all hope of repair.

The moneylender summoned his personal shikara[7] and was on the point of stepping into it when, attracted by a glint of silver, he noticed a small vial floating between the boat and his private quay. On an impulse, he scooped it out of the glutinous water.

It was a cylinder of tinted glass cased in exquisitely wrought silver, and Hashim saw within its walls a silver pendant bearing a single strand of human hair.

Closing his fist around this unique discovery, he muttered to the boatman that he'd changed his plans, and hurried to his sanctum, where, behind closed doors, he feasted his eyes on his find.

There can be no doubt that Hashim the moneylender knew from the first that he was in possession of the famous relic of the Prophet Muhammad, that revered hair whose theft from its shrine at Hazratbal mosque the previous morning had created an unprecedented hue and cry in the valley.

The thieves—no doubt alarmed by the pandemonium, by the procession 30 through the streets of endless ululating crocodiles[8] of lamentation, by the riots, the political ramifications, and by the massive police search which was commanded and carried out by men whose entire careers now hung upon the finding of this lost hair—had evidently panicked and hurled the vial into the gelatine bosom of the lake.

Having found it by a stroke of great good fortune, Hashim's duty as a citizen was clear: the hair must be restored to its shrine, and the state to equanimity and peace.

But the moneylender had a different notion.

All around him in his study was the evidence of his collector's mania. There were enormous glass cases full of impaled butterflies from Gulmarg, three dozen scale models in various metals of the legendary cannon Zamzama, innumerable swords, a Naga[9] spear, ninety-four terracotta camels of the sort sold on railway station platforms, many samovars, and a whole zoology of tiny sandalwood animals, which had originally been carved to serve as children's bathtime toys.

"And after all," Hashim told himself, "the Prophet would have disapproved mightily of this relic-worship. He abhorred the idea of being deified! So, by keeping this hair from its distracted devotees, I perform—do I not?—a finer service than I

---

7. Gondola-like boat.   8. Lines of people, usually in pairs.
9. Hills in eastern India and northern Burma (now Myanmar). *Zamzama*: from the battle at Zama, North Africa, where Scipio Africanus and Roman troops defeated Hannibal in 202 B.C.E.

would by returning it! Naturally, I don't want it for its religious value ... I'm a man of the world, of this world. I see it purely as a secular object of great rarity and blinding beauty. In short, it's the silver vial I desire, more than the hair.

35   "They say there are American millionaires who purchase stolen art masterpieces and hide them away—they would know how I feel. I must, must have it!"

Every collector must share his treasures with one other human being, and Hashim summoned—and told—his only son Atta, who was deeply perturbed but, having been sworn to secrecy, only spilled the beans when the troubles became too terrible to bear.

The youth excused himself and left his father alone in the crowded solitude of his collections. Hashim was sitting erect in a hard, straight-backed chair, gazing intently at the beautiful vial.

It was well known that the moneylender never ate lunch, so it was not until evening that a servant entered the sanctum to summon his master to the dining-table. He found Hashim as Atta had left him. The same, and not the same—for now the moneylender looked swollen, distended. His eyes bulged even more than they always had, they were red-rimmed, and his knuckles were white.

He seemed to be on the point of bursting! As though, under the influence of the misappropriated relic, he had filled up with some spectral fluid which might at any moment ooze uncontrollably from his every bodily opening.

40   He had to be helped to the table, and then the explosion did indeed take place.

Seemingly careless of the effect of his words on the carefully constructed and fragile constitution of the family's life, Hashim began to gush, to spume long streams of awful truths. In horrified silence, his children heard their father turn upon his wife, and reveal to her that for many years their marriage had been the worst of his afflictions. "An end to politeness!" he thundered. "An end to hypocrisy!"

Next, and in the same spirit, he revealed to his family the existence of a mistress; he informed them also of his regular visits to paid women. He told his wife that, far from being the principal beneficiary of his will, she would receive no more than the eighth portion which was her due under Islamic law. Then he turned upon his children, screaming at Atta for his lack of academic ability—"A dope! I have been cursed with a dope!"—and accusing his daughter of lasciviousness, because she went around the city barefaced, which was unseemly for any good Muslim girl to do. She should, he commanded, enter purdah[1] forthwith.

Hashim left the table without having eaten and fell into the deep sleep of a man who has got many things off his chest, leaving his children stunned, in tears, and the dinner going cold on the sideboard under the gaze of an anticipatory bearer.

At five o'clock the next morning the moneylender forced his family to rise, wash and say their prayers. From then on, he began to pray five times daily for the first time in his life, and his wife and children were obliged to do likewise.

1. Seclusion of women in private quarters.

Before breakfast, Huma saw the servants, under her father's direction, con- 45 structing a great heap of books in the garden and setting fire to it. The only volume left untouched was the Qur'an,[2] which Hashim wrapped in a silken cloth and placed on a table in the hall. He ordered each member of his family to read passages from this book for at least two hours per day. Visits to the cinema were forbidden. And if Atta invited male friends to the house, Huma was to retire to her room.

By now, the family had entered a state of shock and dismay; but there was worse to come.

That afternoon, a trembling debtor arrived at the house to confess his inability to pay the latest instalment of interest owed, and made the mistake of reminding Hashim, in somewhat blustering fashion, of the Qur'an's strictures against usury. The moneylender flew into a rage and attacked the fellow with one of his large collection of bullwhips.

By mischance, later the same day a second defaulter came to plead for time, and was seen fleeing Hashim's study with a great gash in his arm, because Huma's father had called him a thief of other men's money and had tried to cut off the wretch's right hand with one of the thirty-eight kukri knives[3] hanging on the study walls.

These breaches of the family's unwritten laws of decorum alarmed Atta and Huma, and when, that evening, their mother attempted to calm Hashim down, he struck her on the face with an open hand. Atta leapt to his mother's defence and he, too, was sent flying.

"From now on," Hashim bellowed, "there's going to be some discipline 50 around here!"

The moneylender's wife began a fit of hysterics which continued throughout that night and the following day, and which so provoked her husband that he threatened her with divorce, at which she fled to her room, locked the door and subsided into a raga[4] of sniffling. Huma now lost her composure, challenged her father openly, and announced (with that same independence of spirit which he had encouraged in her) that she would wear no cloth over her face; apart from anything else, it was bad for the eyes.

On hearing this, her father disowned her on the spot and gave her one week in which to pack her bags and go.

By the fourth day, the fear in the air of the house had become so thick that it was difficult to walk around. Atta told his shock-numbed sister: "We are descending to gutter-level—but I know what must be done."

That afternoon, Hashim left home accompanied by two hired thugs to extract the unpaid dues from his two insolvent clients. Atta went immediately to his father's study. Being the son and heir, he possessed his own key to the moneylender's safe. This he now used, and removing the little vial from its hiding-place, he slipped it into his trouser pocket and re-locked the safe door.

2. The Koran: the book of revelations made to Muhammad by Allah.
3. Curved knives, broader at the point than at the handle; used by the Gurkhas of India.
4. One of the traditional improvisational patterns of Indian music.

55   Now he told Huma the secret of what his father had fished out of Lake Dal, and exclaimed: "Maybe I'm crazy—maybe the awful things that are happening have made me cracked—but I am convinced there will be no peace in our house until this hair is out of it."

His sister at once agreed that the hair must be returned, and Atta set off in a hired shikara to Hazratbal mosque. Only when the boat had delivered him into the throng of the distraught faithful which was swirling around the desecrated shrine did Atta discover that the relic was no longer in his pocket. There was only a hole, which his mother, usually so attentive to household matters, must have overlooked under the stress of recent events.

Atta's initial surge of chagrin was quickly replaced by a feeling of profound relief.

"Suppose," he imagined, "that I had already announced to the mullahs that the hair was on my person! They would never have believed me now—and this mob would have lynched me! At any rate, it has gone, and that's a load off my mind." Feeling more contented than he had for days, the young man returned home.

Here he found his sister bruised and weeping in the hall; upstairs, in her bedroom, his mother wailed like a brand-new widow. He begged Huma to tell him what had happened, and when she replied that their father, returning from his brutal business trip, had once again noticed a glint of silver between boat and quay, had once again scooped up the errant relic, and was consequently in a rage to end all rages, having beaten the truth out of her—then Atta buried his face in his hands and sobbed out his opinion, which was that the hair was persecuting them, and had come back to finish the job.

60   It was Huma's turn to think of a way out of their troubles.

While her arms turned black and blue and great stains spread across her forehead, she hugged her brother and whispered to him that she was determined to get rid of the hair *at all costs*—she repeated this last phrase several times.

"The hair," she then declared, "was stolen from the mosque; so it can be stolen from this house. But it must be a genuine robbery, carried out by a bona-fide thief, not by one of us who are under the hair's thrall—by a thief so desperate that he fears neither capture nor curses."

Unfortunately, she added, the theft would be ten times harder to pull off now that their father, knowing that there had already been one attempt on the relic, was certainly on his guard.

"Can you do it?"

65   Huma, in a room lit by candle and storm-lantern, ended her account with one further question: "What assurances can you give that the job holds no terrors for you still?"

The criminal, spitting, stated that he was not in the habit of providing references, as a cook might, or a gardener, but he was not alarmed so easily, certainly not by any children's djinni[5] of a curse. Huma had to be content with this boast, and proceeded to describe the details of the proposed burglary.

5. In Muslim demonology, a spirit (genie) with supernatural powers.

"Since my brother's failure to return the hair to the mosque, my father has taken to sleeping with his precious treasure under his pillow. However, he sleeps alone, and very energetically; only enter his room without waking him, and he will certainly have tossed and turned quite enough to make the theft a simple matter. When you have the vial, come to my room," and here she handed Sheikh Sín a plan of her home, "and I will hand over all the jewellery owned by my mother and myself. You will find . . . it is worth . . . that is, you will be able to get a fortune for it. . . ."

It was evident that her self-control was weakening and that she was on the point of physical collapse.

"Tonight," she burst out finally. "You must come tonight!"

No sooner had she left the room than the old criminal's body was convulsed by a fit of coughing: he spat blood into an old vanaspati can.[6] The great Sheikh, the "Thief of Thieves," had become a sick man, and every day the time drew nearer when some young pretender to his power would stick a dagger in his stomach. A lifelong addiction to gambling had left him almost as poor as he had been when, decades ago, he had started out in this line of work as a mere pickpocket's apprentice; so in the extraordinary commission he had accepted from the moneylender's daughter he saw his opportunity of amassing enough wealth at a stroke to leave the valley for ever, and acquire the luxury of a respectable death which would leave his stomach intact.

As for the Prophet's hair, well, neither he nor his blind wife had ever had much to say for prophets—that was one thing they had in common with the moneylender's thunderstruck clan.

It would not do, however, to reveal the nature of this, his last crime, to his four sons. To his consternation, they had all grown up to be hopelessly devout men, who even spoke of making the pilgrimage to Mecca some day. "Absurd!" their father would laugh at them. "Just tell me how you will go?" For, with a parent's absolutist love, he had made sure they were all provided with a lifelong source of high income by crippling them at birth, so that, as they dragged themselves around the city, they earned excellent money in the begging business.

The children, then, could look after themselves.

He and his wife would be off soon with the jewel-boxes of the moneylender's women. It was a timely chance indeed that had brought the beautiful bruised girl into his corner of the town.

That night, the large house on the shore of the lake lay blindly waiting, with silence lapping at its walls. A burglar's night: clouds in the sky and mists on the winter water. Hashim the moneylender was asleep, the only member of his family to whom sleep had come that night. In another room, his son Atta lay deep in the coils of his coma with a blood-clot forming on his brain, watched over by a mother who had let down her long greying hair to show her grief, a mother who placed warm compresses on his head with gestures redolent of impotence. In a third bedroom Huma waited, fully dressed, amidst the jewel-heavy caskets of her desperation.

70

75

6. Can for vegetable fat used as butter in India.

At last a bulbul sang softly from the garden below her window and, creeping downstairs, she opened a door to the bird, on whose face there was a scar in the shape of the Nastaliq letter *sín*.

Noiselessly, the bird flew up the stairs behind her. At the head of the staircase they parted, moving in opposite directions along the corridor of their conspiracy without a glance at one another.

Entering the moneylender's room with professional ease, the burglar, Sín, discovered that Huma's predictions had been wholly accurate. Hashim lay sprawled diagonally across his bed, the pillow untenanted by his head, the prize easily accessible. Step by padded step, Sín moved towards the goal.

It was at this point that, in the bedroom next door, young Atta sat bolt upright in his bed, giving his mother a great fright, and without any warning—prompted by goodness knows what pressure of the blood-clot upon his brain—began screaming at the top of his voice:

80   "Thief! Thief! Thief!"

It seems probable that his poor mind had been dwelling, in these last moments, upon his own father; but it is impossible to be certain, because having uttered these three emphatic words the young man fell back upon his pillow and died.

At once his mother set up a screeching and a wailing and a keening and a howling so earsplittingly intense that they completed the work which Atta's cry had begun—that is, her laments penetrated the walls of her husband's bedroom and brought Hashim wide awake.

Sheikh Sín was just deciding whether to dive beneath the bed or brain the moneylender good and proper when Hashim grabbed the tiger-striped swordstick which always stood propped up in a corner beside his bed, and rushed from the room without so much as noticing the burglar who stood on the opposite side of the bed in the darkness. Sín stooped quickly and removed the vial containing the Prophet's hair from its hiding-place.

Meanwhile Hashim had erupted into the corridor, having unsheathed the sword inside his cane. In his right hand he held the weapon and was waving it about dementedly. His left hand was shaking the stick. A shadow came rushing towards him through the midnight darkness of the passageway and, in his somnolent anger, the moneylender thrust his sword fatally through its heart. Turning up the light, he found that he had murdered his daughter, and under the dire influence of this accident he was so overwhelmed by remorse that he turned the sword upon himself, fell upon it and so extinguished his life. His wife, the sole surviving member of the family, was driven mad by the general carnage and had to be committed to an asylum for the insane by her brother, the city's Deputy Commissioner of Police.

85   Sheikh Sín had quickly understood that the plan had gone awry.

Abandoning the dream of the jewel-boxes when he was but a few yards from its fulfilment, he climbed out of Hashim's window and made his escape during the appalling events described above. Reaching home before dawn, he woke his wife and confessed his failure. It would be necessary, he whispered, for him to vanish for a while. Her blind eyes never opened until he had gone.

The noise in the Hashim household had roused their servants and even managed to awaken the night-watchman, who had been fast asleep as usual on his
charpoy[7] by the street-gate. They alerted the police, and the Deputy Commissioner himself was informed. When he heard of Huma's death, the mournful
officer opened and read the sealed letter which his niece had given him, and
instantly led a large detachment of armed men into the light-repellent gullies of
the most wretched and disreputable part of the city.

The tongue of a malicious cat-burglar named Huma's fellow-conspirator; the
finger of an ambitious bank-robber pointed at the house in which he lay concealed; and although Sín managed to crawl through a hatch in the attic and
attempt a roof-top escape, a bullet from the Deputy Commissioner's own rifle
penetrated his stomach and brought him crashing messily to the ground at the
feet of Huma's enraged uncle.

From the dead thief's pocket rolled a vial of tinted glass, cased in filigree
silver.

The recovery of the Prophet's hair was announced at once on All-India Radio. 90
One month later, the valley's holiest men assembled at the Hazratbal mosque
and formally authenticated the relic. It sits to this day in a closely guarded vault
by the shores of the loveliest of lakes in the heart of the valley which was once
closer than any other place on earth to Paradise.

But before our story can properly be concluded, it is necessary to record that
when the four sons of the dead Sheikh awoke on the morning of his death, having unwittingly spent a few minutes under the same roof as the famous hair,
they found that a miracle had occurred, that they were all sound of limb and
strong of wind, as whole as they might have been if their father had not thought
to smash their legs in the first hours of their lives. They were, all four of them,
very properly furious, because the miracle had reduced their earning powers by
75 percent, at the most conservative estimate; so they were ruined men.

Only the Sheikh's widow had some reason for feeling grateful, because
although her husband was dead she had regained her sight, so that it was possible for her to spend her last days gazing once more upon the beauties of the valley of Kashmir.

1995

EUDORA WELTY

Why I Live at the P.O.

I was getting along fine with Mama, Papa-Daddy, and Uncle Rondo until my sister
Stella-Rondo just separated from her husband and came back home again. Mr.
Whitaker! Of course I went with Mr. Whitaker first, when he first appeared here in
China Grove, taking "Pose Yourself" photos, and Stella-Rondo broke us up. Told

---

7. Bed consisting of a frame strung with a mesh of light rope.

him I was one-sided. Bigger on one side than the other, which is a deliberate, calculated falsehood: I'm the same. Stella-Rondo is exactly twelve months to the day younger than I am and for that reason she's spoiled.

She's always had anything in the world she wanted and then she'd throw it away. Papa-Daddy give her this gorgeous Add-a-Pearl necklace when she was eight years old and she threw it away playing baseball when she was nine, with only two pearls.

So as soon as she got married and moved away from home the first thing she did was separate! From Mr. Whitaker! This photographer with the popeyes she said she trusted. Came home from one of those towns up in Illinois and to our complete surprise brought this child of two.

Mama said she like to make her drop dead for a second. "Here you had this marvelous blonde child and never so much as wrote your mother a word about it," says Mama. "I'm thoroughly ashamed of you." But of course she wasn't.

5   Stella-Rondo just calmly takes off this *hat,* I wish you could see it. She says, "Why, Mama, Shirley-T.'s adopted, I can prove it."

"How?" says Mama, but all I says was, "H'm!" There I was over the hot stove, trying to stretch two chickens over five people and a completely unexpected child into the bargain without one moment's notice.

"What do you mean—'H'm'?" says Stella-Rondo, and Mama says, "I heard that, Sister."

I said that oh, I didn't mean a thing, only that whoever Shirley-T. was, she was the spit-image of Papa-Daddy if he'd cut off his beard, which of course he'd never do in the world. Papa-Daddy's Mama's papa and sulks.

Stella-Rondo got furious! She said, "Sister, I don't need to tell you you got a lot of nerve and always did have and I'll thank you to make no future reference to my adopted child whatsoever."

10   "Very well," I said. "Very well, very well. Of course I noticed at once she looks like Mr. Whitaker's side too. That frown. She looks like a cross between Mr. Whitaker and Papa-Daddy."

"Well, all I can say is she isn't."

"She looks exactly like Shirley Temple to me," says Mama, but Shirley-T. just ran away from her.

So the first thing Stella-Rondo did at the table was turn Papa-Daddy against me.

"Papa-Daddy," she says. He was trying to cut up his meat. "Papa-Daddy!" I was taken completely by surprise. Papa-Daddy is about a million years old and's got this long-long beard. "Papa-Daddy, Sister says she fails to understand why you don't cut off your beard."

15   So Papa-Daddy l-a-y-s down his knife and fork! He's real rich. Mama says he is, he says he isn't. So he says, "Have I heard correctly? You don't understand why I don't cut off my beard?"

"Why," I says, "Papa-Daddy, of course I understand, I did not say any such a thing, the idea!"

He says, "Hussy!"

I says, "Papa-Daddy, you know I wouldn't any more want you to cut off your beard than the man in the moon. It was the farthest thing from my mind! Stella-Rondo sat there and made that up while she was eating breast of chicken."

But he says, "So the postmistress fails to understand why I don't cut off my beard. Which job I got you through my influence with the government. 'Bird's nest'—is that what you call it?"

Not that it isn't the next to smallest P.O. in the entire state of Mississippi.   20

I says, "Oh, Papa-Daddy," I says, "I didn't say any such a thing, I never dreamed it was a bird's nest, I have always been grateful though this is the next to smallest P.O. in the state of Mississippi, and I do not enjoy being referred to as a hussy by my own grandfather."

But Stella-Rondo says, "Yes, you did say it too. Anybody in the world could of heard you, that had ears."

"Stop right there," says Mama, looking at *me*.

So I pulled my napkin straight back through the napkin ring and left the table.

As soon as I was out of the room Mama says, "Call her back, or she'll starve to   25
death," but Papa-Daddy says, "This is the beard I started growing on the Coast when I was fifteen years old." He would of gone on till nightfall if Shirley-T. hadn't lost the Milky Way she ate in Cairo.

So Papa-Daddy says, "I am going out and lie in the hammock, and you can all sit here and remember my words: I'll never cut off my beard as long as I live, even one inch, and I don't appreciate it in you at all." Passed right by me in the hall and went straight out and got in the hammock.

It would be a holiday. It wasn't five minutes before Uncle Rondo suddenly appeared in the hall in one of Stella-Rondo's flesh-colored kimonos, all cut on the bias, like something Mr. Whitaker probably thought was gorgeous.

"Uncle Rondo!" I says. "I didn't know who that was! Where are you going?"

"Sister," he says, "get out of my way, I'm poisoned."

"If you're poisoned stay away from Papa-Daddy," I says. "Keep out of the ham-   30
mock. Papa-Daddy will certainly beat you on the head if you come within forty miles of him. He thinks I deliberately said he ought to cut off his beard after he got me the P.O., and I've told him and told him and told him, and he acts like he just don't hear me. Papa-Daddy must of gone stone deaf."

"He picked a fine day to do it then," says Uncle Rondo, and before you could say "Jack Robinson" flew out in the yard.

What he'd really done, he'd drunk another bottle of that prescription. He does it every single Fourth of July as sure as shooting, and it's horribly expensive. Then he falls over in the hammock and snores. So he insisted on zigzagging right on out to the hammock, looking like a half-wit.

Papa-Daddy woke with this horrible yell and right there without moving an inch he tried to turn Uncle Rondo against me. I heard every word he said. Oh, he told Uncle Rondo I didn't learn to read till I was eight years old and he didn't see how in the world I ever got the mail put up at the P.O., much less read it all, and he said if Uncle Rondo could only fathom the lengths he had gone to get me that job! And he said on the other hand he thought Stella-Rondo had a brilliant mind and deserved credit for getting out of town. All the time he was just lying there swing-ing as pretty as you please and looping out his beard, and poor Uncle Rondo was *pleading* with him to slow down the hammock, it was making him as dizzy as a witch to watch it. But that's what Papa-Daddy likes about a hammock. So Uncle Rondo was too dizzy to get turned against me for the time being. He's Mama's only brother and is a good case of a one-track mind. Ask anybody. A certified pharmacist.

Just then I heard Stella-Rondo raising the upstairs window. While she was married she got this peculiar idea that it's cooler with the windows shut and locked. So she has to raise the window before she can make a soul hear her outdoors.

35   So she raises the window and says, "*Oh!*" You would have thought she was mortally wounded.

Uncle Rondo and Papa-Daddy didn't even look up, but kept right on with what they were doing. I had to laugh.

I flew up the stairs and threw the door open! I says, "What in the wide world's the matter, Stella-Rondo? You mortally wounded?"

"No," she says, "I am not mortally wounded but I wish you would do me the favor of looking out that window there and telling me what you see."

So I shade my eyes and look out the window.

40   "I see the front yard," I says.

"Don't you see any human beings?"

"I see Uncle Rondo trying to run Papa-Daddy out of the hammock," I says. "Nothing more. Naturally, it's so suffocating-hot in the house, with all the windows shut and locked, everybody who cares to stay in their right mind will have to go out and get in the hammock before the Fourth of July is over."

"Don't you notice anything different about Uncle Rondo?" asks Stella-Rondo.

"Why, no, except he's got on some terrible-looking flesh-colored contraption I wouldn't be found dead in, is all I can see," I says.

45   "Never mind, you won't be found dead in it, because it happens to be part of my trousseau, and Mr. Whitaker took several dozen photographs of me in it," says Stella-Rondo. "What on earth could Uncle Rondo *mean* by wearing part of my trousseau out in the broad open daylight without saying so much as 'Kiss my foot,' *knowing* I only got home this morning after my separation and hung my negligee up on the bathroom door, just as nervous as I could be?"

"I'm sure I don't know, and what do you expect me to do about it?" I says. "Jump out the window?"

"No, I expect nothing of the kind. I simply declare that Uncle Rondo looks like a fool in it, that's all," she says. "It makes me sick to my stomach."

"Well, he looks as good as he can," I says. "As good as anybody in reason could." I stood up for Uncle Rondo, please remember. And I said to Stella-Rondo, "I think I would do well not to criticize so freely if I were you and came home with a two-year-old child I had never said a word about, and no explanation whatever about my separation."

"I asked you the instant I entered this house not to refer one more time to my adopted child, and you gave me your word of honor you would not," was all Stella-Rondo would say, and started pulling out every one of her eyebrows with some cheap Kress tweezers.

50   So I merely slammed the door behind me and went down and made some green-tomato pickle. Somebody had to do it. Of course Mama had turned both the Negroes loose; she always said no earthly power could hold one anyway on the Fourth of July, so she wouldn't even try. It turned out that Jaypan fell in the lake and came within a very narrow limit of drowning.

So Mama trots in. Lifts up the lid and says, "H'm! Not very good for your Uncle Rondo in his precarious condition, I must say. Or poor little adopted Shirley-T. Shame on you!"

That made me tired. I says, "Well, Stella-Rondo had better thank her lucky stars it was her instead of me came trotting in with that very peculiar-looking child. Now if it had been me that trotted in from Illinois and brought a peculiar-looking child or two, I shudder to think of the reception I'd of got, much less controlled the diet of an entire family."

"But you must remember, Sister, that you were never married to Mr. Whitaker in the first place and didn't go up to Illinois to live," says Mama, shaking a spoon in my face. "If you had I would of been just as overjoyed to see you and your little adopted girl as I was to see Stella-Rondo, when you wound up with your separation and came on back home."

"You would not," I says.

"Don't contradict me, I would," says Mama.

But I said she couldn't convince me though she talked till she was blue in the face. Then I said, "Besides, you know as well as I do that that child is not adopted."

"She most certainly is adopted," says Mama, stiff as a poker.

I says, "Why, Mama, Stella-Rondo had her just as sure as anything in this world, and just too stuck up to admit it."

"Why, Sister," said Mama. "Here I thought we were going to have a pleasant Fourth of July, and you start right out not believing a word your own baby sister tells you!"

"Just like Cousin Annie Flo. Went to her grave denying the facts of life," I reminded Mama.

"I told you if you ever mentioned Annie Flo's name I'd slap your face," says Mama, and slaps my face.

"All right, you wait and see," I says.

"I," says Mama, "*I* prefer to take my children's word for anything when it's humanly possible." You ought to see Mama, she weighs two hundred pounds and has real tiny feet.

Just then something perfectly horrible occurred to me.

"Mama," I says, "can that child talk?" I simply had to whisper! "Mama, I wonder if that child can be—you know—in any way? Do you realize?" I says, "that she hasn't spoke one single, solitary word to a human being up to this minute? This is the way she looks," I says, and I looked like this.

Well, Mama and I just stood there and stared at each other. It was horrible!

"I remember well that Joe Whitaker frequently drank like a fish," says Mama. "I believed to my soul he drank *chemicals*." And without another word she marches to the foot of the stairs and calls Stella-Rondo.

"Stella-Rondo? O-o-o-o-o! Stella-Rondo!"

"What?" says Stella-Rondo from upstairs. Not even the grace to get up off the bed.

"Can that child of yours talk?" asks Mama.

Stella-Rondo says, "Can she what?"

"Talk! Talk!" says Mama. "Burdyburdyburdyburdy!"

So Stella-Rondo yells back, "Who says she can't talk?"

"Sister says so," says Mama.

"You didn't have to tell me, I know whose word of honor don't mean a thing in this house," says Stella-Rondo.

And in a minute the loudest Yankee voice I ever heard in my life yells out, "OE'm Pop-OE the Sailor-r-r-r Ma-a-an!" and then somebody jumps up and down in the upstairs hall. In another second the house would of fallen down.

"Not only talks, she can tap-dance!" calls Stella-Rondo. "Which is more than some people I won't name can do."

"Why, the little precious darling thing!" Mama says, so surprised. "Just as smart as she can be!" Starts talking baby talk right there. Then she turns on me. "Sister, you ought to be thoroughly ashamed! Run upstairs this instant and apologize to Stella-Rondo and Shirley-T."

"Apologize for what?" I says. "I merely wondered if the child was normal, that's all. Now that she's proved she is, why, I have nothing further to say."

80   But Mama just turned on her heel and flew out, furious. She ran right upstairs and hugged the baby. She believed it was adopted. Stella-Rondo hadn't done a thing but turn her against me from upstairs while I stood there helpless over the hot stove. So that made Mama, Papa-Daddy, and the baby all on Stella-Rondo's side.

Next, Uncle Rondo.

I must say that Uncle Rondo has been marvelous to me at various times in the past and I was completely unprepared to be made to jump out of my skin, the way it turned out. Once Stella-Rondo did something perfectly horrible to him—broke a chain letter from Flanders Field—and he took the radio back he had given her and gave it to me. Stella-Rondo was furious! For six months we all had to call her Stella instead of Stella-Rondo, or she wouldn't answer. I always thought Uncle Rondo had all the brains of the entire family. Another time he sent me to Mammoth Cave with all expenses paid.

But this would be the day he was drinking that prescription, the Fourth of July.

So at supper Stella-Rondo speaks up and says she thinks Uncle Rondo ought to try to eat a little something. So finally Uncle Rondo said he would try a little cold biscuits and ketchup, but that was all. So *she* brought it to him.

85   "Do you think it wise to disport with ketchup in Stella-Rondo's flesh-colored kimono?" I says. Trying to be considerate! If Stella-Rondo couldn't watch out for her trousseau, somebody had to.

"Any objections?" asks Uncle Rondo, just about to pour out all of the ketchup.

"Don't mind what she says, Uncle Rondo," says Stella-Rondo. "Sister has been devoting this solid afternoon to sneering out my bedroom window at the way you look."

"What's that?" says Uncle Rondo. Uncle Rondo has got the most terrible temper in the world. Anything is liable to make him tear the house down if it comes at the wrong time.

So Stella-Rondo says, "Sister says, 'Uncle Rondo certainly does look like a fool in that pink kimono!'"

90   Do you remember who it was really said that?

Uncle Rondo spills out all the ketchup and jumps out of his chair and tears off the kimono and throws it down on the dirty floor and puts his foot on it. It had to be sent all the way to Jackson to the cleaners and re-pleated.

"So that's your opinion of your Uncle Rondo, is it?" he says. "I look like a fool, do I? Well, that's the last straw. A whole day in this house with nothing to do, and then to hear you come out with a remark like that behind my back!"

"I didn't say any such of a thing, Uncle Rondo," I says, "and I'm not saying who did, either. Why, I think you look all right. Just try to take care of yourself and not talk and eat at the same time," I says. "I think you better go lie down."

"Lie down my foot," says Uncle Rondo. I ought to of known by that he was fixing to do something perfectly horrible.

So he didn't do anything that night in the precarious state he was in—just 95 played Casino with Mama and Stella-Rondo and Shirley-T. and gave Shirley-T. a nickel with a head on both sides. It tickled her nearly to death, and she called him "Papa." But at 6:30 A.M. the next morning, he threw a whole five-cent package of some unsold one-inch firecrackers from the store as hard as he could into my bedroom and they every one went off. Not one bad one in the string. Anybody else, there'd be one that wouldn't go off.

Well, I'm just terribly susceptible to noise of any kind, the doctor has always told me I was the most sensitive person he had ever seen in his whole life, and I was simply prostrated. I couldn't eat! People tell me they heard it as far as the cemetery, and old Aunt Jep Patterson, that had been holding her own so good, thought it was Judgment Day and she was going to meet her whole family. It's usually so quiet here.

And I'll tell you it didn't take me any longer than a minute to make up my mind what to do. There I was with the whole entire house on Stella-Rondo's side and turned against me. If I have anything at all I have pride.

So I just decided I'd go straight down to the P.O. There's plenty of room there in the back, I says to myself.

Well! I made no bones about letting the family catch on to what I was up to. I didn't try to conceal it.

The first thing they knew, I marched in where they were all playing Old Maid 100 and pulled the electric oscillating fan out by the plug, and everything got real hot. Next I snatched the pillow I'd done the needlepoint on right off the davenport from behind Papa-Daddy. He went "Ugh!" I beat Stella-Rondo up the stairs and finally found my charm bracelet in her bureau drawer under a picture of Nelson Eddy.[1]

"So that's the way the land lies," says Uncle Rondo. There he was, piecing on the ham. "Well, Sister, I'll be glad to donate my army cot if you got any place to set it up, providing you'll leave right this minute and let me get some peace." Uncle Rondo was in France.

"Thank you kindly for the cot and 'peace' is hardly the word I would select if I had to resort to firecrackers at 6:30 A.M. in a young girl's bedroom," I says to him. "And as to where I intend to go, you seem to forget my position as postmistress of China Grove, Mississippi," I says. "I've always got the P.O.".

Well, that made them all sit up and take notice.

I went out front and started digging up some four-o'clocks to plant around the P.O.

"Ah-ah-ah!" says Mama, raising the window. "Those happen to be my four- 105 o'clocks. Everything planted in that star is mine. I've never known you to make anything grow in your life."

---

1. Opera singer (1901–67) who enjoyed phenomenal popularity in the 1930s and 1940s when he costarred in numerous film musicals with Jeanette MacDonald. The two were known as "America's Singing Sweethearts."

"Very well," I says. "But I take the fern. Even you, Mama, can't stand there and deny that I'm the one watered that fern. And I happen to know where I can send in a box top and get a packet of one thousand mixed seeds, no two the same kind, free."

"Oh, where?" Mama wants to know.

But I says, "Too late. You 'tend to your house, and I'll 'tend to mine. You hear things like that all the time if you know how to listen to the radio. Perfectly marvelous offers. Get anything you want free."

So I hope to tell you I marched in and got that radio, and they could of all bit a nail in two, especially Stella-Rondo, that it used to belong to, and she well knew she couldn't get it back, I'd sue for it like a shot. And I very politely took the sewing-machine motor I helped pay the most on to give Mama for Christmas back in 1929, and a good big calendar, with the first-aid remedies on it. The thermometer and the Hawaiian ukulele certainly were rightfully mine, and I stood on the step-ladder and got all my watermelon-rind preserves and every fruit and vegetable I'd put up, every jar. Then I began to pull the tacks out of the bluebird wall vases on the archway to the dining room.

110   "Who told you you could have those, Miss Priss?" says Mama, fanning as hard as she could.

"I bought 'em and I'll keep track of 'em," I says. "I'll tack 'em up one on each side of the post-office window, and you can see 'em when you come to ask me for your mail, if you're so dead to see 'em."

"Not I! I'll never darken the door to that post office again if I live to be a hundred," Mama says. "Ungrateful child! After all the money we spent on you at the Normal."[2]

"Me either," says Stella-Rondo. "You can just let my mail lie there and *rot,* for all I care. I'll never come and relieve you of a single, solitary piece."

"I should worry," I says. "And who you think's going to sit down and write you all those big fat letters and postcards, by the way? Mr. Whitaker? Just because he was the only man ever dropped down in China Grove and you got him—unfairly—is he going to sit down and write you a lengthy correspondence after you come home giving no rhyme nor reason whatsoever for your separation and no explanation for the presence of that child? I may not have your brilliant mind, but I fail to see it."

115   So Mama says, "Sister, I've told you a thousand times that Stella-Rondo simply got homesick, and this child is far too big to be hers," and she says, "Now, why don't you just sit down and play Casino?"

Then Shirley-T. sticks out her tongue at me in this perfectly horrible way. She has no more manners than the man in the moon. I told her she was going to cross her eyes like that some day and they'd stick.

"It's too late to stop me now," I says. "You should have tried that yesterday. I'm going to the P.O. and the only way you can possibly see me is to visit me there."

So Papa-Daddy says, "You'll never catch me setting foot in that post office, even if I should take a notion into my head to write a letter some place." He says, "I won't have you reachin' out of that little old window with a pair of shears and cuttin' off any beard of mine. I'm too smart for you!"

"We all are," says Stella-Rondo.

---

2. That is, normal school (teachers' college).

But I said, "If you're so smart, where's Mr. Whitaker?" 120

So then Uncle Rondo says, "I'll thank you from now on to stop reading all the orders I get on postcards and telling everybody in China Grove what you think is the matter with them," but I says, "I draw my own conclusions and will continue in the future to draw them." I says, "If people want to write their innermost secrets on penny postcards, there's nothing in the wide world you can do about it, Uncle Rondo."

"And if you think we'll ever *write* another postcard you're sadly mistaken," says Mama.

"Cutting off your nose to spite your face then," I says. "But if you're all determined to have no more to do with the U.S. mail, think of this: What will Stella-Rondo do now, if she wants to tell Mr. Whitaker to come after her?"

"Wah!" says Stella-Rondo. I knew she'd cry. She had a conniption fit right there in the kitchen.

"It will be interesting to see how long she holds out," I says. "And now—I am 125
leaving."

"Good-bye," says Uncle Rondo.

"Oh, I declare," says Mama, "to think that a family of mine should quarrel on the Fourth of July, or the day after, over Stella-Rondo leaving old Mr. Whitaker and having the sweetest little adopted child! It looks like we'd all be glad!"

"Wah!" says Stella-Rondo, and has a fresh conniption fit.

"He left *her*—you mark my words," I says. "That's Mr. Whitaker. I know Mr. Whitaker. After all, I knew him first. I said from the beginning he'd up and leave her. I foretold every single thing that's happened."

"Where did he go?" asks Mama. 130

"Probably to the North Pole, if he knows what's good for him," I says.

But Stella-Rondo just bawled and wouldn't say another word. She flew to her room and slammed the door.

"Now look what you've gone and done, Sister," says Mama. "You go apologize."

"I haven't the time, I'm leaving," I says.

"Well, what are you waiting around for?" asks Uncle Rondo. 135

So I just picked up the kitchen clock and marched off, without saying, "Kiss my foot," or anything, and never did tell Stella-Rondo good-bye.

There was a girl going along on a little wagon right in front.

"Girl," I says, "come help me haul these things down the hill, I'm going to live in the post office."

Took her nine trips in her express wagon. Uncle Rondo came out on the porch and threw her a nickel.

And that's the last I've laid eyes on any of my family or my family laid eyes on 140
me for five solid days and nights. Stella-Rondo may be telling the most horrible tales in the world about Mr. Whitaker, but I haven't heard them. As I tell everybody, I draw my own conclusions.

But oh, I like it here. It's ideal, as I've been saying. You see, I've got everything cater-cornered, the way I like it. Hear the radio? All the war news. Radio, sewing machine, book ends, ironing board and that great big piano lamp—peace, that's what I like. Butter-bean vines planted all along the front where the strings are.

Of course, there's not much mail. My family are naturally the main people in China Grove, and if they prefer to vanish from the face of the earth, for all the mail they get or the mail they write, why, I'm not going to open my mouth. Some of the folks here in town are taking up for me and some turned against me. I know which is which. There are always people who will quit buying stamps just to get on the right side of Papa-Daddy.

But here I am, and here I'll stay. I want the world to know I'm happy.

And if Stella-Rondo should come to me this minute, on bended knees, and *attempt* to explain the incidents of her life with Mr. Whitaker, I'd simply put my fingers in both my ears and refuse to listen.

1941

WILLIAM CARLOS WILLIAMS

The Use of Force

They were new patients to me, all I had was the name, Olson. Please come down as soon as you can, my daughter is very sick. When I arrived I was met by the mother, a big startled looking woman, very clean and apologetic who merely said, Is this the doctor? and let me in. In the back, she added. You must excuse us, doctor, we have her in the kitchen where it is warm. It is very damp here sometimes.

The child was fully dressed and sitting on her father's lap near the kitchen table. He tried to get up, but I motioned for him not to bother, took off my overcoat and started to look things over. I could see that they were all very nervous, eyeing me up and down distrustfully. As often, in such cases, they weren't telling me more than they had to, it was up to me to tell them; that's why they were spending three dollars on me.

The child was fairly eating me up with her cold, steady eyes, and no expression to her face whatever. She did not move and seemed, inwardly, quiet; an unusually attractive little thing, and as strong as a heifer in appearance. But her face was flushed, she was breathing rapidly, and I realized that she had a high fever. She had magnificent blonde hair, in profusion. One of those picture children often reproduced in advertising leaflets and the photogravure[1] sections of the Sunday papers.

She's had a fever for three days, began the father and we don't know what it comes from. My wife has given her things, you know, like people do, but it don't do no good. And there's been a lot of sickness around. So we tho't you'd better look her over and tell us what is the matter.

5   As doctors often do I took a trial shot at it as a point of departure. Has she had a sore throat?

Both parents answered me together, No . . . No, she says her throat don't hurt her.

Does your throat hurt you? added the mother to the child. But the little girl's expression didn't change nor did she move her eyes from my face.

Have you looked?

I tried to, said the mother, but I couldn't see.

1. Process for printing photographs.

As it happens we had been having a number of cases of diphtheria in the 10
school to which this child went during that month and we were all, quite apparently, thinking of that, though no one had as yet spoken of the thing.

Well, I said, suppose we take a look at the throat first. I smiled in my best professional manner and asking for the child's first name I said, come on, Mathilda,
open your mouth and let's take a look at your throat.

Nothing doing.

Aw, come on, I coaxed, just open your mouth wide and let me take a look.
Look, I said opening both hands wide, I haven't anything in my hands. Just open
up and let me see.

Such a nice man, put in the mother. Look how kind he is to you. Come on, do
what he tells you to. He won't hurt you.

At that I ground my teeth in disgust. If only they wouldn't use the word 15
"hurt" I might be able to get somewhere. But I did not allow myself to be hurried
or disturbed but speaking quietly and slowly I approached the child again.

As I moved my chair a little nearer suddenly with one catlike movement both
her hands clawed instinctively for my eyes and she almost reached them too. In
fact she knocked my glasses flying and they fell, though unbroken, several feet
away from me on the kitchen floor.

Both the mother and father almost turned themselves inside out in embarrassment and apology. You bad girl, said the mother, taking her and shaking her
by one arm. Look what you've done. The nice man . . .

For heaven's sake, I broke in. Don't call me a nice man to her. I'm here to look
at her throat on the chance that she might have diphtheria[2] and possibly die of
it. But that's nothing to her. Look here, I said to the child, we're going to look at
your throat. You're old enough to understand what I'm saying. Will you open it
now by yourself or shall we have to open it for you?

Not a move. Even her expression hadn't changed. Her breaths however were
coming faster and faster. Then the battle began. I had to do it. I had to have a
throat culture for her own protection. But first I told the parents that it was
entirely up to them. I explained the danger but said that I would not insist on a
throat examination so long as they would take the responsibility.

If you don't do what the doctor says you'll have to go to the hospital, the 20
mother admonished her severely.

Oh yeah? I had to smile to myself. After all, I had already fallen in love with
the savage brat, the parents were contemptible to me. In the ensuing struggle
they grew more and more abject, crushed, exhausted while she surely rose to
magnificent heights of insane fury of effort bred of her terror of me.

The father tried his best, and he was a big man but the fact that she was his
daughter, his shame at her behavior and his dread of hurting her made him
release her just at the critical times when I had almost achieved success, till I
wanted to kill him. But his dread also that she might have diphtheria made him
tell me to go on, go on though he himself was almost fainting, while the mother
moved back and forth behind us raising and lowering her hands in an agony of
apprehension.

---

2. Bacterial disease that killed millions, mostly children, in the era before antibiotic medicines and effective programs of immunization. The most common sign of infection is a thick, bluish-white membrane
coating the tonsils and throat.

Put her in front of you on your lap, I ordered, and hold both her wrists.

But as soon as he did the child let out a scream. Don't, you're hurting me. Let go of my hands. Let them go I tell you. Then she shrieked terrifyingly, hysterically. Stop it! Stop it! You're killing me!

25   Do you think she can stand it, doctor! said the mother.

You get out, said the husband to his wife. Do you want her to die of diphtheria?

Come on now, hold her, I said.

Then I grasped the child's head with my left hand and tried to get the wooden tongue depressor between her teeth. She fought, with clenched teeth, desperately! But now I also had grown furious—at a child. I tried to hold myself down but I couldn't. I know how to expose a throat for inspection. And I did my best. When finally I got the wooden spatula behind the last teeth and just the point of it into the mouth cavity, she opened up for an instant but before I could see anything she came down again and gripping the wooden blade between her molars she reduced it to splinters before I could get it out again.

Aren't you ashamed, the mother yelled at her. Aren't you ashamed to act like that in front of the doctor?

30   Get me a smooth-handled spoon of some sort, I told the mother. We're going through with this. The child's mouth was already bleeding. Her tongue was cut and she was screaming in wild hysterical shrieks. Perhaps I should have desisted and come back in an hour or more. No doubt it would have been better. But I have seen at least two children lying dead in bed of neglect in such cases, and feeling that I must get a diagnosis now or never I went at it, again. But the worst of it was that I too had got beyond reason. I could have torn the child apart in my own fury and enjoyed it. It was a pleasure to attack her. My face was burning with it.

The damned little brat must be protected against her own idiocy, one says to one's self at such times. Others must be protected against her. It is a social necessity. And all these things are true. But a blind fury, a feeling of adult shame, bred of a longing for muscular release are the operatives. One goes on to the end.

In the final unreasoning assault I overpowered the child's neck and jaws. I forced the heavy silver spoon back of her teeth and down her throat till she gagged. And there it was—both tonsils covered with membrane. She had fought valiantly to keep me from knowing her secret. She had been hiding that sore throat for three days at least and lying to her parents in order to escape just such an outcome as this.

Now truly she was furious. She had been on the defensive before but now she attacked. Tried to get off her father's lap and fly at me while tears of defeat blinded her eyes.

1938

Biographical Sketches
Fiction Writers

AESOP

(c. 620 B.C.E.–c. 560 B.C.E.)

Little is known for certain about the ancient Greek fabulist Aesop. Because the name *Aesop* is itself a Greek reference to Ethiopia and because many of the fables today attributed to Aesop feature characters very like the trickster figures in African tales, scholars today speculate that Aesop himself may well have been of African birth or descent. The first recorded mention of Aesop came some one hundred years after his supposed death, in the work of the Greek historian Herodotus, who indicated only that the storyteller had lived around 550 B.C., had once been a slave, and ultimately died at Delphi. Over the centuries, this and a few other sketchy ancient references grew into a full-fledged legend: Aesop was a slave who earned his freedom through his talent as a storyteller, served King Croesus as an ambassador, and yet was ultimately framed for the theft of a gold cup from Apollo's temple at Delphi and was thrown off the cliffs to his death. Whatever the truth of this story, it is almost certainly true that Aesop was an oral storyteller who never wrote down the tales first attributed to him in 320 B.C. when a Greek writer compiled the first known anthology of the fables, which eventually made their way to medieval Europe through a fifth-century Latin verse translation.

SHERMAN ALEXIE

(b. 1966)

Born on an Indian reservation near Spokane, Washington, Sherman Alexie attended high school in nearby Reardan, where he was the only Native American other than the school mascot. Shortly after graduating in American Studies from Washington State University, Alexie received the Washington State Arts Commission Poetry Fellowship in 1991 and the National Endowment for the Arts Poetry Fellowship in 1992. The first of eleven collections of poetry, *The Business of Fancydancing* (1991), was named a *New York Times* Notable Book of the Year in 1992. *The Lone Ranger and Tonto Fistfight in Heaven* (1993), a collection of short stories, received a PEN/Hemingway Award for Best First Book of Fiction. Alexie is also the author of four novels, including *Reservation Blues* (1995) and *Flight* (2007), as well as screenplays: *Smoke Signals* (1998) was featured at the Sundance Film Festival. A stand-up comedian and four-time champion of the World Heavyweight Poetry Bout, he lives in Seattle, Washington with his wife and two sons.

MAX (ISAAC) APPLE

(b. 1941)

Max Apple grew up speaking Yiddish in a kosher household in Grand Rapids, Michigan, a town where, in his words, "There were no movies, no dancing," and "being Jewish was just a different kind of craziness." A graduate of the University of Michigan (B.A., 1963; Ph.D. 1970), Apple has taught literature at Rice University in Houston, Texas, since 1972, yet labels himself "a Texan but not an academic." Labeled by his reviewers as a playfully imaginative, witty, "utterly cynicism-free," and "rarely sentimental" satirist, Apple is the author of three short-story collections—*The Oranging of America and Other Stories* (1976), *Free Agents* (1984), which also includes essays, and *The Jew of Home Depot and Other Stories* (2007). His other works include two novels—*Zip: A Novel of the Left and Right* (1978) and *The Propheteers* (1986)—and two much-praised memoirs—*Roommates: My Grandfather's Story* (1994) and *I Love Gootie: My Grandmother's Story* (1998).

MARGARET ATWOOD
(b. 1939)

Canada's Pre-eminent novelist and poet spent her first eleven years in sparsely populated areas of northern Ontario and Quebec, where her father worked as an entomologist. Educated at the University of Toronto and Harvard, Margaret Atwood published her first poem at nineteen and has won numerous prizes for her poetry as well as her fiction. Her many novels include *The Edible Woman* (1969), *Surfacing* (1972), *Life before Man* (1979), *Bodily Harm* (1982), *The Handmaid's Tale* (1985), *Cat's Eye* (1988), *The Robber Bride* (1993), *Alias Grace* (1996), the Booker Prize—winning *The Blind Assassin* (2000), and *Oryx and Crake* (2003); her story collections include *Murder in the Dark* (1983), *Bluebeard's Egg* (1983), *Wilderness Tips* (1991), and *Good Bones* (1992). *The Door* (2007) is her most recent collection of poems. Atwood has also authored two children's books, *For the Birds* (1990) and *Princess Prunella and the Purple Peanut* (1995), an influential book of critical essays, *Strange Things: The Malevolent North in Canadian Literature* (1995), and *Negotiating with the Dead: A Writer on Writing* (2002).

JAMES BALDWIN
(1924–1987)

For much of his life, James Baldwin was a leading literary spokesman for civil rights and racial equality in America. Born in New York City but long a resident of France, he first attracted critical attention with two extraordinary novels, *Go Tell It on the Mountain* (1953), drawing upon his past as a teenage preacher in the Fireside Pentecostal Church, and *Giovanni's Room* (1956), which dealt with the anguish of being black and homosexual in a largely white and heterosexual society. Other works include the novels *Another Country* (1962) and *If Beale Street Could Talk* (1974), the play *Blues for Mr. Charlie* (1964), and a story collection, *Going to Meet the Man* (1965). Baldwin is perhaps best remembered as a perceptive and eloquent essayist, the author of *Notes of a Native Son* (1955), *Nobody Knows My Name* (1961), *The Fire Next Time* (1963), *No Name in the Street* (1972), and *The Price of a Ticket* (1985).

TONI CADE BAMBARA
(1939–1995)

Born in New York City, Toni Cade Bambara grew up in Harlem and Bedford-Stuyvesant, two of New York's poorest neighborhoods. She began writing as a child and took her last name from a signature on a sketchbook she found in a trunk belonging to her great-grandmother. (The Bambara are a people of northwest Africa.) After graduating from Queens College, she wrote fiction in "the predawn in-betweens" while studying for her MA at the City College of New York and working at a great variety of jobs: dancer, social worker, recreation director, psychiatric counselor, college English teacher, literary critic, and film producer. Bambara began to publish her stories in 1962. Her fiction includes two collections of stories, *Gorilla, My Love* (1972) and *The Sea Birds Are Still Alive* (1977), as well as two novels, *The Salt Eaters* (1980) and *If Blessing Comes* (1987). Bambara also edited two anthologies, *The Black Woman* (1970) and *Stories for Black Folks* (1971).

ANN BEATTIE (b. 1947)

Ann Beattie grew up in the Washington suburb of Chevy Chase, Maryland. She received a B.A. from American University and went on to graduate study in English at the University of Connecticut. After publishing "A Rose for Judy Garland" in 1972, she began placing stories in such magazines as *The New Yorker,* becoming a kind of spokesperson for the generation that came of age in the 1960s. Many of her stories are collected in (among other books) *Distortions* (1976), *Jacklighting* (1981), *The Burning House* (1982), *What Was Mine: Stories* (1990), *Park City: New and Selected Stories* (1999) and *Follies* (2005). Her novels include *Chilly Scenes of Winter* (1976), *Falling in Place* (1980), *Love Always* (1985), *Picturing Will* (1990), *Another You* (1995), *My Life, Starring Dara Falcon* (1997), *Park City* (1998), and *The Doctor's House* (2002). In 2000 Beattie received the PEN/Malamud Prize for Excellence in Short Fiction. She teaches at the University of Virginia, where she is Edgar Allan Poe Professor of Creative Writing.

AMBROSE BIERCE
(1842–1914?)

The tenth child of a poor Ohio family, Ambrose Bierce served with distinction in the Union Army during the Civil War, rising to the rank of major. After the war he worked as a journalist in California and London, where his boisterous western mannerisms and savage wit made him a celebrity and earned him the name "Bitter Bierce." He is probably best known as the author of *The Cynic's Word Book* (1906; later called *The Devil's Dictionary*), but his finest achievement may be his two volumes of short stories—*Tales of Soldiers and Civilians* (1891; later called *In the Midst of Life*) and *Can Such Things Be?* (1893)—and *The Monk and the Hangman's Daughter* (1892), an adaptation of a German story. Disillusioned and depressed after his divorce and the deaths of his two sons, Bierce went to Mexico in 1913, where he reportedly rode with Pancho Villa's revolutionaries. He disappeared and is presumed to have died there.

JORGE LUIS BORGES
(1899–1986)

Often considered Latin America's foremost author, Jorge Luis Borges was born and raised in Argentina, where he learned both Spanish and English. Traveling in Europe, his family was trapped in Geneva at the outbreak of World War I, and Borges attended the Collège de Genève, where he learned French, German, and Latin. He then spent two years in Spain, writing his first poems under the influence of the Ultraists, an "art for art's sake" movement that Borges established in Argentina upon his return in 1921. Despite his persistent and outspoken opposition to the military dictatorship of Juan Perón, he eventually became the director of the national library of Argentina. His many publications include *Ficciones, 1935–1944* (1944), *El Aleph* (1949), *El Libro de Arena* (1955), and *El Libro de los Seres Imaginarios* (1967). English translations of his works include *Labyrinths: Selected Stories and Other Writings* (1988), *Ficciones* (1989), *Collected Fictions* (1999), *Selected Non-Fictions* (1999), and *Selected Poems* (2000).

LINDA BREWER (b. 1946)

Western writer Linda Brewer grew up in Oregon's Siuslaw and now lives in the Sonora Desert of southern Arizona, where she works in a medical lab and writes features and food articles for a Tucson publication, *The Desert Leaf.* A finalist in the World's Best Short Story Contest, she won the 2002 Raymond Carver Short Story Contest. Her story "20/20" was featured in *Micro Fiction: An Anthology of Really Short Stories* (1996).

A. S. BYATT (b. 1936)

The oldest of four children (and half-sister of novelist Margaret Drabble), Antonia Susan Byatt was born in Sheffield, England, graduated from Newnham College, Cambridge, and worked toward her doctorate in seventeenth-century English literature at Bryn Mawr College in Pennsylvania and at Somerville College, Oxford. In 1964 Byatt began teaching at the University of London and published her first work, *Shadow of a Sun,* a novel about a young woman attempting to escape the influence of her novelist father. Byatt has drawn on her rich academic background in novels such as *The Game* (1967), *The Virgin in the Garden* (1978), *Still Life* (1985), the Booker Prize-winning *Possession* (1989), *Babel Tower* (1996), *The Biographer's Tale* (2001), and *A Whistling Woman* (2002), and such story collections as *Sugar and Other Stories* (1989) and *Little Black Book of Stories* (2004). She has also published many works of literary criticism, including two studies of novelist Iris Murdoch and *Wordsworth and Coleridge in Their Time* (1970). Made a Dane Commander of the British Empire in 1999, Dame Byatt lives in London.

RAYMOND CARVER
(1938–1988)

Born in the logging town of Clatskanie, Oregon, to a working-class family, Raymond Carver married at nineteen and had two children by the time he was twenty-one. Despite these early responsibilities and a struggle with alcoholism that was to continue for the rest of his life, Carver published his first story in 1961 and graduated from Humboldt State College in 1963.

He published his first book, *Near Klamath,* a collection of poems, in 1968 and thereafter supported himself with visiting lectureships at the University of California at Berkeley, Syracuse University, and the Iowa Writer's Workshop, among other institutions. His short-story collections include *What We Talk About When We Talk About Love* (1981), *Will You Please Be Quiet, Please?* (1976), *Cathedral* (1983), *My Father's Life* (1986), and *Where I'm Calling From* (1989). His poetry is collected in *All of Us* (2000).

MICHAEL CHABON
(b. 1963)

Maryland-born Michael Chabon was still a graduate student at the University of California, Irvine, when his MFA thesis became a bestselling novel, *The Mysteries of Pittsburgh* (1988). Two collections of short stories followed: *A Model World* (1990) and *Werewolves in Their Youth* (1999). Chabon's second novel, *Wonder Boys* (1995), was adapted into a movie starring Michael Douglas. *The Amazing Adventures of Kavalier and Clay* (2000), a novel about two boy geniuses who start a comic-strip business during WWII, earned Chabon the Pulitzer Prize in 2001. His stories have appeared in *The New Yorker, Playboy, Harper's,* and *Esquire.* In 2002 Chabon wrote a novel for children, *Summerland.* His novella *The Final Solution* appeared in 2004; his latest novel, *The Yiddish Policeman's Union* (2007), won both the Nebula and Hugo awards. Chabon lives with his wife and children in Berkeley, California.

JOHN CHEEVER
(1912–1982)

John Cheever was born in Quincy, Massachusetts. His formal education ended when he was expelled from Thayer Academy at seventeen; and he moved to New York City and devoted himself to fiction writing, except for brief interludes of writing scripts for television and of teaching at Barnard College and the University of Iowa. Cheever published his first story when he was sixteen, and even after his first novel, *The Wapshot Chronicle,* won the National Book Award in 1958, he was known primarily as a prolific writer of superb short stories. Collections include *The Way Some People Live* (1943), *The Enormous Radio* (1953), and

The Stories of John Cheever (1978), which won the Pulitzer Prize. Known as "the Chekhov of the suburbs," Cheever was awarded the National Medal for Literature by the American Academy of Arts and Letters shortly before his death in 1982.

ANTON CHEKHOV
(1860–1904)

The grandson of an emancipated serf, Anton Chekhov was born in the Russian town of Taganrog. In 1875, his father, a grocer facing bankruptcy and imprisonment, fled to Moscow, and soon the rest of the family lost their house to a former friend and lodger, a situation that Chekhov would revisit in his play *The Cherry Orchard.* In 1884, Chekhov received his M.D. from the University of Moscow. He purchased an estate near Moscow in the early 1890s and became both an industrious landowner and doctor to the local peasants. After contributing stories to magazines and journals throughout the 1880s, he began writing for the stage in 1887. His plays, now regarded as classics, were generally ill-received in his lifetime. *The Wood Demon* (later rewritten as *Uncle Vanya*) was performed only a few times in 1889 before closing, while the 1896 premiere of *The Seagull* sparked a riot when an audience expecting comedy was confronted with an experimental tragedy.

KATE CHOPIN
(1850–1904)

Katherine O'Flaherty was born in St. Louis, Missouri, to a Creole-Irish family that enjoyed a high place in society. Her father died when she was four, and Kate was raised by her mother, grandmother, and great-grandmother. Very well read at a young age, she received her formal education at the St. Louis Academy of the Sacred Heart. In 1870, she married Oscar Chopin, a Louisiana businessman, and lived with him in Natchitoches parish and New Orleans, where she became a close observer of Creole and Cajun life. Following her husband's sudden death in 1884, she returned to St. Louis, where she raised her six children and began her literary career. In slightly more than a decade she produced a substantial body of work, including the story collections *Bayou Folk* (1894) and *A Night in Acadie*

(1897) and the classic novella *The Awakening* (1899), which was greeted with a storm of criticism for its frank treatment of female sexuality.

STEPHEN CRANE
(1871–1900)

One of fourteen children, Stephen Crane and his family moved frequently before settling, after his father's death in 1880, in Asbury Park, New Jersey. Crane sporadically attended various preparatory schools and colleges without excelling at much besides baseball. Determined to be a journalist, he left school for the last time in 1891 and began contributing pieces to New York newspapers. His city experiences led him to write *Maggie: A Girl of the Streets,* a realist social-reform novel published in 1893 at his own expense. His next novel, *The Red Badge of Courage* (1895), presented a stark picture of the Civil War and brought him widespread fame; many of his stories were published in the collections *The Open Boat and Other Tales of Adventure* (1898) and *The Monster and Other Stories* (1899). Crane served as a foreign correspondent, reporting on conflicts in Cuba and Greece, and lived his last years abroad, dying of tuberculosis at the age of 28.

EDWIDGE DANTICAT
(b. 1969)

When she was twelve, Edwidge Danticat moved from Port-au-Prince, Haiti, to Brooklyn, New York, where her parents had relocated eight years before. Danticat published her first writing in English two years later, a newspaper article about her immigration to the United States that developed into her first novel, *Breath, Eyes, Memory* (1994). Danticat received a degree in French literature from Barnard College and an MFA from Brown University. *Krik? Krak!* (1991), a collection of short stories, was nominated for the National Book Award. Her second novel, *The Farming of Bones* (1998), is based on the 1937 massacre of Haitians at the border of the Dominican Republic. In 2002 Danticat published *After the Dance: A Walk through Carnival in Jacmel, Haiti,* an account of her travels. More recent publications include *The Dew Breaker* (2004), a collection of stories that examine the life of a Haitian torturer, and *Brother, I'm Dying*

(2007), winner of the National Book Critics Circle Award for Autobiography.

RALPH ELLISON
(1914–1994)

After the early death of his father, Ralph Ellison was raised by his mother and by a close-knit African American community in Oklahoma City. He grew up loving jazz and began to study music at Tuskegee Institute in 1933. In 1936, Ellison moved to New York, where, with the novelist Richard Wright's encouragement, he wrote short stories, essays, and book reviews. In the years after his monumental novel *Invisible Man* (1952) won the National Book Award and earned him international acclaim, Ellison lectured and taught at various institutions, including New York University, and published *Shadow and Act* (1964), a collection of critical essays on the novelist's art. Upon his death from cancer in 1994, the literary world learned that he had been working steadily on a second major novel, begun in 1952, seemingly lost in a fire in 1967. The nearly completed manuscript was edited by Ellison's friend John F. Callahan and published as *Juneteenth* (1999).

LOUISE ERDRICH
(b. 1954)

Born in Minnesota of German-American and French-Chippewa descent, Louise Erdrich grew up in Wahpeton, North Dakota, as a member of the Turtle Mountain Band of Chippewa. She attended Dartmouth College and received an MFA in creative writing from Johns Hopkins University. Her first novel, *Love Medicine* (1984), a collection of linked stories, won the National Book Critics Circle Award. In her subsequent publications—*The Beet Queen* (1986), *Tracks* (1988), *The Bingo Palace* (1993), and *Tales of Burning Love* (1996)—she pursued her focus on the lives of Native Americans in contemporary North Dakota. In 1991, she jointly authored the best-selling novel *The Crown of Columbus* with her husband, Michael Dorris. Her recent works include the novels *The Last Report on the Miracles at Little No Horse* (2001), *Four Souls* (2004), *The Plague of Doves* (2008), and a series of novels for young readers. She lives in Minnesota with her family and dogs.

WILLIAM FAULKNER
(1897–1962)

A native of Oxford, Mississippi, William Faulkner left high school without graduating, joined the Royal Canadian Air Force in 1918, and in the mid-1920s lived briefly in New Orleans, where he was encouraged as a writer by Sherwood Anderson. He then spent a few miserable months as a clerk in a New York bookstore, published a collection of poems, *The Marble Faun*, in 1924, and took a long walking tour of Europe in 1925 before returning to Mississippi. With the publication of *Sartoris* in 1929, Faulkner began a cycle of works, featuring recurrent characters and set in fictional Yoknapatawpha County, including *The Sound and the Fury* (1929), *As I Lay Dying* (1930), *Light in August* (1932), *Absalom, Absalom!* (1936), *The Hamlet* (1940), and *Go Down, Moses* (1942). He spent time in Hollywood, writing screenplays for *The Big Sleep* and other films, and lived his last years in Charlottesville, Virginia. Faulkner received the Nobel Prize for Literature in 1950.

GABRIEL GARCÍA MÁRQUEZ (b. 1928)

Born in Aracataca, Colombia, a remote town near the Caribbean coast, Gabriel García Márquez studied law at the University of Bogotá and then worked as a journalist in Latin America, Europe, and the United States. In 1967, he took up permanent residence in Barcelona, Spain. His first published book, *Leaf Storm* (1955), set in the fictional small town of Macondo, is based on the myths and legends of his childhood home. His most famous novel, *One Hundred Years of Solitude* (1967), fuses magic, reality, fable, and fantasy to present six generations of one Macondo family, a microcosm of many of the social, political, and economic problems of Latin America. Among his many works are *The Autumn of the Patriarch* (1975), *Chronicle of a Death Foretold* (1981), *Love in the Time of Cholera* (1987), *Of Love and Other Demons* (1994), and *Living to Tell the Tale* (2003), a three-volume set of memoirs. Márquez won the Nobel Prize for Literature in 1982.

F. SCOTT FITZGERALD
(1896–1940)

Born in Minnesota into a solidly upper-middle-class Catholic family, Francis Scott Key Fitzgerald started writing at a young age and continued even after dropping out of Princeton to join the army. At twenty-one he submitted his first novel for publication; it was rejected, but with the kind of encouragement that led to his revising it for years. In 1918, while stationed in Alabama, he met Zelda Sayre, whom he married after the publication of that first novel, *This Side of Paradise* (1920), which became an immediate best-seller and established Fitzgerald as a spokesperson for his generation. Extravagant living, in New York and later in Europe, took its toll on both of them, as he succumbed to alcoholism and she to mental illness. Much of Fitzgerald's semiautobiographical work depicts the privileged lives of wealthy, aspiring socialites of the Roaring Twenties. His novels include *The Beautiful and the Damned* (1922), *The Great Gatsby* (1925), and *Tender Is the Night* (1934).

CHARLOTTE PERKINS GILMAN (1860–1935)

Charlotte Anna Perkins was born in Hartford, Connecticut. After a painful, lonely childhood and several years of supporting herself as a governess, art teacher, and designer of greeting cards, Perkins married the artist Charles Stetson. Following Gilman's several extended periods of depression, her husband put her in the care of a doctor who "sent me home with the solemn advice to 'live as domestic a life as . . . possible,' to 'have but two hours' intellectual life a day,' and 'never to touch pen, brush, or pencil again' as long as I lived." Three months of this regimen brought her "near the borderline of utter mortal ruin" and inspired her masterpiece, "The Yellow Wallpaper." In 1900, she married George Houghton Gilman, having divorced Stetson in 1892. Her nonfiction works, springing from the early women's movement, include *Women and Economics* (1898) and *Man-Made World* (1911). She also wrote several utopian novels, including *Moving the Mountain* (1911) and *Herland* (1915).

SUSAN GLASPELL
(1876–1948)

Born and raised in Davenport, Iowa, Susan Glaspell graduated from Drake University and worked on the staff of the *Des Moines Daily News* until her stories began appearing in magazines such as *Harper's* and the *Ladies' Home Journal*. In 1911, Glaspell moved to New York City, where, two years later, she married the theater director George Cram Cook. In 1915, they founded the Provincetown Playhouse on Cape Cod, an extraordinary gathering of actors, directors, and playwrights, including Eugene O'Neill, Edna St. Vincent Millay, and John Reed; among the many plays she wrote to be performed by this company are *Trifles* (1916), *The Verge* (1921), *Bernice* (1924), and *Alison's House* (1931), a Pulitzer Prize–winning drama based on the life of Emily Dickinson. Glaspell spent the last part of her life in Provincetown, devoting herself to writing fiction; among her books are *Visioning* (1911), *Lifted Masks: Stories* (1912), *Fidelity* (1915), and *The Morning Is Near Us* (1940).

JACOB AND WILHELM
GRIMM (1785–1863, 1786–1859)

Among the world's first, as well as most famous, folklorists, the German "Brothers Grimm" were only two of nine children born into the family of a lawyer and judge. After what they described as an idyllic childhood was cut short by the death of their father in 1796, both brothers studied law only to become fascinated with medieval German literature and history. With the death of their mother in 1808, the brothers became the sole support of their four surviving siblings. For the next 23 years, both would work as private librarians even as they began to collect the traditional legends and tales they published in the famed two-volume *Nursery and Household Tales* (1812, 1816). Appointed university librarians and lecturers, the brothers, along with Wilhelm's wife and growing brood of children, moved first to Göttingen (1830) and then to Berlin (1840). Here, they not only revised their *Tales* but also undertook important research into the history of German law, customs, and mythology, as well as grammar and historical linguistics. Modern scholars estimate that their tales have been translated into

some 160 languages, rivaling the Bible in overall sales.

HA JIN (b. 1956)

Born Xuefei Jin, Ha Jin grew up in mainland China. During his teenage years, he served in the People's Army. He then worked for a railroad company while teaching himself English, before receiving degrees from Heilongjiang and Shandong universities in China. While earning his Ph.D. from Brandeis, Jin watched television coverage of the Tiananmen Square massacre and decided to remain, with his wife and son, in the United States, where he now teaches English and creative writing at Emory University. He has published the poetry collections *Between Silences* (1990), *Facing Shadows* (1996), and *Wreckage* (2001); the short-story collections *Ocean of Words: Army Stories* (1996), *Under the Red Flag* (1997), and *The Bridegroom* (2000); and the novels *In the Pond* (1998) and *Waiting* (1999), which won both the National Book Award and the 2000 PEN/Faulkner Award for Fiction. Ha Jin's most recent novels are *The Crazed* (2002), *War Trash* (2004), which also won the PEN/Faulkner Award, and *A Free Life* (2007). Jin's opera *The First Emperor*, co-authored with composer Tan Dun, opened at New York's Metropolitan Opera in 2006.

NATHANIEL HAW-
THORNE (1804–1864)

Nathaniel Hawthorne was born in Salem, Massachusetts, a descendant of Puritan immigrants. Educated at Bowdoin College, he was agonizingly slow in winning recognition for his work and supported himself from time to time in government service—working in the customhouses of Boston and Salem and serving as the United States consul in Liverpool. His early collections of stories, *Twice-Told Tales* (1837) and *Mosses from an Old Manse* (1846), did not sell well, and it was not until the publication of his most famous novel, *The Scarlet Letter* (1850), that his fame spread beyond a discerning few. His other novels include *The House of the Seven Gables* (1851) and *The Blithedale Romance* (1852). Burdened by a deep sense of guilt for his family's role in the notorious Salem witchcraft trials over a century before he was born (one ancestor had been a judge), Hawthorne used fiction as a means of exploring the moral dimensions of sin and the human soul.

ERNEST HEMINGWAY
(1899–1961)

Born in Oak Park, Illinois, Ernest Hemingway became a reporter after graduating from high school. During World War I, he served as an ambulance-service volunteer in France and an infantryman in Italy, where he was wounded and decorated for valor. After the war, he lived for a time in Paris, part of the "Lost Generation" of American expatriates that also included Gertrude Stein and F. Scott Fitzgerald. Two volumes of stories, *In Our Time* (1925) and *Death in the Afternoon* (1932), and two major novels, *The Sun Also Rises* (1926) and *A Farewell to Arms* (1929), established his international reputation. Hemingway supported the Loyalists in the Spanish Civil War—the subject of *For Whom the Bell Tolls* (1940)—served as a war correspondent during World War II, and from 1950 until his death lived in Cuba. His novel *The Old Man and the Sea* (1952) won a Pulitzer Prize, and Hemingway was awarded the Nobel Prize for Literature in 1954.

JAMES JOYCE
(1882–1941)

In 1902, after graduating from University College, Dublin, James Joyce left Ireland for Paris, returning a year later. In October 1904, he eloped with Nora Barnacle and settled in Trieste, where he taught English for the Berlitz school. Though he lived as an expatriate for the rest of his life, all of his fiction is set in his native Dublin. Joyce had more than his share of difficulties with publication and censorship. His volume of short stories, *Dubliners*, completed in 1905, was not published until 1914. His novel *Portrait of the Artist as a Young Man*, dated "Dublin 1904, Trieste 1914," appeared first in America, in 1916. His great novel *Ulysses* (1921) was banned for a dozen years in the United States and as long or longer elsewhere. In addition, Joyce published a play, *Exiles* (1918); two collec-

tions of poetry, *Chamber Music* (1907) and *Pomes Penyeach* (1927); and the monumental, experimental, and puzzling novel *Finnegans Wake* (1939).

FRANZ KAFKA
(1883–1924)

Born into a middle-class Jewish family in Prague, Franz Kafka earned a doctorate in law from the German University in that city and held an inconspicuous position in the civil service for many years. Emotionally and physically ill for the last seven or eight years of his short life, he died of tuberculosis in Vienna, never having married (though he was twice engaged to the same woman and lived with an actress in Berlin for some time before he died) and not having published his three major novels, *The Trial* (1925), *The Castle* (1926), and *Amerika* (1927). Indeed, he ordered his friend Max Brod to destroy them and other works he had left in manuscript. Fortunately, Brod did not; and not long after Kafka's death, his sometimes-dreamlike, sometimes-nightmarish work was known and admired all over the world. His stories in English translation are collected in *The Great Wall of China* (1933), *The Penal Colony* (1948), and *The Complete Stories* (1976).

YASUNARI KAWABATA
(1899–1972)

Born in Osaka, Japan, to a prosperous family, Yasunari Kawabata graduated from Tokyo Imperial University in 1924 and had his first literary success with the semiautobiographical novella *The Izu Dancer* (1926). He cofounded the journal *Contemporary Literature* in support of the Neosensualist movement, which had much in common with the European literary movements of Dadaism, Expressionism, and Cubism. His best-known works include *Snow Country* (1937), *Thousand Cranes* (1952), *The Sound of the Mountain* (1954), *The Lake* (1955), *The Sleeping Beauty* (1960), *The Old Capital* (1962), and the collection *Palm-of-the-Hand Stories* (translated in 1988). Kawabata was awarded the Nobel Prize for Literature in 1968. After long suffering from poor health, he committed suicide in 1972.

JAMAICA KINCAID
(b. 1949)

Born in St. John's, Antigua, Elaine Potter Richardson left her native island and her family at seventeen. Changing her name to Jamaica Kincaid, she worked in New York City as an au pair and a receptionist before studying photography at the New School for Social Research, then briefly continuing her studies at Franconia College in New Hampshire. After returning to New York, she became a regular contributor to *The New Yorker*, for which she wrote from 1976 until 1995. Her publications include a collection of short stories, *At the Bottom of the River* (1983); a book-length essay about Antigua, *A Small Place* (1988); a book for children, *Annie, Gwen, Lilly, Pam, and Tulip* (1986); the novels *Annie John* (1985), *Lucy* (1990), and *The Autobiography of My Mother* (1996); the memoir *My Brother* (1997); and a collection of her *New Yorker* pieces, *Talk Stories* (2001). Her most recent novel, *Mr. Potter* (2002), takes place on the island of Antigua.

HANIF KUREISHI
(b. 1954)

The son of a Pakistani father and an English mother, Hanif Kureishi was born and raised in the London suburb of Bromley. Though he began writing novels while still in his teens, he majored in philosophy at London University before rising from usher to writer-in-residence at London's Royal Court Theater. His first play, *Soaking up the Heat*, debuted at London's Theatre Upstairs in 1976 to be followed by *The Mother Country* (1980), *Borderline*, and *Outskirts* (both 1981), among others. Turning his hand to screenwriting, Kureishi earned critical acclaim, fame, and both a New York Film Critics Circle Award and an Academy Award nomination with his controversial *My Beautiful Launderette* (1985). Later films include *Sammy and Rosie Get Laid* (1987), *London Kills Me* (1991), which he also directed, and *Venus* (2006). Having won the prestigious Whitbread Award for his first novel, *The Buddha of Suburbia*, in 1990, he has since published five more—including *The Black Album* (1995), *Intimacy* (1999), and *The Body* (2004)—as well as three short-story collections and a novella. A frequent contributor to periodicals ranging

from the *London Review of Books* to *Harper's* and *The New Statesman*, he also co-edited *The Faber Book of Pop*, a music-oriented anthology that appeared in 1995.

JHUMPA LAHIRI
(b. 1967)

Born in London and raised in Rhode Island, Jhumpa Lahiri is the daughter of Bengali parents; much of her fiction addresses the difficulty of reconciling an Indian heritage with life in the United States. Lahiri earned a B.A. from Barnard College and several degrees from Boston University: an M.A. in English, an MFA in creative writing, an M.A. in comparative studies in literature and the arts, and a Ph.D. in Renaissance Studies. She has published many stories in well-known periodicals such as *The New Yorker* and won the 2000 Pulitzer Prize for her first collection, *Interpreter of Maladies* (1999), a best-seller that has been translated into 29 languages. *The Namesake,* her first novel, was published in 2003 and made into a film in 2006. Lahiri lives in New York City with her husband and two children.

D. H. LAWRENCE
(1885–1930)

The son of a coal miner and a schoolteacher, David Herbert Lawrence was able to attend high school only briefly. He worked for a surgical-appliance manufacturer, attended Nottingham University College, and taught school in Croydon, near London. After publishing his first novel, *The White Peacock* (1911), he devoted his time exclusively to writing; *Sons and Lovers* (1913) established him as a major literary figure. In 1912, he eloped with Frieda von Richthofen, and in 1914, after her divorce, they were married. During World War I, both his novels and his wife's German nationality gave him trouble: *The Rainbow* was published in September 1915 and suppressed in November. In 1919, the Lawrences left England and began years of wandering: first to Italy, then Ceylon, Australia, Mexico, and New Mexico, then back to England and Italy. Lawrence published *Women in Love* in 1920 and *Lady Chatterley's Lover,* his most sexually explicit novel, in 1928. Through it all he suffered from tuberculosis, eventually dying from the disease.

URSULA K. LE GUIN
(b. 1929)

Born in Berkeley, California, to a writer/folklorist mother and an anthropologist father, Ursula Kroeber earned a B.A. from Radcliffe College and an M.A. from Columbia University. In 1952, she married the historian Charles Le Guin. Although she began publishing fiction in the early 1960s, Le Guin established her literary reputation with the philosophical fantasy *A Wizard of Earthsea* (1968), which formed a trilogy with *The Tombs of Atuan* (1971) and *The Farthest Shore* (1972). Read by both adolescents and adults, her work often depicts complex fictional societies with a folklorist's or anthropologist's eye for detail. Her novels include *The Left Hand of Darkness* (1969), *The Dispossessed* (1974), *Malafrena* (1979), *The Compass Rose* (1982), *The Telling* (2000), and *Gifts* (2004). Short story collections include *The Birthday of the World* (2002) and *Changing Planes* (2003). In addition, Le Guin has written essays, children's books, and poetry; collaborated on multimedia work; and edited collections of science fiction.

TOBY LITT (b. 1968)

Named one of the Twenty Best Young British Novelists by *Granta* magazine in 2003, Toby Litt attended Oxford University's Worcester College before entering the creative writing program at the University of East Anglia. The short stories he wrote there formed the kernel of his first collection, *Adventures in Capitalism* (1996); a second, *Exhibitionism*, appeared in 2002. Litt has also published four novels—*Beatniks: An English Road Movie* (1997), an updated and distinctly British reworking of Jack Kerouac's American classic *On the Road*; *Corpsing* (2000), a thriller featuring a television editor; *Deadkidsongs* (2001), about a gang of boys in 1970s England anxious to save their town from a possible Russian invasion; and *Finding Myself* (2003), a parody of both "chick lit" and reality television. He has also contributed reviews, essays, stories, and poetry to London's *Guardian* and *Independent* newspapers, as well as *Poetry Review*, *Punch*, and *New Statesman*.

KATHERINE MANSFIELD
(1888–1923)

Born in Wellington, New Zealand, Katherine Mansfield Beauchamp was an accomplished cellist who studied music at Queen's College, London. At her parents' urging she returned to New Zealand, where, instead of settling down as they wished, she turned to writing at the age of 20. She moved back to London, dropped her last name, and began publishing story collections including *In a German Pension* (1911); *Bliss* (1920), which established her reputation; *The Garden-Party* (1922); and *The Dove's Nest* (1923). A longtime companion of John Middleton Murry, she was friends with (and a literary rival of) D.H. Lawrence and Virginia Woolf. She died suddenly in 1923, while in France trying to cure her tuberculosis. A final volume of stories, *Something Childish,* was published shortly thereafter. *Novels and Novelists*, a collection of essays, appeared in 1930 and her *Collected Stories* in 1937.

BOBBIE ANN MASON
(b. 1940)

Bobbie Ann Mason was born and raised in Mayfield, Kentucky, where her parents were dairy farmers. She received a B.A. from the University of Kentucky, an M.A. from the State University of New York at Binghamton, and a Ph.D. in English from the University of Connecticut. After her stories appeared in such magazines as *The New Yorker* and *Redbook,* Mason published her first collection, *Shiloh and Other Stories* (1982), which won the Ernest Hemingway Foundation Award and established her literary reputation. Her works include the novels *In Country* (1985), *Feather Crowns* (1993), and *Atomic Romance* (2005); a short novel, *Spence and Lila* (1988); three collections of stories—*Love Life* (1989); *Midnight Magic* (1998), and *Zigzagging Down a Wild Trail* (2001); and a memoir, *Clear Springs* (1999), which was a finalist for the Pulitzer Prize.

GUY DE MAUPASSANT
(1850–1893)

Born Henri René Albert in Normandy, France, Maupassant was expelled at sixteen from a Rouen seminary and finished his education at a public high school. After serving in the Franco-Prussian War, he worked as a government clerk in Paris for ten years. A protégé of Flaubert, he published during the 1880s some three hundred stories, half a dozen novels, and plays. The short stories, which appeared regularly in popular periodicals, sampled military and peasant life, the decadent world of politics and journalism, prostitution, the supernatural, and the hypocrisies of solid citizens; with Chekhov, he may be said to have created the modern short story. His life ended somewhat like one of his own stories: he died of syphilis in an asylum. His novels include *Une Vie* (*A Life,* 1883), *Bel Ami* (*Handsome Friend,* 1885), and *Pierre et Jean* (1888).

HERMAN MELVILLE
(1819–1891)

When his father died in debt, twelve-year-old Herman Melville's life of privilege became one of struggle. At eighteen, he left his native New York to teach in a backwoods Massachusetts school, then trained as a surveyor; finding no work, he became a sailor in 1839. After five years in the South Seas, he wrote *Typee* (1846) and *Omoo* (1847), sensationalized and wildly popular accounts of his voyages. They proved the pinnacle of Melville's career in his lifetime, however; *Mardi* (1849) was judged too abstruse, the travel narratives *Redburn* (1849) and *White-Jacket* (1850) too listless. Melville's magnum opus, *Moby-Dick* (1851), was alternately shunned and condemned. His later novels—*Pierre* (1852), *Israel Potter* (1853), and *The Confidence-Man* (1856)—as well as his poetry collection *Battle-Pieces* (1866) were all but ignored. Melville's reputation as one of the giants of American literature was established only after his death; the novella *Billy Budd, Sailor* (not published until 1924), like *Moby-Dick,* is judged a masterpiece.

LORRIE MOORE (b. 1957)

Marie Lorena Moore was born in Glens Falls, New York. At nineteen, while attending St. Lawrence University, she published her first story in *Seventeen* magazine; after graduating, she worked as a paralegal in New York City before earning her MFA in creative writ-ing from Cornell. In 1989 her story "You're Ugly, Too" was published in the *New Yorker* and included in *The Best American Short Stories.* Her first book, *Self-Help* (1985), a collection of short stories, was followed by the novels *Anagrams* (1986) and *Who Will Run the Frog Hospital?* (1994) and the short-story collections *Like Life* (1990) and *Birds of America* (1998). Since 1984, she has been a professor of English at the University of Wisconsin at Madison.

TONI MORRISON
(b. 1931)

Born in Lorain, Ohio, a steel town on the shores of Lake Erie, Chloe Anthony Wofford was the first member of her family to go to college, graduat-ing from Howard University in 1953 and earning an M.A. from Cornell. She taught at both Texas Southern University and at Howard before becoming an editor at Random House, where she worked for nearly twenty years. In such novels as *The Bluest Eye* (1969), *Sula* (1973), *Song of Solomon* (1977), *Beloved* (1987), and *Paradise* (1998), Morrison traces the problems and possibilities faced by black Americans struggling with slavery and its aftermath in the United States. More recent work includes her eighth novel, *Love* (2003); two picture books for children co-authored with her son, Slade—*The Bog Box* (1999) and *Book of Mean People* (2002); a book for young adults, *Remember: The Journey to School Integration* (2004); and *What Moves at the Margin: Selected Nonfiction* (2008). In 1993 she became the first African American author to win the Nobel Prize for literature.

BHARATI MUKHERJEE
(b. 1940)

Born to wealthy parents in Calcutta, Bharati Mukherjee attended pri-vate schools in India, London, and Switzerland before studying at the University of Iowa, where she earned both an MFA in creative writing and a Ph.D. in English and Comparative Literature. At Iowa she met and married Canadian novel-ist Clark Blaise, with whom she has lived in Canada and the United States, and with whom she wrote *Days and Nights in Calcutta* (1977), an acclaimed account of their 1972 visit to her native India. In addition to her novels *The Tiger's Daughter* (1971), *Wife* (1975), *Jasmine* (1989), *The Holder of the World* (1993), *Leave It to Me* (1997), *Desirable Daughters* (2002), and *The Tree Bride* (2004), Mukherjee has published the short-story collections *Darkness* (1985) and *The Middleman* (1988). She teaches at the University of California, Berkeley.

ALICE MUNRO (b. 1931)

Widely considered Canada's best short-story writer, Alice Laidlaw was born on a farm in Wingham, Ontario, near Lake Huron. She began publishing stories while attending the University of Western Ontario. When her two-year scholarship ran out, she left the university, married James Munro, and moved to Vancouver. Her stories appeared sporadically during the 1950s, and she did not publish her first collection, the Governor General's Award–winning *Dance of the Happy Shades*, until 1968. Divorced and remarried, she returned to Ontario and went on to publish the novel *Lives of Girls and Women* (1971) and the collections *Something I've Been Meaning to Tell You* (1974), *Who Do You Think You Are?* (1978, published in the United States as *The Beggar Maid* in 1979), *The Moons of Jupiter* (1983), *The Progress of Love* (1986), *Friend of My Youth* (1990), *Open Secrets* (1994), *Selected Stories* (1996), *The Love of a Good Woman* (1998), *Hateship, Friendship, Courtship, Loveship, and Marriage* (2001), *Runaway* (2004), and *The View from Castle Rock* (2006).

JOYCE CAROL OATES

(b. 1938)

A remarkably prolific writer of short stories, poems, novels, and non-fiction, Joyce Carol Oates was born in Lockport, New York, and graduated from Syracuse University. She received an M.A. in English from the University of Wisconsin but abandoned doctoral studies at Rice University in order to devote herself to writing. The recipient of numerous awards, including the O. Henry Award for continuing achievement (1970, 1986), the Rea Award for the Short Story, the Alan Swallow Award for Fiction, and the National Book Award for the novel *them* (1969), Oates has taught at the University of Detroit and the University of Windsor, Ontario, and currently teaches cre-

ative writing at Princeton University. Her recent novels include *We Were the Mulvaneys* (1996), *Blonde* (2000), *The Tattooed Girl* (2003), *Rape: A Love Story* (2003), *Take Me, Take Me With You* (2004), and *The Falls* (2004). *The Faith of A Writer: Life, Craft, Art,* a collection of personal essays, was published in 2003. *I am No One You Know: Stories* appeared in 2004.

FLANNERY O'CONNOR

(1925–1964)

Mary Flannery O'Connor was born in Savannah, Georgia, studied at the Georgia State College for Women, and won a fellowship to the Writer's Workshop of the University of Iowa, from which she received her MFA. In 1950, she was first diagnosed with lupus, a painful autoimmune disorder that had killed her father and would trouble her for the rest of her brief life. Her first novel, *Wise Blood,* was published in 1952, and her first collection of stories, *A Good Man Is Hard to Find,* in 1955. She was able to complete only one more novel, *The Violent Bear It Away* (1960), and a second collection of stories, *Everything That Rises Must Converge* (1965), before dying of lupus in Milledgeville, Georgia. Her posthumously published *Complete Stories* won the National Book Award in 1972. A collection of letters, edited by Sally Fitzgerald under the title *The Habit of Being,* appeared in 1979.

GRACE PALEY

(1922–2007)

Born to Russian immigrants in the Bronx, New York, Grace Paley attended Hunter College and New York University but never finished college because she was too busy reading and writing poetry before she turned to fiction. Her short stories, first published in *The Little Disturbances of Man: Stories of Men and Women at Love* (1959), *Enormous Changes at the Last Minute* (1974), and *Later the Same Day* (1985), are assembled in *The Collected Stories* (1994); her poetry, in *Begin Again: Collected Poems* (2000); and her essays, reviews, and lectures, in *Just as I Thought* (1998). In 1987, she was awarded a Senior Fellowship by the National Endowment for the Arts, in recognition of her lifetime contribution to literature. In 1988, she was named the first New York State Author. Always politically engaged, she was an outspoken critic of the Vietnam War and had been a lifelong anti-nuclear activist and feminist.

EDGAR ALLAN POE
(1809–1849)

Orphaned before he was three, Edgar Poe was adopted by John Allan, a wealthy Richmond businessman. Poe received his early schooling in Richmond and in England before a brief, unsuccessful stint at the University of Virginia. After serving for two years in the army, he was appointed to West Point in 1830 but expelled within the year for cutting classes. Living in Baltimore with his grandmother, aunt, and cousin Virginia (whom he married in 1835, when she was thirteen), Poe eked out a precarious living as an editor; his keen-edged reviews earned him numerous literary enemies. His two-volume *Tales of the Grotesque and Arabesque* received little critical attention when published in 1839, but his poem "The Raven" (1845) made him a literary celebrity. After his wife's death of tuberculosis in 1847, Poe, already an alcoholic, became increasingly erratic; two years later he died mysteriously in Baltimore.

KATHERINE ANNE
PORTER (1890–1980)

A native of Indian Creek, Texas, and a descendant of Daniel Boone, Katherine Anne Porter was raised by her grandmother and educated in convent schools. Forced by tuberculosis to abandon an acting career, she worked as a journalist in Denver, Chicago, and Mexico. She published her first short story in 1922; her first collection, *Flowering Judas* (1930), won critical acclaim. Porter's only full-length novel, *Ship of Fools* (1962), established her as a major American writer and made her rich. She won numerous awards for her work, including both a Pulitzer Prize and a National Book Award for her *Collected Short Stories* (1965) and a Gold Medal from the National Institute of Arts and Letters. Among her works are the story collections *Pale Horse, Pale Rider* (1939) and *The Leaning Tower and Other Stories* (1944); a volume of essays, *The Days Before* (1952); and an account of the controversial Sacco and Vanzetti murder trial, *The Never-Ending Wrong* (1977).

SALMAN RUSHDIE
(b. 1947)

Born in Bombay, India, Salman Rushdie was educated in England at Rugby School and Cambridge University. He published his first novel, *Grimus* (1975), while working as an advertising copywriter; his second novel, the Booker Prize–winning *Midnight's Children* (1981), established his literary reputation. Rushdie received international attention when Muslim clerics issued a *fatwa* (or edict—in this case, a death sentence) against him following the publication of his novel *The Satanic Verses* (1988), which allegedly blasphemes Islam. Obliged to go into hiding, Rushdie continued to write and to make unannounced public appearances. In 1998, the Iranian government revoked the *fatwa*, and Rushdie ended his hiding. His works include the children's book *Haroun and the Sea of Stories* (1990); the novels *Shame* (1983), *The Moor's Last Sigh* (1995), *The Ground Beneath Her Feet* (1999), *Fury* (2001), and *The Enchantress of Florence* (2008); a collection of short stories, *East, West* (1994); and two volumes of essays: *Imaginary Homelands: Essays and Criticism* (1991); and *Step Across This Line: Collected Nonfiction 1992–2002* (2002). Rushdie was made a Knight of the British Empire in 2007 and in 2008 won the Best of the Booker Award for *Midnight's Children*.

WILLIAM SAIDI
(b. 1937)

Raised in a suburb of Harare, the capital of Zimbabwe, William Saidi launched his career as a journalist in 1957, working for various papers in Zambia and Zimbabwe and serving as editor and columnist for Zimbabwe's independent *Daily News* until the paper was banned by Robert Mugabe's government in 2003. (The newspaper's printing press was bombed in 2001.) Until July 2008, he worked as deputy editor of *The Standard*. Saidi published his first short story in 1956 and has since published stories in South Africa, Zambia, Sweden, Egypt, the United States, and the former Soviet Union. He is also the author of five novels—*The Hanging* (1975), *Day of the Baboons* (1980), *The Old Bricks Lives* (1988), *Gwebede's Wars* (1989), and *The Brothers of Chatima Road*(1990), as well as *Who's Who in Zimbabwe* (1992).

MARJANE SATRAPI
(b. 1969)

As the granddaughter of Nasreddine Shah, the last Quadjar emperor of Iran, Iranian-born Marjane Satrapi is a princess by birth and a self-declared pacifist by inclination. Only 10 years old at the time of the 1979 Islamist revolution, she was reportedly expelled at age 14 from her French-language school after hitting a principal who demanded she stop wearing jewelry. Fearing for her safety, Satrapi's secularist parents sent her to Vienna, Austria, where she would remain until age 18, when she returned to Iran to attend college. After a brief marriage ended in divorce, Satrapi moved to France in 1994, where her graphic memoir, *Persepolis*, was published to great acclaim in 2000. Subsequently translated into numerous languages, it appeared in the United States as *Persepolis: The Story of a Childhood* (2003) and *Persepolis 2: The Story of a Return* (2004). A 2007 animated movie version garnered the Jury Prize at the Cannes Film Festival and was nominated for an Academy Award in 2008. Satrapi's other works are *Embroideries* (2005), which explores Iranian women's views of sex and love through a conversation among Satrapi's female relatives; *Chicken with Plums* (2006), which tells the story of both the 1953 CIA-backed Iranian coup d'etat and the last days of Satrapi's great-uncle, a musician who committed suicide; and several children's books.

AMY TAN (b. 1952)

Amy Tan was born in Oakland, California, just two and a half years after her parents immigrated from China. She received her M.A. in linguistics from San Jose State University and has worked on programs for disabled children and as a freelance writer. In 1987, she visited China for the first time—"As soon as my feet touched China, I became Chinese"—and returned to write her first book, *The Joy Luck Club* (1989). Tan has since published four more novels—*The Kitchen God's Wife* (1991), *The Hundred Secret Senses* (1995), *The Bonesetter's Daughter* (2000) and *Saving Fish from Drowning* (2006)—and has co-authored two children's books. Her first book of nonfiction, *The Opposite of Fate: A Book of Musings* (2003), explores lucky accidents, choice, and

memory. Tan is also the lead singer for the Rock Bottom Remainders, a rock band made up of fellow writers, including Stephen King and Dave Barry; they make appearances at benefits that support literacy programs for children.

GARRY TRUDEAU
(b. 1948)

A New York native of Canadian descent, Garry Trudeau began his career as a cartoonist while still a student at Yale University. His popular comic strip *Doonesbury* debuted nationally in 1970. In the almost forty years since, the controversial, often-political strip has earned Trudeau a Pulitzer Prize (1975) and spawned an Academy Award–nominated animated film (1977), a Broadway musical (1983), and numerous books—all written by Trudeau. (His most recent books are *The Revolt of the English Majors* [2001] and The *Long Road Home* [2005], a collection of strips inspired by the war in Iraq.) The cartoonist—who calls drama his "earliest passion"—is also the author of *Rap Master Ronnie* (1984), a Broadway musical about President Ronald Reagan; and, with famed film director Robert Altman, the HBO series *Tanner 88* (1988), which portrayed the ongoing presidential campaign through the eyes of a fictional Democratic candidate, as well as a 2004 sequel for the Sundance Channel. Known as something of a recluse, the father of three has been married to journalist and television personality Jane Pauley since 1980.

JOHN UPDIKE
(1932–2009)

The man *The Oxford Encyclopedia of American Literature* dubs "perhaps America's most versatile, prolific, and distinguished man of letters of the second half of the twentieth century" spent the early years of his life in Reading and rural Shillington, Pennsylvania. John Updike went on to study English literature at Harvard, where he also contributed cartoons and articles to the famous *Lampoon*. Marrying a Radcliffe fine-arts student in 1953, Updike the next year graduated summa cum laude and sold both his first poem and his first story to *The New Yorker*, whose staff he joined in 1955. Though he would continue to contribute essays, poems, and fiction to *The New Yorker*

for the rest of his life, in 1957 Updike moved with his young family from Manhattan to rural Massachusetts. In the two years following the move, he published both his first book, a collection of poems (1958), and his first novel (1959). Updike went on to publish some 21 novels, 13 short-story collections, seven volumes of poetry (including *Collected Poems, 1953–1993* [1993]), as well as seven collections of essays, a play, and a memoir. He is best known for the tetralogy tracing the life of high-school basketball star turned car salesman Harry C. Rabbit Angstrom. Begun with *Rabbit, Run* in 1960, the series of novels includes *Rabbit Is Rich* (1981) and *Rabbit at Rest* (1990), both of which were awarded Pulitzer Prizes.

LARA VAPNYAR (b. 1971)

Born in Moscow, Russia, Lara Vapnyar emigrated to New York with her husband in 1994, reportedly learning English via television and the fiction of Jane Austen and Alice Munro. A Ph.D. student in Comparative Literature at the City University of New York, Vapnyar in 2002 began publishing short stories in her adopted language. Her first collection, *There Are Jews in My House*, appeared in 2003 and focuses mainly on the experiences of Russian and Russian American characters. Vapnyar's 2004 novel *Memoirs of a Muse* draws on her doctoral research, interweaving the story of the woman who was the muse of nineteenth-century Russian novelist Fyodor Dostoevsky with the story of a contemporary Russian American graduate student who becomes fascinated with them both. Originally appearing in filmmaker Francis Ford Coppola's *Zoetrope: All Story*, "Puffed Rice and Meatballs" was selected to appear alongside a story by Alice Munro, as well as 18 others, in the 2006 *O. Henry Prize Stories: The Best Stories of the Year*. It is also one of the six stories collected in Vapnyar's *Broccoli and Other Tales of Food and Love* (2008).

EUDORA WELTY

(1909–2001)

Known as the "First Lady of Southern Literature," Eudora Welty was born and raised in Jackson, Mississippi, attended Mississippi State College for Women, and earned a B.A. from the University of Wisconsin. Among the countless awards she received were two Guggenheim Fellowships, six O. Henry Awards, a Pulitzer Prize, the French Legion of Honor, the National Medal for Literature, and the Presidential Medal of Freedom. Although she wrote five novels, including *The Robber Bridegroom* (1942), *Ponder Heart* (1954), and *The Optimist's Daughter* (1972), she is best known for her short stories, many of which appear in *The Collected Stories of Eudora Welty* (1980). Among her nonfiction works are *One Writer's Beginnings* (1984), *A Writer's Eye: Collected Book Reviews* (1994), and five collections of her photographs, including *One Place, One Time* (1978) and *Photographs* (1989). In 1998 the Library of America published a two-volume edition of her selected works, making her the first living author they had published.

EDITH WHARTON

(1862–1937)

Edith Jones was born into a distinguished New York family. Educated by private tutors and governesses, she published a book of her poems privately but did not begin to write for a public audience until after her marriage, to Edward Wharton, in 1885. The author of more than fifty volumes of poetry, essays, fiction, travelogues, and criticism, she was the first woman to receive an honorary doctorate from Yale University, in 1923. Although she emigrated to France in 1907 (and later was awarded the Legion of Honor for her philanthropic work during World War I), she continued to write about the New England of her youth in novels such as the popular *Ethan Frome* (1911). Among her many works are *The Valley of Decision* (1902), *The House of Mirth* (1905), *A Son at the Front* (1923), *Twilight Sleep* (1927), the autobiographical *A Backward Glance* (1934), and *The Buccaneers* (1938). She received a Pulitzer Prize for *The Age of Innocence* (1920).

WILLIAM CARLOS WILLIAMS

(1883–1963)

Born in Rutherford, New Jersey, William Carlos Williams attended school in Switzerland and New York and studied medicine at the University of Pennsylvania and the University of Leipzig in Germany. He spent most of his life in Rutherford, practicing medicine and gradually establishing himself as one of the great figures in American poetry. Early in his writing career he left the European-inspired Imagist movement in favor of a more uniquely American poetic style comprised of vital, local language, and "no ideas but in things." His shorter poems have been published in numerous collected editions and other volumes, including the Pulitzer Prize–winning *Brueghel,*

and Other Poems (1963); his five-volume philosophical poem, *Paterson,* was published in 1963. Among his other works are plays such as *A Dream of Love* (1948) and *Many Loves* (1950); a trilogy of novels—*White Mules* (1937), *In the Money* (1940), and *The Build-Up* (1952); his *Autobiography* (1951); his *Selected Essays* (1954); and his *Selected Letters* (1957).

READING, RESPONDING, WRITING

Poetry

Poetry: Reading, Responding, Writing

If you're a reader of poetry, you already know that poetry reading is not just an intellectual and bookish activity; it is about feeling. Reading poetry well means responding to it. If you respond emotionally, you are likely to read more accurately, with deeper understanding, and with greater pleasure. Conversely, if you read poetry accurately and with attention to detail, you will almost certainly respond to it—or learn how to respond—on an emotional level. Reading and responding come to be, for experienced readers of poetry, very nearly one. But those who teach poetry have discovered something else: Writing about poetry helps both the reading and the responding processes.

Responding involves remembering and reflecting as well. As you recall your own past and make associations between things in the text and things you already know and feel, you will not only respond more fully to a particular poem but also improve your general reading skills. Your knowledge and life experience inform your reading of what is before you and allow you to connect elements within the text—events, images, words, sounds—so that meanings and feelings develop and accumulate. Prior learning creates expectations: of pattern, repetition, association, or causality. Reflecting on the text—and on expectations produced by the text—re-creates old feelings but directs them in new, often unusual ways. Poems, even when they are about things we have no experience of, connect to things we do know and order our memories, thoughts, and feelings in new and newly challenging ways.

A course in reading poetry can enrich your life by helping you become more articulate and more sensitive to both ideas and feelings; that's the larger goal. But the more immediate goal—and the route to the larger one—is to become a better reader of texts and a more precise and careful writer. Close attention to one text makes you appreciate and understand textuality and its possibilities more generally. Texts may be complex and even unstable in some ways; they do not affect all readers the same way, and they work through language that has its own volatilities and complexities. But paying attention to how you read—developing specific questions to ask and working on your reading skills systematically—can take a lot of the guesswork out of reading texts and make your interpretations more satisfying.

READING POETRY

Poems, perhaps even more than other texts, can sharpen your reading skills because they tend to be so compact, so fully dependent on concise expression of feeling. In poems, ideas and feelings may be packed tightly into just a few lines.

The experiences of life are very concentrated here, and meanings emerge quickly, word by word.

Poems often show us the very process of putting feelings into a language that can be shared with others. Poetry can be intellectual, too, explaining and exploring ideas, but its focus is more often on how people feel than on how they think. Poems work out a shareable language for feeling, and one of poetry's most insistent virtues arises from its attempt to express the inexpressible. How can anyone, for example, put into words what it means to be in love or how it feels to lose someone one cares about? Poetry tries, and it often captures a shade of emotion that feels just right to a reader. No single poem can be said to represent all the things that love or death feels like or means, but one of the joys of poetry comes when we read a poem and want to say, "Yes, that is just what it is like; I know exactly what that line means, but I've never been able to express it so well." Poetry can be the voice of our feelings even when our minds are speechless with grief or joy. Reading is no substitute for living, but it can make living more abundant and more available. At the same time, poetry does not always celebrate or make us feel better. Sometimes, it questions easy expectations about how we are supposed to feel. Even the most appealing subjects may be handled very differently than we expect, challenging our assumptions and understanding.

READING POEMS: FOUR EXAMPLES

The following four poems talk about the love between two people—a familiar poetic subject and something we all have our own ideas and expectations about. Each poem is written as if it were spoken by one person to his or her lover, and each powerfully conveys the intensity, sincerity, and depth of the love. But the poems work in different ways. As you read these poems, make mental (or actual) notes about what you think makes them alike and different, both in terms of what they suggest about love and how they suggest it.

ELIZABETH BARRETT BROWNING
How Do I Love Thee?

How do I love thee? Let me count the ways.
I love thee to the depth and breadth and height
My soul can reach, when feeling out of sight
For the ends of Being and ideal Grace.
5 I love thee to the level of every day's
Most quiet need, by sun and candlelight.
I love thee freely, as men strive for Right;
I love thee purely, as they turn from Praise;
I love thee with the passion put to use
10 In my old griefs, and with my childhood's faith.
I love thee with a love I seemed to lose
With my lost saints—I love thee with the breath,

Smiles, tears of all my life!—and, if God choose,
I shall but love thee better after death.

1850

JAROLD RAMSEY

The Tally Stick

Here from the start, from our first of days, look:
I have carved our lives in secret on this stick
of mountain mahogany the length of your arms
outstretched, the wood clear red, so hard and rare.
5   It is time to touch and handle what we know we share.

Near the butt, this intricate notch where the grains
converge and join: it is our wedding.
I can read it through with a thumb and tell you now
who danced, who made up the songs, who meant us joy.
10 These little arrowheads along the grain,
they are the births of our children. See,
they make a kind of design with these heavy crosses,
the deaths of our parents, the loss of friends.

Over it all as it goes, of course, I
15 have chiseled Events, History—random
hashmarks cut against the swirling grain.
See, here is the Year the World Went Wrong,
we thought, and here the days the Great Men fell.
The lengthening runes of our lives run through it all.

20 See, our tally stick is whittled nearly end to end;
delicate as scrimshaw, it would not bear you up.
Regrets have polished it, hand over hand.
Yet let us take it up, and as our fingers
like children leading on a trail cry back
25 our unforgotten wonders, sign after sign,
we will talk softly as of ordinary matters,
and in one another's blameless eyes go blind.

1977

LINDA PASTAN

love poem

I want to write you
a love poem as headlong
as our creek

```
        after thaw
     5  when we stand
        on its dangerous
        banks and watch it carry
        with it every twig
        every dry leaf and branch
    10  in its path
        every scruple
        when we see it
        so swollen
        with runoff
    15  that even as we watch
        we must grab
        each other
        and step back
        we must grab each
    20  other or
        get our shoes
        soaked we must
        grab each other
```

1988

"How Do I Love Thee?" is direct but fairly abstract. It lists several ways the poet feels love and connects them to some noble ideas of higher obligations—to justice (line 7), for example, and to spiritual aspiration (lines 2–4). It suggests a wide range of things that love can mean and evokes a variety of emotions. It does not say much about the everyday relationship between the two lovers, the experiences they have had together, or the ways in which their relationship is unlike those of other devoted or ideal lovers. Its appeal is to our general sense of what love is like and of how intense feelings can be; it does not offer details.

"The Tally Stick" is much more concrete. The whole poem concentrates on a single object that "counts" or "tallies" the ways in which this couple love one another, as does "How Do I Love Thee?" This stick stands for their love and becomes a kind of physical totem for it: The stick's natural features (lines 4, 6–7, 10, and 16) and the marks carved on it (lines 6, 10, 12 15–16, 20–21) indicate events in the story of the relationship—their wedding and the births of their children, for example. We could say that the stick *symbolizes* their love, but for now it is enough to notice that the stick serves the lovers as a marker and a reminder of some specific details of their love. It is a special kind of reminder because its language is "secret" (line 2), something they can share privately. The stick itself becomes a very personal object, and in the last stanza of the poem it is as if we watch the lovers touching the stick together and reminiscing over it, gradually dissolving into their emotions and each other as they recall the "unforgotten wonders" (line 25) of their lives together.

Linda Pastan's direct and seemingly simple "love poem" suggests as much about the art and craft of poetry as it does about love. The poem expresses the desire to write a love poem even as the love poem itself materializes before our eyes; the desire and the resultant poem exist side by side, and in reading the poem we seem to watch and hear the poet's creative process at work in developing appropriate metaphors and means of expression. The poem must be "headlong" (line 2) to match the power of a love comparable to the irresistible forces of nature. The poem should, like the love it expresses and the swollen creek it describes, sweep everything along, and it should represent (and reproduce) the sense of watching that the lovers have when they observe natural processes at work. The poem, like the action it represents, suggests to readers the kind of desire that propels the lovers.

The poem suggests that love straddles a border between safety and danger. Instead of bringing passivity and peace, it requires activity and boldness and deep passion. Everything—twigs, leaves, branches, scruples—is carried along by the powerful currents of love and the creek, and the poem replicates the repeated action of the lovers as if to power along observant readers, too, just as the lovers are powered along by what they see. Love here is no quiet or simple matter even if the expression of it in poems can be direct and can stem from a simple observation of experience. The "love poem" itself—linked as it is with the headlong currents of the creek from which the lovers are protecting themselves even as they step close—seems to represent that which is beyond love and that which, therefore, both threatens love and at the same time is love's source. The poem thus affirms the power of poetry, but it also suggests that the subject of poetry—love and life—is what matters most.

Of course, love does not always go smoothly, and poems are not always about emotional fulfillment. Many poems are about disappointment, suggesting the contradictions and uncertainties in relationships. The following poem is a kind of **monologue**, recording the complex longings of a married woman whose attitudes toward marriage are quite different from those of Barrett Browning or Ramsay. How are they different? What emotions are expressed in the poem? How might this poem challenge your assumptions about what married love might feel like?

LIZ ROSENBERG

Married Love

The trees are uncurling their first
green messages: Spring, and some man
lets his arm brush my arm in a darkened
theatre. Faint-headed, I fight the throb.
5 Later I dream
the gas attendant puts a cool hand
on my breast, asking a question.
Slowly I rise through the surface of the dream,
brushing his hand and my own heat away.

10 Young, I burned to marry. Married,
the smolder goes on underground;
clutching at weeds, writhing everywhere.
I'm trying to talk to a friend on burning
issues, flaming from the feet up,
15 drinking in his breath, touching his wrist.

I want to grab the pretty woman
on the street, seize the falcon
by its neck, beat my way into whistling steam.

I turn to you in the dark, oh husband,
20 watching your lit breath circle the pillow.
Then you turn to me, throwing first one limb
and then another over me, in the easy brotherly
lust of marriage. I cling to you
as if I were a burning ship and you
25 could save me, as if I won't go sliding down
beneath you soon; as if our lives are made of rise
and fall, and we could ride this out forever,
with longing's thunder rolling heavy in our arms.

1986

The initial expectations of springtime and newness here quickly turn into signs, both conscious and unconscious, of desire ("throb") for anonymous sex ("some man"). Reality and fantasy are nearly one here, as the woman tries to repress arousal she does not wish to feel. The poem is full of fire and burning, in fact, which the speaker cannot ignore, subdue, or quench; there is hurt here and bewilderment and fear, and the easy habitual comforts of married love are not exactly reassuring ("brotherly lust"), nor do they seem to satisfy desire. The woman feels herself to be a burning (and sinking) ship, and her marital clinging seems an act of desperation; she hopes for salvation (or at least a "rid[ing] out"), but "longing's thunder" remains far more powerful than any sense of satisfaction or solution.

RESPONDING TO POETRY

Various readers will respond differently to the same poem; some will prefer one poem and some another. Personal preference does not mean that objective standards for poetry cannot be found—some poems *are* better than others, and in later chapters we will look in detail at features that help us evaluate and interpret poems—but there are no unquestionable standards as to what poetry must be or how it must work. Some good poems are quite abstract, others quite specific. Some deal with familiar, comfortable feelings, others with more difficult ones. Any poem that helps us articulate and clarify human feelings and ideas has a legitimate claim on us as readers. Watching how poems discover a language for feeling can help us discover a language for our own feelings, but the process is also reciprocal: Being conscious of feelings we already have can lead us into poems more surely and with more satisfaction. Readers with a strong romantic bent—and with strong yearnings or positive memories of desire—will be likely to find a poem like "The Tally Stick" easy to respond to and admire, while those more skeptical of human institutions and male behavior may find the wifely despair of "Married Love" more compelling.

You may also come across poems about events or feelings you have never experienced—or even ones you can hardly imagine. But sharing unfamiliar experiences through language often enables us to uncover feelings—of love or anger, fear or confidence—we did not know we had, or could have, thus increasing what some people call our *emotional literacy*. We don't have to be a person who has been married for years or a parent who has lost a child to respond emotionally to a poem that describes such an experience: Our own experiences give us some idea of what such a love or loss would feel like. And the words and strategies of the poem may arouse expectations created by our previous experiences.

Indeed, poets often write about experiences and feelings that they have not themselves had. Like a dramatist or writer of fiction, the poet may simply *imagine* an event in order to analyze and articulate how it might feel. A work of literature can be *true* without being *actual*.

RESPONDING TO POEMS: TWO EXAMPLES

In the following poems, a father and a husband struggle to deal with the death of a loved one, though each poem handles the subject quite differently.

BEN JONSON

On My First Son

Farewell, thou child of my right hand,[1] and joy;
My sin was too much hope of thee, loved boy:
Seven years thou wert lent to me, and I thee pay,
Exacted by thy fate, on the just[2] day.
5 O could I lose all father now! for why
Will man lament the state he should envý,
To have so soon 'scaped world's and flesh's rage,
And, if no other misery, yet age?
Rest in soft peace, and asked, say, "Here doth lie
10 Ben Jonson his[3] best piece of poetry."
For whose sake henceforth all his vows be such
As what he loves may never like too much.

                                                    1616

HOWARD NEMEROV

The Vacuum

The house is so quiet now
The vacuum cleaner sulks in the corner closet,
Its bag limp as a stopped lung, its mouth

---

1. A literal translation of the son's name, Benjamin.
2. Exact; the son died on his seventh birthday, in 1603.
3. That is, Ben Jonson's (this was a common Renaissance form of the possessive).

Grinning into the floor, maybe at my
5   Slovenly life, my dog-dead youth.

I've lived this way long enough,
But when my old woman died her soul
Went into that vacuum cleaner, and I can't bear
To see the bag swell like a belly, eating the dust
10   And the woolen mice, and begin to howl

Because there is old filth everywhere
She used to crawl, in the corner and under the stair.
I know now how life is cheap as dirt,
And still the hungry, angry heart
15   Hangs on and howls, biting at air.

1955

The first poem's attempts to rationalize the boy's death are quite conventional. Although the father tries to be comforted by pious thoughts, his feelings keep showing through. The poem's beginning—with its formal "farewell" and the rather distant-sounding address to his dead son ("child of my right hand")—cannot be sustained for long: Both of the first two lines end with bursts of emotion. It is as if the father is trying to explain the death to himself and to keep his emotions under control, but he cannot quite manage it. Even the punctuation suggests the way his feelings compete with conventional attempts to put the death into some sort of perspective that will soften the grief, and the comma near the end of each of the first two lines marks a pause that cannot quite hold back the overflowing emotion. But finally the only "idea" that the poem supports is that the father wishes he did not feel so intensely; in the fifth line he fairly blurts that he wishes he could lose his fatherly emotions, and in the final lines he resolves never again to "like" so much that he can be this deeply hurt. Philosophy and religion offer their useful counsels in this poem, but they prove far less powerful than feeling. Rather than drawing some kind of moral about what death means, the poem presents the actuality of feeling as inevitable and nearly all-consuming.

The husband in the second poem also tries to suppress the rawness of his feelings, but this survivor is haunted by memories of his loved one when he sees a physical object—a vacuum cleaner—that he associates with her. The poem's title refers most obviously to the vacuum cleaner that, like the tally stick in Ramsey's poem, seems to stand for many of the things that were once important in the life he had together with his wife. Yet the poem is ultimately more about the vacuum in the husband's life created by his wife's death. The machine is a reminder of the dead wife ("my old woman," line 7) because of her devotion to cleanliness. But to the surviving husband buried in the filth of his life it seems as if the machine has become almost human, a kind of ghost of her: it "sulks" (line 2), it has lungs and a mouth (line 3), and it seems to grin, making fun of what has become of him. He "can't bear" (line 8) to see it in action because it then seems too much alive, too much a reminder of her life.

The poem records his paralysis, his inability to do more than discover that life is "cheap as dirt" without her ordering and cleansing presence for him. At the end it is *his* angry heart that acts like the haunting machine, howling and biting at air as if he has merged with her spirit and the physical object that memorializes her. This poem puts a strong emphasis on the stillness of death and the way it makes things seem to stop; it captures in words the hurt, the anger, the inability to understand, the vacuum that remains when a loved one dies and leaves a vacant space. But here we do not see the body or hear a direct good-bye to the dead person; rather we encounter the feeling that lingers and won't go away, recalled through memory by an especially significant object, a mere thing but one that has been personalized to the point of becoming nearly human itself. (The event described here is, by the way, fictional; the poet's wife did not actually die.)

Responding to Poems: An Exercise

Though you may never have been in love or lost a loved one, you were once a child, and adult memories of childhood are the subject of the following poems. In the first, written as if the person speaking the poem were in the fifth grade, a child's sense of death is portrayed through the speaker's exploration of a photograph that makes her grandfather's presence vivid to her memory—a memory that lingers primarily through smell and touch. In the second poem, another childhood memory—this time of overshoes—takes an adult almost physically back into childhood. In the third poem, a man remembers an even more traumatic event—the aftermath of his brother's death. As you read the three poems, jot down your responses. How much are your responses shaped by your own past experiences? In what specific places did these experiences occur? What family photographs do you remember most vividly? What feelings do they evoke that make them so memorable? Which feelings expressed in each poem are similar to your own? Where do your feelings differ most strongly? How would you articulate your responses to such memories differently? In what ways does an awareness of your similar—and different—experiences and feelings make you a better reader of the poem?

RITA DOVE

Fifth Grade Autobiography

I was four in this photograph fishing
with my grandparents at a lake in Michigan.
My brother squats in poison ivy.
His Davy Crockett cap
5   sits squared on his head so the raccoon tail
flounces down the back of his sailor suit.

My grandfather sits to the far right
in a folding chair,

(Continued on next page)

(Continued)

    and I know his left hand is on
10 the tobacco in his pants pocket
    because I used to wrap it for him
    every Christmas. Grandmother's hips
    bulge from the brush, she's leaning
    into the ice chest, sun through the trees
15 printing her dress with soft
    luminous paws.

    I am staring jealously at my brother;
    the day before he rode his first horse, alone.
    I was strapped in a basket
20 behind my grandfather.
    He smelled of lemons. He's died—

    but I remember his hands.

                    1989

ANNE SEXTON

The Fury of Overshoes

    They sit in a row
    outside the kindergarten,
    black, red, brown, all
    with those brass buckles.
5 Remember when you couldn't
    buckle your own
    overshoe
    or tie your own
    shoe
10 or cut your own meat
    and the tears
    running down like mud
    because you fell off your
    tricycle?
15 Remember, big fish,
    when you couldn't swim
    and simply slipped under
    like a stone frog?
    The world wasn't
20 yours.
    It belonged to
    the big people.

(Continued on next page)

(Continued)

Under your bed
sat the wolf
25 and he made a shadow
when cars passed by
at night.
They made you give up
your nightlight
30 and your teddy
and your thumb.
Oh overshoes,
don't you
remember me,
35 pushing you up and down
in the winter snow?
Oh thumb,
I want a drink,
it is dark,
40 where are the big people,
when will I get there,
taking giant steps
all day,
each day
45 and thinking
nothing of it?

1974

SEAMUS HEANEY

Mid-Term Break

I sat all morning in the college sick bay
Counting bells knelling classes to a close.
At two o'clock our neighbors drove me home.

In the porch I met my father crying—
5 He had always taken funerals in his stride—
And Big Jim Evans saying it was a hard blow.

The baby cooed and laughed and rocked the pram
When I came in, and I was embarrassed
By old men standing up to shake my hand

10 And tell me they were "sorry for my trouble,"
Whispers informed strangers I was the eldest,
Away at school, as my mother held my hand

(Continued on next page)

(Continued)

In hers and coughed out angry tearless sighs.
At ten o'clock the ambulance arrived
15 With the corpse, stanched and bandaged by the nurses.

Next morning I went up into the room. Snowdrops
And candles soothed the bedside; I saw him
For the first time in six weeks. Paler now,

Wearing a poppy bruise on his left temple,
20 He lay in the four foot box as in his cot.
No gaudy scars, the bumper knocked him clear.

A four foot box, a foot for every year.

1966

Not all poems are as accessible as those in this chapter, and even the accessible ones yield themselves to us more readily and more fully if we approach them systematically by developing specific reading habits and skills—just as someone learning to play tennis or to make pottery systematically learns the rules, the techniques, the things to watch out for that are distinctive to that activity. It helps if you develop a sense of what to expect, and the chapters that follow will show you the things that poets can do—and thus what you can do with poetry.

But knowing what to expect isn't everything. As a reader of poetry, you should always be open—to new experiences, new feelings, new ideas. Every poem is a potential new experience, and no matter how sophisticated you become, you can still be surprised (and delighted) by new poems—and by re-reading old ones. Good poems bear many, many re-readings, and you may often discover something new with every reading: There is no such thing as "mastering" a poem. Let poems surprise you when you come to them, let them come on their own terms, let them be themselves. If you are open to poetry, you are also open to much more that the world can offer you.

Reading and Responding: Three General Tips

1. *Take a poem on its own terms.* Adjust to the poem; don't make the poem adjust to you. Be prepared to hear things you do not want to hear. Not all poems are about your ideas, nor will they always present emotions you want to feel. But be tolerant and listen to the poem's ideas first; later you can explore the ways you do or don't agree with the poem.
2. *Assume there is a reason for everything.* Poets do make mistakes, but when a poem shows some degree of verbal control it is usually safest to assume that the poet chose each word carefully; if the choice seems peculiar, you may be missing something. Try to account for everything in a poem, see what kind of sense you can make of it, and figure out a coherent pattern that explains the text as it stands.

(Continued on next page)

(Continued)

3. *Remember that poems exist in time, and times change.* Not only the meanings of words, but whole ways of looking at the universe vary in different ages. Consciousness of time works two ways: Your knowledge of history provides a context for reading the poem, and the poem's use of a word or idea may modify your notion of a particular age.

RESPONDING TO POETRY: EIGHT CONCRETE STEPS AND AN EXAMPLE

No one can give you a method that will offer you total experience of all poems. But because individual poems often share characteristics with other poems, taking certain steps can prompt you to ask the right questions. If you are relatively new to poetry or are faced with a poem that seems especially difficult, you may need to tackle these steps one at a time, pausing to write even as you read and respond. With more accessible poems and with further experience, though, you will find that you can skip steps or run through them quickly and almost automatically.

The following list and description of the steps shows you how this process might work in practice. First, though, we need a poem to work on.

APHRA BEHN

On Her Loving Two Equally

I

How strongly does my passion flow,
Divided equally twixt[4] two?
Damon had ne'er subdued my heart
Had not Alexis took his part;
5 Nor could Alexis powerful prove,
Without my Damon's aid, to gain my love.

II

When my Alexis present is,
Then I for Damon sigh and mourn;
But when Alexis I do miss,
10 Damon gains nothing but my scorn.
But if it chance they both are by,
For both alike I languish, sigh, and die.

III

Cure then, thou mighty wingèd god,[5]
This restless fever in my blood;

4. Between.
5. Cupid, who, according to myth, shot darts of lead and of gold at the hearts of lovers, corresponding to false love and true love, respectively.

15 One golden-pointed dart take back:
      But which, O Cupid, wilt thou take?
      If Damon's, all my hopes are crossed;
      Or that of my Alexis, I am lost.

1684

Now that you've read Behn's poem, read through the steps below and see how one reader used them as a guide for responding. Later, you may want to return to these steps as you read and respond to other poems.

1. **Articulate your expectations, starting with the title.** Poets often use false leads and try to surprise readers, but defining your expectations makes you more conscious of where you are when you begin. As you read the poem, pay attention to what you expect and where, when, and how the poem fulfills, or perhaps frustrates, your expectations.

   The title of Aphra Behn's "On Her Loving Two Equally" both creates certain expectations and defies other expectations about love, as well as love poems. Can someone really "love two equally"? Perhaps this will be the question the poem seeks to answer.

2. **Read the syntax literally.** What the sentences literally say is only a starting point, but it is vital. Not all poems use normal prose syntax, but most of them do, and you can save yourself from going astray by first "translating" the poem accurately and not simply free-associating from an isolated word or phrase. To do this, especially with poems written before the twentieth century, you may need to break this step down into the following smaller steps:

   a. *Identify sentences.* For now, ignore the line breaks and look for sentences or independent clauses (word groups that can function as complete sentences). These will typically be preceded and followed by a period (.), a semicolon (;), a colon (:), or a dash (—).

   The 18 lines of Aphra Behn's "On Her Loving Two Equally" can be broken down into nine sentences.

   1. How strongly does my passion flow, Divided equally twixt two?
   2. Damon had ne'er subdued my heart Had not Alexis took his part;
   3. Nor could Alexis powerful prove, Without my Damon's aid, to gain my love.
   4. When my Alexis present is, Then I for Damon sigh and mourn;
   5. But when Alexis I do miss, Damon gains nothing but my scorn.
   6. But if it chance they both are by, For both alike I languish, sigh, and die.
   7. Cure then, thou mighty wingèd god, This restless fever in my blood;
   8. One golden-pointed dart take back: But which, O Cupid, wilt thou take?
   9. If Damon's, all my hopes are crossed; Or that of my Alexis, I am lost.

   b. *Reorder sentences.* Identify the main elements—subject(s), verb(s), object(s)—of each sentence or independent clause, and if necessary rearrange them in normative word order. (By "normative word order," we mean the normal way words are ordered. In English, that is usually *subject*, then *verb*, then *object*, with dependent clauses at the beginning or end of the main clause and next to whatever main element they modify.) Have you clarified which subjects and verbs belong together, what pronouns refer to what nouns, and so on?

In the following sentences, the reordered words appear in italics:

1. How strong does my passion flow, Divided equally twixt two?
2. Damon had ne'er subdued my heart Had not Alexis took his part;
3. Nor *Without my Damon's aid* could Alexis *prove* powerful *to gain my love.*
4. When my Alexis *is* present, Then I *sigh and mourn* for Damon;
5. But when *I do miss* Alexis, Damon gains nothing but my scorn.
6. But if it chance they both are by, *I languish, sigh, and die* For both alike.
7. *thou mighty wingèd god,* Cure then This restless fever in my blood;
8. *take back* One golden-pointed dart: But which wilt thou take, *O Cupid*?
9. If Damon's, all my hopes are crossed; Or that of my Alexis, I am lost.

c. *Translate sentences into modern prose, defining unfamiliar or ambiguous words.* **Be sure to link the parts of the sentence logically and to link one sentence logically to the sentence that comes before it by adding any implied words necessary to make the connection. At this stage, don't move to outright paraphrase; instead, stick closely to the original.**

Below, added words appear in brackets, definitions of words in parentheses:

1. How strongly does my passion flow [when it is] divided equally between two [people]?
2. Damon would never have (*conquered* or *tamed*) my heart if Alexis had not taken his [own] (portion) [of my heart].
3. Nor without my Damon's aid could Alexis have proven powerful [enough] to gain my love.
4. When my Alexis is present, then I sigh and mourn for Damon;
5. But when I miss Alexis, Damon doesn't gain anything (except) my scorn.
6. But if it (so happens) that [Damon and Alexis] are both (near) [me], I languish, sigh, and die for both [Damon and Alexis] alike.
7. [Cupid,] (you) mighty wingèd god, cure then this restless fever in my blood;
8. Take back one [of your two] darts [with] pointed gold [tips]: But which [of these arrows] will you take, O Cupid?
9. If [on the one hand, you take away] Damon's [arrow], all my hopes are (*opposed, invalidated, spoiled*); Or [if, on the other hand, you take away] Alexis's arrow, I am lost.

d. *Note any ambiguities in the original language that might be ignored in your translation.* **Look for modifiers that might modify more than one thing, verbs that might have multiple subjects and objects, words that have multiple, relevant meanings:**

The translation of lines 3 and 4—"Damon would never have (*conquered* or *tamed*) my heart if Alexis had not taken his [own] (portion) [of my heart]"—ignores the ambiguity of the phrase "Alexis took his part." *His* could refer to Alexis or Damon because both are mentioned in the first part of the sentence, so this phrase could be translated as "Alexis took Damon's part" or "Alexis took his own part." But what about the word *part*? At least three different meanings of this word make equal sense in this context:

- "one of the . . . subdivisions into which something is . . . divided," the most obvious "something" here being the "heart" mentioned in the last line and in exactly the same place in the line that *part* comes in this line.
- "the role of a character in a play" or "one's . . . allotted task (as in an action)."
- "one of the opposing sides in a conflict or dispute," which in this case could be the "conflict" over the speaker's love.

On the one hand, then, this phrase could mean something like "Alexis took his own portion of my heart"; "Alexis played his own role in my life or in this three-way courtship drama"; "Alexis defended his own side in the battle for my love." On the other hand, it could mean "Alexis took *Damon's* part of my heart"; "Alexis played *Damon's* role"; or even "Alexis defended *Damon's* side in the battle for my love."

3. **Use your dictionary, other reference books, and reliable Web sites.** Look up anything that you either don't understand or that you suspect might be ambiguous: an unfamiliar word, a word used in an unfamiliar way, a word that seems to have multiple meanings, a place, a person, a myth, an idea—anything the poem uses. When you can't find what you need or don't know where to look, ask the reference librarian to help.

   This step has been addressed above to get at the precise meanings of *part* and other words, but you could also consult a source to find out more about Cupid, for example.

4. **Figure out who, where, when, and what happens.** Once you have gotten a sense of the literal meaning of each sentence, ask the following very general factual questions about the whole poem. Remember that not all of the questions will suit every poem. At this point, stick to the facts. What do you know for sure?

   Who?
   - Who is, or who are, the poem's **speaker(s)**?
   - Who is the **auditor**? That is, whom does the speaker address in the poem?
   - Which other **characters**, if any, appear within the poem?

The title "On *Her* Loving Two Equally" suggests that the speaker is a woman who equally loves two people. In the body of the poem, she identifies these as two men—Damon and Alexis. At the beginning of the poem, the woman doesn't seem to be addressing anyone in particular (certainly not the two men she talks *about*). But in the third stanza, she addresses Cupid—first through the epithet "mighty wingèd god" (line 13) and then by name (line 16). (Because Cupid isn't present, this is an apostrophe.)

   Where? When?
   Where is the speaker and when are the events he or she describes? That is, what is the poem's temporal and physical **setting**?

No place or time is specified in Behn's poem. The antiquated diction ("twixt," line 2; "wilt," line 16) implies that the poem wasn't written recently, and the publication date is 1684. But there is nothing in the poem to limit the situation or feelings it describes to any specific time or place.

What?

- What is the **situation** described in the poem?
- What, if anything, literally happens over the course of it, or what **action**, if any, does it describe?
- Or, if the poem doesn't tell a story, then how is it structured internally? Does the speaker's subject or focus shift over the course of the poem? When and how?

The basic situation is that the speaker loves two men equally. Beyond that, the poem doesn't say much about what has happened. Instead, the speaker alludes in the second stanza to general situations—when she is with one of the men and not the other or when she is with both of them at once—and the feelings that result. Then, in the third stanza, she imagines what would happen if she stopped loving one of them. The topic or subject essentially remains the same throughout, though there are two subtle shifts. First is the shift from addressing anyone in stanzas one and two to addressing Cupid in stanza three. Second, there are shifts in verb tense and time: The first stanza floats among various tenses ("does," line 1; "took," line 4), the second sticks to the present tense ("is," "sigh," "mourn," etc.), and the third shifts to future ("wilt," line 16).

5. **Formulate tentative answers to the questions, Why does it matter? What does it all mean?**

- Why should the poem matter to anyone other than the poet, or what might the poem show and say to readers?
- What problems, issues, questions, or conflicts does the poem explore that might be relevant to people other than the speaker(s) or the poet— to humanity in general, to the poet's contemporaries, to people of a certain type or in a certain situation, and so forth?
- How is each problem or conflict developed and resolved over the course of the poem, or how is each question answered? What conclusions does the poem seem to reach about these, or what are its **themes**?

The title and first two lines pose a question: How strong is our love if we love two people instead of one? We tend to assume that anything that is "divided" is less strong than something unified. The use of the word *flow* in the first line reinforces that assumption because it implicitly compares love to something that flows: A river, for example, "flows," and when a river divides into two streams, each is smaller and its flow less strong than the river's. So the way the speaker articulates the question implies an answer: Love, like a river, isn't strong and sure when divided.

But the rest of the poem undermines that answer. In the first stanza, the speaker points out that each lover and his love has "aided" and added to the "power" of the other: Neither man would have "gain[ed her] love" if the other hadn't. The second stanza gives a more concrete sense of why this might happen: Since we tend to yearn for what we don't have at the moment, being with one of these men makes her miss the other one. But if both men are present, she feels the same about both and perhaps even feels *more* complete and satisfied.

As if realizing she can't solve the problem herself, she turns in the third stanza to Cupid and asks him to solve it by taking away her love for either Damon or Alexis. As soon as she asks for this, though, she indicates that the result would be unhappiness. In the end, the poem seems to say (or its theme is) that love *doesn't* flow or work like a river because love can actually be stronger when we love more than one person, as if it's multiplied instead of lessened by division.

6. **Consider how the poem's form contributes to its effect and meaning.**

   • How is the poem put together? What are its formal features?
   • How do the poem's overall form and its various specific formal features contribute to its meaning?
   • In other words, what gets lost when you translate the poem into modern prose?

   Formal features to consider include **diction** (or word choice) and **syntax** (or word order), **figures of speech** (**metaphor, simile**, etc.), **symbolism**, sound patterns (**rhyme, alliteration, assonance, meter**), and the organization of lines and stanzas—the length, shape, and arrangement of lines (as opposed to sentences). Here, you might note where you see a **caesura, end-stopped lines, enjambment**, and so on.

   The stanza organization underscores shifts in the speaker's approach to her situation. But organization reinforces meaning in other ways as well. On the one hand, the division into three stanzas and the choice to number them, plus the fact that each stanza has three sentences, mirror the three-way struggle or "love triangle" described in the poem. On the other hand—as the fact that the poem has 18 *lines* and 9 *sentences* suggests—every sentence is "divided equally twixt two" *lines*. Sound and especially rhyme reinforce this pattern since the two lines that make up one sentence usually rhyme with each other (to form a couplet). The only lines that aren't couplets are those that begin the second stanza, where we instead have alternating rhyme—*is* (line 7) rhymes with *miss* (line 9), *mourn* (line 8) rhymes with *scorn* (line 10). Notice, though, the content of these lines: They describe how the speaker "miss[es]" one man when the other is "by," a sensation she arguably reproduces in readers by ensuring that they twice "miss" the rhyme that the rest of the poem leads us to expect.

7. **Investigate and consider the ways the poem draws on and departs from poetic tradition, especially (but not exclusively) in terms of its formal features.** Find out whether the poem conforms to any traditional poetic formal patterns or what particular subgenre or kind of poem it might be—a **sonnet**, an **ode**, a **ballad**, and so forth—and ask why and how that affects the meaning of the poem. Certain patterns of rhythm and rhyme, particular verse forms, and poetic genres and kinds have traditionally been used in certain ways and to certain ends. As a result, they generate particular expectations for readers familiar with such traditions, and poems gain additional meaning by both fulfilling and defying those expectations, following and departing from tradition. For example, **anapestic** meter (two unstressed syllables followed by a stressed one, as in *Tennessee*) is usually used for comic poems, so when poets use it in a serious poem they are probably making a point.

8. **Argue.** Discussion with others—both out loud and in writing—usually results in clarification and keeps you from being too dependent on personal biases and preoccupations that sometimes mislead even the best readers. Discussing a poem with someone else (especially someone who

thinks very differently) or sharing what you've written about the poem can expand your perspective and enrich your experience.

WRITING ABOUT POETRY

If you have followed the steps outlined above and kept notes on your personal responses to the poems you've read, you have already taken an important step toward more formal writing about them. Two examples of such writing appear in this chapter: an informal student response paper on W. H. Auden's "[Stop all the clocks]," a poem included in "Romantic Love: An Album," and a more formal essay on Aphra Behn's "On Her Loving Two Equally," based on the notes on the poem presented in the previous section. There are many different ways to write about poems, just as there are many different things to say. (The section of the anthology called "Writing about Literature" suggests some ways to come up with and develop a good topic.) But all writing begins with a clear sense of the poem itself and your responses to it, so the first steps (long before formally sitting down to write) are to read the poem several times and take notes on the things that strike you and the questions that remain.

* * *

What *is* poetry? Let your definition be cumulative as you read more and more poems. No dictionary definition will cover all that you find, and it is better to discover for yourself poetry's many ingredients, its many effects, its many ways of acting. What can it do for you? Wait and see. Add up its effects after you have read carefully—after you have re-read and studied—a hundred or so poems; then continue to read new poems or re-read old ones.

SAMPLE WRITING

In the response paper that follows, Stephen Bordland works through Auden's poem "[Stop all the clocks, cut off the telephone]" more or less line-by-line, writing down whatever ideas come to him. The form of this paper is less important than the process of thinking carefully about the poem's music, emotions, and meanings. As you can see, by the time Stephen reaches the end of his response, he has decided on a topic for the more formal paper that he will write later.

Stephen Bordland
Professor O'Connor
English 157
2 February 2005

Response Paper on
W. H. Auden's "[Stop all the clocks, cut off the telephone]"

I first heard this poem read aloud when I saw the movie *Four Weddings and a Funeral* on cable. The character who read the poem was reading it at the funeral of his lover. It was perfectly suited to the story and was very moving. I was struck by the actor's reading because the poem seemed to have a steady rhythm for several lines and then suddenly hit what sounded like a dead end—"I thought that love would last forever: I was wrong." Hearing the actor's reading of this poem made me want to read it myself, to see if the poem would still affect me if I read/heard it outside of the context of an emotional scene in a movie. It did, and I think that the "I was wrong" line is the key—a turning point, I guess.

In the anthology, the poem seems to have no actual title (at least that's how I interpret the fact that the first line is in brackets where the title usually goes), but I did some searching on the Internet and found that this poem was once called "Funeral Blues." If I were reading the poem for the first time under that title, I would at least know that the poem has something to do with death right from the start. But this title makes the poem sound irreverent rather than sincerely painful. I wonder if that would have been true in the 1930s, when Auden wrote the poem. There were lots of blues and jazz songs of that era whose titles ended in "Blues" (like Robert Johnson's "Kindhearted Woman Blues"), so maybe the title wasn't meant to be read the way that I'm reading it. Anyway, I don't know if Auden himself changed the title, or if there's another story there, but I think it's a better poem without the title.

   The poem starts with a request to an unknown person (everyone?) to make some common aspects of daily life go away: "Stop all the clocks," presumably because time seems to be standing still; "cut off the telephone," presumably because the speaker wants to be alone and undisturbed, cut off from human contact. I'm not sure what's implied by "Prevent the dog from barking with a juicy bone," mainly because I'm confused about the literal meaning: Are we supposed to prevent the dog from barking by giving him a juicy bone (one way to interpret "with a juicy bone"), or are we supposed to prevent the dog with a juicy bone in his mouth (another way of interpreting "with a juicy bone") from barking at all? I don't think I really have a handle on what this line means in relation to the other ones, but I'll leave it for now. In the next line, "Silence the pianos" clearly means that the speaker wants no music now that his lover is dead, except for the "muffled drum" that will accompany the coffin and mourners in the fourth line. It's interesting that all of these things so far are sounds—the tick-tock of the clock, the ring of the telephone, a barking dog, music. They all seem to stand in for something, too—for the passing of time, contact with other people (and with pets?), joy as expressed by music.

   The image of "aeroplanes" circling overhead (and "moaning"—that's a really good choice of words) writing "He is Dead" is very strong and would have been a very modern reference at the time of this poem (1936). A *Christian Science Monitor* article about a "skywriting" pilot says that "Skywriting's heyday was from the 1930s to the early 1950s when Pepsi Cola used skywriting as its main way of advertising," so the reference here is to a commercial medium being used to make as many people as possible aware of the speaker's loss. If a poet tried to make a reference to something equivalent today, it would have to be a television advertisement or a blog, maybe. I wonder if a modern poet could really pull off a reference to a TV ad and still make it sound sincerely sad.

   I'm not sure what the "crepe bows round the white necks of the public doves" means. Would the bows even be visible? Does "crepe" imply a color, or is it just a type of fabric? And what is a public dove? I'm not sure I like the repetition in this line of three adjective/noun pairs: "crepe bows," "white necks," "public doves." It seems too precious or "poetic." The "traffic policemen" that I've seen all wear white gloves so that their hand movements can be seen clearly. The speaker wants them all to wear "black cotton gloves," the appropriate color for mourning, but that would probably create real problems for the drivers trying to see what the policemen are directing them to do. So, I wonder if the bows on doves and black gloves on cops are both there to show us that the speaker is feeling not just the sort of grief that moves him to write poetry, but also the sort of intense pain that makes him want to throw the rest of the world into the same confusion and chaos he's experiencing. Or at least, he's not only asking to be alone, but also wanting the rest of the world to share his grief.

   In the next four lines, the speaker turns to himself and his lover: "He was my North, my South, my East and West / My working week and my Sunday rest."

Bordland 3

These lines flow so smoothly, with a soothing, regular rhythm; they're almost sing-songy. But they don't seem sappy or wrong in this poem; they seem painfully sincere. The author uses place (as described by the compass) and time (the whole week, the reference to noon and midnight) to make very clear, in case we hadn't figured it out from the preceding lines, that his lover was everything to him. In the fourth line of this section, this regular rhythm is interrupted, or even stopped dead: "I thought that love would last for ever: I was wrong." This is a very true and moving conclusion to reach, but it also seems ironic, once we read to the end of the poem. If the speaker was wrong to believe (before the death of his lover) that love would last forever, isn't it possible that he's wrong about the conclusion "nothing now can ever come to any good"—that grief will last forever.

I think that Auden probably intended us to be aware of this irony. It seems to me that the poem is broken into three major parts. First, we sympathize with the speaker's grief and sense of loss. Then we're supposed to stop at the point where the speaker makes a judgment about his understanding of the world prior to that loss ("I thought that love would last for ever: I was wrong") and to spend a moment absorbing the meaning of that judgment. Finally, as we read the most extreme expression of the speaker's loss ("Pack up the moon and dismantle the sun"), we can see that although we sympathize and understand, we also know something that the speaker doesn't know at the moment. Just as his love apparently blinded the speaker to love's inevitable end, his profound grief is probably blinding him to grief's inevitable end. Also, it may just be me, but it seems that this last part is almost too dramatic or theatrical, as if maybe the speaker has made some sort of transition from being unself-consciously mournful to being self-consciously aware that the way he's expressing himself is poetic.

Back to the idea about the irony: The poem itself seems to be arguing against the notion that love cannot last forever (or, okay, a very long time). After all, people are still reading this poem, and I bet people will continue to read it for as long as people read poetry. That's about as close to forever as we get on this earth, so even though the lovers of this poem are long dead, their love lives on, in a way. Auden must have been aware of this when he was writing the poem. I wonder if he ever said anything in letters, essays, or speeches about art and immortality? If so, I think I'll write a paper on that topic as addressed in this poem.

SAMPLE WRITING

The following sample essay develops the observations about Aphra Behn's "On Her Loving Two Equally" in this chapter, demonstrating how you can turn notes about a poem into a coherent, well-structured essay. As this essay also shows, however, you will often discover new ways of looking at a poem (or any literary text) in the very process of writing about it. (For guidelines on correctly quoting and citing poetry, see "Writing about Literature," chapter 36.)

The writer begins by considering why she is drawn to the poem, even though it does not express her ideal of love. She then uses her personal response to the poem as a starting point for analyzing it in greater depth.

Multiplying by Dividing in Aphra Behn's "On Her Loving Two Equally"

My favorite poem in "Reading, Responding, Writing" is Aphra Behn's "On Her Loving Two Equally"—not because it expresses my ideal of love, but because it challenges conventional ideals. The main ideal or assumption explored in the poem is that true love is exclusive and monogamous, as the very titles of two other poems in the chapter and the "Romantic Love" album insist: "How Do *I* [singular] Love *Thee* [singular]?" or "To *My* Dear and Loving [and One and Only] Husband." The mere title of Behn's poem upsets that idea by insisting that at least one woman is capable of "Loving Two Equally." In fact, one thing that is immediately interesting about Behn's poem is that, though it poses and explores a question, its question is not "Can a woman love two equally?" The title and the poem take it for granted that she can. Instead, the poem asks whether equally loving two people lessens the power or quality of love—or, as the speaker puts it in the first two lines, "How strongly does my passion flow, / Divided equally twixt two?" Every aspect of this poem suggests that when it comes to love, as opposed to math, "division" leads to multiplication.

This answer grabs attention because it is so counterintuitive and unconventional. Forget love for just a minute: It's common sense that anything that is "divided" is smaller and weaker than something unified. In math, for example, division is the opposite of multiplication; if we divide one number by another, we get a number smaller than the first number, if not the second. Although Behn's use of the word *flow* to frame her question compares love to a river instead of a number, the implication is the same: When a river divides into two streams, each of them is smaller than the river, and its flow less strong; as a result, each stream is more easily dammed up or diverted than the undivided river. So the way the speaker initially poses her question seems to support the conventional view: Love is stronger when it "flows" toward one person, weaker when divided between two.

However conventional and comforting that implied answer, however, it's one the poem immediately rejects. In the remaining lines of the first stanza, the speaker insists that each of her two lovers and the love she feels for him has *not* lessened the strength of her feelings for the other, but the reverse. Each lover and each love has "aid[ed]" (line 6) the other, making him and it more "powerful" (line 5). Indeed, she says, neither man would have "subdued [her] heart" (line 3) or "gain[ed her] love" (line 6) at all if the other hadn't done so as well.

In the second stanza, the speaker gives us a somewhat more concrete sense of why and how this might be the case. On the one hand, being with either one of these men ("When Alexis present is," line 7) actually makes her both "scorn" him (line 10) and "miss" (line 9) the man who's not there ("I for Damon sigh and mourn," line 8). This isn't really a paradox; we often yearn more for the person or thing we don't have (the grass is always greener on the *other* side of the fence), and we often lose our appreciation for nearby, familiar things and people. What is far away and inaccessible is often dearer to us because its absence either makes us aware of what it means to us or allows us to forget its flaws and idealize it.

Perhaps because all of this makes the speaker feel that she can't possibly solve the problem by herself, the speaker turns in the third stanza to Cupid—the deity who is supposed to control these things by shooting a "golden-pointed dart" (line 15) into the heart of each lover. She asks him to solve her dilemma for her by "tak[ing] back" her love for either Damon or Alexis (line 15). As with her question in the first stanza, however, this plea is taken back as soon as it's formulated, for if she loses Damon, "all [her] hopes are crossed"; if she loses Alexis, she is "lost" (lines 17–18).

Here and throughout the poem, the speaker's main preoccupation seems to be what *she* feels and what this situation is like for *her*—"*my* passion" (line 1), "*my* heart" (line 3), "*my* Damon's aid, . . . *my* love" (line 6), "*my* Alexis" (line 7), "*I* . . . sigh and mourn" (line 8), "*I* do miss" (line 9), "*my* scorn" (line 10), "*I* languish, sigh, and die" (line 12), "This restless fever in *my* blood" (line 14), "*my* hopes" (line 17), "*my* Alexis" and "*I* am lost" (line 18). Yet the poem implies that the payoff here is not hers alone and that her feelings are not purely selfish. Both times the word *gain* appears in the poem, for example, her lovers' gains and feelings are the focus—the fact that Alexis is able "to gain [her] love" thanks to "Damon's aid" (line 6) and that "Damon gains nothing but my scorn" when she is missing Alexis (line 10). Moreover, ambiguous wording in the first stanza suggests that the men here may be actively, intentionally helping to create this situation and even themselves acting in contradictory, selfish and unselfish, ways. For when the speaker says that "Damon had ne'er subdued my heart / Had not Alexis took his part" (lines 3–4), *his* could refer to Alexis or Damon and *part* could mean "a portion" (of her "heart," presumably), "a role" (in her life or in this courtship drama), or a "side in a dispute or conflict" (over and for her love). Thus, she could be saying that Alexis (unselfishly) defended Damon's suit; (selfishly) fought against Damon or took a share or role that properly belonged to Damon; and/or (neutrally) took his (Alexis's) own share or role or defended his (Alexis's) own cause. Perhaps all of this *has* been the case at various times; people do behave in contradictory ways when they are in love, especially when they perceive that they have a rival. It's also true that men and women alike often more highly prize something or someone that someone else prizes, too. So perhaps each lover's "passion" for her also "flow[s]" more strongly than it would otherwise precisely because he has a rival.

In the end, the poem thus seems to say that love *doesn't* flow or work like a river because love isn't a tangible or quantifiable thing. As a result, love is also different from the sort of battle conjured up by the martial language of the first stanza in which someone wins only if someone else loses. The poem attributes this to the perversity of the human heart—especially our tendency to yearn for what we can't have and what we think other people want, too.

Through its form, the poem demonstrates that division can increase instead of lessen meaning, as well as love. On the one hand, just as the poem's content stresses the power of the love among *three people,* so the poem's form also stresses "threeness" as well as "twoness." It is after all divided into *three* distinctly numbered stanzas, and each stanza consists of *three* sentences. On the other hand, every *sentence* is "divided equally twixt two" *lines,* just as the speaker's "passion" is divided equally between two men. Formally, then, the poem mirrors the kinds of division it describes. Sound and especially rhyme reinforce this pattern since the two lines that make up one sentence usually rhyme with each other to form a couplet. The only lines that don't conform to this pattern come at the beginning of the second stanza where we instead have alternating rhyme—*is* (line 7) rhymes with *miss* (line 9), *mourn* (line 8) rhymes with *scorn* (line 10). But here, again, form reinforces content. For these lines describe how the speaker "miss[es]" one man when the other is "by," a sensation that she arguably reproduces in us as we read by ensuring we twice "miss" the rhyme that the rest of the poem leads us to expect.

Because of the way it challenges our expectations and our conventional ideas about romantic love, the poem might well make us uncomfortable, perhaps all the more so because the speaker and poet here are female. For though we tend to think all true lovers should be loyal and monogamous, this has been expected even more of women than of men. What the poem says about love might make more sense and seem less strange and even objectionable, however, if we think of other, nonromantic kinds of love: After all, do we really think that our mother and father love us less if their love is "divided equally twixt" ourselves and our siblings, or do we love each of our parents less because there are two of *them*? If we think of these familial kinds of love, it becomes much easier to accept Behn's suggestion that love multiplies when we spread it around.

WORK CITED

Behn, Aphra. "On Her Loving Two Equally." *The Norton Introduction to Literature.* Eds. Alison Booth and Kelly J. Mays. 10th ed. New York: Norton, 2010. Print.

Romantic Love: An Album

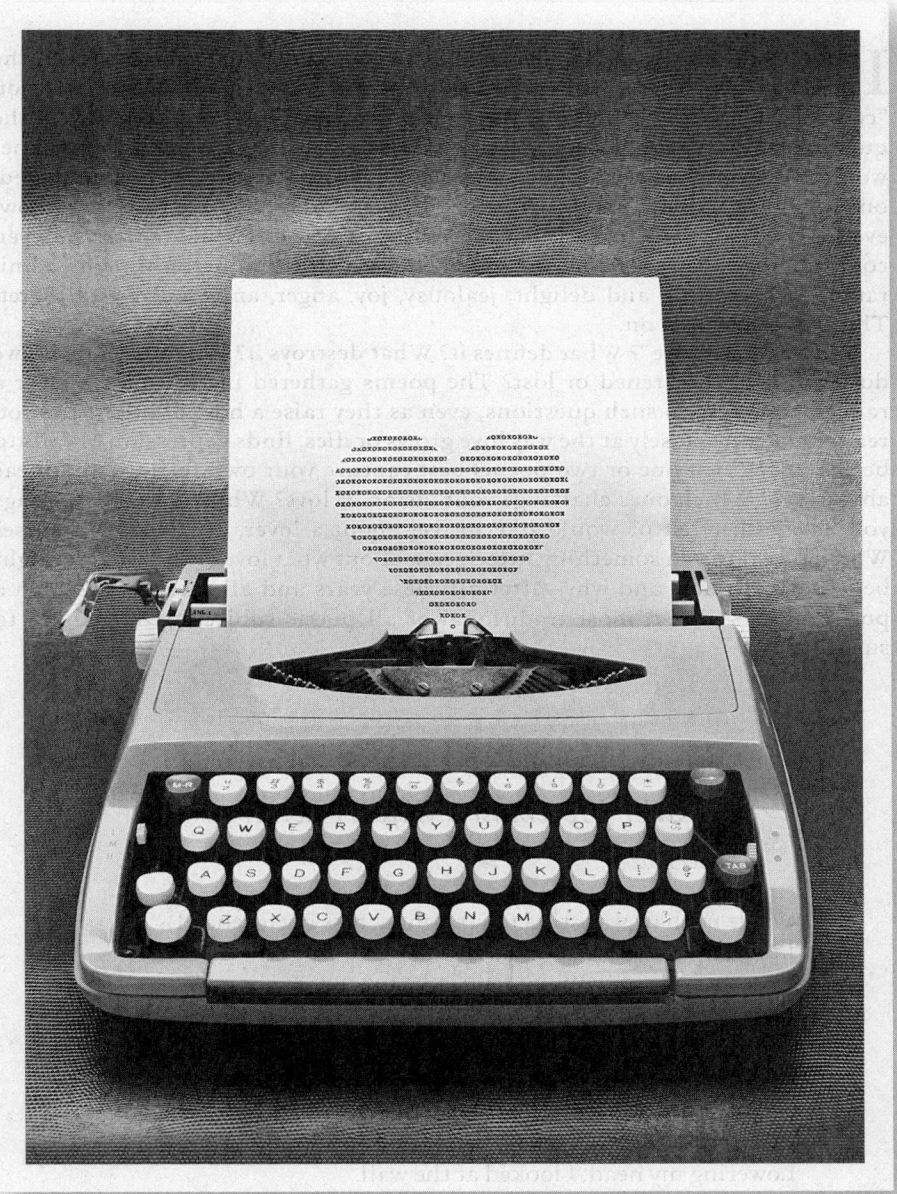

Said Elizabeth . . . , "I wonder who first discovered the efficacy of poetry in driving away love!"
"I have been used to consider poetry as the food of love," said Darcy.
"Of a fine, stout, healthy love it may. Everything nourishes what is strong already. But if it be only a slight, thin sort of inclination, I am convinced that one good sonnet will starve it entirely away."

—JANE AUSTEN, *Pride and Prejudice*

If poetry is a way to probe, understand, and express our emotions, then the emotion most readily associated with poetry is love. Whether or not you "consider poetry as the food of love" (as does Jane Austen's Mr. Darcy) or the quickest way to starve it right out of existence (as Austen's Elizabeth Bennet would have it), there is no doubt that poetry has, over the ages, fed, even feasted, on the feeling we call *love*. What some of the greatest poetry reminds us, however, is that romantic love is not one emotion but innumerable different, even contradictory ones—desire, lust, excitement, and affection; astonishment, admiration, desperation, and delight; jealousy, joy, anger, annoyance, and regret. The list goes on and on.

What is "true love"? What defines it? What destroys it? What on earth do we do when it is threatened or lost? The poems gathered in this album offer a range of answers to such questions, even as they raise a host of others. As you read them, look closely at the way love grows or dies, finds expression or fails to be shared. Which one or two poems best capture your own feelings and ideas about love? Which ones challenge your vision of love? Which describe feelings you have either felt or would like to feel about a lover, a partner, a spouse? Which reveal to you something utterly new about what love is and what it might be? Above all, how and why—after all these years and all these words—can a poem on this oldest, most traditional of all poetic subjects still manage to surprise?

EZRA POUND

The River-Merchant's Wife: A Letter

(after Rihaku)[1]

While my hair was still cut straight across my forehead
I played about the front gate, pulling flowers.
You came by on bamboo stilts, playing horse,
You walked about my seat, playing with blue plums.
5 And we went on living in the village of Chokan:
Two small people, without dislike or suspicion.

At fourteen I married My Lord you.
I never laughed, being bashful.
Lowering my head, I looked at the wall.
10 Called to, a thousand times, I never looked back.

---

1. The Japanese name for Li Po, an eighth-century Chinese poet. Pound's poem is a loose paraphrase of one by Li Po.

At fifteen I stopped scowling,
I desired my dust to be mingled with yours
For ever and for ever and for ever.
Why should I climb the look out?

15 At sixteen you departed,
You went into far Ku-to-yen, by the river of swirling eddies,
And you have been gone five months.
The monkeys make sorrowful noise overhead.

You dragged your feet when you went out.
20 By the gate now, the moss is grown, the different mosses,
Too deep to clear them away!

The leaves fall early this autumn, in wind.
The paired butterflies are already yellow with August
Over the grass in the West garden;
25 They hurt me. I grow older.
If you are coming down through the narrows of the river Kiang,
Please let me know beforehand,
And I will come out to meet you
      As far as Cho-fu-Sa.

                                                              1915

- How have the speaker's feelings about her husband changed over
  time? How do you know?

W. H. AUDEN

[*Stop all the clocks, cut off the telephone*]

Stop all the clocks, cut off the telephone,
Prevent the dog from barking with a juicy bone,
Silence the pianos and with muffled drum
Bring out the coffin, let the mourners come.

5 Let aeroplanes circle moaning overhead
Scribbling on the sky the message He Is Dead,
Put crêpe bows round the white necks of the public doves,
Let the traffic policemen wear black cotton gloves.

He was my North, my South, my East and West,
10 My working week and my Sunday rest,
My noon, my midnight, my talk, my song;
I thought that love would last for ever: I was wrong.

The stars are not wanted now: put out every one;
Pack up the moon and dismantle the sun;
15 Pour away the ocean and sweep up the wood;
For nothing now can ever come to any good.

                                                    ca. 1936

- Whom does the speaker of this poem seem to be addressing? Why might the poet have proclaimed his grief with such a public declaration as this poem?

ANNE BRADSTREET

To My Dear and Loving Husband

If ever two were one, then surely we.
If ever man were loved by wife, then thee;
If ever wife was happy in a man,
Compare with me ye women if you can.
5 I prize thy love more than whole mines of gold,
Or all the riches that the East doth hold.
My love is such that rivers cannot quench,
Nor aught but love from thee give recompense.
Thy love is such I can no way repay;
10 The heavens reward thee manifold, I pray.
Then while we live, in love let's so persever,
That when we live no more we may live ever.

1678

- How does Bradstreet's strategy of characterizing her love through a series of comparisons compare with Barrett Browning's strategy in "How Do I Love Thee?"

WILLIAM SHAKESPEARE

[Let me not to the marriage of true minds]

Let me not to the marriage of true minds
Admit impediments.[2] Love is not love
Which alters when it alteration finds,
Or bends with the remover to remove:
5 Oh, no! it is an ever-fixèd mark,
That looks on tempests and is never shaken;
It is the star to every wandering bark,
Whose worth's unknown, although his height be taken.[3]
Love's not Time's fool, though rosy lips and cheeks
10 Within his bending sickle's compass come;
Love alters not with his brief hours and weeks,
But bears it out even to the edge of doom.

2. The Church of England's Marriage Service contains this address to the witnesses: "If any of you know cause or just impediments why these persons should not be joined together. . . ."
3. That is, measuring the altitude of stars (for purposes of navigation) is not a way to measure value.

If this be error and upon me proved,
I never writ, nor no man ever loved.

1609

- What might the speaker mean when he says that love doesn't "ben[d] with the remover to remove" (line 4)? How might the rest of the poem explain and develop this statement?

SHARON OLDS

Last Night

The next day, I am almost afraid.
Love? It was more like dragonflies
in the sun, 100 degrees at noon,
the ends of their abdomens stuck together, I
5 close my eyes when I remember. I hardly
knew myself, like something twisting and
twisting out of a chrysalis,
enormous, without language, all
head, all shut eyes, and the humming
10 like madness, the way they writhe away,
and do not leave, back, back,
away, back. Did I know you? No kiss,
no tenderness—more like killing, death-grip
holding to life, genitals
15 like violent hands clasped tight
barely moving, more like being closed
in a great jaw and eaten, and the screaming
I groan to remember it, and when we started
to die, then I refuse to remember,
20 the way a drunkard forgets. After,
you held my hands extremely hard as my
body moved in shudders like the ferry when its
axle is loosed past engagement, you kept me
sealed exactly against you, our hairlines
25 wet as the arc of a gateway after
a cloudburst, you secured me in your arms till I slept—
that was love, and we woke in the morning
clasped, fragrant, buoyant, that was
the morning after love.

1996

- What comparison is the speaker of this poem making between "dragonflies / in the sun" and a night of love-making (lines 2–3)? What other comparisons are made in the poem? How do they work together?

JOHN DONNE

The Sun Rising

Busy old fool, unruly sun,
   Why dost thou thus,
Through windows, and through curtains, call on us?
Must to thy motions lovers' seasons run?
5   Saucy pedantic wretch, go chide
      Late schoolboys, and sour prentices,[4]
   Go tell court-huntsmen that the king will ride,
   Call country ants[5] to harvest offices;
Love, all alike, no season knows, nor clime,
10 Nor hours, days, months, which are the rags of time.
      Thy beams, so reverend and strong
      why shouldst thou think?
   I could eclipse and cloud them with a wink,
   But that I would not lose her sight so long:
15   If her eyes have not blinded thine,
      Look, and tomorrow late, tell me
   Whether both the Indias[6] of spice and mine
   Be where thou left'st them, or lie here with me.
Ask for those kings whom thou saw'st yesterday,
20 And thou shalt hear, all here in one bed lay.

      She is all states, and all princes I,
      Nothing else is.
   Princes do but play us; compared to this,
   All honor's mimic,[7] all wealth alchemy.
25   Thou, sun, art half as happy as we,
      In that the world's contracted thus;
   Thine age asks[8] ease, and since thy duties be
   To warm the world, that's done in warming us.
Shine here to us, and thou art every where;
30 This bed thy center[9] is, these walls thy sphere.

                                        1633

- **What does the poem as a whole suggest about how and why the
  world has "contracted" for the speaker (line 26)?**

EDNA ST. VINCENT MILLAY

[Women have loved before as I love now]

Women have loved before as I love now;
At least, in lively chronicles of the past—

---

4. Apprentices.   5. Farmworkers.   6. The East and West Indies, commercial sources of spices and gold.
7. Hypocritical.   8. Requires.   9. Of orbit.

Of Irish waters by a Cornish prow
Or Trojan waters by a Spartan mast
5 Much to their cost invaded—here and there,
Hunting the amorous line, skimming the rest,
I find some woman bearing as I bear
Love like a burning city in the breast.
I think however that of all alive
10 I only in such utter, ancient way
Do suffer love; in me alone survive
The unregenerate passions of a day
When treacherous queens, with death upon the tread,
Heedless and wilful, took their knights to bed.

1931

- What does this poem imply about the difference between ancient and modern ways of loving?

[*I, being born a woman and distressed*]

I, being born a woman and distressed
By all the needs and notions of my kind,
Am urged by your propinquity to find
Your person fair, and feel a certain zest
5 To bear your body's weight upon my breast:
So subtly is the fume of life designed,
To clarify the pulse and cloud the mind,
And leave me once again undone, possessed.
Think not for this, however, the poor treason
10 Of my stout blood against my staggering brain,
I shall remember you with love, or season
My scorn with pity,—let me make it plain:
I find this frenzy insufficient reason
For conversation when we meet again.

1923

- What feelings are expressed here? What does the poem imply about the source or cause of these feelings?

ROBERT BROWNING

Porphyria's Lover[1]

The rain set early in tonight,
The sullen wind was soon awake,
It tore the elm-tops down for spite,

1. Monologue originally published under the title *Madhouse Cells*.

        And did its worst to vex the lake:
5   I listened with heart fit to break.
      When glided in Porphyria; straight
         She shut the cold out and the storm,
      And kneeled and made the cheerless grate
         Blaze up, and all the cottage warm;
10   Which done, she rose, and from her form
      Withdrew the dripping cloak and shawl,
         And laid her soiled gloves by, untied
      Her hat and let the damp hair fall,
         And, last, she sat down by my side
15   And called me. When no voice replied,
      She put my arm about her waist,
         And made her smooth white shoulder bare,
      And all her yellow hair displaced,
         And, stooping, made my cheek lie there,
20   And spread, o'er all, her yellow hair,
      Murmuring how she loved me—she
         Too weak, for all her heart's endeavor,
      To set its struggling passion free
         From pride, and vainer ties dissever,
25   And give herself to me forever.
      But passion sometimes would prevail,
         Nor could tonight's gay feast restrain
      A sudden thought of one so pale
         For love of her, and all in vain:
30   So, she was come through wind and rain.
      Be sure I looked up at her eyes
         Happy and proud; at last I knew
      Porphyria worshiped me: surprise
         Made my heart swell, and still it grew
35   While I debated what to do.
      That moment she was mine, mine, fair,
         Perfectly pure and good: I found
      A thing to do, and all her hair
         In one long yellow string I wound
40   Three times her little throat around,
      And strangled her. No pain felt she;
         I am quite sure she felt no pain.
      As a shut bud that holds a bee,
         I warily oped her lids: again
45   Laughed the blue eyes without a stain.
      And I untightened next the tress
         About her neck; her cheek once more
      Blushed bright beneath my burning kiss:
         I propped her head up as before,
50   Only, this time my shoulder bore
      Her head, which droops upon it still:
         The smiling rosy little head,

So glad it has its utmost will,
    That all it scorned at once is fled,
55   And I, its love, am gained instead!
Porphyria's love: she guessed not how
    Her darling one wish would be heard.
And thus we sit together now,
    And all night long we have not stirred
60   And yet God has not said a word!

1836, 1842

- At what point in the poem did you first suspect that the speaker might harm his love? Why does he do it?

MARGARET CAVENDISH, DUCHESS OF NEWCASTLE

Of the Theme of Love

O Love, how thou art tired out with rhyme!
Thou art a tree whereon all poets climb;
And from thy branches every one takes some
Of thy sweet fruit, which fancy feeds upon.
5 But now thy tree is left so bare and poor
That they can hardly gather one plum more.

late 17th century

- Why does the speaker complain that "thy tree is left so bare and poor" (line 5)?

SUGGESTIONS FOR WRITING

1. Of all the love poems in this album, which one would you most like to have addressed to you? which least? Write an essay in which you answer the author of either poem you have chosen, explaining what seemed to you most (or least) complimentary in what the poem said about you.
2. Which of the poems in this album or in the preceding chapter ("Poetry: Reading, Responding, Writing") do you find most moving, and why? Write a short response paper or essay in which you explore your response and explain when, how, and why the poem evoked it. What about the situation, relationship, or feelings described in the poem do you find especially moving? What aspects of the poem itself do you find most moving, and why?
3. Consider your responses to all the poems in this album. Which one most accurately expresses your ideal of love? Why do you think so? What does your choice say about you? Write an essay in which you reflect on how these poems reinforce, refine, or perhaps challenge your views of love.

Understanding the Text

13 THEME AND TONE

Poetry is full of surprises. Poems express anger or outrage just as effectively as love or sadness, and good poems can be written about going to a rock concert or having lunch or mowing the lawn, as well as about making love or smelling flowers or listening to Beethoven. Even poems on "predictable" subjects can surprise us with unpredicted attitudes, unusual events, or sudden twists. Knowing that a poem is about some particular subject or topic—love, for example, or death—may give us a general idea of what to expect, but it never tells us altogether what we will find in a particular poem. Labeling a poem a "love poem" or a "death poem" is a convenient way to speak of its topic. But poems that may be loosely called "love poems" or "death poems" may have little else in common, may express utterly different attitudes or ideas, and may concentrate on very different aspects of the subject. Letting a poem speak to us means more than merely figuring out its topic; it means listening to *how* the poem says what it says. *What* a poem says involves its **theme**. *How* a poem makes that statement involves its **tone**—the poem's attitude or feelings toward the theme. No two poems on the same subject affect us in exactly the same way; their themes and tones vary, and even similar themes may be expressed in various ways, creating different tones and effects.

Tone, a term borrowed from acoustics and music, refers to the qualities of the language a speaker uses in social situations or in a poem, and it also refers to a speaker's intended effect. Tone is closely related to style and diction; it is an effect of the speaker's expressions, *as if* showing a real person's feelings, manner, and attitude or relationship to a listener and to the particular subject or situation. (Note that the speaker of a poem does not necessarily represent the voice of the author, as we discuss in chapter 14.) Thus, the speaker may use angry or mocking words, may address the listener intimately or distantly, may sincerely confess or coolly observe, may paint a grand picture or narrate a legend. Our response to the tone of the poem, however it surprises or jars or stirs us, becomes a starting point for a clearer restatement of the poem's subject and theme(s).

The tone of a poem thus guides us to understand its theme (or themes): what the poem expresses about its topic. A theme is not simply a work's subject or its topic; it is a statement *about* that topic. Although we can usually agree on what a poem is about without much difficulty, it is harder to determine how to state a poem's theme. Not only may a theme be expressed in several different ways, but also many poems arguably have more than one theme. Sometimes the poet explicitly states a poem's theme, and such a statement may clarify why the author chose a particular mode of presentation and how the poem fits into the author's own patterns of thinking and growing. However, the author's words may give a misleading view of how most people read the poem, just as a person's self-assessment may not be all we need in order to understand his or her character. Further study of the poem is necessary to understand how it fulfills—or fails to fulfill—the author's intentions. Despite the difficulty of identifying and expressing themes, doing so is an important step in understanding and writing about poetry.

LISTENING TO TONE

Reading two or more poems with similar topics side by side may suggest how each is distinctive in what it has to say and how it does so—its theme and tone. The following poems differ widely from those in the previous chapter and from each other. Each focuses on a striking topic that pushes the limits of what was commonly considered polite for conversation—or poetry—at the time it was written. The tones of these poems vary according to the situation and the implied attitude of the speaker and the reader. Arguably, some have similar topics, and some could be said to include themes such as *Love is dangerous* or *Desire can be deadly*. But each unique poem makes its own statements about specific topics that have broad significance.

MARGE PIERCY

Barbie Doll

This girlchild was born as usual
and presented dolls that did pee-pee
and miniature GE stoves and irons
and wee lipsticks the color of cherry candy.
5 Then in the magic of puberty, a classmate said:
You have a great big nose and fat legs.

She was healthy, tested intelligent,
possessed strong arms and back,
abundant sexual drive and manual dexterity.
10 She went to and fro apologizing.
Everyone saw a fat nose on thick legs.

She was advised to play coy,
exhorted to come on hearty,
exercise, diet, smile and wheedle.
15 Her good nature wore out
like a fan belt.
So she cut off her nose and her legs
and offered them up.

In the casket displayed on satin she lay
20 with the undertaker's cosmetics painted on,
a turned-up putty nose,
dressed in a pink and white nightie.
Doesn't she look pretty? everyone said.
Consummation at last.
25 To every woman a happy ending.

1973

W. D. SNODGRASS

Leaving the Motel

Outside, the last kids holler
Near the pool: they'll stay the night.
Pick up the towels; fold your collar
Out of sight.

5   Check: is the second bed
Unrumpled, as agreed?
Landlords have to think ahead
In case of need,

Too. Keep things straight: don't take
10 The matches, the wrong keyrings—
We've nowhere we could keep a keepsake—
Ashtrays, combs, things

That sooner or later others
Would accidentally find.
15 Check: take nothing of one another's
And leave behind

Your license number only,
Which they won't care to trace;
We've paid. Still, should such things get lonely,
20 Leave in their vase

An aspirin to preserve
Our lilacs, the wayside flowers
We've gathered and must leave to serve
A few more hours;

25 That's all. We can't tell when
We'll come back, can't press claims,
We would no doubt have other rooms then,
Or other names.

                                        1968

THOM GUNN

In Time of Plague

My thoughts are crowded with death
and it draws so oddly on the sexual
that I am confused
confused to be attracted
5   by, in effect, my own annihilation.
Who are these two, these fiercely attractive men

who want me to stick their needle in my arm?
They tell me they are called Brad and John,
one from here, one from Denver, sitting the same
10 on the bench as they talk to me,
their legs spread apart, their eyes attentive.
I love their daring, their looks, their jargon,
and what they have in mind.
Their mind is the mind of death.

15 They know it, and do not know it,
and they are like me in that
(I know it, and do not know it)
and like the flow of people through this bar.
Brad and John thirst heroically together
20 for euphoria—for a state of ardent life
in which we could all stretch ourselves
and lose our differences. I seek
to enter their minds: am I a fool,
and they direct and right, properly
25 testing themselves against risk,
as a human must, and does,
or are they the fools, their alert faces
mere death's heads lighted glamorously?

I weigh possibilities
30 till I am afraid of the strength
of my own health
and of their evident health.

They get restless at last with my indecisiveness
and so, first one, and then the other,
35 move off into the moving concourse of people
who are boisterous and bright
carrying in their faces and throughout their bodies
the news of life and death.

1992

ETHERIDGE KNIGHT

Hard Rock Returns to Prison from the Hospital
for the Criminal Insane

Hard Rock was "known not to take no shit
From nobody," and he had the scars to prove it:
Split purple lips, lumped ears, welts above
His yellow eyes, and one long scar that cut
5 Across his temple and plowed through a thick
Canopy of kinky hair.

The WORD was that Hard Rock wasn't a mean nigger
Anymore, that the doctors had bored a hole in his head,
Cut out part of his brain, and shot electricity
10 Through the rest. When they brought Hard Rock back,
Handcuffed and chained, he was turned loose,
Like a freshly gelded stallion, to try his new status.
And we all waited and watched, like indians at a corral,
To see if the WORD was true.

15 As we waited we wrapped ourselves in the cloak
Of his exploits: "Man, the last time, it took eight
Screws to put him in the Hole."[1] "Yeah, remember when he
Smacked the captain with his dinner tray?" "He set
The record for time in the Hole—67 straight days!"
20 "Ol Hard Rock! man, that's one crazy nigger."
And then the jewel of a myth that Hard Rock had once bit
A screw on the thumb and poisoned him with syphilitic spit.

The testing came, to see if Hard Rock was really tame.
A hillbilly called him a black son of a bitch
25 And didn't lose his teeth, a screw who knew Hard Rock
From before shook him down and barked in his face.
And Hard Rock did *nothing*. Just grinned and looked silly,
His eyes empty like knot holes in a fence.

And even after we discovered that it took Hard Rock
30 Exactly 3 minutes to tell you his first name,
We told ourselves that he had just wised up,
Was being cool; but we could not fool ourselves for long,
And we turned away, our eyes on the ground. Crushed.
He had been our Destroyer, the doer of things
35 We dreamed of doing but could not bring ourselves to do,
The fears of years, like a biting whip,
Had cut grooves too deeply across our backs.

                                                1968

These poems approach a range of topics from unusual angles (and situations) and using different tones. "Barbie Doll" has an objective or distant speaker who retells a kind of legend (albeit with familiar twentieth-century toys) about the grotesque life and early death of a "girlchild" who is expected to embody the perfect beauty of a Barbie doll. The title and details of "Leaving the Motel" indicate that two secret lovers are at the end of an afternoon sexual encounter in a motel room (perhaps one is speaking for both of them), reminding themselves not to leave or take with them any clues for "others"—their spouses?—to find. The speaker of "In the Time of Plague" is a participant in the action of the poem; he describes his attraction to two gay men who entice him to share both sex and drugs during the AIDS epidemic in American gay culture—a new manifestation of the plagues that ravaged medieval Europe, as the title suggests. "Hard Rock Returns to Prison

1. Solitary confinement. *Screws*: guards

from the Hospital for the Criminal Insane" tells a story of defeat not unlike "Barbie Doll," but this time the speaker of the poem appears to be the spokesman for a group of fellow African American prisoners who looked up to one unconquerable prisoner as a hero for doing the things they "dreamed of doing," until a lobotomy left him brain damaged.

The set of topics these poems offer us—from illicit and deadly sexuality to the potentially destructive forces of gender, race, and class—is hardly cheerful. But the tone of these poems varies significantly, in keeping with their themes, the ideas or feelings that they express on their subjects.

"Barbie Doll," as the title suggests, satirizes romance plots with happy endings and the commercialized standards of femininity represented by Barbie. However we choose to state the theme—*Girls are willing to kill themselves to live up to the unrealistic body images society pushes on them*, perhaps—that theme is expressed with humor, particularly in the comparisons between a doll and a baby ("did pee-pee," [line 2]) and between the girl and an object of a scientific study ("tested intelligent, / possessed strong arms and back, / abundant sexual drive and manual dexterity," [lines 7–9]). The outcome is also ironically neat: In her pretty coffin (like Sleeping Beauty), she gets the nose and the "consummation" of her dreams, if not with the missing Prince Charming. The playful tone parodying these sinister stereotypes is probably more effective in conveying the theme than a sincere and overt statement of political protest would be. A reader knows the final "happy ending" is ironic, just as the made-up corpse sugar-coats the sad life.

Whereas many poems on the topic of love confirm an enduring attachment or express desire or suggest erotic experience, "Leaving the Motel" focuses on the effort to erase a stolen encounter. Like the "she" of "Barbie Doll," the two lovers in this poem have no names; indeed, they have registered under false names. They have already paid for this temporary shelter, can't stay the night like other guests or build a home with children of their own, and are running through a checklist of their agreements and duties ("Check." "Keep things straight." "Check" [lines 5, 9, 15]). Other than the "wayside" lilacs, the objects are daily trivia (with some hints of association with weddings and marriage), from matches and keyrings to license numbers. The matter-of-fact but hurried tone suggests that they wish to hide any deep feelings (hinted at in the last two stanzas in the wish to make "claims" or preserve flowers). The failure to express love—or guilt—enhances the effect when the tone shifts, at the word "still" (line 19), to the second thoughts about leaving something behind. The poem's short rhyming lines, sounding brisk and somewhat impersonal, contrast with the situation and add to the tone of subdued regret that nothing lasts.

The speaker in Gunn's "In the Time of the Plague" seems to address himself in the present tense—"My thoughts are crowded with death" (line 1)—as if writing a diary while simultaneously experiencing an encounter in a gay bar that ends without incident. The tone of doubt and contradiction, set up by the first lines with the repetition of "confused / confused" (lines 3 and 4), requires that the debate go on silently in his own mind and that words be frequently repeated and balanced with their opposites. "Who are these two," a fearful or even hostile rhetorical question (line 6), receives a hesitant response, weighing "possibilities" (line 29). Both the pair of similar men and the speaker "know" and "do not know" (lines 15 and 17) that their proposition is a deadly idea, an invitation to death. Imagery such as the "death's heads" or skulls suggests a medieval worldview in which the flesh is sinful, corrupt, and transitory. The mixture of grand thoughts about mortality with an informal manner of speech ("one from here, one from Denver, sitting the same") complements the speaker's mixed feelings. He is tempted by the two men and "what they have in mind" (line 13), but the poem is about a mental state rather than a physical action. The tone is carefully poised between excitement and fear—so much so that the two emotions are nearly one; here, lust for life and attraction to death are closely related. The speaker realizes that he is "attracted by . . . my own annihilation" (lines 4–5), and he vacillates in an internal debate between desire and self-protection.

Etheridge Knight's "Hard Rock Returns to Prison from the Hospital for the Criminal Insane" identifies with those who wait; they are hopeful that Hard Rock's spirit has not been broken by lobotomy or shock treatments, and the lines crawl almost to a stop with disappointment in stanza 4. The "*nothing*" (line 27) of Hard Rock's response to taunting and the emptiness of his eyes ("like knot holes in a fence," line 28) reduce the speaker's hopes to despair. The final stanza recounts the observers' attempts to reinterpret, to hang onto hope for their symbol of heroism. But the spirit has gone out of the hero-worshipers, too. The tone of street slang and gossip about an undefeated fighter, which makes the first stanzas so rapid-fire, becomes tame within the single word "Crushed" (line 33). The poem records despair and vain resistance in the grip of a system that can quash even a defiant figure such as Hard Rock.

SETTING AS THEME

The **setting** of a work of literature often makes a powerful statement, serving as the subject of a poem (or story or play) and shaping its theme as well as its tone. Setting is abstract in "Barbie Doll," but in "Leaving the Motel" it determines the title and situation as well as the theme. Certain kinds of setting, such as *the country* or *the city*, have a broad significance in literary tradition. The great metropolises such as Rome, Paris, London, and New York have inspired a large body of poetry as well as visual art, while certain landscapes or natural scenes (the Lake District in England, the West in North America, for example) and certain familiar types of places like the country estate or the family farm have similarly inspired literary themes. Some poems devote many lines to evocative descriptions of setting. In other poems, we can quickly recognize the setting and fill in the details, so the poem may not need to devote much space to description.

In the following poem, the speaker responds to setting as a record of social and political changes—that is, setting develops the poem's theme of protest against injustice and suffering; the tone of the poem conveys outrage and grief, while the author's historical context informs the poem's depiction of the London streets. How does Blake use place to develop the speaker's protest against violence? Does the speaker address a companion, or does he walk alone through the places he wishes the reader to imagine?

WILLIAM BLAKE

London

I wander through each chartered street,
Near where the chartered Thames does flow,
And mark in every face I meet
Marks of weakness, marks of woe.

5 In every cry of every man,
In every Infant's cry of fear,
In every voice, in every ban,
The mind-forged manacles I hear.

How the Chimney-sweeper's cry
10 Every black'ning Church appalls;
And the hapless Soldier's sigh
Runs in blood down Palace walls.

But most through midnight streets I hear
How the youthful Harlot's curse
15 Blasts the new-born Infant's tear,
And blights with plagues the Marriage hearse.

1794

Whereas Etheridge Knight's poem about Hard Rock is set in an actual prison, Blake's "London" envisions an entire metropolis as a kind of mental prison. Blake's speaker appears to be taking a walk through that city ("I wander," line 1), though it might be a repeated action over many occasions. The time (around midnight?) as well as the specific locations (river, church, palace) are unspecific, but everything observed implies multitudes of individuals (*every* infant, lines 5–7; the typical chimney-sweep or prostitute, lines 9 and 14).

The word "chartered," used twice (lines 1 and 2), implies strong feelings, too. The streets, instead of seeming alive with people or bustling with movement, are rigidly, coldly determined, controlled, cramped. Likewise the river seems as if it were planned, programmed, and laid out by an oppressor. In fact, the course of the Thames through the city had been altered (slightly) by the government before Blake's time, but most important is the word's emotional force, the sense it projects of constriction and artificiality: The speaker experiences London as if human artifice had usurped nature. Moreover, according to the poem, people are victimized, "marked" (lines 3 and 4) by their confrontations with the city and its faceless institutions. The "Soldier's sigh" that "runs in blood down Palace walls" (lines 11–12) vividly suggests, through metaphor, both the powerlessness of the individual and the headless violence of power. This description of the city is clearly a subjective, highly emotional, and vivid expression of how the speaker feels about London and what it represents to him. The unidentified, formal speaker at first looks at the miserable people and then listens to a worsening series of voices expressing the social wrongs, from economic to gender oppression. The time of a lifespan is compressed into single lines. The infant is cursed by the "Harlot" (line 14), whose disease infects even those who legitimately marry, making weddings into funerals ("Marriage hearse," line 16).

COMPARING TWO OR MORE POEMS ON SIMILAR TOPICS

The following two poems are about animals, although both of them place their final emphasis on human beings: The animal in each case is only the means to the end of exploring human nature. The poems share the assumption that animal behavior may appear to reflect human habits and conduct, and that it may reveal much about ourselves; in each case the character central to the poem is revealed to be surprisingly unlike the way she thinks of herself. But the poems differ in their tones, in the specific relationship between the woman and the animals, and in their themes.

MAXINE KUMIN

Woodchucks

Gassing the woodchucks didn't turn out right.
The knockout bomb from the Feed and Grain Exchange
was featured as merciful, quick at the bone
and the case we had against them was airtight,
5 both exits shoehorned shut with puddingstone,[2]
but they had a sub-sub-basement out of range.

Next morning they turned up again, no worse
for the cyanide than we for our cigarettes
and state-store Scotch, all of us up to scratch.
10 They brought down the marigolds as a matter of course
and then took over the vegetable patch
nipping the broccoli shoots, beheading the carrots.

The food from our mouths, I said, righteously thrilling
to the feel of the .22, the bullets' neat noses.
15 I, a lapsed pacifist fallen from grace
puffed with Darwinian pieties for killing,
now drew a bead on the littlest woodchuck's face.
He died down in the everbearing roses.

Ten minutes later I dropped the mother. She
20 flipflopped in the air and fell, her needle teeth
still hooked in a leaf of early Swiss chard.
Another baby next. O one-two-three
the murderer inside me rose up hard,
the hawkeye killer came on stage forthwith.

2. A mixture of cement, pebbles, and gravel.

25 There's one chuck left. Old wily fellow, he keeps
me cocked and ready day after day after day.
All night I hunt his humped-up form. I dream
I sight along the barrel in my sleep.
If only they'd all consented to die unseen
30 gassed underground the quiet Nazi way.

1972

ADRIENNE RICH

Aunt Jennifer's Tigers

Aunt Jennifer's tigers prance across a screen,
Bright topaz denizens of a world of green.
They do not fear the men beneath the tree;
They pace in sleek chivalric certainty.

5 Aunt Jennifer's fingers fluttering through her wool
Find even the ivory needle hard to pull.
The massive weight of Uncle's wedding band
Sits heavily upon Aunt Jennifer's hand.

When Aunt is dead, her terrified hands will lie
10 Still ringed with ordeals she was mastered by.
The tigers in the panel that she made
Will go on prancing, proud and unafraid.

1951

Authors on their Work: ADRIENNE RICH

From "When We Dead Awaken" (1971)*

Twenty years after writing "Aunt Jennifer's Tigers," Adrienne Rich said this
about the poem:

> In writing this poem, composed and apparently cool as it is, I thought I
> was creating a portrait of an imaginary woman. But this woman suffers
> from the opposition of her imagination, worked out in tapestry, and her
> lifestyle, "ringed with ordeals she was mastered by." It was important to
> me that Aunt Jennifer was a person as distinct from myself as possible—
> distanced by the formalism of the poem, by its objective, observant
> tone—even by putting the woman in a different generation. In those
> years formalism was part of the strategy—like asbestos gloves, it allowed
> me to handle materials I couldn't pick up bare-handed.

*From "When We Dead Awaken: Writing As Re-Vision," a talk given in December 1971 at the
Women's Forum of the Modern Language Association.

Questions for Comparing Two Poems

Here are some questions and steps for identifying, interpreting, and comparing the topic, theme, and tone of more than one poem. Some of these steps will be familiar to you already, and you may discover other ways to illuminate poetic themes and tones in addition to the guidelines offered here. As you respond to these questions or prompts, be sure to note line numbers to cite your evidence, according to this format: "puddingstone" (line 5) or "her terrified hands will lie / Still ringed with ordeals" (lines 9–10).

1. Read each poem through slowly and carefully.
2. Compare the titles. How do the titles point to the topics and possible themes, and are these similar or different? Take "Woodchucks" and "Aunt Jennifer's Tigers," for example. What different qualities do we associate with woodchucks or tigers, animals rarely kept as pets?
3. What is the situation and setting in each poem? Make a list of the words in each poem that name objects or state physical actions. Which things or scenes are most significant, and how would you visualize or imagine them? Compare and contrast your notes on situation, setting, objects, and actions in both poems.
4. Who are the speakers? Is there an "I" present in the action of either poem, or are the speakers external and unidentified? Are there other people in the poems? Is anyone identified as a listener or auditor? Are any things or beings (such as animals) personified or given human traits? Compare and contrast the speakers and other personalities in the poems.
5. What happens in each poem? Look closely at each stanza. Could the stanzas or lines be rearranged without making a difference? Does one poem tell of a single event or short passage of time, whereas another describes repeated actions or longer periods? Is one poem more eventful than the other?
6. Write down four or five words that describe the tone of first one poem and then the other. Do these words also describe the language or style of each poem? Can you use all or some of the same words for both poems? What is different about the two styles and forms, including length? Notice the rhythms and sounds, any regular or irregular patterns of meter or rhyme, and the shape of the stanzas.
7. Reread the poems and try to express their themes in sentences or phrases. Then try to combine the two themes in a statement that notes similarities and differences between them. Does your statement comparing the themes resemble your comparison of the tone and style of the two poems? Do the themes relate to similar or different historical, political, and social issues or contexts featured in the poems? Do the poems develop their themes with comparable allusions to myth, religion, literature, art, or other familiar or traditional ideas or associations?
8. Combining your notes and responses to the other questions, outline and write an essay comparing the two poems. Your argument on how and why the two poems are different or similar may be chosen from responses to the questions above, and you will be able to cite some of the evidence that you noted in your answers.

As you read "Woodchucks" aloud, how does your tone of voice change from beginning to end? What tone do you use to read the ending? How does the hunter feel about her increasing attraction to violence? Why does the poem begin by calling the gassing of the woodchucks "merciful" and end by describing it as "the quiet Nazi way"? What names does the hunter call herself? How does the name-calling affect your feelings about her? Exactly when does the hunter begin to *enjoy* the feel of the gun and the idea of killing? How does the poet make that clear?

In the second poem, why are tigers a particularly appropriate contrast to the woman embroidering or cross-stitching a hunting scene? What words describing the tigers seem particularly significant? Why are Aunt Jennifer's hands described as "terrified"? What clues does the poem give about why Aunt Jennifer is so afraid? How does the poem make you feel about Aunt Jennifer's life and death? How would you describe the tone of the poem? Why does the poem begin and end with the tigers?

SUGGESTIONS FOR WRITING

1. Choose any two poems in this chapter that associate positive and negative feelings on their topics—for example, the death of a loved one. How do the tones of the poems combine or contrast the feelings about these topics? Is there a shift in tone in each poem? If so, where? How is the shift revealed through language? Write an essay in which you compare and contrast the way each poet accomplishes this shifting of tone.

2. Write an essay in which you consider the use of language to create tone in any two or more poems on the same subject. How do the tones suit the themes of these poems?

3. Write an essay on Maxine Kumin's "Woodchucks" in which you show that the speaker's conflict between sympathy and murderous instinct is reflected in the mixed tone and varied vocabulary. Focus on formal and informal tone, noting phrases from law or religion—"the case we had against them"; "fallen from grace"— or from everyday speech—"up to scratch," "food from our mouths." How does the diction, or word choice, of the poem affect its tone?

4. Imagine W. D. Snodgrass's "Leaving the Motel" as a poem in which the speaker and lover are happy and delighted with each other and certain that the relationship will last forever. What details and phrases would need to be changed for the poem to express a positive feeling about the relationship? Write an essay in which you relate the tone of the poem to the subject of secret and short-lived sexual relationships.

Family: An Album

F amilies are the groundwork of society, and most people's earliest memories
involve family members. Families may be nuclear or extended, biological or
adoptive, emotionally demonstrative or distant. Families may pass down traditions, or younger generations may choose to abandon them. Adults who have
left home may dwell on memories, good or bad, of their mothers, fathers, brothers, or sisters. Each renewed contact with family can spark conflicted thoughts
and feelings. Hope, disappointment, or grief for one's child can find expression as
a concentrated moment in a poem. A spouse or a child can remind the speaker of
the passage of time and mortality.

Because the family is such a basic unit of social interaction, many poems explore
family relations. The following poems are all, in different ways, about families.
What do these poems have in common? How do they differ? Which have the
most unusual situations or relationships compared with the rest? Can you find
two poems that address the same theme—in other words, can you accurately state
their themes in the same way? How do any two poems differ in tone, whether or
not they have similar themes? Which poems have surprising shifts in tone? Do
any poems express surprising or disturbing attitudes toward loved ones? Are
some relatives not beloved?

GALWAY KINNELL

After Making Love We Hear Footsteps

For I can snore like a bullhorn
or play loud music
or sit up talking with any reasonably sober Irishman
and Fergus will only sink deeper
5 into his dreamless sleep, which goes by all in one flash,
but let there be that heavy breathing
or a stifled come-cry anywhere in the house
and he will wrench himself awake
and make for it on the run—as now, we lie together,
10 after making love, quiet, touching along the length of our bodies,
familiar touch of the long-married,
and he appears—in his baseball pajamas, it happens,
the neck opening so small
he has to screw them on, which one day may make him wonder
15 about the mental capacity of baseball players—
and says, "Are you loving and snuggling? May I join?"
He flops down between us and hugs us and snuggles himself to sleep,
his face gleaming with satisfaction at being this very child.

In the half darkness we look at each other
20 and smile
and touch arms across his little, startlingly muscled body—
this one whom habit of memory propels to the ground of his making,
sleeper only the mortal sounds can sing awake,
this blessing love gives again into our arms.

1980

- How does the language in lines 1–5 establish the poem's tone? Do the last lines (starting with line 22) alter the tone in any way?

EMILY GROSHOLZ

Eden

In lurid cartoon colors, the big baby
dinosaur steps backwards under the shadow
of an approaching tyrannosaurus rex.
"His mommy going to fix it," you remark,
5   serenely anxious, hoping for the best.

After the big explosion, after the lights
go down inside the house and up the street,
we rush outdoors to find a squirrel stopped
in straws of half-gnawed cable. I explain,
10   trying to fit the facts, "The squirrel is dead."

No, you explain it otherwise to me.
"He's sleeping. And his mommy going to come."
Later, when the squirrel has been removed,
"His mommy fix him," you insist, insisting
15   on the right to know what you believe.

The world is truly full of fabulous
great and curious small inhabitants,
and you're the freshly minted, unashamed
Adam in this garden. You preside,
20   appreciate, and judge our proper names.

Like God, I brought you here.
Like God, I seem to be omnipotent,
mostly helpful, sometimes angry as hell.
I fix whatever minor faults arise
25   with bandaids, batteries, masking tape, and pills.

But I am powerless, as you must know,
to chase the serpent sliding in the grass,
or the tall angel with the flaming sword
who scares you when he rises suddenly
30   behind the gates of sunset.

1992

- How does Grosholz use language to elevate the poem's subject matter from the trivial and childish to the biblical and profound?

PAUL MULDOON

Milkweed and Monarch

As he knelt by the grave of his mother and father
the taste of dill, or tarragon—
he could barely tell one from the other—

filled his mouth. It seemed as if he might smother.
5   Why should he be stricken
with grief, not for his mother and father,

but a woman slinking from the fur of a sea-otter
in Portland, Maine, or, yes, Portland, Oregon—
he could barely tell one from the other—

10 and why should he now savor
the tang of her, her little pickled gherkin,
as he knelt by the grave of his mother and father?

He looked about. He remembered her palaver
on how both earth and sky would darken—
15 "You could barely tell one from the other"—

while the Monarch butterflies passed over
in their milkweed-hunger: "A wing-beat, some reckon,
may trigger off the mother and father

of all storms, striking your Irish Cliffs of Moher[1]
20 with the force of a hurricane."
Then: "Milkweed and Monarch 'invented' each other."

He looked about. Cow's-parsley[2] in a samovar.
He'd mistaken his mother's name, "Regan," for "Anger":
as he knelt by the grave of his mother and father
25 he could barely tell one from the other.

                                                          1999

- What is the effect of the repeating words "father" and "other" on the tone of the poem? What is the feeling of the poem's final stanza?

ROBERT HAYDEN

Those Winter Sundays

Sundays too my father got up early
and put his clothes on in the blueblack cold,
then with cracked hands that ached

---

1. Tall, rocky cliffs on the coast of western Ireland that are constantly buffeted by the Atlantic.
2. Another name for Queen Anne's lace, a flowering plant with disks of many small, white blossoms, that grows in fields and on roadsides.

from labor in the weekday weather made
5   banked fires blaze. No one ever thanked him.

I'd wake and hear the cold splintering, breaking.
When the rooms were warm, he'd call,
and slowly I would rise and dress,
fearing the chronic angers of that house,

10 Speaking indifferently to him,
who had driven out the cold
and polished my good shoes as well.
What did I know, what did I know
of love's austere and lonely offices?

                                                                1966

- Why does the poem begin with the words "Sundays too" (rather
  than, say, "On Sundays")? What are the "austere and lonely offices"
  of love in the poem's final line?

CLAUDIA EMERSON

Driving Glove

I was unloading groceries from the trunk
of what had been her car, when the glove floated
up from underneath the shifting junk—
a crippled umbrella, the jack, ragged
5   maps. I knew it was not one of yours,
this more delicate, soft, made from the hide
of a kid or lamb. It still remembered
her hand, the creases where her fingers

had bent to hold the wheel, the turn
10 of her palm, smaller than mine. There was
nothing else to do but return it—
let it drift, sink, slow as a leaf through water
to rest on the bottom where I have not
forgotten it remains—persistent in its loss.

                                                                2005

- Given that this poem is part of a collection titled *Late Wife*, what
  can you infer about the three people alluded to in the poem? What
  feelings are revealed by the discovery of the glove?

SEAMUS HEANEY

Mother of the Groom

What she remembers
Is his glistening back
In the bath, his small boots
In the ring of boots at her feet.

5   Hands in her voided lap,
She hears a daughter welcomed.
It's as if he kicked when lifted
And slipped her soapy hold.

Once soap would ease off
10   The wedding ring
That's bedded forever now
In her clapping hand.

                                    1966

- Which words in the poem appear to have double meanings? How does this use of language affect the poem's tone?

JIMMY SANTIAGO BACA

Green Chile

I prefer red chile over my eggs
and potatoes for breakfast.
Red chile *ristras*[3] decorate my door,
dry on my roof, and hang from eaves.
5   They lend open-air vegetable stands
historical grandeur, and gently swing
with an air of festive welcome.
I can hear them talking in the wind,
haggard, yellowing, crisp, rasping
10   tongues of old men, licking the breeze.

        But grandmother loves green chile.
When I visit her,
she holds the green chile pepper
in her wrinkled hands.
15   Ah, voluptuous, masculine,
an air of authority and youth simmers
from its swan-neck stem, tapering to a flowery

---

3. Braided strings of peppers.

collar, fermenting resinous spice.
A well-dressed gentleman at the door
20 my grandmother takes sensuously in her hand,
rubbing its firm glossed sides,
caressing the oily rubbery serpent,
with mouth-watering fulfillment,
fondling its curves with gentle fingers.
25 Its bearing magnificent and taut
as flanks of a tiger in mid-leap,
she thrusts her blade into
and cuts it open, with lust
on her hot mouth, sweating over the stove,
30 bandanna round her forehead,
mysterious passion on her face
and she serves me green chile con carne
between soft warm leaves of corn tortillas,
with beans and rice—her sacrifice
35 to her little prince.
I slurp from my plate
with last bit of tortilla, my mouth burns
and I hiss and drink a tall glass of cold water.

All over New Mexico, sunburned men and women
40 drive rickety trucks stuffed with gunny-sacks
of green chile, from Belen, Veguita, Willard, Estancia,
San Antonio y Socorro, from fields
to roadside stands, you see them roasting green chile
in screen-sided homemade barrels, and for a dollar a bag,
45 we relive this old, beautiful ritual again and again.

                                                              1989

- What different qualities do the red and green chiles have? Which
  words in the poem help personify the chiles? How fully do these
  words reflect the differences between the speaker and the grandmother?

KELLY CHERRY

Alzheimer's

He stands at the door, a crazy old man
Back from the hospital, his mind rattling
Like the suitcase, swinging from his hand,
That contains shaving cream, a piggy bank,
5 A book he sometimes pretends to read,
His clothes. On the brick wall beside him
Roses and columbine slug it out for space, claw the mortar.
The sun is shining, as it does late in the afternoon

In England, after rain.
10 Sun hardens the house, reifies it,
    Strikes the iron grillwork like a smithy
    And sparks fly off, burning in the bushes—
    The rosebushes—
    While the white wood trim defines solidity in space.
15 This is his house. He remembers it as his,
    Remembers the walkway he built between the front room
    And the garage, the rhododendron he planted in back,
    The car he used to drive. He remembers himself,
    A younger man, in a tweed hat, a man who loved
20 Music. There is no time for that now. No time for music,
    The peculiar screeching of strings, the luxurious
    Fiddling with emotion.
    Other things have become more urgent.
    Other matters are now of greater import, have more
25 Consequence, must be attended to. The first
    Thing he must do, now that he is home, is decide who
    This woman is, this old, white-haired woman
    Standing here in the doorway,
    Welcoming him in.

                                                            1997

- How do phrases like "a crazy old man" and "a book he sometimes
  pretends to read" indicate the speaker's feelings toward her father?
  Does her attitude shift at some point? Where?

ANDREW HUDGINS

Begotten

I've never, as some children do,
looked at my folks and thought, I *must*
have come from someone else—
rich parents who'd misplaced me, but
5 who would, as in a myth or novel,
return and claim me. Hell, no. I saw
my face in cousins' faces, heard
my voice in their high drawls. And Sundays,
after the dinner plates were cleared,
10 I lingered, elbow propped on red
oilcloth, and studied great-uncles, aunts,
and cousins new to me. They squirmed.
I stared till I discerned the features
they'd gotten from the family larder:
15 eyes, nose, lips, hair? I stared until,
uncomfortable, they'd snap, "Hey, boy—

what are you looking at? At me?"
"No, sir," I'd lie. "No, ma'am." I'd count ten
and then continue staring at them.
20   I never had to ask, What am I?
I stared at my blood-kin, and thought,
So *this*, dear God, is what I am.

1994

- What can you infer from the language in this poem about the speaker's attitude toward his life? What does the poem's title evoke?

SIMON J. ORTIZ

My Father's Song

Wanting to say things,
I miss my father tonight.
His voice, the slight catch,
the depth from his thin chest,
5   the tremble of emotion
in something he has just said
to his son, his song:

We planted corn one Spring at Aču—
we planted several times
10   but this one particular time
I remember the soft damp sand
in my hand.

My father had stopped at one point
to show me an overturned furrow;
15   the plowshare had unearthed
the burrow nest of a mouse
in the soft moist sand.

Very gently, he scooped tiny pink animals
into the palm of his hand
20   and told me to touch them.
We took them to the edge
of the field and put them in the shade
of a sand moist clod.

I remember the very softness
25   of cool and warm sand and tiny alive mice
and my father saying things.

1976

- What are the "things" that the speaker wants to say? Are they the same things he remembers his father saying? Does the poem itself say these things?

ALBERTO ÁLVARO RÍOS

Mi Abuelo[4]

Where my grandfather is is in the ground
where you can hear the future like an
Indian with his ear at the tracks. A
pipe leads down to him so that sometimes
5 he whispers what will happen to a man
in town or how he will meet the best-
dressed woman tomorrow and how the best
man at her wedding will chew the ground
next to her. Mi abuelo is the man
10 who talks through all the mouths in my house. An
echo of me hitting the pipe sometimes
to stop him from saying "my hair is a
sieve" is the only other sound. It is a
phrase that among all others is the best,
15 he says, and "my hair is a sieve" is sometimes
repeated for hours out of the ground
when I let him, but mostly I don't. "An
abuelo should be much more than a man
like you!" He stops then, and speaks: "I am a man
20 who has served ants with the attitude of a
waiter, who has made each smile as only an
ant who is fat can, and they liked me best,
but there is nothing left." Yet, I know he ground
green coffee beans as a child, and sometimes
25 he will talk about his wife, and sometimes
about when he was deaf and a man
cured him by mail and he heard ground
hogs talking, or about how he walked with a
cane he chewed on when he got hungry. At best,
30 mi abuelo is a liar. I see an
old picture of him at nani's with an
off-white yellow center mustache and sometimes
that's all I know for sure. He talks best
about these hills, slowest waves, and where this man
35 is going, and I'm convinced his hair is a
sieve, that his fever is cool now in the ground.
Mi abuelo is an ordinary man.
I look down the pipe, sometimes, and see a
ripple-topped stream in its best suit, in the ground.

1980

- What is the "pipe" in this poem? What might it mean that "my hair is a sieve"? What are some of the speaker's attitudes toward his grandfather?

---

4. My grandfather.

CHARLES R. FELDSTEIN

Gravity

In the photograph,
my father is about twenty-three,
kneeling in the white sand of some beach.
    He is handsome,
5 like my middle brother,
and surrounded by a quorum of
four young women.

I gently lift the photograph,
stiff with age,
10 from the scrapbook
    and with scissors
rearrange my father's past.
I snip at the woman on his right,
her arm hooked inside his.

15 She is hard to get at,
wedged between my father
and the woman on her right,
    the one with large breasts ready
to tumble from her bathing suit,
20 her mouth open,
turned to his open mouth.

The woman with large breasts
drops, like the other shoe,
along with the woman hooked arm in arm with my father.
25   The third woman, the one on my father's immediate left, is
      bending over,
hands on her knees.
She is looking directly into the camera,
eyes black and turbulent.

Her hair is black, too,
30 scattered like
strips of burned paper.
    Almost certainly my father ran his sandy fingers through that
      hair.
Made promises he did not keep.
I imagine her giving birth to me,
35 the doctor holding me up, handing me to her.

I see the eyes,
scream till my lungs shrivel into two small balloons,
feel the weight of her hands on my back, the weight of a mistake.
    I come out of my daze with a jolt,

40 cut around the eyes first,
then snip away the rest of her.
Cut up, she resembles a tiny tree falling.

The woman remaining squints into the sun and stands
a little back of the others,
45 as if uncertain of her place in the picture,
　　or whether she belongs at all.
She is about twenty and so delicate
she seems the absence of someone, someone
about to perish in the painful light.

50 I stare into this wisp of a woman,
and slip the photograph of my father and her into the scrapbook.
She will not perish on the beach.
　　She will marry my father,
bear him four children,
55 and, always standing in the background,
unseen like gravity, she will hold our world together.

2008

- What is the situation in the present of the poem? What relationships are revealed in the photograph? How does the speaker "rearrange" his own past as well as his father's?

SUGGESTIONS FOR WRITING

1. Choose any two poems in this album that associate positive and negative feelings of one family member toward another. How do the tones shift from one tone to another? Where, in each poem, is this shift of tone? How is the shift revealed through language? Write an essay in which you compare and contrast the way each poet accomplishes this shifting tone.
2. What words in Robert Hayden's "Those Winter Sundays" suggest the son's feelings toward his father and his home? What words indicate that the poet's attitudes have changed since the time depicted in the poem? Write an essay in which you compare the speaker's feelings, as a youth and then later as a man, about his father and his home.
3. Kelly Cherry's "Alzheimer's" uses contrasts—especially before and after—to characterize the ravages of Alzheimer's disease. What evidence does the poem provide about what the man used to be like? What specific changes have come about? How does the setting of the poem suggest some of those changes? In what ways do the stabilities of house, landscape, and other people clarify what has happened? Write an essay about the function of the poem's setting.
4. Write an essay in which you consider the use of language to create tone in two or more poems on the same subject. How do the tones suit the themes of these poems?

14 SPEAKER: WHOSE VOICE DO WE HEAR?

Poems are personal. The thoughts and feelings they express belong to a specific person, and however general or universal their sentiments seem to be, poems come to us as the expression of an individual human voice. That voice is often the voice of the poet, but not always. Poets sometimes create "characters" just as writers of fiction or drama do—people who speak for them only indirectly. A character may, in fact, be very different from the poet, just as a character in a play or story is not necessarily the author, and that person, the **speaker** of the poem, may express ideas or feelings very different from the poet's own. In the following poem, rather than speaking directly to us himself, the poet has created two speakers, both female, each of whom has a distinctive voice, personality, and character. A third speaker here acts as a **narrator**, telling us who said what. (We can thus describe this poem as a **narrative poem** rather than a **lyric**.)

THOMAS HARDY

The Ruined Maid

"O 'Melia,[1] my dear, this does everything crown!
Who could have supposed I should meet you in Town?
And whence such fair garments, such prosperi-ty?"—
"O didn't you know I'd been ruined?" said she.

5 —"You left us in tatters, without shoes or socks,
Tired of digging potatoes, and spudding up docks;[2]
And now you've gay bracelets and bright feathers three!"—
"Yes: that's how we dress when we're ruined," said she.

—"At home in the barton[3] you said 'thee' and 'thou,'
10 And 'thik oon,' and 'theäs oon,' and 't'other'; but now
Your talking quite fits 'ee for high compa-ny!"—
"Some polish is gained with one's ruin," said she.

—"Your hands were like paws then, your face blue and bleak
But now I'm bewitched by your delicate cheek,
15 And your little gloves fit as on any la-dy!"—
"We never do work when we're ruined," said she.

---

1. Short for Amelia.   2. Spading up weeds.   3. Farmyard.

—"You used to call home-life a hag-ridden dream,
And you'd sigh, and you'd sock;[4] but at present you seem
To know not of megrims[5] or melancho-ly!"—
20 "True. One's pretty lively when ruined," said she.

—"I wish I had feathers, a fine sweeping gown,
And a delicate face, and could strut about Town!"—
"My dear—a raw country girl, such as you be,
Cannot quite expect that. You ain't ruined," said she.

1866

The first voice, that of a young woman who has remained back on the farm, is designated typographically (that is, by the way the poem is printed): There are dashes at the beginning and end of all but the first of her speeches. She speaks the first part of each **stanza** (a stanza is a section of a poem designated by spacing), usually the first three lines. The second young woman, a companion and coworker on the farm in years gone by, regularly gets the last line in each stanza (and in the last stanza, two lines), so it is clear who is talking at every point.

The two women are just as clearly distinguished by what they say, how they say it, and what sort of person each proves to be. The nameless stay-at-home shows little knowledge of the world, and everything surprises her: seeing her former companion at all, but especially seeing her well clothed, cheerful, and polished. And as the poem develops she shows increasing envy of her more worldly friend. She is the "raw country girl" (line 23) that the other speaker says she is, and she still speaks the country dialect ("fits 'ee," line 11, for example) that she notices her friend has lost (lines 9–11). The "ruined" young woman ('Melia), on the other hand, says little except the refrain about having been ruined, but even the slight variations she plays on that theme suggest her sophistication and amusement at her rural friend, although she still uses a country "ain't" at the end.

We are not told the full story of their lives (Was the "ruined" young woman thrown out? Did she run away from home or work?), but we know enough (that they've been separated for some time, that the stay-at-home did not know where the other had gone) to allow the dialogue to articulate the contrast between them: One is still rural, inexperienced, and innocent; the other is sophisticated, citified—and "ruined." Each speaker's style of speech then does the rest.

It is equally obvious that there are two speakers (or, in this case, a speaker and a singer) in the following poem: The first functions as a narrator, the second speaks in stanzas 2 through 9.

---

4. Deliver angry blows.   5. Migraine headaches.

X. J. KENNEDY

In a Prominent Bar in Secaucus One Day

To the tune of "The Old Orange Flute" or the tune of
"Sweet Betsy from Pike"

In a prominent bar in Secaucus[6] one day
Rose a lady in skunk with a topheavy sway,
Raised a knobby red finger—all turned from their beer—
While with eyes bright as snowcrust she sang high and clear:

5 "Now who of you'd think from an eyeload of me
That I once was a lady as proud as could be?
Oh I'd never sit down by a tumbledown drunk
If it wasn't, my dears, for the high cost of junk.

"All the gents used to swear that the white of my calf
10 Beat the down of a swan by a length and a half.
In the kerchief of linen I caught to my nose
Ah, there never fell snot, but a little gold rose.

"I had seven gold teeth and a toothpick of gold.
My Virginia cheroot was a leaf of it rolled
15 And I'd light it each time with a thousand in cash—
Why the bums used to fight if I flicked them an ash.

"Once the toast of the Biltmore,[7] the belle of the Taft,
I would drink bottle beer at the Drake, never draft,
And dine at the Astor on Salisbury steak
20 With a clean tablecloth for each bite I did take.

"In a car like the Roxy[8] I'd roll to the track,
A steel-guitar trio, a bar in the back,
And the wheels made no noise, they turned over so fast,
Still it took you ten minutes to see me go past.

25 "When the horses bowed down to me that I might choose,
I bet on them all, for I hated to lose.
Now I'm saddled each night for my butter and eggs
And the broken threads race down the backs of my legs.

"Let you hold in mind, girls, that your beauty must pass
30 Like a lovely white clover that rusts with its grass.
Keep your bottoms off barstools and marry you young
Or be left—an old barrel with many a bung.

"For when time takes you out for a spin in his car
You'll be hard-pressed to stop him from going too far

---

6. Small town on the Hackensack River in New Jersey, a few miles west of Manhattan.
7. Like the Taft, Drake, and Astor, a once-fashionable New York hotel.
8. Luxurious old New York theater and movie house, the site of many "world premieres" in the heyday of Hollywood.

35 And be left by the roadside, for all your good deeds,
Two toadstools for tits and a face full of weeds."

All the house raised a cheer, but the man at the bar
Made a phonecall and up pulled a red patrol car
And she blew us a kiss as they copped her away
40 From that prominent bar in Secaucus, N.J.

1961

Again, we learn about the singer primarily through her own words, although we may not believe everything she tells us about her past. From her introduction in the first stanza we get some general notion of her appearance and condition, but it is she who tells us that she is a junkie (line 8) and a prostitute (lines 27, 32) and that her face and figure have seen better days (lines 32, 36). That information could make her a sad case, and the poem might lament her state or encourage us to lament it, but instead she presents herself in a light, friendly, and theatrical way. The comedy is bittersweet, perhaps, but she is allowed to present herself, through her own words and attitudes, as a likable character—someone who has survived life's disappointments and retained her dignity. The self-portrait accumulates almost completely through how she talks about herself, and the poet develops our attitude toward her by allowing her to recount her story herself, in her own words—or rather in words he has chosen for her.

Sometimes poets "borrow" a character from history and ask readers to factor in historical facts and contexts. In the following poem, for example, the Canadian poet Margaret Atwood draws heavily on facts and traditions about a nineteenth-century émigré from Scotland to Canada. The poem is a lyric spoken in the first person, but its speaker is a fictional character based on a real woman.

MARGARET ATWOOD

Death of a Young Son by Drowning

He, who navigated with success
the dangerous river of his own birth
once more set forth

on a voyage of discovery
5 into the land I floated on
but could not touch to claim.

His feet slid on the bank,
the currents took him;
he swirled with ice and trees in the swollen water

10 and plunged into distant regions,
his head a bathysphere;
through his eyes' thin glass bubbles

he looked out, reckless adventurer
on a landscape stranger than Uranus
15 we have all been to and some remember.

There was an accident; the air locked,
he was hung in the river like a heart.
They retrieved the swamped body,

cairn of my plans and future charts,
20 with poles and hooks
from among the nudging logs.

It was spring, the sun kept shining, the new grass
leapt to solidity;
my hands glistened with details.

25 After the long trip I was tired of waves.
My foot hit rock. The dreamed sails
collapsed, ragged.

I planted him in this country
like a flag.
                                                              1970

The poem comes from a volume called *The Journals of Susanna Moodie: Poems by Margaret Atwood* (1970). A frontier pioneer, Moodie herself wrote two books about Canada, *Roughing It in the Bush* and *Life in the Clearings,* and Atwood found their observations rather stark and disorganized. She wrote her Susanna Moodie poems to refocus the "character" and to reconstruct Moodie's actual geographical exploration and self-discovery. To fully understand these thoughts and meditations, then, we need to know something of the history behind them. Yet even without such knowledge, we can appreciate the poem's powerful evocation of the speaker's situation and feelings.

Some speakers in poems are not nearly so heroic or attractive, and some poems create a speaker we are made to dislike, as the following poem does. A **dramatic monologue**, it consists entirely of the words of a single, fictional speaker in a specific time, place, and dramatic situation, very like a character in a play.

ROBERT BROWNING

Soliloquy of the Spanish Cloister

Gr-r-r—there go, my heart's abhorrence!
    Water your damned flower-pots, do!
If hate killed men, Brother Lawrence,
    God's blood, would not mine kill you!
5 What? your myrtle-bush wants trimming?
    Oh, that rose has prior claims—

Needs its leaden vase filled brimming?
  Hell dry you up with its flames!

At the meal we sit together:
10   *Salve tibi!*[9] I must hear
Wish talk of the kind of weather,
  Sort of season, time of year:
Not a plenteous cork-crop: scarcely
  Dare we hope oak-galls,[1] *I doubt:*
15 *What's the Latin name for "parsley"?*
  What's the Greek name for Swine's Snout?

Whew! We'll have our platter burnished,
  Laid with care on our own shelf!
With a fire-new spoon we're furnished,
20   And a goblet for ourself,
Rinsed like something sacrificial
  Ere 'tis fit to touch our chaps[2]—
Marked with L. for our initial!
  (He-he! There his lily snaps!)

25 *Saint,* forsooth! While brown Dolores
  —Squats outside the Convent bank
With Sanchicha, telling stories,
  Steeping tresses in the tank,
Blue-black, lustrous, thick like horsehairs,
30 —Can't I see his dead eye glow,
Bright as 'twere a Barbary corsair's?[3]
  (That is, if he'd let it show!)

When he finishes refection,
  Knife and fork he never lays
35 Cross-wise, to my recollection,
  As do I, in Jesu's praise.
I the Trinity illustrate,
  Drinking watered orange-pulp—
In three sips the Arian[4] frustrate;
40 —While he drains his at one gulp.

Oh, those melons? If he's able
  We're to have a feast! so nice!
One goes to the Abbot's table,
  All of us get each a slice.
45 How go on your flowers? None double?
  Not one fruit-sort can you spy?
Strange!—And I, too, at such trouble,
  —Keep them close-nipped on the sly!

---

9. Hail to thee (Latin). Italics usually indicate the words of Brother Lawrence.
1. Abnormal growth on oak trees, used for tanning.   2. Jaws.   3. African pirate's.
4. Heretical sect that denied the Trinity.

There's a great text in Galatians,
50   Once you trip on it, entails
Twenty-nine distinct damnations,[5]
     One sure, if another fails:
If I trip him just a-dying,
     Sure of heaven as sure can be,
55 Spin him round and send him flying
     Off to hell, a Manichee?[6]

Or, my scrofulous French novel
     On gray paper with blunt type!
Simply glance at it, you grovel
60   Hand and foot in Belial's gripe:[7]
If I double down its pages
     At the woeful sixteenth print,
When he gathers his greengages,
     Ope a sieve and slip it in't?

65 Or, there's Satan!—one might venture
     Pledge one's soul to him, yet leave
Such a flaw in the indenture
     —As he'd miss till, past retrieve,
Blasted lay that rose-acacia
70   We're so proud of! _Hy, Zy, Hine_ ...[8]
'St, there's Vespers! _Plena gratiâ_
     Ave, Virgo.[9] Gr-r-r—you swine!

1842

Not many poems begin with a growl, and this harsh sound turns out to be fair warning that we are about to meet a real beast, even though he is in the clothing of a religious man. In line 1 he shows himself to hold a most uncharitable attitude toward his fellow monk, Brother Lawrence, and by line 4 he has uttered two profanities and admitted his intense feelings of hatred and vengefulness. His ranting and roaring is full of exclamation points (four in the first stanza!), and he reveals his own personality and character when he imagines curses and unflattering nicknames for Brother Lawrence or plots malicious jokes on him. By the end, we have accumulated no knowledge of Brother Lawrence that makes him seem a fit target for such rage (except that he is pious, dutiful, and pleasant— perhaps enough to make this sort of speaker despise him), but we should have discovered much about the speaker's character and habits.

The speaker characterizes himself; the details accumulate into a fairly full portrait, and here we do not have even an opening and closing "objective" narrator's description (as in Kennedy's "In a Prominent Bar") or another speaker (as

---

5. Galatians 5.15–23 provides a long list of possible offenses, though they do not add up to twenty-nine.
6. Heretic. According to the Manichean heresy, the world was divided into the forces of good and evil, each equally powerful.   7. That is, in the devil's clutches.
8. Possibly the beginning of an incantation or curse.
9. Opening words of the _Ave Maria,_ here reversed: "Full of grace, Hail, Virgin" (Latin).

in Hardy's "The Ruined Maid") to give us perspective. Except for the moments when the speaker mimics or parodies Brother Lawrence (usually in italic type), we have only the speaker's own words and thoughts. But that is enough; the poet has controlled them so carefully that we know what he thinks of the speaker. The whole poem has been about the speaker and his attitudes; the point has been to characterize the speaker and develop in us a dislike of him and what he stands for.

In reading a poem like this aloud, we would want our voice to suggest all the speaker's unlikable features. We would also need to suggest, through tone of voice, the author's contemptuous mocking of them, and we would want, like an actor, to create strong disapproval in the hearer. The poem's words (the ones the author has given to the speaker) clearly imply those attitudes, and we would want our voice to express them.

Usually there is much more to a poem than the characterization of the speaker, but often it is necessary first to identify the speaker and determine his or her character before we can appreciate what else goes on in the poem. And sometimes, as here, in looking for the speaker of the poem, we discover the gist of the entire poem.

Analyzing Speakers: An Exercise

In the following poem, we do not get a full sense of the speaker until well into the poem. As you read, try to imagine the tone of voice you think this person would use. Exactly when do you begin to know what she sounds like?

DOROTHY PARKER

A Certain Lady

Oh, I can smile for you, and tilt my head,
    And drink your rushing words with eager lips,
And paint my mouth for you a fragrant red,
    And trace your brows with tutored finger-tips.
5 When you rehearse your list of loves to me,
    Oh, I can laugh and marvel, rapturous-eyed.
And you laugh back, nor can you ever see
    The thousand little deaths my heart has died.
And you believe, so well I know my part,
10   That I am gay as morning, light as snow,
And all the straining things within my heart
    You'll never know.

(Continued on next page)

(Continued)

Oh, I can laugh and listen, when we meet,
 And you bring tales of fresh adventurings—
15 Of ladies delicately indiscreet,
 Of lingering hands, and gently whispered things.
And you are pleased with me, and strive anew
 To sing me sagas of your late delights.
Thus do you want me—marveling, gay, and true—
20 Nor do you see my staring eyes of nights.
And when, in search of novelty, you stray,
 Oh, I can kiss you blithely as you go . . .
And what goes on, my love, while you're away,
 You'll never know.

1937

To whom does the speaker seem to be talking? What sort of person is he? How do you feel about him? Which habits and attitudes of his do you like least? How soon can you tell that the speaker is not altogether happy about his conversation and conduct? In what tone of voice would you read the first twenty-two lines aloud? What attitude would you try to express toward the person spoken to? What tone would you use for the last two lines? How would you describe the speaker's personality? What aspects of her behavior are most crucial to the poem's effect?

AUTHOR VERSUS SPEAKER

It is easy to assume that the speaker in a poem is an extension of the poet, especially when the voice is as distinctively self-assured as in "A Certain Lady." So, is the speaker in the poem above Dorothy Parker? Maybe. A lot of Parker's poems present a similar world-weary posture and a wry cynicism about romantic love. But the poem is hardly a case of self-revelation, a giving away of personal secrets. If it were, it would be silly, not to say risky, to address her lover in a way that gives damaging facts about a pose she has been so careful to set up.

In poems such as "The Ruined Maid," "In a Prominent Bar," and "Soliloquy of the Spanish Cloister," we are in no danger of mistaking the speaker for the poet, once we recognize that poets may create speakers who participate in specific situations, much as in fiction or drama. When there is a pointed discrepancy between the speaker and what we know of the poet—when the speaker is a woman, for example, and the poet is a man—we know we have a created speaker to contend with and that the point (or at least *one* point) in the poem is to observe the characterization carefully. In "A Certain Lady" we may be less sure, and in other poems the discrepancy between speaker and poet may be even more uncertain. What are we to make, for example, of the speaker in "Woodchucks" in the previous chapter? Is that speaker the real Maxine Kumin? At best (without knowing something quite specific about the author) we can only say "maybe" to that question. What we can be sure of is the sort of person the speaker is portrayed to be—someone (a man? a woman?) surprised to discover feelings and attitudes that contradict values apparently held with confidence. And that is exactly what we need to know for the poem to have its effect.

Even when poets present themselves as if they were speaking directly to us in their own voices, their poems present only a partial portrait, something considerably less than the full personality and character of the poet. Even when there is not an obviously created character—someone with distinct characteristics that are different from those of the poet—strategies of characterization are used to present the person speaking in one way and not another. Even when reading a poem like the following one, which contains identifiable autobiographical details, you should still think of the speaker instead of the poet, although here the poet is probably writing about a personal, actual experience, and he is certainly making a character of himself—that is, characterizing himself in a certain way, emphasizing some parts of himself and not others.

WILLIAM WORDSWORTH

She Dwelt among the Untrodden Ways

> She dwelt among the untrodden ways
>   Beside the springs of Dove,[1]
> A Maid whom there were none to praise
>   And very few to love:
>
> 5   A violet by a mossy stone
>   Half hidden from the eye!
> —Fair as a star, when only one
>   Is shining in the sky.
>
> She lived unknown, and few could know
> 10   When Lucy ceased to be;
> But she is in her grave, and, oh,
>   The difference to me!

1800

Is this poem more about Lucy or about the speaker's feelings concerning her death? Her simple life, far removed from fame and known only to a few, is said to have been beautiful, but we know little about her beyond her name and where she lived, in a beautiful but then-isolated section of northern England. We don't know if she was young or old, only that the speaker thinks of her as "fair" and compares her to a "violet by a mossy stone." We do know that the speaker is deeply pained by her death, so deeply that he is almost inarticulate with grief, lapsing into simple exclamation ("oh," line 11) and hardly able to articulate the "difference" that her death makes.

1. Small stream in the Lake District in northern England, near where Wordsworth lived.

Did Lucy actually live? Was she a friend of the poet? We don't know; the poem doesn't tell us, and even biographers of Wordsworth are unsure. What we do know is that Wordsworth was able to represent grief very powerfully. Whether the speaker is the historical Wordsworth or not, that speaker is a major focus of the poem, and it is his feelings that the poem isolates and expresses. We need to recognize some characteristics of the speaker and be sensitive to his feelings for the poem to work.

The poems we have looked at in this chapter—and the group that follows—all suggest the value of beginning the reading of any poem with three simple questions: Who is speaking? What do we know about him or her? What kind of person is she or he? Putting together the evidence that the poem presents in answer to such questions can often take us a long way into the poem. For some poems, such questions won't help a great deal because the speaking voice is too indistinct or the character behind the poem too scantily presented. But starting with such questions will often lead you toward the central experience the poem offers. At the very least, the question of speaker helps clarify the tone of voice, and it often provides guidance to the larger situation the poem explores.

• • •

AUDRE LORDE

Hanging Fire

I am fourteen
and my skin has betrayed me
the boy I cannot live without
still sucks his thumb
5   in secret
how come my knees are
always so ashy
what if I die
before morning
10   and momma's in the bedroom
with the door closed.

I have to learn how to dance
in time for the next party
my room is too small for me
15   suppose I die before graduation
they will sing sad melodies
but finally
tell the truth about me
There is nothing I want to do
20   and too much
that has to be done
and momma's in the bedroom
with the door closed.

Nobody even stops to think
25   about my side of it

I should have been on Math Team
my marks were better than his
why do I have to be
the one
30 wearing braces
I have nothing to wear tomorrow
will I live long enough
to grow up
and momma's in the bedroom
35 with the door closed.

1978

- What, precisely, do we know about the speaker? How does she feel
  about herself? How can you tell?

ROBERT BURNS

To a Louse

On Seeing One on a Lady's Bonnet at Church

Ha! whare ya gaun, ye crowlan ferlie![2]
Your impudence protects you sairly:[3]
I canna say but ye strunt[4] rarely,
        Owre gauze and lace;
5 Tho' faith, I fear ye dine but sparely,
        On sic a place.

Ye ugly, creepan, blastit wonner,[5]
Detested, shunn'd, by saunt an' sinner,
How daur ye set your fit[6] upon her,
10   Sae fine a Lady!
Gae somewhere else and seek your dinner,
        On some poor body.

Swith, in some beggar's haffet squattle;[7]
There ye may creep, and sprawl, and sprattle,[8]
15 Wi'ither kindred, jumping cattle,
        In shoals and, nations;
Whare horn nor bane[9] ne'er daur unsettle,
        Your thick plantations.

Now haud you there ye're out o'sight,
20 Below the fatt'rels,[1] snug and tight,
Na faith ye yet![2] ye'll no be right,
        Till ye've got on it,
The vera tapmost, towrin height
        O' Miss's bonnet.

2. Crawling miracle! (The speaker uses Scots dialect.)   3. Sorely.   4. Strut.   5. Wonder.   6. Foot.
7. Swift, in some beggar's hair sprawl.   8. Struggle.   9. Bone.   1. Ribbon ends.   2. No matter!

25 My sooth! right bauld ye set your nose out,
   As plump an' gray as onie grozet:[3]
   O for some rank, mercurial rozet,[4]
         Or fell, red smeddum,[5]
   I'd gie you sic a hearty dose o't,
30   Wad dress your droddum![6]

   I wad na been surpriz'd to spy
   You on an auld wife's flainen toy,[7]
   Or aiblins some bit duddie boy,[8]
         On 's wylecoat;[9]
35 But Miss's fine Lunardi,[1] fye!
         How daur ye do't?

   O Jenny dinna toss your head,
   An' set your beauties a' abread![2]
   Ye little ken what cursed speed
40   The blastie's[3] makin!
   Thae[4] winks and finger-ends, I dread,
         Are notice takin!

   O wad some Pow'r the giftie gie us
   To see oursels as others see us!
45 It wad frae monie a blunder free us
         An foolish notion:
   What airs in dress an' gait wad lea'e us,
         And ev'n Devotion![5]

                                1785

• What is the speaker's attitude toward the louse? toward Jenny?
  How do the speaker's attitude and focus change in the last two
  stanzas? What lines best summarize the speaker's main point?

GWENDOLYN BROOKS

We Real Cool

THE POOL PLAYERS,
SEVEN AT THE GOLDEN SHOVEL.

We real cool. We
Left school. We

Lurk late. We
Strike straight. We

5 Sing sin. We
Thin gin. We

---

3. Gooseberry.   4. Rosin.   5. Or sharp, red powder.   6. Buttocks.   7. Flannel cap.
8. Or perhaps some small ragged boy.   9. Undershirt.   1. Bonnet.   2. Abroad.   3. Creature's.
4. Those.   5. Piety.

Jazz June. We
Die soon.
                    1950

- Who are "we" in this poem? Do you think that the speaker and the
  poet share the same idea of what is "cool"?

Authors on Their Work: GWENDOLYN BROOKS (1917–2000)*

From "An Interview with Gwendolyn Brooks" (1970)*

Q. Are your characters literally true to your experience
   or do you set out to change experience?

A. Some of them are, are invented, some of them are
   very real people.

                • • •

Q. How about the seven pool players in the poem "We
   Real Cool"?

A. They have no pretensions to any glamor. They are supposedly dropouts, or
   at least they're in the poolroom when they should possibly be in school,
   since they're probably young enough, or at least those I saw were when I
   looked in a poolroom. . . . First of all, let me tell you how that's supposed to
   be said, because there's a reason why I set it out as I did. These are people
   who are essentially saying, "Kilroy is here. We are." But they're a little
   uncertain of the strength of their identity. . . .

   The "We"—you're supposed to stop after the "We" and think about their
   validity, and of course there's no way for you to tell whether it should be
   said softly or not, I suppose, but I say it rather softly because I want to represent their basic uncertainty, which they don't bother to question every
   day, of course.

Q. Are you saying that the form of this poem, then, was determined by the
   colloquial rhythm you were trying to catch?

A. No, determined by my feeling about these boys, these young men.

*Gwendolyn Brooks and George Stavros, "An Interview with Gwendolyn Brooks." *Contemporary
Literature* 11.1 (Winter 1970), 7, 9–10.

WALT WHITMAN

[*I celebrate myself, and sing myself*]

I celebrate myself, and sing myself,
And what I assume you shall assume,

For every atom belonging to me as good belongs to you.
I loafe and invite my soul,
5 I lean and loafe at my ease observing a spear of summer grass.

My tongue, every atom of my blood, form'd from this soil, this air,
Born here of parents born here from parents the same, and their
    parents the same,
I, now thirty-seven years old in perfect health begin,
Hoping to cease not till death.
10 Creeds and schools in abeyance,
Retiring back a while suffced at what they are, but never forgotten,
I harbor for good or bad, I permit to speak at every hazard,
Nature without check with original energy.

1855, 1881

- What is characteristically American about the speaker of this poem?

YUSEF KOMUNYAKAA

Tu Do Street

Searching for love, a woman,
someone to help ease down the cocked hammer
of my nerves & senses. The music
divides the evening into black
5 & white—soul, country & western,
acid rock, & Frank Sinatra.
I close my eyes & can see
men drawing lines in the dust,
daring each other to step across.
10 America pushes through the membrane
of mist & smoke, & I'm a small boy
again in Bogalusa[6] skirting tough talk
coming out of bars with *White Only*
signs & Hank Snow. But tonight,
15 here in Saigon, just for the hell of it,
I walk into a place with Hank Williams
calling from the jukebox. The bar girls
fade behind a smokescreen, fluttering
like tropical birds in a cage, not
20 speaking with their eyes & usual
painted smiles. I get the silent
treatment. We have played Judas
for each other out in the boonies
but only enemy machinegun fire
25 can bring us together again.

---

6. Industrial city in southeastern Louisiana.

When I order a beer, the mama-san
behind the counter acts as if she
can't understand, while her
eyes caress a white face;
30 down the street the black GIs
hold to their turf also.
An off-limits sign pulls me
deeper into alleys; I look
for a softness behind these voices
35 wounded by their beauty & war.
Back in the bush at Dak To
& Khe Sahn, we fought
the brothers of these women
we now run to hold in our arms.
40 There's more than a nation divided
inside us, as black & white
soldiers touch the same lovers
minutes apart, tasting
each other's breath,
45 without knowing these rooms
run into each other like tunnels
leading to the underworld.

1988

- At what point in the poem do you become aware of the speaker's racial identity? What might the poem suggest about war and race?

SUGGESTIONS FOR WRITING

1. Several of the poems in this chapter create characters and imply situations, as in drama. Write an essay in which you describe and analyze the main speaker of "The Ruined Maid" by Thomas Hardy, "In a Prominent Bar in Secaucus One Day" by X. J. Kennedy, "Soliloquy of the Spanish Cloister" by Robert Browning, or "A Certain Lady" by Dorothy Parker.
2. Write an essay in which you compare the speakers in "Hanging Fire" by Audre Lord and "We Real Cool" by Gwendolyn Brooks. What kinds of self-image do they have? In each poem, what is the implied distance between the speaker and the poet?
3. Choose any of the poems in this or the previous chapter and write an essay about the way a poet can create irony and humor through the use of a speaker who is clearly distinct from the poet himself or herself.
4. Write a poem, short story, or personal essay in which the speaker or narrator is a character mentioned by a speaker in any of the poems in this chapter—for example, Amelia in Hardy's "The Ruined Maid," someone who hears the song sung in X. J. Kennedy's "In a Prominent Bar in Secaucus One Day," the lover in Dorothy Parker's "A Certain Lady," Jenny in Robert Burns's "To a Louse," or any of the women to whom Yusef Komunyakaa's "Tu Do Street" alludes. How might the same situation, as well as the main speaker of these poems, look and sound different when viewed from another speaker's point of view and described in another speaker's voice?

Exploring Gender: An Album

As far as I'm concerned, being any gender is a drag.
—PATTI SMITH

I n poetry, as in life, the meaning of what is said to us depends in great part on who says it. In both contexts, too, our sense of who a speaker (or any person) is has much to do with gender, even when we aren't aware of it. Is this person a *he* or a *she*? Those little pronouns make all the difference.

As an experiment, look back at one or two of the poems in the last chapter. At what point, and for what reason, did you first decide that a poem's speaker was male or female? Did you ever change your mind? Does any speaker's gender seem more ambiguous now, on a second reading of the poem, than it did on the first reading? What difference does the speaker's gender make to your response to both the speaker and the poem? What difference does it make to the poem's tone? How might your response to the poem relate to the ways the poem does or doesn't conform to your expectations of men and women? What is the effect of the correspondence (or lack thereof) between the author's gender and the speaker's?

Despite all we have said about the danger of confusing the author of a poem with its speaker(s), in practice we usually use our knowledge of, or assumptions about, an author's gender in determining a speaker's gender, particularly when the latter is ambiguous. For example, consider William Wordsworth's poem "She Dwelt among the Untrodden Ways." Already the title has told us that the poem describes a "she," who we later learn is "A Maid"—that is, an unmarried woman, probably young and virginal, named Lucy (lines 3, 10). But what about the speaker? On the one hand, we know that Lucy's death and burial make all "The difference" to this person (line 12), and the poem also gives us plenty of reasons to suspect that the speaker is among the "very few" who "love[d]" Lucy (line 4), at the very least finding her flowerlike and "Fair" (lines 5, 7). On the other hand, you might be surprised to discover that nothing in the poem establishes the speaker's gender "beyond a reasonable doubt." Yet based on these few cues—on the fact that the poem is written by *William* Wordsworth, on our experience of the ways men and women tend to feel and talk about each other, and on the ways a lyric is likely to portray the lost beloved—we almost inevitably assume as we read that the speaker is a man. (Notice that we have ourselves done just that in avowing of the speaker, in the paragraph following the poem, "*he* is almost inarticulate with grief" [page 887; emphasis added]).

In the absence of definitive textual cues about a speaker's gender, such assumptions are perfectly acceptable and conventional, perhaps even inevitable. But it is nonetheless important (and just plain interesting) to notice that when we assign gender to the speaker of some poems, we *are* making an assumption—one that greatly affects our reading and response. Notice, too, that in assigning gender we often draw on assumptions about sexuality as well, often taking it for granted that people are heterosexual. When it comes to gender we need to pay attention to all the details that a poem gives us, as well as to those it withholds. We also need to be ready for surprises and to look for evidence that might overturn, or at least complicate, our assumptions. For example, Shakespeare's sonnets famously include some addressed to a young man, others addressed to a woman, and still others that are ambiguous, especially when read independently of the rest of the sonnets in the **sequence**. In some cases, the erotic charge of the poems, combined with our own tendency to believe that love poems must be addressed from a man to a woman or vice versa, might well lead us to make problematic assumptions about the gender of the speaker or the lover.

To help you think more about these issues, this album gathers poems that vary widely in terms of their tone and their speakers. In one way or another, however, all of these poems invite us to explore our ideas and feelings about gender and, to a lesser extent, sexuality. What does it mean to be a man or a woman? What has it meant in other times and places? Might gender be more complex than the phrases *man or woman* and *he or she* suggest? When, where, and how do we acquire our ideas about gender-appropriate roles, qualities, behavior, and appearance? Are some or all of these "ideas" not learned at all, but rather innate or instinctual? When and why might having a gender be a burden? a pleasure? How does gender shape our experience? our sense of ourselves and others? our interactions with, and our emotional responses to, poems and people?

RICHARD LOVELACE

Song: To Lucasta, Going to the Wars

> Tell me not, sweet, I am unkind,
>   That from the nunnery
> Of thy chaste breast and quiet mind
>   To war and arms I fly.
>
> 5 True: a new mistress now I chase,
>   The first foe in the field;
> And with a stronger faith embrace
>   A sword, a horse, a shield.
>
> Yet this inconstancy is such
> 10   As you too shall adore;
> I could not love thee, dear, so much,
>   Loved I not honor more.

1649

- What might this poem imply about men's and women's attitudes toward love and war?

MARY, LADY CHUDLEIGH

To the Ladies

> Wife and servant are the same,
>   But only differ in the name:
> For when that fatal knot is tied,
>   Which nothing, nothing can divide,
> 5 When she the word *Obey* has said,
>   And man by law supreme has made,
>   Then all that's kind is laid aside,

And nothing left but state[1] and pride.
Fierce as an eastern prince he grows,
10 And all his innate rigor shows:
Then but to look, to laugh, or speak,
Will the nuptial contract break.
Like mutes, she signs alone must make,
And never any freedom take,
15 But still be governed by a nod,
And fear her husband as her god:
Him still must serve, him still obey,
And nothing act, and nothing say,
But what her haughty lord thinks fit,
20 Who, with the power, has all the wit.
Then shun, oh! shun that wretched state,
And all the fawning flatterers hate.
Value yourselves, and men despise:
You must be proud, if you'll be wise.

1703

• What might the speaker mean when she says a husband "with the power, has all the wit" (line 20)? How might that statement multiply the meanings of the poem's last line?

WILFRED OWEN

Disabled

He sat in a wheeled chair, waiting for dark,
And shivered in his ghastly suit of grey,
Legless, sewn short at elbow. Through the park
Voices of boys rang saddening like a hymn,
5 Voices of play and pleasure after day,
Till gathering sleep had mothered them from him.

About this time Town used to swing so gay
When glow-lamps budded in the light blue trees,
And girls glanced lovelier as the air grew dim,—
10 In the old times, before he threw away his knees.
Now he will never feel again how slim
Girls' waists are, or how warm their subtle hands;
All of them touch him like some queer disease.

There was an artist silly for his face,
15 For it was younger than his youth, last year.
Now, he is old; his back will never brace;
He's lost his color very far from here,
Poured it down shell-holes till the veins ran dry,

And half his lifetime lapsed in the hot race,
20 And leap of purple spurted from his thigh.

* * *

One time he liked a blood-smear down his leg,
After the matches,[2] carried shoulder-high.
It was after football, when he'd drunk a peg,[3]
He thought he'd better join.—He wonders why.
25 Someone had said he'd look a god in kilts,
That's why; and may be, too, to please his Meg;
Aye, that was it, to please the giddy jilts
He asked to join. He didn't have to beg;
Smiling they wrote his lie; aged nineteen years.

30 Germans he scarcely thought of; all their guilt,
And Austria's, did not move him. And no fears
Of Fear came yet. He thought of jeweled hilts
For daggers in plaid socks; of smart salutes;
And care of arms; and leave; and pay arrears;
35 *Esprit de corps;* and hints for young recruits.
And soon, he was drafted out with drums and cheers.

Some cheered him home, but not as crowds cheer Goal.
Only a solemn man who brought him fruits
Thanked him; and then inquired about his soul.
40 Now, he will spend a few sick years in Institutes,
And do what things the rules consider wise,
And take whatever pity they may dole.
Tonight he noticed how the women's eyes
Passed from him to the strong men that were whole.
45 How cold and late it is! Why don't they come
And put him into bed? Why don't they come?

1917

- How might you respond differently to this poem if the soldier himself were the speaker? if the poem described the events of his life in
  the order in which they happened? if the poem lacked its last two
  lines?

AMY LOWELL

The Lonely Wife[4]

The mist is thick. On the wide river, the water-plants float smoothly.
No letters come; none go.
There is only the moon, shining through the clouds of a hard, jade-
  green sky,

---

2. Soccer games.   3. A drink, usually brandy and soda.
4. A translation/adaptation of a poem by the Chinese poet Li Po (701–762 C.E.).

Looking down at us so far divided, so anxiously apart.
All day, going about my affairs, I suffer and grieve, and press the
5   thought of you closely to my heart.
My eyebrows are locked in sorrow, I cannot separate them.
Nightly, nightly, I keep ready half the quilt,
And wait for the return of that divine dream which is my Lord.

Beneath the quilt of the Fire-Bird, on the bed of the Silver-Crested
        Love-Pheasant,
10 Nightly, nightly, I drowse alone.
The red candles in the silver candlesticks melt, and the wax runs from
        them,
As the tears of your so Unworthy One escape and continue constantly
        to flow.
A flower face endures but a short season,
Yet still he drifts along the river Hsiao and the river Hsiang.
As I toss on my pillow, I hear the cold, nostalgic sound of the water-
15   clock:
Shêng! Shêng! it drips, cutting my heart in two.

I rise at dawn. In the Hall of Pictures
They come and tell me that the snow-flowers are falling.
The reed-blind is rolled high, and I gaze at the beautiful, glittering,
        primeval snow,
20 Whitening the distance, confusing the stone steps and the courtyard.
The air is filled with its shining, it blows far out like the smoke of a
        furnace.
The grass-blades are cold and white, like jade girdle pendants.
Surely the Immortals in Heaven must be crazy with wine to cause such
        disorder,
Seizing the white clouds, crumpling them up, destroying them.

                                                          1921

- To what extent does this poem's speaker portray herself as subservient to her husband? as contented or discontented with her situation? Does her reference to her husband as her "Lord" (line 8) have
  the same implications in this poem as in Mary, Lady Chudleigh's
  "To the Ladies" (line 19)?

ELIZABETH BISHOP

Exchanging Hats

Unfunny uncles who insist
in trying on a lady's hat,
—oh, even if the joke falls flat,
we share your slight transvestite twist

5 in spite of our embarrassment.
Costume and custom are complex.

The headgear of the other sex
inspires us to experiment.

Anandrous⁵ aunts, who, at the beach
10 with paper plates upon your laps,
keep putting on the yachtsmen's caps
with exhibitionistic screech,

the visors hanging o'er the ear
so that the golden anchors drag,
15 —the tides of fashion never lag.
Such caps may not be worn next year.

Or you who don the paper plate
itself, and put some grapes upon it,
or sport the Indian's feather bonnet,
20 —perversities may aggravate

the natural madness of the hatter.
And if the opera hats collapse
and crowns grow drafty, then, perhaps,
he thinks what might a miter matter?

25 Unfunny uncle, you who wore a
hat too big, or one too many,
tell us, can't you, are there any
stars inside your black fedora?

Aunt exemplary and slim,
30 with avernal⁶ eyes, we wonder
what slow changes they see under
their vast, shady, turned-down brim.

1956

- The speaker in this poem uses the first-person plural ("we," line 4;
  "our," line 5; "us," line 8). Who might "we" be? How might your
  response to the poem change if the speaker instead used the first-
  person singular ("I") or the third-person plural ("they")?

PAULETTE JILES

Paper Matches

My aunts washed dishes while the uncles
squirted each other on the lawn with
    garden hoses. Why are we in here,
I said, and they are out there.
5   That's the way it is,

---

5. Literally, "husbandless."   6. Infernal.

said Aunt Hetty, the shrivelled-up one.
I have the rages that small animals have,
being small, being animal.
Written on me was a message,
10 "At Your Service" like a book of
paper matches. One by one we were
taken out and struck.
We come bearing supper,
our heads on fire.

1973

• What is the significance of the way pronouns are used in this
  poem—"we" (line 3), "I" (line 4), "it" (line 5), and so on? How does
  the speaker's tone shift over the course of the poem? Why?

MARGE PIERCY

What's That Smell in the Kitchen?

All over America women are burning dinners.
It's lambchops in Peoria; it's haddock
in Providence; it's steak in Chicago;
tofu delight in Big Sur; red
5 rice and beans in Dallas.
All over America women are burning
food they're supposed to bring with calico
smile on platters glittering like wax.
Anger sputters in her brainpan, confined
10 but spewing out missiles of hot fat.
Carbonized despair presses like a clinker
from a barbecue against the back of her eyes.
If she wants to grill anything, it's
her husband spitted over a slow fire.
15 If she wants to serve him anything
it's a dead rat with a bomb in its belly
ticking like the heart of an insomniac.
Her life is cooked and digested,
nothing but leftovers in Tupperware.
20 Look, she says, once I was roast duck
on your platter with parsley but now I am Spam.
Burning dinner is not incompetence but war.

1983

• What does the poem's last line mean? How does the rest of the
  poem prepare us for, and explain, that statement? What is the
  effect of the poem's references to specific sorts of food and to specific places?

DAVID WAGONER

My Father's Garden

On his way to the open hearth where white-hot steel
Boiled against furnace walls in wait for his lance
To pierce the fireclay and set loose demons
And dragons in molten tons, blazing
5 Down to the huge satanic caldrons,
Each day he would pass the scrapyard, his kind of garden.

In rusty rockeries of stoves and brake drums,
In grottoes of sewing machines and refrigerators,
He would pick flowers for us: small gears and cogwheels
10 With teeth like petals, with holes for anthers,
Long stalks of lead to be poured into toy soldiers,
Ball bearings as big as grapes to knock them down.

He was called a melter. He tried to keep his brain
From melting in those tyger-mouthed mills
15 Where the same steel reappeared over and over
To be reborn in the fire as something better
Or worse: cannons or cars, needles or girders,
Flagpoles, swords, or plowshares.

But it melted. His classical learning ran
20 Down and away from him, not burning bright.[7]
His fingers culled a few cold scraps of Latin
And Greek, *magna sine laude*,[8] for crosswords
And brought home lumps of tin and sewer grills
As if they were his ripe prize vegetables.

                                                    1987

- What facts do we learn here about the speaker's father and his life?
  What are the speaker's feelings about both?

JUDITH ORTIZ COFER

The Changeling

                    As a young girl
vying for my father's attention,
I invented a game that made him look up
from his reading and shake his head
5 as if both baffled and amused.

---

7. Like "tyger-mouthed" (line 14), an allusion to William Blake's poem "The Tyger" (1790).
8. Without great distinction; a reversal of the usual *magna cum laude*.

In my brother's closet, I'd change
into his dungarees—the rough material
molding me into boy shape; hide
my long hair under an army helmet
10 he'd been given by Father, and emerge
transformed into the legendary Ché[9]
of grown-up talk.

Strutting around the room,
I'd tell of life in the mountains,
15 of carnage and rivers of blood,
and of manly feasts with rum and music
to celebrate victories *para la libertad*.[1]
He would listen with a smile
to my tales of battles and brotherhood
20 until Mother called us to dinner.

She was not amused
by my transformations, sternly forbidding me
from sitting down with them as a man.
She'd order me back to the dark cubicle
25 that smelled of adventure, to shed
my costume, to braid my hair furiously
with blind hands, and to return invisible,
as myself,
to the real world of her kitchen.

1993

- Why do you think the speaker's father is amused by her "transformation," and why does her mother forbid it? What does this poem imply about all three of them?

LIZ ROSENBERG

The Silence of Women

Old men, as time goes on, grow softer, sweeter,
while their wives get angrier.
You see them hauling the men across the mall
or pushing them down on chairs,
5 "Sit there! and don't you move!"
A lifetime of *yes* has left them
hissing bent as snakes.
It seems even their bones will turn
against them, once the fruitful years are gone.
10 Something snaps off the houselights,

9. Ernesto "Che" Guevara (1928–67), Argentinian-born Cuban revolutionary leader.
1. For freedom (Spanish).

and the cells go dim;
the chicken hatching back into the egg.

Oh lifetime of silence!
words scattered like a sibyl's leaves.
15 Voice thrown into a baritone storm—
whose shrilling is a soulful wind
blown through an instrument
that cannot beat time

but must make music
20 any way it can.

1994

- What is implied by the image at the end of the first stanza? What is implied by the musical imagery in the second and third stanzas?

TONY HOAGLAND

Dickhead

To whomever taught me the word *dickhead*,
I owe a debt of thanks.
It gave me a way of being in the world of men
when I most needed one,

5 when I was pale and scrawny,
naked, goosefleshed
as a plucked chicken
in a supermarket cooler, a poor

forked thing stranded in the savage
10 universe of puberty, where wild
jockstraps flew across the steamy

skies of locker rooms,
and everybody fell down laughing
at jokes I didn't understand.

15 But *dickhead* was a word as dumb
and democratic as a hammer, an object
you could pick up in your hand,
and swing,

saying *dickhead* this and *dickhead* that,
20 a song that meant the world
was yours enough at least
to bang on like a garbage can,

and knowing it, and having that
beautiful ugliness always

25 cocked and loaded in my mind,
   protected me and calmed me like a psalm.

   Now I have myself become
   a beautiful ugliness,
   and my weakness is a fact
30 so well established that
   it makes me calm,

   and I am calm enough
   to be grateful for the lives I
   never have to live again;

35 but I remember all the bad old days
   back in the world of men,
   when everything was serious, mysterious, scary,
   hairier and bigger than I was;

   I recall when flesh
40 was what I hated, feared
   and was excluded from:

   Hardly knowing what I did,
   or what would come of it,
   I made a word my friend.

                                                    1998

- How is "the world of men" (line 36) characterized in this poem? Why and how did the word *dickhead* help the speaker navigate that world?

MARIE HOWE

Practicing

I want to write a love poem for the girls I kissed in seventh grade,
a song for what we did on the floor in the basement

of somebody's parents' house, a hymn for what we didn't say but
         thought:
That feels good or *I like that*, when we learned how to open each other's
         mouths

how to move our tongues to make somebody moan. We called it
5   practicing, and
one was the boy, and we paired off—maybe six or eight girls—and
         turned out

the lights and kissed and kissed until we were stoned on kisses, and
         lifted our
nightgowns or let the straps drop, and, Now you be the boy:

concrete floor, sleeping bag or couch, playroom, game room, train
    room, laundry.
10   Linda's basement was like a boat with booths and portholes

instead of windows. Gloria's father had a bar downstairs with stools
    that spun,
plush carpeting. We kissed each other's throats.

We sucked each other's breasts, and we left marks, and never spoke of
    it upstairs
outdoors, in daylight, not once. We did it, and it was

practicing, and slept, sprawled so our legs still locked or crossed, a
15   hand still lost
in someone's hair . . . and we grew up and hardly mentioned who

the first kiss really was—a girl like us, still sticky with the moisturizer
    we'd
shared in the bathroom. I want to write a song

for that thick silence in the dark, and the first pure thrill of unreluc-
    tant desire,
20   just before we made ourselves stop.

1998

- What does the speaker of this poem imply about why her memories
  of "practicing" matter to her now that she is an adult? What does
  she imply about how being a girl compares to being a woman?

Authors on Their Work: MARIE HOWE

From "Marie Howe" (1997)*

M[ARIE] H[OWE]: . . . I was interested in what it means to be a
woman, what it means to be a man. . . .
   In this culture, our mothers don't tell us about their first
sexual experience, they don't tell us about their marriage,
their lives, their sexual life in marriage, they don't tell us
anything. My mother told us nothing. . . . So, I've been really
aware lately, at forty-six years old, that I still need my sisters
and my friends to teach me and help me figure out how to
be a "girl."

[INTERVIEWER]: So much of our time as girls and women is spent trying to figure
out what is allowed, by men and by other women as well. What is not talked
about and what is talked about. How we can have an authentic sexuality.

*Victoria Redel, "Marie Howe," *Bomb: A Quarterly Arts & Culture Magazine* (Fall 1997). Web.
17 June 2009.

(Continued on next page)

(Continued)

MH: In learning how to be a girl in this culture, we are learning how to be objects. . . .

So in the poems, I was trying to find places in my young life where I was actually the subject, and I found it was in practicing how to kiss, which I did with other girls. I got to be a boy-girl and a girl-girl—I got to kiss the girl and kiss the boy. I loved that. . . .

It was wonderful to go back and try and remember the way it felt to be a girl. In order to write about what it means to be a woman in love with a man, I had to go back and find that girl who is still in the attic.

From "The Complexity of the Human Heart: A Conversation with Marie Howe" (2004)**

[INTERVIEWER]: I was interested in your saying you don't want to write personal poems anymore. Is one of the dangers having people confuse your poetry with your life? Once I heard someone say to Sharon Olds, "Tell me, how old are your son and daughter now?" And she said, "I have no son or daughter. Those are fictitious children."

MH: I understand what she means. For example, with that poem "Practicing," . . . *The New Yorker* legal department called up and said, "Are those girls identifiable?" I said, well, Linda's basement was like a boat and Gloria's father did have a bar downstairs with plush carpeting, but I didn't kiss those girls. So, yes, they're identifiable, because the poem has great, great details from my childhood, but that to me is the answer to the question of whether it is autobiographical. It's all constructed. I didn't kiss those two girls. They were my best friends when I was a kid. I kissed other girls, but how could you give up those gorgeous details with those basements, and it poured into the poems. They still made me change the names. But what comes together in a poem isn't true. . . .

I'm making something, like [the artist] Joseph Cornell makes his boxes and everyone looks into them, but it's the box you look into; it's not the man or the woman. It's alchemy of language and memory and imagination and time and music and sounds that gets made, and that's different from "Here is what happened to me when I was ten." That poem is a good example. Linda's boat basement and Gloria's plush carpeting were there, but they weren't *there* there.

**David Elliott, "The Complexity of the Human Heart: A Conversation with Marie Howe," *AGNI Online* (2004). Web. 17 June 2009.

VICTORIA REDEL

Bedecked

Tell me it's wrong the scarlet nails my son sports or the toy store rings
　　he clusters four jewels to each finger.

He's bedecked. I see the other mothers looking at the star choker, the
　　rhinestone strand he fastens over a sock.
Sometimes I help him find sparkle clip-ons when he says sticker ear-
　　rings look too fake.

Tell me I should teach him it's wrong to love the glitter that a boy's
　　only a boy who'd love a truck with a remote that revs,
battery slamming into corners or Hot Wheels loop-de-looping off
　　tracks into the tub.

5　Then tell me it's fine—really—maybe even a good thing—a boy who's
　　got some girl to him,
and I'm right for the days he wears a pink shirt on the seesaw in the
　　park.

Tell me what you need to tell me but keep far away from my son who
　　still loves a beautiful thing not for what it means—
this way or that—but for the way facets set off prisms and prisms spin
　　up everywhere

10　and from his own jeweled body he's cast rainbows—made every shining
　　true color.

Now try to tell me—man or woman—your heart was ever once that brave.

2003

- **What is the effect of the way the speaker addresses the reader in this poem? How does she feel about her son's behavior, and why?**

BOB HICOK

O my pa-pa

Our fathers have formed a poetry workshop.
They sit in a circle of disappointment over our fastballs
and wives. We thought they didn't read our stuff,
whole anthologies of poems that begin, My father never,
5　or those that end, and he was silent as a carp,
or those with middles which, if you think
of the right side as a sketch, look like a paunch
of beer and worry, but secretly, with flashlights
in the woods, they've read every word and noticed
10　that our nine happy poems have balloons and sex

and giraffes inside, but not one dad waving hello
from the top of a hill at dusk. Theirs
is the revenge school of poetry, with titles like
"My Yellow Sheet Lad" and "Given Your Mother's Taste
15   for Vodka, I'm Pretty Sure You're Not Mine."
They're not trying to make the poems better
so much as sharper or louder, more like a fishhook
or electrocution, as a group
they overcome their individual senilities,
20   their complete distaste for language, how cloying
it is, how like tears it can be, and remember
every mention of their long hours at the office
or how tired they were when they came home,
when they were dragged through the door
25   by their shadows. I don't know why it's so hard
to write a simple and kind poem to my father, who worked,
not like a dog, dogs sleep most of the day in a ball
of wanting to chase something, but like a man, a man
with seven kids and a house to feed, whose absence
30   was his presence, his present, the Cheerios,
the PF Flyers, who taught me things about trees,
that they're the most intricate version of standing up,
who built a grandfather clock with me so I would know
that time is a constructed thing, a passing, ticking fancy.
35   A bomb. A bomb that'll go off soon for him, for me,
and I notice in our fathers' poems a reciprocal dwelling
on absence, that they wonder why we disappeared
as soon as we got our licenses, why we wanted
the rocket cars, as if running away from them
40   to kiss girls who looked like mirrors of our mothers
wasn't fast enough, and it turns out they did
start to say something, to form the words hey
or stay, but we'd turned into a door full of sun,
into the burning leave, and were gone
45   before it came to them that it was all right
to shout, that they should have knocked us down
with a hand on our shoulders, that they too are mystified
by the distance men need in their love.

2007

- What does the speaker seem to discover about fathers, sons, and
  men by imagining the poems "Our fathers" might write (line 1)?
  What does the poem imply about the relationship between poetry,
  "language" (line 20), and gender?

AFAA MICHAEL WEAVER

American Income

The survey says all groups can make more money
if they lose weight except black men . . . men of other colors
and women of all colors have more gold, but black men
are the summary of weight, a lead thick thing on the scales,
5   meters spinning until they ring off the end of the numbering
of accumulation, how things grow heavy, fish on the
ends of lines that become whales, then prehistoric sea life
beyond all memories, the billion days of human hands
working, doing all the labor one can imagine, hands
10   now the population of cactus leaves on a papyrus moon
waiting for the fire, the notes from all their singing gone
up into the salt breath of tears of children that dry, rise
up to be the crystalline canopy of promises, the infinite
gone fishing days with the apologies for not being able to love
15   anymore, gone down inside earth somewhere where
women make no demands, have fewer dreams of forever,
these feet that marched and ran and got cut off, these hearts
torn out of chests by nameless thieves, this thrashing
until the chaff is gone out and black men know the gold
20   of being the dead center of things, where pain is the gateway
to Jerusalems, Bodhi trees,[2] places for meditation and howling,
keeping the weeping heads of gods in their eyes.

2007

- How does this poem play with the idea of "weight" (line 2)? What
  does it imply about how black men behave and why they do so?

SUGGESTIONS FOR WRITING

1. Identify the poem in this album that moves you the most, whether to anger, frustration, sadness, delight, or any other emotion. Write an essay exploring why and how
   the poem evokes the emotions it does, focusing especially on the way your emotional
   response relates, on the one hand, to the poem's representation of gender and, on the
   other hand, to either your own experience of being a certain gender or your own ideas
   about gender. Alternatively, choose any poem in the album that you find especially
   good or interesting, and write an essay exploring what it shows about gender and
   how it does so.
2. Some of the poems in this album explore the relationship between parents and
   children, whether from the parent's perspective (Victoria Redel's "Bedecked"), the
   grown-up child's (David Wagoner's "My Father's Garden," Judith Ortiz Cofer's
   "The Changeling"), or both (Bob Hicok's "O my pa-pa"). Write an essay comparing
   the way at least two of these poems portray either these relationships or the role of

2. Trees native to South Asia; according to tradition, the Buddha became enlightened while sitting in
meditation under a Bodhi tree.

parents in teaching their children what it means to be a boy or a girl, a man or a woman. What feelings do the poems express about these relationships or roles?

3. Richard Lovelace's "Song: To Lucasta, Going to the Wars," Wilfred Owen's "Disabled," and Judith Ortiz Cofer's "The Changeling" all deal with war and men's and women's attitude toward it and role in it. Write an essay in which you compare these poems and their implications about the role of war in defining masculinity and femininity.

4. Elizabeth Bishop's "Exchanging Hats," Judith Ortiz Cofer's "The Changeling," and Marie Howe's "Practicing" all describe games or experiments that involve trying on different roles, sometimes by trying on different clothes. Write an essay in which you compare at least two of these poems and the games they describe. What does each game and each poem illustrate about social roles and rules? about the difference between "play" and "real life" or between childhood and adulthood? If you focus on "Practicing," feel free to draw on the excerpts from the Howe interviews, as well as the poem itself.

5. Choose any poem from another chapter or album in this book, and write an essay exploring how the poem's meaning and emotional impact are affected by the fact that its speaker is, or is not, clearly male or female.

15 SITUATION AND SETTING: WHAT HAPPENS? WHERE? WHEN?

Questions about the speaker (*Who* questions) in a poem lead to questions about *What?* and *Why?* as well as *Where?* and *When?* First you identify the imagined **situation** in the poem: Who is speaking? To whom is the speaker speaking? Is there an auditor in the poem, or simply an audience outside of it? Is anyone else present or referred to in the poem? What is happening? Why is this event or communication occurring, and why is it significant? As soon as you zoom in on answers to such questions about persons and actions, you also encounter questions about place (Where does the action or communication take place?) and time (When is the poem set?). In other words, situation entails **setting**.

The place involved in a poem is its *spatial setting*, and the time is its *temporal setting*. The temporal setting may be a specific date or an era, a season of the year or a time of day. We tend, for example, to think of spring as a time of discovery and growth, and poems set in spring are likely to make use of that association. Similarly, morning usually suggests discovery—beginnings, vitality, the world fresh and new—even to those of us who in reality take our waking slow. Temporal or spatial setting often influences our expectations of theme and tone, although a poet may surprise us by making something very different from what we had thought was familiar.

Not all poems have an identifiable situation or setting, just as not all poems have a speaker who is entirely distinct from the author. Poems that simply present a series of thoughts and feelings directly, in a reflective way, may not present anything resembling a scene with action and dialogue. But many poems depend crucially on a sense of place, a sense of time, and an understanding of human interaction in scenes that resemble those in plays or films. And questions about these matters will often lead you to define not only the "facts" but also the feelings central to the design a poem has on its readers.

To understand the dialogue in Hardy's "The Ruined Maid" (chapter 14), for example, we need to recognize that the two women are meeting after an extended period of separation, and that they meet in a town setting rather than the rural area in which they grew up together. We infer (from the opening lines) that the meeting is accidental and that no other friends are present for the conversation. The poem's whole "story" depends on their situation: After leading separate lives for a while, they have some catching up to do. We don't know what specific town they are in or what year, season, or time of day it is—and those details are not important to the poem's effect.

More specific settings matter in other poems. X. J. Kennedy's "lady in skunk" sings her life story "in a prominent bar in Secaucus," a working-class town in New Jersey, but on no particular occasion ("one day"). In Browning's "Soliloquy of the Spanish Cloister," the setting, a monastery, adds to the irony because of the gross inappropriateness of the speaker's sentiments and attitudes in a supposedly holy place.

Situation and setting may be treated in various ways in a text, ranging from silence to the barest hints of description to full photographic detail. Often it is relatively easy to identify the situation at the beginning of a poem, but the implications of setting, and what happens as the poem unfolds, may be subtler. Poets often rely on readers to fill in the gaps in what is mentioned, drawing on their knowledge of circumstances and familiar experiences in the present or in the past. The poem may specify only a few aspects of a *kind* of setting, such as a motel room in the afternoon.

Frequently a poem's setting draws on common notions of a particular time or place. Setting a poem in a garden, for example, or writing about apples almost inevitably reminds many readers of the Garden of Eden because it is an important and widely recognized part of the Western heritage of belief and knowledge. Even people who don't read at all or who lack Judeo-Christian religious commitments are likely to know about Eden, and poets writing in Western cultures can count on that knowledge. A reference to something outside the poem that carries a history of meaning and strong emotional associations is called an **allusion**. For example, gardens may carry suggestions of innocence and order, or temptation and the Fall, or both, depending on how the poem handles the allusion.

Specific, well-known places from history or myth may similarly be associated with particular ideas or values or ways of life. The titles of many poems refer directly to specific places or times. Or the poem itself may indicate a well-known place such as Paris, or a historic event or period such as D-Day or the Great Depression. Indeed, while much of the poetry in this anthology expresses personal feelings, and while some of it is tied to the poet's autobiographical circumstances, a great deal of poetry written over the centuries has focused not on individuals but on political or historical topics and themes. The "setting" of epic poetry may be as broad as a nation or even the cosmos. Poems have been written to instruct readers about religion, science, philosophy, and the art of poetry, among many other themes, with an appropriate range of settings and situations. The poet may wish to influence readers' sympathies or loyalties toward different sides in a conflict, or to record and honor a specific event such as an inauguration. A poem written about or for a specific occasion is called an *occasional poem,* and such a poem is *referential*; that is, it *refers* to a certain historical time or event.

Sometimes it is hard to place ourselves fully in another time or place in order to imagine sympathetically what a particular historical moment would have been like, and even the best poetic efforts, by themselves, do not necessarily transport us there. For such poems we need, at the least, specific historical information—plus a willingness to be transported by a name, a date, or a dramatic situation.

SITUATIONS: CARING FOR CHILDREN

RITA DOVE

Daystar

She wanted a little room for thinking:
but she saw diapers steaming on the line,
a doll slumped behind the door.

So she lugged a chair behind the garage
5 to sit out the children's naps.

Sometimes there were things to watch—
the pinched armor of a vanished cricket,
a floating maple leaf. Other days
she stared until she was assured
10 when she closed her eyes
she'd see only her own vivid blood.

She had an hour, at best, before Liza appeared
pouting from the top of the stairs.
And just *what* was mother doing
15 out back with the field mice? Why,
building a palace. Later
that night when Thomas rolled over and
lurched into her, she would open her eyes
and think of the place that was hers
20 for an hour—where
she was nothing,
pure nothing, in the middle of the day.

1986

LINDA PASTAN

To a Daughter Leaving Home

When I taught you
at eight to ride
a bicycle, loping along
beside you
5 as you wobbled away
on two round wheels,
my own mouth rounding
in surprise when you pulled
ahead down the curved
10 path of the park,

> I kept waiting
> for the thud
> of your crash as I
> sprinted to catch up,
> 15 while you grew
> smaller, more breakable
> with distance,
> pumping, pumping
> for your life, screaming
> 20 with laughter,
> the hair flapping
> behind you like a
> handkerchief waving
> goodbye.
>
>   1988

Both of these poems involve motherhood, but they take entirely different stances about it and have very different tones. The mother in Dove's "Daystar," overwhelmed by the demands of young children, needs a room of her own. All she can manage, however, is a brief hour of respite. The situation is virtually the whole story here. Nothing really happens except that daily events (washing diapers, picking up toys, looking at crickets and leaves, explaining the world to children, having sex) surround her brief private hour and make it precious. Being "nothing" (lines 21 and 22) takes on great value in these circumstances, and the poem makes much of the setting: an isolated chair behind the garage. Setting in poems often means something much more specific about a particular culture or social history, but here time and place get their value from the circumstances of the situation for one frazzled mother.

The particulars of time and place in Pastan's "To a Daughter Leaving Home" are even less specific; the incident the poem describes happened a long time ago, and its vividness is a function of memory. The speaker here thinks back nostalgically to a moment when her daughter made an earlier (but briefer) departure. Though we learn very little about the speaker, at least directly, we may infer quite a bit about her—her affection for her daughter, the kind of mother she has been, her anxiety at the new departure that seems to reflect the earlier wobbly ride into the distance. The daughter is now, the poem implies, old enough to "leave" home in a full sense, but we do not know the specific reason or what the present circumstances are. Only the title tells us the situation, and (like "Daystar") the poem is all situation.

SETTINGS: HISTORICAL CONTEXTS

JOHN MILTON

On the Late Massacre in Piedmont

Avenge, O Lord, thy slaughtered saints, whose bones
　　Lie scattered on the Alpine mountains cold;
　　Even them who kept thy truth so pure of old
　　When all our fathers worshiped stocks and stones,[1]
5　Forget not: in thy book record their groans
　　Who were thy sheep and in their ancient fold
　　Slain by the bloody Piemontese that rolled
　　Mother with infant down the rocks. Their moans
　The vales redoubled to the hills, and they
10　　To heaven. Their martyred blood and ashes sow
　　O'er all th' Italian fields, where still doth sway
　　The triple tyrant:[2] that from these may grow
　　A hundredfold, who having learnt thy way
　　Early may fly the Babylonian woe.[3]

1655

MATTHEW ARNOLD

Dover Beach[4]

The sea is calm tonight.
The tide is full, the moon lies fair
Upon the straits; on the French coast the light
Gleams and is gone; the cliffs of England stand,
5　Glimmering and vast, out in the tranquil bay.
Come to the window, sweet is the night-air!
Only, from the long line of spray
Where the sea meets the moon-blanched land,
Listen! you hear the grating roar
10　Of pebbles which the waves draw back, and fling,
At their return, up the high strand,
Begin, and cease, and then again begin,
With tremulous cadence slow, and bring
The eternal note of sadness in.

---

1. Idols of wood and stone.　　2. The pope's tiara featured three crowns.
3. In Milton's day, Protestants often likened the Roman Church to Babylonian decadence, calling the church "the whore of Babylon," and they read Revelation 17 and 18 as an allegory of its coming destruction.
4. At the narrowest point on the English Channel. The light on the French coast (lines 3–4) would be about twenty miles away.

15 Sophocles long ago
Heard it on the Aegean, and it brought
Into his mind the turbid ebb and flow
Of human misery;⁵ we
Find also in the sound a thought,
20 Hearing it by this distant northern sea.

The Sea of Faith
Was once, too, at the full, and round earth's shore
Lay like the folds of a bright girdle furled.
But now I only hear
25 Its melancholy, long, withdrawing roar,
Retreating, to the breath
Of the night-wind, down the vast edges drear
And naked shingles⁶ of the world.

Ah, love, let us be true
30 To one another! for the world, which seems
To lie before us like a land of dreams,
So various, so beautiful, so new,
Hath really neither joy, nor love, nor light,
Nor certitude, nor peace, nor help for pain;
35 And we are here as on a darkling plain
Swept with confused alarms of struggle and flight,
Where ignorant armies clash by night.

ca. 1851

JOHN BETJEMAN

*In Westminster Abbey*⁷

Let me take this other glove off
　As the *vox humana*⁸ swells,
And the beauteous fields of Eden
　Bask beneath the Abbey bells.
5 Here, where England's statesmen lie,
　Listen to a lady's cry.

Gracious Lord, oh bomb the Germans.
　Spare their women for Thy Sake,
And if that is not too easy
10 　We will pardon Thy Mistake.
But, gracious Lord, whate'er shall be,
　Don't let anyone bomb me.

5. In Sophocles' *Antigone*, lines 637–46, the chorus compares the fate of the house of Oedipus to the waves of the sea.
6. Pebble-strewn beaches.
7. Gothic church in London in which English monarchs are crowned and many famous Englishmen are buried (see lines 5, 39–40).　8. Organ tones that resemble the human voice.

Keep our Empire undismembered
    Guide our Forces by Thy Hand,
15 Gallant blacks from far Jamaica,
    Honduras and Togoland;
Protect them Lord in all their fights,
And, even more, protect the whites.

Think of what our Nation stands for,
20   Books from Boots[9] and country lanes,
Free speech, free passes, class distinction,
    Democracy and proper drains.
Lord, put beneath Thy special care
One-eighty-nine Cadogan Square.[1]

25 Although dear Lord I am a sinner,
    I have done no major crime;
Now I'll come to Evening Service
    Whensoever I have the time.
So, Lord, reserve for me a crown,[2]
30 And do not let my shares go down.

I will labor for Thy Kingdom,
    Help our lads to win the war,
Send white feathers to the cowards[3]
    Join the Women's Army Corps,[4]
35 Then wash the Steps around Thy Throne
In the Eternal Safety Zone.

Now I feel a little better,
    What a treat to hear Thy Word
Where the bones of leading statesmen,
40   Have so often been interred.
And now, dear Lord, I cannot wait
Because I have a luncheon date.

                1940

    These three poems, with their distinctive meter and rhyme and varied tones, would be difficult to interpret without reference to specific English perspectives on European traditions, to specific events such as war, and to specific places such as Dover (where many British travelers embarked for tours of the European continent) and Westminster Abbey (the church near the Houses of Parliament in London where many famous Englishmen, including writers as well as leaders, are buried). The poems were written at different times—1655, 1851, and 1940—but

9. A chain of British pharmacies.
1. Presumably where the speaker lives, in a fashionable section of central London.
2. Coin worth five shillings (but also an afterlife reward).
3. White feathers were sometimes given or sent to men not in uniform to suggest that they were cowards and should join the armed forces.
4. The speaker uses the old World War I name (Women's Army Auxiliary Corps) of the Auxiliary Territorial Service, an organization that performed domestic (and some foreign) defense duties.

each reflects the latest news and outlook at the time of writing. Milton's speaker is scarcely identified, and the sonnet resembles a public prayer addressed to God on current religious and political conflicts. Arnold's speaker closely resembles the poet himself, and eventually addresses a companion in a room overlooking the sea at Dover, contemplating the history of the West since Sophocles. Betjeman, in contrast, creates an ironic or unreliable speaker who is, unlike the poet, an upper-class woman praying for special favors in the abbey during World War II.

What does the reader need to know in order to understand the situations and settings in these poems? Milton's occasional poem requires the most explanation, largely because it is the most historically removed from what is familiar to readers today. (Imagine a poem written about the Hurricane Katrina disaster when the evacuation of New Orleans was still in the news; few details would need to be explained for contemporary readers.) Milton wrote the poem when the news reached England that many of the Waldensians, a heretical sect living in southern France and northern Italy (the Piedmont), had been massacred. Until 1655, they had been allowed freedom of worship, but when their legal protection was withdrawn, local Catholics attacked them. Milton's readers would have perceived parallels between events in the Piedmont and current English politics. "Saints" was the term then regularly used by English Protestants of the Puritan stamp to describe all individual Christian believers, in contrast with the few saints worshipped by Catholics. Milton was warning his fellow Puritans that, if the Stuart monarchy were reestablished, what had just happened to the Waldensians could happen to them as well. The heir to the English throne, who would be crowned as Charles II in 1660, was suspected of being a Catholic—anathema to the Protestant English. Indeed, following the Restoration in 1660, tight restrictions were placed on the Puritan "sects" under the new British monarchy. In lines 12 and 14, the poem alludes to dangers of religious rule by dominant groups by invoking standard images of Catholic power and persecution.

The situation and setting of "Dover Beach" are more concrete and specific. It is night by the seashore, and the speaker is gazing at the view from a room with someone he invites to "come to the window" (line 6) and "listen" (line 9); later he says to this person, "Ah, love, let us be true / To one another!" (lines 29–30). Most readers have assumed that the speaker and his companion are about to travel from Dover across the sea to France and that the situation is a honeymoon, or at least that the couple is young and married; after all the "world . . . seems to lie before us . . . so new" (lines 30–32). Although this poem is not a prayer, it is a kind of plea for hope despite the modern loss of faith. The tide is now full, but the poet hears a destructive repetition of rising and falling waves (the pebbles will be worn down eventually), and he dwells on the "withdrawing" side of this pattern. For centuries, Christian belief ("the Sea of Faith") was at high tide, beholding the world as a glorious whole, but both the ancient Greeks and the Victorians took a longer view of the recurring calamities of history. England had been at war with France throughout most of the eighteenth century and until 1815; a wave of European revolutions (as recently as 1848 in France), as well as colonial conflicts, made the shore of England feel vulnerable enough. In 1854, England was to embroil itself in the disastrous Crimean War. As an island, England had some protection; as an imperial power, it depended on its navy and was coming close to ruling the majority of the world's territories. Yet the sea and its rocky shore suggest both time that extends beyond empires and the exposed fossil evidence of deep time before human history. The speaker, at this threshold, is moved to cling to love as the only refuge from a nightmarish vision of the history of the world.

Instead of a melancholy ode, "In Westminster Abbey" is a mocking satire of British imperialism during World War II (with allusions to World War I), spoken in the voice of a patriotic, snobbish, self-centered woman; of these three historical poems, its time and place are the most specific. The supposed prayer is uttered during a morning service amid the tombs of great statesmen, before the speaker hurries off to lunch. Her wishes are racist and chauvinistic, imagining a deity that takes her side in the war against the Germans and will prevent the speaker's own house (she gives the exact address) from being bombed, as many buildings in London were during the Blitz. The repeated references to the setting emphasize the political target of the satire: the nationalism and narrow materialism of the official state religion of Britain, in which statesmen are worshiped like saints and the worshipers ask for a good return on their investments.

SETTINGS: IN THE MORNING

The setting of the following poems is clearly temporal as well as spatial. All six of these poems identify the early time of day in their titles. August Kleinzahler's "Aubade on East 12th Street" may at first appear not to state its topic, "morning," in the title, but an **aubade** is a morning song or poem (from the French term for dawn). Although morning suggests fresh beginnings and hope, an aubade often expresses sadness because the new day means that two lovers must part—time has moved on. Do you detect a sad or a hopeful tone in each of these poems? Some of the poems refer to times of day metaphorically or more abstractly. Do the poems help you visualize a particular day? How do some of these poems use space, such as the idea of the earth and the sun? How does the specific place in some of these poems, such as a city or the writer's home, affect the speaker's response to the time of day? What references to darkness or light, to sleep or waking, or to other times of day do you notice in these poems?

WILLIAM SHAKESPEARE

[*Full many a glorious morning have I seen*]

Full many a glorious morning have I seen
Flatter the mountain-tops with sovereign eye,
Kissing with golden face the meadows green,
Gilding pale streams with heavenly alchymy;
5   Anon permit the basest clouds to ride
With ugly rack[5] on his celestial face,
And from the forlorn world his visage hide,
Stealing unseen to west with this disgrace:
Even so my sun one early morn did shine,
10   With all-triumphant splendor on my brow;

5. Moss.

But, out! alack! he was but one hour mine,
The region cloud hath mask'd him from me now.
   Yet him for this my love no whit disdaineth;
   Suns of the world may stain when heaven's sun staineth.

1609

- What words and phrases mark the shifts of the clouds back and forth across the face of the sun in "Full many a glorious morning"? What distinction is Shakespeare making between "suns of the world" and "heaven's sun"?

JOHN DONNE

The Good-Morrow

   I wonder, by my troth, what thou and I
      Did, till we loved? were we not weaned till then?
   But sucked on country pleasures, childishly?
   Or snorted we in the Seven Sleepers' den?[6]
5   'Twas so; but[7] this, all pleasures fancies be.
   If ever any beauty I did see,
Which I desired, and got,[8] twas but a dream of thee.

   And now good-morrow to our waking souls,
      Which watch not one another out of fear;
10   For love, all love of other sights controls,
      And makes one little room an everywhere.
   Let sea-discoverers to new worlds have gone,
   Let maps to other,[9] worlds on worlds have shown,
Let us possess one world, each hath one, and is one.

15   My face in thine eye, thine in mine appears,[1]
      And true plain hearts do in the faces rest;
   Where can we find two better hemispheres,
      Without sharp north, without declining west?
   Whatever dies was not mixed equally,[2]
20   If our two loves be one, or, thou and I
Love so alike that none do slacken, none can die.

1633

- Like so many of Donne's poems, this one attempts to persuade. What is the situation of this poem? What does the speaker wish to demonstrate?

6. According to legend, seven Christian youths escaped Roman persecution by sleeping in a cave for 187 years. *Snorted*: snored.   7. Except for.   8. Sexually possessed.   9. Other people.
1. That is, each is reflected in the other's eyes.
2. Perfectly mixed elements, according to scholastic philosophy, were stable and immortal.

SYLVIA PLATH

Morning Song

Love set you going like a fat gold watch.
The midwife slapped your footsoles, and your bald cry
Took its place among the elements.

Our voices echo, magnifying your arrival. New statue.
5 In a drafty museum, your nakedness
Shadows our safety. We stand round blankly as walls.

I'm no more your mother
Than the cloud that distils a mirror to reflect its own slow
Effacement at the wind's hand.

10 All night your moth-breath
Flickers among the flat pink roses. I wake to listen:
A far sea moves in my ear.

One cry, and I stumble from bed, cow-heavy and floral
In my Victorian nightgown.
15 Your mouth opens clean as a cat's. The window square

Whitens and swallows its dull stars. And now you try
Your handful of notes;
The clear vowels rise like balloons.

                                                        1961

- How does this poem's language emphasize the distinctions between
  the speaker and her baby? How does the poem's setting in time—
  morning—affect its meaning?

BILLY COLLINS

Morning

Why do we bother with the rest of the day,
the swale of the afternoon,
the sudden dip into evening,

then night with his notorious perfumes,
5 his many-pointed stars?

This is the best—
throwing off the light covers,
feet on the cold floor,
and buzzing around the house on espresso—

10 maybe a splash of water on the face,
a palmful of vitamins—
but mostly buzzing around the house on espresso,

dictionary and atlas open on the rug,
the typewriter waiting for the key of the head,
15   a cello on the radio,

and, if necessary, the windows—
trees fifty, a hundred years old
out there,
heavy clouds on the way
20   and the lawn steaming like a horse
in the early morning.

1998

- What words and phrases help color the reader's perceptions of the
  various times of day mentioned in this poem? Why is morning "the
  best" (line 6)?

AUGUST KLEINZAHLER

Aubade on East 12th Street

The skylight silvers
and a faint shudder from the underground
travels up the building's steel.
Dawn breaks across this wilderness
5   of roofs with their old wooden storage tanks
and caps of louvered cowlings

moving in the wind. Your back,
raised hip and thigh
well-tooled as a rounded baluster
10   on a lathe of shadow and light.

1996

- Paraphrase the simile that concludes this poem. How does "a lathe
  of shadow and light" figure into the comparison?

JONATHAN SWIFT

A Description of the Morning

Now hardly here and there a hackney-coach[3]
Appearing, showed the ruddy morn's approach.
Now Betty[4] from her master's bed had flown,

---

3. Hired coach. *Hardly:* scarcely; that is, they are just beginning to appear.
4. A stock name for a servant girl. Moll (lines 7, 14) is a frequent lower-class nickname.

And softly stole to discompose her own.
5   The slip shod 'prentice from his master's door
Had pared the dirt, and sprinkled round the floor.
Now Moll had whirled her mop with dext'rous airs,
Prepared to scrub the entry and the stairs.
The youth with broomy stumps began to trace
10 The kennel-edge[5] where wheels had worn the place.
The small-coal man[6] was heard with cadence deep,
Till drowned in shriller notes of chimney-sweep:
Duns[7] at his lordship's gate began to meet;
And brick-dust Moll had screamed through half the street.[8]
15 The turnkey now his flock returning sees,
Duly let out a-nights to steal for fees.[9]
The watchful bailiffs take their silent stands,[1]
And schoolboys lag with satchels in their hands.

                                                      1709

- From the poem's brief descriptions of morning routines, what do
  we know about its various characters and the kind of community
  they inhabit? Could a similar poem be written today?

SITUATION AND SETTING: PREPARING A RESPONSE PAPER

The title of the following poem suggests that place may be important, and it is,
although you may be surprised to discover exactly what exists at this address and
what uses the speaker makes of it. What happens in "Cherrylog Road" is fairly
easy to sort out, but its effect is more complex than the simple story suggests,
largely because of the wealth of details the poem provides about setting. First,
read the poem through once, pausing only when you come to a period and allowing your immediate personal impressions to form on their own. Then, reread the
poem, following the steps provided for analyzing and taking notes on specific
elements, which will help you understand—and write about—the centrality of its
setting.

JAMES DICKEY

Cherrylog Road

Off Highway 106
At Cherrylog Road I entered
The '34 Ford without wheels,

---

5. Edge of the gutter that ran down the middle of the street. *Trace:* To find old nails [Swift's note].
6. A seller of coal and charcoal.   7. Bill collectors.
8. Selling powdered brick that was used to clean knives.
9. Jailers collected fees from prisoners for their keep and often let them out at night so they could steal to
pay expenses.   1. Looking for those on their "wanted" lists.

Smothered in kudzu,
5 With a seat pulled out to run
Corn whiskey down from the hills,

And then from the other side
Crept into an Essex
With a rumble seat of red leather
10 And then out again, aboard
A blue Chevrolet, releasing
The rust from its other color,

Reared up on three building blocks.
None had the same body heat;
15 I changed with them inward, toward
The weedy heart of the junkyard,
For I knew that Doris Holbrook
Would escape from her father at noon

And would come from the farm
20 To seek parts owned by the sun
Among the abandoned chassis,
Sitting in each in turn
As I did, leaning forward
As in a wild stock-car race

25 In the parking lot of the dead.
Time after time, I climbed in
And out the other side, like
An envoy or movie star
Met at the station by crickets.
30 A radiator cap raised its head,

Become a real toad or a kingsnake
As I neared the hub of the yard,
Passing through many states,
Many lives, to reach
35 Some grandmother's long Pierce-Arrow
Sending platters of blindness forth

From its nickel hubcaps
And spilling its tender upholstery
On sleepy roaches,
40 The glass panel in between
Lady and colored driver
Not all the way broken out,

The back-seat phone
Still on its hook.
45 I got in as though to exclaim,
"Let us go to the orphan asylum,
John; I have some old toys
For children who say their prayers."

I popped with sweat as I thought
50   I heard Doris Holbrook scrape
Like a mouse in the southern-state sun
That was eating the paint in blisters
From a hundred car tops and hoods.
She was tapping like code,

55   Loosening the screws,
Carrying off headlights,
Sparkplugs, bumpers,
Cracked mirrors and gear-knobs,
Getting ready, already,
60   To go back with something to show

Other than her lips' new trembling
I would hold to me soon, soon,
Where I sat in the ripped back seat
Talking over the interphone,
65   Praying for Doris Holbrook
To come from her father's farm

And to get back there
With no trace of me on her face
To be seen by her red-haired father
70   Who would change, in the squalling barn,
Her back's pale skin with a strop,
Then lay for me

In a bootlegger's roasting car
With a string-triggered 12-gauge shotgun
75   To blast the breath from the air.
Not cut by the jagged windshields,
Through the acres of wrecks she came
With a wrench in her hand,

Through dust where the blacksnake dies
80   Of boredom, and the beetle knows
The compost has no more life.
Someone outside would have seen
The oldest car's door inexplicably
Close from within:

85   I held her and held her and held her,
Convoyed at terrific speed
By the stalled, dreaming traffic around us,
So the blacksnake, stiff
With inaction, curved back
90   Into life, and hunted the mouse

With deadly overexcitement,
The beetles reclaimed their field
As we clung, glued together,

With the hooks of the seat springs
95 Working through to catch us red-handed
Amidst the gray breathless batting

That burst from the seat at our backs.
We left by separate doors
Into the changed, other bodies
100 Of cars, she down Cherrylog Road
And I to my motorcycle
Parked like the soul of the junkyard

Restored, a bicycle fleshed
With power, and tore off
105 Up Highway 106, continually
Drunk on the wind in my mouth,
Wringing the handlebar for speed,
Wild to be wreckage forever.

1964

Now consider your response to Dickey's poem.
1. First, answer the basic questions at the beginning of this chapter: Who is
   speaking? To whom is the speaker speaking? Is there an auditor in the
   poem, or simply an audience outside of it? Is anyone else present or referred
   to in the poem?
2. Underline or list the words or lines in which setting is first indicated.
3. Underline (perhaps in a different color) or list the words or lines that gave
   you your first impression of the situation. What do you notice about the
   connection between setting and situation? Could the action occur in a
   different place or kind of place?
4. Similarly, list the proper or improper nouns that fill in your sense of the
   setting. Sort these into different kinds of entities: plants, animals, machines,
   real or imaginary people. Consider and compare the items you list under
   each category. How do they contribute to the specific spatial setting and
   temporal setting of the poem? How do they contribute to the situation of
   the poem?
5. Make a similar inventory of the verbs in the poem in order to understand
   the action step by step. Which actions are real? Which are remembered?
   Which are repeated? Which are imagined?
6. As your inventories show, the poem relies on personification (attributing
   human qualities to natural or inanimate things). Find lines in which
   insects, reptiles, or mammals interact with the parts of cars, either helping destroy them or making them come back to life. Find lines in which
   creatures and humans are compared.
7. Now that you have comprehended the details of the poem, try to summarize
   each stanza in a phrase and to place it in time and place, whether within the
   scene or within the twentieth century in the United States. What is the significance of "Time after time" (line 26)? Of "Passing through many states, /
   Many lives" (lines 33–34)? Of "the southern-state sun" (line 51)? What is

implied about the region and the time period in two references to illegal alcohol: "run / Corn whiskey down from the hills" (lines 5–6) and "a boot-legger's roasting car" (line 73)? What is implied about local social rules in the scenario of the "Lady and colored driver" with her plans to donate toys to orphans (lines 40–48)? Or in the idea of the menacing father who would whip his daughter in the barn and gun down her seducer (lines 65–75)?

8. Review the action of the poem and your answers in number 1 above. Why does the speaker arrive at the junkyard first and explore the cars before Doris Holbrook arrives? Why does the poem begin with the names of two roads in the first two lines and end with Doris departing "down Cherrylog Road" in the next-to-last stanza, followed by the speaker speeding on his motorcycle "up Highway 106" in the final stanza (lines 100, 105)? What does the last line suggest not only about the speaker's desire but also about the temporal and spatial setting?

9. Did the sexual experience happen once, a few times, or many times? Is the memory of the encounter recent? Is the speaker still a young boy? Find specific evidence in the poem for your answers to these questions.

10. What is the significance of the title "Cherrylog Road"? (There is a real Cherrylog Road in North Georgia, but no Highway 106 near it.)

Based on your answers and discoveries, write a short response paper on "Cherry-log Road" in which you argue that the poem's specific, richly detailed setting is essential to its situation, theme, and tone, finding your own way to express the theme and tone. Support your claim by showing that James Dickey uses personi-fication to bring to life a particular setting, a car junkyard in the heat of a south-ern summer, as a metaphor for the situation—the reckless, instinctive, and fleeting lovemaking of teenagers.

TWO CARPE DIEM POEMS

The following two poems from the 1600s could be said to represent a similar situ-ation to that in "Cherrylog Road": The male speaker desires a woman who also appears in the scene represented in the poem. As in Dickey's poem, their possible sexual acts and the delay or foreplay are described figuratively in relation to natu-ral or other objects—in Donne's poem through the symbol of the flea that has bit-ten both lovers, and in Marvell's poem through the series of metaphors of the history of the world and cosmos, birds of prey, and a ball bombarding iron gates. The poems belong to the tradition of **carpe diem** (Latin for *seize the day*) because the speaker is urging his auditor, his lover, to enjoy pleasures now, before they die. The woman is resisting because of her concern for chastity ("That long pre-served virginity" in Marvell's poem, line 28) or social rules ("parents grudge" in Donne's poem, line 14). The most significant differences from "Cherrylog Road" emerge from the situation (the speaker is directly appealing to the woman, who has not yet agreed to have sex) and from the setting (we learn little about the place, time of day, weather, or other details of the scene in either poem). The action of these poems is implied in the shifts in what the speaker is saying. What does the woman do in "The Flea"? Can you imagine the woman's response in "To His Coy Mistress"? How do the images in the poems create a sense of time and space?

JOHN DONNE

The Flea

Mark but this flea, and mark in this[2]
How little that which thou deny'st me is;
It sucked me first, and now sucks thee,
And in this flea our two bloods mingled be;
5 Thou know'st that this cannot be said
A sin, nor shame, nor loss of maidenhead.
    Yet this enjoys before it woo,
    And pampered[3] swells with one blood made of two,
    And this, alas, is more than we would do.[4]

10 Oh stay,[5] three lives in one flea spare,
Where we almost, yea more than, married are.
This flea is you and I, and this
Our marriage bed, and marriage temple is;
Though parents grudge, and you, we're met
15 And cloistered in these living walls of jet.
    Though use[6] make you apt to kill me,
    Let not to that, self-murder added be,
    And sacrilege, three sins in killing three.

Cruel and sudden, hast thou since
20 Purpled thy nail in blood of innocence?
Wherein could this flea guilty be,
Except in that drop which it sucked from thee?
Yet thou triumph'st, and say'st that thou
Find'st not thyself, nor me, the weaker now;
25   'Tis true; then learn how false, fears be;
    Just so much honor, when thou yield'st to me,
    Will waste, as this flea's death took life from thee.

                      1633

- Is the setting of the encounter between the speaker and the woman
  described or hinted at? What lines help you imagine where they are
  and what the woman does or says?

---

2. Medieval preachers and rhetoricians asked their hearers to "mark" (look at) an object that illustrated a
moral or philosophical lesson they wished to emphasize.
3. Fed luxuriously.
4. According to the medical theory of Donne's era, conception involved the literal mingling of the lovers'
blood.   5. Desist.   6. Habit.

ANDREW MARVELL

To His Coy Mistress

    Had we but world enough, and time,
This coyness,[7] lady, were no crime.
We would sit down, and think which way
To walk, and pass our long love's day.
5 Thou by the Indian Ganges' side
Shouldst rubies[8] find: I by the tide
Of Humber would complain.[9] I would
Love you ten years before the Flood,
And you should if you please refuse
10 Till the conversion of the Jews.[1]
My vegetable love[2] should grow
Vaster than empires, and more slow;
An hundred years should go to praise
Thine eyes, and on thy forehead gaze;
15 Two hundred to adore each breast,
But thirty thousand to the rest.
An age at least to every part,
And the last age should show your heart.
For, lady, you deserve this state;[3]
20 Nor would I love at lower rate.
    But at my back I always hear
Time's wingèd chariot hurrying near;
And yonder all before us lie
Deserts of vast eternity.
25 Thy beauty shall no more be found,
Nor, in thy marble vault, shall sound
My echoing song; then worms shall try
That long preserved virginity,
And your quaint honor turn to dust,
30 And into ashes all my lust:
The grave's a fine and private place,
But none, I think, do there embrace.
    Now therefore, while the youthful hue
Sits on thy skin like morning dew,[4]
35 And while thy willing soul transpires[5]
At every pore with instant fires,
Now let us sport us while we may,

7. Hesitancy, modesty (not necessarily suggesting calculation).
8. Talismans that are supposed to preserve virginity.
9. Write love complaints, conventional songs lamenting the cruelty of love. *Humber*: a river and estuary in Marvell's hometown of Hull.
1. Which, according to popular Christian belief, will occur just before the end of the world.
2. Which is capable only of passive growth, not of consciousness. The "vegetable soul" is lower than the other two divisions of the soul, "animal" and "rational."   3. Dignity.
4. The text reads "glew." "Lew" (warmth) has also been suggested as an emendation.   5. Breathes forth.

And now, like am'rous birds of prey,
Rather at once our time devour
40 Than languish in his slow-chapped[6] pow'r.
Let us roll all our strength and all
Our sweetness up into one ball,
And tear our pleasures with rough strife
Thorough[7] the iron gates of life.
45 Thus, though we cannot make our sun
Stand still,[8] yet we will make him run.[9]

1681

- Whom is the speaker trying to persuade in this poem? Is his argument persuasive?

POEMS OF VARIED SITUATIONS AND SETTINGS

Consider the *Who? What? Why? Where?* and *When?* questions as you read the following poems.

EMILY BRONTË

The Night-Wind

In summer's mellow midnight,
A cloudless moon shone through
Our open parlor window
And rosetrees wet with dew.

5 I sat in silent musing,
The soft wind waved my hair:
It told me Heaven was glorious,
And sleeping Earth was fair.

I needed not its breathing
10 To bring such thoughts to me,
But still it whispered lowly,
"How dark the woods will be!

"The thick leaves in my murmur
Are rustling like a dream,
15 And all their myriad voices
Instinct[1] with spirit seem."

I said, "Go, gentle singer,
Thy wooing voice is kind,

---

6. Slow-jawed. Chronos (Time), ruler of the world in early Greek myth, devoured all of his children except Zeus, who was hidden. Later, Zeus seized power (see line 46 and note).   7. Through.
8. To lengthen his night of love with Alcmene, Zeus made the sun stand still.
9. Each sex act was believed to shorten life by one day.   1. Infused.

But do not think its music
20 Has power to reach my mind.

"Play with the scented flower,
The young tree's supple bough,
And leave my human feelings
In their own course to flow."

25 The wanderer would not leave me;
Its kiss grew warmer still—
"O come," it sighed so sweetly,
"I'll win thee 'gainst thy will.

"Have we not been from childhood friends?
30 Have I not loved thee long?
As long as thou hast loved the night
Whose silence wakes my song.

"And when thy heart is laid at rest
Beneath the church-yard stone
35 I shall have time enough to mourn
And thou to be alone."

September 11, 1840

- What might it mean that the speaker feels tempted by the wind to go wandering in the darkness? What might she find there?

SYLVIA PLATH

Point Shirley

From Water-Tower Hill to the brick prison
The shingle booms, bickering under
The sea's collapse.
Snowcakes break and welter. This year
5 The gritted wave leaps
The seawall and drops onto a bier
Of quahog chips,[2]
Leaving a salty mash of ice to whiten

In my grandmother's sand yard. She is dead,
10 Whose laundry snapped and froze here, who
Kept house against
What the sluttish, rutted sea could do.
Squall waves once danced
Ship timbers in through the cellar window;
15 A thresh-tailed, lanced
Shark littered in the geranium bed—

2. Chips from quahog clamshells, common on the New England coast.

Such collusion of mulish elements
She wore her broom straws to the nub.
Twenty years out
20 Of her hand; the house still hugs in each drab
Stucco socket
The purple egg-stones: from Great Head's knob
To the filled-in Gut
The sea in its cold gizzard ground those rounds.

25 Nobody wintering now behind
The planked-up windows where she set
Her wheat loaves
And apple cakes to cool. What is it
Survives, grieves
30 So, over this battered, obstinate spit
Of gravel? The waves'
Spewed relics clicker masses in the wind,

Gray waves the stub-necked eiders ride.
A labor of love, and that labor lost.
35 Steadily the sea
Eats at Point Shirley. She died blessed,
And I come by
Bones, bones only, pawed and tossed,
A dog-faced sea.
40 The sun sinks under Boston, bloody red.

I would get from these dry-papped stones
The milk your love instilled in them.
The black ducks dive.
And though your graciousness might stream,
45 And I contrive,
Grandmother, stones are nothing of home
To that spumiest dove.
Against both bar and tower the black sea runs.

                                                        1960

- How important is the specific setting of Point Shirley near Boston?
  How are memories mixed with the specific "now" of the poem?

MARY JO SALTER

Welcome to Hiroshima

is what you first see, stepping off the train:
a billboard brought to you in living English
by Toshiba Electric. While a channel
silent in the TV of the brain

5   projects those flickering re-runs of a cloud
that brims its risen columnful like beer
and, spilling over, hangs its foamy head,
you feel a thirst for history: what year

it started to be safe to breathe the air,
10 and when to drink the blood and scum afloat
on the Ohta River. But no, the water's clear,
they pour it for your morning cup of tea

in one of the countless sunny coffee shops
whose plastic dioramas advertise
15 mutations of cuisine behind the glass:
a pancake sandwich; a pizza someone tops

with a maraschino cherry. Passing by
the Peace Park's floral hypocenter (where
how bravely, or with what mistaken cheer,
20 humanity erased its own erasure),

you enter the memorial museum
and through more glass are served, as on a dish
of blistered grass, three mannequins. Like gloves
a mother clips to coatsleeves, strings of flesh

25 hang from their fingertips; or as if tied
to recall a duty for us, *Reverence
the dead whose mourners too shall soon be dead*,
but all commemoration's swallowed up

in questions of bad taste, how re-created
30 horror mocks the grim original,
and thinking at last *They should have left it all*
you stop. This is the wristwatch of a child.

Jammed on the moment's impact, resolute
to communicate some message, although mute,
35 it gestures with its hands at eight-fifteen
and eight-fifteen and eight-fifteen again

while tables of statistics on the wall
update the news by calling on a roll
of tape, death gummed on death, and in the case
40 adjacent, an exhibit under glass

is glass itself: a shard the bomb slammed in
a woman's arm at eight-fifteen, but some
three decades on—as if to make it plain
hope's only as renewable as pain

45 and as if all the unsung
debasements of the past may one day come
rising to the surface once again—
worked its filthy way out like a tongue

1984

- What arrests the speaker's attention to see beyond the "bad taste" (line 29) of the museum's displays? What is it that "worked its filthy way out like a tongue" (line 48)?

JOSHUA CLOVER

The Nevada Glassworks

Ka-Boom! They're making glass in Nevada![3]
Figure August, 1953,
mom's 13, it's hot as a simile.
Ker-Pow! Transmutation in Nevada!
5 Imagine mom: pre-PostModern new teen,
innocent for Elvis, ditto "Korean
conflict," John Paul George Ringo[4] Viet Nam.
Mom's 1 state west of the glassworks, she's
in a tree / K*I*S*S*I*N*G,
10 lurid cartoon-colored kisses. Ka-Blam!
They're blowing peacock-tinted New World glass
in southern Nevada, the alchemists
& architects of mom's duck-&-cover[5]
adolescence, they're making Las Vegas
15 turn to gold—real neon gold—in the blast
furnace heat that reaches clear to Clover
Ranch in dry Central Valley: O the dust—
It is the Golden State! O the landscape—
dreaming of James Dean! O mom in a tree
20 close-range kissing as in Nevada just
now they're making crazy ground-zero shapes
of radiant see-through geography.
What timing! What kisses! What a fever
this day's become, humming hundred degree
25 California afternoon that she's
sure she could never duplicate, never,
she feels transparent, gone—isn't this heat
suffocating?—no, she forgot to breathe
for a flash while in the Nevada flats
30 factory glassblowers exhale . . . exhale . . .
a philosopher's stone,[6] a crystal ball,
a spectacular machine. Hooray! Hats
off—they're making a window in the sand!
Mom's in the tree—picture this—all alone!

3. Sand fused into glass in the intense heat of the atomic bombs tested in Nevada in the 1950s.
4. The four Beatles, whose musical career would help define the 1960s.
5. During the Cold War era, American school children were trained to "duck and cover" in case of nuclear attack.
6. Legendary substance long sought by alchemists, who believed it would transmute base metals to gold and confer immortal life.

35 Unforgettable kisses, comic book
    mnemonic kisses, O something's coming
    out of the ranch road heat mirage. That drone—
    an engine? Mom quits practice & looks
    east, cups an ear to the beloved humming,
40 the hazy gold dust kicked wildly west
    ahead of something almost . . . in . . . sight. Vroom!
    It's the Future, hot like nothing else, dressed
    as a sonic-boom Cadillac. O mom!
    This land is your land / This land Amnesia—
45 they're dropping some new science out there,
    a picture-perfect hole blown clear to Asia:
    everything in the desert—Shazam!—turns
    to glass, gold glass, a picture-window where
    the bomb-dead kids are burned & burn & burn

                                                      1997

- In what line do you discover that the speaker is not himself a boy in
  1953, but is writing from his mother's teenage perspective? What
  words especially convey the place and time period?

DEREK WALCOTT

Midsummer

Certain things here[7] are quietly American—
that chain-link fence dividing the absent roars
of the beach from the empty ball park, its holes
muttering the word umpire instead of empire;
5   the gray, metal light where an early pelican
coasts, with its engine off, over the pink fire
of a sea whose surface is as cold as Maine's.
The light warms up the sides of white, eager Cessnas[8]
parked at the airstrip under the freckling hills
10 of St. Thomas. The sheds, the brown, functional hangar,
are like those of the Occupation in the last war.
The night left a rank smell under the casuarinas,
the villas have fenced-off beaches where the natives walk,
illegal immigrants from unlucky islands
15 who envy the smallest polyp its right to work.
Here the wetback crab and the mollusc are citizens,
and the leaves have green cards. Bulldozers jerk
and gouge out a hill, but we all know that the dust
is industrial and must be suffered. Soon—
20 the sea's corrugations are sheets of zinc
soldered by the sun's steady acetylene. This

---

7. Trinidad.   8. Small airplanes.

drizzle that falls now is American rain,
stitching stars in the sand. My own corpuscles
are changing as fast. I fear what the migrant envies:
25 the starry pattern they make—the flag on the post office—
the quality of the dirt, the fealty changing under my foot.

1984

- What is "American" (line 22) about the images described in this
  poem? Why does the speaker say he fears "the starry pattern" made
  by the raindrops in the sand (line 25)?

MARY OLIVER

Singapore

In Singapore, in the airport,
a darkness was ripped from my eyes.
In the women's restroom, one compartment stood open.
A woman knelt there, washing something in the white bowl.

5 Disgust argued in my stomach
and I felt, in my pocket, for my ticket.

A poem should always have birds in it.
Kingfishers, say, with their bold eyes and gaudy wings.
Rivers are pleasant, and of course trees.
10 A waterfall, or if that's not possible, a fountain rising and falling.
A person wants to stand in a happy place, in a poem.

When the woman turned I could not answer her face.
Her beauty and her embarrassment struggled together, and neither
    could win.
She smiled and I smiled. What kind of nonsense is this?
15 Everybody needs a job.

Yes, a person wants to stand in a happy place, in a poem.
But first we must watch her as she stares down at her labor, which is
    dull enough.
She is washing the tops of the airport ashtrays, as big as hubcaps, with
    a blue rag.
Her small hands turn the metal, scrubbing and rinsing.
20 She does not work slowly, nor quickly, but like a river.
Her dark hair is like the wing of a bird.

I don't doubt for a moment that she loves her life.
And I want her to rise up from the crust and the slop and fly down to
    the river.
This probably won't happen.
25 But maybe it will.
If the world were only pain and logic, who would want it?

Of course, it isn't.
Neither do I mean anything miraculous, but only
the light that can shine out of a life. I mean
30   the way she unfolded and refolded the blue cloth,
the way her smile was only for my sake; I mean
the way this poem is filled with trees, and birds.

1990

- What "darkness was ripped" from the speaker's eyes (line 2)? Does it
  matter that the poem is set in (and named after) a particular city?

EARLE BIRNEY

Irapuato[9]

For reasons any
                brigadier
                        could tell
this is a favorite nook for
5   massacre
Toltex by Mixtex Mixtex by Aztex
Aztex by Spanishtex Spanishtex by
Mexitex by Mexitex by Mexitex by Texaco[1]
So any farmer can see how the strawberries
10 are the biggest and reddest
    in the whole damn continent

but why
        when arranged under
                        the market flies
15 do they look like small clotting hearts?

1962

- What connects "Toltex" and "Texaco" in the speaker's mind (lines
  6–8)?

SUGGESTIONS FOR WRITING

1. Matthew Arnold's "Dover Beach" is a meditation on history and human destiny
   derived from the poet's close observation of the ebb and flow of the sea. Write an
   essay in which you examine the poem's descriptive language and the way it creates
   a suitable setting for Arnold's philosophical musings.
2. Certain seventeenth-century poets, such as John Donne and Andrew Marvell, have
   been called "metaphysical poets" for their ingenuity in using apparently far-fetched
   analogies to create apt and insightful comparisons, usually intended to persuade.

9. A city in central Mexico, northwest of Mexico City.
1. The Toltec, Mixtec, and Aztec peoples lived in pre-Columbian Mexico.

What is the line of reasoning in Donne's "The Flea" or Marvell's "To His Coy Mistress?" Who is the intended audience for each poem? Write an essay in which you discuss the way that either or both of these poems uses situation as the basis for comparison and persuasion.

3. Mary Jo Salter's "Welcome to Hiroshima" and Mary Oliver's "Singapore" both use a similar situation—a visit to a site in Asia—to confront the reader with a clash between traditional and contemporary things and values. How does each speaker respond to the painful or disgusting scenes she witnesses? Write an essay in which you examine the way either of these poems draws on situation and setting to develop a theme about global economics, the relations of East and West, or the destruction or preservation of the past.

4. This chapter contains a number of poems that, in both obvious and subtle ways, associate love with the morning—Shakespeare's "[Full many a glorious morning have I seen]," Donne's "The Good-Morrow," Sylvia Plath's "Morning Song," Billy Collins's "Morning," August Kleinzahler's "Aubade on East 12th Street," and Jonathan Swift's "A Description of the Morning." Write an essay in which you compare and contrast the poetic use of the morning setting in any two of these poems.

5. Choose any of the poems in this or the previous chapters and write an essay about the way a poet can use situation and setting to evoke a rich intermingling of language, subject, and feeling.

Cultural Homelands: An Album

Rosemary Woods, *Africa Collage*

One of the most ancient topics of literature is the quest or journey away from home. Sacred literature, including the Bible, tells of exile and a long period of suffering before returning to or reaching a homeland. Epic poems and romances may concern the hero's wanderings or adventures to reach or to defend a realm that is deeply associated with his birth, inheritance, or fate. Since the 1500s, global exploration, colonialism, slavery, mass migration, and economic transformation have meant that many of the world's populations have experienced dislocation and loss of roots. Those who find themselves displaced try to remember where they came from; they may seek to honor their heritage or yearn for a sense of belonging. The poems in this album were written at different times in different cultural contexts. Each speaker suggests some kind of double vision on the past and present, on a more modern or recent location and the former place. What is the role of dislocation or altered identity in these poems? How do these poems represent the speaker's divided loyalties or distance from home? How do they indicate the passage of time, whether in history, over generations, or within one person's life?

PHILLIS WHEATLEY

On Being Brought from Africa to America

'Twas mercy brought me from my Pagan land,
Taught my benighted soul to understand
That there's a God, that there's a Saviour too:
Once I redemption neither sought nor knew.
5 Some view our sable race with scornful eye,
"Their colour is a diabolic die."
Remember, Christians, Negroes, black as Cain,[1]
May be refin'd, and join th' angelic train.

1773

- How does this compressed poem appeal to "Christians" (line 7)? If Africa was "Pagan" and "benighted" (lines 1, 2), why are "some" people wrong to see Africans as "diabolic" or dark because of devilish sin (lines 5, 6)?

MAYA ANGELOU

Africa

Thus she had lain
sugar cane sweet
deserts her hair
golden her feet
5 mountains her breasts
two Niles her tears

---

1. One of Adam's sons, who killed his brother Abel. See Genesis 4.

Thus she has lain
Black through the years.

Over the white seas
10 rime white and cold
brigands ungentled
icicle bold
took her young daughters
sold her strong sons
15 churched her with Jesus
bled her with guns.
Thus she has lain.

Now she is rising
remember her pain
20 remember the losses
her screams loud and vain
remember her riches
her history slain
now she is striding
25 although she had lain.

1975

- Why do the phrases describing Africa's action—"had lain," "is rising," and so forth—repeat with variations throughout the poem?

DEREK WALCOTT

A Far Cry from Africa

A wind is ruffling the tawny pelt
Of Africa. Kikuyu,[2] quick as flies,
Batten upon the bloodstreams of the veldt.[3]
Corpses are scattered through a paradise.
5 Only the worm, colonel of carrion, cries:
"Waste no compassion on these separate dead!"
Statistics justify and scholars seize
The salients of colonial policy.
What is that to the white child hacked in bed?
10 To savages, expendable as Jews?

Threshed out by beaters,[4] the long rushes break
In a white dust of ibises whose cries

2. An East African tribe whose members, as Mau Mau fighters, conducted an eight-year insurrection
against British colonial settlers in Kenya.
3. Open plains, neither cultivated nor thickly forested (Afrikaans).
4. In big-game hunting, natives are hired to beat the brush, driving birds—such as ibises—and other animals into the open.

Have wheeled since civilization's dawn
From the parched river or beast-teeming plain.
15 The violence of beast on beast is read
As natural law, but upright man
Seeks his divinity by inflicting pain.
Delirious as these worried beasts, his wars
Dance to the tightened carcass of a drum,
20 While he calls courage still that native dread
Of the white peace contracted by the dead.

Again brutish necessity wipes its hands
Upon the napkin of a dirty cause, again
A waste of our compassion, as with Spain,[5]
25 The gorilla wrestles with the superman.
I who am poisoned with the blood of both,
Where shall I turn, divided to the vein?
I who have cursed
The drunken officer of British rule, how choose
30 Between this Africa and the English tongue I love?
Betray them both, or give back what they give?
How can I face such slaughter and be cool?
How can I turn from Africa and live?

                                        1962

- How does the speaker express his divided loyalties in the questions that conclude the poem? Can be choose a homeland to return to?

Authors on Their Work: DEREK WALCOTT

From "An Interview with Derek Walcott" (1979)*

Q. ... "A Far Cry from Africa" ... closes with "How can I turn from Africa and live?" And yet at another juncture you speak of the African revival as a kind of simplification, although a glamorous one, for the Caribbean writer. Do you want to talk about the Caribbean writer's special relationship to Africa?

A. ... I have been British; I have been a citizen of the Caribbean federation; now I'm supposed to be either a Trinidadian or a St. Lucian but with a British passport. I find that I am able to make a living in America (and I owe America a great deal for its recognition and the fact that I can work here); and there is the same danger, the same seduction in saying I really am

(Continued on next page)

5. The Spanish Civil War (1936–39), in which the Republican loyalists were supported politically by liberals in the West and militarily by Soviet Communists, and the Nationalist rebels by Nazi Germany and Fascist Italy.

(Continued)

African and should be in Africa, or that my whole experience is African. This can be simply another longing, even a slave longing, for another master. There is no West Indian who is black, or even one who is not black, who is not aware of the existence of Africa in all of us. I was writing against the African influence during a period when the political nostalgia seemed to be a deceit because it meant that if one was lifting up a spade or fork, all one had to do was to throw it down and turn and look toward Africa and say, well, I shouldn't be digging up the ground in St. Lucia, or I shouldn't be doing whatever job I am doing in any one of the islands. I should really be in some sort of pastoral idealized place where I won't have to work, or where I may be working for Mother Africa. The fact is that every West Indian has been severed from a continent, whether he be Indian, Chinese, Portuguese, or black. To have the population induced into a mass nostalgia to be somewhere else seemed to me about as ennobling as wishing that the whole population was in Brooklyn. . . . What I think was especially irritating to me was the fact that this idea was continually being dramatized in poems being offered to the masses—mainly the urban masses—as an escape. It would be equally abhorrent to me to say "I wish we were English again" as to say "I wish we were African again." The reality is that one has to build in the West Indies. But that is not to say one doesn't know who one is: our music, our speech—all the things that are organic in the way we live—are African.

• • •

I . . . felt that it was a privilege to grow up as an English colonial child [in the West Indies] because politically and culturally the British heritage was supposed to be mine. It was no problem for me to feel that since I was writing in English, I was in tune with the growth of the language. I was the contemporary of anyone writing in English anywhere in the world. What is more important, however—and I'm still working on this—was to find a voice that was not inflected by influences. One didn't develop an English accent in speech; one kept as close as possible to an inflection that was West Indian. The aim was that a West Indian or an Englishman could read a single poem, each with his own accent, without either one feeling that it was written in dialect.

*Edward Hirsch and Derek Walcott, "An Interview with Derek Walcott," *Contemporary Literature* 20.3 (Summer 1979): 279–292.

ELIZABETH ALEXANDER

West Indian Primer

for Clifford L. Alexander, Sr.
1898–1989

"On the road between Spanish Town
and Kingston," my grandfather said,
"I was born." His father a merchant,
Jewish, from Italy or Spain

5   In the great earthquake the ground split
clean, and great-grandfather fell
in the fault with his goat. I don't know
how I got this tale and do not ask.

His black mother taught my grand-
10   father figures, fixed codfish cakes
and fried plantains, drilled cleanliness,
telling the truth, punctuality.

"There is no man more honest,"
my father says. Years later
15   I read that Jews passed through my
grandfather's birthplace frequently.

I know more about Toussaint[6]
and Hispaniola[7] than my own
Jamaica and my family tales.
20   I finger the stories like genie

lamps. I write this West Indian primer.

                                        1990

- Why do you think this poem is presented as a "primer"—that is, a basic introduction—for the speaker's native Jamaica? Does the poem fulfill that function?

AGHA SHAHID ALI

Postcard from Kashmir

(for Pavan Sahgal)

Kashmir shrinks into my mailbox,
my home a neat four by six inches.

---

6. Self-educated Haitian black soldier and liberator (1783–1803).
7. The first island claimed by Columbus for Spain in 1492, now divided into the nations of Haiti and the Dominican Republic.

I always loved neatness. Now I hold
the half-inch Himalayas in my hand.
5 This is home. And this the closest
I'll ever be to home. When I return,
the colors won't be so brilliant,
the Jhelum's waters[8] so clean,
so ultramarine. My love
10 so overexposed.

And my memory will be a little
out of focus, in it
a giant negative, black
and white, still undeveloped.

1987

- What words characterize the speaker's dreams of home in this poem?
  What words reveal a more realistic attitude?

SUGGESTIONS FOR WRITING

1. How does the form of a poem reveal divided attachments to two cultures or the experience of leaving a cultural homeland? How do some poets adapt the art forms of the new country? Phillis Wheatley's "On Being Brought from Africa to America" uses the heroic couplet, and June Jordan's "Something Like a Sonnet for Phillis Miracle Wheatley" (chapter 19) uses both the sonnet and an unusual dactylic tetrameter (see chapter 17). Write an essay in which you compare these two poems that both honor traditions and challenge them. How does Jordan pay her respects to Wheatley and make it clear that she and Wheatley were protesting slavery?

2. Look closely at the three stanzas of "A Far Cry from Africa" by Derek Walcott. Be sure to note any changes—rhyme patterns or meter, subject matter or tone—across the three stanzas. Where does the speaker clarify who he is and where his loyalties lie? Why is the last part of the poem a series of questions? Write an essay in which you interpret the form and theme of the poem as itself a kind of "far cry from Africa," in every sense: far from that homeland, part of non-African tradition, "crying" for connection.

3. How many generations, how many locations, and how many races or ethnic groups are featured in Elizabeth Alexander's "A West Indian Primer"? Write an essay in which you begin with the last line of the poem and explain that the speaker is writing a sort of back-to-basics lesson in the history of the West Indies and her own connection to that cultural homeland.

4. Imagine receiving in your mailbox a postcard from the place where you or your parents were born. (You may imagine receiving digital pictures or messages in other formats.) Write a poem or a short prose description in which you express a response similar to the speaker's in Agha Shahid Ali's "Postcard from Kashmir": How would the place be changed if you could visit, and how would it differ from the way you or your family think about it now?

8. The river Jhelum runs through Kashmir and Pakistan.

16 LANGUAGE

Fiction and drama depend on language just as poetry does, but in a poem almost everything comes down to the particular meanings and implications, as well as sound and shape, of individual words. When we read stories and plays, we generally focus our attention on character and plot, and although words determine how we imagine those characters and how we respond to what happens to them, we are not as likely to pause over any one word as we may need to when reading a poem. Because poems are often short, much depends on every word in them. Sometimes, as though they were distilled prose, poems contain only the essential words. They say just barely enough to communicate in the most basic way, using elemental signs—each of which is chosen for exactly the right shade of meaning or feeling or both. But elemental does not necessarily mean simple, and these signs may be very rich in their meanings and complex in their effects. The poet's word choice—the **diction** of a poem—determines not only meaning but just about every effect the poem produces.

PRECISION AND AMBIGUITY, DENOTATION AND CONNOTATION

Let's look first at poems that create some of their effects by examining—or playing with—a single word. Often multiple meanings or shiftiness and uncertainty of a word are at issue. The following short poem, for example, depends almost entirely on the ways we use the word *play*.

SARAH CLEGHORN

[The golf links lie so near the mill]

The golf links lie so near the mill
That almost every day
The laboring children can look out
And see the men at play.

1915

While traveling in the American South, Cleghorn had seen, right next to a golf course, a textile mill that employed quite young children. Her poem doesn't *say* that we expect men to work and children to play; it just assumes our expectation and builds an effect of *dramatic* **irony**—an incongruity between what we expect and what actually occurs—out of the observation. The poem saves almost all of its devastating effect for the final word, after the situation has been carefully described and the irony set up.

In the following two poems, a word used over and over acquires multiple meanings and refuses to be limited to a single one.

ANNE FINCH, COUNTESS OF WINCHELSEA

There's No To-morrow

A Fable imitated from Sir Roger L'Estrange

Two long had Lov'd, and now the Nymph desir'd,
The Cloak of Wedlock, as the Case requir'd;
Urg'd that, the Day he wrought her to this Sorrow,
He Vow'd, that he wou'd marry her To-Morrow.
5   Agen he Swears, to shun the present Storm,
That he, To-Morrow, will that Vow perform.
The Morrows in their due Successions came;
Impatient still on Each, the pregnant Dame
Urg'd him to keep his Word, and still he swore the same.
10   When tir'd at length, and meaning no Redress,
But yet the Lye not caring to confess,
He for his Oath this Salvo chose to borrow,
That he was Free, since there was no To-Morrow;
For when it comes in Place to be employ'd,
15   'Tis then To-Day; To-Morrow's ne'er enjoy'd.
The Tale's a Jest, the Moral is a Truth;
To-Morrow and To-Morrow, cheat our Youth:
In riper Age, To-Morrow still we cry,
Not thinking, that the present Day we Dye;
20   Unpractis'd all the Good we had Design'd;
There's No To-Morrow to a Willing Mind.

1713

CHARLES BERNSTEIN

Of Time and the Line

George Burns[1] likes to insist that he always
takes the straight lines; the cigar in his mouth
is a way of leaving space between the

---

1. American comedian (1896–1996) who played straight man to his wife, Gracie Allen.

lines for a laugh. He weaves lines together
5 by means of a picaresque narrative;
not so Hennie Youngman,[2] whose lines are strictly paratactic. My father pushed a
line of ladies' dresses—not down the street
in a pushcart but upstairs in a fact'ry
10 office. My mother has been more concerned
with her hemline. Chairman Mao[3] put forward
Maoist lines, but that's been abandoned (mostly) for the East-West line of malarkey
so popular in these parts. The prestige
15 of the iambic line has recently
suffered decline, since it's no longer so
clear who "I" am, much less who *you* are. When
making a line, better be double sure
what you're lining in & what you're lining
20 out & which side of the line you're on; the
world is made up so (Adam didn't so much
name as delineate). Every poem's got
a prosodic lining, some of which will
unzip for summer wear. The lines of an
25 imaginary are inscribed on the
social flesh by the knifepoint of history.
Nowadays, you can often spot a work
of poetry by whether it's in lines
or no; if it's in prose, there's a good chance
30 it's a poem. While there is no lesson in
the line more useful than that of the picket line, the line that has caused the most adversity is the bloodline. In Russia
everyone is worried about long lines;
35 back in the USA, it's strictly soup-
lines. "Take a chisel to write," but for an
actor a line's got to be cued. Or, as
they say in math, it takes two lines to make
an angle but only one lime to make
40 a Margarita.

1991

In these poems, the importance of a word involves its ambiguity (that is, its having more than one possible meaning) rather than its precision or exactness. The Finch poem repeatedly explores the shifting sands of the word *tomorrow*, first noting how different people may think of its meanings differently, and then showing how these shifts are anchored in time and the whole process of meaning. The Bernstein poem finds a great variety of completely different meanings of the

2. American stand-up comedian (1906–98), king of the one-liner.
3. Mao Zedong (1893–1976), leader of the revolution that established China as a communist nation.

word *line*. How many different meanings can you distinguish in the poem? What does "Time" (in the title) have to do with the poem?

Although the unambiguous or "dictionary" meaning of words—that is, what words denote, their **denotation**—is certainly important, words are more than hard blocks of meaning on whose sense everyone agrees. They also have a more personal side, and they carry emotional force and shades of suggestion. The words we use indicate not only what we mean but how we feel about it, and we choose words that we hope will engage others emotionally and persuasively, in conversation and daily usage as well as in poems. A person who holds office is, quite literally (and unemotionally), an *officeholder*—the word denotes what he or she does. But if we want to convey that a particular officeholder is wise, trustworthy, and deserving of political support we may call that person a *civil servant*, a *political leader*, or an *elected official*, whereas if we want to promote distrust or contempt of that same officeholder we might say *politician* or *bureaucrat* or *political hack*. These terms have clear **connotations**—suggestions of emotional coloration that imply our attitude and invite a similar one from our hearers. What words connote can be just as important to a poem as what they denote; some poems work primarily through denotation and some more through connotation.

The following **epitaph**, for example, which describes one person's mixed feelings about another, depends heavily on the connotations of fairly common words.

WALTER DE LA MARE

Slim Cunning Hands

Slim cunning hands at rest, and cozening eyes—
Under this stone one loved too wildly lies;
How false she was, no granite could declare;
    Nor all earth's flowers, how fair.

1950

What the speaker in "Slim Cunning Hands" remembers about the dead woman—her hands, her eyes—tells part of the story; her physical presence was clearly important to him. The poem's other nouns—stone, granite, flowers—all remind us of her death and its finality. All these words denote objects having to do with the rituals that memorialize a departed life. Granite and stone connote finality as well, and flowers connote fragility and suggest the shortness of life (which is why they have become the symbolic language of funerals). The way the speaker talks about the woman expresses, in just a few words, the complexity of his love for her. She was loved, he says, too "wildly"—by him perhaps, and apparently by others. The excitement she offered is suggested by the word, and also the lack of control. The words *cunning* and *cozening* help us interpret both her wildness and her falsity; they suggest her calculation, cleverness, and untrustworthiness as well as her skill, persuasiveness, and ability to please. Moreover, coming at the end of the second line, the word *lies* has more than one meaning. The body "lies" under the stone, but the woman's falsity has by now become too prominent to ignore as a second meaning. And the word *fair*, a simple yet very inclusive word, suggests how totally attractive the speaker finds her: Her beauty can no more be expressed by flowers than her fickleness can be expressed by something as permanent as words in stone. But the word *fair*, in the emphatic position as the final word, also implies two other meanings that seem to resonate, ironically, with what we have already learned about her from the speaker: "impartial" and "just." "Impartial" she may be in her preferences (as the word *false* suggests), but to the speaker she is hardly "just," and the final defining word speaks both to her appearance and (ironically) to her character. Simple words here tell us perhaps all we need to know of a long story—or at least the speaker's version of it.

Words like *fair* and *cozening* are clearly loaded. They imply more emotionally than they mean literally. They have strong, clear connotations; they tell us what to think, what evaluation to make; and they suggest the basis for the evaluation.

Sometimes word choice in poems is less dramatic and less obviously significant but equally important. Often, in fact, simple appropriateness makes the words in a poem work, and words that do not call special attention to themselves can be the most effective. Precision of denotation may be just as impressive and productive of specific effects as the resonance or ambiguous suggestiveness of connotation. Often poems achieve their power by a combination of verbal effects, setting off elaborate figures of speech or other complicated strategies with simple words chosen to mark exact actions, moments, or states of mind.

Words are the starting point for all poetry, of course, and almost every word is likely to be significant, either denotatively or connotatively or both. Poets who know their craft pick each word with care to express exactly what needs to be expressed and to suggest every emotional shade that the poem is calculated to evoke in us.

Word Choice: An Example and an Exercise

Before you read the following poem, notice the three words in the title. What do they lead you to expect? What questions do they raise? Jot down your thoughts on a piece of paper. Then, as you read the poem, take note of key words and try to be conscious of the emotional effects and impressions they create.

THEODORE ROETHKE

My Papa's Waltz

The whiskey on your breath
Could make a small boy dizzy;
But I hung on like death:
Such waltzing was not easy.

5 We romped until the pans
Slid from the kitchen shelf;

(Continued on next page)

(Continued)

My mother's countenance
Could not unfrown itself.

The hand that held my wrist
10　Was battered on one knuckle;
At every step you missed
My right ear scraped a buckle.

You beat time on my head
With a palm caked hard by dirt,
15　Then waltzed me off to bed
Still clinging to your shirt.

1948

Exactly how does the situation in "My Papa's Waltz" and the poem itself
fulfill or deny your expectations? How does it answer your questions? How
does it characterize the waltz and the speaker's feelings about it? Which
words are most suggestive in these terms? What clues are there in the word
choice that an adult is remembering a childhood experience? How scared
was the boy at the time? How does the grown adult now evaluate his emotions when he was a boy?

WORD ORDER AND WORD PLACEMENT

Often individual words qualify and amplify one another—suggestions clarify
other suggestions, and meanings grow upon meanings—and thus how words are
put together and where individual words are located can be important, too.
Notice, for example, that in "Slim Cunning Hands" the final emphasis is on how
fair in appearance the woman was; the speaker's last word describes the quality
he can't forget despite her lack of a different kind of fairness and his distrust of
her. Even though it doesn't justify everything else, her beauty mitigates all the
disappointment and hurt. Putting the word *fair* at the end of the line and of the
poem gives it special emphasis and meaning.

That one word, *fair*, does not stand all by itself, however, any more than any
other word in a poem can be considered all alone. Every word exists within larger
units of meaning—sentences, patterns of comparisons and contrasts, the whole
poem—and where the word is and how it is used are often important. The final
word or words may be especially emphatic (as in "Slim Cunning Hands"), and
words that are repeated take on a special intensity, as *line* does in "Of Time and
the Line," or as *chartered* and *cry* do in "London" (chapter 13), or *what did I know?* in
"Those Winter Sundays" (Family: An Album). Certain words may stand out
because they are used in an unusual way (like *chartered* in "London") or because
they are given an artificial prominence—through unusual sentence structure, for
example, or because the title calls special attention to them. In a poem, as opposed

to a prose work, moreover, the number and placement of words in a line and the spacing of the words and lines stays the same in every printed version. Where words come—in a line, in a stanza—and how they are spatially and visually related to other words also helps determine their force and meaning.

The subtlety and force of word choice are sometimes strongly affected by **syntax**—the way the sentences are put together. When you find unusual syntax or spacing, you can be pretty sure that something there merits special attention. Notice the odd sentence constructions in the second and third stanzas of "My Papa's Waltz"—the way the speaker talks about the abrasion of buckle on ear in line 12, for example. He does not say that the buckle scraped his ear, but rather "My right ear scraped a buckle." Reversing the more common expression makes a big difference in the effect created; the speaker avoids placing blame and refuses to specify any unpleasant effect. Had he said that the buckle scraped his ear, we would have to worry about the fragile ear. The syntax of the poem channels our feeling and helps control what we think of the "waltz."

In the most curious part of the poem, the second stanza, the silent mother appears, and the syntax on both sides of the semicolon is peculiar. In lines 5–6, the connection between the romping and the pans falling is stated oddly: "We romped *until* the pans / Slid from the kitchen shelf" (emphasis added). The speaker does not say that they knocked down the pans or imply awkwardness, but he does suggest energetic activity and duration. He implies intensity, almost intention— as though the romping would not be complete until the pans fell. And the clause about the mother—odd but effective—makes her position clear. A silent bystander in this male ritual, she doesn't seem frightened or angry. She seems to be holding a frown, or to have it molded on her face, as though it were part of her own ritual, and perhaps a facet of her stern character as well. The syntax implies that she *has to* maintain the frown, and the falling of the pans almost seems to be for her benefit. She disapproves, but she remains their audience.

Sometimes poems create, as well, a powerful sense of the way minds and emotions work by varying normal syntactical order in special ways. Listen and watch, for example, what happens a few lines into the following poem. What does it suggest about what is happening inside the speaker?

SHARON OLDS

Sex without Love

How do they do it, the ones who make love
without love? Beautiful as dancers,
gliding over each other like ice-skaters
over the ice, fingers hooked
5 inside each other's bodies, faces
red as steak, wine, wet as the
children at birth whose mothers are going to
give them away. How do they come to the
come to the   come to the   God   come to the
10 still waters, and not love

the one who came there with them, light
rising slowly as steam off their joined
skin? These are the true religious,
the purists, the pros, the ones who will not
15 accept a false Messiah, love the
priest instead of the God. They do not
mistake the lover for their own pleasure,
they are like great runners: they know they are alone
with the road surface, the cold, the wind,
20 the fit of their shoes, their over-all cardio-
vascular health—just factors, like the partner
in the bed, and not the truth, which is the
single body alone in the universe
against its own best time.

1984

The poem starts calmly enough, with a simple rhetorical question implying that the speaker just cannot understand sex without love. Lines 2–4 carefully compare such sexual activity with two other artful activities, and the speaker—although plainly disapproving—seems coolly in control of the analysis and evaluation. But by the end of the fourth line, something begins to seem odd: "Hooked" seems too ugly and extreme a way to characterize the lovers' fingers, however much the speaker may disapprove, and by line 6 the syntax seems to break down. How does "wine" fit the syntax of the line? Is it parallel with "steak," another example of redness? Or is it somehow related to the last part of the sentence, parallel with "faces"? Neither of these possibilities quite works. At best, the punctuation is inadequate; at worst, the speaker's mind is working too fast for the language it generates, scrambling its images. We can't yet be sure what is going on, but by the ninth line the lack of control is manifest with the compulsive repeating (three times) of "come to the" and the interjected "God."

Such verbal behavior—here concretized by the way the poem orders its words and spaces them on the page—invites us to reevaluate the speaker's moralizing relative to her emotional involvement with the issues and with her representation of sexuality itself. The speaker's own values, as well as those who have sex without love, become a subject for evaluation.

Words, the basic materials of poetry, come in many kinds and can be used in many different ways and in different—sometimes surprising—combinations. They are seldom simple or transparent, even when we know their meanings and recognize their syntactical combinations as ordinary and conventional. Carefully examining them, individually and collectively, is a crucial part of reading poems, and being able to ask good questions about the words that poems use and the way they use them is one of the most basic—and rewarding—skills a reader of poetry can develop.

. . .

YVOR WINTERS

At the San Francisco Airport

to my daughter, 1954

This is the terminal: the light
Gives perfect vision, false and hard;
The metal glitters, deep and bright.
Great planes are waiting in the yard—
5 They are already in the night.

And you are here beside me, small,
Contained and fragile, and intent
On things that I but half recall—
Yet going whither you are bent.
10 I am the past, and that is all.

But you and I in part are one:
The frightened brain, the nervous will,
The knowledge of what must be done,
The passion to acquire the skill
15 To face that which you dare not shun.

The rain of matter upon sense
Destroys me momently. The score:
There comes what will come. The expense
Is what one thought, and something more—
20 One's being and intelligence.

This is the terminal, the break.
Beyond this point, on lines of air,
You take the way that you must take;
And I remain in light and stare—
25 In light, and nothing else, awake.

                                    1954

• How does this poem use the ambiguity of the word *terminal*?

MARTHA COLLINS

Lies

Anyone can get it wrong, laying low
when she ought to lie, but is it a lie
for her to say she laid him when we know
he wouldn't lie still long enough to let
5 her do it? A good lay is not a song,
not anymore; a good lie is something

else: lyrics, lines, what if you say *dear sister*
when you have no sister, what if you say *guns*
when you saw no guns, though you know
10 they're there? *She laid down her arms; she lay*
down, her arms by her sides. If we don't know,
do we lie if we say? If we don't say, do we lie
down on the job? To arms! in any case
dear friends. If we must lie, let's not lie around.

1999

• How many different meanings of "lie" and "lay" does this poem
  contain? What would you say is the poem's real subject?

EMILY DICKINSON

[*I dwell in Possibility—*]

I dwell in Possibility—
A fairer House than Prose—
More numerous of Windows—
Superior—for Doors—

5 Of Chambers as the Cedars—
Impregnable of Eye—
And for an Everlasting Roof
The Gambrels[4] of the Sky—

Of Visitors—the fairest—
10 For Occupation—This—
The spreading wide my narrow Hands
To gather Paradise—

ca. 1862

• What does Dickinson seem to mean by "Possibility"? How does the
  poem's ending broaden this meaning?

WILLIAM CARLOS WILLIAMS

The Red Wheelbarrow

so much depends
upon

a red wheel
barrow

---

4. Roofs with double slopes.

5 glazed with rain
water

beside the white
chickens.
                    1923

- How does setting the words *barrow, water,* and *chickens* on lines of
  their own help to substantiate the poem's first line?

This Is Just to Say

I have eaten
the plums
that were in
the icebox

5 and which
you were probably
saving
for breakfast

Forgive me
10 they were delicious
so sweet
and so cold
                    1934

- What is meant by "This" in the poem's title? What is the apparent
  occasion for this poem?

Authors on Their Work: WILLIAM CARLOS WILLIAMS

From reading and commentary at Princeton
University (1952)*

I've . . . gotten some fame, but I should probably say notoriety,
from a very brief little poem called "The Red Wheelbarrow." . . .
I had a letter from a lady in Boston after that appearance
that said, "I love it. It's perfectly wonderful. But what does it
mean?" [audience laughs] In the first place, I say modestly it's
a perfect poem. [laughs] . . . It means just the same as the opening lines of [John
Keats's] *Endymion,* "A thing of beauty is a joy forever." And so much depends
upon it. But instead of saying "A thing of beauty," I say, "a red wheel / barrow
// glazed with rain / water // beside the white / chickens." Isn't that beautiful?

* * *

(Continued on next page)

(Continued)

From interview with John W. Gerber (1950)**

WILLIAMS: It actually took place just as it . . . says here [in "This Is Just to Say"]. And my wife being out, I left a note for her just that way, and she replied very beautifully. Unfortunately, I lost it. . . . I think what she wrote was quite as good as this, a little more complex, but quite as good. Perhaps the virtue of this is its simplicity.

INTERVIEWER: Now, what I want to ask you about that [is], What makes that a poem?

WILLIAMS: In the first place, it's metrically absolutely regular. . . . [reads poem] So, dogmatically speaking, it has to be a poem because it goes that way, don't you see?

INTERVIEWER: Well, this goes against so many preconceived ideas of the poem, though, because it's the kind of thing that almost anybody might say.

WILLIAMS: Yes, because no one believes that poetry can exist in its own light. That's one of our immediate fallacies. . . . Imagine reading a poem in the American dialects, how impossible! That's the first hazard, that's the first hurdle. We have to get over that. . . . It can't be that we poor colonials, as we have been ever since the Revolution, we poor people who are not living in the centers of Europe can have anything happen in our lives important enough to be put down in words and given a form. But everything in our lives, if it's sufficiently authentic to our lives and touches us deeply enough, with a certain amount of feeling, is capable of being organized into a form which can be a poem. . . . Your wife, . . . the woman who's there with whom you are supposed to be in love and sometimes are . . . had these things saved for supper, and here you come along and raid it. Why, it's practically rape of the icebox, and there you are. So I think that's material for a poem. [laughs] That's a definite poem—without even writing it. But then if you can give it conventional metrical form, why . . . you're just simply superb, that's all. [laughs] You've done a great deed.

* Reading and commentary at Princeton University, March 19, 1952. *Penn Sound*. Web. 17 June 2009.
** Interview with John W. Gerber, Rutherford, New Jersey, June 1950. *Penn Sound*. Web. 17 June 2009.

GERARD MANLEY HOPKINS

Pied Beauty[5]

Glory be to God for dappled things—
    For skies of couple-color as a brinded[6] cow;
        For rose-moles all in stipple[7] upon trout that swim;
Fresh-firecoal chestnut-falls;[8] finches' wings;
5   Landscape plotted and pieced—fold, fallow, and plow;
        And all trades, their gear and tackle and trim.
All things counter, original, spare, strange;
    Whatever is fickle, freckled (who knows how?)
        With swift, slow; sweet, sour; adazzle, dim;
10 He fathers-forth whose beauty is past change;
        Praise him.

1887

- How many ways of expressing mixed color can you find in this poem? How does Hopkins expand the meaning of "pied beauty"?

E. E. CUMMINGS

[*in Just-*][9]

in Just-
spring   when the world is mud-
luscious the little
lame balloonman

5 whistles   far   and wee

and eddieandbill come
running from marbles and
piracies and it's
spring

10 when the world is puddle-wonderful

the queer
old balloonman whistles
far   and   wee
and bettyandisbel come dancing

15 from hop-scotch and jump-rope and
it's
spring

---

5. Particolored beauty: having patches or sections of more than one color.   6. Streaked or spotted.
7. Rose-colored dots or flecks.   8. Fallen chestnuts as red as burning coals.
9. First poem in the series *Chansons innocentes*.

and
    the
20   goat-footed

balloonMan   whistles
far
and
wee[1]

1923

- What are some connotations of "mud-luscious" and "puddle-wonderful" (lines 2–3, 10)? What are some of the ways in which this poem challenges a reader's expectations of diction and syntax?

BOB PERELMAN

The Masque of Rhyme

Adding my pee to the sea
of rhyme, it's time I admit sameness

is a bit of a hoax.
Yes, my body lies over social oceans

5 like yours and slightly like Rover's,
except he barks to speak and we

speak to bargain and intermingle. All's
translation in love and war. Do you

hear the joke about the marriage of
10 true mind to impediment after impediment?

That's what we call "language," at
least around here. What rhymes with "rhythm"?

"Mythic"? You have to squint to
hear it. Squint and scatter letters to

15 the five senses, shake off circumstance, and
find yourself in words: squatting amid

ashes while the wicked affluent legislators
dress for the ball. Your feet ache

and stink. The thought-track wakes and thinks:
20 novelty again, the same old novelty.

It's almost worse than royalty. My biographic
foot in the glass shoe—fate

---

1. Pan, whose Greek name means "everything," is traditionally represented with a syrinx (or the pipes of Pan). The upper half of his body is human, the lower half goat, and as the father of Silenus he is associated with the spring rites of Dionysus.

or déjà vu? The rhythm of
days produces chill, stupor, and after considerable

25   training, a bunch of personal pronouns.
It's Thursday, history's late as usual. Meanwhile,

some sort of sexual traffic jam
has been goading us all into public

revelation. Offstage, Fact slapped Value on the
30   butt, and said, Break a leg,

make a killing, show these suckers
where to suck. And Value answered, Don't

be vulgar, Fact, unless you're speaking personally.
As for me, where the bee

35   sucks, there suck I, a mean-er,
a be-er, an arriviste tooling down that

divided highway heading where none, they say,
ever returns. And when I don't

come back, say I told you
40   everything about yourself except the future, lie

alone in our bed of roses
whence, they say, poems arise, to amuse

the students when we've gone to prose.
I'd say more but you hear

45   those stuck horns blaring: that's been
my cue ever since I can remember.

                                            1998

• How many puns and tricks of sound can you find in this poem?

LI-YOUNG LEE

Persimmons

In sixth grade Mrs. Walker
slapped the back of my head
and made me stand in the corner
for not knowing the difference
5   between *persimmon* and *precision*.
How to choose
persimmons. This is precision.
Ripe ones are soft and brown-spotted.
Sniff the bottoms. The sweet one
10   will be fragrant. How to eat:

put the knife away, lay down newspaper.
Peel the skin tenderly, not to tear the meat.
Chew the skin, suck it,
and swallow. Now, eat
15 the meat of the fruit,
so sweet,
all of it, to the heart.

Donna undresses, her stomach is white.
In the yard, dewy and shivering
20 with crickets, we lie naked,
face-up, face-down.
I teach her Chinese.
Crickets: *chiu chiu.* Dew: I've forgotten.
Naked: I've forgotten.
25 *Ni, wo:*   you and me.
I part her legs,
remember to tell her
she is beautiful as the moon.

Other words
30 that got me into trouble were
fight and *fright, wren* and *yarn.*
Fight was what I did when I was frightened,
fright was what I felt when I was fighting.
Wrens are small, plain birds,
35 yarn is what one knits with.
Wrens are soft as yarn.
My mother made birds out of yarn.
I loved to watch her tie the stuff;
a bird, a rabbit, a wee man.

40 Mrs. Walker brought a persimmon to class
and cut it up
so everyone could taste
a *Chinese apple.* Knowing
it wasn't ripe or sweet, I didn't eat
45 but watched the other faces.

My mother said every persimmon has a sun
inside, something golden, glowing,
warm as my face.

Once, in the cellar, I found two wrapped in newspaper,
50 forgotten and not yet ripe.
I took them and set both on my bedroom windowsill,
where each morning a cardinal
sang, *The sun, the sun.*
Finally understanding
55 he was going blind,
my father sat up all one night
waiting for a song, a ghost.

I gave him the persimmons,
swelled, heavy as sadness,
60 and sweet as love.

This year, in the muddy lighting
of my parents' cellar, I rummage, looking
for something I lost.
My father sits on the tired, wooden stairs,
65 black cane between his knees,
hand over hand, gripping the handle.

He's so happy that I've come home.
I ask how his eyes are, a stupid question.
All gone, he answers.

70 Under some blankets, I find a box.
Inside the box I find three scrolls.
I sit beside him and untie
three paintings by my father:
Hibiscus leaf and a white flower.
75 Two cats preening.
Two persimmons, so full they want to drop from the cloth.

He raises both hands to touch the cloth,
asks, *Which is this?*

This is persimmons, Father.

80 *Oh, the feel of the wolftail on the silk,*
the strength, the tense
precision in the wrist.
I painted them hundreds of times
eyes closed. These I painted blind.
85 *Some things never leave a person:*
scent of the hair of one you love,
the texture of persimmons,
in your palm, the ripe weight.

1986

• How does the poem play on the words *precision* and *persimmons*?
  What different kinds of precision are discussed and demonstrated
  in the poem?

BARBARA HAMBY

Ode to American English

I was missing English one day, American, really,
    with its pill-popping Hungarian goulash of everything
from Anglo-Saxon to Zulu, because British English
    is not the same, if the paperback dictionary

5   I bought at Brentano's on the Avenue de l'Opéra[2]
        is any indication, too cultured by half. Oh, the English
    know their dahlias, but what about doowop, donuts,
        Dick Tracy, Tricky Dick?[3] With their elegant Oxfordian
    accents, how could they understand my yearning for the hotrod,
10   hotdog, hot flash vocabulary of the U. S. of A.,
    the fragmented fandango of Dagwood's[4] everyday flattening
        of Mr. Beasley on the sidewalk, fetuses floating
    on billboards, drive-by monster hip-hop stereos shaking
        the windows of my dining room like a 7.5 earthquake,
15 Ebonics,[5] Spanglish, "you know" used as comma and period,
        the inability of 90% of the population to get the past perfect:
    I have went, I have saw, I have tooken Jesus into my heart,
        the battle cry of the Bible Belt, but no one uses
    the King James anymore, only plain-speak versions,
20   in which Jesus, raising Lazarus from the dead, says,
    "Dude, wake up," and the L-man bolts up like a B-movie
        mummy. "Whoa, I was toasted." Yes, ma'am,
    I miss the mongrel plenitude of American English, its fall-guy,
        rat-terrier, dog-pound neologisms, the bomb of it all,
25 the rushing River Jordan backwoods mutability of it, the low-rider,
        boom-box cruise of it, from New Joisey to Ha-wah-ya
    with its sly dog, malasada[6]-scarfing beach blanket lingo
        to the ubiquitous Valley Girl's *like-like* stuttering,
    shopaholic rant. I miss its quotidian beauty, its querulous
30   back-biting righteous indignation, its preening rotgut
    flag-waving cowardice. *Suffering Succotash*, sputters
        Sylvester the Cat; *sine die*,[7] say the pork-bellied legislators
    of the swamps and plains. I miss all those guys, their Tweety-bird
        resilience, their Doris Day[8] optimism, the candid unguent
35 of utter unhappiness on every channel, the midnight televangelist
        euphoric stew, the junk mail, voice mail vernacular.
    On every *boulevard* and *rue*[9] I miss the Tarzan cry of Johnny
        Weismueller,[1] Johnny Cash, Johnny B. Goode,[2]
    and all the smart-talking, gum-snapping hard-girl dialogue,
40   finger-popping x-rated street talk, sports babble,

---

2. In Paris, France. *Brentano's*: the "American bookstore in Paris" since 1895.
3. Pejorative nickname for U.S. President Richard Nixon (1913–94), who resigned from office three years into his second term (in 1974) because of his involvement in the infamous Watergate scandal.
4. Husband of Blondie Bumstead in *Blondie*, a comic strip that debuted in 1930 and also featured Mr. Beasley, the mailman.   5. African American vernacular English.
6. Deep-fried confection, a Portuguese invention that is today a popular snack in Hawaii.
7. Literally, "without day" (Latin); words that officially end a legislative session.
8. American singer and actress (b. 1922) with a wholesome, "girl-next-door" reputation; her biggest hit—and television theme song—was "Que Sera, Sera (Whatever will be, will be)."   9. Street (French).
1. American swimming champion (1904–84); after winning five Olympic gold medals in the 1920s, he starred in many Hollywood movies, most famously playing the role of Tarzan.
2. 1958 rock-and-roll classic by Chuck Berry.

Cheetoes, Cheerios, chili dog diatribes. Yeah, I miss them all,
 sitting here on my sidewalk throne sipping champagne
 verses lined up like hearses, metaphors juking, nouns zipping
 in my head like Corvettes on Dexedrine,[3] French verbs
45 slitting my throat, yearning for James Dean to jump my curb.

                 2004

- What qualities does Hamby's poem attribute to American English?
  How is each quality illustrated by the way she uses that language in
  the poem?

PICTURING: THE LANGUAGES OF DESCRIPTION

The language of poetry is often visual and pictorial. Rather than depending primarily on abstract ideas and elaborate reasoning, poems depend more on concrete and specific words that create images in our minds. Poems thus help us see things afresh or feel them suggestively through our other physical senses, such as hearing or touch. Sound is, as we will see, a vital aspect of poetry. But most poems use the sense of sight to help us form, in our minds, visual impressions, images that communicate more directly than concepts. We "see" yellow leaves on a branch, a father and son waltzing precariously, or two lovers sitting together on the bank of a stream, so that our response begins from a vivid visual impression of exactly what is happening. Some people think that those media and arts that challenge the imagination of a hearer or reader—radio drama, for example, or poetry—allow us to respond more fully than those (such as television or theater) that actually show things more fully to our physical senses. Certainly these media leave more to our imagination, to our mind's eye.

Poems are sometimes quite abstract—they can even be *about* abstractions. But usually they are quite concrete in what they ask us to see. One reason is that they often begin in a poet's mind with a picture or an image: of a person, a place, an event, or an object of observation. That image may be based on something the poet has seen—that is, it may be a picture of something remembered by the poet—but it may also be totally imaginary and only based on the "real world" in the sense that it draws on the poet's physical sense of what the world is like, including the people and things in it. Even when a poet begins with an idea that draws on visual experience, however, the reader still has to *imagine* (through the poem's words) an image, some person or thing or action that the poem describes. The poet must rely on words to help the reader to flesh out that mental image. In a sense, then, the reader becomes a visual artist, but the poet directs the visualization by evoking specific responses through words. *How* that happens can involve quite complicated verbal strategies—or even *visual* ones that draw on the possibilities of print (see chapter 19).

The languages of description are quite varied. The visual qualities of poetry result partly from the two aspects of poetic language described in the previous section: on the one hand, the precision of individual words, and, on the other hand, precision's opposite—the reach, richness, and ambiguity of suggestion that words sometimes accrue. Visualization can also derive from sophisticated rhetorical and literary devices (**figures of speech** and **symbols,** for example, as we will see later in

3. Amphetamine.

this chapter). But often description begins simply with naming—providing the word (noun, verb, adjective, or adverb) that will trigger images familiar from a reader's own experience. A reader can readily imagine a *dog* or *cat* or *house* or *flower* when each word is named, but not all readers will envision the same kind of dog or flower (because of our individual experiences) until the word is qualified in some way. So the poet may specify that the dog is a greyhound or poodle, or that the flower is a daffodil or a lilac or Queen Anne's lace; or the poet may provide colors, sizes, specific movements, or particular identifying features. Such description can involve either narrowing by category or expanding through detail, and often comparisons are either explicitly or implicitly involved. In Richard Wilbur's "The Beautiful Changes" (later in this chapter), for example, the similarity between wading through flowers in a meadow and wading among waves in the sea both suggests how the first experience feels and etches it visually in our minds. More than just a matter of naming, using precise words, and providing basic information, description involves qualification and comparison; sometimes the poet needs to tell us what not to picture, dissociating what the poem describes from other possible images we may have in mind. Different features in the language of description add up to something that describes a whole—a picture or scene—as well as a series of individualized objects.

Seeing in the mind's eye—the re-creation of visual experience—requires different skills from poets and readers. Poets use all the languistic strategies they can think of to re-create for us something they have already "seen." Poets depend on our having had a rich variety of visual experiences and try to draw on those experiences by using common, evocative words and then refining the process through more elaborate verbal devices. We as readers inhabit the process the other way around, trying to draw on our previous knowledge so that we can "see" by following verbal clues. In the poems that follow, notice the ways that description inspires specific images, and pay attention to how shape, color, relationship, and perspective become clear, not only through individual words but also through combinations of words and phrases that suggest appearance and motion.

• • •

JEANNE MARIE BEAUMONT

Rorschach

Snow patches along the creek bank.
Too simple. Wings melting there.

The tops of two maples
beside the window of my childhood bedroom.

5   Stain on a linen napkin left by lipstick—why it's called that. *Go on.*

A man's tattered bow tie
put through the wash cycle—by accident.

A dress, haunted by the child who wore it,
10   standing by itself in the center of a room.

A face. *Whose?* A woman's face, lathered up
with soap except around the eyes.

A fluke. *A flute?* A fluke
with two eyes on one side of its head.

15 The cigarette ground into the floor
by Bette Davis in *All About Eve.*

Next. A house that can't be seen
from the road—no, what hides it.

Graffiti of the nearsighted
20 painted by mouth.

And if I say "tree"?
I'd say—death by wood.

Cabinet? Casket.
Tell me again.

25 A map. A map of the island
where I asked to be born.

                              1997

- **What is the meaning of the poem's title, "Rorschach"? What does
  that meaning reveal about the nature of the dialogue that follows?**

OSCAR WILDE

Symphony in Yellow

An omnibus across the bridge
    Crawls like a yellow butterfly,
    And, here and there, a passer-by
Shows like a little restless midge.[4]

5 Big barges full of yellow hay
    Are moored against the shadowy wharf,
    And, like a yellow silken scarf,
The thick fog hangs along the quay.

The yellow leaves begin to fade
10   And flutter from the Temple[5] elms,
    And at my feet the pale green Thames
Lies like a rod of rippled jade.

                              1909

- **What can you infer about London, its climate, and the season from
  each of the yellow images in this poem?**

4. Tiny mosquito-like insect.   5. The law-courts area of London.

RICHARD WILBUR

The Beautiful Changes

One wading a Fall meadow finds on all sides
The Queen Anne's Lace[6] lying like lilies
On water; it glides
So from the walker, it turns
5   Dry grass to a lake, as the slightest shade of you
Valleys my mind in fabulous blue Lucernes.[7]

The beautiful changes as a forest is changed
By a chameleon's tuning his skin to it;
As a mantis, arranged
10 On a green leaf, grows
Into it, makes the leaf leafier, and proves
Any greenness is deeper than anyone knows.

Your hands hold roses always in a way that says
They are not only yours; the beautiful changes
15 In such kind ways,
Wishing ever to sunder
Things and things' selves for a second finding, to lose
For a moment all that it touches back to wonder.

                                                              1947

- What part of speech is "Beautiful" in the poem's title and lines
  7 and 14? What part of speech is "Changes"? What is meant by "the
  beautiful changes / In such kind ways" (lines 14–15)?

JAMES MERRILL

body

Look closely at the letters. Can you see,
entering (stage right), then floating full,
then heading off—so soon—
how like a little kohl-rimmed moon
5   o plots her course from b to d

—as y, unanswered, knocks at the stage door?
Looked at too long, words fail,
phase out. Ask, now that body shines

---

6. Plant sometimes called "wild carrot," with delicate, finger-like leaves and flat clusters of small white
flowers.
7. Alfalfa, a plant resembling clover, with small purple flowers. Lake Lucerne is famed for its deep blue
color and picturesque Swiss setting amid limestone mountains.

no longer, by what light you learn these lines
10 and what the *b* and *d* stood for.

1995

- Why might *y* be described as "unanswered" in the word *body*? What is meant by "Looked at too long, words fail" (line 7)?

ANDREW MARVELL

On a Drop of Dew

See how the orient[8] dew
Shed from the bosom of the morn
   Into the blowing roses,
Yet careless of its mansion new
5   For[9] the clear region where 'twas born
     Round in itself incloses,
     And in its little globe's extent
      Frames as it can its native element;
       How it the purple flow'r does slight,
10   Scarce touching where it lies,
But gazing back upon the skies,
   Shines with a mournful light
     Like its own tear,
Because so long divided from the sphere.[1]
15   Restless it rolls and unsecure,
   Trembling lest it grow impure,

   Till the warm sun pity its pain,
And to the skies exhale it back again.
     So the soul, that drop, that ray
20 Of the clear fountain of eternal day,
Could it within the human flower be seen,
     Rememb'ring still its former height,
     Shuns the sweet leaves and blossoms green;
     And, recollecting its own light,
25 Does, in its pure and circling thoughts, express
The greater Heaven in an Heaven less.
     In how coy[2] a figure wound,
     Every way it turns away;
     So the world excluding round,
30   Yet receiving in the day:
     Dark beneath, but bright above,
     Here disdaining, there in love.

     How loose and easy hence to go,
     How girt and ready to ascend;

---

8. Shining.   9. By reason of.   1. Of heaven.   2. Reserved, withdrawn, modest.

35   Moving but on a point below,
        It all about does upwards bend.
    Such did the manna's sacred dew distill,
    White and entire, though congealed and chill;[3]
    Congealed on earth, but does, dissolving, run
    Into the glories of th' almighty sun.

                                        1681

- How does the sun "exhale" (line 17) the drop of dew? "Back again" to where? Explain the comparison between the dewdrop and the human soul.

LYNN POWELL

Kind of Blue

Not Delft or
delphinium, not Wedgewood[4]
among the knickknacks, not wide-eyed chicory
evangelizing in the devil strip—

5   But way on down in the moonless
            octave below midnight, honey,
                way down where you can't tell cerulean
                    from teal.

    Not Mason jars of moonshine, not
    waverings of silk, not the long-legged hunger
10 of a heron or the peacock's
    iridescent id—

            But Delilahs of darkness, darling,
            and the muscle of the mind
            giving in.

15 Not sullen snow slumped
    against the garden, not the first instinct of flame,
    not small, stoic ponds, or the cold derangement
    of a jealous sea—

            But bluer than the lips of Lazarus, baby,
20   before Sweet Jesus himself could figure out
            what else in the world to do but weep.

                                        2004

---

3. In the wilderness, the Israelites fed upon manna from heaven (distilled from the dew; see Exodus 16.10–21); manna became a traditional symbol for divine grace.

4. Wedgwood pottery, often of a distinctive blue, manufactured by a company founded in England. *Delft*: city in southern Holland renowned for the manufacture of ceramics.

- How does this poem help us envision a certain "kind of blue" by creating images of what it isn't? How do the images develop over the course of the poem?

METAPHOR AND PERSONIFICATION

Being visual does not just mean describing; telling us facts; indicating shapes, colors, and specific details; and giving us precise discriminations through exacting verbs, nouns, adverbs, and adjectives. Often the vividness of the picture in our minds depends on comparisons made through figures of speech. What we are trying to imagine is pictured in terms of something else familiar to us, and we are asked to think of one thing as if it were something else. Many such comparisons, in which something is pictured or figured forth in terms of something already familiar to us, are taken for granted in daily life. Things we can't see or that aren't familiar to us are imaged as things we already know; for example, God is said to be like a father; Italy is said to be shaped like a boot; life is compared to a forest, a journey, or a sea. When the comparison is implicit, describing something as if it were something else, it is called a **metaphor.**

Poems use **figurative language** much of the time. A poem may insist that death is like a sunset or sex like an earthquake or that the way to imagine how it feels to be spiritually secure is to think of the way a sheep is taken care of by a shepherd. The pictorialness of our imagination may *clarify* things for us—scenes, states of mind, ideas—but at the same time it stimulates us to think of how those pictures make us *feel*. Pictures, even when they are mental pictures or imagined visions, may be both denotative and connotative, just as individual words are: They may clarify and make precise, and they may evoke a range of feelings.

In the poem that follows, the poet helps us visualize old age and approaching death by making comparisons with familiar things—the coming of winter, the approach of sunset, and the dying embers of a fire.

WILLIAM SHAKESPEARE

[*That time of year thou mayst in me behold*]

That time of year thou mayst in me behold
When yellow leaves, or none, or few, do hang
Upon those boughs which shake against the cold,
Bare ruined choirs, where late the sweet birds sang.
5 In me thou see'st the twilight of such day
As after sunset fadeth in the west;
Which by and by[5] black night doth take away,
Death's second self,[6] that seals up all in rest.
In me thou see'st the glowing of such fire,
10 That on the ashes of his youth doth lie,
As the deathbed whereon it must expire,

5. Shortly.   6. Sleep.

Consumed with that which it was nourished by.
This thou perceiv'st, which makes thy love more strong,
To love that well which thou must leave ere long.

                              1609

The first four lines of "That time of year" evoke images of the late autumn, but notice that the poet does not have the speaker say directly that his physical condition and age make him resemble autumn. He draws the comparison without stating it as a comparison: You can see my own state, he says, in the coming of winter, when almost all the leaves have fallen from the trees. The speaker portrays himself *indirectly* by talking about the passing of the year. The poem uses metaphor; that is, one thing is pictured *as if* it were something else. "That time of year" goes on to another metaphor in lines 5–8 and still another in lines 9–12, and each metaphor contributes to our understanding of the speaker's sense of his old age and approaching death. More important, however, is the way the metaphors give us feelings, an emotional sense of the speaker's age and of his own attitude toward aging. Through the metaphors we come to understand, appreciate, and to some extent share the increasing sense of urgency that the poem expresses. Our emotional sense of the poem depends largely on the way each metaphor is developed and by the way each metaphor leads, with its own kind of internal logic, to another.

The images of late autumn in the first four lines all suggest loneliness, loss, and nostalgia for earlier times. As in the rest of the poem, the speaker presents our eyes as the main vehicle for noticing his age and condition; in the phrase "thou mayst in me behold" (line 1), he introduces what he is asking us to see, and in both lines 5 and 9 he tells us similarly, "In me thou see'st. . . ." The picture of the trees shedding their leaves suggests that autumn is nearly over, and we can imagine trees either with yellow leaves, or without leaves, or with just a trace of foliage remaining—the latter perhaps most feelingly suggesting the bleakness and loneliness that characterize the change of seasons, the ending of the life cycle. But other senses are invoked, too. The boughs shaking against the cold represent an appeal to our tactile sense, and the next line appeals to our sense of hearing, although only by the silence of birds no longer singing. (Notice how exact the visual representation is of the bare, or nearly bare, limbs, even as the speaker notes the cold and the lack of birds; birds lined up like a choir on risers would have made a striking visual image on the barren limbs one above the other, but now there is only the *reminder* of what used to be. The present is quiet, bleak, and lonely; it is the absence of color, song, and life that underscores the visual impression, a reminder of what formerly was.)

The next four lines have a slightly different tone, and the color changes. From a black-and-white landscape with a few yellow leaves, we come upon a rich and almost warm reminder of a faded sunset. But a somber note enters the poem in these lines through another figure of speech, **personification,** which involves treating an abstraction, such as death or justice or beauty, as if it were a person. As the poem talks about the coming of night and of sleep, Sleep is personified as the "second self" of Death (that is, as a kind of "double" for death). The main emphasis is on how night and sleep close in on the twilight, and only secondarily does a reminder of death enter the poem. But it does enter.

The third metaphor—that of the dying embers of a fire—begins in line 9 and continues to color and warm the bleak cold that the poem began with, but it also sharpens the reminder of death. The three main metaphors in the poem work to make our sense of old age and approaching death not only more familiar but also more immediate: Moving from barren trees, to fading twilight, to dying embers suggests a sensuous increase of color and warmth—and an increasing urgency. The first metaphor involves a whole season, or at least a segment of one, a matter of days or possibly weeks; the second involves the passing of a single day, reducing the time scale to a matter of minutes, and the third draws our attention to that split second when a glowing ember dies into a gray ash. The final part of the fire metaphor introduces the most explicit sense of death so far, as the metaphor of embers shifts into a direct reminder of death. Embers, which had been a metaphor of the speaker's aging body, now themselves become, metaphorically, a deathbed; the vitality that nourishes youth is used up just as a log in a fire is. The urgency of the reminder of coming death has now peaked. It is friendlier but now seems immediate and inevitable, a natural part of the life process, and the final two lines offer an explicit plea to make good and intense use of the remaining moments of human relationship.

"That time of year" represents an unusually intricate use of images to organize a poem and focus its emotional impact. Not all poems are so skillfully made, and not all depend on such a full and varied use of metaphor. But most poems use metaphors for at least part of their effect. Sometimes a single metaphor extends over a section of a poem (in which it is called an *extended metaphor*) or even over the whole poem (in which case it is called a *controlling metaphor*). The following poem depends from the beginning—even from its title—on a single controlling metaphor.

LINDA PASTAN

Marks

My husband gives me an A
for last night's supper,
an incomplete for my ironing,
a B plus in bed.
5   My son says I am average,
an average mother, but if
I put my mind to it
I could improve.
My daughter believes
10   in Pass/Fail and tells me
I pass. Wait 'til they learn
I'm dropping out.

1978

The speaker in "Marks" is obviously less than pleased with the idea of continually being judged, and the metaphor of marks (or grades) as a way of talking about her performance of family duties suggests her irritation. The list of the roles implies the many things expected of her, and the three different systems of marking (letter grades, categories to be checked off on a chart, and pass/fail) detail the difficulties of multiple standards. The poem retains the language of schooldays all the way to the end ("learn," line 11; "dropping out," line 12), and the major effect of the poem depends on the irony of the speaker's surrendering to the metaphor the family has thrust upon her; if she is to be judged as if she were a student, she retains the right to leave the system. Ironically, she joins the system (adopts the metaphor for herself) in order to defeat it.

SIMILE AND ANALOGY

Sometimes, in poetry as in prose, comparisons are made explicitly, as in the following poem:

ROBERT BURNS

A Red, Red Rose

O, my luve's like a red, red rose
That's newly sprung in June.
O, my luve is like the melodie
That's sweetly played in tune.

5   As fair art thou, my bonnie lass,
So deep in luve am I;
And I will luve thee still, my dear,
Till a' the seas gang[7] dry.

Till a' the seas gang dry, my dear,
10 And the rocks melt wi' the sun;
And I will luve thee still, my dear,
While the sands o' life shall run.

And fare thee weel, my only luve,
And fare thee weel a while!
15 And I will come again, my luve,
Though it were ten thousand mile.

1796

The first four lines make two explicit comparisons: The speaker says that his love is "like a . . . rose" and "like [a] melodie." Such *explicit* comparisons are called **similes**, and usually (as here) the comparison involves the word *like* or the word *as*. Similes work much as do metaphors, except that usually they are used more passingly, more incidentally; they make a quick comparison and usually do not elaborate.

The two similes in "A Red, Red Rose" assume that we already have a favorable opinion of roses and of melodies. Here the poet does not develop the comparison

7. Go.

or even remind us of attractive details about roses or tunes. He pays the quick compliment and moves on. Similes sometimes develop more elaborate comparisons than this and occasionally, as in Marvell's "On a Drop of Dew," even govern long sections of a poem (in which case they are called *analogies*). Usually, though, a simile is briefer and relies more fully on something we already know. The speaker in "My Papa's Waltz" says that he hung on "like death." He doesn't have to explain or elaborate on the comparison: We know the anxiety he refers to.

Like metaphors, similes may imply both meaning and feeling; they may both explain something and invoke feelings about it. All figurative language involves an attempt to clarify something *and* to prompt readers to feel a certain way about it. Saying that one's love is like a rose implies a delicate and fragile beauty and invites our senses into play so that we can share sensuously a response to appealing fragrance and soft touch, just as the shivering boughs and dying embers in "That time of year" suggest separation and loss at the same time that they invite us to share both the cold sense of loneliness and the warmth of old friendship.

Once you start looking for them, you will find figures of speech in poem after poem; they are among the most common devices through which poets share their visions with us.

WILLIAM SHAKESPEARE

[*Shall I compare thee to a summer's day?*]

Shall I compare thee to a summer's day?
Thou art more lovely and more temperate.
Rough winds do shake the darling buds of May,
And summer's lease hath all too short a date.
5 Sometime too hot the eye of heaven shines,
And often is his gold complexion dimmed;
And every fair from fair sometime declines,
By chance or nature's changing course untrimmed.
But thy eternal summer shall not fade,
10 Nor lose possession of that fair thou ow'st,
Nor shall Death brag thou wand'rest in his shade,
When in eternal lines to time thou grow'st.
   So long as men can breathe or eyes can see,
   So long lives this,[8] and this gives life to thee.

                                    1609

- What sort of promise does the speaker make with this poem? Why can he boast that "thy eternal summer shall not fade" (line 9)?

8. This poem.

ANONYMOUS[9]

The Twenty-third Psalm

The Lord is my shepherd; I shall not want.
He maketh me to lie down in green pastures: he leadeth me beside
    the still waters.
He restoreth my soul: he leadeth me in the paths of righteousness
    for his name's sake.
Yea, though I walk through the valley of the shadow of death,
    I will fear no evil: for thou art with me;
    thy rod and thy staff they comfort me.
5 Thou preparest a table before me in the presence of mine enemies:
    thou anointest my head with oil; my cup runneth over.
Surely goodness and mercy shall follow me all the days of my life:
    and I will dwell in the house of the Lord for ever.

- What is the controlling metaphor in this poem? At what point in
  the psalm does the controlling metaphor shift?

JOHN DONNE

[Batter my heart, three-personed God][1]

Batter my heart, three-personed God; for You
As yet but knock, breathe, shine, and seek to mend;
That I may rise and stand, o'erthrow me, and bend
Your force, to break, blow, burn, and make me new.
5 I, like an usurped town, to another due,
Labor to admit You, but Oh, to no end!
Reason, Your viceroy[2] in me, me should defend,
But is captived, and proves weak or untrue.
Yet dearly I love You, and would be loved fain,[3]
10 But am betrothed unto Your enemy:
Divorce me, untie or break that knot again,
Take me to You, imprison me, for I,
Except You enthrall me, never shall be free,
Nor ever chaste, except You ravish me.

                          1633

- In the poem's controlling metaphor, who is the speaker? Who, or
  what, is God? To whom is the speaker "betrothed" (line 10)?

9. Traditionally attributed to King David. This English translation is from the King James Version of the
Bible (1611).   1. From the sequence *Holy Sonnets,* 14.
2. One who rules as the representative of a higher power.   3. Gladly.

The Canonization

For God's sake hold your tongue and let me love!
   Or [4] chide my palsy or my gout,
My five gray hairs or ruined fortune flout;
With wealth your state, your mind with arts improve,
5   Take you a course, get you a place,
     Observe his Honor or his Grace,
Or the king's real or his stampèd face [5]
     Contemplate; what you will, approve,
       So you will let me love.

10 Alas, alas, who's injured by my love?
     What merchant's ships have my sighs drowned?
Who says my tears have overflowed his ground?
When did my colds a forward spring remove?
     When did the heats which my veins fill
15   Add one man to the plaguy bill? [6]
Soldiers find wars, and lawyers find out still
     Litigious men which quarrels move,
       Though she and I do love.

Call us what you will, we are made such by love.
20   Call her one, me another fly,
We're tapers too, and at our own cost die; [7]
And we in us find th' eagle and the dove. [8]
     The phoenix riddle hath more wit [9]
     By us; we two, being one, are it.
25 So to one neutral thing both sexes fit,
     We die and rise the same, and prove
       Mysterious by this love.

We can die by it, if not live by love;
     And if unfit for tombs and hearse
30 Our legend be, it will be fit for verse; [1]
     And if no piece of chronicle we prove,
     We'll build in sonnets pretty rooms [2]
(As well a well-wrought urn becomes [3]
The greatest ashes, as half-acre tombs),
35   And by these hymns all shall approve
       Us canonized for love.

---

4. Either.   5. On coins.   6. List of plague victims.
7. Tapers (candles) consume themselves. To "die" is Renaissance slang for consummating the sexual act, which was popularly believed to shorten life by one day. *Fly*: a traditional symbol of transitory life.
8. Traditional symbols of strength and purity.
9. Meaning. According to tradition, only one phoenix existed at a time, dying in a funeral pyre of its own making and being reborn from its own ashes. The bird's existence was thus a riddle akin to a religious mystery (line 27), and a symbol sometimes fused with Christian representations of immortality.
1. That is, if we don't turn out to be an authenticated piece of historical narrative.
2. In Italian, *stanza* means "room."   3. Befits.

And thus invoke us: "You whom reverent love
     Made one another's hermitage,
You to whom love was peace, that now is rage,
40 Who did the whole world's soul extract, and drove[1]
     Into the glasses of your eyes
     (So made such mirrors and such spies
That they did all to you epitomize)
     Countries, towns, courts; beg from above
45   A pattern of your love!"
                                                        1633

- Whom does the speaker address in the first line, "hold your tongue"?
  Why does the speaker concede that he and his lover may not "prove"
  a "piece of chronicle" (line 31)?

DAVID FERRY

At the Hospital

She was the sentence the cancer spoke at last,
Its blurred grammar finally clarified.
                                                        1983

- What, exactly, has "clarified" the cancer's "blurred grammar"?

RANDALL JARRELL

The Death of the Ball Turret Gunner[2]

From my mother's sleep I fell into the State,
And I hunched in its belly till my wet fur froze.
Six miles from earth, loosed from its dream of life,
5 I woke to black flak and the nightmare fighters.
When I died they washed me out of the turret with a hose.
                                                        1945

- What is meant by "I fell into the State"? What do the words "sleep,"
  "dream," and "nightmare" suggest about the poem's basic situation?

4. Compressed.
5. A ball turret was a plexiglass sphere set into the belly of a B-17 or B-24 and inhabited by two .50 caliber
machine-guns and one short, small man. When this gunner tracked with his machine-guns a fighter
attacking his bomber from below, he revolved with the turret; hunched upside-down in his little sphere,
he looked like the foetus in the womb. The fighters which attacked him were armed with cannon firing
explosive shells. The hose was a steam hose. [Jarrell's note was erased.]

WILFRED OWEN

Dulce et Decorum Est [6]

Bent double, like old beggars under sacks,
Knock-kneed, coughing like hags, we cursed through sludge,
Till on the haunting flares we turned our backs
And towards our distant rest began to trudge.
5 Men marched asleep. Many had lost their boots
But limped on, blood-shod. All went lame; all blind;
Drunk with fatigue; deaf even to the hoots
Of disappointed shells that dropped behind.

Gas! Gas! Quick, boys!—An ecstasy of fumbling,
10 Fitting the clumsy helmets just in time;
But someone still was yelling out and stumbling
And floundering like a man in fire or lime.—
Dim, through the misty panes and thick green light
As under a green sea, I saw him drowning.

15 In all my dreams, before my helpless sight,
He plunges at me, guttering, choking, drowning.

If in some smothering dreams you too could pace
Behind the wagon that we flung him in,
And watch the white eyes writhing in his face,
20 His hanging face, like a devil's sick of sin;
If you could hear, at every jolt, the blood
Come gargling from the froth-corrupted lungs,
Obscene as cancer, bitter as the cud
Of vile, incurable sores on innocent tongues,—
25 My friend, you would not tell with such high zest
To children ardent for some desperate glory,
The old Lie: Dulce et decorum est
Pro patria mori.

1917

- Note all the similes in this poem. What patterns do you see here?
  What do the similes individually and collectively contribute to the
  poem, especially in terms of undermining the "lie" to which Owen
  alludes?

6. Part of a phrase from Horace (Roman poet and satirist, 65–8 B.C.E.), quoted in full in the last lines: "It is sweet and proper to die for one's country."

HARRYETTE MULLEN

Wipe That Simile Off Your Aphasia[7]

as horses as for
as purple as we go
as heartbeat as if
as silverware as it were
5 as onion as I can
as cherries as feared
as combustion as want
as dog collar as expected
as oboes as anyone
10 as umbrella as catch can
as penmanship as it gets
as narcosis as could be
as hit parade as all that
as ice box as far as I know
15 as fax machine as one can imagine
as cyclones as hoped
as dictionary as you like
as shadow as promised
as drinking fountain as well
20 as grassfire as myself
as mirror as is
as never as this

1996

• Why might Mullen's similes seem "wrong" or refuse to make literal sense? How might they be "right"? What might the poem reveal about why and how similes work in both poetry and everyday speech?

SYMBOL

Properly used, the term *symbol* suggests one of the most basic things about poems—their ability to get beyond what words signify and to make larger claims about meanings in the verbal world. All words go beyond themselves. They are not simply a collection of sounds: They signify something beyond their sounds, often things or actions or ideas. Words describe not only a verbal universe but also a world in which actions occur, acts have implications, and events have meaning. Sometimes words signify something beyond themselves, say, *rock* or *tree* or *cloud*, and symbolize something as well, such as solidity or life or dreams. Words can—when their implications are agreed on by tradition, convention, or habit—stand for things beyond their most immediate meanings or significations and become symbols, and even simple words that have accumulated no special power from previous use may be given special significance in special circumstances—in poetry as in life itself.

7. Impairment or loss of the ability to comprehend or use words.

A **symbol** is, put simply, something that stands for something else. The every-day world is full of common examples; a flag, a logo, a trademark, or a skull and crossbones all suggest things beyond themselves, and everyone likely understands what their display indicates, whether or not each viewer shares a commitment to what is thus represented. In common usage a prison symbolizes confinement, constriction, and loss of freedom, and in specialized traditional usage a cross may symbolize oppression, cruelty, suffering, death, resurrection, triumph, or an intersection of some kind (as in *crossroads* and *crosscurrents*). The specific symbolic significance depends on the context; for example, a reader might determine significance by looking at contiguous details in a poem and by examining the poem's attitude toward a particular tradition or body of beliefs. A star means one thing to a Jewish poet and something else to a Christian poet, still something else to a sailor or an actor. In a very literal sense, words themselves are all symbols (they stand for objects, actions, or qualities, not just for letters or sounds), but symbols in poetry are those words and phrases that have a range of reference beyond their literal signification or denotation.

Poems sometimes create a symbol out of a thing, action, or event that has no previously agreed-upon symbolic significance. The following poem, for example, gives an action symbolic significance.

JAMES DICKEY

The Leap

The only thing I have of Jane MacNaughton
Is one instant of a dancing-class dance.
She was the fastest runner in the seventh grade,
My scrapbook says, even when boys were beginning
5 To be as big as the girls,
But I do not have her running in my mind,
Though Frances Lane is there, Agnes Fraser,
Fat Betty Lou Black in the boys-against-girls
Relays we ran at recess: she must have run

10 Like the other girls, with her skirts tucked up
So they would be like bloomers,
But I cannot tell; that part of her is gone.
What I do have is when she came,
With the hem of her skirt where it should be
15 For a young lady, into the annual dance
Of the dancing class we all hated, and with a light
Grave leap, jumped up and touched the end
Of one of the paper-ring decorations

To see if she could reach it. She could,
20 And reached me now as well, hanging in my mind
From a brown chain of brittle paper, thin
And muscular, wide-mouthed, eager to prove

Whatever it proves when you leap
In a new dress, a new womanhood, among the boys
25   Whom you easily left in the dust
Of the passionless playground. If I said I saw
In the paper where Jane MacNaughton Hill,

Mother of four, leapt to her death from a window
Of a downtown hotel, and that her body crushed-in
30   The top of a parked taxi, and that I held
Without trembling a picture of her lying cradled
In that papery steel as though lying in the grass,
One shoe idly off, arms folded across her breast,
I would not believe myself. I would say
35   The convenient thing, that it was a bad dream
Of maturity, to see that eternal process

Most obsessively wrong with the world
Come out of her light, earth-spurning feet
Grown heavy: would say that in the dusty heels
40   Of the playground some boy who did not depend
On speed of foot, caught and betrayed her.
Jane, stay where you are in my first mind:
It was odd in that school, at that dance.
I and the other slow-footed yokels sat in corners
45   Cutting rings out of drawing paper

Before you leapt in your new dress
And touched the end of something I began,
Above the couples struggling on the floor,
New men and women clutching at each other
50   And prancing foolishly as bears: hold on
To that ring I made for you, Jane—
My feet are nailed to the ground
By dust I swallowed thirty years ago—
While I examine my hands.

                                        1967

Memory is crucial to "The Leap." The fact that Jane MacNaughton's graceful leap in dancing class has stuck in the speaker's mind all these years means that this leap was important to him, meant something to him, stood for something in his mind. For the speaker, the leap is an "instant" and the "only thing" he has of Jane. He remembers its grace and ease, and he struggles at several points to articulate its meaning (lines 16–26, 44–50), but even without articulation or explanation it remains in his head as a visual memory, a symbol of something beyond himself, something he cannot do, something he wanted to be. What that leap stood for, or symbolized, was boldness, confidence, accomplishment, maturity, Jane's ability to go beyond her fellow students in dancing class—the transcending of childhood by someone entering adulthood. Her feet now seem "earth-spurning" (line 38) in that original leap, and they separate her from everyone else. Jane MacNaughton was beyond the speaker's abilities and any attempt he could make to articulate his hopes, but she was not beyond his dreams. And even before he could say so, she symbolized a dream.

The leap to her death seems cruelly wrong and ironic after the grace of her earlier leap. In memory she is suspended in air, as if there were no gravity, no coming back to earth, as if life could exist as dream. And so the photograph, re-created in precise detail, is a cruel dashing of the speaker's dream—a detailed record of the ending of a leap, a denial of the suspension in which his memory had held her. His dream is grounded; her mortality is insistent. But the speaker still wants to hang on to that symbolic moment (line 42), which he confronts in a more mature context but will never altogether replace or surrender.

The leap is ultimately symbolic in the *poem*, too, not just in the speaker's mind. In the poem (and for us as readers) its symbolism is double: The first leap symbolizes aspiration, and the second symbolizes the frustration and grounding of high hopes; the two are complementary, one impossible to imagine without the other. The poem is horrifying in some ways, a dramatic reminder that human beings don't ultimately transcend their mortality, their limits, no matter how heroic or unencumbered by gravity they may once have seemed. But the poem is not altogether sad and despairing, partly because it still affirms the validity of the original leap and partly because it creates and elaborates another symbol: the paper chain.

The chain connects Jane to the speaker both literally and figuratively. It is, in part, *his* paper chain that she had leaped to touch in dancing class (lines 18–19), and he thinks of her first leap as "touch[ing] the end of something I began" (line 47). He and the other earthbound, "slow-footed yokels" (line 44) made the chain, and it connects them to her original leap, just as a photograph glimpsed in the newspaper connects the speaker to her second leap. The paper in the chain is "brittle" (line 21), and its creators seem dull artisans compared to the artistic performer that Jane was. They are heavy and "left in the dust" (lines 25, 52–53), but she is "light" (line 16) and able to transcend them, even in transcendence touching their lives. And so the paper chain becomes the poem's symbol of linkage, connecting lower accomplishment to higher possibility, the artisan to the artist, material substance to the act of imagination. And at the end the speaker examines the hands that made the chain because those hands certify his connection to her and the imaginative leap she had made for him. The chain thus symbolizes not only the lower capabilities of those who cannot leap like the budding Jane could, but (later) the connection with her leap as both transcendence and mortality. Like the leap, the chain is elevated to special meaning, given symbolic significance, by the poet's treatment of it. A leap and a chain have no necessary significance in themselves to most of us—at least no significance that we have all agreed upon—but they may take on significance in specific circumstances or a specific text.

Other objects and acts have a built-in significance because of past usage in literature, or tradition, or the stories a culture develops to explain itself and its beliefs. Over the years some things have acquired an agreed-upon significance, an accepted value in our minds. They already stand for something before the poet cites them; they are *traditional symbols*. Poets assume that their readers will recognize the traditional meanings of these symbols, and the poem does not have to propose or argue a particular symbolic value. Birds, for example, traditionally symbolize flight, freedom from confinement, detachment from earthbound limits, the ability to soar beyond rationality and transcend mortal limits. Traditionally, birds have also been linked with imagination, especially poetic imagination, and poets often identify with them as pure and ideal singers of songs, as in Keats's "Ode to a Nightingale" (see "Reading More Poetry").

One traditional symbol, the rose, may be a simple and fairly plentiful flower in its season, but it has so long stood for particular qualities that merely to name it raises predictable expectations. Its beauty, delicacy, fragrance, shortness of life, and depth of color have made it a symbol of the transitoriness of beauty, and countless poets have counted on its accepted symbolism—sometimes to compliment a friend (as Burns does in "A Red, Red Rose") or sometimes to make a point about the nature of symbolism. The following poem draws, in quite a traditional way, on the traditional meanings.

EDMUND WALLER

Song

    Go, lovely rose!
Tell her that wastes her time and me
    That now she knows,
When I resemble[8] her to thee,
5 How sweet and fair she seems to be.

    Tell her that's young,
And shuns to have her graces spied,
    That hadst thou sprung
In deserts, where no men abide,
10 Thou must have uncommended died.

    Small is the worth
Of beauty from the light retired;
    Bid her come forth,
Suffer herself to be desired,
15 And not blush so to be admired.

    Then die! that she
The common fate of all things rare
    May read in thee;
How small a part of time they share
That are so wondrous sweet and fair!
                  1645

The speaker in "Song" sends the rose to his love in order to have it speak its traditional meanings of beauty and transitoriness. He counts on accepted symbolism to make his point and hurry her into accepting his advances. Likewise, the poet does not elaborate or argue these things because he does not need to; he counts on the familiarity of the tradition (though, of course, readers unfamiliar with the tradition will not respond in the same way—that is one reason it is difficult to fully appreciate texts from another linguistic or cultural tradition).

8. Compare.

Poets may use traditional symbols to invoke predictable responses—in effect using shortcuts to meaning by repeating acts of signification sanctioned by time and cultural habit. But often poets examine the tradition even as they employ it, and sometimes they revise or reverse meanings built into the tradition. Symbols do not necessarily stay the same over time, and poets often turn even the most traditional symbols to their own original uses. Knowing the traditions of poetry— reading a lot of poems and observing how they tend to use certain words, meta- phors, and symbols—can be very useful in reading new poems, but traditions evolve and individual poems do highly individual things. Knowing the past never means being able to interpret new texts with certainty. Symbolism makes things happen, but individual poets and texts determine what will happen and how. The following two poems work important variations on the traditional associa- tions of roses.

D. H. LAWRENCE

I Am Like a Rose

I am myself at last; now I achieve
My very self. I, with the wonder mellow,
Full of fine warmth, I issue forth in clear
And single me, perfected from my fellow.

5 Here I am all myself. No rose-bush heaving
Its limpid sap to culmination has brought
Itself more sheer and naked out of the green
In stark-clear roses, than I to myself am brought.

1917

DOROTHY PARKER

One Perfect Rose

A single flow'r he sent me, since we met.
    All tenderly his messenger he chose;
Deep-hearted, pure, with scented dew still wet—
    One perfect rose.

5 I knew the language of the floweret;
    "My fragile leaves," it said, "his heart enclose."
Love long has taken for his amulet
    One perfect rose.

Why is it no one ever sent me yet
10   One perfect limousine, do you suppose?
Ah no, it's always just my luck to get
    One perfect rose.

1937

Sometimes symbols—traditional or not—become so insistent in the world of a poem that the larger referential world is left almost totally behind. In such cases the symbol is everything, and the poem does not just *use* symbols but becomes a **symbolic poem**, usually a highly individualized one dependent on an internal system introduced by the individual poet.

Here is an example of such a poem:

WILLIAM BLAKE

The Sick Rose [9]

O rose, thou art sick.
The invisible worm
That flies in the night
In the howling storm

5 Has found out thy bed
Of crimson joy,
And his dark secret love
Does thy life destroy.

1794

The poem does not seem to be about a rose, but about what the rose represents—not in this case something altogether understandable through the traditional meanings of *rose*.

We usually associate the rose with beauty and love, often with sex; and here several key terms have sexual connotations: "worm," "bed," and "crimson joy." The violation of the rose by the worm is the poem's main concern; the violation seems to have involved secrecy, deceit, and "dark" motives, and the result is sickness rather than the joy of love. The poem is sad; it involves a sense of hurt and tragedy, nearly of despair. The poem cries out against the misuse of the rose, against its desecration, implying that instead of a healthy joy in sensuality and sexuality, there has been in this case destruction and hurt, perhaps because of misunderstanding and repression and lack of sensitivity.

But to say so much about this poem we have to extrapolate from other poems by Blake, and we have to introduce information from outside the poem. Fully symbolic poems often require that we thus go beyond the formal procedures of reading that we have discussed so far. As presented in this poem, the rose is not part of the normal world that we ordinarily see, and it is symbolic in a special sense. The poet does not simply take an object from our everyday world and give it special significance, making it a symbol in the same sense that the leap becomes a symbol for James Dickey. Here the rose seems to belong to its own world, a world made entirely inside the poem or the poet's head. The rose is not referential, or not primarily so. The whole poem is symbolic; it is not paraphrasable; it lives in its own world. But

9. In Renaissance emblem books, the scarab beetle, worm, and rose are closely associated: The beetle feeds on dung, and the smell of the rose is fatal to it.

what is the rose here a symbol of? In general terms, we can say from what the poem tells us; but we may not be as confident as we can be in the more nearly recognizable world of "The Leap" or "I Am Like a Rose." In "The Sick Rose," it seems inappropriate to ask the standard questions: What rose? Where? Which worm? What are the particulars here? In the world of this poem worms can fly and may be invisible. We are altogether in a world of meanings that have been formulated according to a special system of knowledge and code of belief. We will feel comfortable and confident in that world only if we read many poems written by the poet (in this case, William Blake) within the same symbolic system.

Negotiation of meanings in symbolic poems can be very difficult indeed. Reading symbolic poems is an advanced skill that depends on knowledge of context, especially the lives and work of authors and the special literary and cultural traditions they work from (see chapters 21–25). But usually the symbols you will find in poems *are* referential of meanings we all share, and you can readily discover these meanings by carefully studying the poems themselves.

. . .

SHARON OLDS

Leningrad Cemetery, Winter of 1941[1]

That winter, the dead could not be buried.
The ground was frozen, the gravediggers weak from hunger,
the coffin wood used for fuel. So they were covered with something
and taken on a child's sled to the cemetery
5 in the sub-zero air. They lay on the soil,
some of them wrapped in dark cloth
bound with rope like the tree's ball of roots
when it waits to be planted; others wound in sheets,
their pale, gauze, tapered shapes
10 stiff as cocoons that will split down the center
when the new life inside is prepared;
but most lay like corpses, their coverings
coming undone, naked calves
hard as corded wood spilling
15 from under a cloak, a hand reaching out
with no sign of peace, wanting to come back
even to the bread made of glue and sawdust,
even to the icy winter, and the siege.

1979

- What does the "hand reaching out" (line 15) come to symbolize in the poem? Might the poem turn the corpses themselves into symbols?

1. The 900-day siege of Leningrad (now Saint Petersburg) during World War II began in September 1941.

ROBERT FROST

Fireflies in the Garden

Here come real stars to fill the upper skies,
And here on earth come emulating flies,
That though they never equal stars in size,
(And they were never really stars at heart)
5   Achieve at times a very star-like start.
Only, of course, they can't sustain the part.
                                          1928

- What is the tone of this poem? What does the poem say about the limits of symbolism?

STEPHEN DUNN

Dancing with God

At first the surprise
of being singled out,
the dance floor crowded
and me not looking my best,
5   a too-often-worn dress
and the man with me
a budding casualty
of one repetition too much.
God just touched his shoulder
10 and he left.
Then the confirmation of
an old guess.
God was a wild god,
into the most mindless rock,
15 but graceful,
looking—this excited me—
like no one I could love,
cruel mouth, eyes evocative
of promises unkept.
20 I never danced better, freer,
as if dancing were my way
of saying how easily
I could be with him, or apart.
When the music turned slow
25 God held me close
and I felt for a moment
I'd mistaken him,
that he was Death

and this the famous embrace
30 before the lights go out.
But God kept holding me
and I him
until the band stopped
and I stood looking at a figure
35 I wanted to slap
or forgive for something,
I couldn't decide which.
He left then, no thanks,
no sign
40 that he'd felt anything
more than an earthly moment
with someone who could've been
anyone on earth.
To this day I don't know why
45 I thought he was God,
though it was clear
there was no going back
to the man who brought me,
nice man
50 with whom I'd slept
and grown tired,
who danced wrong,
who never again
could do anything right.

1989

- Does the poem finally state definitively whether or not the dance
  partner really was God, at least in the speaker's mind? How does
  the ambiguity serve the poem?

ADRIENNE RICH

Diving into the Wreck

First having read the book of myths,
and loaded the camera,
and checked the edge of the knife-blade,
I put on
5 the body-armor of black rubber
the absurd flippers
the grave and awkward mask.
I am having to do this
not like Cousteau[2] with his

2. Jacques-Yves Cousteau (1910–97), French underwater explorer and writer.

10   assiduous team
      aboard the sun-flooded schooner
      but here alone.

      There is a ladder.
      The ladder is always there
15   hanging innocently
      close to the side of the schooner.
      We know what it is for,
      we who have used it.
      Otherwise
20   it's a piece of maritime floss
      some sundry equipment.

      I go down.
      Rung after rung and still
      the oxygen immerses me
25   the blue light
      the clear atoms
      of our human air.
      I go down.
      My flippers cripple me,
30   I crawl like an insect down the ladder
      and there is no one
      to tell me when the ocean
      will begin.

      First the air is blue and then
35   it is bluer and then green and then
      black I am blacking out and yet
      my mask is powerful
      it pumps my blood with power
      the sea is another story
40   the sea is not a question of power
      I have to learn alone
      to turn my body without force
      in the deep element.

      And now: it is easy to forget
45   what I came for
      among so many who have always
      lived here
      swaying their crenellated fans
      between the reefs
50   and besides
      you breathe differently down here.

      I came to explore the wreck.
      The words are purposes.
      The words are maps.
55   I came to see the damage that was done

and the treasures that prevail.
I stroke the beam of my lamp
slowly along the flank
of something more permanent
60 than fish or weed

the thing I came for:
the wreck and not the story of the wreck
the thing itself and not the myth
the drowned face always staring
65 toward the sun
the evidence of damage
worn by salt and sway into this threadbare beauty
the ribs of the disaster
curving their assertion
70 among the tentative haunters.

This is the place.
And I am here, the mermaid whose dark hair
streams black, the merman in his armored body
We circle silently
75 about the wreck
we dive into the hold.
I am she: I am he

whose drowned face sleeps with open eyes
whose breasts still bear the stress
80 whose silver, copper, vermeil cargo lies
obscurely inside barrels
half-wedged and left to rot
we are the half-destroyed instruments
that once held to a course
85 the water-eaten log
the fouled compass

We are, I am, you are
by cowardice or courage
the one who find our way
90 back to this scene
carrying a knife, a camera
a book of myths
in which
our names do not appear.
1972   1973

- What word or phrase first signals that "Diving into the Wreck" is to be understood symbolically, not literally? What are some possible symbolic interpretations of the wreck and the dive?

ROO BORSON

After a Death

Seeing that there's no other way,
I turn his absence into a chair.
I can sit in it,
gaze out through the window.
5 I can do what I do best
and then go out into the world.
And I can return then with my useless love,
to rest,
because the chair is there.

1989

- Why do you think the speaker chooses to symbolize her absent
  loved one with a chair?

DENISE LEVERTOV

Wedding-Ring

My wedding-ring lies in a basket
as if at the bottom of a well.
Nothing will come to fish it back up
and onto my finger again.
5   It lies
among keys to abandoned houses,
nails waiting to be needed and hammered
into some wall,
telephone numbers with no names attached,
10 idle paperclips.
                    It can't be given away
for fear of bringing ill-luck.
                    It can't be sold
for the marriage was good in its own
15 time, though that time is gone.
                    Could some artificer
beat into it bright stones, transform it
into a dazzling circlet no one could take
for solemn betrothal or to make promises
20 living will not let them keep? Change it
into a simple gift I could give in friendship?

1978

- How does the wedding ring's situation—lying "in a basket /
  as if at the bottom of a well" (lines 1–2)—embody the marriage symbolized
  by the ring?

SUGGESTIONS FOR WRITING

1. Choose one poem you have read in this book in which a single word seems crucial to that poem's total effect. Write an essay in which you work out carefully how the poem's meaning and tone depend on that one word.

2. Choose any poem in this chapter and explore the meaning and effect of its metaphor(s). Does the poem make use of an extended or controlling metaphor or of multiple metaphors? If the latter, how do the metaphors relate to and build on each other?

3. Consider the poems about roses in this chapter and write a paragraph about each poem showing how it establishes specific symbolism for the rose. What generalizations can you draw about the rose's traditional meanings in poetry? If you can, find other poems about roses outside of this book to determine if your generalizations still apply.

4. Is there a "correct" interpretation of Adrienne Rich's "Diving into the Wreck"? If one interpretation seems to fit all the particulars of the poem, does that mean it's better than other possible interpretations? Write an essay in which you explore the poem's symbolism and argue for or against the idea that there is a single best way to understand this poem. Can ambiguity serve a poet's purpose, or does it ultimately undercut a poem's meaning and significance?

5. Research the design of World War II bombers like the B-17 and the B-24. Try to find a picture of the gunner in the ball turret of such an airplane, and note carefully his body position. Write an essay in which you explain how Randall Jarrell's "The Death of the Ball Turret Gunner" uses visual details to create its fetal and birth metaphors.

17 THE SOUNDS OF POETRY

Much of what happens in a poem happens in your mind's eye, but some of it happens in your "mind's ear" and in your voice. Poems are full of meaningful sounds and silences as well as words and sentences. Besides choosing words for their meanings, poets choose words because they have certain sounds, and poems use sound effects to create a mood or establish a tone, just as films do.

Historically, poetry began as an oral phenomenon. Early bards in many cultures chanted or recited their verses, often accompanied by a musical instrument of some kind—and poetry remains a vocal art, dependent on the human voice. Often poems that seem very difficult when looked at silently come alive when turned into sound. The music and rhythms become clearer, and saying the words aloud or hearing them spoken is very good practice for learning to hear in your mind's ear when you read silently.

Sometimes the sounds in poems just provide special effects, rather like a musical score behind a film, setting the mood and getting us into an appropriate frame of mind. But often sound and meaning go hand in hand, and the poet finds words whose sounds echo the action. A word that captures or approximates the sound of what it describes, such as "splash" or "squish" or "murmur," is an *onomatopoeic* word, and the device itself is **onomatopoeia**. Poets can do similar things with pacing and rhythm, sounds and pauses. The punctuation, the length of vowels, and the combination of consonant sounds help control the way we read so that our voices imitate what is being described.

SOUND POEMS: SOME EXAMPLES

HELEN CHASIN

The Word Plum

The word *plum* is delicious

pout and push, luxury of
self-love, and savoring murmur

full in the mouth and falling
5   like fruit

taut skin
pierced, bitten, provoked into
juice, and tart flesh

question
10 and reply, lip and tongue
of pleasure.

1968

MONA VAN DUYN

What the Motorcycle Said

Br-r-r-am-m-m, rackety-am-m, OM, *Am:*
All—r-r-room, r-r-ram, ala-bas-ter—
Am, the world's my oyster.

I hate plastic, wear it black and slick,
5 hate hardhats, wear one on my head,
that's what the motorcycle said.

Passed phonies in Fords, knocked down billboards, landed
on the other side of The Gap, and Whee,
bypassed history.

10 When I was born (The Past), baby knew best.
They shook when I bawled, took Freud's path,
threw away their wrath.

R-r-rackety-am-m. *Am.* War, rhyme,
soap, meat, marriage, the Phantom Jet
15 are shit, and like that.

Hate pompousness, punishment, patience, am into Love,
hate middle-class moneymakers, live on Dad,
that's what the motorcycle said.

Br-r-r-am-m-m. It's Nowsville, man. Passed Oldies, Uglies,
20 Straighties, Honkies. I'll never be
mean, tired or unsexy.

Passed cigarette suckers, souses, mother-fuckers,
losers, went back to Nature and found
how to get VD, stoned.

25 Passed a cow, too fast to hear her moo, "*I* rolled
our leaves of grass into one ball.
I am the grassy All."

Br-r-r-am-m-m, rackety-am-m, OM, *Am:*
All—gr-r-rin, oooohgah, gl-l-utton—
30 *Am,* the world's my smilebutton.

1973

KENNETH FEARING

Dirge

1-2-3 was the number he played but today the number came 3-2-1;
Bought his Carbide at 30, and it went to 29; had the favorite at Bowie[1]
  but the track was slow—

O executive type, would you like to drive a floating-power, knee-action,
  silk-upholstered six? Wed a Hollywood star? Shoot the course in 58?
  Draw to the ace, king, jack?
O fellow with a will who won't take no, watch out for three cigarettes
  on the same, single match; O democratic voter born in August under
  Mars, beware of liquidated rails—

5 Denouement to denouement, he took a personal pride in the certain,
  certain way he lived his own, private life,
But nevertheless, they shut off his gas; nevertheless, the bank fore-
  closed; nevertheless, the landlord called; nevertheless, the radio
  broke,

And twelve o'clock arrived just once too often,
Just the same he wore one gray tweed suit, bought one straw hat, drank
  one straight Scotch, walked one short step, took one long look, drew
  one deep breath,
Just one too many,

10 And wow he died as wow he lived,
Going whop to the office and blooie home to sleep and biff got mar-
  ried and bam had children and oof got fired,
Zowie did he live and zowie did he die,

With who the hell are you at the corner of his casket, and where the
  hell're we going on the right-hand silver knob, and who the hell cares
  walking second from the end with an American Beauty[2] wreath
  from why the hell not,

Very much missed by the circulation staff of the New York Evening
  Post; deeply, deeply mourned by the B.M.T.[3]

15 Wham, Mr. Roosevelt; pow, Sears Roebuck; awk, big dipper; bop, summer rain;

Bong, Mr., bong, Mr., bong, Mr., bong.

1935

---

1. A racetrack in Maryland. *Carbide:* stock in the Union Carbide Corporation.   2. A variety of rose.
3. A New York City subway line.

ALEXANDER POPE

Sound and Sense[4]

337 But most by numbers[5] judge a poet's song,
    And smooth or rough, with them, is right or wrong;
    In the bright muse though thousand charms conspire,[6]
340 Her voice is all these tuneful fools admire,
    Who haunt Parnassus[7] but to please their ear,
    Not mend their minds; as some to church repair,
    Not for the doctrine, but the music there.
    These, equal syllables[8] alone require,
345 Though oft the ear the open vowels tire,
    While expletives[9] their feeble aid do join,
    And ten low words oft creep in one dull line,
    While they ring round the same unvaried chimes,
    With sure returns of still expected rhymes.
350 Where'er you find "the cooling western breeze,"
    In the next line, it "whispers through the trees";
    If crystal streams "with pleasing murmurs creep,"
    The reader's threatened (not in vain) with "sleep."
    Then, at the last and only couplet fraught
355 With some unmeaning thing they call a thought,
    A needless Alexandrine[1] ends the song,
    That, like a wounded snake, drags its slow length along.
    Leave such to tune their own dull rhymes, and know
    What's roundly smooth, or languishingly slow;
360 And praise the easy vigor of a line,
    Where Denham's strength and Waller's[2] sweetness join.
    True ease in writing comes from art, not chance,
    As those move easiest who have learned to dance.
    'Tis not enough no harshness gives offense,
365 The sound must seem an echo to the sense:
    Soft is the strain when Zephyr[3] gently blows,
    And the smooth stream in smoother numbers flows;
    But when loud surges lash the sounding shore,
    The hoarse, rough verse should like the torrent roar.
370 When Ajax[4] strives, some rock's vast weight to throw,

---

4. From *An Essay on Criticism,* Pope's poem on the art of poetry and the problems of literary criticism. The passage excerpted here follows a discussion of several common weaknesses of critics—failure to regard an author's intention, for example, or overemphasis on clever metaphors and ornate style.
5. Meter, rhythm, sound.   6. Unite.
7. A mountain in Greece, traditionally associated with the Muses and considered the seat of poetry and music.   8. Regular accents.   9. Filler words, such as "do."
1. A line of six metrical feet, sometimes used in pentameter poems to vary the pace mechanically. Line 357 is an alexandrine.
2. Sir John Denham and Edmund Waller, seventeenth-century poets credited with perfecting the heroic couplet.   3. The west wind.   4. A Greek hero of the Trojan War, noted for his strength.

The line too labors, and the words move slow;
Not so, when swift Camilla[5] scours the plain,
Flies o'er th' unbending corn, and skims along the main.
Hear how Timotheus'[6] varied lays surprise,
375   And bid alternate passions fall and rise!
While, at each change, the son of Libyan Jove[7]
Now burns with glory, and then melts with love;
Now his fierce eyes with sparkling fury glow,
Now sighs steal out, and tears begin to flow:
380   Persians and Greeks like turns of nature[8] found,
And the world's victor stood subdued by sound!
The pow'r of music all our hearts allow,
And what Timotheus was, is DRYDEN now.

1711

Helen Chasin's poem "The Word *Plum*" savors the sounds of the word as well as the taste and feel of the fruit itself. It is almost as if the poem is tasting the sounds and rolling them slowly on the tongue. The second and third lines even replicate the *p, l, uh,* and *m* sounds of the word while imitating the squishy sounds of eating the fruit. Words like "delicious" and "luxury" sound juicy, and other words, such as "murmur," imitate sounds of satisfaction and pleasure. Even the process of eating is in part re-created aurally. The tight, clipped sounds of "taut skin / pierced" suggest the way teeth sharply break the skin and slice quickly into the soft flesh of a plum, and the words describing the tartness ("provoked," "question") force the lips to pucker and the tongue and palate to meet and hold, as if the mouth were savoring a tart fruit. The poet is having fun here refashioning the sensual appeal of a plum, teasing the sounds and meanings out of available words. The words must mean something appropriate and describe something accurately first of all, of course, but when they also imitate the sounds and feel of the process, they do double duty.

Read Mona Van Duyn's poem aloud as if you were a motorcycle with the power of speech. The rich, loud sounds of a motorcycle revving up concentrate and intensify the effect. The speaking motorcycle seems to take on the values of some of its riders, the noisy and obtrusive ones that readers may associate with motorcycles. The types of riders made fun of here are themselves somewhat mindless and mechanical; they have cult feelings about their group, they travel in packs, and they seem to have no life beyond their machines. The speaking motorcycle, like such riders, exults in power and speed, lives for the moment, and has little respect for people, the past, or anything beyond its own small world. It is self-centered, trendy, and ignorant, but it is proud of the mighty thunder of its own sounds. That's what the motorcycle says.

5. A woman warrior in Virgil's *Aeneid*.
6. The court musician of Alexander the Great, celebrated in a famous poem by John Dryden (see line 383) for the power of his music over Alexander's emotions.
7. In Greek tradition, the chief god of any people was often given the name Zeus (Jove), and the chief god of Libya (the Greek name for all of Africa) was called Zeus Ammon. Alexander visited his oracle and was proclaimed son of the god.   8. Similar alternations of emotion.

As the title implies, Kenneth Fearing's "Dirge" is a musical lament, in this case for a businessman who took many chances and saw his investments and life go down the drain in the Great Depression of the early 1930s. The expressive cartoon words here, like "oof" and "blooie," echo the action. Reading aloud, you will notice that the poem employs rhythms much as a song would and that it frequently shifts its pace and mood. Notice how carefully the first two lines are balanced, and then how quickly the rhythm shifts as the "executive type" is addressed directly in line 3. (Especially long lines, like line 2, and irregular line lengths here create some of the poem's special sound effects.) In the direct address, the poem first picks up the rapid lingo of advertising. In stanza 3, the rhythm shifts again, but the poem gives us helpful clues about how to read. Line 5 sounds like prose and is long, drawn out, and rather dull (rather like its subject), but line 6 sets up a regular (and monotonous) rhythm with its repeated "nevertheless," which punctuates the rhythm like a drumbeat: "But nevertheless, *tuh-tuh-tuh-tuh-tuh;* nevertheless, *tuh-tuh-tuh-tuh;* nevertheless, *tuh-tuh-tuh-tuh;* nevertheless, *tuh-tuh-tuh-tuh-tuh.*" In the next stanza comes more repetitive phrasing, this time guided by the word "one" in conjunction with other one-syllable words: "wore *one* gray tweed suit, bought *one* straw hat, *tuh* one *tuh-tuh, tuh* one *tuh-tuh, tuh* one *tuh-tuh, tuh* one *tuh-tuh.*" And then a new rhythm and a new technique begin in stanza 5, which again imitates the language of comic books. You have to say words like "whop" and "zowie" aloud and in the rhythm of the whole sentence to get the full effect of how boring his life is, no matter how he tries to jazz it up. And so it goes—the repeating rhythms of routine—until the final bell ("Bong . . . bong . . . bong . . . bong") tolls rhythmically for the dead man in the final clanging line.

Written in a very different era and style, Pope's "Sound and Sense" uses a number of echoic or onomatopoeic words. In some lines pleasant and unpleasant consonant sounds underline a particular point or emphasize a mood. When the poet talks about a particular weakness in poetry, he illustrates it at the same time—by using open vowels (line 345), expletives (line 346), monosyllabic words (line 347), predictable rhymes (lines 350–53), or long, slow lines (line 357). He similarly illustrates the good qualities of poetry as well (line 360, for example). But the main effects of the passage come from an interaction of several ingenious strategies at once. In lines 339 and 340, for example, Pope produces complex sound effects in addition to the harmony of a rhyming couplet ("conspire," "admire"). Assonance echoes in the *oo* vowel sounds in "muse," "tuneful," and "fools"; alliteration repeats consonants in "*r*ight or *wr*ong" and "tune*f*ul *f*ools." Ironically, the *muse*-ical voice here is a bit out of tune to those who have good poetic taste: Pope intends the *r* and *f* sounds to feel both cute and awkward, as a comment on people who only want easy listening and miss poetry's other "charms," including its meaning (compared to the "doctrine" that is the real purpose of a church service, in line 343).

With a similar technique of demonstrating principles of poetic style and taste, the pace of lines 347, 357, and 359 is controlled by clashing consonant sounds as well as long vowels. Line 347 seems much longer than it is because almost every one-syllable word ends in a consonant that refuses to blend with the beginning of the next word, making the words hard to say without distinct, awkward pauses between them. In lines 357 and 359, long vowels such as those in "wounded," "snake," "slow," "along," "roundly," and "smooth" slow down the pace, and awkward, hard-to-pronounce consonants are again juxtaposed. The commas also provide nearly full stops in the middle of these lines to slow us down still more.

Similarly, the harsh lashing of the shore in lines 368–69 is accomplished partly by onomatopoeia, partly by a shift in the pattern of stress, which creates irregular waves in line 368, and partly by the dominance of rough consonants in line 369. (In Pope's time, the English *r* was still trilled gruffly so that it could be made to sound extremely *rrr*ough and ha*rrr*sh.) Almost every line in this passage demonstrates how to make sound echo sense.

POETIC METER

In the Western world, we can thank the ancient Greeks for systematizing an understanding of meter and providing a vocabulary (including the words **rhythm** and **meter**) that enables us to discuss the art of poetry. *Meter* comes from a Greek word meaning "measure": What we measure in the English language are the patterns of stressed (or accented) syllables that occur naturally when we speak, and, just as when we measure length, the unit we use in measuring poetry is the **foot**. Most traditional poetry in English uses the accentual-syllabic form of meter—meaning that its rhythmic pattern is based on both a set number of syllables per line and a regular pattern of accents in each line. Not all poems have a regular metrical pattern, and not all metered poems follow only one pattern throughout. But like everyday speech, the language of poetry always has *some* accents (as in this italic emphasis on "some"), and poets arrange that rhythm for effect. Thus in nonmetrical as well as metrical poetry, a reader should "listen" for patterns of stress.

The Basic Metrical Feet of Poetry in English

iamb: an unstressed or unaccented syllable followed by a stressed or accented one ("she wént," "belíeve"). This meter is called *iambic*.

trochee: a stressed syllable followed by an unstressed one ("méter," "Hómer"). This meter is called *trochaic*.

anapest: two unstressed syllables followed by a stressed one ("comprehénd," "after yóu"). This meter is called *anapestic*.

dactyl: a stressed syllable followed by two unstressed ones ("róundabout," "dínnertime"). This meter is called *dactylic*.

long or **short, strong** or **weak**: various terms that have been used for the syllables that we call stressed and unstressed.

rising or **falling**: the above feet either begin or end with the stressed syllable, as if they lose or gain momentum or "height." Hence iambic and anapestic are called rising meters, and trochaic and dactylic are called falling meters.

Other Kinds of Feet

spondee: two stressed syllables. Spondaic feet vary or interrupt the prevailing rhythm, emphasizing a syllable that we would expect to be unstressed ("Lást cáll," "Dón't gó").

pyrrhic: two unstressed syllables. Pyrrhic feet similarly interrupt the expected rising or falling beats, placing an unstressed syllable where we expect an emphasis ("ŭntŏ," "ĭs ă").

(Continued on next page)

(Continued)

Spondees and pyrrhic feet depend on prevailing meter and usually appear singly or only a few times in a row. It is difficult to imagine (or to write or speak) a line or sentence either that has no unstressed syllables—a constant strong beat (spondaic)—or one that lacks stressed syllables—a rippling monotone (pyrrhic).

Because the concept of meter derives from poetic traditions in Greek and Latin that counted syllables rather than accents, other possible combinations of syllables acquired names, for instance, *amphibrach* (unstressed, stressed, unstressed—noted by Coleridge in his demonstration of meter, "Metrical Feet," below). But since most meter in poetry in English depends on accents rather than the number of syllables, the terms above cover most of the variations that you will encounter.

Counting Feet, or Meter

A line of poetry is subdivided into feet in order to "measure" its meter. The terms are easy enough to understand if you recall geometry or other numeric terminology. Remember that this is a count *not* of the number of syllables but of stresses; thus, for example, monometer could have two or three syllables per line.

monometer:	one foot
dimeter:	two feet
trimeter:	three feet
tetrameter:	four feet
pentameter:	five feet
hexameter:	six feet
heptameter:	seven feet
octameter:	eight feet

Counting the number of feet, that is, the number of accents, stresses, or strong beats per line, helps you identify the *kind* of feet in the line. Thus the terms are combined: *Iambic pentameter* has five iambs per line; *trochaic tetrameter* has four trochees per line, and so on.

Although scanning lines of poetry by reading them aloud, marking syllables as "short" or "long" (unstressed or stressed), and adding up feet may seem like a counting game that has little to do with the meaning of poetry, it is an important way to understand the sound effects of a poem. Like different styles of music, different meters tend to express different moods or to be appropriate to different themes. When you know the basic meter of a poem, you are more alert to subtle variations in the pattern. Poets avoid the predictable or the lulling by using certain "change-ups" in the dominant meter or line length, such as substitution of a different foot (e.g., a trochee or spondee instead of an iamb); **caesura**, a short pause within a line often signaled by punctuation; or **enjambment**, extending the end of the grammatical sentence beyond the end of the poetic line.

(Continued on next page)

(Continued)

Here are the first two lines of Alexander Pope's "Sound and Sense," marked to show the stressed syllables:

But móst | by núm- | bers júdge | a pó- | et's sóng,
And smóoth | or róugh, | with thém, | is ríght | or wróng.

These lines, like so many in English literature, provide an example of *iambic pentameter*—that is, the lines are written in a meter consisting of five iambic feet. Notice that there is nothing forced or artificial in the sound of these lines; the words flow easily. In fact, linguists contend that English is naturally iambic, and even the most ordinary, "unpoetic" utterances often fall into this pattern: "Please tell me if you've heard this one before." "They said she had a certain way with words." "The baseball game was televised at nine."

> **iambic pentameter**: "In sé- | quent tóil | all fór- | wards dó | con- | ténd . . ." (William Shakespeare)
> **trochaic octameter**: "Ónce u- | pón a | mídnight | dréary, | whíle I | póndered, | wéak and | wéary . . ." (Edgar Allan Poe)
> **anapestic tetrameter**: "There are mán- | y who sáy | that a dóg | has his dáy . . ." (Dylan Thomas)
> **dactylic hexameter**: "Thís is the | fórest pri- | méval. The | múrmuring | pínes and the | hémlocks . . ." (Henry Wadsworth Longfellow)

Notice that this final example is perfectly regular until the final foot, a trochee. Also notice that Poe and Longfellow have placed a caesura within a long line. Substitution of one metrical foot for another—to accommodate idioms and conversational habits or to create a special effect or emphasis—is quite common, especially in the first foot of a line. Shakespeare often begins an iambic line with a trochee:

Líke as | the wáves | make towárds | the péb- | bled shóre . . .

Or consider this line from John Milton's *Paradise Lost,* a poem written mainly in iambic pentameter:

Rócks, cáves, | lákes, féns, | bógs, déns, | and Shádes | of Déath . . .

Here Milton substitutes three spondees for the first three iambs in a pentameter line. John Dryden's "To the Memory of Mr. Oldham" arguably begins with two spondees, a pyrrhic, and an iamb before settling into a regular iambic pentameter (here the slashes mark the feet):

Fárewéll, | tóo lít | tle, and | tóo láte | ly knówn,

As Dryden's poem shows, meter does leave room for discussion; some readers might read the line above as iambic throughout, and others might read the last three feet as iambic: The natural emphasis on the first word after the caesura, "and," could make the predictable word "too" unstressed.

In the following poem, Samuel Taylor Coleridge playfully names and illustrates many types of meter.

SAMUEL TAYLOR COLERIDGE

Metrical Feet

Lesson for a Boy

Trōchĕe trīps frŏm lōng tŏ shōrt;[9]
From long to long in solemn sort
Slōw Spōndēe stālks; strōng fōōt! yet ill able
Ĕvĕr tŏ cōme ŭp wĭth Dāctÿl trĭsÿllăblĕ.
5 Ĭāmbĭcs mārch frŏm shōrt tŏ lōng—
With ă lēap ănd ă bōūnd thĕ swĭft Ānăpĕsts thrōng;
One syllable long, with one short at each side,
Ămphībrăchÿs hāstes wĭth ă stātelÿ stride—
Fīrst ănd lāst bēing lōng, mĭddlĕ shōrt, Amphĭmācer
10 Strīkes hĭs thūndērĭng hōōfs līke ă prōud hīgh-brĕd Rācer.
If Derwent[1] be innocent, steady, and wise,
And delight in the things of earth, water, and skies;
Tender warmth at his heart, with these meters to show it,
With sound sense in his brains, may make Derwent a poet—
15 May crown him with fame, and must win him the love
Of his father on earth and his Father above.
           My dear, dear child!
Could you stand upon Skiddaw,[2] you would not from its whole ridge
See a man who so loves you as your fond S. T. COLERIDGE.

1806

PRACTICING SCANSION (READING METER)

Scansion is the technique of listening to and marking stressed and unstressed syllables, counting the syllables and feet, and checking the rhyme patterns. Often, you will need to scan several lines before you can be sure of the "controlling" metrical pattern of a poem. Though there is no easy substitute for this work, it will help you appreciate the subtleties of a poet's craft.

Hearing a poem properly involves practice—listening to others read poetry and especially to yourself as you read poems aloud. Your dictionary will show you the stresses for every word of more than one syllable, and the governing stress of individual words will largely control the patterns in a line: If you read a line for its sense (almost as if it were prose), you will usually see the line's basic pattern. But

9. The long and short marks over syllables are Coleridge's.
1. Written originally for Coleridge's son Hartley, the poem was later adapted for his younger son, Derwent.
2. A mountain in the lake country of northern England (where Coleridge lived in his early years), near the town of Derwent.

single-syllable words can be a challenge because they may or may not be stressed, depending on their syntactic function and the full meaning of the sentence. Normally, important functional words, such as one-syllable nouns and verbs, are stressed (as in normal conversation or in prose), but conjunctions (such as *and* or *but*), prepositions (such as *on* or *with*), and articles (such as *an* or *the*) are not.

The way you actually read a line, once you have "heard" the basic rhythm, is influenced by two factors: normal pronunciation and prose sense (on the one hand) and the predominant pattern of the poem (on the other). Since these two forces are constantly in tension and are sometimes contradictory, you can almost never fully predict the actual reading of a line, and good reading aloud (like every other art) depends less on formula than on subtlety and flexibility. Sometimes very good readers plausibly disagree about whether or not to stress certain syllables. We have noted the use of substitution, and many poems since around 1900 have taken liberties with meter and rhyme. Some poets (such as Marianne Moore) have favored counting syllables rather than accents. Even more widespread is **free verse**, which does without any governing pattern of stresses or line lengths.

Each of the following poems is written in a different meter. Using the terms defined in "Poetic Meter" (on pp. 1000–02) as well as in Coleridge's poem "Metrical Feet," pair the following poems with their corresponding meter. (The answers are on p. 1006.)

1. ANONYMOUS

[*There was a young girl from St. Paul*]

There was a young girl from St. Paul,
Wore a newspaper-dress to a ball.
   The dress caught on fire
   And burned her entire
Front page, sporting section and all.

2. ALFRED, LORD TENNYSON

From *The Charge of the Light Brigade*

1.

Half a league, half a league,
   Half a league onward,
All in the valley of Death
   Rode the six hundred.
5 "Forward, the Light Brigade!
   "Charge for the guns!" he said:
Into the valley of Death
   Rode the six hundred.

2.
"Forward, the Light Brigade!"
10 Was there a man dismay'd?
   Not tho' the soldier knew
      Someone had blunder'd:
   Theirs not to make reply,
   Theirs not to reason why,
15 Theirs but to do and die:
   Into the valley of Death
      Rode the six hundred.

                              1854

3. SIR JOHN SUCKLING

Song

Why so pale and wan, fond Lover?
   Prithee why so pale?
Will, when looking well can't move her,
   Looking ill prevail?
5   Prithee why so pale?

Why so dull and mute, young Sinner?
   Prithee why so mute?
Will, when speaking well can't win her,
   Saying nothing do 't?
10   Prithee why so mute?

Quit, quit, for shame, this will not move,
   This cannot take her;
If of her self she will not love,
   Nothing can make her,
15   The Devil take her.

                              1646

4. JOHN DRYDEN

To the Memory of Mr. Oldham[3]

Farewell, too little, and too lately known,
Whom I began to think and call my own;
For sure our souls were near allied, and thine
Cast in the same poetic mold with mine.
5 One common note on either lyre did strike,

---

3. John Oldham (1653–83), like Dryden (see lines 3–6), wrote satiric poetry.

And knaves and fools we both abhorred alike.
To the same goal did both our studies drive;
The last set out the soonest did arrive.
Thus Nisus fell upon the slippery place,
10 While his young friend performed and won the race.[4]
O early ripe! to thy abundant store
What could advancing age have added more?
It might (what nature never gives the young)
Have taught the numbers[5] of thy native tongue.
15 But satire needs not those, and wit will shine
Through the harsh cadence of a rugged line.[6]
A noble error, and but seldom made,
When poets are by too much force betrayed.
Thy generous fruits, though gathered ere their prime,
20 Still showed a quickness; and maturing time
But mellows what we write to the dull sweets of rhyme.
Once more, hail and farewell; farewell, thou young,
But ah too short, Marcellus[7] of our tongue;
Thy brows with ivy, and with laurels bound;
25 But fate and gloomy night encompass thee around.

1684

• • •

SCANNING METER: A SELECTION OF POEMS

EDGAR ALLAN POE

The Raven

Once upon a midnight dreary, while I pondered, weak and weary,
Over many a quaint and curious volume of forgotten lore,
While I nodded, nearly napping, suddenly there came a tapping,
As of some one gently rapping, rapping at my chamber door.
5   " 'Tis some visitor," I muttered, "tapping at my chamber door—
           Only this, and nothing more."

Ah, distinctly I remember it was in the bleak December,
And each separate dying ember wrought its ghost upon the floor.
Eagerly I wished the morrow;—vainly I had sought to borrow
10 From my books surcease of sorrow—sorrow for the lost Lenore—
For the rare and radiant maiden whom the angels name Lenore—
           Nameless here for evermore.

*ANSWERS: 1. anapestic, 2. dactylic, 3. trochaic, 4. iambic.
4. In Virgil's *Aeneid* (Book 5), Nisus (who is leading the race) falls and then trips the second runner so that his friend Euryalus can win.   5. Rhythms.
6. In Dryden's time, the English *r* was pronounced with a harsh, trilling sound.
7. Nephew of the Roman emperor Augustus who died at twenty, celebrated by Virgil in the *Aeneid,* Book 6.

And the silken sad uncertain rustling of each purple curtain
Thrilled me—filled me with fantastic terrors never felt before;
15 So that now, to still the beating of my heart, I stood repeating
" 'Tis some visitor entreating entrance at my chamber door;—
Some late visitor entreating entrance at my chamber door;
               This it is, and nothing more."

Presently my soul grew stronger; hesitating then no longer,
20 "Sir," said I, "or Madam, truly your forgiveness I implore;
But the fact is I was napping, and so gently you came rapping,
And so faintly you came tapping, tapping at my chamber door,
That I scarce was sure I heard you"—here I opened wide the door;—
               Darkness there, and nothing more.

25 Deep into that darkness peering, long I stood there wondering, fearing,
Doubting, dreaming dreams no mortal ever dared to dream before;
But the silence was unbroken, and the darkness gave no token,
And the only word there spoken was the whispered word, "Lenore!"
This I whispered, and an echo murmured back the word, "Lenore!"—
30   Merely this, and nothing more.

Back into the chamber turning, all my soul within me burning,
Soon I heard again a tapping somewhat louder than before.
"Surely," said I, "surely that is something at my window lattice;
Let me see, then, what thereat is, and this mystery explore—
35 Let my heart be still a moment and this mystery explore;—
               'Tis the wind and nothing more!"

Open here I flung the shutter, when, with many a flirt and flutter,
In there stepped a stately raven of the saintly days of yore;
Not the least obeisance made he; not an instant stopped or stayed he;
40 But, with mien of lord or lady, perched above my chamber door—
Perched upon a bust of Pallas[8] just above my chamber door—
               Perched, and sat, and nothing more.

Then this ebony bird beguiling my sad fancy into smiling,
By the grave and stern decorum of the countenance it wore,
45 "Though thy crest be shorn and shaven, thou," I said, "art sure no craven,
Ghastly grim and ancient raven wandering from the Nightly shore—
Tell me what thy lordly name is on the Night's Plutonian[9] shore!"
               Quoth the raven, "Nevermore."

Much I marvelled this ungainly fowl to hear discourse so plainly,
50 Though its answer little meaning—little relevancy bore,
For we cannot help agreeing that no living human being
Ever yet was blessed with seeing bird above his chamber door—
Bird or beast upon the sculptured bust above his chamber door,
               With such name as "Nevermore."

55 But the raven, sitting lonely on the placid bust, spoke only
That one word, as if his soul in that one word he did outpour.

8. Athena, the Greek goddess of wisdom.   9. Dark; Pluto was god of the underworld.

Nothing farther then he uttered—not a feather then he fluttered—
Till I scarcely more than muttered "Other friends have flown before—
On the morrow *he* will leave me, as my hopes have flown before."
60   Then the bird said "Nevermore."

Startled at the stillness broken by reply so aptly spoken,
"Doubtless," said I, "what it utters is its only stock and store
Caught from some unhappy master whom unmerciful Disaster
Followed fast and followed faster till his songs one burden bore—
65 Till the dirges of his Hope that melancholy burden bore
                   Of 'Never—nevermore.' "

But the raven still beguiling all my sad soul into smiling,
Straight I wheeled a cushioned seat in front of bird and bust and door;
Then, upon the velvet sinking, I betook myself to linking
70 Fancy unto fancy, thinking what this ominous bird of yore—
What this grim, ungainly, ghastly, gaunt, and ominous bird of yore
                 Meant in croaking "Nevermore."

This I sat engaged in guessing, but no syllable expressing
To the fowl whose fiery eyes now burned into my bosom's core;
75 This and more I sat divining, with my head at ease reclining
On the cushion's velvet lining that the lamplight gloated o'er,
But whose velvet violet lining with the lamplight gloating o'er,
                 She shall press, ah, nevermore!

Then, methought, the air grew denser, perfumed from an unseen censer
80 Swung by angels whose faint foot-falls tinkled on the tufted floor.
"Wretch," I cried, "thy God hath lent thee—by these angels he hath sent
    thee
Respite—respite and nepenthe[1] from thy memories of Lenore!
Quaff, oh quaff this kind nepenthe and forget this lost Lenore!"
                 Quoth the raven, "Nevermore."

85 "Prophet!" said I, "thing of evil!—prophet still, if bird or devil!—
Whether Tempter sent, or whether tempest tossed thee here ashore,
Desolate, yet all undaunted, on this desert land enchanted—
On this home by Horror haunted—tell me truly, I implore—
Is there—*is* there balm in Gilead?[2]—tell me—tell me, I implore!"
90   Quoth the raven, "Nevermore."

"Prophet!" said I, "thing of evil—prophet still, if bird or devil!
By that Heaven that bends above us—by that God we both adore—
Tell this soul with sorrow laden if, within the distant Aidenn,[3]
It shall clasp a sainted maiden whom the angels name Lenore—
95 Clasp a rare and radiant maiden whom the angels name Lenore."
                 Quoth the raven, "Nevermore."

---

1. A drug reputed by the Greeks to cause forgetfulness or sorrow (pronounced "ne-PEN-thee").
2. See Jeremiah 8.22.   3. Eden.

"Be that word our sign of parting, bird or fiend!" I shrieked upstarting—
"Get thee back into the tempest and the Night's Plutonian shore!
Leave no black plume as a token of that lie thy soul hath spoken!
100 Leave my loneliness unbroken!—quit the bust above my door!
Take thy beak from out my heart, and take thy form from off my door!"
Quoth the raven, "Nevermore."

And the raven, never flitting, still is sitting, still is sitting
On the pallid bust of Pallas just above my chamber door;
105 And his eyes have all the seeming of a demon's that is dreaming,
And the lamp-light o'er him streaming throws his shadow on the floor;
And my soul from out that shadow that lies floating on the floor
Shall be lifted—nevermore!

1844

- Describing the composition of "The Raven," Poe wrote of the need
  to use sounds "in the fullest possible keeping with that melancholy
  which I had predetermined as the tone of the poem." List at least
  five of the sound effects (e.g., rhyme, alliteration, etc.) that Poe uses
  in "The Raven." How does each of these contribute to the poem's
  tone of "melancholy"?

WILLIAM SHAKESPEARE

[*Like as the waves make towards the pebbled shore*]

Like as the waves make towards the pebbled shore,
So do our minutes hasten to their end,
Each changing place with that which goes before,
In sequent toil all forwards do contend.[4]
5 Nativity, once in the main[5] of light,
Crawls to maturity, wherewith being crowned,
Crooked[6] eclipses 'gainst his glory fight,
And Time that gave doth now his gift confound.[7]
Time doth transfix[8] the flourish set on youth
10 And delves the parallels[9] in beauty's brow,
Feeds on the rarities of nature's truth,
And nothing stands but for his scythe to mow.
And yet to times in hope[1] my verse shall stand,
Praising thy worth, despite his cruel hand.

1609

- Which lines in this poem vary the basic iambic metric scheme?
  What is the effect of these variations?

4. Struggle. *Sequent:* successive.   5. High seas. *Nativity:* newborn life.   6. Perverse.
7. Bring to nothing.   8. Pierce.   9. Lines, wrinkles.   1. In the future.

JAMES MERRILL

Watching the Dance

1. BALANCHINE'S[2]

Poor savage, doubting that a river flows
But for the myriad eddies made
By unseen powers twirling on their toes,

Here in this darkness it would seem
5 You had already died, and were afraid.
Be still. Observe the powers. Infer the stream.

2. DISCOTHÈQUE

Having survived entirely your own youth,
Last of your generation, purple gloom
Investing you, sit, Jonah,[3] beyond speech,

10 And let towards the brute volume VOOM whale mouth
VAM pounding viscera VAM VOOM
A teenage plankton luminously twitch.

1967

- When you read this poem aloud, which lines flow most easily, and which contain abrupt pauses? If the first stanza of the poem is an imitation of a dance choreographed by Balanchine, what might this dance look like?

GERARD MANLEY HOPKINS

Spring and Fall

to a young child

Márgarét áre you gríeving[4]
Over Goldengrove unleaving?
Leáves, like the things of man, you
With your fresh thoughts care for, can you?
5 Áh! ás the heart grows older
It will come to such sights colder
By and by, nor spare a sigh
Though worlds of wanwood leafmeal[5] lie;
And yet you wíll weep and know why.

2. George Balanchine (1904–83), Russian-born ballet choreographer and teacher.
3. According to Jonah 4, Jonah sat in gloom near Nineveh after its residents repented and God decided to spare the city from destruction.   4. Hopkins's own accent markings.
5. Broken up, leaf by leaf (analogous to "piecemeal"). *Wanwood*: pale, gloomy woods.

10 Now no matter, child, the name:
Sórrow's spríngs áre the same.
Nor mouth had, no nor mind, expressed
What heart heard of, ghost[6] guessed:
It ís the blight man was born for,
15 It is Margaret you mourn for.

1880

- How does this poem's heavy use of alliteration serve its themes of youth and age, life and death?

LEE ANN BROWN

Foolproof Loofah

Lo! I fill prol pills
Poof! I rail pro lolls
Fool! I ill for lips
O Pale! I foil frail profs
5 Fop! I frill pale roils—
So! I proof oil spills

April Fool's!

1999

- Do the lines of this poem have meaning outside of their sound? How do the poem's first six lines set up the final one?

EMILY DICKINSON

[*A narrow Fellow in the Grass*]

A narrow Fellow in the Grass
Occasionally rides—
You may have met Him—did you not
His notice sudden is—

5 The Grass divides as with a Comb—
A spotted shaft is seen—
And then it closes at your feet
And opens further on—

He likes a Boggy Acre
10 A Floor too cool for Corn—

6. Soul.

Yet when a Boy, and Barefoot—
I more than once at Noon

Have passed, I thought, a Whip lash
Unbraiding in the Sun
15 When stooping to secure it
It wrinkled, and was gone—

Several of Nature's People
I know, and they know me—
I feel for them a transport
20 Of cordiality—

But never met this Fellow
Attended, or alone
Without a tighter breathing
And Zero at the Bone—

1866

- How does Dickinson use sound devices such as alliteration to
  underscore the images and themes of the poem?

CATHERINE BOWMAN

Mr. X

All my Ex's
live in Texas,[7] so the country song says and no excuses,
it's mostly true for me too that the spade-shaped extra
big state with its cotton lints and Ruby Reds holds the crux
5 of my semi-truck-I've-never-had-any-kind-of-luck-deluxe-
super-high-jinx-born-to-be-unhappy-if-it-ain't-broken-don't-fix-

it loves, for example, there was the snakebit mudlogger who fixed
himself forever diving off that hexed bridge, and that foxy ex-
patriot who imported exotic parrots, he'd pump me up with his deluxe
10 stuff, the salesman who felt so guilty for the wide-eyed excuses
he told his wife that at the Big Six Motel just outside Las Cruces
he spent the afternoon hunched over Exodus, bemoaning the sin of extra-

marital sex, and the harmonica player, his mouth organ could extract
an oily bended blues, on sticky nights we'd hit the 12th hole pond with a fix
15 of Dos Equis and a hit of Ecstasy and I'd wrap my legs around his lanky
        crux,
as moonlight cut through the water like a giant X-ray, his Hohner ax
glistened in and out. And then there was the feckless shrink. No excuse
for his fixation, the tax man, the cute butcher from the Deluxe,

7. The opening line and title of a song by country singer George Strait and Sanger D. Shafer (1987).

the Kilim[8] dealer, the defrocked priest. So what if my mother was a deluxe
20 lush, my father Baptist and weak, I can't blame them, I was born just extra
    affectionate. Don't ask about the abortions, and who can ever make
        excuses
    for the time I spent holed up with the Port-O-Can tycoon my friend fixed
    me up with, or the Mexican sculptor who made cathedral-sized onyx Xs,
    twisted crucifixes. Art, he quoted Marx, was history at its crux.[9]

25 Then there was the Ph.D. who took me to Peru and showed me Crux
    (the Southern Cross), Centaurus, Musca, Vela, Lupus,[1] and another
        deluxe
    equatorial constellation that I forgot. For fun I ascribed each sparkly X
    a name and date, so now I have a star chart to exalt each of my extra-
    ordinary, heavenly bodies. But that night I dreamed the stars were
        fixed
30 on stacks of pages: pica asterisks to indicate omission, footnotes, excuses,

    explanations. I stood there, Ms. D. Giovanni,[2] with a million excuses.
    Now in exile I journey on the Styx with Mr. X in our boat the *Crux
    Criticorum*.[3] I wear an aqua slicker, he a sharkskin suit. He's non-fiction,
    never incognito. We've got our sextant and spy manual open on our
        deluxe
35 waterbed. I can just make out the tattoo above his boxers in this extra
    dark, there's the curve of his back. Now we'll break the code and go
        beyond X

                                                                    1993

- What rules has Bowman set for this poem's line length, stanzas,
  and rhyme? How does she create an effect of breaking rules?

SUGGESTIONS FOR WRITING

1. Read Pope's "Sound and Sense" carefully twice—once silently and once aloud—and
   then mark the stressed and unstressed syllables. Single out all the lines that have
   major variations from the basic iambic pentameter pattern. Pick out six lines with
   variations that seem to you worthy of comment, and write a paragraph on each in
   which you show how the varied metrical pattern contributes to the specific effects
   achieved in that line and the corresponding point Pope conveys about poetic style.
2. Try your hand at writing limericks in imitation of "There was a young girl from St.
   Paul"; study the rhythmic patterns and line lengths carefully, and imitate them
   exactly in your poem. Begin your limerick with "There once was a _____ from
   _____" (using a place for which you think you can find a comic rhyme).
3. Read Poe's "The Raven" aloud, paying particular attention to pacing. Do you find
   yourself speeding up as you continue through the poem? Does a quickening pace
   suit the speaker's growing exasperation and madness? Write an essay in which you
   examine the way that Poe underlines the poem's story and emotional flow with a

8. Fine carpets produced in a number of Asian countries.
9. "Art is always and everywhere the secret confession, and at the same time the immortal movement of its
time" (Karl Marx).   1. Constellations visible south of the equator.
2. Don Juan (*Giovanni* in Italian) was damned for sexual exploitation of many women.
3. Puzzle of the critics (Latin). *Styx*: in Greek mythology, the chief river of Hades.

range of poetic devices: line length, punctuation, rhyme, meter, and the sounds of words.

4. Pope's "Sound and Sense" contains this advice for poets: "But when loud surges lash the sounding shore, / The hoarse, rough verse should like the torrent roar" (lines 368–69). In other words, he counsels that the sound of the poet's description should match the sense of what the poem is describing. Write an essay in which you examine the sound and sense in Shakespeare's "[Like as the waves make towards the pebbled shore]. How does the poem achieve a harmony of meaning and sound?

5. Write an essay in which you discuss any of the poems you have read in this book in which sound seems a more important element than anything else, even the meaning of words. What is the point of writing and reading this kind of poetry? Can it achieve its effects through silent reading, or must it be experienced aloud?

Words and Music: An Album

People often associate poetry with music, for good reason. The word **lyric**—the standard term for a short, harmonious, pleasant, and often romantic poem—derives from the ancient Greeks' practice of reciting certain poems to the accompaniment of a harplike instrument, the lyre. Throughout history, poems have been set to music and many "lyrics" have been created specifically to fit musical compositions. Many poems, especially during the Renaissance, were simply called "Song" (or "Chanson" or "Lied" or similar terms in other languages), and some were constructed in hybrid musical-poetic forms such as the madrigal, the dirge, and the hymn.

The most fundamental link between poetry and music involves their almost equal dependence on the principles of rhythm. Both art forms have a basis in mathematics: A regular beat or syncopated sound pattern shapes their phrasing and formal movement. Performers of both arts must keep count and consider quantities as well as qualities of sounds. Just as good musicians learn to listen and count so easily that it seems "natural," poets often develop an ear for rhythm that makes their sound choices seem effortless. Readers, too, can develop such an ear.

Both poetry and music use representational or imitative strategies to create the illusion of sounds—bells, waves, motorcycles, for example—but words operate referentially in a way that sounds normally do not, and their syntax is of a different kind from that in musical composition. The referential fact of language almost always alters the "pure" effects of sound (though in nonsense lyrics or in poems like "What the Motorcycle Said," sounds or tonal expressions seem to be merely recorded in letters).

Poems composed to or for music obviously rely on rhythmic or harmonic effects even more than those created solely by words. Reading the lyrics of a song you know well is quite different from reading words that have for you no musical association or history. But the "music" created by a poem itself can work in a similar way when there is no musical "source" or co-creation.

The poems that follow were all written for, in conjunction with, or to imitate music. Can you add your own song lyrics from your favorite contemporary singers and groups? Are the words as effective without the music? Do they make good poems? Can you, in the lyrics you know well, separate the actual musical implications from those of the words alone?

THOMAS CAMPION

When to Her Lute Corinna Sings

When to her lute Corinna sings,
Her voice revives the leaden[1] strings,
And doth in highest notes appear
As any challenged[2] echo clear;
5 But when she doth of mourning speak,
Ev'n with her sighs the strings do break.

1. Heavy. 2. Aroused.

And as her lute doth live or die,
Led by her passion, so must I:
For when of pleasure she doth sing,
10 My thoughts enjoy a sudden spring;
But if she doth of sorrow speak,
Ev'n from my heart the strings do break.

1601

- How does Campion mimic an "echo" in this poem? What is the
  effect of this echoing?

WILLIAM SHAKESPEARE

Spring[3]

When daisies pied[4] and violets blue
   And ladysmocks all silver-white
And cuckoobuds of yellow hue
   Do paint the meadows with delight,
5 The cuckoo then, on every tree,
Mocks married men;[5] for thus sings he,
           Cuckoo;
Cuckoo, cuckoo: Oh word of fear,
Unpleasing to a married ear!

10 When shepherds pipe on oaten straws,
   And merry larks are plowmen's clocks,
When turtles tread,[6] and rooks, and daws,
   And maidens bleach their summer smocks,
The cuckoo then, on every tree,
15 Mocks married men; for thus sings he,
           Cuckoo;
Cuckoo, cuckoo: Oh word of fear,
Unpleasing to a married ear!

ca. 1595

- What words or phrases might a singer emphasize in order to enhance
  this poem's comic effect?

---

3. Song from *Love's Labour's Lost*.   4. Of varied colors.
5. That is, by the resemblance of its call to the word *cuckold*.   6. Turtledoves copulate.

AUGUSTUS MONTAGUE TOPLADY

A Prayer, Living and Dying

I

ROCK of ages, cleft for me,
Let me hide myself in Thee!
Let the Water and the Blood,
From thy riven Side which flow'd,
5 Be of sin the double cure;
Cleanse me from its guilt and pow'r.

II

Not the labors of my hands
Can fulfill thy Law's demands:
Could my zeal no respite know,
10 Could my tears for ever flow,
All for sin could not atone;
Thou must save, and Thou alone.

III

Nothing in my hand I bring;
Simply to thy Cross I cling;
15 Naked, come to Thee for dress;
Helpless, look to Thee for grace;
Foul, I to the Fountain fly:
Wash me, SAVIOR, or I die!

IV

While I draw this fleeting breath—
20 When my eye-strings break in death—
When I soar to worlds unknown—
See Thee on thy judgment-throne—
ROCK of ages, cleft for me,
Let me hide myself in Thee!

1776

- What aspects of this poem might make it suitable for communal singing by untrained singers?

ROBERT HAYDEN

Homage to the Empress of the Blues[7]

Because there was a man somewhere in a candystripe silk shirt,
gracile and dangerous as a jaguar and because a woman moaned
for him in sixty-watt gloom and mourned him Faithless Love
Twotiming Love Oh Love Oh Careless Aggravating Love,

5   She came out on the stage in yards of pearls, emerging like
     a favorite scenic view, flashed her golden smile and sang.

Because grey laths began somewhere to show from underneath
torn hurdygurdy[8] lithographs of dollfaced heaven;
and because there were those who feared alarming fists of snow
10 on the door and those who feared the riot-squad of statistics,

     She came out on the stage in ostrich feathers, beaded satin,
     and shone that smile on us and sang.

                                                    1962

- How do the two short stanzas beginning with "She came out" complete the thoughts of the longer stanzas that start with "Because"?

MICHAEL HARPER

Dear John, Dear Coltrane

         a love supreme, a love supreme
         a love supreme, a love supreme[9]

     Sex fingers toes
     in the marketplace
     near your father's church
     in Hamlet, North Carolina—[1]
5   witness to this love
     in this calm fallow
     of these minds,
     there is no substitute for pain:
     genitals gone or going,
10   seed burned out,
     you tuck the roots in the earth,

---

7. Bessie Smith (1894 [or 1898?]–1937); legendary blues singer whose theatrical style grew out of the black American vaudeville tradition.   8. A disreputable kind of dance hall.
9. Coltrane wrote "A Love Supreme" in response to a spiritual experience in 1957 that also led to his quitting heroin and alcohol. Mainly an instrumental improvisation featuring Coltrane's saxophone, the piece begins with the repeated chant of "a love supreme." The record was released in 1965.
1. Coltrane's birthplace. His family shared a house with Coltrane's grandfather, who was the minister of St. Stephen's AME Zion Church.

turn back, and move
by river through the swamps,
singing: *a love supreme, a love supreme;*
15   what does it all mean?
Loss, so great each black
woman expects your failure
in mute change, the seed gone.
You plod up into the electric city—
20   your song now crystal and
the blues. You pick up the horn
with some will and blow
into the freezing night:
a love supreme, a love supreme—

25   Dawn comes and you cook
up the thick sin 'tween
impotence and death, fuel
the tenor sax cannibal
heart, genitals and sweat
30   that makes you clean—
a love supreme, a love supreme—

Why you so black?
cause I am
why you so funky?
35   *cause I am*
why you so black
cause I am
why you so sweet?
cause I am
40   *why you so black?*
cause I am
a love supreme, a love supreme:

So sick
you couldn't play *Naima,*[2]
45   so flat we ached
for song you'd concealed
with your own blood,
your diseased liver gave
out its purity,
50   the inflated heart
pumps out, the tenor kiss,
tenor love:
a love supreme, a love supreme—
a love supreme, a love supreme—

1970

- In what ways is this poem, as suggested by the title, both a "Dear
John" letter and a poem of praise?

2. A song Coltrane wrote for and named after his wife, recorded in 1959.

BOB DYLAN

Mr. Tambourine Man

Hey! Mr. Tambourine Man, play a song for me,
I'm not sleepy and there is no place I'm going to.
Hey! Mr. Tambourine Man, play a song for me,
In the jingle jangle morning I'll come followin' you.

5   Though I know that evenin's empire has returned into sand,
Vanished from my hand,
Left me blindly here to stand but still not sleeping.
My weariness amazes me, I'm branded on my feet,
I have no one to meet
10 And the ancient empty street's too dead for dreaming.

Hey! Mr. Tambourine Man, play a song for me,
I'm not sleepy and there is no place I'm going to.
Hey! Mr. Tambourine Man, play a song for me,
In the jingle jangle morning I'll come followin' you.

15 Take me on a trip upon your magic swirlin' ship,
My senses have been stripped, my hands can't feel to grip,
My toes too numb to step, wait only for my boot heels
To be wanderin'.
I'm ready to go anywhere, I'm ready for to fade
20 Into my own parade, cast your dancing spell my way,
I promise to go under it.

Hey! Mr. Tambourine Man, play a song for me,
I'm not sleepy and there is no place I'm going to.
Hey! Mr. Tambourine Man, play a song for me,
25 In the jingle jangle morning I'll come followin' you.

Though you might hear laughin', spinnin', swingin' madly across the
       sun,
It's not aimed at anyone, it's just escapin' on the run
And but for the sky there are no fences facin'.
And if you hear vague traces of skippin' reels of rhyme
30 To your tambourine in time, it's just a ragged clown behind,
I wouldn't pay it any mind, it's just a shadow you're
Seein' that he's chasing.

Hey! Mr. Tambourine Man, play a song for me,
I'm not sleepy and there is no place I'm going to.
35 Hey! Mr. Tambourine Man, play a song for me,
In the jingle jangle morning I'll come followin' you.

Then take me disappearin' through the smoke rings of my mind,
Down the foggy ruins of time, far past the frozen leaves,
The haunted, frightened trees, out to the windy beach,
40 Far from the twisted reach of crazy sorrow.
Yes, to dance beneath the diamond sky with one hand waving free,

Silhouetted by the sea, circled by the circus sands,
With all memory and fate driven deep beneath the waves,
Let me forget about today until tomorrow.

45 Hey! Mr. Tambourine Man, play a song for me,
I'm not sleepy and there is no place I'm going to.
Hey! Mr. Tambourine Man, play a song for me,
In the jingle jangle morning I'll come followin' you.

1964

- How does familiarity with "Mr. Tambourine Man" as a song affect
  our sense of it as a poem? Do successful song lyrics necessarily work
  as poetry?

WILLIE PERDOMO

123rd Street Rap

A day on
123rd Street

goes a little
something like
5 this:

Automatic bullets bounce
off stoop steps

It's about time to pay
all my debts

10 Church bells bong for
for drunken mourners

Baby men growing on
all the corners

Money that
15 ain't mine

Sun that
don't shine

Trees that
don't grow

20 Wind that
won't blow

Drug posses
ready to rumble

Ceilings starting
25 to crumble

Abuelas[3] close
eyes and pray

While they watch
the children play

30　Not much I
can say

Except day turns
to night

And I can't tell what's
35　wrong from what's right

on 123rd Street

1996

- Read "123rd Street Rap" first silently and then aloud. Does it "work"
  better one way or the other? Does reading it aloud change your
  opinion of it?

SUGGESTIONS FOR WRITING

1. Is there a meaningful difference between poetry and song lyrics? between poetry
   and rap? Is hip-hop a form of literature? Write an essay in which you explore the
   definitions of "poetry" and "lyrics." Be sure to cite enough examples to illustrate
   your ideas.
2. Find on the Internet the lyrics of a song (of any genre) that in your opinion uses
   words well, and download or print out one or more versions. First, notice any variations between the text(s) you find and the words you hear when listening to the
   song. Using a correct version of the lyrics (as you determine it), scan the lines for
   meter and rhyme. Are any words or syllables used to keep the beat without adding
   to the meaning (like the word "do," in Pope's "Sound and Sense")? Are any rhymes
   dependent on vowel sounds rather than consonants (that is, do they not quite
   rhyme in print)? How does the refrain (if any) vary from the rest of the lyrics, and
   how does it relate to the title or theme of the song? Which lines or verses are most
   important in the "story" or the feeling relayed by the song? How would you describe
   the diction and tone of the "speaker" of the words, and how does it compare with
   the vocal style of the singer? Write a descriptive response paper on these words as a
   poem without music, and as lyrics within the song. Are they equally successful in
   print as they are when performed with music?

---

3. Grandmothers.

18

INTERNAL STRUCTURE

"Proper words in proper places": That is how one great writer of English prose, Jonathan Swift, described good writing. A good poet finds appropriate words, and already we have looked at some implications for readers of the verbal choices a poet makes. But the poet must also decide where to put those words—how to arrange them for maximum effect—because individual words, metaphors, and symbols exist not only within phrases and sentences and rhythmic patterns, but also within the larger whole of the poem. How should the words be arranged and the poem organized? What comes first and what last? Will the poem have a "plot"? What principle or idea of organization will inform it? How can words, sentences, images, ideas, and feelings be combined into a structure that holds together, seems complete, and affects readers?

Considering these questions from the poet's point of view (What is my plan? Where shall I begin?) can help us notice the effects of structural choices. Every poem works in its own unique way, and therefore every poet must make independent decisions about how to organize an individual poem. But poems do fall into patterns of organization, sometimes because of subject matter, sometimes because of effects intended, sometimes for other reasons. A poet may consciously decide on a particular strategy, may reach instinctively for one, or may happen into one that suits the needs of the moment—a framework onto which words and sentences will hang, one by one and group by group.

NARRATIVE POEMS

A **narrative poem** tells a story, and its organization may be fairly straightforward. The following poem, for example, tells a simple story largely in chronological order:

EDWIN ARLINGTON ROBINSON

Mr. Flood's Party

Old Eben Flood, climbing alone one night
Over the hill between the town below
And the forsaken upland hermitage
That held as much as he should ever know
5 On earth again of home, paused warily.
The road was his and not a native near;

And Eben, having leisure, said aloud,
For no man else in Tilbury Town to hear:

"Well, Mr. Flood, we have the harvest moon
10 Again, and we may not have many more;
The bird is on the wing, the poet says,[1]
And you and I have said it here before.
Drink to the bird." He raised up to the light
The jug that he had gone so far to fill,
15 And answered huskily: "Well, Mr. Flood,
Since you propose it, I believe I will."

Alone, as if enduring to the end
A valiant armor of scarred hopes outworn
He stood there in the middle of the road
20 Like Roland's ghost winding a silent horn.[2]
Below him, in the town among the trees,
Where friends of other days had honored him,
A phantom salutation of the dead
Rang thinly till old Eben's eyes were dim.

25 Then, as a mother lays her sleeping child
Down tenderly, fearing it may awake
He set the jug down slowly at his feet
With trembling care, knowing that most things break;
And only when assured that on firm earth
30 It stood, as the uncertain lives of men
Assuredly did not, he paced away,
And with his hand extended paused again:

"Well, Mr. Flood, we have not met like this
In a long time; and many a change has come
35 To both of us, I fear, since last it was
We had a drop together. Welcome home!"
Convivially returning with himself,
Again he raised the jug up to the light;
And with an acquiescent quaver said:
40 "Well, Mr. Flood, if you insist, I might.

"Only a very little, Mr. Flood—
For auld lang syne. No more, sir; that will do."
So, for the time, apparently it did,
And Eben evidently thought so too;
45 For soon amid the silver loneliness
Of night he lifted up his voice and sang,
Secure, with only two moons listening,
Until the whole harmonious landscape rang—

1. Edward FitzGerald, in "The Rubáiyát of Omar Khayyám" (more or less a translation of an Arab original), so describes the "Bird of Time."
2. According to French legend, the hero Roland used his powerful ivory horn to warn his allies of impending attack.

"For auld lang syne." The weary throat gave out,
50 The last word wavered, and the song was done.
He raised again the jug regretfully
And shook his head, and was again alone.
There was not much that was ahead of him,
And there was nothing in the town below—
55 Where strangers would have shut the many doors
That many friends had opened long ago.

1921

The fairly simple narrative structure here is based on the gradual unfolding of the story. After old Eben is introduced and situated in relation to the town and his home, the "plot" unfolds: He sits down in the road, reviews his life, reflects on the present, and has a drink—several drinks, in fact, as he thinks about passing time and growing old; then he sings and considers going "home." Not much happens, really; we get a vignette of Mr. Flood between two places and two times. But there *is* **action**, and the poem's movement—its organization and structure—depends on it: Mr. Flood in motion, in stasis, and then, again, contemplating motion. This counts as action, and a certain, limited chronological movement. We could say that a spare sort of story takes place, like that in Dickey's "Cherrylog Road" (chapter 15). The poem's organization—its structural principle—involves the passing of time, action moving forward, a larger story being revealed by the few moments depicted here.

"Mr. Flood's Party" presents about as much story as a short poem ever does, but like many poems it doesn't really emphasize the developing action—which all seems fairly predictable once we "get" who Eben is, how old he is, and what place he occupies in the communal memory of Tilbury Town and vice versa. Rather, the movement forward in time dictates the shape of the poem, determines the way it presents its images, ideas, themes. Nearly everything occurs within an easy-to-follow chronology.

But even here, in this most simple narrative structure, we note complications. One complication is in the use of time itself, for "old" time and "present" time seem posed against each other as a structural principle, too, one in tension with the chronological movement: Eben's past, as contrasted with his present and limited future, focuses the poem's attention, and in some ways the contrast between what was and what is seems even more important than the brief movement through present time that gets the most obvious attention in the poem. Then, too, "character"—Eben's character and that of the townspeople of later generations—gets a lot of attention, even as the chronology moves forward. More than one structural principle is at work here. We may identify the main movement of the poem as chronological and its principal structure as narrative, but to be fair and full in our discussion we have to note several other competing organizational forces at work—principles of comparison and contrast, for example, and of descriptive elaboration.

Most poems work with this kind of complexity, and identifying a single structure behind any poem involves a sense of the organizational principle that makes it work; at the same time, other principles repeatedly, perhaps continually, compete for our attention. A poem's structure involves its conceptual framework—what principle best explains its organization and movement—and it is often useful to identify one dominating kind of structure, such as narrative structure, that gives the poem its shape. But we need to recognize from the start that most poems follow structural models loosely. Finding an appropriate label to describe the structure of a particular poem can help us analyze the poem's other aspects, but the label itself has no magic.

Purely narrative poems are often very long and often include many features that are not, strictly speaking, closely connected to the narrative or linked to a strict chronology. Very often a poem moves from a narrative of an event to some sort of commentary or reflection on it, as in Philip Larkin's "Church Going" (later in this chapter). Reflection can be included along the way or may be implicit in the way the story is narrated, as in Maxine Kumin's "Woodchucks" (chapter 13), where we focus more on the narrator and her responses than on the events in the story.

The following poem represents a composite of several similar experiences (compare Blake's "London" [chapter 13] and Dickey's "Cherrylog Road" [chapter 15]) rather than a single event—another fairly common pattern:

PHILIP LARKIN

Church Going

Once I am sure there's nothing going on
I step inside, letting the door thud shut.
Another church: matting, seats, and stone,
And little books; sprawlings of flowers, cut
5 For Sunday, brownish now; some brass and stuff
Up at the holy end; the small neat organ;
And a tense, musty, unignorable silence,
Brewed God knows how long. Hatless, I take off
My cycle-clips in awkward reverence,

10 Move forward, run my hand around the font.
From where I stand, the roof looks almost new—
Cleaned, or restored? Someone would know: I don't.
Mounting the lectern, I peruse a few
Hectoring large-scale verses, and pronounce
15 "Here endeth" much more loudly than I'd meant.
The echoes snigger briefly. Back at the door
I sign the book, donate an Irish sixpence,
Reflect the place was not worth stopping for.

Yet stop I did: in fact I often do,
20 And always end much at a loss like this,
Wondering what to look for; wondering, too,
When churches fall completely out of use
What we shall turn them into, if we shall keep
A few cathedrals chronically on show,
25 Their parchment, plate and pyx in locked cases,
And let the rest rent-free to rain and sheep.
Shall we avoid them as unlucky places?

Or, after dark, will dubious women come
To make their children touch a particular stone;
30 Pick simples[3] for a cancer; or on some
Advised night see walking a dead one?
Power of some sort or other will go on
In games, in riddles, seemingly at random;
But superstition, like belief, must die,
35 And what remains when disbelief has gone?
Grass, weedy pavement, brambles, buttress, sky,

A shape less recognizable each week,
A purpose more obscure. I wonder who
Will be the last, the very last, to seek
40 This place for what it was; one of the crew
That tap and jot and know what rood-lofts[4] were?
Some ruin-bibber,[5] randy for antique,
Or Christmas-addict, counting on a whiff
Of gown-and-bands and organ-pipes and myrrh?
45 Or will he be my representative,

Bored, uninformed, knowing the ghostly silt
Dispersed, yet tending to this cross of ground
Through suburb scrub because it held unspilt
So long and equably what since is found
50 Only in separation—marriage, and birth,
And death, and thoughts of these—for whom was built
This special shell? For, though I've no idea
What this accoutered frowsty barn is worth,
It pleases me to stand in silence here;

55 A serious house on serious earth it is,
In whose blent[6] air all our compulsions meet,
Are recognized, and robed as destinies.
And that much never can be obsolete,
Since someone will forever be surprising
60 A hunger in himself to be more serious,
And gravitating with it to this ground,
Which, he once heard, was proper to grow wise in,
If only that so many dead lie round.

1955

Ultimately, Larkin's poem focuses on what it means to visit churches, what it might be that church buildings represent, and what we should make of the fact that "church going" (in the usual sense of the word) has declined so much. The poem

3. Medicinal herbs.
4. Galleries atop the screens (on which crosses are mounted) that divide the naves or main bodies of churches from the choirs or chancels.
5. Literally, ruin-drinker: someone extremely attracted to antiquarian objects.   6. Blended.

uses a *different* sort of church going (visitation by tourists) to consider larger questions about the relationship of religion to culture and history. The poem is, finally, a rather philosophical one about the directions of English culture, and through an enumeration of religious objects and rituals it reviews part of the history of that culture. It tells a kind of story first, through one lengthy dramatized scene, in order to comment later on what the place and the experience may mean, and the larger conclusion derives from the particulars of what the speaker does and touches. By the end of stanza 2 the action is over, but that action, we are told, stands for many such visits to similar churches; after that, the next five stanzas present reflection and discussion. Thus the relatively brief story provides a context for the rambling reflections that grow out of the speaker's dramatic experience.

DRAMATIC POEMS

Just as poems sometimes take on a structure like that of a story, they sometimes borrow the structure of plays. Indeed, some plays *are* written in verse and are thus examples of **verse drama**. What we here call **dramatic poems** are instead merely modeled on drama. The following poem has a dramatic structure; although it, too, is technically a narrative poem insofar as its speaker narrates what happens to the characters in it, the poem consists wholly of a series of scenes, each of which is presented vividly and in detail, as if on stage.

HOWARD NEMEROV

The Goose Fish

On the long shore, lit by the moon
To show them properly alone,
Two lovers suddenly embraced
So that their shadows were as one.
5 The ordinary night was graced
For them by the swift tide of blood
That silently they took at flood.
And for a little time they prized
    Themselves emparadised.

10 Then, as if shaken by stage-fright
Beneath the hard moon's bony light,
They stood together on the sand
Embarrassed in each other's sight
But still conspiring hand in hand,
15 Until they saw, there underfoot,
As though the world had found them out,
The goose fish turning up, though dead,
    His hugely grinning head.

There in the china light he lay,
20 Most ancient and corrupt and gray.

They hesitated at his smile,
Wondering what it seemed to say
To lovers who a little while
Before had thought to understand,
25   By violence upon the sand,
The only way that could be known
     To make a world their own.

It was a wide and moony grin
Together peaceful and obscene;
30   They knew not what he would express,
So finished a comedian
He might mean failure or success,
But took it for an emblem of
Their sudden, new and guilty love
35   To be observed by, when they kissed,
     That rigid optimist.

So he became their patriarch,
Dreadfully mild in the half-dark.
His throat that the sand seemed to choke,
40   His picket teeth, these left their mark
But never did explain the joke
That so amused him, lying there
While the moon went down to disappear
Along the still and tilted track
45   That bears the zodiac.

                    1955

    The first stanza sets the scene—a sandy shore in moonlight—and presents, in fact, the major action of the poem. The rest of the poem dramatizes the lovers' reactions: their initial embarrassment and feelings of guilt (stanza 2); their attempt to interpret the goose fish's smile (stanza 3); their decision to make him, whatever his meaning, the "emblem" of their love (stanza 4); and their acceptance of the fish's ambiguity and of their own relationship (stanza 5). The five stanzas do not exactly present five different scenes or angles on the action, but they do present separate dramatic moments, even if little time has elapsed between them. Almost like a play of five very short acts, the poem traces the drama of the lovers' discovery of themselves and their coming to terms with the meaning of their action. As in many plays, the central event (their lovemaking) is not the focus of the drama, although the drama is based on that event and could not take place without it. The poem depicts the event swiftly but very vividly through figurative language: "they took at flood" the "swift tide of blood" (lines 7, 6). The lovers then briefly feel "emparadised" (line 9), but the poem concentrates on their later reactions.

    Their sudden discovery of the fish, a rude shock, injects a grotesque, almost macabre, note into the poem. From a vision of paradise, the poem seems for a moment to turn toward gothic horror when the lovers discover that they have, after all, been seen—and by such a ghoulish spectator. The last three stanzas gradually re-create the intruder in their minds, as they admit that their act of love exists not in isolation, but rather as part of a continuum, as part of their relationship to the larger world, even (at the end) within the context of the earth itself, and the moon, and the stars. In retrospect, we can see that even at the moment of passion the lovers were in touch with larger processes controlled by the presiding moon ("the swift *tide* of blood"), but neither they nor we had understood their act as such then, and the poem is about this gradual recognition of their "place" in time and space.

Stages of feeling and knowing rather than specific visual scenes determine the poem's progress, and its dramatic structure depends on internal perceptions and internal states of mind rather than dialogue and events. Visualization and images help organize the poem, too. Notice in particular how the two most striking visual features—the fish and the moon—are presented stanza by stanza. In stanza 1, the fish does not appear; the moon is only mentioned, not described, and its light provides a stage spotlight to assure not center-stage attention, but rather total privacy: The moon serves as a lookout for the lovers. The stage imagery, barely suggested by the light in stanza 1, is articulated in stanza 2, and there the moon is "hard" and its light "bony"; its characteristics seem more appropriate to the fish, which has now become visible. In stanza 3, the moon's light comes to seem fragile ("china") as it exposes the fish directly; the moon's role as lookout and protector seems abandoned, or at least endangered. No moon appears in stanza 4, but the fish's grin is "wide and moony," almost as if the two onlookers, one earthly and dead, the other heavenly and eternal, have merged, as they nearly were by the imagery in stanza 2. And in stanza 5, the fish becomes a friend, a comedian, an optimist, an emblem, and a patriarch of their love—and his new position in collaboration with the lovers is presided over by the moon going about its eternal business. The moon—providing the stage light for the poem and the means by which not only the fish but also the meaning of the lovers' act is discovered—has also helped to organize the poem, partly as a dramatic accessory, partly as imagery.

OTHER TYPES OF POETIC STRUCTURE

Some poems are also (or instead) organized by contrasts, and they conveniently set one thing up against another that is quite different. Notice, for example, how the following poem carefully contrasts two worlds:

PAT MORA

Sonrisas

I live in a doorway
between two rooms, I hear
quiet clicks, cups of black
coffee, *click, click* like facts
5   budgets, tenure, curriculum,
from careful women in crisp beige
suits, quick beige smiles
that seldom sneak into their eyes.

I peek
10   in the other room señoras
  in faded dresses stir sweet
  milk coffee, laughter whirls
  with steam from fresh *tamales*
  sh, sh, mucho ruido,[7]
15   they scold one another,
  press their lips, trap smiles
  in their dark, Mexican eyes.

1986

Here different words, habits, sights, sounds, and values characterize the worlds of the two sets of characters, and the poem is organized largely by the contrasts between them. The meaning of the poem (the difference between the two worlds) is very nearly the same as the structure.

Poems can have **discursive structures**; that is, they may be organized like a treatise, an argument, or an essay. "First," they say, "and second . . . and third . . ." This sort of 1-2-3 structure takes a variety of forms depending on what is being enumerated or argued. Discursive structures help organize poems such as Shelley's "Ode to the West Wind" (later in this chapter), where the wind drives a leaf in part I, a cloud in part II, a wave in part III, and then, after a summary and statement of the speaker's ambitious hope in part IV, is asked to make the speaker a lyre in part V.

Poems may borrow their organizational strategies from many places, imitating chronological, visual, or discursive shapes in reality or in other works of art. Sometimes poems strive to be almost purely descriptive of someone or something (using **descriptive structures**), in which case poets have to make organizational decisions much as painters or photographers would, deciding first how a whole scene should look, then putting the parts into proper place for the whole. Of course, poems must present their details sequentially, not all at once as actual pictures more or less can, so poets must decide where to start a description (at the left? center? top?) and what sort of movement to use (linear across the scene? clockwise?). But if using words instead of paint or film has some drawbacks, it also has particular advantages: **Figurative language** can be a part of description, or an adjunct to it. Poets can insert comparisons at any point without necessarily disturbing the unity of their descriptions.

Some poems use **imitative structures,** mirroring as exactly as possible the structure of something that already exists as an object and can be seen—another poem, perhaps, as in Koch's "Variations on a Theme by William Carlos Williams" (chapter 23). Other poems use **reflective** (or *meditative*) **structures,** pondering a subject, theme, or event, and letting the mind play with it, skipping (logically or not) from one sound to another, or to related thoughts or objects as the mind encounters them.

SHIFTS OF TONE AND SUBJECT

Most poems, regardless of which structure or mix of structures they use, depend on shifts of focus, attitude, tone, or subject that are sometimes subtle but always important. Such shifts divide the poem into parts, even when those parts aren't

---

7. A lot of noise.

marked by line or stanza breaks or changes in sound or rhythm. Being attuned to such shifts is key to fully responsive reading, and explaining them is often equally key to effective interpretation.

Although the following poem employs several organizational principles, it ultimately takes its structure from an important shift in the speaker's attitude as she reviews, ponders, and rethinks events of long ago.

SHARON OLDS

The Victims

When Mother divorced you, we were glad. She took it and
took it, in silence, all those years and then
kicked you out, suddenly, and her
kids loved it. Then you were fired, and we
5 grinned inside, the way people grinned when
Nixon's helicopter lifted off the South
Lawn for the last time.[8] We were tickled
to think of your office taken away,
your secretaries taken away,
10 your lunches with three double bourbons,
your pencils, your reams of paper. Would they take your
suits back, too, those dark
carcasses hung in your closet, and the black
noses of your shoes with their large pores?
15 She had taught us to take it, to hate you and take it
until we pricked with her for your
annihilation, Father. Now I
pass the bums in doorways, the white
slugs of their bodies gleaming through slits in their
20 suits of compressed silt, the stained
flippers of their hands, the underwater
fire of their eyes, ships gone down with the
lanterns lit, and I wonder who took it and
took it from them in silence until they had
25 given it all away and had nothing
left but this.

1984

"The Victims" divides basically into two parts. In the first two-thirds of the poem (from line 1 to the middle of line 17), the speaker evokes her father (the "you" of lines 1, 3, and so forth), who had been guilty of terrible behavior during the speaker's youth and was kicked out suddenly and divorced by the speaker's mother (lines 1–3). The father seems to have led a luxurious and insensitive life, with lots of

8. When Richard Nixon resigned the U.S. presidency on August 8, 1974, his exit from the White House (by helicopter from the lawn) was televised live.

support in his office (lines 8–11), fancy clothes (lines 12–14), and decadent lunches (line 10); his artificial identity seemed haunting and frightening (lines 11–14) to the speaker as child. He was then fired from his job (line 4) and lost his whole way of life (lines 8–12), and the speaker (taught by the mother, lines 15–17) recalls celebrating every defeat and every loss ("we pricked with her for your annihilation," lines 16–17). The mother is regarded as a victim ("She took it and took it, in silence, all those years" [lines 1–2]), and the speaker forms an indivisible unit with her and the other children ("her kids," lines 3–4). They are the "we" of the first part of the poem. They were "glad" (line 1) at the divorce; they "loved it" (line 4) when the mother kicked out the father; they "grinned" (line 5) when the father was fired; they were "tickled" (line 7) when he lost his job, his secretaries, and his daily life. Only at the end of the first section does the speaker (now older but remembering what it was like to be a child) recognize that the mother was responsible for the easy, childish vision of the father's guilt ("She had taught us to take it, to hate you and take it" [line 15]); nevertheless, all sympathy in this part of the poem is with the mother and her children, while all of the imagery is entirely unfavorable to the father. The family reacted to the father's misfortunes the way observers responded to the retreat in disgrace of Richard Nixon from the U.S. presidency.

But in line 17, the poem shifts its focus and tone. The "you" in the poem is now, suddenly, "Father." A bit of sympathy begins to surface for "bums in doorways" (line 18), who begin to seem like victims, too; their bodies are "slugs" (line 19), their suits are made of residual waste (lines 19–20), and their hands are reduced to nearly useless "flippers" (line 21). Their eyes contain fire (line 22), but it is as if they retain only a spark of life in their submerged and dying state. The speaker has not forgotten the cruelty and insensitivity recalled in the first part of the poem, but the blame seems to have shifted somewhat, and the father is not the only villain, nor are the mother and children the only victims. Look carefully at how the existence of street people recalls earlier details about the father, how sympathy for his plight is elicited from us, and how the definition of *victim* shifts.

Imagery, words, attitudes, and narrative are different in the two parts of the poem, and the second half carefully qualifies the first, as if to illustrate the more mature and considered attitudes of the speaker in her older years—a qualification of the easy imitation of the earlier years, when the mother's views dominated and set the tone. Change has governed the poem's structure here; differences in age and attitude are supported by an entirely different point of view and frame of reference.

• • •

The paradigms (or models) for organizing poems are, finally, not all that different from those of prose. It may be easier to organize something short (like many a poem) rather than something long (like a short story or biography), but the question of intensity becomes comparatively more important in shorter works. Basically, the problem of how to organize one's material is, for the writer, first of all a matter of deciding what kind of thing one wants to create, of having its purposes and effects clearly in mind. That means that every poem will differ somewhat from every other, but it also means that purposeful patterns—narrative, dramatic, descriptive, imitative, or reflective—may help writers organize and develop their ideas. A consciousness of purpose and effect can help the reader see *how* a poem proceeds toward its goal. And seeing how a poem is organized is, in turn, often a good way of seeing where it is going and what its real concerns, purposes, and **themes** may be. Often a poem's organization helps clarify the particular effects that the poet wishes to generate. In a good poem, means and ends are closely related, and a reader who is a good observer of one will be rewarded with the other.

• • •

ANONYMOUS

Sir Patrick Spens

The king sits in Dumferling toune,[9]
    Drinking the blude-reid[1] wine:
"O whar will I get guid sailor,
    To sail this ship of mine?"

5 Up and spake an eldern knicht,
    Sat at the king's richt knee:
"Sir Patrick Spens is the best sailor
    That sails upon the sea."

The king has written a braid[2] letter
10   And signed it wi' his hand,
And sent it to Sir Patrick Spens,
    Was walking on the sand.

The first line that Sir Patrick read,
    A loud lauch[3] lauched he;
15 The next line that Sir Patrick read,
    The tear blinded his ee.[4]

"O wha is this has done this deed,
    This il deed done to me,
To send me out this time o' the year,
20   To sail upon the sea?

"Make haste, make haste, my merry men all,
    Our guid ship sails the morn."
"O say na sae,[5] my master dear,
    For I fear a deadly storm.

25 "Late, late yestre'en I saw the new moon
    Wi' the auld moon in her arm,
And I fear, I fear, my dear mastér,
    That we will come to harm."

O our Scots nobles were richt laith[6]
30   To weet their cork-heeled shoon,[7]

---

9. Town.   1. Blood-red.   2. Broad: explicit.   3. Laugh.   4. Eye.   5. Not so.
6. Right loath: very reluctant.
7. To wet their cork-heeled shoes. Cork was expensive, and therefore such shoes were a mark of wealth and status.

But lang owre a'[8] the play were played
    Their hats they swam aboon.[9]

O lang, lang, may their ladies sit,
    Wi' their fans into their hand,
35 Or ere they see Sir Patrick Spens
    Come sailing to the land.

O lang, lang, may the ladies stand
    Wi' their gold kems[1] in their hair,
Waiting for their ain[2] dear lords,
40   For they'll see them na mair.

Half o'er, half o'er to Aberdour
    It's fifty fadom deep,
And there lies guid Sir Patrick Spens
    Wi' the Scots lords at his feet.

               ca. 13th century

- What event is hinted at in line 32 ("Their hats they swam aboon") and in the poem's final stanza? What is the effect of depicting the poem's principal action indirectly?

WILLIAM CARLOS WILLIAMS

The Dance

In Brueghel's great picture, The Kermess,[3]
the dancers go round, they go round and
around, the squeal and the blare and the
tweedle of bagpipes, a bugle and fiddles
5 tipping their bellies (round as the thick-
sided glasses whose wash they impound)
their hips and their bellies off balance
to turn them. Kicking and rolling about
the Fair Grounds, swinging their butts, those
10 shanks must be sound to bear up under such
rollicking measures, prance as they dance
in Brueghel's great picture, The Kermess.

               1944

- Why is it appropriate to the subject, a painting, to begin and end the poem with the same line? In what ways is the poem like the dance it depicts?

---

8. Before all.   9. Their hats swam above them.   1. Combs.   2. Own.
3. A painting by Pieter Brueghel the Elder (1525?–69).

EMILY DICKINSON

[*The Wind begun to knead the Grass—*]

The Wind begun to knead the Grass—
As Women do a Dough—
He flung a Hand full at the Plain—
A Hand full at the Sky—
5 The Leaves unhooked themselves from Trees—
And started all abroad—
The Dust did scoop itself like Hands—
And throw away the Road—
The Wagons quickened on the Street—
10 The Thunders gossiped low—
The Lightning showed a Yellow Head—
And then a livid Toe—
The Birds put up the Bars to Nests—
The Cattle flung to Barns—
15 Then came one drop of Giant Rain—
And then, as if the Hands
That held the Dams—had parted hold—
The Waters Wrecked the Sky—
20 But overlooked my Father's House—
Just Quartering a Tree—

1864

• How would you describe this poem's structure? What happens in this
   poem's final line? How is this the work of "the Hands" (line 16)?

WILLIAM SHAKESPEARE

[*Th'expense of spirit in a waste of shame*]

Th'expense of spirit in a waste[4] of shame
Is lust in action; and, till action, lust
Is perjured, murderous, bloody, full of blame,
Savage, extreme, rude, cruel, not to trust;
5 Enjoyed no sooner but despisèd straight:
Past reason hunted; and no sooner had,
Past reason hated, as a swallowed bait,
On purpose laid to make the taker mad:
Mad in pursuit, and in possession so;
10 Had, having, and in quest to have, extreme;
A bliss in proof;[5] and proved, a very woe;

---

4. Using up; also, desert. *Expense:* expending   5. In the act.

Before, a joy proposed; behind, a dream.
All this the world well knows; yet none knows well
To shun the heaven that leads men to this hell.

                                                    1609

- Paraphrase this poem. What emotional stages accompany the carrying out of a violent or lustful act? What is the poem's major insight
  about how lust works? How does the poem's structure contribute to
  its effect and meaning?

CATHY SONG

Heaven

He thinks when we die we'll go to China.
Think of it—a Chinese heaven
where, except for his blond hair,
the part that belongs to his father,
5   everyone will look like him.
China, that blue flower on the map,
bluer than the sea
his hand must span like a bridge
to reach it.
10 An octave away.

I've never seen it.
It's as if I can't sing that far.
But look—
on the map, this black dot.
15 Here is where we live,
on the pancake plains
just east of the Rockies,
on the other side of the clouds.
A mile above the sea,
20 the air is so thin, you can starve on it.
No bamboo trees
But the alpine equivalent,
reedy aspen with light, fluttering leaves.
Did a boy in Guangzhou[6] dream of this
25 as his last stop?
I've heard the trains at night
whistling past our yards,
what we've come to own,
the broken fences, the whiny dog, the rattletrap cars.
30 It's still the wild west,
mean and grubby,
the shootouts and fistfights in the back alley.

6. Usually called Canton, a seaport city in southeastern China.

With my son the dreamer
and my daughter, who is too young to walk,
35 I've sat in this spot
and wondered why here?
Why in this short life,
this town, this creek they call a river?

He had never planned to stay,
40 the boy who helped to build
the railroads for a dollar a day.[7]
He had always meant to go back.
When did he finally know
that each mile of track led him further away,
45 that he would die in his sleep,
dispossessed,
having seen Gold Mountain,[8]
the icy wind tunneling through it,
these landlocked, makeshift ghost towns?

50 It must be in the blood,
this notion of returning.
It skipped two generations, lay fallow,
the garden an unmarked grave.
On a spring sweater day
55 it's as if we remember him.
I call to the children.
We can see the mountains
shimmering blue above the air.
If you look really hard
60 says my son the dreamer,
leaning out from the laundry's rigging,
the work shirts fluttering like sails,
you can see all the way to heaven.

1988

- Who is "He" in this poem's first line? What family history is
  recounted in the poem? How does the poem make use of contrast?

STEPHEN DUNN

Poetry

It makes no difference where one starts,
doesn't every beginning subvert
the tyrannies of time and place?

---

7. The railroads used immigrant day laborers (mostly Chinese) to lay the tracks in the nineteenth century.   8. Chinese term for America, especially common in the nineteenth century.

New Jersey or Vermont, it's the gray zone
5 where I mostly find myself
with little purpose or design.
An apple orchard, an old hotel—
when I introduce them
I feel I've been taken somewhere
10 I've been before; such comfort,
like the sound of consecutive iambs
to the nostalgic ear.
Yet it helps as well
here in the middle, somewhat amused,
15 to have a fast red car
and a winding, country road.
To forget oneself can be an art.
"Frost was wrong about free verse,"[9]
she said to me. "Tear the net down,
20 turn the court into a dance floor."
She happened to be good looking, too,
which seemed to further enliven her remark.
It always makes a difference
how one ends, aren't endings where you
25 shut but don't lock the door?
Strange music beginning,
the dance floor getting crowded now.

                                                1996

• In what way is this poem an *ars poetica*—that is, a declaration of a poet's
  aims and practices? What might the poem demonstrate about poetic
  structure and parts, especially beginnings, middles, and ends?

PERCY BYSSHE SHELLEY

Ode to the West Wind

I

O wild West Wind, thou breath of Autumn's being,
Thou, from whose unseen presence the leaves dead
Are driven, like ghosts from an enchanter fleeing,

Yellow, and black, and pale, and hectic red,
5 Pestilence-stricken multitudes: O thou,
Who chariotest to their dark wintry bed

The wingèd seeds, where they lie cold and low,
Each like a corpse within its grave, until
Thine azure sister of the Spring shall blow

---

9. Poet Robert Frost famously compared writing free verse to "playing tennis with the net down."

10　Her clarion[1] o'er the dreaming earth, and fill
　　(Driving sweet buds like flocks to feed in air)
　　With living hues and odors plain and hill:

　　Wild Spirit, which art moving everywhere;
　　Destroyer and preserver; hear, oh, hear!

　　　　　　II

15　Thou on whose stream, mid the steep sky's commotion,
　　Loose clouds like earth's decaying leaves are shed,
　　Shook from the tangled boughs of Heaven and Ocean,

　　Angels[2] of rain and lightning: there are spread
　　On the blue surface of thine aëry surge,
20　Like the bright hair uplifted from the head

　　Of some fierce Maenad,[3] even from the dim verge
　　Of the horizon to the zenith's height,
　　The locks of the approaching storm. Thou dirge

　　Of the dying year, to which this closing night
25　Will be the dome of a vast sepulcher,
　　Vaulted with all thy congregated might

　　Of vapors, from whose solid atmosphere
　　Black rain, and fire, and hail will burst: oh, hear!

　　　　　　III

　　Thou who didst waken from his summer dreams
30　The blue Mediterranean, where he lay,
　　Lulled by the coil of his crystàlline streams,

　　Beside a pumice isle in Baiae's bay,[4]
　　And saw in sleep old palaces and towers
　　Quivering within the wave's intenser day,

35　All overgrown with azure moss and flowers
　　So sweet, the sense faints picturing them! Thou
　　For whose path the Atlantic's level powers

　　Cleave themselves into chasms, while far below
　　The sea-blooms and the oozy woods which wear
40　The sapless foliage of the ocean, know

　　Thy voice, and suddenly grow gray with fear,
　　And tremble and despoil themselves:[5] oh, hear!

---

1. Trumpet call.　　2. Messengers.
3. Frenzied female votary of Dionysus, the Greek god of vegetation and fertility who was supposed to die in the fall and rise again each spring.
4. Where Roman emperors had erected villas, west of Naples.
5. The vegetation at the bottom of the sea . . . sympathizes with that of the land in the change of seasons. [Shelley's note]

IV

If I were a dead leaf thou mightest bear;
If I were a swift cloud to fly with thee;
45 A wave to pant beneath thy power, and share

The impulse of thy strength, only less free
Than thou, O uncontrollable! If even
I were as in my boyhood, and could be

The comrade of thy wanderings over Heaven,
50 As then, when to outstrip thy skyey speed
Scarce seemed a vision; I would ne'er have striven

As thus with thee in prayer in my sore need.
Oh, lift me as a wave, a leaf, a cloud!
I fall upon the thorns of life! I bleed!

55 A heavy weight of hours has chained and bowed
One too like thee: tameless, and swift, and proud.

V

Make me thy lyre, even as the forest is:
What if my leaves are falling like its own!
The tumult of thy mighty harmonies

60 Will take from both a deep, autumnal tone,
Sweet though in sadness. Be thou, Spirit fierce,
My spirit! Be thou me, impetuous one!

Drive my dead thoughts over the universe
Like withered leaves to quicken a new birth!
65 And, by the incantation of this verse,

Scatter, as from an unextinguished hearth
Ashes and sparks, my words among mankind!
Be through my lips to unawakened earth

The trumpet of a prophecy! O Wind,
70 If Winter comes, can Spring be far behind?

1820

- What attributes of the West Wind does the speaker want his poetry
  to embody? In what ways is this poem like the wind it describes?
  What is the effect of its structure?

PAUL CELAN

Deathfugue[6]

Black milk of daybreak we drink it at evening
we drink it at midday and morning we drink it at night
we drink and we drink
we shovel a grave in the air where you won't lie too cramped
5 A man lives in the house he plays with his vipers he writes
he writes when it grows dark to Deutschland your golden hair
    Margareta[7]
he writes it and steps out of doors and the stars are all sparkling he
    whistles his hounds to stay close
he whistles his Jews into rows has them shovel a grave in the ground
he commands us play up for the dance[8]

10 Black milk of daybreak we drink you at night
we drink you at morning and midday we drink you at evening
we drink and we drink
A man lives in the house he plays with his vipers he writes
he writes when it grows dark to Deutschland your golden hair
    Margareta
15 Your ashen hair Shulamith[9] we shovel a grave in the air where you
    won't lie too cramped

He shouts dig this earth deeper you lot there you others sing up and
    play
he grabs for the rod in his belt he swings it his eyes are so blue
stick your spades deeper you lot there you others play on for the
    dancing

Black milk of daybreak we drink you at night
20 we drink you at midday and morning we drink you at evening
we drink and we drink
a man lives in the house your goldenes Haar Margareta
your aschenes Haar[1] Shulamith he plays with his vipers

He shouts play death more sweetly this Death is a master from
    Deutschland

---

6. Translated from the German by John Felstiner. *Fugue:* a particularly complex and highly regarded genre
of classical musical in which repeated variations on a single or central theme are interwoven.
7. Name of the tragic heroine in German poet Johann Wolfgang von Goethe's *Faust* (1808, 1832). The protagonist of Goethe's poem sells his soul to the devil, who then introduces him to Margarete; after Faust
seduces and impregnates her, and then kills her brother in a swordfight, Margarete goes insane, drowns
her child, and is sentenced to death. *Deutschland:* Germany (German); also, the first word of Germany's
national anthem.
8. During World War II, Jewish musicians in concentration camps were forced to perform for their German captors and fellow prisoners.
9. Biblical character from the Song of Songs; she is traditionally regarded as a symbol of the Jewish people. 1. Respectively, "golden hair" and "ashen hair" in German.

25　he shouts scrape your strings darker you'll rise up as smoke to the sky
　　you'll then have a grave in the clouds where you won't lie too cramped

　　Black milk of daybreak we drink you at night
　　we drink you at midday Death is a master aus Deutschland
　　we drink you at evening and morning we drink and we drink
30　this Death is ein Meister aus Deutschland his eye it is blue
　　he shoots you with shot made of lead shoots you level and true
　　a man lives in the house your goldenes Haar Margarete
　　he looses his hounds on us grants us a grave in the air
　　he plays with his vipers and daydreams der Tod ist ein Meister aus
　　　　Deutschland[2]

35　dein[3] goldenes Haar Margarete
　　dein aschenes Haar Sulamith
　　c. 1944–45　　　　　　　　　　　　　　　　　　　　　　1952
　　　　　　　　　　　　　　　　　　　　　　　　　　　(trans. 1995)

- **How is each stanza like and different from preceding stanzas?
  What is the effect of both the repetition and the changes?**

Prisoners' orchestra during a Sunday concert for the SS-men in Auschwitz in 1941.
The orchestra was probably conducted by the inmate Franciszek Nierychlo.

2. Death is a master from Germany (German).　3. Your (German).

The Translator on His Work: JOHN FELSTINER

From *Paul Celan: Poet, Survivor, Jew* (1995)

Out of those months that saw the war [World War II] ending and its Jewish catastrophe revealed, Paul Antschel [later Celan] wrote . . . *"Todesfuge."* Its title in English might be "Fugue of Death," "Death's Fugue," "Death Fugue," or "Deathfugue."

When Celan . . . crossed out *tango* in a typescript and substituted *fuge* . . . , this small change made an immense difference. It was to bring on decades of debate, the term *Todesfuge* offending against acceptable modes of meaning. What is this absurd genitive, this irreconcilable compound? "Fugue of Death," a correct translation, loses the accentual (and atrocious) symmetry of *Tó-des fú-ge*, while loosening the German possessive's compactness—the compact between death and music, nullity and order, which are the word's two sides. Yet "Death Fugue" does not convey the sense of belonging, a train of events belonging to death. "Death's Fugue" sounds disjointed, and "Deathsfugue" coins too strange an equivalent.

For the first line of *"Todesfuge"* I would like to say "Black milk of daybreak we drink it at dusk," so as to let alliteration imprint the day-in, day-out fatality of camp existence. But "evening" rather than "dusk" for *abends* keeps Celan's rhythm and leads familiarly to "morning" in the next line. . . .
. . . In the beginning I [also] hear—or persuade myself I hear—the creation sequence from Genesis: "And God called the light Day, and the darkness he called Night. And there was evening and there was morning: one day." If the Bible reverberates through Celan's opening lines, "day . . . night . . . evening . . . morning," then the word "dusk" cannot parody Scripture as does "evening . . . and morning."
For forty years now, what Celan wrote has imprinted itself on readers and audiences through a relentless cadence that cannot be gainsaid. As his only poem not stopped by punctuation, "Todesfuge" finds a beat by the first line—

> *wir* trink*en sie* ab*ends*
>
> we *drink* it at *ev*ening

. . . *Wir trinken und trinken*: "we drink it and drink it," or "we're drinking and drinking," a rollicking beat that calls up much-loved German songs—from the Munich beer-hall, let us say, where Nazism arose.

Another reverberation occurs three times over: *da liegt man nicht eng* ("there one doesn't lie narrowly"). . . .
For years I have tried one way after another to bring *da liegt man nicht eng* into rhythmic, idiomatic English: "there you won't lie too tight"—but this makes an unwanted rhyme with "we drink it at night," in a poem where rhyme would

(Continued on next page)

(Continued)

prettify. Celan's laconic phrase gives a proverbial ring to the notion that these prisoners will not be jammed into rough narrow bunks anymore, once they have gone up in smoke. Or else: "there you won't lie crammed in," but I would rather end on a hard consonant as Celan does on *eng* . . . . Hence "there you won't lie too cramped," with its harsh cutoff.

Verse translators are always weighing whether to try for musical effects at the spots where such effects occur in the original. "A man lives in the house," we hear, then the treble alliteration in *der spielt mit den Schlangen der schreibt*, which connects playing, snakes, and writing. To say "he plays with his snakes he writes" creates some resonance, but "he plays with his vipers he writes" moves the rhythm along and ties "vipers" to "writes," uncovering something deadly in the act of writing.

Celan's sounds sometimes defy any English equivalent: *der schreibt wenn es dunkelt nach Deutschland*. Rather than "he writes when it grows dark to Germany," we can keep the jolt of *dunkelt* and *Deutschland* by extraditing the name into English: "he writes when it grows dark to Deutschland." Those two syllables grip the rhythm better than "Germany," and, after all, why translate *Deutschland*, drilled into everyone by Nazism's "Deutschland, Deutschland, über Alles." The word occurs this once in Celan's poetry, then never again.

With this poem's longest line, English syllables can equal the German: *er schreibt es und tritt vor das Haus und es blitzen die Sterne er pfeift seine Rüden herbei*: "he writes it and steps out of doors and the stars are all sparkling he whistles his hounds to come close." To catch in *blitzen* a glimpse of Hitler's *Blitzkrieg*, [Hitler's] lightning war, the stars could be "flashing." But "sparkling," a hackneyed poeticism, fits this nocturne better. And *es blitzen die Sterne* half-quotes a song popular during (and after) the Third Reich, *Heimat, deine Sterne*: "Homeland, thy stars / shine on me even in distant climes." This nostalgic tune, which SS officers demanded from the Auschwitz orchestra, brings a bitter taste to Celan's poem. . . .

A sharp counterpoint follows on the sparkling stars: *er pfeift sein Rüden herbei / er pfeift seine Juden hervor*. Literally, "He whistles his hounds to come near / he whistles his Jews to appear." This matches the German, but its smooth rhyme on "near" and "appear" distracts from Celan's abrasive off-rhyme of *Rüden* ("hounds") and *Juden* ("Jews"), one word with an umlaut, the other not. Making a slight change—"he whistles his hounds to come close / he whistles his Jews into rows"—the voiced *s* in "rows" grinds against the unvoiced *s* in "close." Nazi guards used to call their Jews "dogs" and their German shepherds "men."

Celan's *spielt süsser den Tod* ("play death more sweetly") brings into earshot Bach's aria *"Komm süsser Tod"* (Come sweet death). . . . Celan articulates a twist of thought that English cannot manage:

(Continued on next page)

(Continued)

spielt	süsser	den Tod	der Tod ist ein Meister
play	more sweetly	death	death is a master

At the line's midpoint, *den Tod der Tod,* "death" as the object of sweet playing pivots directly on "death" as the subject of mastery. *Tod* wedges up against itself, making death both outcome and origin.

Now the poem confirms its title: *der Tod ist ein Meister aus Deutschland.* . . . It translates readily, yet *Meister* can designate God, Christ, rabbi, teacher, champion, captain, owner, guildsman, master of arts or theology, labor-camp overseer, musical maestro, "master" race, not to mention Goethe's *Wilhelm Meister* and Wagner's *Meistersinger von Nürnberg,* which carries overtones of the 1935 Nuremberg racial laws and the postwar trials. Any other choice but "master" would lose the loaded sense of *Meister.*

As this motif takes over, the verse itself falls into step and turns up the poem's only rhyme:

> *der Tod ist ein Meister aus Deutschland sein Auge ist blau*
> *er trifft dich mit bleierner Kugel er trifft dich genau*

> this death is ein Meister aus Deutschland his eye it is blue
> he shoots you with shot made of lead shoots you level and true

The celebrated purity of that icy Nordic eye calls for a folk idiom, a singsong wordiness to bring out the childlike tone, and a hackneyed rhyme. . . .

By the time this "master from Deutschland" is named three and then four times, *"Todesfuge"* has evolved its own span of real time. Rhythm and repetition have become systemic, there is no escaping them. . . .

Then suddenly this mind-emptying repetitiveness makes the poem easier to translate: *wir trinken dich mittags*—I've solved this already, and this: *der Tod ist ein Meister aus Deutschland.* The next time they come round I've got my version, then the next and the next. There's no use in thinking anymore, and that points to a rare option, given the poem's *fugue* of death: that is, to drive home its motifs as Celan himself does. The catch phrase *der Tod ist ein Meister aus Deutschland* appears four times. Let this sentence gradually revert to German. First, so that the reader comprehends, say "Death is a master from Deutschland." The second time, "Death is a master aus Deutschland." Then "Death is ein Meister aus Deutschland." And finally, "der Tod ist ein Meister aus Deutschland"—a German contagion of English.

What makes it possible to do this is the logic of *"Todesfuge"*—its musicality, for better or worse. By veering more and more to the original, my version gets a ring of truth, an identity with verse written by Paul Celan. In this gradual reversion, unavailable to German readers, we re-enter the darkness of death-bringing speech.

Finally, I leave the litany of appeals to Margaret and Shulamith wholly in German. The translator's voice moves into unison with the poet's, recouping a little of what has been lost in translation. . . .

SUGGESTIONS FOR WRITING

1. How many different "scenes" can you identify in "Sir Patrick Spens"? Write an essay in which you first summarize the story recounted by the poem, and then discuss the methods of storytelling employed by the poem. Consider the transitions from one scene to another and the almost cinematic "fading" effect between scenes.

2. What words and patterns are repeated in the different stanzas of Shelley's "Ode to the West Wind"? What differences are there from stanza to stanza? What "progress" does the poem make? Write an essay in which you discuss the ways that meaning and structure are intertwined in Shelley's poem.

3. Write an essay that explores the use of contrast in Pat Mora's "Sonrisas." How is each of the two rooms in the poem characterized by way of contrast with the other? What do they individually and jointly symbolize? What does the poem show through this contrast?

4. Write an essay that explores the structure of "Deathfugue" and especially the effect and significance of the repetition and change within and across the poem's various parts. In what way might the poem's structure mimic that of a fugue, and why and how is that mimicking meaningful? Based on John Felstiner's comments on his own translation, as well on as your experience of it, how does this translation enhance or underscore the poem's structure and its effects?

5. Pick out any poem you have read in this book that seems particularly effective in the way it is put together. Write an essay in which you consider how the poem is organized—that is, what structural principles it employs. What do the choices of speaker, situation, and setting have to do with the poem's structure? What other artistic decisions contribute to its structure?

SAMPLE WRITING

The following piece of writing by student Lindsay Gibson was originally just one section of a longer essay on multiple poems by Philip Larkin. Though the beginning and middle of the piece work fine out of that context, you'll notice that we haven't supplied either the complete title or the real conclusion that the piece needs to be an entire, effective essay. What should the piece be titled? How might it be brought to a more satisfying conclusion?

You will notice, too, that the essay focuses only in part and somewhat unevenly on issues related to internal structure. How might the essay make more of the poem's structure? More generally, what are the weakest and strongest moments and aspects of the essay? How might its argument be improved or expanded? Answering such questions for yourself or discussing them with your classmates might be a useful way to better understand the qualities of a good argument, a good title, and a good conclusion.

Lindsay Gibson
Modern British Poetry
Dr. Nick Lolordo
Spring 2007

Philip Larkin's "Church Going"

Philip Larkin is one of the semester's most fascinating poets. His use of colloquial language, regular meter, and rhyme sets him slightly apart from other poets of his day, many of whom write in varying forms of verse, use nearly indecipherable language, and rarely, if ever, make use of rhyme at all. Many of his poems are fraught with existential crises, the nature of which only someone living in the post-modern world could understand; consequently, his poems contain a lot of meaning for the contemporary reader.

Larkin's most fascinating poem, "Church Going," embodies many of Larkin's best attributes as a poet: it uses everyday, standard English and is therefore easy to read and understand, yet its stanzas contain a real search for meaning that its simple language might not immediately invite the reader to ponder. The poem also addresses one of Larkin's main preoccupations: religion, and specifically the role of religion in a post-modern world. Even with all of this, the most engaging aspect of the poem is the duality reflected in its structure: at first and on the one hand, the speaker makes quiet fun out of religion; later and on the other hand, he

---

reveals to us his own search for meaning and the answers that he realizes religion may or may not be able to give him.

The first two stanzas of "Church Going" contain a narrative of a seemingly secular man entering a church he has passed along his way. The speaker observes the layout of the building, the various accoutrements common to a church, and views it all with a mild sense of sarcasm or awkward reverence. His language almost insists on his self-proclaimed ignorance: "someone would know; I don't" (line 12), and he foreshadows the rest of the poem when appraising the roof of the church as one would an antique: "Cleaned, or restored?" (line 12). At the end of the second stanza, the speaker reflects that "the place was not worth stopping for" (line 18). Yet stop he did, and that tells us volumes about what the rest of the poem is about.

In the third stanza, the poem's tone and the speaker's attitude shift as the speaker begins to ponder big questions about religion in today's world: Does it have any meaning left? Should it? The speaker reveals to us that he often stops at churches like these, searching for meaning, yet "Wondering what to look for" (line 21), not even knowing what the questions are that he wants answered. His use of words like "parchment, plate, and pyx" (line 25) reveals to us that he is not as ignorant about religious liturgy as he would have us believe—which, in turn, is further evidence of the dual nature of the poem: The speaker wants us to believe he doesn't know or care about anything to do with religion, yet he has been on his quest for meaning long enough to know the names of things he claims he does not. The last line of the third stanza poses another compelling question, this time about the future: After churches fall out of use, "Shall we avoid them as unlucky places?" (line 27). The question of whether, when faith is finally dead, people will still cling to superstitions such as luck and supernatural powers of whatever nature is a fascinating one.

The speaker goes on to explore this question in the next few stanzas by imagining some specific ways in which superstition might persist after religion is gone: Women might take their children to "touch a particular stone" (line 29) or pick herbs around the church to use for medicinal purposes. But in all these imagined examples, no one actually goes to the church to worship anymore. In stanza 4, the speaker presents various tableaus of people using the church for more and more mundane uses, such as a student of architecture, someone else who only likes to see the ruins of old buildings simply because they're old, and finally, and somewhat paradoxically, a "Christmas-addict" who (presumably) wants to see the last religious remnants of his beloved, commoditized, and commercialized holiday. The last person who might visit the church in this post-religion world might even be a doppelganger of the speaker himself, who, though claiming to be "bored" and "uninformed" (line 46), visits the church because "it held unspilt / So long and equably what since is found / Only in separation—marriage, and birth, / And death, and thoughts of these" (lines 48-51). Once again the speaker insists that he is ignorant and careless of religion, but goes on to betray the fact that even if he does not believe in the religion itself, he is fascinated by the idea that it held "unspilt" what people now only find in marriages, births, and deaths: meaning. It is at

Gibson 3

this point that the reader can truly appreciate the point and purpose of this whole poem: meaning, and the search for it. It seems poignant that the speaker realizes there is more *meaning* in the church itself than any other place, whether actual belief in religion is there or not.

The last stanza seems to be an attempt on the speaker's part to reconcile the opposing forces of the poem—the speaker's insistence that he cares nothing for religion and that religion is meaningless anyway versus his existential need to find some kind of meaning that will justify his existence and maybe even the beliefs of others. The speaker finally respects what the church does for people, including himself: one's "compulsions meet, / Are recognised, and robed as destinies" (lines 56-57). When one wonders if compulsions are merely that, one can go to church and be told that he or she is part of a larger whole—one's destiny. And if compulsions can be transformed into destinies, at least in the mind of the wonderer, then there will always be value in such a service: "that much never can be obsolete" (line 58), according to the speaker of the poem.

The last stanzas of the poem are devoted to a man who gravitates to the church because he "once heard [it] was proper to grow wise in, / If only that so many dead lie round" (lines 62-63). Once again, the speaker shows us that even when belief in the religion associated with the church is completely gone, a sense of reverence, if only for the dead, will remain. The belief may be gone, but the sense of a community among people searching for, and perhaps finding, meaning will remain, and people will always be drawn to that, no matter what their belief system (or lack thereof).

The poem itself has another overarching concern that merits discussion: death. There are many images of or mentions of death throughout the poem: There are "flowers, cut / For Sunday, brownish now" (lines 4-5), the words "Here endeth" (line 15) echoing through the small church, the possibility of someone seeing a "walking dead one" (line 31), the assertion that "superstition, like belief, must die" (line 34), talk of the "ghostly silt / Dispersed" (lines 46-47), thoughts of "marriage, and birth, / And death" (lines 50-51). And finally, the last image in the poem is the abandoned church's graveyard in which "so many dead lie round" (line 62). Throughout the poem there is death: death of people, death of ideas, death of faith. Death's pervasiveness is one more way the poem struggles with its dual nature: the poem narrates a serious search for meaning, yet the very definition of death is that there *is* no meaning. Death is the end, there is nothing more. Any search for meaning is rendered meaningless anyway upon one's death. The speaker implies that there is even an end to the search for meaning itself. The speaker asks in line 35, perhaps the most powerful line of the whole poem: "And what remains when disbelief has gone?" What is left over when even "disbelief" has died? Is it the beginning of another cycle in the search for meaning, or has even the "faith" that there is nothing out there died as well?

The poem "Church Going" is a very layered, intensive look at all the things that matter to us as human beings: meaning, death, hope, hopelessness, and the way all of these things blend together in the perpetual existential crisis that is man's very existence.

19

EXTERNAL FORM

The previous chapters have discussed many of the *internal* features of a poem that make it unique: the tone and characteristics of its speaker; its situation and setting and its themes; its diction, imagery, and sounds. This chapter ventures into what is called the *external* form of a poem. These formal aspects are external in being recognizable; like the fashion and fabric of clothing that expresses the personality of an individual, the external form is an appropriate garb or guise for the unique internal action and meaning of the poem. When reading a poem, you might immediately notice its stanza breaks and even its rhyme scheme before you comprehend the words and meaning. Or you might quickly recognize that the poem takes a traditional form such as the sonnet. These forms guide readers as well as the poet. They help readers feel and appreciate repetitions and connections, changes and gaps, in the language as well as the meaning of the poem.

RHYME

Early English poetry used **alliteration**, instead of rhyming words at the end of the poetic lines, to balance the first and second half of each line (see Earle Birney's "Anglosaxon Street" later in this chapter for a modern imitation of this principle). From the later Middle Ages until the twentieth century, the music of **rhyme** was central to both the sound and the formal conception of most poems in the Western world. Because poetry was originally an oral art (many poems were only later written down, if at all), various kinds of memory devices (sometimes called mnemonic devices) were built into poems to help reciters remember them. Rhyme was one such device, and most people still find it easier to memorize poetry that rhymes. The simple pleasure of hearing familiar sounds repeated at regular intervals may help account for the traditional popularity of rhyme. Rhyme also gives poetry a special aural quality that distinguishes it from prose. According to the established taste in eras before our own, there was a decorum or proper behavior in poetry as in other things: A poem should not in any way be mistaken for prose (though it might serve prosaic functions). Hence, the literary critics in those ages made extraordinary efforts to distinguish poetry, which was thought to be artistically superior, from prose, which was thought to be primarily utilitarian.

Some English poets (especially in the Renaissance) did experiment—often very successfully—with **blank verse** (that is, verse that does not rhyme but that nevertheless conforms to strict metrical requirements), but the cultural pressure for rhyme was almost constant. Why? Custom combined with the sense of proper decorum accounted in part for the assumption that rhyme was necessary to poetry, but there was probably more to it than that. Rather, the poets' sense that poetry was an imitation of larger relationships in the universe made it seem natural to use rhyme to represent or re-create a sense of pattern, harmony, correspondence, symmetry, and order. The sounds of poetry were thus, they reasoned, reminders of the harmonious cosmos, of the music of the spheres that animated all creation. In a modern world increasingly perceived as fragmented and chaotic, there may be less of a tendency to assert a sense of harmony and symmetry. It would be too simple to say that rhyme in a poem specifically means that the poet has a firm sense of cosmic order, or that an unrhymed poem testifies to chaos. Unrhymed medieval alliterative poetry certainly presupposed a divinely ordered universe, for instance. In different ways, the norms of poetry and the cultural assumptions of the time interact to influence the expectations of both poets and readers.

Rhyme also provides a kind of discipline for the poet, a way of harnessing poetic talents and keeping a rein on the imagination, so that the results have a recognizable form. Robert Frost said that writing **free verse**—that is, poems without rhyme or regular meter—was pointless, like playing tennis without a net. Frost speaks for many (perhaps most) traditional poets in suggesting that writing good poetry requires discipline and great care with formal elements such as rhyme or rhythm. More recent poets have often chosen to play by new rules or to invent their own as they go along, preferring the sparer tones that unrhymed poetry provides. Contemporary poets of course still care about the sounds of their poetry, but they may replace rhyme and meter with other aural and metrical devices and other strategies for organizing stanzas. Nevertheless, some contemporary poets mix regular rhyme and meter with more flexible lines to suggest a tribute to tradition as well as the unexpectedness of experience; even the search for rhyming words may lead to surprising discoveries.

STANZAS

Most poems of more than a few lines are divided into **stanzas**—groups of lines divided from other groups by white space on the page. Putting some space between groupings of lines has the effect of sectioning a poem, giving its physical appearance a series of divisions that often mark turns of thought, changes of scene or image, or other shifts in structure or direction. In Donne's "The Flea" (chapter 15), for example, the stanza divisions mark distinct stages in the action: Between the first and second stanzas, the speaker stops his companion from killing the flea; between the second and third stanzas, the companion follows through on her intention and kills the flea. In Nemerov's "The Goose Fish" (chapter 18), the stanzas mark stages in the self-perception of the lovers: Each stanza is a more or less distinct scene, and the scenes unfold almost like a series of slides. Any formal division of a poem into stanzas is important to consider; what appear to be gaps or silences may be structural markers.

Historically, stanzas have most often been organized by patterns of rhyme, and thus stanza divisions have traditionally been a visual indicator of patterns in sound. Highly elaborate verse forms have been developed that set up stanzas as part of a scheme for the whole poem. The poets of medieval Provence were especially inventive, subtle, and elaborate in their construction of complex verse forms, such as the sestina; some of these forms have been adapted by poets ever since. Different cultures develop their own patterns and measures, and they vary from age to age as well as from region to region. In most traditional stanza forms, the pattern of rhyme is repeated in stanza after stanza throughout the poem, until voice and ear become familiar with the pattern and come to expect it. The repetition of pattern allows us to hear deviations from the pattern as well, just as we do in music.

STANZAS AND RHYME SCHEMES: SOME EXAMPLES

In Shelley's "Ode to the West Wind," the first and third lines in each stanza rhyme, and the middle line then rhymes with the first and third lines of the next stanza. (In indicating rhyme, we conventionally use a different letter of the alphabet to represent each rhyme sound. Remember to reuse a letter if the same sound repeats in later lines or stanzas; for instance, a poem may return to *a* and *b* rhymes for the last lines after *g* and *h*, to bring a feeling of closure and coherence. In the following example, if we begin with "being" as *a* and "dead" as *b*, then "fleeing" is also *a*, "red" and "bed" are *b*, and so forth.)

O wild West Wind, thou breath of Autumn's being,	*a*
Thou, from whose unseen presence the leaves dead	*b*
Are driven, like ghosts from an enchanter fleeing,	*a*
Yellow, and black, and pale, and hectic red,	*b*
Pestilence-stricken multitudes: O thou,	*c*
Who chariotest to their dark wintry bed	*b*
The wingèd seeds, where they lie cold and low,	*c*
Each like a corpse within its grave, until	*d*
Thine azure sister of the Spring shall blow	*c*

In this stanza form, known as **terza rima**, the stanzas are linked to each other by a common sound: One rhyme sound from each stanza is picked up in the next stanza, and so on to the end of the poem (though sometimes poems in this form have sections that use varied rhyme schemes). This stanza form was used by Dante in *The Divine Comedy*, written in Italian in the early 1300s. Terza rima requires many rhymes, and thus many different rhyme words, and therefore it is not very common in English, a relatively rhyme-poor language (not as rich in rhyme possibilities as Italian or French). English is derived from so many different language families that it has fewer similar word endings than languages that mainly derive from a single language family.

The **Spenserian stanza** is even more rhyme-rich than terza rima, using only three rhyme sounds in nine rhymed lines, as in Keats's *The Eve of St. Agnes*:

Her falt'ring hand upon the balustrade,	*a*
Old Angela was feeling for the stair,	*b*
When Madeline, St. Agnes' charmèd maid,	*a*
Rose, like a missioned spirit, unaware:	*b*
With silver taper's light, and pious care,	*b*
She turned, and down the agèd gossip led	*c*
To a safe level matting. Now prepare,	*b*
Young Porphyro, for gazing on that bed;	*c*
She comes, she comes again, like ring dove frayed and fled	*c*

On the other hand, the **ballad stanza** (as in "Sir Patrick Spens") has only one set of rhymes in four lines; lines 1 and 3 in each stanza do not rhyme at all:

The king sits in Dumferling toune,   *a*
  Drinking the blude-reid wine: *b*
"O whar will I get guid sailor,   *c*
  To sail this ship of mine?"   *b*

Most stanza forms use a metrical pattern as well as a rhyme scheme. Terza rima, like most English stanza and verse forms, involves **iambic** meter (unstressed and stressed syllables alternating regularly), and each line has five beats (**pentameter**). The first eight lines of a Spenserian stanza are also in iambic pentameter, but the ninth line in each stanza has one extra foot (iambic **hexameter**). The ballad stanza, also iambic, alternates three-beat and four-beat lines; lines 1 and 3 are unrhymed iambic **tetrameter** (four beats), and lines 2 and 4 are rhymed iambic **trimeter** (three beats).

You can probably deduce the principles involved in each of the following stanza or verse forms by looking carefully at a poem that uses it; if you have trouble, look at the definitions in the glossary. Some examples of these and other forms follow.

heroic couplet	"Sound and Sense"	chapter 17
tetrameter couplet	"To His Coy Mistress"	chapter 15
limerick	"[There was a young girl from St. Paul]"	chapter 17
free verse	"Dirge"	chapter 17
blank verse	"Lines Written a Few Miles above Tintern Abbey"	
		Reading More Poetry
sestina	"Sestina"	chapter 19
villanelle	"Do Not Go Gentle into That Good Night"	chapter 19

• • •

DYLAN THOMAS

Do Not Go Gentle into That Good Night[1]

Do not go gentle into that good night,
Old age should burn and rave at close of day;
Rage, rage against the dying of the light.

Though wise men at their end know dark is right,
5 Because their words had forked no lightning they
Do not go gentle into that good night.

Good men, the last wave by, crying how bright
Their frail deeds might have danced in a green bay,
Rage, rage against the dying of the light.

10 Wild men who caught and sang the sun in flight,
And learn, too late, they grieved it on its way,
Do not go gentle into that good night.

---

1. Written during the final illness of the poet's father.

Grave men, near death, who see with blinding sight
Blind eyes could blaze like meteors and be gay,
15 Rage, rage against the dying of the light.

And you, my father, there on the sad height,
Curse, bless, me now with your fierce tears, I pray.
Do not go gentle into that good night.
Rage, rage against the dying of the light.

1952

- What do the wise, good, wild, and grave men have in common with the speaker's father? Why do you think Thomas chose such a strict form, the villanelle, for such an emotionally charged subject?

MARIANNE MOORE

Poetry

I, too, dislike it: there are things that are important beyond all this
    fiddle.
    Reading it, however, with a perfect contempt for it, one discovers in
    it after all, a place for the genuine.
        Hands that can grasp, eyes
5   that can dilate, hair that can rise
            if it must, these things are important not because a

high-sounding interpretation can be put upon them but because they
    are
    useful. When they become so derivative as to become unintelligible,
    the same thing may be said for all of us, that we
10   do not admire what
        we cannot understand: the bat
            holding on upside down or in quest of something to

eat, elephants pushing, a wild horse taking a roll, a tireless wolf under
    a tree, the immovable critic twitching his skin like a horse that feels a
    flea, the base-
15   ball fan, the statistician—
        nor is it valid
            to discriminate against "business documents and

school-books";[2] all these phenomena are important. One must make a
    distinction
    however: when dragged into prominence by half poets, the result is
    not poetry,

2. *Diary of Tolstoy* (Dutton), p. 84. "Where the boundary between prose and poetry lies, I shall never be able to understand. The question is raised in manuals of style, yet the answer to it lies beyond me. Poetry is verse: Prose is not verse. Or else poetry is everything with the exception of business documents and school books" [Moore's note].

20   nor till the poets among us can be
            "literalists of
               the imagination"[3]—above
                  insolence and triviality and can present

for inspection, "imaginary gardens with real toads in them," shall we have
25   it. In the meantime, if you demand on the one hand,
         the raw material of poetry in
            all its rawness and
               that which is on the other hand
                  genuine, you are interested in poetry.

                                                                                    1921

• In what ways does this poem resemble prose? Does it follow any
rules of line endings or stanza forms? Is there a regular meter?
(Hint: The first line of each stanza has nineteen syllables.)

ELIZABETH BISHOP

Sestina

September rain falls on the house.
In the failing light, the old grandmother
sits in the kitchen with the child
beside the Little Marvel Stove,
5   reading the jokes from the almanac,
laughing and talking to hide her tears.

She thinks that her equinoctial tears
and the rain that beats on the roof of the house
were both foretold by the almanac,
10 but only known to a grandmother.
The iron kettle sings on the stove.
She cuts some bread and says to the child,

It's time for tea now; but the child
is watching the teakettle's small hard tears
15 dance like mad on the hot black stove,
the way the rain must dance on the house.
Tidying up, the old grandmother
hangs up the clever almanac

on its string. Birdlike, the almanac
20 hovers half open above the child,

3. Yeats, *Ideas of Good and Evil* (A. H. Bullen, 1903), p. 182. "The limitation of [William Blake's] view was
from the very intensity of his vision; he was a too literal realist of imagination, as others are of nature;
and because he believed that the figures seen by the mind's eye, when exalted by inspiration, were 'eternal
existences,' symbols of divine essences, he hated every grace of style that might obscure their lineaments"
[Moore's note]. The phrase "imaginary . . . in them," in the next stanza, has no known source.

hovers above the old grandmother
and her teacup full of dark brown tears.
She shivers and says she thinks the house
feels chilly, and puts more wood in the stove.

25 *It was to be*, says the Marvel Stove.
I know what I know, says the almanac.
With crayons the child draws a rigid house
and a winding pathway. Then the child
puts in a man with buttons like tears
30 and shows it proudly to the grandmother.

But secretly, while the grandmother
busies herself about the stove,
the little moons fall down like tears
from between the pages of the almanac
35 into the flower bed the child
has carefully placed in the front of the house.

Time to plant tears, says the almanac.
The grandmother sings to the marvellous stove
and the child draws another inscrutable house.

1965

- Try to derive from "Sestina" the "rules" that govern the sestina form. Why do you think Bishop chose this form for her poem?

ISHMAEL REED

beware : do not read this poem

tonite   ,   thriller was
abt an ol woman   ,   so vain she
surrounded herself w /
   many mirrors
it got so bad that finally she
5 locked herself indoors & her
whole life became the
   mirrors

one day the villagers broke
10 into her house   ,   but she was too
swift for them   .   she disappeared
   into a mirror

each tenant who bought the house
after that   ,   lost a loved one to
15   the ol woman in the mirror :
   first a little girl
   then a young woman
   then the young woman / s husband

the hunger of this poem is legendary
20 it has taken in many victims
back off from this poem
it has drawn in yr feet
back off from this poem
it has drawn in yr legs

25 back off from this poem
it is a greedy mirror
you are into this poem   .   from
    the waist down
nobody can hear you can they   ?
30 this poem has had you up to here
       belch
this poem aint got no manners
you cant call out frm this poem
relax now & go w /   this poem
35 move & roll on to this poem
do not resist this poem
this poem has yr eyes
this poem has his head
this poem has his arms
40 this poem has his fingers
this poem has his fingertips
this poem is the reader & the
reader this poem

statistic   :   the us bureau of missing persons reports
45   that in 1968 over 100,000 people disappeared
                    leaving no solid clues
                         nor trace   only
        a space   in the lives of their friends

                                                1970

- How does the speaker's repeated use of the word *mirror* help determine the form of this poem? How (and why) does the form evolve in
  the course of the poem?

ARCHIBALD MacLEISH

Ars Poetica[4]

A poem should be palpable and mute
As a globed fruit,

Dumb
As old medallions to the thumb,

---

4. "The Art of Poetry," title of a poetical treatise by the Roman poet Horace (65–8 B.C.E.).

5 Silent as the sleeve-worn stone
Of casement ledges where the moss has grown—

A poem should be wordless
As the flight of birds.

A poem should be motionless in time
10 As the moon climbs.

Leaving, as the moon releases
Twig by twig the night-entangled trees,

Leaving, as the moon behind the winter leaves,
Memory by memory the mind—

15 A poem should be motionless in time
As the moon climbs.

A poem should be equal to:
Not true.

For all the history of grief
20 An empty doorway and a maple leaf.

For love
The leaning grasses and two lights above the sea—

A poem should not mean
But be.

                                                1926

- Can you summarize this poem's ideas about what poetry should
  be? How does the poem itself illustrate these principles?

DUDLEY RANDALL

Ballad of Birmingham

(On the bombing of a church in Birmingham, Alabama, 1963)

"Mother dear, may I go downtown
Instead of out to play,
And march the streets of Birmingham
In a Freedom March today?"

5 "No, baby, no, you may not go,
For the dogs are fierce and wild,
And clubs and hoses, guns and jails
Aren't good for a little child."

"But, mother, I won't be alone.
10 Other children will go with me,
And march the streets of Birmingham
To make our country free."

"No, baby, no, you may not go,
For I fear those guns will fire.
15   But you may go to church instead
And sing in the children's choir."

She has combed and brushed her night-dark hair,
And bathed rose petal sweet,
And drawn white gloves on her small brown hands,
20   And white shoes on her feet.

The mother smiled to know her child
Was in the sacred place,
But that smile was the last smile
To come upon her face.

25   For when she heard the explosion,
Her eyes grew wet and wild.
She raced through the streets of Birmingham
Calling for her child.

She clawed through bits of glass and brick,
30   Then lifted out a shoe.
"Oh, here's the shoe my baby wore,
But, baby, where are you?"

1969

- Compare this poem to other ballads in this volume and elsewhere.
  Why is the form appropriate for commemorating this violent event?

THE SONNET

The **sonnet**, one of the most persistent verse forms, originated in the Middle
Ages in Italian and French poetry. It dominated English poetry in the late sixteenth and early seventeenth centuries and then was revived several times from
the early nineteenth century onward. Except for some early experiments with
length, the sonnet has always been fourteen lines long, and it usually is written
in iambic pentameter. It is most often printed as if it were a single stanza,
although it actually has formal divisions defined by its various rhyme schemes
and structures. (In discussions of poetry, the word *formal* simply means "relating
to form.") For more than four centuries, the sonnet has been surprisingly resil-
ient, and it continues to attract a variety of poets. As a verse form, the sonnet is
contained, compact, demanding; whatever it does, it must do concisely. It is best
suited to intensity of feeling and concentration of figurative language and
expression.

Most sonnets are structured according to one of two principles of division.
The *English*, or *Shakespearean*, *sonnet* is divided into three units of four lines
each and a final unit of two lines, and sometimes the line spacing reflects this
division. Ordinarily its rhyme scheme reflects the structure: The scheme of
abab cdcd efef gg is the classic one, but many variations from that pattern still
reflect the basic 4-4-4-2 division. In the *Italian*, or *Petrarchan*, *sonnet* (the Italian
poet Petrarch was an early master of this structure), the fundamental break is
between the first eight lines (called an **octave**) and the last six (called a **sestet**).

Its "typical" rhyme scheme is *abbaabba cdecde*, although it too produces many variations that still reflect the basic division into two parts, an octave and a sestet.

The two kinds of sonnet structures are useful for different sorts of argument. The 4-4-4-2 structure works very well for constructing a poem that makes a three-step argument (with a quick summary at the end) or for setting up brief, cumulative images. Shakespeare's "[That time of year thou mayst in me behold]" (chapter 16), for example, uses the 4-4-4-2 structure to mark the progressive steps toward death and the parting of lovers by using three distinct images and then summarizing. In the two-part structure of the Italian sonnet, the octave states a proposition or generalization and the sestet provides a particular example, consequence, or application of it; alternatively, the second part may turn away from the first to present a new position or response. The final lines may, for example, reverse the first eight and achieve a paradox or irony in the poem, or the poem may nearly balance two comparable arguments. Basically, the 8-6 structure lends itself to poems with two points to make, or to those that make one point and then illustrate it.

During the Renaissance, poets regularly employed the sonnet for love poems; many modern sonnets continue to be about love or private life, and many poets continue to use a personal, apparently open and sincere tone in their sonnets. But poets often find the sonnet's compact form and rigid demands equally useful for a variety of subjects and tones. Sonnets may be about subjects other than love: politics, philosophy, discovery. And their tones vary widely, too, from the anger and remorse of "[Th' expense of spirit in a waste of shame]" (chapter 18) and righteous outrage of "On the Late Massacre in Piedmont" (chapter 15) to the tender awe of "How Do I Love Thee?" ("Poetry: Reading, Responding, Writing"). Many poets seem to take the kind of comfort in the careful limits of the form that William Wordsworth describes in "Nuns Fret Not" (below), finding in its two basic variations, the English sonnet and the Italian sonnet, a wealth of ways to organize their materials into coherent structures.

TWO SONNETS: PRACTICING

Can you identify the rhyme scheme in each of these poems and the type of sonnet each poem is?

HENRY CONSTABLE

[My lady's presence makes the roses red]

My lady's presence makes the roses red,
Because to see her lips they blush for shame.
The lily's leaves, for envy, pale became,
And her white hands in them this envy bred.
5   The marigold the leaves abroad doth spread,
Because the sun's and her power is the same.
The violet of purple colour came,

Dyed in the blood she made my heart to shed.
In brief: all flowers from her their virtue take;
10   From her sweet breath their sweet smells do proceed;
The living heat which her eyebeams doth make
Warmeth the ground and quickeneth the seed.
The rain, wherewith she watereth the flowers,
Falls from mine eyes, which she dissolves in showers.

1594

WILLIAM WORDSWORTH

Nuns Fret Not

Nuns fret not at their convent's narrow room;
And hermits are contented with their cells;
And students with their pensive citadels;
Maids at the wheel, the weaver at his loom,
5   Sit blithe and happy; bees that soar for bloom,
High as the highest Peak of Furness-fells,[5]
Will murmur by the hour in foxglove bells:
In truth the prison, unto which we doom
Ourselves, no prison is: and hence for me,
10   In sundry moods, 'twas pastime to be bound
Within the sonnet's scanty plot of ground;
Pleased if some souls (for such there needs must be)
Who have felt the weight of too much liberty,
Should find brief solace there, as I have found.

1807

Mark with letters of the alphabet the rhyme sounds at the end of all fourteen lines of both sonnets. Then decide whether each poem is an Italian or an English sonnet. Do you notice any variations from the descriptions above of these two sonnet forms?

Do the last two lines of Wordsworth's sonnet rhyme? In which line do you first see or hear a third end-rhyme sound? What feelings might be expressed by the sound as well as sense of the last words in each line? For instance, "room," "loom," and "bloom" rhyme with "gloom" and "tomb"; not all these words have dark or haunting meanings, but readers may vaguely sense such associations, especially when they anticipate and then hear the sound again, in "doom" (line 8). Where do you first notice the speaker referring to himself and his views ("me")? Can you summarize two or more basic points this sonnet makes?

What is the rhyme scheme of Constable's sonnet? How many of the end-rhymes (last words of the lines) end with the letter *d*? How many of the end-rhymes have a

---

5. Mountains in England's Lake District, where Wordsworth lived.

long *a* vowel sound, as in "shame"? Which end rhymes have a single syllable? Which have two syllables? Are these word patterns meaningful, or do they simply enhance the pleasing sounds of this poem about love? Why do the new rhyme sounds begin in line 9? What do the first eight lines argue? How do the next four lines add to or follow from the argument? What happens to rhyme and meaning in the final couplet?

Sometimes a neat and precise structure is altered—either slightly, as in Wordsworth's "Nuns Fret Not," or more radically as particular needs or effects may demand. And the two basic structures, Shakespearean and Petrarchan, certainly do not define all the structural possibilities within a fourteen-line poem, even if they are the most traditional ways of taking advantage of the sonnet's compact and contained form.

THE SONNET: EXAMPLES

DANTE GABRIEL ROSSETTI

A Sonnet Is a Moment's Monument

A Sonnet is a moment's monument—
  Memorial from the Soul's eternity
  To one dead deathless hour. Look that it be,
Whether for lustral[6] rite or dire portent,
5 Of its own arduous fullness reverent.
  Carve it in ivory or in ebony,
  As Day or Night may rule; and let Time see
Its flowering crest impearled and orient.[7]

A Sonnet is a coin: its face reveals
10 The soul—its converse, to what Power 'tis due—
Whether for tribute to the august appeals
  Of Life or dower in Love's high retinue,

It serve; or 'mid the dark wharf's cavernous breath,
In Charon's palm it pay the toll to Death.[8]

                             1881

- In Rossetti's metaphor comparing the sonnet to a coin (lines 9–14), what are the two "sides" of a sonnet?

6. Purificatory.   7. Sparkling.
8. In classical myth, Charon was the boatman who rowed the souls of the dead across the river Styx. Ancient Greeks put a small coin in the hand of the dead to pay his fee.

JOHN KEATS

On the Sonnet

If by dull rhymes our English must be chained,
And like Andromeda,[9] the sonnet sweet
Fettered, in spite of painèd loveliness,
Let us find, if we must be constrained,
5 Sandals more interwoven and complete
To fit the naked foot of Poesy:[1]
Let us inspect the lyre, and weigh the stress
Of every chord,[2] and see what may be gained
By ear industrious, and attention meet;
10 Misers of sound and syllable, no less
Than Midas[3] of his coinage, let us be
Jealous of dead leaves in the bay-wreath crown;[4]
So, if we may not let the Muse be free,
She will be bound with garlands of her own.

1819

- What is the rhyme scheme of this poem? How well does this unusual structure meet the challenge implied by the poem?

On the Grasshopper and the Cricket

The poetry of earth is never dead:
When all the birds are faint with the hot sun,
And hide in cooling trees, a voice will run
From hedge to hedge about the new-mown mead;
5 That is the grasshopper's—he takes the lead
In summer luxury—he has never done
With his delights; for when tired out with fun
He rests at ease beneath some pleasant weed.
The poetry of earth is ceasing never:
10 On a lone winter evening, when the frost
Has wrought a silence, from the stove there shrills
The cricket's song, in warmth increasing ever,

---

9. According to Greek myth, Andromeda was chained to a rock so that she would be devoured by a sea monster. She was rescued by Perseus, who married her. When she died she was placed among the stars.
1. In a letter that contained this sonnet, Keats expressed impatience with the traditional Petrarchan and Shakespearean sonnet forms: "I have been endeavoring to discover a better sonnet stanza than we have."
2. Lyre string. *Meet:* proper.
3. The legendary king of Phrygia who asked, and got, the power to turn all he touched to gold.
4. The bay tree was sacred to Apollo, god of poetry, and bay wreaths came to symbolize true poetic achievement. The withering of the bay tree is sometimes considered an omen of death. *Jealous:* suspiciously watchful.

And seems to one in drowsiness half lost,
The grasshopper's among some grassy hills.
                              December 30, 1816

- How does this sonnet connect and compare two scenes and two "singers" in its two-part "Italian" form?

On Seeing the Elgin Marbles[5]

My spirit is too weak—mortality
Weighs heavily on me like unwilling sleep,
And each imagined pinnacle and steep
Of godlike hardship tells me I must die
5   Like a sick eagle looking at the sky.
Yet 'tis a gentle luxury to weep
That I have not the cloudy winds to keep
Fresh for the opening of the morning's eye.
Such dim-conceivèd glories of the brain
10 Bring round the heart an indescribable feud;
So do these wonders a most dizzy pain,
That mingles Grecian grandeur with the rude
Wasting of old Time—with a billowy main—
A sun—a shadow of a magnitude.

                                   1817

- Most of the octet and the beginning of the sestet describe the speaker's desire for imagined "pinnacles" of vision. Why are the carved stone ruins referred to so late and so obliquely in the poem?

GWENDOLYN BROOKS

First Fight. Then Fiddle.

First fight. Then fiddle. Ply the slipping string
With feathery sorcery; muzzle the note
With hurting love; the music that they wrote
Bewitch, bewilder. Qualify to sing
5   Threadwise. Devise no salt, no hempen thing
For the dear instrument to bear. Devote
The bow to silks and honey. Be remote
A while from malice and from murdering.
But first to arms, to armor. Carry hate

---

5. Figures and friezes from the Athenian Parthenon, they were taken from the site by Lord Elgin, brought to England in 1806, and then sold to the British Museum, where Keats saw them.

10 In front of you and harmony behind.
Be deaf to music and to beauty blind.
Win war. Rise bloody, maybe not too late
For having first to civilize a space
Wherein to play your violin with grace.

1949

- After advising "First fight. Then fiddle," the speaker discusses first music, then conflict. Why do you think the poet has arranged her argument this way?

EMMA LAZARUS

The New Colossus[6]

Not like the brazen giant of Greek fame,[7]
With conquering limbs astride from land to land;
Here at our sea-washed, sunset gates shall stand
A mighty woman with a torch, whose flame
5 Is the imprisoned lightning, and her name
Mother of Exiles. From her beacon-hand
Glows world-wide welcome; her mild eyes command
The air-bridged harbor that twin cities[8] frame.
"Keep ancient lands, your storied pomp!" cries she
10 With silent lips. "Give me your tired, your poor,
Your huddled masses yearning to breathe free,
The wretched refuse of your teeming shore.
Send these, the homeless, tempest-tost to me,
I lift my lamp beside the golden door!"

November 1883

- What comparison is the speaker making between the old and new worlds?

ROBERT FROST

Range-Finding

The battle rent a cobweb diamond-strung
And cut a flower beside a groundbird's nest
Before it stained a single human breast.

---

6. The poem was written to commemorate the opening of the Statue of Liberty, in New York harbor.
7. The Colossus of Rhodes, one of the seven wonders of the ancient world, a 100-foot statue of Helios, the sun god. 8. Manhattan and Brooklyn.

The stricken flower bent double and so hung.
5 And still the bird revisited her young.
A butterfly its fall had dispossessed,
A moment sought in air his flower of rest,
Then slightly stooped to it and fluttering clung.
On the bare upland pasture there had spread
10 O'ernight 'twixt mullein stalks a wheel of thread
And straining cables wet with silver dew.
A sudden passing bullet shook it dry.
The indwelling spider ran to greet the fly,
But finding nothing, sullenly withdrew.

1916

- What is the "battle" of line 1? What is the poem's actual subject?

Design

I found a dimpled spider, fat and white,
On a white heal-all,[9] holding up a moth
Like a white piece of rigid satin cloth—
Assorted characters of death and blight
5 Mixed ready to begin the morning right,
Like the ingredients of a witches' broth—
A snow-drop spider, a flower like a froth,
And dead wings carried like a paper kite.

What had that flower to do with being white,
10 The wayside blue and innocent heal-all?
What brought the kindred spider to that height,
Then steered the white moth thither in the night?
What but design of darkness to appall?—
If design govern in a thing so small.

1936

- How does this poem confound our usual preconceptions about "light" and "darkness"? How does its elaborate form complement its theme?

WILLIAM WORDSWORTH

London, 1802

Milton! thou should'st be living at this hour:
England hath need of thee: she is a fen
Of stagnant waters: altar, sword, and pen,

9. A plant, also called the "all-heal" and "self-heal," with tightly clustered violet-blue flowers.

Fireside, the heroic wealth of hall and bower,
5 Have forfeited their ancient English dower
Of inward happiness. We are selfish men;
Oh! raise us up, return to us again;
And give us manners, virtue, freedom, power.
Thy soul was like a star, and dwelt apart:
10 Thou hadst a voice whose sound was like the sea:
Pure as the naked heavens, majestic, free,
So didst thou travel on life's common way,
In cheerful godliness; and yet thy heart
The lowliest duties on herself did lay.

1802

- What is Wordsworth asserting about the power of poetry in this sonnet? Why do you think he chose the sonnet form for this poem?

JOHN MILTON

[*When I consider how my light is spent*]

When I consider how my light is spent,
  Ere half my days, in this dark world and wide,
  And that one talent which is death to hide[1]
  Lodged with me useless, though my soul more bent
5 To serve therewith my Maker, and present
  My true account, lest he returning chide;
  "Doth God exact day-labor, light denied?"
  I fondly ask; but Patience to prevent[2]
That murmur, soon replies, "God doth not need
10 Either man's work or his own gifts; who best
  Bear his mild yoke, they serve him best. His state
Is kingly. Thousands at his bidding speed
  And post o'er land and ocean without rest:
  They also serve who only stand and wait."

ca. 1652

- Paraphrase the speaker's question and Patience's reply. Does knowing that Milton was blind alter your interpretation of this poem?

---

1. In the parable of the talents (Matthew 25), the servants who earned interest on their master's money (his talents) while he was away were called "good and faithful"; the one who simply hid the money and then returned it was condemned and sent away.   2. Forestall. *Fondly:* foolishly.

ELIZABETH BARRETT BROWNING

[When our two souls stand up]

When our two souls stand up erect and strong,
Face to face, silent, drawing nigh and nigher,
Until the lengthening wings break into fire
At either curvèd point,—what bitter wrong
5 Can the earth do to us, that we should not long
Be here contented? Think. In mounting higher,
The angels would press on us and aspire
To drop some golden orb of perfect song
Into our deep, dear silence. Let us stay
10 Rather on earth, Belovèd,—where the unfit
Contrarious moods of men recoil away
And isolate pure spirits, and permit
A place to stand and love in for a day,
With darkness and the death-hour rounding it.

1897

- Explain the metaphor of this poem's first four lines. What will cause "the lengthening wings" to "break into fire"?

CHRISTINA ROSSETTI

In an Artist's Studio

One face looks out from all his canvases,
  One selfsame figure sits or walks or leans;
  We found her hidden just behind those screens,
That mirror gave back all her loveliness.
5 A queen in opal or in ruby dress,
  A nameless girl in freshest summer-greens,
  A saint, an angel—every canvas means
The same one meaning, neither more nor less.
He feeds upon her face by day and night,
10 And she with true kind eyes looks back on him
Fair as the moon and joyful as the light:
  Not wan with waiting, not with sorrow dim;
Not as she is, but was when hope shone bright;
  Not as she is, but as she fills his dream.

1856

- Does this sonnet show a single view of "the same one meaning" the speaker sees in every portrait in the studio, or is there a shift or turn at line 9 or line 13?

EDNA ST. VINCENT MILLAY

[*What lips my lips have kissed, and where, and why*]

What lips my lips have kissed, and where, and why,
I have forgotten, and what arms have lain
Under my head till morning; but the rain
Is full of ghosts tonight, that tap and sigh
5   Upon the glass and listen for reply,
And in my heart there stirs a quiet pain
For unremembered lads that not again
Will turn to me at midnight with a cry.
Thus in the winter stands the lonely tree,
10 Nor knows what birds have vanished one by one,
Yet knows its boughs more silent than before:
I cannot say what loves have come and gone;
I only know that summer sang in me
A little while, that in me sings no more.

                                        1923

- What are the poem's principal parts? Why does the Petrarchan
  model suit this sonnet?

[*I shall forget you presently, my dear*]

I shall forget you presently, my dear,
So make the most of this, your little day,
Your little month, your little half a year,
Ere I forget, or die, or move away,
5   And we are done forever; by and by
I shall forget you, as I said, but now,
If you entreat me with your loveliest lie
I will protest you with my favorite vow.
I would indeed that love were longer-lived,
10 And oaths were not so brittle as they are,
But so it is, and nature has contrived
To struggle on without a break thus far,—
Whether or not we find what we are seeking
Is idle, biologically speaking.

                                        1922

- What is the meaning of this poem's final couplet? What does it
  indicate about the poem's tone?

GWEN HARWOOD

In the Park

She sits in the park. Her clothes are out of date.
Two children whine and bicker, tug her skirt.
A third draws aimless patterns in the dirt.
Someone she loved once passes by—too late

5 to feign indifference to that casual nod.
"How nice," et cetera. "Time holds great surprises."
From his neat head unquestionably rises
a small balloon . . . "but for the grace of God . . ."

They stand a while in flickering light, rehearsing
10 the children's names and birthdays. "It's so sweet
to hear their chatter, watch them grow and thrive,"
she says to his departing smile. Then, nursing
the youngest child, sits staring at her feet.
To the wind she says, "They have eaten me alive."

                                                    1963

- What is the implication of the "small balloon" that rises from the
  head of the man who passes by?

WILLIAM SHAKESPEARE

[My mistress' eyes are nothing like the sun]

My mistress' eyes are nothing like the sun;
Coral is far more red than her lips' red;
If snow be white, why then her breasts are dun;[3]
If hairs be wires, black wires grow on her head.
5 I have seen roses damasked[4] red and white,
But no such roses see I in her cheeks;
And in some perfumes is there more delight
Than in the breath that from my mistress reeks.
I love to hear her speak, yet well I know
10 That music hath a far more pleasing sound;
I grant I never saw a goddess go;[5]
My mistress, when she walks, treads on the ground.
And yet, by heaven, I think my love as rare
As any she belied with false compare.

                                                    1609

- In addition to the speaker's mistress, what might be another subject of this poem?

---

3. Mouse-colored.   4. Variegated.   5. Walk

DIANE ACKERMAN

Sweep Me through Your Many-Chambered Heart

Sweep me through your many-chambered heart
if you like, or leave me here, flushed
amid the sap-ooze and blossom: one more dish
in the banquet called April, or think me hard-
5   won all your days full of women. Weeks
later, till I felt your arms around
me like a shackle, heard all the sundown
wizardries the fired body speaks.
Tell me why, if it was no more than this,
10 the unmuddled tumble, the renegade kiss,
today, rapt in a still life and unaware,
my paintbrush dropped like an amber hawk;
thinking I'd heard your footfall on the stair,
I listened, heartwise, for the knock.

1978

- How does the poet make the poem seem off-balance? How is this technique appropriate to the speaker's state of mind?

BILLY COLLINS

Sonnet

All we need is fourteen lines, well, thirteen now,
and after this one just a dozen
to launch a little ship on love's storm-tossed seas,
then only ten more left like rows of beans.
5   How easily it goes unless you get Elizabethan
and insist the iambic bongos must be played
and rhymes positioned at the ends of lines,
one for every station of the cross.
But hang on here while we make the turn
10 into the final six where all will be resolved,
where longing and heartache will find an end,
where Laura will tell Petrarch[6] to put down his pen,
take off those crazy medieval tights,
blow out the lights, and come at last to bed.

1999

- In what respects is Collins's poem a traditional sonnet? In what respects is it not?

6. Italian poet Francesco Petrarca (1304–74), regarded as a father of the sonnet form. Many of his love poems were inspired by Laura, who may have been the wife of a local nobleman.

JUNE JORDAN

Something Like a Sonnet for
Phillis Miracle Wheatley

Girl from the realm of birds florid and fleet
flying full feather in far or near weather
Who fell to a dollar lust coffled[7] like meat
Captured by avarice and hate spit together
5   Trembling asthmatic alone on the slave block
built by a savagery travelling by carriage
viewed like a species of flaw in the livestock
A child without safety of mother or marriage

Chosen by whimsy but born to surprise
10 They taught you to read but you learned how to write
Begging the universe into your eyes:
They dressed you in light but you dreamed with the night.
From Africa singing of justice and grace,
Your early verse sweetens the fame of our Race.

1989

- Phillis Wheatley herself usually wrote in "heroic couplets"—
  couplets of iambic pentameter. Why does Jordan choose dactylic
  meter, unusual for a sonnet?

SANDRA GILBERT

Sonnet: The Ladies' Home Journal

The brilliant stills of food, the cozy
glossy, bygone life—mashed potatoes
posing as whipped cream, a neat mom
conjuring shapes from chaos, trimming the flame—
5   how we ached for all that,
that dance of love in the living room,
those paneled walls, that kitchen golden
as the inside of a seed: how we leaned
on those shiny columns of advice,
10 stroking the *thank yous*, the firm thighs, the wise
closets full of soap.

7. Chained together in a line.

But even then
we knew it was the lies we loved, the lies
we wore like Dior coats,[8] the clean-cut airtight
lies that laid out our lives in black and white.

                                        1984

- How does this poem vary the traditional meter and rhyme scheme
  of an English sonnet? Why does the "turn" come late and in mid-
  line?

THE WAY A POEM LOOKS

Like stanza breaks, other arrangements of print and space help guide the voice and
the mind to a clearer sense of sound and meaning. But sometimes poems are written to be seen rather than heard, and their appearance on the page is crucial to their
effect. E. E. Cummings's poem "l(a," for example, tries to visualize typographically
what the poet asks you to see in your mind's eye.

E. E. CUMMINGS

l(a

l(a

le

af

fa

ll

s)

one

l

iness

                1958

Occasionally, too, poems are composed in a specific shape so that they look
like physical objects. The idea that poems can be related to the visual arts is an
old one. Theodoric in ancient Greece is credited with inventing *technopaegnia*—
that is, the construction of poems with visual appeal. Once, the shaping of words
to resemble an object was thought to have mystical power, but more recent
attempts at **concrete poetry**, or shaped verse, are usually playful exercises (such
as Hollander's "You Too? Me Too—Why Not? Soda Pop" in chapter 23) that
attempt to supplement (or replace) verbal meanings with devices from painting
and sculpture.

The following poem depends on recognition of some standard typographical
symbols and knowledge of their names. We have to say those names to read the
poem, for example, making the word "periodic" out of ".ic" or "high Phoenician"
out of "-ician" or "daguerreotype" out of "†eotype."

8. Designer coats by Christian Dior.

FRANKLIN P. ADAMS

Composed in the Composing Room

At stated .ic times
I love to sit and — off rhymes
Till ,tose at last I fall
Exclaiming "I don't ∧ all."

5   Though I'm an * objection
By running this in this here §
This ☞ of the Fleeting Hour,
This lofty -ician Tower—

A ¶er's hope dispels
10   All fear of deadly ||.
You think these [ ] are a pipe?
Well, not on your †eotype.

                    1914

The unusual spacing of words in the following poem, with some run together and others widely separated, provides a guide to reading, regulating both speed and sense, so that the poem can capture aloud some of the boy's wide-eyed enthusiasm, remembered now from a later perspective (notice how the word "defunct" helps set the time and point of view).

E. E. CUMMINGS

[Buffalo Bill   's][9]

Buffalo Bill 's
defunct
            who used to
            ride a watersmooth-silver
5   stallion
and break onetwothreefourfive pigeonsjustlikethat
                                                    Jesus
    he was a handsome man
                    and what i want to know is
    how do you like your blueeyed boy
    Mister Death

                    1923

---

9. From Cummings's *Portraits* XXI.

In poetry as well as prose, syntax and punctuation are the main guides to the voice of a reader, providing indicators of emphasis, pace, and speed. Silence as well as sound is part of any poem, and reading punctuation is as important as knowing how to say the words. The placement and spacing of lines on the page may be helpful to a reader even when that placement is not as radical as it is in "Buffalo Bill." The fact that poetry looks different from prose is not an accident; decisions to make lines one length instead of another have as much to do with vocal breaks and phrasing as with functions of syntax or meaning.

The eye also may help us notice repeated sounds by spotting repeated visual patterns in letters. The most common rhymes in poems occur at the ends of lines, and the arrangement of lines (the typography of the poem) often calls attention to the pattern of sounds. Many poems hint at their stanza patterns and verse forms by their spatial arrangements and repeated patterns at ends of lines. The following poem plays with such expectations in various ways.

STEVIE SMITH

The Jungle Husband

Dearest Evelyn, I often think of you
Out with the guns in the jungle stew
Yesterday I hittapotamus
I put the measurements down for you but they got lost in the fuss
5   It's not a good thing to drink out here
You know, I've practically given it up dear.
Tomorrow I am going alone a long way
Into the jungle. It is all grey
But green on top
10   Only sometimes when a tree has fallen
The sun comes down plop, it is quite appalling.
You never want to go in a jungle pool
In the hot sun, it would be the act of a fool
Because it's always full of anacondas, Evelyn, not looking ill-fed
15   I'll say. So no more now, from your loving husband, Wilfred.

1957

- How does this "letter" playfully force or miss the expected rhymes and meter? Why is it fifteen lines long?

• • •

GEORGE HERBERT

Easter Wings

Lord, who createdst man in wealth and store,[1]
Though foolishly he lost the same,
Decaying more and more
Till he became
Most poor:
                With thee
            O let me rise
        As larks,[2] harmoniously,
    And sing this day thy victories:
Then shall the fall further the flight in me.

My tender age in sorrow did begin;
And still with sicknesses and shame
Thou didst so punish sin,
That I became
Most thin.
                With thee
            Let me combine,
        And feel this day thy victory;
    For, if I imp[3] my wing on thine,
Affliction shall advance the flight in me.

1633

- How do this poem's decreasing and increasing line lengths correspond to the meaning of the words? Why do you think Herbert has chosen to present the poem "sideways"?

1. In plenty.   2. Which herald the morning.
3. Engraft. In falconry, to engraft feathers in a damaged wing, so as to restore the powers of flight (*OED*).

CHARLES H. WEBB

The Shape of History

Turning and turning in the widening gyre . . . [4]

Today's paper is crammed full of news: pages and pages on the Somalia Famine,
the Balkan Wars, Gays in the Military. On this date a year ago, only 1/365
of "The Year's Top Stories" happened. *Time* magazine fits a decade into
one thin retrospective. Barely enough occurred a century ago to fill one
sub-chapter in a high school text. 500 years ago, one or two things
happened every 50 years. 5000 years ago, a city was founded,
a grain cultivated, a civilization toppled every other century.
Still farther back, the years march by in groups like grad-
uates at a big state university: 10,000 to 20,000 BC;
50,000–100,000 BC; 1–10 million BC. Before
that, things happened once an Era: Mammals in
the Cenozoic, Dinosaurs in the Mesozoic,
Forests in the Paleozoic, Protozoans in
the Pre-Cambrian. Below that, at the
very base of time's twisting gyre,
its cornucopia, its ram's-horn
trumpet, its tornado tracking
across eternity, came what
Christians call Creation,
astrophysicists call the
Big Bang. Then, for
trillions of years,
nothing at
all.

1994

- A gyre is a conical spiral. How does Webb vary the vocabulary as
  the lines get shorter?

---

4. Allusion to W. B. Yeats, "The Second Coming" ("W. B. Yeats: An Album").

MAY SWENSON

Women

Women	Or they
should be	should be
pedestals	little horses
moving	those wooden
pedestals	sweet
moving	oldfashioned
to the	painted
motions	rocking
of men	horses

the gladdest things in the toyroom

The	feelingly
pegs	and then
of their	unfeelingly
ears	To be
so familiar	joyfully
and dear	ridden
to the trusting	rockingly
fists	ridden until
To be chafed	the restored

egos dismount and the legs stride away

Immobile	willing
sweetlipped	to be set
sturdy	into motion
and smiling	Women
women	should be
should always	pedestals
be waiting	to men

1978

- What shapes do you see in this poem? How are repeating words or sounds significant to the speaker's apparent statements about what women "should be" or should do?

EARLE BIRNEY

Anglosaxon Street

Dawn drizzle ended   dampness steams from
blotching brick and   blank plasterwaste
Faded housepatterns   hoary and finicky
unfold stuttering   stick like a phonograph

5 Here is a ghetto   gotten for goyim
O with care denuded   of nigger and kike
No coonsmell rankles   reeks only cellarrot
Ottar[5] of carexhaust   catcorpse and cookinggrease

Imperial hearts   heave in this haven
10 Cracks across windows   are welded with slogans
There'll Always Be An England   enhances geraniums
and V's for Victory   vanquish the housefly

Ho! with climbing sun   march the bleached beldames[6]
festooned with shopping bags   farded[7] flatarched
15 bigthewed Saxonwives   stepping over buttrivers
waddling back wienerladen   to suckle smallfry

Hoy! with sunslope   shrieking over hydrants
flood from learninghall   the lean fingerlings
Nordic nobblecheeked[8]   not all clean of nose
20 leaping Commandowise   into leprous lanes

What![9] after whistleblow!   spewed from wheelboat
after daylight doughtiness   dire handplay
in sewertrench or sandpit   come Saxonthegns
Junebrown Jutekings[1]   jawslack for meat

25 Sit after supper   on smeared doorsteps
not humbly swearing   hatedeeds on Huns
profiteers politicians   pacifists Jews

Then by twobit magic   to muse in movie
unlock picturehoard   or lope to alehall
30 soaking bleakly   in beer skittleless

Home again to hotbox   and humid husbandhood
in slumbertrough adding   sleepily to Anglekin
Alongside in lanenooks   carling and leman[2]
caterwaul and clip[3]   careless of Saxonry
35 with moonglow and   haste and a higher heartbeat

5. Roselike fragrance.   6. Aged women.   7. Rouged.   8. Pimpled.
9. Allusion to the eighth-century Anglo-Saxon (Old English) epic poem *Beowulf*, which begins with the word *Hwæt!* "Anglosaxon Street" closely imitates the manner of *Beowulf* and other Old English poems.
1. The Jutes were the German tribe that invaded England in the fifth century and spearheaded the Anglo-Saxon conquest. *Saxonthegns:* freemen who provided military services for the Saxon lords.
2. Lover. *Carling:* old woman.   3. Embrace.

Slumbers now slumtrack   unstinks cooling
waiting brief for milkmaid   mornstar and worldrise

1942, revised 1966

- Read this poem aloud. How does the poem's appearance help determine the tone and pacing of your reading?

SUGGESTIONS FOR WRITING

1. Trace the variations on imagery of light and darkness in Thomas's "Do Not Go
   Gentle into That Good Night." How do we know that light represents life and darkness death (rather than, say, sight and blindness)? How does the poet use the strict
   formal requirements of the villanelle to emphasize this interplay of light and darkness? Write an essay in which you discuss the interaction of form and content in
   "Do Not Go Gentle into That Good Night."
2. Chart the rhyme scheme of Keats's "On the Sonnet"; then, after reading the poem
   aloud, mark the major structural divisions of the poem. At what points do these
   structural divisions and the breaks in rhyme coincide? At what points do they conflict? Write an essay in which you discuss how these patterns and variations relate
   to the poem's meaning.
3. Consider carefully the structure of and sequencing in Brooks's "First Fight. Then
   Fiddle." How do various uses of sound in the poem (rhyme, onomatopoeia, and
   alliteration, for example) reinforce its themes and tones? Write an essay in which
   you explore the relationship between "sound and sense" in the poem.
4. Some of the sonnets in this book, such as those by Shakespeare, adhere closely to
   the classic English model; others, such as Milton's "[When I consider how my light
   is spent]," follow the Italian model; and some, such as Sandra Gilbert's "Sonnet:
   The Ladies' Home Journal," bear only slight resemblance to either of the traditional sonnet models. Take any four sonnets in this book as the basis for an essay
   in which you compare and contrast the various ways poets have used the sonnet
   form to achieve their unique artistic purposes.
5. Every poem has a structure, whether or not it adheres to a traditional form or to
   conventional ideas about line, rhythm, or spacing. Examine closely the structure
   of any poem or group of poems in this book. How does the poet use form to shape
   sound, emotion, and meaning? Write an essay in which you examine the structural
   choices that determine both the form and the content of these poems.
6. Research Anglo-Saxon poetry and look at classic examples, such as *Beowulf* and
   "The Seafarer." What are the principles of sound and the function of poetry that
   inform these Old English poems? Now consider Birney's "Anglosaxon Street." How
   successful is Birney in applying these principles to a modern poem? Is Birney's
   poem "serious"? Is it a parody? Write an essay in which you discuss the sound patterns and the form of "Anglosaxon Street" in light of your findings.

20   THE LONGER WORK

Poetry is often described as the art of brevity, compactness, and compression. Its sentences are usually divided into relatively short lines, its lines into stanzas that are generally much shorter than prose paragraphs. And many poems are very short overall. As we've seen, too, some subgenres or forms of poetry are short by definition: A **sonnet**, for example, generally has precisely fourteen lines, a **haiku** only three. As a result, poets have to "load every rift . . . with ore," as poet John Keats once put it.

Even so, there have been long poems for as long as there has been poetry. Indeed, some of the world's most famous poems—Homer's *Odyssey* (c. eighth century B.C.E.), Geoffrey Chaucer's *Canterbury Tales* (fourteenth century), Dante's *Divine Comedy* (fourteenth century), John Milton's *Paradise Lost* (1674), and Goethe's *Faust* (1808, 1832), to name a few—are long enough to be published on their own as stand-alone books. Others such as Edgar Allan's Poe's "The Raven" (chapter 17), Walt Whitman's "Song of Myself" (1855), and T. S. Eliot's "The Waste Land" (1922) take up many pages in volumes that also include shorter works by the same author.

Most book-length poems are themselves divided into smaller, often numbered, units variously called *cantos* (Dante's *Inferno*), *books* (the *Odyssey, Paradise Lost*), *chapters*, or simply *sections* or *parts* (Whitman's "Song of Myself"). These units are sometimes, in turn, divided into **stanzas** or **verse paragraphs**. Additionally, the long-poem category includes book-length works composed of a carefully ordered sequence of poems that can themselves be long, as in the case of *The Canterbury Tales* and Alfred, Lord Tennyson's *Idylls of the King* (1859–89). (The latter poem relates the story of King Arthur and his knights in twelve books, each of which can stand alone and has its own title, such as "The Coming of Arthur" and "The Passing of Arthur.") Other long poems are instead assembled of very short units that might work as individual poems, but together tell a story of sorts. Tennyson's *In Memoriam A. H. H.* (1850), for instance, consists of more than 130 short lyrics plus a verse introduction and an epilogue; collectively, they detail the speaker's response—over several years—to the death of a dear friend. (For more on poem collections and **sequences**, see chapter 22.) Regardless of a poem's length, however, the steps involved in reading, responding to, and writing about it are essentially the same.

THE LONG POEM AND THE QUESTION OF GENRE

Length makes a difference in our experience of a poem and in the way a poem works—so much so that Edgar Allan Poe famously declared that there is in fact no such thing as a "long poem" because a long work ceases to be "poetic" after a certain point. Sometimes the long poem is treated as a distinct poetic genre or subgenre in its own right, though there is little agreement about how long a poem must be to qualify: Some scholars and critics maintain that only book-length works should count; others apply the label to any poem over, say, 100 lines (as we do in this chapter). This debate is reflected in the inconsistent way the titles of long poems are formatted. While everyone agrees that the titles of book-length works such as *Paradise Lost* should be italicized and that those of shorter works such as "Stopping by Woods on a Snowy Evening" should appear in quotation marks, you will often see titles of shorter long poems formatted both ways—as "The Waste Land" or *The Waste Land*, for example.

Regardless of which definition of *long poem* we use, however, the category embraces works that vary widely in terms of both content and form. Long poems include **dramatic poems** and verse drama, **narrative poems** (in which a speaker relates a series of events just as a fictional **narrator** would), or even **lyrics** in the broadest sense (poems in which a speaker describes, in the first person, his or her feelings or thoughts rather than telling a "story" per se). Long poems can tackle almost any subject and situation and feature any sort of speaker and setting.

Long poems can be written in **free verse** ("Song of Myself") or follow any other formal pattern. The lyrics that make up *In Memoriam*, for instance, contain a varied number of stanzas, but each stanza has precisely the same **rhyme scheme**, meter, and number of lines; though this unusual stanza form had been used before, it is now widely known as "the *In Memoriam* stanza." Similarly, Edmund Spenser's *Faerie Queene* uses a stanza form now known as the **Spenserian stanza**: a stanza of nine lines in which eight lines are iambic pentameter, the ninth an **Alexandrine** (a line in **iambic hexameter**); the rhyme scheme is *ababbcbcc*.

The long-poem category might thus be seen as a kind of catchall, or at least "catch-a-lot," including long works that don't fit easily into any other generic category, as well as long works that do fit. Below is a list and description of some of the genre categories into which many long poems fall (including those in this chapter).

Long Poem Genres

ballad: a narrative poem using relatively simple, sometimes archaic language to relate an often well-known story. Ballads conventionally feature ordinary, socially lowly characters, on the one hand, and, on the other, extraordinary action, often involving supernatural occurrences, tragic love, and/or semihistorical, legendary subjects such as Robin Hood. A ballad usually consists of short stanzas, has a simple rhyme scheme and meter, and makes much use of dialogue, repetition (often, a refrain), simple syntax, and stock imagery ("milk-white steed," "red as blood"). Many ballads use the particular stanza form known as **ballad stanza**, with alternating three-beat and four-beat lines. Not all ballads are long, especially folk ballads such as "Sir Patrick Spens" (chapter 18) or poems modeled on folk ballads such as Dudley Randall's "Ballad of Birmingham" (chapter 19). But some later, written (versus oral) ballads are long, including Samuel Taylor Coleridge's "The Rime of the Ancient Mariner" (later in this chapter). Though perhaps not designed to

(Continued on next page)

(Continued)

be sung, this poem does use a version of ballad stanza and can be sung to the tune of the *Gilligan's Island* theme song, "The Ballad of Gilligan's Island."

The ballad is one of the oldest poetic forms in the English-language tradition: It is also, in origin, a "popular" form in the sense of being "of the (common) people," not least because ballads were traditionally composed and disseminated orally and, later, via cheap "broadsides" sold in the streets. Thus a person did not have to be wealthy or even literate to compose or enjoy a ballad.

dramatic monologue: a poem in which, in the words of literary critic M. H. Abrams, "(1) A single person, who is patently *not* the poet" (and often not a person with whom the poet encourages us to identify or sympathize) "utters the entire poem in a specific situation at a critical moment.... (2) This person addresses and interacts with one or more other people; but we know of the auditors' presence and what they say and do only from clues in the discourse of the single speaker. (3) The principle controlling the poet's selection and organization of what the ... speaker says is the speaker's unintentional revelation of his or her temperament and character" (*A Glossary of Literary Terms*, 6th ed. [Harcourt Brace, 1993], 48). Examples include Robert Browning's "Porphyria's Lover" ("Romantic Love: An Album"), "Soliloquy of the Spanish Cloister" (chapter 14), and "My Last Duchess" ("Reading More Poetry"); Alfred Tennyson's "Ulysses" (chapter 23); and T. S. Eliot's "The Love Song of J. Alfred Prufrock" (later in this chapter).

The dramatic monologue is sometimes described both as a kind of lyric and as a kind of closet drama. Even the acknowledged master of the form, Robert Browning, labeled his own poems "dramatic lyrics," describing them as "dramatic in principle" and "lyric in expression." The dramatic monologue is thus best understood as a hybrid form.

Lyrics like John Donne's "The Good-Morrow" and Matthew Arnold's "Dover Beach" (both in chapter 15) resemble dramatic monologues but aren't usually classed as such because neither focuses primarily on "the speaker's unintentional revelation of his or her temperament and character."

elegy: In the most specific sense, a lyric in which the speaker laments the death of a particular person, praises that person, expresses his or her personal grief and often that of the community, and seeks both to find and to offer consolation. Examples include W. H. Auden's "In Memory of W. B. Yeats" ("W. B. Yeats: An Album") and Walt Whitman's poem on the death of Abraham Lincoln, "When Lilacs Last in the Dooryard Bloom'd" (1865). More broadly, an elegy can be any lyric in sorrowful mood that is inspired by, and is about, death in general. A famous English-language example is Thomas Gray's "Elegy Written in a Country Churchyard" ("Reading More Poetry").

epic: a long narrative poem in elevated language that celebrates the achievements of one or more heroic (often male) personages of history or legend. Epic

(Continued on next page)

(Continued)

heroes conventionally possess both high social rank and high office (so that their actions directly affect an entire society), as well as extraordinary, even superhuman, qualities and skills. Epic plots typically involve extraordinary events of major significance to an entire society—Homer's *Iliad* focuses on the Trojan War, Milton's *Paradise Lost* on the fall of Adam and Eve. Other epic **conventions** include

- an opening that states the poem's major subject, or what is conventionally called its *argument*; contains an *invocation of the Muse* or other source of inspiration, usually addressed directly in the second person ("thou" or "you") and asked to help the poet in his work; and begins to recount the **action** *in medias res* (Latin for "in the middle of things"), thus requiring the use of **flashbacks** later in the poem;
- a spatially and temporally vast, but often vaguely defined or described, **setting** that is usually much earlier than the time in which the poem was first written and read;
- lengthy *catalogs*, or lists (Book II of *The Iliad*, for example, lists the captains of all the ships that sailed to Troy);
- epic similes—long, complex comparisons;
- a scene describing the arming of the hero for battle;
- at least one battle requiring extraordinary feats of derring-do (described vividly and at great length);
- a journey, often to a literal or figurative underworld, requiring further extraordinary feats of derring-do. (The *Odyssey*, for example, focuses on Odysseus' journey home from the Trojan War and includes an episode in which Odysseus travels to the Underworld to meet with the shades of the dead.)

Long considered one of the most demanding and revered of literary forms, the epic originated in the ancient world as an oral form. In addition to the works of Homer, the ancient world's greatest epics include the Babylonian *Epic of Gilgamesh*, the Roman poet Virgil's *Aeneid*, and the Hindu *Mahabharata* and *Ramayana*. Later epics in the English-language tradition include *Beowulf* (excerpted later in this chapter), John Milton's *Paradise Lost*, and Derek Walcott's *Omeros* (1990, a reworking of *The Odyssey* set in the Caribbean).

mock epic: a poem that uses epic language and conventions to depict subject matter—settings, characters, action—that usually wouldn't make it into traditional epics. The overall goal or effect is typically to "mock" or ridicule the particular social milieu represented in the poem (and the values or worldview of that milieu). However, a very few mock epics instead mock the grandeur and heroism of the epic itself (and the values or worldview associated with it). Alexander Pope's *The Rape of the Lock* (1714) is a famous and funny English-language mock epic.

pastoral elegy: a specific type of elegy that uses conventions associated with **pastoral literature**. Examples include John Milton's "Lycidas" (1638) and Percy Bysshe Shelley's poem on the death of John Keats, "Adonais" (1821).

(Continued on next page)

(Continued)

verse novel: a narrative poem that is like a **novel** but written in verse. Unlike epics and like most novels, verse novels tend to have more contemporary, familiar, and often vividly described settings and to focus on more ordinary characters and actions. Examples include Elizabeth Barrett Browning's *Aurora Leigh* (1857), which also has certain epic features; Alexander Pushkin's Russian-language *Eugene Onegin* (1823–31); and Vikram Seth's *The Golden Gate* (1986).

verse drama: a play or plays written entirely or mainly in verse, whether designed for performance (like all of Shakespeare's plays, including *A Midsummer Night's Dream* and *Hamlet*, chapter 28), or as **closet drama** to be read (like Percy Bysshe's Shelley's *Prometheus Unbound* [1820] and Goethe's *Faust*). (See also *dramatic monologue* above.)

BEOWULF

Beowulf is the oldest and probably best-known long poem in the English-language tradition, its 3,100-plus lines composed in Old English by an unknown poet sometime between the early eighth and the tenth centuries. (The following excerpt comes from a modern English translation by Irish poet Seamus Heaney.) The action in the poem, however, takes place centuries before the poem was written and concerns not the English but the Danes (or Shieldings) and the Geats, two Scandinavian peoples from whom the English descended. Though the Danes and Geats were pagan, the poem's chief speaker is apparently a Christian.

The 1,309 lines of the poem that precede the excerpt are set mainly in Heorot, the mead-hall or chief gathering place of the Danish tribe led by a good but elderly king named Hrothgar. The peace and prosperity of Hrothgar's kingdom are threatened when Heorot is attacked by the monster Grendel, who lives in a nearby swamp. After many years of suffering, however, a young Geat prince named Beowulf—nephew of the Geat king, Hygelac—hears of Hrothgar's troubles and travels to Denmark with a group of warriors. Inspired both by the challenge of defeating Grendel and by a sense of debt for the great favors Hrothgar once did his father, Beowulf vows to avenge the Danes by fighting Grendel in hand-to-hand, unarmed combat. He carries through on his promise that very night, when Grendel again attacks Heorot; the battle ends with a mortally wounded Grendel slouching off to die. Beowulf's victory is celebrated the next night in a great communal feast, but as soon as the Danes fall asleep, Grendel's mother attacks, carrying off both Beowulf's battle trophy (her son's "bloodied hand") and Aeschere, one of Hrothgar's greatest warriors.

ANONYMOUS

From *Beowulf*

1310   Beowulf was quickly brought to the chamber:
the winner of fights, the arch-warrior,
came first-footing in with his fellow-troops
to where the king in his wisdom waited,
still wondering whether Almighty God
1315   would ever turn the tide of his misfortunes.
So Beowulf entered with his band in attendance
and the wooden floorboards banged and rang
as he advanced, hurrying to address
the prince of the Ingwins, asking if he'd rested
1320   since the urgent summons had come as a surprise.
       Then Hrothgar, the Shieldings' helmet, spoke:
"Rest? What is rest? Sorrow has returned.
Alas for the Danes! Aeschere is dead.
He was Yrmenlaf's elder brother
1325   and a soul-mate to me, a true mentor,
my right-hand man when the ranks clashed
and our boar-crests had to take a battering
in the line of action. Aeschere was everything
the world admires in a wise man and a friend.
1330   Then this roaming killer came in a fury
and slaughtered him in Heorot. Where she is hiding,
glutting on the corpse and glorying in her escape,
I cannot tell; she has taken up the feud
because of last night, when you killed Grendel,
1335   wrestled and racked him in ruinous combat
since for too long he had terrorized us
with his depredations. He died in battle,
paid with his life; and now this powerful
other one arrives, this force for evil
1340   driven to avenge her kinsman's death.
Or so it seems to thanes in their grief,
in the anguish every thane endures
at the loss of a ring-giver,[1] now that the hand
that bestowed so richly has been stilled in death.
1345   "I have heard it said by my people in hall,
counselors who live in the upland country,
that they have seen two such creatures
prowling the moors, huge marauders
from some other world. One of these things,
1350   as far as anyone can ever discern,
looks like a woman; the other, warped
in the shape of a man, moves beyond the pale[2]

---

1. The thane's lord, a "ring-giver" because he distributes booty.   2. That is, beyond what is known.

bigger than any man, an unnatural birth
called Grendel by the country people
1355 in former days. They are fatherless creatures,
and their whole ancestry is hidden in a past
of demons and ghosts. They dwell apart
among wolves on the hills, on windswept crags
and treacherous keshes,[3] where cold streams
1360 pour down the mountain and disappear
under mist and moorland.
                    A few miles from here
a frost-stiffened wood waits and keeps watch
above a mere;[4] the overhanging bank
is a maze of tree-roots mirrored in its surface.
1365 At night there, something uncanny happens:
the water burns. And the mere bottom
has never been sounded by the sons of men.
On its bank, the heather-stepper halts:
the hart in flight from pursuing hounds
1370 will turn to face them with firm-set horns
and die in the wood rather than dive
beneath its surface. That is no good place.
When wind blows up and stormy weather
makes clouds scud and the skies weep,
1375 out of its depths a dirty surge
is pitched toward the heavens. Now help depends
again on you and on you alone.
The gap of danger where the demon waits
is still unknown to you. Seek it if you dare.
1380 I will compensate you for settling the feud
as I did the last time with lavish wealth,
coffers of coiled gold, if you come back."
      Beowulf, son of Ecgtheow, spoke:
"Wise sir, do not grieve. It is always better
1385 to avenge dear ones than to indulge in mourning.
For every one of us, living in this world
means waiting for our end. Let whoever can
win glory before death. When a warrior is gone,
that will be his best and only bulwark.
1390 So arise, my lord, and let us immediately
set forth on the trail of this troll-dam.[5]
I guarantee you: she will not get away,
not to dens under ground nor upland groves
nor the ocean floor. She'll have nowhere to flee to.
1395 Endure your troubles today. Bear up
and be the man I expect you to be."
      With that the old lord sprang to his feet

---

3. Causeway built up of wicker baskets of stone or earth (Irish).   4. Lake or pool (British).
5. That is, troll's mother.

and praised God for Beowulf's pledge.
Then a bit and halter were brought for his horse
1400 with the plaited mane. The wise king mounted
the royal saddle and rode out in style
with a force of shield-bearers. The forest paths
were marked all over with the monster's tracks,
her trail on the ground wherever she had gone
1405 across the dark moors, dragging away
the body of that thane, Hrothgar's best
counselor and overseer of the country.
So the noble prince proceeded undismayed
up fells and screes,[6] along narrow footpaths
1410 and ways where they were forced into single file,
ledges on cliffs above lairs of water-monsters.
He went in front with a few men,
good judges of the lie of the land,
and suddenly discovered the dismal wood,
1415 mountain trees growing out at an angle
above gray stones: the bloodshot water
surged underneath. It was a sore blow
to all of the Danes, friends of the Shieldings,
a hurt to each and every one
1420 of that noble company when they came upon
Aeschere's head at the foot of the cliff.
    Everybody gazed as the hot gore
kept wallowing up and an urgent war-horn
repeated its notes: the whole party
1425 sat down to watch. The water was infested
with all kinds of reptiles. There were writhing sea-dragons
and monsters slouching on slopes by the cliff,
serpents and wild things such as those that often
surface at dawn to roam the sail-road[7]
1430 and doom the voyage. Down they plunged,
lashing in anger at the loud call
of the battle-bugle. An arrow from the bow
of the Geat chief got one of them
as he surged to the surface: the seasoned shaft
1435 went in deep and his freedom in the water
got less and less. It was his last swim.
He was swiftly overwhelmed in the shallows,
prodded by barbed boar-spears,
cornered, beaten, pulled up on the bank,
1440 a strange lake-birth, a loathsome catch
men gazed at in awe.
                    Beowulf got ready,
donned his war-gear, indifferent to death;
his mighty, hand-forged, fine-webbed mail

---

6. Mountains and rocky slopes.   7. That is, the road traveled by sailing ships—the ocean.

would soon meet with the menace underwater.
1445 It would keep the bone-cage of his body safe:
no enemy's clasp could crush him in it,
no vicious armlock choke his life out.
To guard his head he had a glittering helmet
that was due to be muddied on the mere bottom
1450 and blurred in the upswirl. It was of beaten gold,
princely headgear hooped and hasped
by a weapon-smith who had worked wonders
in days gone by and embellished it with boar-shapes;
since then it had resisted every sword.
1455 And another item lent by Unferth
at that moment of need was of no small importance:
the brehon[8] handed him a hilted weapon,
a rare and ancient sword named Hrunting.
The iron blade with its ill-boding patterns
1460 had been tempered in blood. It had never failed
the hand of anyone who hefted it in battle,
anyone who had fought and faced the worst
in the gap of danger. This was not the first time
it had been called to perform heroic feats.
1465   When he lent that blade to the better swordsman,
Unferth, the strong-built son of Ecglaf,
could hardly have remembered the ranting speech
he had made in his cups. He was not man enough
to face the turmoil of a fight under water
1470 and the risk to his life. So there he lost
fame and repute. It was different for the other
rigged out in his gear, ready to do battle.
    Beowulf, son of Ecgtheow, spoke:
"Wisest of kings, now that I have come
1475 to the point of action, I ask you to recall
what we said earlier: that you, son of Halfdane
and gold-friend to retainers, that you, if I should fall
and suffer death while serving your cause,
would act like a father to me afterward.
1480 If this combat kills me, take care
of my young company, my comrades in arms.
And be sure also, my beloved Hrothgar,
to send Hygelac the treasures I received.
Let the lord of the Geats gaze on that gold,
1485 let Hrethel's son take note of it and see
that I found a ring-giver of rare magnificence
and enjoyed the good of his generosity.
And Unferth is to have what I inherited:
to that far-famed man I bequeath my own
1490 sharp-honed, wave-sheened wonder-blade.

---

8. One of an ancient class of lawyers in Ireland [Translator's note].

With Hrunting I shall gain glory or die."
     After these words, the prince of the Weather-Geats
was impatient to be away and plunged suddenly:
without further ado he dived into the heaving
1495 depths of the lake. It was the best part of a day
before he could see the solid bottom.
     Quickly the one who haunted those waters,
who had scavenged and gone her gluttonous rounds
for a hundred seasons, sensed a human
1500 observing her outlandish lair from overhead.
So she lunged and clutched and managed to catch him
in her brutal grip; but his body, for all that,
remained unscathed: the mesh of the chain-mail
saved him on the outside. Her savage talons
1505 failed to rip the web of his war-shirt.
Then once she touched bottom, that wolfish swimmer
carried the ring-mailed prince to her court
so that for all his courage he could never use
the weapons he carried; and a bewildering horde
1510 came at him from the depths, droves of sea-beasts
who attacked with tusks and tore at his chain-mail
in a ghastly onslaught. The gallant man
could see he had entered some hellish turn-hole
and yet the water there did not work against him
1515 because the hall-roofing held off
the force of the current; then he saw firelight,
a gleam and flare-up, a glimmer of brightness.
     The hero observed that swamp-thing from hell,
the tarn-hag in all her terrible strength,
1520 then heaved his war-sword and swung his arm:
the decorated blade came down ringing
and singing on her head. But he soon found
his battle-torch extinguished; the shining blade
refused to bite. It spared her and failed
1525 the man in his need. It had gone through many
a hand-to-hand fight, had hewed the armor
and helmets of the doomed, but here at last
the fabulous powers of that heirloom failed.
     Hygelac's kinsman kept thinking about
1530 his name and fame: he never lost heart.
Then, in a fury, he flung his sword away.
The keen, inlaid, worm-loop-patterned steel
was hurled to the ground: he would have to rely
on the might of his arm. So must a man do
1535 who intends to gain enduring glory
in a combat. Life doesn't cost him a thought.
Then the prince of War-Geats, warming to this fight
with Grendel's mother, gripped her shoulder
and laid about him in a battle frenzy:

1540   he pitched his killer opponent to the floor
      but she rose quickly and retaliated,
      grappled him tightly in her grim embrace.
      The sure-footed fighter felt suddenly daunted,
      the strongest of warriors stumbled and fell.
1545   So she pounced upon him and pulled out
      a broad, whetted knife: now she would avenge
      her only child. But the mesh of chain-mail
      on Beowulf's shoulder shielded his life,
      turned the edge and tip of the blade.
1550   The son of Ecgtheow would have surely perished
      and the Geats lost their warrior under the wide earth
      had the strong links and locks of his war-gear
      not helped to save him: holy God
      decided the victory. It was easy for the Lord,
1555   the Ruler of Heaven, to redress the balance
      once Beowulf got back up on his feet.
         Then he saw a blade that boded well,
      a sword in her armory, an ancient heirloom
      from the days of the giants, an ideal weapon,
1560   one that any warrior would envy,
      but so huge and heavy of itself
      only Beowulf could wield it in a battle.
      So the Shieldings' hero hard-pressed and enraged,
      took a firm hold of the hilt and swung
1565   the blade in an arc, a resolute blow
      that bit deep into her neck-bone
      and severed it entirely, toppling the doomed
      house of her flesh; she fell to the floor.
      The sword dripped blood, the swordsman was elated.
1570   A light appeared and the place brightened
      the way the sky does when heaven's candle
      is shining clearly. He inspected the vault:
      with sword held high, its hilt raised
      to guard and threaten, Hygelac's thane
1575   scouted along the wall in Grendel's wake.
      Now the weapon was to prove its worth.
      The warrior determined to take revenge
      for every gross act Grendel had committed—
      and not only for that one occasion
1580   when he'd come to slaughter the sleeping troops,
      fifteen of Hrothgar's house-guards
      surprised on their benches and ruthlessly devoured,
      and as many again carried away,
      a brutal plunder. Beowulf in his fury
1585   now settled that score: he saw the monster
      in his resting place, war-weary and wrecked,
      a lifeless corpse, a casualty
      of the battle in Heorot. The body gaped

at the stroke dealt to it after death:
1590 Beowulf cut the corpse's head off.

  Immediately the counselors keeping a lookout
with Hrothgar, watching the lake water,
saw a heave-up and surge of waves
and blood in the backwash. They bowed gray heads,
1595 spoke in their sage, experienced way
about the good warrior, how they never again
expected to see that prince returning
in triumph to their king. It was clear to many
that the wolf of the deep had destroyed him forever.
1600   The ninth hour of the day arrived.
The brave Shieldings abandoned the cliff-top
and the king went home; but sick at heart,
staring at the mere, the strangers held on.
They wished, without hope, to behold their lord,
Beowulf himself.
1605   Meanwhile, the sword
began to wilt into gory icicles
to slather and thaw. It was a wonderful thing,
the way it all melted as ice melts
when the Father eases the fetters off the frost
1610 and unravels the water-ropes. He who wields power
over time and tide: He is the true Lord.

  The Geat captain saw treasure in abundance
but carried no spoils from those quarters
except for the head and the inlaid hilt
1615 embossed with jewels; its blade had melted
and the scrollwork on it burned, so scalding was the blood
of the poisonous fiend who had perished there.
Then away he swam, the one who had survived
the fall of his enemies, flailing to the surface.
1620 The wide water, the waves and pools,
were no longer infested once the wandering fiend
let go of his life and this unreliable world.

  The seafarers' leader made for land,
resolutely swimming, delighted with his prize,
1625 the mighty load he was lugging to the surface.
His thanes advanced in a troop to meet him,
thanking God and taking great delight
in seeing their prince safe and sound.
Quickly the hero's helmet and mail-shirt
1630 were loosed and unlaced. The lake settled,
clouds darkened above the bloodshot depths.

  With high hearts they headed away
along footpaths and trails through the fields,
roads that they knew, each of them wrestling
1635 with the head they were carrying from the lakeside cliff,
men kingly in their courage and capable
of difficult work. It was a task for four

to hoist Grendel's head on a spear
and bear it under strain to the bright hall.
1640 But soon enough they neared the place,
fourteen Geats in fine fettle,
striding together across the outlying ground
in a delighted throng around their leader.
        In he came then, the thanes' commander,
1645 the arch-warrior, to address Hrothgar:
his courage was proven, his glory was secure.
Grendel's head was hauled by the hair,
dragged across the floor where the people were drinking,
a horror for both queen and company to behold.
1650 They stared in awe. It was an astonishing sight.
        Beowulf, son of Ecgtheow, spoke:
"So, son of Halfdane, prince of the Shieldings,
we are glad to bring this booty from the lake.
It is a token of triumph and we tender it to you.
1655 I barely survived the battle under water.
It was hard fought, a desperate affair
that could have gone badly; if God had not helped me,
the outcome would have been quick and fatal.
Although Hrunting is hard-edged,
1660 I could never bring it to bear in battle.
But the Lord of Men allowed me to behold
an ancient sword shining on the wall—
for he often helps the unbefriended—
a weapon made for giants, there for the wielding.
1665 Then my moment came in the combat and I struck
the dwellers in that den. Next thing the damascened[9]
sword blade melted; it bloated and it burned
in their rushing blood. I have wrested the hilt
from the enemies' hand, avenged the evil
1670 done to the Danes; it is what was due.
And this I pledge, O prince of the Shieldings:
you can sleep secure with your company of troops
in Heorot Hall. Never need you fear
for a single thane of your sept[1] or nation,
1675 young warriors or old, that laying waste of life
that you and your people endured of yore."
        Then the golden hilt was handed over
to the old lord, a relic from long ago
for the venerable ruler. That rare smithwork
1680 was passed on to the prince of the Danes
when those devils perished; once death removed
that murdering, guilt-steeped, God-cursed fiend,
eliminating his unholy life
and his mother's as well, it was willed to that king

---

9. Ornamented with wavy patterns resembling watered silk or with inlaid filigree of precious metals.
1. Branch of a family or clan.

1685 who of all the lavish gift-lords of the north
      was the best regarded between the two seas.

        Hrothgar spoke; he examined the hilt,
      that relic of old times. It was engraved all over
      and showed how war first came into the world
1690 and the flood destroyed the tribe of giants.
      They suffered a terrible severance from the Lord;
      the Almighty made the waters rise
      and drowned them in the deluge for retribution.
      In pure gold inlay on the sword-guards
1695 there were rune-markings correctly incised,
      stating and recording for whom the sword
      had been first made and ornamented
      with its scrollworked hilt. Then everyone hushed
      as the son of Halfdane spoke this wisdom:
1700 "A protector of his people, pledged to uphold
      truth and justice and to respect tradition,
      is entitled to affirm that this man
      was born to distinction. Beowulf, my friend,
      your fame has gone far and wide,
1705 you are known everywhere. In all things you are even-tempered,
      prudent and resolute. So I stand firm by the promise of friendship
      we exchanged before. Forever you will be
      your people's mainstay and your own warriors'
      helping hand.
                Heremod[2] was different,
1710 the way he behaved to Ecgwela's sons.
      His rise in the world brought little joy
      to the Danish people, only death and destruction.
      He vented his rage on men he caroused with,
      killed his own comrades, a pariah king
1715 who cut himself off from his own kind,
      even though Almighty God had made him
      eminent and powerful and marked him from the start
      for a happy life. But a change happened,
      he grew bloodthirsty, gave no more rings
1720 to honor the Danes. He suffered in the end
      for having plagued his people for so long:
      his life lost happiness.
                 So learn from this
      and understand true values. I who am telling you
      have wintered into wisdom.
                    It is a great wonder
1725 how Almighty God in His magnificence
      favors our race with rank and scope
      and the gift of wisdom; His sway is wide.
      Sometimes He allows the mind of a man

---

2. Ruler in an age long before that depicted in the poem: Hrothgar is using this legendary king to teach a lesson.

of distinguished birth to follow its bent,
1730 grants him fulfillment and felicity on earth
and forts to command in his own country.
He permits him to lord it in many lands
until the man in his unthinkingness
forgets that it will ever end for him.
1735 He indulges his desires; illness and old age
mean nothing to him; his mind is untroubled
by envy or malice or the thought of enemies
with their hate-honed swords. The whole world
conforms to his will, he is kept from the worst
1740 until an element of overweening
enters into him and takes hold
while the soul's guard, its sentry, drowses,
grown too distracted. A killer stalks him,
an archer who draws a deadly bow.
1745 And then the man is hit in the heart,
the arrow flies beneath his defenses,
the devious promptings of the demon start.
His old possessions seem paltry to him now.
He covets and resents; dishonors custom
1750 and bestows no gold; and because of good things
that the Heavenly Powers gave him in the past
he ignores the shape of things to come.
Then finally the end arrives
when the body he was lent collapses and falls
1755 prey to its death; ancestral possessions
and the goods he hoarded are inherited by another
who lets them go with a liberal hand.
      "O flower of warriors, beware of that trap.
Choose, dear Beowulf, the better part,
1760 eternal rewards. Do not give way to pride.
For a brief while your strength is in bloom
but it fades quickly; and soon there will follow
illness or the sword to lay you low,
or a sudden fire or surge of water
1765 or jabbing blade or javelin from the air
or repellent age. Your piercing eye
will dim and darken; and death will arrive,
dear warrior, to sweep you away.
      "Just so I ruled the Ring-Danes' country
1770 for fifty years, defended them in wartime
with spear and sword against constant assaults
by many tribes: I came to believe
my enemies had faded from the face of the earth.
Still, what happened was a hard reversal
1775 from bliss to grief. Grendel struck
after lying in wait. He laid waste to the land
and from that moment my mind was in dread
of his depredations. So I praise God

in His heavenly glory that I lived to behold
1780 this head dripping blood and that after such harrowing
I can look upon it in triumph at last.
Take your place, then, with pride and pleasure,
and move to the feast. Tomorrow morning
our treasure will be shared and showered upon you."
1785   The Geat was elated and gladly obeyed
the old man's bidding; he sat on the bench.
And soon all was restored, the same as before.
Happiness came back, the hall was thronged,
and a banquet set forth; black night fell
and covered them in darkness.
1790   Then the company rose
for the old campaigner: the gray-haired prince
was ready for bed. And a need for rest
came over the brave shield-bearing Geat.
He was a weary seafarer, far from home,
1795 so immediately a house-guard guided him out,
one whose office entailed looking after
whatever a thane on the road in those days
might need or require. It was noble courtesy.

- Like all epics, *Beowulf* features a protagonist who is also quite
  clearly a hero. According to the poem, what are the chief qualities
  and motives of a true hero? What epic conventions are used here,
  and how do they help characterize the hero?

SAMUEL TAYLOR COLERIDGE
The Rime of the Ancient Mariner

IN SEVEN PARTS

*Facile credo, plures esse Naturas invisibiles quam visibiles in rerum universitate.
Sed horum* [sic] *omnium familiam quis nobis enarrabit? et gradus et cognationes et
discrimina et singulorum munera? Quid agunt? quae loca habitant? Harum rerum
notitiam semper ambivit ingenium humanum, nunquam attigit. Juvat, interea,
non diffiteor, quandoque in animo, tanquam in tabulâ, majoris et melioris mundi
imaginem contemplari: ne mens assuefacta hodiernae vitae minutiis se contrahat
nimis, et tota subsidat in pusillas cogitationes. Sed veritati interea invigilandum
est, modusque servandus, ut certa ab incertis, diem a nocte, distinguamus.*

T. BURNET, *Archaeol. Phil.* p. 68.[3]

3. "I readily believe that there are more invisible than visible Natures in the universe. But who will explain
for us the family of all these beings, and the ranks and relations and distinguishing features and functions of each? What do they do? What places do they inhabit? The human mind has always sought the
knowledge of these things, but never attained it. Meanwhile I do not deny that it is helpful sometimes to

Argument

How a Ship, having first sailed to the Equator, was driven by storms to the cold Country towards the South Pole; how the Ancient Mariner cruelly and in contempt of the laws of hospitality killed a Seabird and how he was followed by many and strange Judgments: and in what manner he came back to his own Country.

Part 1

An ancient Mariner meeteth three Gallants bidden to a wedding feast, and detaineth one.

It is an ancient Mariner
And he stoppeth one of three.
—"By thy long gray beard and glittering eye,
Now wherefore stopp'st thou me?

The Bridegroom's doors are opened wide,   5
And I am next of kin;
The guests are met, the feast is set:
May'st hear the merry din."

He holds him with his skinny hand,
"There was a ship," quoth he.   10
"Hold off! unhand me, graybeard loon!"
Eftsoons[4] his hand dropped he.

The Wedding-Guest is spellbound by the eye of the old seafaring man, and constrained to hear his tale.

He holds him with his glittering eye—
The Wedding-Guest stood still,
And listens like a three years' child: 15
The Mariner hath his will.

The Wedding-Guest sat on a stone;
He cannot choose but hear;
And thus spake on that ancient man,
The bright-eyed Mariner.   20

"The ship was cheered, the harbor cleared,
Merrily did we drop
Below the kirk,[5] below the hill,
Below the lighthouse top.

The Mariner tells how the ship sailed southward with a good wind and fair weather, till it reached the Line.

The Sun came up upon the left,   25
Out of the sea came he!
And he shone bright, and on the right
Went down into the sea.

---

contemplate in the mind, as on a tablet, the image of a greater and better world, lest the intellect, habituated to the petty things of daily life, narrow itself and sink wholly into trivial thoughts. But at the same time we must be watchful for the truth and keep a sense of proportion, so that we may distinguish the certain from the uncertain, day from night." Adapted by Coleridge from Thomas Burnet, *Archaeologiae Philosophicae* (1692).   4. At once.   5. Church.

Higher and higher every day,
Till over the mast at noon[6]—"
The Wedding-Guest here beat his breast,   30
For he heard the loud bassoon.

The bride hath paced into the hall,
Red as a rose is she;
Nodding their heads before her goes   35
The merry minstrelsy.

The Wedding-Guest he beat his breast,
Yet he cannot choose but hear;
And thus spake on that ancient man,
The bright-eyed Mariner.   40

"And now the STORM-BLAST came, and he
Was tyrannous and strong;
He struck with his o'ertaking wings,
And chased us south along.

With sloping masts and dipping prow,   45
As who pursued with yell and blow
Still treads the shadow of his foe,
And forward bends his head,
The ship drove fast, loud roared the blast,
And southward aye we fled.   50

And now there came both mist and snow,
And it grew wondrous cold:
And ice, mast-high, came floating by,
As green as emerald.

And through the drifts the snowy clifts   55
Did send a dismal sheen:
Nor shapes of men nor beasts we ken[7]—
The ice was all between.

The ice was here, the ice was there,
The ice was all around: 60
It cracked and growled, and roared and howled,
Like noises in a swound![8]

At length did cross an Albatross,
Thorough the fog it came;
As if it had been a Christian soul,   65
We hailed it in God's name.

It ate the food it ne'er had eat,
And round and round it flew.
The ice did split with a thunder-fit;
The helmsman steered us through!   70

6. Indicating that the ship had reached the equator ("the Line").   7. Saw   8. Swoon.

And lo! the Albatross proveth a bird of good omen, and followeth the ship as it returned northward through fog and floating ice.

And a good south wind sprung up behind;
The Albatross did follow,
And every day, for food or play,
Came to the mariners' hollo!

In mist or cloud, on mast or shroud,[9]   75
It perched for vespers nine;
Whiles all the night, through fog-smoke white,
Glimmered the white Moon-shine."

The ancient Mariner inhospitably killeth the pious bird of good omen.

"God save thee, ancient Mariner!
From the fiends, that plague thee thus!—   80
Why look'st thou so?"—With my crossbow
I shot the ALBATROSS.

Part 2

The Sun now rose upon the right:[1]
Out of the sea came he,
Still hid in mist, and on the left   85
Went down into the sea.

And the good south wind still blew behind,
But no sweet bird did follow,
Nor any day for food or play
Came to the mariners' hollo!   90

His shipmates cry out against the ancient Mariner, for killing the bird of good luck.

And I had done a hellish thing,
And it would work 'em woe:
For all averred, I had killed the bird
That made the breeze to blow.
Ah wretch! said they, the bird to slay,   95
That made the breeze to blow!

But when the fog cleared off, they justify the same, and thus make themselves accomplices in the crime.

Nor dim nor red, like God's own head,
The glorious Sun uprist:
Then all averred, I had killed the bird
That brought the fog and mist.   100
'Twas right, said they, such birds to slay,
That bring the fog and mist.

The fair breeze continues; the ship enters the Pacific Ocean, and sails northward, even till it reaches the Line.

The fair breeze blew, the white foam flew,
The furrow followed free;
We were the first that ever burst   105
Into that silent sea.

The ship hath been suddenly becalmed.

Down dropped the breeze, the sails dropped down,
'Twas sad as sad could be;
And we did speak only to break
The silence of the sea!   110

9. Stout, tarred rope supporting the mast.
1. That is, the ship has now rounded Cape Horn and is headed northward.

All in a hot and copper sky,
The bloody Sun, at noon,
Right up above the mast did stand,
No bigger than the Moon.

Day after day, day after day,   115
We stuck, nor breath nor motion;
As idle as a painted ship
Upon a painted ocean.

And the Albatross begins to be avenged.

Water, water, everywhere,
And all the boards did shrink;   120
Water, water, everywhere,
Nor any drop to drink.

The very deep did rot: O Christ!
That ever this should be!
Yea, slimy things did crawl with legs   125
Upon the slimy sea.

About, about, in reel and rout
The death-fires[2] danced at night;
The water, like a witch's oils,
Burnt green, and blue and white.   130

A Spirit had followed them; one of the invisible inhabitants of this planet, neither departed souls nor angels; concerning whom the learned Jew, Josephus, and the Platonic Constaninopolitan, Michael Psellus, may be consulted. They are very numerous, and there is no climate or element without one or more.

And some in dreams assured were
Of the Spirit that plagued us so;
Nine fathom deep he had followed us
From the land of mist and snow.

And every tongue, through utter drought,   135
Was withered at the root;
We could not speak, no more than if
We had been choked with soot.

The shipmates, in their sore distress, would fain throw the whole guilt on the ancient Mariner: in sign whereof they hang the dead sea bird round his neck.

Ah! well-a-day! what evil looks
Had I from old and young!   140
Instead of the cross, the Albatross
About my neck was hung.

Part 3

There passed a weary time. Each throat
Was parched, and glazed each eye.
A weary time! a weary time!   145
How glazed each weary eye,

---

2. Perhaps St. Elmo's fire—discharges of atmospheric electricity on a ship's spars or rigging—believed by superstitious sailors to portend disaster.

When looking westward, I beheld
A something in the sky.

The ancient Mariner beholdeth a sign in the element afar off.

At first it seemed a little speck,
And then it seemed a mist;
It moved and moved, and took at last
A certain shape, I wist.[3]

150

A speck, a mist, a shape, I wist!
And still it neared and neared:
As if it dodged a water-sprite,
It plunged and tacked and veered.

155

At its nearer approach, it seemeth him to be a ship; and at a dear ransom he freeth his speech from the bonds of thirst.

With throats unslaked, with black lips baked,
We could nor laugh nor wail;
Through utter drought all dumb we stood!
I bit my arm, I sucked the blood,
And cried, A sail! a sail!

160

A flash of joy;

With throats unslaked, with black lips baked,
Agape they heard me call:
Gramercy![4] they for joy did grin,
And all at once their breath drew in,
As they were drinking all.

165

And horror follows. For can it be a ship that comes onward without wind or tide?

See! see! (I cried) she tacks no more!
Hither to work us weal;[5]
Without a breeze, without a tide,
She steadies with upright keel!

170

The western wave was all aflame.
The day was well nigh done!
Almost upon the western wave
Rested the broad bright Sun;
When that strange shape drove suddenly
Betwixt us and the Sun.

175

It seemeth him but the skeleton of a ship.

And straight the Sun was flecked with bars,
(Heaven's Mother send us grace!)
As if through a dungeon grate he peered
With broad and burning face.

180

Alas! (thought I, and my heart beat loud)
How fast she nears and nears!
Are those *her* sails that glance in the Sun,
Like restless gossameres?[6]

And its ribs are seen as bars on the face of the setting Sun.

The Specter-Woman and her Deathmate, and no other on board the skeleton ship.

Are those *her* ribs through which the Sun
Did peer, as through a grate?
And is that Woman all her crew?

185

---

3. Knew.   4. From *grand-merci*, French for "great thanks."   5. Benefit.   6. Floating cobwebs.

Is that a DEATH? and are there two?
Is DEATH that woman's mate?

Like vessel, like crew!

Her lips were red, *her* looks were free,
Her locks were yellow as gold:
Her skin was as white as leprosy,
The Night-mare LIFE-IN-DEATH was she,
Who thicks man's blood with cold.   190

Death and Life-in-Death have diced for the ship's crew, and she (the latter) winneth the ancient Mariner.

The naked hulk alongside came,   195
And the twain were casting dice;
"The game is done! I've won! I've won!"
Quoth she, and whistles thrice.

No twilight within the courts of the Sun.

The Sun's rim dips; the stars rush out:
At one stride comes the dark;   200
With far-heard whisper, o'er the sea,
Off shot the spectre-bark.

At the rising of the Moon,

We listened and looked sideways up!
Fear at my heart, as at a cup,
My lifeblood seemed to sip!   205
The stars were dim, and thick the night,
The steersman's face by his lamp gleamed white;
From the sails the dew did drip—
Till clomb above the eastern bar
The hornèd Moon, with one bright star   210
Within the nether tip.[7]

One after another,

One after one, by the star-dogged Moon,
Too quick for groan or sigh,
Each turned his face with a ghastly pang,
And cursed me with his eye.   215

His shipmates drop down dead.

Four times fifty living men,
(And I heard nor sigh nor groan)
With heavy thump, a lifeless lump,
They dropped down one by one.

But Life-in-Death begins her work on the ancient Mariner.

The souls did from their bodies fly—   220
They fled to bliss or woe!
And every soul, it passed me by,
Like the whizz of my crossbow!

Part 4

The Wedding-Guest feareth that a Spirit is talking to him;

"I fear thee, ancient Mariner!
I fear thy skinny hand!   225
And thou art long, and lank, and brown,
As is the ribbed sea-sand.

7. An ill omen.

But the ancient Mariner assureth him of his bodily life, and pro- ceedeth to relate his horrible penance.	I fear thee and thy glittering eye, And thy skinny hand, so brown."— Fear not, fear not, thou Wedding-Guest! 230 This body dropped not down.
	Alone, alone, all, all alone, Alone on a wide wide sea! And never a saint took pity on My soul in agony. 235
He despiseth the creatures of the calm,	The many men, so beautiful! And they all dead did lie: And a thousand thousand slimy things Lived on; and so did I.
And envieth that they should live, and so many lie dead.	I looked upon the rotting sea, And drew my eyes away; I looked upon the rotting deck, And there the dead men lay.
	I looked to heaven, and tried to pray; But or[8] ever a prayer had gushed, 245 A wicked whisper came, and made My heart as dry as dust.
	I closed my lids, and kept them close, And the balls like pulses beat; For the sky and the sea, and the sea and the sky 250 Lay like a load on my weary eye, And the dead were at my feet.
But the curse liv- eth for him in the eye of the dead men.	The cold sweat melted from their limbs, Nor rot nor reek did they: The look with which they looked on me 255 Had never passed away.
	An orphan's curse would drag to hell A spirit from on high; But oh! more horrible than that Is the curse in a dead man's eye! 260 Seven days, seven nights, I saw that curse, And yet I could not die.
In his loneliness and fixedness he yearneth towards the journeying Moon, and the stars that still sojourn, yet still move onward; and everywhere the blue sky belongs to them, and is	The moving Moon went up the sky, And nowhere did abide: Softly she was going up, 265 And a star or two beside— Her beams bemocked the sultry main, Like April hoar-frost spread; But where the ship's huge shadow lay,

8. Before.

<table>
<tr><td>their appointed rest, and their native country</td><td>The charmèd water burnt alway
A still and awful red.</td><td>270</td></tr>
</table>

and their own natural homes, which they enter unannounced, as lords that are certainly expected and yet there is a silent joy at their arrival.

| By the light of the Moon he beholdeth God's creatures of the great calm. | Beyond the shadow of the ship,
I watched the water snakes:
They moved in tracks of shining white,
And when they reared, the elfish light
Fell off in hoary flakes. | 275 |

Within the shadow of the ship
I watched their rich attire:
Blue, glossy green, and velvet black,
They coiled and swam; and every track
Was a flash of golden fire.

| Their beauty and their happiness. | O happy living things! no tongue
Their beauty might declare: | |
| He blesseth them in his heart. | A spring of love gushed from my heart,
And I blessed them unaware:
Sure my kind saint took pity on me,
And I blessed them unaware. | 285 |

| The spell begins to break. | The self-same moment I could pray;
And from my neck so free
The Albatross fell off, and sank
Like lead into the sea. | 290 |

Part 5

Oh sleep! it is a gentle thing,
Beloved from pole to pole!
To Mary Queen the praise be given!
She sent the gentle sleep from Heaven,
That slid into my soul.   295

| By grace of the holy Mother, the ancient Mariner is refreshed with rain. | The silly[9] buckets on the deck,
That had so long remained,
I dreamt that they were filled with dew;
And when I awoke, it rained. | 300 |

My lips were wet, my throat was cold,
My garments all were dank;
Sure I had drunken in my dreams,
And still my body drank.

I moved, and could not feel my limbs: 305
I was so light—almost
I thought that I had died in sleep,
And was a blessed ghost.

9. Plain, simple.

He heareth sounds and seeth strange sights and commotions in the sky and the element.

And soon I heard a roaring wind:
It did not come anear;
But with its sound it shook the sails,
That were so thin and sere.   310

The upper air burst into life!
And a hundred fire-flags sheen,[1]
To and fro they were hurried about!   315
And to and fro, and in and out,
The wan stars danced between.

And the coming wind did roar more loud,
And the sails did sigh like sedge;[2]
And the rain poured down from one black cloud;   320
The Moon was at its edge.

The thick black cloud was cleft, and still
The Moon was at its side:
Like waters shot from some high crag,
The lightning fell with never a jag,   325
A river steep and wide.

The bodies of the ship's crew are inspirited, and the ship moves on;

The loud wind never reached the ship,
Yet now the ship moved on!
Beneath the lightning and the Moon
The dead men gave a groan.   330

They groaned, they stirred, they all uprose,
Nor spake, nor moved their eyes;
It had been strange, even in a dream,
To have seen those dead men rise.

The helmsman steered, the ship moved on;   335
Yet never a breeze up-blew;
The mariners all 'gan work the ropes,
Where they were wont to do;
They raised their limbs like lifeless tools—
We were a ghastly crew.   340

The body of my brother's son
Stood by me, knee to knee:
The body and I pulled at one rope,

But not by the souls of the men, nor by dæmons[3] of earth or middle air, but by a blessed troop of angelic spirits, sent down by the invocation of the guardian saint.

But he said nought to me.

"I fear thee, ancient Mariner!"   345
Be calm, thou Wedding Guest!
'Twas not those souls that fled in pain,

---

1. Shone. These fire-flags are probably St. Elmo's fire (see line 128n) but may be the Aurora Australis, or Southern Lights, and possibly also lightning.   2. Rushlike plant growing in wet soil.
3. Supernatural beings neither wholly mortal nor spiritual; see Coleridge's gloss beside lines 131–34.

Which to their corses⁴ came again,
But a troop of spirits blest:

For when it dawned—they dropped their arms,   350
And clustered round the mast;
Sweet sounds rose slowly through their mouths,
And from their bodies passed.

Around, around, flew each sweet sound,
Then darted to the Sun;   355
Slowly the sounds came back again,
Now mixed, now one by one.

Sometimes a-dropping from the sky
I heard the sky-lark sing;
Sometimes all little birds that are,   360
How they seemed to fill the sea and air
With their sweet jargoning!⁵

And now 'twas like all instruments,
Now like a lonely flute;
And now it is an angel's song,   365
That makes the heavens be mute.

It ceased; yet still the sails made on
A pleasant noise till noon,
A noise like of a hidden brook
In the leafy month of June,   370
That to the sleeping woods all night
Singeth a quiet tune.

Till noon we quietly sailed on,
Yet never a breeze did breathe:
Slowly and smoothly went the ship,   375
Moved onward from beneath.

The lonesome Spirit from the South Pole carries on the ship as far as the Line, in obedience to the angelic troop, but still requireth vengeance.

Under the keel nine fathom deep,
From the land of mist and snow,
The spirit slid: and it was he
That made the ship to go.   380
The sails at noon left off their tune,
And the ship stood still also.

The Sun, right up above the mast,
Had fixed her to the ocean:
But in a minute she 'gan stir,   385
With a short uneasy motion—
Backwards and forwards half her length
With a short uneasy motion.

Then like a pawing horse let go,
She made a sudden bound: 390

4. Corpses.   5. Warbling.

It flung the blood into my head,
And I fell down in a swound.

The Polar Spirit's fellow dæmons, the invisible inhabitants of the element, take part in his wrong; and two of them relate, one to the other, that penance long and heavy for the ancient Mariner hath been accorded to the Polar Spirit, who returneth southward.

How long in that same fit I lay,
I have not[6] to declare;
But ere my living life returned,   395
I heard and in my soul discerned
Two voices in the air.

"Is it he?" quoth one, "Is this the man?
By him who died on cross,
With his cruel bow he laid full low   400
The harmless Albatross.

The spirit who bideth by himself
In the land of mist and snow,
He loved the bird that loved the man
Who shot him with his bow."   405

The other was a softer voice,
As soft as honeydew:
Quoth he, "The man hath penance done,
And penance more will do."

Part 6

FIRST VOICE

"But tell me, tell me! speak again,   410
Thy soft response renewing—
What makes that ship drive on so fast?
What is the ocean doing?"

SECOND VOICE

"Still as a slave before his lord,
The ocean hath no blast;   415
His great bright eye most silently
Up to the Moon is cast—

If he may know which way to go;
For she guides him smooth or grim.
See, brother, see! how graciously   420
She looketh down on him."

The Mariner hath been cast into a trance; for the angelic power causeth the vessel to drive northward faster than human life could endure.

FIRST VOICE

"But why drives on that ship so fast,
Without or[7] wave or wind?"

SECOND VOICE

"The air is cut away before,
And closes from behind.   425

Fly, brother, fly! more high, more high!

6. That is, do not have the ability.   7. Either.

Or we shall be belated:
For slow and slow that ship will go,
When the Mariner's trance is abated."

The supernatural motion is retarded; the Mariner awakes, and his penance begins anew.

I woke, and we were sailing on   430
As in a gentle weather:
'Twas night, calm night, the moon was high;
The dead men stood together.

All stood together on the deck,
For a charnel-dungeon fitter: 435
All fixed on me their stony eyes,
That in the Moon did glitter.

The pang, the curse, with which they died,
Had never passed away:
I could not draw my eyes from theirs,   440
Nor turn them up to pray.

The curse is finally expiated.

And now this spell was snapped: once more
I viewed the ocean green,
And looked far forth, yet little saw
Of what had else been seen—   445

Like one, that on a lonesome road
Doth walk in fear and dread,
And having once turned round walks on,
And turns no more his head;
Because he knows, a frightful fiend   450
Doth close behind him tread.

But soon there breathed a wind on me,
Nor[8] sound nor motion made:
Its path was not upon the sea,
In ripple or in shade.   455

It raised my hair, it fanned my cheek
Like a meadow-gale of spring—
It mingled strangely with my fears,
Yet it felt like a welcoming.

Swiftly, swiftly flew the ship,   460
Yet she sailed softly too:
Sweetly, sweetly blew the breeze—
On me alone it blew.

And the ancient Mariner beholdeth his native country.

Oh! dream of joy! is this indeed
The lighthouse top I see?   465
Is this the hill? is this the kirk?
Is this mine own countree?

We drifted o'er the harbor bar,
And I with sobs did pray—

8. Neither.

O let me be awake, my God!   470
Or let me sleep alway.

The harbor bay was clear as glass,
So smoothly it was strewn!
And on the bay the moonlight lay,
And the shadow of the Moon.   475

The rock shone bright, the kirk no less,
That stands above the rock:
The moonlight steeped in silentness
The steady weathercock.

And the bay was white with silent light,   480
Till rising from the same,
The angelic spirits Full many shapes, that shadows were,
leave the dead In crimson colors came.
bodies,

And appear in A little distance from the prow
their own forms of Those crimson shadows were: 485
light. I turned my eyes upon the deck—
Oh, Christ! what saw I there!

Each corse lay flat, lifeless and flat,
And, by the holy rood!
A man all light, a seraph[9] man,   490
On every corse there stood.

This seraph band, each waved his hand:
It was a heavenly sight!
They stood as signals to the land,
Each one a lovely light;   495

This seraph band, each waved his hand,
No voice did they impart—
No voice; but oh! the silence sank
Like music on my heart.

But soon I heard the dash of oars,   500
I heard the Pilot's cheer;[1]
My head was turned perforce away
And I saw a boat appear.

The Pilot and the Pilot's boy,
I heard them coming fast: 505
Dear Lord in Heaven! it was a joy
The dead men could not blast.

I saw a third—I heard his voice:
It is the Hermit good!
He singeth loud his godly hymns   510
That he makes in the wood.

9. Angel. *Rood*: cross.   1. Shout of encouragement.

> He'll shrieve my soul, he'll wash away
> The Albatross's blood.

Part 7

The Hermit of the Wood,

> This Hermit good lives in that wood
> Which slopes down to the sea.
> How loudly his sweet voice he rears!
> He loves to talk with marineres
> That come from a far countree.

515

> He kneels at morn, and noon, and eve—
> He hath a cushion plump:
> It is the moss that wholly hides
> The rotted old oak-stump.

520

> The skiff-boat neared: I heard them talk,
> "Why, this is strange, I trow!²
> Where are those lights so many and fair,
> That signal made but now?"

525

Approacheth the ship with wonder.

> "Strange, by my faith!" the Hermit said—
> "And they answered not our cheer!
> The planks looked warped! and see those sails,
> How thin they are and sere!
> I never saw aught like to them,
> Unless perchance it were

530

> Brown skeletons of leaves that lag
> My forest-brook along;
> When the ivy tod³ is heavy with snow,
> And the owlet whoops to the wolf below,
> That eats the she-wolf's young."

535

> "Dear Lord! it hath a fiendish look,"
> (The Pilot made reply)
> "I am a-feared"—"Push on, push on!"
> Said the Hermit cheerily.

540

> The boat came closer to the ship,
> But I nor spake nor stirred;
> The boat came close beneath the ship,
> And straight a sound was heard.

545

The ship suddenly sinketh.

> Under the water it rumbled on,
> Still louder and more dread:
> It reached the ship, it split the bay;
> The ship went down like lead.

The ancient Mariner is saved in the Pilot's boat.

> Stunned by that loud and dreadful sound,
> Which sky and ocean smote,
> Like one that hath been seven days drowned
> My body lay afloat;

550

2. Think or believe.   3. Clump.

But swift as dreams, myself I found
Within the Pilot's boat.   555

Upon the whirl, where sank the ship,
The boat spun round and round;
And all was still, save that the hill
Was telling of the sound.

I moved my lips—the Pilot shrieked   560
And fell down in a fit;
The holy Hermit raised his eyes,
And prayed where he did sit.

I took the oars: the Pilot's boy,
Who now doth crazy go,   565
Laughed loud and long, and all the while
His eyes went to and fro.
"Ha! ha!" quoth he, "full plain I see,
The Devil knows how to row."

And now, all in my own countree,   570
I stood on the firm land!
The Hermit stepped forth from the boat,
And scarcely he could stand.

The ancient Mari-
ner earnestly
entreateth the
Hermit to shrieve
him; and the pen-
ance of life falls
on him.

"O shrieve me, shrieve me, holy man!"
The Hermit crossed his brow.[4]   575
"Say quick," quoth he, "I bid thee say—
What manner of man art thou?"

Forthwith this frame of mine was wrenched
With a woeful agony,
Which forced me to begin my tale;   580
And then it left me free.

And ever and
anon throughout
his future life an
agony con-
straineth him to
travel from land to
land;

Since then, at an uncertain hour,
That agony returns:
And till my ghastly tale is told,
This heart within me burns.   585

I pass, like night, from land to land;
I have strange power of speech;
That moment that his face I see,
I know the man that must hear me:
To him my tale I teach.   590

What loud uproar bursts from that door!
The wedding-guests are there:
But in the garden-bower the bride
And bride-maids singing are:

---

4. That is, made the sign of the cross on his forehead. *Shrieve me*: hear my confession and grant me absolution.

And hark the little vesper bell,   595
Which biddeth me to prayer!

O Wedding-Guest! this soul hath been
Alone on a wide wide sea:
So lonely 'twas, that God himself
Scarce seemèd there to be.   600

O sweeter than the marriage feast,
'Tis sweeter far to me,
To walk together to the kirk
With a goodly company!—

To walk together to the kirk,   605
And all together pray,
While each to his great Father bends,
Old men, and babes, and loving friends
And youths and maidens gay!

And to teach, by his own example, love and reverence to all things that God made and loveth.

Farewell, farewell! but this I tell   610
To thee, thou Wedding-Guest!
He prayeth well, who loveth well
Both man and bird and beast.

He prayeth best, who loveth best
All things both great and small;   615
For the dear God who loveth us,
He made and loveth all.[5]

The Mariner, whose eye is bright,
Whose beard with age is hoar,
Is gone: and now the Wedding-Guest   620
Turned from the bridegroom's door.

He went like one that hath been stunned,
And is of sense forlorn:[6]
A sadder and a wiser man,
He rose the morrow morn.   625
1797   1798

- Coleridge's poem has often been described as a tale of sin, punishment, and redemption. How is the killing of the albatross represented as a sin rather than simply a wrong or a crime? Why are *all* the mariners punished along with the ancient mariner? How does the mariner redeem himself?

5. Coleridge said in 1830, in response to the poet Anna Barbauld's objection that the poem "lacked a moral": "I told her that in my own judgment the poem had too much; and that the only, or chief fault, if I might say so, was the obtrusion of the moral sentiment so openly on the reader as a principle or cause of action in a work of pure imagination. It ought to have had no more moral than the *Arabian Nights'* tale of the merchant's sitting down to eat dates by the side of a well and throwing the shells aside, and lo! a genie starts up and says he *must* kill the aforesaid merchant *because* one of the date shells had, it seems, put out the eye of the genie's son."   6. Forsaken.

> ### Connections: Contemporary Songs Based on *The Rime of the Ancient Mariner*
>
> Perhaps because it is such a haunting ballad, Coleridge's poem has inspired a number of songs and albums by a range of contemporary artists, including
>
> - Fleetwood Mac's instrumental "Albatross," on the album *The Pious Bird of Good Omen* (1969)
> - David Bedford's album *The Rime of the Ancient Mariner* (1975)
> - Iron Maiden's "The Rime of the Ancient Mariner" (1984)
> - The Pogues' "Turkish Song of the Damned" (1988)
> - The Pogues' "Fiesta" (1988)
> - Slint's "Good Morning Captain" (1991)
> - Corrosion of Conformity's "Albatross" (1994)
> - Flogging Molly's "Rebels of the Sacred Heart" (2002)
> - Captain Dan & the Scurvy Crew's "Rime of the Hip-Hop Mariners" (2007)

T. S. ELIOT

The Love Song of J. Alfred Prufrock

> *S'io credessi che mia risposta fosse*
> *a persona che mai tornasse al mondo,*
> *questa fiamma staria senza più scosse.*
> *Ma per ciò che giammai di questo fondo*
> *non tornò vivo alcun, s'i'odo il vero,*
> *senza tema d'infamia ti rispondo.*[7]

Let us go then, you and I,
When the evening is spread out against the sky
Like a patient etherised upon a table;
Let us go, through certain half-deserted streets,
5   The muttering retreats
Of restless nights in one-night cheap hotels
And sawdust restaurants with oyster-shells:
Streets that follow like a tedious argument
Of insidious intent
10 To lead you to an overwhelming question . . .

---

7. From Dante, *Inferno* (27.61–66): "If I thought that my reply would be / to one who would ever return to the world, / this flame would stay without further movement; / but since none has ever returned alive from this depth, / if what I hear is true, / I answer you without fear of infamy." The words are spoken by the character Guido da Montefeltro—imprisoned in flame in the depths of hell as a punishment for giving false counsel—to Dante, whom da Montefeltro believes will never return from his journey into the inferno.

Oh, do not ask, 'What is it?'
Let us go and make our visit.

In the room the women come and go
Talking of Michelangelo.[8]

15 The yellow fog that rubs its back upon the window-panes,
The yellow smoke that rubs its muzzle on the window-panes,
Licked its tongue into the corners of the evening,
Lingered upon the pools that stand in drains,
Let fall upon its back the soot that falls from chimneys,
20 Slipped by the terrace, made a sudden leap,
And seeing that it was a soft October night,
Curled once about the house, and fell asleep.

And indeed there will be time[9]
For the yellow smoke that slides along the street
25 Rubbing its back upon the window-panes;
There will be time, there will be time
To prepare a face to meet the faces that you meet;
There will be time to murder and create,
And time for all the works and days[1] of hands
30 That lift and drop a question on your plate;
Time for you and time for me,
And time yet for a hundred indecisions,
And for a hundred visions and revisions,
Before the taking of a toast and tea.

35 In the room the women come and go
Talking of Michelangelo.

And indeed there will be time
To wonder, 'Do I dare?' and, 'Do I dare?'
Time to turn back and descend the stair,
40 With a bald spot in the middle of my hair—
(They will say: 'How his hair is growing thin!')
My morning coat, my collar mounting firmly to the chin,
My necktie rich and modest, but asserted by a simple pin—
(They will say: 'But how his arms and legs are thin!')
45 Do I dare
Disturb the universe?
In a minute there is time
For decisions and revisions which a minute will reverse.

---

8. Italian artist Michelangelo Buonarroti (1475–1564).
9. Echo of Andrew Marvell's "To His Coy Mistress" (1681), which famously begins, "Had we but world enough, and time / This coyness, lady, were no crime."
1. *Works and Days* is a poem composed about 700 B.C.E. by the Greek writer Hesiod; lamenting the moral decay of the present, it celebrates simple life and hard work, especially agricultural labor.

For I have known them all already, known them all—
50 Have known the evenings, mornings, afternoons,
I have measured out my life with coffee spoons;
I know the voices dying with a dying fall
Beneath the music from a farther room.
    So how should I presume?

55 And I have known the eyes already, known them all—
The eyes that fix you in a formulated phrase,
And when I am formulated, sprawling on a pin,
When I am pinned and wriggling on the wall,
Then how should I begin
60 To spit out all the butt-ends of my days and ways?
    And how should I presume?

And I have known the arms already, known them all—
Arms that are braceleted and white and bare
(But in the lamplight, downed with light brown hair!)
65 Is it perfume from a dress
That makes me so digress?
Arms that lie along a table, or wrap about a shawl.
    And should I then presume?
    And how should I begin?

70 Shall I say, I have gone at dusk through narrow streets
And watched the smoke that rises from the pipes
Of lonely men in shirt-sleeves, leaning out of windows? . . .

I should have been a pair of ragged claws
Scuttling across the floors of silent seas.
                        . . . . .
75 And the afternoon, the evening, sleeps so peacefully!
Smoothed by long fingers,
Asleep . . . tired . . . or it malingers,
Stretched on the floor, here beside you and me.
Should I, after tea and cakes and ices,
80 Have the strength to force the moment to its crisis?
But though I have wept and fasted, wept and prayed,
Though I have seen my head (grown slightly bald) brought in
        upon a platter,[2]
I am no prophet—and here's no great matter;
I have seen the moment of my greatness flicker,
85 And I have seen the eternal Footman hold my coat, and snicker,
And in short, I was afraid.

---

2. Like John the Baptist; at a banquet, King Herod has the prophet's head delivered on a plate to Salome, the woman who requested his execution (Mark 6.17–28; Matthew 14.3–11).

And would it have been worth it, after all,
After the cups, the marmalade, the tea,
Among the porcelain, among some talk of you and me,
90   Would it have been worth while,
To have bitten off the matter with a smile,
To have squeezed the universe into a ball[3]
To roll it towards some overwhelming question,
To say: 'I am Lazarus, come from the dead,[4]
95   Come back to tell you all, I shall tell you all'—
If one, settling a pillow by her head,
        Should say: 'That is not what I meant at all.
        That is not it, at all.'

And would it have been worth it, after all,
100   Would it have been worth while,
After the sunsets and the dooryards and the sprinkled streets,
After the novels, after the teacups, after the skirts that trail along
        the floor—
And this, and so much more?—
It is impossible to say just what I mean!
105   But as if a magic lantern threw the nerves in patterns on a
        screen:
Would it have been worth while
If one, settling a pillow or throwing off a shawl,
And turning toward the window, should say:
        'That is not it at all,
110   That is not what I meant, at all.'

          · · · · ·

No! I am not Prince Hamlet,[5] nor was meant to be;
Am an attendant lord, one that will do
To swell a progress,[6] start a scene or two,
Advise the prince; no doubt, an easy tool,
115   Deferential, glad to be of use,
Politic, cautious, and meticulous;
Full of high sentence,[7] but a bit obtuse;
At times, indeed, almost ridiculous—
Almost, at times, the Fool.

120   I grow old . . . I grow old . . .
I shall wear the bottoms of my trousers rolled.

3. Another echo of "To His Coy Mistress": "Let us roll all our strength and all / Our sweetness up into one ball, / And tear our pleasures with rough strife / Through the iron gates of life" (lines 41–44).
4. The New Testament relates the story of Jesus raising Lazarus from the dead in John 11.1–44.
5. Protagonist of Shakespeare's tragedy *Hamlet*, who is indecisive for much of the play.
6. Journey of a royal or noble person, or the representation of such a journey onstage as part of a play (as was common in the age of Shakespeare).
7. In either of its two archaic senses: official opinion, as of a judge; maxim, general truth, or proverbial saying.

Shall I part my hair behind? Do I dare to eat a peach?
I shall wear white flannel trousers, and walk upon the beach.
125 I have heard the mermaids singing, each to each.

I do not think that they will sing to me.

I have seen them riding seaward on the waves
Combing the white hair of the waves blown back
When the wind blows the water white and black.

130 We have lingered in the chambers of the sea
By sea-girls wreathed with seaweed red and brown
Till human voices wake us, and we drown.

1915

- Like the speakers in all dramatic monologues, Prufrock intentionally and unintentionally reveals much about his temperament and
  character through both what he says and how he says it. How is
  Prufrock characterized? What do we learn about him, for example,
  through his allusions to Shakespeare's *Hamlet* (line 111)? to John
  the Baptist and Lazarus (lines 82, 94)?

SUGGESTIONS FOR WRITING

1. One of the many features that distinguishes Coleridge's *Rime of the Ancient Mariner* from traditional folk ballads (and makes the poem so long) is its use of a frame narrative—the story of how the ancient mariner tells the story of his experience at sea to a man on his way to a wedding. Write an essay explaining what the frame narrative contributes to the poem's effect and meaning.

2. Like most poems by T. S. Eliot, *The Love Song of J. Alfred Prufrock* contains many allusions. Write an essay exploring how the allusions contribute to the effect and meaning of the poem. Alternatively, focus your essay on the significance of Eliot's allusions to one poem—Andrew Marvell's "To His Coy Mistress." One theme of Marvell's seduction poem is *carpe diem*, or "seize the day." To what extent is this also a theme or a key to the theme of Eliot's poem?

3. Write an essay comparing the protagonists of at least two of the three poems in this chapter—one straightforwardly a hero, another who arguably learns to be heroic through his mistakes, and a third who perhaps yearns, but fails, to be a hero. What is similar and what is different about each poem's vision or definition of heroism?

4. Write an essay exploring how the internal structure and external form, as well as genre, of any one poem in this chapter contribute to its effect and meaning. For example, how does the fact that *The Rime of the Ancient Mariner* is a ballad (and in ballad stanzas) shape its meaning and effect? How would "Prufrock" work differently if it weren't a dramatic monologue but rather a narrative poem with the sort of third-person speaker-narrator we get in *Beowulf*? Conversely, how would *Beowulf* be different if it were a dramatic monologue?

5. Write an essay comparing *The Rime of the Ancient Mariner* to one or both of the shorter ballads in this anthology—"Sir Patrick Spens" (chapter 18) or Dudley Randall's "The Ballad of Birmingham" (chapter 19). What is similar and different about the shorter and longer ballads? Why does the ballad seem an appropriate or effective form for each of these poems? What might these poems together suggest about the nature and uses of the ballad?

SAMPLE WRITING

The following essay on *The Rime of the Ancient Mariner* was originally written for an upper-division Romantic poetry course, but it answers the questions posed in the first and fourth of this chapter's "Suggestions for Writing." In it, student writer Dan Douglas uses only literary terms and reading strategies covered in this book, though he draws—perhaps too heavily and less effectively than he might—on a relatively reliable Internet source for his information about the ballad genre. As you read the essay, identify its strongest and weakest moments and aspects. How, for example, might Douglas better use the material from his secondary source? How might his essay be improved were he to draw on a different kind of source or on multiple sources? What kind of source would be best? (On Internet sources and evaluating sources, see "Writing about Literature," 35.3.2–3.)

Dan Douglas
ENG 434: Romantic Poets.
Dr. Kelly Mays
Nov. 10, 2006

The Form of *The Rime of the Ancient Mariner*

The Norton Anthology of English Literature explains that when another poet, Anna Letitia Barbauld, complained to Samuel Taylor Coleridge that *The Rime of the Ancient Mariner* "lacked a moral," he responded that the poem's "chief fault" was in fact the very opposite: "I told her that in my own judgment the poem had too much" moral, he is quoted as saying, and one too "openly" "obtru[ded] . . . on the reader" (446, n. 6). The poem does seem to state its own moral when the mariner says near its end,

> He prayeth best, who loveth best
> All things both great and small;
> For the dear God who loveth us,
> He made and loveth all. (lines 614–617)

This is the lesson that the mariner learns when he is first punished for killing one animal (an extreme form of not "loving all") and then released only after he "blessed . . . unaware" (line 285) other animals he had only seconds before negatively labeled "slimy things" (line 238).

Douglas 2

What is not so obvious, though, is why Coleridge chose to teach this moral in a ballad and why he chose not to follow ballad convention by using a frame narrative. Or, in other words, how is the moral about treasuring all God's creatures "both great and small" affected by these choices? In this paper, I will argue that both devices are brilliant additions to the poem because they ensure (1) that we apply the poem's lesson to human beings as well as animals; (2) that we are clear about the poem's attitude toward organized religion versus its attitude toward God.

The frame narrative tells the story of the mariner's telling of the story of what happened with the albatross to a man on his way to a wedding. What's especially important is the auditor's initial response to the mariner. In the first stanza, when the mariner first "stoppeth" him (line 2), he is pretty shocked and maybe mad, asking, "By thy long grey beard and glittering eye, / Now wherefore stopp'st thou me?" (lines 3–4). Later, he practically screams, "Hold off! unhand me, grey-beard loon!" (line 11). The auditor's words imply that he wants to get away not just because he doesn't want to be late to the wedding of his "next of kin" (line 6), but because he's not happy about being held up and even touched by *this particular person*—a man so "ancient" he has a "grey beard" (notice he mentions the color of the beard twice), whom he maybe sees as badly groomed just because of the beard, and whom he definitely dismisses as a "loon" or crazy person. What we have here is age discrimination and a prejudice against people who have facial hair and seem "loony." Though we don't know much about the auditor, I wonder if we also have social prejudice here—after all, the ancient mariner is just a mariner, a common sailor. By dismissing the mariner, the auditor is arguably just doing to the mariner what the mariner did to the albatross. The auditor may not go so far as to kill the mariner, but he doesn't value him or what he's got to say, and I think that might be the reason that, as the mariner says later, he knows that this particular man is someone who "must hear" his story and learn what it "teach[es]" (lines 589–590).

The man is changed by what he hears. Almost immediately (by the third stanza), he is (maybe literally) "mesmerized" (431) by the mariner and his tale: "He holds him with his glittering eye— / The wedding guest stood still, / And listens like a three years' child" (lines 13–15). He might "beat his breast" in anger or frustration when he hears the wedding music start in the church (line 31–32), but "he cannot choose but hear" (line 38). And by the end of the first part, he even actually starts to think and care about what's going on with the mariner, how he feels, and why he feels that way, saying, "God save thee, ancient Mariner! / From the fiends, that plague thee thus!— / Why look'st thou so?" (lines 79–81). At this point, he's *asking* to hear the story. He's hooked, and he's hooked not just because the story is exciting (the mariner hasn't even gotten to the exciting part of the story yet), but because he's interested in the mariner himself. At least to some extent, the auditor has already started to learn what the mariner's story is supposed to teach: that we need to listen to, and value, the *people* we usually think of as "small," as well as the ones who are obviously "great," even "grey-beard loon[s]." And the word "loon"—which is literally a kind of bird—connects the albatross and the mariner.

The idea that we need to place more value on the people, as well as animals, we usually think of as "small" and unimportant is reinforced by Coleridge's choice to make the poem a ballad. On his website, Ted Nellen says,

> Of all the types of poetry, perhaps the one making the most direct appeal to all classes of readers and listeners from the Middle Ages to our own day is the popular ballad. It is essentially a narrative poem, that is, a poem that tells a story. And herein lies one of the reasons for its almost universal appeal; children and adults, educated and uneducated people, sophisticated and unsophisticated people—all like stories.

However, it's not just *that* ballads tell stories but *how* they tell stories that matters in this poem:

> So many ballads are cast into a four-line stanza of alternating four stress and three stress lines rhyming abcb that this stanza has come to be known as the ballad stanza. Ballads not composed in this stanza use one or another adaptation of it that is still essentially simple in structure
>
> Just as the form is simple, so is the language. And this is what we might expect, since ballads originally were composed to be sung—frequently enough by the "folk" themselves as well as by professional ballad singers—to essentially simple music. Ballads use the vocabulary of everyday speech. . . . Dialogue does not normally distinguish between speakers, even though one may be a king and the other a commoner. Again, since ballads are folk literature, we do not find highly figurative language, learned allusions, or a highly literary vocabulary.

In other words, ballads are accessible to everyone, "both great and small," so by writing in this simple way, Coleridge makes his poem accessible, too, and he shows the value of listening to ordinary people and even telling stories their way.

As Nellen points out, there are lots of ways that Coleridge's poem isn't like folk ballads: Its "incidents are developed in far more detail," it is "rich in imagery," and it has "a complex system of symbols" and "significant philosophical content." However, another way Coleridge's ballad *is* like "a popular ballad" is that its plot includes "stirring and dramatic" and specifically "supernatural" "action" (Nellen)—"The Night-mare Life-in-Death" actually appears in the poem to punish the mariner, after he prays the albatross miraculously falls off his neck, and then *something* reanimates the sailors' bodies so that they can sail the ship home. According to *The Norton*

Douglas 4

Anthology of English Literature, there is also the implication that the mariner might mesmerize the wedding guest in some magical way (431, n. 4). But none of these supernatural events or characters come from the Bible or from any organized religion I know of, though the mariner does refer to the virgin Mary (line 294) and Christ (line 487). Although the mariner also refers to "God" when he delivers the poem's moral (line 616), the moral doesn't say anything about actually going to church or participating in religion in any way. Instead, it stresses that we "prayeth well" by simply "lov[ing] well / Both man and bird and beast" (lines 612–613)—something we can't actually do in church since "bird[s] and beast[s]" are not allowed in.

This theme—that we don't really need organized religion or churches—is highlighted in the frame narrative because the wedding guest *never makes it to the church* or to the wedding ceremony. At the end of the poem, though he missed the wedding, he could still make it to the feast, as the mariner describes,

> What loud uproar bursts from that door!
> The wedding-guests are there:
> But in the garden-bower the bride
> And bride-maids singing are:
> And hark the little vesper bell,
> Which biddeth me to prayer! (lines 591–596)

However, the wedding guest doesn't go in, instead "Turn[ing] from the bridegroom's door" and presumably going home, where the next day "He rose" "A sadder and a wiser man" (lines 625, 624). The mariner also actually says that he thinks "walk[ing] together to the kirk [church] / With a goodly company" (lines 602–603) is "sweeter far" than "the marriage-feast" (lines 601–602), and even when he goes on to talk about going into the church and "all together pray[ing]," he emphasizes the relationship and relating between the people rather than the sermon or between the people and the minister. And here, too, he reinforces the point that that relationship has to be one in which *all* people, "great and small" and every age, class, etc. participate "all together"—"Old men, and babes, and loving friends, / And youths and maidens gay!" (lines 608–609).

This poem wouldn't be the same without the ballad form or the story about the wedding that frames the story of the albatross. Coleridge uses both to make sure that we don't take this story as only being about animals and the way we should value them and that we also don't take it as an endorsement of any particular religion or even organized religion at all. We can love God without going to church just by loving each other, but only if we love everyone of every species, age, looks, and class.

WORKS CITED

Coleridge, Samuel Taylor. *The Rime of the Ancient Mariner. The Norton Anthology of English Literature,* Vol. 2a: *The Romantic Period.* 8th ed. New York: Norton, 2006. 430–446.

Nellen, Ted. "The Ballad." <www.tnellen.com/cybereng/ballad.html>. 9 November 2001.

Exploring Contexts

The more knowledge you have—both general knowledge and knowledge of poetic and literary traditions—the better a reader of poetry you are likely to be. Poems often draw on a fund of human knowledge about all sorts of things, asking us to bring to bear facts and values we have acquired from earlier reading or from our experiences in the world. In the previous chapters, we have looked at how practice, specific skills, and a knowledge of basic literary terms make interpretation easier and better. This contextual section, however, focuses on other types of information you need to read richly and fully: information about authors and their work, about events that influenced authors or inspired their writing, about literary traditions that inform the work, and about how other readers and critics have interpreted the work. Poets always write in a specific time and place, under unique circumstances, and with some awareness of the world around them and the literature that came before them, whether or not they explicitly refer to contemporary matters or earlier literature in a particular poem. Poems not only *refer* to people, places, and events—things that exist in time—but also *reflect* given moments; they are the products of both the potentialities and the limitations of the times in which they are created. Many poems—like many works of drama and fiction—also have something to say about their times, as well as human qualities, habits, and relationships that seem timeless.

Beyond simply understanding that a particular poem is about an event or place or idea, you often must develop a full sense of historical context, a sense of the larger significance and resonance of the historical background. A poet may expect readers to have some sense of that significance already, but just as often, a poem works to educate you further, in both your understanding and your feelings.

What we need to bring to our reading varies from poem to poem. For example, to understand Wilfred Owen's "Dulce et Decorum Est" (chapter 16) we need to know that poison gas was used in World War I; the green tint through which the speaker sees the world in lines 13–14 comes from the green glass in the goggles of the gas mask he has just put on. But some broader issues matter as well, such as the climate of opinion that surrounded the war and the way war had been represented in earlier literary works. No doubt you will read a poem more intelligently—and with more feeling—the more you know about its cultural or historical and literary contexts. But at the same time, your sense of these subjects will grow as a result of reading the poems themselves sensitively and thoughtfully. Reading poetry can be a way to gain knowledge as well as an aesthetic experience. Although we don't generally turn to poetry for information as such, poems often give us more than we expect, insofar as we are aware of real-world contexts.

To get at appropriate factual, cultural, and historical information, we need to ask three kinds of questions of ourselves. The first is obvious: Do I understand all (or most) of the references in the poem? When events, places, or people unfamiliar to you come up, you will need to find out what, where, or who they are. The second question is more difficult: How do I know, in a poem that does *not* refer specifically to events, people, or ideas that I do not recognize, that I need to know more? That is, when a poem has no specific references to look up, no people or events to identify, how do I know that it has a specific context? Usually, good poets will not puzzle you more than necessary, so you can safely assume that anything that is not self-explanatory will merit close attention and possibly some digging in the library. References that are not in themselves clear provide a strong clue that you need more information. When something doesn't click, when the information given does not seem enough, you need to trust your puzzlement and try to find the missing facts that will allow the poem to make sense. But how? Often the date of the poem helps; sometimes the title gives a clue or a point of departure; sometimes you can uncover, by reading about the author, some of the things he or she was interested in or concerned about. There is no single all-purpose way to discover what to look for, but that kind of research—looking for clues, adding up the evidence—can be interesting in itself and very rewarding when it is successful. The third question for every factual reference is *Why*? Why does the poem refer to this particular person instead of some other? What function does the reference serve?

21 THE AUTHOR'S WORK AS CONTEXT: ADRIENNE RICH

Even though all poets share the medium of language and usually have some common notions about their craft, they put the unique resources of their individual personalities, experiences, and outlooks into every poem they create. A poet may rely on tradition extensively and use devices that others have developed without surrendering his or her individuality, just as any individual shares certain characteristics with others—political affiliations, religious beliefs, tastes in clothes and music—without compromising his or her integrity and uniqueness. Sometimes a person's uniqueness is hard to define. But it is always there, and we recognize and depend on it in our relationships with other people. And so with poets: Most don't make a conscious effort to put an individual stamp on their work; they don't have to. The stamp is there in the very subjects, words, images, and forms they choose. Every individual's unique consciousness marks what it records and imagines.

Experienced readers can often identify a poem as the distinctive work of an individual poet even though they may never have seen that poem before, much as experienced listeners can identify a new piece of music as the work of a particular composer, singer, or group after hearing only a few phrases. This ability depends on a lot of reading or a lot of listening to music, and any reasonably sensitive reader can learn, over time, to do it with remarkable accuracy. Yet this ability is not really an end in itself; rather, it is a by-product of learning to appreciate the particular, distinctive qualities of any poet's work. Once you've read several poems by the same poet, you will usually see some features that the poems all share, and gradually you may come to think of those features as characteristic. Many people have favorite poets, just as they have favorite rock groups or rap artists. In both cases, we are attracted to the artist's work precisely because, consciously or not, we recognize and appreciate that artist's distinctive style and outlook.

IDENTIFYING CHARACTERISTICS OF AN AUTHOR'S WORK

To perform an experiment, consult the Index of Authors at the back of this book to locate the following poems by Howard Nemerov: "The Vacuum," "The Goose Fish," and "Boom!" (You can also do this experiment with other poets whose work appears in the book several times, such as John Donne.) After reading these poems, list the similarities you find, perhaps by concentrating on each of the literary elements in turn. What are the distinctive features of the poems?

The concern with contemporary life, the tendency to concentrate on modern conveniences and luxuries, and the interest in isolating and defining aspects of a distinctively modern sensibility are all characteristic of Nemerov. So, too, is the tendency to create a short drama, with a speaker who is not altogether admirable.

Several of Nemerov's poems also share an attitude—a kind of antiromanticism that emerges when someone tries to sound or feel *too* proud or cheerful and is shown, by events in the poem, to be part of a grimmer reality instead. The concentration on one or more physical objects is also characteristic, and often (as in "The Vacuum") the main object is a mechanical one that symbolizes modernity and our modern dependency on things. Americanness is emphasized here, too, through a concern with defining not only our time but also our culture, its habits, and its values. The mood of loneliness is typical of Nemerov, and so is a witty conversational style, which often seems to derive from the language of commercials and street speech. Regular stanzas, rhymed in a nontraditional or irregular way and using a number of near-rhymes, are also typical.

The work of any writer will display a characteristic way of thinking. It will have certain identifiable *tendencies*. But this does not mean that every poem by a particular author will be predictable and contain all of the same features. Poets test their talents and their views—as well as their readers—by experimenting with various subjects and points of view, formal structures and devices. Like all of us, poets also grow and change over time. As readers, then, we want to strive to recognize differences, as well as similarities, among individual poems and to appreciate the ways an author's work does and doesn't change over the years.

Of what practical use is it to learn to recognize and understand the distinctive voice and mind of a particular poet? One use is the pleasant surprise that occurs when you recognize something familiar. Reading a new poem by a familiar poet can be like meeting an old friend whose face or conversation reminds you of experiences you have had together. Just as novelty—meeting something or someone altogether new to you—provides one kind of pleasure, so revisiting the familiar provides another, equal and opposite kind. Just *knowing* and *recognizing* often feel good in and of themselves.

In addition, just as you learn from watching other people, seeing how they react and respond to various situations and events, so you can learn from watching poets at work—seeing how they learn and develop, how they change their minds or test alternative points of view, how they discover the reach and limits of their imaginations and talents, how they find their distinctive voices and come to terms with their own identities. Each poem exists separately and individually, but at the same time the whole body of a poet's work records the evolution of a distinctive artistic consciousness as it confronts a world that is itself perpetually changing.

Finally, the more you know about a poet and the more of his or her poems you read, the better a reader you will likely be of any individual poem by the poet. External facts of the writer's life may inform whatever he or she writes—be it a poem, an essay, a letter, or an autobiography. But beyond that, when you grow accustomed to a writer's habits and manners and means of expression, you learn what to expect. Coming to a new poem by a poet you already are familiar with, you know what to look for and have clear expectations for the poem. At the same time, you are better prepared to appreciate the surprises each poem holds in store.

THE POETRY OF ADRIENNE RICH

You will find both continuity and change, similarities and differences, in the work of any good poet, and this chapter introduces you to a great one. Adrienne Rich (born in 1929) remains an active, prolific poet, and many readers and critics regard her as the best poet writing today. A careful reader of her work will find similarities of interest and strategy from her earliest poems—published shortly after World War II, in 1951—to her newest ones. A distinctive mind and orientation are at work.

But over the years Rich's work has changed quite a lot, too, and she has modified her views on a number of issues. Such changes were the result both of her personal experiences and of those shared experiences that help define her era. Many of the changes in Rich's ideas and attitudes, for example, reflect changing concerns among American intellectuals (especially women) in the second half of the twentieth century, and her poems represent both changed social conditions and sharply altered social, political, and philosophical attitudes. But her poems also reflect altered personal circumstances. Rich married in her early twenties and had three children by the time she was thirty; many of her early poems are about heterosexual love, and some of them are quite explicitly about sex. (See, for example, "Two Songs," later in this chapter.) More recently, she has been involved in a long-term lesbian relationship and has written, again quite explicitly, about sex between women. (See, for example, "My mouth hovers across your breasts" later in this chapter.) In Rich's poems, then, we may not only trace the contours of an evolving personal life and outlook but also—and even more important for the study of poetry generally—see how changes *within* the poet and in her social and cultural context alter the subjects and themes of her poetry, as well as its formal structure.

Just as information about an author's life and times can help us in this enterprise, so, too, can the essays, letters, and interviews in which an author reflects on the character and aims of his or her poetry and on the subjects the poetry explores. In the case of Rich, we have a bounty of such material from a poet who has also been a remarkably prolific and articulate prose writer. Gathered at the end of this chapter are excerpts from these writings, including both essays that express the author's outlook at a particular moment and retrospective pieces in which the poet gives us her interpretation of the character and development of her work over time.

It is fitting that two of Adrienne Rich's books—*A Change of World* (1951) and *The Will to Change* (1971)—bear titles that prominently feature the word *change*. For change has, indeed, been both a continuing concern of her poetry and a hallmark of her poetic career. Published when their author was just twenty-one, poems such as "At a Bach Concert," "Storm Warnings," and "Aunt Jennifer's Tigers" seem, at first glance, preternaturally mature. With their tightly controlled structure, their regular rhythm (and, often, rhyme), and their coolly observant tone, these early poems both embody and celebrate the "discipline" that "masters feelings" and the "proud restraining purity" by which art lends order to life ("At a Bach Concert"). (Versions of the word *master*, in fact, appear in all three poems.) Explaining why he chose *A Change of World* for the Yale Younger Poets Series, poet W. H. Auden singled out just such qualities and attitudes, praising Rich for a "craftsmanship" based in that "capacity for detachment from the self and its emotions without which no art is possible." If "poems are analogous to persons," Auden continued, then these poems are "neatly and modestly dressed, speak quietly but do not mumble, respect their elders but are not cowed by them, and do not tell fibs."

Less than a decade later, however, Rich began to see the very "neatness" and "detachment" of these poems as itself a kind of "fib." As she put it in 1964, the early poems, "even the ones I liked best and in which I felt I'd said most, were queerly limited; . . . in many cases I . . . suppressed, omitted, falsified even, certain disturbing elements to gain the perfection of order." From this point forward, Rich's work is very much an attempt to do the very opposite—to, in Matthew Arnold's words, "see life steadily and see it whole," in all its disturbing, disorderly imperfection. Indeed, one of the major themes of the later poems is both the necessity and the difficulty of breaking through the web of "myth" and illusion in order to get to "the thing itself" ("Diving into the Wreck," chapter 16).

In its attempt to do just that, Rich's work has itself become less neat and orderly, less quiet, modest, and respectful. Beginning with *Snapshots of a Daughter-in-Law* and its title poem, the poems speak in many radically different voices and tones and are cast in many different forms. Rich's evolution as a poet has not been a matter of pursuing any kind of single-minded mastery over her materials. "I find that I can no longer go to write a poem with a neat handful of materials and express those materials according to a prior plan," Rich explained in 1964; "the poem itself engenders new sensations, new awareness in me as it progresses." What results are "poems that *are* experiences" rather than "poems *about* experiences."

Adrienne Rich, circa 1970

In becoming more informal, exploratory, and emotional, Rich's poems have also become more personal and autobiographical, more willing to enter and lay bare what "Storm Warnings" calls the "troubled regions" of the poet's own life, heart, and mind. In fact, Rich has suggested that her artistic growth has been, in part, a matter of closing the gap between "the woman in the poem and the woman writing the poem." And in "Roofwalker," a 1961 poem that articulates her new poetic ideal, Rich compares herself both to a roofer standing atop a half-built house and to "a naked man fleeing / across" those very roofs. Like both, she now dares to be "exposed, larger than life, / and due to break my neck."

At the same time, Rich's work has also become steadily more social, political, and historical. "History" is, in fact, the title of one poem in this chapter and the subject of many others. Quite a few allude to, or take as their focus, specific women in history—from poet Emily Dickinson to astronomer Caroline Herschel and photographer Tina Modotti. As early as 1956, moreover, Rich began to insist on the historicity of her own poems by dating each one. "It seems to me now that this was an oblique political statement," Rich insists in the 1984 essay "Blood, Bread, and Poetry": "It was a declaration that placed poetry in a historical continuity, not above or outside history." "For Rich," as one critic argues, "a deepening subjectivity does not mean withdrawal, as it did for [Emily] Dickinson, but, on the contrary, a more searching engagement with people and with social forces."

In Rich's life, as in her work, the movement into the self has fueled the movement outward—into the world and back into the past—and vice versa. On the one hand, it was in part her personal feelings and experiences—the fact that she felt "unfit, disempowered, adrift" as a housewife and mother in the mid-1950s—that sent her to the work of "political" writers like Mary Wollstonecraft, Simone de Beauvoir, and James Baldwin, and, later, into the antiwar, civil rights, and women's movements. On the other hand, it was these writers and movements that eventually encouraged her to see her "private turmoil"—indeed, her consciousness itself—as the product of historically specific social and political forces. As she explains in "Blood, Bread, and Poetry,"

> my personal world view . . . was . . . created by political conditions. I was not a man; I was white in a white-supremacist society; I was . . . educated from the perspective of a particular class; my father was an "assimilated" Jew in an anti-Semitic world, my mother a white southern Protestant; there were particular historical currents on which my consciousness would come together, piece by piece. . . . My personal world view, which like so many young people I carried as a conviction of my own uniqueness, was not original with me, but was, rather, my untutored and half-conscious rendering of the facts of blood and bread, the social and political forces of my time and place.

Rich's mature poetry is, in many ways, an attempt to scrutinize the "social and political forces" that shape our lives and our relationships with one another and with the planet we inhabit. In this way, "the personal is political" for and in Rich—and so, too, is the literary. Yet her poetry works as poetry largely because in it the converse is always equally and palpably true. Her "poems compel us," as critic Albert Gelpi suggests, "precisely because . . . the politics [are] not abstracted and depersonalized but tested on the nerve-ends."

Despite—or even because of—all the changes, Rich's work also demonstrates a real and rare sort of consistency. From the very beginning of her career, Rich has conceived poems with a powerful sense of functional structure and cast them in **lyric** modes that sensitively reflect their moods and tones. She has engaged readers viscerally and intellectually through vivid images. And certain images and objects—knives and coffee pots, ruins and rubble, maps and monsters, wintry weather—recur in multiple poems, binding the poems together even as they help us track a process of evolution and change that, Rich reminds us, isn't either simple or complete. "If you think you can grasp me, think again," she warns us in "Delta"; "my story flows in more than one direction."

At a Bach Concert

Coming by evening through the wintry city
We said that art is out of love with life.
Here we approach a love that is not pity.

This antique discipline, tenderly severe,
5   Renews belief in love yet masters feeling,
Asking of us a grace in what we bear.

Form is the ultimate gift that love can offer—
The vital union of necessity
With all that we desire, all that we suffer.

10   A too-compassionate art is half an art.
        Only such proud restraining purity
        Restores the else-betrayed, too-human heart.

                                                    1951

Storm Warnings

        The glass has been falling all the afternoon,
        And knowing better than the instrument
        What winds are walking overhead, what zone
        Of gray unrest is moving across the land,
5   I leave the book upon a pillowed chair
        And walk from window to closed window, watching
        Boughs strain against the sky

        And think again, as often when the air
        Moves inward toward a silent core of waiting,
10   How with a single purpose time has traveled
        By secret currents of the undiscerned
        Into this polar realm. Weather abroad
        And weather in the heart alike come on
        Regardless of prediction.

15   Between foreseeing and averting change
        Lies all the mastery of elements
        Which clocks and weatherglasses cannot alter.
        Time in the hand is not control of time,
        Nor shattered fragments of an instrument
20   A proof against the wind; the wind will rise,
        We can only close the shutters.

        I draw the curtains as the sky goes black
        And set a match to candles sheathed in glass
        Against the keyhole draught, the insistent whine
25   Of weather through the unsealed aperture.
        This is our sole defense against the season;
        These are the things that we have learned to do
        Who live in troubled regions.

                                                    1951

Living in Sin

        She had thought the studio would keep itself;
        no dust upon the furniture of love.
        Half heresy, to wish the taps less vocal,
        the panes relieved of grime. A plate of pears,

5 a piano with a Persian shawl, a cat
   stalking the picturesque amusing mouse
   had risen at his urging.
   Not that at five each separate stair would writhe
   under the milkman's tramp; that morning light
10 so coldly would delineate the scraps
   of last night's cheese and three sepulchral bottles;
   that on the kitchen shelf among the saucers
   a pair of beetle-eyes would fix her own—
   envoy from some village in the moldings . . .
15 Meanwhile, he, with a yawn,
   sounded a dozen notes upon the keyboard,
   declared it out of tune, shrugged at the mirror,
   rubbed at his beard, went out for cigarettes;
   while she, jeered by the minor demons,
20 pulled back the sheets and made the bed and found
   a towel to dust the table-top,
   and let the coffee-pot boil over on the stove.
   By evening she was back in love again,
   though not so wholly but throughout the night
25 she woke sometimes to feel the daylight coming
   like a relentless milkman up the stairs.

                                                    1955

Snapshots of a Daughter-in-Law

1

You, once a belle in Shreveport,
with henna-colored hair, skin like a peachbud,
still have your dresses copied from that time,
and play a Chopin prelude
5 called by Cortot:[1] *"Delicious recollections*
float like perfume through the memory."

Your mind now, mouldering like wedding-cake,
heavy with useless experience, rich
with suspicion, rumor, fantasy,
10 crumbling to pieces under the knife-edge
of mere fact. In the prime of your life.
Nervy, glowering, your daughter
wipes the teaspoons, grows another way.

2

Banging the coffee-pot into the sink
15 she hears the angels chiding, and looks out

1. Alfred Cortot (1877–1962), Franco-Swiss pianist and conductor.

past the raked gardens to the sloppy sky.
Only a week since They said: *Have no patience.*

The next time it was: *Be insatiable.*
Then: *Save yourself; others you cannot save.*[2]
20 Sometimes she's let the tapstream scald her arm,
a match burn to her thumbnail,

or held her hand above the kettle's snout
right in the woolly steam. They are probably angels,
since nothing hurts her anymore, except
25 each morning's grit blowing into her eyes.

3

A thinking woman sleeps with monsters.
The beak that grips her, she becomes. And Nature,
that sprung-lidded, still commodious
steamer-trunk of *tempora* and *mores*[3]
30 gets stuffed with it all: the mildewed orange-flowers,
the female pills, the terrible breasts
of Boadicea[4] beneath flat foxes' heads and orchids.

Two handsome women, gripped in argument,
each proud, acute, subtle, I hear scream
35 across the cut glass and majolica
like Furies[5] cornered from their prey:
The argument *ad feminam*,[6] all the old knives
that have rusted in my back, I drive in yours,
ma semblable, ma soeur![7]

4

40 Knowing themselves too well in one another:
their gifts no pure fruition, but a thorn,
the prick filed sharp against a hint of scorn . . .
Reading while waiting
for the iron to heat,
45 writing, *My Life had stood—a Loaded Gun—*[8]
in that Amherst pantry while the jellies boil and scum,
or, more often,

---

2. According to Matthew 27.42, the chief priests, scribes, and elders mocked the crucified Jesus by saying, "He saved others; himself he cannot save." 3. Times and customs (Latin).

4. Queen of the ancient Britons. When her husband died, the Romans seized the territory he ruled and scourged Boadicea; she then led a heroic but ultimately unsuccessful revolt. *Female pills:* medicines for menstrual ailments.

5. In Roman mythology, the three sisters were the avenging spirits of retributive justice.

6. To the woman (Latin). The *argumentum ad hominem* (literally, "argument to the man") is (in classical rhetoric) an argument aimed at a person's individual prejudices or special interests.

7. My mirror-image or "double," my sister (French). Baudelaire, in the prefatory poem to *Les Fleurs du Mal*, addresses (and attacks) his "hypocrite reader" as "mon semblable, mon frère" (my double, my brother).

8. "My Life had stood—a Loaded Gun—" [Poem No. 754], Emily Dickinson, *Complete Poems*, ed. T. H. Johnson, 1960, p. 369 [Rich's note]. It is reprinted in the Emily Dickson album that follows this chapter.

iron-eyed and beaked and purposed as a bird,
dusting everything on the whatnot every day of life.

5

50 *Dulce ridens, dulce loquens,*[9]
she shaves her legs until they gleam
like petrified mammoth-tusk.

6

When to her lute Corinna sings[1]
neither words nor music are her own;
55 only the long hair dipping
over her cheek, only the song
of silk against her knees
and these
adjusted in reflections of an eye.

60 Poised, trembling and unsatisfied, before
an unlocked door, that cage of cages,
tell us, you bird, you tragical machine—
is this *fertilisante douleur?*[2] Pinned down
by love, for you the only natural action,
65 are you edged more keen
to prise the secrets of the vault? has Nature shown
her household books to you, daughter-in-law,
that her sons never saw?

7

"To have in this uncertain world some stay
70 *which cannot be undermined, is*
of the utmost consequence."[3]
          Thus wrote
a woman, partly brave and partly good,
who fought with what she partly understood.
75 Few men about her would or could do more,
hence she was labeled harpy, shrew and whore.

8

"You all die at fifteen," said Diderot,[4]
and turn part legend, part convention.

---

9. Sweet laughter, sweet chatter (Latin). The phrase (slightly modified here) concludes Horace's *Ode* 1.22, describing the appeal of a mistress.
1. Opening line of a lyric by Thomas Campion (1567–1620). It is reprinted in the "Words and Music" album following chapter 17. 2. Enriching pain (French).
3. ". . . is of the utmost consequence," from Mary Wollstonecraft, *Thoughts on the Education of Daughters,* London, 1787 [Rich's note].
4. "Vous mourez toutes a quinze ans," from the *Lettres à Sophie Volland,* quoted by Simone de Beauvoir in *Le Deuxième Sexe,* vol. II, pp. 123–4 [Rich's note]. Editor of the *Encyclopédie* (the central document of the French Enlightenment), Denis Diderot (1713–84) became disillusioned with the traditional education of women and undertook an experimental education for his own daughter.

Still, eyes inaccurately dream
80   behind closed windows blankening with steam.
Deliciously, all that we might have been,
all that we were—fire, tears,
wit, taste, martyred ambition—
stirs like the memory of refused adultery
85   the drained and flagging bosom of our middle years.

9

Not that it is done well, but
that it is done at all?[5] Yes, think
of the odds! or shrug them off forever.
This luxury of the precocious child,
90   Time's precious chronic invalid,—
would we, darlings, resign it if we could?
Our blight has been our sinecure:
mere talent was enough for us—
glitter in fragments and rough drafts.

95   Sigh no more, ladies.
                              Time is male
and in his cups drinks to the fair.
Bemused by gallantry, we hear
our mediocrities over-praised,
100   indolence read as abnegation,
slattern thought styled intuition,
every lapse forgiven, our crime
only to cast too bold a shadow
or smash the mould straight off.

105   For that, solitary confinement,
tear gas, attrition shelling.
Few applicants for that honor.

10

                              Well,
she's long about her coming, who must be
110   more merciless to herself than history.[6]
Her mind full to the wind, I see her plunge
breasted and glancing through the currents,
taking the light upon her
at least as beautiful as any boy

---

5. Samuel Johnson's comment on women preachers: "Sir, a woman's preaching is like a dog's walking on his hinder legs. It is not done well, but you are surprised to find it done at all" (Boswell's *Life of Johnson*, ed. L. F. Powell and G. B. Hill [Oxford: Clarendon, 1934–64], 1.463).
6. Cf. *Le Deuxième Sexe*, vol. II, p. 574: "… elle arrive du fond des ages, de Thèbes, de Minos, de Chichen Itza; et elle est aussi le totem planté au coeur de la brousse africaine; c'est un helicoptère et c'est un oiseau; et voilà la plus grande merveille: sous ses cheveux peints le bruissement des feuillages devient une pensée et des paroles s'échappent de ses seins" [Rich's note].

115 or helicopter,
                    poised, still coming,
          her fine blades making the air wince

          but her cargo
          no promise then:
120 delivered
          palpable
          ours.

                                        1958–60

Authors on Their Work: ADRIENNE RICH*

Over two years I wrote a 10-part poem called "Snapshots of a Daughter-in-Law," in a longer, looser mode than I'd ever trusted myself with before. It was an extraordinary relief to write that poem. It strikes me now as too literary, too dependent on allusion; I hadn't found the courage yet to do without authorities, or even to use the pronoun "I"—the woman in the poem is always "she." One section of it, #2, concerns a woman who thinks she is going mad; she is haunted by voices telling her to resist and rebel, voices which she can hear but not obey.

*Adrienne Rich, "When We Dead Awaken," *On Lies, Secrets, and Silence: Selected Prose: 1966–1978* (New York: W. W. Norton, 1979).

Planetarium

> *(Thinking of Caroline Herschel, 1750–1848, astronomer, sister of William; and others)*

          A woman in the shape of a monster
          a monster in the shape of a woman
          the skies are full of them

          a woman   "in the snow
5   among the Clocks and instruments
          or measuring the ground with poles"

          in her 98 years to discover
          8 comets
          she whom the moon ruled
10   like us
          levitating into the night sky
          riding the polished lenses

Galaxies of women, there
doing penance for impetuousness
15 ribs chilled
in those spaces   of the mind

An eye,
        "virile, precise and absolutely certain"
            from the mad webs of Uranisborg[7]
20   encountering the NOVA
every impulse of light exploding
from the core
as life flies out of us

        Tycho whispering at last
25   "Let me not seem to have lived in vain"

What we see, we see
and seeing is changing

the light that shrivels a mountain
and leaves a man alive

30 Heartbeat of the pulsar
heart sweating through my body

The radio impulse
pouring in from Taurus
    I am bombarded yet   I stand

35 I have been standing all my life in the
direct path of a battery of signals
the most accurately transmitted most
untranslatable language in the universe
I am a galactic cloud so deep   so invo-
40 luted that a light wave could take 15
years to travel through me   And has
taken   I am an instrument in the shape
of a woman trying to translate pulsations
into images   for the relief of the body
45 and the reconstruction of the mind.

                                        1968

Two Songs

                    I

Sex, as they harshly call it,
I fell into this morning
at ten o'clock, a drizzling hour

---

7. Actually Uraniborg, the elaborate palace-laboratory-observatory of Danish astronomer Tycho Brahe (1546–1601), whose cosmology tried to fuse the Ptolemaic and Copernican systems. Brahe discovered and described (in *De Nova Stella*, 1574) a new star in what had previously been considered a fixed-star system.

of traffic and wet newspapers.
5 I thought of him who yesterday
clearly didn't
turn me to a hot field
ready for plowing,
and longing for that young man
10 piercéd me to the roots
bathing every vein, etc.[8]
All day he appears to me
touchingly desirable,
a prize one could wreck one's peace for.
15 I'd call it love if love
didn't take so many years
but lust too is a jewel
a sweet flower and what
pure happiness to know
20 all our high-toned questions
breed in a lively animal.

      II
That "old last act"!
And yet sometimes
all seems post coitum triste[9]
25 and I a mere bystander.
Somebody else is going off,
getting shot to the moon.
Or, a moon-race!
Split seconds after
30 my opposite number lands
I make it—
we lie fainting together
at a crater-edge
heavy as mercury in our moonsuits
35 till he speaks
in a different language
yet one I've picked up
through cultural exchanges . . .
we murmur the first moonwords:
40 *Spasibo.*[1] *Thanks. O.K.*

        1964

---

8. See the opening lines of the Prologue to Chaucer's *Canterbury Tales* (ca. 1380).
9. Sadness after sexual union (Latin).　　1. Russian for "thanks."`

For the Record

The clouds and the stars didn't wage this war
the brooks gave no information
if the mountain spewed stones of fire into the river
it was not taking sides
5   the raindrop faintly swaying under the leaf
had no political opinions

and if here or there a house
filled with backed-up raw sewage
or poisoned those who lived there
10 with slow fumes, over years
the houses were not at war
nor did the tinned-up buildings

intend to refuse shelter
to homeless old women and roaming children
15 they had no policy to keep them roaming
or dying, no, the cities were not the problem
the bridges were non-partisan
the freeways burned, but not with hatred

Even the miles of barbed-wire
20 stretched around crouching temporary huts
designed to keep the unwanted
at a safe distance, out of sight
even the boards that had to absorb
year upon year, so many human sounds

25 so many depths of vomit, tears
slow-soaking blood
had not offered themselves for this
The trees didn't volunteer to be cut into boards
nor the thorns for tearing flesh
30 Look around at all of it

and ask whose signature
is stamped on the orders, traced
in the corner of the building plans
Ask where the illiterate, big-bellied
35 women were, the drunks and crazies,
the ones you fear most of all: ask where you were.

1983

[*My mouth hovers across your breasts*][2]

My mouth hovers across your breasts
in the short grey winter afternoon
in this bed   we are delicate
and tough   so hot with joy we amaze ourselves
5 tough   and delicate   we play rings
around each other   our daytime candle burns
with its peculiar light   and if the snow
begins to fall outside   filling the branches
and if the night falls   without announcement
10 these are the pleasures of winter
sudden, wild and delicate   your fingers
exact   my tongue exact at the same moment
stopping to laugh at a joke
my love   hot on your scent   on the cusp of winter
                                                        1986

History[3]

Should I simplify my life for you?
Don't ask how I began to love men.
Don't ask how I began to love women.
Remember the forties songs, the slowdance numbers
5 the small sex-filled gas-rationed Chevrolet?
Remember walking in the snow and who was gay?
Cigarette smoke of the movies, silver-and-gray
profiles, dreaming the dreams of he-and-she
breathing the dissolution of the wisping silver plume?
10 Dreaming that dream we leaned applying lipstick
by the gravestone's mirror when we found ourselves
playing in the cemetery. In Current Events she said
the war in Europe is over, the Allies
and she wore no lipstick have won the war
15 and we raced screaming out of Sixth Period.

Dreaming that dream
we had to maze our ways through a wood
where lips were knives breasts razors and I hid
in the cage of my mind scribbling
20 *this map stops where it all begins*
into a red-and-black notebook.

2. This is poem 3 in Rich's sequence "Tracking Poems."
3. This is poem 4 in Rich's sequence "Inscriptions."

Remember after the war when peace came down
as plenty for some and they said we were saved
in an eternal present and we knew the world could end?
25 —Remember after the war when peace rained down
on the winds from Hiroshima Nagasaki Utah Nevada?[4]
and the socialist queer Christian teacher jumps from the hotel
window?[5]
and L.G. saying *I want to sleep with you but not for sex*
and the red-and-black enamelled coffee-pot dripped slow through the
dark grounds
30 —appetite terror power tenderness
the long kiss in the stairwell the switch thrown
on two Jewish Communists[6] married to each other
the definitive crunch of glass at the end of the wedding?[7]
(When shall we learn, what should be clear as day,
35 *We cannot choose what we are free to love?)*[8]

1995

Modotti [9]

Your footprints of light on sensitive paper
that typewriter you made famous
my footsteps following you up stair-
wells of scarred oak and shredded newsprint
5 these windowpanes smeared with stifled breaths
corridors of tile and jaundiced plaster
if this is where I must look for you
then this is where I'll find you

From a streetlamp's wet lozenge bent
10 on a curb plastered with newsprint
the headlines aiming straight at your eyes
to a room's dark breath-smeared light

4. Sites of atomic bomb explosions, the first two in Japan near the end of World War II, the last two at test sites in the American desert.
5. This line alludes to the critic Francis Otto Matthiessen (1902–50), who taught at Harvard while Rich was an undergraduate there.   6. Julius and Ethel Rosenberg, executed as spies by the U.S. in 1953.
7. Reference to the custom at Jewish weddings in which the groom breaks a glass to commemorate the loss of Jerusalem and the Temple.
8. The italicized last two lines are the opening lines of W. H. Auden's poem "Canzone."
9. Tina Modotti (1896–1942): photographer, political activist, revolutionary. Her most significant artistic work was done in Mexico in the 1920s, including a study of the typewriter belonging to her lover, the Cuban revolutionary Julio Antonio Mella. Framed for his murder by the fascists in 1929, she was expelled from Mexico in 1930. After some years of political activity in Berlin, the Soviet Union, and Spain, she returned incognito to Mexico, where she died in 1942.
    In my search for Modotti I had to follow clues she left; I did not want to iconize her but to imagine critically the traps and opportunities of her life and choices [Rich's note].

these footsteps I'm following you with
down tiles of a red corridor
15 if this is a way to find you
of course this is how I'll find you

Your negatives pegged to dry in a darkroom
rigged up over a bathtub's lozenge
your footprints of light on sensitive paper
20 stacked curling under blackened panes
the always upstairs of your hideout
the stern exposure of your brows
—these footsteps I'm following you with
aren't to arrest you

25 The bristling hairs of your eyeflash
that typewriter you made famous
your enormous will to arrest and frame
what was, what is, still liquid, flowing
your exposure of manifestos, your
30 lightbulb in a scarred ceiling
well if this is how I find you
Modotti so I find you

In the red wash of your darkroom
from your neighborhood of volcanoes
35 to the geranium nailed in a can
on the wall of your upstairs hideout
in the rush of breath a window
of revolution allowed you
on this jaundiced stair in this huge lashed eye
40   these
footsteps I'm following you with

1996   1999

PERSONAL REFLECTIONS

From *When We Dead Awaken:*
*Writing as Re-Vision**

Most, if not all, human lives are full of fantasy—passive daydreaming which
need not be acted on. But to write poetry or fiction, or even to think well, is not
to fantasize, or to put fantasies on paper. For a poem to coalesce, for a character
or an action to take shape, there has to be an imaginative transformation of

*First published in *College English* in 1972; this version, slightly revised, is included in *On Lies, Secrets, and
Silence: Selected Prose: 1966-1978* (New York: W. W. Norton, 1979), pp. 33-49.

Adrienne Rich, circa 1978

reality which is in no way passive. And a certain freedom of the mind is needed—freedom to press on, to enter the currents of your thought like a glider pilot, knowing that your motion can be sustained, that the buoyancy of your attention will not be suddenly snatched away. Moreover, if the imagination is to transcend and transform experience it has to question, to challenge, to conceive of alternatives, perhaps to the very life you are living at that moment. You have to be free to play around with the notion that day might be night, love might be hate; nothing can be too sacred for the imagination to turn into its opposite or to call experimentally by another name. For writing is re-naming.

Now, to be maternally with small children all day in the old way, to be with a man in the old way of marriage, requires a holding-back, a putting-aside of that imaginative activity, and demands instead a kind of conservatism. I want to make it clear that I am *not* saying that in order to write well, or think well, it is necessary to become unavailable to others, or to become a devouring ego. This has been the myth of the masculine artist and thinker; and I do not accept it. But to be a female human being trying to fulfill traditional female functions in a traditional way *is* in direct conflict with the subversive function of the imagination. The word traditional is important here. There must be ways, and we will be finding out more and more about them, in which the energy of creation and the energy of relation can be united. But in those earlier years I always felt the conflict as a failure of love in myself. I had thought I was choosing a full life: the life available to most men, in which sexuality, work, and parenthood could coexist. But I felt, at twenty-nine, guilt toward the people closest to me, and guilty toward my own being.

I wanted, then, more than anything, the one thing of which there was never enough: time to think, time to write. The fifties and early sixties were years of rapid revelations: the sit-ins and marches in the South, the Bay of Pigs, the early antiwar movement, raised large questions—questions for which the masculine world of the academy around me seemed to have expert and fluent answers. But I needed to think for myself—about pacifism and dissent and violence, about poetry and society, and about my own relationship to all these things. For about ten years I was reading in fierce snatches, scribbling in notebooks, writing poetry in fragments; I was looking desperately for clues, because if there were no clues then I thought I might be insane. I wrote in a notebook about this time:

> Paralyzed by the sense that there exists a mesh of relationships—e.g., between my anger at the children, my sensual life, pacifism, sex (I mean sex in its broadest significance, not merely sexual desire)—an interconnectedness which, if I could see it, make it valid, would give me back myself, make it possible to function lucidly and passionately. Yet I grope in and out among these dark webs.

I think I began at this point to feel that politics was not something "out there" but something "in here" and of the essence of my condition.

In the late fifties I was able to write, for the first time, directly about experiencing myself as a woman. The poem was jotted in fragments during children's naps, brief hours in a library, or at 3 A.M. after rising with a wakeful child. I despaired of doing any continuous work at this time. Yet I began to feel that my fragments and scraps had a common consciousness and a common theme, one which I would have been very unwilling to put on paper at an earlier time because I had been taught that poetry should be "universal," which meant, of course, nonfemale. Until then I had tried very much *not* to identify myself as a female poet.

How Does a Poet Put Bread on the Table?*

But how does a poet put bread on the table? Rarely, if ever, by poetry alone. Of the four lesbian poets at the Nuyorican Poets Café about whose lives I know something, one directs an underfunded community arts project, two are untenured college teachers, one an assistant dean of students at a state university. Of other poets I know, most teach, often part-time, without security but year round; two are on disability; one does clerical work; one cleans houses; one is a paid organizer; one has a paid editing job. Whatever odd money comes in erratically from readings and workshops, grants, permissions fees, royalties, prizes can be very odd money indeed, never to be counted on and almost always small: checks have to be chased down, grants become fewer and more competitive in a worsening political and economic climate. Most poets who teach at universities are untenured, without pension plans or group health insurance, or are employed at public and community colleges with heavy teaching loads and low salaries. Many give unpaid readings and workshops as part of their political "tithe."

Inherited wealth accounts for the careers of some poets: to inherit wealth is to inherit time. Most of the poets I know, hearing of a sum of money, translate it not into possessions, but into time—that precious immaterial necessity of our lives. It's true that a poem can be attempted in brief interstitial moments, pulled out of the pocket and worked on while waiting for a bus or riding a train or while children nap or while waiting for a new batch of clerical work or blood samples to come in. But only certain kinds of poems are amenable to these conditions. Sometimes the very knowledge of coming interruption dampens the flicker. And there is a difference between the ordinary "free" moments stolen from exhausting family strains, from alienating labor, from thought chained by material anxiety, and those other moments that sometimes arrive in a life being lived at its height though under extreme tension; perhaps we are waiting to initiate some act we believe will catalyze change but whose outcome is uncertain; perhaps we are facing personal or communal crisis in which everything

*From *What Is Found There: Notebooks on Poetry and Politics* (New York: W. W. Norton, 1993), pp. 41–43. Print.

unimportant seems to fall away and we are left with our naked lives, the brevity of life itself, and words. At such times we may experience a speeding-up of our imaginative powers, images and voices rush together in a kind of inevitability, what was externally fragmented is internally recognized, and the hand can barely keep pace.

But such moments presuppose other times: when we could simply stare into the wood grain of a door, or the trace of bubbles in a glass of water as long as we wanted to, *almost* secure in the knowledge that there would be no interruption—times of slowness, or purposelessness.

Often such time feels like a luxury, guiltily seized when it can be had, fearfully taken because it does not seem like work, this abeyance, but like "wasting time" in a society where personal importance—even job security—can hinge on acting busy, where the phrase "keeping busy" is a common idiom, where there is, for activists, so much to be done.

Most, if not all, of the names we know in North American poetry are the names of people who have had some access to freedom in time—that privilege of some which is actually a necessity for all. The struggle to limit the working day is a sacred struggle for the worker's freedom in time. To feel herself or himself, for a few hours or a weekend, as a free being with choices—to plant vegetables and later sit on the porch with a cold beer, to write poetry or build a fence or fish or play cards, to walk without a purpose, to make love in the daytime. To sleep late. Ordinary human pleasures, the self's re-creation. Yet every working generation has to reclaim that freedom in time, and many are brutally thwarted in the effort. Capitalism is based on the abridgment of that freedom.

Poets in the United States have either had some kind of private means, or help from people with private means, have held full-time, consuming jobs, or have chosen to work in low-paying, part-time sectors of the economy, saving their creative energies for poetry, keeping their material wants simple. Interstitial living, where the art itself is not expected to bring in much money, where the artist may move from a clerical job to part-time, temporary teaching to subsistence living on the land to waitressing or doing construction or translating, typesetting, or ghostwriting. In the 1990s this kind of interstitial living is more difficult, risky, and wearing than it has ever been, and this is a loss to all the arts—as much as the shrinkage of arts funding, the censorship-by-clique, the censorship by the Right, the censorship by distribution.

From *A Communal Poetry*[*]

One day in New York in the late 1980s, I had lunch with a poet I'd known for more than twenty years. Many of his poems were—are—embedded in my life. We had read together at the antiwar events of the Vietnam years. Then, for a long time, we hardly met. As a friend, he had seemed to me withheld, defended in a certain way I defined as masculine and with which I was becoming in general impatient; yet

*From *What Is Found There: Notebooks on Poetry and Politics* (New York: W. W. Norton, 1993), pp. 164–180. Print.

often, in their painful beauty, his poems told another story. On this day, he was as I had remembered him: distant, stiff, shy perhaps. The conversation stumbled along as we talked about our experiences with teaching poetry, which seemed a safe ground. I made some remark about how long it was since last we'd talked. Suddenly, his whole manner changed: *You disappeared! You simply disappeared.* I realized he meant not so much from his life as from a landscape of poetry to which he thought we both belonged and were in some sense loyal.

Adrienne Rich, circa 1990s

If anything, those intervening years had made me feel more apparent, more visible— to myself and to others—as a poet. The powerful magnet of the women's liberation movement—and the women's poetry movement it released—had drawn me to coffeehouses where women were reading new kinds of poems; to emerging "journals of liberation" that published women's poems, often in a context of political articles and the beginnings of feminist criticism; to bookstores selling chapbooks and pamphlets from the new women's presses; to a woman poet's workshops with women in prison; to meetings with other women poets in Chinese restaurants, coffee shops, apartments, where we talked not only of poetry, but of the conditions that make it possible or impossible. It had never occurred to me that I was disappearing—rather, that I was, along with other women poets, beginning to appear. In fact, we were taking part in an immense shift in human consciousness.

My old friend had, I believe, not much awareness of any of this. It was, for him, so off-to-the-edge, so out-of-the-way; perhaps so dangerous, it seemed I had sunk, or dived, into a black hole. Only later, in a less constrained and happier meeting, were we able to speak of the different ways we had perceived that time.

He thought there had been a known, defined poetic landscape and that as poetic contemporaries we simply shared it. But whatever poetic "generation" I belonged to, in the 1950s I was a mother, under thirty, raising three small children. Notwithstanding the prize and the fellowship to Europe that my first book of poems had won me, there was little or no "appearance" I then felt able to claim as a poet, against that other profound and as yet unworded reality.

Why I Refused the National Medal for the Arts*

July 3, 1997

Jane Alexander, Chair
The National Endowment for the Arts
1100 Pennsylvania Avenue
Washington, D.C. 20506

Dear Jane Alexander,

I just spoke with a young man from your office, who informed me that I had been chosen to be one of twelve recipients of the National Medal for the Arts at a ceremony at the White House in the fall. I told him at once that I could not accept such an award from President Clinton or this White House because the very meaning of art, as I understand it, is incompatible with the cynical politics of this administration. I want to clarify to you what I meant by my refusal.

Anyone familiar with my work from the early sixties on knows that I believe in art's social presence—as breaker of official silences, as voice for those whose voices are disregarded, and as a human birthright. In my lifetime I have seen the space for the arts opened by movements for social justice, the power of art to break despair. Over the past two decades I have witnessed the increasingly brutal impact of racial and economic injustice in our country.

There is no simple formula for the relationship of art to justice. But I do know that art—in my own case the art of poetry—means nothing if it simply decorates the dinner table of power that holds it hostage. The radical disparities of wealth and power in America are widening at a devastating rate. A president cannot meaningfully honor certain token artists while the people at large are so dishonored.

I know you have been engaged in a serious and disheartening struggle to save government funding for the arts, against those whose fear and suspicion of art is nakedly repressive. In the end, I don't think we can separate art from overall human dignity and hope. My concern for my country is inextricable from my concerns as an artist. I could not participate in a ritual that would feel so hypocritical to me.

Sincerely,
Adrienne Rich

cc: President Clinton

The invitation from the White House came by telephone on July 3. After several years' erosion of arts funding and hostile propaganda from the religious right

*From *Arts of the Possible: Essays and Conversations* (New York: W. W. Norton, 2001), pp. 98–105. Print.
    After the text of my letter to Jane Alexander, then chair of the National Endowment for the Arts, had been fragmentarily quoted in various news stories, Steve Wasserman, editor of the *Los Angeles Times Book Review*, asked me for an article expanding on my reasons. Herewith the letter and the article [Rich's note].

and the Republican Congress, the House vote to end the National Endowment for the Arts was looming. That vote would break as news on July 10; my refusal of the National Medal for the Arts would run as a sidebar story in the *New York Times* and the *San Francisco Chronicle*.

In fact, I was unaware of the timing. My refusal came directly out of my work as a poet and essayist and citizen drawn to the interfold of personal and public experience. I had recently been thinking and writing about the shrinking of the social compact, of whatever it was this country had ever meant when it called itself a democracy: the shredding of the vision of *government of the people, by the people, for the people*.

"We the people—still an excellent phrase," said the playwright Lorraine Hansberry in 1962, well aware who had been excluded, yet believing the phrase might someday come to embrace us all. And I had for years been feeling both personal and public grief, fear, hunger, and the need to render this, my time, in the language of my art.

Whatever was "newsworthy" about my refusal was not about a single individual—not myself, not President Clinton. Nor was it about a single political party. Both major parties have displayed a crude affinity for the interests of corporate power, while deserting the majority of the people, especially the most vulnerable. Like so many others, I've watched the dismantling of our public education, the steep rise in our incarceration rates, the demonization of our young black men, the accusations against our teen-age mothers, the selling of health care—public and private—to the highest bidders, the export of subsistence-level jobs in the United States to even lower-wage countries, the use of below-minimum-wage prison labor to break strikes and raise profits, the scapegoating of immigrants, the denial of dignity and minimal security to working and poor people. At the same time, we've witnessed the acquisition of publishing houses, once risk-taking conduits of creativity, by conglomerates driven single-mindedly to fast profits, the acquisition of major communications and media by those same interests, the sacrifice of the arts and public libraries in stripped-down school and civic budgets, and, most recently, the evisceration of the National Endowment for the Arts. Piece by piece the democratic process has been losing ground to the accumulation of private wealth.

There is no political leadership in the White House or the Congress that has spoken to and for the people who, in a very real sense, have felt abandoned by their government.

Lorraine Hansberry spoke her words about government during the Cuban missile crisis, at a public meeting in New York to abolish the House Un-American Activities Committee. She also said in that speech, "My government is wrong." She did not say, I abhor all government. She claimed her government as a citizen, African American, and female, and she challenged it. (I listened to her words again, on an old vinyl recording, this past Fourth of July.)

In a similar spirit many of us today might wish to hold government accountable, to challenge the agendas of private power and wealth that have displaced historical tendencies toward genuinely representative government in the United States. We might still wish to claim our government, to say, *This belongs to us*—we, the people, as we are now.

We would have to start asking questions that have been defined as nonquestions—or as naive, childish questions. In the recent official White House focus on race, it goes consistently unsaid that the all-embracing enterprise of our early history was the slave trade, which left nothing, no single life, untouched, and was, along with the genocide of the native population and the seizure of their lands, the foundation of our national prosperity and power. Promote dialogues on race? apologize for slavery? We would need to perform an autopsy on capitalism itself.

Marxism has been declared dead. Yet the questions Marx raised are still alive and pulsing, however the language and the labels have been co-opted and abused. What is social wealth? How do the conditions of human labor infiltrate other social relationships? What would it require for people to live and work together in conditions of radical equality? How much inequality will we tolerate in the world's richest and most powerful nation? Why and how have these and similar questions become discredited in public discourse?

And what about art? Mistrusted, adored, pietized, condemned, dismissed as entertainment, commodified, auctioned at Sotheby's, purchased by investment-seeking celebrities, it dies into the "art object" of a thousand museum basements. It's also reborn hourly in prisons, women's shelters, small-town garages, community-college workshops, halfway houses, wherever someone picks up a pencil, a wood-burning tool, a copy of *The Tempest*, a tag-sale camera, a whittling knife, a stick of charcoal, a pawnshop horn, a video of *Citizen Kane*, whatever lets you know again that this deeply instinctual yet self-conscious expressive language, this regenerative process, could help you save your life. "If there were no poetry on any day in the world," the poet Muriel Rukeyser wrote, "poetry would be invented that day. For there would be an intolerable hunger." In an essay on the Caribbean poet Aimé Césaire, Clayton Eshleman names this hunger as "the desire, the need, for a more profound and ensouled world." There is a continuing dynamic between art repressed and art reborn, between the relentless marketing of the superficial and the "spectral and vivid reality that employs all means" (Rukeyser again) to reach through armoring, resistances, resignation, to recall us to desire.

Art is both tough and fragile. It speaks of what we long to hear and what we dread to find. Its source and native impulse, the imagination, may be shackled in early life, yet may find release in conditions offering little else to the spirit. For a recent document on this, look at Phyllis Kornfeld's *Cellblock Visions: Prison Art in America*, notable for the variety and emotional depth of the artworks reproduced, the words of the inmate artists, and for Kornfeld's unsentimental and lucid text. Having taught art to inmates for fourteen years, in eighteen institutions (including maximum-security units), she sees recent incarceration policy as rapidly devolving from rehabilitation to dehumanization, including the dismantling of prison arts programs.

Art can never be totally legislated by any system, even those that reward obedience and send dissident artists to hard labor and death; nor can it, in our specifically compromised system, be really free. It may push up through cracked macadam, by the merest means, but it needs breathing space, cultivation, protection to fulfill itself. Just as people do. New artists, young or old, need education in their art, the tools of their craft, chances to study examples from the past and meet practitioners in the present, get the criticism and encouragement of mentors, learn that they are not alone. As the social compact withers, fewer and fewer people will be told *Yes, you can do this; this also belongs to you.* Like government, art needs the participation of the many in order not to become the property of a powerful and narrowly self-interested few.

Art is our human birthright, our most powerful means of access to our own and another's experience and imaginative life. In continually rediscovering and recovering the humanity of human beings, art is crucial to the democratic vision. A government tending further and further away from the search for democracy will see less and less "use" in encouraging artists, will see art as obscenity or hoax.

In 1987, the late Justice William Brennan spoke of "formal reason severed from the insights of passion" as a major threat to due-process principles. "Due process asks whether government has treated someone fairly, whether individual dignity has been honored, whether the worth of an individual has been acknowledged. Officials cannot always silence these questions by pointing to rational action taken according to standard rules. They must plumb their conduct more deeply, seeking answers in the more complex equations of human nature and experience."

It is precisely where fear and hatred of art join the pull toward quantification and abstraction, where the human face is mechanically deleted, that human dignity disappears from the social equation. Because it is to those "complex equations of human nature and experience" that art addresses itself.

In a society tyrannized by the accumulation of wealth as Eastern Europe was tyrannized by its own false gods of concentrated power, recognized artists have, perhaps, a new opportunity: to work out our connectedness, *as artists*, with other people who are beleaguered, suffering, disenfranchised—precariously employed workers, trashed elders, rejected youth, the "unsuccessful," and the art they too are nonetheless making and seeking.

I wish I didn't feel the necessity to say here that none of this is about imposing ideology or style or content on artists; it's about the inseparability of art from acute social crisis in this century and the one now approaching.

We have a short-lived model, in our history, for the place of art in relation to government. During the Depression of the 1930s, under New Deal legislation, thousands of creative and performing artists were paid modest stipends to work in the Federal Writers Project, the Federal Theatre Project, the Federal Art Project. Their creativity, in the form of novels, murals, plays, performances, public monuments, the providing of music and theater to new audiences, seeded the art and the consciousness of succeeding decades. By 1939 this funding was discontinued.

Federal funding for the arts, like the philanthropy of private arts patrons, can be given and taken away. In the long run art needs to grow organically out of a social compost nourishing to everyone, a literate citizenry, a free, universal, public education complex with art as an integral element, a society honoring both human individuality and the search for a decent, sustainable common life. In such conditions, art would still be a voice of hunger, desire, discontent, passion, reminding us that the democratic project is never-ending.

For that to happen, what else would have to change?

Adrienne Rich: A Chronology

1929	Born in Baltimore, Maryland, May 16. Begins writing poetry as a child with the encouragement of her father, Dr. Arnold Rich, from whose "very Victorian, pre-Raphaelite" library, Rich read Tennyson, Keats, Arnold, Blake, Rossetti, Swinburne, Carlyle, and Pater.
1951	A.B., Radcliffe College. *A Change of World* chosen by W. H. Auden for publication in the Yale Younger Poets series.
1952–53	Guggenheim Fellowship; travel in Europe and England. Marriage to Alfred H. Conrad, an economist teaching at Harvard. Residence in Cambridge, Massachusetts, 1953–66.
1955	Birth of David Conrad. Publication of *The Diamond Cutters and Other Poems*.
1957	Birth of Paul Conrad.
1959	Birth of Jacob Conrad.
1960	National Institute of Arts and Letters Award for poetry.
1961–62	Guggenheim Fellowship; residence with family in the Netherlands.
1962	Bollingen Foundation grant for translation of Dutch poetry.
1962–63	Amy Lowell Travelling Fellowship.
1963	*Snapshots of a Daughter-in-Law* published. Bess Hokin Prize of *Poetry* magazine.
1966	*Necessities of Life* published. Moves to New York City; residence there from 1966 on. Increasingly active in protests against the war in Vietnam.
1966–68	Lecturer at Swarthmore College.
1967–69	Adjunct Professor of Writing in the Graduate School of the Arts, Columbia University.
1968	Begins teaching in the SEEK and Open Admissions Programs at City College of New York.
1969	*Leaflets* published.
1970	Death of Alfred Conrad.
1971	*The Will to Change* published. Increasingly active in the women's movement.
1972–73	Fannie Hurst Visiting Professor of Creative Literature at Brandeis University.
1973	*Diving into the Wreck* published.
1974	National Book Award for *Diving into the Wreck*. Rich rejects the award as an individual, but accepts it, in a statement written with Audre Lorde and Alice Walker, two other nominees, in the name of all women. Professor of English, City College of New York.

1975   *Poems: Selected and New* published.

1976   Professor of English at Douglass College. *Of Woman Born: Motherhood as Experience and Institution* published. *Twenty-one Love Poems* published.

1978   *The Dream of a Common Language: Poems 1974–1977* published.

1979   *On Lies, Secrets, and Silence: Selected Prose 1966–1978* published. Leaves Douglass College and New York City; moves to Montague, Massachusetts; edits, with Michelle Cliff, the lesbian-feminist journal *Sinister Wisdom.*

1981   *A Wild Patience Has Taken Me This Far: Poems 1978–1981* published.

1984   *The Fact of a Doorframe: Poems Selected and New 1950–1984* published. Moves to Santa Cruz, California. Professor of English, San Jose State University.

1986   *Blood, Bread, and Poetry: Selected Prose 1979–1985* published. Professor of English, Stanford University.

1989   *Time's Power: Poems 1985–1988* published.

1991   *An Atlas of the Difficult World: Poems 1988–1991* published.

1992   Wins *Los Angeles Times* Book Prize for *An Atlas of the Difficult World: Poems 1988–1991,* the Lenore Marshall/*Nation* Prize for Poetry, and Nicholas Roerich Museum Poet's Prize; is co-winner of the Frost Silver Medal for distinguished lifetime achievement.

1993   *What Is Found There: Notebooks on Poetry and Politics* published.

1994   Awarded MacArthur fellowship.

1995   *Dark Fields of the Republic: Poems 1991–1995* published.

1996   Awarded the Dorothea Tanning Prize, given by the Academy of American Poets.

1999   Elected a chancellor of the Academy. Received Lannan Foundation's Lifetime Achievement Award. *Midnight Salvage: Poems 1995–1998* published.

2001   *Fox: Poems 1998–2000* and *Arts of the Possible: Essays and Conversations* published.

2002   *The Fact of a Doorframe: Poems Selected and New 1950–2000* published.

2005   *The School among the Ruins: Poems 2000–2004* published.

2006   Awarded the National Book Foundation's Medal for Distinguished Contribution to American Letters.

2007   *Telephone Ringing in the Labyrinth: Poems 2004–2006* and (with Mark Doty) *Poetry and Commitment* published.

2009   *A Human Eye: Essays on Art in Society, 1997–2008* published.

SUGGESTIONS FOR WRITING

1. In her 1951 poem "At a Bach Concert," Adrienne Rich writes that "Form is the ultimate gift that love can offer" (line 7). What, exactly, is the case for the "discipline" of formal art argued by this poem (line 4)? How has Rich's later work both embodied and rejected formalism? Considering as evidence the selections of Rich's poetry

and prose in this and previous chapters, write an essay in which you discuss how Rich's thoughts about formality and form have evolved throughout her career.

2. Carefully considering plot, characterization, and structure, write an essay in which you detail the ways "Diving into the Wreck" (chapter 16) is and is not typical of Rich's work.

3. In poems such as "Snapshots of a Daughter-in-Law," "Planetarium," and "Modotti," Rich considers the creative accomplishments of women throughout history. What role do these women play, separately and together? How is that role both constrained and unconstrained by their gender? Write an essay in which you examine the way Rich portrays creative women. Are they role models in her work, or something else?

4. Rich once said of her college days in the late 1940s, "I had no political ideas of my own, only the era's vague and hallucinatory anti-Communism and the encroaching privatism of the 1950s. Drenched in invisible assumptions of my class and race, unable to fathom the pervasive ideology of gender, I felt 'politics' as distant, vaguely sinister, the province of powerful older men or of people I saw as fanatics. It was in poetry that I sought a grasp on the world and on interior events, 'ideas of order,' even power." Using the poems by Rich included in this book, write an essay that charts the development of the poet's political consciousness.

5. In the prose writings excerpted in this chapter, Rich describes and defends the political passions that, she says, animate her life as an artist. How fully do Rich's poems embody her political beliefs, particularly her commitment to feminism? Write an essay in which you explore Rich's poetry in light of her feminist politics.

6. Choose two or more poems in this book by one author, and write an essay in which you draw on those poems to demonstrate either the distinctive, characteristic qualities and features of that author's work or the way your understanding of one poem by the author is altered or enhanced when you read it in conjunction with the other poem or poems. Poets whose work you might consider include those featured in the albums that follow this chapter (Emily Dickinson, W. B. Yeats, and Pat Mora), as well as Gwendolyn Brooks, Elizabeth Barrett Browning, Robert Browning, Countee Cullen, James Dickey, John Donne, Paul Laurence Dunbar, Robert Frost, Robert Hayden, Gerard Manley Hopkins, Langston Hughes, John Keats, Andrew Marvell, Claude McKay, Edna St. Vincent Millay, Howard Nemerov, Sharon Olds, Wilfred Owen, Linda Pastan, Sylvia Plath, William Shakespeare, Wallace Stevens, Alfred Tennyson, Walt Whitman, and William Carlos Williams.

SAMPLE WRITING

The student essay below was written in response to the following assignment (a more elaborate version of the last writing suggestion in this chapter):

> Your second essay for the course should be 6–9 pages long and should analyze two or more poems included in *The Norton Introduction to Literature*. The poems must be by the same author.

> You are *strongly* encouraged to pay attention to how the poems' meaning and effect are shaped by some aspect or aspects of their form. Those aspects might include specific formal features such as lineation, rhyme, meter, alliteration, or assonance, and/or external form or subgenre—the fact that a poem is a Shakespearean/English or Petrarchan/Italian sonnet, a haiku, or a dramatic monologue, for example. (In terms of the latter, you might consider how the poem's effect and meaning are shaped by the very fact that it takes a particular form, by the poet uses the specific conventions of that genre to create particular effects and meanings, and by specific departures from convention.)

In her essay, student writer Melissa Makolin draws on three English sonnets by William Shakespeare to argue for the distinctiveness and radicalism of the views expressed in two English sonnets by another author, Edna St. Vincent Millay. In a sense, then, Makolin's essay focuses simultaneously on external form (chapter 19), the author's work (chapters 21 and 22), and literary tradition (chapter 23), even as it explores gender ("Exploring Gender: An Album") and engages in a kind of feminist criticism ("Critical Approaches"). That's a lot to tackle in a relatively short essay, and you will no doubt find things both to admire and to criticize about Makolin's argument. At what points do you find yourself agreeing with her interpretation? disagreeing? wanting more evidence or more analysis of the evidence provided? more contextual information—about literary tradition, the author, or the author's historical and cultural context? Where and how might the essay's logic seem faulty or its claims contradictory? In the end, what might you take away from this sample essay about how to craft an effective, persuasive argument about an author's work?

Melissa Makolin
Dr. Mays
English 298X
13 April 2007

Out-Sonneting Shakespeare: An Examination of Edna St. Vincent Millay's
Use of the Shakespearean Sonnet Form

Edna St. Vincent Millay is known not only for her poetry, but also for the feminist ideals she represents therein. She was an extremely talented poet who turned the sonnet form on its head, using the traditionally restrictive form previously used almost exclusively by male poets to express feminist ideas that were radical for her time. Shakespearean sonnets are often about the physical beauty of an idealized but also objectified woman, and they implicitly emphasize the man's dominance over her. Millay uses Shakespeare's form to assert a much different view of femininity, sexuality, and biological dominance. She uses a form known for its poetic limitations to reject social limitations. She uses a form previously used to objectify women to portray them as sexual beings with power and control over their own bodies and lives. The paradox of Millay's poetry is that she uses a poetically binding, male-dominated form to show that she will not be bound either by literary tradition or societal mores regarding inter-gender relations.

The idea of a woman seeking physical pleasure in defiance of societal constraints is one that was revolutionary when "[Women have loved before as I love now]" and "[I shall forget you presently, my dear]" were published, in 1931 and 1922 respectively. They are poems about a woman's lust leading her to select a sexual partner based on her physical needs rather than on the desire for love. This is a concept that Shakespeare would have found very contentious for three reasons. First, Shakespeare did not agree with acting on lust of any kind; in fact, this is the topic of his sonnet "[Th' expense of spirit in a waste of shame]." It is a fourteen-line treatise on the evils that result from acting on lustful urges in which Shakespeare declares,

> Th' expense of spirit in a waste of shame
> Is lust in action; and, till action, lust
> Is perjured, murderous, bloody, full of blame,
> Savage, extreme, rude, cruel, not to trust. . . . (lines 1–4)

Lust, sexual or otherwise, is a pathway to a hell both religious and secular. Seventeenth-century society dramatically constricted the liberties of women in particular and didn't encourage sexual freedom for either gender.

Second, the majority of Shakespeare's sonnets simultaneously idealize and trivialize the two things they celebrate: women and love. In poems such as "[My mistress' eyes are nothing like the sun]," he treats women either as objects of an ordered, almost courtly love or as objects of mild ridicule. In this poem's first twelve lines, he mocks his mistress by describing her halitosis (lines 7–8), referring to her breasts as "dun" (line 3) and her hair as "black wires" (line 4), references to all the contemporary conventions of beauty to which she does not conform. He not only tells her what the ideal of feminine beauty is, but also makes light of the various ways in which she does not live up to it. He justifies these hurtful insults by reassuring the poor woman that his love for her is "as rare / As any she belied with false compare" (lines 13–14). He mocks her appearance by telling her that she is special and beautiful in her own way only because he loves her. Insulting someone, breaking down her self-esteem, and convincing her that she could be loved by no one else are tactics used in abusive relationships to subjugate one partner. This is not love, and the role of women in the traditional Shakespearean sonnet is far from empowered.

Third and finally, in addition to idealizing while simultaneously trivializing women, Shakespeare's sonnets also demean the concept of love. To Shakespeare, a woman is worthy of love either because she is an ideal of physical beauty or because he is noble enough to love her despite her disgusting flaws (as in "[My mistress' eyes are nothing like the sun]"). He takes this warped concept one step further, though, by creating an ideal of love that is egotistical and unhealthy for both parties. In "[Shall I compare thee to a summer's day?]," he spends the first twelve lines describing the ways in which this particular woman fulfills the contemporary ideals of beauty. It is clear that he ardently reveres her physical appearance, and the poem ends with the kind of declaration of personal devotion consistent with love. The turn, however, exhibits a malignant narcissism when it reassures the beloved that "So long as men can breathe or eyes can see, / So long lives this, and this gives life to thee" (lines 13–4). The object of the speaker's affection is just that, an object that only exists as an appendage to him. Shakespeare makes it clear that it is only because of his poetic greatness that their love will persist through the ages. He uses the poetic form to relegate women to the position of objects.

The Shakespearean sonnets of Edna St. Vincent Millay use the form to offer quite a different view of the role of women. She sees herself as a liberated woman, and she is not afraid to defy social conventions by taking lovers and discarding them when necessary. In writing sonnets about actively satisfying her lust, she also defies literary conventions, completely changing the male-female power dynamic of past sonnets by male writers. In "[Women have loved before as I love now]," Millay discusses how women throughout history have felt the same lust that she feels, but unlike other more timid and traditional women, she is willing to join the ranks of the brave women of antiquity and to satisfy her passions despite the potential cost. This poem celebrates the women who choose to act against the standards set for them. Describing them as "treacherous queens, with death upon the tread, / Heedless and wilful, [who] took their knights to bed" makes them sound heroic, and it shifts control in the sexual relationship from the man to the woman (lines 13–14). In Millay's version, the women sexually dominate the men and temporarily free themselves from the constraints of an oppressive society. Further, by alluding to the famous females of the "lively chronicles of the past" (line 2), she shows not only that this behavior is natural and heroic, but also that it is historically valid. The specific women she alludes to when referring to "Irish waters by a Cornish prow" (line 3) and "Trojan waters by a Spartan mast" (line 4) are respectively Iseult, the adulteress of the classic work of medieval passion *The Romance of Tristan and Iseult*, and Helen of Troy (or any of the other libidinous women) of the Homeric epics.

The fact that Millay uses the sonnet form to illustrate sexual liberation is significant for several reasons. First, it shows that she understands the restrictions placed upon her, both as a poet and as a woman. Second, using the sonnet shows that she can hold her own against the great male poets and write within the boundaries that they have erected; the subject matter of her poetry shows that she chooses not to. Lastly, it is significant because, in using his form for her own feminist purposes, she directly confronts Shakespeare's one-dimensional portrayal of women by proposing her own view of ideal femininity.

The second of Edna St. Vincent Millay's Shakespearean sonnets that defies the ideals set forth by Shakespeare is "[I shall forget you presently, my dear]." It is a poem about the impermanence of love and lust. The speaker tells her lover that he or she will be forgotten because love does not last forever, and "biologically speaking" (line 14) it is not necessary for it to do so because emotional and physical needs are two things which need not be dependent on, or even related to, each other. Consummation of a relationship was never discussed in the time of Shakespeare as a tenet of courtly love because women were supposed to be angelic ideals rather than real people with carnal desires. Millay's speaker defies these unrealistic and unattainable ideals of eternal adoration by stating repeatedly, "I shall forget you" (lines 1, 6), illustrating that she does not need to be monogamous to be fulfilled physically and emotionally. In fact, the statement that "I would indeed that love were longer-lived, / And oaths were not so brittle as they are, / But it is so . . ." (lines 9–11) offers a cynical view of love. The love of Millay's world is fleeting, whereas the love of Shakespeare's world is final and complete once the man conquers all and the woman takes her place on his arm. Still, Millay's poem represents a more realistic view of female and male interactions; life and love are transitory and to be enjoyed in the moment because sexual urges can be sated, are biologically determined, and essential to survival, while emotional ones are (relatively) inconsequential and satisfied in other ways.

Millay draws on Shakespeare as a kind of foil by using the form that bears his name as a vehicle for her very different views on the same topics. Millay brings sexual relationships to a far more terrestrial level with her assertions that women have primal urges that must be satisfied and that submission to ascribed gender roles is not necessary in order to obtain this satisfaction. She presents a radically modern view of relationships. She lambastes the Shakespearean paradigm of the idealized woman, a traditionally beautiful possession of the egotistical man. By using the Shakespearean sonnet form to propose her own revamped vision of the modern woman, a self-aware person who fearlessly relishes the idea of her own emotional and sexual independence, Millay redefines both "woman" and "love."

WORKS CITED

Booth, Alison, J. Paul Hunter, and Kelly J. Mays, eds. *The Norton Introduction to Literature.* 9th ed. New York: W. W. Norton, 2005.

Millay, Edna St. Vincent. "[I shall forget you presently, my dear.]" Booth, Hunter, and Mays 1031.

———. "[Women have loved before as I love now]." Booth, Hunter, and Mays 878-9.

Shakespeare, William. "[Th'expense of spirit in a waste of shame]." Booth, Hunter, and Mays 1011.

———. "[My mistress' eyes are nothing like the sun]." Booth, Hunter, and Mays 1034.

———. "[Shall I compare thee to a summer's day?]" Booth, Hunter, and Mays 948.

Emily Dickinson: An Album

The bee himself did not evade the schoolboy more than she evaded me; and even at this day I still stand somewhat bewildered, like the boy.

—THOMAS WENTWORTH HIGGINSON

The woman many regard as America's most original poet was born in her family's home in Amherst, Massachusetts, on December 10, 1830. She would die in the same home at the age of fifty-five, having anonymously published only ten of the almost 1,800 poems that her sister was surprised to discover after her death, poems that have since made her a legend. Because she never married and rarely, if ever, ventured outside her home in the last twenty years of her life, biographers and critics are fond of contrasting the narrowness of Emily Dickinson's life with the tremendous breadth of her posthumous reputation and influence, and the brevity and emotional intensity of her poetry, with its sheer formal, emotional, and intellectual audacity and range.

Yet Dickinson's life was not quite as uneventful or narrow as it might outwardly appear. She received a fairly extensive education for a woman of her era, studying classics, as well as science and other subjects, at both Amherst Academy, which she attended for seven years, and the Mount Holyoke Female Seminary (later, Mount Holyoke College), which she attended for one. She also read both widely and deeply throughout her life. Moreover, she had a great deal of indirect knowledge of public and literary affairs, including the abolitionist, feminist, and Transcendentalist movements, prominent as well as the various theological controversies of her day. Her father was a lawyer, college administrator, and politician; Emily herself maintained an avid correspondence with some ninety people and included among her friends the clergyman Charles Wadsworth, journalists Samuel Bowles and Thomas Higginson, and novelist Helen Hunt Jackson. Dickinson's friendships also ensured her a select, but astute, audience for her letters and the poems she often included in them.

Dickinson nonetheless did cultivate her privacy and independence, bequeathing us a body of a poetry that is in some ways as deliberately elusive, enigmatic, and eccentric as the woman herself apparently was, even to those who knew her best. As a result, hers is also a poetry that holds especially rich rewards for readers willing both to read individual poems multiple times and to read multiple poems with an eye on the light each sheds on the others.

As you read the ten Dickinson poems gathered in the following album as well as those in chapters 16, 17, and 18, try to identify the various formal features and strategies that seem to you most characteristic of Dickinson's poetry, including its **diction**, **syntax**, punctuation, **meter**, and **rhyme**. Pay attention, too, to the varying **tone** of the poems and the persona Dickinson creates in and through them. To what extent and how and why do the speakers of these varied **lyrics** seem like versions of the same person? what sort of person or persons? What patterns do you notice in the objects depicted and the topics or questions explored in these poems? What sorts of feelings are communicated, and what might the poems have to say about feeling, as well as thought and imagination? Why might (or might not) Dickinson's poems seem "torn up by the roots, with rain and dew and earth still clinging to them," as Higginson once declared? Or how might the poems help you understand what Dickinson meant when she wrote, "Tell all the truth but tell it slant / Success in Circuit lies"?

As you work to answer these questions for yourself, you may—like countless other readers before you—find yourself as intrigued by the poet behind the work as by the work itself. In "Writing about Literature" (chapters 32–37), you will find a sample research paper in which one student interprets three poems by Dickinson in light of both biographical and historical context. Interesting and persuasive though that paper is, critic Molly McQuade's cautionary words are perhaps worth keeping in mind: "Because [Dickinson] lived in seclusion by choice, and because her poetry also steadfastly reflects the author's coveting of privacy, to read the life in the poetry is perilous, if not impossible. Likewise, to search the life for the origins of her poetry would be treacherous."

Another factor that may make both a biographical approach to Dickinson's poetry, as well as claims about how it changed over time, somewhat more diffi-cult than in the case of poets such as Adrienne Rich, W. B. Yeats, or Pat Mora is the fact that we cannot precisely date Dickinson's individual poems. Instead, we have to rely on the approximate dates scholars assign the poems based on a study of the letters and hand-sewn books that hold the only surviving copies. In a way, then, the case of Emily Dickinson is a bit like that of William Shakespeare— one in which all that we *don't* know about the author makes his or her work even more intriguing.

EMILY DICKINSON

[Because I could not stop for Death—]

Because I could not stop for Death—
He kindly stopped for me—
The Carriage held but just Ourselves—
And Immortality.

5   We slowly drove—He knew no haste
And I had put away
My labor and my leisure too,
For His Civility—

We passed the School, where Children strove
10 At Recess—in the Ring—
We passed the Fields of Gazing Grain—
We passed the Setting Sun—

Or rather—He passed Us—
The Dews drew quivering and chill—
15 For only Gossamer,[1] my Gown—
My Tippet—only Tulle[2]—

We paused before a House that seemed
A Swelling of the Ground—
The Roof was scarcely visible—
20 The Cornice—in the Ground—

---

1. Soft, sheer fabric.   2. Fine net fabric. *Tippet*: shawl.

Since then—'tis Centuries—and yet
Feels shorter than the Day
I first surmised the Horses' Heads
Were toward Eternity—

ca. 1863

- What vision of death and the afterlife is implied by the way death is personified and characterized in the poem? by the details the speaker offers about the carriage ride she takes with him?

[*I stepped from Plank to Plank*]

I stepped from Plank to Plank
A slow and cautious way
The Stars about my Head I felt
About my Feet the Sea.

5 I knew not but the next
Would be my final inch—
This gave me that precarious Gait
Some call Experience.

ca. 1864

- For what does "stepp[ing] from Plank to Plank" become a metaphor in the poem (line 1)? Is this experience a positive or a negative one?

[*We do not play on Graves—*]

We do not play on Graves—
Because there isn't Room—
Besides—it isn't even—it slants
And People come—

5 And put a Flower on it—
And hang their faces so—
We're fearing that their Hearts will drop—
And crush our pretty play—

And so we move as far
10 As Enemies—away—
Just looking round to see how far
It is—Occasionally—

ca. 1862

- What can we infer about the speaker's age and experience? Who are "We"? Why do the speaker and her companions "loo[k] round . . . / Occasionally" (lines 11–12)?

[The Brain—is wider than the Sky—]

The Brain—is wider than the Sky—
For—put them side by side—
The one the other will contain
With ease—and You—beside—

5   The Brain is deeper than the sea—
For—hold them—Blue to Blue—
The one the other will absorb—
As Sponges—Buckets—do—

The Brain is just the weight of God—
10 For—Heft them—Pound for Pound—
And they will differ—if they do—
As Syllable from Sound—

                                        ca. 1862

- What does this poem imply about the human brain by focusing on its width, depth, and weight? by comparing it to the sky, the sea, and God?

[She dealt her pretty words like Blades—]

She dealt her pretty words like Blades—
How glittering they shone—
And every One unbared a Nerve
Or wantoned with a Bone—

5   She never deemed—she hurt—
That—is not Steel's Affair—
A vulgar grimace in the Flesh—
How ill the Creatures bear—

To Ache is human—not polite—
10 The Film upon the eye
Mortality's old Custom—
Just locking up—to Die.

                                        1862

- What kind of person and situation might the poem describe? What does the end of the poem imply about how someone should respond to such a situation and person?

[*Wild Nights—Wild Nights!*]

Wild Nights—Wild Nights!
Were I with thee
Wild Nights should be
Our luxury!

5 Futile—the Winds—
To a Heart in port—
Done with the Compass—
Done with the Chart!

Rowing in Eden—
10 Ah, the Sea!
Might I but moor—Tonight—
In Thee!

ca. 1861

- Whom might the speaker be addressing? What might it mean to be "Done with the Chart" (line 8)?

[*My Life had stood—a Loaded Gun—*]

My Life had stood—a Loaded Gun—
In Corners—till a Day
The Owner passed—identified—
And carried Me away—

5 And now We roam in Sovereign Woods—
And now We hunt the Doe—
And every time I speak for Him—
The Mountains straight reply—

And do I smile, such cordial light
10 Upon the Valley glow—
It is as a Vesuvian face
Had let its pleasure through—

And when at Night—Our good Day done—
I guard My Master's Head—
15 'Tis better than the Eider-Duck's
Deep Pillow—to have shared—

To foe of His—I'm deadly foe—
None stir the second time—
On whom I lay a Yellow Eye—
20 Or an emphatic Thumb—

Though I than He—may longer live
He longer must—than I—

For I have but the power to kill,
Without—the power to die—
                    ca. 1863

• How does Dickinson set up and then defy the reader's expectations through the poem's controlling metaphor—the speaker's life as a loaded gun? How do the poem's quirks (e.g., the jerky rhythm, the strange syntax, the slant rhymes) contribute to its overall effect?

[After great pain, a formal feeling comes—]

After great pain, a formal feeling comes—
The Nerves sit ceremonious, like Tombs—
The stiff Heart questions was it He, that bore,
And Yesterday, or Centuries before?

5   The Feet, mechanical, go round—
Of Ground, or Air, or Ought—
A Wooden way
Regardless grown,
A Quartz contentment, like a stone—

10   This is the Hour of Lead—
Remembered, if outlived,
As Freezing Persons recollect the Snow—
First—Chill—then Stupor—then the letting go—
                    ca. 1862

• What different metaphors and similes are used here, and what does each contribute to the poem's portrayal of how we feel "After great pain"?

WENDY COPE

Emily Dickinson

Higgledy-piggledy
Emily Dickinson
Liked to use dashes
Instead of full stops.

5   Nowadays, faced with such
Idiosyncrasy,
Critics and editors
Send for the cops.
                    1986

- What does the use of dactyls (each metrical foot consisting of a stressed syllable followed by two unstressed syllables) contribute to this poem? How do this meter and the poem's other formal features underscore its depiction of both Dickinson's poetry and the attitudes of modern poetry's "Critics and editors"? (line 7)

HART CRANE

To Emily Dickinson

You who desired so much—in vain to ask—
Yet fed you hunger like an endless task,
Dared dignify the labor, bless the quest—
Achieved that stillness ultimately best,

5   Being, of all, least sought for: Emily, hear!
O sweet, dead Silencer, most suddenly clear
When singing that Eternity possessed
And plundered momently in every breast;

—Truly no flower yet withers in your hand.
10 The harvest you described and understand
Needs more than wit to gather, love to bind.
Some reconcilement of remotest mind—

Leaves Ormus rubyless, and Ophir[3] chill.
Else tears heap all within one clay-cold hill.

1927

- How does the speaker characterize Emily Dickinson in the first five lines of the poem? What does the second stanza suggest about the nature of her poetry? How does the poem's form contribute to its characterization of Dickinson and her work?

Emily Dickinson: A Chronology

1830   Dickinson is born on December 10 in Amherst, Massachusetts, second of the three children of Emily Norcross Dickinson and Edward Dickinson, son of the founder of Amherst College and himself a treasurer of the college, as well as a lawyer.

1841   After attending two local primary schools, Dickinson enters Amherst Academy; one of her teachers will later describe her "as a very bright, but rather delicate and frail-looking girl; an excellent scholar; of exemplary deportment, faithful in all school duties; but somewhat shy and nervous." "Her compositions," he added, "were strikingly original."

---

3. Both Ormus and Ophir were cities in the Middle East legendary for their wealth and luxury.

1842–43 Dickinson's father serves two terms as a state senator, later serving on the Governor's Executive Council (1846–47).

1844 After the death of a cousin, a distraught thirteen-year-old Dickinson is sent on a monthlong visit to her aunt in Boston.

1847 Dickinson leaves Amherst Academy for one year at Mount Holyoke Female Seminary (later Mount Holyoke College).

1852 Dickinson publishes the first of seven of her poems to appear anonymously in the local *Springfield Daily Republican*, a newspaper with Liberal, abolitionist leanings.

1853–55 Dickinson's father serves in the U.S. Congress; in Spring 1855, Dickinson visits Washington, DC, with her father and sister, spending time with a cousin in Philadelphia on the way home. In 1855, her elder brother, Austin, declares himself "saved," and Emily becomes the only member of her immediate family not to undergo a similar religious experience.

1856 Austin Dickinson marries Susan Huntington Gilbert, who will become one of Dickinson's most intimate friends and the recipient of many letters and approximately 90 of her poems—by far the most of any correspondent.

1858 Dickinson meets *Springfield Daily Republican* editor Samuel Bowles, who will become a frequent visitor.

1862 Dickinson initiates a lifelong correspondence with *Atlantic Monthly* literary editor, abolitionist, and feminist Thomas Wentworth Higginson; though she will send many of her poems to Higginson, he advises against their immediate publication.

1864–65 Eye trouble twice sends Dickinson on two extended (six- to seven-month) stays in Cambridgeport, where she is treated by a Boston ophthalmologist. After her return, Dickinson will seldom leave the family home, though she will receive visits from a select group of intimates that includes Higginson, Bowles, and the Reverend Charles Wadsworth.

1874 Dickinson's father dies.

1875 Dickinson's always-frail mother suffers a major stroke; Dickinson (with the help of her younger sister) becomes her bedridden mother's primary caretaker.

1877 After the death of his wife, Judge Otis P. Lord, an old friend, engages Dickinson in what one journalist calls "an astonishingly candid, erotic correspondence," though Dickinson apparently turns down his marriage proposal.

1886 Dickinson dies at age fifty-five in her family's Amherst home on May 15. In an obituary, sister-in-law Susan Dickinson observes, "Very few in the village, except among older inhabitants, knew Miss Emily personally, although the facts of her seclusion and her intellectual brilliancy were familiar Amherst traditions." After Dickinson's death, her sister discovers a cache of almost 1,800 poems, as well as three volumes of letters.

1890 Austin Dickinson's mistress, Mabel Loomis Todd, and Thomas Higginson coedit and publish a posthumous collection of selected poems by Emily Dickinson.

1891   Responding to what he describes as "a constant and earnest demand by [Dickinson's] readers for further information in regard to her," Higginson publishes in *Atlantic Monthly* excerpts from selected letters written by Dickinson.

SUGGESTIONS FOR WRITING

1. One immediately apparent feature of Dickinson's poetry is her rather odd use of punctuation, especially her frequent use of the dash. Write an essay that explains how punctuation contributes to the effect and meaning of at least two of Dickinson's poems.

2. As the introduction to this album notes, Dickinson begins one poem with the command, "Tell all the truth but tell it slant / Success in Circuit lies." Write an essay that explores the various kinds of "circuits" or "circuitousness" at work in at least two of Dickinson's poems and the way such "circuits" contribute to the poems' success.

3. Write an essay explaining the way Dickinson's poetry is characterized in either Wendy Cope's or Hart Crane's poem; be sure to draw on at least one of Dickinson's poems to assess whether, why, and how that characterization seems apt.

W. B. Yeats: An Album

Mad Ireland hurt you into poetry.
—W. H. AUDEN

If it is difficult to make claims about either biographical elements in Emily Dickinson's poems or her poetry's development over time, the opposite seems true of the work of W. B. Yeats. Whereas Dickinson left us guessing about her inner life, the timing and revision of her poems, and her ideas about the nature and goals of her craft, Yeats left us a treasure trove of memoirs, essays, and manuscripts on which to draw. As such, his poetry may well move and speak to us more as we discover more about the author's personal life, experience, ideas, and beliefs; about the order in which the poems were written (and often rewritten); and about the historical events that helped shape both the author and his work. Whereas Dickinson published few poems in her lifetime and soared to fame only after her death, Yeats was a prolific and celebrated, if controversial, public figure who received the Nobel Prize for Literature some 25 years before his death.

William Butler Yeats was born in Dublin in 1865. Though he spent much of his youth in London and is today regarded as one of the greatest **lyric** poets in the English language, he is best known as the preeminent Irish poet of the twentieth century. Well-versed and thoroughly immersed in Irish history, folklore, and politics, Yeats attended art school for a time before devoting himself to writing poetry that was, early in his career, self-consciously dreamy and ethereal. (A great admirer of Percy Bysshe Shelley and William Blake, Yeats once labeled himself "the last Romantic.") Yeats's poems became tighter, more concrete, direct, and passionate with his involvement (mainly through theater) with the Irish nationalist cause, his desperate love for the actress and nationalist Maud Gonne, his exposure to the work of the German philosopher Friedrich Nietzsche, and his friendship with the American poet Ezra Pound. Yeats served as a senator in the newly independent Irish government before withdrawing from active public life to Thoor Ballylee, a crumbling, ancient tower fashioned into a home by Yeats and Georgie Hyde-Lees, the young Englishwoman he ultimately married.

Both Yeats and his work were profoundly shaped by shifts in the character and fortunes of Irish nationalism—both the political movement to liberate Ireland from British control and its cultural cousin, the Irish (or Celtic) Revival, which sought to rejuvenate a distinctively Irish literature and culture. Deeply involved in both movements in a way that his younger countryman, James Joyce, never was (see chapter 9), Yeats nonetheless—at various times and in various ways—found himself in profound conflict with their aims, their methods, and their vision of both art and Ireland. Though he was particularly averse to the idea of art as propaganda, his early poetry and plays draw heavily on the oral folk traditions (and rhythms) to which he was first introduced during childhood visits to County Sligo and which he began to research more seriously after his introduction to Irish nationalists. Though such folk sources would become less important to his later work, Yeats strove throughout his life to preserve and reinvigorate Irish culture.

Yeats was also deeply influenced by events and movements that stretched well beyond his native country, including World War I (1914–18), the spiritualist movement, and the birth of psychology. As Yeats himself recognized, his deep immersion in the occult, as well as his lifelong search for a satisfactory belief system to replace or rejuvenate the Protestant Christianity of his ancestors, was at once a reaction to the materialistic, rationalistic spirit of his age (or what he called "the despotism of fact" that for him culminated in the First World War) and a reaction exceedingly common among the artists and intellectuals of his day. Ultimately, Yeats came to believe fervently in what his contemporary Carl Jung (1875–1961) labeled the "collective unconscious"—a sort of universal memory shared by all human beings—and in the idea that the poet, like the priest, the prophet, and the magician, tapped into the collective unconscious and moved his audience through **symbols**. The comparison between priest and poet is no accident, for Yeats also believed that the arts, including poetry, should perform a quasi-religious function. He claimed in his essay "The Autumn of the Body" (1898) that "The arts are . . . about to take upon their shoulders the burdens that have fallen from the shoulders of priests, and to lead us back upon our journey by filling our thoughts with the essence of things, and not with things." Elsewhere, he declared that he "made a new religion, almost an infallible church of poetic tradition."

Such beliefs shape not only the complex symbolism of Yeats's verse but also its external form. Yeats eschewed the **free verse** popular with his contemporaries at least in part because, as he explains in "The Symbolism of Poetry" (1900),

> The purpose of rhythm . . . is to prolong the moment . . . when we are both asleep and awake, . . . by hushing us with an alluring monotony, which holds us waking by variety, to keep us in that state of perhaps real trance, in which the mind liberated from the pressure of the will is unfolded in symbols. . . . In the making and in the understanding of a work of art, and the more easily if it is full of patterns and symbols and music, we are lured to the threshold of sleep, and it may be far beyond it, without knowing that we have ever set our feet upon the steps of horn or of ivory.

To achieve those incantatory rhythms, Yeats experimented with various meters and verse forms, ranging from **ballad stanza** to **ottava rima**.

The chronology below and the footnotes that accompany the poems will provide you with more information about Yeats, and you may find much more online and in the library. Even without that information, however, you will learn much about Yeats, his art, his beliefs, and the way all three changed over time by closely and carefully reading the poems in this album one by one, paying attention to all that you observe, and talking about them with other readers. As you do so, keep in mind the following questions:

- What patterns can you detect in the poems' rhythm and form, as well as internal structure?
- Where do symbols occur and recur, and what role do they play?
- What vision of art and the artist is conveyed by both the content and the form of these poems?
- Do you agree with those scholars who see dramatic shifts of both form and content from early poems such as "The Lake Isle of Innisfree" (1890) to mid-career poems such as "All Things Can Tempt Me" (1910) and "Easter 1916" (1916) to late poems such as "Leda and the Swan" (1923) and the companion poems "Sailing to Byzantium" (1923) and "Byzantium" (1927)?
- If you do detect three distinct phases and kinds of poems here, then do you think "The Second Coming" (1919) fits more with the poems of Yeats's

second or middle phase, or more with those of his third or late phase? Why and how so?

• If you see all the poems as more alike than different, what are the features that make them both alike and distinctive?

The Lake Isle of Innisfree[1]

I will arise and go now, and go to Innisfree,
And a small cabin build there, of clay and wattles made,
Nine bean-rows will I have there, a hive for the honey-bee,
And live alone in the bee-loud glade.

5 And I shall have some peace there, for peace comes dropping slow,
Dropping from the veils of the morning to where the cricket sings;
There midnight's all a glimmer, and noon a purple glow,
And evening full of the linnet's wings.

I will arise and go now, for always night and day
10 I hear lake water lapping with low sounds by the shore;
While I stand on the roadway, or on the pavements grey,
I hear it in the deep heart's core.

1890

• Why does the speaker vow to go to Innisfree, and how does the life he imagines living there compare to the one he is now living? In what ways might his imagined future seem like a return to the past (his own or humanity's)?

Authors on Their Work: W. B. YEATS

From *The Trembling of the Veil* (1922)*

Sometimes I told myself very adventurous love-stories with myself for hero, and at other times I planned out a life of lonely austerity, and at other times mixed the ideals and planned a life of lonely austerity mitigated by periodical lapses. I had still the ambition, formed in Sligo in my teens, of living in imitation of Thoreau on Innisfree, a little island in Lough Gill, and when walking through Fleet Street very homesick I heard a little tinkle of water and saw a fountain in a shop-window which balanced a little ball upon its jet, and began to remember lake water. From the sudden remembrance came my poem *Innisfree*, my first

(Continued on next page)

---

1. Island in Lough Gill, County Sligo, Ireland.

(Continued)

lyric with anything in its rhythm of my own music. I had begun to loosen rhythm as an escape from rhetoric and from that emotion of the crowd that rhetoric brings, but I only understood vaguely and occasionally that I must for my special purpose use nothing but the common syntax. A couple of years later I would not have written that first line with its conventional archaism—"Arise and go"—nor the inversion in the last stanza. Passing another day by the new Law Courts . . . I grew suddenly oppressed by the great weight of stone, and thought, "There are miles and miles of stone and brick all round me," and presently added, "If John the Baptist or his like were to come again and had his mind set upon it, he could make all these people go out into some wilderness leaving their buildings empty," and that thought, which does not seem very valuable now, so enlightened the day that it is still vivid in the memory. . . .

* W. B. Yeats, *The Autobiography of William Butler Yeats* (New York: Macmillan, 1953), p. 94. Print. In this excerpt from his autobiography, Yeats describes the period in the 1880s when he was in his twenties and living in London with his family.

All Things Can Tempt Me

All things can tempt me from this craft of verse:
One time it was a woman's face, or worse—
The seeming needs of my fool-driven land;
Now nothing but comes readier to the hand
5 Than this accustomed toil. When I was young,
I had not given a penny for a song
Did not the poet sing it with such airs
That one believed he had a sword upstairs;
Yet would be now, could I but have my wish,
10 Colder and dumber and deafer than a fish.

1910

- In his commentary on "The Lake Isle of Innisfree" (see "Authors on Their Work," above), Yeats suggests that over time he abandoned the archaic language and syntax, as well as subject matter, of his early verse. How might (or might not) "All Things Can Tempt Me" both exemplify and comment on that shift? How do diction and syntax contribute to the poem's effect?

Easter 1916[2]

I have met them at close of day
Coming with vivid faces
From counter or desk among gray
Eighteenth-century houses.
5 I have passed with a nod of the head
Or polite meaningless words,
Or have lingered awhile and said
Polite meaningless words,
And thought before I had done
10 Of a mocking tale or a gibe
To please a companion
Around the fire at the club,
Being certain that they and I
But lived where motley is worn:
15 All changed, changed utterly:
A terrible beauty is born.

That woman's[3] days were spent
In ignorant good-will,
Her nights in argument
20 Until her voice grew shrill.
What voice more sweet than hers
When, young and beautiful,
She rode to harriers?
This man[4] had kept a school
25 And rode our wingèd horse;[5]
This other[6] his helper and friend
Was coming into his force;
He might have won fame in the end,
So sensitive his nature seemed,
30 So daring and sweet his thought.
This other man[7] I had dreamed
A drunken, vainglorious lout.
He had done most bitter wrong

2. On Easter Monday, 1916, nationalist leaders proclaimed an Irish Republic. After a week of street fighting, the British government put down the Easter Rebellion and executed a number of prominent nationalists, including the four mentioned in lines 75–76, all of whom Yeats knew personally.
3. Countess Constance Georgina Markiewicz, a beautiful and well-born young woman from County Sligo who became a vigorous and bitter nationalist. At first she was condemned to death, but her sentence was later commuted to life imprisonment, and she was granted amnesty in 1917.
4. Patrick Pearse, who led the assault on the Dublin Post Office, from which the proclamation of a republic was issued. A schoolmaster by profession, he had vigorously supported the restoration of the Gaelic language in Ireland and was an active political writer and poet.
5. The mythological Pegasus, a traditional symbol of poetic inspiration.
6. Thomas MacDonagh, also a writer and teacher.
7. Major John MacBride, who had married Yeats's beloved Maud Gonne in 1903 but separated from her two years later.

To some who are near my heart,
35　Yet I number him in the song;
He, too, has resigned his part
In the casual comedy;
He, too, has been changed in his turn,
Transformed utterly:
40　A terrible beauty is born.

Hearts with one purpose alone
Through summer and winter seem
Enchanted to a stone
To trouble the living stream.
45　The horse that comes from the road,
The rider, the birds that range
From cloud to tumbling cloud,
Minute by minute they change;
A shadow of cloud on the stream
50　Changes minute by minute;
A horse-hoof slides on the brim,
And a horse plashes within it;
The long-legged moor-hens dive,
And hens to moor-cocks call;
55　Minute by minute they live:
The stone's in the midst of all.

Too long a sacrifice
Can make a stone of the heart.
O when may it suffice?
60　That is Heaven's part, our part
To murmur name upon name,
As a mother names her child
When sleep at last has come
On limbs that had run wild.
65　What is it but nightfall?
No, no, not night but death;
Was it needless death after all?
For England may keep faith[8]
For all that is done and said.
70　We know their dream; enough
To know they dreamed and are dead;
And what if excess of love
Bewildered them till they died?
I write it out in a verse—
75　MacDonagh and MacBride
And Connolly[9] and Pearse
Now and in time to be,
Wherever green is worn,

8. Before the uprising, the English had promised eventual home rule to Ireland.
9. James Connolly, the leader of the Easter uprising.

Are changed, changed utterly;
80　A terrible beauty is born.

1916

- The phrase "A terrible beauty is born" becomes a kind of **refrain** in this poem. What does the poem suggest about why the events of Easter 1916 and the kind of political passion and commitment that went into it were both "terrible" and "beautiful" at the same time? What do the stone and the stream seem to symbolize?

The Second Coming[1]

Turning and turning in the widening gyre[2]
The falcon cannot hear the falconer;
Things fall apart; the center cannot hold;
Mere anarchy is loosed upon the world,
5　The blood-dimmed tide is loosed, and everywhere
The ceremony of innocence is drowned;
The best lack all conviction, while the worst
Are full of passionate intensity.
Surely some revelation is at hand;
10　Surely the Second Coming is at hand.
The Second Coming! Hardly are those words out
When a vast image out of *Spiritus Mundi*[3]
Troubles my sight: somewhere in sands of the desert
A shape with lion body and the head of a man,
15　A gaze blank and pitiless as the sun,
Is moving its slow thighs, while all about it
Reel shadows of the indignant desert birds.[4]
The darkness drops again; but now I know
That twenty centuries of stony sleep
20　Were vexed to nightmare by a rocking cradle,
And what rough beast, its hour come round at last,
Slouches towards Bethlehem to be born?

January 1919

1. The Second Coming of Christ, according to Matthew 24.29–44, will follow a time of "tribulation." Disillusioned by Ireland's continued civil strife, Yeats saw his time as the end of another historical cycle. In *A Vision* (1937), Yeats describes his view of history as dependent on cycles of about two thousand years: the birth of Christ had ended the cycle of Greco-Roman civilization, and now the Christian cycle seemed near an end, to be followed by an antithetical cycle, ominous in its portents.
2. Literally, the widening spiral of a falcon's flight. "Gyre" is Yeats's term for a cycle of history, which he diagrammed as a series of interpenetrating cones.
3. Or *Anima Mundi* (Latin), the spirit or soul of the world. Yeats considered this universal consciousness or memory a fund from which poets drew their images and symbols.
4. Yeats later wrote of the "brazen winged beast . . . described in my poem *The Second Coming*" as "associated with laughing, ecstatic destruction."

- What vision of the contemporary world is implied by the metaphors in the poem's first half? What vision of its future is suggested in the poem's second half?

Leda and the Swan[5]

A sudden blow: the great wings beating still
Above the staggering girl, her thighs caressed
By the dark webs, her nape caught in his bill,
He holds her helpless breast upon his breast.

5　How can those terrified vague fingers push
The feathered glory from her loosening thighs?
And how can body, laid in that white rush,
But feel the strange heart beating where it lies?

A shudder in the loins engenders there
10　The broken wall, the burning roof and tower
And Agamemnon dead.
　　　　　　　　　　Being so caught up,
So mastered by the brute blood of the air,
Did she put on his knowledge with his power
Before the indifferent beak could let her drop?

　　　　　　　　　　　　　　1923

- If "The Second Coming" predicts the end of one historical cycle and its governing (Christian) myth, "Leda and the Swan" imagines the beginning of the preceding cycle. How does the poem characterize that beginning? Might we again have here a kind of "terrible beauty"? How would you paraphrase the question the speaker poses at the end? Why might questions in general loom so large in this poem?

Sailing to Byzantium[6]

I

That[7] is no country for old men. The young
In one another's arms, birds in the trees
—Those dying generations—at their song,

---

5. According to Greek myth, Zeus took the form of a swan to rape Leda, who became the mother of Helen of Troy; of Castor; and also of Clytemnestra, Agamemnon's wife and murderer. Helen's abduction from her husband, Menelaus, brother of Agamemnon, began the Trojan War (line 10). Yeats described the visit of Zeus to Leda as an annunciation like that to Mary (see Luke 1.26–38); "I imagine the annunciation that founded Greece as made to Leda" (*A Vision*).

6. Ancient name of Istanbul, the capital and holy city of Eastern Christendom from the late fourth century until 1453. It was famous for its stylized and formal mosaics; its symbolic, nonnaturalistic art; and its highly developed intellectual life. Yeats repeatedly uses it to symbolize a world of artifice and timelessness, free from the decay and death of the natural and sensual world.

7. Ireland, as an instance of the natural, temporal world.

The salmon-falls, the mackerel-crowded seas,
5   Fish, flesh, or fowl, commend all summer long
Whatever is begotten, born, and dies.
Caught in that sensual music all neglect
Monuments of unaging intellect.

II

An aged man is but a paltry thing,
10 A tattered coat upon a stick, unless
Soul clap its hands and sing, and louder sing
For every tatter in its mortal dress,
Nor is there singing school but studying
Monuments of its own magnificence;
15 And therefore I have sailed the seas and come
To the holy city of Byzantium.

III

O sages standing in God's holy fire
As in the gold mosaic of a wall,
Come from the holy fire, perne in a gyre,[8]
20 And be the singing-masters of my soul.
Consume my heart away; sick with desire
And fastened to a dying animal
It knows not what it is; and gather me
Into the artifice of eternity.

IV

25 Once out of nature I shall never take
My bodily form from any natural thing,
But such a form as Grecian goldsmiths make
Of hammered gold and gold enameling
To keep a drowsy Emperor awake;[9]
30 Or set upon a golden bough[1] to sing
To lords and ladies of Byzantium
Of what is past, or passing, or to come.

                                        1927

- Like "The Lake Isle of Innisfree," this poem focuses on an imaginary journey and on a contrast between then and there versus here and now, yet this poem deals much more directly with the subject of art and especially of poetry or song: what it might be like, where it might come from, what it might do for us. How does this poem both pose and answer those questions?

---

8. That is, whirl in a coiling motion, so that his soul may merge with its motion as the timeless world invades the cycles of history and nature. "Perne" is Yeats's coinage (from the noun *pirn*): to spin around in the kind of spiral pattern that thread makes as it comes off a bobbin or spool.
9. "I have read somewhere that in the Emperor's palace at Byzantium was a tree made of gold and silver, and artificial birds that sang" [Yeats's note].
1. In Book 6 of the *Aeneid,* the sibyl tells Aeneas that he must pluck a golden bough from a nearby tree in order to descend to Hades. Each time Aeneas plucks the one such branch there, an identical one takes its place.

Byzantium

The unpurged images of day recede;
The Emperor's drunken soldiery are abed;
Night resonance recedes, night-walkers' song
After great cathedral gong;
5 A starlit or a moonlit dome[2] disdains
All that man is,
All mere complexities,
The fury and the mire of human veins.

Before me floats an image, man or shade,
10 Shade more than man, more image than a shade;
For Hades' bobbin bound in mummy-cloth
May unwind the winding path;
A mouth that has no moisture and no breath
Breathless mouths may summon;
15 I hail the superhuman;
I call it death-in-life and life-in-death.

Miracle, bird or golden handiwork,
More miracle than bird or handiwork,
Planted on the star-lit golden bough
20 Can like the cocks of Hades crow,[3]
Or, by the moon embittered, scorn aloud
In glory of changeless metal
Common bird or petal
And all complexities of mire or blood.

25 At midnight on the Emperor's pavement flit
Flames that no faggot[4] feeds, nor steel has lit,
Nor storm disturbs, flames begotten of flame,
Where blood-begotten spirits come
And all complexities of fury leave,
30 Dying into a dance,
An agony of trance,
An agony of flame that cannot singe a sleeve.

Astraddle on the dolphin's mire and blood,[5]
Spirit after spirit! The smithies break the flood,
35 The golden smithies of the Emperor!
Marbles of the dancing floor
Break bitter furies of complexity,
Those images that yet

2. According to Yeats's philosophy, the full moon ("moonlit") represents the mind "completely absorbed in being."   3. As the bird of dawn, the cock has from antiquity symbolized rebirth and resurrection.
4. Bundle of sticks used as fuel.
5. In ancient art, dolphins symbolize the soul moving from one state to another, and sometimes they provide a vehicle for the dead.

Fresh images beget,
40 That dolphin-torn, that gong-tormented sea.

1932

• What might this poem suggest about the nature, sources, and functions of art? Why might it be important that it begins as "day
recede[s]" (line 1)? that the mechanical bird that also appears in
"Sailing to Byzantium" is here described as "More miracle than bird
or handiwork" (line 18)?

W. H. AUDEN

In Memory of W. B. Yeats

(d. January, 1939)

I

He disappeared in the dead of winter:
The brooks were frozen, the airports almost deserted,
And snow disfigured the public statues;
The mercury sank in the mouth of the dying day.
5 What instruments we have agree
The day of his death was a dark cold day.

Far from his illness
The wolves ran on through the evergreen forests,
The peasant river was untempted by the fashionable quays;
10 By mourning tongues
The death of the poet was kept from his poems.

But for him it was his last afternoon as himself,
An afternoon of nurses and rumors;
The provinces of his body revolted,
15 The squares of his mind were empty,
Silence invaded the suburbs,
The current of his feeling failed; he became his admirers.

Now he is scattered among a hundred cities
And wholly given over to unfamiliar affections,
20 To find his happiness in another kind of wood
And be punished under a foreign code of conscience.
The words of a dead man
Are modified in the guts of the living.

But in the importance and noise of tomorrow
25 When the brokers are roaring like beasts on the floor of the Bourse,[6]
And the poor have the sufferings to which they are fairly accustomed,
And each in the cell of himself is almost convinced of his freedom,

6. The Paris stock exchange.

A few thousand will think of this day
As one thinks of a day when one did something slightly unusual.
30 What instruments we have agree
The day of his death was a dark cold day.

II

You were silly like us; your gift survived it all:
The parish of rich women, physical decay,
Yourself. Mad Ireland hurt you into poetry.
35 Now Ireland has her madness and her weather still,
For poetry makes nothing happen: it survives
In the valley of its making where executives
Would never want to tamper, flows on south
From ranches of isolation and the busy griefs,
40 Raw towns that we believe and die in; it survives,
A way of happening, a mouth.

III

Earth, receive an honored guest:
William Yeats is laid to rest.
Let the Irish vessel lie
45 Emptied of its poetry.

In the nightmare of the dark
All the dogs of Europe bark,
And the living nations wait,
Each sequestered in its hate;

50 Intellectual disgrace
Stares from every human face,
And the seas of pity lie
Locked and frozen in each eye.

Follow, poet, follow right
55 To the bottom of the night,
With your unconstraining voice
Still persuade us to rejoice;

With the farming of a verse
Make a vineyard of the curse,
60 Sing of human unsuccess
In a rapture of distress;

In the deserts of the heart
Let the healing fountain start,
In the prison of his days
65 Teach the free man how to praise.

1939

• **Does Auden's *elegy* as a whole affirm that "poetry makes nothing happen" (line 36)? Why does the death of Yeats specifically seem to inspire the speaker to reflect on this possibility?**

W. B. Yeats and His Times: A Chronology

1865   William Butler Yeats is born on June 13 in Dublin, Ireland, the eldest child of Susan Pollexfen Yeats, the daughter of a successful merchant, and the well-known, but often financially strapped, lawyer-turned-painter John Butler Yeats; though both of his parents are of Protestant descent, W. B. Yeats's father is a religious skeptic who adopts the "religion of art."

1867   To further his career as an artist, John Yeats moves his family to London.

1872   Yeats, with his mother and siblings, spends two years at his maternal grandparents' home in Sligo, on Ireland's rural west coast.

1874   Yeats returns to London with his family and attends the Godolphin School.

1880   Financial difficulties force John Yeats to move his family back to Dublin, where his eldest son attends a local high school.

1884   Yeats enters Dublin's Metropolitan School of Art, where he will study until 1886. With fellow writer and art student George Russell (known as "A.E."), Yeats will begin his research into spiritualism and the occult and go on to found the Dublin Hermetic Society.

1885   Yeats meets Irish nationalist leader John O'Leary and, in part with O'Leary's help, publishes his first poems in the *Dublin University Review*. (In a 1907 essay, Yeats will describe O'Leary as championing the "romantic" and "idealistic" "conception of Irish nationality . . . in whose service I labour.")

1887   Yeats returns to London with his family and edits the anthology *Poems and Ballads of Young Ireland*.

1888   Yeats joins the spiritualist Theosophical Society and edits *Fairy and Folk Tales of the Irish Peasantry*.

1889   Yeats publishes his first volume of poetry, *The Wanderings of Oisin and Other Poems*, and meets and falls in love with the actress and Irish revolutionary Maud Gonne.

1891   Gonne rejects the first of at least three marriage proposals from Yeats.

1892   Yeats and others found the London-based Irish Literary Society, and Yeats publishes *The Countess Cathleen and Various Legends and Lyrics*, a collection of plays and poems.

1893   Yeats publishes an edition of the poems of William Blake and a prose work, *The Celtic Twilight*.

1895   Yeats publishes *Poems*, which includes a thorough revision of works previously published in his first two collections and which is sometimes said to mark the end of his early period.

1896   Yeats meets fellow writer and Irish Revivalist Lady Augusta Gregory and begins to spend holidays at her estate, Coole Park, in rural County Galway, Ireland.

1899   Yeats and Lady Gregory found the Irish Literary Theatre, later called the Abbey Theatre, in Dublin, which produces his *Countess Cathleen*.

1902 Maud Gonne stars in Yeats's *Cathleen ni Houlihan*.

1903 Gonne marries war veteran John MacBride.

1904 Yeats's so-called middle period arguably begins with the publication of the collection *In the Seven Woods*. He begins a six-year stint as manager of the Abbey Theatre, a position that brings him in conflict both with conservative, especially middle-class, Catholics offended by the supposed immorality and impiety of Abbey productions and also with Irish nationalists who believe Abbey plays should promote a wholly positive view of Irish people, history, and culture.

1907 An Abbey performance of J. M. Synge's *The Playboy of the Western World* sparks riots over its supposedly negative portrayal of the Irish.

1913 Yeats spends the first of three winters with the young American poet Ezra Pound.

1914 World War I begins (in August). Yeats publishes *Responsibilities*, his first pointedly modernist, as well as avowedly public and political, poetry collection.

1916 In London, Yeats debuts *At the Hawk's Well*, the first of his plays influenced by Japanese Noh drama (rather than Irish history and legend), and publishes *Reveries of Childhood and Youth*, the first volume of his autobiography. In April, Irish nationalists stage the Easter Uprising in Dublin. Proclaiming Ireland an independent republic, the 700 volunteers are defeated by British troops after a week of bloody fighting; their leaders, including John MacBride, are executed for treason in May. Yeats proposes to Maud Gonne for the last time.

1917 The Russian Revolution begins, and T. S. Eliot publishes his first poetry collection, which includes *The Love Song of J. Afred Prufrock* and which, Yeats later claimed, announces the birth of a new, self-consciously "modern" poetry that he "disliked" and yet admired for its "satiric intensity." Yeats marries Georgie Hyde-Lees; while still on their honeymoon, Georgie begins to perform the spirit-inspired automatic writing that will be the basis for the cosmology that Yeats would later elaborate in *A Vision* (1925; see below).

1918 World War I ends. Yeats and his wife move to Thoor (literally, "Castle") Ballylee, an ancient Norman tower near Lady Gregory's estate; the tower and its winding staircase will become a central symbol in his later poetry.

1919 In January, Russian revolutionaries kill four grand dukes, bringing to 17 the number of members of the former Russian emperor's family to die in the revolution. Yeats writes "The Second Coming" and publishes *The Wild Swans at Coole*, the last collection of his so-called middle period. His first child, a daughter, is born in Dublin. Ireland enters a period of civil unrest.

1921 A truce brings temporary peace to Ireland. Yeats's second child, a son, is born, and Yeats publishes the poetry collection *Michael Robartes and the Dancer* (1921).

1922 The Irish Civil War begins. Yeats's father dies. Yeats publishes *The Trembling of the Veil*, the second volume of his autobiography, and begins his six-year stint as a senator in the first Irish government, defending the rights of the Protestant minority, championing preservation of Ireland's cultural heritage, and opposing censorship.

1923 Yeats receives the Nobel Prize for Literature.

1925 Yeats publishes *A Vision*, a work of nonfiction, based on his wife's spirit-inspired automatic writing, that explains his system of symbols and cyclical vision of history.

1928 Yeats publishes *The Tower* and resigns from the Irish Senate.

1933 Yeats publishes *The Winding Stair and Other Poems*.

1939 At 73, Yeats dies in France on January 28. World War II begins.

1948 Yeats's remains are returned to Ireland and buried in County Sligo under a stone bearing the epitaph he composed: "Cast a cold eye / On Life, on Death. / Horseman, pass by!"

SUGGESTIONS FOR WRITING

1. Write an essay in which you compare "The Lake Isle of Innisfree" (the earliest poem in the album) and "Sailing to Byzantium" (one of the last) in order to show how Yeats's poetry both did and didn't change over the course of his career. How might the first of these poems seem like the work of a young man and poet, and the latter like that of a mature one?

2. Write an essay that explains the significance of any one recurring image or symbol, or set of related images or symbols, in at least two Yeats poems. Alternatively, use your essay to explore why terror and beauty seem to go together in Yeats's poems.

3. Drawing on at least three poems by Yeats, write an essay explaining whether and how his poetry seems distinctly "Irish." How, for example, might the troubled history of his native country or his own troubled relationship to Irish nationalism, as well as the middle-class Irish public, be explored in the poems, including the later ones that outwardly seem resolutely non-Irish in content and form?

4. Write an essay comparing the way W. H. Auden's poem about Yeats portrays the nature, source, and function of poetry to the way Yeats's poems, such as "Sailing to Byzantium," do. Alternatively, compare the way each poet handles the contrast between physical, mortal life and "decay" (Auden, line 33), on the one hand, and the life lived in the imagination and poetry. Do both poets seem to agree about the immortality and importance of poetry?

Pat Mora: An Album

A ward-winning contemporary writer Pat Mora was born in 1942 in El Paso, Texas, a city on the Mexican border to which all four of her Spanish-speaking grandparents migrated during the Mexican Revolution. After earning a B.A. and M.A. from the University of Texas, El Paso, she taught both high-school and college English but did not devote herself seriously to writing until after her 1981 divorce, when, as she once joked to an interviewer, "I saw the age of forty coming at me." In the years since, she has seen her three children into adulthood, remarried, and left Texas for Cincinnati, Ohio, and Santa Fe, New Mexico (her two current homes). She has also flourished as a writer, publishing six collections of poetry, including *Chants* (1984), *Borders* (1986), *Agua Santa/Holy Water* (1995), *Aunt Carmen's Book of Practical Saints* (1997), and *Adobe Odes* (2007); a book of essays, *Nepantla: Essays from the Land in the Middle* (1993); a family memoir, *House of Houses* (1997); and some twenty-five books for children and young adults, including poetry, picture books, biographies, and retellings of Mayan folktales.

Avowing that she "take[s] pride in being a Hispanic writer," Mora sees her work for both children and adults as bound up with the effort to promote literacy, a wider knowledge and appreciation of Hispanic culture and heritage, and cross-cultural understanding. In *Nepantla* she likens the work of the poet to that of the *curandera*, or traditional healer, sounding not unlike the Irish poet W. B. Yeats when she argues that

> The Chicana writer seeks to heal cultural wounds of historical neglect by providing opportunities to remember the past, to share and ease bitterness, to describe what has been viewed as unworthy of description, to cure by incantations and rhythms, by listening with her entire being and responding. She then gathers the tales and myths, weaves them together, and, if lucky, casts spells.

Though she makes frequent use of Spanish terms and phrases in all her work, Mora writes primarily in English largely because she is, in her own words, "bilingual, though English-dominant," living on the figurative border between languages and cultures or in what she calls "the land in the middle." Much of her work explores that land. Yet in interviews, Mora roundly rejects the idea that the experience of living "in the middle" is necessarily negative. Rather she insists that, while "there are situations where, yes, it's plenty difficult" or where she is uncertain about where she belongs or who she is, there is also a flip side: "it's double pleasure in a way," and she enjoys "the advantage of moving back and forth." As Mora also suggests, people from all backgrounds "experience borders of many kinds throughout life." And by exploring some of these divides—between, for example, men and women or different generations—Mora's work stresses the ubiquity and even universality of the border experience, as well as the pleasures and conflicts it entails.

Literal, physical borders and space and place in general also intrigue Mora— all the more, she suggests, since a 1989 move from the Southwest to the Midwest heightened her awareness of the distinctiveness of her native landscape and her own relationship to it. Whenever she flew West, she explained to one interviewer,

> I would look out at this tremendous space and think how totally I felt at home there. Many of my Midwestern friends would confide to me that they found the desert sometimes even terrifying. I remember one of the brightest women I know who is an academic in Cincinnati said to me that the first time she came to the Southwest she

was afraid she would fall off because she was so used to the protection of trees. . . .
Our early geography shapes us in complex ways.

Geography, landscape, and the immigrant experience are only some of the
many things you will find to explore in Mora's poems, including those gathered
in this album and "Sonrisas" (chapter 18). What might her poems individually
and collectively suggest about what both is and isn't unique about the Mexican
American experience? about the positive and negative aspects of living "in the
land of the middle"? about what unites and divides Mexican Americans of different classes, generations, and genders? about family? about the power and the
limits of language? In what ways might Mora's poems perform the *curandera*-like
work she ascribes to the poet in *Nepantla*?

Elena

My Spanish isn't enough.
I remember how I'd smile
listening to my little ones,
understanding every word they'd say,
5   their jokes, their songs, their plots.
 Vamos a pedirle dulces a mamá. Vamos.[1]
But that was in Mexico.
Now my children go to American high schools.
They speak English. At night they sit around
10 the kitchen table, laugh with one another.
I stand by the stove and feel dumb, alone.
I bought a book to learn English.
My husband frowned, drank more beer.
My oldest said, "*Mamá*, he doesn't want you
15 to be smarter than he is." I'm forty,
embarrassed at mispronouncing words,
embarrassed at the laughter of my children,
the grocer, the mailman. Sometimes I take
my English book and lock myself in the bathroom,
20 say the thick words softly,
for if I stop trying, I will be deaf
when my children need my help.

1985

- What does the speaker mean by the first line—"My Spanish isn't
  enough"? What other words in the poem address the inadequacy of
  language?

1. "Let's go ask mama for sweets. Let's go" (Spanish).

Gentle Communion

Even the long-dead are willing to move.
Without a word, she came with me from the desert.
Mornings she wanders through my rooms
making beds, folding socks.

5 Since she can't hear me anymore,
Mamande[2] ignores the questions I never knew
to ask, about her younger days, her red
hair, the time she fell and broke her nose
in the snow. I will never know.

10 When I try to make her laugh,
to disprove her sad album face, she leaves
the room, resists me as she resisted
grinning for cameras, make-up, English.

While I write, she sits and prays,
15 feet apart, legs never crossed,
the blue housecoat buttoned high
as her hair dries white, girlish
around her head and shoulders.

She closes her eyes, bows her head,
20 and like a child presses her hands together,
her patient flesh steeple, the skin
worn, like the pages of her prayer book.

Sometimes I sit in her wide-armed
chair as I once sat in her lap.
25 Alone, we played a quiet I Spy.
She peeled grapes I still taste.

She removes the thin skin, places
the luminous coolness on my tongue.
I know not to bite or chew. I wait
30 for the thick melt,
our private green honey.

1991

- How does this poem draw on the various meanings of the word
  communion? Why might it be significant that the grandmother comes
  "Without a word" (line 2)?

---

2. Child's conflation of *mama grande* (Spanish for "grandmother").

Mothers and Daughters

The arm-in-arm-mother-daughter-stroll
in villages and shopping malls
evenings and weekends
the w a l k - t a l k slow,
5   arm-in-arm
            around the world.

Sometimes they feed one another
memories sweet as hot bread
and lemon tea. Sometimes it's mother-stories
the young one can't remember:

10   "When you were new, I'd nest you
in one arm, while I cooked,
whisper, what am I to do with you?"

Sometimes it's tug
-of-war that started in the womb
15   the fight for space
the sharp jab deep inside
as the weight shifts,
arm-in-arm
            around the world

always the bodytalk thick,
20   always the recipes
hints for feeding
more with less.

                                    1991

- How does the poem's form, especially its visual appearance and
  rhythm, contribute to its characterization of the mother–daughter
  relationship?

La Migra

                    I
Let's play *La Migra*[3]
I'll be the Border Patrol.
You be the Mexican maid.
I get the badge and sunglasses.
5   You can hide and run,
but you can't get away
because I have a jeep

3. Mexican slang for U.S. border patrol agents (an abbreviation of the word "immigration").

I can take you wherever
I want, but don't ask
10 questions because
I don't speak Spanish.
I can touch you wherever
I want but don't complain
too much because I've got
15 boots and kick—if I have to,
and I have handcuffs.
Oh, and a gun.
Get ready, get set, run.

II

Let's play *La Migra*
20 You be the Border Patrol.
I'll be the Mexican woman.
Your jeep has a flat,
and you have been spotted
by the sun.
25 All you have is heavy: hat,
glasses, badge, shoes, gun.
I know this desert,
where to rest,
where to drink.
30 Oh, I am not alone.
You hear us singing
and laughing with the wind,
Agua dulce brota aquí,
aquí, aquí,[4] but since you
35 can't speak Spanish,
you do not understand.
Get ready.

1993

• Who seems to be the speaker of this poem, or are there more than
one? What is the game of "hide and run" the speaker proposes (line
5)? Who will win?

Ode to Adobe

Your blue mouth,
door of a thousand river-rolled stories,
opens.
Walls whisper,
5   voices of earth and straw.

4. Sweet water springs here, here, here.

Clay flower,
each of your rooms welcomes
  like a wish,
tastes a different color—
10   mango, papaya, persimmon, quince.
In your nichos,[5] Santa Rita and San Judas,
  patron saints of the impossible,
shake their heads,
    gossip
15 about an aunt's pastel
  lust, while they pretend to pray.

Mud song,
growing to your interior music,
  dream cave,
20 honey-hive shaped by a choir
  of muddy hands,
ballad of eloquent bricks,
  kitchen of unending banquets,
beans simmering for centuries,
25   sun-baked loaf, you rise
    from the desert into a luminaria.[6]

Traditional adobe dwelling found in the Southwestern United States
and northern Mexico.

5. Small shelves carved into a wall. *Santa Rita*: Known as the patroness of impossible causes, Italian-born Saint Rita (1381–1457) was mistreated for twenty years by the husband her parents forced her to marry and entered a convent after both he and her two sons died. *Saint Judas*: One of Jesus's twelve apostles, St. Jude Thaddeus is considered the patron saint of desperate causes because his New Testament letter stresses that the faithful should persevere in the face of harsh, difficult circumstances.
6. Traditional Mexican Christmas lantern originally made by setting a candle inside a paper bag weighted with sand.

Serenata de barro,
cantadora de la tierra,[7]
    our hands stroke you, wrinkled
      and delicious,
30 smell the layered legacy
      that shelters us in the arms
        of candle and piñon smoke.

Your melodies, washed and ironed
    by generations of mothers,
35   drift out,
  lure departed spirits home again
    to dream in the crackle
      of kiva[8] fireplaces
warmed by sips of humor
40 and old desires, the taste
    of guacamole, the silk
      of skin.

In your candlelit mirror,
eternal vanity:
45 a spirit powders her bony nose.

                        2006

- To what is the adobe compared in the poem? How do these comparisons together characterize both the adobe and the life lived within it?

Pat Mora: A Chronology

1942   Pat Mora is born on January 19 in El Paso, Texas, to Raul Antonio Mora, an optician, and his wife, Estela; both are bilingual, second-generation El Pasoans of Mexican descent.

1963   Mora marries William H. Burnside Jr., with whom she will ultimately have a son and two daughters; earns her B.A. from Texas Western College (now the University of Texas, El Paso); and begins a three-year stint teaching in the El Paso Independent School District.

1967   Mora earns her M.A. from the University of Texas, El Paso (UTEP).

1971   Mora begins working as a part-time English and communications instructor at El Paso Community College.

1979   Mora begins working as a part-time English instructor at UTEP.

---

7. Serenader of mud, singer of the popular songs of the earth, land, or soil.
8. Traditional adobe dwellings of the various Pueblo Indian peoples of the Southwestern United States and northern Mexico.

1981   After her first marriage ends in divorce, Mora starts to devote more time to writing, while also working as assistant to UTEP's vice president of academic affairs.

1984   Mora marries Vernon Lee Scarborough, an archaeologist teaching at UTEP.

1988   Mora becomes director of UTEP's natural history museum and assistant to the university's president.

1989   Mora leaves UTEP to devote herself full-time to writing, lecturing, and promoting literacy; she also moves to the Cincinnati/Northern Kentucky area when her husband joins the anthropology department of the University of Cincinnati. (The couple will make a second home in Santa Fe, New Mexico.)

SUGGESTIONS FOR WRITING

1. Food, cooking, and related imagery figure in many of Mora's poems. Write an essay exploring the significance of such references. What might the poems suggest about the roles food, cooking, and eating play in our lives?
2. Drawing on at least three of Mora's poems, write an essay that explores her vision of the role of language. When, how, and why does language both unite and divide people? When, why, and how might nonverbal forms of communication serve us better?
3. As the introduction to this album suggests, Pat Mora takes pride in being a Latina writer and identifies one of her goals as chronicling the experience and feelings of contemporary Latinos and Latinas. Write an essay in which you compare at least two of Mora's poems, exploring what they together imply about what it is like to be Latino and how that experience differs across generations, classes, and/or genders.
4. The poems reprinted here were originally included in various collections, each of which has a distinct focus and flavor. "Gentle Communion," for example, appears in Mora's third volume, *Communion* (1991), which some critics see as the culmination of the earliest phase of her career and as the reflection of both a widening of the world depicted in her work (through poems inspired by her travels to other countries) and a greater concentration on the situation of women and the relationships among women and between women and men. Pick the Mora poem you like most, identify the collection in which it originally appeared, and read some other poems in that collection. Then write an essay that either compares your chosen poem to others in the collection or that explains how your interpretation of the original poem changes when you read it in the context of the other.

22 THE AUTHOR'S WORK AS CONTEXT: WILLIAM BLAKE'S *SONGS OF INNOCENCE AND OF EXPERIENCE*

Throughout history and across the globe, poets have collected their poems into **sequences** or cycles. The type of poem we today call **haiku**, for instance, emerged out of a tradition in Japanese culture dating back to the middle ages, whereby a single poet would produce a poem of three lines to which other poets would add poems of two and three lines each to create a sequence of thirty-six, one hundred, or even a thousand or more linked poems. Over time, people began to lift out the three-line verse that began such a sequence and to treat it as a poem in its own right, often gathering a number of these to create an anthology of sorts. The popularity of such anthologies in turn inspired poets to begin writing stand-alone poems of this type, which eventually came to be known as haiku. Even Bashō (1644–94), the acknowledged master of the form, published most of his haiku as part of a sequence embedded within a lengthy prose memoir of his extensive travels.

In the Western literary tradition, one common type of poetic sequence is the **sonnet** sequence. Many of the most famous sonnets—from those of Francesco Petrarch (1304–74) and William Shakespeare to those of Elizabeth Barrett Browning and Edna St. Vincent Millay—are part of such sequences. These poems often lack titles; instead we conventionally either use the poems' first lines as titles ("[My mistress's eyes are nothing like the sun]") or number them according to their place in the sequence (Sonnet 130).

Each of the poems in a sequence is itself an independent literary work that can be, and often is, enjoyed and understood on its own. Yet each also functions as part of the larger literary work that is the sequence. We can thus enjoy and understand the poem in quite a different way when we read it in the context of other poems in the sequence, and in light of the traditions of poetic sequences generally.

Today, most poems are too short to be published singly, even if they are not part of a sequence. They may first appear in magazines, newspapers, Web sites, and so forth, and later in books, including both collections of poems by a single writer and anthologies (like the one you are reading) that include the work of various poets. The poems in one poet's collection may be less intimately related to each other than the poems in a sequence, but they usually were written around the same time and provide a window of sorts onto a particular phase of the author's life and career. Further, poems in a collection—even, in rare cases, a collection by multiple authors—often share other features, depicting comparable situations or speakers, or having a similar external form, for example. Though not the same as sequences, such collections can also offer an illuminating context for a particular poem—slightly altering, perhaps expanding, our response and interpretation.

For example, a reader might be tempted to read Margaret Atwood's lyric "Death of a Young Son by Drowning" (chapter 14) as an autobiographical account of the poet's own son's demise unless that reader came to the poem armed with the knowledge that it originally appeared in *The Journals of Susanna Moodie* (1970), a sequence of poems by Atwood that traces the experiences of Susanna Moodie, a nineteenth-century Canadian pioneer. Likewise, Harryette Mullen's wacky and wonderful "Wipe That Simile Off Your Aphasia" (chapter 16) might make a different kind of sense when considered in the context of the collection in which it appeared. Titled *Sleeping with the Dictionary*, that volume is, to quote its publisher, "the . . . offspring of [Mullen's] collaboration with two of the poet's most seductive writing partners, *Roget's Thesaurus* and *The American Heritage Dictionary*." Like entries in both of these reference works, the poems in Mullen's collection are arranged in alphabetical order, and they engage in elaborate word games—acrostic, anagram, homophone, parody, pun—in order to humorously explore the pleasures and perversities of language and the sense and nonsense we make of it. Knowing these facts and even reading other poems in *Sleeping with the Dictionary* might well help you make more sense of a poem that might otherwise prove elusive or even intimidating.

The Importance of the Collection as Context: An Example and Exercise

Samuel Taylor Coleridge's *The Rime of the Ancient Mariner* (chapter 20) and William Wordsworth's "Tintern Abbey" ("Reading More Poetry") originally appeared together in a book titled *Lyrical Ballads* (1798)—among the most famous and influential poetry collections in the English-language tradition. A collaborative project of the two poets, the book was intended—as Wordsworth explained in the preface to the second and subsequent editions—as "an experiment" in creating a kind of poetry very different in both content and form from the poetry admired in the late-eighteenth century. (Largely because of its artistic radicalism, *Lyrical Ballads* was initially published anonymously.) One of the many distinctive features of the collection is indicated by its title: Many of the poems it includes are **ballads**, highly personal **lyrics**, or some unprecedented combination of the two. When the book was published in 1798, moreover, both the ballad and the lyric were considered relatively undignified and even "lowly" literary genres, just as the sorts of people who feature as speakers or characters in many Wordsworth and Coleridge poems were considered undignified and lowly in a social sense.

Each of the two poets contributed a different sort of poem to this shared project, however. As Coleridge explains in his autobiography, his poems set out to give "a human interest and a semblance of truth" to events and

(Continued on next page)

(Continued)

"characters supernatural" and extraordinary; Wordsworth's instead sought to "excite a feeling analogous to the supernatural" about natural, everyday things. Together, then, the two sets of poems took opposite approaches to a single, common end: "awakening the mind's attention . . . to the loveliness and the wonders of the world before us" and revealing the interconnections between the natural, human, ordinary aspect of that world and its supernatural, divine, and extraordinary aspect.

Read or re-read "Tintern Abbey" and *The Rime of the Ancient Mariner*, and then write a response paper explaining why you think these poems belong together. Different as they are outwardly, what commonalities can you discover? What might make them fit together as part of a single collection? How are your response and interpretation affected by what you now know about *Lyrical Ballads*?

WILLIAM BLAKE'S *SONGS OF INNOCENCE AND OF EXPERIENCE*

The rest of this chapter focuses on William Blake's *Songs of Innocence and of Experience*, one of the English-language tradition's most extraordinary poetry collections (and published around the same time as Wordsworth and Coleridge's *Lyrical Ballads*). One unique aspect of this collection is the fact that its creator—a professional painter and illustrator—not only wrote all the poems but also illustrated and printed the book himself, using a method of his own invention. (For a very brief description of that method, see the excerpt from Morton Paley later in this chapter.) As a result, Blake should indeed be regarded as the *creator* rather than the mere *author* of a book that is simultaneously a visual and verbal experience—a collection of interlinked paintings and poems.

The fact that the book was etched, printed, painted, and then sewn together by hand, moreover, had at least two important effects. First, Blake produced few copies of *Songs of Innocence and of Experience*; to date, only twenty-four are known to exist. Second, each of those twenty-four copies differs slightly from all the others: The order of the poems varies somewhat, and so, too, does the coloring of individual pages and illustrations.

In all its versions, however, the book combines two distinct yet intimately related sequences of poems. Blake first produced the book *Songs of Innocence* in 1789. Five years later, in 1794, he added other poems and pages to that book in order to create a new one: *Songs of Innocence and of Experience*. As its title suggests, the book is divided into two sections—"Songs of Innocence" and "Songs of Experience," each with its own title page and introductory poem.

Together, the two sections and sequences portray the world from two different, even opposite, perspectives, or what the book's title page labels "Two Contrary States of the Human Soul." An individual poem in "Songs of Innocence" thus often has a direct companion or counterpart poem in "Songs of Experience." In some cases, those two poems, though dramatically different, have precisely the same title and depict the same character or situation: There are, for example, two poems called "Holy Thursday" and two called "The Chimney Sweeper." In other cases, the connection between the two poems is less direct: The poem "The Lamb," in "Songs of Innocence," for example, is typically viewed as the companion to "The Tyger," in "Songs of Experience." And the same holds true for "The Ecchoing Green" (in "Innocence") and "The Garden of Love" (in "Experience"). A few poems, however, do not have any obvious counterpart; the two most famous examples are "London" and "The Sick Rose," which originally appeared in "Songs of Experience" and which you will find in, respectively, chapters 13 and 16 of this book.

In this chapter, we include ten poems from *Songs of Innocence and of Experience*, along with color reproductions of some of the volume's actual pages to give you a sense of how it looks. (To see all of Blake's work, including various versions of the poems in this album, visit the impressive *Blake Archive* at http://www.blakearchive .org/blake/.) To provide more insight into how *Songs of Innocence and of Experience* was produced, how its various parts might be seen to fit together into a whole, and what was happening in Blake's life and world when he created it, a chronology and excerpts from four critical essays follow the poems.

SONGS OF INNOCENCE

Introduction

Piping down the valleys wild
Piping songs of pleasant glee
On a cloud I saw a child.
And he laughing said to me.

5   Pipe a song about a Lamb;
So I piped with merry chear,
Piper pipe that song again—
So I piped, he wept to hear.

Drop thy pipe thy happy pipe
10   Sing thy songs of happy chear,
So I sung the same again
While he wept with joy to hear

Piper sit thee down and write
In a book that all may read—
15   So he vanish'd from my sight.
And I pluck'd a hollow reed.

And I made a rural pen,
And I stain'd the water clear,
And I wrote my happy songs
20   Every child may joy to hear

The Ecchoing Green

The Sun does arise,
And make happy the skies.
The merry bells ring,
To welcome the Spring.
5 The sky-lark and thrush,
The birds of the bush,
Sing louder around,
To the bells chearful sound.
While our sports shall be seen
10 On the Ecchoing Green.

Old John with white hair
Does laugh away care,
Sitting under the oak,
Among the old folk.
15 They laugh at our play,
And soon they all say,
Such such were the joys.
When we all girls & boys,
In our youth time were seen,
20 On the Ecchoing Green.

Till the little ones weary
No more can be merry
The sun does descend,
And our sports have an end:
25 Round the laps of their mothers,
Many sisters and brothers,
Like birds in their nest,
Are ready for rest;
And sport no more seen,
30 On the darkening Green.

Holy Thursday[1]

'Twas on a Holy Thursday, their innocent faces clean,
The children walking two & two, in red & blue & green;
Grey headed beadles walkd before with wands as white as snow,
Till into the high dome of Paul's they like Thames' waters flow.

5 O what a multitude they seemd, these flowers of London town!
Seated in companies they sit with radiance all their own.

1. In the English Church, the Thursday celebrating Christ's ascension, thirty-nine days after Easter. It was customary on this day to march the poor, frequently orphaned, children from the charity schools of London to a service at St. Paul's Cathedral.

The hum of multitudes was there, but multitudes of lambs,
Thousands of little boys & girls raising their innocent hands.

Now like a mighty wind they raise to heaven the voice of song,
10   Or like harmonious thunderings the seats of heaven among.
Beneath them sit the agèd men, wise guardians of the poor;
Then cherish pity, lest you drive an angel from your door.[2]

The Lamb

    Little Lamb, who made thee?
    Dost thou know who made thee?
Gave thee life, and bid thee feed
By the stream and o'er the mead;
5 Gave thee clothing of delight,
Softest clothing woolly bright;
Gave thee such a tender voice,
Making all the vales rejoice?
    Little Lamb, who made thee?
10   Dost thou know who made thee?

    Little Lamb, I'll tell thee!
    Little Lamb, I'll tell thee:
He is callèd by thy name,
For he calls himself a Lamb,
15 He is meek and he is mild;
He became a little child.
I a child and thou a lamb,
We are callèd by his name.
    Little Lamb, God bless thee!
20   Little Lamb, God bless thee!

The Chimney Sweeper

When my mother died I was very young,
And my father sold me while yet my tongue,
Could scarcely cry weep weep weep weep.
So your chimneys I sweep & in soot I sleep.

5 Theres little Tom Dacre, who cried when his head
That curl'd like a lambs back, was shav'd, so I said.
Hush Tom never mind it, for when your head's bare,
You know that the soot cannot spoil your white hair.

2. See Hebrews 13.2: "Be not forgetful to entertain strangers: for thereby some have entertained angels
unawares."

And so he was quiet, & that very night,
10 As Tom was a sleeping he had such a sight,
    That thousands of sweepers Dick, Joe Ned & Jack
    Were all of them lock'd up in coffins of black

    And by came an Angel who had a bright key,
    And he open'd the coffins & set them all free.
15 Then down a green plain leaping laughing they run
    And wash in a river and shine in the Sun.

    Then naked & white, all their bags left behind,
    They rise upon clouds, and sport in the wind.
    And the Angel told Tom if he'd be a good boy,
20 He'd have God for his father & never want[3] joy.

    And so Tom awoke and we rose in the dark
    And got with our bags & our brushes to work.
    Tho' the morning was cold, Tom was happy & warm,
    So if all do their duty, they need not fear harm.

                                        1789

SONGS OF EXPERIENCE

Introduction

    Hear the voice of the Bard!
    Who Present, Past, & Future sees
    Whose ears have heard,
    The Holy Word,
5   That walk'd among the ancient trees.

    Calling the lapsed Soul
    And weeping in the evening dew;
    That might controll,
    The starry pole;
10 And fallen fallen light renew!

    O Earth O Earth return!
    Arise from out the dewy grass;
    Night is worn,
    And the morn
15 Rises from the slumberous mass.

    Turn away no more:
    Why wilt thou turn away
    The starry floor
    The watry shore
20 Is giv'n thee till the break of day.

3. Lack.

The Tyger

Tyger! Tyger! burning bright
In the forests of the night,
What immortal hand or eye
Could frame thy fearful symmetry?

5   In what distant deeps or skies
Burnt the fire of thine eyes?
On what wings dare he aspire?
What the hand dare seize the fire?

And what shoulder, & what art,
10 Could twist the sinews of thy heart?
And when thy heart began to beat,
What dread hand? & what dread feet?

What the hammer? what the chain?
In what furnace was thy brain?
15 What the anvil? what dread grasp
Dare its deadly terrors clasp?

When the stars threw down their spears
And water'd heaven with their tears,
Did he smile his work to see?
20 Did he who made the Lamb make thee?

Tyger! Tyger! burning bright
In the forests of the night,
What immortal hand or eye
Dare frame thy fearful symmetry?

The Garden of Love

I went to the Garden of Love,
And saw what I never had seen:
A Chapel was built in the midst,
Where I used to play on the green.

5   And the gates of this Chapel were shut,
And Thou shalt not, writ over the door;
So I turn'd to the Garden of Love,
That so many sweet flowers bore,

And I saw it was filled with graves,
10 And tomb-stones where flowers should be:
And Priests in black gowns, were walking their rounds,
And binding with briars, my joys & desires.

The Chimney Sweeper

A little black thing among the snow:
Crying weep, weep, in notes of woe!
Where are thy father & mother? say?
They are both gone up to the church to pray.

5 Because I was happy upon the heath,
And smil'd among the winters snow:
They clothed me in the clothes of death,
And taught me to sing the notes of woe.

And because I am happy, & dance & sing,
10 They think they have done me no injury:
And are gone to praise God & his Priest & King
Who make up a heaven of our misery.

Holy Thursday

Is this a holy thing to see,
In a rich and fruitful land,
Babes reduced to misery,
Fed with cold and usurous hand?

5 Is that trembling cry a song?
Can it be a song of joy?
And so many children poor?
It is a land of poverty!

And their sun does never shine,
10 And their fields are bleak & bare,
And their ways are fill'd with thorns;
It is eternal winter there.

For where-e'er the sun does shine,
And where-e'er the rain does fall,
15 Babe can never hunger there,
Nor poverty the mind appall.
                                        1794

William Blake and His Times: A Chronology

1757   William Blake is born in London on November 28, one of the seven
        children of Catherine and James Blake (a maker and seller of stockings
        and gloves); only five of the children will survive infancy.

1765–67 Blake has his first angelic visions and, at age ten (1767), enters drawing
        school.

1772   At age fourteen, Blake is apprenticed to a master engraver.

1776   The American Revolution, or War of Independence, begins.

1779   His apprenticeship complete, the twenty-one-year-old Blake begins his studies at the Royal Academy of Art.

1780   Blake begins to read and sing his own poems to friends and to earn his living by giving drawing lessons and by engraving prints and book illustrations for other authors and artists. (One such work is Anna Letitia Barbauld's *Hymns in Prose for Children* [1781].) While sketching near a river, Blake and two fellow artists are detained by British soldiers, who suspect them of being French spies; the prisoners are released only after other Royal Academy members testify on their behalf.

1782   Blake (at 24) marries Catherine Boucher, an illiterate former domestic servant and one of the thirteen children of a market gardener. (Blake will teach his wife not only to read and write but also to engrave and print books, and she will eventually help with the engraving, printing, coloring, and assembly of all his self-published works.)

1783   A friend finances the publication of *Poetical Sketches*, the only book by Blake to be published in the conventional manner by another publisher. The American War of Independence ends in a British defeat.

1784   After the death of Blake's father, Blake's younger brother comes to live and study engraving with Blake and his wife; Blake uses his small inheritance to open a small print-selling and publishing business with a friend and writes (but does not publish) *An Island in the Moon*, a work of prose satire containing drafts of three poems later included in *Songs of Innocence*.

1785   When Blake's business folds, he returns to his work as an engraver for other publishers.

1787   After his brother's death, Blake begins to see him in visions, including one that reveals to him a new method of "illuminated printing" or relief etching.

1788   Blake produces *All Religions Are One* and *There Is No Natural Religion*, the first works produced using his "illuminated printing" technique; Blake will use the same method to self-publish all of his subsequent work.

1789   Blake etches *Songs of Innocence* and *The Book of Thel*. The French Revolution begins in July with the storming of the Bastille, a Parisian prison.

1790–91   Blake etches *The Marriage of Heaven and Hell* and *The French Revolution*.

1792   Blake's friend and fellow radical Thomas Paine is sentenced to death in absentia for publishing his two-part political treatise *Rights of Man*, though the sentence is never carried out.

1793   In France, Louis XVI and Marie Antoinette are executed as part of the "Reign of Terror." Britain and France go to war. Blake etches *America*.

1794   Several London radicals well known to Blake are tried for high treason, a capital crime, but they are ultimately acquitted. Blake produces *Songs* of Innocence and of Experience, Visions of the Daughters of Albion, and The Book of Urizen.

1795–96 Blake produces *The Book of Los* and begins *The Four Zoas*.

1800 Blake and his wife move from London to the Sussex seaside to be near his new patron, William Hayley, whom Blake will later describe as "the enemy of my Spiritual Life while he pretends to be the Friend of my Corporeal."

1802–1804 A scuffle with a soldier leads to Blake's trial and acquittal on charges of sedition, a capital crime. Blake and Catherine move back to London.

1809–10 Blake self-publishes *Milton*.

1815 British forces defeat Napoleon at Waterloo.

1818–20 Blake self-publishes *Jerusalem*.

1820–25 Blake produces (on commission) watercolor illustrations for the Book of Job.

1825 Blake begins work on another commission, illustrations for Dante's *Divine Comedy*.

1827 Blake dies on August 12 at the age of 69.

MORTON D. PALEY

From *Twentieth-Century Interpretations of Songs of Innocence and of Experience**

In 1789, William Blake published a book unique in several ways. Other poets, such as Isaac Watts . . . , had produced volumes of religious poems for children in the eighteenth century; and some books of this type . . . were emblem books with an illustration for each poem. Blake was alone, however, in producing *Songs of Innocence* as a total work of art comprising both design and text (including calligraphy). Even the process of relief etching by which the book was published was developed by Blake himself—with, according to a tradition established by Blake's contemporary John Thomas Smith, visionary assistance:

> Blake, after deeply perplexing himself as to the mode of accomplishing the publication of his illustrated songs, without their being subject to the expense of letter-press, his brother Robert stood before him in one of his visionary imaginations, and so decidedly directed him in the way in which he ought to proceed, that he immediately followed his advice, by writing his poetry, and drawing his marginal subjects of embellishments in outline upon the copper-plate with an impervious liquid, and then eating the plain parts or lights away with aquafortis[1]

*From the introduction to *Twentieth-Century Interpretations of* Songs of Innocence and of Experience: A Collection of Critical Essays, ed. Morton D. Paley (Englewood Cliffs, NJ: Prentice Hall, 1969), pp. 1–9. Some of Paley's footnotes have been omitted.
1. Nitric acid, used in etching.

considerably below them, so that the outlines were left as a stereotype. The plates in this state were then printed in any tint that he wished, to enable him or Mrs. Blake to colour the marginal figures up by hand in imitation of the drawings.[2]

As Alexander Gilchrist, author of the first book-length biography of Blake, said, "Never before so surely was a man literally the author of his own book."[3] A sequel, produced in the same way, was advertised in 1793, but no separate copy of *Songs of Experience* is known to exist. Instead, it was issued as part of a single volume with the earlier *Songs*, with a combined title page, etched in 1794: *Songs of Innocence and of Experience / Shewing the Two Contrary States of the Human Soul.* Clearly, Blake regarded the two sets of *Songs* as an artistic whole, and we shall increase our appreciation of the poems if we follow him in this.

What are the two Contrary States and what is the relationship between them? . . . Both are phases in the spiritual development of man and, at the same time, perennial ways of looking at the world.

The state of Innocence is compounded of the pagan Age of Gold and the Judeo-Christian Eden. Externally and generically, it applies to the condition of man before the Fall; internally and psychologically to the child who has not yet experienced the inner divisions of human life. Its literary forebears are the worlds of the pastoral and the Psalms. Blake's Innocence also has a special relationship to the thought of the Swedish visionary Emanuel Swedenborg,[4] . . . who conceived of Innocence in terms peculiarly appropriate to Blake's:

> Afterwards genuine innocence was represented by a most beautiful child, naked and full of life; for the really innocent, who are in the inmost heaven and thus nearest to the Lord, always appear before the eyes of the other angels as children, and some of them naked; for innocence is represented by nakedness unaccompanied by shame, as is said of the first man and his wife in Paradise (*Gen.* ii, 25); so when their state of innocence perished they were ashamed of their nakedness and hid themselves. . . . In a word, the wiser the angels are, and the more innocent they are the more they appear to themselves as little children. This is why the Word "childhood" signifies innocence. . . .[5]

. . . [For] both Blake and Swedenborg the state of Innocence is projected in terms of images corresponding to an inner, spiritual condition:

> This World is also full of Correspondences. . . . To give only a Hint by Way of Illustration. To two Angels conversing together, supposing on Love or Innocence, the corresponding visible Scene presented to them may be delightful Fields with sporting Lambs, little Children playing in Flower-Gardens, . . . and the like pleasing Imagery. To Infernal Spirits, according to their different States . . . are represented Scenes of Wildness, Barrenness, Dismay, or Horror.[6]

---

2. *Nollekens and His Times,* ed. Wilfred Whitten (London and New York, 1920), II, 372. [Author's note]

3. *The Life of William Blake,* ed. Ruthven Todd, rev. ed. (London and New York, 1945), p. 61. (Gilchrist's *Life* . . . was first published in 1863.) [Author's note]

4. Swedish scientist, philosopher, and Christian mystic (1688–1772), best known for theological works, especially *Heaven and Hell* (1758).

5. *Heaven and Its Wonders and Hell* (New York, 1956), pp. 218–19. The book, first published in English translation in 1784, was owned and annotated by Blake. [Author's note]

6. Emanuel Swedenborg, *A Treatise of the Nature of Influx,* 3ᵈ ed. (London, 1788), p. 59n. [Author's note]

SONGS
of
INNOCENCE
and Of
EXPERIENCE

Shewing the Two Contrary States
of the Human Soul

SONGS OF Innocence

The Author & Printer W Blake

Introduction

Piping down the valleys wild
Piping songs of pleasant glee
On a cloud I saw a child.
And he laughing said to me

Pipe a song about a Lamb:
So I piped with merry chear,
Piper pipe that song again—
So I piped, he wept to hear.

Drop thy pipe thy happy pipe
Sing thy songs of happy chear.
So I sung the same again
While he wept with joy to hear

Piper sit thee down and write
In a book that all may read—
So he vanish'd from my sight.
And I pluck'd a hollow reed.

And I made a rural pen,
And I stain'd the water clear,
And I wrote my happy songs
Every child may joy to hear

The Ecchoing Green

The Sun does arise,
And make happy the skies.
The merry bells ring,
To welcome the Spring.
The sky-lark and thrush,
The birds of the bush,
Sing louder around,
To the bells cheerful sound.
While our sports shall be seen
On the Ecchoing Green.

Old John with white hair
Does laugh away care,
Sitting under the oak,
Among the old folk.

They

They laugh at our play,
And soon they all say,
Such, such were the joys,
When we all girls & boys,
In our youth time were seen,
On the Echoing Green.

Till the little ones weary
No more can be merry
The sun does descend,
And our sports have an end:
Round the laps of their mothers,
Many sisters and brothers,
Like birds in their nest,
Are ready for rest:
And sport no more seen,
On the darkening Green.

HOLY THURSDAY

Twas on a Holy Thursday their innocent faces clean
The children walking two & two in red & blue & green
Grey headed beadles walkd before with wands as white as snow
Till into the high dome of Pauls they like Thames waters flow

O what a multitude they seemd these flowers of London town
Seated in companies they sit with radiance all their own
The hum of multitudes was there but multitudes of lambs
Thousands of little boys & girls raising their innocent hands

Now like a mighty wind they raise to heaven the voice of song
Or like harmonious thunderings the seats of heaven among
Beneath them sit the aged men wise guardians of the poor
Then cherish pity, lest you drive an angel from your door

The Lamb

Little Lamb who made thee
Dost thou know who made thee
Gave thee life & bid thee feed.
By the stream & o'er the mead;
Gave thee clothing of delight,
Softest clothing wooly bright;
Gave thee such a tender voice,
Making all the vales rejoice;
    Little Lamb who made thee
    Dost thou know who made thee

Little Lamb I'll tell thee,
Little Lamb I'll tell thee;
He is called by thy name,
For he calls himself a Lamb;
He is meek & he is mild,
He became a little child:
I a child & thou a lamb,
We are called by his name.
    Little Lamb God bless thee.
    Little Lamb God bless thee.

The Chimney Sweeper.

When my mother died I was very young,
And my father sold me while yet my tongue.
Could scarcely cry weep weep weep weep.
So your chimneys I sweep & in soot I sleep.

Theres little Tom Dacre who cried when his head,
That curl'd like a lambs back, was shav'd, so I said.
Hush Tom never mind it, for when your heads bare,
You know that the soot cannot spoil your white hair.

And so he was quiet, & that very night,
As Tom was a sleeping he had such a sight,
That thousands of sweepers Dick, Joe Ned & Jack
Were all of them lock'd up in coffins of black,

And by came an Angel who had a bright key
And he opend the coffins & set them all free.
Then down a green plain leaping laughing they run
And wash in a river and shine in the Sun.

Then naked & white, all their bags left behind,
They rise upon clouds, and sport in the wind.
And the Angel told Tom if he'd be a good boy,
He'd have God for his father & never want joy.

And so Tom awoke and we rose in the dark
And got with our bags & our brushes to work.
Tho' the morning was cold, Tom was happy & warm,
So if all do their duty, they need not fear harm.

SONGS
of
EXPERIENCE

The Author & Printer W Blake

Introduction.

Hear the voice of the Bard!
Who Present, Past, & Future sees
Whose ears have heard,
The Holy Word,
That walk'd among the ancient trees.

Calling the lapsed Soul,
And weeping in the evening dew:
That might controll.
The starry pole;
And fallen fallen light renew!

O Earth O Earth return!
Arise from out the dewy grass;
Night is worn.
And the morn
Rises from the slumberous mass.

Turn away no more:
Why wilt thou turn away
The starry floor
The watry shore
Is giv'n thee till the break of day.

The Tyger.

Tyger Tyger, burning bright,
In the forests of the night;
What immortal hand or eye,
Could frame thy fearful symmetry?

In what distant deeps or skies.
Burnt the fire of thine eyes?
On what wings dare he aspire?
What the hand, dare seize the fire?

And what shoulder, & what art,
Could twist the sinews of thy heart?
And when thy heart began to beat,
What dread hand? & what dread feet?

What the hammer? what the chain,
In what furnace was thy brain?
What the anvil? what dread grasp,
Dare its deadly terrors clasp?

When the stars threw down their spears
And water'd heaven with their tears:
Did he smile his work to see?
Did he who made the Lamb make thee?

Tyger Tyger burning bright,
In the forests of the night:
What immortal hand or eye,
Dare frame thy fearful symmetry?

The GARDEN of LOVE

I went to the Garden of Love.
And saw what I never had seen:
A Chapel was built in the midst,
Where I used to play on the green.

And the gates of this Chapel were shut,
And Thou shalt not. writ over the door;
So I turn'd to the Garden of Love,
That so many sweet flowers bore.

And I saw it was filled with graves,
And tomb-stones where flowers should be;
And Priests in black gowns, were walking their
rounds,
And binding with briars, my joys & desires.

THE Chimney Sweeper

A little black thing among the snow:
Crying weep, weep, in notes of woe!
Where are thy father & mother? say?
They are both gone up to the church to pray.

Because I was happy upon the heath,
And smil'd among the winters snow:
They clothed me in the clothes of death,
And taught me to sing the notes of woe.

And because I am happy, & dance & sing,
They think they have done me no injury:
And are gone to praise God & his Priest & King,
Who make up a heaven of our misery.

HOLY THURSDAY

Is this a holy thing to see,
In a rich and fruitful land,
Babes reduced to misery,
Fed with cold and usurous hand?

Is that trembling cry a song?
Can it be a song of joy?
And so many children poor?
It is a land of poverty!

And their sun does never shine,
And their fields are bleak & bare,
And their ways are fill'd with thorns,
It is eternal winter there.

For where-e'er the sun does shine,
And where-e'er the rain does fall:
Babe can never hunger there,
Nor poverty the mind appall.

Experience, too, is an inner state externalized in a world of images—chain, thorns, spears, graves, briars, blood, and roots, to name a few—all of which correspond to felt qualities in life. . . . In experience, which is the world of normal adult life, people try to analyze and codify their feelings, and as a result they become incapable of spontaneity. . . . They suppress their real selves out of fear; . . . they defer gratification. . . . The traditional hierarchy of society, seen as benevolent in *Innocence*, is now regarded as a vast exploitative deceit: "God & his Priest & King / Who make up a heaven of our misery."[7] The pastoral landscape of Innocence is replaced by . . . wartime London, a city of victims. With all this suffering, however, Experience also brings a bitter wisdom. . . . In the wisdom of Experience, as embodied in the voice of the prophetic Bard at the beginning and again at the end of the second group of *Songs*, lies the possibility of reorganizing man's divided self and, if not of regaining the lost world of Innocence, then of forging a new unity. "Man is so created," Swedenborg wrote, "as to be during his childhood in external innocence, and when he becomes old in internal innocence, to the end that he may come by means of the former into the latter, and from the latter return into the former" (*Heaven and Hell*, p. 171). . . .

The transition from Innocence to Experience may be seen as a version of what medieval theologians called the Fortunate Fall—the idea that the fall of Adam and Eve was in a paradoxical sense a "happy sin," in that otherwise Christ would not have been born to save mankind. For Blake, the fall into Experience was if not happy at least necessary. . . .

In his *Life Against Death: The Psychoanalytical Meaning of History* (Middletown, Conn., 1959), Norman O. Brown remarks:

> It is one of the great romantic visions . . . that the history of mankind consists
> in a departure from a condition of undifferentiated primal unity with himself
> and with nature, an intermediate period in which man's powers are developed
> through differentiation and antagonism (alienation) with himself and with
> nature, and a final return to a unity on a higher level or harmony. . . . (p. 86)

Blake's *Songs* is one of the first literary works to deliberately embody this pattern. Innocence and Experience are Contraries, and, as Blake tells us in *The Marriage of Heaven and Hell* (1790–93), "without Contraries is no progression." In this case, progression is toward a condition of being in which the harmony lost in the fall from Innocence is regained. The agent of regeneration is Energy. . . . In the fallen world of Experience, this Energy is present as the wrath of the Tyger. . . .

7. *The Poetry and Prose of William Blake,* ed. David V. Erdman (Garden City, N.Y., 1965), p. 23. [Author's note].

ANDREW LINCOLN

From *William Blake: Songs of Innocence and of Experience**

In his own lifetime Blake's *Songs of Innocence and of Experience* was known only to those lucky enough to own, or have access to, one of the rare illuminated copies produced by the author himself.[1] Some twenty-four copies of the combined *Songs* have survived, and four copies of *Songs of Experience*, while twenty-six copies of the separate *Songs of Innocence* are known—one recently discovered . . . in the Bavarian State Museum at Munich. The total is much higher than for any other work Blake published himself, but seems small given the reputation the songs now hold. No doubt Blake's limited means of advertising and the method of production tended to restrict sales. Although the songs were addressed to "Every child," they were expensive [and eventually took up to six months each to produce]. . . . The contents might also have deterred some potential customers: the songs challenge traditional assumptions, sometimes obliquely, sometimes with a daring directness. From the outset of his career as a self-publishing author, Blake was radically at odds with much of the public he sought to reach.

The Two Contrary States of the Human Soul

Blake's "Contrary States" of Innocence and Experience illuminate many areas of thought and feeling. Among other things, they direct attention to dualities at the heart of the Christian tradition. In the Bible there are many contrasting ideas and images which interpreters usually seek to harmonise. Divine power is associated with terror and with joy. God is presented as a transcendent being who demands obedience to moral law, and as a loving merciful being who becomes human. . . . In the *Songs* Blake presents comparable contrasts, not as elements of a coherent and unified system of belief, but as aspects of two contrary modes of vision that illuminate each other dialectically.

. . .

The *Songs of Innocence and of Experience* rarely offer simple choices—as between moral absolutes—but tend to emphasize the relativity of particular images and points of view. "Mercy Pity Love and Peace" can reveal the innate divinity in human life, or mask the selfishness of the natural heart. To accept one view and refuse the alternative would be to turn away from an unpleasant truth or to accept a reductive view of human feeling. Some poems contain contradictory views within them. . . . Blake's technique generates ambiguities that repeatedly

---

*From the introduction to *William Blake:* Songs of Innocence and of Experience, ed. Andrew Lincoln (Princeton: The William Blake Trust/Princeton UP, 1991). Some of Lincoln's footnotes have been omitted.
1. Seven songs were published separately in Blake's lifetime[: "Laughing Song," "Holy Thursday" (from *Innocence*), "The Divine Image," "The Tyger," "The Garden of Love," part of the "Introduction" to *Innocence,* and "The Chimney Sweeper" from *Innocence.* "The Tyger" appeared in two separate publications, "Holy Thursday" in three]. . . . [Author's note]

complicate interpretations. Few books offer such challenges with such a disarming appearance of simplicity. . . .

• • •

Songs of Innocence

. . . As many critics have noted, in the variety of its contents *Songs of Innocence* invites comparison with a range of other children's books available at the time, including collections of hymns for children, such as those by Isaac Watts, Charles Wesley, or Anna Barbauld. . . .

In the later eighteenth century, children's books were often illustrated, usually with an engraving or simple woodcut. Some pictures were even coloured with watercolours. . . . But Blake's integration of text and design goes far beyond the capacities of conventional printing methods. The relief etching process seems to have encouraged him to avoid blank spaces, to fill his margins with decorative motifs, to add the tiny leaves and figures that appear in or around the text of his songs.[2] This embellishment invites close exploration of each plate, and helps to make the hand coloured copies of the work look more like illuminated manuscripts than printed books.[3]

• • •

Songs of Experience

As the sequel to the Innocence series, *Songs of Experience* differs considerably in mood and perspective. . . . The bitterly ironical references to "God & his Priest & King" show a new outspokenness in Blake's work, a new drive to expose the social consequences of error, which was no doubt prompted by the course of events in revolutionary France, and by the political turmoil in England. . . . But Blake's concern with social and religious tyranny here is an extension of his interest in the habits of thought that imprison individuals in "the same dull round." . . . Cruelty and repression are seen to be rooted in mental passivity; the conventional association of goodness with conformity and restraint is seen as both a symptom and a source of error. . . . The use of "Contrary States" was intended to make readers think "for themselves."

• • •

The Combined Songs

In the combined work the parallel between the two series helps to focus attention on the differences: Innocence poems may be linked to their counterparts in Experience by identical or contrasting titles, while visual contrasts reinforce

2. Viscomi notes a "tightly composed design needs to be etched less deeply than one with open areas," *The Art of William Blake's Illuminated Books* [Manchester, 1983], p. 9. [Author's note]

3. Bindman suggests that Blake may have had an acquaintance with the inheritors of the medieval tradition of illumination, such as the prayer books and devotional works of John Sturt. *Blake as an Artist* [Oxford, 1977], p. 61. [Author's note]

those in the text. The designs of Innocence make more use of flowing, curving lines, protective spaces, exuberant vegetation; in Experience spaces are often defined and fractured by bare branches. The etched images on the Innocence plates are usually delicate and finely detailed. . . . The etched images on the Experience plates generally have fewer details and show less concern with texture. The leafless trees are represented in bold outlines, their trunks shaded with a few unbroken patches. . . .

. . .

VARIATIONS: ADDITIONS, TRANSFERS, ORDERING

Blake's conception of the *Songs* seems to have evolved through several stages. . . . When Blake combined the two series into a single collection in 1794, he transferred "The Little Girl Lost" and "The Little Girl Found" (plates 34–36) from Innocence to Experience. . . . These transfers give a clear indication that the boundaries between the two "States of the Human Soul" were not hard and fast in Blake's view. . . .

. . . [T]here is considerable variation in the arrangement of the poems [across different copies of *Songs of Innocence and of Experience*]. Blake seems to have tried a different order for the plates with each new copy until about 1815, when he began to favour one arrangement, shared by six copies. . . .

ROBERT F. GLECKNER

From *Point of View and Context in Blake's* Songs*

For the serious reader of Blake's songs, . . . a constant awareness of the context or state in which a poem appears is indispensable; and since each state is made up of many poems, the other poems in that state must be consulted to grasp the full significance of any one poem. Each song out of its context means a great deal less than Blake expected of his total invention, and occasionally it may be taken to mean something quite different from what he intended. Blake created a system of which innocence and experience are vital parts. . . . Without the system, Blake is the simplest of lyric poets and every child may joy to hear the songs. . . . [But t]he states are separate, the two contrary states of the human soul, and the songs were written not merely for our enjoyment, or even for our edification, but for our salvation.

Closely related to the necessity of reading each song in terms of its state is the vital importance of point of view. Often it is unobtrusive, but many times upon a correct determination of speaker and perspective depends a faithful interpretation of the poem. Blake himself suggests this by his organization of the songs into series, *Innocence* introduced and sung by the piper, *Experience* by the Bard. Superfi-

*From "Point of View and Context in Blake's *Songs*," *Bulletin of the New York Public Library* 61 (Nov. 1957).

cially there seems to be little to distinguish one from the other since the piper clearly exhibits imaginative vision and the Bard "Present, Past, & Future sees." Yet for each, the past, present, and future are different: for the piper the past can only be the primal unity, for the present is innocence and the immediate future is experience; for the Bard the past is innocence, the present experience, the future a higher innocence. It is natural, then, that the piper's point of view is prevailingly happy; he is conscious of the child's essential divinity and assured of his present protection. But into that joyous context the elements of experience constantly insinuate themselves so that the note of sorrow is never completely absent from the piper's pipe. In experience, on the other hand, the Bard's voice is solemn and more deeply resonant, for the high-pitched joy of innocence is now only a memory. Within this gloom, though, lies the ember which can leap into flame at any moment to light the way to the higher innocence. . . . Though one singer uses "mild and gentle numbers" and the other more "terrific" tones, both see the imaginative (and symbolic) significance of all the activity in the songs. The inexplicit, Blake said, "rouzes the faculties to act." The reader of Blake, then, must rouse his faculties to consider this imaginative point of view always no matter who is speaking or seeing or acting in a poem.

. . . [A] good example is "Holy Thursday" of *Songs of Innocence*. . . . From a conventional point of view it is thoughtful and kind of the "wise guardians of the poor" to run charity schools and to take the children occasionally to St. Paul's to give thanks for all their so-called blessings. But from the piper's point of view (and Blake's of course) the children clearly are disciplined, regimented, marched in formation to church in the uniforms of their respective schools—mainly to advertise the charitable souls of their supposed guardians. The point here (seen only through the piper's vision) is that in the state of innocence there is, or ought to be, no discipline, no regimentation, no marching, no uniforms, and no guardians—merely free, uninhibited, irresponsible, thoughtless play on the echoing green. Accordingly the children in "Holy Thursday" assert and preserve their essential innocence, not by going to church, but by freely and spontaneously, "like a mighty wind," raising to "heaven the voice of song." This simple act raises them to a level far above their supposed benefactors, who are without vision, without innocence, without love. . . . The irony is severe, but lost upon us unless we are aware of context and point of view.

In addition, many of Blake's symbols are recurrent, so that once a symbol's basic significance is revealed in a kind of archetypal context, each successive context adds association to association within the song series. When the beadle's wand appears in the first stanza of "Holy Thursday" of *Innocence*, for example, its immediate connotation is authority. But since a *beadle* wields the symbol, it is also religious authority, the organized church, institutionalized religion. It also represents an act of restraint which forces the children to act according to rule rather than impulse. The wand is "white as snow" to suggest the frigidity of man-made moral purity as opposed to the warmth of young, energetic, exuberant innocence. And finally, it suggests the worldly, non-innocent concept of duty (and its corollary, harm), the duty of worship which clashes with all of Blake's ideas of freedom and spontaneity. But all of this, it will be said, strongly suggests the world of experience, and "Holy Thursday" *is* a Song of Innocence; the overall point of view is the piper's. The point to be made here is simply this. If we do not read the poem as a Song of Innocence, about the *state* of innocence and its major symbol, the joyous child, we *can* read it as a rather pleasant picture of nicely dressed charity children being led to church by a gentle beadle to sing hymns; or as a terrible view of unfortunate, exploited charity children under the thumbs of their elders. And we would *not* see that despite outward appearance the children *are* innocent, essentially free and happy, as they spontaneously sing their songs. Without an awareness of context the symbols do not work as Blake intended them to, and the song becomes a fairly inconsequential bit of sentimental social comment.

Considering, then, the care Blake took with point of view, recurring symbols, and symbolic action, we can see that gradually many of Blake's characters merge. The final products of these mergers are what I have called the major symbols. Kindred points of view tend to unite the holders of these points of view; characters who are associated continually with the same or similar symbols tend to melt into one another; and a similar pattern of action reveals a fundamental affinity among the actors. In these ways the significance and value of any one character in any one song are intensified and expanded beyond the immediate context. The physical identity may shift, but the symbolic value remains constant—or better, is constantly enriched. When the beadle's wand in "Holy Thursday" is recognized as part of the basic scepter motif, the beadle's identity, while being retained as representative of church law, merges with that of . . . the father—and ultimately with the "selfish father of men" in "Earth's Answer," the pebble in "The Clod and the Pebble"; the "cold and usurous hand" of "Holy Thursday"; God in "The Chimney Sweeper"; . . . [and] Cruelty, Humility, and the Human Brain in "The Human Abstract". . . . Within the identity are inherent all the other identities which combine to make up the major symbol of the context. The priests of "The Garden of Love" may bind with briars love and desire, but they do so because they are selfish, fatherly, cold and usurous, worldly, cruel, humble, hypocritical, and so forth.

One serious question remains: how does one distinguish along all these characters, or are they all precisely alike and hence redundant? Professor Mark Schorer answers the question this way . . . : "The point is," he says, "that the individuality of these creations lies not in their rich diversity but in the outline that separates them from their backgrounds." That is, each individual identity in its specific context is at once a part of the whole context and the whole of which it is a part. Both the priest of "The Garden of Love" and the flower in "My Pretty Rose-Tree" are self-sufficient for some understandings of these two poems. Blake simply asked his reader to do more than merely understand: that, he said, is a "corporeal" function. He wanted them to imagine as he imagined, to see as he saw, even to re-create as he created. Only then does his method make sense, only then can one see the minor symbol as part of a major symbol, only then can the individual song take its rightful place as a Song of Innocence or Song of Experience.

ALICIA OSTRIKER

From *Vision and Verse in William Blake**

There is a Buddhist proverb which explains the three stages of wisdom as follows. When you are unenlightened, mountains are mountains and rivers are

*From *Vision and Verse in William Blake* (Madison: U of Wisconsin P, 1965). Some of Ostriker's footnotes have been omitted.

rivers. As you approach Enlightenment, mountains are not mountains and rivers are not rivers. When you have achieved Enlightenment, mountains are mountains and rivers are rivers.

. . . It is the same with Blake's versification. The immediate impression his verse makes on an unprepared reader will resemble that of jingle. It will seem extremely simple and obvious, providing the same sensuous pleasure which children's rhymes provide. Then the reader will discover that the poetry contains a good deal of formal variation and irregularity, and that the variations not only keep the verse from cloying, but contribute as far as rhythm and sound can do to the establishment of precise meanings. We must analyze their deviations from rhythmic norm. Yet this sort of analysis does not complete our understanding, since we must always return at last to the physical and emotional appeal of Blake's simplicity. . . . Blake's lyric rightness depends on a continual interplay between a primitive regularity which identifies Blake's world with the child's, and a functional irregularity which is the man's work.

The surface naïveté in Blake's metrics associates naturally with the same quality in his language. In diction, simplicity asserts itself through his plain Anglo-Saxon vocabulary, his uncomplicated sentence-structure, and his very heavy use of repetition. Metrically, it is revealed in the two areas of stanza-form and rhythmic beat.

First we can consider the naïveté of language. The most conspicuous stylistic feature of the *Songs* is their extraordinary use of repetition and parallel phrasing. Josephine Miles has found that in a thousand lines taken from Blake's whole poetic work some seventy or eighty nouns, adjectives, and verbs will appear more than ten times, instead of the thirty or forty common to other poets.[1] . . .

. . . You cannot look anywhere in *Songs of Innocence* without finding these hypnotic repetitions. Then, reinforcing them, you find parallel structures of phrase. "So I piped . . . So I sung . . . And I made . . . And I stain'd . . . And I wrote" defines the process of creation in the "Introduction," and things are typically this simple for Blake. . . . These are the beads he strings together to make the *Songs*. It is a world of plain identities, progressions, and contrasts. Only rarely does *Innocence* have a construction even so complicated as "wrath by his meekness / And by his health, sickness."

In *Experience*, which is a briefer group, only love, weep, and night appear more than ten times, although variations of self, father, hand, and fear follow close behind. *Experience* is slightly less mesmeric than *Innocence*, less restricted. As befits its broader world, where the symbols can be more diverse, fewer terms repeat from song to song. Within the poems there is still a fairly high degree of repetition. . . . The rule of parallel phrasing also still holds.

In brevity of sentence structure, which is almost as significant a feature of these songs as verbal repetition, the two groups are virtually identical. The typical complete sentence time and again takes only one or two lines. . . . In longer sentences the common lengtheners are "and" and "but," "if" and "when." Clauses remain brief. As a result, the single unit of the line almost becomes the unit of perception. The line is vivid, compact, complete, a moment of vision; each song composed of such lines is a chain of such moments; and each set of songs is constructed like a mosaic out of these innumerable tiny independent parts.

1. Josephine Miles, *Eras and Modes in English Poetry* (Berkeley, 1957), p. 79. [Author's note]

The metrical form of the songs both reinforces these traits of diction and structure, and is reinforced by them. In both *Innocence* and *Experience* the stanzaic patterns are extremely plain. The lines are usually short, seldom longer than a tetrameter, so that the rhymes come thick and fast. The stanzas themselves are brief units, most commonly quatrains in couplets or cross-rhyme. Only one poem of *Innocence* is in pentameter, one in septenary, and one in dimeter quatrains with a single-line pentameter refrain. In *Experience*, only the "Introduction" and "Earth's Answer," less simple than the rest in diction and more abstract in theme, use complex stanzas. Except for the pentameter refrain of "A Little Girl Lost," no line in *Experience* is longer than four beats. The lines are almost invariably end-stopped in both books, and because the line-unit is also the unit of meaning, we are not allowed to leap ahead or to suspend our thought from line to line. Blake makes us take baby steps, and we feel that each line affords a finished, if minute, esthetic satisfaction.

The use of pause in these poems adds symmetry to simplicity. Consider one of Blake's most famous quatrains:

Tyger Tyger, / burning bright
In the forests / of the night;
What immortal / hand or eye
Could frame / thy fearful symmetry.

The first two lines each split roughly in half, with the same number of beats before and after the pause. The third line can really be read without a pause, but if there were a break, it would come after "immortal," again dividing the line down the middle. Only the fourth line is asymmetrical. The remainder of "The Tyger" contains only one other asymmetrical line. This pattern is the norm for the *Songs*. . . .

Lines of two or four feet either split evenly or do not split at all, with few exceptions. Only some of the more rhetorical pieces like . . . "London" . . . in *Experience*, have more than three asymmetrical lines. . . .

These stanza forms of three and four beats, symmetrically divided, are like nursery rhymes, folk songs, and ballads. . . . This line . . . has historically acquired an aura of naturalness, primitiveness, and artlessness. . . . Because of all these factors, we can intone Blake's songs with the kind of regular jingle or thump which children enjoy, without severe distortion. Most poetry cannot be read in this way. . . .

Short lines are easier to accent regularly. Alliterated words are easier to accent strongly. A central pause emphasizes the accents. Parallel construction, brief phrases, images without surface difficulty, all encourage reading with a fixed beat. This is the form of rhythm the human ear can perceive. It remains the most accessible, since it is associated with regular organic processes like heartbeat, with semivoluntary activities like breathing and walking, and with simple exercises like foot-tapping and hand-clapping. Blake's *Songs* are so constructed that we will hear in them, with a part of our ear, the unsophisticated succession of regular beats, even while our conscious reading accents more subtly. This undercurrent of simple rhythm must be allowed to go its way, affecting us kinetically rather than mentally, or we will miss a good part of Blake's message.

Yet we cannot ignore the superstructure Blake erects on his primitive rhythmical base. The drawback of children's songs is that they all sound rather alike, lacking the "minute particulars" which induce the more refined mental and emotional satisfactions in poetry. One lullaby, one comic jingle, one counting-out rhyme, is like another. The tune counts more than the words. This is not so in Blake's *Songs*.

To help him fit his measures to his meanings, Blake began with a command of more meters than were dreamt of in the current prosodic philosophy. Iambs, of course, were standard fare. . . . About a fourth of the lyrics in *Innocence*, and a third in *Experience*, are iambic. They are the soberer pieces in each book: . . . "Holy Thursday" in *Innocence*, the didactic "London" . . . in *Experience*. . . .

The trochaic line . . . was a favorite of Blake's, from which he elicited diverse effects. Several of his best-known pieces are trochaic. One student of metrics finds this "the chief technical means by which Blake obtains his characteristic infantine effect, and gives the impression of speaking through the lips of a child,"[2] as in "The Lamb." . . . This childlike effect comes from the fact that trochaic rhythms, since they start on the downbeat and are usually subject to less variation than iambs, give a more emphatic feeling. They have a quality of directness which lends itself well to Blake's "infant" style. . . . Between one-half and one-third of the poems in *Innocence*, including many of the longer ones, are trochaic; somewhat fewer in *Experience*.

Finally, the uses of anapestic meters, e.g., in . . . "The Chimney Sweeper" . . . in *Innocence* . . . were virtually his own discovery.

. . . Anapest is well suited to a cheerful, rapid run, in waltz or polka time. But he is not limited to such relatively obvious music. The anapest darkens, with him, to form the strangely grave beat of the first "Chimney Sweeper," the ironic spriteliness of "The Garden of Love," and the terrible, gyring "Rose thou art sick" of *Experience*, where the waltz has become a *danse macabre*.

The poet's facility with trochaic and anapestic measures permits him a greater range of expressiveness than confinement to iambs alone would allow. The iambic poems are closest to normal discursive or argumentative speech. The trochaic poems are barer, more emphatic, purer. The poems in anapest resemble music, and carry the reader along more by the swing and sway of rhythm than by any rational content. Blake had another advantage over his contemporaries: a willingness to vary his lines internally in a manner which had not been practised since the seventeenth century. These irregularities have the double function of avoiding metrical monotony, and of helping him realize his ideas and emotions with as much precision as possible.

The importance of variation in English metrics cannot be overemphasized. If a poet has established enough of a regular metric pattern to set some beat going in our heads, the next most important thing for him is to know how to ring changes on it. These changes will form a counterpoint to the steady beat underneath, and the combination of base-beat and counterpoint will create the unique rhythm of a poem, which a reader always feels whether he knows what is happening or not, and will also help create its unique mood. . . .

A[n] . . . instance is "The Sick Rose," which gives the impression of strictest unity where Blake is in fact being most free. In my reading, only the fourth and eight lines scan identically. . . .

These poems illustrate what is perhaps most characteristically Blakean in the metric of the *Songs*, their repeated use of mixed measures. About one-third of the *Songs* are in mixed iamb-anapest meters; some like "The Sick Rose" . . .

2. Enid Hamer, *The Metres of English Poetry* (London, 1930), p. 242 [Author's note].

combining the two kinds of feet in almost every line, a few . . . juxtaposing whole lines of each. Another third mix iambic and trochaic lines, usually with the trochees dominating. . . .

A fin[e] example of how Blake employed mixed meters for expressive ends is "The Tyger," where an iambic line serves at several points like a water boy among the hammering trochees and spondees.

T. S. Eliot has paid Blake a high compliment by finding in him "merely a peculiar honesty, which, in a world too frightened to be honest, is peculiarly terrifying. It is an honesty against which the whole world conspires, because it is unpleasant. . . . And this honesty never exists without great technical accomplishment."[3] The technical accomplishment of Blake's candid lyrics involved a double temerity. In the first place, he dared to write serious poetry with the basic rhythmical and linguistic tools of a prattling child. In the second, he dared to think thoughts and hear melodies whose precise expression required breaking some universally accepted metrical conventions. The latter achievement . . . should not obscure the former, which was at least as essential to Blake's lyric gift. They dovetail, one defining the particulars of emotion and idea, the other the generalities of simplicity and purity.

SUGGESTIONS FOR WRITING

1. Write an essay analyzing Blake's two "Holy Thursday" poems or any other pair of counterpart poems from *Songs of Innocence and of Experience*. What different views of the same person, place, situation, and so on are offered in your two poems? What conclusions does each poem seem to reach about, and through, the subject it depicts? How do the poems' formal qualities—syntax, diction, rhythm, rhyme, and so on—contribute to their distinctive tone and theme(s)?

2. Drawing on evidence from various poems in the "Songs of Experience" section of *Songs of Innocence and of Experience*, write an essay explaining how "London" or "The Sick Rose" works as a "Song of Experience" poem. What similarities do you see between "London" or "The Sick Rose" and other "Experience" poems? What does either of these poems add to the "Experience" sequence?

3. Robert F. Gleckner suggests that one thing that binds the "Innocence" and "Experience" poems to each other is Blake's use of recurring or similar symbols and characters. Alicia Ostriker argues the same of various formal features such as diction, syntax, and meter. Write an essay exploring a particular symbol or set of symbols, characters, or formal techniques that you see as important to the effect and meaning of Blake's *Songs* as a sequence.

4. Choose any poem in this anthology and use library or Internet resources to research the collection or sequence of which it is a part. Write a response paper or essay reflecting on how your interpretation of the poem changes when you read it as part of a particular collection or sequence rather than on its own.

5. Write an essay analyzing at least two poems in this book that are part of the same sequence or collection. You might choose two sonnets by Elizabeth Barrett Browning, Edna St. Vincent Millay, or William Shakespeare; two of the poems from Robert Browning's *Dramatic Lyrics* (1842): "My Last Duchess" ("Reading More Poetry"), "Soliloquy of the Spanish Cloister" (chapter 14), or "Porphyria's Lover" ("Romantic Love: An Album"); or two poems from the sequence of odes by John Keats that includes "Ode to a Nightingale," "Ode on a Grecian Urn," and "To Autumn" (all in

---

3. T. S. Eliot, *The Sacred Wood* (London, 1934), p. 151 [Author's note].

"Reading More Poetry"). How do your two poems make sense together, as parts of a single, unified sequence or collection? If you know how the poems are ordered in the collection, what difference might their order make to their meaning?

6. Write two poems that, like Blake's "Holy Thursday" or "Chimney Sweeper" poems, depict the same object, person, or situation from two dramatically different perspectives.

Reading More Poetry. How do your two poems make sense together as parts of a larger "unit" sequence or collection? If you know how the poems are ordered in the collection, what difference might their order make to their meaning?

Look at two poems that, like Blake's "Holy Thursday" or "Spring" sweeper poems depict the same object, person, or situation from two dramatically different points of view.

23 LITERARY TRADITION AS CONTEXT

The more poetry you read, the better a reader of poetry you are likely to become—not just because your skills will improve and develop but also because you will come to know more about poetic traditions—the ever-growing body of poetic customs and practices. A poet's consciousness of what others have done leads to a sense of tradition that is often hard to articulate and that may present a problem for a new reader of poetry. How can I possibly read a poem intelligently, you might ask yourself in exasperation, until I've read all the other poems that inspired it? What is the point of poets' relentless consciousness of what has already been done by others? Why do they repeatedly answer, allude to, and echo other poems? Why does tradition matter?

Tradition matters to a poet or other artist much as the history of a sport matters to an athlete. There are former stars to honor and records to break in order to enter that tradition. But literature has had much longer to evolve its rules and standards than most sports played today. Contemporary poets rarely write new poems *strictly* by rules of writing that were current in, say, the sixteenth century. Rather, they refer to one another's work or use it as a starting point for their own. Sometimes they compete; at other times they playfully echo or imitate one another. And sometimes poets simply want to pay tribute to predecessors.

Often poets set themselves a particular task to see what they can do. One way of doing so is to introduce a standard **motif** (a recurrent device, formula, or situation that deliberately connects a poem with traditional thought) and then to play variations on it much as a musician might do. Another way is to provide an alternative answer to a question that has repeatedly been asked and answered in a traditional way. Poetic playfulness by no means excludes serious intention—the poems in this chapter often make important statements about their subjects, however humorous they may be in their method, and they illustrate some of the ways that the tradition energizes individual poets to make the most of their heritage.

ECHO AND ALLUSION

You have probably noticed, in the poems you have read so far, a number of allusions—glances at the tradition or at individual expressions of it. The more poems you read, the more such allusions you will grasp and the more you will become a comfortable member of the audience poets write for. The poems in this group employ this familiar poetic strategy of echoing or alluding to other texts as a way of importing meaning into a poem, similar to the strategy of "sampling" words or sounds in contemporary music. An echo may simply recall a word, phrase, or sound in another text as a way of associating what is going on in *this* poem with something in another, already familiar text. An **allusion** more insistently connects a particular word, phrase, or section of a poem with some similar formulation in a previous text; it explicitly *invokes* the reader's recognition of the previous text and asks for interpretation based on the implied similarity. Often poets quote—or echo with variations—a passage from another text in order to suggest some thematic, ideological, tonal, or stylistic link. Sometimes the purpose is simply to invoke an idea or attitude from another text, another place, or another culture.

The following poems recall individual passages, poems, or traditions in order to establish a particular stance or attitude. As you read them, ask yourself how the allusion affects your interpretation and how it changes the meaning of the poem.

BEN JONSON

[Come, my Celia, let us prove][1]

Come, my Celia, let us prove,[2]
While we can, the sports of love;
Time will not be ours forever:
He at length our good will sever.
5 Spend not, then, his gifts in vain;
Suns that set may rise again,
But if once we lose this light,
'Tis with us perpetual night.
Why should we defer our joys?
10 Fame and rumor are but toys.
Cannot we delude the eyes
Of a few poor household spies?
Or his easier ears beguile,
Thus removèd by our wile?
15 'Tis no sin love's fruits to steal,
But the sweet thefts to reveal;
To be taken, to be seen,
These have crimes accounted been.

1606

HOWARD NEMEROV

Boom!

Sees Boom in Religion, too

Atlantic City, June 23, 1957 (AP)—President Eisenhower's pastor said tonight that Americans are living in a period of "unprecedented religious activity" caused partially by paid vacations, the eight-hour day and modern conveniences.

---

1. A song from *Volpone*, sung by the play's villain and would-be seducer. Part of the poem paraphrases Catullus, poem 5. The speaker's invitation echoes Satan's temptation of Eve in Genesis. 2. Experience.

"These fruits of material progress," said the Rev. Edward L. R. Elson of the National
Presbyterian Church, Washington, *"have provided the leisure, the energy, and the
means for a level of human and spiritual values never before reached."*

Here at the Vespasian-Carlton,[3] it's just one
religious activity after another; the sky
is constantly being crossed by cruciform
airplanes, in which nobody disbelieves
5   for a second and the tide, the tide
of spiritual progress and prosperity
miraculously keeps rising, to a level
never before attained. The churches are full,
the beaches are full, and the filling-stations
10   are full, God's great ocean is full
of paid vacationers praying an eight-hour day
to the human and spiritual values, the fruits,[4]
the leisure, the energy, and the means, Lord,
the means for the level, the unprecedented level,
15   and the modern conveniences, which also are full.
Never before, O Lord, have the prayers and praises
from belfry and phonebooth, from ballpark and barbecue
the sacrifices,[5] so endlessly ascended.

It was not thus when Job in Palestine
20   sat in the dust and cried, cried bitterly;[6]
when Damien kissed the lepers on their wounds
it was not thus;[7] it was not thus
when Francis worked a fourteen-hour day
strictly for the birds;[8] when Dante took
25   a week's vacation without pay and it rained
part of the time,[9] O Lord, it was not thus.

But now the gears mesh and the tires burn
and the ice chatters in the shaker and the priest
in the pulpit and Thy Name, O Lord,
30   is kept before the public, while the fruits
ripen and religion booms and the level rises

3. Vespasian was emperor of Rome 69–79 C.E., shortly after the reign of Nero. In French, *vespasienne* means "public toilet." Carlton is a familiar hotel name.
4. "Fruits" echoes biblical language about the fruit of our labor as well as the beginning of John Milton's biblical epic, *Paradise Lost.*
5. Allusion to the burnt offerings of livestock commanded in the Hebrew Bible. The rising smoke was said to please God.
6. According to the Book of Job, he was afflicted with the loss of prosperity, children, and health as a test of his faith. His name means, in Hebrew, "he cries"; see especially Job 2.7–13.
7. "Father Damien" (Joseph Damien de Veuster, 1840–89), a Roman Catholic missionary from Belgium, was known for his work among lepers in Hawaii; he ultimately contracted leprosy himself and died there.
8. St. Francis of Assisi, thirteenth-century founder of the Franciscan order, was noted for his love of all living things, and one of the most famous stories about him tells of his preaching to the birds.
9. Dante's journey through Hell, Purgatory, and Paradise (in *The Divine Comedy*) takes a week, beginning on Good Friday, 1300. It rains in the third chasm of Hell.

and every modern convenience runneth over,[1]
that it may never be with us as it hath been
with Athens and Karnak and Nagasaki,[2]
35 nor Thy sun for one instant refrain from shining
on the rainbow Buick by the breezeway
or the Chris Craft with the uplift life raft;
that we may continue to be the just folks we are,
plain people with ordinary superliners and
40 disposable diaperliners, people of the stop'n'shop
'n'pray as you go, of hotel, motel, boatel,
the humble pilgrims of no deposit no return
and please adjust thy clothing, who will give to Thee,
if Thee will keep us going, our annual
45 Miss Universe, for Thy Name's Sake, Amen.

                                                    1960

MARIANNE MOORE

Love in America?

Whatever it is, it's a passion—
a benign dementia that should be
engulfing America, fed in a way
    the opposite of the way
5   in which the Minotaur[3] was fed.
It's a Midas[4] of tenderness;
    from the heart;
nothing else. From one with ability
to bear being misunderstood—
10   take the blame, with "nobility
    that is action,"[5] identifying itself with
    pioneer unperfunctoriness

    without brazenness or
    bigness of overgrown
15   undergrown shallowness.

    Whatever it is, let it be without
        affection.

    Yes, yes, yes, *yes.*

                                                    1967

1. Alludes to Psalm 23:5, King James version of the Bible: "my cup runneth over," i.e., I have abundance.
2. Large Japanese port city, virtually destroyed by a U.S. atomic bomb in 1945. *Athens:* the cultural center of ancient Greek civilization. *Karnak:* a village on the Nile, built on the site of ancient Thebes.
3. The Minotaur demanded a virgin to devour once a year [Moore's note; notes 4–6 are also Moore's].
4. Midas, who had the golden touch, was inconvenienced when eating or picking things up.
5. Unamuno said that what we need as a cure for unruly youth is "nobility that is action."

ROBERT HOLLANDER

You Too? Me Too—Why Not? Soda Pop

```
              I am
              look
              ing at
              the Co
              caCola
              bottle
              which is
              green wi
              th ridges
              just-like
              c     c     c
              o     o     o
              l     l     l
              u     u     u
              m     m     m
              n     n     n
              s     s     s
          and on itself it says

              COCA-COLA
              reg.u.s.pat.off.
```

exactly like an art pop
statue of that kind of
bottle but not so green
that the juice inside
gives other than the co-
lor it has when I pour
it out in a clear glass
glass on this table top
(It's making me thirsty
all this winking and
beading of Hippocrene[6]
please let me pause drinking   the   fluid   in)
ah! it is enticing how each
color   is   the   same
brown   in   green   bottle
brown   in   uplifted   glass
making each utensil on
the table laid a brown
fork in a brown shade[7]
making me long to watch
them harvesting the crop
which makes the deep-aged
rich brown wine of America
that is to say which makes
soda   pop

1968

---

6. In Greek mythology, a fountain created by the hooves of the winged horse Pegasus, said to be a source of inspiration to the poets who drink from it. The speaker in "Ode to a Nightingale" by John Keats ("Reading More Poetry") refers to Hippocrene.

7. A paraphrase of "a green thought in a green shade" in Andrew Marvell's "The Garden."

WILLIAM SHAKESPEARE

[*Not marble, nor the gilded monuments*]

Not marble, nor the gilded monuments
Of princes, shall outlive this powerful rhyme;
But you shall shine more bright in these contènts
Than unswept stone, besmeared with sluttish time.
5 When wasteful war shall statues overturn,
And broils[8] root out the work of masonry,
Nor[9] Mars his sword nor war's quick fire shall burn
The living record of your memory.
'Gainst death and all-oblivious enmity
10 Shall you pace forth; your praise shall still find room
Even in the eyes of all posterity
That wear this world out to the ending doom.[1]
So, till the judgment that yourself arise,
You live in this, and dwell in lovers' eyes.

                                                         1609

IMITATING AND ANSWERING

A poem will often respond directly—sometimes point by point or even line by line or word by word—to another poem. The tactic may be teasing or comic, but often, too, a real challenge exists behind such a facetious answer, perhaps a serious criticism of the first poem's point or the tradition it represents, or an attempt to provide a different perspective. While it may follow its model slavishly, the poem may also alter key words or details so that readers will easily notice the differences in tone or attitude.

The following two poems, by Christopher Marlowe and Sir Walter Raleigh, provide a famous example of one poem responding to another. Both are **pastoral** poems, concerned with the simple life of country folk and describing that life in stylized, idealized terms. The people in a pastoral poem are usually shepherds, although they may be fishermen or other rustics who lead an outdoor life and tend to basic human needs in a simplified world of beauty, music, and love. Pastoral thus is an interlude apart from civic, adult, mortal life. To present a certain tone, attitude, and wholeness, poets self-consciously construct this vision of a self-contained world, at the same time alluding to previous works in the pastoral tradition. Raleigh's pastoral poem is only one of many "replies" to Marlowe's poem.

CHRISTOPHER MARLOWE

The Passionate Shepherd to His Love

Come live with me and be my love,
And we will all the pleasures prove[2]
That valleys, groves, hills, and fields,
Woods, or steepy mountain yields.

8. Riots.   9. Neither. *Mars his*: Mars's.   1. Judgment Day.   2. Experience.

5 And we will sit upon the rocks,
Seeing the shepherds feed their flocks,
By shallow rivers to whose falls
Melodious birds sing madrigals.

And I will make thee beds of roses
10 And a thousand fragrant posies,
A cap of flowers, and a kirtle[3]
Embroidered all with leaves of myrtle;

A gown made of the finest wool
Which from our pretty lambs we pull;
15 Fair linèd slippers for the cold,
With buckles of the purest gold;

A belt of straw and ivy buds,
With coral clasps and amber studs:
And if these pleasures may thee move,
20 Come live with me, and be my love.

The shepherd swains[4] shall dance and sing
For thy delight each May morning:
If these delights thy mind may move,
Then live with me and be my love.

1600

SIR WALTER RALEIGH

The Nymph's Reply to the Shepherd

If all the world and love were young,
And truth in every shepherd's tongue,
These pretty pleasures might me move
To live with thee and be thy love.

5 Time drives the flocks from field to fold,
When rivers rage, and rocks grow cold,
And Philomel[5] becometh dumb;
The rest complain of cares to come.

The flowers do fade, and wanton fields
10 To wayward winter reckoning yields:
A honey tongue, a heart of gall,
Is fancy's spring, but sorrow's fall.

Thy gowns, thy shoes, thy beds of roses,
Thy cap, thy kirtle, and thy posies

---

3. Gown.   4. Youths.   5. The nightingale.

15 Soon break, soon wither, soon forgotten;
In folly ripe, in reason rotten.

Thy belt of straw and ivy buds,
Thy coral clasps and amber studs,
All these in me no means can move
20 To come to thee and be thy love.

But could youth last, and love still breed,
Had joys no date,[6] nor age no need,
Then these delights my mind might move
To live with thee and be thy love.

1600

The selections that follow similarly play on well-known poems. Strictly speaking, only one of these poems that follows (the one by Koch) is a **parody**—that is, it pretends to write in the style of the original poem but exaggerates that style and changes the content for comic effect. The others make fun of an original in less direct ways, but they share the objective of answering an original, even though they use very different styles to alter the poetic intention of that original.

HARRYETTE MULLEN

Dim Lady[7]

My honeybunch's peepers are nothing like neon. Today's
special at Red Lobster is redder than her kisser. If Liquid Paper
is white, her racks are institutional beige. If her mop were
Slinkys, dishwater Slinkys would grow on her noggin. I have
seen tablecloths in Shakey's Pizza Parlors, red and white, but   5
no such picnic colors do I see in her mug. And in some minty-
fresh mouthwashes there is more sweetness than in the garlic
breeze my main squeeze wheezes. I love to hear her rap, yet
I'm aware that Muzak has a hipper beat. I don't know any
Marilyn Monroes. My ball and chain is plain from head to toe.   10
And yet, by gosh, my scrumptious Twinkie has as much sex
appeal for me as any lanky model or platinum movie idol
who's hyped beyond belief.

2002

6. End.
7. Mullen's poem parodies each descriptive idea in Shakespeare's "[My mistress' eyes are nothing like the sun]" (chapter 19). Shakespeare's sonnets frequently address or refer to the so-called Dark Lady.

ANNE LAUINGER

Marvell Noir[8]

Sweetheart, if we had the time,
A week in bed would be no crime.
I'd light your Camels, pour your Jack;
You'd do shiatsu[9] on my back.
5 When you got up to scramble eggs,
I'd write a sonnet to your legs,
And you could watch my stubble grow.
Yes, gorgeous, we'd take it slow.
I'd hear the whole sad tale again:
10 A roadhouse band; you can't trust men;
He set you up; you had to eat,
And bitter with the bittersweet
Was what they dished you; Ginger lied;
You weren't there when Sanchez died;
15 You didn't know the pearls were fake . . .
Aw, can it, sport! Make no mistake,
You're in it, doll, up to your eyeballs!
Tears? Please! You'll dilute our highballs,
And make that angel face a mess
20 For the nice Lieutenant. I confess
I'm nuts for you—but take the rap?[1]
You must think I'm some other sap!
And, precious, I kind of wish I was.
Well, when they spring[2] you, give a buzz;
25 Guess I'll get back to Archie's wife,
And you'll get twenty-five to life.[3]
You'll have time there, more than enough,
To reminisce about the stuff
That dreams are made of,[4] and the men
30 You suckered. Sadly, in the pen
Your kind of talent goes to waste.
But Irish bars are more my taste
Than Iron ones: stripes ain't my style.
You're going down; I promise I'll
35 Come visit every other year.
Now kiss me, sweet—the squad car's here.

2005

---

8. This poem directly echoes and parodies Andrew Marvell's "To His Coy Mistress" (chapter 15) as well as "noir" films (*noir* means "black" in French) in which a tough guy in the end reveals that the sexy woman is guilty of conspiring to commit murder or other crimes.   9. Japanese style of massage.

1. Confess and take the punishment in someone's stead.
2. Release from prison.   3. A 25-year or lifetime sentence.
4. Allusion to Shakespeare, *The Tempest*, act 4, scene 1: "we are such stuff as dreams are made on."

The following poem, by E. E. Cummings, is not a direct response to a single poem but a playful pastiche: a sampling of poetic materials and conventions. Instead of pastoral, it refers to the literary convention of fallen monuments or ruins, as many neoclassical and Romantic poets "pondered" the remains of the Roman Empire. It parodies **carpe diem** poems such as Andrew Marvell's "To His Coy Mistress" (chapter 15), in which the speaker urges the lady to make love before time passes. It is also a fragmentary meditation on the situation and themes of Matthew Arnold's "Dover Beach" (chapter 15).

E. E. CUMMINGS

[(*ponder, darling, these busted statues*]

(ponder,darling,these busted statues
of yon motheaten forum be aware
notice what hath remained
—the stone cringes
5 clinging to the stone, how obsolete

lips utter their extant smile. . . .
remark

a few deleted of texture
or meaning monuments and dolls

10 resist Them Greediest Paws of careful
time all of which is extremely
unimportant)whereas Life

matters if or

when the your- and my-
15 idle vertical worthless
self unite in a peculiarly
momentary

partnership(to instigate
constructive
20   Horizontal
business. . . . even so, let us make haste
—consider well this ruined aqueduct

lady,
which used to lead something into somewhere)
              1926

KENNETH KOCH

Variations on a Theme by William Carlos Williams[5]

1

I chopped down the house that you had been saving to live in next
      summer.
I am sorry, but it was morning, and I had nothing to do
and its wooden beams were so inviting.

2

We laughed at the hollyhocks together
5 and then I sprayed them with lye.
Forgive me. I simply do not know what I am doing.

3

I gave away the money that you had been saving to live on for the next
      ten years.
The man who asked for it was shabby
and the firm March wind on the porch was so juicy and cold.

4

10 Last evening we went dancing and I broke your leg.
Forgive me. I was clumsy, and
I wanted you here in the wards, where I am the doctor!

1962

DESMOND SKIRROW

Ode on a Grecian Urn Summarized[6]

Gods chase
Round vase.
What say?
What play?
5 Don't know.
Nice, though.

1960

---

5. Koch presents four variations on "This Is Just to Say" (chapter 16).
6. Skirrow's six lines of dimeter condense Keats's poem ("Reading More Poetry").

ANTHONY HECHT

The Dover Bitch

A Criticism of Life[7]

for Andrews Wanning[8]

So there stood Matthew Arnold and this girl
With the cliffs of England crumbling away behind them,
And he said to her, "Try to be true to me,
And I'll do the same for you, for things are bad
5 All over, etc., etc."
Well now, I knew this girl. It's true she had read
Sophocles in a fairly good translation
And caught that bitter allusion to the sea,[9]
But all the time he was talking she had in mind
10 The notion of what his whiskers would feel like
On the back of her neck. She told me later on
That after a while she got to looking out
At the lights across the channel, and really felt sad,
Thinking of all the wine and enormous beds
15 And blandishments in French and the perfumes.
And then she got really angry. To have been brought
All the way down from London, and then be addressed
As a sort of mournful cosmic last resort
Is really tough on a girl, and she was pretty.
20 Anyway, she watched him pace the room
And finger his watch-chain and seem to sweat a bit,
And then she said one or two unprintable things.
But you mustn't judge her by that. What I mean to say is,
She's really all right. I still see her once in a while
25 And she always treats me right. We have a drink
And I give her a good time, and perhaps it's a year
Before I see her again, but there she is,
Running to fat, but dependable as they come.
And sometimes I bring her a bottle of *Nuit d'Amour.*[1]

                                                        1968

POETIC "KINDS"

Poems may be classified in a variety of ways—by subject or theme; by their length,
appearance, and formal features; by the way they are organized; by the level of
language they use; by the poet's intention and the kinds of effects the poem tries
to generate. We can experience a poem more fully if we understand early on what

---

7. Matthew Arnold, critic as well as poet, famously wrote that poetry should be "a criticism of life."
8. Andrews Wanning, a contemporary of Hecht's, was a professor of literature at Bard College.
9. In Sophocles' *Antigone*, lines 583–91. See "Dover Beach," lines 9–18 (chapter 15).
1. French for "Night of Love," presumably a bottle of perfume.

Poetic Kinds

aubade	a morning song in which the coming of dawn is either celebrated or denounced as a nuissance	Donne, "The Good-Morrow" (ch. 15)
ballad	a narrative poem characterized by short lines, regular meter, and a repeated refrain; ballads were originally orally transmitted	Anonymous, "Sir Patrick Spens" (ch. 18)
carpe diem	from the Latin phrase meaning "seize the day," a poem written in contemplation of human mortality and the passing of time	Cummings, "[(ponder, darling, these busted statues)]" (ch. 23)
confessional	a relatively recent kind in which the speaker describes a state of mind that becomes a metaphor for the larger world	Lowell, "Skunk Hour" (ch. 25)
dramatic monologue	a monologue set in a specific situation and spoken to an imaginary audience	Browning, "My Last Duchess" (ch. 14)
elegy	usually a formal lament on the death of a particular person	Auden, "In Memory of Yeats" (ch. 21)
epic	a narrative poem using elevated language and a grand, high style to celebrate the achievements of heroes and heroines, and usually with grand historic or national themes	Anonymous, *Beowulf* (ch. 20)
epigram	a very short, usually witty verse with a quick turn at the end	Coleridge, Parker, Wilde (ch. 23)
haiku	an unrhymed poetic form, Japanese in origin, arranged in three lines of five, seven, and five syllables, respectively	Buson, "[Coolness—]" (ch. 23)
lyric	any short poem in which the speaker expresses intense personal emotion rather than describing a narrative or dramatic situation	Blake, "The Lamb" (ch. 22)
meditation	a contemplation of some physical object as a way of reflecting upon some larger truth, often (but not necessarily) a spiritual one	Wilbur, "Love Calls Us to the Things of This World" (ch. 25)
occasional	a poem written about or for a specific occasion, public or private	Tennyson, "The Charge of the Light Brigade" (ch. 17)
ode	a lyric poem characterized by a serious topic and formal tone but no prescribed formal pattern	Keats, "Ode on a Grecian Urn" (Reading More Poetry)
parody	a work that imitates another work for comic effect by exaggerating the style and changing the content of the original	Hecht, "The Dover Bitch" (ch. 23)
pastoral	describes the simple life of country folk, usually shepherds, who live in a world of beauty, music, and love (also called an eclogue, a bucolic, or an idyll)	Marlowe, "The Passionate Shepherd to His Love" (ch. 23)
protest	a poetic attack, usually quite direct, on allegedly unjust institutions or social injustices	Blake, "London" (ch. 13)
satire	a literary work that holds up human failings to ridicule and censure	Kennedy, "In a Prominent Bar in Secaucus" (ch. 14)
soliloquy	a monologue in which the character in a play is alone and speaking only to him- or herself	Browning, "Soliloquy of the Spanish Cloister" (ch. 14)

kind of poem it is, and if we know that the poet has consciously adhered to certain conventions, standard ways of saying things that achieve certain expected effects or responses.

HAIKU

The **haiku**, an import into the English poetic tradition, has a long history in Japanese poetry. Originally, the haiku (then called *hokku*) was a short section of a longer poem (called a *renga* or *haikai*) composed by several poets who wrote segments in response to one another. Traditionally, the Japanese haiku was an unrhymed poem consisting of seventeen sounds (or, rather, characters representing seventeen sounds) and distributed over three lines in a five-seven-five pattern—that is, five distinctive sounds in the first line, seven in the second, and five in the third. "Sounds" in the Japanese language are not exactly the same as "syllables" in English, but when English writers began to compose haiku about a century ago, they ordinarily translated the sound requirement into syllables.

Haiku aim for compression; they leave a lot unsaid. Typically, haiku describe a natural object and imply a state of mind. They usually have a "seasonal" requirement, so that each poem associates itself with one season of the year in a revolving pattern of change. This seasonal association may be quite subtle and indirect through, for example, a seasonal flower. Haiku more generally involve descriptions of nature, reflecting the Buddhist sense of nature as orderly and benign but also contingent and transient.

When adapted into other languages and cultures, haiku cannot rely on the same spiritual assumptions or worldview, but these poems usually retain a sense of the human and natural as being mutually reflective and interdependent. Haiku often combine observation and imagination, blurring the Western distinction between seeing something literally and having some "vision" of its end or meaning.

Some of the traditional Japanese "masters" of haiku from the seventeenth to the early twentieth century—Bashō, Issa, and Buson, for example—are represented (in English translations) in the examples that follow. Later poets and translators have not always observed the seventeen-syllable and three-line requirements. Moreover, haiku has become an international form, and poets around the world have created a haiku tradition in at least fifty languages. As in any other poetic kind, the conventions prove both demanding and adaptable to the particular needs of different situations, different languages, and different individual poets.

CHIYOJO

[*Whether astringent*][2]

Whether astringent
I do not know. This is my first
Persimmon picking.

2. Chiyojo (1703–75) is probably the most famous Japanese woman haiku poet. Tradition has it that she wrote this poem at the time of (and about) her engagement. Translation by Daniel C. Buchanan.

BASHŌ

[A village without bells—][3]

A village without bells—
   how do they live?
      spring dusk.

[This road—]

This road—
no one goes down it,
   autumn evening.

BUSON

[Coolness—][4]

Coolness—
   the sound of the bell
      as it leaves the bell.

[Listening to the moon]

Listening to the moon,
gazing at the croaking of frogs
   in a field of ripe rice.

SEIFŪ

[The faces of dolls][5]

The faces of dolls.
In unavoidable ways
I must have grown old.

---

3. Matsuo Bashō (1644–94) is usually considered the first great master poet of haiku. Translations by Robert Hass.   4. Yosa Buson (1716–83). Translations by Robert Hass.
5. Seifū (1650–1721) was a nun. Translation by Daniel C. Buchanan.

Perhaps the single most famous haiku poem is by Bashō. Here are four different translations into English of that poem. (The source of these poems, Hiroaki Sato's *One Hundred Frogs: From Matsu [i.e. Matsuo] Basho to Allen Ginsberg*, contains an even greater variety of examples.)

LAFCADIO HEARN

[*Old pond—*]

Old pond—frogs jumped in—sound of water.
                                        1898

CLARA A. WALSH

[*An old-time pond*]

An old-time pond, from off whose shadowed depth
Is heard the splash where some lithe frog leaps in.
                                        1910

EARL MINER

[*The still old pond*]

   The still old pond
and as a frog leaps in it
   the sound of a splash.
                                        1979

ALLEN GINSBERG

[*The old pond*]

The old pond—a frog jumps in, kerplunk!
                                        1979

The following haiku were all written in English:

BABETTE DEUTSCH

[*The falling flower*]⁶

The falling flower
I saw drift back to the branch
Was a butterfly.

                    1957

ETHERIDGE KNIGHT

[*Eastern guard tower*]

Eastern guard tower
glints in sunset; convicts rest
like lizards on rocks.

                    1960

ALLEN GINSBERG

[*Looking over my shoulder*]

Looking over my shoulder
my behind was covered
with cherry blossoms.

                    1955

RICHARD WRIGHT

[*In the falling snow*]

In the falling snow
A laughing boy holds out his palms
Until they are white.

                    1960

---

6. An adaptation of a poem by Arakida Moritake (1473–1549).

JAMES A. EMANUEL

Ray Charles

His get-aboard smile,
picnic knees, back-up bounce: JAZZ,
all there, ounce by ounce.

1999

A Handful of Epigrams

Like the haiku, the **epigram** in the English-language literary tradition is characterized by brevity and compression. Epigrams, however, are short witty statements, whether in prose or poetry, involving play on words or doubled or paradoxical meaning. (*Epigraphs*, often confused with epigrams, are short quotations attached to other texts, usually at the beginning.) An epigram does not have to be written down; some great talkers are known for inventing clever epigrams in conversation. But prose writers may be known for an epigrammatic style—that is, for frequently producing gem-like turns of phrase that will be remembered and quoted. Thus epigrams may be confused with any kind of famous quotation of a sentence or two, and they resemble cartoon captions or one-liner jokes. They may be just the sort of thing for public speeches, stand-up comedy, blogs, or Twitter!

There is a long tradition of epigrams as rhyming couplets:

SAMUEL TAYLOR COLERIDGE
What is an Epigram? A dwarfish whole;
Its body brevity, and wit its soul.

*

Swans sing before they die—'twere no bad thing
Should certain people die before they sing!

ALEXANDER POPE
I am His Highness' dog at Kew;
Pray tell me, sir, whose dog are you?

DOROTHY PARKER
Dorothy Parker's style in prose, poetry, and personal conversation had the quick perverse twists that are called epigrammatic.

I'd rather have a bottle in front of me than a frontal lobotomy.

*

If, with the literate, I am
Impelled to try an epigram,

(Continued on next page)

(Continued)

> I never seek to take the credit;
> We all assume that Oscar said it.

OSCAR WILDE

As Parker suggests, however, no one outdid Oscar Wilde in epigrams. Some of his epigrams are lines spoken by his characters; indeed, The Importance of Being Earnest (chapter 27) is crammed with epigrammatic speeches.

> All women become like their mothers. That is their tragedy. No man does. That's his.

*

> To love oneself is the beginning of a life-long romance.

MARK TWAIN

> Man is the only animal that blushes. Or needs to.

*

> When I was a boy of fourteen, my father was so ignorant I could hardly stand to have the old man around. But when I got to be twenty-one, I was astonished at how much the old man had learned in seven years.

OGDEN NASH

> Poets aren't very useful
> Because they aren't consumeful or produceful.

CULTURAL BELIEF AND TRADITION

Culture is a broad, flexible term. Culture generally is contrasted with nature, and always entails practices shared by more than one person or family. Often we think of a nation as a culture (and so, for example, speak of American culture), and we may make smaller and larger divisions—as long as the group has some common history and a somewhat cohesive purpose. We speak of Southern culture, or of urban culture, or of the drug culture, or of the various popular-music cultures, or of a culture associated with a particular political belief, economic class, or social group. Most of us belong, willingly or not, to a number of such cultures at one time, and to some extent our identities and destinies are linked to the distinctive features of those cultures and the ways each culture perceives its identity, values, and history. Some of these cultures we choose to join; some are thrust upon us by birth and circumstances. It is these larger and more persistent forms of culture—not those chosen by an individual—that we illustrate in this section.

Poets aware of their heritage often like to probe its history and beliefs and plumb its depths, just as they like to articulate and play variations on the poetic tradition they feel a part of. For poetry written in the English language over the last four hundred years or so, both the Judeo-Christian frame of reference and the classical frame of reference (drawing on the civilizations of ancient Greece and Rome) have been important. Western culture, a broad culture that includes many nations and many religious and social groups, is largely defined within these two frames of reference—or it has been until quite recently. More recently, poets in Europe and North America have drawn on other cultural myths—Native American, African, and Asian, for example—to expand our sense of common heritage and give new meaning to the "American" and "Western" experience.

Every culture develops stories to explain itself; these stories are often called **myths**. A myth may be fictitious but not untrue, and in fact may encompass great truths and shared cultural beliefs. A myth is a frame of reference that people within the culture understand and share. The poems that follow draw on different myths in a variety of ways and tones.

MIRIAM WADDINGTON

Ulysses Embroidered

You've come
at last from
all your journeying
to the old blind woman
5   in the tower,
Ulysses.[7]

After all adventurings
through seas and
mountains through
10   giant battles,
storms and death,
from pinnacles
to valleys;

Past sirens
15   naked on rocks
between Charybdis
and Scylla, from
dragons' teeth,
from sleep in
20   stables choking
on red flowers
walking through weeds
and through shipwreck.

And now you are
25   climbing the stairs,

7. After the Trojan War, Ulysses (or Odysseus), king of Ithaca and one of the Greek heroes of the war, journeyed for ten years to return to his island home and to his wife, Penelope. To ward off suitors, Penelope had craftily been weaving and unraveling a tapestry that had to be finished before she would remarry. See Homer's *Odyssey* for accounts of these events and others mentioned in the poem.

taking shape,
a figure in shining
thread rising from
a golden shield:
30 a medallion
emblazoned in
tapestry you grew
from the blind hands
of Penelope.

35 Her tapestry
saw everything,
her stitches
embroidered the
painful colors
40 of her breath the
long sighing touch
of her hands.

She made many
journeys.

1992

ALFRED, LORD TENNYSON

Ulysses[8]

It little profits that an idle king,
By this still hearth, among these barren crags,
Matched with an agèd wife,[9] I mete and dole
Unequal laws unto a savage race,
5   That hoard, and sleep, and feed, and know not me.

I cannot rest from travel; I will drink
Life to the lees.[1] All times I have enjoyed
Greatly, have suffered greatly, both with those
That loved me, and alone; on shore, and when
10 Through scudding drifts the rainy Hyades[2]
Vexed the dim sea. I am become a name;
For always roaming with a hungry heart
Much have I seen and known—cities of men
And manners, climates, councils, governments,
15 Myself not least, but honored of them all—
And drunk delight of battle with my peers,

8. After the end of the Trojan War, Ulysses (or Odysseus), king of Ithaca and one of the war's Greek heroes, returned to his island home (line 34). Homer's account of the situation is in book 11 of *The Odyssey*, but Dante's account of Ulysses in canto 26 of the *Inferno* is the more immediate background of the poem.
9. Penelope.   1. That is, all the way down to the bottom of the cup.
2. Group of stars that were supposed to predict the rain when they rose at the same time as the sun.

Far on the ringing plains of windy Troy.
I am a part of all that I have met;
Yet all experience is an arch wherethrough
20 Gleams that untraveled world, whose margin fades
For ever and for ever when I move.
How dull it is to pause, to make an end,
To rust unburnished, not to shine in use!
As though to breathe were life. Life piled on life
25 Were all too little, and of one to me
Little remains; but every hour is saved
From that eternal silence, something more,
A bringer of new things; and vile it were
For some three suns to store and hoard myself,
30 And this gray spirit yearning in desire
To follow knowledge like a sinking star,
Beyond the utmost bound of human thought.

This is my son, mine own Telemachus,
To whom I leave the scepter and the isle—
35 Well-loved of me, discerning to fulfill
This labor by slow prudence to make mild
A rugged people, and through soft degrees
Subdue them to the useful and the good.
Most blameless is he, centered in the sphere
40 Of common duties, decent not to fail
In offices of tenderness, and pay
Meet adoration to my household gods,
When I am gone. He works his work, I mine.

There lies the port; the vessel puffs her sail:
45 There gloom the dark, broad seas. My mariners,
Souls that have toiled, and wrought, and thought with me—
That ever with a frolic welcome took
The thunder and the sunshine, and opposed
Free hearts, free foreheads—you and I are old;
50 Old age hath yet his honor and his toil.
Death closes all; but something ere the end,
Some work of noble note, may yet be done,
Not unbecoming men that strove with Gods.
The lights begin to twinkle from the rocks;
55 The long day wanes; the slow moon climbs; the deep
Moans round with many voices. Come, my friends.
'Tis not too late to seek a newer world.
Push off, and sitting well in order smite
The sounding furrows; for my purpose holds
60 To sail beyond the sunset, and the baths
Of all the western stars, until I die.
It may be that the gulfs will wash us down;[3]

3. Beyond the Gulf of Gibraltar was supposed to lie a chasm that led to Hades.

It may be we shall touch the Happy Isles,[4]
And see the great Achilles, whom we knew.
65 Though much is taken, much abides; and though
We are not now that strength which in old days
Moved earth and heaven, that which we are, we are:
One equal temper of heroic hearts,
Made weak by time and fate, but strong in will
70 To strive, to seek, to find, and not to yield.

1833

SYLVIA PLATH

Lady Lazarus

I have done it again.
One year in every ten
I manage it—

A sort of walking miracle, my skin
5 Bright as a Nazi lampshade,
My right foot

A paperweight,
My face a featureless, fine
Jew linen.[5]

10 Peel off the napkin
O my enemy.
Do I terrify?—

The nose, the eye pits, the full set of teeth?
The sour breath
15 Will vanish in a day.

Soon, soon the flesh
The grave cave ate will be
At home on me

And I a smiling woman.
20 I am only thirty.
And like the cat I have nine times to die.

This is Number Three.
What a trash
To annihilate each decade.

25 What a million filaments.
The peanut-crunching crowd
Shoves in to see

4. Elysium, the Islands of the Blessed, where heroes like Achilles (line 64) go after death.
5. During World War II, prisoners in some Nazi camps were gassed to death and their body parts then turned into objects such as lampshades and paperweights.

Them unwrap me hand and foot—
The big strip tease.
30 Gentlemen, ladies

These are my hands
My knees.
I may be skin and bone,

Nevertheless, I am the same, identical woman.
35 The first time it happened I was ten.
It was an accident.

The second time I meant
To last it out and not come back at all.
I rocked shut

40 As a seashell.
They had to call and call
And pick the worms off me like sticky pearls.

Dying
Is an art, like everything else.
45 I do it exceptionally well.

I do it so it feels like hell.
I do it so it feels real.
I guess you could say I've a call.

It's easy enough to do it in a cell.
50 It's easy enough to do it and stay put.
It's the theatrical

Comeback in broad day
To the same place, the same face, the same brute
Amused shout:

55 "A miracle!"
That knocks me out.
There is a charge

For the eyeing of my scars, there is a charge
For the hearing of my heart—
60 It really goes.

And there is a charge, a very large charge
For a word or a touch
Or a bit of blood

Or a piece of my hair or my clothes.
65 So, so Herr Doktor.
So, Herr Enemy.

I am your opus,
I am your valuable,
The pure gold baby

70 That melts to a shriek.
   I turn and burn.
   Do not think I underestimate your great concern

   Ash, ash—
   You poke and stir.
75 Flesh, bone, there is nothing there—

   A cake of soap,
   A wedding ring,
   A gold filling.

   Herr God, Herr Lucifer
80 Beware
   Beware.

   Out of the ash
   I rise with my red hair
   And I eat men like air.

                                    1965

WILLIAM CARLOS WILLIAMS

Landscape with the Fall of Icarus[6]

According to Brueghel
when Icarus fell
it was spring

   a farmer was ploughing
5 his field
   the whole pageantry

   of the year was
   awake tingling
   near

10 the edge of the sea
   concerned
   with itself

   sweating in the sun
   that melted
15 the wings' wax

   unsignificantly
   off the coast
   there was

6. The painting *Landscape with the Fall of Icarus* was long thought to be the work of Flemish master Pieter Bruegel the Elder (c. 1525–69); the name was spelled Brueghel by his painter sons. It is now believed to be a copy or version of a now-lost Bruegel original.

a splash quite unnoticed
20 this was
Icarus drowning

1962

EAVAN BOLAND

Atlantis—A Lost Sonnet

How on earth did it happen, I used to wonder
that a whole city—arches, pillars, colonnades,
not to mention vehicles and animals—had all
one fine day gone under?

5 I mean, I said to myself, the world was small then.
Surely a great city must have been missed?
I miss our old city—

white pepper, white pudding, you and I meeting
under fanlights and low skies to go home in it. Maybe
10 what really happened is

this: the old fable-makers searched hard for a word
to convey that what is gone is gone forever and
never found it. And so, in the best traditions of

where we come from, they gave their sorrow a name
15 and drowned it.

2007

ALBERTO ÁLVARO RÍOS

Advice to a First Cousin

The way the world works is like this:
for the bite of scorpions, she says,
my grandmother to my first cousin,
because I might die and someone must know,
5 go to the animal jar
the one with the soup of green herbs
mixed with the scorpions I have been putting in
still alive. Take one out
put it on the bite. It has had time to think
10 there with the others—put the lid back tight—
and knows that a biting is not the way to win
a finger or a young girl's foot.
It will take back into itself the hurting
the redness and the itching and its marks.

15 But the world works like this, too:
look out for the next scorpion you see,
she says, and makes a big face to scare me
thereby instructing my cousin, look out!
for one of the scorpion's many
20 illegitimate and unhappy sons.
It will be smarter, more of the devil.
It will have lived longer than these dead ones.
It will know from them something more
about the world, in the way mothers know
25 when something happens to a child, or how
I knew from your sadness you had been bitten.
It will learn something stronger than biting.
Look out most for that scorpion, she says,
making a big face to scare me again and it works
30 I go—crying—she lets me go—they laugh,
the way you must look out for men
who have not yet bruised you.

1985

LOUISE ERDRICH

Jacklight

The same Chippewa word is used both for flirting and hunting game, while another Chippewa word connotes both using force in intercourse and also killing a bear with one's bare hands.

—DUNNING 1959

We have come to the edge of the woods,
out of brown grass where we slept, unseen,
out of knotted twigs, out of leaves creaked shut,
out of hiding.

5 At first the light wavered, glancing over us.
Then it clenched to a fist of light that pointed,
searched out, divided us.
Each took the beams like direct blows the heart answers.
Each of us moved forward alone.

10 We have come to the edge of the woods,
drawn out of ourselves by this night sun,
this battery of polarized acids,
that outshines the moon.

We smell them behind it
15 but they are faceless, invisible,
We smell the raw steel of their gun barrels,
mink oil on leather, their tongues of sour barley.
We smell their mother buried chin-deep in wet dirt.

We smell their fathers with scoured knuckles,
20 teeth cracked from hot marrow.
We smell their sisters of crushed dogwood, bruised apples,
of fractured cups and concussions of burnt hooks.

We smell their breath steaming lightly behind the jacklight.
We smell the itch underneath the caked guts on their clothes.
25 We smell their minds like silver hammers
cocked back, held in readiness
for the first of us to step into the open.

We have come to the edge of the woods,
out of brown grass where we slept, unseen,
30 out of leaves creaked shut, out of our hiding.
We have come here too long.

It is their turn now,
their turn to follow us. Listen,
they put down their equipment.
35 It is useless in the tall brush.
And now they take the first steps, not knowing
how deep the woods are and lightless.
How deep the woods are.

1984

SUGGESTIONS FOR WRITING

1. What does Howard Nemerov's "Boom!" allude to in its language and its form? What picture of American politics and culture does the poem paint? Write an essay in which you analyze the satire of "Boom!"

2. Consider Christopher Marlowe's "The Passionate Shepherd to His Love" and one "answer" that poem has inspired: Sir Walter Raleigh's "The Nymph's Reply to the Shepherd." Compare it to other pastoral or *carpe diem* poems in this chapter. Write an essay examining the phenomenon of Marlowe's original poem and the poems responding to it on relying on similar conventions.

3. What is gained, and what is lost, when an artistic tradition like Japanese haiku is imported, through translation, imitation, and inspiration, into another culture? Using the poems in this chapter and your own research, write an essay in which you analyze the way that haiku has established itself as a part of English-language literary culture.

4. How closely do E. E. Cummings's "(ponder,darling,these busted statues" and Anne Lauinger's "Marvell Noir" echo Andrew Marvell's "To His Coy Mistress" (chapter 15)? What images are derived from Marvell? In what specific ways do Cummings's and Lauinger's poems undercut Marvell's argument, or their own? Write an essay in which you compare and contrast the three poems. What seem to be Marvell's real intentions? What are Cummings's and Lauinger's?

5. Write an essay in which you discuss the adaptation of Greek myth in Miriam Waddington's "Ulysses Embroidered." What details of Waddington's poem seem consistent with Homer's account in the *Odyssey*? What details seem to challenge Homer's account? What might be Waddington's purpose in adapting the myth in this way?

6. Using research and your own analysis, write an essay in which you examine the cultural traditions and historical background behind any poem or group of poems in this book.

The Garden of Eden: An Album

It would be difficult to find a story that has had a greater influence on literature and art than the account of Creation in the Bible. Jews, Christians, and Muslims all look back to Adam and Eve as the first man and woman, the parents of humanity. In Genesis, the first book of the Hebrew and Christian Bible, Adam and Eve are placed in the Garden of Eden, also known as Paradise (from the Persian and Greek words denoting walled park or garden).

Genesis in the King James Bible

Until the twentieth century, most writers in English grew up knowing the Bible intimately, usually in the King James version, a translation from Hebrew and Greek into English sponsored by King James I of England and completed in 1611. No matter what our beliefs, as readers of literature we can benefit from knowing the beautiful language of this key text.

7: And the LORD God formed man of the dust of the ground, and breathed into his nostrils the breath of life; and man became a living soul.

8: And the LORD God planted a garden eastward in Eden; and there he put the man whom he had formed.

9: And out of the ground made the LORD God to grow every tree that is pleasant to the sight, and good for food; the tree of life also in the midst of the garden, and the tree of knowledge of good and evil.

10: And a river went out of Eden to water the garden; and from thence it was parted, and became into four heads. . . .

15: And the LORD God took the man, and put him into the garden of Eden to dress it and to keep it.

16: And the LORD God commanded the man, saying, Of every tree of the garden thou mayest freely eat:

17: But of the tree of the knowledge of good and evil, thou shalt not eat of it: for in the day that thou eatest thereof thou shalt surely die.

18: And the LORD God said, It is not good that the man should be alone; I will make him an help meet[1] for him.

19: And out of the ground the LORD God formed every beast of the field, and every fowl of the air; and brought them unto Adam to see what he would call them: and whatsoever Adam called every living creature, that was the name thereof.

20: And Adam gave names to all cattle, and to the fowl of the air, and to every beast of the field; but for Adam there was not found an help meet for him.

21: And the LORD God caused a deep sleep to fall upon Adam and he slept: and he took one of his ribs, and closed up the flesh instead thereof;

22: And the rib, which the LORD God had taken from man, made he a woman, and brought her unto the man.

23: And Adam said, This is now bone of my bones, and flesh of my flesh: she shall be called Woman, because she was taken out of Man.

24: Therefore shall a man leave his father and his mother, and shall cleave unto his wife: and they shall be one flesh.

25: And they were both naked, the man and his wife, and were not ashamed. (Genesis 2.7–25)

1. That is, a helpmate or partner.

This remarkable text has stirred and inspired writers and artists for many centuries. There have been countless **allusions**, retellings, and visual or dramatic representations of the fundamental ideas and images: an enclosed garden with flowing rivers, two symbolic fruit trees, the first use of language in naming the creatures, and the creation of the two sexes, at first naked and unashamed.

And of course the story continues: The "edenic" paradise is overthrown. The Fall, as it is called, occurs in the next chapter of Genesis. The serpent speaks to the woman and tempts her to break the law against eating of the tree of the knowledge of good and evil. He says it isn't true that anyone who eats the forbidden fruit will die; God simply wants to keep the man and woman in ignorance and submission.

6: And when the woman saw that the tree was good for food, and that it was pleasant to the eyes, and a tree to be desired to make one wise, she took of the fruit thereof, and did eat, and gave also unto her husband with her; and he did eat.

7: And the eyes of them both were opened, and they knew that they were naked; and they sewed fig leaves together, and made themselves aprons.

8: And they heard the voice of the LORD God walking in the garden in the cool of the day: and Adam and his wife hid themselves from the presence of the LORD God amongst the trees of the garden.

9: And the LORD God called unto Adam, and said unto him, Where art thou?

10: And he said, I heard thy voice in the garden, and I was afraid, because I was naked; and I hid myself.

11: And he said, Who told thee that thou wast naked? Hast thou eaten of the tree, whereof I commanded thee that thou shouldest not eat?

12: And the man said, The woman whom thou gavest to be with me, she gave me of the tree, and I did eat.

13: And the LORD God said unto the woman, What is this that thou hast done? And the woman said, The serpent beguiled me, and I did eat. . . .

16: Unto the woman [God] said, I will greatly multiply thy sorrow and thy conception; in sorrow thou shalt bring forth children; and thy desire shall be to thy husband, and he shall rule over thee.

17: And unto Adam he said, . . .

19: In the sweat of thy face shalt thou eat bread, till thou return unto the ground; for out of it wast thou taken: for dust thou art, and unto dust shalt thou return.

20: And Adam called his wife's name Eve; because she was the mother of all living.

21: Unto Adam also and to his wife did the LORD God make coats of skins, and clothed them.

22: And the LORD God said, Behold, the man is become as one of us, to know good and evil: and now, lest he put forth his hand, and take also of the tree of life, and eat, and live for ever:

23: Therefore the LORD God sent him forth from the garden of Eden, to till the ground from whence he was taken.

24: So he drove out the man; and he placed at the east of the garden of Eden Cherubims,[2] and a flaming sword which turned every way, to keep the way of the tree of life. (Genesis 3.4–24)

2. Angels (Hebrew).

Adam and Eve Expelled from Paradise, an illustration from a mid-19th century copy
of *Grand Catechisme des familles (Christian Doctrine for Families)*

The details of these verses likewise have served countless works of literature
and art to this day. For instance, in an art museum or illustrated book you might
see a picture of a naked couple fleeing from a gateway guarded by spirits or angels
and a flaming sword, and recognize it as depicting Genesis 3.24. Or you might
read a poem or a prose work in which a happy, innocent couple is destroyed by the

Adam and Eve by William Strang, 1899

Animals and Birds in the Garden of Eden by school of Ferdinand van Kessel, ca. 17th century

woman's yielding to the arguments of a tempter, and consider whether the writer intends to present a version of the story of Adam and Eve and the serpent or Satan.

Adam and Eve have been painted and characterized in many different guises. Eden has been depicted as a golden age of childhood or a rural past. Beautiful and protected natural scenes and gardens have often been associated with the first garden, or Paradise. Any loss of innocence might be compared to the Fall. Destruction of the environment or rude awakenings into shame, suffering, and the hard work of adulthood have all been expressed through allusions to these chapters in Genesis.

This album presents some versions, ironic or humorous or otherwise, of the conflict between men and women associated with the Garden of Eden, including some protests against blaming the woman for the Fall. The album also presents some responses to the idea of the dawn of language in the naming of the living things that God had created. Can you find other recent uses of the motif of the Garden of Eden? Do they take sides in interpreting the moral of the Garden of Eden story? What parts of that story and what characters are included, emphasized, or excluded in each version—in this album and elsewhere? What do you think is the connection between acquiring language, knowledge of good and evil, and shame about nakedness? Could Adam and Eve have remained in Eden?

JOHN HOLLANDER

Adam's Task

And Adam gave names to all cattle, and to the fowl of the air, and to every beast of the field . . .

—Gen. 2.20

Thou, paw-paw-paw; thou, glurd; thou, spotted
  Glurd; thou, whitestap, lurching through
The high-grown brush; thou, pliant-footed,
  Implex; thou, awagabu.

5 Every burrower, each flier
  Came for the name he had to give:
Gay, first work, ever to be prior,
  Not yet sunk to primitive.

Thou, verdle; thou, McFleery's pomma;
10   Thou; thou; thou—three types of grawl;
Thou, flisket; thou, kabasch; thou, comma-
  Eared mashawk; thou, all; thou, all.

Were, in a fire of becoming,
  Laboring to be burned away,
15 Then work, half-measuring, half-humming,
  Would be as serious as play.

Thou, pambler; thou, rivarn; thou, greater
  Wherret, and thou, lesser one;
Thou, sproal; thou, zant; thou, lily-eater.
20   Naming's over. Day is done.

1971

- The speaker of the poem is Adam performing the "task" of naming. How does Hollander play with the sounds of words, including rhymes? Are real nouns or meanings suggested in the invented ones? What happens in the two stanzas that do not begin with "Thou"?

MARJORIE PICKTHALL

Adam and Eve

When the first dark had fallen around them
And the leaves were weary of praise,
In the clear silence Beauty found them
And shewed them all her ways.

5 In the high noon of the heavenly garden
Where the angels sunned with the birds,

Beauty, before their hearts could harden,
Had taught them heavenly words.

When they fled in the burning weather
10   And nothing dawned but a dream,
Beauty fasted their hands together
And cooled them at her stream.

And when day wearied and night grew stronger,
And they slept as the beautiful must,
15   Then she bided a little longer,
And blossomed from their dust.

                                              1922

- How does Pickthall adapt or modify the story of Adam and Eve? What happens to time in the stanzas of this poem? Is Beauty comparable to the serpent or Satan, or to a different idea or character?

SUSAN DONNELLY

Eve Names the Animals

To me, *lion* was sun on a wing
over the garden. *Dove,*
a burrowing, blind creature.

I swear that man
5   never knew animals. Words
he lined up according to size,

while elephants slipped flat-eyed
through water

and trout
10   hurtled from the underbrush, tusked
and ready for battle.

The name he gave me stuck
me to him. He did it to comfort me,
for not being first.

15   Mornings, while he slept,
I got away. Pickerel
hopped on the branches above me.
Only spider accompanied me,
nosing everywhere,
20   running up to lick my hand.

Poor finch. I suppose I was
woe to him—
the way he'd come looking for me,

not wanting either of us
25 to be ever alone

But to myself I was
palomino
    raven
        fox . . .

30 I strung words
by their stems and wore them
as garlands on my long walks.

The next day
I'd find them withered.
35 I liked change.

                  1985

- The speaker in the poem uses words in her own way. How is this way similar to or different from the speaker's use of words in "Adam's Task"? Why does Donnelly's poem use the word "man" instead of the name "Adam"? What does the final line suggest about the rest of the poem?

URSULA K. LE GUIN

She Unnames Them

Most of them accepted namelessness with the perfect indifference with which they had so long accepted and ignored their names. Whales and dolphins, seals and sea otters consented with particular grace and alacrity, sliding into anonymity as into their element. A faction of yaks, however, protested. They said that "yak" sounded right, and that almost everyone who knew they existed called them that. Unlike the ubiquitous creatures such as rats and fleas, who had been called by hundreds or thousands of different names since Babel, the yaks could truly say, they said, that they had a *name*. They discussed the matter all summer. The councils of the elderly females finally agreed that though the name might be useful to others it was so redundant from the yak point of view that they never spoke it themselves and hence might as well dispense with it. After they presented the argument in this light to their bulls, a full consensus was delayed only by the onset of severe early blizzards. Soon after the beginning of the thaw, their agreement was reached and the designation "yak" was returned to the donor.

Among the domestic animals, few horses had cared what anybody called them since the failure of Dean Swift's attempt to name them from their own vocabulary.[3] Cattle, sheep, swine, asses, mules, and goats, along with chickens,

---

3. In *Gulliver's Travels* (1726), part IV, Jonathan Swift (1667–1745), dean of St. Patrick's Cathedral, Dublin, gave the name *Houyhnhnms*—meant to sound like a horse neighing—to a race of rational, talking horses.

geese, and turkeys, all agreed enthusiastically to give their names back to the people to whom—as they put it—they belonged.

A couple of problems did come up with pets. The cats, of course, steadfastly denied ever having had any name other than those self-given, unspoken, effanin-effably personal names which, as the poet named Eliot[4] said, they spend long hours daily contemplating—though none of the contemplators has ever admitted that what they contemplate is their names and some onlookers have wondered if the object of that meditative gaze might not in fact be the Perfect, or Platonic, Mouse.[5] In any case, it is a moot point now. It was with the dogs, and with some parrots, lovebirds, ravens, and mynahs, that the trouble arose. These verbally talented individuals insisted that their names were important to them, and flatly refused to part with them. But as soon as they understood that the issue was precisely one of individual choice, and that anybody who wanted to be called Rover, or Froufrou, or Polly, or even Birdie in the personal sense, was perfectly free to do so, not one of them had the least objection to parting with the lowercase (or, as regards German creatures, uppercase)[6] generic appellations "poodle," "parrot," "dog," or "bird," and all the Linnaean qualifiers[7] that had trailed along behind them for two hundred years like tin cans tied to a tail.

The insects parted with their names in vast clouds and swarms of ephemeral syllables buzzing and stinging and humming and flitting and crawling and tunneling away.

5   As for the fish of the sea, their names dispersed from them in silence throughout the oceans like faint, dark blurs of cuttlefish ink, and drifted off on the currents without a trace.

None were left now to unname, and yet how close I felt to them when I saw one of them swim or fly or trot or crawl across my way or over my skin, or stalk me in the night, or go along beside me for a while in the day. They seemed far closer than when their names had stood between myself and them like a clear barrier: so close that my fear of them and their fear of me became one same fear. And the attraction that many of us felt, the desire to smell one another's smells, feel or rub or caress one another's scales or skin or feathers or fur, taste one another's blood or flesh, keep one another warm—that attraction was now all one with the fear, and the hunter could not be told from the hunted, nor the eater from the food.

This was more or less the effect I had been after. It was somewhat more powerful than I had anticipated, but I could not now, in all conscience, make an exception for myself. I resolutely put anxiety away, went to Adam,[8] and said, "You and your father lent me this—gave it to me, actually. It's been really useful,

---

4. American-born British poet T. S. Eliot (1888–1965), in *The Naming of Cats* (1939), where he coined the word *effanineffable*.
5. That is, the ideal form of a mouse; the Greek philosopher Plato (ca. 428–348 or 347 B.C.E.) argued that archetypes existed for all material things.   6. In the German language, most nouns are capitalized.
7. Swedish botanist and taxonomist Carolus Linnaeus (1707–78) originated the modern scientific classification of plants and animals.
8. See Genesis, esp. 2.19 ("And out of the ground the Lord God formed every beast of the field, and every fowl of the air; and brought them unto Adam to see what he would call them") and 3.20 ("Adam called his wife's name Eve; because she was the mother of all living").

but it doesn't exactly seem to fit very well lately. But thanks very much! It's really been very useful."

It is hard to give back a gift without sounding peevish or ungrateful, and I did not want to leave him with that impression of me. He was not paying much attention, as it happened, and said only, "Put it down over there, O.K.?" and went on with what he was doing.

One of my reasons for doing what I did was that talk was getting us nowhere, but all the same I felt a little let down. I had been prepared to defend my decision. And I thought that perhaps when he did notice he might be upset and want to talk. I put some things away and fiddled around a little, but he continued to do what he was doing and to take no notice of anything else. At last I said, "Well, goodbye, dear. I hope the garden key turns up."

He was fitting parts together, and said, without looking around, "O.K., fine, 10
dear. When's dinner?"

"I'm not sure," I said. "I'm going now. With the—" I hesitated, and finally said, "With them, you know," and went on out. In fact, I had only just then realized how hard it would have been to explain myself. I could not chatter away as I used to do, taking it all for granted. My words now must be as slow, as new, as single, as tentative as the steps I took going down the path away from the house, between the dark-branched, tall dancers motionless against the winter shining.

1985

- The narrator (Eve) recalls the characteristic reactions of various animal groups to losing their names. How are the situation and plot of this story different from the verses of Genesis 2 and 3? What is the effect of personifying the animals and describing their different social organizations? What is the gift that the narrator returns to Adam?

ANI DIFRANCO

Adam and Eve

Tonight you stooped to my level
I am your mangy little whore
Now you're trying to find your underwear
And then your socks and then the door
5 And you're trying to find a reason
Why you have to leave
But I know it's 'cuz you think you're Adam
And you think I'm Eve

You rhapsodize about beauty
10 And my eyes glaze
Everything I love is ugly
I mean really, you would be amazed
Just do me a favor
It's the least that you can do

15 Just don't treat me like I am
    Something that happened to you

    I am truly sorry about all this

    You put a tiny pin prick
    In my big red balloon
20 And as I slowly start to exhale
    That's when you leave the room
    I did not design this game
    I did not name the stakes
    I just happen to like apples
25 And I am not afraid of snakes

    I am truly sorry about all this
    I envy you your ignorance
    I hear that it's bliss

    So I let go the ratio
30 Of things said to things heard
    As I leave you to your garden
    And the beauty you preferred
    And I wonder what of this
    Will have meaning for you
35 When you've left it all behind
    I guess I'll even wonder
    If you meant it
    At the time
                                        1996

- What is the situation in DiFranco's lyrics? How does it differ from
  the situation in the other works in this album? What is implied
  when the woman says, "I am not afraid of snakes"?

SUGGESTIONS FOR WRITING

1. How does naming, and the use of language in general, help shape and define our
   perception of ourselves and the world around us? With reference to "Adam's Task"
   by John Hollander and "Eve Names the Animals" by Susan Donnelly, as well as the
   story "She Unnames Them" by Ursula K. LeGuin, write an essay discussing the way
   writers have regarded naming as emblematic of our power to see and understand
   our experience.

2. The man in DiFranco's song is said to be ignorant, in a garden, praising beauty.
   Adam and Eve in Pickthall's poem are accompanied by beauty. How are these two
   ideas of beauty similar or different? How does each verse in DiFranco's and Pickthall's "Adam and Eve" vary or change the time of day or the images of the man and
   woman's relationship? Write an essay in which you compare and contrast the lyrics
   and the poem, noting their different time periods (1996 and 1922) and different
   forms, styles, and tones.

3. Ursula K. LeGuin's parents were anthropologists, and much of her writing is considered science fiction in which the "science" focuses on linguistics and anthropology
   or sociology—the study of languages, cultures, and social organizations. Write an

essay in which you discuss "She Unnames Them" as not only a rewriting of the idea of Adam's naming Eve and the animals but also, more significantly, a fable (with talking animals) about the uses of language and the differences among cultures.

4. Genesis is utterly serious about the establishment of the order of the world and the beginning not only of the wonders but also of the pains and losses of human existence. How and why do any of the writers in this album turn this subject into humor? Can you find other funny versions of the Garden of Eden material? Can you find any treatments of this tradition that are unintentionally funny? Write an essay on any one or two parodies or humorous adaptations of the early chapters of Genesis, considering what is gained or lost in changing the perspective or tone from the original.

5. Search for allusions and adaptations of the Garden of Eden story in various genres or media and from different perspectives. Select two works that would reward comparison as versions of the Garden of Eden story because of the particular perspectives they take, and write a comparative essay in which you show the effect of that chosen perspective—and any other similar or different features of the works—on the significance of the story. For instance, does one version portray Satan as a sympathetic fallen angel and another portray him as a cynical snake or a human seducer of Eve? Or do otherwise similar versions take the side of either Adam or Eve, showing only the thoughts of one or the other person in the couple? Are any versions presented from the perspective of the Cherubim or archangel or of God?

24

CULTURAL AND HISTORICAL CONTEXTS:
THE HARLEM RENAISSANCE

Poetry may be read in private moments or experienced in a great variety of communal settings—in classrooms or theaters, for example, or at poetry slams or public readings. But it is almost always *written* in solitude by a single author. Collaboration is rare in poetry, even rarer than in other arts, though artistic creation in general (with a few exceptions like film) is usually a lonely process. Still, there is a sense in which many poems represent collaborative acts. Traditions, group identities, shared experiences, desires, and communal needs may come together in a particular moment and location to produce poetry (and other arts and artifacts) that has a distinctive stamp of time, place, and vision. One such phenomenon was the "Harlem Renaissance," a period of ten or fifteen years early in the twentieth century when an extraordinary (and extraordinarily talented) group of people came together in uptown Manhattan to celebrate (and embody) the awakening of a new African American consciousness. It was an unprecedented moment in American poetry and in American culture more generally, and it produced some of the twentieth century's most dramatic, compelling, and original poems, as well as significant works of art in a variety of other categories.

The Harlem Renaissance was not exactly a movement in the usual sense of structure and leadership; no one originated it or called it to order, and in fact it was not consciously planned or organized by any person or group. There was no founder, no architect, no leader, and it is hard to say why or how—or even exactly when—it began or ended. It happened, as needs and desires of African American intellectuals and artists became manifest and began to coalesce in a particular time and place, and it ended—or rather scattered its energy—when conditions in the world at large dictated that other priorities, especially economic ones, began to trump the forces that had brought it together. But it was not, of course, independent of history or without cause. It was a product of many circumstances, most of them involving the long-term aftereffects of slavery and the increasingly articulated desire of African Americans to produce a distinctive black American culture within the larger national culture that they had been introduced into forcibly. The Harlem Renaissance represented powerful assertions: that America had to include the voices of black Americans in order to find its own full definition, and, equally, that artistic creativity—including literary creativity—had to be fully realized and recognized if black Americans were to find their full human identity in their American homeland. To live in Harlem and to be black and creative was not an altogether happy experience, and the poetry that exploded out of that time and place was a poetry of anger, resentment, conflict, and torn loyalties. But it was also a poetry of energy, sensitivity, humanity, and high ideals.

The Cotton Club, circa 1930

What was the Harlem Renaissance? To call it a movement is to make it seem more coherent, goal-centered, and idealistic than it appeared to be at the time, but out of leaderless and haphazard beginnings it focused needs and desires in a forceful and effective way. It was first of all a migration or, rather, part of a migration: Around the end of World War I (the "War to End All Wars"), American blacks relocated in large numbers from the South to the North and from rural agricultural areas to cities. New York was only one of many destinations; Chicago, Philadelphia, Detroit, Washington, Cleveland, Buffalo, and other urban centers all received huge numbers of black migrants. But New York was the largest and most vibrant seat of culture in America, beginning to rival European capitals as a site where active artistic communities produced and consumed culture of all kinds—high, low, and in between. More than 100,000 blacks migrated to Harlem during the 1920s, taking over and transforming a Manhattan neighborhood north of Central Park and turning it into a distinctive, creative, independent, and infectious center of art and performance activities that drew the rest of New York City to it. For most of the 1920s—called "the Roaring 20s" throughout the Western world because of the era's daring, rebellious attitudes and booming economic growth—Harlem was a magnet for avant-garde whites in New York to take their pleasures. They flocked to speakeasies, nightclubs, and theaters (see map, pp. 1260–61), and they were fascinated by the kinds of music, dance, and performance art they could find there—productions quite different from those on Broadway or in other parts of the city, though increasingly the white venues tried to capture, in their own productions, something of the life and energy that patrons sought in Harlem. White readers, and many white artists, showed enormous—sometimes mawkish or even ghoulish—curiosity about black life in America. Before the Harlem Renaissance had ended, a large number

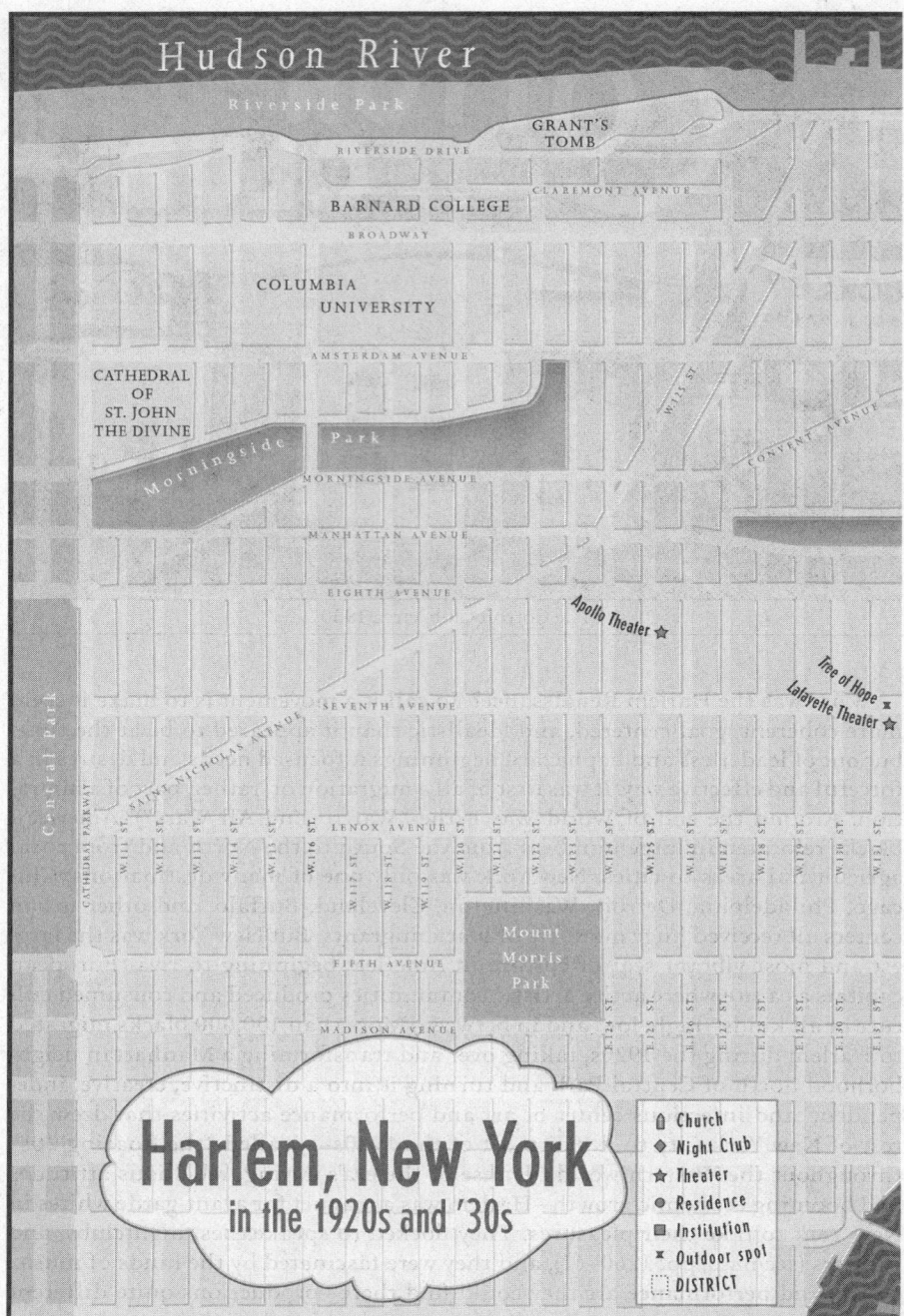

Hudson River

Riverside Park

GRANT'S TOMB

RIVERSIDE DRIVE

BARNARD COLLEGE

CLAREMONT AVENUE

BROADWAY

COLUMBIA UNIVERSITY

AMSTERDAM AVENUE

W. 133 ST.

CONVENT AVENUE

CATHEDRAL OF ST. JOHN THE DIVINE

Morningside Park

MORNINGSIDE AVENUE

MANHATTAN AVENUE

EIGHTH AVENUE

Apollo Theater ☆

Tree of Hope ✕
Lafayette Theater ☆

SEVENTH AVENUE

SAINT NICHOLAS AVENUE

Central Park

CATHEDRAL PARKWAY

W. 111 ST.
W. 112 ST.
W. 113 ST.
W. 114 ST.
W. 115 ST.
W. 116 ST.
W. 117 ST.
W. 118 ST.
W. 119 ST.

LENOX AVENUE

W. 120 ST.
W. 121 ST.
W. 122 ST.
W. 123 ST.
W. 124 ST.
W. 125 ST.
W. 126 ST.
W. 127 ST.
W. 128 ST.
W. 129 ST.
W. 130 ST.
W. 131 ST.

Mount Morris Park

FIFTH AVENUE

E. 124 ST.
E. 125 ST.
E. 126 ST.
E. 127 ST.
E. 128 ST.
E. 129 ST.
E. 130 ST.
E. 131 ST.

MADISON AVENUE

Harlem, New York
in the 1920s and '30s

🏠 Church
◆ Night Club
☆ Theater
● Residence
■ Institution
✕ Outdoor spot
⬚ DISTRICT

who wanted to capture, in their own productions, something of the life and energy that patrons sought in Harlem. White readers, and many white artists, showed enormous—sometimes mawkish or even ghoulish—curiosity about black life in America. Before the Harlem Renaissance had ended, a large number

A dancer entertains a crowd at Small's Paradise Club, 1929. As at many of Harlem's best-known nightclubs, the entertainers and staff at Small's were primarily African American, and the clientele was mainly white.

of Broadway productions—Marc Connelly's *Green Pastures*, Eugene O'Neill's *The Emperor Jones* and *All God's Chillun Got Wings*, for example—and many novels tried to represent the black experience for white audiences. Black artists and writers (and their readers) were not always happy with the way white writers portrayed black experience and black concerns, but the widespread curiosity—some of it piqued by the flourishing of the Harlem group and some by "intruders" from the white establishment—provided a wider audience for black literature and arts than had existed in earlier generations.

The height of the Harlem Renaissance was the 1920s, though it is hard to pin down just when the period began and ended. Some historians, pointing to the political ferment caused by U.S. entry into the war in 1917, date the beginnings in the mid to late teens, and some regard it as lasting until the outbreak of World War II in the late 1930s. But

Prominent African Americans (including W. E. B. Du Bois, third from the right in the second row) parade down New York's Fifth Avenue on July 28, 1917, to protest a race riot in East St. Louis, Illinois. Thirty-nine African Americans were killed and hundreds were seriously injured in that melee, one of the deadliest outbreaks of racial violence in America.

the decade of the 1920s saw most of the productivity and creative energy that we associate with the flourishing of Harlem. And it was in the early 1920s when most of the leading writers in the group actually moved to New York. Many historians regard the stock-market crash of 1929 and the depression that followed as signs of the end. Certainly the mood of the whole nation changed rapidly then, and by the early 1930s most of the leading figures had moved away from New York, forming smaller communities elsewhere or becoming individually isolated. The Harlem neighborhood itself began a slow economic decline.

Between the wars, though, Harlem's productivity and impact were dramatic. Before 1917, there had been few publishing outlets hospitable to young black writers; only Paul Lawrence Dunbar among African American poets was widely read or known, and he had died in 1906. But rising political and social concerns during and immediately after World War I produced several new periodicals: *The Messenger*, founded in 1917 by A. Philip Randolph and Chandler Owen, claimed to be "The only Radical Negro Magazine in America," and in 1923 the Urban League started its own magazine,

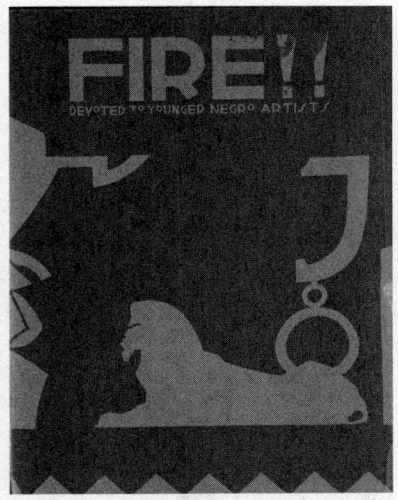

The cover of Volume I, Number 1 of *Fire!!*, a journal "Devoted to Younger Negro Artists," established by the self-designated "niggerati," the younger generation of African American intellectuals and writers—including Wallace Thurman, Langston Hughes, Zora Neale Hurston, and others—who wanted to (in Hughes's words) "burn up a lot of the old, dead, conventional Negro-white ideas of the past."

Claude McKay, photographed circa 1930 by Carl Van Vechten

Portrait of Alain Locke, by Betsy G. Reyneau

Langston Hughes, circa 1925, in a pastel portrait by Winold Reiss. The original hangs in the National Portrait Gallery in Washington, D.C.

Opportunity. Both of these new journals saw themselves as activist alternatives to the NAACP's official journal, *Crisis*, edited by W. E. B. Du Bois. Other magazines came and went. *Fire!!* managed only a single issue, but brought verbal and visual art spectacularly together. Meanwhile—and perhaps just as important in a different way—mainstream magazines (*Vanity Fair*, for example) and publishers (Knopf, Macmillan, Harper, and Harcourt Brace) began to feature younger black writers who soon developed a growing readership.

Some historians date the Harlem Renaissance from the composition of Claude McKay's fiery sonnet "If We Must Die," written in the summer of 1919. McKay later denied that the poem referred specifically to blacks and whites, but the many antiblack riots that broke out in several American cities that summer—sometimes called "the Red Summer"—certainly inspired and contextualized the poem. Another milestone was the publication in 1922 of James Weldon Johnson's *Book of American Negro Poetry*, which, in the words of the editors of the *Norton Anthology of African American Literature*, "emphasized the youthful promise of the new writers and established some of the terms of the emerging movement." But it was Alain Locke's landmark anthology, *The New Negro*, that, in 1925, effectively announced the significance of the Harlem Renaissance. Locke, a sociology professor at Howard University and an Oxford graduate as the first African American Rhodes Scholar, gathered all kinds of material—poems, fiction, essays, visual art—by authors old and young, black and white—into a working definition of what the "new Negro" was all about.

Countee Cullen, circa 1935

The major figures of the Harlem Renaissance were, however, highly individual, and (although they shared many ideals and aspirations) never confined themselves to a creed or hardened into a "school." Langston Hughes, with a wonderful lyric voice and an eye for telling details, pursued the relationship of poetry to black music and experimented with a variety of forms and rhythms; look, for example, at the award-winning "Weary Blues." Countee Cullen, on the other hand, was deeply committed to conventional poetic forms and felt most at home poetically when he was working in traditional fixed formal structures. Claude McKay, born in Jamaica, lived briefly in New York but mostly in Greenwich Village rather than Harlem, and spent much of his career abroad (Russia, France, North Africa). He always followed his own star in poetry too; his poetry was sometimes violent and incendiary, but equally strong was his sense of nostalgia and natural spiritualism. "The Tropics in New York" shows his sensuous and romantic side, and despite setting a militant tone in a founding poem of the Harlem Renaissance, "If We Must Die," he wrote only two poems that were directly about Harlem experiences and themes. Likewise, novelists like Zora Neale Hurston, Jean Toomer, Jesse Fauset, and Nella Larsen pursued individual styles and themes in their fiction. What held the group together conceptually was a dedica-

Vendor selling books and pamphlets from a cart on 125th Street in Harlem, June 1943

tion to producing first-rate writing, on the one hand, and, on the other hand, a commitment to raising the aspirations of American blacks of all backgrounds and abilities.

The question of who was to benefit from the ambitious art of the Harlem Renaissance was hotly debated. Was it ordinary people, who could stretch the horizons of their reading and their own ambitions? African Americans generally? Or was it primarily intellectuals and artists who might raise expectations for black thought and art? W. E. B. Du Bois, who was a lightning rod for many members of the militant and radical new generation, had famously championed the "talented tenth," a select group whose natural gifts authoritatively raised them above others, and opinions split over whether the beneficiaries of the Harlem Renaissance were to be ordinary

The Dark Tower, a forum for African American intellectuals, met frequently in the home of A'Lelia Walker, a prominent Harlem heiress and socialite. Countee Cullen's poem "From the Dark Tower" is painted on the wall.

Carl Van Vechten, 1926

readers and viewers or the creative geniuses themselves, in the service of a higher aesthetic quite distinct from social progress. It's fair to say that the writers themselves remained divided, alternately championing the triumph of art and hoping for a larger cultural impact that would benefit readers (especially black readers) more generally.

The role of whites in the Harlem Renaissance is a matter of some dispute. The most controversial (though undeniably influential) figure was Carl Van Vechten, whose parties legendarily brought young black writers into the company of famous and powerful white celebrities, many of whom could be helpful to the black writers' careers. Van Vechten was a gifted photographer whose portraits of many rising figures chronicle the Harlem years brilliantly (see the photo of Arna Bontemps on p. 1267), and he unde-

niably fostered many useful connections that resulted in publication and fame. But some felt his motives were self-serving and meretricious, and his well-meaning novel about everyday Harlem life, *Nigger Heaven*, was widely disparaged, though critics equally suspected "realistic" accounts of everyday life by black writers. (See, for example, the Du Bois review of a Claude McKay novel on pp. 1285–86). There is no doubt that figures like Van Vechten fostered considerable interaction between prominent whites and rising figures in the black artistic community, but not everyone regarded the results as helpful to the black cause overall. Some historians view white participation in the Harlem Renaissance more generally as exploitative, others as sincere but bumbling; still others view black-white collaboration then as an early demonstration of racial unity on behalf of art and communal relations.

A second set of questions involves elitism—whether the renaissance had truly salutary effects on the larger black community. Du Bois insisted on the obligation of "the talented tenth" to use their artistic and intellectual gifts to improve the lot of others. Critics of Du Bois find his position divisive and patronizing toward the majority of the black community; defenders see the idea as a strategy for community improvement by emphasizing the responsibility of potential leaders. At the heart of this controversy is disagreement about how leadership works to promote both improved social conditions and audience engagement. (Similar arguments rage today over the stardom of African American athletes and entertainers.)

Two related controversies concern the influence of the church on black culture and the relationship of the ambitious new "high art" of poetry, novels, and painting to popular-culture phenomena such as jazz, blues, and dance. There is little doubt that religion was a powerful force in the black community, but observers continue to debate, as the artists themselves then did, whether it fostered and furthered artistic expression or served as a restraining and discouraging force. Often readers can see in poetry about even the most secular subjects traces of religious ideas and traditions; you will have to decide for yourself whether the effects are positive or not. The relationship of radical art to popular culture was even more vexed. Some central figures in the Harlem Renaissance regarded their own aims as "above" the "attractions" and "spectacles" that drew large numbers of whites to Harlem, and they regarded the performance arts as, at best, distractions from or dilutions of the main flow of radical artistic expression. And while nearly everyone agrees that the quality of various theatrical arts in the many venues of Harlem was very high, the question of whether, beyond jazz and blues, the influence of popular arts on poetry was good or bad remains open.

. . .

No easy summary of the Harlem Renaissance will do. Its ambitions—often radical, sometimes revolutionary—made enormous waves in both the black urban community and the world of art. However one measures the Harlem Renaissance in terms of its impact on later writers, black and white, the poems themselves continue to speak to readers across divides of time and culture. You will find that some of the poems can hardly be understood without knowledge of the specific circumstances and conditions that produced them; you will also find that many of the poems reach insistently for connections both to the past and to the enduring concerns of poets and readers in far-flung times and places.

Known as the "Empress of the Blues," Bessie Smith was one of the most popular entertainers in America during the 1920s. A protégé of the legendary Ma Rainey, Smith spent much of the mid-1920s touring the United States as the star attraction on the vaudeville circuit.

Arna Bontemps, photographed by Carl Van Vechten, 1939

ARNA BONTEMPS

A Black Man Talks of Reaping

I have sown beside all waters in my day.
I planted deep, within my heart the fear
That wind or fowl would take the grain away.
I planted safe against this stark, lean year.

5   I scattered seed enough to plant the land
In rows from Canada to Mexico
But for my reaping only what the hand
Can hold at once is all that I can show.

Yet what I sowed and what the orchard yields
10 My brother's sons are gathering stalk and root,

Small wonder then my children glean in fields
They have not sown, and feed on bitter fruit.

1926

COUNTEE CULLEN

Yet Do I Marvel

I doubt not God is good, well-meaning, kind,
And did He stoop to quibble could tell why
The little buried mole continues blind,
Why flesh that mirrors Him must some day die,
5 Make plain the reason tortured Tantalus[1]
Is baited by the fickle fruit, declare
If merely brute caprice dooms Sisyphus[2]
To struggle up a never-ending stair.
Inscrutable His ways are, and immune
10 To catechism by a mind too strewn
With petty cares to slightly understand
What awful brain compels His awful hand.
Yet do I marvel at this curious thing:
To make a poet black, and bid him sing!

1925

Saturday's Child [3]

Some are teethed on a silver spoon,
    With the stars strung for a rattle;
I cut my teeth as the black raccoon—
    For implements of battle.

5 Some are swaddled in silk and down,
    And heralded by a star;[4]
They swathed my limbs in a sackcloth gown
    On a night that was black as tar.

For some, godfather and goddame
10   The opulent fairies be;
Dame Poverty gave me my name,
    And Pain godfathered me.

For I was born on Saturday—
    "Bad time for planting a seed,"

---

1. In Greek myth he was condemned, for ambiguous reasons, to stand up to his neck in water he couldn't drink and to be within sight of fruit he couldn't reach to eat.
2. The king of Corinth who, in Greek myth, was condemned eternally to roll a huge stone uphill.
3. According to a popular nursery rhyme, "Saturday's child works hard for his living."
4. According to Matthew 2.7–10, Jesus' birth was accompanied by the appearance of a new star.

15 Was all my father had to say,
And, "One mouth more to feed."

Death cut the strings that gave me life,
And handed me to Sorrow,
The only kind of middle wife
20   My folks could beg or borrow.

1925

From the Dark Tower

(To Charles S. Johnson)[5]

We shall not always plant while others reap
The golden increment of bursting fruit,
Not always countenance, abject and mute,
That lesser men should hold their brothers cheap;
5 Not everlastingly while others sleep
Shall we beguile their limbs with mellow flute,
Not always bend to some more subtle brute;
We were not made eternally to weep.

The night whose sable breast relieves the stark,
10 White stars is no less lovely being dark,
And there are buds that cannot bloom at all
In light, but crumple, piteous, and fall;
So in the dark we hide the heart that bleeds,
And wait, and tend our agonizing seeds.

1927

ANGELINA GRIMKÉ

The Black Finger

I have just seen a beautiful thing
  Slim and still,
Against a gold, gold sky,
  A straight cypress,
5   Sensitive
  Exquisite,
A black finger
Pointing upwards.
Why, beautiful, still finger are you
  black?
10 And why are you pointing upwards?

1925

Angelina Grimké, circa 1905

5. Founder and editor of *Opportunity* magazine.

Tenebris[6]

There is a tree, by day,
That, at night,
Has a shadow,
A hand huge and black,
5 With fingers long and black.
   All through the dark,
Against the white man's house,
   In the little wind,
The black hand plucks and plucks
10   At the bricks.
The bricks are the color of blood and very small.
   Is it a black hand,
   Or is it a shadow?

1927

LANGSTON HUGHES

Harlem

What happens to a dream deferred?

   Does it dry up
   Like a raisin in the sun?
   Or fester like a sore—
5 And then run?
   Does it stink like rotten meat?
   Or crust and sugar over—
   Like a syrupy sweet?
   Maybe it just sags
10 Like a heavy load.

   Or does it explode?

1951

The Weary Blues

Droning a drowsy syncopated tune,
Rocking back and forth to a mellow croon,
   I heard a Negro play.
Down on Lenox Avenue[7] the other night
5 By the pale dull pallor of an old gas light
   He did a lazy sway. . . .
   He did a lazy sway. . . .

---

6. In darkness (Latin).   7 Major Harlem thoroughfare, now Malcolm X Boulevard.

To the tune o' those Weary Blues.
With his ebony hands on each
    ivory key
10 He made that poor piano moan
    with melody.
    O Blues!
Swaying to and fro on his rickety
    stool
He played that sad raggy tune like
    a musical fool.
    Sweet Blues!
15 Coming from a black man's soul.
    O Blues!
In a deep song voice with a
    melancholy tone
I heard that Negro sing, that old
    piano moan—
    "Ain't got nobody in all this
    world,
20   Ain't got nobody but ma self.
    I's gwine to quit ma frownin'
    And put ma troubles on the shelf."
Thump, thump, thump, went his foot on the floor.
He played a few chords then he sang some more—
25   "I got the Weary Blues
    And I can't be satisfied.
    Got the Weary Blues
    And can't be satisfied—
    I ain't happy no mo'
30   And I wish that I had died."
And far into the night he crooned that tune.
The stars went out and so did the moon.
The singer stopped playing and went to bed
While the Weary Blues echoed through his head.
35 He slept like a rock or a man that's dead.
1923   1925

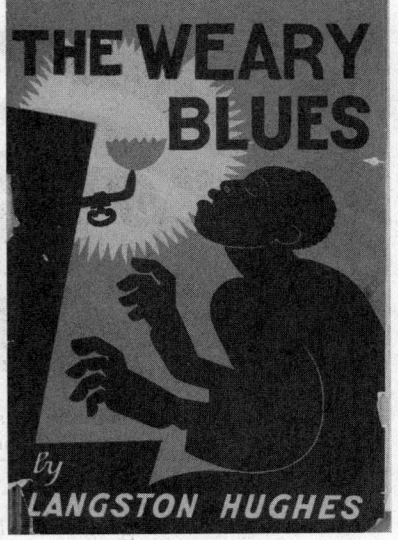

The Negro Speaks of Rivers

I've known rivers:
I've known rivers ancient as the world and older than the flow of
    human blood in human veins.

My soul has grown deep like the rivers.

I bathed in the Euphrates when dawns were young.
5 I built my hut near the Congo and it lulled me to sleep.
I looked upon the Nile and raised the pyramids above it.

A pen-and-ink illustration by the artist Aaron Douglas made specifically to accompany Hughes's "The Negro Speaks of Rivers"

I heard the singing of the Mississippi when Abe Lincoln went down to
     New Orleans, and I've seen its muddy bosom turn all golden in
     the sunset.

I've known rivers:
Ancient, dusky rivers.

10 My soul has grown deep like the rivers.

                                                              1926

I, Too

I, too, sing America.

I am the darker brother.
They send me to eat in the kitchen
When company comes,
5 But I laugh,
And eat well,
And grow strong.

Tomorrow,
I'll sit at the table.
10 When company comes
Nobody'll dare
Say to me,
"Eat in the kitchen,"
Then.

15 Besides,
They'll see how beautiful I am
And be ashamed—

I, too, am America.

                    1932

HELENE JOHNSON

Sonnet to a Negro in Harlem

You are disdainful and magnificent—
Your perfect body and your pompous gait,
Your dark eyes flashing solemnly with hate,
Small wonder that you are incompetent
5 To imitate those whom you so despise—
Your shoulders towering high above the throng,
Your head thrown back in rich, barbaric song,
Palm trees and mangoes stretched before your eyes.
Let others toil and sweat for labor's sake
10 And wring from grasping hands their meed[8] of gold.
Why urge ahead your supercilious feet?
Scorn will efface each footprint that you make.
I love your laughter arrogant and bold.
You are too splendid for this city street.

1927

CLAUDE McKAY

Harlem Shadows

I hear the halting footsteps of a lass
    In Negro Harlem when the night lets fall
Its veil. I see the shapes of girls who pass
    To bend and barter at desire's call.
5 Ah, little dark girls who in slippered feet
Go prowling through the night from street to street!

Through the long night until the silver break
    Of day the little gray feet know no rest;
Through the lone night until the last snow-flake
10   Has dropped from heaven upon the earth's white breast,
The dusky, half-clad girls of tired feet
Are trudging, thinly shod, from street to street.

Ah, stern harsh world, that in the wretched way
    Of poverty, dishonor and disgrace,
15 Has pushed the timid little feet of clay,
    The sacred brown feet of my fallen race!
Ah, heart of me, the weary, weary feet
In Harlem wandering from street to street.

1918

8. Reward.

If We Must Die

If we must die, let it not be like hogs
Hunted and penned in an inglorious spot,
While round us bark the mad and hungry dogs,
Making their mock at our accursed lot.
5   If we must die, O let us nobly die,
So that our precious blood may not be shed
In vain; then even the monsters we defy
Shall be constrained to honor us though dead!
O kinsmen! we must meet the common foe!
10   Though far outnumbered let us show us brave,
And for their thousand blows deal one deathblow!
What though before us lies the open grave?
Like men we'll face the murderous, cowardly pack,
Pressed to the wall, dying, but fighting back!

                                                        1919

The Tropics in New York

Bananas ripe and green, and ginger-root,
    Cocoa in pods and alligator pears,
And tangerines and mangoes and grape fruit,
    Fit for the highest prize at parish fairs,

5   Set in the window, bringing memories
    Of fruit-trees laden by low-singing rills,
And dewy dawns, and mystical blue skies
    In benediction over nun-like hills.

My eyes grew dim, and I could no more gaze;
10   A wave of longing through my body swept,
And, hungry for the old, familiar ways,
    I turned aside and bowed my head and wept.

                                                        1920

The Harlem Dancer

Applauding youths laughed with young prostitutes
And watched her perfect, half-clothed body sway;
Her voice was like the sound of blended flutes
Blown by black players upon a picnic day.
5   She sang and danced on gracefully and calm,
The light gauze hanging loose about her form;
To me she seemed a proudly-swaying palm

Grown lovelier for passing through a storm.
Upon her swarthy neck black shiny curls
10 Luxuriant fell; and tossing coins in praise,
The wine-flushed, bold-eyed boys, and even the girls,
Devoured her shape with eager, passionate gaze;
But looking at her falsely-smiling face,
I knew her self was not in that strange place.

1922

The White House

Your door is shut against my tightened face,
And I am sharp as steel with discontent;
But I possess the courage and the grace
To bear my anger proudly and unbent.
5 The pavement slabs burn loose beneath my feet,
And passion rends my vitals as I pass,
A chafing savage, down the decent street,
Where boldly shines your shuttered door of glass.
Oh, I must search for wisdom every hour,
10 Deep in my wrathful bosom sore and raw,
And find in it the superhuman power
To hold me to the letter of your law!
Oh, I must keep my heart inviolate
Against the poison of your deadly hate.

1937

JAMES WELDON JOHNSON

From the preface to *The Book of American Negro Poetry* (1921)

* * *

This preface has gone far beyond what I had in mind when I started. It was my intention to gather together the best verses I could find by Negro poets and present them with a bare word of introduction. It was not my plan to make this collection inclusive nor to make the book in any sense a book of criticism. I planned to present only verses by contemporary writers; but,

James Weldon Johnson, circa 1920

perhaps, because this is the first collection of its kind, I realized the absence of a starting-point and was led to provide one and to fill in with historical data what I felt to be a gap.

It may be surprising to many to see how little of the poetry being written by Negro poets today is being written in Negro dialect. The newer Negro poets show a tendency to discard dialect; much of the subject-matter which went into the making of traditional dialect poetry, 'possums, watermelons, etc., they have discarded altogether, at least, as poetic material. This tendency will, no doubt, be regretted by the majority of white readers; and, indeed, it would be a distinct loss if the American Negro poets threw away this quaint and musical folk speech as a medium of expression. And yet, after all, these poets are working through a problem not realized by the reader, and, perhaps, by many of these poets themselves not realized consciously. They are trying to break away from, not Negro dialect itself, but the limitations on Negro dialect imposed by the fixing effects of long convention.

The Negro in the United States has achieved or been placed in a certain artistic niche. When he is thought of artistically, it is as a happy-go-lucky, singing, shuffling, banjo-picking being or as a more or less pathetic figure. The picture of him is in a log cabin amid fields of cotton or along the levees. Negro dialect is naturally and by long association the exact instrument for voicing this phase of Negro life; and by that very exactness it is an instrument with but two full stops, humor and pathos. So even when he confines himself to purely racial themes, the Aframerican poet realizes that there are phases of Negro life in the United States which cannot be treated in the dialect either adequately or artistically. Take, for example, the phases rising out of life in Harlem, that most wonderful Negro city in the world. I do not deny that a Negro in a log cabin is more picturesque than a Negro in a Harlem flat, but the Negro in the Harlem flat is here, and he is but part of a group growing everywhere in the country, a group whose ideals are becoming increasingly more vital than those of the traditionally artistic group, even if its members are less picturesque.

What the colored poet in the United States needs to do is something like what Synge[9] did for the Irish; he needs to find a form that will express the racial spirit by symbols from within rather than by symbols from without, such as the mere mutilation of English spelling and pronunciation. He needs a form that is freer and larger than dialect, but which will still hold the racial flavor; a form expressing the imagery, the idioms, the peculiar turns of thought, and the distinctive humor and pathos, too, of the Negro, but which will also be capable of voicing the deepest and highest emotions and aspirations, and allow of the widest range of subjects and the widest scope of treatment.

Negro dialect is at present a medium that is not capable of giving expression to the varied conditions of Negro life in America, and much less is it capable of giving the fullest interpretation of Negro character and psychology. This is no indictment against the dialect as dialect, but against the mold of convention in which Negro dialect in the United States has been set. In time these conventions may become lost, and the colored poet in the United States may sit down to write in dialect without feeling that his first line will put the general reader in a frame of mind which demands that the poem be humorous or pathetic. In the

9. John Middleton Synge (1871–1909), Irish dramatist whose works celebrate Irish traditions.

meantime, there is no reason why these poets should not continue to do the beautiful things that can be done, and done best, in the dialect.

In stating the need for Aframerican poets in the United States to work out a new and distinctive form of expression I do not wish to be understood to hold any theory that they should limit themselves to Negro poetry, to racial themes; the sooner they are able to write *American* poetry spontaneously, the better. Nevertheless, I believe that the richest contribution the Negro poet can make to the American literature of the future will be the fusion into it of his own individual artistic gifts.

ALAIN LOCKE

From *The New Negro* (1925)

The tide of Negro migration, northward and city-ward, is not to be fully explained as a blind flood started by the demands of war industry coupled with the shutting off of foreign migration, or by the pressure of poor crops coupled with increased social terrorism in certain sections of the South and Southwest. Neither labor demand, the bollweevil,[1] nor the Ku Klux Klan is a basic factor, however contributory any or all of them may have been. The wash and rush of this human tide on the beach line of the northern city centers is to be explained primarily in terms of a new vision of opportunity, of social and economic freedom, of a spirit to seize, even in the face of an extortionate and heavy toll, a chance for the improvement of conditions. With each successive wave of it, the movement of the Negro becomes more and more a mass movement toward the larger and the more democratic chance—in the Negro's case a deliberate flight not only from countryside to city, but from medieval America to modern.

Take Harlem as an instance of this. Here in Manhattan is not merely the largest Negro community in the world, but the first concentration in history of so many diverse elements of Negro life. It has attracted the African, the West Indian, the Negro American; has brought together the Negro of the North and the Negro of the South; the man from the city and the man from the town and village; the peasant, the student, the business man, the professional man, artist, poet, musician, adventurer and worker, preacher and criminal, exploiter and social outcast. Each group has come with its own separate motives and for its own special ends, but their greatest experience has been the finding of one another. Proscription and prejudice have thrown these dissimilar elements into a common area of contact and interaction. Within this area, race sympathy and unity have determined a further fusing of sentiment and experience. So what began in terms of segregation becomes more and more, as its elements mix and react, the laboratory of a great race-welding. Hitherto, it must be admitted that American Negroes have been a race more in name than in fact, or to be exact, more in sentiment than in experience. The chief bond between them has been that of a common condition rather than a common consciousness; a problem in common rather than a life in common. In Harlem, Negro life is seizing upon its

1. A snout beetle notorious for destroying cotton crops.

first chances for group expression and self-determination. It is—or promises at least to be—a race capital. That is why our comparison is taken with those nascent centers of folk-expression and self-determination which are playing a creative part in the world today. Without pretense to their political significance, Harlem has the same role to play for the New Negro as Dublin has had for the New Ireland or Prague for the New Czechoslovakia.

Harlem, I grant you, isn't typical—but it is significant, it is prophetic. No sane observer, however sympathetic to the new trend, would contend that the great masses are articulate as yet, but they stir, they move, they are more than physically restless. The challenge of the new intellectuals among them is clear enough—the "race radicals" and realists who have broken with the old epoch of philanthropic guidance, sentimental appeal and protest. But are we after all only reading into the stirrings of a sleeping giant the dreams of an agitator? The answer is in the migrating peasant. It is the "man farthest down" who is most active in getting up. One of the most characteristic symptoms of this is the professional man, himself migrating to recapture his constituency after a vain effort to maintain in some Southern corner what for years back seemed an established living and clientele. The clergyman following his errant flock, the physician or lawyer trailing his clients, supply the true clues. In a real sense it is the rank and file who are leading, and the leaders who are following. A transformed and transforming psychology permeates the masses.

When the racial leaders of twenty years ago spoke of developing race-pride and stimulating race-consciousness, and of the desirability of race solidarity, they could not in any accurate degree have anticipated the abrupt feeling that has surged up and now pervades the awakened centers.... It is a social disservice to blunt the fact that the Negro of the Northern centers has reached a stage where tutelage, even of the most interested and well-intentioned sort, must give place to new relationships, where positive self-direction must be reckoned with in ever increasing measure. The American mind must reckon with a fundamentally changed Negro.

The Negro too, for his part, has idols of the tribe to smash. If on the one hand the white man has erred in making the Negro appear to be that which would excuse or extenuate his treatment of him, the Negro, in turn, has too often unnecessarily excused himself because of the way he has been treated. The intelligent Negro of today is resolved not to make discrimination an extenuation for his shortcomings in performance, individual or collective; he is trying to hold himself at par, neither inflated by sentimental allowances nor depreciated by current social discounts. For this he must know himself and be known for precisely what he is, and for that reason he welcomes the new scientific rather than the old sentimental interest. Sentimental interest in the Negro has ebbed. We used to lament this as the falling off of our friends; now we rejoice and pray to be delivered both from self-pity and condescension. The mind of each racial group has had a bitter weaning, apathy or hatred on one side matching disillusionment or resentment on the other; but they face each other today with the possibility at least of entirely new mutual attitudes....

The fiction is that the life of the races is separate, and increasingly so. The fact is that they have touched too closely at the unfavorable and too lightly at the favorable levels.

While inter-racial councils have sprung up in the South, drawing on forward elements of both races, in the Northern cities manual laborers may brush elbows in their everyday work, but the community and business leaders have experienced no such interplay or far too little of it. These segments must achieve contact or the race situation in America becomes desperate. Fortunately this is happening. There is a growing realization that in social effort the cooperative basis must supplant long-distance philanthropy, and that the only safeguard for mass relations in the future must be provided in the carefully maintained contacts of the enlightened minorities of both race groups. In the intellectual realm a renewed and keen curiosity is replacing the recent apathy; the Negro is being carefully studied, not just talked about and discussed. In art and letters, instead of being wholly caricatured, he is being seriously portrayed and painted.

To all of this the New Negro is keenly responsive as an augury of a new democracy in American culture. He is contributing his share to the new social understanding. But the desire to be understood would never in itself have been sufficient to have opened so completely the protectively closed portals of the thinking Negro's mind. There is still too much possibility of being snubbed or patronized for that. It was rather the necessity for fuller, truer self-expression, the realization of the unwisdom of allowing social discrimination to segregate him mentally, and a counter-attitude to cramp and fetter his own living—and so the "spite-wall" that the intellectuals built over the "color-line" has happily been taken down. Much of this reopening of intellectual contacts has centered in New York and has been richly fruitful not merely in the enlarging of personal experience, but in the definite enrichment of American art and letters and in the clarifying of our common vision of the social tasks ahead.

The particular significance in the re-establishment of contact between the more advanced and representative classes is that it promises to offset some of the unfavorable reactions of the past, or at least to re-surface race contacts somewhat for the future. Subtly the conditions that are molding a New Negro are molding a new American attitude.

However, this new phase of things is delicate; it will call for less charity but more justice; less help, but infinitely closer understanding. This is indeed a critical stage of race relationships because of the likelihood, if the new temper is not understood, of engendering sharp group antagonism and a second crop of more calculated prejudice. In some quarters, it has already done so. Having weaned the Negro, public opinion cannot continue to paternalize. The Negro today is inevitably moving forward under the control largely of his own objectives. What are these objectives? Those of his outer life are happily already well and finally formulated, for they are none other than the ideals of American institutions and democracy. Those of his inner life are yet in process of formation, for the new psychology at present is more of a consensus of feeling than of opinion, of attitude rather than of program. Still some points seem to have crystallized.

Up to the present one may adequately describe the Negro's "inner objectives" as an attempt to repair a damaged group psychology and reshape a warped social perspective. Their realization has required a new mentality for the American Negro. And as it matures we begin to see its effects; at first, negative, iconoclastic, and then positive and constructive. In this new group psychology we note the lapse of sentimental appeal, then the development of a more positive self-respect and self-reliance; the repudiation of social dependence, and then the gradual recovery from hyper-sensitiveness and "touchy" nerves, the repudiation of the double standard of judgment with its special philanthropic allowances and then the sturdier desire for objective and scientific appraisal; and finally the rise from social disillusionment to race pride, from the sense of social debt to the responsibilities of social contribution, and offsetting the necessary working and commonsense acceptance of restricted conditions, the belief in ultimate esteem and recognition. . . .

The Negro mind reaches out as yet to nothing but American wants, American ideas. But this forced attempt to build his Americanism on race values is a unique social experiment, and its ultimate success is impossible except through the fullest sharing of American culture and institutions. There should be no delusion about this. American nerves in sections unstrung with race hysteria are often fed the opiate that the trend of Negro advance is wholly separatist, and that the effect of its operation will be to encyst the Negro as a benign foreign body in the body politic. This cannot be—even if it were desirable. The racialism of the Negro is no limitation or reservation with respect to American life; it is only a constructive effort to build the obstructions in the stream of his progress into an efficient dam of social energy and power. Democracy itself is obstructed and stagnated to the extent that any of its channels are closed. Indeed they cannot be selectively closed. So the choice is not between one way for the Negro and another way for the rest, but between American institutions frustrated on the one hand and American ideals progressively fulfilled and realized on the other. . . .

More and more, however, an intelligent realization of the great discrepancy between the American social creed and the American social practice forces upon the Negro the taking of the moral advantage that is his. Only the steadying and sobering effect of a truly characteristic gentleness of spirit prevents the rapid rise of a definite cynicism and counter-hate and a defiant superiority feeling. Human as this reaction would be, the majority still deprecate its advent, and would gladly see it forestalled by the speedy amelioration of its causes. We wish our race pride to be a healthier, more positive achievement than a feeling based upon a realization of the shortcomings of others. But all paths toward the attainment of a sound social attitude have been difficult; only a relatively few enlightened minds have been able as the phrase puts it "to rise above" prejudice. The ordinary man has had until recently only a hard choice between the alternatives of supine and humiliating submission and stimulating but hurtful counter-prejudice. Fortunately from some inner, desperate resourcefulness has recently sprung up the simple expedient of fighting prejudice by mental passive resistance, in other words by trying to ignore it. For the few, this manna may perhaps be effective, but the masses cannot thrive upon it.

Fortunately there are constructive channels opening out into which the balked social feelings of the American Negro can flow freely.

Without them there would be much more pressure and danger than there is. These compensating interests are racial but in a new and enlarged way. One is the consciousness of acting as the advance-guard of the African peoples in their contact with Twentieth Century civilization; the other, the sense of a mission of rehabilitating the race in world esteem from that loss of prestige for which the fate and conditions of slavery have so largely been responsible. Harlem, as we shall see, is the center of both these movements; she is the home of the Negro's "Zionism."[2] The pulse of the Negro world has begun to beat in Harlem. A Negro newspaper

2. An international movement aimed at securing a homeland for the Jewish people.

carrying news material in English, French, and Spanish, gathered from all quarters of America, the West Indies, and Africa has maintained itself in Harlem for over five years. Two important magazines,[3] both edited from New York, maintain their news and circulation consistently on a cosmopolitan scale. Under American auspices and backing, three pan-African congresses have been held abroad for the discussion of common interests, colonial questions, and the future cooperative development of Africa. In terms of the race question as a world problem, the Negro mind has leapt, so to speak, upon the parapets of prejudice and extended its cramped horizons. In so doing it has linked up with the growing group consciousness of the dark-peoples and is gradually learning their common interests. As one of our writers has recently put it: "It is imperative that we understand the white world in its relations to the non-white world." As with the Jew, persecution is making the Negro international.

As a world phenomenon this wider race consciousness is a different thing from the much asserted rising tide of color. Its inevitable causes are not of our making. The consequences are not necessarily damaging to the best interests of civilization. Whether it actually brings into being new Armadas of conflict or argosies[4] of cultural exchange and enlightenment can only be decided by the attitude of the dominant races in an era of critical change. With the American Negro, his new internationalism is primarily an effort to recapture contact with the scattered peoples of African derivation. Garveyism[5] may be a transient, if spectacular, phenomenon, but the possible role of the American Negro in the future development of Africa is one of the most constructive and universally helpful missions that any modern people can lay claim to.

RUDOLPH FISHER

The Caucasian Storms Harlem (1927)

I

It might not have been such a jolt had my five years' absence from Harlem been spent otherwise. But the study of medicine includes no courses in cabareting; and, anyway, the Negro cabarets in Washington, where I studied, are all uncompromisingly black. Accordingly I was entirely unprepared for what I found when I returned to Harlem recently.

I remembered one place especially where my own crowd used to hold forth; and, hoping to find some old-timers there still, I sought it out one midnight. The old, familiar plunkety-plunk welcomed me from below as I entered. I descended the same old narrow stairs, came into the same smoke-misty basement, and found myself a chair at one of the ancient white-porcelain, mirror-smooth tables. I drew a deep breath and looked about, seeking familiar faces. "What a lot of 'fays!"[6] I thought, as I noticed the number of white guests. Presently I grew puzzled and began to stare, then I gaped—and gasped. I found myself wondering if

3. Probably *Opportunity* and *The Crisis*.   4. Merchant ships. *Armadas*: fleets of warships.
5. The Back to Africa movement of Marcus Garvey (1887–1940).
6. Short for "ofays," a derogatory term for whites.

this was the right place—if, indeed, this was Harlem at all. I suddenly became aware that, except for the waiters and members of the orchestra, I was the only Negro in the place.

After a while I left it and wandered about in a daze from night-club to night-club. I tried the Nest, Small's, Connie's Inn, the Capitol, Happy's, the Cotton Club. There was no mistake; my discovery was real and was repeatedly confirmed. No wonder my old crowd was not to be found in any of them. The best of Harlem's black cabarets have changed their names and turned white.

Such a discovery renders a moment's recollection irresistible. As irresistible as were the cabarets themselves to me seven or eight years ago. Just out of college in a town where cabarets were something only read about. A year of graduate work ahead. A Summer of rest at hand. Cabarets. Cabarets night after night, and one after another. There was no cover-charge then, and a fifteen-cent bottle of Whistle lasted an hour. It was just after the war[7]—the heroes were home—cabarets were the thing.

How the Lybia prospered in those happy days! It was the gathering place of the swellest Harlem set: if you didn't go to the Lybia, why, my dear, you just didn't belong. The people you saw at church in the morning you met at the Lybia at night. What romance in those war-tinged days and nights! Officers from Camp Upton,[8] with pretty maids from Brooklyn! Gay lieutenants, handsome captains—all whirling the lively onestep. Poor non-coms[9] completely ignored; what sensible girl wanted a corporal or even a sergeant? That white, old-fashioned house, standing alone in 138th street, near the corner of Seventh avenue—doomed to be torn down a few months thence—how it shook with the dancing and laughter of the dark merry crowds!

But the first place really popular with my friends was a Chinese restaurant in 136th street, which had been known as Hayne's Café and then became the Oriental. It occupied an entire house of three stories, and had carpeted floors and a quiet, superior air. There was excellent food and incredibly good tea and two unusual entertainers: a Cuban girl, who could so vary popular airs that they sounded like real music, and a slender little "brown" with a voice of silver and a way of singing a song that made you forget your food. One could dance in the Oriental if one liked, but one danced to a piano only, and wound one's way between linen-clad tables over velvety, noiseless floors.

Here we gathered: Fritz Pollard, All-American halfback,[1] selling Negro stock to prosperous Negro physicians; Henry Creamer and Turner Layton, who had written "After You've Gone" and a dozen more songs, and were going to write "Strut, Miss Lizzie;" Paul Robeson,[2] All-American end, on the point of tackling law, quite unaware that the stage would intervene; Preacher Harry Bragg, Harvard Jimmie MacLendon and a half a dozen others. Here at a little table, just inside the door, Bert Williams[3] had supper every night, and afterward sometimes joined us upstairs and sang songs with us and lampooned the Actors'

7. I.e., World War I. *Whistle*: a beverage.   8. A military facility near Manhattan.
9. Noncommissioned officers.
1. In 1916 at Brown University. He was the first black professional football player (Akron Indians, 1919).
2. A star football player at Rutgers before entering the Columbia University Law School in 1919 (1898–1976); he would later gain international renown as a singer and civil rights spokesman.
3. Popular black comedian and actor (ca. 1874–1922).

Equity Association, which had barred him because of his color. Never did white guests come to the Oriental except as guests of Negroes. But the manager soon was stricken with a psychosis of some sort, became a black Jew, grew himself a bushy, square-cut beard, donned a skull-cap and abandoned the Oriental. And so we were robbed of our favorite resort, and thereafter became mere rounders.

II

Such places, those real Negro cabarets that we met in the course of our rounds! There was Edmonds' in Fifth avenue at 130th street. It was a sure-enough honky-tonk, occupying the cellar of a saloon. It was the social center of what was then, and still is, Negro Harlem's kitchen. Here a tall brown-skin girl, unmistakably the one guaranteed in the song to make a preacher lay his Bible down, used to sing and dance her own peculiar numbers, vesting them with her own original-ity. She was known simply as Ethel,[4] and was a genuine drawing-card. She knew her importance, too. Other girls wore themselves ragged trying to rise above the inattentive din of conversation, and soon, literally, yelled themselves hoarse; eventually they lost whatever music there was in their voices and acquired that familiar throaty roughness which is so frequent among blues singers, and which, though admired as characteristically African, is as a matter of fact nothing but a form of chronic laryngitis. Other girls did these things, but not Ethel. She took it easy. She would stride with great leisure and self-assurance to the center of the floor, stand there with a half-contemptuous nonchalance, and wait. All would become silent at once. Then she'd begin her song, genuine blues, which, for all their humorous lines, emanated tragedy and heartbreak:

> Woke up this mawnin'
> The day was dawnin'
> And I was sad and blue, so blue, Lord—
> Didn' have nobody
> To tell my troubles to—

It was Ethel who first made popular the song, "Tryin' to Teach My Good Man Right from Wrong," in the slow, meditative measures in which she complained:

> I'm gettin' sick and tired of my railroad man
> I'm gettin' sick and tired of my railroad man—
> Can't get him when I want him—
> I get him when I can.

It wasn't long before this song-bird escaped her dingy cage. Her name is a vaude-ville attraction now, and she uses it all—Ethel Waters. Is there anyone who hasn't heard her sing "Shake That Thing!"? . . .

There were the Lybia, then, and Hayne's, Connor's, the Oriental, Edmonds' and the Garden of Joy, each distinctive, standing for a type, some living up to their names, others living down to them, but all predominantly black. Regularly I made the rounds among these places and saw only incidental white people. I have seen them occasionally in numbers, but such parties were out on a lark. They weren't in their natural habitat and they often weren't any too comfortable.

---

4. Ethel Waters (1896–1977).

But what of Barron's, you say? Certainly they were at home there. Yes, I know about Barron's. I have been turned away from Barron's because I was too dark to be welcome. I have been a member of a group that was told, "No more room," when we could see plenty of room. Negroes were never actually wanted in Barron's save to work. Dark skins were always discouraged or barred. In short, the fact about Barron's was this: it simply wasn't a Negro cabaret; it was a cabaret run by Negroes for whites. It wasn't even on the lists of those who lived in Harlem—they'd no more think of going there than of going to the Winter Garden Roof.[5] But these other places were Negro through and through. Negroes supported them, not merely in now-and-then parties, but steadily, night after night.

IV

Some think it's just a fad. White people have always more or less sought Negro entertainment as diversion. The old shows of the early nineteen hundreds, Williams and Walker[6] and Cole and Johnson, are brought to mind as examples. The howling success—literally that—of J. Leubrie Hill[7] around 1913 is another; on the road his "Darktown Follies" played in numerous white theatres. In Harlem it played at the black Lafayette and, behold, the Lafayette temporarily became white. And so now, it is held, we are observing merely one aspect of a meteoric phenomenon, which simply presents itself differently in different circumstances: Roland Hayes and Paul Robeson, Jean Toomer and Walter White, Charles Gilpin and Florence Mills[8]—"Green Thursday," "Porgy," "In Abraham's Bosom"[9]— Negro spirituals—the startling new African groups proposed for the Metropolitan Museum of Art. Negro stock is going up, and everybody's buying.

V

It may be a season's whim, then, this sudden, contagious interest in everything Negro. If so, when I go into a familiar cabaret, or the place where a familiar cabaret used to be, and find it transformed and relatively colorless, I may be observing just one form that the season's whim has taken.

But suppose it is a fad—to say that explains nothing. How came the fad? What occasions the focusing of attention on this particular thing—rounds up and gathers these seasonal whims, and centers them about the Negro? Cabarets are peculiar, mind you. They're not like theatres and concert halls. You don't just go to a cabaret and sit back and wait to be entertained. You get out on the floor and join the pow-wow and help entertain yourself. Granted that white people have long enjoyed the Negro entertainment as a diversion, is it not something different, something more, when they bodily throw themselves into Negro entertainment in cabarets? "Now Negroes go to their own cabarets to see how white people act."

And what do we see? Why, we see them actually playing Negro games. I watch them in that epidemic Negroism, the Charleston. I look on and envy them. They camel and fish-tail and turkey, they geche and black-bottom and scronch, they

5. A prominent Manhattan night club.
6. Bert Williams and George Nash Walker formed an immensely popular vaudeville team in 1895.
7. Songwriter (1869–1916).
8. Performer (1895–1927). Hayes (1887–1976), singer. Toomer (1894–1967), author of *Cane*. White (1893–1955), writer and civil rights leader. Gilpin (1878–1930), actor.
9. A 1926 play by white writer Paul Green. *Porgy* (1925) is a novel by Du Bose Heyward.

skate and buzzard and mess-around[1]—and they do them all better than I! This interest in the Negro is an active and participating interest. It is almost as if a traveler from the North stood watching an African tribe-dance, then suddenly found himself swept wildly into it, caught in its tidal rhythm.

Willingly would I be an outsider in this if I could know that I read it aright— that out of this change in the old familiar ways some finer thing may come. Is this interest akin to that of the Virginians on the veranda of a plantation's big-house—sitting genuinely spellbound as they hear the lugubrious strains floating up from the Negro quarters? Is it akin to that of the African explorer, Stanley,[2] leaving a village far behind, but halting in spite of himself to catch the boom of its distant drum? Is it significant of basic human responses, the effect of which, once admitted, will extend far beyond cabarets? Maybe these Nordics at last have tuned in on our wave-length. Maybe they are at last learning to speak our language.

W. E. B. DU BOIS

From *Two Novels* (1928)

Nella Larsen[3] *Quicksand* (Knopf)
Claude McKay *Home to Harlem* (Harper and Brothers)

[Discussion of *Quicksand* omitted here]
Claude McKay's *Home to Harlem* . . . for the most part nauseates me, and after the dirtier parts of its filth I feel distinctly like taking a bath. This does not mean that the book is wholly bad. McKay is too great a poet to make any complete failure in writing. There are bits of *Home to Harlem* beautiful and fascinating: the continued changes upon the theme of the beauty of colored skins; the portrayal of the fascination of their new yearnings for each other which Negroes are developing. The chief character, Jake, has something appealing, and the glimpses of the Haitian, Ray, have all the materials of a great piece of fiction.

But it looks as though, despite this, McKay has set out to cater for that prurient demand on the part of white folk for a portrayal in Negroes of that utter licentiousness which conventional civilization holds white folk back from enjoying—if

The cover of the first edition of McKay's *Home to Harlem*

1. Various popular dances.   2. Sir Henry Morgan Stanley (1841–1904), English explorer of Africa.
3. Novelist (1891–1964).

enjoyment it can be called. That which a certain decadent section of the white American world, centered particularly in New York, longs for with fierce and unrestrained passions, it wants to see written out in black and white, and saddled on black Harlem. This demand, as voiced by a number of New York publishers, McKay has certainly satisfied, and added much for good measure. He has used every art and emphasis to paint drunkenness, fighting, lascivious sexual promiscuity, and utter absence of restraint in as bold and as bright colors as he can.

If this had been done in the course of a well-conceived plot or with any artistic unity, it might have been understood if not excused. But *Home to Harlem* is padded. Whole chapters here and there are inserted with no connection to the main plot, except that they are on the same dirty subject. As a picture of Harlem life or of Negro life anywhere, it is, of course, nonsense. Untrue, not so much as on account of its facts, but on account of its emphasis and glaring colors. I am sorry that the author of *Harlem Shadows* stooped to this. I sincerely hope that he will some day rise above it and give us in fiction the strong, well-knit as well as beautiful theme, that it seems to me he might do. . . .

ZORA NEALE HURSTON

How It Feels to Be Colored Me (1928)

I am colored but I offer nothing in the way of extenuating circumstances except the fact that I am the only Negro in the United States whose grandfather on the mother's side was *not* an Indian chief.

I remember the very day that I became colored. Up to my thirteenth year I lived in the little Negro town of Eatonville, Florida. It is exclusively a colored town. The only white people I knew passed through the town going to or coming from Orlando. The native whites rode dusty horses, the Northern tourists chugged down the sandy village road in automobiles. The town knew the Southerners and never stopped cane chewing when they passed. But the Northerners were something else again. They were peered at cautiously from behind curtains by the timid. The more venturesome would come out on the porch to watch them go past and got just as much pleasure out of the tourists as the tourists got out of the village. . . .

During this period, white people differed from colored to me only in that they rode through town and never lived there. They liked to hear me "speak pieces" and sing and wanted to see me dance the parse-me-la, and gave me generously of their

Zora Neale Hurston

small silver for doing these things, which seemed strange to me for I wanted to do them so much that I needed bribing to stop. Only they didn't know it. The colored people gave no dimes. They deplored any joyful tendencies in me, but I was their Zora nevertheless. I belonged to them, to the nearby hotels, to the county—everybody's Zora.

But changes came in the family when I was thirteen, and I was sent to school in Jacksonville. I left Eatonville, the town of the oleanders, as Zora. When I disembarked from the river-boat at Jacksonville, she was no more. It seemed that I had suffered a sea change. I was not Zora of Orange County any more, I was now a little colored girl. I found it out in certain ways. In my heart as well as in the mirror, I became a fast[4] brown—warranted not to rub nor run.

But I am not tragically colored. There is no great sorrow dammed up in my soul, nor lurking behind my eyes. I do not mind at all. I do not belong to the sobbing school of Negrohood who hold that nature somehow has given them a lowdown dirty deal and whose feelings are all hurt about it. Even in the helter-skelter skirmish that is my life, I have seen that the world is to the strong regardless of a little pigmentation more or less. No, I do not weep at the world—I am too busy sharpening my oyster knife.[5]

Someone is always at my elbow reminding me that I am the grand-daughter of slaves. It fails to register depression with me. Slavery is sixty years in the past. The operation was successful and the patient is doing well, thank you. The terrible struggle that made me an American out of a potential slave said "On the line!" The Reconstruction said "Get set!"; and the generation before said "Go!" I am off to a flying start and I must not halt in the stretch to look behind and weep. Slavery is the price I paid for civilization, and the choice was not with me. It is a bully adventure and worth all that I have paid through my ancestors for it. No one on earth ever had a greater chance for glory. The world to be won and nothing to be lost. It is thrilling to think—to know that for any act of mine, I shall get twice as much praise or twice as much blame. It is quite exciting to hold the center of the national stage, with the spectators not knowing whether to laugh or to weep.

The position of my white neighbor is much more difficult. No brown specter pulls up a chair beside me when I sit down to eat. No dark ghost thrusts its leg against mine in bed. The game of keeping what one has is never so exciting as the game of getting.

I do not always feel colored. Even now I often achieve the unconscious Zora of Eatonville before the Hegira.[6] I feel most colored when I am thrown against a sharp white background.

For instance at Barnard.[7] "Beside the waters of the Hudson" I feel my race. Among the thousand white persons, I am a dark rock surged upon, and overswept, but through it all, I remain myself. When covered by the waters, I am; and the ebb but reveals me again.

---

4. That is, colorfast.
5. An allusion to Shakespeare's *The Merry Wives of Windsor* 2.2.4–5: "Why, then the world's mine oyster, / Which I with sword will open."
6. In Islam, Muhammad's emigration from Mecca to Medina in 622 C.E.; here, the journey to Jacksonville.
7. Barnard College in Manhattan, then a private women's school, now part of Columbia University.

Sometimes it is the other way around. A white person is set down in our midst, but the contrast is just as sharp for me. For instance, when I sit in the drafty basement that is The New World Cabaret with a white person, my color comes. We enter chatting about any little nothing that we have in common and are seated by the jazz waiters. In the abrupt way that jazz orchestras have, this one plunges into a number. It loses no time in circumlocutions, but gets right down to business. It constricts the thorax and splits the heart with its tempo and narcotic harmonies. This orchestra grows rambunctious, rears on its hind legs and attacks the tonal veil with primitive fury, rending it, clawing it until it breaks through to the jungle beyond. I follow those heathen—follow them exultingly. I dance wildly inside myself; I yell within, I whoop; I shake my assegai[8] above my head, I hurl it true to the mark *yeeeeooww!* I am in the jungle and living in the jungle way. My face is painted red and yellow and my body is painted blue. My pulse is throbbing like a war drum. I want to slaughter something—give pain, give death to what, I do not know. But the piece ends. The men of the orchestra wipe their lips and rest their fingers. I creep back slowly to the veneer we call civilization with the last tone and find the white friend sitting motionless in his seat, smoking calmly.

"Good music they have here," he remarks, drumming the table with his fingertips.

Music. The great blobs of purple and red emotion have not touched him. He has only heard what I felt. He is far away and I see him but dimly across the ocean and the continent that have fallen between us. He is so pale with his whiteness then and I am *so* colored. . . .

I have no separate feeling about being an American citizen and colored. I am merely a fragment of the Great Soul that surges within the boundaries. My country, right or wrong.

Sometimes, I feel discriminated against, but it does not make me angry. It merely astonishes me. How *can* any deny themselves the pleasure of my company? It's beyond me.

But in the main, I feel like a brown bag of miscellany propped against a wall. Against a wall in company with other bags, white, red and yellow. Pour out the contents, and there is discovered a jumble of small things priceless and worthless. A first-water diamond,[9] an empty spool, bits of broken glass, lengths of string, a key to a door long since crumbled away, a rusty knife-blade, old shoes saved for a road that never was and never will be, a nail bent under the weight of things too heavy for any nail, a dried flower or two still a little fragrant. In your hand is the brown bag. On the ground before you is the jumble it held—so much like the jumble in the bags, could they be emptied, that all might be dumped in a single heap and the bags refilled without altering the content of any greatly. A bit of colored glass more or less would not matter. Perhaps that is how the Great Stuffer of Bags filled them in the first place—who knows?

8. Spear.   9. That is, a diamond of the highest quality.

LANGSTON HUGHES

From *The Big Sea* (1940)

Harlem Literati

The summer of 1926, I lived in a rooming house on 137th Street, where Wallace Thurman and Harcourt Tynes[1] also lived. Thurman was then managing editor of the *Messenger*, a Negro magazine that had a curious career. It began by being very radical, racial, and socialistic, just after the war. I believe it received a grant from the Garland Fund[2] in its early days. Then it later became a kind of Negro society magazine and a plugger for Negro business, with photographs of prominent colored ladies and their nice homes in it. A. Phillip Randolph, now President of the Brotherhood of Sleeping Car Porters, Chandler Owen, and George S. Schuyler were connected with it. Schuyler's editorials, à la Mencken,[3] were the most interesting things in the magazine, verbal brickbats that said sometimes one thing, sometimes another, but always vigorously. I asked Thurman what kind of magazine the *Messenger* was, and he said it reflected the policy of whoever paid off best at the time.

Anyway, the *Messenger* bought my first short stories. They paid me ten dollars a story. Wallace Thurman wrote me that they were very bad stories, but better than any others they could find, so he published them.

Thurman had recently come from California to New York. He was a strangely brilliant black boy, who had read everything, and whose critical mind could find something wrong with everything he read. I have no critical mind, so I usually either like a book or don't. But I am not capable of liking a book and then finding a million things wrong with it, too—as Thurman was capable of doing.

Thurman had read so many books because he could read eleven lines at a time. He would get from the library a great pile of volumes that would have taken me a year to read. But he would go through them in less than a week, and be able to discuss each one at great length with anybody. That was why, I suppose, he was later given a job as a reader at Macaulay's—the only Negro reader, so far as I know, to be employed by any of the larger publishing firms. . . .

Wallace Thurman wanted to be a great writer, but none of his own work ever made him happy. *The Blacker the Berry*,[4] his first book, was an important novel on a subject little dwelt upon in Negro fiction—the plight of the very dark Negro woman, who encounters in some communities a double wall of color prejudice within and without the race. His play, *Harlem*, considerably distorted for box office purposes, was, nevertheless, a compelling study—and the only one in the theater—of the impact of Harlem on a Negro family fresh from the South. And his *Infants of the Spring*, a superb and bitter study of the bohemian fringe of Harlem's literary and artistic life, is a compelling book.

---

1. A friend of Thurman's. *House on 137th Street*: the rooming house appears in Thurman's *Infants of the Spring* as "Niggerati Manor."

2. The American Fund for Public Service, established in 1920 by Charles Garland.

3. Henry Louis Mencken (1880–1956), prominent Baltimore essayist, critic, and editor who was a friend of Schuyler's. Randolph (1889–1976) and Owen (1889–1967), editors at the *Messenger*, who hired Schuyler as a writer in 1923. Schuyler (1895–1977), conservative black writer. 4. Published in 1929.

But none of these things pleased Wallace Thurman. He wanted to be a *very* great writer, like Gorki or Thomas Mann,[5] and he felt that he was merely a journalistic writer. His critical mind, comparing his pages to the thousands of other pages he had read, by Proust, Melville, Tolstoy, Galsworthy, Dostoyevski, Henry James, Sainte-Beuve, Taine, Anatole France,[6] found his own pages vastly wanting. So he contented himself by writing a great deal for money, laughing bitterly at his fabulously concocted "true stories," creating two bad motion pictures[7] of the "Adults Only" type for Hollywood, drinking more and more gin, and then threatening to jump out of windows at people's parties and kill himself.

During the summer of 1926, Wallace Thurman, Zora Neale Hurston, Aaron Douglas, John P. Davis, Bruce Nugent, Gwendolyn Bennett,[8] and I decided to publish "a Negro quarterly of the arts" to be called *Fire*—the idea being that it would burn up a lot of the old, dead conventional Negro-white ideas of the past, *épater le bourgeois*[9] into a realization of the existence of the younger Negro writers and artists, and provide us with an outlet for publication not available in the limited pages of the small Negro magazines then existing, the *Crisis, Opportunity*, and the *Messenger*—the first two being house organs of inter-racial organizations, and the latter being God knows what.

Sweltering summer evenings we met to plan *Fire*. Each of the seven of us agreed to give fifty dollars to finance the first issue. Thurman was to edit it, John P. Davis to handle the business end, and Bruce Nugent to take charge of distribution. The rest of us were to serve as an editorial board to collect material, contribute our own work, and act in any useful way that we could. . . .

I don't know how Thurman persuaded the printer to let us have all the copies to distribute, but he did. I think Alain Locke, among others, signed notes guaranteeing payments. But since Thurman was the only one of the seven of us with a regular job, for the next three or four years his checks were constantly being attached and his income seized to pay for *Fire*. And whenever I sold a poem, mine went there, too—to *Fire*.

None of the older Negro intellectuals would have anything to do with *Fire*. Dr. DuBois[1] in the *Crisis* roasted it. The Negro press called it all sorts of bad names, largely because of a green and purple story by Bruce Nugent, in the Oscar Wilde[2] tradition, which we had included. Rean Graves, the critic for the *Baltimore Afro-American*, began his review by saying: "I have just tossed the first issue of *Fire* into the fire." Commenting upon various of our contributors, he said: "Aaron Douglas

---

5. German novelist (1875–1955). Maxim Gorki was the pen name of Russian writer Aleksey Maksimovich Pyeshkov (1868–1936).
6. Pen name of French novelist and essayist Jacques Antole Francois Thibault (1844–1924). Marcel Proust (1871–1922), French novelist. Herman Melville (1819–91), U.S. writer. Leo Tolstoy (1828–1910), Russian novelist and social critic. John Galsworthy (1867–1933), English novelist. Fyodor Dostoyevski (1821–81), Russian novelist. James (1843–1916), U.S. novelist and critic. Charles Augustin Sainte-Beuve (1804–69), French critic and poet. Hippolyte Adolphe Taine (1828–93), French critic and historian.
7. *Tomorrow's Children* (1934) and *High School Girl* (1935).
8. Poet (1902–81). Hurston (1891–1960), novelist and folklore collector. Douglas (1898–1979), artist. Davis (1905–73), lawyer and prominent leftist. Nugent (1906–87), illustrator and writer.
9. Shock the middle class (French).
1. W. E. B. Du Bois (1868–1963), African American writer, editor of *Crisis*, and cofounder of the NAACP.
2. Irish poet, novelist, and playwright (1854–1900), a proponent of the Art for Art's Sake movement. *Green and purple story:* the first installment of a novel called *Smoke, Lilies and Jade.*

who, in spite of himself and the meaningless grotesqueness of his creations, has gained a reputation as an artist, is permitted to spoil three perfectly good pages and a cover with his pen and ink hudge pudge. Countee Cullen has written a beautiful poem in his 'From a Dark Tower,' but tries his best to obscure the thought in superfluous sentences. Langston Hughes displays his usual ability to say nothing in many words."

So *Fire* had plenty of cold water thrown on it by the colored critics. The white critics (except for an excellent editorial in the *Bookman* for November, 1926) scarcely noticed it at all. We had no way of getting it distributed to bookstands or news stands. Bruce Nugent took it around New York on foot and some of the Greenwich Village bookshops put it on display, and sold it for us. But then Bruce, who had no job, would collect the money and, on account of salary, eat it up before he got back to Harlem.

Finally, irony of ironies, several hundred copies of *Fire* were stored in the basement of an apartment where an actual fire occurred and the bulk of the whole issue was burned up. Even after that Thurman had to go on paying the printer.

Now *Fire* is a collector's item, and very difficult to get, being mostly ashes.

That taught me a lesson about little magazines. But since white folks had them, we Negroes thought we could have one, too. But we didn't have the money. . . .

About the future of Negro literature [Wallace] Thurman was very pessimistic. He thought the Negro vogue had made us all too conscious of ourselves, had flattered and spoiled us, and had provided too many easy opportunities for some of us to drink gin and more gin, on which he thought we would always be drunk. With his bitter sense of humor, he called the Harlem literati, the "niggerati."

Of this "niggerati," Zora Neale Hurston was certainly the most amusing. Only to reach a wider audience, need she ever write books—because she is a perfect book of entertainment in herself. In her youth she was always getting scholarships and things from wealthy white people, some of whom simply paid her just to sit around and represent the Negro race for them, she did it in such a racy fashion. She was full of side-splitting anecdotes, humorous tales, and tragicomic stories, remembered out of her life in the South as a daughter of a travelling minister of God. She could make you laugh one minute and cry the next. To many of her white friends, no doubt, she was a perfect "darkie," in the nice meaning they give the term—that is a naïve, childlike, sweet, humorous, and highly colored Negro.

But Miss Hurston was clever, too—a student who didn't let college give her a broad *a* and who had great scorn for all pretensions, academic or otherwise. That is why she was such a fine folk-lore collector,[3] able to go among the people and never act as if she had been to school at all. Almost nobody else could stop the average Harlemite on Lenox Avenue and measure his head with a strange-looking, anthropological device and not get bawled out for the attempt, except Zora, who used to stop anyone whose head looked interesting, and measure it. . . .

Harlem was like a great magnet for the Negro intellectual, pulling him from everywhere. Or perhaps the magnet was New York—but once in New York, he had to live in Harlem, for rooms were hardly to be found elsewhere unless one

---

3. Hurston published two such collections: *Mules and Men* (1935) and *Tell My Horse* (1938).

could pass for white or Mexican or Eurasian and perhaps live in the Village—which always seemed to me a very arty locale, in spite of the many real artists and writers who lived there. Only a few of the New Negroes lived in the Village, Harlem being their real stamping ground. . . .

SUGGESTIONS FOR WRITING

1. Many poets of the Harlem Renaissance made extensive use of the sonnet form; this chapter contains such examples as Countee Cullen's "From the Dark Tower," Helene Johnson's "Sonnet to a Negro in Harlem," and Claude McKay's "If We Must Die." Write an essay in which you compare and contrast some of the sonnets written during the Harlem Renaissance. How do different approaches to the sonnet form signal different thematic concerns?

2. In 1921, James Weldon Johnson wrote of "the need for Aframerican poets in the United States to work out a new and distinctive form of expression." Judging from the selections in this chapter, do you think that poets such as Langston Hughes and Claude McKay met the need articulated by Johnson? Write an essay in which you examine both traditionalism and innovation in the poetry of the Harlem Renaissance. How distinct are the works of black and white poets during this period?

3. In *The New Negro*, Alain Locke declared, "In Harlem, Negro life is seizing upon its first chances for group expression and self-determination." Do poems such as Arna Bontemps's "A Black Man Talks of Reaping," Angelina Grimké's "The Black Finger," and Langston Hughes's "I, Too" achieve a common social consciousness—Locke's "group expression"? What political effect do you think these poets hoped to achieve through their work? Write an essay in which you analyze the political ideas in the poetry of the Harlem Renaissance.

4. Some poems of the Harlem Renaissance—Langston Hughes's "The Weary Blues" and Claude McKay's "The Harlem Dancer," for example—are explicitly about music; others, such as Countee Cullen's "Saturday's Child," with its ballad form, and Angelina Grimke's improvisational "Tenebris," take a distinctly musical approach. Write an essay about the interplay of words and music in the poetry of this period.

5. In his review of Claude McKay's *Home to Harlem*, W. E. B. Du Bois laments that McKay "stooped" to betraying the black cause by portraying "drunkenness, fighting, lascivious sexual promiscuity, and utter absence of restraint" in his novel's black characters. Do writers have a particular duty to portray positive role models? Do writers from ethnic groups engaged in social struggle have a particular duty to participate in that struggle? Citing evidence from the selections in this chapter, write an essay in which you weigh the demands of artistic duty against the demands of artistic freedom.

6. What does it mean for a group of artists to be considered a "school"—that is, a group whose work appears to share common themes, styles, and goals? Write an essay in which you discuss whether or not the writers of the Harlem Renaissance spoke with a unified voice. Does a grouping like "the Harlem Renaissance" help our understanding of this period and the art it produced, or does it obscure the individual achievements of the artists themselves?

25

CRITICAL CONTEXTS:
SYLVIA PLATH'S "DADDY"

As the previous context chapters have suggested, poems draw on all kinds of earlier texts, experiences, and events. But they also produce new contexts of discussion and interpretation, ongoing conversations about the poems themselves. Different readers of poems see different things in them, so naturally a variety of interpretations and evaluations develop around any poem that is read repeatedly by various readers. Many of those interpretations are published in specialized journals and books (the selections that follow are all reprinted from published sources), and a kind of dialogue develops among readers, producing a body of commentary about the poem. Professional interpreters of texts are called *literary critics,* and the textual analysis they provide is called **literary criticism**—not because their work is necessarily negative or corrective, but because they ask hard, analytical, "critical" questions and interpret texts through a wide variety of literary, historical, biographical, psychological, aesthetic, moral, political, or social perspectives.

Your own interpretive work may seem to you more private and far removed from such "professional" writing about poems. But once you engage in class discussion or talk informally about a poem, you are in effect practicing literary criticism—offering comments, analyzing, judging, putting the poem into some kind of perspective that makes it more intelligible. You are, in effect, joining the ongoing conversation about the poem. And when you *write* about the poem, you may often engage specifically the opinions of others—your teacher, fellow students, or published "criticism." You may not have the experience or specific expertise of professional critics, but you can modify or answer the work of others and use it in your own work.

There are many ways to engage literary criticism and put it to work for you. The most common is to draw on published work for specific information about the poem: glossings of particular terms; explanations of references or situations you don't recognize; accounts of how, when, and under what circumstances the poem was written. Another common use of such material is as a springboard for your own interpretation, either building on what someone else has said or, if you disagree, using it as a point of departure to launch a different view. When you use the work of others, you must give full credit, carefully detailing the sources of all direct quotations and all borrowed ideas. You must always tell your reader exactly how to find the material you have quoted or summarized. Usually, you do this through careful notes and a list of citations (that is, a bibliography) at the end of your paper. (See chapter 36 for help with citation and documentation.) Your instructor may also guide you to handbooks—for example, the *MLA Handbook* or *The Chicago Manual of Style*—that provide more detail.

1293

It is usually best to do your own extensive analysis of a poem *before* consulting what other critics have said. Your own reading experience gives you a legitimate perspective. You always want to take in new information and to challenge both your first impressions and your considered analyses—but don't be too quick to adopt somebody else's ideas. The best way to test the views of others is to compare them critically to your own conclusions, which you might then want to supplement, refine, extend, or even scrap altogether. You can sharpen your skills by articulating your views against those of people with extensive interpretive experience. Besides, even the experts disagree. In fact, one measure of a poem's greatness is its ability to stimulate disagreement and a broad range of interpretation.

SYLVIA PLATH

Daddy[1]

You do not do, you do not do
Any more, black shoe
In which I have lived like a foot
For thirty years, poor and white,
5 Barely daring to breathe or Achoo.

Daddy, I have had to kill you.
You died before I had time—
Marble-heavy, a bag full of God,
Ghastly statue with one gray toe[2]
10 Big as a Frisco seal

And a head in the freakish Atlantic
Where it pours bean green over blue
In the waters off beautiful Nauset.[3]
I used to pray to recover you.
15 Ach, du.[4]

In the German tongue, in the Polish town[5]
Scraped flat by the roller
Of wars, wars, wars.
But the name of the town is common.
20 My Polack friend

Says there are a dozen or two.
So I never could tell where you
Put your foot, your root,
I never could talk to you.
25 The tongue stuck in my jaw.

---

1. First published in *Ariel*, a volume of poems that appeared two years after Plath's suicide.
2. Otto Plath, Sylvia's father, lost a toe to gangrene that resulted from diabetes.
3. Inlet on Cape Cod.
4. Oh, you (German). Plath often portrays herself as Jewish and her oppressors as German.
5. Otto Plath, an ethnic German, was born in Grabow, Poland.

It stuck in a barb wire snare.
Ich,[6] ich, ich, ich,
I could hardly speak.
I thought every German was you.
30 And the language obscene

An engine, an engine
Chuffing me off like a Jew.
A Jew to Dachau, Auschwitz, Belsen.[7]
I began to talk like a Jew.
35 I think I may well be a Jew.

The snows of the Tyrol, the clear beer of Vienna[8]
Are not very pure or true.
With my gypsy-ancestress and my weird luck
And my Taroc[9] pack and my Taroc pack
40 I may be a bit of a Jew.

I have always been scared of *you*,
With your Luftwaffe,[1] your gobbledygoo.
And your neat moustache
And your Aryan[2] eye, bright blue.
45 Panzer[3]-man, panzer-man, O You—

Not God but a swastika
So black no sky could squeak through.
Every woman adores a Fascist,
The boot in the face, the brute
50 Brute heart of a brute like you.

You stand at the blackboard, daddy,
In the picture I have of you,
A cleft in your chin instead of your foot
But no less a devil for that, no not
55 Any less the black man who

Bit my pretty red heart in two.
I was ten when they buried you.
At twenty I tried to die
And get back, back, back to you.
60 I thought even the bones would do.

But they pulled me out of the sack,
And they stuck me together with glue.[4]
And then I knew what to do.

---

6. German for "I."   7. Sites of World War II Nazi death camps.
8. The snow in the Tyrol (an Alpine region in Austria and northern Italy) is, legendarily, as pure as the beer
is clear in Vienna.   9. Tarot, playing cards used mainly for fortune-telling.   1. German air force.
2. People of Germanic lineage, often blond-haired and blue-eyed.
3. Literally "panther," the Nazi tank corps' term for an armored vehicle.
4. Allusion to Plath's recovery from her first suicide attempt.

      I made a model of you,
65 A man in black with a Meinkampf[5] look

      And a love of the rack and the screw.
      And I said I do, I do.
      So daddy, I'm finally through.
      The black telephone's off at the root,
70 The voices just can't worm through.

      If I've killed one man, I've killed two—
      The vampire who said he was you
      And drank my blood for a year,
      Seven years, if you want to know.
75 Daddy, you can lie back now.

      There's a stake in your fat black heart
      And the villagers never liked you.
      They are dancing and stamping on you.
      They always *knew* it was you.
80 Daddy, daddy, you bastard, I'm through.

                              1966

PREPARING A RESPONSE TO CRITICAL CONTEXTS

Before you read the criticism on Sylvia Plath's "Daddy" reprinted in this chapter, carefully read the poem itself several times. Ask all the analytical questions you have found useful in other cases: Who is speaking? To whom? When? Under what conditions? What is the full situation? What kind of language does the poem use? How does the poem use metaphor? allusion? historical reference? What strategies of rhythm and sound does the poem use? What is the poem's tone? When was the poem written and how does it reflect its time? What do you know about the person who wrote it? In what ways is this poem like others you have read by this poet or by this poet's contemporaries?

Once you have a "reading" of your own and have noted answers to these questions, look at the selections that follow. In order to come up with ideas for an essay incorporating the selections, you might follow these basic steps:

1. Read each critical piece carefully and keep close track of all the things with which you agree and (even more important) disagree.
2. Look specifically for information and facts that are new to you; examine and question the information carefully.
3. Look for points of disagreement in the different interpretations, make a list of the most important issues raised, and look for the crucial parts of the poem where the basis for the disagreements occurs.
4. Once you have prepared your notes and absorbed some of the criticism, how do you participate in the debate about Sylvia Plath's poem? Here are some possible topics for an essay on the criticism that has been published about "Daddy":

5. The title of Adolf Hitler's autobiography and manifesto (1925–27); German for "my struggle."

Sylvia Plath

Otto Plath

- *Your essay could show that others have overlooked or misinterpreted something significant for a better understanding of the poem.* Note the sources the critics cite. Which articles or works by or about Sylvia Plath come up in more than one of the essays below? Find in your library or on the Internet a copy of the cited sources and read and interpret them in your own way.
- *Your essay could be an overview of critical trends in the study of this poem, making clear which positions you find helpful, and where your own critical position differs from others.* Sort the critics into two or three groups according to their interpretation of "Daddy." Which critics place the most emphasis on Plath's psychology, experience, and self-expression? Which critics stress her development as a poet with a specific style? Which critics highlight her social criticism, either of anti-Semitism and the Holocaust or of sexism and women's oppression, or both? (See the section "Critical Approaches" for help identifying and describing the approaches of these critics or groups of critics.)

5. In one or two sentences, write a thesis statement expressing your views on various critical approaches, such as the following:

- Criticism of Sylvia Plath's "Daddy" has gone too far with a biographical approach, whereas myth criticism would facilitate a better understanding of the poem.
- The life of Sylvia Plath provides a key to a reading of her poem "Daddy." As suggested by critics (including Steiner, Alvarez, and Axelrod) and biographical sources, the poem expresses violent emotional aspects of her life, including her unresolved attachment to her father, Otto Plath; her power struggle with her husband, Ted Hughes; and her suicide attempt.
- Feminist readings of Sylvia Plath's "Daddy" have taken different approaches: Some focus on biographical evidence of Plath's experience as a woman, whereas others, such as Margaret Homans's "A Feminine

Tradition," consider a "literal" identification of the woman poet with the female speaker of the poem to be a reinforcement of the idea that women can never escape their personal, physical lives. This essay balances these feminist approaches to "Daddy," examining it as a semiautobiographical dramatic monologue: The speaker responds to some experiences Plath had as a daughter and wife, but the poem is not wholly autobiographical.

- The many critical studies of Sylvia Plath's "Daddy" focus on allusions to Nazis without fully considering an international context and setting. Instead of reading the references to places in Europe as shorthand for political ideas, this essay reads the poem as more descriptive, comparing it to such poems of place as "Point Shirley." The essay focuses on the image of the fallen colossus that extends from San Francisco ("frisco seal") to Cape Cod ("beautiful Nauset").

See also the writing suggestions at the end of this chapter.

GEORGE STEINER

From *Dying Is an Art**

Sylvia Plath's last poems have already passed into legend as both representative of our present tone of emotional life and unique in their implacable, harsh brilliance. . . .

The spell does not lie wholly in the poems themselves. The suicide of Sylvia Plath at the age of thirty-one in 1963, and the personality of this young woman who had come from Massachusetts to study and live in England (where she married Ted Hughes, himself a gifted poet), are vital parts of it. To those who knew her and to the greatly enlarged circle who were electrified by her last poems and sudden death, she had come to signify the specific honesties and risks of the poet's condition. Her personal style, and the price in private harrowing she so obviously paid to achieve the intensity and candor of her principal poems, have taken on their own dramatic authority.

All this makes it difficult to judge the poems. I mean that the vehemence and intimacy of the verse is such as to constitute a very powerful rhetoric of sincerity. The poems play on our nerves with their own proud nakedness, making claims so immediate and sharply urged that the reader flinches, embarrassed by the routine discretions and evasions of his own sensibility. Yet if these poems are to take life among us, if they are to be more than exhibits in the history of modern psychological stress, they must be read with all the intelligence and scruple we can muster. They are too honest, they have cost too much, to be yielded to myth.

. . . It requires no biographical impertinence to realize that Sylvia Plath's life was harried by bouts of physical pain, that she sometimes looked on the accumulated

---

* From George Steiner, *Language and Silence: Essays on Language, Literature, and the Inhuman* (1967; New York: Atheneum, 1974), pp. 295–302.

exactions of her own nerve and body as "a trash / To annihilate each decade." She was haunted by the piecemeal, strung-together mechanics of the flesh. . . . The hospital ward was her exemplary ground:

> My patent leather overnight case like a black pillbox,
> My husband and child smiling out of the family photo;
> Their smiles catch onto my skin, little smiling hooks.

This brokenness, so sharply feminine and contemporary, is, I think, her principal realization. . . . Sylvia Plath carries forward, in an intensely womanly and aggravated note, from Robert Lowell's *Life Studies,* a book that obviously had a great impact on her. This new frankness of women about the specific hurts and tangles of their nervous-physiological makeup is as vital to the poetry of Sylvia Plath as it is to the tracts of Simone de Beauvoir or to the novels of Edna O'Brien and Brigid Brophy. Women speak out as never before:

> I shall take no bite of your body,
> Bottle in which I live,
>
> Ghastly Vatican.
> I am sick to death of hot salt.
> Green as eunuchs, your wishes
> Hiss at my sin.
> Off, off, eely tentacle!
>
> There is nothing between us.

The ambiguity and dual flash of insight in this final line are of a richness and obviousness that only a very great poem can carry off.

The progress registered between the early and the mature poems is one of concretion. The general Gothic means with which Sylvia Plath was so fluently equipped become singular to herself and therefore fiercely honest. What had been style passes into need. It is the need of a superbly intelligent, highly literate young woman to cry out about her especial being, about the tyrannies of blood and gland, of . . . sex and childbirth in which a woman is still compelled to be wholly of her organic condition. Where Emily Dickinson could—indeed was obliged to—shut the door on the riot and humiliations of the flesh, thus achieving her particular dry lightness, Sylvia Plath "fully assumed her own condition." This alone would assure her of a place in modern literature. But she took one step further, assuming a burden that was not naturally or necessarily hers.

Born in Boston in 1932 of German and Austrian parents, Sylvia Plath had no personal, immediate contact with the world of the concentration camps. I may be mistaken, but so far as I know there was nothing Jewish in her background. But her last, greatest poems culminate in an act of identification, of total communion with those tortured and massacred. [Here Steiner quotes lines 31–40 of "Daddy."]

. . . Sylvia Plath is only one of a number of young contemporary poets, novelists, and playwrights, themselves in no way implicated in the actual holocaust, who have done most to counter the general inclination to forget the death camps. Perhaps it is only those who had no part in the events who *can* focus on them rationally and imaginatively; to those who experienced the thing, it has lost the hard edges of possibility, it has stepped outside the real.

Committing the whole of her poetic and formal authority to the metaphor, to the mask of language, Sylvia Plath *became* a woman being transported to Auschwitz on the death trains. The notorious shards of massacre seemed to enter into her own being:

> A cake of soap,
> A wedding ring,
> A gold filling.

In "Daddy" she wrote one of the very few poems I know of in any language to come near the last horror. It achieves the classic act of generalization, translating a private, obviously intolerable hurt into a code of plain statement, of instantaneously public images which concern us all. It is the "Guernica"[6] of modern poetry. And it is both histrionic and, in some ways, "arty," as is Picasso's outcry.

Are these final poems entirely legitimate? In what sense does anyone, himself uninvolved and long after the event, commit a subtle larceny when he invokes the echoes and trappings of Auschwitz and appropriates an enormity of ready emotion to his own private design? Was there latent in Sylvia Plath's sensibility, as in that of many of us who remember only by fiat of imagination, a fearful envy, a dim resentment at not having been there, of having missed the rendezvous with hell? In "Lady Lazarus" and "Daddy" the realization seems to me so complete, the sheer rawness and control so great, that only irresistible need could have brought it off. These poems take tremendous risks, extending Sylvia Plath's essentially austere manner to the very limit. They are a bitter triumph, proof of the capacity of poetry to give to reality the greater permanence of the imagined. She could not return from them.

IRVING HOWE

From *The Plath Celebration: A Partial Dissent**

Sylvia Plath's most famous poem, adored by many sons and daughters, is "Daddy." It is a poem with an affecting theme, the feelings of the speaker as she regathers the pain of her father's premature death and her persuasion that he has betrayed her by dying:

> I was ten when they buried you.
> At twenty I tried to die
> And get back, back, back to you.

In the poem Sylvia Plath identifies the father (we recall his German birth) with the Nazis ("Panzer-man, panzer-man, O You") and flares out with assaults for which nothing in the poem (nor, so far as we know, in Sylvia Plath's own life) offers any warrant: "A cleft in your chin instead of your foot / But no less a devil for that. . . ." Nor does anything in the poem offer warrant, other than the free-

---

6. Pablo Picasso's famous painting (1937) depicting the brutalities of war.
* From Irving Howe, *The Critical Point of Literature and Culture* (1973; New York: Horizon Press, 1977), pp. 231–33.

flowing hysteria of the speaker, for the assault of such lines as, "There's a stake in your fat black heart / And the villagers never liked you." . . .

What we have here is a revenge fantasy, feeding upon filial love-hatred, and thereby mostly of clinical interest. But seemingly aware that the merely clinical can't provide the materials for a satisfying poem, Sylvia Plath tries to enlarge upon the personal plight, give meaning to the personal outcry, by fancying the girl as victim of a Nazi father: "An engine, an engine / Chuffing me off like a Jew. . . ."

The more sophisticated admirers of this poem may say that I fail to see it as a dramatic presentation, a monologue spoken by a disturbed girl not necessarily to be identified with Sylvia Plath, despite the similarities of detail between the events of the poem and the events of her life. I cannot accept this view. The personal-confessional element, strident and undisciplined, is simply too obtrusive to suppose the poem no more than a dramatic picture of a certain style of disturbance. If, however, we did accept such a reading of "Daddy," we would fatally narrow its claims to emotional or moral significance, for we would be confining it to a mere vivid imagining of pathological state. That, surely, is not how its admirers really take the poem.

It is clearly not how the critic George Steiner takes the poem when he calls it "the 'Guernica' of modern poetry." But then, in an astonishing turn, he asks: "In what sense does anyone, himself uninvolved and long after the event, commit a subtle larceny when he invokes the echoes and trappings of Auschwitz and appropriates an enormity of ready emotion to his own private design?" The question is devastating to his early comparison with "Guernica." Picasso's painting objectifies the horrors of Guernica, through the distancing of art; no one can suppose that he shares or participates in them. Plath's poem aggrandizes on the "enormity of ready emotion" invoked by references to the concentration camps, in behalf of an ill-controlled if occasionally brilliant outburst. There is something monstrous, utterly disproportionate, when tangled emotions about one's father are deliberately compared with the historical fate of the European Jews; something sad, if the comparison is made spontaneously. "Daddy" persuades once again, through the force of negative example, of how accurate T. S. Eliot was in saying, "The more perfect the artist, the more completely separate in him will be the man who suffers and the mind which creates."

A. ALVAREZ

From *Sylvia Plath**

The reasons for Sylvia Plath's images are always there, though sometimes you have to work hard to find them. She is, in short, always in intelligent control of her feelings. Her work bears out her theories:

> I think my poems come immediately out of the sensuous and emotional experiences I have, but I must say I cannot sympathise with these cries from the heart that are informed by nothing except a needle or a knife or whatever it is. I believe that one should be able to control and manipulate experiences, even the

* From A. Alvarez, *Beyond All This Fiddle* (London: Penguin, 1968), pp. 56–57.

most terrifying—like madness, being tortured, this kind of experience—and one should be able to manipulate these experiences with an informed and intelligent mind. I think that personal experience shouldn't be a kind of shut box and mirror-looking narcissistic experience. I believe it should be generally relevant, to such things as Hiroshima and Dachau, and so on.

It seems to me that it was only by her determination both to face her most inward and terrifying experiences and to use her intelligence in doing so—so as not to be overwhelmed by them—that she managed to write these extraordinary last poems, which are at once deeply autobiographical and yet detached, generally relevant.

. . . She assumes the suffering of all the modern victims. Above all, she becomes an imaginary Jew. I think this is a vitally important element in her work. For two reasons. First, because anyone whose subject is suffering has a ready-made modern example of hell on earth in the concentration camps. And what matters in them is not so much the physical torture—since sadism is general and perennial—but the way modern, as it were industrial, techniques can be used to destroy utterly the human identity. . . . This anonymity of pain, which makes all dignity impossible, was Sylvia Plath's subject. Second, she seemed convinced, in these last poems, that the root of her suffering was the death of her father, whom she loved, who abandoned her, and who dragged her after him into death. And in her fantasies her father was pure German, pure Aryan, pure anti-semite.

It all comes together in the most powerful of her last poems, "Daddy," . . . about which she wrote the following bleak note:

> The poem is spoken by a girl with an Electra complex. Her father died while she thought he was God. Her case is complicated by the fact that her father was also a Nazi and her mother very possibly part Jewish. In the daughter the two strains marry and paralyse each other—she has to act out the awful little allegory once over before she is free of it.[7]

. . . What comes through most powerfully, I think, is the terrible *unforgivingness* of her verse, the continual sense not so much of violence—although there is a good deal of that—as of violent resentment that this should have been done to *her*. What she does in the poem is, with a weird detachment, to turn the violence against herself so as to show that she can equal her oppressors with her self-inflicted oppression. And this is the strategy of the concentration camps. When suffering is there whatever you do, by inflicting it upon yourself you achieve your identity, you set yourself free.

Yet the tone of the poem, like its psychological mechanisms, is not single or simple, and she uses a great deal of skill to keep it complex. Basically, her trick is to tell this horror story in a verse form as insistently jaunty and ritualistic as a nursery rhyme. And this helps her to maintain towards all the protagonists—her father, her husband and herself—a note of hard and sardonic anger, as though she were almost amused that her own suffering should be so extreme, so grotesque. . . . When she first read me the poem a few days after she wrote it, she called it a piece of "light verse." It obviously isn't, yet equally obviously it also isn't

7. From the introductory notes to "New Poems," a reading prepared for the BBC Third Programme but never broadcast [Alvarez's note].

the racking personal confession that a mere description or précis of it might make it sound.

Yet neither is it unchangingly vindictive or angry. The whole poem works on one single, returning note and rhyme, echoing from start to finish:

> You do not do, you do not do . . .
> . . . I used to pray to recover you.
> Ach, du . . .

There is a kind of cooing tenderness in this which complicates the other, more savage note of resentment. It brings in an element of pity, less for herself and her own suffering than for the person who made her suffer. Despite everything, "Daddy" is a love poem.

JUDITH KROLL

From *Rituals of Exorcism: "Daddy"**

Poems explicitly about the protagonist's father, read in order of composition, show that the attitude toward him evolves from nostalgic mournfulness, regret, and guilt, to resentment and a bitter resolve to break his hold on her. . . .

The recital of the myth in "Daddy" ends in a ritual intended to cancel the earlier "sacred marriage" which has suffocated her:

> You do not do, you do not do
> Any more, black shoe
> In which I have lived like a foot
> For thirty years, poor and white,
> Barely daring to breathe or Achoo.[8]

In this image of passive and victimized domesticity, the speaker implicitly compares her past self to the "old woman who lived in a shoe" who "didn't know what to do"; now, however, she makes it clear that she does know what to do.

As a preamble to the exorcism, . . . Daddy must be cast in this new light, transformed from god to devil, if he is to be successfully expelled, but there must also be some real basis for it. To be effectively exposed, he must first appear as godly. But the speaker soon shows that she now attributes his godliness in part to his authoritarianism and personal inaccessibility—qualities which became intensified through his death, and which later became transferred to "a model of you"— her husband. . . . Loving a man literally or metaphorically dead . . . becomes a kind of persecution or punishment; and so, by the end of the incantation, Daddy

---

* From Judith Kroll, *Chapters in a Mythology: The Poetry of Sylvia Plath* (New York: Harper & Row, 1976), pp. 122–26. Unless otherwise specified, all notes are Kroll's.

8. When Plath introduced "Daddy" as being about "a girl with an Electra complex" (with, in effect, the female version of an Oedipus complex), she gave a clue to what may be a play on words in the poem. "Oedipus" means "swell-foot," and therefore the speaker's identification of herself as a "foot" may be a private way of saying "I am Oedipus" and incorporating into the poem an allusion to the Electra complex.

deserves to be cast out. The "black telephone . . . off at the root," conveys the finality of the intended exorcism.

The "venomousness," ambiguous from the beginning, is not the whole story. "Daddy" is not primarily a poem of "father-hatred" or abuse as Robert Lowell, Elizabeth Hardwick, and others have contended. The need for exorcising her father's ghost lies, after all, in the extremity of her attachment to him. Alvarez very justly remarks that . . . "'Daddy' is a love poem."[9] . . . The love is not merely conveyed by the rhythm and sound of the poem, it is a necessary part of the poem's meaning, a part of the logic of its act.

The exorcism serves another purpose because through it she attempts to reject the pattern of being abandoned and made to suffer by a god, a man who is "chock-full of power": she creates "a model of you"—an image of her father—and marries this proxy. Then she kills both father and husband at once, magically using each as the other's representative.[1] Each death entails that of the other: the stake in her father's heart also kills the "vampire who said he was you"; and the killing of her marriage (for which she now claims to take responsibility, as she does for having allowed her marriage to perpetuate, by proxy, her relationship to her father) finally permits Daddy to "lie back." The marriage to and killing of her father by proxy are acts of what Frazer[2] calls "sympathetic magic," in which "things act on each other at a distance through a secret sympathy." . . .

Plath was familiar with and used such ideas. . . . The notion that "as the image suffers, so does the man"—affecting the real subject through a proxy—nicely describes marriage to a model of Daddy, and explains why "If I've killed one man, I've killed two." The earlier attempt of the speaker in "Daddy" to recover her father also involved sympathetic magic; she had tried to rejoin him by dying and becoming like him:

> At twenty I tried to die
> And get back, back, back to you.

She finally exorcises her father as if he were a scapegoat invested with the evils of her spoiled history. Frazer's discussion of rituals in which the dying god is also a scapegoat is germane here. He conjectures that two originally separate rituals merged. . . . [T]he father in "Daddy" may well be described as such a divine scapegoat figure. . . .

The logic of sympathetic magic, which appears widely in Plath's late poetry, might well be called one of the physical laws of her poems. . . . Such a logic seems poetically appropriate for a mythology: that the Moon-muse (or one of her agents, such as "The Rival") governs and affects her by a "secret sympathy" seems natural to a mythic drama.

The motifs "released"—or triggered—in her late poems contain the potential for a sympathetic association of those details which express the same motif. Because the details are not incidental, called forth as they are by her mythology, the sympathy is in a sense guaranteed. The images of blood, violent death, and red poppies, all of which release the death and rebirth motif, have the

---

9. Alvarez, "Sylvia Plath" [see pp. 1301–03].

1. The biographical basis for this identification is evident in *Letters Home*. . . .

2. Sir James George Frazer (1854–1941), Scottish anthropologist whose book *The Golden Bough* analyzes early religious and magical practices [Editor's note].

potential for sympathetically affecting one another through their family resemblance.

MARY LYNN BROE

From *Protean Poetic**

Among the other poems that display the performing self, "Daddy" and "Lady Lazarus" are two of the most often quoted, but most frequently misunderstood, poems in the Plath canon. The speaker in "Daddy" performs a mock poetic exorcism of an event that has already happened—the death of her father, who she feels withdrew his love from her by dying prematurely: "Daddy, I have had to kill you. / You died before I had time—."

The speaker attempts to exorcise not just the memory of her father but her own *Mein Kampf* model of him as well as her inherited behavioral traits that lead her graveward under the Freudian banner of death instinct or Thanatos's libido. But her ritual reenactment simply does not take. The event comically backfires as pure self-parody: the metaphorical murder of the father dwindles into Hollywood spectacle, while the poet is lost in the clutter of the collective unconscious.

Early in the poem, the ritual gets off on the wrong foot both literally and figuratively. A sudden rhythmic break midway through the first stanza interrupts the insistent and mesmeric chant of the poet's own freedom:

> You do not do, you do not do
> Any more, black shoe
> In which I have lived like a foot
> For thirty years, poor and white,
> Barely daring to breathe or Achoo.

The break suggests, on the one hand, that the nursery-rhyme world of contained terror is here abandoned; on the other, that the poet-exorcist's mesmeric control is superficial, founded in a shaky faith and an unsure heart—the worst possible state for the strong, disciplined exorcist.

At first she kills her father succinctly with her own words, demythologizing him to a ludicrous piece of statuary that is hardly a Poseidon or the Colossus of Rhodes.[3] . . .

Then as she tries to patch together the narrative of him, his tribal myth (the "common" town, the "German tongue," the war-scraped culture), she begins to lose her own powers of description to a senseless Germanic prattle ("The tongue stuck in my jaw. / It stuck in a barb wire snare. / Ich, ich, ich, ich"). The individual man is absorbed by his inhuman archetype, the "panzer man," "an engine / Chuffing me off like a Jew." Losing the exorcist's power that binds the spirit and then casts out the demon, she is the classic helpless victim of the swastika man.

---

* From Mary Lynn Broe, *Protean Poetic: The Poetry of Sylvia Plath* (Columbia and London: University of Missouri Press, 1980), pp. 172–75.
3. One of the seven wonders of the ancient world, a gigantic statue of the Greek sun god, Helios; *Poseidon:* the chief sea god in the Greek pantheon [Editor's note].

As she calls up her own picture of him as a devil, he refuses to adopt this stereo-type. Instead he jumbles his trademark:

> A cleft in your chin instead of your foot
> But no less a devil for that, no not
> Any less the black man who
>
> Bit my pretty red heart in two.

The overt Nazi-Jew allegory throughout the poem suggests that, by a simple inversion of power, father and daughter grow more alike. But when she tries to imitate his action of dying, making all the appropriate grand gestures, she once again fails: "but they pulled me out of the sack, / And they stuck me together with glue." She retreats to a safe world of icons and replicas, but even the doll image she constructs turns out to be "the vampire who said he was you." At last, she abandons her father to the collective unconscious where it is *he* who is finally recognized ("they always *knew* it was you"). *She* is lost, impersonally absorbed by his irate persecutors, bereft of both her power and her conjuror's discipline, and possessed by the incensed villagers. The exorcist's ritual, one of purifying, cleansing, commanding silence and then ordering the evil spirit's departure, has dwindled to a comic picture from the heart of darkness. Mad villagers stamp on the devil-vampire creation. . . .

. . . It would seem that the real victim is the poet-performer who, despite her straining toward identification with the public events of holocaust and destruc-tion of World War II, becomes more murderously persecuting than the "panzer-man" who smothered her, and who abandoned her with a paradoxical love, guilt, and fear. . . .

The failure of the exorcism and the emotional ambivalence are echoed in the curious rhythm. The incantatory safety of the nursery-rhyme thump (seemingly one of controlled, familiar terrors) also suggests some sinister brooding by its repetition. The poem opens with a suspiciously emphatic protest, a kind of psychological whistling-in-the-dark. As it proceeds, "Daddy"'s continuous life-rhythms—the assonance, consonance, and especially the sustained *oo* sounds—triumph over either the personal or the cultural-historical imagery. The sheer sense of organic life in the interwoven sounds carries the verse forward in boister-ous spirit and communicates an underlying feeling of comedy that is also echoed in the repeated failure of the speaker to perform her exorcism.

Ultimately, "Daddy" is like an emotional, psychological, and historical autopsy, a final report. There is no real progress. The poet is in the same place in the beginning as in the end. . . . Although it seems that the speaker has moved from identification with the persecuted to identity as persecutor, Jew to vampire-killer, powerless to powerful, she has simply enacted a performance that allows her to live with what is unchangeable. She has used her art to stave off suffocation, and performs her self-contempt with a degree of bravado.[4]

---

4. What remains the most thorough and enlightening account of the poem is A. R. Jones, "On 'Daddy,'" *The Art of Sylvia Plath,* [ed. Newman], pp. 230–36 [Broe's note].

MARGARET HOMANS

From *A Feminine Tradition**

To place an exclusive valuation on the literal, especially to identify the self as literal, is simply to ratify women's age-old and disadvantageous position as the other and the object. Contemporary poetry by women that takes up this self-defeating strategy risks encounters with death that are destructive both poetically and actually. The current belief in a literal "I" present in poetry is responsible for the popular superstition that Sylvia Plath's death was the purposeful completion of her poetry's project, the assumption being that if the speaker is precisely the same as the biographical Plath, the poetry's self-destructive violence is directed toward Plath herself, not toward an imagined speaker. This reading of Plath is unfair to the woman and, by calling it merely unmediated self-expression, obscures her poetry's real power. In poem after poem depicting or wishing for physical violence, the imagery of violence is part of a symmetrical figurative system, and death is figured as a way of achieving rebirth or some other transcendence.[5] Plath's project may not thus be very different from that of Dickinson, who speaks quite often from beyond the grave, reimagining and repossessing death as her own in order to dispel the terrors of literal death. However, within that figurative system the poet embraces a self-destructive program that must soon have been poetically terminal, even if it did not bring about the actual death.

Several of Plath's late poems come to terms with a father figure (who may include the poetic fathers she acknowledges in *The Colossus*), whose crime, no different from that identified by nineteenth-century women, is of attempting to transform the feminine self into objects. "Lady Lazarus" borrows the most appalling of Nazi imagery to accuse a generalized figure of male power of the ultimate reification. . . .

Though the poet is here objecting to literalization, not embracing it, the poetic myth of suicide through which the oppression may be lifted amounts to the same thing: the speaker must submit to this literalization in order to transcend it.

> Out of the ash
> I rise with my red hair
> And I eat men like air.

Their death costs her death, and powerful though the poem is, this is an extraordinarily high price for retribution. And as always, it is the process of objectification that makes up the poem, not the final, scarcely articulable transcendence.

"Daddy" uses Nazi imagery to make the same accusation about objectification brought against men as oppressors in "Lady Lazarus" and makes the corollary accusation against the father (and the husband modelled after him) that objectification has silenced her: "I never could talk to you./. . . I could hardly

* From Margaret Homans, *Women Writers and Poetic Identity: Dorothy Wordsworth, Emily Brontë, and Emily Dickinson* (Princeton: Princeton University Press, 1982), pp. 218–21.

5. I am indebted here, for their persuasively positive readings of Plath, to Judith Kroll, *Chapters in a Mythology: The Poetry of Sylvia Plath* (New York: Harper & Row, 1976), and to Stacy Pies, "Coming Clear of the Shadow: The Poetry of Sylvia Plath," unpublished essay (Yale University, 1979) [Homans's note].

speak." In this context defiance and retribution take the form of her speaking, but again this counterattack is counterproductive. Punning on the expression "being through" to mean both establishing a telephone connection and being finished, she at once makes and conclusively severs communication:

> So daddy, I'm finally through.
> The black telephone's off at the root,
> The voices just can't worm through.

The poem concludes, "Daddy, daddy, you bastard, I'm through." Suppressing the power of the one who silenced her, she simultaneously returns herself to the silence that the poem came into being to protest.

PAMELA J. ANNAS

From *A Disturbance in Mirrors**

... The particular sexual metaphor in "Daddy" is sado-masochism, which stands for the authority structure of a partriarchal and war-making society.... "Daddy" is an analysis of the structure of the society in which the individual is enmeshed. Intertwined with the image of sadist and masochist in "Daddy" is a parallel image of vampire and victim. In "Daddy," father, husband, and a larger patriarchal and competitive authority structure, which the speaker of the poem sees as having been responsible for the various imperialisms of the twentieth century, all melt together and become demonic, finally a gigantic vampire figure. In the modulation from one image to another to form an accumulated image that is characteristic of many of Plath's late poems, the male figure at the center of "Daddy" takes four major forms: the statue, the Gestapo officer, the professor, and the vampire. The poem begins, however, with an image of a black shoe, an image which, like the black shoe in "The Munich Mannequins" and like the black suit in "The Applicant," can be seen to stand for corporate man. The second stanza of the poem refers back to the title poem of *The Colossus,* where the speaker's father, representative of a gigantic male other, so dominated her world that her horizon was bounded by his scattered pieces.... Between "The Colossus" and "Daddy" there has been a movement from a mythic and natural landscape to one with social and political boundaries. Here the image of her father, grown larger than the earlier Colossus of Rhodes, stretches across and subsumes the whole of the United States, from the Pacific to the Atlantic ocean.

The next seven stanzas of "Daddy" construct the image of the Gestapo officer, using her family background—her parents were both of German origin—to mediate between her personal sense of suffocation and the social history of the Nazi invasions. The black shoe of the first stanza in which she says she has been wedged like a foot "barely daring to breathe" becomes in stanza ten, at the end of the Nazi section, a larger social image of suffocation: "Not God but a

---

* From Pamela J. Annas, *A Disturbance in Mirrors: The Poetry of Sylvia Plath,* Contributions in Women's Studies no. 89 (New York, Westport, and London: Greenwood Press, 1988), pp. 139–43. All notes are Annas's.

swastika / So black no sky could squeak through." The Gestapo figure recurs briefly three stanzas later as the speaker of the poem transfers the image from father to husband and incidentally suggests that the victim has some control in a brutalized association—at least to the extent she chooses to be there.[6] "I made a model of you, . . . And I said I do, I do." The Gestapo figure becomes "Herr Professor" in stanza eleven, an actual image of Plath's father, and also an image of what has for centuries been seen as the prototypical and even ideal relationship between a man and a woman.[7] The professor, who is a man, talks and is active; the woman, who is a student, listens and is passive. . . . But Plath places this image between the images of Nazi/Jew and vampire/victim so that it becomes the center of a series. Indeed, the image of daddy as teacher turns almost immediately into a devil/demon/vampire. . . .

The last two stanzas of "Daddy" are like the conclusion of "Lady Lazarus" in their assertion that the speaker of the poem is breaking out of the cycle and that, in order to do so, she must turn on and kill Herr God, Herr Lucifer in the one poem, and Daddy in his final metamorphosis as vampire in the other poem. . . .

The cycle of victim/vampire is, left alone, a closed and repetitious cycle, like the repeated suicides of "Lady Lazarus." According to the legends and the Hollywood film versions of these legends we all grew up on, once consumed by a vampire, one dies and is reborn a vampire and preys upon others, who in their turn die and become vampires. The vampire imagery in Sylvia Plath's poetry intersects on one level with her World War II imagery and its exploitation and victimization and on another level intersects with her images of a bureaucratic, fragmented, and dead—in the sense of numbed and unaware—society. The connections are sometimes confused, but certainly World War II is often imaged in her poetry as a kind of grisly, vampiric feast. . . .

The whole of "Daddy" is an exorcism to banish the demon, put a stake through the vampire's heart, and thus break the cycle of vampire→victim. It is crucial to the poem that the exorcism is accomplished through communal action by the "villagers." The rhythm of the poem is powerfully and deliberately primitive: a child's chant, a formal curse. The hard sounds, short lines, and repeated rhymes of "do," "you," "Jew," and "through" give a hard pounding quality to the poem that is close to the sound of a heart beat. . . .

Purity, which is what exorcism aims at, is for Plath an ambiguous concept. On the one hand it means integrity of self, wholeness rather than fragmentation, as unspoiled state of being, rest, perfection, aesthetic beauty, and loss of self through transformation into some reborn other. On the other hand, it also means absence, isolation, blindness, a kind of autism which shuts out the world, stasis and death, and a loss of self through dispersal into some other. In "Lady

6. See Wilhelm Reich's *The Mass Psychology of Fascism* (New York: Simon and Schuster, 1969), particularly his chapter on "The Authoritarian Personality," for an analysis of how an oppressed class can contribute to its own oppression. Judith Lewis Herman, in *Father-Daughter Incest* (Cambridge, Mass.: Harvard University Press, 1981), discusses the history of the suppression of incest beginning with Freud and continuing into contemporary psychological literature, the attribution of reports of incest to hysterical female oedipal fantasizing or, when the fact of incest is impossible to deny, assigning blame to the victim: what Herman calls the Seductive Daughter and/or the Collusive Mother (Chapter 1, "A Common Occurrence"). Writing in the early 1960s and familiar with some of these attitudes, . . . Plath [not surprisingly] assigns some culpability to the victim.

7. This photograph of Otto Plath is reproduced on page 17 of *Letters Home*.

Lazarus" and "Fever 103°" the emphasis is on exorcising the poet's previous selves, though within a social context that makes that unlikely. "Daddy," however, is a purification of the world; in "Daddy" it is the various avatars of the other—the male figure who represents the patriarchal society she lives in—that are being exorcised. . . . The more the speaker of the poems defines her situation as desperate, the more violent and vengeful becomes the agent of purification and transformation. . . .

STEVEN GOULD AXELROD

From *Jealous Gods**

[Although "Daddy"] has traditionally been read as "personal" (Aird 78)[8] or "confessional" (M. L. Rosenthal 82),[9] Margaret Homans has more recently suggested that it concerns a woman's dislocated relations to speech (*Women Writers* 220–21).[1] Plath herself introduced it on the BBC as the opposite of confession, as a constructed fiction: "Here is a poem spoken by a girl with an Electra complex. . . . [quoted in Alvarez, p. 1302]" (*CP* 293).[2] We might interpret this preface as an accurate retelling of the poem; or we might regard it as a case of an author's estrangement from her text, on the order of Coleridge's preface to "Kubla Khan" in which he claims to be unable to finish the poem, having forgotten what it was about. However we interpret Plath's preface, we must agree that "Daddy" is dramatic and allegorical, since its details depart freely from the facts of her biography. In this poem she again figures her unresolved conflicts with paternal authority as a textual issue. Significantly, her father was a published writer, and his successor, her husband, was also a writer. Her preface asserts that the poem concerns a young woman's paralyzing self-division, which she can defeat only through allegorical representation. Recalling that paralysis was one of Plath's main tropes for literary incapacity, we begin to see that the poem evokes the female poet's anxiety of authorship and specifically Plath's strategy of delivering herself from that anxiety by making it the topic of her discourse. Viewed from this perspective, "Daddy" enacts the woman poet's struggle with "daddy-poetry." It represents her effort to eject the "buried male muse" from her invention process and the "jealous gods" from her audience (*J* 223;[3] *CP* 179).

Plath wrote "Daddy" several months after Hughes left her, on the day she learned that he had agreed to a divorce (October 12, 1962). George Brown and Tirril Harris have shown that early loss makes one especially vulnerable to subsequent loss (Bowlby 250–59),[4] and Plath seems to have defended against

---

*From Steven Gould Axelrod, *Sylvia Plath: The Wound and the Cure of Words* (Baltimore: Johns Hopkins University Press, 1990), pp. 51–70, 237. Unless otherwise indicated, all notes are Axelrod's.

8. Eileen Aird, *Sylvia Plath: Her Life and Work* (New York: Harper & Row, 1973).

9. M. L. Rosenthal, *The New Poets: American and British Poetry since World War II* (London: Oxford University Press, 1967).

1. Margaret Homans, *Women Writers and Poetic Identity: Dorothy Wordsworth, Emily Brontë, and Emily Dickinson* (Princeton: Princeton University Press, 1980).   2. *CP* = *The Collected Poems*.   3. *J* = *The Journals*.

4. John Bowlby, *Attachment and Loss*, III: *Loss: Sadness and Depression* (London: Hogarth, 1980).

depression by almost literally throwing herself into her poetry. She followed "Daddy" with a host of poems that she considered her greatest achievement to date: "Medusa," "The Jailer," "Lady Lazarus," "Ariel," the bee sequence, and others. The letters she wrote to her mother and brother on the day of "Daddy," and then again four days later, brim with a sense of artistic self-discovery: "Writing like mad. . . . Terrific stuff, as if domesticity had choked me" (*LH* 466).[5] Composing at the "still blue, almost eternal hour before the baby's cry, before the glassy music of the milkman, settling his bottles" (quoted in Alvarez, *Savage God* 21),[6] she experienced an "enormous" surge in creative energy (*LH* 467). Yet she also expressed feelings of misery: "The half year ahead seems like a lifetime, and the half behind an endless hell" (*LH* 468). She was again contemplating things German: a trip to the Austrian Alps, a renewed effort to learn the language. . . . Desperately eager to sacrifice her "flesh," which was "wasted," to her "mind and spirit," which were "fine" (*LH* 470), she wrote "Daddy" to demonstrate the existence of her voice, which had been silent or subservient for so long. She wrote it to prove her "genius" (*LH* 468).

Plath projected her struggle for textual identity onto the figure of a partly Jewish young woman who learns to express her anger at the patriarch and at his language of male mastery, which is as foreign to her as German, as "obscene" as murder (st. 6), and as meaningless as "gobbledygoo" (st. 9). The patriarch's death "off beautiful Nauset" (st. 3) recalls Plath's journal entry in which she associated the "green seaweeded water" at "Nauset Light" with "the deadness of a being . . . who no longer creates" (*J* 164). Daddy's deadness—suggesting Plath's unwillingness to let her father, her education, her library, or her husband inhibit her any longer—inspires the poem's speaker to her moment of illumination. At a basic level, "Daddy" concerns its own violent, transgressive birth as a text, its origin in a culture that regards it as illegitimate—a judgment the speaker hurls back on the patriarch himself when she labels *him* a bastard (st. 16). Plath's unaccommodating worldview . . . led her to understand literary tradition . . . as a closed universe in which every addition required a corresponding subtraction. If Plath's speaker was to be born as a poet, a patriarch must die.

As in "The Colossus," the father here appears as a force or an object rather than as a person. . . .

The poem emphasizes [Daddy's] feet and, implicitly, his phallus. He is a "black shoe" (st. 1), a statue with "one gray toe" (st. 2), a "boot" (st. 10). . . . Appropriately, Daddy can be killed only by being stamped on: he lives and dies by force, not language. If "The Colossus" tells a tale of the patriarch's speech, his grunts and brays, "Daddy" tells a tale of the daughter's effort to speak.

Thus we are led to another important difference between the two poems. The "I" of "The Colossus" acquires her identity only through serving her "father," whereas the "I" of "Daddy" actuates her gift only through opposition to him. . . . Otto Rank's *Beyond Psychology*,[7] which had a lasting influence on her, explicitly compares women to Jews, since "woman . . . has suffered from the very beginning a fate similar to that of the Jew, namely, suppression, slavery, confinement, and subsequent persecution" (287–88). Rank, whose discourse I would consider tainted by anti-Semitism, argues that Jews speak a language of pessimistic "self-hatred"

---

5. *LH* = *Letters Home.*   6. A. Alvarez, *The Savage God: A Study of Suicide* (1971; New York, Bantam, 1973).
7. Otto Rank, *Beyond Psychology* (Baltimore: Johns Hopkins University Press, 1990).

that differs essentially from the language of the majority cultures in which they find themselves (191, 281–84). He analogously, though more sympathetically, argues that woman speaks in a language different from man's, and that as a result of man's denial of woman's world, "woman's 'native tongue' has hitherto been unknown or at least unheard" (248). . . . Rank's . . . idea of linguistic difference based on gender and his analogy between Jewish and female speech seem to have embedded themselves in the substructure of "Daddy" (and in many of Plath's other texts as well). For Plath, as later for Adrienne Rich, the Holocaust and the patriarchy's silencing of women were linked outcomes of the masculinist interpretation of the world. Political insurrection and female self-assertion also interlaced symbolically. . . .

. . . The language of "Daddy," beginning with its title, is often regressive. The "I" articulates herself by moving backward in time, using the language of nursery rhymes and fairy tales (the little old woman who lived in a shoe, the black man of the forest). Such language accords with a child's conception of the world, not an adult's. Plath's assault on the language of "daddy-poetry" has turned inward, on the language of her own poem, which teeters precariously on the edge of a preverbal abyss—represented by the eerie, keening "oo" sound with which a majority of the verses end. And then let us consider the play on "through" at the poem's conclusion. Although that last line allows for multiple readings, one interpretation is that the "I" has unconsciously carried out her father's wish: her discourse, by transforming itself into cathartic oversimplifications, has undone itself.

Yet the poem does contain its verbal violence by means more productive than silence. In a letter to her brother, Plath referred to "Daddy" as "gruesome" (LH 472), while on almost the same day she described it to A. Alvarez as a piece of "light verse" (Alvarez, Beyond 56).[8] She later read it on the BBC in a highly ironic tone of voice. The poem's unique spell derives from its rhetorical complexity: its variegated and perhaps bizarre fusion of the horrendous and the comic. As Uroff has remarked, it both shares and remains detached from the fixation of its protagonist (159).[9] . . . Plath's speaker uses potentially self-mocking melodramatic terms to describe both her opponent ("so black no sky could squeak through" [st. 10]) and herself ("poor and white" [st. 1]). . . . The poem expresses feelings that it simultaneously parodies—it may be parodying the very idea of feeling. The tension between erudition and simplicity in the speaker's voice appears in her pairings that juxtapose adult with childlike diction: "breathe or Achoo," "your Luftewaffe, your gobbledygoo" (st. 1, 9). . . . She oscillates between calm reflection ("You stand at the blackboard, daddy, / In the picture I have of you" [st. 11]) and mad incoherence ("Ich, ich, ich, ich" [st. 6]). Her sophisticated language puts her wild language in an ironic perspective, removing the discourse from the control of the archaic self who understands experience only in extreme terms.

The ironies in "Daddy" proliferate in unexpected ways, however. When the speaker proclaims categorically that "every woman adores a Fascist" (st. 10), she is subjecting her victimization to irony by suggesting that sufferers choose, or at least accommodate themselves to, their suffering. But she is also subjecting her authority to irony, since her claim about "every woman" is transparently false. It

8. A. Alvarez, Beyond All This Fiddle (London: Allen Lane–Penguin, 1968).
9. Margaret Dickie Uroff, Sylvia Plath and Ted Hughes (Urbana: University of Illinois Press, 1979).

simply parodies patriarchal commonplaces, such as those advanced by Helene Deutsch concerning "feminine masochism" (192–99, 245–85).[1] . . .

Plath's irony cuts both ways. At the same time that the speaker's sophisticated voice undercuts her childish voice, reducing its melodrama to comedy, the childish or maddened voice undercuts the pretensions of the sophisticated voice, revealing the extremity of suffering masked by its ironies. While demonstrating the inadequacy of thinking and feeling in opposites, the poem implies that such a mode can locate truths denied more complex cognitive and affective systems. The very moderation of the normal adult intelligence, its tolerance of ambiguity, its defenses against the primal energies of the id, results in falsification. Reflecting Schiller's idea that the creative artist experiences a "momentary and passing madness" (quoted by Freud in a passage of *The Interpretation of Dreams* [193][2] that Plath underscored), "Daddy" gives voice to that madness. Yet the poem's sophisticated awareness, its comic vision, probably wins out in the end, since the poem concludes by curtailing the power of its extreme discourse. . . .

Plath's poetic revolt in "Daddy" liberated her pent-up creativity, but the momentary success sustained her little more than self-sacrifice had done. "Daddy" became another stage in her development, an unrepeatable experiment, a vocal opening that closed itself at once. The poem is not only an elegy for the power of "daddy-poetry" but for the powers of speech Plath discovered in composing it.

When we consider "Daddy" generically, a further range of implications presents itself. Although we could profitably consider the poem as the dramatic monologue Plath called it in her BBC broadcast, let us regard it instead as the kind of poem most readers have taken it to be: a domestic poem. I have chosen this term, rather than M. L. Rosenthal's better-known "confessional poem" or the more neutral "autobiographical poem." . . . I shall define the domestic poem as one that represents and comments on a protagonist's relationship to one or more family members, usually a parent, child, or spouse. To focus our discussion even further, I shall emphasize poetry that specifically concerns a father.

. . . In the 1950s the "domestic poem" proper appeared on the scene, with its own conventions and expectations, and with its own complex cultural and literary reasons for being. Perhaps the precursive poems made the genre's eventual flowering inevitable, while its precise timing depended on a reaction against modernism's aesthetic of impersonality. Theodore Roethke wrote several early poems that initiated the genre: "My Papa's Waltz" (1948), "The Lost Son" (1948), and "Where Knock Is Open Wide" (1951). Lowell's "Life Studies" sequence (1959) was, and is, the genre's most prominent landmark. Other poems in the genre include John Berryman's *The Dream Songs* (1969); Frank Bidart's "Golden State" (1973) and "Confessional" (1983); Robert Duncan's "My Mother Would Be a Falconress" (1968); Allen Ginsberg's *Kaddish* (1960); Randall Jarrell's "The Lost World" (1965); Maxine Kumin's "The Thirties Revisited" (1975), "My Father's Neckties" (1978), and "Marianne, My Mother, and Me" (1989); Stanley Kunitz's "Father and Son" (1958) and "The Testing Tree" (1971); Lowell's "To Mother" (1977), "Robert T. S. Lowell" (1977), and "Unwanted" (1977); James Merrill's "Scenes of Childhood"

1. Helen Deutsch, *The Psychology of Women*, I: *Girlhood* (1944; repr. New York: Bantam, 1973).
2. Sigmund Freud, *The Interpretation of Dreams,* ed. James Strachey, Standard Edition, IV (1900; New York: Norton, 1976).

(1962); Adrienne Rich's "After Dark" (1966); Anne Sexton's "Division of the Parts" (1960) and "The Death of the Fathers" (1972); W. D. Snodgrass' "Heart's Needle" (1959); Diane Wakoski's "The Father of My Country" (1968); and of course Sylvia Plath's "Daddy" (1962). In all these poems, the parent-child relationship serves as a locus for psychological investigation. In many of them it also serves as a means of representing the acquisition of poetic identity and of exploring the bounds of textuality itself. Because later writers were conscious of the Roethke-Lowell domestic poem as at least a genre in embryo, they chose to use its features, or perhaps the power of the genre was such that the features chose them. The "domestic poem" became a system of signs in which each individual text's adherence to the system and deviations within the system produced its particular literary meaning.

In 1959 Plath did not consciously attempt to write in the domestic poem genre. . . . But by fall 1962, when she had already lost so much, she was ready to chance tackling poetic tradition, and specifically her chief male instructors, Roethke and Lowell. In "Daddy" she achieved her victory. . . . The father whose power she attacks is not simply Roethke or Lowell, or even Hughes or Otto Plath, but a literary character who includes reference to all of them as categories of masculine authority. Although the Daddy of poetry has already "died" (st. 2)—the fate of all published texts in Plath's postromantic perspective—the speaker must symbolically "kill" him from her own discourse. The poem ironically depicts poetry as both an aggression and a suicide. . . .

. . . Taking a genre established by Roethke and Lowell, "Daddy" fundamentally alters it through antithesis and parody. Like all strong poems, it transforms its genre and therefore the way we perceive the precursive examples, making them seem not fulfillments but anticipations. Thus the later work projects its anxiety retrospectively back through its predecessors. . . .

This point comes clearer if we compare "Daddy" with two analogues, Roethke's "The Lost Son" (1948) and Lowell's "Commander Lowell" (1959). In the Freudian drama of "The Lost Son," the protagonist subjectively relives his childhood fears and fantasies. Like the speaker of the companion piece, "My Papa's Waltz," he is still enmeshed in the family romance, remembering the father ambivalently as powerful, protective, and threatening. After locating himself at his father's grave, where he feels both grief and estrangement (in a scene that adumbrates "Electra on Azalea Path"), he descends into his unconscious, seeking, as Roethke later explained, "some clue to existence" (*Poet* 38).[3] He encounters his death wish, his memory of his father as "Father Fear," his sexual anxieties, and finally the "dark swirl" of a blackout, after which a childhood memory of his "Papa" shouting "order" in German returns him to consciousness. Although the figure of "Papa" blends earthly and heavenly father (*Poet* 39), he also symbolizes the superego, restoring order to a psyche and a poem that had fallen into chaos. At the poem's conclusion, as the "lost son" waits for his "understandable spirit" to revive, he appears to be purged, though not cured, of the conflicts that incapacitated him.

The speaker of "Commander Lowell," in contrast, is objective, precise, and witty. His discourse reflects a detached perspective on the past rather than a

3. *On the Poet and His Craft: Selected Prose of Theodore Roethke,* ed. Ralph J. Mills, Jr. (Seattle and London: University of Washington Press, 1965).

psychic reimmersion in it. He portrays his father as one who threatened him only through weakness. This father "was nothing to shout / about to the summer colony at 'Matt'"; took "four shots with his putter to sink his putt"; sang "Anchors Aweigh" in the bathtub; was fired from his job; and squandered his inheritance. Whereas Roethke's poem represents a cathartic experience, Lowell's converts chaotic feelings into intellectual irony. Whereas Roethke's poem can be read as an allegory of man's relationship to God or as a model of the Freudian psyche, Lowell's remains a realistic narrative, though it does suggest the cultural and financial decline of a social class.

Plath's poem combines features of both of these precursors: Roethke's evocation of a German-speaking authoritarian with Lowell's sarcastic deflation of a man without qualities; Roethke's subjective anguish with Lowell's social comedy. Like Roethke's Papa, Plath's title character is an intimidating patriarch; like Lowell's Father, he is a buffoon ("big as a Frisco seal"). Finally, Plath's poem, like those of her predecessors, has little to do with psychological cure: the speaker's defenses remain in place. But in a deeper sense, "Daddy" swerves sharply from its precursors, curtailing their power. It turns the psychological depth of Roethke's poem and the ironically detached surface of Lowell's poem into a fury of denunciation, an extravagance of emotion, an exaggeration of acts and effects, perhaps revealing the subtexts of both precursors. If in a sense the texts by Roethke and Lowell constitute what Ned Lukacher[4] might term the primal scene of "Daddy," the latter poem's raw intensity succeeds in reversing the relationship, making itself resemble *their* primal scene. It unmasks Roethke's implicitly oppressive father figure as a monster and Lowell's sophisticated comedy as slapstick. It transforms the domestic genre alternately into a horror show, encapsulating every political, cultural, and familial atrocity of the age, and a theater of cruelty, evoking nervous laughter. "Daddy" takes the genre as far as it can go—and then further.

SUGGESTIONS FOR WRITING

1. In his essay "Dying Is an Art," George Steiner argues that Plath's poems "are too honest, they have cost too much, to be yielded to myth." Do you think that "Daddy" is an "honest" poem? Write an essay exploring what "honesty" means in modern poetry and whether or not "Daddy" is an "honest" poem. Draw on the critical essays found in this chapter, and be sure to cite them as appropriate.

2. Several of the critics in this chapter make competing claims about the meaning and significance of the form of "Daddy," particularly its nursery-rhyme-like qualities. Using those claims as a springboard, write an essay in which you make your own argument about the relationship between form and content in "Daddy."

3. In "The Plath Celebration: A Partial Dissent," Irving Howe argues, "There is something monstrous, utterly disproportionate, when tangled emotions about one's father are deliberately compared with the historical fate of the European Jews." Is Plath's personal, artistic use of a great historical tragedy truly "monstrous," as Howe says, or is it simply a case of what George Steiner calls "subtle larceny"? Write an essay in which you discuss whether or not it is appropriate for an artist to use the sufferings of others as material for personal artistic expression.

4. Ned Lukacher, *Primal Scenes: Literature, Philosophy, Psychoanalysis* (Ithaca and London: Cornell University Press, 1986).

4. Broe, Kroll, Homans, Annas, and Axelrod all claim that "Daddy" portrays the speaker's attempt to successfully "exorcise" one demon or another, though they disagree rather dramatically both about what that demon is and about whether and how that exorcism (not the poem) succeeds. Using their arguments as a starting point, write an essay in which you offer your own interpretation of the process of exorcism enacted in the poem.

5. In "Sylvia Plath," A. Alvarez quotes Plath's own interpretation of "Daddy" as a poem "spoken by a girl with an Electra complex." (Other articles mention this statement.) Research the term "Electra complex," which originated with Sigmund Freud. Is it useful to interpret "Daddy" through the lens of the Electra complex? Citing critics included in this chapter, write an essay in which you discuss Plath's Freudian explanation of "Daddy" and, more generally, the reliability of artists' interpretations of their own works.

6. Write an essay comparing Plath's "Daddy" to at least two of the "domestic poems" mentioned by Axelrod in "Jealous Gods." To what extent do you agree and disagree with Axelrod's interpretation of the similarities and differences between "Daddy" and these other poems by Plath's contemporaries?

7. Is "Daddy" a "feminist" poem? Does examination of the poem from a feminist viewpoint, like that of Margaret Homans, help illuminate the poem, or does it obscure understanding? Citing the essays by Homans and other critics in this chapter, write an essay in which you discuss a feminist reading of "Daddy" and then argue for or against its validity.

Reading More Poetry

W. H. AUDEN

Musée des Beaux Arts[1]

About suffering they were never wrong,
The Old Masters: how well they understood
Its human position; how it takes place
While someone else is eating or opening a window or just walking
     dully along;
5 How, when the aged are reverently, passionately waiting
For the miraculous birth, there always must be
Children who did not specially want it to happen, skating
On a pond at the edge of the wood:
They never forgot
10 That even the dreadful martyrdom must run its course
Anyhow in a corner, some untidy spot
Where the dogs go on with their doggy life and the torturer's horse
Scratches its innocent behind on a tree.

In Brueghel's *Icarus*,[2] for instance: how everything turns away
15 Quite leisurely from the disaster; the plowman may
Have heard the splash, the forsaken cry,
But for him it was not an important failure; the sun shone
As it had to on the white legs disappearing into the green
Water; and the expensive delicate ship that must have seen
20 Something amazing, a boy falling out of the sky,
Had somewhere to get to and sailed calmly on.

1938

1. The Museum of the Fine Arts, in Brussels.
2. *Landscape with the Fall of Icarus*, by Pieter Bruegel the Elder (1525?–1569), located in the Brussels museum. According to Greek myth, Daedalus and his son, Icarus, escaped from imprisonment by using home-made wings of feathers and wax; but Icarus flew too near the sun, the wax melted, and he fell into the sea and drowned. In the Bruegel painting the central figure is a peasant plowing, and several other figures are more immediately noticeable than Icarus, who, disappearing into the sea, is easy to miss in the lower right-hand corner.

GWENDOLYN BROOKS

To the Diaspora

you did not know you were Afrika

When you set out for Afrika
you did not know you were going.
Because
you did not know you were Afrika.
5   You did not know the Black continent
that had to be reached
was you.

I could not have told you then that some sun
would come,
10   somewhere over the road,
would come evoking the diamonds
of you, the Black continent—
somewhere over the road.
You would not have believed my mouth.

15   When I told you, meeting you somewhere close
to the heat and youth of the road,
liking my loyalty, liking belief,
you smiled and you thanked me but very little believed me.

Here is some sun. Some.
20   Now off into the places rough to reach.
Though dry, though drowsy, all unwillingly a-wobble,
into the dissonant and dangerous crescendo.
Your work, that was done, to be done to be done to be done.

1981

ROBERT BROWNING

My Last Duchess

Ferrara[3]

That's my last Duchess painted on the wall,
Looking as if she were alive. I call
That piece a wonder, now: Frà Pandolf's hands[4]

---

3. Alfonso II, duke of Ferrara in Italy in the mid-sixteenth century, is the presumed speaker of the poem, which is loosely based on historical events. The duke's first wife—whom he had married when she was fourteen—died under suspicious circumstances at seventeen, and he then negotiated through an agent (to whom the poem is spoken) for the hand of the niece of the count of Tyrol in Austria.
4. Frà Pandolf is, like Claus (line 56), fictitious.

Worked busily a day, and there she stands.
5 Will't please you sit and look at her? I said
"Frà Pandolf" by design, for never read
Strangers like you that pictured countenance,
The depth and passion of its earnest glance,
But to myself they turned (since none puts by
10 The curtain I have drawn for you, but I)
And seemed as they would ask me, if they durst,
How such a glance came there; so, not the first
Are you to turn and ask thus. Sir, 'twas not
Her husband's presence only, called that spot
15 Of joy into the Duchess' cheek: perhaps
Frà Pandolf chanced to say "Her mantle laps
Over my lady's wrist too much," or "Paint
Must never hope to reproduce the faint
Half-flush that dies along her throat": such stuff
20 Was courtesy, she thought, and cause enough
For calling up that spot of joy. She had
A heart—how shall I say?—too soon made glad,
Too easily impressed; she liked whate'er
She looked on, and her looks went everywhere.
25 Sir, 'twas all one! My favor at her breast,
The dropping of the daylight in the West,
The bough of cherries some officious fool
Broke in the orchard for her, the white mule
She rode with round the terrace—all and each
30 Would draw from her alike the approving speech,
Or blush, at least. She thanked men,—good! but thanked
Somehow—I know not how—as if she ranked
My gift of a nine-hundred-years-old name
With anybody's gift. Who'd stoop to blame
35 This sort of trifling? Even had you skill
In speech—which I have not—to make your will
Quite clear to such an one, and say, "Just this
Or that in you disgusts me; here you miss,
Or there exceed the mark"—and if she let
40 Herself be lessoned so, nor plainly set
Her wits to yours, forsooth, and made excuse,
—E'en then would be some stooping; and I choose
Never to stoop. Oh sir, she smiled, no doubt,
Whene'er I passed her; but who passed without
45 Much the same smile? This grew; I gave commands;
Then all smiles stopped together. There she stands
As if alive. Will't please you rise? We'll meet
The company below, then. I repeat,
The Count your master's known munificence
50 Is ample warrant that no just pretense
Of mine for dowry will be disallowed;
Though his fair daughter's self, as I avowed

At starting, is my object. Nay, we'll go
Together down, sir. Notice Neptune, though,
55   Taming a sea-horse, thought a rarity,
Which Claus of Innsbruck cast in bronze for me!

1842

SAMUEL TAYLOR COLERIDGE

Kubla Khan

Or, a Vision in a Dream[5]

In Xanadu did Kubla Khan
A stately pleasure-dome decree:
Where Alph, the sacred river, ran
Through caverns measureless to man
5   Down to a sunless sea.
So twice five miles of fertile ground
With walls and towers were girdled round:
And here were gardens bright with sinuous rills
Where blossomed many an incense-bearing tree;
10   And here were forests ancient as the hills,
Enfolding sunny spots of greenery.

But oh! that deep romantic chasm which slanted
Down the green hill athwart a cedarn cover![6]
A savage place! as holy and enchanted
15   As e'er beneath a waning moon was haunted
By woman wailing for her demon-lover![7]
And from this chasm, with ceaseless turmoil seething,
As if this earth in fast thick pants were breathing,
A mighty fountain momently[8] was forced,
20   Amid whose swift half-intermitted burst
Huge fragments vaulted like rebounding hail,
Or chaffy grain beneath the thresher's flail:
And 'mid these dancing rocks at once and ever
It flung up momently the sacred river.
25   Five miles meandering with a mazy motion
Through wood and dale the sacred river ran,
Then reached the caverns measureless to man,
And sank in tumult to a lifeless ocean:
And 'mid this tumult Kubla heard from far
30   Ancestral voices prophesying war!

5. Coleridge said that he wrote this fragment immediately after waking from an opium dream and that after he was interrupted by a caller he was unable to finish the poem.
6. That is, from side to side beneath a cover of cedar trees.
7. In a famous and often-imitated German ballad, the lady Lenore is carried off on horseback by the specter of her lover and married to him at his grave.   8. Suddenly.

The shadow of the dome of pleasure
Floated midway on the waves;
Where was heard the mingled measure
From the fountain and the caves.
35 It was a miracle of rare device,
A sunny pleasure-dome with caves of ice!

A damsel with a dulcimer
In a vision once I saw:
It was an Abyssinian maid,
40 And on her dulcimer she played,
Singing of Mount Abora.
Could I revive within me
Her symphony and song,
To such a deep delight 'twould win me,
45 That with music loud and long,
I would build that dome in air,
That sunny dome! those caves of ice!
And all who heard should see them there,
And all should cry, Beware! Beware!
50 His flashing eyes, his floating hair!
Weave a circle round him thrice,
And close your eyes with holy dread,
For he on honey-dew hath fed,
And drunk the milk of Paradise.

1798

JOHN DONNE

[*Death, be not proud*]

Death be not proud, though some have callèd thee
Mighty and dreadful, for thou art not so;
For those whom thou think'st thou dost overthrow
Die not, poor Death, nor yet canst thou kill me.
5 From rest and sleep, which but thy pictures[9] be,
Much pleasure; then from thee much more must flow,
And soonest[1] our best men with thee do go,
Rest of their bones, and soul's delivery.[2]
Thou art slave to Fate, Chance, kings, and desperate men,
10 And dost with Poison, War, and Sickness dwell;
And poppy or charms can make us sleep as well,
And better than thy stroke; why swell'st[3] thou then?
One short sleep past, we wake eternally
And death shall be no more; Death, thou shalt die.

1633

---

9. Likenesses.   1. Most willingly.   2. Deliverance.   3. Puff with pride.

Song

Go, and catch a falling star,
  Get with child a mandrake root,[4]
Tell me, where all past years are,
  Or who cleft the devil's foot,
5 Teach me to hear mermaids singing
  Or to keep off envy's stinging,
      And find
      What wind
Serves to advance an honest mind.

10 If thou beest born to strange sights,[5]
  Things invisible to see,
Ride ten thousand days and nights,
  Till age snow white hairs on thee;
Thou, when thou return'st, wilt tell me
15 All strange wonders that befell thee,
      And swear
      No where
Lives a woman true, and fair.

If thou find'st one, let me know:
20   Such a pilgrimage were sweet.
Yet do not, I would not go,
    Though at next door we might meet:
Though she were true when you met her,
And last till you write your letter,
25   Yet she
      Will be
False, ere I come, to two, or three.

1633

A Valediction: Forbidding Mourning

As virtuous men pass mildly away,
  And whisper to their souls to go,
Whilst some of their sad friends do say,
  "The breath goes now," and some say, "No,"

5 So let us melt, and make no noise,
  No tear-floods, nor sigh-tempests move;
'Twere profanation of our joys
  To tell the laity our love.

4. The forked mandrake root looks vaguely like a pair of human legs.
5. That is, if you have supernatural powers.

Moving of the earth[6] brings harms and fears,
10   Men reckon what it did and meant;
But trepidation of the spheres,[7]
    Though greater far, is innocent.

Dull sublunary[8] lovers' love
    (Whose soul is sense) cannot admit
15 Absence, because it doth remove
    Those things which elemented[9] it.

But we, by a love so much refined
    That our selves know not what it is,
Inter-assured of the mind,
20   Care less, eyes, lips, and hands to miss.

Our two souls therefore, which are one,
    Though I must go, endure not yet
A breach, but an expansion,
    Like gold to airy thinness beat.

25 If they be two, they are two so
    As stiff twin compasses are two:
Thy soul, the fixed foot, makes no show
    To move, but doth, if the other do;

And though it in the center sit,
30   Yet when the other far doth roam,
It leans, and hearkens after it,
    And grows erect, as that comes home.

Such wilt thou be to me, who must,
    Like the other foot, obliquely run;
35 Thy firmness makes my circle[1] just,
    And makes me end where I begun.

1611?

PAUL LAURENCE DUNBAR

Sympathy

I know what the caged bird feels, alas!
    When the sun is bright on the upland slopes;
When the wind stirs soft through the springing grass,
    And the river flows like a stream of glass;

6. Earthquakes.
7. Renaissance theory that the celestial spheres trembled and thus caused unexpected variations in their orbits. Such movements are "innocent" because earthlings do not observe or fret about them.
8. Below the moon—that is, changeable. According to the traditional cosmology that Donne invokes here, the moon is the dividing line between the immutable celestial world and the mutable earthly one.
9. Comprised.   1. Traditional symbol of perfection.

5   When the first bird sings and the first bud opens,
       And the faint perfume from its chalice steals—
       I know what the caged bird feels!

       I know why the caged bird beats his wing
           Till its blood is red on the cruel bars;
10   For he must fly back to his perch and cling
       When he fain[2] would be on the bough a-swing;
           And a pain still throbs in the old, old scars
       And they pulse again with a keener sting—
       I know why he beats his wing!

15   I know why the caged bird sings, ah me,
           When his wing is bruised and his bosom sore,—
       When he beats his bars and he would be free;
       It is not a carol of joy or glee,
           But a prayer that he sends from his heart's deep core,
20   But a plea, that upward to Heaven he flings—
       I know why the caged bird sings!

                                                        1893

We Wear the Mask

       We wear the mask that grins and lies,
       It hides our cheeks and shades our eyes,—
       This debt we pay to human guile;
       With torn and bleeding hearts we smile,
5   And mouth with myriad subtleties.

       Why should the world be over-wise,
       In counting all our tears and sighs?
       Nay, let them only see us, while
           We wear the mask.

10   We smile, but, O great Christ, our cries
       To thee from tortured souls arise.
       We sing, but oh the clay is vile
       Beneath our feet, and long the mile;
       But let the world dream otherwise,
15   We wear the mask!

                                                        1895

2. Gladly.

ROBERT FROST

The Road Not Taken

Two roads diverged in a yellow wood,
And sorry I could not travel both
And be one traveler, long I stood
And looked down one as far as I could
5 To where it bent in the undergrowth;

Then took the other, as just as fair,
And having perhaps the better claim,
Because it was grassy and wanted wear;
Though as for that the passing there
10 Had worn them really about the same,

And both that morning equally lay
In leaves no step had trodden black.
Oh, I kept the first for another day!
Yet knowing how way leads on to way,
15 I doubted if I should ever come back.

I shall be telling this with a sigh
Somewhere ages and ages hence:
Two roads diverged in a wood, and I—
I took the one less traveled by,
20 And that has made all the difference.

1916

Stopping by Woods on a Snowy Evening

Whose woods these are I think I know.
His house is in the village, though;
He will not see me stopping here
To watch his woods fill up with snow.

5 My little horse must think it queer
To stop without a farmhouse near
Between the woods and frozen lake
The darkest evening of the year.

He gives his harness bells a shake
10 To ask if there is some mistake.
The only other sound's the sweep
Of easy wind and downy flake.

The woods are lovely, dark, and deep,
But I have promises to keep,
15 And miles to go before I sleep,
And miles to go before I sleep.

1923

Home Burial

He saw her from the bottom of the stairs
Before she saw him. She was starting down,
Looking back over her shoulder at some fear.
She took a doubtful step and then undid it
5   To raise herself and look again. He spoke
Advancing toward her: "What is it you see
From up there always?—for I want to know."
She turned and sank upon her skirts at that,
And her face changed from terrified to dull.
10   He said to gain time: "What is it you see?"
Mounting until she cowered under him.
"I will find out now—you must tell me, dear."
She, in her place, refused him any help,
With the least stiffening of her neck and silence.
15   She let him look, sure that he wouldn't see,
Blind creature; and awhile he didn't see.
But at last he murmured, "Oh," and again, "Oh."

"What is it—what?" she said.

                              "Just that I see."

"You don't," she challenged. "Tell me what it is."

20   "The wonder is I didn't see at once.
I never noticed it from here before.
I must be wonted to it—that's the reason.
The little graveyard where my people are!
So small the window frames the whole of it.
25   Not so much larger than a bedroom, is it?
There are three stones of slate and one of marble,
Broad-shouldered little slabs there in the sunlight
On the sidehill. We haven't to mind *those*.
But I understand: it is not the stones,
But the child's mound——"

                              "Don't, don't, don't,
30   don't," she cried.

She withdrew, shrinking from beneath his arm
That rested on the banister, and slid downstairs;
And turned on him with such a daunting look,
He said twice over before he knew himself:
35   "Can't a man speak of his own child he's lost?"

"Not you!—Oh, where's my hat? Oh, I don't need it!
I must get out of here. I must get air.—
I don't know rightly whether any man can."

"Amy! Don't go to someone else this time.
40   Listen to me. I won't come down the stairs."

He sat and fixed his chin between his fists.
"There's something I should like to ask you, dear."

"You don't know how to ask it."

                                 "Help me, then."

45 Her fingers moved the latch for all reply.

"My words are nearly always an offense.
I don't know how to speak of anything
So as to please you. But I might be taught,
I should suppose. I can't say I see how.
50 A man must partly give up being a man
With womenfolk. We could have some arrangement
By which I'd bind myself to keep hands off
Anything special you're a-mind to name.
Though I don't like such things 'twixt those that love.
55 Two that don't love can't live together without them.
But two that do can't live together with them."
She moved the latch a little. "Don't—don't go.
Don't carry it to someone else this time.
Tell me about it if it's something human.
Let me into your grief. I'm not so much
60 Unlike other folks as your standing there
Apart would make me out. Give me my chance.
I do think, though, you overdo it a little.
What was it brought you up to think it the thing
To take your mother-loss of a first child
65 So inconsolably—in the face of love.
You'd think his memory might be satisfied——"

"There you go sneering now!"

                              "I'm not, I'm not!
You make me angry. I'll come down to you.
God, what a woman! And it's come to this,
70 A man can't speak of his own child that's dead."

"You can't because you don't know how to speak.
If you had any feelings, you that dug
With your own hand—how could you?—his little grave;
I saw you from that very window there,
75 Making the gravel leap and leap in air,
Leap up, like that, like that, and land so lightly
And roll back down the mound beside the hole.
I thought, Who is that man? I didn't know you.
And I crept down the stairs and up the stairs
80 To look again, and still your spade kept lifting.
Then you came in. I heard your rumbling voice
Out in the kitchen, and I don't know why,
But I went near to see with my own eyes.
You could sit there with the stains on your shoes
85 Of the fresh earth from your own baby's grave

And talk about your everyday concerns.
You had stood the spade up against the wall
Outside there in the entry, for I saw it."

"I shall laugh the worst laugh I ever laughed.
90   I'm cursed. God, if I don't believe I'm cursed."

"I can repeat the very words you were saying:
'Three foggy mornings and one rainy day
Will rot the best birch fence a man can build.'
Think of it, talk like that at such a time!
95   What had how long it takes a birch to rot
To do with what was in the darkened parlor?
You *couldn't* care! The nearest friends can go
With anyone to death, comes so far short
They might as well not try to go at all.
100   No, from the time when one is sick to death,
One is alone, and he dies more alone.
Friends make pretense of following to the grave,
But before one is in it, their minds are turned
And making the best of their way back to life
105   And living people, and things they understand.
But the world's evil. I won't have grief so
If I can change it. Oh, I won't, I won't!"

"There, you have said it all and you feel better.
You won't go now. You're crying. Close the door.
110   The heart's gone out of it: why keep it up?
Amy! There's someone coming down the road!"

"*You*——oh, you think the talk is all. I must go—
Somewhere out of this house. How can I make you——"

"If—you—do!" She was opening the door wider.
115   "Where do you mean to go? First tell me that.
I'll follow and bring you back by force. I *will*!—"

1915

ALLEN GINSBERG

Velocity of Money

For Lee Berton

I'm delighted by the velocity of money as it whistles through windows
    of Lower East Side
Delighted skyscrapers rise grungy apartments fall on 84th Street's
    pavement
Delighted this year inflation drives me out on the street
with double digit interest rates in Capitalist worlds

5 I always was a communist, now we'll win
  as usury makes walls thinner, books thicker & dumber
  Usury makes my poetry more valuable
  Manuscripts worth their weight in useless gold—
  The velocity's what counts as the National Debt gets trillions higher
10 Everybody running after the rising dollar
  Crowds of joggers down Broadway past City Hall on the way to the
      Fed[3]
  Nobody reads Dostoyevsky books anymore so they'll have to give pass-
      ing ear
  to my fragmented ravings in between President's speeches
  Nothing's happening but the collapse of the Economy
15 so I can go back to sleep till the landlord wins his eviction suit in court

February 18, 1986, 10:00 A.M.

THOMAS GRAY

Elegy Written in a Country Churchyard

The curfew tolls the knell of parting day,
  The lowing herd wind slowly o'er the lea,
The plowman homeward plods his weary way,
  And leaves the world to darkness and to me.

5 Now fades the glimmering landscape on the sight,
  And all the air a solemn stillness holds,
Save where the beetle wheels his droning flight,
  And drowsy tinklings lull the distant folds;

Save that from yonder ivy-mantled tower
10   The moping owl does to the moon complain
Of such, as wandering near her secret bower,
  Molest her ancient solitary reign.

Beneath those rugged elms, that yew tree's shade,
  Where heaves the turf in many a moldering heap,
15 Each in his narrow cell forever laid,
  The rude[4] forefathers of the hamlet sleep.

The breezy call of incense-breathing Morn,
  The swallow twittering from the straw-built shed,
The cock's shrill clarion, or the echoing horn,[5]
20   No more shall rouse them from their lowly bed.

For them no more the blazing hearth shall burn,
  Or busy housewife ply her evening care;

---

3. The Federal Reserve Bank of New York, part of the Federal Reserve System, which controls the money supply in the United States.   4. Unlearned.   5. Hunter's horn.

No children run to lisp their sire's return,
   Or climb his knees the envied kiss to share.

25 Oft did the harvest to their sickle yield,
   Their furrow oft the stubborn glebe[6] has broke;
How jocund did they drive their team afield!
   How bowed the woods beneath their sturdy stroke!

Let not Ambition mock their useful toil,
30   Their homely joys, and destiny obscure;
Nor Grandeur hear with a disdainful smile
   The short and simple annals of the poor.

The boast of heraldry,[7] the pomp of power,
   And all that beauty, all that wealth e'er gave,
35 Awaits alike the inevitable hour.
   The paths of glory lead but to the grave.

Nor you, ye proud, impute to these the fault,
   If Memory o'er their tomb no trophies[8] raise,
Where through the long-drawn aisle and fretted[9] vault
40   The pealing anthem swells the note of praise

Can storied urn or animated[1] bust
   Back to its mansion call the fleeting breath?
Can Honor's voice provoke the silent dust,
   Or Flattery soothe the dull cold ear of Death?

45 Perhaps in this neglected spot is laid
   Some heart once pregnant with celestial fire;
Hands that the rod of empire might have swayed,
   Or waked to ecstasy the living lyre.

But Knowledge to their eyes her ample page
50   Rich with the spoils of time did ne'er unroll;
Chill Penury repressed their noble rage,
   And froze the genial current of the soul.

Full many a gem of purest ray serene,
   The dark unfathomed caves of ocean bear:
55 Full many a flower is born to blush unseen,
   And waste its sweetness on the desert air.

Some village Hampden,[2] that with dauntless breast
   The little tyrant of his fields withstood;

6. Soil.   7. That is, noble birth.
8. Ornamental or symbolic groups of figures depicting the achievements of the deceased.
9. Decorated with intersecting lines in relief.
1. Lifelike. *Storied urn*: a funeral urn with an epitaph or pictured story inscribed on it.
2. John Hampden (1594–1643), both as a private citizen and as a member of Parliament, zealously defended the rights of the people against the autocratic policies of King Charles I.

Some mute inglorious Milton[3] here may rest,
60   Some Cromwell[4] guiltless of his country's blood.

The applause of listening senates to command,
    The threats of pain and ruin to despise,
To scatter plenty o'er a smiling land,
    And read their history in a nation's eyes,

65 Their lot forbade: nor circumscribed alone
    Their growing virtues, but their crimes confined;
Forbade to wade through slaughter to a throne,
    And shut the gates of mercy on mankind,

The struggling pangs of conscious truth to hide,
70   To quench the blushes of ingenuous shame,
Or heap the shrine of Luxury and Pride
    With incense kindled at the Muse's flame.

Far from the madding crowd's ignoble strife,
    Their sober wishes never learned to stray;
75 Along the cool sequestered vale of life
    They kept the noiseless tenor of their way.

Yet even these bones from insult to protect
    Some frail memorial still erected nigh,
With uncouth rhymes and shapeless sculpture decked,[5]
80   Implores the passing tribute of a sigh.

Their name, their years, spelt by the unlettered Muse,
    The place of fame and elegy supply:
And many a holy text around she strews,
    That teach the rustic moralist to die.

85 For who to dumb Forgetfulness a prey,
    This pleasing anxious being e'er resigned,
Left the warm precincts of the cheerful day,
    Nor cast one longing lingering look behind?

On some fond breast the parting soul relies,
90   Some pious drops the closing eye requires;
Even from the tomb the voice of Nature cries,
    Even in our ashes live their wonted fires.

For thee, who mindful of the unhonored dead
    Dost in these lines their artless tale relate;
95 If chance, by lonely contemplation led,
    Some kindred spirit shall inquire thy fate,

3. John Milton (1608–74), great English poet.
4. Oliver Cromwell (1599–1658), Lord Protector of England during the Commonwealth, or Interregnum, noted for military genius but also cruelty and intolerance.
5. Cf. the "storied urn or animated bust" (line 41) dedicated inside the church to the "proud" (line 37).

Haply[6] some hoary-headed swain may say,
    "Oft have we seen him at the peep of dawn
Brushing with hasty steps the dews away
100   To meet the sun upon the upland lawn.

"There at the foot of yonder nodding beech
    That wreathes its old fantastic roots so high,
His listless length at noontide would he stretch,
    And pore upon the brook that babbles by.

105 "Hard by yon wood, now smiling as in scorn,
    Muttering his wayward fancies he would rove,
Now drooping, woeful wan, like one forlorn,
    Or crazed with care, or crossed in hopeless love.

"One morn I missed him on the customed hill,
110   Along the heath and near his favorite tree;
Another came; nor[7] yet beside the rill,
    Nor up the lawn, nor at the wood was he;

"The next with dirges due in sad array
    Slow through the churchway path we saw him borne.
115 Approach and read (for thou canst read) the lay,
    Graved on the stone beneath yon aged thorn."

The Epitaph

Here rests his head upon the lap of Earth
    A youth to Fortune and to Fame unknown.
Fair Science[8] frowned not on his humble birth,
120   *And Melancholy marked him for her own.*

Large was his bounty, and his soul sincere,
    Heaven did a recompense as largely send:
He gave to Misery all he had, a tear,
    He gained from Heaven ('twas all he wished) a friend.

125 *No farther seek his merits to disclose,*
    Or draw his frailties from their dread abode
(There they alike in trembling hope repose),
    The bosom of his Father and his God.

1751

---

6. Perhaps.   7. Neither.   8. Learning.

ROBERT HAYDEN

The Whipping

The old woman across the way
    is whipping the boy again
and shouting to the neighborhood
    her goodness and his wrongs.

5 Wildly he crashes through elephant ears,
    pleads in dusty zinnias,
while she in spite of crippling fat
    pursues and corners him.

She strikes and strikes the shrilly circling
10 boy till the stick breaks
in her hand. His tears are rainy weather
    to woundlike memories:

My head gripped in bony vise
    of knees, the writhing struggle
15 to wrench free, the blows, the fear
    worse than blows that hateful

Words could bring, the face that I
    no longer knew or loved. . . .
Well, it is over now, it is over,
20 and the boy sobs in his room,

And the woman leans muttering against
    a tree, exhausted, purged—
avenged in part for lifelong hidings
    she has had to bear.

                          1962, 1966

Frederick Douglass

When it is finally ours, this freedom,[9] this liberty, this beautiful
and terrible thing, needful to man as air,
usable as earth; when it belongs at last to all,
when it is truly instinct, brain matter, diastole, systole,
5 reflex action; when it is finally won; when it is more
than the gaudy mumbo jumbo of politicians:
this man, this Douglass, this former slave, this Negro
beaten to his knees, exiled, visioning a world
where none is lonely, none hunted, alien,

---

9. Frederick Douglass (1817–95), an escaped slave, was involved in the Underground Railroad and became publisher of the famous abolitionist newspaper the *North Star*, in Rochester, New York.

10 this man, superb in love and logic, this man
shall be remembered. Oh, not with statues' rhetoric,
not with legends and poems and wreaths of bronze alone,
but with the lives grown out of his life, the lives
fleshing his dream of the beautiful, needful thing.

1966

SEAMUS HEANEY

Digging

Between my finger and my thumb
The squat pen rests; snug as a gun.

Under my window, a clean rasping sound
When the spade sinks into gravelly ground:
5 My father, digging. I look down

Till his straining rump among the flowerbeds
Bends low, comes up twenty years away
Stooping in rhythm through potato drills[1]
Where he was digging.

10 The coarse boot nestled on the lug, the shaft
Against the inside knee was levered firmly.
He rooted out tall tops, buried the bright edge deep
To scatter new potatoes that we picked
Loving their cool hardness in our hands.

15 By God, the old man could handle a spade.
Just like his old man.

My grandfather cut more turf[2] in a day
Than any other man on Toner's bog.
Once I carried him milk in a bottle
20 Corked sloppily with paper. He straightened up
To drink it, then fell to right away.
Nicking and slicing neatly, heaving sods
Over his shoulder, going down and down
For the good turf. Digging.

25 The cold smell of potato mould, the squelch and slap
Of soggy peat, the curt cuts of an edge
Through living roots awaken in my head.
But I've no spade to follow men like them.

---

1. Small furrows in which seeds are sown.
2. Peat cut into slabs and dried to be used as fuel in stoves and furnaces.

Between my finger and my thumb
30 The squat pen rests.
I'll dig with it.

1966

Punishment[3]

I can feel the tug
of the halter at the nape
of her neck, the wind
on her naked front.

5 It blows her nipples
to amber beads,
it shakes the frail rigging
of her ribs.

I can see her drowned
10 body in the bog,
the weighing stone,
the floating rods and boughs.

Under which at first
she was a barked sapling
15 that is dug up
oak-bone, brain-firkin:

her shaved head
like a stubble of black corn,
her blindfold a soiled bandage,
20 her noose a ring

to store
the memories of love.
Little adulteress,
before they punished you

25 you were flaxen-haired,
undernourished, and your
tar-black face was beautiful.
My poor scapegoat,

I almost love you
30 but would have cast, I know,

---

3. According to the Roman historian Tacitus (ca. 56–ca. 120 C.E.), Germanic peoples punished adulterous women by first shaving their heads and then banishing or killing them. In 1951, in Windeby, Germany, the naked body of a young girl from the first century C.E. was pulled from the bog where she had been murdered. In contemporary Ireland, "betraying sisters" (38) have sometimes been punished by the Irish Republican Army (IRA) for associating with British soldiers.

the stones of silence.
I am the artful voyeur

of your brain's exposed
and darkened combs,
35   your muscles' webbing
and all your numbered bones:

I who have stood dumb
when your betraying sisters,
cauled[4] in tar,
40   wept by the railings,

who would connive
in civilized outrage
yet understand the exact
and tribal, intimate revenge.

1975

GERARD MANLEY HOPKINS

God's Grandeur

The world is charged with the grandeur of God.
    It will flame out, like shining from shook foil;[5]
    It gathers to a greatness, like the ooze of oil
Crushed. Why do men then now not reck his rod?[6]
5   Generations have trod, have trod, have trod;
    And all is seared with trade; bleared, smeared with toil;
    And wears man's smudge and shares man's smell: the soil
Is bare now, nor can foot feel, being shod.

And for all this, nature is never spent;
10   There lives the dearest freshness deep down things;
And though the last lights off the black West went
    Oh, morning, at the brown brink eastward, springs—
Because the Holy Ghost over the bent
    World broods with warm breast and with ah! bright wings.

ca. 1877

---

4. Wrapped or enclosed as if in a caul (the inner fetal membrane of higher vertebrates that sometimes covers the head at birth).
5. "I mean foil in its sense of leaf or tinsel. . . . Shaken goldfoil gives off broad glares like sheet lightning and also, and this is true of nothing else, owing to its zig-zag dints and creasings and network of small many cornered facets, a sort of fork lightning too" (*Letters of Gerard Manley Hopkins to Robert Bridges,* ed. C. C. Abbott [1955], p. 169).   6. Heed his authority.

The Windhover[7]

To Christ our Lord

I caught this morning morning's minion,[8] king-
    dom of daylight's dauphin,[9] dapple-dawn-drawn Falcon, in his riding
  Of the rolling level underneath him steady air, and striding
High there, how he rung upon the rein of a wimpling[1] wing
5 In his ecstasy! then off, off forth on swing,
    As a skate's heel sweeps smooth on a bow-bend: the hurl and gliding
  Rebuffed the big wind. My heart in hiding
Stirred for a bird,—the achieve of, the mastery of the thing!

Brute beauty and valor and act, oh, air, pride, plume, here
10 Buckle![2] AND the fire that breaks from thee then, a billion
Times told lovelier, more dangerous, O my chevalier![3]

No wonder of it: shéer plód makes plow down sillion[4]
Shine, and blue-bleak embers, ah my dear,
  Fall, gall themselves, and gash gold-vermilion.

1877

JOHN KEATS

Ode to a Nightingale

I

My heart aches, and a drowsy numbness pains
  My sense, as though of hemlock I had drunk,
Or emptied some dull opiate to the drains
  One minute past, and Lethe-wards[5] had sunk:
5 'Tis not through envy of thy happy lot,
    But being too happy in thine happiness,
      That thou, light-wingèd Dryad[6] of the trees,
        In some melodious plot
  Of beechen green, and shadows numberless,
10   Singest of summer in full-throated ease.

II

O, for a draught of vintage! that hath been
  Cooled a long age in the deep-delvèd earth,
Tasting of Flora[7] and the country green,

---

7. Small hawk, the kestrel, which habitually hovers in the air, headed into the wind.
8. Favorite, beloved.   9. Heir to regal splendor.   1. Rippling.
2. Several meanings may apply: to join closely, to prepare for battle, to grapple with, to collapse.
3. Horseman, knight.
4. Narrow strip of land between furrows in an open field divided for separate cultivation.
5. Toward the river of forgetfulness (Lethe) in Hades.   6. Wood nymph.   7. Roman goddess of flowers.

        Dance, and Provençal song,[8] and sunburnt mirth!
15 O for a beaker full of the warm South,
        Full of the true, the blushful Hippocrene,[9]
          With beaded bubbles winking at the brim,
            And purple-stainèd mouth;
        That I might drink, and leave the world unseen,
20   And with thee fade away into the forest dim:

        III

Fade far away, dissolve, and quite forget
        What thou among the leaves hast never known,
The weariness, the fever, and the fret
        Here, where men sit and hear each other groan;
25 Where palsy shakes a few, sad, last gray hairs,
        Where youth grows pale, and specter-thin, and dies;
          Where but to think is to be full of sorrow
            And leaden-eyed despairs,
        Where Beauty cannot keep her lustrous eyes,
30   Or new Love pine at them beyond tomorrow.

        IV

Away! away! for I will fly to thee,
        Not charioted by Bacchus and his pards,[1]
But on the viewless[2] wings of Poesy,
        Though the dull brain perplexes and retards:
35 Already with thee! tender is the night,
        And haply the Queen-Moon is on her throne,
          Clustered around by all her starry Fays;[3]
            But here there is no light,
        Save what from heaven is with the breezes blown
40   Through verdurous glooms and winding mossy ways.

        V

I cannot see what flowers are at my feet,
        Nor what soft incense hangs upon the boughs,
But, in embalmèd[4] darkness, guess each sweet
        Wherewith the seasonable month endows
45 The grass, the thicket, and the fruit-tree wild;
        White hawthorn, and the pastoral eglantine;[5]
          Fast fading violets covered up in leaves;
            And mid-May's eldest child,
        The coming musk-rose, full of dewy wine,
50   The murmurous haunt of flies on summer eves.

8. The medieval troubadours of Provence were famous for their love songs.
9. The fountain of the Muses on Mt. Helicon, whose waters bring poetic inspiration.
1. The Roman god of wine was sometimes portrayed in a chariot drawn by leopards.   2. Invisible.
3. Fairies.   4. Fragrant, aromatic.   5. Sweetbriar or honeysuckle.

VI

Darkling[6] I listen; and, for many a time
    I have been half in love with easeful Death,
Called him soft names in many a musèd rhyme,
    To take into the air my quiet breath;
55 Now more than ever seems it rich to die,
    To cease upon the midnight with no pain,
        While thou art pouring forth thy soul abroad
           In such an ecstasy!
    Still wouldst thou sing, and I have ears in vain—
60   To thy high requiem become a sod.

VII

Thou wast not born for death, immortal Bird!
    No hungry generations tread thee down;
The voice I hear this passing night was heard
    In ancient days by emperor and clown:
65 Perhaps the selfsame song that found a path
    Through the sad heart of Ruth,[7] when, sick for home,
        She stood in tears amid the alien corn;
           The same that ofttimes hath
    Charmed magic casements, opening on the foam
70   Of perilous seas, in faery lands forlorn.

VIII

Forlorn! the very word is like a bell
    To toll me back from thee to my sole self!
Adieu! the fancy cannot cheat so well
    As she is famed to do, deceiving elf.
75 Adieu! adieu! thy plaintive anthem fades
    Past the near meadows, over the still stream,
        Up the hillside; and now 'tis buried deep
           In the next valley-glades:
    Was it a vision, or a waking dream?
80   Fled is that music:—Do I wake or sleep?

                        May 1819

Ode on a Grecian Urn

I

Thou still unravished bride of quietness,
    Thou foster-child of silence and slow time,

---

6. In the dark.
7. A virtuous Moabite widow who, according to the Old Testament Book of Ruth, left her own country to accompany her mother-in-law, Naomi, back to Naomi's native land. She supported herself as a gleaner.

Sylvan historian, who canst thus express
    A flowery tale more sweetly than our rhyme:
5   What leaf-fringed legend haunts about thy shape
        Of deities or mortals, or of both,
            In Tempe or the dales of Arcady?[8]
    What men or gods are these? What maidens loath?
    What mad pursuit? What struggle to escape?
10   What pipes and timbrels? What wild ecstasy?

            II

Heard melodies are sweet, but those unheard
    Are sweeter; therefore, ye soft pipes, play on;
Not to the sensual[9] ear, but, more endeared,
    Pipe to the spirit ditties of no tone:
15 Fair youth, beneath the trees, thou canst not leave
        Thy song, nor ever can those trees be bare;
            Bold Lover, never, never canst thou kiss,
    Though winning near the goal—yet, do not grieve;
        She cannot fade, though thou hast not thy bliss,
20   For ever wilt thou love, and she be fair!

            III

Ah, happy, happy boughs! that cannot shed
    Your leaves, nor ever bid the Spring adieu;
And, happy melodist, unwearièd,
    For ever piping songs for ever new;
25 More happy love! more happy, happy love!
        For ever warm and still to be enjoyed,
            For ever panting, and for ever young;
All breathing human passion far above,
        That leaves a heart high-sorrowful and cloyed,
30   A burning forehead, and a parching tongue.

            IV

Who are these coming to the sacrifice?
    To what green altar, O mysterious priest,
Lead'st thou that heifer lowing at the skies,
    And all her silken flanks with garlands dressed?
35 What little town by river or sea shore,
        Or mountain-built with peaceful citadel,
            Is emptied of this folk, this pious morn?
And, little town, thy streets for evermore
        Will silent be; and not a soul to tell
40   Why thou art desolate, can e'er return.

---

8. Arcadia. Tempe is a beautiful valley near Mt. Olympus in Greece, and the valleys ("dales") of Arcadia
are a picturesque section of the Peloponnesus; both came to be associated with the pastoral ideal.
9. Of the senses, as distinguished from the "ear" of the spirit or imagination.

V

O Attic shape! Fair attitude! with brede[1]
    Of marble men and maidens overwrought,[2]
With forest branches and the trodden weed;
    Thou, silent form, dost tease us out of thought
45 As doth eternity: Cold Pastoral!
    When old age shall this generation waste,
        Thou shalt remain, in midst of other woe
Than ours, a friend to man, to whom thou say'st,
    Beauty is truth, truth beauty[3]—that is all
50   Ye know on earth, and all ye need to know.

                       May 1819

To Autumn

I

Season of mists and mellow fruitfulness,
    Close bosom-friend of the maturing sun;
Conspiring with him how to load and bless
    With fruit the vines that round the thatch-eves run;
5 To bend with apples the mossed cottage-trees,
    And fill all fruit with ripeness to the core;
        To swell the gourd, and plump the hazel shells
With a sweet kernel; to set budding more,
    And still more, later flowers for the bees,
10   Until they think warm days will never cease,
        For Summer has o'er-brimmed their clammy cells.

II

Who hath not seen thee oft amid thy store?
    Sometimes whoever seeks abroad may find
Thee sitting careless on a granary floor,
15   Thy hair soft-lifted by the winnowing wind;[4]
Or on a half-reaped furrow sound asleep,
    Drowsed with the fume of poppies, while thy hook[5]
        Spares the next swath and all its twinèd flowers:
And sometimes like a gleaner thou dost keep
20   Steady thy laden head across a brook;
    Or by a cider-press, with patient look,
        Thou watchest the last oozings hours by hours.

---

1. Woven pattern. *Attic*: Attica was the district of ancient Greece surrounding Athens.
2. Ornamented all over.
3. In some texts of the poem, "Beauty is truth, truth beauty" is in quotation marks, and in some texts it is not, leading to critical disagreements about whether the last line and a half are also inscribed on the urn or spoken by the poet.   4. Which sifts the grain from the chaff.   5. Scythe or sickle.

III

Where are the songs of Spring? Ay, where are they?
 Think not of them, thou hast thy music too—
25 While barrèd clouds bloom the soft-dying day,
 And touch the stubble-plains with rosy hue;
Then in a wailful choir the small gnats mourn
 Among the river sallows,[6] borne aloft
  Or sinking as the light wind lives or dies;
30 And full-grown lambs loud bleat from hilly bourn;[7]
 Hedge-crickets sing; and now with treble soft
 The red-breast whistles from a garden-croft;[8]
 And gathering swallows twitter in the skies.

September 19, 1819

GALWAY KINNELL

Blackberry Eating

I love to go out in late September
among the fat, overripe, icy, black blackberries
to eat blackberries for breakfast,
the stalks very prickly, a penalty
5 they earn for knowing the black art
of blackberry-making; and as I stand among them
lifting the stalks to my mouth, the ripest berries
fall almost unbidden to my tongue,
as words sometimes do, certain peculiar words
10 like *strengths* or *squinched*,
many-lettered, one-syllabled lumps,
which I squeeze, squinch open, and splurge well
in the silent, startled, icy, black language
of blackberry-eating in late September.

1980

ROBERT LOWELL

Skunk Hour

for Elizabeth Bishop

Nautilus Island's hermit
heiress still lives through winter in her Spartan cottage;
her sheep still graze above the sea.

---

6. Shallows. 7. Domain. 8. Enclosed garden near a house.

Her son's a bishop. Her farmer
5 is first selectman[9] in our village,
she's in her dotage.

Thirsting for
the hierarchic privacy
of Queen Victoria's century,
10 she buys up all
the eyesores facing her shore,
and lets them fall.

The season's ill—
we've lost our summer millionaire,
15 who seemed to leap from an L. L. Bean[1]
catalogue. His nine-knot yawl
was auctioned off to lobstermen.
A red fox stain covers Blue Hill.

And now our fairy
20 decorator brightens his shop for fall,
his fishnet's filled with orange cork,
orange, his cobbler's bench and awl,
there is no money in his work,
he'd rather marry.

25 One dark night,
my Tudor Ford climbed the hill's skull,
I watched for love-cars. Lights turned down,
they lay together, hull to hull,
where the graveyard shelves on the town. . . .
30 My mind's not right.

A car radio bleats,
"Love, O careless Love. . . ."[2] I hear
my ill-spirit sob in each blood cell,
as if my hand were at its throat. . . .
35 I myself am hell;
nobody's here—

only skunks, that search
in the moonlight for a bite to eat.
They march on their soles up Main Street:
40 white stripes, moonstruck eyes' red fire
under the chalk-dry and spar spire
of the Trinitarian Church.

I stand on top
of our back steps and breathe the rich air—
45 a mother skunk with her column of kittens swills the garbage pail.

---

9. Elected New England town official.   1. Famous old Maine sporting goods firm.
2. Popular folk song recorded many times, as by Frankie Laine (1959).

She jabs her wedge head in a cup
of sour cream, drops her ostrich tail,
and will not scare.

1959

ANDREW MARVELL

The Garden

How vainly men themselves amaze[3]
To win the palm, the oak, or bays,[4]
And their incessant labors see
Crowned from some single herb, or tree,
5 Whose short and narrow-vergèd[5] shade
Does prudently their toils upbraid;
While all flowers and all trees do close[6]
To weave the garlands of repose!

Fair Quiet, have I found thee here,
10 And Innocence, thy sister dear?
Mistaken long, I sought you then
In busy companies of men.
Your sacred plants,[7] if here below,
Only among the plants will grow;
15 Society is all but rude[8]
To[9] this delicious solitude.

No white nor red was ever seen
So am'rous as this lovely green.
Fond lovers, cruel as their flame,
20 Cut in these trees their mistress' name:
Little, alas, they know, or heed
How far these beauties hers exceed!
Fair trees, wheresoe'er your barks I wound,
No name shall but your own be found.

25 When we have run our passion's heat,
Love hither makes his best retreat.
The gods, that mortal beauty chase,
Still in a tree did end their race:
Apollo hunted Daphne so,
30 Only that she might laurel grow;
And Pan did after Syrinx speed,
Not as a nymph, but for a reed.[1]

---

3. Become frenzied.   4. Awards for athletic, civic, and literary achievements, respectively.
5. Narrowly cropped.   6. Unite.   7. Cuttings.   8. Barbarous.   9. Compared to.
1. In Ovid's *Metamorphoses*, Daphne, pursued by Apollo, is turned into a laurel, and Syrinx, pursued by Pan, into a reed that Pan makes into a flute.

What wondrous life is this I lead!
Ripe apples drop about my head;
35 The luscious clusters of the vine
Upon my mouth do crush their wine;
The nectarine and curious[2] peach
Into my hands themselves do reach;
Stumbling on melons, as I pass,
40 Insnared with flowers, I fall on grass.

Meanwhile the mind, from pleasure less,
Withdraws into its happiness;[3]
The mind, that ocean where each kind
Does straight its own resemblance find;[4]
45 Yet it creates, transcending these,
Far other worlds and other seas,
Annihilating[5] all that's made
To a green thought in a green shade.

Here at the fountain's sliding foot,
50 Or at some fruit tree's mossy root,
Casting the body's vest[6] aside,
My soul into the boughs does glide:
There, like a bird, it sits and sings,
Then whets[7] and combs its silver wings,
55 And, till prepared for longer flight,
Waves in its plumes the various[8] light.

Such was that happy garden-state,
While man there walked without a mate:
After a place so pure, and sweet,
60 What other help could yet be meet![9]
But 'twas beyond a mortal's share
To wander solitary there:
Two paradises 'twere in one
To live in paradise alone.

65   How well the skillful gardener drew
Of flowers and herbs this dial[1] new,
Where, from above, the milder sun
Does through a fragrant zodiac run;
And as it works, th' industrious bee
70 Computes its time as well as we!
How could such sweet and wholesome hours
Be reckoned but with herbs and flowers?

1681

2. Exquisite.   3. That is, the mind withdraws from lesser-sense pleasure into contemplation.
4. All land creatures supposedly had corresponding sea creatures.
5. Reducing to nothing by comparison.
6. Vestment, clothing; the flesh is being considered as simply clothing for the soul.
7. Preens.   8. Many-colored.   9. Appropriate.
1. Garden planted in the shape of a sundial, complete with zodiac.

SYLVIA PLATH

Barren Woman

Empty, I echo to the least footfall,
Museum without statues, grand with pillars, porticoes, rotundas.
In my courtyard a fountain leaps and sinks back into itself,
Nun-hearted and blind to the world. Marble lilies
5   Exhale their pallor like scent.

I imagine myself with a great public,
Mother of a white Nike and several bald-eyed Apollos.[2]
Instead, the dead injure me with attentions, and nothing can happen.
The moon lays a hand on my forehead,
10   Blank-faced and mum as a nurse.

February 21, 1963

Black Rook in Rainy Weather

On the stiff twig up there
Hunches a wet black rook
Arranging and rearranging its feathers in the rain.
I do not expect a miracle
5   Or an accident

To set the sight on fire
In my eye, nor seek
Any more in the desultory weather some design,
But let spotted leaves fall as they fall,
10   Without ceremony, or portent

Although, I admit, I desire,
Occasionally, some backtalk
From the mute sky, I can't honestly complain:
A certain minor light may still
15   Leap incandescent

Out of kitchen table or chair
As if a celestial burning took
Possession of the most obtuse objects now and then—
Thus hallowing an interval
20   Otherwise inconsequent

By bestowing largesse, honor,
One might say love. At any rate, I now walk
Wary (for it could happen

---

2. That is, gods of poetic inspiration. Nike: goddess of victory.

Even in this dull, ruinous landscape); skeptical,
25 Yet politic; ignorant

Of whatever angel may choose to flare
Suddenly at my elbow. I only know that a rook
Ordering its black feathers can so shine
As to seize my senses, haul
30 My eyelids up, and grant

A brief respite from fear
Of total neutrality. With luck,
Trekking stubborn through this season
Of fatigue, I shall
35 Patch together a content

Of sorts. Miracles occur,
If you care to call those spasmodic
Tricks of radiance miracles. The wait's begun again,
The long wait for the angel,
40 For that rare, random descent.[3]

                                            1960

EZRA POUND

In a Station of the Metro[4]

The apparition of these faces in the crowd;
Petals on a wet, black bough.

                                            1913

A Virginal

No, no! Go from me. I have left her lately.
I will not spoil my sheath with lesser brightness,
For my surrounding air hath a new lightness;
Slight are her arms, yet they have bound me straitly
5 And left me cloaked as with a gauze of aether;
As with sweet leaves; as with a subtle clearness.
Oh, I have picked up magic in her nearness
To sheathe me half in half the things that sheathe her.
No, no! Go from me, I have still the flavor,
10 Soft as spring wind that's come from birchen bowers.
Green come the shoots, aye April in the branches,

---

3. According to Acts 2, the Holy Ghost at Pentecost descended like a tongue of fire upon Jesus' disciples.
4. Paris subway.

As winter's wound with her sleight hand she staunches,
Hath of the trees a likeness of the savor:
As white their bark, so white this lady's hours.

1912

JOHN CROWE RANSOM

Bells for John Whiteside's Daughter

There was such speed in her little body,
And such lightness in her footfall,
It is no wonder her brown study[5]
Astonishes us all.

5   Her wars were bruited in our high window.
We looked among orchard trees and beyond
Where she took arms against her shadow,
Or harried unto the pond

The lazy geese, like a snow cloud
10 Dripping their snow on the green grass,
Tricking and stopping, sleepy and proud,
Who cried in goose, Alas,

For the tireless heart within the little
Lady with rod that made them rise
15 From their noon apple-dreams and scuttle
Goose-fashion under the skies!

But now go the bells, and we are ready,
In one house we are sternly stopped
To say we are vexed at her brown study,
20 Lying so primly propped.

1924

THEODORE ROETHKE

I Knew a Woman

I knew a woman, lovely in her bones,
When small birds sighed, she would sigh back at them;
Ah, when she moved, she moved more ways than one:
The shapes a bright container can contain!
Of her choice virtues only gods should speak;

---

5. Stillness, as if in meditation or deep thought.

Or English poets who grew up on Greek
(I'd have them sing in chorus, cheek to cheek).

How well her wishes went! She stroked my chin,
She taught me Turn, and Counter-turn, and Stand;[6]
10 She taught me Touch, that undulant white skin;
I nibbled meekly from her proffered hand;
She was the sickle; I, poor I, the rake,
Coming behind her for her pretty sake
(But what prodigious mowing we did make).

15 Love likes a gander, and adores a goose:
Her full lips pursed, the errant note to seize;
She played it quick, she played it light and loose;
My eyes, they dazzled at her flowing knees;
Her several parts could keep a pure repose,
20 Or one hip quiver with a mobile nose
(She moved in circles, and those circles moved).

Let seed be grass, and grass turn into hay:
I'm martyr to a motion not my own;
What's freedom for? To know eternity.
25 I swear she cast a shadow white as stone.
But who would count eternity in days?
These old bones live to learn her wanton ways:
(I measure time by how a body sways).

1958

The Waking

I wake to sleep, and take my waking slow.
I feel my fate in what I cannot fear.
I learn by going where I have to go.

We think by feeling. What is there to know?
5 I hear my being dance from ear to ear.
I wake to sleep, and take my waking slow.

Of those so close beside me, which are you?
God bless the Ground! I shall walk softly there,
And learn by going where I have to go.

10 Light takes the Tree; but who can tell us how?
The lowly worm climbs up a winding stair;
I wake to sleep, and take my waking slow.

Great Nature has another thing to do
To you and me; so take the lively air,
15 And, lovely, learn by going where to go.

6. Literary terms for the parts of a Pindaric ode.

This shaking keeps me steady. I should know.
What falls away is always. And is near.
I wake to sleep, and take my waking slow.
I learn by going where I have to go.

1953

WALLACE STEVENS

The Idea of Order at Key West

She sang beyond the genius of the sea.
The water never formed to mind or voice,
Like a body wholly body, fluttering
Its empty sleeves; and yet its mimic motion
5 Made constant cry, caused constantly a cry,
That was not ours although we understood,
Inhuman, of the veritable ocean.

The sea was not a mask. No more was she.
The song and water were not medleyed sound
10 Even if what she sang was what she heard,
Since what she sang was uttered word by word.
It may be that in all her phrases stirred
The grinding water and the gasping wind;
But it was she and not the sea we heard.

15 For she was the maker of the song she sang.
The ever-hooded, tragic-gestured sea
Was merely a place by which she walked to sing.
Whose spirit is this? we said, because we knew
It was the spirit that we sought and knew
20 That we should ask this often as she sang.

If it was only the dark voice of the sea
That rose, or even colored by many waves;
If it was only the outer voice of sky
And cloud, of the sunken coral water-walled,
25 However clear, it would have been deep air,
The heaving speech of air, a summer sound
Repeated in a summer without end
And sound alone. But it was more than that,
More even than her voice, and ours, among
30 The meaningless plungings of water and the wind,
Theatrical distances, bronze shadows heaped
On high horizons, mountainous atmospheres
Of sky and sea.
                    It was her voice that made
The sky acutest at its vanishing.
35 She measured to the hour its solitude.

She was the single artificer of the world
In which she sang. And when she sang, the sea,
Whatever self it had, became the self
That was her song, for she was the maker. Then we,
40 As we beheld her striding there alone,
Knew that there never was a world for her
Except the one she sang and, singing, made.

Ramon Fernandez,[7] tell me, if you know,
Why, when the singing ended and we turned
45 Toward the town, tell why the glassy lights,
The lights in the fishing boats at anchor there,
As the night descended, tilting in the air,
Mastered the night and portioned out the sea,
Fixing emblazoned zones and fiery poles,
50 Arranging, deepening, enchanting night.

Oh! Blessed rage for order, pale Ramon,
The maker's rage to order words of the sea,
Words of the fragrant portals, dimly-starred,
And of ourselves and of our origins,
55 In ghostlier demarcations, keener sounds.

                                                    1935

The Emperor of Ice-Cream

Call the roller of big cigars,
The muscular one, and bid him whip
In kitchen cups concupiscent curds.[8]
Let the wenches dawdle in such dress
5 As they are used to wear, and let the boys
Bring flowers in last month's newspapers.
Let be be finale of seem.[9]
The only emperor is the emperor of ice-cream.

Take from the dresser of deal,
10 Lacking the three glass knobs, that sheet

7. French classicist and critic (1894–1944), who emphasized the ordering role of a writer's consciousness upon the materials he or she used. Stevens denied that he had Fernandez in mind, saying that he combined a Spanish first name and surname at random: "I knew of Ramon Fernandez, the critic, and had read some of his criticisms, but I did not have him in mind" (*Letters of Wallace Stevens*, ed. Holly Stevens [1966], p. 798). Later, Stevens wrote to another correspondent that he did not have the critic "consciously" in mind (*Letters*, p. 823).

8. "The words 'concupiscent curds' have no genealogy; they are merely expressive: at least, I hope they are expressive. They express the concupiscence of life, but, by contrast with the things in relation in the poem, they express or accentuate life's destitution, and it is this that gives them something more than a cheap lustre" (*Letters*, p. 500).

9. "The true sense of Let be be the finale of seem is let being become the conclusion or denouement of appearing to be: in short, ice cream is an absolute good. The poem is obviously not about ice cream, but about being as distinguished from seeming to be" (*Letters*, p. 341).

On which she embroidered fantails[1] once
And spread it so as to cover her face.
If her horny feet protrude, they come
To show how cold she is, and dumb.
15 Let the lamp affix its beam.
The only emperor is the emperor of ice-cream.

                                        1923

Anecdote of the Jar

I placed a jar in Tennessee,
And round it was, upon a hill.
It made the slovenly wilderness
Surround that hill.

5 The wilderness rose up to it,
And sprawled around, no longer wild.
The jar was round upon the ground
And tall and of a port in air.

It took dominion everywhere.
10 The jar was gray and bare.
It did not give of bird or bush,
Like nothing else in Tennessee.

                                        1923

ALFRED, LORD TENNYSON

The Lotos-Eaters[2]

"Courage!" he[3] said, and pointed toward the land,
"This mounting wave will roll us shoreward soon."
In the afternoon they came unto a land
In which it seemèd always afternoon.
5 All round the coast the languid air did swoon,
Breathing like one that hath a weary dream.
Full-faced above the valley stood the moon;
And, like a downward smoke, the slender stream
Along the cliff to fall and pause and fall did seem.

---

1. Fantail pigeons.
2. In the *Odyssey* (9.82–97), the weary Greek veterans of the Trojan War are tempted to abandon their long voyage homeward. As Odysseus later reported: "On the tenth day we set foot on the land of the lotos-eaters who eat a flowering food. . . . I sent forth certain of my company [who] . . . mixed with the men of the lotos-eaters who gave . . . them of the lotos to taste. Now whosoever of them did eat the honey-sweet fruit of the lotos had no more wish to bring tidings nor to come back, but there he chose to abide . . . forgetful of his homeward way."   3. Odysseus (or Ulysses).

10 A land of streams! some, like a downward smoke,
    Slow-dropping veils of thinnest lawn,[4] did go;
    And some through wavering lights and shadows broke,
    Rolling a slumbrous sheet of foam below.
    They saw the gleaming river seaward flow
15 From the inner land; far off, three mountaintops
    Three silent pinnacles of aged snow,
    Stood sunset-flushed; and, dewed with showery drops,
    Up-clomb the shadowy pine above the woven copse.

    The charmèd sunset lingered low adown
20 In the red West; through mountain clefts the dale
    Was seen far inland, and the yellow down[5]
    Bordered with palm, and many a winding vale
    And meadow, set with slender galingale;[6]
    A land where all things always seemed the same!
25 And round about the keel with faces pale,
    Dark faces pale against that rosy flame,
    The mild-eyed melancholy Lotos-eaters came.

    Branches they bore of that enchanted stem,
    Laden with flower and fruit, whereof they gave
30 To each, but whoso did receive of them
    And taste, to him the gushing of the wave
    Far far away did seem to mourn and rave
    On alien shores; and if his fellow spake,
    His voice was thin, as voices from the grave;
35 And deep-asleep he seemed, yet all awake,
    And music in his ears his beating heart did make.

    They sat them down upon the yellow sand,
    Between the sun and moon upon the shore;
    And sweet it was to dream of Fatherland,
40 Of child, and wife, and slave; but evermore
    Most weary seemed the sea, weary the oar,
    Weary the wandering fields of barren foam,
    Then some one said, "We will return no more";
    And all at once they sang, "Our island home[7]
45 Is far beyond the wave; we will no longer roam."

Choric Song[8]

1

    There is sweet music here that softer falls
    Than petals from blown roses on the grass,
    Or night-dews on still waters between walls
    Of shadowy granite, in a gleaming pass;

---

4. Fine, sheer linen.   5. Grassy, treeless highland.   6. Type of sedge used in basket-making.
7. That is, Ithaca, the Greek island ruled by Odysseus.   8. Sung by Odysseus's sailors.

50 Music that gentlier on the spirit lies,
   Than tired eyelids upon tired eyes;
   Music that brings sweet sleep down from the blissful skies.
   Here are cool mosses deep,
   And through the moss the ivies creep,
55 And in the stream the long-leaved flowers weep,
   And from the craggy ledge the poppy hangs in sleep.

2

   Why are we weighed upon with heaviness,
   And utterly consumed with sharp distress,
   While all things else have rest from weariness?
60 All things have rest: why should we toil alone,
   We only toil, who are the first of things,
   And make perpetual moan,
   Still from one sorrow to another thrown;
   Nor ever fold our wings,
65 And cease from wanderings,
   Nor steep our brows in slumber's holy balm;
   Nor harken what the inner spirit sings,
   "There is no joy but calm!"—
   Why should we only toil, the roof and crown of things?

3

70 Lo! in the middle of the wood,
   The folded leaf is wooed from out the bud
   With winds upon the branch, and there
   Grows green and broad, and takes no care,
   Sun-steeped at noon, and in the moon
75 Nightly dew-fed; and turning yellow
   Falls, and floats adown the air.
   Lo! sweetened with summer light,
   The full-juiced apple, waxing over-mellow,
   Drops in a silent autumn night.
80 All its allotted length of days
   The flower ripens in its place,
   Ripens and fades, and falls, and hath no toil,
   Fast-rooted in the fruitful soil.

4

   Hateful is the dark blue sky,
85 Vaulted o'er the dark blue sea.
   Death is the end of life; ah, why
   Should life all labor be?
   Let us alone. Time driveth onward fast,
   And in a little while our lips are dumb.
90 Let us alone. What is it that will last?
   All things are taken from us, and become
   Portions and parcels of the dreadful past.

Let us alone. What pleasure can we have
To war with evil? Is there any peace
95 In ever climbing up the climbing wave?
All things have rest, and ripen toward the grave
In silence—ripen, fall, and cease:
Give us long rest or death, dark death, or dreamful ease

5

How sweet it were, hearing the downward stream,
100 With half-shut eyes ever to seem
Falling asleep in a half-dream!
To dream and dream, like yonder amber light,
Which will not leave the myrrh-bush on the height;
To hear each other's whispered speech;
105 Eating the Lotos day by day,
To watch the crisping[9] ripples on the beach,
And tender curving lines of creamy spray;
To lend our hearts and spirits wholly
To the influence of mild-minded melancholy;
110 To muse and brood and live again in memory,
With those old faces of our infancy
Heaped over with a mound of grass,
Two handfuls of white dust, shut in an urn of brass!

6

Dear is the memory of our wedded lives,
115 And dear the last embraces of our wives
And their warm tears; but all hath suffered change;
For surely now our household hearths are cold,
Our sons inherit us, our looks are strange,
And we should come like ghosts to trouble joy.
120 Or else the island princes[1] overbold
Have eat our substance, and the minstrel sings
Before them of the ten years' war in Troy,
And our great deeds, as half-forgotten things.
Is there confusion in the little isle?
125 Let what is broken so remain.
The Gods are hard to reconcile;
'Tis hard to settle order once again.
There is confusion worse than death,
Trouble on trouble, pain on pain,
130 Long labor unto aged breath,
Sore tasks to hearts worn out by many wars
And eyes grown dim with gazing on the pilot-stars.

9. Curling.   1. That is, Penelope's suitors.

7

But, propped on beds of amaranth and moly,[2]
How sweet—while warm airs lull us, blowing lowly—
135   With half-dropped eyelid still,
Beneath a heaven dark and holy,
To watch the long bright river drawing slowly
His waters from the purple hill—
To hear the dewy echoes calling
140   From cave to cave through the thick-twined vine—
To watch the emerald-colored water falling
Through many a woven acanthus[3] wreath divine!
Only to hear and see the far-off sparkling brine,
Only to hear were[4] sweet, stretched out beneath the pine.

8

145   The Lotos blooms below the barren peak,
The Lotos blows by every winding creek;
All day the wind breathes low with mellower tone;
Through every hollow cave and alley lone
Round and round the spicy downs the yellow Lotos dust is blown.
150   We have had enough of action, and of motion we,
Rolled to starboard, rolled to larboard, when the surge was seething
    free,
Where the wallowing monster spouted his foam-fountains in the sea.
Let us swear an oath, and keep it with an equal mind,
In the hollow Lotos land to live and lie reclined
155   On the hills like Gods together, careless of mankind.
For they lie beside their nectar, and the bolts[5] are hurled
Far below them in the valleys, and the clouds are lightly curled
Round their golden houses, girdled with the gleaming world;
Where they smile in secret, looking over wasted lands,
160   Blight and famine, plague and earthquake, roaring deeps and fiery
    sands,
Clanging fights, and flaming towns, and sinking ships, and praying
    hands.
But they smile, they find a music centered in a doleful song
Steaming up, a lamentation and an ancient tale of wrong,
Like a tale of little meaning though the words are strong;
165   Chanted from an ill-used race of men that cleave the soil,
Sow the seed, and reap the harvest with enduring toil,
Storing yearly little dues of wheat, and wine and oil;
Till they perish and they suffer—some, 'tis whispered—down in hell
Suffer endless anguish, others in Elysian valleys dwell,
170   Resting weary limbs at last on beds of asphodel.[6]
Surely, surely, slumber is more sweet than toil, the shore

2. Magical flowers.   3. Herb with prickly leaves.   4. Would be.   5. Thunderbolts.
6. Type of lily.

Than labor in the deep mid-ocean, wind and wave and oar;
O, rest ye, brother mariners, we will not wander more.

1832, 1842

Tears, Idle Tears[7]

Tears, idle tears, I know not what they mean,
Tears from the depth of some divine despair
Rise in the heart, and gather to the eyes,
In looking on the happy autumn-fields,
5   And thinking of the days that are no more.

Fresh as the first beam glittering on a sail,
That brings our friends up from the underworld,
Sad as the last which reddens over one
That sinks with all we love below the verge;
10   So sad, so fresh, the days that are no more.

Ah, sad and strange as in dark summer dawns
The earliest pipe of half-awakened birds
To dying ears, when unto dying eyes
The casement slowly grows a glimmering square;
15   So sad, so strange, the days that are no more.

Dear as remembered kisses after death,
And sweet as those by hopeless fancy feigned
On lips that are for others; deep as love,
Deep as first love, and wild with all regret;
20   O Death in Life, the days that are no more!

1847

DYLAN THOMAS

Fern Hill

Now as I was young and easy under the apple boughs
About the lilting house and happy as the grass was green,
    The night above the dingle starry,
        Time let me hail and climb
5   Golden in the heydays of his eyes,
And honored among wagons I was prince of the apple towns
And once below a time I lordly had the trees and leaves
        Trail with daisies and barley
    Down the rivers of the windfall light.

7. One of the songs from Tennyson's book-length narrative poem *The Princess*.

10 And as I was green and carefree, famous among the barns
   About the happy yard and singing as the farm was home,
      In the sun that is young once only,
         Time let me play and be
      Golden in the mercy of his means,
15 And green and golden I was huntsman and herdsman, the calves
   Sang to my horn, the foxes on the hills barked clear and cold,
         And the sabbath rang slowly
      In the pebbles of the holy streams.

   All the sun long it was running, it was lovely, the hay
20 Fields high as the house, the tunes from the chimneys, it was air
         And playing, lovely and watery
            And fire green as grass.
         And nightly under the simple stars
      As I rode to sleep the owls were bearing the farm away,
25 All the moon long I heard, blessed among stables, the nightjars[8]
      Flying with the ricks,[9] and the horses
            Flashing into the dark.

   And then to awake, and the farm, like a wanderer white
   With the dew, come back, the cock on his shoulder: it was all
30   Shining, it was Adam and maiden,
         The sky gathered again
         And the sun grew round that very day.
   So it must have been after the birth of the simple light
   In the first, spinning place, the spellbound horses walking warm
35   Out of the whinnying green stable
         On to the fields of praise.

   And honored among foxes and pheasants by the gay house
   Under the new made clouds and happy as the heart was long,
      In the sun born over and over,
40   I ran my heedless ways,
      My wishes raced through the house-high hay
   And nothing I cared, at my sky-blue trades, that time allows
      In all his tuneful turning so few and such morning songs
         Before the children green and golden
45   Follow him out of grace,

   Nothing I cared, in the lamb white days, that time would take me
   Up to the swallow-thronged loft by the shadow of my hand,
      In the moon that is always rising,
         Nor that riding to sleep
50   I should hear him fly with the high fields
   And wake to the farm forever fled from the childless land.
   Oh as I was young and easy in the mercy of his means,
         Time held me green and dying
      Though I sang in my chains like the sea.

                                                            1946

8. Birds also known as goatsuckers.   9. Haystacks.

WALT WHITMAN

Facing West from California's Shores

Facing west, from California's shores,
Inquiring, tireless, seeking what is yet unfound,
I, a child, very old, over waves, towards the house of maternity,[1] the
    land of migrations, look afar,
Look off the shores of my Western sea, the circle almost circled:
5 For starting westward from Hindustan, from the vales of Kashmere,
From Asia, from the north, from the God, the sage, and the hero,
From the south, from the flowery peninsulas and the spice islands,
Long having wandered since, round the earth having wandered,
Now I face home again, very pleased and joyous;
10 (But where is what I started for, so long ago?
And why is it yet unfound?)

                                      1860

I Hear America Singing

I hear America singing, the varied carols I hear,
Those of mechanics, each one singing his as it should be blithe and
    strong,
The carpenter singing his as he measures his plank or beam,
The mason singing his as he makes ready for work, or leaves off work,
5 The boatman singing what belongs to him in his boat, the deckhand
    singing on the steamboat deck,
The shoemaker singing as he sits on his bench, the hatter singing as he
    stands,
The wood-cutter's song, the ploughboy's on his way in the morning, or
    at noon intermission or at sundown,
The delicious singing of the mother, or of the young wife at work, or of
    the girl sewing or washing,
Each singing what belongs to him or her and to none else,
10 The day what belongs to the day—at night the party of young fellows,
    robust, friendly,
Singing with open mouths their strong melodious songs.

                                        1860

A Noiseless Patient Spider

A noiseless patient spider,
I marked where on a little promontory it stood isolated,
Marked how to explore the vacant vast surrounding,

---

1. Asia, as the supposed birthplace of the human race.

It launched forth filament, filament, filament, out of itself,
5 Ever unreeling them, ever tirelessly speeding them.

And you O my soul where you stand,
Surrounded, detached, in measureless oceans of space,
Ceaselessly musing, venturing, throwing, seeking the spheres to
    connect them,
Till the bridge you will need be formed, till the ductile anchor hold,
10 Till the gossamer thread you fling catch somewhere, O my soul.

                                                                1881

RICHARD WILBUR

Love Calls Us to the Things of This World

The eyes open to a cry of pulleys,
And spirited from sleep, the astounded soul
Hangs for a moment bodiless and simple
As false dawn.
5   Outside the open window
The morning air is all awash with angels.

Some are in bed-sheets, some are in blouses,
Some are in smocks: but truly there they are.
Now they are rising together in calm swells
10 Of halcyon² feeling, filling whatever they wear
With the deep joy of their impersonal breathing;
    Now they are flying in place, conveying
The terrible speed of their omnipresence, moving
And staying like white water; and now of a sudden
15 They swoon down into so rapt a quiet
That nobody seems to be there.
                                        The soul shrinks

    From all that it is about to remember,
From the punctual rape of every blessed day,
20 And cries,
            "Oh, let there be nothing on earth but laundry,
Nothing but rosy hands in the rising steam
And clear dances done in the sight of heaven."

Yet, as the sun acknowledges
25 With a warm look the world's hunks and colors,
The soul descends once more in bitter love
To accept the waking body, saying now
In a changed voice as the man yawns and rises,

2. Serene.

"Bring them down from their ruddy gallows;
30 Let there be clean linen for the backs of thieves;
Let lovers go fresh and sweet to be undone,
And the heaviest nuns walk in a pure floating
Of dark habits,
                keeping their difficult balance."

                                      1956

WILLIAM WORDSWORTH

Lines Written a Few Miles above Tintern Abbey, On Revisiting the Banks of the Wye during a Tour, July 13, 1798 [3]

Five years have passed; five summers, with the length
Of five long winters! and again I hear
These waters, rolling from their mountain-springs
With a soft inland murmur. Once again
5 Do I behold these steep and lofty cliffs,
That on a wild secluded scene impress
Thoughts of more deep seclusion; and connect
The landscape with the quiet of the sky.
The day is come when I again repose
10 Here, under this dark sycamore, and view
These plots of cottage-ground, these orchard tufts,
Which at this season, with their unripe fruits,
Are clad in one green hue, and lose themselves
'Mid groves and copses.[4] Once again I see
15 These hedge-rows, hardly hedge-rows, little lines
Of sportive wood run wild: these pastoral farms,
Green to the very door; and wreaths of smoke
Sent up, in silence, from among the trees!
With some uncertain notice, as might seem
20 Of vagrant dwellers in the houseless woods,
Or of some hermit's cave, where by his fire
The hermit sits alone.
                    These beauteous forms,
Through a long absence, have not been to me
As is a landscape to a blind man's eye;
25 But oft, in lonely rooms, and 'mid the din
Of towns and cities, I have owed to them,

---

3. Wordsworth had first visited the Wye valley in Wales and the ruins of the medieval abbey there in 1793, while on a solitary walking tour. He was twenty-three then, twenty-eight when he wrote this poem.
4. Thickets.

In hours of weariness, sensations sweet,
Felt in the blood, and felt along the heart;
And passing even into my purer mind,
30 With tranquil restoration—feelings too
Of unremembered pleasure: such, perhaps,
As have no slight or trivial influence
On that best portion of a good man's life,
His little, nameless, unremembered acts
35 Of kindness and of love. Nor less, I trust,
To them I may have owed another gift,
Of aspect more sublime; that blessèd mood,
In which the burthen[5] of the mystery,
In which the heavy and the weary weight
40 Of all this unintelligible world,
Is lightened—that serene and blessèd mood,
In which the affections gently lead us on—
Until, the breath of this corporeal frame
And even the motion of our human blood
45 Almost suspended, we are laid asleep
In body, and become a living soul;
While with an eye made quiet by the power
Of harmony, and the deep power of joy,
We see into the life of things.

                     If this
50 Be but a vain belief, yet, oh! how oft—
In darkness and amid the many shapes
Of joyless daylight; when the fretful stir
Unprofitable, and the fever of the world,
Have hung upon the beatings of my heart—
55 How oft, in spirit, have I turned to thee,
O sylvan Wye! thou wanderer through the woods,
How often has my spirit turned to thee!

    And now, with gleams of half-extinguished thought,
With many recognitions dim and faint,
60 And somewhat of a sad perplexity,
The picture of the mind revives again;
While here I stand, not only with the sense
Of present pleasure, but with pleasing thoughts
That in this moment there is life and food
65 For future years. And so I dare to hope,
Though changed, no doubt, from what I was when first
I came among these hills; when like a roe
I bounded o'er the mountains, by the sides
Of the deep rivers, and the lonely streams,
70 Wherever nature led: more like a man
Flying from something that he dreads than one

5. Burden.

Who sought the thing he loved. For nature then
(The coarser[6] pleasures of my boyish days,
And their glad animal movements all gone by)
75 To me was all in all—I cannot paint
What then I was. The sounding cataract
Haunted me like a passion; the tall rock,
The mountain, and the deep and gloomy wood,
Their colors and their forms, were then to me
80 An appetite; a feeling and a love,
That had no need of a remoter charm,
By thought supplied, nor any interest
Unborrowed from the eye. That time is past,
And all its aching joys are now no more,
85 And all its dizzy raptures. Not for this
Faint I,[7] nor mourn nor murmur; other gifts
Have followed; for such loss, I would believe,
Abundant recompense. For I have learned
To look on nature, not as in the hour
90 Of thoughtless youth; but hearing oftentimes
The still, sad music of humanity,
Nor[8] harsh nor grating, though of ample power
To chasten and subdue. And I have felt
A presence that disturbs me with the joy
95 Of elevated thoughts, a sense sublime
Of something far more deeply interfused,
Whose dwelling is the light of setting suns,
And the round ocean and the living air,
And the blue sky, and in the mind of man:
100 A motion and a spirit, that impels
All thinking things, all objects of all thought,
And rolls through all things. Therefore am I still
A lover of the meadows and the woods
And mountains; and of all that we behold
105 From this green earth; of all the mighty world
Of eye, and ear—both what they half create,
And what perceive; well pleased to recognize
In nature and the language of the sense
The anchor of my purest thoughts, the nurse,
110 The guide, the guardian of my heart, and soul
Of all my moral being.

                        Nor perchance,
If I were not thus taught, should I the more
Suffer my genial spirits[9] to decay:
For thou art with me here upon the banks
115 Of this fair river; thou my dearest Friend,[1]

---

6. Physical.   7. Am I discouraged.   8. Neither.
9. Natural disposition; that is, the spirits are part of his individual genius.   1. His sister Dorothy.

My dear, dear Friend; and in thy voice I catch
The language of my former heart, and read
My former pleasures in the shooting lights
Of thy wild eyes. Oh! yet a little while
120 May I behold in thee what I was once,
My dear, dear Sister! and this prayer I make,
Knowing that Nature never did betray
The heart that loved her; 'tis her privilege,
Through all the years of this our life, to lead
125 From joy to joy: for she can so inform
The mind that is within us, so impress
With quietness and beauty, and so feed
With lofty thoughts, that neither evil tongues,
Rash judgments, nor the sneers of selfish men,
130 Nor greetings where no kindness is, nor all
The dreary intercourse of daily life,
Shall e'er prevail against us, or disturb
Our cheerful faith that all which we behold
Is full of blessings. Therefore let the moon
135 Shine on thee in thy solitary walk;
And let the misty mountain-winds be free
To blow against thee: and, in after years,
When these wild ecstasies shall be matured
Into a sober pleasure; when thy mind
140 Shall be a mansion for all lovely forms,
Thy memory be as a dwelling-place
For all sweet sounds and harmonies; oh! then,
If solitude, or fear, or pain, or grief,
Should be thy portion, with what healing thoughts
145 Of tender joy wilt thou remember me,
And these my exhortations! No, perchance—
If I should be where I no more can hear
Thy voice, nor catch from thy wild eyes these gleams
Of past existence—wilt thou then forget
150 That on the banks of this delightful stream
We stood together; and that I, so long
A worshiper of Nature, hither came
Unwearied in that service; rather say
With warmer love—oh! with far deeper zeal
155 Of holier love. Nor wilt thou then forget,
That after many wanderings, many years
Of absence, these steep woods and lofty cliffs,
And this green pastoral landscape, were to me
More dear, both for themselves and for thy sake!

1798

Biographical Sketches
Poets

Sketches are included for all poets represented by two or more poems.

W. H. AUDEN
(1907–1973)

Wystan Hugh Auden was born in York, England, to a medical officer and a nurse. Intending at first to become a scientist, Auden studied at Oxford, where he became the center of the "Oxford Group" of poets and leftist intellectuals. His travels during the 1930s led him to Germany, Iceland, China, Spain (where he was an ambulance driver in the civil war), and the United States (where he taught at various universities and, in 1946, became a naturalized citizen). A prolific writer of poems, plays, essays, and criticism, Auden won the Pulitzer Prize in 1948 for his collection of poems *The Age of Anxiety*, set in a New York City bar. Late in life he returned to Christ Church College, Oxford, where he was writer in residence. He is regarded as a masterly poet of political and intellectual conscience as well as one of the twentieth century's greatest lyric craftsmen.

BASHŌ (1644–1694)

Born Matsuo Munefusa, the second son of a low-ranking provincial samurai, the haiku poet who came to be known as Bashō at first put aside his literary interests and entered into service with the local ruling military house. In 1666, following the feudal lord's death, Bashō left for Edo (now Tokyo), the military capital of the shogun's new government, to pursue a career as a professional poet. He supported himself as a teacher and editor of other people's poetry but ultimately developed a following and a sizable group of students. A seasoned traveler, Bashō maintained an austere existence on the road as well as at home, casting himself in travel narratives such as *Oku no hosomichi* (*The Narrow Road to the Interior*, 1694) as a pilgrim devoted to nature and Zen.

EARLE BIRNEY
(1904–1995)

Born in Calgary, Alberta, Earle Birney was educated in Canada and earned a Ph.D. from the University of Toronto before teaching at the University of Utah. After serving as a major in the Canadian army during World War II, Birney returned to the University of British Columbia, where he had received his B.A. twenty years earlier, and developed the first course there in creative writing. Birney's many books include novels and criticism, but he is best known as a poet. His first collection, *David and Other Poems*, won the Governor General's Medal for Poetry in 1942; many volumes and many awards later, his final collection, *Last Makings*, appeared in 1991.

ELIZABETH BISHOP
(1911–1979)

Born in Worcester, Massachusetts, Elizabeth Bishop endured the death of her father before she was a year old and the institutionalization of her mother four years later. Bishop was raised by her maternal grandmother in Nova Scotia, then by her paternal grandparents back in Worcester. At Vassar College she met the poet Marianne Moore, who encouraged her to give up plans for medical school and pursue a career in poetry. Bishop traveled through Canada, Europe, and South America, finally settling in Rio de Janeiro, where she lived for nearly twenty years. Her four volumes of poetry are *North and South* (1946); *A Cold Spring* (1955), which won the Pulitzer Prize; *Questions of Travel* (1965); and *Geography III* (1976), which won the National Book Critics' Circle Award. *Complete Poems 1929–1979* and *Collected Prose* gather most of her published work.

WILLIAM BLAKE
(1757–1828)

The son of a London haberdasher and his wife, William Blake studied drawing at ten and at fourteen was apprenticed to an engraver for seven years. After a first book of poems, *Poetical Sketches* (1783), he began experimenting with what he called "illuminated printing"—the words and pictures of each page were engraved in relief on copper, which was used to print sheets that were then partly colored by hand—a laborious and time-consuming process that resulted in books of singular beauty, no two of which are exactly alike. His great *Songs of Innocence and of Experience* (1794) were produced in this manner, as were his increasingly mythic and prophetic books, including *The Marriage of Heaven and Hell* (1793), *The Four Zoas* (1803), *Milton* (1804), and *Jerusalem* (1809). Blake devoted his later life to pictorial art, illustrating *The Canterbury Tales*, the Book of Job, and *The Divine Comedy*, on which he was hard at work when he died.

GWENDOLYN BROOKS
(1917–2000)

Gwendolyn Brooks was born in Topeka, Kansas, and raised in Chicago, where she began writing poetry at the age of seven, and where she graduated from Wilson Junior College in 1936. Shortly after beginning her formal study of modern poetry at Chicago's Southside Community Art Center, Brooks produced her first book of poems, *A Street in Bronzeville* (1945). With her second volume, *Annie Allen* (1949), she became the first African American to win the Pulitzer Prize. Though her early work focused on what Langston Hughes called the "ordinary aspects of black life," during the mid-1960s she devoted her poetry to raising African American consciousness and to social activism. In 1968, she was named the Poet Laureate of Illinois; from 1985 to 1986, she served as poetry consultant to the Library of Congress. Her *Selected Poems* appeared in 1999.

ELIZABETH BARRETT BROWNING
(1806–1861)

Elizabeth Barrett was born into a wealthy family in Durham, England, and raised in Herefordshire. She received no formal schooling, but was very well educated at home in the classics and in English literature, and published her first volume of poetry at the age of thirteen. Despite her status as a prominent woman of letters, deteriorating health forced Barrett to live in semi-seclusion. Her collection *Poems* (1844) inspired the poet Robert Browning to write to her in May 1845, and thus began a courtship that resulted in their eloping to Italy in 1846. Following the publication of *Sonnets from the Portuguese* (1850), Barrett Browning received serious consideration to succeed Wordsworth as Poet Laureate (although the laureateship went instead to Tennyson); one critic hailed her as "the greatest female poet that England has produced." Her most admired work is *Aurora Leigh* (1857), a nine-book verse novel.

ROBERT BROWNING
(1812–1889)

Born in London, Robert Browning attended London University but was largely self-educated, learning Latin, Greek, French, and Italian by the time he was fourteen. He was an accomplished but little-known poet and playwright when he began courting the already famous poet Elizabeth Barrett. After they eloped to Italy in 1846, the Brownings enjoyed a period of happiness during which they produced most of their best-known work. Following Elizabeth's death in 1861, Robert returned to England with their son and for the rest of his life enjoyed great literary and social success. His major collections are *Men and Women* (1855), dedicated to his wife, and *Dramatis Personae* (1864), which contains some of his finest dramatic monologues. Lionized as one of England's greatest poets by the time of his death, Browning is buried in Poets' Corner at Westminster Abbey.

ROBERT BURNS
(1759–1796)

Robert Burns was born and raised in Ayrshire, Scotland. The son of impoverished tenant farmers, he attended school sporadically but was largely self-taught. He collected subscriptions to publish his first collection, *Poems, Chiefly in the Scottish Dialect* (1786), which made his reputation in both Edinburgh and London. These poems were new in their rebellious individualism and in their pre-Romantic sensitivity to nature, yet they seemed to speak in an authentic "auld Scots" voice. A perennial failure as a farmer, Burns became a tax inspector and settled in the country town of Dumfries. Despite financial difficulties and failing health, he continued to write poems and songs (including "Auld Lang Syne") and devoted his last years to collecting Scottish folk songs for a cultural-preservation project. His work, frequently bawdy, politically zealous, and critical of organized religion, remains deeply loved throughout the world.

BUSON (1716–1784)

Born into a wealthy family in Kemu, Settsu province, Japan, Taniguchi Buson renounced a life of privilege to pursue a career in the arts. In 1751, after several years of traveling and studying under haiku masters in northeastern Japan, he settled in Kyoto and established himself as a professional painter. Known in later life as Yosa Buson, or simply Buson, he was responsible for a revival of the work of his prominent predecessor, Bashō. His own poems, regarded in Japan as second only to those of Bashō, display a subtle complexity and painterly attention to visual detail.

SAMUEL TAYLOR COLE-RIDGE (1772–1834)

Born in the small town of Ottery St. Mary in rural Devonshire, England, Samuel Taylor Coleridge is among the greatest and most original of the nineteenth-century Romantic poets. He wrote three of the most haunting and powerful poems in English—*The Rime of the Ancient Mariner* (1798), *Christabel* (1816), and "Kubla Khan" (1816)—as well as immensely influential literary criticism and a treatise on biology. In 1795, in the midst of a failed experiment to establish a "Pantisocracy" (his form of ideal community), he met William Wordsworth, and in 1798 they jointly published their enormously influential *Lyrical Ballads*. Coleridge's physical ailments, addiction to opium, and profound sense of despair made his life difficult and tumultuous and certainly affected his work. Still, he remains a central figure in English literature.

BILLY COLLINS (b. 1941)

Born in New York, Billy Collins received a B.A. from the College of the Holy Cross in Massachusetts and a Ph.D. from the University of California at Riverside before becoming a professor of English at Lehman College, City University of New York. His publications, several of which have broken sales records for poetry, include *Pokerface* (1977), *Video Poems* (1980), *The Apple That Astonished Paris* (1988), *Questions about Angels* (1991), *The Art of Drowning* (1995), *Picnic, Lightning* (1998), *Sailing Alone around the Room: New and Selected Poems* (2000), *Taking off Emily Dickinson's Clothes* (2000), *The Trouble with Poetry* (2005), and *Ballistics* (2008). He reads regularly on National Public Radio, performs live, and has recorded two spoken-word CDs, *The Best Cigarette* (1997) and *Billy Collins Live* (2005). He served two terms as Poet Laureate of the United States (2001–2003).

COUNTEE CULLEN (1903–1946)

During his own lifetime, Countee Cullen was the most celebrated and honored poet of the Harlem Renaissance, and he claimed New York City as his birthplace. In fact, he may have been born in Louisville, Kentucky, and the circumstances of his childhood adoption by the Reverend Frederick Cullen remain obscure. It is certain, though, that the poet received a good education at New York's DeWitt Clinton High School and then New York University. After receiving his M.A. at Harvard, Cullen returned to New York in 1926 and soon established himself as the leading figure in the Harlem literary world, winning numerous awards for his poetry and editing the influential monthly column "The Dark Tower" for *Opportunity: Journal of Negro Life*. A playwright, novelist, translator, and anthologist, Cullen is best remembered as a poet; his work has been collected in the volume *My Soul's High Song: The Collected Writings of Countee Cullen, Voice of the Harlem Renaissance* (1991).

E. E. CUMMINGS (1894–1962)

Born in Cambridge, Massachusetts, the son of a Congregationalist minister, Edward Estlin Cummings attended Harvard University, where he wrote poetry in the Pre-Raphaelite and Metaphysical traditions. He joined the ambulance corps in France the day after the United States entered World War I but was imprisoned by the French due to his outspokenness against the war; he transmuted the experience into his first literary success, the novel *The Enormous*

Room (1922). After the war, Cummings established himself as a poet and artist in New York City's Greenwich Village, made frequent trips to France and New Hampshire, and showed little interest in wealth or his growing celebrity. His variety of modernism was distinguished by its playfulness, its formal experimentation, its lyrical directness, and above all its celebration of the individual. His poetry is collected in *Complete Poems 1904–62* (1991).

JAMES DICKEY
(1923–1997)

James Dickey did not become seriously interested in poetry until he joined the Air Force in 1942. When he returned from World War II, he earned a B.A. and an M.A. at Vanderbilt University, publishing his first poem in *Sewanee Review* in his senior year. Following the publication of his first volume of poems, *Into the Stone* (1960), Dickey, while primarily a poet, worked in advertising, wrote novels, and taught at various universities. His 1965 collection, *Buckdancer's Choice*, received the National Book Award, and from 1967 to 1969 Dickey was Consultant in Poetry to the Library of Congress. He is widely known for his best-selling novel *Deliverance* (1970), which he later adapted for Hollywood. Other publications include *The Whole Motion: Collected Poems 1949–1992* (1992) and another novel, *To the White Sea* (1993).

EMILY DICKINSON
(1830–1886)

From childhood on, Emily Dickinson led a sequestered and obscure life. Yet her verse has traveled far beyond the cultured yet relatively circumscribed environment in which she lived: her room, her father's house, her family, a few close friends, and the small town of Amherst, Massachusetts. Indeed, along with Walt Whitman, her far more public contemporary, she all but invented American poetry. Born in Amherst, the daughter of a respected lawyer whom she revered ("His heart was pure and terrible," she once wrote), Dickinson studied for less than a year at the Mount Holyoke Female Seminary, returning permanently to her family home. She became more and more reclusive, dressing only in white, seeing no visitors, yet working

ceaselessly at her poems—nearly eighteen hundred in all, only a few of which were published during her lifetime. After her death, her sister Lavinia discovered the rest in a trunk, neatly bound into packets with blue ribbons—among the most important bodies of work in all of American literature.

JOHN DONNE
(1572–1631)

The first and greatest of the English writers who came to be known as the Metaphysical poets, John Donne wrote in a revolutionary style that combined highly intellectual conceits with complex, compressed phrasing. Born into an old Roman Catholic family at a time when Catholics were subject to constant harassment, Donne quietly abandoned his religion and had a promising legal career until a politically disastrous marriage ruined his worldly hopes. He struggled for years to support a large family; impoverished and despairing, he even wrote a treatise (*Biathanatos*) on the lawfulness of suicide. King James (who had ambitions for him as a preacher) eventually pressured Donne to take Anglican orders in 1615, and Donne became one of the great sermonizers of his day, rising to the position of dean of St. Paul's Cathedral in 1621. Donne's private devotions ("Meditations") were published in 1624, and he continued to write poetry until a few years before his death.

RITA DOVE (b. 1952)

A native of Akron, Ohio, Rita Dove attended Miami University in Ohio, studied for a year in West Germany as a Fulbright scholar, and received an M.F.A. in creative writing from the University of Iowa. She is now a professor of English at the University of Virginia as well as associate editor of *Callaloo*, a journal of African American arts and letters. In 1987, Dove became the second African American poet (after Gwendolyn Brooks, in 1950) to win the Pulitzer Prize (for *Thomas and Beulah*). In 1993, she was appointed Poet Laureate of the United States, ultimately serving two terms. Her books include *The Yellow House on the Corner* (1980), *Museum* (1983), *Grace Notes* (1989), *Mother Love* (1995), *On the Bus with Rosa Parks* (1999), and, most recently, *American Smooth* (2004). A tireless advocate for poetry, Dove edited *The Best American Poetry 2000*

and, from 2000 to 2002, authored the weekly column "Poet's Choice" in the *Washington Post Book World*.

PAUL LAURENCE DUNBAR (1872–1906)

The son of former slaves, Paul Laurence Dunbar was born in Dayton, Ohio. He attended a white high school, where he showed an early talent for writing and was elected class president. Unable to afford further education, he then worked as an elevator operator, writing poems and newspaper articles in his spare time. Dunbar took out a loan to subsidize the printing of his first book, *Oak and Ivy* (1893), but with the publication of *Majors and Minors* (1895) and *Lyrics of Lowly Life* (1896), his growing reputation enabled him to support himself by writing and lecturing. Though acclaimed during his lifetime for his lyrical use of rural black dialect in volumes such as *Candle-Lightin' Time* (1902), Dunbar was later criticized for adopting "white" literary conventions and accused of pandering to racist images of slaves and ex-slaves. He wrote novels and short stories in addition to poetry and dealt frankly with racial injustice in works such as *The Sport of the Gods* (1903) and *The Fourth of July and Race Outrages* (1903).

STEPHEN DUNN (b. 1939)

Born in New York, Stephen Dunn received a B.A. in history from Hofstra University, served in the armed forces, played professional basketball in Pennsylvania for a year, and afterward worked in advertising. In 1966, Dunn went to Spain "to try to change my life and see if I could write poetry"; in 1970, he earned an M.A. in creative writing from Syracuse University. Known for his clear, quietly powerful poems, Dunn has taught poetry at several universities, including Columbia, and has published many collections. Some of these are *Five Impersonations* (1971), *Full of Lust and Good Usage* (1976), *Work and Love* (1981), *Local Time* (1986), *Between Angels* (1989), *New and Selected Poems: 1974–1994* (1994), *Loosestrife* (1996), *Different Hours* (2000), which won the Pulitzer Prize, and *Everything Else in the World* (2008). *What Goes On: New and Selected Poems: 1995–2009* is due out in 2009.

T. S. ELIOT (1888–1965)

Thomas Stearns Eliot—from his formally experimental and oblique writings to his brilliant arguments in defense of "orthodoxy" and "tradition"—dominated the world of English poetry between the world wars. Born in St. Louis, Missouri, into a family that hailed from New England, Eliot studied literature and philosophy at Harvard and later in France and Germany. He went to England in 1914, read Greek philosophy at Oxford, and published his first major poem, "The Love Song of J. Alfred Prufrock," the next year. In 1922, with the help of Ezra Pound, Eliot published *The Waste Land*, which profoundly influenced a generation of poets and became a cornerstone of literary modernism. In his later work, particularly the *Four Quartets* (completed in 1945), Eliot explored religious questions in a quieter, more controlled idiom. By the middle of the twentieth century, Eliot was regarded as a towering figure in modern literature, renowned as a poet, critic, essayist, editor, and dramatist. He was awarded the Nobel Prize for Literature in 1948.

ROBERT FROST (1874–1963)

Though his poetry identifies Frost with rural New England, he was born and lived to the age of eleven in San Francisco. Moving to New England after his father's death, Frost studied classics in high school, entered and dropped out of both Dartmouth and Harvard, and spent difficult years as an unrecognized poet before his first book, *A Boy's Will* (1913), was accepted and published in England. Frost's character was full of contradiction—he held "that we get forward as much by hating as by loving"—yet by the end of his long life he was one of the most honored poets of his time, and the most widely read. In 1961, two years before his death, he was invited to read a poem at John F. Kennedy's presidential inauguration ceremony. Frost's poems—masterfully crafted, sometimes deceptively simple—are collected in *The Poetry of Robert Frost* (1969).

ALLEN GINSBERG
(1926–1997)

After a childhood in Paterson, New Jersey, overshadowed by his mother's mental illness, Allen Ginsberg enrolled at Columbia University, intent upon following his father's advice and becoming a labor lawyer. At the center of a circle that included Lucien Carr, Jack Kerouac, William S. Burroughs, and Neal Cassady, Ginsberg became interested in experimental poetry and alternative lifestyles. He graduated in 1948 and then joined the literary scene in San Francisco. In 1956, he published *Howl and Other Poems*, with an introduction by his mentor William Carlos Williams. The title poem, which condemned bourgeois culture and celebrated the emerging counterculture, became a manifesto for the Beat movement and catapulted Ginsberg to fame. Deeply involved in radical politics and Eastern spiritualism, Ginsberg went on to write such prose works as *Declaration of Independence for Dr. Timothy Leary* (1971) in addition to many volumes of poetry. His *Collected Poems, 1947–1980* appeared in 1984 and *Selected Poems 1947–1995* in 1996.

ANGELINA GRIMKÉ
(1880–1958)

Born in Boston, Angelina Grimké was the descendent of black slaves, white slaveholders, free blacks, and prominent white abolitionists, including her namesake, Angelina Weld Grimké. As a child, Angelina was abandoned by her white mother, whose middle-class family disapproved of her marriage to Archibald Grimké, a biracial lawyer and author who eventually became vice president of the NAACP. Grimké graduated from the Boston Normal School of Gymnastics in 1902 and then moved with her father to Washington, DC, where she worked as a teacher and began to write poetry, essays, short stories, and plays. By the 1920s, she was publishing her work in the leading journals and anthologies of the Harlem Renaissance—*The Crisis, Opportunity,* Alain Locke's *The New Negro* (1925), Countee Cullen's *Caroling Dusk* (1927), and Robert Kerlin's *Negro Poets and Their Poems* (1928). Much of her finest writing can be found in *Selected Works of Angelina Weld Grimké* (1991).

ROBERT HAYDEN
(1913–1980)

Robert Hayden was born Asa Bundy Sheffey, in Detroit, Michigan, and raised by foster parents. He studied at Detroit City College (later Wayne State University), but left in 1936 to work for the Federal Writers' Project, where he researched black history and folk culture. He received an M.A. from the University of Michigan, taught at Fisk University from 1949 until 1969, and then taught at Michigan until his retirement. Although he published ten volumes of poetry, he did not receive acclaim until late in life. His collections include *Heart-Shape in the Dust* (1940), *The Lion and the Archer, Figures of Time* (1955), *A Ballad of Remembrance* (1962), *Selected Poems* (1966), *Words in the Mourning Time* (1970), *Night-Blooming Cereus* (1972), *Angle of Ascent* (1975), *American Journal* (1978 and 1982), and *Collected Poems* (1985).

SEAMUS HEANEY
(b. 1939)

Seamus Heaney, whose poems explore themes of rural life, memory, and history, was born on a farm in Mossbawn, County Derry (Castledawson, Londonderry), Northern Ireland. Educated at Queen's University in Belfast, he has taught at the University of California at Berkeley, Carysfort College in Dublin, Oxford University and Harvard. Once called by Robert Lowell "the most important Irish poet since Yeats," Heaney received the 1995 Nobel Prize for Literature. His poetry collections include *Eleven Poems* (1965), *Death of a Naturalist* (1966), *Wintering Out* (1972), *The Haw Lantern* (1987), *Seeing Things* (1991), *The Spirit Level* (1996), *Electric Light* (2001), and *District and Circle* (2006). Heaney's translation of *Beowulf* (2000) from Anglo-Saxon into modern English gave new life to the oldest of English poems; it not only won Britain's prestigious Whitbread Award but also become a best-seller.

GERARD MANLEY HOPKINS (1844–1889)

Born the eldest of eight children of a marine-insurance adjuster and his wife, Gerard Manley Hopkins attended Oxford, where his ambition was to become a painter—until, at the age of 22, he converted to Roman Catholicism and burned all his early poetry as too worldly. Not until after his seminary training and ordination as a Jesuit priest, in 1877, did he resume writing poetry, though he made few attempts to publish his verse, which many of his contemporaries found nearly incomprehensible. Near the end of his life, Hopkins was appointed professor of Greek at University College, Dublin, where—out of place, deeply depressed, and all but unknown—he died of typhoid. His poetry, collected and published by his friends, has been championed by modern poets, who admire its controlled tension, strong rhythm, and sheer exuberance.

LANGSTON HUGHES
(1902–1967)

Born in Joplin, Missouri, Langston Hughes was raised mainly by his maternal grandmother, though he lived intermittently with each of his parents. He studied at Columbia University, but left to travel and work at a variety of jobs. Having already published poems in periodicals, anthologies, and his own first collection, *The Weary Blues* (1926), he graduated from Lincoln University; published a successful novel, *Not without Laughter* (1930); and became a major writer in the intellectual and literary movement called the Harlem Renaissance. During the 1930s, he became involved in radical politics and traveled the world as a correspondent and columnist; during the 1950s, though, the FBI classified him as a security risk and limited his ability to travel. In addition to poems and novels, he wrote essays, plays, screenplays, and an autobiography; he also edited anthologies of literature and folklore. His *Collected Poems* appeared in 1994.

BEN JONSON
(1572?–1637)

Poet, playwright, actor, scholar, critic, and translator, Ben Jonson was the posthumous son of a clergyman and the stepson of a master bricklayer of Westminster. Jonson had an eventful early life, going to war against the Spanish, working as an actor, killing an associate in a duel, and converting to Roman Catholicism. Meanwhile, Jonson wrote a number of plays that have remained popular to this day, including *Every Man in His Humour* (in which Shakespeare acted a leading role; 1598), *Volpone* (1606), and *The Alchemist* (1610). He was named Poet Laureate in 1616 and spent the latter part of his life at the center of a large circle of friends and admirers known as the "Tribe of Ben." Often considered the first English author to deem writing his primary career, he published *The Works of Benjamin Jonson* in 1616.

JOHN KEATS (1795–1821)

Because John Keats was the son of a London livery stable owner and his wife, reviewers would later disparage him as a working-class "Cockney poet." At fifteen he was apprenticed to a surgeon, and at twenty-one he became a licensed pharmacist—in the same year that his first two published poems, including the sonnet "On First Looking into Chapman's Homer," appeared in *The Examiner*, a journal edited by the critic and poet Leigh Hunt. Hunt introduced Keats to such literary figures as the poet Percy Bysshe Shelley and helped him publish his *Poems by John Keats* (1817). When his second book, the long poem *Endymion* (1818), was fiercely attacked by critics, Keats, suffering from a steadily worsening case of tuberculosis, knew that he would not live to realize his poetic promise. In July 1820, he published *Lamia, Isabella, The Eve of St. Agnes, and Other Poems*, which contained the poignant "To Autumn" and three other great odes: "Ode on a Grecian Urn," "Ode on Melancholy," and "Ode to a Nightingale"; early the next year, he died in Rome. In the years after Keats's death, his letters became almost as famous as his poetry.

GALWAY KINNELL
(b. 1927)

Born in Providence, Rhode Island, Galway Kinnell earned a B.A. from Princeton and an M.A. from the University of Rochester. He served in the navy and has been a journalist, a civil-rights field-worker, and a teacher at numerous colleges and universities. His early poetry, collected in *What a Kingdom It Was* (1960) and *First Poems 1946–1954* (1970), is highly formal; his subsequent work employs a more colloquial style. "Poetry," he has said, "is the attempt to find a language that can speak the unspeakable." He received both a Pulitzer Prize and the American Book Award for *Selected Poems* (1982), and in 2000 he culled *A New Selected Poems* from eight collections spanning twenty-four years. He lives in New York and Vermont.

ETHERIDGE KNIGHT
(1931–1991)

A native of Corinth, Mississippi, Etheridge Knight spent much of his adolescence carousing in pool halls, bars, and juke joints, developing a skillful oratorical style in an environment that prized verbal agility. During this time he also became addicted to narcotics. He served in the U.S. Army from 1947 to 1951; in 1960 he was sentenced to eight years in prison for robbery. At the Indiana State Prison in Michigan City, he began to write poetry and in 1968 published his first collection, *Poems from Prison*. After his release, Knight joined the Black Arts movement, taught at a number of universities, and published works including *Black Voices from Prison* (1970), *Belly Song and Other Poems* (1973), and *Born of a Woman* (1980).

ANDREW MARVELL
(1621–1678)

The son of a clergyman and his wife, Andrew Marvell was born in Yorkshire, England, and educated at Trinity College, Cambridge. There is no evidence that he fought in the English Civil War, which broke out in 1642, but his poem "An Horatian Ode upon Cromwell's Return from Ireland" appeared in 1650, shortly after the beheading of King Charles I in 1649, and may represent straightforward praise of England's new Puritan leader. Some regard it as strong satire, however—Marvell was known in his day for his satirical prose and verse. Today he is better known for lyric poems such as the *carpe diem* manifesto "To His Coy Mistress," which he probably wrote while serving as tutor to a Yorkshire nobleman's daughter. In 1657, on the recommendation of John Milton, Marvell accepted a position in Cromwell's government that he held until his election to Parliament in 1659. After helping restore the monarchy in 1660, he continued to write and to serve as a member of Parliament until the end of his life.

CLAUDE MCKAY
(1889–1948)

Festus Claudius McKay was born and raised in Sunny Ville, Clarendon Parish, Jamaica, the youngest of eleven children. He worked as a wheelwright and cabinetmaker, then briefly as a police constable, before writing and publishing two books of poetry in Jamaican dialect. In 1912, he emigrated to the United States, where he attended Booker T. Washington's Tuskegee Institute in Alabama, studied agricultural science at Kansas State College, and then moved to New York City. McKay supported himself through various jobs while becoming a prominent literary and political figure. The oldest Harlem Renaissance writer, McKay was also the first to publish, with the poetry collection *Harlem Shadows* (1922). His other works include the novels *Home to Harlem* (1928) and *Banana Bottom* (1933), and his autobiography, *A Long Way from Home* (1937).

JAMES MERRILL
(1926–1995)

Born to wealth in New York City (his father co-founded the Merrill Lynch brokerage house), James Merrill was a precocious poet whose first collection, *Jim's Book*, was printed privately when he was only sixteen. After college at Amherst, which was interrupted by a year of military service, Merrill began teaching at Bard College and soon started publishing poetry, plays, and fiction. *First Poems* (1951) was followed by many other verse collections, including two National Book Award–winners, *Nights and Days* (1966) and *Mirabell* (1979); the Pulitzer Prize–winning *Divine Comedies* (1976); *From the First Nine: Poems 1946–1976* (1982); and *The Inner Room* (1988). His masterpiece, *The Changing Light at Sandover* (1982), grew out of spiritualist sessions with a Ouija board that Merrill conducted with his partner, David Jackson. Merrill served as Chancellor of the Academy of American Poets from 1979 until his death.

EDNA ST. VINCENT MILLAY (1892–1950)

Born in Rockland, Maine, Edna St. Vincent Millay published her first poem at twenty, her first poetry collection at twenty-five. After graduating from

Vassar College, she moved to New York City's Greenwich Village, where she both gained a reputation as a brilliant poet and became notorious for her bohemian life and her association with prominent artists, writers, and radicals. In 1923, she won the Pulitzer Prize for her collection *The Ballad of the Harp-Weaver*; in 1925, growing weary of fame, she and her husband moved to Austerlitz, New York, where she lived for the rest of her life. Although her work fell out of favor with mid-twentieth century modernists, who rejected her formalism as old-fashioned, her poetry—witty, acerbic, and superbly crafted—has found many new admirers today.

JOHN MILTON
(1608–1674)

Born in London, the elder son of a self-made businessman and his wife, John Milton exhibited unusual literary and scholarly gifts at an early age; before entering Cambridge University, he was adept at Latin and Greek and was well on his way to mastering Hebrew and a number of European languages. After graduation, he spent six more years of intense study and composed, among other works, his great pastoral elegy, "Lycidas" (1637). After a year of travel in Europe, Milton return to England and found his country embroiled in religious strife and civil war. Milton took up the Puritan cause and, in 1641, began writing pamphlets defending everything from free speech to Cromwell's execution of Charles I; Milton also served as Cromwell's Latin secretary until, in 1651, he lost his sight. After the monarchy was restored in 1660, Milton was briefly imprisoned, and his property confiscated. Blind, impoverished, and isolated, he devoted himself to the great spiritual epics of his later years: *Paradise Lost* (1667), *Paradise Regained* (1671), and *Samson Agonistes* (1671).

MARIANNE MOORE
(1887–1972)

Born in Kirkwood, Missouri, Marianne Moore was raised in Carlisle, Pennsylvania. After receiving a degree in biology from Bryn Mawr College, she studied business at Carlisle Commercial College, taught stenography at the U.S. Industrial Indian School in Carlisle, and traveled to Europe. She and her mother moved first to

New Jersey and then to New York's Greenwich Village before settling, in 1918, in Brooklyn, New York. From 1921 to 1925, Moore was a librarian at the New York Public Library. She had written and published poetry while still in college, but did not publish her first collection until 1921. A prolific critic, she also edited the influential modernist magazine *Dial* from 1926 to 1929. Her *Collected Poems* (1951) won the Bollingen Prize, the Pulitzer Prize, and a National Book Award and made her a public figure. Her *Complete Poems* appeared in 1967.

PAT MORA (b. 1942)

Born to Mexican American parents in El Paso, Texas, Pat Mora earned a B.A. and an M.A. from the University of Texas at El Paso. She has been a consultant on U.S.–Mexico youth exchanges; a museum director and administrator at her alma mater; and a teacher of English at all levels. Her poetry—collected in *Chants* (1985), *Borders* (1986), *Communion* (1991), *Agua Santa* (1995), and *Aunt Carmen's Book of Practical Saints* (1997)—reflects and addresses her Chicana and southwestern background. Mora's other publications include *Nepantla: Essays from the Land in the Middle* (1993); a family memoir, *House of Houses* (1997); and many works for children and young adults.

HARRYETTE MULLEN
(b. 1953)

Born in Alabama, but raised mostly in Texas, Harryette Mullen had her first poem published in the local paper when she was still in high school. "Writing became important to me when I was very young," she has said. "It was the only way I could communicate with my father after my parents were divorced." She was also encouraged by a mother who passionately "believed in educating the whole child," and her "sense of poetry was awakened," she says, "by the formal and informal, written and oral rhymes and rhythms of family, church, and school." Her first collection, *Tree Tall Woman*, appeared in 1981, six years after her graduation from the University of Texas at Austin, and many of these poems are reprinted in her 2002 collection *Blues Baby: Early Poems*. Her four other books of poetry are *Trimmings*

(1991), dubbed by *Partisan Review* "an ebulliently feminist, black and bluesy, bebop, wicked, scatty, addictive sequence of mazy prose poems"; *S*PeRM**K*T* (1992), a serious and funny exploration of the American consumer culture; *Muse and Drudge* (1995); and *Sleeping with the Dictionary* (2002), a finalist for the National Book Award for Poetry, the National Book Critics Circle Award, and the *Los Angeles Times* Book Award. Mullen, who earned her Ph.D. at the University of California, Santa Cruz in 1990, has also published essays in journals such as *Callaloo*, *Antioch Review*, and *MELUS*, which awarded her its Katherine Newman Award for Best Essay in 1996. Currently a professor at UCLA, Mullen teaches creative writing and African-American literature.

HOWARD NEMEROV
(1920–1991)

Born and raised in New York City, Howard Nemerov graduated from Harvard University, served in the U.S. Army Air Corps during World War II, and returned to New York to complete his first book, *The Image and the Law* (1948). He taught at a number of colleges and universities and published books of poetry, plays, short stories, novels, and essays. His *Collected Poems* won the Pulitzer Prize and the National Book Award in 1978. He served as Consultant in Poetry to the Library of Congress from 1963 to 1964, and Poet Laureate of the United States from 1988 to 1990. *Trying Conclusions: New and Selected Poems 1961–1991* was published in 1991.

SHARON OLDS (b. 1942)

Born in San Francisco, Sharon Olds earned a B.A. from Stanford University and a Ph.D. from Columbia University. She was founding chair of the Writing Program at Goldwater Hospital (a public facility for the severely physically disabled), and she currently teaches in New York University's Creative Writing Program. She has received a National Endowment for the Arts Grant and a Guggenheim Fellowship, and served as New York State Poet Laureate from 1998 to 2000. Her books include *Satan Says* (1980); the National Book Critics Circle Award–winning *The Dead and the Living* (1983); *The Gold Cell* (1987); *The Father* (1992); *The*

Wellspring (1997); *Blood, Tin, Straw* (1999); and *The Unswept Room*, a National Book Award nominee in 2002. Her *Strike Sparks: Selected Poems: 1980–2002* appeared in 2004.

WILFRED OWEN
(1893–1918)

Born in Oswestry, Shropshire, England, Wilfred Owen left school in 1911, having failed to win a scholarship to London University. He served as assistant to a vicar in Oxfordshire until 1913, when he left to teach English at a Berlitz school in Bordeaux. In 1915, Owen returned to England to enlist in the army and was sent to the front lines in France. Suffering from shell shock two years later, he was evacuated to Craiglockhart War Hospital, where he met the poets Siegfried Sassoon and Robert Graves. Five of Owen's poems were published in 1918, the year he returned to combat; he was killed one week before the signing of the armistice. His poems, which portray the horror of trench warfare and satirize the unthinking patriotism of those who cheered the war from their armchairs, are collected in the two-volume *Complete Poems and Fragments* (1983).

DOROTHY PARKER
(1893–1967)

Born in West End, New Jersey, Dorothy Rothschild worked for both *Vogue* and *Vanity Fair* magazines before becoming a freelance writer. In 1917, she married Edwin Pond Parker II, whom she divorced in 1928. Her first book of verse, *Enough Rope* (1926), was a best-seller and was followed by *Sunset Gun* (1928), *Death and Taxes* (1931), and *Collected Poems: Not So Deep as a Well* (1936). In 1927, Parker became a book reviewer for *The New Yorker*, to which she contributed for most of her career. In 1933, Parker and her second husband, Alan Campbell, moved to Hollywood, where they collaborated as film writers. In addition, Parker wrote criticism, two plays, short stories, and news reports from the Spanish Civil War. She is probably best remembered, though, as the reigning wit at the "Round Table" at Manhattan's Algonquin Hotel, where, in the 1920s and '30s, she traded barbs with other prominent writers and humorists.

LINDA PASTAN (b. 1932)

Linda Pastan was born in New York City and raised in nearby Westchester County. After graduating from Radcliffe College, she received an M.A. in literature from Brandeis University. Although her first published poems appeared in *Mademoiselle* in 1955, Pastan spent many years concentrating on her husband and children—indeed, much of her poetry deals with her own family life. Her many collections include *A Perfect Circle of Sun* (1971), *The Five Stages of Grief* (1978), American Book Award nominee *PM/AM: New and Selected Poems* (1982), *Carnival Evening: New and Selected Poems 1968–1998* (1998), and *Queen of a Rainy Country* (2006). She lives in Potomac, Maryland, and was named Poet Laureate of Maryland in 1991.

MARGE PIERCY (b. 1936)

Born and raised in Detroit, Marge Piercy received a B.A. from the University of Michigan and an M.A. from Northwestern University. She taught for some time before the success of her novels allowed her to move to Cape Cod. While her well-known early poetry is vigorously feminist and political, her later work draws more upon her love of nature and her Jewish heritage. Her many poetry collections include *Living in the Open* (1976), *The Moon Is Always Female* (1980), *Stone, Paper, Knife* (1983), *Available Light* (1988), *Mars and Her Children* (1992), *What Are Big Girls Made Of?* (1997), and *The Art of Blessing the Day: Poems with a Jewish Theme* (2000). Even more widely known as a novelist, Piercy's most recent fictional works are *Three Women* (1999) and *Sex Wars: A Novel of Gilded Age New York* (2005).

SYLVIA PLATH

(1932–1963)

Sylvia Plath was born in Boston; her father, a Polish immigrant, died when she was eight. After graduating from Smith College, Plath attended Cambridge University on a Fulbright scholarship, and there she met and married the poet Ted Hughes, with whom she had two children. As she documented in her novel *The Bell Jar* (1963), in 1953—between her junior and senior years of college—Plath became seriously depressed, attempted suicide, and was hospitalized. In 1963, the break-up of her marriage led to another suicide attempt, this time successful. Plath has attained cult status as much for her poems as for her "martyrdom" to art and life. In addition to her first volume of poetry, *The Colossus* (1960), Plath's work has been collected in *Ariel* (1966), *Crossing the Water* (1971), and *Winter Trees* (1972). Her selected letters were published in 1975; her expurgated journals in 1983; and her unabridged journals in 2000.

EZRA POUND

(1885–1972)

Born in Hailey, Idaho, Ezra Pound studied at the University of Pennsylvania and Hamilton College before traveling to Europe in 1908. He remained there, living in Ireland, England, France, and Italy, for much of his life. Pound's tremendous ambition—to succeed in his own work and to influence the development of poetry and Western culture in general—led him to found the Imagist school of poetry, to advise and assist many great writers (Eliot, Joyce, Williams, Frost, and Hemingway, to name a few), and to write a number of highly influential critical works. His increasingly fiery and erratic behavior led to a charge of treason (he served as a propagandist for Mussolini during World War II), a diagnosis of insanity, and twelve years at St. Elizabeth's, an institution for the criminally insane. His verse is collected in *Personae: The Collected Poems* (1949) and *The Cantos* (1976).

ADRIENNE RICH

(b. 1929)

Adrienne Rich was born in Baltimore. Since the selection of her first volume by W. H. Auden for the Yale Series of Younger Poets (1951), her work has continually evolved, from the tightly controlled early poems to the politically and personally charged verse for which she is known today. Rich's books of poetry include *Collected Early Poems 1950–1970* (1993), *The Dream of a Common Language* (1978), *Your Native Land, Your Life* (1986), *Time's Power* (1988), *An Atlas of the Difficult World* (1991), *Dark Fields of the Republic* (1995), *Midnight Salvage* (1999), *Fox* (2001), and

The School among the Ruins (2004). Her prose works include *Of Woman Born: Motherhood as Experience and Institution* (1976), *On Lies, Secrets, and Silence* (1979), and *Blood, Bread, and Poetry* (1986), all influential feminist texts; *What Is Found There: Notebooks on Poetry and Politics* (1993); and *Arts of the Possible: Essays and Conversations* (2001). Her many awards include a Mac-Arthur Fellowship and a Lanning Foundation Lifetime Achievement Award.

ALBERTO ÁLVARO RÍOS
(b. 1952)

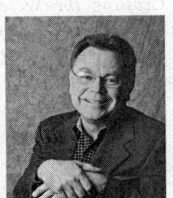

Born in the border city of Nogales, Arizona to an English mother and a Mexican father, Alberto Ríos grew up speaking both Spanish and English, though today he recalls being punished for speaking Spanish in school. Ríos attended the University of Arizona, earning a B.A. in literature and another in psychology, as well as an M.F.A. in creative writing. The author of three short-story collections and an award-winning memoir, Ríos has also published nine books of poetry, including, most recently, *The Smallest Muscle in the Human Body* (a finalist for the 2002 National Book Award) and *The Theater of Night* (2007). In addition to fellowships from the Guggenheim Foundation and National Endowment for the Arts, Ríos's numerous awards include the Western Literature Association Distinguished Achievement Award, the Academy of American Poets Walt Whitman Award, and six Pushcart Prizes (for both poetry and fiction). His work has also appeared in a range of prestigious periodicals and in more than 200 anthologies. For more than twenty-five years Ríos has taught at Arizona State, where he currently serves as a Regents' Professor and holds an endowed chair. Married to Lupita Barron since 1979, he has one son.

THEODORE ROETHKE
(1908–1963)

Born in Saginaw, Michigan, Theodore Roethke grew up around his father's twenty-five-acre greenhouse complex; plants and their associations with nurture and growth were an important subject in his later poetry. He worked for a time at Lafayette College, where he was professor of English and tennis coach, and later at the University of Washington, which appointed him poet-in-residence one year before he died. Roethke suffered from periodic mental breakdowns, yet the best of his poetry, with its reverence for and fear of the physical world, seems destined to last. His books include *Open House* (1942), *Praise to the End!* (1951), *The Far Field* (1964), which received a posthumous National Book Award, and *Collected Poems* (1966).

LIZ ROSENBERG
(b. 1956)

A native of Long Island, New York, Liz Rosenberg received a B.A. from Bennington College, an M.A. from Johns Hopkins University, and a Ph.D. from the State University of New York at Binghamton, where she teaches creative writing. She has published several books of poetry, including *The Angel Poems* (1984), *The Fire Music* (1985), *Children of Paradise* (1994), *These Happy Days* (2000) and *17* (2002); a novel, *Heart and Soul* (1996); and numerous children's books such as *Eli's Night-Light*, illustrated by Joanna Yardley (2001), and *We Wanted You*, illustrated by Peter Catalanotto (2002). In addition, she is a book columnist for *The Boston Globe*.

CHRISTINA ROSSETTI
(1830–1894)

The daughter of Italian political refugees, Christina Rossetti was born in London and educated at home. Though associated with the Pre-Raphaelite group of artists and writers through her brother, Dante Gabriel Rossetti, Christina withdrew into the more personal world of her quiet but intense devotion to poetry and Anglican spirituality. Published under the pseudonym "Ellen Alleyn," her first poems appeared when she was only eighteen; her first adult collection, *Goblin Market and Other Poems* (1862), was a popular and critical success. Never marrying, Rossetti instead devoted herself to her writing and to a variety of moral and educational causes. Her collected *Poetical Works* (1904) was published a decade after her death.

WILLIAM SHAKESPEARE
(1554–1616)

Considering the great fame of his work, surprisingly little is known of William Shakespeare's life. Between 1585 and 1592, he left his birthplace of

Stratford-upon-Avon for London to begin a career as playwright and actor. No dates of his professional career are recorded, however, nor can the order in which he composed his plays and poetry be determined with any certainty. By 1594, he had established himself as a poet with two long works—*Venus and Adonis* and *The Rape of Lucrece*—and his more than 150 sonnets are supreme expressions of the form. His reputation, though, rests on the works he wrote for the theater. Shakespeare produced perhaps thirty-five plays in twenty-five years, proving himself a master of every dramatic genre: tragedy (in works such as *Macbeth*, *Hamlet*, *King Lear*, and *Othello*); historical drama (for example, *Richard III* and *Henry IV*); comedy (*Twelfth Night*, *As You Like It*, and many more); and romance (in plays such as *The Tempest* and *Cymbaline*). Without question, Shakespeare is the most quoted, discussed, and beloved English writer.

WALLACE STEVENS
(1879–1955)

Born and raised in Reading, Pennsylvania, Wallace Stevens attended Harvard University and New York Law School. In New York City, he worked for a number of law firms, published poems in magazines, and befriended such literary figures as William Carlos Williams and Marianne Moore. In 1916, Stevens moved to Connecticut and began working for the Hartford Accident and Indemnity Company, where he became a vice-president in 1934 and where he worked for the rest of his life, writing poetry at night and during vacations. He published his first collection, *Harmonium*, in 1923, and followed it with a series of volumes from 1935 until 1950, establishing himself as one of the twentieth century's most important poets. His lectures were collected in *The Necessary Angel: Essays on Reality and Imagination* (1951); his *Collected Poems* appeared in 1954.

ALFRED, LORD TENNY-
SON (1809–1892)

Certainly the most popular and perhaps the most important of the Victorian poets, Alfred, Lord Tennyson demonstrated his talents at an early age; he published his first volume in 1827. Encouraged to devote his life to poetry by a group of undergraduates at Cambridge University known as the "Apostles," Tennyson was particularly close to Arthur Hallam, whose sudden death in 1833 inspired the long elegy *In Memoriam* (1850). With that poem he achieved lasting fame and recognition; he was appointed Poet Laureate the year of its publication, succeeding Wordsworth. Despite the great popularity of his "journalistic" poems—"The Charge of the Light Brigade" (1854) is perhaps the best known—Tennyson's great theme was the past, both personal (*In the Valley of Cauteretz*, 1864) and national (*Idylls of the King*, 1869). Tennyson was made a baron in 1884; when he died, eight years later, he was buried in Poets' Corner in Westminster Abbey.

DYLAN THOMAS
(1914–1953)

Born in Swansea, Wales, into what he called "the smug darkness of a provincial town," Dylan Thomas published his first book, *Eighteen Poems* (1934), at twenty, in the same year that he moved to London. Thereafter he had a successful, though turbulent, career publishing poetry, short stories, and plays, including the highly successful *Under Milk Wood* (1954). In his last years he supported himself with lecture tours and poetry readings in the United States, but his excessive drinking caught up with him, and he died in New York City of chronic alcoholism. His *Collected Poems, 1934–1952* (1952) was the last book he published during his short lifetime; his comic novel, *Adventures in the Skin Trade*, was never completed.

DEREK WALCOTT
(b. 1930)

Born of mixed heritage on the West Indian island of St. Lucia, Derek Walcott grew up speaking French and patois but was educated in English. In 1953, he earned his B.A. in English, French, and Latin from the University College of the West Indies in Jamaica. In 1950, with his twin brother, Roderick, he founded the St. Lucia Arts Guild, a dramatic society; nine years later, he founded the Little Carib Theatre Workshop in Trinidad, which he ran until 1976, writing many plays for production there. Walcott has published many volumes of poetry, including *In a Green Night* (1962), *The Castaway* (1965), *Another Life* (1973), *Sea Grapes* (1976), *The Fortunate Traveller* (1981), *Omeros* (1990), *The Bounty* (1997), *Tiepolo's Hound* (2000), and *The Prodigal: A Poem* (2004).

His work draws on diverse influences, from West Indian folk tales to Homer to Yeats. The first Caribbean poet to win the Nobel Prize (in 1992), Walcott now lives and teaches in the United States.

WALT WHITMAN
(1819–1892)

Walt Whitman was born on a farm in West Hills, Long Island, to a British father and a Dutch mother. After working as a journalist throughout New York for many years, he taught for a time and founded his own newspaper, *The Long Islander*, in 1838; he then left journalism to work on *Leaves of Grass*, originally intended as a poetic treatise on American democratic idealism. Published privately in multiple editions from 1855 to 1874, the book at first failed to reach a mass audience. In 1881, Boston's Osgood and Company published another edition of *Leaves of Grass*, which sold well until the district attorney called it "obscene literature" and stipulated that Whitman remove certain poems and phrases. He refused, and it was many years before his works were again published, this time in Philadelphia. By the time Whitman died, his work was revered, as it still is today, for its greatness of spirit and its exuberant American voice.

RICHARD WILBUR
(b. 1921)

Born in New York City and raised in New Jersey, Richard Wilbur received his B.A. from Amherst College and his M.A. from Harvard. He started to write while serving as an army cryptographer during World War II, and his collections *The Beautiful Changes* (1947) and *Ceremony* (1950) established his reputation as a serious poet. In addition to subsequent volumes such as the Pulitzer Prize–winning *Things of This World* (1956), *Walking to Sleep* (1969), *The Mind Reader* (1976), the Pulitzer Prize–winning *New and Collected Poems* (1988), and *Mayflies: New Poems and Translations* (2000), he has published children's books, critical essays, and numerous translations of classic French works by Racine and Molière. He has taught at various colleges and universities, including Harvard, Wellesley, Wesleyan, and Smith. In 1987, he was named Poet Laureate of the United States.

WILLIAM CARLOS WILLIAMS
(1883–1963)

Born in Rutherford, New Jersey, William Carlos Williams attended school in Switzerland and New York and studied medicine at the University of Pennsylvania and the University of Leipzig in Germany. He spent most of his life in Rutherford, practicing medicine and gradually establishing himself as one of the great figures in American poetry. Early in his writing career he left the European-inspired Imagist movement in favor of a more uniquely American poetic style comprised of vital, local language, and "no ideas but in things." His shorter poems have been published in numerous collected editions and other volumes, including the Pulitzer Prize-winning *Brueghel, and Other Poems* (1963); his five-volume philosophical poem, *Paterson*, was published in 1963. Among his other works are plays such as *A Dream of Love* (1948) and *Many Loves* (1950); a trilogy of novels—*White Mules* (1937), *In the Money* (1940), and *The Build-Up* (1952); his *Autobiography* (1951); his *Selected Essays* (1954); and his *Selected Letters* (1957).

WILLIAM WORDS-
WORTH (1770–1850)

Regarded by many as the greatest of the Romantic poets, William Wordsworth was born in Cockermouth in the English Lake District, a beautiful, mountainous region that his poetry helped make a popular tourist destination even in his own lifetime. He studied at Cambridge and then spent a year in France, hoping to witness the French Revolution firsthand; as the Revolution's "glorious renovation" dissolved into anarchy and then tyranny, Wordsworth was forced to return to England. Remarkably, he managed to establish "a saving intercourse with my true self" and to write some of his finest poetry, including the early version of his masterpiece, *The Prelude*, which first appeared in 1805 and then again, much altered, in 1850. In 1798, Wordsworth and his friend Samuel Taylor Coleridge published *Lyrical Ballads*, which contained many of their greatest poems and can be considered the founding document of English Romanticism. Wordsworth was revered by the reading public and in 1843 was named Poet Laureate.

WILLIAM BUTLER YEATS
(1865–1939)

William Butler Yeats was born in Dublin and, though he spent most of his youth in London, became the pre-eminent Irish poet of the twentieth century. Immersed in Irish history, folklore, and politics, as well as spiritualism and the occult, he attended art school for a time but left to devote himself to poetry that was, early in his career, self-consciously dreamy and ethereal. Yeats's poems became tighter and more passionate with his reading of philoso-phers such as Nietzsche, his involvement (mainly through theater) with the Irish nationalist cause, and his desperate love for the actress and nationalist Maud Gonne. He was briefly a senator in the newly independent Irish government before withdrawing from active public life to Thoor Ballylee, a crumbling Norman tower that Yeats and his wife fashioned into a home. There he developed an elaborate mythology (published as *A Vision* in 1925) and wrote poems that explored fundamental questions of history and identity. He was awarded the Nobel Prize for Literature in 1923. His works, in many genres, have been selected and collected in various editions.

Drama: Reading, Responding, Writing

READING, RESPONDING, WRITING

Drama

Drama: Reading, Responding, Writing

As noted in the introduction, many cultures have had oral literatures: histories, romances, poems to be recited or sung. Our own era has its share of oral art forms, of course, but "literary" fiction and poetry are now most often read privately, silently, from the printed page. Most contemporary fiction writers and poets write with an understanding that their work will be experienced and enjoyed this way.

In contrast, **drama** is written primarily to be performed—by actors, on a stage, for an audience. Playwrights work with an understanding that the words on the page are just the first step—a map of sorts—toward the ultimate goal: a collaborative, publicly performed work of art. They create plays fully aware of the possibilities that go beyond printed words and extend to physical actions, stage devices, and other theatrical techniques for creating special effects and modifying audience responses. Although the script of a play may be the most essential piece in the puzzle that makes up the final work of art, the play text is not the final, complete work.

To attend a play—that is, to be part of an audience—represents a very different kind of experience from the usually solitary act of reading. On the stage, real human beings, standing for imaginary characters, deliver lines and perform actions for you to see and hear. In turn, the actors adapt in subtle ways to the reactions of the people who attend the performance and whose responses are no longer wholly private but have become, in part, communal.

When you attend the performance of a play, then, you become a collaborator in the creation of a unique work of art: not the play *text* but instead a specific *interpretation* of that text. No two performances of a play can ever be identical, just as no two interpretations of a play can be exactly the same.

READING DRAMA

In many respects, of course, reading drama is similar to reading fiction. In both cases we anticipate what will happen next; we imagine the characters, settings, and actions; we respond to the symbolic suggestiveness of images; and we notice thematic patterns that are likely to matter in the end. But because most plays are written to be performed, reading plays is also somewhat different from reading fiction or poetry on the printed page. In narrative fiction, for example, there is a mediator or narrator, someone standing between us and the events to help us relate to the characters, actions, and meanings. In contrast, drama rarely has such an interpreter or mediator to tell us what is happening or to shape our responses. Play texts instead rely on **stage directions** (the italicized descriptions of the set, characters, and actions), while **exposition** (the explanation of the past and current situation) emerges only here and there in the dialogue.

For this reason, reading drama may place a greater demand on the imagination than reading fiction does: The reader must be his or her own narrator and interpreter. Such an exercise for the imagination can prove rewarding, however, for it has much in common with the imaginative work that a director, actors, and other artists involved in a staged production bring to their performance of a play. In re-creating a play as we read it, we are essentially imagining the play as if it were being performed by live actors in real time. We "cast" the characters, we design the set with its furniture and props, and we choreograph or "block" the physical action, according to the cues in the text.

In reading drama even more than in reading fiction, we construct our ideas of character and personality from what a character says. In some plays, especially those with a modernist or experimental bent, certain lines of dialogue can be mystifying; other characters, as well as the audience or readers, can be left wondering what a speech meant. On the one hand, such puzzling lines can become clearer in performance, in which actors physically express the intentions and interactions of the characters. On the other hand, plays that call for several characters to speak at once or to talk at cross purposes can be much easier to understand from the printed script than in performance. In interpreting dialogue, you will naturally draw on your own experiences of comparable situations or similar personalities, as well as your familiarity with other plays or stories.

QUESTIONS TO ASK WHEN READING A PLAY

As mentioned above, reading drama has much in common with reading fiction. You can begin to understand a play by asking some basic questions about the elements of drama, similar to those in fiction. Most critics would agree that plays, as well as most films and television shows, generally have no narrator. At times there may be a voiceover or an actor onstage or offstage telling us something, but usually this device will be dropped as the action gets under way and the actors perform what happens. Again, your questions will be somewhat different when you attend a performance of a play from your questions when you read a printed play.

- **Expectations:** What do you expect:
  ∘ from the title? from the first sentence, paragraph, or speech?
  ∘ after the first events or interactions of characters? as the conflict is resolved?
- **Characterization:** Who are the characters? Is there a list of characters printed after the title of the play? What do you notice about their names or any identification of their roles, character types, or relationships?
  ∘ Who is/are the **protagonist**(s) (hero, heroine)?
  ∘ Who is/are the **antagonist**(s) (villain, opponent, obstacle)?
  ∘ Who are the other characters?
  ∘ What does each character know at any moment in the action? What does each character expect at any point? What does the audience know or expect that is different from what the characters know or expect?

- **Plot:** What happens in the play?
  - Do the characters or situations change during the play?
  - What are the differences between the beginning, middle, and end of the play? Is it divided into acts? Would there be an intermission in a performance?
  - Can you summarize the plot? Is it a recognizable kind or genre such as tragedy, comedy, farce, or mystery?
- **Setting:** What is the setting of the play?
  - What is the *time* of the play? Is it contemporary or set in the past? Do the stage directions specify a day of the week, a season, a time of day?
  - Are there any time changes during the play? Are the scenes in chronological order, or are there any scenes that are supposed to take place earlier or simultaneously? Does the passage of time in the lives of the characters correspond with the passage of time onstage during the performance? Or do we understand that time has passed and events have occurred offstage and between scenes?
  - *Where* does it take place? Is it in the United States or another country, or in a specific town or region? Do the stage directions describe the scene that an audience would see on stage, and does this remain the same or does it change during the play? How many scene changes are there?
- **Style:** What do you notice about how the play is written?
  - What is the **style** of the dialogue? Are the sentences and speeches short or long? Is the vocabulary simple or complex? Do characters ever speak at the same time, or do they always take turns? Does the play instruct actors to be silent for periods of time? Which characters speak most often?
  - Are there any **images** or figures of speech?
  - What is the **tone** or mood? Does the play make the reader or audience feel sad, amused, worried, curious?
- **Theme:** What does the play mean? Can you express its theme or themes?
  - Answers to these big questions may be found in many instances by returning to your answers to the questions above. The play's meaning or theme depends on all its features.

Later in this chapter you will find an example of responses to these questions in the form of reading notes on Susan Glaspell's play *Trifles*.

As you read a play, you should not only make mental or written notes but also raise some of the questions an actor might ask in preparing a role, or that a director might ask before choosing a cast: How should this line be spoken? What kind of person is this character, and what are his or her motives in each scene? What does the play imply or state about what made the character this way—family, environment, experience? Which characters are present or absent (onstage or off) in which scenes, and how do the characters onstage or off influence one another?

Besides trying to understand the characters, you should consider ways that the play could be produced, designed, staged, and acted. How might a set designer create a kitchen, drawing room, garden, woods, or other space for the actors to move in, and how many set changes are there in the play? What would the audience see through any windows or doors in an imaginary building? How would lighting give an impression of the time of day or season? Would sound effects or music be necessary (such as a gunshot, radio, or telephone)? What sort of costumes are specified in the stage directions, and how would costumes help express character types and their relationships, as well as the historical time period? What essential props must be provided for the actors to use, and what other props are optional? Would you, as "director" of an imaginary performance, tell the actors to move in certain directions, together or apart; to express certain emotions and intentions; to speak in quiet, angry, sarcastic, or agonized tones?

As you read Susan Glaspell's *Trifles* and Tom Stoppard's *The Real Inspector Hound*, below, keep these kinds of questions in mind. Try to create a mental image of the settings and of each character, and think about different ways the lines might be delivered that would affect an audience's response.

SUSAN GLASPELL

Trifles

CHARACTERS

SHERIFF	MRS. PETERS, *Sheriff's wife*
COUNTY ATTORNEY	MRS. HALE
HALE	

SCENE: *The kitchen in the now abandoned farmhouse of* JOHN WRIGHT, *a gloomy kitchen, and left without having been put in order—unwashed pans under the sink, a loaf of bread outside the bread-box, a dish-towel on the table—other signs of incompleted work. At the rear the outer door opens and the* SHERIFF *comes in followed by the* COUNTY ATTORNEY *and* HALE. *The* SHERIFF *and* HALE *are men in middle life, the* COUNTY ATTORNEY *is a young man; all are much bundled up and go at once to the stove. They are followed by the two women—the* SHERIFF'S *wife first; she is a slight wiry woman, a thin nervous face.* MRS. HALE *is larger and would ordinarily be called more comfortable looking, but she is disturbed now and looks fearfully about as she enters. The women have come in slowly, and stand close together near the door.*

COUNTY ATTORNEY: [*Rubbing his hands.*] This feels good. Come up to the fire, ladies.

MRS. PETERS: [*After taking a step forward.*] I'm not—cold.

SHERIFF: [*Unbuttoning his overcoat and stepping away from the stove as if to mark the beginning of official business.*] Now, Mr. Hale, before we move things about, you explain to Mr. Henderson just what you saw when you came here yesterday morning.

COUNTY ATTORNEY: By the way, has anything been moved? Are things just as you left them yesterday?

SHERIFF: [*Looking about.*] It's just the same. When it dropped below zero last night I thought I'd better send Frank out this morning to make a fire for us—no use getting pneumonia with a big case on, but I told him not to touch anything except the stove—and you know Frank.

COUNTY ATTORNEY: Somebody should have been left here yesterday.

SHERIFF: Oh—yesterday. When I had to send Frank to Morris Center for that man who went crazy—I want you to know I had my hands full yesterday. I knew you could get back from Omaha by today and as long as I went over everything here myself—

COUNTY ATTORNEY: Well, Mr. Hale, tell just what happened when you came here yesterday morning.

HALE: Harry and I had started to town with a load of potatoes. We came along the road from my place and as I got here I said, "I'm going to see if I can't get John Wright to go in with me on a party telephone."[1] I spoke to Wright about it once before and he put me off, saying folks talked too much anyway, and all he asked was peace and quiet—I guess you know about how much he talked himself; but I thought maybe if I went to the house and talked about it before his wife, though I said to Harry that I didn't know as what his wife wanted made much difference to John—

COUNTY ATTORNEY: Let's talk about that later, Mr. Hale. I do want to talk about that, but tell now just what happened when you got to the house.

HALE: I didn't hear or see anything; I knocked at the door, and still it was all quiet inside. I knew they must be up, it was past eight o'clock. So I knocked again, and I thought I heard somebody say, "Come in." I wasn't sure, I'm not sure yet, but I opened the door—this door [*Indicating the door by which the two women are still standing.*] and there in that rocker—[*Pointing to it.*] sat Mrs. Wright.

[*They all look at the rocker.*]

COUNTY ATTORNEY: What—was she doing?

HALE: She was rockin' back and forth. She had her apron in her hand and was kind of—pleating it.

COUNTY ATTORNEY: And how did she—look?

HALE: Well, she looked queer.

COUNTY ATTORNEY: How do you mean—queer?

HALE: Well, as if she didn't know what she was going to do next. And kind of done up.

COUNTY ATTORNEY: How did she seem to feel about your coming?

HALE: Why, I don't think she minded—one way or other. She didn't pay much attention. I said, "How do, Mrs. Wright, it's cold, ain't it?" And she said, "Is it?"—and went on kind of pleating at her apron. Well, I was surprised; she didn't ask me to come up to the stove, or to set down, but just sat there, not even looking at me, so I said, "I want to see John." And then she—laughed. I guess you would call it a laugh. I thought of Harry and the team outside, so I said a little sharp: "Can't I see John?" "No," she says, kind o' dull like. "Ain't he home?" says I. "Yes," says she, "he's home." "Then why can't I see him?" I asked her, out of patience. "'Cause he's dead," says she. *Dead?* says I. She just nodded her head, not getting a bit excited, but rockin' back and forth. "Why—where is he?" says I, not knowing what to say. She just pointed upstairs—like that. [*Himself pointing to the room above.*] I got up, with the idea of going up there. I walked from there to here—then I says, "Why, what did he die of?" "He died of a rope round his neck," says she, and just went on pleatin' at her apron. Well,

---

1. That is, a party line in which a number of households each have extensions of a single line, a common arrangement in the early twentieth century, especially in rural areas.

I went out and called Harry. I thought I might—need help. We went upstairs and there he was lyin'—

COUNTY ATTORNEY: I think I'd rather have you go into that upstairs, where you can point it all out. Just go on now with the rest of the story.

HALE: Well, my first thought was to get that rope off. It looked . . . [*Stops, his face twitches.*] . . . but Harry, he went up to him, and he said, "No, he's dead all right, and we'd better not touch anything." So we went back downstairs. She was still sitting that same way. "Has anybody been notified?" I asked. "No," says she unconcerned. "Who did this, Mrs. Wright?" said Harry. He said it business-like—and she stopped pleatin' of her apron. "I don't know," she says. "You don't *know*?" says Harry. "No," says she. "Weren't you sleepin' in the bed with him?" says Harry. "Yes," says she, "but I was on the inside." "Somebody slipped a rope round his neck and strangled him and you didn't wake up?" says Harry. "I didn't wake up," she said after him. We must 'a looked as if we didn't see how that could be, for after a minute she said, "I sleep sound." Harry was going to ask her more questions but I said maybe we ought to let her tell her story first to the coroner, or the sheriff, so Harry went fast as he could to Rivers' place, where there's a telephone.

COUNTY ATTORNEY: And what did Mrs. Wright do when she knew that you had gone for the coroner?

HALE: She moved from that chair to this one over here [*Pointing to a small chair in the corner.*] and just sat there with her hands held together and looking down. I got a feeling that I ought to make some conversation, so I said I had come in to see if John wanted to put in a telephone, and at that she started to laugh, and then she stopped and looked at me—scared. [*The* COUNTY ATTORNEY, *who has had his notebook out, makes a note.*] I dunno, maybe it wasn't scared. I wouldn't like to say it was. Soon Harry got back, and then Dr. Lloyd came, and you, Mr. Peters, and so I guess that's all I know that you don't.

COUNTY ATTORNEY: [*Looking around.*] I guess we'll go upstairs first—and then out to the barn and around there. [*To the* SHERIFF.] You're convinced that there was nothing important here—nothing that would point to any motive?

SHERIFF: Nothing here but kitchen things.

[*The* COUNTY ATTORNEY, *after again looking around the kitchen, opens the door of a cupboard closet. He gets up on a chair and looks on a shelf. Pulls his hand away, sticky.*]

COUNTY ATTORNEY: Here's a nice mess.

[*The women draw nearer.*]

MRS. PETERS: [*To the other woman.*] Oh, her fruit; it did freeze. [*To the* LAWYER.] She worried about that when it turned so cold. She said the fire'd go out and her jars would break.

SHERIFF: Well, can you beat the women! Held for murder and worryin' about her preserves.

COUNTY ATTORNEY: I guess before we're through she may have something more serious than preserves to worry about.

HALE: Well, women are used to worrying over trifles.

[*The two women move a little closer together.*]

COUNTY ATTORNEY: [*With the gallantry of a young politician.*] And yet, for all their worries, what would we do without the ladies? [*The women do not unbend. He goes to the sink, takes a dipperful of water from the pail and pouring it into a basin, washes his hands. Starts to wipe them on the roller towel, turns it for a cleaner place.*] Dirty towels! [*Kicks his foot against the pans under the sink.*] Not much of a housekeeper, would you say, ladies?

MRS. HALE: [*Stiffly.*] There's a great deal of work to be done on a farm.

COUNTY ATTORNEY: To be sure. And yet [*With a little bow to her.*] I know there are some Dickson county farmhouses which do not have such roller towels. [*He gives it a pull to expose its length again.*]

MRS. HALE: Those towels get dirty awful quick. Men's hands aren't always as clean as they might be.

COUNTY ATTORNEY: Ah, loyal to your sex, I see. But you and Mrs. Wright were neighbors. I suppose you were friends, too.

MRS. HALE: [*Shaking her head.*] I've not seen much of her of late years. I've not been in this house—it's more than a year.

COUNTY ATTORNEY: And why was that? You didn't like her?

MRS. HALE: I liked her all well enough. Farmers' wives have their hands full, Mr. Henderson. And then—

COUNTY ATTORNEY: Yes—?

MRS. HALE: [*Looking about.*] It never seemed a very cheerful place.

COUNTY ATTORNEY: No—it's not cheerful. I shouldn't say she had the homemaking instinct.

MRS. HALE: Well, I don't know as Wright had, either.

COUNTY ATTORNEY: You mean that they didn't get on very well?

MRS. HALE: No, I don't mean anything. But I don't think a place'd be any cheerfuller for John Wright's being in it.

COUNTY ATTORNEY: I'd like to talk more of that a little later. I want to get the lay of things upstairs now. [*He goes to the left, where three steps lead to a stair door.*]

SHERIFF: I suppose anything Mrs. Peters does'll be all right. She was to take in some clothes for her, you know, and a few little things. We left in such a hurry yesterday.

COUNTY ATTORNEY: Yes, but I would like to see what you take, Mrs. Peters, and keep an eye out for anything that might be of use to us.

MRS. PETERS: Yes, Mr. Henderson. [*The women listen to the men's steps on the stairs, then look about the kitchen.*]

MRS. HALE: I'd hate to have men coming into my kitchen, snooping around and criticizing. [*She arranges the pans under sink which the* LAWYER *had shoved out of place.*]

MRS. PETERS: Of course it's no more than their duty.

MRS. HALE: Duty's all right, but I guess that deputy sheriff that came out to make the fire might have got a little of this on. [*Gives the roller towel a pull.*] Wish I'd thought of that sooner. Seems mean to talk about her for not having things slicked up when she had to come away in such a hurry.

MRS. PETERS: [*Who has gone to a small table in the left rear corner of the room, and lifted one end of a towel that covers a pan.*] She had bread set. [*Stands still.*]

MRS. HALE: [*Eyes fixed on a loaf of bread beside the bread box, which is on a low shelf at the other side of the room. Moves slowly toward it.*] She was going to put this in there. [*Picks up loaf, then abruptly drops it. In a manner of returning to familiar things.*] It's a shame about her fruit. I wonder if it's all gone. [*Gets up on the chair and looks.*] I think there's some here that's all right, Mrs. Peters. Yes—here; [*Holding it toward the window.*] this is cherries, too. [*Looking again.*] I declare I believe that's the only one. [*Gets down, bottle in her hand. Goes to the sink and wipes it off on the outside.*] She'll feel awful bad after all her hard work in the hot weather. I remember the afternoon I put up my cherries last summer. [*She puts the bottle on the big kitchen table, center of the room. With a sigh, is about to sit down in the rocking-chair. Before she is seated realizes what chair it is; with a slow look at it, steps back. The chair, which she has touched, rocks back and forth.*]

MRS. PETERS: Well, I must get those things from the front room closet. [*She goes to the door at the right, but after looking into the other room, steps back.*] You coming with me, Mrs. Hale? You could help me carry them. [*They go in the other room; reappear,* MRS. PETERS *carrying a dress and skirt,* MRS. HALE *following with a pair of shoes.*] My, it's cold in there. [*She puts the clothes on the big table, and hurries to the stove.*]

MRS. HALE: [*Examining the skirt.*] Wright was close. I think maybe that's why she kept so much to herself. She didn't even belong to the Ladies Aid. I suppose she felt she couldn't do her part, and then you don't enjoy things when you feel shabby. She used to wear pretty clothes and be lively, when she was Minnie Foster, one of the town girls singing in the choir. But that—oh, that was thirty years ago. This all you was to take in?

MRS. PETERS: She said she wanted an apron. Funny thing to want, for there isn't much to get you dirty in jail, goodness knows. But I suppose just to make her feel more natural. She said they was in the top drawer in this cupboard. Yes, here. And then her little shawl that always hung behind the door. [*Opens stair door and looks.*] Yes, here it is. [*Quickly shuts door leading upstairs.*]

MRS. HALE: [*Abruptly moving toward her.*] Mrs. Peters?

MRS. PETERS: Yes, Mrs. Hale?

MRS. HALE: Do you think she did it?

MRS. PETERS: [*In a frightened voice.*] Oh, I don't know.

MRS. HALE: Well, I don't think she did. Asking for an apron and her little shawl. Worrying about her fruit.

MRS. PETERS: [*Starts to speak, glances up, where footsteps are heard in the room above. In a low voice.*] Mr. Peters says it looks bad for her. Mr. Henderson is awful sarcastic in a speech and he'll make fun of her sayin' she didn't wake up.

MRS. HALE: Well, I guess John Wright didn't wake when they was slipping that rope under his neck.

MRS. PETERS: No, it's strange. It must have been done awful crafty and still. They say it was such a—funny way to kill a man, rigging it all up like that.

MRS. HALE: That's just what Mr. Hale said. There was a gun in the house. He says that's what he can't understand.

MRS. PETERS: Mr. Henderson said coming out that what was needed for the case was a motive; something to show anger, or—sudden feeling.

MRS. HALE: [*Who is standing by the table.*] Well, I don't see any signs of anger around here. [*She puts her hand on the dish towel which lies on the table, stands looking down at table, one half of which is clean, the other half messy.*] It's wiped to here. [*Makes a move as if to finish work, then turns and looks at loaf of bread outside the bread box. Drops towel. In that voice of coming back to familiar things.*] Wonder how they are finding things upstairs. I hope she had it a little more red-up[2] up there. You know, it

2. Tidied up.

seems kind of *sneaking*. Locking her up in town and then coming out here and trying to get her own house to turn against her!

MRS. PETERS: But Mrs. Hale, the law is the law.

MRS. HALE: I s'pose 'tis. [*Unbuttoning her coat.*] Better loosen up your things, Mrs. Peters. You won't feel them when you go out.

[MRS. PETERS *takes off her fur tippet, goes to hang it on hook at back of room, stands looking at the under part of the small corner table.*]

MRS. PETERS: She was piecing a quilt. [*She brings the large sewing basket and they look at the bright pieces.*]

MRS. HALE: It's log cabin pattern. Pretty, isn't it? I wonder if she was goin' to quilt it or just knot it?

[*Footsteps have been heard coming down the stairs. The* SHERIFF *enters followed by* HALE *and the* COUNTY ATTORNEY.]

SHERIFF: They wonder if she was going to quilt it or just knot it!

[*The men laugh, the women look abashed.*]

COUNTY ATTORNEY: [*Rubbing his hands over the stove.*] Frank's fire didn't do much up there, did it? Well, let's go out to the barn and get that cleared up.

[*The men go outside.*]

MRS. HALE: [*Resentfully.*] I don't know as there's anything so strange, our takin' up our time with little things while we're waiting for them to get the evidence. [*She sits down at the big table smoothing out a block with decision.*] I don't see as it's anything to laugh about.

MRS. PETERS: [*Apologetically.*] Of course they've got awful important things on their minds. [*Pulls up a chair and joins* MRS. HALE *at the table.*]

MRS. HALE: [*Examining another block.*] Mrs. Peters, look at this one. Here, this is the one she was working on, and look at the sewing! All the rest of it has been so nice and even. And look at this! It's all over the place! Why, it looks as if she didn't know what she was about! [*After she has said this they look at each other, then start to glance back at the door. After an instant* MRS. HALE *has pulled at a knot and ripped the sewing.*]

MRS. PETERS: Oh, what are you doing, Mrs. Hale?

MRS. HALE: [*Mildly.*] Just pulling out a stitch or two that's not sewed very good. [*Threading the needle.*] Bad sewing always made me fidgety.

MRS. PETERS: [*Nervously.*] I don't think we ought to touch things.

MRS. HALE: I'll just finish up this end. [*Suddenly stopping and leaning forward.*] Mrs. Peters?

MRS. PETERS: Yes, Mrs. Hale?

MRS. HALE: What do you suppose she was so nervous about?

MRS. PETERS: Oh—I don't know. I don't know as she was nervous. I sometimes sew awful queer when I'm just tired. [MRS. HALE *starts to say something, looks at* MRS. PETERS, *then goes on sewing.*] Well, I must get these things wrapped up. They may be through sooner than we think. [*Putting apron and other things together.*] I wonder where I can find a piece of paper, and string.

MRS. HALE: In that cupboard, maybe.

MRS. PETERS: [*Looking in cupboard.*] Why, here's a bird-cage. [*Holds it up.*] Did she have a bird, Mrs. Hale?

MRS. HALE: Why, I don't know whether she did or not—I've not been here for so long. There was a man around last year selling canaries cheap, but I don't know as she took one; maybe she did. She used to sing real pretty herself.

MRS. PETERS: [*Glancing around.*] Seems funny to think of a bird here. But she must have had one, or why would she have a cage? I wonder what happened to it.

MRS. HALE: I s'pose maybe the cat got it.

MRS. PETERS: No, she didn't have a cat. She's got that feeling some people have about cats—being afraid of them. My cat got in her room and she was real upset and asked me to take it out.

MRS. HALE: My sister Bessie was like that. Queer, ain't it?

MRS. PETERS: [*Examining the cage.*] Why, look at this door. It's broke. One hinge is pulled apart.

MRS. HALE: [*Looking too.*] Looks as if someone must have been rough with it.

MRS. PETERS: Why, yes. [*She brings the cage forward and puts it on the table.*]

MRS. HALE: I wish if they're going to find any evidence they'd be about it. I don't like this place.

MRS. PETERS: But I'm awful glad you came with me, Mrs. Hale. It would be lonesome for me sitting here alone.

MRS. HALE: It would, wouldn't it? [*Dropping her sewing.*] But I tell you what I do wish, Mrs. Peters. I wish I had come over sometimes when *she* was here. I—[*Looking around the room.*]—wish I had.

MRS. PETERS: But of course you were awful busy, Mrs. Hale—your house and your children.

MRS. HALE: I could've come. I stayed away because it weren't cheerful—and that's why I ought to have come. I—I've never liked this place. Maybe because it's down in a hollow and you don't see the road. I dunno what it is, but it's a lonesome place and always was. I wish I had come over to see Minnie Foster sometimes. I can see now—[*Shakes her head.*]

MRS. PETERS: Well, you mustn't reproach yourself, Mrs. Hale. Somehow we just don't see how it is with other folks until—something comes up.

MRS. HALE: Not having children makes less work—but it makes a quiet house, and Wright out to work all day, and no company when he did come in. Did you know John Wright, Mrs. Peters?

MRS. PETERS: Not to know him; I've seen him in town. They say he was a good man.

MRS. HALE: Yes—good; he didn't drink, and kept his word as well as most, I guess, and paid his debts. But he was a hard man, Mrs. Peters. Just to pass the time of day with him—[*Shivers.*] Like a raw wind that gets to the bone. [*Pauses, her eye falling on the cage.*] I should think she would 'a wanted a bird. But what do you suppose went with it?

MRS. PETERS: I don't know, unless it got sick and died. [*She reaches over and swings the broken door, swings it again, both women watch it.*]

MRS. HALE: You weren't raised round here, were you? [MRS. PETERS *shakes her head.*] You didn't know—her?

MRS. PETERS: Not till they brought her yesterday.

MRS. HALE: She—come to think of it, she was kind of like a bird herself—real sweet and pretty, but kind of timid and—fluttery. How—she—did—change. [*Silence; then as if struck by a happy thought and relieved to get back to everyday things.*] Tell you what, Mrs. Peters, why don't you take the quilt in with you? It might take up her mind.

MRS. PETERS: Why, I think that's a real nice idea, Mrs. Hale. There couldn't possibly be any objection to it, could there? Now, just what would I take? I wonder if her patches are in here—and her things. [*They look in the sewing basket.*]

MRS. HALE: Here's some red. I expect this has got sewing things in it. [*Brings out a fancy box.*] What a pretty box. Looks like something somebody would give you. Maybe her scissors are in here. [*Opens box. Suddenly puts her hand to her nose.*] Why—[MRS. PETERS *bends nearer, then turns her face away.*] There's something wrapped up in this piece of silk.

MRS. PETERS: Why, this isn't her scissors.

MRS. HALE: [*Lifting the silk.*] Oh, Mrs. Peters—it's—

[MRS. PETERS *bends closer.*]

MRS. PETERS: It's the bird.

MRS. HALE: [*Jumping up.*] But, Mrs. Peters—look at it! Its neck! Look at its neck! It's all—other side *to.*

MRS. PETERS: Somebody—wrung—its—neck.

[*Their eyes meet. A look of growing comprehension, of horror. Steps are heard outside.* MRS. HALE *slips box under quilt pieces, and sinks into her chair. Enter* SHERIFF *and* COUNTY ATTORNEY. MRS. PETERS *rises.*]

COUNTY ATTORNEY: [*As one turning from serious things to little pleasantries.*] Well ladies, have you decided whether she was going to quilt it or knot it?

MRS. PETERS: We think she was going to—knot it.

COUNTY ATTORNEY: Well, that's interesting, I'm sure. [*Seeing the bird-cage.*] Has the bird flown?

MRS. HALE: [*Putting more quilt pieces over the box.*] We think the—cat got it.

COUNTY ATTORNEY: [*Preoccupied.*] Is there a cat?

[MRS. HALE *glances in a quick covert way at* MRS. PETERS.]

MRS. PETERS: Well, not *now.* They're superstitious, you know. They leave.

COUNTY ATTORNEY: [*To* SHERIFF PETERS, *continuing an interrupted conversation.*] No sign at all of anyone having come from the outside. Their own rope. Now let's go up again and go over it piece by piece. [*They start upstairs.*] It would have to have been someone who knew just the—

[MRS. PETERS *sits down. The two women sit there not looking at one another, but as if peering into something and at the same time holding back. When they talk now it is in the manner of feeling their way over strange ground, as if afraid of what they are saying, but as if they cannot help saying it.*]

MRS. HALE: She liked the bird. She was going to bury it in that pretty box.

MRS. PETERS: [*In a whisper.*] When I was a girl—my kitten—there was a boy took a hatchet, and before my eyes—and before I could get there—[*Covers her face an instant.*] If they hadn't held me back I would have—[*Catches herself, looks upstairs where steps are heard, falters weakly.*]—hurt him.

MRS. HALE: [*With a slow look around her.*] I wonder how it would seem never to have had any children around. [*Pause.*] No, Wright wouldn't like the bird—a thing that sang. She used to sing. He killed that, too.

MRS. PETERS: [*Moving uneasily.*] We don't know who killed the bird.

MRS. HALE: I knew John Wright.

MRS. PETERS: It was an awful thing was done in this house that night, Mrs. Hale. Killing a man while he slept, slipping a rope around his neck that choked the life out of him.

MRS. HALE: His neck. Choked the life out of him. [*Her hand goes out and rests on the bird-cage.*]

MRS. PETERS: [*With rising voice.*] We don't know who killed him. We don't *know.*

MRS. HALE: [*Her own feeling not interrupted.*] If there's been years and years of nothing, then a bird to sing to you, it would be awful—still, after the bird was still.

MRS. PETERS: [*Something within her speaking.*] I know what stillness is. When we homesteaded in Dakota, and my first baby died—after he was two years old, and me with no other then—

MRS. HALE: [*Moving.*] How soon do you suppose they'll be through, looking for the evidence?

MRS. PETERS: I know what stillness is. [*Pulling herself back.*] The law has got to punish crime, Mrs. Hale.

MRS. HALE: [*Not as if answering that.*] I wish you'd seen Minnie Foster when she wore a white dress with blue ribbons and stood up there in the choir and sang. [*A look around the room.*] Oh, I *wish* I'd come over here once in a while! That was a crime! That was a crime! Who's going to punish that?

MRS. PETERS: [*Looking upstairs.*] We mustn't—take on.

MRS. HALE: I might have known she needed help! I know how things can be—for women. I tell you, it's queer, Mrs. Peters. We live close together and we live far apart. We all go through the same things—it's all just a different kind of the same thing. [*Brushes her eyes, noticing the bottle of fruit, reaches out for it.*] If I was you, I wouldn't tell her her fruit was gone. Tell her it *ain't.* Tell her it's all right. Take this in to prove it to her. She—she may never know whether it was broke or not.

MRS. PETERS: [*Takes the bottle, looks about for something to wrap it in; takes petticoat from the clothes brought from the other room, very nervously begins winding this around the bottle. In a false voice.*] My, it's a good thing the men couldn't hear us. Wouldn't they just laugh! Getting all stirred up over a little thing like a—dead canary. As if that could have anything to do with—with—wouldn't they *laugh!*

[*The men are heard coming down stairs.*]

MRS. HALE: [*Under her breath.*] Maybe they would—maybe they wouldn't.

COUNTY ATTORNEY: No, Peters, it's all perfectly clear except a reason for doing it. But you know juries when it comes to women. If there was some definite thing. Something to show—something to make a story about—a thing that would connect up with this strange way of doing it—

[*The women's eyes meet for an instant. Enter* HALE *from outer door.*]

HALE: Well, I've got the team around. Pretty cold out there.

COUNTY ATTORNEY: I'm going to stay here a while by myself. [*To the* SHERIFF.] You can send Frank out for me, can't you? I want to go over everything. I'm not satisfied that we can't do better.

SHERIFF: Do you want to see what Mrs. Peters is going to take in?

[*The* LAWYER *goes to the table, picks up the apron, laughs.*]

COUNTY ATTORNEY: Oh, I guess they're not very dangerous things the ladies have picked out. [*Moves a few things about, disturbing the quilt pieces which cover the box.*

Steps back.] No, Mrs. Peters doesn't need supervising. For that matter, a sheriff's wife is married to the law. Ever think of it that way, Mrs. Peters?

MRS. PETERS: Not—just that way.

SHERIFF: [*Chuckling.*] Married to the law. [*Moves toward the other room.*] I just want you to come in here a minute, George. We ought to take a look at these windows.

COUNTY ATTORNEY: [*Scoffingly.*] Oh, windows!

SHERIFF: We'll be right out, Mr. Hale.

[HALE *goes outside. The* SHERIFF *follows the* COUNTY ATTORNEY *into the other room. Then* MRS. HALE *rises, hands tight together, looking intensely at* MRS. PETERS, *whose eyes make a slow turn, finally meeting* MRS. HALE's. *A moment* MRS. HALE *holds her, then her own eyes point the way to where the box is concealed. Suddenly* MRS. PETERS *throws back quilt pieces and tries to put the box in the bag she is wearing. It is too big. She opens box, starts to take bird out, cannot touch it, goes to pieces, stands there helpless. Sound of a knob turning in the other room.* MRS. HALE *snatches the box and puts it in the pocket of her big coat. Enter* COUNTY ATTORNEY *and* SHERIFF.]

COUNTY ATTORNEY: [*Facetiously.*] Well, Henry, at least we found out that she was not going to quilt it. She was going to—what is it you call it, ladies?

MRS. HALE: [*Her hand against her pocket.*] We call it—knot it, Mr. Henderson.

CURTAIN

1916

QUESTIONS

1. If we were watching a production of *Trifles* and had no cast list, how would we gradually piece together the fact that Mrs. Peters is the sheriff's wife? What are the earliest lines of dialogue that allow an audience to infer this fact?
2. What lines in the play characterize Mrs. Hale's reaction to the men's behavior and attitudes? What lines characterize Mrs. Peters's reaction to the men early in the play, and what lines show her feelings changing later in the play? What might account for both their initial differences and then their evolving solidarity with Mrs. Wright?
3. What are the "trifles" that the men ignore and the two women notice? Why do the men dismiss them, and why do the women see these things as significant clues? What is the thematic importance of these "trifles"?
4. How would you stage the key moment of the play, Mrs. Hale's discovery of the bird in the sewing basket? What facial expression would she have, what body language? Where would you place Mrs. Peters, and what would she be doing? How would you use lighting to heighten the effectiveness of the scene?
5. To what degree is each of the characters in the play "round," or well developed? To what degree are any of them stereotypes?
6. If a twenty-first-century playwright were to write an updated version of *Trifles*, what details of plot, character, and setting would be different from those in Glaspell's play? What would be the same? What are some possible "trifles" that might serve the same dramatic functions as those in Glaspell's play?

TOM STOPPARD

The Real Inspector Hound

CHARACTERS

MOON	SIMON	MAGNUS
BIRDBOOT	FELICITY	INSPECTOR HOUND
MRS. DRUDGE	CYNTHIA	

The first thing is that the audience appear to be confronted by their own reflection in a huge mirror. Impossible. However, back there in the gloom—not at the footlights—a bank of plush seats and pale smudges of faces. The total effect having been established, it can be progressively faded out as the play goes on, until the front row remains to remind us of the rest and then, finally, merely two seats in that row—one of which is now occupied by MOON. *Between* MOON *and the auditorium is an acting area which represents, in as realistic an idiom as possible, the drawing-room of Muldoon Manor. French windows at one side. A telephone fairly well upstage (i.e. towards* MOON*). The body of a man lies sprawled face down on the floor in front of a large settee. This settee must be of a size and design to allow it to be wheeled over the body, hiding it completely. Silence. The room. The body.* MOON.

MOON *stares blankly ahead. He turns his head to one side then the other, then up, then down—waiting. He picks up his programme and reads the front cover. He turns over the page and reads.*

He turns over the page and reads.

He turns over the page and reads.

He turns over the page and reads.

He looks at the back cover and reads.

He puts it down and crosses his legs and looks about. He stares front. Behind him and to one side, barely visible, a man enters and sits down: BIRDBOOT.

Pause. MOON *picks up his programme, glances at the front cover and puts it down impatiently. Pause . . . Behind him there is the crackle of a chocolate-box, absurdly loud.* MOON *looks round. He and* BIRDBOOT *see each other. They are clearly known to each other. They acknowledge each other with constrained waves.* MOON *looks straight ahead.* BIRDBOOT *comes down to join him.*

Note: Almost always, MOON *and* BIRDBOOT *converse in tones suitable for an auditorium, sometimes a whisper. However good the acoustics might be, they will have to have microphones where they are sitting. The effect must be not of sound picked up, amplified and flung out at the audience, but of sound picked up, carried and gently dispersed around the auditorium.*

Anyway, BIRDBOOT, *with a box of Black Magic,[1] makes his way down to join* MOON *and plumps himself down next to him, plumpish middle-aged* BIRDBOOT *and younger, taller, less-relaxed* MOON.

BIRDBOOT: [*sitting down; conspiratorially*] Me and the lads have had a meeting in the bar and decided it's first-class family entertainment but if it goes on beyond half-past ten it's self-indulgent—pass it on . . . [*and laughs jovially*] I'm on my own tonight, don't mind if I join you?

MOON: Hello, Birdboot.

BIRDBOOT: Where's Higgs?

---

1. Popular brand of chocolates sold in London theaters.

MOON: I'm standing in.

MOON AND BIRDBOOT: Where's Higgs?

MOON: Every time.

BIRDBOOT: What?

MOON: It is as if we only existed one at a time, combining to achieve continuity. I keep space warm for Higgs. My presence defines his absence, his absence confirms my presence, his presence precludes mine. . . . When Higgs and I walk down this aisle together to claim our common seat, the oceans will fall into the sky and the trees will hang with fishes.

BIRDBOOT: [*he has not been paying attention, looking around vaguely, now catches up*] Where's Higgs?

MOON: The very sight of me with a complimentary ticket is enough. The streets are impassable tonight, the country is rising and the cry goes up from hill to hill—Where—is—Higgs? [*Small pause.*] Perhaps he's dead at last, or trapped in a lift[2] somewhere, or succumbed to amnesia, wandering the land with his turn-ups stuffed with ticket-stubs.

[BIRDBOOT *regards him doubtfully for a moment.*]

BIRDBOOT: Yes. . . . Yes, well I didn't bring Myrtle tonight—not exactly her cup of tea, I thought, tonight.

MOON: Over her head, you mean?

BIRDBOOT: Well, no—I mean it's a sort of a *thriller*, isn't it?

MOON: Is it?

BIRDBOOT: That's what I heard. Who killed thing?—no one will leave the house.

MOON: I suppose so. Underneath.

BIRDBOOT: *Underneath*?!? It's a whodunnit, man!—Look at it!

[*They look at it. The room. The body. Silence.*]

Has it started yet?

MOON: Yes.

[*Pause. They look at it.*]

BIRDBOOT: Are you sure?

MOON: It's a pause.

BIRDBOOT: You can't start with a *pause*! If you want my opinion there's total panic back there. [*Laughs and subsides.*] Where's Higgs tonight, then?

MOON: It will follow me to the grave and become my epitaph—Here lies Moon the second string: where's Higgs? . . . Sometimes I dream of revolution, a bloody *coup d'etat* by the second rank—troupes of actors slaughtered by their understudies, magicians sawn in half by indefatigably smiling glamour girls, cricket teams wiped out by marauding bands of twelfth men[3]—I dream of champions chopped down by rabbit-punching sparring partners while eternal bridesmaids turn and rape the bridegrooms over the sausage rolls and parliamentary private secretaries plant bombs in the Minister's Humber[4]—comedians die on provincial stages, robbed of their feeds by mutely triumphant stooges—

2. Elevator. *Turn-ups*: trouser cuffs.
3. Substitutes. A cricket team ("side") fields eleven players at a time.
4. A car once manufactured in Britain. *Feeds*: cues provided to comedians by straight men, "stooges."

and—march—an army of assistants and deputies, the seconds-in-command, the runners-up, the right-hand men—storming the palace gates wherein the second son has already mounted the throne having committed regicide with a croquet-mallet—stand-ins of the world stand up!—

[*Beat.*][5] Sometimes I dream of Higgs.

[*Pause.* BIRDBOOT *regards him doubtfully. He is at a loss, and grasps reality in the form of his box of chocolates.*]

BIRDBOOT: [*Chewing into mike.*] Have a chocolate!
MOON: What kind?
BIRDBOOT: [*Chewing into mike.*] Black Magic.
MOON: No thanks.

[*Chewing stops dead.*]
[*Of such tiny victories and defeats. . . .*]

BIRDBOOT: I'll give you a tip, then. Watch the girl.
MOON: You think she did it?
BIRDBOOT: No, no—the *girl*, watch her.
MOON: What girl?
BIRDBOOT: You won't know her, I'll give you a nudge.
MOON: *You* know her, do you?
BIRDBOOT: [*suspiciously, bridling*] What's *that* supposed to mean?
MOON: I beg your pardon?
BIRDBOOT: I'm trying to tip you a wink—give you a nudge as good as a tip—for God's sake, Moon, what's the matter with you?—you could do yourself some good, spotting her first time out—she's new, from the provinces, going straight to the top. I don't want to put words into your mouth but a word from us and we could make her.
MOON: I suppose you've made dozens of them, like that.
BIRDBOOT: [*Instantly outraged.*] I'll have you know I'm a family man devoted to my homely but good-natured wife, and if you're suggesting—
MOON: No, no—
BIRDBOOT: —A man of my scrupulous morality—
MOON: I'm sorry—
BIRDBOOT: —falsely besmirched.
MOON: Is that her?

[*For* MRS. DRUDGE *has entered.*]

BIRDBOOT: —don't be absurd, wouldn't be seen dead with the old—ah.

[MRS. DRUDGE *is the char,*[6] *middle-aged, turbanned. She heads straight for the radio, dusting on the trot.*]

MOON: [*reading his programme*] Mrs. Drudge the Help.
RADIO: [*without preamble, having been switched on by* MRS. DRUDGE] We interrupt our programme for a special police message.

---

5. In drama, a "beat" is a pause.
6. British term for cleaning lady or maid who does not live in the house.

[MRS. DRUDGE *stops to listen.*]

The search still goes on for the escaped madman who is on the run in Essex.

MRS. DRUDGE: [*fear and dismay*] Essex!

RADIO: County police led by Inspector Hound have received a report that the man has been seen in the desolate marshes around Muldoon Manor.

[*Fearful gasp from* MRS. DRUDGE.]

The man is wearing a darkish suit with a lightish shirt. He is of medium height and build and youngish. Anyone seeing a man answering to this description and acting suspiciously, is advised to phone the nearest police station.

[*A man answering this description has appeared behind* MRS. DRUDGE. *He is acting suspiciously. He creeps in. He creeps out.* MRS. DRUDGE *does not see him. He does not see the body.*]

That is the end of the police message.

[MRS. DRUDGE *turns off the radio and resumes her cleaning. She does not see the body. Quite fortuitously, her view of the body is always blocked, and when it isn't she has her back to it. However, she is dusting and polishing her way towards it.*]

BIRDBOOT: So that's what they say about me, is it?

MOON: What?

BIRDBOOT: Oh, I know what goes on behind my back—sniggers—slanders—hole-in-corner innuendo—What have you heard?

MOON: Nothing.

BIRDBOOT: [*urbanely*] Tittle tattle. Tittle, my dear fellow, tattle. I take no notice of it—the sly envy of scandal mongers—I can afford to ignore them, I'm a respectable married man—

MOON: Incidentally—

BIRDBOOT: Water off a duck's back, I assure you.

MOON: Who was that lady I saw you with last night?

BIRDBOOT: [*unexpectedly stung into fury*] How dare you! [*More quietly*] How dare you. Don't you come here with your slimy insinuations! My wife Myrtle understands perfectly well that a man of my critical standing is obliged occasionally to mingle with the world of the footlights, simply by way of keeping *au fait*[7] with the latest——

MOON: I'm sorry——

BIRDBOOT: That a critic of my scrupulous integrity should be vilified and pilloried in the stocks of common gossip——

MOON: Ssssh——

BIRDBOOT: I have nothing to hide!—why, if this should reach the ears of my beloved Myrtle——

MOON: Can I have a chocolate?

BIRDBOOT: What? Oh——[*Mollified.*] Oh yes—my dear fellow—yes, let's have a chocolate——No point in—yes, good show. [*Pops chocolate into his mouth and chews.*]

---

7. In touch; knowledgeable (French).

Which one do you fancy?—Cherry? Strawberry? Coffee cream? Turkish delight?

MOON: I'll have montelimar.

[*Chewing stops.*]

BIRDBOOT: Ah. Sorry. [*Just missed that one.*]

MOON: Gooseberry fondue?

BIRDBOOT: No.

MOON: Pistacchio fudge? Nectarine cluster? Hickory nut praline? Chateau Neuf du Pape '55 cracknell?[8]

BIRDBOOT: I'm afraid not . . . Caramel?

MOON: Yes, all right.

BIRDBOOT: Thanks very much. [*He gives* MOON *a chocolate. Pause.*] Incidentally, old chap, I'd be grateful if you didn't mention—I mean, you know how these misunderstandings get about. . . .

MOON: What?

BIRDBOOT: The fact is, Myrtle simply doesn't *like* the theatre. . . .

[*He tails off hopelessly.* MRS. DRUDGE, *whose discovery of the body has been imminent, now—by way of tidying the room—slides the couch over the corpse, hiding it completely. She resumes dusting and humming.*]

MOON: By the way, congratulations, Birdboot.

BIRDBOOT: What?

MOON: At the Theatre Royal. Your entire review reproduced in neon!

BIRDBOOT: [*pleased.*] Oh . . . that old thing.

MOON: You've seen it, of course.

BIRDBOOT: [*vaguely.*] Well, I was passing. . . .

MOON: I definitely intend to take a second look when it has settled down.

BIRDBOOT: As a matter of fact I have a few colour transparencies—I don't know whether you'd care to . . . ?

MOON: Please, please—love to, love to. . . .

[BIRDBOOT *hands over a few colour slides and a battery-powered viewer which* MOON *holds up to his eyes as he speaks.*]

Yes . . . yes . . . lovely . . . awfully sound. It has scale, it has colour, it is, in the best sense of the word, electric. Large as it is, it is a small masterpiece—I would go so far as to say—kinetic without being pop, and having said that, I think it must be said that here we have a review that adds a new dimension to the critical scene. I urge you to make haste to the Theatre Royal, for this is the stuff of life itself. [*Handing back the slides, morosely*]: All I ever got was "Unforgettable" on the posters for . . . What was it?

BIRDBOOT: Oh—yes—I know. . . . Was that you? I thought it was Higgs.

[*The phone rings.* MRS. DRUDGE *seems to have been waiting for it to do so and for the last few seconds has been dusting it with an intense concentration. She snatches it up.*]

8. A hard, sweet biscuit. *Chateau Neuf du Pape '55*: a fine wine in an excellent vintage year. The flavors that Moon requests, after "montelimar," are all fanciful—not found in any Black Magic box.

MRS. DRUDGE: [*into phone*] Hello, the drawing-room of Lady Muldoon's country residence one morning in early spring? . . . He*llo!*—the draw— Who? Who did you wish to speak to? I'm afraid there is no one of that name here, this is all very mysterious and I'm sure it's leading up to something. I hope nothing is amiss for we, that is Lady Muldoon and her houseguests, are here cut off from the world, including Magnus, the wheelchair-ridden half-brother of her ladyship's husband Lord Albert Muldoon who ten years ago went out for a walk on the cliffs and was never seen again—and all alone, for they had no children.

MOON: Derivative, of course.

BIRDBOOT: But quite sound.

MRS. DRUDGE: Should a stranger enter our midst, which I very much doubt, I will tell him you called. Good-bye.

[*She puts down the phone and catches sight of the previously seen suspicious character who has now entered again, more suspiciously than ever, through the french windows. He senses her stare, freezes, and straightens up.*]

SIMON: Ah!—hello there! I'm Simon Gascoyne, I hope you don't mind, the door was open so I wandered in. I'm a friend of Lady Muldoon, the lady of the house, having made her acquaintance through a mutual friend, Felicity Cunningham, shortly after moving into this neighbourhood just the other day.

MRS. DRUDGE: I'm Mrs. Drudge. I don't live in but I pop in on my bicycle when the weather allows to help in the running of charming though somewhat isolated Muldoon Manor. Judging by the time [*she glances at the clock*] you did well to get here before high water cut us off for all practical purposes from the outside world.

SIMON: I took the short cut over the cliffs and followed one of the old smugglers' paths through the treacherous swamps that surround this strangely inaccessible house.

MRS. DRUDGE: Yes, many visitors have remarked on the topographical quirk in the local strata whereby there are no roads leading from the Manor, though there *are* ways of getting *to* it, weather allowing.

SIMON: Yes, well I must say it's a lovely day so far.

MRS. DRUDGE: Ah, but now that the cuckoo-beard is in bud there'll be fog before the sun hits Foster's Ridge.

SIMON: I say, it's wonderful how you country people really know weather.

MRS. DRUDGE: [*suspiciously*] Know whether what?

SIMON: [*glancing out of the window.*] Yes, it does seem to be coming on a bit foggy.

MRS. DRUDGE: The fog is very treacherous around here—it rolls off the sea without warning, shrouding the cliffs in a deadly mantle of blind man's buff.

SIMON: Yes, I've heard it said.

MRS. DRUDGE: I've known whole week-ends when Muldoon Manor, as this lovely old Queen Anne House is called, might as well have been floating on the pack ice for all the good it would have done phoning the police. It was on such a week-end as this that Lord Muldoon who had lately brought his beautiful bride back to the home of his ancestors, walked out of this house ten years ago, and his body was never found.

SIMON: Yes, indeed, poor Cynthia.

MRS. DRUDGE: His name was Albert.

SIMON: Yes indeed, poor Albert. But tell me, is Lady Muldoon about?

MRS. DRUDGE: I believe she is playing tennis on the lawn with Felicity Cunningham.

SIMON: [*startled*] Felicity Cunningham?

MRS. DRUDGE: A mutual friend, I believe you said. A happy chance. I will tell them you are here.

SIMON: Well, I can't really stay as a matter of fact—please don't disturb them—I really should be off.

MRS. DRUDGE: They would be very disappointed. It is some time since we have had a four for pontoon bridge at the Manor, and I don't play cards myself.

SIMON: There is another guest, then?

MRS. DRUDGE: Major Magnus, the crippled half-brother of Lord Muldoon who turned up out of the blue from Canada just the other day, completes the house-party.

[MRS. DRUDGE *leaves on this,* SIMON *is undecided.*]

MOON: [*ruminating quietly*] I think I must be waiting for Higgs to die.

BIRDBOOT: What?

MOON: Half afraid that I will vanish when he does.

[*The phone rings.* SIMON *picks it up.*]

SIMON: Hello?

MOON: I wonder if it's the same for Puckeridge?

BIRDBOOT AND SIMON: [*together*] Who?

MOON: Third string.

BIRDBOOT: Your stand-in?

MOON: Does he wait for Higgs and I to write each other's obituary—does he dream——?

SIMON: To whom did you wish to speak?

BIRDBOOT: What's he like?

MOON: Bitter.

SIMON: There is no one of that name here.

BIRDBOOT: No—as a critic, what's Puckeridge like as a critic?

MOON: [*laughs poisonously*] Nobody knows——

SIMON: You must have got the wrong number!

MOON: —there's always been me and Higgs.

[SIMON *replaces the phone and paces nervously. Pause.* BIRDBOOT *consults his programme.*]

BIRDBOOT: Simon Gascoyne. It's not him, of course.

MOON: What?

BIRDBOOT: I said it's not him.

MOON: Who is it, then?

BIRDBOOT: My guess is Magnus.

MOON: In disguise, you mean?

BIRDBOOT: What?

MOON: You think he's Magnus in disguise?

BIRDBOOT: I don't think you're concentrating, Moon.

MOON: I thought you said——

BIRDBOOT: You keep chattering on about Higgs and Puckeridge—what's the matter with you?

MOON: [*thoughtfully*] I wonder if they talk about me . . . ?

[*A strange impulse makes* SIMON *turn on the radio.*]

RADIO: Here is another police message. Essex county police are still searching in vain for the madman who is at large in the deadly marshes of the coastal region. Inspector Hound who is masterminding the operation, is not available for comment but it is widely believed that he has a secret plan. . . . Meanwhile police and volunteers are combing the swamps with loud-hailers, shouting, "Don't be a madman, give yourself up." That is the end of the police message.

[SIMON *turns off the radio. He is clearly nervous.* MOON *and* BIRDBOOT *are on separate tracks.*]

BIRDBOOT: [*knowingly*] Oh yes . . .

MOON: Yes, I should think my name is seldom off Puckeridge's lips . . . sad, really. I mean, it's no life at all, a stand-in's stand-in.

BIRDBOOT: Yes . . . yes . . .

MOON: Higgs never gives me a second thought. I can tell by the way he nods.

BIRDBOOT: Revenge, of course.

MOON: What?

BIRDBOOT: Jealousy.

MOON: Nonsense—there's nothing *personal* in it——

BIRDBOOT: The paranoid grudge——

MOON: [*sharply first, then starting to career . . .*] It is merely that it is not enough to wax at another's wane, to be held in reserve, to be on hand, on call, to step in or not at all, the substitute—the near offer—the temporary-acting—for I am Moon, continuous Moon, in my own shoes, Moon in June, April, September and no member of the human race keeps warm my bit of space—yes, I can tell by the way he nods.

BIRDBOOT: Quite mad, of course.

MOON: What?

BIRDBOOT: The answer lies out there in the swamps.

MOON: Oh.

BIRDBOOT: The skeleton in the cupboard is coming home to roost.

MOON: Oh yes. [*He clears his throat . . . for both he and* BIRDBOOT *have a "public" voice, a critic voice which they turn on for sustained pronouncements of opinion.*] Already in the opening stages we note the classic impact of the catalystic figure—the outsider—plunging through to the centre of an ordered world and setting up the disruptions—the shock waves—which unless I am much mistaken, will strip these comfortable people—these crustaceans in the rock pool of society—strip them of their shells and leave them exposed as the trembling raw meat which, at heart, is all of us. But there is more to it than that——

BIRDBOOT: I agree—keep your eye on Magnus.

[*A tennis ball bounces through the french windows, closely followed by* FELICITY, *who is in her 20's. She wears a pretty tennis outfit, and carries a racket.*]

FELICITY: [*calling behind her*] Out!

[*It takes her a moment to notice* SIMON *who is standing shiftily to one side.* MOON *is stirred by a memory.*]

MOON: I say, Birdboot . . .

BIRDBOOT: That's the one.

FELICITY: [*catching sight of* SIMON] You!

[FELICITY'*s manner at the moment is one of great surprise but some pleasure.*]

SIMON: [*nervously*] Er, yes—hello again.

FELICITY: What are you doing here?

SIMON: Well, I . . .

MOON: She's—

BIRDBOOT: Sssh . . .

SIMON: No doubt you're surprised to see me.

FELICITY: Honestly, darling, you really are extraordinary.

SIMON: Yes, well, here I am.

FELICITY: You must have been desperate to see me—I mean, I'm *flattered*, but couldn't it wait till I got back?

SIMON: [*bravely*] There is something you don't know.

FELICITY: What is it?

SIMON: Look, about the things I said—it may be that I got carried away a little— we both did—

FELICITY: [*stiffly*] What are you trying to say?

SIMON: I love another!

FELICITY: I see.

SIMON: I didn't make any promises—I merely—

FELICITY: You don't have to say any more—

SIMON: Oh, I didn't want to hurt you—

FELICITY: Of all the nerve!

SIMON: Well, I—

FELICITY: You philandering coward—

SIMON: Let me explain—

FELICITY: This is hardly the time and place—you think you can barge in anywhere, whatever I happen to be doing—

SIMON: But I want you to know that my admiration for you is sincere—I don't want you to think that I didn't mean those things I said—

FELICITY: I'll kill you for this, Simon Gascoyne!

[*She leaves in tears, passing* MRS. DRUDGE *who has entered in time to overhear her last remark.*]

MOON: It was her.

BIRDBOOT: I told you—straight to the top—

MOON: No, no—

BIRDBOOT: Sssh . . .

SIMON: [*to* MRS. DRUDGE] Yes, what is it?

MRS. DRUDGE: I have come to set up the card table, sir.

SIMON: I don't think I can stay.

MRS. DRUDGE: Oh, Lady Muldoon *will* be disappointed.

SIMON: Does she know I'm here?

MRS. DRUDGE: Oh yes, sir, I just told her and it put her in quite a tizzy.

SIMON: Really? . . . Well, I suppose now that I've cleared the air. . . . Quite a tizzy, you say . . . really . . . really . . .

[*He and* MRS. DRUDGE *start setting up for card game.* MRS. DRUDGE *leaves when this is done.*]

MOON: Felicity!—she's the one.

BIRDBOOT: Nonsense—red herring.

MOON: I mean, it was *her*!

BIRDBOOT: [*exasperated*] *What* was?

MOON: That lady I saw you with last night!

BIRDBOOT: [*inhales with fury*] Are you suggesting that a man of my scrupulous integrity would trade his pen for a mess of potage?![9] Simply because in the course of my profession I happen to have struck up an acquaintance—to have, that is, a warm regard, if you like, for a fellow toiler in the vineyard of greasepaint—I find it simply intolerable to be pillified and villoried——

MOON: I never implied——

BIRDBOOT: —to find myself the object of uninformed malice, the petty slanders of little men——

MOON: I'm sorry——

BIRDBOOT: —to suggest that my good opinion in a journal of unimpeachable integrity is at the disposal of the first coquette who gives me what I want——

MOON: Ssssh——

BIRDBOOT: A ladies' man! . . . Why, Myrtle and I have been together now for— Christ!—who's *that*?

[*Enter* LADY CYNTHIA MULDOON *through french windows. A beautiful woman in her thirties. She wears a cocktail dress, is formally coiffured, and carries a tennis racket.*]
[*Her effect on* BIRDBOOT *is also impressive. He half rises and sinks back agape.*]

CYNTHIA: [*entering*] Simon!

[*A dramatic freeze between her and* SIMON].

MOON: Lady Muldoon.

BIRDBOOT: No, I mean—who *is* she?

SIMON: [*coming forward*] Cynthia!

CYNTHIA: Don't say anything for a moment—just hold me.

[*He seizes her and glues his lips to hers, as they say. While their lips are glued——*]

BIRDBOOT: She's *beautiful*—a vision of eternal grace, a poem . . .

MOON: I think she's got her mouth open.

[CYNTHIA *breaks away dramatically.*]

CYNTHIA: We can't go on meeting like this!

SIMON: We have nothing to be ashamed of!

9. In the Bible, Jacob persuades his elder brother Esau to give up his right of inheritance in exchange for a "mess of potage" or dish of stew—that is, for a very cheap price. *Toiler in the vineyard of greasepaint*: theater professional. *Pillified and villoried*: vilified and pilloried.

CYNTHIA: But darling, this is madness!

SIMON: Yes!—I am mad with love for you!

CYNTHIA: Please—remember where we are!

SIMON: Cynthia, I love you!

CYNTHIA: Don't—I love Albert!

SIMON: He's dead! [*Shaking her.*] Do you understand me—Albert's dead!

CYNTHIA: No—I'll never give up hope! Let me go! We are not free!

SIMON: I don't care, we were meant for each other—had we but met in time.

CYNTHIA: You're a cad, Simon! You will use me and cast me aside as you have cast aside so many others.

SIMON: No, Cynthia!—you can make me a better person!

CYNTHIA: You're ruthless—so strong, so cruel—

[*Ruthlessly he kisses her.*]

MOON: The son she never had, now projected in this handsome stranger and transformed into lover—youth, vigour, the animal, the athlete as aesthete—breaking down the barriers at the deepest level of desire.

BIRDBOOT: By jove, I think you're right. Her mouth *is* open.

[CYNTHIA *breaks away.* MRS. DRUDGE *has entered.*]

CYNTHIA: Stop—can't you see you're making a fool of yourself!

SIMON: I'll kill anyone who comes between us!

CYNTHIA: Yes, what is it, Mrs. Drudge?

MRS. DRUDGE: Should I close the windows, my lady? The fog is beginning to roll off the sea like a deadly—

CYNTHIA: Yes, you'd better. It looks as if we're in for one of those days. Are the cards ready?

MRS. DRUDGE: Yes, my lady.

CYNTHIA: Would you tell Miss Cunningham we are waiting.

MRS. DRUDGE: Yes, my lady.

CYNTHIA: And fetch the Major down.

MRS. DRUDGE: I think I hear him coming downstairs now [*as she leaves*].

[*She does: the sound of a wheelchair approaching down several flights of stairs with landings in between. It arrives bearing* MAGNUS *at about 15 m.p.h., knocking* SIMON *over violently.*]

CYNTHIA: Simon!

MAGNUS: [*roaring*] Never had a chance! Ran under the wheels!

CYNTHIA: Darling, are you all right?

MAGNUS: I have witnesses!

CYNTHIA: Oh, Simon—say something!

SIMON: [*sitting up suddenly*] I'm most frightfully sorry.

MAGNUS: [*shouting yet*] How long have you been a pedestrian?

SIMON: Ever since I could walk.

CYNTHIA: Can you walk now . . . ?

[SIMON *rises and walks.*]

Thank God! Magnus, this is Simon Gascoyne.

MAGNUS: What's he doing here?

CYNTHIA: He just turned up.

MAGNUS: Really? How do you like it here?

SIMON: [to CYNTHIA] I could stay forever.

[FELICITY enters.]

FELICITY: So—you're still here.

CYNTHIA: Of course he's still here. We're going to play cards. There's no need to introduce you two, is there, for I recall now that you, Simon, met me through Felicity, our mutual friend.

FELICITY: Yes, Simon is an old friend, though not as old as you, Cynthia dear.

SIMON: Yes, I haven't seen Felicity since——

FELICITY: Last night.

CYNTHIA: Indeed? Well, you deal, Felicity. Simon, you help me with the sofa. Will you partner Felicity, Magnus, against Simon and me?

MAGNUS: [aside] Will Simon and you always be partnered against me, Cynthia?

CYNTHIA: What do you mean, Magnus?

MAGNUS: You are a damned attractive woman, Cynthia.

CYNTHIA: Please! Please! Remember Albert!

MAGNUS: Albert's dead, Cynthia—and you are still young. I'm sure he would have wished that you and I——

CYNTHIA: No, Magnus, this is not to be!

MAGNUS: It's Gascoyne, isn't it? I'll kill him if he comes between us!

CYNTHIA: [calling] Simon!

[The sofa is shoved towards the card table, once more revealing the corpse, though not to the players.]

BIRDBOOT: Simon's for the chop[1] all right.

CYNTHIA: Right! Who starts?

MAGNUS: I do. No bid.

CYNTHIA: Did I hear you say you saw Felicity last night, Simon?

SIMON: Did I?—Ah yes, yes, quite—your turn, Felicity.

FELICITY: I've had my turn, haven't I, Simon?—now, it seems, it's Cynthia's turn.

CYNTHIA: That's my trick, Felicity dear.

FELICITY: Hell hath no fury like a woman scorned,[2] Simon.

SIMON: Yes, I've heard it said.

FELICITY: So I hope you have not been cheating, Simon.

SIMON: [standing up and throwing down his cards] No, Felicity, it's just that I hold the cards!

CYNTHIA: Well done, Simon!

[MAGNUS pays SIMON, while CYNTHIA deals.]

FELICITY: Strange how Simon appeared in the neighborhood from nowhere. We know so little about him.

SIMON: It doesn't always pay to show your hand!

CYNTHIA: Right! Simon, it's your opening on the minor bid.

1. In danger; slated for execution.
2. A saying adapted from a line in William Congreve's play *The Mourning Bride* (1697), warning that rejected or jealous women are roused to overwhelming, violent revenge.

[SIMON *plays.*]

CYNTHIA: Hm, let's see . . . [*Plays.*]

FELICITY: I hear there's a dangerous madman on the loose.

CYNTHIA: Simon?

SIMON: Yes—yes—sorry. [*Plays.*]

CYNTHIA: I meld.

· FELICITY: Yes—personally, I think he's been hiding out in the deserted cottage [*plays*] on the cliffs.

SIMON: Flush!

CYNTHIA: No! Simon—your luck's in tonight!

FELICITY: We shall see—the night is not over yet, Simon Gascoyne! [*She exits.*]

[MAGNUS *pays* SIMON *again.*]

SIMON: [*to* MAGNUS] So you're the crippled half-brother of Lord Muldoon who turned up out of the blue from Canada just the other day, are you? It's taken you a long time to get here. What did you do—walk? Oh, I say, I'm most frightfully sorry!

MAGNUS: Care for a spin round the rose garden, Cynthia?

CYNTHIA: No, Magnus, I must talk to Simon.

SIMON: My round, I think, Major.

MAGNUS: You think so?

SIMON: Yes, Major—I do.

MAGNUS: There's an old Canadian proverb handed down from the Bladfoot Indians, which says: He who laughs last laughs longest.[3]

SIMON: Yes, I've heard it said.

[SIMON *turns away to* CYNTHIA.]

MAGNUS: Well, I think I'll go and oil my gun. [*He exits.*]

CYNTHIA: I think Magnus suspects something. And Felicity . . . Simon, was there anything between you and Felicity?

SIMON: No, no—it's over between her and me, Cynthia—it was a mere passing fleeting thing we had—but now that I have found you——

CYNTHIA: If I find that you have been untrue to me—if I find that you have falsely seduced me from my dear husband Albert—I will kill you, Simon Gascoyne!

[MRS. DRUDGE *has entered silently to witness this. On this tableau, pregnant with significance, the act ends, the body still undiscovered. Perfunctory applause.*]
[MOON *and* BIRDBOOT *seem to be completely preoccupied, becoming audible, as it were.*]

MOON: Camps it around the Old Vic in his opera cloak and passes me the tat.[4]

BIRDBOOT: Do you believe in love at first sight?

MOON: It's not that I think I'm a better critic——

BIRDBOOT: I feel my whole life changing——

MOON: I am but it's not that.

---

3. The usual proverb, possibly of Italian origin, is "He who laughs last laughs best." The Bladfoot Indians, like Magnus's association with Canada, are fictitious.

4. That is, puts on a grand act when he goes to the Old Vic (a prestigious London theater) and treats Moon as an underling.

BIRDBOOT: Oh, the world will laugh at me, I know. . . .

MOON: It is not that they are much in the way of shoes to step into. . . .

BIRDBOOT: . . . call me an infatuated old fool . . .

MOON: . . . They are not.

BIRDBOOT: . . . condemn me . . .

MOON: He is standing in my light, that is all.

BIRDBOOT: . . . betrayer of my class . . .

MOON: . . . an almost continuous eclipse, interrupted by the phenomenon of moonlight.

BIRDBOOT: I don't care, I'm a goner.

MOON: And I dream . . .

BIRDBOOT: The Blue Angel[5] all over again.

MOON: . . . of the day his temperature climbs through the top of his head . . .

BIRDBOOT: Ah, the sweet madness of love . . .

MOON: . . . of the spasm on the stairs . . .

BIRDBOOT: Myrtle, farewell . . .

MOON: . . . dreaming of the stair he'll never reach—

BIRDBOOT: . . . for I only live but once. . . .

MOON: Sometimes I dream that I've killed him.

BIRDBOOT: What?

MOON: What?

[*They pull themselves together.*]

BIRDBOOT: Yes . . . yes. . . . A beautiful performance, a collector's piece. I shall say so.

MOON: A very promising debut. I'll put in a good word.

BIRDBOOT: It would be as hypocritical of me to withhold praise on grounds of personal feelings, as to withhold censure.

MOON: You're right. Courageous.

BIRDBOOT: Oh, I know what people will say— There goes Birdboot buttering up his latest—

MOON: Ignore them—

BIRDBOOT: But I rise above that— The fact is I genuinely believe her performance to be one of the summits in the range of contemporary theatre.

MOON: Trim-buttocked, that's the word for her.

BIRDBOOT: —the radiance, the inner sadness—

MOON: Does she actually come across with it?

BIRDBOOT: The part as written is a mere cypher but she manages to make Cynthia a real person—

MOON: *Cynthia?*

BIRDBOOT: And should she, as a result, care to meet me over a drink, simply by way of er—thanking me, as it were—

MOON: Well, you fickle old bastard!

BIRDBOOT: [*aggressively*] Are you suggesting . . . ?

[BIRDBOOT *shudders to a halt and clears his throat.*]

---

5. A 1931 film directed by Josef von Sternberg and starring Marlene Dietrich and Emil Jennings; it tells the story of a middle-aged professor falling for a nightclub performer.

BIRDBOOT: Well now—shaping up quite nicely, wouldn't you say?

MOON: Oh yes, yes. A nice trichotomy of forces. One must reserve judgement of course, until the confrontation, but I think it's pretty clear where we're heading.

BIRDBOOT: I agree. It's Magnus a mile off.

[*Small pause.*]

MOON: What's Magnus a mile off?

BIRDBOOT: If we knew that we wouldn't be here.

MOON: [*clears throat*] Let me at once say that it has *élan*[6] while at the same time avoiding *éclat*. Having said that, and I think it must be said, I am bound to ask—does this play know where it is going?

BIRDBOOT: Well, it seems open and shut to me, Moon—Magnus is not what he pretends to be and he's got his next victim marked down—

MOON: Does it, I repeat, declare its affiliations? There are moments, and I would not begrudge it this, when the play, if we can call it that, and I think on balance we can, aligns itself uncompromisingly on the side of life. *Je suis*, it seems to be saying, *ergo sum*.[7] But is that enough? I think we are entitled to ask. For what in fact is this play concerned with? It is my belief that here we are concerned with what I have referred to elsewhere as the nature of identity. I think we are entitled to ask—and here one is irresistibly reminded of Voltaire's cry, "*Violà!*"—I think we are entitled to ask—*Where is God?*

BIRDBOOT: [*stunned*] Who?

MOON: Go-od.

BIRDBOOT: [*peeping furtively into his programme*] God?

MOON: I think we are entitled to ask.

[*The phone rings.*]
[*The set re-illumines to reveal* CYNTHIA, FELICITY *and* MAGNUS *about to take coffee, which is being taken round by* MRS. DRUDGE. SIMON *is missing. The body lies in position.*]

MRS. DRUDGE: [*into phone*] The same, half an hour later? . . . No, I'm sorry—there's no one of that name here. [*She replaces phone and goes round with coffee. To* CYNTHIA]: Black or white, my lady?

CYNTHIA: White please.

[MRS. DRUDGE *pours.*]

MRS. DRUDGE: [*to* FELICITY] Black or white, miss?

FELICITY: White please.

[MRS. DRUDGE *pours.*]

MRS. DRUDGE: [*to* MAGNUS] Black or white, Major?

MAGNUS: White please.

---

6. Flair; grace (French). *Éclat*: a public sensation; a splashy production (French).

7. Moon misquotes and misapplies the French philosopher Descartes's principle *Cogito, ergo sum*, Latin for "I think, therefore I am." *"Je suis"* means "I am" in French; that is, Moon says, "I am . . . therefore I am." *Voilà*: French expression meaning "Look!" or "You see!" There is no common reference to the French philosopher Voltaire (1694–1778) ever saying this.

[*Ditto.*]

MRS. DRUDGE: [*to* CYNTHIA] Sugar, my lady?
CYNTHIA: Yes please.

[*Puts sugar in.*]

MRS. DRUDGE: [*to* FELICITY] Sugar, miss?
FELICITY: Yes please.

[*Ditto.*]

MRS. DRUDGE: [*to* MAGNUS] Sugar, Major?
MAGNUS: Yes please.

[*Ditto.*]

MRS. DRUDGE: [*to* CYNTHIA] Biscuit, my lady?
CYNTHIA: No thank you.
BIRDBOOT: [*writing elaborately in his notebook*] The second act, however, fails to fulfil the promise. . . .
FELICITY: If you ask me, there's something funny going on.

[MRS. DRUDGE*'s approach to* FELICITY *makes* FELICITY *jump to her feet in impatience. She goes to the radio while* MAGNUS *declines his biscuit, and* MRS. DRUDGE *leaves.*]

RADIO: We interrupt our programme for a special police message. The search for the dangerous madman who is on the loose in Essex has now narrowed to the immediate vicinity of Muldoon Manor. Police are hampered by the deadly swamps and the fog, but believe that the madman spent last night in a deserted cottage on the cliffs. The public is advised to stick together and make sure none of their number is missing. That is the end of the police message.

[FELICITY *turns off the radio nervously. Pause.*]

CYNTHIA: Where's Simon?
FELICITY: Who?
CYNTHIA: Simon. Have you seen him?
FELICITY: No.
CYNTHIA: Have you, Magnus?
MAGNUS: No.
CYNTHIA: Oh.
FELICITY: Yes, there's something foreboding in the air, it is as if one of *us*—
CYNTHIA: Oh, Felicity, the house is locked up tight—no one can get in—and the police are practically on the doorstep.
FELICITY: I don't know—it's just a feeling.
CYNTHIA: It's only the fog.
MAGNUS: Hound will never get through on a day like this.
CYNTHIA: [*shouting at him*] Fog!
FELICITY: He means the Inspector.
CYNTHIA: Is he bringing a dog?
FELICITY: Not that I know of.
MAGNUS: —never get through the swamps. Yes, I'm afraid the madman can show his hand in safety now.

[*A mournful baying hooting is heard in the distance, scary.*]

CYNTHIA: What's that?!

FELICITY: [*tensely*] It sounded like the cry of a gigantic hound!

MAGNUS: Poor devil!

CYNTHIA: Sssh!

[*They listen. The sound is repeated, nearer.*]

FELICITY: There it is again!

CYNTHIA: It's coming this way—it's right outside the house!

[MRS. DRUDGE *enters.*]

MRS. DRUDGE: Inspector Hound!

CYNTHIA: A *police* dog?

[*Enter* INSPECTOR HOUND. *On his feet are his swamp boots. These are two inflatable— and inflated—pontoons with flat bottoms about two feet across. He carries a foghorn.*]

HOUND: Lady Muldoon?

CYNTHIA: Yes.

HOUND: I came as soon as I could. Where shall I put my foghorn and my swamp boots?

CYNTHIA: Mrs. Drudge will take them out. Be prepared, as the Force's motto has it, eh, Inspector? How very resourceful!

HOUND: [*divesting himself of boots and foghorn*] It takes more than a bit of weather to keep a policeman from his duty.

[MRS. DRUDGE *leaves with chattels. A pause.*]

CYNTHIA: Oh—er, Inspector Hound—Felicity Cunningham, Major Magnus Muldoon.

HOUND: Good evening.

[*He and* CYNTHIA *continue to look expectantly at each other.*]

CYNTHIA AND HOUND: [*together*] Well?—Sorry—

CYNTHIA: No, do go on.

HOUND: Thank you. Well, tell me about it in your own words—take your time, begin at the beginning and don't leave anything out.

CYNTHIA: I beg your pardon?

HOUND: Fear nothing. You are in safe hands now. I hope you haven't touched anything.

CYNTHIA: I'm afraid I don't understand.

HOUND: I'm Inspector Hound.

CYNTHIA: Yes.

HOUND: Well, what's it all about?

CYNTHIA: I really have no idea.

HOUND: How did it begin?

CYNTHIA: What?

HOUND: The . . . thing.

CYNTHIA: What thing?

HOUND: [*rapidly losing confidence but exasperated*] The trouble!

CYNTHIA: There hasn't *been* any trouble!

HOUND: Didn't you phone the police?

CYNTHIA: No.

FELICITY: I didn't.

MAGNUS: What for?

HOUND: I see. [*Pause.*] This puts me in a very difficult position. [*A steady pause.*] Well, I'll be getting along, then. [*He moves towards the door.*]

CYNTHIA: I'm terribly sorry.

HOUND: [*stiffly*] That's perfectly all right.

CYNTHIA: Thank you so much for coming.

HOUND: Not at all. You never know, there might have been a serious matter.

CYNTHIA: Drink?

HOUND: More serious than that, even.

CYNTHIA: [*correcting*] Drink before you go?

HOUND: No thank you. [*Leaves.*]

CYNTHIA: [*through the door*] I do hope you find him.

HOUND: [*reappearing at once*] Find who, Madam?—out with it!

CYNTHIA: I thought you were looking for the lunatic.

HOUND: And what do you know about that?

CYNTHIA: It was on the radio.

HOUND: Was it, indeed? Well, that's what I'm here about, really. I didn't want to mention it because I didn't know how much you knew. No point in causing unnecessary panic, even with a murderer in our midst.

FELICITY: Murderer, did you say?

HOUND: Ah—so that was not on the radio?

CYNTHIA: Whom has he murdered, Inspector?

HOUND: Perhaps no one—yet. Let us hope we are in time.

MAGNUS: You believe he is in our midst, Inspector?

HOUND: I do. If anyone of you have recently encountered a youngish good-looking fellow in a smart suit, white shirt, hatless, well-spoken—someone possibly claiming to have just moved into the neighbourhood, someone who on the surface seems as sane as you or I, then now is the time to speak!

FELICITY: I——

HOUND: Don't interrupt!

FELICITY: Inspector——

HOUND: Very well.

CYNTHIA: No. Felicity!

HOUND: Please, Lady Cynthia, we are all in this together. I must ask you to put yourself completely in my hands.

CYNTHIA: Don't, Inspector. I love Albert.

HOUND: I don't think you quite grasp my meaning.

MAGNUS: Is one of us in danger, Inspector?

HOUND: Didn't it strike you as odd that on his escape the madman made a bee-line for Muldoon Manor? It is my guess that he bears a deep-seated grudge against someone in this very house! Lady Muldoon—where is your husband?

CYNTHIA: My husband?—you don't mean——?

HOUND: I don't know—but I have a reason to believe that one of you is the real McCoy![8]

---

8. This expression, meaning the genuine original, the real article among fakes, has many possible origins, none of which has anything to do with the fanciful explanation in Inspector Hound's next speech.

FELICITY: The real what?

HOUND: William Herbert McCoy who as a young man, meeting the madman in the street and being solicited for sixpence for a cup of tea, replied, "Why don't you do a decent day's work, you shifty old bag of horse manure," in Canada all those many years ago and went on to make his fortune. [*He starts to pace intensely.*] The madman was a mere boy at the time but he never forgot that moment, and thenceforth carried in his heart the promise of revenge! [*At which point he finds himself standing on top of the corpse. He looks down carefully.*]

HOUND: Is there anything you have forgotten to tell me?

[*They all see the corpse for the first time.*]

FELICITY: So the madman has struck!

CYNTHIA: Oh—it's horrible—horrible——

HOUND: Yes, just as I feared. Now you see the sort of man you are protecting.

CYNTHIA: I can't believe it!

FELICITY: I'll have to tell him, Cynthia—Inspector, a stranger of that description has indeed appeared in our midst—Simon Gascoyne. Oh, he had charm, I'll give you that, and he took me in completely. I'm afraid I made a fool of myself over him, and so did Cynthia.

HOUND: Where is he now?

MAGNUS: He must be around the house—he couldn't get away in these conditions.

HOUND: You're right. Fear naught, Lady Muldoon—I shall apprehend the man who killed your husband.

CYNTHIA: My husband? I don't understand.

HOUND: Everything points to Gascoyne.

CYNTHIA: But who's that? [*The corpse.*]

HOUND: Your husband.

CYNTHIA: No, it's not.

HOUND: Yes, it is.

CYNTHIA: I tell you it's not.

HOUND: *I'm* in charge of this case!

CYNTHIA: But that's not my husband.

HOUND: Are you sure?

CYNTHIA: For goodness sake!

HOUND: Then who is it?

CYNTHIA: I don't know.

HOUND: Anybody?

FELICITY: I've never seen him before.

MAGNUS: Quite unlike anybody I've ever met.

HOUND: This case is becoming an utter shambles.

CYNTHIA: But what are we going to do?

HOUND: [*snatching the phone*] I'll phone the police!

CYNTHIA: But you are the police!

HOUND: Thank God I'm here—the lines have been cut!

CYNTHIA: You mean——?

HOUND: Yes!—we're on our own, cut off from the world and in grave danger!

FELICITY: You mean——?

HOUND: Yes!—I think the killer will strike again!

MAGNUS: You mean——?

HOUND: Yes! One of us ordinary mortals thrown together by fate and cut off by the elements, is the murderer! He must be found—search the house!

[*All depart speedily in different directions leaving a momentarily empty stage.* SIMON *strolls on.*]

SIMON: [*entering, calling*] Anyone about?—funny . . .

[*He notices the corpse and is surprised. He approaches it and turns it over. He stands up and looks about in alarm.*]

BIRDBOOT: This is where Simon gets the chop.

[*There is a shot.* SIMON *falls dead.*]
[INSPECTOR HOUND *runs on and crouches down by* SIMON'*s body.* CYNTHIA *appears at the french windows. She stops there and stares.*]

CYNTHIA: What happened, Inspector?!

[HOUND *turns to face her.*]

HOUND: He's dead . . . Simon Gascoyne, I presume. Rough justice even for a killer— unless—unless—We assumed that the body could not have been lying there before Simon Gascoyne entered the house . . . but . . . [*he slides the sofa over the body*] there's your answer. And now—who killed Simon Gascoyne? And why?

["*Curtain*", *freeze, applause, exeunt.*[9]]

MOON: Why not?
BIRDBOOT: Exactly. Good riddance.
MOON: Yes, getting away with murder must be quite easy provided that one's motive is sufficiently inscrutable.
BIRDBOOT: Fickle young pup! He was deceiving her right, left and centre.
MOON: [*thoughtfully*] Of course. I'd still have Puckeridge behind *me*—
BIRDBOOT: She needs someone steadier, more mature—
MOON: —And if I could, so could he—
BIRDBOOT: Yes, I know of this rather nice hotel, very discreet, run by a man of the world—
MOON: Uneasy lies the head that wears the crown.[1]
BIRDBOOT: Breakfast served in one's room and no questions asked.
MOON: Does Puckeridge dream of me?
BIRDBOOT: [*pause*] Hello—what's happened?
MOON: What? Oh yes—what do you make of it, so far?
BIRDBOOT: [*clears throat*] It is at this point that the play for me comes alive. The groundwork has been well and truly laid, and the author has taken the trouble to learn from the masters of the genre. He has created a real situation, and few will doubt his ability to resolve it with a startling denouement. Certainly that is what it so far lacks, but it has a beginning, a middle and I have no doubt it will prove to have an end. For this let us give thanks, and double thanks for a

9. Literally, "They go out" (Latin).
1. Shakespeare, *2 Henry IV* 3.1.31. The king is lamenting his insomnia, in contrast with a poor sailor boy's ability to sleep soundly during a storm at sea.

good clean show without a trace of smut. But perhaps even all this would be for nothing were it not for a performance which I consider to be one of the summits in the range of contemporary theatre. In what is possibly the finest Cynthia since the war——

MOON: If we examine this more closely, and I think close examination is the least tribute that this play deserves, I think we will find that within the austere framework of what is seen to be on one level a country-house week-end, and what a useful symbol that is, the author has given us—yes, I will go so far—he has given us the human condition——

BIRDBOOT: More talent in her little finger——

MOON: An uncanny ear that might have belonged to a Van Gogh[2]——

BIRDBOOT: —a public scandal that the Birthday Honours[3] to date have neglected——

MOON: Faced as we are with such ubiquitous obliquity, it is hard, it is hard indeed, and therefore I will not attempt, to refrain from invoking the names of Kafka, Sartre, Shakespeare, St. Paul, Beckett, Birkett, Pinero, Pirandello, Dante and Dorothy L. Sayers.[4]

BIRDBOOT: A rattling good evening out. I was held.

[*The phone starts to ring on the empty stage.* MOON *tries to ignore it.*]

MOON: Harder still—— Harder still if possible—— Harder still if it is possible to be—— Neither do I find it easy—— Dante and Dorothy L. Sayers. Harder still——

BIRDBOOT: Others taking part included—*Moon!*

[*For* MOON *has lost patience and is bearing down on the ringing phone. He is frankly irritated.*]

MOON: [*picking up phone, barks*] Hel-lo! [*Pause, turns to* BIRDBOOT, *quietly.*] It's for you. [*Pause.*]

[BIRDBOOT *gets up. He approaches cautiously.* MOON *gives him the phone and moves back to his seat.* BIRDBOOT *watches him go. He looks round and smiles weakly, expiating himself.*]

BIRDBOOT: [*into phone*] Hello . . . [*Explosion.*] Oh, for God's sake, Myrtle!—I've told you never to phone me at work! [*He is naturally embarrassed, looking about with surreptitious fury.*] What? Last night? Good God, woman, this is hardly the time to—I assure you, Myrtle, there is absolutely nothing going on between me and—I took her to dinner simply by way of keeping *au fait* with the world of the paint and the motley[5]—— Yes, I promise—— Yes, I do—— Yes, I *said* yes—I *do*—and you are mine too, Myrtle—darling—I can't—[*whispers*] *I'm not alone*—[*up*]. No, she's not!—[*he looks around furtively, licks his lips and mumbles*]. All *right*! I love your little pink ears and you are my own fluffy bunny-boo—— Now for God's sake—— Good-bye, Myrtle—[*puts down phone*].

---

2. Dutch artist (1853–90); Van Gogh cut off his ear, possibly because of suffering from Meniere's disease, which causes ringing in the inner ear and loss of balance.

3. A list of honorees for public service in various fields; the list is issued yearly in Britain to mark Queen Elizabeth's birthday.

4. A range of writers' names, biblical, classic, and modern, ending with one of the most famous detective novelists. "Birkett" apparently is an invention to chime with "Beckett."

5. That is, the world of the theater. ("Motley" refers to a jester's patchwork costume.)

[BIRDBOOT *mops his brow with his handkerchief. As he turns, a tennis ball bounces in through the french windows, followed by* FELICITY, *as before, in tennis outfit. The lighting is as it was. Everything is as it was. It is, let us say, the same moment of time.*]

FELICITY: [*calling*] Out! [*She catches sight of* BIRDBOOT *and is amazed.*] You!

BIRDBOOT: Er, yes—hello again.

FELICITY: What are you doing here?!

BIRDBOOT: Well, I . . .

FELICITY: Honestly, darling, you really are extraordinary——

BIRDBOOT: Yes, well, here I am. [*He looks round sheepishly.*]

FELICITY: You must have been desperate to see me—I mean, I'm flattered, but couldn't it wait till I got back?

BIRDBOOT: No, no, you've got it all wrong——

FELICITY: What is it?

BIRDBOOT: And about last night—perhaps I gave you the wrong impression—got carried away a bit, perhaps——

FELICITY: [*stiffly*] What are you trying to say?

BIRDBOOT: I want to call it off.

FELICITY: I see.

BIRDBOOT: I didn't promise anything—and the fact is, I have my reputation—people do talk——

FELICITY: You don't have to say any more——

BIRDBOOT: And my wife, too—I don't know how she got to hear of it, but——

FELICITY: Of all the nerve! To march in here and——

BIRDBOOT: I'm sorry you had to find out like this—the fact is I didn't mean it this way——

FELICITY: You philandering coward!

BIRDBOOT: I'm sorry—but I want you to know that I meant those things I said—oh yes—shows brilliant promise—I shall say so——

FELICITY: I'll kill you for this, Simon Gascoyne!

[*She leaves in tears, passing* MRS. DRUDGE *who has entered in time to overhear her last remark.*]

BIRDBOOT: [*wide-eyed*] Good God. . . .

MRS. DRUDGE: I have come to set up the card table, sir.

BIRDBOOT: [*wildly*] I can't stay for a game of *cards*!

MRS. DRUDGE: Oh, Lady Muldoon *will* be disappointed.

BIRDBOOT: You mean . . . you mean, she wants to meet me . . . ?

MRS. DRUDGE: Oh yes, sir, I just told her and it put her in quite a tizzy.

BIRDBOOT: Really? Yes, well, a man of my influence is not to be sneezed at—I think I have some small name for the making of reputations—mmm, yes, quite a tizzy, you say?

[MRS. DRUDGE *is busied with the card table.* BIRDBOOT *stands marooned and bemused for a moment.*]

MOON: [*from his seat*] Birdboot!—[*a tense whisper*]. Birdboot!

[BIRDBOOT *looks round vaguely.*]

What the hell are you doing?

BIRDBOOT: Nothing.

MOON: Stop making an ass of yourself. Come back.

BIRDBOOT: Oh, I know what you're thinking—but the fact is I genuinely consider her performance to be one of the summits——

[CYNTHIA *enters as before.* MRS. DRUDGE *has gone.*]

CYNTHIA: Darling!

BIRDBOOT: Ah, good evening—may I say that I genuinely consider——

CYNTHIA: Don't say anything for a moment—just hold me.

[*She falls into his arms.*]

BIRDBOOT: All right! [*They kiss.*] My God!—she *does* have her mouth open! Dear lady, from the first moment I saw you, I felt my whole life changing——

CYNTHIA: [*breaking free*] We can't go on meeting like this!

BIRDBOOT: I am not ashamed to proclaim nightly my love for you!—but fortunately that will not be necessary—— I know of a very good hotel, discreet—run by a man of the world——

CYNTHIA: But darling, this is madness!

BIRDBOOT: Yes! I am mad with love.

CYNTHIA: Please!—remember where we are!

BIRDBOOT: I don't care! Let them think what they like, I love you!

CYNTHIA: Don't—I love Albert!

BIRDBOOT: He's dead. [*Shaking her.*] Do you understand me—Albert's dead!

CYNTHIA: No—I'll never give up hope! Let me go! We are not free!

BIRDBOOT: You mean Myrtle? She means nothing to me—nothing!—she's all cocoa and blue nylon fur slippers—not a spark of creative genius in her whole slumping knee-length-knickered body——

CYNTHIA: You're a cad, Simon! You will use me and cast me aside as you have cast aside so many others!

BIRDBOOT: No, Cynthia—now that I have found you——

CYNTHIA: You're ruthless—so strong—so cruel——

[BIRDBOOT *seizes her in an embrace, during which* MRS. DRUDGE *enters, and* MOON's *fevered voice is heard.*]

MOON: Have you taken leave of your tiny mind?

[CYNTHIA *breaks free.*]

CYNTHIA: Stop—can't you see you're making a fool of yourself!

MOON: She's right.

BIRDBOOT: [*to* MOON] You keep out of this.

CYNTHIA: Yes, what is it, Mrs. Drudge?

MRS. DRUDGE: Should I close the windows, my lady? The fog——

CYNTHIA: Yes, you'd better.

MOON: Look, they've got your number——

BIRDBOOT: I'll leave in my own time, thank you very much.

MOON: It's the finish of you, I suppose you know that——

BIRDBOOT: I don't need your twopenny Grubb Street prognostications[6]—I have found something bigger and finer——

---

6. Cheap predictions from hack journalists. Grubb Street, in London, was once home to low-market writers and publishers.

MOON: [*bemused, to himself*] If only it were Higgs. . . .

CYNTHIA: . . . And fetch the Major down.

MRS. DRUDGE: I think I hear him coming downstairs now.

[*She leaves. The sound of a wheelchair's approach as before.* BIRDBOOT *prudently keeps out of the chair's former path but it enters from the next wing down and knocks him flying. A babble of anguish and protestation.*]

CYNTHIA: Simon—say something!

BIRDBOOT: That reckless bastard [*as he sits up*].

CYNTHIA: Thank God!——

MAGNUS: What's *he* doing here?

CYNTHIA: He just turned up.

MAGNUS: Really? How do you like it here?

BIRDBOOT: I couldn't take it night after night.

[FELICITY *enters.*]

FELICITY: So—you're still here.

CYNTHIA: Of course he's still here. We're going to play cards. There is no need to introduce you two, is there, for I recall now that you, Simon, met me through Felicity, our mutual friend.

FELICITY: Yes, Simon is an old friend——

BIRDBOOT: Ah—yes—well, I like to give young up and comers the benefit of my— er—Of course, she lacks technique as yet——

FELICITY: Last night.

BIRDBOOT: I'm not talking about last night!

CYNTHIA: Indeed? Well, you deal, Felicity. Simon, you help me with the sofa.

BIRDBOOT: [*to* MOON] Did you see that? Tried to kill me. I told you it was Magnus— not that it *is* Magnus.

MOON: Who did it, you mean?

BIRDBOOT: What?

MOON: You think it's not Magnus who did it?

BIRDBOOT: Get a grip on yourself, Moon—the facts are staring you in the face. He's after Cynthia for one thing.

MAGNUS: It's Gascoyne, isn't it?

BIRDBOOT: Over my dead body!

MAGNUS: If he comes between us . . .

MOON: [*angrily*] For God's sake sit down!

CYNTHIA: Simon!

BIRDBOOT: She needs me, Moon. I've got to make up a four.

[CYNTHIA *and* BIRDBOOT *move the sofa as before, and they all sit at the table.*]

CYNTHIA: Right! Who starts?

MAGNUS: I do. I'll dummy for a no-bid ruff and double my holding on South's queen.[7] [*While he moves cards.*]

CYNTHIA: Did I hear you say you saw Felicity last night, Simon?

BIRDBOOT: Er—er——

FELICITY: Pay twenty-ones or trump my contract. [*Discards.*] Cynthia's turn.

---

7. Like much of the dialogue that follows, a fanciful mishmash of card-game and chess terminology.

CYNTHIA: I'll trump your contract with five dummy no-trumps there [*discards*], and I'll move West's rook for the re-bid with a banker ruff on his second trick there. [*Discards.*] Simon?

BIRDBOOT: Would you mind doing that again?

CYNTHIA: And I'll ruff your dummy with five no-bid trumps there, [*discards*] and I support your re-bid with a banker for the solo ruff in the dummy trick there. [*Discards.*]

BIRDBOOT: [*standing up and throwing down his cards*] And I call your bluff!

CYNTHIA: Well done, Simon!

[MAGNUS *pays* BIRDBOOT *while* CYNTHIA *deals.*]

FELICITY: Strange how Simon appeared in the neighbourhood from nowhere, we know so little about him.

CYNTHIA: Right, Simon, it's your opening on the minor bid. Hmm. Let's see. I think I'll overbid the spade convention with two no-trumps and King's gambit offered there—[*discards*] and West's dummy split double to Queen's Bishop four there!

MAGNUS: [*as he plays cards*] Faites vos jeux.[8] Rien ne va plus. Rouge et noir. Zero.

CYNTHIA: Simon?

BIRDBOOT: [*triumphant, leaping to his feet*] And I call your bluff!

CYNTHIA: [*imperturbably*] I meld.

FELICITY: I huff.

MAGNUS: I ruff.

BIRDBOOT: I bluff.

CYNTHIA: Twist.

FELICITY: Bust.

MAGNUS: Check.

BIRDBOOT: Snap.

CYNTHIA: How's that?

FELICITY: Not out.

MAGNUS: Double top.

BIRDBOOT: Bingo!

CYNTHIA: No! Simon—your luck's in tonight.

FELICITY: We shall see—the night is not over yet, Simon Gascoyne! [*She quickly exits.*]

BIRDBOOT: [*looking after* FELICITY] Red herring[9]—smell it a mile off. [*To* MAGNUS.] Oh, yes, she's as clean as a whistle, I've seen it a thousand times. And I've seen you before too, haven't I? Strange—there's something about you—

MAGNUS: Care for a spin round the rose garden, Cynthia?

CYNTHIA: No, Magnus, I must talk to Simon.

BIRDBOOT: There's nothing for you there, you know.

MAGNUS: You think so?

BIRDBOOT: Oh, yes, she knows which side her bread is buttered. I am a man not without a certain influence among those who would reap the limelight—she's not going to throw me over for a heavily disguised cripple.

---

8. Place your bets. *Rien ne va plus:* The betting is closed. (Literally: "No more.") *Rouge et noir:* Red and black. These are all French phrases that would be used at a roulette table (though not a card table) by a croupier—a casino employee in charge of table games like blackjack and roulette.

9. False lead; distraction.

MAGNUS: There's an old Canadian proverb——

BIRDBOOT: Don't give me that—I tumbled to you[1] right from the start—oh, yes, you chaps are not as clever as you think. . . . Sooner or later you make your mistake. . . . Incidentally, where was it I saw you? . . . I've definitely——

MAGNUS: [*leaving*] Well, I think I'll go and oil my gun. [*Exit.*]

BIRDBOOT: [*after* MAGNUS] Double bluff!—[*to* CYNTHIA] I've seen it a thousand times.

CYNTHIA: I think Magnus suspects something. And Felicity? Simon, was there anything between you and Felicity?

BIRDBOOT: No, no—that's all over now. I merely flattered her a little over a drink, told her she'd go far, that sort of thing. Dear me, the fuss that's been made over a simple flirtation——

CYNTHIA: [*as* MRS. DRUDGE *enters behind*] If I find you have falsely seduced me from my dear husband Albert, I will kill you, Simon Gascoyne!

[*The* "CURTAIN" *as before.* MRS. DRUDGE *and* CYNTHIA *leave.* BIRDBOOT *starts to follow them.*]

MOON: *Birdboot!*

[BIRDBOOT *stops.*]

MOON: For God's sake pull yourself together.

BIRDBOOT: I can't help it.

MOON: What do you think you're doing? You're turning it into a complete farce!

BIRDBOOT: I know, I know—but I can't live without her. [*He is making erratic neurotic journeys about the stage.*] I shall resign my position, of course. I don't care I'm a goner, I tell you—— [*He has arrived at the body. He looks at it in surprise, hesitates, bends and turns it over.*]

MOON: Birdboot, think of your family, your friends—your high standing in the world of letters—I say, what are you doing?

[BIRDBOOT *is staring at the body's face.*]

Birdboot . . . leave it alone. Come and sit down—what's the matter with you?

BIRDBOOT: [*dead-voiced*] It's Higgs.

MOON: What?

BIRDBOOT: It's Higgs.

[*Pause.*]

MOON: Don't be silly.

BIRDBOOT: I tell you it's Higgs!

[MOON *half rises. Bewildered.*]

I don't understand. . . . He's dead.

MOON: Dead?

BIRDBOOT: Who would want to . . . ?

MOON: He must have been lying there all the time . . .

BIRDBOOT: . . . kill Higgs?

---

1. That is, I was on to you; I suspected you.

MOON: But what's he doing here? I was standing in tonight. . . .

BIRDBOOT: [*turning*] Moon? . . .

MOON: [*in wonder, quietly*] So it's me and Puckeridge now.

BIRDBOOT: *Moon* . . . ?

MOON: [*faltering*] But I swear I. . . .

BIRDBOOT: I've got it—

MOON: But I didn't—

BIRDBOOT: [*quietly*] My God . . . so that was it . . . [*Up.*] Moon—now I see—

MOON: —I swear I didn't—

BIRDBOOT: Now—finally—I see it all—

[*There is a shot and* BIRDBOOT *falls dead.*]

MOON: Birdboot! [*He runs on, to* BIRDBOOT's *body.*]

[CYNTHIA *appears at the french windows. She stops and stares. All as before.*]

CYNTHIA: Oh my God—what happened, Inspector?

MOON: [*almost to himself*] He's dead. . . . [*He rises.*] That's a bit rough, isn't it?—A bit extreme!—He may have had his faults—I admit he was a fickle old . . . Who did this, and why?

[MOON *turns to face her. He stands up and makes swiftly for his seat. Before he gets there he is stopped by the sound of voices.*]
[SIMON *and* HOUND *are occupying the critics' seats.*]
[MOON *freezes.*]

SIMON: To say that it is without pace, point, focus, interest, drama, wit or originality is to say simply that it does not happen to be my cup of tea. One has only to compare this ragbag with the masters of the genre to see that here we have a trifle that is not my cup of tea at all.

HOUND: I'm sorry to be blunt but there is no getting away from it. It lacks pace. A complete ragbag.

SIMON: I will go further. Those of you who were fortunate enough to be at the Comedie Française on Wednesday last, will not need to be reminded that hysterics are no substitute for *éclat*.

HOUND: It lacks *élan*.

SIMON: Some of the cast seem to have given up acting altogether, apparently aghast, with every reason, at finding themselves involved in an evening that would, and indeed will, make the angels weep.

HOUND: I am not a prude but I fail to see any reason for the shower of filth and sexual allusion foisted on to an unsuspecting public in the guise of modernity at all costs. . . .

[*Behind* MOON, FELICITY, MAGNUS *and* MRS. DRUDGE *have made their entrances, so that he turns to face their semicircle.*]

MAGNUS: [*pointing to* BIRDBOOT's *body*] Well, Inspector, is this your man?

MOON: [*warily*] . . . Yes. . . . Yes. . . .

CYNTHIA: It's Simon . . .

MOON: Yes . . . yes . . . poor. . . . [*Up.*] Is this some kind of joke?

MAGNUS: If it is, Inspector, it's in very poor taste.

[MOON *pulls himself together and becomes galvanic, a little wild, in grief for* BIRDBOOT.]

MOON: All right! I'm going to find out who did this! I want everyone to go to the positions they occupied when the shot was fired—[*they move; hysterically*]: No one will leave the house! [*They move back.*]

MAGNUS: I think we all had the opportunity to fire the shot, Inspector—

MOON: [*furious*] I am not—

MAGNUS: —but which of us would want to?

MOON: Perhaps you, Major Magnus!

MAGNUS: Why should I want to kill him?

MOON: Because he was on to you—yes, he tumbled you right from the start—and you shot him just when he was about to reveal that you killed—[MOON *points, pauses and then crosses to Higgs's body and falters*]—killed—[*he turns Higgs over*]—this . . . chap.

MAGNUS: But what motive would there be for killing him? [*Pause.*] Who *is* this chap? [*Pause.*] Inspector?

MOON: [*rising*] I don't know. Quite unlike anyone I've ever met. [*Long pause.*] Well . . . now . . .

MRS. DRUDGE: Inspector?

MOON: [*eagerly*] Yes? Yes, what is it, dear lady?

MRS. DRUDGE: Happening to enter this room earlier in the day to close the windows, I chanced to overhear a remark made by the deceased Simon Gascoyne to her ladyship, viz.[2]—"I will kill anyone who comes between us."

MOON: Ah—yes—well, that's it, then. This . . . chap . . . [*pointing*] was obviously killed by [*pointing*] er . . . by [*pause*] Simon.

CYNTHIA: But he didn't come between us!

MAGNUS: And who, then, killed Simon?

MRS. DRUDGE: Subsequent to that reported remark, I also happened to be in earshot of a remark made by Lady Muldoon to the deceased, to the effect, "I will kill you, Simon Gascoyne!" I hope you don't mind my mentioning it.

MOON: Not at all. I'm glad you did. It is from these chance remarks that we in the force build up our complete picture before moving in to make the arrest. It will not be long now, I fancy, and I must warn you, Lady Muldoon that anything you say—

CYNTHIA: Yes!—I hated Simon Gascoyne, for he had me in his power!—But I didn't kill him!

MRS. DRUDGE: Prior to that, Inspector, I also chanced to overhear a remark made by Miss Cunningham, no doubt in the heat of the moment, but it stuck in my mind as these things do, viz., "I will kill you for this, Simon Gascoyne!"

MOON: Ah! The final piece of the jigsaw! I think I am now in a position to reveal the mystery. This man [*the corpse*] was, of course, McCoy, the Canadian who, as we heard, meeting Gascoyne in the street and being solicited for sixpence for a toffee apple, smacked him across the ear, with the cry, "How's that for a grudge to harbour, you sniffling little workshy!"[3] all those many years ago. Gascoyne bided his time, but in due course tracked McCoy down to this house, having, on the way, met, in the neighbourhood, a simple ambitious girl from the provinces. He was charming, persuasive—told her, I have no doubt,

---

2. Common abbreviation of *videlicet*, a Latin term meaning "namely" or "that is to say."   3. Shirker.

that she would go straight to the top—and she, flattered by his sophistication, taken in by his promises to see her all right on the night, gave in to his simple desires. Perhaps she loved him. We shall never know. But in the very hour of her promised triumph, his eye fell on another—yes, I refer to Lady Cynthia Muldoon. From the moment he caught sight of her there was no other woman for him—he was in her spell, willing to sacrifice anything, even you, Felicity Cunningham. It was only today—unexpectedly finding him here—that you learned the truth. There was a bitter argument which ended with your promise to kill him—a promise that you carried out in this very room at your first opportunity! And I must warn you that anything you say——

FELICITY: But it doesn't make sense!

MOON: Not at first glance, *perhaps*.

MAGNUS: Could not Simon have been killed by the same person who killed McCoy?

FELICITY: But why should any of us want to kill a perfect stranger?

MAGNUS: Perhaps he was not a stranger to *one* of us.

MOON: [*faltering*] But Simon was the madman, wasn't he?

MAGNUS: We only have your word for that, Inspector. We only have your word for a lot of things. For instance—McCoy. Who is he? Is his name McCoy? Is there any truth in that fantastic and implausible tale of the insult inflicted in the Canadian streets? Or is there something else, something quite unknown to us, behind all this? Suppose for a moment that the madman, having killed this unknown stranger for private and inscrutable reasons of his own, was disturbed before he could dispose of the body, so having cut the telephone wires he decided to return to the scene of the crime, masquerading as—Police Inspector Hound!

MOON: But . . . I'm not mad . . . I'm almost sure I'm not mad . . .

MAGNUS: . . . only to discover that in the house was a man, Simon Gascoyne, who recognized the corpse as a man against whom you had held a deep-seated grudge——!

MOON: But I didn't kill—I'm almost sure I——

MAGNUS: I put it to you!—are you the real Inspector Hound?!

MOON: You know damn well I'm not! What's it all about?

MAGNUS: I thought as much.

MOON: I only dreamed . . . sometimes I dreamed——

CYNTHIA: So it was you!

MRS. DRUDGE: The madman!

FELICITY: The killer!

CYNTHIA: Oh, it's horrible, horrible.

MRS. DRUDGE: The stranger in our midst!

MAGNUS: Yes, we had a shrewd suspicion he would turn up here—and he walked into the trap!

MOON: What *trap*?

MAGNUS: I am not the real Magnus Muldoon!—It was a mere subterfuge!—and [*standing up and removing his mustaches.*] I now reveal myself as——

CYNTHIA: You mean——?

MAGNUS: Yes!—I am the real Inspector Hound!

MOON: [*pause*] Puckeridge!

MAGNUS: [*with pistol*] Stand where you are, or I shoot!

MOON: [*backing*] Puckeridge! You killed Higgs—and Birdboot tried to tell me—

MAGNUS: Stop in the name of the law!

[MOON *turns to run.* MAGNUS *fires.* MOON *drops to his knees.*]

I have waited a long time for this moment.

CYNTHIA: So you are the real Inspector Hound.

MAGNUS: Not only that!—I have been leading a double life—at *least*!

CYNTHIA: You mean——?

MAGNUS: Yes!—It's been ten long years, but don't you know me?

CYNTHIA: You mean——?

MAGNUS: Yes!—it is me, Albert!—who lost his memory and joined the force, rising by merit to the rank of Inspector, his past blotted out—until fate cast him back into the home he left behind, back to the beautiful woman he had brought here as his girlish bride—in short, my darling, my memory has returned and your long wait is over!

CYNTHIA: Oh, Albert!

[*They embrace.*]

MOON: [*with a trace of admiration*] Puckeridge . . . you cunning bastard.

[MOON *dies.*]

THE END

1968

QUESTIONS

1. How does Stoppard differentiate Moon from Birdboot? What can the reader infer about their respective characters—education and class background, attitude toward drama, and so forth—from their speeches in the play?
2. If you were the set designer for a production of *The Real Inspector Hound*, how would you create the illusion that the audience is actually backstage, looking out over the stage and the "audience" that includes the critics Moon and Birdboot? How would you position the actors onstage so that their faces could be seen clearly by the real audience?
3. When does the imaginary barrier between the critics and the actors onstage first become blurred? When does it disappear entirely?
4. What is the dramatic function of Mrs. Drudge in the play? Is she a "static" character or "dynamic"—that is, does her character change over the course of the play?
5. For the comedy of *The Real Inspector Hound* to "work," what conventions of fiction and drama (standard settings, plots, characters) must be familiar to the audience? What must an audience know about the theater world of critics and reviews?

RESPONDING TO DRAMA

When reading a play in order to write about it, you will need to keep a record of your responses and insights as the action unfolds. Recording your thoughts before you've finished a play may help you clarify your expectations, much as Moon and Birdboot in *The Real Inspector Hound* guess out loud who the murderer is and rehearse the reviews they will write. Below you will find examples showing two ways of responding to a play. The first example, in response to *The Real Inspector Hound*, shows how you might jot down your initial impressions in the margins of a play as you read. The second example shows how one reader used the questions on pages 1385–86 to take more comprehensive, methodical notes on *Trifles*. Each of these methods of note-taking has certain advantages, and you might find that using a combination of the two works best.

SAMPLE WRITING: ANNOTATING A PLAY

Any passage in *The Real Inspector Hound* would reward close analysis. The passage chosen here comes after the two main characters, Moon and Birdboot, continue their parallel monologues, daydreaming about murder and romance, respectively. They have been ignoring each other and the play, although they both try out some lines for the different reviews they will write for tomorrow's papers. In this passage, just at the beginning of the third act of the mystery at Muldoon Manor, Moon and Birdboot unwillingly become part of the action, which includes comic repetition of dialogue from the first act.

BIRDBOOT: A rattling good evening out. I was held. — Birdboot's review appeals to popular audience.

[*The phone starts to ring on the empty stage.* MOON *tries to ignore it.*]

MOON: Harder still— Harder still if possible— Harder still if it is possible to be— Neither do I find it easy—Dante and Dorothy L. Sayers. Harder still—

Moon struggles to impress a sophisticated audience.

BIRDBOOT: Others taking part included—*Moon!*

Double meaning: At this point, Moon does start to take part.

[*For* MOON *has lost patience and is bearing down on the ringing phone. He is frankly irritated.*]

MOON: [*picking up phone, barks*] Hel-lo! [*Pause, turns to* BIRDBOOT, *quietly.*] It's for you. [*Pause.*]

Now Birdboot takes part.

[BIRDBOOT *gets up. He approaches cautiously.* MOON *gives him the phone and moves back to his seat.* BIRDBOOT *watches him go. He looks round and smiles weakly, expiating himself.*]

BIRDBOOT: [*into phone*] Hello . . . [*Explosion.*] Oh, for God's sake, Myrtle!— I've told you never to phone me at work! [*He is naturally embarrassed, looking about with surreptitious fury.*] What? Last night? Good God, woman, this is hardly the time to—I assure you, Myrtle, there is absolutely nothing going on between me and—I took her to dinner simply by way of keeping *au fait* with the world of the paint and the motley— Yes, I promise— Yes, I do— Yes, I *said* yes—I *do*—and you are mine too, Myrtle—darling—I can't—[*whispers*] I'm not alone—[*up*]. No, she's

Hypocrisy.

not!—[*he looks around furtively, licks his lips and mumbles*]. All *right!* I love your little pink ears and you are my own fluffy bunny-boo—— Now for God's sake—— Good-bye, Myrtle—[*puts down phone*].

> Has to use embarrassing baby talk to get off the hook.

[BIRDBOOT *mops his brow with his handkerchief. As he turns, a tennis ball bounces in through the french windows, followed by* FELICITY, *as before, in tennis outfit. The lighting is as it was. Everything is as it was. It is, let us say, the same moment of time.*]

> Stage direction seems intended to be read.

FELICITY: [*calling*] Out! [*She catches sight of* BIRDBOOT *and is amazed.*] You!

> Haven't we heard this before?

BIRDBOOT: Er, yes—hello again.

FELICITY: What are you doing here?!

> Birdboot "becomes" Simon. Blurs line between "reality" and play.

BIRDBOOT: Well, I . . .

FELICITY: Honestly, darling, you really are extraordinary——

BIRDBOOT: Yes, well, here I am. [*He looks round sheepishly.*]

FELICITY: You must have been desperate to see me—I mean, I'm flattered, but couldn't it wait till I got back?

BIRDBOOT: No, no, you've got it all wrong——

> Here he breaks from earlier dialogue. Why?

FELICITY: What is it?

BIRDBOOT: And about last night—perhaps I gave you the wrong impression—got carried away a bit, perhaps——

FELICITY: [*stiffly*] What are you trying to say?

BIRDBOOT: I want to call it off.

> Why doesn't he say he loves another? Simon did.

FELICITY: I see.

BIRDBOOT: I didn't promise anything—and the fact is, I have my reputation—people do talk——

FELICITY: You don't have to say any more——

BIRDBOOT: And my wife, too—I don't know how she got to hear of it, but——

FELICITY: Of all the nerve! To march in here and——

BIRDBOOT: I'm sorry you had to find out like this—the fact is I didn't mean it this way——

FELICITY: You philandering coward!

BIRDBOOT: I'm sorry—but I want you to know that I meant those things I said—oh yes—shows brilliant promise—I shall say so——

> Birdboot is talking to the actress, but the character replies to Simon.

FELICITY: I'll kill you for this, Simon Gascoyne!

[*She leaves in tears, passing* MRS. DRUDGE *who has entered in time to over-hear her last remark.*]

SAMPLE WRITING: READING NOTES ON *TRIFLES*

Below are examples of the questions an experienced reader might ask when reading the play *Trifles* for the first time, as well as responses to those questions. (See pp. 1385–86.) Any of these notes might inspire ideas for essay topics on *Trifles*. This is just a selection of the many details that could be observed about this lasting play, in which details certainly matter.

Expectations

Do you know anything about the playwright or other works by her or him? Chapter 10 provides some information about Susan Glaspell, and her story "A Jury of Her Peers" also appears there. I could check the short biography in this anthology or do a Google search if I wanted to know more. I expect a realistic play about everyday people; I expect neither old-fashioned poetic language nor abstract and ironic dialogue.

When was it written? According to the date at the end of the play, it was written and first staged in 1916, during World War I.

Does the title suggest anything? "Trifles" sounds like a comedy (a trifle is something trivial), but it might be ironic. But why does Hale say that "women are used to worrying over trifles"? I expect to find out that the title is significant in some way.

Characterization

Who are the characters? What are they like? Three men and two women in the cast of characters. After I read the stage directions and part of the dialogue, I check the list again to keep straight who is who. What kind of situation would bring together a sheriff, a county attorney, a farmer, and two wives? No actors are needed to play either Mr. Wright or Mrs. Wright. Some men who help Mr. Hale (Harry) and Mr. Peters (deputy Frank) are mentioned as coming and going but are never on stage.

The "county attorney" acts like a detective; he seems businesslike and thinks he's smarter than farmers and women. The stage directions specify that he speaks "With the gallantry of a young politician," but his flattery toward the women doesn't work. We find out his name is Mr. Henderson.

According to the stage directions, Mrs. Peters, the sheriff's wife, is "a slight wiry woman, a thin nervous face"; Mrs. Hale, the farmer's wife, is "larger and would ordinarily be called more comfortable looking." The casting of the two women would be important for contrast; a wider range of physical types would be suitable for the men. Everyone is cold, but only the men take comfort by the fire in the kitchen; the women are upset.

Is there a protagonist, an antagonist, or other types? There isn't a young hero or heroine of this play, and I wouldn't call anyone the villain unless it's the dead man.

Are the characters' names significant? There's nothing especially meaningful or unusual about the names, although "Hale" means healthy (as in "hale and hearty"), and "Wright" sounds just like "right," though obviously something's wrong in this house where the woman has no rights?

Plot

What happens? The big event has already happened; this is the scene of the crime. The men are looking for clues and leave the women in the kitchen, where they discover possible causes or motives for the crime, such as the uneven sewing on the quilt piece, a broken birdcage, and the dead bird in the box. The women decide not to tell the men about their suspicion that John Wright wrung the bird's neck and Minnie Wright strangled him in revenge; instead they hide the bird.

Are there scene changes? The whole scene is a fairly short uninterrupted time in one part of a farmhouse. Characters go offstage to other rooms or outdoors to the barn.

How is exposition handled? The county attorney asks Hale to "tell just what happened"; Hale explains what happened before the play started, describing how Mrs. Wright behaved. It comes as a shock to learn that Mrs. Wright told Hale he couldn't see John Wright " 'Cause [he was] dead." Shouldn't she have run to tell someone about the murder or have told Hale as soon as he arrived? When Hale reports that Mrs. Wright said her husband "died of a rope around his neck," it sounds suspicious. Could she have slept so soundly that she didn't realize someone had strangled Mr. Wright?

What events mark the rising action? When the men go upstairs and Mrs. Hale says "I'd hate to have men coming into my kitchen, and snooping and criticizing," the women have a chance to notice more in the kitchen. Mrs. Hale recalls her relationship to Mrs. Wright, and the women discuss whether the wife really murdered her husband.

The men return to the kitchen on their way out to the barn just after the women discover the quilt pieces with the bad stitching. The next dialogue between the women is more open and brings out Mrs. Hale's regret for not having visited and supported Mrs. Wright in her unhappy marriage. They notice the empty birdcage.

What is the climax? Mrs. Hale finds the dead bird in the pretty box, and the two women understand what it means just before the men return to the kitchen briefly. From then on the women utter small lies to the men. Mrs. Peters for the first time reveals her own memories that suggest she can imagine Mrs. Wright's motives.

What is the resolution? As everyone prepares to leave, Mrs. Peters pretends the bird is insignificant, joining Mrs. Hale in protecting Mrs. Wright and playing along with the men's idea that there's nothing to notice in the kitchen. The women collaborate in hiding the bird.

What kind of play or plot is it? Like some detective stories, the play doesn't ask "whodunnit?" but asks why the murder was committed. Its mode of representation is a familiar type—domestic realism—in which the places, people, things, and even events are more or less ordinary. (Unfortunately, domestic violence is quite common.)

Setting

When does the action occur? The play appears to be contemporary with 1916 (a stove heater, party-line telephones, a horse-drawn wagon). It is a winter morning, and the scene takes perhaps an hour.

Where does the action occur? It is obviously farm country, perhaps in the Midwest, where farms are very far apart. The Dickson County attorney has just returned from Omaha—so it may be Nebraska, though the original event took place in Iowa. There's a Dickson County in Nebraska, a Dickinson County in Iowa.

What is the atmosphere? The freezing weather reflects the feeling of the play and gives the characters a motivation for gathering in the kitchen. John Wright is described as a chilly wind. The frozen house has ruined Mrs. Wright's preserves of summer fruit. The mess in the kitchen, especially the sticky spill of red fruit in the cupboard, seems related to the unhappiness and horror of the marriage and the crime.

Are there scene changes? Instead of several scenes over a longer time, showing the deteriorating marriage, the crisis over the bird, the murder itself, Mrs. Wright's sleepless night, and Mr. Hale's visit, the story unfolds in a single scene, in one room, on the second morning after the murder, between the entrance and exit of Mrs. Hale and Mrs. Peters. It is essential that the play focus on "kitchen things" and what the women visitors notice and think.

Style, Tone, Imagery

What is the style of the dialogue? The dialogue seems similar to everyday speech. There are some differences in speaking style that show the Hales are more rustic

1430 DRAMA: READING, RESPONDING, WRITING

than the Peters and the county attorney. Hale has a relaxed way of telling a story: "then I says," etc. Mrs. Hale: "Those towels get dirty awful quick" and "If I was you, I wouldn't tell her the fruit was gone. Tell her it *ain't*."

How do nonverbal gestures and actions convey meaning? Many specific actions given in the stage directions are crucial to the play: everyone looking at the rocking chair, pointing to the room upstairs, looking at the loaf of bread that should have been put back in the bread box, etc.

Do any of the props seem to have symbolic meaning? Some objects in the play are so important they seem symbolic, though the play tries not to be too heavily poetic. All kinds of "trifles" are clues. For instance, the women get Mrs. Wright's clothes to bring to her in jail. "MRS. HALE: [*Examining the skirt.*] Wright was close," meaning stingy. Mrs. Hale's words convey a quick impression: The skirt looks "shabby" because John Wright didn't give his wife any money for clothes (he was "good" but stingy and cold).

There would be some colorful props on stage—the jar of cherries, the red cloth and other quilt material, the pretty box—all of them signs of what has gone wrong. The room itself is "gloomy" and has some dirty and messy things in plain sight; other things in the cupboards are eventually revealed. These props would add to the uncomfortable feeling of the play.

The closest thing to a symbol is the caged songbird. Even the men notice the broken door and missing bird. Mrs. Hale underlines the comparison to Mrs. Wright twice: "she was kind of like a bird," and later, "No, Wright wouldn't like the bird—a thing that sang. She used to sing. He killed that, too."

Theme

What is the theme of the play? The title calls attention to what the play is about. Glaspell didn't call it *The Caged Songbird* or *Murder in the Midwest* or something heavy-handed. The main action is a search for a motive to confirm what everyone believes, that Minnie Wright must have strangled her husband while he was sleeping in bed. But the underlying theme of the play seems to be about men's and women's different perspectives. How can women's everyday things be important? Why would anyone charged with murder worry about preserves? Even the women hope that Mrs. Wright's worry about having her apron and shawl in jail means she didn't commit the crime. The kitchen things—the trifles in her own house—"turn against her," but the women are able to hide evidence that the men consider insignificant.

WRITING ABOUT DRAMA

Writing an essay about drama, like writing about fiction or poetry, can sharpen your responses and focus your reading; at the same time, it can demonstrate effects in the work that other readers may have missed. When you write about drama, in a very real sense you perform the role that directors and actors take on in a stage performance: You offer your "reading" of the text, interpreting it in order to guide other readers' responses. But you also shape and refine your own response by attempting to express it clearly.

Using the notes you have taken while reading a play, try to locate the specific lines that have contributed to your expectations or your discoveries. Are these lines at the beginning, the middle, or the end of the play? Who gives most of the hints or misleading information? If there is one character who is especially unseeing, especially devious, or especially insightful, you might decide to write an essay describing the function of that character in the play. A good way to undertake such a study of a character in drama (as in fiction) is to imagine the work without that character. Mrs. Hale in *Trifles* is certainly the cleverest "detective," so why do we need Mrs. Peters as well? Similarly, Moon is cleverer than Birdboot, but *The Real Inspector Hound* would be incomplete without Moon's more conservative and complacent counterpart. Why? One answer is that plays need dialogue, and we would find it artificial if Mrs. Hale and Moon talked mainly to themselves. But a more interesting answer is that in each play the audience learns by witnessing characters with different temperaments responding to a situation. Mrs. Peters speaks for our misgivings about protecting a murderer, and Birdboot stands in for our ordinary appetites, whether for chocolates or romance. As these remarks suggest, you can also develop essays that compare characters with similar roles in two plays. To do so, however, you need to take into account the different styles and forms of the respective plays. A brief essay comparing two characters is usually best limited to a single play.

In addition to character studies, essays on drama can focus on the kinds of observations made above: expectations and plot structure; the presence and absence of characters or actions onstage; the different degrees of awareness of characters and audience at various points in the action; titles, stage directions, and other stylistic details, including metaphors or other imagery; and, of course, themes such as the importance of feminine "trifles" or the illusoriness of reality, onstage or off. As you write, you will probably discover that you can imagine directing or acting in a performance of the play, and you'll realize that interpreting a play is a crucial step in bringing it to life.

SUGGESTIONS FOR WRITING

1. How do your sympathies for Mrs. Peters change over the course of *Trifles*? What might Mrs. Peters be said to represent in the clash of attitudes at the heart of the play? Write an essay in which you examine both Mrs. Peters's evolving character as it is revealed in *Trifles* and her dramatic function in relation to the other characters and to the plot.

2. How would you characterize Susan Glaspell's feminism as revealed in *Trifles*—does it seem radical or moderate? How does it compare to feminist political and social

ideas of our own time? (Consult three or more educational or library Web sites for biographical background on Glaspell; there are several sites offering teaching materials on *Trifles* as well. If time allows, you might also pursue sources that provide an overview of women's movements in the United States in the twentieth century.) Write an essay in which you explore the political leanings apparent in *Trifles*, both in the context of Glaspell's play (published in 1920) and in the broader historical context of the struggle for women's rights over the past century.

3. Write an essay in which you propose a production of *Trifles,* complete with details of how you would handle the casting, costumes, set design, lighting, and direction of the actors. What would be your overall controlling vision for the production? Would you attempt to reproduce faithfully the look and feel of the play as it might have been in 1916, or would you introduce innovations? How would you justify your choices in terms of dramatic effectiveness?

4. Write an essay in which you compare and contrast the way Glaspell presents the same material in the short story "A Jury of Her Peers" (in chapter 10) as in the play *Trifles*. In what ways is the play more or less effective than the short story? What might make Glaspell's material better suited to one medium than the other?

5. Can a farce like *The Real Inspector Hound* be considered a "serious" play? What is *Inspector Hound* really about—drama? illusion? identity? Write an essay in which you argue that Stoppard's play should be taken seriously, that his aim is more than mere entertainment. What would you say is the play's main theme?

6. In *The Real Inspector Hound*, what does it mean that Moon and Birdboot seem to have formulated their reviews of the play-within-a-play in advance, or that they become more and more involved in the action onstage? Write an essay in which you examine the different critical approaches of Moon and Birdboot, as well as Stoppard's depiction of the relationship between drama and drama criticism.

7. How would you stage *The Real Inspector Hound*? Write a proposal for all aspects of a production—casting, direction, costumes, set design, lighting, sound, etc. What special challenges and opportunities does *Inspector Hound* present? What would be your overarching vision for a production of the play?

8. Glaspell's play has the manner of domestic realism that was current when the play was first performed in 1916, whereas Stoppard's play, which premiered in 1968, is an absurdist or postmodern farce. Yet each play uses a single set that represents a house in the country in which a murder has taken place. Write an essay in which you compare the setting, style, and tone of the realist and the farcical "whodunnit?" plots of these plays.

SAMPLE WRITING

In the following short essay, Linda Durai writes about the repetition and the stage directions in *The Real Inspector Hound* and argues that these elements make it a play that is better appreciated when read than when seen in a theater. Consider this essay as an example of good student work that needs to be edited in order to correct some common errors and enhance its effect. As you read it, note what works well and what could be improved. Notice, on the positive side, that the thesis is significant—beyond what anyone would simply agree on about the play. The author supports her thesis with specific evidence, quoting accurately from the text. She strengthens her argument by acknowledging other perspectives—as when she notes that some of the humor of the play would work better in a performance than on the page.

What other positive qualities can you observe in Durai's essay? How might you revise it to make it even stronger? For example, could she organize her essay differently? Are there places in the essay that could be clearer and more focused? How might you edit Durai's choices of words or the structure of her sentences to be more precise or economical? Like many student essays, this one has a few common errors that are easy to catch on rereading. Can you find where the antecedent or reference for a pronoun is unclear? Can you locate where a plural pronoun is used for a singular subject (the number should be consistent)? Are there any incomplete sentences?

Linda Durai
Professor Paul Ridgeway
English 282

Reading a "Whodunnit?": Stage Directions and Repetition
in *The Real Inspector Hound*

Most plays have stage directions to guide the director and actors as well as readers. Comedies use repetition to make the audience laugh. Tom Stoppard's *The Real Inspector Hound* (1968) uses both stage directions and repetition in unusual and funny ways. In this play, different kinds of stage directions add to the humor, usually with repetitions that don't seem to make sense. Further, the stage directions go beyond what is necessary for performing the play. Some of the italicized words crack jokes for the reader, and sometimes what would usually be

---

in the printed script is spoken aloud by characters. One of the characters, Mrs. Drudge, is a major source of this ridiculous repetition, as to what she says and the stage directions of what she does. *The Real Inspector Hound* is a really complicated play that needs to be read again and again to be fully understood. A reader can reread and compare the stage directions that connect the murder mystery at Muldoon Manor with the play about the theater critics Moon and Birdboot.

The Real Inspector Hound is a parody of Agatha Christie's *The Mousetrap*, and it also makes fun of theater critics and plays that have a "play-within-the-play" (Ridgeway, Hodgson, Stoppard, "Conversation"). This is a device that Shakespeare used in *Hamlet* and *A Midsummer Night's Dream* (Ridgeway). A frame and an inner play usually mirror each other, with comic results. The printed play of *The Real Inspector Hound* makes it more obvious that there is a frame or a mirroring of an inside and an outside play. This is something that you wouldn't notice in a theater. It begins with several paragraphs in italics that no one in the theater would read. What a live audience would *see* is something like "their own reflection." Stoppard's note declares: "Impossible" (1395; all page references are to *The Norton Introduction to Literature*, 10th edition); no mirror could really reflect everyone sitting in the actual seats. The reader knows that Stoppard describes the set of the play-within-the-play as a realistic drawing room, and knows that Stoppard instructs directors to cast two different types, "plumpish middle-aged Birdboot and younger taller, less-relaxed Moon" (1395). Theatergoers would probably be slower to realize that this play is not going to proceed like other plays do, though they would know the play has started, whereas the reader sees continuing stage directions.

Alone on stage, Moon follows directions that Stoppard drags out to entertain the reader; it could be summarized "*Moon stares around the stage for several minutes and then reads the program cover to cover.*" Instead the prose is dramatic: "*Silence. The room. The body.* MOON. . . . *He turns over the page and reads.* . . . *Pause.* MOON *picks up his programme.* . . . *Pause . . .*" I count seven sentences that tell us how Moon reads the program. When performed, this would make the audience impatient like Moon, and laugh at seeing him act the way they might feel. But it is also a funny imitation of a reader *reading* the play and waiting to find out the plot. We feel like Birdboot objecting when Moon says the play has started with a pause, "You can't start with a *pause*!" (1396). That's already a joke about the kind of experimental theater that Stoppard writes.

There are many "straight" stage directions not meant for laughs. These help the reader put themselves in the place of actors, directors, and crew. I can't note all of the fun effects here. But Moon and Birdboot are always talking over and over about the same themes, Moon about his jealousy of the lead reviewer and wanting to murder him, Birdboot about his affairs and his lusting after actresses. There are lots of jokes about the way the two reviewers see the same thing differently, one very intellectual and fancy and the other crude or vulgar. It's interesting that most of the dialogue directions are about Birdboot, who is always shifting his tone to keep up appearances: "conspiratorially," "suspiciously," "instantly outraged," "urbanely." His repeated loud chewing on chocolates would be funnier onstage. But the reader can enjoy the stage-direction descriptions, and only a reader knows that Stoppard thinks Birdboot "grasps reality in the form of his box of chocolates" (1397). The audience would just see him as a lover of candy, a kind of big baby, and he even uses baby talk to his wife.

Besides the beginning with a "pause," the play has a bunch of jokes, out loud and in the written play, about stage directions, programs, and exposition—information that you might find in a program or printed stage directions. Many of these jokes are around Mrs. Drudge, who is always repeating things in a crazy overdone way. We read that "the char" comes in to dust the room "on the trot," giving a very English picture of a servant (familiar from lots of comedies and farces). And then Moon reads out loud from the program: "Mrs. Drudge the Help"—a little like labeling her Mrs. Clean the Maid, to be really sure everyone gets it. Her job is obviously to "help" the play, doing the chores of getting information across and making the audience laugh because she doesn't see what the audience sees. It's like a game where she's blind-folded and can't see the corpse *and* the suspicious intruder. She is the one who turns on the radio announcement that sounds like a warning in an old scary movie. And she is the one who answers the phone by saying aloud the information about the scene, what ought to be in the program. It's especially funny to read what is happening while Mrs. Drudge keeps waiting for the sound technician to make the phone ring. Her answer makes no sense only as a parody of stage directions: "Hello, the drawing-room of Lady Muldoon's country residence one morning in early spring?" Most of Mrs. Drudge's speeches rattle off the background about all the people and the time and place of the play that is happening on the stage. Sometimes they sound like a silly idea of the country life: "now that the cuckoo-beard is in bud" (1400).

The play gets incredibly ridiculous as things repeat more and more. Especially with the repeating of Mrs. Drudge's stage business and speeches. She is the center of several scenes that seem to go nowhere, especially in the episode where she serves coffee (beginning of "act two"). Again she seems to *ask* the person on the telephone what would actually be the information about the next scene: "the same, half an hour later?" (1409). Then she sets up a silly round of asking characters how they take their coffee. Stoppard winks at the reader by first spelling it all out and then getting impatient: "[*Mrs. Drudge pours.*]" becomes "[*Ditto.*]" and so on through cream, sugar, and starting to offer biscuits. Birdboot writes a note out loud about how dull the beginning of the second act is, and Felicity jumps up and says, "If you ask me, there's something funny going on." This is a double irony that is easier to catch on paper because you can stop and read it again. That is, if Mrs. Drudge *asks her* about a biscuit, it's ridiculous, *and* Felicity thinks there's something suspicious like a crime going on. This meaning comes out when Felicity turns on the radio so the warning is broadcast again. Felicity is another character type, the romantic leading lady, as much as Mrs. Drudge is the type of a wise servant, and she also mostly repeats whatever she says or does, including her threats to kill Simon Gascoyne. A lot of times Mrs. Drudge happens to come onstage "in time to overhear" such remarks.

There are scenes that repeat as if the actors have gotten stuck in the first act, and the stage directions seem to be aware of this. When "[a tennis ball bounces in through the french windows, followed by FELICITY . . .]," for the second time, things are a little different because Birdboot is onstage. The stage directions make a big deal of the idea that the scene is being acted over again: "as before. . . . The lighting is as it was. Everything is as it was. It is, let us say, the same moment in time."] (1416). The last two sentences just can't be staged. Stoppard seems to be talking to us as readers. We can turn back the pages to check that the words are almost identical, and that the actress who plays Felicity says her lines the same no matter which man is playing "Simon."

The inner play is obviously a "whodunnit" or murder mystery. It is also a farce, a kind of play with lots of coincidences, running in and out of entrances, disguises, and funny repetitions and discoveries that get people in trouble. The whole play depends on physical situation, the kind of thing viewers see, even though a character like Mrs. Drudge ignores it. But at the same time it involves puns and wordplay, also noticed by the audience while the characters may not be aware. The audience and readers are going to enjoy the way the Moon's long speeches about theater are also comments by the playwright about his own work. Although some actions, for instance the two times that Magnus runs over characters in a wheelchair, are probably funnier live than reading about it, other repetitions are going to be more obvious to a reader than if we were watching in a real theater. I think the stage directions make all the repetitions in *The Real Inspector Hound* funnier than they would be in performance. As a parody of all sorts of theater conventions, it is a play that should be read and reread.

Works Cited

Hodgson, Terry. "The Plays of Tom Stoppard." As quoted in "*The Real Inspector Hound*: Drama Criticism of the Play by Tom Stoppard." *Theatre Database*. Web. http://www.theatredatabase.com/20th_century/real_inspector_hound.htm. Accessed 7 March 2009.

Ridgeway, Paul. Class lecture, English 282 Introduction to Literature, February 10, 2009.

Stoppard, Tom. "Tom Stoppard in Conversation." As quoted in "*The Real Inspector Hound*: Drama Criticism of the Play by Tom Stoppard." *Theatre Database*. Web. http://www.theatredatabase.com/20th_century/real_inspector_hound.htm. Accessed 7 March 2009.

Understanding the Text

26 ELEMENTS OF DRAMA

Most of us read more fiction than drama and are likely to encounter drama by watching filmed versions of it. Nonetheless, the skills you have developed in reading stories and poems come in handy when you read plays. And just as with fiction and poetry, you will understand and appreciate drama more fully by becoming familiar with the various elements of the genre.

CHARACTER

Character is possibly the most familiar and accessible of the elements; both fiction and drama feature one or more imaginary persons who take part in the action. The word "character" refers not only to a person represented in an imagined plot, whether narrated or acted out, but also to the unique qualities that make up a personality. From one point of view, "character" as a part in a plot and "character" as a kind of personality are both predictions: This sort of person is likely to see things from a certain angle and behave in certain ways. Notice that the idea of character includes both the individual differences among people and the classification of similar people into types. Whereas much realistic fiction emphasizes unique individuals rather than general character types, drama often compresses and simplifies personalities—a play has only about two hours in which to show situations, appearances, and behaviors, without description or background other than exposition spoken by the actors. The advantage of portraying character in broader strokes is that it heightens the contrasts between character types, adding to the drama: Differences provoke stronger reactions.

Plays are especially concerned with characters because of the concrete manner in which they portray people on the stage. With a few exceptions (such as experiments in multimedia performance), the only words in the performance of a play are spoken by actors, and usually these actors are *in character*—that is, speaking as though they really were the people they play in the drama. (Some plays have a narrator who observes and comments on the action from the sidelines, and in some plays a character may address the audience directly, but even when the actors apparently step outside of the imaginary frame, they are still part of the play and are still playing characters.) In fiction, the narrator's description and commentary can guide a reader's judgment about characters. Reading a play, you will have no such guide because most drama relies almost exclusively on *indirect characterization* (see chapter 3). Apart from some clues about characters in the stage directions, you will need to imagine the appearance, manners, and movement of someone speaking the lines assigned to any one character. You can do this even as you read through a play for the first time, discovering the characters' attitudes and motivations as the scenes unfold. This ability to predict character and then to revise expectations as situations change is based not only on our experiences of people in real life but also on our familiarity with types of characters or roles that occur in many dramatic forms.

Consider the patterns of characters in many stories that are narrated or acted out, whether in novels, comic books, television series, Hollywood films, or even some video games. In many of these forms, there is a leading role, a main character: the **protagonist**. The titles of plays such as *Hamlet*, *Antigone*, or, a little less obviously, *Death of a Salesman* imply that the play will be about a central character, the chief object of the playwright's and the reader's or audience's concern. Understanding the character of the protagonist—sometimes in contrast with an **antagonist**, the opponent of the main character—becomes the consuming interest of such a play. Especially in more traditional or popular genres, the protagonist may be called a **hero** or **heroine**, and the antagonist may be called the **villain**. Most characterization in professional theater, however, avoids depicting pure good and pure evil in a fight to the death. Most characters possess both negative and redeeming qualities.

As in other genres that represent people in action, in drama there are minor characters or supporting roles. At least since ancient Rome, romantic comedies have been structured around a leading man and woman, along with a comparable pair (often the "buddies" of the leads) whose problems may be less serious, whose characters may be less complex, or who in other ways support rather than lead the action. Sometimes a minor character can be said to be a **foil**, a character designed to bring out qualities in another character by contrast. The main point to remember is that all the characters in a drama are interdependent and help characterize each other. Through dialogue and behavior, each brings out what is characteristic in the others.

Like movies and other "shows," plays must respect certain limitations: the time an audience can be expected to sit and watch, the attention and sympathy an audience is likely to give to various characters, the amount of **exposition** that can be shown rather than spoken aloud. Because of these constraints, playwrights, screenwriters, casting directors, and actors must rely on shortcuts to convey character. Everyone involved, including the audience, consciously or unconsciously relies on stereotypes of various social roles to flesh out the dramatic action that is concentrated into two hours, more or less. Even a play that seeks to undermine stereotypes must still invoke them. In the United States today, casting—or typecasting—usually relies on an actor's social identity, from gender and race to occupation, region, and age. However, plays or other dramatic forms can rely too much on stereotypes, positive or negative, and the familiarity leaves everyone disappointed (or offended); a role that defies stereotypes can be more interesting to perform and to watch. Alternatively, a character can be so exceptional and unfamiliar that audiences will fail to recognize any connection to people they might meet, and their responses will fall flat. All dramatic roles, then, must have some connection to types of personality, and good roles modify such types just enough to make the character deeper and more interesting. Playwrights often overturn or modify expectations of character in order to surprise an audience. So, too, do the actors who play those parts.

Every performance of a given character, like every production of a play, is an interpretation. Not just "adaptations"—Greek or Elizabethan plays set in modern times and performed in modern dress, for example—but even productions that seek to adhere faithfully to the written play are interpretations of what is vital or essential in it. John Malkovich, in the 1983–84 production of *Death of a*

Salesman, did not project Biff Loman as an outgoing, successful, hail-fellow-well-met jock, though that is what Arthur Miller intended and how he wanted the part played. Malkovich saw Biff as only pretending to be a jock. Big-time athletes, he insisted, don't glad-hand people; they wait for people to come to them. The actor did not change the author's words, but by intonation, body language, and "stage business" (wordless gestures and actions) he suggested his own view of the character's nature. In other words, he broke with the expectations associated with the character's type. As you read and develop your own interpretation of a play, try adding unexpected qualities to one or more of the characters in order to reveal different possible meanings in the drama.

Questions about Character

1. Who is the protagonist? Why and how so? Which other characters, if any, are main or major characters? Which are minor characters?

2. What are the protagonist's most distinctive traits, and what is most distinctive about his or her outlook and values? What motivates the character? What is it about the character that creates internal and/or external conflict? Which lines or stage directions reveal most about the character?

3. What are the roles of other characters? Which, if any, functions as an antagonist? Which, if any, serves as a foil? Does any character function as a narrator or chorus, providing background information and commentary? Why and how so?

4. To what extent are any of the characters in the play "types"? How might this affect an audience's experience of the play? In what ways might a director or actor choose to go against the expected types, and how would this complicate the overall effect of the play?

5. Which of the characters, or which aspects of the characters, does the play encourage us to sympathize with or to admire? to view negatively? Why and how so? Are there characters who might be more or less sympathetic, depending on how the role is cast and interpreted?

6. If you were directing a production of this play, whom among your friends and acquaintances would you cast in each role, and why? If you were directing a movie version, what professional actors would you cast?

PLOT AND STRUCTURE

An important part of any storyteller's task, whether in narrative or dramatic genres, is the invention, selection, and arrangement of some **action**. Even carefully structured action cannot properly be called a full-scale **plot** without some unifying sense of purpose. That is, what happens should seem to happen for meaningful reasons. This does not mean, of course, that characters or the audience must be satisfied in their hopes or expectations, or that effective plays need to wrap up every loose end. It does mean that a reader or theatergoer should feel that the playwright has completed *this* play—that nothing essential is missing—though the play's outcome or overall effect may be difficult to sum up.

Conflict is the engine that drives plot, and the presentation of conflict shapes the dramatic structure of a play. A conflict whose outcome is never in doubt may have other kinds of interest, but it is not truly dramatic. In a dramatic conflict, each of the opposing forces must at some point seem likely to triumph or worthy of such triumph—whether it is *external* (one character versus another, or one group of characters versus another group, each of whom may represent a different worldview) or *internal* (within a single character torn between competing views, duties, needs, or desires), or even one idea or ideology versus another one. In *Hamlet*, for example, our interest in the struggle between Hamlet and Claudius depends on their being evenly matched, though few viewers would ever wish that the new king would defeat the young hero. Claudius has possession of the throne and the queen, but Hamlet's role as the heir to the late king and his popularity with the people offset his opponent's strength.

The typical plot in drama, as in fiction, involves five stages: exposition, rising action, climax, falling action, and conclusion. **Exposition**, the first phase of plot, provides essential background information about the characters and situation as they exist at the beginning of a play and perhaps also about the events that got the characters to this point—as when, early in *Trifles*, Mr. Hale describes what happened before the play opens. The second phase, **rising action**, begins when an **inciting incident** leads to open conflict either within a single character or among two or more characters—as when, in *Trifles*, the men leave the women alone with what the latter soon discover to be crucial evidence. The moment when the conflict reaches its greatest pitch of intensity and its outcome is decided is the plot's third phase, its **climax** or **turning point**—in *Trifles*, perhaps the discovery of the dead bird and the act of covering up the evidence. The fourth stage, **falling action**, brings a release of emotional tension and moves the characters toward the **resolution** of their conflict and the plot itself toward its fifth and final stage, the **conclusion**. In *Trifles*, the men's return to the kitchen because, they believe, no evidence has been found can be called the falling action. The women's apparent decision to remain mute about what they have discovered can be called the resolution. The play concludes as the characters leave the Wrights' house with a few things for Mrs. Wright in the jailhouse. *Trifles*, then, contains all five stages, while some lengthy plays (Shakespeare's *Hamlet* and *A Midsummer Night's Dream*, for example) feature more than one plot. In such cases, the plot to which less time and attention is devoted is called the **subplot**.

Many older plays in the Western tradition, such as Shakespeare's, have five acts, each act roughly corresponding to—and thus emphasizing—a particular phase of plot. Acts are often further subdivided into scenes, each of which usually takes place in a somewhat different time and place and features a somewhat different combination of characters. Ancient Greek plays such as *Oedipus the King* are structured differently, such that individual scenes or *episodes* are separated by choral songs—that is, odes spoken or sung by the group of characters known as the chorus. Modern plays tend to have fewer acts and scenes than those of earlier eras, and plays such as *Trifles* and *The Real Inspector Hound*—in which the action unfolds continuously and, usually, in a single time and place—have become so common that they have their own name: the *one-act play*.

In the performance of a play longer than one act, it has become customary to have at least one intermission, in part for the practical reason that the audience may need restrooms or refreshments. Breaks may be signaled by turning down stage lights, turning up the house lights, and lowering the curtain (if there is one).

On rare occasions, very long plays (such as Tony Kushner's *Angels in America*) are performed over more than one evening, with the obvious challenge of finding an audience willing and able to pay and find the time for more than one performance; those who read such play "cycles" or **sequences** at their own pace at home have a certain advantage.

The key point is that the form of a play and the breaks between scenes or acts result from the nature of the play. Breaks can create suspense—a curtain comes down after an unexplained gunshot—or they can provide relief from tension or an emotional crisis.

Questions about Plot

1. Read the first scene or the first few pages and then stop. What potential for conflict do you see here? What do you expect to happen in the rest of the play?

2. How is the play divided into acts, scenes, or episodes, if at all? What is the effect of this division? Does the division of the play correspond, more or less, to the five stages of plot development—exposition, rising action, climax, resolution, conclusion?

3. Does the play show a relatively clear progression through the traditional stages of plot development, or does it seem to defy such conventions? If so, how, and what might the playwright achieve through these departures from tradition?

4. What is the inciting incident or destabilizing event? How and why does this event destabilize the initial situation? How would you describe the conflict that develops? To what extent is it external, internal, or both?

5. What is the climax, or turning point? Why and how so? How is the conflict resolved? How and why might this resolution fulfill or defy your expectations?

STAGES, SETS, AND SETTING

Most of us have been to a theater at one time or another, if only for a school play, and we know what a conventional modern stage (the **proscenium stage**) looks like: a room with the wall missing between us and it (the so-called *fourth wall*). So when we read a modern play—that is, one written during the past two or three hundred years—and imagine it taking place before us, we think of it as happening on this kind of stage. But there are also other modern types of stages—the **thrust stage**, where the audience sits around three sides of the major acting area, and the **arena stage**, where the audience sits all the way around the acting area and players make their entrances and their exits through the auditorium—but most plays today are performed on a proscenium stage. Most of the plays in this book can be readily imagined as taking place on such a stage.

Ancient Greek plays and the plays of Shakespeare were originally staged quite differently from most modern plays, and although they may be played today on a proscenium stage, we might be confused as we read if we are unaware of the layout of the theaters for which they were first written. In the Greek theater, the audience sat on a raised semicircle of seats (**amphitheater**) halfway around a circular area (**orchestra**) used primarily for dancing by the chorus. At the back of the orchestra was the **skene**, or stage house, representing the palace or temple before which the action took place. Shakespeare's stage, in contrast, basically involved a rectangular area built inside one end of a large enclosure like a circular walled-in yard; the audience stood on the ground or sat in stacked balconies around three sides of the principal acting area (rather like a thrust stage). There were additional acting areas on either side of this stage, as well as a recessed area at its back (which could represent Gertrude's chamber in *Hamlet,* for example) and an upper acting area (which could serve as Juliet's balcony). A trap door in the stage floor was used for occasional effects; the ghost of Hamlet's father probably entered and exited this way. Until three centuries ago—and certainly in Shakespeare's time—plays for large paying audiences were performed outdoors in daylight because of the difficulty and expense of lighting. If you are curious about Shakespeare's stage, you can visit a reconstruction of his Globe Theatre in Southwark, London, England, either in person or online at <www.shakespeares-globe.org>. Every summer, plays by Shakespeare are performed there for large international audiences willing to sit on hard benches around the arena or to stand as "groundlings" (a lucky few of whom can lean on the stage near the feet of the actors). The walls in the background of the stage are beautifully carved and painted, but there is no painted scenery, minimal furniture, few costume changes, no lighting, and no curtain around the stage (a cloth hanging usually covers the recessed area at the back of the stage). Three or four musicians may play period instruments on the balcony.

As the design of the Globe suggests, the conventions of dramatic writing and stage production have changed considerably over the centuries. Certainly this is true of the way playwrights convey a sense of place—one of the two key ingredients that make up a play's **setting**. Usually the audience is asked to imagine that the featured section of the auditorium is actually a particular place somewhere else. The audience of course knows it is a stage, more or less bare or elaborately disguised, but they accept it as a kitchen, a public square, a wooded park, an open road, or a room in a castle or a hut. *Oedipus the King* takes place entirely before the palace at Thebes. Following the general convention of ancient Greek drama, the play's setting never changes. When the action demands the presence of Teiresias, for example, the scene does not shift to him; instead, escorts bring him to the front of the palace. Similarly, important events that take place elsewhere are described by witnesses who arrive on the scene.

In Shakespeare's theater the conventions of place are quite different: The acting arena does not represent a single specific place but assumes a temporary identity according to the characters who inhabit it, their costumes, and their speeches. At the opening of *Hamlet* we know we are at a sentry station because a man dressed as a soldier challenges two others. By line 15, we know that we are in Denmark because the actors profess to be "liegemen to the Dane." At the end of the scene the actors leave the stage and in a sense take the sentry station with them. Shortly thereafter, a group of people dressed in court costumes and a man and a woman wearing crowns appear. As a theater audience, we must surmise from the costumes and dialogue that the acting area has now become a royal court; when we read the play, the stage directions give us a cue that the place has changed.

In a modern play, there are likely to be several changes of scene, each marked by the lowering of the curtain or the darkening of the stage while different sets and props are arranged. **Sets** (the design, decoration, and scenery) and **props** (articles or objects used on stage) vary greatly in modern productions of plays written in any period. Sometimes space is merely suggested—a circle of sand at one end of the stage, a blank wall behind—to emphasize abstraction and universal themes, or to stimulate the audience's imagination. More typically, a set uses realistic aids to the imagination. The set of *Trifles*, for example, must include at least a sink, a cupboard, a stove, a small table, a large kitchen table, and a rocking chair, as well as certain props: a bird cage, quilting pieces, and an ornamental box.

Time is the second key ingredient of setting, and conventions for representing time have also altered across the centuries. Three or four centuries ago, European dramatists and critics admired the conventions of classical Greek drama which, they believed, dictated that the action of a play should represent a very short time—sometimes as short as the actual performance time (two or three hours), and certainly no longer than a single day. This unity of time, one of the so-called **classical unities**, impels a dramatist to select the moment when a stable situation should change and to fill in the necessary prior details by exposition. (These same critics maintained that a play should be unified in place and action as well; the kind of leaping from Denmark to England, or from court to forest, that happens in Shakespeare's plays was off-limits according to such standards.) Thus, in *Trifles*, all the action before the investigators' visit to the farmhouse is summarized by characters during their brief visit, and the kitchen is the only part of the house seen by the audience.

When there are gaps and shifts in time, they are often indicated between scenes with the help of scenery, sound effects, stage directions, or notes in the program. An actor must assist in conveying the idea of time if his or her character appears at different ages, as in *How I Learned to Drive*. Various conventions of classical or Elizabethan drama have also worked effectively to communicate to the audience the idea of the passage of time, from the choral odes in *Oedipus the King* to the breaks between scenes in Shakespeare plays. There is a short time between Hamlet's departure to see his mother at the end of act 3, scene 2, and the entrance of the king with Rosencrantz and Guildenstern at the beginning of the next scene; in other parts of the play, the elapsed time might be as long as that between scenes 4 and 5 of act 4, during which the news of Polonius's death reaches Paris and Laertes returns to Denmark and there rallies his friends.

Action within a play thus can take place in a wide range of locations and over many years rather than in the one place and the twenty-four-hour period demanded by critics who believed in the classical unities. And we can learn much about how a particular play works and what it means by paying attention to the way it handles setting and sets.

Questions about Setting and Staging

1. Does all the action occur in one time and place, or in more than one? If the latter, what are those times and places? How much time tends to pass between scenes or episodes?

2. How important do the general time and place seem to be, and in what ways are they important? What about the plot and characters would remain the

(Continued on next page)

(Continued)

same if a director chose to set the play in a different time and place? What wouldn't?

3. What patterns do you notice regarding where and when things happen? Which characters are associated with each setting? How do different characters relate to the same setting? When, how, and why do scenes change from one setting to another? Are there significant deviations?

4. Do the stage directions describe particular settings and props in detail? If so, what seems significant about the details? How might they establish mood, reveal character, and affect individual characters and the characters' interactions with one another? Is there anything in the stage directions that seems to be intended more for readers than for a director staging a production?

5. Does the date of the play tell you anything about the way it was originally intended to be staged? Does the representation of time and place in the play implicitly call for a certain type of stage? If you were staging the play today, what kind of stage, sets, and props might you use, and why? How might your choices affect how the play works on audiences and what it means to them?

TONE, LANGUAGE, AND SYMBOL

In plays as in other literary genres, the **tone**—that is, the style or manner of expression—is difficult to specify or explain. Perhaps tone is more important in drama than in other genres because it is, in performance, a spoken form, and vocal tone always affects the meaning of spoken words to some extent, in any culture or language. The actor—and any reader who wishes to imagine a play as spoken aloud—must infer from the written language just how to read a line, what tone of voice to use. The choice of tone must be a negotiation between the words of the playwright and the interpretation and skill of the actor or reader. At times stage directions will specify the tone of a line of dialogue, though even that must be only a hint, since there are many ways of speaking "intensely" or "angrily." Find a line in one of the plays printed here that has a stage direction telling the actor how to deliver it, and with one or two other people take turns saying it that way. (*Trifles* and *The Real Inspector Hound* have many such instructions on tone.) If nothing else, such an experiment may help you appreciate the talent of good actors who can put on a certain tone of voice and make it seem natural and convincing. But it will also show you the many options for interpreting tone.

Dramatic **irony**, in which a character's perception is contradicted by what the audience knows, and even *situational irony*, in which a character's (and the audience's) expectations about what will happen are contradicted by what actually does happen, are relatively easy to detect. But *verbal irony*, in which a statement implies a meaning quite different from its obvious, literal meaning, can be fairly subtle and easy to miss. In the absence of clear stage directions, verbal irony—like other aspects of tone—can also be a matter of interpretation. That is, directors and actors, as well as readers and audiences, will often have to decide which lines in a play should be interpreted ironically. All three types of irony are nonetheless crucial to drama. As the very term *dramatic irony* suggests, drama—even more than fiction—depends for its effects on gaps between what the various characters and the audience know.

And situational irony—the gap between expectations and outcomes and even between what characters seem to deserve and what they get—is an especially key component and even a characteristic element of **tragedy**.

Never hesitate to apply the skills you have developed in interpreting poetry to drama; after all, most early plays were written in some form of verse. Aspects of poetry often emerge in modern plays; for example, **monologues** or extended speeches by one character, while they rarely rhyme or have regular meter, may allow greater eloquence than is usual in everyday speech and may include revealing imagery and **figures of speech**. Moon in *The Real Inspector Hound*, for instance, often embarks on strange fantasy monologues, as in his description of his dream of the violent uprising of "the stand-ins of the world," or more briefly, his comment on his name and role: "It is merely that it is not enough to wax at another's wane, to be held in reserve . . . to step in or not at all, the substitute . . . for I am Moon, continuous Moon, in my own shoes, Moon in June, April, September and no member of the human race keeps warm my bit of space. . . ." Without line breaks, you may not notice that "moon" and "June," "September" and "member," "race" and "space" rhyme, and you may miss at first the point that Moon, like the moon itself, is in shadow (or wanes) when the first-string critic is in place. Stoppard is not using poetic devices seriously, but in parodic fun. Tennessee Williams and other playwrights may use these resources more straightforwardly, as in the names of characters and places (*Blanche DuBois*, or "White of the Woods"; *Belle Reve*, or "Beautiful Dream").

Simple actions or objects, too, often have metaphorical significance or turn into **symbols**. Effective plays often use props in this way, as *Trifles* does with the bird and its cage. And some plays, like some poems, may even be organized around *controlling metaphors*—such as the driving lessons in Paula Vogel's *How I Learned to Drive* (in "Reading More Drama") or the piano lessons in August Wilson's *The Piano Lesson* (later in this chapter). As you read, pay close attention to metaphors or images, whether in language or more concrete form.

Allusions, too, can enrich the text in similar ways. In *Wit*, the doctor who signs Professor Bearing's "DNR" (do not resuscitate) order is named Kelekian. Although there are many doctors of Armenian descent in the United States, this appears to be a reference to the famous Dr. Kevorkian, who has defied the law against assisted suicide; by alluding to him in this way, the playwright clearly encourages us to connect the world of the play with our own. Awareness of all the stylistic choices in the work can help you reach a clearer interpretation of the whole play.

Questions about Tone, Language, and Symbol

1. Which lines in the play strike you as most ambiguous when it comes to the tone in which they should be spoken? Why and how so? What is the effect of that ambiguity, or how might an actor's or reader's decision about tone here affect the play as a whole?

2. How would you describe the overall tone of the whole play? Do any moments or entire scenes or acts in the play seem interestingly different in terms of their tone?

(Continued on next page)

(Continued)

3. How do the play's characters differ from one another in terms of their tone? Does any character's tone change over the course of the play?

4. Are any details—such as names; actions or statements; references to objects, props, or other details of setting; or allusions, metaphors, or other figures of speech—repeated throughout the play? Do any of these repeated details seem to have special significance? If so, what might that significance be?

5. What types of irony, if any, are at work in the play? What is the effect of the irony?

THEME

Theme—usually defined as a statement a work seems to make about a given issue or subject—is by its very nature the most comprehensive of the elements, embracing the impact of the entire work. Indeed, theme is not part of the work but is abstracted from it by the reader or audience. Since we, as interpreters, infer the theme and put it in our own words, we understandably often disagree about it. To arrive at your own statement of a theme, you need to consider all the elements of a play together: character, structure, setting (including time and place), tone, and other aspects of the style or the potential staging that create the entire effect.

Above all, try to understand a play on its own terms and to separate interpretation from evaluation. You may dislike symbolic or unrealistic drama until you get more used to it; if a play is not supposed to represent what real people would do in everyday life in that place and time, then it should not be criticized for failing to do so. Or you may find realistic plays about ordinary adults in middle America in the mid-twentieth century to be lacking in excitement or appeal. Yet if you read carefully, you may discover vigorous, moving portrayals of people trapped in situations all too familiar to them, if alien to you. Tastes may vary as widely as tones of speech, but if you are familiar with the elements of drama and the ways dramatic **conventions** vary over time and across cultures, you can become a good judge of theatrical literature, and you will notice more and more of the fine effects it can achieve. Nothing replaces the exhilaration and immediacy of a live theater performance, but reading and rereading plays can yield a rich and rewarding appreciation of the dramatic art.

Tips for Identifying Theme

Because theme emerges from a work in its entirety and from all the other elements working together, there's no one-size-fits-all method for discovering theme. Here, however, are some things to look for and consider as you read and reread a play.

(Continued on next page)

(Continued)

1. Pay attention to the title. A title will seldom indicate a play's theme directly, but some titles do suggest a central topic or a key question. Probe the rest of the play to see what insights, if any, about that topic or answers to that question it ultimately seems to offer.

2. Identify any statements that the characters make about a general concept, issue, or topic such as human nature, the natural world, and so on, particularly in monologues or in debates between major characters. Look, too, for statements that potentially have a general meaning or application beyond the play, even if they refer to a specific situation. Then consider whether and how the play as a whole corroborates, overturns, or complicates any one such view or statement.

3. If a character changes over the course of the play, try to articulate the truth or insight that he or she seems to discover. Then consider whether and how the play as a whole corroborates or complicates that insight.

4. Identify a conflict depicted in the play and state it in general terms or turn it into a general question, leaving out any reference to specific characters, setting, and so on. Then think about the insight or theme that might be implied by the way the conflict is resolved.

HENRIK IBSEN

A Doll House[1]

CHARACTERS

TORVALD HELMER, *a lawyer*	THE HELMERS' THREE SMALL CHILDREN
NORA, *his wife*	ANNE-MARIE, *their nurse*
DR. RANK	HELENE, *a maid*
MRS. LINDE	A DELIVERY BOY
NILS KROGSTAD, *a bank clerk*	

The action takes place in HELMER'*s residence.*

ACT I

A comfortable room, tastefully but not expensively furnished. A door to the right in the back wall leads to the entryway; another to the left leads to HELMER'*s study. Between these doors, a piano. Midway in the left-hand wall a door, and further back a window. Near the window a round table with an armchair and a small sofa. In the right-hand wall, toward the rear, a door, and nearer the foreground a porcelain stove with two armchairs and a rocking chair beside it. Between the stove and the side door, a small table. Engravings on the walls. An etagère with china figures and other small art objects; a small bookcase with richly bound books; the floor carpeted; a fire burning in the stove. It is a winter day.*

A bell rings in the entryway; shortly after we hear the door being unlocked. NORA *comes into the room, humming happily to herself; she is wearing street clothes and carries an*

1. Translated by Rolf Fjelde.

armload of packages, which she puts down on the table to the right. She has left the hall door open; and through it a DELIVERY BOY *is seen, holding a Christmas tree and a basket, which he gives to the* MAID *who let them in.*

NORA: Hide the tree well, Helene. The children mustn't get a glimpse of it till this evening, after it's trimmed. [*To the* DELIVERY BOY, *taking out her purse.*] How much?

DELIVERY BOY: Fifty, ma'am.

NORA: There's a crown. No, keep the change. [*The* BOY *thanks her and leaves.* NORA *shuts the door. She laughs softly to herself while taking off her street things. Drawing a bag of macaroons from her pocket, she eats a couple, then steals over and listens at her husband's study door.*] Yes, he's home. [*Hums again as she moves to the table right.*]

HELMER: [*From the study.*] Is that my little lark twittering out there?

NORA: [*Busy opening some packages.*] Yes, it is.

HELMER: Is that my squirrel rummaging around?

NORA: Yes!

HELMER: When did my squirrel get in?

NORA: Just now. [*Putting the macaroon bag in her pocket and wiping her mouth.*] Do come in, Torvald, and see what I've bought.

HELMER: Can't be disturbed. [*After a moment he opens the door and peers in, pen in hand.*] Bought, you say? All that there? Has the little spendthrift been out throwing money around again?

NORA: Oh, but Torvald, this year we really should let ourselves go a bit. It's the first Christmas we haven't had to economize.

HELMER: But you know we can't go squandering.

NORA: Oh yes, Torvald, we can squander a little now. Can't we? Just a tiny, wee bit. Now that you've got a big salary and are going to make piles and piles of money.

HELMER: Yes—starting New Year's. But then it's a full three months till the raise comes through.

NORA: Pooh! We can borrow that long.

HELMER: Nora! [*Goes over and playfully takes her by the ear.*] Are your scatterbrains off again? What if today I borrowed a thousand crowns, and you squandered them over Christmas week, and then on New Year's Eve a roof tile fell on my head, and I lay there—

NORA: [*Putting her hand on his mouth.*] Oh! Don't say such things!

HELMER: Yes, but what if it happened—then what?

NORA: If anything so awful happened, then it just wouldn't matter if I had debts or not.

HELMER: Well, but the people I'd borrowed from?

NORA: Them? Who cares about them! They're strangers.

HELMER: Nora, Nora, how like a woman! No, but seriously, Nora, you know what I think about that. No debts! Never borrow! Something of freedom's lost—and something of beauty, too—from a home that's founded on borrowing and debt. We've made a brave stand up to now, the two of us; and we'll go right on like that the little while we have to.

NORA: [*Going toward the stove.*] Yes, whatever you say, Torvald.

HELMER: [*Following her.*] Now, now, the little lark's wings mustn't droop. Come on, don't be a sulky squirrel. [*Taking out his wallet.*] Nora, guess what I have here.

NORA: [*Turning quickly.*] Money!

HELMER: There, see. [*Hands her some notes.*] Good grief, I know how costs go up in a house at Christmastime.

NORA: Ten—twenty—thirty—forty. Oh, thank you, Torvald; I can manage no end on this.

HELMER: You really will have to.

NORA: Oh yes, I promise I will. But come here so I can show you everything I bought. And so cheap! Look, new clothes for Ivar here—and a sword. Here a horse and a trumpet for Bob. And a doll and a doll's bed here for Emmy; they're nothing much, but she'll tear them to bits in no time anyway. And here I have dress material and handkerchiefs for the maids. Old Anne-Marie really deserves something more.

HELMER: And what's in that package there?

NORA: [*With a cry.*] Torvald, no! You can't see that till tonight!

HELMER: I see. But tell me now, you little prodigal, what have you thought of for yourself?

NORA: For myself? Oh, I don't want anything at all.

HELMER: Of course you do. Tell me just what—within reason—you'd most like to have.

NORA: I honestly don't know. Oh, listen, Torvald—

HELMER: Well?

NORA: [*Fumbling at his coat buttons, without looking at him.*] If you want to give me something, then maybe you could—you could—

HELMER: Come, on, out with it.

NORA: [*Hurriedly.*] You could give me money, Torvald. No more than you think you can spare; then one of these days I'll buy something with it.

HELMER: But Nora—

NORA: Oh, please, Torvald darling, do that! I beg you, please. Then I could hang the bills in pretty gilt paper on the Christmas tree. Wouldn't that be fun?

HELMER: What are those little birds called that always fly through their fortunes?

NORA: Oh yes, spendthrifts; I know all that. But let's do as I say, Torvald; then I'll have time to decide what I really need most. That's very sensible, isn't it?

HELMER: [*Smiling.*] Yes, very—that is, if you actually hung onto the money I give you, and you actually used it to buy yourself something. But it goes for the house and for all sorts of foolish things, and then I only have to lay out some more.

NORA: Oh, but Torvald—

HELMER: Don't deny it, my dear little Nora. [*Putting his arm around her waist.*] Spendthrifts are sweet, but they use up a frightful amount of money. It's incredible what it costs a man to feed such birds.

NORA: Oh, how can you say that! Really, I save everything I can.

HELMER: [*Laughing.*] Yes, that's the truth. Everything you can. But that's nothing at all.

NORA: [*Humming, with a smile of quiet satisfaction.*] Hm, if you only knew what expenses we larks and squirrels have, Torvald.

HELMER: You're an odd little one. Exactly the way your father was. You're never at a loss for scaring up money; but the moment you have it, it runs right out through your fingers; you never know what you've done with it. Well, one takes you as you are. It's deep in your blood. Yes, these things are hereditary, Nora.

NORA: Ah, I could wish I'd inherited many of Papa's qualities.

HELMER: And I couldn't wish you anything but just what you are, my sweet little lark. But wait; it seems to me you have a very—what should I call it?—a very suspicious look today—

NORA: I do?

HELMER: You certainly do. Look me straight in the eye.

NORA: [Looking at him.] Well?

HELMER: [Shaking an admonitory finger.] Surely my sweet tooth hasn't been running riot in town today, has she?

NORA: No. Why do you imagine that?

HELMER: My sweet tooth really didn't make a little detour through the confectioner's?

NORA: No, I assure you, Torvald—

HELMER: Hasn't nibbled some pastry?

NORA: No, not at all.

HELMER: Not even munched a macaroon or two?

NORA: No, Torvald, I assure you, really—

HELMER: There, there now. Of course I'm only joking.

NORA: [Going to the table, right.] You know I could never think of going against you.

HELMER: No, I understand that; and you *have* given me your word. [Going over to her.] Well, you keep your little Christmas secrets to yourself, Nora darling. I expect they'll come to light this evening, when the tree is lit.

NORA: Did you remember to ask Dr. Rank?

HELMER: No. But there's no need for that; it's assumed he'll be dining with us. All the same, I'll ask him when he stops by here this morning. I've ordered some fine wine. Nora, you can't imagine how I'm looking forward to this evening.

NORA: So am I. And what fun for the children, Torvald!

HELMER: Ah, it's so gratifying to know that one's gotten a safe, secure job, and with a comfortable salary. It's a great satisfaction, isn't it?

NORA: Oh, it's wonderful!

HELMER: Remember last Christmas? Three whole weeks before, you shut yourself in every evening till long after midnight, making flowers for the Christmas tree, and all the other decorations to surprise us. Ugh, that was the dullest time I've ever lived through.

NORA: It wasn't at all dull for me.

HELMER: [Smiling.] But the outcome *was* pretty sorry, Nora.

NORA: Oh, don't tease me with that again. How could I help it that the cat came in and tore everything to shreds.

HELMER: No, poor thing, you certainly couldn't. You wanted so much to please us all, and that's what counts. But it's just as well that the hard times are past.

NORA: Yes, it's really wonderful.

HELMER: Now I don't have to sit here alone, boring myself, and you don't have to tire your precious eyes and your fair little delicate hands—

NORA: [Clapping her hands.] No, is it really true, Torvald, I don't have to? Oh, how wonderfully lovely to hear! [Taking his arm.] Now I'll tell you just how I've thought we should plan things. Right after Christmas—[The doorbell rings.] Oh, the bell. [Straightening the room up a bit.] Somebody would have to come. What a bore!

HELMER: I'm not at home to visitors, don't forget.

MAID: [*From the hall doorway.*] Ma'am, a lady to see you—

NORA: All right, let her come in.

MAID: [*To* HELMER.] And the doctor's just come too.

HELMER: Did he go right to my study?

MAID: Yes, he did.

> [HELMER *goes into his room. The* MAID *shows in* MRS. LINDE, *dressed in traveling clothes, and shuts the door after her.*]

MRS. LINDE: [*In a dispirited and somewhat hesitant voice.*] Hello, Nora.

NORA: [*Uncertain.*] Hello—

MRS. LINDE: You don't recognize me.

NORA: No, I don't know—but wait, I think—[*Exclaiming.*] What! Kristine! Is it really you?

MRS. LINDE: Yes, it's me.

NORA: Kristine! To think I didn't recognize you. But then, how could I? [*More quietly.*] How you've changed, Kristine!

MRS. LINDE: Yes, no doubt I have. In nine—ten long years.

NORA: Is it so long since we met! Yes, it's all of that. Oh, these last eight years have been a happy time, believe me. And so now you've come in to town, too. Made the long trip in the winter. That took courage.

MRS. LINDE: I just got here by ship this morning.

NORA: To enjoy yourself over Christmas, of course. Oh, how lovely! Yes, enjoy ourselves, we'll do that. But take your coat off. You're not still cold? [*Helping her.*] There now, let's get cozy here by the stove. No, the easy chair there! I'll take the rocker here. [*Seizing her hands.*] Yes, now you have your old look again; it was only in that first moment. You're a bit more pale, Kristine—and maybe a bit thinner.

MRS. LINDE: And much, much older, Nora.

NORA: Yes, perhaps a bit older; a tiny, tiny bit; not much at all. [*Stopping short; suddenly serious.*] Oh, but thoughtless me, to sit here, chattering away. Sweet, good Kristine, can you forgive me?

MRS. LINDE: What do you mean, Nora?

NORA: [*Softly.*] Poor Kristine, you've become a widow.

MRS. LINDE: Yes, three years ago.

NORA: Oh, I knew it, of course; I read it in the papers. Oh, Kristine, you must believe me; I often thought of writing you then, but I kept postponing it, and something always interfered.

MRS. LINDE: Nora dear, I understand completely.

NORA: No, it was awful of me, Kristine. You poor thing, how much you must have gone through. And he left you nothing?

MRS. LINDE: No.

NORA: And no children?

MRS. LINDE: No.

NORA: Nothing at all, then?

MRS. LINDE: Not even a sense of loss to feed on.

NORA: [*Looking incredulously at her.*] But Kristine, how could that be?

MRS. LINDE: [*Smiling wearily and smoothing her hair.*] Oh, sometimes it happens, Nora.

NORA: So completely alone. How terribly hard that must be for you. I have three lovely children. You can't see them now; they're out with the maid. But now you must tell me everything—

MRS. LINDE: No, no, no, tell me about yourself.

NORA: No, you begin. Today I don't want to be selfish. I want to think only of you today. But there *is* something I must tell you. Did you hear of the wonderful luck we had recently?

MRS. LINDE: No, what's that?

NORA: My husband's been made manager in the bank, just think!

MRS. LINDE: Your husband? How marvelous!

NORA: Isn't it? Being a lawyer is such an uncertain living, you know, especially if one won't touch any cases that aren't clean and decent. And of course Torvald would never do that, and I'm with him completely there. Oh, we're simply delighted, believe me! He'll join the bank right after New Year's and start getting a huge salary and lots of commissions. From now on we can live quite differently—just as we want. Oh, Kristine, I feel so light and happy! Won't it be lovely to have stacks of money and not a care in the world?

MRS. LINDE: Well, anyway, it would be lovely to have enough for necessities.

NORA: No, not just for necessities, but stacks and stacks of money!

MRS. LINDE: [*Smiling.*] Nora, Nora, aren't you sensible yet? Back in school you were such a free spender.

NORA: [*With a quiet laugh.*] Yes, that's what Torvald still says. [*Shaking her finger.*] But "Nora, Nora" isn't as silly as you all think. Really, we've been in no position for me to go squandering. We've had to work, both of us.

MRS. LINDE: You too?

NORA: Yes, at odd jobs—needlework, crocheting, embroidery, and such—[*Casually.*] and other things too. You remember that Torvald left the department when we were married? There was no chance of promotion in his office, and of course he needed to earn more money. But that first year he drove himself terribly. He took on all kinds of extra work that kept him going morning and night. It wore him down, and then he fell deathly ill. The doctors said it was essential for him to travel south.

MRS. LINDE: Yes, didn't you spend a whole year in Italy?

NORA: That's right. It wasn't easy to get away, you know. Ivar had just been born. But of course we had to go. Oh, that was a beautiful trip, and it saved Torvald's life. But it cost a frightful sum, Kristine.

MRS. LINDE: I can well imagine.

NORA: Four thousand, eight hundred crowns it cost. That's really a lot of money.

MRS. LINDE: But it's lucky you had it when you needed it.

NORA: Well, as it was, we got it from Papa.

MRS. LINDE: I see. It was just about the time your father died.

NORA: Yes, just about then. And, you know, I couldn't make that trip out to nurse him. I had to stay here, expecting Ivar any moment, and with my poor sick Torvald to care for. Dearest Papa, I never saw him again, Kristine. Oh, that was the worst time I've known in all my marriage.

MRS. LINDE: I know how you loved him. And then you went off to Italy?

NORA: Yes. We had the means now, and the doctors urged us. So we left a month after.

MRS. LINDE: And your husband came back completely cured?

NORA: Sound as a drum!

MRS. LINDE: But—the doctor?

NORA: Who?

MRS. LINDE: I thought the maid said he was a doctor, the man who came in with me.

NORA: Yes, that was Dr. Rank—but he's not making a sick call. He's our closest friend, and he stops by at least once a day. No, Torvald hasn't had a sick moment since, and the children are fit and strong, and I am, too. [*Jumping up and clapping her hands.*] Oh, dear God, Kristine, what a lovely thing to live and be happy! But how disgusting of me—I'm talking of nothing but my own affairs. [*Sits on a stool close by* KRISTINE, *arms resting across her knees.*] Oh, don't be angry with me! Tell me, is it really true that you weren't in love with your husband? Why did you marry him, then?

MRS. LINDE: My mother was still alive, but bedridden and helpless—and I had my two younger brothers to look after. In all conscience, I didn't think I could turn him down.

NORA: No, you were right there. But was he rich at the time?

MRS. LINDE: He was very well off, I'd say. But the business was shaky, Nora. When he died, it all fell apart, and nothing was left.

NORA: And then—?

MRS. LINDE: Yes, so I had to scrape up a living with a little shop and a little teaching and whatever else I could find. The last three years have been like one endless workday without a rest for me. Now it's over, Nora. My poor mother doesn't need me, for she's passed on. Nor the boys, either; they're working now and can take care of themselves.

NORA: How free you must feel—

MRS. LINDE: No—only unspeakably empty. Nothing to live for now. [*Standing up anxiously.*] That's why I couldn't take it any longer out in that desolate hole. Maybe here it'll be easier to find something to do and keep my mind occupied. If I could only be lucky enough to get a steady job, some office work—

NORA: Oh, but Kristine, that's so dreadfully tiring, and you already look so tired. It would be much better for you if you could go off to a bathing resort.

MRS. LINDE: [*Going toward the window.*] I have no father to give me travel money, Nora.

NORA: [*Rising.*] Oh, don't be angry with me.

MRS. LINDE: [*Going to her.*] Nora dear, don't you be angry with me. The worst of my kind of situation is all the bitterness that's stored away. No one to work for, and yet you're always having to snap up your opportunities. You have to live; and so you grow selfish. When you told me the happy change in your lot, do you know I was delighted less for your sakes than for mine?

NORA: How so? Oh, I see. You think maybe Torvald could do something for you.

MRS. LINDE: Yes, that's what I thought.

NORA: And he will, Kristine! Just leave it to me; I'll bring it up so delicately—find something attractive to humor him with. Oh, I'm so eager to help you.

MRS. LINDE: How very kind of you, Nora, to be so concerned over me—doubly kind, considering you really know so little of life's burdens yourself.

NORA: I—? I know so little—?

MRS. LINDE: [*Smiling.*] Well, my heavens—a little needlework and such—Nora, you're just a child.

NORA: [*Tossing her head and pacing the floor.*] You don't have to act so superior.

MRS. LINDE: Oh?

NORA: You're just like the others. You all think I'm incapable of anything serious—

MRS. LINDE: Come now—

NORA: That I've never had to face the raw world.

MRS. LINDE: Nora dear, you've just been telling me all your troubles.

NORA: Hm! Trivia! [*Quietly.*] I haven't told you the big thing.

MRS. LINDE: Big thing? What do you mean?

NORA: You look down on me so, Kristine, but you shouldn't. You're proud that you worked so long and hard for your mother.

MRS. LINDE: I don't look down on a soul. But it *is* true: I'm proud—and happy, too—to think it was given to me to make my mother's last days almost free of care.

NORA: And you're also proud thinking of what you've done for your brothers.

MRS. LINDE: I feel I've a right to be.

NORA: I agree. But listen to this, Kristine—I've also got something to be proud and happy for.

MRS. LINDE: I don't doubt it. But whatever do you mean?

NORA: Not so loud. What if Torvald heard! He mustn't, not for anything in the world. Nobody must know, Kristine. No one but you.

MRS. LINDE: But what is it, then?

NORA: Come here. [*Drawing her down beside her on the sofa.*] It's true—I've also got something to be proud and happy for. I'm the one who saved Torvald's life.

MRS. LINDE: Saved—? Saved how?

NORA: I told you about the trip to Italy. Torvald never would have lived if he hadn't gone south—

MRS. LINDE: Of course; your father gave you the means—

NORA: [*Smiling.*] That's what Torvald and all the rest think, but—

MRS. LINDE: But—?

NORA: Papa didn't give us a pin. I was the one who raised the money.

MRS. LINDE: You? That whole amount?

NORA: Four thousand, eight hundred crowns. What do you say to that?

MRS. LINDE: But Nora, how was it possible? Did you win the lottery?

NORA: [*Disdainfully.*] The lottery? Pooh! No art to that.

MRS. LINDE: But where did you get it from then?

NORA: [*Humming, with a mysterious smile.*] Hmm, tra-la-la-la.

MRS. LINDE: Because you couldn't have borrowed it.

NORA: No? Why not?

MRS. LINDE: A wife can't borrow without her husband's consent.

NORA: [*Tossing her head.*] Oh, but a wife with a little business sense, a wife who knows how to manage—

MRS. LINDE: Nora, I simply don't understand—

NORA: You don't have to. Whoever said I *borrowed* the money? I could have gotten it other ways. [*Throwing herself back on the sofa.*] I could have gotten it from some admirer or other. After all, a girl with my ravishing appeal—

MRS. LINDE: You lunatic.

NORA: I'll bet you're eaten up with curiosity, Kristine.

MRS. LINDE: Now listen here, Nora—you haven't done something indiscreet?

NORA: [*Sitting up again.*] Is it indiscreet to save your husband's life?

MRS. LINDE: I think it's indiscreet that without his knowledge you—

NORA: But that's the point: he mustn't know! My Lord, can't you understand? He mustn't ever know the close call he had. It was to *me* the doctors came to say his life was in danger—that nothing could save him but a stay in the south. Didn't I try strategy then! I began talking about how lovely it would be for me to travel abroad like other young wives; I begged and I cried; I told him please to remember my condition, to be kind and indulge me; and then I dropped a hint that he could easily take out a loan. But at that, Kristine, he nearly exploded. He said I was frivolous, and it was his duty as man of the house not to indulge me in whims and fancies—as I think he called them. Aha, I thought, now you'll just have to be saved—and that's when I saw my chance.

MRS. LINDE: And your father never told Torvald the money wasn't from him?

NORA: No, never. Papa died right about then. I'd considered bringing him into my secret and begging him never to tell. But he was too sick at the time—and then, sadly, it didn't matter.

MRS. LINDE: And you've never confided in your husband since?

NORA: For heaven's sake, no! Are you serious? He's so strict on that subject. Besides—Torvald, with all his masculine pride—how painfully humiliating for him if he ever found out he was in debt to me. That would just ruin our relationship. Our beautiful, happy home would never be the same.

MRS. LINDE: Won't you ever tell him?

NORA: [*Thoughtfully.*] Yes—maybe sometime years from now, when I'm no longer so attractive. Don't laugh! I only mean when Torvald loves me less than now, when he stops enjoying my dancing and dressing up and reciting for him. Then it might be wise to have something in reserve—[*Breaking off.*] How ridiculous! That'll never happen—Well, Kristine, what do you think of my big secret? I'm capable of something too, hm? You can imagine, of course, how this thing hangs over me. It really hasn't been easy meeting the payments on time. In the business world there's what they call quarterly interest and what they call amortization, and these are always so terribly hard to manage. I've had to skimp a little here and there, wherever I could, you know. I could hardly spare anything from my house allowance, because Torvald has to live well. I couldn't let the children go poorly dressed; whatever I got for them, I felt I had to use up completely—the darlings!

MRS. LINDE: Poor Nora, so it had to come out of your own budget, then?

NORA: Yes, of course. But I was the one most responsible, too. Every time Torvald gave me money for new clothes and such, I never used more than half; always bought the simplest, cheapest outfits. It was a godsend that everything looks so well on me that Torvald never noticed. But it did weigh me down at times, Kristine. It *is* such a joy to wear fine things. You understand.

MRS. LINDE: Oh, of course.

NORA: And then I found other ways of making money. Last winter I was lucky enough to get a lot of copying to do. I locked myself in and sat writing every evening till late in the night. Ah, I was tired so often, dead tired. But still it was wonderful fun, sitting and working like that, earning money. It was almost like being a man.

MRS. LINDE: But how much have you paid off this way so far?

NORA: That's hard to say, exactly. These accounts, you know, aren't easy to figure. I only know that I've paid out all I could scrape together. Time and again I haven't known where to turn. [*Smiling.*] Then I'd sit here dreaming of a rich old gentleman who had fallen in love with me—

MRS. LINDE: What! Who is he?

NORA: Oh, really! And that he'd died, and when his will was opened, there in big letters it said, "All my fortune shall be paid over in cash, immediately, to that enchanting Mrs. Nora Helmer."

MRS. LINDE: But Nora dear—who *was* this gentleman?

NORA: Good grief, can't you understand? The old man never existed; that was only something I'd dream up time and again whenever I was at my wits' end for money. But it makes no difference now; the old fossil can go where he pleases for all I care; I don't need him or his will—because now I'm free. [*Jumping up.*] Oh, how lovely to think of that, Kristine! Carefree! To know you're carefree, utterly carefree; to be able to romp and play with the children, and to keep up a beautiful, charming home—everything just the way Torvald likes it! And think, spring is coming, with big blue skies. Maybe we can travel a little then. Maybe I'll see the ocean again. Oh yes, it *is* so marvelous to live and be happy!

[*The front doorbell rings.*]

MRS. LINDE: [*Rising.*] There's the bell. It's probably best that I go.

NORA: No, stay. No one's expected. It must be for Torvald.

MAID: [*From the hall doorway.*] Excuse me, ma'am—there's a gentleman here to see Mr. Helmer, but I didn't know—since the doctor's with him—

NORA: Who is the gentleman?

KROGSTAD: [*From the doorway.*] It's me, Mrs. Helmer.

[MRS. LINDE *starts and turns away toward the window.*]

NORA: [*Stepping toward him, tense, her voice a whisper.*] You? What is it? Why do you want to speak to my husband?

KROGSTAD: Bank business—after a fashion. I have a small job in the investment bank, and I hear now your husband is going to be our chief—

NORA: In other words, it's—

KROGSTAD: Just dry business, Mrs. Helmer. Nothing but that.

NORA: Yes, then please be good enough to step into the study. [*She nods indifferently as she sees him out by the hall door, then returns and begins stirring up the stove.*]

MRS. LINDE: Nora—who was that man?

NORA: That was a Mr. Krogstad—a lawyer.

MRS. LINDE: Then it really was him.

NORA: Do you know that person?

MRS. LINDE: I did once—many years ago. For a time he was a law clerk in our town.

NORA: Yes, he's been that.

MRS. LINDE: How he's changed.

NORA: I understand he had a very unhappy marriage.

MRS. LINDE: He's a widower now.

NORA: With a number of children. There now, it's burning. [*She closes the stove door and moves the rocker a bit to one side.*]

MRS. LINDE: They say he has a hand in all kinds of business.

NORA: Oh? That may be true; I wouldn't know. But let's not think about business. It's so dull.

[DR. RANK *enters from* HELMER'S *study.*]

RANK: [*Still in the doorway.*] No, no, really—I don't want to intrude, I'd just as soon talk a little while with your wife. [*Shuts the door, then notices* MRS. LINDE.] Oh, beg pardon. I'm intruding here too.

NORA: No, not at all. [*Introducing him.*] Dr. Rank, Mrs. Linde.

RANK: Well now, that's a name much heard in this house. I believe I passed the lady on the stairs as I came.

MRS. LINDE: Yes, I take the stairs very slowly. They're rather hard on me.

RANK: Uh-hm, some touch of internal weakness?

MRS. LINDE: More overexertion, I'd say.

RANK: Nothing else? Then you're probably here in town to rest up in a round of parties?

MRS. LINDE: I'm here to look for work.

RANK: Is that the best cure for overexertion?

MRS. LINDE: One has to live, Doctor.

RANK: Yes, there's a common prejudice to that effect.

NORA: Oh, come on, Dr. Rank—you really do want to live yourself.

RANK: Yes, I really do. Wretched as I am, I'll gladly prolong my torment indefinitely. All my patients feel like that. And it's quite the same, too, with the morally sick. Right at this moment there's one of those moral invalids in there with Helmer—

MRS. LINDE: [*Softly.*] Ah!

NORA: Who do you mean?

RANK: Oh, it's a lawyer, Krogstad, a type you wouldn't know. His character is rotten to the root—but even he began chattering all-importantly about how he had to *live.*

NORA: Oh? What did he want to talk to Torvald about?

RANK: I really don't know. I only heard something about the bank.

NORA: I didn't know that Krog—that this man Krogstad had anything to do with the bank.

RANK: Yes, he's gotten some kind of berth down there. [*To* MRS. LINDE.] I don't know if you also have, in your neck of the woods, a type of person who scuttles about breathlessly, sniffing out hints of moral corruption, and then maneuvers his victim into some sort of key position where he can keep an eye on him. It's the healthy these days that are out in the cold.

MRS. LINDE: All the same, it's the sick who most need to be taken in.

RANK: [*With a shrug.*] Yes, there we have it. That's the concept that's turning society into a sanatorium.

[NORA, *lost in her thoughts, breaks out into quiet laughter and claps her hands.*]

RANK: Why do you laugh at that? Do you have any real idea of what society is?

NORA: What do I care about dreary old society? I was laughing at something quite different—something terribly funny. Tell me, Doctor—is everyone who works in the bank dependent now on Torvald?

RANK: Is that what you find so terribly funny?

NORA: [*Smiling and humming.*] Never mind, never mind [*Pacing the floor.*] Yes, that's really immensely amusing: that we—that Torvald has so much power now over all those people. [*Taking the bag out of her pocket.*] Dr. Rank, a little macaroon on that?

RANK: See here, macaroons! I thought they were contraband here.

NORA: Yes, but these are some that Kristine gave me.

MRS. LINDE: What? I—?

NORA: Now, now, don't be afraid. You couldn't possibly know that Torvald had forbidden them. You see, he's worried they'll ruin my teeth. But hmp! Just this once! Isn't that so, Dr. Rank? Help yourself! [*Puts a macaroon in his mouth.*] And you too, Kristine. And I'll also have one, only a little one—or two, at the most. [*Walking about again.*] Now I'm really tremendously happy. Now there's just one last thing in the world that I have an enormous desire to do.

RANK: Well! And what's that?

NORA: It's something I have such a consuming desire to say so Torvald could hear.

RANK: And why can't you say it?

NORA: I don't dare. It's quite shocking.

MRS. LINDE: Shocking?

RANK: Well, then it isn't advisable. But in front of us you certainly can. What do you have such a desire to say so Torvald could hear?

NORA: I have such a huge desire to say—to hell and be damned!

RANK: Are you crazy?

MRS. LINDE: My goodness, Nora!

RANK: Go on, say it. Here he is.

NORA: [*Hiding the macaroon bag.*] Shh, shh, shh!

[HELMER *comes in from his study, hat in hand, overcoat over his arm.*]

NORA: [*Going toward him.*] Well, Torvald dear, are you through with him?

HELMER: Yes, he just left.

NORA: Let me introduce you—this is Kristine, who's arrived here in town.

HELMER: Kristine—? I'm sorry, but I don't know—

NORA: Mrs. Linde, Torvald dear. Mrs. Kristine Linde.

HELMER: Of course. A childhood friend of my wife's, no doubt?

MRS. LINDE: Yes, we knew each other in those days.

NORA: And just think, she made the long trip down here in order to talk with you.

HELMER: What's this?

MRS. LINDE: Well, not exactly—

NORA: You see, Kristine is remarkably clever in office work, and so she's terribly eager to come under a capable man's supervision and add more to what she already knows—

HELMER: Very wise, Mrs. Linde.

NORA: And then when she heard that you'd become a bank manager—the story was wired out to the papers—then she came in as fast as she could and—Really, Torvald, for my sake you can do a little something for Kristine, can't you?

HELMER: Yes, it's not at all impossible. Mrs. Linde, I suppose you're a widow?

MRS. LINDE: Yes.

HELMER: Any experience in office work?

MRS. LINDE: Yes, a good deal.

HELMER: Well, it's quite likely that I can make an opening for you—

NORA: [*Clapping her hands.*] You see, you see!

HELMER: You've come at a lucky moment, Mrs. Linde.

MRS. LINDE: Oh, how can I thank you?

HELMER: Not necessary. [*Putting his overcoat on.*] But today you'll have to excuse me—

RANK: Wait, I'll go with you. [*He fetches his coat from the hall and warms it at the stove.*]

NORA: Don't stay out long, dear.

HELMER: An hour; no more.

NORA: Are you going too, Kristine?

MRS. LINDE: [*Putting on her winter garments.*] Yes, I have to see about a room now.

HELMER: Then perhaps we can all walk together.

NORA: [*Helping her.*] What a shame we're so cramped here, but it's quite impossible for us to—

MRS. LINDE: Oh, don't even think of it! Good-bye, Nora dear, and thanks for everything.

NORA: Good-bye for now. Of course you'll be back this evening. And you too, Dr. Rank. What? If you're well enough? Oh, you've got to be! Wrap up tight now.

[*In a ripple of small talk the company moves out into the hall; children's voices are heard outside on the steps.*]

NORA: There they are! There they are! [*She runs to open the door. The children come in with their nurse,* ANNE-MARIE.] Come in, come in! [*Bends down and kisses them.*] Oh, you darlings—! Look at them, Kristine. Aren't they lovely!

RANK: No loitering in the draft here.

HELMER: Come, Mrs. Linde—this place is unbearable now for anyone but mothers.

[DR. RANK, HELMER, *and* MRS. LINDE *go down the stairs.* ANNE-MARIE *goes into the living room with the children.* NORA *follows, after closing the hall door.*]

NORA: How fresh and strong you look. Oh, such red cheeks you have! Like apples and roses. [*The children interrupt her throughout the following.*] And it was so much fun? That's wonderful. Really? You pulled both Emmy and Bob on the sled? Imagine, all together! Yes, you're a clever boy, Ivar. Oh, let me hold her a bit, Anne-Marie. My sweet little doll baby! [*Takes the smallest from the nurse and dances with her.*] Yes, yes, Mama will dance with Bob as well. What? Did you throw snowballs? Oh, if I'd only been there! No, don't bother, Anne-Marie— I'll undress them myself. Oh yes, let me. It's such fun. Go in and rest; you look half frozen. There's hot coffee waiting for you on the stove. [*The nurse goes into the room to the left.* NORA *takes the children's winter things off, throwing them about, while the children talk to her all at once.*] Is that so? A big dog chased you? But it didn't bite? No, dogs never bite little, lovely doll babies. Don't peek in the packages, Ivar! What is it? Yes, wouldn't you like to know. No, no, it's an ugly something. Well? Shall we play? What shall we play? Hide-and-seek? Yes, let's play hide-and-seek. Bob must hide first. I must? Yes, let me hide first. [*Laughing and shouting, she and the children play in and out of the living room and the adjoining room to the right. At last* NORA *hides under the table. The children come storming in, search, but cannot find her, then hear her muffled laughter, dash over to the table, lift the cloth up and find her. Wild shouting. She creeps forward as if to scare them. More shouts. Meanwhile, a knock at the hall door; no one has noticed it. Now the door half opens, and* KROGSTAD *appears. He waits a moment; the game goes on.*]

KROGSTAD: Beg pardon, Mrs. Helmer—

NORA: [*With a strangled cry, turning and scrambling to her knees.*] Oh! What do you want?

KROGSTAD: Excuse me. The outer door was ajar; it must be someone forgot to shut it—

NORA: [*Rising.*] My husband isn't home, Mr. Krogstad.

KROGSTAD: I know that.

NORA: Yes—then what do you want here?

KROGSTAD: A word with you.

NORA: With—? [*To the children, quietly.*] Go in to Anne-Marie. What? No, the strange man won't hurt Mama. When he's gone, we'll play some more. [*She leads the children into the room to the left and shuts the door after them. Then, tense and nervous:*] You want to speak to me?

KROGSTAD: Yes, I want to.

NORA: Today? But it's not yet the first of the month—

KROGSTAD: No, it's Christmas Eve. It's going to be up to you how merry a Christmas you have.

NORA: What is it you want? Today I absolutely can't—

KROGSTAD: We won't talk about that till later. This is something else. You do have a moment to spare, I suppose?

NORA: Oh yes, of course—I do, except—

KROGSTAD: Good. I was sitting over at Olsen's Restaurant when I saw your husband go down the street—

NORA: Yes?

KROGSTAD: With a lady.

NORA: Yes. So?

KROGSTAD: If you'll pardon my asking: wasn't that lady a Mrs. Linde?

NORA: Yes.

KROGSTAD: Just now come into town?

NORA: Yes, today.

KROGSTAD: She's a good friend of yours?

NORA: Yes, she is. But I don't see—

KROGSTAD: I also knew her once.

NORA: I'm aware of that.

KROGSTAD: Oh? You know all about it. I thought so. Well, then let me ask you short and sweet: is Mrs. Linde getting a job in the bank?

NORA: What makes you think you can cross-examine me, Mr. Krogstad—you, one of my husband's employees? But since you ask, you might as well know— yes, Mrs. Linde's going to be taken on at the bank. And I'm the one who spoke for her, Mr. Krogstad. Now you know.

KROGSTAD: So I guessed right.

NORA: [*Pacing up and down.*] Oh, one does have a tiny bit of influence, I should hope. Just because I am a woman, don't think it means that—When one has a subordinate position, Mr. Krogstad, one really ought to be careful about pushing somebody who—hm—

KROGSTAD: Who has influence?

NORA: That's right.

KROGSTAD: [*In a different tone.*] Mrs. Helmer, would you be good enough to use your influence on my behalf?

NORA: What? What do you mean?

KROGSTAD: Would you please make sure that I keep my subordinate position in the bank?

NORA: What does that mean? Who's thinking of taking away your position?

KROGSTAD: Oh, don't play the innocent with me. I'm quite aware that your friend would hardly relish the chance of running into me again; and I'm also aware now whom I can thank for being turned out.

NORA: But I promise you—

KROGSTAD: Yes, yes, yes, to the point: there's still time, and I'm advising you to use your influence to prevent it.

NORA: But Mr. Krogstad, I have absolutely no influence.

KROGSTAD: You haven't? I thought you were just saying—

NORA: You shouldn't take me so literally. I! How can you believe that I have any such influence over my husband?

KROGSTAD: Oh, I've known your husband from our student days. I don't think the great bank manager's more steadfast than any other married man.

NORA: You speak insolently about my husband, and I'll show you the door.

KROGSTAD: The lady has spirit.

NORA: I'm not afraid of you any longer. After New Year's, I'll soon be done with the whole business.

KROGSTAD: [*Restraining himself.*] Now listen to me, Mrs. Helmer. If necessary, I'll fight for my little job in the bank as if it were life itself.

NORA: Yes, so it seems.

KROGSTAD: It's not just a matter of income; that's the least of it. It's something else—All right, out with it! Look, this is the thing. You know, just like all the others, of course, that once, a good many years ago, I did something rather rash.

NORA: I've heard rumors to that effect.

KROGSTAD: The case never got into court; but all the same, every door was closed in my face from then on. So I took up those various activities you know about. I had to grab hold somewhere; and I dare say I haven't been among the worst. But now I want to drop all that. My boys are growing up. For their sakes, I'll have to win back as much respect as possible here in town. That job in the bank was like the first rung in my ladder. And now your husband wants to kick me right back down in the mud again.

NORA: But for heaven's sake, Mr. Krogstad, it's simply not in my power to help you.

KROGSTAD: That's because you haven't the will to—but I have the means to make you.

NORA: You certainly won't tell my husband that I owe you money?

KROGSTAD: Hm—what if I told him that?

NORA: That would be shameful of you. [*Nearly in tears.*] This secret—my joy and my pride—that he should learn it in such a crude and disgusting way—learn it from you. You'd expose me to the most horrible unpleasantness—

KROGSTAD: Only unpleasantness?

NORA: [*Vehemently.*] But go on and try. It'll turn out the worse for you, because then my husband will really see what a crook you are, and then you'll *never* be able to hold your job.

KROGSTAD: I asked if it was just domestic unpleasantness you were afraid of?

NORA: If my husband finds out, then of course he'll pay what I owe at once, and then we'd be through with you for good.

KROGSTAD: [*A step closer.*] Listen, Mrs. Helmer—you've either got a very bad memory, or else no head at all for business. I'd better put you a little more in touch with the facts.

NORA: What do you mean?

KROGSTAD: When your husband was sick, you came to me for a loan of four thousand, eight hundred crowns.

NORA: Where else could I go?

KROGSTAD: I promised to get you that sum—

NORA: And you got it.

KROGSTAD: I promised to get you that sum, on certain conditions. You were so involved in your husband's illness, and so eager to finance your trip, that I guess you didn't think out all the details. It might just be a good idea to remind you. I promised you the money on the strength of a note I drew up.

NORA: Yes, and that I signed.

KROGSTAD: Right. But at the bottom I added some lines for your father to guarantee the loan. He was supposed to sign down there.

NORA: Supposed to? He did sign.

KROGSTAD: I left the date blank. In other words, your father would have dated his signature himself. Do you remember that?

NORA: Yes, I think—

KROGSTAD: Then I gave you the note for you to mail to your father. Isn't that so?

NORA: Yes.

KROGSTAD: And naturally you sent it at once—because only some five, six days later you brought me the note, properly signed. And with that, the money was yours.

NORA: Well, then; I've made my payments regularly, haven't I?

KROGSTAD: More or less. But—getting back to the point—those were hard times for you then, Mrs. Helmer.

NORA: Yes, they were.

KROGSTAD: Your father was very ill, I believe.

NORA: He was near the end.

KROGSTAD: He died soon after?

NORA: Yes.

KROGSTAD: Tell me, Mrs. Helmer, do you happen to recall the date of your father's death? The day of the month, I mean.

NORA: Papa died the twenty-ninth of September.

KROGSTAD: That's quite correct; I've already looked into that. And now we come to a curious thing—[*Taking out a paper.*] which I simply cannot comprehend.

NORA: Curious thing? I don't know—

KROGSTAD: This is the curious thing: that your father co-signed the note for your loan three days after his death.

NORA: How—? I don't understand.

KROGSTAD: Your father died the twenty-ninth of September. But look. Here your father dated his signature October second. Isn't that curious, Mrs. Helmer? [NORA *is silent.*] Can you explain it to me? [NORA *remains silent.*] It's also remarkable that the words "October second" and the year aren't written in your father's hand, but rather in one that I think I know. Well, it's easy to understand. Your father forgot perhaps to date his signature, and then someone or other added it, a bit sloppily, before anyone knew of his death. There's nothing wrong in that. It all comes down to the signature. And there's no question about *that*, Mrs. Helmer. It really *was* your father who signed his own name here, wasn't it?

NORA: [*After a short silence, throwing her head back and looking squarely at him.*] No, it wasn't. *I* signed papa's name.

KROGSTAD: Wait, now—are you fully aware that this is a dangerous confession?

NORA: Why? You'll soon get your money.

KROGSTAD: Let me ask you a question—why didn't you send the paper to your father?

NORA: That was impossible. Papa was so sick. If I'd asked him for his signature, I also would have had to tell him what the money was for. But I couldn't tell him, sick as he was, that my husband's life was in danger. That was just impossible.

KROGSTAD: Then it would have been better if you'd given up the trip abroad.

NORA: I couldn't possibly. The trip was to save my husband's life. I couldn't give that up.

KROGSTAD: But didn't you ever consider that this was a fraud against me?

NORA: I couldn't let myself be bothered by that. You weren't any concern of mine. I couldn't stand you, with all those cold complications you made, even though you knew how badly off my husband was.

KROGSTAD: Mrs. Helmer, obviously you haven't the vaguest idea of what you've involved yourself in. But I can tell you this: it was nothing more and nothing worse that I once did—and it wrecked my whole reputation.

NORA: You? Do you expect me to believe that you ever acted bravely to save your wife's life?

KROGSTAD: Laws don't inquire into motives.

NORA: Then they must be very poor laws.

KROGSTAD: Poor or not—if I introduce this paper in court, you'll be judged according to law.

NORA: This I refuse to believe. A daughter hasn't a right to protect her dying father from anxiety and care? A wife hasn't a right to save her husband's life? I don't know much about laws, but I'm sure that somewhere in the books these things are allowed. And you don't know anything about it—you who practice the law? You must be an awful lawyer, Mr. Krogstad.

KROGSTAD: Could be. But business—the kind of business we two are mixed up in—don't you think I know about that? All right. Do what you want now. But I'm telling you *this*: if I get shoved down a second time, you're going to keep me company. [*He bows and goes out through the hall.*]

NORA: [*Pensive for a moment, then tossing her head.*] Oh, really! Trying to frighten me! I'm not so silly as all that. [*Begins gathering up the children's clothes, but soon stops.*] But—? No, but that's impossible! I did it out of love.

THE CHILDREN: [*In the doorway, left.*] Mama, that strange man's gone out the door.

NORA: Yes, yes, I know it. But don't tell anyone about the strange man. Do you hear? Not even Papa!

THE CHILDREN: No, Mama. But now will you play again?

NORA: No, not now.

THE CHILDREN: Oh, but Mama, you promised.

NORA: Yes, but I can't now. Go inside; I have too much to do. Go in, go in, my sweet darlings. [*She herds them gently back in the room and shuts the door after them. Settling on the sofa, she takes up a piece of embroidery and makes some stitches, but soon stops abruptly.*] No! [*Throws the work aside, rises, goes to the hall door and calls out.*] Helene! Let me have the tree in here. [*Goes to the table, left, opens the table drawer, and stops again.*] No, but that's utterly impossible!

MAID: [*With the Christmas tree.*] Where should I put it, ma'am?

NORA: There. The middle of the floor.

MAID: Should I bring anything else?

NORA: No, thanks. I have what I need.

[*The* MAID, *who has set the tree down, goes out.*]

NORA: [*Absorbed in trimming the tree.*] Candles here—and flowers here. That terrible creature! Talk, talk, talk! There's nothing to it at all. The tree's going to be lovely. I'll do anything to please you, Torvald. I'll sing for you, dance for you—

[HELMER *comes in from the hall, with a sheaf of papers under his arm.*]

NORA: Oh! You're back so soon?

HELMER: Yes. Has anyone been here?

NORA: Here? No.

HELMER: That's odd. I saw Krogstad leaving the front door.

NORA: So? Oh yes, that's true. Krogstad was here a moment.

HELMER: Nora, I can see by your face that he's been here, begging you to put in a good word for him.

NORA: Yes.

HELMER: And it was supposed to seem like your own idea? You were to hide it from me that he'd been here. He asked you that, too, didn't he?

NORA: Yes, Torvald, but—

HELMER: Nora, Nora, and you could fall for that? Talk with that sort of person and promise him anything? And then in the bargain, tell me an untruth.

NORA: An untruth—?

HELMER: Didn't you say that no one had been here? [*Wagging his finger.*] My little songbird must never do that again. A songbird needs a clean beak to warble with. No false notes. [*Putting his arm about her waist.*] That's the way it should be, isn't it? Yes, I'm sure of it. [*Releasing her.*] And so, enough of that. [*Sitting by the stove.*] Ah, how snug and cozy it is here. [*Leafing among his papers.*]

NORA: [*Busy with the tree, after a short pause.*] Torvald!

HELMER: Yes.

NORA: I'm so much looking forward to the Stenborgs' costume party, day after tomorrow.

HELMER: And I can't wait to see what you'll surprise me with.

NORA: Oh, that stupid business!

HELMER: What?

NORA: I can't find anything that's right. Everything seems so ridiculous, so inane.

HELMER: So my little Nora's come to *that* recognition?

NORA: [*Going behind his chair, her arms resting on its back.*] Are you very busy, Torvald?

HELMER: Oh—

NORA: What papers are those?

HELMER: Bank matters.

NORA: Already?

HELMER: I've gotten full authority from the retiring management to make all necessary changes in personnel and procedure. I'll need Christmas week for that. I want to have everything in order by New Year's.

NORA: So that was the reason this poor Krogstad—

HELMER: Hm.

NORA: [*Still leaning on the chair and slowly stroking the nape of his neck.*] If you weren't so very busy, I would have asked you an enormous favor, Torvald.

HELMER: Let's hear. What is it?

NORA: You know, there isn't anyone who has your good taste—and I want so much to look well at the costume party. Torvald, couldn't you take over and decide what I should be and plan my costume?

HELMER: Ah, is my stubborn little creature calling for a lifeguard?

NORA: Yes, Torvald, I can't get anywhere without your help.

HELMER: All right—I'll think it over. We'll hit on something.

NORA: Oh, how sweet of you. [*Goes to the tree again. Pause.*] Aren't the red flowers pretty—? But tell me, was it really such a crime that this Krogstad committed?

HELMER: Forgery. Do you have any idea what that means?

NORA: Couldn't he have done it out of need?

HELMER: Yes, or thoughtlessness, like so many others. I'm not so heartless that I'd condemn a man categorically for just one mistake.

NORA: No, of course not, Torvald!

HELMER: Plenty of men have redeemed themselves by openly confessing their crimes and taking their punishment.

NORA: Punishment—?

HELMER: But now Krogstad didn't go that way. He got himself out by sharp practices, and that's the real cause of his moral breakdown.

NORA: Do you really think that would—?

HELMER: Just imagine how a man with that sort of guilt in him has to lie and cheat and deceive on all sides, has to wear a mask even with the nearest and dearest he has, even with his own wife and children. And with the children, Nora—that's where it's most horrible.

NORA: Why?

HELMER: Because that kind of atmosphere of lies infects the whole life of a home. Every breath the children take in is filled with the germs of something degenerate.

NORA: [*Coming closer behind him.*] Are you sure of that?

HELMER: Oh, I've seen it often enough as a lawyer. Almost everyone who goes bad early in life has a mother who's a chronic liar.

NORA: Why just—the mother?

HELMER: It's usually the mother's influence that's dominant, but the father's works in the same way, of course. Every lawyer is quite familiar with it. And still this Krogstad's been going home year in, year out, poisoning his own children with lies and pretense; that's why I call him morally lost. [*Reaching his hands out toward her.*] So my sweet little Nora must promise me never to plead his cause. Your hand on it. Come, come, what's this? Give me your hand. There, now. All settled. I can tell you it'd be impossible for me to work alongside of him. I literally feel physically revolted when I'm anywhere near such a person.

NORA: [*Withdraws her hand and goes to the other side of the Christmas tree.*] How hot it is here! And I've got so much to do.

HELMER: [*Getting up and gathering his papers.*] Yes, and I have to think about getting some of these read through before dinner. I'll think about your costume, too. And something to hang on the tree in gilt paper, I may even see about that. [*Putting his hand on her head.*] Oh you, my darling little songbird. [*He goes into his study and closes the door after him.*]

NORA: [*Softly, after a silence.*] Oh, really! it isn't so. It's impossible. It must be impossible.

MARIE: [*In the doorway, left.*] The children are begging so hard to come in to
Mama.

NORA: No, no, no, don't let them in to me! You stay with them, Anne-Marie.

ANNE-MARIE: Of course, ma'am. [*Closes the door.*]

NORA: [*Pale with terror*]. Hurt my children—! Poison my home? [*A moment's pause;
then she tosses her head.*] That's not true. Never. Never in all the world.

ACT II

*Same room. Beside the piano the Christmas tree now stands stripped of ornament,
burned-down candle stubs on its ragged branches.* NORA'*s street clothes lie on the sofa.* NORA,
*alone in the room, moves restlessly about; at last she stops at the sofa and picks up her
coat.*

NORA: [*Dropping the coat again.*] Someone's coming! [*Goes toward the door, listens.*]
No—there's no one. Of course—nobody's coming today, Christmas Day—or
tomorrow, either. But maybe—[*Opens the door and looks out.*] No, nothing in the
mailbox. Quite empty. [*Coming forward.*] What nonsense! He won't do anything
serious. Nothing terrible could happen. It's impossible. Why, I have three small
children.

[ANNE-MARIE, *with a large carton, comes in from the room to the left.*]

ANNE-MARIE: Well, at last I found the box with the masquerade clothes.

NORA: Thanks. Put it on the table.

ANNE-MARIE: [*Does so.*] But they're all pretty much of a mess.

NORA: Ahh! I'd love to rip them in a million pieces!

ANNE-MARIE: Oh, mercy, they can be fixed right up. Just a little patience.

NORA: Yes, I'll go get Mrs. Linde to help me.

ANNE-MARIE: Out again now? In this nasty weather? Miss Nora will catch cold—
get sick.

NORA: Oh, worse things could happen—How are the children?

ANNE-MARIE: The poor mites are playing with their Christmas presents, but—

NORA: Do they ask for me much?

ANNE-MARIE: They're so used to having Mama around, you know.

NORA: Yes, but Anne-Marie, I *can't* be together with them as much as I was.

ANNE-MARIE: Well, small children get used to anything.

NORA: You think so? Do you think they'd forget their mother if she was gone for
good?

ANNE-MARIE: Oh, mercy—gone for good!

NORA: Wait, tell me, Anne-Marie—I've wondered so often—how could you ever
have the heart to give your child over to strangers?

ANNE-MARIE: But I had to, you know, to become little Nora's nurse.

NORA: Yes, but how could you *do* it?

ANNE-MARIE: When I could get such a good place? A girl who's poor and who's
gotten in trouble is glad enough for that. Because that slippery fish, he didn't
do a thing for me, you know.

NORA: But your daughter's surely forgotten you.

ANNE-MARIE: Oh, she certainly has not. She's written to me, both when she was
confirmed and when she was married.

NORA: [*Clasping her about the neck.*] You old Anne-Marie, you were a good mother for me when I was little.

ANNE-MARIE: Poor little Nora, with no other mother but me.

NORA: And if the babies didn't have one, then I know that you'd—What silly talk! [*Opening the carton.*] Go in to them. Now I'll have to—Tomorrow you can see how lovely I'll look.

ANNE-MARIE: Oh, there won't be anyone at the party as lovely as Miss Nora. [*She goes off into the room, left.*]

NORA: [*Begins unpacking the box, but soon throws it aside.*] Oh, if I dared to go out. If only nobody would come. If only nothing would happen here while I'm out. What craziness—nobody's coming. Just don't think. This muff—needs a brushing. Beautiful gloves, beautiful gloves. Let it go. Let it go! One, two, three, four, five, six—[*With a cry.*] Oh, there they are! [*Poises to move toward the door, but remains irresolutely standing.* MRS. LINDE *enters from the hall, where she has removed her street clothes.*]

NORA: Oh, it's you, Kristine. There's no one else out there? How good that you've come.

MRS. LINDE: I hear you were up asking for me.

NORA: Yes, I just stopped by. There's something you really can help me with. Let's get settled on the sofa. Look, there's going to be a costume party tomorrow evening at the Stenborgs' right above us, and now Torvald wants me to go as a Neapolitan peasant girl and dance the tarantella[2] that I learned in Capri.

MRS. LINDE: Really, are you giving a whole performance?

NORA: Torvald says yes, I should. See, here's the dress. Torvald had it made for me down there; but now it's all so tattered that I just don't know—

MRS. LINDE: Oh, we'll fix that up in no time. It's nothing more than the trimmings—they're a bit loose here and there. Needle and thread? Good, now we have what we need.

NORA: Oh, how sweet of you!

MRS. LINDE: [*Sewing.*] So you'll be in disguise tomorrow, Nora. You know what? I'll stop by then for a moment and have a look at you all dressed up. But listen, I've absolutely forgotten to thank you for that pleasant evening yesterday.

NORA: [*Getting up and walking about.*] I don't think it was as pleasant as usual yesterday. You should have come to town a bit sooner, Kristine—Yes, Torvald really knows how to give a home elegance and charm.

MRS. LINDE: And you do, too, if you ask me. You're not your father's daughter for nothing. But tell me, is Dr. Rank always so down in the mouth as yesterday?

NORA: No, that was quite an exception. But he goes around critically ill all the time—tuberculosis of the spine, poor man. You know, his father was a disgusting thing who kept mistresses and so on—and that's why the son's been sickly from birth.

MRS. LINDE: [*Lets her sewing fall to her lap.*] But my dearest Nora, how do you know about such things?

NORA: [*Walking more jauntily.*] Hmp! When you've had three children, then you've had a few visits from—from women who know something of medicine, and they tell you this and that.

MRS. LINDE: [*Resumes sewing; a short pause.*] Does Dr. Rank come here every day?

---

2. Lively folk dance of southern Italy, thought to cure the bite of the tarantula.

NORA: Every blessed day. He's Torvald's best friend from childhood, and *my* good friend, too. Dr. Rank almost belongs to this house.

MRS. LINDE: But tell me—is he quite sincere? I mean, doesn't he rather enjoy flattering people?

NORA: Just the opposite. Why do you think that?

MRS. LINDE: When you introduced us yesterday, he was proclaiming that he'd often heard my name in this house; but later I noticed that your husband hadn't the slightest idea who I really was. So how could Dr. Rank—?

NORA: But it's all true, Kristine. You see, Torvald loves me beyond words, and, as he puts it, he'd like to keep me all to himself. For a long time he'd almost be jealous if I even mentioned any of my old friends back home. So of course I dropped that. But with Dr. Rank I talk a lot about such things, because he likes hearing about them.

MRS. LINDE: Now listen, Nora; in many ways you're still like a child. I'm a good deal older than you, with a little more experience. I'll tell you something: you ought to put an end to all this with Dr. Rank.

NORA: What should I put an end to?

MRS. LINDE: Both parts of it, I think. Yesterday you said something about a rich admirer who'd provide you with money—

NORA: Yes, one who doesn't exist—worse luck. So?

MRS. LINDE: Is Dr. Rank well off?

NORA: Yes, he is.

MRS. LINDE: With no dependents?

NORA: No, no one. But—

MRS. LINDE: And he's over here every day?

NORA: Yes, I told you that.

MRS. LINDE: How can a man of such refinement be so grasping?

NORA: I don't follow you at all.

MRS. LINDE: Now don't try to hide it, Nora. You think I can't guess who loaned you the forty-eight hundred crowns?

NORA: Are you out of your mind? How could you think such a thing! A friend of ours, who comes here every single day. What an intolerable situation that would have been!

MRS. LINDE: Then it really wasn't him.

NORA: No, absolutely not. It never even crossed my mind for a moment—And he had nothing to lend in those days; his inheritance came later.

MRS. LINDE: Well, I think that was a stroke of luck for you, Nora dear.

NORA: No, it never would have occurred to me to ask Dr. Rank—Still, I'm quite sure that if I had asked him—

MRS. LINDE: Which you won't, of course.

NORA: No, of course not. I can't see that I'd ever need to. But I'm quite positive that if I talked to Dr. Rank—

MRS. LINDE: Behind your husband's back?

NORA: I've got to clear up this other thing; *that's* also behind his back. I've *got* to clear it all up.

MRS. LINDE: Yes, I was saying that yesterday, but—

NORA: [*Pacing up and down.*] A man handles these problems so much better than a woman—

MRS. LINDE: One's husband does, yes.

NORA: Nonsense. [*Stopping.*] When you pay everything you owe, then you get your note back, right?

MRS. LINDE: Yes, naturally.

NORA: And can rip it into a million pieces and burn it up—that filthy scrap of paper!

MRS. LINDE: [*Looking hard at her, laying her sewing aside, and rising slowly.*] Nora, you're hiding something from me.

NORA: You can see it in my face?

MRS. LINDE: Something's happened to you since yesterday morning. Nora, what is it?

NORA: [*Hurrying toward her.*] Kristine! [*Listening.*] Shh! Torvald's home. Look, go in with the children a while. Torvald can't bear all this snipping and stitching. Let Anne-Marie help you.

MRS. LINDE: [*Gathering up some of the things.*] All right, but I'm not leaving here until we've talked this out. [*She disappears into the room, left, as* TORVALD *enters from the hall.*]

NORA: Oh, how I've been waiting for you, Torvald dear.

HELMER: Was that the dressmaker?

NORA: No, that was Kristine. She's helping me fix up my costume. You know, it's going to be quite attractive.

HELMER: Yes, wasn't that a bright idea I had?

NORA: Brilliant! But then wasn't I good as well to give in to you?

HELMER: Good—because you give in to your husband's judgment? All right, you little goose, I know you didn't mean it like that. But I won't disturb you. You'll want to have a fitting, I suppose.

NORA: And you'll be working?

HELMER: Yes. [*Indicating a bundle of papers.*] See. I've been down to the bank. [*Starts toward his study.*]

NORA: Torvald.

HELMER: [*Stops.*] Yes.

NORA: If your little squirrel begged you, with all her heart and soul, for something—?

HELMER: What's that?

NORA: Then would you do it?

HELMER: First, naturally, I'd have to know what it was.

NORA: Your squirrel would scamper about and do tricks, if you'd only be sweet and give in.

HELMER: Out with it.

NORA: Your lark would be singing high and low in every room—

HELMER: Come on, she does that anyway.

NORA: I'd be a wood nymph and dance for you in the moonlight.

HELMER: Nora—don't tell me it's that same business from this morning?

NORA: [*Coming closer.*] Yes, Torvald, I beg you, please!

HELMER: And you actually have the nerve to drag that up again?

NORA: Yes, yes, you've got to give in to me; you *have* to let Krogstad keep his job in the bank.

HELMER: My dear Nora, I've slated his job for Mrs. Linde.

NORA: That's awfully kind of you. But you could just fire another clerk instead of Krogstad.

HELMER: This is the most incredible stubbornness! Because you go and give an impulsive promise to speak up for him, I'm expected to—

NORA: That's not the reason, Torvald. It's for your own sake. That man does writing for the worst papers; you said it yourself. He could do you any amount of harm. I'm scared to death of him—

HELMER: Ah, I understand. It's the old memories haunting you.

NORA: What do you mean by that?

HELMER: Of course, you're thinking about your father.

NORA: Yes, all right. Just remember how those nasty gossips wrote in the papers about Papa and slandered him so cruelly. I think they'd have had him dismissed if the department hadn't sent you up to investigate, and if you hadn't been so kind and open-minded toward him.

HELMER: My dear Nora, there's a notable difference between your father and me. Your father's official career was hardly above reproach. But mine is; and I hope it'll stay that way as long as I hold my position.

NORA: Oh, who can ever tell what vicious minds can invent? We could be so snug and happy now in our quiet, carefree home—you and I and the children, Torvald! That's why I'm pleading with you so—

HELMER: And just by pleading for him you make it impossible for me to keep him on. It's already known at the bank that I'm firing Krogstad. What if it's rumored around now that the new bank manager was vetoed by his wife—

NORA: Yes, what then—?

HELMER: Oh yes—as long as our little bundle of stubbornness gets her way—! I should go and make myself ridiculous in front of the whole office—give people the idea I can be swayed by all kinds of outside pressure. Oh, you can bet I'd feel the effects of that soon enough! Besides—there's something that rules Krogstad right out at the bank as long as I'm the manager.

NORA: What's that?

HELMER: His moral failings I could maybe overlook if I had to—

NORA: Yes, Torvald, why not?

HELMER: And I hear he's quite efficient on the job. But he was a crony of mine back in my teens—one of those rash friendships that crop up again and again to embarrass you later in life. Well, I might as well say it straight out: we're on a first-name basis. And that tactless fool makes no effort at all to hide it in front of others. Quite the contrary—he thinks that entitles him to take a familiar air around me, and so every other second he comes booming out with his "Yes, Torvald!" and "Sure thing, Torvald!" I tell you, it's been excruciating for me. He's out to make my place in the bank unbearable.

NORA: Torvald, you can't be serious about all this.

HELMER: Oh no? Why not?

NORA: Because these are such petty considerations.

HELMER: What are you saying? Petty? You think I'm petty!

NORA: No, just the opposite, Torvald dear. That's exactly why—

HELMER: Never mind. You call my motives petty; then I might as well be just that. Petty! All right! We'll put a stop to this for good. [Goes to the hall door and calls.] Helene!

NORA: What do you want?

HELMER: [Searching among his papers.] A decision. [The MAID comes in.] Look here; take this letter; go out with it at once. Get hold of a messenger and have him deliver it. Quick now. It's already addressed. Wait, here's some money.

MAID: Yes, sir. [*She leaves with the letter.*]

HELMER: [*Straightening his papers.*] There, now, little Miss Willful.

NORA: [*Breathlessly.*] Torvald, what was that letter?

HELMER: Krogstad's notice.

NORA: Call it back, Torvald! There's still time. Oh, Torvald, call it back! Do it for my sake—for your sake, for the children's sake! Do you hear, Torvald; do it! You don't know how this can harm us.

HELMER: Too late.

NORA: Yes, too late.

HELMER: Nora dear, I can forgive you this panic, even though basically you're insulting me. Yes, you are! Or isn't it an insult to think that *I* should be afraid of a courtroom hack's revenge? But I forgive you anyway, because this shows so beautifully how much you love me. [*Takes her in his arms.*] This is the way it should be, my darling Nora. Whatever comes, you'll see: when it really counts, I have strength and courage enough as a man to take on the whole weight myself.

NORA: [*Terrified.*] What do you mean by that?

HELMER: The whole weight, I said.

NORA: [*Resolutely.*] No, never in all the world.

HELMER: Good. So we'll share it, Nora, as man and wife. That's as it should be. [*Fondling her.*] Are you happy now? There, there, there—not these frightened dove's eyes. It's nothing at all but empty fantasies—Now you should run through your tarantella and practice your tambourine. I'll go to the inner office and shut both doors, so I won't hear a thing; you can make all the noise you like. [*Turning in the doorway.*] And when Rank comes, just tell him where he can find me. [*He nods to her and goes with his papers into the study, closing the door.*]

NORA: [*Standing as though rooted, dazed with fright, in a whisper.*] He really could do it. He will do it. He'll do it in spite of everything. No, not that, never, never! Anything but that! Escape! A way out—[*The doorbell rings.*] Dr. Rank! Anything but that! *Anything,* whatever it is! [*Her hands pass over her face, smoothing it; she pulls herself together, goes over and opens the hall door.* DR. RANK *stands outside, hanging his fur coat up. During the following scene, it begins getting dark.*]

NORA: Hello, Dr. Rank. I recognized your ring. But you mustn't go in to Torvald yet; I believe he's working.

RANK: And you?

NORA: For you, I always have an hour to spare—you know that. [*He has entered, and she shuts the door after him.*]

RANK: Many thanks. I'll make use of these hours while I can.

NORA: What do you mean by that? While you can?

RANK: Does that disturb you?

NORA: Well, it's such an odd phrase. Is anything going to happen?

RANK: What's going to happen is what I've been expecting so long—but I honestly didn't think it would come so soon.

NORA: [*Gripping his arm.*] What is it you've found out? Dr. Rank, you have to tell me!

RANK: [*Sitting by the stove.*] It's all over with me. There's nothing to be done about it.

NORA: [*Breathing easier.*] Is it you—then—?

RANK: Who else? There's no point in lying to one's self. I'm the most miserable of all my patients, Mrs. Helmer. These past few days I've been auditing my internal accounts. Bankrupt! Within a month I'll probably be laid out and rotting in the churchyard.

NORA: Oh, what a horrible thing to say.

RANK: The thing itself is horrible. But the worst of it is all the other horror before it's over. There's only one final examination left; when I'm finished with that, I'll know about when my disintegration will begin. There's something I want to say. Helmer with his sensitivity has such a sharp distaste for anything ugly. I don't want him near my sickroom.

NORA: Oh, but Dr. Rank—

RANK: I won't have him in there. Under no condition. I'll lock my door to him—As soon as I'm completely sure of the worst, I'll send you my calling card marked with a black cross, and you'll know then the wreck has started to come apart.

NORA: No, today you're completely unreasonable. And I wanted you so much to be in a really good humor.

RANK: With death up my sleeve? And then to suffer this way for somebody else's sins. Is there any justice in that? And in every single family, in some way or another, this inevitable retribution of nature goes on—

NORA: [*Her hands pressed over her ears.*] Oh, stuff! Cheer up! Please—be gay!

RANK: Yes, I'd just as soon laugh at it all. My poor, innocent spine, serving time for my father's gay army days.

NORA: [*By the table, left.*] He was so infatuated with asparagus tips and *pâté de foie gras,* wasn't that it?

RANK: Yes—and with truffles.

NORA: Truffles, yes. And then with oysters, I suppose?

RANK: Yes, tons of oysters, naturally.

NORA: And then the port and champagne to go with it. It's so sad that all these delectable things have to strike at our bones.

RANK: Especially when they strike at the unhappy bones that never shared in the fun.

NORA: Ah, that's the saddest of all.

RANK: [*Looks searchingly at her.*] Hm.

NORA: [*After a moment.*] Why did you smile?

RANK: No, it was you who laughed.

NORA: No, it was you who smiled, Dr. Rank!

RANK: [*Getting up.*] You're even a bigger tease than I'd thought.

NORA: I'm full of wild ideas today.

RANK: That's obvious.

NORA: [*Putting both hands on his shoulders.*] Dear, dear Dr. Rank, you'll never die for Torvald and me.

RANK: Oh, that loss you'll easily get over. Those who go away are soon forgotten.

NORA: [*Looks fearfully at him.*] You believe that?

RANK: One makes new connections, and then—

NORA: Who makes new connections?

RANK: Both you and Torvald will when I'm gone. I'd say you're well under way already. What was that Mrs. Linde doing here last evening?

NORA: Oh, come—you can't be jealous of poor Kristine?

RANK: Oh yes, I am. She'll be my successor here in the house. When I'm down under, that woman will probably—

NORA: Shh! Not so loud. She's right in there.

RANK: Today as well. So you see.

NORA: Only to sew on my dress. Good gracious, how unreasonable you are. [*Sitting on the sofa.*] Be nice now, Dr. Rank. Tomorrow you'll see how beautifully

I'll dance; and you can imagine then that I'm dancing only for you—yes, and of course for Torvald, too—that's understood. [*Takes various items out of the carton.*] Dr. Rank, sit over here and I'll show you something.

RANK: [*Sitting.*] What's that?

NORA: Look here. Look.

RANK: Silk stockings.

NORA: Flesh-colored. Aren't they lovely? Now it's so dark here, but tomorrow— No, no, no, just look at the feet. Oh well, you might as well look at the rest.

RANK: Hm—

NORA: Why do you look so critical? Don't you believe they'll fit?

RANK: I've never had any chance to form an opinion on that.

NORA: [*Glancing at him a moment.*] Shame on you. [*Hits him lightly on the ear with the stockings.*] That's for you. [*Puts them away again.*]

RANK: And what other splendors am I going to see now?

NORA: Not the least bit more, because you've been naughty. [*She hums a little and rummages among her things.*]

RANK: [*After a short silence.*] When I sit here together with you like this, completely easy and open, then I don't know—I simply can't imagine—whatever would have become of me if I'd never come into this house.

NORA: [*Smiling.*] Yes, I really think you feel completely at ease with us.

RANK: [*More quietly, staring straight ahead.*] And then to have to go away from it all—

NORA: Nonsense, you're not going away.

RANK: [*His voice unchanged.*]—and not even be able to leave some poor show of gratitude behind, scarcely a fleeting regret—no more than a vacant place that anyone can fill.

NORA: And if I asked you now for—? No—

RANK: For what?

NORA: For a great proof of your friendship—

RANK: Yes, yes?

NORA: No, I mean—for an exceptionally big favor—

RANK: Would you really, for once, make me so happy?

NORA: Oh, you haven't the vaguest idea what it is.

RANK: All right, then tell me.

NORA: No, but I can't, Dr. Rank—it's all out of reason. It's advice and help, too— and a favor—

RANK: So much the better. I can't fathom what you're hinting at. Just speak out. Don't you trust me?

NORA: Of course. More than anyone else. You're my best and truest friend, I'm sure. That's why I want to talk to you. All right, then, Dr. Rank: there's something you can help me prevent. You know how deeply, how inexpressibly dearly Torvald loves me; he'd never hesitate a second to give up his life for me.

RANK: [*Leaning close to her.*] Nora—do you think he's the only one—

NORA: [*With a slight start.*] Who—?

RANK: Who'd gladly give up his life for you.

NORA: [*Heavily.*] I see.

RANK: I swore to myself you should know this before I'm gone. I'll never find a better chance. Yes, Nora, now you know. And also you know now that you can trust me beyond anyone else.

NORA: [*Rising, natural and calm.*] Let me by.

RANK: [*Making room for her, but still sitting.*] Nora—

NORA: [*In the hall doorway.*] Helene, bring the lamp in. [*Goes over to the stove.*] Ah, dear Dr. Rank, that was really mean of you.

RANK: [*Getting up.*] That I've loved you just as deeply as somebody else? Was *that* mean?

NORA: No, but that you came out and told me. That was quite unnecessary—

RANK: What do you mean? Have you known—?

[*The* MAID *comes in with the lamp, sets it on the table, and goes out again.*]

RANK: Nora—Mrs. Helmer—I'm asking you: have you known about it?

NORA: Oh, how can I tell what I know or don't know? Really, I don't know what to say—Why did you have to be so clumsy, Dr. Rank! Everything was so good.

RANK: Well, in any case, you now have the knowledge that my body and soul are at your command. So won't you speak out?

NORA: [*Looking at him.*] After that?

RANK: Please, just let me know what it is.

NORA: You can't know anything now.

RANK: I have to. You mustn't punish me like this. Give me the chance to do whatever is humanly possible for you.

NORA: Now there's nothing you can do for me. Besides, actually, I don't need any help. You'll see—it's only my fantasies. That's what it is. Of course! [*Sits in the rocker, looks at him, and smiles.*] What a nice one you are, Dr. Rank. Aren't you a little bit ashamed, now that the lamp is here?

RANK: No, not exactly. But perhaps I'd better go—for good?

NORA: No, you certainly can't do that. You must come here just as you always have. You know Torvald can't do without you.

RANK: Yes, but *you?*

NORA: You know how much I enjoy it when you're here.

RANK: That's precisely what threw me off. You're a mystery to me. So many times I've felt you'd almost rather be with me than with Helmer.

NORA: Yes—you see, there are some people that one loves most and other people that one would almost prefer being with.

RANK: Yes, there's something to that.

NORA: When I was back home, of course I loved Papa most. But I always thought it was so much fun when I could sneak down to the maids' quarters, because they never tried to improve me, and it was always so amusing, the way they talked to each other.

RANK: Aha, so it's *their* place that I've filled.

NORA: [*Jumping up and going to him.*] Oh, dear, sweet Dr. Rank, that's not what I meant at all. But you can understand that with Torvald it's just the same as with Papa—

[*The* MAID *enters from the hall.*]

MAID: Ma'am—please! [*She whispers to* NORA *and hands her a calling card.*]

NORA: [*Glancing at the card.*] Ah! [*Slips it into her pocket.*]

RANK: Anything wrong?

NORA: No, no, not at all. It's only some—it's my new dress—

RANK: Really? But—there's your dress.

NORA: Oh, that. But this is another one—I ordered it—Torvald mustn't know—

RANK: Ah, now we have the big secret.

NORA: That's right. Just go in with him—he's back in the inner study. Keep him there as long as—

RANK: Don't worry. He won't get away. [*Goes into the study.*]

NORA: [*To the* MAID.] And he's standing waiting in the kitchen?

MAID: Yes, he came up by the back stairs.

NORA: But didn't you tell him somebody was here?

MAID: Yes, but that didn't do any good.

NORA: He won't leave?

MAID: No, he won't go till he's talked with you, ma'am.

NORA: Let him come in, then—but quietly. Helene, don't breathe a word about this. It's a surprise for my husband.

MAID: Yes, yes, I understand—[*Goes out.*]

NORA: This horror—it's going to happen. No, no, no, it can't happen, it mustn't.

[*She goes and bolts* HELMER's *door. The* MAID *opens the hall door for* KROGSTAD *and shuts it behind him. He is dressed for travel in a fur coat, boots, and a fur cap.*]

NORA: [*Going toward him.*] Talk softly. My husband's home.

KROGSTAD: Well, good for him.

NORA: What do you want?

KROGSTAD: Some information.

NORA: Hurry up, then. What is it?

KROGSTAD: You know, of course, that I got my notice.

NORA: I couldn't prevent it, Mr. Krogstad. I fought for you to the bitter end, but nothing worked.

KROGSTAD: Does your husband's love for you run so thin? He knows everything I can expose you to, and all the same he dares to—

NORA: How can you imagine he knows anything about this?

KROGSTAD: Ah, no—I can't imagine it either, now. It's not at all like my fine Torvald Helmer to have so much guts—

NORA: Mr. Krogstad, I demand respect for my husband!

KROGSTAD: Why, of course—all due respect. But since the lady's keeping it so carefully hidden, may I presume to ask if you're also a bit better informed than yesterday about what you've actually done?

NORA: More than you ever could teach me.

KROGSTAD: Yes, I *am* such an awful lawyer.

NORA: What is it you want from me?

KROGSTAD: Just a glimpse of how you are, Mrs. Helmer. I've been thinking about you all day long. A cashier, a night-court scribbler, a—well, a type like me also has a little of what they call a heart, you know.

NORA: Then show it. Think of my children.

KROGSTAD: Did you or your husband ever think of mine? But never mind. I simply wanted to tell you that you don't need to take this thing too seriously. For the present, I'm not proceeding with any action.

NORA: Oh no, really! Well—I knew that.

KROGSTAD: Everything can be settled in a friendly spirit. It doesn't have to get around town at all; it can stay just among us three.

NORA: My husband must never know anything of this.

KROGSTAD: How can you manage that? Perhaps you can pay me the balance?

NORA: No, not right now.

KROGSTAD: Or you know some way of raising the money in a day or two?

NORA: No way that I'm willing to use.

KROGSTAD: Well, it wouldn't have done you any good, anyway. If you stood in front of me with a fistful of bills, you still couldn't buy your signature back.

NORA: Then tell me what you're going to do with it.

KROGSTAD: I'll just hold onto it—keep it on file. There's no outsider who'll even get wind of it. So if you've been thinking of taking some desperate step—

NORA: I have.

KROGSTAD: Been thinking of running away from home—

NORA: I have!

KROGSTAD: Or even of something worse—

NORA: How could you guess that?

KROGSTAD: You can drop those thoughts.

NORA: How could you guess I was thinking of *that*?

KROGSTAD: Most of us think about *that* at first. I thought about it too, but I discovered I hadn't the courage—

NORA: [*Lifelessly.*] I don't either.

KROGSTAD: [*Relieved.*] That's true, you haven't the courage? You too?

NORA: I don't have it—I don't have it.

KROGSTAD: It would be terribly stupid, anyway. After that first storm at home blows out, why, then—I have here in my pocket a letter for your husband—

NORA: Telling everything?

KROGSTAD: As charitably as possible.

NORA: [*Quickly.*] He mustn't ever get that letter. Tear it up. I'll find some way to get money.

KROGSTAD: Beg pardon, Mrs. Helmer, but I think I just told you—

NORA: Oh, I don't mean the money I owe you. Let me know how much you want from my husband, and I'll manage it.

KROGSTAD: I don't want any money from your husband.

NORA: What do you want, then?

KROGSTAD: I'll tell you what. I want to recoup, Mrs. Helmer; I want to get on in the world—and there's where your husband can help me. For a year and a half I've kept myself clean of anything disreputable—all that time struggling with the worst conditions; but I was satisfied, working my way up step by step. Now I've been written right off, and I'm just not in the mood to come crawling back. I tell you, I want to move on. I want to get back in the bank—in a better position. Your husband can set up a job for me—

NORA: He'll never do that!

KROGSTAD: He'll do it. I know him. He won't dare breathe a word of protest. And once I'm in there together with him, you just wait and see! Inside of a year, I'll be the manager's right-hand man. It'll be Nils Krogstad, not Torvald Helmer, who runs the bank.

NORA: You'll never see the day!

KROGSTAD: Maybe you think you can—

NORA: I have the courage now—for *that*.

KROGSTAD: Oh, you don't scare me. A smart, spoiled lady like you—

NORA: You'll see; you'll see!

KROGSTAD: Under the ice, maybe? Down in the freezing, coal-black water? There, till you float up in the spring, ugly, unrecognizable, with your hair falling out—

NORA: You don't frighten me.

KROGSTAD: Nor do you frighten me. One doesn't do these things, Mrs. Helmer. Besides, what good would it be? I'd still have him safe in my pocket.

NORA: Afterwards? When I'm no longer—?

KROGSTAD: Are you forgetting that *I'll* be in control then over your final reputation? [NORA *stands speechless, staring at him.*] Good; now I've warned you. Don't do anything stupid. When Helmer's read my letter, I'll be waiting for his reply. And bear in mind that it's your husband himself who's forced me back to my old ways. I'll never forgive him for that. Good-bye, Mrs. Helmer. [*He goes out through the hall.*]

NORA: [*Goes to the hall door, opens it a crack, and listens.*] He's gone. Didn't leave the letter. Oh no, no, that's impossible too! [*Opening the door more and more.*] What's that? He's standing outside—not going downstairs. He's thinking it over? Maybe he'll—? [*A letter falls in the mailbox; then* KROGSTAD's *footsteps are heard, dying away down a flight of stairs.* NORA *gives a muffled cry and runs over toward the sofa table. A short pause.*] In the mailbox. [*Slips warily over to the hall door.*] It's lying there. Torvald, Torvald—now we're lost!

MRS. LINDE: [*Entering with the costume from the room, left.*] There now, I can't see anything else to mend. Perhaps you'd like to try—

NORA: [*In a hoarse whisper.*] Kristine, come here.

MRS. LINDE: [*Tossing the dress on the sofa.*] What's wrong? You look upset.

NORA: Come here. See that letter? *There!* Look—through the glass in the mailbox.

MRS. LINDE: Yes, yes, I see it.

NORA: That letter's from Krogstad—

MRS. LINDE: Nora—it's Krogstad who loaned you the money!

NORA: Yes, and now Torvald will find out everything.

MRS. LINDE: Believe me, Nora, it's best for both of you.

NORA: There's more you don't know. I forged a name.

MRS. LINDE: But for heaven's sake—?

NORA: I only want to tell you that, Kristine, so that you can be my witness.

MRS. LINDE: Witness? Why should I—?

NORA: If I should go out of my mind—it could easily happen—

MRS. LINDE: Nora!

NORA: Or anything else occurred—so I couldn't be present here—

MRS. LINDE: Nora, Nora, you aren't yourself at all!

NORA: And someone should try to take on the whole weight, all of the guilt, you follow me—

MRS. LINDE: Yes, of course, but why do you think—?

NORA: Then you're the witness that it isn't true, Kristine. I'm very much myself; my mind right now is perfectly clear; and I'm telling you: nobody else has known about this; I alone did everything. Remember that.

MRS. LINDE: I will. But I don't understand all this.

NORA: Oh, how could you ever understand it? It's the miracle now that's going to take place.

MRS. LINDE: The miracle?

NORA: Yes, the miracle. But it's so awful, Kristine. It mustn't take place, not for anything in the world.

MRS. LINDE: I'm going right over and talk with Krogstad.

NORA: Don't go near him; he'll do you some terrible harm!

MRS. LINDE: There was a time once when he'd gladly have done anything for me.

NORA: He?

MRS. LINDE: Where does he live?

NORA: Oh, how do I know? Yes. [*Searches in her pocket.*] Here's his card. But the letter, the letter—!

HELMER: [*From the study, knocking on the door.*] Nora!

NORA: [*With a cry of fear.*] Oh! What is it? What do you want?

HELMER: Now, now, don't be so frightened. We're not coming in. You locked the door—are you trying on the dress?

NORA: Yes, I'm trying it. I'll look just beautiful, Torvald.

MRS. LINDE: [*Who has read the card.*] He's living right around the corner.

NORA: Yes, but what's the use? We're lost. The letter's in the box.

MRS. LINDE: And your husband has the key?

NORA: Yes, always.

MRS. LINDE: Krogstad can ask for his letter back unread; he can find some excuse—

NORA: But it's just this time that Torvald usually—

MRS. LINDE: Stall him. Keep him in there. I'll be back as quick as I can. [*She hurries out through the hall entrance.*]

NORA: [*Goes to* HELMER's *door, opens it, and peers in.*] Torvald!

HELMER: [*From the inner study.*] Well—does one dare set foot in one's own living room at last? Come on, Rank, now we'll get a look—[*In the doorway.*] But what's this?

NORA: What, Torvald dear?

HELMER: Rank had me expecting some grand masquerade.

RANK: [*In the doorway.*] That was my impression, but I must have been wrong.

NORA: No one can admire me in my splendor—not till tomorrow.

HELMER: But Nora dear, you look so exhausted. Have you practiced too hard?

NORA: No, I haven't practiced at all yet.

HELMER: You know, it's necessary—

NORA: Oh, it's absolutely necessary, Torvald. But I can't get anywhere without your help. I've forgotten the whole thing completely.

HELMER: Ah, we'll soon take care of that.

NORA: Yes, take care of me, Torvald, please! Promise me that? Oh, I'm so nervous. That big party—You must give up everything this evening for me. No business—don't even touch your pen. Yes? Dear Torvald, promise?

HELMER: It's a promise. Tonight I'm totally at your service—you little helpless thing. Hm—but first there's one thing I want to—[*Goes toward the hall door.*]

NORA: What are you looking for?

HELMER: Just to see if there's any mail.

NORA: No, no, don't do that, Torvald!

HELMER: Now what?

NORA: Torvald, please. There isn't any.

HELMER: Let me look, though. [*Starts out.* NORA, *at the piano, strikes the first notes of the tarantella.* HELMER, *at the door, stops.*] Aha!

NORA: I can't dance tomorrow if I don't practice with you.

HELMER: [*Going over to her.*] Nora dear, are you really so frightened?

NORA: Yes, so terribly frightened. Let me practice right now; there's still time before dinner. Oh, sit down and play for me, Torvald. Direct me. Teach me, the way you always have.

HELMER: Gladly, if it's what you want. [*Sits at the piano.*]

NORA: [*Snatches the tambourine up from the box, then a long, varicolored shawl, which she throws around herself, whereupon she springs forward and cries out:*] Play for me now! Now I'll dance!

[HELMER *plays and* NORA *dances.* RANK *stands behind* HELMER *at the piano and looks on.*]

HELMER: [*As he plays.*] Slower. Slow down.

NORA: Can't change it.

HELMER: Not so violent, Nora!

NORA: Has to be just like this.

HELMER: [*Stopping.*] No, no, that won't do at all.

NORA: [*Laughing and swinging her tambourine.*] Isn't that what I told you?

RANK: Let me play for her.

HELMER: [*Getting up.*] Yes, go on. I can teach her more easily then.

[RANK *sits at the piano and plays;* NORA *dances more and more wildly.* HELMER *has stationed himself by the stove and repeatedly gives her directions; she seems not to hear them; her hair loosens and falls over her shoulders; she does not notice, but goes on dancing.* MRS. LINDE *enters.*]

MRS. LINDE: [*Standing dumbfounded at the door.*] Ah—!

NORA: [*Still dancing.*] See what fun, Kristine!

HELMER: But Nora darling, you dance as if your life were at stake.

NORA: And it is.

HELMER: Rank, stop! This is pure madness. Stop it, I say!

[RANK *breaks off playing, and* NORA *halts abruptly.*]

HELMER: [*Going over to her.*] I never would have believed it. You've forgotten everything I taught you.

NORA: [*Throwing away the tambourine.*] You see for yourself.

HELMER: Well, there's certainly room for instruction here.

NORA: Yes, you see how important it is. You've got to teach me to the very last minute. Promise me that, Torvald?

HELMER: You can bet on it.

NORA: You mustn't, either today or tomorrow, think about anything else but me; you mustn't open any letters—or the mailbox—

HELMER: Ah, it's still the fear of that man—

NORA: Oh yes, yes, that too.

HELMER: Nora, it's written all over you—there's already a letter from him out there.

NORA: I don't know. I guess so. But you mustn't read such things now; there mustn't be anything ugly between us before it's all over.

RANK: [*Quietly to* HELMER.] You shouldn't deny her.

HELMER: [*Putting his arm around her.*] The child can have her way. But tomorrow night, after you've danced—

NORA: Then you'll be free.

MAID: [*In the doorway, right.*] Ma'am, dinner is served.

NORA: We'll be wanting champagne, Helene.

MAID: Very good, ma'am. [*Goes out.*]

HELMER: So—a regular banquet, hm?

NORA: Yes, a banquet—champagne till daybreak! [*Calling out.*] And some maca-roons, Helene. Heaps of them—just this once.

HELMER: [*Taking her hands.*] Now, now, now—no hysterics. Be my own little lark again.

NORA: Oh, I will soon enough. But go on in—and you, Dr. Rank. Kristine, help me put up my hair.

RANK: [*Whispering, as they go.*] There's nothing wrong—really wrong, is there?

HELMER: Oh, of course not. It's nothing more than this childish anxiety I was tell-ing you about. [*They go out, right.*]

NORA: Well?

MRS. LINDE: Left town.

NORA: I could see by your face.

MRS. LINDE: He'll be home tomorrow evening. I wrote him a note.

NORA: You shouldn't have. Don't try to stop anything now. After all, it's a won-derful joy, this waiting here for the miracle.

MRS. LINDE: What is it you're waiting for?

NORA: Oh, you can't understand that. Go in to them; I'll be along in a moment.

[MRS. LINDE *goes into the dining room.* NORA *stands a short while as if composing herself; then she looks at her watch.*]

NORA: Five. Seven hours to midnight. Twenty-four hours to the midnight after, and then the tarantella's done. Seven and twenty-four? Thirty-one hours to live.

HELMER: [*In the doorway, right.*] What's become of the little lark?

NORA: [*Going toward him with open arms.*] Here's your lark!

ACT III

Same scene. The table, with chairs around it, has been moved to the center of the room. A lamp on the table is lit. The hall door stands open. Dance music drifts down from the floor above. MRS. LINDE *sits at the table, absently paging through a book, trying to read, but appar-ently unable to focus her thoughts. Once or twice she pauses, tensely listening for a sound at the outer entrance.*

MRS. LINDE: [*Glancing at her watch.*] Not yet—and there's hardly any time left. If only he's not—[*Listening again.*] Ah, there he is. [*She goes out in the hall and cau-tiously opens the outer door. Quiet footsteps are heard on the stairs. She whispers:*] Come in. Nobody's here.

KROGSTAD: [*In the doorway.*] I found a note from you at home. What's back of all this?

MRS. LINDE: I just *had* to talk to you.

KROGSTAD: Oh? And it just *had* to be here in this house?

MRS. LINDE: At my place it was impossible; my room hasn't a private entrance. Come in; we're all alone. The maid's asleep, and the Helmers are at the dance upstairs.

KROGSTAD: [*Entering the room.*] Well, well, the Helmers are dancing tonight? Really?

MRS. LINDE: Yes, why not?

KROGSTAD: How true—why not?

MRS. LINDE: All right, Krogstad, let's talk.

KROGSTAD: Do we two have anything more to talk about?

MRS. LINDE: We have a great deal to talk about.

KROGSTAD: I wouldn't have thought so.

MRS. LINDE: No, because you've never understood me, really.

KROGSTAD: Was there anything more to understand—except what's all too common in life? A calculating woman throws over a man the moment a better catch comes by.

MRS. LINDE: You think I'm so thoroughly calculating? You think I broke it off lightly?

KROGSTAD: Didn't you?

MRS. LINDE: Nils—is that what you really thought?

KROGSTAD: If you cared, then why did you write me the way you did?

MRS. LINDE: What else could I do? If I had to break off with you, then it was my job as well to root out everything you felt for me.

KROGSTAD: [*Wringing his hands.*] So that was it. And this—all this, simply for money!

MRS. LINDE: Don't forget I had a helpless mother and two small brothers. We couldn't wait for you, Nils; you had such a long road ahead of you then.

KROGSTAD: That may be; but you still hadn't the right to abandon me for somebody else's sake.

MRS. LINDE: Yes—I don't know. So many, many times I've asked myself if I did have that right.

KROGSTAD: [*More softly.*] When I lost you, it was as if all the solid ground dissolved from under my feet. Look at me; I'm a half-drowned man now, hanging onto a wreck.

MRS. LINDE: Help may be near.

KROGSTAD: It was near—but then you came and blocked it off.

MRS. LINDE: Without my knowing it, Nils. Today for the first time I learned that it's you I'm replacing at the bank.

KROGSTAD: All right—I believe you. But now that you know, will you step aside?

MRS. LINDE: No, because that wouldn't benefit you in the slightest.

KROGSTAD: Not "benefit" me, hm! I'd step aside anyway.

MRS. LINDE: I've learned to be realistic. Life and hard, bitter necessity have taught me that.

KROGSTAD: And life's taught me never to trust fine phrases.

MRS. LINDE: Then life's taught you a very sound thing. But you do have to trust in actions, don't you?

KROGSTAD: What does that mean?

MRS. LINDE: You said you were hanging on like a half-drowned man to a wreck.

KROGSTAD: I've good reason to say that.

MRS. LINDE: I'm also like a half-drowned woman on a wreck. No one to suffer with; no one to care for.

KROGSTAD: You made your choice

MRS. LINDE: There wasn't any choice then.

KROGSTAD: So—what of it?

MRS. LINDE: Nils, if only we two shipwrecked people could reach across to each other.

KROGSTAD: What are you saying?

MRS. LINDE: Two on one wreck are at least better off than each on his own.

KROGSTAD: Kristine!

MRS. LINDE: Why do you think I came into town?

KROGSTAD: Did you really have some thought of me?

MRS. LINDE: I have to work to go on living. All my born days, as long as I can remember, I've worked, and it's been my best and my only joy. But now I'm completely alone in the world; it frightens me to be so empty and lost. To work for yourself—there's no joy in that. Nils, give me something—someone to work for.

KROGSTAD: I don't believe all this. It's just some hysterical feminine urge to go out and make a noble sacrifice.

MRS. LINDE: Have you ever found me to be hysterical?

KROGSTAD: Can you honestly mean this? Tell me—do you know everything about my past?

MRS. LINDE: Yes.

KROGSTAD: And you know what they think I'm worth around here.

MRS. LINDE: From what you were saying before, it would seem that with me you could have been another person.

KROGSTAD: I'm positive of that.

MRS. LINDE: Couldn't it happen still?

KROGSTAD: Kristine—you're saying this in all seriousness? Yes, you are! I can see it in you. And do you really have the courage, then—?

MRS. LINDE: I need to have someone to care for; and your children need a mother. We both need each other. Nils, I have faith that you're good at heart—I'll risk everything together with you.

KROGSTAD: [Gripping her hands.] Kristine, thank you, thank you—Now I know I can win back a place in their eyes. Yes—but I forgot—

MRS. LINDE: [Listening.] Shh! The tarantella. Go now! Go on!

KROGSTAD: Why? What is it?

MRS. LINDE: Hear the dance up there? When that's over, they'll be coming down.

KROGSTAD: Oh, then I'll go. But—it's all pointless. Of course, you don't know the move I made against the Helmers.

MRS. LINDE: Yes, Nils, I know.

KROGSTAD: And all the same, you have the courage to—?

MRS. LINDE: I know how far despair can drive a man like you.

KROGSTAD: Oh, if I only could take it all back.

MRS. LINDE: You easily could—your letter's still lying in the mailbox.

KROGSTAD: Are you sure of that?

MRS. LINDE: Positive. But—

KROGSTAD: [Looks at her searchingly.] Is that the meaning of it, then? You'll save your friend at any price. Tell me straight out. Is that it?

MRS. LINDE: Nils—anyone who's sold herself for somebody else once isn't going to do it again.

KROGSTAD: I'll demand my letter back.

MRS. LINDE: No, no.

KROGSTAD: Yes, of course. I'll stay here till Helmer comes down; I'll tell him to give me my letter again—that it only involves my dismissal—that he shouldn't read it—

MRS. LINDE: No, Nils, don't call the letter back.

KROGSTAD: But wasn't that exactly why you wrote me to come here?

MRS. LINDE: Yes, in that first panic. But it's been a whole day and night since then, and in that time I've seen such incredible things in this house. Helmer's got to learn everything; this dreadful secret has to be aired; those two have to come to a full understanding; all these lies and evasions can't go on.

KROGSTAD: Well, then, if you want to chance it. But at least there's one thing I can do, and do right away—

MRS. LINDE: [*Listening.*] Go now, go, quick! The dance is over. We're not safe another second.

KROGSTAD: I'll wait for you downstairs.

MRS. LINDE: Yes, please do; take me home.

KROGSTAD: I can't believe it; I've never been so happy. [*He leaves by way of the outer door; the door between the room and the hall stays open.*]

MRS. LINDE: [*Straightening up a bit and getting together her street clothes.*] How different now! How different! Someone to work for, to live for—a home to build. Well, it is worth the try! Oh, if they'd only come! [*Listening.*] Ah, there they are. Bundle up. [*She picks up her hat and coat.* NORA's *and* HELMER's *voices can be heard outside; a key turns in the lock, and* HELMER *brings* NORA *into the hall almost by force. She is wearing the Italian costume with a large black shawl about her; he has on evening dress, with a black domino*[3] *open over it.*]

NORA: [*Struggling in the doorway.*] No, no, no, not inside! I'm going up again. I don't want to leave so soon.

HELMER: But Nora dear—

NORA: Oh, I beg you, please, Torvald. From the bottom of my heart, *please*—only an hour more!

HELMER: Not a single minute, Nora darling. You know our agreement. Come on, in we go; you'll catch cold out here. [*In spite of her resistance, he gently draws her into the room.*]

MRS. LINDE: Good evening.

NORA: Kristine!

HELMER: Why, Mrs. Linde—are you here so late?

MRS. LINDE: Yes, I'm sorry, but I did want to see Nora in costume.

NORA: Have you been sitting here, waiting for me?

MRS. LINDE: Yes. I didn't come early enough; you were all upstairs; and then I thought I really couldn't leave without seeing you.

HELMER: [*Removing* NORA's *shawl.*] Yes, take a good look. She's worth looking at, I can tell you that, Mrs. Linde. Isn't she lovely?

MRS. LINDE: Yes, I should say—

HELMER: A dream of loveliness, isn't she? That's what everyone thought at the party, too. But she's horribly stubborn—this sweet little thing. What's to be done with her? Can you imagine, I almost had to use force to pry her away.

NORA: Oh, Torvald, you're going to regret you didn't indulge me, even for just a half hour more.

HELMER: There, you see. She danced her tarantella and got a tumultuous hand—which was well earned, although the performance may have been a bit too naturalistic—I mean it rather overstepped the proprieties of art. But never mind—what's important is, she made a success, an overwhelming success. You think I could let her stay on after that and spoil the effect? Oh no; I took my

---

3. Hood worn by members of some religious orders.

lovely little Capri girl—my capricious little Capri girl, I should say—took her under my arm; one quick tour of the ballroom, a curtsy to every side, and then—as they say in novels—the beautiful vision disappeared. An exit should always be effective, Mrs. Linde, but that's what I can't get Nora to grasp. Phew, it's hot in here. [*Flings the domino on a chair and opens the door to his room.*] Why's it dark in here? Oh yes, of course. Excuse me. [*He goes in and lights a couple of candles.*]

NORA: [*In a sharp, breathless whisper.*] So?

MRS. LINDE: [*Quietly.*] I talked with him.

NORA: And—?

MRS. LINDE: Nora—you must tell your husband everything.

NORA: [*Dully.*] I knew it.

MRS. LINDE: You've got nothing to fear from Krogstad, but you have to speak out.

NORA: I won't tell.

MRS. LINDE: Then the letter will.

NORA: Thanks, Kristine. I know now what's to be done. Shh!

HELMER: [*Reentering.*] Well, then, Mrs. Linde—have you admired her?

MRS. LINDE: Yes, and now I'll say good night.

HELMER: Oh, come, so soon? Is this yours, this knitting?

MRS. LINDE: Yes, thanks. I nearly forgot it.

HELMER: Do you knit, then?

MRS. LINDE: Oh yes.

HELMER: You know what? You should embroider instead.

MRS. LINDE: Really? Why?

HELMER: Yes, because it's a lot prettier. See here, one holds the embroidery so, in the left hand, and then one guides the needle with the right—so—in an easy, sweeping curve—right?

MRS. LINDE: Yes, I guess that's—

HELMER: But, on the other hand, knitting—it can never be anything but ugly. Look, see here, the arms tucked in, the knitting needles going up and down— there's something Chinese about it. Ah, that was really a glorious champagne they served.

MRS. LINDE: Yes, good night, Nora, and don't be stubborn anymore.

HELMER: Well put, Mrs. Linde!

MRS. LINDE: Good night, Mr. Helmer.

HELMER: [*Accompanying her to the door.*] Good night, good night. I hope you get home all right. I'd be very happy to—but you don't have far to go. Good night, good night. [*She leaves. He shuts the door after her and returns.*] There, now, at last we got her out the door. She's a deadly bore, that creature.

NORA: Aren't you pretty tired, Torvald?

HELMER: No, not a bit.

NORA: You're not sleepy?

HELMER: Not at all. On the contrary, I'm feeling quite exhilarated. But you? Yes, you really look tired and sleepy.

NORA: Yes, I'm very tired. Soon now I'll sleep.

HELMER: See! You see! I was right all along that we shouldn't stay longer.

NORA: Whatever you do is always right.

HELMER: [*Kissing her brow.*] Now my little lark talks sense. Say, did you notice what a time Rank was having tonight?

NORA: Oh, was he? I didn't get to speak with him.

HELMER: I scarcely did either, but it's a long time since I've seen him in such high spirits. [*Gazes at her a moment, then comes nearer her.*] Hm—it's marvelous, though, to be back home again—to be completely alone with you. Oh, you bewitchingly lovely young woman!

NORA: Torvald, don't look at me like that!

HELMER: Can't I look at my richest treasure? At all that beauty that's mine, mine alone—completely and utterly.

NORA: [*Moving around to the other side of the table.*] You mustn't talk to me that way tonight.

HELMER: [*Following her.*] The tarantella is still in your blood, I can see—and it makes you even more enticing. Listen. The guests are beginning to go. [*Dropping his voice.*] Nora—it'll soon be quiet through this whole house.

NORA: Yes, I hope so.

HELMER: You do, don't you, my love? Do you realize—when I'm out at a party like this with you—do you know why I talk to you so little, and keep such a distance away; just send you a stolen look now and then—you know why I do it? It's because I'm imagining then that you're my secret darling, my secret young bride-to-be, and that no one suspects there's anything between us.

NORA: Yes, yes; oh, yes, I know you're always thinking of me.

HELMER: And then when we leave and I place the shawl over those fine young rounded shoulders—over that wonderful curving neck—then I pretend that you're my young bride, that we're just coming from the wedding, that for the first time I'm bringing you into my house—that for the first time I'm alone with you—completely alone with you, your trembling young beauty! All this evening I've longed for nothing but you. When I saw you turn and sway in the tarantella—my blood was pounding till I couldn't stand it—that's why I brought you down here so early—

NORA: Go away, Torvald! Leave me alone. I don't want all this.

HELMER: What do you mean? Nora, you're teasing me. You will, won't you? Aren't I your husband—?

[*A knock at the outside door.*]

NORA: [*Startled.*] What's that?

HELMER: [*Going toward the hall.*] Who is it?

RANK: [*Outside.*] It's me. May I come in a moment?

HELMER: [*With quiet irritation.*] Oh, what does he want now? [*Aloud.*] Hold on. [*Goes and opens the door.*] Oh, how nice that you didn't just pass us by!

RANK: I thought I heard your voice, and then I wanted so badly to have a look in. [*Lightly glancing about.*] Ah, me, these old familiar haunts. You have it snug and cozy in here, you two.

HELMER: You seemed to be having it pretty cozy upstairs, too.

RANK: Absolutely. Why shouldn't I? Why not take in everything in life? As much as you can, anyway, and as long as you can. The wine was superb—

HELMER: The champagne especially.

RANK: You noticed that too? It's amazing how much I could guzzle down.

NORA: Torvald also drank a lot of champagne this evening.

RANK: Oh?

NORA: Yes, and that always makes him so entertaining.

RANK: Well, why shouldn't one have a pleasant evening after a well-spent day?

HELMER: Well spent? I'm afraid I can't claim that.

RANK: [*Slapping him on the back.*] But I can, you see!

NORA: Dr. Rank, you must have done some scientific research today.

RANK: Quite so.

HELMER: Come now—little Nora talking about scientific research!

NORA: And can I congratulate you on the results?

RANK: Indeed you may.

NORA: Then they were good?

RANK: The best possible for both doctor and patient—certainty.

NORA: [*Quickly and searchingly.*] Certainty?

RANK: Complete certainty. So don't I owe myself a gay evening afterwards?

NORA: Yes, you're right, Dr. Rank.

HELMER: I'm with you—just so long as you don't have to suffer for it in the morning.

RANK: Well, one never gets something for nothing in life.

NORA: Dr. Rank—are you very fond of masquerade parties?

RANK: Yes, if there's a good array of odd disguises—

NORA: Tell me, what should we two go as at the next masquerade?

HELMER: You little featherhead—already thinking of the next!

RANK: We two? I'll tell you what: you must go as Charmed Life—

HELMER: Yes, but find a costume for *that!*

RANK: Your wife can appear just as she looks every day.

HELMER: That was nicely put. But don't you know what you're going to be?

RANK: Yes, Helmer, I've made up my mind.

HELMER: Well?

RANK: At the next masquerade I'm going to be invisible.

HELMER: That's a funny idea.

RANK: They say there's a hat—black, huge—have you never heard of the hat that makes you invisible? You put it on, and then no one on earth can see you.

HELMER: [*Suppressing a smile.*] Ah, of course.

RANK: But I'm quite forgetting what I came for. Helmer, give me a cigar, one of the dark Havanas.

HELMER: With the greatest pleasure. [*Holds out his case.*]

RANK: Thanks. [*Takes one and cuts off the tip.*]

NORA: [*Striking a match*] Let me give you a light.

RANK: Thank you. [*She holds the match for him; he lights the cigar.*] And now good-bye.

HELMER: Good-bye, good-bye, old friend.

NORA: Sleep well, Doctor.

RANK: Thanks for that wish.

NORA: Wish me the same.

RANK: You? All right, if you like—Sleep well. And thanks for the light. [*He nods to them both and leaves.*]

HELMER: [*His voice subdued.*] He's been drinking heavily.

NORA: [*Absently.*] Could be. [HELMER *takes his keys from his pocket and goes out in the hall.*] Torvald—what are you after?

HELMER: Got to empty the mailbox; it's nearly full. There won't be room for the morning papers.

NORA: Are you working tonight?

HELMER: You know I'm not. Why—what's this? Someone's been at the lock.

NORA: At the lock—?

HELMER: Yes, I'm positive. What do you suppose—? I can't imagine one of the maids—? Here's a broken hairpin. Nora, it's yours—

NORA: [*Quickly.*] Then it must be the children—

HELMER: You'd better break them of that. Hm, hm—well, opened it after all. [*Takes the contents out and calls into the kitchen.*] Helene! Helene, would you put out the lamp in the hall. [*He returns to the room, shutting the hall door, then displays the handful of mail.*] Look how it's piled up. [*Sorting through them.*] Now what's this?

NORA: [*At the window.*] The letter! Oh, Torvald, no!

HELMER: Two calling cards—from Rank.

NORA: From Dr. Rank?

HELMER: [*Examining them.*] "Dr. Rank, Consulting Physician." They were on top. He must have dropped them in as he left.

NORA: Is there anything on them?

HELMER: There's a black cross over the name. See? That's a gruesome notion. He could almost be announcing his own death.

NORA: That's just what he's doing.

HELMER: What! You've heard something? Something he's told you?

NORA: Yes. That when those cards came, he'd be taking his leave of us. He'll shut himself in now and die.

HELMER: Ah, my poor friend! Of course I knew he wouldn't be here much longer. But so soon—And then to hide himself away like a wounded animal.

NORA: If it has to happen, then it's best it happens in silence—don't you think so, Torvald?

HELMER: [*Pacing up and down.*] He'd grown right into our lives. I simply can't imagine him gone. He with his suffering and loneliness—like a dark cloud setting off our sunlit happiness. Well, maybe it's best this way. For him, at least. [*Standing still.*] And maybe for us too, Nora. Now we're thrown back on each other, completely. [*Embracing her.*] Oh you, my darling wife, how can I hold you close enough? You know what, Nora—time and again I've wished you were in some terrible danger, just so I could stake my life and soul and everything, for your sake.

NORA: [*Tearing herself away, her voice firm and decisive.*] Now you must read your mail, Torvald.

HELMER: No, no, not tonight. I want to stay with you, dearest.

NORA: With a dying friend on your mind?

HELMER: You're right. We've both had a shock. There's ugliness between us— these thoughts of death and corruption. We'll have to get free of them first. Until then—we'll stay apart.

NORA: [*Clinging about his neck.*] Torvald—good night! Good night!

HELMER: [*Kissing her on the cheek.*] Good night, little songbird. Sleep well, Nora. I'll be reading my mail now. [*He takes the letters into his room and shuts the door after him.*]

NORA: [*With bewildered glances, groping about, seizing* HELMER's *domino, throwing it around her, and speaking in short, hoarse, broken whispers.*] Never see him again. Never, never. [*Putting her shawl over her head.*] Never see the children either— them, too. Never, never. Oh, the freezing black water! The depths—down—Oh, I wish it were over—He has it now; he's reading it—now. Oh no, no, not yet.

Torvald, good-bye, you and the children—[*She starts for the hall; as she does,* HELMER *throws open his door and stands with an open letter in his hand.*]

HELMER: Nora!

NORA: [*Screams.*] Oh—!

HELMER: What is this? You know what's in this letter?

NORA: Yes, I know. Let me go! Let me out!

HELMER: [*Holding her back.*] Where are you going?

NORA: [*Struggling to break loose.*] You can't save me, Torvald!

HELMER: [*Slumping back.*] True! Then it's true what he writes? How horrible! No, no, it's impossible—it can't be true.

NORA: It *is* true. I've loved you more than all this world.

HELMER: Ah, none of your slippery tricks.

NORA: [*Taking one step toward him.*] Torvald—!

HELMER: What *is* this you've blundered into!

NORA: Just let me loose. You're not going to suffer for my sake. You're not going to take on my guilt.

HELMER: No more playacting. [*Locks the hall door.*] You stay right here and give me a reckoning. You understand what you've done? Answer! You understand?

NORA: [*Looking squarely at him, her face hardening.*] Yes. I'm beginning to understand everything now.

HELMER: [*Striding about.*] Oh, what an awful awakening! In all these eight years—she who was my pride and joy—a hypocrite, a liar—worse, worse—a criminal! How infinitely disgusting it all is! The shame! [NORA *says nothing and goes on looking straight at him. He stops in front of her.*] I should have suspected something of the kind. I should have known. All your father's flimsy values—Be still! All your father's flimsy values have come out in you. No religion, no morals, no sense of duty—Oh, how I'm punished for letting him off! I did it for your sake, and you repay me like this.

NORA: Yes, like this.

HELMER: Now you've wrecked all my happiness—ruined my whole future. Oh, it's awful to think of. I'm in a cheap little grafter's hands; he can do anything he wants with me, ask for anything, play with me like a puppet—and I can't breathe a word. I'll be swept down miserably into the depths on account of a featherbrained woman.

NORA: When I'm gone from this world, you'll be free.

HELMER: Oh, quit posing. Your father had a mess of those speeches too. What good would that ever do me if you were gone from this world, as you say? Not the slightest. He can still make the whole thing known; and if he does, I could be falsely suspected as your accomplice. They might even think that I was behind it—that I put you up to it. And all that I can thank you for—you that I've coddled the whole of our marriage. Can you see now what you've done to me?

NORA: [*Icily calm.*] Yes.

HELMER: It's so incredible, I just can't grasp it. But we'll have to patch up whatever we can. Take off the shawl. I said, take it off! I've got to appease him somehow or other. The thing has to be hushed up at any cost. And as for you and me, it's got to seem like everything between us is just as it was—to the outside world, that is. You'll go right on living in this house, of course. But you can't be allowed to bring up the children; I don't dare trust you with them—Oh, to have to say this to someone I've loved so much, and that I still—! Well, that's done with. From now on happiness doesn't matter; all that matters is saving the bits and pieces, the appearance—[*The doorbell rings.* HELMER *starts.*] What's that? And so late. Maybe the worst—? You think he'd—? Hide, Nora! Say you're sick. [NORA *remains standing motionless.* HELMER *goes and opens the door.*]

MAID: [*Half dressed, in the hall.*] A letter for Mrs. Helmer.

HELMER: I'll take it. [*Snatches the letter and shuts the door.*] Yes, it's from him. You don't get it; I'm reading it myself.

NORA: Then read it.

HELMER: [*By the lamp.*] I hardly dare. We may be ruined, you and I. But—I've got to know. [*Rips open the letter, skims through a few lines, glances at an enclosure, then cries out joyfully.*] Nora! [NORA *looks inquiringly at him.*] Nora! Wait—better check it again—Yes, yes, it's true. I'm saved. Nora, I'm saved!

NORA: And I?

HELMER: You too, of course. We're both saved, both of us. Look. He's sent back your note. He says he's sorry and ashamed—that a happy development in his life—oh, who cares what he says! Nora, we're saved! No one can hurt you. Oh, Nora, Nora—but first, this ugliness all has to go. Let me see—[*Takes a look at the note.*] No, I don't want to see it; I want the whole thing to fade like a dream. [*Tears the note and both letters to pieces, throws them into the stove and watches them burn.*] There—now there's nothing left—He wrote that since Christmas Eve you—Oh, they must have been three terrible days for you, Nora.

NORA: I fought a hard fight.

HELMER: And suffered pain and saw no escape but—No, we're not going to dwell on anything unpleasant. We'll just be grateful and keep on repeating: it's over now, it's over! You hear me, Nora? You don't seem to realize—it's over. What's it mean—that frozen look? Oh, poor little Nora, I understand. You can't believe I've forgiven you. But I have, Nora; I swear I have. I know that what you did, you did out of love for me.

NORA: That's true.

HELMER: You loved me the way a wife ought to love her husband. It's simply the means that you couldn't judge. But you think I love you any the less for not knowing how to handle your affairs? No, no—just lean on me; I'll guide you and teach you. I wouldn't be a man if this feminine helplessness didn't make you twice as attractive to me. You mustn't mind those sharp words I said— that was all in the first confusion of thinking my world had collapsed. I've forgiven you, Nora; I swear I've forgiven you.

NORA: My thanks for your forgiveness. [*She goes out through the door, right.*]

HELMER: No, wait—[*Peers in.*] What are you doing in there?

NORA: [*Inside.*] Getting out of my costume.

HELMER: [*By the open door.*] Yes, do that. Try to calm yourself and collect your thoughts again, my frightened little songbird. You can rest easy now; I've got wide wings to shelter you with. [*Walking about close by the door.*] How snug and nice our home is, Nora. You're safe here; I'll keep you like a hunted dove I've rescued out of a hawk's claws. I'll bring peace to your poor, shuddering heart. Gradually it'll happen, Nora; you'll see. Tomorrow all this will look differ- ent to you; then everything will be as it was. I won't have to go on repeating I forgive you; you'll feel it for yourself. How can you imagine I'd ever conceiv- ably want to disown you—or even blame you in any way? Ah, you don't know a man's heart, Nora. For a man there's something indescribably sweet and satisfying in knowing he's forgiven his wife—and forgiven her out of a full and open heart. It's as if she belongs to him in two ways now: in a sense he's given her fresh into the world again, and she's become his wife and his child as well. From now on that's what you'll be to me—you little, bewildered, help-less thing. Don't be afraid of anything, Nora; just open your heart to me, and I'll be conscience and will to you both—[NORA *enters in her regular clothes.*] What's this? Not in bed? You've changed your dress?

NORA: Yes, Torvald, I've changed my dress.

HELMER: But why now, so late?

NORA: Tonight I'm not sleeping.

HELMER: But Nora dear—

NORA: [*Looking at her watch.*] It's still not so very late. Sit down, Torvald; we have a lot to talk over. [*She sits at one side of the table.*]

HELMER: Nora—what is this? That hard expression—

NORA: Sit down. This'll take some time. I have a lot to say.

HELMER: [*Sitting at the table directly opposite her.*] You worry me, Nora. And I don't understand you.

NORA: No, that's exactly it. You don't understand me. And I've never understood you either—until tonight. No, don't interrupt. You can just listen to what I say. We're closing out accounts, Torvald.

HELMER: How do you mean that?

NORA: [*After a short pause.*] Doesn't anything strike you about our sitting here like this?

HELMER: What's that?

NORA: We've been married now eight years. Doesn't it occur to you that this is the first time we two, you and I, man and wife, have ever talked seriously together?

HELMER: What do you mean—seriously?

NORA: In eight whole years—longer even—right from our first acquaintance, we've never exchanged a serious word on any serious thing.

HELMER: You mean I should constantly go and involve you in problems you couldn't possibly help me with?

NORA: I'm not talking of problems. I'm saying that we've never sat down seriously together and tried to get to the bottom of anything.

HELMER: But dearest, what good would that ever do you?

NORA: That's the point right there: you've never understood me. I've been wronged greatly, Torvald—first by Papa, and then by you.

HELMER: What! By us—the two people who've loved you more than anyone else?

NORA: [*Shaking her head.*] You never loved me. You've thought it fun to be in love with me, that's all.

HELMER: Nora, what a thing to say!

NORA: Yes, it's true now, Torvald. When I lived at home with Papa, he told me all his opinions, so I had the same ones too; or if they were different I hid them, since he wouldn't have cared for that. He used to call me his doll-child, and he played with me the way I played with my dolls. Then I came into your house—

HELMER: How can you speak of our marriage like that?

NORA: [*Unperturbed.*] I mean, then I went from Papa's hands into yours. You arranged everything to your own taste, and so I got the same taste as you—or I pretended to; I can't remember. I guess a little of both, first one, then the other. Now when I look back, it seems as if I'd lived here like a beggar—just from hand to mouth. I've lived by doing tricks for you, Torvald. But that's the way you wanted it. It's a great sin what you and Papa did to me. You're to blame that nothing's become of me.

HELMER: Nora, how unfair and ungrateful you are! Haven't you been happy here?

NORA: No, never. I thought so—but I never have.

HELMER: Not—not happy!

NORA: No, only lighthearted. And you've always been so kind to me. But our home's been nothing but a playpen. I've been your doll-wife here, just as at home I was Papa's doll-child. And in turn the children have been my dolls. I thought it was fun when you played with me, just as they thought it fun when I played with them. That's been our marriage, Torvald.

HELMER: There's some truth in what you're saying—under all the raving exaggeration. But it'll all be different after this. Playtime's over; now for the schooling.

NORA: Whose schooling—mine or the children's?

HELMER: Both yours and the children's, dearest.

NORA: Oh, Torvald, you're not the man to teach me to be a good wife to you.

HELMER: And you can say that?

NORA: And I—how am I equipped to bring up children?

HELMER: Nora!

NORA: Didn't you say a moment ago that that was no job to trust me with?

HELMER: In a flare of temper! Why fasten on that?

NORA: Yes, but you were so very right. I'm not up to the job. There's another job I have to do first. I have to try to educate myself. You can't help me with that. I've got to do it alone. And that's why I'm leaving you now.

HELMER: [*Jumping up.*] What's that?

NORA: I have to stand completely alone, if I'm ever going to discover myself and the world out there. So I can't go on living with you.

HELMER: Nora, Nora!

NORA: I want to leave right away. Kristine should put me up for the night—

HELMER: You're insane! You've no right! I forbid you!

NORA: From here on, there's no use forbidding me anything. I'll take with me whatever is mine. I don't want a thing from you, either now or later.

HELMER: What kind of madness is this!

NORA: Tomorrow I'm going home—I mean, home where I came from. It'll be easier up there to find something to do.

HELMER: Oh, you blind, incompetent child!

NORA: I must learn to be competent, Torvald.

HELMER: Abandon your home, your husband, your children! And you're not even thinking what people will say.

NORA: I can't be concerned about that. I only know how essential this is.

HELMER: Oh, it's outrageous. So you'll run out like this on your most sacred vows.

NORA: What do you think are my most sacred vows?

HELMER: And I have to tell you that! Aren't they your duties to your husband and children?

NORA: I have other duties equally sacred.

HELMER: That isn't true. What duties are they?

NORA: Duties to myself.

HELMER: Before all else, you're a wife and a mother.

NORA: I don't believe in that anymore. I believe that, before all else, I'm a human being, no less than you—or anyway, I ought to try to become one. I know the majority thinks you're right, Torvald, and plenty of books agree with you, too. But I can't go on believing what the majority says, or what's written in books. I have to think over these things myself and try to understand them.

HELMER: Why can't you understand your place in your own home? On a point like that, isn't there one everlasting guide you can turn to? Where's your religion?

NORA: Oh, Torvald, I'm really not sure what religion is.

HELMER: What—?

NORA: I only know what the minister said when I was confirmed. He told me religion was this thing and that. When I get clear and away by myself, I'll go into that problem too. I'll see if what the minister said was right, or, in any case, if it's right for me.

HELMER: A young woman your age shouldn't talk like that. If religion can't move you, I can try to rouse your conscience. You do have some moral feeling? Or, tell me—has that gone too?

NORA: It's not easy to answer that, Torvald. I simply don't know. I'm all confused about these things. I just know I see them so differently from you. I find out, for one thing, that the law's not at all what I'd thought—but I can't get it through my head that the law is fair. A woman hasn't a right to protect her dying father or save her husband's life! I can't believe that.

HELMER: You talk like a child. You don't know anything of the world you live in.

NORA: No, I don't. But now I'll begin to learn for myself. I'll try to discover who's right, the world or I.

HELMER: Nora, you're sick; you've got a fever. I almost think you're out of your head.

NORA: I've never felt more clearheaded and sure in my life.

HELMER: And—clearheaded and sure—you're leaving your husband and children?

NORA: Yes.

HELMER: Then there's only one possible reason.

NORA: What?

HELMER: You no longer love me.

NORA: No. That's exactly it.

HELMER: Nora! You can't be serious!

NORA: Oh, this is so hard, Torvald—you've been so kind to me always. But I can't help it. I don't love you anymore.

HELMER: [Struggling for composure.] Are you also clearheaded and sure about that?

NORA: Yes, completely. That's why I can't go on staying here.

HELMER: Can you tell me what I did to lose your love?

NORA: Yes, I can tell you. It was this evening when the miraculous thing didn't come—then I knew you weren't the man I'd imagined.

HELMER: Be more explicit; I don't follow you.

NORA: I've waited now so patiently eight long years—for, my Lord, I know miracles don't come every day. Then this crisis broke over me, and such a certainty filled me: *now* the miraculous event would occur. While Krogstad's letter was lying out there, I never for an instant dreamed that you could give in to his terms. I was so utterly sure you'd say to him: go on, tell your tale to the whole wide world. And when he'd done that—

HELMER: Yes, what then? When I'd delivered my own wife into shame and disgrace—!

NORA: When he'd done that, I was so utterly sure that you'd step forward, take the blame on yourself and say: I am the guilty one.

HELMER: Nora—!

NORA: You're thinking I'd never accept such a sacrifice from you? No, of course not. But what good would my protests be against you? That was the miracle I was waiting for, in terror and hope. And to stave that off, I would have taken my life.

HELMER: I'd gladly work for you day and night, Nora—and take on pain and deprivation. But there's no one who gives up honor for love.

NORA: Millions of women have done just that.

HELMER: Oh, you think and talk like a silly child.

NORA: Perhaps. But you neither think nor talk like the man I could join myself to. When your big fright was over—and it wasn't from any threat against me, only for what might damage you—when all the danger was past, for you it was just as if nothing had happened. I was exactly the same, your little lark, your doll, that you'd have to handle with double care now that I'd turned out so brittle and frail. [*Gets up.*] Torvald—in that instant it dawned on me that for eight years I've been living here with a stranger, and that I'd even conceived three children—oh, I can't stand the thought of it! I could tear myself to bits.

HELMER: [*Heavily.*] I see. There's a gulf that's opened between us—that's clear. Oh, but Nora, can't we bridge it somehow?

NORA: The way I am now, I'm no wife for you.

HELMER: I have the strength to make myself over.

NORA: Maybe—if your doll gets taken away.

HELMER: But to part! To part from you! No, Nora, no—I can't imagine it.

NORA: [*Going out, right.*] All the more reason why it has to be. [*She reenters with her coat and a small overnight bag, which she puts on a chair by the table.*]

HELMER: Nora, Nora, not now! Wait till tomorrow.

NORA: I can't spend the night in a strange man's room.

HELMER: But couldn't we live here like brother and sister—

NORA: You know very well how long that would last. [*Throws her shawl about her.*] Good-bye, Torvald. I won't look in on the children. I know they're in better hands than mine. The way I am now, I'm no use to them.

HELMER: But someday, Nora—someday—?

NORA: How can I tell? I haven't the least idea what'll become of me.

HELMER: But you're my wife, now and wherever you go.

NORA: Listen, Torvald—I've heard that when a wife deserts her husband's house just as I'm doing, then the law frees him from all responsibility. In any case, I'm freeing you from being responsible. Don't feel yourself bound, any more than I will. There has to be absolute freedom for us both. Here, take your ring back. Give me mine.

HELMER: That too?

NORA: That too.

HELMER: There it is.

NORA: Good. Well, now it's all over. I'm putting the keys here. The maids know all about keeping up the house—better than I do. Tomorrow, after I've left town, Kristine will stop by to pack up everything that's mine from home. I'd like those things shipped up to me.

HELMER: Over! All over! Nora, won't you ever think about me?

NORA: I'm sure I'll think of you often, and about the children and the house here.

HELMER: May I write you?

NORA: No—never. You're not to do that.

HELMER: Oh, but let me send you—

NORA: Nothing. Nothing.

HELMER: Or help you if you need it.

NORA: No. I accept nothing from strangers.

HELMER: Nora—can I never be more than a stranger to you?

NORA: [Picking up the overnight bag.] Ah, Torvald—it would take the greatest miracle of all—

HELMER: Tell me the greatest miracle!

NORA: You and I both would have to transform ourselves to the point that—Oh, Torvald, I've stopped believing in miracles.

HELMER: But I'll believe. Tell me! Transform ourselves to the point that—?

NORA: That our living together could be a true marriage. [She goes out down the hall.]

HELMER: [Sinks down on a chair by the door, face buried in his hands.] Nora! Nora! [Looking about and rising.] Empty. She's gone. [A sudden hope leaps in him.] The greatest miracle—?

[From below, the sound of a door slamming shut.]

1879

QUESTIONS

1. Though the three acts of *A Doll House* are not formally divided into scenes, each does unfold as a series of relatively discreet, though continuous, episodes. In the first act, for example, the initial encounter between Nora and Helmer is followed by Nora's conversation with Mrs. Linde; a conversation among Mrs. Linde, Dr. Rank, and Nora, and then Torvald as well; a brief interlude in which Nora plays with her children; and, finally, her conversations first with Krogstad and then with her husband. What might the episodic structure itself tell us about Nora's character and situation? How is each of these episodes both similar to and different from the others, especially in terms of justifying or complicating Nora's assertion that everyone sees her the same way? What does each episode contribute to your impression of Nora's character and situation? to your degree of sympathy with her? In these terms, why and how does the order of the episodes matter? For example, what is the effect of Ibsen's choice to delay exposition regarding past events until the second episode (the conversation between Nora and Mrs. Linde)? By the end of this act, what do you see as the play's central conflict or conflicts?

2. How, if at all, has Nora or Torvald, or your impression of their characters and their marriage, changed by the beginning of act II? by its end? How has your interpretation of the conflict changed by this point? In these terms, what is the effect and significance of the way this act is plotted and structured? Why does Nora decide not to confide everything to Dr. Rank and seek his help? What can you surmise at this stage about Nora's plans and expectations for the immediate future? For what "miracle" is she "waiting" (p. 1480)?

3. Act III begins with the first and only episode in which Nora does not appear. What is the effect and significance of her absence? of the scene itself? How might this scene compare to the later one between Nora and Torvald? More generally, how does the relationship between Mrs. Linde and Krogstad compare to, and comment on, that between Nora and Torvald?

4. At the end of the play, Nora declares, "It's a great sin what you and Papa did to me. You're to blame that nothing's become of me" (p. 1491). How does the play as a whole both endorse and complicate Nora's assessment?

5. To what extent and how might the play as a whole suggest that Nora is right or wrong—or both—to leave her family at the play's end? Why is or isn't this an appropriate or satisfying resolution of the conflict?

6. In what various ways might one interpret the very end of the play? That is, what "sudden hope leaps in" Helmer? What might he mean when he says, "The greatest miracle—"? What is the effect and significance of the fact that we then hear "the sound of a door slamming shut"? Based on evidence from the rest of the play, what interpretation seems most valid to you? How does your interpretation of these words and actions affect your interpretation of the play's theme(s)?

7. In what way does *A Doll House* make use of dramatic or situational irony? By the end of the play, what statements in earlier acts might seem like instances of verbal irony?

8. In act III, Mrs. Linde tells Krogstad that she believes he "could have been another person" had he married her (p. 1482), implying that it is, at least in part, forces outside ourselves that shape who we are and how we behave, regardless of our gender. Does the play as a whole seem to endorse that view? If so, what are the most important forces? What role, for example, do different characters—and the play as a whole—assign to heredity or parentage, to parenting, and to economics? In terms of the latter, why might it matter that characters in the play tend to use economic language and metaphors, as when, in act II, Dr. Rank tells Nora, "I've been auditing my internal accounts. Bankrupt!" (p. 1471)?

9. What is the effect and significance of Ibsen's choice to have all the action in *A Doll House* take place in one location? to make that location the interior of the Helmer home? to describe this interior as he does in the stage directions that begin each act? What is the effect and significance of the fact that the play opens on Christmas Eve? that each act takes place on a different day? that the play ends 48 hours after it began? What other aspects of setting seem especially effective or important?

10. In terms of the play's conflict, theme(s), and characterization of Nora, Torvald, and their marriage, what role is played by each of the minor characters—Dr. Rank, Anne-Marie, and the Helmer children?

SUGGESTIONS FOR WRITING

1. Do any characters besides Nora change over the course of the play, or is it merely our perception of them that changes? Write an essay that answers this question with regard to Torvald, Mrs. Linde, or Krogstad, making sure to explain precisely when, how, and why either the character or your perception of the character changes and why and how that change affects how the play as a whole works and what it means.

2. Write an essay exploring the symbolic or metaphorical significance of the masquerade and/or tarantella.

3. In a brief essay, explore the validity and significance of Nora's claim that Dr. Rank is her "best and truest friend" (p. 1473).

4. Write an essay that draws on evidence from Ibsen's play to make an argument about what most likely happens after the play ends, either to Mrs. Linde and

Mr. Krogstad or to Nora and/or Torvald. What reasons, if any, for example, might the play give you for believing that Mrs. Linde and Krogstad will enjoy what Nora calls "a true marriage" (p. 1496), or that "Those who go away are soon forgotten" and, perhaps, replaced (p. 1474)?

5. *A Doll House* was first performed in 1879, and its portrait of women's roles as daughters, wives, and mothers is in certain ways specific to the late nineteenth century, when—for example—a woman couldn't legally borrow money without her father's or husband's consent and seldom got custody of her children in cases of separation or divorce. Write an essay in which you analyze both how the play characterizes the role nineteenth-century women were expected to play as daughters, wives, *or* mothers, and why and how that characterization is and/or isn't relevant or accurate today.

6. Religion is explicitly discussed only at the very end of the play, when Torvald asks, "Where's your religion?" and Nora answers him (p. 1494). Yet the play takes place during a Christian holiday, and there is frequent talk of "miracles." Write an essay exploring what the play as a whole ultimately seems to suggest about Christianity, its status in the social world depicted in the play, and its role in generating conflict.

AUGUST WILSON
The Piano Lesson

> Gin my cotton
> Sell my seed
> Buy my baby
> Everything she need
> —Skip James[1]

CHARACTERS

DOAKER   MARETHA
BOY WILLIE   AVERY
LYMON   WINING BOY
BERNIECE   GRACE

Romare Bearden, *Piano Lesson*, 1983. Collage of various papers with paint, ink, and graphite on paper. Art © Romare Bearden Foundation/Licensed by VAGA, New York NY.

THE SETTING: *The action of the play takes place in the kitchen and parlor of the house where* DOAKER CHARLES *lives with his niece,* BERNIECE, *and her eleven-year-old daughter,* MARETHA. *The house is sparsely furnished, and although there is evidence of a woman's touch, there is a lack of warmth and vigor.* BERNIECE *and* MARETHA *occupy the upstairs rooms.*

DOAKER's *room is prominent and opens onto the kitchen. Dominating the parlor is an old upright piano. On the legs of the piano, carved in the manner of African sculpture, are mask-like figures resembling totems. The carvings are rendered with a grace and power of invention that lifts them out of the realm of craftsmanship and into the realm of art. At left is a staircase leading to the upstairs.*

---

1. Mississippi-born blues musician and minister (1902–69); the quoted lines come from his "Illinois Blues."

ACT I

Scene 1

[*The lights come up on the Charles household. It is five o'clock in the morning. The dawn is beginning to announce itself, but there is something in the air that belongs to the night. A stillness that is a portent, a gathering, a coming together of something akin to a storm. There is a loud knock at the door.*]

BOY WILLIE: [*Off stage, calling.*] Hey, Doaker . . . Doaker! [*He knocks again and calls.*] Hey, Doaker! Hey, Berniece! Berniece!

[DOAKER *enters from his room. He is a tall, thin man of forty-seven, with severe features, who has for all intents and purposes retired from the world though he works full-time as a railroad cook.*]

DOAKER: Who is it?

BOY WILLIE: Open the door, nigger! It's me . . . Boy Willie!

DOAKER: Who?

BOY WILLIE: Boy Willie! Open the door!

[DOAKER *opens the door and* BOY WILLIE *and* LYMON *enter.* BOY WILLIE *is thirty years old. He has an infectious grin and a boyishness that is apt for his name. He is brash and impulsive, talkative and somewhat crude in speech and manner.* LYMON *is twenty-nine.* BOY WILLIE's *partner, he talks little, and then with a straightforwardness that is often disarming.*]

DOAKER: What you doing up here?

BOY WILLIE: I told you, Lymon. Lymon talking about you might be sleep. This is Lymon. You remember Lymon Jackson from down home? This my Uncle Doaker.

DOAKER: What you doing up here? I couldn't figure out who that was. I thought you was still down in Mississippi.

BOY WILLIE: Me and Lymon selling watermelons. We got a truck out there. Got a whole truckload of watermelons. We brought them up here to sell. Where's Berniece? [*Calls.*] Hey, Berniece!

DOAKER: Berniece up there sleep.

BOY WILLIE: Well, let her get up. [*Calls.*] Hey, Berniece!

DOAKER: She got to go to work in the morning.

BOY WILLIE: Well she can get up and say hi. It's been three years since I seen her. [*Calls.*] Hey, Berniece! It's me . . . Boy Willie.

DOAKER: Berniece don't like all that hollering now. She got to work in the morning.

BOY WILLIE: She can go on back to bed. Me and Lymon been riding two days in that truck . . . the least she can do is get up and say hi.

DOAKER: [*Looking out the window.*] Where you all get that truck from?

BOY WILLIE: It's Lymon's. I told him let's get a load of watermelons and bring them up here.

LYMON: Boy Willie say he going back, but I'm gonna stay. See what it's like up here.

BOY WILLIE: You gonna carry me down there first.

LYMON: I told you I ain't going back down there and take a chance on that truck breaking down again. You can take the train. Hey, tell him Doaker, he can take the train back. After we sell them watermelons he have enough money he can buy him a whole railroad car.

DOAKER: You got all them watermelons stacked up there no wonder the truck broke down. I'm surprised you made it this far with a load like that. Where you break down at?

BOY WILLIE: We broke down three times! It took us two and a half days to get here. It's a good thing we picked them watermelons fresh.

LYMON: We broke down twice in West Virginia. The first time was just as soon as we got out of Sunflower. About forty miles out she broke down. We got it going and got all the way to West Virginia before she broke down again.

BOY WILLIE: We had to walk about five miles for some water.

LYMON: It got a hole in the radiator but it runs pretty good. You have to pump the brakes sometime before they catch. Boy Willie have his door open and be ready to jump when that happens.

BOY WILLIE: Lymon think that's funny. I told the nigger I give him ten dollars to get the brakes fixed. But he thinks that funny.

LYMON: They don't need fixing. All you got to do is pump them till they catch.

[BERNIECE *enters on the stairs. Thirty-five years old, with an eleven-year-old daughter, she is still in mourning for her husband after three years.*]

BERNIECE: What you doing all that hollering for?

BOY WILLIE: Hey, Berniece. Doaker said you was sleep. I said at least you could get up and say hi.

BERNIECE: It's five o'clock in the morning and you come in here with all this noise. You can't come like normal folks. You got to bring all that noise with you.

BOY WILLIE: Hell, I ain't done nothing but come in and say hi. I ain't got in the house good.

BERNIECE: That's what I'm talking about. You start all that hollering and carry on as soon as you hit the door.

BOY WILLIE: Aw hell, woman, I was glad to see Doaker. You ain't had to come down if you didn't want to. I come eighteen hundred miles to see my sister I figure she might want to get up and say hi. Other than that you can go back upstairs. What you got, Doaker? Where your bottle? Me and Lymon want a drink. [*To* BERNIECE.] This is Lymon. You remember Lymon Jackson from down home.

LYMON: How you doing, Berniece. You look just like I thought you looked.

BERNIECE: Why you all got to come in hollering and carrying on? Waking the neighbors with all that noise.

BOY WILLIE: They can come over and join the party. We fixing to have a party. Doaker, where your bottle? Me and Lymon celebrating. The Ghosts of the Yellow Dog got Sutter.

BERNIECE: Say what?

BOY WILLIE: Ask Lymon, they found him the next morning. Say he drowned in his well.

DOAKER: When this happen, Boy Willie?

BOY WILLIE: About three weeks ago. Me and Lymon was over in Stoner County when we heard about it. We laughed. We thought it was funny. A great big old three-hundred-and-forty-pound man gonna fall down his well.

LYMON: It remind me of Humpty Dumpty.

BOY WILLIE: Everybody say the Ghosts of the Yellow Dog pushed him.

BERNIECE: I don't want to hear that nonsense. Somebody down there pushing them people in their wells.

DOAKER: What was you and Lymon doing over in Stoner County?

BOY WILLIE: We was down there working. Lymon got some people down there.

LYMON: My cousin got some land down there. We was helping him.

BOY WILLIE: Got near about a hundred acres. He got it set up real nice. Me and Lymon was down there chopping down trees. We was using Lymon's truck to haul the wood. Me and Lymon used to haul wood all around them parts. [*To* BERNIECE.] Me and Lymon got a truckload of watermelons out there.

[BERNIECE *crosses to the window to the parlor.*]

Doaker, where your bottle? I know you got a bottle stuck up in your room. Come on, me and Lymon want a drink.

[DOAKER *exits into his room.*]

BERNIECE: Where you all get that truck from?

BOY WILLIE: I told you it's Lymon's.

BERNIECE: Where you get the truck from, Lymon?

LYMON: I bought it.

BERNIECE: Where he get that truck from, Boy Willie?

BOY WILLIE: He told you he bought it. Bought it for a hundred and twenty dollars. I can't say where he got that hundred and twenty dollars from . . . but he bought that old piece of truck from Henry Porter. [*To* LYMON.] Where you get that hundred and twenty dollars from, nigger?

LYMON: I got it like you get yours. I know how to take care of money.

[DOAKER *brings a bottle and sets it on the table.*]

BOY WILLIE: Aw hell, Doaker got some of that good whiskey. Don't give Lymon none of that. He ain't used to good whiskey. He liable to get sick.

LYMON: I done had good whiskey before.

BOY WILLIE: Lymon bought that truck so he have him a place to sleep. He down there wasn't doing no work or nothing. Sheriff looking for him. He bought that truck to keep away from the sheriff. Got Stovall looking for him too. He down there sleeping in that truck ducking and dodging both of them. I told him come on let's go up and see my sister.

BERNIECE: What the sheriff looking for you for, Lymon?

BOY WILLIE: The man don't want you to know all his business. He's my company. He ain't asking you no questions.

LYMON: It wasn't nothing. It was just a misunderstanding.

BERNIECE: He in my house. You say the sheriff looking for him, I wanna know what he looking for him for. Otherwise you all can go back out there and be where nobody don't have to ask you nothing.

LYMON: It was just a misunderstanding. Sometimes me and the sheriff we don't think alike. So we just got crossed on each other.

BERNIECE: Might be looking for him about that truck. He might have stole that truck.

BOY WILLIE: We ain't stole no truck, woman. I told you Lymon bought it.

DOAKER: Boy Willie and Lymon got more sense than to ride all the way up here in a stolen truck with a load of watermelons. Now they might have stole them watermelons, but I don't believe they stole that truck.

BOY WILLIE: You don't even know the man good and you calling him a thief. And we ain't stole them watermelons either. Them old man Pitterford's watermelons. He give me and Lymon all we could load for ten dollars.

DOAKER: No wonder you got them stacked up out there. You must have five hundred watermelons stacked up out there.

BERNIECE: Boy Willie, when you and Lymon planning on going back?

BOY WILLIE: Lymon say he staying. As soon as we sell them watermelons I'm going on back.

BERNIECE: [*Starts to exit up the stairs.*] That's what you need to do. And you need to do it quick. Come in here disrupting the house. I don't want all that loud carrying on around here. I'm surprised you ain't woke Maretha up.

BOY WILLIE: I was fixing to get her now. [*Calls.*] Hey, Maretha!

DOAKER: Berniece don't like all that hollering now.

BERNIECE: Don't you wake that child up!

BOY WILLIE: You going up there . . . wake her up and tell her her uncle's here. I ain't seen her in three years. Wake her up and send her down here. She can go back to bed.

BERNIECE: I ain't waking that child up . . . and don't you be making all that noise. You and Lymon need to sell them watermelons and go on back.

[BERNIECE *exits up the stairs.*]

BOY WILLIE: I see Berniece still try to be stuck up.

DOAKER: Berniece alright. She don't want you making all that noise. Maretha up there sleep. Let her sleep until she get up. She can see you then.

BOY WILLIE: I ain't thinking about Berniece. You hear from Wining Boy? You know Cleotha died?

DOAKER: Yeah, I heard that. He come by here about a year ago. Had a whole sack of money. He stayed here about two weeks. Ain't offered nothing. Berniece asked him for three dollars to buy some food and he got mad and left.

LYMON: Who's Wining Boy?

BOY WILLIE: That's my uncle. That's Doaker's brother. You heard me talk about Wining Boy. He play piano. He done made some records and everything. He still doing that, Doaker?

DOAKER: He made one or two records a long time ago. That's the only ones I ever known him to make. If you let him tell it he a big recording star.

BOY WILLIE: He stopped down home about two years ago. That's what I hear. I don't know. Me and Lymon was up on Parchman Farm[2] doing them three years.

DOAKER: He don't never stay in one place. Now, he been here about eight months ago. Back in the winter. Now, you subject not to see him for another two years. It's liable to be that long before he stop by.

BOY WILLIE: If he had a whole sack of money he liable never to see him. You ain't gonna see him until he get broke. Just as soon as that sack of money is gone you look up and he be on your doorstep.

LYMON: [*Noticing the piano.*] Is that the piano?

BOY WILLIE: Yeah . . . look here, Lymon. See how it's carved up real nice and polished and everything? You never find you another piano like that.

LYMON: Yeah, that look real nice.

---

2. Former name of the Mississippi State Penitentiary, a work farm operated with the labor of convicts.

BOY WILLIE: I told you. See how it's polished? My mama used to polish it every day. See all them pictures carved on it? That's what I was talking about. You can get a nice price for that piano.

LYMON: That's all Boy Willie talked about the whole trip up here. I got tired of hearing him talk about the piano.

BOY WILLIE: All you want to talk about is women. You ought to hear this nigger, Doaker. Talking about all the women he gonna get when he get up here. He ain't had none down there but he gonna get a hundred when he get up here.

DOAKER: How your people doing down there, Lymon?

LYMON: They alright. They still there. I come up here to see what it's like up here. Boy Willie trying to get me to go back and farm with him.

BOY WILLIE: Sutter's brother selling the land. He say he gonna sell it to me. That's why I come up here. I got one part of it. Sell them watermelons and get me another part. Get Berniece to sell that piano and I'll have the third part.

DOAKER: Berniece ain't gonna sell that piano.

BOY WILLIE: I'm gonna talk to her. When she see I got a chance to get Sutter's land she'll come around.

DOAKER: You can put that thought out your mind. Berniece ain't gonna sell that piano.

BOY WILLIE: I'm gonna talk to her. She been playing on it?

DOAKER: You know she won't touch that piano. I ain't never known her to touch it since Mama Ola died. That's over seven years now. She say it got blood on it. She got Maretha playing on it though. Say Maretha can go on and do everything she can't do. Got her in an extra school down at the Irene Kaufman Settlement House. She want Maretha to grow up and be a schoolteacher. Say she good enough she can teach on the piano.

BOY WILLIE: Maretha don't need to be playing on no piano. She can play on the guitar.

DOAKER: How much land Sutter got left?

BOY WILLIE: Got a hundred acres. Good land. He done sold it piece by piece, he kept the good part for himself. Now he got to give that up. His brother come down from Chicago for the funeral . . . he up there in Chicago got some kind of business with soda fountain equipment. He anxious to sell the land, Doaker. He don't want to be bothered with it. He called me to him and said cause of how long our families done known each other and how we been good friends and all, say he wanted to sell the land to me. Say he'd rather see me with it than Jim Stovall. Told me he'd let me have it for two thousand dollars cash money. He don't know I found out the most Stovall would give him for it was fifteen hundred dollars. He trying to get that extra five hundred out of me telling me he doing me a favor. I thanked him just as nice. Told him what a good man Sutter was and how he had my sympathy and all. Told him to give me two weeks. He said he'd wait on me. That's why I come up here. Sell them watermelons. Get Berniece to sell that piano. Put them two parts with the part I done saved. Walk in there. Tip my hat. Lay my money down on the table. Get my deed and walk on out. This time I get to keep all the cotton. Hire me some men to work it for me. Gin my cotton. Get my seed. And I'll see you again next year. Might even plant some tobacco or some oats.

DOAKER: You gonna have a hard time trying to get Berniece to sell that piano. You know Avery Brown from down there don't you? He up here now. He followed

Berniece up here trying to get her to marry him after Crawley got killed. He been up here about two years. He call himself a preacher now.

BOY WILLIE: I know Avery. I know him from when he used to work on the Willshaw place. Lymon know him too.

DOAKER: He after Berniece to marry him. She keep telling him no but he won't give up. He keep pressing her on it.

BOY WILLIE: Avery think all white men is bigshots. He don't know there some white men ain't got as much as he got.

DOAKER: He supposed to come past here this morning. Berniece going down to the bank with him to see if he can get a loan to start his church. That's why I know Berniece ain't gonna sell that piano. He tried to get her to sell it to help him start his church. Sent the man around and everything.

BOY WILLIE: What man?

DOAKER: Some white fellow was going around to all the colored people's houses looking to buy up musical instruments. He'd buy anything. Drums. Guitars. Harmonicas. Pianos. Avery sent him past here. He looked at the piano and got excited. Offered her a nice price. She turned him down and got on Avery for sending him past. The man kept on her about two weeks. He seen where she wasn't gonna sell it, he gave her his number and told her if she ever wanted to sell it to call him first. Say he'd go one better than what anybody else would give her for it.

BOY WILLIE: How much he offer her for it?

DOAKER: Now you know me. She didn't say and I didn't ask. I just know it was a nice price.

LYMON: All you got to do is find out who he is and tell him somebody else wanna buy it from you. Tell him you can't make up your mind who to sell it to, and if he like Doaker say, he'll give you anything you want for it.

BOY WILLIE: That's what I'm gonna do. I'm gonna find out who he is from Avery.

DOAKER: It ain't gonna do you no good. Berniece ain't gonna sell that piano.

BOY WILLIE: She ain't got to sell it. I'm gonna sell it. I own just as much of it as she does.

BERNIECE: [Offstage, hollers.] Doaker! Go on get away. Doaker!

DOAKER: [Calling.] Berniece?

[DOAKER and BOY WILLIE rush to the stairs, BOY WILLIE runs up the stairs, passing BERNIECE as she enters, running.]

DOAKER: Berniece, what's the matter? You alright? What's the matter?

[BERNIECE tries to catch her breath. She is unable to speak.]

DOAKER: That's alright. Take your time. You alright. What's the matter? [He calls.] Hey, Boy Willie?

BOY WILLIE: [Offstage.] Ain't nobody up here.

BERNIECE: Sutter . . . Sutter's standing at the top of the steps.

DOAKER: [Calls.] Boy Willie!

[LYMON crosses to the stairs and looks up. BOY WILLIE enters from the stairs.]

BOY WILLIE: Hey Doaker, what's wrong with her? Berniece, what's wrong? Who was you talking to?

DOAKER: She say she seen Sutter's ghost standing at the top of the stairs.

BOY WILLIE: Seen what? Sutter? She ain't seen no Sutter.

BERNIECE: He was standing right up there.

BOY WILLIE: [*Entering on the stairs.*] That's all in Berniece's head. Ain't nobody up there. Go on up there, Doaker.

DOAKER: I'll take your word for it. Berniece talking about what she seen. She say Sutter's ghost standing at the top of the steps. She ain't just make all that up.

BOY WILLIE: She up there dreaming. She ain't seen no ghost.

LYMON: You want a glass of water, Berniece? Get her a glass of water, Boy Willie.

BOY WILLIE: She don't need no water. She ain't seen nothing. Go on up there and look. Ain't nobody up there but Maretha.

DOAKER: Let Berniece tell it.

BOY WILLIE: I ain't stopping her from telling it.

DOAKER: What happened, Berniece?

BERNIECE: I come out my room to come back down here and Sutter was standing there in the hall.

BOY WILLIE: What he look like?

BERNIECE: He look like Sutter. He look like he always look.

BOY WILLIE: Sutter couldn't find his way from Big Sandy to Little Sandy. How he gonna find his way all the way up here to Pittsburgh? Sutter ain't never even heard of Pittsburgh.

DOAKER: Go on, Berniece.

BERNIECE: Just standing there with the blue suit on.

BOY WILLIE: The man ain't never left Marlin County when he was living . . . and he's gonna come all the way up here now that he's dead?

DOAKER: Let her finish. I want to hear what she got to say.

BOY WILLIE: I'll tell you this. If Berniece had seen him like she think she seen him she'd still be running.

DOAKER: Go on, Berniece. Don't pay Boy Willie no mind.

BERNIECE: He was standing there . . . had his hand on top of his head. Look like he might have thought if he took his hand down his head might have fallen off.

LYMON: Did he have on a hat?

BERNIECE: Just had on that blue suit . . . I told him to go away and he just stood there looking at me . . . calling Boy Willie's name.

BOY WILLIE: What he calling my name for?

BERNIECE: I believe you pushed him in the well.

BOY WILLIE: Now what kind of sense that make? You telling me I'm gonna go out there and hide in the weeds with all them dogs and things he got around there . . . I'm gonna hide and wait till I catch him looking down his well just right . . . then I'm gonna run over and push him in. A great big old three-hundred-and-forty-pound man.

BERNIECE: Well, what he calling your name for?

BOY WILLIE: He bending over looking down his well, woman . . . how he know who pushed him? It could have been anybody. Where was you when Sutter fell in his well? Where was Doaker? Me and Lymon was over in Stoner County. Tell her, Lymon. The Ghosts of the Yellow Dog got Sutter. That's what happened to him.

BERNIECE: You can talk all that Ghosts of the Yellow Dog stuff if you want. I know better.

LYMON: The Ghosts of the Yellow Dog pushed him. That's what the people say. They found him in his well and all the people say it must be the Ghosts of the Yellow Dog. Just like all them other men.

BOY WILLIE: Come talking about he looking for me. What he come all the way up here for? If he looking for me all he got to do is wait. He could have saved himself a trip if he looking for me. That ain't nothing but in Berniece's head. Ain't no telling what she liable to come up with next.

BERNIECE: Boy Willie, I want you and Lymon to go ahead and leave my house. Just go on somewhere. You don't do nothing but bring trouble with you everywhere you go. If it wasn't for you Crawley would still be alive.

BOY WILLIE: Crawley what? I ain't had nothing to do with Crawley getting killed. Crawley three time seven.[3] He had his own mind.

BERNIECE: Just go on and leave. Let Sutter go somewhere else looking for you.

BOY WILLIE: I'm leaving. Soon as we sell them watermelons. Other than that I ain't going nowhere. Hell, I just got here. Talking about Sutter looking for me. Sutter was looking for that piano. That's what he was looking for. He had to die to find out where that piano was at . . . If I was you I'd get rid of it. That's the way to get rid of Sutter's ghost. Get rid of that piano.

BERNIECE: I want you and Lymon to go on and take all this confusion out of my house!

BOY WILLIE: Hey, tell her, Doaker. What kind of sense that make? I told you, Lymon, as soon as Berniece see me she was gonna start something. Didn't I tell you that? Now she done made up that story about Sutter just so she could tell me to leave her house. Well, hell, I ain't going nowhere till I sell them watermelons.

BERNIECE: Well why don't you go out there and sell them! Sell them and go on back!

BOY WILLIE: We waiting till the people get up.

LYMON: Boy Willie say if you get out there too early and wake the people up they get mad at you and won't buy nothing from you.

DOAKER: You won't be waiting long. You done let the sun catch up with you. This the time everybody be getting up around here.

BERNIECE: Come on, Doaker, walk up here with me. Let me get Maretha up and get her started. I got to get ready myself. Boy Willie, just go on out there and sell them watermelons and you and Lymon leave my house.

[BERNIECE and DOAKER exit up the stairs.]

BOY WILLIE: [Calling after them.] If you see Sutter up there . . . tell him I'm down here waiting on him.

LYMON: What if she see him again?

BOY WILLIE: That's all in her head. There ain't no ghost up there. [Calls.] Hey, Doaker . . . I told you ain't nothing up there.

LYMON: I'm glad he didn't say he was looking for me.

BOY WILLIE: I wish I would see Sutter's ghost. Give me a chance to put a whupping on him.

LYMON: You ought to stay up here with me. You be down there working his land . . . he might come looking for you all the time.

3. That is, Crawley was 21 years old—an adult.

BOY WILLIE: I ain't thinking about Sutter. And I ain't thinking about staying up here. You stay up here. I'm going back and get Sutter's land. You think you ain't got to work up here. You think this the land of milk and honey. But I ain't scared of work. I'm going back and farm every acre of that land.

[DOAKER *enters from the stairs.*]

I told you there ain't nothing up there, Doaker. Berniece dreaming all that.

DOAKER: I believe Berniece seen something. Berniece levelheaded. She ain't just made all that up. She say Sutter had on a suit. I don't believe she ever seen Sutter in a suit. I believe that's what he was buried in, and that's what Berniece saw.

BOY WILLIE: Well, let her keep on seeing him then. As long as he don't mess with me.

[DOAKER *starts to cook his breakfast.*]

I heard about you, Doaker. They say you got all the women looking out for you down home. They be looking to see you coming. Say you got a different one every two weeks. Say they be fighting one another for you to stay with them. [*To* LYMON.] Look at him, Lymon. He know it's true.

DOAKER: I ain't thinking about no women. They never get me tied up with them. After Coreen I ain't got no use for them. I stay up on Jack Slattery's place when I be down there. All them women want is somebody with a steady payday.

BOY WILLIE: That ain't what I hear. I hear every two weeks the women all put on their dresses and line up at the railroad station.

DOAKER: I don't get down there but once a month. I used to go down there every two weeks but they keep switching me around. They keep switching all the fellows around.

BOY WILLIE: Doaker can't turn that railroad loose. He was working the railroad when I was walking around crying for sugartit. My mama used to brag on him.

DOAKER: I'm cooking now, but I used to line track. I pieced together the Yellow Dog stitch by stitch. Rail by rail. Line track all up around there. I lined track all up around Sunflower and Clarksdale. Wining Boy worked with me. He helped put in some of that track. He'd work it for six months and quit. Go back to playing piano and gambling.

BOY WILLIE: How long you been with the railroad now?

DOAKER: Twenty-seven years. Now, I'll tell you something about the railroad. What I done learned after twenty-seven years. See, you got North. You got West. You look over here you got South. Over there you got East. Now, you can start from anywhere. Don't care where you at. You got to go one of them four ways. And whichever way you decide to go they got a railroad that will take you there. Now, that's something simple. You think anybody would be able to understand that. But you'd be surprised how many people trying to go North get on a train going West. They think the train's supposed to go where they going rather than where it's going.

Now, why people going? Their sister's sick. They leaving before they kill somebody . . . and they sitting across from somebody who's leaving to keep from getting killed. They leaving cause they can't get satisfied. They going to meet someone. I wish I had a dollar for every time that someone wasn't at the station to meet them. I done seen that a lot. In between the time they sent the telegram and the time the person get there . . . they done forgot all about them.

They got so many trains out there they have a hard time keeping them from running into each other. Got trains going every whichaway. Got people on all of them. Somebody going where somebody just left. If everybody stay in one place I believe this would be a better world. Now what I done learned after twenty-seven years of railroading is this . . . if the train stays on the track . . . it's going to get where it's going. It might not be where you going. If it ain't, then all you got to do is sit and wait cause the train's coming back to get you. The train don't never stop. It'll come back every time. Now I'll tell you another thing . . .

BOY WILLIE: What you cooking over there, Doaker? Me and Lymon's hungry.

DOAKER: Go on down there to Wylie and Kirkpatrick to Eddie's restaurant. Coffee cost a nickel and you can get two eggs, sausage, and grits for fifteen cents. He even give you a biscuit with it.

BOY WILLIE: That look good what you got. Give me a little piece of that grilled bread.

DOAKER: Here . . . go on take the whole piece.

BOY WILLIE: Here you go, Lymon . . . you want a piece?

[*He gives* LYMON *a piece of toast.* MARETHA *enters from the stairs.*]

BOY WILLIE: Hey, sugar. Come here and give me a hug. Come on give Uncle Boy Willie a hug. Don't be shy. Look at her, Doaker. She done got bigger. Ain't she got big?

DOAKER: Yeah, she getting up there.

BOY WILLIE: How you doing, sugar?

MARETHA: Fine.

BOY WILLIE: You was just a little old thing last time I seen you. You remember me, don't you? This your Uncle Boy Willie from down South. That there's Lymon. He my friend. We come up here to sell watermelons. You like watermelons?

[MARETHA *nods.*]

We got a whole truckload out front. You can have as many as you want. What you been doing?

MARETHA: Nothing.

BOY WILLIE: Don't be shy now. Look at you getting all big. How old is you?

MARETHA: Eleven. I'm gonna be twelve soon.

BOY WILLIE: You like it up here? You like the North?

MARETHA: It's alright.

BOY WILLIE: That there's Lymon. Did you say hi to Lymon?

MARETHA: Hi.

LYMON: How you doing? You look just like your mama. I remember you when you was wearing diapers.

BOY WILLIE: You gonna come down South and see me? Uncle Boy Willie gonna get him a farm. Gonna get a great big old farm. Come down there and I'll teach you how to ride a mule. Teach you how to kill a chicken, too.

MARETHA: I seen my mama do that.

BOY WILLIE: Ain't nothing to it. You just grab him by his neck and twist it. Get you a real good grip and then you just wring his neck and throw him in the pot. Cook him up. Then you got some good eating. What you like to eat? What kind of food you like?

MARETHA: I like everything . . . except I don't like no black-eyed peas.

BOY WILLIE: Uncle Doaker tell me your mama got you playing that piano. Come on play something for me.

[BOY WILLIE *crosses over to the piano followed by* MARETHA.]

Show me what you can do. Come on now. Here . . . Uncle Boy Willie give you a dime . . . show me what you can do. Don't be bashful now. That dime say you can't be bashful.

[MARETHA *plays. It is something any beginner first learns.*]

Here, let me show you something.

[BOY WILLIE *sits and plays a simple boogie-woogie.*]

See that? See what I'm doing? That's what you call the boogie-woogie. See now . . . you can get up and dance to that. That's how good it sound. It sound like you wanna dance. You can dance to that. It'll hold you up. Whatever kind of dance you wanna do you can dance to that right there. See that? See how it go? Ain't nothing to it. Go on you do it.

MARETHA: I got to read it on the paper.

BOY WILLIE: You don't need no paper. Go on. Do just like that there.

BERNIECE: Maretha! You get up here and get ready to go so you be on time. Ain't no need you trying to take advantage of company.

MARETHA: I got to go.

BOY WILLIE: Uncle Boy Willie gonna get you a guitar. Let Uncle Doaker teach you how to play that. You don't need to read no paper to play the guitar. Your mama told you about that piano? You know how them pictures got on there?

MARETHA: She say it just always been like that since she got it.

BOY WILLIE: You hear that, Doaker? And you sitting up here in the house with Berniece.

DOAKER: I ain't got nothing to do with that. I don't get in the way of Berniece's raising her.

BOY WILLIE: You tell your mama to tell you about that piano. You ask her how them pictures got on there. If she don't tell you I'll tell you.

BERNIECE: Maretha!

MARETHA: I got to get ready to go.

BOY WILLIE: She getting big, Doaker. You remember her, Lymon?

LYMON: She used to be real little.

[*There is a knock on the door.* DOAKER *goes to answer it.* AVERY *enters. Thirty-eight years old, honest and ambitious, he has taken to the city like a fish to water, finding in it opportunities for growth and advancement that did not exist for him in the rural South. He is dressed in a suit and tie with a gold cross around his neck. He carries a small Bible.*]

DOAKER: Hey, Avery, come on in. Berniece upstairs.

BOY WILLIE: Look at him . . . look at him . . . he don't know what to say. He wasn't expecting to see me.

AVERY: Hey, Boy Willie. What you doing up here?

BOY WILLIE: Look at him, Lymon.

AVERY: Is that Lymon? Lymon Jackson?

BOY WILLIE: Yeah, you know Lymon.

DOAKER: Berniece be ready in a minute, Avery.

BOY WILLIE: Doaker say you a preacher now. What . . . we supposed to call you Reverend? You used to be plain old Avery. When you get to be a preacher, nigger?

LYMON: Avery say he gonna be a preacher so he don't have to work.

BOY WILLIE: I remember when you was down there on the Willshaw place planting cotton. You wasn't thinking about no Reverend then.

AVERY: That must be your truck out there. I saw that truck with them watermelons, I was trying to figure out what it was doing in front of the house.

BOY WILLIE: Yeah, me and Lymon selling watermelons. That's Lymon's truck.

DOAKER: Berniece say you all going down to the bank.

AVERY: Yeah, they give me a half day off work. I got an appointment to talk to the bank about getting a loan to start my church.

BOY WILLIE: Lymon say preachers don't have to work. Where you working at, nigger?

DOAKER: Avery got him one of them good jobs. He working at one of them skyscrapers downtown.

AVERY: I'm working down there at the Gulf Building running an elevator. Got a pension and everything. They even give you a turkey on Thanksgiving.

LYMON: How you know the rope ain't gonna break? Ain't you scared the rope's gonna break?

AVERY: That's steel. They got steel cables hold it up. It take a whole lot of breaking to break that steel. Naw, I ain't worried about nothing like that. It ain't nothing but a little old elevator. Now, I wouldn't get in none of them airplanes. You couldn't pay me to do nothing like that.

LYMON: That be fun. I'd rather do that than ride in one of them elevators.

BOY WILLIE: How many of them watermelons you wanna buy?

AVERY: I thought you was gonna give me one seeing as how you got a whole truck full.

BOY WILLIE: You can get one, get two. I'll give you two for a dollar.

AVERY: I can't eat but one. How much are they?

BOY WILLIE: Aw, nigger, you know I'll give you a watermelon. Go on, take as many as you want. Just leave some for me and Lymon to sell.

AVERY: I don't want but one.

BOY WILLIE: How you get to be a preacher, Avery? I might want to be a preacher one day. Have everybody call me Reverend Boy Willie.

AVERY: It come to me in a dream. God called me and told me he wanted me to be a shepherd for his flock. That's what I'm gonna call my church . . . The Good Shepherd Church of God in Christ.

DOAKER: Tell him what you told me. Tell him about the three hobos.

AVERY: Boy Willie don't want to hear all that.

LYMON: I do. Lots a people say your dreams can come true.

AVERY: Naw. You don't want to hear all that.

DOAKER: Go on. I told him you was a preacher. He didn't want to believe me. Tell him about the three hobos.

AVERY: Well, it come to me in a dream. See . . . I was sitting out in this railroad yard watching the trains go by. The train stopped and these three hobos got off. They told me they had come from Nazareth and was on their way to Jerusalem. They had three candles. They gave me one and told me to light it . . . but to be careful that it didn't go out. Next thing I knew I was standing in front of this house. Something told me to go knock on the door. This old woman opened the door and said they had been waiting on me. Then she led me into this room. It was a big room and it was full of all kinds of different people. They looked like anybody else except they all had sheep heads and was making noise like sheep make. I heard somebody call my name. I looked around and there was these same three hobos. They told me to take off my clothes and they give me a blue robe with gold thread. They washed my feet and combed my hair. Then they showed me these three doors and told me to pick one.

I went through one of them doors and that flame leapt off that candle and it seemed like my whole head caught fire. I looked around and there was four or five other men standing there with these same blue robes on. Then we heard a voice tell us to look out across this valley. We looked out and saw the valley was full of wolves. The voice told us that these sheep people that I had seen in the other room had to go over to the other side of this valley and somebody had to take them. Then I heard another voice say, "Who shall I send?" Next thing I knew I said, "Here I am. Send me." That's when I met Jesus. He say, "If you go, I'll go with you." Something told me to say, "Come on. Let's go." That's when I woke up. My head still felt like it was on fire . . . but I had a peace about myself that was hard to explain. I knew right then that I had been filled with the Holy Ghost and called to be a servant of the Lord. It took me a while before I could accept that. But then a lot of little ways God showed me that it was true. So I became a preacher.

LYMON: I see why you gonna call it the Good Shepherd Church. You dreaming about them sheep people. I can see that easy.

BOY WILLIE: Doaker say you sent some white man past the house to look at that piano. Say he was going around to all the colored people's houses looking to buy up musical instruments.

AVERY: Yeah, but Berniece didn't want to sell that piano. After she told me about it . . . I could see why she didn't want to sell it.

BOY WILLIE: What's this man's name?

AVERY: Oh, that's a while back now. I done forgot his name. He give Berniece a card with his name and telephone number on it, but I believe she throwed it away.

[BERNIECE *and* MARETHA *enter from the stairs.*]

BERNIECE: Maretha, run back upstairs and get my pocketbook. And wipe that hair grease off your forehead. Go ahead, hurry up.

[MARETHA *exits up the stairs.*]

How you doing, Avery? You done got all dressed up. You look nice. Boy Willie, I thought you and Lymon was going to sell them watermelons.

BOY WILLIE: Lymon done got sleepy. We liable to get some sleep first.

LYMON: I ain't sleepy.

DOAKER: As many watermelons as you got stacked up on that truck out there, you ought to have been gone.

BOY WILLIE: We gonna go in a minute. We going.

BERNIECE: Doaker. I'm gonna stop down there on Logan Street. You want anything?

DOAKER: You can pick up some ham hocks if you going down there. See if you can get the smoked ones. If they ain't got that get the fresh ones. Don't get the ones that got all that fat under the skin. Look for the long ones. They nice and lean. [*He gives her a dollar.*] Don't get the short ones lessen they smoked. If you got to get the fresh ones make sure that they the long ones. If they ain't got them smoked then go ahead and get the short ones. [*Pause.*] You may as well get some turnip greens while you down there. I got some buttermilk . . . if you pick up some cornmeal I'll make me some cornbread and cook up them turnip greens.

[MARETHA *enters from the stairs.*]

MARETHA: We gonna take the streetcar?

BERNIECE: Me and Avery gonna drop you off at the settlement house. You mind them people down there. Don't be going down there showing your color. Boy Willie, I done told you what to do. I'll see you later, Doaker.

AVERY: I'll be seeing you again, Boy Willie.

BOY WILLIE: Hey, Berniece . . . what's the name of that man Avery sent past say he want to buy the piano?

BERNIECE: I knew it. I knew it when I first seen you. I knew you was up to something.

BOY WILLIE: Sutter's brother say he selling the land to me. He waiting on me now. Told me he'd give me two weeks. I got one part. Sell them watermelons get me another part. Then we can sell that piano and I'll have the third part.

BERNIECE: I ain't selling that piano, Boy Willie. If that's why you come up here you can just forget about it. [*To* DOAKER.] Doaker, I'll see you later. Boy Willie ain't nothing but a whole lot of mouth. I ain't paying him no mind. If he come up here thinking he gonna sell that piano then he done come up here for nothing.

[BERNIECE, AVERY, *and* MARETHA *exit the front door.*]

BOY WILLIE: Hey, Lymon! You ready to go sell these watermelons.

[BOY WILLIE *and* LYMON *start to exit. At the door* BOY WILLIE *turns to* DOAKER.]

Hey, Doaker . . . if Berniece don't want to sell that piano . . . I'm gonna cut it in half and go on and sell my half.

[BOY WILLIE *and* LYMON *exit.*]

[*The lights go down on the scene.*]

Scene 2

[*The lights come up on the kitchen. It is three days later.* WINING BOY *sits at the kitchen table. There is a half-empty pint bottle on the table.* DOAKER *busies himself washing pots.* WINING BOY *is fifty-six years old.* DOAKER's *older brother, he tries to present the image of a successful musician and gambler, but his music, his clothes, and even his manner of presentation are old. He is a man who looking back over his life continues to live it with an odd mixture of zest and sorrow.*]

WINING BOY: So the Ghosts of the Yellow Dog got Sutter. That just go to show you I believe I always lived right. They say every dog gonna have his day and time it go around it sure come back to you. I done seen that a thousand times. I know the truth of that. But I'll tell you outright . . . if I see Sutter's ghost I'll be on the first thing I find that got wheels on it.

[DOAKER *enters from his room.*]

DOAKER: Wining Boy!

WINING BOY: And I'll tell you another thing . . . Berniece ain't gonna sell that piano.

DOAKER: That's what she told him. He say he gonna cut it in half and go on and sell his half. They been around here three days trying to sell them watermelons. They trying to get out to where the white folks live but the truck keep breaking down. They go a block or two and it break down again. They trying to get out to Squirrel Hill and can't get around the corner. He say soon as he can get that truck empty to where he can set the piano up in there he gonna take it out of here and go sell it.

WINING BOY: What about them boys Sutter got? How come they ain't farming that land?

DOAKER: One of them going to school. He left down there and come North to school. The other one ain't got as much sense as that frying pan over yonder. That is the dumbest white man I ever seen. He'd stand in the river and watch it rise till it drown him.

WINING BOY: Other than seeing Sutter's ghost how's Berniece doing?

DOAKER: She doing alright. She still got Crawley on her mind. He been dead three years but she still holding on to him. She need to go out here and let one of these fellows grab a whole handful of whatever she got. She act like it done got precious.

WINING BOY: They always told me any fish will bite if you got good bait.

DOAKER: She stuck up on it. She think it's better than she is. I believe she messing around with Avery. They got something going. He a preacher now. If you let him tell it the Holy Ghost sat on his head and heaven opened up with thunder and lightning and God was calling his name. Told him to go out and preach and tend to his flock. That's what he gonna call his church. The Good Shepherd Church.

WINING BOY: They had that joker down in Spear walking around talking about he Jesus Christ. He gonna live the life of Christ. Went through the Last Supper and everything. Rented him a mule on Palm Sunday and rode through the town. Did everything . . . talking about he Christ. He did everything until they got up to that crucifixion part. Got up to that part and told everybody to go home and quit pretending. He got up to the crucifixion part and changed his mind. Had a whole bunch of folks come down there to see him get nailed to the cross. I don't know who's the worse fool. Him or them. Had all them folks come down there . . . even carried the cross up this little hill. People standing around waiting to see him get nailed to the cross and he stop everything and preach a little sermon and told everybody to go home. Had enough nerve to tell them to come to church on Easter Sunday to celebrate his resurrection.

DOAKER: I'm surprised Avery ain't thought about that. He trying every little thing to get him a congregation together. They meeting over at his house till he get him a church.

WINING BOY: Ain't nothing wrong with being a preacher. You got the preacher on one hand and the gambler on the other. Sometimes there ain't too much difference in them.

DOAKER: How long you been in Kansas City?

WINING BOY: Since I left here. I got tied up with some old gal down there. [*Pause.*] You know Cleotha died.

DOAKER: Yeah, I heard that last time I was down there. I was sorry to hear that.

WINING BOY: One of her friends wrote and told me. I got the letter right here. [*He takes the letter out of his pocket.*] I was down in Kansas City and she wrote and told me Cleotha had died. Name of Willa Bryant. She say she know cousin Rupert. [*He opens the letter and reads.*] Dear Wining Boy: I am writing this letter to let you know Miss Cleotha Holman passed on Saturday the first of May she departed this world in the loving arms of her sister Miss Alberta Samuels. I know you would want to know this and am writing as a friend of Cleotha. There have been many hardships since last you seen her but she survived them all and to the end was a good woman whom I hope have God's grace and is in His Paradise. Your cousin Rupert Bates is my friend also and he give me your address and I pray this reaches you about Cleotha. Miss Willa Bryant. A friend. [*He folds the letter and returns it to his pocket.*] They was nailing her coffin shut by the time I heard about it. I never knew she was sick. I believe it was that yellow jaundice. That's what killed her mama.

DOAKER: Cleotha wasn't but forty-some.

WINING BOY: She was forty-six. I got ten years on her. I met her when she was sixteen. You remember I used to run around there. Couldn't nothing keep me still. Much as I loved Cleotha I loved to ramble. Couldn't nothing keep me still. We got married and we used to fight about it all the time. Then one day she asked me to leave. Told me she loved me before I left. Told me, Wining Boy, you got a home as long as I got mine. And I believe in my heart I always felt that and that kept me safe.

DOAKER: Cleotha always did have a nice way about her.

WINING BOY: Man that woman was something. I used to thank the Lord. Many a night I sat up and looked out over my life. Said, well, I had Cleotha. When it didn't look like there was nothing else for me, I said, thank God, at least I had that. If ever I go anywhere in this life I done known a good woman. And that used to hold me till the next morning. [*Pause.*] What you got? Give me a little nip. I know you got something stuck up in your room.

DOAKER: I ain't seen you walk in here and put nothing on the table. You done sat there and drank up your whiskey. Now you talking about what you got.

WINING BOY: I got plenty money. Give me a little nip.

[DOAKER *carries a glass into his room and returns with it half-filled. He sets it on the table in front of* WINING BOY.]

WINING BOY: You hear from Coreen?

DOAKER: She up in New York. I let her go from my mind.

WINING BOY: She was something back then. She wasn't too pretty but she had a way of looking at you made you know there was a whole lot of woman there. You got married and snatched her out from under us and we all got mad at you.

DOAKER: She up in New York City. That's what I hear.

[*The door opens and* BOY WILLIE *and* LYMON *enter.*]

BOY WILLIE: Aw hell . . . look here! We was just talking about you. Doaker say you left out of here with a whole sack of money. I told him we wasn't going see you till you got broke.

WINING BOY: What you mean broke? I got a whole pocketful of money.

DOAKER: Did you all get that truck fixed?

BOY WILLIE: We got it running and got halfway out there on Centre and it broke down again. Lymon went out there and messed it up some more. Fellow told us we got to wait till tomorrow to get it fixed. Say he have it running like new. Lymon going back down there and sleep in the truck so the people don't take the watermelons.

LYMON: Lymon nothing. You go down there and sleep in it.

BOY WILLIE: You was sleeping in it down home, nigger! I don't know nothing about sleeping in no truck.

LYMON: I ain't sleeping in no truck.

BOY WILLIE: They can take all the watermelons. I don't care. Wining Boy, where you coming from? Where you been?

WINING BOY: I been down in Kansas City.

BOY WILLIE: You remember Lymon? Lymon Jackson.

WINING BOY: Yeah, I used to know his daddy.

BOY WILLIE: Doaker say you don't never leave no address with nobody. Say he got to depend on your whim. See when it strike you to pay a visit.

WINING BOY: I got four or five addresses.

BOY WILLIE: Doaker say Berniece asked you for three dollars and you got mad and left.

WINING BOY: Berniece try and rule over you too much for me. That's why I left. It wasn't about no three dollars.

BOY WILLIE: Where you getting all these sacks of money from? I need to be with you. Doaker say you had a whole sack of money . . . turn some of it loose.

WINING BOY: I was just fixing to ask you for five dollars.

BOY WILLIE: I ain't got no money. I'm trying to get some. Doaker tell you about Sutter? The Ghosts of the Yellow Dog got him about three weeks ago. Berniece done seen his ghost and everything. He right upstairs. [*Calls.*] Hey Sutter! Wining Boy's here. Come on, get a drink!

WINING BOY: How many that make the Ghosts of the Yellow Dog done got?

BOY WILLIE: Must be about nine or ten, eleven or twelve. I don't know.

DOAKER: You got Ed Saunders. Howard Peterson. Charlie Webb.

WINING BOY: Robert Smith. That fellow that shot Becky's boy . . . say he was stealing peaches . . .

DOAKER: You talking about Bob Mallory.

BOY WILLIE: Berniece say she don't believe all that about the Ghosts of the Yellow Dog.

WINING BOY: She ain't got to believe. You go ask them white folks in Sunflower County if they believe. You go ask Sutter if he believe. I don't care if Berniece believe or not. I done been to where the Southern cross the Yellow Dog and called out their names. They talk back to you, too.

LYMON: What they sound like? The wind or something?

BOY WILLIE: You done been there for real, Wining Boy?

WINING BOY: Nineteen thirty. July of nineteen thirty I stood right there on that spot. It didn't look like nothing was going right in my life. I said everything can't go wrong all the time . . . let me go down there and call on the Ghosts of the Yellow Dog, see if they can help me. I went down there and right there where them two railroads cross each other . . . I stood right there on that spot and called out their names. They talk back to you, too.

LYMON: People say you can ask them questions. They talk to you like that?

WINING BOY: A lot of things you got to find out on your own. I can't say how they talked to nobody else. But to me it just filled me up in a strange sort of way to be standing there on that spot. I didn't want to leave. It felt like the longer I stood there the bigger I got. I seen the train coming and it seem like I was bigger than the train. I started not to move. But something told me to go ahead and get on out the way. The train passed and I started to go back up there and stand some more. But something told me not to do it. I walked away from there feeling like a king. Went on and had a stroke of luck that run on for three years. So I don't care if Berniece believe or not. Berniece ain't got to believe. I know cause I been there. Now Doaker'll tell you about the Ghosts of the Yellow Dog.

DOAKER: I don't try and talk that stuff with Berniece. Avery got her all tied up in that church. She just think it's a whole lot of nonsense.

BOY WILLIE: Berniece don't believe in nothing. She just think she believe. She believe in anything if it's convenient for her to believe. But when that convenience run out then she ain't got nothing to stand on.

WINING BOY: Let's not get on Berniece now. Doaker tell me you talking about selling that piano.

BOY WILLIE: Yeah . . . hey, Doaker, I got the name of that man Avery was talking about. The man what's fixing the truck gave me his name. Everybody know him. Say he buy up anything you can make music with. I got his name and his telephone number. Hey, Wining Boy, Sutter's brother say he selling the land to me. I got one part. Sell them watermelons get me the second part. Then . . . soon as I get them watermelons out that truck I'm gonna take and sell that piano and get the third part.

DOAKER: That land ain't worth nothing no more. The smart white man's up here in these cities. He cut the land loose and step back and watch you and the dumb white man argue over it.

WINING BOY: How you know Sutter's brother ain't sold it already? You talking about selling the piano and the man's liable to sold the land two or three times.

BOY WILLIE: He say he waiting on me. He say he give me two weeks. That's two weeks from Friday. Say if I ain't back by then he might gonna sell it to somebody else. He say he wanna see me with it.

WINING BOY: You know as well as I know the man gonna sell the land to the first one walk up and hand him the money.

BOY WILLIE: That's just who I'm gonna be. Look, you ain't gotta know he waiting on me. I know. Okay. I know what the man told me. Stovall already done tried to buy the land from him and he told him no. The man say he waiting on me . . . he waiting on me. Hey, Doaker . . . give me a drink. I see Wining Boy got his glass.

[DOAKER *exits into his room.*]

Wining Boy, what you doing in Kansas City? What they got down there?

LYMON: I hear they got some nice-looking women in Kansas City. I sure like to go down there and find out.

WINING BOY: Man, the women down there is something else.

[DOAKER *enters with a bottle of whiskey. He sets it on the table with some glasses.*]

DOAKER: You wanna sit up here and drink up my whiskey, leave a dollar on the table when you get up.

BOY WILLIE: You ain't doing nothing but showing your hospitality. I know we ain't got to pay for your hospitality.

WINING BOY: Doaker say they had you and Lymon down on the Parchman Farm. Had you on my old stomping grounds.

BOY WILLIE: Me and Lymon was down there hauling wood for Jim Miller and keeping us a little bit to sell. Some white fellows tried to run us off of it. That's when Crawley got killed. They put me and Lymon in the penitentiary.

LYMON: They ambushed us right there where that road dip down and around that bend in the creek. Crawley tried to fight them. Me and Boy Willie got away but the sheriff got us. Say we was stealing wood. They shot me in my stomach.

BOY WILLIE: They looking for Lymon down there now. They rounded him up and put him in jail for not working.

LYMON: Fined me a hundred dollars. Mr. Stovall come and paid my hundred dollars and the judge say I got to work for him to pay him back his hundred dollars. I told them I'd rather take my thirty days but they wouldn't let me do that.

BOY WILLIE: As soon as Stovall turned his back, Lymon was gone. He down there living in that truck dodging the sheriff and Stovall. He got both of them looking for him. So I brought him up here.

LYMON: I told Boy Willie I'm gonna stay up here. I ain't going back with him.

BOY WILLIE: Ain't nobody twisting your arm to make you go back. You can do what you want to do.

WINING BOY: I'll go back with you. I'm on my way down there. You gonna take the train? I'm gonna take the train.

LYMON: They treat you better up here.

BOY WILLIE: I ain't worried about nobody mistreating me. They treat you like you let them treat you. They mistreat me I mistreat them right back. Ain't no difference in me and the white man.

WINING BOY: Ain't no difference as far as how somebody supposed to treat you. I agree with that. But I'll tell you the difference between the colored man and the white man. Alright. Now you take and eat some berries. They taste real good to you. So you say I'm gonna go out and get me a whole pot of these berries and cook them up to make a pie or whatever. But you ain't looked to see them berries is sitting in the white fellow's yard. Ain't got no fence around them. You figure anybody want something they'd fence it in. Alright. Now the white man come along and say that's my land. Therefore everything that grow on it belong to me. He tell the sheriff, "I want you to put this nigger in jail as a warning to all the other niggers. Otherwise first thing you know these niggers have everything that belong to us."

BOY WILLIE: I'd come back at night and haul off his whole patch while he was sleep.

WINING BOY: Alright. Now Mr. So and So, he sell the land to you. And he come to you and say, "John, you own the land. It's all yours now. But them is my berries. And come time to pick them I'm gonna send my boys over. You got the land . . . but them berries, I'm gonna keep them. They mine." And he go and fix it with the law that them is his berries. Now that's the difference between the colored man and the white man. The colored man can't fix nothing with the law.

BOY WILLIE: I don't go by what the law say. The law's liable to say anything. I go by if it's right or not. It don't matter to me what the law say. I take and look at it for myself.

LYMON: That's why you gonna end up back down there on the Parchman Farm.

BOY WILLIE: I ain't thinking about no Parchman Farm. You liable to go back before me.

LYMON: They work you too hard down there. All that weeding and hoeing and chopping down trees. I didn't like all that.

WINING BOY: You ain't got to like your job on Parchman. Hey, tell him, Doaker, the only one got to like his job is the waterboy.

DOAKER: If he don't like his job he need to set that bucket down.

BOY WILLIE: That's what they told Lymon. They had Lymon on water and everybody got mad at him cause he was lazy.

LYMON: That water was heavy.

BOY WILLIE: They had Lymon down there singing:

[*Sings.*]

O Lord Berta Berta O Lord gal oh-ah
O Lord Berta Berta O Lord gal well

[LYMON *and* WINING BOY *join in.*]

Go 'head marry don't you wait on me oh-ah
Go 'head marry don't you wait on me well
Might not want you when I go free oh-ah
Might not want you when I go free well

BOY WILLIE: Come on, Doaker. Doaker know this one.

[As DOAKER *joins in the men stamp and clap to keep time. They sing in harmony with great fervor and style.*]

O Lord Berta Berta O Lord gal oh-ah
O Lord Berta Berta O Lord gal well

Raise them up higher, let them drop on down oh-ah
Raise them up higher, let them drop on down well
Don't know the difference when the sun go down oh-ah
Don't know the difference when the sun go down well

Berta in Meridan and she living at ease oh-ah
Berta in Meridan and she living at ease well
I'm on old Parchman, got to work or leave oh-ah
I'm on old Parchman, got to work or leave well

O Alberta, Berta, O Lord gal oh-ah
O Alberta, Berta, O Lord gal well

When you marry, don't marry no farming man oh-ah
When you marry, don't marry no farming man well
Everyday Monday, hoe handle in your hand oh-ah
Everyday Monday, hoe handle in your hand well

When you marry, marry a railroad man, oh-ah
When you marry, marry a railroad man, well
Everyday Sunday, dollar in your hand oh-ah
Everyday Sunday, dollar in your hand well

O Alberta, Berta, O Lord gal oh-ah
O Alberta, Berta, O Lord gal well

BOY WILLIE: Doaker like that part. He like that railroad part.

LYMON: Doaker sound like Tangleye.[4] He can't sing a lick.

BOY WILLIE: Hey, Doaker, they still talk about you down on Parchman. They ask me, "You Doaker Boy's nephew?" I say, "Yeah, me and him is family." They treated me alright soon as I told them that. Say, "Yeah, he my uncle."

DOAKER: I don't never want to see none of them niggers no more.

BOY WILLIE: I don't want to see them either. Hey, Wining Boy, come on play some piano. You a piano player, play some piano. Lymon wanna hear you.

WINING BOY: I give that piano up. That was the best thing that ever happened to me, getting rid of that piano. That piano got so big and I'm carrying it around on my back. I don't wish that on nobody. See, you think it's all fun being a recording star. Got to carrying that piano around and man did I get slow. Got just like molasses. The world just slipping by me and I'm walking around with that piano. Alright. Now, there ain't but so many places you can go. Only so many road wide enough for you and that piano. And that piano get heavier and heavier. Go to a place and they find out you play piano, the first thing they want to do is give you a drink, find you a piano, and sit you right down. And that's where you gonna be for the next eight hours. They ain't gonna let you get up! Now, the first three or four years of that is fun. You can't get enough whiskey and you can't get enough women and you don't never get tired of playing that piano. But that only last so long. You look up one day and you hate the whiskey, and you hate the women, and you hate the piano. But that's all you got. You can't do nothing else. All you know how to do is play that piano. Now, who am I? Am I me? Or am I the piano player? Sometime it seem like the only thing to do is shoot the piano player cause he the cause of all the trouble I'm having.

DOAKER: What you gonna do when your troubles get like mine?

---

4. Or Tangle Eye, one of the prisoners field-recorded at Parchman Farm by Alan Lomax in the 1930s and 1940s.

LYMON: If I knew how to play it, I'd play it. That's a nice piano.

BOY WILLIE: Whoever playing better play quick. Sutter's brother say he waiting on me. I sell them watermelons. Get Berniece to sell that piano. Put them two parts with the part I done saved . . .

WINING BOY: Berniece ain't gonna sell that piano. I don't see why you don't know that.

BOY WILLIE: What she gonna do with it? She ain't doing nothing but letting it sit up there and rot. That piano ain't doing nobody no good.

LYMON: That's a nice piano. If I had it I'd sell it. Unless I knew how to play like Wining Boy. You can get a nice price for that piano.

DOAKER: Now I'm gonna tell you something, Lymon don't know this . . . but I'm gonna tell you why me and Wining Boy say Berniece ain't gonna sell that piano.

BOY WILLIE: She ain't got to sell it! I'm gonna sell it! Berniece ain't got no more rights to that piano than I do.

DOAKER: I'm talking to the man . . . let me talk to the man. See, now . . . to understand why we say that . . . to understand about that piano . . . you got to go back to slavery time. See, our family was owned by a fellow named Robert Sutter. That was Sutter's grandfather. Alright. The piano was owned by a fellow named Joel Nolander. He was one of the Nolander brothers from down in Georgia. It was coming up on Sutter's wedding anniversary and he was looking to buy his wife . . . Miss Ophelia was her name . . . he was looking to buy her an anniversary present. Only thing with him . . . he ain't had no money. But he had some niggers. So he asked Mr. Nolander to see if maybe he could trade off some of his niggers for that piano. Told him he would give him one and a half niggers for it. That's the way he told him. Say he could have one full grown and one half grown. Mr. Nolander agreed only he say he had to pick them. He didn't want Sutter to give him just any old nigger. He say he wanted to have the pick of the litter. So Sutter lined up his niggers and Mr. Nolander looked them over and out of the whole bunch he picked my grandmother . . . her name was Berniece . . . same like Berniece . . . and he picked my daddy when he wasn't nothing but a little boy nine years old. They made the trade off and Miss Ophelia was so happy with that piano that it got to be just about all she would do was play on that piano.

WINING BOY: Just get up in the morning, get all dressed up and sit down and play on that piano.

DOAKER: Alright. Time go along. Time go along. Miss Ophelia got to missing my grandmother . . . the way she would cook and clean the house and talk to her and what not. And she missed having my daddy around the house to fetch things for her. So she asked to see if maybe she could trade back that piano and get her niggers back. Mr. Nolander said no. Said a deal was a deal. Him and Sutter had a big falling out about it and Miss Ophelia took sick to the bed. Wouldn't get out of the bed in the morning. She just lay there. The doctor said she was wasting away.

WINING BOY: That's when Sutter called our granddaddy up to the house.

DOAKER: Now, our granddaddy's name was Boy Willie. That's who Boy Willie's named after . . . only they called him Willie Boy. Now, he was a worker of wood. He could make you anything you wanted out of wood. He'd make you a desk. A table. A lamp. Anything you wanted. Them white fellows around there used to come up to Mr. Sutter and get him to make all kinds of things for them. Then they'd pay Mr. Sutter a nice price. See, everything my granddaddy made Mr. Sutter owned cause he owned him. That's why when Mr. Nolander offered to buy him to keep the family together Mr. Sutter wouldn't sell him. Told Mr. Nolander he didn't have enough money to buy him. Now . . . am I telling it right, Wining Boy?

WINING BOY: You telling it.

DOAKER: Sutter called him up to the house and told him to carve my grandmother and my daddy's picture on the piano for Miss Ophelia. And he took and carved this . . .

[DOAKER *crosses over to the piano.*]

See that right there? That's my grandmother, Berniece. She looked just like that. And he put a picture of my daddy when he wasn't nothing but a little boy the way he remembered him. He made them up out of his memory. Only thing . . . he didn't stop there. He carved all this. He got a picture of his mama . . . Mama Esther . . . and his daddy, Boy Charles.

WINING BOY: That was the first Boy Charles.

DOAKER: Then he put on the side here all kinds of things. See that? That's when him and Mama Berniece got married. They called it jumping the broom. That's how you got married in them days. Then he got here when my daddy was born . . . and here he got Mama Esther's funeral . . . and down here he got Mr. Nolander taking Mama Berniece and my daddy away down to his place in Georgia. He got all kinds of things what happened with our family. When Mr. Sutter seen the piano with all them carvings on it he got mad. He didn't ask for all that. But see . . . there wasn't nothing he could do about it. When Miss Ophelia seen it . . . she got excited. Now she had her piano and her niggers too. She took back to playing it and played on it right up till the day she died. Alright . . . now see, our brother Boy Charles . . . that's Berniece and Boy Willie's daddy . . . he was the oldest of us three boys. He's dead now. But he would have been fifty-seven if he had lived. He died in 1911 when he was thirty-one years old. Boy Charles used to talk about that piano all the time. He never could get it off his mind. Two or three months go by and he be talking about it again. He be talking about taking it out of Sutter's house. Say it was the story of our whole family and as long as Sutter had it . . . he had us. Say we was still in slavery. Me and Wining Boy tried to talk him out of it but it wouldn't do any good. Soon as he quiet down about it he'd start up again. We seen where he wasn't gonna get it off his mind . . . so, on the Fourth of July, 1911 . . . when Sutter was at the picnic what the county give every year . . . me and Wining Boy went on down there with him and took that piano out of Sutter's house. We put it on a wagon and me and Wining Boy carried it over into the next county with Mama Ola's people. Boy Charles decided to stay around there and wait until Sutter got home to make it look like business as usual.

Now, I don't know what happened when Sutter came home and found that piano gone. But somebody went up to Boy Charles's house and set it on fire. But he wasn't in there. He must have seen them coming cause he went down and caught the 3:57 Yellow Dog. He didn't know they was gonna come down and stop the train. Stopped the train and found Boy Charles in the boxcar with four of them hobos. Must have got mad when they couldn't find the piano cause they set the boxcar afire and killed everybody. Now, nobody know who done that. Some people say it was Sutter cause it was his piano. Some people say it was Sheriff Carter. Some people say it was Robert Smith and Ed Saunders. But don't nobody know for sure. It was about two months after that that Ed Saunders fell down his well. Just upped and fell down his well for no reason. People say it was the ghost of them men who burned up in the boxcar that pushed him in his well. They started calling them the Ghosts of the Yellow Dog. Now, that's how all that got started and that why we say Berniece ain't gonna sell that piano. Cause her daddy died over it.

BOY WILLIE: All that's in the past. If my daddy had seen where he could have traded that piano in for some land of his own, it wouldn't be sitting up here now. He spent his whole life farming on somebody else's land. I ain't gonna do that. See, he couldn't do no better. When he come along he ain't had nothing he could build on. His daddy ain't had nothing to give him. The only thing my daddy had to give me was that piano. And he died over giving me that. I ain't gonna let it sit up there and rot without trying to do something with it. If Berniece can't see that, then I'm gonna go ahead and sell my half. And you and Wining Boy know I'm right.

DOAKER: Ain't nobody said nothing about who's right and who's wrong. I was just telling the man about the piano. I was telling him why we say Berniece ain't gonna sell it.

LYMON: Yeah, I can see why you say that now. I told Boy Willie he ought to stay up here with me.

BOY WILLIE: You stay! I'm going back! That's what I'm gonna do with my life! Why I got to come up here and learn to do something I don't know how to do when I already know how to farm? You stay up here and make your own way if that's what you want to do. I'm going back and live my life the way I want to live it.

[WINING BOY *gets up and crosses to the piano.*]

WINING BOY: Let's see what we got here. I ain't played on this thing for a while.

DOAKER: You can stop telling that. You was playing on it the last time you was through here. We couldn't get you off of it. Go on and play something.

[WINING BOY *sits down at the piano and plays and sings. The song is one which has put many dimes and quarters in his pocket, long ago, in dimly remembered towns and way stations. He plays badly, without hesitation, and sings in a forceful voice.*]

WINING BOY: [*Singing.*]

I am a rambling gambling man
I gambled in many towns
I rambled this wide world over
I rambled this world around
I had my ups and downs in life
And bitter times I saw
But I never knew what misery was
Till I lit on old Arkansas.

I started out one morning
To meet that early train
He said, "You better work for me
I have some land to drain.
I'll give you fifty cents a day,
Your washing, board and all
And you shall be a different man
In the state of Arkansas."

I worked six months for the rascal
Joe Herrin was his name
He fed me old corn dodgers[5]
They was hard as any rock
My tooth is all got loosened
And my knees begin to knock
That was the kind of hash I got
In the state of Arkansas.

Traveling man
I've traveled all around this world
Traveling man
I've traveled from land to land
Traveling man
I've traveled all around this world
Well it ain't no use
Writing no news
I'm a traveling man.

[*The door opens and* BERNIECE *enters with* MARETHA.]

BERNIECE: Is that . . . Lord, I know that ain't Wining Boy sitting there.

WINING BOY: Hey, Berniece.

BERNIECE: You all had this planned. You and Boy Willie had this planned.

WINING BOY: I didn't know he was gonna be here. I'm on my way down home. I stopped by to see you and Doaker first.

DOAKER: I told the nigger he left out of here with that sack of money, we thought we might never see him again. Boy Willie say he wasn't gonna see him till he got broke. I looked up and seen him sitting on the doorstep asking for two dollars. Look at him laughing. He know it's the truth.

BERNIECE: Boy Willie, I didn't see that truck out there. I thought you was out selling watermelons.

BOY WILLIE: We done sold them all. Sold the truck too.

BERNIECE: I don't want to go through none of your stuff. I done told you to go back where you belong.

BOY WILLIE: I was just teasing you, woman. You can't take no teasing?

BERNIECE: Wining Boy, when you get here?

WINING BOY: A little while ago. I took the train from Kansas City.

BERNIECE: Let me go upstairs and change and then I'll cook you something to eat.

BOY WILLIE: You ain't cooked me nothing when I come.

5. Cornbread dumplings.

BERNIECE: Boy Willie, go on and leave me alone. Come on, Maretha, get up here and change your clothes before you get them dirty.

[BERNIECE *exits up the stairs, followed by* MARETHA.]

WINING BOY: Maretha sure getting big, ain't she, Doaker. And just as pretty as she want to be. I didn't know Crawley had it in him.

[BOY WILLIE *crosses to the piano.*]

BOY WILLIE: Hey, Lymon . . . get up on the other side of this piano and let me see something.

WINING BOY: Boy Willie, what is you doing?

BOY WILLIE: I'm seeing how heavy this piano is. Get up over there, Lymon.

WINING BOY: Go on and leave that piano alone. You ain't taking that piano out of here and selling it.

BOY WILLIE: Just as soon as I get them watermelons out that truck.

WINING BOY: Well, I got something to say about that.

BOY WILLIE: This my daddy's piano.

WINING BOY: He ain't took it by himself. Me and Doaker helped him.

BOY WILLIE: He died by himself. Where was you and Doaker at then? Don't come telling me nothing about this piano. This is me and Berniece's piano. Am I right, Doaker?

DOAKER: Yeah, you right.

BOY WILLIE: Let's see if we can lift it up, Lymon. Get a good grip on it and pick it up on your end. Ready? Lift!

[*As they start to move the piano, the sound of* SUTTER'S GHOST *is heard.* DOAKER *is the only one to hear it. With difficulty they move the piano a little bit so it is out of place.*]

BOY WILLIE: What you think?

LYMON: It's heavy . . . but you can move it. Only it ain't gonna be easy.

BOY WILLIE: It wasn't that heavy to me. Okay, let's put it back.

[*The sound of* SUTTER'S GHOST *is heard again. They all hear it as* BERNIECE *enters on the stairs.*]

BERNIECE: Boy Willie . . . you gonna play around with me one too many times. And then God's gonna bless you and West is gonna dress you. Now set that piano back over there. I done told you a hundred times I ain't selling that piano.

BOY WILLIE: I'm trying to get me some land, woman. I need that piano to get me some money so I can buy Sutter's land.

BERNIECE: Money can't buy what that piano cost. You can't sell your soul for money. It won't go with the buyer. It'll shrivel and shrink to know that you ain't taken on to it. But it won't go with the buyer.

BOY WILLIE: I ain't talking about all that, woman. I ain't talking about selling my soul. I'm talking about trading that piece of wood for some land. Get something under your feet. Land the only thing God ain't making no more of. You can always get you another piano. I'm talking about some land. What you get something out the ground from. That's what I'm talking about. You can't do nothing with that piano but sit up there and look at it.

BERNIECE: That's just what I'm gonna do. Wining Boy, you want me to fry you some pork chops?

BOY WILLIE: Now, I'm gonna tell you the way I see it. The only thing that make that piano worth something is them carvings Papa Willie Boy put on there. That's what make it worth something. That was my great-grandaddy. Papa Boy Charles brought that piano into the house. Now, I'm supposed to build on what they left me. You can't do nothing with that piano sitting up here in the house. That's just like if I let them watermelons sit out there and rot. I'd be a fool. Alright now, if you say to me, Boy Willie, I'm using that piano. I give out lessons on it and that help me make my rent or whatever. Then that be something else. I'd have to go on and say, well, Berniece using that piano. She building on it. Let her go on and use it. I got to find another way to get Sutter's land. But Doaker say you ain't touched that piano the whole time it's been up here. So why you wanna stand in my way? See, you just looking at the sentimental value. See, that's good. That's alright. I take my hat off whenever somebody say my daddy's name. But I ain't gonna be no fool about no sentimental value. You can sit up here and look at the piano for the next hundred years and it's just gonna be a piano. You can't make more than that. Now I want to get Sutter's land with that piano. I get Sutter's land and I can go down and cash in the crop and get my seed. As long as I got the land and the seed then I'm alright. I can always get me a little something else. Cause that land give back to you. I can make me another crop and cash that in. I still got the land and the seed. But that piano don't put out nothing else. You ain't got nothing working for you. Now, the kind of man my daddy was he would have understood that. I'm sorry you can't see it that way. But that's why I'm gonna take that piano out of here and sell it.

BERNIECE: You ain't taking that piano out of my house. [*She crosses to the piano.*] Look at this piano. Look at it. Mama Ola polished this piano with her tears for seventeen years. For seventeen years she rubbed on it till her hands bled. Then she rubbed the blood in . . . mixed it up with the rest of the blood on it. Every day that God breathed life into her body she rubbed and cleaned and polished and prayed over it. "Play something for me, Berniece. Play something for me, Berniece." Every day. "I cleaned it up for you, play something for me, Berniece." You always talking about your daddy but you ain't never stopped to look at what his foolishness cost your mama. Seventeen years' worth of cold nights and an empty bed. For what? For a piano? For a piece of wood? To get even with somebody? I look at you and you're all the same. You, Papa Boy Charles, Wining Boy, Doaker, Crawley . . . you're all alike. All this thieving and killing and thieving and killing. And what it ever lead to? More killing and more thieving. I ain't never seen it come to nothing. People getting burned up. People getting shot. People falling down their wells. It don't never stop.

DOAKER: Come on now, Berniece, ain't no need in getting upset.

BOY WILLIE: I done a little bit of stealing here and there, but I ain't never killed nobody. I can't be speaking for nobody else. You all got to speak for yourself, but I ain't never killed nobody.

BERNIECE: You killed Crawley just as sure as if you pulled the trigger.

BOY WILLIE: See, that's ignorant. That's downright foolish for you to say something like that. You ain't doing nothing but showing your ignorance. If the nigger was here I'd whup his ass for getting me and Lymon shot at.

BERNIECE: Crawley ain't knew about the wood.

BOY WILLIE: We told the man about the wood. Ask Lymon. He knew all about the wood. He seen we was sneaking it. Why else we gonna be out there at night?

Don't come telling me Crawley ain't knew about the wood. Them fellows come up on us and Crawley tried to bully them. Me and Lymon seen the sheriff with them and give in. Wasn't no sense in getting killed over fifty dollars' worth of wood.

BERNIECE: Crawley ain't knew you stole that wood.

BOY WILLIE: We ain't stole no wood. Me and Lymon was hauling wood for Jim Miller and keeping us a little bit on the side. We dumped our little bit down there by the creek till we had enough to make a load. Some fellows seen us and we figured we better get it before they did. We come up there and got Crawley to help us load it. Figured we'd cut him in. Crawley trying to keep the wolf from his door . . . we was trying to help him.

LYMON: Me and Boy Willie told him about the wood. We told him some fellows might be trying to beat us to it. He say let me go back and get my thirty-eight. That's what caused all the trouble.

BOY WILLIE: If Crawley ain't had the gun he'd be alive today.

LYMON: We had it about half loaded when they come up on us. We seen the sheriff with them and we tried to get away. We ducked around near the bend in the creek . . . but they was down there too. Boy Willie say let's give in. But Crawley pulled out his gun and started shooting. That's when they started shooting back.

BERNIECE: All I know is Crawley would be alive if you hadn't come up there and got him.

BOY WILLIE: I ain't had nothing to do with Crawley getting killed. That was his own fault.

BERNIECE: Crawley's dead and in the ground and you still walking around here eating. That's all I know. He went off to load some wood with you and ain't never come back.

BOY WILLIE: I told you, woman . . . I ain't had nothing to do with . . .

BERNIECE: He ain't here, is he? He ain't here!

[BERNIECE *hits* BOY WILLIE.]

I said he ain't here. Is he?

[BERNIECE *continues to hit* BOY WILLIE, *who doesn't move to defend himself, other than back up and turning his head so that most of the blows fall on his chest and arms.*]

DOAKER: [*Grabbing* BERNIECE.] Come on, Berniece . . . let it go, it ain't his fault.

BERNIECE: He ain't here, is he? Is he?

BOY WILLIE: I told you I ain't responsible for Crawley.

BERNIECE: He ain't here.

BOY WILLIE: Come on now, Berniece . . . don't do this now. Doaker get her. I ain't had nothing to do with Crawley . . .

BERNIECE: You come up there and got him!

BOY WILLIE: I done told you now. Doaker, get her. I ain't playing.

DOAKER: Come on. Berniece.

[MARETHA *is heard screaming upstairs. It is a scream of stark terror.*]

MARETHA: Mama! . . . Mama!

[*The lights go down to black. End of Act One.*]

ACT II

Scene 1

[*The lights come up on the kitchen. It is the following morning.* DOAKER *is ironing the pants to his uniform. He has a pot cooking on the stove at the same time. He is singing a song. The song provides him with the rhythm for his work and he moves about the kitchen with the ease born of many years as a railroad cook.*]

DOAKER:

Gonna leave Jackson Mississippi
And go to Memphis
And double back to Jackson
Come on down to Hattiesburg
Change cars on the Y.D.
Coming through the territory to
Meridian
And Meridian to Greenville
And Greenville to Memphis
I'm on my way and I know where

Change cars on the Katy
Leaving Jackson
And going through Clarksdale
Hello Winona!
Courtland!
Bateville!
Como!
Senitobia!
Lewisberg!
Sunflower!
Glendora!
Sharkey!
And double back to Jackson
Hello Greenwood
I'm on my way Memphis
Clarksdale
Moorhead
Indianola
Can a highball pass through?
Highball on through sir
Grand Carson!
Thirty First Street Depot
Fourth Street Depot
Memphis!

[WINING BOY *enters carrying a suit of clothes.*]

DOAKER: I thought you took that suit to the pawnshop?
WINING BOY: I went down there and the man tell me the suit is too old. Look at this suit. This is one hundred percent silk! How a silk suit gonna get too old?

I know what it was he just didn't want to give me five dollars for it. Best he wanna give me is three dollars. I figure a silk suit is worth five dollars all over the world. I wasn't gonna part with it for no three dollars so I brought it back.

DOAKER: They got another pawnshop up on Wylie.

WINING BOY: I carried it up there. He say he don't take no clothes. Only thing he take is guns and radios. Maybe a guitar or two. Where's Berniece?

DOAKER: Berniece still at work. Boy Willie went down there to meet Lymon this morning. I guess they got that truck fixed, they had been out there all day and ain't come back yet. Maretha scared to sleep up there now. Berniece don't know, but I seen Sutter before she did.

WINING BOY: Say what?

DOAKER: About three weeks ago. I had just come back from down there. Sutter couldn't have been dead more than three days. He was sitting over there at the piano. I come out to go to work . . . and he was sitting right there. Had his hand on top of his head just like Berniece said. I believe he broke his neck when he fell in the well. I kept quiet about it. I didn't see no reason to upset Berniece.

WINING BOY: Did he say anything? Did he say he was looking for Boy Willie?

DOAKER: He was just sitting there. He ain't said nothing. I went on out the door and left him sitting there. I figure as long as he was on the other side of the room everything be alright. I don't know what I would have done if he had started walking toward me.

WINING BOY: Berniece say he was calling Boy Willie's name.

DOAKER: I ain't heard him say nothing. He was just sitting there when I seen him. But I don't believe Boy Willie pushed him in the well. Sutter here cause of that piano. I heard him playing on it one time. I thought it was Berniece but then she don't play that kind of music. I come out here and ain't seen nobody, but them piano keys was moving a mile a minute. Berniece need to go on and get rid of it. It ain't done nothing but cause trouble.

WINING BOY: I agree with Berniece. Boy Charles ain't took it to give it back. He took it cause he figure he had more right to it than Sutter did. If Sutter can't understand that . . . then that's just the way that go. Sutter dead and in the ground . . . don't care where his ghost is. He can hover around and play on the piano all he want. I want to see him carry it out the house. That's what I want to see. What time Berniece get home? I don't see how I let her get away from me this morning.

DOAKER: You up there sleep. Berniece leave out of here early in the morning. She out there in Squirrel Hill cleaning house for some bigshot down there at the steel mill. They don't like you to come late. You come late they won't give you your carfare. What kind of business you got with Berniece?

WINING BOY: My business. I ain't asked you what kind of business you got.

DOAKER: Berniece ain't got no money. If that's why you was trying to catch her. She having a hard enough time trying to get by as it is. If she go ahead and marry Avery . . . he working every day . . . she go ahead and marry him they could do alright for themselves. But as it stands she ain't got no money.

WINING BOY: Well, let me have five dollars.

DOAKER: I just give you a dollar before you left out of here. You ain't gonna take my five dollars out there and gamble and drink it up.

WINING BOY: Aw, nigger, give me five dollars. I'll give it back to you.

DOAKER: You wasn't looking to give me five dollars when you had that sack of money. You wasn't looking to throw nothing my way. Now you wanna come in here and borrow five dollars. If you going back with Boy Willie you need to be trying to figure out how you gonna get train fare.

WINING BOY: That's why I need the five dollars. If I had five dollars I could get me some money.

[DOAKER *goes into his pocket.*]

Make it seven.

DOAKER: You take this five dollars . . . and you bring my money back here too.

[BOY WILLIE *and* LYMON *enter. They are happy and excited. They have money in all of their pockets and are anxious to count it.*]

DOAKER: How'd you do out there?

BOY WILLIE: They was lining up for them.

LYMON: Me and Boy Willie couldn't sell them fast enough. Time we got one sold we'd sell another.

BOY WILLIE: I seen what was happening and told Lymon to up the price on them.

LYMON: Boy Willie say charge them a quarter more. They didn't care. A couple of people give me a dollar and told me to keep the change.

BOY WILLIE: One fellow bought five. I say now what he gonna do with five watermelons? He can't eat them all. I sold him the five and asked him did he want to buy five more.

LYMON: I ain't never seen nobody snatch a dollar fast as Boy Willie.

BOY WILLIE: One lady asked me say, "Is they sweet?" I told her say, "Lady, where we grow these watermelons we put sugar in the ground." You know, she believed me. Talking about she had never heard of that before. Lymon was laughing his head off. I told her, "Oh, yeah, we put the sugar right in the ground with the seed." She say, "Well, give me another one." Them white folks is something else . . . ain't they, Lymon?

LYMON: Soon as you holler watermelons they come right out their door. Then they go and get their neighbors. Look like they having a contest to see who can buy the most.

WINING BOY: I got something for Lymon.

[WINING BOY *goes to get his suit.* BOY WILLIE *and* LYMON *continue to count their money.*]

BOY WILLIE: I know you got more than that. You ain't sold all them watermelons for that little bit of money.

LYMON: I'm still looking. That ain't all you got either. Where's all them quarters?

BOY WILLIE: You let me worry about the quarters. Just put the money on the table.

WINING BOY: [*Entering with his suit.*] Look here, Lymon . . . see this? Look at his eyes getting big. He ain't never seen a suit like this. This is one hundred percent silk. Go ahead . . . put it on. See if it fit you.

[LYMON *tries the suit coat on.*]

Look at that. Feel it. That's one hundred percent genuine silk. I got that in Chicago. You can't get clothes like that nowhere but New York and Chicago.

You can't get clothes like that in Pittsburgh. These folks in Pittsburgh ain't never seen clothes like that.

LYMON: This is nice, feel real nice and smooth.

WINING BOY: That's a fifty-five-dollar suit. That's the kind of suit the bigshots wear. You need a pistol and a pocketful of money to wear that suit. I'll let you have it for three dollars. The women will fall out their windows they see you in a suit like that. Give me three dollars and go on and wear it down the street and get you a woman.

BOY WILLIE: That looks nice, Lymon. Put the pants on. Let me see it with the pants.

[LYMON *begins to try on the pants.*]

WINING BOY: Look at that . . . see how it fits you? Give me three dollars and go on and take it. Look at that, Doaker . . . don't he look nice?

DOAKER: Yeah . . . that's a nice suit.

WINING BOY: Got a shirt to go with it. Cost you an extra dollar. Four dollars you got the whole deal.

LYMON: How this look, Boy Willie?

BOY WILLIE: That look nice . . . if you like that kind of thing. I don't like them dress-up kind of clothes. If you like it, look real nice.

WINING BOY: That's the kind of suit you need for up here in the North.

LYMON: Four dollars for everything? The suit and the shirt?

WINING BOY: That's cheap. I should be charging you twenty dollars. I give you a break cause you a homeboy. That's the only way I let you have it for four dollars.

LYMON: [*Going into his pocket.*] Okay . . . here go the four dollars.

WINING BOY: You got some shoes? What size you wear?

LYMON: Size nine.

WINING BOY: That's what size I got! Size nine. I let you have them for three dollars.

LYMON: Where they at? Let me see them.

WINING BOY: They real nice shoes, too. Got a nice tip to them. Got pointy toe just like you want.

[WINING BOY *goes to get his shoes.*]

LYMON: Come on, Boy Willie, let's go out tonight. I wanna see what it looks like up here. Maybe we go to a picture show. Hey, Doaker, they got picture shows up here?

DOAKER: The Rhumba Theater. Right down there on Fullerton Street. Can't miss it. Got the speakers outside on the sidewalk. You can hear it a block away. Boy Willie know where it's at.

[DOAKER *exits into his room.*]

LYMON: Let's go to the picture show, Boy Willie. Let's go find some women.

BOY WILLIE: Hey, Lymon, how many of them watermelons would you say we got left? We got just under a half a load . . . right?

LYMON: About that much. Maybe a little more.

BOY WILLIE: You think that piano will fit up in there?

LYMON: If we stack them watermelons you can sit it up in the front there.

BOY WILLIE: I'm gonna call that man tomorrow.

WINING BOY: [*Returns with his shoes.*] Here you go . . . size nine. Put them on. Cost you three dollars. That's a Florsheim shoe. That's the kind Staggerlee[6] wore.

LYMON: [*Trying on the shoes.*] You sure these size nine?

WINING BOY: You can look at my feet and see we wear the same size. Man, you put on that suit and them shoes and you got something there. You ready for whatever's out there. But is they ready for you? With them shoes on you be the King of the Walk. Have everybody stop to look at your shoes. Wishing they had a pair. I'll give you a break. Go on and take them for two dollars.

[LYMON *pays* WINING BOY *two dollars.*]

LYMON: Come on, Boy Willie . . . let's go find some women. I'm gonna go upstairs and get ready. I'll be ready to go in a minute. Ain't you gonna get dressed?

BOY WILLIE: I'm gonna wear what I got on. I ain't dressing up for these city niggers.

[LYMON *exits up the stairs.*]

That's all Lymon think about is women.

WINING BOY: His daddy was the same way. I used to run around with him. I know his mama too. Two strokes back and I would have been his daddy! His daddy's dead now . . . but I got the nigger out of jail one time. They was fixing to name him Daniel and walk him through the Lion's Den.[7] He got in a tussle with one of them white fellows and the sheriff lit on him like white on rice. That's how the whole thing come about between me and Lymon's mama. She knew me and his daddy used to run together and he got in jail and she went down there and took the sheriff a hundred dollars. Don't get me to lying about where she got it from. I don't know. The sheriff looked at that hundred dollars and turned his nose up. Told her, say, "That ain't gonna do him no good. You got to put another hundred on top of that." She come up there and got me where I was playing at this saloon . . . said she had all but fifty dollars and asked me if I could help. Now the way I figured it . . . without that fifty dollars the sheriff was gonna turn him over to Parchman. The sheriff turn him over to Parchman it be three years before anybody see him again. Now I'm gonna say it right . . . I will give anybody fifty dollars to keep them out of jail for three years. I give her the fifty dollars and she told me to come over to the house. I ain't asked her. I figure if she was nice enough to invite me I ought to go. I ain't had to say a word. She invited me over just as nice. Say, "Why don't you come over to the house?" She ain't had to say nothing else. Them words rolled off her tongue just as nice. I went on down there and sat about three hours. Started to leave and changed my mind. She grabbed hold to me

---

6. In African American folklore, a flashy figure (also called Stagger Lee, Stagolee, Stagalee, Stackolee, Stack O'Lee, Stack-o-lee, and so on) who murdered the man who stole his Stetson hat. The story is frequently retold (and reinterpreted) in song.

7. See Daniel 6.23: "My God has sent his angel and closed the lions' mouths so that they have not hurt me."

and say, "Baby, it's all night long." That was one of the shortest nights I have ever spent on this earth! I could have used another eight hours. Lymon's daddy didn't even say nothing to me when he got out. He just looked at me funny. He had a good notion something had happened between me an' her. L. D. Jackson. That was one bad-luck nigger. Got killed at some dance. Fellow walked in and shot him thinking he was somebody else.

[DOAKER *enters from his room.*]

Hey, Doaker, you remember L. D. Jackson?

DOAKER: That's Lymon's daddy. That was one bad-luck nigger.

BOY WILLIE: Look like you ready to railroad some.

DOAKER: Yeah, I got to make that run.

[LYMON *enters from the stairs. He is dressed in his new suit and shoes, to which he has added a cheap straw hat.*]

LYMON: How I look?

WINING BOY: You look like a million dollars. Don't he look good, Doaker? Come on, let's play some cards. You wanna play some cards?

BOY WILLIE: We ain't gonna play no cards with you. Me and Lymon gonna find some women. Hey, Lymon, don't play no cards with Wining Boy. He'll take all your money.

WINING BOY: [*To* LYMON.] You got a magic suit there. You can get you a woman easy with that suit . . . but you got to know the magic words. You know the magic words to get you a woman?

LYMON: I just talk to them to see if I like them and they like me.

WINING BOY: You just walk right up to them and say, "If you got the harbor I got the ship." If that don't work ask them if you can put them in your pocket. The first thing they gonna say is, "It's too small." That's when you look them dead in the eye and say, "Baby, ain't nothing small about me." If that don't work then you move on to another one. Am I telling him right, Doaker?

DOAKER: That man don't need you to tell him nothing about no women. These women these days ain't gonna fall for that kind of stuff. You got to buy them a present. That's what they looking for these days.

BOY WILLIE: Come on, I'm ready. You ready, Lymon? Come on, let's go find some women.

WINING BOY: Here, let me walk out with you. I wanna see the women fall out their window when they see Lymon.

[*They all exit and the lights go down on the scene.*]

Scene 2

[*The lights come up on the kitchen. It is late evening of the same day.* BERNIECE *has set a tub for her bath in the kitchen. She is heating up water on the stove. There is a knock at the door.*]

BERNIECE: Who is it?

AVERY: It's me, Avery.

[BERNIECE *opens the door and lets him in.*]

BERNIECE: Avery, come on in. I was just fixing to take my bath.

AVERY: Where Boy Willie? I see that truck out there almost empty. They done sold almost all them watermelons.

BERNIECE: They was gone when I come home. I don't know where they went off to. Boy Willie around here about to drive me crazy.

AVERY: They sell them watermelons . . . he'll be gone soon.

BERNIECE: What Mr. Cohen say about letting you have the place?

AVERY: He say he'll let me have it for thirty dollars a month. I talked him out of thirty-five and he say he'll let me have it for thirty.

BERNIECE: That's a nice spot next to Benny Diamond's store.

AVERY: Berniece . . . I be at home and I get to thinking you up here an' I'm down there. I get to thinking how that look to have a preacher that ain't married. It makes for a better congregation if the preacher was settled down and married.

BERNIECE: Avery . . . not now. I was fixing to take my bath.

AVERY: You know how I feel about you, Berniece. Now . . . I done got the place from Mr. Cohen. I get the money from the bank and I can fix it up real nice. They give me a ten cents a hour raise down there on the job . . . now Berniece, I ain't got much in the way of comforts. I got a hole in my pockets near about as far as money is concerned. I ain't never found no way through life to a woman I care about like I care about you. I need that. I need somebody on my bond side. I need a woman that fits in my hand.

BERNIECE: Avery, I ain't ready to get married now.

AVERY: You too young a woman to close up, Berniece.

BERNIECE: I ain't said nothing about closing up. I got a lot of woman left in me.

AVERY: Where's it at? When's the last time you looked at it?

BERNIECE: [*Stunned by his remark.*] That's a nasty thing to say. And you call yourself a preacher.

AVERY: Anytime I get anywhere near you . . . you push me away.

BERNIECE: I got enough on my hands with Maretha. I got enough people to love and take care of.

AVERY: Who you got to love you? Can't nobody get close enough to you. Doaker can't half say nothing to you. You jump all over Boy Willie. Who you got to love you, Berniece?

BERNIECE: You trying to tell me a woman can't be nothing without a man. But you alright, huh? You can just walk out of here without me—without a woman—and still be a man. That's alright. Ain't nobody gonna ask you, "Avery, who you got to love you?" That's alright for you. But everybody gonna be worried about Berniece. "How Berniece gonna take care of herself? How she gonna raise that child without a man? Wonder what she do with herself. How she gonna live like that?" Everybody got all kinds of questions for Berniece. Everybody telling me I can't be a woman unless I got a man. Well, you tell me, Avery—you know—how much woman am I?

AVERY: It wasn't me, Berniece. You can't blame me for nobody else. I'll own up to my own shortcomings. But you can't blame me for Crawley or nobody else.

BERNIECE: I ain't blaming nobody for nothing. I'm just stating the facts.

AVERY: How long you gonna carry Crawley with you, Berniece? It's been over three years. At some point you got to let go and go on. Life's got all kinds of twists and turns. That don't mean you stop living. That don't mean you cut yourself off from life. You can't go through life carrying Crawley's ghost with you. Crawley's been dead three years. Three years, Berniece.

BERNIECE: I know how long Crawley's been dead. You ain't got to tell me that. I just ain't ready to get married right now.

AVERY: What is you ready for, Berniece? You just gonna drift along from day to day. Life is more than making it from one day to another. You gonna look up one day and it's all gonna be past you. Life's gonna be gone out of your hands—there won't be enough to make nothing with. I'm standing here now, Berniece—but I don't know how much longer I'm gonna be standing here waiting on you.

BERNIECE: Avery, I told you . . . when you get your church we'll sit down and talk about this. I got too many other things to deal with right now. Boy Willie and the piano . . . and Sutter's ghost. I thought I might have been seeing things, but Maretha done seen Sutter's ghost, too.

AVERY: When this happen, Berniece?

BERNIECE: Right after I came home yesterday. Me and Boy Willie was arguing about the piano and Sutter's ghost was standing at the top of the stairs. Maretha scared to sleep up there now. Maybe if you bless the house he'll go away.

AVERY: I don't know, Berniece. I don't know if I should fool around with something like that.

BERNIECE: I can't have Maretha scared to go to sleep up there. Seem like if you bless the house he would go away.

AVERY: You might have to be a special kind of preacher to do something like that.

BERNIECE: I keep telling myself when Boy Willie leave he'll go on and leave with him. I believe Boy Willie pushed him in the well.

AVERY: That's been going on down there a long time. The Ghosts of the Yellow Dog been pushing people in their wells long before Boy Willie got grown.

BERNIECE: Somebody down there pushing them people in their wells. They ain't just upped and fell. Ain't no wind pushed nobody in their well.

AVERY: Oh, I don't know. God works in mysterious ways.

BERNIECE: He ain't pushed nobody in their wells.

AVERY: He caused it to happen. God is the Great Causer. He can do anything. He parted the Red Sea.[8] He say I will smite my enemies. Reverend Thompson used to preach on the Ghosts of the Yellow Dog as the hand of God.

BERNIECE: I don't care who preached what. Somebody down there pushing them people in their wells. Somebody like Boy Willie. I can see him doing something like that. You ain't gonna tell me that Sutter just upped and fell in his well. I believe Boy Willie pushed him so he could get his land.

AVERY: What Doaker say about Boy Willie selling the piano?

BERNIECE: Doaker don't want no part of that piano. He ain't never wanted no part of it. He blames himself for not staying behind with Papa Boy Charles. He washed his hands of that piano a long time ago. He didn't want me to bring it up here—but I wasn't gonna leave it down there.

AVERY: Well, it seems to me somebody ought to be able to talk to Boy Willie.

8. See Exodus 14.21: "Then Moses stretched out his hand over the sea, and the Lord swept the sea with a strong east wind throughout the night and so turned it into dry land."

BERNIECE: You can't talk to Boy Willie. He been that way all his life. Mama Ola had her hands full trying to talk to him. He don't listen to nobody. He just like my daddy. He get his mind fixed on something and can't nobody turn him from it.

AVERY: You ought to start a choir at the church. Maybe if he seen you was doing something with it—if you told him you was gonna put it in my church—maybe he'd see it different. You ought to put it down in the church and start a choir. The Bible say "Make a joyful noise unto the Lord." Maybe if Boy Willie see you was doing something with it he'd see it different.

BERNIECE: I done told you I don't play on that piano. Ain't no need in you to keep talking this choir stuff. When my mama died I shut the top on that piano and I ain't never opened it since. I was only playing it for her. When my daddy died seem like all her life went into that piano. She used to have me playing on it . . . had Miss Eula come in and teach me . . . say when I played it she could hear my daddy talking to her. I used to think them pictures came alive and walked through the house. Sometime late at night I could hear my mama talking to them. I said that wasn't gonna happen to me. I don't play that piano cause I don't want to wake them spirits. They never be walking around in this house.

AVERY: You got to put all that behind you, Berniece.

BERNIECE: I got Maretha playing on it. She don't know nothing about it. Let her go on and be a schoolteacher or something. She don't have to carry all of that with her. She got a chance I didn't have. I ain't gonna burden her with that piano.

AVERY: You got to put all of that behind you. Berniece. That's the same thing like Crawley. Everybody got stones in their passway. You got to step over them or walk around them. You picking them up and carrying them with you. All you got to do is set them down by the side of the road. You ain't got to carry them with you. You can walk over there right now and play that piano. You can walk over there right now and God will walk over there with you. Right now you can set that sack of stones down by the side of the road and walk away from it. You don't have to carry it with you. You can do it right now.

[AVERY *crosses over to the piano and raises the lid.*]

Come on, Berniece . . . set it down and walk away from it. Come on, play "Old Ship of Zion." Walk over here and claim it as an instrument of the Lord. You can walk over here right now and make it into a celebration.

[BERNIECE *moves toward the piano.*]

BERNIECE: Avery . . . I done told you I don't want to play that piano. Now or no other time.

AVERY: The Bible say, "The Lord is my refuge . . . and my strength!" With the strength of God you can put the past behind you, Berniece. With the strength of God you can do anything! God got a bright tomorrow. God don't ask what you done . . . God ask what you gonna do. The strength of God can move mountains! God's got a bright tomorrow for you . . . all you got to do is walk over here and claim it.

BERNIECE: Avery, just go on and let me finish my bath. I'll see you tomorrow.

AVERY: Okay, Berniece. I'm gonna go home. I'm gonna go home and read up on my Bible. And tomorrow . . . if the good Lord give me strength tomorrow . . . I'm gonna come by and bless the house . . . and show you the power of the Lord.

[AVERY *crosses to the door.*]

It's gonna be alright, Berniece. God say he will soothe the troubled waters. I'll come by tomorrow and bless the house.

[*The lights go down to black.*]

Scene 3

[*Several hours later. The house is dark.* BERNIECE *has retired for the night.* BOY WILLIE *enters the darkened house with* GRACE.]

BOY WILLIE: Come on in. This is my sister's house. My sister live here. Come on, I ain't gonna bite you.

GRACE: Put some light on. I can't see.

BOY WILLIE: You don't need to see nothing, baby. This here is all you need to see. All you need to do is see me. If you can't see me you can feel me in the dark. How's that, sugar? [*He attempts to kiss her.*]

GRACE: Go on now . . . wait!

BOY WILLIE: Just give me one little old kiss.

GRACE: [*Pushing him away.*] Come on, now. Where I'm gonna sleep at?

BOY WILLIE: We got to sleep out here on the couch. Come on, my sister don't mind. Lymon come back he just got to sleep on the floor. He run off with Dolly somewhere he better stay there. Come on, sugar.

GRACE: Wait now . . . you ain't told me nothing about no couch. I thought you had a bed. Both of us can't sleep on that little old couch.

BOY WILLIE: It don't make no difference. We can sleep on the floor. Let Lymon sleep on the couch.

GRACE: You ain't told me nothing about no couch.

BOY WILLIE: What difference it make? You just wanna be with me.

GRACE: I don't want to be with you on no couch. Ain't you got no bed?

BOY WILLIE: You don't need no bed, woman. My granddaddy used to take women on the backs of horses. What you need a bed for? You just want to be with me.

GRACE: You sure is country. I didn't know you was this country.

BOY WILLIE: There's a lot of things you don't know about me. Come on, let me show you what this country boy can do.

GRACE: Let's go to my place. I got a room with a bed if Leroy don't come back there.

BOY WILLIE: Who's Leroy? You ain't said nothing about no Leroy.

GRACE: He used to be my man. He ain't coming back. He gone off with some other gal.

BOY WILLIE: You let him have your key?

GRACE: He ain't coming back.

BOY WILLIE: Did you let him have your key?

GRACE: He got a key but he ain't coming back. He took off with some other gal.

BOY WILLIE: I don't wanna go nowhere he might come. Let's stay here. Come on, sugar. [*He pulls her over to the couch.*] Let me heist your hood and check your oil. See if your battery needs charged. [*He pulls her to him. They kiss and tug at each other's clothing. In their anxiety they knock over a lamp.*]

BERNIECE: Who's that . . . Wining Boy?

BOY WILLIE: It's me . . . Boy Willie. Go on back to sleep. Everything's alright. [*To* GRACE.] That's my sister. Everything's alright, Berniece. Go on back to sleep.

BERNIECE: What you doing down there? What you done knocked over?

BOY WILLIE: It wasn't nothing. Everything's alright. Go on back to sleep. [*To* GRACE.] That's my sister. We alright. She gone back to sleep.

[*They begin to kiss.* BERNIECE *enters from the stairs dressed in a nightgown. She cuts on the light.*]

BERNIECE: Boy Willie, what you doing down here?

BOY WILLIE: It was just that there lamp. It ain't broke. It's okay. Everything's alright. Go on back to bed.

BERNIECE: Boy Willie, I don't allow that in my house. You gonna have to take your company someplace else.

BOY WILLIE: It's alright. We ain't doing nothing. We just sitting here talking. This here is Grace. That's my sister Berniece.

BERNIECE: You know I don't allow that kind of stuff in my house.

BOY WILLIE: Allow what? We just sitting here talking.

BERNIECE: Well, your company gonna have to leave. Come back and talk in the morning.

BOY WILLIE: Go on back upstairs now.

BERNIECE: I got an eleven-year-old girl upstairs. I can't allow that around here.

BOY WILLIE: Ain't nobody said nothing about that. I told you we just talking.

GRACE: Come on . . . let's go to my place. Ain't nobody got to tell me to leave but once.

BOY WILLIE: You ain't got to be like that, Berniece.

BERNIECE: I'm sorry, Miss. But he know I don't allow that in here.

GRACE: You ain't got to tell me but once. I don't stay nowhere I ain't wanted.

BOY WILLIE: I don't know why you want to embarrass me in front of my company.

GRACE: Come on, take me home.

BERNIECE: Go on, Boy Willie. Just go on with your company.

[BOY WILLIE *and* GRACE *exit.* BERNIECE *puts the light on in the kitchen and puts on the teakettle. Presently there is a knock at the door.* BERNIECE *goes to answer it.* BERNIECE *opens the door.* LYMON *enters.*]

LYMON: How you doing, Berniece? I thought you'd be asleep. Boy Willie been back here?

BERNIECE: He just left out of here a minute ago.

LYMON: I went out to see a picture show and never got there. We always end up doing something else. I was with this woman she just wanted to drink up all my money. So I left her there and came back looking for Boy Willie.

BERNIECE: You just missed him. He just left out of here.

LYMON: They got some nice-looking women in this city. I'm gonna like it up here real good. I like seeing them with their dresses on. Got them high heels. I like that. Make them look like they real precious. Boy Willie met a real nice one today. I wish I had met her before he did.

BERNIECE: He come by here with some woman a little while ago. I told him to go on and take all that out of my house.

LYMON: What she look like, the woman he was with? Was she a brown-skinned woman about this high? Nice and healthy? Got nice hips on her?

BERNIECE: She had on a red dress.

LYMON: That's her! That's Grace. She real nice. Laugh a lot. Lot of fun to be with. She don't be trying to put on. Some of these woman act like they the Queen of Sheba. I don't like them kind. Grace ain't like that. She real nice with herself.

BERNIECE: I don't know what she was like. He come in here all drunk knocking over the lamp, and making all kind of noise. I told them to take that somewhere else. I can't really say what she was like.

LYMON: She real nice. I seen her before he did. I was trying not to act like I seen her. I wanted to look at her a while before I said something. She seen me when I come into the saloon. I tried to act like I didn't see her. Time I looked around Boy Willie was talking to her. She was talking to him kept looking at me. That's when her friend Dolly came. I asked her if she wanted to go to the picture show. She told me to buy her a drink while she thought about it. Next thing I knew she done had three drinks talking about she too tired to go. I bought her another drink, then I left. Boy Willie was gone and I thought he might have come back here. Doaker gone, huh? He say he had to make a trip.

BERNIECE: Yeah, he gone on his trip. This is when I can usually get me some peace and quiet, Maretha asleep.

LYMON: She look just like you. Got them big eyes. I remember her when she was in diapers.

BERNIECE: Time just keep on. It go on with or without you. She going on twelve.

LYMON: She sure is pretty. I like kids.

BERNIECE: Boy Willie say you staying . . . what you gonna do up here in this big city? You thought about that?

LYMON: They never get me back down there. The sheriff looking for me. All because they gonna try and make me work for somebody when I don't want to. They gonna try and make me work for Stovall when he don't pay nothing. It ain't like that up here. Up here you more or less do what you want to. I figure I find me a job and try to get set up and then see what the year brings. I tried to do that two or three times down there . . . but it never would work out. I was always in the wrong place.

BERNIECE: This ain't a bad city once you get to know your way around.

LYMON: Up here is different. I'm gonna get me a job unloading boxcars or something. One fellow told me say he know a place. I'm gonna go over there with him next week. Me and Boy Willie finish selling them watermelons I'll have enough money to hold me for a while. But I'm gonna go over there and see what kind of jobs they have.

BERNIECE: You shouldn't have too much trouble finding a job. It's all in how you present yourself. See now, Boy Willie couldn't get no job up here. Somebody hire him they got a pack of trouble on their hands. Soon as they find that out they fire him. He don't want to do nothing unless he do it his way.

LYMON: I know. I told him let's go to the picture show first and see if there was any women down there. They might get tired of sitting at home and walk down to the picture show. He say he wanna look around first. We never did get down there. We tried a couple of places and then we went to this saloon where he met Grace. I tried to meet her before he did but he beat me to her. We left Wining Boy sitting down there running his mouth. He told me if I wear this suit I'd find me a woman. He was almost right.

BERNIECE: You don't need to be out there in them saloons. Ain't no telling what you liable to run into out there. This one liable to cut you as quick as that one shoot you. You don't need to be out there. You start out that fast life you can't keep it up. It makes you old quick. I don't know what them women out there be thinking about.

LYMON: Mostly they be lonely and looking for somebody to spend the night with them. Sometimes it matters who it is and sometimes it don't. I used to be the same way. Now it got to matter. That's why I'm here now. Dolly liable not to even recognize me if she sees me again. I don't like women like that. I like my women to be with me in a nice and easy way. That way we can both enjoy ourselves. The way I see it we the only two people like us in the world. We got to see how we fit together. A woman that don't want to take the time to do that I don't bother with. Used to. Used to bother with all of them. Then I woke up one time with this woman and I didn't know who she was. She was the prettiest woman I had ever seen in my life. I spent the whole night with her and didn't even know it. I had never taken the time to look at her. I guess she kinda knew I ain't never really looked at her. She must have known that cause she ain't wanted to see me no more. If she had wanted to see me I believe we might have got married. How come you ain't married? It seem like to me you would be married. I remember Avery from down home. I used to call him plain old Avery. Now he Reverend Avery. That's kinda funny about him becoming a preacher. I like when he told about how that come to him in a dream about them sheep people and them hobos. Nothing ever come to me in a dream like that. I just dream about women. Can't never seem to find the right one.

BERNIECE: She out there somewhere. You just got to get yourself ready to meet her. That's what I'm trying to do. Avery's alright. I ain't really got nobody in mind.

LYMON: I get me a job and a little place and get set up to where I can make a woman comfortable I might get married. Avery's nice. You ought to go ahead and get married. You be a preacher's wife you won't have to work. I hate living by myself. I didn't want to be no strain on my mama so I left home when I was about sixteen. Everything I tried seem like it just didn't work out. Now I'm trying this.

BERNIECE: You keep trying it'll work out for you.

LYMON: You ever go down there to the picture show?

BERNIECE: I don't go in for all that.

LYMON: Ain't nothing wrong with it. It ain't like gambling and sinning. I went to one down in Jackson once. It was fun.

BERNIECE: I just stay home most of the time. Take care of Maretha.

LYMON: It's getting kind of late. I don't know where Boy Willie went off to. He's liable not to come back. I'm gonna take off these shoes. My feet hurt. Was you in bed? I don't mean to be keeping you up.

BERNIECE: You ain't keeping me up. I couldn't sleep after that Boy Willie woke me up.

LYMON: You got on that nightgown. I likes women when they wear them fancy nightclothes and all. It makes their skin look real pretty.

BERNIECE: I got this at the five-and-ten-cents store. It ain't so fancy.

LYMON: I don't too often get to see a woman dressed like that. [*There is a long pause.* LYMON *takes off his suit coat.*] Well, I'm gonna sleep here on the couch. I'm supposed to sleep on the floor but I don't reckon Boy Willie's coming back tonight. Wining Boy sold me this suit. Told me it was a magic suit. I'm gonna put it on again tomorrow. Maybe it bring me a woman like he say. [*He goes into his coat pocket and takes out a small bottle of perfume.*] I almost forgot I had this. Some man sold me this for a dollar. Say it come from Paris. This is the same kind of perfume the Queen of France wear. That's what he told me. I don't know if it's true or not. I smelled it. It smelled good to me. Here ... smell it see if you like it. I was gonna give it to Dolly. But I didn't like her too much.

BERNIECE: [*Takes the bottle.*] It smells nice.

LYMON: I was gonna give it to Dolly if she had went to the picture with me. Go on, you take it.

BERNIECE: I can't take it. Here ... go on you keep it. You'll find somebody to give it to.

LYMON: I wanna give it to you. Make you smell nice. [*He takes the bottle and puts perfume behind* BERNIECE'*s ear.*] They tell me you supposed to put it right here behind your ear. Say if you put it there you smell nice all day.

[BERNIECE *stiffens at his touch.* LYMON *bends down to smell her.*]

There ... you smell real good now. [*He kisses her neck.*] You smell real good for Lymon.

[*He kisses her again.* BERNIECE *returns the kiss, then breaks the embrace and crosses to the stairs. She turns and they look silently at each other.* LYMON *hands her the bottle of perfume.* BERNIECE *exits up the stairs.* LYMON *picks up his suit coat and strokes it lovingly with the full knowledge that it is indeed a magic suit. The lights go down on the scene.*]

Scene 4

[*It is late the next morning. The lights come up on the parlor.* LYMON *is asleep on the sofa.* BOY WILLIE *enters the front door.*]

BOY WILLIE: Hey, Lymon! Lymon, come on get up.

LYMON: Leave me alone.

BOY WILLIE: Come on, get up, nigger! Wake up, Lymon.

LYMON: What you want?

BOY WILLIE: Come on, let's go. I done called the man about the piano.

LYMON: What piano?

BOY WILLIE: [*Dumps* LYMON *on the floor.*] Come on, get up!

LYMON: Why you leave, I looked around and you was gone.

BOY WILLIE: I come back here with Grace, then I went looking for you. I figured you'd be with Dolly.

LYMON: She just want to drink and spend up your money. I come on back here looking for you to see if you wanted to go to the picture show.

BOY WILLIE: I been up at Grace's house. Some nigger named Leroy come by but I had a chair up against the door. He got mad when he couldn't get in. He went off somewhere and I got out of there before he could come back. Berniece got mad when we came here.

LYMON: She say you was knocking over the lamp busting up the place.

BOY WILLIE: That was Grace doing all that.

LYMON: Wining Boy seen Sutter's ghost last night.

BOY WILLIE: Wining Boy's liable to see anything. I'm surprised he found the right house. Come on, I done called the man about the piano.

LYMON: What he say?

BOY WILLIE: He say to bring it on out. I told him I was calling for my sister, Miss Berniece Charles. I told him some man wanted to buy it for eleven hundred dollars and asked him if he would go any better. He said yeah, he would give me eleven hundred and fifty dollars for it if it was the same piano. I described it to him again and he told me to bring it out.

LYMON: Why didn't you tell him to come and pick it up?

BOY WILLIE: I didn't want to have no problem with Berniece. This way we just take it on out there and it be out the way. He want to charge twenty-five dollars to pick it up.

LYMON: You should have told him the man was gonna give you twelve hundred for it.

BOY WILLIE: I figure I was taking a chance with that eleven hundred. If I had told him twelve hundred he might have run off. Now I wish I had told him twelve-fifty. It's hard to figure out white folks sometimes.

LYMON: You might have been able to tell him anything. White folks got a lot of money.

BOY WILLIE: Come on, let's get it loaded before Berniece come back. Get that end over there. All you got to do is pick it up on that side. Don't worry about this side. You wanna stretch you' back for a minute?

LYMON: I'm ready.

BOY WILLIE: Get a real good grip on it now.

[*The sound of* SUTTER'S GHOST *is heard. They do not hear it.*]

LYMON: I got this end. You get that end.

BOY WILLIE: Wait till I say ready now. Alright. You got it good? You got a grip on it?

LYMON: Yeah, I got it. You lift up on that end.

BOY WILLIE: Ready? Lift!

[*The piano will not budge.*]

LYMON: Man, this piano is heavy! It's gonna take more than me and you to move this piano.

BOY WILLIE: We can do it. Come on—we did it before.

LYMON: Nigger—you crazy! That piano weighs five hundred pounds!

BOY WILLIE: I got three hundred pounds of it! I know you can carry two hundred pounds! You be lifting them cotton sacks! Come on lift this piano!

[*They try to move the piano again without success.*]

LYMON: It's stuck. Something holding it.

BOY WILLIE: How the piano gonna be stuck? We just moved it. Slide you' end out.

LYMON: Naw—we gonna need two or three more people. How this big old piano get in the house?

BOY WILLIE: I don't know how it got in the house. I know how it's going out though! You get on this end. I'll carry three hundred and fifty pounds of it. All you got to do is slide your end out. Ready?

[*They switch sides and try again without success.* DOAKER *enters from his room as they try to push and shove it.*]

LYMON: Hey, Doaker . . . how this piano get in the house?

DOAKER: Boy Willie, what you doing?

BOY WILLIE: I'm carrying this piano out the house. What it look like I'm doing? Come on, Lymon, let's try again.

DOAKER: Go on let the piano sit there till Berniece come home.

BOY WILLIE: You ain't got nothing to do with this, Doaker. This my business.

DOAKER: This is my house, nigger! I ain't gonna let you or nobody else carry nothing out of it. You ain't gonna carry nothing out of here without my permission!

BOY WILLIE: This is my piano. I don't need your permission to carry my belongings out of your house. This is mine. This ain't got nothing to do with you.

DOAKER: I say leave it over there till Berniece come home. She got part of it too. Leave it set there till you see what she say.

BOY WILLIE: I don't care what Berniece say. Come on, Lymon. I got this side.

DOAKER: Go on and cut it half in two if you want to. Just leave Berniece's half sitting over there. I can't tell you what to do with your piano. But I can't let you take her half out of here.

BOY WILLIE: Go on, Doaker. You ain't got nothing to do with this. I don't want you starting nothing now. Just go on and leave me alone. Come on, Lymon. I got this end.

[DOAKER *goes into his room.* BOY WILLIE *and* LYMON *prepare to move the piano.*]

LYMON: How we gonna get it in the truck?

BOY WILLIE: Don't worry about how we gonna get it on the truck. You got to get it out the house first.

LYMON: It's gonna take more than me and you to move this piano.

BOY WILLIE: Just lift up on that end, nigger!

[DOAKER *comes to the doorway of his room and stands.*]

DOAKER: [*Quietly with authority.*] Leave that piano set over there till Berniece come back. I don't care what you do with it then. But you gonna leave it sit over there right now.

BOY WILLIE: Alright. . . . I'm gonna tell you this, Doaker. I'm going out of here . . . I'm gonna get me some rope . . . find me a plank and some wheels . . . and I'm coming back. Then I'm gonna carry that piano out of here . . . sell it and give Berniece half the money. See . . . now that's what I'm gonna do. And you . . . or nobody else is gonna stop me. Come on, Lymon . . . let's go get some rope and stuff. I'll be back, Doaker.

[BOY WILLIE *and* LYMON *exit. The lights go down on the scene.*]

Scene 5

[*The lights come up.* BOY WILLIE *sits on the sofa, screwing casters on a wooden plank.* MARETHA *is sitting on the piano stool.* DOAKER *sits at the table playing solitaire.*]

BOY WILLIE: [*To* MARETHA.] Then after that them white folks down around there started falling down their wells. You ever seen a well? A well got a wall around it. It's hard to fall down a well. You got to be leaning way over. Couldn't nobody figure out too much what was making these fellows fall down their well . . . so everybody says the Ghosts of the Yellow Dog must have pushed them. That's what everybody called them four men what got burned up in the boxcar.

MARETHA: Why they call them that?

BOY WILLIE: Cause the Yazoo Delta railroad got yellow boxcars. Sometime the way the whistle blow sound like an old dog howling so the people call it the Yellow Dog.

MARETHA: Anybody ever see the Ghosts?

BOY WILLIE: I told you they like the wind. Can you see the wind?

MARETHA: No.

BOY WILLIE: They like the wind you can't see them. But sometimes you be in trouble they might be around to help you. They say if you go where the Southern cross the Yellow Dog . . . you go to where them two railroads cross each other . . . and call out their names . . . they say they talk back to you. I don't know, I ain't never done that. But Uncle Wining Boy he say he been down there and talked to them. You have to ask him about that part.

[BERNIECE *has entered from the front door.*]

BERNIECE: Maretha, you go on and get ready for me to do your hair.

[MARETHA *crosses to the steps.*]

Boy Willie, I done told you to leave my house. [*To* MARETHA.] Go on, Maretha.

[MARETHA *is hesitant about going up the stairs.*]

BOY WILLIE: Don't be scared. Here, I'll go up there with you. If we see Sutter's ghost I'll put a whupping on him. Come on, Uncle Boy Willie going with you.

[BOY WILLIE *and* MARETHA *exit up the stairs.*]

BERNIECE: Doaker—what is going on here?

DOAKER: I come home and him and Lymon was moving the piano. I told them to leave it over there till you got home. He went out and got that board and them wheels. He say he gonna take that piano out of here and ain't nobody gonna stop him.

BERNIECE: I ain't playing with Boy Willie. I got Crawley's gun upstairs. He don't know but I'm through with it. Where Lymon go?

DOAKER: Boy Willie sent him for some rope just before you come in.

BERNIECE: I ain't studying Boy Willie or Lymon—or the rope. Boy Willie ain't taking that piano out this house. That's all there is to it.

[BOY WILLIE *and* MARETHA *enter on the stairs.* MARETHA *carries a hot comb and a can of hair grease.* BOY WILLIE *crosses over and continues to screw the wheels on the board.*]

MARETHA: Mama, all the hair grease is gone. There ain't but this little bit left.

BERNIECE: [*Gives her a dollar.*] Here . . . run across the street and get another can. You come straight back, too. Don't you be playing around out there. And watch the cars. Be careful when you cross the street.

[MARETHA *exits out the front door.*]

Boy Willie, I done told you to leave my house.

BOY WILLIE: I ain't in you' house. I'm in Doaker's house. If he ask me to leave then I'll go on and leave. But consider me done left your part.

BERNIECE: Doaker, tell him to leave. Tell him to go on.

DOAKER: Boy Willie ain't done nothing for me to put him out of the house. I told you if you can't get along just go on and don't have nothing to do with each other.

BOY WILLIE: I ain't thinking about Berniece. [*He gets up and draws a line across the floor with his foot.*] There! Now I'm out of your part of the house. Consider me done left your part. Soon as Lymon come back with that rope. I'm gonna take that piano out of here and sell it.

BERNIECE: You ain't gonna touch that piano.

BOY WILLIE: Carry it out of here just as big and bold. Do like my daddy would have done come time to get Sutter's land.

BERNIECE: I got something to make you leave it over there.

BOY WILLIE: It's got to come better than this thirty-two-twenty.[9]

DOAKER: Why don't you stop all that! Boy Willie, go on and leave her alone. You know how Berniece get. Why you wanna sit there and pick with her?

BOY WILLIE: I ain't picking with her. I told her the truth. She the one talking about what she got. I just told her what she better have.

BERNIECE: That's alright, Doaker. Leave him alone.

BOY WILLIE: She trying to scare me. Hell, I ain't scared of dying. I look around and see people dying every day. You got to die to make room for somebody else. I had a dog that died. Wasn't nothing but a puppy. I picked it up and put it in a bag and carried it up there to Reverend C. L. Thompson's church. I carried it up there and prayed and asked Jesus to make it live like he did the man in the Bible.[1] I prayed real hard. Knelt down and everything. Say ask in Jesus' name. Well, I must have called Jesus' name two hundred times. I called his name till my mouth got sore. I got up and looked in the bag and the dog still dead. It ain't moved a muscle! I say, "Well, ain't nothing precious." And then I went out and killed me a cat. That's when I discovered the power of death. See, a nigger that ain't afraid to die is the worse kind of nigger for the white man. He can't hold that power over you. That's what I learned when I killed that cat. I got the power of death too. I can command him. I can call him up. The white man don't like to see that. He don't like for you to stand up and look him square in the eye and say, "I got it too." Then he got to deal with you square up.

BERNIECE: That's why I don't talk to him, Doaker. You try and talk to him and that's the only kind of stuff that comes out his mouth.

---

9. That is, this thirty-two-twenty-caliber gun I'm (figuratively) holding.

1. Lazarus, who was raised from the dead by Jesus; see John 11.1–44.

DOAKER: You say Avery went home to get his Bible?

BOY WILLIE: What Avery gonna do? Avery can't do nothing with me. I wish Avery would say something to me about this piano.

DOAKER: Berniece ain't said about that. Avery went home to get his Bible. He coming by to bless the house see if he can get rid of Sutter's ghost.

BOY WILLIE: Ain't nothing but a house full of ghosts down there at the church. What Avery look like chasing away somebody's ghost?

[MARETHA *enters the front door.*]

BERNIECE: Light that stove and set that comb over there to get hot. Get something to put around your shoulders.

BOY WILLIE: The Bible say an eye for an eye, a tooth for a tooth, and a life for a life.[2] Tit for tat. But you and Avery don't want to believe that. You gonna pass up that part and pretend it ain't in there. Everything else you gonna agree with. But if you gonna agree with part of it you got to agree with all of it. You can't do nothing halfway. You gonna go at the Bible halfway. You gonna act like that part ain't in there. But you pull out the Bible and open it and see what it say. Ask Avery. He a preacher. He'll tell you it's in there. He the Good Shepherd. Unless he gonna shepherd you to heaven with half the Bible.

BERNIECE: Maretha, bring me that comb. Make sure it's hot.

[MARETHA *brings the comb.* BERNIECE *begins to do her hair.*]

BOY WILLIE: I will say this for Avery. He done figured out a path to go through life. I don't agree with it. But he done fixed it so he can go right through it real smooth. Hell, he liable to end up with a million dollars that he done got from selling bread and wine.

MARETHA: OWWWWWW!

BERNIECE: Be still, Maretha. If you was a boy I wouldn't be going through this.

BOY WILLIE: Don't you tell that girl that. Why you wanna tell her that?

BERNIECE: You ain't got nothing to do with this child.

BOY WILLIE: Telling her you wished she was a boy. How's that gonna make her feel?

BERNIECE: Boy Willie, go on and leave me alone.

DOAKER: Why don't you leave her alone? What you got to pick with her for? Why don't you go on out and see what's out there in the streets? Have something to tell the fellows down home.

BOY WILLIE: I'm waiting on Lymon to get back with that truck. Why don't you go on out and see what's out there in the streets? You ain't got to work tomorrow. Talking about me . . . why don't you go out there? It's Friday night.

DOAKER: I got to stay around here and keep you all from killing one another.

BOY WILLIE: You ain't got to worry about me. I'm gonna be here just as long as it takes Lymon to get back here with that truck. You ought to be talking to Berniece. Sitting up there telling Maretha she wished she was a boy. What kind of thing is that to tell a child? If you want to tell her something tell her about that piano. You ain't even told her about that piano. Like that's

2. See Exodus 21. 23–25.

something to be ashamed of. Like she supposed to go off and hide somewhere about that piano. You ought to mark down on the calendar the day that Papa Boy Charles brought that piano into the house. You ought to mark that day down and draw a circle around it . . . and every year when it come up throw a party. Have a celebration. If you did that she wouldn't have no problem in life. She could walk around here with her head held high. I'm talking about a big party!

Invite everybody! Mark that day down with a special meaning. That way she know where she at in the world. You got her going out here thinking she wrong in the world. Like there ain't no part of it belong to her.

BERNIECE: Let me take care of my child. When you get one of your own then you can teach it what you want to teach it.

[DOAKER *exits into his room.*]

BOY WILLIE: What I want to bring a child into this world for? Why I wanna bring somebody else into all this for? I'll tell you this . . . If I was Rockefeller[3] I'd have forty or fifty. I'd make one every day. Cause they gonna start out in life with all the advantages. I ain't got no advantages to offer nobody. Many is the time I looked at my daddy and seen him staring off at his hands. I got a little older I know what he was thinking. He sitting there saying, "I got these big old hands but what I'm gonna do with them? Best I can do is make a fifty-acre crop for Mr. Stovall. Got these big old hands capable of doing anything. I can take and build something with these hands. But where's the tools? All I got is these hands. Unless I go out here and kill me somebody and take what they got . . . it's a long row to hoe for me to get something of my own. So what I'm gonna do with these big old hands? What would you do?"

See now . . . if he had his own land he wouldn't have felt that way. If he had something under his feet that belonged to him he could stand up taller. That's what I'm talking about. Hell, the land is there for everybody. All you got to do is figure out how to get you a piece. Ain't no mystery to life. You just got to go out and meet it square on. If you got a piece of land you'll find everything else fall right into place. You can stand right up next to the white man and talk about the price of cotton . . . the weather, and anything else you want to talk about. If you teach that girl that she living at the bottom of life, she's gonna grow up and hate you.

BERNIECE: I'm gonna teach her the truth. That's just where she living. Only she ain't got to stay there. [*To* MARETHA.] Turn you' head over to the other side.

BOY WILLIE: This might be your bottom but it ain't mine. I'm living at the top of life. I ain't gonna just take my life and throw it away at the bottom. I'm in the world like everybody else. The way I see it everybody else got to come up a little taste to be where I am.

BERNIECE: You right at the bottom with the rest of us.

BOY WILLIE: I'll tell you this . . . and ain't a living soul can put a come back on it. If you believe that's where you at then you gonna act that way. If you act that way then that's where you gonna be. It's as simple as that. Ain't no mystery to

3. John D. Rockefeller (1839–1937), American oil magnate and philanthropist; the Rockefeller family is known for its wealth.

life. I don't know how you come to believe that stuff. Crawley didn't think like that. He wasn't living at the bottom of life. Papa Boy Charles and Mama Ola wasn't living at the bottom of life. You ain't never heard them say nothing like that. They would have taken a strap to you if they heard you say something like that.

[DOAKER *enters from his room.*]

Hey, Doaker . . . Berniece say the colored folks is living at the bottom of life. I tried to tell her if she think that . . . that's where she gonna be. You think you living at the bottom of life? Is that how you see yourself?

DOAKER: I'm just living the best way I know how. I ain't thinking about no top or no bottom.

BOY WILLIE: That's what I tried to tell Berniece. I don't know where she got that from. That sound like something Avery would say. Avery think cause the white man give him a turkey for Thanksgiving that makes him better than everybody else. That's gonna raise him out of the bottom of life. I don't need nobody to give me a turkey. I can get my own turkey. All you have to do is get out my way. I'll get me two or three turkeys.

BERNIECE: You can't even get a chicken let alone two or three turkeys. Talking about get out your way. Ain't nobody in your way. [*To* MARETHA.] Straighten your head, Maretha! Don't be bending down like that. Hold your head up! [*To* BOY WILLIE.] All you got going for you is talk. You' whole life that's all you ever had going for you.

BOY WILLIE: See now . . . I'll tell you something about me. I done strung along and strung along. Going this way and that. Whatever way would lead me to a moment of peace. That's all I want. To be as easy with everything. But I wasn't born to that. I was born to a time of fire.

The world ain't wanted no part of me. I could see that since I was about seven. The world say it's better off without me. See, Berniece accept that. She trying to come up to where she can prove something to the world. Hell, the world a better place cause of me. I don't see it like Berniece. I got a heart that beats here and it beats just as loud as the next fellow's. Don't care if he black or white. Sometime it beats louder. When it beats louder, then everybody can hear it. Some people get scared of that. Like Berniece. Some people get scared to hear a nigger's heart beating. They think you ought to lay low with that heart. Make it beat quiet and go along with everything the way it is. But my mama ain't birthed me for nothing. So what I got to do? I got to mark my passing on the road. Just like you write on a tree, "Boy Willie was here."

That's all I'm trying to do with that piano. Trying to put my mark on the road. Like my daddy done. My heart say for me to sell that piano and get me some land so I can make a life for myself to live in my own way. Other than that I ain't thinking about nothing Berniece got to say.

[*There is a knock at the door.* BOY WILLIE *crosses to it and yanks it open thinking it is* LYMON. AVERY *enters. He carries a Bible.*]

BOY WILLIE: Where you been, nigger? Aw . . . I thought you was Lymon. Hey, Berniece, look who's here.

BERNIECE: Come on in, Avery. Don't you pay Boy Willie no mind.

BOY WILLIE: Hey . . . Hey, Avery . . . tell me this . . . can you get to heaven with half the Bible?

BERNIECE: Boy Willie . . . I done told you to leave me alone.

BOY WILLIE: I just ask the man a question. He can answer. He don't need you to speak for him. Avery . . . if you only believe on half the Bible and don't want to accept the other half . . . you think God let you in heaven? Or do you got to have the whole Bible? Tell Berniece . . . if you only believe in part of it . . . when you see God he gonna ask you why you ain't believed in the other part . . . then he gonna send you straight to Hell.

AVERY: You got to be born again. Jesus say unless a man be born again he cannot come unto the Father and who so ever heareth my words and believeth them not shall be cast into a fiery pit.[4]

BOY WILLIE: That's what I was trying to tell Berniece. You got to believe in it all. You can't go at nothing halfway. She think she going to heaven with half the Bible. [*To* BERNIECE.] You hear that . . . Jesus say you got to believe in it all.

BERNIECE: You keep messing with me.

BOY WILLIE: I ain't thinking about you.

DOAKER: Come on in, Avery, and have a seat. Don't pay neither one of them no mind. They been arguing all day.

BERNIECE: Come on in, Avery.

AVERY: How's everybody in here?

BERNIECE: Here, set this comb back over there on that stove. [*To* AVERY.] Don't pay Boy Willie no mind. He been around here bothering me since I come home from work.

BOY WILLIE: Boy Willie ain't bothering you. Boy Willie ain't bothering nobody. I'm just waiting on Lymon to get back. I ain't thinking about you. You heard the man say I was right and you still don't want to believe it. You just wanna go and make up anythin'. Well there's Avery . . . there's the preacher . . . go on and ask him.

AVERY: Berniece believe in the Bible. She been baptized.

BOY WILLIE: What about that part that say an eye for an eye a tooth for a tooth and a life for a life? Ain't that in there?

DOAKER: What they say down there at the bank, Avery?

AVERY: Oh, they talked to me real nice. I told Berniece . . . they say maybe they let me borrow the money. They done talked to my boss down at work and everything.

DOAKER: That's what I told Berniece. You working every day you ought to be able to borrow some money.

AVERY: I'm getting more people in my congregation every day. Berniece says she gonna be the Deaconess. I get me my church I can get married and settled down. That's what I told Berniece.

DOAKER: That be nice. You all ought to go ahead and get married. Berniece don't need to be by herself. I tell her that all the time.

BERNIECE: I ain't said nothing about getting married. I said I was thinking about it.

4. See John 3.3.

DOAKER: Avery get him his church you all can make it nice. [*To* AVERY.] Berniece said you was coming by to bless the house.

AVERY: Yeah, I done read up on my Bible. She asked me to come by and see if I can get rid of Sutter's ghost.

BOY WILLIE: Ain't no ghost in this house. That's all in Berniece's head. Go on up there and see if you see him. I'll give you a hundred dollars if you see him. That's all in her imagination.

DOAKER: Well, let her find that out then. If Avery blessing the house is gonna make her feel better . . . what you got to do with it?

AVERY: Berniece say Maretha seen him too. I don't know, but I found a part in the Bible to bless the house. If he is here then that ought to make him go.

BOY WILLIE: You worse than Berniece believing all that stuff. Talking about . . . if he here. Go on up there and find out. I been up there I ain't seen him. If you reading from that Bible gonna make him leave out of Berniece imagination, well, you might be right. But if you talking about . . .

DOAKER: Boy Willie, why don't you just be quiet? Getting all up in the man's business. This ain't got nothing to do with you. Let him go ahead and do what he gonna do.

BOY WILLIE: I ain't stopping him. Avery ain't got no power to do nothing.

AVERY: Oh, I ain't got no power. God got the power! God got power over everything in His creation. God can do anything. God say, "As I commandeth so it shall be." God said, "Let there be light," and there was light.[5] He made the world in six days and rested on the seventh. God's got a wonderful power. He got power over life and death. Jesus raised Lazareth from the dead. They was getting ready to bury him and Jesus told him say, "Rise up and walk." He got up and walked and the people made great rejoicing at the power of God. I ain't worried about him chasing away a little old ghost!

[*There is a knock at the door.* BOY WILLIE *goes to answer it.* LYMON *enters carrying a coil of rope.*]

BOY WILLIE: Where you been? I been waiting on you and you run off somewhere.

LYMON: I ran into Grace. I stopped and bought her drink. She say she gonna go to the picture show with me.

BOY WILLIE: I ain't thinking about no Grace nothing.

LYMON: Hi, Berniece.

BOY WILLIE: Give me that rope and get up on this side of the piano.

DOAKER: Boy Willie, don't start nothing now. Leave the piano alone.

BOY WILLIE: Get that board there, Lymon. Stay out of this, Doaker.

[BERNIECE *exits up the stairs.*]

DOAKER: You just can't take the piano. How you gonna take the piano? Berniece ain't said nothing about selling that piano.

BOY WILLIE: She ain't got to say nothing. Come on, Lymon. We got to lift one end at a time up on the board. You got to watch so that the board don't slide up under there.

LYMON: What we gonna do with the rope?

5. See Genesis 1.3. *Lazareth:* Lazarus.

BOY WILLIE: Let me worry about the rope. You just get up on this side over here with me.

[BERNIECE *enters from the stairs. She has her hand in her pocket where she has Crawley's gun.*]

AVERY: Boy Willie . . . Berniece . . . why don't you all sit down and talk this out now?

BERNIECE: Ain't nothing to talk out.

BOY WILLIE: I'm through talking to Berniece. You can talk to Berniece till you get blue in the face, and it don't make no difference. Get up on that side, Lymon. Throw that rope around there and tie it to the leg.

LYMON: Wait a minute . . . wait a minute, Boy Willie. Berniece got to say. Hey, Berniece . . . did you tell Boy Willie he could take this piano?

BERNIECE: Boy Willie ain't taking nothing out of my house but himself. Now you let him go ahead and try.

BOY WILLIE: Come on, Lymon, get up on this side with me.

[LYMON *stands undecided.*]

Come on, nigger! What you standing there for?

LYMON: Maybe Berniece is right, Boy Willie. Maybe you shouldn't sell it.

AVERY: You all ought to sit down and talk it out. See if you can come to an agreement.

DOAKER: That's what I been trying to tell them. Seem like one of them ought to respect the other one's wishes.

BERNIECE: I wish Boy Willie would go on and leave my house. That's what I wish. Now, he can respect that. Cause he's leaving here one way or another.

BOY WILLIE: What you mean one way or another? What's that supposed to mean? I ain't scared of no gun.

DOAKER: Come on, Berniece, leave him alone with that.

BOY WILLIE: I don't care what Berniece say. I'm selling my half. I can't help it if her half got to go along with it. It ain't like I'm trying to cheat her out of her half. Come on, Lymon.

LYMON: Berniece . . . I got to do this . . . Boy Willie say he gonna give you half of the money . . . say he want to get Sutter's land.

BERNIECE: Go on, Lymon. Just go on . . . I done told Boy Willie what to do.

BOY WILLIE: Here, Lymon . . . put that rope up over there.

LYMON: Boy Willie, you sure you want to do this? The way I figure it . . . I might be wrong . . . but I figure she gonna shoot you first.

BOY WILLIE: She just gonna have to shoot me.

BERNIECE: Maretha, get on out the way. Get her out the way, Doaker.

DOAKER: Go on, do what your mama told you.

BERNIECE: Put her in your room.

[MARETHA *exits to Doaker's room.* BOY WILLIE *and* LYMON *try to lift the piano. The door opens and* WINING BOY *enters. He has been drinking.*]

WINING BOY: Man, these niggers around here! I stopped down there at Seefus. . . . These folks standing around talking about Patchneck Red's coming. They jumping back and getting off the sidewalk talking about Patchneck Red this and Patchneck Red that. Come to find out . . . you know who they was talking about? Old John D. from up around Tyler! Used to run around with Otis

Smith. He got everybody scared of him. Calling him Patchneck Red. They don't know I whupped the nigger's head in one time.

BOY WILLIE: Just make sure that board don't slide, Lymon.

LYMON: I got this side. You watch that side.

WINING BOY: Hey, Boy Willie, what you got? I know you got a pint stuck up in your coat.

BOY WILLIE: Wining Boy, get out the way!

WINING BOY: Hey, Doaker. What you got? Gimme a drink. I want a drink.

DOAKER: It look like you had enough of whatever it was. Come talking about "What you got?" You ought to be trying to find somewhere to lay down.

WINING BOY: I ain't worried about no place to lay down. I can always find me a place to lay down in Berniece's house. Ain't that right, Berniece?

BERNIECE: Wining Boy, sit down somewhere. You been out there drinking all day. Come in here smelling like an old polecat. Sit on down there, you don't need nothing to drink.

DOAKER: You know Berniece don't like all that drinking.

WINING BOY: I ain't disrespecting Berniece. Berniece, am I disrespecting you? I'm just trying to be nice. I been with strangers all day and they treated me like family. I come in here to family and you treat me like a stranger. I don't need your whiskey. I can buy my own. I wanted your company, not your whiskey.

DOAKER: Nigger, why don't you go upstairs and lay down? You don't need nothing to drink.

WINING BOY: I ain't thinking about no laying down. Me and Boy Willie fixing to party. Ain't that right, Boy Willie? Tell him. I'm fixing to play me some piano. Watch this.

[WINING BOY *sits down at the piano.*]

BOY WILLIE: Come on, Wining Boy! Me and Lymon fixing to move the piano.

WINING BOY: Wait a minute . . . wait a minute. This a song I wrote for Cleotha. I wrote this song in memory of Cleotha. [*He begins to play and sing.*]

Hey little woman what's the matter with you now
Had a storm last night and blowed the line all down

Tell me how long
Is I got to wait
Can I get it now
Or must I hesitate

It takes a hesitating stocking in her hesitating shoe
It takes a hesitating woman wanna sing the blues

Tell me how long
Is I got to wait
Can I kiss you now
Or must I hesitate.

BOY WILLIE: Come on, Wining Boy, get up! Get up, Wining Boy! Me and Lymon's fixing to move the piano.

WINING BOY: Naw . . . Naw . . . you ain't gonna move this piano!

BOY WILLIE: Get out the way, Wining Boy.

[WINING BOY, *his back to the piano, spreads his arms out over the piano.*]

WINING BOY: You ain't taking this piano out the house. You got to take me with it!
BOY WILLIE: Get on out the way, Wining Boy! Doaker get him!

[*There is a knock on the door.*]

BERNIECE: I got him, Doaker. Come on, Wining Boy. I done told Boy Willie he ain't taking the piano.

[BERNIECE *tries to take* WINING BOY *away from the piano.*]

WINING BOY: He got to take me with it!

[DOAKER *goes to answer the door.* GRACE *enters.*]

GRACE: Is Lymon here?
DOAKER: Lymon.
WINING BOY: He ain't taking that piano.
BERNIECE: I ain't gonna let him take it.
GRACE: I thought you was coming back. I ain't gonna sit in that truck all day.
LYMON: I told you I was coming back.
GRACE: [Sees BOY WILLIE.] Oh, hi, Boy Willie. Lymon told me you was gone back down South.
LYMON: I said he was going back. I didn't say he had left already.
GRACE: That's what you told me.
BERNIECE: Lymon, you got to take your company someplace else.
LYMON: Berniece, this is Grace. That there is Berniece. That's Boy Willie's sister.
GRACE: Nice to meet you. [To LYMON.] I ain't gonna sit out in that truck all day. You told me you was gonna take me to the movie.
LYMON: I told you I had something to do first. You supposed to wait on me.
BERNIECE: Lymon, just go on and leave. Take Grace or whoever with you. Just go on get out my house.
BOY WILLIE: You gonna help me move this piano first, nigger!
LYMON: [To GRACE.] I got to help Boy Willie move the piano first.

[*Everybody but* GRACE *suddenly senses* SUTTER'S *presence.*]

GRACE: I ain't waiting on you. Told me you was coming right back. Now you got to move a piano. You just like all the other men. [GRACE *now senses something.*] Something ain't right here. I knew I shouldn't have come back up in this house. [GRACE *exits.*]
LYMON: Hey, Grace! I'll be right back, Boy Willie.
BOY WILLIE: Where you going, nigger?
LYMON: I'll be back. I got to take Grace home.
BOY WILLIE: Come on, let's move the piano first!
LYMON: I got to take Grace home. I told you I'll be back.

[LYMON *exits.* BOY WILLIE *exits and calls after him.*]

BOY WILLIE: Come on, Lymon! Hey . . . Lymon! Lymon . . . come on!

[*Again, the presence of* SUTTER *is felt.*]

WINING BOY: Hey, Doaker, did you feel that? Hey, Berniece . . . did you get cold? Hey, Doaker . . .

DOAKER: What you calling me for?

WINING BOY: I believe that's Sutter.

DOAKER: Well, let him stay up there. As long as he don't mess with me.

BERNIECE: Avery, go on and bless the house.

DOAKER: You need to bless that piano. That's what you need to bless. It ain't done nothing but cause trouble. If you gonna bless anything go on and bless that.

WINING BOY: Hey, Doaker, if he gonna bless something let him bless everything. The kitchen . . . the upstairs. Go on and bless it all.

BOY WILLIE: Ain't no ghost in this house. He need to bless Berniece's head. That's what he need to bless.

AVERY: Seem like that piano's causing all the trouble. I can bless that. Berniece, put me some water in that bottle.

[AVERY *takes a small bottle from his pocket and hands it to* BERNIECE, *who goes into the kitchen to get water.* AVERY *takes a candle from his pocket and lights it. He gives it to* BERNIECE *as she gives him the water.*]

Hold this candle. Whatever you do make sure it don't go out.

O Holy Father we gather here this evening in the Holy Name to cast out the spirit of one James Sutter. May this vial of water be empowered with thy spirit. May each drop of it be a weapon and a shield against the presence of all evil and may it be a cleansing and blessing of this humble abode.

Just as Our Father taught us how to pray so He say, "I will prepare a table for you in the midst of mine enemies,"[6] and in His hands we place ourselves to come unto his presence. Where there is Good so shall it cause Evil to scatter to the Four Winds. [*He throws water at the piano at each commandment.*] Get thee behind me, Satan! Get thee behind the face of Righteousness as we Glorify His Holy Name! Get thee behind the Hammer of Truth that breaketh down the Wall of Falsehood! Father. Father. Praise. Praise. We ask in Jesus' name and call forth the power of the Holy Spirit as it is written. . . . [*He opens the Bible and reads from it.*] I will sprinkle clean water upon thee and ye shall be clean.

BOY WILLIE: All this old preaching stuff. Hell, just tell him to leave.

[AVERY *continues reading throughout* BOY WILLIE'*s outburst.*]

AVERY: I will sprinkle clean water upon you and you shall be clean: from all your uncleanliness, and from all your idols, will I cleanse you. A new heart also will I give you, and a new spirit will I put within you: and I will take out of your flesh the heart of stone, and I will give you a heart of flesh. And I will put my spirit within you, and cause you to walk in my statutes, and ye shall keep my judgments, and do them.

[BOY WILLIE *grabs a pot of water from the stove and begins to fling it around the room.*]

BOY WILLIE: Hey Sutter! Sutter! Get your ass out this house! Sutter! Come on and get some of this water! You done drowned in the well, come on and get some more of this water!

[BOY WILLIE *is working himself into a frenzy as he runs around the room throwing water and calling* SUTTER'*s name.* AVERY *continues reading.*]

6. Psalm 23.5.

BOY WILLIE: Come on, Sutter! [*He starts up the stairs.*] Come on, get some water! Come on, Sutter!

> [*The sound of* SUTTER'S GHOST *is heard. As* BOY WILLIE *approaches the steps he is suddenly thrown back by the unseen force, which is choking him. As he struggles he frees himself, then dashes up the stairs.*]

BOY WILLIE: Come on, Sutter!

AVERY: [*Continuing.*] A new heart also will I give you and a new spirit will I put within you: and I will take out of your flesh the heart of stone, and I will give you a heart of flesh. And I will put my spirit within you, and cause you to walk in my statutes, and ye shall keep my judgments, and do them.

> [*There are loud sounds heard from upstairs as* BOY WILLIE *begins to wrestle with* SUTTER'S GHOST. *It is a life-and-death struggle fraught with perils and faultless terror.* BOY WILLIE *is thrown down the stairs.* AVERY *is stunned into silence.* BOY WILLIE *picks himself up and dashes back upstairs.*]

AVERY: Berniece, I can't do it.

> [*There are more sounds heard from upstairs.* DOAKER *and* WINING BOY *stare at one another in stunned disbelief. It is in this moment, from somewhere old, that* BERNIECE *realizes what she must do. She crosses to the piano. She begins to play. The song is found piece by piece. It is an old urge to song that is both a commandment and a plea. With each repetition it gains in strength. It is intended as an exorcism and a dressing for battle. A rustle of wind blowing across two continents.*]

BERNIECE: [*Singing.*]

I want you to help me
I want you to help me
I want you to help me
I want you to help me
I want you to help me
I want you to help me
Mama Berniece
I want you to help me
Mama Esther
I want you to help me
Papa Boy Charles
I want you to help me
Mama Ola
I want you to help me

I want you to help me
I want you to help me
I want you to help me
I want you to help me
I want you to help me
I want you to help me
I want you to help me
I want you to help me

[*The sound of a train approaching is heard. The noise upstairs subsides.*]

BOY WILLIE: Come on, Sutter! Come back, Sutter!

[BERNIECE *begins to chant:*]

BERNIECE:

Thank you.
Thank you.
Thank you.

[*A calm comes over the house.* MARETHA *enters from* DOAKER'*s room.* BOY WILLIE *enters on the stairs. He pauses a moment to watch* BERNIECE *at the piano.*]

BERNIECE:

Thank you.
Thank you.
Thank you.

BOY WILLIE: Wining Boy, you ready to go back down home? Hey, Doaker, what time the train leave?

DOAKER: You still got time to make it.

[MARETHA *crosses and embraces* BOY WILLIE.]

BOY WILLIE: Hey Berniece . . . if you and Maretha don't keep playing on that piano . . . ain't no telling . . . me and Sutter both liable to be back. [*He exits.*]

BERNIECE: Thank you.

[*The lights go down to black.*]

1987

QUESTIONS

1. What, specifically, do the carvings on the piano represent? What different past does the piano represent for each of the characters? How important is the past ownership of the piano? What is the significance of the way the family acquired it? In what ways do different characters' attitudes toward the piano reveal their feelings about the past?

2. Why is Boy Willie portrayed in the first scene as so loud and intrusive? What does this behavior achieve for the play dramatically? What aspects of Boy Willie's character does the opening scene illustrate? What aspects of his character are revealed later? What does "land" represent to him?

3. How would you describe Doaker's role in the play? Is he a minor character? How does he contribute to the play thematically? How does he affect the way events unfold, or the dramatic climax? Given the importance of family in this play and his role as the family's acting patriarch, could we call him a hero?

4. What functions does Maretha have in the play? In what ways is her age important? If you were directing the play, how would you have Maretha behave? How would she be costumed?

5. In what ways is geography important to the play? What does Mississippi represent to the different characters? What does Pittsburgh represent to the different characters? What does Doaker's continued employment with the railroad symbolize,

and what is the significance of his description of how the railroad works (in the play's opening scene)?

6. What does the truckload of watermelons represent to Boy Willie? to Lymon? In what sense does the offstage presence of the watermelons keep time for the play and mark the progression of the plot? Describe the rising action and climax of the play in relation to the truck's load.

7. Describe the the conflict between Berniece and Boy Willie and the way it develops throughout the play. Where do other characters fit into the opposition? What role might gender, as well as race, play in this conflict?

8. What plot functions does Grace perform? In what ways does her presence complicate the play's portrayal of African American women's experience and options?

9. What does Avery represent to Berniece? What attracts her to him, and what, on the other hand, makes her hesitate in accepting his offer of marriage? If you were directing the play, how would you present the critical scene of Avery preaching? Of the exorcism?

10. What does "Lesson" in the title mean? What lesson does the piano teach each of the characters?

SUGGESTIONS FOR WRITING

1. What is the role of music in *The Piano Lesson*? How does the music function to reveal character and to provide a counterpoint to the action? What is the thematic importance of the music? Write an essay in which you explore the many uses of music in Wilson's play.

2. What is the legacy of slavery in the lives of the African American characters in *The Piano Lesson*? How fully does each character acknowledge slavery's influence on the mid-twentieth-century lives depicted in the play? How does each character try to break free of this influence? Write an essay in which you explore slavery's lingering power to shape the attitudes and behavior of the characters in *The Piano Lesson*.

3. How does *The Piano Lesson* present gender roles and sexual politics? What expectations do the men and women in the play have of each other? Write an essay in which you discuss the play's representation of gender differences.

4. Were you surprised by the play's ending? A longstanding "rule" for playwrights is that if a gun appears onstage, it must be fired by the end of the play. *The Piano Lesson*, though, seems to build steadily toward a violent climax that is averted at the last moment. Write an essay in which you examine the way August Wilson both uses and subverts the audience's conventional expectation that drama is resolved by violence.

5. Write an essay exploring Sutter's role in and significance to the play, especially in terms of conflict and theme. Why might it matter that we aren't informed about Sutter's race until the second act? What is the significance of the timing of his appearances and of the way other characters respond to and interpret them? Why is Berniece able to rid the house of Sutter by playing the piano whereas Avery's approach proves ineffectual?

6. Write a series of "newsy" letters from Boy Willie, Berniece, Maretha, and Lymon, in which each character, in turn, describes the conflict over the piano. How would they describe their own feelings and actions? How would they account for the values and motivations of the other characters? What resolution of the conflict would each character hope for?

Authors on Their Work: AUGUST WILSON (1945–2005)

From "August Wilson: The Art of Theater XIV" (1999)*

INTERVIEWER

Can you talk about the genesis of a work? *The Piano Lesson?*

WILSON

I started with the idea from one of Romare Bearden's paintings—*The Piano Lesson*, the subtitle of which was *Homage to Mary Lou Williams*, who was a jazz pianist in Pittsburgh. I started with a question: Can you acquire a sense of self worth by denying your past, or is implicit in that denial a repudiation of the worth of the self? Once deciding that, I had to construct a series of events that posed that question and illustrated some possible answers. I started by having four guys carry the piano into the house. I wrote eight pages of dialogue. . . . Once they got it in the house they began arguing about where to put it. I thought, Wait a minute, where am I going? What am I doing? So I threw those pages out and started over. And then I got the idea of the brother coming into the house like a tornado, bringing in the past that his sister is trying to deny. I usually start with a line of dialogue, which contains elements of the plot, character, and the thematic idea.

From "An Interview with August Wilson" (1999)**

Q. Is *The Piano Lesson* a kind of debate between Berniece and Boy Willie?

A. That play sets up the question of whether you can develop a sense of self-worth by denying the past. Everyone sees the play differently than I do. Because Boy Willie wants to sell the piano, they think he is trying to deny the past. But Berniece cannot even touch the piano—she's the one who is denying everything, she's the one trying to run away from the past. (15–16)

• • •

Q. One playwright has said that drama is made up of sound and silence. Do you see drama that way?

A. No doubt drama is made up of sound and silence, but I see conflict at the center. What you do is set up a character who has certain beliefs and you establish a situation where those beliefs are challenged and that character is forced to examine those beliefs and perhaps change them. That's the kind of dramatic situation which engages an audience.

Q. Then is the conflict primarily internal rather than external, between characters?

A. Internal, right, where the character has to reexamine his whole body of beliefs. The play has to shake the very foundation of his whole system of beliefs and force him to make a choice. Then I think you as a playwright

(Continued on next page)

(Continued)

have accomplished something, because that process also forces the audience to go through the same inner struggle.

*From George Plimpton and August Wilson, "August Wilson: The Art of Theater XIV," *The Paris Review* 41.153 (Winter 1999): 67–94.

**Bonnie Lyons, "An Interview with August Wilson," *Contemporary Literature* 40.1 (Spring 1999): 1–21.

27 TRAGEDY AND COMEDY

Classifying literary texts serves a variety of purposes for literary critics, who may need to "place" a work in history, suggest its relationship to other texts, or assess its literary quality or cultural value. But classification is not just an activity for "professionals." Classification can also be important to students and ordinary readers; a knowledge of categories and what they stand for can aid in the enjoyment and interpretation of individual texts.

Authors sometimes label their texts specifically to help readers know what to expect, thereby entering into a kind of contract with readers. When fiction writers call their books "romances," for example, they tell readers to expect stories that are romantic, idealistic, improbable, full of fantasy, and characterized by love and emotional fulfillment. Playwrights, similarly, have historically labeled their texts to inform both audiences and readers about what they may experience during a performance or reading of a work. **Pastoral** plays promise to be about shepherds living in an idealized world reminiscent of some primitive golden age. **Farces** promise broad humor and wild antics, perhaps slapstick, pratfalls, or other physical humor or perhaps easy puns and verbal high jinks, but certainly something entertaining, not too taxing, and not too serious. **Satires** promise critical commentary on a person or situation or event, often political or involving a specific cultural or social situation. Not all satires, farces, and pastoral plays do exactly what their labels promise, but those labels do lead readers to expect a certain kind of text—one that will treat predictable subject matter and progress in predictable fashion. Often these labels imply a certain kind of structure, language, and value system.

Not all plays (or texts of any other kind) are labeled by their authors, but many unlabeled texts draw on previous practice and traditional classifications and are therefore placed by critics or by viewers and readers within traditional categories. We might, for example, describe a film as a whodunnit or a "spaghetti Western," or we might call a TV program a sitcom or a soap, and reasonably expect that others will know, at least roughly, what kind of film or show we are describing.

Tragedy and **comedy** are two of the oldest dramatic forms, and many contemporary playwrights and critics continue to apply these terms. Many people believe that tragedy and comedy still provide convenient ways to organize and present experience because they reflect basic ways of viewing human history. You can sometimes get into a pretty lively argument about whether a particular play should be called a tragedy; all kinds of critics, students, theatergoers, and readers argued with Arthur Miller and with one another about whether *Death of a Salesman* was truly tragic, for example. But while individuals often disagree about how to label particular texts, and about exactly what each label implies, most people admit the necessity of labels and believe that general agreement about definition is possible, despite quibbling over details.

The broad parameters of comedy and tragedy have been around since the time of Aristotle, the fourth century B.C.E.; in his *Poetics* Aristotle defined tragedy in terms of contemporary examples. Aristotle's definition depends on three things—the order of values implicit in the play, the nature of character in the play, and the nature of the conclusion.

In a tragedy like *Oedipus the King*, values are universal and beyond the control of humankind. Right and wrong stem not from any agreement between individuals but from the will of the gods or from some other extrahuman authority. When the oracle tells Oedipus that he is fated to kill his father and marry his mother, Oedipus is horrified. In human terms he must try to avoid this fate—but in terms of the value system that rules the play, his attempt to circumvent the will of the gods must destroy him. In a comedy like *The Importance of Being Earnest*, on the other hand, values are social and determined by the general opinion of society. In moral terms, Jack and Gwendolen, being healthy and single, might marry and establish a family. They face a social problem, however, in that Gwendolen's children cannot achieve their "proper" place in society unless her husband is a man of good family, some social position, and adequate means. Indeed, comedy tends to endorse the values of society, sometimes at the expense of individual needs or values.

Tragedy and comedy also differ in their treatment of character. Tragedy tends to focus on a person of high rank who confronts the universe and his or her fate as an individual. The tragic figure is ultimately doomed because, although good and noble, he or she has a flaw of character or a limitation of knowledge—some mark of humanity—that offsets all his or her greatness. Oedipus wishes to know and to control his own destiny, but he learns too much and is destroyed. Had Oedipus been the son of a shepherd rather than of a king, perhaps the gods would not have taken such an unfortunate interest in his fate.

By contrast, being concerned largely with society, comedies often define their characters in terms of social roles. In *The Importance of Being Earnest*, both Jack and Algernon are, for plot purposes, unmarried young men but not eminently eligible husbands-to-be, Jack because of his uncertain parentage and Algernon because of his lack of money. They have individual traits—Algernon eats too much and is somewhat pretentious; Jack tries to be more straightforward—but what distinguishes them is not so important as what they have in common according to prevailing societal standards. Many comic characters become stereotypes. Lady Bracknell, for example, is a middle-aged, meddling matron, ideally placed by age and position to exert decisive social influence. Other stereotypes in the play include Miss Prism, the desperate spinster, and Dr. Chasuble, the slightly dim clergyman.

Finally, tragedy and comedy can be defined by their endings. In most tragedies, the hero is enlightened, coming to understand the meaning of his or her deeds and to accept an appropriate punishment. At the end of *Oedipus the King*, the blind hero sees and understands. Accepting his ostracism, he leaves Thebes a chastened and humbled but wiser man. Many tragic heroes die, as Hamlet does, but understanding, rather than death itself, ends the tragedy. Hamlet understands what has happened and in his last moments tries to restore order to the kingdom, asking for himself only that people may know the truth about what he has done. In comedy, on the other hand, the resolution occurs when one or more characters take on a proper social role. Most frequently, this means the marriage of an eligible young woman and an equally eligible young man. The society of *Earnest* believes that young men like Jack and Algernon and young women like Gwendolen and

Cecily should marry and get about the business of having children and raising them to perpetuate the society. Even the marriage of Miss Prism and Dr. Chasuble serves social purposes. The society of the play prefers married clergymen to celibates and has no really useful function for a middle-aged spinster.

Oedipus the King and *The Importance of Being Earnest* clearly display the assumptions and features of tragedy and comedy, respectively. Many good plays provide less clear-cut examples of these genres, and many other categories have been used over the centuries to describe the shape and conventions of groups of dramatic texts. Still, *tragedy* and *comedy* are two of the most important genres to explore in any study of the various classifications of drama.

SOPHOCLES

Oedipus the King[1]

CHARACTERS

OEDIPUS, *King of Thebes*	FIRST MESSENGER
JOCASTA, *His Wife*	SECOND MESSENGER
CREON, *His Brother-in-Law*	A HERDSMAN
TEIRESIAS, *an Old Blind Prophet*	A CHORUS *of Old Men of Thebes*
A PRIEST	

SCENE: *In front of the palace of* OEDIPUS *at Thebes. To the right of the stage near the altar stands the* PRIEST *with a crowd of children.* OEDIPUS *emerges from the central door.*

OEDIPUS: Children, young sons and daughters of old Cadmus,[2]
why do you sit here with your suppliant crowns?
The town is heavy with a mingled burden
of sounds and smells, of groans and hymns and incense;
I did not think it fit that I should hear   5
of this from messengers but came myself,—
I Oedipus whom all men call the Great.

[*He turns to the* PRIEST.]

You're old and they are young; come, speak for them.
What do you fear or want, that you sit here
suppliant? Indeed I'm willing to give all   10
that you may need; I would be very hard
should I not pity suppliants like these.
PRIEST: O ruler of my country, Oedipus,
you see our company around the altar;
you see our ages; some of us, like these,   15
who cannot yet fly far, and some of us
heavy with age; these children are the chosen
among the young, and I the priest of Zeus.

1. Translated by David Grene.   2. The founder of Thebes.

Within the market place sit others crowned

20 with suppliant garlands, at the double shrine
of Pallas[3] and the temple where Ismenus
gives oracles by fire. King, you yourself
have seen our city reeling like a wreck
already; it can scarcely lift its prow

25 out of the depths, out of the bloody surf.
A blight is on the fruitful plants of the earth,
a blight is on the cattle in the fields,
a blight is on our women that no children
are born to them; a God that carries fire,

30 a deadly pestilence, is on our town,
strikes us and spares not, and the house of Cadmus
is emptied of its people while black Death
grows rich in groaning and in lamentation.
We have not come as suppliants to this altar

35 because we thought of you as of a God,
but rather judging you the first of men
in all the chances of this life and when
we mortals have to do with more than man.
You came and by your coming saved our city,

40 freed us from tribute which we paid of old
to the Sphinx, cruel singer.[4] This you did
in virtue of no knowledge we could give you,
in virtue of no teaching; it was God
that aided you, men say, and you are held

45 with God's assistance to have saved our lives.
Now Oedipus, Greatest in all men's eyes,
here falling at your feet we all entreat you,
find us some strength for rescue.
Perhaps you'll hear a wise word from some God,

50 perhaps you will learn something from a man
(for I have seen that for the skilled of practice
the outcome of their counsels live the most).
Noblest of men, go, and raise up our city,
go,—and give heed. For now this land of ours

55 calls you its savior since you saved it once.
So, let us never speak about your reign
as of a time when first our feet were set
secure on high, but later fell to ruin.
Raise up our city, save it and raise it up.

60 Once you have brought us luck with happy omen;
be no less now in fortune.
If you will rule this land, as now you rule it,

---

3. *Athena*, the goddess of wisdom. *Zeus*: principal god and father of Athena.
4. Thebes was in the thrall of the monstrous sphinx—part human, part lion, part eagle, part serpent—until Oedipus was able to answer a riddle; freed at last from the monster's cruelty, the grateful citizens of Thebes made Oedipus their king.

better to rule it full of men than empty.
For neither tower nor ship is anything
when empty, and none live in it together.   65

OEDIPUS: I pity you, children. You have come full of longing,
but I have known the story before you told it
only too well. I know you are all sick,
yet there is not one of you, sick though you are,
that is as sick as I myself.   70
Your several sorrows each have single scope
and touch but one of you. My spirit groans
for city and myself and you at once.
You have not roused me like a man from sleep;
know that I have given many tears to this,   75
gone many ways wandering in thought,
but as I thought I found only one remedy
and that I took. I sent Menoeceus' son
Creon, Jocasta's brother, to Apollo,[5]
to his Pythian temple,   80
that he might learn there by what act or word
I could save this city. As I count the days,
it vexes me what ails him; he is gone
far longer than he needed for the journey.
But when he comes, then, may I prove a villain,   85
if I shall not do all the God commands.

PRIEST: Thanks for your gracious words. Your servants here
signal that Creon is this moment coming.

OEDIPUS: His face is bright. O holy Lord Apollo,
grant that his news too may be bright for us   90
and bring us safety.

PRIEST: It is happy news,
I think, for else his head would not be crowned
with sprigs of fruitful laurel.

OEDIPUS: We will know soon,
he's within hail. Lord Creon, my good brother,   95
what is the word you bring us from the God?

[CREON *enters.*]

CREON: A good word,—for things hard to bear themselves
if in the final issue all is well
I count complete good fortune.

OEDIPUS: What do you mean?
What you have said so far   100
leaves me uncertain whether to trust or fear.

CREON: If you will hear my news before these others
I am ready to speak, or else to go within.

OEDIPUS: Speak it to all;

---

5. God of truth and of light, worshipped at many shrines, most famously that at Pytho (an ancient name
for Delphi), where an oracle was believed to speak for the god.

105 the grief I bear, I bear it more for these
  than for my own heart.

CREON: I will tell you, then,
  what I heard from the God.
  King Phoebus[6] in plain words commanded us
  to drive out a pollution from our land,
110 pollution grown ingrained within the land;
  drive it out, said the God, not cherish it,
  till it's past cure.

OEDIPUS: What is the rite
  of purification? How shall it be done?

CREON: By banishing a man, or expiation
115 of blood by blood, since it is murder guilt
  which holds our city in this destroying storm.

OEDIPUS: Who is this man whose fate the God pronounces?

CREON: My Lord, before you piloted the state
  we had a king called Laius.

120 OEDIPUS: I know of him by hearsay. I have not seen him.

CREON: The God commanded clearly: let someone
  punish with force this dead man's murderers.

OEDIPUS: Where are they in the world? Where would a trace
  of this old crime be found? It would be hard
  to guess where.

125 CREON: The clue is in this land;
  that which is sought is found;
  the unheeded thing escapes:
  so said the God.

OEDIPUS: Was it at home,
  or in the country that death came upon him,
130 or in another country travelling?

CREON: He went, he said himself, upon an embassy,
  but never returned when he set out from home.

OEDIPUS: Was there no messenger, no fellow traveller
  who knew what happened? Such a one might tell
135 something of use.

CREON: They were all killed save one. He fled in terror
  and he could tell us nothing in clear terms
  of what he knew, nothing, but one thing only.

OEDIPUS: What was it?
140 If we could even find a slim beginning
  in which to hope, we might discover much.

CREON: This man said that the robbers they encountered
  were many and the hands that did the murder
  were many; it was no man's single power.

145 OEDIPUS: How could a robber dare a deed like this
  were he not helped with money from the city,
  money and treachery?

---

6. Another name for Apollo.

CREON: That indeed was thought.
    But Laius was dead and in our trouble
    there was none to help.

OEDIPUS: What trouble was so great to hinder you   150
    inquiring out the murder of your king?

CREON: The riddling Sphinx induced us to neglect
    mysterious crimes and rather seek solution
    of troubles at our feet.

OEDIPUS: I will bring this to light again. King Phoebus   155
    fittingly took this care about the dead,
    and you too fittingly.
    And justly you will see in me an ally,
    a champion of my country and the God.
    For when I drive pollution from the land   160
    I will not serve a distant friend's advantage,
    but act in my own interest. Whoever
    he was that killed the king may readily
    wish to dispatch me with his murderous hand;
    so helping the dead king I help myself.   165

    Come, children, take your suppliant boughs and go;
    up from the altars now. Call the assembly
    and let it meet upon the understanding
    that I'll do everything. God will decide
    whether we prosper or remain in sorrow.   170

PRIEST: Rise, children—it was this we came to seek,
    which of himself the king now offers us.
    May Phoebus who gave us the oracle
    come to our rescue and stay the plague.

        [*Exeunt*[7] *all but the* CHORUS.]

CHORUS: [*Strophe.*] What is the sweet spoken word of God from the shrine of 175
    Pytho, rich in gold
    that has come to glorious Thebes?
    I am stretched on the rack of doubt, and terror and trembling hold
    my heart, O Delian Healer,[8] and I worship full of fears
    for what doom you will bring to pass, new or renewed in the revolving years.
    Speak to me, immortal voice,   180
    child of golden Hope.

      [*Antistrophe.*]

    First I call on you, Athene,[9] deathless daughter of Zeus,
    and Artemis, Earth Upholder,

---

7. Exit the stage (Latin for "they go out"). *Strophe* (line 175): in Greek stagecraft, a choral song and the corresponding dance of the chorus to one side. *Antistrophe* (stage direction following line 181): after the strophe, the chorus's answering song and returning dance.
8. Apollo was also god of healing; one of his principal shrines was located on the island of Delos.
9. Goddess of both war and peace as well as wisdom. *Artemis*: goddess of the earth and the hunt, twin sister of Apollo.

who sits in the midst of the marketplace in the throne which men call Fame,
185   and Phoebus, the Far Shooter, three averters of Fate,
come to us now, if ever before, when ruin rushed upon the state,
you drove destruction's flame away
out of our land.

[*Strophe.*]

Our sorrows defy number;
190   all the ship's timbers are rotten;
taking of thought is no spear for the driving away of the plague.
There are no growing children in this famous land;
there are no women bearing the pangs of childbirth.
You may see them one with another, like birds swift on the wing,
195   quicker than fire unmastered,
speeding away to the coast of the Western God.

[*Antistrophe.*]

In the unnumbered deaths
of its people the city dies;
those children that are born lie dead on the naked earth
200   unpitied, spreading contagion of death; and grey haired mothers and wives
everywhere stand at the altar's edge, suppliant, moaning;
the hymn to the healing God rings out but with it the wailing voices are blended.
From these our sufferings grant us, O golden Daughter of Zeus,
glad-faced deliverance.

[*Strophe.*]

205   There is no clash of brazen shields but our fight is with the War God,
a War God ringed with the cries of men, a savage God who burns us;
grant that he turn in racing course backwards out of our country's bounds
to the great palace of Amphitrite[1] or where the waves of the Thracian sea
deny the stranger safe anchorage.
210   Whatsoever escapes the night
at last the light of day revisits;
so smite the War God, Father Zeus,
beneath your thunderbolt,
for you are the Lord of the lightning, the lightning that carries fire.

[*Antistrophe.*]

215   And your unconquered arrow shafts, winged by the golden corded bow,
Lycean King, I beg to be at our side for help;[2]
and the gleaming torches of Artemis with which she scours the Lycean hills,
and I call on the God with the turban of gold, who gave his name to this
country of ours,
the Bacchic God with the wind flushed face,

---

1. Queen of the sea and wife of Poseidon, sometimes said to dwell in the Atlantic Ocean. *War God*: Ares, a son of Zeus and half-brother to Athena.
2. That is, Apollo, a major shrine to whom was located at Lycia in Anatolia, modern-day Turkey.

Evian One, who travel   220
with the Maenad[3] company,
combat the God that burns us
with your torch of pine;
for the God that is our enemy is a God unhonoured among the Gods.

[OEDIPUS *returns.*]

OEDIPUS: For what you ask me—if you will hear my words,   225
and hearing welcome them and fight the plague,
you will find strength and lightening of your load
Hark to me; what I say to you, I say
as one that is a stranger to the story
as stranger to the deed. For I would not   230
be far upon the track if I alone
were tracing it without a clue. But now,
since after all was finished, I became
a citizen among you, citizens—
now I proclaim to all the men of Thebes: 235
who so among you knows the murderer
by whose hand Laius, son of Labdacus,
died—I command him to tell everything
to me,—yes, though he fears himself to take the blame
on his own head; for bitter punishment   240
he shall have none, but leave this land unharmed.
Or if he knows the murderer, another,
a foreigner, still let him speak the truth.
For I will pay him and be grateful, too.
But if you shall keep silence, if perhaps   245
some one of you, to shield a guilty friend,
or for his own sake shall reject my words—
hear what I shall do then:
I forbid that man, whoever he be, my land,
my land where I hold sovereignty and throne;   250
and I forbid any to welcome him
or cry him greeting or make him a sharer
in sacrifice or offering to the gods,
or give him water for his hands to wash.
I command all to drive him from their homes,   255
since he is our pollution, as the oracle
of Pytho's god proclaimed him now to me.
So I stand forth a champion of the god
and of the man who died.
Upon the murderer I invoke this curse—   260
whether he is one man and all unknown,
or one of many—may he wear out his life
in misery to miserable doom!

---

3. Female worshipers of Dionysus (Bacchus to the Romans; see line 219), god of fertility and wine. *Evian one*: Dionysus (also known as Evius).

If with my knowledge he lives at my hearth
265   I pray that I myself may feel my curse.
On you I lay my charge to fulfill all this
for me, for the god, and for this land of ours
destroyed and blighted, by the god forsaken.

Even were this no matter of God's ordinance
270   it would not fit you so to leave it lie,
unpurified, since a good man is dead
and one that was a king. Search it out.
Since I am now the holder of his office,
and have his bed and wife that once was his,
275   and had his line not been unfortunate
we would have common children—(fortune leaped
upon his head)—because of all these things,
I fight in his defence as for my father,
and I shall try all means to take the murderer
280   of Laius the son of Labdacus
the son of Polydorus and before him
of Cadmus and before him of Agenor.
Those who do not obey me, may the Gods
grant no crops springing from the ground they plough
285   nor children to their women! May a fate
like this, or one still worse than this consume them!
For you whom these words please, the other Thebans,
may Justice as your ally and all the Gods
live with you, blessing you now and for ever!

290   CHORUS: As you have held me to my oath, I speak:
I neither killed the king nor can declare
the killer; but since Phoebus set the quest
it is his part to tell who the man is.
OEDIPUS: Right; but to put compulsion on the Gods
295   against their will—no man can do that.
CHORUS: May I then say what I think second best?
OEDIPUS: If there's a third best, too, spare not to tell it.
CHORUS: I know that what the Lord Teiresias
sees, is most often what the Lord Apollo
300   sees. If you should inquire of this from him
you might find out most clearly.
OEDIPUS: Even in this my actions have not been sluggard.
On Creon's word I have sent two messengers
and why the prophet is not here already
I have been wondering.
305   CHORUS: His skill apart
there is besides only an old faint story.
OEDIPUS: What is it?
I look at every story.
CHORUS: It was said
that he was killed by certain wayfarers.

OEDIPUS: I heard that, too, but no one saw the killer.   310
CHORUS: Yet if he has a share of fear at all,
   his courage will not stand firm, hearing your curse.
OEDIPUS: The man who in the doing did not shrink
   will fear no word.
CHORUS: Here comes his prosecutor:
   led by your men the godly prophet comes   315
   in whom alone of mankind truth is native.

    [*Enter* TEIRESIAS, *led by a* LITTLE BOY.]

OEDIPUS: Teiresias, you are versed in everything,
   things teachable and things not to be spoken,
   things of the heaven and earth-creeping things.
   You have no eyes but in your mind you know   320
   with what a plague our city is afflicted.
   My lord, in you alone we find a champion,
   in you alone one that can rescue us.
   Perhaps you have not heard the messengers,
   but Phoebus sent in answer to our sending   325
   an oracle declaring that our freedom
   from this disease would only come when we
   should learn the names of those who killed King Laius,
   and kill them or expel from our country.
   Do not begrudge us oracles from birds,   330
   or any other way of prophecy
   within your skill; save yourself and the city,
   save me; redeem the debt of our pollution
   that lies on us because of this dead man.
   We are in your hands; pains are most nobly taken   335
   to help another when you have means and power.
TEIRESIAS: Alas, how terrible is wisdom when
   it brings no profit to the man that's wise!
   This I knew well, but had forgotten it,
   else I would not have come here.
OEDIPUS: What is this?   340
   How sad you are now you have come!
TEIRESIAS: Let me
   go home. It will be easiest for us both
   to bear our several destinies to the end
   if you will follow my advice.
OEDIPUS: You'd rob us
   of this your gift of prophecy? You talk   345
   as one who had no care for law nor love
   for Thebes who reared you.
TEIRESIAS: Yes, but I see that even your own words
   miss the mark; therefore I must fear for mine.
OEDIPUS: For God's sake if you know of anything,   350
   do not turn from us; all of us kneel to you,
   all of us here, your suppliants.

TEIRESIAS: All of you here know nothing. I will not
    bring to the light of day my troubles, mine—
    rather than call them yours.

355 OEDIPUS: What do you mean?
    You know of something but refuse to speak.
    Would you betray us and destroy the city?

TEIRESIAS: I will not bring this pain upon us both,
    neither on you nor on myself. Why is it
360 you question me and waste your labour? I
    will tell you nothing.

OEDIPUS: You would provoke a stone! Tell us, you villain,
    tell us, and do not stand there quietly
    unmoved and balking at the issue.

365 TEIRESIAS: You blame my temper but you do not see
    your own that lives within you; it is me
    you chide.

OEDIPUS: Who would not feel his temper rise
    at words like these with which you shame our city?

370 TEIRESIAS: Of themselves things will come, although I hide them
    and breathe no word of them.

OEDIPUS: Since they will come
    tell them to me.

TEIRESIAS: I will say nothing further.
    Against this answer let your temper rage
    as wildly as you will.

OEDIPUS: Indeed I am
375 so angry I shall not hold back a jot
    of what I think. For I would have you know
    I think you were complotter of the deed
    and doer of the deed save in so far
    as for the actual killing. Had you had eyes
380 I would have said alone you murdered him.

TEIRESIAS: Yes? Then I warn you faithfully to keep
    the letter of your proclamation and
    from this day forth to speak no word of greeting
    to these nor me; you are the land's pollution.

385 OEDIPUS: How shamelessly you started up this taunt!
    How do you think you will escape?

TEIRESIAS: I have.
    I have escaped; the truth is what I cherish
    and that's my strength.

OEDIPUS: And who has taught you truth?
    Not your profession surely!

TEIRESIAS: You have taught me,
390 for you have made me speak against my will.

OEDIPUS: Speak what? Tell me again that I may learn it better.

TEIRESIAS: Did you not understand before or would you
    provoke me into speaking?

OEDIPUS: I did not grasp it,

not so to call it known. Say it again.

TEIRESIAS: I say you are the murderer of the king   395
   whose murderer you seek.

OEDIPUS: Not twice you shall
   say calumnies like this and stay unpunished.

TEIRESIAS: Shall I say more to tempt your anger more?

OEDIPUS: As much as you desire; it will be said
   in vain.

TEIRESIAS: I say that with those you love best   400
   you live in foulest shame unconsciously
   and do not see where you are in calamity.

OEDIPUS: Do you imagine you can always talk
   like this, and live to laugh at it hereafter?

TEIRESIAS: Yes, if the truth has anything of strength.   405

OEDIPUS: It has, but not for you; it has no strength
   for you because you are blind in mind and ears
   as well as in your eyes.

TEIRESIAS: You are a poor wretch
   to taunt me with the very insults which
   everyone soon will heap upon yourself.   410

OEDIPUS: Your life is one long night so that you cannot
   hurt me or any other who sees the light.

TEIRESIAS: It is not fate that I should be your ruin,
   Apollo is enough; it is his care
   to work this out.

OEDIPUS: Was this your own design   415
   or Creon's?

TEIRESIAS: Creon is no hurt to you,
   but you are to yourself.

OEDIPUS: Wealth, sovereignty and skill outmatching skill
   for the contrivance of an envied life!
   Great store of jealousy fill your treasury chests,   420
   if my friend Creon, friend from the first and loyal,
   thus secretly attacks me, secretly
   desires to drive me out and secretly
   suborns this juggling, trick devising quack,
   this wily beggar who has only eyes   425
   for his own gains, but blindness in his skill.
   For, tell me, where have you seen clear, Teiresias,
   with your prophetic eyes? When the dark singer,
   the Sphinx, was in your country, did you speak
   word of deliverance to its citizens?   430
   And yet the riddle's answer was not the province
   of a chance comer. It was a prophet's task
   and plainly you had no such gift of prophecy
   from birds nor otherwise from any God
   to glean a word of knowledge. But I came,   435
   Oedipus, who knew nothing, and I stopped her.
   I solved the riddle by my wit alone.

Mine was no knowledge got from birds.[4] And now
you would expel me,
440　because you think that you will find a place
by Creon's throne. I think you will be sorry,
both you and your accomplice, for your plot
to drive me out. And did I not regard you
as an old man, some suffering would have taught you
445　that what was in your heart was treason.

CHORUS: We look at this man's words and yours, my king,
and we find both have spoken them in anger.
We need no angry words but only thought
how we may best hit the God's meaning for us.

450　TEIRESIAS: If you are king, at least I have the right
no less to speak in my defence against you.
Of that much I am master. I am no slave
of yours, but Loxias',[5] and so I shall not
enroll myself with Creon for my patron.
455　Since you have taunted me with being blind,
here is my word for you.
You have your eyes but see not where you are
in sin, nor where you live, nor whom you live with.
Do you know who your parents are? Unknowing
460　you are an enemy to kith and kin
in death, beneath the earth, and in this life.
A deadly footed, double striking curse,
from father and mother both, shall drive you forth
out of this land, with darkness on your eyes,
465　that now have such straight vision. Shall there be
a place will not be harbour to your cries,
a corner of Cithaeron[6] will not ring
in echo to your cries, soon, soon,—
when you shall learn the secret of your marriage,
470　which steered you to a haven in this house,—
haven no haven, after lucky voyage?
And of the multitude of other evils
establishing a grim equality
between you and your children, you know nothing.
475　So, muddy with contempt my words and Creon's!
Misery shall grind no man as it will you.

OEDIPUS: Is it endurable that I should hear
such words from him? Go and a curse go with you!
Quick, home with you! Out of my house at once!
480　TEIRESIAS: I would not have come either had you not called me.
OEDIPUS: I did not know then you would talk like a fool—
or it would have been long before I called you.

---

4. Prophetic knowledge derived from observing the flight of birds, or sometimes from inspecting bird
entrails.　5. Yet another name for Apollo.　6. The mountain where Oedipus was abandoned as a child.

TEIRESIAS: I am a fool then, as it seems to you—
    but to the parents who have bred you, wise.
OEDIPUS: What parents? Stop! Who are they of all the world?   485
TEIRESIAS: This day will show your birth and will destroy you.
OEDIPUS: How needlessly your riddles darken everything.
TEIRESIAS: But it's in riddle answering you are strongest.
OEDIPUS: Yes. Taunt me where you will find me great.
TEIRESIAS: It is this very luck that has destroyed you.   490
OEDIPUS: I do not care, if it has saved this city.
TEIRESIAS: Well, I will go. Come, boy, lead me away.
OEDIPUS: Yes, lead him off. So long as you are here,
    you'll be a stumbling block and a vexation;
    once gone, you will not trouble me again.
TEIRESIAS: I have said   495
    what I came here to say not fearing your
    countenance: there is no way you can hurt me.
    I tell you, king, this man, this murderer
    (whom you have long declared you are in search of,
    indicting him in threatening proclamation   500
    as murderer of Laius)—he is here.
    In name he is a stranger among citizens
    but soon he will be shown to be a citizen
    true native Theban, and he'll have no joy
    of the discovery: blindness for sight   505
    and beggary for riches his exchange,
    he shall go journeying to a foreign country
    tapping his way before him with a stick.
    He shall be proved father and brother both
    to his own children in his house; to her   510
    that gave him birth, a son and husband both;
    a fellow sower in his father's bed
    with that same father that he murdered.
    Go within, reckon that out, and if you find me
    mistaken, say I have no skill in prophecy.   515

        [*Exeunt separately* TEIRESIAS *and* OEDIPUS.]

CHORUS: [*Strophe.*] Who is the man proclaimed
    by Delphi's[7] prophetic rock
    as the bloody handed murderer,
    the doer of deeds that none dare name?
    Now is the time for him to run   520
    with a stronger foot
    than Pegasus[8]
    for the child of Zeus leaps in arms upon him
    with fire and the lightning bolt,

---

7. Location of Greece's most important shrine to Apollo, renowned for its oracle.
8. Winged horse.

525   and terribly close on his heels
are the Fates[9] that never miss.

    [*Antistrophe.*]

Lately from snowy Parnassus[1]
clearly the voice flashed forth,
bidding each Theban track him down,
530   the unknown murderer.
In the savage forests he lurks and in
the caverns like
the mountain bull.
He is sad and lonely, and lonely his feet
535   that carry him far from the navel of earth;
but its prophecies, ever living,
flutter around his head.

    [*Strophe.*]

The augur has spread confusion,
terrible confusion;
540   I do not approve what was said
nor can I deny it.
I do not know what to say;
I am in a flutter of foreboding;
I never heard in the present
545   nor past of a quarrel between
the sons of Labdacus and Polybus,[2]
that I might bring as proof
in attacking the popular fame
of Oedipus, seeking
550   to take vengeance for undiscovered
death in the line of Labdacus.

    [*Antistrophe.*]

Truly Zeus and Apollo are wise
and in human things all knowing;
but amongst men there is no
555   distinct judgment, between the prophet
and me—which of us is right.
One man may pass another in wisdom
but I would never agree
with those that find fault with the king
560   till I should see the word
proved right beyond doubt. For once
in visible form the Sphinx
came on him and all of us
saw his wisdom and in that test
565   he saved the city. So he will not be condemned by my mind.

---

9. Goddesses who decide the course of human life.   1. Mountain sacred to Apollo.
2. King who adopted Oedipus.

[*Enter* CREON.]

CREON: Citizens, I have come because I heard
   deadly words spread about me, that the king
   accuses me. I cannot take that from him.
   If he believes that in these present troubles
   he has been wronged by me in word or deed   570
   I do not want to live on with the burden
   of such a scandal on me. The report
   injures me doubly and most vitally—
   for I'll be called a traitor to my city
   and traitor also to my friends and you.   575
CHORUS: Perhaps it was a sudden gust of anger
   that forced that insult from him, and no judgment.
CREON: But did he say that it was in compliance
   with schemes of mine that the seer told him lies?
CHORUS: Yes, he said that, but why, I do not know.   580
CREON: Were his eyes straight in his head? Was his mind right
   when he accused me in this fashion?
CHORUS: I do not know; I have no eyes to see
   what princes do. Here comes the king himself.

[*Enter* OEDIPUS.]

OEDIPUS: You, sir, how is it you come here? Have you so much   585
   brazen-faced daring that you venture in
   my house although you are proved manifestly
   the murderer of that man, and though you tried,
   openly, highway robbery of my crown?
   For God's sake, tell me what you saw in me,   590
   what cowardice or what stupidity,
   that made you lay a plot like this against me?
   Did you imagine I should not observe
   the crafty scheme that stole upon me or
   seeing it, take no means to counter it?   595
   Was it not stupid of you to make the attempt,
   to try to hunt down royal power without
   the people at your back or friends? For only
   with the people at your back or money can
   the hunt end in the capture of a crown.   600
CREON: Do you know what you're doing? Will you listen
   to words to answer yours, and then pass judgment?
OEDIPUS: You're quick to speak, but I am slow to grasp you,
   for I have found you dangerous,—and my foe.
CREON: First of all hear what I shall say to that.   605
OEDIPUS: At least don't tell me that you are not guilty.
CREON: If you think obstinacy without wisdom
   a valuable possession, you are wrong.
OEDIPUS: And you are wrong if you believe that one,
   a criminal, will not be punished only   610
   because he is my kinsman.

CREON: This is but just—
  but tell me, then, of what offense I'm guilty?
OEDIPUS: Did you or did you not urge me to send
  to this prophetic mumbler?
CREON: I did indeed,
615 and I shall stand by what I told you.
OEDIPUS: How long ago is it since Laius . . .
CREON: What about Laius? I don't understand.
OEDIPUS: Vanished—died—was murdered?
CREON: It is long,
  a long, long time to reckon.
OEDIPUS: Was this prophet
  in the profession then?
620 CREON: He was, and honoured
  as highly as he is today.
OEDIPUS: At that time did he say a word about me?
CREON: Never, at least when I was near him.
OEDIPUS: You never made a search for the dead man?
625 CREON: We searched, indeed, but never learned of anything.
OEDIPUS: Why did our wise old friend not say this then?
CREON: I don't know; and when I know nothing, I
  usually hold my tongue.
OEDIPUS: You know this much,
  and can declare this much if you are loyal.
630 CREON: What is it? If I know, I'll not deny it.
OEDIPUS: That he would not have said that I killed Laius
  had he not met you first.
CREON: You know yourself
  whether he said this, but I demand that I
  should hear as much from you as you from me.
635 OEDIPUS: Then hear,—I'll not be proved a murderer.
CREON: Well, then. You're married to my sister.
OEDIPUS: Yes,
  that I am not disposed to deny.
CREON: You rule
  this country giving her an equal share
  in the government?
OEDIPUS: Yes, everything she wants
  she has from me.
640 CREON: And I, as thirdsman to you,
  am rated as the equal of you two?
OEDIPUS: Yes, and it's there you've proved yourself false friend.
CREON: Not if you will reflect on it as I do.
  Consider, first, if you think anyone
645 would choose to rule and fear rather than rule
  and sleep untroubled by a fear if power
  were equal in both cases. I, at least,
  I was not born with such a frantic yearning
  to be a king—but to do what kings do.

And so it is with everyone who has learned 650
wisdom and self-control. As it stands now,
the prizes are all mine—and without fear.
But if I were the king myself, I must
do much that went against the grain.
How should despotic rule seem sweeter to me 655
than painless power and an assured authority?
I am not so besotted yet that I
want other honours than those that come with profit.
Now every man's my pleasure; every man greets me;
now those who are your suitors fawn on me,— 660
success for them depends upon my favour.
Why should I let all this go to win that?
My mind would not be traitor if it's wise;
I am no treason lover, of my nature,
nor would I ever dare to join a plot. 665
Prove what I say. Go to the oracle
at Pytho and inquire about the answers,
if they are as I told you. For the rest,
if you discover I laid any plot
together with the seer, kill me, I say, 670
not only by your vote but by my own.
But do not charge me on obscure opinion
without some proof to back it. It's not just
lightly to count your knaves as honest men,
nor honest men as knaves. To throw away 675
an honest friend is, as it were, to throw
your life away, which a man loves the best.
In time you will know all with certainty;
time is the only test of honest men,
one day is space enough to know a rogue. 680
CHORUS: His words are wise, king, if one fears to fall.
Those who are quick of temper are not safe.
OEDIPUS: When he that plots against me secretly
moves quickly, I must quickly counterplot.
If I wait taking no decisive measure 685
his business will be done, and mine be spoiled.
CREON: What do you want to do then? Banish me?
OEDIPUS: No, certainly; kill you, not banish you.[3]
CREON: I do not think that you've your wits about you.
OEDIPUS: For my own interests, yes.
CREON: But for mine, too, 690
you should think equally.
OEDIPUS: You are a rogue.

---

3. *Translator's note*: Two lines omitted here owing to the confusion in the dialogue consequent on the loss of a third line. The lines as they stand in Jebb's edition (1902) are: OED: That you may show what manner of thing is envy. / CREON: You speak as one that will not yield or trust. / [OED: *lost line*.]

CREON: Suppose you do not understand?

OEDIPUS: But yet
I must be ruler.

CREON: Not if you rule badly.

OEDIPUS: O, city, city!

CREON: I too have some share
695   in the city; it is not yours alone.

CHORUS: Stop, my lords! Here—and in the nick of time
I see Jocasta coming from the house;
with her help lay the quarrel that now stirs you.

[*Enter* JOCASTA.]

JOCASTA: For shame! Why have you raised this foolish squabbling
700   brawl? Are you not ashamed to air your private
griefs when the country's sick? Go in, you, Oedipus,
and you, too, Creon, into the house. Don't magnify
your nothing troubles.

CREON: Sister, Oedipus,
your husband, thinks he has the right to do
705   terrible wrongs—he has but to choose between
two terrors: banishing or killing me.

OEDIPUS: He's right, Jocasta; for I find him plotting
with knavish tricks against my person.

CREON: That God may never bless me! May I die
710   accursed, if I have been guilty of
one tittle of the charge you bring against me!

JOCASTA: I beg you, Oedipus, trust him in this,
spare him for the sake of this his oath to God,
for my sake, and the sake of those who stand here.

715 CHORUS: Be gracious, be merciful,
we beg of you.

OEDIPUS: In what would you have me yield?

CHORUS: He has been no silly child in the past.
He is strong in his oath now.
720   Spare him.

OEDIPUS: Do you know what you ask?

CHORUS: Yes.

OEDIPUS: Tell me then.

CHORUS: He has been your friend before all men's eyes; do not cast him
725   away dishonoured on an obscure conjecture.

OEDIPUS: I would have you know that this request of yours
really requests my death or banishment.

CHORUS: May the Sun God,[4] king of Gods, forbid! May I die without God's
blessing, without friends' help, if I had any such thought. But my
730   spirit is broken by my unhappiness for my wasting country; and
this would but add troubles amongst ourselves to the other troubles.

OEDIPUS: Well, let him go then—if I must die ten times for it,

---

4. Helios, closely associated with Apollo, the god of light.

or be sent out dishonoured into exile.
It is your lips that prayed for him I pitied,
not his; wherever he is, I shall hate him.   735
CREON: I see you sulk in yielding and you're dangerous
when you are out of temper; natures like yours
are justly heaviest for themselves to bear.
OEDIPUS: Leave me alone! Take yourself off, I tell you.
CREON: I'll go, you have not known me, but they have,   740
and they have known my innocence.

    [*Exit.*]

CHORUS: Won't you take him inside, lady?
JOCASTA: Yes, when I've found out what was the matter.
CHORUS: There was some misconceived suspicion of a story, and on the other
side the sting of injustice.   745
JOCASTA: So, on both sides?
CHORUS: Yes.
JOCASTA: What was the story?
CHORUS: I think it best, in the interests of the country, to leave it where it ended.
OEDIPUS: You see where you have ended, straight of judgment   750
although you are, by softening my anger.
CHORUS: Sir, I have said before and I say again—be sure that I would have been
proved a madman, bankrupt in sane council, if I should put you away, you
who steered the country I love safely when she was crazed with troubles. God
grant that now, too, you may prove a fortunate guide for us. 755
JOCASTA: Tell me, my lord, I beg of you, what was it
that roused your anger so?
OEDIPUS: Yes, I will tell you.
I honour you more than I honour them.
It was Creon and the plots he laid against me.
JOCASTA: Tell me—if you can clearly tell the quarrel—   760
OEDIPUS: Creon says
that I'm the murderer of Laius.
JOCASTA: Of his own knowledge or on information?
OEDIPUS: He sent this rascal prophet to me, since
he keeps his own mouth clean of any guilt.
JOCASTA: Do not concern yourself about this matter;   765
listen to me and learn that human beings
have no part in the craft of prophecy.
Of that I'll show you a short proof.
There was an oracle once that came to Laius,—
I will not say that it was Phoebus' own,   770
but it was from his servants—and it told him
that it was fate that he should die a victim
at the hands of his own son, a son to be born
of Laius and me. But, see now, he,
the king, was killed by foreign highway robbers   775
at a place where three roads meet—so goes the story;
and for the son—before three days were out

after his birth King Laius pierced his ankles
and by the hands of others cast him forth
780   upon a pathless hillside. So Apollo
failed to fulfill his oracle to the son,
that he should kill his father, and to Laius
also proved false in that the thing he feared,
death at his son's hands, never came to pass.
785   So clear in this case were the oracles,
so clear and false. Give them no heed, I say;
what God discovers need of, easily
he shows to us himself.

OEDIPUS: O dear Jocasta,
as I hear this from you, there comes upon me
790   a wandering of the soul—I could run mad.

JOCASTA: What trouble is it, that you turn again
and speak like this?

OEDIPUS: I thought I heard you say
that Laius was killed at a crossroads.

JOCASTA: Yes, that was how the story went and still
that word goes round.

795   OEDIPUS: Where is this place, Jocasta,
where he was murdered?

JOCASTA: Phocis is the country
and the road splits there, one of two roads from Delphi,
another comes from Daulia.

OEDIPUS: How long ago is this?

JOCASTA: The news came to the city just before
800   you became king and all men's eyes looked to you.
What is it, Oedipus, that's in your mind?

OEDIPUS: What have you designed, O Zeus, to do with me?

JOCASTA: What is the thought that troubles your heart?

OEDIPUS: Don't ask me yet—tell me of Laius—
805   How did he look? How old or young was he?

JOCASTA: He was a tall man and his hair was grizzled
already—nearly white—and in his form
not unlike you.

OEDIPUS: O God, I think I have
called curses on myself in ignorance.

810   JOCASTA: What do you mean? I am terrified
when I look at you.

OEDIPUS: I have a deadly fear
that the old seer had eyes. You'll show me more
if you can tell me one more thing.

JOCASTA: I will.
I'm frightened,—but if I can understand,
I'll tell you all you ask.

815   OEDIPUS: How was his company?
Had he few with him when he went this journey,
or many servants, as would suit a prince?

JOCASTA: In all there were but five, and among them
    a herald; and one carriage for the king.

OEDIPUS: It's plain—it's plain—who was it told you this?   820

JOCASTA: The only servant that escaped safe home.

OEDIPUS: Is he at home now?

JOCASTA: No, when he came home again
    and saw you king and Laius was dead,
    he came to me and touched my hand and begged
    that I should send him to the fields to be   825
    my shepherd and so he might see the city
    as far off as he might. So I
    sent him away. He was an honest man,
    as slaves go, and was worthy of far more
    than what he asked of me.   830

OEDIPUS: O, how I wish that he could come back quickly!

JOCASTA: He can. Why is your heart so set on this?

OEDIPUS: O dear Jocasta, I am full of fears
    that I have spoken far too much; and therefore
    I wish to see this shepherd.

JOCASTA: He will come;   835
    but, Oedipus, I think I'm worthy too
    to know what it is that disquiets you.

OEDIPUS: It shall not be kept from you, since my mind
    has gone so far with its forebodings. Whom
    should I confide in rather than you, who is there   840
    of more importance to me who have passed
    through such a fortune?
    Polybus was my father, king of Corinth,
    and Merope, the Dorian, my mother.
    I was held greatest of the citizens   845
    in Corinth till a curious chance befell me
    as I shall tell you—curious, indeed,
    but hardly worth the store I set upon it.
    There was a dinner and at it a man,
    a drunken man, accused me in his drink   850
    of being bastard. I was furious
    but held my temper under for that day.
    Next day I went and taxed my parents with it;
    they took the insult very ill from him,
    the drunken fellow who had uttered it.   855
    So I was comforted for their part, but
    still this thing rankled always, for the story
    crept about widely. And I went at last
    to Pytho, though my parents did not know.
    But Phoebus sent me home again unhonoured   860
    in what I came to learn, but he foretold
    other and desperate horrors to befall me,
    that I was fated to lie with my mother,
    and show to daylight an accursed breed

865   which men would not endure, and I was doomed
        to be murderer of the father that begot me.
        When I heard this I fled, and in the days
        that followed I would measure from the stars
        the whereabouts of Corinth—yes, I fled
870   to somewhere where I should not see fulfilled
        the infamies told in that dreadful oracle.
        And as I journeyed I came to the place
        where, as you say, this king met with his death.
        Jocasta, I will tell you the whole truth.
875   When I was near the branching of the crossroads,
        going on foot, I was encountered by
        a herald and a carriage with a man in it,
        just as you tell me. He that led the way
        and the old man himself wanted to thrust me
880   out of the road by force. I became angry
        and struck the coachman who was pushing me.
        When the old man saw this he watched his moment,
        and as I passed he struck me from his carriage,
        full on the head with his two pointed goad.
885   But he was paid in full and presently
        my stick had struck him backwards from the car
        and he rolled out of it. And then I killed them
        all. If it happened there was any tie
        of kinship twixt this man and Laius,
890   who is then now more miserable than I,
        what man on earth so hated by the Gods,
        since neither citizen nor foreigner
        may welcome me at home or even greet me,
        but drive me out of doors? And it is I,
895   I and no other have so cursed myself.
        And I pollute the bed of him I killed
        by the hands that killed him. Was I not born evil?
        Am I not utterly unclean? I had to fly
        and in my banishment not even see
900   my kindred nor set foot in my own country,
        or otherwise my fate was to be yoked
        in marriage with my mother and kill my father,
        Polybus who begot me and had reared me.
        Would not one rightly judge and say that on me
905   these things were sent by some malignant God?
        O no, no, no—O holy majesty
        of God on high, may I not see that day!
        May I be gone out of men's sight before
        I see the deadly taint of this disaster
910   come upon me.

CHORUS: Sir, we too fear these things. But until you see this man face to face and
    hear his story, hope.

OEDIPUS: Yes, I have just this much of hope—to wait until the herdsman comes.

JOCASTA: And when he comes, what do you want with him?

OEDIPUS: I'll tell you; if I find that his story is the same as yours, I at least will be 915
clear of this guilt.

JOCASTA: Why what so particularly did you learn from my story?

OEDIPUS: You said that he spoke of highway *robbers* who killed Laius. Now if he
uses the same number, it was not I who killed him. One man cannot be the
same as many. But if he speaks of a man travelling alone, then clearly the bur- 920
den of the guilt inclines towards me.

JOCASTA: Be sure, at least, that this was how he told the story. He cannot unsay
it now, for everyone in the city heard it—not I alone. But, Oedipus, even if
he diverges from what he said then, he shall never prove that the murder of
Laius squares rightly with the prophecy—for Loxias declared that the king 925
should be killed by his own son. And that poor creature did not kill him
surely,—for he died himself first. So as far as prophecy goes, henceforward I
shall not look to the right hand or the left.

OEDIPUS: Right. But yet, send someone for the peasant to bring him here; do
not neglect it. 930

JOCASTA: I will send quickly. Now let me go indoors. I will do nothing except
what pleases you.

[*Exeunt.*]

CHORUS: [*Strophe.*] May destiny ever find me
pious in word and deed
prescribed by the laws that live on high: 935
laws begotten in the clear air of heaven,
whose only father is Olympus;
no mortal nature brought them to birth,
no forgetfulness shall lull them to sleep;
for God is great in them and grows not old. 940

[*Antistrophe.*]

Insolence breeds the tyrant, insolence
if it is glutted with a surfeit, unseasonable, unprofitable,
climbs to the roof-top and plunges
sheer down to the ruin that must be,
and there its feet are no service. 945
But I pray that the God may never
abolish the eager ambition that profits the state.
For I shall never cease to hold the God as our protector.

[*Strophe.*]

If a man walks with haughtiness
of hand or word and gives no heed 950
to Justice and the shrines of Gods
despises—may an evil doom
smite him for his ill-starred pride of heart!—
if he reaps gains without justice
and will not hold from impiety 955
and his fingers itch for untouchable things.
When such things are done, what man shall contrive
to shield his soul from the shafts of the God?

When such deeds are held in honour,
960   why should I honour the Gods in the dance?

[*Antistrophe.*]

No longer to the holy place,
to the navel of earth I'll go
to worship, nor to Abae[5]
nor to Olympia,
965   unless the oracles are proved to fit,
for all men's hands to point at.
O Zeus, if you are rightly called
the sovereign lord, all-mastering,
let this not escape you nor your ever-living power!
970   The oracles concerning Laius
are old and dim and men regard them not.
Apollo is nowhere clear in honour; God's service perishes.

[*Enter* JOCASTA, *carrying garlands.*]

JOCASTA: Princes of the land, I have had the thought to go
to the Gods' temples, bringing in my hand
975   garlands and gifts of incense, as you see.
For Oedipus excites himself too much
at every sort of trouble, not conjecturing,
like a man of sense, what will be from what was,
but he is always at the speaker's mercy,
980   when he speaks terrors. I can do no good
by my advice, and so I came as suppliant
to you, Lycaean Apollo, who are nearest.
These are the symbols of my prayer and this
my prayer: grant us escape free of the curse.
985   Now when we look to him we are all afraid;
he's pilot of our ship and he is frightened.

[*Enter* MESSENGER.]

MESSENGER: Might I learn from you, sirs, where is the house of Oedipus? Or best
of all, if you know, where is the king himself?
CHORUS: This is his house and he is within doors. This lady is his wife and
990   mother of his children.
MESSENGER: God bless you, lady, and God bless your household! God bless Oedi-
pus' noble wife!
JOCASTA: God bless you, sir, for your kind greeting! What do you want of us that
you have come here? What have you to tell us?
995   MESSENGER: Good news, lady. Good for your house and for your husband.
JOCASTA: What is your news? Who sent you to us?
MESSENGER: I come from Corinth and the news I bring will give you pleasure.
Perhaps a little pain too.

5. Site of one of Apollo's oracles. *Olympia*: mountain in Greece said to be the home of Zeus and the other
principal gods.

JOCASTA: What is this news of double meaning?

MESSENGER: The people of the Isthmus[6] will choose Oedipus to be their king.   1000
    That is the rumour there.

JOCASTA: But isn't their king still old Polybus?

MESSENGER: No. He is in his grave. Death has got him.

JOCASTA: Is that the truth? Is Oedipus' father dead?

MESSENGER: May I die myself if it be otherwise!   1005

JOCASTA: [*To a* SERVANT.] Be quick and run to the King with the news! O oracles
    of the Gods, where are you now? It was from this man Oedipus fled, lest he
    should be his murderer! And now he is dead, in the course of nature, and not
    killed by Oedipus.

    [*Enter* OEDIPUS.]

OEDIPUS: Dearest Jocasta, why have you sent for me?   1010

JOCASTA: Listen to this man and when you hear reflect what is the outcome of the
    holy oracles of the Gods.

OEDIPUS: Who is he? What is his message for me?

JOCASTA: He is from Corinth and he tells us that your father Polybus is dead and
    gone.   1015

OEDIPUS: What's this you say, sir? Tell me yourself.

MESSENGER: Since this is the first matter you want clearly told: Polybus has gone
    down to death. You may be sure of it.

OEDIPUS: By treachery or sickness?

MESSENGER: A small thing will put old bodies asleep.   1020

OEDIPUS: So he died of sickness, it seems,—poor old man!

MESSENGER: Yes, and of age—the long years he had measured.

OEDIPUS: Ha! Ha! O dear Jocasta, why should one
    look to the Pythian hearth?[7] Why should one look
    to the birds screaming overhead? They prophesied   1025
    that I should kill my father! But he's dead,
    and hidden deep in earth, and I stand here
    who never laid a hand on spear against him,—
    unless perhaps he died of longing for me,
    and thus I am his murderer. But they,   1030
    the oracles, as they stand—he's taken them
    away with him, they're dead as he himself is,
    and worthless.

JOCASTA: That I told you before now.

OEDIPUS: You did, but I was misled by my fear.

JOCASTA: Then lay no more of them to heart, not one.   1035

OEDIPUS: But surely I must fear my mother's bed?

JOCASTA: Why should man fear since chance is all in all
    for him, and he can clearly foreknow nothing?
    Best to live lightly, as one can, unthinkingly.
    As to your mother's marriage bed,—don't fear it.   1040
    Before this, in dreams too, as well as oracles,

---

6. That is, Corinth, the city-state located on the isthmus connecting the Peloponnesian peninsula with
mainland Greece.   7. Delphi.

many a man has lain with his own mother.
But he to whom such things are nothing bears
his life most easily.

1045 OEDIPUS: All that you say would be said perfectly
if she were dead; but since she lives I must
still fear, although you talk so well, Jocasta.

JOCASTA: Still in your father's death there's light of comfort?

OEDIPUS: Great light of comfort; but I fear the living.

1050 MESSENGER: Who is the woman that makes you afraid?

OEDIPUS: Merope, old man, Polybus' wife.

MESSENGER: What about her frightens the queen and you?

OEDIPUS: A terrible oracle, stranger, from the Gods.

MESSENGER: Can it be told? Or does the sacred law

1055 forbid another to have knowledge of it?

OEDIPUS: O no! Once on a time Loxias said
that I should lie with my own mother and
take on my hands the blood of my own father.
And so for these long years I've lived away

1060 from Corinth; it has been to my great happiness;
but yet it's sweet to see the face of parents.

MESSENGER: This was the fear which drove you out of Corinth?

OEDIPUS: Old man, I did not wish to kill my father.

MESSENGER: Why should I not free you from this fear, sir,

1065 since I have come to you in all goodwill?

OEDIPUS: You would not find me thankless if you did.

MESSENGER: Why, it was just for this I brought the news,—
to earn your thanks when you had come safe home.

OEDIPUS: No, I will never come near my parents.

MESSENGER: Son,

1070 it's very plain you don't know what you're doing.

OEDIPUS: What do you mean, old man? For God's sake, tell me.

MESSENGER: If your homecoming is checked by fears like these.

OEDIPUS: Yes, I'm afraid that Phoebus may prove right.

MESSENGER: The murder and the incest?

OEDIPUS: Yes, old man;
that is my constant terror.

1075 MESSENGER: Do you know
that all your fears are empty?

OEDIPUS: How is that,
if they are father and mother and I their son?

MESSENGER: Because Polybus was no kin to you in blood.

OEDIPUS: What, was not Polybus my father?

MESSENGER: No more than I but just so much.

1080 OEDIPUS: How can
my father be my father as much as one
that's nothing to me?

MESSENGER: Neither he nor I
begat you.

OEDIPUS: Why then did he call me son?

MESSENGER: A gift he took you from these hands of mine.
OEDIPUS: Did he love so much what he took from another's hand?   1085
MESSENGER: His childlessness before persuaded him.
OEDIPUS: Was I a child you bought or found when I
    was given to him?
MESSENGER: On Cithaeron's slopes
    in the twisting thickets you were found.
OEDIPUS: And why
    were you a traveller in those parts?
MESSENGER: I was   1090
    in charge of mountain flocks.
OEDIPUS: You were a shepherd?
    A hireling vagrant?
MESSENGER: Yes, but at least at that time
    the man that saved your life, son.
OEDIPUS: What ailed me when you took me in your arms?
MESSENGER: In that your ankles should be witnesses.   1095
OEDIPUS: Why do you speak of that old pain?
MESSENGER: I loosed you;
    the tendons of your feet were pierced and fettered,—
OEDIPUS: My swaddling clothes brought me a rare disgrace.
MESSENGER: So that from this you're called your present name.[8]
OEDIPUS: Was this my father's doing or my mother's?   1100
    For God's sake, tell me.
MESSENGER: I don't know, but he
    who gave you to me has more knowledge than I.
OEDIPUS: You yourself did not find me then? You took me
    from someone else?
MESSENGER: Yes, from another shepherd.
OEDIPUS: Who was he? Do you know him well enough   1105
    to tell?
MESSENGER: He was called Laius' man.
OEDIPUS: You mean the king who reigned here in the old days?
MESSENGER: Yes, he was that man's shepherd.
OEDIPUS: Is he alive
    still, so that I could see him?
MESSENGER: You who live here
    would know that best.
OEDIPUS: Do any of you here   1110
    know of this shepherd whom he speaks about
    in town or in the fields? Tell me. It's time
    that this was found out once for all.
CHORUS: I think he is none other than the peasant
    whom you have sought to see already; but   1115
    Jocasta here can tell us best of that.
OEDIPUS: Jocasta, do you know about this man
    whom we have sent for? Is he the man he mentions?

8. *Oedipus* means, literally, "swollen foot" (cf. lines 777–80).

JOCASTA: Why ask of whom he spoke? Don't give it heed;
1120   nor try to keep in mind what has been said.
         It will be wasted labour.

OEDIPUS: With such clues
         I could not fail to bring my birth to light.

JOCASTA: I beg you—do not hunt this out—I beg you,
         if you have any care for your own life.
         What I am suffering is enough.

1125 OEDIPUS: Keep up
         your heart, Jocasta. Though I'm proved a slave,
         thrice slave, and though my mother is thrice slave,
         you'll not be shown to be of lowly lineage.

JOCASTA: O be persuaded by me, I entreat you;
1130   do not do this.

OEDIPUS: I will not be persuaded to let be
         the chance of finding out the whole thing clearly.

JOCASTA: It is because I wish you well that I
         give you this counsel—and it's the best counsel.

1135 OEDIPUS: Then the best counsel vexes me, and has
         for some while since.

JOCASTA: O Oedipus, God help you!
         God keep you from the knowledge of who you are!

OEDIPUS: Here, someone, go and fetch the shepherd for me;
         and let her find her joy in her rich family!

1140 JOCASTA: O Oedipus, unhappy Oedipus!
         that is all I can call you, and the last thing
         that I shall ever call you.

         [*Exit.*]

CHORUS: Why has the queen gone, Oedipus, in wild
         grief rushing from us? I am afraid that trouble
1145   will break out of this silence.

OEDIPUS: Break out what will! I at least shall be
         willing to see my ancestry, though humble.
         Perhaps she is ashamed of my low birth,
         for she has all a woman's high-flown pride.
1150   But I account myself a child of Fortune,
         beneficent Fortune, and I shall not be
         dishonoured. She's the mother from whom I spring;
         the months, my brothers, marked me, now as small,
         and now again as mighty. Such is my breeding,
1155   and I shall never prove so false to it,
         as not to find the secret of my birth.

CHORUS: [*Strophe.*] If I am a prophet and wise of heart
         you shall not fail, Cithaeron,
         by the limitless sky, you shall not!—
1160   to know at tomorrow's full moon
         that Oedipus honours you,
         as native to him and mother and nurse at once;

and that you are honoured in dancing by us, as finding favour in sight of
our king.
Apollo, to whom we cry, find these things pleasing!

[*Antistrophe.*]

Who was it bore you, child? One of   1165
the long-lived nymphs who lay with Pan[9]—
the father who treads the hills?
Or was she a bride of Loxias, your mother? The grassy slopes
are all of them dear to him. Or perhaps Cyllene's[1] king
or the Bacchants' God[2] that lives on the tops   1170
of the hills received you a gift from some
one of the Helicon Nymphs,[3] with whom he mostly plays?

[*Enter an* OLD MAN, *led by* OEDIPUS' *servants.*]

OEDIPUS: If someone like myself who never met him
may make a guess,—I think this is the herdsman,
whom we were seeking. His old age is consonant   1175
with the other. And besides, the men who bring him
I recognize as my own servants. You
perhaps may better me in knowledge since
you've seen the man before.
CHORUS: You can be sure
I recognize him. For if Laius   1180
had ever an honest shepherd, this was he.
OEDIPUS: You, sir, from Corinth, I must ask you first,
is this the man you spoke of?
MESSENGER: This is he
before your eyes.
OEDIPUS: Old man, look here at me
and tell me what I ask you. Were you ever   1185
a servant of King Laius?
HERDSMAN: I was,—
no slave he bought but reared in his own house.
OEDIPUS: What did you do as work? How did you live?
HERDSMAN: Most of my life was spent among the flocks.
OEDIPUS: In what part of the country did you live?   1190
HERDSMAN: Cithaeron and the places near to it.
OEDIPUS: And somewhere there perhaps you knew this man?
HERDSMAN: What was his occupation? Who?
OEDIPUS: This man here,
have you had any dealings with him?
HERDSMAN: No—
not such that I can quickly call to mind.   1195

9. God of nature; half man, half goat.
1. Mountain reputed to be the birthplace of Hermes, the messenger god. 2. Dionysus.
3. The Muses; nine sister goddesses who presided over poetry, music, and the arts.

MESSENGER: That is no wonder, master. But I'll make him remember what he
does not know. For I know, that he well knows the country of Cithaeron, how
he with two flocks, I with one kept company for three years—each year half a
year—from spring till autumn time and then when winter came I drove my
1200 flocks to our fold home again and he to Laius' steadings. Well—am I right or
not in what I said we did?

HERDSMAN: You're right—although it's a long time ago.

MESSENGER: Do you remember giving me a child
to bring up as my foster child?

HERDSMAN: What's this?
Why do you ask this question?

1205 MESSENGER: Look old man,
here he is—here's the man who was that child!

HERDSMAN: Death take you! Won't you hold your tongue?

OEDIPUS: No, no,
do not find fault with him, old man. Your words
are more at fault than his.

HERDSMAN: O best of masters,
how do I give offense?

1210 OEDIPUS: When you refuse
to speak about the child of whom he asks you.

HERDSMAN: He speaks out of his ignorance, without meaning.

OEDIPUS: If you'll not talk to gratify me, you
will talk with pain to urge you.

HERDSMAN: O please, sir,
don't hurt an old man, sir.

1215 OEDIPUS: [To the SERVANTS.] Here, one of you,
twist his hands behind him.

HERDSMAN: Why, God help me, why?
What do you want to know?

OEDIPUS: You gave a child
to him,—the child he asked you of?

HERDSMAN: I did.
I wish I'd died the day I did.

OEDIPUS: You will
unless you tell me truly.

1220 HERDSMAN: And I'll die
far worse if I should tell you.

OEDIPUS: This fellow
is bent on more delays, as it would seem.

HERDSMAN: O no, no! I have told you that I gave it.

OEDIPUS: Where did you get this child from? Was it your own or did you get it
from another?

1225 HERDSMAN: Not
my own at all; I had it from someone.

OEDIPUS: One of these citizens? or from what house?

HERDSMAN: O master, please—I beg you, master, please don't ask me more.

OEDIPUS: You're a dead man if I
ask you again.

HERDSMAN: It was one of the children   1230
    of Laius.
OEDIPUS: A slave? Or born in wedlock?
HERDSMAN: O God, I am on the brink of frightful speech.
OEDIPUS: And I of frightful hearing. But I must hear.
HERDSMAN: The child was called his child; but she within,
    your wife would tell you best how all this was.   1235
OEDIPUS: *She* gave it to you?
HERDSMAN: Yes, she did, my lord.
OEDIPUS: To do what with it?
HERDSMAN: Make away with it.
OEDIPUS: She was so hard—its mother?
HERDSMAN: Aye, through fear
    of evil oracles.
OEDIPUS: Which?
HERDSMAN: They said that he
    should kill his parents.
OEDIPUS: How was it that you   1240
    gave it away to this old man?
HERDSMAN: O master,
    I pitied it, and thought that I could send it
    off to another country and this man
    was from another country. But he saved it
    for the most terrible troubles. If you are   1245
    the man he says you are, you're bred to misery.
OEDIPUS: O, O, O, they will all come,
    all come out clearly! Light of the sun, let me
    look upon you no more after today!
    I who first saw the light bred of a match   1250
    accursed, and accursed in my living
    with them I lived with, cursed in my killing.

    [*Exeunt all but the* CHORUS.]

CHORUS: [*Strophe.*] O generations of men, how I
    count you as equal with those who live
    not at all!   1255
    What man, what man on earth wins more
    of happiness than a seeming
    and after that turning away?
    Oedipus, you are my pattern of this,
    Oedipus, you and your fate!   1260
    Luckless Oedipus, whom of all men
    I envy not at all.

    [*Antistrophe.*]

    In as much as he shot his bolt
    beyond the others and won the prize
    of happiness complete—   1265
    O Zeus—and killed and reduced to nought

the hooked taloned maid of the riddling speech,[4]
standing a tower against death for my land:
hence he was called my king and hence
1270   was honoured the highest of all
honours; and hence he ruled
in the great city of Thebes.

[*Strophe.*]

But now whose tale is more miserable?
Who is there lives with a savager fate?
1275   Whose troubles so reverse his life as his?

O Oedipus, the famous prince
for whom a great haven
the same both as father and son
sufficed for generation,
1280   how, O how, have the furrows ploughed
by your father endured to bear you, poor wretch,
and hold their peace so long?

[*Antistrophe.*]

Time who sees all has found you out
against your will; judges your marriage accursed,
1285   begetter and begot at one in it.

O child of Laius,
would I had never seen you.
I weep for you and cry
a dirge of lamentation.

1290   To speak directly, I drew my breath
from you at the first and so now I lull
my mouth to sleep with your name.

[*Enter a* SECOND MESSENGER.]

SECOND MESSENGER: O Princes always honoured by our country,
what deeds you'll hear of and what horrors see,
1295   what grief you'll feel, if you as true born Thebans
care for the house of Labdacus' sons.[5]
Phasis nor Ister cannot purge this house,
I think, with all their streams, such things
it hides, such evils shortly will bring forth
1300   into the light, whether they will or not;
and troubles hurt the most
when they prove self-inflicted.

---

4. The Sphinx, who killed herself when Oedipus was the first to give a correct answer to her riddle: "What walks on four feet in the morning, on two at noon, and on three in the evening?" (cf. line 41n.)
5. Labdacus, king of Thebes, was father of Laïus and grandfather of Oedipus. *Phasis ... Ister*: rivers near Thebes.

CHORUS: What we had known before did not fall short
    of bitter groaning's worth; what's more to tell?

SECOND MESSENGER: Shortest to hear and tell—our glorious queen   1305
    Jocasta's dead.

CHORUS: Unhappy woman! How?

SECOND MESSENGER: By her own hand. The worst of what was done
    you cannot know. You did not see the sight.
    Yet in so far as I remember it
    you'll hear the end of our unlucky queen.   1310
    When she came raging into the house she went
    straight to her marriage bed, tearing her hair
    with both her hands, and crying upon Laius
    long dead—Do you remember, Laius,
    that night long past which bred a child for us   1315
    to send you to your death and leave
    a mother making children with her son?
    And then she groaned and cursed the bed in which
    she brought forth husband by her husband, children
    by her own child, an infamous double bond.   1320
    How after that she died I do not know,—
    for Oedipus distracted us from seeing.
    He burst upon us shouting and we looked
    to him as he paced frantically around,
    begging us always: Give me a sword, I say,   1325
    to find this wife no wife, this mother's womb,
    this field of double sowing whence I sprang
    and where I sowed my children! As he raved
    some god showed him the way—none of us there.
    Bellowing terribly and led by some   1330
    invisible guide he rushed on the two doors,—
    wrenching the hollow bolts out of their sockets,
    he charged inside. There, there, we saw his wife
    hanging, the twisted rope around her neck.
    When he saw her, he cried out fearfully   1335
    and cut the dangling noose. Then, as she lay,
    poor woman, on the ground, what happened after,
    was terrible to see. He tore the brooches—
    the gold chased[6] brooches fastening her robe—
    away from her and lifting them up high   1340
    dashed them on his own eyeballs, shrieking out
    such things as: they will never see the crime
    I have committed or had done upon me!
    Dark eyes, now in the days to come look on
    forbidden faces, do not recognize   1345
    those whom you long for—with such imprecations
    he struck his eyes again and yet again
    with the brooches. And the bleeding eyeballs gushed

6. Decorated with ornamental indentations.

and stained his beard—no sluggish oozing drops
1350   but a black rain and bloody hail poured down.
So it has broken—and not on one head
but troubles mixed for husband and for wife.
The fortune of the days gone by was true
good fortune—but today groans and destruction
1355   and death and shame—of all ills can be named
not one is missing.
CHORUS: Is he now in any ease from pain?
SECOND MESSENGER: He shouts
for someone to unbar the doors and show him
to all the men of Thebes, his father's killer,
1360   his mother's—no I cannot say the word,
it is unholy—for he'll cast himself,
out of the land, he says, and not remain
to bring a curse upon his house, the curse
he called upon it in his proclamation. But
1365   he wants for strength, aye, and someone to guide him;
his sickness is too great to bear. You, too,
will be shown that. The bolts are opening.
Soon you will see a sight to waken pity
even in the horror of it.

[*Enter the blinded* OEDIPUS.]

1370 CHORUS: This is a terrible sight for men to see!
I never found a worse!
Poor wretch, what madness came upon you!
What evil spirit leaped upon your life
to your ill-luck—a leap beyond man's strength!
1375   Indeed I pity you, but I cannot
look at you, though there's much I want to ask
and much to learn and much to see.
I shudder at the sight of you.
OEDIPUS: O, O,
1380   where am I going? Where is my voice
borne on the wind to and fro?
Spirit, how far have you sprung?
CHORUS: To a terrible place whereof men's ears
may not hear, nor their eyes behold it.
1385 OEDIPUS: Darkness!
Horror of darkness enfolding, resistless, unspeakable visitant sped by an ill
   wind in haste!
Madness and stabbing pain and memory
of evil deeds I have done!
CHORUS: In such misfortunes it's no wonder
1390   if double weighs the burden of your grief.
OEDIPUS: My friend,
you are the only one steadfast, the only one that attends on me;
you still stay nursing the blind man.
Your care is not unnoticed. I can know

your voice, although this darkness is my world.   1395

CHORUS: Doer of dreadful deeds, how did you dare
    so far to do despite to your own eyes?
    what spirit urged you to it?

OEDIPUS: It was Apollo, friends, Apollo,
    that brought this bitter bitterness, my sorrows to completion.   1400
    But the hand that struck me
    was none but my own.
    Why should I see
    whose vision showed me nothing sweet to see?

CHORUS: These things are as you say.   1405

OEDIPUS: What can I see to love?
    What greeting can touch my ears with joy?
    Take me away, and haste—to a place out of the way!
    Take me away, my friends, the greatly miserable,
    the most accursed, whom God too hates   1410
    above all men on earth!

CHORUS: Unhappy in your mind and your misfortune,
    would I had never known you!

OEDIPUS: Curse on the man who took
    the cruel bonds from off my legs, as I lay in the field.   1415
    He stole me from death and saved me,
    no kindly service.
    Had I died then
    I would not be so burdensome to friends.

CHORUS: I, too, could have wished it had been so.   1420

OEDIPUS: Then I would not have come
    to kill my father and marry my mother infamously.
    Now I am godless and child of impurity,
    begetter in the same seed that created my wretched self.
    If there is any ill worse than ill,   1425
    that is the lot of Oedipus.

CHORUS: I cannot say your remedy was good;
    you would be better dead than blind and living.

OEDIPUS: What I have done here was best done—don't tell me
    otherwise, do not give me further counsel.   1430
    I do not know with what eyes I could look
    upon my father when I die and go
    under the earth, nor yet my wretched mother—
    those two to whom I have done things deserving
    worse punishment than hanging. Would the sight   1435
    of children, bred as mine are, gladden me?
    No, not these eyes, never. And my city,
    its towers and sacred places of the Gods,
    of these I robbed my miserable self
    when I commanded all to drive *him* out,   1440
    the criminal since proved by God impure
    and of the race of Laius.
    To this guilt I bore witness against myself—
    with what eyes shall I look upon my people?

1445   No. If there were a means to choke the fountain
of hearing I would not have stayed my hand
from locking up my miserable carcase,
seeing and hearing nothing; it is sweet
to keep our thoughts out of the range of hurt.

1450   Cithaeron, why did you receive me? why
having received me did you not kill me straight?
And so I had not shown to men my birth.

O Polybus and Corinth and the house,
the old house that I used to call my father's—
1455   what fairness you were nurse to, and what foulness
festered beneath! Now I am found to be
a sinner and a son of sinners. Crossroads,
and hidden glade, oak and the narrow way
at the crossroads, that drank my father's blood
1460   offered you by my hands, do you remember
still what I did as you looked on, and what
I did when I came here? O marriage, marriage!
you bred me and again when you had bred
bred children of your child and showed to men
1465   brides, wives and mothers and the foulest deeds
that can be in this world of ours.

Come—it's unfit to say what is unfit
to do.—I beg of you in God's name hide me
somewhere outside your country, yes, or kill me,
1470   or throw me into the sea, to be forever
out of your sight. Approach and deign to touch me
for all my wretchedness, and do not fear.
No man but I can bear my evil doom.

CHORUS: Here Creon comes in fit time to perform
1475   or give advice in what you ask of us.
Creon is left sole ruler in your stead.

OEDIPUS: Creon! Creon! What shall I say to him?
How can I justly hope that he will trust me?
In what is past I have been proved towards him
an utter liar.

    [*Enter* CREON.]

1480 CREON: Oedipus, I've come
not so that I might laugh at you nor taunt you
with evil of the past. But if you still
are without shame before the face of men
reverence at least the flame that gives all life,
1485   our Lord the Sun, and do not show unveiled
to him pollution such that neither land
nor holy rain nor light of day can welcome.

    [*To a* SERVANT.]

Be quick and take him in. It is most decent
that only kin should see and hear the troubles
of kin.

OEDIPUS: I beg you, since you've torn me from   1490
my dreadful expectations and have come
in a most noble spirit to a man
that has used you vilely—do a thing for me.
I shall speak for your own good, not for my own.

CREON: What do you need that you would ask of me?   1495

OEDIPUS: Drive me from here with all the speed you can
to where I may not hear a human voice.

CREON: Be sure, I would have done this had not I
wished first of all to learn from the God the course
of action I should follow.

OEDIPUS: But his word   1500
has been quite clear to let the parricide,
the sinner, die.

CREON: Yes, that indeed was said.
But in the present need we had best discover
what we should do.

OEDIPUS: And will you ask about
a man so wretched?

CREON: Now even you will trust   1505
the God.

OEDIPUS: So. I command you—and will beseech you—
to her that lies inside that house give burial
as you would have it; she is yours and rightly
you will perform the rites for her. For me—
never let this my father's city have me   1510
living a dweller in it. Leave me live
in the mountains where Cithaeron is, that's called
my mountain, which my mother and my father
while they were living would have made my tomb.
So I may die by their decree who sought   1515
indeed to kill me. Yet I know this much:
no sickness and no other thing will kill me.
I would not have been saved from death if not
for some strange evil fate. Well, let my fate
go where it will.

         Creon, you need not care   1520
about my sons; they're men and so wherever
they are, they will not lack a livelihood.
But my two girls—so sad and pitiful—
whose table never stood apart from mine,
and everything I touched they always shared—   1525
O Creon, have a thought for them! And most
I wish that you might suffer me to touch them
and sorrow with them.

[*Enter* ANTIGONE *and* ISMENE, OEDIPUS' *two daughters.*]

O my lord! O true noble Creon! Can I
1530   really be touching them, as when I saw?
What shall I say?
Yes, I can hear them sobbing—my two darlings!
and Creon has had pity and has sent me
what I loved most?
1535   Am I right?
CREON: You're right: it was I gave you this
because I knew from old days how you loved them
as I see now.
OEDIPUS: God bless you for it, Creon,
and may God guard you better on your road
than he did me!
1540   O children,
where are you? Come here, come to my hands,
a brother's hands which turned your father's eyes,
those bright eyes you knew once, to what you see,
a father seeing nothing, knowing nothing,
1545   begetting you from his own source of life.
I weep for you—I cannot see your faces—
I weep when I think of the bitterness
there will be in your lives, how you must live
before the world. At what assemblages
1550   of citizens will you make one? to what
gay company will you go and not come home
in tears instead of sharing in the holiday?
And when you're ripe for marriage, who will he be,
the man who'll risk to take such infamy
1555   as shall cling to my children, to bring hurt
on them and those that marry with them? What
curse is not there? "Your father killed his father
and sowed the seed where he had sprung himself
and begot you out of the womb that held him."
1560   These insults you will hear. Then who will marry you?
No one, my children; clearly you are doomed
to waste away in barrenness unmarried.
Son of Menoeceus,[7] since you are all the father
left these two girls, and we, their parents, both
1565   are dead to them—do not allow them wander
like beggars, poor and husbandless.
They are of your own blood.
And do not make them equal with myself
in wretchedness; for you can see them now
1570   so young, so utterly alone, save for you only.
Touch my hand, noble Creon, and say yes.
If you were older, children, and were wiser,
there's much advice I'd give you. But as it is,
let this be what you pray: give me a life

7. Father of Creon and Jocasta.

wherever there is opportunity   1575
 to live, and better life than was my father's.
CREON: Your tears have had enough of scope; now go within the house.
OEDIPUS: I must obey, though bitter of heart.
CREON: In season, all is good.
OEDIPUS: Do you know on what conditions I obey?
CREON: You tell me them,   1580
 and I shall know them when I hear.
OEDIPUS: That you shall send me out
 to live away from Thebes.
CREON: That gift you must ask of the Gods.
OEDIPUS: But I'm now hated by the Gods.
CREON: So quickly you'll obtain your prayer.
OEDIPUS: You consent then?
CREON: What I do not mean, I do not use to say.
OEDIPUS: Now lead me away from here.
CREON: Let go the children, then, and come.   1585
OEDIPUS: Do not take them from me.
CREON: Do not seek to be master in everything,
 for the things you mastered did not follow you throughout your life.

    [*As* CREON *and* OEDIPUS *go out.*]

CHORUS: You that live in my ancestral Thebes, behold this Oedipus,—
 him who knew the famous riddles and was a man most masterful;
 not a citizen who did not look with envy on his lot—
 see him now and see the breakers of misfortune swallow him!   1590
 Look upon that last day always. Count no mortal happy till
 he has passed the final limit of his life secure from pain.

ca. 429 B.C.E.

OSCAR WILDE

The Importance of Being Earnest

CHARACTERS

ALGERNON MONCRIEFF	LADY AUGUSTA BRACKNELL	CECILY CARDEW
LANE	GWENDOLEN FAIRFAX	CANON CHASUBLE
ERNEST WORTHING	MISS PRISM	MERRIMAN

ACT I

    SCENE: *Morning room in* ALGERNON'*s flat in Half-Moon Street.*[1]
    The room is luxuriously and artistically furnished. The sound of a piano is heard in the adjoining room.

---

1. Like many of the addresses in the play, Half-Moon Street is in Mayfair, a very fashionable section of London. It runs north from Piccadilly near Hyde Park.

[LANE *is arranging afternoon tea on the table, and after the music has ceased,* ALGERNON *enters.*]

ALGERNON: Did you hear what I was playing, Lane?

LANE: I didn't think it polite to listen, sir.

ALGERNON: I'm sorry for that, for your sake. I don't play accurately—anyone can play accurately—but I play with wonderful expression. As far as the piano is concerned, sentiment is my forte. I keep science for Life.

LANE: Yes, sir.

ALGERNON: And, speaking of the science of Life, have you got the cucumber sandwiches cut for Lady Bracknell?

LANE: Yes, sir. [*Hands them on a salver.*]

ALGERNON: [*Inspects them, takes two, and sits down on the sofa.*] Oh! . . . by the way, Lane, I see from your book that on Thursday night, when Lord Shoreham and Mr. Worthing were dining with me, eight bottles of champagne are entered as having been consumed.

LANE: Yes, sir; eight bottles and a pint.

ALGERNON: Why is it that at a bachelor's establishment the servants invariably drink the champagne? I ask merely for information.

LANE: I attribute it to the superior quality of the wine, sir. I have often observed that in married households the champagne is rarely of a first-rate brand.

ALGERNON: Good heavens! Is marriage so demoralizing as that?

LANE: I believe it *is* a very pleasant state, sir. I have had very little experience of it myself up to the present. I have only been married once. That was in consequence of a misunderstanding between myself and a young person.

ALGERNON: [*Languidly.*] I don't know that I am much interested in your family life, Lane.

LANE: No, sir; it is not a very interesting subject. I never think of it myself.

ALGERNON: Very natural, I am sure. That will do, Lane, thank you.

LANE: Thank you, sir. [LANE *goes out.*]

ALGERNON: Lane's views on marriage seem somewhat lax. Really, if the lower orders don't set us a good example, what on earth is the use of them? They seem, as a class, to have absolutely no sense of moral responsibility.

[*Enter* LANE.]

LANE: Mr. Ernest Worthing.

[*Enter* JACK. LANE *goes out.*]

ALGERNON: How are you, my dear Ernest? What brings you up to town?

JACK: Oh, pleasure, pleasure! What else should bring one anywhere? Eating as usual, I see, Algy!

ALGERNON: [*Stiffly.*] I believe it is customary in good society to take some slight refreshment at five o'clock. Where have you been since last Thursday?

JACK: [*Sitting down on the sofa.*] In the country.

ALGERNON: What on earth do you do there?

JACK: [*Pulling off his gloves.*] When one is in town one amuses oneself. When one is in the country one amuses other people. It is excessively boring.

ALGERNON: And who are the people you amuse?

JACK: [*Airily.*] Oh, neighbors, neighbors.

ALGERNON: Got nice neighbors in your part of Shropshire?

JACK: Perfectly horrid! Never speak to one of them.

ALGERNON: How immensely you must amuse them! [*Goes over and takes sandwich.*] By the way, Shropshire is your county, is it not?

JACK: Eh? Shropshire?[2] Yes, of course. Hallo! Why all these cups? Why cucumber sandwiches? Why such reckless extravagance in one so young? Who is coming to tea?

ALGERNON: Oh! merely Aunt Augusta and Gwendolen.

JACK: How perfectly delightful!

ALGERNON: Yes, that is all very well; but I am afraid Aunt Augusta won't quite approve of your being here.

JACK: May I ask why?

ALGERNON: My dear fellow, the way you flirt with Gwendolen is perfectly disgraceful. It is almost as bad as the way Gwendolen flirts with you.

JACK: I am in love with Gwendolen. I have come up to town expressly to propose to her.

ALGERNON: I thought you had come up for pleasure? . . . I call that business.

JACK: How utterly unromantic you are!

ALGERNON: I really don't see anything romantic in proposing. It is very romantic to be in love. But there is nothing romantic about a definite proposal. Why, one may be accepted. One usually is, I believe. Then the excitement is all over. The very essence of romance is uncertainty. If ever I get married, I'll certainly try to forget the fact.

JACK: I have no doubt about that, dear Algy. The divorce court was specially invented for people whose memories are so curiously constituted.

ALGERNON: Oh! there is no use speculating on that subject. Divorces are made in heaven— [JACK *puts out his hand to take a sandwich.* ALGERNON *at once interferes.*] Please don't touch the cucumber sandwiches. They are ordered specially for Aunt Augusta. [*Takes one and eats it.*]

JACK: Well, you have been eating them all the time.

ALGERNON: That is quite a different matter. She is my aunt. [*Takes plate from below.*] Have some bread and butter. The bread and butter is for Gwendolen. Gwendolen is devoted to bread and butter.

JACK: [*Advancing to table and helping himself.*] And very good bread and butter it is too.

ALGERNON: Well, my dear fellow, you need not eat as if you were going to eat it all. You behave as if you were married to her already. You are not married to her already, and I don't think you ever will be.

JACK: Why on earth do you say that?

ALGERNON: Well, in the first place, girls never marry the men they flirt with. Girls don't think it right.

JACK: Oh, that is nonsense!

ALGERNON: It isn't. It is a great truth. It accounts for the extraordinary number of bachelors that one sees all over the place. In the second place, I don't give my consent.

JACK: Your consent!

---

2. County on the Welsh border, to the west of London; Jack's country place is actually in Hertfordshire, to the north of London.

ALGERNON: My dear fellow, Gwendolen is my first cousin. And before I allow you to marry her, you will have to clear up the whole question of Cecily. [*Rings bell*.]

JACK: Cecily! What on earth do you mean? What do you mean, Algy, by Cecily? I don't know anyone of the name of Cecily.

[*Enter* LANE.]

ALGERNON: Bring me that cigarette case Mr. Worthing left in the smoking-room the last time he dined here.

LANE: Yes, sir. [LANE *goes out*.]

JACK: Do you mean to say you have had my cigarette case all this time? I wish to goodness you had let me know. I have been writing frantic letters to Scotland Yard about it. I was very nearly offering a large reward.

ALGERNON: Well, I wish you would offer one. I happen to be more than usually hard up.

JACK: There is no good offering a large reward now that the thing is found.

[*Enter* LANE *with the cigarette case on a salver.* ALGERNON *takes it at once.* LANE *goes out*.]

ALGERNON: I think that is rather mean of you, Ernest, I must say. [*Opens case and examines it*.] However, it makes no matter, for, now that I look at the inscription inside, I find that the thing isn't yours after all.

JACK: Of course it's mine. [*Moving to him*.] You have seen me with it a hundred times, and you have no right whatsoever to read what is written inside. It is a very ungentlemanly thing to read a private cigarette case.

ALGERNON: Oh! it is absurd to have a hard-and-fast rule about what one should read and what one shouldn't. More than half of modern culture depends on what one shouldn't read.

JACK: I am quite aware of the fact, and I don't propose to discuss modern culture. It isn't the sort of thing one should talk of in private. I simply want my cigarette case back.

ALGERNON: Yes; but this isn't your cigarette case. This cigarette case is a present from someone of the name of Cecily, and you said you didn't know anyone of that name.

JACK: Well, if you want to know, Cecily happens to be my aunt.

ALGERNON: Your aunt!

JACK: Yes. Charming old lady she is, too. Lives at Tunbridge Wells.[3] Just give it back to me, Algy.

ALGERNON: [*Retreating to back of sofa*.] But why does she call herself Cecily if she is your aunt and lives at Tunbridge Wells? [*Reading*.] "From little Cecily with her fondest love."

JACK: [*Moving to sofa and kneeling upon it*.] My dear fellow, what on earth is there in that? Some aunts are tall, some aunts are not tall. That is a matter that surely an aunt may be allowed to decide for herself. You seem to think that every aunt should be exactly like your aunt! That is absurd! For heaven's sake give me back my cigarette case. [*Follows* ALGY *round the room*.]

---

3. Resort town in Kent, southeast of London.

ALGERNON: Yes. But why does your aunt call you her uncle? "From little Cecily, with her fondest love to her dear Uncle Jack." There is no objection, I admit, to an aunt being a small aunt, but why an aunt, no matter what her size may be, should call her own nephew her uncle, I can't quite make out. Besides, your name isn't Jack at all; it is Ernest.

JACK: It isn't Ernest; it's Jack.

ALGERNON: You have always told me it was Ernest. I have introduced you to everyone as Ernest. You answer to the name of Ernest. You look as if your name was Ernest. You are the most earnest looking person I ever saw in my life. It is perfectly absurd your saying that your name isn't Ernest. It's on your cards. Here is one of them. [*Taking it from case.*] "Mr. Ernest Worthing, B. 4, The Albany."[4] I'll keep this as a proof that your name is Ernest if ever you attempt to deny it to me, or to Gwendolen, or to anyone else. [*Puts the card in his pocket.*]

JACK: Well, my name is Ernest in town and Jack in the country, and the cigarette case was given to me in the country.

ALGERNON: Yes, but that does not account for the fact that your small Aunt Cecily, who lives at Tunbridge Wells, calls you her dear uncle. Come, old boy, you had much better have the thing out at once.

JACK: My dear Algy, you talk exactly as if you were a dentist. It is very vulgar to talk like a dentist when one isn't a dentist. It produces a false impression.

ALGERNON: Well, that is exactly what dentists always do. Now, go on! Tell me the whole thing. I may mention that I have always suspected you of being a confirmed and secret Bunburyist; and I am quite sure of it now.

JACK: Bunburyist? What on earth do you mean by a Bunburyist?

ALGERNON: I'll reveal to you the meaning of that incomparable expression as soon as you are kind enough to inform me why you are Ernest in town and Jack in the country.

JACK: Well, produce my cigarette case first.

ALGERNON: Here it is. [*Hands cigarette case.*] Now produce your explanation, and pray make it improbable. [*Sits on sofa.*]

JACK: My dear fellow, there is nothing improbable about my explanation at all. In fact it's perfectly ordinary. Old Mr. Thomas Cardew, who adopted me when I was a little boy, made me in his will guardian to his granddaughter, Miss Cecily Cardew. Cecily, who addresses me as her uncle from motives of respect that you could not possibly appreciate, lives at my place in the country under the charge of her admirable governess, Miss Prism.

ALGERNON: Where is that place in the country, by the way?

JACK: That is nothing to you, dear boy. You are not going to be invited. . . . I may tell you candidly that the place is not in Shropshire.

ALGERNON: I suspected that, my dear fellow! I have Bunburyed all over Shropshire on two separate occasions. Now, go on. Why are you Ernest in town and Jack in the country?

JACK: My dear Algy, I don't know whether you will be able to understand my real motives. You are hardly serious enough. When one is placed in the position of guardian, one has to adopt a very high moral tone on all subjects. It's one's duty to do so. And as a high moral tone can hardly be said to conduce very

---

4. Apartment building for single gentlemen on Piccadilly, east of Algernon's flat.

much to either one's health or one's happiness, in order to get up to town I
have always pretended to have a younger brother of the name of Ernest, who
lives in the Albany, and gets into the most dreadful scrapes. That, my dear
Algy, is the whole truth pure and simple.

ALGERNON: The truth is rarely pure and never simple. Modern life would be very
tedious if it were either, and modern literature a complete impossibility!

JACK: That wouldn't be at all a bad thing.

ALGERNON: Literary criticism is not your forte, my dear fellow. Don't try it. You
should leave that to people who haven't been at a university. They do it so well
in the daily papers. What you really are is a Bunburyist. I was quite right in
saying you were a Bunburyist. You are one of the most advanced Bunburyists
I know.

JACK: What on earth do you mean?

ALGERNON: You have invented a very useful young brother called Ernest, in order
that you may be able to come up to town as often as you like. I have invented
an invaluable permanent invalid called Bunbury, in order that I may be able
to go down into the country whenever I choose. Bunbury is perfectly invaluable. If it wasn't for Bunbury's extraordinary bad health, for instance, I wouldn't
be able to dine with you at Willis's[5] tonight, for I have been really engaged to
Aunt Augusta for more than a week.

JACK: I haven't asked you to dine with me anywhere tonight.

ALGERNON: I know. You are absurdly careless about sending out invitations. It
is very foolish of you. Nothing annoys people so much as not receiving
invitations.

JACK: You had much better dine with your Aunt Augusta.

ALGERNON: I haven't the smallest intention of doing anything of the kind. To
begin with, I dined there on Monday, and once a week is quite enough to
dine with one's own relations. In the second place, whenever I do dine there I
am always treated as a member of the family, and sent down with either no
woman at all, or two. In the third place, I know perfectly well whom she will
place me next to, tonight. She will place me next Mary Farquhar, who always
flirts with her own husband across the dinner table. That is not very pleasant. Indeed, it is not even decent . . . and that sort of thing is enormously on
the increase. The amount of women in London who flirt with their own husbands is perfectly scandalous. It looks so bad. It is simply washing one's
clean linen in public. Besides, now that I know you to be a confirmed Bunburyist, I naturally want to talk to you about Bunburying. I want to tell you
the rules.

JACK: I'm not a Bunburyist at all. If Gwendolen accepts me, I am going to kill my
brother, indeed I think I'll kill him in any case. Cecily is a little too much
interested in him. It is rather a bore. So I am going to get rid of Ernest. And I
strongly advise you to do the same with Mr. . . . with your invalid friend who
has the absurd name.

ALGERNON: Nothing will induce me to part with Bunbury, and if you ever get
married, which seems to me extremely problematic, you will be very glad to
know Bunbury. A man who marries without knowing Bunbury has a very
tedious time of it.

---

5. Well-known restaurant on King Street, off St. James's Street, near Piccadilly.

JACK: That is nonsense. If I marry a charming girl like Gwendolen, and she is the only girl I ever saw in my life that I would marry, I certainly won't want to know Bunbury.

ALGERNON: Then your wife will. You don't seem to realize, that in married life three is company and two is none.

JACK: [*Sententiously.*] That, my dear young friend, is the theory that the corrupt French drama has been propounding for the last fifty years.[6]

ALGERNON: Yes; and that the happy English home has proved in half the time.

JACK: For heaven's sake, don't try to be cynical. It's perfectly easy to be cynical.

ALGERNON: My dear fellow, it isn't easy to be anything nowadays. There's such a lot of beastly competition about. [*The sound of an electric bell is heard.*] Ah! that must be Aunt Augusta. Only relatives, or creditors, ever ring in that Wagnerian manner.[7] Now, if I get her out of the way for ten minutes, so that you can have an opportunity for proposing to Gwendolen, may I dine with you tonight at Willis's?

JACK: I suppose so, if you want to.

ALGERNON: Yes, but you must be serious about it. I hate people who are not serious about meals. It is so shallow of them.

    [*Enter* LANE.]

LANE: Lady Bracknell and Miss Fairfax.

    [ALGERNON *goes forward to meet them. Enter* LADY BRACKNELL *and* GWENDOLEN.]

LADY BRACKNELL: Good afternoon, dear Algernon, I hope you are behaving very well.

ALGERNON: I'm feeling very well, Aunt Augusta.

LADY BRACKNELL: That's not quite the same thing. In fact the two things rarely go together. [*Sees* JACK *and bows to him with icy coldness.*]

ALGERNON: [*To* GWENDOLEN.] Dear me, you are smart![8]

GWENDOLEN: I am always smart! Aren't I, Mr. Worthing?

JACK: You're quite perfect, Miss Fairfax.

GWENDOLEN: Oh! I hope I am not that. It would leave no room for developments, and I intend to develop in many directions. [GWENDOLEN *and* JACK *sit down together in the corner.*]

LADY BRACKNELL: I'm sorry if we are a little late, Algernon, but I was obliged to call on dear Lady Harbury. I hadn't been there since her poor husband's death. I never saw a woman so altered; she looks quite twenty years younger. And now I'll have a cup of tea, and one of those nice cucumber sandwiches you promised me.

ALGERNON: Certainly, Aunt Augusta. [*Goes over to teatable.*]

LADY BRACKNELL: Won't you come and sit here, Gwendolen?

GWENDOLEN: Thanks, mamma, I'm quite comfortable where I am.

---

6. Starting in the mid-nineteenth century, the French produced plays dealing with such subjects as adultery, prostitution, and illegitimacy. The heavily censored English theater either avoided such subjects or dealt with them more cautiously.

7. Many early listeners to the music of Richard Wagner found it extremely loud and, consequently, unpleasantly demanding.   8. That is, neat and stylish in appearance.

ALGERNON: [*Picking up empty plate in horror.*] Good heavens! Lane! Why are there no cucumber sandwiches? I ordered them specially.

LANE: [*Gravely.*] There were no cucumbers in the market this morning, sir. I went down twice.

ALGERNON: No cucumbers!

LANE: No, sir. Not even for ready money.

ALGERNON: That will do, Lane, thank you.

LANE: Thank you, sir.

ALGERNON: I am greatly distressed, Aunt Augusta, about there being no cucumbers, not even for ready money.

LADY BRACKNELL: It really makes no matter, Algernon. I had some crumpets with Lady Harbury, who seems to me to be living entirely for pleasure now.

ALGERNON: I hear her hair has turned quite gold from grief.

LADY BRACKNELL: It certainly has changed its color. From what cause I, of course, cannot say. [ALGERNON *crosses and hands tea.*] Thank you. I've quite a treat for you tonight, Algernon. I am going to send you down with Mary Farquhar. She is such a nice woman, and so attentive to her husband. It's delightful to watch them.

ALGERNON: I am afraid, Aunt Augusta, I shall have to give up the pleasure of dining with you tonight after all.

LADY BRACKNELL: [*Frowning.*] I hope not, Algernon. It would put my table completely out. Your uncle would have to dine upstairs. Fortunately he is accustomed to that.

ALGERNON: It is a great bore, and, I need hardly say, a terrible disappointment to me, but the fact is I have just had a telegram to say that my poor friend Bunbury is very ill again. [*Exchanges glances with* JACK.] They seem to think I should be with him.

LADY BRACKNELL: It is very strange. This Mr. Bunbury seems to suffer from curiously bad health.

ALGERNON: Yes; poor Bunbury is a dreadful invalid.

LADY BRACKNELL: Well, I must say, Algernon, that I think it is high time that Mr. Bunbury made up his mind whether he was going to live or to die. This shilly-shallying with the question is absurd. Nor do I in any way approve of the modern sympathy with invalids. I consider it morbid. Illness of any kind is hardly a thing to be encouraged in others. Health is the primary duty of life. I am always telling that to your poor uncle, but he never seems to take much notice . . . as far as any improvement in his ailments goes. I should be obliged if you would ask Mr. Bunbury, from me, to be kind enough not to have a relapse on Saturday, for I rely on you to arrange my music for me. It is my last reception, and one wants something that will encourage conversation, particularly at the end of the season when everyone has practically said whatever they had to say, which, in most cases, was probably not much.

ALGERNON: I'll speak to Bunbury, Aunt Augusta, if he is still conscious, and I think I can promise you he'll be all right by Saturday. Of course the music is a great difficulty. You see, if one plays good music, people don't listen, and if one plays bad music, people don't talk. But I'll run over the program I've drawn out, if you will kindly come into the next room for a moment.

LADY BRACKNELL: Thank you, Algernon. It is very thoughtful of you. [*Rising, and following* ALGERNON.] I'm sure the program will be delightful, after a few expurgations. French songs I cannot possibly allow. People always seem to think that they are improper, and either look shocked, which is vulgar, or laugh, which is worse. But German sounds a thoroughly respectable language, and indeed, I believe is so. Gwendolen, you will accompany me.

GWENDOLEN: Certainly, mamma.

[LADY BRACKNELL *and* ALGERNON *go into the music room,* GWENDOLEN *remains behind.*]

JACK: Charming day it has been, Miss Fairfax.

GWENDOLEN: Pray don't talk to me about the weather, Mr. Worthing. Whenever people talk to me about the weather, I always feel quite certain that they mean something else. And that makes me so nervous.

JACK: I do mean something else.

GWENDOLWN: I thought so. In fact, I am never wrong.

JACK: And I would like to be allowed to take advantage of Lady Bracknell's temporary absence . . .

GWENDOLEN: I would certainly advise you to do so. Mamma has a way of coming back suddenly into a room that I have often had to speak to her about.

JACK: [*Nervously.*] Miss Fairfax, ever since I met you I have admired you more than any girl . . . I have ever met since . . . I met you.

GWENDOLEN: Yes, I am quite aware of the fact. And I often wish that in public, at any rate, you had been more demonstrative. For me you have always had an irresistible fascination. Even before I met you I was far from indifferent to you. [JACK *looks at her in amazement.*] We live, as I hope you know, Mr. Worthing, in an age of ideals. The fact is constantly mentioned in the more expensive monthly magazines, and has reached the provincial pulpits, I am told: and my ideal has always been to love someone of the name of Ernest. There is something in that name that inspires absolute confidence. The moment Algernon first mentioned to me that he had a friend called Ernest, I knew I was destined to love you.

JACK: You really love me, Gwendolen?

GWENDOLEN: Passionately!

JACK: Darling! You don't know how happy you've made me.

GWENDOLEN: My own Ernest!

JACK: But you don't really mean to say that you couldn't love me if my name wasn't Ernest?

GWENDOLEN: But your name is Ernest.

JACK: Yes, I know it is. But supposing it was something else? Do you mean to say you couldn't love me then?

GWENDOLEN: [*Glibly.*] Ah! that is clearly a metaphysical speculation, and like most metaphysical speculations has very little reference at all to the actual facts of real life, as we know them.

JACK: Personally, darling, to speak quite candidly, I don't much care about the name of Ernest . . . I don't think the name suits me at all.

GWENDOLEN: It suits you perfectly. It is a divine name. It has a music of its own. It produces vibrations.

JACK: Well, really, Gwendolen, I must say that I think there are lots of other much nicer names. I think Jack, for instance, a charming name.

GWENDOLEN: Jack? . . . No, there is very little music in the name Jack, if any at all, indeed. It does not thrill. It produces absolutely no vibrations. . . . I have known several Jacks, and they all, without exception, were more than usually plain.

Besides, Jack is a notorious domesticity for John! And I pity any woman who is married to a man called John. She would probably never be allowed to know the entrancing pleasure of a single moment's solitude. The only really safe name is Ernest.

JACK: Gwendolen, I must get christened at once—I mean we must get married at once. There is no time to be lost.

GWENDOLEN: Married, Mr. Worthing?

JACK: [*Astounded.*] Well . . . surely. You know that I love you, and you led me to believe, Miss Fairfax, that you were not absolutely indifferent to me.

GWENDOLEN: I adore you. But you haven't proposed to me yet. Nothing has been said at all about marriage. The subject has not even been touched on.

JACK: Well . . . may I propose to you now?

GWENDOLEN: I think it would be an admirable opportunity. And to spare you any possible disappointment, Mr. Worthing, I think it only fair to tell you quite frankly beforehand that I am fully determined to accept you.

JACK: Gwendolen!

GWENDOLEN: Yes, Mr. Worthing, what have you got to say to me?

JACK: You know what I have got to say to you.

GWENDOLEN: Yes, but you don't say it.

JACK: Gwendolen, will you marry me? [*Goes on his knees.*]

GWENDOLEN: Of course I will, darling. How long you have been about it! I am afraid you have had very little experience in how to propose.

JACK: My own one, I have never loved anyone in the world but you.

GWENDOLEN: Yes, but men often propose for practice. I know my brother Gerald does. All my girlfriends tell me so. What wonderfully blue eyes you have, Ernest! They are quite, quite blue. I hope you will always look at me just like that, especially when there are other people present.

[*Enter* LADY BRACKNELL.]

LADY BRACKNELL: Mr. Worthing! Rise, sir, from this semi-recumbent posture. It is most indecorous.

GWENDOLEN: Mamma! [*He tries to rise; she restrains him.*] I must beg you to retire. This is no place for you. Besides, Mr. Worthing has not quite finished yet.

LADY BRACKNELL: Finished what, may I ask?

GWENDOLEN: I am engaged to Mr. Worthing, mamma.

[*They rise together.*]

LADY BRACKNELL: Pardon me, you are not engaged to anyone. When you do become engaged to someone, I, or your father, should his health permit him, will inform you of the fact. An engagement should come on a young girl as a surprise, pleasant or unpleasant, as the case may be. It is hardly a matter that she could be allowed to arrange for herself. . . . And now I have a few questions to put to you, Mr. Worthing. While I am making these inquiries, you, Gwendolen, will wait for me below in the carriage.

GWENDOLEN: [*Reproachfully.*] Mamma!

LADY BRACKNELL: In the carriage, Gwendolen! [GWENDOLEN *goes to the door. She and* JACK *blow kisses to each other behind* LADY BRACKNELL'S *back.* LADY BRACKNELL *looks vaguely about as if she could not understand what the noise was. Finally turns round.*] Gwendolen, the carriage!

GWENDOLEN: Yes, mamma. [*Goes out, looking back at* JACK.]

LADY BRACKNELL: [*Sitting down.*] You can take a seat, Mr. Worthing.

[*Looks in her pocket for notebook and pencil.*]

JACK: Thank you, Lady Bracknell, I prefer standing.

LADY BRACKNELL: [*Pencil and notebook in hand.*] I feel bound to tell you that you are not down on my list of eligible young men, although I have the same list as the dear Duchess of Bolton has. We work together, in fact. However, I am quite ready to enter your name, should your answers be what a really affectionate mother requires. Do you smoke?

JACK: Well, yes, I must admit I smoke.

LADY BRACKNELL: I am glad to hear it. A man should always have an occupation of some kind. There are far too many idle men in London as it is. How old are you?

JACK: Twenty-nine.

LADY BRACKNELL: A very good age to be married at. I have always been of opinion that a man who desires to get married should know either everything or nothing. Which do you know?

JACK: [*After some hesitation.*] I know nothing, Lady Bracknell.

LADY BRACKNELL: I am pleased to hear it. I do not approve of anything that tampers with natural ignorance. Ignorance is like a delicate exotic fruit; touch it and the bloom is gone. The whole theory of modern education is radically unsound. Fortunately in England, at any rate, education produces no effect whatsoever. If it did, it would prove a serious danger to the upper classes, and probably lead to acts of violence in Grosvenor Square.[9] What is your income?

JACK: Between seven and eight thousand a year.[1]

LADY BRACKNELL: [*Makes a note in her book.*] In land, or in investments?

JACK: In investments, chiefly.

LADY BRACKNELL: That is satisfactory. What between the duties expected of one during one's lifetime, and the duties exacted from one after one's death, land has ceased to be either a profit or a pleasure. It gives one position, and prevents one from keeping it up. That's all that can be said about land.

JACK: I have a country house with some land, of course, attached to it, about fifteen hundred acres, I believe; but I don't depend on that for my real income. In fact, as far as I can make out, the poachers are the only people who make anything out of it.

LADY BRACKNELL: A country house! How many bedrooms? Well, that point can be cleared up afterwards. You have a town house, I hope? A girl with a simple, unspoiled nature, like Gwendolen, could hardly be expected to reside in the country.

JACK: Well, I own a house in Belgrave Square,[2] but it is let by the year to Lady Bloxham. Of course, I can get it back whenever I like, at six months' notice.

LADY BRACKNELL: Lady Bloxham? I don't know her.

JACK: Oh, she goes about very little. She is a lady considerably advanced in years.

---

9. Fashionable location in Mayfair. 1. Nearly $1,000,000 annually in today's U.S. currency.
2. Near the southeast corner of Hyde Park in Belgravia, another fashionable section of London.

LADY BRACKNELL: Ah, nowadays that is no guarantee of respectability of character. What number in Belgrave Square?

JACK: 149.

LADY BRACKNELL: [*Shaking her head.*] The unfashionable side. I thought there was
something. However, that could easily be altered.

JACK: Do you mean the fashion, or the side?

LADY BRACKNELL: [*Sternly.*] Both, if necessary, I presume. What are your politics?

JACK: Well, I am afraid I really have none. I am a Liberal Unionist.

LADY BRACKNELL: Oh, they count as Tories.[3] They dine with us. Or come in the
evening, at any rate. Now to minor matters. Are your parents living?

JACK: I have lost both my parents.

LADY BRACKNELL: Both? To lose one parent may be regarded as a misfortune—to
lose *both* seems like carelessness. Who was your father? He was evidently a
man of some wealth. Was he born in what the Radical papers call the purple
of commerce, or did he rise from the ranks of aristocracy?

JACK: I am afraid I really don't know. The fact is, Lady Bracknell, I said I had lost
my parents. It would be nearer the truth to say that my parents seem to have
lost me.... I don't actually know who I am by birth. I was ... well, I was
found.

LADY BRACKNELL: Found!

JACK: The late Mr. Thomas Cardew, an old gentleman of a very charitable and
kindly disposition, found me, and gave me the name of Worthing, because he
happened to have a first-class ticket for Worthing in his pocket at the time.
Worthing is a place in Sussex. It is a seaside resort.

LADY BRACKNELL: Where did the charitable gentleman who had a first-class ticket
for this seaside resort find you?

JACK: [*Gravely.*] In a handbag.

LADY BRACKNELL: A handbag?

JACK: [*Very seriously.*] Yes, Lady Bracknell. I was in a handbag—a somewhat large,
black leather handbag, with handles to it—an ordinary handbag, in fact.

LADY BRACKNELL: In what locality did this Mr. James, or Thomas, Cardew come
across this ordinary handbag?

JACK: In the cloak room at Victoria Station.[4] It was given to him in mistake for
his own.

LADY BRACKNELL: The cloak room at Victoria Station?

JACK: Yes. The Brighton line.

LADY BRACKNELL: The line is immaterial. Mr. Worthing, I confess I feel somewhat
bewildered by what you have just told me. To be born, or at any rate, bred in a
handbag, whether it had handles or not, seems to me to display a contempt
for the ordinary decencies of family life that reminds one of the worst excesses
of the French Revolution. And I presume you know what that unfortunate
movement led to? As for the particular locality in which the handbag was
found, a cloak room at a railway station might serve to conceal a social
indiscretion—has probably, indeed, been used for that purpose before now—

---

3. Members of the Conservative party. Opposed to home rule for Ireland, they joined forces with the
Liberal Unionists, who had split from the Liberal party over the issue.
4. Major railroad station in London.

but it could hardly be regarded as an assured basis for a recognized position in good society.

JACK: May I ask you then what you would advise me to do? I need hardly say I would do anything in the world to ensure Gwendolen's happiness.

LADY BRACKNELL: I would strongly advise you, Mr. Worthing, to try and acquire some relations as soon as possible, and to make a definite effort to produce at any rate one parent, of either sex, before the season is quite over.

JACK: Well, I don't see how I could possibly manage to do that. I can produce the handbag at any moment, it is in my dressing room at home. I really think that should satisfy you, Lady Bracknell.

LADY BRACKNELL: Me, sir! What has it to do with me? You can hardly imagine that I and Lord Bracknell would dream of allowing our only daughter—a girl brought up with the utmost care—to marry into a cloak room, and form an alliance with a parcel? Good morning, Mr. Worthing!

[LADY BRACKNELL *sweeps out in majestic indignation*.]

JACK: Good morning! [ALGERNON, *from the other room, strikes up the Wedding March.* JACK *looks perfectly furious, and goes to the door*.] For goodness' sake don't play that ghastly tune, Algy! How idiotic you are!

[*The music stops, and* ALGERNON *enters cheerily*.]

ALGERNON: Didn't it go off all right, old boy? You don't mean to say Gwendolen refused you? I know it is a way she has. She is always refusing people. I think it is most ill-natured of her.

JACK: Oh, Gwendolen is as right as a trivet.[5] As far as she is concerned, we are engaged. Her mother is perfectly unbeatable. Never met such a Gorgon[6] . . . I don't really know what a Gorgon is like, but I am quite sure that Lady Bracknell is one. In any case, she is a monster, without being a myth, which is rather unfair. . . . I beg your pardon, Algy, I suppose I shouldn't talk about your own aunt in that way before you.

ALGERNON: My dear boy, I love hearing my relations abused. It is the only thing that makes me put up with them at all. Relations are simply a tedious pack of people who haven't got the remotest knowledge of how to live, nor the smallest instinct about when to die.

JACK: Oh, that is nonsense!

ALGERNON: It isn't!

JACK: Well, I won't argue about the matter. You always want to argue about things.

ALGERNON: That is exactly what things were originally made for.

JACK: Upon my word, if I thought that, I'd shoot myself. . . . [*A pause*.] You don't think there is any chance of Gwendolen becoming like her mother in about a hundred and fifty years, do you, Algy?

ALGERNON: All women become like their mothers. That is their tragedy. No man does. That's his.

JACK: Is that clever?

5. Proverbial expression, referring to the solidity of a tripod on its three legs.
6. Mythological creature with a horrible face, the Gorgon had snakes in place of hair. According to myth, those who looked on a Gorgon were turned to stone.

ALGERNON: It is perfectly phrased! and quite as true as any observation in civilized life should be.

JACK: I am sick to death of cleverness. Everybody is clever nowadays. You can't go anywhere without meeting clever people. The thing has become an absolute public nuisance. I wish to goodness we had a few fools left.

ALGERNON: We have.

JACK: I should extremely like to meet them. What do they talk about?

ALGERNON: The fools? Oh! about the clever people, of course.

JACK: What fools!

ALGERNON: By the way, did you tell Gwendolen the truth about your being Ernest in town, and Jack in the country?

JACK: [*In a very patronizing manner.*] My dear fellow, the truth isn't quite the sort of thing one tells to a nice sweet refined girl. What extraordinary ideas you have about the way to behave to a woman!

ALGERNON: The only way to behave to a woman is to make love to her, if she is pretty, and to someone else if she is plain.

JACK: Oh, that is nonsense.

ALGERNON: What about your brother? What about the profligate Ernest?

JACK: Oh, before the end of the week I shall have got rid of him. I'll say he died in Paris of apoplexy. Lots of people die of apoplexy, quite suddenly, don't they?

ALGERNON: Yes, but it's hereditary, my dear fellow. It's a sort of thing that runs in families. You had much better say a severe chill.

JACK: You are sure a severe chill isn't hereditary, or anything of that kind?

ALGERNON: Of course it isn't!

JACK: Very well, then. My poor brother Ernest is carried off suddenly in Paris, by a severe chill. That gets rid of him.

ALGERNON: But I thought you said that . . . Miss Cardew was a little too much interested in your poor brother Ernest? Won't she feel his loss a good deal?

JACK: Oh, that is all right. Cecily is not a silly romantic girl, I am glad to say. She has got a capital appetite, goes on long walks, and pays no attention at all to her lessons.

ALGERNON: I would rather like to see Cecily.

JACK: I will take very good care you never do. She is excessively pretty, and she is only just eighteen.

ALGERNON: Have you told Gwendolen yet that you have an excessively pretty ward who is only just eighteen?

JACK: Oh! one doesn't blurt these things out to people. Cecily and Gwendolen are perfectly certain to be extremely great friends. I'll bet you anything you like that half an hour after they have met, they will be calling each other sister.

ALGERNON: Women only do that when they have called each other a lot of other things first. Now, my dear boy, if we want to get a good table at Willis's, we really must go and dress. Do you know it is nearly seven?

JACK: [*Irritably.*] Oh! it always is nearly seven.

ALGERNON: Well, I'm hungry.

JACK: I never knew you when you weren't. . . .

ALGERNON: What shall we do after dinner? Go to the theater?

JACK: Oh no! I loathe listening.

ALGERNON: Well, let us go to the club?

JACK: Oh, no! I hate talking.

ALGERNON: Well, we might trot around to the Empire[7] at ten?

JACK: Oh no! I can't bear looking at things. It is so silly.

ALGERNON: Well, what shall we do?

JACK: Nothing!

ALGERNON: It is awfully hard work doing nothing. However, I don't mind hard work where there is no definite object of any kind.

[*Enter* LANE.]

LANE: Miss Fairfax.

[*Enter* GWENDOLEN. LANE *goes out.*]

ALGERNON: Gwendolen, upon my word!

GWENDOLEN: Algy, kindly turn your back. I have something very particular to say to Mr. Worthing.

ALGERNON: Really, Gwendolen, I don't think I can allow this at all.

GWENDOLEN: Algy, you always adopt a strictly immoral attitude towards life. You are not quite old enough to do that.

[ALGERNON *retires to the fireplace.*]

JACK: My own darling!

GWENDOLEN: Ernest, we may never be married. From the expression on mamma's face I fear we never shall. Few parents nowadays pay any regard to what their children say to them. The old-fashioned respect for the young is fast dying out. Whatever influence I ever had over mamma, I lost at the age of three. But although she may prevent us from becoming man and wife, and I may marry someone else, and marry often, nothing that she can possibly do can alter my eternal devotion to you.

JACK: Dear Gwendolen!

GWENDOLEN: The story of your romantic origin, as related to me by mamma, with unpleasing comments, has naturally stirred the deeper fibers of my nature. Your Christian name has an irresistible fascination. The simplicity of your character makes you exquisitely incomprehensible to me. Your town address at the Albany I have. What is your address in the country?

JACK: The Manor House, Woolton, Hertfordshire.

[ALGERNON, *who has been carefully listening, smiles to himself, and writes the address on his shirt-cuff. Then picks up the Railway Guide.*]

GWENDOLEN: There is a good postal service, I suppose? It may be necessary to do something desperate. That of course will require serious consideration. I will communicate with you daily.

JACK: My own one!

GWENDOLEN: How long do you remain in town?

JACK: Till Monday.

GWENDOLEN: Good! Algy, you may turn round now.

ALGERNON: Thanks, I've turned round already.

GWENDOLEN: You may also ring the bell.

JACK: You will let me see you to your carriage, my own darling?

---

7. The Empire Theatre of Varieties, a music hall on Leicester Square.

GWENDOLEN: Certainly.

JACK: [*To* LANE, *who now enters.*] I will see Miss Fairfax out.

LANE: Yes, sir.

> [JACK *and* GWENDOLEN *go off.* LANE *presents several letters on a salver to* ALGERNON. *It is to be surmised that they are bills, as* ALGERNON, *after looking at the envelopes, tears them up.*]

ALGERNON: A glass of sherry, Lane.

LANE: Yes, sir.

ALGERNON: Tomorrow, Lane, I'm going Bunburying.

LANE: Yes, sir.

ALGERNON: I shall probably not be back till Monday. You can put up my dress clothes, my smoking jacket, and all the Bunbury suits. . . .

LANE: Yes, sir. [*Handing sherry.*]

ALGERNON: I hope tomorrow will be a fine day, Lane.

LANE: It never is, sir.

ALGERNON: Lane, you're a perfect pessimist.

LANE: I do my best to give satisfaction, sir.

> [*Enter* JACK. LANE *goes off.*]

JACK: There's a sensible, intellectual girl! the only girl I ever cared for in my life. [ALGERNON *is laughing immoderately.*] What on earth are you so amused at?

ALGERNON: Oh, I'm a little anxious about poor Bunbury, that is all.

JACK: If you don't take care, your friend Bunbury will get you into a serious scrape some day.

ALGERNON: I love scrapes. They are the only things that are never serious.

JACK: Oh, that's nonsense, Algy. You never talk anything but nonsense.

ALGERNON: Nobody ever does.

> [JACK *looks indignantly at him, and leaves the room.* ALGERNON *lights a cigarette, reads his shirt-cuff, and smiles.*]

ACT-DROP[8]

ACT II

SCENE: *Garden at the Manor House. A flight of gray stone steps leads up to the house. The garden, an old-fashioned one, full of roses. Time of year, July. Basket chairs, and a table covered with books, are set under a large yew tree.*

> [MISS PRISM *discovered seated at the table.* CECILY *is at the back watering flowers.*]

MISS PRISM: [*Calling.*] Cecily, Cecily! Surely such a utilitarian occupation as the watering of flowers is rather Moulton's duty than yours? Especially at a moment when intellectual pleasures await you. Your German grammar is on the table. Pray open it at page fifteen. We will repeat yesterday's lesson.

CECILY: [*Coming over very slowly.*] But I don't like German. It isn't at all a becoming language. I know perfectly well that I look quite plain after my German lesson.

---

8. That is, a lowering of the curtain to permit a scene change.

MISS PRISM: Child, you know how anxious your guardian is that you should improve yourself in every way. He laid particular stress on your German, as he was leaving for town yesterday. Indeed, he always lays stress on your German when he is leaving for town.

CECILY: Dear Uncle Jack is so very serious! Sometime he is so serious that I think he cannot be quite well.

MISS PRISM: [*Drawing herself up.*] Your guardian enjoys the best of health, and his gravity of demeanor is especially to be commended in one so comparatively young as he is. I know no one who has a higher sense of duty and responsibility.

CECILY: I suppose that is why he often looks a little bored when we three are together.

MISS PRISM: Cecily! I am surprised at you. Mr. Worthing has many troubles in his life. Idle merriment and triviality would be out of place in his conversation. You must remember his constant anxiety about that unfortunate young man his brother.

CECILY: I wish Uncle Jack would allow that unfortunate young man, his brother, to come down here sometimes. We might have a good influence over him, Miss Prism. I am sure you certainly would. You know German, and geology, and things of that kind influence a man very much. [CECILY *begins to write in her diary.*]

MISS PRISM: [*Shaking her head.*] I do not think that even I could produce any effect on a character that according to his own brother's admission is irretrievably weak and vacillating. Indeed I am not sure that I would desire to reclaim him. I am not in favor of this modern mania for turning bad people into good people at a moment's notice. As a man sows so let him reap. You must put away your diary, Cecily. I really don't see why you should keep a diary at all.

CECILY: I keep a diary in order to enter the wonderful secrets of my life. If I didn't write them down I should probably forget all about them.

MISS PRISM: Memory, my dear Cecily, is the diary that we all carry about with us.

CECILY: Yes, but it usually chronicles the things that have never happened, and couldn't possibly have happened. I believe that memory is responsible for nearly all the three-volume novels that Mudie sends us.[9]

MISS PRISM: Do not speak slightingly of the three-volume novel, Cecily. I wrote one myself in earlier days.

CECILY: Did you really, Miss Prism? How wonderfully clever you are! I hope it did not end happily? I don't like novels that end happily. They depress me so much.

MISS PRISM: The good ended happily, and the bad unhappily. That is what fiction means.

CECILY: I suppose so. But it seems very unfair. And was your novel ever published?

MISS PRISM: Alas! no. The manuscript unfortunately was abandoned. I use the word in the sense of lost or mislaid. To your work, child—these speculations are profitless.

---

9. From the 1840s to the 1890s, most novels were published in three volumes. Because of the price, most readers could not afford to buy copies and so obtained them by subscription from lending libraries, of which Mudie's in London was by far the largest.

CECILY: [*Smiling.*] But I see dear Dr. Chasuble coming up through the garden.

MISS PRISM: [*Rising and advancing.*] Dr. Chasuble! This is indeed a pleasure.

[*Enter* CANON CHASUBLE.]

CHASUBLE: And how are we this morning? Miss Prism, you are, I trust, well?

CECILY: Miss Prism has just been complaining of a slight headache. I think it would do her so much good to have a short stroll with you in the park, Dr. Chasuble.

MISS PRISM: Cecily, I have not mentioned anything about a headache.

CECILY: No, dear Miss Prism, I know that, but I felt instinctively that you had a headache. Indeed I was thinking about that, and not about my German lesson, when the Rector came in.

CHASUBLE: I hope, Cecily, you are not inattentive.

CECILY: Oh, I am afraid I am.

CHASUBLE: That is strange. Were I fortunate enough to be Miss Prism's pupil, I would hang upon her lips. [MISS PRISM *glares.*] I spoke metaphorically.—My metaphor was drawn from bees.[1] Ahem! Mr. Worthing, I suppose, has not returned from town yet?

MISS PRISM: We do not expect him till Monday afternoon.

CHASUBLE: Ah yes, he usually likes to spend his Sunday in London. He is not one of those whose sole aim is enjoyment, as, by all accounts, that unfortunate young man his brother seems to be. But I must not disturb Egeria[2] and her pupil any longer.

MISS PRISM: Egeria? My name is Laetitia, Doctor.

CHASUBLE: [*Bowing.*] A classical allusion merely, drawn from the Pagan authors. I shall see you both no doubt at Evensong?[3]

MISS PRISM: I think, dear Doctor, I will have a stroll with you. I find I have a headache after all, and a walk might do it good.

CHASUBLE: With pleasure, Miss Prism, with pleasure. We might go as far as the schools and back.

MISS PRISM: That would be delightful. Cecily, you will read your Political Economy[4] in my absence. The chapter on the Fall of the Rupee you may omit. It is somewhat too sensational. Even these metallic problems have their melodramatic side. [*Goes down the garden with* CANON CHASUBLE.]

CECILY: [*Picks up books and throws them back on table.*] Horrid Political Economy! Horrid Geography! Horrid, horrid German!

[*Enter* MERRIMAN *with a card on a salver.*]

MERRIMAN: Mr. Ernest Worthing has just driven over from the station. He has brought his luggage with him.

CECILY: [*Takes the card and reads it.*] "Mr. Ernest Worthing, B. 4, The Albany, W." Uncle Jack's brother! Did you tell him Mr. Worthing was in town?

MERRIMAN: Yes, Miss. He seemed very much disappointed. I mentioned that you and Miss Prism were in the garden. He said he was anxious to speak to you privately for a moment.

---

1. Reference to the "honey" of Miss Prism's instruction.
2. In classical mythology, a nymph famous as the wise counselor of Numa Pompilius, the second of the legendary kings of Rome.   3. Evening church services.   4. That is, book about economics.

CECILY: Ask Mr. Ernest Worthing to come here. I suppose you had better talk to the housekeeper about a room for him.

MERRIMAN: Yes, Miss. [MERRIMAN *goes off.*]

CECILY: I have never met any really wicked person before. I feel rather frightened. I am so afraid he will look just like everyone else. [*Enter* ALGERNON, *very gay and debonair.*] He does!

ALGERNON: [*Raising his hat.*] You are my little cousin Cecily, I'm sure.

CECILY: You are under some strange mistake. I am not little. In fact, I believe I am more than usually tall for my age. [ALGERNON *is rather taken aback.*] But I am your cousin Cecily. You, I see from your card, are Uncle Jack's brother, my cousin Ernest, my wicked cousin Ernest.

ALGERNON: Oh! I am not really wicked at all, cousin Cecily. You mustn't think that I am wicked.

CECILY: If you are not, then you have certainly been deceiving us all in a very inexcusable manner. I hope you have not been leading a double life, pretending to be wicked and being really good all the time. That would be hypocrisy.

ALGERNON: [*Looks at her in amazement.*] Oh! Of course I have been rather reckless.

CECILY: I am glad to hear it.

ALGERNON: In fact, now you mention the subject, I have been very bad in my own small way.

CECILY: I don't think you should be so proud of that, though I am sure it must have been very pleasant.

ALGERNON: It is much pleasanter being here with you.

CECILY: I can't understand how you are here at all. Uncle Jack won't be back till Monday afternoon.

ALGERNON: That is a great disappointment. I am obliged to go up by the first train on Monday morning. I have a business appointment that I am anxious . . . to miss.

CECILY: Couldn't you miss it anywhere but in London?

ALGERNON: No: the appointment is in London.

CECILY: Well, I know, of course, how important it is not to keep a business engagement, if one wants to retain any sense of the beauty of life, but still I think you had better wait till Uncle Jack arrives. I know he wants to speak to you about your emigrating.

ALGERNON: About my what?

CECILY: Your emigrating. He has gone up to buy your outfit.

ALGERNON: I certainly wouldn't let Jack buy my outfit. He has no taste in neckties at all.

CECILY: I don't think you will require neckties. Uncle Jack is sending you to Australia.[5]

ALGERNON: Australia? I'd sooner die.

CECILY: Well, he said at dinner on Wednesday night, that you would have to choose between this world, the next world, and Australia.

ALGERNON: Oh, well! The accounts I have received of Australia and the next world are not particularly encouraging. This world is good enough for me, cousin Cecily.

5. Though no longer a British penal colony in Wilde's day, Australia was still widely believed to be a place where disreputable family members might be sent.

CECILY: Yes, but are you good enough for it?

ALGERNON: I'm afraid I'm not that. That is why I want you to reform me. You might make that your mission, if you don't mind, cousin Cecily.

CECILY: I'm afraid I've no time, this afternoon.

ALGERNON: Well, would you mind my reforming myself this afternoon?

CECILY: It is rather Quixotic of you. But I think you should try.

ALGERNON: I will. I feel better already.

CECILY: You are looking a little worse.

ALGERNON: That is because I am hungry.

CECILY: How thoughtless of me. I should have remembered that when one is going to lead an entirely new life, one requires regular and wholesome meals. Won't you come in?

ALGERNON: Thank you. Might I have a buttonhole[6] first? I never have any appetite unless I have a buttonhole first.

CECILY: A Maréchal Niel? [*Picks up scissors.*]

ALGERNON: No, I'd sooner have a pink rose.

CECILY: Why? [*Cuts a flower.*]

ALGERNON: Because you are like a pink rose, cousin Cecily.

CECILY: I don't think it can be right for you to talk to me like that. Miss Prism never says such things to me.

ALGERNON: Then Miss Prism is a shortsighted old lady. [CECILY *puts the rose in his buttonhole.*] You are the prettiest girl I ever saw.

CECILY: Miss Prism says that all good looks are a snare.

ALGERNON: They are a snare that every sensible man would like to be caught in.

CECILY: Oh! I don't think I would care to catch a sensible man. I shouldn't know what to talk to him about.

[*They pass into the house.* MISS PRISM *and* DR. CHASUBLE *return.*]

MISS PRISM: You are too much alone, dear Dr. Chasuble. You should get married. A misanthrope I can understand—a womanthrope, never!

CHASUBLE: [*With a scholar's shudder.*] Believe me, I do not deserve so neologistic a phrase. The precept as well as the practice of the Primitive Church[7] was distinctly against matrimony.

MISS PRISM: [*Sententiously.*] That is obviously the reason why the Primitive Church has not lasted up to the present day. And you do not seem to realize, dear Doctor, that by persistently remaining single, a man converts himself into a permanent public temptation. Men should be more careful; this very celibacy leads weaker vessels astray.

CHASUBLE: But is a man not equally attractive when married?

MISS PRISM: No married man is ever attractive except to his wife.

CHASUBLE: And often, I've been told, not even to her.

MISS PRISM: That depends on the intellectual sympathies of the woman. Maturity can always be depended on. Ripeness can be trusted. Young women are green. [DR. CHASUBLE *starts.*] I spoke horticulturally. My metaphor was drawn from fruits. But where is Cecily?

CHASUBLE: Perhaps she followed us to the schools.

6. A flower to be worn on the lapel of a man's coat, in this case the Maréchal Niel, a popular yellow rose of the period.   7. Early Christian Church.

[*Enter* JACK *slowly from the back of the garden. He is dressed in the deepest mourning, with crape hat-band and black gloves.*]

MISS PRISM: Mr. Worthing!

CHASUBLE: Mr. Worthing?

MISS PRISM: This is indeed a surprise. We did not look for you till Monday afternoon.

JACK: [*Shakes* MISS PRISM'*s hand in a tragic manner.*] I have returned sooner than I expected. Dr. Chasuble, I hope you are well?

CHASUBLE: Dear Mr. Worthing, I trust this garb of woe does not betoken some terrible calamity?

JACK: My brother.

MISS PRISM: More shameful debts and extravagance?

CHASUBLE: Still leading his life of pleasure?

JACK: [*Shaking his head.*] Dead!

CHASUBLE: Your brother Ernest dead?

JACK: Quite dead.

MISS PRISM: What a lesson for him! I trust he will profit by it.

CHASUBLE: Mr. Worthing, I offer you my sincere condolence. You have at least the consolation of knowing that you were always the most generous and forgiving of brothers.

JACK: Poor Ernest! He had many faults, but it is a sad, sad blow.

CHASUBLE: Very sad indeed. Were you with him at the end?

JACK: No. He died abroad; in Paris, in fact. I had a telegram last night from the manager of the Grand Hotel.

CHASUBLE: Was the cause of death mentioned?

JACK: A severe chill, it seems.

MISS PRISM: As a man sows, so shall he reap.

CHASUBLE: [*Raising his hand.*] Charity, dear Miss Prism, charity! None of us are perfect. I myself am peculiarly susceptible to drafts. Will the interment take place here?

JACK: No. He seemed to have expressed a desire to be buried in Paris.

CHASUBLE: In Paris! [*Shakes his head.*] I fear that hardly points to any very serious state of mind at the last. You would no doubt wish me to make some slight allusion to this tragic domestic affliction next Sunday. [JACK *presses his hand convulsively.*] My sermon on the meaning of the manna in the wilderness can be adapted to almost any occasion, joyful, or, as in the present case, distressing. [*All sigh.*] I have preached it at harvest celebrations, christenings, confirmations, on days of humiliation and festal days. The last time I delivered it was in the Cathedral, as a charity sermon on behalf of the Society for the Prevention of Discontent among the Upper Orders. The Bishop, who was present, was much struck by some of the analogies I drew.

JACK: Ah! That reminds me, you mentioned christenings, I think, Dr. Chasuble? I suppose you know how to christen all right? [DR. CHASUBLE *looks astounded.*] I mean, of course, you are continually christening, aren't you?

MISS PRISM: It is, I regret to say, one of the Rector's most constant duties in this parish. I have often spoken to the poorer classes on the subject. But they don't seem to know what thrift is.

CHASUBLE: But is there any particular infant in whom you are interested, Mr. Worthing? Your brother was, I believe, unmarried, was he not?

JACK: Oh yes.

MISS PRISM: [*Bitterly.*] People who live entirely for pleasure usually are.

JACK: But it is not for any child, dear Doctor. I am very fond of children. No! the fact is, I would like to be christened myself, this afternoon, if you have nothing better to do.

CHASUBLE: But surely, Mr. Worthing, you have been christened already?

JACK: I don't remember anything about it.

CHASUBLE: But have you any grave doubts on the subject?

JACK: I certainly intend to have. Of course I don't know if the thing would bother you in any way, or if you think I am a little too old now.

CHASUBLE: Not at all. The sprinkling, and, indeed, the immersion of adults is a perfectly canonical practice.

JACK: Immersion!

CHASUBLE: You need have no apprehensions. Sprinkling is all that is necessary, or indeed I think advisable. Our weather is so changeable. At what hour would you wish the ceremony performed?

JACK: Oh, I might trot round about five if that would suit you.

CHASUBLE: Perfectly, perfectly! In fact I have two similar ceremonies to perform at that time. A case of twins that occurred recently in one of the outlying cottages on your own estate. Poor Jenkins the carter, a most hard-working man.

JACK: Oh! I don't see much fun in being christened along with other babies. It would be childish. Would half-past five do?

CHASUBLE: Admirably! Admirably! [*Takes out watch.*] And now, dear Mr. Worthing, I will not intrude any longer into a house of sorrow. I would merely beg you not to be too much bowed down by grief. What seem to us bitter trials are often blessings in disguise.

MISS PRISM: This seems to me a blessing of an extremely obvious kind.

[*Enter* CECILY *from the house.*]

CECILY: Uncle Jack! Oh, I am pleased to see you back. But what horrid clothes you have got on! Do go and change them.

MISS PRISM: Cecily!

CHASUBLE: My child! my child!

[CECILY *goes towards* JACK; *he kisses her brow in a melancholy manner.*]

CECILY: What is the matter, Uncle Jack? Do look happy! You look as if you had toothache, and I have got such a surprise for you. Who do you think is in the dining room? Your brother!

JACK: Who?

CECILY: Your brother Ernest. He arrived about half an hour ago.

JACK: What nonsense! I haven't got a brother!

CECILY: Oh, don't say that. However badly he may have behaved to you in the past he is still your brother. You couldn't be so heartless as to disown him. I'll tell him to come out. And you will shake hands with him, won't you, Uncle Jack? [*Runs back into the house.*]

CHASUBLE: These are very joyful tidings.

MISS PRISM: After we had all been resigned to his loss, his sudden return seems to me peculiarly distressing.

JACK: My brother is in the dining room? I don't know what it all means. I think it is perfectly absurd. [*Enter* ALGERNON *and* CECILY *hand in hand. They come slowly up to* JACK.] Good heavens! [*Motions* ALGERNON *away.*]

ALGERNON: Brother John, I have come down from town to tell you that I am very sorry for all the trouble I have given you, and that I intend to lead a better life in the future. [JACK *glares at him and does not take his hand.*]

CECILY: Uncle Jack, you are not going to refuse your own brother's hand?

JACK: Nothing will induce me to take his hand. I think his coming down here disgraceful. He knows perfectly well why.

CECILY: Uncle Jack, do be nice. There is some good in everyone. Ernest has just been telling me about his poor invalid friend Mr. Bunbury whom he goes to visit so often. And surely there must be much good in one who is kind to an invalid, and leaves the pleasures of London to sit by a bed of pain.

JACK: Oh! he has been talking about Bunbury, has he?

CECILY: Yes, he has told me all about poor Mr. Bunbury, and his terrible state of health.

JACK: Bunbury! Well, I won't have him talk to you about Bunbury or about anything else. It is enough to drive one perfectly frantic.

ALGERNON: Of course I admit that the faults were all on my side. But I must say that I think that Brother John's coldness to me is peculiarly painful. I expected a more enthusiastic welcome, especially considering it is the first time I have come here.

CECILY: Uncle Jack, if you don't shake hands with Ernest, I will never forgive you.

JACK: Never forgive me?

CECILY: Never, never, never!

JACK: Well, this is the last time I shall ever do it. [*Shakes hands with* ALGERNON *and glares.*]

CHASUBLE: It's pleasant, is it not, to see so perfect a reconciliation? I think we might leave the two brothers together.

MISS PRISM: Cecily, you will come with us.

CECILY: Certainly, Miss Prism. My little task of reconciliation is over.

CHASUBLE: You have done a beautiful action today, dear child.

MISS PRISM: We must not be premature in our judgments.

CECILY: I feel very happy.

[*They all go off.*]

JACK: You young scoundrel, Algy, you must get out of this place as soon as possible. I don't allow any Bunburying here.

[*Enter* MERRIMAN.]

MERRIMAN: I have put Mr. Ernest's things in the room next to yours, sir. I suppose that is all right?

JACK: What?

MERRIMAN: Mr. Ernest's luggage, sir. I have unpacked it and put it in the room next to your own.

JACK: His luggage?

MERRIMAN: Yes, sir. Three portmanteaus, a dressing case, two hat-boxes, and a large luncheon basket.

ALGERNON: I am afraid I can't stay more than a week this time.

JACK: Merriman, order the dogcart[8] at once. Mr. Ernest has been suddenly called back to town.

MERRIMAN: Yes, sir. [*Goes back into the house.*]

ALGERNON: What a fearful liar you are, Jack. I have not been called back to town at all.

JACK: Yes, you have.

ALGERNON: I haven't heard anyone call me.

JACK: Your duty as a gentleman calls you back.

ALGERNON: My duty as a gentleman has never interfered with my pleasures in the smallest degree.

JACK: I can quite understand that.

ALGERNON: Well, Cecily is a darling.

JACK: You are not to talk of Miss Cardew like that. I don't like it.

ALGERNON: Well, I don't like your clothes. You look perfectly ridiculous in them. Why on earth don't you go up and change? It is perfectly childish to be in deep mourning for a man who is actually staying for a whole week with you in your house as a guest. I call it grotesque.

JACK: You are certainly not staying with me for a whole week as a guest or anything else. You have got to leave . . . by the four-five train.

ALGERNON: I certainly won't leave you so long as you are in mourning. It would be most unfriendly. If I were in mourning you would stay with me, I suppose. I should think it very unkind if you didn't.

JACK: Well, will you go if I change my clothes?

ALGERNON: Yes, if you are not too long. I never saw anybody take so long to dress, and with such little result.

JACK: Well, at any rate, that is better than being always overdressed as you are.

ALGERNON: If I am occasionally a little overdressed, I make up for it by being always immensely overeducated.

JACK: Your vanity is ridiculous, your conduct an outrage, and your presence in my garden utterly absurd. However, you have got to catch the four-five, and I hope you will have a pleasant journey back to town. This Bunburying, as you call it, has not been a great success for you. [*Goes into the house.*]

ALGERNON: I think it has been a great success. I'm in love with Cecily, and that is everything. [*Enter* CECILY *at the back of the garden. She picks up the can and begins to water the flowers.*] But I must see her before I go, and make arrangements for another Bunbury. Ah, there she is.

CECILY: Oh, I merely came back to water the roses. I thought you were with Uncle Jack.

ALGERNON: He's gone to order the dogcart for me.

CECILY: Oh, is he going to take you for a nice drive?

ALGERNON: He's going to send me away.

CECILY: Then have we got to part?

ALGERNON: I am afraid so. It's very painful parting.

CECILY: It is always painful to part from people whom one has known for a very brief space of time. The absence of old friends one can endure with equanimity. But even a momentary separation from anyone to whom one has just been introduced is almost unbearable.

ALGERNON: Thank you.

---

8. A light, two-wheeled carriage, usually drawn by one horse.

[*Enter* MERRIMAN.]

MERRIMAN: The dogcart is at the door, sir. [ALGERNON *looks appealingly at* CECILY.]

CECILY: It can wait, Merriman . . . for . . . five minutes.

MERRIMAN: Yes, Miss. [*Exit* MERRIMAN.]

ALGERNON: I hope, Cecily, I shall not offend you if I state quite frankly and openly that you seem to me to be in every way the visible personification of absolute perfection.

CECILY: I think your frankness does you great credit, Ernest. If you will allow me I will copy your remarks into my diary. [*Goes over to table and begins writing in diary.*]

ALGERNON: Do you really keep a diary? I'd give anything to look at it. May I?

CECILY: Oh no. [*Puts her hand over it.*] You see, it is simply a very young girl's record of her own thoughts and impressions, and consequently meant for publication. When it appears in volume form I hope you will order a copy. But pray, Ernest, don't stop. I delight in taking down from dictation. I have reached "absolute perfection." You can go on. I am quite ready for more.

ALGERNON: [*Somewhat taken aback.*] Ahem! Ahem!

CECILY: Oh, don't cough, Ernest. When one is dictating one should speak fluently and not cough. Besides, I don't know how to spell a cough. [*Writes as* ALGERNON *speaks.*]

ALGERNON: [*Speaking very rapidly.*] Cecily, ever since I first looked upon your wonderful and incomparable beauty, I have dared to love you wildly, passionately, devotedly, hopelessly.

CECILY: I don't think that you should tell me that you love me wildly, passionately, devotedly, hopelessly. Hopelessly doesn't seem to make much sense, does it?

ALGERNON: Cecily!

[*Enter* MERRIMAN.]

MERRIMAN: The dogcart is waiting, sir.

ALGERNON: Tell it to come round next week, at the same hour.

MERRIMAN: [*Looks at* CECILY, *who makes no sign.*] Yes, sir. [MERRIMAN *retires.*]

CECILY: Uncle Jack would be very much annoyed if he knew you were staying on till next week, at the same hour.

ALGERNON: Oh, I don't care about Jack. I don't care for anybody in the whole world but you. I love you, Cecily. You will marry me, won't you?

CECILY: You silly boy! Of course. Why, we have been engaged for the last three months.

ALGERNON: For the last three months?

CECILY: Yes, it will be exactly three months on Thursday.

ALGERNON: But how did we become engaged?

CECILY: Well, ever since dear Uncle Jack first confessed to us that he had a younger brother who was very wicked and bad, you of course have formed the chief topic of conversation between myself and Miss Prism. And of course a man who is much talked about is always very attractive. One feels there must be something in him after all. I daresay it was foolish of me, but I fell in love with you, Ernest.

ALGERNON: Darling! And when was the engagement actually settled?

CECILY: On the 14th of February last. Worn out by your entire ignorance of my existence, I determined to end the matter one way or the other, and after a long struggle with myself I accepted you under this dear old tree here. The next day I bought this little ring in your name, and this is the little bangle with the true lovers' knot I promised you always to wear.

ALGERNON: Did I give you this? It's very pretty, isn't it?

CECILY: Yes, you've wonderfully good taste, Ernest. It's the excuse I've always given for your leading such a bad life. And this is the box in which I keep all your dear letters. [*Kneels at table, opens box, and produces letters tied up with blue ribbon.*]

ALGERNON: My letters! But my own sweet Cecily, I have never written you any letters.

CECILY: You need hardly remind me of that, Ernest. I remember only too well that I was forced to write your letters for you. I always wrote three times a week, and sometimes oftener.

ALGERNON: Oh, do let me read them, Cecily?

CECILY: Oh, I couldn't possibly. They would make you far too conceited. [*Replaces box.*] The three you wrote me after I had broken off the engagement are so beautiful, and so badly spelled, that even now I can hardly read them without crying a little.

ALGERNON: But was our engagement ever broken off?

CECILY: Of course it was. On the 22nd of last March. You can see the entry if you like. [*Shows diary.*] "Today I broke off my engagement with Ernest. I feel it is better to do so. The weather still continues charming."

ALGERNON: But why on earth did you break it off? What had I done? I had done nothing at all. Cecily, I am very much hurt indeed to hear you broke it off. Particularly when the weather was so charming.

CECILY: It would hardly have been a really serious engagement if it hadn't been broken off at least once. But I forgave you before the week was out.

ALGERNON: [*Crossing to her, and kneeling.*] What a perfect angel you are, Cecily.

CECILY: You dear romantic boy. [*He kisses her, she puts her fingers through his hair.*] I hope your hair curls naturally, does it?

ALGERNON: Yes, darling, with a little help from others.

CECILY: I am so glad.

ALGERNON: You'll never break off our engagement again, Cecily?

CECILY: I don't think I could break it off now that I have actually met you. Besides, of course, there is the question of your name.

ALGERNON: Yes, of course. [*Nervously.*]

CECILY: You must not laugh at me, darling, but it had always been a girlish dream of mine to love someone whose name was Ernest. [ALGERNON *rises,* CECILY *also.*] There is something in that name that seems to inspire absolute confidence. I pity any poor married woman whose husband is not called Ernest.

ALGERNON: But, my dear child, do you mean to say you could not love me if I had some other name?

CECILY: But what name?

ALGERNON: Oh, any name you like—Algernon—for instance . . .

CECILY: But I don't like the name of Algernon.

ALGERNON: Well, my own dear, sweet, loving little darling, I really can't see why you should object to the name of Algernon. It is not at all a bad name. In fact, it is rather an aristocratic name. Half of the chaps who get into the Bankruptcy Court are called Algernon. But seriously, Cecily . . . [*Moving to her.*] . . . if my name was Algy, couldn't you love me?

CECILY: [*Rising.*] I might respect you, Ernest, I might admire your character, but I fear that I should not be able to give you my undivided attention.

ALGERNON: Ahem! Cecily! [*Picking up hat.*] Your Rector here is, I suppose, thoroughly experienced in the practice of all the rites and ceremonials of the Church?

CECILY: Oh, yes. Dr. Chasuble is a most learned man. He has never written a single book, so you can imagine how much he knows.

ALGERNON: I must see him at once on a most important christening—I mean on most important business.

CECILY: Oh!

ALGERNON: I shan't be away more than half an hour.

CECILY: Considering that we have been engaged since February the 14th, and that I only met you today for the first time, I think it is rather hard that you should leave me for so long a period as half an hour. Couldn't you make it twenty minutes?

ALGERNON: I'll be back in no time. [*Kisses her and rushes down the garden.*]

CECILY: What an impetuous boy he is! I like his hair so much. I must enter his proposal in my diary.

[*Enter* MERRIMAN.]

MERRIMAN: A Miss Fairfax has just called to see Mr. Worthing. On very important business, Miss Fairfax states.

CECILY: Isn't Mr. Worthing in his library?

MERRIMAN: Mr. Worthing went over in the direction of the rectory some time ago.

CECILY: Pray ask the lady to come out here; Mr. Worthing is sure to be back soon. And you can bring tea.

MERRIMAN: Yes, Miss. [*Goes out.*]

CECILY: Miss Fairfax! I suppose one of the many good elderly women who are associated with Uncle Jack in some of his philanthropic work in London. I don't quite like women who are interested in philanthropic work. I think it is so forward of them.

[*Enter* MERRIMAN.]

MERRIMAN: Miss Fairfax.

[*Enter* GWENDOLEN. *Exit* MERRIMAN.]

CECILY: [*Advancing to meet her.*] Pray let me introduce myself to you. My name is Cecily Cardew.

GWENDOLEN: Cecily Cardew? [*Moving to her and shaking hands.*] What a very sweet name! Something tells me that we are going to be great friends. I like you already more than I can say. My first impressions of people are never wrong.

CECILY: How nice of you to like me so much after we have known each other such a comparatively short time. Pray sit down.

GWENDOLEN: [*Still standing up.*] I may call you Cecily, may I not?

CECILY: With pleasure!

GWENDOLEN: And you will always call me Gwendolen, won't you?

CECILY: If you wish.

GWENDOLEN: Then that is all quite settled, is it not?

CECILY: I hope so. [*A pause. They both sit down together.*]

GWENDOLEN: Perhaps this might be a favorable opportunity for my mentioning who I am. My father is Lord Bracknell. You have never heard of papa, I suppose?

CECILY: I don't think so.

GWENDOLEN: Outside the family circle, papa, I am glad to say, is entirely unknown. I think that is quite as it should be. The home seems to me to be the proper sphere for the man. And certainly once a man begins to neglect his domestic duties he becomes painfully effeminate, does he not? And I don't like that. It makes men so very attractive. Cecily, mamma, whose views on education are remarkably strict, has brought me up to be extremely shortsighted; it is part of her system; so do you mind my looking at you through my glasses?

CECILY: Oh! not at all, Gwendolen. I am very fond of being looked at.

GWENDOLEN: [*After examining* CECILY *carefully through a lorgnette.*] You are here on a short visit, I suppose.

CECILY: Oh no! I live here.

GWENDOLEN: [*Severely.*] Really? Your mother, no doubt, or some female relative of advanced years, resides here also?

CECILY: Oh no! I have no mother, nor, in fact, any relations.

GWENDOLEN: Indeed?

CECILY: My dear guardian, with the assistance of Miss Prism, has the arduous task of looking after me.

GWENDOLEN: Your guardian?

CECILY: Yes, I am Mr. Worthing's ward.

GWENDOLEN: Oh! It is strange he never mentioned to me that he had a ward. How secretive of him! He grows more interesting hourly. I am not sure, however, that the news inspires me with feelings of unmixed delight. [*Rising and going to her.*] I am very fond of you, Cecily; I have liked you ever since I met you! But I am bound to state that now that I know that you are Mr. Worthing's ward, I cannot help expressing a wish you were—well just a little older than you seem to be—and not quite so very alluring in appearance. In fact, if I may speak candidly—

CECILY: Pray do! I think that whenever one has anything unpleasant to say, one should always be quite candid.

GWENDOLEN: Well, to speak with perfect candor, Cecily, I wish that you were fully forty-two, and more than usually plain for your age. Ernest has a strong upright nature. He is the very soul of truth and honor. Disloyalty would be as impossible to him as deception. But even men of the noblest possible moral character are extremely susceptible to the influence of the physical charms of others. Modern, no less than ancient history, supplies us with many most painful examples of what I refer to. If it were not so, indeed, history would be quite unreadable.

CECILY: I beg your pardon, Gwendolen, did you say Ernest?

GWENDOLEN: Yes.

CECILY: Oh, but it is not Mr. Ernest Worthing who is my guardian. It is his brother—his elder brother.

GWENDOLEN: [*Sitting down again.*] Ernest never mentioned to me that he had a brother.

CECILY: I am sorry to say they have not been on good terms for a long time.

GWENDOLEN: Ah! that accounts for it. And now that I think of it I have never heard any man mention his brother. The subject seems distasteful to most men. Cecily, you have lifted a load from my mind. I was growing almost anxious. It would have been terrible if any cloud had come across a friendship like ours, would it not? Of course you are quite, quite sure that it is not Mr. Ernest Worthing who is your guardian?

CECILY: Quite sure. [*A pause.*] In fact, I am going to be his.

GWENDOLEN: [*Inquiringly.*] I beg your pardon?

CECILY: [*Rather shy and confidingly.*] Dearest Gwendolen, there is no reason why I should make a secret of it to you. Our little county newspaper is sure to chronicle the fact next week. Mr. Ernest Worthing and I are engaged to be married.

GWENDOLEN: [*Quite politely, rising.*] My darling Cecily, I think there must be some slight error. Mr. Ernest Worthing is engaged to me. The announcement will appear in the *Morning Post* on Saturday at the latest.

CECILY: [*Very politely, rising.*] I am afraid you must be under some misconception. Ernest proposed to me exactly ten minutes ago. [*Shows diary.*]

GWENDOLEN: [*Examines diary through her lorgnette carefully.*] It is certainly very curious, for he asked me to be his wife yesterday afternoon at 5:30. If you would care to verify the incident, pray do so. [*Produces diary of her own.*] I never travel without my diary. One should always have something sensational to read in the train. I am so sorry, dear Cecily, if it is any disappointment to you, but I am afraid *I* have the prior claim.

CECILY: It would distress me more than I can tell you, dear Gwendolen, if it caused you any mental or physical anguish, but I feel bound to point out that since Ernest proposed to you he clearly has changed his mind.

GWENDOLEN: [*Meditatively.*] If the poor fellow has been entrapped into any foolish promise I shall consider it my duty to rescue him at once, and with a firm hand.

CECILY: [*Thoughtfully and sadly.*] Whatever unfortunate entanglement my dear boy may have got into, I will never reproach him with it after we are married.

GWENDOLEN: Do you allude to me, Miss Cardew, as an entanglement? You are presumptuous. On an occasion of this kind it becomes more than a moral duty to speak one's mind. It becomes a pleasure.

CECILY: Do you suggest, Miss Fairfax, that I entrapped Ernest into an engagement? How dare you? This is no time for wearing the shallow mask of manners. When I see a spade I call it a spade.

GWENDOLEN: [*Satirically.*] I am glad to say that I have never seen a spade. It is obvious that our social spheres have been widely different.

[*Enter* MERRIMAN, *followed by the footman. He carries a salver, tablecloth, and plate stand.* CECILY *is about to retort. The presence of the servants exercises a restraining influence, under which both girls chafe.*]

MERRIMAN: Shall I lay tea here as usual, Miss?

CECILY: [*Sternly, in a calm voice.*] Yes, as usual.

[MERRIMAN *begins to clear table and lay cloth. A long pause.* CECILY *and* GWENDOLEN *glare at each other.*]

GWENDOLEN: Are there many interesting walks in the vicinity, Miss Cardew?

CECILY: Oh! yes! a great many. From the top of one of the hills quite close one can see five counties.

GWENDOLEN: Five counties! I don't think I should like that. I hate crowds.

CECILY: [*Sweetly.*] I suppose that is why you live in town?

[GWENDOLEN *bites her lip, and beats her foot nervously with her parasol.*]

GWENDOLEN: [*Looking round.*] Quite a well-kept garden this is, Miss Cardew.

CECILY: So glad you like it, Miss Fairfax.

GWENDOLEN: I had no idea there were any flowers in the country.

CECILY: Oh, flowers are as common here, Miss Fairfax, as people are in London.

GWENDOLEN: Personally I cannot understand how anybody manages to exist in the country, if anybody who is anybody does. The country always bores me to death.

CECILY: Ah! This is what the newspapers call agricultural depression, is it not? I believe the aristocracy are suffering very much from it just at present. It is almost an epidemic amongst them, I have been told. May I offer you some tea, Miss Fairfax?

GWENDOLEN: [*With elaborate politeness.*] Thank you. [*Aside.*] Detestable girl! But I require tea!

CECILY: [*Sweetly.*] Sugar?

GWENDOLEN: [*Superciliously.*] No, thank you. Sugar is not fashionable anymore.

[CECILY *looks angrily at her, takes up the tongs and puts four lumps of sugar into the cup.*]

CECILY: [*Severely.*] Cake or bread and butter?

GWENDOLEN: [*In a bored manner.*] Bread and butter, please. Cake is rarely seen at the best houses nowadays.

CECILY: [*Cuts a very large slice of cake, and puts it on the tray.*] Hand that to Miss Fairfax.

[MERRIMAN *does so, and goes out with footman.* GWENDOLEN *drinks the tea and makes a grimace. Puts down cup at once, reaches out her hand to the bread and butter, looks at it, and finds it is cake. Rises in indignation.*]

GWENDOLEN: You have filled my tea with lumps of sugar, and though I asked most distinctly for bread and butter, you have given me cake. I am known for the gentleness of my disposition, and the extraordinary sweetness of my nature, but I warn you, Miss Cardew, you may go too far.

CECILY: [*Rising.*] To save my poor, innocent, trusting boy from the machinations of any other girl there are no lengths to which I would not go.

GWENDOLEN: From the moment I saw you I distrusted you. I felt that you were false and deceitful. I am never deceived in such matters. My first impressions of people are invariably right.

CECILY: It seems to me, Miss Fairfax, that I am trespassing on your valuable time. No doubt you have many other calls of a similar character to make in the neighborhood.

[*Enter* JACK.]

GWENDOLEN: [*Catching sight of him.*] Ernest! My own Ernest!

JACK: Gwendolen! Darling! [*Offers to kiss her.*]

GWENDOLEN: [*Drawing back.*] A moment! May I ask if you are engaged to be married to this young lady? [*Points to* CECILY.]

JACK: [*Laughing.*] To dear little Cecily! Of course not! What could have put such an idea into your pretty little head?

GWENDOLEN: Thank you. You may! [*Offers her cheek.*]

CECILY: [*Very sweetly.*] I knew there must be some misunderstanding, Miss Fairfax. The gentleman whose arm is at present round your waist is my dear guardian, Mr. John Worthing.

GWENDOLEN: I beg your pardon?

CECILY: This is Uncle Jack.

GWENDOLEN: [*Receding.*] Jack! Oh!

[*Enter* ALGERNON.]

CECILY: Here is Ernest.

ALGERNON: [*Goes straight over to* CECILY *without noticing anyone else.*] My own love! [*Offers to kiss her.*]

CECILY: [*Drawing back.*] A moment, Ernest! May I ask you—are you engaged to be married to this young lady?

ALGERNON: [*Looking round.*] To what young lady? Good heavens! Gwendolen!

CECILY: Yes! to good heavens, Gwendolen, I mean to Gwendolen.

ALGERNON: [*Laughing.*] Of course not! What could have put such an idea into your pretty little head?

CECILY: Thank you. [*Presenting her cheek to be kissed.*] You may. [ALGERNON *kisses her.*]

GWENDOLEN: I felt there was some slight error, Miss Cardew. The gentleman who is now embracing you is my cousin, Mr. Algernon Moncrieff.

CECILY: [*Breaking away from* ALGERNON.] Algernon Moncrieff! Oh! [*The two girls move towards each other and put their arms round each other's waists as if for protection.*] Are you called Algernon?

ALGERNON: I cannot deny it.

CECILY: Oh!

GWENDOLEN: Is your name really John?

JACK: [*Standing rather proudly.*] I could deny it if I liked, I could deny anything if I liked. But my name certainly is John. It has been John for years.

CECILY: [*To* GWENDOLEN.] A gross deception has been practiced on both of us.

GWENDOLEN: My poor wounded Cecily!

CECILY: My sweet wronged Gwendolen!

GWENDOLEN: [*Slowly and seriously.*] You will call me sister, will you not?

[*They embrace.* JACK *and* ALGERNON *groan and walk up and down.*]

CECILY: [*Rather brightly.*] There is just one question I would like to be allowed to ask my guardian.

GWENDOLEN: An admirable idea! Mr. Worthing, there is just one question I would like to be permitted to put to you. Where is your brother Ernest? We are both engaged to be married to your brother Ernest, so it is a matter of some importance to us to know where your brother Ernest is at present.

JACK: [*Slowly and hesitatingly.*] Gwendolen—Cecily—it is very painful for me to be forced to speak the truth. It is the first time in my life that I have ever been reduced to such a painful position, and I am really quite inexperienced in doing anything of the kind. However I will tell you quite frankly that I have no brother Ernest. I have no brother at all. I never had a brother in my life, and certainly have not the smallest intention of ever having one in the future.

CECILY: [*Surprised.*] No brother at all?

JACK: [*Cheerily.*] None!

GWENDOLEN: [*Severely.*] Had you never a brother of any kind?

JACK: [*Pleasantly.*] Never. Not even of any kind.

GWENDOLEN: I am afraid it is quite clear, Cecily, that neither of us is engaged to be married to anyone.

CECILY: It is not a very pleasant position for a young girl suddenly to find herself in. Is it?

GWENDOLEN: Let us go into the house. They will hardly venture to come after us there.

CECILY: No, men are so cowardly, aren't they?

[*They retire into the house with scornful looks.*]

JACK: This ghastly state of things is what you call Bunburying, I suppose?

ALGERNON: Yes, and a perfectly wonderful Bunbury it is. The most wonderful Bunbury I have ever had in my life.

JACK: Well, you've no right whatsoever to Bunbury here.

ALGERNON: That is absurd. One has a right to Bunbury anywhere one chooses. Every serious Bunburyist knows that.

JACK: Serious Bunburyist! Good heavens!

ALGERNON: Well, one must be serious about something, if one wants to have any amusement in life. I happen to be serious about Bunburying. What on earth you are serious about I haven't got the remotest idea. About everything, I should fancy. You have such an absolutely trivial nature.

JACK: Well, the only small satisfaction I have in the whole of this wretched business is that your friend Bunbury is quite exploded. You won't be able to run down to the country quite so often as you used to do, dear Algy. And a very good thing too.

ALGERNON: Your brother is a little off-color,[9] isn't he, dear Jack? You won't be able to disappear to London quite so frequently as your wicked custom was. And not a bad thing either.

JACK: As for your conduct towards Miss Cardew, I must say that your taking in a sweet, simple, innocent girl like that is quite inexcusable. To say nothing of the fact that she is my ward.

ALGERNON: I can see no possible defense at all for your deceiving a brilliant, clever, thoroughly experienced young lady like Miss Fairfax. To say nothing of the fact that she is my cousin.

JACK: I wanted to be engaged to Gwendolen, that is all. I love her.

ALGERNON: Well, I simply wanted to be engaged to Cecily. I adore her.

JACK: There is certainly no chance of your marrying Miss Cardew.

ALGERNON: I don't think there is much likelihood, Jack, of you and Miss Fairfax being united.

JACK: Well, that is no business of yours.

ALGERNON: If it was my business, I wouldn't talk about it. [*Begins to eat muffins.*] It is very vulgar to talk about one's business. Only people like stockbrokers do that, and then merely at dinner parties.

---

9. In poor health.

JACK: How can you sit there, calmly eating muffins when we are in this horrible trouble, I can't make out. You seem to me to be perfectly heartless.

ALGERNON: Well, I can't eat muffins in an agitated manner. The butter would probably get on my cuffs. One should always eat muffins quite calmly. It is the only way to eat them.

JACK: I say it's perfectly heartless your eating muffins at all, under the circumstances.

ALGERNON: When I am in trouble, eating is the only thing that consoles me. Indeed, when I am in really great trouble, as anyone who knows me intimately will tell you, I refuse everything except food and drink. At the present moment I am eating muffins because I am unhappy. Besides, I am particularly fond of muffins. [*Rising.*]

JACK: [*Rising.*] Well, that is no reason why you should eat them all in that greedy way. [*Takes muffins from* ALGERNON.]

ALGERNON: [*Offering tea cake.*] I wish you would have tea cake instead. I don't like tea cake.

JACK: Good heavens! I suppose a man may eat his own muffins in his own garden.

ALGERNON: But you have just said it was perfectly heartless to eat muffins.

JACK: I said it was perfectly heartless of you, under the circumstances. That is a very different thing.

ALGERNON: That may be. But the muffins are the same. [*He seizes the muffin dish from* JACK.]

JACK: Algy, I wish to goodness you would go.

ALGERNON: You can't possibly ask me to go without having some dinner. It's absurd. I never go without my dinner. No one ever does, except vegetarians and people like that. Besides I have just made arrangements with Dr. Chasuble to be christened at a quarter to six under the name of Ernest.

JACK: My dear fellow, the sooner you give up that nonsense the better. I made arrangements this morning with Dr. Chasuble to be christened myself at 5:30, and I naturally will take the name of Ernest. Gwendolen would wish it. We can't both be christened Ernest. It's absurd. Besides, I have a perfect right to be christened if I like. There is no evidence at all that I ever have been christened by anybody. I should think it extremely probable I never was, and so does Dr. Chasuble. It is entirely different in your case. You have been christened already.

ALGERNON: Yes, but I have not been christened for years.

JACK: Yes, but you have been christened. That is the important thing.

ALGERNON: Quite so. So I know my constitution can stand it. If you are not quite sure about your ever having been christened, I must say I think it rather dangerous your venturing on it now. It might make you very unwell. You can hardly have forgotten that someone very closely connected with you was very nearly carried off this week in Paris by a severe chill.

JACK: Yes, but you said yourself that a severe chill was not hereditary.

ALGERNON: It usen't to be, I know—but I daresay it is now. Science is always making wonderful improvements in things.

JACK: [*Picking up the muffin dish.*] Oh, that is nonsense; you are always talking nonsense.

ALGERNON: Jack, you are at the muffins again! I wish you wouldn't. There are only two left. [*Takes them.*] I told you I was particularly fond of muffins.

JACK: But I hate tea cake.

ALGERNON: Why on earth then do you allow tea cake to be served up for your guests? What ideas you have of hospitality!

JACK: Algernon! I have already told you to go. I don't want you here. Why don't you go!

ALGERNON: I haven't quite finished my tea yet! and there is still one muffin left.

[JACK *groans, and sinks into a chair.* ALGERNON *still continues eating.*]

ACT-DROP

ACT III

SCENE: *Morning room at the Manor House.*

[GWENDOLEN *and* CECILY *are at the window, looking out into the garden.*]

GWENDOLEN: The fact that they did not follow us at once into the house, as anyone else would have done, seems to me to show that they have some sense of shame left.

CECILY: They have been eating muffins. That looks like repentance.

GWENDOLEN: [*After a pause.*] They don't seem to notice us at all. Couldn't you cough?

CECILY: But I haven't got a cough.

GWENDOLEN: They're looking at us. What effrontery!

CECILY: They're approaching. That's very forward of them.

GWENDOLEN: Let us preserve a dignified silence.

CECILY: Certainly. It's the only thing to do now.

[*Enter* JACK *followed by* ALGERNON. *They whistle some dreadful popular air from a British Opera.*]

GWENDOLEN: This dignified silence seems to produce an unpleasant effect.

CECILY: A most distasteful one.

GWENDOLEN: But we will not be the first to speak.

CECILY: Certainly not.

GWENDOLEN: Mr. Worthing, I have something very particular to ask you. Much depends on your reply.

CECILY: Gwendolen, your common sense is invaluable. Mr. Moncrieff, kindly answer me the following question. Why did you pretend to be my guardian's brother?

ALGERNON: In order that I might have an opportunity of meeting you.

CECILY: [*To* GWENDOLEN.] That certainly seems a satisfactory explanation, does it not?

GWENDOLEN: Yes, dear, if you can believe him.

CECILY: I don't. But that does not affect the wonderful beauty of his answer.

GWENDOLEN: True. In matters of grave importance, style, not sincerity, is the vital thing. Mr. Worthing, what explanation can you offer to me for pretending to have a brother? Was it in order that you might have an opportunity of coming up to town to see me as often as possible?

JACK: Can you doubt it, Miss Fairfax?

GWENDOLEN: I have the gravest doubts upon the subject. But I intend to crush them. This is not the moment for German skepticism.[1] [*Moving to* CECILY.] Their explanations appear to be quite satisfactory, especially Mr. Worthing's. That seems to me to have the stamp of truth upon it.

CECILY: I am more than content with what Mr. Moncrieff said. His voice alone inspires one with absolute credulity.

GWENDOLEN: Then you think we should forgive them?

CECILY: Yes. I mean no.

GWENDOLEN: True! I had forgotten. There are principles at stake that one cannot surrender. Which of us should tell them? The task is not a pleasant one.

CECILY: Could we not both speak at the same time?

GWENDOLEN: An excellent idea! I nearly always speak at the same time as other people. Will you take the time from me?

CECILY: Certainly. [GWENDOLEN *beats time with uplifted finger.*]

GWENDOLEN AND CECILY: [*Speaking together.*] Your Christian names are still an insuperable barrier. That is all!

JACK AND ALGERNON: [*Speaking together.*] Our Christian names! Is that all? But we are going to be christened this afternoon.

GWENDOLEN: [*To* JACK.] For my sake you are prepared to do this terrible thing?

JACK: I am.

CECILY: [*To* ALGERNON.] To please me you are ready to face this fearful ordeal?

ALGERNON: I am!

GWENDOLEN: How absurd to talk of the equality of the sexes! Where questions of self-sacrifice are concerned, men are infinitely beyond us.

JACK: We are. [*Clasps hands with* ALGERNON.]

CECILY: They have moments of physical courage of which we women know absolutely nothing.

GWENDOLEN: [*To* JACK.] Darling!

ALGERNON: [*To* CECILY.] Darling. [*They fall into each other's arms.*]

[*Enter* MERRIMAN. *When he enters he coughs loudly, seeing the situation.*]

MERRIMAN: Ahem! Ahem! Lady Bracknell!

JACK: Good heavens!

[*Enter* LADY BRACKNELL. *The couples separate in alarm. Exit* MERRIMAN.]

LADY BRACKNELL: Gwendolen! What does this mean?

GWENDOLEN: Merely that I am engaged to be married to Mr. Worthing, mamma.

LADY BRACKNELL: Come here. Sit down. Sit down immediately. Hesitation of any kind is a sign of mental decay in the young, of physical weakness in the old. [*Turns to* JACK.] Apprised, sir, of my daughter's sudden flight by her trusty maid, whose confidence I purchased by means of a small coin, I followed her at once by a luggage train. Her unhappy father is, I am glad to say, under the impression that she is attending a more than usually lengthy lecture by the

---

1. A reference to such philosophical movements as the Materialism of Ludwig Feuerbach (1804–72) and such theological movements as the "Higher Criticism," which promoted studying the Bible in the same way as other books.

University Extension Scheme[2] on the Influence of a Permanent Income on Thought. I do not propose to undeceive him. Indeed I have never undeceived him on any question. I would consider it wrong. But of course, you will clearly understand that all communication between yourself and my daughter must cease immediately from this moment. On this point, as indeed on all points, I am firm.

JACK: I am engaged to be married to Gwendolen, Lady Bracknell!

LADY BRACKNELL: You are nothing of the kind, sir. And now, as regards Algernon! . . . Algernon!

ALGERNON: Yes, Aunt Augusta.

LADY BRACKNELL: May I ask if it is in this house that your invalid friend Mr. Bunbury resides?

ALGERNON: [Stammering.] Oh! No! Bunbury doesn't live here. Bunbury is somewhere else at present. In fact, Bunbury is dead.

LADY BRACKNELL: Dead! When did Mr. Bunbury die? His death must have been extremely sudden.

ALGERNON: [Airily.] Oh! I killed Bunbury this afternoon. I mean poor Bunbury died this afternoon.

LADY BRACKNELL: What did he die of?

ALGERNON: Bunbury? Oh, he was quite exploded.

LADY BRACKNELL: Exploded! Was he the victim of a revolutionary outrage? I was not aware that Mr. Bunbury was interested in social legislation. If so, he is well punished for his morbidity.

ALGERNON: My dear Aunt Augusta, I mean he was found out! The doctors found out that Bunbury could not live, that is what I mean—so Bunbury died.

LADY BRACKNELL: He seems to have had great confidence in the opinion of his physicians. I am glad, however, that he made up his mind at the last to some definite course of action, and acted under proper medical advice. And now that we have finally got rid of this Mr. Bunbury, may I ask, Mr. Worthing, who is that young person whose hand my nephew Algernon is now holding in what seems to me a peculiarly unnecessary manner?

JACK: That lady is Miss Cecily Cardew, my ward.

[LADY BRACKNELL bows coldly to CECILY.]

ALGERNON: I am engaged to be married to Cecily, Aunt Augusta.

LADY BRACKNELL: I beg your pardon?

CECILY: Mr. Moncrieff and I are engaged to be married, Lady Bracknell.

LADY BRACKNELL: [With a shiver, crossing to the sofa and sitting down.] I do not know whether there is anything peculiarly exciting in the air of this particular part of Hertfordshire, but the number of engagements that go on seems to me considerably above the proper average that statistics have laid down for our guidance. I think some preliminary inquiry on my part would not be out of place. Mr. Worthing, is Miss Cardew at all connected with any of the larger railway stations in London? I merely desire information. Until yesterday I had no idea that there were any families or persons whose origin was a terminus.

[JACK looks perfectly furious, but restrains himself.]

2. Program of public lectures delivered by university professors.

JACK: [*In a clear, cold voice.*] Miss Cardew is the granddaughter of the late Mr. Thomas Cardew of 149, Belgrave Square, S.W.; Gervase Park, Dorking, Surrey; and the Sporran, Fifeshire, N.B.[3]

LADY BRACKNELL: That sounds not unsatisfactory. Three addresses always inspire confidence, even in tradesmen. But what proof have I of their authenticity?

JACK: I have carefully preserved the Court Guides[4] of the period. They are open to your inspection, Lady Bracknell.

LADY BRACKNELL: [*Grimly.*] I have known strange errors in that publication.

JACK: Miss Cardew's family solicitors are Messrs.[5] Markby, Markby, and Markby.

LADY BRACKNELL: Markby, Markby, and Markby? A firm of the very highest position in their profession. Indeed I am told that one of the Mr. Markbys is occasionally to be seen at dinner parties. So far I am satisfied.

JACK: [*Very irritably.*] How extremely kind of you, Lady Bracknell! I have also in my possession, you will be pleased to hear, certificates of Miss Cardew's birth, baptism, whooping cough, registration, vaccination, confirmation, and the measles; both the German and the English variety.

LADY BRACKNELL: Ah! A life crowded with incident, I see; though perhaps somewhat too exciting for a young girl. I am not myself in favor of premature experiences. [*Rises, looks at her watch.*] Gwendolen! the time approaches for our departure. We have not a moment to lose. As a matter of form, Mr. Worthing, I had better ask you if Miss Cardew has any little fortune?

JACK: Oh! about a hundred and thirty thousand pounds in the Funds.[6] That is all. Good-bye, Lady Bracknell. So pleased to have seen you.

LADY BRACKNELL: [*Sitting down again.*] A moment, Mr. Worthing. A hundred and thirty thousand pounds! And in the Funds! Miss Cardew seems to me a most attractive young lady, now that I look at her. Few girls of the present day have any really solid qualities, any of the qualities that last, and improve with time. We live, I regret to say, in an age of surfaces. [*To* CECILY.] Come over here, dear. [CECILY *goes across.*] Pretty child! your dress is sadly simple, and your hair seems almost as Nature might have left it. But we can soon alter all that. A thoroughly experienced French maid produces a really marvelous result in a very brief space of time. I remember recommending one to young Lady Lancing, and after three months her own husband did not know her.

JACK: [*Aside.*] And after six months nobody knew her.

LADY BRACKNELL: [*Glares at* JACK *for a few moments. Then bends, with a practiced smile, to* CECILY.] Kindly turn round, sweet child. [CECILY *turns completely round.*] No, the side view is what I want. [CECILY *presents her profile.*] Yes, quite as I expected. There are distinct social possibilities in your profile. The two weak points in our age are its want of principle and its want of profile. The chin a little higher, dear. Style largely depends on the way the chin is worn. They are worn very high, just at present. Algernon!

ALGERNON: Yes, Aunt Augusta!

LADY BRACKNELL: There are distinct social possibilities in Miss Cardew's profile.

---

3. In addition to his London residence in Belgrave Square (referred to in act I), Mr. Cardew has homes in the south of England (Dorking, Surrey) and in Scotland (Fifeshire; N.B.: North Britain).

4. Records of civil and legal proceedings.   5. That is, "Messieurs" ("Misters" in French).

6. Nearly $20,000,000 in today's U.S. currency, invested in stock of the British National Debt.

ALGERNON: Cecily is the sweetest, dearest, prettiest girl in the whole world. And I don't care twopence about social possibilities.

LADY BRACKNELL: Never speak disrespectfully of Society, Algernon. Only people who can't get into it do that. [*To* CECILY.] Dear child, of course you know that Algernon has nothing but his debts to depend upon. But I do not approve of mercenary marriages. When I married Lord Bracknell I had no fortune of any kind. But I never dreamed for a moment of allowing that to stand in my way. Well, I suppose I must give my consent.

ALGERNON: Thank you, Aunt Augusta.

LADY BRACKNELL: Cecily, you may kiss me!

CECILY: [*Kisses her.*] Thank you, Lady Bracknell.

LADY BRACKNELL: You may also address me as Aunt Augusta for the future.

CECILY: Thank you, Aunt Augusta.

LADY BRACKNELL: The marriage, I think, had better take place quite soon.

ALGERNON: Thank you, Aunt Augusta.

CECILY: Thank you, Aunt Augusta.

LADY BRACKNELL: To speak frankly, I am not in favor of long engagements. They give people the opportunity of finding out each other's character before marriage, which I think is never advisable.

JACK: I beg your pardon for interrupting you, Lady Bracknell, but this engagement is quite out of the question. I am Miss Cardew's guardian, and she cannot marry without my consent until she comes of age. That consent I absolutely decline to give.

LADY BRACKNELL: Upon what grounds may I ask? Algernon is an extremely, I may almost say an ostentatiously, eligible young man. He has nothing, but he looks everything. What more can one desire?

JACK: It pains me very much to have to speak frankly to you, Lady Bracknell, about your nephew, but the fact is that I do not approve at all of his moral character. I suspect him of being untruthful.

[ALGERNON *and* CECILY *look at him in indignant amazement.*]

LADY BRACKNELL: Untruthful! My nephew Algernon? Impossible! He is an Oxonian.[7]

JACK: I fear there can be no possible doubt about the matter. This afternoon, during my temporary absence in London on an important question of romance, he obtained admission to my house by means of the false pretense of being my brother. Under an assumed name he drank, I've just been informed by the butler, an entire pint bottle of my Perrier-Jouet, Brut, '89;[8] a wine I was specially reserving for myself. Continuing his disgraceful deception, he succeeded in the course of the afternoon in alienating the affections of my only ward. He subsequently stayed to tea, and devoured every single muffin. And what makes his conduct all the more heartless is, that he was perfectly well aware from the first that I have no brother, that I never had a brother, and that I don't intend to have a brother, not even any kind. I distinctly told him so myself yesterday afternoon.

LADY BRACKNELL: Ahem! Mr. Worthing, after careful consideration I have decided entirely to overlook my nephew's conduct to you.

---

7. Graduate of Oxford University.   8. Very fine champagne.

JACK: That is very generous of you, Lady Bracknell. My own decision, however, is unalterable. I decline to give my consent.

LADY BRACKNELL: [*To* CECILY.] Come here, sweet child. [CECILY goes over.] How old are you, dear?

CECILY: Well, I am really only eighteen, but I always admit to twenty when I go to evening parties.

LADY BRACKNELL: You are perfectly right in making some slight alteration. Indeed, no woman should ever be quite accurate about her age. It looks so calculating. . . . [*In a meditative manner.*] Eighteen, but admitting to twenty at evening parties. Well, it will not be very long before you are of age and free from the restraints of tutelage. So I don't think your guardian's consent, after all, a matter of any importance.

JACK: Pray excuse me, Lady Bracknell, for interrupting you again, but it is only fair to tell you that according to the terms of her grandfather's will Miss Cardew does not come legally of age till she is thirty-five.

LADY BRACKNELL: That does not seem to me to be a grave objection. Thirty-five is a very attractive age. London society is full of women of the very highest birth who have, of their own free choice, remained thirty-five for years. Lady Dumbleton is an instance in point. To my own knowledge she has been thirty-five ever since she arrived at the age of forty, which was many years ago now. I see no reason why our dear Cecily should not be even still more attractive at the age you mention than she is at present. There will be a large accumulation of property.

CECILY: Algy, could you wait for me till I was thirty-five?

ALGERNON: Of course I could, Cecily. You know I could.

CECILY: Yes, I felt it instinctively, but I couldn't wait all that time. I hate waiting even five minutes for anybody. It always makes me rather cross. I am not punctual myself, I know, but I do like punctuality in others, and waiting, even to be married, is quite out of the question.

ALGERNON: Then what is to be done, Cecily?

CECILY: I don't know, Mr. Moncrieff.

LADY BRACKNELL: My dear Mr. Worthing, as Miss Cardew states positively that she cannot wait till she is thirty-five—a remark which I am bound to say seems to me to show a somewhat impatient nature—I would beg of you to reconsider your decision.

JACK: But my dear Lady Bracknell, the matter is entirely in your own hands. The moment you consent to my marriage with Gwendolen, I will most gladly allow your nephew to form an alliance with my ward.

LADY BRACKNELL: [*Rising and drawing herself up.*] You must be quite aware that what you propose is out of the question.

JACK: Then a passionate celibacy is all that any of us can look forward to.

LADY BRACKNELL: This is not the destiny I propose for Gwendolen. Algernon, of course, can choose for himself. [*Pulls out her watch.*] Come, dear; [GWENDOLEN *rises.*] we have already missed five, if not six, trains. To miss any more might expose us to comment on the platform.

    [*Enter* CANON CHASUBLE.]

CHASUBLE: Everything is quite ready for the christenings.

LADY BRACKNELL: The christenings, sir! Is not that somewhat premature!

CHASUBLE: [_looking rather puzzled, and pointing to_ JACK _and_ ALGERNON.] Both these gentlemen have expressed a desire for immediate baptism.

LADY BRACKNELL: At their age? The idea is grotesque and irreligious! Algernon, I forbid you to be baptized. I will not hear of such excesses. Lord Bracknell would be highly displeased if he learned that that was the way in which you wasted your time and money.

CHASUBLE: Am I to understand then that there are to be no christenings at all this afternoon?

JACK: I don't think that, as things are now, it would be of much practical value to either of us, Dr. Chasuble.

CHASUBLE: I am grieved to hear such sentiments from you, Mr. Worthing. They savor of the heretical views of the Anabaptists,[1] views that I have completely refuted in four of my unpublished sermons. However, as your present mood seems to be one peculiarly secular, I will return to the church at once. Indeed, I have just been informed by the pew-opener[2] that for the last hour and a half Miss Prism has been waiting for me in the vestry.

LADY BRACKNELL: [_Starting._] Miss Prism! Did I hear you mention a Miss Prism?

CHASUBLE: Yes, Lady Bracknell. I am on my way to join her.

LADY BRACKNELL: Pray allow me to detain you for a moment. This matter may prove to be one of vital importance to Lord Bracknell and myself. Is this Miss Prism a female of repellent aspect, remotely connected with education?

CHASUBLE: [_Somewhat indignantly._] She is the most cultivated of ladies, and the very picture of respectability.

LADY BRACKNELL: It is obviously the same person. May I ask what position she holds in your household?

CHASUBLE: [_Severely._] I am a celibate, madam.

JACK: [_Interposing._] Miss Prism, Lady Bracknell, has been for the last three years Miss Cardew's esteemed governess and valued companion.

LADY BRACKNELL: In spite of what I hear of her, I must see her at once. Let her be sent for.

CHASUBLE: [_Looking off._] She approaches; she is nigh.

[_Enter_ MISS PRISM _hurriedly._]

MISS PRISM: I was told you expected me in the vestry, dear Canon. I have been waiting for you there for an hour and three quarters. [_Catches sight of_ LADY BRACKNELL, _who has fixed her with a stony glare._ MISS PRISM _grows pale and quails. She looks anxiously round as if desirous to escape._]

LADY BRACKNELL: [_In a severe, judicial voice._] Prism! [MISS PRISM _bows her head in shame._] Come here, Prism! [MISS PRISM _approaches in a humble manner._] Prism! Where is that baby? [_General consternation._ THE CANON _starts back in horror._ ALGERNON _and_ JACK _pretend to be anxious to shield_ CECILY _and_ GWENDOLEN _from hearing the details of a terrible public scandal._] Twenty-eight years ago, Prism, you left Lord Bracknell's house, Number 104, Upper Grosvenor Street, in charge of a perambulator that

---

9. Sixteenth-century religious group, somewhat like contemporary Mennonites. Dr. Chasuble, however, is probably using the term loosely to apply to a group more like contemporary Baptists.

1. Usher. Since most pews were enclosed, his duties would have included opening the gate that allowed worshipers to enter. In addition, since most pews were rented for the use of specific persons, he would have been responsible for seeing that worshipers were seated in the correct pews.

contained a baby, of the male sex. You never returned. A few weeks later, through the elaborate investigations of the Metropolitan police, the perambulator was discovered at midnight, standing by itself in a remote corner of Bayswater.[3] It contained the manuscript of a three-volume novel of more than usually revolting sentimentality. [MISS PRISM *starts in involuntary indignation*.] But the baby was not there! [*Everyone looks at* MISS PRISM.] Prism! Where is that baby? [*A pause*.]

MISS PRISM: Lady Bracknell, I admit with shame that I do not know. I only wish I did. The plain facts of the case are these. On the morning of the day you mention, a day that is forever branded on my memory, I prepared as usual to take the baby out in its perambulator. I had also with me a somewhat old, but capacious handbag, in which I had intended to place the manuscript of a work of fiction that I had written during my few unoccupied hours. In a moment of mental abstraction, for which I never can forgive myself, I deposited the manuscript in the bassinette, and placed the baby in the handbag.

JACK: [*Who has been listening attentively*.] But where did you deposit the handbag?

MISS PRISM: Do not ask me, Mr. Worthing.

JACK: Miss Prism, this is a matter of no small importance to me. I insist on knowing where you deposited the handbag that contained that infant.

MISS PRISM: I left it in the cloak room of one of the larger railway stations in London.

JACK: What railway station?

MISS PRISM: [*Quite crushed*.] Victoria. The Brighton line. [*Sinks into a chair*.]

JACK: I must retire to my room for a moment. Gwendolen, wait here for me.

GWENDOLEN: If you are not too long, I will wait here for you all my life.

[*Exit* JACK *in great excitement*.]

CHASUBLE: What do you think this means, Lady Bracknell?

LADY BRACKNELL: I dare not even suspect, Dr. Chasuble. I need hardly tell you that in families of high position strange coincidences are not supposed to occur. They are hardly considered the thing.

[*Noises heard overhead as if someone was throwing trunks about. Everyone looks up*.]

CECILY: Uncle Jack seems strangely agitated.

CHASUBLE: Your guardian has a very emotional nature.

LADY BRACKNELL: This noise is extremely unpleasant. It sounds as if he was having an argument. I dislike arguments of any kind. They are always vulgar, and often convincing.

CHASUBLE: [*Looking up*.] It has stopped now. [*The noise is redoubled*.]

LADY BRACKNELL: I wish he would arrive at some conclusion.

GWENDOLEN: This suspense is terrible. I hope it will last.

[*Enter* JACK *with a handbag of black leather in his hand*.]

JACK: [*Rushing over to* MISS PRISM.] Is this the handbag, Miss Prism? Examine it carefully before you speak. The happiness of more than one life depends on your answer.

MISS PRISM: [*Calmly*.] It seems to be mine. Yes, here is the injury it received through the upsetting of a Gower Street omnibus in younger and happier days. Here is

---

2. Fashionable residential section north of Hyde Park and Kensington Gardens.

the stain on the lining caused by the explosion of a temperance beverage,[4] an incident that occurred at Leamington. And here, on the lock, are my initials. I had forgotten that in an extravagant mood I had had them placed there. The bag is undoubtedly mine. I am delighted to have it so unexpectedly restored to me. It has been a great inconvenience being without it all these years.

JACK: [*In a pathetic voice.*] Miss Prism, more is restored to you than this handbag. I was the baby you placed in it.

MISS PRISM: [*Amazed.*] You!

JACK: [*Embracing her.*] Yes . . . mother!

MISS PRISM: [*Recoiling in indignant astonishment.*] Mr. Worthing! I am unmarried!

JACK: Unmarried! I do not deny that is a serious blow. But after all, who has the right to cast a stone against one who has suffered? Cannot repentance wipe out an act of folly? Why should there be one law for men, and another for women? Mother, I forgive you. [*Tries to embrace her again.*]

MISS PRISM: [*Still more indignant.*] Mr. Worthing, there is some error. [*Pointing to* LADY BRACKNELL.] There is the lady who can tell you who you really are.

JACK: [*After a pause.*] Lady Bracknell, I hate to seem inquisitive, but would you kindly inform me who I am?

LADY BRACKNELL: I am afraid that the news I have to give you will not altogether please you. You are the son of my poor sister, Mrs. Moncrieff, and consequently Algernon's elder brother.

JACK: Algy's elder brother! Then I have a brother after all. I knew I had a brother! I always said I had a brother! Cecily—how could you have ever doubted that I had a brother? [*Seizes hold of* ALGERNON.] Dr. Chasuble, my unfortunate brother. Miss Prism, my unfortunate brother. Gwendolen, my unfortunate brother. Algy, you young scoundrel, you will have to treat me with more respect in the future. You have never behaved to me like a brother in all your life.

ALGERNON: Well, not till today, old boy, I admit. I did my best, however, though I was out of practice. [*Shakes hands.*]

GWENDOLEN: [*To* JACK.] My own! But what own are you? What is your Christian name, now that you have become someone else?

JACK: Good heavens! . . . I had quite forgotten that point. Your decision on the subject of my name is irrevocable, I suppose?

GWENDOLEN: I never change, except in my affections.

CECILY: What a noble nature you have, Gwendolen!

JACK: Then the question had better be cleared up at once. Aunt Augusta, a moment. At the time when Miss Prism left me in the handbag, had I been christened already?

LADY BRACKNELL: Every luxury that money could buy, including christening, had been lavished on you by your fond and doting parents.

JACK: Then I was christened! That is settled. Now, what name was I given? Let me know the worst.

LADY BRACKNELL: Being the eldest son you were naturally christened after your father.

JACK: [*Irritably.*] Yes, but what was my father's Christian name?

---

3. Carbonated soda drinks were marketed, in the 1890s, as "temperance beverages" (healthy alternatives to alcohol).

LADY BRACKNELL: [*Meditatively.*] I cannot at the present moment recall what the
   General's Christian name was. But I have no doubt he had one. He was eccen-
   tric, I admit. But only in later years. And that was the result of the Indian
   climate, and marriage, and indigestion, and other things of that kind.
JACK: Algy! Can't you recollect what our father's Christian name was?
ALGERNON: My dear boy, we were never even on speaking terms. He died before I
   was a year old.
JACK: His name would appear in the Army Lists of the period, I suppose, Aunt
   Augusta?
LADY BRACKNELL: The General was essentially a man of peace, except in his domes-
   tic life. But I have no doubt his name would appear in any military directory.
JACK: The Army Lists of the last forty years are here. These delightful records
   should have been my constant study. [*Rushes to bookcase and tears the books out.*]
   M. Generals . . . Mallam, Maxbohm, Magley, what ghastly names they have—
   Markby, Migsby, Mobbs, Moncrieff! Lieutenant 1840, Captain, Lieutenant
   Colonel, Colonel, General 1869, Christian names, Ernest John. [*Puts book very
   quietly down and speaks quite calmly.*] I always told you, Gwendolen, my name
   was Ernest, didn't I? Well, it is Ernest after all. I mean it naturally is Ernest.
LADY BRACKNELL: Yes, I remember now that the General was called Ernest. I knew
   I had some particular reason for disliking the name.
GWENDOLEN: Ernest! My own Ernest! I felt from the first that you could have no
   other name!
JACK: Gwendolen, it is a terrible thing for a man to find out suddenly that all his
   life he has been speaking nothing but the truth. Can you forgive me?
GWENDOLEN: I can. For I feel that you are sure to change.
JACK: My own one!
CHASUBLE: [*To* MISS PRISM.] Laetitia! [*Embraces her.*]
MISS PRISM: [*Enthusiastically.*] Frederick! At last!
ALGERNON: Cecily! [*Embraces her.*] At last!
JACK: Gwendolen! [*Embraces her.*] At last!
LADY BRACKNELL: My nephew, you seem to be displaying signs of triviality.
JACK: On the contrary, Aunt Augusta, I've now realized for the first time in my
   life the vital Importance of Being Earnest.

   CURTAIN

1895   1899

SUGGESTIONS FOR WRITING

1. *Oedipus the King* poses intriguing questions about the mysteries of sight and blindness, light and darkness. Why, for example, is it significant that Apollo, the sun
   god, is also a god of prophecy? Why is Teiresias, a prophet inspired by Apollo,
   blind? How does his blindness compare to that of Oedipus? What distinction does
   Sophocles draw between sight and insight? Using specific actions, images, and passages, write an essay in which you examine what *seeing* means in *Oedipus the King.*
   With what kinds of enlightenment and darkness is the play concerned?

2. What is "tragic," and what is "heroic," about a tragic hero? To the modern sensibility, Oedipus's poor judgment and stubborn unwillingness to face facts are what bring down upon him, and upon his family and the people of Thebes, the fate shown in the play. But to the ancients, Oedipus was the model of nobility in his innate sense of justice, selfless concern for the well-being of his people, and ultimate embrace of his destiny. What, then, is the nature of Oedipus's responsibility for his fate and the fate of Thebes? Write an essay in which you discuss the role of the "tragic hero" in *Oedipus the King*. What is the play's intended "lesson"?

3. In his *Poetics*, Aristotle praised *Oedipus the King* as a model tragedy—nearly perfect in the simplicity of its plot, the nobility of its characterization, and the decorousness of its poetry. Write an essay in which you compare and contrast the dramatic elements of *Oedipus the King* with those of at least one other play by Sophocles, such as *Antigone* (chapter 31). How does Sophocles define and vary his dramatic formula?

4. In its traditional form as practiced, for example, by Shakespeare, a comedy nearly always depicts lovers who must overcome obstacles (such as misunderstandings, unjust laws, or family interference) in order to unite in marriage and in this way ensure the continuation of their society. By such a definition, is *The Importance of Being Earnest* a traditional "comedy"? Or might it instead be labeled an "anti-comedy," a play that subverts traditional social mores? Using research if necessary, write an essay in which you trace the ways in which *The Importance of Being Earnest* does and does not adhere to the classic comic formula.

5. Oscar Wilde was famous in his time as a champion of aestheticism—that is, the belief that art exists solely for its own sake and that artists should be free from any religious, political, or social interference. "All art," he declared, "is quite useless." Nevertheless, in its own witty way, *The Importance of Being Earnest* seems to address many of the same matters that concern moralists—the proper ordering of society, the use and abuse of language, the relations between men and women. Is Wilde's play truly "useless"? Write an essay in which you argue that the play either is or is not a mere entertainment. Does *The Importance of Being Earnest* have a "moral"?

Exploring Contexts

28 THE AUTHOR'S WORK AS CONTEXT: WILLIAM SHAKESPEARE

When we read, we inevitably compare. We compare the writer's style to the styles of other writers; we compare characters within a story or play to one another and to people we know; we compare our life experiences to the many imaginary experiences that unfold before us as we read. Our interpretations of literature are fueled by such comparisons.

Reading several works by a single author is one of the most rewarding and enlightening types of comparison we can employ as active readers of literature. Such comparisons serve a variety of purposes: They help us develop a sense of the overall shape of the writer's work (that is, the writer's **oeuvre**, or **canon**); they reveal the kinds of characters, plots, and dramatic situations the author likes to create; they offer a glimpse into the author's particular way of looking at the world. At the same time, such comparisons can enrich our understanding of any one work by drawing our attention to features we might not have thought much about otherwise.

THE LIFE OF SHAKESPEARE: A BIOGRAPHICAL MYSTERY

This chapter offers you the opportunity to compare two plays by one of history's most vital and versatile playwrights: William Shakespeare. Shakespeare is a particularly enticing subject for this kind of comparative study in part because we know so little about him. While we can facilitate and enhance our reading of many writers by studying the letters, essays, diaries, and other documents in which the writers comment directly on their lives and works, Shakespeare left behind no such record. The only records that exist are a handful of official ones—marriage licenses, property deeds, and wills.

Those records tell a brief story. Shakespeare's origins were humble: His grandfather, Richard, rented the land he farmed, near Stratford-upon-

William Shakespeare

1641

Shakespeare's birthplace

Avon, a market town in the English midlands. Richard's son, John, married the daughter of one of Richard's former landlords and moved to town. There he became a tradesman prosperous and respected enough to buy quite a bit of property and to hold several civic offices, including that of mayor. The family's star was on the rise by the time William was born (sometime in April 1564). Though most likely neither of Shakespeare's parents could read or write (certainly they had no formal schooling), his father's involvement in city government brought with it the privilege of enrolling William in the local free grammar school. Here Shakespeare learned how to read and write, not only in English but also in Latin and perhaps Greek. His schoolmasters also probably required him to read such standard classical works as Ovid's *Metamorphoses* and the plays of Plautus and Terence (which greatly influenced the plays he would later write). In 1582, Shakespeare married Anne Hathaway, the daughter of a local farmer; in the next three years, the couple had three children, including a set of twins.

From the time of the twins' birth in 1585 until 1592, Shakespeare's life becomes—for us—a blank: All we know is that by the latter date he was a successful actor and playwright spending most of his time in London. (We know this, in part, because Shakespeare was prominent enough to be called an "upstart crow" in a book published by a rival playwright in 1592; apparently, this London-born, university-educated author felt a bit threatened by the undereducated provincial.) Though, in 1594, the "upstart crow" achieved a measure of renown as a poet by publishing two lengthy narrative poems (*Venus and Adonis* and *The Rape of Lucrece*), his career from this time until his death centered mainly on his work with the Lord Chamberlain's (later King's) Men—one of the two most prominent acting companies of his day. Shakespeare's work with the company was multifaceted: An actor with the troupe and its chief dramatist, he was also a shareholder who helped manage the troupe's affairs (including the building of the Globe Theater, on the South Bank of the River Thames, in 1599). Being a shareholder ensured that he prospered along with the company (especially after they secured the patronage of the king in 1603). As a result, Shakespeare enjoyed a level of economic prosperity and a kind of status that wouldn't have been possible to a mere actor, playwright, or poet. The Crown granted Shakespeare's father (and thus the playwright) the title of "gentleman" in the late 1590s. And at his death in 1616, Shakespeare left his family substantial property in both London and Stratford (where the family had continued to live).

The Globe Theater

Such facts remind us that Shakespeare was, after all, a real and in some ways rather ordinary person—who ultimately convinced audiences and rivals alike that he was more than an "upstart crow," but who did not, as a recent biographer reminds us, "in his own day inspire the mysterious veneration that afterwards came to surround him." These mundane facts tell us almost nothing, however, about the man's or the artist's inner life—his personal opinions, his motives, his loves, his dislikes, his politics, his "philosophy." These we can only infer, guess at, or imagine by reading and comparing his poems and plays. Luckily, Shakespeare left us a lot of these, including 154 sonnets (some of which are included in the poetry section of this book) and at least thirty-eight plays. Scholars believe Shakespeare cowrote at least one more play, and others may yet be discovered and authenticated.

EXPLORING TWO CLASSICS: *A MIDSUMMER NIGHT'S DREAM* AND *HAMLET*

Given that his plays include thirteen comedies, ten tragedies, ten English histories, and five romances, variety is a distinctive feature of Shakespeare's work as a playwright. It is fitting, then, that the two plays included in this chapter—*A Midsummer Night's Dream* and *Hamlet*—seem, at first glance, so different. *A Midsummer Night's Dream*, written in about 1595, is generally considered one of the last of Shakespeare's "apprentice" plays—the work of a young writer just beginning to find his own voice and dramatic style, but still quite dependent on classical models. Though written only a few years later (ca. 1599–1601), *Hamlet* is nonetheless regarded as one of the greatest works of a seasoned writer. Differences proliferate: *Dream*, a comedy, culminates in marriage (several marriages, in fact); *Hamlet*, a tragedy, concludes with the death and destruction of an entire royal family. *Dream* is among Shakespeare's shortest plays; *Hamlet*, among his longest. *Hamlet* focuses squarely—almost relentlessly—on its title character, whom we leave the play feeling that we know inside and out. *Dream*, in contrast, flits among many characters. Though we may fall in love with some of them, we probably will not feel that we truly know any of them. (Indeed, part of the play's humor comes from our having as hard a time as the characters themselves do remembering who is who and who loves whom.)

But while the plays have important and revealing differences, they have equally significant similarities, and by attending to these similarities we may come to understand and appreciate Shakespeare's particular way of looking at the world. To begin with, we may approach such similarities (within these or any plays) by concentrating on their basic elements, looking for patterns in character, setting, structure, tone, and theme, remembering that these elements ultimately combine to shape our experience of any one play.

In thinking about character, for example, notice that both the protagonists and the antagonists of *A Midsummer Night's Dream* and *Hamlet* are persons of high birth and position. These characters' choices and behavior deeply affect the communities that they lead. In fact, both plays repeatedly remind us of the general effects and communal significance of such characters' actions, as when, for example, we are told in *A Midsummer Night's Dream* of the "progeny of evils" that come of the "debate" and "dissension" between Titania and Oberon (2.1.115–16). Like all Shakespeare's plays, this comedy and tragedy both take for granted the idea that "on [a leader's] choice depends / The safety and health of th[e] whole state" (*Hamlet* 1.3.20–21), and both trace the effects of the particular, often bad, choices made by kings, princes, and dukes.

Shakespeare and his contemporaries often compared the relationship between a king and his subjects to that between a father and his children or between a husband and his wife. For example, an early Shakespeare comedy, *The Taming of the Shrew*, concludes with a speech in which the tamed shrew declares, "Thy husband is thy lord, thy life, thy keeper, / Thy head, thy sovereign." Building on this idea, she argues both that a woman's duty to her husband is the same "as the subject owes the prince" and that a woman who refuses to obey her husband is exactly like "a foul contending rebel / And graceless traitor." We can see similar analogies at work in *A Midsummer Night's Dream* and *Hamlet*: One begins with a duke and a father provoking a group of young Athenians to rebel against them; the other shows us a son who is also a prince struggling to choose the right response to the murder of a father who was also a king.

We pay attention to the effects of these high-born characters on their environments in part because Shakespeare's plays also include characters who occupy positions much lower on the social scale than the main characters do. In addition to Titania, Oberon, Theseus, and Hippolyta (rulers of the divine and human realms), *A Midsummer Night's Dream* introduces us to the Athenian craftsmen (or "mechanicals") led by the fittingly named Bottom. And while *Hamlet* focuses predominantly on members of the Danish royal court, one of the most memorable scenes in the play features a lowly gravedigger and the skeletal remains of a court jester named Yorick. As a result, the two plays demonstrate Shakespeare's tendency to people his plays with a socially diverse cast of characters and to thereby create a socially inclusive dramatic world.

As inclusive as Shakespeare's dramatic world is, it is far from *democratic* (as the speech from *The Taming of the Shrew* suggests). As you read more plays by Shakespeare, you will probably become more attuned to the different ways in which they depict "high" and "low" characters. *A Midsummer Night's Dream* is typical, for example, in the way it associates socially low characters with **low** or **physical comedy** (as opposed to **high** or **verbal comedy**). Bottom, after all, wears an ass's head for much of the play. Yet Bottom is also typical of Shakespeare's socially humble characters because he possesses a kind of wisdom lacking in his social betters. Certainly, he has more imagination and a much greater appreciation of art's power than Duke Theseus, who refuses to believe in "fables," thinks lovers and poets are no better than madmen (5.1.2–8), and rather heartlessly ridicules the mechanicals' creative efforts.

Despite the tendency to distinguish high from low, then, Shakespearean drama draws our attention to fundamental human experiences that cut across social lines. *A Midsummer Night's Dream* reminds us that a fairy queen is no more immune to love's magic or foolishness than the lowliest of mortals;

Bottom, from *A Midsummer Night's Dream*

Hamlet, that a king's life lasts no longer than a court jester's. The joys of love, the pain of death—these experiences link us and remind us of our common humanity.

Shakespeare suggests such links, in part, by structuring each play so that the main plot is complemented by parallel, yet often contrasting, secondary plots. *A Midsummer Night's Dream* offers at least four plots, each featuring a pair of lovers whose happiness is, or has been, threatened by their own failures to understand each other or by others' opposition to their relationship. *Hamlet* revolves around three intersecting, but distinct, plots featuring Hamlet, Laertes, and Fortinbras— three very different young men who must each figure out how to respond to, and perhaps avenge, his father's murder. In these, as in other Shakespeare plays, the secondary plots can be divided into **underplots**, which are romantic or parodic versions of the main plot, and **overplots**, which foreground its political dimensions. In *A Midsummer Night's Dream*, Bottom becomes the protagonist of the underplot, Theseus and Hippolyta (and, perhaps, Titania and Oberon) of the overplot(s). In *Hamlet*, the underplot focuses on Laertes; the overplot, on Fortinbras. However, all the secondary plots encourage us—and sometimes, as in *Hamlet*, the characters themselves—to compare the ways different people handle similar situations and thus to evaluate various choices and various responses. The parallel plots serve simultaneously as a structural device, a potent means of characterization, and a way of drawing our attention to general issues and themes.

Reading *Hamlet* and *A Midsummer Night's Dream* side by side may also help us appreciate the tonal complexity of Shakespeare's plays—their incorporation of both comic and tragic elements. While *A Midsummer Night's Dream* plunges us into a nighttime world dominated by the intertwining forces of magic, love, and humor, it also continually reminds us of the dangerous aspects of the night, of the struggles that human beings endure in their pursuit of love and happiness, of the

Sir Laurence Olivier as Hamlet

brevity and fragility of human joy and life, of what Hamlet calls the "thousand natural shocks / That flesh is heir to" (3.1.62–63). The specter of death hovers in the background of *A Midsummer Night's Dream* as surely as it occupies the foreground of *Hamlet*. And while *Hamlet*, like most tragedies, focuses primarily on mortality, violence, and time's destructive force, it also shows us the comic side of the human condition. In fact, one of the things that makes Hamlet such a sympathetic character is his sense of humor; he proves so adept at wordplay that we wish he could stick to that instead of having to resort to swordplay.

Turning from tone to theme, we find that both *Hamlet* and *A Midsummer Night's Dream* say something about the order of things and the rhythm of life. Although *Hamlet* ends with a body-strewn stage, the play encourages us to see those deaths as the necessary prelude to a restoration of order and health to a kingdom diseased and disordered as a result of a sovereign's choices. Claudius's crimes ultimately infect and poison everything and everyone, even innocent bystanders like Ophelia. Both to us and to Hamlet, Claudius's reign represents the triumph of humanity's worst impulses. By embracing his role as heaven's "scourge and minister" even at the risk of his own life (3.4.179–81), however, Hamlet reaffirms our faith in humanity's noblest qualities as he strives to set right all that is "rotten in Denmark" (1.4.90). In *A Midsummer Night's Dream*, we again see the actions of a sovereign turn the world upside down: The young rebel against the old, women chase men, old friends turn on each other, an ass consorts with a queen. Clearly, the kinds of dissension and disorder at work in *A Midsummer Night's Dream* make us laugh, while those in *Hamlet* make us cringe or cry. Yet the rhythm of both plays turns out to be surprisingly similar, tracing the movement from disorder to order, from dissension to harmony. In the process, both plays ask us to think about the nature and causes of social, political, and moral disorder, of dissension within states and families.

As you read *Hamlet* and *A Midsummer Night's Dream*, you will discover many more parallels of theme, character, setting, and structure whose significance you will want to ponder and investigate. But you may also want to think about another, perhaps more elusive element: language. Shakespeare is justly celebrated for his use of language, and we pay homage to it, unwittingly or not, every time we use any one of the many idiomatic expressions that originated in the plays. (If, for example, you conclude that Shakespeare is "Greek to me," you have proved otherwise by quoting directly from his play *Julius Caesar*.) In Shakespearean drama, language is never an end in itself but instead establishes character and tone, structures the play, shapes our emotional response to it, and enunciates theme. *Hamlet*, for example, characterizes both Polonius and Hamlet in part through their penchant for wordplay. But as Polonius suggests, Hamlet's wordplay is "pregnant" with significance in a way that his own is not (2.2.201). While Polonius's use of language arguably demonstrates both his pompous nature and his fondness for sham and trickery, Hamlet's displays his preoccupation with probing beneath the surface of language and much else.

In both *Hamlet* and *A Midsummer Night's Dream*, the musical and visual qualities of Shakespeare's language are integral to its meaning. Though written mainly in verse, Shakespeare's plays include prose passages; and though most of the poetry is **blank verse** (unrhymed iambic pentameter), Shakespeare also uses rhyme and rhythmic variation to great effect. As you read the plays, then, you will want to pay attention to the texture and rhythm of the language—to the effect of *sound* on *sense*. You will also want to attend to the way Shakespeare uses language to appeal to your eye, as well as your ear. Visual imagery, like sound, consistently serves both structural and thematic ends, linking various moments and ideas, actions and themes. In *A Midsummer Night's Dream*, for example, characters frequently refer to their eyes. Such references begin in the very first scene: When Hermia wishes that her father "look'd but with my eyes," Theseus responds that "your eyes must with his judgment look" (lines 56–57). These lines prepare us for a drama in which eyes will play a major part, in which love and vision tend to go hand in hand, in which both love and vision often conflict with "judgment." Oberon's love potion, after all, works through the eyes, while Puck initially misapplies the potion largely because his eyes have deceived him. The characters' talk of eyes thus connects directly to the plot; through both, the play asks us to think about the tremendous power of vision and the dangers of relying too heavily on it.

Reading many plays by a single playwright will help you better recognize stylistic as well as structural and thematic patterns within each play: Each additional Shakespeare play you read will bring you closer to an understanding and appreciation of his unique way of looking at the world and of the way his views and his technique changed over time. You will gain a sense of Shakespeare's development as a dramatist even as, ideally, you develop your own skills as a reader of drama.

WILLIAM SHAKESPEARE

A Midsummer Night's Dream[1]

CHARACTERS

THESEUS, *Duke of Athens*
HIPPOLYTA, *Queen of the Amazons, betrothed to Theseus*
PHILOSTRATE, *Master of the Revels to Theseus*
EGEUS, *father to Hermia*
HERMIA, *daughter to Egeus, in love with Lysander*
LYSANDER, } *in love with Hermia*
DEMETRIUS,

HELENA, *in love with Demetrius*
OBERON, *King of the Fairies*
TITANIA, *Queen of the Fairies*
PUCK, *or Robin Goodfellow*
PEASEBLOSSOM,
COBWEB,
MOTH, } *fairies*
MUSTARDSEED
QUINCE, *a carpenter*
SNUG, *a joiner*

1. Edited and annotated by David Bevington (except footnotes set in brackets).

BOTTOM, *a weaver*
FLUTE, *a bellows-maker*
SNOUT, *a tinker*

STARVELING, *a tailor*
Other FAIRIES *attending their king and queen*
ATTENDANTS *on Theseus and Hippolyta*

SCENE: *Athens, and a wood near it.*

ACT I

Scene 1[2]

Enter THESEUS, HIPPOLYTA, PHILOSTRATE, *with others.*

THESEUS: Now, fair Hippolyta, our nuptial hour
  Draws on apace. Four happy days bring in
  Another moon; but, O, methinks, how slow
  This old moon wanes! She lingers[3] my desires,
5 Like to a step-dame or a dowager[4]
  Long withering out a young man's revenue.
HIPPOLYTA: Four days will quickly steep themselves in night,
  Four nights will quickly dream away the time;
  And then the moon, like to a silver bow
10 New-bent in heaven, shall behold the night
  Of our solemnities.
THESEUS: Go, Philostrate,
  Stir up the Athenian youth to merriments,
  Awake the pert and nimble spirit of mirth,
  Turn melancholy forth to funerals;
15 The pale companion is not for our pomp.[5] [*Exit* PHILOSTRATE.]
  Hippolyta, I woo'd thee with my sword,[6]
  And won thy love doing thee injuries;
  But I will wed thee in another key,
  With pomp, with triumph,[7] and with reveling.

[*Enter* EGEUS *and his daughter* HERMIA, *and* LYSANDER, *and* DEMETRIUS.]

20 EGEUS: Happy be Theseus, our renowned Duke!
THESEUS: Thanks, good Egeus. What's the news with thee?
EGEUS: Full of vexation come I, with complaint
  Against my child, my daughter Hermia.
  Stand forth, Demetrius. My noble lord,
25 This man hath my consent to marry her.
  Stand forth, Lysander. And, my gracious Duke,
  This man hath bewitch'd the bosom of my child.
  Thou, thou, Lysander, thou hast given her rhymes

2. Location: Athens. The palace of Theseus. 3. Lengthens, protracts.
4. Widow with a jointure or dower. *Step-dame*: stepmother.
5. Ceremonial magnificence. *Companion*: fellow.
6. That is, in a military engagement against the Amazons, when Hippolyta was taken captive.
7. Public festivity.

And interchang'd love-tokens with my child.
Thou hast by moonlight at her window sung   30
With feigning[8] voice verses of feigning love,
And stol'n the impression of her fantasy[9]
With bracelets of thy hair, rings, gauds, conceits,[1]
Knacks,[2] trifles, nosegays, sweetmeats—messengers
Of strong prevailment in unhardened youth.   35
With cunning hast thou filch'd my daughter's heart,
Turn'd her obedience, which is due to me,
To stubborn harshness. And, my gracious Duke,
Be it so she will not here before your Grace
Consent to marry with Demetrius,   40
I beg the ancient privilege of Athens:
As she is mine, I may dispose of her,
Which shall be either to this gentleman
Or to her death, according to our law
Immediately[3] provided in that case.   45
THESEUS: What say you, Hermia? Be advis'd, fair maid.
   To you your father should be as a god—
   One that compos'd your beauties, yea, and one
   To whom you are but as a form in wax
   By him imprinted and within his power   50
   To leave the figure or disfigure[4] it.
   Demetrius is a worthy gentleman.
HERMIA: So is Lysander.
THESEUS: In himself he is;
   But in this kind, wanting your father's voice,[5]
   The other must be held the worthier.   55
HERMIA: I would my father look'd but with my eyes.
THESEUS: Rather your eyes must with his judgment look.
HERMIA: I do entreat your Grace to pardon me.
   I know not by what power I am made bold,
   Nor how it may concern[6] my modesty,   60
   In such a presence here to plead my thoughts;
   But I beseech your Grace that I may know
   The worst that may befall me in this case,
   If I refuse to wed Demetrius.
THESEUS: Either to die the death, or to abjure   65
   Forever the society of men.
   Therefore, fair Hermia, question your desires,
   Know of your youth, examine well your blood,[7]
   Whether, if you yield not to your father's choice,

---

8. (1) Counterfeiting; (2) faining, desirous.
9. Made her fall in love with you (imprinting your image on her imagination) by stealthy and dishonest
means.   1. Fanciful trifles. *Gauds*: playthings.   2. Knickknacks.   3. Expressly.
4. Obliterate. *Leave*: that is, leave unaltered.   5. Approval. *Kind*: respect. *Wanting*: lacking.
6. Befit.   7. Passions.

70   You can endure the livery[8] of a nun,
       For aye to be in shady cloister mew'd,[9]
       To live a barren sister all your life,
       Chanting faint hymns to the cold fruitless moon.
       Thrice blessed they that master so their blood
75   To undergo such maiden pilgrimage;
       But earthlier happy[1] is the rose distill'd,
       Than that which withering on the virgin thorn
       Grows, lives, and dies in single blessedness.
       HERMIA: So will I grow, so live, so die, my lord,
80   Ere I will yield my virgin patent[2] up
       Unto his lordship, whose unwished yoke
       My soul consents not to give sovereignty.
       THESEUS: Take time to pause; and, by the next new moon—
       The sealing-day betwixt my love and me,
85   For everlasting bond of fellowship—
       Upon that day either prepare to die
       For disobedience to your father's will,
       Or[3] else to wed Demetrius, as he would,
       Or on Diana's altar to protest[4]
90   For aye austerity and single life.
       DEMETRIUS: Relent, sweet Hermia, and, Lysander, yield
       Thy crazed[5] title to my certain right.
       LYSANDER: You have her father's love, Demetrius;
       Let me have Hermia's. Do you marry him.
95   EGEUS: Scornful Lysander! True, he hath my love,
       And what is mine my love shall render him.
       And she is mine, and all my right of her
       I do estate unto[6] Demetrius.
       LYSANDER: I am, my lord, as well deriv'd[7] as he,
100   As well possess'd;[8] my love is more than his;
       My fortunes every way as fairly[9] rank'd,
       If not with vantage,[1] as Demetrius';
       And, which is more than all these boasts can be,
       I am belov'd of beauteous Hermia.
105   Why should not I then prosecute my right?
       Demetrius, I'll avouch it to his head,[2]
       Made love to Nedar's daughter, Helena,
       And won her soul; and she, sweet lady, dotes,
       Devoutly dotes, dotes in idolatry,
110   Upon this spotted[3] and inconstant man.
       THESEUS: I must confess that I have heard so much,
       And with Demetrius thought to have spoke thereof;
       But, being over-full of self-affairs,

---

8. Habit.   9. Shut in (said of a hawk, poultry, and so on). *Aye:* ever.
1. Happier as respects this world.   2. Privilege.   3. Either.   4. Vow.   5. Cracked, unsound.
6. Settle or bestow upon.   7. Descended; that is, as well born.   8. Endowed with wealth.
9. Handsomely.   1. Superiority.   2. That is, face.   3. That is, morally stained.

My mind did lose it. But, Demetrius, come,
And come, Egeus, you shall go with me;   115
I have some private schooling for you both.
For you, fair Hermia, look you arm[4] yourself
To fit your fancies[5] to your father's will;
Or else the law of Athens yields you up—
Which by no means we may extenuate[6]—   120
To death, or to a vow of single life.
Come, my Hippolyta. What cheer, my love?
Demetrius and Egeus, go[7] along.
I must employ you in some business
Against[8] our nuptial, and confer with you   125
Of something nearly that[9] concerns yourselves.
EGEUS: With duty and desire we follow you.

                              [Exeunt (all but LYSANDER *and* HERMIA*).]*

LYSANDER: How now, my love, why is your cheek so pale?
  How chance the roses there do fade so fast?
HERMIA: Belike[1] for want of rain, which I could well   130
  Beteem[2] them from the tempest of my eyes.
LYSANDER: Ay me! For aught that I could ever read,
  Could ever hear by tale or history,
  The course of true love never did run smooth;
  But either it was different in blood[3]—   135
HERMIA: O cross,[4] too high to be enthrall'd to low!
LYSANDER: Or else misgraffed[5] in respect of years—
HERMIA: O spite, too old to be engag'd to young!
LYSANDER: Or else it stood upon the choice of friends[6]—
HERMIA: O hell, to choose love by another's eyes!   140
LYSANDER: Or, if there were a sympathy in choice,
  War, death, or sickness did lay siege to it,
  Making it momentany[7] as a sound,
  Swift as a shadow, short as any dream,
  Brief as the lightning in the collied[8] night,   145
  That, in a spleen, unfolds[9] both heaven and earth,
  And ere a man hath power to say "Behold!"
  The jaws of darkness do devour it up.
  So quick bright things come to confusion.[1]
HERMIA: If then true lovers have been ever cross'd,[2]   150
  It stands as an edict in destiny.
  Then let us teach our trial patience,[3]
  Because it is a customary cross,
  As due to love as thoughts and dreams and sighs,

---

4. Take care you prepare.   5. Likings, thoughts of love.   6. Mitigate.   7. That is, come.
8. In preparation for.   9. That closely.   1. Very likely.   2. Grant, afford.   3. Hereditary station.
4. Vexation.   5. Ill grafted, badly matched.   6. Relatives.   7. Lasting but a moment.
8. Blackened (as with coal dust), darkened.
9. Discloses. *In a spleen*: in a swift impulse, in a violent flash.
1. Ruin. *Quick*: quickly; or, perhaps, living, alive.   2. Always thwarted.
3. That is, teach ourselves patience in this trial.

155   Wishes and tears, poor fancy's[4] followers.
     LYSANDER: A good persuasion. Therefore, hear me, Hermia.
            I have a widow aunt, a dowager
            Of great revenue, and she hath no child.
            From Athens is her house remote seven leagues;
160   And she respects[5] me as her only son.
            There, gentle Hermia, may I marry thee,
            And to that place the sharp Athenian law
            Cannot pursue us. If thou lovest me, then,
            Steal forth thy father's house tomorrow night;
165   And in the wood, a league without the town,
            Where I did meet thee once with Helena
            To do observance to a morn of May,[6]
            There will I stay for thee.
     HERMIA: My good Lysander!
            I swear to thee, by Cupid's strongest bow,
170   By his best arrow[7] with the golden head,
            By the simplicity of Venus' doves,[8]
            By that which knitteth souls and prospers loves,
            And by that fire which burn'd the Carthage queen,
            When the false Troyan[9] under sail was seen,
175   By all the vows that ever men have broke,
            In number more than ever women spoke,
            In that same place thou hast appointed me
            Tomorrow truly will I meet with thee.
     LYSANDER: Keep promise, love. Look, here comes Helena.

            [Enter HELENA.]

180 HERMIA: God speed fair[1] Helena, whither away?
     HELENA: Call you me fair? That fair again unsay.
            Demetrius loves your fair. O happy fair![2]
            Your eyes are lodestars, and your tongue's sweet air[3]
            More tuneable[4] than lark to shepherd's ear
185   When wheat is green, when hawthorn buds appear.
            Sickness is catching. O, were favor[5] so,
            Yours would I catch, fair Hermia, ere I go;
            My ear should catch your voice, my eye your eye,
            My tongue should catch your tongue's sweet melody.
190   Were the world mine, Demetrius being bated,[6]
            The rest I'd give to be to you translated.[7]

4. Amorous passion's.   5. Regards.   6. Perform the ceremonies of May Day.
7. [Cupid's best gold-pointed arrows were supposed to induce love; his blunt leaden arrows, aversion.]
8. That is, those that drew Venus's chariot. *Simplicity*: innocence.
9. [Dido, queen of Carthage, immolated herself on a funeral pyre after having been deserted by the Trojan hero Aeneas.]
1. Fair-complexioned (a fair complexion was generally regarded by the Elizabethans as more beautiful than a dark complexion).   2. Lucky fair one! *Fair*: beauty (even though Hermia is dark-complexioned).
3. Music. *Lodestars*: guiding stars.   4. Tuneful, melodious.   5. Appearance, looks.   6. Excepted.
7. Transformed.

O, teach me how you look, and with what art
You sway the motion[8] of Demetrius' heart.
HERMIA: I frown upon him, yet he loves me still.
HELENA: O that your frowns would teach my smiles such skill! 195
HERMIA: I give him curses, yet he gives me love.
HELENA: O that my prayers could such affection move![9]
HERMIA: The more I hate, the more he follows me.
HELENA: The more I love, the more he hateth me.
HERMIA: His folly, Helena, is no fault of mine. 200
HELENA: None, but your beauty. Would that fault were mine!
HERMIA: Take comfort. He no more shall see my face.
Lysander and myself will fly this place.
Before the time I did Lysander see,
Seem'd Athens as a paradise to me. 205
O, then, what graces in my love do dwell,
That he hath turn'd a heaven unto a hell!
LYSANDER: Helen, to you our minds we will unfold.
Tomorrow night, when Phoebe[1] doth behold
Her silver visage in the wat'ry glass,[2] 210
Decking with liquid pearl the bladed grass,
A time that lovers' flights doth still[3] conceal,
Through Athens' gates have we devis'd to steal.
HERMIA: And in the wood, where often you and I
Upon faint[4] primrose beds were wont to lie, 215
Emptying our bosoms of their counsel[5] sweet,
There my Lysander and myself shall meet;
And thence from Athens turn away our eyes,
To seek new friends and stranger companies.
Farewell, sweet playfellow. Pray thou for us, 220
And good luck grant thee thy Demetrius!
Keep word, Lysander. We must starve our sight
From lovers' food till morrow deep midnight.
LYSANDER: I will, my Hermia.   [*Exit* HERMIA.]
                    Helena, adieu.
As you on him, Demetrius dote on you!   [*Exit.*] 225
HELENA: How happy some o'er other some can be![6]
Through Athens I am thought as fair as she.
But what of that? Demetrius thinks not so;
He will not know what all but he do know.
And as he errs, doting on Hermia's eyes, 230
So I, admiring of[7] his qualities.
Things base and vile, holding no quantity,[8]
Love can transpose to form and dignity.
Love looks not with the eyes, but with the mind,
And therefore is wing'd Cupid painted blind. 235

---

8. Impulse.   9. Arouse. *Affection*: passion.   1. Diana, the moon.   2. Mirror.   3. Always.   4. Pale.
5. Secret thought.   6. Can be in comparison to some others.   7. Wondering at.
8. That is, unsubstantial, unshapely.

Nor hath Love's mind of any judgment taste;[9]
Wings, and no eyes, figure[1] unheedy haste.
And therefore is Love said to be a child,
Because in choice he is so oft beguil'd.
240   As waggish boys in game[2] themselves forswear,
So the boy Love is perjur'd everywhere.
For ere Demetrius look'd on Hermia's eyne,[3]
He hail'd down oaths that he was only mine;
And when this hail some heat from Hermia felt,
245   So he dissolv'd, and show'rs of oaths did melt.
I will go tell him of fair Hermia's flight.
Then to the wood will he tomorrow night
Pursue her; and for this intelligence[4]
If I have thanks, it is a dear expense.[5]
250   But herein mean I to enrich my pain,
To have his sight thither and back again.   [*Exit.*]

Scene 2[6]

Enter QUINCE *the Carpenter, and* SNUG *the Joiner, and* BOTTOM *the Weaver, and* FLUTE
the Bellows-mender, and SNOUT *the Tinker, and* STARVELING *the Tailor.*

QUINCE: Is all our company here?
BOTTOM: You were best to call them generally,[7] man by man, according to the
      scrip.[8]
5   QUINCE: Here is the scroll of every man's name which is thought fit, through all
      Athens, to play in our interlude before the Duke and the Duchess on his
      wedding-day at night.
BOTTOM: First, good Peter Quince, say what the play treats on, then read the
      names of the actors, and so grow to[9] a point.
10   QUINCE: Marry,[1] our play is "The most lamentable comedy and most cruel death
      of Pyramus and Thisby."
BOTTOM: A very good piece of work, I assure you, and a merry. Now, good Peter
      Quince, call forth your actors by the scroll. Masters, spread yourselves.
QUINCE: Answer as I call you. Nick Bottom, the weaver.
BOTTOM: Ready. Name what part I am for, and proceed.
15   QUINCE: You, Nick Bottom, are set down for Pyramus.
BOTTOM: What is Pyramus? A lover, or a tyrant?
QUINCE: A lover, that kills himself most gallant for love.
BOTTOM: That will ask some tears in the true performing of it. If I do it, let the
      audience look to their eyes. I will move storms; I will condole[2] in some mea-
20   sure. To the rest—yet my chief humor[3] is for a tyrant. I could play Ercles rarely,
      or a part to tear a cat in, to make all split.[4]

9. That is, nor has Love, which dwells in the fancy or imagination, any taste or least bit of judgment or
reason.   1. Are a symbol of.   2. Sport, jest.   3. Eyes (old form of plural).   4. Information.
5. That is, a trouble worth taking. *Dear*: costly.   6. Location: Athens. Quince's house (?).
7. [Bottom's blunder for *individually*.]   8. Script, written list.   9. Come to.
1. [A mild oath, originally the name of the Virgin Mary.]   2. Lament, arouse pity.   3. Inclination, whim.
4. That is, cause a stir, bring the house down. *Ercles*: Hercules (the tradition of ranting came from Seneca's
Hercules Furens). *Tear a cat*: that is, rant.

"The raging rocks
And shivering shocks
Shall break the locks
    Of prison gates;
And Phibbus' car[5]
Shall shine from far
And make and mar
    The foolish Fates." 25

This was lofty! Now name the rest of the players. This is Ercles' vein, a tyrant's 30
vein. A lover is more condoling.

QUINCE: Francis Flute, the bellows-mender.

FLUTE: Here, Peter Quince.

QUINCE: Flute, you must take Thisby on you.

FLUTE: What is Thisby? A wand'ring knight? 35

QUINCE: It is the lady that Pyramus must love.

FLUTE: Nay, faith, let not me play a woman. I have a beard coming.

QUINCE: That's all one.[6] You shall play it in a mask, and you may speak as small[7]
as you will.

BOTTOM: An[8] I may hide my face, let me play Thisby too. I'll speak in a monstrous 40
little voice, "Thisne, Thisne!" "Ah, Pyramus, my lover dear! Thy Thisby dear,
and lady dear!"

QUINCE: No, no; you must play Pyramus; and, Flute, you Thisby.

BOTTOM: Well, proceed.

QUINCE: Robin Starveling, the tailor. 45

STARVELING: Here, Peter Quince.

QUINCE: Robin Starveling, you must play Thisby's mother. Tom Snout, the tinker.

SNOUT: Here, Peter Quince.

QUINCE: You, Pyramus' father; myself, Thisby's father; Snug, the joiner, you, the 50
lion's part; and I hope here is a play fitted.

SNUG: Have you the lion's part written? Pray you, if it be, give it me, for I am slow
of study.

QUINCE: You may do it extempore, for it is nothing but roaring.

BOTTOM: Let me play the lion too. I will roar that I will do any man's heart good 55
to hear me. I will roar that I will make the Duke say, "Let him roar again, let
him roar again."

QUINCE: An you should do it too terribly, you would fright the Duchess and the
ladies, that they would shriek; and that were enough to hang us all.

ALL: That would hang us, every mother's son. 60

BOTTOM: I grant you, friends, if you should fright the ladies out of their wits,
they would have no more discretion but to hang us; but I will aggravate[9] my
voice so that I will roar[1] you as gently as any sucking dove; I will roar you an
'twere any nightingale.

QUINCE: You can play no part but Pyramus; for Pyramus is a sweet-fac'd man, a 65
proper[2] man as one shall see in a summer's day, a most lovely gentlemanlike
man. Therefore you must needs play Pyramus.

---

5. Phoebus's, the sun-god's, chariot.   6. It makes no difference.   7. High-pitched.   8. If.
9. [Bottom's blunder for *diminish*.]   1. That is, roar for you.   2. Handsome.

BOTTOM: Well, I will undertake it. What beard were I best to play it in?

QUINCE: Why, what you will.

70 BOTTOM: I will discharge it in either your[3] straw-color beard, your orange-tawny beard, your purple-in-grain beard, or your French-crown-color[4] beard, your perfect yellow.

QUINCE: Some of your French crowns[5] have no hair at all, and then you will play barefac'd. But, masters, here are your parts. [*He distributes parts.*] And I am to
75 entreat you, request you, and desire you, to con[6] them by tomorrow night; and meet me in the palace wood, a mile without the town, by moonlight. There will we rehearse; for if we meet in the city, we shall be dogg'd with company, and our devices[7] known. In the meantime I will draw a bill[8] of properties, such as our play wants. I pray you, fail me not.

80 BOTTOM: We will meet, and there we may rehearse most obscenely[9] and courageously. Take pains, be perfect;[1] adieu.

QUINCE: At the Duke's oak we meet.

BOTTOM: Enough. Hold, or cut bow-strings.[2]   [*Exeunt.*]

ACT II

Scene 1[3]

Enter a FAIRY *at one door, and Robin Goodfellow* (PUCK) *at another.*

PUCK: How now, spirit! Whither wander you?

FAIRY: Over hill, over dale,
      Thorough[4] bush, thorough brier,
      Over park, over pale,[5]
5   Thorough flood, thorough fire,
      I do wander every where,
      Swifter than the moon's sphere;
      And I serve the Fairy Queen,
      To dew her orbs[6] upon the green.
10   The cowslips tall her pensioners[7] be.
      In their gold coats spots you see;
      Those be rubies, fairy favors,[8]
      In those freckles live their savors.[9]
      I must go seek some dewdrops here
15   And hang a pearl in every cowslip's ear.
      Farewell, thou lob[1] of spirits; I'll be gone.

---

3. That is, you know the kind I mean. *Discharge*: perform.
4. That is, color of a French crown, a gold coin. *Purple-in-grain*: dyed a very deep red (from *grain*, the name applied to the dried insect used to make the dye).   5. Heads bald from syphilis, the "French disease."
6. Learn by heart.   7. Plans.   8. List.
9. [An unintentionally funny blunder, whatever Bottom meant to say.]
1. That is, letter-perfect in memorizing your parts.
2. [An archer's expression not definitely explained, but probably meaning here "keep your promises, or give up the play."]   3. Location: a wood near Athens.   4. Through.   5. Enclosure.
6. Circles; that is, fairy rings.   7. Retainers, members of the royal bodyguard.   8. Love tokens.
9. Sweet smells.   1. Country bumpkin.

Our Queen and all her elves come here anon.[2]
PUCK: The King doth keep his revels here tonight.
Take heed the Queen come not within his sight.
For Oberon is passing fell and wrath,[3]   20
Because that she as her attendant hath
A lovely boy, stolen from an Indian king;
She never had so sweet a changeling.[4]
And jealous Oberon would have the child
Knight of his train, to trace[5] the forests wild.   25
But she perforce[6] withholds the loved boy,
Crowns him with flowers and makes him all her joy.
And now they never meet in grove or green,
By fountain[7] clear, or spangled starlight sheen,
But they do square,[8] that all their elves for fear   30
Creep into acorn-cups and hide them there.
FAIRY: Either I mistake your shape and making quite,
Or else you are that shrewd and knavish sprite[9]
Call'd Robin Goodfellow. Are not you he
That frights the maidens of the villagery,   35
Skim milk, and sometimes labor in the quern,[1]
And bootless[2] make the breathless huswife churn,
And sometime make the drink to bear no barm,[3]
Mislead night-wanderers, laughing at their harm?
Those that Hobgoblin call you and sweet Puck,   40
You do their work, and they shall have good luck.
Are you not he?
PUCK: Thou speakest aright;
I am that merry wanderer of the night.
I jest to Oberon and make him smile
When I a fat and bean-fed horse beguile,   45
Neighing in likeness of a filly foal;
And sometime lurk I in a gossip's[4] bowl,
In very likeness of a roasted crab,[5]
And when she drinks, against her lips I bob
And on her withered dewlap[6] pour the ale.   50
The wisest aunt, telling the saddest[7] tale,
Sometime for three-foot stool mistaketh me;
Then slip I from her bum, down topples she,
And "tailor"[8] cries, and falls into a cough;
And then the whole quire[9] hold their hips and laugh,   55
And waxen in their mirth and neeze[1] and swear
A merrier hour was never wasted there.

---

2. At once.   3. Wrathful. *Fell*: exceedingly angry.   4. Child exchanged for another by the fairies.
5. Range through.   6. Forcibly.   7. Spring.   8. Quarrel.   9. Spirit. *Shrewd*: mischievous.
1. Handmill.   2. In vain.   3. Yeast, head on the ale.   4. Old woman's.   5. Crab apple.
6. Loose skin on neck.   7. Most serious. *Aunt*: old woman.
8. [Possibly because she ends up sitting cross-legged on the floor, looking like a tailor.]
9. Company.   1. Sneeze. *Waxen*: increase.

But, room, fairy! Here comes Oberon.

FAIRY: And here my mistress. Would that he were gone!

[*Enter* OBERON, *the King of Fairies, at one door, with his train; and* TITANIA, *the Queen, at another, with hers.*]

60 OBERON: Ill met by moonlight, proud Titania.

TITANIA: What, jealous Oberon? Fairies, skip hence.
  I have forsworn his bed and company.

OBERON: Tarry, rash wanton.[2] Am not I thy lord?

TITANIA: Then I must be thy lady; but I know

65 When thou hast stolen away from fairy land,
  And in the shape of Corin[3] sat all day,
  Playing on pipes of corn[4] and versing love
  To amorous Phillida. Why art thou here,
  Come from the farthest steep[5] of India,

70 But that, forsooth, the bouncing Amazon,
  Your buskin'd[6] mistress and your warrior love,
  To Theseus must be wedded, and you come
  To give their bed joy and prosperity.

OBERON: How canst thou thus for shame, Titania,

75 Glance at my credit with Hippolyta,[7]
  Knowing I know thy love to Theseus?
  Didst not thou lead him through the glimmering night
  From Perigenia,[8] whom he ravished?
  And make him with fair Aegles[9] break his faith,

80 With Ariadne and Antiopa?[1]

TITANIA: These are the forgeries of jealousy;
  And never, since the middle summer's spring,[2]
  Met we on hill, in dale, forest, or mead,
  By paved fountain or by rushy[3] brook,

85 Or in the beached margent[4] of the sea,
  To dance our ringlets[5] to the whistling wind,
  But with thy brawls thou hast disturb'd our sport.
  Therefore the winds, piping to us in vain,
  As in revenge, have suck'd up from the sea

90 Contagious[6] fogs; which falling in the land
  Hath every pelting[7] river made so proud

2. Headstrong creature.   3. Corin and Phillida are conventional names of pastoral lovers.
4. [Here, oat stalks.]   5. Mountain range.   6. Wearing half boots called buskins.
7. Make insinuations about my favored relationship with Hippolyta.
8. That is, Perigouna, one of Theseus's conquests. (This and the following women are named in Thomas North's translation of Plutarch's *Life of Theseus*.)
9. That is, Aegle, for whom Theseus deserted Ariadne, according to some accounts.
1. Queen of the Amazons and wife of Theseus; elsewhere identified with Hippolyta, but here thought of as a separate woman. *Ariadne:* the daughter of Minos, king of Crete, who helped Theseus to escape the labyrinth after killing the Minotaur; later she was abandoned by Theseus.
2. Beginning of midsummer.   3. Bordered with rushes. *Paved:* with pebbled bottom.
4. Edge, border. *In:* on.   5. Dances in a ring. (See *orbs* in 2.1.9.)   6. Noxious.
7. Paltry; or striking, moving forcefully.

That they have overborne their continents.[8]
The ox hath therefore stretch'd his yoke in vain,
The ploughman lost his sweat, and the green corn[9]
Hath rotted ere his youth attain'd a beard;   95
The fold[1] stands empty in the drowned field,
And crows are fatted with the murrion[2] flock;
The nine men's morris[3] is fill'd up with mud,
And the quaint mazes in the wanton[4] green
For lack of tread are undistinguishable.   100
The human mortals want their winter[5] here;
No night is now with hymn or carol bless'd.
Therefore[6] the moon, the governess of floods,
Pale in her anger, washes all the air,
That rheumatic[7] diseases do abound.   105
And thorough this distemperature[8] we see
The seasons alter: hoary-headed frosts
Fall in the fresh lap of the crimson rose,
And on old Hiems'[9] thin and icy crown
An odorous chaplet of sweet summer buds   110
Is, as in mockery, set. The spring, the summer,
The childing[1] autumn, angry winter, change
Their wonted liveries, and the mazed[2] world,
By their increase,[3] now knows not which is which.
And this same progeny of evils comes   115
From our debate,[4] from our dissension;
We are their parents and original.[5]

OBERON: Do you amend it then; it lies in you.
  Why should Titania cross her Oberon?
  I do but beg a little changeling boy,   120
  To be my henchman.[6]

TITANIA: Set your heart at rest.
  The fairy land buys not the child of me.
  His mother was a vot'ress of my order,
  And, in the spiced Indian air, by night,
  Full often hath she gossip'd by my side,   125
  And sat with me on Neptune's yellow sands,
  Marking th' embarked traders on the flood,[7]
  When we have laugh'd to see the sails conceive

8. Banks that contain them.   9. Grain of any kind.   1. Pen for sheep or cattle.
2. Having died of the murrain, plague.
3. That is, portion of the village green marked out in a square for a game played with nine pebbles or pegs.
4. Luxuriant. *Mazes:* that is, intricate paths marked out on the village green to be followed rapidly on foot as a kind of contest.
5. That is, regular winter season; or proper observances of winter, such as the *hymn* or *carol* in the next line. *Want:* lack.   6. That is, as a result of our quarrel.   7. Colds, flu, and other respiratory infections.
8. Disturbance in nature.   9. The winter god's.   1. Fruitful, pregnant.
2. Bewildered. *Liveries:* usual apparel.   3. Their yield, what they produce.   4. Quarrel.   5. Origin.
6. Attendant, page.   7. Flood tide. *Traders:* trading vessels.

And grow big-bellied with the wanton[8] wind;
130   Which she, with pretty and with swimming gait,
      Following—her womb then rich with my young squire—
      Would imitate, and sail upon the land
      To fetch me trifles, and return again,
      As from a voyage, rich with merchandise.
135   But she, being mortal, of that boy did die;
      And for her sake do I rear up her boy,
      And for her sake I will not part with him.
OBERON: How long within this wood intend you stay?
TITANIA: Perchance till after Theseus' wedding-day.
140   If you will patiently dance in our round[9]
      And see our moonlight revels, go with us;
      If not, shun me, and I will spare[1] your haunts.
OBERON: Give me that boy, and I will go with thee.
TITANIA: Not for thy fairy kingdom. Fairies, away!
145   We shall chide downright, if I longer stay.   [*Exeunt* TITANIA *with her train.*]
OBERON: Well, go thy way. Thou shalt not from[2] this grove
      Till I torment thee for this injury.
      My gentle Puck, come hither. Thou rememb'rest
      Since[3] once I sat upon a promontory,
150   And heard a mermaid on a dolphin's back
      Uttering such dulcet and harmonious breath[4]
      That the rude sea grew civil at her song
      And certain stars shot madly from their spheres,
      To hear the sea-maid's music.
PUCK: I remember.
155 OBERON: That very time I saw, but thou couldst not,
      Flying between the cold moon and the earth,
      Cupid all[5] arm'd. A certain aim he took
      At a fair vestal[6] throned by the west,
      And loos'd his love-shaft smartly from his bow,
160   As[7] it should pierce a hundred thousand hearts;
      But I might[8] see young Cupid's fiery shaft
      Quench'd in the chaste beams of the wat'ry moon,
      And the imperial vot'ress passed on,
      In maiden meditation, fancy-free.[9]
165   Yet mark'd I where the bolt of Cupid fell:
      It fell upon a little western flower,
      Before milk-white, now purple with love's wound,
      And maidens call it love-in-idleness.[1]
      Fetch me that flow'r; the herb I showed thee once.
170   The juice of it on sleeping eyelids laid
      Will make or man or[2] woman madly dote

---

8. Sportive.   9. Circular dance.   1. Shun.   2. Go from.   3. When.   4. Voice, song.   5. Fully.
6. Vestal virgin (contains a complimentary allusion to Queen Elizabeth as a votaress of Diana and probably refers to an actual entertainment in her honor at Elvetham in 1591).   7. As if.   8. Could.
9. Free of love's spell.   1. Pansy, heartsease.   2. Either . . . or.

Upon the next live creature that it sees.
Fetch me this herb, and be thou here again
Ere the leviathan³ can swim a league.

PUCK: I'll put a girdle round about the earth   175
  In forty⁴ minutes.   [*Exit.*]

OBERON: Having once this juice,
  I'll watch Titania when she is asleep,
  And drop the liquor of it in her eyes.
  The next thing then she waking looks upon,
  Be it on lion, bear, or wolf, or bull,   180
  On meddling monkey, or on busy ape,
  She shall pursue it with the soul of love.
  And ere I take this charm from off her sight,
  As I can take it with another herb,
  I'll make her render up her page to me.   185
  But who comes here? I am invisible,
  And I will overhear their conference.

    [*Enter* DEMETRIUS, HELENA *following him.*]

DEMETRIUS: I love thee not, therefore pursue me not.
  Where is Lysander and fair Hermia?
  The one I'll slay, the other slayeth me.   190
  Thou told'st me they were stol'n unto this wood;
  And here am I, and wode⁵ within this wood,
  Because I cannot meet my Hermia.
  Hence, get thee gone, and follow me no more.

HELENA: You draw me, you hard-hearted adamant;⁶   195
  But yet you draw not iron, for my heart
  Is true as steel. Leave⁷ you your power to draw,
  And I shall have no power to follow you.

DEMETRIUS: Do I entice you? Do I speak you fair?⁸
  Or, rather, do I not in plainest truth   200
  Tell you I do not nor I cannot love you?

HELENA: And even for that do I love you the more.
  I am your spaniel; and, Demetrius,
  The more you beat me, I will fawn on you.
  Use me but as your spaniel, spurn me, strike me,   205
  Neglect me, lose me; only give me leave,
  Unworthy as I am, to follow you.
  What worser place can I beg in your love—
  And yet a place of high respect with me—
  Than to be used as you use your dog?   210

DEMETRIUS: Tempt not too much the hatred of my spirit,
  For I am sick when I do look on thee.

---

3. Sea monster, whale.   4. [The time parameters are used indefinitely here.]
5. Mad (pronounced *wood* and often spelled so).
6. Lodestone, magnet (with pun on *hard-hearted*, since adamant was also thought to be the hardest of all
stones and was confused with the diamond).   7. Give up.   8. Courteously.

HELENA: And I am sick when I look not on you.

DEMETRIUS: You do impeach[9] your modesty too much

215   To leave the city and commit yourself
    Into the hands of one that loves you not,
    To trust the opportunity of night
    And the ill counsel of a desert[1] place
    With the rich worth of your virginity.

220 HELENA: Your virtue is my privilege. For that[2]
    It is not night when I do see your face,
    Therefore I think I am not in the night;
    Nor doth this wood lack worlds of company,
    For you in my respect[3] are all the world.

225   Then how can it be said I am alone,
    When all the world is here to look on me?

DEMETRIUS: I'll run from thee and hide me in the brakes,[4]
    And leave thee to the mercy of wild beasts.

HELENA: The wildest hath not such a heart as you.

230   Run when you will, the story shall be chang'd:
    Apollo flies and Daphne holds the chase,[5]
    The dove pursues the griffin, the mild hind[6]
    Makes speed to catch the tiger—bootless[7] speed,
    When cowardice pursues and valor flies.

235 DEMETRIUS: I will not stay thy questions.[8] Let me go!
    Or if thou follow me, do not believe
    But I shall do thee mischief in the wood.

HELENA: Ay, in the temple, in the town, the field,
    You do me mischief. Fie, Demetrius!

240   Your wrongs do set a scandal on my sex.
    We cannot fight for love, as men may do;
    We should be woo'd and were not made to woo.   [*Exit* DEMETRIUS.]
    I'll follow thee and make a heaven of hell,
    To die upon[9] the hand I love so well.   [*Exit.*]

245 OBERON: Fare thee well, nymph. Ere he do leave this grove,
    Thou shalt fly him and he shall seek thy love.

      [*Enter* PUCK.]

    Hast thou the flower there? Welcome, wanderer.

PUCK: Ay, there it is.   [*Offers the flower.*]

OBERON: I pray thee, give it me.
    I know a bank where the wild thyme blows,[1]

250   Where oxlips[2] and the nodding violet grows,

---

9. Call into question.   1. Deserted.

2. Because. *Virtue*: goodness or power to attract. *Privilege*: safeguard, warrant.

3. As far as I am concerned.   4. Thickets.

5. [In the ancient myth, Daphne fled from Apollo and was saved from rape by being transformed into a laurel tree; here it is the female who *holds the chase*, or pursues, instead of the male.]

6. Female deer. *Griffin*: a fabulous monster with the head of an eagle and the body of a lion.

7. Fruitless.   8. Talk or argument. *Stay*: wait for.   9. By.   1. Blooms.

2. Flowers resembling cowslip and primrose.

Quite over-canopied with luscious woodbine,[3]
With sweet musk-roses and with eglantine.[4]
There sleeps Titania sometime of the night,
Lull'd in these flowers with dances and delight;
And there the snake throws[5] her enamel'd skin,   255
Weed[6] wide enough to wrap a fairy in.
And with the juice of this I'll streak[7] her eyes,
And make her full of hateful fantasies.
Take thou some of it, and seek through this grove.   [*Gives some love-juice.*]
A sweet Athenian lady is in love   260
With a disdainful youth. Anoint his eyes,
But do it when the next thing he espies
May be the lady. Thou shalt know the man
By the Athenian garments he hath on.
Effect it with some care, that he may prove   265
More fond on[8] her than she upon her love;
And look thou meet me ere the first cock crow.
PUCK: Fear not, my lord, your servant shall do so.   [*Exeunt.*]

Scene 2[9]

Enter TITANIA, *Queen of Fairies, with her train.*

TITANIA: Come, now a roundel[1] and a fairy song;
    Then, for the third part of a minute, hence—
    Some to kill cankers[2] in the musk-rose buds,
    Some war with rere-mice[3] for their leathern wings,
    To make my small elves coats, and some keep back   5
    The clamorous owl, that nightly hoots and wonders
    At our quaint[4] spirits. Sing me now asleep.
    Then to your offices and let me rest.

    [FAIRIES *sing.*]

[FIRST FAIRY:]

    You spotted snakes with double[5] tongue,
        Thorny hedgehogs, be not seen;   10
    Newts[6] and blindworms, do no wrong,
        Come not near our fairy queen.
[*Chorus.*] Philomel,[7] with melody
        Sing in our sweet lullaby;
    Lulla, lulla, lullaby, lulla, lulla, lullaby.   15
        Never harm,

---

3. Honeysuckle.   4. Sweetbriar, a kind of rose. *Musk-rose*: a kind of large, sweet-scented rose.
5. Sloughs off, sheds.   6. Garment.   7. Anoint, touch gently.   8. Doting on.
9. Location: the wood.   1. Dance in a ring.   2. Cankerworms.   3. Bats.   4. Dainty.   5. Forked.
6. Water lizards (considered poisonous, as were *blindworms*—small snakes with tiny eyes—and spiders).
7. The nightingale (Philomela, daughter of King Pandion, was transformed into a nightingale, according
to Ovid's *Metamorphoses* 6, after she had been raped by her sister Procne's husband, Tereus).

> Nor spell nor charm,
> Come our lovely lady nigh.
> So, good night, with lullaby.

[FIRST FAIRY:]

20   Weaving spiders, come not here;
         Hence, you long-legg'd spinners, hence!
         Beetles black, approach not near;
         Worm nor snail, do no offense.
       [*Chorus.*] Philomel, with melody, etc.

                                        [TITANIA *sleeps.*]

[SECOND FAIRY:]

25   Hence, away! Now all is well.
         One aloof stand sentinel.

                                        [*Exeunt* FAIRIES.]

   [*Enter* OBERON *and squeezes the flower on* TITANIA's *eyelids.*]

OBERON: What thou seest when thou dost wake,
   Do it for thy true-love take;
   Love and languish for his sake.
30 Be it ounce,[8] or cat, or bear,
   Pard,[9] or boar with bristled hair,
   In thy eye that shall appear
   When thou wak'st, it is thy dear.
   Wake when some vile thing is near.   [*Exit.*]

   [*Enter* LYSANDER *and* HERMIA.]

35 LYSANDER: Fair love, you faint with wand'ring in the wood;
   And to speak troth,[1] I have forgot our way.
   We'll rest us, Hermia, if you think it good,
   And tarry for the comfort of the day.
HERMIA: Be 't so, Lysander. Find you out a bed,
40   For I upon this bank will rest my head.
LYSANDER: One turf shall serve as pillow for us both,
   One heart, one bed, two bosoms, and one troth.[2]
HERMIA: Nay, good Lysander; for my sake, my dear,
   Lie further off yet, do not lie so near.
45 LYSANDER: O, take the sense, sweet, of my innocence![3]
   Love takes the meaning in love's conference.[4]
   I mean, that my heart unto yours is knit
   So that but one heart we can make of it;
   Two bosoms interchained with an oath—
50   So then two bosoms and a single troth.
   Then by your side no bed-room me deny,

8. Lynx.   9. Leopard.   1. Truth.   2. Faith, trothplight.   3. That is, interpret my intention as innocent.
4. That is, when lovers confer, love teaches each lover to interpret the other's meaning lovingly.

For lying so, Hermia, I do not lie.[5]
HERMIA: Lysander riddles very prettily.
   Now much beshrew[6] my manners and my pride
   If Hermia meant to say Lysander lied.
   But, gentle friend, for love and courtesy   55
   Lie further off, in human[7] modesty;
   Such separation as may well be said
   Becomes a virtuous bachelor and a maid,
   So far be distant; and, good night, sweet friend.   60
   Thy love ne'er alter till thy sweet life end!
LYSANDER: Amen, amen, to that fair prayer, say I,
   And then end life when I end loyalty!
   Here is my bed. Sleep give thee all his rest!
HERMIA: With half that wish the wisher's eyes be press'd![8]   65

[*They sleep, separated by a short distance. Enter* PUCK.]

PUCK: Through the forest have I gone,
   But Athenian found I none
   On whose eyes I might approve[9]
   This flower's force in stirring love.
   Night and silence.—Who is here?   70
   Weeds of Athens he doth wear.
   This is he, my master said,
   Despised the Athenian maid;
   And here the maiden, sleeping sound,
   On the dank and dirty ground.   75
   Pretty soul! She durst not lie
   Near this lack-love, this kill-courtesy.
   Churl, upon thy eyes I throw
   All the power this charm doth owe.[1]   [*Applies the love-juice.*]
   When thou wak'st, let love forbid   80
   Sleep his seat on thy eyelid.
   So awake when I am gone,
   For I must now to Oberon.   [*Exit.*]

[*Enter* DEMETRIUS *and* HELENA, *running.*]

HELENA: Stay, though thou kill me, sweet Demetrius.
   DEMETRIUS:I charge thee, hence, and do not haunt me thus.   85
HELENA: O, wilt thou darkling[2] leave me? Do not so.
DEMETRIUS: Stay, on thy peril![3] I alone will go.   [*Exit.*]
HELENA: O, I am out of breath in this fond[4] chase!
   The more my prayer, the lesser is my grace.[5]
   Happy is Hermia, wheresoe'er she lies,[6]   90
   For she hath blessed and attractive eyes.

5. Tell a falsehood (with a pun on *lie,* recline).   6. Curse (but mildly meant).   7. Courteous.
8. That is, may we share your wish, so that your eyes too are *press'd,* closed, in sleep.   9. Test.   1. Own.
2. In the dark.   3. That is, on pain of danger to you if you don't obey me and stay.   4. Doting.
5. The favor I obtain.   6. Dwells.

How came her eyes so bright? Not with salt tears;
If so, my eyes are oft'ner wash'd than hers.
No, no, I am as ugly as a bear;
95 For beasts that meet me run away for fear.
Therefore no marvel though Demetrius
Do, as a monster, fly my presence thus.
What wicked and dissembling glass of mine
Made me compare with Hermia's sphery eyne?[7]
100 But who is here? Lysander, on the ground?
Dead, or asleep? I see no blood, no wound.
Lysander, if you live, good sir, awake.
LYSANDER: [*Awaking.*] And run through fire I will for thy sweet sake.
Transparent[8] Helena! Nature shows art,
105 That through thy bosom makes me see thy heart.
Where is Demetrius? O, how fit a word
Is that vile name to perish on my sword!
HELENA: Do not say so, Lysander, say not so.
What though he love your Hermia? Lord, what though?
110 Yet Hermia still loves you. Then be content.
LYSANDER: Content with Hermia? No! I do repent
The tedious minutes I with her have spent.
Not Hermia but Helena I love.
Who will not change a raven for a dove?
115 The will of man is by his reason sway'd,
And reason says you are the worthier maid.
Things growing are not ripe until their season;
So I, being young, till now ripe not to reason.[9]
And touching now the point of human skill,[1]
120 Reason becomes the marshal to my will
And leads me to your eyes, where I o'erlook[2]
Love's stories written in love's richest book.
HELENA: Wherefore was I to this keen mockery born?
When at your hands did I deserve this scorn?
125 Is 't not enough, is 't not enough, young man,
That I did never, no, nor never can,
Deserve a sweet look from Demetrius' eye,
But you must flout my insufficiency?
Good troth, you do me wrong, good sooth,[3] you do,
130 In such disdainful manner me to woo.
But fare you well. Perforce I must confess
I thought you lord of more true gentleness.[4]
O, that a lady, of [5] one man refus'd,
Should of another therefore be abus'd![6]   [*Exit.*]
135 LYSANDER: She sees not Hermia. Hermia, sleep thou there,
And never mayst thou come Lysander near!

---

7. Eyes as bright as stars in their spheres.   8. (1) Radiant; (2) able to be seen through.
9. Mature enough to be reasonable.   1. Judgment. *Touching*: reaching. *Point*: summit.   2. Read.
3. That is, indeed, truly.   4. Courtesy. *Lord of*: that is, possessor of.   5. By.   6. Ill treated.

For as a surfeit of the sweetest things
The deepest loathing to the stomach brings,
Or as the heresies that men do leave
Are hated most of those they did deceive,   140
So thou, my surfeit and my heresy,
Of all be hated, but the most of me!
And, all my powers, address your love and might
To honor Helen and to be her knight!   [*Exit.*]
HERMIA:[*Awaking.*] Help me, Lysander, help me! Do thy best   145
To pluck this crawling serpent from my breast!
Ay me, for pity! What a dream was here!
Lysander, look how I do quake with fear.
Methought a serpent eat[7] my heart away,
And you sat smiling at his cruel prey.[8]   150
Lysander! What, remov'd? Lysander! Lord!
What, out of hearing? Gone? No sound, no word?
Alack, where are you? Speak, an if you hear.
Speak, of all loves![9] I swoon almost with fear.
No? Then I well perceive you are not nigh.   155
Either death, or you, I'll find immediately.

[*Exit. Manet*[1] TITANIA *lying asleep.*]

ACT III

Scene 1[2]

Enter the Clowns (QUINCE, SNUG, BOTTOM, FLUTE, SNOUT, *and* STARVELING.)

BOTTOM: Are we all met?
QUINCE: Pat, pat; and here's a marvailes convenient place for our rehearsal. This
   green plot shall be our stage, this hawthorn brake our tiring-house,[3] and we
   will do it in action as we will do it before the Duke.
BOTTOM: Peter Quince?   5
QUINCE: What sayest thou, bully[4] Bottom?
BOTTOM: There are things in this comedy of Pyramus and Thisby that will never
   please. First, Pyramus must draw a sword to kill himself, which the ladies
   cannot abide. How answer you that?
SNOUT: By 'r lakin, a parlous[5] fear.   10
STARVELING: I believe we must leave the killing out, when all is done.[6]
BOTTOM: Not a whit. I have a device to make all well. Write me[7] a prologue; and
   let the prologue seem to say, we will do no harm with our swords and that
   Pyramus is not kill'd indeed; and, for the more better assurance, tell them
   that I Pyramus am not Pyramus, but Bottom the weaver. This will put them 15
   out of fear.

---

7. Ate (pronounced *et*).   8. Act of preying.   9. For all love's sake.   1. [Remains (Latin).]
2. Location: scene continues.   3. Attiring area, hence backstage. *Brake*: thicket.
4. That is, worthy, jolly, fine fellow.   5. Perilous. *By 'r lakin*: by our ladykin; that is, the Virgin Mary.
6. That is, when all is said and done.   7. That is, write at my suggestion.

QUINCE: Well, we will have such a prologue, and it shall be written in eight and six.[8]

BOTTOM: No, make it two more; let it be written in eight and eight.

20 SNOUT: Will not the ladies be afeard of the lion?

STARVELING: I fear it, I promise you.

BOTTOM: Masters, you ought to consider with yourselves, to bring in—God shield us!—a lion among ladies,[9] is a most dreadful thing. For there is not a more fearful[1] wild-fowl than your lion living; and we ought to look to 't.

25 SNOUT: Therefore another prologue must tell he is not a lion.

BOTTOM: Nay, you must name his name, and half his face must be seen through the lion's neck, and he himself must speak through, saying thus, or to the same defect:[2] "Ladies"—or "Fair ladies—I would wish you"—or "I would request you"—or "I would entreat you—not to fear, not to tremble; my life for yours. If you think I come hither as a lion, it were pity of my life.[3] No, I am no such thing; I am a man as other men are." And there indeed let him name his name, and tell them plainly he is Snug the joiner.

QUINCE: Well, it shall be so. But there is two hard things: that is, to bring the moonlight into a chamber; for, you know, Pyramus and Thisby meet by moonlight.

35 SNOUT: Doth the moon shine that night we play our play?

BOTTOM: A calendar, a calendar! Look in the almanac. Find out moonshine, find out moonshine. [They consult an almanac.]

QUINCE: Yes, it doth shine that night.

40 BOTTOM: Why then may you leave a casement of the great chamber window, where we play, open, and the moon may shine in at the casement.

QUINCE: Ay; or else one must come in with a bush of thorns and a lantern, and say he comes to disfigure,[4] or to present,[5] the person of Moonshine. Then there is another thing: we must have a wall in the great chamber; for Pyramus and Thisby, says the story, did talk through the chink of a wall.

SNOUT: You can never bring in a wall. What say you, Bottom?

BOTTOM: Some man or other must present Wall. And let him have some plaster, or some loam, or some roughcast[6] about him, to signify wall; and let him hold his fingers thus, and through that cranny shall Pyramus and Thisby whisper.

QUINCE: If that may be, then all is well. Come, sit down, every mother's son, and rehearse your parts. Pyramus, you begin. When you have spoken your speech, enter into that brake, and so every one according to his cue.

[Enter Robin (PUCK).]

8. Alternate lines of eight and six syllables, a common ballad measure.
9. [A contemporary pamphlet tells how at the christening in 1594 of Prince Henry, eldest son of King James VI of Scotland, later James I of England, a "blackmoor" instead of a lion drew the triumphal chariot since the lion's presence might have "brought some fear to the nearest."]   1. Fear-inspiring.
2. [Bottom's blunder for *effect*.]
3. My life would be endangered. *My life for yours:* I pledge my life to make your lives safe.
4. [Quince's blunder for *prefigure*.] *Bush of thorns:* bundle of thornbush faggots (part of the accoutrements of the man in the moon, according to the popular notions of the time, along with his lantern and his dog).   5. Represent.   6. A mixture of lime and gravel used to plaster the outside of buildings.

PUCK: What hempen home-spuns have we swagg'ring here,
So near the cradle of the Fairy Queen?   55
What, a play toward?[7] I'll be an auditor;
An actor too perhaps, if I see cause.
QUINCE: Speak, Pyramus. Thisby, stand forth.
BOTTOM: "Thisby, the flowers of odious savors sweet,"—
QUINCE: Odors, odors.   60
BOTTOM: —"Odors savors sweet;
So hath thy breath, my dearest Thisby dear.
But hark, a voice! Stay thou but here awhile,
And by and by I will to thee appear."   [*Exit.*]
PUCK: A stranger Pyramus than e'er played here.[8]   [*Exit.*]   65
FLUTE: Must I speak now?
QUINCE: Ay, marry, must you; for you must understand he goes but to see a noise
that he heard, and is to come again.
FLUTE: "Most radiant Pyramus, most lily-white of hue,
Of color like the red rose on triumphant brier,   70
Most brisky juvenal and eke most lovely Jew,[9]
As true as truest horse that yet would never tire.
I'll meet thee, Pyramus, at Ninny's tomb."
QUINCE: "Ninus'[1] tomb," man. Why, you must not speak that yet. That you   75
answer to Pyramus. You speak all your part at once, cues and all. Pyramus,
enter. Your cue is past; it is, "never tire."
FLUTE: O—"As true as truest horse, that yet would never tire."

[*Enter* PUCK, *and* BOTTOM *as Pyramus with the ass head.*][2]

BOTTOM: "If I were fair,[3] Thisby, I were only thine."
QUINCE: O monstrous! O strange! We are haunted. Pray, masters! Fly, masters!
Help!   [*Exeunt* QUINCE, SNUG, FLUTE, SNOUT, and STARVELING.]   80
PUCK: I'll follow you, I'll lead you about a round,[4]
Through bog, through bush, through brake, through brier.
Sometime a horse I'll be, sometime a hound,
A hog, a headless bear, sometime a fire;[5]
And neigh, and bark, and grunt, and roar, and burn,   85
Like horse, hound, hog, bear, fire, at every turn.   [*Exit.*]
BOTTOM: Why do they run away? This is a knavery of them to make me afeard.

[*Enter* SNOUT.]

SNOUT: O Bottom, thou art chang'd! what do I see on thee?
BOTTOM: What do you see? You see an ass-head of your own, do you?
                                                               [*Exit* SNOUT.]

[*Enter* QUINCE.]

---

7. About to take place.   8. That is, in this theater (?).
9. [Probably an absurd repetition of the first syllable of *juvenal*.] *Briskly juvenal*: brisk youth. *Eke*: also.
1. Mythical founder of Nineveh (whose wife, Semiramis, was supposed to have built the walls of Babylon,
where the story of Pyramis and Thisbe takes place).
2. [This stage direction, taken from the Folio, presumably refers to a standard stage property.]
3. Handsome.   4. Roundabout.   5. Will-o'-the-wisp.

90   QUINCE: Bless thee, Bottom, bless thee! Thou art translated.[6]   [*Exit.*]
      BOTTOM: I see their knavery. This is to make an ass of me, to fright me, if they
            could. But I will not stir from this place, do what they can. I will walk up and
            down here, and will sing, that they shall hear I am not afraid.

[*Sings.*]

            The woosel cock[7] so black of hue,
95   With orange-tawny bill,
            The throstle[8] with his note so true,
                 The wren with little quill[9]—

TITANIA: [*Awaking.*] What angel wakes me from my flow'ry bed?

[BOTTOM *sings.*]

            The finch, the sparrow, and the lark,
100   The plain-song[1] cuckoo grey,
            Whose note full many a man doth mark,
                 And dares not answer nay[2]—

      For, indeed, who would set his wit to so foolish a bird? Who would give a bird
      the lie,[3] though he cry "cuckoo" never so?[4]
105 TITANIA: I pray thee, gentle mortal, sing again.
            Mine ear is much enamored of thy note;
            So is mine eye enthralled to thy shape;
            And thy fair virtue's force[5] perforce doth move me
            On the first view to say, to swear, I love thee.
110 BOTTOM: Methinks, mistress, you should have little reason for that. And yet, to
            say the truth, reason and love keep little company together nowadays. The
            more the pity that some honest neighbors will not make them friends. Nay, I
            can gleek[6] upon occasion.
      TITANIA: Thou art as wise as thou art beautiful.
115 BOTTOM: Not so, neither. But if I had wit enough to get out of this wood, I have
            enough to serve mine own turn.[7]
      TITANIA: Out of this wood do not desire to go.
            Thou shalt remain here, whether thou wilt or no.
            I am a spirit of no common rate.[8]
120   The summer still doth tend upon my state;[9]
            And I do love thee. Therefore, go with me.
            I'll give thee fairies to attend on thee,
            And they shall fetch thee jewels from the deep,
            And sing while thou on pressed flowers dost sleep.
125   And I will purge thy mortal grossness so
            That thou shalt like an airy spirit go.
            Peaseblossom, Cobweb, Moth,[1] and Mustardseed!

---

6. Transformed.   7. Male ousel or ouzel, blackbird.   8. Song thrush.
9. [Literally, a reed pipe; hence, the bird's piping song.]   1. Singing a melody without variations.
2. That is, cannot deny that he is a cuckold.   3. Call the bird a liar.   4. Ever so much.
5. The power of your beauty.   6. Scoff, jest.   7. Answer my purpose.   8. Rank, value.
9. Waits upon me as a part of my royal retinue. *Still*: ever, always.
1. That is, mote, speck. (The two words *moth* and *mote* were pronounced alike.)

[*Enter four* FAIRIES (PEASEBLOSSOM, COBWEB, MOTH, *and* MUSTARDSEED).]

PEASEBLOSSOM: Ready.

COBWEB: And I.

MOTH: And I.

MUSTARDSEED: And I.

ALL: Where shall we go?

TITANIA: Be kind and courteous to this gentleman.
    Hop in his walks and gambol in his eyes;   130
    Feed him with apricocks and dewberries,
    With purple grapes, green figs, and mulberries;
    The honey-bags steal from the humble-bees,
    And for night-tapers crop their waxen thighs
    And light them at the fiery glow-worm's eyes,   135
    To have my love to bed and to arise;
    And pluck the wings from painted butterflies
    To fan the moonbeams from his sleeping eyes.
    Nod to him, elves, and do him courtesies.

PEASEBLOSSOM: Hail, mortal!   140

COBWEB: Hail!

MOTH: Hail!

MUSTARDSEED: Hail!

BOTTOM: I cry your worships mercy, heartily. I beseech your worship's name.

COBWEB: Cobweb.   145

BOTTOM: I shall desire you of more acquaintance, good Master Cobweb. If I cut my finger, I shall make bold with you.[2] Your name, honest gentleman?

PEASEBLOSSOM: Peaseblossom.

BOTTOM: I pray you, commend me to Mistress Squash,[3] your mother, and to Master Peascod,[4] your father. Good Master Peaseblossom, I shall desire you of   150
more acquaintance too. Your name, I beseech you, sir?

MUSTARDSEED: Mustardseed.

BOTTOM: Good Master Mustardseed, I know your patience well.[5] That same cowardly, giant-like ox-beef hath devour'd many a gentleman of your house. I
promise you your kindred hath made my eyes water ere now. I desire you of   155
more acquaintance, good Master Mustardseed.

TITANIA: Come wait upon him; lead him to my bower.
    The moon methinks looks with a wat'ry eye;
    And when she weeps,[6] weeps every little flower,
    Lamenting some enforced[7] chastity.   160
    Tie up my lover's tongue, bring him silently.   [*Exeunt.*]

---

2. [Cobwebs were used to stanch bleeding.]   3. Unripe pea pod.   4. Ripe pea pod.
5. What you have endured.   6. That is, she causes dew.
7. Forced, violated, or, possibly, constrained (since Titania at this moment is hardly concerned about chastity).

Scene 2[8]

Enter OBERON, *King of Fairies.*

OBERON: I wonder if Titania be awak'd;
    Then, what it was that next came in her eye,
    Which she must dote on in extremity.

    [*Enter Robin Goodfellow (*PUCK*).*]

    Here comes my messenger. How now, mad spirit?
5   What night-rule now about this haunted[9] grove?
    PUCK: My mistress with a monster is in love.
    Near to her close[1] and consecrated bower,
    While she was in her dull[2] and sleeping hour,
    A crew of patches, rude mechanicals,[3]
10   That work for bread upon Athenian stalls,
    Were met together to rehearse a play
    Intended for great Theseus' nuptial day.
    The shallowest thick-skin of that barren sort,[4]
    Who Pyramus presented,[5] in their sport
15   Forsook his scene[6] and ent'red in a brake.
    When I did him at this advantage take,
    An ass's nole[7] I fixed on his head.
    Anon his Thisby must be answered,
    And forth my mimic[8] comes. When they him spy,
20   As wild geese that the creeping fowler eye,
    Or russet-pated choughs, many in sort,[9]
    Rising and cawing at the gun's report,
    Sever[1] themselves and madly sweep the sky,
    So, at his sight, away his fellows fly;
25   And, at our stamp, here o'er and o'er one falls;
    He murder cries and help from Athens calls.
    Their sense thus weak, lost with their fears thus strong,
    Made senseless things begin to do them wrong,
    For briers and thorns at their apparel snatch;
30   Some, sleeves—some, hats; from yielders all things catch.
    I led them on in this distracted fear
    And left sweet Pyramus translated there,
    When in that moment, so it came to pass,
    Titania wak'd and straightway lov'd an ass.
35 OBERON: This falls out better than I could devise.
    But hast thou yet latch'd[2] the Athenian's eyes
    With the love-juice, as I did bid thee do?
    PUCK: I took him sleeping—that is finish'd too—

---

8. Location: the wood.   9. Much frequented. *Night-rule*: diversion for the night.   1. Secret, private.
2. Drowsy.   3. Ignorant artisans. *Patches*: clowns, fools.   4. Stupid company or crew.   5. Acted.
6. Playing area.   7. Noddle, head.   8. Burlesque actor.
9. In a flock. *Russet-pated choughs*: gray-headed jackdaws.   1. That is, scatter.   2. Moistened, anointed.

And the Athenian woman by his side,
That, when he wak'd, of force[3] she must be ey'd.   40

[*Enter* DEMETRIUS *and* HERMIA.]

OBERON: Stand close. This is the same Athenian.
PUCK: This is the woman, but not this the man.   [*They stand aside.*]
DEMETRIUS: O, why rebuke you him that loves you so?
    Lay breath so bitter on your bitter foe.
HERMIA: Now I but chide; but I should use thee worse,   45
    For thou, I fear, hast given me cause to curse.
    If thou hast slain Lysander in his sleep,
    Being o'er shoes in blood, plunge in the deep,
    And kill me too.
    The sun was not so true unto the day   50
    As he to me. Would he have stolen away
    From sleeping Hermia? I'll believe as soon
    This whole[4] earth may be bor'd and that the moon
    May through the center creep and so displease
    Her brother's noontide with th' Antipodes.[5]   55
    It cannot be but thou hast murd'red him;
    So should a murderer look, so dead,[6] so grim.
DEMETRIUS: So should the murdered look, and so should I,
    Pierc'd through the heart with your stern cruelty.
    Yet you, the murderer, look as bright, as clear,   60
    As yonder Venus in her glimmering sphere.
HERMIA: What's this to my Lysander? Where is he?
    Ah, good Demetrius, wilt thou give him me?
DEMETRIUS: I had rather give his carcass to my hounds.
HERMIA: Out, dog! Out, cur! Thou driv'st me past the bounds   65
    Of maiden's patience. Hast thou slain him, then?
    Henceforth be never numb'red among men!
    O, once tell true, tell true, even for my sake!
    Durst thou have look'd upon him being awake,
    And hast thou kill'd him sleeping? O brave touch![7]   70
    Could not a worm,[8] an adder, do so much?
    An adder did it; for with doubler tongue
    Than thine, thou serpent, never adder stung.
DEMETRIUS: You spend your passion on a mispris'd mood.[9]
    I am not guilty of Lysander's blood,   75
    Nor is he dead, for aught that I can tell.
HERMIA: I pray thee, tell me then that he is well.
DEMETRIUS: An if I could, what should I get therefore?
HERMIA: A privilege never to see me more.
    And from thy hated presence part I so.   80
    See me no more, whether he be dead or no.   [*Exit.*]

---

3. Perforce.   4. Solid.   5. The people on the opposite side of the Earth. *Her brother's*: that is, the sun's.
6. Deadly, or deathly pale.   7. Noble exploit (said ironically).   8. Serpent.
9. Anger based on misconception. *Passion*: violent feelings.

DEMETRIUS: There is no following her in this fierce vein.
   Here therefore for a while I will remain.
   So sorrow's heaviness doth heavier[1] grow
85   For debt that bankrupt[2] sleep doth sorrow owe;
   Which now in some slight measure it will pay,
   If for his tender here I make some stay.[3]   *[He lies down and sleeps.]*
OBERON: What hast thou done? Thou hast mistaken quite
   And laid the love-juice on some true-love's sight.
90   Of thy misprision[4] must perforce ensue
   Some true love turn'd and not a false turn'd true.
PUCK: Then fate o'er-rules that, one man holding troth,[5]
   A million fail, confounding[6] oath on oath.
OBERON: About the wood go swifter than the wind,
95   And Helena of Athens look thou find.
   All fancy-sick she is and pale of cheer,[7]
   With sighs of love, that cost the fresh blood[8] dear.
   By some illusion see thou bring her here.
   I'll charm his eyes against she do appear.[9]
100 PUCK: I go, I go; look how I go,
   Swifter than arrow from the Tartar's bow.[1]   *[Exit.]*
OBERON: Flower of this purple dye,
   Hit with Cupid's archery.
   Sink in apple of his eye.   *[Applies love-juice to DEMETRIUS's eyes.]*
105   When his love he doth espy,
   Let her shine as gloriously
   As the Venus of the sky.
   When thou wak'st, if she be by,
   Beg of her for remedy.

   [Enter PUCK.]

110 PUCK: Captain of our fairy band,
   Helena is here at hand,
   And the youth, mistook by me,
   Pleading for a lover's fee.[2]
   Shall we their fond pageant[3] see?
115   Lord, what fools these mortals be!
OBERON: Stand aside. The noise they make
   Will cause Demetrius to awake.
PUCK: Then will two at once woo one;
   That must needs be sport alone[4];

1. (1) Harder to bear; (2) more drowsy.
2. [Demetrius is saying that his sleepiness adds to the weariness caused by sorrow.]
3. That is, to a small extent I will be able to "pay back" and hence find some relief from sorrow, if I pause here a while (*make some stay*) while sleep "tenders" or offers itself by way of paying the debt owed to sorrow.
4. Mistake.   5. Faith.   6. That is, invalidating one oath with another.   7. Face. *Fancy-sick*: lovesick.
8. [An allusion to the physiological theory that each sigh costs the heart a drop of blood.]
9. In anticipation of her coming.   1. [Tartars were famed for their skill with the bow.]
2. Privilege, reward.   3. Foolish exhibition.   4. Unequaled.

And those things do best please me   120
That befall prepost'rously.[5]   [*They stand aside.*]

[*Enter* LYSANDER *and* HELENA.]

LYSANDER: Why should you think that I should woo in scorn?
    Scorn and derision never come in tears.
    Look when[6] I vow, I weep; and vows so born,
    In their nativity all truth appears.[7]   125
    How can these things in me seem scorn to you,
    Bearing the badge[8] of faith, to prove them true?
HELENA: You do advance[9] your cunning more and more.
    When truth kills truth,[1] O devilish-holy fray!
    These vows are Hermia's. Will you give her o'er?   130
    Weigh oath with oath, and you will nothing weigh.
    Your vows to her and me, put in two scales,
    Will even weigh, and both as light as tales.[2]
LYSANDER: I had no judgment when to her I swore.
HELENA: Nor none, in my mind, now you give her o'er.   135
LYSANDER: Demetrius loves her, and he loves not you.
DEMETRIUS: [*Awaking.*] O Helen, goddess, nymph, perfect, divine!
    To what, my love, shall I compare thine eyne?
    Crystal is muddy. O, how ripe in show[3]
    Thy lips, those kissing cherries, tempting grow!   140
    That pure congealed white, high Taurus'[4] snow,
    Fann'd with the eastern wind, turns to a crow[5]
    When thou hold'st up thy hand. O, let me kiss
    This princess of pure white, this seal[6] of bliss!
HELENA: O spite! O hell! I see you all are bent   145
    To set against me for your merriment.
    If you were civil and knew courtesy,
    You would not do me thus much injury.
    Can you not hate me, as I know you do,
    But you must join in souls to mock me too?   150
    If you were men, as men you are in show,
    You would not use a gentle lady so—
    To vow, and swear, and superpraise my parts,[7]
    When I am sure you hate me with your hearts.
    You both are rivals, and love Hermia;   155
    And now both rivals, to mock Helena.
    A trim[8] exploit, a manly enterprise,
    To conjure tears up in a poor maid's eyes
    With your derision! None of noble sort

5. Out of the natural order.   6. Whenever.
7. That is, vows made by one who is weeping give evidence thereby of their sincerity.
8. Identifying device such as that worn on servants' livery.   9. Carry forward, display.
1. That is, one of Lysander's vows must invalidate the other.   2. Lies.   3. Appearance.
4. A lofty mountain range in Asia Minor.   5. That is, seems black by contrast.   6. Pledge.
7. Qualities. *Superpraise*: overpraise.   8. Pretty, fine (said ironically).

160   Would so offend a virgin and extort[9]
      A poor soul's patience, all to make you sport.
      LYSANDER: You are unkind, Demetrius. Be not so;
         For you love Hermia; this you know I know.
         And here, with all good will, with all my heart,
165   In Hermia's love I yield you up my part;
         And yours of Helena to me bequeath,
         Whom I do love and will do till my death.
      HELENA: Never did mockers waste more idle breath.
      DEMETRIUS: Lysander, keep thy Hermia; I will none.[1]
170   If e'er I lov'd her, all that love is gone.
         My heart to her but as guest-wise sojourn'd,
         And now to Helen is it home return'd,
         There to remain.
      LYSANDER: Helen, it is not so.
      DEMETRIUS: Disparage not the faith thou dost not know,
175   Lest, to thy peril, thou aby[2] it dear.
         Look, where thy love comes; yonder is thy dear.

      [Enter HERMIA.]

      HERMIA: Dark night, that from the eye his[3] function takes,
         The ear more quick of apprehension makes;
         Wherein it doth impair the seeing sense,
180   It pays the hearing double recompense.
         Thou art not by mine eye, Lysander, found;
         Mine ear, I thank it, brought me to thy sound.
         But why unkindly didst thou leave me so?
      LYSANDER: Why should he stay, whom love doth press to go?
185   HERMIA: What love could press Lysander from my side?
      LYSANDER: Lysander's love, that would not let him bide,
         Fair Helena, who more engilds the night
         Than all yon fiery oes[4] and eyes of light.
         Why seek'st thou me? Could not this make thee know,
190   The hate I bear thee made me leave thee so?
      HERMIA: You speak not as you think. It cannot be.
      HELENA: Lo, she is one of this confederacy!
         Now I perceive they have conjoin'd all three
         To fashion this false sport, in spite of me.[5]
195   Injurious Hermia, most ungrateful maid!
         Have you conspir'd, have you with these contriv'd[6]
         To bait[7] me with this foul derision?
         Is all the counsel[8] that we two have shar'd,
         The sisters' vows, the hours that we have spent,
200   When we have chid the hasty-footed time
         For parting us—O, is all forgot?

___

9. Twist, torture.   1. That is, wish none of her.   2. Pay for.   3. Its.   4. That is, circles, orbs, stars.
5. To vex me.   6. Plotted.   7. Torment, as one sets on dogs to bait a bear.   8. Confidential talk.

All school-days friendship, childhood innocence?
We, Hermia, like two artificial[9] gods,
Have with our needles created both one flower,
Both on one sampler, sitting on one cushion,   205
Both warbling of one song, both in one key,
As if our hands, our sides, voices, and minds
Had been incorporate. So we grew together,
Like to a double cherry, seeming parted,
But yet an union in partition;   210
Two lovely[1] berries molded on one stem;
So, with two seeming bodies, but one heart;
Two of the first, like coats in heraldry,
Due but to one and crowned with one crest.[2]
And will you rent[3] our ancient love asunder,   215
To join with men in scorning your poor friend?
It is not friendly, 'tis not maidenly.
Our sex, as well as I, may chide you for it,
Though I alone do feel the injury.
HERMIA: I am amazed at your passionate words.   220
　　　I scorn you not. It seems that you scorn me.
HELENA: Have you not set Lysander, as in scorn,
　　　To follow me and praise my eyes and face?
　　　And made your other love, Demetrius,
　　　Who even but now did spurn me with his foot,   225
　　　To call me goddess, nymph, divine and rare,
　　　Precious, celestial? Wherefore speaks he this
　　　To her he hates? And wherefore doth Lysander
　　　Deny your love, so rich within his soul,
　　　And tender[4] me, forsooth, affection,   230
　　　But by your setting on, by your consent?
　　　What though I be not so in grace[5] as you,
　　　So hung upon with love, so fortunate,
　　　But miserable most, to love unlov'd?
　　　This you should pity rather than despise.   235
HERMIA: I understand not what you mean by this.
HELENA: Ay, do! Persever, counterfeit sad[6] looks,
　　　Make mouths upon[7] me when I turn my back,
　　　Wink each at other, hold the sweet jest up.
　　　This sport, well carried,[8] shall be chronicled.   240
　　　If you have any pity, grace, or manners,
　　　You would not make me such an argument.[9]
　　　But fare ye well. 'Tis partly my own fault,
　　　Which death, or absence, soon shall remedy.

---

9. Skilled in art or creation.　　1. Loving.
2. That is, we have two separate bodies, just as a coat of arms in heraldry can be represented twice on
a shield but surmounted by a single crest.　　3. Rend.　　4. Offer.　　5. Favor.　　6. Grave, serious.
7. That is, makes mows, faces, grimaces at.　　8. Managed.　　9. Subject for a jest.

245 LYSANDER: Stay, gentle Helena; hear my excuse,
　　My love, my life, my soul, fair Helena!
HELENA: O excellent!
HERMIA: 　　　　　　Sweet, do not scorn her so.
DEMETRIUS: If she cannot entreat,[1] I can compel.
LYSANDER: Thou canst compel no more than she entreat.
250 　　Thy threats have no more strength than her weak prayers.
　　Helen, I love thee, by my life, I do!
　　I swear by that which I will lose for thee,
　　To prove him false that says I love thee not.
DEMETRIUS: I say I love thee more than he can do.
255 LYSANDER: If thou say so, withdraw, and prove it too.
DEMETRIUS: Quick, come!
HERMIA: 　　　　　　Lysander, whereto tends all this?
LYSANDER: Away, you Ethiope![2] 　　　[*He tries to break away from* HERMIA.]
DEMETRIUS: 　　　　　No, no; he'll
　　Seem to break loose; take on as you would follow,
　　But yet come not. You are a tame man, go!
260 LYSANDER: Hang off,[3] thou cat, thou burr! Vile thing, let loose,
　　Or I will shake thee from me like a serpent!
HERMIA: Why are you grown so rude? What change is this,
　　Sweet love?
LYSANDER: 　　Thy love? Out, tawny Tartar, out!
　　Out, loathed med'cine![4] O hated potion, hence!
HERMIA: Do you not jest?
265 HELENA: 　　　　　　Yes, sooth,[5] and so do you.
LYSANDER: Demetrius, I will keep my word with thee.
DEMETRIUS: I would I had your bond, for I perceive
　　A weak bond[6] holds you. I'll not trust your word.
LYSANDER: What, should I hurt her, strike her, kill her dead?
270 　　Although I hate her, I'll not harm her so.
HERMIA: What, can you do me greater harm than hate?
　　Hate me? Wherefore? O me, what news,[7] my love?
　　Am not I Hermia? Are not you Lysander?
　　I am as fair now as I was erewhile.[8]
275 　　Since night you lov'd me; yet since night you left me.
　　Why, then you left me—O, the gods forbid!—
　　In earnest, shall I say?
LYSANDER: 　　　　　　Ay, by my life!
　　And never did desire to see thee more.
　　Therefore be out of hope, of question, of doubt;
280 　　Be certain, nothing truer. 'Tis no jest
　　That I do hate thee and love Helena.

---

1. That is, succeed by entreaty.
2. [Referring to Hermia's relatively dark hair and complexion; see also *tawny Tartar* six lines later.]
3. Let go. 　4. That is, poison. 　5. Truly.
6. That is, Hermia's arm (with a pun on *bond*, oath, in the previous line). 　7. What is the matter.
8. Just now.

HERMIA: O me! You juggler! You cankerblossom![9]
　　You thief of love! What, have you come by night
　　And stol'n my love's heart from him?

HELENA: 　　　　　　　　　　　Fine, i' faith!
　　Have you no modesty, no maiden shame, 285
　　No touch of bashfulness? What, will you tear
　　Impatient answers from my gentle tongue?
　　Fie, fie! You counterfeit, you puppet,[1] you!

HERMIA: Puppet? Why so? Ay, that way goes the game.
　　Now I perceive that she hath made compare 290
　　Between our statures; she hath urg'd her height,
　　And with her personage, her tall personage,
　　Her height, forsooth, she hath prevail'd with him.
　　And are you grown so high in his esteem,
　　Because I am so dwarfish and so low? 295
　　How low am I, thou painted maypole? Speak!
　　How low am I? I am not yet so low
　　But that my nails can reach unto thine eyes.

　　　　　　　　[*She flails at* HERMIA, *but is restrained.*]

HELENA: I pray you, though you mock me, gentlemen,
　　Let her not hurt me. I was never curst;[2] 300
　　I have no gift at all in shrewishness;
　　I am a right[3] maid for my cowardice.
　　Let her not strike me. You perhaps may think,
　　Because she is something[4] lower than myself,
　　That I can match her.

HERMIA: 　　　　　　Lower! Hark, again! 305

HELENA: Good Hermia, do not be so bitter with me.
　　I evermore did love you, Hermia,
　　Did ever keep your counsels, never wrong'd you;
　　Save that, in love unto Demetrius,
　　I told him of your stealth[5] unto this wood. 310
　　He followed you; for love I followed him.
　　But he hath chid me hence and threat'ned me
　　To strike me, spurn me, nay, to kill me too.
　　And now, so[6] you will let me quiet go,
　　To Athens will I bear my folly back 315
　　And follow you no further. Let me go.
　　You see how simple and how fond[7] I am.

HERMIA: Why, get you gone. Who is 't that hinders you?

HELENA: A foolish heart, that I leave here behind.

HERMIA: What, with Lysander?

HELENA: 　　　　　　　　With Demetrius. 320

LYSANDER: Be not afraid; she shall not harm thee, Helena.

DEMETRIUS: No, sir, she shall not, though you take her part.

---

9. Worm that destroys the flower bud (?).
1. (1) Counterfeit; (2) dwarfish woman (in reference to Hermia's smaller stature). 　2. Shrewish.
3. True. 　4. Somewhat. 　5. Stealing away. 　6. If only. 　7. Foolish.

HELENA: O, when she is angry, she is keen and shrewd![8]
    She was a vixen when she went to school;
325   And though she be but little, she is fierce.
HERMIA: "Little" again! Nothing but "low" and "little"!
    Why will you suffer her to flout me thus?
    Let me come to her.
LYSANDER: Get you gone, you dwarf!
    You minimus, of hind'ring knot-grass[9] made!
    You bead, you acorn!
330 DEMETRIUS: You are too officious
    In her behalf that scorns your services.
    Let her alone. Speak not of Helena;
    Take not her part. For, if thou dost intend[1]
    Never so little show of love to her,
    Thou shalt aby[2] it.
335 LYSANDER: Now she holds me not;
    Now follow, if thou dar'st, to try whose right,
    Of thine or mine, is most in Helena.[Exit.]
DEMETRIUS: Follow? Nay, I'll go with thee, cheek by jowl.[3]
                           [Exit, following LYSANDER.]
HERMIA: You, mistress, all this coil is 'long of[4] you.
    Nay, go not back.[5]
340 HELENA: I will not trust you, I,
    Nor longer stay in your curst company.
    Your hands than mine are quicker for a fray;
    My legs are longer, though, to run away.   [Exit.]
HERMIA: I am amaz'd, and know not what to say.   [Exit.]
345 OBERON: This is thy negligence. Still thou mistak'st,
    Or else committ'st thy knaveries willfully.
PUCK: Believe me, king of shadows, I mistook.
    Did not you tell me I should know the man
    By the Athenian garments he had on?
350   And so far blameless proves my enterprise
    That I have 'nointed an Athenian's eyes;
    And so far am I glad it so did sort[6]
    As this their jangling I esteem a sport.
OBERON: Thou see'st these lovers seek a place to fight.
355   Hie therefore, Robin, overcast the night;
    The starry welkin[7] cover thou anon
    With drooping fog as black as Acheron,[8]
    And lead these testy rivals so astray
    As[9] one come not within another's way.
360   Like to Lysander sometime frame thy tongue,

---

8. Shrewish.
9. A weed, an infusion of which was thought to stunt the growth. *Minimus:* diminutive creature.
1. Give sign of.   2. Pay for.   3. That is, side by side.   4. On account of. *Coil:* turmoil, dissension.
5. That is, don't retreat (Hermia is again proposing a fight).   6. Turn out.   7. Sky.
8. River of Hades (here representing Hades itself).   9. That.

Then stir Demetrius up with bitter wrong;[1]
And sometime rail thou like Demetrius.
And from each other look thou lead them thus,
Till o'er their brows death-counterfeiting sleep
With leaden legs and batty[2] wings doth creep.   365
Then crush this herb[3] into Lysander's eye,   *[Gives herb.]*
Whose liquor hath this virtuous[4] property,
To take from thence all error with his[5] might
And make his eyeballs roll with wonted[6] sight.
When they next wake, all this derision[7]   370
Shall seem a dream and fruitless vision,
And back to Athens shall the lovers wend
With league whose date[8] till death shall never end.
Whiles I in this affair do thee employ,
I'll to my queen and beg her Indian boy;   375
And then I will her charmed eye release
From monster's view, and all things shall be peace.
PUCK: My fairy lord, this must be done with haste,
For night's swift dragons[9] cut the clouds full fast,
And yonder shines Aurora's harbinger,[1]   380
At whose approach, ghosts, wand'ring here and there,
Troop home to churchyards. Damned spirits all,
That in crossways and floods have burial,[2]
Already to their wormy beds are gone.
For fear lest day should look their shames upon,   385
They willfully themselves exile from light
And must for aye[3] consort with black-brow'd night.
OBERON: But we are spirits of another sort.
I with the Morning's love[4] have oft made sport,
And, like a forester,[5] the groves may tread   390
Even till the eastern gate, all fiery-red,
Opening on Neptune with fair blessed beams,
Turns into yellow gold his salt green streams.
But, notwithstanding, haste; make no delay.
We may effect this business yet ere day.   *[Exit.]* 395
PUCK: Up and down, up and down,
I will lead them up and down.
I am fear'd in field and town.
Goblin, lead them up and down.

---

1. Insults.   2. Batlike.   3. That is, the antidote (mentioned in 2.1.184) to love-in-idleness.
4. Efficacious.   5. Its.   6. Accustomed.   7. Laughable business.   8. Term of existence.
9. [Supposed by Shakespeare to be yoked to the car of the goddess of night.]
1. The morning star, precursor of dawn.
2. [Those who had committed suicide were buried at crossways, with a stake driven through them; those
drowned, that is, buried in floods or great waters, would be condemned to wander disconsolate for want
of burial rites.]   3. Forever.
4. Cephalus, a beautiful youth beloved by Aurora; or perhaps the goddess of the dawn herself.
5. Keeper of a royal forest.

400   Here comes one.

      [*Enter* LYSANDER.]

LYSANDER: Where art thou, proud Demetrius? Speak thou now.
PUCK: [*Mimicking* DEMETRIUS.] Here, villain, drawn[6] and ready. Where art thou?
LYSANDER: I will be with thee straight.[7]
PUCK: Follow me, then,
    To plainer[8] ground.

      [LYSANDER *wanders about,*[9] *following the voice. Enter* DEMETRIUS.]

DEMETRIUS: Lysander! Speak again!
405   Thou runaway, thou coward, art thou fled?
    Speak! In some bush? Where dost thou hide thy head?
PUCK: [*Mimicking* LYSANDER.] Thou coward, art thou bragging to the stars,
    Telling the bushes that thou look'st for wars,
    And wilt not come? Come, recreant;[1] come, thou child,
410   I'll whip thee with a rod. He is defil'd
    That draws a sword on thee.
DEMETRIUS: Yea, art thou there?
PUCK: Follow my voice. We'll try[2] no manhood here.   [*Exeunt.*]

      [LYSANDER *returns.*]

LYSANDER: He goes before me and still dares me on.
    When I come where he calls, then he is gone.
415   The villain is much lighter-heel'd than I.
    I followed fast, but faster he did fly,
    That fallen am I in dark uneven way,
    And here will rest me. [*Lies down.*] Come, thou gentle day!
    For if but once thou show me thy grey light,
420   I'll find Demetrius and revenge this spite.   [*Sleeps.*]

      [*Enter Robin* (PUCK) *and* DEMETRIUS.]

PUCK: Ho, ho, ho! Coward, why com'st thou not?
DEMETRIUS: Abide me, if thou dar'st; for well I wot[3]
    Thou runn'st before me, shifting every place,
    And dar'st not stand nor look me in the face.
    Where art thou now?
425 PUCK: Come hither. I am here.
DEMETRIUS: Nay, then, thou mock'st me. Thou shalt buy this dear,[4]
    If ever I thy face by daylight see.
    Now, go thy way. Faintness constraineth me
    To measure out my length on this cold bed.
430   By day's approach look to be visited.   [*Lies down and sleeps.*]

      [*Enter* HELENA.]

---

6. With drawn sword.   7. Immediately.   8. Smoother.
9. [It is not clearly necessary that Lysander exit at this point; neither exit nor reentrance is indicated in the early texts.]   1. Cowardly wretch.   2. Test.   3. Know.   4. Pay dearly for this.

HELENA: O weary night, O long and tedious night,
    Abate⁵ thy hours! Shine, comforts, from the east,
    That I may back to Athens by daylight,
    From these that my poor company detest;
    And sleep, that sometimes shuts up sorrow's eye,   435
    Steal me awhile from mine own company.   [*Lies down and sleeps.*]
PUCK: Yet but three? Come one more;
    Two of both kinds makes up four.
    Here she comes, curst and sad.
    Cupid is a knavish lad,   440
    Thus to make poor females mad.

    [*Enter* HERMIA.]

HERMIA: Never so weary, never so in woe,
    Bedabbled with the dew and torn with briers,
    I can no further crawl, no further go;
    My legs can keep no pace with my desires.   445
    Here will I rest me till the break of day.
    Heavens shield Lysander, if they mean a fray!   [*Lies down and sleeps.*]
PUCK: On the ground
    Sleep sound.
    I'll apply   450
    To your eye,
    Gentle lover, remedy.   [*Squeezing the juice on* LYSANDER*'s eyes.*]
    When thou wak'st,
    Thou tak'st
    True delight   455
    In the sight
    Of thy former lady's eye;
    And the country proverb known,
    That every man should take his own,
    In your waking shall be shown: 460
    Jack shall have Jill;
    Nought shall go ill;
    The man shall have his mare again, and all
    shall be well.   [*Exit. Manent the four lovers.*]

ACT IV

Scene 1⁶

Enter TITANIA, *Queen of Fairies, and* BOTTOM *the Clown, and* FAIRIES: *and* OBERON, *the King, behind them.*

TITANIA: Come, sit thee down upon this flow'ry bed,
    While I thy amiable cheeks do coy,⁷

5. Lessen, shorten.   6. Location: scene continues. The four lovers are still asleep on stage.
7. Caress. *Amiable:* lovely.

And stick musk-roses in thy sleek smooth head,
And kiss thy fair large ears, my gentle joy.

[*They recline.*]

5 BOTTOM: Where's Peaseblossom?
PEASEBLOSSOM: Ready.
BOTTOM: Scratch my head, Peaseblossom. Where's Mounsieur Cobweb?
COBWEB: Ready.
BOTTOM: Mounsieur Cobweb, good mounsier, get you your weapons in your
10 hand, and kill me a red-hipp'd humble-bee on the top of a thistle; and, good
mounsieur, bring me the honey-bag. Do not fret yourself too much in the
action, mounsieur; and, good mounsieur, have a care the honey-bag break
not; I would be loath to have you overflown with a honey-bag, signior. Where's
Mounsieur Mustardseed?   [*Exit* COBWEB.]
15 MUSTARDSEED: Ready.
BOTTOM: Give me your neaf,[8] Mounsieur Mustardseed. Pray you, leave your
curtsy,[9] good mounsieur.
MUSTARDSEED: What's your will?
20 BOTTOM: Nothing, good mounsieur, but to help Cavalery Cobweb[1] to scratch. I
must to the barber's, mounsieur; for methinks I am marvailes hairy about
the face; and I am such a tender ass, if my hair do but tickle me, I must
scratch.
TITANIA: What, wilt thou hear some music, my sweet love?
BOTTOM: I have a reasonable good ear in music. Let's have the tongs and the
bones.[2]

[*Music: tongs, rural music.*][3]

25 TITANIA: Or say, sweet love, what thou desirest to eat.
BOTTOM: Truly, a peck of provender. I could munch your good dry oats. Methinks
I have a great desire to a bottle of hay. Good hay, sweet hay, hath no fellow.[4]
TITANIA: I have a venturous fairy that shall seek
30 The squirrel's hoard, and fetch thee new nuts.
BOTTOM: I had rather have a handful or two of dried peas. But, I pray you, let
none of your people stir me. I have an exposition[5] of sleep come upon me.
TITANIA: Sleep thou, and I will wind thee in my arms.
Fairies, be gone, and be all ways[6] away.   [*Exeunt* FAIRIES.]
35 So doth the woodbine the sweet honeysuckle
Gently entwist; the female ivy so
Enrings the barky fingers of the elm.
Oh, how I love thee! How I dote on thee!   [*They sleep.*]

[*Enter Robin Goodfellow (*PUCK*).*]

---

8. Fist.   9. That is, put on your hat.
1. [Seemingly an error since Cobweb has been sent to bring honey while Peaseblossom has been asked to
scratch. *Cavalery*: form of address for a gentleman.]
2. Instruments for rustic music. (The tongs were played like a triangle, whereas the bones were held
between the fingers and used as clappers.)   3. [This stage direction is added from the Folio.]
4. Equal. *Bottle*: bundle.   5. [Bottom's word for *disposition*.]   6. In all directions.

OBERON: [*Advancing.*] Welcome, good Robin. See'st thou this sweet sight?
Her dotage now I do begin to pity. 40
For, meeting her of late behind the wood,
Seeking sweet favors⁷ for this hateful fool,
I did upbraid her and fall out with her.
For she his hairy temples then had rounded
With coronet of fresh and fragrant flowers; 45
And that same dew, which sometime⁸ on the buds
Was wont to swell like round and orient pearls,⁹
Stood now within the pretty flouriets'¹ eyes
Like tears that did their own disgrace bewail.
When I had at my pleasure taunted her, 50
And she in mild terms begg'd my patience,
I then did ask of her her changeling child;
Which straight she gave me, and her fairy sent
To bear him to my bower in fairy land.
And, now I have the boy, I will undo 55
This hateful imperfection of her eyes.
And, gentle Puck, take this transformed scalp
From off the head of this Athenian swain,
That he, awaking when the other² do,
May all to Athens back again repair, 60
And think no more of this night's accidents
But as the fierce vexation of a dream.
But first I will release the Fairy Queen. [*Squeezes juice in her eyes.*]
　Be as thou wast wont to be;
　See as thou wast wont to see. 65
　Dian's bud³ o'er Cupid's flower
　Hath such force and blessed power.
Now, my Titania, wake you, my sweet queen.
TITANIA: [*Waking.*] My Oberon! What visions have I seen!
Methought I was enamor'd of an ass. 70
OBERON: There lies your love.
TITANIA:　　　　　　　　　How came these things to pass?
O, how mine eyes do loathe his visage now!
OBERON: Silence awhile. Robin, take off this head.
Titania, music call, and strike more dead
Than common sleep of all these five⁴ the sense. 75
TITANIA: Music, ho! Music, such as charmeth sleep!

　[*Music.*]

7. That is, gifts of flowers.　8. Formerly.
9. That is, the most beautiful of all pearls, those coming from the Orient.
1. Flowerets'.　2. Others.
3. [Perhaps the flower of the *agnus castus*, or chaste-tree, supposed to preserve chastity; or perhaps referring simply to the herb by which Oberon can undo the effects of "Cupid's flower," the love-in-idleness of
2.1.166 f.]　4. That is, the four lovers and Bottom.

PUCK: [*Removing the ass's head.*] Now, when thou wak'st, with thine own fool's eyes
    peep.
OBERON: Sound, music! Come, my queen, take hands with me,
80   And rock the ground whereon these sleepers be.

      [*Dance.*]

    Now thou and I are new in amity,
    And will tomorrow midnight solemnly[5]
    Dance in Duke Theseus' house triumphantly
    And bless it to all fair prosperity.
85   There shall the pairs of faithful lovers be
    Wedded, with Theseus, all in jollity.
PUCK: Fairy King, attend, and mark:
    I do hear the morning lark.
OBERON: Then, my queen, in silence sad,[6]
90   Trip we after night's shade.
    We the globe can compass soon,
    Swifter than the wand'ring moon.
TITANIA: Come, my lord, and in our flight
    Tell me how it came this night
95   That I sleeping here was found
    With these mortals on the ground.   [*Exeunt.*]

    [*Wind horn within. Enter* THESEUS *and all his train;* HIPPOLYTA, EGEUS.]

THESEUS: Go, one of you, find out the forester,
    For now our observation[7] is perform'd;
    And since we have the vaward[8] of the day,
100   My love shall hear the music of my hounds.
    Uncouple in the western valley; let them go.
    Dispatch, I say, and find the forester.   [*Exit an Attendant.*]
    We will, fair queen, up to the mountain's top
    And mark the musical confusion
105   Of hounds and echo in conjunction.
HIPPOLYTA: I was with Hercules and Cadmus[9] once,
    When in a wood of Crete they bay'd[1] the bear
    With hounds of Sparta.[2] Never did I hear
    Such gallant chiding; for, besides the groves,
110   The skies, the fountains, every region near
    Seem'd all one mutual cry. I never heard
    So musical a discord, such sweet thunder.
THESEUS: My hounds are bred out of the Spartan kind,
    So flew'd, so sanded;[3] and their heads are hung
115   With ears that sweep away the morning dew;

---

5. Ceremoniously.   6. Sober.   7. That is, observance to a morn of May (1.1.167).
8. Vanguard, that is, earliest part.
9. Mythical founder of Thebes. (This story about him is unknown.)
1. Brought to bay.   2. [A breed famous in antiquity for its hunting skill.]
3. Of sandy color. *So flew'd*: similarly having large hanging chaps or fleshy covering of the jaw.

Crook-knee'd, and dewlapp'd[4] like Thessalian bulls;
Slow in pursuit, but match'd in mouth like bells,
Each under each. A cry more tuneable[5]
Was never holla'd to, nor cheer'd with horn,
In Crete, in Sparta, nor in Thessaly.   120
Judge when you hear. [*Sees the sleepers.*] But, soft! What nymphs are these?
EGEUS: My lord, this' my daughter here asleep;
    And this, Lysander; this Demetrius is;
    This Helena, old Nedar's Helena.
    I wonder of their being here together.   125
THESEUS: No doubt they rose up early to observe
    The rite of May, and, hearing our intent,
    Came here in grace of our solemnity.[6]
    But speak, Egeus. Is not this the day
    That Hermia should give answer of her choice?   130
EGEUS: It is, my lord.
THESEUS: Go, bid the huntsmen wake them with their horns.
                                                    [*Exit an Attendant.*]

    [*Shout within. Wind horns. They all start up.*]

Good morrow, friends. Saint Valentine[7] is past.
Begin these wood-birds but to couple now?
LYSANDER: Pardon, my lord   [*They kneel.*]
THESEUS: I pray you all, stand up.   135
    I know you two are rival enemies;
    How comes this gentle concord in the world,
    That hatred is so far from jealousy
    To sleep by hate and fear no enmity?
LYSANDER: My lord, I shall reply amazedly,   140
    Half sleep, half waking; but as yet, I swear,
    I cannot truly say how I came here.
    But, as I think—for truly would I speak,
    And now I do bethink me, so it is—
    I came with Hermia hither. Our intent   145
    Was to be gone from Athens, where[8] we might,
    Without[9] the peril of the Athenian law—
EGEUS: Enough, enough, my lord; you have enough.
    I beg the law, the law, upon his head.
    They would have stol'n away; they would, Demetrius,   150
    Thereby to have defeated you and me,
    You of your wife and me of my consent,
    Of my consent that she should be your wife.

---

4. Having pendulous folds of skin under the neck.
5. Well tuned, melodious. *Match'd . . . each*: that is, harmoniously matched in their various cries like a set of
bells, from treble down to bass. *Cry*: pack of hounds.   6. That is, observance of these same rites of May.
7. [Birds were supposed to choose their mates on St. Valentine's Day.]   8. Wherever, or to where.
9. Outside of, beyond.

DEMETRIUS: My lord, fair Helen told me of their stealth,
155   Of this their purpose hither to this wood,
And I in fury hither followed them,
Fair Helena in fancy following me.
But, my good lord, I wot not by what power—
But by some power it is—my love to Hermia,
160   Melted as the snow, seems to me now
As the remembrance of an idle gaud[1]
Which in my childhood I did dote upon;
And all the faith, the virtue of my heart,
The object and the pleasure of mine eye,
165   Is only Helena. To her, my lord,
Was I betroth'd ere I saw Hermia,
But like a sickness did I loathe this food;
But, as in health, come to my natural taste,
Now I do wish it, love it, long for it,
170   And will for evermore be true to it.
THESEUS: Fair lovers, you are fortunately met.
Of this discourse we more will hear anon.
Egeus, I will overbear your will;
For in the temple, by and by, with us
175   These couples shall eternally be knit.
And, for the morning now is something[2] worn,
Our purpos'd hunting shall be set aside.
Away with us to Athens. Three and three,
We'll hold a feast in great solemnity.
180   Come, Hippolyta.   [*Exeunt* THESEUS, HIPPOLYTA, EGEUS, *and train.*]
DEMETRIUS: These things seem small and undistinguishable,
Like far-off mountains turned into clouds.
HERMIA: Methinks I see these things with parted[3] eye,
When every thing seems double.
HELENA: So methinks;
185   And I have found Demetrius like a jewel,
Mine own, and not mine own.[4]
DEMETRIUS: Are you sure
That we are awake? It seems to me
That yet we sleep, we dream. Do not you think
The Duke was here, and bid us follow him?
HERMIA: Yea, and my father.
190 HELENA: And Hippolyta.
LYSANDER: And he did bid us follow to the temple.
DEMETRIUS: Why, then, we are awake. Let's follow him,
And by the way let us recount our dreams.   [*Exeunt.*]
BOTTOM: [*Awaking.*] When my cue comes, call me, and I will answer. My next is,
195   "Most fair Pyramus." Heigh-ho! Peter Quince! Flute, the bellows-mender!

1. Worthless trinket.   2. Somewhat. *For*: since.   3. Improperly focused.
4. That is, like a jewel that one finds by chance and, therefore, possesses but cannot certainly consider one's own property.

Snout, the tinker! Starveling! God's my life, stol'n hence, and left me asleep! I
have had a most rare vision. I have had a dream, past the wit of man to say
what dream it was. Man is but an ass, if he go about[5] to expound this dream.
Methought I was—there is no man can tell what. Methought I was—and methought I had—but man is but a patch'd fool, if he will offer[6] to say what me-   200
thought I had. The eye of man hath not heard, the ear of man hath not seen,
man's hand is not able to taste, his tongue to conceive, nor his heart to report,
what my dream was. I will get Peter Quince to write a ballad of this dream. It
shall be called "Bottom's Dream," because it hath no bottom; and I will sing it   205
in the latter end of a play, before the Duke. Peradventure, to make it the more
gracious, I shall sing it at her[7] death.   [*Exit.*]

Scene 2[8]

Enter QUINCE, FLUTE, SNOUT, *and* STARVELING.

QUINCE: Have you sent to Bottom's house? Is he come home yet?
STARVELING: He cannot be heard of. Out of doubt he is transported.[9]
FLUTE: If he come not, then the play is marr'd. It goes not forward, doth it?
QUINCE: It is not possible. You have not a man in all Athens able to discharge[1]
   Pyramus but he.   5
FLUTE: No, he hath simply the best wit of any handicraft man in Athens.
QUINCE: Yea, and the best person too; and he is a very paramour for a sweet
   voice.
FLUTE: You must say "paragon." A paramour is, God bless us, a thing of naught.

   [*Enter* SNUG *the Joiner.*]

SNUG: Masters, the Duke is coming from the temple, and there is two or three   10
   lords and ladies more married. If our sport had gone forward, we had all been
   made men.
FLUTE: O sweet bully Bottom! Thus hath he lost sixpence a day[2] during his life;
   he could not have scap'd sixpence a day. An the Duke had not given him sixpence a day for playing Pyramus, I'll be hang'd. He would have deserv'd it.   15
   Sixpence a day in Pyramus, or nothing.

   [*Enter* BOTTOM.]

BOTTOM: Where are these lads? Where are these hearts?[3]
QUINCE: Bottom! O most courageous day! O most happy hour!
BOTTOM: Masters, I am to discourse wonders.[4] But ask me not what; for if I tell
   you, I am no true Athenian. I will tell you everything, right as it fell out.   20
QUINCE: Let us hear, sweet Bottom.
BOTTOM: Not a word of[5] me. All that I will tell you is, that the Duke hath din'd.
   Get your apparel together, good strings to your beards, new ribands[6] to your
   pumps; meet presently[7] at the palace; every man look o'er his part; for the

---

5. Attempt.   6. Venture. *Patch'd*: wearing motley, that is, a dress of various colors.
7. Thisby's (?).   8. Location: Athens. Quince's house (?).   9. Carried off by fairies or, possibly, transformed.   1. Perform.   2. That is, as a royal pension.   3. Good fellows.   4. Have wonders to relate.
5. Out of.   6. Ribbons. *Strings*: that is, to attach the beards.   7. Immediately.

25   short and the long is, our play is preferr'd.[8] In any case, let Thisby have clean
    linen; and let not him that plays the lion pare his nails, for they shall hang
    out for the lion's claws. And, most dear actors, eat no onions nor garlic, for we
    are to utter sweet breath; and I do not doubt but to hear them say, it is a sweet
    comedy. No more words. Away! Go away!   [*Exeunt.*]

ACT V

Scene 1[9]

Enter THESEUS, HIPPOLYTA, *and* PHILOSTRATE, *Lords, and Attendants.*

HIPPOLYTA: 'Tis strange, my Theseus, that[1] these lovers speak of.
THESEUS: More strange than true. I never may[2] believe
    These antic fables, nor these fairy toys.[3]
    Lovers and madmen have such seething brains,
5   Such shaping fantasies,[4] that apprehend
    More than cool reason ever comprehends.
    The lunatic, the lover, and the poet
    Are of imagination all compact.[5]
    One sees more devils than vast hell can hold;
10   That is the madman. The lover, all as frantic,
    Sees Helen's beauty in a brow of Egypt.[6]
    The poet's eye, in a fine frenzy rolling,
    Doth glance from heaven to earth, from earth to heaven;
    And as imagination bodies forth
15   The forms of things unknown, the poet's pen
    Turns them to shapes and gives to airy nothing
    A local habitation and a name.
    Such tricks hath strong imagination
    That, if it would but apprehend some joy,
20   It comprehends some bringer[7] of that joy;
    Or in the night, imagining some fear,[8]
    How easy is a bush suppos'd a bear!
HIPPOLYTA: But all the story of the night told over,
    And all their minds transfigur'd so together,
25   More witnesseth than fancy's images[9]
    And grows to something of great constancy;[1]
    But, howsoever, strange and admirable.[2]

    [*Enter lovers:* LYSANDER, DEMETRIUS, HERMIA, *and* HELENA.]

---

8. Selected for consideration.   9. Location: Athens. The palace of Theseus.   1. That which.
2. Can.
3. Trifling stories about fairies. *Antic*: strange, grotesque (with additional punning sense of *antique*,
ancient).   4. Imaginations.   5. Formed, composed.
6. That is, face of a gypsy. *Helen's*: that is, of Helen of Troy, pattern of beauty.
7. That is, source.   8. Object of fear.
9. Testifies to something more substantial than mere imaginings.   1. Certainty.
2. Source of wonder. *Howsoever*: in any case.

THESEUS: Here come the lovers, full of joy and mirth.
 Joy, gentle friends! Joy and fresh days of love
 Accompany your hearts!
LYSANDER: More than to us   30
 Wait in your royal walks, your board, your bed!
THESEUS: Come now, what masques, what dances shall we have,
 To wear away this long age of three hours
 Between our after-supper and bed-time?
 Where is our usual manager of mirth?   35
 What revels are in hand? Is there no play,
 To ease the anguish of a torturing hour?
 Call Philostrate.
PHILOSTRATE: Here, mighty Theseus.
THESEUS: Say, what abridgement[3] have you for this evening?
 What masque? What music? How shall we beguile   40
 The lazy time, if not with some delight?
PHILOSTRATE: There is a brief[4] how many sports are ripe.
 Make choice of which your Highness will see first.   [*Giving a paper.*]
THESEUS: [*Reads.*] "The battle with the Centaurs,[5] to be sung
 By an Athenian eunuch to the harp."   45
 We'll none of that. That have I told my love,
 In glory of my kinsman[6] Hercules.
 [*Reads.*] "The riot of the tipsy Bacchanals,
 Tearing the Thracian singer in their rage."[7]
 That is an old device; and it was play'd   50
 When I from Thebes came last a conqueror.
 [*Reads.*] "The thrice three Muses mourning for the death
 Of Learning, late deceas'd in beggary."[8]
 That is some satire, keen and critical,
 Not sorting with[9] a nuptial ceremony.   55
 [*Reads.*] "A tedious brief scene of young Pyramus
 And his love Thisby; very tragical mirth."
 Merry and tragical? Tedious and brief?
 That is, hot ice and wondrous strange[1] snow.
 How shall we find the concord of this discord?   60
PHILOSTRATE: A play there is, my lord, some ten words long,
 Which is as brief as I have known a play;
 But by ten words, my lord, it is too long,
 Which makes it tedious. For in all the play

3. Pastime (to abridge or shorten the evening). 4. Short written statement, list.
5. [Probably refers to the battle of the Centaurs and the Lapithae, when the Centaurs attempted to carry off Hippodamia, bride of Theseus's friend Pirothous.]
6. [Plutarch's *Life of Theseus* states that Hercules and Theseus were near kinsmen. Theseus is referring to a version of the battle of the Centaurs in which Hercules was said to be present.]
7. [This was the story of the death of Orpheus, as told in *Metamorphoses* 11.]
8. [Possibly an allusion to Spenser's *Teares of the Muses* (1591), though "satires" deploring the neglect of learning and the creative arts were commonplace.] 9. Befitting.
1. [Seemingly an error for some adjective that would contrast with *snow*, just as *hot* contrasts with *ice*.]

65   There is not one word apt, one player fitted.
        And tragical, my noble lord, it is,
        For Pyramus therein doth kill himself.
        Which, when I saw rehears'd, I must confess,
        Made mine eyes water; but more merry tears
70   The passion of loud laughter never shed.
        THESEUS: What are they that do play it?
        PHILOSTRATE: Hard-handed men that work in Athens here,
        Which never labor'd in their minds till now,
        And now have toil'd their unbreathed[2] memories
75   With this same play, against[3] your nuptial.
        THESEUS: And we will hear it.
        PHILOSTRATE: No, my noble lord,
        It is not for you. I have heard it over,
        And it is nothing, nothing in the world;
        Unless you can find sport in their intents,
80   Extremely stretch'd and conn'd[4] with cruel pain,
        To do you service.
        THESEUS: I will hear that play;
        For never anything can be amiss
        When simpleness and duty tender it.
        Go, bring them in; and take your places, ladies.

        [PHILOSTRATE *goes to summon the players.*]

85   HIPPOLYTA: I love not to see wretchedness o'ercharg'd[5]
        And duty in his service[6] perishing.
        THESEUS: Why, gentle sweet, you shall see no such thing.
        HIPPOLYTA: He says they can do nothing in this kind.[7]
        THESEUS: The kinder we, to give them thanks for nothing.
90   Our sport shall be to take what they mistake;
        And what poor duty cannot do, noble respect
        Takes it in might, not merit.[8]
        Where I have come, great clerks[9] have purposed
        To greet me with premeditated welcomes;
95   Where I have seen them shiver and look pale,
        Make periods in the midst of sentences,
        Throttle their practic'd accent[1] in their fears,
        And in conclusion dumbly have broke off,
        Not paying me a welcome. Trust me, sweet,
100   Out of this silence yet I pick'd a welcome;
        And in the modesty of fearful duty
        I read as much as from the rattling tongue
        Of saucy and audacious eloquence.
        Love, therefore, and tongue-tied simplicity

---

2. Unexercised. *Toil'd*: taxed.   3. In preparation for.   4. Memorized. *Stretch'd*: strained.
5. Incompetence overburdened.   6. Its attempt to serve.   7. Kind of thing.
8. Values it for the effort made rather than for the excellence achieved.   9. Learned men.
1. That is, rehearsed speech, or usual way of speaking.

In least speak most, to my capacity.[2]   105

    [PHILOSTRATE *returns.*]

PHILOSTRATE: So please your Grace, the Prologue is address'd.[3]
THESEUS: Let him approach.

    [*Flourish of trumpets. Enter the Prologue* (QUINCE).]

PROLOGUE: If we offend, it is with our good will.
    That you should think, we come not to offend,
    But with good will. To show our simple skill,   110
    That is the true beginning of our end.
    Consider, then, we come but in despite.
    We do not come, as minding[4] to content you,
    Our true intent is. All for your delight
    We are not here. That you should here repent you,   115
    The actors are at hand; and, by their show,
    You shall know all that you are like to know.
THESEUS: This fellow doth not stand upon points.[5]
LYSANDER: He hath rid his prologue like a rough[6] colt; he knows not the stop.[7]
    A good moral, my lord: it is not enough to speak, but to speak true.   120
HIPPOLYTA: Indeed he hath play'd on his prologue like a child on a recorder; a
    sound, but not in government.[8]
THESEUS: His speech was like a tangled chain, nothing[9] impair'd, but all disorder'd.
    Who is next?

    [*Enter* PYRAMUS *and* THISBY, *and* WALL, *and* MOONSHINE, *and* LION.]

PROLOGUE: Gentles, perchance you wonder at this show;   125
    But wonder on, till truth make all things plain.
    This man is Pyramus, if you would know;
    This beauteous lady Thisby is certain.
    This man, with lime and rough-cast, doth present
    Wall, that vile Wall which did these lovers sunder;   130
    And through Wall's chink, poor souls, they are content
    To whisper. At the which let no man wonder.
    This man, with lantern, dog, and bush of thorn,
    Presenteth Moonshine; for, if you will know,
    By moonshine did these lovers think no scorn[1]   135
    To meet at Ninus' tomb, there, there to woo.
    This grisly beast, which Lion hight[2] by name,
    The trusty Thisby, coming first by night,
    Did scare away, or rather did affright;

---

2. In my judgment and understanding. *Least*: that is, saying least.
3. Ready. *Prologue*: speaker of the prologue.   4. Intending.
5. (1) Heed niceties or small points; (2) pay attention to punctuation in his reading. (The humor of Quince's speech is in the blunders of its punctuation.)   6. Unbroken.
7. (1) The stopping of a colt by reining it in; (2) punctuation mark.
8. Control. *Recorder*: a wind instrument like a flute or flageolet.   9. Not at all.
1. Think it no disgraceful matter.   2. Is called.

140   And, as she fled, her mantle she did fall,[3]
       Which Lion vile with bloody mouth did stain.
       Anon comes Pyramus, sweet youth and tall,[4]
       And finds his trusty Thisby's mantle slain;
       Whereat, with blade, with bloody blameful blade,
145   He bravely broach'd[5] his boiling bloody breast.
       And Thisby, tarrying in mulberry shade,
       His dagger drew, and died. For all the rest,
       Let Lion, Moonshine, Wall, and lovers twain
       At large[6] discourse, while here they do remain.

                              [*Exeunt* LION, THISBY, *and* MOONSHINE.]

150   THESEUS: I wonder if the lion be to speak.
       DEMETRIUS: No wonder, my lord. One lion may, when many asses do.
       WALL: In this same interlude it doth befall
           That I, one Snout by name, present a wall;
           And such a wall, as I would have you think,
155   That had in it a crannied hole or chink,
           Through which the lovers, Pyramus and Thisby,
           Did whisper often very secretly.
           This loam, this rough-cast, and this stone doth show
           That I am that same wall; the truth is so.
160   And this the cranny is, right and sinister,[7]
           Through which the fearful lovers are to whisper.
       THESEUS: Would you desire lime and hair to speak better?
       DEMETRIUS: It is the wittiest partition[8] that ever I heard discourse, my lord.

           [PYRAMUS *comes forward.*]

       THESEUS: Pyramus draws near the wall. Silence!
165   PYRAMUS: O grim-look'd[9] night! O night with hue so black!
           O night, which ever art when day is not!
           O night, O night! Alack, alack, alack,
           I fear my Thisby's promise is forgot.
           And thou, O wall, O sweet, O lovely wall,
170   That stand'st between her father's ground and mine,
           Thou wall, O wall, O sweet and lovely wall,
           Show me thy chink, to blink through with mine eyne!

           [WALL *holds up his fingers.*]

           Thanks, courteous Wall. Jove shield thee well for this!
           But what see I? No Thisby do I see.
175   O wicked wall, through whom I see no bliss!
           Curs'd be thy stones for thus deceiving me!
       THESEUS: The wall, methinks, being sensible,[1] should curse again.

---

3. Let fall.   4. Courageous.   5. Stabbed.   6. In full, at length.
7. That is, the right side of it and the left; or running from right to left, horizontally.
8. (1) Wall; (2) section of a learned treatise or oration.   9. Grim-looking.   1. Capable of feeling.

PYRAMUS: No, in truth, sir, he should not. "Deceiving me" is Thisby's cue: she is
to enter now, and I am to spy her through the wall. You shall see, it will fall
pat as I told you. Yonder she comes.   180

    [*Enter* THISBY.]

THISBY: O wall, full often hast thou heard my moans,
    For parting my fair Pyramus and me.
    My cherry lips have often kiss'd thy stones,
    Thy stones with lime and hair knit up in thee.
PYRAMUS: I see a voice. Now will I to the chink,   185
    To spy an[2] I can hear my Thisby's face.
    Thisby!
THISBY: My love! Thou art my love, I think.
PYRAMUS: Think what thou wilt, I am thy lover's grace;[3]
    And, like Limander, am I trusty still.   190
THISBY: And I like Helen,[4] till the Fates me kill.
PYRAMUS: Not Shafalus to Procrus[5] was so true.
THISBY: As Shafalus to Procrus, I to you.
PYRAMUS: O, kiss me through the hole of this vile wall!
THISBY: I kiss the wall's hole, not your lips at all.   195
PYRAMUS: Wilt thou at Ninny's tomb meet me straightway?
THISBY: 'Tide[6] life, 'tide death, I come without delay.

                                        [*Exeunt* PYRAMUS *and* THISBY.]

WALL: Thus have I, Wall, my part discharged so;
    And, being done, thus Wall away doth go.   [*Exit.*]
THESEUS: Now is the mural down between the two neighbors.   200
DEMETRIUS: No remedy, my lord, when walls are so willful to hear without
    warning.[7]
HIPPOLYTA: This is the silliest stuff that ever I heard.
THESEUS: The best in this kind are but shadows;[8] and the worst are no worse, if
    imagination amend them.   205
HIPPOLYTA: It must be your imagination then, and not theirs.
THESEUS: If we imagine no worse of them than they of themselves, they may pass
    for excellent men. Here come two noble beasts in, a man and a lion.

    [*Enter* LION *and* MOONSHINE.]

LION: You, ladies, you, whose gentle hearts do fear
    The smallest monstrous mouse that creeps on floor,   210
    May now perchance both quake and tremble here,
    When lion rough in widest rage doth roar.
    Then know that I, as Snug the joiner, am
    A lion fell,[9] nor else no lion's dam;

---

2. If.   3. That is, gracious lover.   4. [Blunders for "Leander" (*Limander*) and "Hero."]
5. [Blunders for "Cephalus" (*Shafalus*) and "Procris," also famous lovers.]   6. Betide, come.
7. That is, without warning the parents. *To hear*: as to hear.
8. Likenesses, representations. *In this kind*: of this sort.
9. Fierce lion (with a play on the idea of *lion skin*).

215   For, if I should as lion come in strife
      Into this place, 'twere pity on my life.
      THESEUS: A very gentle beast, and of a good conscience.
      DEMETRIUS: The very best at a beast, my lord, that e'er I saw.
      LYSANDER: This lion is a very fox for his valor.[1]
220   THESEUS: True; and a goose for his discretion.[2]
      DEMETRIUS: Not so, my lord; for his valor cannot carry his discretion; and the fox
          carries the goose.
      THESEUS: His discretion, I am sure, cannot carry his valor; for the goose carries
          not the fox. It is well. Leave it to his discretion, and let us listen to the moon.
225   MOON: This lanthorn[3] doth the horned moon present—
      DEMETRIUS: He should have worn the horns on his head.[4]
      THESEUS: He is no crescent, and his horns are invisible within the circumference.
      MOON: This lanthorn doth the horned moon present;
          Myself the man i' th' moon do seem to be.
230   THESEUS: This is the greatest error of all the rest. The man should be put into the
          lanthorn. How is it else the man i' th' moon?
      DEMETRIUS: He dares not come there for the[5] candle; for, you see, it is already in
          snuff.[6]
      HIPPOLYTA: I am aweary of this moon. Would he would change!
235   THESEUS: It appears, by his small light of discretion, that he is in the wane; but
          yet, in courtesy, in all reason, we must stay the time.
      LYSANDER: Proceed, Moon.
      MOON: All that I have to say is to tell you that the lanthorn is the moon, I, the
          man in the moon, this thorn-bush my thorn-bush, and this dog my dog.
240   DEMETRIUS: Why, all these should be in the lanthorn; for all these are in the
          moon. But silence! Here comes Thisby.

          [Enter THISBY.]

      THISBY: This is old Ninny's tomb. Where is my love?
      LION: [Roaring.] Oh—   [THISBY runs off, dropping her mantle.]
      DEMETRIUS: Well roar'd, Lion.
245   THESEUS: Well run, Thisby.
      HIPPOLYTA: Well shone, Moon. Truly, the moon shines with a good grace.

          [The LION shakes THISBY's mantle, and exits.]

      THESEUS: Well mous'd,[7] Lion.
      DEMETRIUS: And then came Pyramus.

          [Enter PYRAMUS.]

      LYSANDER: And so the lion vanish'd.
250   PYRAMUS: Sweet Moon, I thank thee for thy sunny beams;

---

1. That is, his valor consists of craftiness and discretion.
2. That is, as discreet as a goose, meaning more foolish than discreet.
3. [This original spelling, *lanthorn*, may suggest a play on the *horn* of which lanterns were made, and also on a cuckold's horns; but the spelling *lanthorn* is not used consistently for comic effect in this play or elsewhere. At 5.1.133, for example, the word is *lantern* in the original.]   4. [As a sign of cuckoldry.]
5. Because of the.   6. (1) Offended; (2) in need of snuffing.   7. Shaken.

I thank thee, Moon, for shining now so bright;
  For, by thy gracious, golden, glittering gleams,
  I trust to take of truest Thisby sight.

    But stay, O spite!
    But mark, poor knight,   255
  What dreadful dole[8] is here!
    Eyes, do you see?
    How can it be?
  O dainty duck! O dear!
    Thy mantle good,   260
    What, stain'd with blood!
  Approach, ye Furies fell![9]
    O Fates, come, come,
    Cut thread and thrum;[1]
  Quail, crush, conclude, and quell![2]   265

THESEUS: This passion, and the death of a dear friend, would go near to make a
  man look sad.[3]
HIPPOLYTA: Beshrew my heart, but I pity the man.
PYRAMUS: O wherefore, Nature, didst thou lions frame?
  Since lion vile hath here deflow'r'd my dear,   270
  Which is—no, no—which was the fairest dame
  That liv'd, that lov'd, that lik'd, that look'd with cheer.[4]

    Come, tears, confound,
    Out, sword, and wound
    The pap of Pyramus;   275
    Ay, that left pap,
    Where heart doth hop.   *[Stabs himself.]*
    Thus die I, thus, thus, thus.
    Now am I dead,
    Now am I fled;   280
    My soul is in the sky.
    Tongue, lose thy light;
    Moon, take thy flight.   *[Exit* MOONSHINE.*]*
    Now die, die, die, die, die.   *[Dies.]*

DEMETRIUS: No die, but an ace,[5] for him; for he is but one.[6]   285
LYSANDER: Less than an ace, man; for he is dead, he is nothing.
THESEUS: With the help of a surgeon he might yet recover, and yet prove an ass.[7]
HIPPOLYTA: How chance Moonshine is gone before Thisby comes back and finds
  her lover?

8. Grievous event.   9. Fierce.   1. The warp in weaving and the loose end of the warp.
2. Kill, destroy. *Quail*: overpower.
3. That is, if one had other reason to grieve, one might be sad, but not from this absurd portrayal of
passion.   4. Countenance.
5. The side of the die featuring the single pip, or spot. (The pun is on *die* as a singular of *dice*; Bottom's
performance is not worth a whole *die* but rather one single face of it, one small portion.)
6. (1) An individual person; (2) unique.   7. [With a pun on *ace.*]

290   THESEUS: She will find him by starlight. Here she comes; and her passion ends the
play.

[*Enter* THISBY.]

HIPPOLYTA: Methinks she should not use a long one for such a Pyramus. I hope
she will be brief.

DEMETRIUS: A mote will turn the balance, which Pyramus, which[8] Thisby, is the
295   better: he for a man, God warr'nt us; she for a woman, God bless us.

LYSANDER: She hath spied him already with those sweet eyes.

DEMETRIUS: And thus she means, videlicet:[9]

THISBY: Asleep, my love?
What, dead, my dove?
300   O Pyramus, arise!
Speak, speak. Quite dumb?
Dead, dead? A tomb
Must cover thy sweet eyes.
These lily lips,
305   This cherry nose,
These yellow cowslip cheeks,
Are gone, are gone!
Lovers, make moan.
His eyes were green as leeks.
310   O Sisters Three,[1]
Come, come to me,
With hands as pale as milk;
Lay them in gore,
Since you have shore[2]
315   With shears his thread of silk.
Tongue, not a word.
Come, trusty sword,
Come, blade, my breast imbrue![3]   [*Stabs herself.*]
And farewell, friends.
320   Thus Thisby ends.
Adieu, adieu, adieu.   [*Dies.*]

THESEUS: Moonshine and Lion are left to bury the dead.

DEMETRIUS: Ay, and Wall too.

BOTTOM: [*Starting up.*] No, I assure you; the wall is down that parted their fathers.
325   Will it please you to see the epilogue, or to hear a Bergomask dance[4] between
two of our company?

THESEUS: No epilogue, I pray you; for your play needs no excuse. Never excuse; for
when the players are all dead, there need none to be blam'd. Marry, if he that
writ it had play'd Pyramus and hang'd himself in Thisby's garter, it would
330   have been a fine tragedy; and so it is, truly, and very notably discharg'd. But,
come, your Bergomask. Let your epilogue alone.

[*A dance.*]

8. Whether . . . or.   9. [Namely (Latin). *Means*: moans, laments.]   1. The Fates.   2. Shorn.
3. Stain with blood.   4. A rustic dance named from Bergamo, a province in the state of Venice.

The iron tongue of midnight hath told[5] twelve.
Lovers, to bed; 'tis almost fairy time.
I fear we shall outsleep the coming morn
As much as we this night have overwatch'd.[6]   335
This palpable-gross[7] play hath well beguil'd
The heavy[8] gait of night. Sweet friends, to bed.
A fortnight hold we this solemnity,
In nightly revels and new jollity.   *[Exeunt.]*

    [Enter PUCK, *carrying a broom.]*

PUCK: Now the hungry lion roars,   340
    And the wolf behowls the moon;
Whilst the heavy ploughman snores,
    All with weary task fordone.[9]
Now the wasted brands[1] do glow,
    Whilst the screech-owl, screeching loud,   345
Puts the wretch that lies in woe
    In remembrance of a shroud.
Now it is the time of night
    That the graves, all gaping wide,
Every one lets forth his sprite,[2]   350
    In the churchway paths to glide.
And we fairies, that do run
    By the triple Hecate's[3] team
From the presence of the sun,
    Following darkness like a dream,   355
Now are frolic.[4] Not a mouse
Shall disturb this hallowed house.
I am sent with broom before,
To sweep the dust behind[5] the door.

    [Enter OBERON *and* TITANIA, *King and Queen of Fairies, with all their train.]*

OBERON: Through the house give glimmering light,   360
    By the dead and drowsy fire;
Every elf and fairy sprite
    Hop as light as bird from brier;
And this ditty, after me,
Sing, and dance it trippingly.   365
TITANIA: First, rehearse your song by rote,
    To each word a warbling note.
Hand in hand, with fairy grace,
Will we sing, and bless this place.

---

5. Counted, struck ("tolled").   6. Stayed up too late.   7. Palpably gross, obviously crude.
8. Drowsy, dull.   9. Exhausted.   1. Burned-out logs.   2. Every grave lets forth its ghost.
3. [Hecate ruled as Luna or Cynthia in Heaven, as Diana on Earth, and as Proserpina in Hell.]
4. Merry.
5. From behind. (Robin Goodfellow was a household spirit who helped good housemaids and punished lazy ones.)

[*Song and dance.*]

370 OBERON: Now, until the break of day,
Through this house each fairy stray.
To the best bride-bed will we,
Which by us shall blessed be;
And the issue there create[6]
375 Ever shall be fortunate.
So shall all the couples three
Ever true in loving be;
And the blots of Nature's hand
Shall not in their issue stand;
380 Never mole, hare lip, nor scar,
Nor mark prodigious,[7] such as are
Despised in nativity,
Shall upon their children be.
With this field-dew consecrate,[8]
385 Every fairy take his gait,[9]
And each several[1] chamber bless,
Through this palace, with sweet peace;
And the owner of it blest
Ever shall in safety rest.
390 Trip away; make no stay;
Meet me all by break of day.   [*Exeunt* OBERON, TITANIA, *and train.*]
PUCK: If we shadows have offended,
Think but this, and all is mended,
That you have but slumb'red here[2]
395 While these visions did appear.
And this weak and idle theme,
No more yielding but[3] a dream,
Gentles, do not reprehend.
If you pardon, we will mend.
400 And, as I am an honest Puck,
If we have unearned luck
Now to scape the serpent's tongue,[4]
We will make amends ere long;
Else the Puck a liar call.
405 So, good night unto you all.
Give me your hands,[5] if we be friends,
And Robin shall restore amends.   [*Exit.*]

ca. 1594–95

6. Created. 7. Monstrous, unnatural. 8. Consecrated. 9. Go his way. 1. Separate.
2. That is, that it is a "midsummer night's dream." 3. Yielding no more than. 4. That is, hissing.
5. Applaud.

Hamlet

CHARACTERS

CLAUDIUS, *King of Denmark*
HAMLET, *son of the former king and*
   nephew to the present king
POLONIUS, *Lord Chamberlain*
HORATIO, *friend of Hamlet*
LAERTES, *son of Polonius*
VOLTEMAND
CORNELIUS
ROSENCRANTZ
GUILDENSTERN } *courtiers*
OSRIC
A GENTLEMAN
A PRIEST

MARCELLUS
BERNARDO } *officers*
FRANCISCO, *a soldier*
REYNALDO, *servant to Polonius*
PLAYERS
TWO CLOWNS, *gravediggers*
FORTINBRAS, *Prince of Norway*
A NORWEGIAN CAPTAIN
ENGLISH AMBASSADORS
GERTRUDE, *Queen of Denmark, and*
   mother of Hamlet
OPHELIA, *daughter of Polonius*
GHOST OF HAMLET'S FATHER

LORDS, LADIES, OFFICERS, SOLDIERS, SAILORS, MESSENGERS, AND ATTENDANTS

SCENE: *The action takes place in or near the royal castle of Denmark at Elsinore.*

ACT I

Scene 1

A guard station atop the castle. Enter BERNARDO *and* FRANCISCO, *two sentinels.*

BERNARDO: Who's there?
FRANCISCO: Nay, answer me. Stand and unfold yourself.
BERNARDO: Long live the king!
FRANCISCO: Bernardo?
BERNARDO: He.
FRANCISCO: You come most carefully upon your hour.   5
BERNARDO: 'Tis now struck twelve. Get thee to bed, Francisco.
FRANCISCO: For this relief much thanks. 'Tis bitter cold,
   And I am sick at heart.
BERNARDO: Have you had quiet guard?
FRANCISCO: Not a mouse stirring.   10
BERNARDO: Well, good night.
   If you do meet Horatio and Marcellus,
   The rivals[5] of my watch, bid them make haste.

     [*Enter* HORATIO *and* MARCELLUS.]

FRANCISCO: I think I hear them. Stand, ho! Who is there?
HORATIO: Friends to this ground.
MARCELLUS: And liegemen to the Dane.[6]   15

---

1. Companions.
2. The "Dane" is the king of Denmark, who is also called "Denmark," as in line 48 of this scene. In line 61 a similar reference is used for the king of Norway.

FRANCISCO: Give you good night.

MARCELLUS: O, farewell, honest soldier!
 Who hath relieved you?

FRANCISCO: Bernardo hath my place.
 Give you good night.   [*Exit* FRANCISCO.]

MARCELLUS: Holla, Bernardo!

BERNARDO: Say—
 What, is Horatio there?

HORATIO: A piece of him.

20 BERNARDO: Welcome, Horatio. Welcome, good Marcellus.

HORATIO: What, has this thing appeared again tonight?

BERNARDO: I have seen nothing.

MARCELLUS: Horatio says 'tis but our fantasy,
 And will not let belief take hold of him

25 Touching this dreaded sight twice seen of us.
 Therefore I have entreated him along
 With us to watch the minutes of this night,
 That if again this apparition come,
 He may approve[7] our eyes and speak to it.

HORATIO: Tush, tush, 'twill not appear.

30 BERNARDO: Sit down awhile,
 And let us once again assail your ears,
 That are so fortified against our story,
 What we have two nights seen.

HORATIO: Well, sit we down.
 And let us hear Bernardo speak of this.

35 BERNARDO: Last night of all,
 When yond same star that's westward from the pole[8]
 Had made his course t' illume that part of heaven
 Where now it burns, Marcellus and myself,
 The bell then beating one—

  [*Enter* GHOST.]

40 MARCELLUS: Peace, break thee off. Look where it comes again.

BERNARDO: In the same figure like the king that's dead.

MARCELLUS: Thou art a scholar; speak to it, Horatio.

BERNARDO: Looks 'a[9] not like the king? Mark it, Horatio.

HORATIO: Most like. It harrows me with fear and wonder.

BERNARDO: It would be spoke to.

45 MARCELLUS: Speak to it, Horatio.

HORATIO: What art thou that usurp'st this time of night
 Together with that fair and warlike form
 In which the majesty of buried Denmark
 Did sometimes march? By heaven I charge thee, speak.

MARCELLUS: It is offended.

50 BERNARDO: See, it stalks away.

HORATIO: Stay. Speak, speak. I charge thee, speak.   [*Exit* GHOST.]

3. Confirm the testimony of. 4. Polestar. 5. He.

MARCELLUS: 'Tis gone and will not answer.
BERNARDO: How now, Horatio! You tremble and look pale.
    Is not this something more than fantasy?
    What think you on't?   55
HORATIO: Before my God, I might not this believe
    Without the sensible[6] and true avouch
    Of mine own eyes.
MARCELLUS: It is not like the king?
HORATIO: As thou art to thyself.
    Such was the very armor he had on   60
    When he the ambitious Norway combated.
    So frowned he once when, in an angry parle,[7]
    He smote the sledded Polacks on the ice.
    'Tis strange.
MARCELLUS: Thus twice before, and jump[8] at this dead hour,   65
    With martial stalk hath he gone by our watch.
HORATIO: In what particular thought to work I know not,
    But in the gross and scope of mine opinion,
    This bodes some strange eruption to our state.
MARCELLUS: Good now, sit down, and tell me he that knows,   70
    Why this same strict and most observant watch
    So nightly toils the subject[9] of the land,
    And why such daily cast of brazen cannon
    And foreign mart for implements of war;
    Why such impress of shipwrights, whose sore task   75
    Does not divide the Sunday from the week.
    What might be toward that this sweaty haste
    Doth make the night joint-laborer with the day?
    Who is't that can inform me?
HORATIO: That can I.
    At least, the whisper goes so. Our last king,   80
    Whose image even but now appeared to us,
    Was as you know by Fortinbras of Norway,
    Thereto pricked on by a most emulate pride,
    Dared to the combat; in which our valiant Hamlet
    (For so this side of our known world esteemed him)   85
    Did slay this Fortinbras; who by a sealed compact
    Well ratified by law and heraldry,
    Did forfeit, with his life, all those his lands
    Which he stood seized of,[1] to the conqueror;
    Against the which a moiety competent[2]   90
    Was gagèd[3] by our king; which had returned
    To the inheritance of Fortinbras,
    Had he been vanquisher; as, by the same covenant
    And carriage of the article designed,
    His fell to Hamlet. Now, sir, young Fortinbras,   95

6. Perceptible.   7. Parley.   8. Precisely.   9. People.   1. Possessed.   2. Portion of similar value.
3. Pledged.

Of unimprovèd mettle hot and full,
Hath in the skirts of Norway here and there
Sharked up a list of lawless resolutes
For food and diet to some enterprise
100 That hath a stomach in't; which is no other,
As it doth well appear unto our state,
But to recover of us by strong hand
And terms compulsatory, those foresaid lands
So by his father lost; and this, I take it,
105 Is the main motive of our preparations,
The source of this our watch, and the chief head
Of this post-haste and romage[4] in the land.
BERNARDO: I think it be no other but e'en so.
Well may it sort[5] that this portentous figure
110 Comes armèd through our watch so like the king
That was and is the question of these wars.
HORATIO: A mote[6] it is to trouble the mind's eye.
In the most high and palmy state of Rome,
A little ere the mightiest Julius fell,
115 The graves stood tenantless, and the sheeted dead
Did squeak and gibber in the Roman streets;
As stars with trains of fire, and dews of blood,
Disasters in the sun; and the moist star,
Upon whose influence Neptune's empire stands,[7]
120 Was sick almost to doomsday with eclipse.
And even the like precurse[8] of feared events,
As harbingers preceding still the fates
And prologue to the omen coming on,
Have heaven and earth together demonstrated
125 Unto our climatures[9] and countrymen.

[*Enter* GHOST.]

But soft, behold, lo where it comes again!
I'll cross it[1] though it blast me.—Stay, illusion.

[*It spreads (its) arms.*]

If thou hast any sound or use of voice,
Speak to me.
130 If there be any good thing to be done,
That may to thee do ease, and grace to me,
Speak to me.
If thou art privy to thy country's fate,
Which happily foreknowing may avoid,

4. Stir.   5. Chance.   6. Speck of dust.
7. Neptune was the Roman sea god; the "moist star" is the moon.   8. Precursor.   9. Regions.
1. Horatio means either that he will move across the ghost's path in order to stop him or that he will
make the sign of the cross to gain power over him. The stage direction that follows is somewhat ambiguous. "It" seems to refer to the ghost, but the movement would be appropriate to Horatio.

O, speak! 135
Or if thou hast uphoarded in thy life[1]
Extorted treasure in the womb of earth,
For which, they say, you spirits oft walk in death,

    [*The cock crows.*]

    Speak of it. Stay, and speak. Stop it, Marcellus.
MARCELLUS: Shall I strike at it with my partisan?[2] 140
HORATIO: Do, if it will not stand.
BERNARDO: 'Tis here.
HORATIO: 'Tis here.
MARCELLUS: 'Tis gone.   [*Exit* GHOST.]
    We do it wrong, being so majestical,
To offer it the show of violence;
For it is as the air, invulnerable, 145
And our vain blows malicious mockery.
BERNARDO: It was about to speak when the cock crew.
HORATIO: And then it started like a guilty thing
Upon a fearful summons. I have heard
The cock, that is the trumpet to the morn, 150
Doth with his lofty and shrill-sounding throat
Awake the god of day, and at his warning,
Whether in sea or fire, in earth or air,
Th' extravagant and erring[3] spirit hies
To his confine; and of the truth herein 155
This present object made probation.[4]
MARCELLUS: It faded on the crowing of the cock.
Some say that ever 'gainst that season comes
Wherein our Savior's birth is celebrated,
This bird of dawning singeth all night long, 160
And then, they say, no spirit dare stir abroad,
The nights are wholesome, then no planets strike,
No fairy takes,[5] nor witch hath power to charm,
So hallowed and so gracious is that time.
HORATIO: So have I heard and do in part believe it. 165
But look, the morn in russet mantle clad
Walks o'er the dew of yon high eastward hill.
Break we our watch up, and by my advice
Let us impart what we have seen tonight
Unto young Hamlet, for upon my life 170
This spirit, dumb to us, will speak to him.
Do you consent we shall acquaint him with it,
As needful in our loves, fitting our duty?
MARCELLUS: Let's do't, I pray, and I this morning know
Where we shall find him most conveniently.   [*Exeunt.*] 175

---

2. Halbert.   3. Errant, wandering out of bounds.   4. Proof.   5. Enchants.

Scene 2

A chamber of state. Enter KING CLAUDIUS, QUEEN GERTRUDE, HAMLET, POLONIUS, LAERTES, VOLTEMAND, CORNELIUS *and other members of the court.*

KING: Though yet of Hamlet our dear brother's death
    The memory be green, and that it us befitted
    To bear our hearts in grief, and our whole kingdom
    To be contracted in one brow of woe,
5   Yet so far hath discretion fought with nature
    That we with wisest sorrow think on him,
    Together with remembrance of ourselves.
    Therefore our sometime sister, now our queen,
    Th' imperial jointress[6] to this warlike state,
10   Have we, as 'twere with a defeated joy,
    With an auspicious and a dropping eye,
    With mirth in funeral, and with dirge in marriage,
    In equal scale weighing delight and dole,
    Taken to wife; nor have we herein barred
15   Your better wisdoms, which have freely gone
    With this affair along. For all, our thanks.
    Now follows that you know young Fortinbras,
    Holding a weak supposal of our worth,
    Or thinking by our late dear brother's death
20   Our state to be disjoint and out of frame,
    Colleaguèd with this dream of his advantage,
    He hath not failed to pester us with message
    Importing the surrender of those lands
    Lost by his father, with all bonds of law,
25   To our most valiant brother. So much for him.
    Now for ourself, and for this time of meeting,
    Thus much the business is: we have here writ
    To Norway, uncle of young Fortinbras—
    Who, impotent and bedrid, scarcely hears
30   Of this his nephew's purpose—to suppress
    His further gait[7] herein, in that the levies,
    The lists, and full proportions are all made
    Out of his subject; and we here dispatch
    You, good Cornelius, and you, Voltemand,
35   For bearers of this greeting to old Norway,
    Giving to you no further personal power
    To business with the king, more than the scope
    Of these dilated[8] articles allow.
    Farewell, and let your haste commend your duty.
40 CORNELIUS: ⎫
    VOLTEMAND: ⎭ In that, and all things will we show our duty.

6. A "jointress" is a widow who holds a *jointure* or life interest in the estate of her deceased husband.
7. Progress.   8. Fully expressed.

KING: We doubt it nothing, heartily farewell.

                                                [*Exeunt* VOLTEMAND *and* CORNELIUS.]

    And now, Laertes, what's the news with you?

    You told us of some suit. What is't, Laertes?

    You cannot speak of reason to the Dane

    And lose your voice. What wouldst thou beg, Laertes,   45

    That shall not be my offer, not thy asking?

    The head is not more native to the heart,

    The hand more instrumental[9] to the mouth,

    Than is the throne of Denmark to thy father.

    What wouldst thou have, Laertes?

LAERTES: My dread lord,   50

    Your leave and favor to return to France,

    From whence, though willingly, I came to Denmark

    To show my duty in your coronation,

    Yet now I must confess, that duty done,

    My thoughts and wishes bend again toward France,   55

    And bow them to your gracious leave and pardon.

KING: Have you your father's leave? What says Polonius?

POLONIUS: He hath, my lord, wrung from me my slow leave

    By laborsome petition, and at last

    Upon his will I sealed my hard consent.   60

    I do beseech you give him leave to go.

KING: Take thy fair hour, Laertes. Time be thine,

    And thy best graces spend it at thy will.

    But now, my cousin[1] Hamlet, and my son—

HAMLET: [*Aside.*] A little more than kin, and less than kind.   65

KING: How is it that the clouds still hang on you?

HAMLET: Not so, my lord. I am too much in the sun.

QUEEN: Good Hamlet, cast thy nighted color off,

    And let thine eye look like a friend on Denmark.

    Do not for ever with thy vailèd lids[2]   70

    Seek for thy noble father in the dust.

    Thou know'st 'tis common—all that lives must die,

    Passing through nature to eternity.

HAMLET: Ay, madam, it is common.

QUEEN: If it be,

    Why seems it so particular with thee?   75

HAMLET: Seems, madam? Nay, it is. I know not "seems."

    'Tis not alone my inky cloak, good mother,

    Nor customary suits of solemn black,

    Nor windy suspiration of forced breath,

    No, nor the fruitful river in the eye,   80

    Nor the dejected havior[3] of the visage,

    Together with all forms, moods, shapes of grief,

    That can denote me truly. These indeed seem,

---

9. Serviceable.   1. "Cousin" is used here as a general term of kinship.   2. Lowered eyes.
3. Appearance.

For they are actions that a man might play,
85   But I have that within which passes show—
These but the trappings and the suits of woe.
KING: 'Tis sweet and commendable in your nature, Hamlet,
To give these mourning duties to your father,
But you must know your father lost a father,
90   That father lost, lost his, and the survivor bound
In filial obligation for some term
To do obsequious[4] sorrow. But to persever
In obstinate condolement is a course
Of impious stubbornness. 'Tis unmanly grief.
95   It shows a will most incorrect to[5] heaven,
A heart unfortified, a mind impatient,
An understanding simple and unschooled.
For what we know must be, and is as common
As any the most vulgar thing to sense,
100   Why should we in our peevish opposition
Take it to heart? Fie, 'tis a fault to heaven,
A fault against the dead, a fault to nature,
To reason most absurd, whose common theme
Is death of fathers, and who still hath cried,
105   From the first corse[6] till he that died today,
"This must be so." We pray you throw to earth
This unprevailing woe, and think of us
As of a father, for let the world take note
You are the most immediate[7] to our throne,
110   And with no less nobility of love
Than that which dearest father bears his son
Do I impart toward you. For your intent
In going back to school in Wittenberg,
It is most retrograde[8] to our desire,
115   And we beseech you, bend you to remain
Here in the cheer and comfort of our eye,
Our chiefest courtier, cousin, and our son.
QUEEN: Let not thy mother lose her prayers, Hamlet.
I pray thee stay with us, go not to Wittenberg.
120   HAMLET: I shall in all my best obey you, madam.
KING: Why, 'tis a loving and a fair reply.
Be as ourself in Denmark. Madam, come.
This gentle and unforced accord of Hamlet
Sits smiling to my heart, in grace whereof,
125   No jocund health that Denmark drinks today
But the great cannon to the clouds shall tell,
And the king's rouse the heaven shall bruit[9] again,
Respeaking earthly thunder. Come away.   [*Flourish. Exeunt all but* HAMLET.]
HAMLET: O, that this too too solid flesh would melt,

4. Suited for funeral obsequies.   5. Unsubmissive toward.   6. Corpse.   7. Next in line.
8. Contrary.   9. Echo. *Rouse*: carousal.

Thaw, and resolve itself into a dew, 130
Or that the Everlasting had not fixed
His canon[1] 'gainst self-slaughter. O God, God,
How weary, stale, flat, and unprofitable
Seem to me all the uses of this world!
Fie on't, ah, fie, 'tis an unweeded garden 135
That grows to seed. Things rank and gross in nature
Possess it merely.[2] That it should come to this,
But two months dead, nay, not so much, not two.
So excellent a king, that was to this
Hyperion to a satyr,[3] so loving to my mother, 140
That he might not beteem[4] the winds of heaven
Visit her face too roughly. Heaven and earth,
Must I remember? Why, she would hang on him
As if increase of appetite had grown
By what it fed on, and yet, within a month— 145
Let me not think on't. Frailty, thy name is woman—
A little month, or ere those shoes were old
With which she followed my poor father's body
Like Niobe,[5] all tears, why she, even she—
O God, a beast that wants discourse of reason 150
Would have mourned longer—married with my uncle,
My father's brother, but no more like my father
Than I to Hercules.[6] Within a month,
Ere yet the salt of most unrighteous tears
Had left the flushing in her gallèd eyes, 155
She married. O, most wicked speed, to post
With such dexterity to incestuous sheets!
It is not, nor it cannot come to good.
But break my heart, for I must hold my tongue.

[*Enter* HORATIO, MARCELLUS, *and* BERNARDO.]

HORATIO: Hail to your lordship!
HAMLET: I am glad to see you well. 160
   Horatio—or I do forget myself.
HORATIO: The same, my lord, and your poor servant ever.
HAMLET: Sir, my good friend, I'll change that name with you.
   And what make you from[7] Wittenberg, Horatio?
   Marcellus? 165
MARCELLUS: My good lord!
HAMLET: I am very glad to see you. [*To* BERNARDO.] Good even, sir.—

---

1. Law. 2. Entirely.
3. Hyperion, a Greek god, stands here for beauty in contrast to the monstrous satyr, a lecherous creature, half man and half goat. 4. Permit.
5. In Greek mythology, Niobe was turned to stone after a tremendous fit of weeping over the death of her fourteen children, a misfortune brought about by her boasting over her fertility.
6. The demigod Hercules was noted for his strength and the series of spectacular labors that he accomplished. 7. What are you doing away from? *Change*: exchange.

But what, in faith, make you from Wittenberg?
HORATIO: A truant disposition, good my lord.
170   HAMLET: I would not hear your enemy say so,
Nor shall you do my ear that violence
To make it truster of your own report
Against yourself. I know you are no truant.
But what is your affair in Elsinore?
175   We'll teach you to drink deep ere you depart.
HORATIO: My lord, I came to see your father's funeral.
HAMLET: I prithee do not mock me, fellow-student,
I think it was to see my mother's wedding.
HORATIO: Indeed, my lord, it followed hard upon.
180   HAMLET: Thrift, thrift, Horatio. The funeral-baked meats
Did coldly furnish forth the marriage tables.
Would I had met my dearest[8] foe in heaven
Or ever I had seen that day, Horatio!
My father—methinks I see my father.
HORATIO: Where, my lord?
185   HAMLET: In my mind's eye, Horatio.
HORATIO: I saw him once, 'a was a goodly king.
HAMLET: 'A was a man, take him for all in all,
I shall not look upon his like again.
HORATIO: My lord, I think I saw him yesternight.
190   HAMLET: Saw who?
HORATIO: My lord, the king your father.
HAMLET: The king my father?
HORATIO: Season your admiration[9] for a while
With an attent ear till I may deliver[1]
Upon the witness of these gentlemen
This marvel to you.
195   HAMLET: For God's love, let me hear!
HORATIO: Two nights together had these gentlemen,
Marcellus and Bernardo, on their watch
In the dead waste and middle of the night
Been thus encountered. A figure like your father,
200   Armèd at point exactly, cap-a-pe,[2]
Appears before them, and with solemn march
Goes slow and stately by them. Thrice he walked
By their oppressed and fear-surprisèd eyes
Within his truncheon's[3] length, whilst they, distilled
205   Almost to jelly with the act of fear,
Stand dumb and speak not to him. This to me
In dreadful secrecy impart they did,
And I with them the third night kept the watch,
Where, as they had delivered, both in time,
210   Form of the thing, each word made true and good,

8. Bitterest.   9. Moderate your wonder.   1. Relate. *Attent*: attentive.
2. From head to toe. *Exactly*: completely.   3. Baton of office.

The apparition comes. I knew your father.
These hands are not more like.

HAMLET: But where was this?

MARCELLUS: My lord, upon the platform where we watch.

HAMLET: Did you not speak to it?

HORATIO: My lord, I did,
But answer made it none. Yet once methought   215
It lifted up it head and did address
Itself to motion, like as it would speak;
But even then the morning cock crew loud,
And at the sound it shrunk in haste away
And vanished from our sight.

HAMLET: 'Tis very strange.   220

HORATIO: As I do live, my honored lord, 'tis true,
And we did think it writ down in our duty
To let you know of it.

HAMLET: Indeed, sirs, but
This troubles me. Hold you the watch tonight?

ALL: We do, my lord.

HAMLET: Armed, say you?

ALL: Armed, my lord.   225

HAMLET: From top to toe?

ALL: My lord, from head to foot.

HAMLET: Then saw you not his face.

HORATIO: O yes, my lord, he wore his beaver[4] up.

HAMLET: What, looked he frowningly?

HORATIO: A countenance more in sorrow than in anger.   230

HAMLET: Pale or red?

HORATIO: Nay, very pale.

HAMLET: And fixed his eyes upon you?

HORATIO: Most constantly.

HAMLET: I would I had been there.

HORATIO: It would have much amazed you.

HAMLET: Very like.
Stayed it long?   235

HORATIO: While one with moderate haste might tell[5] a hundred.

BOTH: Longer, longer.

HORATIO: Not when I saw't.

HAMLET: His beard was grizzled, no?

HORATIO: It was as I have seen it in his life,
A sable silvered.

HAMLET: I will watch tonight.   240
Perchance 'twill walk again.

HORATIO: I warr'nt it will.

HAMLET: If it assume my noble father's person,
I'll speak to it though hell itself should gape
And bid me hold my peace. I pray you all,

---

4. Hinged face protector.   5. Count.

245   If you have hitherto concealed this sight,
    Let it be tenable[6] in your silence still,
    And whatsomever else shall hap tonight,
    Give it an understanding but no tongue.
    I will requite your loves. So fare you well.
250   Upon the platform 'twixt eleven and twelve
    I'll visit you.
ALL: Our duty to your honor.
HAMLET: Your loves, as mine to you. Farewell.   [*Exeunt all but* HAMLET.]
    My father's spirit in arms? All is not well.
    I doubt[7] some foul play. Would the night were come!
255   Till then sit still, my soul. Foul deeds will rise,
    Though all the earth o'erwhelm them, to men's eyes.   [*Exit.*]

Scene 3

The dwelling of POLONIUS. *Enter* LAERTES *and* OPHELIA.

LAERTES: My necessaries are embarked. Farewell.
    And, sister, as the winds give benefit
    And convoy is assistant,[8] do not sleep,
    But let me hear from you.
OPHELIA: Do you doubt that?
5 LAERTES: For Hamlet, and the trifling of his favor,
    Hold it a fashion and a toy in blood,
    A violet in the youth of primy[9] nature,
    Forward, not permanent, sweet, not lasting,
    The perfume and suppliance of a minute,
    No more.
OPHELIA: No more but so?
10 LAERTES: Think it no more.
    For nature crescent[1] does not grow alone
    In thews and bulk, but as this temple[2] waxes
    The inward service of the mind and soul
    Grows wide withal. Perhaps he loves you now,
15   And now no soil nor cautel[3] doth besmirch
    The virtue of his will, but you must fear,
    His greatness weighted,[4] his will is not his own,
    For he himself is subject to his birth.
    He may not, as unvalued persons do,
20   Carve for himself, for on his choice depends
    The safety and health of this whole state,
    And therefore must his choice be circumscribed
    Unto the voice[5] and yielding of that body
    Whereof he is the head. Then if he says he loves you,
25   It fits your wisdom so far to believe it

6. Held.   7. Suspect.   8. Means of transport is available.   9. Of the spring.   1. Growing.
2. Body. *Thews*: muscles.   3. Deceit.   4. Rank considered.   5. Assent.

As he in his particular act and place
May give his saying deed, which is no further
Than the main voice of Denmark goes withal.
Then weigh what loss your honor may sustain
If with too credent ear you list[6] his songs,   30
Or lose your heart, or your chaste treasure open
To his unmastered importunity.
Fear it, Ophelia, fear it, my dear sister,
And keep you in the rear of your affection,
Out of the shot and danger of desire.   35
The chariest[7] maid is prodigal enough
If she unmask her beauty to the moon.
Virtue itself scapes not calumnious strokes.
The canker[8] galls the infants of the spring
Too oft before their buttons[9] be disclosed,   40
And in the morn and liquid dew of youth
Contagious blastments[1] are most imminent.
Be wary then; best safety lies in fear.
Youth to itself rebels, though none else near.
OPHELIA: I shall the effect of this good lesson keep   45
As watchman to my heart. But, good my brother,
Do not as some ungracious pastors do,
Show me the steep and thorny way to heaven,
Whiles like a puffed and reckless libertine
Himself the primrose path of dalliance treads   50
And recks not his own rede.[2]
LAERTES: O, fear me not.

    [*Enter* POLONIUS.]

I stay too long. But here my father comes.
A double blessing is a double grace;
Occasion smiles upon a second leave.
POLONIUS: Yet here, Laertes? Aboard, aboard, for shame!   55
The wind sits in the shoulder of your sail,
And you are stayed for. There—my blessing with thee,
And these few precepts in thy memory
Look thou character.[3] Give thy thoughts no tongue,
Nor any unproportioned thought his act.   60
Be thou familiar, but by no means vulgar.
Those friends thou hast, and their adoption tried,
Grapple them unto thy soul with hoops of steel;
But do not dull[4] thy palm with entertainment
Of each new-hatched, unfledged comrade. Beware   65
Of entrance to a quarrel, but being in,
Bear't that th' opposèd[5] may beware of thee.

---

6. Too credulous an ear you listen to.   7. Most circumspect.   8. Cankerworm.   9. Buds.
1. Blights.   2. Heeds not his own advice.   3. Write.   4. Make callous.
5. Conduct it so that the opponent.

Give every man thy ear, but few thy voice;[6]
Take each man's censure, but reserve thy judgment.
70   Costly thy habit as thy purse can buy,
But not expressed in fancy; rich not gaudy,
For the apparel oft proclaims the man,
And they in France of the best rank and station
Are of a most select and generous chief[7] in that.
75   Neither a borrower nor a lender be,
For loan oft loses both itself and friend,
And borrowing dulls th' edge of husbandry.
This above all, to thine own self be true,
And it must follow as the night the day
80   Thou canst not then be false to any man.
Farewell. My blessing season this in thee!
LAERTES: Most humbly do I take my leave, my lord.
POLONIUS: The time invests you. Go, your servants tend.[8]
LAERTES: Farewell, Ophelia, and remember well
What I have said to you.
85 OPHELIA: 'Tis in my memory locked,
And you yourself shall keep the key of it.
LAERTES: Farewell.   [Exit.]
POLONIUS: What is't, Ophelia, he hath said to you?
OPHELIA: So please you, something touching the Lord Hamlet.
90 POLONIUS: Marry, well bethought.
'Tis told me he hath very oft of late
Given private time to you, and you yourself
Have of your audience been most free and bounteous.
If it be so—as so 'tis put on me,
95   And that in way of caution—I must tell you,
You do not understand yourself so clearly
As it behooves my daughter and your honor.
What is between you? Give me up the truth.
OPHELIA: He hath, my lord, of late made many tenders
100   Of his affection to me.
POLONIUS: Affection? Pooh! You speak like a green girl,
Unsifted in such perilous circumstance.
Do you believe his tenders, as you call them?
OPHELIA: I do not know, my lord, what I should think.
105 POLONIUS: Marry, I will teach you. Think yourself a baby
That you have ta'en these tenders for true pay
Which are not sterling. Tender yourself more dearly,
Or (not to crack the wind of the poor phrase,
Running it thus) you'll tender me a fool.
110 OPHELIA: My lord, he hath importuned me with love
In honorable fashion.
POLONIUS: Ay, fashion you may call it. Go to, go to.
OPHELIA: And hath given countenance[9] to his speech, my lord,

6. Approval.   7. Eminence.   8. Await.   9. Confirmation.

With almost all the holy vows of heaven.
POLONIUS: Ay, springs[1] to catch woodcocks. I do know, 115
    When the blood burns, how prodigal the soul
    Lends the tongue vows. These blazes, daughter,
    Giving more light than heat, extinct in both
    Even in their promise, as it is a-making,
    You must not take for fire. From this time 120
    Be something scanter of your maiden presence.
    Set your entreatments[2] at a higher rate
    Than a command to parle. For Lord Hamlet,
    Believe so much in him that he is young,
    And with a larger tether may he walk 125
    Than may be given you. In few, Ophelia,
    Do not believe his vows, for they are brokers,[3]
    Not of that dye which their investments[4] show,
    But mere implorators[5] of unholy suits,
    Breathing like sanctified and pious bawds, 130
    The better to beguile. This is for all:
    I would not, in plain terms, from this time forth
    Have you so slander any moment leisure
    As to give words or talk with the Lord Hamlet.
    Look to't, I charge you. Come your ways. 135
OPHELIA: I shall obey, my lord.   *[Exeunt.]*

Scene 4

The guard station. Enter HAMLET, HORATIO *and* MARCELLUS.

HAMLET: The air bites shrewdly;[6] it is very cold.
HORATIO: It is a nipping and an eager[7] air.
HAMLET: What hour now?
HORATIO: I think it lacks of twelve.
MARCELLUS: No, it is struck.
HORATIO: Indeed? I heard it not.
    It then draws near the season 5
    Wherein the spirit held his wont to walk.

      [A flourish of trumpets, and two pieces go off.]

    What does this mean, my lord?
HAMLET: The king doth wake tonight and takes his rouse,
    Keeps wassail, and the swagg'ring up-spring reels,
    And as he drains his draughts of Rhenish[8] down, 10
    The kettledrum and trumpet thus bray out
    The triumph of his pledge.
HORATIO: Is it a custom?
HAMLET: Ay, marry, is't,
    But to my mind, though I am native here

---

1. Snares.   2. Negotiations before a surrender.   3. Panderers.   4. Garments.   5. Solicitors.
6. Sharply.   7. Keen.   8. Rhine wine. *Up-spring*: a German dance.

15   And to the manner born, it is a custom
More honored in the breach than the observance.
This heavy-headed revel east and west
Makes us traduced and taxed of other nations.
They clepe[9] us drunkards, and with swinish phrase
20   Soil our addition,[1] and indeed it takes
From our achievements, though performed at height,
The pith and marrow of our attribute.[2]
So oft it chances in particular men,
That for some vicious mole of nature in them,
25   As in their birth, wherein they are not guilty
(Since nature cannot choose his origin),
By their o'ergrowth of some complexion,
Oft breaking down the pales[3] and forts of reason,
Or by some habit that too much o'er-leavens
30   The form of plausive[4] manners—that these men,
Carrying, I say, the stamp of one defect,
Being nature's livery or fortune's star,
His virtues else, be they as pure as grace,
As infinite as man may undergo,
35   Shall in the general censure take corruption
From that particular fault. The dram of evil
Doth all the noble substance often doubt[5]
To his own scandal.

          [*Enter* GHOST.]

HORATIO: Look, my lord, it comes.
HAMLET: Angels and ministers of grace defend us!
40   Be thou a spirit of health or goblin damned,
Bring with thee airs from heaven or blasts from hell,
Be thy intents wicked or charitable,
Thou com'st in such a questionable[6] shape
That I will speak to thee. I'll call thee Hamlet,
45   King, father, royal Dane. O, answer me!
Let me not burst in ignorance, but tell
Why thy canonized[7] bones, hearsèd in death,
Have burst their cerements;[8] why the sepulchre
Wherein we saw thee quietly inurned
50   Hath oped his ponderous and marble jaws
To cast thee up again. What may this mean
That thou, dead corse, again in complete steel[9]
Revisits thus the glimpses of the moon,
Making night hideous, and we fools of nature
55   So horridly to shake our disposition
With thoughts beyond the reaches of our souls?
Say, why is this? Wherefore? What should we do?

          [GHOST *beckons*.]

9. Call.   1. Reputation.   2. Honor.   3. Barriers.   4. Pleasing.   5. Extinguish.
6. Prompting question.   7. Buried in accordance with church canons.   8. Gravecloths.   9. Armor.

HORATIO: It beckons you to go away with it,
  As if it some impartment[1] did desire
  To you alone.
MARCELLUS: Look with what courteous action   60
  It waves you to a more removèd[2] ground.
  But do not go with it.
HORATIO: No, by no means.
HAMLET: It will not speak; then I will follow it.
HORATIO: Do not, my lord.
HAMLET: Why, what should be the fear?
  I do not set my life at a pin's fee,[3]   65
  And for my soul, what can it do to that,
  Being a thing immortal as itself?
  It waves me forth again. I'll follow it.
HORATIO: What if it tempt you toward the flood, my lord,
  Or to the dreadful summit of the cliff   70
  That beetles[4] o'er his base into the sea,
  And there assume some other horrible form,
  Which might deprive your sovereignty of reason[5]
  And draw you into madness? Think of it.
  The very place puts toys of desperation,[6]   75
  Without more motive, into every brain
  That looks so many fathoms to the sea
  And hears it roar beneath.
HAMLET: It wafts me still.
  Go on. I'll follow thee.
MARCELLUS: You shall not go, my lord.
HAMLET: Hold off your hands.   80
HORATIO: Be ruled. You shall not go.
HAMLET: My fate cries out
  And makes each petty artere in this body
  As hardy as the Nemean lion's nerve.[7]
  Still am I called. Unhand me, gentlemen.
  By heaven, I'll make a ghost of him that lets[8] me.   85
  I say, away! Go on. I'll follow thee.   [*Exeunt* GHOST *and* HAMLET.]
HORATIO: He waxes desperate with imagination.
MARCELLUS: Let's follow. 'Tis not fit thus to obey him.
HORATIO: Have after. To what issue will this come?
MARCELLUS: Something is rotten in the state of Denmark.   90
HORATIO: Heaven will direct it.
MARCELLUS: Nay, let's follow him.   [*Exeunt.*]

---

1. Communication.   2. Beckons you to a more distant.   3. Price.   4. Juts out.
5. Rational power. *Deprive*: take away.   6. Desperate fancies.
7. The Nemean lion was a mythological monster slain by Hercules as one of his twelve labors. *Artere*:
artery.   8. Hinders.

Scene 5

Near the guard station. Enter GHOST *and* HAMLET.

HAMLET: Whither wilt thou lead me? Speak. I'll go no further.
GHOST: Mark me.
HAMLET: I will.
GHOST: My hour is almost come,
  When I to sulph'rous and tormenting flames
  Must render up myself.
HAMLET: Alas, poor ghost!
5 GHOST: Pity me not, but lend thy serious hearing
  To what I shall unfold.
HAMLET: Speak. I am bound to hear.
GHOST: So art thou to revenge, when thou shalt hear.
HAMLET: What?
GHOST: I am thy father's spirit,
10 Doomed for a certain term to walk the night,
  And for the day confined to fast in fires,
  Till the foul crimes done in my days of nature[9]
  Are burnt and purged away. But that I am forbid
  To tell the secrets of my prison house,
15 I could a tale unfold whose lightest word
  Would harrow up thy soul, freeze thy young blood,
  Make thy two eyes like stars start from their spheres,
  Thy knotted and combinèd[1] locks to part,
  And each particular hair to stand an end,
20 Like quills upon the fretful porpentine.[2]
  But this eternal blazon[3] must not be
  To ears of flesh and blood. List, list, O, list!
  If thou didst ever thy dear father love—
HAMLET: O God!
25 GHOST: Revenge his foul and most unnatural murder.
HAMLET: Murder!
GHOST: Murder most foul, as in the best it is,
  But this most foul, strange, and unnatural.
HAMLET: Haste me to know't, that I, with wings as swift
30 As meditation or the thoughts of love,
  May sweep to my revenge.
GHOST: I find thee apt.
  And duller shouldst thou be than the fat weed
  That rots itself in ease on Lethe[4] wharf,—
  Wouldst thou not stir in this. Now, Hamlet, hear.
35 'Tis given out that, sleeping in my orchard,

9. That is, while I was alive. 1. Tangled. 2. Porcupine. 3. Description of eternity.
4. The waters of the Lethe, one of the rivers of the classical underworld, when drunk, induced forgetfulness. The "fat weed" is the asphodel that grew there; some texts have "roots" for "rots."

A serpent stung me. So the whole ear of Denmark
Is by a forgèd process[5] of my death
Rankly abused. But know, thou noble youth,
The serpent that did sting thy father's life
Now wears his crown.

HAMLET: O my prophetic soul!   40
    My uncle!

GHOST: Ay, that incestuous, that adulterate beast,
    With witchcraft of his wits, with traitorous gifts—
    O wicked wit and gifts that have the power
    So to seduce!—won to his shameful lust   45
    The will of my most seeming virtuous queen.
    O Hamlet, what a falling off was there,
    From me, whose love was of that dignity
    That it went hand in hand even with the vow
    I made to her in marriage, and to decline[6]   50
    Upon a wretch whose natural gifts were poor
    To those of mine!
    But virtue, as it never will be moved,
    Though lewdness court it in a shape of heaven,
    So lust, though to a radiant angel linked,   55
    Will sate itself in a celestial bed
    And prey on garbage.
    But soft, methinks I scent the morning air.
    Brief let me be. Sleeping within my orchard,
    My custom always of the afternoon,   60
    Upon my secure hour thy uncle stole,
    With juice of cursed hebona[7] in a vial,
    And in the porches of my ears did pour
    The leperous distilment, whose effect
    Holds such an enmity with blood of man   65
    That swift as quicksilver it courses through
    The natural gates and alleys of the body,
    And with a sudden vigor it doth posset[8]
    And curd, like eager[9] droppings into milk,
    The thin and wholesome blood. So did it mine,   70
    And a most instant tetter barked about[1]
    Most lazar-like[2] with vile and loathsome crust
    All my smooth body.
    Thus was I sleeping by a brother's hand
    Of life, of crown, of queen at once dispatched,   75
    Cut off even in the blossoms of my sin,
    Unhouseled, disappointed, unaneled,[3]
    No reck'ning made, but sent to my account

5. False report.   6. Sink.   7. A poison.   8. Coagulate.   9. Acid. *Curd*: curdle.
1. Covered like bark. *Tetter*: a skin disease.   2. Leperlike.
3. The ghost means that he died without the customary rites of the church, that is, without receiving the
Sacrament, without confession, and without Extreme Unction.

With all my imperfections on my head.
80   O, horrible! O, horrible, most horrible!
If thou hast nature in thee, bear it not.
Let not the royal bed of Denmark be
A couch of luxury[4] and damnèd incest.
But howsomever thou pursues this act,
85   Taint not thy mind, nor let thy soul contrive
Against thy mother aught. Leave her to heaven,
And to those thorns that in her bosom lodge
To prick and sting her. Fare thee well at once.
The glowworm shows the matin[5] to be near,
90   And gins to pale his uneffectual fire.
Adieu, adieu, adieu. Remember me.   [Exit.]
HAMLET: O all you host of heaven! O earth! What else?
And shall I couple hell? O, fie! Hold, hold, my heart,
And you, my sinews, grow not instant old,
95   But bear me stiffly up. Remember thee?
Ay, thou poor ghost, whiles memory holds a seat
In this distracted globe.[6] Remember thee?
Yea, from the table[7] of my memory
I'll wipe away all trivial fond[8] records,
100 All saws of books, all forms, all pressures past
That youth and observation copied there,
And thy commandment all alone shall live
Within the book and volume of my brain,
Unmixed with baser matter. Yes, by heaven!
105 O most pernicious woman!
O villain, villain, smiling, damnèd villain!
My tables—meet it is I set it down
That one may smile, and smile, and be a villain.
At least I am sure it may be so in Denmark.
110 So, uncle, there you are. Now to my word:[9]
It is "Adieu, adieu. Remember me."
I have sworn't.

[Enter HORATIO and MARCELLUS.]

HORATIO: My lord, my lord!
MARCELLUS: Lord Hamlet!
HORATIO: Heavens secure him!
HAMLET: So be it!
115 MARCELLUS: Illo, ho, ho,[1] my lord!
HAMLET: Hillo, ho, ho, boy! Come, bird, come.
MARCELLUS: How is't, my noble lord?
HORATIO: What news, my lord?
HAMLET: O, wonderful!
HORATIO: Good my lord, tell it.

4. Lust.   5. Morning.   6. Skull.   7. Writing tablet.   8. Foolish.   9. For my motto.
1. A falconer's cry.

HAMLET:	No, you will reveal it.
HORATIO: Not I, my lord, by heaven.	
MARCELLUS:	Nor I, my lord.	120

HAMLET: How say you then, would heart of man once think it?
But you'll be secret?

BOTH: Ay, by heaven, my lord.

HAMLET: There's never a villain dwelling in all Denmark
But he's an arrant knave.

HORATIO: There needs no ghost, my lord, come from the grave   125
To tell us this.

HAMLET: Why, right, you are in the right,
And so without more circumstance at all
I hold it fit that we shake hands and part,
You, as your business and desire shall point you,
For every man hath business and desire   130
Such as it is, and for my own poor part,
Look you, I'll go pray.

HORATIO: These are but wild and whirling words, my lord.

HAMLET: I am sorry they offend you, heartily;
Yes, faith, heartily.

HORATIO: There's no offence, my lord.   135

HAMLET: Yes, by Saint Patrick, but there is, Horatio,
And much offence too. Touching this vision here,
It is an honest ghost, that let me tell you.
For your desire to know what is between us,
O'ermaster't as you may. And now, good friends,   140
As you are friends, scholars, and soldiers,
Give me one poor request.

HORATIO: What is't, my lord? We will.

HAMLET: Never make known what you have seen tonight.

BOTH: My lord, we will not.

HAMLET: Nay, but swear't.

HORATIO: In faith,   145
My lord, not I.

MARCELLUS: Nor I, my lord, in faith.

HAMLET: Upon my sword.

MARCELLUS: We have sworn, my lord, already.

HAMLET: Indeed, upon my sword, indeed.

[GHOST *cries under the stage.*]

GHOST: Swear.

HAMLET: Ha, ha, boy, say'st thou so? Art thou there, truepenny?[2]
Come on. You hear this fellow in the cellarage.[3]   150
Consent to swear.

HORATIO: Propose the oath, my lord.

HAMLET: Never to speak of this that you have seen,
Swear by my sword.

2. Trusty old fellow.   3. Below.

GHOST: [*Beneath.*] Swear.

155 HAMLET: Hic et ubique?[4] Then we'll shift our ground.
    Come hither, gentlemen,
    And lay your hands again upon my sword.
    Swear by my sword
    Never to speak of this that you have heard.

160 GHOST: [*Beneath.*] Swear by his sword.

HAMLET: Well said, old mole! Canst work i' th' earth so fast?
    A worthy pioneer![5] Once more remove, good friends.

HORATIO: O day and night, but this is wondrous strange!

HAMLET: And therefore as a stranger give it welcome.
165   There are more things in heaven and earth, Horatio,
    Than are dreamt of in your philosophy.
    But come.
    Here as before, never, so help you mercy,
    How strange or odd some'er I bear myself
170   (As I perchance hereafter shall think meet
    To put an antic[6] disposition on),
    That you, at such times, seeing me, never shall,
    With arms encumbered[7] thus, or this head-shake,
    Or by pronouncing of some doubtful phrase,
175   As "Well, we know," or "We could, and if we would"
    Or "If we list to speak," or "There be, and if they might"
    Or such ambiguous giving out, to note
    That you know aught of me—this do swear,
    So grace and mercy at your most need help you.

180 GHOST: [*Beneath.*] Swear.   [*They swear.*]

HAMLET: Rest, rest, perturbèd spirit! So, gentlemen,
    With all my love I do commend me to you,
    And what so poor a man as Hamlet is
    May do t'express his love and friending[8] to you,
185   God willing, shall not lack. Let us go in together,
    And still your fingers on your lips, I pray.
    The time is out of joint. O cursèd spite
    That ever I was born to set it right!
    Nay, come, let's go together.   [*Exeunt.*]

ACT II

Scene 1

The dwelling of POLONIUS. *Enter* POLONIUS *and* REYNALDO.

POLONIUS: Give him this money and these notes, Reynaldo.

REYNALDO: I will, my lord.

POLONIUS: You shall do marvellous wisely, good Reynaldo,

---

4. Here and everywhere? (Latin).   5. Soldier who digs trenches.   6. Mad.   7. Folded.
8. Friendship.

Before you visit him, to make inquire[9]
Of his behavior.

REYNALDO: My lord, I did intend it.   5

POLONIUS: Marry, well said, very well said. Look you, sir.
Enquire me first what Danskers[1] are in Paris,
And how, and who, what means, and where they keep,[2]
What company, at what expense; and finding
By this encompassment[3] and drift of question   10
That they do know my son, come you more nearer
Than your particular demands[4] will touch it.
Take you as 'twere some distant knowledge of him,
As thus, "I know his father and his friends,
And in part him." Do you mark this, Reynaldo?   15

REYNALDO: Ay, very well, my lord.

POLONIUS: "And in part him, but," you may say, "not well,
But if't be he I mean, he's very wild,
Addicted so and so." And there put on him
What forgeries you please; marry, none so rank[5]   20
As may dishonor him. Take heed of that.
But, sir, such wanton, wild, and usual slips
As are companions noted and most known
To youth and liberty.

REYNALDO: As gaming, my lord.

POLONIUS: Ay, or drinking, fencing, swearing,   25
Quarrelling, drabbing[6]—you may go so far.

REYNALDO: My lord, that would dishonor him.

POLONIUS: Faith, no, as you may season it in the charge.[7]
You must not put another scandal on him,
That he is open to incontinency.[8]   30
That's not my meaning. But breathe his faults so quaintly[9]
That they may seem the taints of liberty,[1]
The flash and outbreak of a fiery mind,
A savageness in unreclaimèd[2] blood,
Of general assault.[3]

REYNALDO: But, my good lord—   35

POLONIUS: Wherefore should you do this?

REYNALDO: Ay, my lord,
I would know that.

POLONIUS: Marry, sir, here's my drift,
And I believe it is a fetch of warrant.[4]
You laying these slight sullies on my son,
As 'twere a thing a little soiled wi' th' working,   40
Mark you,
Your party in converse,[5] him you would sound,
Having ever seen in the prenominate[6] crimes

9. Inquiry.   1. Danes.   2. Live.   3. Indirect means.   4. Direct questions.   5. Foul. *Forgeries*: lies.
6. Whoring.   7. Soften the accusation.   8. Sexual excess.   9. With delicacy.   1. Faults of freedom.
2. Untamed.   3. Touching everyone.   4. Permissible trick.   5. Conversation.   6. Already named.

The youth you breathe[7] of guilty, be assured
45   He closes with you in this consequence,
"Good sir," or so, or "friend," or "gentleman,"
According to the phrase or the addition
Of man and country.

REYNALDO: Very good, my lord.

POLONIUS: And then, sir, does 'a this—'a does—What was I about to say?
50   By the mass, I was about to say something.
Where did I leave?

REYNALDO: At "closes in the consequence."

POLONIUS: At "closes in the consequence"—ay, marry,
He closes thus: "I know the gentleman.
55   I saw him yesterday, or th' other day,
Or then, or then, with such, or such, and as you say,
There was 'a gaming, there o'ertook in's rouse,
There falling out at tennis," or perchance
"I saw him enter such a house of sale,"
60   Videlicet,[8] a brothel, or so forth.
See you, now—
Your bait of falsehood takes this carp of truth,
And thus do we of wisdom and of reach,[9]
With windlasses and with assays of bias,[1]
65   By indirections find directions out;
So by my former lecture and advice
Shall you my son. You have me, have you not?

REYNALDO: My lord, I have.

POLONIUS: God b'wi' ye; fare ye well.

REYNALDO: Good my lord.

70 POLONIUS: Observe his inclination in yourself.

REYNALDO: I shall, my lord.

POLONIUS: And let him ply[2] his music.

REYNALDO: Well, my lord.

POLONIUS: Farewell.   [*Exit* REYNALDO.]

[*Enter* OPHELIA.]

                    How now, Ophelia, what's the matter?

OPHELIA: O my lord, my lord, I have been so affrighted!

75 POLONIUS: With what, i' th' name of God?

OPHELIA: My lord, as I was sewing in my closet,[3]
Lord Hamlet with his doublet all unbraced,[4]
No hat upon his head, his stockings fouled,
Ungartered and down-gyvèd[5] to his ankle,
80   Pale as his shirt, his knees knocking each other,
And with a look so piteous in purport
As if he had been loosèd out of hell
To speak of horrors—he comes before me.

7. Speak.   8. Namely.   9. Ability.   1. Indirect tests.   2. Practice.   3. Chamber.
4. Unlaced. *Doublet*: jacket.   5. Fallen down like fetters.

POLONIUS: Mad for thy love?

OPHELIA: My lord, I do not know,
　　But truly I do fear it.

POLONIUS: What said he?　　　　　　　　　85

OPHELIA: He took me by the wrist, and held me hard,
　　Then goes he to the length of all his arm,
　　And with his other hand thus o'er his brow,
　　He falls to such perusal of my face
　　As 'a would draw it. Long stayed he so.　　　90
　　At last, a little shaking of mine arm,
　　And thrice his head thus waving up and down,
　　He raised a sigh so piteous and profound
　　As it did seem to shatter all his bulk,[6]
　　And end his being. That done, he lets me go,　　95
　　And with his head over his shoulder turned
　　He seemed to find his way without his eyes,
　　For out adoors he went without their helps,
　　And to the last bended[7] their light on me.

POLONIUS: Come, go with me. I will go seek the king.　　100
　　This is the very ecstasy of love,
　　Whose violent property fordoes[8] itself,
　　And leads the will to desperate undertakings
　　As oft as any passion under heaven
　　That does afflict our natures. I am sorry.　　105
　　What, have you given him any hard words of late?

OPHELIA: No, my good lord, but as you did command
　　I did repel[9] his letters, and denied
　　His access to me.

POLONIUS: That hath made him mad.
　　I am sorry that with better heed and judgment　　110
　　I had not quoted[1] him. I feared he did but trifle,
　　And meant to wrack[2] thee; but beshrew my jealousy.
　　By heaven, it is as proper to our age
　　To cast beyond ourselves in our opinions
　　As it is common for the younger sort　　　115
　　To lack discretion. Come, go we to the king.
　　This must be known, which being kept close, might move
　　More grief to hide than hate to utter love.
　　Come.　　　　　　　　　　　　　　　[*Exeunt.*]

Scene 2

A public room. Enter KING, QUEEN, ROSENCRANTZ *and* GUILDENSTERN.

KING: Welcome, dear Rosencrantz and Guildenstern.
　　Moreover that[3] we much did long to see you,

---

6. Body.　7. Directed.　8. Destroys. *Property*: character.　9. Refuse.　1. Observed.　2. Harm.
3. In addition to the fact that.

      The need we have to use you did provoke
      Our hasty sending. Something have you heard
5   Of Hamlet's transformation—so call it,
      Sith[4] nor th' exterior nor the inward man
      Resembles that it was. What it should be,
      More than his father's death, that thus hath put him
      So much from th' understanding of himself,
10   I cannot deem of. I entreat you both
      That, being of so young days[5] brought up with him,
      And sith so neighbored[6] to his youth and havior,
      That you vouchsafe your rest here in our court
      Some little time, so by your companies
15   To draw him on to pleasures, and to gather
      So much as from occasion you may glean,
      Whether aught to us unknown afflicts him thus,
      That opened lies within our remedy.
    QUEEN: Good gentlemen, he hath much talked of you,
20   And sure I am two men there are not living
      To whom he more adheres. If it will please you
      To show us so much gentry[7] and good will
      As to expend your time with us awhile
      For the supply and profit of our hope,
25   Your visitation shall receive such thanks
      As fits a king's remembrance.
    ROSENCRANTZ: Both your majesties
      Might, by the sovereign power you have of us,
      Put your dread pleasures more into command
      Than to entreaty.
    GUILDENSTERN: But we both obey,
30   And here give up ourselves in the full bent[8]
      To lay our service freely at your feet,
      To be commanded.
    KING: Thanks, Rosencrantz and gentle Guildenstern.
    QUEEN: Thanks, Guildenstern and gentle Rosencrantz.
35   And I beseech you instantly to visit
      My too much changed son. Go, some of you,
      And bring these gentlemen where Hamlet is.
    GUILDENSTERN: Heavens make our presence and our practices
      Pleasant and helpful to him!
    QUEEN: Ay, amen!
                    [*Exeunt* ROSENCRANTZ *and* GUILDENSTERN.]

    [*Enter* POLONIUS.]

40   POLONIUS: Th' ambassadors from Norway, my good lord,
      Are joyfully returned.

---

4. Since.   5. From childhood.   6. Closely allied.   7. Courtesy.   8. Completely.

KING: Thou still[9] hast been the father of good news.

POLONIUS: Have I, my lord? I assure you, my good liege,
   I hold my duty as I hold my soul,
   Both to my God and to my gracious king;   45
   And I do think—or else this brain of mine
   Hunts not the trail of policy[1] so sure
   As it hath used to do—that I have found
   The very cause of Hamlet's lunacy.

KING: O, speak of that, that do I long to hear.   50

POLONIUS: Give first admittance to th' ambassadors.
   My news shall be the fruit[2] to that great feast.

KING: Thyself do grace to them, and bring them in.   [*Exit* POLONIUS.]
   He tells me, my dear Gertrude, he hath found
   The head and source of all your son's distemper.

QUEEN: I doubt it is no other but the main,   55
   His father's death and our o'erhasty marriage.

KING: Well, we shall sift[3] him.

[*Enter Ambassadors (*VOLTEMAND *and* CORNELIUS*) with* POLONIUS.]

                          Welcome, my good friends,
   Say, Voltemand, what from our brother Norway?

VOLTEMAND: Most fair return of greetings and desires.   60
   Upon our first,[4] he sent out to suppress
   His nephew's levies, which to him appeared
   To be a preparation 'gainst the Polack,
   But better looked into, he truly found
   It was against your highness, whereat grieved,   65
   That so his sickness, age, and impotence
   Was falsely borne in hand, sends out arrests[5]
   On Fortinbras, which he in brief obeys,
   Receives rebuke from Norway, and in fine,
   Makes vow before his uncle never more   70
   To give th' assay[6] of arms against your majesty.
   Whereon old Norway, overcome with joy,
   Gives him three thousand crowns in annual fee,
   And his commission to employ those soldiers,
   So levied as before, against the Polack,   75
   With an entreaty, herein further shown,   [*Gives* CLAUDIUS *a paper.*]
   That it might please you to give quiet pass[7]
   Through your dominions for this enterprise,
   On such regards of safety and allowance
   As therein are set down.

KING: It likes[8] us well,   80
   And at our more considered time[9] we'll read,

---

9. Ever.   1. Statecraft.   2. Dessert.   3. Examine.   4. That is, first appearance.
5. Orders to stop. *Falsely borne in hand*: deceived.   6. Trial.   7. Safe conduct.   8. Pleases.
9. Time for more consideration.

Answer, and think upon this business.
Meantime we thank you for your well-took[1] labor.
Go to your rest; at night we'll feast together.
Most welcome home! [*Exeunt* AMBASSADORS.]

85 POLONIUS: This business is well ended.
My liege and madam, to expostulate[2]
What majesty should be, what duty is,
Why day is day, night night, and time is time,
Were nothing but to waste night, day, and time.
90 Therefore, since brevity is the soul of wit,
And tediousness the limbs and outward flourishes,[3]
I will be brief. Your noble son is mad.
Mad call I it, for to define true madness,
What is't but to be nothing else but mad?
But let that go.

95 QUEEN: More matter with less art.
POLONIUS: Madam, I swear I use no art at all.
That he is mad, 'tis true: 'tis true 'tis pity,
And pity 'tis 'tis true. A foolish figure,
But farewell it, for I will use no art.
100 Mad let us grant him, then, and now remains
That we find out the cause of this effect,
Or rather say the cause of this defect,
For this effect defective comes by cause.
Thus it remains, and the remainder thus.
105 Perpend.[4]
I have a daughter—have while she is mine—
Who in her duty and obedience, mark,
Hath given me this. Now gather, and surmise.
[*Reads*] the letter.
"To the celestial, and my soul's idol, the most beautified Ophelia."—That's
110 an ill phrase, a vile phrase, "beautified" is a vile phrase. But you shall hear.
Thus:
"In her excellent white bosom, these, etc."
QUEEN: Came this from Hamlet to her?
POLONIUS: Good madam, stay awhile. I will be faithful.
115 "Doubt thou the stars are fire,
Doubt that the sun doth move;
Doubt truth to be a liar;
But never doubt I love.

O dear Ophelia, I am ill at these numbers.[5] I have not art to reckon my groans,
120 but that I love thee best, O most best, believe it. Adieu.
Thine evermore, most dear lady,
whilst this machine[6] is to him, Hamlet."
This in obedience hath my daughter shown me,
And more above, hath his solicitings,

---

1. Successful. 2. Discuss. 3. Adornments. 4. Consider. 5. Verses. 6. Body.

As they fell out by time, by means, and place,   125
    All given to mine ear.
KING: But how hath she
    Received his love?
POLONIUS: What do you think of me?
KING: As of a man faithful and honorable.
POLONIUS: I would fain prove so. But what might you think,
    When I had seen this hot love on the wing.   130
    (As I perceived it, I must tell you that,
    Before my daughter told me), what might you,
    Or my dear majesty your queen here, think,
    If I had played the desk or table-book,
    Or given my heart a winking, mute and dumb,   135
    Or looked upon this love with idle sight,[7]
    What might you think? No, I went round[8] to work,
    And my young mistress thus I did bespeak:
    "Lord Hamlet is a prince out of thy star.[9]
    This must not be." And then I prescripts[1] gave her,   140
    That she should lock herself from his resort,
    Admit no messengers, receive no tokens.
    Which done, she took[2] the fruits of my advice;
    And he repelled, a short tale to make,
    Fell into a sadness, then into a fast,   145
    Thence to a watch, thence into a weakness,
    Thence to a lightness, and by this declension,
    Into the madness wherein now he raves,
    And all we mourn for.
KING: Do you think 'tis this?
QUEEN: It may be, very like.   150
POLONIUS: Hath there been such a time—I would fain know that—
    That I have positively said "'Tis so,"
    When it proved otherwise?
KING: Not that I know.
POLONIUS: [*Pointing to his head and shoulder.*] Take this from this, if this be
    otherwise.
    If circumstances lead me, I will find   155
    Where truth is hid, though it were hid indeed
    Within the centre.[3]
KING: How may we try it further?
POLONIUS: You know sometimes he walks four hours together
    Here in the lobby.
QUEEN: So he does, indeed.
POLONIUS: At such a time I'll loose[4] my daughter to him.   160
    Be you and I behind an arras[5] then.

7. Polonius means that he would have been at fault if, having seen Hamlet's attention to Ophelia, he had winked at it or not paid attention, an "idle sight," and if he had remained silent and kept the information to himself, as if it were written in a "desk" or "table-book." 8. Directly. 9. Beyond your sphere.
1. Orders. 2. Followed. 3. Of the earth. 4. Let loose. 5. Tapestry.

Mark the encounter. If he love her not,
And be not from his reason fall'n thereon,
Let me be no assistant for a state,
But keep a farm and carters.

165   KING: We will try it.

[*Enter* HAMLET *reading a book.*]

QUEEN: But look where sadly the poor wretch comes reading.
POLONIUS: Away, I do beseech you both away,
I'll board[6] him presently.   [*Exeunt* KING *and* QUEEN.]
                    O, give me leave.
How does my good Lord Hamlet?

170   HAMLET: Well, God-a-mercy.
POLONIUS: Do you know me, my lord?
HAMLET: Excellent well, you are a fishmonger.
POLONIUS: Not I, my lord.
HAMLET: Then I would you were so honest a man.
175   POLONIUS: Honest, my lord?
HAMLET: Ay, sir, to be honest as this world goes, is to be one man picked out of
    ten thousand.
POLONIUS: That's very true, my lord.
HAMLET: For if the sun breed maggots in a dead dog, being a god kissing
180   carrion[7]—Have you a daughter?
POLONIUS: I have, my lord.
HAMLET: Let her not walk i' th' sun. Conception is a blessing, but as your daugh-
    ter may conceive—friend, look to't.
POLONIUS: How say you by that? [*Aside.*] Still harping on my daughter. Yet he
185   knew me not at first. 'A said I was a fishmonger. 'A is far gone. And truly in my
    youth I suffered much extremity for love. Very near this. I'll speak to him
    again.—What do you read, my lord?
HAMLET: Words, words, words.
POLONIUS: What is the matter, my lord?
190   HAMLET: Between who?
POLONIUS: I mean the matter that you read, my lord.
HAMLET: Slanders, sir; for the satirical rogue says here that old men have grey
    beards, that their faces are wrinkled, their eyes purging thick amber and
    plumtree gum, and that they have a plentiful lack of wit, together with most
195   weak hams[8]—all which, sir, though I most powerfully and potently believe,
    yet I hold it not honesty to have it thus set down, for yourself, sir, shall grow
    old as I am, if like a crab you could go backward.
POLONIUS: [*Aside.*] Though this be madness, yet there is method in't.—Will you
    walk out of the air, my lord?
200   HAMLET: Into my grave?

6. Accost.
7. A reference to the belief of the period that maggots were produced spontaneously by the action of sunshine on carrion.   8. Limbs.

POLONIUS: [*Aside.*] Indeed, that's out of the air. How pregnant sometime his replies are! a happiness that often madness hits on, which reason and sanity could not so prosperously be delivered of. I will leave him, and suddenly contrive the means of meeting between him and my daughter.—My honorable lord. I will most humbly take my leave of you.   205

HAMLET: You cannot take from me anything that I will more willingly part withal—except my life, except my life, except my life.

[*Enter* GUILDENSTERN *and* ROSENCRANTZ.]

POLONIUS: Fare you well, my lord.

HAMLET: These tedious old fools!

POLONIUS: You go to seek the Lord Hamlet. There he is.   210

ROSENCRANTZ: [*To* POLONIUS.] God save you, sir!   [*Exit* POLONIUS.]

GUILDENSTERN: My honored lord!

ROSENCRANTZ: My most dear lord!

HAMLET: My excellent good friends! How dost thou, Guildenstern?   215
Ah, Rosencrantz! Good lads, how do you both?

ROSENCRANTZ: As the indifferent[9] children of the earth.

GUILDENSTERN: Happy in that we are not over-happy;
On Fortune's cap we are not the very button.[1]

HAMLET: Nor the soles of her shoe?

ROSENCRANTZ: Neither, my lord.   220

HAMLET: Then you live about her waist, or in the middle of her favors?

GUILDENSTERN: Faith, her privates we.

HAMLET: In the secret parts of Fortune? O, most true, she is a strumpet.[2] What news?

ROSENCRANTZ: None, my lord, but that the world's grown honest.   225

HAMLET: Then is doomsday near. But your news is not true. Let me question more in particular. What have you, my good friends, deserved at the hands of Fortune, that she sends you to prison hither?

GUILDENSTERN: Prison, my lord?

HAMLET: Denmark's a prison.   230

ROSENCRANTZ: Then is the world one.

HAMLET: A goodly one, in which there are many confines, wards[3] and dungeons. Denmark being one o' th' worst.

ROSENCRANTZ: We think not so, my lord.

HAMLET: Why then 'tis none to you; for there is nothing either good or bad, but 235
thinking makes it so. To me it is a prison.

ROSENCRANTZ: Why then your ambition makes it one. 'Tis too narrow for your mind.

HAMLET: O God, I could be bounded in a nutshell and count myself a king of infinite space, were it not that I have bad dreams.   240

GUILDENSTERN: Which dreams indeed are ambition; for the very substance of the ambitious is merely the shadow of a dream.

9. Ordinary.   1. That is, on top.
2. Prostitute. Hamlet is indulging in characteristic ribaldry. Guildenstern means that they are "privates" = ordinary citizens, but Hamlet takes him to mean "privates" = sexual organs and "middle of her favors" = waist = sexual organs.   3. Cells.

HAMLET: A dream itself is but a shadow.

ROSENCRANTZ: Truly, and I hold ambition of so airy and light a quality that it is
245   but a shadow's shadow.

HAMLET: Then are our beggars bodies, and our monarchs and outstretched
    heroes the beggars' shadows. Shall we to th' court? for, by my fay,[4] I cannot
    reason.

BOTH: We'll wait upon you.

250 HAMLET: No such matter. I will not sort[5] you with the rest of my servants; for to
    speak to you like an honest man, I am most dreadfully attended. But in the
    beaten way of friendship, what make you at Elsinore?

ROSENCRANTZ: To visit you, my lord; no other occasion.

HAMLET: Beggar that I am, I am even poor in thanks, but I thank you; and sure,
255   dear friends, my thanks are too dear a halfpenny.[6] Were you not sent for? Is it
    your own inclining? Is it a free visitation? Come, come, deal justly with me.
    Come, come, nay speak.

GUILDENSTERN: What should we say, my lord?

HAMLET: Anything but to th' purpose. You were sent for, and there is a kind of
260   confession in your looks, which your modesties have not craft enough to
    color. I know the good king and queen have sent for you.

ROSENCRANTZ: To what end, my lord?

HAMLET: That you must teach me. But let me conjure you by the rights of our fel-
    lowship, by the consonancy of our youth, by the obligation of our ever pre-
265   served love, and by what more dear a better proposer can charge you withal,
    be even and direct[7] with me whether you were sent for or no.

ROSENCRANTZ: [Aside to GUILDENSTERN.] What say you?

HAMLET: [Aside.] Nay, then, I have an eye of you.—If you love me, hold not off.

GUILDENSTERN: My lord, we were sent for.

270 HAMLET: I will tell you why; so shall my anticipation prevent your discovery,[8] and
    your secrecy to the king and queen moult no feather. I have of late—but
    wherefore I know not—lost all my mirth, forgone all custom of exercises; and
    indeed it goes so heavily with my disposition, that this goodly frame the
    earth seems to me a sterile promontory, this most excellent canopy the air,
275   look you, this brave o'er-hanging firmament, this majestical roof fretted[9]
    with golden fire, why it appeareth nothing to me but a foul and pestilent con-
    gregation of vapors. What a piece of work is a man, how noble in reason, how
    infinite in faculties, in form and moving, how express[1] and admirable in
    action, how like an angel in apprehension, how like a god: the beauty of the
280   world, the paragon of animals. And yet to me, what is this quintessence of
    dust? Man delights not me, nor woman neither, though by your smiling you
    seem to say so.

ROSENCRANTZ: My lord, there was no such stuff in my thoughts.

HAMLET: Why did ye laugh, then, when I said "Man delights not me"?

285 ROSENCRANTZ: To think, my lord, if you delight not in man, what lenten enter-
    tainment the players shall receive from you. We coted[2] them on the way, and
    hither are they coming to offer you service.

---

4. Faith.   5. Include.   6. Not worth a halfpenny.   7. Straightforward.   8. Disclosure.
9. Ornamented with fretwork.   1. Well built.   2. Passed. *Lenten*: scanty.

HAMLET: He that plays the king shall be welcome—his majesty shall have tribute
of me; the adventurous knight shall use his foil and target; the lover shall not
sigh gratis; the humorous[3] man shall end his part in peace; the clown shall 290
make those laugh whose lungs are tickle o' th' sere;[4] and the lady shall say her
mind freely, or the blank verse shall halt for't. What players are they?

ROSENCRANTZ: Even those you were wont to take such delight in, the tragedians
of the city. 295

HAMLET: How chances it they travel? Their residence, both in reputation and
profit, was better both ways.

ROSENCRANTZ: I think their inhibition comes by the means of the late innovation.

HAMLET: Do they hold the same estimation they did when I was in the city? Are 300
they so followed?

ROSENCRANTZ: No, indeed, are they not.

HAMLET: How comes it? Do they grow rusty?

ROSENCRANTZ: Nay, their endeavor keeps in the wonted pace; but there is, sir, an
eyrie of children, little eyases,[5] that cry out on the top of question,[6] and are 305
most tyrannically clapped for't. These are now the fashion, and so berattle
the common stages (so they call them) that many wearing rapiers are afraid
of goose quills[7] and dare scarce come thither.[8]

HAMLET: What, are they children? Who maintains 'em? How are they escoted?[9]
Will they pursue the quality no longer than they can sing? Will they not say 310
afterwards, if they should grow themselves to common players (as it is most
like, if their means are no better), their writers do them wrong to make them
exclaim against their own succession?[1]

ROSENCRANTZ: Faith, there has been much todo on both sides; and the nation
holds it no sin to tarre[2] them to controversy. There was for a while no money bid 315
for argument,[3] unless the poet and the player went to cuffs[4] in the question.

HAMLET: Is't possible?

GUILDENSTERN: O, there has been much throwing about of brains.

HAMLET: Do the boys carry it away? 320

ROSENCRANTZ: Ay, that they do, my lord. Hercules and his load too.[5]

HAMLET: It is not very strange, for my uncle is King of Denmark, and those that
would make mouths[6] at him while my father lived give twenty, forty, fifty, a
hundred ducats apiece for his picture in little.[7] 'Sblood, there is something in
this more than natural, if philosophy could find it out. 325

[*A flourish.*]

---

3. Eccentric. *Foil and target*: sword and shield.   4. Easily set off.   5. Little hawks.
6. With a loud, high delivery.   7. Pens of satirical writers.
8. The passage refers to the emergence at the time of the play of theatrical companies made up of children from London choir schools. Their performances became fashionable and hurt the business of the established companies. Hamlet says that if they continue to act, "pursue the quality," when they are grown, they will find that they have been damaging their own future careers.   9. Supported.
1. Future careers.   2. Urge.   3. Paid for a play plot.   4. Blows.
5. During one of his labors Hercules assumed for a time the burden of the Titan Atlas, who supported the heavens on his shoulders. Also a reference to the effect on business at Shakespeare's theater, the Globe.
6. Sneer.   7. Miniature.

GUILDENSTERN: There are the players.

HAMLET: Gentlemen, you are welcome to Elsinore. Your hands. Come then, th'
appurtenance of welcome is fashion and ceremony. Let me comply with you
in this garb, lest my extent[8] to the players, which I tell you must show fairly
330   outwards should more appear like entertainment[9] than yours. You are welcome. But my uncle-father and aunt-mother are deceived.

GUILDENSTERN: In what, my dear lord?

HAMLET: I am but mad north-north-west; when the wind is southerly I know a
hawk from a handsaw.[1]

[*Enter* POLONIUS.]

335   POLONIUS: Well be with you, gentlemen.

HAMLET: Hark you, Guildenstern—and you too—at each ear a hearer. That great
baby you see there is not yet out of his swaddling clouts.[2]

ROSENCRANTZ: Happily he is the second time come to them, for they say an old
man is twice a child.

340   HAMLET: I will prophesy he comes to tell me of the players. Mark it.—You say
right, sir, a Monday morning, 'twas then indeed.

POLONIUS: My lord, I have news to tell you.

HAMLET: My lord, I have news to tell you. When Roscius was an actor in Rome—[3]

POLONIUS: The actors are come hither, my lord.

345   HAMLET: Buzz, buzz.

POLONIUS: Upon my honor—

HAMLET: Then came each actor on his ass—

POLONIUS: The best actors in the world, either for tragedy, comedy, history, pastoral, pastoral-comical, historical-pastoral, tragical-historical, tragical-comical
350   historical-pastoral, scene individable, or poem unlimited. Seneca cannot be
too heavy nor Plautus too light. For the law of writ and the liberty, these are
the only men.[4]

HAMLET: O Jephtha, judge of Israel, what a treasure hadst thou![5]

POLONIUS: What a treasure had he, my lord?

355   HAMLET: Why—

"One fair daughter, and no more,
The which he loved passing well."

POLONIUS: [*Aside.*] Still on my daughter.

HAMLET: Am I not i' th' right, old Jephtha?

360   POLONIUS: If you call me Jephtha, my lord, I have a daughter that I love passing
well.

HAMLET: Nay, that follows not.

8. Fashion. *Comply with*: welcome.   9. Cordiality.
1. A "hawk" is a plasterer's tool; Hamlet may also be using "handsaw" = hernshaw = heron.
2. Wrappings for an infant.   3. Roscius was the most famous actor of classical Rome.
4. Seneca and Plautus were Roman writers of tragedy and comedy, respectively. The "law of writ" refers to
plays written according to such rules as the three unities; the "liberty" to those written otherwise.
5. To ensure victory, Jephtha promised to sacrifice the first creature to meet him on his return. Unfortunately, his only daughter outstripped his dog and was the victim of his vow. The biblical story is told in
Judges 11.

POLONIUS: What follows then, my lord?

HAMLET: Why—

> "As by lot, God wot"   365

and then, you know,

> "It came to pass, as most like it was."

The first row of the pious chanson[6] will show you more, for look where my abridgement[7] comes.

[*Enter the* PLAYERS.]

You are welcome, masters; welcome, all.—I am glad to see thee well.—Welcome, 370 good friends.—O, old friend! Why, thy face is valanced[8] since I saw thee last. Com'st thou to beard me in Denmark?—What, my young lady and mistress? By'r lady, your ladyship is nearer to heaven than when I saw you last by the altitude of a chopine.[9] Pray God your voice, like a piece of uncurrent gold, be not cracked within the ring.—Masters, you are all welcome. We'll e'en to't like 375 French falconers, fly at anything we see. We'll have a speech straight. Come give us a taste of your quality,[1] come a passionate speech.

FIRST PLAYER: What speech, my good lord?

HAMLET: I heard thee speak me a speech once, but it was never acted, or if it was, not above once, for the play, I remember, pleased not the million; 'twas caviary 380 to the general.[2] But it was—as I received it, and others whose judgments in such matters cried in the top of[3] mine—an excellent play, well digested[4] in the scenes, set down with as much modesty as cunning. I remember one said there were no sallets[5] in the lines to make the matter savory, nor no matter in the phrase that might indict the author of affectation, but called it an honest 385 method, as wholesome as sweet, and by very much more handsome than fine. One speech in't I chiefly loved. 'Twas Æneas' tale to Dido, and thereabout of it especially where he speaks of Priam's slaughter.[6] If it live in your memory, begin at this line—let me see, let me see:

> "The rugged Pyrrhus, like th' Hyrcanian beast"[7]—   390

'tis not so; it begins with Pyrrhus—

> "The rugged Pyrrhus, he whose sable arms,
> Black as his purpose, did the night resemble
> When he lay couchèd in th' ominous horse,[8]
> Hath now this dread and black complexion smeared   395
> With heraldry more dismal; head to foot

---

6. Song. *Row*: stanza.   7. That which cuts short by interrupting.   8. Fringed (with a beard).
9. A reference to the contemporary theatrical practice of using boys to play women's parts. The company's "lady" has grown in height by the size of a woman's thick-soled shoe, "chopine," since Hamlet saw him last. The next sentence refers to the possibility, suggested by his growth, that the young actor's voice may soon begin to change.   1. Trade.   2. Caviar to the masses (i.e., pearls before swine).
3. Were weightier than.   4. Arranged.   5. Spicy passages.
6. Aeneas, fleeing with his band from fallen Troy (Ilium), arrives in Carthage, where he tells Dido, the queen of Carthage, of the fall of Troy. Here he is describing the death of Priam, the aged king of Troy, at the hands of Pyrrhus, the son of the slain Achilles.   7. Tiger.   8. That is, the Trojan horse.

Now is he total gules, horridly tricked[9]
With blood of fathers, mothers, daughters, sons,
Baked and impasted with the parching[1] streets,
400   That lend a tyrannous and a damnèd light
To their lord's murder. Roasted in wrath and fire,
And thus o'er-sizèd with coagulate[2] gore,
With eyes like carbuncles, the hellish Pyrrhus
Old grandsire Priam seeks."

405   So proceed you.
POLONIUS: Fore God, my lord, well spoken, with good accent and good
discretion.
FIRST PLAYER: "Anon he finds him[3]
Striking too short at Greeks. His antique[4] sword,
410   Rebellious[5] to his arm, lies where it falls,
Repugnant to command. Unequal matched,
Pyrrhus at Priam drives, in rage strikes wide.
But with the whiff and wind of his fell sword
Th' unnervèd father falls. Then senseless[6] Ilium,
415   Seeming to feel this blow, with flaming top
Stoops[7] to his base, and with a hideous crash
Takes prisoner Pyrrhus' ear. For, lo! his sword,
Which was declining[8] on the milky head
Of reverend Priam, seemed i' th' air to stick.
420   So as a painted tyrant Pyrrhus stood,
And like a neutral to his will and matter,[9]
Did nothing.
But as we often see, against some storm,
A silence in the heavens, the rack[1] stand still,
425   The bold winds speechless, and the orb below
As hush as death, anon the dreadful thunder
Doth rend the region; so, after Pyrrhus' pause,
A rousèd vengeance sets him new awork,[2]
And never did the Cyclops' hammers fall
430   On Mars's armor, forged for proof eterne,[3]
With less remorse than Pyrrhus' bleeding sword
Now falls on Priam.
Out, out, thou strumpet, Fortune! All you gods,
In general synod take away her power,
435   Break all the spokes and fellies[4] from her wheel,
And bowl the round nave[5] down the hill of heaven
As low as to the fiends."
POLONIUS: This is too long.

9. Adorned. *Total gules*: completely red.   1. Burning. *Impasted*: crusted.   2. Clotted. *O'er-sizèd*: glued over.
3. That is, Pyrrhus finds Priam.   4. Which he used when young.   5. Refractory.   6. Without feeling.
7. Falls.   8. About to fall.   9. Between his will and the fulfillment of it.   1. Clouds.   2. To work.
3. Mars, as befits a Roman war god, had armor made for him by the blacksmith god Vulcan and his assistants, the Cyclopes. It was suitably impenetrable, of "proof eterne."   4. Parts of the rim.
5. Hub. *Bowl*: roll.

HAMLET: It shall to the barber's with your beard.—Prithee say on. He's for a jig,[6]
or a tale of bawdry, or he sleeps. Say on; come to Hecuba.[7]   440

FIRST PLAYER: "But who, ah woe! had seen the moblèd[8] queen—"

HAMLET: "The mobled queen"?

POLONIUS: That's good. "Mobled queen" is good.

FIRST PLAYER: "Run barefoot up and down, threat'ning the flames
With bisson rheum, a clout[9] upon that head   445
Where late the diadem stood, and for a robe,
About her lank and all o'er-teemèd loins,
A blanket, in the alarm of fear caught up—
Who this had seen, with tongue in venom steeped,
'Gainst Fortune's state[1] would treason have pronounced.   450
But if the gods themselves did see her then,
When she saw Pyrrhus make malicious sport
In mincing[2] with his sword her husband's limbs,
The instant burst of clamor that she made,
Unless things mortal move them not at all,   455
Would have made milch[3] the burning eyes of heaven,
And passion in the gods."

POLONIUS: Look whe'r[4] he has not turned his color, and has tears in's eyes. Prithee
no more.

HAMLET: 'Tis well. I'll have thee speak out the rest of this soon.—Good my lord,   460
will you see the players well bestowed?[5] Do you hear, let them be well used, for
they are the abstract[6] and brief chronicles of the time; after your death you
were better have a bad epitaph than their ill report while you live.

POLONIUS: My lord, I will use them according to their desert.

HAMLET: God's bodkin, man, much better. Use every man after his desert, and   465
who shall 'scape whipping? Use them after your own honor and dignity. The
less they deserve, the more merit is in your bounty. Take them in.

POLONIUS: Come, sirs.

HAMLET: Follow him, friends. We'll hear a play tomorrow.
                                                                   [*Aside to* FIRST PLAYER.]

Dost thou hear me, old friend, can you play "The Murder of Gonzago"?   470

FIRST PLAYER: Ay, my lord.

HAMLET: We'll ha't tomorrow night. You could for a need study a speech of some
dozen or sixteen lines which I would set down and insert in't, could you not?

FIRST PLAYER: Ay, my lord.

HAMLET: Very well. Follow that lord, and look you mock him not.   475
                                                       [*Exeunt* POLONIUS *and* PLAYERS.]

My good friends, I'll leave you till night. You are welcome to Elsinore.

ROSENCRANTZ: Good my lord.   [*Exeunt* ROSENCRANTZ *and* GUILDENSTERN.]

HAMLET: Ay, so God b'wi'ye. Now I am alone.
O, what a rogue and peasant slave am I!

---

6. A comic act.
7. Hecuba was the wife of Priam and queen of Troy. Her "loins" are described below as "o'erteemèd"
because of her unusual fertility. The number of her children varies in different accounts, but twenty is a
safe minimum.   8. Muffled (in a hood).   9. Cloth. *Bisson rheum*: blinding tears.   1. Government.
2. Cutting up.   3. Tearful (literally, milk-giving).   4. Whether.   5. Provided for.   6. Summary.

480   Is it not monstrous that this player here,
         But in a fiction, in a dream of passion,
         Could force his soul so to his own conceit[7]
         That from her working all his visage wanned;[8]
         Tears in his eyes, distraction in his aspect[9]
485   A broken voice, and his whole function suiting
         With forms to his conceit? And all for nothing,
         For Hecuba!
         What's Hecuba to him or he to Hecuba,
         That he should weep for her? What would he do
490   Had he the motive and the cue for passion
         That I have? He would drown the stage with tears,
         And cleave the general ear with horrid speech,
         Make mad the guilty, and appal the free,
         Confound the ignorant, and amaze indeed
495   The very faculties of eyes and ears.
         Yet I,
         A dull and muddy-mettled rascal, peak[1]
         Like John-a-dreams, unpregnant[2] of my cause,
         And can say nothing; no, not for a king
500   Upon whose property and most dear life
         A damned defeat was made. Am I a coward?
         Who calls me villain, breaks my pate across,
         Plucks off my beard and blows it in my face,
         Tweaks me by the nose, gives me the lie i' th' throat
505   As deep as to the lungs? Who does me this?
         Ha, 'swounds, I should take it; for it cannot be
         But I am pigeon-livered and lack gall[3]
         To make oppression bitter, or ere this
         I should 'a fatted all the region kites[4]
510   With this slave's offal. Bloody, bawdy villain!
         Remorseless, treacherous, lecherous, kindless[5] villain!
         O, vengeance!
         Why, what an ass am I! This is most brave,
         That I, the son of a dear father murdered,
515   Prompted to my revenge by heaven and hell,
         Must like a whore unpack[6] my heart with words,
         And fall a-cursing like a very drab,
         A scullion![7] Fie upon't! foh!
         About, my brains. Hum—I have heard
520   That guilty creatures sitting at a play,
         Have by the very cunning of the scene
         Been struck so to the soul that presently

---

7. Imagination.   8. Grew pale.   9. Face.   1. Mope. *Muddy-mettled*: dull-spirited.
2. Not quickened by. *John-a-dreams*: a man dreaming.   3. Bitterness.   4. Birds of prey of the area.
5. Unnatural.   6. Relieve.
7. In some versions of the play, the word "stallion," a slang term for a prostitute, appears in place of "scullion."

They have proclaimed⁸ their malefactions;
For murder, though it have no tongue, will speak
With most miraculous organ. I'll have these players   525
Play something like the murder of my father
Before mine uncle. I'll observe his looks.
I'll tent him to the quick. If 'a do blench,⁹
I know my course. The spirit that I have seen
May be a devil, and the devil hath power   530
T' assume a pleasing shape, yea, and perhaps
Out of my weakness and my melancholy,
As he is very potent with such spirits,
Abuses me to damn me. I'll have grounds
More relative¹ than this. The play's the thing   535
Wherein I'll catch the conscience of the king.   [*Exit.*]

ACT III

Scene 1

A room in the castle. Enter KING, QUEEN, POLONIUS, OPHELIA, ROSENCRANTZ *and*
GUILDENSTERN.

KING: And can you by no drift of conference²
  Get from him why he puts on this confusion,
  Grating so harshly all his days of quiet
  With turbulent³ and dangerous lunacy?
ROSENCRANTZ: He does confess he feels himself distracted,   5
  But from what cause 'a will by no means speak.
GUILDENSTERN: Nor do we find him forward to be sounded,⁴
  But with a crafty madness keeps aloof
  When we would bring him on to some confession
  Of his true state.
QUEEN: Did he receive you well?   10
ROSENCRANTZ: Most like a gentleman.
GUILDENSTERN: But with much forcing of his disposition.⁵
ROSENCRANTZ: Niggard of question, but of our demands⁶
  Most free in his reply.
QUEEN: Did you assay⁷ him
  To any pastime?   15
ROSENCRANTZ: Madam, it so fell out that certain players
  We o'er-raught⁸ on the way. Of these we told him,
  And there did seem in him a kind of joy
  To hear of it. They are here about the court,
  And as I think, they have already order   20
  This night to play before him.
POLONIUS: 'Tis most true,

---

8. Admitted.   9. Turn pale. *Tent*: try.   1. Conclusive.   2. Line of conversation.   3. Disturbing.
4. Questioned. *Forward*: eager.   5. Mood.   6. To our questions.   7. Tempt.   8. Passed.

And he beseeched me to entreat your majesties
To hear and see the matter.[9]

KING: With all my heart, and it doth much content me
25   To hear him so inclined.
      Good gentlemen, give him a further edge,
      And drive his purpose[1] into these delights.

ROSENCRANTZ: We shall, my lord.   [*Exeunt* ROSENCRANTZ *and* GUILDENSTERN.]

KING: Sweet Gertrude, leave us too,
      For we have closely sent for Hamlet hither,
30   That he, as 'twere by accident, may here
      Affront[2] Ophelia.
      Her father and myself (lawful espials[3])
      Will so bestow ourselves that, seeing unseen,
      We may of their encounter frankly judge,
35   And gather by him, as he is behaved,
      If't be th' affliction of his love or no
      That thus he suffers for.

QUEEN: I shall obey you.—
      And for your part, Ophelia, I do wish
      That your good beauties be the happy cause
40   Of Hamlet's wildness. So shall I hope your virtues
      Will bring him to his wonted[4] way again,
      To both your honors.

OPHELIA: Madam, I wish it may.   [*Exit* QUEEN.]

POLONIUS: Ophelia, walk you here.—Gracious,[5] so please you,
      We will bestow ourselves.—[*To* OPHELIA.] Read on this book,
45   That show of such an exercise may color[6]
      Your loneliness.—We are oft to blame in this,
      'Tis too much proved, that with devotion's visage
      And pious action we do sugar o'er
      The devil himself.

50 KING: [*Aside.*]   O, 'tis too true.
      How smart a lash that speech doth give my conscience!
      The harlot's cheek, beautied with plast'ring[7] art,
      Is not more ugly to the thing that helps it
      Than is my deed to my most painted word.
      O heavy burden!

55 POLONIUS: I hear him coming. Let's withdraw, my lord.

                               [*Exeunt* KING *and* POLONIUS.]

      [*Enter* HAMLET.]

HAMLET: To be, or not to be, that is the question:
      Whether 'tis nobler in the mind to suffer
      The slings and arrows of outrageous fortune,
      Or to take arms against a sea of troubles,
60   And by opposing end them. To die, to sleep—

---

9. Performance.   1. Sharpen his intention.   2. Confront.   3. Justified spies.   4. Usual.
5. Majesty.   6. Explain. *Exercise*: act of devotion.   7. Thickly painted.

No more; and by a sleep to say we end
The heartache, and the thousand natural shocks
That flesh is heir to. 'Tis a consummation
Devoutly to be wished—to die, to sleep—
To sleep, perchance to dream, ay there's the rub;   65
For in that sleep of death what dreams may come
When we have shuffled off this mortal coil[8]
Must give us pause—there's the respect[9]
That makes calamity of so long life.
For who would bear the whips and scorns of time,   70
Th' oppressor's wrong, the proud man's contumely,[1]
The pangs of despised love, the law's delay,
The insolence of office, and the spurns[2]
That patient merit of th' unworthy takes,
When he himself might his quietus[3] make   75
With a bare bodkin? Who would fardels[4] bear,
To grunt and sweat under a weary life,
But that the dread of something after death,
The undiscovered country, from whose bourn[5]
No traveller returns, puzzles the will,   80
And makes us rather bear those ills we have
Than fly to others that we know not of?
Thus conscience does make cowards of us all;
And thus the native[6] hue of resolution
Is sicklied o'er with the pale cast of thought,   85
And enterprises of great pitch and moment[7]
With this regard their currents turn awry
And lose the name of action.—Soft you now,
The fair Ophelia.—Nymph, in thy orisons[8]
Be all my sins remembered.
OPHELIA: Good my lord,   90
  How does your honor for this many a day?
HAMLET: I humbly thank you, well, well, well.
OPHELIA: My lord, I have remembrances of yours
  That I have longèd long to re-deliver.
  I pray you now receive them.
HAMLET: No, not I,   95
  I never gave you aught.
OPHELIA: My honored lord, you know right well you did,
  And with them words of so sweet breath composed
  As made the things more rich. Their perfume lost,
  Take these again, for to the noble mind   100
  Rich gifts wax[9] poor when givers prove unkind.
  There, my lord.
HAMLET: Ha, ha! are you honest?[1]

8. Turmoil. 9. Consideration. 1. Insulting behavior. 2. Rejections. 3. Settlement.
4. Burdens. *Bodkin*: dagger. 5. Boundary. 6. Natural. 7. Importance. *Pitch*: height. 8. Prayers.
9. Become. 1. Chaste.

OPHELIA: My lord?

105 HAMLET: Are you fair?

OPHELIA: What means your lordship?

HAMLET: That if you be honest and fair, your honesty should admit no discourse
to your beauty.

OPHELIA: Could beauty, my lord, have better commerce[2] than with honesty?

110 HAMLET: Ay, truly, for the power of beauty will sooner transform honesty from
what it is to a bawd than the force of honesty can translate beauty into his
likeness. This was sometimes a paradox, but now the time gives it proof. I did
love you once.

OPHELIA: Indeed, my lord, you made me believe so.

115 HAMLET: You should not have believed me, for virtue cannot so inoculate[3] our
old stock but we shall relish of it. I loved you not.

OPHELIA: I was the more deceived.

HAMLET: Get thee to a nunnery.[4] Why wouldst thou be a breeder of sinners? I am
myself indifferent[5] honest, but yet I could accuse me of such things that it
120 were better my mother had not borne me: I am very proud, revengeful, ambitious, with more offences at my beck[6] than I have thoughts to put them in,
imagination to give them shape, or time to act them in. What should such
fellows as I do crawling between earth and heaven? We are arrant[7] knaves all;
believe none of us. Go thy ways to a nunnery. Where's your father?

125 OPHELIA: At home, my lord.

HAMLET: Let the doors be shut upon him, that he may play the fool nowhere but
in's own house. Farewell.

OPHELIA: O, help him, you sweet heavens!

HAMLET: If thou dost marry, I'll give thee this plague for thy dowry: be thou as
130 chaste as ice, as pure as snow, thou shalt not escape calumny. Get thee to a
nunnery, farewell. Or if thou wilt needs marry, marry a fool, for wise men
know well enough what monsters[8] you make of them. To a nunnery, go, and
quickly too. Farewell.

OPHELIA: Heavenly powers, restore him!

135 HAMLET: I have heard of your paintings, too, well enough. God hath given you
one face, and you make yourselves another. You jig, you amble, and you lisp;[9]
you nickname God's creatures, and make your wantonness your ignorance.[1]
Go to, I'll no more on't, it hath made me mad. I say we will have no more marriage. Those that are married already, all but one, shall live. The rest shall
140 keep as they are. To a nunnery, go.   [Exit.]

OPHELIA: O, what a noble mind is here o'erthrown!
    The courtier's, soldier's, scholar's, eye, tongue, sword,
    Th' expectancy and rose[2] of the fair state,
    The glass of fashion and the mould[3] of form,
145   Th' observed of all observers, quite quite down!

---

2. Intercourse.   3. Change by grafting.
4. With typical ribaldry Hamlet uses "nunnery" in two senses, the second as a slang term for brothel.
5. Moderately.   6. Command.   7. Thorough.   8. Horned because cuckolded.
9. Walk and talk affectedly.
1. Hamlet means that women call things by pet names and then blame the affectation on ignorance.
2. Ornament. *Expectancy*: hope.   3. Model. *Glass*: mirror.

And I of ladies most deject and wretched,
That sucked the honey of his music[4] vows,
Now see that noble and most sovereign reason
Like sweet bells jangled, out of time and harsh;
That unmatched form and feature of blown[5] youth   150
Blasted with ecstasy. O, woe is me
T' have seen what I have seen, see what I see!

[*Enter* KING *and* POLONIUS.]

KING: Love! His affections do not that way tend,
    Nor what he spake, though it lacked form a little,
    Was not like madness. There's something in his soul   155
    O'er which his melancholy sits on brood,[6]
    And I do doubt the hatch and the disclose[7]
    Will be some danger; which to prevent,
    I have in quick determination
    Thus set it down: he shall with speed to England   160
    For the demand of our neglected tribute.
    Haply the seas and countries different,
    With variable objects, shall expel
    This something-settled matter in his heart
    Whereon his brains still beating puts him thus   165
    From fashion of himself. What think you on't?
POLONIUS: It shall do well. But yet do I believe
    The origin and commencement of his grief
    Sprung from neglected love.—How now, Ophelia?
    You need not tell us what Lord Hamlet said,   170
    We heard it all.—My lord, do as you please,
    But if you hold it fit, after the play
    Let his queen-mother all alone entreat him
    To show his grief. Let her be round[8] with him,
    And I'll be placed, so please you, in the ear[9]   175
    Of all their conference. If she find him not,[1]
    To England send him; or confine him where
    Your wisdom best shall think.
KING: It shall be so.
    Madness in great ones must not unwatched go.   [*Exeunt.*]

Scene 2

A public room in the castle. Enter HAMLET *and three of the* PLAYERS.

HAMLET: Speak the speech, I pray you, as I pronounced it to you, trippingly on
the tongue; but if you mouth it as many of our players do, I had as lief the
town-crier spoke my lines. Nor do not saw the air too much with your hand
thus, but use all gently, for in the very torrent, tempest, and as I may say,

---

4. Musical.   5. Full-blown.   6. That is, like a hen.   7. Result. *Doubt:* fear.   8. Direct.   9. Hearing.
1. Does not discover his problem.

5   whirlwind of your passion, you must acquire and beget a temperance that
     may give it smoothness. O, it offends me to the soul to hear a robustious
     periwig-pated[2] fellow tear a passion to tatters, to very rags, to split the ears of
     the groundlings, who for the most part are capable of [3] nothing but inexpli-
     cable dumb shows and noise. I would have such a fellow whipped for o'erdoing
10   Termagant. It out-herods Herod.[4] Pray you avoid it.
FIRST PLAYER: I warrant your honor.
HAMLET: Be not too tame neither, but let your own discretion be your tutor. Suit
     the action to the word, the word to the action, with this special observance,
     that you o'erstep not the modesty of nature; for anything so o'erdone is from[5]
15   the purpose of playing, whose end both at the first, and now, was and is, to
     hold as 'twere the mirror up to nature, to show virtue her own feature, scorn
     her own image, and the very age and body of the time his form and pressure.[6]
     Now this overdone, or come tardy off, though it makes the unskilful[7] laugh,
     cannot but make the judicious grieve, the censure[8] of the which one must in
20   your allowance o'erweigh a whole theatre of others. O, there be players that I
     have seen play—and heard others praise, and that highly—not to speak it pro-
     fanely, that neither having th' accent of Christians, nor the gait of Christian,
     pagan, nor man, have so strutted and bellowed that I have thought some of
     nature's journeymen[9] had made men, and not made them well, they imitated
25   humanity so abominably.
FIRST PLAYER: I hope we have reformed that indifferently[1] with us, sir.
HAMLET: O, reform it altogether. And let those that play your clowns speak no
     more than is set down for them, for there be of them that will themselves
     laugh, to set on some quantity of barren[2] spectators to laugh too, though in
30   the meantime some necessary question of the play be then to be considered.
     That's villainous, and shows a most pitiful ambition in the fool that uses it.
     Go, make you ready.   [Exeunt PLAYERS.]

     [Enter POLONIUS, GUILDENSTERN, and ROSENCRANTZ.]

     How now, my lord? Will the king hear this piece of work?
POLONIUS: And the queen too, and that presently.
35   HAMLET: Bid the players make haste.   [Exit POLONIUS.]
     Will you two help to hasten them?
ROSENCRANTZ: Ay, my lord.   [Exeunt they two.]
HAMLET: What, ho, Horatio!

     [Enter HORATIO.]

HORATIO: Here, sweet lord, at your service.
40   HAMLET: Horatio, thou art e'en as just a man
     As e'er my conversation coped[3] withal.
HORATIO: O my dear lord!
HAMLET: Nay, do not think I flatter,

---

2. Bewigged. *Robustious*: noisy.
3. That is, capable of understanding. *Groundlings*: the spectators who paid least.
4. Termagant, a "Saracen" deity, and the biblical Herod were stock characters in popular drama noted for
the excesses of sound and fury used by their interpreters.   5. Contrary to.   6. Shape.   7. Ignorant.
8. Judgment.   9. Inferior craftsmen.   1. Somewhat.   2. Dull-witted.   3. Encountered.

For what advancement may I hope from thee,
That no revenue hast but thy good spirits
To feed and clothe thee? Why should the poor be flattered?   45
No, let the candied tongue lick absurd pomp,
And crook the pregnant[4] hinges of the knee
Where thrift[5] may follow fawning. Dost thou hear?
Since my dear soul was mistress of her choice
And could of men distinguish her election,   50
S'hath sealed thee for herself, for thou hast been
As one in suff'ring all that suffers nothing,
A man that Fortune's buffets and rewards
Hast ta'en with equal thanks; and blest are those
Whose blood and judgment are so well commingled   55
That they are not a pipe[6] for Fortune's finger
To sound what stop[7] she please. Give me that man
That is not passion's slave, and I will wear him
In my heart's core, ay, in my heart of heart,
As I do thee. Something too much of this.   60
There is a play tonight before the king.
One scene of it comes near the circumstance
Which I have told thee of my father's death.
I prithee, when thou seest that act afoot,
Even with the very comment[8] of thy soul   65
Observe my uncle. If his occulted[9] guilt
Do not itself unkennel[1] in one speech,
It is a damnèd ghost that we have seen,
And my imaginations are as foul
As Vulcan's stithy. Give him heedful note,[2]   70
For I mine eyes will rivet to his face,
And after we will both our judgments join
In censure of his seeming.[3]
HORATIO: Well, my lord.
If 'a steal aught the whilst this play in playing,
And 'scape detecting, I will pay[4] the theft.   75

[*Enter Trumpets and Kettledrums,* KING, QUEEN, POLONIUS, OPHELIA, ROSEN-
CRANTZ, GUILDENSTERN, *and other* LORDS *attendant.*]

HAMLET: They are coming to the play. I must be idle.
    Get you a place.
KING: How fares our cousin Hamlet?
HAMLET: Excellent, i' faith, of the chameleon's dish. I eat the air, promise-
    crammed. You cannot feed capons[5] so.
KING: I have nothing with this answer, Hamlet. These words are not mine.   80

---

4. Quick to bend.   5. Profit.   6. Musical instrument.   7. Note. *Sound:* play.   8. Keenest observation.
9. Hidden.   1. Break loose.   2. Careful attention. *Stithy:* smithy.   3. Manner.   4. Repay.
5. Castrated male chickens fattened for slaughter; also a term for fool. *Chameleon's dish:* a reference to a
popular belief that the chameleon subsisted on a diet of air. Hamlet has deliberately misunderstood the
king's question.

HAMLET: No, nor mine now. [*To* POLONIUS.] My lord, you played once i' th' university, you say?

POLONIUS: That did I, my lord, and was accounted a good actor.

HAMLET: What did you enact?

85 POLONIUS: I did enact Julius Cæsar. I was killed i' th' Capitol; Brutus killed me.[6]

HAMLET: It was a brute part of him to kill so capital a calf there. Be the players ready?

ROSENCRANTZ: Ay, my lord, they stay upon your patience.[7]

QUEEN: Come hither, my dear Hamlet, sit by me.

90 HAMLET: No, good mother, here's metal more attractive.

POLONIUS: [*To the* KING.] O, ho! do you mark that?

HAMLET: Lady, shall I lie in your lap?

[*Lying down at* OPHELIA's *feet.*]

OPHELIA: No, my lord.

HAMLET: I mean, my head upon your lap?

95 OPHELIA: Ay, my lord.

HAMLET: Do you think I meant country matters?[8]

OPHELIA: I think nothing, my lord.

HAMLET: That's a fair thought to lie between maids' legs.

OPHELIA: What is, my lord?

100 HAMLET: Nothing.

OPHELIA: You are merry, my lord.

HAMLET: Who, I?

OPHELIA: Ay, my lord.

HAMLET: O God, your only jig-maker![9] What should a man do but be merry? For
105 look you how cheerfully my mother looks, and my father died within's two
hours.

OPHELIA: Nay, 'tis twice two months, my lord.

HAMLET: So long? Nay then, let the devil wear black, for I'll have a suit of sables.
O heavens! die two months ago, and not forgotten yet? Then there's hope a
110 great man's memory may outlive his life half a year, but by'r lady 'a must build
churches then, or else shall 'a suffer not thinking on, with the hobby-horse,
whose epitaph is "For O, for O, the hobby-horse is forgot!"[1]

The trumpets sound. Dumb Show follows. Enter a KING *and a* QUEEN *very lovingly;
the* QUEEN *embracing him and he her. She kneels, and makes show of protestation
unto him. He takes her up, and declines[2] his head upon her neck. He lies him down
upon a bank of flowers; she, seeing him asleep, leaves him. Anon come in another
man, takes off his crown, kisses it, pours poison in the sleeper's ears, and leaves him.
The* QUEEN *returns, finds the* KING *dead, makes passionate action. The* POISONER
*with some three or four come in again, seem to condole with her. The dead body is
carried away. The* POISONER *woos the* QUEEN *with gifts; she seems harsh awhile, but
in the end accepts love.*
[*Exeunt.*]

6. The assassination of Julius Caesar by Brutus and others is the subject of another play by Shakespeare.
7. Leisure. *Stay*: wait.
8. Presumably, rustic misbehavior, but here and elsewhere in this exchange Hamlet treats Ophelia to
some ribald double meanings.   9. Writer of comic scenes.
1. In traditional games and dances one of the characters was a man represented as riding a horse. The
horse was made of something like cardboard and was worn about the "rider's" waist.   2. Lays.

OPHELIA: What means this, my lord?
HAMLET: Marry, this is miching mallecho;[3] it means mischief.
OPHELIA: Belike this show imports the argument[4] of the play.   115

[*Enter* PROLOGUE.]

HAMLET: We shall know by this fellow. The players cannot keep counsel; they'll tell all.
OPHELIA: Will 'a tell us what this show meant?
HAMLET: Ay, or any show that you will show him. Be not you ashamed to show, he'll not shame to tell you what it means.   120
OPHELIA: You are naught, you are naught. I'll mark[5] the play.
PROLOGUE: *For us, and for our tragedy,*
    Here stooping to your clemency,
    We beg your hearing patiently.   [*Exit.*]

HAMLET: Is this a prologue, or the posy[6] of a ring?   125
OPHELIA: 'Tis brief, my lord.
HAMLET: As woman's love.

[*Enter the* PLAYER KING *and* QUEEN.]

PLAYER KING: *Full thirty times hath Phœbus' cart gone round*
    Neptune's salt wash and Tellus' orbèd ground,
    And thirty dozen moons with borrowed sheen[7]   130
    About the world have times twelve thirties been,
    Since love our hearts and Hymen did our hands
    Unite comutual in most sacred bands.[8]

PLAYER QUEEN: *So many journeys may the sun and moon*
    Make us again count o'er ere love be done!   135
    But woe is me, you are so sick of late,
    So far from cheer and from your former state,
    That I distrust[9] you. Yet though I distrust,
    Discomfort you, my lord, it nothing must.
    For women's fear and love hold quantity,[1]   140
    In neither aught, or in extremity.[2]
    Now what my love is proof hath made you know,
    And as my love is sized,[3] my fear is so.
    Where love is great, the littlest doubts are fear;
    Where little fears grow great, great love grows there.   145

PLAYER KING: *Faith, I must leave thee, love, and shortly too;*
    My operant powers their functions leave[4] to do.
    And thou shalt live in this fair world behind,
    Honored, beloved, and haply one as kind
    For husband shalt thou—

---

3. Sneaking crime (from the Spanish *malhecho*, "evil deed").   4. Plot. *Imports*: explains.
5. Attend to. *Naught*: obscene.   6. Motto engraved inside.   7. Light.
8. The speech contains several references to Greek mythology. Phoebus was the sun god, and his chariot or "cart" is the sun. The "salt wash" of Neptune is the ocean; Tellus was an earth goddess, and her "orbed ground" is the Earth, or globe. Hymen was the god of marriage. *Comutual*: mutually.   9. Fear for.
1. Agree in weight.   2. Without regard to too much or too little.   3. In size.
4. Cease. *Operant powers*: active forces.

150   PLAYER QUEEN: *O, confound the rest!*
        Such love must needs be treason in my breast.
        In second husband let me be accurst!
        None wed the second but who killed the first.[5]
      HAMLET: That's wormwood.[6]
155   PLAYER QUEEN: *The instances[7] that second marriage move*
        Are base respects[8] of thrift, but none of love.
        A second time I kill my husband dead,
        When second husband kisses me in bed.
      PLAYER KING: *I do believe you think what now you speak,*
160   *But what we do determine oft we break.*
        Purpose is but the slave to memory,
        Of violent birth, but poor validity;
        Which now, like fruit unripe, sticks on the tree,
        But fall unshaken when they mellow be.
165   *Most necessary 'tis that we forget*
        To pay ourselves what to ourselves is debt.
        What to ourselves in passion we propose,
        The passion ending, doth the purpose lose.
        The violence of either grief or joy
170   *Their own enactures[9] with themselves destroy.*
        Where joy most revels, grief doth most lament;
        Grief joys, joy grieves, on slender accident.
        This world is not for aye,[1] nor 'tis not strange
        That even our loves should with our fortunes change;
175   *For 'tis a question left us yet to prove,*
        Whether love lead fortune, or else fortune love.
        The great man down, you mark his favorite flies;
        The poor advanced makes friends of enemies;
        And hitherto doth love on fortune tend,
180   *For who not needs shall never lack a friend,*
        And who in want a hollow[2] friend doth try,
        Directly seasons him[3] his enemy.
        But orderly to end where I begun,
        Our wills and fates do so contrary run
185   *That our devices[4] still are overthrown;*
        Our thoughts are ours, their ends none of our own.
        So think thou wilt no second husband wed,
        But die thy thoughts when thy first lord is dead.
      PLAYER QUEEN: *Nor earth to me give food, nor heaven light,*
190   *Sport and repose lock from me day and night,*
        To desperation turn my trust and hope,
        An anchor's cheer[5] in prison be my scope,
        Each opposite that blanks[6] the face of joy

---

5. Though there is some ambiguity, she seems to mean that the only kind of woman who would remarry is one who has killed or would kill her first husband.   6. *Wormwood*: bitter medicine.   7. Causes.
8. Concerns.   9. Actions.   1. Eternal.   2. False.   3. Ripens him into.   4. Plans.
5. Anchorite's (hermit's) food.   6. Blanches.

Meet what I would have well, and it destroy,
Both here and hence[7] *pursue me lasting strife,*   195
If once a widow, ever I be wife!

HAMLET: If she should break it now!

PLAYER KING: *'Tis deeply sworn. Sweet, leave me here awhile.*
My spirits grow dull, and fain I would beguile
The tedious day with sleep.   [*Sleeps.*]

PLAYER QUEEN: *Sleep rock thy brain,*   200
And never come mischance between us twain!   [*Exit.*]

HAMLET: Madam, how like you this play?

QUEEN: The lady doth protest too much, methinks.

HAMLET: O, but she'll keep her word.

KING: Have you heard the argument? Is there no offence in't?   205

HAMLET: No, no, they do but jest, poison in jest; no offence i' th' world.

KING: What do you call the play?

HAMLET: "The Mouse-trap." Marry, how? Tropically.[8] This play is the image of a
murder done in Vienna. Gonzago is the duke's name; his wife, Baptista. You
shall see anon. 'Tis a knavish piece of work, but what of that? Your majesty,   210
and we that have free souls, it touches us not. Let the galled jade wince, our
withers are unwrung.[9]

[*Enter* LUCIANUS.]

This is one Lucianus, nephew to the king.

OPHELIA: You are as good as a chorus, my lord.

HAMLET: I could interpret between you and your love, if I could see the puppets   215
dallying.

OPHELIA: You are keen, my lord, you are keen.

HAMLET: It would cost you a groaning to take off mine edge.

OPHELIA: Still better, and worse.

HAMLET: So you mistake your husbands.—Begin, murderer. Leave thy damnable   220
faces and begin. Come, the croaking raven doth bellow for revenge.

LUCIANUS: *Thoughts black, hands apt, drugs fit, and time agreeing,*
Confederate season,[1] *else no creature seeing,*
Thou mixture rank, of midnight weeds collected,
With Hecate's ban thrice blasted, thrice infected,[2]   225
Thy natural magic[3] *and dire property*
On wholesome life usurp immediately.   [*Pours the poison in his ears.*]

HAMLET: 'A poisons him i' th' garden for his estate. His name's Gonzago. The
story is extant, and written in very choice Italian. You shall see anon how the
murderer gets the love of Gonzago's wife.   230

OPHELIA: The king rises.

HAMLET: What, frighted with false fire?

QUEEN: How fares my lord?

POLONIUS: Give o'er the play.

---

7. In the next world.   8. Figuratively.
9. A "galled jade" is a horse, particularly one of poor quality, with a sore back. The "withers" are the ridge
between a horse's shoulders; "unwrung withers" are not chafed by the harness.
1. A helpful time for the crime.   2. Hecate was a classical goddess of witchcraft.   3. Native power.

235   KING: Give me some light. Away!
   POLONIUS: Lights, lights, lights!   [*Exeunt all but* HAMLET *and* HORATIO.]
   HAMLET:

> Why, let the strucken deer go weep,
>   The hart ungallèd[4] play.
> For some must watch while some must sleep;

240 >   Thus runs the world away.

Would not this, sir, and a forest of feathers[5]—if the rest of my fortunes turn
Turk with me—with two Provincial roses on my razed shoes, get me a fellowship in a cry of players?[6]

HORATIO: Half a share.

245   HAMLET: A whole one, I.

> For thou dost know, O Damon dear,[7]
>   This realm dismantled was
> Of Jove himself, and now reigns here
> A very, very—peacock.

250   HORATIO: You might have rhymed.
   HAMLET: O good Horatio, I'll take the ghost's word for a thousand pound. Didst
      perceive?
   HORATIO: Very well, my lord.
   HAMLET: Upon the talk of the poisoning.
255   HORATIO: I did very well note[8] him.
   HAMLET: Ah, ha! Come, some music. Come, the recorders.[9]

> For if the king like not the comedy.
> Why then, belike he likes it not, perdy.[1]

Come, some music.

[*Enter* ROSENCRANTZ *and* GUILDENSTERN.]

260   GUILDENSTERN: Good my lord, vouchsafe me a word with you.
   HAMLET: Sir, a whole history.
   GUILDENSTERN: The king, sir—
   HAMLET: Ay, sir, what of him?
   GUILDENSTERN: Is in his retirement marvellous distempered.[2]
265   HAMLET: With drink, sir?
   GUILDENSTERN: No, my lord, with choler.[3]
   HAMLET: Your wisdom should show itself more richer to signify this to the doc-
      tor, for for me to put him to his purgation[4] would perhaps plunge him into
      more choler.

---

4. Uninjured.   5. Plumes.
6. Hamlet asks Horatio if "this" recitation, accompanied with a player's costume, including plumes and
rosettes on shoes that have been slashed for decorative effect, might not entitle him to become a shareholder in a theatrical company in the event that Fortune goes against him, "turn Turk." *Cry*: company.
7. Damon was a common name for a young man or a shepherd in lyric, especially pastoral poetry. Jove
was the chief god of the Romans. Readers may supply for themselves the rhyme referred to by Horatio.
8. Observe.   9. Wooden, end-blown flutes.   1. *Perdy*, that is, *par Dieu* (French for "by God").
2. Vexed. *Retirement*: place to which he has retired.   3. Bile (anger).   4. Treatment with a laxative.

GUILDENSTERN: Good my lord, put your discourse into some frame,[5] and start 270
not so wildly from my affair.

HAMLET: I am tame, sir. Pronounce.

GUILDENSTERN: The queen your mother, in most great affliction of spirit, hath
sent me to you.

HAMLET: You are welcome. 275

GUILDENSTERN: Nay, good my lord, this courtesy is not of the right breed. If it
shall please you to make me a wholesome[6] answer, I will do your mother's
commandment. If not, your pardon and my return[7] shall be the end of my
business.

HAMLET: Sir, I cannot. 280

ROSENCRANTZ: What, my lord?

HAMLET: Make you a wholesome answer; my wit's diseased. But, sir, such answer
as I can make, you shall command, or rather, as you say, my mother. Therefore no more, but to the matter. My mother, you say—

ROSENCRANTZ: Then thus she says: your behavior hath struck her into amaze- 285
ment and admiration.[8]

HAMLET: O wonderful son, that can so stonish a mother! But is there no sequel at
the heels of his mother's admiration? Impart.[9]

ROSENCRANTZ: She desires to speak with you in her closet[1] ere you go to bed.

HAMLET: We shall obey, were she ten times our mother. Have you any further 290
trade[2] with us?

ROSENCRANTZ: My lord, you once did love me.

HAMLET: And do still, by these pickers and stealers.[3]

ROSENCRANTZ: Good my lord, what is your cause of distemper? You do surely bar
the door upon your own liberty, if you deny your griefs to your friend. 295

HAMLET: Sir, I lack advancement.

ROSENCRANTZ: How can that be, when you have the voice of the king himself for
your succession in Denmark?

HAMLET: Ay, sir, but "while the grass grows"—the proverb[4] is something musty.

[*Enter the* PLAYERS *with recorders.*]

O, the recorders! Let me see one. To withdraw with you[5]—why do you 300
go about to recover the wind of me, as if you would drive me into a toil?[6]

GUILDENSTERN: O my lord, if my duty be too bold, my love is too unmannerly.

HAMLET: I do not well understand that. Will you play upon this pipe?[7]

GUILDENSTERN: My lord, I cannot. 305

HAMLET: I pray you.

GUILDENSTERN: Believe me, I cannot.

HAMLET: I do beseech you.

GUILDENSTERN: I know no touch of it,[8] my lord.

HAMLET: It is as easy as lying. Govern these ventages[9] with your fingers and 310

5. Order. *Discourse*: speech.   6. Reasonable.   7. That is, to the queen.   8. Wonder.   9. Tell me.
1. Bedroom.   2. Business.   3. Hands.   4. The proverb ends "the horse starves."
5. Let me step aside.
6. The figure is from hunting. Hamlet asks why Guildenstern is attempting to get windward of him, as if
he would drive him into a net.   7. Recorder.   8. Have no ability.
9. Holes. *Govern*: cover and uncover.

thumb, give it breath with your mouth, and it will discourse most eloquent music. Look you, these are the stops.[1]

GUILDENSTERN: But these cannot I command to any utt'rance of harmony. I have not the skill.

315 HAMLET: Why, look you now, how unworthy a thing you make of me! You would play upon me, you would seem to know my stops, you would pluck out the heart of my mystery, you would sound[2] me from my lowest note to the top of my compass;[3] and there is much music, excellent voice, in this little organ, yet cannot you make it speak. 'Sblood, do you think I am easier to be played on

320 than a pipe? Call me what instrument you will, though you can fret[4] me, you cannot play upon me.

    [*Enter* POLONIUS.]

    God bless you, sir!

POLONIUS: My lord, the queen would speak with you, and presently.[5]

HAMLET: Do you see yonder cloud that's almost in shape of a camel?

325 POLONIUS: By th' mass, and 'tis like a camel indeed.

HAMLET: Methinks it is like a weasel.

POLONIUS: It is backed like a weasel.

HAMLET: Or like a whale.

POLONIUS: Very like a whale.

330 HAMLET: Then I will come to my mother by and by. [*Aside.*] They fool me to the top of my bent.[6]—I will come by and by.

POLONIUS: I will say so.   [*Exit.*]

HAMLET: "By and by" is easily said. Leave me, friends.   [*Exeunt all but* HAMLET.]
    'Tis now the very witching time of night,

335   When churchyards yawn, and hell itself breathes out
    Contagion to this world. Now could I drink hot blood,
    And do such bitter business as the day
    Would quake to look on. Soft, now to my mother.
    O heart, lose not thy nature; let not ever

340   The soul of Nero[7] enter this firm bosom.
    Let me be cruel, not unnatural;
    I will speak daggers to her, but use none.
    My tongue and soul in this be hypocrites—
    How in my words somever she be shent,[8]

345   To give them seals[9] never, my soul, consent!   [*Exit.*]

Scene 3

A room in the castle. Enter KING, ROSENCRANTZ *and* GUILDENSTERN.

KING: I like him not,[1] nor stands it safe with us
    To let his madness range.[2] Therefore prepare you.

---

1. Wind-holes. 2. Play. 3. Range.
4. "Fret" is used in a double sense, to annoy and to play a guitar or similar instrument using the "frets" or small bars on the neck. 5. At once. 6. Treat me as an utter fool.
7. The Roman emperor Nero, known for his excesses, was believed to have been responsible for the death of his mother. 8. Shamed. 9. Fulfillment in action. 1. Distrust him. 2. Roam freely.

I your commission will forthwith dispatch,
And he to England shall along with you.
The terms of our estate[3] may not endure   5
Hazard so near's as doth hourly grow
Out of his brows.
GUILDENSTERN: We will ourselves provide,[4]
   Most holy and religious fear it is
   To keep those many many bodies safe
   That live and feed upon your majesty.   10
ROSENCRANTZ: The single and peculiar[5] life is bound
   With all the strength and armor of the mind
   To keep itself from noyance,[6] but much more
   That spirit upon whose weal[7] depends and rests
   The lives of many. The cess[8] of majesty   15
   Dies not alone, but like a gulf[9] doth draw
   What's near it with it. It is a massy[1] wheel
   Fixed on the summit of the highest mount,
   To whose huge spokes ten thousand lesser things
   Are mortised and adjoined,[2] which when it falls,   20
   Each small annexment, petty consequence,
   Attends[3] the boist'rous ruin. Never alone
   Did the king sigh, but with a general groan.
KING: Arm you, I pray you, to this speedy voyage,
   For we will fetters put about this fear,   25
   Which now goes too free-footed.
ROSENCRANTZ: We will haste us.
            [*Exeunt* ROSENCRANTZ *and* GUILDENSTERN.]

   [*Enter* POLONIUS.]

POLONIUS: My lord, he's going to his mother's closet.
   Behind the arras I'll convey[4] myself
   To hear the process. I'll warrant she'll tax him home,[5]
   And as you said, and wisely was it said,   30
   'Tis meet that some more audience than a mother,
   Since nature makes them partial, should o'erhear
   The speech, of vantage.[6] Fare you well, my liege.
   I'll call upon you ere you go to bed,
   And tell you what I know.
KING: Thanks, dear my lord. [*Exit* POLONIUS.] 35
   O, my offence is rank, it smells to heaven;
   It hath the primal eldest curse[7] upon't,
   A brother's murder. Pray can I not,
   Though inclination be as sharp as will.
   My stronger guilt defeats my strong intent,   40

---

3. Condition of the state.   4. Equip (for the journey).   5. Individual.   6. Harm.   7. Welfare.
8. Cessation.   9. Whirlpool.   1. Massive.   2. Attached.   3. Joins in.   4. Station.
5. Sharply. *Process*: proceedings.   6. From a position of vantage.   7. That is, of Cain.

And like a man to double business[8] bound,
I stand in pause where I shall first begin,
And both neglect. What if this cursèd hand
Were thicker than itself with brother's blood,

45 Is there not rain enough in the sweet heavens
To wash it white as snow? Whereto serves mercy
But to confront the visage of offence?
And what's in prayer but this twofold force,
To be forestallèd[9] ere we come to fall,

50 Or pardoned being down?[1] Then I'll look up.
My fault is past. But, O, what form of prayer
Can serve my turn? "Forgive me my foul murder"?
That cannot be, since I am still possessed
Of those effects[2] for which I did the murder—

55 My crown, mine own ambition, and my queen.
May one be pardoned and retain th' offence?[3]
In the corrupted currents of this world
Offence's gilded[4] hand may shove by justice,
And oft 'tis seen the wicked prize itself

60 Buys out the law. But 'tis not so above.
There is no shuffling; there the action[5] lies
In his true nature, and we ourselves compelled,
Even to the teeth and forehead of[6] our faults,
To give in evidence. What then? What rests?[7]

65 Try what repentance can. What can it not?
Yet what can it when one cannot repent?
O wretched state! O bosom black as death!
O limèd[8] soul, that struggling to be free
Art more engaged! Help, angels! Make assay.

70 Bow, stubborn knees, and heart with strings of steel,
Be soft as sinews of the new-born babe.
All may be well.   [He kneels.]

[Enter HAMLET.]

HAMLET: Now might I do it pat,[9] now 'a is a-praying,
And now I'll do't—and so 'a goes to heaven,
75 And so am I revenged. That would be scanned.[1]
A villain kills my father, and for that,
I, his sole son, do this same villain send
To heaven.
Why, this is hire and salary, not revenge.
80 'A took my father grossly, full of bread,[2]
With all his crimes broad blown, as flush[3] as May;
And how his audit stands who knows save heaven?

---

8. Two mutually opposed interests.   9. Prevented (from sin).   1. Having sinned.   2. Gains.
3. That is, benefits of the offense.   4. Bearing gold as a bribe.   5. Case at law.   6. Face-to-face with.
7. Remains.   8. Caught as with birdlime.   9. Easily.   1. Deserves consideration.
2. In a state of sin and without fasting.   3. Vigorous. *Broad blown*: full-blown.

But in our circumstance and course of thought
'Tis heavy with him; and am I then revenged
To take him in the purging of his soul,   85
When he is fit and seasoned[4] for his passage?
No.
Up, sword, and know thou a more horrid hent.[5]
When he is drunk, asleep, or in his rage,
Or in th' incestuous pleasure of his bed,   90
At game a-swearing, or about some act
That has no relish[6] of salvation in't—
Then trip him, that his heels may kick at heaven,
And that his soul may be as damned and black
As hell, whereto it goes. My mother stays.   95
This physic[7] but prolongs thy sickly days.   [*Exit.*]
KING: [*Rising.*] My words fly up, my thoughts remain below.
Words without thoughts never to heaven go.   [*Exit.*]

Scene 4

The Queen's chamber. Enter QUEEN *and* POLONIUS.

POLONIUS: 'A will come straight. Look you lay home to[8] him.
Tell him his pranks have been too broad[9] to bear with,
And that your grace hath screen'd[1] and stood between
Much heat and him. I'll silence me even here.
Pray you be round with him.   5
HAMLET: [*Within.*] Mother, mother, mother!
QUEEN: I'll warrant you. Fear[2] me not.
Withdraw, I hear him coming.

[POLONIUS *goes behind the arras. Enter* HAMLET.]

HAMLET: Now, mother, what's the matter?
QUEEN: Hamlet, thou hast thy father much offended.   10
HAMLET: Mother, you have my father much offended.
QUEEN: Come, come, you answer with an idle tongue.
HAMLET: Go, go, you question with a wicked tongue.
QUEEN: Why, how now, Hamlet?
HAMLET: What's the matter now?
QUEEN: Have you forgot me?
HAMLET: No, by the rood,[3] not so.   15
You are the queen, your husband's brother's wife,
And would it were not so, you are my mother.
QUEEN: Nay, then I'll set those to you that can speak.
HAMLET: Come, come, and sit you down. You shall not budge.
You go not till I set you up a glass[4]   20
Where you may see the inmost part of you.

---

4. Ready. 5. Opportunity. 6. Flavor. 7. Medicine. 8. Be sharp with. 9. Outrageous.
1. Acted as a fire screen. 2. Doubt. 3. Cross. 4. Mirror.

QUEEN: What wilt thou do? Thou wilt not murder me?
    Help, ho!
POLONIUS: [*Behind.*] What, ho! help!
25 HAMLET: [*Draws.*] How now, a rat?
    Dead for a ducat, dead!

[*Kills* POLONIUS *with a pass through the arras.*]

POLONIUS: [*Behind.*] O, I am slain!
QUEEN: O me, what hast thou done?
HAMLET: Nay, I know not.
    Is it the king?
30 QUEEN: O, what a rash and bloody deed is this!
HAMLET: A bloody deed!—almost as bad, good mother,
    As kill a king and marry with his brother.
QUEEN: As kill a king?
HAMLET: Ay, lady, it was my word.   [*Parting the arras.*]
    Thou wretched, rash, intruding fool, farewell!
35   I took thee for thy better. Take thy fortune.
    Thou find'st to be too busy[5] is some danger.—
    Leave wringing of your hands. Peace, sit you down
    And let me wring your heart, for so I shall
    If it be made of penetrable stuff,
40   If damnèd custom have not brazed it[6] so
    That it be proof and bulwark against sense.[7]
QUEEN: What have I done that thou dar'st wag thy tongue
    In noise so rude against me?
HAMLET: Such an act
    That blurs the grace and blush of modesty,
45   Calls virtue hypocrite, takes off the rose
    From the fair forehead of an innocent love.
    And sets a blister[8] there, makes marriage-vows
    As false as dicers' oaths. O, such a deed
    As from the body of contraction[9] plucks
50   The very soul, and sweet religion makes
    A rhapsody of words. Heaven's face does glow
    O'er this solidity and compound mass[1]
    With heated visage, as against the doom[2]—
    Is thought-sick at the act.
QUEEN: Ay me, what act
55   That roars so loud and thunders in the index?[3]
HAMLET: Look here upon this picture[4] and on this,
    The counterfeit presentment of two brothers.
    See what a grace was seated on this brow:
    Hyperion's curls, the front[5] of Jove himself,
60   An eye like Mars, to threaten and command,

5. Officious.   6. Plated it with brass.   7. Feeling. *Proof*: armor.   8. Brand.
9. The marriage contract.   1. Meaningless mass (Earth).   2. Judgment Day.
3. Table of contents.   4. Portrait.   5. Forehead.

A station like the herald Mercury[6]
New lighted[7] on a heaven-kissing hill—
A combination and a form indeed
Where every god did seem to set his seal,[8]
To give the world assurance of a man.   65
This was your husband. Look you now what follows.
Here is your husband, like a mildewed ear
Blasting his wholesome brother. Have you eyes?
Could you on this fair mountain leave to feed,
And batten[9] on this moor? Ha! have you eyes?   70
You cannot call it love, for at your age
The heyday in the blood is tame, it's humble,
And waits upon the judgment, and what judgment
Would step from this to this? Sense sure you have
Else could you not have motion, but sure that sense   75
Is apoplexed[1] for madness would not err,
Nor sense to ecstasy was ne'er so thralled
But it reserved some quantity[2] of choice
To serve in such a difference. What devil was't
That thus hath cozened you at hoodman-blind?[3]   80
Eyes without feeling, feeling without sight,
Ears without hands or eyes, smelling sans[4] all,
Or but a sickly part of one true sense
Could not so mope.[5] O shame! where is thy blush?
Rebellious hell,   85
If thou canst mutine[6] in a matron's bones,
To flaming youth let virtue be as wax
And melt in her own fire. Proclaim no shame
When the compulsive ardor gives the charge,[7]
Since frost itself as actively doth burn,   90
And reason panders[8] will.

QUEEN: O Hamlet, speak no more!
  Thou turn'st my eyes into my very soul;
  And there I see such black and grainèd[9] spots
  As will not leave their tinct.[1]

HAMLET: Nay, but to live
  In the rank sweat of an enseamèd[2] bed,   95
  Stewed in curruption, honeying and making love
  Over the nasty sty—

QUEEN: O, speak to me no more!
  These words like daggers enter in my ears;
  No more, sweet Hamlet.

HAMLET: A murderer and a villain,
  A slave that is not twentieth part the tithe[3]   100

6. In Roman mythology, Mercury served as the messenger of the gods. *Station*: bearing.
7. Newly alighted. 8. Mark of approval. 9. Feed greedily. 1. Paralyzed. 2. Power.
3. Blindman's buff. *Cozened*: cheated. 4. Without. 5. Be stupid. 6. Commit mutiny. 7. Attacks.
8. Pimps for. 9. Ingrained. 1. Lose their color. 2. Greasy. 3. One-tenth.

Of your precedent lord, a vice of kings,[4]
A cutpurse[5] of the empire and the rule,
That from a shelf the precious diadem stole
And put it in his pocket—

105 QUEEN: No more.

[*Enter* GHOST.]

HAMLET: A king of shreds and patches—
    Save me and hover o'er me with your wings,
    You heavenly guards! What would your gracious figure?
QUEEN: Alas, he's mad.
110 HAMLET: Do you not come your tardy[6] son to chide,
    That lapsed in time and passion lets go by
    Th' important acting of your dread command?
    O, say!
GHOST: Do not forget. This visitation
115   Is but to whet thy almost blunted purpose.
    But look, amazement on thy mother sits.
    O, step between her and her fighting soul!
    Conceit[7] in weakest bodies strongest works.
    Speak to her, Hamlet.
HAMLET: How is it with you, lady?
120 QUEEN: Alas, how is't with you,
    That you do bend[8] your eye on vacancy,
    And with th' incorporal air do hold discourse?
    Forth at your eyes your spirits wildly peep,
    And as the sleeping soldiers in th' alarm,
125   Your bedded hairs like life in excrements[9]
    Start up and stand an end. O gentle son,
    Upon the heat and flame of thy distemper
    Sprinkle cool patience. Whereon do you look?
HAMLET: On him, on him! Look you how pale he glares.
130   His form and cause conjoined,[1] preaching to stones,
    Would make them capable.[2]—Do not look upon me,
    Lest with this piteous action you convert
    My stern effects.[3] Then what I have to do
    Will want true color—tears perchance for blood.
135 QUEEN: To whom do you speak this?
HAMLET: Do you see nothing there?
QUEEN: Nothing at all, yet all that is I see.
HAMLET: Nor did you nothing hear?
QUEEN: No, nothing but ourselves.
140 HAMLET: Why, look you there. Look how it steals away.
    My father, in his habit[4] as he lived!
    Look where he goes even now out at the portal.   [*Exit* GHOST.]

4. The "Vice," a common figure in the popular drama, was a clown or buffoon. *Precedent lord*: first
husband.   5. Pickpocket.   6. Slow to act.   7. Imagination.   8. Turn.   9. Nails and hair.
1. Working together.   2. Of responding.   3. Deeds.   4. Clothing.

QUEEN: This is the very coinage[5] of your brain.
    This bodiless creation ecstasy[6]
    Is very cunning[7] in.
HAMLET: Ecstasy?   145
    My pulse as yours doth temperately keep time,
    And makes as healthful music. It is not madness
    That I have uttered. Bring me to the test,
    And I the matter will re-word, which madness
    Would gambol[8] from. Mother, for love of grace,   150
    Lay not that flattering unction[9] to your soul,
    That not your trespass but my madness speaks.
    It will but skin and film the ulcerous place
    Whiles rank corruption, mining[1] all within,
    Infects unseen. Confess yourself to heaven,   155
    Repent what's past, avoid what is to come.
    And do not spread the compost on the weeds,
    To make them ranker. Forgive me this my virtue,
    For in the fatness of these pursy[2] times
    Virtue itself of vice must pardon beg,   160
    Yea, curb[3] and woo for leave to do him good.
QUEEN: O Hamlet, thou hast cleft my heart in twain.
HAMLET: O, throw away the worser part of it,
    And live the purer with the other half.
    Good night—but go not to my uncle's bed.   165
    Assume a virtue, if you have it not.
    That monster custom[4] who all sense doth eat
    Of habits devil, is angel yet in this,
    That to the use of actions fair and good
    He likewise gives a frock or livery   170
    That aptly[5] is put on. Refrain tonight,
    And that shall lend a kind of easiness
    To the next abstinence; the next more easy;
    For use almost can change the stamp of nature,
    And either curb the devil, or throw him out   175
    With wondrous potency. Once more, good night,
    And when you are desirous to be blest,
    I'll blessing beg of you. For this same lord
    I do repent; but heaven hath pleased it so,
    To punish me with this, and this with me,   180
    That I must be their scourge and minister.
    I will bestow[6] him and will answer well
    The death I gave him. So, again, good night.
    I must be cruel only to be kind.
    Thus bad begins and worse remains behind.   185
    One word more, good lady.
QUEEN: What shall I do?

---

5. Invention.   6. Madness.   7. Skilled.   8. Shy away.   9. Ointment.   1. Undermining.
2. Bloated.   3. Bow.   4. Habit.   5. Easily.   6. Dispose of.

HAMLET: Not this, by no means, that I bid you do:
   Let the bloat[7] king tempt you again to bed,
   Pinch wanton[8] on your cheek, call you his mouse,
190   And let him, for a pair of reechy[9] kisses,
   Or paddling in your neck with his damned fingers,
   Make you to ravel[1] all this matter out,
   That I essentially am not in madness,
   But mad in craft. 'Twere good you let him know,
195   For who that's but a queen, fair, sober, wise,
   Would from a paddock, from a bat, a gib,[2]
   Such dear concernings hide? Who would so do?
   No, in despite of sense and secrecy,
   Unpeg the basket on the house's top,
200   Let the birds fly, and like the famous ape,
   To try conclusions, in the basket creep
   And break your own neck down.[3]
QUEEN: Be thou assured, if words be made of breath
   And breath of life, I have no life to breathe
205   What thou hast said to me.
HAMLET: I must to England; you know that?
QUEEN: Alack,
   I had forgot. 'Tis so concluded on.
HAMLET: There's letters sealed, and my two school-fellows,
   Whom I will trust as I will adders fanged,
210   They bear the mandate; they must sweep[4] my way
   And marshal me to knavery. Let it work,
   For 'tis the sport to have the enginer
   Hoist with his own petard;[5] and't shall go hard
   But I will delve[6] one yard below their mines
215   And blow them at the moon. O, 'tis most sweet
   When in one line two crafts directly meet.
   This man shall set me packing.
   I'll lug the guts into the neighbor room.
   Mother, good night. Indeed, this counsellor
220   Is now most still, most secret, and most grave,
   Who was in life a foolish prating knave.
   Come sir, to draw toward an end with you.
   Good night, mother.   [*Exit the* QUEEN. *Then exit* HAMLET *tugging* POLONIUS.]

---

7. Bloated.   8. Lewdly.   9. Foul.   1. Reveal.   2. Tomcat. *Paddock*: toad.
3. Apparently a reference to a now-lost fable in which an ape, finding a basket containing a cage of birds on a housetop, opens the cage. The birds fly away. The ape, thinking that if he were in the basket he too could fly, enters, jumps out, and breaks his neck.   4. Prepare. *Mandate*: command.
5. The "enginer," or engineer, is a military man who is here described as being blown up by a bomb of his own construction, "hoist with his own petard." The military figure continues in the succeeding lines where Hamlet describes himself as digging a countermine or tunnel beneath the one Claudius is digging to defeat Hamlet. In line 216 the two tunnels unexpectedly meet.   6. Dig.

ACT IV

Scene 1

A room in the castle. Enter KING, QUEEN, ROSENCRANTZ *and* GUILDENSTERN.

KING: There's matter in these sighs, these profound heaves,
    You must translate;[7] 'tis fit we understand them.
    Where is your son?
QUEEN: Bestow this place on us a little while.

                   [*Exeunt* ROSENCRANTZ *and* GUILDENSTERN.]
    Ah, mine own lord, what have I seen tonight!   5
KING: What, Gertrude? How does Hamlet?
QUEEN: Mad as the sea and wind when both contend
    Which is the mightier. In his lawless fit,
    Behind the arras hearing something stir,
    Whips out his rapier, cries "A rat, a rat!"   10
    And in this brainish apprehension[8] kills
    The unseen good old man.
KING: O heavy deed!
    It had been so with us had we been there.
    His liberty is full of threats to all—
    To you yourself, to us, to every one.   15
    Alas, how shall this bloody deed be answered?
    It will be laid to us, whose providence[9]
    Should have kept short, restrained, and out of haunt,[1]
    This mad young man. But so much was our love,
    We would not understand what was most fit;   20
    But, like the owner of a foul disease,
    To keep it from divulging, let it feed
    Even on the pith of life. Where is he gone?
QUEEN: To draw apart the body he hath killed,
    O'er whom his very madness, like some ore   25
    Among a mineral of metals base,
    Shows itself pure: 'a weeps for what is done.
KING: O Gertrude, come away!
    The sun no sooner shall the mountains touch
    But we will ship him hence, and this vile deed   30
    We must with all our majesty and skill
    Both countenance and excuse. Ho, Guildenstern!

    [*Enter* ROSENCRANTZ *and* GUILDENSTERN.]

    Friends both, go join you with some further aid.
    Hamlet in madness hath Polonius slain,
    And from his mother's closet hath he dragged him.   35
    Go seek him out; speak fair, and bring the body

---

7. Explain.   8. Insane notion.   9. Prudence.   1. Away from public gatherings.

Into the chapel. I pray you haste in this.

                                  [*Exeunt* ROSENCRANTZ *and* GUILDENSTERN.]

Come, Gertrude, we'll call up our wisest friends

And let them know both what we mean to do

40 And what's untimely done;

Whose whisper o'er the world's diameter,

As level as the cannon to his blank,[2]

Transports his poisoned shot—may miss our name,

And hit the woundless air. O, come away!

45 My soul is full of discord and dismay.   [*Exeunt*.]

Scene 2

A passageway. Enter HAMLET.

HAMLET: Safely stowed.

ROSENCRANTZ *and* GUILDENSTERN: [*Within*.] Hamlet! Lord Hamlet!

HAMLET: But soft, what noise? Who calls on Hamlet?

    O, here they come.

[*Enter* ROSENCRANTZ, GUILDENSTERN, *and* OTHERS.]

5   ROSENCRANTZ: What have you done, my lord, with the dead body?

HAMLET: Compounded it with dust, whereto 'tis kin.

ROSENCRANTZ: Tell us where 'tis, that we may take it thence

    And bear it to the chapel.

HAMLET: Do not believe it.

10 ROSENCRANTZ: Believe what?

HAMLET: That I can keep your counsel and not mine own. Besides, to be demanded of a sponge—what replication[3] should be made by the son of a king?

ROSENCRANTZ: Take you me for a sponge, my lord?

15 HAMLET: Ay, sir, that soaks up the king's countenance,[4] his rewards, his authorities. But such officers do the king best service in the end. He keeps them like an apple in the corner of his jaw, first mouthed to be last swallowed. When he needs what you have gleaned, it is but squeezing you and, sponge, you shall be dry again.

20 ROSENCRANTZ: I understand you not, my lord.

HAMLET: I am glad of it. A knavish speech sleeps in a foolish ear.

ROSENCRANTZ: My lord, you must tell us where the body is, and go with us to the king.

HAMLET: The body is with the king, but the king is not with the body.

25   The king is a thing—

GUILDENSTERN: A thing, my lord!

HAMLET: Of nothing. Bring me to him. Hide fox, and all after.[5]   [*Exeunt*.]

---

2. Mark. *Level*: direct.   3. Answer. *Demanded of*: questioned by.   4. Favor.

5. Apparently a reference to a children's game like hide-and-seek.

Scene 3

A room in the castle. Enter KING.

KING: I have sent to seek him, and to find the body.
How dangerous is it that this man goes loose!
Yet must not we put the strong law on him.
He's loved of the distracted[6] multitude,
Who like not in their judgment but their eyes,   5
And where 'tis so, th' offender's scourge[7] is weighed,
But never the offence. To bear all smooth and even,
This sudden sending him away must seem
Deliberate pause.[8] Diseases desperate grown
By desperate appliance are relieved,   10
Or not at all.

[*Enter* ROSENCRANTZ, GUILDENSTERN, *and all the rest.*]

　　　　　　　How now! what hath befall'n?
ROSENCRANTZ: Where the dead body is bestowed, my lord,
　We cannot get from him.
KING:　　　　　　　　But where is he?
ROSENCRANTZ: Without, my lord; guarded, to know[9] your pleasure.
KING: Bring him before us.
ROSENCRANTZ:　　　　　Ho! bring in the lord.   15

[*They enter with* HAMLET.]

KING: Now, Hamlet, where's Polonius?
HAMLET: At supper.
KING: At supper? Where?
HAMLET: Not where he eats, but where 'a is eaten. A certain convocation of
　politic[1] worms are e'en at him. Your worm is your only emperor for diet. We   20
　fat all creatures else to fat us, and we fat ourselves for maggots. Your fat king
　and your lean beggar is but variable service—two dishes, but to one table.
　That's the end.
KING: Alas, alas!
HAMLET: A man may fish with the worm that hath eat of a king, and eat of the   25
　fish that hath fed of that worm.
KING: What dost thou mean by this?
HAMLET: Nothing but to show you how a king may go a progress through the
　guts of a beggar.
KING: Where is Polonius?   30
HAMLET: In heaven. Send thither to see. If your messenger find him not there,
　seek him i' th' other place yourself. But if, indeed, you find him not within
　this month, you shall nose[2] him as you go up the stairs into the lobby.
KING: [*To* ATTENDANTS.] Go seek him there.
HAMLET: 'A will stay till you come.　　　　　　　　　　[*Exeunt* ATTENDANTS.]   35

---

6. Confused.　　7. Punishment.　　8. That is, not an impulse.　　9. Await.
1. Scheming. *Convocation*: gathering.　　2. Smell.

KING: Hamlet, this deed, for thine especial safety—
    Which we do tender, as we dearly[3] grieve
    For that which thou hast done—must send thee hence
    With fiery quickness. Therefore prepare thyself.
40   The bark is ready, and the wind at help,
    Th' associates tend, and everything is bent
    For England.
HAMLET: For England?
KING: Ay, Hamlet.
HAMLET: Good.
KING: So it is, if thou knew'st our purposes.
HAMLET: I see a cherub that sees them. But come, for England!
45   Farewell, dear mother.
KING: Thy loving father, Hamlet.
HAMLET: My mother. Father and mother is man and wife, man and wife is one
    flesh. So, my mother. Come, for England.   [*Exit.*]
KING: Follow him at foot;[4] tempt him with speed aboard.
50   Delay it not; I'll have him hence tonight.
    Away! for everything is sealed and done
    That else leans on th' affair. Pray you make haste. [*Exeunt all but the* KING.]
    And, England, if my love thou hold'st at aught—
    As my great power thereof may give thee sense,[5]
55   Since yet thy cicatrice[6] looks raw and red
    After the Danish sword, and thy free awe
    Pays homage to us—thou mayst not coldly set[7]
    Our sovereign process,[8] which imports at full
    By letters congruing[9] to that effect
60   The present death of Hamlet. Do it, England,
    For like the hectic[1] in my blood he rages,
    And thou must cure me. Till I know 'tis done,
    Howe'er my haps, my joys were ne'er begun.   [*Exit.*]

Scene 4

Near Elsinore. Enter FORTINBRAS *with his army.*

FORTINBRAS: Go, captain, from me greet the Danish king.
    Tell him that by his license Fortinbras
    Craves the conveyance[2] of a promised march
    Over his kingdom. You know the rendezvous.
5   If that his majesty would aught with us,
    We shall express our duty in his eye,[3]
    And let him know so.
CAPTAIN: I will do't, my lord.
FORTINBRAS: Go softly on.   [*Exeunt all but the* CAPTAIN.]

[*Enter* HAMLET, ROSENCRANTZ, GUILDENSTERN, *and* OTHERS.]

---

3. Deeply. *Tender*: consider.   4. Closely.   5. Of its value.   6. Wound scar.   7. Set aside.
8. Mandate.   9. Agreeing.   1. Chronic fever.   2. Escort.   3. Presence.

HAMLET: Good sir, whose powers are these?
CAPTAIN: They are of Norway, sir.   10
HAMLET: How purposed, sir, I pray you?
CAPTAIN: Against some part of Poland.
HAMLET: Who commands them, sir?
CAPTAIN: The nephew to old Norway, Fortinbras.
HAMLET: Goes it against the main[4] of Poland, sir,   15
  Or for some frontier?
CAPTAIN: Truly to speak, and with no addition,[5]
  We go to gain a little patch of ground
  That hath in it no profit but the name.
  To pay five ducats,[6] five, I would not farm it;   20
  Nor will it yield to Norway or the Pole
  A ranker rate should it be sold in fee.[7]
HAMLET: Why, then the Polack never will defend it.
CAPTAIN: Yes, it is already garrisoned.
HAMLET: Two thousand souls and twenty thousand ducats   25
  Will not debate the question of this straw.
  This is th' imposthume[8] of much wealth and peace,
  That inward breaks, and shows no cause without
  Why the man dies. I humbly thank you, sir.
CAPTAIN: God b'wi'ye, sir.   [*Exit.*]
ROSENCRANTZ: Will't please you go, my lord?   30
HAMLET: I'll be with you straight. Go a little before.   [*Exeunt all but* HAMLET.]
  How all occasions do inform against me,
  And spur my dull revenge! What is a man,
  If his chief good and market[9] of his time
  Be but to sleep and feed? A beast, no more.   35
  Sure he that made us with such large discourse,[1]
  Looking before and after, gave us not
  That capability and godlike reason
  To fust[2] in us unused. Now, whether it be
  Bestial oblivion, or some craven scruple   40
  Of thinking too precisely on th' event[3]—
  A thought which, quartered, hath but one part wisdom
  And ever three parts coward—I do not know
  Why yet I live to say "This thing's to do,"
  Sith[4] I have cause, and will, and strength, and means,   45
  To do't. Examples gross as earth exhort me.
  Witness this army of such mass and charge,[5]
  Led by a delicate and tender prince,
  Whose spirit, with divine ambition puffed,
  Makes mouths at[6] the invisible event,   50
  Exposing what is mortal and unsure
  To all that fortune, death, and danger dare,

4. Central part.   5. Exaggeration.   6. That is, in rent.   7. Outright. *Ranker*: higher.   8. Abscess.
9. Occupation.   1. Ample reasoning power.   2. Grow musty.   3. Outcome.   4. Since.
5. Expense.   6. Scorns.

Even for an eggshell. Rightly to be great
Is not to stir without great argument,
55   But greatly to find quarrel in a straw
When honor's at the stake. How stand I then,
That have a father killed, a mother stained,
Excitements of my reason and my blood,
And let all sleep, while to my shame I see
60   The imminent death of twenty thousand men
That for a fantasy and trick of fame
Go to their graves like beds, fight for a plot
Whereon the numbers cannot try the cause,
Which is not tomb enough and continent
65   To hide the slain?[7] O, from this time forth,
My thoughts be bloody, or be nothing worth!   [*Exit.*]

Scene 5

A room in the castle. Enter QUEEN, HORATIO *and a* GENTLEMAN.

QUEEN: I will not speak with her.
GENTLEMAN: She is importunate, indeed distract.
Her mood will needs to be pitied.
QUEEN: What would she have?
GENTLEMAN: She speaks much of her father, says she hears
5   There's tricks i' th' world, and hems, and beats her heart,
Spurns enviously at straws,[8] speaks things in doubt
That carry but half sense. Her speech is nothing,
Yet the unshapèd use of it doth move
The hearers to collection;[9] they yawn at it,
10   And botch the words up fit to their own thoughts,
Which, as her winks and nods and gestures yield them,
Indeed would make one think there might be thought,
Though nothing sure, yet much unhappily.
HORATIO: 'Twere good she were spoken with, for she may strew
15   Dangerous conjectures in ill-breeding minds.
QUEEN: Let her come in.   [*Exit* GENTLEMAN.]
[*Aside.*] To my sick soul, as sin's true nature is,
Each toy seems prologue to some great amiss.[1]
So full of artless jealousy is guilt,
20   It spills itself in fearing to be spilt.

          [*Enter* OPHELIA *distracted.*]

OPHELIA: Where is the beauteous majesty of Denmark?
QUEEN: How now, Ophelia!

---

7. The plot of ground involved is so small that it cannot contain the number of men involved in fighting
or furnish burial space for the number of those who will die.   8. Takes offense at trifles.
9. An attempt to order.   1. Catastrophe. *Toy:* trifle.

OPHELIA:

> [*Sings.*]
>
> How should I your true love know
>> From another one?
>
> By his cockle hat and staff,[2]
>> And his sandal shoon.[3]

QUEEN: Alas, sweet lady, what imports this song?

OPHELIA: Say you? Nay, pray you mark.   25

> [*Sings.*]
>
> He is dead and gone, lady,
>> He is dead and gone;
>
> At his head a grass-green turf,   30
>> At his heels a stone.

O, ho!

QUEEN: Nay, but Ophelia—

OPHELIA: Pray you mark.

> [*Sings.*]
>
> White his shroud as the mountain snow—

[*Enter* KING.]

QUEEN: Alas, look here, my lord.   35

OPHELIA:

> [*Sings.*]
>
> Larded all with sweet flowers;
> Which bewept to the grave did not go
>> With true-love showers.

KING: How do you, pretty lady?

OPHELIA: Well, God dild you! They say the owl was a baker's daughter.[4] Lord, we   40
know what we are, but know not what we may be. God be at your table!

KING: Conceit[5] upon her father.

OPHELIA: Pray let's have no words of this, but when they ask you what it means,
say you this:

> [*Sings.*]
>
> Tomorrow is Saint Valentine's day,   45
>> All in the morning betime,
>
> And I a maid at your window,
>> To be your Valentine.
>
> Then up he rose, and donn'd his clo'es,
>> And dupped[6] the chamber-door,   50

---

2. A cockle hat, one decorated with a shell, indicated that the wearer had made a pilgrimage to the shrine of St. James at Compostela in Spain. The staff also marked the carrier as a pilgrim.   3. Shoes.
4. Reference to a folktale about a young woman who was transformed into an owl when she failed to offer generosity to Jesus, who had asked for bread in her father's shop. *Dild*: yield, repay.   5. Thought.
6. Opened.

Let in the maid, that out a maid
   Never departed more.

KING: Pretty Ophelia!
OPHELIA: Indeed, without an oath, I'll make an end on't.

   [*Sings.*]

55   By Gis[7] and by Saint Charity,
      Alack, and fie for shame!
   Young men will do't, if they come to't;
      By Cock,[8] they are to blame.
   Quoth she "before you tumbled me,
60   You promised me to wed."

   He answers:

   "So would I'a done, by yonder sun,
   An thou hadst not come to my bed."

KING: How long hath she been thus?
65 OPHELIA: I hope all will be well. We must be patient, but I cannot choose but
   weep to think they would lay him i' th' cold ground. My brother shall know of
   it, and so I thank you for your good counsel. Come, my coach! Good night,
   ladies, good night. Sweet ladies, good night, good night.   [*Exit.*]
KING: Follow her close; give her good watch, I pray you.
                              [*Exeunt* HORATIO *and* GENTLEMAN.]
70   O, this is the poison of deep grief; it springs
   All from her father's death, and now behold!
   O Gertrude, Gertrude!
   When sorrows come, they come not single spies,
   But in battalions: first, her father slain;
75   Next, your son gone, and he most violent author
   Of his own just remove; the people muddied,[9]
   Thick and unwholesome in their thoughts and whispers
   For good Polonius' death; and we have done but greenly[1]
   In hugger-mugger[2] to inter him; poor Ophelia
80   Divided from herself and her fair judgment,
   Without the which we are pictures, or mere beasts;
   Last, and as much containing as all these,
   Her brother is in secret come from France,
   Feeds on his wonder, keeps himself in clouds,
85   And wants not buzzers to infect his ear
   With pestilent speeches of his father's death,
   Wherein necessity, of matter beggared,[3]
   Will nothing stick our person to arraign[4]
   In ear and ear.[5] O my dear Gertrude, this,
90   Like to a murd'ring piece,[6] in many places
   Gives me superfluous death.   [*A noise within.*]

7. Jesus.   8. Corruption of "God," with a sexual pun.   9. Disturbed.   1. Without judgment.
2. Haste.   3. Short on facts.   4. Accuse. *Stick*: hesitate.   5. From both sides.
6. A weapon designed to scatter its shot.

QUEEN: Alack, what noise is this?
KING: Attend!
    Where are my Switzers?[7] Let them guard the door.
    What is the matter?
MESSENGER: Save yourself, my lord.   95
    The ocean, overpeering of his list,[8]
    Eats not the flats with more impiteous[9] haste
    Than young Laertes, in a riotous head,[1]
    O'erbears your officers. The rabble call him lord,
    And as the world were now but to begin,   100
    Antiquity forgot, custom not known,
    The ratifiers and props of every word,
    They cry "Choose we, Laertes shall be king."
    Caps, hands, and tongues, applaud it to the clouds,
    "Laertes shall be king, Laertes king."   105
QUEEN: How cheerfully on the false trail they cry![2]

    [*A noise within.*]

    O, this is counter,[3] you false Danish dogs!
KING: The doors are broke.

    [*Enter* LAERTES, *with* OTHERS.]

LAERTES: Where is this king?—Sirs, stand you all without.
ALL: No, let's come in.
LAERTES: I pray you give me leave.   110
ALL: We will, we will.
LAERTES: I thank you. Keep[4] the door.   [*Exeunt his followers.*]
                O thou vile king,
    Give me my father!
QUEEN: Calmly, good Laertes.
LAERTES: That drop of blood that's calm proclaims me bastard,
    Cries cuckold to my father, brands the harlot   115
    Even here between the chaste unsmirchèd brow
    Of my true mother.
KING: What is the cause, Laertes,
    That thy rebellion looks so giant-like?
    Let him go, Gertrude. Do not fear[5] our person.
    There's such divinity doth hedge a king   120
    That treason can but peep to[6] what it would,
    Acts little of his will. Tell me, Laertes.
    Why thou art thus incensed. Let him go, Gertrude.
    Speak, man.
LAERTES: Where is my father?
KING: Dead.
QUEEN: But not by him.
KING: Let him demand[7] his fill.   125

---

7. Swiss guards.   8. Towering above its limits.   9. Pitiless.   1. With an armed band.
2. As if following the scent.   3. Backward.   4. Guard.   5. Fear for.
6. Look at over or through a barrier.   7. Question.

LAERTES: How came he dead? I'll not be juggled with.
 To hell allegiance, vows to the blackest devil,
 Conscience and grace to the profoundest pit!
 I dare damnation. To this point I stand,
130 That both the worlds I give to negligence,[8]
 Let come what comes, only I'll be revenged
 Most throughly for my father.
KING: Who shall stay you?
LAERTES: My will, not all the world's.
 And for my means, I'll husband[9] them so well
 They shall go far with little.
135 KING: Good Laertes,
 If you desire to know the certainty
 Of your dear father, is't writ in your revenge
 That, swoopstake,[1] you will draw both friend and foe,
 Winner and loser?
LAERTES: None but his enemies.
140 KING: Will you know them, then?
LAERTES: To his good friends thus wide I'll ope my arms,
 And like the kind life-rend'ring pelican,[2]
 Repast them with my blood.
KING: Why, now you speak
 Like a good child and a true gentleman.
145 That I am guiltless of your father's death,
 And am most sensibly in grief for it,
 It shall as level[3] to your judgment 'pear
 As day does to your eye.

  [*A noise within:* "Let her come in."]

LAERTES: How now? What noise is that?

  [*Enter* OPHELIA.]

150 O, heat dry up my brains! tears seven times salt
 Burn out the sense and virtue[4] of mine eye!
 By heaven, thy madness shall be paid with weight
 Till our scale turn the beam. O rose of May,
 Dear maid, kind sister, sweet Ophelia!
155 O heavens, is't possible a young maid's wits
 Should be as mortal as an old man's life?
 Nature is fin[5] in love, and where 'tis fine
 It sends some precious instances of itself
 After the thing it loves.[6]

---

8. Disregard. *Both the worlds*: that is, this and the next. 9. Manage. 1. Sweeping the board.
2. The pelican was believed to feed her young with her own blood. 3. Plain.
4. Function. *Sense*: feeling. 5. Refined.
6. Laertes means that Ophelia, because of her love for her father, gave up her sanity as a token of grief at his death.

OPHELIA:

[*Sings.*]

They bore him barefac'd on the bier;   160
  Hey non nonny, nonny, hey nonny;
  And in his grave rain'd many a tear—

Fare you well, my dove!
LAERTES: Hadst thou thy wits, and didst persuade revenge,
  It could not move thus.   165
OPHELIA: You must sing "A-down, a-down, and you call him a-down-a." O, how
  the wheel becomes it! It is the false steward, that stole his master's daughter.[7]
LAERTES: This nothing's more than matter.
OPHELIA: There's a rosemary, that's for remembrance. Pray you, love, remember.
  And there is pansies, that's for thoughts.   170
LAERTES: A document[8] in madness, thoughts and remembrance fitted.
OPHELIA: There's fennel for you, and columbines. There's rue for you, and here's
  some for me. We may call it herb of grace a Sundays. O, you must wear your
  rue with a difference. There's a daisy. I would give you some violets, but they
  withered all when my father died. They say 'a made a good end.   175

[*Sings.*]

For bonny sweet Robin is all my joy.
LAERTES: Thought and affliction, passion, hell itself,
  She turns to favor[9] and to prettiness.
OPHELIA:

[*Sings.*]

And will 'a not come again?
And will 'a not come again?   180
  No, no, he is dead,
  Go to thy death-bed,
He never will come again.

His beard was as white as snow,   185
All flaxen was his poll;[1]
  He is gone, he is gone,
  And we cast away moan:
God-a-mercy on his soul!

And of all Christian souls, I pray God. God b'wi'you.   [*Exit.*]
LAERTES: Do you see this, O God?   190
KING: Laertes, I must commune with your grief,
  Or you deny me right. Go but apart,
  Make choice of whom your wisest friends you will,
  And they shall hear and judge 'twixt you and me.
  If by direct or by collateral[2] hand   195

---

7. The "wheel" refers to the "burden" or refrain of a song, in this case "A-down, a-down, and you call him a-down-a." The ballad to which she refers was about a false steward. Others have suggested that the "wheel" is the Wheel of Fortune, a spinning wheel to whose rhythm such a song might have been sung or a kind of dance movement performed by Ophelia as she sings.   8. Lesson.   9. Beauty.   1. Head.   2. Indirect.

They find us touched,[3] we will our kingdom give,
Our crown, our life, and all that we call ours,
To you in satisfaction; but if not,
Be you content to lend your patience to us,
200   And we shall jointly labor with your soul
To give it due content.
LAERTES: Let this be so.
His means of death, his obscure funeral—
No trophy, sword, nor hatchment,[4] o'er his bones,
No noble rite nor formal ostentation[5]—
205   Cry to be heard, as 'twere from heaven to earth,
That I must call't in question.
KING: So you shall;
And where th' offence is, let the great axe fall.
I pray you go with me.   [*Exeunt.*]

Scene 6

Another room in the castle. Enter HORATIO *and a* GENTLEMAN.

HORATIO: What are they that would speak with me?
GENTLEMAN: Sea-faring men, sir. They say they have letters for you.
HORATIO: Let them come in.   [*Exit* GENTLEMAN.]
    I do not know from what part of the world
5   I should be greeted, if not from Lord Hamlet.

        [*Enter* SAILORS.]

SAILOR: God bless you, sir.
HORATIO: Let him bless thee too.
SAILOR: 'A shall, sir, an't please him. There's a letter for you, sir—it came from th'
    ambassador that was bound for England—if your name be Horatio, as I am
10   let to know[6] it is.
HORATIO: [*Reads.*] "Horatio, when thou shalt have overlooked[7] this, give these
    fellows some means[8] to the king. They have letters for him. Ere we were two
    days old at sea, a pirate of very warlike appointment[9] gave us chase. Finding
    ourselves too slow of sail, we put on a compelled valor, and in the grapple I
15   boarded them. On the instant they got clear of our ship, so I alone became
    their prisoner. They have dealt with me like thieves of mercy, but they knew
    what they did; I am to do a good turn for them. Let the king have the letters I
    have sent, and repair thou to me with as much speed as thou wouldest fly
    death. I have words to speak in thine ear will make thee dumb; yet are they
20   much too light for the bore of the matter.[1] These good fellows will bring thee
    where I am. Rosencrantz and Guildenstern hold their course for England. Of
    them I have much to tell thee. Farewell.
                    He that thou knowest thine, Hamlet."

---

3. By guilt.   4. Coat of arms.   5. Pomp.   6. Informed.   7. Read through.   8. Access.
9. Equipment.
1. A figure from gunnery, referring to shot that is too small for the size of the weapons to be fired.

Come, I will give you way[2] for these your letters,
And do't the speedier that you may direct me   25
To him from whom you brought them.   [*Exeunt.*]

Scene 7

Another room in the castle. Enter KING *and* LAERTES.

KING: Now must your conscience my acquittance seal,[3]
  And you must put me in your heart for friend,
  Sith you have heard, and with a knowing ear,
  That he which hath your noble father slain
  Pursued my life.
LAERTES: It well appears. But tell me   5
  Why you proceeded not against these feats,
  So criminal and so capital in nature,
  As by your safety, greatness, wisdom, all things else,
  You mainly were stirred up.
KING: O, for two special reasons,
  Which may to you, perhaps, seem much unsinewed,[4]   10
  But yet to me th' are strong. The queen his mother
  Lives almost by his looks, and for myself—
  My virtue or my plague, be it either which—
  She is so conjunctive[5] to my life and soul
  That, as the star moves not but in his sphere,[6]   15
  I could not but by her. The other motive,
  Why to a public count[7] I might not go,
  Is the great love the general gender[8] bear him,
  Who, dipping all his faults in their affection,
  Work like the spring that turneth wood to stone,[9]   20
  Convert his gyves[1] to graces; so that my arrows,
  Too slightly timbered[2] for so loud a wind,
  Would have reverted to my bow again,
  But not where I had aimed them.
LAERTES: And so have I a noble father lost,   25
  A sister driven into desp'rate terms,
  Whose worth, if praises may go back again,
  Stood challenger on mount of all the age
  For her perfections. But my revenge will come.
KING: Break not your sleeps for that. You must not think 30
  That we are made of stuff so flat and dull
  That we can let our beard be shook with danger,
  And think it pastime. You shortly shall hear more.
  I loved your father, and we love our self,

2. Means of delivery.   3. Grant me innocent.   4. Weak.   5. Closely joined.
6. A reference to the Ptolemaic cosmology, in which planets and stars were believed to revolve in crystalline spheres concentrically about the Earth.   7. Reckoning.   8. Common people.
9. Certain English springs contain so much lime that a limestone covering will be deposited on a log placed in one of them for a length of time.   1. Fetters.   2. Shafted.

35　　And that, I hope, will teach you to imagine—

　　　[*Enter a* MESSENGER *with letters.*]

　　How now? What news?
MESSENGER:　　　　　　　Letters, my lord, from Hamlet.
　　These to your majesty; this to the queen.
KING: From Hamlet! Who brought them?
MESSENGER: Sailors, my lord, they say. I saw them not.
40　　They were given me by Claudio; he received them
　　Of him that brought them.
KING:　　　　　　　　　Laertes, you shall hear them.—
　　Leave us.　　　　　　　　　　　　　　　[*Exit* MESSENGER.]
　　　[*Reads.*] "High and mighty, you shall know I am set naked on your kingdom.
　　Tomorrow shall I beg leave to see your kingly eyes; when I shall, first asking
　　your pardon thereunto, recount the occasion of my sudden and more strange
45　　return.
　　　　　　Hamlet."
　　What should this mean? Are all the rest come back?
　　Or is it some abuse,[3] and no such thing?
LAERTES: Know you the hand?
50　KING: 'Tis Hamlet's character.[4] "Naked"!
　　And in a postscript here, he says "alone."
　　Can you devise[5] me?
LAERTES: I am lost in it, my lord. But let him come.
　　It warms the very sickness in my heart
55　　That I shall live and tell him to his teeth
　　"Thus didest thou."
KING:　　　　　　　If it be so, Laertes—
　　As how should it be so, how otherwise?—
　　Will you be ruled by me?
LAERTES:　　　　　　　Ay, my lord,
　　So you will not o'errule me to a peace.
60　KING: To thine own peace. If he be now returned,
　　As checking at[6] his voyage, and that he means
　　No more to undertake it, I will work him
　　To an exploit now ripe in my device,
　　Under the which he shall not choose but fall;
65　　And for his death no wind of blame shall breathe
　　But even his mother shall uncharge[7] the practice
　　And call it accident.
LAERTES:　　　　　　My lord, I will be ruled;
　　The rather if you could devise it so
　　That I might be the organ.[8]
KING:　　　　　　　It falls right.
70　　You have been talked of since your travel much,
　　And that in Hamlet's hearing, for a quality

---

3. Trick.　4. Handwriting.　5. Explain it to.　6. Turning aside from.　7. Not accuse.
8. Instrument.

Wherein they say you shine. Your sum of parts
Did not together pluck such envy from him
As did that one, and that, in my regard,
Of the unworthiest siege.[9]
LAERTES: What part is that, my lord?   75
KING: A very riband in the cap of youth,
    Yet needful too, for youth no less becomes
    The light and careless livery that it wears
    Than settled age his sables and his weeds,[1]
    Importing health and graveness. Two months since   80
    Here was a gentleman of Normandy.
    I have seen myself, and served against, the French,
    And they can[2] well on horseback, but this gallant
    Had witchcraft in't. He grew unto his seat,
    And to such wondrous doing brought his horse,   85
    As had he been incorpsed and demi-natured
    With the brave beast. So far he topped my thought
    That I, in forgery[3] of shapes and tricks,
    Come short of what he did.[4]
LAERTES: A Norman was't?
KING: A Norman.   90
LAERTES: Upon my life, Lamord.
KING: The very same.
LAERTES: I know him well. He is the brooch indeed
    And gem of all the nation.
KING: He made confession[5] of you,
    And gave you such a masterly report   95
    For art and exercise in your defence,[6]
    And for your rapier most especial,
    That he cried out 'twould be a sight indeed
    If one could match you. The scrimers[7] of their nation
    He swore had neither motion, guard, nor eye,   100
    If you opposed them. Sir, this report of his
    Did Hamlet so envenom with his envy
    That he could nothing do but wish and beg
    Your sudden coming o'er, to play with you.
    Now out of this—
LAERTES: What out of this, my lord?   105
KING: Laertes, was your father dear to you?
    Or are you like the painting of a sorrow,
    A face without a heart?
LAERTES: Why ask you this?
KING: Not that I think you did not love your father,

9. Lowest rank.   1. Dignified clothing.   2. Perform.   3. Imagination.
4. The gentleman referred to was so skilled in horsemanship that he seemed to share one body with the horse, "incorpsed." The king further extends the compliment by saying that he appeared like the mythical centaur, a creature who was man from the waist up and horse from the waist down, therefore "demi-natured."   5. Gave a report.   6. Skill in fencing.   7. Fencers.

110 But that I know love is begun by time,
And that I see in passages of proof,[8]
Time qualifies the spark and fire of it.
There lives within the very flame of love
A kind of wick or snuff that will abate it,
115 And nothing is at a like goodness still,
For goodness, growing to a plurisy,[9]
Dies in his own too much.[1] That we would do,
We should do when we would; for this "would" changes,
And hath abatements and delays as many
120 As there are tongues, are hands, are accidents,
And then this "should" is like a spendthrift's sigh
That hurts by easing. But to the quick of th' ulcer—[2]
Hamlet comes back; what would you undertake
To show yourself in deed your father's son
More than in words?

125 LAERTES: To cut his throat i' th' church.
KING: No place indeed should murder sanctuarize;[3]
Revenge should have no bounds. But, good Laertes,
Will you do this? Keep close within your chamber.
Hamlet returned shall know you are come home.
130 We'll put on those shall praise your excellence,
And set a double varnish on the fame
The Frenchman gave you, bring you in fine[4] together,
And wager on your heads. He, being remiss,[5]
Most generous, and free from all contriving,
135 Will not peruse[6] the foils, so that with ease,
Or with a little shuffling, you may choose
A sword unbated,[7] and in a pass of practice
Requite him for your father.
LAERTES: I will do't,
And for that purpose I'll anoint my sword.
140 I bought an unction of a mountebank
So mortal that but dip a knife in it,
Where it draws blood no cataplasm[8] so rare,
Collected from all simples[9] that have virtue
Under the moon, can save the thing from death
145 That is but scratched withal. I'll touch my point
With this contagion, that if I gall[1] him slightly,
It may be death.
KING: Let's further think of this,
Weigh what convenience both of time and means
May fit us to our shape. If this should fail,
150 And that our drift look[2] through our bad performance,
'Twere better not assayed. Therefore this project

8. Tests of experience.   9. Fullness.   1. Excess.
2. Heart of the matter. *Spendthrift's sigh:* a sigh was believed to draw a drop of blood from the heart and thus to "hurt" by "easing" sadness.   3. Provide sanctuary for murder.   4. In short.   5. Careless.
6. Examine.   7. Not blunted.   8. Poultice.   9. Herbs.   1. Scratch.   2. Intent become obvious.

Should have a back or second that might hold
If this did blast in proof.[3] Soft, let me see.
We'll make a solemn wager on your cunnings—
I ha't.   155
When in your motion you are hot and dry—
As make your bouts more violent to that end—
And that he calls for drink, I'll have prepared him
A chalice for the nonce, whereon but sipping,
If he by chance escape your venomed stuck,[4]   160
Our purpose may hold there.—But stay, what noise?

    [*Enter* QUEEN.]

QUEEN: One woe doth tread upon another's heel,
  So fast they follow. Your sister's drowned, Laertes.
LAERTES: Drowned? O, where?
QUEEN: There is a willow grows aslant the brook   165
  That shows his hoar leaves in the glassy stream.
  Therewith fantastic garlands did she make
  Of crowflowers, nettles, daisies, and long purples
  That liberal shepherds give a grosser[5] name,
  But our cold[6] maids do dead men's fingers call them.   170
  There on the pendent boughs her coronet weeds
  Clamb'ring to hang, an envious[7] sliver broke,
  When down her weedy trophies and herself
  Fell in the weeping brook. Her clothes spread wide,
  And mermaid-like awhile they bore her up,   175
  Which time she chanted snatches of old tunes,
  As one incapable[8] of her own distress,
  Or like a creature native and indued[9]
  Unto that element. But long it could not be
  Till that her garments, heavy with their drink,   180
  Pulled the poor wretch from her melodious lay
  To muddy death.
LAERTES: Alas, then she is drowned?
QUEEN: Drowned, drowned.
LAERTES: Too much of water hast thou, poor Ophelia,
  And therefore I forbid my tears; but yet   185
  It is our trick; nature her custom holds,
  Let shame say what it will. When these are gone,
  The woman will be out. Adieu, my lord.
  I have a speech o' fire that fain would blaze
  But that this folly drowns it.   [*Exit.*]
KING: Let's follow, Gertrude.   190
  How much I had to do to calm his rage!
  Now fear I this will give it start again;
  Therefore let's follow.   [*Exeunt.*]

3. Fail when tried.   4. Thrust.
5. Coarser. The "long purples" are purple orchises, a type of orchid known as "dog's cullions" (testicles)
or "goat's cullions." *Liberal*: vulgar.   6. Chaste.   7. Malicious.   8. Unaware.   9. Habituated.

ACT V

Scene 1

A churchyard. Enter two CLOWNS.[1]

CLOWN: Is she to be buried in Christian burial when she wilfully seeks her own salvation?

OTHER: I tell thee she is. Therefore make her grave straight. The crowner hath sat on her,[2] and finds it Christian burial.

5 CLOWN: How can that be, unless she drowned herself in her own defence?

OTHER: Why, 'tis found so.

CLOWN: It must be "se offendendo";[3] it cannot be else. For here lies the point: if I drown myself wittingly, it argues an act, and an act hath three branches—it is to act, to do, to perform; argal,[4] she drowned herself wittingly.

10 OTHER: Nay, but hear you, Goodman Delver.

CLOWN: Give me leave. Here lies the water; good. Here stands the man; good. If the man go to this water and drown himself, it is, will he, nill he, he goes— mark you that. But if the water come to him and drown him, he drowns not himself. Argal, he that is not guilty of his own death shortens not his own

15 life.

OTHER: But is this law?

CLOWN: Ay, marry, is't; crowner's quest[5] law.

OTHER: Will you ha' the truth on't? If this had not been a gentlewoman, she should have been buried out o' Christian burial.

20 CLOWN: Why, there thou say'st. And the more pity that great folk should have count'nance[6] in this world to drown or hang themselves more than their even-Christen.[7] Come, my spade. There is no ancient gentlemen but gard'ners, ditchers, and grave-makers. They hold up Adam's profession.

OTHER: Was he a gentleman?

25 CLOWN: 'A was the first that ever bore arms.

OTHER: Why, he had none.

CLOWN: What, art a heathen? How dost thou understand the Scripture? The Scripture says Adam digged. Could he dig without arms? I'll put another question to thee. If thou answerest me not to the purpose, confess thyself—

30 OTHER: Go to.

CLOWN: What is he that builds stronger than either the mason, the shipwright, or the carpenter?

OTHER: The gallows-maker, for that frame outlives a thousand tenants.

CLOWN: I like thy wit well, in good faith. The gallows does well. But how does it

35 well? It does well to those that do ill. Now thou dost ill to say the gallows is built stronger than the church. Argal, the gallows may do well to thee. To't again,[8] come.

OTHER: Who builds stronger than a mason, a shipwright, or a carpenter?

CLOWN: Ay tell me that, and unyoke.[9]

40 OTHER: Marry, now I can tell.

CLOWN: To't.

---

1. Rustics.   2. Held an inquest. *Crowner*: coroner.   3. An error for *se defendendo*, in self-defense.
4. "Ergo," therefore.   5. Inquest.   6. Approval.   7. Fellow Christians.   8. Guess again.
9. Finish the matter.

OTHER: Mass, I cannot tell.

CLOWN: Cudgel thy brains no more about it, for your dull ass will not mend his pace with beating. And when you are asked this question next, say "a grave maker." The houses he makes lasts till doomsday. Go, get thee in, and fetch me a stoup[1] of liquor. *[Exit OTHER CLOWN.]* 45

[Enter HAMLET and HORATIO as CLOWN digs and sings.]

In youth, when I did love, did love,
    Methought it was very sweet,
To contract the time for-a my behove,[2]
    O, methought there-a was nothing-a meet.[3] 50

HAMLET: Has this fellow no feeling of his business, that 'a sings in grave-making?

HORATIO: Custom hath made it in him a property of easiness.

HAMLET: 'Tis e'en so. The hand of little employment hath the daintier sense.

CLOWN:

[Sings.]

But age, with his stealing steps,
    Hath clawed me in his clutch, 55
And hath shipped me into the land,
    As if I had never been such.

[Throws up a skull.]

HAMLET: That skull had a tongue in it, and could sing once. How the knave jowls[4] it to the ground, as if 'twere Cain's jawbone, that did the first murder! This might be the pate of a politician, which this ass now o'erreaches;[5] one 60 that would circumvent God, might it not?

HORATIO: It might, my lord.

HAMLET: Or of a courtier, which could say, "Good morrow, sweet lord! How does thou, sweet lord?" This might be my Lord Such-a-one, that praised my Lord Such-a-one's horse, when 'a meant to beg it, might it not? 65

HORATIO: Ay, my lord.

HAMLET: Why, e'en so, and now my Lady Worm's, chapless,[6] and knock'd about the mazzard with a sexton's spade. Here's fine revolution,[7] an we had the trick to see't. Did these bones cost no more the breeding but to play at loggets with them?[8] Mine ache to think on't. 70

CLOWN:

[Sings.]

A pick-axe and a spade, a spade,
    For and a shrouding sheet:
O, a pit of clay for to be made
    For such a guest is meet.

[Throws up another skull.]

1. Mug.   2. Advantage. *Contract*: shorten.
3. The gravedigger's song is a free version of "The aged lover renounceth love" by Thomas, Lord Vaux, published in *Tottel's Miscellany*, 1557.   4. Hurls.   5. Gets the better of.   6. Lacking a lower jaw.
7. Skill. *Mazzard*: head.   8. "Loggets" were small pieces of wood thrown as part of a game.

75 HAMLET: There's another. Why may not that be the skull of a lawyer? Where be his quiddities now, his quillets, his cases, his tenures, and his tricks? Why does he suffer this mad knave now to knock him about the sconce[9] with a dirty shovel, and will not tell him of his action of battery? Hum! This fellow might be in's time a great buyer of land, with his statutes, his recognizances, his
80 fines, his double vouchers, his recoveries. Is this the fine[1] of his fines, and the recovery of his recoveries, to have his fine pate full of fine dirt? Will his vouchers vouch him no more of his purchases, and double ones too, than the length and breadth of a pair of indentures?[2] The very conveyances of his lands will scarcely lie in this box, and must th' inheritor himself have no more, ha?[3]
85 HORATIO: Not a jot more, my lord.
    HAMLET: Is not parchment made of sheepskins?
    HORATIO: Ay, my lord, and of calves' skins too.
    HAMLET: They are sheep and calves which seek out assurance in that. I will speak to this fellow. Whose grave's this, sirrah?
90 CLOWN: Mine, sir.

            [Sings.]

        O, a pit of clay for to be made
            For such a guest is meet.

    HAMLET: I think it be thine indeed, for thou liest in't.
    CLOWN: You lie out on't, sir, and therefore 'tis not yours. For my part, I do not lie
95   in't, yet it is mine.
    HAMLET: Thou dost lie in't, to be in't and say it is thine. 'Tis for the dead, not for the quick;[4] therefore thou liest.
    CLOWN: 'Tis a quick lie, sir; 'twill away again from me to you.
    HAMLET: What man dost thou dig it for?
100 CLOWN: For no man, sir.
    HAMLET: What woman, then?
    CLOWN: For none neither.
    HAMLET: Who is to be buried in't?
    CLOWN: One that was a woman, sir; but, rest her soul, she's dead.
105 HAMLET: How absolute the knave is! We must speak by the card,[5] or equivocation will undo us. By the Lord, Horatio, this three years I have took note of it, the age is grown so picked[6] that the toe of the peasant comes so near the heel of the courtier, he galls his kibe.[7] How long hast thou been a grave-maker?
    CLOWN: Of all the days i' th' year, I came to't that day that our last King Hamlet
110   overcame Fortinbras.
    HAMLET: How long is that since?
    CLOWN: Cannot you tell that? Every fool can tell that. It was that very day that young Hamlet was born—he that is mad, and sent into England.
    HAMLET: Ay, marry, why was he sent into England?
115 CLOWN: Why, because 'a was mad. 'A shall recover his wits there; or, if 'a do not, 'tis no great matter there.
    HAMLET: Why?

---

9. Head.   1. End.   2. Contracts.
3. In this speech Hamlet reels off a list of legal terms relating to property transactions.   4. Living.
5. Exactly. *Absolute:* precise.   6. Refined.   7. Rubs a blister on his heel.

CLOWN: 'Twill not be seen in him there. There the men are as mad as he.

HAMLET: How came he mad?

CLOWN: Very strangely, they say.   120

HAMLET: How strangely?

CLOWN: Faith, e'en with losing his wits.

HAMLET: Upon what ground?

CLOWN: Why, here in Denmark. I have been sexton here, man and boy, thirty
years.   125

HAMLET: How long will a man lie i' th' earth ere he rot?

CLOWN: Faith, if 'a be not rotten before 'a die—as we have many pocky[8] corses
now-a-days that will scarce hold the laying in—'a will last you some eight year
or nine year. A tanner will last you nine year.

HAMLET: Why he more than another?   130

CLOWN: Why, sir, his hide is so tanned with his trade that 'a will keep out water a
great while; and your water is a sore decayer of your whoreson dead body.
Here's a skull now hath lien[9] you i' th' earth three and twenty years.

HAMLET: Whose was it?

CLOWN: A whoreson mad fellow's it was. Whose do you think it was?   135

HAMLET: Nay, I know not.

CLOWN: A pestilence on him for a mad rogue! 'A poured a flagon of Rhenish on
my head once. This same skull, sir, was, sir, Yorick's skull, the king's jester.

HAMLET: [*Takes the skull.*] This?

CLOWN: E'en that.   140

HAMLET: Alas, poor Yorick! I knew him, Horatio—a fellow of infinite jest, of most
excellent fancy. He hath bore me on his back a thousand times, and now how
abhorred in my imagination it is! My gorg[1] rises at it. Here hung those lips
that I have kissed I know not how oft. Where be your gibes now, your gam-
bols, your songs, your flashes of merriment that were wont to set the table on 145
a roar? Not one now to mock your own grinning? Quite chap-fall'n?[2] Now get
you to my lady's chamber, and tell her, let her paint an inch thick, to this
favor[3] she must come. Make her laugh at that. Prithee, Horatio, tell me one
thing.

HORATIO: What's that, my lord?   150

HAMLET: Dost thou think Alexander looked o' this fashion i' th' earth?

HORATIO: E'en so.

HAMLET: And smelt so? Pah!   [*Throws down the skull.*]

HORATIO: E'en so, my lord.

HAMLET: To what base uses we may return, Horatio! Why may not imagination 155
trace the noble dust of Alexander till 'a find it stopping a bung-hole?[4]

HORATIO: 'Twere to consider too curiously[5] to consider so.

HAMLET: No, faith, not a jot, but to follow him thither with modesty[6] enough,
and likelihood to lead it. Alexander died, Alexander was buried, Alexander
returneth to dust; the dust is earth; of earth we make loam; and why of that 160
loam whereto he was converted might they not stop a beerbarrel?

> Imperious Cæsar, dead and turned to clay,
> Might stop a hole to keep the wind away.

---

8. Corrupted by syphilis.   9. Lain. *Whoreson*: bastard (not literally).   1. Throat.
2. Lacking a lower jaw.   3. Appearance.   4. Used as a cork in a cask.   5. Precisely.   6. Moderation.

O, that that earth which kept the world in awe
165   Should patch a wall t'expel the winter's flaw![7]

But soft, but soft awhile! Here comes the king,
The queen, the courtiers.

[*Enter* KING, QUEEN, LAERTES, *and the Corse with a* PRIEST *and* LORDS *attendant.*]

Who is this they follow?
And with such maimèd[8] rites? This doth betoken
The corse they follow did with desperate hand
170   Fordo its own life. 'Twas of some estate.[9]
Couch[1] we awhile and mark.   [*Retires with* HORATIO.]

LAERTES: What ceremony else?[2]
HAMLET: That is Laertes, a very noble youth. Mark.
LAERTES: What ceremony else?
175 PRIEST: Here obsequies have been as far enlarged[3]
As we have warranty. Her death was doubtful,
And but that great command o'ersways the order,[4]
She should in ground unsanctified been lodged
Till the last trumpet. For charitable prayers,
180   Shards, flints, and pebbles, should be thrown on her.
Yet here she is allowed her virgin crants,[5]
Her maiden strewments,[6] and the bringing home
Of bell and burial.
LAERTES: Must there no more be done?
PRIEST: No more be done.
185   We should profane the service of the dead
To sing a requiem and such rest to her
As to peace-parted souls.
LAERTES: Lay her i' th' earth,
And from her fair and unpolluted flesh
May violets spring! I tell thee, churlish priest,
190   A minist'ring angel shall my sister be
When thou liest howling.[7]
HAMLET: What, the fair Ophelia!
QUEEN: Sweets to the sweet. Farewell!   [*Scatters flowers.*]
I hoped thou shouldst have been my Hamlet's wife.
I thought thy bride-bed to have decked, sweet maid,
And not t' have strewed thy grave.
195 LAERTES: O, treble woe
Fall ten times treble on that cursèd head
Whose wicked deed thy most ingenious sense[8]
Deprived thee of! Hold off the earth awhile,
Till I have caught her once more in mine arms.   [*Leaps into the grave.*]
200   Now pile your dust upon the quick and dead,

---

7. Gusty wind.   8. Shortened.   9. Rank. *Fordo*: destroy.   1. Conceal ourselves.   2. More.
3. Extended.   4. Usual rules.   5. Wreaths.   6. Flowers strewn on the grave.   7. In Hell.
8. Lively mind.

Till of this flat a mountain you have made
T' o'er-top old Pelion or the skyish head
Of blue Olympus.[9]

HAMLET: [*Coming forward.*] What is he whose grief
    Bears such an emphasis, whose phrase of sorrow
    Conjures[1] the wand'ring stars, and makes them stand   205
    Like wonder-wounded hearers? This is I,
    Hamlet the Dane.

[HAMLET *leaps into the grave and they grapple.*]

LAERTES: The devil take thy soul!
HAMLET: Thou pray'st not well.
    I prithee take thy fingers from my throat,
    For though I am not splenitive[2] and rash,   210
    Yet have I in me something dangerous,
    Which let thy wisdom fear. Hold off thy hand.
KING: Pluck them asunder.
QUEEN: Hamlet! Hamlet!
ALL: Gentlemen!   215
HORATIO: Good my lord, be quiet.

[*The* ATTENDANTS *part them, and they come out of the grave.*]

HAMLET: Why, I will fight with him upon this theme
    Until my eyelids will no longer wag.[3]
QUEEN: O my son, what theme?
HAMLET: I loved Ophelia. Forty thousand brothers   220
    Could not with all their quantity of love
    Make up my sum. What wilt thou do for her?
KING: O, he is mad, Laertes.
QUEEN: For love of God, forbear[4] him.
HAMLET: 'Swounds, show me what th'owt do.   225
    Woo't[5] weep, woo't fight, woo't fast, woo't tear thyself,
    Woo't drink up eisel,[6] eat a crocodile?
    I'll do't. Dost come here to whine?
    To outface[7] me with leaping in her grave?
    Be buried quick with her, and so will I.   230
    And if thou prate of mountains, let them throw
    Millions of acres on us, till our ground,
    Singeing his pate against the burning zone,[8]
    Make Ossa like a wart! Nay, an thou'lt mouth,
    I'll rant as well as thou.
QUEEN: This is mere madness   235
    And thus awhile the fit will work on him.

---

9. The rivalry between Laertes and Hamlet in this scene extends even to their rhetoric. Pelion and Olympus, mentioned here by Laertes, and Ossa, mentioned below by Hamlet, are Greek mountains noted in mythology for their height. Olympus was the reputed home of the gods, and the other two were piled one on top of the other by the Giants in an attempt to reach the top of Olympus and overthrow the gods.
1. Casts a spell on.   2. Hot-tempered.   3. Move.   4. Bear with.   5. Will you.   6. Vinegar.
7. Get the best of.   8. Sky in the torrid zone.

Anon, as patient as the female dove
When that her golden couplets[9] are disclosed,
His silence will sit drooping.

HAMLET: Hear you, sir.
240   What is the reason that you use me thus?
I loved you ever. But it is no matter.
Let Hercules himself do what he may,
The cat will mew, and dog will have his day.   [*Exit.*]
KING: I pray thee, good Horatio, wait upon[1] him.

        [*Exit* HORATIO.]

245   [*To* LAERTES.] Strengthen your patience in our last night's speech.
We'll put the matter to the present push.[2]—
Good Gertrude, set some watch over your son.—
This grave shall have a living monument.
An hour of quiet shortly shall we see;
250   Till then in patience our proceeding be.   [*Exeunt.*]

Scene 2

A hall or public room. Enter HAMLET *and* HORATIO.

HAMLET: So much for this, sir; now shall you see the other.
You do remember all the circumstance?
HORATIO: Remember it, my lord!
HAMLET: Sir, in my heart there was a kind of fighting
5   That would not let me sleep. Methought I lay
Worse than the mutines in the bilboes.[3] Rashly,
And praised be rashness for it—let us know,
Our indiscretion sometime serves us well,
When our deep plots do pall; and that should learn[4] us
10   There's a divinity that shapes our ends,
Rough-hew them how we will—
HORATIO: That is most certain.
HAMLET: Up from my cabin,
My sea-gown scarfed[5] about me, in the dark
Groped I to find out them, had my desire,
15   Fingered their packet, and in fine[6] withdrew
To mine own room again, making so bold,
My fears forgetting manners, to unseal
Their grand commission; where I found, Horatio—
Ah, royal knavery!—an exact[7] command,
20   Larded[8] with many several sorts of reasons,
Importing Denmark's health, and England's too,
With, ho! such bugs and goblins in my life,[9]
That on the supervise,[1] no leisure bated,
No, not to stay the grinding of the axe,

9. Pair of eggs.   1. Attend.   2. Immediate trial.   3. Stocks. *Mutines:* mutineers.   4. Teach.
5. Wrapped.   6. Quickly. *Fingered:* stole.   7. Precisely stated.   8. Garnished.
9. Such dangers if I remained alive.   1. As soon as the commission was read.

My head should be struck off.

HORATIO: Is't possible?   25

HAMLET: Here's the commission; read it at more leisure.
   But wilt thou hear now how I did proceed?

HORATIO: I beseech you.

HAMLET: Being thus benetted[2] round with villainies,
   Ere I could make a prologue to my brains,   30
   They had begun the play. I sat me down,
   Devised a new commission, wrote it fair.[3]
   I once did hold it, as our statists[4] do,
   A baseness to write fair, and labored much
   How to forget that learning; but sir, now   35
   It did me yeoman's service.[5] Wilt thou know
   Th' effect[6] of what I wrote?

HORATIO: Ay, good my lord.

HAMLET: An earnest conjuration from the king,
   As England was his faithful tributary,[7]
   As love between them like the palm might flourish,   40
   As peace should still her wheaten garland wear
   And stand a comma 'tween their amities[8]
   And many such like as's of great charge,[9]
   That on the view and knowing of these contents,
   Without debatement[1] further more or less,   45
   He should those bearers put to sudden death,
   Not shriving-time allowed.[2]

HORATIO: How was this sealed?

HAMLET: Why, even in that was heaven ordinant,[3]
   I had my father's signet in my purse,
   Which was the model of that Danish seal,   50
   Folded the writ up in the form of th' other,
   Subscribed it, gave't th' impression,[4] placed it safely,
   The changeling[5] never known. Now, the next day
   Was our sea-fight, and what to this was sequent[6]
   Thou knowest already.   55

HORATIO: So Guildenstern and Rosencrantz go to't.

HAMLET: Why, man, they did make love to this employment.
   They are not near my conscience; their defeat[7]
   Does by their own insinuation grow.
   'Tis dangerous when the baser nature comes   60
   Between the pass and fell[8] incensèd points
   Of mighty opposites.

HORATIO: Why, what a king is this!

HAMLET: Does it not, think thee, stand me now upon—
   He that hath killed my king and whored my mother,
   Popped in between th' election and my hopes,   65

2. Caught in a net.   3. Legibly. *Devised*: made.   4. Politicians.   5. Served me well.   6. Contents.
7. Vassal.   8. Link friendships.   9. Import.   1. Consideration.   2. Without time for confession.
3. Operative.   4. With the seal.   5. Replacement.   6. Followed.
7. Death. *Are not near*: do not touch.   8. Cruel. *Pass*: thrust.

Thrown out his angle[9] for my proper life,
And with such coz'nage[1]—is't not perfect conscience
To quit[2] him with this arm? And is't not to be damned
To let this canker of our nature come
70 In further evil?
HORATIO: It must be shortly known to him from England
What is the issue[3] of the business there.
HAMLET: It will be short;[4] the interim is mine.
And a man's life's no more than to say "one."
75 But I am very sorry, good Horatio,
That to Laertes I forgot myself;
For by the image of my cause I see
The portraiture of his. I'll court his favors.
But sure the bravery[5] of his grief did put me
Into a tow'ring passion.
80 HORATIO: Peace; who comes here?

     [Enter OSRIC.]

OSRIC: Your lordship is right welcome back to Denmark.
HAMLET: I humbly thank you, sir. [Aside to HORATIO.] Dost know this water-fly?
HORATIO: [Aside to HAMLET.] No, my good lord.
HAMLET: [Aside to HORATIO.] Thy state is the more gracious, for 'tis a vice to know
85   him. He hath much land, and fertile. Let a beast be lord of beasts, and his crib
     shall stand at the king's mess. 'Tis a chough,[6] but as I say, spacious in the pos-
     session of dirt.
OSRIC: Sweet lord, if your lordship were at leisure, I should impart a thing to you
     from his majesty.
90 HAMLET: I will receive it, sir, with all diligence of spirit. Put your bonnet to his
     right use. 'Tis for the head.[7]
OSRIC: I thank your lordship, it is very hot.
HAMLET: No, believe me, 'tis very cold; the wind is northerly.
OSRIC: It is indifferent[8] cold, my lord, indeed.
95 HAMLET: But yet methinks it is very sultry and hot for my complexion.[9]
OSRIC: Exceedingly, my lord; it is very sultry, as 'twere—I cannot tell how. My lord,
     his majesty bade me signify to you that 'a has laid a great wager on your head.
     Sir, this is the matter—
HAMLET: I beseech you, remember.   [Moves him to put on his hat.]
100 OSRIC: Nay, good my lord; for my ease, in good faith. Sir, here is newly come to
     court Laertes; believe me, an absolute[1] gentleman, full of most excellent dif-
     ferences of very soft society and great showing.[2] Indeed, to speak feelingly of
     him, he is the card or calendar of gentry, for you shall find in him the conti-
     nent[3] of what part a gentleman would see.
105 HAMLET: Sir, his definement[4] suffers no perdition in you, though I know to
     divide him inventorially would dozy[5] th' arithmetic of memory, and yet but

9. Fishhook.   1. Trickery.   2. Repay.   3. Outcome.   4. Soon.   5. Exaggerated display.
6. Jackdaw.   7. Osric has evidently removed his hat in deference to the prince.   8. Moderately.
9. Temperament.   1. Perfect.   2. Good manners. *Excellent differences*: qualities.
3. Sum total. *Calendar*: measure.   4. Description.   5. Steer wildly. *Dozy*: daze. *Divide him inventorially*:
examine bit by bit.

yaw neither in respect of his quick sail. But in the verity of extolment, I take him to be a soul of great article,[6] and his infusion of such dearth and rareness as, to make true diction of him, his semblage is his mirror,[7] and who else would trace him, his umbrage,[8] nothing more. 110

OSRIC: Your lordship speaks most infallibly of him.

HAMLET: The concernancy,[9] sir? Why do we wrap the gentleman in our more rawer breath?[1]

OSRIC: Sir?

HORATIO: Is't not possible to understand in another tongue? You will to't, sir, 115 really.

HAMLET: What imports the nomination[2] of this gentleman?

OSRIC: Of Laertes?

HORATIO: [*Aside.*] His purse is empty already. All's golden words are spent.

HAMLET: Of him, sir. 120

OSRIC: I know you are not ignorant—

HAMLET: I would you did, sir; yet, in faith, if you did, it would not much approve me. Well, sir.

OSRIC: You are not ignorant of what excellence Laertes is—

HAMLET: I dare not confess that, lest I should compare[3] with him in excellence; 125 but to know a man well were to know himself.

OSRIC: I mean, sir, for his weapon; but in the imputation[4] laid on him by them, in his meed he's unfellowed.[5]

HAMLET: What's his weapon?

OSRIC: Rapier and dagger. 130

HAMLET: That's two of his weapons—but well.

OSRIC: The king, sir, hath wagered with him six Barbary horses, against the which he has impawned,[6] as I take it, six French rapiers and poniards, with their assigns, as girdle, hangers,[7] and so. Three of the carriages, in faith, are very dear to fancy,[8] very responsive to the hilts, most delicate carriages, and of 135 very liberal conceit.[9]

HAMLET: What call you the carriages?

HORATIO: [*Aside to* HAMLET.] I knew you must be edified by the margent[1] ere you had done.

OSRIC: The carriages, sir, are the hangers. 140

HAMLET: The phrase would be more germane to the matter if we could carry a cannon by our sides. I would it might be hangers till then. But on! Six Barbary horses against six French swords, their assigns, and three liberal conceited carriages; that's the French bet against the Danish. Why is this all impawned, as you call it? 145

OSRIC: The king, sir, hath laid, sir, that in a dozen passes between yourself and him he shall not exceed you three hits; he hath laid on twelve for nine, and it would come to immediate trial if your lordship would vouchsafe the answer.

HAMLET: How if I answer no?

OSRIC: I mean, my lord, the opposition of your person in trial. 150

---

6. Nature. *Article*: scope.

7. That is, his likeness ("semblage") is (only) his own mirror image; he is unrivaled. *Diction*: telling.

8. Shadow. *Trace*: keep pace with. 9. Meaning. (Hamlet is mocking Osric's affected speech.)

1. Cruder words. 2. Naming. 3. That is, compare myself. 4. Reputation.

5. Unequaled in his excellence. 6. Staked. 7. Sword belts. *Assigns*: appurtenances.

8. Finely designed. 9. Elegant design. *Delicate*: well adjusted. 1. Marginal gloss.

HAMLET: Sir, I will walk here in the hall. If it please his majesty, it is the breathing time[2] of day with me. Let the foils be brought, the gentleman willing, and the king hold his purpose; I will win for him an I can. If not, I will gain nothing but my shame and the odd hits.

155 OSRIC: Shall I deliver you so?

HAMLET: To this effect, sir, after what flourish your nature will.

OSRIC: I commend my duty to your lordship.

HAMLET: Yours, yours. [*Exit* OSRIC.] He does well to commend it himself; there are no tongues else for's turn.

160 HORATIO: This lapwing runs away with the shell on his head.[3]

HAMLET: 'A did comply, sir, with his dug[4] before 'a sucked it. Thus has he, and many more of the same bevy that I know the drossy age dotes on, only got the tune of the time; and out of an habit of encounter, a king of yesty[5] collection which carries them through and through the most fanned and winnowed

165 opinions; and do but blow them to their trial, the bubbles are out.

[*Enter a* LORD.]

LORD: My lord, his majesty commended him to you by young Osric, who brings back to him that you attend[6] him in the hall. He sends to know if your pleasure hold to play with Laertes, or that you will take longer time.

HAMLET: I am constant to my purposes; they follow the king's pleasure. If his fit-
170 ness speaks, mine is ready; now or whensoever, provided I be so able as now.

LORD: The king and queen and all are coming down.

HAMLET: In happy time.

LORD: The queen desires you to use some gentle entertainment[7] to Laertes before you fall to play.

175 HAMLET: She well instructs me.   [*Exit* LORD.]

HORATIO: You will lose this wager, my lord.

HAMLET: I do not think so. Since he went into France I have been in continual practice. I shall win at the odds. But thou wouldst not think how ill[8] all's here about my heart. But it's no matter.

180 HORATIO: Nay, good my lord—

HAMLET: It is but foolery, but it is such a kind of gaingiving[9] as would perhaps trouble a woman.

HORATIO: If your mind dislike anything, obey it. I will forestall their repair[1] hither, and say you are not fit.

185 HAMLET: Not a whit, we defy augury. There is special providence in the fall of a sparrow. If it be now, 'tis not to come; if it be not to come, it will be now; if it be not now, yet it will come. The readiness is all. Since no man of aught he leaves knows, what is't to leave betimes? Let be.

[*A table prepared. Enter* TRUMPETS, DRUMS, *and* OFFICERS *with cushions;* KING, QUEEN, OSRIC *and* ATTENDANTS *with foils, daggers, and* LAERTES.]

KING: Come, Hamlet, come and take this hand from me.

---

2. Time for exercise.
3. The lapwing was thought to be so precocious that it could run immediately after being hatched, even, as here, with bits of the shell still on its head.   4. Mother's breast. *Comply*: deal formally.   5. Yeasty.
6. Await.   7. Cordiality.   8. Uneasy.   9. Misgiving.   1. Coming.

[*The* KING *puts* LAERTES' *hand into* HAMLET'*s*.]

HAMLET: Give me your pardon, sir. I have done you wrong,   190
  But pardon 't as you are a gentleman.
  This presence[2] knows, and you must needs have heard,
  How I am punished with a sore distraction.
  What I have done
  That might your nature, honor, and exception,[3]   195
  Roughly awake, I here proclaim was madness.
  Was 't Hamlet wronged Laertes? Never Hamlet.
  If Hamlet from himself be ta'en away,
  And when he's not himself does wrong Laertes,
  Then Hamlet does it not, Hamlet denies it.   200
  Who does it then? His madness. If 't be so,
  Hamlet is of the faction that is wronged;
  His madness is poor Hamlet's enemy.
  Sir, in this audience,
  Let my disclaiming from[4] a purposed evil   205
  Free[5] me so far in your most generous thoughts
  That I have shot my arrow o'er the house
  And hurt my brother.
LAERTES: I am satisfied in nature,
  Whose motive in this case should stir me most
  To my revenge. But in my terms of honor   210
  I stand aloof, and will no reconcilement
  Till by some elder masters of known honor
  I have a voice[6] and precedent of peace
  To keep my name ungored.[7] But till that time
  I do receive your offered love like love,   215
  And will not wrong it.
HAMLET: I embrace it freely,
  And will this brother's wager frankly[8] play.
  Give us the foils. Come on.
LAERTES: Come, one for me.
HAMLET: I'll be your foil, Laertes. In mine ignorance
  Your skill shall, like a star i' th' darkest night,   220
  Stick fiery off[9] indeed.
LAERTES: You mock me, sir.
HAMLET: No, by this hand.
KING: Give them the foils, young Osric. Cousin Hamlet,
  You know the wager?
HAMLET: Very well, my lord;
  Your Grace has laid the odds o' th' weaker side.   225
KING: I do not fear it, I have seen you both;
  But since he is bettered[1] we have therefore odds.
LAERTES: This is too heavy; let me see another.
HAMLET: This likes me well. These foils have all a[2] length?

2. Company.   3. Resentment.   4. Denying of.   5. Absolve.   6. Authority.   7. Unshamed.
8. Freely.   9. Shine brightly.   1. Reported better.   2. The same. *Likes*: suits.

[*They prepare to play.*]

230 OSRIC: Ay, my good lord.
     KING: Set me the stoups of wine upon that table.
         If Hamlet give the first or second hit,
         Or quit in answer of[3] the third exchange,
         Let all the battlements their ordnance fire.
235   The king shall drink to Hamlet's better breath,
         And in the cup an union[4] shall he throw,
         Richer than that which four successive kings
         In Denmark's crown have worn. Give me the cups,
         And let the kettle[5] to the trumpet speak,
240   The trumpet to the cannoneer without,
         The cannons to the heavens, the heaven to earth,
         "Now the king drinks to Hamlet." Come, begin—

         [*Trumpets the while.*]

         And you, the judges, bear a wary eye.
     HAMLET: Come on, sir.
     LAERTES: Come, my lord.

         [*They play.*]

     HAMLET: One.
     LAERTES: No.
     HAMLET: **Judgment?**
245 OSRIC: A hit, a very palpable hit.

         [*Drums, trumpets, and shot. Flourish; a piece goes off.*]

     LAERTES: Well, again.
     KING: Stay, give me drink. Hamlet, this pearl is thine.
         Here's to thy health. Give him the cup.
     HAMLET: I'll play this bout first; set it by awhile.
250 Come.

         [*They play.*]

         Another hit; what say you?
     LAERTES: A touch, a touch, I do confess't.
     KING: Our son shall win.
     QUEEN: He's fat,[6] and scant of breath.
         Here, Hamlet, take my napkin, rub thy brows.
255   The queen carouses to thy fortune, Hamlet.
     HAMLET: Good madam!
     KING: Gertrude, do not drink.
     QUEEN: I will, my lord; I pray you pardon me.
     KING: [*Aside.*] It is the poisoned cup; it is too late.
260 HAMLET: I dare not drink yet, madam; by and by.
     QUEEN: Come, let me wipe thy face.
     LAERTES: My lord, I'll hit him now.

3. Repay.   4. Pearl.   5. Kettledrum.   6. Out of shape.

KING: I do not think't.

LAERTES: [*Aside.*] And yet it is almost against my conscience.

HAMLET: Come, for the third, Laertes. You do but dally.
I pray you pass[7] with your best violence;   265
I am afeard you make a wanton of me.[8]

LAERTES: Say you so? Come on.

[*They play.*]

OSRIC: Nothing, neither way.

LAERTES: Have at you now!

[LAERTES *wounds* HAMLET: *then, in scuffling, they change rapiers, and* HAMLET *wounds* LAERTES.]

KING: Part them. They are incensed.   270

HAMLET: Nay, come again.

[*The* QUEEN *falls.*]

OSRIC: Look to the queen there, ho!

HORATIO: They bleed on both sides. How is it, my lord?

OSRIC: How is't, Laertes?

LAERTES: Why, as a woodcock to mine own springe,[9] Osric.   275
I am justly killed with mine own treachery.

HAMLET: How does the queen?

KING: She swoons to see them bleed.

QUEEN: No, no, the drink, the drink! O my dear Hamlet!
The drink, the drink! I am poisoned.   [*Dies.*]

HAMLET: O, villainy! Ho! let the door be locked.   280
Treachery! seek it out.

LAERTES: It is here, Hamlet. Hamlet, thou art slain;
No med'cine in the world can do thee good.
In thee there is not half an hour's life.
The treacherous instrument is in thy hand,   285
Unbated[1] and envenomed. The foul practice
Hath turned itself on me. Lo, here I lie,
Never to rise again. Thy mother's poisoned.
I can no more. The king, the king's to blame.

HAMLET: The point envenomed too?   290
Then, venom, to thy work.   [*Hurts the* KING.]

ALL: Treason! treason!

KING: O, yet defend me, friends. I am but hurt.[2]

HAMLET: Here, thou incestuous, murd'rous, damnèd Dane,
Drink off this potion. Is thy union here?   295
Follow my mother.

[*The* KING *dies.*]

LAERTES: He is justly served.
It is a poison tempered[3] by himself.

7. Attack.   8. Trifle with me.   9. Snare.   1. Unblunted.   2. Wounded.   3. Mixed.

Exchange forgiveness with me, noble Hamlet.
Mine and my father's death come not upon thee,
300   Nor thine on me!   *[Dies.]*
HAMLET: Heaven make thee free of[4] it! I follow thee.
    I am dead, Horatio. Wretched queen, adieu!
    You that look pale and tremble at this chance,[5]
    That are but mutes or audience to this act,
305   Had I but time, as this fell sergeant Death
    Is strict in his arrest,[6] O, I could tell you—
    But let it be. Horatio, I am dead:
    Thou livest; report me and my cause aright
    To the unsatisfied.[7]
HORATIO: Never believe it.
310   I am more an antique Roman than a Dane.
    Here's yet some liquor left.
HAMLET: As th'art a man,
    Give me the cup. Let go. By heaven, I'll ha't.
    O God, Horatio, what a wounded name,
    Things standing thus unknown, shall live behind me!
315   If thou didst ever hold me in thy heart,
    Absent thee from felicity awhile,
    And in this harsh world draw thy breath in pain,
    To tell my story.

       [A march afar off.]

                 What warlike noise is this?
OSRIC: Young Fortinbras, with conquest come from Poland,
320   To th' ambassadors of England gives
    This warlike volley.[8]
HAMLET: O, I die, Horatio!
    The potent poison quite o'er-crows[9] my spirit.
    I cannot live to hear the news from England,
    But I do prophesy th' election[1] lights
325   On Fortinbras. He has my dying voice.[2]
    So tell him, with th' occurrents,[3] more and less,
    Which have solicited[4]—the rest is silence.   *[Dies.]*
HORATIO: Now cracks a noble heart. Good night, sweet prince,
    And flights of angels sing thee to thy rest!

      [March within.]

330   Why does the drum come hither?

      [Enter FORTINBRAS, *with the* AMBASSADORS *and with drum, colors, and* ATTEN-
    DANTS.]

---

4. Forgive.   5. Circumstance.   6. Summons to court.   7. Uninformed.
8. The staging presents some difficulties here. Unless Osric is clairvoyant, he must have left the stage at
some point and returned. One possibility is that he might have left to carry out Hamlet's order to lock the
door (line 280) and returned when the sound of the distant march is heard.   9. Overcomes.
1. (Of a new king for Denmark.)   2. Support.   3. Circumstances.   4. Brought about this scene.

FORTINBRAS: Where is this sight?

HORATIO: What is it you would see?
   If aught of woe or wonder, cease your search.

FORTINBRAS: This quarry cries on havoc.[5] O proud death,
   What feast is toward[6] in thine eternal cell
   That thou so many princes at a shot   335
   So bloodily hast struck?

AMBASSADORS: The sight is dismal;
   And our affairs from England come too late.
   The ears are senseless[7] that should give us hearing
   To tell him his commandment is fulfilled,
   That Rosencrantz and Guildenstern are dead.   340
   Where should we have our thanks?

HORATIO: Not from his mouth,
   Had it th' ability of life to thank you.
   He never gave commandment for their death.
   But since, so jump[8] upon this bloody question,
   You from the Polack wars, and you from England,   345
   Are here arrived, give orders that these bodies
   High on a stage be placèd to the view,
   And let me speak to th' yet unknowing world
   How these things came about. So shall you hear
   Of carnal, bloody, and unnatural acts;   350
   Of accidental judgments, casual[9] slaughters;
   Of deaths put on by cunning and forced cause;
   And, in this upshot,[1] purposes mistook
   Fall'n on th' inventors' heads. All this can I
   Truly deliver.

FORTINBRAS: Let us haste to hear it,   355
   And call the noblest to the audience.[2]
   For me, with sorrow I embrace my fortune.
   I have some rights of memory[3] in this kingdom,
   Which now to claim my vantage[4] doth invite me.

HORATIO: Of that I shall have also cause to speak,   360
   And from his mouth whose voice will draw on more.
   But let this same be presently performed,
   Even while men's minds are wild, lest more mischance
   On plots and errors happen.

FORTINBRAS: Let four captains
   Bear Hamlet like a soldier to the stage,   365
   For he was likely, had he been put on,[5]
   To have proved most royal; and for his passage
   The soldier's music and the rite of war
   Speak loudly for him.
   Take up the bodies. Such a sight as this   370

5. The game killed in the hunt proclaims a slaughter.   6. In preparation.
7. Without sense of hearing.   8. Exactly.   9. Brought about by apparent accident.   1. Result.
2. Hearing.   3. Succession.   4. Position.   5. Elected king.

Becomes the field,[6] but here shows much amiss.
Go, bid the soldiers shoot.   [*Exeunt marching. A peal of ordnance shot off.*]

ca. 1600

SUGGESTIONS FOR WRITING

1. In *A Midsummer Night's Dream*'s best-known speech, Theseus asserts that "The luna-tic, the lover, and the poet / Are of imagination all compact" (5.1.7–8). Citing evi-dence from the play, write an essay analyzing Shakespeare's characterization of love—not only in the play's action but also in the words of the love-obsessed char-acters. Is Shakespearean love merely a kind of madness, or does it contain hints of a guiding wisdom beyond the awareness of lovers themselves?

2. Early in *A Midsummer Night's Dream*, Helena remarks, "Love looks not with the eyes, but with the mind" (1.1.234). The play is filled with references to eyes and vision; indeed, the plot hinges on the differences between what characters see and what they think they see. Using specific examples, write an essay exploring the signifi-cance of eyes, sight, and seeing in this play. What does the play suggest about the power and the limitations of human vision?

3. In ancient Greek tragedy, misfortune is often the result of *hubris*—the excessive pride that leads a hero to overstep the bounds of his destiny and thus to offend the gods. More recent writing about tragedy develops the concept of *hamartia*—the notion that the protagonist's fate is brought about by a tragic flaw or failing of character. What propels *Hamlet*—the prince's proud wish to avenge his father's death and assert his rights? A tragic flaw in Hamlet's otherwise noble character? Or something else altogether? Write an essay examining the circumstances and moti-vations that lead to Hamlet's death and the fall of Denmark.

4. Some critics have focused on the psychological underpinnings of *Hamlet*; others have seen the play as political commentary. In 1600 (the approximate date of *Ham-let*'s first performance), Queen Elizabeth I was sixty-seven and had no direct heirs, a situation that promised no end to the wars and rebellions over succession to the throne that had plagued England for the preceding two centuries. Drawing on the play and, if need be, your own research into the politics of Shakespeare's era, write an essay showing how England's historical circumstances may be reflected in *Hamlet*.

5. In both *A Midsummer Night's Dream* and *Hamlet*, characters perform a play. What are the functions and effects of this device? What might the plays within plays suggest about the value of drama—including the value of plays like Shakespeare's own? What different attitudes toward drama are displayed by various characters in *A Midsummer Night's Dream* and *Hamlet*? Write an essay exploring the function and significance of these plays within plays. What attitudes toward drama does Shake-speare encourage us to adopt?

6. For centuries Shakespeare's plays have been celebrated for their originality and variety. Samuel Johnson, the great eighteenth-century literary critic, once wrote of Shakespeare that "Each change of many-colour'd life he drew." T. S. Eliot claimed that, of all writers, "Shakespeare gives the greatest width of human passion." Still, for all their variety, most of Shakespeare's plays follow fairly rigid formulas for either comedy or tragedy. Write an essay in which you discuss either (a) how *A Mid-summer Night's Dream* and at least one other Shakespeare play (for example, *The Merchant of Venice, As You Like It,* or *Twelfth Night*) typify Shakespearean comedy, or (b) how *Hamlet* and at least one other Shakespeare play (for example, *Romeo and Juliet, Julius Caesar,* or *Macbeth*) typify Shakespearean tragedy.

---

6. Battlefield.

29   PERFORMANCE AS CONTEXT

What is the relationship between a printed play or script and a play performed onstage? Can we fully absorb and understand *Hamlet* in the heat of performance, as the actors quickly speak their lines? Alternatively, might we lose a sense of the drama if we do not witness it in person but instead silently read the speeches of Ophelia or Polonius or Hamlet? The difference between reading and watching a play is only one factor that influences our understanding and judgment of drama. There are also the differences, subtle and marked, between any two productions of the same play, and even between any two performances of the same production. A performing art like dance or music, live drama unfolds in real time through the collaboration of various people. This collaboration, which includes the design of the stage or set, the lighting, the costumes and props, and the sound, is always the result of an interpretation of the play. With the guidance of a director, the actors make decisions, consciously or not, about how to perform the lines and actions required by the play. In its entirety, a performance is a unique interpretation, created by a group of people, of the text of a play.

Because reading and performance provide different insights into drama, many theatergoers like to read a play before or after they see it performed. In turn, a perceptive reading of any play requires you to imagine what it might be like in performance. As you read a play, consider its title, the cast of characters and stage directions, and the representation of time and place (in terms of both the historical period and geographical setting as well as the timing and location of the scenes shown on stage). Imagine the appearance, costumes, vocal styles, and movements of each of the characters throughout each scene: Who is on stage, who is claiming the attention or yielding to whom, who walks, who sits, who busies himself or herself with a book, a game, or a chore? Are any sound or lighting effects needed? Are any props picked up, brought on stage, or carried off?

Once you have a good idea of what happens step by step in a performance of a play, you are in a better position to raise questions about what it all means. If you know you will write about or even perform the play, you should make notes on the first reading. Mark passages directly on the page as you read, or use post-it flags that can be removed. Then write down your observations and questions, using the boxes in chapter 26 as a guide. Which differences between the characters seem most important? What causes the decisive conflict that must be resolved, or at least eased, by the play's end? For the sake of analysis, pinpoint which portion of the play corresponds with each of the five stages of plot: exposition, rising action, climax, falling action, and conclusion. Are there surprises, delays, or disappointments in how the conflict is set up, how it is brought out in the open, how it is resolved? What does each character know at the end that he or she did not know earlier? Has power shifted from one character to another at the end? Once you understand the characters and the plot or structure, look again more closely at specific scenes and lines. What tone of voice should an actor use, and what gestures should he or she make while speaking the lines?

Just as you should consider the possibilities for performance when you read a play, you should ask whether any live performance of a play that you attend fulfills the expectations or understanding of the play you formed when you read it. How does seeing the play performed enhance your understanding of it? What choices did the director and actors make that affected your experience of the play? What would you have done differently? Is the play itself written according to standards and customs of an earlier era, or does it represent a more modern or an innovative style? And are the production and acting traditional or experimental, whether in keeping with the original manner of the play or not?

Tastes and styles in drama, as in other genres, have changed over the centuries. Indeed, attitudes toward the theater in general have changed drastically over the years. Today, fine acting, particularly in classic and dramatic roles, is widely recognized as an art. The most successful actors (who are, arguably, not always the best actors) are compensated generously for their work, and their personal lives are scrutinized and glamorized by the public and the media. But in some periods of history, theater had a bad reputation as popular entertainment that attracted rough crowds. Actors and especially actresses were not respectable and they usually led a wandering, impoverished life.

As recently as the nineteenth century, some critics, such as the writer Charles Lamb, believed that the theater was a vulgar spectacle. Lamb felt that reading a play by Shakespeare in private was a loftier pursuit of great literature than going to see it performed in public. For Lamb, the performer merely mimics passions with tricks of expression and gestures to please the ear and eye. It is Shakespeare the playwright who has the genius to comprehend the range of the human spirit, yet the audience often gives the actor the credit for the qualities that the playwright wrote into the character. Although Lamb conceded that a performance can provide a "juvenile pleasure" to the viewers, he cautioned that "When the novelty is past, we find to our cost that, instead of realising an idea, we have only materialised and brought down a fine vision to the standard of flesh and blood." Lamb protests against having his mind's "free conceptions thus cramped and pressed down to . . . actuality," preferring his own imagining of all the possible ways to perform the lines over a single version that was staged on one occasion.

Few would take Lamb's position against performance today. Opinions of the theater have changed, just as plays written across the centuries have varied in their appeal to readers of drama as well as audiences. You may find it easier to appreciate a recent play with a contemporary style and current themes. Or you may prefer classics written forty or one hundred years ago—or even four centuries ago, if Shakespeare's plays are your favorites. Or you may enjoy plays of all different types.

Your response to a performance will also depend a great deal on how the play is interpreted, which in turn is influenced by the artistic standards of the playwright's time as well as our own. By the middle of the twentieth century, many actors were influenced by Russian acting techniques associated with Anton Chekhov and Konstantin Stanislavsky (1863–1938), the Russian actor and producer.

The final scene of the original Broadway production of Tennessee Williams's play *A Streetcar Named Desire* is shown on December 17, 1947, in New York City. The cast includes Marlon Brando as Stanley Kowalski, Kim Hunter as Stella, and Jessica Tandy as Blanche. (AP Photo)

Stanislavsky recommended that an actor prepare a role by reconstructing a history for the character and drawing on memories of similar experiences to arouse the feelings and physical responses needed to perform the part. Stanislavsky's "Method" became the standard training for actors in the United States by the middle of the twentieth century. Method acting was popularized, in fact, by Marlon Brando, who played Stanley in Elia Kazan's stage and movie versions of Tennessee Williams's *A Streetcar Named Desire*. (Tributes to Brando when he died in 2004 gave him credit for transforming the way actors act.) Actors today will usually have learned some Method techniques, though schools of acting in other countries approach the art quite differently. When you read a play from an earlier century, though, you should bear in mind that the style of acting then would probably strike us as mannered and artificial, if we could see it now. But even today's stage acting may seem too "theatrical" to viewers who are accustomed to film and television, which have fostered quieter, more subtle styles of speech and gesture suited to camera close-ups.

Great Roles, Great Performances

Some famous actors have put their stamp on certain roles, making it difficult for any other actor to play that character without responding to the precedent. This is especially true of performances in the premiere, or first production, of a play or musical, such as Rex Harrison's performance as Professor Higgins in *My Fair Lady*. Some roles are so famous and challenging that every ambitious performer wants to have a chance at them, hoping to create something memorable, as Sir Laurence Olivier created a memorable Hamlet or Dame Maggie Smith created a famous Hedda Gabler.

Arthur Miller's *Death of a Salesman* is a modern American play that has built up a history of famous performances in "revivals" or new productions. It began as a successful Broadway production that led to a film version. Below are some images of famous actors in the leading tragic role of Willy Loman in *Death of a Salesman*. Compare the personalities and scenes captured in these stills. How might each actor bring out different nuances in the role?

Mark Bazeley (as Happy Loman), Brian Dennehy (as Willy Loman), and Douglas Henshall (as Biff Loman) in the production *Death of a Salesman* at the Lyric Theater in London

Lee J. Cobb, Mildred Dunnock, and Arthur Kennedy, scene from *Death of a Salesman*

Styles of production and staging, like styles of acting, follow historical trends. *A Streetcar Named Desire* and *Death of a Salesman* were first staged within two years of each other. Both plays express the harshness of the competitive postwar world. In the original Broadway productions, the sets of *Streetcar* and *Salesman* showed the inside and outside of cramped, low-income homes; both plays used invasive shadows and sounds to convey the characters' confinement. And with their intermixing of symbolic staging, poetic monologues, realistic everyday action, and explicit psychological and sexual motivation, Williams and Miller together influenced theater across the globe.

Different dramatic styles have developed to express different themes and different conceptions of character and experience. Realistic theater, such as the production of Susan Glaspell's *Trifles* at the Provincetown Playhouse in 1916, allows us to pretend that we are observing real people who would behave the same way even if we were not watching. Experimental plays from the 1950s and 1960s, such as Tom Stoppard's *The Real Inspector Hound* as performed in London, do little to hide their fictionality; they often use the effect of "breaking down the fourth wall," reminding us that we are sitting in a theater watching a performance on a set that represents only three sides of a room or other location.

More recent innovators in the theater world have gone even farther, viewing the text or script as a kind of straitjacket on the mad genius of performance. Some advocates of performance art and performance studies since the 1960s have looked down on the staging of written dramas as a restrictive, predictable, outmoded practice. Within the broad potential of theatrical performance, is a text necessary at all? Must actors speak at all, or must they speak words already written down? Today, while plays continue to be written, produced, and performed more or less by traditional rules, there is also a thriving world of experimental performance: autobiographical or conceptual performance art that occurs unannounced on city streets or on the Internet; group improvisation on a stage before a paying audience; or "devised" theater, rehearsed from a plan or script, sometimes combining dance, music, mime, puppetry, electronic media, and perhaps some written or improvised speech. The meanings of theatricality and performance have been stretched, and the twenty-first century will undoubtedly see a continuing transformation of drama and theater.

The plays in this chapter were all written down and have all been published. They have also been staged in various ways. Williams's *A Streetcar Named Desire* first appeared in 1947 and relied on traditional expectations for staging and performance. The play represents a version of everyday contemporary reality in a real city; the emotional communication between characters is the center of the action. Realistic dialogue also prevails in Suzan-Lori Parks's recent experiment in playwriting, *365 Days / 365 Plays* (2006), but the situations are more obviously fictitious than in *Streetcar*, and the characters are simply types. In contrast, Samuel Beckett's 1956 *Act Without Words* extended the possibilities for a short play: One unnamed character interacts with unseen "agents" of movement and sound that create the effects and events onstage without ever appearing as human characters. The written text, without dialogue, consists entirely of stage directions for the actor and for everyone else behind the scenes.

Mikhail Baryshnikov in JoAnne Akalaitis's 2007 production of *Act Without Words I*

SAMUEL BECKETT

Act Without Words I

Desert. Dazzling light.

The man is flung backwards on stage from right wing.[1] He falls, gets up immediately, dusts himself, turns aside, reflects.

Whistle from right wing.

He reflects, goes out right.

Immediately flung back on stage he falls, gets up immediately, dusts himself, turns aside, reflects.

Whistle from left wing.

He reflects, goes out left.

Immediately flung back on stage he falls, gets up immediately, dusts himself, turns aside, reflects.

Whistle from left wing.

He reflects, goes towards left wing, hesitates, thinks better of it, halts, turns aside, reflects.

A little tree descends from flies,[2] lands. It has a single bough some three yards from ground and at its summit a meagre tuft of palms casting at its foot a circle of shadow.

---

1. That is, from offstage, right side.   2. Space above the stage where lights, scenery, etc. can be hung.

He continues to reflect.

Whistle from above.

He turns, sees tree, reflects, goes to it, sits down in its shadow, looks at his hands.

A pair of tailor's scissors descends from flies, comes to rest before tree, a yard from ground.

He continues to look at his hands.

Whistle from above.

He looks up, sees scissors, takes them and starts to trim his nails.

The palms close like a parasol, the shadow disappears.

He drops scissors, reflects.

A tiny carafe, to which is attached a huge label inscribed WATER, descends from flies, comes to rest some three yards from ground.

He continues to reflect.

Whistle from above.

He looks up, sees carafe, reflects, gets up, goes and stands under it, tries in vain to reach it, renounces, turns aside, reflects.

A big cube descends from flies, lands.

He continues to reflect.

Whistle from above.

He turns, sees cube, looks at it, at carafe, reflects, goes to cube, takes it up, carries it over and sets it down under carafe, tests its stability, gets up on it, tries in vain to reach carafe, renounces, gets down, carries cube back to its place, turns aside, reflects.

A second smaller cube descends from flies, lands.

He continues to reflect.

Whistle from above.

He turns, sees second cube, looks at it, at carafe, goes to second cube, takes it up, carries it over and sets it down under carafe, tests its stability, gets up on it, tries in vain to reach carafe, renounces, gets down, takes up second cube to carry it back to its place, hesitates, thinks better of it, sets it down, goes to big cube, takes it up, carries it over and puts it on small one, tests their stability, gets up on them, the cubes collapse, he falls, gets up immediately, brushes himself, reflects.

He takes up small cube, puts it on big one, tests their stability, gets up on them and is about to reach carafe when it is pulled up a little way and comes to rest beyond his reach.

He gets down, reflects, carries cubes back to their place, one by one, turns aside, reflects.

A third still smaller cube descends from flies, lands.

He continues to reflect.

Whistle from above.

He turns, sees third cube, looks at it, reflects, turns aside, reflects.

The third cube is pulled up and disappears in flies.

Beside carafe a rope descends from flies, with knots to facilitate ascent.

He continues to reflect.

Whistle from above.

He turns, sees rope, reflects, goes to it, climbs up it and is about to reach carafe when rope is let out and deposits him back on ground.

He reflects, looks around for scissors, sees them, goes and picks them up, returns to rope and starts to cut it with scissors.

The rope is pulled up, lifts him off ground, he hangs on, succeeds in cutting rope, falls back on ground, drops scissors, gets up again immediately, brushes himself, reflects.

The rope is pulled up quickly and disappears in flies.

With length of rope in his possession he makes a lasso with which he tries to lasso the carafe.

The carafe is pulled up quickly and disappears in flies.

He turns aside, reflects.

He goes with lasso in his hand to tree, looks at bough, turns and looks at cubes, looks again at bough, drops lasso, goes to cubes, takes up small one, carries it over and sets it down under bough, goes back for big one, takes it up and carries it over under bough, makes to put it on small one, hesitates, thinks better of it, sets it down, takes up small one and puts it on big one, tests their stability, turns aside and stoops to pick up lasso.

The bough folds down against trunk.

He straightens up with lasso in his hand, turns and sees what has happened.

He drops lasso, turns aside, reflects.

He carries back cubes to their place, one by one, goes back for lasso, carries it over to the cubes and lays it in a neat coil on small one.

He turns aside, reflects.

Whistle from right wing.

He reflects, goes out right.

Immediately flung back on stage he falls, gets up immediately, brushes himself, turns aside, reflects.

Whistle from left wing.

He does not move.

He looks at his hands, looks round for scissors, sees them, goes and picks them up, starts to trim his nails, stops, reflects, runs his finger along blade of scissors, goes and lays them on small cube, turns aside, opens his collar, frees his neck and fingers it.

The small cube is pulled up and disappears in flies, carrying away rope and scissors.

He turns to take scissors, sees what has happened.

He turns aside, reflects.

He goes and sits down on big cube.

The big cube is pulled from under him. He falls. The big cube is pulled up and disappears in flies.

He remains lying on his side, his face towards auditorium, staring before him.

The carafe descends from flies and comes to rest a few feet from his body.

He does not move.

Whistle from above.

He does not move.

The carafe descends further, dangles and plays about his face.

He does not move.

The carafe is pulled up and disappears in flies.

The bough returns to horizontal, the palms open, the shadow returns.

Whistle from above.
He does not move.
The tree is pulled up and disappears in flies.
He looks at his hands.

CURTAIN

1956

QUESTIONS

1. What would be added or lost in *Act Without Words I* if "the man" had a name? if he were described in the stage directions? if he made sounds? if he talked to himself?
2. What is the plot of Beckett's one-act play? Is there more than one character?
3. Why is "water" the only word the audience perceives in a theatrical performance of this play?

SUGGESTIONS FOR WRITING

1. The man in Beckett's play "reflects" again and again. Write a short essay in which you analyze what the man is apparently thinking about or realizing, based each time on what he does next. Why does the play not specify what the man should think? Would an actor change expression or behavior to show changing reactions and expectations? What reflection does the audience have by the end of the play (that is, what is the theme of the play)?
2. Write an essay in which you compare one or more of Suzan-Lori Parks's plays with Samuel Beckett's *Act Without Words I.* Does each play work with audience expectations in a similar way? What is the significance of objects or sounds caused by something offstage in one or more of the plays? What similar or different acting styles seem appropriate? How do the plays use the space of the stage? Be sure to take into account (briefly) the different historical contexts and careers of the two playwrights.
3. Repetition is often a source of comedy. In *Act Without Words I,* there is a certain humor in the whistles, checks, and assorted instructions, temptations, or taunts. Why is it not a comedy altogether? How much or how little should a performance invite the audience to laugh? Write an essay defending your interpretation of the appropriate tone of the play, specifying how and when the performance would avoid or encourage amusement.
4. Find reviews of *Act Without Words I* or other Beckett plays. (The *New York Times* and the *London Times* or other newspapers are available online.) Search for criticism on Beckett and his style of drama. Write a research essay on changing responses to Beckett's plays since the 1950s. What other writers is he compared to? How do reviewers and critics express Beckett's view of the world, and how do they respond to his style of writing and to specific performances?

TENNESSEE WILLIAMS

A Streetcar Named Desire

> And so it was I entered the broken world
> To trace the visionary company of love,
> its voice
> An instant in the wind (I know not
> whither hurled)
> But not for long to hold each desperate
> choice.
>
> —"THE BROKEN TOWER" BY HART
> CRANE[1]

CHARACTERS

BLANCHE	EUNICE	A DOCTOR
STELLA	STEVE	A NURSE (MATRON)
STANLEY	PABLO	A YOUNG COLLECTOR
MITCH	A NEGRO WOMAN	A MEXICAN WOMAN

Scene 1

The exterior of a two-story corner building on a street in New Orleans which is named Elysian Fields and runs between the L & N tracks and the river.[2] The section is poor but, unlike corresponding sections in other American cities, it has a raffish charm. The houses are mostly white frame, weathered grey, with rickety outside stairs and galleries and quaintly ornamented gables. This building contains two flats, upstairs and down. Faded white stairs ascend to the entrances of both.

It is first dark of an evening early in May. The sky that shows around the dim white building is a peculiarly tender blue, almost a turquoise, which invests the scene with a kind of lyricism and gracefully attenuates the atmosphere of decay. You can almost feel the warm breath of the brown river beyond the river warehouses with their faint redolences of bananas and coffee. A corresponding air is evoked by the music of Negro entertainers at a barroom around the corner. In this part of New Orleans you are practically always just around the corner, or a few doors down the street, from a tinny piano being played with the infatuated fluency of brown fingers. This "Blue Piano" expresses the spirit of the life which goes on here.

Two women, one white and one colored, are taking the air on the steps of the building. The white woman is EUNICE, who occupies the upstairs flat; the NEGRO WOMAN, a neighbor, for New Orleans is a cosmopolitan city where there is a relatively warm and easy intermingling of races in the old part of town.

Above the music of the "Blue Piano" the voices of people on the street can be heard overlapping.

---

1. American poet (1899–1932).

2. Elysian Fields is in fact a New Orleans street at the northern tip of the French Quarter, between the Louisville & Nashville railroad tracks and the Mississippi River. In Greek mythology, the Elysian Fields are the abode of the blessed in the afterlife; in Paris, the Champs-Élysées ("Elysian Fields") is a grand boulevard.

[*Two men come around the corner,* STANLEY KOWALSKI *and* MITCH. *They are about twenty-eight, or thirty years old, roughly dressed in blue denim work clothes.* STANLEY *carries his bowling jacket and a red-stained package from a butcher's. They stop at the foot of the steps.*]

STANLEY: [*Bellowing.*] Hey there! Stella, baby!

[STELLA *comes out on the first floor landing, a gentle young woman, about twenty-five, and of a background obviously quite different from her husband's.*]

STELLA: [*Mildly.*] Don't holler at me like that. Hi, Mitch.

STANLEY: Catch!

STELLA: What?

STANLEY: Meat!

[*He heaves the package at her. She cries out in protest but manages to catch it: then she laughs breathlessly. Her husband and his companion have already started back around the corner.*]

STELLA: [*Calling after him.*] Stanley! Where are you going?

STANLEY: Bowling!

STELLA: Can I come watch?

STANLEY: Come on. [*He goes out.*]

STELLA: Be over soon. [*To the* WHITE WOMAN.] Hello, Eunice. How are you?

EUNICE: I'm all right. Tell Steve to get him a poor boy's sandwich[3] 'cause nothing's left here.

[*They all laugh; the* NEGRO WOMAN *does not stop.* STELLA *goes out.*]

NEGRO WOMAN: What was that package he th'ew at 'er? [*She rises from steps, laughing louder.*]

EUNICE: You hush, now!

NEGRO WOMAN: Catch *what!*

[*She continues to laugh.* BLANCHE *comes around the corner, carrying a valise. She looks at a slip of paper, then at the building, then again at the slip and again at the building. Her expression is one of shocked disbelief. Her appearance is incongruous to this setting. She is daintily dressed in a white suit with a fluffy bodice, necklace and earrings of pearl, white gloves and hat, looking as if she were arriving at a summer tea or cocktail party in the garden district.[4] She is about five years older than* STELLA. *Her delicate beauty must avoid a strong light. There is something about her uncertain manner, as well as her white clothes, that suggests a moth.*]

EUNICE: [*Finally.*] What's the matter, honey? Are you lost?

BLANCHE: [*With faintly hysterical humor.*] They told me to take a street-car named Desire, and then transfer to one called Cemeteries[5] and ride six blocks and get off at—Elysian Fields!

EUNICE: That's where you are now.

BLANCHE: At Elysian Fields?

EUNICE: This here is Elysian Fields.

BLANCHE: They mustn't have—understood—what number I wanted. . . .

---

3. Usually called just "poor boy" or "po' boy"; similar to a hero or submarine sandwich.

4. Wealthy, fashionable section of New Orleans.

5. Desire is a street in New Orleans; Cemeteries is the end of a streetcar line that stopped at a cemetery.

EUNICE: What number you lookin' for?

[BLANCHE *wearily refers to the slip of paper.*]

BLANCHE: Six thirty-two.

EUNICE: You don't have to look no further.

BLANCHE: [*Uncomprehendingly.*] I'm looking for my sister, Stella DuBois, I mean—Mrs. Stanley Kowalski.

EUNICE: That's the party.—You just did miss her, though.

BLANCHE: This—can this be—her home?

EUNICE: She's got the downstairs here and I got the up.

BLANCHE: Oh. She's—out?

EUNICE: You noticed that bowling alley around the corner?

BLANCHE: I'm—not sure I did.

EUNICE: Well, that's where she's at, watchin' her husband bowl. [*There is a pause.*] You want to leave your suitcase here an' go find her?

BLANCHE: No.

NEGRO WOMAN: I'll go tell her you come.

BLANCHE: Thanks.

NEGRO WOMAN: You welcome. [*She goes out.*]

EUNICE: She wasn't expecting you?

BLANCHE: No. No, not tonight.

EUNICE: Well, why don't you just go in and make yourself at home till they get back.

BLANCHE: How could I—do that?

EUNICE: We own this place so I can let you in.

[*She gets up and opens the downstairs door. A light goes on behind the blind, turning it light blue. BLANCHE slowly follows her into the downstairs flat. The surrounding areas dim out as the interior is lighted. Two rooms can be seen, not too clearly defined. The one first entered is primarily a kitchen but contains a folding bed to be used by BLANCHE. The room beyond this is a bedroom. Off this room is a narrow door to a bathroom.*]

EUNICE: [*Defensively, noticing BLANCHE's look.*] It's sort of messed up right now but when it's clean it's real sweet.

BLANCHE: Is it?

EUNICE: Uh-huh, I think so. So you're Stella's sister?

BLANCHE: Yes. [*Wanting to get rid of her.*] Thanks for letting me in.

EUNICE: *Por nada,* as the Mexicans say, *por nada!*[6] Stella spoke of you.

BLANCHE: Yes?

EUNICE: I think she said you taught school.

BLANCHE: Yes.

EUNICE: And you're from Mississippi, huh?

BLANCHE: Yes.

EUNICE: She showed me a picture of your home-place, the plantation.

BLANCHE: Belle Reve?[7]

EUNICE: A great big place with white columns.

BLANCHE: Yes . . .

---

6. It's nothing.   7. Beautiful Dream.

EUNICE: A place like that must be awful hard to keep up.

BLANCHE: If you will excuse me, I'm just about to drop.

EUNICE: Sure, honey. Why don't you set down?

BLANCHE: What I meant was I'd like to be left alone.

EUNICE: [*Offended.*] Aw. I'll make myself scarce, in that case.

BLANCHE: I didn't mean to be rude, but—

EUNICE: I'll drop by the bowling alley an' hustle her up. [*She goes out the door.*]

[BLANCHE *sits in a chair very stiffly with her shoulders slightly hunched and her legs pressed close together and her hands tightly clutching her purse as if she were quite cold. After a while the blind look goes out of her eyes and she begins to look slowly around. A cat screeches. She catches her breath with a startled gesture. Suddenly she notices something in a half opened closet. She springs up and crosses to it, and removes a whiskey bottle. She pours a half tumbler of whiskey and tosses it down. She carefully replaces the bottle and washes out the tumbler at the sink. Then she resumes her seat in front of the table.*]

BLANCHE: [*Faintly to herself.*] I've got to keep hold of myself!

[STELLA *comes quickly around the corner of the building and runs to the door of the downstairs flat.*]

STELLA: [*Calling out joyfully.*] Blanche!

[*For a moment they stare at each other. Then* BLANCHE *springs up and runs to her with a wild cry.*]

BLANCHE: Stella, oh, Stella, Stella! Stella for Star![8] [*She begins to speak with feverish vivacity as if she feared for either of them to stop and think. They catch each other in a spasmodic embrace.*] Now, then, let me look at you. But don't you look at me, Stella, no, no, no, not till later, not till I've bathed and rested! And turn that over-light off! Turn that off! I won't be looked at in this merciless glare! [STELLA *laughs and complies.*] Come back here now! Oh, my baby! Stella! Stella for Star! [*She embraces her again.*] I thought you would never come back to this horrible place! What am I saying? I didn't mean to say that. I meant to be nice about it and say—Oh, what a convenient location and such—Ha-a-ha! Precious lamb! You haven't said a *word* to me.

STELLA: You haven't given me a chance to, honey! [*She laughs, but her glance at* BLANCHE *is a little anxious.*]

BLANCHE: Well, now you talk. Open your pretty mouth and talk while I look around for some liquor! I know you must have some liquor on the place! Where could it be, I wonder? Oh, I spy, I spy! [*She rushes to the closet and removes the bottle; she is shaking all over and panting for breath as she tries to laugh. The bottle nearly slips from her grasp.*]

STELLA: [*Noticing.*] Blanche, you sit down and let me pour the drinks. I don't know what we've got to mix with. Maybe a Coke in the icebox. Look'n see, honey, while I'm—

BLANCHE: No Coke, honey, not with my nerves tonight! Where—where—where is—?

---

8. *Stella* is "star" in Latin.

STELLA: Stanley? Bowling! He loves it. They're having a—found some soda!—tournament. . . .

BLANCHE: Just water, baby, to chase it! Now don't get worried, your sister hasn't turned into a drunkard, she's just all shaken up and hot and tired and dirty! You sit down, now, and explain this place to me! What are you doing in a place like this?

STELLA: Now, Blanche—

BLANCHE: Oh, I'm not going to be hypocritical, I'm going to be honestly critical about it! Never, never, never in my worst dreams could I picture—Only Poe! Only Mr. Edgar Allan Poe!—could do it justice! Out there I suppose is the ghoul-haunted woodland of Weir![9] [*She laughs.*]

STELLA: No, honey, those are the L & N tracks.

BLANCHE: No, now seriously, putting joking aside. Why didn't you tell me, why didn't you write me, honey, why didn't you let me know?

STELLA: [*Carefully, pouring herself a drink.*] Tell you what, Blanche?

BLANCHE: Why, that you had to live in these conditions!

STELLA: Aren't you being a little intense about it? It's not that bad at all! New Orleans isn't like other cities.

BLANCHE: This has got nothing to do with New Orleans. You might as well say—forgive me, blessed baby! [*She suddenly stops short.*] The subject is closed!

STELLA: [*A little drily.*] Thanks.

[*During the pause,* BLANCHE *stares at her. She smiles at* BLANCHE.]

BLANCHE: [*Looking down at her glass, which shakes in her hand.*] You're all I've got in the world, and you're not glad to see me!

STELLA: [*Sincerely.*] Why, Blanche, you know that's not true.

BLANCHE: No?—I'd forgotten how quiet you were.

STELLA: You never did give me a chance to say much, Blanche. So I just got in the habit of being quiet around you.

BLANCHE: [*Vaguely.*] A good habit to get into . . . [*Then, abruptly.*] You haven't asked me how I happened to get away from the school before the spring term ended.

STELLA: Well, I thought you'd volunteer that information—if you wanted to tell me.

BLANCHE: You thought I'd been fired?

STELLA: No, I—thought you might have—resigned. . . .

BLANCHE: I was so exhausted by all I'd been through my—nerves broke. [*Nervously tamping cigarette.*] I was on the verge of—lunacy, almost! So Mr. Graves—Mr. Graves is the high school superintendent—he suggested I take a leave of absence. I couldn't put all of those details into the wire.[1] . . . [*She drinks quickly.*] Oh, this buzzes right through me and feels so *good*!

STELLA: Won't you have another?

BLANCHE: No, one's my limit.

STELLA: Sure?

BLANCHE: You haven't said a word about my appearance.

STELLA: You look just fine.

---

9. From the refrain of Poe's gothic ballad "Ulalume" (1847).   1. Telegram.

BLANCHE: God love you for a liar! Daylight never exposed so total a ruin! But you—you've put on some weight, yes, you're just as plump as a little partridge! And it's so becoming to you!

STELLA: Now, Blanche—

BLANCHE: Yes, it is, it is or I wouldn't say it! You just have to watch around the hips a little. Stand up.

STELLA: Not now.

BLANCHE: You hear me? I said stand up! [STELLA *complies reluctantly.*] You messy child, you, you've spilt something on that pretty white lace collar! About your hair—you ought to have it cut in a feather bob with your dainty features. Stella, you have a maid, don't you?

STELLA: No. With only two rooms it's—

BLANCHE: What? *Two* rooms, did you say?

STELLA: This one and— [*She is embarrassed.*]

BLANCHE: The other one? [*She laughs sharply. There is an embarrassed silence.*] I am going to take just one little tiny nip more, sort of to put the stopper on, so to speak. . . . Then put the bottle away so I won't be tempted. [*She rises.*] I want you to look at *my* figure! [*She turns around.*] You know I haven't put on one ounce in ten years, Stella? I weigh what I weighed the summer you left Belle Reve. The summer Dad died and you left us. . . .

STELLA: [*A little wearily.*] It's just incredible, Blanche, how well you're looking.

BLANCHE: [*They both laugh uncomfortably.*] But, Stella, there's only two rooms, I don't see where you're going to put me!

STELLA: We're going to put you in here.

BLANCHE: What kind of bed's this—one of those collapsible things? [*She sits on it.*]

STELLA: Does it feel all right?

BLANCHE: [*Dubiously.*] Wonderful, honey. I don't like a bed that gives much. But there's no door between the two rooms, and Stanley—will it be decent?

STELLA: Stanley is Polish, you know.

BLANCHE: Oh, yes. They're something like Irish, aren't they?

STELLA: Well—

BLANCHE: Only not so—highbrow? [*They both laugh again in the same way.*] I brought some nice clothes to meet all your lovely friends in.

STELLA: I'm afraid you won't think they are lovely.

BLANCHE: What are they like?

STELLA: They're Stanley's friends.

BLANCHE: Polacks?

STELLA: They're a mixed lot, Blanche.

BLANCHE: Heterogeneous—types?

STELLA: Oh, yes. Yes, types is right!

BLANCHE: Well—anyhow—I brought nice clothes and I'll wear them. I guess you're hoping I'll say I'll put up at a hotel, but I'm not going to put up at a hotel. I want to be *near* you, got to be *with* somebody, I *can't* be *alone*! Because—as you must have noticed—I'm—*not* very *well*. . . . [*Her voice drops and her look is frightened.*]

STELLA: You seem a little bit nervous or overwrought or something.

BLANCHE: Will Stanley like me, or will I be just a visiting in-law, Stella? I couldn't stand that.

STELLA: You'll get along fine together, if you'll just try not to—well—compare him with men that we went out with at home.

BLANCHE: Is he so—different?

STELLA: Yes. A different species.

BLANCHE: In what way; what's he like?

STELLA: Oh, you can't describe someone you're in love with! Here's a picture of him! [*She hands a photograph to* BLANCHE.]

BLANCHE: An officer?

STELLA: A Master Sergeant in the Engineers' Corps. Those are decorations!

BLANCHE: He had those on when you met him?

STELLA: I assure you I wasn't just blinded by all the brass.

BLANCHE: That's not what I—

STELLA: But of course there were things to adjust myself to later on.

BLANCHE: Such as his civilian background! [STELLA *laughs uncertainly.*] How did he take it when you said I was coming?

STELLA: Oh, Stanley doesn't know yet.

BLANCHE: [*Frightened.*] You—haven't told him?

STELLA: He's on the road a good deal.

BLANCHE: Oh. Travels?

STELLA: Yes.

BLANCHE: Good. I mean—isn't it?

STELLA: [*Half to herself.*] I can hardly stand it when he is away for a night . . .

BLANCHE: Why, Stella!

STELLA: When he's away for a week I nearly go wild!

BLANCHE: Gracious!

STELLA: And when he comes back I cry on his lap like a baby. . . . [*She smiles to herself.*]

BLANCHE: I guess that is what is meant by being in love. . . . [STELLA *looks up with a radiant smile.*] Stella—

STELLA: What?

BLANCHE: [*In an uneasy rush.*] I haven't asked you the things you probably thought I was going to ask. And so I'll expect you to be understanding about what *I* have to tell *you.*

STELLA: What, Blanche? [*Her face turns anxious.*]

BLANCHE: Well, Stella—you're going to reproach me, I know that you're bound to reproach me—but before you do—take into consideration—you left! I stayed and struggled! You came to New Orleans and looked out for yourself! *I* stayed at Belle Reve and tried to hold it together! I'm not meaning this in any reproachful way, but *all* the burden descended on *my* shoulders.

STELLA: The best I could do was make my own living, Blanche.

[BLANCHE *begins to shake again with intensity.*]

BLANCHE: I know, I know. But you are the one that abandoned Belle Reve, not I! I stayed and fought for it, bled for it, almost died for it!

STELLA: Stop this hysterical outburst and tell me what's happened? What do you mean fought and bled? What kind of—

BLANCHE: I knew you would, Stella. I knew you would take this attitude about it!

STELLA: About—what?—please!

BLANCHE: [*Slowly.*] The loss—the loss . . .

STELLA: Belle Reve? Lost, is it? No!

BLANCHE: Yes, Stella.

[*They stare at each other across the yellow-checked linoleum of the table.* BLANCHE *slowly nods her head and* STELLA *looks slowly down at her hands folded on the table. The music of the "Blue Piano" grows louder.* BLANCHE *touches her handkerchief to her forehead.*]

STELLA: But how did it go? What happened?

BLANCHE: [*Springing up.*] You're a fine one to ask me how it went!

STELLA: Blanche!

BLANCHE: You're a fine one to sit there *accusing me* of it!

STELLA: *Blanche!*

BLANCHE: I, I, *I* took the blows in my face and my body! All of those deaths! The long parade to the graveyard! Father, Mother! Margaret, that dreadful way! So big with it, it couldn't be put in a coffin! But had to be burned like rubbish! You just came home in time for the funerals, Stella. And funerals are pretty compared to deaths. Funerals are quiet, but deaths—not always. Sometimes their breathing is hoarse, and sometimes it rattles, and sometimes they even cry out to you, "Don't let me go!" Even the old, sometimes, say, "Don't let me go." As if you were able to stop them! But funerals are quiet, with pretty flowers. And, oh, what gorgeous boxes they pack them away in! Unless you were there at the bed when they cried out, "Hold me!" you'd never suspect there was the struggle for breath and bleeding. You didn't dream, but I saw! Saw! Saw! And now you sit there telling me with your eyes that I let the place go! How in hell do you think all that sickness and dying was paid for? Death is expensive, Miss Stella! And old Cousin Jessie's right after Margaret's, hers! Why, the Grim Reaper[2] had put up his tent on our doorstep! . . . Stella. Belle Reve was his headquarters! Honey—that's how it slipped through my fingers! Which of them left us a fortune? Which of them left a cent of insurance even? Only poor Jessie—one hundred to pay for her coffin. That was all, Stella! And I with my pitiful salary at the school. Yes, accuse me! Sit there and stare at me, thinking I let the place go! *I* let the place go? Where were *you*! In bed with your— Polack!

STELLA: [*Springing.*] Blanche! You be still! That's enough! [*She starts out.*]

BLANCHE: Where are you going?

STELLA: I'm going into the bathroom to wash my face.

BLANCHE: Oh, Stella, Stella, you're crying!

STELLA: Does that surprise you?

BLANCHE: Forgive me—I didn't mean to—

[*The sound of men's voices is heard.* STELLA *goes into the bathroom, closing the door behind her. When the men appear, and* BLANCHE *realizes it must be* STANLEY *returning, she moves uncertainly from the bathroom door to the dressing table, looking apprehensively toward the front door.* STANLEY *enters, followed by* STEVE *and* MITCH. STANLEY *pauses near his door,* STEVE *by the foot of the spiral stair, and* MITCH *is slightly above and to the right of them, about to go out. As the men enter, we hear some of the following dialogue.*]

STANLEY: Is that how he got it?

2. Death.

STEVE: Sure that's how he got it. He hit the old weather-bird for 300 bucks on a six-number-ticket.[3]

MITCH: Don't tell him those things; he'll believe it. [MITCH *starts out.*]

STANLEY: [*Restraining* MITCH.] Hey, Mitch—come back here.

[BLANCHE, *at the sound of voices, retires in the bedroom. She picks up* STANLEY's *photo from dressing table, looks at it, puts it down. When* STANLEY *enters the apartment, she darts and hides behind the screen at the head of bed.*]

STEVE: [*To* STANLEY *and* MITCH.] Hey, are we playin' poker tomorrow?

STANLEY: Sure—at Mitch's.

MITCH: [*Hearing this, returns quickly to the stair rail.*] No—not at my place. My mother's still sick!

STANLEY: Okay, at my place . . . [MITCH *starts out again.*] But you bring the beer!

[MITCH *pretends not to hear—calls out "Good night, all," and goes out, singing.* EUNICE's *voice is heard, above.*]

EUNICE: Break it up down there! I made the spaghetti dish and ate it myself.

STEVE: [*Going upstairs.*] I told you and phoned you we was playing. [*To the men.*] Jax[4] beer!

EUNICE: You never phoned me once.

STEVE: I told you at breakfast—and phoned you at lunch. . . .

EUNICE: Well, never mind about that. You just get yourself home here once in a while.

STEVE: You want it in the papers?

[*More laughter and shouts of parting come from the men.* STANLEY *throws the screen door of the kitchen open and comes in. He is of medium height, about five feet eight or nine, and strongly, compactly built. Animal joy in his being is implicit in all his movements and attitudes. Since earliest manhood the center of his life has been pleasure with women, the giving and taking of it, not with weak indulgence, dependently, but with the power and pride of a richly feathered male bird among hens. Branching out from this complete and satisfying center are all the auxiliary channels of his life, such as his heartiness with men, his appreciation of rough humor, his love of good drink and food and games, his car, his radio, everything that is his, that bears his emblem of the gaudy seed-bearer. He sizes women up at a glance, with sexual classifications, crude images flashing into his mind and determining the way he smiles at them.*]

BLANCHE: [*Drawing involuntarily back from his stare.*] You must be Stanley. I'm Blanche.

STANLEY: Stella's sister?

BLANCHE: Yes.

STANLEY: H'lo. Where's the little woman?

BLANCHE: In the bathroom.

STANLEY: Oh. Didn't know you were coming in town.

BLANCHE: I—uh—

STANLEY: Where you from, Blanche?

---

3. That is, he won $300 in a lottery. To "hit the weather-bird" in target shooting, means to shoot at a barn and hit the ornamental rooster on the weathervane—an extraordinarily lucky shot.

4. A local brand.

BLANCHE: Why, I—live in Laurel.

[*He has crossed to the closet and removed the whiskey bottle.*]

STANLEY: In Laurel, huh? Oh, yeah. Yeah, in Laurel, that's right. Not in my territory. Liquor goes fast in hot weather. [*He holds the bottle to the light to observe its depletion.*] Have a shot?

BLANCHE: No, I—rarely touch it.

STANLEY: Some people rarely touch it, but it touches them often.

BLANCHE: [*Faintly.*] Ha-ha.

STANLEY: My clothes're stickin' to me. Do you mind if I make myself comfortable?

[*He starts to remove his shirt.*]

BLANCHE: Please, please do.

STANLEY: Be comfortable is my motto.

BLANCHE: It's mine, too. It's hard to stay looking fresh. I haven't washed or even powdered my face and—here you are!

STANLEY: You know you can catch cold sitting around in damp things, especially when you been exercising hard like bowling is. You're a teacher, aren't you?

BLANCHE: Yes.

STANLEY: What do you teach, Blanche?

BLANCHE: English.

STANLEY: I never was a very good English student. How long you here for, Blanche?

BLANCHE: I—don't know yet.

STANLEY: You going to shack up here?

BLANCHE: I thought I would if it's not inconvenient for you all.

STANLEY: Good.

BLANCHE: Traveling wears me out.

STANLEY: Well, take it easy.

[*A cat screeches near the window.* BLANCHE *springs up.*]

BLANCHE: What's that?

STANLEY: Cats, . . . Hey, Stella!

STELLA: [*Faintly, from the bathroom.*] Yes, Stanley.

STANLEY: Haven't fallen in, have you? [*He grins at* BLANCHE. *She tries unsuccessfully to smile back. There is a silence.*] I'm afraid I'll strike you as being the unrefined type. Stella's spoke of you a good deal. You were married once, weren't you?

[*The music of the polka rises up, faint in the distance.*]

BLANCHE: Yes. When I was quite young.

STANLEY: What happened?

BLANCHE: The boy—the boy died. [*She sinks back down.*] I'm afraid I'm—going to be sick! [*Her head falls on her arms.*]

Scene 2

It is six o'clock the following evening. BLANCHE *is bathing.* STELLA *is completing her toilette.* BLANCHE's *dress, a flowered print, is laid out on* STELLA's *bed.*

STANLEY *enters the kitchen from outside, leaving the door open on the perpetual "Blue Piano" around the corner.*

STANLEY: What's all this monkey doings?

STELLA: Oh, Stan! [*She jumps up and kisses him, which he accepts with lordly composure.*] I'm taking Blanche to Galatoire's[5] for supper and then to a show, because it's your poker night.

STANLEY: How about my supper, huh? I'm not going to no Galatoire's for supper!

STELLA: I put you a cold plate on ice.

STANLEY: Well, isn't that just dandy!

STELLA: I'm going to try to keep Blanche out till the party breaks up because I don't know how she would take it. So we'll go to one of the little places in the Quarter afterward and you'd better give me some money.

STANLEY: Where is she?

STELLA: She's soaking in a hot tub to quiet her nerves. She's terribly upset.

STANLEY: Over what?

STELLA: She's been through such an ordeal.

STANLEY: Yeah?

STELLA: Stan, we've—lost Belle Reve!

STANLEY: The place in the country?

STELLA: Yes.

STANLEY: How?

STELLA: [*Vaguely.*] Oh, it had to be—sacrificed or something. [*There is a pause while* STANLEY *considers.* STELLA *is changing into her dress.*] When she comes in be sure to say something nice about her appearance. And, oh! Don't mention the baby. I haven't said anything yet, I'm waiting until she gets in a quieter condition.

STANLEY: [*Ominously.*] So?

STELLA: And try to understand her and be nice to her, Stan.

BLANCHE: [*Singing in the bathroom.*] "From the land of the sky blue water, They brought a captive maid!"[6]

STELLA: She wasn't expecting to find us in such a small place. You see I'd tried to gloss things over a little in my letters.

STANLEY: So?

STELLA: And admire her dress and tell her she's looking wonderful. That's important with Blanche. Her little weakness!

STANLEY: Yeah. I get the idea. Now let's skip back a little to where you said the country place was disposed of.

STELLA: Oh!—yes . . .

STANLEY: How about that? Let's have a few more details on that subjeck.

STELLA: It's best not to talk much about it until she's calmed down.

STANLEY: So that's the deal, huh? Sister Blanche cannot be annoyed with business details right now!

STELLA: You saw how she was last night.

STANLEY: Uh-hum, I saw how she was. Now let's have a gander at the bill of sale.

5. A famous old restaurant on Bourbon Street, the principal street in the French Quarter.
6. From the song "From the Land of Sky-Blue Water" (1908), by Nelle Richmond Eberhart (1871–1944) and Charles Wakefield Cadman (1881–1946), popularized by the Andrews Sisters in the late 1930s.

STELLA: I haven't seen any.

STANLEY: She didn't show you no papers, no deed of sale or nothing like that, huh?

STELLA: It seems like it wasn't sold.

STANLEY: Well, what in hell was it then, give away? To charity?

STELLA: Shhh! She'll hear you.

STANLEY: I don't care if she hears me. Let's see the papers!

STELLA: There weren't any papers, she didn't show any papers, I don't care about papers.

STANLEY: Have you ever heard of the Napoleonic code?[7]

STELLA: No, Stanley, I haven't heard of the Napoleonic code and if I have, I don't see what it—

STANLEY: Let me enlighten you on a point or two, baby.

STELLA: Yes?

STANLEY: In the state of Louisiana we have the Napoleonic code according to which what belongs to the wife belongs to the husband and vice versa. For instance if I had a piece of property, or you had a piece of property—

STELLA: My head is swimming!

STANLEY: All right. I'll wait till she gets through soaking in a hot tub and then I'll inquire if *she* is acquainted with the Napoleonic code. It looks to me like you have been swindled, baby, and when you're swindled under the Napoleonic code I'm swindled *too*. And I don't like to be *swindled*.

STELLA: There's plenty of time to ask her questions later but if you do now she'll go to pieces again. I don't understand what happened to Belle Reve but you don't know how ridiculous you are being when you suggest that my sister or I or anyone of our family could have perpetrated a swindle on anyone else.

STANLEY: Then where's the money if the place was sold?

STELLA: Not sold—*lost, lost!* [*He stalks into bedroom, and she follows him.*] Stanley!

[*He pulls open the wardrobe trunk standing in middle of room and jerks out an armful of dresses.*]

STANLEY: Open your eyes to this stuff! You think she got them out of a teacher's pay?

STELLA: Hush!

STANLEY: Look at these feathers and furs that she come here to preen herself in! What's this here? A solid-gold dress, I believe! And this one! What is these here? Fox-pieces! [*He blows on them.*] Genuine fox fur-pieces, a half a mile long! Where are your fox-pieces, Stella? Bushy snowwhite ones, no less! Where are your white fox-pieces?

STELLA: Those are inexpensive summer furs that Blanche has had a long time.

STANLEY: I got an acquaintance who deals in this sort of merchandise. I'll have him in here to appraise it. I'm willing to bet you there's thousands of dollars invested in this stuff here!

STELLA: Don't be such an idiot, Stanley!

[*He hurls the furs to the day bed. Then he jerks open a small drawer in the trunk and pulls up a fistful of costume jewelry.*]

---

7. This codification of French law (1802), made by Napoleon as emperor, is the basis for Louisiana's civil law.

STANLEY: And what have we here? The treasure chest of a pirate!

STELLA: Oh, Stanley!

STANLEY: Pearls! Ropes of them! What is this sister of yours, a deep-sea diver? Bracelets of solid gold, too! Where are your pearls and gold bracelets?

STELLA: Shhh! Be still, Stanley!

STANLEY: And diamonds! A crown for an empress!

STELLA: A rhinestone tiara she wore to a costume ball.

STANLEY: What's rhinestone?

STELLA: Next door to glass.

STANLEY: Are you kidding? I have an acquaintance that works in a jewelry store. I'll have him in here to make an appraisal of this. Here's your plantation, or what was left of it, here!

STELLA: You have no idea how stupid and horrid you're being! Now close that trunk before she comes out of the bathroom!

[*He kicks the trunk partly closed and sits on the kitchen table.*]

STANLEY: The Kowalskis and the DuBoises have different notions.

STELLA: [*Angrily.*] Indeed they have, thank heavens!—*I'm* going outside. [*She snatches up her white hat and gloves and crosses to the outside door.*] You come out with me while Blanche is getting dressed.

STANLEY: Since when do you give me orders?

STELLA: Are you going to stay here and insult her?

STANLEY: You're damn tootin' I'm going to stay here.

[STELLA *goes out to the porch.* BLANCHE *comes out of the bathroom in a red satin robe.*]

BLANCHE: [*Airily.*] Hello, Stanley! Here I am, all freshly bathed and scented, and feeling like a brand new human being!

[*He lights a cigarette.*]

STANLEY: That's good.

BLANCHE: [*Drawing the curtains at the windows.*] Excuse me while I slip on my pretty new dress!

STANLEY: Go right ahead, Blanche.

[*She closes the drapes between the rooms.*]

BLANCHE: I understand there's to be a little card party to which we ladies are cordially *not* invited!

STANLEY: [*Ominously.*] Yeah?

[BLANCHE *throws off her robe and slips into a flowered print dress.*]

BLANCHE: Where's Stella?

STANLEY: Out on the porch.

BLANCHE: I'm going to ask a favor of you in a moment.

STANLEY: What could that be, I wonder?

BLANCHE: Some buttons in back! You may enter! [*He crosses through drapes with a smoldering look.*] How do I look?

STANLEY: You look all right.

BLANCHE: Many thanks! Now the buttons!

STANLEY: I can't do nothing with them.

BLANCHE: You men with your big clumsy fingers. May I have a drag on your cig?

STANLEY: Have one for yourself.

BLANCHE: Why, thanks! . . . It looks like my trunk has exploded.

STANLEY: Me an' Stella were helping you unpack.

BLANCHE: Well, you certainly did a fast and thorough job of it!

STANLEY: It looks like you raided some stylish shops in Paris.

BLANCHE: Ha-ha! Yes—clothes are my passion!

STANLEY: What does it cost for a string of fur-pieces like that?

BLANCHE: Why, those were a tribute from an admirer of mine!

STANLEY: He must have had a lot of—admiration!

BLANCHE: Oh, in my youth I excited some admiration. But look at me now! [*She smiles at him radiantly.*] Would you think it possible that I was once considered to be—attractive?

STANLEY: Your looks are okay.

BLANCHE: I was fishing for a compliment, Stanley.

STANLEY: I don't go in for that stuff.

BLANCHE: What—stuff?

STANLEY: Compliments to women about their looks. I never met a woman that didn't know if she was good-looking or not without being told, and some of them give themselves credit for more than they've got. I once went out with a doll who said to me, "I am the glamorous type, I am the glamorous type!" I said, "So what?"

BLANCHE: And what did she say then?

STANLEY: She didn't say nothing. That shut her up like a clam.

BLANCHE: Did it end the romance?

STANLEY: It ended the conversation—that was all. Some men are took in by this Hollywood glamor stuff and some men are not.

BLANCHE: I'm sure you belong in the second category.

STANLEY: That's right.

BLANCHE: I cannot imagine any witch of a woman casting a spell over you.

STANLEY: That's—right.

BLANCHE: You're simple, straightforward and honest, a little bit on the primitive side I should think. To interest you a woman would have to— [*She pauses with an indefinite gesture.*]

STANLEY: [*Slowly.*] Lay . . . her cards on the table.

BLANCHE: [*Smiling.*] Well, I never cared for wishy-washy people. That was why, when you walked in here last night, I said to myself—"My sister has married a man!"—Of course that was all that I could tell about you.

STANLEY: [*Booming.*] Now let's cut the re-bop![8]

BLANCHE: [*Pressing hands to her ears.*] Ouuuuu!

STELLA: [*Calling from the steps.*] Stanley! You come out here and let Blanche finish dressing!

BLANCHE: I'm through dressing, honey.

STELLA: Well, you come out, then.

STANLEY: Your sister and I are having a little talk.

---

8. Nonsense (from "bop," a form of jazz).

BLANCHE: [*Lightly.*] Honey, do me a favor. Run to the drugstore and get me a lemon Coke with plenty of chipped ice in it!—Will you do that for me, sweetie?

STELLA: [*Uncertainly.*] Yes. [*She goes around the corner of the building.*]

BLANCHE: The poor little thing was out there listening to us, and I have an idea she doesn't understand you as well as I do. . . . All right; now, Mr. Kowalski, let us proceed without any more double-talk. I'm ready to answer all questions. I've nothing to hide. What is it?

STANLEY: There is such a thing in this state of Louisiana as the Napoleonic code, according to which whatever belongs to my wife is also mine—and vice versa.

BLANCHE: My, but you have an impressive judicial air!

[*She sprays herself with her atomizer; then playfully sprays him with it. He seizes the atomizer and slams it down on the dresser. She throws back her head and laughs.*]

STANLEY: If I didn't know that you was my wife's sister I'd get ideas about you!

BLANCHE: Such as what!

STANLEY: Don't play so dumb. You know what!

BLANCHE: [*She puts the atomizer on the table.*] All right. Cards on the table. That suits me. [*She turns to* STANLEY.] I know I fib a good deal. After all, a woman's charm is fifty per cent illusion, but when a thing is important I tell the truth, and this is the truth: I haven't cheated my sister or you or anyone else as long as I have lived.

STANLEY: Where's the papers? In the trunk?

BLANCHE: Everything that I own is in that trunk. [STANLEY *crosses to the trunk, shoves it roughly open and begins to open compartments.*] What in the name of heaven are you thinking of! What's in the back of that little boy's mind of yours? That I am absconding with something, attempting some kind of treachery on my sister?—Let me do that! It will be faster and simpler. . . . [*She crosses to the trunk and takes out a box.*] I keep my papers mostly in this tin box. [*She opens it.*]

STANLEY: What's them underneath? [*He indicates another sheaf of paper.*]

BLANCHE: These are love-letters, yellowing with antiquity, all from one boy. [*He snatches them up. She speaks fiercely.*] Give those back to me!

STANLEY: I'll have a look at them first!

BLANCHE: The touch of your hands insults them!

STANLEY: Don't pull that stuff!

[*He rips off the ribbon and starts to examine them.* BLANCHE *snatches them from him, and they cascade to the floor.*]

BLANCHE: Now that you've touched them I'll burn them!

STANLEY: [*Staring, baffled.*] What in hell are they?

BLANCHE: [*On the floor gathering them up.*] Poems a dead boy wrote. I hurt him the way that you would like to hurt me, but you can't! I'm not young and vulnerable any more. But my young husband was and I—never mind about that! Just give them back to me!

STANLEY: What do you mean by saying you'll have to burn them?

BLANCHE: I'm sorry, I must have lost my head for a moment. Everyone has something he won't let others touch because of their—intimate nature. . . . [*She now seems faint with exhaustion and she sits down with the strong box and puts on a pair of glasses and goes methodically through a large stack of papers.*] Ambler & Ambler. Hmmmmm. . . . Crabtree. . . . More Ambler & Ambler.

STANLEY: What is Ambler & Ambler?

BLANCHE: A firm that made loans on the place.

STANLEY: Then it *was* lost on a mortgage?

BLANCHE: [*Touching her forehead.*] That must've been what happened.

STANLEY: I don't want no ifs, ands or buts! What's all the rest of them papers?

[*She hands him the entire box. He carries it to the table and starts to examine the papers.*]

BLANCHE: [*Picking up a large envelope containing more papers.*] There are thousands of papers, stretching back over hundreds of years, affecting Belle Reve as, piece by piece, our improvident grandfathers and father and uncles and brothers exchanged the land for their epic fornications—to put it plainly! [*She removes her glasses with an exhausted laugh.*] The four-letter word deprived us of our plantation, till finally all that was left—and Stella can verify that!—was the house itself and about twenty acres of ground, including a graveyard, to which now all but Stella and I have retreated. [*She pours the contents of the envelope on the table.*] Here all of them are, all papers! I hereby endow you with them! Take them, peruse them—commit them to memory, even! I think it's wonderfully fitting that Belle Reve should finally be this bunch of old papers in your big, capable hands! . . . I wonder if Stella's come back with my lemon Coke. . . . [*She leans back and closes her eyes.*]

STANLEY: I have a lawyer acquaintance who will study these out.

BLANCHE: Present them to him with a box of aspirin tablets.

STANLEY: [*Becoming somewhat sheepish.*] You see, under the Napoleonic code—a man has to take an interest in his wife's affairs—especially now that she's going to have a baby.

[BLANCHE *opens her eyes. The "Blue Piano" sounds louder.*]

BLANCHE: Stella? Stella going to have a baby? [*Dreamily.*] I didn't know she was going to have a baby! [*She gets up and crosses to the outside door.* STELLA *appears around the corner with a carton from the drugstore.* STANLEY *goes into the bedroom with the envelope and the box. The inner rooms fade to darkness and the outside wall of the house is visible.* BLANCHE *meets* STELLA *at the foot of the steps to the sidewalk.*] Stella, Stella for star! How lovely to have a baby! It's all right. Everything's all right.

STELLA: I'm sorry he did that to you.

BLANCHE: Oh, I guess he's just not the type that goes for jasmine perfume, but maybe he's what we need to mix with our blood now that we've lost Belle Reve. We thrashed it out. I feel a bit shaky, but I think I handled it nicely, I laughed and treated it all as a joke. [STEVE *and* PABLO *appear, carrying a case of beer.*] I called him a little boy and laughed and flirted. Yes, I was flirting with your husband! [*As the men approach.*] The guests are gathering for the poker party. [*The two men pass between them, and enter the house.*] Which way do we go now, Stella—this way?

STELLA: No, this way. [*She leads* BLANCHE *away.*]

BLANCHE: [*Laughing.*] The blind are leading the blind![9]

---

9. See Matthew 15.14—"If a blind person leads a blind person, both will fall into a pit." *Red-hot!*: Hot dog!

[*A tamale* VENDOR *is heard calling.*]

VENDOR'S VOICE: Red-hot!

Scene 3. The Poker Night

*There is a picture of Van Gogh's of a billiard-parlor at night.[1] The kitchen now suggests that sort of lurid nocturnal brilliance, the raw colors of childhood's spectrum. Over the yellow linoleum of the kitchen table hangs an electric bulb with a vivid green glass shade. The poker players—*STANLEY, STEVE, MITCH *and* PABLO*—wear colored shirts, solid blues, a purple, a red-and-white check, a light green, and they are men at the peak of their physical manhood, as coarse and direct and powerful as the primary colors. There are vivid slices of watermelon on the table, whiskey bottles and glasses. The bedroom is relatively dim with only the light that spills between the portieres and through the wide window on the street.*

For a moment, there is absorbed silence as a hand is dealt.

STEVE: Anything wild this deal?

PABLO: One-eyed jacks are wild.

STEVE: Give me two cards.

PABLO: You, Mitch?

MITCH: I'm out.

PABLO: One.

MITCH: Anyone want a shot?

STANLEY: Yeah. Me.

PABLO: Why don't somebody go to the Chinaman's and bring back a load of chop suey?

STANLEY: When I'm losing you want to eat! Ante up! Openers? Openers! Get y'r ass off the table, Mitch. Nothing belongs on a poker table but cards, chips and whiskey. [*He lurches up and tosses some watermelon rinds to the floor.*]

MITCH: Kind of on your high horse, ain't you?

STANLEY: How many?

STEVE: Give me three.

STANLEY: One.

MITCH: I'm out again. I oughta go home pretty soon.

STANLEY: Shut up.

MITCH: I gotta sick mother. She don't go to sleep until I come in at night.

STANLEY: Then why don't you stay home with her?

MITCH: She says to go out, so I go, but I don't enjoy it. All the while I keep wondering how she is.

STANLEY: Aw, for the sake of Jesus, go home, then!

PABLO: What've you got?

STEVE: Spade flush.

MITCH: You all are married. But I'll be alone when she goes.—I'm going to the bathroom.

STANLEY: Hurry back and we'll fix you a sugar-tit.[2]

MITCH: Aw, go rut. [*He crosses through the bedroom into the bathroom.*]

---

1. *The Night Café,* by Vincent van Gogh (1853–90), Dutch Postimpressionist painter. *The Poker Night* was Williams's first working title for *A Streetcar Named Desire.*   2. Baby's pacifier dipped in sugar.

STEVE: [*Dealing a hand.*] Seven card stud. [*Telling his joke as he deals.*] This ole farmer is out in back of his house sittin' down th'owing corn to the chickens when all at once he hears a loud cackle and this young hen comes lickety split around the side of the house with the rooster right behind her and gaining on her fast.

STANLEY: [*Impatient with the story.*] Deal!

STEVE: But when the rooster catches sight of the farmer th'owing the corn he puts on the brakes and lets the hen get away and starts pecking corn. And the old farmer says, "Lord God, I hopes I never gits *that* hungry!"

[STEVE *and* PABLO *laugh. The sisters appear around the corner of the building.*]

STELLA: The game is still going on.

BLANCHE: How do I look?

STELLA: Lovely, Blanche.

BLANCHE: I feel so hot and frazzled. Wait till I powder before you open the door. Do I look done in?

STELLA: Why no. You are as fresh as a daisy.

BLANCHE: One that's been picked a few days.

[STELLA *opens the door and they enter.*]

STELLA: Well, well, well. I see you boys are still at it?

STANLEY: Where you been?

STELLA: Blanche and I took in a show. Blanche, this is Mr. Gonzales and Mr. Hubbell.

BLANCHE: Please don't get up.

STANLEY: Nobody's going to get up, so don't be worried.

STELLA: How much longer is this game going to continue?

STANLEY: Till we get ready to quit.

BLANCHE: Poker is so fascinating. Could I kibitz?[3]

STANLEY: You could not. Why don't you women go up and sit with Eunice?

STELLA: Because it is nearly two-thirty. [BLANCHE *crosses into the bedroom and partially closes the portieres.*] Couldn't you call it quits after one more hand?

[*A chair scrapes.* STANLEY *gives a loud whack of his hand on her thigh.*]

STELLA: [*Sharply.*] That's not fun, Stanley. [*The men laugh.* STELLA *goes into the bedroom.*] It makes me so mad when he does that in front of people.

BLANCHE: I think I will bathe.

STELLA: Again?

BLANCHE: My nerves are in knots. Is the bathroom occupied?

STELLA: I don't know.

[BLANCHE *knocks.* MITCH *opens the door and comes out, still wiping his hands on a towel.*]

BLANCHE: Oh!—good evening.

MITCH: Hello. [*He stares at her.*]

STELLA: Blanche, this is Harold Mitchell. My sister, Blanche DuBois.

MITCH: [*With awkward courtesy.*] How do you do, Miss DuBois.

3. That is, watch a card player from behind and offer advice.

STELLA: How is your mother now, Mitch?

MITCH: About the same, thanks. She appreciated your sending over that custard.—Excuse me, please.

[*He crosses slowly back into the kitchen, glancing back at* BLANCHE *and coughing a little shyly. He realizes he still has the towel in his hands and with an embarrassed laugh hands it to* STELLA. BLANCHE *looks after him with a certain interest.*]

BLANCHE: That one seems—superior to the others.

STELLA: Yes, he is.

BLANCHE: I thought he had a sort of sensitive look.

STELLA: His mother is sick.

BLANCHE: Is he married?

STELLA: No.

BLANCHE: Is he a wolf?

STELLA: Why, Blanche! [BLANCHE *laughs.*] I don't think he would be.

BLANCHE: What does—what does he do? [*She is unbuttoning her blouse.*]

STELLA: He's on the precision bench in the spare parts department. At the plant Stanley travels for.

BLANCHE: Is that something much?

STELLA: No. Stanley's the only one of his crowd that's likely to get anywhere.

BLANCHE: What makes you think Stanley will?

STELLA: Look at him.

BLANCHE: I've looked at him.

STELLA: Then you should know.

BLANCHE: I'm sorry, but I haven't noticed the stamp of genius even on Stanley's forehead.

[*She takes off the blouse and stands in her pink silk brassiere and white skirt in the light through the portieres. The game has continued in undertones.*]

STELLA: It isn't on his forehead and it isn't genius.

BLANCHE: Oh. Well, what is it, and where? I would like to know.

STELLA: It's a drive that he has. You're standing in the light, Blanche!

BLANCHE: Oh, am I!

[*She moves out of the yellow streak of light.* STELLA *has removed her dress and put on a light blue satin kimona.*[4]]

STELLA: [*With girlish laughter.*] You ought to see their wives.

BLANCHE: [*Laughingly.*] I can imagine. Big, beefy things, I suppose.

STELLA: You know that one upstairs? [*More laughter.*] One time [*Laughing.*] the plaster— [*Laughing.*] cracked—

STANLEY: You hens cut out that conversation in there!

STELLA: You can't hear us.

STANLEY: Well, you can hear me and I said to hush up!

STELLA: This is my house and I'll talk as much as I want to!

BLANCHE: Stella, don't start a row.

STELLA: He's half drunk!—I'll be out in a minute.

4. Kimono.

[*She goes into the bathroom.* BLANCHE *rises and crosses leisurely to a small white radio and turns it on.*]

STANLEY: Awright, Mitch, you in?
MITCH: What? Oh!—No, I'm out!

[BLANCHE *moves back into the streak of light. She raises her arms and stretches, as she moves indolently back to the chair. Rhumba music comes over the radio.* MITCH *rises at the table.*]

STANLEY: Who turned that on in there?
BLANCHE: I did. Do you mind?
STANLEY: Turn it off!
STEVE: Aw, let the girls have their music.
PABLO: Sure, that's good, leave it on!
STEVE: Sounds like Xavier Cugat![5] [STANLEY *jumps up and, crossing to the radio, turns it off. He stops short at the sight of* BLANCHE *in the chair. She returns his look without flinching. Then he sits again at the poker table. Two of the men have started arguing hotly.*] I didn't hear you name it.
PABLO: Didn't I name it, Mitch?
MITCH: I wasn't listenin'.
PABLO: What were you doing, then?
STANLEY: He was looking through them drapes. [*He jumps up and jerks roughly at curtains to close them.*] Now deal the hand over again and let's play cards or quit. Some people get ants when they win.

[MITCH *rises as* STANLEY *returns to his seat.*]

STANLEY: [*Yelling.*] Sit down!
MITCH: I'm going to the "head." Deal me out.
PABLO: Sure he's got ants now. Seven five-dollar bills in his pants pocket folded up tight as spitballs.
STEVE: Tomorrow you'll see him at the cashier's window getting them changed into quarters.
STANLEY: And when he goes home he'll deposit them one by one in a piggy bank his mother give him for Christmas. [*Dealing.*] This game is Spit in the Ocean.

[MITCH *laughs uncomfortably and continues through the portieres. He stops just inside.*]

BLANCHE: [*Softly.*] Hello! The Little Boys' Room is busy right now.
MITCH: We've—been drinking beer.
BLANCHE: I hate beer.
MITCH: It's—a hot weather drink.
BLANCHE: Oh, I don't think so; it always makes me warmer. Have you got any cigs?

[*She has slipped on the dark red satin wrapper.*]

MITCH: Sure.
BLANCHE: What kind are they?
MITCH: Luckies.

5. Spanish-born Cuban bandleader (1900–90), well known for composing and playing rhumbas.

BLANCHE: Oh, good. What a pretty case. Silver?

MITCH: Yes. Yes; read the inscription.

BLANCHE: Oh, is there an inscription? I can't make it out. [*He strikes a match and moves closer.*] Oh! [*Reading with feigned difficulty.*] "And if God choose,/I shall but love thee better—after—death!" Why, that's from my favorite sonnet by Mrs. Browning![6]

MITCH: You know it?

BLANCHE: Certainly I do!

MITCH: There's a story connected with that inscription.

BLANCHE: It sounds like a romance.

MITCH: A pretty sad one.

BLANCHE: Oh?

MITCH: The girl's dead now.

BLANCHE: [*In a tone of deep sympathy.*] Oh!

MITCH: She knew she was dying when she give me this. A very strange girl, very sweet—very!

BLANCHE: She must have been fond of you. Sick people have such deep, sincere attachments.

MITCH: That's right, they certainly do.

BLANCHE: Sorrow makes for sincerity, I think.

MITCH: It sure brings it out in people.

BLANCHE: The little there is belongs to people who have experienced some sorrow.

MITCH: I believe you are right about that.

BLANCHE: I'm positive that I am. Show me a person who hasn't known any sorrow and I'll show you a shuperficial—Listen to me! My tongue is a little—thick! You boys are responsible for it. The show let out at eleven and we couldn't come home on account of the poker game so we had to go somewhere and drink. I'm not accustomed to having more than one drink. Two is the limit— and *three*! [*She laughs.*] Tonight I had three.

STANLEY: Mitch!

MITCH: Deal me out. I'm talking to Miss—

BLANCHE: DuBois.

MITCH: Miss DuBois?

BLANCHE: It's a French name. It means woods and Blanche means white, so the two together mean white woods. Like an orchard in spring! You can remember it by that.

MITCH: You're French?

BLANCHE: We are French by extraction. Our first American ancestors were French Huguenots.[7]

MITCH: You are Stella's sister, are you not?

BLANCHE: Yes, Stella is my precious little sister. I call her little in spite of the fact she's somewhat older than I. Just slightly. Less than a year. Will you do something for me?

6. Elizabeth Barrett Browning (1806–61), British poet, famous for her sequence of love poems, *Sonnets from the Portuguese,* which includes the poem quoted here, "How Do I Love Thee?"
7. Protestants who fled persecution in Catholic France after the Edict of Nantes (1685); many settled in the American South.

MITCH: Sure. What?

BLANCHE: I bought this adorable little colored paper lantern at a Chinese shop on Bourbon. Put it over the light bulb! Will you, please?

MITCH: Be glad to.

BLANCHE: I can't stand a naked light bulb, any more than I can a rude remark or a vulgar action.

MITCH: [*Adjusting the lantern.*] I guess we strike you as being a pretty rough bunch.

BLANCHE: I'm very adaptable—to circumstances.

MITCH: Well, that's a good thing to be. You are visiting Stanley and Stella?

BLANCHE: Stella hasn't been so well lately, and I came down to help her for a while. She's very run down.

MITCH: You're not—?

BLANCHE: Married? No, no. I'm an old maid schoolteacher!

MITCH: You may teach school but you're certainly not an old maid.

BLANCHE: Thank you, sir! I appreciate your gallantry!

MITCH: So you are in the teaching profession?

BLANCHE: Yes. Ah, yes . . .

MITCH: Grade school or high school or—

STANLEY: [*Bellowing.*] Mitch!

MITCH: Coming!

BLANCHE: Gracious, what lung-power! . . . I teach high school. In Laurel.

MITCH: What do you teach? What subject?

BLANCHE: Guess!

MITCH: I bet you teach art or music? [BLANCHE *laughs delicately.*] Of course I could be wrong. You might teach arithmetic.

BLANCHE: Never arithmetic, sir; never arithmetic! [*With a laugh.*] I don't even know my multiplication tables! No, I have the misfortune of being an English instructor. I attempt to instill a bunch of bobby-soxers and drugstore Romeos with reverence for Hawthorne and Whitman and Poe!

MITCH: I guess that some of them are more interested in other things.

BLANCHE: How very right you are! Their literary heritage is not what most of them treasure above all else! But they're sweet things! And in the spring, it's touching to notice them making their first discovery of love! As if nobody had ever known it before! [*The bathroom door opens and* STELLA *comes out.* BLANCHE *continues talking to* MITCH.] Oh! Have you finished? Wait—I'll turn on the radio.

> [*She turns the knobs on the radio and it begins to play* "Wien, Wien, nur du allein."[8] BLANCHE *waltzes to the music with romantic gestures.* MITCH *is delighted and moves in awkward imitation like a dancing bear.* STANLEY *stalks fiercely through the portieres into the bedroom. He crosses to the small white radio and snatches it off the table. With a shouted oath, he tosses the instrument out the window.*]

STELLA: Drunk—drunk—animal thing, you! [*She rushes through to the poker table.*] All of you—please go home! If any of you have one spark of decency in you—

BLANCHE: [*Wildly.*] Stella, watch out, he's—

---

8. "Vienna, Vienna, you are my only," a waltz from an operetta by Franz Lehár (1870–1948).

[STANLEY *charges after* STELLA.]

MEN: [*Feebly.*] Take it easy, Stanley. Easy, fellow.—Let's all—
STELLA: You lay your hands on me and I'll—

[*She backs out of sight. He advances and disappears. There is the sound of a blow,* STELLA *cries out.* BLANCHE *screams and runs into the kitchen. The men rush forward and there is grappling and cursing. Something is overturned with a crash.*]

BLANCHE: [*Shrilly.*] My sister is going to have a baby!
MITCH: This is terrible.
BLANCHE: Lunacy, absolute lunacy!
MITCH: Get him in here, men.

[STANLEY *is forced, pinioned by the two men, into the bedroom. He nearly throws them off. Then all at once he subsides and is limp in their grasp. They speak quietly and lovingly to him and he leans his face on one of their shoulders.*]

STELLA: [*In a high, unnatural voice, out of sight.*] I want to go away, I want to go away!
MITCH: Poker shouldn't be played in a house with women.

[BLANCHE *rushes into the bedroom.*]

BLANCHE: I want my sister's clothes! We'll go to that woman's upstairs!
MITCH: Where is the clothes?
BLANCHE: [*Opening the closet.*] I've got them! [*She rushes through to* STELLA.] Stella, Stella, precious! Dear, dear little sister, don't be afraid!

[*With her arm around* STELLA, BLANCHE *guides her to the outside door and upstairs.*]

STANLEY: [*Dully.*] What's the matter; what's happened?
MITCH: You just blew your top, Stan.
PABLO: He's okay, now.
STEVE: Sure, my boy's okay!
MITCH: Put him on the bed and get a wet towel.
PABLO: I think coffee would do him a world of good, now.
STANLEY: [*Thickly.*] I want water.
MITCH: Put him under the shower!

[*The men talk quietly as they lead him to the bathroom.*]

STANLEY: Let the rut go of me, you sons of bitches!

[*Sounds of blows are heard. The water goes on full tilt.*]

STEVE: Let's get quick out of here!

[*They rush to the poker table and sweep up their winnings on their way out.*]

MITCH: [*Sadly but firmly.*] Poker should not be played in a house with women.

[*The door closes on them and the place is still. The Negro entertainers in the bar around the corner play "Paper Doll"[9] slow and blue. After a moment* STANLEY *comes out of the bathroom dripping water and still in his clinging wet polka dot drawers.*]

9. Song by Johnny S. Black (1915), popularized by the Mills Brothers in the early 1940s.

STANLEY: Stella! [*There is a pause.*] My baby doll's left me! [*He breaks into sobs. Then he goes to the phone and dials, still shuddering with sobs.*] Eunice? I want my baby! [*He waits a moment; then he hangs up and dials again.*] Eunice! I'll keep on ringin' until I talk with my *baby*! [*An indistinguishable shrill voice is heard. He hurls phone to floor. Dissonant brass and piano sounds as the rooms dim out to darkness and the outer walls appear in the night light. The "Blue Piano" plays for a brief interval. Finally,* STANLEY *stumbles half-dressed out to the porch and down the wooden steps to the pavement before the building. There he throws back his head like a baying hound and bellows his wife's name:* "STELLA! STELLA, *sweetheart!* STELLA!"] Stell-*lahhhh*!

EUNICE: [*Calling down from the door of her upper apartment.*] Quit that howling out there an' go back to bed!

STANLEY: I want my baby down here. Stella, Stella!

EUNICE: She ain't comin' down so you quit! Or you'll git th' law on you!

STANLEY: Stella!

EUNICE: You can't beat on a woman an' then call 'er back! She won't come! And her goin' t' have a baby! . . . You stinker! You whelp of a Polack, you! I hope they do haul you in and turn the fire hose on you, same as the last time!

STANLEY: [*Humbly.*] Eunice, I want my girl to come down with me!

EUNICE: Hah! [*She slams her door.*]

STANLEY: [*With heaven-splitting violence.*] STELL-LAHHHHH!

[*The low-tone clarinet moans. The door upstairs opens again.* STELLA *slips down the rickety stairs in her robe. Her eyes are glistening with tears and her hair loose about her throat and shoulders. They stare at each other. Then they come together with low, animal moans. He falls to his knees on the steps and presses his face to her belly, curving a little with maternity. Her eyes go blind with tenderness as she catches his head and raises him level with her. He snatches the screen door open and lifts her off her feet and bears her into the dark flat.* BLANCHE *comes out the upper landing in her robe and slips fearfully down the steps.*]

BLANCHE: Where is my little sister? Stella? Stella?

[*She stops before the dark entrance of her sister's flat. Then catches her breath as if struck. She rushes down to the walk before the house. She looks right and left as if for a sanctuary. The music fades away.* MITCH *appears from around the corner.*]

MITCH: Miss DuBois?

BLANCHE: Oh!

MITCH: All quiet on the Potomac now?[1]

BLANCHE: She ran downstairs and went back in there with him.

MITCH: Sure she did.

BLANCHE: I'm terrified!

MITCH: Ho-ho! There's nothing to be scared of. They're crazy about each other.

BLANCHE: I'm not used to such—

MITCH: Naw, it's a shame this had to happen when you just got here. But don't take it serious.

BLANCHE: Violence! Is so—

MITCH: Set down on the steps and have a cigarette with me.

---

1. "All Quiet on the Potomac" was a Civil War catchphrase, attributed to Union general George McClellan, who pushed the Confederate army back over the Potomac River in 1862.

BLANCHE: I'm not properly dressed.

MITCH: That don't make no difference in the Quarter.

BLANCHE: Such a pretty silver case.

MITCH: I showed you the inscription, didn't I?

BLANCHE: Yes. [*During the pause, she looks up at the sky.*] There's so much—so much confusion in the world. . . . [*He coughs diffidently.*] Thank you for being so kind! I need kindness now.

Scene 4

It is early the following morning. There is a confusion of street cries like a choral chant.

STELLA *is lying down in the bedroom. Her face is serene in the early morning sunlight. One hand rests on her belly, rounding slightly with new maternity. From the other dangles a book of colored comics. Her eyes and lips have that almost narcotized tranquility that is in the faces of Eastern idols.*

The table is sloppy with remains of breakfast and the debris of the preceding night, and STANLEY's *gaudy pyjamas lie across the threshold of the bathroom. The outside door is slightly ajar on a sky of summer brilliance.*

BLANCHE *appears at this door. She has spent a sleepless night and her appearance entirely contrasts with* STELLA's. *She presses her knuckles nervously to her lips as she looks through the door, before entering.*

BLANCHE: Stella?

STELLA: [*Stirring lazily.*] Hmmh?

[BLANCHE *utters a moaning cry and runs into the bedroom, throwing herself down beside* STELLA *in a rush of hysterical tenderness.*]

BLANCHE: Baby, my baby sister!

STELLA: [*Drawing away from her.*] Blanche, what is the matter with you?

[BLANCHE *straightens up slowly and stands beside the bed looking down at her sister with knuckles pressed to her lips.*]

BLANCHE: He's left?

STELLA: Stan? Yes.

BLANCHE: Will he be back?

STELLA: He's gone to get the car greased. Why?

BLANCHE: Why! I've been half crazy, Stella! When I found out you'd been insane enough to come back in here after what happened—I started to rush in after you!

STELLA: I'm glad you didn't.

BLANCHE: What were you thinking of? [STELLA *makes an indefinite gesture.*] Answer me! What? What?

STELLA: Please, Blanche! Sit down and stop yelling.

BLANCHE: All right, Stella. I will repeat the question quietly now. How could you come back in this place last night? Why, you must have slept with him!

[STELLA *gets up in a calm and leisurely way.*]

STELLA: Blanche, I'd forgotten how excitable you are. You're making much too much fuss about this.

BLANCHE: Am I?

STELLA: Yes, you are, Blanche. I know how it must have seemed to you and I'm awful sorry it had to happen, but it wasn't anything as serious as you seem to take it. In the first place, when men are drinking and playing poker anything can happen. It's always a powder-keg. He didn't know what he was doing. . . . He was as good as a lamb when I came back and he's really very, very ashamed of himself.

BLANCHE: And that—that makes it all right?

STELLA: No, it isn't all right for anybody to make such a terrible row, but—people do sometimes. Stanley's always smashed things. Why, on our wedding night—soon as we came in here—he snatched off one of my slippers and rushed about the place smashing light bulbs with it.

BLANCHE: He did—*what*?

STELLA: He smashed all the lightbulbs with the heel of my slipper! [*She laughs.*]

BLANCHE: And you—you *let* him? Didn't *run*, didn't *scream*?

STELLA: I was—sort of—thrilled by it. [*She waits for a moment.*] Eunice and you had breakfast?

BLANCHE: Do you suppose I wanted any breakfast?

STELLA: There's some coffee left on the stove.

BLANCHE: You're so—matter-of-fact about it, Stella.

STELLA: What other can I be? He's taken the radio to get it fixed. It didn't land on the pavement so only one tube was smashed.

BLANCHE: And you are standing there smiling!

STELLA: What do you want me to do?

BLANCHE: Pull yourself together and face the facts.

STELLA: What are they, in your opinion?

BLANCHE: In my opinion? You're married to a madman!

STELLA: No!

BLANCHE: Yes, you are, your fix is worse than mine is! Only you're not being sensible about it. I'm going to *do* something. Get hold of myself and make myself a new life!

STELLA: Yes?

BLANCHE: But you've given in. And that isn't right, you're not old! You can get out.

STELLA: [*Slowly and emphatically.*] I'm not in anything I want to get out of.

BLANCHE: [*Incredulously.*] What—Stella?

STELLA: I said I am not in anything that I have a desire to get out of. Look at the mess in this room! And those empty bottles! They went through two cases last night! He promised this morning that he was going to quit having these poker parties, but you know how long such a promise is going to keep. Oh, well, it's his pleasure, like mine is movies and bridge. People have got to tolerate each other's habits, I guess.

BLANCHE: I don't understand you. [STELLA *turns toward her.*] I don't understand your indifference. Is this a Chinese philosophy you've—cultivated?

STELLA: Is what—what?

BLANCHE: This—shuffling about and mumbling—"One tube smashed—beer bottles—mess in the kitchen!"—as if nothing out of the ordinary has happened! [STELLA *laughs uncertainly and picking up the broom, twirls it in her hands.*] Are you deliberately shaking that thing in my face?

STELLA: No.

BLANCHE: Stop it. Let go of that broom. I won't have you cleaning up for him!

STELLA: Then who's going to do it? Are you?

BLANCHE: I? I!

STELLA: No, I didn't think so.

BLANCHE: Oh, let me think, if only my mind would function! We've got to get hold of some money, that's the way out!

STELLA: I guess that money is always nice to get hold of.

BLANCHE: Listen to me. I have an idea of some kind. [*Shakily she twists a cigarette into her holder.*] Do you remember Shep Huntleigh? [STELLA *shakes her head.*] Of course you remember Shep Huntleigh. I went out with him at college and wore his pin for a while. Well—

STELLA: Well?

BLANCHE: I ran into him last winter. You know I went to Miami during the Christmas holidays?

STELLA: No.

BLANCHE: Well, I did. I took the trip as an investment, thinking I'd meet someone with a million dollars.

STELLA: Did you?

BLANCHE: Yes. I ran into Shep Huntleigh—I ran into him on Biscayne Boulevard, on Christmas Eve, about dusk . . . getting into his car—Cadillac convertible; must have been a block long!

STELLA: I should think it would have been—inconvenient in traffic!

BLANCHE: You've heard of oil wells?

STELLA: Yes—remotely.

BLANCHE: He has them, all over Texas. Texas is literally spouting gold in his pockets.

STELLA: My, my.

BLANCHE: Y'know how indifferent I am to money. I think of money in terms of what it does for you. But he could do it, he could certainly do it!

STELLA: Do what, Blanche?

BLANCHE: Why—set us up in a—shop!

STELLA: What kind of shop?

BLANCHE: Oh, a—shop of some kind! He could do it with half what his wife throws away at the races.

STELLA: He's married?

BLANCHE: Honey, would I be here if the man weren't married? [STELLA *laughs a little. BLANCHE suddenly springs up and crosses to phone. She speaks shrilly.*] How do I get Western Union?[2]—Operator! Western Union!

STELLA: That's a dial phone, honey.

BLANCHE: I can't dial, I'm too—

STELLA: Just dial O.

BLANCHE: O?

STELLA: Yes, "O" for Operator!

[BLANCHE *considers a moment; then she puts the phone down.*]

---

2. The largest American telegraph company throughout most of the twentieth century.

BLANCHE: Give me a pencil. Where is a slip of paper? I've got to write it down first—the message, I mean. . . . [*She goes to the dressing table, and grabs up a sheet of Kleenex and an eyebrow pencil for writing equipment.*] Let me see now. . . . [*She bites the pencil.*] "Darling Shep. Sister and I in desperate situation."

STELLA: I beg your pardon!

BLANCHE: "Sister and I in desperate situation. Will explain details later. Would you be interested in—?" [*She bites the pencil again.*] "Would you be—interested—in . . ." [*She smashes the pencil on the table and springs up.*] You never get anywhere with direct appeals!

STELLA: [*With a laugh.*] Don't be so ridiculous, darling!

BLANCHE: But I'll think of something, I've *got* to think of—*something*! Don't laugh at me, Stella! Please, please don't—I—I want you to look at the contents of my purse! Here's what's in it! [*She snatches her purse open.*] Sixty-five measly cents in coin of the realm!

STELLA: [*Crossing to bureau.*] Stanley doesn't give me a regular allowance, he likes to pay bills himself, but—this morning he gave me ten dollars to smooth things over. You take five of it, Blanche, and I'll keep the rest.

BLANCHE: Oh, no. No, Stella.

STELLA: [*Insisting.*] I know how it helps your morale just having a little pocket-money on you.

BLANCHE: No, thank you—I'll take to the streets!

STELLA: Talk sense! How did you happen to get so low on funds?

BLANCHE: Money just goes—it goes places. [*She rubs her forehead.*] Sometime today I've got to get hold of a Bromo![3]

STELLA: I'll fix you one now.

BLANCHE: Not yet—I've got to keep thinking!

STELLA: I wish you'd just let things go, at least for a—while.

BLANCHE: Stella, I can't live with him! You can, he's your husband. But how could I stay here with him, after last night, with just those curtains between us?

STELLA: Blanche, you saw him at his worst last night.

BLANCHE: On the contrary, I saw him at his best! What such a man has to offer is animal force and he gave a wonderful exhibition of that! But the only way to live with such a man is to—go to bed with him! And that's your job—not mine!

STELLA: After you've rested a little, you'll see it's going to work out. You don't have to worry about anything while you're here. I mean—expenses . . .

BLANCHE: I have to plan for us both, to get us both—out!

STELLA: You take it for granted that I am in something that I want to get out of.

BLANCHE: I take it for granted that you still have sufficient memory of Belle Reve to find this place and these poker players impossible to live with.

STELLA: Well, you're taking entirely too much for granted.

BLANCHE: I can't believe you're in earnest.

STELLA: No?

BLANCHE: I understand how it happened—a little. You saw him in uniform, an officer, not here but—

STELLA: I'm not sure it would have made any difference where I saw him.

---

3. Short for "Bromo Seltzer," a headache remedy.

BLANCHE: Now don't say it was one of those mysterious electric things between people! If you do I'll laugh in your face.

STELLA: I am not going to say anything more at all about it!

BLANCHE: All right, then, don't!

STELLA: But there are things that happen between a man and a woman in the dark—that sort of make everything else seem—unimportant. [*Pause.*]

BLANCHE: What you are talking about is brutal desire—just—Desire!—the name of that rattle-trap streetcar that bangs through the Quarter, up one old narrow street and down another. . . .

STELLA: Haven't you ever ridden on that streetcar?

BLANCHE: It brought me here.—Where I'm not wanted and where I'm ashamed to be. . . .

STELLA: Then don't you think your superior attitude is a bit out of place?

BLANCHE: I am not being or feeling at all superior, Stella. Believe me I'm not! It's just this. This is how I look at it. A man like that is someone to go out with—once—twice—three times when the devil is in you. But live with? Have a child by?

STELLA: I have told you I love him.

BLANCHE: Then I *tremble* for you! I just—*tremble* for you. . . .

STELLA: I can't help your trembling if you insist on trembling!

[*There is a pause.*]

BLANCHE: May I—speak—*plainly*?

STELLA: Yes, do. Go ahead. As plainly as you want to.

[*Outside, a train approaches. They are silent till the noise subsides. They are both in the bedroom. Under cover of the train's noise* STANLEY *enters from outside. He stands unseen by the women, holding some packages in his arms, and overhears their following conversation. He wears an undershirt and grease-stained seersucker pants.*]

BLANCHE: Well—if you'll forgive me—he's *common*!

STELLA: Why, yes, I suppose he is.

BLANCHE: Suppose! You can't have forgotten that much of our bringing up, Stella, that you just *suppose* that any part of a gentleman's in his nature! *Not one particle, no!* Oh, if he was just—*ordinary*! Just plain—but good and wholesome, but—*no*. There's something downright—*bestial*—about him! You're hating me saying this, aren't you?

STELLA: [*Coldly.*] Go on and say it all, Blanche.

BLANCHE: He acts like an animal, has an animal's habits! Eats like one, moves like one, talks like one! There's even something—sub-human—something not quite to the stage of humanity yet! Yes, something—ape-like about him, like one of those pictures I've seen in—anthropological studies! Thousands and thousands of years have passed him right by, and there he is—Stanley Kowalski—survivor of the Stone Age! Bearing the raw meat home from the kill in the jungle! And you—*you* here—*waiting* for him! Maybe he'll strike you or maybe grunt and kiss you! That is, if kisses have been discovered yet! Night falls and the other apes gather! There in the front of the cave, all grunting like him, and swilling and gnawing and hulking! His poker night! you call it—this party of apes! Somebody growls—some creature snatches at something—the fight is on! *God!* Maybe we are a long way from being made in

God's image, but Stella—my sister—there has been *some* progress since then! Such things as art—as poetry and music—such kinds of new light have come into the world since then! In some kinds of people some tenderer feelings have had some little beginning! That we have got to make *grow*! And *cling* to, and hold as our flag! In this dark march toward whatever it is we're approaching. . . . *Don't—don't hang back with the brutes!*

[*Another train passes outside.* STANLEY *hesitates, licking his lips. Then suddenly he turns stealthily about and withdraws through front door. The women are still unaware of his presence. When the train has passed he calls through the closed front door.*]

STANLEY: Hey! Hey, Stella!
STELLA: [*Who has listened gravely to* BLANCHE.] Stanley!
BLANCHE: Stell, I—

[*But* STELLA *has gone to the front door.* STANLEY *enters casually with his packages.*]

STANLEY: Hiyuh, Stella. Blanche back?
STELLA: Yes, she's back.
STANLEY: Hiyuh, Blanche. [*He grins at her.*]
STELLA: You must've got under the car.
STANLEY: Them darn mechanics at Fritz's don't know their ass fr'm—*Hey!*

[STELLA *has embraced him with both arms, fiercely, and full in the view of* BLANCHE. *He laughs and clasps her head to him. Over her head he grins through the curtains at* BLANCHE. *As the lights fade away, with a lingering brightness on their embrace, the music of the "Blue Piano" and trumpet and drums is heard.*]

Scene 5

BLANCHE *is seated in the bedroom fanning herself with a palm leaf as she reads over a just-completed letter. Suddenly she bursts into a peal of laughter.* STELLA *is dressing in the bedroom.*

STELLA: What are you laughing at, honey?
BLANCHE: Myself, myself, for being such a liar! I'm writing a letter to Shep. [*She picks up the letter.*] "Darling Shep. I am spending the summer on the wing, making flying visits here and there. And who knows, perhaps I shall take a sudden notion to *swoop* down on *Dallas*! How would you feel about that? Ha-ha! [*She laughs nervously and brightly, touching her throat as if actually talking to Shep.*] Forewarned is forearmed, as they say!"—How does that sound?
STELLA: Uh-huh . . .
BLANCHE: [*Going on nervously.*] "Most of my sister's friends go north in the summer but some have homes on the Gulf and there has been a continued round of entertainments, teas, cocktails, and luncheons—"

[*A disturbance is heard upstairs at the Hubbells' apartment.*]

STELLA: Eunice seems to be having some trouble with Steve. [EUNICE's *voice shouts in terrible wrath.*]
EUNICE: I heard about you and that blonde!
STEVE: That's a damn lie!

EUNICE: You ain't pulling the wool over my eyes! I wouldn't mind if you'd stay down at the Four Deuces, but you always going up.

STEVE: Who ever seen me up?

EUNICE: I seen you chasing her 'round the balcony—I'm gonna call the vice squad!

STEVE: Don't you throw that at me!

EUNICE: [*Shrieking.*] You hit me! I'm gonna call the police!

[*A clatter of aluminum striking a wall is heard, followed by a man's angry roar, shouts, and overturned furniture. There is a crash; then a relative hush.*]

BLANCHE: [*Brightly.*] Did he *kill* her?

[EUNICE *appears on the steps in daemonic disorder.*]

STELLA: No! She's coming downstairs.

EUNICE: Call the police, I'm going to call the police! [*She rushes around the corner.*]

[*They laugh lightly.* STANLEY *comes around the corner in his green and scarlet silk bowling shirt. He trots up the steps and bangs into the kitchen.* BLANCHE *registers his entrance with nervous gestures.*]

STANLEY: What's a matter with Eun-uss?

STELLA: She and Steve had a row. Has she got the police?

STANLEY: Naw. She's gettin' a drink.

STELLA: That's much more practical!

[STEVE *comes down nursing a bruise on his forehead and looks in the door.*]

STEVE: She here?

STANLEY: Naw, naw. At the Four Deuces.

STEVE: That rutting hunk! [*He looks around the corner a bit timidly, then turns with affected boldness and runs after her.*]

BLANCHE: I must jot that down in my notebook. Ha-ha! I'm compiling a notebook of quaint little words and phrases I've picked up here.

STANLEY: You won't pick up nothing here you ain't heard before.

BLANCHE: Can I count on that?

STANLEY: You can count on it up to five hundred.

BLANCHE: That's a mighty high number. [*He jerks open the bureau drawer, slams it shut and throws shoes in a corner. At each noise* BLANCHE *winces slightly. Finally she speaks.*] What sign were you born under?

STANLEY: [*While he is dressing.*] Sign?

BLANCHE: Astrological sign. I bet you were born under Aries. Aries people are forceful and dynamic. They dote on noise! They love to bang things around! You must have had lots of banging around in the army and now that you're out, you make up for it by treating inanimate objects with such a fury!

[STELLA *has been going in and out of closet during this scene. Now she pops her head out of the closet.*]

STELLA: Stanley was born just five minutes after Christmas.

BLANCHE: Capricorn—the Goat!

STANLEY: What sign were *you* born under?

BLANCHE: Oh, my birthday's next month, the fifteenth of September; that's under Virgo.

STANLEY: What's Virgo?

BLANCHE: Virgo is the Virgin.

STANLEY: [*Contemptuously.*] Hah! [*He advances a little as he knots his tie.*] Say, do you happen to know somebody named Shaw?

[*Her face expresses a faint shock. She reaches for the cologne bottle and dampens her handkerchief as she answers carefully.*]

BLANCHE: Why, everybody knows somebody named Shaw!

STANLEY: Well, this somebody named Shaw is under the impression he met you in Laurel, but I figure he must have got you mixed up with some other party because this other party is someone he met at a hotel called the Flamingo.

[BLANCHE *laughs breathlessly as she touches the cologne-dampened handkerchief to her temples.*]

BLANCHE: I'm afraid he does have me mixed up with this "other party." The Hotel Flamingo is not the sort of establishment I would dare to be seen in!

STANLEY: You know of it?

BLANCHE: Yes, I've seen it and smelled it.

STANLEY: You must've got pretty close if you could smell it.

BLANCHE: The odor of cheap perfume is penetrating.

STANLEY: That stuff you use is expensive?

BLANCHE: Twenty-five dollars an ounce! I'm nearly out. That's just a hint if you want to remember my birthday! [*She speaks lightly but her voice has a note of fear.*]

STANLEY: Shaw must've got you mixed up. He goes in and out of Laurel all the time so he can check on it and clear up any mistake.

[*He turns away and crosses to the portieres.* BLANCHE *closes her eyes as if faint. Her hand trembles as she lifts the handkerchief again to her forehead.* STEVE *and* EUNICE *come around corner.* STEVE'*s arm is around* EUNICE'*s shoulder and she is sobbing luxuriously and he is cooing love-words. There is a murmur of thunder as they go slowly upstairs in a tight embrace.*]

STANLEY: [*To* STELLA.] I'll wait for you at the Four Deuces!

STELLA: Hey! Don't I rate one kiss?

STANLEY: Not in front of your sister.

[*He goes out.* BLANCHE *rises from her chair. She seems faint; looks about her with an expression of almost panic.*]

BLANCHE: Stella! What have you heard about me?

STELLA: Huh?

BLANCHE: What have people been telling you about me?

STELLA: Telling?

BLANCHE: You haven't heard any—unkind—gossip about me?

STELLA: Why, no, Blanche, of course not!

BLANCHE: Honey, there was—a good deal of talk in Laurel.

STELLA: About *you*, Blanche?

BLANCHE: I wasn't so good the last two years or so, after Belle Reve had started to slip through my fingers.

STELLA: All of us do things we—

BLANCHE: I never was hard or self-sufficient enough. When people are soft—soft people have got to shimmer and glow—they've got to put on soft colors, the colors of butterfly wings, and put a—paper lantern over the light. . . . It isn't enough to be soft *and attractive*. And I—I'm fading now! I don't know how much longer I can turn the trick. [*The afternoon has faded to dusk.* STELLA *goes into the bedroom and turns on the light under the paper lantern. She holds a bottled soft drink in her hand.*] Have you been listening to me?

STELLA: I don't listen to you when you are being morbid! [*She advances with the bottled Coke.*]

BLANCHE: [*With abrupt change to gaiety.*] Is that Coke for me?

STELLA: Not for anyone else!

BLANCHE: Why, you precious thing, you! Is it just Coke?

STELLA: [*Turning.*] You mean you want a shot in it!

BLANCHE: Well, honey, a shot never does a Coke any harm! Let me! You mustn't wait on me!

STELLA: I like to wait on you, Blanche. It makes it seem more like home. [*She goes into the kitchen, finds a glass and pours a shot of whiskey into it.*]

BLANCHE: I have to admit I love to be waited on . . . [*She rushes into the bedroom.* STELLA *goes to her with the glass.* BLANCHE *suddenly clutches* STELLA's *free hand with a moaning sound and presses the hand to her lips.* STELLA *is embarrassed by her show of emotion.* BLANCHE *speaks in a choked voice.*] You're—you're—so *good* to me! And I—

STELLA: Blanche.

BLANCHE: I know, I won't! You hate me to talk sentimental! But honey, *believe* I feel things more than I *tell* you! I *won't* stay long! I won't, I *promise* I—

STELLA: Blanche!

BLANCHE: [*Hysterically.*] I won't, I promise, *I'll* go! Go *soon*! I will *really*! I *won't* hang around until he—throws me out. . . .

STELLA: Now will you stop talking foolish?

BLANCHE: Yes, honey. Watch how you pour—that fizzy stuff foams over!

[BLANCHE *laughs shrilly and grabs the glass, but her hand shakes so it almost slips from her grasp.* STELLA *pours the Coke into the glass. It foams over and spills.* BLANCHE *gives a piercing cry.*]

STELLA: [*Shocked by the cry.*] Heavens!

BLANCHE: Right on my pretty white skirt!

STELLA: Oh . . . Use my hanky. Blot gently.

BLANCHE: [*Slowly recovering.*] I know—gently—gently . . .

STELLA: Did it stain?

BLANCHE: Not a bit. Ha-ha! Isn't that lucky? [*She sits down shakily, taking a grateful drink. She holds the glass in both hands and continues to laugh a little.*]

STELLA: Why did you scream like that?

BLANCHE: I don't know why I screamed! [*Continuing nervously.*] Mitch—Mitch is coming at seven. I guess I am just feeling nervous about our relations. [*She begins to talk rapidly and breathlessly.*] He hasn't gotten a thing but a good-night kiss, that's all I have given him, Stella. I want his respect. And men don't want anything they get too easy. But on the other hand men lose interest quickly. Especially when the girl is over—thirty. They think a girl over thirty ought to— the vulgar term is—"put out." . . . And I—I'm not "putting out." Of course he—he doesn't know—I mean I haven't informed him—of my real age!

STELLA: Why are you sensitive about your age?

BLANCHE: Because of hard knocks my vanity's been given. What I mean is—he thinks I'm sort of—prim and proper, you know! [*She laughs out sharply.*] I want to *deceive* him enough to make him—want me . . .

STELLA: Blanche, do you want *him*?

BLANCHE: I want to *rest*! I want to breathe quietly again! Yes—I *want* Mitch . . . *very badly*! Just think! If it happens! I can leave here and not be anyone's problem. . . .

[STANLEY *comes around the corner with a drink under his belt.*]

STANLEY: [*Bawling.*] Hey, Steve! Hey, Eunice! Hey, Stella!

[*There are joyous calls from above. Trumpet and drums are heard from around the corner.*]

STELLA: [*Kissing* BLANCHE *impulsively.*] It *will* happen!

BLANCHE: [*Doubtfully.*] It will?

STELLA: It *will*! [*She goes across into the kitchen, looking back at* BLANCHE.] It will, honey, *it will.* . . . But don't take another drink! [*Her voice catches as she goes out the door to meet her husband.*]

[BLANCHE *sinks faintly back in her chair with her drink.* EUNICE *shrieks with laughter and runs down the steps.* STEVE *bounds after her with goat-like screeches and chases her around corner.* STANLEY *and* STELLA *twine arms as they follow, laughing. Dusk settles deeper. The music from the Four Deuces is slow and blue.*]

BLANCHE: Ah, me, ah, me, ah, me . . . [*Her eyes fall shut and the palm leaf fan drops from her fingers. She slaps her hand on the chair arm a couple of times. There is a little glimmer of lightning about the building. A* YOUNG MAN *comes along the street and rings the bell.*] Come in. [*The* YOUNG MAN *appears through the portieres. She regards him with interest.*] Well, well! What can I do for *you*?

YOUNG MAN: I'm collecting for *The Evening Star*.

BLANCHE: I didn't know that stars took up collections.

YOUNG MAN: It's the paper.

BLANCHE: I know, I was joking—feebly! Will you—have a drink?

YOUNG MAN: No, ma'am. No, thank you. I can't drink on the job.

BLANCHE: Oh, well, now, let's see. . . . No, I don't have a dime! I'm not the lady of the house. I'm her sister from Mississippi. I'm one of those poor relations you've heard about.

YOUNG MAN: That's all right. I'll drop by later. [*He starts to go out. She approaches a little.*]

BLANCHE: Hey! [*He turns back shyly. She puts a cigarette in a long holder.*] Could you give me a light? [*She crosses toward him. They meet at the door between the two rooms.*]

YOUNG MAN: Sure. [*He takes out a lighter.*] This doesn't always work.

BLANCHE: It's temperamental? [*It flares.*] Ah!—thank you. [*He starts away again.*] Hey! [*He turns again, still more uncertainly. She goes close to him.*] Uh—what time is it?

YOUNG MAN: Fifteen of seven, ma'am.

BLANCHE: So late? Don't you just love these long rainy afternoons in New Orleans when an hour isn't just an hour—but a little piece of eternity dropped into your hands—and who knows what to do with it? [*She touches his shoulders.*] You—uh—didn't get wet in the rain?

YOUNG MAN: No, ma'am. I stepped inside.

BLANCHE: In a drugstore? And had a soda?

YOUNG MAN: Uh-huh.

BLANCHE: Chocolate?

YOUNG MAN: No, ma'am. Cherry.

BLANCHE: [*Laughing.*] Cherry!

YOUNG MAN: A cherry soda.

BLANCHE: You make my mouth water. [*She touches his cheek lightly, and smiles. Then she goes to the trunk.*]

YOUNG MAN: Well, I'd better be going—

BLANCHE: [*Stopping him.*] Young man! [*He turns. She takes a large, gossamer scarf from the trunk and drapes it about her shoulders. In the ensuing pause, the "Blue Piano" is heard. It continues through the rest of this scene and the opening of the next. The* YOUNG MAN *clears his throat and looks yearningly at the door.*] Young man! Young, young, young man! Has anyone ever told you that you look like a young Prince out of the Arabian Nights?[4] [*The* YOUNG MAN *laughs uncomfortably and stands like a bashful kid.* BLANCHE *speaks softly to him.*] Well, you do, honey lamb! Come here. I want to kiss you, just once, softly and sweetly on your mouth! [*Without waiting for him to accept, she crosses quickly to him and presses her lips to his.*] Now run along, now, quickly! It would be nice to keep you, but I've got to be good—and keep my hands off children.

[*He stares at her a moment. She opens the door for him and blows a kiss at him as he goes down the steps with a dazed look. She stands there a little dreamily after he has disappeared. Then* MITCH *appears around the corner with a bunch of roses.*]

BLANCHE: [*Gaily.*] Look who's coming! My Rosenkavalier! Bow to me first . . . now present them! Ahhhh—Merciiii![5] [*She looks at him over them, coquettishly pressing them to her lips. He beams at her self-consciously.*]

Scene 6

It is about two a.m. on the same evening. The outer wall of the building is visible. BLANCHE *and* MITCH *come in. The utter exhaustion which only a neurasthenic personality[6] can know is evident in* BLANCHE's *voice and manner.* MITCH *is stolid but depressed. They have probably been out to the amusement park on Lake Pontchartrain,[7] for* MITCH *is bearing, upside down, a plaster statuette of Mae West, the sort of prize won at shooting galleries and carnival games of chance.*

BLANCHE: [*Stopping lifelessly at the steps.*] Well—[MITCH *laughs uneasily.*] Well . . .

MITCH: I guess it must be pretty late—and you're tired.

4. *The Arabian Nights* is a collection of Persian, Indian, and Arabic folktales.
5. *Merci*: thank you (French). *Rosenkavalier*: *Knight of the Rose* (German), title of a romantic opera (1911) by Richard Strauss (1864–1949).
6. Nineteenth-century diagnostic term for a psychological disorder characterized by nervous exhaustion and other physical symptoms.
7. Large coastal inlet in southern Louisiana; New Orleans is located on its south shore. *Mae West*: American star of stage and film (1892–1980).

BLANCHE: Even the hot tamale man has deserted the street, and he hangs on till the end. [MITCH *laughs uneasily again.*] How will you get home?

MITCH: I'll walk over to Bourbon and catch an owl-car.[8]

BLANCHE: [*Laughing grimly.*] Is that street-car named Desire still grinding along the tracks at this hour?

MITCH: [*Heavily.*] I'm afraid you haven't gotten much fun out of this evening, Blanche.

BLANCHE: I spoiled it for *you*.

MITCH: No, you didn't, but I felt all the time that I wasn't giving you much— entertainment.

BLANCHE: I simply couldn't rise to the occasion. That was all. I don't think I've ever tried so hard to be gay and made such a dismal mess of it. I get ten points for trying!—I *did* try.

MITCH: Why did you try if you didn't feel like it, Blanche?

BLANCHE: I was just obeying the law of nature.

MITCH: Which law is that?

BLANCHE: The one that says the lady must entertain the gentleman—or no dice! See if you can locate my door key in this purse. When I'm so tired my fingers are all thumbs!

MITCH: [*Rooting in her purse.*] This it?

BLANCHE: No, honey, that's the key to my trunk which I must soon be packing.

MITCH: You mean you are leaving here soon?

BLANCHE: I've outstayed my welcome.

MITCH: This it?

[*The music fades away.*]

BLANCHE: Eureka! Honey, you open the door while I take a last look at the sky. [*She leans on the porch rail. He opens the door and stands awkwardly behind her.*] I'm looking for the Pleiades,[9] the Seven Sisters, but these girls are not out tonight. Oh, yes they are, there they are! God bless them! All in a bunch going home from their little bridge party. . . . Y' get the door open? Good boy! I guess you—want to go now. . . .

[*He shuffles and coughs a little.*]

MITCH: Can I—uh—kiss you—good night?

BLANCHE: Why do you always ask me if you may?

MITCH: I don't know whether you want me to or not.

BLANCHE: Why should you be so doubtful?

MITCH: That night when we parked by the lake and I kissed you, you—

BLANCHE: Honey, it wasn't the kiss I objected to. I liked the kiss very much. It was the other little—familiarity—that I—felt obliged to—discourage. . . . I didn't resent it! Not a bit in the world! In fact, I was somewhat flattered that you— desired me! But, honey, you know as well as I do that a single girl, a girl alone in the world, has got to keep a firm hold on her emotions or she'll be lost!

MITCH: [*Solemnly.*] Lost?

8. All-night streetcar.
9. Constellation named for the seven daughters of Atlas who were changed into stars.

BLANCHE: I guess you are used to girls that like to be lost. The kind that get lost immediately, on the first date!

MITCH: I like you to be exactly the way that you are, because in all my—experience—I have never known anyone like you. [BLANCHE *looks at him gravely; then she bursts into laughter and then claps a hand to her mouth.*] Are you laughing at me?

BLANCHE: No, honey. The lord and lady of the house have not yet returned, so come in. We'll have a nightcap. Let's leave the lights off. Shall we?

MITCH: You just—do what you want to.

[BLANCHE *precedes him into the kitchen. The outer wall of the building disappears and the interiors of the two rooms can be dimly seen.*]

BLANCHE: [*Remaining in the first room.*] The other room's more comfortable—go on in. This crashing around in the dark is my search for some liquor.

MITCH: You want a drink?

BLANCHE: I want *you* to have a drink! You have been so anxious and solemn all evening, and so have I; we have both been anxious and solemn and now for these few last remaining moments of our lives together—I want to create—*joie de vivre*![1] I'm lighting a candle.

MITCH: That's good.

BLANCHE: We are going to be very Bohemian. We are going to pretend that we are sitting in a little artists' cafe on the Left Bank in Paris! [*She lights a candle stub and puts it in a bottle.*] Je suis la Dame aux Camellias! Vous êtes—Armand![2] Understand French?

MITCH: [*Heavily.*] Naw. Naw, I—

BLANCHE: *Voulez-vous couchez avec moi ce soir? Vous ne comprenez pas? Ah, quelle dommage!*[3]—I mean it's a damned good thing. . . . I've found some liquor! Just enough for two shots without any dividends, honey. . . .

MITCH: [*Heavily.*] That's—good.

[*She enters the bedroom with the drinks and the candle.*]

BLANCHE: Sit down! Why don't you take off your coat and loosen your collar?

MITCH: I better leave it on.

BLANCHE: No. I want you to be comfortable.

MITCH: I am ashamed of the way I perspire. My shirt is sticking to me.

BLANCHE: Perspiration is healthy. If people didn't perspire they would die in five minutes. [*She takes his coat from him.*] This is a nice coat. What kind of material is it?

MITCH: They call that stuff alpaca.

BLANCHE: Oh. Alpaca.

MITCH: It's very light-weight alpaca.

1. Joy of life (French).
2. I am the Lady of the Camellias! You are—Armand! (French) Both are characters in the popular romantic play *La Dame aux Camélias* (1852) by the French author Alexandre Dumas (1824–95); she is a courtesan who gives up her true love, Armand. *Left Bank*: section of Paris on the westward ("left") bank of the river Seine, long associated with students and artists.
3. Would you like to sleep with me this evening? You don't understand? Ah, what a pity! (French).

BLANCHE: Oh. Light-weight alpaca.

MITCH: I don't like to wear a wash-coat[4] even in summer because I sweat through it.

BLANCHE: Oh.

MITCH: And it don't look neat on me. A man with a heavy build has got to be careful of what he puts on him so he don't look too clumsy.

BLANCHE: You are not too heavy.

MITCH: You don't think I am?

BLANCHE: You are not the delicate type. You have a massive bone-structure and a very imposing physique.

MITCH: Thank you. Last Christmas I was given a membership to the New Orleans Athletic Club.

BLANCHE: Oh, good.

MITCH: It was the finest present I ever was given. I work out there with the weights and I swim and I keep myself fit. When I started there, I was getting soft in the belly but now my belly is hard. It is so hard now that a man can punch me in the belly and it don't hurt me. Punch me! Go on! See? [*She pokes lightly at him.*]

BLANCHE: Gracious. [*Her hand touches her chest.*]

MITCH: Guess how much I weigh, Blanche?

BLANCHE: Oh, I'd say in the vicinity of—one hundred and eighty?

MITCH: Guess again.

BLANCHE: Not that much?

MITCH: No. More.

BLANCHE: Well, you're a tall man and you can carry a good deal of weight without looking awkward.

MITCH: I weigh two hundred and seven pounds and I'm six feet one and one half inches tall in my bare feet—without shoes on. And that is what I weigh stripped.

BLANCHE: Oh, my goodness, me! It's awe-inspiring.

MITCH: [*Embarrassed.*] My weight is not a very interesting subject to talk about. [*He hesitates for a moment.*] What's yours?

BLANCHE: My weight?

MITCH: Yes.

BLANCHE: Guess!

MITCH: Let me lift you.

BLANCHE: Samson![5] Go on, lift me. [*He comes behind her and puts his hands on her waist and raises her lightly off the ground.*] Well?

MITCH: You are light as a feather.

BLANCHE: Ha-ha! [*He lowers her but keeps his hands on her waist.* BLANCHE *speaks with an affectation of demureness.*] You may release me now.

MITCH: Huh?

BLANCHE: [*Gaily.*] I said unhand me, sir. [*He fumblingly embraces her. Her voice sounds gently reproving.*] Now, Mitch. Just because Stanley and Stella aren't at home is no reason why you shouldn't behave like a gentleman.

MITCH: Just give me a slap whenever I step out of bounds.

---

4. Light washable jacket.   5. Legendary strong man, an Israelite in the Old Testament.

BLANCHE: That won't be necessary. You're a natural gentleman, one of the very few that are left in the world. I don't want you to think that I am severe and old maid school-teacherish or anything like that. It's just—well—

MITCH: Huh?

BLANCHE: I guess it is just that I have—old-fashioned ideals! [*She rolls her eyes, knowing he cannot see her face.* MITCH *goes to the front door. There is a considerable silence between them.* BLANCHE *sighs and* MITCH *coughs self-consciously.*]

MITCH: [*Finally.*] Where's Stanley and Stella tonight?

BLANCHE: They have gone out. With Mr. and Mrs. Hubbell upstairs.

MITCH: Where did they go?

BLANCHE: I think they were planning to go to a midnight prevue at Loew's State.

MITCH: We should all go out together some night.

BLANCHE: No. That wouldn't be a good plan.

MITCH: Why not?

BLANCHE: You are an old friend of Stanley's?

MITCH: We was together in the Two-forty-first.[6]

BLANCHE: I guess he talks to you frankly?

MITCH: Sure.

BLANCHE: Has he talked to you about me?

MITCH: Oh—not very much.

BLANCHE: The way you say that, I suspect that he has.

MITCH: No, he hasn't said much.

BLANCHE: But what he *has* said. What would you say his attitude toward me was?

MITCH: Why do you want to ask that?

BLANCHE: Well—

MITCH: Don't you get along with him?

BLANCHE: What do you think?

MITCH: I don't think he understands you.

BLANCHE: That is putting it mildly. If it weren't for Stella about to have a baby, I wouldn't be able to endure things here.

MITCH: He isn't—nice to you?

BLANCHE: He is insufferably rude. Goes out of his way to offend me.

MITCH: In what way, Blanche?

BLANCHE: Why, in every conceivable way.

MITCH: I'm surprised to hear that.

BLANCHE: Are you?

MITCH: Well, I—don't see how anybody could be rude to you.

BLANCHE: It's really a pretty frightful situation. You see, there's no privacy here. There's just these portieres between the two rooms at night. He stalks through the rooms in his underwear at night. And I have to ask him to close the bathroom door. That sort of commonness isn't necessary. You probably wonder why I don't move out. Well, I'll tell you frankly. A teacher's salary is barely sufficient for her living expenses. I didn't save a penny last year and so I had to come here for the summer. That's why I have to put up with my sister's husband. And he has to put up with me, apparently so much against his wishes. . . . Surely he must have told you how much he hates he!

MITCH: I don't think he hates you.

6. Battalion of engineers, in World War II.

BLANCHE: He hates me. Or why would he insult me? The first time I laid eyes on him I thought to myself, that man is my executioner! That man will destroy me, unless—

MITCH: Blanche—

BLANCHE: Yes, honey?

MITCH: Can I ask you a question?

BLANCHE: Yes. What?

MITCH: How old are you?

[*She makes a nervous gesture.*]

BLANCHE: Why do you want to know?

MITCH: I talked to my mother about you and she said, "How old is Blanche?" And I wasn't able to tell her. [*There is another pause.*]

BLANCHE: You talked to your mother about me?

MITCH: Yes.

BLANCHE: Why?

MITCH: I told my mother how nice you were, and I liked you.

BLANCHE: Were you sincere about that?

MITCH: You know I was.

BLANCHE: Why did your mother want to know my age?

MITCH: Mother is sick.

BLANCHE: I'm sorry to hear it. Badly?

MITCH: She won't live long. Maybe just a few months.

BLANCHE: Oh.

MITCH: She worries because I'm not settled.

BLANCHE: Oh.

MITCH: She wants me to be settled down before she— [*His voice is hoarse and he clears his throat twice, shuffling nervously around with his hands in and out of his pockets.*]

BLANCHE: You love her very much, don't you?

MITCH: Yes.

BLANCHE: I think you have a great capacity for devotion. You will be lonely when she passes on, won't you? [MITCH *clears his throat and nods.*] I understand what that is.

MITCH: To be lonely?

BLANCHE: I loved someone, too, and the person I loved I lost.

MITCH: Dead? [*She crosses to the window and sits on the sill, looking out. She pours herself another drink.*] A man?

BLANCHE: He was a boy, just a boy, when I was a very young girl. When I was sixteen, I made the discovery—love. All at once and much, much too completely. It was like you suddenly turned a blinding light on something that had always been half in shadow, that's how it struck the world for me. But I was unlucky. Deluded. There was something different about the boy, a nervousness, a softness and tenderness which wasn't like a man's, although he wasn't the least bit effeminate looking—still—that thing was there. . . . He came to me for help. I didn't know that. I didn't find out anything till after our marriage when we'd run away and come back and all I knew was I'd failed him in some mysterious way and wasn't able to give the help he needed but couldn't speak of! He was in the quicksands and clutching at me—but I wasn't holding him out, I was slipping in with him! I didn't know that. I didn't know anything except I loved him unendurably but without being able to help him or help myself. Then I found out. In the worst of all possible ways. By coming suddenly into a room that I thought was empty—which wasn't empty, but had two people in it ... the boy I had married and an older man who had been his friend for years. . . . [*A locomotive is heard approaching outside. She claps her hands to her ears and crouches over. The headlight of the locomotive glares into the room as it thunders past. As the noise recedes she straightens slowly and continues speaking.*] Afterward we pretended that nothing had been discovered. Yes, the three of us drove out to Moon Lake Casino,[7] very drunk and laughing all the way. [*Polka music sounds, in a minor key faint with distance.*] We danced the "Varsouviana!"[8] Suddenly in the middle of the dance the boy I had married broke away from me and ran out of the casino. A few moments later—a shot! [*The polka stops abruptly.* BLANCHE *rises stiffly. Then, the polka resumes in a major key.*] I ran out—all did!—all ran and gathered about the terrible thing at the edge of the lake! I couldn't get near for the crowding. Then somebody caught my arm. "Don't go any closer! Come back! You don't want to see!" See? See what! Then I heard voices say—Allan! Allan! The Grey boy! He'd stuck the revolver into his mouth, and fired—so that the back of his head had been—blown away! [*She sways and covers her face.*] It was because—on the dance floor—unable to stop myself—I'd suddenly said—"I saw! I know! You disgust me. . . ." And then the searchlight which had been turned on the world was turned off again and never for one moment since has there been any light that's stronger than this—kitchen—candle. . . .

[MITCH *gets up awkwardly and moves toward her a little. The polka music increases.* MITCH *stands beside her.*]

MITCH: [*Drawing her slowly into his arms.*] You need somebody. And I need some-body, too. Could it be—you and me, Blanche?

[*She stares at him vacantly for a moment. Then with a soft cry huddles in his embrace. She makes a sobbing effort to speak but the words won't come. He kisses her forehead and her eyes and finally her lips. The polka tune fades out. Her breath is drawn and released in long, grateful sobs.*]

BLANCHE: Sometimes—there's God—so quickly!

Scene 7

It is late afternoon in mid-September.
The portieres are open and a table is set for a birthday supper, with cake and flowers.
STELLA *is completing the decorations as* STANLEY *comes in.*

STANLEY: What's all this stuff for?
STELLA: Honey, it's Blanche's birthday.
STANLEY: She here?
STELLA: In the bathroom.
STANLEY: [*Mimicking.*] "Washing out some things"?

7. Casino and night club in Dundee, Mississippi, popular during the 1940s.
8. Fast Polish dance, similar to the polka.

STELLA: I reckon so.

STANLEY: How long she been in there?

STELLA: All afternoon.

STANLEY: [*Mimicking.*] "Soaking in a hot tub"?

STELLA: Yes.

STANLEY: Temperature 100 on the nose, and she soaks herself in a hot tub.

STELLA: She says it cools her off for the evening.

STANLEY: And you run out an' get her cokes, I suppose? And serve 'em to Her Majesty in the tub? [STELLA *shrugs.*] Set down here a minute.

STELLA: Stanley, I've got things to do.

STANLEY: Set down! I've got th' dope on your big sister, Stella.

STELLA: Stanley, stop picking on Blanche.

STANLEY: That girl calls *me* common!

STELLA: Lately you been doing all you can think of to rub her the wrong way, Stanley, and Blanche is sensitive and you've got to realize that Blanche and I grew up under very different circumstances than you did.

STANLEY: So I been told. And told and told and told! You know she's been feeding us a pack of lies here?

STELLA: No, I don't and—

STANLEY: Well, she has, however. But now the cat's out of the bag! I found out some things!

STELLA: What—things?

STANLEY: Things I already suspected. But now I got proof from the most reliable sources—which I have checked on!

[BLANCHE *is singing in the bathroom a saccharine[9] popular ballad which is used contrapuntally with* STANLEY'S *speech.*]

STELLA: [*To* STANLEY.] Lower your voice!

STANLEY: Some canary bird, huh!

STELLA: Now please tell me quietly what you think you've found out about my sister.

STANLEY: Lie Number One: All this squeamishness she puts on! You should just know the line she's been feeding to Mitch. He thought she had never been more than kissed by a fellow! But Sister Blanche is no lily! Ha-ha! Some lily she is!

STELLA: What have you heard and who from?

STANLEY: Our supply-man down at the plant has been going through Laurel for years and he knows all about her and everybody else in the town of Laurel knows all about her. She is as famous in Laurel as if she was the President of the United States, only she is not respected by any party! This supply-man stops at a hotel called the Flamingo.

BLANCHE: [*Singing blithely.*] "Say, it's only a paper moon, Sailing over a cardboard sea /—But it wouldn't be make-believe If you believed in me!"[1]

STELLA: What about the—Flamingo?

STANLEY: She stayed there, too.

---

9. Cloyingly sweet; overly sentimental. *Contrapuntally*: musical term meaning "in an alternating or contrasting manner."

1. From "It's Only a Paper Moon" (1933), a popular song by Harold Arlen (1905–86).

STELLA: My sister lived at Belle Reve.

STANLEY: This is after the home-place had slipped through her lily-white fingers! She moved to the Flamingo! A second-class hotel which has the advantage of not interfering in the private social life of the personalities there! The Flamingo is used to all kinds of goings-on. But even the management of the Flamingo was impressed by Dame Blanche! In fact they was so impressed by Dame Blanche that they requested her to turn in her room key—for permanently! This happened a couple of weeks before she showed here.

BLANCHE: [*Singing.*] "It's a Barnum and Bailey[2] world, Just as phony as it can be—/ But it wouldn't be make-believe If you believed in me!"

STELLA: What—contemptible—lies!

STANLEY: Sure, I can see how you would be upset by this. She pulled the wool over your eyes as much as Mitch's!

STELLA: It's pure invention! There's not a word of truth in it and if I were a man and this creature had dared to invent such things in my presence—

BLANCHE: [*Singing.*] "Without your love, / it's a honky-tonk parade! / Without your love, / It's a melody played / In a penny arcade . . ."

STANLEY: Honey, I told you I thoroughly checked on these stories! Now wait till I finish. The trouble with Dame Blanche was that she couldn't put on her act anymore in Laurel! They got wised up after two or three dates with her and then they quit, and she goes on to another, the same old line, same old act, same old hooey! But the town was too small for this to go on forever! And as time went by she became a town character. Regarded as not just different but downright loco—nuts. [STELLA *draws back.*] And for the last year or two she has been washed up like poison. That's why she's here this summer, visiting royalty, putting on all this act—because she's practically told by the mayor to get out of town! Yes, did you know there was an army camp near Laurel and your sister's was one of the places called "Out-of-Bounds"?

BLANCHE: "It's only a paper moon, / Just as phony as it can be— / But it wouldn't be make-believe / If you believed in me!"

STANLEY: Well, so much for her being such a refined and particular type of girl. Which brings us to Lie Number Two.

STELLA: I don't want to hear any more!

STANLEY: She's not going back to teach school! In fact I am willing to bet you that she never had no idea of returning to Laurel! She didn't resign temporarily from the high school because of her nerves! No, siree, Bob! She didn't. They kicked her out of that high school before the spring term ended—and I hate to tell you the reason that step was taken! A seventeen-year-old boy—she'd gotten mixed up with!

BLANCHE: "It's a Barnum and Bailey world, / Just as phony as it can be—"

[*In the bathroom the water goes on loud; little breathless cries and peals of laughter are heard as if a child were frolicking in the tub.*]

STELLA: This is making me—sick!

STANLEY: The boy's dad learned about it and got in touch with the high school superintendent. Boy, oh, boy, I'd like to have been in that office when Dame

2. P. T. Barnum (1810–91) and James Bailey (1847–1906), circus promoters of "The Greatest Show on Earth."

Blanche was called on the carpet! I'd like to have seen her trying to squirm out of that one! But they had her on the hook good and proper that time and she knew that the jig was all up! They told her she better move on to some fresh territory. Yep, it was practickly a town ordinance passed against her!

[*The bathroom door is opened and* BLANCHE *thrusts her head out, holding a towel about her hair.*]

BLANCHE: Stella!

STELLA: [*Faintly.*] Yes, Blanche?

BLANCHE: Give me another bath-towel to dry my hair with. I've just washed it.

STELLA: Yes, Blanche. [*She crosses in a dazed way from the kitchen to the bathroom door with a towel.*]

BLANCHE: What's the matter, honey?

STELLA: Matter? Why?

BLANCHE: You have such a strange expression on your face!

STELLA: Oh—[*She tries to laugh.*] I guess I'm a little tired!

BLANCHE: Why don't you bathe, too, soon as I get out?

STANLEY: [*Calling from the kitchen.*] How soon is that going to be?

BLANCHE: Not so terribly long! Possess your soul in patience![3]

STANLEY: It's not my soul, it's my kidneys I'm worried about! [BLANCHE *slams the door.* STANLEY *laughs harshly.* STELLA *comes slowly back into the kitchen.*] Well, what do you think of it?

STELLA: I don't believe all of those stories and I think your supply-man was mean and rotten to tell them. It's possible that some of the things he said are partly true. There are things about my sister I don't approve of—things that caused sorrow at home. She was always—flighty!

STANLEY: Flighty!

STELLA: But when she was young, very young, she married a boy who wrote poetry. . . . He was extremely good-looking. I think Blanche didn't just love him but worshipped the ground he walked on! Adored him and thought him almost too fine to be human! But then she found out—

STANLEY: What?

STELLA: This beautiful and talented young man was a degenerate. Didn't your supply-man give you that information?

STANLEY: All we discussed was recent history. That must have been a pretty long time ago.

STELLA: Yes, it was—a pretty long time ago. . . .

[STANLEY *comes up and takes her by the shoulders rather gently. She gently withdraws from him. Automatically she starts sticking little pink candles in the birthday cake.*]

STANLEY: How many candles you putting in that cake?

STELLA: I'll stop at twenty-five.

STANLEY: Is company expected?

STELLA: We asked Mitch to come over for cake and ice-cream.

[STANLEY *looks a little uncomfortable. He lights a cigarette from the one he has just finished.*]

---

3. "In your patience you will possess your souls" (Luke 21.19).

STANLEY: I wouldn't be expecting Mitch over tonight.

[STELLA *pauses in her occupation with candles and looks slowly around at* STANLEY.]

STELLA: *Why?*

STANLEY: Mitch is a buddy of mine. We were in the same outfit together—Two-forty-first Engineers. We work in the same plant and now on the same bowling team. You think I could face him if—

STELLA: Stanley Kowalski, did you—did you repeat what that—?

STANLEY: You're goddam right I told him! I'd have that on my conscience the rest of my life if I knew all that stuff and let my best friend get caught!

STELLA: Is Mitch through with her?

STANLEY: Wouldn't you be if—?

STELLA: I said, *Is Mitch through with her?*

[BLANCHE's *voice is lifted again, serenely as a bell. She sings* "But it wouldn't be make-believe / If you believed in me."]

STANLEY: No, I don't think he's necessarily through with her—just wised up!

STELLA: Stanley, she thought Mitch was—going to—going to marry her. I was hoping so, too.

STANLEY: Well, he's not going to marry her. Maybe he *was*, but he's not going to jump in a tank with a school of sharks—now! [*He rises.*] Blanche! Oh, Blanche! Can I please get in my bathroom? [*There is a pause.*]

BLANCHE: Yes, indeed, sir! Can you wait one second while I dry?

STANLEY: Having waited one hour I guess one second ought to pass in a hurry.

STELLA: And she hasn't got her job? Well, what will she do!

STANLEY: She's not stayin' here after Tuesday. You know that, don't you? Just to make sure I bought her ticket myself. A bus ticket.

STELLA: In the first place, Blanche wouldn't go on a bus.

STANLEY: She'll go on a bus and like it.

STELLA: No, she won't, no, she won't, Stanley!

STANLEY: *She'll go!* Period. P.S. She'll go *Tuesday*!

STELLA: [*Slowly.*] What'll—she—do? What on earth will she—*do*!

STANLEY: Her future is mapped out for her.

STELLA: What do you mean?

[BLANCHE *sings.*]

STANLEY: Hey, canary bird! Toots! Get *OUT* of the *BATHROOM*!

[*The bathroom door flies open and* BLANCHE *emerges with a gay peal of laughter, but as* STANLEY *crosses past her, a frightened look appears in her face, almost a look of panic. He doesn't look at her but slams the bathroom door shut as he goes in.*]

BLANCHE: [*Snatching up a hairbrush.*] Oh, I feel so good after my long, hot bath, I feel so good and cool and—rested!

STELLA: [*Sadly and doubtfully from the kitchen.*] Do you, Blanche?

BLANCHE: [*Snatching up a hairbrush.*] Yes, I do, so refreshed! [*She tinkles her highball glass.*] A hot bath and a long, cold drink always give me a brand new outlook on life! [*She looks through the portieres at* STELLA, *standing between them, and slowly stops brushing.*] Something has happened!—What is it?

STELLA: [*Turning away quickly.*] Why, nothing has happened, Blanche.

BLANCHE: You're lying! Something has! [*She stares fearfully at* STELLA, *who pretends to be busy at the table. The distant piano goes into a hectic breakdown.*]

Scene 8

Three quarters of an hour later.

The view through the big windows is fading gradually into a still-golden dusk. A torch of sunlight blazes on the side of a big water-tank or oil-drum across the empty lot toward the business district which is now pierced by pinpoints of lighted windows or windows reflecting the sunset.

The three people are completing a dismal birthday supper. STANLEY *looks sullen.* STELLA *is embarrassed and sad.*

BLANCHE *has a tight, artificial smile on her drawn face. There is a fourth place at the table which is left vacant.*

BLANCHE: [*Suddenly.*] Stanley, tell us a joke, tell us a funny story to make us all laugh. I don't know what's the matter, we're all so solemn. Is it because I've been stood up by my beau? [STELLA *laughs feebly.*] It's the first time in my entire experience with men, and I've had a good deal of all sorts, that I've actually been stood up by anybody! Ha-ha! I don't know how to take it. . . . Tell us a funny little story, Stanley! Something to help us out.

STANLEY: I didn't think you liked my stories, Blanche.

BLANCHE: I like them when they're amusing but not indecent.

STANLEY: I don't know any refined enough for your taste.

BLANCHE: Then let me tell one.

STELLA: Yes, you tell one, Blanche. You used to know lots of good stories.

[*The music fades.*]

BLANCHE: Let me see, now. . . . I must run through my repertoire! Oh, yes—I love parrot stories! Do you all like parrot stories? Well, this one's about the old maid and the parrot. This old maid, she had a parrot that cursed a blue streak and knew more vulgar expressions than Mr. Kowalski!

STANLEY: Huh.

BLANCHE: And the only way to hush the parrot up was to put the cover back on its cage so it would think it was night and go back to sleep. Well, one morning the old maid had just uncovered the parrot for the day—when who should she see coming up the front walk but the preacher! Well, she rushed back to the parrot and slipped the cover back on the cage and then she let in the preacher. And the parrot was perfectly still, just as quiet as a mouse, but just as she was asking the preacher how much sugar he wanted in his coffee—the parrot broke the silence with a loud— [*She whistles.*] —and said—"God *damn,* but that was a short day!" [*She throws back her head and laughs.* STELLA *also makes an ineffectual effort to seem amused.* STANLEY *pays no attention to the story but reaches way over the table to spear his fork into the remaining chop which he eats with his fingers.*] Apparently Mr. Kowalski was not amused.

STELLA: Mr. Kowalski is too busy making a pig of himself to think of anything else!

STANLEY: That's right, baby.

STELLA: Your face and your fingers are disgustingly greasy. Go and wash up and then help me clear the table.

[*He hurls a plate to the floor.*]

STANLEY: That's how I'll clear the table! [*He seizes her arm.*] Don't ever talk that way to me! "Pig—Polack—disgusting—vulgar—greasy!"—them kind of words have been on your tongue and your sister's too much around here! What do you two think you are? A pair of queens? Remember what Huey Long[4] said— "Every Man is a King!" And I am the king around here, so don't forget it! [*He hurls a cup and saucer to the floor.*] My place is cleared! You want me to clear your places?

> [STELLA *begins to cry weakly.* STANLEY *stalks out on the porch and lights a cigarette. The Negro entertainers around the corner are heard.*]

BLANCHE: What happened while I was bathing? What did he tell you, Stella?

STELLA: Nothing, nothing, nothing!

BLANCHE: I think he told you something about Mitch and me! You know why Mitch didn't come but you won't tell me! [STELLA *shakes her head helplessly.*] I'm going to call him!

STELLA: I wouldn't call him, Blanche.

BLANCHE: I am, I'm going to call him on the phone.

STELLA: [*Miserably.*] I wish you wouldn't.

BLANCHE: I intend to be given some explanation from someone!

> [*She rushes to the phone in the bedroom.* STELLA *goes out on the porch and stares reproachfully at her husband. He grunts and turns away from her.*]

STELLA: I hope you're pleased with your doings. I never had so much trouble swallowing food in my life, looking at that girl's face and the empty chair! [*She cries quietly.*]

BLANCHE: [*At the phone.*] Hello. Mr. Mitchell, please.... Oh.... I would like to leave a number if I may. Magnolia 9047. And say it's important to call.... Yes, very important.... Thank you. [*She remains by the phone with a lost, frightened look.*]

> [STANLEY *turns slowly back toward his wife and takes her clumsily in his arms.*]

STANLEY: Stell, it's gonna be all right after she goes and after you've had the baby. It's gonna be all right again between you and me the way that it was. You remember the way that it was? Them nights we had together? God, honey, it's gonna be sweet when we can make noise in the night the way that we used to and get the colored lights going with nobody's sister behind the curtains to hear us! [*Their upstairs neighbors are heard in bellowing laughter at something.* STANLEY *chuckles.*] Steve an' Eunice ...

STELLA: Come on back in. [*She returns to the kitchen and starts lighting the candles on the white cake.*] Blanche?

BLANCHE: Yes. [*She returns from the bedroom to the table in the kitchen.*] Oh, those pretty, pretty little candles! Oh, don't burn them, Stella.

STELLA: I certainly will.

> [STANLEY *comes back in.*]

BLANCHE: You ought to save them for baby's birthdays. Oh, I hope candles are going to glow in his life and I hope that his eyes are going to be like candles, like two blue candles lighted in a white cake!

---

4. Louisiana political leader, governor, and senator (1893–1935); a fiery and flamboyant populist.

STANLEY: [*Sitting down.*] What poetry!

BLANCHE: [*She pauses reflectively for a moment.*] I shouldn't have called him.

STELLA: There's lots of things could have happened.

BLANCHE: There's no excuse for it, Stella. I don't have to put up with insults. I won't be taken for granted.

STANLEY: Goddamn, it's hot in here with the steam from the bathroom.

BLANCHE: I've said I was sorry three times. [*The piano fades out.*] I take hot baths for my nerves. Hydrotherapy, they call it. You healthy Polack, without a nerve in your body, of course you don't know what anxiety feels like!

STANLEY: I am not a Polack. People from Poland are Poles, not Polacks. But what I am is a one-hundred-per-cent American, born and raised in the greatest country on earth and proud as hell of it, so don't ever call me a Polack.

[*The phone rings.* BLANCHE *rises expectantly.*]

BLANCHE: Oh, that's for me, I'm sure.

STANLEY: *I'm* not sure. Keep your seat. [*He crosses leisurely to phone.*] H'lo. Aw, yeh, hello, Mac.

[*He leans against wall, staring insultingly in at* BLANCHE. *She sinks back in her chair with a frightened look.* STELLA *leans over and touches her shoulder.*]

BLANCHE: Oh, keep your hands off me, Stella. What is the matter with you? Why do you look at me with that pitying look?

STANLEY: [*Bawling.*] QUIET IN THERE!—We've got a noisy woman on the place.— Go on, Mac. At Riley's? No, I don't wanta bowl at Riley's. I had a little trouble with Riley last week. I'm the team captain, ain't I? All right, then, we're not gonna bowl at Riley's, we're gonna bowl at the West Side or the Gala! All right, Mac. See you! [*He hangs up and returns to the table.* BLANCHE *fiercely controls herself, drinking quickly from her tumbler of water. He doesn't look at her but reaches in a pocket. Then he speaks slowly and with false amiability.*] Sister Blanche, I've got a little birthday remembrance for you.

BLANCHE: Oh, have you, Stanley? I wasn't expecting any, I—I don't know why Stella wants to observe my birthday! I'd much rather forget it—when you— reach twenty-seven! Well—age is a subject that you'd prefer to—ignore!

STANLEY: Twenty-seven?

BLANCHE: [*Quickly.*] What is it? Is it for *me*?

[*He is holding a little envelope toward her.*]

STANLEY: Yes, I hope you like it!

BLANCHE: Why, why—Why, it's a—

STANLEY: Ticket! Back to Laurel! On the Greyhound![5] Tuesday! [*The "Varsouviana" music steals in softly and continues playing.* STELLA *rises abruptly and turns her back.* BLANCHE *tries to smile. Then she tries to laugh. Then she gives both up and springs from the table and runs into the next room. She clutches her throat and then runs into the bathroom. Coughing, gagging sounds are heard.*] Well!

STELLA: You didn't need to do that.

STANLEY: Don't forget all that I took off her.

STELLA: You needn't have been so cruel to someone alone as she is.

5. Long-distance bus company.

STANLEY: Delicate piece she is.

STELLA: She is. She was. You didn't know Blanche as a girl. Nobody, nobody, was tender and trusting as she was. But people like you abused her, and forced her to change. [*He crosses into the bedroom, ripping off his shirt, and changes into a brilliant silk bowling shirt. She follows him.*] Do you think you're going bowling now?

STANLEY: Sure.

STELLA: You're not going bowling. [*She catches hold of his shirt.*] Why did you do this to her?

STANLEY: I done nothing to no one. Let go of my shirt. You've torn it.

STELLA: I want to know why. Tell me why.

STANLEY: When we first met, me and you, you thought I was common. How right you was, baby. I was common as dirt. You showed me the snapshot of the place with the columns. I pulled you down off them columns and how you loved it, having them colored lights going! And wasn't we happy together, wasn't it all okay till she showed here? [STELLA *makes a slight movement. Her look goes suddenly inward as if some interior voice had called her name. She begins a slow, shuffling progress from the bedroom to the kitchen, leaning and resting on the back of the chair and then on the edge of a table with a blind look and listening expression.* STANLEY, *finishing with his shirt, is unaware of her reaction.*] And wasn't we happy together? Wasn't it all okay? Till she showed here. Hoity-Toity, describing me as an ape. [*He suddenly notices the change in* STELLA.] Hey, what is it, Stell? [*He crosses to her.*]

STELLA: [*Quietly.*] Take me to the hospital.

  [*He is with her now, supporting her with his arm, murmuring indistinguishably as they go outside.*]

Scene 9

A while later that evening. BLANCHE *is seated in a tense hunched position in a bedroom chair that she has recovered with diagonal green and white stripes. She has on her scarlet satin robe. On the table beside chair is a bottle of liquor and a glass. The rapid, feverish polka tune, the "Varsouviana," is heard. The music is in her mind; she is drinking to escape it and the sense of disaster closing in on her, and she seems to whisper the words of the song. An electric fan is turning back and forth across her.*

  MITCH *comes around the corner in work clothes: blue denim shirt and pants. He is unshaven. He climbs the steps to the door and rings.* BLANCHE *is startled.*

BLANCHE: Who is it, please?

MITCH: [*Hoarsely.*] Me. Mitch.

  [*The polka tune stops.*]

BLANCHE: Mitch!—Just a minute. [*She rushes about frantically, hiding the bottle in a closet, crouching at the mirror and dabbing her face with cologne and powder. She is so excited that her breath is audible as she dashes about. At last she rushes to the door in the kitchen and lets him in.*] Mitch!—Y'know, I really shouldn't let you in after the treatment I have received from you this evening! So utterly uncavalier! But hello, beautiful! [*She offers him her lips. He ignores it and pushes past her into the flat. She looks fearfully after him as he stalks into the bedroom.*] My, my, what a cold shoulder! And such uncouth apparel! Why, you haven't even shaved! The unforgivable insult to a lady! But I forgive you. I forgive you because it's such a relief to see you. You've stopped that polka tune that I had caught in my head. Have you ever had anything caught in your head? No, of course you haven't, you dumb angel-puss, you'd never get anything awful caught in your head!

[*He stares at her while she follows him while she talks. It is obvious that he has had a few drinks on the way over.*]

MITCH: Do we have to have that fan on?

BLANCHE: No!

MITCH: I don't like fans.

BLANCHE: Then let's turn it off, honey. I'm not partial to them! [*She presses the switch and the fan nods slowly off. She clears her throat uneasily as* MITCH *plumps himself down on the bed in the bedroom and lights a cigarette.*] I don't know what there is to drink. I—haven't investigated.

MITCH: I don't want Stan's liquor.

BLANCHE: It isn't Stan's. Everything here isn't Stan's. Some things on the premises are actually mine! How is your mother? Isn't your mother well?

MITCH: Why?

BLANCHE: Something's the matter tonight, but never mind. I won't cross-examine the witness. I'll just— [*She touches her forehead vaguely. The polka tune starts up again.*]—pretend I don't notice anything different about you! That—music again . . .

MITCH: What music?

BLANCHE: The "Varsouviana"! The polka tune they were playing when Allan— Wait! [*A distant revolver shot is heard.* BLANCHE *seems relieved.*] There now, the shot! It always stops after that. [*The polka music dies out again.*] Yes, now it's stopped.

MITCH: Are you boxed out of your mind?

BLANCHE: I'll go and see what I can find in the way of—[*She crosses into the closet, pretending to search for the bottle.*] Oh, by the way, excuse me for not being dressed. But I'd practically given you up! Had you forgotten your invitation to supper?

MITCH: I wasn't going to see you anymore.

BLANCHE: Wait a minute. I can't hear what you're saying and you talk so little that when you do say something, I don't want to miss a single syllable of it. . . . What am I looking around here for? Oh, yes—liquor! We've had so much excitement around here this evening that I *am* boxed out of my mind! [*She pretends suddenly to find the bottle. He draws his foot up on the bed and stares at her contemptuously.*] Here's something. Southern Comfort![6] What is that, I wonder?

MITCH: If you don't know, it must belong to Stan.

BLANCHE: Take your foot off the bed. It has a light cover on it. Of course you boys don't notice things like that. I've done so much with this place since I've been here.

MITCH: I bet you have.

BLANCHE: You saw it before I came. Well, look at it now! This room is almost— dainty! I want to keep it that way. I wonder if this stuff ought to be mixed with something? Ummm, it's sweet! It's terribly, terribly sweet! Why, it's a *liqueur,*

---

6. Peach-flavored bourbon liqueur.

I believe! Yes, that's what it *is*, a liqueur! [MITCH *grunts.*] I'm afraid you won't like it, but try it, and maybe you will.

MITCH: I told you already I don't want none of his liquor and I mean it. You ought to lay off his liquor. He says you been lapping it up all summer like a wild cat!

BLANCHE: What a fantastic statement! Fantastic of him to say it, fantastic of you to repeat it! I won't descend to the level of such cheap accusations to answer them, even!

MITCH: Huh.

BLANCHE: What's in your mind? I see something in your eyes!

MITCH: [*Getting up.*] It's dark in here.

BLANCHE: I like it dark. The dark is comforting to me.

MITCH: I don't think I ever seen you in the light. [BLANCHE *laughs breathlessly.*] That's a fact!

BLANCHE: Is it?

MITCH: I've never seen you in the afternoon.

BLANCHE: Whose fault is that?

MITCH: You never want to go out in the afternoon.

BLANCHE: Why, Mitch, you're at the plant in the afternoon!

MITCH: Not Sunday afternoon. I've asked you to go out with me sometimes on Sundays but you always make an excuse. You never want to go out till after six and then it's always some place that's not lighted much.

BLANCHE: There is some obscure meaning in this but I fail to catch it.

MITCH: What it means is I've never had a real good look at you, Blanche. Let's turn the light on here.

BLANCHE: [*Fearfully.*] Light? Which light? What for?

MITCH: This one with the paper thing on it.

[*He tears the paper lantern off the light bulb. She utters a frightened gasp.*]

BLANCHE: What did you do that for?

MITCH: So I can take a look at you good and plain!

BLANCHE: Of course you don't really mean to be insulting!

MITCH: No, just realistic.

BLANCHE: I don't want realism. I want magic! [MITCH *laughs.*] Yes, yes, magic! I try to give that to people. I misrepresent things to them. I don't tell truth, I tell what *ought* to be truth. And if that is sinful, then let me be damned for it!— Don't turn the light on!

[MITCH *crosses to the switch. He turns the light on and stares at her. She cries out and covers her face. He turns the lights off again.*]

MITCH: [*Slowly and bitterly.*] I don't mind you being older than what I thought. But all the rest of it—Christ! That pitch about your ideals being so old-fashioned and all the malarkey that you've dished out all summer. Oh, I knew you weren't sixteen anymore. But I was a fool enough to believe you was straight.

BLANCHE: Who told you I wasn't—"straight"? My loving brother-in-law. And you believed him.

MITCH: I called him a liar at first. And then I checked on the story. First I asked our supply-man who travels through Laurel. And then I talked directly over long-distance to this merchant.

BLANCHE: Who is this merchant?

MITCH: Kiefaber.

BLANCHE: The merchant Kiefaber of Laurel! I know the man. He whistled at me. I put him in his place. So now for revenge he makes up stories about me.

MITCH: Three people, Kiefaber, Stanley, and Shaw, swore to them!

BLANCHE: Rub-a-dub-dub, three men in a tub! And such a filthy tub!

MITCH: Didn't you stay at a hotel called The Flamingo?

BLANCHE: Flamingo? No! Tarantula was the name of it! I stayed at a hotel called The Tarantula Arms!

MITCH: [*Stupidly.*] Tarantula?

BLANCHE: Yes, a big spider! That's where I brought my victims. [*She pours herself another drink.*] Yes, I had many intimacies with strangers. After the death of Allan—intimacies with strangers was all I seemed able to fill my empty heart with. . . . I think it was panic, just panic, that drove me from one to another, hunting for some protection—here and there, in the most—unlikely places— even, at last, in a seventeen-year-old boy but—somebody wrote the superin- tendent about it—"This woman is morally unfit for her position!" [*She throws back her head with convulsive, sobbing laughter. Then she repeats the statement, gasps, and drinks.*] True? Yes, I suppose—unfit somehow—anyway. . . . So I came here. There was nowhere else I could go. I was played out. You know what played out is? My youth was suddenly gone up the water-spout, and—I met you. You said you needed somebody. Well, I needed somebody, too. I thanked God for you, because you seemed to be gentle—a cleft in the rock of the world that I could hide in! But I guess I was asking, hoping—too much! Kiefaber, Stanley, and Shaw have tied an old tin can to the tail of the kite.

[*There is a pause.* MITCH *stares at her dumbly.*]

MITCH: You lied to me, Blanche.

BLANCHE: Don't say I lied to you.

MITCH: Lies, lies, inside and out, all lies.

BLANCHE: Never inside, I didn't lie in my heart. . . .

[*A vendor comes around the corner. She is a blind* MEXICAN WOMAN *in a dark shawl, carrying bunches of those gaudy tin flowers that lower-class Mexicans display at funerals and other festive occasions. She is calling barely audibly. Her figure is only faintly visible outside the building.*]

MEXICAN WOMAN: *Flores. Flores, Flores para los muertos.*[7] *Flores. Flores.*

BLANCHE: What? Oh! Somebody outside . . . [*She goes to the door, opens it and stares at the* MEXICAN WOMAN.]

MEXICAN WOMAN: [*She is at the door and offers* BLANCHE *some of her flowers.*] *Flores? Flores para los muertos?*

BLANCHE: [*Frightened.*] No, no! Not now! Not now! [*She darts back into the apart- ment, slamming the door.*]

MEXICAN WOMAN: [*She turns away and starts to move down the street.*] *Flores para los muertos.*

[*The polka tune fades in.*]

7. Flowers for the dead (Spanish).

BLANCHE: [*As if to herself.*] Crumble and fade and—regrets—recriminations . . . "If you'd done this, it wouldn't've cost me that!"

MEXICAN WOMAN: *Corones*[8] *para los muertos. Corones* . . .

BLANCHE: Legacies! Huh. . . . And other things such as bloodstained pillow-slips—"Her linen needs changing"—"Yes, Mother. But couldn't we get a colored girl to do it?" No, we couldn't of course. Everything gone but the—

MEXICAN WOMAN: *Flores.*

BLANCHE: Death—I used to sit here and she used to sit over there and death was as close as you are. . . . We didn't dare even admit we had ever heard of it!

MEXICAN WOMAN: *Flores para los muertos, flores—flores* . . .

BLANCHE: The opposite is desire. So do you wonder? How could you possibly wonder! Not far from Belle Reve, before we had lost Belle Reve, was a camp where they trained young soldiers. On Sunday nights they would go in town to get drunk—

MEXICAN WOMAN: [*Softly.*] *Corones* . . .

BLANCHE: —and on the way back they would stagger onto my lawn and call—"Blanche! Blanche!"—the deaf old lady remaining suspected nothing. But sometimes I slipped outside to answer their calls. . . . Later the paddy-wagon[9] would gather them up like daisies . . . the long way home. . . . [*The* MEXICAN WOMAN *turns slowly and drifts back off with her soft mournful cries.* BLANCHE *goes to the dresser and leans forward on it. After a moment,* MITCH *rises and follows her purposefully. The polka music fades away. He places his hands on her waist and tries to turn her about.*] What do you want?

MITCH: [*Fumbling to embrace her.*] What I been missing all summer.

BLANCHE: Then marry me, Mitch!

MITCH: I don't think I want to marry you anymore.

BLANCHE: No?

MITCH: [*Dropping his hands from her waist.*] You're not clean enough to bring in the house with my mother.

BLANCHE: Go away, then. [*He stares at her.*] Get out of here quick before I start screaming fire! [*Her throat is tightening with hysteria.*] Get out of here quick before I start screaming fire. [*He still remains staring. She suddenly rushes to the big window with its pale blue square of the soft summer light and cries wildly.*] Fire! Fire! Fire!

[*With a startled gasp,* MITCH *turns and goes out the outer door, clatters awkwardly down the steps and around the corner of the building.* BLANCHE *staggers back from the window and falls to her knees. The distant piano is slow and blue.*]

Scene 10

It is a few hours later that night.

BLANCHE *has been drinking fairly steadily since* MITCH *left. She has dragged her wardrobe trunk into the center of the bedroom. It hangs open with flowery dresses thrown across it. As the drinking and packing went on, a mood of hysterical exhilaration came into her and she has decked herself out in a somewhat soiled and crumpled white satin evening gown and a pair of scuffed silver slippers with brilliants*[1] *set in their heels.*

---

8. Wreaths (Spanish).   9. Police van.   1. Sparkling gems.

Now she is placing the rhinestone tiara on her head before the mirror of the dressing-table and murmuring excitedly as if to a group of spectral admirers.

BLANCHE: How about taking a swim, a moonlight swim at the old rock-quarry? If anyone's sober enough to drive a car! Ha-ha! Best way in the world to stop your head buzzing! Only you've got to be careful to dive where the deep pool is—if you hit a rock you don't come up till tomorrow . . . [*Tremblingly she lifts the hand mirror for a closer inspection. She catches her breath and slams the mirror face down with such violence that the glass cracks. She moans a little and attempts to rise.* STANLEY *appears around the corner of the building. He still has on the vivid green silk bowling shirt. As he rounds the corner the honky-tonk music is heard. It continues softly throughout the scene. He enters the kitchen, slamming the door. As he peers in at* BLANCHE, *he gives a low whistle. He has had a few drinks on the way and has brought some quart beer bottles home with him.*] How is my sister?

STANLEY: She is doing okay.

BLANCHE: And how is the baby?

STANLEY: [*Grinning amiably.*] The baby won't come before morning so they told me to go home and get a little shut-eye.

BLANCHE: Does that mean we are to be alone in here?

STANLEY: Yep. Just me and you, Blanche. Unless you got somebody hid under the bed. What've you got on those fine feathers for?

BLANCHE: Oh, that's right. You left before my wire came.

STANLEY: You got a wire?

BLANCHE: I received a telegram from an old admirer of mine.

STANLEY: Anything good?

BLANCHE: I think so. An invitation.

STANLEY: What to? A fireman's ball?

BLANCHE: [*Throwing back her head.*] A cruise of the Caribbean on a yacht!

STANLEY: Well, well. What do you know?

BLANCHE: I have never been so surprised in my life.

STANLEY: I guess not.

BLANCHE: It came like a bolt from the blue!

STANLEY: Who did you say it was from?

BLANCHE: An old beau of mine.

STANLEY: The one that give you the white fox-pieces?

BLANCHE: Mr. Shep Huntleigh. I wore his ATO[2] pin my last year at college. I hadn't seen him again until last Christmas. I ran in to him on Biscayne Boulevard. Then—just now—this wire—inviting me on a cruise of the Caribbean! The problem is clothes. I tore into my trunk to see what I have that's suitable for the tropics!

STANLEY: And come up with that—gorgeous—diamond—tiara?

BLANCHE: This old relic? Ha-ha! It's only rhinestones.

STANLEY: Gosh. I thought it was Tiffany diamonds. [*He unbuttons his shirt.*]

BLANCHE: Well, anyhow, I shall be entertained in style.

STANLEY: Uh-huh. It goes to show, you never know what is coming.

BLANCHE: Just when I thought my luck had begun to fail me—

STANLEY: Into the picture pops this Miami millionaire.

2. Probably Alpha Tau Omega, a college fraternity.

BLANCHE: This man is not from Miami. This man is from Dallas.

STANLEY: This man is from Dallas?

BLANCHE: Yes, this man is from Dallas where gold spouts out of the ground!

STANLEY: Well, just so he's from somewhere! [*He starts removing his shirt.*]

BLANCHE: Close the curtains before you undress any further.

STANLEY: [*Amiably.*] This is all I'm going to undress right now. [*He rips the sack off a quart beer bottle.*] Seen a bottle-opener? [*She moves slowly toward the dresser, where she stands with her hands knotted together.*] I used to have a cousin who could open a beer bottle with his teeth. [*Pounding the bottle cap on the corner of table.*] That was his only accomplishment, all he could do—he was just a human bottle-opener. And then one time, at a wedding party, he broke his front teeth off! After that he was so ashamed of himself he used t' sneak out of the house when company came . . . [*The bottle cap pops off and a geyser of foam shoots up. STANLEY laughs happily, holding up the bottle over his head.*] Ha-ha! Rain from heaven! [*He extends the bottle toward her.*] Shall we bury the hatchet and make it a loving-cup? Huh?

BLANCHE: No, thank you.

STANLEY: Well, it's a red-letter night for us both. You having an oil millionaire and me having a baby. [*He goes to the bureau in the bedroom and crouches to remove something from the bottom drawer.*]

BLANCHE: [*Drawing back.*] What are you doing in here?

STANLEY: Here's something I always break out on special occasions like this. The silk pyjamas I wore on my wedding night!

BLANCHE: Oh.

STANLEY: When the telephone rings and they say, "You've got a son!" I'll tear this off and wave it like a flag! [*He shakes out a brilliant pyjama coat.*] I guess we are both entitled to put on the dog. [*He goes back to the kitchen with the coat over his arm.*]

BLANCHE: When I think of how divine it is going to be to have such a thing as privacy once more—I could weep with joy!

STANLEY: This millionaire from Dallas is not going to interfere with your privacy any?

BLANCHE: It won't be the sort of thing you have in mind. This man is a gentleman and he respects me. [*Improvising feverishly.*] What he wants is my companionship. Having great wealth sometimes makes people lonely! A cultivated woman, a woman of intelligence and breeding, can enrich a man's life—immeasurably! I have those things to offer, and this doesn't take them away. Physical beauty is passing. A transitory possession. But beauty of the mind and richness of the spirit and tenderness of the heart—and I have all of those things—aren't taken away, but grow! Increase with the years! How strange that I should be called a destitute woman! When I have all of these treasures locked in my heart. [*A choked sob comes from her.*] I think of myself as a very, very rich woman! But I have been foolish—casting my pearls before swine![3]

STANLEY: Swine, huh?

BLANCHE: Yes, swine! Swine! And I'm thinking not only of you but of your friend, Mr. Mitchell. He came to see me tonight. He dared to come here in his work

---

3. See Matthew 7.6: "Do not give what is holy to dogs, or throw your pearls before swine, lest they trample them underfoot, and turn and tear you to pieces."

clothes! And to repeat slander to me, vicious stories that he had gotten from you! I gave him his walking papers . . .

STANLEY: You did, huh?

BLANCHE: But then he came back. He returned with a box of roses to beg my forgiveness! He implored my forgiveness. But some things are not forgivable. Deliberate cruelty is not forgivable. It is the one unforgivable thing in my opinion and it is the one thing of which I have never, ever been guilty. And so I told him, I said to him, "Thank you," but it was foolish of me to think that we could ever adapt ourselves to each other. Our ways of life are too different. Our attitudes and our backgrounds are incompatible. We have to be realistic about such things. So farewell, my friend! And let there be no hard feelings. . . .

STANLEY: Was this before or after the telegram came from the Texas oil millionaire?

BLANCHE: What telegram? No! No, after! As a matter of fact, the wire came just as—

STANLEY: As a matter of fact there wasn't no wire at all!

BLANCHE: Oh, oh!

STANLEY: There isn't no millionaire! And Mitch didn't come back with roses 'cause I know where he is—

BLANCHE: Oh!

STANLEY: There isn't a goddam thing but imagination!

BLANCHE: Oh!

STANLEY: And lies and conceit and tricks!

BLANCHE: Oh!

STANLEY: And look at yourself! Take a look at yourself in that worn-out Mardi Gras[4] outfit, rented for fifty cents from some ragpicker! And with the crazy crown on! What queen do you think you are?

BLANCHE: Oh—God . . .

STANLEY: I've been on to you from the start! Not once did you pull any wool over this boy's eyes! You come in here and sprinkle the place with powder and spray perfume and cover the light-bulb with a paper lantern, and lo and behold the place has turned into Egypt and you are the Queen of the Nile![5] Sitting on your throne and swilling down my liquor! I say—Ha!—Ha! Do you hear me? Ha—ha—ha! [*He walks into the bedroom.*]

BLANCHE: Don't come in here! [*Lurid reflections appear on the walls around* BLANCHE. *The shadows are of a grotesque and menacing form. She catches her breath, crosses to the phone and jiggles the hook.* STANLEY *goes into the bathroom and closes the door.*] Operator, operator! Give me long-distance, please. . . . I want to get in touch with Mr. Shep Huntleigh of Dallas. He's so well known he doesn't require any address. Just ask anybody who—Wait!!—No, I couldn't find it right now. . . . Please understand, I—No! No, wait! . . . One moment! Someone is—Nothing! Hold on, please! [*She sets the phone down and crosses warily into the kitchen. The night is filled with inhuman voices like cries in a jungle. The shadows and lurid reflections move sinuously as flames along the wall spaces. Through the back wall of the rooms, which have become transparent, can be seen the sidewalk. A prostitute has rolled[6] a drunkard. He pursues her along the walk, overtakes her and there is a struggle. A policeman's whistle*

---

4. Literally, "Fat Tuesday" (French), the carnival before Lent, the Christian period of self-denial, which begins on Ash Wednesday.   5. Cleopatra, Queen of Egypt.   6. Robbed.

breaks it up. The figures disappear. Some moments later the NEGRO WOMAN *appears around the corner with a sequined bag which the prostitute had dropped on the walk. She is rooting excitedly through it.* BLANCHE *presses her knuckles to her lips and returns slowly to the phone. She speaks in a hoarse whisper.*] Operator! Operator! Never mind long-distance. Get Western Union. There isn't time to be—Western—Western Union! [*She waits anxiously.*] Western Union? Yes! I—want to—Take down this message! "In desperate, desperate circumstances! Help me! Caught in a trap. Caught in—" *Oh!*

[*The bathroom door is thrown open and* STANLEY *comes out in the brilliant silk pyjamas. He grins at her as he knots the tassled sash about his waist. She gasps and backs away from the phone. He stares at her for a count of ten. Then a clicking becomes audible from the telephone, steady and rasping.*]

STANLEY: You left th' phone off th' hook.

[*He crosses to it deliberately and sets it back on the hook. After he has replaced it, he stares at her again, his mouth slowly curving into a grin, as he weaves between* BLANCHE *and the outer door. The barely audible "Blue Piano" begins to drum up louder. The sound of it turns into the roar of an approaching locomotive.* BLANCHE *crouches, pressing her fists to her ears until it has gone by.*]

BLANCHE: [*Finally straightening.*] Let me—let me get by you!
STANLEY: Get by me? Sure. Go ahead. [*He moves back a pace in the doorway.*]
BLANCHE: You—you stand over there! [*She indicates a further position.*]
STANLEY: You got plenty of room to walk by me now.
BLANCHE: Not with you there! But I've got to get out somehow!
STANLEY: You think I'll interfere with you? Ha-ha! [*The "Blue Piano" goes softy. She turns confusedly and makes a faint gesture. The inhuman jungle voices rise up. He takes a step toward her, biting his tongue, which protrudes between his lips. Softly.*] Come to think of it—maybe you wouldn't be bad to—interfere with. . . .

[BLANCHE *moves backward through the door into the bedroom.*]

BLANCHE: Stay back! Don't you come toward me another step or I'll—
STANLEY: What?
BLANCHE: Some awful thing will happen! It will!
STANLEY: What are you putting on now?

[*They are now both inside the bedroom.*]

BLANCHE: I warn you, don't, I'm in danger!

[*He takes another step. She smashes a bottle on the table and faces him, clutching the broken top.*]

STANLEY: What did you do that for?
BLANCHE: So I could twist the broken end in your face!
STANLEY: I bet you would do that!
BLANCHE: I would! I will if you—
STANLEY: Oh! So you want some roughhouse! All right, let's have some roughhouse! [*He springs toward her, overturning the table. She cries out and strikes at him with the bottle top but he catches her wrist.*] Tiger—tiger! Drop the bottle-top! Drop it! We've had this date with each other from the beginning!

[*She moans. The bottle-top falls. She sinks to her knees: He picks up her inert figure and carries her to the bed. The hot trumpet and drums from the Four Deuces sound loudly.*]

Scene 11

It is some weeks later. STELLA *is packing* BLANCHE'*s things. Sounds of water can be heard running in the bathroom.*

*The portieres are partly open on the poker players—*STANLEY, STEVE, MITCH *and* PAB-LO—*who sit around the table in the kitchen. The atmosphere of the kitchen is now the same raw, lurid one of the disastrous poker night.*

The building is framed by the sky of turquoise. STELLA *has been crying as she arranges the flowery dresses in the open trunk.*

EUNICE *comes down the steps from her flat above and enters the kitchen. There is an outburst from the poker table.*

STANLEY: Drew to an inside straight and made it, by God.
PABLO: *Maldita sea tu suerto!*
STANLEY: Put it in English, greaseball.
PABLO: I am cursing your rutting luck.
STANLEY: [*Prodigiously elated.*] You know what luck is? Luck is believing you're lucky. Take at Salerno.[7] I believed I was lucky. I figured that 4 out of 5 would not come through but I would . . . and I did. I put that down as a rule. To hold front position in this rat-race you've got to believe you are lucky.
MITCH: You . . . you . . . you . . . Brag . . . brag . . . bull . . . bull.

[STELLA *goes into the bedroom and starts folding a dress.*]

STANLEY: What's the matter with him?
EUNICE: [*Walking past the table.*] I always did say that men are callous things with no feelings but this does beat anything. Making pigs of yourselves. [*She comes through the portieres into the bedroom.*]
STANLEY: What's the matter with her?
STELLA: How is my baby?
EUNICE: Sleeping like a little angel. Brought you some grapes. [*She puts them on a stool and lowers her voice.*] Blanche?
STELLA: Bathing.
EUNICE: How is she?
STELLA: She wouldn't eat anything but asked for a drink.
EUNICE: What did you tell her?
STELLA: I—just told her that—we'd made arrangements for her to rest in the country. She's got it mixed in her mind with Shep Huntleigh.

[BLANCHE *opens the bathroom door slightly.*]

BLANCHE: Stella.
STELLA: Yes.

---

7. Important beachhead in the Allied invasion of Italy in World War II.

BLANCHE: That cool yellow silk—the bouclé.[8] See if it's crushed. If it's not too crushed I'll wear it and on the lapel that silver and turquoise pin in the shape of a seahorse. You will find them in the heart-shaped box I keep my accessories in. And Stella . . . Try and locate a bunch of artificial violets in that box, too, to pin with the seahorse on the lapel of the jacket.

[*She closes the door.* STELLA *turns to* EUNICE.]

STELLA: I don't know if I did the right thing.

EUNICE: What else could you do?

STELLA: I couldn't believe her story and go on living with Stanley.

EUNICE: Don't ever believe it. Life has got to go on. No matter what happens, you've got to keep on going.

[*The bathroom door opens a little.*]

BLANCHE: [*Looking out.*] Is the coast clear?

STELLA: Yes, Blanche. [*To* EUNICE.] Tell her how well she's looking.

BLANCHE: Please close the curtains before I come out.

STELLA: They're closed.

STANLEY: —How many for you?

PABLO: Two.

STEVE: Three.

[BLANCHE *appears in the amber light of the door. She has a tragic radiance in her red satin robe following the sculptural lines of her body. The "Varsouviana" rises audibly as* BLANCHE *enters the bedroom.*]

BLANCHE: [*With faintly hysterical vivacity.*] I have just washed my hair.

STELLA: Did you?

BLANCHE: I'm not sure I got the soap out.

EUNICE: Such fine hair!

BLANCHE: [*Accepting the compliment.*] It's a problem. Didn't I get a call?

STELLA: Who from, Blanche?

BLANCHE: Shep Huntleigh . . .

STELLA: Why, not yet, honey!

BLANCHE: How strange! I—

[*At the sound of* BLANCHE'S *voice* MITCH'S *arm supporting his cards has sagged and his gaze is dissolved into space.* STANLEY *slaps him on the shoulder.*]

STANLEY: Hey, Mitch, come to!

[*The sound of this new voice shocks* BLANCHE. *She makes a shocked gesture, forming his name with her lips.* STELLA *nods and looks quickly away.* BLANCHE *stands quite still for some moments—the silver-backed mirror in her hand and a look of sorrowful perplexity as though all human experience shows on her face.* BLANCHE *finally speaks but with sudden hysteria.*]

BLANCHE: What's going on here? [*She turns from* STELLA *to* EUNICE *and back to* STELLA. *Her rising voice penetrates the concentration of the game.* MITCH *ducks his head lower but* STANLEY *shoves back his chair as if about to rise.* STEVE *places a restraining hand on*

---

8. Textile woven with uneven yarn to produce a rough, uneven surface.

his arm. Continuing.] What's happened here? I want an explanation of what's happened here.

STELLA: [*Agonizingly.*] Hush! Hush!

EUNICE: Hush! Hush! Honey.

STELLA: Please, Blanche.

BLANCHE: Why are you looking at me like that? Is something wrong with me?

EUNICE: You look wonderful, Blanche. Don't she look wonderful?

STELLA: Yes.

EUNICE: I understand you are going on a trip.

STELLA: Yes, Blanche *is.* She's going on a vacation.

EUNICE: I'm green with envy.

BLANCHE: Help me, help me get dressed!

STELLA: [*Handing her dress.*] Is this what you—

BLANCHE: Yes, it will do! I'm anxious to get out of here—this place is a trap!

EUNICE: What a pretty blue jacket.

STELLA: It's lilac colored.

BLANCHE: You're both mistaken. It's Della Robbia blue.[9] The blue of the robe in the old Madonna pictures. Are these grapes washed? [*She fingers the bunch of grapes which* EUNICE *had brought in.*]

EUNICE: Huh?

BLANCHE: Washed, I said. Are they washed?

EUNICE: They're from the French Market.

BLANCHE: That doesn't mean they've been washed. [*The cathedral bells chime.*] Those cathedral bells—they're the only clean thing in the Quarter. Well, I'm going now. I'm ready to go.

EUNICE: [*Whispering.*] She's going to walk out before they get here.

STELLA: Wait, Blanche.

BLANCHE: I don't want to pass in front of those men.

EUNICE: Then wait'll the game breaks up.

STELLA: Sit down and . . .

[BLANCHE *turns weakly, hesitantly about. She lets them push her into a chair.*]

BLANCHE: I can smell the sea air. The rest of my time I'm going to spend on the sea. And when I die, I'm going to die on the sea. You know what I shall die of? [*She plucks a grape.*] I shall die of eating an unwashed grape one day out on the ocean. I will die—with my hand in the hand of some nice-looking ship's doctor, a very young one with a small blond mustache and a big silver watch. "Poor lady," they'll say, "the quinine[1] did her no good. That unwashed grape has transported her soul to heaven." [*The cathedral chimes are heard.*] And I'll be buried at sea sewn up in a clean white sack and dropped overboard—at noon—in the blaze of summer—and into an ocean as blue as [*Chimes again.*] my first lover's eyes!

[A DOCTOR *and a* MATRON[2] *have appeared around the corner of the building and climbed the steps to the porch. The gravity of their profession is exaggerated—the*

---

9. A shade of light blue seen in terra cottas made by the Della Robbia family during the Italian Renaissance.   1. Medicinal salt used to treat malaria.

2. Female supervisor at a hospital or other institution.

unmistakable aura of the state institution with its cynical detachment. The DOCTOR *rings the doorbell. The murmur of the game is interrupted.*]

EUNICE: [*Whispering to* STELLA.] That must be them.

[STELLA *presses her fists to her lips.*]

BLANCHE: [*Rising slowly.*] What is it?
EUNICE: [*Affectedly casual.*] Excuse me while I see who's at the door.
STELLA: Yes.

[EUNICE *goes into the kitchen.*]

BLANCHE: [*Tensely.*] I wonder if it's for me.

[*A whispered colloquy takes place at the door.*]

EUNICE: [*Returning, brightly.*] Someone is calling for Blanche.
BLANCHE: It *is* for me, then! [*She looks fearfully from one to the other and then to the portieres. The "Varsouviana" faintly plays.*] Is it the gentleman I was expecting from Dallas?
EUNICE: I think it is, Blanche.
BLANCHE: I'm not quite ready.
STELLA: Ask him to wait outside.
BLANCHE: I . . .

[EUNICE *goes back to the portieres. Drums sound very softly.*]

STELLA: Everything packed?
BLANCHE: My silver toilet articles are still out.
STELLA: Ah!
EUNICE: [*Returning.*] They're waiting in front of the house.
BLANCHE: They! Who's "they"?
EUNICE: There's a lady with him.
BLANCHE: I cannot imagine who this "lady" could be! How is she dressed?
EUNICE: Just—just a sort of a—plain-tailored outfit.
BLANCHE: Possibly she's—[*Her voice dies out nervously.*]
STELLA: Shall we go, Blanche?
BLANCHE: Must we go through that room?
STELLA: I will go with you.
BLANCHE: How do I look?
STELLA: Lovely.
EUNICE: [*Echoing.*] Lovely.

[BLANCHE *moves fearfully to the portieres.* EUNICE *draws them open for her.* BLANCHE *goes into the kitchen.*]

BLANCHE: [*To the men.*] Please don't get up. I'm only passing through.

[*She crosses quickly to outside door.* STELLA *and* EUNICE *follow. The poker players stand awkwardly at the table—all except* MITCH, *who remains seated, looking down at the table.* BLANCHE *steps out on a small porch at the side of the door. She stops short and catches her breath.*]

DOCTOR: How do you do?

BLANCHE: You are not the gentleman I was expecting. [*She suddenly gasps and starts back up the steps. She stops by* STELLA, *who stands just outside the door, and speaks in a frightening whisper.*] That man isn't Shep Huntleigh.

[*The "Varsouviana" is playing distantly.* STELLA *stares back at* BLANCHE. EUNICE *is holding* STELLA'*s arm. There is a moment of silence—no sound but that of* STANLEY *steadily shuffling the cards.* BLANCHE *catches her breath again and slips back into the flat. She enters the flat with a peculiar smile, her eyes wide and brilliant. As soon as her sister goes past her,* STELLA *closes her eyes and clenches her hands.* EUNICE *throws her arms comfortingly about her. Then she starts up to her flat.* BLANCHE *stops just inside the door.* MITCH *keeps staring down at his hands on the table, but the other men look at her curiously. At last she starts around the table toward the bedroom. As she does,* STANLEY *suddenly pushes back his chair and rises as if to block her way. The* MATRON *follows her into the flat.*]

STANLEY: Did you forget something?

BLANCHE: [*Shrilly.*] Yes! Yes, I forgot something!

[*She rushes past him into the bedroom. Lurid reflections appear on the walls in odd, sinuous shapes. The "Varsouviana" is filtered into a weird distortion, accompanied by the cries and noises of the jungle.* BLANCHE *seizes the back of a chair as if to defend herself.*]

STANLEY: [*Sotto voce.*[3]] Doc, you better go in.

DOCTOR: [*Sotto voce, motioning to the* MATRON.] Nurse, bring her out.

[*The* MATRON *advances on one side,* STANLEY *on the other. Divested of all the softer properties of womanhood, the* MATRON *is a peculiarly sinister figure in her severe dress. Her voice is bold and toneless as a firebell.*]

MATRON: Hello, Blanche.

[*The greeting is echoed and re-echoed by other mysterious voices behind the walls, as if reverberated through a canyon of rock.*]

STANLEY: She says that she forgot something.

[*The echo sounds in threatening whispers.*]

MATRON: That's all right.

STANLEY: What did you forget, Blanche?

BLANCHE: I—I—

MATRON: It don't matter. We can pick it up later.

STANLEY: Sure. We can send it along with the trunk.

BLANCHE: [*Retreating in panic.*] I don't know you—I don't know you. I want to be—left alone—please!

MATRON: Now, Blanche!

ECHOES: [*Rising and falling.*] Now, Blanche—now, Blanche—now, Blanche!

STANLEY: You left nothing here but spilt talcum and old empty perfume bottles—unless it's the paper lantern you want to take with you. You want the lantern?

---

3. In an undertone (Italian).

[*He crosses to dressing table and seizes the paper lantern, tearing it off the light bulb, and extends it toward her. She cries out as if the lantern was herself. The* MATRON *steps boldly toward her. She screams and tries to break past the* MATRON. *All the men spring to their feet.* STELLA *runs out to the porch, with* EUNICE *following to comfort her, simultaneously with the confused voices of the men in the kitchen.* STELLA *rushes into* EUNICE'*s embrace on the porch.*]

STELLA: Oh, my God, Eunice help me! Don't let them do that to her, don't let them hurt her! Oh, God, oh, please God, don't hurt her! What are they doing to her? What are they doing? [*She tries to break from* EUNICE'*s arms.*]

EUNICE: No, honey, no, no, honey. Stay here. Don't go back in there. Stay with me and don't look.

STELLA: What have I done to my sister? Oh, God, what have I done to my sister?

EUNICE: You done the right thing, the only thing you could do. She couldn't stay here; there wasn't no other place for her to go.

[*While* STELLA *and* EUNICE *are speaking on the porch the voices of the men in the kitchen overlap them.* MITCH *has started toward the bedroom.* STANLEY *crosses to block him.* STANLEY *pushes him aside.* MITCH *lunges and strikes at* STANLEY. STANLEY *pushes* MITCH *back.* MITCH *collapses at the table, sobbing. During the preceding scenes, the* MATRON *catches hold of* BLANCHE'*s arm and prevents her flight.* BLANCHE *turns wildly and scratches at the* MATRON. *The heavy woman pinions her arms.* BLANCHE *cries out hoarsely and slips to her knees.*]

MATRON: These fingernails have to be trimmed. [*The* DOCTOR *comes into the room and she looks at him.*] Jacket,[4] Doctor?

DOCTOR: Not unless necessary. [*He takes off his hat and now he becomes personalized. The unhuman quality goes. His voice is gentle and reassuring as he crosses to* BLANCHE *and crouches in front of her. As he speaks her name, her terror subsides a little. The lurid reflections fade from the walls, the inhuman cries and noises die out and her own hoarse crying is calmed.*] Miss DuBois. [*She turns her face to him and stares at him with desperate pleading. He smiles; then he speaks to the* MATRON.] It won't be necessary.

BLANCHE: [*Faintly.*] Ask her to let go of me.

DOCTOR: [*To the* MATRON.] Let go.

[*The* MATRON *releases her.* BLANCHE *extends her hands toward the* DOCTOR. *He draws her up gently and supports her with his arm and leads her through the portieres.*]

BLANCHE: [*Holding tight to his arm.*] Whoever you are—I have always depended on the kindness of strangers.

[*The poker players stand back as* BLANCHE *and the* DOCTOR *cross the kitchen to the front door. She allows him to lead her as if she were blind. As they go out on the porch,* STELLA *cries out her sister's name from where she is crouched a few steps up on the stairs.*]

STELLA: Blanche! Blanche, Blanche!

[BLANCHE *walks on without turning, followed by the* DOCTOR *and the* MATRON. *They go around the corner of the building.* EUNICE *descends to* STELLA *and places the*

---

4. That is, straitjacket, used to restrain the mentally ill from violence.

child in her arms. It is wrapped in a pale blue blanket. STELLA *accepts the child, sobbingly.* EUNICE *continues downstairs and enters the kitchen where the men, except for* STANLEY, *are returning silently to their places about the table.* STANLEY *has gone out on the porch and stands at the foot of the steps looking at* STELLA.]

STANLEY: [*A bit uncertainly.*] Stella? [*She sobs with inhuman abandon. There is something luxurious in her complete surrender to crying now that her sister is gone. Voluptuously, soothingly.*] Now, honey. Now, love. Now, now, love. [*He kneels beside her and his fingers find the opening of her blouse.*] Now, now, love. Now, love. . . .

[*The luxurious sobbing, the sensual murmur fade away under the swelling music of the "Blue Piano" and the muted trumpet.*]

STEVE: This game is seven-card stud.

CURTAIN

1947

QUESTIONS

1. Why do you think Williams divided the play into eleven scenes rather than three or five acts? Consider the staging of the play. Would the actors go offstage between these scenes? Would a curtain hide the stage? Would the audience need to read abbreviated stage directions such as "early the following morning" in the program, or is this unnecessary?

2. Twelve roles are listed under "Characters" at the beginning of *A Streetcar Named Desire.* Could more than one of the roles be assigned to one female or male actor? In other words, are there smaller parts in different scenes that could be played by someone who exits, changes costumes and character, and comes back onstage in the new role?

3. *A Streetcar Named Desire* centers on the conflict between Blanche DuBois and Stanley Kowalski. Why and how are their personalities and values in conflict? Can either of them be called a "hero" or a "villain" in the traditional senses of those words? Why or why not? Of these two characters, whom do you most sympathize with and/or admire at different moments of the play? At which point are you most aware of the faults of one or the other?

4. What is the full significance of Stella's line, in scene 11, that she couldn't believe Blanche's story "and go on living with Stanley"? Might this line or any other lines make Stella a less sympathetic character? How might an actress make Stella seem manipulative and powerful instead of submissive to Stanley or Blanche?

5. What is the significance of Stanley's allusion in scene 8 to Huey Long's remark that "Every Man is a King"? How might this remark resonate with the references to class sprinkled throughout the play, including the initial description of Stella as "of a background obviously quite different from her husband's" and Stanley's reference to how he "pulled [Stella] down off them columns"?

6. Much of the action of the play centers on the process whereby Stanley discovers and reveals what he sees as the truth about Blanche and about Blanche's past, and he more than once refers to her as a liar. Yet Blanche offers us a very different reading of her lies, particularly in her encounter with Mitch in scene 9. In what sense is or is not Blanche a liar? How might an actress indicate whether or not Blanche really knows the truth?

7. A key moment in Blanche's past and one that we get both from her point of view and from Stella's is the night when her young husband shot himself. Why does that moment figure so largely, not only in Blanche's mind but also in the play? What does this long-dead character represent in the play?

8. What is the significance of the play's title? How did Williams change the play by naming it *A Streetcar Named Desire* rather than *The Poker Night*? What different kinds or notions of "desire" are at issue in the play? (Consider such references as when Blanche rebukes Stella for "talking about . . . brutal desire—just—Desire!" [scene 4] or when Blanche tells Mitch that desire is "the opposite" of death [scene 9]).

9. To what extent does Williams draw on stereotypes of New Orleans, or the South? How do the setting and the set enhance the conflict between the characters? What details of space, sound, lighting, and color seem most significant to the play's effect?

10. How are Williams's stage directions unlike those of other plays you have read? What are some examples of stage directions in *A Streetcar Named Desire* that go beyond what is necessary for staging a performance and indicate that Williams intended the play to be read as literature as well as performed?

SUGGESTIONS FOR WRITING

1. Is *A Streetcar Named Desire* a "realistic" play—that is, are the characters, setting, and situation plausible, recognizable? Do the characters speak in a natural idiom, or do they seem to be "speechifying" for the sake of the play? Write an essay in which you argue that the mode of the play is or is not one suited to "Method" or realistic acting style, and be sure to support your position with specifics from the text.

2. Although *A Streetcar Named Desire* is set in New Orleans, the DuBois family plantation, Belle Reve, has critical significance in the play. What is evoked—about history, about social class—by the offstage presence of a Southern plantation? How does the story of Belle Reve affect each character and propel the plot? Write an essay in which you discuss the dramatic and thematic significance of Belle Reve in the play.

3. *A Streetcar Named Desire* is filled with paper and references to paper: the paper lantern, the deed to Belle Reve, the song "Paper Moon," among others. What is the effect of such accumulating details? How do they acquire thematic significance? How might you reflect these references in designing a production of the play? Write an essay in which you examine the recurrence of paper imagery in the play. Why is it important?

4. Gender roles and sexuality are central to the drama of *A Streetcar Named Desire*. To what extent are Stanley Kowalski and Blanche DuBois caricatures of masculinity and femininity? Could the performers play against caricature by revealing a more feminine side of Stanley and a more masculine quality in Blanche, or would that be a misreading of the play? Write an essay in which you discuss the play's depiction of gender roles.

5. At one point Blanche tells Mitch, "The first time I laid eyes on [Stanley] I thought to myself, that man is my executioner! That man will destroy me." And indeed, at the play's climactic moment Stanley declares, "We've had this date with each other from the beginning!" Are the play's characters pawns of fate, acting out destinies over which they have little control, or are they fully conscious of and responsible for their actions? Write an essay in which you examine the role of free will in *A Streetcar Named Desire*.

Rachel Holmes and Joan MacIntosh in The Public Theater production
of *365 Days / 365 Plays*, 2006

SUZAN-LORI PARKS
From 365 Days/365 Plays

From the Author's "Elements of Style"

I'm continuing the use of my slightly unconventional theatrical elements. Here's
a road map.

- *(Rest)*
  Take a little time, a pause, a breather; make a transition.

- A Spell
  An elongated and heightened *(Rest)*. Denoted by repetition of figures' names
  with no dialogue. Has sort of an architectural look:

  KRISHNA

  ARJUNA

  KRISHNA

  ARJUNA

  This is a place where the figures experience their pure true simple state. While
  no action or stage business is necessary, directors should fill this moment as
  they best see fit.

- (Parentheses around dialogue indicate softly spoken passages (asides; sotto
  voce)).

- Some plays for two characters use no character names. The performers should
  alternate lines. Other plays for two or more characters use no character names,
  but each new speech is preceded by a dash. Each dash indicates when a new
  speaker begins. The lines below would be read by two different speakers:

  —She dont talk.
  —I do so talk.

THE 3 CONSTANTS

For 365 Days / 365 Plays, I'm inviting everybody to perform these 3 Constants along with your selected plays—sprinkle them where you like.

—XOXOXOX S-L P

THE 1ST CONSTANT (Remember Who You Are)

2 benches or 2 chairs. Someone on the bench (or chair). Someone Else comes in.

SOMEONE ELSE: This seat taken?
SOMEONE: Nope.
SOMEONE ELSE: You sleep?
SOMEONE: Yep.
SOMEONE ELSE: Oh. Sorry.

Someone Else goes through an elaborate before-sleep ritual. Feel free, do whatever you want. Brush yr teeth, floss maybe, pray maybe. You could stretch or gargle. Take out yr contacts, oil yr feet and hands, cold-creme yr face, roll up yr hair in curlers or wrap it in a doo-rag. Lock up yr belongings. Kiss yr beloved's image. Thank God. Do whatcha gotta do.

SOMEONE ELSE
SOMEONE ELSE

(Rest)

SOMEONE ELSE: Yr sleeping with one eye open.
SOMEONE: Yes.
SOMEONE ELSE: How come?
SOMEONE: To watch over you.
SOMEONE ELSE: But—. But you dont even know me!!!!
SOMEONE: I am That, you are That, all this is That, and Thats all there is.

SOMEONE
SOMEONE ELSE

(Rest)

They sleep.

THE 2ND CONSTANT (Action in Inaction)

Someone standing still. They could be dressed in mourning. The sound of wind or whales forever.

THE 3RD CONSTANT (Inaction in Action)

Onstage are 365 things to do, that is, 365 tasks. What are the tasks? Yr choice. Lights up. Dart around trying to do all the tasks. Make it clear that you desire to complete all the tasks. Dart around as fast as possible. Do yr best. Dont be shy about going all out. There isnt anything to hold out for. This is it. Hurry hurry hurry. Lights go out long before yr done.

January

1 HERE WE GO

> *4 People wearing 4 different historical hats.*
> *Maybe a Lincoln hat, a Napoléon hat,*
> *a President Mobuto leopard-skin pillbox-style hat,*[1]
> *a Jackie Kennedy hat. A 5th Person wears a wig.*

5TH PERSON: Ready?
4 PEOPLE WITH HATS: Ready.
ONE OF THE PEOPLE WITH HATS: Wait!

> *Someone turns on music and there is a mad scramble,*
> *they exchange their hats with an intensity as yet unseen.*
> *For the most part the exchange is kindly, well-intentioned,*
> *but sometimes there is a violent outburst, nothing fatal, nothing*
> *verbal. During this exchange, The 5th Person can change or*
> *groom the wig and apply makeup or shave face.*
> *The music stops as suddenly as it started.*
> *The 5th Person puts away grooming supplies and*
> *the 4 People with Hats (or Hates) sit contentedly,*
> *wearing whatever hat they have as if theyve always worn it*
> *and will wear it forever.*

(Rest)

5TH PERSON: Ready?
4 PEOPLE WITH HATS: Ready!
5TH PERSON: All right. Here we go:

> *Everybody leans forward—the lean takes forever*
> *and is performed with great enthusiasm.*

2 WE ARE FRESH OUT OF CANNED LAUGHTER, GET SOME OFF THE TELEVISION

> *A Kid (an adult with a doll, sucking her finger) sits on a Man's*
> *knee. They watch tv. A comedy show. Canned laughter.*
> *Every so often they laugh. When the Man laughs he slaps his*
> *knee (the one the Kid isnt sitting on). Then he jiggles*
> *his other knee (the one the Kid is sitting on). He jiggles his knee*
> *out of laughter, and then for no apparent reason. More canned*
> *laughter. The Kid laughs. The Man jiggles his knee.*

MAN: Horsey.

> *He jiggles his knee some more. The Kid laughs then—*

---

1. Hats made of real leopard skin became a signature of Mobuto Sese Seko (1930–97), longtime president of Zaire, now the Democratic Republic of the Congo.

KID: Ouch.
MAN: Whats the matter?
KID: Im going to bed.
MAN: Good idea.

The Man straightens his leg.

MAN: Slide down.
KID: No thanks.

She hops down instead of sliding and walks offstage.
He sits there staring at the tv with its canned laughter.
After a moment, the Kid comes back onstage.

KID: The door's locked.

MAN

MAN

KID: The door's locked. Will you unlock—

MAN

KID

MAN

KID

He makes a grab at her and she runs around the room,
screaming with delight or fear—it should be hard to tell which.
A door opens. A Woman stands there. The Kid hides.

MAN: How was yr day?
WOMAN: Shitty. What are you doing?
MAN: Stretching my legs.

WOMAN

MAN

(Rest)

WOMAN: Im going to hang up my coat.
MAN: Sounds like a plan.

She goes offstage to hang up her coat. The Man resumes
chasing the Kid. The Woman reappears. The Kid hides.

WOMAN: Wheres Clara?
MAN: Clara?
WOMAN: Where is she?
MAN: Clara's in bed.

The Woman looks in the direction of where the Kid is hiding.

WOMAN: All in bed and tucked in?
MAN: Yep.
WOMAN: And you read her a story?
MAN: Am I the man of the house, or am I the man of the house?
WOMAN: Yr the man of the house.
MAN: And I read her a story.

WOMAN
MAN

WOMAN: Whats on tv?
MAN: The Comedy Hour.
WOMAN: Im not in the mood for comedy.
MAN: Watch it with me, whydontcha. A little laughter wont kill you.

> *The Woman sits. After a beat, the Man sits. They watch tv.*
> *The Kid watches tv from her hiding place.*

3 2 MARYS

> *1st Woman sits in a lawn chair. 2nd Woman comes up*
> *and sits in a lawn chair some distance away.*

2ND WOMAN: How was yr vacation?

1ST WOMAN
1ST WOMAN

(Rest)

2ND WOMAN: How was—
1ST WOMAN: Hello there.
2ND WOMAN: Hello. You were away. I kept an eye on yr house. The whole time.
Nothing bad happened. To yr house, I mean.
1ST WOMAN: I dont think weve met.
2ND WOMAN: Im yr neighbor. Ive been living over here for 3 years now. Ask anybody.
(Rest)
How was yr vacation?
1ST WOMAN: Nice.
2ND WOMAN: Good for you. A nice vacation. Yr lucky. Do you know how hard it is
to have a nice vacation these days, what with the world the way it is and—
MAN'S VOICE *(From inside)*: WHAT IN THE HELL ARE YOU DOING?
2ND WOMAN: IM TALKING. TO THE NEIGHBOR.
MAN'S VOICE: WHAT IN THE HELL ARE YOU DOING THAT FOR?

(Rest)

2ND WOMAN: IM BEING—NEIGHBORLY. *(Back to 1st Woman)* "Being neighborly."
Thats one of my New Year's resolutions. Whats one of yrs?
1ST WOMAN: Not to have any New Year's resolutions.
2ND WOMAN: Really?
1ST WOMAN: Really.
2ND WOMAN: Thats unpatriotic. I could have you reported.

1ST WOMAN
2ND WOMAN

1ST WOMAN: What if I told you Im hoping to lose 20 pounds?
2ND WOMAN: A health kick, huh? Good for you. "Be more neighborly" and "Quit
kicking the dog." "Quit kicking the dog" is my 2nd one. Whats yr 2nd one?

MAN'S VOICE: WHAT IN THE FUCK ARE YOU TELLING HER?!

2ND WOMAN: WE'RE EXCHANGING—*PLEASANTRIES.*

MAN'S VOICE: IM GOING TO COME OUT THERE AND GIVE YOU A PIECE OF MY MIND. AND THEN, AND THEN, AND THEN YOU KNOW WHAT I'LL DO THEN? I'LL BEAT YOU WITH A STICK.

2ND WOMAN

2ND WOMAN

2ND WOMAN

(Rest)

2ND WOMAN: Excuse me.

1ST WOMAN: Should I call the police?

2ND WOMAN: Why would you wanna do that?

2nd Woman goes inside.

MAN'S VOICE: DONT HURT ME! PLEASE! AAAAAAHHEEEEE!

2ND WOMAN: I didnt touch him. I just gave him a look.

(Rest)

They used to call me "Bloody Mary." On account of the way I handled myself. You can fill in the blanks on yr own, right? You know what Im talking about, dontcha? You get my drift without me drifting too far into it, yes?

1ST WOMAN: You worked in the—meat business.

2ND WOMAN: Im retired now. But back in the day, lemmie tell ya, I could carve them up—in my sleep. "Bloody Mary" they called me. Back in the day.

1ST WOMAN: My name's Mary too.

2ND WOMAN: No shit.

1ST WOMAN: No shit.

2ND WOMAN: How about that. 2 Marys. Side by side. This is what you call an event of great singularity.

1ST WOMAN: This is going to be a great year.

2ND WOMAN: You think?

1ST WOMAN: I know. I can tell.

4 THE NEWS IS *HERE*

WOMAN: Look at them. Fighting in the streets. When will it end?

(Rest)

Get yr head out of that newspaper, honey. Come take a look.

MAN: What are they fighting over?

WOMAN: Hard to tell.

The Man gets up. Looks.

MAN: Looks like a child.

(Rest)

Im going out there and Im going to do something about that.

WOMAN: What?

MAN: Watch me. And, hey take a few pictures or, you know, work the video. This could be my moment.

> *The Man dashes out. The Woman watches, takes a picture or 2,*
> *looks for the video camera and finally finds it.*
> *The Man comes back in with something.*

WOMAN: Dont bring it in here, huh?

MAN: To the victor go the spoils.

WOMAN: Please.

MAN: Have a heart. They woulda torn him limb from limb.

WOMAN: Its a he?

MAN: Its got a thingy. Take a look.

WOMAN: Spare me. Is he white?

MAN: Yup.

WOMAN: We're talking money.

MAN: Yup yup.

WOMAN: We're talking a house in Lush Valley. Or at least a quonset hut in Mountain View. Away from all this action. We're talking food in the winter. We're talking—

MAN: Dont even say it.

WOMAN: Ima say it.

MAN: You say it youll jinx it.

WOMAN: Ima say it anyway cause what the fuck.

> *The Man puts the Baby down on the floor. The Man sticks*
> *his fingers in his own ears and sings. The Woman just watches him.*

MAN: I dont hear you I dont hear you I dont hear you I cant hear you so even if you did say it which you probably are doing right now I cant even hear you saying it so you wont jinx the good things that we might get by saying them and I cant even read yr lips saying it cause I got my eyes closed.

> *The Man peeps open his eyes and then unplugs his ears.*

WOMAN: Yr too sensitive.

MAN: Did you say it?

WOMAN: Yeah, several times over and over, so any chance of getting anything from that baby is—

MAN: Over.

WOMAN: Sorry.

MAN: Thats ok. Its not like we woulda moved anyhow. I mean, could you see me and you living in the mountains with all those—*Mountainites* or whatever the fuck theyre called?

WOMAN: Not in a million.

MAN: The baby's probably a Mountainite.

WOMAN: You think?

MAN: Yeah. Look at his ears. Theyre hairy like the back of my hand.

WOMAN: Shit. So, even if we could sell him, we'd be responsible for the carnage he'd cause.

MAN: Yep. Turn on the camera.

The Woman turns on the camera. The Man walks to the window,
holds the Baby over the ledge, lets go. The Baby falls.

MAN: Hit the ground and ran away. A Mountainite.
(Rest)
That was almost our chance at the brass ring.
WOMAN: A better chance will come.
MAN: I feel a little crestfallen.
WOMAN: Itll fade.

The Man goes back to reading the newspaper. The Woman
goes back to sitting at the window. Everything as before.

5 THE STAR OF INDIA

MASTER OF CEREMONIES: . . . Lets have a big hand for The Cassanova Sword Swallowing Family Circus!!!!

Amazing canned applause.

MASTER OF CEREMONIES: Theyre quite something, arent they? Do you know, I had a chance—before they went on—I had a chance to talk with Mamma Cassanova. Each Cassanova kid, on his or her first birthday is given a sword and, you know how most of us have marks on the walls where our kids grow taller and taller each year, you know, "Thats how tall Junior was on his 8th birthday!"? Well the Cassanovas *mark the sword.* Heres how much Cheeky Cassanova could swallow when he was only one, and see, the marks by his 5th birthday, already 2 inches away from the hilt! Im not kidding, they really do that. On each kid's 7th birthday, when they can swallow up to the hilt, the sword is set aflame—and then, from then on out, its not how deep but how hot, and how *many.* What a life, huh? Anyway, up next we have a male contortionist called "The Star of India." Lets give him a big hand, shall we?

If applause from the audience is tepid,
the Master of Ceremonies should turn on applause from
canned applause machine by stomping on a foot pedal,
to produce a great swell of artificial enthusiasm.
The Star walks on. He's Anglo American, dressed in the style
of a middle management person from the middle of
the Continental United States. He stands there as
the Master of Ceremonies looks on expectantly.

MASTER OF CEREMONIES
STAR

(Rest)

MASTER OF CEREMONIES: Do you need music?
STAR: No, sir, I dont.

MASTER OF CEREMONIES
STAR

(Rest)

STAR: Theres a misprint in the program, sir. It should read: "Indiana." "The Star of Indiana."

MASTER OF CEREMONIES: Yr not "The Star of India"?

STAR: Im the Star of *Indiana*.

(Rest)

MASTER OF CEREMONIES: Can you put yr feet behind yr head and balance on the tip of yr nose?

STAR: Ive never tried, but I dont think I'd be able to, no sir. You see, Ive got this back condition. My doctor says its not serious. "Sciatica" he calls it and he says theres lots of ways to get it. I got mine from putting in long hours at my desk with my fat wallet in my hip pocket.

MASTER OF CEREMONIES: Isnt that something, folks!

Applause.

STAR: I carry my wallet in the breast pocket of my suit coat now. But lets keep that *entre nous*, K?? Wouldnt want the unscrupulous types knowing where Big Daddy keeps his greenbacks. Plus the pictures of my wife and kids: Dorothy just had our latest baby—he's huge and I mean huge. And of course he looks just like—

MASTER OF CEREMONIES: Star! Of *Indiana*! How did you get that name?

STAR: Ive been top salesman in my group statewide for 3 years running. I can sell almost anything.

MASTER OF CEREMONIES: Wellwellwellwell.

STAR: Thats nothing to sneeze at.

MASTER OF CEREMONIES: Certainly not. Ladies and gentlemen: The Star of Indiana!

> *Massive canned applause. The Star opens his wallet and an accordian flood of plastic-encased family photos spills out. The Master of Ceremonies thinks (to himself), Hasn't this Indiana guy heard of birth control? But he acts as if he's very impressed.*

6 THE BIRTH OF TRAGEDY[2]

> *People gathered around a Child, Tragedy. He wears a robe, a crown on his head, and he holds a scepter. The Child sits on a Man's back. The Man is on all 4s, to make a chair.*

HERALD: 4 years ago today we gathered to celebrate the birth of Tragedy. And now we celebrate Tragedy's 4th birthday.

Polite applause.

TRAGEDY: Where are my presents?

HERALD: Theyll be presented one by one.

TRAGEDY: What about my cake?

CHAIR-MAN: Made with the finest ingredients. The finest we could find.

---

2. This is also the title of a book first published in 1872 by German philosopher Friedrich Nietzsche.

MIDWIFE: I remember when you were born. Yr mother was green with pain. A dark cloud passed over the sun. And its been there ever since.

Several people begin to cry quietly.

TRAGEDY: What did you bring me?
MIDWIFE: A sliver from the Root of All Evil.
HERALD: Place it in the gift pile.
TRAGEDY: Now can I eat cake?
HERALD: We have dignitaries from all over the world here to see you.

The Dignitaries smile and bow.

TRAGEDY: I want my cake!
HERALD: Bring the cake!
TRAGEDY: And—kill the dignitaries!
HERALD: And kill the dignitaries!

The cake is brought in. The Dignitaries are ushered out.

8 THERES NOTHING HERE

DICK
JANE

JANE: Theres nothing here.
DICK: No?
DICK
JANE
DICK
JANE

(Rest)

JANE: Im jumping out the window.

She turns to go. At the last possible moment, Dick reaches out and grabs her hand, or arm, or the hem of her coat— his arm is fully extended, the muscles straining. Her arm, or whatever he holds onto, is straining—near the breaking point. Neither of them look at each other.

JANE: I saw pictures of Hiroshima. I could barely look. I thought, "No wonder they hate us." And then—that wasnt even me who did it—it wasnt me and it wasnt no one like me—my people didnt pull the trigger. We were the targets back then too. Still are. I pay first-class taxes and get second-class treatment.
(Rest)
The entire city was devastated. The whole city. There was nothing left.
(Rest)
But I cant kid myself. If we had been in power back then, we woulda been just as bad.
DICK: Come back inside.

He pulls her to him. They hug.

JANE: Look, theres Spot. He's coming down the road. He didnt run away after all.
DICK: He probably had a night on the town.
JANE: Here, Spot! Here, boy!
DICK: Come on in, you old rascal, you!

They clap and call for Spot as the lights fade.

. . .

10 THINGS ARE TOUGH ALL OVER

A Woman leads a Man by the hand.
Theyve been walking for several days.

MAN: Where are you taking me?
WOMAN: I said you shouldnt ask.
MAN: Im asking.
WOMAN: Im taking you to see yr parents.
MAN: Liar!
WOMAN: Im taking you to the cemetery.
MAN: Im not dead. Not yet.
WOMAN: But you will be. And ever since they took the car and the house and the cart and the cow and the horse and the meadow—I lay awake at night for a whole month thinking, "When he goes, I'll have to carry him there, to the cemetery, on my back." This way, when we put you in the ground theyll say: "Here lies a man who came here on his own 2 feet."
MAN: I can dig the hole too.
WOMAN: We'll do it together, howbout.
MAN: Hop up. On my back.
WOMAN: Dont be silly.
MAN: Hop up, Im telling you. I'll give you a piggy.
WOMAN: You wont last 10 steps.
MAN: Try me.

She hops on his back. He looks as if he'll die—
but then the look passes.
Then the look comes back.

MAN: Oh.

She jumps to the ground as he collapses.

WOMAN: Oh?

MAN

WOMAN

(Rest)

MAN: Did you miss me?
WOMAN: Terribly.
MAN: Piggyback ride?
WOMAN: No thanks.

MAN: Im still a man.
WOMAN: Sure you are. Come on.

She takes him by the hand and they continue walking.

· · ·

12 HAMLET/THE HAMLET

Somewhere in William Faulkner's Yoknapatawpha County.[3]

HAMLET SNOPES:
That barn there
I could burn it down
or I could leave it standing.
Burn it
or leave it.
But then what?
Either way Ive taken a step.
Either way Ive done something
and by that something
Ive made myself known:
Barn burner.[4] Outlaw.
Or the kind of fella wholl take an insult
from a rich man
and not pay that rich man no mind
but let that rich man—that rich bastard—
with all the money of the world in his pockets,
use my back
and the backs of every child coming out of me,
and me and mines,
and the likes of me and me and mines
to scrape the cow and mule shit from his fancy boots.
And underneath all that,
not on top of it, but underneath all of it,
a dead father in the ground.
And up above the father,
up above the dead and rotting corpse of a man,
who is more use now than he was useful living,
still alive, an uncle walks.
My daddy's own brother,
eating supper off of my dead daddy's plate.
(Rest)
Help me God, cause life is and seems
particularly complicated just right now.

Mother Snopes enters.

---

3. The name of the imaginary county in Mississippi that is the setting of many Faulkner stories and novels. *The Hamlet* (1940) is the first in a trilogy of novels about the Snopes family, who also appear in other works by Faulkner.   4. Faulkner's short story, "Barn Burning," features a similar character.

MOTHER SNOPES: You gonna come in and eat or you gonna stand out there all night looking at that barn and talking to yrself?

HAMLET SNOPES: I'll come in and eat.

MOTHER SNOPES: Come on in then, before yr uncle eats up all the grits.

HAMLET SNOPES: See that barn, Ma?

MOTHER SNOPES: I see it but I dont see it. I see you seeing it and I dont see you seeing it neither. Folks say yr a barn burner. I call them liars.

HAMLET SNOPES: Yep.

MOTHER SNOPES: Are they liars? Are they liars, son?

HAMLET SNOPES

HAMLET SNOPES

(Rest)

HAMLET SNOPES: Ima get me some of them grits.

He goes inside.

MOTHER SNOPES: God help us. Every one.

She goes inside too.

2006

QUESTIONS

1. Write one or two sentences about each of the 3 Constants to express what you believe each means or shows: What idea, state of being, or feeling is expressed in each Constant? Why do you think Suzan-Lori Parks asks all groups to add these to the selection of the plays that they choose to perform?

2. Do you find any similarities between two or more of the "January" plays in this chapter? Can you sort them into different kinds of plays by characters, situations, events, language? Would you perform them in a different order to make a different meaningful sequence?

3. Which lines in any of the 365 plays included here might be either comic or gloomy, depending on an actor's interpretation? Could any of the plays have either a hopeful ending or a sad one, according to how it is performed?

———————————

SUGGESTIONS FOR WRITING

1. Imagine you are an actor or actress assigned the leading male or female roles in several or most of the short plays from *365 Days / 365 Plays* reproduced here. Look closely at your parts, noting dialogue, action, and probable feelings or motivation. Write an essay on what you discover about the similarity or differences among your roles in these plays. Do these men or women suggest common themes in Parks's plays?

2. Write an essay on the ways that the 3 Constants might relate to different plays in the chapter. Which plays have the most in common with them, if the Constants might be said to exemplify (1) the opposition between two characters that may or may not be resolved into collaboration or unity ("Thats all there is"); (2) silence or stillness in the face of large abstract forces; or (3) spectacular, fast activity? In your view, are the Constants intended to contrast with, summarize, or comment on the other plays, or do they serve as an intermission or refrain?

3. In some of the selected plays, characters are intimately related to one another, whereas in others they are unfamiliar to one another. The short plays often rely on surprise as the audience learns about the relationship or the stranger turns out to be different than expected. Write an essay in which you show how Parks varies the pattern of relationships, interactions, and surprises or revelations in two or more of the plays.

Plans for a Staged Reading, excerpts from 365 Days / 365 Plays by Suzan-Lori Parks

A "staged reading" is a common step in developing a professional production of a play. Actors may read from scripts or memorize their lines; they may sit down or act out the scene in a provisional way. Props, costumes, and set are kept to a minimum, and the reading, designed to reveal the potential of the play or what would need work, is presented before a small nonpaying audience.

Suzan-Lori Parks wrote one play every day for one year from November 13, 2002, to November 12, 2003. The 365 Festival (produced by Parks and Bonnie Metzgar) was performed from November 13, 2006, through November 12, 2007 at more than 700 theaters across the United States and around the world; participating groups produced seven plays (the plays written during one week) in a kind of "relay" of the plays throughout that year. See the website *365 Days / 365 Plays* at www.365days365plays.com for information about the project. "Tablework Notes," a link on the "About" page, records some of the discussion among actors who read through the entire cycle of plays with the playwright and producer in order to prepare the published book. During the yearlong festival, groups in different locations relied on the book for their scripts.

The plays are clearly designed for adult performers and audiences (there are obscenities and some references to sex and violence that would be inappropriate for young teenagers or children), for inexpensive productions with bare sets, and for actors to play different kinds of roles in quick changes with very few costumes or props. Colleges and universities participated in the festival, and the play cycle is well suited to readings in college classrooms. Ideally the set would include a window and a door, as well as hidden space for offstage and a separation between the audience and performers resembling a proscenium arch.

The author's "Elements of Style" indicate a modern or postmodern style that emphasizes drama *without* words as well as *with* them; silence is an important part of Parks's plays. As she says in "Tablework Notes," she likes Beckett. The stage directions in these plays are minimal, and the spelling imitates everyday speech sounds, such as "yr" for "your" or "you're"; "wont" for "won't"; "K" for "o.k."; "howbout" for "how about," and so forth. This suggests that the style and tone of the performance should be suited to American popular culture in the twenty-first century.

All performances are to include "The 3 Constants," in any order. The plays for the first week of January, minus the 7th, plus the 8th, 10th, and

(Continued on next page)

(Continued)

12th appear here, to give a sense of the variety of the plays. The following notes describe what is needed to perform a staged reading of these selections in a certain order: How many male or female actors, what costumes, what props/set/furniture, and what sound effects there should be. With time and energy, a group of students and a teacher could prepare a production, bringing props and costumes to a classroom or auditorium. Students (perhaps one per play) could be designated as directors to work on the next step: to "block" these scenes, that is, to plan and instruct the actors where to sit or stand and when and where to move or perform an action. Still another step would be to rehearse and advise actors what tone or expression to use to deliver a line. This, too, may be done by consulting in teams.

The text clearly encourages actors to improvise actions in some of the plays, and in all of them there is leeway for interpreting the lines. The cast could be chosen well enough in advance for the actors to memorize their lines. If the goal is to share the wealth, every student in the class might have a leading role, especially if typecasting by identity and appearance is ignored. Males or females, older, younger, of any size or skin color or manner might play any part. Alternatively, the class might decide to follow the model of a professional repertory theater company that rotates several plays during one season by assigning each actor several similar roles in different plays. A few extra, or minor, roles could be given to students who do not enjoy acting. Some class members could be the crew, preparing or obtaining props, costumes, sound, lighting, or other components of a production. The process is intended to encourage cooperative experimentation; it should be eye-opening and fun.

Cast and Staging Requirements

MINIMAL NEEDS FOR ALL PLAYS:

2 women, 2 men, and 3 extras (dignitaries, etc.).
5 chairs, 2 of which could be lawn chairs.
The doll (January 2: "We Are Fresh Out of Canned Laughter . . .") could double as the baby (January 4: "The News Is *Here*").
The suit of mourning for the 2nd Constant could be the Star of India's business suit.
One sound system, to play canned laughter, canned applause, the comic music, and the sound of whales.

The 1st Constant ("Remember Who You Are")

Actors: 2 actors of any kind.
Props/set/furniture: 2 chairs; a toothbrush; a squeeze bottle of lotion.

January 1: "Here We Go"

Actors: 5 actors of any kind.
Props/set/furniture: 5 chairs. 4 different historical hats: a tri-corner George Washington hat, a Nazi helmet, Fidel Castro cap, Indian chief feather

(Continued on next page)

(Continued)

headdress (or whatever headgear the crew members can readily obtain). The wig is an eighteenth century powdered wig (man's or woman's). Makeup or shaver for 5th person wearing the wig. A hand mirror.

Sound: music to play "musical headgear."

January 2: "We Are Fresh Out of Canned Laughter . . ."

Actors: 1 female: Kid, Clara; 1 female: Woman, her mother; 1 male: Man, father and husband.

Props/set/furniture: There must be an exit to offstage as well as a front door to the house or apartment. Two chairs or a sofa so Man and Woman can sit side by side to watch TV; TV or an agreed-on direction to look as if watching TV. A doll.

Costumes: Kid could be wearing pajamas. Woman wears a coat that she goes to hang up.

Sound: recording of a laugh track from a TV comedy.

January 3: "2 Marys"

Actors: 2 females, neighbor-strangers; one of them is more threatening somehow ("bloody Mary"). 1 male to yell offstage.

Props/set/furniture: 2 lawn chairs or 2 of the indoor chairs used in other plays. To show that it is outdoors, one woman could bring a plastic flower pot onstage with her; the other could bring a small barbecue grill or the head of a sprinkler.

January 4: "The News Is *Here*"

Actors: 1 female, 1 male, appearing to be husband and wife and not well off; they should somehow represent a difference from the "white" baby *and* the "mountainites"; for example, they could be an African American or Asian or interracial couple, and they could appear to be bikers, gang members, or somehow urban.

Props/set/furniture: The "window" needs to allow something to be dropped out (in a classroom, it could be a desk at the side of the performing area). 2 chairs. A newspaper. A Caucasian-looking doll wrapped in a blanket (supposedly a male baby with hairy ears). 1 camera, 1 video camera.

January 5: "The Star of India"

Actors: 1 person as a circus "barker" or master of ceremonies; 1 person as an Anglo American businessman from the Midwestern United States.

Props/set/furniture: "applause machine" (could use old tape player with red cord) and foot pump (an attachment of some sort on the floor). Large wallet that can open to let out a long accordion-style plastic picture holder with family photos.

(Continued on next page)

(Continued)

Costumes: bright satin vest and bowtie, top hat for the m.c.; business suit or jacket and tie for the Star.
Sound: recording of applause.

January 6: "The Birth of Tragedy"

Actors: 1 person: male child; 1 male: Chair-man; 1 female: Midwife; 1 person: Herald; 3 people: Dignitaries.
Props/set/furniture: crown and scepter, cake, gifts.
Costumes: robe for Tragedy (toga made out of sheet or red bathrobe made to look like king's robe with "ermine" collar made of cotton balls). Dignitaries could look like prime ministers (business suits). Or everyone including herald and midwife could be wearing togas. Or everyone could appear to be Renaissance courtiers if costumes may be borrowed or rented.

January 8: "There's Nothing Here"

Actors: 1 male, 1 female.
Props/set/furniture: a "window" as above.

January 10: "Things Are Tough All Over"

Actors: 1 male, 1 female.
Props/set/furniture: a suitcase or a carpetbag.
Costumes: They could wear dusty overalls or oversized worn-out boots.

January 12: "Hamlet/The Hamlet"

Actors: 1 male, 1 female.
Props/set/furniture: none necessary, but an area offstage is designated the "inside" of the house; another area in a different direction is imagined as the barn.

The 3rd Constant (Inaction in Action)

Actors: All seven (or more) actors.
Props/set/furniture: Use all of the props from the other plays, repeating and switching: put on hats, shave, do makeup, change a baby's diaper, read a newspaper, take a picture or a video. Add to this any exercise equipment, puzzles, a computer, a cellphone, sewing and art materials, cooking materials, wood or bricks or blocks to build with, shovel or broom, any available tools.
Sound: fast-paced comic music.

The 2nd Constant (Action in Inaction)

Actors: 1 person.
Costumes: black clothing.
Sound: recording of whales.

30 CULTURAL AND HISTORICAL CONTEXT

Three different levels of **time** operate in most literary texts, including plays. First, a text represents a particular time—the temporal **setting**—in which the action takes place. We can call this *plot time*. Second, the text reflects the time when the author was writing, and, inevitably, the conditions and assumptions of that time inform the text's conception and style; this feature of textual time we may call *authorial time*. Third, readers read in a particular *reader time*, when conditions and assumptions may differ from those that obtain in either the text's or the author's present. (If we encounter a play on the stage, we might instead call this *performance time*.)

In some cases, plot, authorial, and reader time all differ. Wole Soyinka's *Death and the King's Horseman* is set in the early 1940s in the British colony of Nigeria. Yet it was written in the early 1970s, more than ten years after Soyinka's country gained its independence. Thus, when we—as readers in the 2000s—read the play, three distinct historical and cultural contexts are operating at once. The play's plot unfolds in a time and a place quite remote from us. And the text also reflects values, writing conditions, habits of language, and dramatic conventions of yet another context—three decades after the events in the play occurred, but still decades earlier than, and thousands of miles away from, the time and place in which we read the text. Values in these three times will not be identical. How we interpret the actions and thoughts of the characters in part depends not only on our own assumptions about what they should or might do, but also on what we know about the conditions that shaped people's lives in quite different historical and cultural milieus. Keeping these three contexts in mind as we read—and consciously making comparisons when we perceive conflicting values—is a vital part of our response and interpretation.

This can be equally true of plays that represent the times in which they were written. When Lorraine Hansberry's *A Raisin in the Sun* debuted in 1959, its audience watched scenes that might well have been unfolding at virtually the same moment just down the street. The stage directions, in fact, indicate that the action in the play occurs "in Chicago's Southside, sometime between World War II and the present." In this case, almost no difference exists between plot time and authorial time. Indeed, the play asked its original audiences to believe that there was no distinction between these times and their own, that they were confronting life exactly as it was happening and being invited to consider issues of immediate consequence. And the play also drew, at least to some extent, on that audience's knowledge of current events, concerns, and issues—knowledge that we, living in a quite different reader time, may have to work to master.

Of course, this does not mean that *A Raisin in the Sun*, *Death and the King's Horseman*, or any great play can't speak to us unless we "study up" on the worlds about and in which they were written. "Inevitably, . . . every [literary] work belongs to a given moment," as Wole Soyinka reminds us. But, he adds, "it transcends this" moment, too. Both of these plays remain relevant because they show us people who are as hopeful, complex, funny, and flawed as we are. Indeed, one of Hansberry's major objectives in writing *A Raisin in the Sun* was, as she explained in a letter, to "help . . . people to understand how we ['Negroes'] are just as complicated as they are—and just as mixed up." And we see these characters confronting questions that we face, too—about family, cultural and personal identity, gender, race and ethnicity, ambition, human dignity and honor, historical change, and generational conflict. Much of what happens in both plays could and does still happen in our world, and in much the same way.

But not everything. Consider the abortion that Ruth Younger contemplates near the end of *A Raisin in the Sun*'s first act. In 1959, abortion was illegal in the United States. Women who sought abortions had either to leave the country, usually traveling to Mexico or Puerto Rico (a relatively expensive option), or to seek out shady, back-alley practitioners like the one Ruth consults. Such abortionists typically had little medical expertise and often operated in highly unsanitary conditions. Disease and mortality rates were high, and some of the horror that the Younger family expresses at the thought of abortion can be attributed to reasonable fears about its physical consequences. But their horror also results from the moral and social stigma surrounding abortion. However individuals might themselves feel about the ethics of abortion, the law prohibited it in 1959, and public opinion—as well as the Christian doctrine so important to Mama and other African Americans of her generation—weighed heavily against the practice. To appreciate Ruth's situation, understand other characters' responses, and imagine the original audience's reactions, it helps to know about the prevailing legal climate, as well as the various social attitudes and concerns of the day, especially within a respectable, proud, and aspiring African American family like the Youngers.

Some plays offer us a good deal of information about setting that is relevant to the interpretation of specific episodes. But sometimes we have to supply facts that the text doesn't give us. People may share some characteristics across ages and cultures, but behavior and motivation are often conditioned by historically and culturally specific circumstances. Often we have to adjust our expectations because the world of the play or that of its author differs greatly from our own. Identifying the play's setting—in time and place—and considering carefully the historical and cultural context in which the play was written can be crucial to understanding what happens and why.

The rest of this chapter seeks to introduce you to the contexts that inspired and shaped both *A Raisin in the Sun* and *Death and the King's Horseman*—two very different plays, yet ones connected, in part, through the complex web of history and culture that both plays explore.

THE HISTORICAL SIGNIFICANCE OF *A RAISIN IN THE SUN*

The debut of *A Raisin in the Sun* was a significant historical and cultural event in its own right. The first play by an African American woman ever produced on Broadway, *A Raisin in the Sun* earned its creator, Lorraine Hansberry (1930–65), the New York Drama Critics Circle Award as the year's best play just two months after it opened. Hansberry thus became—at twenty-nine—the youngest American playwright, the first black writer, and only the fifth woman ever to receive this prestigious award. Yet when Hansberry's friend and fellow writer James Baldwin labeled her play a "historical achievement" of the greatest importance, he had something else in mind—the unprecedented way that *A Raisin in the Sun* brought African Americans into the theater and onto the stage. "I had never in my life seen so many black people in the theater," Baldwin recalled. "And the reason was that never before, in the entire history of the American theater, had so much of the truth of black people's lives been seen on the stage. Black people [had] ignored the theater because the theater had always

Lorraine Hansberry, 1959

ignored them." To Baldwin and others, *A Raisin in the Sun* was a "historical achievement" precisely because of its realism and contemporaneity, its truthful depiction of the lives of many ordinary African Americans in the late 1950s. In a sense, the play made history by accurately reflecting a historical and cultural reality previously ignored by dramatists.

The Great Migration

One factor that undoubtedly made the Younger family seem so realistic was the fact that their situation closely resembled that of the 6.5 million African Americans who moved from the rural South to the urban North between 1910 and 1970 as part of the Great Migration. Though these migrants settled in every northern city, the majority eventually made their homes in New York City and Chicago. By 1960, Chicago's black population had grown to 813,000—twenty-five percent of the city's inhabitants.

Like Lena Younger and her husband, those migrant millions flew north on the wings of hope—hope for better jobs at higher wages and for greater safety and freedom than they enjoyed in the Jim Crow–era South. (By 1914, every southern state had passed "Jim Crow" laws mandating segregated railroad cars, waiting rooms, bathrooms, restaurants, theaters, recreation areas, and even hospitals.) Not coincidentally, migration increased when northern industries were expanding and when conditions in the South were particularly oppressive or violent. In the 1920s, when the Younger family would have arrived in Chicago, a government-sponsored report on race relations in that city pointed out that over 85 percent of the 2,881 lynchings that occurred in the United States between 1885 and 1918 occurred in southern states and "that numbers of migrants from towns where lynchings had occurred registered for jobs in Chicago very shortly after lynchings." The same report also concluded that southern blacks were drawn to the city as much for so-called sentimental reasons as for economic ones. When recent immigrants interviewed for the report were asked, "What do you like about the North?" their responses were remarkably similar:

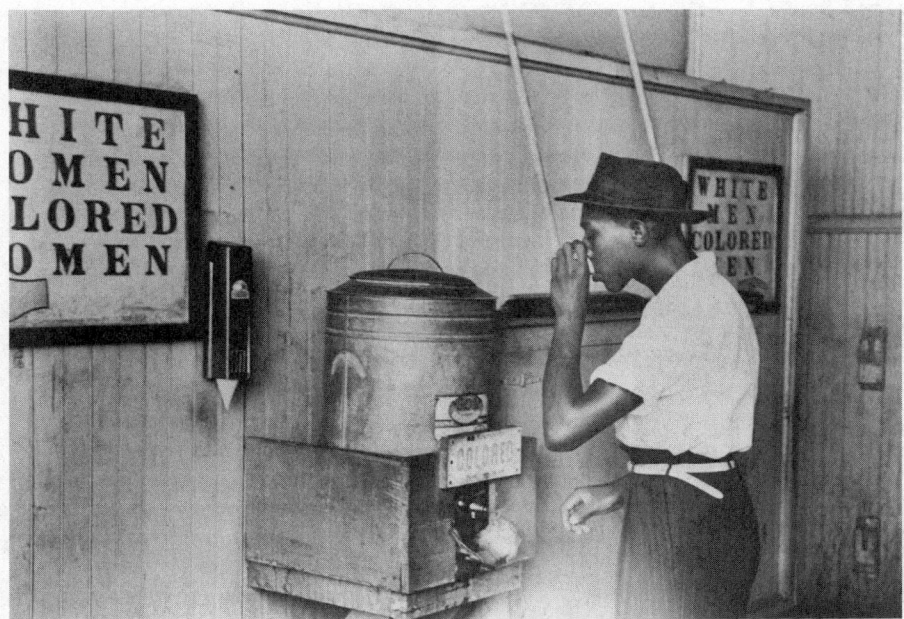

Segregated drinking fountain, Oklahoma City, 1939

1. Freedom in voting and conditions of colored people here.
2. Freedom and chance to make a living; privileges.
3. Freedom and opportunity to acquire something.
   . . .
10. Freedom of speech and action. Can live without fear. No Jim Crow.

Songs and poems of the 1920s, as well as the African American press, fueled such hopes and imbued them with religious significance. The Great Migration was cast as the "Flight out of Egypt"; migrants were encouraged to see themselves as "Bound for the Promised Land," "Going into Canaan."

The "Black Metropolis"

In reality, the vast majority of blacks who came north found themselves not in Canaan, but in the all-black, inner-city enclaves—the "Smoketowns," "Bronzevilles," and "Black Belts"—that had begun to develop in all of the North's major cities before the First World War. In Chicago, that "distinct Negro world" was the South Side, a strip of land extending south along State Street from the Loop (the city's central business district) and bounded by Lake Michigan (to the east), Chicago's famous stockyards (to the west), and white neighborhoods (to the south). By the 1940s, the South Side had become what it remains to this day— "the largest contiguous settlement of African-Americans" (in the words of journalist Nicholas Lemann).

On the one hand, this "Black Metropolis" might well have looked very like the African American Promised Land, a city within a city in which "a black person

Regal Theater, Chicago, 1953

could be somebody." By the 1940s, the South Side boasted bustling shopping districts; a spacious public park and lake-side beach; nationally known institutions such as the Regal Theater, the Savoy Ballroom, and the Hotel Grand; as well as countless movie houses and nightclubs featuring blues masters like Muddy Waters (1915–1983), himself a migrant from the Mississippi Delta. It was also, as Lemann notes,

> home to the heavyweight boxing champion of the world (and the most famous black man in America), Joe Louis; the only black member of Congress, William Dawson; the most prominent black newspaper, the *Defender*; the largest black congregation, J. H. Jackson's Olivet Baptist Church; the greatest black singer, Mahalia Jackson; and a host of lesser-known prosperous people. . . .

Undoubtedly, the presence of so many African American luminaries, as well as the sheer existence of such a large black community, fueled the pride and aspirations of ordinary people like the Youngers.

On the other hand, however, those "prosperous people" were few and far between. And what lay between them were the thousands who, like the Youngers, occupied the lower rungs of the social ladder. For even if northern cities offered African Americans much greater economic opportunities than they enjoyed in the South, they were still paid much lower wages than their white counterparts, barred entirely from many good jobs, fired first in bad economic times, and hired last in good ones. In 1950 (nine years before *A Raisin in the Sun*'s debut), the African American unemployment rate in Chicago was about three times that of white workers. Of those Chicagoans who were employed, 70 percent of black men (vs. 36 percent of white men) and 75 percent of black women (vs. 33 percent of white women) held unskilled jobs. At the same time, 22 percent of black men and almost 36 percent of black women worked, like the Youngers, in the lowest, "service" sector—as cooks, maids, janitors, and chauffeurs; only 14 percent of white men and 11 percent of white women did so.

Housing and Residential Segregation

If the Youngers' jobs make them representative, so, too, does the fact that they live in a small, "tired," roach-infested apartment. In the 1940s, population density on the South Side averaged about 90,000 people per square mile (as compared with 20,000 in white neighborhoods). Landlords often charged South Side residents much higher rents than were charged elsewhere, while doing little to maintain the apartments hastily carved out of existing buildings. In their 1960 study *Housing a Metropolis*, sociologists Beverly Duncan and Philip M. Hauser estimated that Chicago's nonwhite renters were more than twice as likely as whites to live in substandard housing. For home-buyers in the South Side, the situation was even worse. Duncan and Hauser estimated that, in the late 1940s, those buyers paid 28 to 51 percent more than they would in white neighborhoods. And they often got less for their money: In 1960, nonwhite homeowners were, according to the same source, six times as likely as their white counterparts to live in substandard homes.

Though Chicago's Black Belt could and did expand southward and westward throughout the Great Migration, this expansion meant movement into formerly white residential areas—an extraordinarily difficult, slow, and often violent process. This was so, as sociologists St. Clair Drake and Horace R. Cayton explained in their classic *Black Metropolis* (1945), "primarily because of white people's attitudes toward having Negroes as neighbors. Because some white Chicagoans do not wish colored neighbors, formal and informal social controls are used to isolate the latter within congested all-Negro neighborhoods." The major "formal" means of maintaining residential segregation were restrictive covenants preventing property from being sold or rented to blacks. By 1930, about 75 percent of the city's residential property was bound by such agreements, while all agents who belonged to the real-estate trade association were bound by a code of ethics that forbade moving blacks into white areas. The Supreme Court declared such covenants legally unenforceable, though not themselves illegal, in 1948. But both before and after that time—in Chicago and every other northern U.S. city—violence was the chief "informal" means adopted by whites when restrictive covenants and codes failed. According to Drake and Cayton, almost five hundred attacks on black residents were reported in Chicago between 1945 and 1950, most involving arson. In 1956 and 1957 alone, 164 such racial "incidents" occurred.

It is here that Hansberry's personal experience intersects with the historical and cultural context about and in which she wrote, though her family was much more comfortably middle class than the fictional family she created. In 1938, when Lorraine was eight, her father, Carl—a prosperous real-estate broker and founder of one of Chicago's first black-owned banks—decided to test the legality

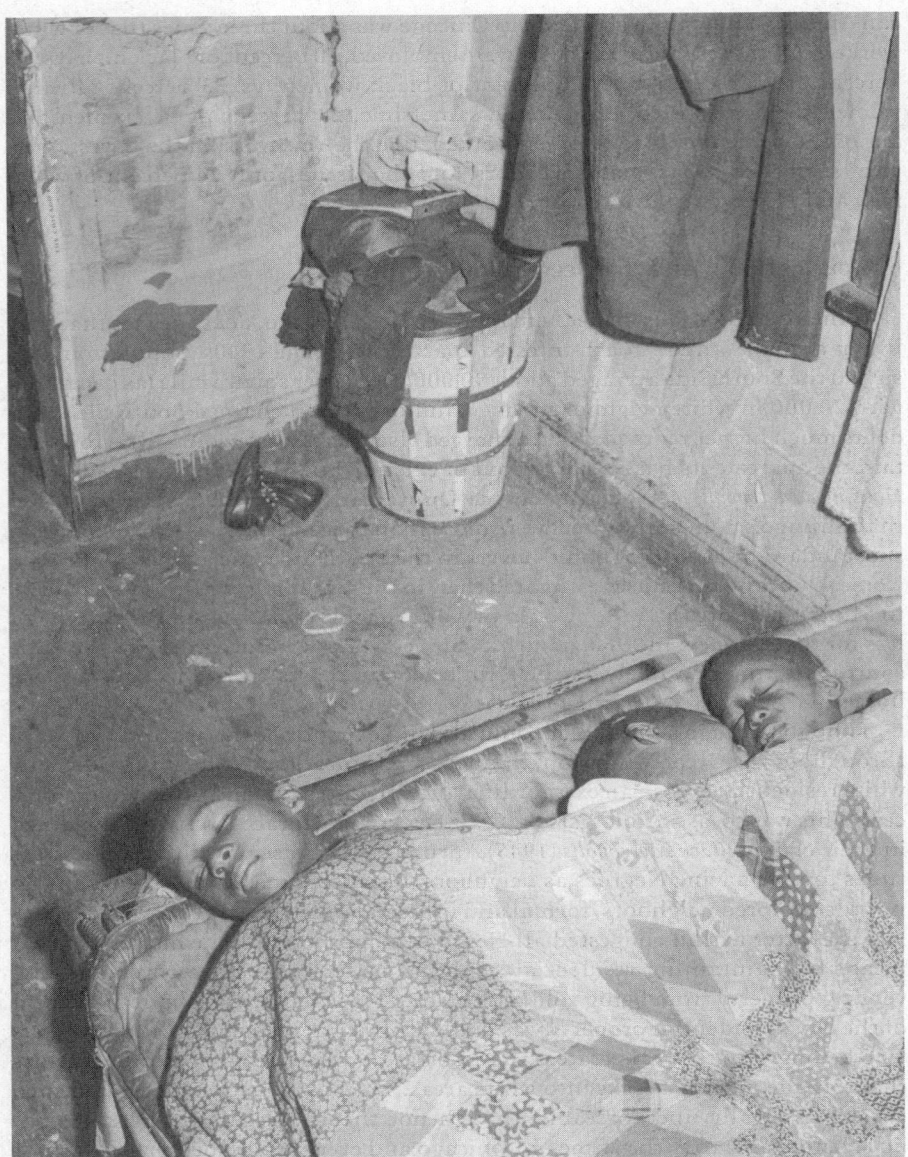

Crowded conditions in a Chicago tenement, 1941

of restrictive covenants by purchasing a house in an all-white neighborhood. When the local neighborhood association secured an injunction prohibiting him from occupying the property, Carl Hansberry, backed by the National Association for the Advancement of Colored People (NAACP), took the case all the way to the Supreme Court. Though he won the case (on a technicality) in 1940, his victory was a limited and costly one. As Lorraine Hansberry later recalled,

That fight . . . required that our family occupy the disputed property in a hellishly hostile "white neighborhood" in which, literally, howling mobs surrounded our house. One of their missiles almost took [my] life. . . . My memories . . . include being spat at, cursed, and pummeled in the daily trek to and from school. And I also remember my desperate and courageous mother, patrolling our house all night with a loaded German luger, doggedly guarding her four children, while my father fought . . . in the Washington court.

. . . The cost, in emotional turmoil, time, and money . . . led to my father's early death as a permanently embittered exile in a foreign country when he saw that after such sacrificial efforts the Negroes of Chicago were as ghetto-locked as ever. . . .

(The disillusioned Carl Hansberry was arranging to move his family to Mexico when he died in 1945.) Among other things, Hansberry's account of her experience might give readers of *A Raisin in the Sun* a deeper appreciation of the play's complex denouement and of the fact that its plot is propelled by a much-loved, hard-working father's death.

The Civil Rights Movement

Hansberry's experiences remind us that the African American civil rights struggle was multifaceted and began well before the 1960s. Yet there is no doubt that it was entering an entirely new phase in 1959. Just five years earlier, in 1954,

The Reverend Ralph Abernathy (center left) and the Reverend Martin Luther King Jr. (center right), leaders of the Southern Christian Leadership Conference (SCLC), are arrested in Birmingham, Alabama, during a peaceful demonstration for civil rights, Good Friday, 1963. Held in solitary confinement for a week, King wrote the famous "Letter from Birmingham Jail" in response to an advertisement in the *Birmingham News*, written by a group of white ministers, in which King was denounced as a troublemaker.

the famous *Brown v. Board of Education* Supreme Court decision declared "separate but equal" education policies unconstitutional, initiating the long, often violent fight to integrate America's schools. One year later, in 1955, the Montgomery Bus Boycott began, eventually forcing full integration of public transportation and launching Martin Luther King Jr. (1929–68) on his career as one of the nation's most famous and influential civil rights leaders. The modern civil rights movement had begun—one in which "gradualism" gave way to direct action, and court battles to marches, sit-ins, and other forms of civil disobedience.

Though the modern civil rights movement involved people of every age, it was in some ways, as Howard Zinn would argue in 1964, the first major social movement in U.S. history "led by youngsters." A political scientist and activist, Zinn was speaking specifically of the college students who, in 1960, began conducting sit-ins throughout the South and eventually formed the Student Non-Violent Coordinating Committee (SNCC). It's worth remembering, too, that Martin Luther King Jr. was himself only twenty-six when he was chosen to lead the Montgomery boycott. In a sense, then, the modern civil rights movement was born out of the kinds of generational attitudes explored in *A Raisin in the Sun*. Hansberry, for example, saw her father as "typical of a generation of Negroes who believed that the 'American way' could successfully be made to work to democratize the United States." But, she said, it was "Negroes my own age and younger" who were beginning to question the "American way" and to advocate a more aggressively confrontational stance, "say[ing] that we must now lie down in the streets, tie up traffic, do whatever we can—take to the hills with guns if necessary—and fight back."

Determined to act on their frustration in ways that their parents wouldn't or couldn't, thousands of young people—many the city-born children of the Great Migration—turned to activism in the 1950s and 1960s. Yet, through Walter's drinking as well as the crime at the heart of her play, Hansberry also subtly reminds us that there were other ways in which that frustration could and did find expression. For as the excerpt from Richard Wright's semiautobiographical *Twelve Million Black Voices* later in this chapter suggests, the very same impulses and emotions that inspired SNCC members to head south led many of their peers in a very different direction.

A poster printed and distributed by the Student Non-Violent Coordinating Committee in the late 1960s

AFRICAN AMERICANS AND AFRICAN DECOLONIZATION

In *A Raisin in the Sun*, differences between and within generations take a variety of shapes, but one such distinction whose meaning and significance may be especially dependent on a knowledge of historical and cultural context involves the character of Joseph Asagai. A Nigerian attending college in Chicago, Joseph plans to return home in order to help liberate his country from British colonial rule. Through him, Hansberry thus highlights connections and parallels between the situation of blacks in the U.S. and in Africa, drawing on her audience's knowledge of contemporary events in Africa even as she points up just how little real knowledge of Africa most Americans possess.

Historically speaking, Hansberry's (and Beneatha's) keen interest in both traditional African culture and contemporary African liberation is no accident. As Earl Thorpe noted in 1959 (in an article excerpted below), various African American intellectuals and activists had worked to spread knowledge about Africa, to forge connections with African leaders, and to improve the situation of colonized Africans since at least the 1920s. But African American interest in Africa was becoming much more widespread and taking on a variety of unprecedented forms in the 1950s. First, between the late 1950s and early 1970s more African Americans than ever before would, like Beneatha, seek to learn about, and embrace, their African cultural heritage. Quite a few made pilgrimages to Africa. Thousands more did so symbolically, sporting dashikis, adopting African names, or giving up hair-straighteners in order to grow Afros. Second, some black activists and intellectuals would, in the early 1960s, begin to argue that the plight of African Americans closely resembled that of colonized peoples elsewhere, even describing African Americans as victims of systematic "domestic" or "internal" colonialism. This controversial argument was popularized through Stokely Carmichael and Charles V. Hamilton's influential *Black Power* (1967, excerpted below). Yet even moderates drew inspiration from events in Africa. In his "Letter from Birmingham Jail" (1963), for example, Martin Luther King Jr. defended civil disobedience and lamented the extremely slow pace of change in the United States by reminding his readers that, while "we still creep at horse and buggy pace toward the gaining of a cup of coffee at a lunch counter," "the nations of Asia and Africa are moving with jet-like speed toward the goal of political independence."

In the 1950s and 1960s, Africa was indeed going through a process of change so rapid and dramatic that it might well have made America seem like a stagnant backwater. Between 1880 and 1912 all of Africa except Liberia and Ethiopia had come under the control of European powers. And for decades the situation changed only in two nations—white-controlled South Africa (which became virtually self-governing in 1910) and Egypt (which achieved a measure of sovereignty in 1922). But in the 1950s, "the winds of change" suddenly began to blow hard across Africa, beginning in the north, where first Libya achieved independence (1951), and then Morocco, Sudan, and Tunisia (1956). One year later the process moved southward into sub-Saharan Africa when Britain's Gold Coast colony became independent Ghana. Thereafter, almost every year saw the birth of at least one new African nation. (See the timeline below.) No wonder, then, that Africa was often in the news and on American minds in the 1950s and 1960s.

The African independence movement drew the West's attention for yet another reason. African independence was, in many cases, the result of hard-fought popular campaigns spearheaded by extraordinarily charismatic men very like Joseph Asagai and Soyinka's Olunde—men educated partially in the West and quite familiar with its culture and ways, yet eager to liberate their people and to embrace and revitalize ancient African folkways. The first presidents of the Republics of Ghana and Nigeria, for example, were Kwame Nkrumah (1909–72) and Benjamin Nnamdi ("Zik") Azikiwe (1904–96), men who returned to their countries only after taking multiple degrees at U.S. and British universities. The first and most famous such leader to emerge on the world stage was Jomo Kenyatta (1893?–1978), whose career led him from an obscure village to the presidency of independent Kenya by way of the London School of Economics; a masterful book on the culture of his own people, the Kikuyu (*Facing Mount Kenya* [1938]); and a seven-year "detainment" for sedition against the British colonial state. At least in African American eyes, such leaders might very well seem like modern versions of the great warriors of African history and myth.

The Impact of World War

For a variety of reasons, change in Africa and the United States was propelled by the shared experience of World War II (1939–45). James Baldwin was only one of many Americans to see that war as marking "a turning point in the Negro's relation to" his country because, as Baldwin wrote in *The Fire Next Time* (1963),

> a certain hope died, a certain respect for white Americans faded. One began to pity them, or to hate them. You must put yourself in the skin of a man who is wearing the uniform of his country, is a candidate for death in its defense, and who is called a "nigger" by his comrades-in-arms and his officers; who is almost always given the hardest, ugliest, most menial work to do; . . . who does not dance at the U.S.O. the night white soldiers dance there . . . ; and who watches German prisoners of war being treated by Americans with more human dignity than he has ever received at their hands. And who, at the same time, as a human being, is far freer in a strange land than he has ever been at home. . . . You must consider what happens to this citizen, after all he has endured, when he returns home: search, in his shoes, for a job, for a place to live; ride, in his skin, on segregated buses; see, with his eyes, the signs saying "White" and "Colored" . . . ; look into the eyes of his wife; look into the eyes of his son; listen, with his ears, to political speeches, North and South; imagine yourself being told to "wait."

Something similar happened to the tens of thousands of African servicemen who fought for the Allies during the war. For, as the authors of *The Making of Modern Africa* suggest, these veterans, too, "came back with new ideas and attitudes" and with stories about Europeans who "worked as [mere] stewards, cooks, cleaners or even lived by begging." Proving that "Europeans were ordinary flesh and blood," such stories did much to undermine "the respect and fear which [colonial] administrators had excited before 1939."

As Baldwin's *The Fire Next Time* emphasizes, too, the revelation of Nazi atrocities—atrocities perpetrated in the very heart of Christian Europe—further undermined the notions of Western civility and superiority so often used to justify segregation in the U.S. and colonialism worldwide:

> . . . The terms "civilized" and "Christian" begin to have a very strange ring, particularly in the ears of those who have been judged to be neither civilized nor

An American soldier of the 12th Armored Division guarding captured German soldiers, Germany, 1945

Christian, when a Christian nation surrenders to a foul and violent orgy, as Germany did during the Third Reich. . . . From my own point of view, the fact of the Third Reich alone makes obsolete forever any question of Christian superiority, except in technological terms.

For these reasons, it seems to be no accident that Hansberry sets her play in the aftermath of World War II or that Wole Soyinka chose to set *Death and the King's Horseman* during the war, even though the events that inspired it in fact occurred after the war's end.

The "Americanness" of *A Raisin in the Sun*

As *A Raisin in the Sun* reminds us, however, the differences between African Americans and Africans are just as deep-seated and significant as their historical and cultural ties. And "domestic colonialism"—if indeed it exists—is not identical to the "classic" variety experienced by Africans. For all its interest in Africa, moreover, *A Raisin in the Sun* is a distinctly American play in terms of both content and style. Hansberry herself was well aware of the way it complemented and contrasted with American classics such as Arthur Miller's *Death of a Salesman*. As she pointed out, "Walter Younger is an American more than he is anything else," and there is "a simple line of descent between" her Walter and Miller's Willy Loman—"the last great hero in American drama to also *accept* the values of his [American] culture."

One way to appreciate the "Americanness" of Hansberry's play—and its distinctly American vision of Africa and Africans—is to compare it with Soyinka's

Newly elected Prime Minister Jomo Kenyatta (right), independent Kenya's first head of state, greets supporters in Nairobi, 1963

Death and the King's Horseman—a play that invites us to explore African culture from the inside and to think about the nature and complex effects of "classic" colonialism.

NIGERIAN CULTURE AND HISTORY

Like the fictional Joseph Asagai, Wole Soyinka and many of his characters are Africans. But they are also Nigerians and, more specifically, Yorubans—a dual (or even triple) identity that Americans like Lena Younger sometimes have difficulty understanding. Here, it is useful to remember that Nigeria, like most modern African nation-states, was itself the product of colonialism—in Soyinka's words, "an artificial creation" whose boundaries were determined by Europeans with little "consideration either [of] the wishes or the will or the interests of" African natives. Among other things, such states "lumped together"—to quote Soyinka again—a number of ethnically, linguistically, and culturally distinct groups. The West African state of Nigeria, for example, didn't exist until the British created it in 1914, in the process bringing together about 250 distinct peoples. The largest of these are the Hausa and Fulani, who dominate northern Nigeria; the Igbo (also known as the Ibo), who live primarily in the southeast; and the Yoruba of the southwest. Today Nigerians certainly see themselves as members of a single nation knit together, as Soyinka puts it, by the "unrolling of historical events, the sharing of certain experiences, political fortunes, economic arrangements, cultural relations, [and] cultural interaction." But cultural differences remain profoundly meaningful. Soyinka speaks of himself as "primarily a Yoruba writer"; his compatriot, novelist Chinua Achebe, sees himself as an Igbo writer.

Yoruban cultural beliefs and traditions inform the style, as well as the content, of all of Soyinka's works, including *Death and the King's Horseman*. And one of the excerpts below—*Yoruba: Nine Centuries of African Art and Thought* by Henry John Drewal, John Pemberton III, and Rowland Abiodun—is included here in order to give you some sense of the unique history and culture of Yorubaland. Yet *Death and the King's Horseman* also draws our attention to the ways in which traditional African cultures have been challenged and changed by three linked forces—Islam, Christianity, and European colonialism.

Islam had become an important force in northern Nigeria as early as the eleventh century. By the early nineteenth century, northern Nigeria had, in fact, become part of a giant Muslim empire known as the Sokoto

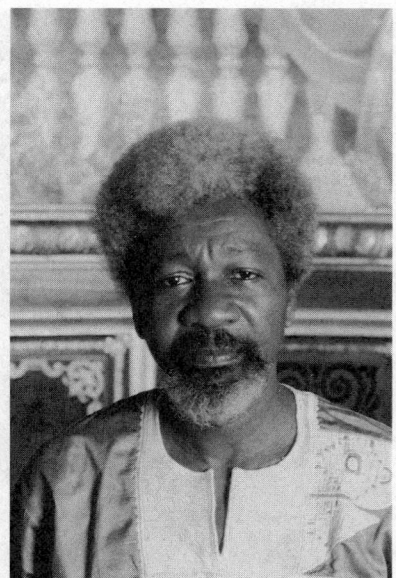

Wole Soyinka of Nigeria, winner of the 1986 Nobel Prize for Literature

Caliphate. Today, almost half of the Nigerian population follows some version of Islam, and the vast majority of them live in the north.

West Africa's contact with European Christians began with the arrival of Portuguese traders in the fifteenth century. By about 1650, West Africa's main export was slaves, and British ships did much of the trafficking. For centuries, however, Europeans seldom ventured beyond the coastline. In the nineteenth century, all of that began to change. Fired with a mixture of economic, humanitarian, and political ambitions, Britons pushed into the interior in order to end the slave trade (declared illegal by Britain in 1807), foster other kinds of commerce, and convert the population to Christianity. Through treaties with local leaders and the use of force, Britain gradually gained control of much of West Africa. Britain's claims to the area were officially recognized at the 1885 Berlin Conference (where Western nations met to settle their ongoing disputes about what portions of Africa each would control).

From around 1900 until independence in 1960, the British governed Nigeria through the system known as "indirect rule." Under this system, a relatively small number of British officials—headed by a governor and several district commissioners—ruled the country through local native leaders. In theory, the latter were men—like the king of Soyinka's play—already recognized as leaders by their communities. In this and other ways, indirect rule ostensibly ensured minimal interference with traditional African culture and society. But in practice, British rule couldn't help but have profoundly disruptive effects. For one thing, the British often found it necessary to supplant defiant native leaders with more compliant ones and to create "warrant chiefs" in communities (like those of the Igbo) that didn't traditionally have them. For another, British governors actively worked to stamp out any traditional practice that they saw as either interfering with trade

British colonial administrators meeting tribal representatives in Lagos, Nigeria, ca. 1900

(and thus with British economic interests) or violating Western notions of civilized, humane behavior. (This policy propels the tragic plot of *Death and the King's Horseman*.) Finally, the British government achieved the latter aim in part by actively encouraging the efforts of both Muslims in northern Nigeria and Christian missionaries in the south to convert and educate the populace. As a result, education and religion went hand in hand in Nigeria, as in much of colonial Africa, and together undermined traditional social structures as well as the beliefs and customs that sustained them. (Today, about 40 percent of Nigerians are Christians, the vast majority living in the south.)

Yet, as *Death and the King's Horseman* demonstrates, African culture has always had a remarkable resilience and capacity to adapt, which Soyinka attributes to its "attitude of philosophic accommodation." Today, both Islam and Christianity often take unique forms in Africa precisely because their doctrines and practices have had to accommodate traditional ones. In northern Nigeria, for example, some Muslim emirs lead prayers for the welfare of the state at the graves of royal ancestors, thus synthesizing Islam with the ancestor-worship at the heart of so many African belief systems. In turn, of course, these indigenous belief systems have themselves evolved: One of Soyinka's examples of this process and of the "accommodative nature" of African culture is the fact that Yorubans have come to regard Sango as the god of electricity, as well as lightning, effectively "extend[ing]" the god's ancient "territory . . . to embrace" a distinctly modern phenomenon. Likewise, Soyinka's own favorite deity, Ogun, has become "not merely the god of war but the god of revolution," a patron saint of sorts to revolutionaries and freedom fighters in Africa and the Americas.

Whatever the aims of educators and missionaries, then, neither a Western-style education nor conversion to Christianity or Islam necessarily led Africans like Soyinka (or his protagonist, Olunde) to completely reject ancient ways and values. Soyinka himself, born in Abeokuta in 1934, grew up in the 1940s—roughly the same time period in which his play is set. And he was, as literary scholar Simon Gikandi notes, raised in "one of the most [Christian] and Westernized families in colonial Nigeria." Soyinka's father was a schoolteacher, his maternal grandfather an Anglican minister, his uncle the principal of the local Anglican grammar school. Yet many in the community, including members of Soyinka's extended family, still embraced traditional Yoruban beliefs and practices. In a 1981 interview, Soyinka describes the world of his childhood as one in which African and European cultural traditions coexisted and combined as often as they conflicted:

Annunciation of the Angel to Mary, carved wood panel by Yoruba sculptor Lamidi Olonade Fakeye. Fakeye converted to Islam as a young man, but his woodwork incorporates Christian and traditional Yoruban imagery.

My family brought together what is generally, simplistically, referred to as the new and the old, the modern and the traditional. . . . My father was a teacher and my mother, who also came from a teaching family, was a petty trader. I grew up among music, performances. I grew up to the sounds of poetry as women hawked their wares. . . . Fruit-sellers or market-women [didn't] just sit but actually s[a]ng their wares to attract customers. . . . I also had the advantage, this is where the question of being born into two societies, two forms, two levels, two patterns of creativity comes in, I had the advantage of actually being raised in a Christian family in the midst of "pagan" manifestations. So it was quite usual for me to be returning from church and suddenly find an *Egungun* masquerade, that's an ancestral masquerade cult, parading with very lively music, drums, etcetera, along the street, to the discomfiture of the Christian worshippers. Discomfiture, because they felt that their Sunday was being desecrated. I don't know what was so desecrating about it. I thought it was a glorious spectacle, and I suppose for following them around once or twice I received the requisite number of lashes or slaps. But I just thought they were all different forms of worship. I don't remember any time when I felt that *that* particular set of worship or belief was sinful. I am afraid that from a very early age I had a rather pagan outlook on the world, let's put it that way, and I think it has stood me in good stead. In any case, to be frank, their music was more enthralling to my ears than the hymns of the Christian church. . . . So I had this advantage of seeing how material belonging to one culture didn't really come to blows with material from another culture.

Moreover, Soyinka's schooling—like Olunde's—reinforced and deepened his knowledge and appreciation of various cultural traditions. Educated in some of Nigeria's most exclusive Western-style schools and at a British university, where the curricula focused on European history, literature, and culture, Soyinka nonetheless also devoted himself to the study of traditional African history and culture (especially drama), as well as East Asian literature.

READING ACROSS CULTURAL CONTEXTS

Having thus "read widely in the world's literature," Soyinka is understandably impatient both with those contemporary African artists and intellectuals who declare that "the literature of Europe has no relevance whatever" to themselves and with those Western readers who find the world portrayed in his plays too "exotic" to enter fully. As he explains,

> I grew up, as many of us did, on the fare of European literature. Even in school we didn't have too much problem understanding the worlds of William Shakespeare, Bernard Shaw, Galsworthy, Moliere, and Ibsen, and, frankly, I'm irritated when people from outside my world say they find it difficult to enter. . . .
> It's laziness, it's intellectual laziness . . . especially today when communication is a matter of course. . . . I find no difficulty at all in entering into Chinese literature, Japanese literature, Russian literature, and this has always been so. I think the barrier is self-induced. "This is a world of the exotic, we cannot enter it." . . . By now it has to be a two-way traffic. There can be no concessions at all; the effort simply has to be made.

Death and the King's Horseman directly challenges us to make that effort, to accept Africans on their own terms in a way that the play's Western characters will not or cannot—or, in Soyinka's words, to approach African people and culture "with some humility," fully "enter[ing] their philosophy, their world view" and "opening" ourselves "up to a new existence, a new scale of values." The play invites us to appreciate the distinctiveness of traditional African culture and the ways in which that culture has been undervalued and undermined by the West. Yet the play issues that invitation in part by itself demonstrating the very same openness toward non-African cultural traditions. Drawing as much on Greek and Shakespearean tragedy as on African ritual and drama, *Death and the King's Horseman* encourages us also to recognize the similarities—or what Soyinka calls the "complementarities"—among widely different literary and cultural traditions. In the process, Soyinka's play, like Hansberry's, offers you the perfect opportunity to think further about both how historical and cultural contexts shape literary texts and how those texts transcend their contexts, showing us everything that connects human beings across the boundaries of time and place, history and culture.

To help you make the most of that opportunity, the rest of this chapter contains a timeline, the text of both plays, and contextual materials. The first is a semiautobiographical account of life in the mid-twentieth century, "Black Metropolis," written by one of the United States' most revered African American writers—Richard Wright (1908–60), who moved from the Mississippi Delta to Chicago's South Side in the 1920s. Connections between Africa and African Americans are the main concern of the four excerpts that follow Wright's. Taken from articles and books published between 1959 and 1969, each of these excerpts offers a very different view of those connections. Finally, the chapter concludes with an excerpt that focuses on Yoruba history and culture.

THE AMERICAN CIVIL RIGHTS AND THE AFRICAN LIBERATION STRUGGLES 1940–70

1943   *U.S.*: In Beaumont, Texas, martial law is declared after a race riot injures 50 and kills two (June); a much larger race riot, in Detroit, kills 34 people (including 25 blacks), injures almost 700, and ends only after President Roosevelt calls in 6,000 National Guardsmen (June); a race riot in Harlem injures 300 and kills six African Americans (August).

1946   *U.S.*: A race riot leads Chicago authorities to abandon efforts to move black families into the Airport Homes housing project.

   Africa: In Kenya, a group of Kikuyus begins what will become known as the Mau Mau rebellion, urging Kenyans to take up arms to regain their rights and lands.

1947   *U.S.*: A race riot occurs in Chicago when local authorities attempt to move blacks into the Fernwood Park housing project.

   Africa: Kwame Nkrumah returns to the Gold Coast from Britain and becomes General Secretary of the colony's most influential political party.

1948   *U.S.*: President Truman issues an executive order integrating the armed forces; the Supreme Court rules restrictive covenants legally unenforceable.

   Africa: The Afrikaner Nationalist Party wins general elections in South Africa after promising to strengthen the system of *apartheid* or racial segregation (which will last until 1991-92); in the Gold Coast, disturbances throughout the colony lead to the arrest and temporary detention of Kwame Nkrumah and several other nationalist political leaders.

1949   *U.S.*: A race riot occurs in Chicago's Park Manor when a black family attempts to move in; another riot breaks out in Englewood Park when a black man is seen visiting the home of a white union organizer.

   Africa: In the Gold Coast, Kwame Nkrumah leads a series of strikes and boycotts to protest British rule and is imprisoned for sedition (until 1952).

1950   *Africa*: British authorities in Kenya outlaw the Mau Mau movement.

1951   *U.S.*: The National Guard is called in to quell a riot after a black family moves into an apartment complex in Cicero, a town bordering Chicago.

   Africa: Libya gains independence from Britain and France.

1952   *Africa*: In response to the Mau Mau rebellion, British authorities in Kenya declare a state of emergency (which will last until 1956) and imprison or exile several African nationalist leaders, including Jomo Kenyatta (who will be detained until 1959); Eritrea, in federation with Ethiopia, gains independence from Britain.

1953   *U.S.*: Two neighborhood associations in Chicago lead a nine-month "campaign of terror" after local authorities try to move a black family into the Trumbull Park Homes housing project.

Africa: British authorities in Kenya outlaw all nationalist political parties and begin a policy of general, forced detention, escalating the Mau Mau rebellion into a full-scale war.

1954   *U.S.*: In *Brown v. Board of Education*, the Supreme Court declares school segregation unconstitutional.

1955   *U.S.*: A year-long bus boycott begins in Montgomery, Alabama.

1956   *U.S.*: The Supreme Court declares segregation on buses unconstitutional.

Africa: Morocco gains independence from Spain and France; Sudan, from Britain; and Tunisia, from France.

1957   *U.S.*: When Arkansas's governor blocks nine black students from attending a Little Rock high school, President Eisenhower sends in federal troops to force compliance with court-ordered desegregation.

Africa: The Gold Coast becomes the independent state (later Republic) of Ghana under the leadership of Nkrumah.

1958   *Africa*: French Guinea becomes the independent state of Guinea.

1960   *U.S.*: Refused service at the lunch counter of a Woolworth's in Greensboro, North Carolina, four black college students stage the first sit-in (February); the Student Non-Violent Coordinating Committee (SNCC) is founded in Raleigh, North Carolina (April).

Africa: The Republic of Congo (formerly the Belgian Congo), Nigeria, Somalia (formerly Italian Somaliland), Togo (formerly French Togoland), and all of France's remaining sub-Saharan colonies gain independence.

1961   *U.S.*: Between May and August, approximately 1,000 volunteer "Freedom Riders" take buses to the South in support of integration.

Africa: Sierra Leone and Tanganyika gain independence from Britain. (In 1964, Tanganyika will join with newly independent Zanzibar to form Tanzania.)

1962   *U.S.*: African American James Meredith is denied admission to the University of Mississippi, resulting in contempt charges against the state's governor and race riots that kill two.

Africa: Algeria gains independence from France; Burundi and Rwanda, from Belgium; and Uganda, from Britain.

1963   *U.S.*: Martin Luther King Jr. is arrested in Birmingham, Alabama, for leading civil rights demonstrations (April); Governor George Wallace attempts to block integration of the University of Alabama but is forced by President Kennedy to allow black enrollment (June); civil rights leader Medgar Evers is assassinated in Mississippi (June); 200,000 people participate in the March on Washington at which Martin Luther King Jr. delivers his "I Have a Dream" speech (August); church bombing in Birmingham, Alabama, kills four black girls attending Sunday School and sparks riots in which two more African Americans are killed (September).

Africa: Kenya gains independence from Britain under the leadership of Kenyatta (president until his death in 1979); Nigeria is declared a republic under the leadership of Nnamdi Azikiwe.

1964   *U.S.*: Twenty-Fourth Amendment to the Constitution is ratified, abolishing the poll tax traditionally used to prevent blacks from voting (January); "Freedom Summer" begins with a massive effort to register black voters throughout the South; Congress overcomes a 75-day filibuster to pass the Civil Rights Act, which outlaws employment discrimination and segregation in public facilities (July); in Mississippi, three people working to register black voters are murdered, their bodies discovered only after President Johnson sends military personnel to aid in the search (June–August); Martin Luther King Jr. wins the Nobel Peace Prize.

   Africa: Former British colonies Northern Rhodesia and Nyasaland become the independent states of Zambia and Malawi.

1965   *U.S.*: Malcolm X is assassinated in Harlem (February); Martin Luther King Jr. leads march from Selma to Montgomery, Alabama, to demand protection of voting rights, and, on "Bloody Sunday," fifty marchers are hospitalized after police use tear gas, whips, and clubs against them (March); the Voting Rights Act makes it easier for southern blacks to register to vote by outlawing requirements such as literacy tests (August); race riots occur in several cities, the worst—in Los Angeles's Watts neighborhood—kills 34 and injures 1,000 (August).

   Africa: Gambia gains independence from Britain.

1966   *U.S.*: In Chicago, Martin Luther King Jr. leads a series of marches to protest housing segregation (July–March); Edward Brooke, of Massachusetts, becomes the first African American elected to the U.S. Senate in 85 years.

   Africa: British Bechuanaland and Basutoland become the independent states of Botswana and Lesotho.

1967   *U.S.*: In the first nine months of the year, 164 race riots occur across the country, the worst in Detroit (43 people killed) and Newark, New Jersey (26 killed, over 1,000 injured); the Supreme Court declares unconstitutional the bans against interracial marriage still enforced in 16 states (June); Thurgood Marshall becomes the first African American Supreme Court justice; Carl Stokes of Cleveland becomes the first elected African American mayor of a major U.S. city.

1968   *U.S.*: Martin Luther King Jr. is assassinated in Memphis, Tennessee, sparking riots in Chicago, Baltimore, Washington, and other cities across the country (April); the Civil Rights Act of 1968 guarantees fair treatment in housing (April).

   Africa: Equatorial Guinea gains independence from Spain; Mauritius and Swaziland, from Britain.

Ruby Dee as Ruth, Sidney Poitier as Walter Lee Younger, and Diana
Sands as Beneatha in the original 1959 Broadway production of
A Raisin in the Sun

LORRAINE HANSBERRY

A Raisin in the Sun

What happens to a dream deferred?

Does it dry up
Like a raisin in the sun?
Or fester like a sore—
And then run?
Does it stink like rotten meat?
Or crust and sugar over—
Like a syrupy sweet?
Maybe it just sags
Like a heavy load.

Or does it explode?
            —LANGSTON HUGHES[1]

---

1. Hughes's poem, published in 1951, is titled "Harlem (A Dream Deferred)."

CAST OF CHARACTERS

RUTH YOUNGER

TRAVIS YOUNGER

WALTER LEE YOUNGER (BROTHER)

BENEATHA YOUNGER

LENA YOUNGER (MAMA)

JOSEPH ASAGAI

GEORGE MURCHISON

KARL LINDNER

BOBO

MOVING MEN

The action of the play is set in Chicago's Southside, sometime between World War II and the present.

ACT I

Scene One

The Younger living room would be a comfortable and well-ordered room if it were not for a number of indestructible contradictions to this state of being. Its furnishings are typical and undistinguished and their primary feature now is that they have clearly had to accommodate the living of too many people for too many years—and they are tired. Still, we can see that at some time, a time probably no longer remembered by the family (except perhaps for MAMA*), the furnishings of this room were actually selected with care and love and even hope—and brought to this apartment and arranged with taste and pride.*

That was a long time ago. Now the once loved pattern of the couch upholstery has to fight to show itself from under acres of crocheted doilies and couch covers which have themselves finally come to be more important than the upholstery. And here a table or a chair has been moved to disguise the worn places in the carpet; but the carpet has fought back by showing its weariness, with depressing uniformity, elsewhere on its surface.

Weariness has, in fact, won in this room. Everything has been polished, washed, sat on, used, scrubbed too often. All pretenses but living itself have long since vanished from the very atmosphere of this room.

Moreover, a section of this room, for it is not really a room unto itself, though the landlord's lease would make it seem so, slopes backward to provide a small kitchen area, where the family prepares the meals that are eaten in the living room proper, which must also serve as dining room. The single window that has been provided for these "two" rooms is located in this kitchen area. The sole natural light the family may enjoy in the course of a day is only that which fights its way through this little window.

At left, a door leads to a bedroom which is shared by MAMA *and her daughter,* BENEATHA. *At right, opposite, is a second room (which in the beginning of the life of this apartment was probably a breakfast room) which serves as a bedroom for* WALTER *and his wife,* RUTH.

Time: Sometime between World War II and the present.

Place: Chicago's Southside.

At Rise: It is morning dark in the living room. TRAVIS *is asleep on the make-down bed at center. An alarm clock sounds from within the bedroom at right, and presently* RUTH *enters from that room and closes the door behind her. She crosses sleepily toward the window. As she passes her sleeping son she reaches down and shakes him a little. At the window she raises the shade and a dusky Southside morning light comes in feebly. She fills a pot with water and puts it on to boil. She calls to the boy, between yawns, in a slightly muffled voice.*

RUTH *is about thirty. We can see that she was a pretty girl, even exceptionally so, but now it is apparent that life has been little that she expected, and disappointment has already begun to hang in her face. In a few years, before thirty-five even, she will be known among her people as a "settled woman."*

She crosses to her son and gives him a good, final, rousing shake.

RUTH: Come on now, boy, it's seven thirty! [*Her son sits up at last, in a stupor of sleepiness.*] I say hurry up, Travis! You ain't the only person in the world got to use a bathroom! [*The child, a sturdy, handsome little boy of ten or eleven, drags himself out of the bed and almost blindly takes his towels and "today's clothes" from drawers and a closet and goes out to the bathroom, which is in an outside hall and which is shared by another family or families on the same floor.* RUTH *crosses to the bedroom door at right and opens it and calls in to her husband.*] Walter Lee! . . . It's after seven thirty! Lemme see you do some waking up in there now! [*She waits.*] You better get up from there, man! It's after seven thirty I tell you. [*She waits again.*] All right, you just go ahead and lay there and next thing you know Travis be finished and Mr. Johnson'll be in there and you'll be fussing and cussing round here like a mad man! And be late too! [*She waits, at the end of patience.*] Walter Lee—it's time for you to get up!

[*She waits another second and then starts to go into the bedroom, but is apparently satisfied that her husband has begun to get up. She stops, pulls the door to, and returns to the kitchen area. She wipes her face with a moist cloth and runs her fingers through her sleep-disheveled hair in a vain effort and ties an apron around her housecoat. The bedroom door at right opens and her husband stands in the doorway in his pajamas, which are rumpled and mismated. He is a lean, intense young man in his middle thirties, inclined to quick nervous movements and erratic speech habits—and always in his voice there is a quality of indictment.*]

WALTER: Is he out yet?

RUTH: What you mean *out*? He ain't hardly got in there good yet.

WALTER: [*Wandering in, still more oriented to sleep than to a new day.*] Well, what was you doing all that yelling for if I can't even get in there yet? [*Stopping and thinking.*] Check coming today?

RUTH: They *said* Saturday and this is just Friday and I hopes to God you ain't going to get up here first thing this morning and start talking to me 'bout no money—'cause I 'bout don't want to hear it.

WALTER: Something the matter with you this morning?

RUTH: No—I'm just sleepy as the devil. What kind of eggs you want?

WALTER: Not scrambled. [RUTH *starts to scramble eggs.*] Paper come? [RUTH *points impatiently to the rolled up* Tribune *on the table, and he gets it and spreads it out and vaguely reads the front page.*] Set off another bomb yesterday.

RUTH: [*Maximum indifference.*] Did they?

WALTER: [*Looking up.*] What's the matter with you?

RUTH: Ain't nothing the matter with me. And don't keep asking me that this morning.

WALTER: Ain't nobody bothering you. [*Reading the news of the day absently again.*] Say Colonel McCormick[2] is sick.

RUTH: [*Affecting tea-party interest.*] Is he now? Poor thing.

2. Robert Rutherford McCormick (1880–1955), owner-publisher of the *Chicago Tribune*.

WALTER: [*Sighing and looking at his watch.*] Oh, me. [*He waits.*] Now what is that boy doing in that bathroom all this time? He just going to have to start getting up earlier. I can't be late to work on account of him fooling around in there.

RUTH: [*Turning on him.*] Oh, no he ain't going to be getting up no earlier no such thing! It ain't his fault that he can't get to bed no earlier nights 'cause he got a bunch of crazy good-for-nothing clowns sitting up running their mouths in what is supposed to be his bedroom after ten o'clock at night . . .

WALTER: That's what you mad about, ain't it? The things I want to talk about with my friends just couldn't be important in your mind, could they?

[*He rises and finds a cigarette in her handbag on the table and crosses to the little window and looks out, smoking and deeply enjoying this first one.*]

RUTH: [*Almost matter of factly, a complaint too automatic to deserve emphasis.*] Why you always got to smoke before you eat in the morning?

WALTER: [*At the window.*] Just look at 'em down there . . . Running and racing to work . . . [*He turns and faces his wife and watches her a moment at the stove, and then, suddenly.*] You look young this morning, baby.

RUTH: [*Indifferently.*] Yeah?

WALTER: Just for a second—stirring them eggs. It's gone now—just for a second it was—you looked real young again. [*Then, drily.*] It's gone now—you look like yourself again.

RUTH: Man, if you don't shut up and leave me alone.

WALTER: [*Looking out to the street again.*] First thing a man ought to learn in life is not to make love to no colored woman first thing in the morning. You all some evil people at eight o'clock in the morning.

[TRAVIS *appears in the hall doorway, almost fully dressed and quite wide awake now, his towels and pajamas across his shoulders. He opens the door and signals for his father to make the bathroom in a hurry.*]

TRAVIS: [*Watching the bathroom.*] Daddy, come on!

[WALTER *gets his bathroom utensils and flies out to the bathroom.*]

RUTH: Sit down and have your breakfast, Travis.

TRAVIS: Mama, this is Friday. [*Gleefully.*] Check coming tomorrow, huh?

RUTH: You get your mind off money and eat your breakfast.

TRAVIS: [*Eating.*] This is the morning we supposed to bring the fifty cents to school.

RUTH: Well, I ain't got no fifty cents this morning.

TRAVIS: Teacher say we have to.

RUTH: I don't care what teacher say. I ain't got it. Eat your breakfast, Travis.

TRAVIS: I *am* eating.

RUTH: Hush up now and just eat!

[*The boy gives her an exasperated look for her lack of understanding, and eats grudgingly.*]

TRAVIS: You think Grandmama would have it?

RUTH: No! And I want you to stop asking your grandmother for money, you hear me?

TRAVIS: [*Outraged.*] Gaaaleee! I don't ask her, she just gimme it sometimes!

RUTH: Travis Willard Younger—I got too much on me this morning to be—

TRAVIS: Maybe Daddy—

RUTH: *Travis!*

[The boy hushes abruptly. They are both quiet and tense for several seconds.]

TRAVIS: *[Presently.]* Could I maybe go carry some groceries in front of the super-market for a little while after school then?

RUTH: Just hush, I said. *[*TRAVIS *jabs his spoon into his cereal bowl viciously, and rests his head in anger upon his fists.]* If you through eating, you can get over there and make up your bed.

[The boy obeys stiffly and crosses the room, almost mechanically, to the bed and more or less carefully folds the covering. He carries the bedding into his mother's room and returns with his books and cap.]

TRAVIS: *[Sulking and standing apart from her unnaturally.]* I'm gone.

RUTH: *[Looking up from the stove to inspect him automatically.]* Come here. *[He crosses to her and she studies his head.]* If you don't take this comb and fix this here head, you better! *[*TRAVIS *puts down his books with a great sigh of oppression, and crosses to the mirror. His mother mutters under her breath about his "slubbornness."]* 'Bout to march out of here with that head looking just like chickens slept in it! I just don't know where you get your slubborn ways . . . And get your jacket, too. Looks chilly out this morning.

TRAVIS: *[With conspicuously brushed hair and jacket.]* I'm gone.

RUTH: Get carfare and milk money—*[Waving one finger.]*—and not a single penny for no caps, you hear me?

TRAVIS: *[With sullen politeness.]* Yes'm.

[He turns in outrage to leave. His mother watches after him as in his frustration he approaches the door almost comically. When she speaks to him, her voice has become a very gentle tease.]

RUTH: *[Mocking; as she thinks he would say it.]* Oh, Mama makes me so mad some-times, I don't know what to do! *[She waits and continues to his back as he stands stock-still in front of the door.]* I wouldn't kiss that woman good-bye for nothing in this world this morning! *[The boy finally turns around and rolls his eyes at her, knowing the mood has changed and he is vindicated; he does not, however, move toward her yet.]* Not for nothing in this world! *[She finally laughs aloud at him and holds out her arms to him and we see that it is a way between them, very old and practiced. He crosses to her and allows her to embrace him warmly but keeps his face fixed with masculine rigidity. She holds him back from her presently and looks at him and runs her fingers over the features of his face. With utter gentleness—]* Now—whose little old angry man are you?

TRAVIS: *[The masculinity and gruffness start to fade at last.]* Aw gaalee—Mama . . .

RUTH: *[Mimicking.]* Aw—gaaaaalleeeee, Mama! *[She pushes him, with rough playful-ness and finality, toward the door.]* Get on out of here or you going to be late.

TRAVIS: *[In the face of love, new aggressiveness.]* Mama, could I *please* go carry groceries?

RUTH: Honey, it's starting to get so cold evenings.

WALTER: *[Coming in from the bathroom and drawing a make-believe gun from a make-believe holster and shooting at his son.]* What is it he wants to do?

RUTH: Go carry groceries after school at the supermarket.

WALTER: Well, let him go . . .

TRAVIS: [*Quickly, to the ally.*] I *have* to—she won't gimme the fifty cents . . .

WALTER: [*To his wife only.*] Why not?

RUTH: [*Simply, and with flavor.*] 'Cause we don't have it.

WALTER: [*To* RUTH *only.*] What you tell the boy things like that for? [*Reaching down into his pants with a rather important gesture.*] Here, son—

[*He hands the boy the coin, but his eyes are directed to his wife's.* TRAVIS *takes the money happily.*]

TRAVIS: Thanks, Daddy.

[*He starts out.* RUTH *watches both of them with murder in her eyes.* WALTER *stands and stares back at her with defiance, and suddenly reaches into his pocket again on an afterthought.*]

WALTER: [*Without even looking at his son, still staring hard at his wife.*] In fact, here's another fifty cents . . . Buy yourself some fruit today—or take a taxicab to school or something!

TRAVIS: Whoopee—

[*He leaps up and clasps his father around the middle with his legs, and they face each other in mutual appreciation; slowly* WALTER LEE *peeks around the boy to catch the violent rays from his wife's eyes and draws his head back as if shot.*]

WALTER: You better get down now—and get to school, man.

TRAVIS: [*At the door.*] O.K. Good-bye.

[*He exits.*]

WALTER: [*After him, pointing with pride.*] That's *my* boy. [*She looks at him in disgust and turns back to her work.*] You know what I was thinking 'bout in the bathroom this morning?

RUTH: No.

WALTER: How come you always try to be so pleasant!

RUTH: What is there to be pleasant 'bout!

WALTER: You want to know what I was thinking 'bout in the bathroom or not!

RUTH: I know what you thinking 'bout.

WALTER: [*Ignoring her.*] 'Bout what me and Willy Harris was talking about last night.

RUTH: [*Immediately—a refrain.*] Willy Harris is a good-for-nothing loud mouth.

WALTER: Anybody who talks to me has got to be a good-for-nothing loud mouth, ain't he? And what you know about who is just a good-for-nothing loud mouth? Charlie Atkins was just a "good-for-nothing loud mouth" too, wasn't he! When he wanted me to go in the dry-cleaning business with him. And now—he's grossing a hundred thousand a year. A hundred thousand dollars a year! You still call *him* a loudmouth!

RUTH: [*Bitterly.*] Oh, Walter Lee . . .

[*She folds her head on her arms over the table.*]

WALTER: [*Rising and coming to her and standing over her.*] You tired, ain't you? Tired of everything. Me, the boy, the way we live—this beat-up hole—everything. Ain't you? [*She doesn't look up, doesn't answer.*] So tired—moaning and groaning all the time, but you wouldn't do nothing to help, would you? You couldn't be on my side that long for nothing, could you?

RUTH: Walter, please leave me alone.

WALTER: A man needs for a woman to back him up . . .

RUTH: Walter—

WALTER: Mama would listen to you. You know she listen to you more than she do me and Bennie. She think more of you. All you have to do is just sit down with her when you drinking your coffee one morning and talking 'bout things like you do and— [*He sits down beside her and demonstrates graphically what he thinks her methods and tone should be.*] —you just sip your coffee, see, and say easy like that you been thinking 'bout that deal Walter Lee is so interested in, 'bout the store and all, and sip some more coffee, like what you saying ain't really that important to you—And the next thing you know, she be listening good and asking you questions and when I come home—I can tell her the details. This ain't no fly-by-night proposition, baby. I mean we figured it out, me and Willy and Bobo.

RUTH: [*With a frown.*] Bobo?

WALTER: Yeah. You see, this little liquor store we got in mind cost seventy-five thousand and we figured the initial investment on the place be 'bout thirty thousand, see. That be ten thousand each. Course, there's a couple of hundred you got to pay so's you don't spend your life just waiting for them clowns to let your license get approved—

RUTH: You mean graft?

WALTER: [*Frowning impatiently.*] Don't call it that. See there, that just goes to show you what women understand about the world. Baby, don't *nothing* happen for you in this world 'less you pay *somebody* off!

RUTH: Walter, leave me alone! [*She raises her head and stares at him vigorously—then says, more quietly.*] Eat your eggs, they gonna be cold.

WALTER: [*Straightening up from her and looking off.*] That's it. There you are. Man say to his woman: I got me a dream. His woman say: Eat your eggs. [*Sadly, but gaining in power.*] Man say: I got to take hold of this here world, baby! And a woman will say: Eat your eggs and go to work. [*Passionately now.*] Man say: I got to change my life, I'm choking to death, baby! And his woman say— [*In utter anguish as he brings his fists down on his thighs.*] —Your eggs is getting cold!

RUTH: [*Softly.*] Walter, that ain't none of our money.

WALTER: [*Not listening at all or even looking at her.*] This morning, I was lookin' in the mirror and thinking about it . . . I'm thirty-five years old; I been married eleven years and I got a boy who sleeps in the living room— [*Very, very quietly.*] —and all I got to give him is stories about how rich white people live . . .

RUTH: Eat your eggs, Walter.

WALTER: *Damn my eggs . . . damn all the eggs that ever was!*

RUTH: Then go to work.

WALTER: [*Looking up at her.*] See—I'm trying to talk to you 'bout myself— [*Shaking his head with the repetition.*] —and all you can say is eat them eggs and go to work.

RUTH: [*Wearily.*] Honey, you never say nothing new. I listen to you every day, every night and every morning, and you never say nothing new. [*Shrugging.*] So you would rather *be* Mr. Arnold than be his chauffeur. So—I would *rather* be living in Buckingham Palace.[3]

3. Where the queen of Great Britain resides in London.

WALTER: That is just what is wrong with the colored woman in this world . . . Don't understand about building their men up and making 'em feel like they somebody. Like they can do something.

RUTH: [*Drily, but to hurt.*] There *are* colored men who do things.

WALTER: No thanks to the colored woman.

RUTH: Well, being a colored woman, I guess I can't help myself none.

[*She rises and gets the ironing board and sets it up and attacks a huge pile of rough-dried clothes, sprinkling them in preparation for the ironing and then rolling them into tight fat balls.*]

WALTER: [*Mumbling.*] We one group of men tied to a race of women with small minds.

[*His sister* BENEATHA *enters. She is about twenty, as slim and intense as her brother. She is not as pretty as her sister-in-law, but her lean, almost intellectual face has a handsomeness of its own. She wears a bright-red flannel nightie, and her thick hair stands wildly about her head. Her speech is a mixture of many things; it is different from the rest of the family's insofar as education has permeated her sense of English—and perhaps the Midwest rather than the South has finally—at last—won out in her inflection; but not altogether, because over all of it is a soft slurring and transformed use of vowels which is the decided influence of the Southside. She passes through the room without looking at either* RUTH *or* WALTER *and goes to the outside door and looks, a little blindly, out to the bathroom. She sees that it has been lost to the Johnsons. She closes the door with a sleepy vengeance and crosses to the table and sits down a little defeated.*]

BENEATHA: I am going to start timing those people.

WALTER: You should get up earlier.

BENEATHA: [*Her face in her hands. She is still fighting the urge to go back to bed.*] Really—would you suggest dawn? Where's the paper?

WALTER: [*Pushing the paper across the table to her as he studies her almost clinically, as though he has never seen her before.*] You a horrible-looking chick at this hour.

BENEATHA: [*Drily.*] Good morning, everybody.

WALTER: [*Senselessly.*] How is school coming?

BENEATHA: [*In the same spirit.*] Lovely. Lovely. And you know, biology is the greatest. [*Looking up at him.*] I dissected something that looked just like you yesterday.

WALTER: I just wondered if you've made up your mind and everything.

BENEATHA: [*Gaining in sharpness and impatience.*] And what did I answer yesterday morning—and the day before that?

RUTH: [*From the ironing board, like someone disinterested and old.*] Don't be so nasty, Bennie.

BENEATHA: [*Still to her brother.*] And the day before that and the day before that!

WALTER: [*Defensively.*] I'm interested in you. Something wrong with that? Ain't many girls who decide—

WALTER AND BENEATHA: [*In unison.*]—"to be a doctor."

[*Silence.*]

WALTER: Have we figured out yet just exactly how much medical school is going to cost?

RUTH: Walter Lee, why don't you leave that girl alone and get out of here to work?

BENEATHA: [*Exits to the bathroom and bangs on the door.*] Come on out of there, please!

[*She comes back into the room.*]

WALTER: [*Looking at his sister intently.*] You know the check is coming tomorrow.

BENEATHA: [*Turning on him with a sharpness all her own.*] That money belongs to Mama, Walter, and it's for her to decide how she wants to use it. I don't care if she wants to buy a house or a rocket ship or just nail it up somewhere and look at it. It's hers. Not ours—*hers.*

WALTER: [*Bitterly.*] Now ain't that fine! You just got your mother's interest at heart, ain't you, girl? You such a nice girl—but if Mama got that money she can always take a few thousand and help you through school too—can't she?

BENEATHA: I have never asked anyone around here to do anything for me.

WALTER: No! And the line between asking and just accepting when the time comes is big and wide—ain't it!

BENEATHA: [*With fury.*] What do you want from me, Brother—that I quit school or just drop dead, which!

WALTER: I don't want nothing but for you to stop acting holy 'round here. Me and Ruth done made some sacrifices for you—why can't you do something for the family?

RUTH: Walter, don't be dragging me in it.

WALTER: You are in it—Don't you get up and go work in somebody's kitchen for the last three years to help put clothes on her back?

RUTH: Oh, Walter—that's not fair . . .

WALTER: It ain't that nobody expects you to get on your knees and say thank you, Brother; thank you, Ruth; thank you, Mama—and thank you, Travis, for wearing the same pair of shoes for two semesters—

BENEATHA: [*Dropping to her knees.*] Well—I *do*—all right?—thank everybody . . . and forgive me for ever wanting to be anything at all . . . forgive me, forgive me!

RUTH: Please stop it! Your mama'll hear you.

WALTER: Who the hell told you you had to be a doctor? If you so crazy 'bout messing 'round with sick people—then go be a nurse like other women—or just get married and be quiet . . .

BENEATHA: Well—you finally got it said . . . it took you three years but you finally got it said. Walter, give up; leave me alone—it's Mama's money.

WALTER: *He was my father, too!*

BENEATHA: So what? He was mine, too—and Travis' grandfather—but the insurance money belongs to Mama. Picking on me is not going to make her give it to you to invest in any liquor stores— [*Underbreath, dropping into a chair.*] —and I for one say, God bless Mama for that!

WALTER: [*To* RUTH.] See—did you hear? Did you hear!

RUTH: Honey, please go to work.

WALTER: Nobody in this house is ever going to understand me.

BENEATHA: Because you're a nut.

WALTER: Who's a nut?

BENEATHA: You—you are a nut. Thee is mad, boy.

WALTER: [*Looking at his wife and his sister from the door, very sadly.*] The world's most backward race of people, and that's a fact.

BENEATHA: [*Turning slowly in her chair.*] And then there are all those prophets who would lead us out of the wilderness—. [WALTER *slams out of the house.*] —into the swamps!

RUTH: Bennie, why you always gotta be pickin' on your brother? Can't you be a little sweeter sometimes? [*Door opens.* WALTER *walks in.*]

WALTER: [*To* RUTH.] I need some money for carfare.

RUTH: [*Looks at him, then warms; teasing, but tenderly.*] Fifty cents? [*She goes to her bag and gets money.*] Here, take a taxi.

[WALTER *exits.* MAMA *enters. She is a woman in her early sixties, full-bodied and strong. She is one of those women of a certain grace and beauty who wear it so unobtrusively that it takes a while to notice. Her dark-brown face is surrounded by the total whiteness of her hair, and, being a woman who has adjusted to many things in life and overcome many more, her face is full of strength. She has, we can see, wit and faith of a kind that keep her eyes lit and full of interest and expectancy. She is, in a word, a beautiful woman. Her bearing is perhaps most like the noble bearing of the women of the Hereros of Southwest Africa—rather as if she imagines that as she walks she still bears a basket or a vessel upon her head. Her speech, on the other hand, is as careless as her carriage is precise—she is inclined to slur everything—but her voice is perhaps not so much quiet as simply soft.*]

MAMA: Who that 'round here slamming doors at this hour?

[*She crosses through the room, goes to the window, opens it, and brings in a feeble little plant growing doggedly in a small pot on the window sill. She feels the dirt and puts it back out.*]

RUTH: That was Walter Lee. He and Bennie was at it again.

MAMA: My children and they tempers. Lord, if this little old plant don't get more sun than it's been getting it ain't never going to see spring again. [*She turns from the window.*] What's the matter with you this morning, Ruth? You looks right peaked. You aiming to iron all them things? Leave some for me. I'll get to 'em this afternoon. Bennie honey, it's too drafty for you to be sitting 'round half dressed. Where's your robe?

BENEATHA: In the cleaners.

MAMA: Well, go get mine and put it on.

BENEATHA: I'm not cold, Mama, honest.

MAMA: I know—but you so thin . . .

BENEATHA: [*Irritably.*] Mama, I'm not cold.

MAMA: [*Seeing the make-down bed as* TRAVIS *has left it.*] Lord have mercy, look at that poor bed. Bless his heart—he tries, don't he?

[*She moves to the bed* TRAVIS *has sloppily made up.*]

RUTH: No—he don't half try at all 'cause he knows you going to come along behind him and fix everything. That's just how come he don't know how to do nothing right now—you done spoiled that boy so.

MAMA: Well—he's a little boy. Ain't supposed to know 'bout housekeeping. My baby, that's what he is. What you fix for his breakfast this morning?

RUTH: [*Angrily.*] I feed my son, Lena!

MAMA: I ain't meddling— [*Underbreath; busy-bodyish.*] I just noticed all last week he had cold cereal, and when it starts getting this chilly in the fall a child ought to have some hot grits or something when he goes out in the cold—

RUTH: [*Furious.*] I gave him hot oats—is that all right!

MAMA: I ain't meddling. [*Pause.*] Put a lot of nice butter on it? [RUTH *shoots her an angry look and does not reply.*] He likes lots of butter.

RUTH: [*Exasperated.*] Lena—

MAMA: [*To* BENEATHA. MAMA *is inclined to wander conversationally sometimes.*] What was you and your brother fussing 'bout this morning?

BENEATHA: It's not important, Mama.

> [*She gets up and goes to look out at the bathroom, which is apparently free, and she picks up her towels and rushes out.*]

MAMA: What was they fighting about?

RUTH: Now you know as well as I do.

MAMA: [*Shaking her head.*] Brother still worrying hisself sick about that money?

RUTH: You know he is.

MAMA: You had breakfast?

RUTH: Some coffee.

MAMA: Girl, you better start eating and looking after yourself better. You almost thin as Travis.

RUTH: Lena—

MAMA: Un-hunh?

RUTH: What are you going to do with it?

MAMA: Now don't you start, child. It's too early in the morning to be talking about money. It ain't Christian.

RUTH: It's just that he got his heart set on that store—

MAMA: You mean that liquor store that Willy Harris want him to invest in?

RUTH: Yes—

MAMA: We ain't no business people, Ruth. We just plain working folks.

RUTH: Ain't nobody business people till they go into business. Walter Lee say colored people ain't never going to start getting ahead till they start gambling on some different kinds of things in the world—investments and things.

MAMA: What done got into you, girl? Walter Lee done finally sold you on investing.

RUTH: No. Mama, something is happening between Walter and me. I don't know what it is—but he needs something—something I can't give him anymore. He needs this chance, Lena.

MAMA: [*Frowning deeply.*] But liquor, honey—

RUTH: Well—like Walter say—I spec people going to always be drinking themselves some liquor.

MAMA: Well—whether they drinks it or not ain't none of my business. But whether I go into business selling it to 'em *is*, and I don't want that on my ledger this late in life. [*Stopping suddenly and studying her daughter-in-law.*] Ruth Younger, what's the matter with you today? You look like you could fall over right there.

RUTH: I'm tired.

MAMA: Then you better stay home from work today.

RUTH: I can't stay home. She'd be calling up the agency and screaming at them, "My girl didn't come in today—send me somebody! My girl didn't come in!" Oh, she just have a fit . . .

MAMA: Well, let her have it. I'll just call her up and say you got the flu—

RUTH: [*Laughing.*] Why the flu?

MAMA: 'Cause it sounds respectable to 'em. Something white people get, too. They know 'bout the flu. Otherwise they think you been cut up or something when you tell 'em you sick.

RUTH: I got to go in. We need the money.

MAMA: Somebody would of thought my children done all but starved to death the way they talk about money here late. Child, we got a great big old check coming tomorrow.

RUTH: [*Sincerely, but also self-righteously.*] Now that's your money. It ain't got nothing to do with me. We all feel like that—Walter and Bennie and me—even Travis.

MAMA: [*Thoughtfully, and suddenly very far away.*] Ten thousand dollars—

RUTH: Sure is wonderful.

MAMA: Ten thousand dollars.

RUTH: You know what you should do, Miss Lena? You should take yourself a trip somewhere. To Europe or South America or someplace—

MAMA: [*Throwing up her hands at the thought.*] Oh, child!

RUTH: I'm serious. Just pack up and leave! Go on away and enjoy yourself some. Forget about the family and have yourself a ball for once in your life—

MAMA: [*Drily.*] You sound like I'm just about ready to die. Who'd go with me? What I look like wandering 'round Europe by myself?

RUTH: Shoot—these here rich white women do it all the time. They don't think nothing of packing up they suitcases and piling on one of them big steamships and—swoosh!—they gone, child.

MAMA: Something always told me I wasn't no rich white woman.

RUTH: Well—what are you going to do with it then?

MAMA: I ain't rightly decided. [*Thinking. She speaks now with emphasis.*] Some of it got to be put away for Beneatha and her schoolin'—and ain't nothing going to touch that part of it. Nothing. [*She waits several seconds, trying to make up her mind about something, and looks at* RUTH *a little tentatively before going on.*] Been thinking that we maybe could meet the notes on a little old two-story somewhere, with a yard where Travis could play in the summertime, if we use part of the insurance for a down payment and everybody kind of pitch in. I could maybe take on a little day work again, few days a week—

RUTH: [*Studying her mother-in-law furtively and concentrating on her ironing, anxious to encourage without seeming to.*] Well, Lord knows, we've put enough rent into this here rat trap to pay for four houses by now . . .

MAMA: [*Looking up at the words "rat trap" and then looking around and leaning back and sighing—in a suddenly reflective mood—*] "Rat trap"—yes, that's all it is. [*Smiling.*] I remember just as well the day me and Big Walter moved in here. Hadn't been married but two weeks and wasn't planning on living here no more than a year. [*She shakes her head at the dissolved dream.*] We was going to set away, little by little, don't you know, and buy a little place out in Morgan Park. We had even picked out the house. [*Chuckling a little.*] Looks right dumpy today. But Lord, child, you should know all the dreams I had 'bout buying that house and fixing it up and making me a little garden in the back— [*She waits and stops smiling.*] And didn't none of it happen.

[*Dropping her hands in a futile gesture.*]

RUTH: [*Keeps her head down, ironing.*] Yes, life can be a barrel of disappointments, sometimes.

MAMA: Honey, Big Walter would come in here some nights back then and slump down on that couch there and just look at the rug, and look at me and look at the rug and then back at me—and I'd know he was down then . . . really down. [*After a second very long and thoughtful pause; she is seeing back to times that only she can see.*] And then, Lord, when I lost that baby—little Claude—I almost thought I was going to lose Big Walter too. Oh, that man grieved hisself! He was one man to love his children.

RUTH: Ain't nothin' can tear at you like losin' your baby.

MAMA: I guess that's how come that man finally worked hisself to death like he done. Like he was fighting his own war with this here world that took his baby from him.

RUTH: He sure was a fine man, all right. I always liked Mr. Younger.

MAMA: Crazy 'bout his children! God knows there was plenty wrong with Walter Younger—hard-headed, mean, kind of wild with women—plenty wrong with him. But he sure loved his children. Always wanted them to have something—be something. That's where Brother gets all these notions, I reckon. Big Walter used to say, he'd get right wet in the eyes sometimes, lean his head back with the water standing in his eyes and say, "Seem like God didn't see fit to give the black man nothing but dreams—but He did give us children to make them dreams seem worthwhile." [*She smiles.*] He could talk like that, don't you know.

RUTH: Yes, he sure could. He was a good man, Mr. Younger.

MAMA: Yes, a fine man—just couldn't never catch up with his dreams, that's all.

[BENEATHA *comes in, brushing her hair and looking up to the ceiling, where the sound of a vacuum cleaner has started up.*]

BENEATHA: What could be so dirty on that woman's rugs that she has to vacuum them every single day?

RUTH: I wish certain young women 'round here who I could name would take inspiration about certain rugs in a certain apartment I could also mention.

BENEATHA: [*Shrugging.*] How much cleaning can a house need, for Christ's sakes.

MAMA: [*Not liking the Lord's name used thus.*] Bennie!

RUTH: Just listen to her—just listen!

BENEATHA: Oh, God!

MAMA: If you use the Lord's name just one more time—

BENEATHA: [*A bit of a whine.*] Oh, Mama—

RUTH: Fresh—just fresh as salt, this girl!

BENEATHA: [*Drily.*] Well—if the salt loses its savor—[4]

MAMA: Now that will do. I just ain't going to have you 'round here reciting the scriptures in vain—you hear me?

BENEATHA: How did I manage to get on everybody's wrong side by just walking into a room?

4. See Matthew 5.13: "You are the salt of the earth. But if the salt loses its taste, with what can it be seasoned? It is no longer good for anything but to be thrown out and trampled underfoot."

RUTH: If you weren't so fresh—

BENEATHA: Ruth, I'm twenty years old.

MAMA: What time you be home from school today?

BENEATHA: Kind of late. [*With enthusiasm.*] Madeline is going to start my guitar lessons today.

[MAMA *and* RUTH *look up with the same expression.*]

MAMA: Your *what* kind of lessons?

BENEATHA: Guitar.

RUTH: Oh, Father!

MAMA: How come you done taken it in your mind to learn to play the guitar?

BENEATHA: I just want to, that's all.

MAMA: [*Smiling.*] Lord, child, don't you know what to do with yourself? How long it going to be before you get tired of this now—like you got tired of that little play-acting group you joined last year? [*Looking at* RUTH.] And what was it the year before that?

RUTH: The horseback-riding club for which she bought that fifty-five-dollar riding habit that's been hanging in the closet ever since!

MAMA: [*To* BENEATHA.] Why you got to flit so from one thing to another, baby?

BENEATHA: [*Sharply.*] I just want to learn to play the guitar. Is there anything wrong with that?

MAMA: Ain't nobody trying to stop you. I just wonders sometimes why you has to flit so from one thing to another all the time. You ain't never done nothing with all that camera equipment you brought home—

BENEATHA: I don't flit! I—I experiment with different forms of expression—

RUTH: Like riding a horse?

BENEATHA: —People have to express themselves one way or another.

MAMA: What is it you want to express?

BENEATHA: [*Angrily.*] Me! [MAMA *and* RUTH *look at each other and burst into raucous laughter.*] Don't worry—I don't expect you to understand.

MAMA: [*To change the subject.*] Who you going out with tomorrow night?

BENEATHA: [*With displeasure.*] George Murchison again.

MAMA: [*Pleased.*] Oh—you getting a little sweet on him?

RUTH: You ask me, this child ain't sweet on nobody but herself— [*Underbreath.*] Express herself!

[*They laugh.*]

BENEATHA: Oh—I like George all right, Mama. I mean I like him enough to go out with him and stuff, but—

RUTH: [*For devilment.*] What does *and stuff* mean?

BENEATHA: Mind your own business.

MAMA: Stop picking at her now, Ruth. [*A thoughtful pause, and then a suspicious sudden look at her daughter as she turns in her chair for emphasis.*] What *does* it mean?

BENEATHA: [*Wearily.*] Oh, I just mean I couldn't ever really be serious about George. He's—he's so shallow.

RUTH: Shallow—what do you mean he's shallow? He's *rich*!

MAMA: Hush, Ruth.

BENEATHA: I know he's rich. He knows he's rich, too.

RUTH: Well—what other qualities a man got to have to satisfy you, little girl?

BENEATHA: You wouldn't even begin to understand. Anybody who married Walter could not possibly understand.

MAMA: [*Outraged.*] What kind of way is that to talk about your brother?

BENEATHA: Brother is a flip—let's face it.

MAMA: [*To* RUTH, *helplessly.*] What's a flip?

RUTH: [*Glad to add kindling.*] She's saying he's crazy.

BENEATHA: Not crazy. Brother isn't really crazy yet—he—he's an elaborate neurotic.

MAMA: Hush your mouth!

BENEATHA: As for George. Well. George looks good—he's got a beautiful car and he takes me to nice places and, as my sister-in-law says, he is probably the richest boy I will ever get to know and I even like him sometimes—but if the Youngers are sitting around waiting to see if their little Bennie is going to tie up the family with the Murchisons, they are wasting their time.

RUTH: You mean you wouldn't marry George Murchison if he asked you someday? That pretty, rich thing? Honey, I knew you was odd—

BENEATHA: No I would not marry him if all I felt for him was what I feel now. Besides, George's family wouldn't really like it.

MAMA: Why not?

BENEATHA: Oh, Mama—The Murchisons are honest-to-God-real-*live*-rich colored people, and the only people in the world who are more snobbish than rich white people are rich colored people. I thought everybody knew that. I've met Mrs. Murchison. She's a scene!

MAMA: You must not dislike people 'cause they well off, honey.

BENEATHA: Why not? It makes just as much sense as disliking people 'cause they are poor, and lots of people do that.

RUTH: [*A wisdom-of-the-ages manner. To* MAMA.] Well, she'll get over some of this—

BENEATHA: Get over it? What are you talking about, Ruth? Listen, I'm going to be a doctor. I'm not worried about who I'm going to marry yet—if I ever get married.

MAMA AND RUTH: *If!*

MAMA: Now, Bennie—

BENEATHA: Oh, I probably will . . . but first I'm going to be a doctor, and George, for one, still thinks that's pretty funny. I couldn't be bothered with that. I am going to be a doctor and everybody around here better understand that!

MAMA: [*Kindly.*] 'Course you going to be a doctor, honey, God willing.

BENEATHA: [*Drily.*] God hasn't got a thing to do with it.

MAMA: Beneatha—that just wasn't necessary.

BENEATHA: Well—neither is God. I get sick of hearing about God.

MAMA: Beneatha!

BENEATHA: I mean it! I'm just tired of hearing about God all the time. What has He got to do with anything? Does He pay tuition?

MAMA: You 'bout to get your fresh little jaw slapped!

RUTH: That's just what she needs, all right!

BENEATHA: Why? Why can't I say what I want to around here, like everybody else?

MAMA: It don't sound nice for a young girl to say things like that—you wasn't brought up that way. Me and your father went to trouble to get you and Brother to church every Sunday.

BENEATHA: Mama, you don't understand. It's all a matter of ideas, and God is just one idea I don't accept. It's not important. I am not going out and be immoral or commit crimes because I don't believe in God. I don't even think about it. It's just that I get tired of Him getting credit for all the things the human race achieves through its own stubborn effort. There simply is no blasted God—there is only man and it is he who makes miracles!

[MAMA *absorbs this speech, studies her daughter and rises slowly and crosses to* BENEATHA *and slaps her powerfully across the face. After, there is only silence and the daughter drops her eyes from her mother's face, and* MAMA *is very tall before her.*]

MAMA: Now—you say after me, in my mother's house there is still God. [*There is a long pause and* BENEATHA *stares at the floor wordlessly.* MAMA *repeats the phrase with precision and cool emotion.*] In my mother's house there is still God.

BENEATHA: In my mother's house there is still God.

[*A long pause.*]

MAMA: [*Walking away from* BENEATHA, *too disturbed for triumphant posture. Stopping and turning back to her daughter.*] There are some ideas we ain't going to have in this house. Not long as I am at the head of this family.

BENEATHA: Yes, ma'am.

[MAMA *walks out of the room.*]

RUTH: [*Almost gently, with profound understanding.*] You think you a woman, Bennie—but you still a little girl. What you did was childish—so you got treated like a child.

BENEATHA: I see. [*Quietly.*] I also see that everybody thinks it's all right for Mama to be a tyrant. But all the tyranny in the world will never put a God in the heavens!

[*She picks up her books and goes out.*]

RUTH: [*Goes to* MAMA's *door.*] She said she was sorry.

MAMA: [*Coming out, going to her plant.*] They frightens me, Ruth. My children.

RUTH: You got good children, Lena. They just a little off sometimes—but they're good.

MAMA: No—there's something come down between me and them that don't let us understand each other and I don't know what it is. One done almost lost his mind thinking 'bout money all the time and the other done commence to talk about things I can't seem to understand in no form or fashion. What is it that's changing, Ruth?

RUTH: [*Soothingly, older than her years.*] Now . . . you taking it all too seriously. You just got strong-willed children and it takes a strong woman like you to keep 'em in hand.

MAMA: [*Looking at her plant and sprinkling a little water on it.*] They spirited all right, my children. Got to admit they got spirit—Bennie and Walter. Like this little old plant that ain't never had enough sunshine or nothing—and look at it . . .

[*She has her back to* RUTH, *who has had to stop ironing and lean against something and put the back of her hand to her forehead.*]

RUTH: [*Trying to keep* MAMA *from noticing.*] You . . . sure . . . loves that little old thing, don't you? . . .

MAMA: Well, I always wanted me a garden like I used to see sometimes at the back of the houses down home. This plant is close as I ever got to having one. [*She looks out of the window as she replaces the plant.*] Lord, ain't nothing as dreary as the view from this window on a dreary day, is there? Why ain't you singing this morning, Ruth? Sing that "No Ways Tired." That song always lifts me up so— [*She turns at last to see that* RUTH *has slipped quietly into a chair, in a state of semiconsciousness.*] Ruth! Ruth honey—what's the matter with you . . . Ruth!

[CURTAIN.]

Scene Two

It is the following morning; a Saturday morning, and house cleaning is in progress at the Youngers. Furniture has been shoved hither and yon and MAMA *is giving the kitchen-area walls a washing down.* BENEATHA, *in dungarees, with a handkerchief tied around her face, is spraying insecticide into the cracks in the walls. As they work, the radio is on and a Southside disk-jockey program is inappropriately filling the house with a rather exotic saxophone blues.* TRAVIS, *the sole idle one, is leaning on his arms, looking out of the window.*

TRAVIS: Grandmama, that stuff Bennie is using smells awful. Can I go downstairs, please?

MAMA: Did you get all them chores done already? I ain't seen you doing much.

TRAVIS: Yes'm—finished early. Where did Mama go this morning?

MAMA: [*Looking at* BENEATHA.] She had to go on a little errand.

TRAVIS: Where?

MAMA: To tend to her business.

TRAVIS: Can I go outside then?

MAMA: Oh, I guess so. You better stay right in front of the house, though . . . and keep a good lookout for the postman.

TRAVIS: Yes'm. [*He starts out and decides to give his aunt* BENEATHA *a good swat on the legs as he passes her.*] Leave them poor little old cockroaches alone, they ain't bothering you none.

[*He runs as she swings the spray gun at him both viciously and playfully.* WALTER *enters from the bedroom and goes to the phone.*]

MAMA: Look out there, girl, before you be spilling some of that stuff on that child!

TRAVIS: [*Teasing.*] That's right—look out now!

[*He exits.*]

BENEATHA: [*Drily.*] I can't imagine that it would hurt him—it has never hurt the roaches.

MAMA: Well, little boys' hides ain't as tough as Southside roaches.

WALTER: [*Into phone.*] Hello—Let me talk to Willy Harris.

MAMA: You better get over there behind the bureau. I seen one marching out of there like Napoleon yesterday.

WALTER: Hello, Willy? It ain't come yet. It'll be here in a few minutes. Did the lawyer give you the papers?

BENEATHA: There's really only one way to get rid of them, Mama—

MAMA: How?

BENEATHA: Set fire to this building.

WALTER: Good. Good. I'll be right over.

BENEATHA: Where did Ruth go, Walter?

WALTER: I don't know.

[*He exits abruptly.*]

BENEATHA: Mama, where did Ruth go?

MAMA: [*Looking at her with meaning.*] To the doctor, I think.

BENEATHA: The doctor? What's the matter? [*They exchange glances.*] You don't think—

MAMA: [*With her sense of drama.*] Now I ain't saying what I think. But I ain't never been wrong 'bout a woman neither.

[*The phone rings.*]

BENEATHA: [*At the phone.*] Hay-lo . . . [*Pause, and a moment of recognition.*] Well—when did you get back! . . . And how was it? . . . Of course I've missed you—in my way . . . This morning? No . . . house cleaning and all that and Mama hates it if I let people come over when the house is like this . . . You *have*? Well, that's different . . . What is it—Oh, what the hell, come on over . . . Right, see you then.

[*She hangs up.*]

MAMA: [*Who has listened vigorously, as is her habit.*] Who is that you inviting over here with this house looking like this? You ain't got the pride you was born with!

BENEATHA: Asagai doesn't care how houses look, Mama—he's an intellectual.

MAMA: *Who?*

BENEATHA: Asagai—Joseph Asagai. He's an African boy I met on campus. He's been studying in Canada all summer.

MAMA: What's his name?

BENEATHA: Asagai, Joseph. Ah-sah-guy . . . He's from Nigeria.

MAMA: Oh, that's the little country that was founded by slaves way back . . .

BENEATHA: No, Mama—that's Liberia.

MAMA: I don't think I never met no African before.

BENEATHA: Well, do me a favor and don't ask him a whole lot of ignorant questions about Africans. I mean, do they wear clothes and all that—

MAMA: Well, now, I guess if you think we so ignorant 'round here maybe you shouldn't bring your friends here—

BENEATHA: It's just that people ask such crazy things. All anyone seems to know about when it comes to Africa is Tarzan—

MAMA: [*Indignantly.*] Why should I know anything about Africa?

BENEATHA: Why do you give money at church for the missionary work?

MAMA: Well, that's to help save people.

BENEATHA: You mean save them from *heathenism*—

MAMA: [*Innocently.*] Yes.

BENEATHA: I'm afraid they need more salvation from the British and the French.

[RUTH *comes in forlornly and pulls off her coat with dejection. They both turn to look at her.*]

RUTH: [*Dispiritedly.*] Well, I guess from all the happy faces—everybody knows.

BENEATHA: You pregnant?

MAMA: Lord have mercy, I sure hope it's a little old girl. Travis ought to have a sister.

[BENEATHA *and* RUTH *give her a hopeless look for this grandmotherly enthusiasm.*]

BENEATHA: How far along are you?

RUTH: Two months.

BENEATHA: Did you mean to? I mean did you plan it or was it an accident?

MAMA: What do you know about planning or not planning?

BENEATHA: Oh, Mama.

RUTH: [*Wearily.*] She's twenty years old, Lena.

BENEATHA: Did you plan it, Ruth?

RUTH: Mind your own business.

BENEATHA: It is my business—where is he going to live, on the roof ? [*There is silence following the remark as the three women react to the sense of it.*] Gee—I didn't mean that, Ruth, honest. Gee, I don't feel like that at all. I—I think it is wonderful.

RUTH: [*Dully.*] Wonderful.

BENEATHA: Yes—really.

MAMA: [*Looking at* RUTH, *worried.*] Doctor say everything going to be all right?

RUTH: [*Far away.*] Yes—she says everything is going to be fine . . .

MAMA: [*Immediately suspicious.*] "She"—What doctor you went to?

[RUTH *folds over, near hysteria.*]

MAMA: [*Worriedly hovering over* RUTH.] Ruth honey—what's the matter with you— you sick?

[RUTH *has her fists clenched on her thighs and is fighting hard to suppress a scream that seems to be rising in her.*]

BENEATHA: What's the matter with her, Mama?

MAMA: [*Working her fingers in* RUTH's *shoulder to relax her.*] She be all right. Women gets right depressed sometimes when they get her way. [*Speaking softly, expertly, rapidly.*] Now you just relax. That's right . . . just lean back, don't think 'bout nothing at all . . . nothing at all—

RUTH: I'm all right . . .

[*The glassy-eyed look melts and then she collapses into a fit of heavy sobbing. The bell rings.*]

BENEATHA: Oh, my God—that must be Asagai.

MAMA: [*To* RUTH.] Come on now, honey. You need to lie down and rest awhile . . . then have some nice hot food.

[*They exit,* RUTH's *weight on her mother-in-law.* BENEATHA, *herself profoundly disturbed, opens the door to admit a rather dramatic-looking young man with a large package.*]

ASAGAI: Hello, Alaiyo—

BENEATHA: [*Holding the door open and regarding him with pleasure.*] Hello . . . [*Long pause.*] Well—come in. And please excuse everything. My mother was very upset about my letting anyone come here with the place like this.

ASAGAI: [*Coming into the room.*] You look disturbed too . . . Is something wrong?

BENEATHA: [*Still at the door, absently.*] Yes . . . we've all got acute ghetto-itus. [*She smiles and comes toward him, finding a cigarette and sitting.*] So—sit down! How was Canada?

ASAGAI: [*A sophisticate.*] Canadian.

BENEATHA: [*Looking at him.*] I'm very glad you are back.

ASAGAI: [*Looking back at her in turn.*] Are you really?

BENEATHA: Yes—very.

ASAGAI: Why—you were quite glad when I went away. What happened?

BENEATHA: You went away.

ASAGAI: Ahhhhhhhh.

BENEATHA: Before—you wanted to be so serious before there was time.

ASAGAI: How much time must there be before one knows what one feels?

BENEATHA: [*Stalling this particular conversation. Her hands pressed together, in a deliberately childish gesture.*] What did you bring me?

ASAGAI: [*Handing her the package.*] Open it and see.

BENEATHA: [*Eagerly opening the package and drawing out some records and the colorful robes of a Nigerian woman.*] Oh, Asagai! . . . You got them for me! . . . How beautiful . . . and the records too! [*She lifts out the robes and runs to the mirror with them and holds the drapery up in front of herself.*]

ASAGAI: [*Coming to her at the mirror.*] I shall have to teach you how to drape it properly. [*He flings the material about her for the moment and stands back to look at her.*] Ah—Oh-pay-gay-day, oh-gbah-mu-shay. [*A Yoruba exclamation for admiration.*] You wear it well . . . very well . . . mutilated hair and all.

BENEATHA: [*Turning suddenly.*] My hair—what's wrong with my hair?

ASAGAI: [*Shrugging.*] Were you born with it like that?

BENEATHA: [*Reaching up to touch it.*] No . . . of course not.

[*She looks back to the mirror, disturbed.*]

ASAGAI: [*Smiling.*] How then?

BENEATHA: You know perfectly well how . . . as crinkly as yours . . . that's how.

ASAGAI: And it is ugly to you that way?

BENEATHA: [*Quickly.*] Oh, no—not ugly . . . [*More slowly, apologetically.*] But it's so hard to manage when it's, well—raw.

ASAGAI: And so to accommodate that—you mutilate it every week?

BENEATHA: It's not mutilation!

ASAGAI: [*Laughing aloud at her seriousness.*] Oh . . . please! I am only teasing you because you are so very serious about these things. [*He stands back from her and folds his arms across his chest as he watches her pulling at her hair and frowning in the mirror.*] Do you remember the first time you met me at school? . . . [*He laughs.*] You came up to me and you said—and I thought you were the most serious little thing I had ever seen—you said: [*He imitates her.*] "Mr. Asagai—I want very much to talk with you. About Africa. You see, Mr. Asagai, I am looking for my *identity!*"

[*He laughs.*]

BENEATHA: [*Turning to him, not laughing.*] Yes—

[*Her face is quizzical, profoundly disturbed.*]

ASAGAI: [*Still teasing and reaching out and taking her face in his hands and turning her profile to him.*] Well . . . it is true that this is not so much a profile of a Hollywood queen as perhaps a queen of the Nile— [*A mock dismissal of the importance of the question.*] But what does it matter? Assimilationism is so popular in your country.

BENEATHA: [*Wheeling, passionately, sharply.*] I am not an assimilationist!

ASAGAI: [*The protest hangs in the room for a moment and* ASAGAI *studies her, his laughter fading.*] Such a serious one. [*There is a pause.*] So—you like the robes? You must take excellent care of them—they are from my sister's personal wardrobe.

BENEATHA: [*With incredulity.*] You—you sent all the way home—for me?

ASAGAI: [*With charm.*] For you—I would do much more . . . Well, that is what I came for. I must go.

BENEATHA: Will you call me Monday?

ASAGAI: Yes . . . We have a great deal to talk about. I mean about identity and time and all that.

BENEATHA: Time?

ASAGAI: Yes. About how much time one needs to know what one feels.

BENEATHA: You never understood that there is more than one kind of feeling which can exist between a man and a woman—or, at least, there should be.

ASAGAI: [*Shaking his head negatively but gently.*] No. Between a man and a woman there need be only one kind of feeling. I have that for you . . . Now even . . . right this moment . . .

BENEATHA: I know—and by itself—it won't do. I can find that anywhere.

ASAGAI: For a woman it should be enough.

BENEATHA: I know—because that's what it says in all the novels that men write. But it isn't. Go ahead and laugh—but I'm not interested in being someone's little episode in America or— [*With feminine vengeance.*] —one of them! [ASAGAI *has burst into laughter again.*] That's funny as hell, huh!

ASAGAI: It's just that every American girl I have known has said that to me. White—black—in this you are all the same. And the same speech, too!

BENEATHA: [*Angrily.*] Yuk, yuk, yuk!

ASAGAI: It's how you can be sure that the world's most liberated women are not liberated at all. You all talk about it too much!

[MAMA *enters and is immediately all social charm because of the presence of a guest.*]

BENEATHA: Oh—Mama—this is Mr. Asagai.

MAMA: How do you do?

ASAGAI: [*Total politeness to an elder.*] How do you do, Mrs. Younger. Please forgive me for coming at such an outrageous hour on a Saturday.

MAMA: Well, you are quite welcome. I just hope you understand that our house don't always look like this. [*Chatterish.*] You must come again. I would love to hear all about— [*Not sure of the name.*] —your country. I think it's so sad the way our American Negroes don't know nothing about Africa 'cept Tarzan and all that. And all that money they pour into these churches when they ought to be helping you people over there drive out them French and Englishmen done taken away your land.

[*The mother flashes a slightly superior look at her daughter upon completion of the recitation.*]

ASAGAI: [*Taken aback by this sudden and acutely unrelated expression of sympathy.*] Yes . . . yes . . .

MAMA: [*Smiling at him suddenly and relaxing and looking him over.*] How many miles is it from here to where you come from?

ASAGAI: Many thousands.

MAMA: [*Looking at him as she would* WALTER.] I bet you don't half look after yourself, being away from your mama either. I spec you better come 'round here from time to time and get yourself some decent home-cooked meals . . .

ASAGAI: [*Moved.*] Thank you. Thank you very much. [*They are all quiet, then—*] Well . . . I must go. I will call you Monday, Alaiyo.

MAMA: What's that he call you?

ASAGAI: Oh—"Alaiyo." I hope you don't mind. It is what you would call a nickname, I think. It is a Yoruba word. I am a Yoruba.

MAMA: [*Looking at* BENEATHA.] I—I thought he was from—

ASAGAI: [*Understanding.*] Nigeria is my country. Yoruba is my tribal origin—

BENEATHA: You didn't tell us what Alaiyo means . . . for all I know, you might be calling me Little Idiot or something . . .

ASAGAI: Well . . . let me see . . . I do not know how just to explain it . . . The sense of a thing can be so different when it changes languages.

BENEATHA: You're evading.

ASAGAI: No—really it is difficult . . . [*Thinking.*] It means . . . it means One for Whom Bread—Food—Is Not Enough. [*He looks at her.*] Is that all right?

BENEATHA: [*Understanding, softly.*] Thank you.

MAMA: [*Looking from one to the other and not understanding any of it.*] Well . . . that's nice . . . You must come see us again—Mr.—

ASAGAI: Ah-sah-guy . . .

MAMA: Yes . . . Do come again.

ASAGAI: Good-bye.

[*He exits.*]

MAMA: [*After him.*] Lord, that's a pretty thing just went out here! [*Insinuatingly, to her daughter.*] Yes, I guess I see why we done commence to get so interested in Africa 'round here. Missionaries my aunt Jenny!

[*She exits.*]

BENEATHA: Oh, Mama! . . .

[*She picks up the Nigerian dress and holds it up to her in front of the mirror again. She sets the headdress on haphazardly and then notices her hair again and clutches at it and then replaces the headdress and frowns at herself. Then she starts to wriggle in front of the mirror as she thinks a Nigerian woman might.* TRAVIS *enters and regards her.*]

TRAVIS: You cracking up?

BENEATHA: Shut up.

[*She pulls the headdress off and looks at herself in the mirror and clutches at her hair again and squinches her eyes as if trying to imagine something. Then, suddenly, she gets her raincoat and kerchief and hurriedly prepares for going out.*]

MAMA: [*Coming back into the room.*] She's resting now. Travis, baby, run next door and ask Miss Johnson to please let me have a little kitchen cleanser. This here can is empty as Jacob's kettle.

TRAVIS: I just came in.

MAMA: Do as you told. [*He exits and she looks at her daughter.*] Where you going?

BENEATHA: [*Halting at the door.*] To become a queen of the Nile!

[*She exits in a breathless blaze of glory.* RUTH *appears in the bedroom doorway.*]

MAMA: Who told you to get up?

RUTH: Ain't nothing wrong with me to be lying in no bed for. Where did Bennie go?

MAMA: [*Drumming her fingers.*] Far as I could make out—to Egypt. [RUTH *just looks at her.*] What time is it getting to?

RUTH: Ten twenty. And the mailman going to ring that bell this morning just like he done every morning for the last umpteen years.

[TRAVIS *comes in with the cleanser can.*]

TRAVIS: She say to tell you that she don't have much.

MAMA: [*Angrily.*] Lord, some people I could name sure is tight-fisted! [*Directing her grandson.*] Mark two cans of cleanser down on the list there. If she that hard up for kitchen cleanser, I sure don't want to forget to get her none!

RUTH: Lena—maybe the woman is just short on cleanser—

MAMA: [*Not listening.*] —Much baking powder as she done borrowed from me all these years, she could of done gone into the baking business!

[*The bell sounds suddenly and sharply and all three are stunned—serious and silent—mid-speech. In spite of all the other conversations and distractions of the morning, this is what they have been waiting for, even* TRAVIS, *who looks helplessly from his mother to his grandmother.* RUTH *is the first to come to life again.*]

RUTH: [*To* TRAVIS.] Get down them steps, boy!

[TRAVIS *snaps to life and flies out to get the mail.*]

MAMA: [*Her eyes wide, her hand to her breast.*] You mean it done really come?

RUTH: [*Excited.*] Oh, Miss Lena!

MAMA: [*Collecting herself.*] Well . . . I don't know what we all so excited about 'round here for. We known it was coming for months.

RUTH: That's a whole lot different from having it come and being able to hold it in your hands . . . a piece of paper worth ten thousand dollars . . . [TRAVIS *bursts back into the room. He holds the envelope high above his head, like a little dancer, his face is radiant and he is breathless. He moves to his grandmother with sudden slow ceremony and puts the envelope into her hands. She accepts it, and then merely holds it and looks at it.*] Come on! Open it . . . Lord have mercy, I wish Walter Lee was here!

TRAVIS: Open it, Grandmama!

MAMA: [*Staring at it.*] Now you all be quiet. It's just a check.

RUTH: Open it . . .

MAMA: [*Still staring at it.*] Now don't act silly . . . We ain't never been no people to act silly 'bout no money—

RUTH: [*Swiftly.*] We ain't never had none before—*open it!*

[MAMA *finally makes a good strong tear and pulls out the thin blue slice of paper and inspects it closely. The boy and his mother study it raptly over* MAMA's *shoulders.*]

MAMA: *Travis!* [*She is counting off with doubt.*] Is that the right number of zeros.

TRAVIS: Yes'm ... ten thousand dollars. Gaalee, Grandmama, you rich.

MAMA: [*She holds the check away from her, still looking at it. Slowly her face sobers into a mask of unhappiness.*] Ten thousand dollars. [*She hands it to* RUTH.] Put it away somewhere, Ruth. [*She does not look at* RUTH; *her eyes seem to be seeing something somewhere very far off.*] Ten thousand dollars they give you. Ten thousand dollars.

TRAVIS: [*To his mother, sincerely.*] What's the matter with Grandmama—don't she want to be rich?

RUTH: [*Distractedly.*] You go on out and play now, baby. [TRAVIS *exits.* MAMA *starts wiping dishes absently, humming intently to herself.* RUTH *turns to her, with kind exasperation.*] You've gone and got yourself upset.

MAMA: [*Not looking at her.*] I spec if it wasn't for you all ... I would just put that money away or give it to the church or something.

RUTH: Now what kind of talk is that. Mr. Younger would just be plain mad if he could hear you talking foolish like that.

MAMA: [*Stopping and staring off.*] Yes ... he sure would. [*Sighing.*] We got enough to do with that money, all right. [*She halts then, and turns and looks at her daughter-in-law hard;* RUTH *avoids her eyes and* MAMA *wipes her hands with finality and starts to speak firmly to* RUTH.] Where did you go today, girl?

RUTH: To the doctor.

MAMA: [*Impatiently.*] Now, Ruth ... you know better than that. Old Doctor Jones is strange enough in his way but there ain't nothing 'bout him make somebody slip and call him "she"—like you done this morning.

RUTH: Well, that's what happened—my tongue slipped.

MAMA: You went to see that woman, didn't you?

RUTH: [*Defensively, giving herself away.*] What woman you talking about?

MAMA: [*Angrily.*] That woman who—

[WALTER *enters in great excitement.*]

WALTER: Did it come?

MAMA: [*Quietly.*] Can't you give people a Christian greeting before you start asking about money?

WALTER: [*To* RUTH.] Did it come? [RUTH *unfolds the check and lays it quietly before him, watching him intently with thoughts of her own.* WALTER *sits down and grasps it close and counts off the zeros.*] Ten thousand dollars— [*He turns suddenly, frantically to his mother and draws some papers out of his breast pocket.*] Mama—look. Old Willy Harris put everything on paper—

MAMA: Son—I think you ought to talk to your wife ... I'll go on out and leave you alone if you want—

WALTER: I can talk to her later—Mama, look—

MAMA: Son—

WALTER: WILL SOMEBODY PLEASE LISTEN TO ME TODAY!

MAMA: [*Quietly.*] I don't 'low no yellin' in this house, Walter Lee, and you know it— [WALTER *stares at them in frustration and starts to speak several times.*] And there ain't going to be no investing in no liquor stores. I don't aim to have to speak on that again.

[*A long pause.*]

WALTER: Oh—so you don't aim to have to speak on that again? So you have decided ... [*Crumpling his papers.*] Well, *you* tell that to my boy tonight when you put him to sleep on the living-room couch . . . [*Turning to* MAMA *and speaking directly to her.*] Yeah—and tell it to my wife, Mama, tomorrow when she has to go out of here to look after somebody else's kids. And tell it to *me*, Mama, every time we need a new pair of curtains and I have to watch *you* go out and work in somebody's kitchen. Yeah, you tell me then!

[WALTER *starts out.*]

RUTH: Where you going?

WALTER: I'm going out!

RUTH: Where?

WALTER: Just out of this house somewhere—

RUTH: [*Getting her coat.*] I'll come too.

WALTER: I don't want you to come!

RUTH: I got something to talk to you about, Walter.

WALTER: That's too bad.

MAMA: [*Still quietly.*] Walter Lee— [*She waits and he finally turns and looks at her.*] Sit down.

WALTER: I'm a grown man, Mama.

MAMA: Ain't nobody said you wasn't grown. But you still in my house and my presence. And as long as you are—you'll talk to your wife civil. Now sit down.

RUTH: [*Suddenly.*] Oh, let him go on out and drink himself to death! He makes me sick to my stomach! [*She flings her coat against him.*]

WALTER: [*Violently.*] And you turn mine too, baby! [RUTH *goes into their bedroom and slams the door behind her.*] That was my greatest mistake—

MAMA: [*Still quietly.*] Walter, what is the matter with you?

WALTER: Matter with me? Ain't nothing the matter with *me*!

MAMA: Yes there is. Something eating you up like a crazy man. Something more than me not giving you this money. The past few years I been watching it happen to you. You get all nervous acting and kind of wild in the eyes—[WALTER *jumps up impatiently at her words.*] I said sit there now, I'm talking to you!

WALTER: Mama—I don't need no nagging at me today.

MAMA: Seem like you getting to a place where you always tied up in some kind of knot about something. But if anybody ask you 'bout it you just yell at 'em and bust out the house and go out and drink somewheres. Walter Lee, people can't live with that. Ruth's a good, patient girl in her way—but you getting to be too much. Boy, don't make the mistake of driving that girl away from you.

WALTER: Why—what she do for me?

MAMA: She loves you.

WALTER: Mama—I'm going out. I want to go off somewhere and be by myself for a while.

MAMA: I'm sorry 'bout your liquor store, son. It just wasn't the thing for us to do. That's what I want to tell you about—

WALTER: I got to go out, Mama—

[*He rises.*]

MAMA: It's dangerous, son.

WALTER: What's dangerous?

MAMA: When a man goes outside his home to look for peace.

WALTER: [*Beseechingly.*] Then why can't there never be no peace in this house then?

MAMA: You done found it in some other house?

WALTER: No—there ain't no woman! Why do women always think there's a woman somewhere when a man gets restless. [*Coming to her.*] Mama—Mama—I want so many things . . .

MAMA: Yes, son—

WALTER: I want so many things that they are driving me kind of crazy . . . Mama— look at me.

MAMA: I'm looking at you. You a good-looking boy. You got a job, a nice wife, a fine boy and—

WALTER: A job. [*Looks at her.*] Mama, a job? I open and close car doors all day long. I drive a man around in his limousine and I say, "Yes, sir; no, sir; very good, sir; shall I take the Drive, sir?" Mama, that ain't no kind of job . . . that ain't nothing at all. [*Very quietly.*] Mama, I don't know if I can make you understand.

MAMA: Understand what, baby?

WALTER: [*Quietly.*] Sometimes it's like I can see the future stretched out in front of me—just plain as day. The future, Mama. Hanging over there at the edge of my days. Just waiting for me—a big, looming blank space—full of *nothing.* Just waiting for *me.* [*Pause.*] Mama—sometimes when I'm downtown and I pass them cool, quiet-looking restaurants where them white boys are sitting back and talking 'bout things . . . sitting there turning deals worth millions of dollars . . . sometimes I see guys don't look much older than me—

MAMA: Son—how come you talk so much 'bout money?

WALTER: [*With immense passion.*] Because it is life, Mama!

MAMA: [*Quietly.*] Oh— [*Very quietly.*] So now it's life. Money is life. Once upon a time freedom used to be life—now it's money. I guess the world really do change . . .

WALTER: No—it was always money, Mama. We just didn't know about it.

MAMA: No . . . something has changed. [*She looks at him.*] You something new, boy. In my time we was worried about not being lynched and getting to the North if we could and how to stay alive and still have a pinch of dignity too . . . Now here come you and Beneatha—talking 'bout things we ain't never even thought about hardly, me and your daddy. You ain't satisfied or proud of nothing we done. I mean that you had a home; that we kept you out of trouble till you was grown; that you don't have to ride to work on the back of nobody's streetcar—You my children—but how different we done become.

WALTER: You just don't understand, Mama, you just don't understand.

MAMA: Son—do you know your wife is expecting another baby? [WALTER *stands, stunned, and absorbs what his mother has said.*] That's what she wanted to talk to you about. [WALTER *sinks down into a chair.*] This ain't for me to be telling—but you ought to know. [*She waits.*] I think Ruth is thinking 'bout getting rid of that child.[5]

WALTER: [*Slowly understanding.*] No—no—Ruth wouldn't do that.

MAMA: When the world gets ugly enough—a woman will do anything for her family. *The part that's already living.*

---

5. Abortions were illegal and dangerous in the United States at that time.

WALTER: You don't know Ruth, Mama, if you think she would do that.

[RUTH *opens the bedroom door and stands there a little limp.*]

RUTH: [*Beaten.*] Yes I would too, Walter. [*Pause.*] I gave her a five-dollar down payment.

[*There is total silence as the man stares at his wife and the mother stares at her son.*]

MAMA: [*Presently.*] Well— [*Tightly.*] Well—son, I'm waiting to hear you say something . . . I'm waiting to hear how you be your father's son. Be the man he was . . . [*Pause.*] Your wife say she going to destroy your child. And I'm waiting to hear you talk like him and say we a people who give children life, not who destroys them— [*She rises.*] I'm waiting to see you stand up and look like your daddy and say we done give up one baby to poverty and that we ain't going to give up nary another one . . . I'm waiting.

WALTER: Ruth—

MAMA: If you a son of mine, tell her! [WALTER *turns, looks at her and can say nothing. She continues, bitterly.*] You . . . you are a disgrace to your father's memory. Somebody get me my hat.

[CURTAIN.]

ACT II

Scene One

Time: Later the same day.

At rise: RUTH *is ironing again. She has the radio going. Presently* BENEATHA's *bedroom door opens and* RUTH's *mouth falls and she puts down the iron in fascination.*

RUTH: What have we got on tonight!

BENEATHA: [*Emerging grandly from the doorway so that we can see her thoroughly robed in the costume* ASAGAI *brought.*] You are looking at what a well-dressed Nigerian woman wears— [*She parades for* RUTH, *her hair completely hidden by the headdress; she is coquettishly fanning herself with an ornate oriental fan, mistakenly more like Butterfly*[6] *than any Nigerian that ever was.*] Isn't it beautiful? [*She promenades to the radio and, with an arrogant flourish, turns off the good loud blues that is playing.*] Enough of this assimilationist junk! [RUTH *follows her with her eyes as she goes to the phonograph and puts on a record and turns and waits ceremoniously for the music to come up. Then, with a shout—*] OCOMOGOSIAY!

[RUTH *jumps. The music comes up, a lovely Nigerian melody.* BENEATHA *listens, enraptured, her eyes far away—"back to the past." She begins to dance.* RUTH *is dumbfounded.*]

RUTH: What kind of dance is that?

BENEATHA: A folk dance.

6. Madame Butterfly, a Japanese woman married to and then abandoned by an American man in the opera *Madama Butterfly* (1904), by the Italian composer Giacomo Puccini (1858–1924).

RUTH: [*Pearl Bailey.*][7] What kind of folks do that, honey?

BENEATHA: It's from Nigeria. It's a dance of welcome.

RUTH: Who you welcoming?

BENEATHA: The men back to the village.

RUTH: Where they been?

BENEATHA: How should I know—out hunting or something. Anyway, they are coming back now ...

RUTH: Well, that's good.

BENEATHA: [*With the record.*]

> Alundi, alundi
> Alundi alunya
> Jop pu a jeepua
> Ang gu sooooooooooo
>
> Ai yai yae ...
> Ayehaye—alundi ...

[WALTER *comes in during this performance; he has obviously been drinking. He leans against the door heavily and watches his sister, at first with distaste. Then his eyes look off—"back to the past"—as he lifts both his fists to the roof, screaming.*]

WALTER: YEAH ... AND ETHIOPIA STRETCH FORTH HER HANDS AGAIN! ...[8]

RUTH: [*Drily, looking at him.*] Yes—and Africa sure is claiming her own tonight. [*She gives them both up and starts ironing again.*]

WALTER: [*All in a drunken, dramatic shout.*] Shut up! ... I'm digging them drums ... them drums move me! ... [*He makes his weaving way to his wife's face and leans in close to her.*] In my *heart of hearts*— [*He thumps his chest.*] —I am much warrior!

RUTH: [*Without even looking up.*] In your heart of hearts you are much drunkard.

WALTER: [*Coming away from her and starting to wander around the room, shouting.*] Me and Jomo ... [*Intently, in his sister's face. She has stopped dancing to watch him in this unknown mood.*] That's my man, Kenyatta.[9] [*Shouting and thumping his chest.*] FLAMING SPEAR! HOT DAMN! [*He is suddenly in possession of an imaginary spear and actively spearing enemies all over the room.*] OCOMOGOSIAY ... THE LION IS WAKING ... OWIMOWEH! [*He pulls his shirt open and leaps up on a table and gestures with his spear. The bell rings.* RUTH *goes to answer.*]

BENEATHA: [*To encourage* WALTER, *thoroughly caught up with this side of him.*] OCOMO-GOSIAY, FLAMING SPEAR!

WALTER: [*On the table, very far gone, his eyes pure glass sheets. He sees what we cannot, that he is a leader of his people, a great chief, a descendant of Chaka,*[1] *and that the hour to march has come.*] Listen, my black brothers—

BENEATHA: OCOMOGOSIAY!

---

7. That is, in the manner of the popular African American singer and entertainer (1918–90).

8. See Psalms 68.31: "Princes shall come out of Egypt; Ethiopia shall soon stretch out her hands unto God."

9. Jomo Kenyatta (1893–1978), African political leader and first president of Kenya (1964–78).

1. Zulu chief (1786–1828), also known as "Shaka" and called "The Black Napoleon" for his strategic and organizational genius.

WALTER: —Do you hear the waters rushing against the shores of the coastlands—

BENEATHA: OCOMOGOSIAY!

WALTER: —Do you hear the screeching of the cocks in yonder hills beyond where the chiefs meet in council for the coming of the mighty war—

BENEATHA: OCOMOGOSIAY!

WALTER: —Do you hear the beating of the wings of the birds flying low over the mountains and the low places of our land—

[RUTH *opens the door.* GEORGE MURCHISON *enters.*]

BENEATHA: OCOMOGOSIAY!

WALTER: —Do you hear the singing of the women, singing the war songs of our fathers to the babies in the great houses . . . singing the sweet war songs? OH, DO YOU HEAR, MY BLACK BROTHERS!

BENEATHA: [*Completely gone.*] We hear you, Flaming Spear—

WALTER: Telling us to prepare for the greatness of the time— [*To* GEORGE.] Black Brother!

[*He extends his hand for the fraternal clasp.*]

GEORGE: Black Brother, hell!

RUTH: [*Having had enough, and embarrassed for the family.*] Beneatha, you got company—what's the matter with you? Walter Lee Younger, get down off that table and stop acting like a fool . . .

[WALTER *comes down off the table suddenly and makes a quick exit to the bathroom.*]

RUTH: He's had a little to drink . . . I don't know what her excuse is.

GEORGE: [*To* BENEATHA.] Look honey, we're going *to* the theatre—we're not going to be *in* it . . . so go change, huh?

RUTH: You expect this boy to go out with you looking like that?

BENEATHA: [*Looking at* GEORGE.] That's up to George. If he's ashamed of his heritage—

GEORGE: Oh, don't be so proud of yourself, Bennie—just because you look eccentric.

BENEATHA: How can something that's natural be eccentric?

GEORGE: That's what being eccentric means—being natural. Get dressed.

BENEATHA: I don't like that, George.

RUTH: Why must you and your brother make an argument out of everything people say?

BENEATHA: Because I hate assimilationist Negroes!

RUTH: Will somebody please tell me what assimila-who-ever means!

GEORGE: Oh, it's just a college girl's way of calling people Uncle Toms—but that isn't what it means at all.

RUTH: Well, what does it mean?

BENEATHA: [*Cutting* GEORGE *off and staring at him as she replies to* RUTH.] It means someone who is willing to give up his own culture and submerge himself completely in the dominant, and in this case, *oppressive* culture!

GEORGE: Oh, dear, dear, dear! Here we go! A lecture on the African past! On our Great West African Heritage! In one second we will hear all about the great Ashanti empires; the great Songhay civilizations; and the great sculpture of Bénin—and then some poetry in the Bantu—and the whole monologue will end with the word *heritage*! [*Nastily.*] Let's face it, baby, your heritage is nothing but a bunch of raggedy-assed spirituals and some grass huts!

BENEATHA: *Grass huts!* [RUTH *crosses to her and forcibly pushes her toward the bedroom.*] See there . . . you are standing there in your splendid ignorance talking about people who were the first to smelt iron on the face of the earth! [RUTH *is pushing her through the door.*] The Ashanti were performing surgical operations when the English— [RUTH *pulls the door to, with* BENEATHA *on the other side, and smiles graciously at* GEORGE. BENEATHA *opens the door and shouts the end of the sentence defiantly at* GEORGE.] —were still tattooing themselves with blue dragons . . . [*She goes back inside.*]

RUTH: Have a seat, George. [*They both sit.* RUTH *folds her hands rather primly on her lap, determined to demonstrate the civilization of the family.*] Warm, ain't it? I mean for September. [*Pause.*] Just like they always say about Chicago weather: If it's too hot or cold for you, just wait a minute and it'll change. [*She smiles happily at this cliché of clichés.*] Everybody say it's got to do with them bombs and things they keep setting off.[2] [*Pause.*] Would you like a nice cold beer?

GEORGE: No, thank you. I don't care for beer. [*He looks at his watch.*] I hope she hurries up.

RUTH: What time is the show?

GEORGE: It's an eight-thirty curtain. That's just Chicago, though. In New York standard curtain time is eight forty.

[*He is rather proud of this knowledge.*]

RUTH: [*Properly appreciating it.*] You get to New York a lot?

GEORGE: [*Offhand.*] Few times a year.

RUTH: Oh—that's nice. I've never been to New York.

[WALTER *enters. We feel he has relieved himself, but the edge of unreality is still with him.*]

WALTER: New York ain't got nothing Chicago ain't. Just a bunch of hustling people all squeezed up together—being "Eastern."

[*He turns his face into a screw of displeasure.*]

GEORGE: Oh—you've been?

WALTER: *Plenty* of times.

RUTH: [*Shocked at the lie.*] Walter Lee Younger!

WALTER: [*Staring her down.*] Plenty! [*Pause.*] What we got to drink in this house? Why don't you offer this man some refreshment. [*To* GEORGE.] They don't know how to entertain people in this house, man.

GEORGE: Thank you—I don't really care for anything.

WALTER: [*Feeling his head; sobriety coming.*] Where's Mama?

RUTH: She ain't come back yet.

WALTER: [*Looking* MURCHISON *over from head to toe, scrutinizing his carefully casual tweed sports jacket over cashmere V-neck sweater over soft eyelet shirt and tie, and soft slacks, finished off with white buckskin shoes.*] Why all you college boys wear them fairyish-looking white shoes?

RUTH: Walter Lee!

---

2. In the 1950s, people commonly blamed weather fluctuations on atomic testing.

[GEORGE MURCHISON *ignores the remark.*]

WALTER: [*To* RUTH.] Well, they look crazy as hell—white shoes, cold as it is.

RUTH: [*Crushed.*] You have to excuse him—

WALTER: No he don't! Excuse me for what? What you always excusing me for! I'll excuse myself when I needs to be excused! [*A pause.*] They look as funny as them black knee socks Beneatha wears out of here all the time.

RUTH: It's the college *style,* Walter.

WALTER: Style, hell. She looks like she got burnt legs or something!

RUTH: Oh, Walter—

WALTER: [*An irritable mimic.*] Oh, Walter! Oh, Walter! [*To* MURCHISON.] How's your old man making out? I understand you all going to buy that big hotel on the Drive?[3] [*He finds a beer in the refrigerator, wanders over to* MURCHISON, *sipping and wiping his lips with the back of his hand, and straddling a chair backwards to talk to the other man.*] Shrewd move. Your old man is all right, man. [*Tapping his head and half winking for emphasis.*] I mean he knows how to operate. I mean he thinks *big,* you know what I mean, I mean for a *home,* you know? But I think he's kind of running out of ideas now. I'd like to talk to him. Listen, man, I got some plans that could turn this city upside down. I mean I think like he does. *Big.* Invest big, gamble big, hell, lose *big* if you have to, you know what I mean. It's hard to find a man on this whole Southside who understands my kind of thinking—you dig? [*He scrutinizes* MURCHISON *again, drinks his beer, squints his eyes and leans in close, confidential, man to man.*] Me and you ought to sit down and talk sometimes, man. Man, I got me some ideas . . .

GEORGE: [*With boredom.*] Yeah—sometimes we'll have to do that, Walter.

WALTER: [*Understanding the indifference, and offended.*] Yeah—well, when you get the time, man. I know you a busy little boy.

RUTH: Walter, please—

WALTER: [*Bitterly, hurt.*] I know ain't nothing in this world as busy as you colored college boys with your fraternity pins and white shoes . . .

RUTH: [*Covering her face with humiliation.*] Oh, Walter Lee—

WALTER: I see you all the time—with the books tucked under your arms—going to your [*British A—a mimic.*] "clahsses." And for what! What the hell you learning over there? Filling up your heads— [*Counting off on his fingers.*] —with the sociology and the psychology—but they teaching you how to be a man? How to take over and run the world? They teaching you how to run a rubber plantation or a steel mill? Naw—just to talk proper and read books and wear white shoes . . .

GEORGE: [*Looking at him with distaste, a little above it all.*] You're all wacked up with bitterness, man.

WALTER: [*Intently, almost quietly, between the teeth, glaring at the boy.*] And you—ain't you bitter, man? Ain't you just about had it yet? Don't you see no stars gleaming that you can't reach out and grab? You happy?—You contented son-of-a-bitch—you happy? You got it made? Bitter? Man, I'm a volcano. Bitter? Here I am a giant—surrounded by ants! Ants who can't even understand what it is the giant is talking about.

RUTH: [*Passionately and suddenly.*] Oh, Walter—ain't you with nobody!

---

3. Lake Shore Drive, a scenic thoroughfare along Lake Michigan.

WALTER: [*Violently.*] No! 'Cause ain't nobody with me! Not even my own mother!
RUTH: Walter, that's a terrible thing to say!

[BENEATHA *enters, dressed for the evening in a cocktail dress and earrings.*]

GEORGE: Well—hey, you look great.
BENEATHA: Let's go, George. See you all later.
RUTH: Have a nice time.
GEORGE: Thanks. Good night. [*To* WALTER, *sarcastically.*] Good night, *Prometheus.*[4]

[BENEATHA *and* GEORGE *exit.*]

WALTER: [*To* RUTH.] Who is Prometheus?
RUTH: I don't know. Don't worry about it.
WALTER: [*In fury, pointing after* GEORGE.] See there—they get to a point where they can't insult you man to man—they got to go talk about something ain't nobody never heard of!
RUTH: How do you know it was an insult? [*To humor him.*] Maybe Prometheus is a nice fellow.
WALTER: Prometheus! I bet there ain't even no such thing! I bet that simple-minded clown—
RUTH: Walter—

[*She stops what she is doing and looks at him.*]

WALTER: [*Yelling.*] Don't start!
RUTH: Start what?
WALTER: Your nagging! Where was I? Who was I with? How much money did I spend?
RUTH: [*Plaintively.*] Walter Lee—why don't we just try to talk about it . . .
WALTER: [*Not listening.*] I been out talking with people who understand me. People who care about the things I got on my mind.
RUTH: [*Wearily.*] I guess that means people like Willy Harris.
WALTER: Yes, people like Willy Harris.
RUTH: [*With a sudden flash of impatience.*] Why don't you all just hurry up and go into the banking business and stop talking about it!
WALTER: Why? You want to know why? 'Cause we all tied up in a race of people that don't know how to do nothing but moan, pray and have babies!

[*The line is too bitter even for him and he looks at her and sits down.*]

RUTH: Oh, Walter . . . [*Softly.*] Honey, why can't you stop fighting me?
WALTER: [*Without thinking.*] Who's fighting you? Who even cares about you?

[*This line begins the retardation of his mood.*]

RUTH: Well— [*She waits a long time, and then with resignation starts to put away her things.*] I guess I might as well go on to bed . . . [*More or less to herself.*] I don't know where we lost it . . . but we have . . . [*Then, to him.*] I—I'm sorry about this new baby, Walter. I guess maybe I better go on and do what I started . . . I guess I just didn't

---

4. In Greek mythology, Prometheus represented the bold creative spirit; he stole fire from Olympus (the locale of the gods) and gave it to humankind.

realize how bad things was with us . . . I guess I just didn't really realize— [*She starts out to the bedroom and stops.*] You want some hot milk?

WALTER: Hot milk?

RUTH: Yes—hot milk.

WALTER: Why hot milk?

RUTH: 'Cause after all that liquor you come home with you ought to have something hot in your stomach.

WALTER: I don't want no milk.

RUTH: You want some coffee then?

WALTER: No, I don't want no coffee. I don't want nothing hot to drink. [*Almost plaintively.*] Why you always trying to give me something to eat?

RUTH: [*Standing and looking at him helplessly.*] What else can I give you, Walter Lee Younger?

> [*She stands and looks at him and presently turns to go out again. He lifts his head and watches her going away from him in a new mood which began to emerge when he asked her "Who cares about you?"*]

WALTER: It's been rough, ain't it, baby? [*She hears and stops but does not turn around and he continues to her back.*] I guess between two people there ain't never as much understood as folks generally thinks there is. I mean like between me and you— [*She turns to face him.*] How we gets to the place where we scared to talk softness to each other. [*He waits, thinking hard himself.*] Why you think it got to be like that? [*He is thoughtful, almost as a child would be.*] Ruth, what is it gets into people ought to be close?

RUTH: I don't know, honey. I think about it a lot.

WALTER: On account of you and me, you mean? The way things are with us. The way something done come down between us.

RUTH: There ain't so much between us, Walter . . . Not when you come to me and try to talk to me. Try to be with me . . . a little even.

WALTER: [*Total honesty.*] Sometimes . . . sometimes . . . I don't even know how to try.

RUTH: Walter—

WALTER: Yes?

RUTH: [*Coming to him, gently and with misgiving, but coming to him.*] Honey . . . life don't have to be like this. I mean sometimes people can do things so that things are better . . . You remember how we used to talk when Travis was born . . . about the way we were going to live . . . the kind of house . . . [*She is stroking his head.*] Well, it's all starting to slip away from us . . .

> [MAMA *enters, and* WALTER *jumps up and shouts at her.*]

WALTER: Mama, where have you been?

MAMA: My—them steps is longer than they used to be. Whew! [*She sits down and ignores him.*] How you feeling this evening, Ruth?

> [RUTH *shrugs, disturbed some at having been prematurely interrupted and watching her husband knowingly.*]

WALTER: Mama, where have you been all day?

MAMA: [*Still ignoring him and leaning on the table and changing to more comfortable shoes.*] Where's Travis?

RUTH: I let him go out earlier and he ain't come back yet. Boy, is he going to get it!

WALTER: Mama!

MAMA: [*As if she has heard him for the first time.*] Yes, son?

WALTER: Where did you go this afternoon?

MAMA: I went downtown to tend to some business that I had to tend to.

WALTER: What kind of business?

MAMA: You know better than to question me like a child, Brother.

WALTER: [*Rising and bending over the table.*] Where were you, Mama? [*Bringing his fists down and shouting.*] Mama, you didn't go do something with that insurance money, something crazy?

[*The front door opens slowly, interrupting him, and* TRAVIS *peeks his head in, less than hopefully.*]

TRAVIS: [*To his mother.*] Mama, I—

RUTH: "Mama I" nothing! You're going to get it, boy! Get on in that bedroom and get yourself ready!

TRAVIS: But I—

MAMA: Why don't you all never let the child explain hisself.

RUTH: Keep out of it now, Lena.

[MAMA *clamps her lips together, and* RUTH *advances toward her son menacingly.*]

RUTH: A thousand times I have told you not to go off like that—

MAMA: [*Holding out her arms to her grandson.*] Well—at least let me tell him something. I want him to be the first one to hear . . . Come here, Travis. [*The boy obeys, gladly.*] Travis— [*She takes him by the shoulder and looks into his face.*] —you know that money we got in the mail this morning?

TRAVIS: Yes'm—

MAMA: Well—what you think your grandmama gone and done with that money?

TRAVIS: I don't know, Grandmama.

MAMA: [*Putting her finger on his nose for emphasis.*] She went out and she bought you a house! [*The explosion comes from* WALTER *at the end of the revelation and he jumps up and turns away from all of them in a fury.* MAMA *continues, to* TRAVIS.] You glad about the house? It's going to be yours when you get to be a man.

TRAVIS: Yeah—I always wanted to live in a house.

MAMA: All right, gimme some sugar then— [TRAVIS *puts his arms around her neck as she watches her son over the boy's shoulder. Then, to* TRAVIS, *after the embrace.*] Now when you say your prayers tonight, you thank God and your grandfather— 'cause it was him who give you the house—in his way.

RUTH: [*Taking the boy from* MAMA *and pushing him toward the bedroom.*] Now you get out of here and get ready for your beating.

TRAVIS: Aw, Mama—

RUTH: Get on in there— [*Closing the door behind him and turning radiantly to her mother-in-law.*] So you went and did it!

MAMA: [*Quietly, looking at her son with pain.*] Yes, I did.

RUTH: [*Raising both arms classically.*] Praise God! [*Looks at* WALTER *a moment, who says nothing. She crosses rapidly to her husband.*] Please, honey—let me be glad . . . you be glad too. [*She has laid her hands on his shoulders, but he shakes himself free of her roughly, without turning to face her.*] Oh, Walter . . . a home . . . *a* home. [*She comes back to* MAMA.] Well—where is it? How big is it? How much it going to cost?

MAMA: Well—

RUTH: When we moving?

MAMA: [Smiling at her.] First of the month.

RUTH: [Throwing back her head with jubilance.] Praise God!

MAMA: [Tentatively, still looking at her son's back turned against her and RUTH.] It's—it's a nice house too . . . [She cannot help speaking directly to him. An imploring quality in her voice, her manner, makes her almost like a girl now.] Three bedrooms—nice big one for you and Ruth . . . Me and Beneatha still have to share our room, but Travis have one of his own—and [With difficulty.] I figure if the—new baby—is a boy, we could get one of them double-decker outfits . . . And there's a yard with a little patch of dirt where I could maybe get to grow me a few flowers . . . And a nice big basement . . .

RUTH: Walter honey, be glad—

MAMA: [Still to his back, fingering things on the table.] 'Course I don't want to make it sound fancier than it is . . . It's just a plain little old house—but it's made good and solid—and it will be ours. Walter Lee—it makes a difference in a man when he can walk on floors that belong to him . . .

RUTH: Where is it?

MAMA: [Frightened at this telling.] Well—well—it's out there in Clybourne Park—[5]

[RUTH's radiance fades abruptly, and WALTER finally turns slowly to face his mother with incredulity and hostility.]

RUTH: Where?

MAMA: [Matter-of-factly.] Four o six Clybourne Street, Clybourne Park.

RUTH: Clybourne Park? Mama, there ain't no colored people living in Clybourne Park.

MAMA: [Almost idiotically.] Well, I guess there's going to be some now.

WALTER: [Bitterly.] So that's the peace and comfort you went out and bought for us today!

MAMA: [Raising her eyes to meet his finally.] Son—I just tried to find the nicest place for the least amount of money for my family.

RUTH: [Trying to recover from the shock.] Well—well—'course I ain't one never been 'fraid of no crackers[6] mind you—but—well, wasn't there no other houses nowhere?

MAMA: Them houses they put up for colored in them areas way out all seem to cost twice as much as other houses. I did the best I could.

RUTH: [Struck senseless with the news, in its various degrees of goodness and trouble, she sits a moment, her fists propping her chin in thought, and then she starts to rise, bringing her fists down with vigor, the radiance spreading from cheek to cheek again.] Well—well!—All I can say is—if this is my time in life—my time—to say good-bye— [And she builds with momentum as she starts to circle the room with an exuberant, almost tearfully happy release.] —to these Goddamned cracking walls!— [She pounds the walls.] —and these marching roaches!— [She wipes at an imaginary army of marching roaches.] —and this cramped little closet which ain't now or never was no kitchen! . . . then I say it loud and good, Hallelujah! and good-bye misery . . . I don't never want to see your ugly face again! [She laughs joyously, having practically destroyed the apartment, and flings her arms up and lets them come down happily,

5. On Chicago's Near North Side.   6. Derogatory term for poor whites.

slowly, reflectively, over her abdomen, aware for the first time perhaps that the life therein pulses with happiness and not despair.] Lena?

MAMA: [*Moved, watching her happiness.*] Yes, honey?

RUTH: [*Looking off.*] Is there—is there a whole lot of sunlight?

MAMA: [*Understanding.*] Yes, child, there's a whole lot of sunlight.

[*Long pause.*]

RUTH: [*Collecting herself and going to the door of the room* TRAVIS *is in.*] Well—I guess I better see 'bout Travis. [*To* MAMA.] Lord, I sure don't feel like whipping nobody today!

[*She exits.*]

MAMA: [*The mother and son are left alone now and the mother waits a long time, considering deeply, before she speaks.*] Son—you—you understand what I done, don't you? [WALTER *is silent and sullen.*] I—I just seen my family falling apart today . . . just falling to pieces in front of my eyes . . . We couldn't of gone on like we was today. We was going backwards 'stead of forwards—talking 'bout killing babies and wishing each other was dead . . . When it gets like that in life—you just got to do something different, push on out and do something bigger . . . [*She waits.*] I wish you say something, son . . . I wish you'd say how deep inside you you think I done the right thing—

WALTER: [*Crossing slowly to his bedroom door and finally turning there and speaking measuredly.*] What you need me to say you done right for? *You* the head of this family. You run our lives like you want to. It was your money and you did what you wanted with it. So what you need for me to say it was all right for? [*Bitterly, to hurt her as deeply as he knows is possible.*] So you butchered up a dream of mine—you—who always talking 'bout your children's dreams . . .

MAMA: Walter Lee—

[*He just closes the door behind him.* MAMA *sits alone, thinking heavily.*]

[CURTAIN.]

Scene Two

Time: Friday night. A few weeks later.

At rise: Packing crates mark the intention of the family to move. BENEATHA *and* GEORGE *come in, presumably from an evening out again.*

GEORGE: O.K. . . . O.K., whatever you say . . . [*They both sit on the couch. He tries to kiss her. She moves away.*] Look, we've had a nice evening; let's not spoil it, huh? . . .

[*He again turns her head and tries to nuzzle in and she turns away from him, not with distaste but with momentary lack of interest; in a mood to pursue what they were talking about.*]

BENEATHA: I'm *trying* to talk to you.

GEORGE: We always talk.

BENEATHA: Yes—and I love to talk.

GEORGE: [*Exasperated; rising.*] I know it and I don't mind it sometimes . . . I want you to cut it out, see—The moody stuff, I mean. I don't like it. You're a nice-looking girl . . . all over. That's all you need, honey, forget the atmosphere. Guys aren't going to go for the atmosphere—they're going to go for what they see. Be glad for that. Drop the Garbo[7] routine. It doesn't go with you. As for myself, I want a nice— [*Groping.*] —simple [*Thoughtfully.*] —sophisticated girl . . . not a poet— O.K.?

[*She rebuffs him again and he starts to leave.*]

BENEATHA: Why are you angry?

GEORGE: Because this is stupid! I don't go out with you to discuss the nature of "quiet desperation"[8] or to hear all about your thoughts—because the world will go on thinking what it thinks regardless—

BENEATHA: Then why read books? Why go to school?

GEORGE: [*With artificial patience, counting on his fingers.*] It's simple. You read books— to learn facts—to get grades—to pass the course—to get a degree. That's all—it has nothing to do with thoughts.

[*A long pause.*]

BENEATHA: I see. [*A longer pause as she looks at him.*] Good night, George.

[GEORGE *looks at her a little oddly, and starts to exit. He meets* MAMA *coming in.*]

GEORGE: Oh—hello, Mrs. Younger.

MAMA: Hello, George, how you feeling?

GEORGE: Fine—fine, how are you?

MAMA: Oh, a little tired. You know them steps can get you after a day's work. You all have a nice time tonight?

GEORGE: Yes—a fine time. Well, good night.

MAMA: Good night. [*He exits.* MAMA *closes the door behind her.*] Hello, honey. What you sitting like that for?

BENEATHA: I'm just sitting.

MAMA: Didn't you have a nice time?

BENEATHA: No.

MAMA: No? What's the matter?

BENEATHA: Mama, George is a fool—honest. [*She rises.*]

MAMA: [*Hustling around unloading the packages she has entered with. She stops.*] Is he, baby?

BENEATHA: Yes.

[BENEATHA *makes up* TRAVIS' *bed as she talks.*]

MAMA: You sure?

BENEATHA: Yes.

MAMA: Well—I guess you better not waste your time with no fools.

[BENEATHA *looks up at her mother, watching her put groceries in the refrigerator. Finally she gathers up her things and starts into the bedroom. At the door she stops and looks back at her mother.*]

BENEATHA: Mama—

7. Greta Garbo (1905–90), Swedish-born American film star whose sultry, remote, and European feminin-ity was widely imitated.
8. In *Walden* (1854), Henry Thoreau asserted that "the mass of men lead lives of quiet desperation."

MAMA: Yes, baby—

BENEATHA: Thank you.

MAMA: For what?

BENEATHA: For understanding me this time.

[*She exits quickly and the mother stands, smiling a little, looking at the place where* BENEATHA *just stood.* RUTH *enters.*]

RUTH: Now don't you fool with any of this stuff, Lena—

MAMA: Oh, I just thought I'd sort a few things out.

[*The phone rings.* RUTH *answers.*]

RUTH: [*At the phone.*] Hello—Just a minute. [*Goes to door.*] Walter, it's Mrs. Arnold. [*Waits. Goes back to the phone. Tense.*] Hello. Yes, this is his wife speaking . . . He's lying down now. Yes . . . well, he'll be in tomorrow. He's been very sick. Yes—I know we should have called, but we were so sure he'd be able to come in today. Yes—yes, I'm very sorry. Yes . . . Thank you very much. [*She hangs up.* WALTER *is standing in the doorway of the bedroom behind her.*] That was Mrs. Arnold.

WALTER: [*Indifferently.*] Was it?

RUTH: She said if you don't come in tomorrow that they are getting a new man . . .

WALTER: Ain't that sad—ain't that crying sad.

RUTH: She said Mr. Arnold has had to take a cab for three days . . . Walter, you ain't been to work for three days! [*This is a revelation to her.*] Where you been, Walter Lee Younger? [WALTER *looks at her and starts to laugh.*] You're going to lose your job.

WALTER: That's right . . .

RUTH: Oh, Walter, and with your mother working like a dog every day—

WALTER: That's sad too—Everything is sad.

MAMA: What you been doing for these three days, son?

WALTER: Mama—you don't know all the things a man what got leisure can find to do in this city . . . What's this—Friday night? Well—Wednesday I borrowed Willy Harris' car and I went for a drive . . . just me and myself and I drove and drove . . . Way out . . . way past South Chicago, and I parked the car and I sat and looked at the steel mills all day long. I just sat in the car and looked at them big black chimneys for hours. Then I drove back and I went to the Green Hat. [*Pause.*] And Thursday—Thursday I borrowed the car again and I got in it and I pointed it the other way and I drove the other way—for hours—way, way up to Wisconsin, and I looked at the farms. I just drove and looked at the farms. Then I drove back and I went to the Green Hat. [*Pause.*] And today— today I didn't get the car. Today I just walked. All over the Southside. And I looked at the Negroes and they looked at me and finally I just sat down on the curb at Thirty-ninth and South Parkway and I just sat there and watched the Negroes go by. And then I went to the Green Hat. You all sad? You all depressed? And you know where I am going right now—

[RUTH *goes out quietly.*]

MAMA: Oh, Big Walter, is this the harvest of our days?

WALTER: You know what I like about the Green Hat? [*He turns the radio on and a steamy, deep blues pours into the room.*] I like this little cat they got there who blows a sax . . . He blows. He talks to me. He ain't but 'bout five feet tall and he's got a conked head[9] and his eyes is always closed and he's all music—

MAMA: [*Rising and getting some papers out of her handbag.*] Walter—

WALTER: And there's this other guy who plays the piano . . . and they got a sound. I mean they can work on some music . . . They got the best little combo in the world in the Green Hat . . . You can just sit there and drink and listen to them three men play and you realize that don't nothing matter worth a damn, but just being there—

MAMA: I've helped do it to you, haven't I, son? Walter, I been wrong.

WALTER: Naw—you ain't never been wrong about nothing, Mama.

MAMA: Listen to me, now. I say I been wrong, son. That I been doing to you what the rest of the world been doing to you. [*She stops and he looks up slowly at her and she meets his eyes pleadingly.*] Walter—what you ain't never understood is that I ain't got nothing, don't own nothing, ain't never really wanted nothing that wasn't for you. There ain't nothing as precious to me . . . There ain't nothing worth holding on to, money, dreams, nothing else—if it means—if it means it's going to destroy my boy. [*She puts her papers in front of him and he watches her without speaking or moving.*] I paid the man thirty-five hundred dollars down on the house. That leaves sixty-five hundred dollars. Monday morning I want you to take this money and take three thousand dollars and put it in a savings account for Beneatha's medical schooling. The rest you put in a checking account—with your name on it. And from now on any penny that come out of it or that go in it is for you to look after. For you to decide. [*She drops her hands a little helplessly.*] It ain't much, but it's all I got in the world and I'm putting it in your hands. I'm telling you to be the head of this family from now on like you supposed to be.

WALTER: [*Stares at the money.*] You trust me like that, Mama?

MAMA: I ain't never stop trusting you. Like I ain't never stop loving you.

[*She goes out, and* WALTER *sits looking at the money on the table as the music continues in its idiom, pulsing in the room. Finally, in a decisive gesture, he gets up, and, in mingled joy and desperation, picks up the money. At the same moment,* TRAVIS *enters for bed.*]

TRAVIS: What's the matter, Daddy? You drunk?

WALTER: [*Sweetly, more sweetly than we have ever known him.*] No, Daddy ain't drunk. Daddy ain't going to never be drunk again. . . .

TRAVIS: Well, good night, Daddy.

[*The father has come from behind the couch and leans over, embracing his son.*]

WALTER: Son, I feel like talking to you tonight.

TRAVIS: About what?

WALTER: Oh, about a lot of things. About you and what kind of man you going to be when you grow up . . . Son—son, what do you want to be when you grow up?

TRAVIS: A bus driver.

WALTER: [*Laughing a little.*] A what? Man, that ain't nothing to want to be!

9. Straightened hair.

TRAVIS: Why not?

WALTER: 'Cause, man—it ain't big enough—you know what I mean.

TRAVIS: I don't know then. I can't make up my mind. Sometimes Mama asks me that too. And sometimes when I tell her I just want to be like you—she says she don't want me to be like that and sometimes she says she does . . .

WALTER: [*Gathering him up in his arms.*] You know what, Travis? In seven years you going to be seventeen years old. And things is going to be very different with us in seven years, Travis . . . One day when you are seventeen I'll come home—home from my office downtown somewhere—

TRAVIS: You don't work in no office, Daddy.

WALTER: No—but after tonight. After what your daddy gonna do tonight, there's going to be offices—a whole lot of offices . . .

TRAVIS: What you gonna do tonight, Daddy?

WALTER: You wouldn't understand yet, son, but your daddy's gonna make a transaction . . . a business transaction that's going to change our lives . . . That's how come one day when you 'bout seventeen years old I'll come home and I'll be pretty tired, you know what I mean, after a day of conferences and secretaries getting things wrong the way they do . . . 'cause an executive's life is hell, man— [*The more he talks the farther away he gets.*] And I'll pull the car up on the driveway . . . just a plain black Chrysler, I think, with white walls—no—black tires. More elegant. Rich people don't have to be flashy . . . though I'll have to get something a little sportier for Ruth—maybe a Cadillac convertible to do her shopping in . . . And I'll come up the steps to the house and the gardener will be clipping away at the hedges and he'll say, "Good evening, Mr. Younger." And I'll say, "Hello, Jefferson, how are you this evening?" And I'll go inside and Ruth will come downstairs and meet me at the door and we'll kiss each other and she'll take my arm and we'll go up to your room to see you sitting on the floor with the catalogues of all the great schools in America around you . . . All the great schools in the world. And—and I'll say, all right son—it's your seventeenth birthday, what is it you've decided? . . . Just tell me where you want to go to school and you'll *go*. Just tell me, what it is you want to be—and you'll *be* it . . . Whatever you want to be—Yessir! [*He holds his arms open for* TRAVIS.] You just name it, son . . . [TRAVIS *leaps into them*.] and I hand you the world!

[WALTER'*s voice has risen in pitch and hysterical promise and on the last line he lifts* TRAVIS *high*.]

[BLACKOUT.]

Scene Three

Time: Saturday, moving day, one week later.

Before the curtain rises, RUTH'*s voice, a strident, dramatic church alto, cuts through the silence.*

It is, in the darkness, a triumphant surge, a penetrating statement of expectation: "Oh, Lord, I don't feel no ways tired! Children, oh, glory hallelujah!"

As the curtain rises we see that RUTH *is alone in the living room, finishing up the family's packing. It is moving day. She is nailing crates and tying cartons.* BENEATHA *enters, carrying a guitar case, and watches her exuberant sister-in-law.*

RUTH: Hey!

BENEATHA: [*Putting away the case.*] Hi.

RUTH: [*Pointing at a package.*] Honey—look in that package there and see what I found on sale this morning at the South Center. [RUTH *gets up and moves to the package and draws out some curtains.*] Lookahere—hand-turned hems!

BENEATHA: How do you know the window size out there?

RUTH: [*Who hadn't thought of that.*] Oh—Well, they bound to fit something in the whole house. Anyhow, they was too good a bargain to pass up. [RUTH *slaps her head, suddenly remembering something.*] Oh, Bennie—I meant to put a special note on that carton over there. That's your mama's good china and she wants 'em to be very careful with it.

BENEATHA: I'll do it.

[BENEATHA *finds a piece of paper and starts to draw large letters on it.*]

RUTH: You know what I'm going to do soon as I get in that new house?

BENEATHA: What?

RUTH: Honey—I'm going to run me a tub of water up to here . . . [*With her fingers practically up to her nostrils.*] And I'm going to get in it—and I am going to sit . . . and sit . . . and sit in that hot water and the first person who knocks to tell *me* to hurry up and come out—

BENEATHA: Gets shot at sunrise.

RUTH: [*Laughing happily.*] You said it, sister! [*Noticing how large* BENEATHA *is absent-mindedly making the note.*] Honey, they ain't going to read that from no airplane.

BENEATHA: [*Laughing herself.*] I guess I always think things have more emphasis if they are big, somehow.

RUTH: [*Looking up at her and smiling.*] You and your brother seem to have that as a philosophy of life. Lord, that man—done changed so 'round here. You know—you know what we did last night? Me and Walter Lee?

BENEATHA: What?

RUTH: [*Smiling to herself.*] We went to the movies. [*Looking at* BENEATHA *to see if she understands.*] We went to the movies. You know the last time me and Walter went to the movies together?

BENEATHA: No.

RUTH: Me neither. That's how long it been. [*Smiling again.*] But we went last night.
   The picture wasn't much good, but that didn't seem to matter. We went—and we held hands.

BENEATHA: Oh, Lord!

RUTH: We held hands—and you know what?

BENEATHA: What?

RUTH: When we come out of the show it was late and dark and all the stores and things was closed up . . . and it was kind of chilly and there wasn't many people on the streets . . . and we was still holding hands, me and Walter.

BENEATHA: You're killing me.

[WALTER *enters with a large package. His happiness is deep in him; he cannot keep still with his new-found exuberance. He is singing and wiggling and snapping his fingers. He puts his package in a corner and puts a phonograph record, which he has brought in with him, on the record player. As the music comes up he dances over to* RUTH *and tries to get her to dance with him. She gives in at last to his raunchiness and in a fit of giggling allows herself to be drawn into his mood and together they deliberately burlesque an old social dance of their youth.*]

BENEATHA: [*Regarding them a long time as they dance, then drawing in her breath for a deeply exaggerated comment which she does not particularly mean.*] Talk about—olddddddddddd-fashioneddddddd—Negroes!

WALTER: [*Stopping momentarily.*] What kind of Negroes?

[*He says this in fun. He is not angry with her today, nor with anyone. He starts to dance with his wife again.*]

BENEATHA: Old-fashioned.

WALTER: [*As he dances with* RUTH.] You know, when these *New Negroes* have their convention— [*Pointing at his sister.*] —that is going to be the chairman of the Committee on Unending Agitation. [*He goes on dancing, then stops.*] Race, race, race! . . . Girl, I do believe you are the first person in the history of the entire human race to successfully brainwash yourself. [BENEATHA *breaks up and he goes on dancing. He stops again, enjoying his tease.*] Damn, even the N double A C P[1] takes a holiday sometimes! [BENEATHA *and* RUTH *laugh. He dances with* RUTH *some more and starts to laugh and stops and pantomimes someone over an operating table.*] I can just see that chick someday looking down at some poor cat on an operating table before she starts to slice him, saying . . . [*Pulling his sleeves back maliciously.*] "By the way, what are your views on civil rights down there? . . ."

[*He laughs at her again and starts to dance happily. The bell sounds.*]

BENEATHA: Sticks and stones may break my bones but . . . words will never hurt me!

[BENEATHA *goes to the door and opens it as* WALTER *and* RUTH *go on with the clowning.* BENEATHA *is somewhat surprised to see a quiet-looking middle-aged white man in a business suit holding his hat and a briefcase in his hand and consulting a small piece of paper.*]

MAN: Uh—how do you do, miss. I am looking for a Mrs.— [*He looks at the slip of paper.*] Mrs. Lena Younger?

BENEATHA: [*Smoothing her hair with slight embarrassment.*] Oh—yes, that's my mother. Excuse me [*She closes the door and turns to quiet the other two.*] Ruth! Brother! Somebody's here. [*Then she opens the door. The* MAN *casts a curious quick glance at all of them.*] Uh—come in please.

MAN: [*Coming in.*] Thank you.

BENEATHA: My mother isn't here just now. Is it business?

MAN: Yes . . . well, of a sort.

WALTER: [*Freely, the Man of the House.*] Have a seat. I'm Mrs. Younger's son. I look after most of her business matters.

[RUTH *and* BENEATHA *exchange amused glances.*]

1. National Association for the Advancement of Colored People, civil rights organization founded in 1909.

MAN: [*Regarding* WALTER, *and sitting.*] Well—My name is Karl Lindner . . .

WALTER: [*Stretching out his hand.*] Walter Younger. This is my wife— [RUTH *nods politely.*] —and my sister.

LINDNER: How do you do.

WALTER: [*Amiably, as he sits himself easily on a chair, leaning with interest forward on his knees and looking expectantly into the newcomer's face.*] What can we do for you, Mr. Lindner!

LINDNER: [*Some minor shuffling of the hat and briefcase on his knees.*] Well—I am a representative of the Clybourne Park Improvement Association—

WALTER: [*Pointing.*] Why don't you sit your things on the floor?

LINDNER: Oh—yes. Thank you. [*He slides the briefcase and hat under the chair.*] And as I was saying—I am from the Clybourne Park Improvement Association and we have had it brought to our attention at the last meeting that you people— or at least your mother—has bought a piece of residential property at— [*He digs for the slip of paper again.*] —four o six Clybourne Street . . .

WALTER: That's right. Care for something to drink? Ruth, get Mr. Lindner a beer.

LINDNER: [*Upset for some reason.*] Oh—no, really. I mean thank you very much, but no thank you.

RUTH: [*Innocently.*] Some coffee?

LINDNER: Thank you, nothing at all.

   [BENEATHA *is watching the man carefully.*]

LINDNER: Well, I don't know how much you folks know about our organization. [*He is a gentle man; thoughtful and somewhat labored in his manner.*] It is one of these community organizations set up to look after—oh, you know, things like block upkeep and special projects and we also have what we call our New Neighbors Orientation Committee . . .

BENEATHA: [*Drily.*] Yes—and what do they do?

LINDNER: [*Turning a little to her and then returning the main force to* WALTER.] Well—it's what you might call a sort of welcoming committee, I guess. I mean they, we, I'm the chairman of the committee—go around and see the new people who move into the neighborhood and sort of give them the lowdown on the way we do things out in Clybourne Park.

BENEATHA: [*With appreciation of the two meanings, which escape* RUTH *and* WALTER.] Un-huh.

LINDNER: And we also have the category of what the association calls— [*He looks elsewhere.*] —uh—special community problems . . .

BENEATHA: Yes—and what are some of those?

WALTER: Girl, let the man talk.

LINDNER: [*With understated relief.*] Thank you. I would sort of like to explain this thing in my own way. I mean I want to explain to you in a certain way.

WALTER: Go ahead.

LINDNER: Yes. Well. I'm going to try to get right to the point. I'm sure we'll all appreciate that in the long run.

BENEATHA: Yes.

WALTER: Be still now!

LINDNER: Well—

RUTH: [*Still innocently.*] Would you like another chair—you don't look comfortable.

LINDNER: [*More frustrated than annoyed.*] No, thank you very much. Please. Well—
to get right to the point I— [*A great breath, and he is off at last.*] I am sure you
people must be aware of some of the incidents which have happened in various parts of the city when colored people have moved into certain areas—
[BENEATHA *exhales heavily and starts tossing a piece of fruit up and down in the air.*]
Well—because we have what I think is going to be a unique type of organization in American community life—not only do we deplore that kind of thing—
but we are trying to do something about it. [BENEATHA *stops tossing and turns
with a new and quizzical interest to the man.*] We feel— [*Gaining confidence in his mission because of the interest in the faces of the people he is talking to.*] —we feel that most
of the trouble in this world, when you come right down to it— [*He hits his knee
for emphasis.*] —most of the trouble exists because people just don't sit down
and talk to each other.
RUTH: [*Nodding as she might in church, pleased with the remark.*] You can say that again,
mister.
LINDNER: [*More encouraged by such affirmation.*] That we don't try hard enough in
this world to understand the other fellow's problem. The other guy's point of
view.
RUTH: Now that's right.

[BENEATHA *and* WALTER *merely watch and listen with genuine interest.*]

LINDNER: Yes—that's the way we feel out in Clybourne Park. And that's why I was
elected to come here this afternoon and talk to you people. Friendly like, you
know, the way people should talk to each other and see if we couldn't find
some way to work this thing out. As I say, the whole business is a matter of
caring about the other fellow. Anybody can see that you are a nice family of
folks, hard working and honest I'm sure. [BENEATHA *frowns slightly, quizzically,
her head tilted regarding him.*] Today everybody knows what it means to be on
the outside of something. And of course, there is always somebody who is out
to take the advantage of people who don't always understand.
WALTER: What do you mean?
LINDNER: Well—you see our community is made up of people who've worked hard
as the dickens for years to build up that little community. They're not rich and
fancy people; just hard-working, honest people who don't really have much but
those little homes and a dream of the kind of community they want to raise
their children in. Now, I don't say we are perfect and there is a lot wrong in some
of the things they want. But you've got to admit that a man, right or wrong, has
the right to want to have the neighborhood he lives in a certain kind of way.
And at the moment the overwhelming majority of our people out there feel
that people get along better, take more of a common interest in the life of the
community, when they share a common background. I want you to believe me
when I tell you that race prejudice simply doesn't enter into it. It is a matter of
the people of Clybourne Park believing, rightly or wrongly, as I say, that for the
happiness of all concerned that our Negro families are happier when they live
in their *own* communities.
BENEATHA: [*With a grand and bitter gesture.*] This, friends, is the Welcoming
Committee!
WALTER: [*Dumfounded, looking at* LINDNER.] Is this what you came marching all the
way over here to tell us?

LINDNER: Well, now we've been having a fine conversation. I hope you'll hear me all the way through.

WALTER: [*Tightly.*] Go ahead, man.

LINDNER: You see—in the face of all things I have said, we are prepared to make your family a very generous offer . . .

BENEATHA: Thirty pieces and not a coin less![2]

WALTER: Yeah?

LINDNER: [*Putting on his glasses and drawing a form out of the briefcase.*] Our association is prepared, through the collective effort of our people, to buy the house from you at a financial gain to your family.

RUTH: Lord have mercy, ain't this the living gall!

WALTER: All right, you through?

LINDNER: Well, I want to give you the exact terms of the financial arrangement—

WALTER: We don't want to hear no exact terms of no arrangements. I want to know if you got any more to tell us 'bout getting together?

LINDNER: [*Taking off his glasses.*] Well—I don't suppose that you feel . . .

WALTER: Never mind how I feel—you got any more to say 'bout how people ought to sit down and talk to each other? . . . Get out of my house, man.

[*He turns his back and walks to the door.*]

LINDNER: [*Looking around at the hostile faces and reaching and assembling his hat and briefcase.*] Well—I don't understand why you people are reacting this way. What do you think you are going to gain by moving into a neighborhood where you just aren't wanted and where some elements—well—people can get awful worked up when they feel that their whole way of life and everything they've ever worked for is threatened.

WALTER: Get out.

LINDNER: [*At the door, holding a small card.*] Well—I'm sorry it went like this.

WALTER: Get out.

LINDNER: [*Almost sadly regarding* WALTER.] You just can't force people to change their hearts, son.

[*He turns and puts his card on a table and exits.* WALTER *pushes the door to with stinging hatred, and stands looking at it.* RUTH *just sits and* BENEATHA *just stands. They say nothing.* MAMA *and* TRAVIS *enter.*]

MAMA: Well—this all the packing got done since I left out of here this morning. I testify before God that my children got all the energy of the dead. What time the moving men due?

BENEATHA: Four o'clock. You had a caller, Mama.

[*She is smiling, teasingly.*]

MAMA: Sure enough—who?

BENEATHA: [*Her arms folded saucily.*] The Welcoming Committee.

[WALTER *and* RUTH *giggle.*]

MAMA: [*Innocently.*] Who?

2. See Matthew 26.15, in which Judas Iscariot is paid 30 pieces of silver to betray Jesus.

BENEATHA: The Welcoming Committee. They said they're sure going to be glad to see you when you get there.

WALTER: [*Devilishly.*] Yeah, they said they can't hardly wait to see your face.

[*Laughter.*]

MAMA: [*Sensing their facetiousness.*] What's the matter with you all?

WALTER: Ain't nothing the matter with us. We just telling you 'bout the gentleman who came to see you this afternoon. From the Clybourne Park Improvement Association.

MAMA: What he want?

RUTH: [*In the same mood as* BENEATHA *and* WALTER.] To welcome you, honey.

WALTER: He said they can't hardly wait. He said the one thing they don't have, that they just *dying* to have out there is a fine family of colored people! [*To* RUTH *and* BENEATHA.] Ain't that right!

RUTH AND BENEATHA: [*Mockingly.*] Yeah! He left his card in case—

[*They indicate the card, and* MAMA *picks it up and throws it on the floor—understanding and looking off as she draws her chair up to the table on which she has put her plant and some sticks and some cord.*]

MAMA: Father, give us strength. [*Knowingly—and without fun.*] Did he threaten us?

BENEATHA: Oh—Mama—they don't do it like that anymore. He talked Brotherhood. He said everybody ought to learn how to sit down and hate each other with good Christian fellowship.

[*She and* WALTER *shake hands to ridicule the remark.*]

MAMA: [*Sadly.*] Lord, protect us . . .

RUTH: You should hear the money those folks raised to buy the house from us. All we paid and then some.

BENEATHA: What they think we going to do—eat 'em?

RUTH: No, honey, marry 'em.

MAMA: [*Shaking her head.*] Lord, Lord, Lord . . .

RUTH: Well—that's the way the crackers crumble. Joke.

BENEATHA: [*Laughingly noticing what her mother is doing.*] Mama, what are you doing?

MAMA: Fixing my plant so it won't get hurt none on the way . . .

BENEATHA: Mama, you going to take *that* to the new house?

MAMA: Un-huh—

BENEATHA: That raggedy-looking old thing?

MAMA: [*Stopping and looking at her.*] It expresses *me.*

RUTH: [*With delight, to* BENEATHA.] So there, Miss Thing!

[WALTER *comes to* MAMA *suddenly and bends down behind her and squeezes her in his arms with all his strength. She is overwhelmed by the suddenness of it and, though delighted, her manner is like that of* RUTH *with* TRAVIS.]

MAMA: Look out now, boy! You make me mess up my thing here!

WALTER: [*His face lit, he slips down on his knees beside her, his arms still about her.*] Mama . . . you know what it means to climb up in the chariot?

MAMA: [*Gruffly, very happy.*] Get on away from me now . . .

RUTH: [*Near the gift-wrapped package, trying to catch* WALTER'S *eye.*] Psst—

WALTER: What the old song say, Mama . . .

RUTH: Walter—Now?

[*She is pointing at the package.*]

WALTER: [*Speaking the lines, sweetly, playfully, in his mother's face.*]

> I got wings . . . you got wings . . .
> All God's Children got wings[3] . . .

MAMA: Boy—get out of my face and do some work . . .

WALTER:
> When I get to heaven gonna put on my wings,
> Gonna fly all over God's heaven . . .

BENEATHA: [*Teasingly, from across the room.*] Everybody talking 'bout heaven ain't going there!

WALTER: [*To* RUTH, *who is carrying the box across to them.*] I don't know, you think we ought to give her that . . . Seems to me she ain't been very appreciative around here.

MAMA: [*Eying the box, which is obviously a gift.*] What is that?

WALTER: [*Taking it from* RUTH *and putting it on the table in front of* MAMA.] Well—what you all think? Should we give it to her?

RUTH: Oh—she was pretty good today.

MAMA: I'll good you—

[*She turns her eyes to the box again.*]

BENEATHA: Open it, Mama.

[*She stands up, looks at it, turns and looks at all of them, and then presses her hands together and does not open the package.*]

WALTER: [*Sweetly.*] Open it, Mama. It's for you. [MAMA *looks in his eyes. It is the first present in her life without its being Christmas. Slowly she opens her package and lifts out, one by one, a brand-new sparkling set of gardening tools.* WALTER *continues, prodding.*] Ruth made up the note—read it . . .

MAMA: [*Picking up the card and adjusting her glasses.*] "To our own Mrs. Miniver[4]— Love from Brother, Ruth and Beneatha." Ain't that lovely . . .

TRAVIS: [*Tugging at his father's sleeve.*] Daddy, can I give her mine now?

WALTER: All right, son. [TRAVIS *flies to get his gift.*] Travis didn't want to go in with the rest of us, Mama. He got his own. [*Somewhat amused.*] We don't know what it is . . .

TRAVIS: [*Racing back in the room with a large hatbox and putting it in front of his grandmother.*] Here!

MAMA: Lord have mercy, baby. You done gone and bought your grandmother a hat?

TRAVIS: [*Very proud.*] Open it!

[*She does and lifts out an elaborate, but very elaborate, wide gardening hat, and all the adults break up at the sight of it.*]

---

3. Lines from an African American spiritual. Walter's and Beneatha's next lines are also from the song.
4. Courageous, charismatic title character of a 1942 film starring Greer Garson.

RUTH: Travis, honey, what is that?

TRAVIS: [*Who thinks it is beautiful and appropriate.*] It's a gardening hat! Like the ladies always have on in the magazines when they work in their gardens.

BENEATHA: [*Giggling fiercely.*] Travis—we were trying to make Mama Mrs. Miniver— not Scarlett O'Hara![5]

MAMA: [*Indignantly.*] What's the matter with you all! This here is a beautiful hat! [*Absurdly.*] I always wanted me one just like it!

[*She pops it on her head to prove it to her grandson, and the hat is ludicrous and considerably oversized.*]

RUTH: Hot dog! Go, Mama!

WALTER: [*Doubled over with laughter.*] I'm sorry, Mama—but you look like you ready to go out and chop you some cotton sure enough!

[*They all laugh except* MAMA, *out of deference to* TRAVIS' *feelings.*]

MAMA: [*Gathering the boy up to her.*] Bless your heart—this is the prettiest hat I ever owned— [WALTER, RUTH *and* BENEATHA *chime in—noisily, festively and insincerely congratulating* TRAVIS *on his gift.*] What are we all standing around here for? We ain't finished packin' yet. Bennie, you ain't packed one book.

[*The bell rings.*]

BENEATHA: That couldn't be the movers . . . it's not hardly two good yet—

[BENEATHA *goes into her room.* MAMA *starts for door.*]

WALTER: [*Turning, stiffening.*] Wait—wait—I'll get it.

[*He stands and looks at the door.*]

MAMA: You expecting company, son?

WALTER: [*Just looking at the door.*] Yeah—yeah . . .

[MAMA *looks at* RUTH, *and they exchange innocent and unfrightened glances.*]

MAMA: [*Not understanding.*] Well, let them in, son.

BENEATHA: [*From her room.*] We need some more string.

MAMA: Travis—you run to the hardware and get me some string cord.

[MAMA *goes out and* WALTER *turns and looks at* RUTH. TRAVIS *goes to a dish for money.*]

RUTH: Why don't you answer the door, man?

WALTER: [*Suddenly bounding across the floor to her.*] 'Cause sometimes it hard to let the future begin! [*Stooping down in her face.*]

I got wings! You got wings!
All God's children got wings!

[*He crosses to the door and throws it open. Standing there is a very slight little man in a not too prosperous business suit and with haunted frightened eyes and a hat pulled down tightly, brim up, around his forehead.* TRAVIS *passes between the men and exits.* WALTER *leans deep in the man's face, still in his jubilance.*]

5. Glamorous, headstrong heroine of Margaret Mitchell's 1936 novel *Gone with the Wind*.

When I get to heaven gonna put on my wings,
Gonna fly all over God's heaven . . .

[*The little man just stares at him.*]

Heaven—

[*Suddenly he stops and looks past the little man into the empty hallway.*] Where's Willy, man?

BOBO: He ain't with me.

WALTER: [*Not disturbed.*] Oh—come on in. You know my wife.

BOBO: [*Dumbly, taking off his hat.*] Yes—h'you, Miss Ruth.

RUTH: [*Quietly, a mood apart from her husband already, seeing* BOBO.] Hello, Bobo.

WALTER: You right on time today . . . Right on time. That's the way! [*He slaps* BOBO *on his back.*] Sit down . . . lemme hear.

[RUTH *stands stiffly and quietly in back of them, as though somehow she senses death, her eyes fixed on her husband.*]

BOBO: [*His frightened eyes on the floor, his hat in his hands.*] Could I please get a drink of water, before I tell you about it, Walter Lee?

[WALTER *does not take his eyes off the man.* RUTH *goes blindly to the tap and gets a glass of water and brings it to* BOBO.]

WALTER: There ain't nothing wrong, is there?

BOBO: Lemme tell you—

WALTER: Man—didn't nothing go wrong?

BOBO: Lemme tell you—Walter Lee. [*Looking at* RUTH *and talking to her more than to* WALTER.] You know how it was. I got to tell you how it was. I mean first I got to tell you how it was all the way . . . I mean about the money I put in, Walter Lee . . .

WALTER: [*With taut agitation now.*] What about the money you put in?

BOBO: Well—it wasn't much as we told you—me and Willy— [*He stops.*] I'm sorry, Walter. I got a bad feeling about it. I got a real bad feeling about it . . .

WALTER: Man, what you telling me about all this for? . . . Tell me what happened in Springfield . . .

BOBO: Springfield.

RUTH: [*Like a dead woman.*] What was supposed to happen in Springfield?

BOBO: [*To her.*] This deal that me and Walter went into with Willy—Me and Willy was going to go down to Springfield and spread some money 'round so's we wouldn't have to wait so long for the liquor license . . . That's what we were going to do. Everybody said that was the way you had to do, you understand, Miss Ruth?

WALTER: Man—what happened down there?

BOBO: [*A pitiful man, near tears.*] I'm trying to tell you, Walter.

WALTER: [*Screaming at him suddenly.*] THEN TELL ME, GODDAMMIT . . . WHAT'S THE MATTER WITH YOU?

BOBO: Man . . . I didn't go to no Springfield, yesterday.

WALTER: [*Halted, life hanging in the moment.*] Why not?

BOBO: [*The long way, the hard way to tell.*] 'Cause I didn't have no reasons to . . .

WALTER: Man, what are you talking about!

BOBO: I'm talking about the fact that when I got to the train station yesterday morning—eight o'clock like we planned . . . Man—*Willy didn't never show up.*

WALTER: Why . . . where was he . . . where is he?

BOBO: That's what I'm trying to tell you . . . I don't know . . . I waited six hours . . . I called his house . . . and I waited . . . six hours . . . I waited in that train station six hours . . . [*Breaking into tears.*] That was all the extra money I had in the world . . . [*Looking up at* WALTER *with the tears running down his face.*] Man, *Willy is gone.*

WALTER: Gone, what you mean Willy is gone? Gone where? You mean he went by himself. You mean he went off to Springfield by himself—to take care of getting the license— [*Turns and looks anxiously at* RUTH.] You mean maybe he didn't want too many people in on the business down there? [*Looks to* RUTH *again, as before.*] You know Willy got his own ways. [*Looks back to* BOBO.] Maybe you was late yesterday and he just went on down there without you. Maybe—maybe—he's been callin' you at home tryin' to tell you what happened or something. Maybe—maybe—he just got sick. He's somewhere—he's got to be somewhere. We just got to find him—me and you got to find him. [*Grabs* BOBO *senselessly by the collar and starts to shake him.*] We got to!

BOBO: [*In sudden angry, frightened agony.*] What's the matter with you, Walter! *When a cat take off with your money he don't leave you no maps!*

WALTER: [*Turning madly, as though he is looking for* WILLY *in the very room.*] Willy! . . . Willy . . . don't do it . . . Please don't do it . . . Man, not with that money . . . Man, please, not with that money . . . Oh, God . . . Don't let it be true . . . [*He is wandering around, crying out for* WILLY *and looking for him or perhaps for help from God.*] Man . . . I trusted you . . . Man, I put my life in your hands . . . [*He starts to crumple down on the floor as* RUTH *just covers her face in horror.* MAMA *opens the door and comes into the room, with* BENEATHA *behind her.*] Man . . . [*He starts to pound the floor with his fists, sobbing wildly.*] *That money is made out of my father's flesh* . . .

BOBO: [*Standing over him helplessly.*] I'm sorry, Walter . . . [*Only* WALTER's *sobs reply.* BOBO *puts on his hat.*] I had my life staked on this deal, too . . .

[*He exits.*]

MAMA: [*To* WALTER.] Son— [*She goes to him, bends down to him, talks to his bent head.*] Son . . . Is it gone? Son, I gave you sixty-five hundred dollars. Is it gone? All of it? Beneatha's money too?

WALTER: [*Lifting his head slowly.*] Mama . . . I never . . . went to the bank at all . . .

MAMA: [*Not wanting to believe him.*] You mean . . . your sister's school money . . . you used that too . . . Walter? . . .

WALTER: Yessss! . . . All of it . . . It's all gone . . . [*There is total silence.* RUTH *stands with her face covered with her hands;* BENEATHA *leans forlornly against a wall, fingering a piece of red ribbon from the mother's gift.* MAMA *stops and looks at her son without recognition and then, quite without thinking about it, starts to beat him senselessly in the face.* BENEATHA *goes to them and stops it.*]

BENEATHA: Mama!

[MAMA *stops and looks at both of her children and rises slowly and wanders vaguely, aimlessly away from them.*]

MAMA: I seen . . . him . . . night after night . . . come in . . . and look at that rug . . . and then look at me . . . the red showing in his eyes . . . the veins moving in his head . . . I seen him grow thin and old before he was forty . . . working and working and working like somebody's old horse . . . killing himself . . . and you—you give it all away in a day . . .

BENEATHA: Mama—

MAMA: Oh, God . . . [*She looks up to Him.*] Look down here—and show me the strength.

BENEATHA: Mama—

MAMA: [*Folding over.*] Strength . . .

BENEATHA: [*Plaintively.*] Mama . . .

MAMA: Strength!

[CURTAIN.]

ACT III

An hour later.

At curtain, there is a sullen light of gloom in the living room, gray light not unlike that which began the first scene of Act I. At left we can see WALTER *within his room, alone with himself. He is stretched out on the bed, his shirt out and open, his arms under his head. He does not smoke, he does not cry out, he merely lies there, looking up at the ceiling, much as if he were alone in the world.*

In the living room BENEATHA *sits at the table, still surrounded by the now almost ominous packing crates. She sits looking off. We feel that this is a mood struck perhaps an hour before, and it lingers now, full of the empty sound of profound disappointment. We see on a line from her brother's bedroom the sameness of their attitudes. Presently the bell rings and* BENEATHA *rises without ambition or interest in answering. It is* ASAGAI, *smiling broadly, striding into the room with energy and happy expectation and conversation.*

ASAGAI: I came over . . . I had some free time. I thought I might help with the packing. Ah, I like the look of packing crates! A household in preparation for a journey! It depresses some people . . . but for me . . . it is another feeling. Something full of the flow of life, do you understand? Movement, progress . . . It makes me think of Africa.

BENEATHA: Africa!

ASAGAI: What kind of a mood is this? Have I told you how deeply you move me?

BENEATHA: He gave away the money, Asagai . . .

ASAGAI: Who gave away what money?

BENEATHA: The insurance money. My brother gave it away.

ASAGAI: Gave it away?

BENEATHA: He made an investment! With a man even Travis wouldn't have trusted.

ASAGAI: And it's gone?

BENEATHA: Gone!

ASAGAI: I'm very sorry . . . And you, now?

BENEATHA: Me? . . . Me? . . . Me, I'm nothing . . . Me. When I was very small . . . we used to take our sleds out in the wintertime and the only hills we had were the ice-covered stone steps of some houses down the street. And we used to fill them in with snow and make them smooth and slide down them all day . . . and it was very dangerous you know . . . far too steep . . . and sure enough one day a kid named Rufus came down too fast and hit the sidewalk . . . and we saw his face just split open right there in front of us . . . And I remember standing there looking at his bloody open face thinking that was the end of Rufus. But the ambulance came and they took him to the hospital and they fixed the broken bones and they sewed it all up . . . and the next time I saw Rufus he just had a little line down the middle of his face . . . I never got over that . . .

[WALTER *sits up, listening on the bed. Throughout this scene it is important that we feel his reaction at all times, that he visibly respond to the words of his sister and* ASAGAI.]

ASAGAI: What?

BENEATHA: That that was what one person could do for another, fix him up—sew up the problem, make him all right again. That was the most marvelous thing in the world . . . I wanted to do that. I always thought it was the one concrete thing in the world that a human being could do. Fix up the sick, you know—and make them whole again. This was truly being God . . .

ASAGAI: You wanted to be God?

BENEATHA: No—I wanted to cure. It used to be so important to me. I wanted to cure. It used to matter. I used to care. I mean about people and how their bodies hurt . . .

ASAGAI: And you've stopped caring?

BENEATHA: Yes—I think so.

ASAGAI: Why?

[WALTER *rises, goes to the door of his room and is about to open it, then stops and stands listening, leaning on the door jamb.*]

BENEATHA: Because it doesn't seem deep enough, close enough to what ails mankind—I mean this thing of sewing up bodies or administering drugs. Don't you understand? It was a child's reaction to the world. I thought that doctors had the secret to all the hurts . . . That's the way a child sees things—or an idealist.

ASAGAI: Children see things very well sometimes—and idealists even better.

BENEATHA: I know that's what you think. Because you are still where I left off—you still care. This is what you see for the world, for Africa. You with the dreams of the future will patch up all Africa—you are going to cure the Great Sore of colonialism with Independence—

ASAGAI: Yes!

BENEATHA: Yes—and you think that one word is the penicillin of the human spirit: "Independence!" But then what?

ASAGAI: That will be the problem for another time. First we must get there.

BENEATHA: And where does it end?

ASAGAI: End? Who even spoke of an end? To life? To living?

BENEATHA: An end to misery!

ASAGAI: [*Smiling.*] You sound like a French intellectual.

BENEATHA: No! I sound like a human being who just had her future taken right out of her hands! While I was sleeping in my bed in there, things were happening in this world that directly concerned me—and nobody asked me, consulted me—they just went out and did things—and changed my life. Don't you see there isn't any real progress, Asagai, there is only one large circle that we march in, around and around, each of us with our own little picture—in front of us— our own little mirage that we think is the future.

ASAGAI: That is the mistake.

BENEATHA: What?

ASAGAI: What you just said—about the circle. It isn't a circle—it is simply a long line—as in geometry, you know, one that reaches into infinity. And because we cannot see the end—we also cannot see how it changes. And it is very odd but those who see the changes are called "idealists"—and those who cannot, or refuse to think, they are the "realists." It is very strange, and amusing too, I think.

BENEATHA: You—you are almost religious.

ASAGAI: Yes . . . I think I have the religion of doing what is necessary in the world— and of worshipping man—because he is so marvelous, you see.

BENEATHA: Man is foul! And the human race deserves its misery!

ASAGAI: You see: *you* have become the religious one in the old sense. Already, and after such a small defeat, you are worshipping despair.

BENEATHA: From now on, I worship the truth—and the truth is that people are puny, small and selfish . . .

ASAGAI: Truth? Why is it that you despairing ones always think that only you have the truth? I never thought to see *you* like that. You! Your brother made a stupid, childish mistake—and you are grateful to him. So that now you can give up the ailing human race on account of it. You talk about what good is struggle; what good is anything? Where are we all going? And why are we bothering?

BENEATHA: *And you cannot answer it!* All your talk and dreams about Africa and Independence. Independence and then what? What about all the crooks and petty thieves and just plain idiots who will come into power to steal and plunder the same as before—only now they will be black and do it in the name of the new Independence—You cannot answer that.

ASAGAI: [*Shouting over her.*] *I live the answer!* [*Pause.*] In my village at home it is the exceptional man who can even read a newspaper . . . or who ever *sees* a book at all. I will go home and much of what I will have to say will seem strange to the people of my village . . . But I will teach and work and things will happen, slowly and swiftly. At times it will seem that nothing changes at all . . . and then again . . . the sudden dramatic events which make history leap into the future. And then quiet again. Retrogression even. Guns, murder, revolution. And I even will have moments when I wonder if the quiet was not better than all that death and hatred. But I will look about my village at the illiteracy and disease and ignorance and I will not wonder long. And perhaps . . . perhaps I will be a great man . . . I mean perhaps I will hold on to the substance of truth and find my way always with the right course . . . and perhaps for it I will be butchered in my bed some night by the servants of empire . . .

BENEATHA: *The martyr!*

ASAGAI: . . . or perhaps I shall live to be a very old man, respected and esteemed in my new nation . . . And perhaps I shall hold office and this is what I'm trying to tell you, Alaiyo; perhaps the things I believe now for my country will be wrong and outmoded, and I will not understand and do terrible things to have things my way or merely to keep my power. Don't you see that there will be young men and women, not British soldiers then, but my own black coun-trymen . . . to step out of the shadows some evening and slit my then useless throat? Don't you see they have always been there . . . that they always will be. And that such a thing as my own death will be an advance? They who might kill me even . . . actually replenish me!

BENEATHA: Oh, Asagai, I know all that.

ASAGAI: Good! Then stop moaning and groaning and tell me what you plan to do.

BENEATHA: Do?

ASAGAI: I have a bit of a suggestion.

BENEATHA: What?

ASAGAI: [*Rather quietly for him.*] That when it is all over—that you come home with me—

BENEATHA: [*Slapping herself on the forehead with exasperation born of misunderstanding.*] Oh—Asagai—at this moment you decide to be romantic!

ASAGAI: [*Quickly understanding the misunderstanding.*] My dear, young creature of the New World—I do not mean across the city—I mean across the ocean; home—to Africa.

BENEATHA: [*Slowly understanding and turning to him with murmured amazement.*] To—to Nigeria?

ASAGAI: Yes! . . . [*Smiling and lifting his arms playfully.*] Three hundred years later the African Prince rose up out of the seas and swept the maiden back across the middle passage[6] over which her ancestors had come—

BENEATHA: [*Unable to play.*] Nigeria?

ASAGAI: Nigeria. Home. [*Coming to her with genuine romantic flippancy.*] I will show you our mountains and our stars; and give you cool drinks from gourds and teach you the old songs and the ways of our people—and, in time, we will pre-tend that— [*Very softly.*] —you have only been away for a day—

[*She turns her back to him, thinking. He swings her around and takes her full in his arms in a long embrace which proceeds to passion.*]

BENEATHA: [*Pulling away.*] You're getting me all mixed up—

ASAGAI: Why?

BENEATHA: Too many things—too many things have happened today. I must sit down and think. I don't know what I feel about anything right this minute.

[*She promptly sits down and props her chin on her fist.*]

ASAGAI: [*Charmed.*] All right, I shall leave you. No—don't get up. [*Touching her, gen-tly, sweetly.*] Just sit awhile and think . . . Never be afraid to sit awhile and think. [*He goes to door and looks at her.*] How often I have looked at you and said, "Ah—so this is what the New World hath finally wrought . . ."[7]

[*He exits.* BENEATHA *sits on alone. Presently* WALTER *enters from his room and starts to rummage through things, feverishly looking for something. She looks up and turns in her seat.*]

---

6. Term denoting the route traveled by slaves transported from Africa to the Americas.
7. Allusion to the biblical exclamation "What hath God wrought!" (Numbers 23.23).

BENEATHA: [*Hissingly.*] Yes—just look at what the New World hath wrought! . . . Just look! [*She gestures with bitter disgust.*] There he is! *Monsieur le petit bourgeois noir*[8]—himself! There he is—Symbol of a Rising Class! Entrepreneur! Titan of the system! [WALTER *ignores her completely and continues frantically and destructively looking for something and hurling things to the floor and tearing things out of their place in his search.* BENEATHA *ignores the eccentricity of his actions and goes on with the monologue of insult.*] Did you dream of yachts on Lake Michigan, Brother? Did you see yourself on that Great Day sitting down at the Conference Table, surrounded by all the mighty bald-headed men in America? All halted, waiting, breathless, waiting for your pronouncements on industry? Waiting for you—Chairman of the Board? [WALTER *finds what he is looking for—a small piece of white paper—and pushes it in his pocket and puts on his coat and rushes out without ever having looked at her. She shouts after him.*] I look at you and I see the final triumph of stupidity in the world!

[*The door slams and she returns to just sitting again.* RUTH *comes quickly out of* MAMA's *room.*]

RUTH: Who was that?
BENEATHA: Your husband.
RUTH: Where did he go?
BENEATHA: Who knows—maybe he has an appointment at U.S. Steel.
RUTH: [*Anxiously, with frightened eyes.*] You didn't say nothing bad to him, did you?
BENEATHA: Bad? Say anything bad to him? No—I told him he was a sweet boy and full of dreams and everything is strictly peachy keen, as the ofay[9] kids say!

[MAMA *enters from her bedroom. She is lost, vague, trying to catch hold, to make some sense of her former command of the world, but it still eludes her. A sense of waste overwhelms her gait; a measure of apology rides on her shoulders. She goes to her plant, which has remained on the table, looks at it, picks it up and takes it to the window sill and sits it outside, and she stands and looks at it a long moment. Then she closes the window, straightens her body with effort and turns around to her children.*]

MAMA: Well—ain't it a mess in here, though? [*A false cheerfulness, a beginning of something.*] I guess we all better stop moping around and get some work done. All this unpacking and everything we got to do. [RUTH *raises her head slowly in response to the sense of the line; and* BENEATHA *in similar manner turns very slowly to look at her mother.*] One of you all better call the moving people and tell 'em not to come.
RUTH: Tell 'em not to come?
MAMA: Of course, baby. Ain't no need in 'em coming all the way here and having to go back. They charges for that too. [*She sits down, fingers to her brow, thinking.*] Lord, ever since I was a little girl, I always remembers people saying, "Lena—Lena Eggleston, you aims too high all the time. You needs to slow down and see life a little more like it is. Just slow down some." That's what they always used to say down home—"Lord, that Lena Eggleston is a high-minded thing. She'll get her due one day!"
RUTH: No, Lena . . .
MAMA: Me and Big Walter just didn't never learn right.

8. Mister Black Middle-Class (French).   9. White.

RUTH: Lena, no! We gotta go. Bennie—tell her . . . [*She rises and crosses to* BENEATHA *with her arms outstretched.* BENEATHA *doesn't respond.*] Tell her we can still move . . . the notes ain't but a hundred and twenty-five a month. We got four grown people in this house—we can work . . .

MAMA: [*To herself.*] Just aimed too high all the time—

RUTH: [*Turning and going to* MAMA *fast—the words pouring out with urgency and desperation.*] Lena—I'll work . . . I'll work twenty hours a day in all the kitchens in Chicago . . . I'll strap my baby on my back if I have to and scrub all the floors in America and wash all the sheets in America if I have to—but we got to move . . . We got to get out of here . . .

[MAMA *reaches out absently and pats* RUTH*'s hand.*]

MAMA: No—I sees things differently now. Been thinking 'bout some of the things we could do to fix this place up some. I seen a second-hand bureau over on Maxwell Street[1] just the other day that could fit right there. [*She points to where the new furniture might go.* RUTH *wanders away from her.*] Would need some new handles on it and then a little varnish and then it look like something brand-new. And—we can put up them new curtains in the kitchen . . . Why this place be looking fine. Cheer us all up so that we forget trouble ever came . . . [*To* RUTH.] And you could get some nice screens to put up in your room round the baby's bassinet . . . [*She looks at both of them, pleadingly.*] Sometimes you just got to know when to give up some things . . . and hold on to what you got.

[WALTER *enters from the outside, looking spent and leaning against the door, his coat hanging from him.*]

MAMA: Where you been, son?

WALTER: [*Breathing hard.*] Made a call.

MAMA: To who, son?

WALTER: To The Man.

MAMA: What man, baby?

WALTER: The Man, Mama. Don't you know who The Man is?

RUTH: Walter Lee?

WALTER: *The Man.* Like the guys in the streets say—The Man. Captain Boss—Mistuh Charley . . . Old Captain Please Mr. Bossman . . .

BENEATHA: [*Suddenly.*] Lindner!

WALTER: That's right! That's good. I told him to come right over.

BENEATHA: [*Fiercely, understanding.*] For what? What do you want to see him for!

WALTER: [*Looking at his sister.*] We going to do business with him.

MAMA: What you talking 'bout, son?

WALTER: Talking 'bout life, Mama. You all always telling me to see life like it is. Well—I laid in there on my back today . . . and I figured it out. Life just like it is. Who gets and who don't get. [*He sits down with his coat on and laughs.*] Mama, you know it's all divided up. Life is. Sure enough. Between the takers and the "tooken." [*He laughs.*] I've figured it out finally. [*He looks around at them.*] Yeah. Some of us always getting "tooken." [*He laughs.*] People like Willy Harris, they don't never get "tooken." And you know why the rest of us do? 'Cause we all mixed up. Mixed up bad. We get to looking 'round for the right and the wrong, and we worry about it and cry about it and stay up nights trying to figure out 'bout

1. Street market southwest of the Loop.

the wrong and the right of things all the time . . . And all the time, man, them takers is out there operating, just taking and taking. Willy Harris? Shoot— Willy Harris don't even count. He don't even count in the big scheme of things. But I'll say one thing for old Willy Harris . . . he's taught me something. He's taught me to keep my eye on what counts in this world. Yeah— [*Shouting out a little.*] Thanks, Willy!

RUTH: What did you call that man for, Walter Lee?

WALTER: Called him to tell him to come on over to the show. Gonna put on a show for the man. Just what he wants to see. You see, Mama, the man came here today and he told us that them people out there where you want us to move—well they so upset they willing to pay us not to move out there. [*He laughs again.*] And—and oh, Mama—you would of been proud of the way me and Ruth and Bennie acted. We told him to get out . . . Lord have mercy! We told the man to get out. Oh, we was some proud folks this afternoon, yeah. [*He lights a cigarette.*] We were still full of that old-time stuff . . .

RUTH: [*Coming toward him slowly.*] You talking 'bout taking them people's money to keep us from moving in that house?

WALTER: I ain't just talking 'bout it, baby—I'm telling you that's what's going to happen.

BENEATHA: Oh, God! Where is the bottom! Where is the real honest-to-God bottom so he can't go any farther!

WALTER: See—that's the old stuff. You and that boy that was here today. You all want everybody to carry a flag and a spear and sing some marching songs, huh? You wanna spend your life looking into things and trying to find the right and the wrong part, huh? Yeah. You know what's going to happen to that boy someday—he'll find himself sitting in a dungeon, locked in forever— and the takers will have the key! Forget it, baby! There ain't no causes—there ain't nothing but taking in this world, and he who takes most is smartest— and it don't make a damn bit of difference *how.*

MAMA: You making something inside me cry, son. Some awful pain inside me.

WALTER: Don't cry, Mama. Understand. That white man is going to walk in that door able to write checks for more money than we ever had. It's important to him and I'm going to help him . . . I'm going to put on the show, Mama.

MAMA: Son—I come from five generations of people who was slaves and sharecroppers—but ain't nobody in my family never let nobody pay 'em no money that was a way of telling us we wasn't fit to walk the earth. We ain't never been that poor. [*Raising her eyes and looking at him.*] We ain't never been that dead inside.

BENEATHA: Well—we are dead now. All the talk about dreams and sunlight that goes on in this house. All dead.

WALTER: What's the matter with you all! I didn't make this world! It was give to me this way! Hell, yes, I want me some yachts someday! Yes, I want to hang some real pearls 'round my wife's neck. Ain't she supposed to wear no pearls? Somebody tell me—tell me, who decides which women is suppose to wear pearls in this world. I tell you I am a *man*—and I think my wife should wear some pearls in this world!

[*This last line hangs a good while and* WALTER *begins to move about the room. The word "Man" has penetrated his consciousness; he mumbles it to himself repeatedly between strange agitated pauses as he moves about.*]

MAMA: Baby, how you going to feel on the inside?

WALTER: Fine! . . . Going to feel fine . . . a man . . .

MAMA: You won't have nothing left then, Walter Lee.

WALTER: [*Coming to her.*] I'm going to feel fine, Mama. I'm going to look that son-of-a-bitch in the eyes and say— [*He falters.*] —and say, "All right, Mr. Lindner— [*He falters even more.*] —that's your neighborhood out there. You got the right to keep it like you want. You got the right to have it like you want. Just write the check and—the house is yours." And, and I am going to say— [*His voice almost breaks.*] And you—you people just put the money in my hand and you won't have to live next to this bunch of stinking niggers! . . . [*He straightens up and moves away from his mother, walking around the room.*] Maybe—maybe I'll just get down on my black knees . . . [*He does so;* RUTH *and* BENNIE *and* MAMA *watch him in frozen horror.*] Captain, Mistuh, Bossman. [*He starts crying.*] A-hee-hee-hee! [*Wringing his hands in profoundly anguished imitation.*] Yassss-suh! Great White Father, just gi' ussen de money, fo' God's sake, and we's ain't gwine come out deh and dirty up yo' white folks neighborhood . . .

[*He breaks down completely, then gets up and goes into the bedroom.*]

BENEATHA: That is not a man. That is nothing but a toothless rat.

MAMA: Yes—death done come in this here house. [*She is nodding, slowly, reflectively.*] Done come walking in my house. On the lips of my children. You what supposed to be my beginning again. You—what supposed to be my harvest. [*To* BENEATHA.] You—you mourning your brother?

BENEATHA: He's no brother of mine.

MAMA: What you say?

BENEATHA: I said that that individual in that room is no brother of mine.

MAMA: That's what I thought you said. You feeling like you better than he is today? [BENEATHA *does not answer.*] Yes? What you tell him a minute ago? That he wasn't a man? Yes? You give him up for me? You done wrote his epitaph too—like the rest of the world? Well, who give you the privilege?

BENEATHA: Be on my side for once! You saw what he just did, Mama! You saw him—down on his knees. Wasn't it you who taught me—to despise any man who would do that. Do what he's going to do.

MAMA: Yes—I taught you that. Me and your daddy. But I thought I taught you something else too . . . I thought I taught you to love him.

BENEATHA: Love him? There is nothing left to love.

MAMA: There is always something left to love. And if you ain't learned that, you ain't learned nothing. [*Looking at her.*] Have you cried for that boy today? I don't mean for yourself and for the family 'cause we lost the money. I mean for him; what he been through and what it done to him. Child, when do you think is the time to love somebody the most; when they done good and made things easy for everybody? Well then, you ain't through learning—because that ain't the time at all. It's when he's at his lowest and can't believe in hisself 'cause the world done whipped him so. When you starts measuring somebody, measure him right, child, measure him right. Make sure you done taken into account what hills and valleys he come through before he got to wherever he is.

[TRAVIS *bursts into the room at the end of the speech, leaving the door open.*]

TRAVIS: Grandmama—the moving men are downstairs! The truck just pulled up.

MAMA: [*Turning and looking at him.*] Are they, baby? They downstairs?

> [*She sighs and sits.* LINDNER *appears in the doorway. He peers in and knocks lightly, to gain attention, and comes in. All turn to look at him.*]

LINDNER: [*Hat and briefcase in hand.*] Uh—hello . . . [RUTH *crosses mechanically to the bedroom door and opens it and lets it swing open freely and slowly as the lights come up on* WALTER *within, still in his coat, sitting at the far corner of the room. He looks up and out through the room to* LINDNER.]

RUTH: He's here.

> [*A long minute passes and* WALTER *slowly gets up.*]

LINDNER: [*Coming to the table with efficiency, putting his briefcase on the table and starting to unfold papers and unscrew fountain pens.*] Well, I certainly was glad to hear from you people. [WALTER *has begun the trek out of the room, slowly and awkwardly, rather like a small boy, passing the back of his sleeve across his mouth from time to time.*] Life can really be so much simpler than people let it be most of the time. Well—with whom do I negotiate? You, Mrs. Younger, or your son here? [MAMA *sits with her hands folded on her lap and her eyes closed as* WALTER *advances.* TRAVIS *goes close to* LINDNER *and looks at the papers curiously.*] Just some official papers, sonny.

RUTH: Travis, you go downstairs.

MAMA: [*Opening her eyes and looking into* WALTER's.] No. Travis, you stay right here. And you make him understand what you doing, Walter Lee. You teach him good. Like Willy Harris taught you. You show where our five generations done come to. Go ahead, son—

WALTER: [*Looks down into his boy's eyes.* TRAVIS *grins at him merrily and* WALTER *draws him beside him with his arm lightly around his shoulders.*] Well, Mr. Lindner. [BENEATHA *turns away.*] We called you— [*There is a profound, simple groping quality in his speech.*] —because, well, me and my family [*He looks around and shifts from one foot to the other.*] Well—we are very plain people . . .

LINDNER: Yes—

WALTER: I mean—I have worked as a chauffeur most of my life—and my wife here, she does domestic work in people's kitchens. So does my mother. I mean—we are plain people . . .

LINDNER: Yes, Mr. Younger—

WALTER: [*Really like a small boy, looking down at his shoes and then up at the man.*] And—uh—well, my father, well, he was a laborer most of his life.

LINDNER: [*Absolutely confused.*] Uh, yes—

WALTER: [*Looking down at his toes once again.*] My father almost beat a man to death once because this man called him a bad name or something, you know what I mean?

LINDNER: No, I'm afraid I don't.

WALTER: [*Finally straightening up.*] Well, what I mean is that we come from people who had a lot of pride. I mean—we are very proud people. And that's my sister over there and she's going to be a doctor—and we are very proud—

LINDNER: Well—I am sure that is very nice, but—

WALTER: [*Starting to cry and facing the man eye to eye.*] What I am telling you is that we called you over here to tell you that we are very proud and that this is—this is my son, who makes the sixth generation of our family in this country, and that we have all thought about your offer and we have decided to move into our house because my father—my father—he earned it. [MAMA *has her eyes closed and is rocking back and forth as though she were in church, with her head nodding the amen yes.*] We don't want to make no trouble for nobody or fight no causes— but we will try to be good neighbors. That's all we got to say. [*He looks the man absolutely in the eyes.*] We don't want your money.

[*He turns and walks away from the man.*]

LINDNER: [*Looking around at all of them.*] I take it then that you have decided to occupy.

BENEATHA: That's what the man said.

LINDNER: [*To* MAMA *in her reverie.*] Then I would like to appeal to you, Mrs. Younger. You are older and wiser and understand things better I am sure . . .

MAMA: [*Rising.*] I am afraid you don't understand. My son said we was going to move and there ain't nothing left for me to say. [*Shaking her head with double meaning.*] You know how these young folks is nowadays, mister. Can't do a thing with 'em. Good-bye.

LINDNER: [*Folding up his materials.*] Well—if you are that final about it . . . There is nothing left for me to say. [*He finishes. He is almost ignored by the family, who are concentrating on* WALTER LEE. *At the door* LINDNER *halts and looks around.*] I sure hope you people know what you're doing.

[*He shakes his head and exits.*]

RUTH: [*Looking around and coming to life.*] Well, for God's sake—if the moving men are here—LET'S GET THE HELL OUT OF HERE!

MAMA: [*Into action.*] Ain't it the truth! Look at all this here mess. Ruth, put Travis' good jacket on him . . . Walter Lee, fix your tie and tuck your shirt in, you look just like somebody's hoodlum. Lord have mercy, where is my plant? [*She flies to get it amid the general bustling of the family, who are deliberately trying to ignore the nobility of the past moment.*] You all start on down . . . Travis child, don't go empty-handed . . . Ruth, where did I put that box with my skillets in it? I want to be in charge of it myself . . . I'm going to make us the biggest dinner we ever ate tonight . . . Beneatha, what's the matter with them stockings? Pull them things up, girl . . .

[*The family starts to file out as two moving men appear and begin to carry out the heavier pieces of furniture, bumping into the family as they move about.*]

BENEATHA: Mama, Asagai—asked me to marry him today and go to Africa—

MAMA: [*In the middle of her getting-ready activity.*] He did? You ain't old enough to marry nobody— [*Seeing the moving men lifting one of her chairs precariously.*] Darling, that ain't no bale of cotton, please handle it so we can sit in it again. I had that chair twenty-five years . . .

[*The movers sigh with exasperation and go on with their work.*]

BENEATHA: [*Girlishly and unreasonably trying to pursue the conversation.*] To go to Africa, Mama—be a doctor in Africa . . .

MAMA: [*Distracted.*] Yes, baby—

WALTER: Africa! What he want you to go to Africa for?

BENEATHA: To practice there . . .

WALTER: Girl, if you don't get all them silly ideas out your head! You better marry yourself a man with some loot . . .

BENEATHA: [*Angrily, precisely as in the first scene of the play.*] What have you got to do with who I marry!

WALTER: Plenty. Now I think George Murchison—

> [*He and* BENEATHA *go out yelling at each other vigorously;* BENEATHA *is heard saying that she would not marry* GEORGE MURCHISON *if he were Adam and she were Eve, etc. The anger is loud and real till their voices diminish.* RUTH *stands at the door and turns to* MAMA *and smiles knowingly.*]

MAMA: [*Fixing her hat at last.*] Yeah—they something all right, my children . . .

RUTH: Yeah—they're something. Let's go, Lena.

MAMA: [*Stalling, starting to look around at the house.*] Yes—I'm coming. Ruth—

RUTH: Yes?

MAMA: [*Quietly, woman to woman.*] He finally come into his manhood today, didn't he? Kind of like a rainbow after the rain . . .

RUTH: [*Biting her lip lest her own pride explode in front of* MAMA.] Yes, Lena.

> [WALTER's *voice calls for them raucously.*]

MAMA: [*Waving* RUTH *out vaguely.*] All right, honey—go on down. I be down directly.

> [RUTH *hesitates, then exits.* MAMA *stands, at last alone in the living room, her plant on the table before her as the lights start to come down. She looks around at all the walls and ceilings and suddenly, despite herself, while the children call below, a great heaving thing rises in her and she puts her fist to her mouth, takes a final desperate look, pulls her coat about her, pats her hat and goes out. The lights dim down. The door opens and she comes back in, grabs her plant, and goes out for the last time.*]

[CURTAIN.]

1959

(Continued)

him. He shares with Willy Loman the acute awareness that *something* is obstructing some abstract progress that he feels he *should* be making; that *something* is in the way of his ascendancy. It does not occur to either of them to question the nature of this desired "ascendancy." Walter accepts, he believes in the "world" as it has been presented to him. When we first meet him, he does not wish to alter *it*; merely to change *his* position in it. His mentors and his associates all take the view that the institutions which frustrate him are somehow impeccable, or, at best, "unfortunate." "Things being as they are," he must look to *himself* as the only source of any rewards he may expect. Within himself, he is encouraged to believe, are the only seeds of defeat or victory within the universe. And Walter believes this and when opportunity, haphazard and rooted in death, prevails, he acts.

Huge Obstacles

But the obstacles . . . are gigantic; the weight of the loss of the money is in fact, the weight of death. In Walter Lee Younger's life, somebody *has* to die for ten thousand bucks to pile up—if then. Elsewhere in the world, in the face of catastrophe, he might be tempted to don the saffron robes of acceptance and sit on a mountain top all day contemplating the divine justice of his misery. Or, history being what it is turning out to be, he might wander down to his first Communist Party meeting. But here in the dynamic and confusing postwar years on the Southside of Chicago, his choices of action are equal to those gestures only in symbolic terms. The American ghetto hero may give up and contemplate his misery in rose-colored bars to the melodies of hypnotic saxophones, but revolution seems alien to him in his circumstances (America), and it is easier to dream of personal wealth than of a communal state wherein universal dignity is supposed to be a corollary. Yet his position in time and space does allow for one other alternative; he may take his place on any one of a number of frontiers of challenge. Challenges (such as helping to break down restricted neighborhoods) which are admittedly limited because they most certainly do not threaten the basic social order.

Not So Small

But why is even this final choice possible . . . ? Well, that is where Walter departs from Willy Loman; there is a second pulse in his still-dual culture. His people have had "somewhere" they have been trying to get for so long that more sophisticated confusions do not yet bind them. . . . Walter is, despite his lack of consciousness of it, inextricably as much wedded to his special mass as Willy was to his, and the moods of each are able to decisively determine the dramatic typicality. Furthermore, the very nature of the situation of American Negroes can force their representative hero to recognize that for his *true* ascendancy he must ultimately be at

(Continued on next page)

(Continued)

cross-purposes with at least certain of his culture's values. It is to the pathos of Willy Loman that his section of American life seems to have momentarily lost that urgency; that he cannot, like Walter, draw on the strength of an incredible people who, historically, have simply refused to give up.

In other words, the symbolism of moving into the new house is quite as small as it seems and quite as significant. For if there are no waving flags and marching songs at the barricades as Walter marches out with his little battalion, it is not because the battle lacks nobility. On the contrary, he has picked up in his way, still imperfect and wobbly in his small view of human destiny, what I believe Arthur Miller once called "the golden thread of history." He becomes, in spite of those who are too intrigued with despair and hatred of man to see it, King Oedipus refusing to tear out his eyes, but attacking the Oracle instead. He is that last Jewish patriot manning his rifle in the burning ghetto at Warsaw; . . . he is the nine small heroes of Little Rock; he is Michelangelo creating David and Beethoven bursting forth with the Ninth Symphony. He is all those things because he has finally reached out in his tiny moment and caught that sweet essence which is human dignity, and it shines like the gold star-touched dream that it is in his eyes. We see, in the moment, I think, what becomes, and not for Negroes alone, but for Willy and all of us, entirely an American responsibility.

Out in the darkness where we watch, most of us are not afraid to cry.

*Lorraine Hansberry, "Willie Loman, Walter Younger, and He Who Must Live," *Village Voice* 12 (Aug. 1959): 7–8.

Norman Matlock (left) as Elesin and Ben Halley Jr. (middle) as the Praise-Singer in the 1979
Kennedy Center production of *Death and the King's Horseman*

WOLE SOYINKA

Death and the King's Horseman

Author's Note

This play is based on events which took place in Oyo, ancient Yoruba city of
Nigeria, in 1946. That year, the lives of Elesin (Olori Elesin), his son, and the
Colonial District Officer intertwined with the disastrous results set out in the
play. The changes I have made are in matters of detail, sequence, and of course
characterisation. The action has also been set back two or three years to while
the war was still on, for minor reasons of dramaturgy.

The factual account still exists in the archives of the British Colonial Administration. It has already inspired a fine play in Yoruba (Oba Wàjà) by Duro Lad-
ipo. It has also misbegotten a film by some German television company.

The bane of themes of this genre is that they are no sooner employed creatively than they acquire the facile tag of "clash of cultures," a prejudicial label
which, quite apart from its frequent misapplication, presupposes a potential
equality *in every given situation* of the alien culture and the indigenous, on the
actual soil of the latter. (In the area of misapplication, the overseas prize for
illiteracy and mental conditioning undoubtedly goes to the blurb-writer for the

American edition of my novel *Season of Anomy* who unblushingly declares that this work portrays the "clash between old values and new ways, between western methods and African traditions"!) It is thanks to this kind of perverse mentality that I find it necessary to caution the would-be producer of this play against a sadly familiar reductionist tendency, and to direct his vision instead to the far more difficult and risky task of eliciting the play's threnodic essence.

One of the more obvious alternative structures of the play would be to make the District Officer the victim of a cruel dilemma. This is not to my taste and it is not by chance that I have avoided dialogue or situation which would encourage this. No attempt should be made in production to suggest it. The Colonial Factor is an incident, a catalytic incident merely. The confrontation in the play is largely metaphysical, contained in the human vehicle which is Elesin and the universe of the Yoruba mind—the world of the living, the dead and the unborn, and the numinous passage which links all: transition. *Death and the King's Horseman* can be fully realised only through an evocation of music from the abyss of transition.

W. S.

CHARACTERS

PRAISE-SINGER	JOSEPH, *houseboy to the Pilkingses*
ELESIN, *Horseman of the King*	BRIDE
IYALOJA, *"Mother"*[1] *of the market*	H.R.H. THE PRINCE
SIMON PILKINGS, *District Officer*	THE RESIDENT[2]
JANE PILKINGS, *his wife*	AIDE-DE-CAMP
SERGEANT AMUSA	OLUNDE, *eldest son of Elesin*
DRUMMERS, WOMEN, YOUNG GIRLS, DANCERS AT THE BALL	

The play should run without an interval. For rapid scene changes, one adjustable outline set is very appropriate.

Scene 1

A passage through a market in its closing stages. The stalls are being emptied, mats folded. A few WOMEN *pass through on their way home, loaded with baskets. On a cloth-stand, bolts of cloth are taken down, display pieces folded and piled on a tray.* ELESIN OBA *enters along a passage before the market, pursued by his* DRUMMERS *and* PRAISE-SINGERS. *He is a man of enormous vitality, speaks, dances, and sings with that infectious enjoyment of life which accompanies all his actions.*

PRAISE-SINGER: Elesin o! Elesin Oba! Howu![3] What tryst is this the cockerel[4] goes to keep with such haste that he must leave his tail behind?

ELESIN: [*Slows down a bit, laughing.*] A tryst where the cockerel needs no adornment.

PRAISE-SINGER: O-oh, you hear that, my companions? That's the way the world goes. Because the man approaches a brand-new bride he forgets the long-faithful mother of his children.

ELESIN: When the horse sniffs the stable does he not strain at the bridle? The market is the long-suffering home of my spirit and the women are packing up

---

1. Leader of the market women.
2. Senior colonial administrator who outranks and oversees the district officer.
3. "Why have you come?"   4. Young domestic rooster.

to go. That Esu[5]-harassed day slipped into the stewpot while we feasted. We ate it up with the rest of the meat. I have neglected my women.

PRAISE-SINGER: We know all that. Still it's no reason for shedding your tail on this day of all days. I know the women will cover you in damask and *alari*[6] but when the wind blows cold from behind, that's when the fowl knows his true friends.

ELESIN: Olohun-iyo![7]

PRAISE-SINGER: Are you sure there will be one like me on the other side?

ELESIN: Olohun-iyo!

PRAISE-SINGER: Far be it for me to belittle the dwellers of that place but, a man is either born to his art or he isn't. And I don't know for certain that you'll meet my father, so who is going to sing these deeds in accents that will pierce the deafness of the ancient ones. I have prepared my going—just tell me: Olohun-iyo, I need you on this journey and I shall be behind you.

ELESIN: You're like a jealous wife. Stay close to me, but only on this side. My fame, my honour are legacies to the living; stay behind and let the world sip its honey from your lips.

PRAISE-SINGER: Your name will be like the sweet berry a child places under his tongue to sweeten the passage of food. The world will never spit it out.

ELESIN: Come then. This market is my roost. When I come among the women I am a chicken with a hundred mothers. I become a monarch whose palace is built with tenderness and beauty.

PRAISE-SINGER: They love to spoil you but beware. The hands of women also weaken the unwary.

ELESIN: This night I'll lay my head upon their lap and go to sleep. This night I'll touch feet with their feet in a dance that is no longer of this earth. But the smell of their flesh, their sweat, the smell of indigo[8] on their cloth, this is the last air I wish to breathe as I go to meet my great forebears.

PRAISE-SINGER: In their time the world was never tilted from its groove, it shall not be in yours.

ELESIN: The gods have said, No.

PRAISE-SINGER: In their time the great wars came and went, the little wars came and went; the white slavers came and went, they took away the heart of our race, they bore away the mind and muscle of our race.[9] The city fell and was rebuilt; the city fell and our people trudged through mountain and forest to found a new home[1] but—Elesin Oba, do you hear me?

ELESIN: I hear your voice, Olohun-iyo.

PRAISE-SINGER: Our world was never wrenched from its true course.

ELESIN: The gods have said, No.

PRAISE-SINGER: There is only one home to the life of a river-mussel; there is only one home to the life of a tortoise; there is only one shell to the soul of man; there is only one world to the spirit of our race. If that world leaves its course and smashes on boulders of the great void, whose world will give us shelter?

5. Yoruba trickster god often associated with doubleness, ambivalence, and duplicity.
6. A rich, woven cloth, brightly coloured [Soyinka's glossary].   7. Praise-singer.
8. Blue dye obtained from plants; it is associated with royalty and power.
9. Reference to the numerous wars among Yoruba kingdoms in the eighteenth and nineteenth centuries and to the transatlantic slave trade and its consequences.
1. As it sought to consolidate its authority in the sixteenth century, the Yoruba kingdom of Oyo had to build and rebuild its capital several times.

ELESIN: It did not in the time of my forebears, it shall not in mine.
PRAISE-SINGER: The cockerel must not be seen without his feathers.
ELESIN: Nor will the Not-I bird[2] be much longer without his nest.
PRAISE-SINGER: [*Stopped in his lyric stride.*] The Not-I bird, Elesin?
ELESIN: I said, The Not-I bird.
PRAISE-SINGER: All respect to our elders but, is there really such a bird?
ELESIN: What! Could it be that he failed to knock on your door?
PRAISE-SINGER: [*Smiling.*] Elesin's riddles are not merely the nut in the kernel[3] that breaks human teeth; he also buries the kernel in hot embers and dares a man's fingers to draw it out.
ELESIN: I am sure he called on you, Olohun-iyo. Did you hide in the loft and push out the servant to tell him you were out?

> [ELESIN *executes a brief, half-taunting dance. The* DRUMMER *moves in and draws a rhythm out of his steps.* ELESIN *dances towards the market-place as he chants the story of the Not-I bird, his voice changing dexterously to mimic his characters. He performs like a born raconteur, infecting his retinue with his humour and energy. More* WOMEN *arrive during his recital, including* IYALOJA.]

Death came calling.
Who does not know his rasp of reeds?
A twilight whisper in the leaves before
The great araba[4] falls? Did you hear it?
Not I! swears the farmer. He snaps
His fingers round his head, abandons
A hard-worn harvest and begins
A rapid dialogue with his legs.
"Not I," shouts the fearless hunter, "but—
It's getting dark, and this night-lamp
Has leaked out all its oil. I think
It's best to go home and resume my hunt
Another day." But now he pauses, suddenly
Lets out a wail: "Oh foolish mouth, calling
Down a curse on your own head! Your lamp
Has leaked out all its oil, has it?"
Forwards or backwards now he dare not move.
To search for leaves and make *etutu*[5]
On that spot? Or race home to the safety
Of his hearth? Ten market-days have passed
My friends, and still he's rooted there
Rigid as the plinth of Orayan.[6]
The mouth of the courtesan barely
Opened wide enough to take a ha'penny *robo*[7]
When she wailed: "Not I." All dressed she was

---

2. Bird whose chirping sounds like it is saying "Not I" in Yoruba.   3. Soft, edible part of a palm nut.
4. Silk cotton tree or kapok.   5. Placatory rites or medicine [Soyinka's glossary].
6. Tall plinth or landmark in Ile-Ife, considered to be the ancestral home of the Yoruba. Orayan was one of the children of Oduduwa, the founding father of the Yoruba people.
7. Delicacy made from crushed melon seeds, fried in tiny balls [Soyinka's glossary].

To call upon my friend the Chief Tax Officer.
But now she sends her go-between instead:
"Tell him I'm ill: my period has come suddenly
But not—I hope—my time."

Why is the pupil crying?
His hapless head was made to taste
The knuckles of my friend the Mallam.[8]
"If you were then reciting the Koran
Would you have ears for idle noises
Darkening the trees, you child of ill omen?"
He shuts down school before its time
Runs home and rings himself with amulets.

And take my good kinsman, Ifawomi.
His hands were like a carver's, strong
And true. I saw them
Tremble like wet wings of a fowl
One day he cast his time-smoothed *opele*[9]
Across the divination board. And all because
The suppliant looked him in the eye and asked,
"Did you hear that whisper in the leaves?"
"Not I," was his reply; "perhaps I'm growing deaf—
Good-day." And Ifa spoke no more that day
The priest locked fast his doors,
Sealed up his leaking roof—but wait!
This sudden care was not for Fawomi[1]
But for Osanyin,[2] courier-bird of Ifa's
Heart of wisdom. I did not know a kite
Was hovering in the sky
And Ifa now a twittering chicken in
The brood of Fawomi the Mother Hen.

Ah, but I must not forget my evening
Courier from the abundant palm, whose groan
Became Not I, as he constipated down
A wayside bush. He wonders if Elegbara[3]
Has tricked his buttocks to discharge
Against a sacred grove. Hear him
Mutter spells to ward off penalties
For an abomination he did not intend.
If any here
Stumbles on a gourd of wine, fermenting
Near the road, and nearby hears a stream
Of spells issuing from a crouching form,

---

8. Muslim teacher.   9. String of beads used in Ifa divination [Soyinka's glossary].
1. Contraction of "Ifawomi," meaning "Ifa watches over me." Ifa is the Yoruba god of divination.
2. Patron deity of diviners and medicine men in Yoruba culture.
3. Another name for Esu, the trickster god.

> Brother to a *sigidi*,[4] bring home my wine,
> Tell my tapper[5] I have ejected
> Fear from home and farm. Assure him,
> All is well.

PRAISE-SINGER: In your time we do not doubt the peace of farmstead and home,
    the peace of road and hearth, we do not doubt the peace of the forest.

ELESIN: There was fear in the forest too.
    Not I was lately heard even in the lair
    Of beasts. The hyena cackled loud: Not I,
    The civet twitched his fiery tail and glared:
    Not I. Not-I became the answering-name
    Of the restless bird, that little one
    Whom Death found nesting in the leaves
    When whisper of his coming ran
    Before him on the wind. Not-I
    Has long abandoned home. This same dawn
    I heard him twitter in the gods' abode.
    Ah, companions of this living world
    What a thing this is, that even those
    We call immortal
    Should fear to die.

IYALOJA: But you, husband of multitudes?

ELESIN: I, when that Not-I bird perched
    Upon my roof, bade him seek his nest again,
    Safe, without care or fear. I unrolled
    My welcome mat for him to see. Not-I
    Flew happily away, you'll hear his voice
    No more in this lifetime—You all know
    What I am.

PRAISE-SINGER: That rock which turns its open lodes
    Into the path of lightning. A gay
    Thoroughbred whose stride disdains
    To falter though an adder reared
    Suddenly in his path.

ELESIN: My rein is loosened.
    I am master of my Fate. When the hour comes
    Watch me dance along the narrowing path
    Glazed by the soles of my great precursors.
    My soul is eager. I shall not turn aside.

WOMEN: You will not delay?

ELESIN: Where the storm pleases, and when, it directs
    The giants of the forest. When friendship summons
    Is when the true comrade goes.

WOMEN: Nothing will hold you back?

ELESIN: Nothing. What! Has no one told you yet?
    I go to keep my friend and master company.

---

4. Squat, carved figure, endowed with the powers of an incubus [Soyinka's glossary]. An incubus is an imaginary evil spirit that descends on sleeping people.

5. Person whose profession is to tap palm trees for their sap, which is fermented into a wine.

Who says the mouth does not believe in
"No, I have chewed all that before?" I say I have.
The world is not a constant honey-pot.
Where I found little I made do with little.
Where there was plenty I gorged myself.
My master's hands and mine have always
Dipped together and, home or sacred feast,
The bowl was beaten bronze, the meats
So succulent our teeth accused us of neglect.
We shared the choicest of the season's
Harvest of yams. How my friend would read
Desire in my eyes before I knew the cause—
However rare, however precious, it was mine.

WOMEN: The town, the very land was yours.

ELESIN: The world was mine. Our joint hands
Raised houseposts of trust that withstood
The siege of envy and the termites of time.
But the twilight hour brings bats and rodents—
Shall I yield them cause to foul the rafters?

PRAISE-SINGER: Elesin Oba! Are you not that man who
Looked out of doors that stormy day
The god of luck[6] limped by, drenched
To the very lice that held
His rags together? You took pity upon
His sores and wished him fortune.
Fortune was footloose this dawn, he replied,
Till you trapped him in a heartfelt wish
That now returns to you. Elesin Oba!
I say you are that man who
Chanced upon the calabash[7] of honour
You thought it was palm wine and
Drained its contents to the final drop.

ELESIN: Life has an end. A life that will outlive
Fame and friendship begs another name.
What elder takes his tongue to his plate,
Licks it clean of every crumb? He will encounter
Silence when he calls on children to fulfill
The smallest errand! Life is honour.
It ends when honour ends.

WOMEN: We know you for a man of honour.

ELESIN: Stop! Enough of that!

WOMEN: [*Puzzled, they whisper among themselves, turning mostly to* IYALOJA.] What is
it? Did we say something to give offence? Have we slighted him in some way?

ELESIN: Enough of that sound I say. Let me hear no more in that vein. I've heard
enough.

6. Possibly a reference to Esu Elegba, the trickster god, who, especially in New World versions, limps because one leg is shorter than the other.
7. Cup or bowl made from half of a gourd, usually used to serve food or drink.

IYALOJA: We must have said something wrong. [*Comes forward a little.*] Elesin Oba, we ask forgiveness before you speak.

ELESIN: I am bitterly offended.

IYALOJA: Our unworthiness has betrayed us. All we can do is ask your forgiveness. Correct us like a kind father.

ELESIN: This day of all days . . .

IYALOJA: It does not bear thinking. If we offend you now we have mortified the gods. We offend heaven itself. Father of us all, tell us where we went astray. [*She kneels, the other women follow.*]

ELESIN: Are you not ashamed? Even a tear-veiled
    Eye preserves its function of sight.
    Because my mind was raised to horizons
    Even the boldest man lowers his gaze
    In thinking of, must my body here
    Be taken for a vagrant's?

IYALOJA: Horseman of the King, I am more baffled than ever.

PRAISE-SINGER: The strictest father unbends his brow when the child is penitent, Elesin. When time is short, we do not spend it prolonging the riddle. Their shoulders are bowed with the weight of fear lest they have marred your day beyond repair. Speak now in plain words and let us pursue the ailment to the home of remedies.

ELESIN: Words are cheap. "We know you for
    A man of honour." Well tell me, is this how
    A man of honour should be seen?
    Are these not the same clothes in which
    I came among you a full half-hour ago?

> [*He roars with laughter and the* WOMEN, *relieved, rise and rush into stalls to fetch rich cloths.*]

WOMEN: The gods are kind. A fault soon remedied is soon forgiven.
    Elesin Oba, even as we match our words with deed, let your heart forgive us completely.

ELESIN: You who are breath and giver of my being
    How shall I dare refuse you forgiveness
    Even if the offence were real.

IYALOJA: [*Dancing round him. Sings.*]
    He forgives us. He forgives us.
    What a fearful thing it is when
    The voyager sets forth
    But a curse remains behind.

WOMEN: For a while we truly feared
    Our hands had wrenched the world adrift
    In emptiness.

IYALOJA: Richly, richly, robe him richly
    The cloth of honour is *alari*
    Sanyan[8] is the band of friendship
    Boa-skin[9] makes slippers of esteem.

WOMEN: For a while we truly feared

---

8. A richly valued woven cloth [Soyinka's glossary].   9. Skin from a boa constrictor.

Our hands had wrenched the world adrift
In emptiness.
PRAISE-SINGER: He who must, must voyage forth
The world will not roll backwards.
It is he who must, with one
Great gesture overtake the world.
WOMEN: For a while we truly feared
Our hands had wrenched the world
In emptiness.
PRAISE-SINGER: The gourd you bear is not for shirking.
The gourd is not for setting down
At the first crossroad or wayside grove.
Only one river may know its contents.
WOMEN: We shall all meet at the great market.[1]
We shall all meet at the great market
He who goes early takes the best bargains
But we shall meet, and resume our banter.

> [ELESIN *stands resplendent in rich clothes, cap, shawl, etc. His sash is of a bright red alari cloth. The* WOMEN *dance round him. Suddenly, his attention is caught by an object off-stage.*]

ELESIN: The world I know is good.
WOMEN: We know you'll leave it so.
ELESIN: The world I know is the bounty
Of hives after bees have swarmed.
No goodness teems with such open hands
Even in the dreams of deities.
WOMEN: And we know you'll leave it so.
ELESIN: I was born to keep it so. A hive
Is never known to wander. An anthill
Does not desert its roots. We cannot see
The still great womb of the world—
No man beholds his mother's womb—
Yet who denies it's there? Coiled
To the navel of the world is that
Endless cord that links us all
To the great origin. If I lose my way
The trailing cord will bring me to the roots.
WOMEN: The world is in your hands.

> [*The earlier distraction, a beautiful* YOUNG GIRL, *comes along the passage through which* ELESIN *first made his entry.*]

ELESIN: I embrace it. And let me tell you, women—
I like this farewell that the world designed,
Unless my eyes deceive me, unless
We are already parted, the world and I,
And all that breeds desire is lodged
Among our tireless ancestors. Tell me, friends,

---

1. That is, in the afterlife.

Am I still earthed in that beloved market
Of my youth? Or could it be my will
Has outleapt the conscious act and I have come
Among the great departed?

PRAISE-SINGER: Elesin-Oba, why do your eyes roll like a bush rat who sees his fate
like his father's spirit, mirrored in the eye of a snake? And all these questions!
You're standing on the same earth you've always stood upon. This voice you
hear is mine, Oluhun-iyo, not that of an acolyte in heaven.

ELESIN: How can that be? In all my life
As Horseman of the King, the juiciest
Fruit on every tree was mine. I saw,
I touched, I wooed, rarely was the answer No.
The honour of my place, the veneration I
Received in the eye of man or woman
Prospered my suit and
Played havoc with my sleeping hours.
And they tell me my eyes were a hawk
In perpetual hunger. Split an iroko[2] tree
In two, hide a woman's beauty in its heartwood
And seal it up again—Elesin, journeying by,
Would make his camp beside that tree
Of all the shades in the forest.

PRAISE-SINGER: Who would deny your reputation, snake-on-the-loose in dark
passages of the market! Bed-bug who wages war on the mat and receives
the thanks of the vanquished! When caught with his bride's own sister he
protested—but I was only prostrating myself to her as becomes a grateful in-
law. Hunter who carries his powder-horn[3] on the hips and fires crouching or
standing! Warrior who never makes that excuse of the whining coward—but
how can I go to battle without my trousers?—trouserless or shirtless it's all
one to him. Oka[4]-rearing-from-a-camouflage-of-leaves, before he strikes the
victim is already prone! Once they told him, Howu, a stallion does not feed
on the grass beneath him: he replied, true, but surely he can roll on it!

WOMEN: Ba-a-a-ba O!

PRAISE-SINGER: Ah, but listen yet. You know there is the leaf-nibbling grub and
there is the cola-chewing beetle; the leaf-nibbling grub lives on the leaf, the
cola-chewing beetle lives in the colanut.[5] Don't we know what our man feeds
on when we find him cocooned in a woman's wrapper?

ELESIN: Enough, enough, you all have cause
To know me well. But, if you say this earth
Is still the same as gave birth to those songs,
Tell me who was that goddess through whose lips
I saw the ivory pebbles of Oya's[6] riverbed.
Iyaloja, who is she? I saw her enter

---

2. An African teak, a large tree believed, in Yoruba folklore, to be inhabited by a roguish fairy or spirit.
The heartwood of the iroko tree is multi-colored.
3. Yoruba hunters carry their gunpowder in a horn.   4. Python.
5. Seed of the cola (kola) nut tree valued by long-distance drivers for its caffeine, but also used as a ritual
symbol of welcome.   6. Oya is the goddess of the Niger River and patron of fishermen and sailors.

Your stall; all your daughters I know well.
No, not even Ogun[7]-of-the-farm toiling.
Dawn till dusk on his tuber patch
Not even Ogun with the finest hoe he ever
Forged at the anvil could have shaped
That rise of buttocks, not though he had
The richest earth between his fingers.
Her wrapper was no disguise
For thighs whose ripples shamed the river's
Coils around the hills of Ilesi.[8] Her eyes
Were new-laid eggs glowing in the dark.
Her skin . . .

IYALOJA: Elesin Oba . . .

ELESIN: What! Where do you all say I am?

IYALOJA: Still among the living.

ELESIN: And that radiance which so suddenly
    Lit up this market I could boast
    I knew so well?

IYALOJA: Has one step already in her husband's home. She is betrothed.

ELESIN: [*Irritated.*] Why do you tell me that?

[IYALOJA *falls silent. The* WOMEN *shuffle uneasily.*]

IYALOJA: Not because we dare give you offence, Elesin. Today is your day and the whole world is yours. Still, even those who leave town to make a new dwelling elsewhere like to be remembered by what they leave behind.

ELESIN: Who does not seek to be remembered?
    Memory is Master of Death, the chink
    In his armour of conceit. I shall leave
    That which makes my going the sheerest
    Dream of an afternoon. Should voyagers
    Not travel light? Let the considerate traveller
    Shed, of his excessive load, all
    That may benefit the living.

WOMEN: [*Relieved.*] Ah Elesin Oba, we knew you for a man of honour.

ELESIN: Then honour me. I deserve a bed of honour to lie upon.

IYALOJA: The best is yours. We know you for a man of honour. You are not one who eats and leaves nothing on his plate for children. Did you not say it yourself? Not one who blights the happiness of others for a moment's pleasure.

ELESIN: Who speaks of pleasure? O women, listen!
    Pleasure palls. Our acts should have meaning.
    The sap of the plantain[9] never dries.
    You have seen the young shoot swelling
    Even as the parent stalk begins to wither.
    Women, let my going be likened to

---

7. God of iron and war, of hunters, soldiers, and blacksmiths; also considered the patron of artists.
8. District and town in Oyo, western Nigeria.
9. A variety of banana, a popular staple of the tropical regions of Africa.

The twilight hour of the plantain.

WOMEN: What does he mean, Iyaloja? This language is the language of our elders, we do not fully grasp it.

IYALOJA: I dare not understand you yet, Elesin.

ELESIN: All you who stand before the spirit that dares
The opening of the last door of passage,
Dare to rid my going of regrets! My wish
Transcends the blotting out of thought
In one mere moment's tremor of the senses.
Do me credit. And do me honour.
I am girded for the route beyond
Burdens of waste and longing.
Then let me travel light. Let
Seed that will not serve the stomach
On the way remain behind. Let it take root
In the earth of my choice, in this earth
I leave behind.

IYALOJA: [*Turns to* WOMEN.] The voice I hear is already touched by the waiting fingers of our departed. I dare not refuse.

WOMAN: But Iyaloja . . .

IYALOJA: The matter is no longer in our hands.

WOMAN: But she is betrothed to your own son. Tell him.

IYALOJA: My son's wish is mine. I did the asking for him, the loss can be remedied. But who will remedy the blight of closed hands on the day when all should be openness and light? Tell him, you say! You wish that I burden him with knowledge that will sour his wish and lay regrets on the last moments of his mind. You pray to him who is your intercessor to the world—don't set this world adrift in your own time; would you rather it was my hand whose sacrilege wrenched it loose?

WOMAN: Not many men will brave the curse of a dispossessed husband.

IYALOJA: Only the curses of the departed are to be feared. The claims of one whose foot is on the threshold of their abode surpasses even the claims of blood. It is impiety even to place hindrances in their ways.

ELESIN: What do my mothers say? Shall I step
Burdened into the unknown?

IYALOJA: Not we, but the very earth says No. The sap in the plantain does not dry. Let grain that will not feed the voyager at his passage drop here and take root as he steps beyond this earth and us. Oh you who fill the home from hearth to threshold with the voices of children, you who now bestride the hidden gulf and pause to draw the right foot across and into the resting-home of the great forebears, it is good that your loins be drained into the earth we know, that your last strength be ploughed back into the womb that gave you being.

PRAISE-SINGER: Iyaloja, mother of multitudes in the teeming market of the world, how your wisdom transfigures you!

IYALOJA: [*Smiling broadly, completely reconciled.*] Elesin, even at the narrow end of the passage I know you will look back and sigh a last regret for the flesh that flashed past your spirit in flight. You always had a restless eye. Your choice has my blessing. [*To the* WOMEN.] Take the good news to our daughter and make her ready. [*Some* WOMEN *go off.*]

ELESIN: Your eyes were clouded at first.

IYALOJA: Not for long. It is those who stand at the gateway of the great change to whose cry we must pay heed. And then, think of this—it makes the mind tremble. The fruit of such a union is rare. It will be neither of this world nor of the next. Nor of the one behind us. As if the timelessness of the ancestor world and the unborn have joined spirits to wring an issue of the elusive being of passage . . . Elesin!

ELESIN: I am here. What is it?

IYALOJA: Did you hear all I said just now?

ELESIN: Yes.

IYALOJA: The living must eat and drink. When the moment comes, don't turn the food to rodents' droppings in their mouth. Don't let them taste the ashes of the world when they step out at dawn to breathe the morning dew.

ELESIN: This doubt is unworthy of you, Iyaloja.

IYALOJA: Eating the awusa[1] nut is not so difficult as drinking water afterwards.

ELESIN: The waters of the bitter stream are honey to a man
Whose tongue has savoured all.

IYALOJA: No one knows when the ants desert their home; they leave the mound intact. The swallow is never seen to peck holes in its nest when it is time to move with the season. There are always throngs of humanity behind the leave-taker. The rain should not come through the roof for them, the wind must not blow through the walls at night.

ELESIN: I refuse to take offence.

IYALOJA: You wish to travel light. Well, the earth is yours. But be sure the seed you leave in it attracts no curse.

ELESIN: You really mistake my person, Iyaloja.

IYALOJA: I said nothing. Now we must go prepare your bridal chamber. Then these same hands will lay your shrouds.

ELESIN: [*Exasperated.*] Must you be so blunt? [*Recovers.*] Well, weave your shrouds, but let the fingers of my bride seal my eyelids with earth and wash my body.

IYALOJA: Prepare yourself, Elesin.

[*She gets up to leave. At that moment the* WOMEN *return, leading the* BRIDE. ELESIN'S *face glows with pleasure. He flicks the sleeves of his agbada[2] with renewed confidence and steps forward to meet the group. As the girl kneels before* IYALOJA, *lights fade out on the scene.*]

Scene 2

The verandah of the District Officer's bungalow. A tango is playing from an old hand-cranked gramophone and, glimpsed through the wide windows and doors which open onto the forestage verandah are the shapes of SIMON PILKINGS *and his wife,* JANE, *tangoing in and out of shadows in the living-room. They are wearing what is immediately apparent as some form of fancy-dress.[3] The dance goes on for some moments and then the figure of a* "NATIVE ADMINISTRATION" POLICEMAN[4] *emerges and climbs up the steps onto the verandah. He peeps through and observes the dancing couple, reacting with what is obviously a*

1. A climbing plant.
2. Large, flowing robe usually worn by men and often embroidered at the neck and chest.
3. Costume, usually representing some historical or fictitious character.
4. African policeman belonging to a unit charged with the policing of Africans and considered inferior to the regular police.

long-standing bewilderment. He stiffens suddenly, his expression changes to one of disbelief and horror. In his excitement he upsets a flowerpot and attracts the attention of the couple. They stop dancing.

PILKINGS: Is there anyone out there?

JANE: I'll turn off the gramophone.

PILKINGS: [*Approaching the verandah.*] I'm sure I heard something fall over. [*The* CONSTABLE *retreats slowly, open-mouthed as* PILKINGS *approaches the verandah.*] Oh, it's you, Amusa. Why didn't you just knock instead of knocking things over?

AMUSA: [*Stammers badly and points a shaky finger at his dress.*] Mista Pirinkin . . . Mista Pirinkin . . .

PILKINGS: What is the matter with you?

JANE: [*Emerging.*] Who is it dear? Oh, Amusa . . .

PILKINGS: Yes, it's Amusa, and acting most strangely.

AMUSA: [*His attention now transferred to* MRS PILKINGS.] Mammadam . . . you too!

PILKINGS: What the hell is the matter with you, man!

JANE: Your costume, darling. Our fancy dress.

PILKINGS: Oh hell, I'd forgotten all about that. [*Lifts the face mask over his head showing his face. His wife follows suit.*]

JANE: I think you've shocked his big pagan heart, bless him.

PILKINGS: Nonsense, he's a Moslem. Come on, Amusa, you don't believe in all this nonsense, do you? I thought you were a good Moslem.

AMUSA: Mista Pirinkin, I beg you sir, what you think you do with that dress? It belong to dead cult, not for human being.

PILKINGS: Oh Amusa, what a let-down you are. I swear by you at the club you know—thank God for Amusa, he doesn't believe in any mumbo-jumbo. And now look at you!

AMUSA: Mista Pirinkin, I beg you, take it off. Is not good for man like you to touch that cloth.

PILKINGS: Well, I've got it on. And what's more, Jane and I have bet on it we're taking first prize at the ball. Now, if you can just pull yourself together and tell me what you wanted to see me about . . .

AMUSA: Sir, I cannot talk this matter to you in that dress. I no fit.

PILKINGS: What's that rubbish again?

JANE: He is dead earnest too, Simon. I think you'll have to handle this delicately.

PILKINGS: Delicately my . . . ! Look here, Amusa, I think this little joke has gone far enough, hm? Let's have some sense. You seem to forget that you are a police officer in the service of His Majesty's Government. I order you to report your business at once or face disciplinary action.

AMUSA: Sir, it is a matter of death. How can man talk against death to person in uniform of death? Is like talking against government to person in uniform of police. Please sir, I go and come back.

PILKINGS: [*Roars.*] Now! [AMUSA *switches his gaze to the ceiling suddenly, remains mute.*]

JANE: Oh Amusa, what is there to be scared of in the costume? You saw it confiscated last month from those *egungun*[5] men who were creating trouble in town.

---

5. Ancestral masquerade [Soyinka's glossary]. The masked figures in the masquerade are considered to be the reincarnated spirits of ancestors; their dress is often a long grass robe and a wooden mask representing the face or head of an animal.

You helped arrest the cult leaders yourself—if the juju[6] didn't harm you at the time how could it possibly harm you now? And merely by looking at it?

AMUSA: [*Without looking down.*] Madam, I arrest the ringleaders who make trouble but me I no touch *egungun*. That *egungun* itself, I no touch. And I no abuse 'am. I arrest ringleader but I treat *egungun* with respect.

PILKINGS: It's hopeless. We'll merely end up missing the best part of the ball. When they get this way there is nothing you can do. It's simply hammering against a brick wall. Write your report or whatever it is on that pad, Amusa, and take yourself out of here. Come on, Jane. We only upset his delicate sensibilities by remaining here.

[AMUSA *waits for them to leave, then writes in the notebook, somewhat laboriously. Drumming from the direction of the town wells up.* AMUSA *listens, makes a movement as if he wants to recall* PILKINGS *but changes his mind. Completes his note and goes. A few moments later* PILKINGS *emerges, picks up the pad and reads.*]

PILKINGS: Jane!

JANE: [*From the bedroom.*] Coming, darling. Nearly ready.

PILKINGS: Never mind being ready, just listen to this.

JANE: What is it?

PILKINGS: Amusa's report. Listen. "I have to report that it come to my information that one prominent chief, namely, the Elesin Oba, is to commit death tonight as a result of native custom. Because this is criminal offence I await further instruction at charge office. Sergeant Amusa."

[JANE *comes out onto the verandah while he is reading.*]

JANE: Did I hear you say commit death?

PILKINGS: Obviously he means murder.

JANE: You mean a ritual murder?

PILKINGS: Must be. You think you've stamped it all out but it's always lurking under the surface somewhere.

JANE: Oh. Does it mean we are not getting to the ball at all?

PILKINGS: No-o. I'll have the man arrested. Everyone remotely involved. In any case there may be nothing to it. Just rumours.

JANE: Really? I thought you found Amusa's rumours generally reliable.

PILKINGS: That's true enough. But who knows what may have been giving him the scare lately. Look at his conduct tonight.

JANE: [*Laughing.*] You have to admit he had his own peculiar logic. [*Deepens her voice.*] How can man talk against death to person in uniform of death? [*Laughs.*] Anyway, you can't go into the police station dressed like that.

PILKINGS: I'll send Joseph with instructions. Damn it, what a confounded nuisance!

JANE: But don't you think you should talk first to the man, Simon?

PILKINGS: Do you want to go to the ball or not?

JANE: Darling, why are you getting rattled? I was only trying to be intelligent. It seems hardly fair just to lock up a man—and a chief at that—simply on the er . . . what is the legal word again?—uncorroborated word of a sergeant.

PILKINGS: Well, that's easily decided. Joseph!

6. Magic, usually attributed to a fetish.

JOSEPH: [*From within.*] Yes, master.

PILKINGS: You're quite right of course, I am getting rattled. Probably the effect of those bloody drums. Do you hear how they go on and on?

JANE: I wondered when you'd notice. Do you suppose it has something to do with this affair?

PILKINGS: Who knows? They always find an excuse for making a noise . . . [*Thoughtfully.*] Even so . . .

JANE: Yes Simon?

PILKINGS: It's different, Jane. I don't think I've heard this particular—sound—before. Something unsettling about it.

JANE: I thought all bush drumming sounded the same.

PILKINGS: Don't tease me now, Jane. This may be serious.

JANE: I'm sorry. [*Gets up and throws her arms around his neck. Kisses him. The* HOUSEBOY *enters, retreats and knocks.*]

PILKINGS: [*Wearily.*] Oh, come in, Joseph! I don't know where you pick up all these elephantine notions of tact. Come over here.

JOSEPH: Sir?

PILKINGS: Joseph, are you a Christian or not?

JOSEPH: Yessir.

PILKINGS: Does seeing me in this outfit bother you?

JOSEPH: No sir, it has no power.

PILKINGS: Thank God for some sanity at last. Now Joseph, answer me on the honour of a Christian—what is supposed to be going on in town tonight?

JOSEPH: Tonight, sir? You mean the chief who is going to kill himself?

PILKINGS: What?

JANE: What do you mean, kill himself?

PILKINGS: You do mean he is going to kill somebody, don't you?

JOSEPH: No, master. He will not kill anybody and no one will kill him. He will simply die.

JANE: But why, Joseph?

JOSEPH: It is native law and custom. The King die last month. Tonight is his burial. But before they can bury him, the Elesin must die so as to accompany him to heaven.

PILKINGS: I seem to be fated to clash more often with that man than with any of the other chiefs.

JOSEPH: He is the King's Chief Horseman.

PILKINGS: [*In a resigned way.*] I know.

JANE: Simon, what's the matter?

PILKINGS: It would have to be him!

JANE: Who is he?

PILKINGS: Don't you remember? He's that chief with whom I had a scrap some three or four years ago. I helped his son get to a medical school in England, remember? He fought tooth and nail to prevent it.

JANE: Oh, now I remember. He was that very sensitive young man. What was his name again?

PILKINGS: Olunde. Haven't replied to his last letter, come to think of it. The old pagan wanted him to stay and carry on some family tradition or the other. Honestly I couldn't understand the fuss he made. I literally had to help the boy escape from close confinement and load him onto the next boat. A most intelligent boy, really bright.

JANE: I rather thought he was much too sensitive, you know. The kind of person you feel should be a poet munching rose petals in Bloomsbury.[7]

PILKINGS: Well, he's going to make a first-class doctor. His mind is set on that. And as long as he wants my help he is welcome to it.

JANE: [*After a pause.*] Simon.

PILKINGS: Yes?

JANE: This boy, he was the eldest son, wasn't he?

PILKINGS: I'm not sure. Who could tell with that old ram?

JANE: Do you know, Joseph?

JOSEPH: Oh yes, madam. He was the eldest son. That's why Elesin cursed master good and proper. The eldest son is not supposed to travel away from the land.

JANE: [*Giggling.*] Is that true, Simon? Did he really curse you good and proper?

PILKINGS: By all accounts I should be dead by now.

JOSEPH: Oh no, master is white man. And good Christian. Black man juju can't touch master.

JANE: If he was his eldest, it means that he would be the Elesin to the next king. It's a family thing, isn't it, Joseph?

JOSEPH: Yes, madam. And if this Elesin had died before the King, his eldest son must take his place.

JANE: That would explain why the old chief was so mad you took the boy away.

PILKINGS: Well, it makes me all the more happy I did.

JANE: I wonder if he knew.

PILKINGS: Who? Oh, you mean Olunde?

JANE: Yes. Was that why he was so determined to get away? I wouldn't stay if I knew I was trapped in such a horrible custom.

PILKINGS: [*Thoughtfully.*] No, I don't think he knew. At least he gave no indication. But you couldn't really tell with him. He was rather close you know, quite unlike most of them. Didn't give much away, not even to me.

JANE: Aren't they all rather close, Simon?

PILKINGS: These natives here? Good gracious. They'll open their mouths and yap with you about their family secrets before you can stop them. Only the other day . . .

JANE: But Simon, do they really give anything away? I mean, anything that really counts. This affair for instance, we didn't know they still practised that custom, did we?

PILKINGS: Ye-e-es, I suppose you're right there. Sly, devious bastards.

JOSEPH: [*Stiffly.*] Can I go now, master? I have to clean the kitchen.

PILKINGS: What? Oh, you can go. Forgot you were still there.

[JOSEPH *goes.*]

JANE: Simon, you really must watch your language. Bastard isn't just a simple swear-word in these parts, you know.

PILKINGS: Look, just when did you become a social anthropologist, that's what I'd like to know.

JANE: I'm not claiming to know anything. I just happen to have overheard quarrels among the servants. That's how I know they consider it a smear.

PILKINGS: I thought the extended family system took care of all that. Elastic family, no bastards.

7. Area of central London next to the British Museum; it is associated with art and high culture.

JANE: [*Shrugs.*] Have it your own way.

[*Awkward silence. The drumming increases in volume.* JANE *gets up suddenly, restless.*]

That drumming, Simon, do you think it might really be connected with this ritual? It's been going on all evening.

PILKINGS: Let's ask our native guide. Joseph! Just a minute, Joseph. [JOSEPH *re-enters.*] What's the drumming about?

JOSEPH: I don't know, master.

PILKINGS: What do you mean, you don't know? It's only two years since your conversion. Don't tell me all that holy water nonsense also wiped out your tribal memory.

JOSEPH: [*Visibly shocked.*] Master!

JANE: Now you've done it.

PILKINGS: What have I done now?

JANE: Never mind. Listen, Joseph, just tell me this. Is that drumming connected with dying or anything of that nature?

JOSEPH: Madam, this is what I am trying to say: I am not sure. It sounds like the death of a great chief and then, it sounds like the wedding of a great chief. It really mix me up.

PILKINGS: Oh, get back to the kitchen. A fat lot of help you are.

JOSEPH: Yes, master. [*Goes.*]

JANE: Simon . . .

PILKINGS: Alright, alright. I'm in no mood for preaching.

JANE: It isn't my preaching you have to worry about, it's the preaching of the missionaries who preceded you here. When they make converts they really convert them. Calling holy water nonsense to our Joseph is really like insulting the Virgin Mary before a Roman Catholic. He's going to hand in his notice tomorrow, you mark my word.

PILKINGS: Now you're being ridiculous.

JANE: Am I? What are you willing to bet that tomorrow we are going to be without a steward-boy?[8] Did you see his face?

PILKINGS: I am more concerned about whether or not we will be one native chief short by tomorrow. Christ! Just listen to those drums. [*He strides up and down, undecided.*]

JANE: [*Getting up.*] I'll change and make us some supper.

PILKINGS: What's that?

JANE: Simon, it's obvious we have to miss this ball.

PILKINGS: Nonsense. It's the first bit of real fun the European club has managed to organise for over a year, I'm damned if I'm going to miss it. And it is a rather special occasion. Doesn't happen every day.

JANE: You know this business has to be stopped, Simon. And you are the only man who can do it.

PILKINGS: I don't have to stop anything. If they want to throw themselves off the top of a cliff or poison themselves for the sake of some barbaric custom what is that to me? If it were ritual murder or something like that I'd be duty-

---

8. Houseboy, servant.

bound to do something. I can't keep an eye on all the potential suicides in this province. And as for that man—believe me, it's good riddance.

JANE: [*Laughs.*] I know you better than that, Simon. You are going to have to do something to stop it—after you've finished blustering.

PILKINGS: [*Shouts after her.*] And suppose after all it's only a wedding. I'd look a proper fool if I interrupted a chief on his honeymoon, wouldn't I? [*Resumes his angry stride, slows down.*] Ah well, who can tell what those chiefs actually do on their honeymoon anyway? [*He takes up the pad and scribbles rapidly on it.*] Joseph! Joseph! Joseph! [*Some moments later* JOSEPH *puts in a sulky appearance.*] Did you hear me call you? Why the hell didn't you answer?

JOSEPH: I didn't hear, master.

PILKINGS: You didn't hear me! How come you are here, then?

JOSEPH: [*Stubbornly.*] I didn't hear, master.

PILKINGS: [*Controls himself with an effort.*] We'll talk about it in the morning. I want you to take this note directly to Sergeant Amusa. You'll find him at the charge office.[9] Get on your bicycle and race there with it. I expect you back in twenty minutes exactly. Twenty minutes, is that clear?

JOSEPH: Yes, master. [*Going.*]

PILKINGS: Oh er . . . Joseph.

JOSEPH: Yes, master?

PILKINGS: [*Between gritted teeth.*] Er . . . forget what I said just now. The holy water is not nonsense. *I* was talking nonsense.

JOSEPH: Yes, master. [*Goes.*]

JANE: [*Pokes her head round the door.*] Have you found him?

PILKINGS: Found who?

JANE: Joseph. Weren't you shouting for him?

PILKINGS: Oh yes, he turned up finally.

JANE: You sounded desperate. What was it all about?

PILKINGS: Oh, nothing. I just wanted to apologise to him. Assure him that the holy water isn't really nonsense.

JANE: Oh? And how did he take it?

PILKINGS: Who the hell gives a damn! I had a sudden vision of our Very Reverend Macfarlane drafting another letter of complaint to the Resident about my unchristian language towards his parishioners.

JANE: Oh, I think he's given up on you by now.

PILKINGS: Don't be too sure. And anyway, I wanted to make sure Joseph didn't "lose" my note on the way. He looked sufficiently full of the holy crusade to do some such thing.

JANE: If you've finished exaggerating, come and have something to eat.

PILKINGS: No, put it all away. We can still get to the ball.

JANE: Simon . . .

PILKINGS: Get your costume back on. Nothing to worry about. I've instructed Amusa to arrest the man and lock him up.

JANE: But that station is hardly secure, Simon. He'll soon get his friends to help him escape.

PILKINGS: A-ah, that's where I have out-thought you. I'm not having him put in the station cell. Amusa will bring him right here and lock him up in my study.

9. Booking office of a police station.

And he'll stay with him till we get back. No one will dare come here to incite him to anything.

JANE: How clever of you, darling. I'll get ready.

PILKINGS: Hey.

JANE: Yes, darling.

PILKINGS: I have a surprise for you. I was going to keep it until we actually got to the ball.

JANE: What is it?

PILKINGS: You know the Prince is on a tour of the colonies, don't you? Well, he docked in the capital only this morning but he is already at the Residency. He is going to grace the ball with his presence later tonight.

JANE: Simon! Not really.

PILKINGS: Yes, he is. He's been invited to give away the prizes and he has agreed. You must admit old Engleton is the best Club Secretary we ever had. Quick off the mark, that lad.

JANE: But how thrilling.

PILKINGS: The other provincials are going to be damned envious.

JANE: I wonder what he'll come as.

PILKINGS: Oh, I don't know. As a coat-of-arms perhaps. Anyway it won't be anything to touch this.

JANE: Well, that's lucky. If we are to be presented I won't have to start looking for a pair of gloves. It's all sewn on.

PILKINGS: [*Laughing.*] Quite right. Trust a woman to think of that. Come on, let's get going.

JANE: [*Rushing off.*] Won't be a second. [*Stops.*] Now I see why you've been so edgy all evening. I thought you weren't handling this affair with your usual brilliance—to begin with that is.

PILKINGS: [*His mood is much improved.*] Shut up, woman, and get your things on.

JANE: Alright, boss—coming.

> [PILKINGS *suddenly begins to hum the tango to which they were dancing before. Starts to execute a few practice steps. Lights fade.*]

Scene 3

A swelling, agitated hum of women's voices rises immediately in the background. The lights come on and we see the frontage of a converted cloth stall in the market. The floor leading up to the entrance is covered in rich velvets and woven cloth. The WOMEN *come on stage, borne backwards by the determined progress of Sergeant* AMUSA *and his two* CONSTABLES, *who already have their batons out and use them as a pressure against the* WOMEN. *At the edge of the cloth-covered floor, however, the* WOMEN *take a determined stand and block all further progress of the men. They begin to tease them mercilessly.*

AMUSA: I am tell you women for last time to commot my road.[1] I am here on official business.

WOMAN: Official business, you white man's eunuch? Official business is taking place where you want to go and it's a business you wouldn't understand.

---

1. "Get out of my way"; literally, "come out of my road" in pidgin English.

WOMAN: [*Makes a quick tug at the* CONSTABLE's *baton.*] That doesn't fool anyone, you know. It's the one you carry under your government knickers[2] that counts. [*She bends low as if to peep under the baggy shorts. The embarrassed* CONSTABLE *quickly puts his knees together. The* WOMEN *roar.*]

WOMAN: You mean there is nothing there at all?

WOMAN: Oh, there was something. You know that handbell which the whiteman uses to summon his servants . . . ?

AMUSA: [*He manages to preserve some dignity throughout.*] I hope you women know that interfering with officer in execution of his duty is criminal offence.

WOMAN: Interfere? He says we're interfering with him. You foolish man, we're telling you there's nothing to interfere with.

AMUSA: I am order you now to clear the road.

WOMAN: What road? The one your father built?

WOMAN: You are a policeman, not so? Then you know what they call trespassing in court. Or— [*Pointing to the cloth-lined steps.*]—do you think that kind of road is built for every kind of feet?

WOMAN: Go back and tell the white man who sent you to come himself.

AMUSA: If I go I will come back with reinforcement. And we will all return carrying weapons.

WOMAN: Oh, now I understand. Before they can put on those knickers the white man first cuts off their weapons.

WOMAN: What a cheek! You mean you come here to show power to women and you don't even have a weapon.

AMUSA: [*Shouting above the laughter.*] For the last time, I warn you women to clear the road.

WOMAN: To where?

AMUSA: To that hut. I know he dey dere.

WOMAN: Who?

AMUSA: The chief who call himself Elesin Oba.

WOMAN: You ignorant man. It is not he who calls himself Elesin Oba, it is his blood that says it. As it called out to his father before him and will to his son after him. And that is in spite of everything your white man can do.

WOMAN: Is it not the same ocean that washes this land and the white man's land? Tell your white man he can hide our son away as long as he likes. When the time comes for him, the same ocean will bring him back.

AMUSA: The government say dat kin' ting[3] must stop.

WOMAN: Who will stop it? You? Tonight our husband and father will prove himself greater than the laws of strangers.

AMUSA: I tell you nobody go prove anything tonight or anytime. Is ignorant and criminal to prove dat kin' prove.

IYALOJA: [*Entering, from the hut. She is accompanied by a group of* YOUNG GIRLS *who have been attending the* BRIDE.] What is it, Amusa? Why do you come here to disturb the happiness of others?

AMUSA: Madame Iyaloja, I glad you come. You know me, I no like trouble but duty is duty. I am here to arrest Elesin for criminal intent. Tell these women to stop obstructing me in the performance of my duty.

2. Women's underpants. The reference here is to the khaki shorts worn by colonial policemen.
3. "That kind of thing" in pidgin English.

IYALOJA: And you? What gives you the right to obstruct our leader of men in the performance of his duty?

AMUSA: What kin' duty be dat one, Iyaloja?

IYALOJA: What kin' duty? What kin' duty does a man have to his new bride?

AMUSA: [*Bewildered, looks at the* WOMEN *and at the entrance to the hut.*] Iyaloja, is it wedding you call dis kin' ting?

IYALOJA: You have wives, haven't you? Whatever the white man has done to you he hasn't stopped you having wives. And if he has, at least he is married. If you don't know what a marriage is, go and ask him to tell you.

AMUSA: This no to wedding.

IYALOJA: And ask him at the same time what he would have done if anyone had come to disturb him on his wedding night.

AMUSA: Iyaloja, I say dis no to wedding.

IYALOJA: You want to look inside the bridal chamber? You want to see for yourself how a man cuts the virgin knot?

AMUSA: Madam . . .

WOMAN: Perhaps his wives are still waiting for him to learn.

AMUSA: Iyaloja, make you tell dese women make den no insult me again. If I hear dat kin' insult once more . . .

GIRL: [*Pushing her way through.*] You will do what?

GIRL: He's out of his mind. It's our mothers you're talking to, do you know that? Not to any illiterate villager you can bully and terrorise. How dare you intrude here anyway?

GIRL: What a cheek, what impertinence!

GIRL: You've treated them too gently. Now let them see what it is to tamper with the mothers of this market.

GIRL: Your betters dare not enter the market when the women say no!

GIRL: Haven't you learnt that yet, you jester in khaki and starch?

IYALOJA: Daughters . . .

GIRL: No no, Iyaloja, leave us to deal with him. He no longer knows his mother, we'll teach him.

> [*With a sudden movement they snatch the batons of the two* CONSTABLES. *They begin to hem them in.*]

GIRL: What next? We have your batons? What next? What are you going to do?

> [*With equally swift movements they knock off their hats.*]

GIRL: Move if you dare. We have your hats, what will you do about it? Didn't the white man teach you to take off your hats before women?

IYALOJA: It's a wedding night. It's a night of joy for us. Peace . . .

GIRL: Not for him. Who asked him here?

GIRL: Does he dare go to the Residency without an invitation?

GIRL: Not even where the servants eat the leftovers.

GIRL: [*In turn. In an "English" accent.*] Well well, it's Mister Amusa. Were you invited? [*Playacting to one another. The older* WOMEN *encourage them with their titters.*]

—Your invitation card please?

—Who are you? Have we been introduced?

—And who did you say you were?

—Sorry, I didn't quite catch your name.

—May I take your hat?
—If you insist. May I take yours? [*Exchanging the* POLICEMEN's *hats.*]
—How very kind of you.
—Not at all. Won't you sit down?
—After you.
—Oh no.
—I insist.
—You're most gracious.
—And how do you find the place?
—The natives are alright.
—Friendly?
—Tractable.
—Not a teeny-weeny bit restless?
—Well, a teeny-weeny bit restless.
—One might even say, difficult?
—Indeed one might be tempted to say, difficult.
—But you do manage to cope?
—Yes, indeed I do. I have a rather faithful ox called Amusa.
—He's loyal?
—Absolutely.
—Lay down his life for you what?
—Without a moment's thought.
—Had one like that once. Trust him with my life.
—Mostly of course they are liars.
—Never known a native to tell the truth.
—Does it get rather close around here?
—It's mild for this time of the year.
—But the rains may still come.
—They are late this year aren't they?
—They are keeping African time.
—Ha ha ha ha
—Ha ha ha ha
—The humidity is what gets me.
—It used to be whisky.
—Ha ha ha ha
—Ha ha ha ha
—What's your handicap, old chap?
—Is there racing by golly?
—Splendid golf course, you'll like it.
—I'm beginning to like it already.
—And a European club, exclusive.
—You've kept the flag flying.
—We do our best for the old country.
—It's a pleasure to serve.
—Another whisky, old chap?
—You are indeed too too kind.
—Not at all sir. Where is that boy? [*With a sudden bellow.*] Sergeant!
AMUSA: [*Snaps to attention.*] Yessir!

[*The* WOMEN *collapse with laughter.*]

GIRL: Take your men out of here.

AMUSA: [*Realising the trick, he rages from loss of face.*] I'm give you warning . . .

GIRL: Alright then. Off with his knickers! [*They surge slowly forward.*]

IYALOJA: Daughters, please.

AMUSA: [*Squaring himself for defence.*] The first woman wey touch me . . .

IYALOJA: My children, I beg of you . . .

GIRL: Then tell him to leave this market. This is the home of our mothers. We don't want the eater of white left-overs at the feast their hands have prepared.

IYALOJA: You heard them, Amusa. You had better go.

GIRL: Now!

AMUSA: [*Commencing his retreat.*] We dey go now, but make you no say we no warn you.

GIRL: Now!

GIRL: Before we read the riot act—you should know all about that.

AMUSA: Make we go. [*They depart, more precipitately.*]

> [*The* WOMEN *strike their palms across in the gesture of wonder.*]

WOMEN: Do they teach you all that at school?

WOMAN: And to think I nearly kept Apinke away from the place.

WOMAN: Did you hear them? Did you see how they mimicked the white man?

WOMAN: The voices exactly. Hey, there are wonders in this world!

IYALOJA: Well, our elders have said it: Dada may be weak, but he has a younger sibling who is truly fearless.[4]

WOMAN: The next time the white man shows his face in this market I will set Wuraola[5] on his tail.

> [*A* WOMAN *bursts into song and dance of euphoria—'Tani l'awa o l'ogbeja? Kayi! A l'ogbeja. Omo Kekere l'ogbeja.'*[6] *The rest of the* WOMEN *join in, some placing the* GIRLS *on their back like infants, others dancing round them. The dance becomes general, mounting in excitement.* ELESIN *appears, in wrapper only. In his hands a white velvet cloth folded loosely as if it held some delicate object. He cries out.*]

ELESIN: Oh, you mothers of beautiful brides! [*The dancing stops. They turn and see him, and the object in his hands.* IYALOJA *approaches and gently takes the cloth from him.*] Take it. It is no mere virgin stain, but the union of life and the seeds of passage. My vital flow, the last from this flesh is intermingled with the promise of future life. All is prepared. Listen! [*A steady drum-beat from the distance.*] Yes. It is nearly time. The King's dog has been killed. The King's favourite horse is about to follow his master. My brother chiefs know their task and perform it well. [*He listens again.*]

> [*The* BRIDE *emerges, stands shyly by the door. He turns to her.*]

Our marriage is not yet wholly fulfilled. When earth and passage wed, the consummation is complete only when there are grains of earth on the eyelids of passage. Stay by me till then. My faithful drummers, do me your last

---

4. Dada, the mythical king of Oyo and patron god of newborns, reputedly abdicated in favor of his fierce younger brother, Shango, the god of thunder and lightning.   5. "Rich gold," a common name for a girl.
6. "Who says we haven't a defender? Silence! We have our defenders. Little children are our champions" [Soyinka's translation].

service. This is where I have chosen to do my leave-taking, in this heart of life, this hive which contains the swarm of the world in its small compass. This is where I have known love and laughter away from the palace. Even the richest food cloys when eaten days on end; in the market, nothing ever cloys. Listen. [*They listen to the drums.*] They have begun to seek out the heart of the King's favourite horse. Soon it will ride in its bolt of raffia[7] with the dog at its feet. Together they will ride on the shoulders of the King's grooms through the pulse centres of the town. They know it is here I shall await them. I have told them. [*His eyes appear to cloud. He passes his hand over them as if to clear his sight. He gives a faint smile.*] It promises well; just then I felt my spirit's eagerness. The kite makes for wide spaces and the wind creeps up behind its tail; can the kite say less than—thank you, the quicker the better? But wait a while my spirit. Wait. Wait for the coming of the courier of the King. Do you know, friends, the horse is born to this one destiny, to bear the burden that is man upon its back. Except for this night, this night alone when the spotless stallion will ride in triumph on the back of man. In the time of my father I witnessed the strange sight. Perhaps tonight also I shall see it for the last time. If they arrive before the drums beat for me, I shall tell them to let the Alafin[8] know I follow swiftly. If they come after the drums have sounded, why then, all is well for I have gone ahead. Our spirits shall fall in step along the great passage. [*He listens to the drums. He seems again to be falling into a state of semi-hypnosis; his eyes scan the sky but it is in a kind of daze. His voice is a little breathless.*] The moon has fed, a glow from its full stomach fills the sky and air, but I cannot tell where is that gateway through which I must pass. My faithful friends, let our feet touch together this last time, lead me into the other market with sounds that cover my skin with down yet make my limbs strike earth like a thoroughbred. Dear mothers, let me dance into the passage even as I have lived beneath your roofs. [*He comes down progressively among them. They make way for him, the* DRUMMERS *playing. His dance is one of solemn, regal motions, each gesture of the body is made with a solemn finality. The* WOMEN *join him, their steps a somewhat more fluid version of his. Beneath the* PRAISE-SINGER's *exhortations the women dirge "Alẹ lẹ lẹ, awo mi lọ."*[9]].

PRAISE-SINGER: Elesin Alafin, can you hear my voice?

ELESIN: Faintly, my friend, faintly.

PRAISE-SINGER: Elesin Alafi, can you hear my call?

ELESIN: Faintly, my king, faintly.

PRAISE-SINGER: Is your memory sound, Elesin?
Shall my voice be a blade of grass and
Tickle the armpit of the past?

ELESIN: My memory needs no prodding but
What do you wish to say to me?

PRAISE-SINGER: Only what has been spoken. Only what concerns
The dying wish of the father of all.

ELESIN: It is buried like seed-yam in my mind.
This is the season of quick rains, the harvest
Is this moment due for gathering.

---

7. Fiber from raffia palms, used in making skirts for masqueraders.   8. King of the Yoruba.
9. "Night has fallen, the seasoned initiate is leaving" (Yoruba).

PRAISE-SINGER: If you cannot come, I said, swear
  You'll tell my favourite horse. I shall
  Ride on through the gates alone.
ELESIN: Elesin's message will be read
  Only when his loyal heart no longer beats.
PRAISE-SINGER: If you cannot come, Elesin, tell my dog.
  I cannot stay the keeper too long
  At the gate.
ELESIN: A dog does not outrun the hand
  That feeds it meat. A horse that throws its rider
  Slows down to a stop. Elesin Alafin
  Trusts no beasts with messages between
  A king and his companion.
PRAISE-SINGER: If you get lost my dog will track
  The hidden path to me.
ELESIN: The seven-way crossroads[1] confuses
  Only the stranger. The Horseman of the King
  Was born in the recesses of the house.
PRAISE-SINGER: I know the wickedness of men. If there is
  Weight on the loose end of your sash, such weight
  As no mere man can shift; if your sash is earthed
  By evil minds who mean to part us at the last . . .
ELESIN: My sash is of the deep purple *alari*;
  It is no tethering-rope. The elephant
  Trails no tethering-rope; that king
  Is not yet crowed who will peg[2] an elephant—
  Not even you, my friend and King.
PRAISE-SINGER: And yet this fear will not depart from me
  The darkness of this new abode is deep—
  Will your human eyes suffice?
ELESIN: In a night which falls before our eyes
  However deep, we do not miss our way.
PRAISE-SINGER: Shall I now not acknowledge I have stood
  Where wonders met their end? The elephant deserves
  Better than that we say, "I have caught
  A glimpse of something." If we see the tamer
  Of the forest let us say plainly, we have seen
  An elephant.
ELESIN: [*His voice is drowsy.*]
  I have freed myself of earth and now
  It's getting dark. Strange voices guide my feet.
PRAISE-SINGER: The river is never so high that the eyes
  Of a fish are covered. The night is not so dark
  That the albino fails to find his way. A child
  Returning homewards craves no leading by the hand.
  Gracefully does the mask regain his grove at the end of the day . . .

---

1. In Yoruba cosmology, Esu Elegba, the god of confusion and doubleness, is often to be found at the crossroads.   2. Confine, pin down.

Gracefully. Gracefully does the mask dance
Homeward at the end of the day, gracefully . . .

[ELESIN's *trance appears to be deepening, his steps heavier.*]

IYALOJA: It is the death of war that kills the valiant,
Death of water is how the swimmer goes.
It is the death of markets that kills the trader
And death of indecision takes the idle away.
The trade of the cutlass blunts its edge
And the beautiful die the death of beauty.
It takes an Elesin to die the death of death . . .
Only Elesin . . . dies the unknowable death of death . . .
Gracefully, gracefully does the horseman regain
The stables at the end of day, gracefully . . .

PRAISE-SINGER: How shall I tell what my eyes have seen? The Horseman gallops on
before the courier, how shall I tell what my eyes have seen? He says a dog may
be confused by new scents of beings he never dreamt of, so he must precede the
dog to heaven. He says a horse may stumble on strange boulders and be lamed,
so he races on before the horse to heaven. It is best, he says, to trust no messenger who may falter at the outer gate; oh how shall I tell what my ears have
heard? But do you hear me still, Elesin, do you hear your faithful one?

[ELESIN *in his motions appears to feel for a direction of sound, subtly, but he only
sinks deeper into his trance-dance.*]

Elesin Alafin, I no longer sense your flesh. The drums are changing now but
you have gone far ahead of the world. It is not yet noon in heaven; let those
who claim it is begin their own journey home. So why must you rush like an
impatient bride: why do you race to desert your Olohun-iyo?

[ELESIN *is now sunk fully deep in his trance, there is no longer sign of any awareness
of his surroundings.*]

Does the deep voice of *gbedu*[3] cover you then, like the passage of royal elephants? Those drums that brook no rivals, have they blocked the passage to
your ears that my voice passes into wind, a mere leaf floating in the night? Is
your flesh lightened, Elesin, is that lump of earth I slid between your slippers
to keep you longer slowly sifting from your feet? Are the drums on the other
side now tuning skin to skin with ours in *osugbo*?[4] Are there sounds there I cannot hear, do footsteps surround you which pound the earth like *gbedu*, roll like
thunder round the dome of the world? Is the darkness gathering in your head,
Elesin? Is there now a streak of light at the end of the passage, a light I dare not
look upon? Does it reveal whose voices we often heard, whose touches we often
felt, whose wisdoms come suddenly into the mind when the wisest have shaken
their heads and murmured: It cannot be done? Elesin Alafin, don't think I do
not know why your lips are heavy, why your limbs are drowsy as palm oil in the
cold of harmattan.[5] I would call you back but when the elephant heads for the
jungle, the tail is too small a handhold for the hunter that would pull him

---

3. A deep-timbred royal drum [Soyinka's glossary].
4. Secret 'executive' cult of the Yoruba; its meeting place [Soyinka's glossary].
5. In west Africa, a dry, parching seasonal breeze carrying dusty winds from the Sahara Desert.

back. The sun that heads for the sea no longer heeds the prayers of the farmer. When the river begins to taste the salt of the ocean, we no longer know what deity to call on, the river-god or Olokun.[6] No arrow flies back to the string, the child does not return through the same passage that gave it birth. Elesin Oba, can you hear me at all? Your eyelids are glazed like a courtesan's, is it that you see the dark groom and master of life? And will you see my father? Will you tell him that I stayed with you to the last? Will my voice ring in your ears awhile, will you remember Olohun-iyo even if the music on the other side surpasses his mortal craft? But will they know you over there? Have they eyes to gauge your worth, have they the heart to love you, will they know what thoroughbred prances towards them in caparisons[7] of honour? If they do not, Elesin, if any there cuts your yam with a small knife, or pours you wine in a small calabash, turn back and return to welcoming hands. If the world were not greater than the wishes of Olohun-iyo, I would not let you go . . .

[*He appears to break down.* ELESIN *dances on, completely in a trance. The dirge wells up louder and stronger.* ELESIN's *dance does not lose its elasticity but his gestures become, if possible, even more weighty. Lights fade slowly on the scene.*]

Scene 4

A Masque.[8] *The front side of the stage is part of a wide corridor around the great hall of the Residency extending beyond vision into the rear and wings. It is redolent of the tawdry decadence of a far-flung but key imperial frontier. The couples in a variety of fancy-dress are ranged around the walls, gazing in the same direction. The guest-of-honour is about to make an appearance. A portion of the local police brass band with its white conductor is just visible. At last, the entrance of Royalty. The band plays "Rule Britannia," badly, beginning long before he is visible. The couples bow and curtsey as he passes by them. Both he and his companions are dressed in seventeenth-century European costume. Following behind are the* RESIDENT *and his partner similarly attired. As they gain the end of the hall where the orchestra dais begins the music comes to an end. The* PRINCE *bows to the guests. The band strikes up a Viennese waltz and the* PRINCE *formally opens the floor. Several bars later the* RESIDENT *and his companion follow suit. Others follow in appropriate pecking order. The orchestra's waltz rendition is not of the highest musical standard.*

Some time later the PRINCE *dances again into view and is settled into a corner by the* RESIDENT *who then proceeds to select couples as they dance past for introduction, sometimes threading his way through the dancers to tap the lucky couple on the shoulder. Desperate efforts from many to ensure that they are recognised in spite of, perhaps, their costume. The ritual of introductions soon takes in* PILKINGS *and his wife. The* PRINCE *is quite fascinated by their costume and they demonstrate the adaptations they have made to it, pulling down the mask to demonstrate how the* egungun *normally appears, then showing the various press-button controls they have innovated for the face flaps, the sleeves, etc. They demonstrate the dance steps and the guttural sounds made by the* egungun, *harass other dancers in the hall,* MRS. PILKINGS *playing the "restrainer"[9] to* PILKINGS' *manic darts. Everyone is highly entertained, the Royal Party especially who lead the applause.*

6. God of the ocean, worshiped by fishermen and sailors.
7. Cloths spread over the saddle or harness of a horse, often gaily ornamented.
8. Formal, European-style costume party with elaborate dress and masks.
9. Person who controls the movements of the dancing mask when its movements seem excessive.

At this point a liveried footman comes in with a note on a salver and is intercepted almost absent-mindedly by the RESIDENT *who takes the note and reads it. After polite coughs he succeeds in excusing the* PILKINGS *from the* PRINCE *and takes them aside. The* PRINCE *considerately offers the* RESIDENT'*s wife his hand and dancing is resumed.*

On their way out the RESIDENT *gives an order to his* AIDE-DE-CAMP.[1] *They come into the side corridor where the* RESIDENT *hands the note to* PILKINGS.

RESIDENT: As you see, it says "emergency" on the outside. I took the liberty of opening it because His Highness was obviously enjoying the entertainment. I didn't want to interrupt unless really necessary.

PILKINGS: Yes, yes of course, sir.

RESIDENT: Is it really as bad as it says? What's it all about?

PILKINGS: Some strange custom they have, sir. It seems because the King is dead some important chief has to commit suicide.

RESIDENT: The King? Isn't it the same one who died nearly a month ago?

PILKINGS: Yes, sir.

RESIDENT: Haven't they buried him yet?

PILKINGS: They take their time about these things, sir. The pre-burial ceremonies last nearly thirty days. It seems tonight is the final night.

RESIDENT: But what has it got to do with the market women? Why are they rioting? We've waived that troublesome tax,[2] haven't we?

PILKINGS: We don't quite know that they are exactly rioting yet, sir. Sergeant Amusa is sometimes prone to exaggerations.

RESIDENT: He sounds desperate enough. That comes out even in his rather quaint grammar. Where is the man, anyway? I asked my aide-de-camp to bring him here.

PILKINGS: They are probably looking in the wrong verandah. I'll fetch him myself.

RESIDENT: No no you stay here. Let your wife go and look for them. Do you mind, my dear . . . ?

JANE: Certainly not, your Excellency. [*Goes.*]

RESIDENT: You should have kept me informed, Pilkings. You realise how disastrous it would have been if things had erupted while His Highness was here.

PILKINGS: I wasn't aware of the whole business until tonight, sir.

RESIDENT: Nose to the ground, Pilkings, nose to the ground. If we all let these little things slip past us, where would the empire be, eh? Tell me that. Where would we all be?

PILKINGS: [*Low voice.*] Sleeping peacefully at home, I bet.

RESIDENT: What did you say, Pilkings?

PILKINGS: It won't happen again, sir.

RESIDENT: It mustn't, Pilkings. It mustn't. Where is that damned sergeant? I ought to get back to His Highness as quickly as possible and offer him some plausible explanation for my rather abrupt conduct. Can you think of one, Pilkings?

PILKINGS: You could tell him the truth, sir.

RESIDENT: I could? No no no, Pilkings, that would never do. What! Go and tell him there is a riot just two miles away from him? This is supposed to be a secure colony of His Majesty, Pilkings.

1. Military assistant to a civilian administrator.
2. Taxes levied on market women were often the cause of riots in colonial West Africa.

PILKINGS: Yes, sir.

RESIDENT: Ah, there they are. No, these are not our native police. Are these the ring-leaders of the riot?

PILKINGS: Sir, these are my police officers.

RESIDENT: Oh, I beg your pardon, officers. You do look a little . . . I say, isn't there something missing in their uniform? I think they used to have some rather colourful sashes. If I remember rightly I recommended them myself in my young days in the service. A bit of colour always appeals to the natives, yes, I remember putting that in my report. Well well well, where are we? Make your report man.

PILKINGS: [*Moves close to* AMUSA, *between his teeth.*] And let's have no more superstitious nonsense from you Amusa or I'll throw you in the guardroom for a month and feed you pork![3]

RESIDENT: What's that? What has pork to do with it?

PILKINGS: Sir, I was just warning him to be brief. I'm sure you are most anxious to hear his report.

RESIDENT: Yes yes yes, of course. Come on man, speak up. Hey, didn't we give them some colourful fez hats with all those wavy things, yes, pink tassels . . .

PILKINGS: Sir, I think if he was permitted to make his report we might find that he lost his hat in the riot.

RESIDENT: Ah yes, indeed. I'd better tell His Highness that. Lost his hat in the riot, ha ha. He'll probably say, Well, as long as he didn't lose his head. [*Chuckles to himself.*] Don't forget to send me a report first thing in the morning, young Pilkings.

PILKINGS: No, sir.

RESIDENT: And whatever you do, don't let things get out of hand. Keep a cool head and—nose to the ground, Pilkings. [*Wanders off in the general direction of the hall.*]

PILKINGS: Yes, sir.

AIDE-DE-CAMP: Would you be needing me, sir?

PILKINGS: No thanks, Bob. I think His Excellency's need of you is greater than ours.

AIDE-DE-CAMP: We have a detachment of soldiers from the capital, sir. They accompanied His Highness up here.

PILKINGS: I doubt if it will come to that but, thanks, I'll bear it in mind. Oh, could you send an orderly[4] with my cloak.

AIDE-DE-CAMP: Very good, sir. [*Goes.*]

PILKINGS: Now, sergeant.

AMUSA: Sir . . . [*Makes an effort, stops dead. Eyes to the ceiling.*]

PILKINGS: Oh, not again.

AMUSA: I cannot against death to dead cult. This dress get power of dead.

PILKINGS: Alright, let's go. You are relieved of all further duty, Amusa. Report to me first thing in the morning.

JANE: Shall I come, Simon?

PILKINGS: No, there's no need for that. If I can get back later I will. Otherwise get Bob to bring you home.

JANE: Be careful, Simon . . . I mean, be clever.

---

3. Muslims consider it a sacrilege to eat pork.
4. Soldier assigned to perform duties for a superior, like carrying orders or messages.

PILKINGS: Sure I will. You two, come with me. [*As he turns to go, the clock in the Residency begins to chime.* PILKINGS *looks at his watch then turns, horror-stricken, to stare at his wife. The same thought clearly occurs to her. He swallows hard. An orderly brings his cloak.*] It's midnight. I had no idea it was that late.

JANE: But surely ... they don't count the hours the way we do. The moon, or something ...

PILKINGS: I am ... not so sure.

[*He turns and breaks into a sudden run. The two* CONSTABLES *follow, also at a run.* AMUSA, *who has kept his eyes on the ceiling throughout waits until the last of the footsteps has faded out of hearing. He salutes suddenly, but without once looking in the direction of the woman.*]

AMUSA: Goodnight, madam.

JANE: Oh. [*She hesitates.*] Amusa ... [*He goes off without seeming to have heard.*] Poor Simon ... [*A figure emerges from the shadows, a young black man dressed in a sober western suit. He peeps into the hall, trying to make out the figures of the dancers.*] Who is that?

OLUNDE: [*Emerging into the light.*] I didn't mean to startle you, madam. I am looking for the District Officer.

JANE: Wait a minute ... don't I know you? Yes, you are Olunde, the young man who ...

OLUNDE: Mrs. Pilkings! How fortunate. I came here to look for your husband.

JANE: Olunde! Let's look at you. What a fine young man you've become. Grand but solemn. Good God, when did you return? Simon never said a word. But you do look well, Olunde. Really!

OLUNDE: You are ... well, you look quite well yourself, Mrs. Pilkings. From what little I can see of you.

JANE: Oh, this. It's caused quite a stir, I assure you, and not all of it very pleasant. You are not shocked, I hope?

OLUNDE: Why should I be? But don't you find it rather hot in there? Your skin must find it difficult to breathe.

JANE: Well, it is a little hot I must confess, but it's all in a good cause.

OLUNDE: What cause, Mrs. Pilkings?

JANE: All this. The ball. And His Highness being here in person and all that.

OLUNDE: [*Mildly.*] And that is the good cause for which you desecrate an ancestral mask?

JANE: Oh, so you are shocked after all. How disappointing.

OLUNDE: No, I am not shocked, Mrs. Pilkings. You forget that I have now spent four years among your people. I discovered that you have no respect for what you do not understand.

JANE: Oh. So you've returned with a chip on your shoulder. That's a pity, Olunde. I am sorry.

[*An uncomfortable silence follows.*]

I take it then that you did not find your stay in England altogether edifying.

OLUNDE: I don't say that. I found your people quite admirable in many ways, their conduct and courage in this war,[5] for instance.

5. World War II.

JANE: Ah yes, the war. Here, of course, it is all rather remote. From time to time we have a black-out drill just to remind us that there is a war on. And the rare convoy passes through on its way somewhere or on manoeuvres. Mind you, there is the occasional bit of excitement like that ship that was blown up in the harbour.

OLUNDE: Here? Do you mean through enemy action?

JANE: Oh no, the war hasn't come that close. The captain did it himself. I don't quite understand it, really. Simon tried to explain. The ship had to be blown up because it had become dangerous to the other ships, even to the city itself. Hundreds of the coastal population would have died.

OLUNDE: Maybe it was loaded with ammunition and had caught fire. Or some of those lethal gases they've been experimenting on.

JANE: Something like that. The captain blew himself up with it. Deliberately. Simon said someone had to remain on board to light the fuse.

OLUNDE: It must have been a very short fuse.

JANE: [*Shrugs.*] I don't know much about it. Only that there was no other way to save lives. No time to devise anything else. The captain took the decision and carried it out.

OLUNDE: Yes . . . I quite believe it. I met men like that in England.

JANE: Oh, just look at me! Fancy welcoming you back with such morbid news. Stale too. It was at least six months ago.

OLUNDE: I don't find it morbid at all. I find it rather inspiring. It is an affirmative commentary on life.

JANE: What is?

OLUNDE: That captain's self-sacrifice.

JANE: Nonsense. Life should never be thrown deliberately away.

OLUNDE: And the innocent people round the harbour?

JANE: Oh, how does one know? The whole thing was probably exaggerated anyway.

OLUNDE: That was a risk the captain couldn't take. But please, Mrs. Pilkings, do you think you could find your husband for me? I have to talk to him.

JANE: Simon? Oh. [*As she recollects for the first time the full significance of* OLUNDE's *presence.*] Simon is . . . there is a little problem in town. He was sent for. But . . . when did you arrive? Does Simon know you're here?

OLUNDE: [*Suddenly earnest.*] I need your help, Mrs. Pilkings. I've always found you somewhat more understanding than your husband. Please find him for me and when you do, you must help me talk to him.

JANE: I'm afraid I don't quite . . . follow you. Have you seen my husband already?

OLUNDE: I went to your house. Your houseboy told me you were here. [*He smiles.*] He even told me how I would recognise you and Mr. Pilkings.

JANE: Then you must know what my husband is trying to do for you.

OLUNDE: For me?

JANE: For you. For your people. And to think he didn't even know you were coming back! But how do you happen to be here? Only this evening we were talking about you. We thought you were still four thousand miles away.

OLUNDE: I was sent a cable.

JANE: A cable? Who did? Simon? The business of your father didn't begin till tonight.

OLUNDE: A relation sent it weeks ago, and it said nothing about my father. All it said was, Our King is dead. But I knew I had to return home at once so as to bury my father. I understood that.

JANE: Well, thank God you don't have to go through that agony. Simon is going to stop it.

OLUNDE: That's why I want to see him. He's wasting his time. And since he has been so helpful to me I don't want him to incur the enmity of our people. Especially over nothing.

JANE: [*Sits down open-mouthed.*] You . . . you Olunde!

OLUNDE: Mrs. Pilkings, I came home to bury my father. As soon as I heard the news I booked my passage home. In fact we were fortunate. We travelled in the same convoy as your Prince, so we had excellent protection.

JANE: But you don't think your father is also entitled to whatever protection is available to him?

OLUNDE: How can I make you understand? He *has* protection. No one can undertake what he does tonight without the deepest protection the mind can conceive. What can you offer him in place of his peace of mind, in place of the honour and veneration of his own people? What would you think of your Prince if he refused to accept the risk of losing his life on this voyage? This . . . showing-the-flag tour of colonial possessions.

JANE: I see. So it isn't just medicine you studied in England.

OLUNDE: Yet another error into which your people fall. You believe that everything which appears to make sense was learnt from you.

JANE: Not so fast, Olunde. You have learnt to argue, I can tell that, but I never said you made sense. However clearly you try to put it, it is still a barbaric custom. It is even worse—it's feudal! The king dies and a chieftain must be buried with him. How feudalistic can you get!

OLUNDE: [*Waves his hand towards the background. The* PRINCE *is dancing past again—to a different step—and all the guests are bowing and curtseying as he passes.*] And this? Even in the midst of a devastating war, look at that. What name would you give to that?

JANE: Therapy, British style. The preservation of sanity in the midst of chaos.

OLUNDE: Others would call it decadence. However, it doesn't really interest me. You white races know how to survive; I've seen proof of that. By all logical and natural laws this war should end with all the white races wiping out one another, wiping out their so-called civilisation for all time and reverting to a state of primitivism the like of which has so far only existed in your imagination when you thought of us. I thought all that at the beginning. Then I slowly realised that your greatest art is the art of survival. But at least have the humility to let others survive in their own way.

JANE: Through ritual suicide?

OLUNDE: Is that worse than mass suicide? Mrs. Pilkings, what do you call what those young men are sent to do by their generals in this war? Of course you have also mastered the art of calling things by names which don't remotely describe them.

JANE: You talk! You people with your long-winded, roundabout way of making conversation.

OLUNDE: Mrs. Pilkings, whatever we do, we never suggest that a thing is the opposite of what it really is. In your newsreels[6] I heard defeats, thorough, murderous defeats described as strategic victories. No wait, it wasn't just on

---

6. Short films of news and other events shown in movie houses before the main features. This was common before the age of television, especially during World War II.

your newsreels. Don't forget I was attached to hospitals all the time. Hordes of your wounded passed through those wards. I spoke to them. I spent long evenings by their bedsides while they spoke terrible truths of the realities of that war. I know now how history is made.

JANE: But surely, in a war of this nature, for the morale of the nation you must expect . . .

OLUNDE: That a disaster beyond human reckoning be spoken of as a triumph? No. I mean, is there no mourning in the home of the bereaved that such blasphemy is permitted?

JANE: [*After a moment's pause.*] Perhaps I can understand you now. The time we picked for you was not really one for seeing us at our best.

OLUNDE: Don't think it was just the war. Before that even started I had plenty of time to study your people. I saw nothing, finally, that gave you the right to pass judgment on other peoples and their ways. Nothing at all.

JANE: [*Hesitantly.*] Was it the . . . colour thing? I know there is some discrimination.

OLUNDE: Don't make it so simple, Mrs. Pilkings. You make it sound as if when I left, I took nothing at all with me.

JANE: Yes . . . and to tell the truth, only this evening, Simon and I agreed that we never really knew what you left with.

OLUNDE: Neither did I. But I found out over there. I am grateful to your country for that. And I will never give it up.

JANE: Olunde, please . . . promise me something. Whatever you do, don't throw away what you have started to do. You want to be a doctor. My husband and I believe you will make an excellent one, sympathetic and competent. Don't let anything make you throw away your training.

OLUNDE: [*Genuinely surprised.*] Of course not. What a strange idea. I intend to return and complete my training. Once the burial of my father is over.

JANE: Oh, please . . . !

OLUNDE: Listen! Come outside. You can't hear anything against that music.

JANE: What is it?

OLUNDE: The drums. Can you hear the changes? Listen.

[*The drums come over, still distant but more distinct. There is a change of rhythm, it rises to a crescendo and then, suddenly, it is cut off. After a silence, a new beat begins, slow and resonant.*]

There, it's all over.

JANE: You mean he's . . .

OLUNDE: Yes, Mrs. Pilkings, my father is dead. His willpower has always been enormous; I know he is dead.

JANE: [*Screams.*] How can you be so callous! So unfeeling! You announce your father's own death like a surgeon looking down on some strange . . . stranger's body! You're just a savage like all the rest.

AIDE-DE-CAMP: [*Rushing out.*] Mrs. Pilkings. Mrs. Pilkings. [*She breaks down, sobbing.*] Are you all right, Mrs. Pilkings?

OLUNDE: She'll be all right. [*Turns to go.*]

AIDE-DE-CAMP: Who are you? And who the hell asked your opinion?

OLUNDE: You're quite right, nobody. [*Going.*]

AIDE-DE-CAMP: What the hell! Did you hear me ask you who you were?

OLUNDE: I have business to attend to.

AIDE-DE-CAMP: I'll give you business in a moment, you impudent nigger. Answer my question!

OLUNDE: I have a funeral to arrange. Excuse me. [*Going.*]

AIDE-DE-CAMP: I said stop! Orderly!

JANE: No, no, don't do that. I'm alright. And for heaven's sake, don't act so foolishly. He's a family friend.

AIDE-DE-CAMP: Well, he'd better learn to answer civil questions when he's asked them. These natives put a suit on and they get high opinions of themselves.

OLUNDE: Can I go now?

JANE: No no, don't go. I must talk to you. I'm sorry about what I said.

OLUNDE: It's nothing, Mrs. Pilkings. And I'm really anxious to go. I couldn't see my father before, it's forbidden for me, his heir and successor, to set eyes on him from the moment of the king's death. But now . . . I would like to touch his body while it is still warm.

JANE: You will. I promise I shan't keep you long. Only, I couldn't possibly let you go like that. Bob, please excuse us.

AIDE-DE-CAMP: If you're sure . . .

JANE: Of course I'm sure. Something happened to upset me just then, but I'm alright now. Really.

[*The* AIDE-DE-CAMP *goes, somewhat reluctantly.*]

OLUNDE: I mustn't stay long.

JANE: Please, I promise not to keep you. It's just that . . . oh, you saw yourself what happens to one in this place. The Resident's man thought he was being helpful, that's the way we all react. But I can't go in among that crowd just now and if I stay by myself somebody will come looking for me. Please, just say something for a few moments and then you can go. Just so I can recover myself.

OLUNDE: What do you want me to say?

JANE: Your calm acceptance, for instance—can you explain that? It was so unnatural. I don't understand that at all. I feel a need to understand all I can.

OLUNDE: But you explained it yourself. My medical training perhaps. I have seen death too often. And the soldiers who returned from the front, they died on our hands all the time.

JANE: No. It has to be more than that. I feel it has to do with the many things we don't really grasp about your people. At least you can explain.

OLUNDE: All these things are part of it. And anyway, my father has been dead in my mind for nearly a month. Ever since I learnt of the King's death. I've lived with my bereavement so long now that I cannot think of him alive. On that journey on the boat, I kept my mind on my duties as the one who must perform the rites over his body. I went through it all again and again in my mind as he himself had taught me. I didn't want to do anything wrong, something which might jeopardise the welfare of my people.

JANE: But he had disowned you. When you left he swore publicly you were no longer his son.

OLUNDE: I told you, he was a man of tremendous will. Sometimes that's another way of saying stubborn. But among our people, you don't disown a child just like that. Even if I had died before him I would still be buried like his eldest son. But it's time for me to go.

JANE: Thank you. I feel calmer. Don't let me keep you from your duties.

OLUNDE: Goodnight, Mrs. Pilkings.

JANE: Welcome home. [*She holds out her hand. As he takes it footsteps are heard approaching the drive. A short while later a woman's sobbing is also heard.*]

PILKINGS: [*Off.*] Keep them here till I get back. [*He strides into view, reacts at the sight of* OLUNDE *but turns to his wife.*] Thank goodness you're still here.

JANE: Simon, what happened?

PILKINGS: Later, Jane, please. Is Bob still here?

JANE: Yes, I think so. I'm sure he must be.

PILKINGS: Try and get him out here as quickly as you can. Tell him it's urgent.

JANE: Of course. Oh Simon, you remember . . .

PILKINGS: Yes yes. I can see who it is. Get Bob out here. [*She runs off.*] At first I thought I was seeing a ghost.

OLUNDE: Mr. Pilkings, I appreciate what you tried to do. I want you to believe that. I can tell you it would have been a terrible calamity if you'd succeeded.

PILKINGS: [*Opens his mouth several times, shuts it.*] You . . . said what?

OLUNDE: A calamity for us, the entire people.

PILKINGS: [*Sighs.*] I see. Hm.

OLUNDE: And now I must go. I must see him before he turns cold.

PILKINGS: Oh ah . . . em . . . but this is a shock to see you. I mean, er, thinking all this while you were in England and thanking God for that.

OLUNDE: I came on the mail boat. We travelled in the Prince's convoy.

PILKINGS: Ah yes, a-ah, hm . . . er, well . . .

OLUNDE: Goodnight. I can see you are shocked by the whole business. But you must know by now there are things you cannot understand—or help.

PILKINGS: Yes. Just a minute. There are armed policemen that way and they have instructions to let no one pass. I suggest you wait a little. I'll, er . . . give you an escort.

OLUNDE: That's very kind of you. But do you think it could be quickly arranged?

PILKINGS: Of course. In fact, yes, what I'll do is send Bob over with some men to the er . . . place. You can go with them. Here he comes now. Excuse me a minute.

AIDE-DE-CAMP: Anything wrong, sir?

PILKINGS: [*Takes him to one side.*] Listen, Bob, that cellar in the disused annexe of the Residency, you know, where the slaves were stored before being taken down to the coast. . . .

AIDE-DE-CAMP: Oh yes, we use it as a storeroom for broken furniture.

PILKINGS: But it's still got the bars on it?

AIDE-DE-CAMP: Oh yes, they are quite intact.

PILKINGS: Get the keys please. I'll explain later. And I want a strong guard over the Residency tonight.

AIDE-DE-CAMP: We have that already. The detachment from the coast . . .

PILKINGS: No, I don't want them at the gates of the Residency. I want you to deploy them at the bottom of the hill, a long way from the main hall so they can deal with any situation long before the sound carries to the house.

AIDE-DE-CAMP: Yes, of course.

PILKINGS: I don't want His Highness alarmed.

AIDE-DE-CAMP: You think the riot will spread here?

PILKINGS: It's unlikely but I don't want to take a chance. I made them believe I was going to lock the man up in my house, which was what I had planned to do in the first place. They are probably assailing it by now. I took a round-about route here so I don't think there is any danger at all. At least not before dawn. Nobody is to leave the premises of course—the native employees I mean. They'll soon smell something is up and they can't keep their mouths shut.

AIDE-DE-CAMP: I'll give instructions at once.

PILKINGS: I'll take the prisoner down myself. Two policemen will stay with him throughout the night. Inside the cell.

AIDE-DE-CAMP: Right, sir. [*Salutes and goes off at the double.*]

PILKINGS: Jane. Bob is coming back in a moment with a detachment. Until he gets back please stay with Olunde. [*He makes an extra warning gesture with his eyes.*]

OLUNDE: Please, Mr. Pilkings . . .

PILKINGS: I hate to be stuffy, old son, but we have a crisis on our hands. It has to do with your father's affair, if you must know. And it happens also at a time when we have His Highness here. I am responsible for security so you'll simply have to do as I say. I hope that's understood. [*Marches off quickly, in the direction from which he made his first appearance.*]

OLUNDE: What's going on? All this can't be just because he failed to stop my father killing himself.

JANE: I honestly don't know. Could it have sparked off a riot?

OLUNDE: No. If he'd succeeded that would be more likely to start the riot. Perhaps there were other factors involved. Was there a chieftancy dispute?

JANE: None that I know of.

ELESIN: [*An animal bellow from off.*[7]] Leave me alone! Is it not enough that you have covered me in shame! White man, take your hand from my body!

[OLUNDE *stands frozen to the spot.* JANE, *understanding at last, tries to move him.*]

JANE: Let's go in. It's getting chilly out here.

PILKINGS: [*Off.*] Carry him.

ELESIN: Give me back the name you have taken away from me, you ghost from the land of the nameless!

PILKINGS: Carry him! I can't have a disturbance here. Quickly! stuff up his mouth.

JANE: Oh God! Let's go in. Please, Olunde. [OLUNDE *does not move.*]

ELESIN: Take your albino's hand from me, you . . .

[*Sounds of a struggle. His voice chokes as he is gagged.*]

OLUNDE: [*Quietly.*] That was my father's voice.

JANE: Oh you poor orphan, what have you come home to?

[*There is a sudden explosion of rage from off-stage and powerful steps come running up the drive.*]

PILKINGS: You bloody fools, after him!

[*Immediately* ELESIN, *in handcuffs, comes pounding in the direction of* JANE *and* OLUNDE, *followed some moments afterwards by* PILKINGS *and the* CONSTABLES. ELESIN, *confronted by the seeming statue of his son, stops dead.* OLUNDE *stares above his head into the distance. The* CONSTABLES *try to grab him.* JANE *screams at them.*]

---

7. The cries of animals, especially cows, were considered to be a feature of the language of *egungun* and other masked figures.

JANE: Leave him alone! Simon, tell them to leave him alone.

PILKINGS: All right, stand aside, you. [*Shrugs.*] Maybe just as well. It might help to calm him down.

> [*For several moments they hold the same position.* ELESIN *moves a step forward, almost as if he's still in doubt.*]

ELESIN: Olunde? [*He moves his head, inspecting him from side to side.*] Olunde! [*He collapses slowly at* OLUNDE's *feet.*] Oh son, don't let the sight of your father turn you blind!

OLUNDE: [*He moves for the first time since he heard his voice, brings his head slowly down to look on him.*] I have no father, eater of leftovers.

> [*He walks slowly down the way his father had run. Light fades out on* ELESIN, *sobbing into the ground.*]

Scene 5

A wide iron-barred gate stretches almost the whole width of the cell in which ELESIN *is imprisoned. His wrists are encased in thick iron bracelets, chained together; he stands against the bars, looking out. Seated on the ground to one side on the outside is his recent* BRIDE, *her eyes bent perpetually to the ground. Figures of the two* GUARDS *can be seen deeper inside the cell, alert to every movement* ELESIN *makes.* PILKINGS *now in a police officer's uniform, enters noiselessly, observes him a while. Then he coughs ostentatiously and approaches. Leans against the bars near a corner, his back to* ELESIN. *He is obviously trying to fall in mood with him. Some moments' silence.*

PILKINGS: You seem fascinated by the moon.

ELESIN: [*After a pause.*] Yes, ghostly one. Your twin-brother up there engages my thoughts.

PILKINGS: It is a beautiful night.

ELESIN: Is that so?

PILKINGS: The light on the leaves, the peace of the night . . .

ELESIN: The night is not at peace, District Officer.

PILKINGS: No? I would have said it was. You know, quiet . . .

ELESIN: And does quiet mean peace for you?

PILKINGS: Well, nearly the same thing. Naturally there is a subtle difference . . .

ELESIN: The night is not at peace, ghostly one. The world is not at peace. You have shattered the peace of the world forever. There is no sleep in the world tonight.

PILKINGS: It is still a good bargain if the world should lose one night's sleep as the price of saving a man's life.

ELESIN: You did not save my life, District Officer. You destroyed it.

PILKINGS: Now come on . . .

ELESIN: And not merely my life but the lives of many. The end of the night's work is not over. Neither this year nor the next will see it. If I wished you well, I would pray that you do not stay long enough on our land to see the disaster you have brought upon us.

PILKINGS: Well, I did my duty as I saw it. I have no regrets.

ELESIN: No. The regrets of life always come later.

[*Some moments' pause.*]

You are waiting for dawn, white man. I hear you saying to yourself: Only so many hours until dawn and then the danger is over. All I must do is to keep him alive tonight. You don't quite understand it all but you know that tonight is when what ought to be must be brought about. I shall ease your mind even more, ghostly one. It is not an entire night but a moment of the night, and that moment is past. The moon was my messenger and guide. When it reached a certain gateway in the sky, it touched that moment for which my whole life has been spent in blessings. Even I do not know the gateway. I have stood here and scanned the sky for a glimpse of that door, but I cannot see it. Human eyes are useless for a search of this nature. But in the house of *osugbo*, those who keep watch through the spirit recognised the moment, they sent word to me through the voice of our sacred drums to prepare myself. I heard them and I shed all thoughts of earth. I began to follow the moon to the abode of the gods . . . servant of the white king, that was when you entered my chosen place of departure on feet of desecration.

PILKINGS: I'm sorry, but we all see our duty differently.

ELESIN: I no longer blame you. You stole from me my first-born, sent him to your country so you could turn him into something in your own image. Did you plan it all beforehand? There are moments when it seems part of a larger plan. He who must follow my footsteps is taken from me, sent across the ocean: Then, in my turn, I am stopped from fulfilling my destiny. Did you think it all out before, this plan to push our world from its course and sever the cord that links us to the great origin?

PILKINGS: You don't really believe that. Anyway, if that was my intention with your son, I appear to have failed.

ELESIN: You did not fail in the main thing, ghostly one. We know the roof covers the rafters, the cloth covers blemishes; who would have known that the white skin covered our future, preventing us from seeing the death our enemies had prepared for us? The world is set adrift and its inhabitants are lost. Around them, there is nothing but emptiness.

PILKINGS: Your son does not take so gloomy a view.

ELESIN: Are you dreaming now, white man? Were you not present at the reunion of shame? Did you not see when the world reversed itself and the father fell before his son, asking forgiveness?

PILKINGS: That was in the heat of the moment. I spoke to him and . . . if you want to know, he wishes he could cut out his tongue for uttering the words he did.

ELESIN: No. What he said must never be unsaid. The contempt of my own son rescued something of my shame at your hands. You have stopped me in my duty but I know now that I did give birth to a son. Once I mistrusted him for seeking the companionship of those my spirit knew as enemies of our race. Now I understand. One should seek to obtain the secrets of his enemies. He will avenge my shame, white one. His spirit will destroy you and yours.

PILKINGS: That kind of talk is hardly called for. If you don't want my consolation . . .

ELESIN: No, white man, I do not want your consolation.

PILKINGS: As you wish. Your son, anyway, sends his consolation. He asks your forgiveness. When I asked him not to despise you his reply was: I cannot judge him, and if I cannot judge him, I cannot despise him. He wants to come to you and say goodbye and to receive your blessing.

ELESIN: Goodbye? Is he returning to your land?

PILKINGS: Don't you think that's the most sensible thing for him to do? I advised him to leave at once, before dawn, and he agrees that is the right course of action.

ELESIN: Yes, it is best. And even if I did not think so, I have lost the father's place of honour. My voice is broken.

PILKINGS: Your son honours you. If he didn't he would not ask your blessing.

ELESIN: No. Even a thoroughbred is not without pity for the turf he strikes with his hoof. When is he coming?

PILKINGS: As soon as the town is a little quieter. I advised it.

ELESIN: Yes, white man, I am sure you advised it. You advise all our lives, although on the authority of what gods, I do not know.

PILKINGS: [*Opens his mouth to reply, then appears to change his mind. Turns to go. Hesitates and stops again.*] Before I leave you, may I ask just one thing of you?

ELESIN: I am listening.

PILKINGS: I wish to ask you to search the quiet of your heart and tell me—do you not find great contradictions in the wisdom of your own race?

ELESIN: Make yourself clear, white one.

PILKINGS: I have lived among you long enough to learn a saying or two. One came to my mind tonight when I stepped into the market and saw what was going on. You were surrounded by those who egged you on with song and praises. I thought, are these not the same people who say: "The elder grimly approaches heaven and you ask him to bear your greetings yonder; do you really think he makes the journey willingly?" After that, I did not hesitate.

[*A pause.* ELESIN *sighs. Before he can speak a sound of running feet is heard.*]

JANE: [*Off.*] Simon! Simon!

PILKINGS: What on earth . . . ! [*Runs off.*]

[ELESIN *turns to his new wife, gazes on her for some moments.*]

ELESIN: My young bride, did you hear the ghostly one? You sit and sob in your silent heart but say nothing to all this. First I blamed the white man, then I blamed my gods for deserting me. Now I feel I want to blame you for the mystery of the sapping of my will. But blame is a strange peace offering for a man to bring a world he has deeply wronged, and to its innocent dwellers. Oh little mother, I have taken countless women in my life but you were more than a desire of the flesh. I needed you as the abyss across which my body must be drawn, I filled it with earth and dropped my seed in it at the moment of preparedness for my crossing. You were the final gift of the living to their emissary to the land of the ancestors, and perhaps your warmth and youth brought new insights of this world to me and turned my feet leaden on this side of the abyss. For I confess to you, daughter, my weakness came not merely from the abomination of the white man who came violently into my fading presence, there was also a weight of longing on my earth-held limbs. I would have shaken it off, already my foot had begun to lift, but then the white ghost entered and all was defiled.

[*Approaching voices of* PILKINGS *and his wife.*]

JANE: Oh Simon, you will let her in, won't you?

PILKINGS: I really wish you'd stop interfering.

[*They come into view.* JANE *is in a dressing-gown.* PILKINGS *is holding a note to which he refers from time to time.*]

JANE: Good gracious, I didn't initiate this. I was sleeping quietly, or trying to anyway, when the servant brought it. It's not my fault if one can't sleep undisturbed even in the Residency.

PILKINGS: He'd have done the same thing if we were sleeping at home, so don't sidetrack the issue. He knows he can get round you or he wouldn't send you the petition in the first place.

JANE: Be fair, Simon. After all, he was thinking of your own interests. He is grateful, you know—you seem to forget that. He feels he owes you something.

PILKINGS: I just wish they'd leave this man alone tonight, that's all.

JANE: Trust him, Simon. He's pledged his word it will all go peacefully.

PILKINGS: Yes, and that's the other thing. I don't like being threatened.

JANE: Threatened? [*Takes the note.*] I didn't spot any threat.

PILKINGS: It's there. Veiled, but it's there. The only way to prevent serious rioting tomorrow—what a cheek!

JANE: I don't think he's threatening you, Simon.

PILKINGS: He's picked up the idiom, alright. Wouldn't surprise me if he's been mixing with commies or anarchists over there. The phrasing sounds too good to be true. Damn! If only the Prince hadn't picked this time for his visit.

JANE: Well, even so, Simon, what have you got to lose? You don't want a riot on your hands, not with the Prince here.

PILKINGS: [*Going up to* ELESIN.] Let's see what he has to say. Chief Elesin, there is yet another person who wants to see you. As she is not a next-of-kin I don't really feel obliged to let her in. But your son sent a note with her, so it's up to you.

ELESIN: I know who that must be. So she found out your hiding-place. Well, it was not difficult. My stench of shame is so strong, it requires no hunter's dog to follow it.

PILKINGS: If you don't want to see her, just say so and I'll send her packing.

ELESIN: Why should I not want to see her? Let her come. I have no more holes in my rag of shame. All is laid bare.

PILKINGS: I'll bring her in. [*Goes off.*]

JANE: [*Hesitates, then goes to* ELESIN.] Please, try and understand. Everything my husband did was for the best.

ELESIN: [*He gives her a long strange stare, as if he is trying to understand who she is.*] You are the wife of the District Officer?

JANE: Yes. My name is Jane.

ELESIN: That is my wife sitting down there. You notice how still and silent she sits? My business is with your husband.

[PILKINGS *returns with* IYALOJA.]

PILKINGS: Here she is. Now first I want your word of honour that you will try nothing foolish.

ELESIN: Honour? White one, did you say you wanted my word of honour?

PILKINGS: I know you to be an honourable man. Give me your word of honour
 you will receive nothing from her.

ELESIN: But I am sure you have searched her clothing as you would never dare
 touch your own mother. And there are these two lizards of yours who roll
 their eyes even when I scratch.

PILKINGS: And I shall be sitting on that tree trunk watching even how you blink.
 Just the same I want your word that you will not let her pass anything to
 you.

ELESIN: You have my honour already. It is locked up in that desk in which you
 will put away your report of this night's events. Even the honour of my people
 you have taken already; it is tied together with those papers of treachery
 which make you masters in this land.

PILKINGS: Alright. I am trying to make things easy but if you must bring in politics we'll have to do it the hard way. Madam, I want you to remain along this
 line and move no nearer to the cell door. Guards! [*They spring to attention.*] If
 she moves beyond this point, blow your whistle. Come on, Jane. [*They go off.*]

IYALOJA: How boldly the lizard struts before the pigeon when it was the eagle
 itself he promised us he would confront.

ELESIN: I don't ask you to take pity on me, Iyaloja. You have a message for me or
 you would not have come. Even if it is the curses of the world, I shall listen.

IYALOJA: You made so bold with the servant of the white king who took your side
 against death. I must tell your brother chiefs when I return how bravely you
 waged war against him. Especially with words.

ELESIN: I more than deserve your scorn.

IYALOJA: [*With sudden anger.*] I warned you, if you must leave a seed behind, be sure
 it is not tainted with the curses of the world. Who are you to open a new life
 when you dared not open the door to a new existence? I say who are you to
 make so bold? [*The* BRIDE *sobs and* IYALOJA *notices her. Her contempt noticeably
 increases as she turns back to* ELESIN.] Oh, you self-vaunted stem of the plantain,
 how hollow it all proves. The pith is gone in the parent stem, so how will it
 prove with the new shoot? How will it go with that earth that bears it? Who
 are you to bring this abomination on us!

ELESIN: My powers deserted me. My charms, my spells, even my voice lacked
 strength when I made to summon the powers that would lead me over the
 last measure of earth into the land of the fleshless. You saw it, Iyaloja. You saw
 me struggle to retrieve my will from the power of the stranger whose shadow
 fell across the doorway and left me floundering and blundering in a maze I
 had never before encountered. My senses were numbed when the touch of
 cold iron came upon my wrists. I could do nothing to save myself.

IYALOJA: You have betrayed us. We fed you sweetmeats[8] such as we hoped awaited
 you on the other side. But you said, No, I must eat the world's leftovers. We
 said you were the hunter who brought the quarry down; to you belonged the
 vital portions of the game. No, you said, I am the hunter's dog and I shall eat
 the entrails of the game and the faeces of the hunter. We said you were the
 hunter returning home in triumph, a slain buffalo pressing down on his neck;
 you said, Wait, I first must turn up this cricket hole with my toes. We said
 yours was the doorway at which we first spy the tapper when he comes down

8. Delicacies made with sugar or honey; pastries or candies.

from the tree, yours was the blessing of the twilight wine,[9] the purl that brings night spirits out of doors to steal their portion before the light of day. We said yours was the body of wine whose burden shakes the tapper like a sudden gust on his perch. You said, No, I am content to lick the dregs from each calabash when the drinkers are done. We said the dew on earth's surface was for you to wash your feet along the slopes of honour. You said, No, I shall step in the vomit of cats and the droppings of mice; I shall fight them for the left-overs of the world.

ELESIN: Enough, Iyaloja, enough.

IYALOJA: We called you leader and oh, how you led us on. What we have no intention of eating should not be held to the nose.

ELESIN: Enough, enough. My shame is heavy enough.

IYALOJA: Wait. I came with a burden.

ELESIN: You have more than discharged it.

IYALOJA: I wish I could pity you.

ELESIN: I need neither your pity nor the pity of the world. I need understanding. Even I need to understand. You were present at my defeat. You were part of the beginnings. You brought about the renewal of my tie to earth, you helped in the binding of the cord.

IYALOJA: I gave you warning. The river which fills up before our eyes does not sweep us away in its flood.

ELESIN: What were warnings beside the moist contact of living earth between my fingers? What were warnings beside the renewal of famished embers lodged eternally in the heart of man? But even that, even if it overwhelmed one with a thousandfold temptations to linger a little while, a man could overcome it. It is when the alien hand pollutes the source of will,[1] when a stranger force of violence shatters the mind's calm resolution, this is when a man is made to commit the awful treachery of relief, commit in his thought the unspeakable blasphemy of seeing the hand of the gods in this alien rupture of his world. I know it was this thought that killed me, sapped my powers and turned me into an infant in the hands of unnamable strangers. I made to utter my spells anew but my tongue merely rattled in my mouth. I fingered hidden charms and the contact was damp; there was no spark left to sever the life-strings that should stretch from every fingertip. My will was squelched in the spittle of an alien race, and all because I had committed this blasphemy of thought— that there might be the hand of the gods in a stranger's intervention.

IYALOJA: Explain it how you will, I hope it brings you peace of mind. The bush rat fled his rightful cause, reached the market and set up a lamentation. "Please save me!"—are these fitting words to hear from an ancestral mask? "There's a wild beast at my heels" is not becoming language from a hunter.

ELESIN: May the world forgive me.

IYALOJA: I came with a burden, I said. It approaches the gates which are so well guarded by those jackals whose spittle will from this day be on your food and drink. But first, tell me, you who were once Elesin Oba, tell me, you who know so well the cycle of the plantain: is it the parent shoot which withers to give sap to the younger, or does your wisdom see it running the other way?

---

9. Palm wine tapped before dawn is considered especially fresh and potent. *Purl*: tonic consisting of alcohol and herbs.   1. In Yoruba cosmology, will is the life source that makes everything happen.

ELESIN: I don't see your meaning, Iyaloja.

IYALOJA: Did I ask you for a meaning? I asked a question. Whose trunk withers to give sap to the other? The parent shoot or the younger?

ELESIN: The parent.

IYALOJA: Ah. So you do know that. There are sights in this world which say different, Elesin. There are some who choose to reverse the cycle of our being. Oh, you emptied bark that the world once saluted for a pith-laden being, shall I tell you what the gods have claimed of you?

> [*In her agitation she steps beyond the line indicated by* PILKINGS *and the air is rent by piercing whistles. The two* GUARDS *also leap forward and place safe-guarding hands on* ELESIN. IYALOJA *stops, astonished.* PILKINGS *comes racing in, followed by* JANE.]

PILKINGS: What is it? Did they try something?

GUARD: She stepped beyond the line.

ELESIN: [*In a broken voice.*] Let her alone. She meant no harm.

IYALOJA: Oh Elesin, see what you've become. Once you had no need to open your mouth in explanation because evil-smelling goats, itchy of hand and foot, had lost their senses. And it was a brave man indeed who dared lay hands on you because Iyaloja stepped from one side of the earth onto another. Now look at the spectacle of your life. I grieve for you.

PILKINGS: I think you'd better leave. I doubt you have done him much good by coming here. I shall make sure you are not allowed to see him again. In any case we are moving him to a different place before dawn, so don't bother to come back.

IYALOJA: We foresaw that. Hence the burden I trudged here to lay beside your gates.

PILKINGS: What was that you said?

IYALOJA: Didn't our son explain? Ask that one. He knows what it is. At least we hope the man we once knew as Elesin remembers the lesser oaths he need not break.

PILKINGS: Do you know what she is talking about?

ELESIN: Go to the gates, ghostly one. Whatever you find there, bring it to me.

IYALOJA: Not yet. It drags behind me on the slow, weary feet of women. Slow as it is, Elesin, it has long overtaken you. It rides ahead of your laggard will.

PILKINGS: What is she saying now? Christ! Must your people forever speak in riddles?

ELESIN: It will come, white man, it will come. Tell your men at the gates to let it through.

PILKINGS: [*Dubiously.*] I'll have to see what it is.

IYALOJA: You will. [*Passionately.*] But this is one oath he cannot shirk. White one, you have a king here, a visitor from your land. We know of his presence here. Tell me, were he to die would you leave his spirit roaming restlessly on the surface of earth? Would you bury him here among those you consider less than human? In your land have you no ceremonies of the dead?

PILKINGS: Yes. But we don't make our chiefs commit suicide to keep him company.

IYALOJA: Child, I have not come to help your understanding. [*Points to* ELESIN.] This is the man whose weakened understanding holds us in bondage to you. But ask him if you wish. He knows the meaning of a king's passage; he was not born yesterday. He knows the peril to the race when our dead father, who goes as intermediary, waits and waits and knows he is betrayed. He knows when the narrow gate was opened and he knows it will not stay for laggards who drag their feet in dung and vomit, whose lips are reeking of the leftovers of lesser men. He knows he has condemned our King to wander in the void of evil with beings who are enemies of life.

PILKINGS: Yes, er . . . but look here . . .

IYALOJA: What we ask is little enough. Let him release our King so he can ride on homewards alone. The messenger is on his way on the backs of women. Let him send word through the heart that is folded up within the bolt. It is the least of all his oaths, it is the easiest fulfilled.

[*The* AIDE-DE-CAMP *runs in.*]

PILKINGS: Bob?

AIDE-DE-CAMP: Sir, there's a group of women chanting up the hill.

PILKINGS: [*Rounding on* IYALOJA.] If you people want trouble . . .

JANE: Simon, I think that's what Olunde referred to in his letter.

PILKINGS: He knows damned well I can't have a crowd here! Damn it, I explained the delicacy of my position to him. I think it's about time I got him out of town. Bob, send a car and two or three soldiers to bring him in. I think the sooner he takes his leave of his father and gets out the better.

IYALOJA: Save your labour, white one. If it is the father of your prisoner you want, Olunde, he who until this night we knew as Elesin's son, he comes soon himself to take his leave. He has sent the women ahead, so let them in.

[PILKINGS *remains undecided.*]

AIDE-DE-CAMP: What do we do about the invasion? We can still stop them far from here.

PILKINGS: What do they look like?

AIDE-DE-CAMP: They're not many. And they seem quite peaceful.

PILKINGS: No men?

AIDE-DE-CAMP: Mm, two or three at the most.

JANE: Honestly, Simon, I'd trust Olunde. I don't think he'll deceive you about their intentions.

PILKINGS: He'd better not. Alright then, let them in, Bob. Warn them to control themselves. Then hurry Olunde here. Make sure he brings his baggage because I'm not returning him into town.

AIDE-DE-CAMP: Very good, sir. [*Goes.*]

PILKINGS: [*To* IYALOJA.] I hope you understand that if anything goes wrong it will be on your head. My men have orders to shoot at the first sign of trouble.

IYALOJA: To prevent one death you will actually make other deaths? Ah, great is the wisdom of the white race. But have no fear. Your Prince will sleep peacefully. So at long last will ours. We will disturb you no further, servant of the white King. Just let Elesin fulfil his oath and we will retire home and pay homage to our King.

JANE: I believe her, Simon, don't you?

PILKINGS: Maybe.

ELESIN: Have no fear, ghostly one. I have a message to send my King and then you have nothing more to fear.

IYALOJA: Olunde would have done it. The chiefs asked him to speak the words but he said no, not while you lived.

ELESIN: Even from the depths to which my spirit has sunk, I find some joy that this little has been left to me.

[*The* WOMEN *enter, intoning the dirge "Ale lee lee" and swaying from side to side. On their shoulders is borne a longish object roughly like a cylindrical bolt, covered in cloth. They set it down on the spot where* IYALOJA *had stood earlier, and form a semi-circle round it. The* PRAISE-SINGER *and* DRUMMER *stand on the inside of the semi-circle but the drum is not used at all. The* DRUMMER *intones under the* PRAISE-SINGER'S *invocations.*]

PILKINGS: [*As they enter.*] What is *that*?

IYALOJA: The burden you have made, white one, but we bring it in peace.

PILKINGS: I said *what* is it?

ELESIN: White man, you must let me out. I have a duty to perform.

PILKINGS: I most certainly will not.

ELESIN: There lies the courier of my King. Let me out so I can perform what is demanded of me.

PILKINGS: You'll do what you need to do from inside there or not at all. I've gone as far as I intend to with this business.

ELESIN: The worshipper who lights a candle in your church to bear a message to his god bows his head and speaks in a whisper to the flame. Have I not seen it, ghostly one? His voice does not ring out to the world. Mine are no words for anyone's ears. They are not words even for the bearers of this load. They are words I must speak secretly, even as my father whispered them in my ears and I in the ears of my first-born. I cannot shout them to the wind and the open night sky.

JANE: Simon . . .

PILKINGS: Don't interfere. Please!

IYALOJA: They have slain the favourite horse of the King and slain his dog. They have borne them from pulse to pulse centre of the land receiving prayers for their King. But the rider has chosen to stay behind. Is it too much to ask that he speak his heart to heart of the waiting courier? [PILKINGS *turns his back on her.*] So be it, Elesin Oba, you see how even the mere leavings are denied you. [*She gestures to the* PRAISE-SINGER.]

PRAISE-SINGER: Elesin Oba! I call you by that name only this last time. Remember when I said, If you cannot come, tell my horse. [*Pause.*] What? I cannot hear you? I said, If you cannot come, whisper in the ears of my horse. Is your tongue severed from the roots, Elesin? I can hear no response. I said, If there are boulders you cannot climb, mount my horse's back, this spotless black stallion, he'll bring you over them. [*Pauses.*] Elesin Oba, once you had a tongue that darted like a drummer's stick. I said, If you get lost my dog will track a path to me. My memory fails me but I think you replied: My feet have found the path, Alafin.

[*The dirge rises and falls.*]

I said at the last, If evil hands hold you back, just tell my horse there is weight on the hem of your smock. I dare not wait too long.

[*The dirge rises and falls.*]

There lies the swiftest ever messenger of a king, so set me free with the errand of your heart. There lie the head and heart of the favourite of the gods, whisper in his ears. Oh my companion, if you had followed when you should, we would not say that the horse preceded its rider. If you had followed when it was time, we would not say the dog has raced beyond and left his master behind. If you had raised your will to cut the thread of life at the summons of the drums, we would not say your mere shadow fell across the gateway and took its owner's place at the banquet. But the hunter, laden with slain buffalo, stayed to root in the cricket's hole with his toes. What now is left? If there is a dearth of bats, the pigeon must serve us for the offering. Speak the words over your shadow which must now serve in your place.

ELESIN: I cannot approach. Take off the cloth. I shall speak my message from heart to heart of silence.

IYALOJA: [*Moves forward and removes the covering.*] Your courier, Elesin, cast your eyes on the favoured companion of the King.

[*Rolled up in the mat, his head and feet showing at either end, is the body of* OLUNDE.]

There lies the honour of your household and of our race. Because he could not bear to let honour fly out of doors, he stopped it with his life. The son has proved the father, Elesin, and there is nothing left in your mouth to gnash but infant gums.

PRAISE-SINGER: Elesin, we placed the reins of the world in your hands yet you watched it plunge over the edge of the bitter precipice. You sat with folded arms while evil strangers tilted the world from its course and crashed it beyond the edge of emptiness—you muttered, There is little that one man can do, you left us floundering in a blind future. Your heir has taken the burden on himself. What the end will be, we are not gods to tell. But this young shoot has poured its sap into the parent stalk, and we know this is not the way of life. Our world is tumbling in the void of strangers, Elesin.

[ELESIN *has stood rock-still, his knuckles taut on the bars, his eyes glued to the body of his son. The stillness seizes and paralyses everyone, including* PILKINGS, *who has turned to look. Suddenly* ELESIN *flings one arm round his neck, once, and with the loop of the chain, strangles himself in a swift, decisive pull. The* GUARDS *rush forward to stop him but they are only in time to let his body down.* PILKINGS *has leapt to the door at the same time and struggles with the lock. He rushes within, fumbles with the handcuffs and unlocks them, raises the body to a sitting position while he tries to give resuscitation. The* WOMEN *continue their dirge, unmoved by the sudden event.*]

IYALOJA: Why do you strain yourself? Why do you labour at tasks for which no one, not even the man lying there, would give you thanks? He is gone at last into the passage but oh, how late it all is. His son will feast on the meat and throw him bones. The passage is clogged with droppings from the King's stallion; he will arrive all stained in dung.

PILKINGS: [*In a tired voice.*] Was this what you wanted?

IYALOJA: No child, it is what you brought to be, you who play with strangers' lives, who even usurp the vestments of our dead, yet believe that the stain of death will not cling to you. The gods demanded only the old expired plantain but you cut down the sap-laden shoot to feed your pride. There is your board, filled to overflowing. Feast on it. [*She screams at him suddenly, seeing that* PILKINGS *is about to close* ELESIN'*s staring eyes.*] Let him alone! However sunk he was in debt he is no pauper's carrion abandoned on the road. Since when have strangers donned clothes of indigo before the bereaved cries out his loss?

[*She turns to the* BRIDE *who has remained motionless throughout.*]

Child.

[*The girl takes up a little earth, walks calmly into the cell and closes* ELESIN'*s eyes. She then pours some earth over each eyelid and comes out again.*]

IYALOJA: Now forget the dead, forget even the living. Turn your mind only to the unborn.

[*She goes off, accompanied by the* BRIDE. *The dirge rises in volume and the* WOMEN *continue their sway. Lights fade to a black-out.*]

THE END

1975

RICHARD WRIGHT

From *Twelve Million Black Voices: A Folk History of the Negro in the United States* (1941)

Perhaps never in history has a more utterly unprepared folk wanted to go to the city; we were barely born as a folk when we headed for the tall and sprawling centers of steel and stone. We, who were landless upon the land; we, who had barely managed to live in family groups; . . . we who had never belonged to any organizations except the church and burial societies; we, who had had our personalities blasted with two hundred years of slavery and had been turned loose to shift for ourselves—we were such a folk as this when we moved into a world that was destined to test all we were, that threw us into the scales of competition to weigh our mettle. And how were we to know that, the moment we landless millions of the land—we men who were struggling to be born—set our awkward feet upon the pavements of the city, life would begin to exact of us a heavy toll in death?

We did not know what would happen, what was in store for us. We went innocently, longing and hoping for a life that the Lords of the Land would not let us live. Our hearts were high as we moved northward to the cities. What emotions, fears, what a complex of sensations we felt when, looking out of a train window at the revolving fields, we first glimpsed the sliding waters of the gleaming Ohio! What memories that river evoked in us, memories black and gloomy, yet tinged with the bright border of a wild and desperate hope! The Ohio is more than a river. It is a symbol, a line that runs through our hearts, dividing hope from despair, just as once it bisected the nation, dividing freedom from slavery.

* * *

[Once in the North] we . . . live in the clinging soot just beyond the factory areas, behind the railroad tracks, near the river banks, under the viaducts, by the steel and iron mills, on the edges of the coal and lumber yards. We live in crowded, barn-like rooms, in old rotting buildings where once dwelt rich native whites of a century ago. . . . When we return home at night from our jobs, we are afraid to venture into other sections of the city, for we fear that the white boys will gang up and molest us. When we do go out into white neighborhoods, we always go in crowds, for that is the best mode of protection.

White people say that they are afraid of us, and it often makes us laugh. When they see one of us, they either smile with contempt or amusement. . . . When they see *six* of us, they become downright apprehensive and alarmed. And because they are afraid of us, we are afraid of them. Especially do we feel fear when we meet the gangs of white boys who have been taught—at home and at school—that we black folk are making their parents lose their homes and life's savings because we have moved into their neighborhoods.

They say our presence in their neighborhoods lowers the value of their property. We do not understand why this should be so. We are poor; but they were once poor, too. They make up their minds, because others tell them to, that they must move at once if we rent an apartment near them. Having been warned against us by the Bosses of the Buildings, having heard tall tales about us, about how "bad" we are, they react emotionally as though we had the plague when we move into their neighborhoods. Is it any wonder, then, that their homes are suddenly and drastically reduced in value? They hastily abandon them, sacrificing them to the Bosses of the Buildings. . . .

And the Bosses of the Buildings take these old houses and convert them into "kitchenettes," and then rent them to us at rates so high that they make fabulous fortunes before the houses are too old for habitation. What they do is this: they take, say, a seven-room apartment, . . . and cut it up into seven small apartments, of one room each; they install one small gas stove and one small sink in each room.

* * *

Sometimes five or six of us live in a one-room kitchenette, a place where simple folk such as we should never be held captive. A war sets up in our emotions: one part of our feelings tells us that it is good to be in the city, that we have a chance at life here, that we need but turn a corner to become a stranger, that we no longer need bow and dodge at the sight of the Lords of the Land. Another part of our feelings tells us that, in terms of worry and strain, the cost of living in the kitchenettes is too high, that the city heaps too much responsibility upon us and gives too little security in return.

The kitchenette is the author of the glad tidings that new suckers are in town, ready to be cheated, plundered, and put in their places.

The kitchenette is our prison, our death sentence without a trial, the new form of mob violence that assaults not only the lone individual, but all of us, in its ceaseless attacks.

The kitchenette, with its filth and foul air, with its one toilet for thirty or more tenants, kills our black babies so fast that in many cities twice as many of them die as white babies.

The kitchenette is the seed bed for scarlet fever, dysentery, typhoid, tuberculosis, gonorrhea, syphilis, pneumonia, and malnutrition.

The kitchenette scatters death so widely among us that our death rate exceeds our birth rate, and if it were not for the trains and autos bringing us daily into the city from the plantations, we black folks who dwell in northern cities would die out entirely over the course of a few years.

The kitchenette, with its crowded rooms and incessant bedlam, provides an enticing place for crimes of all sort—crimes against women and children or any stranger who happens to stray into its dark hallways. The noise of our living, boxed in stone and steel, is so loud that even a pistol shot is smothered.

The kitchenette throws desperate and unhappy people into an unbearable closeness of association, thereby increasing latent friction, giving birth to never-ending quarrels of recrimination, accusation, and vindictiveness, producing warped personalities.

The kitchenette injects pressure and tension into our individual personalities, making many of us give up the struggle, walk off and leave wives, husbands, and even children behind to shift as best they can.

The kitchenette creates thousands of one-room homes where our black mothers sit, deserted, with their children about their knees.

The kitchenette blights the personalities of our growing children, disorganizes them, blinds them to hope, creates problems whose effects can be traced in the characters of its child victims for years afterward.

The kitchenette jams our farm girls, while still in their teens, into rooms with men who are restless and stimulated by the noise and lights of the city; and more of our girls have bastard babies than the girls in any other sections of the city.

The kitchenette fills our black boys with longing and restlessness, urging them to run off from home, to join together with other restless black boys in gangs, that brutal form of city courage.

The kitchenette piles up mountains of profits for the Bosses of the Buildings and makes them ever more determined to keep things as they are.

The kitchenette reaches out with fingers full of golden bribes to the officials of the city, persuading them to allow old firetraps to remain standing and occupied long after they should have been torn down.

The kitchenette is the funnel through which our pulverized lives flow to ruin and death on the city pavements, at a profit. . . .

*   *   *

Despite our new worldliness, . . . we keep our churches alive. In fact, we have built more of them than ever here on the city pavements, for it is only when we are within the walls of our churches that we are wholly ourselves, that we keep alive a sense of our personalities in relation to the total world in which we live, that we maintain a quiet and constant communion with all that is deepest in us. Our going to church of a Sunday is like placing one's ear to another's chest to hear the unquenchable murmur of the human heart. In our collective outpourings of song and prayer, the fluid emotions of others make us feel the strength in ourselves. . . . Our churches are where we dip our tired bodies in cool springs of hope, where we retain our wholeness and humanity. . . .

Our churches are centers of social and community life, for we have virtually no other mode of communion and we are usually forbidden to worship God in the temples of the Bosses of the Buildings. . . .

In the Black Belts of the northern cities, our women are the most circumscribed and tragic objects to be found in our lives, and it is to the churches that our black women cling for emotional security and the release of their personalities. Because their orbit of life is narrow—from their kitchenette to the white folk's kitchen and back home again—they love the church more than do our men, who find a large measure of the expression of their lives in the mills and factories. Surrounding our black women are many almost insuperable barriers: they are black, they are women, they are workers; they are triply anchored and restricted in their movements within and without the Black Belts.

So they keep thousands of Little Bethels and Pilgrims and Calvarys and White Rocks and Good Hopes and Mount Olives going with their nickels and dimes.... Sometimes, even in crowded northern cities, elderly black women, hungry for the South but afraid to return, will cultivate tiny vegetable gardens in the narrow squares of ground in front of their hovels.

* * *

Many of our children scorn us; they say that we still wear the red bandanna about our heads, that we are still Uncle Toms. We lean upon our God and scold our children and try to drag them to church with us, but just as we once, years ago, left the plantation to roam the South, so now they leave us for the city pavements. But deep down in us we are glad that our children feel the world hard enough to yearn to wrestle with it. We, the mothers and fathers of the black children, try to hold them back from death, but if we persuade them to stay, or if they come back because we call them, we will pour out our pity upon them. Always our deepest love is toward those children of ours who turn their backs upon our way of life, for our instincts tell us that those brave ones who struggle against death are the ones who bring new life into the world, even though they die to do so, even though our hearts are broken when they die.

We watch strange moods fill our children, and our hearts swell with pain. The streets, with their noise and flaring lights, the taverns, the automobiles, and the poolrooms claim them, and no voice of ours can call them back. They spend their nights away from home; they forget our ways of life, our language, our God. Their swift speech and impatient eyes make us feel weak and foolish. We cannot keep them in school.... We fall upon our knees and pray for them, but in vain. The city has beaten us, evaded us; but they, with young bodies filled with warm blood, feel bitter and frustrated at the sight of the alluring hopes and prizes denied them. It is not their eagerness to fight that makes us afraid, but that they go to death on the city pavements faster than even disease and starvation can take them.... The courts and the morgues become crowded with our lost children....

EARL E. THORPE

From *Africa in the Thought of Negro Americans* (1959)

The continent of Africa is daily growing in economic, political, and cultural significance. Recently a Negro newspaper in St. Louis, Missouri, contained the statement that the newly independent state of Ghana holds a significance for

Negro Americans which is comparable to that which Israel holds for Jewish Americans. How much truth is there in such a statement? Or better still, what does Africa and its history mean to American Negroes? Opinions on this vary greatly, for in an opposite vein from that contained in the St. Louis newspaper, recently the most eminent of all Negro Sociologists[1] stated that most educated Negroes have little but contempt and disdain for Africa and its peoples.

* * *

What is the truth between these two rather extreme views? While the following does not give a categorical answer to this question, . . . a survey of the statements which Afro-Americans have made from time to time respecting this continent and its peoples may shed light on the question.

* * *

Previous to W. E. B. Du Bois, George Washington Williams was the most distinguished of all Negro historians. Together with the colored abolitionists, and most Negro historians of the nineteenth century, Williams accepted many of the then-current stereotypes about his race. However, Williams and others tended to assign to Afro-Americans only the stereotypes which were favorable and to leave the remainder for Negroes who were still in Africa. . . . Of the African, he declared:

> The Negro type is the result of degradation. It is nothing more than the lowest strata of the African race. . . . His blood infected with the poison of his low habitation, his body shrivelled by disease, his intellect veiled in pagan superstitions, the noblest yearnings of his soul strangled at birth by the savage passions of a nature abandoned to sensuality,—the poor Negro of Africa deserves more our pity than our contempt.

* * *

After the brief flurry of talk in the 1880s and '90s about emigration to Africa, and a mild protest against late nineteenth century imperialism, Afro-American interest in the so-called "Dark Continent" appears to have subsided until the 1920s, when, coincident with the Harlem or Negro Renaissance, interest in Africa burgeoned anew. W. E. B. Du Bois led in the sponsorship of meetings designed to bring Negroid peoples closer together. The first Pan-African Congress, held in Paris in 1919, . . . was attended by fifty-seven delegates from the United States of America, the West Indies, and Africa. Racial concord and advancement were the primary objectives. In 1921 a second Pan-African Congress was held which drew 113 delegates to Europe, two years later a third was held, and the last Congress met in New York City in 1927.

* * *

While most Afro-Americans have wished to be a part of the midstream of [American] national life and culture, not all have wanted this integration. A few, either because they felt that the race actually is inferior and could not compete with whites, or because they went to the opposite extreme and came to believe that Negroes were superior and would lose their distinctive qualities, have desired con-

---

1. E. Franklin Frazier (1894–1962), author of several influential sociological studies of African American life and first black president of the American Sociological Society.

tinued segregation in some form, either here or abroad. Marcus Garvey belonged to the latter group. . . .

The movement of the 1920s with which the West Indian immigrant Marcus Garvey has been prominently identified, revolved around an organization called the Universal Improvement Association. Centered in the North, though by no means limited to it, this movement had its genesis in the World War I stimulus to the desire for equality. But while it originated out of the desire for a full share in democracy, the movement really fed on the lynchings . . . and racial strife which characterized the twenties, and on the growing maturity of the race. Sharing the pessimism and disillusionment, as well as the optimism of the period, Marcus Garvey became convinced that the position of his race within the United States was eternally without hope. Thus he advocated a "back to Africa" movement, and in step with the new appreciation which artists and scholars were beginning to show for African culture, Garvey created a veritable cult of blackness. Reacting against the contempt for dark complexions which many white and Negro Americans held, he proclaimed that black is actually the best and "superior" color. Since it coincided with the efforts of . . . scholars in the social sciences, as well as with . . . trends in art, music, and creative literature, the movement "put steel into the spine of many Negroes who had previously been ashamed of their color." Especially did Garveyism appeal to lower-class Negroes, and even yet it represents the nearest semblance to a mass movement which has existed among Afro-Americans. Most Negro organizations and intellectuals opposed the movement, however.

* * *

With the Depression of the thirties and the events leading to World War II, in many ways Afro-American thought gained a new international concern, and Africa, long the focal point of the international interests of Negro Americans, became more integrated in a larger world setting. . . .

During the thirties Negro historians reflected this continuing interest in Africa. Appearing in this general period were [Carter G.] Woodson's *The African Background Outlined* and *African Heroes and Heroines*. . . . "History should be reconstructed," declared Charles Wesley, "so that Africa . . . shall have its proper place." This was a major theme with Negro historians of the period. . . . About one-third of Du Bois's *Black Folk Then and Now*, published in 1939, deals with the African background of the Afro-American, and in 1947 this same author's *The World and Africa* was published. . . . The author stated that he was seeking to "remind readers of . . . how critical a part Africa has played in human history, past and present, and how impossible it is to forget this and rightly explain the present plight of mankind."

* * *

The prominence of the African theatre of battle during the early years of the war,[2] participation of native African troops in the allied cause, and the possible demise of colonialism as a consequence of the war kept Africa prominent in the thought of Negro Americans. With the return of peace, Afro-American race consciousness and pride were bolstered not only by the phenomenal overthrow of imperialism

2. German forces invaded Libya in 1941; two years later they were driven out of North Africa by Allied forces.

and colonialism by yellow, brown, and black people in Asia and Africa, but by the dramatic achievements in racial integration within their own country. And just as the personality and efforts of Mahatma Gandhi had inspired Afro-Americans in the twenties and thirties, he, Kwame Nkrumah, Jomo Kenyatta, Gamel Nasser,[3] and other nationalist leaders in Asia and Africa were great sources of inspiration to them in the late forties and fifties.

It seems almost paradoxical that rampant nationalism in Asia and Africa have evoked a greater internationalism in the thought of Afro-Americans.

. . . In the fifties, in *Black Power*, Richard Wright lifted his cudgel in defense of nationalist aspirations in Africa, while Era Bell Thompson struck a similar note in her *Land of My Fathers*. . . . Both Wright and Thompson based their convictions on direct observation of conditions in Africa. Indeed, a dominant characteristic of the mid-twentieth century Negro vis-a-vis Africa is the greatly increased number who have visited that continent. . . . This travel is helping to dispel much of the ignorance about Africa and Africans which has been evident among Negro Americans. Thus many of the old stereotypes once commonly accepted are now rapidly being discarded.

* * *

As a consequence of the degradation of slavery, Negroes have been unique among Americans in the rejection of the land of their fathers. Now a greater maturity and developing race pride are bringing an end to this rejection, and it would not be surprising, to the present writer at least, to see the masses of Afro-Americans soon embrace Africa with a force comparable to that which the Irish and Jewish Americans show for the lands of their fathers.

PHAON GOLDMAN

From *The Significance of African Freedom for the Negro American* (1960)

With Africa in the headlines every day it behooves us as alert, adult Americans, to know more about Africa and her peoples and the new nations being born almost monthly on this the world's second largest continent. One of my professors used to say that all we know (as Negro Americans) about Africa was that it was shaped like a "po'k chop"—and it is, too, if you'll notice the map. It's a pork chop that's sizzling nowadays.

Africa is significant not only because it's in the news, but also because we have an ancestral connection with the peoples of Africa—a connection we need to review and re-appraise. We have only heard since we were wee tots about Africa in terms of the exotic, the outlandish—land of cannibals, slithering snakes, and people who go around boiling missionaries in a pot. These are the

---

3. Gamel Nasser (1918–70), first president of the republic of Egypt (1956–70). Kwame Nkrumah (1909–72), first prime minister, then first president, of Ghana (1957–66). Jomo Kenyatta (1893–1978), first president of Kenya (1964–78).

one-sided views of Africa we have been taught; these would furnish material for books and movies that would sell. Seldom, if ever, did we hear the appraisals of Africa made by the most learned scholars of old, such as Ibn Batuda, greatest of the Moslem travelers of the Middle Ages—a man who had traveled throughout most of the then known world, said this of West Africa (in contrast to Spain, Syria, India, China, Turkey, etc.), "Nowhere is there a higher regard for justice or greater security. One can travel throughout the kingdom of the blacks without fear of thieves, robbers, vagabonds, or other evil persons." . . .

* * *

There is also another instance of our background and connection with Africa which we have come to see only in one light, and that is our outlook on the system of slavery—the instrument that brought us to these shores. When we think of slavery we too often visualize happy-go-lucky slaves captured easily and without a struggle. But the truth of the matter is that the Portuguese, Dutch, and British, fought many a pitched battle to capture most of the Africans that were taken into slavery. Those men, sold into the chains of the European slave-traders by other Africans, were most often warriors who had been captured in intervillage battles. Tens of thousands of these men died by their own hand on the long middle passage rather than submit to that day's form of man's inhumanity to man. So you can see that our ancestors represent not a bunch of cringing cowards but the most valiant of men in body and spirit.

* * *

The valor and sense of justice of the ancient peoples of West Africa can most clearly be seen . . . in the determined, forthright, and courageous stand for freedom now being taken by our young Negro youth of the South who in spite of threats, insults, and violence, stand by their right to be accorded the simple human decencies that all other people on earth get in America. The strength of our forefathers is with us still, and make no mistake about it, the students' inspiration came from the fight for freedom now being waged all over the African continent . . .

These are sides of our past which have been deliberately buried, for if a man can convince you that you came from nothing, that you are nothing, and that you never will be anything, he doesn't need to worry about you trying to break down segregation barriers, for he has already convinced you that you are different from other human beings and you will be content with your lot.

There are other ways in which we have come to disrespect ourselves too—subtle ways, ways that affect our subconscious mind and blunt our demand for "Freedom Now," and the human dignity accorded all other peoples.

* * *

[One] subconscious factor causing us to feel we're different from others and therefore perhaps should be treated differently, is the American standard of beauty. . . . The faces we see on TV, in the movies and in the magazine ads, reflect the Anglo-Saxon characteristics of the thin nose, a white skin, and straight hair. Being a minority people of physically diametrically opposite characteristics, but set down in the middle of other values, we begin to subconsciously feel that we need to make ourselves over, physically, in order to become acceptable to the majority. So we're told that certain skin preparations will make us "lighter, brighter, and more acceptable" and similar positive attributes are assigned to hair preparations that give us 'straight' hair instead of the curly variety we have.

* * *

So to sum up, with Africa in the news every day we must re-view our past concepts of Africa and our relations with the African people, we must view their current battle for "Freedom Now" through the pressures of boycotts, strikes, and mass protests as that stage of man's eternal quest for human dignity that brings the issues out into the open and forces a decision. We must keep ever in mind that the cry of "Freedom Now" is but the present-day application of the ideas of men like Thomas Jefferson and Patrick Henry whose cry of "Give me liberty or give me death" brought freedom to this country and still inspires men to fight for freedom around the world.

Perhaps the greatest significance of African freedom for the Negro American is that it may light the way for those of us of African descent here in America to re-vitalize America's conscience by moving together now for our freedom and force America to solve her moral dilemma of the race question and resume her rightful place as a world leader by showing in deed as well as in preachment that she is truly the land of "liberty and justice for all."

NAACP POLITICAL ACTION COMMITTEE

STOKELY CARMICHAEL AND CHARLES V. HAMILTON

From *Black Power: The Politics of Liberation in America* (1967)

. . . Black people in this country form a colony, and it is not in the interest of the colonial power to liberate them. Black people are legal citizens of the United States with, for the most part, the same *legal* rights as other citizens. Yet they stand as colonial subjects in relation to the white society. Thus institutional racism has another name: colonialism.

Obviously, the analogy is not perfect. One normally associates a colony with a land and people subjected to, and physically separated from, the "Mother Country." This is not always the case, however; in South Africa and Rhodesia, black and white inhabit the same land—with blacks subordinated to whites just as in the English, French, Italian, Portuguese, and Spanish colonies. It is the objective relationship which counts, not rhetoric (such as constitutions *articulating* equal rights) or geography.

The analogy is not perfect in another respect. Under classic colonialism, the colony is a source of cheaply produced raw materials (usually agricultural or mineral) which the "Mother Country" then processes into finished goods and sells at high profit—sometimes back to the colony itself. The black communities of the United States do not export anything except human labor. But is the differentiation more than a technicality? Essentially, the African colony is selling its labor; the product itself does not belong to the "subjects" because the land is not theirs. At the same time, let us look at the black people of the South: cultivating cotton at $3.00 for a ten-hour day and from that buying cotton dresses (and food and other goods) from white manufacturers. . . . Black people in the United States have a colonial relationship to the larger society, a relationship characterized by institutional racism. That colonial status operates in three areas—political, economic, social. . . .

Colonial subjects have their political decisions made for them by the colonial masters, and those decisions are handed down directly or through a process of "indirect rule." Politically, decisions which affect black lives have always been made by white people—the "white power structure."

* * *

The black community perceives the "white power structure" in very concrete terms. The man in the ghetto sees his white landlord come only to collect exorbitant rents and fail to make necessary repairs, while both know that the white-dominated city building inspection department will wink at violations or impose only slight fines. The man in the ghetto sees the white policeman on the corner brutally manhandle a black drunkard in a doorway, and at the same time accept a pay-off from one of the agents of the white-controlled rackets. . . . He looks at the absence of a meaningful curriculum in the ghetto schools—for example, the history books that woefully overlook the historical achievements of black people—and he knows that the school board is controlled by whites. He is not about to listen to intellectual discourses on the pluralistic and fragmented nature of political power. He is faced with a "white power structure" as monolithic as Europe's colonial offices have been to African and Asian colonies.

There is another aspect of colonial politics frequently found in colonial Africa and in the United States: the process of indirect rule. . . . In other words, the white power structure rules the black community through local blacks who are responsive to the white leaders, the downtown, white machine, not to the black populace. These black politicians do not exercise effective power. They cannot be relied upon to make forceful demands in behalf of their black constituents, and they become no more than puppets.

* * *

This process of cooptation and a subsequent widening of the gap between the black elites and the masses is common under colonial rule. There has developed in this country an entire class of "captive leaders" in the black communities. These are black people with certain technical and administrative skills who could provide useful leadership roles in the black communities but do not because they have become beholden to the white power structure. These are black school teachers, county agents, junior executives in management positions with companies, etc. . . .

* * *

Historically, colonies have existed for the sole purpose of enriching, in one form or another, the "colonizer"; the consequence is to maintain the economic dependency of the "colonized." All too frequently we hear of the missionary motive behind colonization: to "civilize," to "Christianize" the underdeveloped, backward peoples. . . . One is immediately reminded of the bitter maxim voiced by many black Africans today: the missionaries came for our goods, not for our good. Indeed, the missionaries turned the Africans' eyes toward heaven, and then robbed them blind in the process.

* * *

Professor Kenneth Clark described the economic colonization of the *Dark Ghetto* [1965] as follows:

> The ghetto feeds upon itself; it does not produce goods or contribute to the prosperity of the city. It has few large businesses. . . . Even though the white community has tried to keep the Negro confined in ghetto pockets, the white businessman has not stayed out of the ghetto. A ghetto, too, offers opportunities for profit, and in a competitive society profit is to be made where it can.
>
> In Harlem there is only one large department store and that is owned by whites. Negroes own a savings and loan association; and one Negro-owned bank has recently been organized. The other banks are branches of white-owned downtown banks. Property—apartment houses, stores, businesses, bars, concessions, and theaters—are for the most part owned by persons who live outside the community and take their profits home . . .
>
> When tumult arose in ghetto streets in the summer of 1964, most of the stores broken into and looted belonged to white men. Many of these owners responded to the destruction with bewilderment and anger, for they felt that they had been serving a community that needed them. *They did not realize* that the residents were not grateful for this service but bitter, as natives often feel toward the functionaries of a colonial power who in the very act of service, keep the hated *structure of oppression intact.*

* * *

This is not to say that every single white American consciously oppresses black people. He does not need to. Institutional racism has been maintained deliberately by the power structure and through indifference, inertia, and lack of courage on the part of white masses as well as petty officials. Whenever black demands for change become loud and strong, indifference is replaced by active opposition based on fear and self-interest. The line between purposeful suppression and indifference blurs. One way or another, most whites participate in economic colonialism.

* * *

The social and psychological effects on black people of all their degrading experiences are also very clear. . . . Born into this society today, black people begin to doubt themselves, their worth as human beings. Self-respect becomes almost impossible. Kenneth Clark describes the process in *Dark Ghetto*:

> Human beings who are forced to live under ghetto conditions and whose daily experience tells them that almost nowhere in society are they respected and granted the ordinary dignity and courtesy accorded to others will, as a matter of course, begin to doubt their own worth. Since every human being depends upon his cumulative experiences with others for clues as to how he should view and value himself, children who are consistently rejected understandably begin to question and doubt whether they, their family, and their group really deserve no more respect from the larger society than they receive. These doubts become the

seeds of a pernicious self- and group-hatred, the Negro's complex and debilitating prejudice against himself.

The preoccupation of many Negroes with hair straighteners, skin bleachers, and the like illustrates this tragic aspect of American racial prejudice—Negroes have come to believe in their own inferiority.

There was the same result in Africa. . . .

In a manner similar to that of the colonial powers in Africa, American society indicates avenues of escape from the ghetto for those individuals who adapt to the "mainstream." This adaptation means to disassociate oneself from the black race, its culture, community and heritage, and become immersed (dispersed is another term) in the white world. What actually happens, as Professor E. Franklin Frazier pointed out in his book, *Black Bourgeoisie* [1957], is that the black person ceases to identify himself with black people yet is obviously unable to assimilate with whites. He becomes a "marginal man," living on the fringes of both societies in a world largely of "make believe." This black person is urged to adopt American middle-class standards and values. As with the black African who had to become a "Frenchman" in order to be accepted, so to be an American, the black man must strive to become "white." To the extent that he does, he is considered "well adjusted"—one who has "risen above the race question." These people are frequently held up by the white Establishment as living examples of the progress being made by the society in solving the race problem. Suffice it to say that precisely because they are required to denounce—overtly or covertly—their black race, *they are reinforcing racism in this country.*

ROBERT BLAUNER

From *Internal Colonialism and Ghetto Revolt* (1969)

Classic colonialism involved the control and exploitation of the majority of a nation by a minority of outsiders. Whereas in America the people who are oppressed were themselves originally outsiders and are a numerical minority.

* * *

The essential condition for both American slavery and European colonialism was the power domination and the technological superiority of the Western world in its relation to peoples of non-Western and non-white origins. This objective supremacy in technology and military power buttressed the West's sense of cultural superiority, laying the basis for racist ideologies that were elaborated to justify control and exploitation of non-white people. Thus because classical colonialism and America's internal version developed out of a similar balance of technological, cultural, and power relations, a common *process* of social oppression characterized the racial patterns in the two contexts—despite the variation in political and social structure.

* * *

In present-day America, a major device of Black colonization is the powerless ghetto. . . .

Of course many ethnic groups in America have lived in ghettoes. What make the Black ghettoes an expression of colonized status are three special features. First, the ethnic ghettoes arose more from voluntary choice, both in the sense of the choice to immigrate to America and the decision to live among one's fellow ethnics. Second, the immigrant ghettoes tended to be one and two generation phenomenon; they were actually way-stations in the process of acculturation and assimilation. . . . The Black ghetto on the other hand has been a more permanent phenomenon, although some individuals do escape it. But most relevant is the third point. European ethnic groups like the Poles, Italians, and Jews generally only experienced a brief period, often less than a generation, during which their residential buildings, commercial stores, and other enterprises were owned by outsiders. The Chinese and Japanese faced handicaps of color prejudice that were almost as strong as the Blacks faced, but very soon gained control of their internal communities, because their traditional ethnic culture and social organization had not been destroyed by slavery and internal colonization. But Afro-Americans are distinct in the extent to which their segregated communities have remained controlled economically, politically, and administratively from the outside. . . .

* * *

The most total destruction of culture in the colonization process took place not in traditional colonialism but in America. . . . The integral cultures of the diverse African peoples who furnished the slave trade were destroyed because slaves from different tribes, kingdoms, and linguistic groups were purposely separated to maximize domination and control. Thus language, religion, and national loyalties were lost in North America much more completely than [elsewhere]. . . .

Yet a similar cultural process unfolds in both contexts of colonialism. To the extent that they are involved in the larger society and economy, the colonized are caught up in a conflict between two cultures. Fanon[4] has described how the assimilation-oriented schools of Martinique taught him to reject his own culture and Blackness in favor of Westernized, French, and white values. Both the colonized elites under traditional colonialism and perhaps the majority of Afro-Americans today experience a parallel split in identity, cultural loyalty, and political orientation.

The colonizers use their culture to socialize the colonized elites (intellectuals, politicians, and middle class) into an identification with the colonial system. Because Western culture has the prestige, the power, and the key to open the limited opportunity that a minority of the colonized may achieve, the first reaction seems to be an acceptance of the dominant values.

Cultural revitalization movements play a key role in anti-colonial movements. They follow an inner necessity and logic of their own that comes from the consequences of colonialism on groups and personal identities; they are also essential to provide the solidarity which the political or military phase of the anti-colonial revolution requires. . . . That Afro-Americans are moving toward cultural nationalism in a period when ethnic loyalties tend to be weak (and perhaps on the decline) in this country is another confirmation of the unique colonized position of the Black group.

---

4. Frantz Fanon (1925–61), French West Indian psychiatrist, leader of the Algerian National Front, and author of the influential anticolonial works *Black Skin, White Masks* (1952) and *The Wretched of the Earth* (1961).

HENRY JOHN DREWAL, JOHN PEMBERTON III, AND
ROWLAND ABIODUN

From *Yoruba: Nine Centuries of African Art and Thought* (1989)

The Yoruba-speaking peoples of Nigeria and the Popular Republic of Benin, together with their countless descendants in other parts of Africa and the Americas, have made remarkable contributions to world civilization.[5] Their urbanism is ancient and legendary, probably dating to A.D. 800–1000, according to the results of archeological excavations at two ancient city sites, Oyo and Ife.[6] These were only two of numerous complex city-states headed by sacred rulers (both women and men) and councils of elders and chiefs. Many have flourished up to our own time. The dynasty of kings at Ife, for example, regarded by the Yoruba as the place of origin of life itself and of human civilization, remains unbroken to the present day.

In the arts, the Yoruba are heirs to one of the oldest and finest artistic traditions in Africa, a tradition that remains vital and influential today. By A.D. 1100 the artists at Ife had already developed an exquisitely refined and highly naturalistic sculptural tradition in terracotta and stone that was soon followed by works in copper, brass and bronze. . . .

Of the series of remarkable Yoruba kingdoms over the last nine centuries, one of the earliest was Oyo, sited near the Niger River, the "Nile" of West Africa. Straddling this important trading corridor Oyo and its feared cavalry flourished between 1600 and 1830 and came to dominate a vast territory. . . .

The Ijebu Yoruba kingdoms (1400–1900) . . . were the first Yoruba to establish trading ties with Europeans in the late fifteenth century. Over the next four centuries, the Yoruba kingdoms prospered and then declined as the devastating effects of the slave trade and internecine warfare of the nineteenth century took their toll. The stage was set for the ascendancy of the British and the advent of colonial rule at the end of the nineteenth century.

One of the effects of eighteenth- and nineteenth-century disruptions was the dispersal of millions of Yoruba peoples over the globe, primarily to the Americas—Haiti, Cuba, Trinidad, and Brazil—where their late arrival and enormous numbers ensured a strong Yoruba character in the artistic, religious, and social lives of Africans in the New World. That imprint persists today in many arts and in a variety of African-American faiths that have arisen not only in the Caribbean and South America, but also in urban centers across the United States.[7] Yoruba philosophical, religious, and artistic tenets, ideas, and icons have transformed and continue to transform religious beliefs and practices and the arts of persons far beyond Africa's shores.

5. Throughout this [selection] we use the term Yoruba as shorthand for Yoruba-speaking peoples who historically identified themselves by their independent but interactive city-states, such as Ife, Ijebu, Owo, Ekiti, Oyo, and others. Despite significant cultural diversity, Yoruba-speaking peoples assert their common origins at Ile-Ife and share certain fundamental social, political, religious, philosophical, and artistic concepts that justify the now widely used and accepted designation of Yoruba. [Authors' note]

6. See R. S. Smith, *Kingdoms of the Yoruba* (London: Methuen, 1969). [Authors' note]

7. The African American religious communities include Lucumi, Candomble, Shango, Santeria, Vodun, Umbanda, and Macumba. [Author's note]

There are several fundamental concepts that are distinctive to a Yoruba world view.

The Yoruba Cosmos

The Yoruba conceive of the cosmos as consisting of two distinct yet inseparable realms—*aye* (the visible, tangible world of the living) and *orun* (the invisible, spiritual realm of the ancestors, gods, and spirits) (see the diagram on p. 2033). . . .

. . . The Yoruba conceive of the past as accessible and essential as a model for the present. They believe that persons live, depart, and are reborn and that every individual comes from either the gods or one's ancestors on the mother's or the father's side. In addition, rituals are efficacious only when they are performed regularly according to tenets from the past and creatively re-presented to suit the present.

Orun: The Otherworld

Olodumare (also known as Odumare, Olorun, Eleda, Eleemi) is conceived as the creator of existence, without sexual identity and generally distant, removed from the affairs of both divine and worldly beings. Olodumare is the source of *ase*, the life force possessed by everything that exists. *Orun* (the otherworld), the abode of the sacred, is populated by countless forces such as *orisa* (gods), *ara orun* (ancestors) and *oro, iwin, ajogun,* and *egbe* (various spirits), who are close to the living and frequently involved in human affairs.

The *orisa* are deified ancestors and/or personified natural forces. They are grouped broadly into two categories depending upon their personalities and modes of action—the "cool, temperate, symbolically white gods" (*orisa funfun*), and the "hot, temperamental gods" (*orisa gbigbona*). The former tend to be gentle, soothing, calm, and reflective and include: Obatala/Orisanla, the divine sculptor; Osoosi/Eyinle, hunter and water lord; Osanyin, lord of leaves and medicines; Oduduwa, first monarch at Ile-Ife; Yemoja, Osun, Yewa, and Oba, queens of their respective rivers; Olosa, ruler of the lagoon; and Olokun, goddess of the sea. Many of the "hot gods" are male, although some are female. They include: Ogun, god of Iron; Sango, former king of Oyo and lord of thunder; Obaluaye, lord of pestilence; and Oya, Sango's wife and queen of the whirlwind. The latter tend to be harsh, demanding, aggressive and quick-tempered.

This characterization of the *orisa* has nothing to do with issues of good and evil. All gods, like humans, possess both positive and negative values—strengths as well as foibles. Only their modes of action differ, which is the actualization of their distinctive *ase* (life force), as expressed by their natures or personalities (*iwa*). Furthermore, the gods are not ranked in any hierarchy. Their relative importance in any given part of the Yoruba world reflects their relative local popularity, reputation, and influence, and the order in which they are invoked in ceremonies has to do with their roles in the ritual and their relationships to each other.

The gods regularly enter the world through their mediums—worshippers who have been trained and prepared to receive the spirit of their divinities during possession trances in the course of religious ceremonies. When the gods are made manifest in this way, they speak through their devotees, praying and giving guidance.

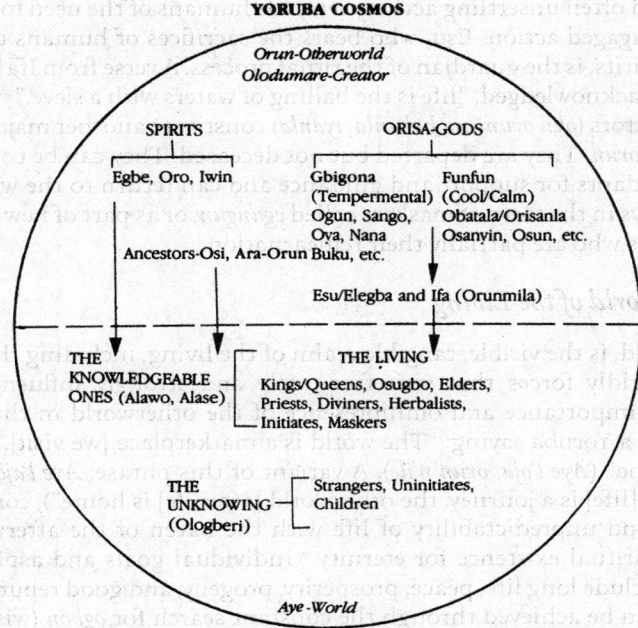

YORUBA COSMOS

Orun-Otherworld
Olodumare-Creator

SPIRITS

Egbe, Oro, Iwin

Ancestors-Osi, Ara-Orun Buku, etc.

ORISA-GODS

Gbigona
(Tempermental)
Ogun, Sango,
Oya, Nana

Funfun
(Cool/Calm)
Obatala/Orisanla
Osanyin, Osun, etc.

Esu/Elegba and Ifa (Orunmila)

THE
KNOWLEDGEABLE
ONES (Alawo, Alase)

THE LIVING
Kings/Queens, Osugbo, Elders,
Priests, Diviners, Herbalists,
Initiates, Maskers

THE
UNKNOWING
(Ologberi)

Strangers, Uninitiates,
Children

Aye -World

A diagram of some of the key elements of the Yoruba cosmos. It consists of two distinct yet interactive realms—*aye*, the tangible world of the living, and *orun*, the invisible realm of spiritual forces such as the gods, ancestors, and spirits. All beings, whether living or spiritual, possess life force, *ase*. Those wise individuals such as priests, initiates, diviners, rulers, and elders who learn to use it for the benefit of themselves and those around them are known as *alase* or *alawo*. Drawing by H. J. Drewal.

While all the gods periodically journey to the world, two sacred powers, Ifa and Esu/Elegba, stand at the threshold between the realms of *orun* and *aye*, assisting in communication between the divine and human realms. Ifa, actually a Yoruba system of divination, is presided over by Orunmila, its deified mythic founder, who is also sometimes called Ifa. . . .

Ifa offers humans the possibility of knowing the forces at work in specific situations in their lives and of influencing the course of events through prayer and sacrifice. The diviner, or *babalawo* ("father of ancient wisdom"), uses the rituals and poetry of Ifa to identify cosmic forces: the gods, ancestors, and spirits, and the machinations of the enemies of humankind personified as Death, Disease, Infirmity, and Loss; . . . and the sometimes evil-intentioned persons known collectively as *araye* ("people-of-the-world") who include *aje* (witches), *oso* (wizards), and others.

While Ifa symbolizes the revealable, Esu/Elegba is the agent of effective action, who also reminds one of the unpredictable nature of human experience. Esu's

2032 CH. 30 / CULTURAL AND HISTORICAL CONTEXT

constant and often unsettling activity reminds humans of the need for guidance in lives of engaged action. Esu, who bears the sacrifices of humans to the *orisa* and other spirits, is the guardian of the ritual process. A verse from Ifa warns that if Esu is not acknowledged, "life is the bailing of waters with a sieve."

The ancestors (*oku orun, osi, babanla, iyanla*) constitute another major category of beings in *orun*. They are departed but not deceased. They can be contacted by their descendants for support and guidance and can return to the world either for short stays in the form of maskers called *egungun*, or as part of new persons in their lineages who are partially their reincarnation.

Aye: The World of the Living

Aye, the world, is the visible, tangible realm of the living, including those invisible otherworldly forces that visit frequently and strongly influence human affairs. The importance and omnipresence of the otherworld in this world is expressed in a Yoruba saying: "The world is a marketplace [we visit], the otherworld is home" (*Aye l'oja, orun n'ile*). A variant of this phrase, *Aye l'ajo, orun n'ile* ("The world [life] is a journey, the otherworld [afterlife] is home"), contrasts the movement and unpredictability of life with the haven of the afterworld that promises spiritual existence for eternity.[8] Individual goals and aspirations in the world include long life, peace, prosperity, progeny, and good reputation. Ideally, these can be achieved through the constant search for *ogbon* (wisdom), *imo* (knowledge), and *oye* (understanding).

Yoruba society is traditionally open, but with a long history of monarchical and hierarchical organization. Nevertheless, decision making is shared widely—consensual rather than autocratic or dictatorial—and an elaborate series of checks and balances ensures an essentially egalitarian system. Just as all the gods are equal in relation to Olodumare, so too all lineages are structurally equal in their relation to the sacred king. At the same time, the possibility of mobility is fundamental, depending on how one marshals the forces in the environment. The situation is remarkably fluid and dynamic. Within this context, there is some recognition of rank, yet distribution of responsibilities and authority are given more importance than hierarchy. Seniority is based on the age of the person, the antiquity of the title, and the person's tenure in office. Such an ideal for social interaction is rooted in the concept of *ase*, the life force possessed by all individuals and unique to each one. Thus *ase* must be acknowledged and used in all social matters and in dealings with divine forces as well.

Ase: Life Force

Ase is given by Olodumare to everything—gods, ancestors, spirits, humans, animals, plants, rocks, rivers, and voiced words such as songs, prayers, praises, curses, or even everyday conversation. Existence, according to Yoruba thought, is dependent upon it; it is the power to make things happen and change. In addition to its

8. For the importance of the metaphor of the "journey" in Yoruba thought and in ritual practice, see M. T. Drewal, "Performer, Play, and Agency: Yoruba Ritual Process." Ph.D. Thesis, New York University, 1989. [Authors' note]

sacred characteristics, *ase* also has important social ramifications, reflected in its translation as "power, authority, command." A person who, through training, experience, and initiation, learns how to use the essential life force of things is called an *alaase*. Theoretically, every individual possesses a unique blend of performative power and knowledge—the potential for certain achievements. Yet because no one can know with certainty the potential of others, *eso* (caution), *ifarabale* (composure), *owo* (respect), and *suuru* (patience) are highly valued in Yoruba society and shape all social interactions and organization.

Social processes encourage the participation of all and the contribution of the *ase* of every person. For example, members of the council of elder men and women, known as Osugbo among the Ijebu Yoruba and Ogboni in the Oyo area, have hereditary titles that rotate among many lineages, and there are other positions that are open to all in the society, as well as honorary titles bestowed on those who have made special contributions to the community. Members stress the equality of such positions in emphasizing their distinctive rights and responsibilities. All are seen as crucial to the successful functioning of the society as evident in Osugbo rituals. The members share kola nut, the drummers play the praises of titles, individuals take turns hosting a series of celebrations, each person has the opportunity to state opinions during debates, and all decisions are consensual. Osugbo members stress the autonomy of their individual roles while at the same time asserting their equality in decision making. At various times some will dominate while others acquiesce, which is entirely in keeping with Yoruba notions of the distinctive *ase* of individuals and the fluid social reality of competing powers that continually shape society.

Rituals to invoke divine forces reflect this same concern for the autonomous *ase* of particular entities. Those invoked first are not more important or higher in rank, rather they are called first in order to perform specific tasks—such as the divine mediator Esu/Elegba who "opens the way" for communication between humans and gods. The recognition of the uniqueness and autonomy of the *ase* of persons and gods is what structures society and its relationship with the otherworld.

SUGGESTIONS FOR WRITING

1. Langston Hughes's poem "Harlem (A Dream Deferred)" poses a question: "What happens to a dream deferred?" Why do you think Lorraine Hansberry chose this poem as the epigraph for *A Raisin in the Sun*? Which of the different "dreams" in the play does the play as a whole endorse? Write an essay in which you discuss the various "dreams" that are so central to the play. Does the play ultimately answer Hughes's question?

2. In *Twelve Million Black Voices: A Folk History of the Negro in the United States*, Richard Wright describes the hopes of black migrants to the North and the sometimes-squalid conditions that awaited them. With reference to Wright's essay and the other primary materials in this chapter, write an essay in which you explore how *A Raisin in the Sun* illustrates various currents in black intellectual thought of the mid-twentieth century.

3. *A Raisin in the Sun* is set in Chicago, but in many ways its heart is in Africa—the Africa of the mythical past, the Africa of the slave trade, and the Africa of the play's own temporal setting. Write an essay in which you explore the many ways in which African history and culture inform Hansberry's play. How African are the play's

African American characters? To what extent does the play illustrate the ideas found in Earl E. Thorpe's *Africa in the Thought of Negro Americans* and Phaon Goldman's *The Significance of African Freedom for the Negro American*?

4. Hansberry's play explores not only the evolving social and economic position of African Americans in the mid-twentieth century, but also their evolving gender roles. On the one hand, we are reminded of the patriarchal nature of traditional African cultures; on the other hand, the Younger household seems to fulfill the more modern stereotype of the African American family dominated by women. Write an essay in which you discuss the crucial role that gender plays in the action of the play. Does *A Raisin in the Sun* seem to endorse any particular family structure as "ideal" for African Americans?

5. In *A Raisin in the Sun*'s third act, Beneatha asserts that "there isn't any real progress . . . there is only one large circle that we march in, around and around, each of us with our own little picture—in front of us—our own little mirage that we think is the future." Asagai counters that progress follows "a long line—as in geometry, you know, one that reaches into infinity." Write an essay in which you compare and contrast these two views of history as they are depicted in *A Raisin in the Sun*. Does the play seem to endorse one view over the other? Does the play seem to contain seeds of the ideas found in Stokely Carmichael and Charles V. Hamilton's *Black Power*, or the essay by Robert Blauner?

6. What must a Western audience know—or be shown—in order to appreciate the Yoruba culture of *Death and the King's Horseman*? Research traditional Yoruba dress, music, and dance, and write an essay in which you discuss how you would stage a production of the play for American or European audiences.

7. How well does Soyinka's play illustrate the ideas about colonialism found in *Black Power* by Stokely Carmichael and Charles V. Hamilton? What evidence of "cooptation" and "captive leaders" do you see in the play? Write an essay in which you discuss the depiction of colonialism in *Death and the King's Horseman*.

8. Soyinka's play offers a rare glimpse into the richly complex traditional culture of the Yoruba. Using the information found in *Yoruba: Nine Centuries of African Art and Thought* by Henry John Drewal, John Pemberton III, and Rowland Abiodun, as well as other materials you might find through research, write a detailed introduction to the play, outlining the Yoruban social and spiritual beliefs at the center of the play's drama.

9. Both Hansberry's *A Raisin in the Sun* and Soyinka's *Death and the King's Horseman* feature characters who are students straddling the very different worlds of traditional Africa and the modern West. Write an essay in which you compare and contrast Hansberry's Asagai and Soyinka's Olunde. How do the characters function dramatically in their respective plays? What different ideas about cultural understanding does each seem to represent? How might they illustrate what Soyinka calls "complementarities" between Western and African cultures?

31 CRITICAL CONTEXTS: SOPHOCLES' *ANTIGONE*

Even more than other forms of literature, drama has a relatively stable **canon**—that is, a select group of plays that the theater community thinks of as especially worthy of frequent performance. New plays join this canon, of course, but theater companies worldwide tend to perform the same ones over and over, especially those by Shakespeare, Ibsen, and Sophocles. The reasons are many, involving the plays' themes and continued appeal across times and cultures as well as their formal literary and theatrical features. But their repeated performance means that a relatively small number of plays become much better known than all the others and that there is a tradition of "talk" about those plays. A lot of this talk is informal and local, resulting from the fact that people see plays communally—that is, they see performances together and often compare responses afterward. But more permanent and more formal records of responses also exist; individual productions of plays are often reviewed in newspapers and magazines, on radio and television, and on the Internet. Such reviews concentrate primarily on evaluating specific performances. But because every production of a play involves a particular interpretation of the text, cumulative accounts of performances add up to a body of interpretive criticism—that is, analytical commentary about many aspects of the play as text and as performance. Scholars add to that body of criticism by publishing their own interpretations of a play in academic journals and books.

Sophocles' *Antigone*, for instance, attracts attention from a wide variety of perspectives—from Greek scholars, who view it in relation to classical myth or the ancient Greek language; from philosophers, who may see in it examinations of classic ideas and ethical problems; from theater historians, who may think about it in relation to traditions of staging and visualization or the particulars of gestures and stage business; and from historians of rhetoric, who may consider the interactions between the chorus and the players.

As a reader of plays in a textbook like this one, you may or may not bring to your reading an awareness of what others have thought about a particular play, but that body of material is available if you choose to use it as a way of getting additional perspectives on the text. You don't have to read this accumulated criticism to understand what happens in a text; indeed, some of this work may seem irrelevant to you. But reading what others have said about a text can help you—by offering historical information that you hadn't known or hadn't considered relevant, by pointing to problems or possibilities of interpretation you had not yet thought of, or by supporting a reading you had already arrived at. In a sense, reading published criticism is like talking with your fellow students or being involved in a class discussion. In general, you shouldn't read "the critics" until after you have read the complete play at least once, just as you should read the text in full before you discuss it with others. That way, your initial responses to the play are your own; if you don't understand some things, you can always discuss them later or read a few pieces of good criticism.

Reading criticism can be especially help-ful when you have to write a paper. Critics will often guide you to crucial points of debate or to a place in the text that is a crux for deciding on a particular interpretation. You will likely get the most help if you read several critics with different perspectives— not because more is better, but because you will see their differences and, more impor-tant, the *grounds* for their differences in the

A bust of Sophocles

kinds of evidence they use. Their disagree-ments will likely be very useful to you as a new interpreter. But don't regard critics as "authorities" (an interpretation is not true simply because it is published or because it is written by somebody famous); instead, look to critics and their work for indicators of what the issues are.

Often, when you're just starting to think about the paper you want to write, reading a few pieces of criticism can help you see some of the critical issues in the play. Critics frequently disagree on the interpretation of particular issues or pas-sages or even on what the issues really are, but reading their work can make your own thoughts concrete, especially when you're just starting to sort things out. Reacting to someone else's view, especially one that is strongly argued, can help you articulate what you think and can suggest a line of interpretation and argu-ment. Sorting out the important issues can be complicated, and issues do shift from era to era and culture to culture. But often the arguments posed in one era interest subsequent critics in whatever age and from whatever perspective.

If you draw on published criticism in your papers, you should acknowledge the critic up front and then work his or her words into your paper the way you have learned to do with lines or phrases from a text. Sometimes a particular critic can be especially helpful in focusing your thoughts because you so clearly dis-agree with what she or he says. In that case, you may well get a good paper out of a rebuttal in which you answer or attack that critic's argument point by point. Pitting one critic against another—sorting out the issues that interpreters dis-agree on and showing what their differences consist of—can also be a good way to focus on your own contribution. But remember that the point of reading criti-cism is to *use* it for your own interpretive purposes, to make your responses more sensitive and resonant, to make you a more informed reader of the play, and to make you a better reader in general.

* * *

Antigone's performance history goes back more than twenty-four centuries, and over that time readers and viewers have recorded many thousands of responses. Following the text of the play below, we reprint only a small sample, all from the

A production of *Antigone*
(New York Shakespeare Festival, 1982)

twentieth century. But earlier views are often referred to and sometimes still argued about. The famous comments of the German philosopher G. W. F. Hegel (1770–1831), for example, continue to set the agenda for an astonishing number of interpreters. Many answer him directly; others use him to sharpen, complicate, or flesh out their views or simply to position themselves in some larger debate about specific issues in the play or about literary criticism or philosophy more generally.

In the following selections, you will find various interpretations of crucial scenes and issues in *Antigone*. Especially prominent are questions about how to read the opinions of the chorus, how to interpret the character of Antigone, and how to assess Creon's flaws. As you read the critics, pay attention to the way they argue—the kinds of textual evidence they use to back up their points and how they structure their arguments—as well as the main interpretive points they make. (Following the chapter is a sample student essay about *Antigone* that draws on one of the critical excerpts in this chapter, as well as other secondary sources.)

SOPHOCLES

Antigone[1]

CHARACTERS

ANTIGONE	HAEMON
ISMENE	TEIRESIAS
CHORUS OF THEBAN ELDERS	A MESSENGER
CREON	EURYDICE
A SENTRY	SECOND MESSENGER

The two sisters ANTIGONE *and* ISMENE *meet in front of the palace gates in Thebes.*

---

1. Translated by David Grene.

ANTIGONE: Ismene, my dear sister,
    whose father was my father, can you think of any
    of all the evils that stem from Oedipus[2]
    that Zeus does not bring to pass for us, while we yet live?
5   No pain, no ruin, no shame, and no dishonor
    but I have seen it in our mischiefs,
    yours and mine.
    And now what is the proclamation that they tell of
    made lately by the commander, publicly,
10   to all the people? Do you know it? Have you heard it?
    Don't you notice when the evils due to enemies
    are headed towards those we love?
ISMENE: Not a word, Antigone, of those we love,
    either sweet or bitter, has come to me since the moment
15   when we lost our two brothers,
    on one day, by their hands dealing mutual death.
    Since the Argive[3] army fled in this past night,
    I know of nothing further, nothing
    of better fortune or of more destruction.
20 ANTIGONE: *I* knew it well; that is why I sent for you
    to come outside the palace gates
    to listen to me, privately.
ISMENE: What is it? Certainly your words
    come of dark thoughts.
25 ANTIGONE: Yes, indeed; for those two brothers of ours, in burial
    has not Creon honored the one, dishonored the other?
    Eteocles, they say he has used justly
    with lawful rites and hid him in the earth
    to have his honor among the dead men there.
30   But the unhappy corpse of Polyneices
    he has proclaimed to all the citizens,
    they say, no man may hide
    in a grave nor mourn in funeral,
    but leave unwept, unburied, a dainty treasure
35   for the birds that see him, for their feast's delight.
    That is what, they say, the worthy Creon
    has proclaimed for you and me—for me, I tell you—
    and he comes here to clarify to the unknowing
    his proclamation; he takes it seriously;
40   for whoever breaks the edict death is prescribed,
    and death by stoning publicly.
    There you have it; soon you will show yourself
    as noble both in your nature and your birth,
    or yourself as base, although of noble parents.

---

2. In Greek legend, Oedipus became king of Thebes by inadvertently fulfilling the prophecy that he was destined to kill his father and marry his mother (as depicted in Sophocles' *Oedipus the King*); for these offenses against nature and the gods, Creon sent Oedipus, along with his daughters Antigone and Ismene, into exile at Colonus. Soon Oedipus's sons, Eteocles and Polyneices, battled to the death for the throne of Thebes.   3. From Argos, a rival Greek city-state.

ISMENE: If things are as you say, poor sister, how   45
    can I better them? how loose or tie the knot?

ANTIGONE: Decide if you will share the work, the deed.

ISMENE: What kind of danger is there? How far have your thoughts gone?

ANTIGONE: Here is this hand. Will you help it to lift the dead man?

ISMENE: Would you bury him, when it is forbidden the city?   50

ANTIGONE: At least he is my brother—and yours, too,
    though you deny him. *I* will not prove false to him.

ISMENE: You are so headstrong. Creon has forbidden it.

ANTIGONE: It is not for him to keep me from my own.

ISMENE: O God!   55
    Consider, sister, how our father died,
    hated and infamous; how he brought to light
    his own offenses; how he himself struck out
    the sight of his two eyes;
    his own hand was their executioner.   60
    Then, mother and wife, two names in one, did shame
    violently on her life, with twisted cords.
    Third, our two brothers, on a single day,
    poor wretches, themselves worked out their mutual doom.
    Each killed the other, hand against brother's hand.   65
    Now there are only the two of us, left behind,
    and see how miserable our end shall be
    if in the teeth of law we shall transgress
    against the sovereign's decree and power.
    You ought to realize we are only women,   70
    not meant in nature to fight against men,
    and that we are ruled, by those who are stronger,
    to obedience in this and even more painful matters.
    I do indeed beg those beneath the earth
    to give me their forgiveness,   75
    since force constrains me,
    that I shall yield in this to the authorities.
    Extravagant action is not sensible.

ANTIGONE: I would not urge you now; nor if you wanted
    to act would I be glad to have you with me.   80
    Be as you choose to be; but for myself
    I myself will bury him. It will be good
    to die, so doing. I shall lie by his side,
    loving him as he loved me; I shall be
    a criminal—but a religious one.   85
    The time in which I must please those that are dead
    is longer than I must please those of this world.
    For there I shall lie forever. You, if you like,
    can cast dishonor on what the gods have honored.

ISMENE: I will not put dishonor on them, but   90
    to act in defiance of the citizenry,
    my nature does not give me means for that.

ANTIGONE: Let that be your excuse. But I will go
    to heap the earth on the grave of my loved brother.

95   ISMENE: How I fear for you, my poor sister!
    ANTIGONE: Do not fear for me. Make straight your own path to destiny.
    ISMENE: At least do not speak of this act to anyone else;
      bury him in secret; I will be silent, too.
    ANTIGONE: Oh, oh, no! shout it out. I will hate you still worse
100   for silence—should you not proclaim it,
      to everyone.
    ISMENE: You have a warm heart for such chilly deeds.
    ANTIGONE: I know I am pleasing those I should please most.
    ISMENE: *If* you can do it. But you are in love
105   with the impossible.
    ANTIGONE: No. When I can no more, then I will stop.
    ISMENE: It is better not to hunt the impossible
      at all.
    ANTIGONE: If you will talk like this I will loathe you,
110   and you will be adjudged an enemy—
      justly—by the dead's decision. Let me alone
      and my folly with me, to endure this terror.
      No suffering of mine will be enough
      to make me die ignobly.
115 ISMENE: Well, if you will, go on.
      Know this; that though you are wrong to go, your friends
      are right to love you.
    CHORUS: Sun's beam, fairest of all
      that ever till now shone
120   on seven-gated Thebes;
      O golden eye of day, you shone
      coming over Dirce's stream;[4]
      You drove in headlong rout
      the whiteshielded man from Argos,
125   complete in arms;
      his bits rang sharper
      under your urging.

      Polyneices brought him here
      against our land, Polyneices,
130   roused by contentious quarrel;
      like an eagle he flew into our country,
      with many men-at-arms,
      with many a helmet crowned with horsehair.

      He stood above the halls, gaping with murderous lances,
135   encompassing the city's
      seven-gated mouth[5]
      But before his jaws would be sated
      with our blood, before the fire,
      pine fed, should capture our crown of towers,

---

4. River near Thebes.
5. Thebes was known throughout the ancient world for having seven gateways through the walls protecting the city.

he went hence— 140
such clamor of war stretched behind his back,
from his dragon foe, a thing he could not overcome.

For Zeus, who hates the most
the boasts of a great tongue,
saw them coming in a great tide, 145
insolent in the clang of golden armor.
The god struck him down with hurled fire,
as he strove to raise the victory cry,
now at the very winning post.

The earth rose to strike him as he fell swinging. 150
In his frantic onslaught, possessed, he breathed upon us
with blasting winds of hate.
Sometimes the great god of war was on one side,
and sometimes he struck a staggering blow on the other;
the god was a very wheel horse[6] on the right trace. 155

At seven gates stood seven captains,
ranged equals against equals, and there left
their brazen suits of armor
to Zeus, the god of trophies.
Only those two wretches born of one father and mother 160
set their spears to win a victory on both sides;
they worked out their share in a common death.

Now Victory, whose name is great, has come
to Thebes of many chariots
with joy to answer her joy, 165
to bring forgetfulness of these wars;
let us go to all the shrines of the gods
and dance all night long.
Let Bacchus lead the dance,
shaking Thebes to trembling. 170

But here is the king of our land,
Creon,[7] son of Menoeceus;
in our new contingencies with the gods,
he is our new ruler.
He comes to set in motion some design— 175
what design is it? Because he has proposed
the convocation of the elders.
He sent a public summons for our discussion.
CREON: Gentlemen: as for our city's fortune,
the gods have shaken her, when the great waves broke, 180
but the gods have brought her through again to safety.

6. Strongest and ablest horse in a team pulling a vehicle, harnessed nearest the front wheels "on the right trace."
7. Brother of Jocasta, mother and wife of Oedipus; he became king of Thebes after the deaths of Oedipus's sons.

For yourselves, I chose you out of all and summoned you
to come to me, partly because I knew you
as always loyal to the throne—at first,
185   when Laïus[8] was king, and then again
when Oedipus saved our city and then again
when he died and you remained with steadfast truth
to their descendants,
until they met their double fate upon one day,
190   striking and stricken, defiled each by a brother's murder.
Now here I am, holding all authority
and the throne, in virtue of kinship with the dead.
It is impossible to know any man—
I mean his soul, intelligence, and judgment—
195   until he shows his skill in rule and law.
I think that a man supreme ruler of a whole city,
if he does not reach for the best counsel for her,
but through some fear, keeps his tongue under lock and key,
him I judge the worst of any;
200   I have always judged so; and anyone thinking
another man more a friend than his own country,
I rate him nowhere. For my part, God is my witness,
who sees all, always, I would not be silent
if I saw ruin, not safety, on the way
205   towards my fellow citizens. I would not count
any enemy of my country as a friend—
because of what I know, that she it is
which gives us our security. If she sails upright
and we sail on her, friends will be ours for the making.
210   In the light of rules like these, I will make her greater still.

In consonance with this, I here proclaim
to the citizens about Oedipus' sons.
For Eteocles, who died this city's champion,
showing his valor's supremacy everywhere,
215   he shall be buried in his grave with every rite
of sanctity given to heroes under earth.
However, his brother, Polyneices, a returned exile,
who sought to burn with fire from top to bottom
his native city, and the gods of his own people;
220   who sought to taste the blood he shared with us,
and lead the rest of us to slavery—
I here proclaim to the city that this man
shall no one honor with a grave and none shall mourn.
You shall leave him without burial; you shall watch him
225   chewed up by birds and dogs and violated.
Such is my mind in the matter; never by me
shall the wicked man have precedence in honor

---

8. Father of Oedipus.

over the just. But he that is loyal to the state
in death, in life alike, shall have my honor.

CHORUS: Son of Menoeceus, so it is your pleasure   230
to deal with foe and friend of this our city.
To use any legal means lies in your power,
both about the dead and those of us who live.

CREON: I understand, then, you will do my bidding.

CHORUS: Please lay this burden on some younger man.   235

CREON: Oh, watchers of the corpse I have already.

CHORUS: What else, then, do your commands entail?

CREON: That you should not side with those who disagree.

CHORUS: There is none so foolish as to love his own death.

CREON: Yes, indeed those are the wages, but often greed   240
has with its hopes brought men to ruin.

[*The* SENTRY *whose speeches follow represents a remarkable experiment in Greek
tragedy in the direction of naturalism of speech. He speaks with marked clumsiness,
partly because he is excited and talks almost colloquially. But also the royal presence
makes him think apparently that he should be rather grand in his show of respect. He
uses odd bits of archaism or somewhat stale poetical passages, particularly in catch
phrases. He sounds something like lower-level Shakespearean characters, e.g. Constable Elbow, with his uncertainty about benefactor and malefactor.*]

SENTRY: My lord, I will never claim my shortness of breath
is due to hurrying, nor were there wings in my feet.
I stopped at many a lay-by in my thinking;
I circled myself till I met myself coming back.   245
My soul accosted me with different speeches.
"Poor fool, yourself, why are you going somewhere
when once you get there you will pay the piper?"
"Well, aren't you the daring fellow! stopping again?
and suppose Creon hears the news from someone else—   250
don't you realize that you will smart for that?"
I turned the whole matter over. I suppose I may say
"I made haste slowly" and the short road became long.
However, at last I came to a resolve:
I must go to you; even if what I say   255
is nothing, really, still I shall say it.
I come here, a man with a firm clutch on the hope
that nothing can betide him save what is fated.

CREON: What is it then that makes you so afraid?

SENTRY: No, I want first of all to tell you my side of it.   260
I didn't do the thing; I never saw who did it.
It would not be fair for me to get into trouble.

CREON: You hedge, and barricade the thing itself.
Clearly you have some ugly news for me.

SENTRY: Well, you know how disasters make a man   265
hesitate to be their messenger.

CREON: For God's sake, tell me and get out of here!

SENTRY: Yes, I *will* tell you. Someone just now

buried the corpse and vanished. He scattered on the skin
270   some thirsty dust; he did the ritual,
duly, to purge the body of desecration.
CREON: What! Now who on earth could have done that?
SENTRY: I do not know. For there was there no mark
of axe's stroke nor casting up of earth
275   of any mattock; the ground was hard and dry,
unbroken; there were no signs of wagon wheels.
The doer of the deed had left no trace.
But when the first sentry of the day pointed it out,
there was for all of us a disagreeable
280   wonder. For the body had disappeared;
not in a grave, of course; but there lay upon him
a little dust as of a hand avoiding
the curse of violating the dead body's sanctity.
There were no signs of any beast nor dog
285   that came there; he had clearly not been torn.
There was a tide of bad words at one another,
guard taunting guard, and it might well have ended
in blows, for there was no one there to stop it.
Each one of us was the criminal but no one
290   manifestly so; all denied knowledge of it.
We were ready to take hot bars in our hands
or walk through fire,[9] and call on the gods with oaths
that we had neither done it nor were privy
to a plot with anyone, neither in planning
295   nor yet in execution.
At last when nothing came of all our searching,
there was one man who spoke, made every head
bow to the ground in fear. For we could not
either contradict him nor yet could we see how
300   if we did what he said we would come out all right.
His word was that we must lay information
about the matter to yourself; we could not cover it.
This view prevailed and the lot of the draw chose me,
unlucky me, to win that prize. So here
305   I am. I did not want to come,
and you don't want to have me. I know that.
For no one likes the messenger of bad news.
CHORUS: My lord: I wonder, could this be God's doing?
This is the thought that keeps on haunting me.
310   CREON: Stop, before your words fill even me with rage,
that you should be exposed as a fool, and you so old.
For what you say is surely insupportable
when you say the gods took forethought for this corpse.

---

9. Ancient legal customs in which an accused person was required to undergo a "trial by ordeal," such as walking through fire; if the resulting injuries were not serious, the person was thought to be innocent and therefore divinely protected.

Is it out of excess of honor for the man,
for the favors that he did them, they should cover him?   315
This man who came to burn their pillared temples,
their dedicated offerings—and this land
and laws he would have scattered to the winds?
Or do you see the gods as honoring
criminals? This is not so. But what I am doing   320
now, and other things before this, some men disliked,
within this very city, and muttered against me,
secretly shaking their heads; they would not bow
justly beneath the yoke to submit to me.
I am very sure that these men hired others   325
to do this thing. I tell you the worse currency
that ever grew among mankind is money. This
sacks cities, this drives people from their homes,
this teaches and corrupts the minds of the loyal
to acts of shame. This displays   330
all kinds of evil for the use of men,
instructs in the knowledge of every impious act.
Those that have done this deed have been paid to do it,
but in the end they will pay for what they have done.

It is as sure as I still reverence Zeus—   335
know this right well—and I speak under oath—
if you and your fellows do not find this man
who with his own hand did the burial
and bring him here before me face to face,
your death alone will not be enough for me.   340
You will hang alive till you open up this outrage.
That will teach you in the days to come from what
you may draw profit—safely—from your plundering.
It's not from anything and everything
you can grow rich. You will find out   345
that ill-gotten gains ruin more than they save.
SENTRY: Have I your leave to say something—or should
    I just turn and go?
CREON: Don't you know your talk is painful enough already?
SENTRY: Is the ache in your ears or in your mind?   350
CREON: Why do you dissect the whereabouts of my pain?
SENTRY: Because it is he who did the deed who hurts your
    mind. I only hurt your ears that listen.
CREON: I am sure you have been a chatterbox since you were born.
SENTRY: All the same, I did not do this thing.   355
CREON: You might have done this, too, if you sold your soul.
SENTRY: It's a bad thing if one judges and judges wrongly.
CREON: You may talk as wittily as you like of judgment.
    Only, if you don't bring to light those men
    who have done this, you will yet come to say   360
    that your wretched gains have brought bad consequences.

SENTRY: [*Aside.*] It were best that he were found, but whether
    the criminal is taken or he isn't—
    for that chance will decide—one thing is certain,
365   you'll never see me coming here again.
    I never hoped to escape, never thought I could.
    But now I have come off safe, I thank God heartily.
CHORUS: Many are the wonders, none
        is more wonderful than what is man.
370   This it is that crosses the sea
      with the south winds storming and the waves swelling,
      breaking around him in roaring surf.
      He it is again who wears away
      the Earth, oldest of gods, immortal, unwearied,
375   as the ploughs wind across her from year to year
      when he works her with the breed that comes from horses.

      The tribe of the lighthearted birds he snares
      and takes prisoner the races of savage beasts
      and the brood of the fish of the sea,
380   with the close-spun web of nets.
      A cunning fellow is man. His contrivances
      make him master of beasts of the field
      and those that move in the mountains.
      So he brings the horse with the shaggy neck
385   to bend underneath the yoke;
      and also the untamed mountain bull;
      and speech and windswift thought
      and the tempers that go with city living
      he has taught himself, and how to avoid
390   the sharp frost, when lodging is cold
      under the open sky
      and pelting strokes of the rain.
      He has a way against everything,
      and he faces nothing that is to come
395   without contrivance.
      Only against death
      can he call on no means of escape;
      but escape from hopeless diseases
      he has found in the depths of his mind.
400   With some sort of cunning, inventive
      beyond all expectation
      he reaches sometimes evil,
      and sometimes good.

      If he honors the laws of earth,
405   and the justice of the gods he has confirmed by oath,
      high is his city; no city
      has he with whom dwells dishonor
      prompted by recklessness.
      He who is so, may he never

share my hearth!   410
may he never think my thoughts!

Is this a portent sent by God?
I cannot tell.
I know her. How can I say
that this is not Antigone?   415
Unhappy girl, child of unhappy Oedipus,
what is this?
Surely it is not you they bring here
as disobedient to the royal edict,
surely not you, taken in such folly.   420

SENTRY: She is the one who did the deed;
   we took her burying him. But where is Creon?

CHORUS: He is just coming from the house, when you most need him.

CREON: What is this? What has happened that I come
   so opportunely?   425

SENTRY: My lord, there is nothing
   that a man should swear he would never do.
   Second thoughts make liars of the first resolution.
   I would have vowed it would be long enough
   before I came again, lashed hence by your threats.   430
   But since the joy that comes past hope, and against all hope,
   is like no other pleasure in extent,
   I have come here, though I break my oath in coming.
   I bring this girl here who has been captured
   giving the grace of burial to the dead man.   435
   This time no lot chose me; this was my jackpot,
   and no one else's. Now, my lord, take her
   and as you please judge her and test her; I
   am justly free and clear of all this trouble.

CREON: This girl—how did you take her and from where?   440

SENTRY: She was burying the man. Now you know all.

CREON: Do you know what you are saying? Do you mean it?

SENTRY: She is the one; I saw her burying
   the dead man you forbade the burial of.
   Now, do I speak plainly and clearly enough?   445

CREON: How was she seen? How was she caught in the act?

SENTRY: This is how it was. When we came there,
   with those dreadful threats of yours upon us,
   we brushed off all the dust that lay upon
   the dead man's body, heedfully   450
   leaving it moist and naked.
   We sat on the brow of the hill, to windward,
   that we might shun the smell of the corpse upon us.
   Each of us wakefully urged his fellow
   with torrents of abuse, not to be careless   455
   in this work of ours. So it went on,
   until in the midst of the sky the sun's bright circle

stood still; the heat was burning. Suddenly
a squall lifted out of the earth a storm of dust,
460   a trouble in the sky. It filled the plain,
ruining all the foliage of the wood
that was around it. The great empty air
was filled with it. We closed our eyes, enduring
this plague sent by the gods. When at long last
465   we were quit of it, why, then we saw the girl.

She was crying out with the shrill cry
of an embittered bird
that sees its nest robbed of its nestlings
and the bed empty. So, too, when she saw
470   the body stripped of its cover, she burst out in groans,
calling terrible curses on those that had done that deed;
and with her hands immediately
brought thirsty dust to the body; from a shapely brazen
urn, held high over it, poured a triple stream
475   of funeral offerings; and crowned the corpse.
When we saw that, we rushed upon her and
caught our quarry then and there, not a bit disturbed.
We charged her with what she had done, then and the first time.
She did not deny a word of it—to my joy,
480   but to my pain as well. It is most pleasant
to have escaped oneself out of such troubles
but painful to bring into it those whom we love.
However, it is but natural for me
to count all this less than my own escape.
485 CREON: You there, that turn your eyes upon the ground,
do you confess or deny what you have done?
ANTIGONE: Yes, I confess; I will not deny my deed.
CREON: [*To the* SENTRY.] You take yourself off where you like.
You are free of a heavy charge.
490   Now, Antigone, tell me shortly and to the point,
did you know the proclamation against your action?
ANTIGONE: I knew it; of course I did. For it was public.
CREON: And did you dare to disobey that law?
ANTIGONE: Yes, it was not Zeus that made the proclamation;
495   nor did Justice, which lives with those below, enact
such laws as that, for mankind. I did not believe
your proclamation had such power to enable
one who will someday die to override
God's ordinances, unwritten and secure.
500   *They* are not of today and yesterday;
they live forever; none knows when first they were.
These are the laws whose penalties I would not
incur from the gods, through fear of any man's temper.

I know that I will die—of course I do—
505   even if you had not doomed me by proclamation.

If I shall die before my time, I count that
a profit. How can such as I, that live
among such troubles, not find a profit in death?
So for such as me, to face such a fate as this
is pain that does not count. But if I dared to leave 510
the dead man, my mother's son, dead and unburied,
that would have been real pain. The other is not.
Now, if you think me a fool to act like this,
perhaps it is a fool that judges so.

CHORUS: The savage spirit of a savage father 515
shows itself in this girl. She does not know
how to yield to trouble.

CREON: I would have you know the most fanatic spirits
fall most of all. It is the toughest iron,
baked in the fire to hardness, you may see 520
most shattered, twisted, shivered to fragments.
I know hot horses are restrained
by a small curb. For he that is his neighbor's slave cannot
be high in spirit. This girl had learned her insolence
before this, when she broke the established laws. 525
But here is still another insolence
in that she boasts of it, laughs at what she did.
I swear I am no man and she the man
if she can win this and not pay for it.
No; though she were my sister's child or closer 530
in blood than all that my hearth god acknowledges
as mine, neither she nor her sister should escape
the utmost sentence—death. For indeed I accuse her,
the sister, equally of plotting the burial.
Summon her. I saw her inside, just now, 535
crazy, distraught. When people plot
mischief in the dark, it is the mind which first
is convicted of deceit. But surely I hate indeed
the one that is caught in evil and then makes
that evil look like good. 540

ANTIGONE: Do you want anything
beyond my taking and my execution?

CREON: Oh, nothing! Once I have that I have everything.

ANTIGONE: Why do you wait, then? Nothing that you say
pleases me; God forbid it ever should. 545
So my words, too, naturally offend you.
Yet how could I win a greater share of glory
than putting my own brother in his grave?
All that are here would surely say that's true,
if fear did not lock their tongues up. A prince's power 550
is blessed in many things, not least in this,
that he can say and do whatever he likes.

CREON: You are alone among the people of Thebes
to see things in that way.

555   ANTIGONE: No, these do, too,
          but keep their mouths shut for the fear of you.
      CREON: Are you not ashamed to think so differently
          from them?
      ANTIGONE: There is nothing shameful in honoring my brother.
560   CREON: Was not he that died on the other side your brother?
      ANTIGONE: Yes, indeed, of my own blood from father and mother.
      CREON: Why then do you show a grace that must be impious
          in *his* sight?
      ANTIGONE: *That* other dead man
565   would never bear you witness in what you say.
      CREON: Yes he would, if you put him only on equality
          with one that was a desecrator.
      ANTIGONE: It was his brother, not his slave, that died.
      CREON: He died destroying the country the other defended.
570   ANTIGONE: The god of death demands these rites for both.
      CREON: But the good man does not seek an *equal* share only,
          with the bad.
      ANTIGONE: Who knows
          if in that other world this is true piety?
      CREON: My enemy is still my enemy, even in death.
574   ANTIGONE: My nature is to join in love, not hate.
      CREON: Go then to the world below, yourself, if you
          must love. Love *them*. When I am alive no woman shall rule.
      CHORUS: Here before the gates comes Ismene
          shedding tears for the love of a brother.
580   A cloud over her brow casts shame
          on her flushed face, as the tears wet
          her fair cheeks.
      CREON: You there, who lurked in my house, viper-like—
          secretly drawing its lifeblood; I never thought
585   that I was raising two sources of destruction,
          two rebels against my throne. Come tell me now,
          will you, too, say you bore a hand in the burial
          or will you swear that you know nothing of it?
      ISMENE: I did it, yes—if she will say I did it
590   I bear my share in it, bear the guilt, too.
      ANTIGONE: Justice will not allow you what you refused
          and I will have none of your partnership.
      ISMENE: But in your troubles I am not ashamed
          to sail with you the sea of suffering.
595   ANTIGONE: Where the act was death, the dead are witnesses.
          I do not love a friend who loves in words.
      ISMENE: Sister, do not dishonor me, denying me
          a common death with you, a common honoring
          of the dead man.
600   ANTIGONE: Don't die with me, nor make your own
          what you have never touched. I that die am enough.
      ISMENE: What life is there for me, once I have lost you?
      ANTIGONE: Ask Creon; all your care was on his behalf.

ISMENE: Why do you hurt me, when you gain nothing by it?
ANTIGONE: I am hurt by my own mockery—if I mock you.   605
ISMENE: Even now—what can I do to help you still?
ANTIGONE: Save yourself; I do not grudge you your escape.
ISMENE: I cannot bear it! Not even to share your death!
ANTIGONE: Life was your choice, and death was mine.
ISMENE: You cannot say I accepted that choice in silence.   610
ANTIGONE: You were right in the eyes of one party, I in the other.
ISMENE: Well then, the fault is equally between us.
ANTIGONE: Take heart; you are alive, but my life died
     long ago, to serve the dead.
CREON: Here are two girls; I think that one of them   615
     has suddenly lost her wits—the other was always so.
ISMENE: Yes, for, my lord, the wits that they are born with
     do not stay firm for the unfortunate.
     They go astray.
CREON: Certainly yours do,
     when you share troubles with the troublemaker.   620
ISMENE: What life can be mine alone without her?
CREON: Do not
     speak of *her. She* isn't, anymore.
ISMENE: Will you kill your son's wife to be?[1]
CREON: Yes, there are other fields for him to plough.
ISMENE: Not with the mutual love of him and her.   625
CREON: I hate a bad wife for a son of mine.
ANTIGONE: Dear Haemon, how your father dishonors you.
CREON: There is too much of you—and of your marriage!
CHORUS: Will you rob your son of this girl?
CREON: Death—it is death that will stop the marriage for me.   630
CHORUS: Your decision it seems is taken: she shall die.
CREON: Both you and I have decided it. No more delay.

          [*He turns to the* SERVANTS.]

     Bring her inside, you. From this time forth,
     these must be women, and not free to roam.
     For even the stout of heart shrink when they see   635
     the approach of death close to their lives.
CHORUS: Lucky are those whose lives
          know no taste of sorrow.
          But for those whose house has been shaken by God
          there is never cessation of ruin;   640
          it steals on generation after generation
          within a breed. Even as the swell
          is driven over the dark deep
          by the fierce Thracian winds
          I see the ancient evils of Labdacus' house[2]   645
          are heaped on the evils of the dead.

1. Antigone, betrothed to Creon's son Haemon.
2. Theban royal lineage that included Labdacus; his son, Laïus; and his grandson, Oedipus.

No generation frees another, some god
strikes them down; there is no deliverance.
Here was the light of hope stretched
650 over the last roots of Oedipus' house,
and the bloody dust due to the gods below
has mowed it down—that and the folly of speech
and ruin's enchantment of the mind.

Your power, O Zeus, what sin of man can limit?
655 All-aging sleep does not overtake it,
nor the unwearied months of the gods; and you,
for whom time brings no age,
you hold the glowing brightness of Olympus.

For the future near and far,
660 and the past, this law holds good:
nothing very great
comes to the life of mortal man
without ruin to accompany it.
For Hope, widely wandering, comes to many of mankind
665 as a blessing,
but to many as the deceiver,
using light-minded lusts;
she comes to him that knows nothing
till he burns his foot in the glowing fire.
670 With wisdom has someone declared
a word of distinction:
that evil seems good to one whose mind
the god leads to ruin,
and but for the briefest moment of time
675 is his life outside of calamity.
Here is Haemon, youngest of your sons.
Does he come grieving
for the fate of his bride to be,
in agony at being cheated of his marriage?

680 CREON: Soon we will know that better than the prophets.
My son, can it be that you have not heard
of my final decision on your betrothed?
Can you have come here in your fury against your father?
Or have I your love still, no matter what I do?
685 HAEMON: Father, I am yours; with your excellent judgment
you lay the right before me, and I shall follow it.
No marriage will ever be so valued by me
as to override the goodness of your leadership.
CREON: Yes, my son, this should always be
690 in your very heart, that everything else
shall be second to your father's decision.
It is for this that fathers pray to have
obedient sons begotten in their halls,
that they may requite with ill their father's enemy

and honor his friend no less than he would himself. 695
If a man have sons that are no use to him,
what can one say of him but that he has bred
so many sorrows to himself, laughter to his enemies?
Do not, my son, banish your good sense
through pleasure in a woman, since you know 700
that the embrace grows cold
when an evil woman shares your bed and home.
What greater wound can there be than a false friend?
No. Spit on her, throw her out like an enemy,
this girl, to marry someone in Death's house. 705
I caught her openly in disobedience
alone out of all this city and I shall not make
myself a liar in the city's sight. No, I will kill her.
So let her cry if she will on the Zeus of kinship;
for if I rear those of my race and breeding 710
to be rebels, surely I will do so with those outside it.
For he who is in his household a good man
will be found a just man, too, in the city.
But he that breaches the law or does it violence
or thinks to dictate to those who govern him 715
shall never have my good word.
The man the city sets up in authority
must be obeyed in small things and in just
but also in their opposites.
I am confident such a man of whom I speak 720
will be a good ruler, and willing to be well ruled.
He will stand on his country's side, faithful and just,
in the storm of battle. There is nothing worse
than disobedience to authority.
It destroys cities, it demolishes homes; 725
it breaks and routs one's allies. Of successful lives
the most of them are saved by discipline.
So we must stand on the side of what is orderly;
we cannot give victory to a woman.
If we must accept defeat, let it be from a man; 730
we must not let people say that a woman beat us.
CHORUS: We think, if we are not victims of Time the Thief,
that you speak intelligently of what you speak.
HAEMON: Father, the natural sense that the gods breed
in men is surely the best of their possessions. 735
I certainly could not declare you wrong—
may I never know how to do so!—Still there might
be something useful that some other than you might think.
It is natural for me to be watchful on your behalf
concerning what all men say or do or find to blame. 740
Your face is terrible to a simple citizen;
it frightens him from words you dislike to hear.
But what *I* can hear, in the dark, are things like these:

the city mourns for this girl; they think she is dying
745   most wrongly and most undeservedly
of all womenkind, for the most glorious acts.
Here is one who would not leave her brother unburied,
a brother who had fallen in bloody conflict,
to meet his end by greedy dogs or by
750   the bird that chanced that way. Surely what she merits
is golden honor, isn't it? That's the dark rumor
that spreads in secret. Nothing I own
I value more highly, father, than your success.
What greater distinction can a son have than the glory
755   of a successful father, and for a father
the distinction of successful children?
Do not bear this single habit of mind, to think
that what you say and nothing else is true.
A man who thinks that he alone is right,
760   or what he says, or what he *is* himself,
unique, such men, when opened up, are seen
to be quite empty. For a man, though he be wise,
it is no shame to learn—learn many things,
and not maintain his views too rigidly.
765   You notice how by streams in wintertime
the trees that yield preserve their branches safely,
but those that fight the tempest perish utterly.
The man who keeps the sheet[3] of his sail tight
and never slackens capsizes his boat
770   and makes the rest of his trip keel uppermost.
Yield something of your anger, give way a little.
If a much younger man, like me, may have
a judgment, I would say it were far better
to be one altogether wise by nature, but,
775   as things incline not to be so, then it is good
also to learn from those who advise well.
CHORUS: My lord, if he says anything to the point,
you should learn from him, and you, too, Haemon,
learn from your father. Both of you
780   have spoken well.
CREON: Should we that are my age learn wisdom
from young men such as he is?
HAEMON: Not learn injustice, certainly. If I am young,
do not look at my years but what I do.
CREON: Is what you do to have respect for rebels?
785   HAEMON: I
would not urge you to be scrupulous
towards the wicked.
CREON: Is *she* not tainted by the disease of wickedness?

---

3. Rope attached to the corner of a sail to hold it at the proper angle to the wind.

HAEMON: The entire people of Thebes says no to that.

CREON: Should the city tell me how I am to rule them? 790

HAEMON: Do you see what a young man's words these are of yours?

CREON: Must I rule the land by someone else's judgment
    rather than my own?

HAEMON: There is no city
    possessed by one man only.

CREON: Is not the city thought to be the ruler's? 795

HAEMON: You would be a fine dictator of a desert.

CREON: It seems this boy is on the woman's side.

HAEMON: If you are a woman—my care is all for you.

CREON: You villain, to bandy words with your own father!

HAEMON: I see your acts as mistaken and unjust. 800

CREON: Am I mistaken, reverencing my own office?

HAEMON: There is no reverence in trampling on God's honor.

CREON: Your nature is vile, in yielding to a woman.

HAEMON: You will not find me yield to what is shameful.

CREON: At least, your argument is all for her. 805

HAEMON: Yes, and for you and me—and for the gods below.

CREON: You will never marry her while her life lasts.

HAEMON: Then she must die—and dying destroy another.

CREON: Has your daring gone so far, to threaten me?

HAEMON: What threat is it to speak against empty judgments? 810

CREON: Empty of sense yourself, you will regret
    your schooling of me in sense.

HAEMON: If you were not
    my father, I would say you are insane.

CREON: You woman's slave, do not try to wheedle me.

HAEMON: You want to talk but never to hear and listen. 815

CREON: Is that so? By the heavens above you will not—
    be sure of that—get off scot-free, insulting,
    abusing me.

        [*He speaks to the* SERVANTS.]

               You people bring out this creature,
    this hated creature, that she may die before
    his very eyes, right now, next her would-be husband. 820

HAEMON: Not at my side! Never think that! She will not
    die by my side. But you will never again
    set eyes upon my face. Go then and rage
    with such of your friends as are willing to endure it.

CHORUS: The man is gone, my lord, quick in his anger. 825
    A young man's mind is fierce when he is hurt.

CREON: Let him go, and do and think things superhuman.
    But these two girls he shall not save from death.

CHORUS: Both of them? Do you mean to kill them both?

CREON: No, not the one that didn't do anything. 830
    You are quite right there.

CHORUS: And by what form of death do you mean to kill her?

CREON: I will bring her where the path is loneliest,
and hide her alive in a rocky cavern there.
835 I'll give just enough of food as shall suffice
for a bare expiation, that the city may avoid pollution.
In that place she shall call on Hades, god of death,
in her prayers. That god only she reveres.
Perhaps she will win from him escape from death
840 or at least in that last moment will recognize
her honoring of the dead is labor lost.
CHORUS: Love undefeated in the fight,
Love that makes havoc of possessions,
Love who lives at night in a young girl's soft cheeks,
845 Who travels over sea, or in huts in the countryside—
there is no god able to escape you
nor anyone of men, whose life is a day only,
and whom you possess is mad.

You wrench the minds of just men to injustice,
850 to their disgrace; this conflict among kinsmen
it is you who stirred to turmoil.
The winner is desire. She gleaming kindles
from the eyes of the girl good to bed.
Love shares the throne with the great powers that rule.
855 For the golden Aphrodite[4] holds her play there
and then no one can overcome her.

Here I too am borne out of the course of lawfulness
when I see these things, and I cannot control
the springs of my tears
860 when I see Antigone making her way
to her bed—but the bed
that is rest for everyone.
ANTIGONE: You see me, you people of my country,
as I set out on my last road of all,
865 looking for the last time on this light of this sun—
never again. I am alive but Hades who gives sleep to everyone
is leading me to the shores of Acheron,[5]
though I have known nothing of marriage songs
nor the chant that brings the bride to bed.
870 My husband is to be the Lord of Death.
CHORUS: Yes, you go to the place where the dead are hidden,
but you go with distinction and praise.
You have not been stricken by wasting sickness;
you have not earned the wages of the sword;
875 it was your own choice and alone among mankind
you will descend, alive,
to that world of death.

---

4. Goddess of love and beauty.   5. River in Hades.

ANTIGONE: But indeed I have heard of the saddest of deaths—
    of the Phrygian stranger,[6] daughter of Tantalus,
    whom the rocky growth subdued, like clinging ivy.   880
    The rains never leave her, the snow never fails,
    as she wastes away. That is how men tell the story.
    From streaming eyes her tears wet the crags;
    most like to her the god brings me to rest.
CHORUS: Yes, but she was a god, and god born,   885
    and you are mortal and mortal born.
    Surely it is great renown
    for a woman that dies, that in life and death
    her lot is a lot shared with demigods.
ANTIGONE: You mock me. In the name of our fathers' gods   890
    why do you not wait till I am gone to insult me?
    Must you do it face to face?
    My city! Rich citizens of my city!
    You springs of Dirce, you holy groves of Thebes,
    famed for its chariots! I would still have you as my witnesses,   895
    with what dry-eyed friends, under what laws
    I make my way to my prison sealed like a tomb.
    Pity me. Neither among the living nor the dead
    do I have a home in common—
    neither with the living nor the dead.   900
CHORUS: You went to the extreme of daring
    and against the high throne of Justice
    you fell, my daughter, grievously.
    But perhaps it was for some ordeal of your father
    that you are paying requital.   905
ANTIGONE: You have touched the most painful of my cares—
    the pity for my father, ever reawakened,
    and the fate of all of our race, the famous Labdacids;
    the doomed self-destruction of my mother's bed
    when she slept with her own son,   910
    my father.
    What parents I was born of, God help me!
    To them I am going to share their home,
    the curse on me, too, and unmarried.
    Brother, it was a luckless marriage you made,   915
    and dying killed my life.
CHORUS: There *is* a certain reverence for piety.
    But for him in authority,
    he cannot see that authority defied;
    it is your own self-willed temper   920
    that has destroyed you.
ANTIGONE: No tears for me, no friends, no marriage. Brokenhearted
    I am led along the road ready before me.

6. Niobe, whose children were slain because of her boastfulness and who was herself turned into a stone
on Mount Siphylus. Her tears became the mountain's streams.

I shall never again be suffered
925   to look on the holy eye of the day.
But my fate claims no tears—
no friend cries for me.

CREON: [*To the* SERVANTS.] Don't you know that weeping and wailing before death
would never stop if one is allowed to weep and wail?
930   Lead her away at once. Enfold her
in that rocky tomb of hers—as I told you to.
There leave her alone, solitary,
to die if she so wishes
or live a buried life in such a home;
935   we are guiltless in respect of her, this girl.
But living above, among the rest of us, this life
she shall certainly lose.

ANTIGONE: Tomb, bridal chamber, prison forever
dug in rock, it is to you I am going
940   to join my people, that great number that have died,
whom in their death Persephone[7] received.
I am the last of them and I go down
in the worst death of all—for I have not lived
the due term of my life. But when I come
945   to that other world my hope is strong
that my coming will be welcome to my father,
and dear to you, my mother, and dear to you,
my brother deeply loved. For when you died,
with my own hands I washed and dressed you all,
950   and poured the lustral offerings on your graves.
And now, Polyneices, it was for such care of your body
that I have earned these wages.
Yet those who think rightly will think I did right
in honoring you. Had I been a mother
955   of children, and my husband been dead and rotten,
I would not have taken this weary task upon me
against the will of the city. What law backs me
when I say this? I will tell you:
If my husband were dead, I might have had another,
960   and child from another man, if I lost the first.
But when father and mother both were hidden in death
no brother's life would bloom for me again.
That is the law under which I gave you precedence,
my dearest brother, and that is why Creon thinks me
965   wrong, even a criminal, and now takes me
by the hand and leads me away,
unbedded, without bridal, without share
in marriage and in nurturing of children;
as lonely as you see me; without friends;

7. Abducted by Pluto (known to the Greeks as Hades), god of the underworld, who made her his queen.

with fate against me I go to the vault of death   970
while still alive. What law of God have I broken?
Why should I still look to the gods in my misery?
Whom should I summon as ally? For indeed
because of piety I was called impious.
If this proceeding is good in the gods' eyes   975
I shall know my sin, once I have suffered.
But if Creon and his people are the wrongdoers
let their suffering be no worse than the injustice
they are meting out to me.

CHORUS: It is the same blasts, the tempests of the soul,   980
   possess her.

CREON: Then for this her guards,
who are so slow, will find themselves in trouble.

ANTIGONE: [*Cries out.*] Oh, that word has come
   very close to death.

CREON: I will not comfort you   985
with hope that the sentence will not be accomplished.

ANTIGONE: O my father's city, in Theban land,
   O gods that sired my race,
   I am led away, I have no more stay.
   Look on me, princes of Thebes,   990
   the last remnant of the old royal line;
   see what I suffer and who makes me suffer
   because I gave reverence to what claims reverence.

CHORUS: Danae suffered, too, when, her beauty lost, she gave
     the light of heaven in exchange for brassbound walls,   995
     and in the tomb-like cell was she hidden and held;
     yet she was honored in her breeding, child,
     and she kept, as guardian, the seed of Zeus
     that came to her in a golden shower.[8]
     But there is some terrible power in destiny   1000
     and neither wealth nor war
     nor tower nor black ships, beaten by the sea,
     can give escape from it.

     The hot-tempered son of Dryas,[9] the Edonian king,
     in fury mocked Dionysus,   1005
     who then held him in restraint
     in a rocky dungeon.
     So the terrible force and flower of his madness
     drained away. He came to know the god
     whom in frenzy he had touched with his mocking tongue,   1010
     when he would have checked the inspired women
     and the fire of Dionysus,

---

8. Danae was locked away because it was prophesized that her son would kill her father. Zeus entered her
cell as a shower of gold, impregnated her, and thus fathered Perseus, the child who fulfilled the prophecy.
9. Stricken with madness by Dionysus.

when he provoked the Muses[1] that love the lyre.
By the black rocks, dividing the sea in two,
1015 are the shores of the Bosporus, Thracian Salmydessus.[2]
There the god of war who lives near the city
saw the terrible blinding wound
dealt by his savage wife
on Phineus' two sons.[3]
1020 She blinded and tore with the points of her shuttle,
and her bloodied hands, those eyes
that else would have looked on her vengefully.
As they wasted away, they lamented
their unhappy fate that they were doomed
1025 to be born of a mother cursed in her marriage.
She traced her descent from the seed
of the ancient Erechtheidae.
In far-distant caves she was raised
among her father's storms, that child of Boreas[4]
1030 quick as a horse, over the steep hills,
a daughter of the gods.
But, my child, the long-lived Fates[5]
bore hard upon her, too.

[*Enter* TEIRESIAS, *the blind prophet, led by a* BOY.]

TEIRESIAS: My lords of Thebes, we have come here together,
1035   one pair of eyes serving us both. For the blind
such must be the way of going, by a guide's leading.
CREON: What is the news, my old Teiresias?
TEIRESIAS: I will tell you; and you, listen to the prophet.
CREON: Never in the past have I turned from your advice.
1040 TEIRESIAS: And so you have steered well the ship of state.
CREON: I have benefited and can testify to that.
TEIRESIAS: Then realize you are on the razor edge
of danger.
CREON: What can that be? I shudder to hear those words.
1045 TEIRESIAS: When you learn the signs recognized by my art
you will understand.
I sat at my ancient place of divination
for watching the birds, where every bird finds shelter;
and I heard an unwonted voice among them;
1050 they were horribly distressed, and screamed unmeaningly.
I knew they were tearing each other murderously;
the beating of their wings was a clear sign.

---

1. Nine sister goddesses of poetry, music, and the arts.
2. City in the land of Thrace, in ancient times erroneously believed to lie on the Bosporus, the strait separating Europe and Asia at the outlet of the Black Sea.
3. King Phineus's second wife blinded the children of his first wife, whom Phineus had imprisoned in a cave.
4. God of the cold north wind, who sometimes took the form of a stallion.
5. Supernatural forces, usually represented as three old women, who determine the quality and length of life.

I was full of fear; at once on all the altars,
as they were fully kindled, I tasted the offerings,
but the god of fire refused to burn from the sacrifice,   1055
and from the thighbones a dark stream of moisture
oozed from the embers, smoked and sputtered.
The gall bladder burst and scattered to the air
and the streaming thighbones lay exposed
from the fat wrapped round them—   1060
so much I learned from this boy here,
the fading prophecies of a rite that failed.
This boy here is my guide, as I am others'.
This is the city's sickness—and your plans are the cause of it.
For our altars and our sacrificial hearths   1065
are filled with the carrion meat of birds and dogs,
torn from the flesh of Oedipus' poor son.
So the gods will not take our prayers or sacrifice
nor yet the flame from the thighbones, and no bird
cries shrill and clear, so glutted   1070
are they with fat of the blood of the killed man.
Reflect on these things, son. All men
can make mistakes; but, once mistaken,
a man is no longer stupid nor accursed
who, having fallen on ill, tries to cure that ill,   1075
not taking a fine undeviating stand.
It is obstinacy that convicts of folly.
Yield to the dead man; do not stab him—
now he is gone—what bravery is this,
to inflict another death upon the dead?   1080
I mean you well and speak well for your good.
It is never sweeter to learn from a good counselor
than when he counsels to your benefit.
CREON: Old man, you are all archers, and I am your mark.
I must be tried by your prophecies as well.   1085
By the breed of you I have been bought and sold
and made a merchandise, for ages now.
But I tell you: make your profit from silver-gold
from Sardis[6] and the gold from India
if you will. But this dead man you shall not hide   1090
in a grave, not though the eagles of Zeus should bear
the carrion, snatching it to the throne of Zeus itself.
Even so, I shall not so tremble at the pollution
to let you bury him.
          No, I am certain
no human has the power to pollute the gods.   1095
They fall, you old Teiresias, those men,
—so very clever—in a bad fall whenever
they eloquently speak vile words for profit.

---

6. Capital of the ancient kingdom of Lydia, part of modern-day Turkey; it was an important trading
center, famed for its wealth.

TEIRESIAS: I wonder if there's a man who dares consider—

1100   CREON: What do you mean? What sort of generalization
      is this talk of yours?

TEIRESIAS: How much the best of possessions is the ability
      to listen to wise advice?

CREON: As I should imagine that the worst

1105   injury must be native stupidity.

TEIRESIAS: Now that is exactly where your mind is sick.

CREON: I do not like to answer a seer with insults.

TEIRESIAS: But you do, when you say my prophecies are lies.

CREON: Well,

1110   the whole breed of prophets certainly loves money.

TEIRESIAS: And the breed that comes from princes loves to take
      advantage—base advantage.

CREON: Do you realize
      you are speaking in such terms of your own prince?

TEIRESIAS: I know. But it is through me you have saved the city.

1115   CREON: You are a wise prophet, but what you love is wrong.

TEIRESIAS: You will force me to declare what should be hidden
      in my own heart.

CREON: Out with it—
      but only if your words are not for gain.

TEIRESIAS: They won't be for *your* gain—that I am sure of.

1120   CREON: But realize you will not make a merchandise
      of my decisions.

TEIRESIAS: And you must realize
      that you will not outlive many cycles more
      of this swift sun before you give in exchange
      one of your own loins bred, a corpse for a corpse,

1125   for you have thrust one that belongs above
      below the earth, and bitterly dishonored
      a living soul by lodging her in the grave;
      while one that belonged indeed to the underworld
      gods you have kept on this earth without due share

1130   of rites of burial, of due funeral offerings,
      a corpse unhallowed. With all of this you, Creon,
      have nothing to do, nor have the gods above.
      These acts of yours are violence, on your part.
      And in requital the avenging Spirits

1135   of Death itself and the gods' Furies shall
      after *your* deeds, lie in ambush for you, and
      in their hands you shall be taken cruelly.
      Now, look at this and tell me I was bribed
      to say it! The delay will not be long

1140   before the cries of mourning in your house,
      of men and women. All the cities will stir in hatred
      against you, because their sons in mangled shreds
      received their burial rites from dogs, from wild beasts
      or when some bird of the air brought a vile stink

to each city that contained the hearths of the dead. 1145
These are the arrows that archer-like I launched—
you vexed me so to anger—at your heart.
You shall not escape their sting. You, boy,
lead me away to my house, so he may discharge
his anger on younger men; so may he come to know 1150
to bear a quieter tongue in his head and a better
mind than that now he carries in him.
CHORUS: That was a terrible prophecy, my lord.
    The man has gone. Since these hairs of mine grew white
    from the black they once were, he has never spoken 1155
    a word of a lie to our city.
CREON: I know, I know.
    My mind is all bewildered. To yield is terrible.
    But by opposition to destroy my very being
    with a self-destructive curse must also be reckoned 1160
    in what is terrible.
CHORUS: You need good counsel, son of Menoeceus,
    and need to take it.
CREON: What must I do, then? Tell me; I shall agree.
CHORUS: The girl—go now and bring her up from her cave, 1165
    and for the exposed dead man, give him his burial.
CREON: That is really your advice? You would have me yield.
CHORUS: And quickly as you may, my lord. Swift harms
    sent by the gods cut off the paths of the foolish.
CREON: Oh, it is hard; I must give up what my heart 1170
    would have me do. But it is ill to fight
    against what must be.
CHORUS: Go now, and do this;
    do not give the task to others.
CREON: I will go, 1175
    just as I am. Come, servants, all of you;
    take axes in your hands; away with you
    to the place you see, there.
    For my part, since my intention is so changed,
    as I bound her myself, myself will free her. 1180
    I am afraid it may be best, in the end
    of life, to have kept the old accepted laws.
CHORUS: You of many names,[7] glory of the Cadmeian
    bride, breed of loud thundering Zeus;
    you who watch over famous Italy; 1185
    you who rule where all are welcome in Eleusis;
    in the sheltered plains of Deo—
    O Bacchus that dwells in Thebes,

---

7. Refers to Dionysus, known also as Bacchus (especially to the later Romans); his father was Zeus and his mortal mother, Semele, was a princess of Thebes. As god of wine, Dionysus presided over frenzied rites known as Bacchanals.

the mother city of Bacchanals,
1190   by the flowing stream of Ismenus,
in the ground sown by the fierce dragon's teeth.

You are he on whom the murky gleam of torches glares,
above the twin peaks of the crag
where come the Corycean nymphs
1195   to worship you, the Bacchanals;
and the stream of Castalia has seen you, too;
and you are he that the ivy-clad
slopes of Nisaean hills,
and the green shore ivy-clustered,
1200   sent to watch over the roads of Thebes,
where the immortal Evoe chant[8] rings out.

It is Thebes which you honor most of all cities,
you and your mother both,
she who died by the blast of Zeus' thunderbolt.
1205   And now when the city, with all its folk,
is gripped by a violent plague,
come with healing foot, over the slopes of Parnassus,[9]
over the moaning strait.
You lead the dance of the fire-breathing stars,
1210   you are master of the voices of the night.
True-born child of Zeus, appear,
my lord, with your Thyiad attendants,
who in frenzy all night long
dance in your house, Iacchus,
1215   dispenser of gifts.

MESSENGER: You who live by the house of Cadmus and Amphion,[1]
hear me. There is no condition of man's life
that stands secure. As such I would not
praise it or blame. It is chance that sets upright;
1220   it is chance that brings down the lucky and the unlucky,
each in his turn. For men, that belong to death,
there is no prophet of established things.
Once Creon was a man worthy of envy—
of my envy, at least. For he saved this city
1225   of Thebes from her enemies, and attained
the throne of the land, with all a king's power.
He guided it right. His race bloomed
with good children. But when a man forfeits joy
I do not count his life as life, but only
1230   a life trapped in a corpse.
Be rich within your house, yes greatly rich,
if so you will, and live in a prince's style.

---

8. Come forth, come forth!
9. Mountain in central Greece sacred to Apollo, Dionysus, and the Muses; Apollo's shrine, Delphi, lies at
the foot of Parnassus.   1. A name for Thebes.

If the gladness of these things is gone, I would not
give the shadow of smoke for the rest,
as against joy. 1235
CHORUS: What is the sorrow of our princes
of which you are the messenger?
MESSENGER: Death; and the living are guilty of their deaths.
CHORUS: But who is the murderer? Who the murdered? Tell us.
MESSENGER: Haemon is dead; the hand that shed his blood 1240
was his very own.
CHORUS: Truly his own hand? Or his father's?
MESSENGER: His own hand, in his anger
against his father for a murder.
CHORUS: Prophet, how truly you have made good your word! 1245
MESSENGER: These things are so; you may debate the rest.
Here I see Creon's wife Eurydice
approaching. Unhappy woman!
Does she come from the house as hearing about her son
or has she come by chance? 1250
EURYDICE: I heard your words, all you men of Thebes, as I
was going out to greet Pallas[2] with my prayers.
I was just drawing back the bolts of the gate
to open it when a cry struck through my ears
telling of my household's ruin. I fell backward 1255
in terror into the arms of my servants; I fainted.
But tell me again, what is the story? I
will hear it as one who is no stranger to sorrow.
MESSENGER: Dear mistress, I will tell you, for I was there,
and I will leave out no word of the truth. 1260
Why should I comfort you and then tomorrow
be proved a liar? The truth is always best.
I followed your husband, at his heels, to the end of the plain
where Polyneices' body still lay unpitied,
and torn by dogs. We prayed to Hecate, goddess 1265
of the crossroads, and also to Pluto[3]
that they might restrain their anger and turn kind.
And him we washed with sacred lustral water
and with fresh-cut boughs we burned what was left of him
and raised a high mound of his native earth; 1270
then we set out again for the hollowed rock,
death's stone bridal chamber for the girl.
Someone then heard a voice of bitter weeping
while we were still far off, coming from that unblest room.
The man came to tell our master Creon of it. 1275
As the king drew nearer, there swarmed about him
a cry of misery but no clear words.
He groaned and in an anguished mourning voice

2. Athena, goddess of wisdom.
3. King of the underworld, known to the Greeks as Hades. *Hecate:* goddess of witchcraft.

cried "Oh, am I a true prophet? Is this the road
1280   that I must travel, saddest of all my wayfaring?
It is my son's voice that haunts my ear. Servants,
get closer, quickly. Stand around the tomb
and look. There is a gap there where the stones
have been wrenched away; enter there, by the very mouth,
1285   and see whether I recognize the voice of Haemon
or if the gods deceive me." On the command
of our despairing master we went to look.
In the furthest part of the tomb we saw her, hanging
by her neck. She had tied a noose of muslin on it.
1290   Haemon's hands were about her waist embracing her,
while he cried for the loss of his bride gone to the dead,
and for all his father had done, and his own sad love.
When Creon saw him he gave a bitter cry,
went in and called to him with a groan: "Poor son!
1295   what have you done? What can you have meant?
What happened to destroy you? Come out, I pray you!"
The boy glared at him with savage eyes, and then
spat in his face, without a word of answer.
He drew his double-hilted sword. As his father
1300   ran to escape him, Haemon failed to strike him,
and the poor wretch in anger at himself
leaned on his sword and drove it halfway in,
into his ribs. Then he folded the girl to him,
in his arms, while he was conscious still,
1305   and gasping poured a sharp stream of bloody drops
on her white cheeks. There they lie,
the dead upon the dead. So he has won
the pitiful fulfillment of his marriage
within death's house. In this human world he has shown
1310   how the wrong choice in plans is for a man
his greatest evil.
  CHORUS: What do you make of this? My lady is gone,
    without a word of good or bad.
  MESSENGER: I, too,
    am lost in wonder. I am inclined to hope
1315   that hearing of her son's death she could not
    open her sorrow to the city, but chose rather
    within her house to lay upon her maids
    the mourning for the household grief. Her judgment
    is good; she will not make any false step.
1320   CHORUS: I do not know. To me this over-heavy silence
    seems just as dangerous as much empty wailing.
  MESSENGER: I will go in and learn if in her passionate
    heart she keeps hidden some secret purpose.
    You are right; there is sometimes danger in too much silence.
1325   CHORUS: Here comes our king himself. He bears in his hands
    a memorial all too clear;

it is a ruin of none other's making,
purely his own if one dare to say that.
CREON: The mistakes of a blinded man
   are themselves rigid and laden with death.   1330
   You look at us the killer and the killed
   of the one blood. Oh, the awful blindness
   of those plans of mine. My son, you were so young,
   so young to die. You were freed from the bonds of life
   through no folly of your own—only through mine.   1335
CHORUS: I think you have learned justice—but too late.
CREON: Yes, I have learned it to my bitterness. At this moment
   God has sprung on my head with a vast weight
   and struck me down. He shook me in my savage ways;
   he has overturned my joy, has trampled it,   1340
   underfoot. The pains men suffer
   are pains indeed.
SECOND MESSENGER: My lord, you have troubles and a store besides;
   some are there in your hands, but there are others
   you will surely see when you come to your house.   1345
CREON: What trouble can there be beside these troubles?
SECOND MESSENGER: The queen is dead. She was indeed true mother
   of the dead son. She died, poor lady,
   by recent violence upon herself.
CREON: Haven of death, you can never have enough.   1350
   Why, why do you destroy me?
   You messenger, who have brought me bitter news,
   what is this tale you tell?
   It is a dead man that you kill again—
   what new message of yours is this, boy?   1355
   Is this new slaughter of a woman
   a doom to lie on the pile of the dead?
CHORUS: You can see. It is no longer
   hidden in a corner.

   [*By some stage device, perhaps the so-called eccyclema,*[4] *the inside of the palace is
   shown, with the body of the dead* QUEEN.]

CREON: Here is yet another horror   1360
   for my unhappy eyes to see.
   What doom still waits for me?
   I have but now taken in my arms my son,
   and again I look upon another dead face.
   Poor mother and poor son!   1365
SECOND MESSENGER: She stood at the altar, and with keen whetted knife
   she suffered her darkening eyes to close.
   First she cried in agony recalling the noble fate of Megareus,[5]
   who died before all this,

4. Wheeled platform rolled forward onto the stage to depict interior scenes; often used in tragedies to
reveal dead bodies.   5. Another son of Creon who died defending Thebes.

1370   and then for the fate of this son; and in the end
    she cursed you for the evil you had done
    in killing her sons.

CREON: I am distracted with fear. Why does not someone
    strike a two-edged sword right through me?

1375   I am dissolved in an agony of misery.

SECOND MESSENGER: You were indeed accused
    by her that is dead
    of Haemon's and of Megareus' death.

CREON: By what kind of violence did she find her end?

1380 SECOND MESSENGER: Her own hand struck her to the entrails
    when she heard of her son's lamentable death.

CREON: These acts can never be made to fit another
    to free me from the guilt. It was I that killed her.
    Poor wretch that I am, I say it is true!

1385   Servants, lead me away, quickly, quickly.
    I am no more a live man than one dead.

CHORUS: What you say is for the best—if there be a best
    in evil such as this. For the shortest way
    is best with troubles that lie at our feet.

1390 CREON: O, let it come, let it come,
    that best of fates that waits on my last day.
    Surely best fate of all. Let it come, let it come!
    That I may never see one more day's light!

CHORUS: These things are for the future. We must deal

1395   with what impends. What in the future is to care for
    rests with those whose duty it is
    to care for them.

CREON: At least, all that *I* want
    is in that prayer of mine.

1400 CHORUS: Pray for no more at all. For what is destined
    for us, men mortal, there is no escape.

CREON: Lead me away, a vain silly man
    who killed you, son, and you, too, lady.
    I did not mean to, but I did.

1405   I do not know where to turn my eyes
    to look to, for support.
    Everything in my hands is crossed. A most unwelcome fate
    has leaped upon me.

CHORUS: Wisdom is far the chief element in happiness

1410   and, secondly, no irreverence towards the gods.
    But great words of haughty men exact
    in retribution blows as great
    and in old age teach wisdom.

       THE END

                            ca. 441 B.C.E.

RICHARD C. JEBB

From *The Antigone of Sophocles**

The issue defined in the opening scene,—the conflict of divine with human law,—remains the central interest throughout. The action, so simple in plan, is varied by masterly character-drawing, both in the two principal figures, and in those lesser persons who contribute gradations of light and shade to the picture. There is no halting in the march of the drama; at each successive step we become more and more keenly interested to see how this great conflict is to end; and when the tragic climax is reached, it is worthy of such a progress.

The simplicity of the plot is due to the clearness with which two principles are opposed to each other. *Creon represents the duty of obeying the State's laws; Antigone, the duty of listening to the private conscience.* The definiteness and the power with which the play puts the case on each side are conclusive proofs that the question had assumed a distinct shape before the poet's mind. It is the only instance in which a Greek play has for its central theme a practical problem of conduct, involving issues, moral and political, which might be discussed on similar grounds in any age and in any country of the world. Greek Tragedy, owing partly to the limitations which it placed on detail, was better suited than modern drama to raise such a question in a general form. The *Antigone*, indeed, raises the question in a form as nearly abstract as is compatible with the nature of drama. The case of Antigone is a thoroughly typical one for the private conscience, because the particular thing which she believes that she ought to do was, in itself, a thing which every Greek of that age recognised as a most sacred duty,—viz.,[1] to render burial rites to kinsfolk. This advantage was not devised by Sophocles; it came to him as part of the story which he was to dramatise; but it forms an additional reason for thinking that, when he dramatised that story in the precise manner which he has chosen, he had a consciously dialectical purpose. Such a purpose was wholly consistent, in this instance, with the artist's first aim,—to produce a work of art. It is because Creon and Antigone are so human that the controversy which they represent becomes so vivid.

But how did Sophocles intend us to view the result? What is the drift of the words at the end, which say that "wisdom is the supreme part of happiness"? If this wisdom, or prudence, means, generally, the observance of due limit, may not the suggested moral be that both the parties to the conflict were censurable? As Creon overstepped the due limit when, by his edict, he infringed the divine law, so Antigone also overstepped it when she defied the edict. The drama would thus be a conflict between two persons, each of whom defends an intrinsically sound principle, but defends it in a mistaken way; and both persons are therefore punished. This view, of which Boeckh[2] is the chief representative, has found several supporters. Among them is Hegel:—"In the view of the Eternal Justice, both were wrong, because they were one-sided, but at the same time both were right."[3]

*From Sir Richard C. Jebb, ed., *The* Antigone *of Sophocles,* abr. by E. S. Shuckburgh (orig. ed., 1902; repr. Cambridge and New York: Cambridge UP, 1984), xvii–xix.
1. Namely (abbreviation of the Latin *videlicet*). [Editor's note]
2. August Boeckh (1785–1867), German classical scholar. [Editor's note]
3. *Religionsphilosophie,* II. 114. [Author's note]

Or does the poet rather intend us to feel that Antigone is wholly in the right,—*i.e.*, that nothing of which the human lawgiver could complain in her was of a moment's account beside the supreme duty which she was fulfilling;—and that Creon was wholly in the wrong,—*i.e.*, that the intrinsically sound maxims of government on which he relies lose all validity when opposed to the higher law which he was breaking? If that was the poet's meaning, then the "wisdom" taught by the issue of the drama means the sense which duly subordinates human to divine law,—teaching that, if the two come into conflict, human law must yield.

A careful study of the play itself will suffice (I think) to show that the second of these two views is the true one. Sophocles has allowed Creon to put his case ably, and (in a measure from which an inferior artist might have shrunk) he has been content to make Antigone merely a nobly heroic woman, not a being exempt from human passion and human weakness; but none the less does he mean us to feel that, in this controversy, the right is wholly with her, and the wrong wholly with her judge.

MAURICE BOWRA

From *Sophoclean Tragedy**

Modern critics who do not share Sophocles' conviction about the paramount duty of burying the dead and who attach more importance than he did to the claims of political authority have tended to underestimate the way in which he justifies Antigone against Creon. To their support they have called in the great name of Hegel, who was fascinated by the play and advanced remarkable views on it. His remarks have been taken out of their context, and he has been made responsible for the opinion that Sophocles dramatized a conflict not between right and wrong but between right and right, that Antigone and Creon are equally justified in their actions and that the tragedy arises out of this irreconcilable conflict. Hegel's own words lend some support to this view: "In the view of eternal justice both were wrong, because they were one-sided; but at the same time both were right." But if we look at Hegel's observations in their own place, we find that this summary hardly conveys his full meaning. He was thinking of something much vaster than the play, of the whole logic of history which is here symbolized in a concrete example. In this the conflict of opposites ends by producing a synthesis which is itself right. The conclusion is what matters, and that is different from saying that both sides in the conflict are themselves right. The tragic conclusion is, so to speak, a lesson of history, a fact which cannot be denied, real and therefore right, but the conflict which precedes it cannot be judged in isolation and neither side in it is right or wrong except in a relative sense. Hegel used the *Antigone* to illustrate his view of tragedy and his view of existence. He drew his own conclusions about the actions portrayed in it, as he was fully entitled to do. But his views are not those of Sophocles, and he should not be thought to maintain that Creon and Antigone were equally right in the eyes of their creator.

*From Maurice Bowra, *Sophoclean Tragedy* (Oxford: Clarendon, 1944), 65–67.

Sophocles leaves no doubt what conclusion should be drawn from the *Antigone*. He closes with a moral on the lips of the Chorus which tells the audience what to think:

> Wisdom has first place in happiness,
> And to fail not in reverence to the gods.
> The big words of the arrogant
> Lay big stripes on the boasters' backs.
> They pay the price
> And learn in old age to be wise.[4]

This can refer to no one but Creon, whose lack of wisdom has brought him to misery, who has shown irreverence to the gods in refusing burial to Polynices, been chastened for his proud words, and learned wisdom in his old age. To this lesson the preceding action in which Creon has lost son and wife and happiness has already made its effective contribution. We may be sure that the Chorus speak for the poet. It is as silent about Antigone as it is emphatic about Creon. There is no hint that she has in any way acted wrongly or that her death should be regarded as a righteous punishment. Of course the final words do not sum up everything important in the play, but we may reasonably assume that they pass judgement on its salient events as they appear in retrospect when the action is finished. There is no real problem about the ethical intention of the *Antigone*. It shows the fall of a proud man, and its lesson is that the gods punish pride and irreverence. But what matters much more than the actual conclusion is the means by which it is reached, the presentation of the different parties in the conflict, the view that we take of each, the feelings that are forced on us. The interest and power of the *Antigone* lie in the tangled issues which are unravelled in it.

A conclusion so clear as this is only worth reaching if it has been preceded by a drama in which the issues are violent and complex. The rights and wrongs of the case must not throughout be so obvious as they are at the end; the audience must feel that the issue is difficult, that there is much to be said on both sides, that the ways of the gods are hard to discern. Without this the play will fail in dramatic and human interest. And Sophocles has taken great care to show the issues in their full difficulty before he provides a solution for them. He makes the two protagonists appear in such a light that at intervals we doubt if all the right is really with Antigone and all the wrong with Creon. To Creon, who defies the divine ordinance of burial, he gives arguments and sentiments which sound convincing enough when they are put forward, and many must feel that he has some good reason to act as he does. On the other hand Antigone, who fearlessly vindicates the laws of the gods, is by no means a gentle womanly creature who suffers martyrdom for the right. She may be right, but there are moments when we qualify our approval of her, when she seems proud and forbidding in her determination to do her duty and to do it alone. For these variations in our feelings Sophocles is responsible. He makes us find some right in Creon, some wrong in Antigone, even if we are misled about both. He built his play on a contrast not between obvious wrong and obvious right but between the real arrogance of Creon and the apparent arrogance of Antigone. The first deceives by its

---

4. Bowra's translation.

fine persuasive sentiments; the second works through Antigone's refusal to offer concessions or to consider any point of view but her own. This contrast runs through much of the play, accounts for misunderstandings of what takes place in it, provides false clues and suggests wrong conclusions, and adds greatly to the intensity of the drama. When a play is written round a moral issue, that issue must be a real problem about which more than one view is tenable until all the relevant facts are known. So the *Antigone* dramatizes a conflict which was familiar to the Periclean age,[5] would excite divergent judgements and feelings, and make some support Antigone, some Creon, until the end makes all clear.

BERNARD KNOX

Introduction to *The Three Theban Plays**

The opening scenes show us the conflicting claims and loyalties of the two adversaries, solidly based, in both cases, on opposed political and religious principles. This is of course the basic insight of Hegel's famous analysis of the play: he sees it as "a collision between the two highest moral powers." What is wrong with them, in his view, is that they are both "one-sided." But Hegel goes much further than that. He was writing in the first half of the nineteenth century, a period of fervent German nationalism in which the foundations of the unified German state were laid: his views on loyalty to the state were very much those of Creon. "Creon," he says, "is not a tyrant, he is really a moral power. He is not in the wrong."

However, as the action develops the favorable impression created by Creon's opening speech is quickly dissipated. His announcement of his decision to expose the corpse, the concluding section of his speech, is couched in violent, vindictive terms—"carrion for the birds and dogs to tear"[6]—which stand in shocking contrast to the ethical generalities that precede it. This hint of a cruel disposition underlying the statesmanlike façade is broadened by the threat of torture leveled at the sentry and the order to execute Antigone in the presence of Haemon, her betrothed. And as he meets resistance from a series of opponents— Antigone's contemptuous defiance, the rational, political advice of his son Haemon, the imperious summons to obedience of the gods' spokesman, Tiresias—he swiftly abandons the temperate rhetoric of his inaugural address for increasingly savage invective. Against the two sanctions invoked by Antigone, the demands of blood relationship, the rights and privileges of the gods below, he rages in terms ranging from near-blasphemous defiance to scornful mockery.

> Sister's child or closer in blood
> than all my family clustered at my altar
> worshiping Guardian Zeus—she'll never escape,
> ... the most barbaric death.

---

5. The height of Athenian culture and political power in the time of the Athenian statesman Pericles (ca. 495–429 B.C.E.).

*From Sophocles, *The Three Theban Plays: Antigone, Oedipus the King, Oedipus at Colonus,* trans. by Robert Fagles, intro. and notes by Bernard Knox (New York: Penguin, 1982), 41–47, 53.

6. Knox's references are to Robert Fagles's translation, printed in *The Three Theban Plays.*

He will live to regret this wholesale denial of the family bond, for it is precisely through that family clustered at his altar that his punishment will be administered, in the suicides of his son and his wife, both of whom die cursing him.

And for Antigone's appeals to Hades, the great god of the underworld to whom the dead belong, Creon has nothing but contempt; for him "Hades" is simply a word meaning "death," a sentence he is prepared to pass on anyone who stands in his way. He threatens the sentry with torture as a prelude: "simple death won't be enough for you." When asked if he really intends to deprive Haemon of his bride he answers sarcastically: "Death will do it for me." He expects to see Antigone and Ismene turn coward "once they see Death coming for their lives." With a derisive comment he tells his son to abandon Antigone: "Spit her out, / . . . Let her find a husband down among the dead [in Hades' house]." And he dismisses Antigone's reverence for Hades and the rights of the dead with mockery as he condemns her to be buried alive: "There let her pray to the one god she worships: / Death." But this Hades is not something to be so lightly referred to, used or mocked. In the great choral ode which celebrated Man's progress and powers this was the one insurmountable obstacle that confronted him:

> ready, Never without man!
> Never without resources
> never an impasse as he marches on the future—
> only Death, from Death alone he will find no rescue . . .

And Creon, in the end, looking at the corpse of his son and hearing the news of his wife's suicide, speaks of Hades for the first time with the fearful respect that is his due, not as an instrument of policy or a subject for sardonic word-play, but as a divine power, a dreadful presence: "harbor of Death, so choked, so hard to cleanse!— / why me? why are you killing me?"

Creon is forced at last to recognize the strength of those social and religious imperatives that Antigone obeys, but long before this happens he has abandoned the principles which he had proclaimed as authority for his own actions. His claim to be representative of the whole community is forgotten as he refuses to accept Haemon's report that the citizens, though they dare not speak out, disapprove of his action; he denies the relevance of such a report even if true— "And is Thebes about to tell me how to rule?"—and finally repudiates his principles in specific terms by an assertion that the city belongs to him—"The city *is* the king's—that's the law!" This autocratic phrase puts the finishing touch to the picture Sophocles is drawing for his audience: Creon has now displayed all the characteristics of the "tyrant," a despotic ruler who seizes power and retains it by intimidation and force. Athens had lived under the rule of a "tyrant" before the democracy was established in 508 B.C., and the name and institution were still regarded with abhorrence. Creon goes on to abandon the gods whose temples crown the city's high places, the gods he once claimed as his own, and his language is even more violent. The blind prophet Tiresias tells him that the birds and dogs are fouling the altars of the city's gods with the carrion flesh of Polynices; he must bury the corpse. His furious reply begins with a characteristic accusation that the prophet has been bribed (the sentry had this same accusation flung at him), but what follows is a hideously blasphemous defiance of those gods Creon once claimed to serve:

> You'll never bury that body in the grave,
> not even if Zeus's eagles rip the corpse
> and wing their rotten pickings off to the throne of god!

At this high point in his stubborn rage (he will break by the end of the scene and try, too late, to avoid the divine wrath), he is sustained by nothing except his tyrannical insistence on his own will, come what may, and his outraged refusal to be defeated by a woman. "No woman," he says, "is going to lord it over me." "I'm not the man, not now: she is the man / if this victory goes to her and she goes free."

Antigone, on her side, is just as indifferent to Creon's principles of action as he is to hers. She mentions the city only in her last agonized laments before she is led off to her living death:

> O my city, all your fine rich sons!
> . . . springs of the Dirce,
> holy grove of Thebes . . .

But here she is appealing for sympathy to the city over the heads of the chorus, the city's symbolic representative on stage. In all her arguments with Creon and Ismene she speaks as one wholly unconscious of the rights and duties membership in the city confers and imposes, as if no unit larger than the family existed. It is a position just as extreme as Creon's insistence that the demands of the city take precedence over all others, for the living and the dead alike.

Like Creon, she acts in the name of gods, but they are different gods. There is more than a little truth in Creon's mocking comment that Hades is "the one god she worships." She is from the beginning "much possessed by death"; together with Ismene she is the last survivor of a doomed family, burdened with such sorrow that she finds life hardly worth living. "Who on earth," she says to Creon, "alive in the midst of so much grief as I, / could fail to find his death a rich reward?" She has performed the funeral rites for mother, father and her brother Eteocles:

> I washed you with my hands,
> I dressed you all, I poured the cups
> across your tombs.

She now sacrifices her life to perform a symbolic burial, a handful of dust sprinkled on the corpse, for Polynices, the brother left to rot on the battlefield. She looks forward to her reunion with her beloved dead in that dark kingdom where Persephone, the bride of Hades, welcomes the ghosts. It is in the name of Hades, one of the three great gods who rule the universe, that she defends the right of Polynices and of all human beings to proper burial. "Death [Hades] longs for the same rites for all," she tells Creon—for patriot and traitor alike; she rejects Ismene's plea to be allowed to share her fate with an appeal to the same stern authority: "Who did the work? / Let the dead and the god of death bear witness!" In Creon's gods, the city's patrons and defenders, she shows no interest at all. Zeus she mentions twice: once as the source of all the calamities that have fallen and are still to fall on the house of Oedipus, and once again at the beginning of her famous speech about the unwritten laws. But the context here suggests strongly that she is thinking about Zeus in his special relationship to the underworld, Zeus *Chthonios* (Underworld Zeus). "It wasn't Zeus," she says,

> who made this proclamation. . . .
> Nor did that Justice, dwelling with the gods
> beneath the earth, ordain such laws for men.

From first to last her religious devotion and duty are to the divine powers of the world below, the masters of that world where lie her family dead, to which she herself, reluctant but fascinated, is irresistibly drawn.

But, like Creon, she ends by denying the great sanctions she invoked to justify her action. In his case the process was spread out over the course of several scenes, as he reacted to each fresh pressure that was brought to bear on him; Antigone turns her back on the claims of blood relationship and the nether gods in one sentence: three lines in Greek, no more. They are the emotional high point of the speech she makes just before she is led off to her death.

> Never, I tell you,
> if I had been the mother of children
> or if my husband died, exposed and rotting—
> I'd never have taken this ordeal upon myself,
> never defied our people's will.

These unexpected words are part of the long speech that concludes a scene of lyric lamentation and is in effect her farewell to the land of the living. They are certainly a total repudiation of her proud claim that she acted as the champion of the unwritten laws and the infernal gods, for, as she herself told Creon, those laws and those gods have no preferences, they long "for the same rites for all." And her assertion that she would not have done for her children what she has done for Polynices is a spectacular betrayal of that fanatical loyalty to blood relationship which she urged on Ismene and defended against Creon, for there is no closer relationship imaginable than that between the mother and the children of her own body. Creon turned his back on his guiding principles step by step, in reaction to opposition based on those principles; Antigone's rejection of her public values is just as complete, but it is the sudden product of a lonely, brooding introspection, a last-minute assessment of her motives, on which the imminence of death confers a merciless clarity. She did it because Polynices was her brother; she would not have done it for husband or child. She goes on to justify this disturbing statement by an argument which is more disturbing still: husband and children, she says, could be replaced by others but, since her parents are dead, she could never have another brother. It so happens that we can identify the source of this strange piece of reasoning; it is a story in the *Histories* of Sophocles' friend Herodotus (a work from which Sophocles borrowed material more than once). Darius the Great King had condemned to death for treason a Persian noble, Intaphrenes, and all the men of his family. The wife of Intaphrenes begged importunately for their lives; offered one, she chose her brother's. When Darius asked her why, she replied in words that are unmistakably the original of Antigone's lines. But what makes sense in the story makes less in the play. The wife of Intaphrenes saves her brother's life, but Polynices is already dead; Antigone's phrase "no brother could ever spring to light again" would be fully appropriate only if Antigone had managed to save Polynices' life rather than bury his corpse.

For this reason, and also because of some stylistic anomalies in this part of the speech, but most of all because they felt that the words are unworthy of the

Antigone who spoke so nobly for the unwritten laws, many great scholars and also a great poet and dramatist, Goethe, have refused to believe that Sophocles wrote them. "I would give a great deal," Goethe told his friend Eckermann in 1827, "if some talented scholar could prove that these lines were interpolated, not genuine." Goethe did not know that the attempt had already been made, six years earlier; many others have tried since—Sir Richard Jebb, the greatest English editor of Sophocles, pronounced against them—and opinion today is still divided. Obviously a decision on this point is of vital significance for the interpretation of the play as a whole: with these lines removed, Antigone goes to her prison-tomb with no flicker of self-doubt, the flawless champion of the family bond and the unwritten laws, "whole as the marble, founded as the rock"—unlike Creon, she is not, in the end, reduced to recognizing that her motive is purely personal.

The gods do not praise Antigone, nor does anyone else in the play—except the young man who loves her so passionately that he cannot bear to live without her. Haemon tells his father what the Thebans are saying behind his back, the "murmurs in the dark": that Antigone deserves not death but "a glowing crown of gold!" Whether this is a true report (and the chorus does not praise Antigone even when they have been convinced that she was right) or just his own feelings attributed to others for the sake of his argument, it is a timely reminder of Antigone's heroic status. In the somber world of the play, against the background of so many sudden deaths and the dark mystery of the divine dispensation, her courage and steadfastness are a gleam of light; she is the embodiment of the only consolation tragedy can offer—that in certain heroic natures unmerited suffering and death can be met with a greatness of soul which, because it is purely human, brings honor to us all.

MARTHA C. NUSSBAUM

From *The Fragility of Goodness: Luck and Ethics in Greek Tragedy and Philosophy**

Almost all interpreters of [*Antigone*] have agreed that the play shows Creon to be morally defective, though they might not agree about the particular nature of his defect. The situation of Antigone is more controversial. Hegel assimilated her defect to Creon's; some more recent writers uncritically hold her up as a blameless heroine. Without entering into an exhaustive study of her role in the tragedy, I should like to claim (with the support of an increasing number of recent critics) that there is at least some justification for the Hegelian assimilation—though the criticism needs to be focused more clearly and specifically than it is in Hegel's brief remarks. I want to suggest that Antigone, like Creon, has engaged in a ruthless simplification of the world of value which effectively eliminates conflicting obligations. Like Creon, she can be blamed for refusal of vision. But there are

*From Martha C. Nussbaum, *The Fragility of Goodness: Luck and Ethics in Greek Tragedy and Philosophy* (Cambridge and New York: Cambridge UP, 1986), 63–67.

important differences, as well, between her project and Creon's. When these are seen, it will also emerge that this criticism of Antigone is not incompatible with the judgment that she is morally superior to Creon.

> O kindred, own-sisterly head of Ismene, do you know that there is not one of the evils left by Oedipus that Zeus does not fulfill for us while we live? . . . Do you grasp anything? Have you heard anything? Or has it escaped your notice that the evils that belong to enemies are advancing against our friends?[7]

A person is addressed with a periphrasis that is both intimate and impersonal. In the most emphatic terms available, it characterizes her as a close relative of the speaker. And yet its attitude towards the addressee is strangely remote. Antigone sees Ismene simply as the form of a close family relation. As such, she presses on her, with anxious insistence, the knowledge of the family: that "loved ones" (*philoi*) are being penalized as if they were enemies (*echthroi*). Loving relatives must "see" the shame and dishonour of "the evils that are yours and mine."

There has been a war. On one side was an army led by Eteocles, brother of Antigone and Ismene. On the other side was an invading army, made up partly of foreigners, but led by a Theban brother, Polynices. This heterogeneity is denied, in different ways, by both Creon and Antigone. Creon's strategy is to draw, in thought, a line between the invading and defending forces. What falls to one side of this line is a foe, bad, unjust; what falls to the other (if loyal to the city's cause) becomes, indiscriminately, friend or loved one. Antigone, on the other hand, denies the relevance of this distinction entirely. She draws, in imagination, a small circle around the members of her family: what is inside (with further restrictions which we shall mention) is family, therefore loved one and friend; what is outside is non-family, therefore, in any conflict with the family, enemy. If one listened only to Antigone, one would not know that a war had taken place or that anything called "city" was ever in danger. To her it is a simple injustice that Polynices should not be treated like a friend.

"Friend" (*philos*) and "enemy," then, are functions solely of family relationship. When Antigone says, "It is my nature to join in loving, not to join in hating," she is expressing not a general attachment to love, but a devotion to the *philia* of the family. It is the nature of these *philia* bonds to make claims on one's commitments and actions regardless of one's occurrent desires. This sort of love is not something one decides about; the relationships involved may have little to do with liking or fondness. We might say (to use terminology borrowed from Kant[8]) that Antigone, in speaking of love, means "practical," not "pathological" love (a love that has its source in fondness or inclination). "He is my own brother," she says to Ismene in explanation of her defiance of the city's decree, "and yours too, even if you don't want it. I certainly will never be found a traitor to him." Relationship is itself a source of obligation, regardless of the feelings involved. When Antigone speaks of Polynices as "my dearest brother," even when she proclaims, "I shall lie with him as a loved one with a loved one," there is no sense of closeness, no personal memory, no particularity animating her speech. Ismene, the one person who ought, historically, to be close to her, is treated from the beginning with remote coldness; she is even called enemy when she takes the

---

7. All translations are Nussbaum's, based on the Oxford Classical Text of A. C. Pearson.
8. Immanuel Kant (1724–1804), German philosopher who uses these terms in his *Critique of Pure Reason*.

wrong stand on matters of pious obligation. It is Ismene whom we see weeping "sister-loving tears," who acts out of commitment to a felt love. "What life is worth living for me, bereft of you?" she asks with an intensity of feeling that never animates her sister's piety. To Haemon, the man who passionately loves and desires her, Antigone never addresses a word throughout the entire play. It is Haemon, not Antigone, whom the Chorus views as inspired by *erōs*. Antigone is as far from *erōs* as Creon. For Antigone, the dead are "those whom it is most important to please." "You have a warm heart for the cold," observes her sister, failing to comprehend this impersonal and single-minded passion.

Duty to the family dead is the supreme law and the supreme passion. And Antigone structures her entire life and her vision of the world in accordance with this simple, self-contained system of duties. Even within this system, should a conflict ever arise, she is ready with a fixed priority ordering that will clearly dictate her choice. The strange speech in which she ranks duties to different family dead, placing duty to brother above duties to husband and children, is in this sense (if genuine) highly revealing: it makes us suspect that she is capable of a strangely ruthless simplification of duties, corresponding not so much to any known religious law as to the exigencies of her own practical imagination.

Other values fall into place, confirming these suspicions. Her single-minded identification with duties to the dead (and only some of these) effects a strange reorganization of piety, as well as of honor and justice. She is truly, in her own words, *hosia panourgēsasa*, one who will do anything for the sake of the pious; and her piety takes in only a part of conventional religion. She speaks of her allegiance to Zeus, but she refuses to recognize his role as guardian of the city and backer of Eteocles. The very expression of her devotion is suspect: "Zeus did not decree this, as far as I am concerned." She sets herself up as the arbiter of what Zeus can and cannot have decreed, just as Creon took it upon himself to say whom the gods could and could not have covered: no other character bears out her view of Zeus as single-mindedly backing the rights of the dead. She speaks, too, of the goddess *Dikē*, Justice; but *Dikē* for her is, simply, "the Justice who lives together with the gods below." The Chorus recognizes another *Dikē*. Later they will say to her, "Having advanced to the utmost limit of boldness, you struck hard against the altar of *Dikē* on high, o child." Justice is up here in the city, as well as below the earth. It is not as simple as she says it is. Antigone, accordingly, is seen by them not as a conventionally pious person, but as one who improvised her piety, making her own decisions about what to honor. She is a "maker of her own law"; her defiance is "self-invented passion." Finally they tell her unequivocally that her pious respect is incomplete: "[This] reverent action is a part of piety." Antigone's rigid adherence to a single narrow set of duties has caused her to misinterpret the nature of piety itself, a virtue within which a more comprehensive understanding would see the possibility of conflict.

Creon's strategy of simplification led him to regard others as material for his aggressive exploitation. Antigone's dutiful subservience to the dead leads to an equally strange, though different (and certainly less hideous) result. Her relation to others in the world above is characterized by an odd coldness. "You are alive," she tells her sister, "but my life is long since dead, to the end of serving the dead." The safely dutiful human life requires, or is, life's annihilation. Creon's attitude towards others is like necrophilia: he aspires to possess the inert and unresisting. Antigone's subservience to duty is, finally, the ambition to be a *nekros*, a corpse beloved of corpses. (Her apparent similarity to martyrs in our own tradition, who expect a fully active life after death, should not conceal from us the strangeness of this goal.) In the world below, there are no risks of failure or wrongdoing.

Neither Creon nor Antigone, then, is a loving or passionate being in anything like the usual sense. Not one of the gods, not one human being escapes the power of *erōs*, says the Chorus; but these two oddly inhuman beings do, it appears, escape. Creon sees loved persons as functions of the civic good, replaceable producers of citizens. For Antigone, they are either dead, fellow servants of the dead, or objects of complete indifference. No living being is loved for his or her personal qualities, loved with the sort of love that Haemon feels and Ismene praises. By altering their beliefs about the nature and value of persons, they have, it seems, altered or restructured the human passions themselves. They achieve harmony in this way; but at a cost. The Chorus speaks of *erōs* as a force as important and obligating as the ancient *thesmoi* or laws of right, a force against which it is both foolish and, apparently, blameworthy to rebel.

Antigone learns too—like Creon, by being forced to recognize a problem that lies at the heart of her single-minded concern. Creon saw that the city itself is pious and loving; that he could not be its champion without valuing what it values, in all its complexity. Antigone comes to see that the service of the dead requires the city, that her own religious aims cannot be fulfilled without civic institutions. By being her own law, she has not only ignored a part of piety, she has also jeopardized the fulfillment of the very pious duties to which she is so attached. Cut off from friends, from the possibility of having children, she cannot keep herself alive in order to do further service to the dead; nor can she guarantee the pious treatment of her own corpse. In her last speeches she laments not so much the fact of imminent death as, repeatedly, her isolation from the continuity of offspring, from friends and mourners. She emphasizes the fact that she will never marry; she will remain childless. Acheron will be her husband, the tomb her bridal chamber. Unless she can successfully appeal to the citizens whose needs as citizens she had refused to consider, she will die without anyone to mourn her death or to replace her as guardian of her family religion. She turns therefore increasingly, in this final scene, to the citizens and the gods of the city, until her last words closely echo an earlier speech made by Creon and blend his concerns with hers:

> O city of my fathers in this land of Thebes. O gods, progenitors of our race. I am led away, and wait no longer. Look, leaders of Thebes, the last of your royal line. Look what I suffer, at whose hands, for having respect for piety.

We have, then, two narrowly limited practical worlds, two strategies of avoidance and simplification. In one, a single human value has become *the* final end; in the other, a single set of duties has eclipsed all others. But we can now acknowledge that we admire Antigone, nonetheless, in a way that we do not admire Creon. It seems important to look for the basis of this difference.

First, in the world of the play, it seems clear that Antigone's actual choice is preferable to Creon's. The dishonour to civic values involved in giving pious burial to an enemy's corpse is far less radical than the violation of religion involved in Creon's act. Antigone shows a deeper understanding of the community and its values than Creon does when she argues that the obligation to bury the dead is an unwritten law, which cannot be set aside by the decree of a particular ruler. The belief that not all values are utility-relative, that there are certain claims whose neglect will prove deeply destructive of communal attunement and individual character, is a part of Antigone's position left untouched by the play's implicit criticism of her single-mindedness.

Furthermore, Antigone's pursuit of virtue is her own. It involves nobody else and commits her to abusing no other person. Rulership must be rulership *of* something; Antigone's pious actions are executed alone, out of a solitary commitment. She may be strangely remote from the world; but she does no violence to it.

Finally, and perhaps most important, Antigone remains ready to risk and to sacrifice her ends in a way that is not possible for Creon, given the singleness of his conception of value. There is a complexity in Antigone's virtue that permits genuine sacrifice *within* the defense of piety. She dies recanting nothing; but still she is torn by a conflict. Her virtue is, then, prepared to admit a contingent conflict, at least in the extreme case where its adequate exercise requires the cancellation of the conditions of its exercise. From within her single-minded devotion to the dead, she recognizes the power of these contingent circumstances and yields to them, comparing herself to Niobe wasted away by nature's snow and rain. (Earlier she had been compared, in her grief, to a mother bird crying out over an empty nest; so she is, while heroically acting, linked with the openness and vulnerability of the female.) The Chorus here briefly tries to console her with the suggestion that her bad luck does not really matter, in view of her future fame; she calls their rationalization a mockery of her loss. This vulnerability in virtue, this ability to acknowledge the world of nature by mourning the constraints that it imposes on virtue, surely contributes to making her the more humanly rational and the richer of the two protagonists: both active and receptive, neither exploiter nor simply victim.

REBECCA W. BUSHNELL

From *Prophesying Tragedy: Sign and Voice in Sophocles' Theban Plays**

It is primarily through the power of speech, against silence, that Creon's suffering is distinguished from Antigone's, as Creon becomes "nothing" in his disaster, whereas Antigone leaves the stage as herself. She has clearly lost in her battle for any kind of political autonomy, in her effort to counteract Creon's *kērygma*[9] (the Chorus, not Antigone, makes him change his mind). Further, neither the other characters in the play nor the gods confer heroic status on her. While the "punishment" of Creon may be seen as her vindication, Creon never mentions her again, nor does Tiresias defend her directly in his prophecy. Yet she leaves the stage, neither abject nor resigned to oblivion, but proclaiming her importance as the last of the Cadmeans. While Creon speaks his "sentence" of death, Antigone responds by invoking the gods and the city of Thebes, calling upon the Chorus

*From Rebecca W. Bushnell, *Prophesying Tragedy: Sign and Voice in Sophocles' Theban Plays* (Ithaca: Cornell UP, 1988), 64–66. All notes are the editor's.   9. Proclamation.

to look on her and acknowledge her right to have buried Polynices. Antigone's last act on stage is thus an act of apostrophe or invocation, meant to establish the presence and power of her own voice. For her, it matters little that neither god nor city responds; for one last time, Antigone relies on her voice to define herself, as she claims her link to her city, her lineage, and the gods of her race. Antigone is denied personal and political autonomy in the city of Thebes—what she cannot have as a woman; yet at the same time Antigone maintains her freedom of speech in public, which was the essence of freedom in Athens, where the worst punishment of exile was considered the loss of *parrēsia* or "free speech." Antigone speaks, too, as the bride of death, both in this world and beyond; like Hector, she has the authority that those on the brink of death possess over the living, and yet she already stands apart from the rest of the citizens, who must find a way to rule in the days to come.

Creon's loss of his power to invoke and command marks the loss of his role in the family and the city. Creon, too, laments his disaster, but his speech lacks the ceremony and self-reflection of Antigone's. Crying forth the ritual sound of wailing, *aiai*, he calls himself wretched (*deilaios*). Creon's penultimate gesture, matching Antigone's, is to utter a prayer for death. It may be addressed to the gods, but it is heard only by the Chorus, who refuse to answer the prayer: "That will come," they say, "but now we must do what is before us." When Creon protests that he prayed for what he desires most, the Chorus answers that he must not pray now. Creon thus ends in the world he created for himself, where "fate" is inflexible, yet there are no gods to hear his prayers. The gods will not help Creon, and he can no longer help himself. His words become meaningless when he himself becomes "nothing," having lost his family and his city. Earlier, Haemon compared Creon to writing tablets which, when unfolded, are blank. In the end, Creon fulfills that image, becoming someone who is nothing, a voice which is *asēmos*, "without significance."

In the *Iliad*, Hector's defiance of prophecy[1] plays out a conflict of discourse in the struggle between man and god for the right to declare *anankē*.[2] In *Antigone*, Sophocles dramatizes that conflict in the context of the city, where the king strives to emulate the gods in making the signs of "fate," and king, prophet, and citizen compete for the right to speak for the city's needs and future. Antigone loses this battle when Creon condemns her to death, just as Hector must die, according to the sentence of "fate." But Creon is silenced by the gods—and by the playwright. Both Creon and Antigone threaten the order of the city and are destroyed, but Sophocles gives the victory to her, in the dramatic authority of her voice. Although the gods themselves never answer her pleas for recognition, her voice commands the audience's and Chorus' attention. Creon, however, trails off in inarticulate confusion, just as he has no recognizable "self" when stripped of his roles of *tyrannos*,[3] husband, and father. Antigone never loses her ability to speak for herself, and in this way, is given her freedom. Thus it is she, not Creon, who is Hector's heir, and she who most closely imitates his defiance of fatal authority. But Antigone is not only Hector's heir; she is also the forerunner[4] of

1. Perhaps a reference to Book 22 of the *Iliad*, in which Hector mistakenly disbelieves Achilles' boast that Zeus will allow Achilles to kill Hector in battle.   2. Necessity, fate.   3. Ruler.
4. In that the play *Antigone* was written and first performed more than ten years before *Oedipus the King*.

her own father, Oedipus, who in *Oedipus the King* masters human speech in his pride and his shame.

MARY WHITLOCK BLUNDELL

From *Helping Friends and Harming Enemies: A Study in Sophocles and Greek Ethics**

Creon and Antigone are alike in several ways, especially the inconsistency of their values and the way they are driven by passion below a surface of rational argument. Both are also one-sided in their commitments. The poet could have given the champion of the *polis*[5] a much stronger case. But he could also have let Antigone meet and conquer Creon on his own ground (for example by arguing that her two brothers were equally responsible for the war). The narrowness of both is revealed by their failure really to engage in argument. Creon's two main statements of principle actually occur in Antigone's absence. When they do confront each other, in the brief passage of stichomythia[6] with which we began, they argue at cross purposes, repeatedly missing each other's point.

This does not mean, however, that they are equally limited in the values to which they adhere. Antigone is sometimes accused of being as narrowly one-sided as Creon in her allegiance to the family and disregard for the interests and *nomoi*[7] of the *polis*: "If one listened only to Antigone, one would not know that a war had taken place or that anything called 'city' was ever in danger" (Nussbaum, p. 2078, above). Nor can it be denied that she ignores competing concepts of *nomos* and justice which have their claims, no matter how shoddily Creon may represent them. Creon's misapplication of his principles does not undermine their claim to consideration, and the rightness of Antigone's cause does not of itself justify the passionate narrowness with which she pursues it. But although she does not acknowledge the authority of the *polis*, she never explicitly rejects it, as Creon does the family. Moreover she acts ultimately to the city's advantage. As Creon himself so ironically puts it, "the man who is worthwhile in family matters will also turn out to be just in the *polis*." It is Creon's own scorn not just for the family but for public opinion which finally brings the *polis* "doom instead of *soteria*."[8] He who began by saving Thebes from its enemies ends by stirring up other cities with enmity. He tells Antigone she is alone in her views, but she retorts that, on the contrary, all those present (namely the chorus of the city's elders) are on her side. Moreover she foresees great glory from her deed, which the context suggests is to derive from none other than her fellow citizens. Creon can make no such claims for himself. Indeed Haemon will hint that his father's behaviour may be destroying a glorious reputation. With the loss of his son's

---

*From Mary Whitlock Blundell, *Helping Friends and Harming Enemies: A Study in Sophocles and Greek Ethics* (Cambridge and New York: Cambridge UP, 1989), 145–48. Print. All notes are the editor's.
5. City-state.   6. Dialogue delivered in alternating lines; often used to show vigorous dispute.
7. Laws, standards (singular, *nomos*).   8. Salvation; the root, *soter*, means "savior."

loyalty, Creon also loses the last shreds of his claim to represent the *polis*. But Antigone's words are vindicated when Haemon reports the admiration of the ordinary citizens, echoing her own evaluation of her deed. Even the chorus, while withholding direct approval of Antigone's actions, promise her praise and glory for the manner of her death.

Antigone does once suggest that she is violating the will of the *polis* as represented by its citizens. But she does so only in the extremity of her isolation, lamenting that she is "friendless" and even questioning her divine support. She has cut herself off from her sister and quarrelled with the chorus, and has not, of course, heard Haemon's report of public sympathy for her fate. Under the circumstances it is not unreasonable that she should now believe she is defying the will of the citizens. But she claims that she would do so under the most extreme provocation, implying respect for the *polis* if not its present king. She restricts her defiance to the drastic circumstances of the present crisis, acknowledging the potential conflict between her own priorities and the demands of civic life.

As Antigone goes to her death, she emphatically calls the city itself, its gods and its most prominent citizens, the chorus, to bear witness to her fate. Does this tell us that she has learned the limitations of her own narrow principles? Or is it a reproach to the apathetic chorus? Surely the latter. She shows no sign of regret or new-found insight into the civic value of obedience. But she addresses the chorus in ways suggesting their special responsibility not just as citizens, but as Theban aristocrats who might be expected to play a role in public life. She calls them "citizens of the fatherland," "wealthy men of the *polis*," "leading men of Thebes." When she refers to herself as "the last remaining daughter of the royal house," she is reasserting her status as a member of the ruling family, to which the chorus are supposedly loyal, and to which Creon is tied only by marriage. This royal status is linked with her reverence for the gods, especially her ancestral gods. Her obligations to the *polis* and her dead family are not mutually exclusive. She has not failed the citizens, for the burial was both in their best interest and called for by their "established laws." But they, intimidated by Creon, have abandoned her. She therefore accuses the chorus of mockery and *hubris*,[9] the same hostile laughter that she inflicted on her sister and (in his view) on Creon.

One-sided and "autonomous" though she may be, Antigone's obsession is less sterile and destructive than Creon's. He, as he so much likes to remind us, is the sole ruler of the *polis*. In order to achieve a just and stable social order, such a ruler must acknowledge and balance competing claims and values. If these are ultimately incommensurable, he must attempt a compromise, however uneasy. As Haemon eloquently insists, he must know how to bend with the storm. He must respect the ties of natural *philia*,[1] and at the same time promote political *philia* by adopting policies that meet the citizens' approval. Antigone abides heroically by the first variety of *philia* as she interprets it, and can make some claim to the second, but Creon is a failure at both.

9. A complex term in Greek ethical thought that implies an impious overreaching of human limits.
1. Love, affinity.

SUGGESTIONS FOR WRITING

1. The first two scenes or episodes of *Antigone* introduce us to each of the play's two main characters—first Antigone herself, then Creon. Write an essay in which you explore what each scene shows us about who these characters are, what motives and values drive them, and why they come into conflict. In these terms, for example, what does Sophocles achieve by showing us Antigone in conversation with her sister, or Creon with a "convocation of the elders" (line 177)? In terms of characterization and conflict, what is the effect and significance of the choral songs that end each episode?

2. As is conventional in Greek drama, *Antigone* ends with a final choral song that articulates the theme of the play, while also leaving a great deal of room for interpretation about just what that theme is. Drawing on evidence from the entire play, explain both how we might and also how we ultimately should interpret the final song and the play's theme.

3. Write an essay that draws on evidence from this ancient Greek play to explore precisely how and why it remains relevant to the world in which you live. Does *Antigone*, for example, depict a type of person or a conflict still common in the twenty-first century, or might it articulate a theme that still applies?

4. Many of the critical excerpts in this chapter focus on the conflict between Antigone and Creon, debating not only how that conflict is ultimately resolved but also what the nature of the conflict is or how best to understand it. To take just two examples, Richard C. Jebb takes the conflict to be one between "*the duty of obeying the State's laws*" (Creon's emphasis; see p. 2069) and "*the duty of listening to the private conscience*" (Antigone's emphasis; see p. 2069), while Maurice Bowra implies that the conflict is instead between duty to the laws of man versus those of the gods and/or between the human tendency toward "arrogance" versus the need for humility and reverence (see p. 2070). Carefully read the other critical excerpts in the chapter, working to understand how each implicitly or explicitly characterizes the conflict between Creon and Antigone. Then, write an essay in which you first describe the views of all the critics and then draw on evidence from the play either to defend one of these views or to offer an alternative interpretation of the nature of the conflict between Antigone and Creon.

5. Though he acknowledges that *Antigone* depicts an external conflict between Antigone and Creon and the views and values each represents, Bernard Knox suggests that the play also presents Creon as internally conflicted. Carefully read the excerpt from Knox's introduction to *The Three Theban Plays*, and write an essay exploring whether and how the play supports his interpretation of Creon's internal conflict and its resolution.

6. Re-read the critical excerpts in this chapter and then make a list of at least three moments in *Antigone* and/or aspects or elements of the play that strike you as important, but that aren't given adequate attention in the critical excerpts. Then write an essay that explores and explains just why and how any one of these moments, aspects, or elements is especially important to the play's effect and meaning.

STUDENT WRITING

The student essay below was written in response to an assignment that asked students to draw on at least five works of literary criticism, including any relevant excerpts in this chapter and at least one journal article *not* included here, in order to develop their own interpretation of any aspect of *Antigone*. Student writer Jackie Izawa decided to explore rival interpretations of Antigone's treatment of her siblings and her fiancé. The resulting essay demonstrates unusual strengths and a few common problems, particularly in terms of the way it uses, presents, and quotes from both primary and secondary sources. The comments that accompany the essay highlight some of those strengths and weaknesses.

Perhaps the weakest moment in the essay is a conclusion that does not fulfill the promise made in the introduction that the essay will ultimately "draw a conclusion" about Antigone's motives. The simplest way to fix that inconsistency would be to change the thesis statement so that it matches up with the conclusion and to devote the conclusion to discussing why it's so "essential that we consider different perspectives" and interpretations rather than simply endorsing one perspective or interpretation. What might the play itself say about that issue, particularly through Haemon's remarks to his father?

Jackie Izawa
ENG 298X
Dr. Mays

The Two Faces of Antigone

Antigone's strong yet harsh nature motivates her to defy Creon's edict, but it also isolates her from those who love her. Throughout the play, Antigone tries to convince Creon that her fallen brother, Polyneices, deserves a proper burial. Her unwavering loyalty to her brother shows she might be capable of love. But if so, why does she only seem to love the person who's dead before the play even begins? She barely shows any affection for her only living sibling, Ismene, and none for her betrothed, Haemon. It is possible that Antigone is so overwhelmed

---

Izawa 2

by a desire for justice for her brother that she becomes blinded to every other person. The other possibility is that she is creating the illusion that she does not love Ismene and Haemon because she wants to spare them. "Namely, that although now Antigone does not mean to be stern and hard, as she is simply being herself, yet all the same she *is* stern and hard" (Simpson 79). Before drawing a conclusion about Antigone's motives, it is important to recognize and acknowledge both positions.

Ismene is Antigone's opposite in every way, in W. H. D. Rouse's words, "a nice girl, soft-hearted and devoted, but a shadow of her strong sister" (41). In the opening scene of *Antigone*, the two sisters have just heard of Creon's edict, and both have different opinions about how to handle it. While Antigone is set on burying her brother, Ismene tries to reason with her. She recalls all the horrible events that happened in their family history. First Oedipus "himself struck out / the sight of his two eyes," and then his wife and mother "did shame / violently on her life, with twisted cords" (lines 58, 59, 61, 62). Ismene continues talking about the family's tragedies, ending with the deaths of her brothers. Both sisters know that the sentence for burying Polyneices is death. Ismene does not want herself or Antigone to follow in the steps of her deceased family members or to "put dishonor on them" by defying Creon (line 90). Ismene is timid and fearful of breaking the law. By nature, Ismene is submissive. She views herself as an obedient woman, a compliant citizen. Naturally, when Antigone asks for Ismene's help in burying their brother, Ismene declines. Ismene would like to bury her brother, but she could not break the law. She tells Antigone, "to act in defiance of the citizenry, / my nature does not give me means for that" (lines 91–93).

In the play's very first line, Antigone calls Ismene "my dear sister." But this is the first and only time that Antigone shows affection

Introduce quotations from sources with a signal phrase that provides the information about the source necessary to understand the quotation and its relationship to your statement. Is Simpson endorsing one of the two possible interpretations you've just offered of Antigone, or does his statement suggest a third possibility? Also, make sure that the quotation makes sense on its own. The sentence fragment you quote here is confusing.

You provide good evidence from your primary source to support your claims about Ismene's natural reluctance to defy the law, but none to back up your other claim—that her reluctance is also due to her sense of her particular position and duties "as an obedient woman."

for Ismene. Because Ismene is afraid to go against Creon's edict, Antigone regards Ismene as a coward and disowns her. Immediately, Antigone verbally attacks her sister, showing that she is unable to view things as others do: "At least he is my brother—and yours, too, / though you deny him. *I* will not prove false to him" (lines 51–52). The emphasis on the "I" shows that Antigone feels a degree of rivalry. It is likely she feels that because *she* is determined to bury Polyneices, she is better than Ismene. This kind of rivalry is common between siblings even today. The idea of proving your superiority is always attractive, especially if you can demonstrate it publicly, to an entire city. Antigone is rather cruel and ruthless to her sister, whether out of pure anger, rivalry, or pain at her betrayal of the family. Towards the end of their first encounter, Ismene promises that she will keep silent, but Antigone retorts, "Oh, oh, no! shout it out. I will hate you still worse / for silence— should you not proclaim it, / to everyone" (lines 99–101). Despite all that both of them have endured because of their shared family history, Antigone is willing to throw it away when Ismene does not help her:

> If you will talk like this I will loathe you,
>
> And you will be adjudged an enemy—
>
> justly—by the dead's decision. Let me alone
>
> and my folly with me, to endure this terror.
>
> No suffering of mine will be enough
>
> To make me die ignobly. (lines 109–14)

The two sisters are seen together only briefly later in the play, but the dynamic between them is much the same. After Antigone attempts to bury Polyneices and both sisters are brought to Creon, Antigone lashes out at Ismene, effectively severing any ties she has with her sister. As Charles Levy argues, " in [a] . . . tense stichomythic exchange with Ismene [shortly after her argument with Creon], she reacts with

---

Interesting observation! Does this introduce a third possible interpretation of Antigone (in addition to the two you introduce early on)?

What exactly do you mean to demonstrate with this quotation? Does this provide evidence for your point about Antigone's desire to publicly demonstrate her superiority? or the point about her cruelty? Or something else?

Izawa 4

still greater vehemence than during their earlier encounter to what she regards as her sister's irremediable betrayal of her, scorning Ismene . . ." (142). Ismene wants to share the sentence of death with her sister, pleading, "Sister, do not dishonor me, denying me / a common death with you, a common honoring / of the dead man." But Antigone refuses to listen, saying, "Don't die with me, nor make your own / what you have never touched . . ." (lines 597–601). Antigone is consistently cold towards her sister.

> This quotation from your secondary source consists mainly of plot summary. It would be more effective to describe the action yourself, while acknowledging that Levy, too, notes its importance.

Showing the same consistency (in the opposite way), Ismene seems to disregard the ill treatment she receives from her sister, continuing to show love for Antigone though Ismene knows that she is no longer welcome in Antigone's eyes. Being the compassionate and devoted sister that she is, Ismene still does her best to save Antigone. Even after being rejected, Ismene tries to reason with Creon. She pleads again that her life would be incomplete without Antigone. When Creon refuses to change his mind, Ismene brings up Haemon, hoping that Creon is not cruel enough to execute his future daughter-in-law. Unfortunately, even that does not budge Creon. Ismene is loving and caring, showing as much loyalty to her sister as Antigone does for their brother, but Ismene's gesture is never acknowledged.

Or might Antigone in fact be making a gesture of love even greater than her sister's? As A. W. Simpson and C. M. H. Millar argue, Antigone's treatment of Ismene could in fact be viewed as liberating Ismene or saving her from death (79). They believe that Antigone is brutal with Ismene because she is "unwillingly" putting up a façade for Creon (80). One of the main driving factors in their argument is the irony in Antigone's decision: "The *irony* of the situation is brought out, because, from love for Ismene, Antigone alienates herself from her, in order to save her, and goes to her death thinking she has failed; and she never finds out that she succeeded after all" (80).

> What evidence from your primary text supports this claim, and what do you think of it? Remember that quoting a critic's interpretive claim isn't enough to prove the claim valid.

Izawa 5

Likewise, there are also two different ways of interpreting Antigone's interaction with her betrothed. Haemon, from the first moment he is introduced, immediately sides with Antigone and is completely devoted to her. He defends his wife-to-be and defies his father, Creon, ironically with as much passion as Antigone shows. When he first appears in the play, he is naturally dedicated to his father. He shows that he respects his father, but at the same time he also reasons with Creon both about the rule of the city and about the punishment of Antigone:

> Haemon: You will not find me yield to what is shameful.
>
> Creon: At least, your argument is all for her.
>
> Haemon: Yes, and for you and me—and for the gods below.
>
> Creon: You will never marry her while her life lasts.
>
> Haemon: Then she must die—and dying destroy another. (lines 804–808)

Haemon is showing his devotion to Antigone as well as foreshadowing his own fate in the play. Even though Creon tells him he can find another wife, Haemon refuses. His love for Antigone dooms him to his death. All of his actions following his argument with his father are undertaken for Antigone. When Haemon finds Antigone dead in the cave, he is consumed with rage and anger. As Walter H. Johns puts it, because "Haemon hears his father's voice and realizes that the cause of all his grief is close at hand," he "turn[s] his sword against himself and d[ies] with his arms about the body of Antigone" (100). Haemon's rage is likely equivalent to his love for Antigone, and for him to kill himself because of his grief over her death only supports this likelihood.

The reader empathizes with and even pities Haemon because although he speaks of great affection for Antigone, she does not do the same for him. In fact, as Martha Nussbaum points out, "Antigone never [even] addresses a word throughout the entire play" to this "man who

Again, this section seems a bit light on evidence (versus secondary source material), while the latter consists of plot summary.

Izawa 6

passionately loves and desires her" (2080). And Antigone says his name only once in the play when she responds to Creon, "Dear Haemon, how your father dishonors you" (line 627). Though "dear" is

Great point! Is it one any other critic makes as well?

usually a term of endearment, the context in which it is used and Antigone's silence about Haemon in the rest of the play suggests that she says it in a pitying manner. Perhaps she felt sympathy for Haemon because he had a father who was willing to kill the love of his life, but that's not the same as loving him as he does her. The relationship is completely one-sided, and Antigone's lack of affection for her betrothed seems to give a new kind of meaning to Ismene's remark much earlier in the play that her sister is "in love / with the impossible" (lines 104–105). Antigone does seem to be more in love with the idea of burying her brother than she is with Haemon.

Again, though, is hard-heartedness or single-heartedness the only explanation for Antigone's behavior? Some critics argue that it isn't, that Antigone's lack of attention to Haemon is inspired by her desire to ensure that he does not share her fate. She could very well love him, but because she is sentenced to death, she breaks off ties with him. Simpson and Millar, for example, conclude that "Antigone has broken the ties between herself and her sister, in order to save her, and is now completely alone in the world. Haemon cannot reach her, as far as she knows, because Creon has just forbidden the marriage" (80). Perhaps Antigone realized that she and Haemon would never have a happy marriage, so she let him go. Unfortunately, Haemon did not realize her intentions.

The true motive behind Antigone's actions will always be debated. There are always at least two sides to everything, and it is essential that we consider different perspectives. Antigone can be viewed as hard-hearted and cruel, able to cut herself off from those who love and cherish her. However, she can also be seen as the type of heroine who

Izawa 7

does everything for the greater good of those she is closest to. In this view, she is compassionate, loyal, and unafraid to make sacrifices. Either way, Antigone remains a heroine who has made a huge impact not only on other characters in the play, but on those who read it as well.

Works Cited

Johns, Walter H. "Dramatic Effect in Sophocles' Antigone 1232." *The Classic Journal* 43.2 (1947): 99–100. JSTOR University of Las Vegas Library. <http://www.jstor.org>. Web. 30 April 2007.

Levy, Charles S. "Antigone's Motives: A Suggested Interpretation." *Transactions and Proceedings of the American Philogical Association* 94 (1963): 137–44. JSTOR University of Las Vegas Library. <http://www.jstor.org>. Web. 30 April 2007.

Nussbaum, Martha C. "From *The Fragility of Goodness: Luck and Ethics in Greek Tragedy and Philosophy.*" 1986. *The Norton Introduction to Literature*. Ed. Alison Booth, J. Paul Hunter and Kelly J. Mays. 9th ed. New York: Norton, 2005. 2113–16.

Rose, J. L. "The Problem of the Second Burial in Sophocles' *Antigone*." *The Classic Journal* 47. 6 (1952): 219–221. JSTOR University of Las Vegas Library. <http://www.jstor.org>. Web. 29 April 2007.

Rouse, W. H. D. "The Two Burials in *Antigone*." *The Classical Review* 25. 2. (1911): 40–42. JSTOR University of Las Vegas Library. <http://www.jstor.org>. Web. 29 April 2007.

Simpson, A. W., and C. M. H. Millar. "A Note on Sophocles' *Antigone,* Lines 531–81." *Greece & Rome* 17.50 (1948): 78–81. JSTOR University of Las Vegas. <http://www.jstor.org>. Web. 29 April 2007.

Reading More Drama

ANTON CHEKHOV

The Cherry Orchard [1]

CHARACTERS IN THE PLAY

MADAME RANEVSKY (LYUBOV ANDREYEVNA), *the owner of the Cherry Orchard*
ANYA, *her daughter, aged 17*
VARYA, *her adopted daughter, aged 24*
SEMYONOV-PISHTCHIK, *a landowner*
CHARLOTTA IVANOVNA, *a governess*
EPIHODOV (SEMYON PANTALEYEVITCH), *a clerk*
DUNYASHA, *a maid*
FIRS, *an old valet, aged 87*

GAEV (LEONID ANDREYEVITCH), *brother of Madame Ranevsky*
LOPAHIN (YERMOLAY ALEXEYEVITCH), *a merchant*
TROFIMOV (PYOTR SERGEYEVITCH), *a student*
YASHA, *a young valet*
A WAYFARER
THE STATION MASTER
A POST-OFFICE CLERK
VISITORS, SERVANTS

The action takes place on the estate of MADAME RANEVSKY.

ACT I

A room, which has always been called the nursery. One of the doors leads into ANYA's *room. Dawn, sun rises during the scene. May, the cherry trees in flower, but it is cold in the garden with the frost of early morning. Windows closed.*

Enter DUNYASHA *with a candle and* LOPAHIN *with a book in his hand.*

LOPAHIN: The train's in, thank God. What time is it?

DUNYASHA: Nearly two o'clock. [*Puts out the candle.*] It's daylight already.

LOPAHIN: The train's late! Two hours, at least. [*Yawns and stretches.*] I'm a pretty one; what a fool I've been. Came here on purpose to meet them at the station and dropped asleep. . . . Dozed off as I sat in the chair. It's annoying. . . . You might have waked me.

DUNYASHA: I thought you had gone. [*Listens.*] There, I do believe they're coming!

LOPAHIN: [*Listens.*] No, what with the luggage and one thing and another. [*A pause.*] Lyubov Andreyevna has been abroad five years; I don't know what she is like now. . . . She's a splendid woman. A good-natured, kind-hearted woman. I remember when I was a lad of fifteen, my poor father—he used to keep a little shop here in the village in those days—gave me a punch in the face with his fist and made my nose bleed. We were in the yard here, I forget what we'd come about—he had had a drop. Lyubov Andreyevna—I can see her now—she was a slim young girl then—took me to wash my face, and then brought me

1. Translated by Constance Garnett.

into this very room, into the nursery. "Don't cry, little peasant," says she, "it will be well in time for your wedding day." . . . [*A pause.*] Little peasant. . . . My father was a peasant, it's true, but here am I in a white waistcoat and brown shoes, like a pig in a bun shop. Yes, I'm a rich man, but for all my money, come to think, a peasant I was, and a peasant I am. [*Turns over the pages of the book.*] I've been reading this book and I can't make head or tail of it. I fell asleep over it. [*A pause.*]

DUNYASHA: The dogs have been awake all night, they feel that the mistress is coming.

LOPAHIN: Why, what's the matter with you, Dunyasha?

DUNYASHA: My hands are all of a tremble. I feel as though I should faint.

LOPAHIN: You're a spoilt soft creature, Dunyasha. And dressed like a lady too, and your hair done up. That's not the thing. One must know one's place.

[*Enter* EPIHODOV *with a nosegay;*[2] *he wears a pea-jacket and highly polished creaking topboots; he drops the nosegay as he comes in.*]

EPIHODOV: [*Picking up the nosegay.*] Here! the gardener's sent this, says you're to put it in the dining-room. [*Gives* DUNYASHA *the nosegay.*]

LOPAHIN: And bring me some kvass.[3]

DUNYASHA: I will. [*Goes out.*]

EPIHODOV: It's chilly this morning, three degrees of frost,[4] though the cherries are all in flower. I can't say much for our climate. [*Sighs.*] I can't. Our climate is not often propitious to the occasion. Yermolay Alexeyevitch, permit me to call your attention to the fact that I purchased myself a pair of boots the day before yesterday, and they creak, I venture to assure you, so that there's no tolerating them. What ought I to grease them with?

LOPAHIN: Oh, shut up! Don't bother me.

EPIHODOV: Every day some misfortune befalls me. I don't complain, I'm used to it, and I wear a smiling face.

[DUNYASHA *comes in, hands* LOPAHIN *the kvass.*]

EPIHODOV: I am going. [*Stumbles against a chair, which falls over.*] There! [*As though triumphant.*] There you see now, excuse the expression, an accident like that among others. . . . It's positively remarkable. [*Goes out.*]

DUNYASHA: Do you know, Yermolay Alexeyevitch, I must confess, Epihodov has made me a proposal.

LOPAHIN: Ah!

DUNYASHA: I'm sure I don't know. . . . He's a harmless fellow, but sometimes when he begins talking, there's no making anything of it. It's all very fine and expressive, only there's no understanding it. I've a sort of liking for him too. He loves me to distraction. He's an unfortunate man; every day there's something. They tease him about it—two and twenty misfortunes they call him.

LOPAHIN: [*Listening.*] There! I do believe they're coming.

DUNYASHA: They are coming! What's the matter with me? . . . I'm cold all over.

LOPAHIN: They really are coming. Let's go and meet them. Will she know me? It's five years since I saw her.

DUNYASHA: [*In a flutter.*] I shall drop this very minute. . . . Ah, I shall drop.

2. Bouquet.   3. Weak homemade beer.   4. That is, 29°F (−2°C).

[*There is a sound of two carriages driving up to the house.* LOPAHIN *and* DUNYASHA *go out quickly. The stage is left empty. A noise is heard in the adjoining rooms.* FIRS, *who has driven to meet* MADAME RANEVSKY, *crosses the stage hurriedly leaning on a stick. He is wearing old-fashioned livery and a high hat. He says something to himself, but not a word can be distinguished. The noise behind the scenes goes on increasing. A voice: "Come, let's go in here." Enter* LYUBOV ANDREYEVNA, ANYA, *and* CHARLOTTA IVANOVNA *with a pet dog on a chain, all in traveling dresses.* VARYA *in an outdoor coat with a kerchief over her head,* GAEV, SEMYONOV-PISHTCHIK, LOPAHIN, DUNYASHA *with bag and parasol, servants with other articles. All walk across the room.*]

ANYA: Let's come in here. Do you remember what room this is, mamma?

LYUBOV: [*Joyfully, through her tears.*] The nursery!

VARYA: How cold it is, my hands are numb. [*To* LYUBOV ANDREYEVNA.] Your rooms, the white room and the lavender one, are just the same as ever, mamma.

LYUBOV: My nursery, dear delightful room. . . . I used to sleep here when I was little. . . . [*Cries.*] And here I am, like a little child. . . . [*Kisses her brother and* VARYA, *and then her brother again.*] Varya's just the same as ever, like a nun. And I knew Dunyasha. [*Kisses* DUNYASHA.]

GAEV: The train was two hours late. What do you think of that? Is that the way to do things?

CHARLOTTA: [*To* PISHTCHIK.] My dog eats nuts, too.

PISHTCHIK: [*Wonderingly.*] Fancy that!

[*They all go out except* ANYA *and* DUNYASHA.]

DUNYASHA: We've been expecting you so long. [*Takes* ANYA'*s hat and coat.*]

ANYA: I haven't slept for four nights on the journey. I feel dreadfully cold.

DUNYASHA: You set out in Lent, there was snow and frost, and now? My darling! [*Laughs and kisses her.*] I *have* missed you, my precious, my joy. I must tell you . . . I can't put it off a minute. . . .

ANYA: [*Wearily.*] What now?

DUNYASHA: Epihodov, the clerk, made me a proposal just after Easter.

ANYA: It's always the same thing with you. . . . [*Straightening her hair.*] I've lost all my hairpins. . . . [*She is staggering from exhaustion.*]

DUNYASHA: I don't know what to think, really. He does love me, he does love me so!

ANYA: [*Looking towards her door, tenderly.*] My own room, my windows just as though I had never gone away. I'm home! To-morrow morning I shall get up and run into the garden. . . . Oh, if I could get to sleep! I haven't slept all the journey, I was so anxious and worried.

DUNYASHA: Pyotr Sergeyevitch came the day before yesterday.

ANYA: [*Joyfully.*] Petya!

DUNYASHA: He's asleep in the bath house, he has settled in there. I'm afraid of being in their way, says he. [*Glancing at her watch.*] I was to have waked him, but Varvara Mihalovna told me not to. Don't you wake him, says she.

[*Enter* VARYA *with a bunch of keys at her waist.*]

VARYA: Dunyasha, coffee and make haste. . . . Mamma's asking for coffee.

DUNYASHA: This very minute. [*Goes out.*]

VARYA: Well, thank God, you've come. You're home again. [*Petting her.*] My little darling has come back! My precious beauty has come back again!

ANYA: I have had a time of it!

VARYA: I can fancy.

ANYA: We set off in Holy Week—it was so cold then, and all the way Charlotta would talk and show off her tricks. What did you want to burden me with Charlotta for?

VARYA: You couldn't have traveled all alone, darling. At seventeen!

ANYA: We got to Paris at last, it was cold there—snow. I speak French shockingly. Mamma lives on the fifth floor, I went up to her and there were a lot of French people, ladies, an old priest with a book. The place smelt of tobacco and so comfortless. I felt sorry, oh! so sorry for mamma all at once, I put my arms round her neck, and hugged her and wouldn't let her go. Mamma was as kind as she could be, and she cried. . . .

VARYA: [*Through her tears.*] Don't speak of it, don't speak of it!

ANYA: She had sold her villa at Mentone, she had nothing left, nothing. I hadn't a farthing left either, we only just had enough to get here. And mamma doesn't understand! When we had dinner at the stations, she always ordered the most expensive things and gave the waiters a whole rouble. Charlotta's just the same. Yasha too must have the same as we do; it's simply awful. You know Yasha is mamma's valet now, we brought him here with us.

VARYA: Yes, I've seen the young rascal.

ANYA: Well, tell me—have you paid the arrears on the mortgage?

VARYA: How could we get the money?

ANYA: Oh, dear! Oh, dear!

VARYA: In August the place will be sold.

ANYA: My goodness!

LOPAHIN: [*Peeps in at the door and moos like a cow.*] Moo! [*Disappears.*]

VARYA: [*Weeping.*] There, that's what I could do to him. [*Shakes her fist.*]

ANYA: [*Embracing* VARYA, *softly.*] Varya, has he made you an offer? [VARYA *shakes her head.*] Why, but he loves you. Why is it you don't come to an understanding? What are you waiting for?

VARYA: I believe that there never will be anything between us. He has a lot to do, he has no time for me . . . and takes no notice of me. Bless the man, it makes me miserable to see him. . . . Everyone's talking of our being married, everyone's congratulating me, and all the while there's really nothing in it; it's all like a dream. [*In another tone.*] You have a new brooch like a bee.

ANYA: [*Mournfully.*] Mamma bought it. [*Goes into her own room and in a lighthearted childish tone.*] And you know, in Paris I went up in a balloon!

VARYA: My darling's home again! My pretty is home again!

[DUNYASHA *returns with the coffee-pot and is making the coffee.*]

VARYA: [*Standing at the door.*] All day long, darling, as I go about looking after the house, I keep dreaming all the time. If only we could marry you to a rich man, then I should feel more at rest. Then I would go off by myself on a pilgrimage to Kiev, to Moscow . . . and so I would spend my life going from one holy place to another. . . . I would go on and on. . . . What bliss!

ANYA: The birds are singing in the garden. What time is it?

VARYA: It must be nearly three. It's time you were asleep, darling. [*Going into* ANYA's *room.*] What bliss!

[YASHA *enters with a rug and a traveling bag.*]

YASHA: [*Crosses the stage, mincingly.*] May one come in here, pray?

DUNYASHA: I shouldn't have known you, Yasha. How you have changed abroad.

YASHA: H'm! . . . And who are you?

DUNYASHA: When you went away, I was that high. [*Shows distance from floor.*] Dunyasha, Fyodor's daughter. . . . You don't remember me!

YASHA: H'm! . . . You're a peach! [*Looks round and embraces her: she shrieks and drops a saucer.* YASHA *goes out hastily.*]

VARYA: [*In the doorway, in a tone of vexation.*] What now?

DUNYASHA: [*Through her tears.*] I have broken a saucer.

VARYA: Well, that brings good luck.

ANYA: [*Coming out of her room.*] We ought to prepare mamma: Petya is here.

VARYA: I told them not to wake him.

ANYA: [*Dreamily.*] It's six years since father died. Then only a month later little brother Grisha was drowned in the river, such a pretty boy he was, only seven. It was more than mamma could bear, so she went away, went away without looking back. [*Shuddering.*] . . . How well I understand her, if only she knew! [*A pause.*] And Petya Trofimov was Grisha's tutor, he may remind her.

[*Enter* FIRS: *he is wearing a pea-jacket and a white waistcoat.*]

FIRS: [*Goes up to the coffee-pot, anxiously.*] The mistress will be served here. [*Puts on white gloves.*] Is the coffee ready? [*Sternly to* DUNYASHA.] Girl! Where's the cream?

DUNYASHA: Ah, mercy on us! [*Goes out quickly.*]

FIRS: [*Fussing round the coffee-pot.*] Ech! you good-for-nothing! [*Muttering to himself.*] Come back from Paris. And the old master used to go to Paris too . . . horses all the way. [*Laughs.*]

VARYA: What is it, Firs?

FIRS: What is your pleasure? [*Gleefully.*] My lady has come home! I have lived to see her again! Now I can die. [*Weeps with joy.*]

[*Enter* LYUBOV ANDREYEVNA, GAEV *and* SEMYONOV-PISHTCHIK; *the latter is in a short-waisted full coat of fine cloth, and full trousers.* GAEV, *as he comes in, makes a gesture with his arms and his whole body, as though he were playing billiards.*]

LYUBOV: How does it go? Let me remember. Cannon off the red!

GAEV: That's it—in off the white! Why, once, sister, we used to sleep together in this very room, and now I'm fifty-one, strange as it seems.

LOPAHIN: Yes, time flies.

GAEV: What do you say?

LOPAHIN: Time, I say, flies.

GAEV: What a smell of patchouli!

ANYA: I'm going to bed. Good-night, mamma. [*Kisses her mother.*]

LYUBOV: My precious darling. [*Kisses her hands.*] Are you glad to be home? I can't believe it.

ANYA: Good-night, uncle.

GAEV: [*Kissing her face and hands.*] God bless you! How like you are to your mother! [*To his sister.*] At her age you were just the same, Lyuba.

[ANYA *shakes hands with* LOPAHIN *and* PISHTCHIK, *then goes out, shutting the door after her.*]

LYUBOV: She's quite worn out.

PISHTCHIK: Aye, it's a long journey, to be sure.

VARYA: [*To* LOPAHIN *and* PISHTCHIK.] Well, gentlemen? It's three o'clock and time to say good-bye.

LYUBOV: [*Laughs.*] You're just the same as ever, Varya. [*Draws her to her and kisses her.*] I'll just drink my coffee and then we will all go and rest. [FIRS *puts a cushion under her feet.*] Thanks, friend. I am so fond of coffee, I drink it day and night. Thanks, dear old man. [*Kisses* FIRS.]

VARYA: I'll just see whether all the things have been brought in. [*Goes out.*]

LYUBOV: Can it really be me sitting here? [*Laughs.*] I want to dance about and clap my hands. [*Covers her face with her hands.*] And I could drop asleep in a moment! God knows I love my country, I love it tenderly; I couldn't look out of the window in the train, I kept crying so. [*Through her tears.*] But I must drink my coffee, though. Thank you, Firs, thanks, dear old man. I'm so glad to find you still alive.

FIRS: The day before yesterday.

GAEV: He's rather deaf.

LOPAHIN: I have to set off for Harkov[5] directly, at five o'clock. . . . It is annoying! I wanted to have a look at you, and a little talk. . . . You are just as splendid as ever.

PISHTCHIK: [*Breathing heavily.*] Handsomer, indeed. . . . Dressed in Parisian style . . . completely bowled me over.

LOPAHIN: Your brother, Leonid Andreyevitch here, is always saying that I'm a low-born knave, that I'm a money-grubber, but I don't care one straw for that. Let him talk. Only I do want you to believe in me as you used to. I do want your wonderful tender eyes to look at me as they used to in the old days. Merciful God! My father was a serf of your father and of your grandfather, but you—you—did so much for me once, that I've forgotten all that; I love you as though you were my kin . . . more than my kin.

LYUBOV: I can't sit still, I simply can't. . . . [*Jumps up and walks about in violent agitation.*] This happiness is too much for me. . . . You may laugh at me, I know I'm silly. . . . My own bookcase. [*Kisses the bookcase.*] My little table.

GAEV: Nurse died while you were away.

LYUBOV: [*Sits down and drinks coffee.*] Yes, the Kingdom of Heaven be hers! You wrote me of her death.

GAEV: And Anastasy is dead. Squinting Petruchka has left me and is in service now with the police captain in the town. [*Takes a box of caramels out of his pocket and sucks one.*]

PISHTCHIK: My daughter, Dashenka, wishes to be remembered to you.

LOPAHIN: I want to tell you something very pleasant and cheering. [*Glancing at his watch.*] I'm going directly . . . there's no time to say much . . . well, I can say it in a couple of words. I needn't tell you your cherry orchard is to be sold to pay your debts; the 22nd of August is the date fixed for the sale; but don't you worry, dearest lady, you may sleep in peace, there is a way of saving it. . . . This is what I propose. I beg your attention! Your estate is not twenty miles from the town, the railway runs close by it, and if the cherry orchard and the land

---

5. Kharkov, the second largest city in the Ukraine, which was part of the Russian Empire at the time of the play.

along the river bank were cut up into building plots and then let on lease for summer villas, you would make an income of at least 25,000 roubles a year out of it.[6]

GAEV: That's all rot, if you'll excuse me.

LYUBOV: I don't quite understand you, Yermolay Alexeyevitch.

LOPAHIN: You will get a rent of at least 25 roubles a year for a three-acre plot from summer visitors, and if you say the word now, I'll bet you what you like there won't be one square foot of ground vacant by the autumn, all the plots will be taken up. I congratulate you; in fact, you are saved. It's a perfect situation with that deep river. Only, of course, it must be cleared—all the old buildings, for example, must be removed, this house too, which is really good for nothing and the old cherry orchard must be cut down.

LYUBOV: Cut down? My dear fellow, forgive me, but you don't know what you are talking about. If there is one thing interesting—remarkable indeed—in the whole province, it's just our cherry orchard.

LOPAHIN: The only thing remarkable about the orchard is that it's a very large one. There's a crop of cherries every alternate year, and then there's nothing to be done with them, no one buys them.

GAEV: This orchard is mentioned in the *Encyclopædia*.[7]

LOPAHIN: [*Glancing at his watch.*] If we don't decide on something and don't take some steps, on the 22nd of August the cherry orchard and the whole estate too will be sold by auction. Make up your minds! There is no other way of saving it, I'll take my oath on that. No, no!

FIRS: In old days, forty or fifty years ago, they used to dry the cherries, soak them, pickle them, make jam too, and they used—

GAEV: Be quiet, Firs.

FIRS: And they used to send the preserved cherries to Moscow and to Harkov by the wagon-load. That brought the money in! And the preserved cherries in those days were soft and juicy, sweet and fragrant. . . . They knew the way to do them then. . . .

LYUBOV: And where is the recipe now?

FIRS: It's forgotten. Nobody remembers it.

PISHTCHIK: [*To* LYUBOV ANDREYEVNA.] What's it like in Paris? Did you eat frogs there?

LYUBOV: Oh, I ate crocodiles.

PISHTCHIK: Fancy that now!

LOPAHIN: There used to be only the gentlefolks and the peasants in the country, but now there are these summer visitors. All the towns, even the small ones, are surrounded nowadays by these summer villas. And one may say for sure, that in another twenty years there'll be many more of these people and that they'll be everywhere. At present the summer visitor only drinks tea in his verandah, but maybe he'll take to working his bit of land too, and then your cherry orchard would become happy, rich, and prosperous. . . .

GAEV: [*Indignant.*] What rot!

6. Nearly $500,000 per year in today's U.S. currency; a rental fee of 25 roubles is the equivalent of about $500.

7. Perhaps the *Great Russian Encyclopedic Dictionary,* an authoritative 86-volume reference work edited by Brockhaus and Efron.

[*Enter* VARYA *and* YASHA.]

VARYA: There are two telegrams for you, mamma. [*Takes out keys and opens an old-fashioned bookcase with a loud crack.*] Here they are.

LYUBOV: From Paris. [*Tears the telegrams, without reading them.*] I have done with Paris.

GAEV: Do you know, Lyuba, how old that bookcase is? Last week I pulled out the bottom drawer and there I found the date branded on it. The bookcase was made just a hundred years ago. What do you say to that? We might have celebrated its jubilee. Though it's an inanimate object, still it is a *book* case.

PISHTCHIK: [*Amazed.*] A hundred years! Fancy that now.

GAEV: Yes. . . . It is a thing. . . . [*Feeling the bookcase.*] Dear, honored, bookcase! Hail to thee who for more than a hundred years hast served the pure ideals of good and justice; thy silent call to fruitful labor has never flagged in those hundred years, maintaining [*In tears.*] in the generations of man, courage and faith in a brighter future and fostering in us ideals of good and social consciousness. [*A pause.*]

LOPAHIN: Yes. . . .

LYUBOV: You are just the same as ever, Leonid.

GAEV: [*A little embarrassed.*] Cannon off the right into the pocket!

LOPAHIN: [*Looking at his watch.*] Well, it's time I was off.

YASHA: [*Handing* LYUBOV ANDREYEVNA *medicine.*] Perhaps you will take your pills now.

PISHTCHIK: You shouldn't take medicines, my dear madam . . . they do no harm and no good. Give them here . . . honored lady. [*Takes the pill-box, pours the pills into the hollow of his hand, blows on them, puts them in his mouth and drinks off some kvass.*] There!

LYUBOV: [*In alarm.*] Why, you must be out of your mind!

PISHTCHIK: I have taken all the pills.

LOPAHIN: What a glutton! [*All laugh.*]

FIRS: His honor stayed with us in Easter week, ate a gallon and a half of cucumbers. . . . [*Mutters.*]

LYUBOV: What is he saying?

VARYA: He has taken to muttering like that for the last three years. We are used to it.

YASHA: His declining years!

[CHARLOTTA IVANOVNA, *a very thin, lanky figure in a white dress with a lorgnette in her belt, walks across the stage.*]

LOPAHIN: I beg your pardon, Charlotta Ivanovna, I have not had time to greet you. [*Tries to kiss her hand.*]

CHARLOTTA: [*Pulling away her hand.*] If I let you kiss my hand, you'll be wanting to kiss my elbow, and then my shoulder.

LOPAHIN: I've no luck to-day! [*All laugh.*] Charlotta Ivanovna, show us some tricks!

LYUBOV: Charlotta, do show us some tricks!

CHARLOTTA: I don't want to. I'm sleepy. [*Goes out.*]

LOPAHIN: In three weeks' time we shall meet again. [*Kisses* LYUBOV ANDREYEVNA's *hand.*] Good-bye till then—I must go. [*To* GAEV.] Good-bye. [*Kisses* PISHTCHIK.]

Good-bye. [*Gives his hand to* VARYA, *then to* FIRS *and* YASHA.] I don't want to go. [*To* LYUBOV ANDREYEVNA.] If you think over my plan for the villas and make up your mind, then let me know; I will lend you 50,000 roubles.[8] Think of it seriously.

VARYA: [*Angrily.*] Well, do go, for goodness sake.

LOPAHIN: I'm going, I'm going. [*Goes out.*]

GAEV: Low-born knave! I beg pardon, though . . . Varya is going to marry him, he's Varya's fiancé.

VARYA: Don't talk nonsense, uncle.

LYUBOV: Well, Varya, I shall be delighted. He's a good man.

PISHTCHIK: He is, one must acknowledge, a most worthy man. And my Dashenka . . . says too that . . . she says . . . various things. [*Snores, but at once wakes up.*] But all the same, honored lady, could you oblige me . . . with a loan of 240 roubles . . . to pay the interest on my mortgage to-morrow?

VARYA: [*Dismayed.*] No, no.

LYUBOV: I really haven't any money.

PISHTCHIK: It will turn up. [*Laughs.*] I never lose hope. I thought everything was over, I was a ruined man, and lo and behold—the railway passed through my land and . . . they paid me for it. And something else will turn up again, if not to-day, then to-morrow . . . Dashenka'll win two hundred thousand . . . she's got a lottery ticket.

LYUBOV: Well, we've finished our coffee, we can go to bed.

FIRS: [*Brushes* GAEV, *reprovingly.*] You have got on the wrong trousers again! What am I to do with you?

VARYA: [*Softly.*] Anya's asleep. [*Softly opens the window.*] Now the sun's risen, it's not a bit cold. Look, mamma, what exquisite trees! My goodness! And the air! The starlings are singing!

GAEV: [*Opens another window.*] The orchard is all white. You've not forgotten it, Lyuba? That long avenue that runs straight, straight as an arrow, how it shines on a moonlight night. You remember? You've not forgotten?

LYUBOV: [*Looking out of the window into the garden.*] Oh, my childhood, my innocence! It was in this nursery I used to sleep, from here I looked out into the orchard, happiness waked with me every morning and in those days the orchard was just the same, nothing has changed. [*Laughs with delight.*] All, all white! Oh, my orchard! After the dark gloomy autumn, and the cold winter; you are young again, and full of happiness, the heavenly angels have never left you. . . . If I could cast off the burden that weighs on my heart, if I could forget the past!

GAEV: H'm! and the orchard will be sold to pay our debts; it seems strange. . . .

LYUBOV: See, our mother walking . . . all in white, down the avenue! [*Laughs with delight.*] It is she!

GAEV: Where?

VARYA: Oh, don't, mamma!

LYUBOV: There is no one. It was my fancy. On the right there, by the path to the arbor, there is a white tree bending like a woman. . . .

[*Enter* TROFIMOV *wearing a shabby student's uniform and spectacles.*]

---

8. The equivalent of nearly $1 million in today's U.S. currency. *A loan of 240 roubles*: a loan of nearly $5,000 in today's U.S. currency.

LYUBOV: What a ravishing orchard! White masses of blossom, blue sky. . . .

TROFIMOV: Lyubov Andreyevna! [*She looks round at him.*] I will just pay my respects to you and then leave you at once. [*Kisses her hand warmly.*] I was told to wait until morning, but I hadn't the patience to wait any longer. . . .

[LYUBOV ANDREYEVNA *looks at him in perplexity.*]

VARYA: [*Through her tears.*] This is Petya Trofimov.

TROFIMOV: Petya Trofimov, who was your Grisha's tutor. . . . Can I have changed so much?

[LYUBOV ANDREYEVNA *embraces him and weeps quietly.*]

GAEV: [*In confusion.*] There, there, Lyuba.

VARYA: [*Crying.*] I told you, Petya, to wait till to-morrow.

LYUBOV: My Grisha . . . my boy . . . Grisha . . . my son!

VARYA: We can't help it, mamma, it is God's will.

TROFIMOV: [*Softly through his tears.*] There . . . there.

LYUBOV: [*Weeping quietly.*] My boy was lost . . . drowned. Why? Oh, why, dear Petya? [*More quietly.*] Anya is asleep in there, and I'm talking loudly . . . making this noise. . . . But, Petya? Why have you grown so ugly? Why do you look so old?

TROFIMOV: A peasant-woman in the train called me a mangy-looking gentleman.

LYUBOV: You were quite a boy then, a pretty little student, and now your hair's thin—and spectacles. Are you really a student still? [*Goes towards the door.*]

TROFIMOV: I seem likely to be a perpetual student.

LYUBOV: [*Kisses her brother, then* VARYA.] Well, go to bed. . . . You are older too, Leonid.

PISHTCHIK: [*Follows her.*] I suppose it's time we were asleep. . . . Ugh! my gout. I'm staying the night! Lyubov Andreyevna, my dear soul, if you could . . . to-morrow morning . . . 240 roubles.

GAEV: That's always his story.

PISHTCHIK: 240 roubles . . . to pay the interest on my mortgage.

LYUBOV: My dear man, I have no money.

PISHTCHIK: I'll pay it back, my dear . . . a trifling sum.

LYUBOV: Oh, well, Leonid will give it you. . . . You give him the money, Leonid.

GAEV: Me give it him! Let him wait till he gets it!

LYUBOV: It can't be helped, give it him. He needs it. He'll pay it back.

[LYUBOV ANDREYEVNA, TROFIMOV, PISHTCHIK *and* FIRS *go out.* GAEV, VARYA *and* YASHA *remain.*]

GAEV: Sister hasn't got out of the habit of flinging away her money. [*To* YASHA.] Get away, my good fellow, you smell of the hen-house.

YASHA: [*With a grin.*] And you, Leonid Andreyevitch, are just the same as ever.

GAEV: What's that? [*To* VARYA.] What did he say?

VARYA: [*To* YASHA.] Your mother has come from the village; she has been sitting in the servants' room since yesterday, waiting to see you.

YASHA: Oh, bother her!

VARYA: For shame!

YASHA: What's the hurry? She might just as well have come to-morrow. [*Goes out.*]

VARYA: Mamma's just the same as ever, she hasn't changed a bit. If she had her own way, she'd give away everything.

GAEV: Yes. [*A pause.*] If a great many remedies are suggested for some disease, it means that the disease is incurable. I keep thinking and racking my brains; I have many schemes, a great many, and that really means none. If we could only come in for a legacy from somebody, or marry our Anya to a very rich man, or we might go to Yaroslavl[9] and try our luck with our old aunt, the Countess. She's very, very rich, you know.

VARYA: [*Weeps.*] If God would help us.

GAEV: Don't blubber. Aunt's very rich, but she doesn't like us. First, sister married a lawyer instead of a nobleman....

[ANYA *appears in the doorway.*]

GAEV: And then her conduct, one can't call it virtuous. She is good, and kind, and nice, and I love her, but, however one allows for extenuating circumstances, there's no denying that she's an immoral woman. One feels it in her slightest gesture.

VARYA: [*In a whisper.*] Anya's in the doorway.

GAEV: What do you say? [*A pause.*] It's queer, there seems to be something wrong with my right eye. I don't see as well as I did. And on Thursday when I was in the district Court ...

[*Enter* ANYA.]

VARYA: Why aren't you asleep, Anya?

ANYA: I can't get to sleep.

GAEV: My pet. [*Kisses* ANYA'S *face and hands.*] My child. [*Weeps.*] You are not my niece, you are my angel, you are everything to me. Believe me, believe....

ANYA: I believe you, uncle. Everyone loves you and respects you ... but, uncle dear, you must be silent ... simply be silent. What were you saying just now about my mother, about your own sister? What made you say that?

GAEV: Yes, yes.... [*Puts his hand over his face.*] Really, that was awful! My God, save me! And to-day I made a speech to the bookcase ... so stupid! And only when I had finished, I saw how stupid it was.

VARYA: It's true, uncle, you ought to keep quiet. Don't talk, that's all.

ANYA: If you could keep from talking, it would make things easier for you, too.

GAEV: I won't speak. [*Kisses* ANYA's *and* VARYA's *hands.*] I'll be silent. Only this is about business. On Thursday I was in the district Court; well, there was a large party of us there and we began talking of one thing and another, and this and that, and do you know, I believe that it will be possible to raise a loan on an I.O.U. to pay the arrears on the mortgage.

VARYA: If the Lord would help us!

GAEV: I'm going on Tuesday; I'll talk of it again. [*To* VARYA.] Don't blubber. [*To* ANYA.] Your mamma will talk to Lopahin; of course, he won't refuse her. And as soon as you're rested you shall go to Yaroslavl to the Countess, your great-aunt. So we shall all set to work in three directions at once, and the business is done. We shall pay off arrears, I'm convinced of it. [*Puts a caramel in his mouth.*] I swear on my honor, I swear by anything you like, the estate shan't be sold. [*Excitedly.*] By my own happiness, I swear it! Here's my hand on it, call me the basest, vilest of men, if I let it come to an auction! Upon my soul I swear it!

9. Major industrial city located on the Volga River, 170 miles northeast of Moscow.

ANYA: [*Her equanimity has returned, she is quite happy.*] How good you are, uncle, and how clever! [*Embraces her uncle.*] I'm at peace now! Quite at peace! I'm happy!

[*Enter* FIRS.]

FIRS: [*Reproachfully.*] Leonid Andreyevitch, have you no fear of God? When are you going to bed?

GAEV: Directly, directly. You can go, Firs. I'll . . . yes, I will undress myself. Come, children, bye-bye. We'll go into details to-morrow, but now go to bed. [*Kisses* ANYA *and* VARYA.] I'm a man of the eighties.[1] They run down that period, but still I can say I have had to suffer not a little for my convictions in my life, it's not for nothing that the peasant loves me. One must know the peasant! One must know how. . . .

ANYA: At it again, uncle!

VARYA: Uncle dear, you'd better be quiet!

FIRS: [*Angrily.*] Leonid Andreyevitch!

GAEV: I'm coming. I'm coming. Go to bed. Potted the shot—there's a shot for you![2] A beauty! [*Goes out,* FIRS *hobbling after him.*]

ANYA: My mind's at rest now. I don't want to go to Yaroslavl, I don't like my great-aunt, but still my mind's at rest. Thanks to uncle. [*Sits down.*]

VARYA: We must go to bed. I'm going. Something unpleasant happened while you were away. In the old servants' quarters there are only the old servants, as you know—Efimyushka, Polya, and Yevstigney—and Karp too. They began letting stray people in to spend the night—I said nothing. But all at once I heard they had been spreading a report that I gave them nothing but pease pudding to eat. Out of stinginess, you know. . . . And it was all Yevstigney's doing. . . . Very well, I said to myself. . . . If that's how it is, I thought, wait a bit. I sent for Yevstigney. . . . [*Yawns.*] He comes. . . . "How's this, Yevstigney," I said, "you could be such a fool as to? . . ." [*Looking at* ANYA.] Anitchka! [*A pause.*] She's asleep. [*Puts her arm around* ANYA.] Come to bed . . . come along! [*Leads her.*] My darling has fallen asleep! Come. . . . [*They go.*]

[*Far away beyond the orchard a shepherd plays on a pipe.* TROFIMOV *crosses the stage and, seeing* VARYA *and* ANYA, *stands still.*]

VARYA: 'Sh! asleep, asleep. Come, my own.

ANYA: [*Softly, half asleep.*] I'm so tired. Still those bells. Uncle . . . dear . . . mamma and uncle. . . .

VARYA: Come, my own, come along.

[*They go into* ANYA's *room.*]

TROFIMOV: [*Tenderly.*] My sunshine! My spring.

CURTAIN.

---

1. That is, the 1880s, a period of reactionary conservatism in Russia under Tsar Alexander III.
2. Gaev is preoccupied with billiards; the terminology is fanciful because Chekhov admittedly knew nothing about the game.

ACT II

The open country. An old shrine,[3] long abandoned and fallen out of the perpendicular; near it a well, large stones that have apparently once been tombstones, and an old garden seat. The road to GAEV's house is seen. On one side rise dark poplars; and there the cherry orchard begins. In the distance a row of telegraph poles and far, far away on the horizon there is faintly outlined a great town, only visible in very fine clear weather. It is near sunset. CHARLOTTA, YASHA and DUNYASHA are sitting on the seat. EPIHODOV is standing near, playing something mournful on a guitar. All sit plunged in thought. CHARLOTTA wears an old forage cap; she has taken a gun from her shoulder and is tightening the buckle on the strap.

CHARLOTTA: [*Musingly.*] I haven't a real passport[4] of my own, and I don't know how old I am, and I always feel that I'm a young thing. When I was a little girl, my father and mother used to travel about to fairs and give performances— very good ones. And I used to dance *salto-mortale*[5] and all sorts of things. And when papa and mamma died, a German lady took me and had me educated. And so I grew up and become a governess. But where I came from, and who I am, I don't know. . . . Who my parents were, very likely they weren't married. . . . I don't know. [*Takes a cucumber out of her pocket and eats.*] I know nothing at all. [*A pause.*] One wants to talk and has no one to talk to. . . . I have nobody.

EPIHODOV: [*Plays on the guitar and sings.*] "What care I for the noisy world! What care I for friends or foes!"[6] How agreeable it is to play on the mandoline!

DUNYASHA: That's a guitar, not a mandoline. [*Looks in a hand-mirror and powders herself.*]

EPIHODOV: To a man mad with love, it's a mandoline. [*Sings.*] "Were her heart but aglow with love's mutual flame." [YASHA *joins in.*]

CHARLOTTA: How shockingly these people sing! Foo! Like jackals!

DUNYASHA: [*To* YASHA.] What happiness, though, to visit foreign lands.

YASHA: Ah, yes! I rather agree with you there. [*Yawns, then lights a cigar.*]

EPIHODOV: That's comprehensible. In foreign lands everything has long since reached full complexion.

YASHA: That's so, of course.

EPIHODOV: I'm a cultivated man, I read remarkable books of all sorts, but I can never make out the tendency I am myself precisely inclined for, whether to live or to shoot myself, speaking precisely, but nevertheless I always carry a revolver. Here it is. . . . [*Shows revolver.*]

CHARLOTTA: I've had enough, and now I'm going. [*Puts on the gun.*] Epihodov, you're a very clever fellow, and a very terrible one too, all the women must be wild about you. Br-r-r! [*Goes.*] These clever fellows are all so stupid; there's not a creature for me to speak to. . . . Always alone, alone, nobody belonging to me . . . and who I am, and why I'm on earth, I don't know. [*Walks away slowly.*]

EPIHODOV: Speaking precisely, not touching upon other subjects, I'm bound to admit about myself, that destiny behaves mercilessly to me, as a storm to a little boat. If, let us suppose, I am mistaken, then why did I wake up this

---

3. That is, a chapel.   4. A document required for travel within Russia.
5. Literally, "deadly leap"; Italian for "somersault."   6. Words of a popular ballad.

morning, to quote an example, and look round, and there on my chest was a spider of fearful magnitude . . . like this. [*Shows with both hands.*] And then I take up a jug of kvass, to quench my thirst, and in it there is something in the highest degree unseemly of the nature of a cockroach. [*A pause.*] Have you read Buckle?[7] [*A pause.*] I am desirous of troubling you, Dunyasha, with a couple of words.

DUNYASHA: Well, speak.

EPIHODOV: I should be desirous to speak with you alone. [*Sighs.*]

DUNYASHA: [*Embarrassed.*] Well—only bring me my mantle first. It's by the cupboard. It's rather damp here.

EPIHODOV: Certainly. I will fetch it. Now I know what I must do with my revolver. [*Takes guitar and goes off playing on it.*]

YASHA: Two and twenty misfortunes! Between ourselves, he's a fool. [*Yawns.*]

DUNYASHA: God grant he doesn't shoot himself! [*A pause.*] I am so nervous, I'm always in a flutter. I was a little girl when I was taken into our lady's house, and now I have quite grown out of peasant ways, and my hands are white, as white as a lady's. I'm such a delicate, sensitive creature, I'm afraid of everything. I'm so frightened. And if you deceive me, Yasha, I don't know what will become of my nerves.

YASHA: [*Kisses her.*] You're a peach! Of course a girl must never forget herself; what I dislike more than anything is a girl being flighty in her behavior.

DUNYASHA: I'm passionately in love with you, Yasha; you are a man of culture—you can give your opinion about anything. [*A pause.*]

YASHA: [*Yawns.*] Yes, that's so. My opinion is this: if a girl loves anyone, that means that she has no principles. [*A pause.*] It's pleasant smoking a cigar in the open air. [*Listens.*] Someone's coming this way . . . it's the gentlefolk. [DUNYASHA *embraces him impulsively.*] Go home, as though you had been to the river to bathe; go by that path, or else they'll meet you and suppose I have made an appointment with you here. That I can't endure.

DUNYASHA: [*Coughing softly.*] The cigar has made my head ache. . . . [*Goes off.*]

[YASHA *remains sitting near the shrine. Enter* LYUBOV ANDREYEVNA, GAEV *and* LOPAHIN.]

LOPAHIN: You must make up your mind once for all—there's no time to lose. It's quite a simple question, you know. Will you consent to letting the land for building or not? One word in answer: Yes or no? Only one word!

LYUBOV: Who is smoking such horrible cigars here? [*Sits down.*]

GAEV: Now the railway line has been brought near, it's made things very convenient. [*Sits down.*] Here we have been over and lunched in town. Cannon off the white! I should like to go home and have a game.

LYUBOV: You have plenty of time.

LOPAHIN: Only one word! [*Beseechingly.*] Give me an answer!

GAEV: [*Yawning.*] What do you say?

LYUBOV: [*Looks in her purse.*] I had quite a lot of money here yesterday, and there's scarcely any left to-day. My poor Varya feeds us all on milk soup for the sake

---

7. Henry Thomas Buckle (1821–61), a learned but eccentric historian known as a freethinker whose *History of Civilization in England* (1857) was the talk of Moscow a generation earlier. His work, initially respected for its empirical methods, quickly fell into disrepute in sophisticated intellectual circles.

2106 READING MORE DRAMA

of economy; the old folks in the kitchen get nothing but pease pudding, while I waste my money in a senseless way. [*Drops purse, scattering gold pieces.*] There, they have all fallen out! [*Annoyed.*]

YASHA: Allow me, I'll soon pick them up. [*Collects the coins.*]

LYUBOV: Pray do, Yasha. And what did I go off to the town to lunch for? Your restaurant's a wretched place with its music and the tablecloth smelling of soap. . . . Why drink so much, Leonid? And eat so much? And talk so much? To-day you talked a great deal again in the restaurant, and all so inappropriately. About the era of the seventies,[8] about the decadents. And to whom? Talking to waiters about decadents!

LOPAHIN: Yes.

GAEV: [*Waving his hand.*] I'm incorrigible; that's evident. [*Irritably to* YASHA.] Why is it you keep fidgeting about in front of us!

YASHA: [*Laughs.*] I can't help laughing when I hear your voice.

GAEV: [*To his sister.*] Either I or he. . . .

LYUBOV: Get along! Go away, Yasha.

YASHA: [*Gives* LYUBOV ANDREYEVNA *her purse.*] Directly. [*Hardly able to suppress his laughter.*] This minute. . . . [*Goes off.*]

LOPAHIN: Deriganov, the millionaire, means to buy your estate. They say he is coming to the sale himself.

LYUBOV: Where did you hear that?

LOPAHIN: That's what they say in town.

GAEV: Our aunt in Yaroslavl has promised to send help; but when, and how much she will send, we don't know.

LOPAHIN: How much will she send? A hundred thousand? Two hundred?

LYUBOV: Oh, well! . . . Ten or fifteen thousand, and we must be thankful to get that.

LOPAHIN: Forgive me, but such reckless people as you are—such queer, unbusiness-like people—I never met in my life. One tells you in plain Russian your estate is going to be sold, and you seem not to understand it.

LYUBOV: What are we to do? Tell us what to do.

LOPAHIN: I do tell you every day. Every day I say the same thing. You absolutely must let the cherry orchard and the land on building leases; and do it at once, as quick as may be—the auction's close upon us! Do understand! Once make up your mind to build villas, and you can raise as much money as you like, and then you are saved.

LYUBOV: Villas and summer visitors—forgive me saying so—it's so vulgar.

GAEV: There I perfectly agree with you.

LOPAHIN: I shall sob, or scream, or fall into a fit. I can't stand it! You drive me mad! [*To* GAEV.] You're an old woman!

GAEV: What do you say?

LOPAHIN: An old woman! [*Gets up to go.*]

LYUBOV: [*In dismay.*] No, don't go! Do stay, my dear friend! Perhaps we shall think of something.

LOPAHIN: What is there to think of?

8. The 1870s, a relatively liberal period in Russia that ended abruptly with the assassination of Alexander II in 1881. *The decadents*: probably a reference to the group of flamboyant French poets of the 1880s who called themselves *les décadents*.

LYUBOV: Don't go, I entreat you! With you here it's more cheerful, anyway. [*A pause.*] I keep expecting something, as though the house were going to fall about our ears.

GAEV: [*In profound dejection.*] Potted the white! It fails—a kiss.

LYUBOV: We have been great sinners. . . .

LOPAHIN: You have no sins to repent of.

GAEV: [*Puts a caramel in his mouth.*] They say I've eaten up my property in caramels. [*Laughs.*]

LYUBOV: Oh, my sins! I've always thrown my money away recklessly like a lunatic. I married a man who made nothing but debts. My husband died of champagne— he drank dreadfully. To my misery I loved another man, and immediately—it was my first punishment—the blow fell upon me, here, in the river . . . my boy was drowned and I went abroad—went away for ever, never to return, not to see that river again . . . I shut my eyes, and fled, distracted, and *he* after me . . . pitilessly, brutally. I bought a villa at Mentone,[9] for *he* fell ill there, and for three years I had no rest day or night. His illness wore me out, my soul was dried up. And last year, when my villa was sold to pay my debts, I went to Paris and there he robbed me of everything and abandoned me for another woman; and I tried to poison myself. . . . So stupid, so shameful! . . . And suddenly I felt a yearning for Russia, for my country, for my little girl. . . . [*Dries her tears.*] Lord, Lord, be merciful! Forgive my sins! Do not chastise me more! [*Takes a telegram out of her pocket.*] I got this to-day from Paris. He implores forgiveness, entreats me to return. [*Tears up the telegram.*] I fancy there is music somewhere. [*Listens.*]

GAEV: That's our famous Jewish orchestra. You remember, four violins, a flute, and a double bass.

LYUBOV: That still in existence? We ought to send for them one evening, and give a dance.

LOPAHIN: [*Listens.*] I can't hear. . . . [*Hums softly.*] "For money the Germans will turn a Russian into a Frenchman." [*Laughs.*] I did see such a piece at the theater yesterday! It was funny!

LYUBOV: And most likely there was nothing funny in it. You shouldn't look at plays, you should look at yourselves a little oftener. How gray your lives are! How much nonsense you talk.

LOPAHIN: That's true. One may say honestly, we live a fool's life. [*Pause.*] My father was a peasant, an idiot; he knew nothing and taught me nothing, only beat me when he was drunk, and always with his stick. In reality I am just such another blockhead and idiot. I've learnt nothing properly. I write a wretched hand. I write so that I feel ashamed before folks, like a pig.

LYUBOV: You ought to get married, my dear fellow.

LOPAHIN: Yes . . . that's true.

LYUBOV: You should marry our Varya, she's a good girl.

LOPAHIN: Yes.

LYUBOV: She's a good-natured girl, she's busy all day long, and what's more, she loves you. And you have liked her for ever so long.

LOPAHIN: Well? I'm not against it. . . . She's a good girl. [*Pause.*]

GAEV: I've been offered a place in the bank: 6,000 roubles a year.[1] Did you know?

9. Resort town on the French Mediterranean coast.
1. Nearly $120,000 per year in today's U.S. currency.

LYUBOV: You would never do for that! You must stay as you are.

[*Enter* FIRS *with overcoat.*]

FIRS: Put it on, sir, it's damp.

GAEV: [*Putting it on.*] You bother me, old fellow.

FIRS: You can't go on like this. You went away in the morning without leaving word. [*Looks him over.*]

LYUBOV: You look older, Firs!

FIRS: What is your pleasure?

LOPAHIN: You look older, she said.

FIRS: I've had a long life. They were arranging my wedding before your papa was born.... [*Laughs.*] I was the head footman before the emancipation came.[2] I wouldn't consent to be set free then; I stayed on with the old master.... [*A pause.*] I remember what rejoicings they made and didn't know themselves what they were rejoicing over.

LOPAHIN: Those were fine old times. There was flogging anyway.

FIRS: [*Not hearing.*] To be sure! The peasants knew their place, and the masters knew theirs; but now they're all at sixes and sevens,[3] there's no making it out.

GAEV: Hold your tongue, Firs. I must go to town to-morrow. I have been promised an introduction to a general, who might let us have a loan.

LOPAHIN: You won't bring that off. And you won't pay your arrears, you may rest assured of that.

LYUBOV: That's all his nonsense. There is no such general.

[*Enter* TROFIMOV, ANYA *and* VARYA.]

GAEV: Here come our girls.

ANYA: There's mamma on the seat.

LYUBOV: [*Tenderly.*] Come here, come along. My darlings! [*Embraces* ANYA *and* VARYA.] If you only knew how I love you both. Sit beside me, there, like that. [*All sit down.*]

LOPAHIN: Our perpetual student is always with the young ladies.

TROFIMOV: That's not your business.

LOPAHIN: He'll soon be fifty, and he's still a student.

TROFIMOV: Drop your idiotic jokes.

LOPAHIN: Why are you so cross, you queer fish?

TROFIMOV: Oh, don't persist!

LOPAHIN: [*Laughs.*] Allow me to ask you what's your idea of me?

TROFIMOV: I'll tell you my idea of you, Yermolay Alexeyevitch: you are a rich man, you'll soon be a millionaire. Well, just as in the economy of nature a wild beast is of use, who devours everything that comes in his way, so you too have your use.

[*All laugh.*]

VARYA: Better tell us something about the planets, Petya.

LYUBOV: No, let us go on with the conversation we had yesterday.

2. In 1861 Tsar Alexander II issued the Edict of Emancipation, which freed the serfs (agricultural workers held in feudal bondage, who represented about one-third of Russia's population).
3. That is, they are confused, unsettled.

TROFIMOV: What was it about?

GAEV: About pride.

TROFIMOV: We had a long conversation yesterday, but we came to no conclusion. In pride, in your sense of it, there is something mystical. Perhaps you are right from your point of view; but if one looks at it simply, without subtlety, what sort of pride can there be, what sense is there in it, if man in his physiological formation is very imperfect, if in the immense majority of cases he is coarse, dull-witted, profoundly unhappy? One must give up glorification of self. One should work, and nothing else.

GAEV: One must die in any case.

TROFIMOV: Who knows? And what does it mean—dying? Perhaps man has a hundred senses, and only the five we know are lost at death, while the other ninety-five remain alive.

LYUBOV: How clever you are, Petya!

LOPAHIN: [*Ironically.*] Fearfully clever!

TROFIMOV: Humanity progresses, perfecting its powers. Everything that is beyond its ken now will one day become familiar and comprehensible; only we must work, we must with all our powers aid the seeker after truth. Here among us in Russia the workers are few in number as yet. The vast majority of the intellectual people I know, seek nothing, do nothing, are not fit as yet for work of any kind. They call themselves intellectual, but they treat their servants as inferiors, behave to the peasants as though they were animals, learn little, read nothing seriously, do practically nothing, only talk about science and know very little about art. They are all serious people, they all have severe faces, they all talk of weighty matters and air their theories, and yet the vast majority of us—ninety-nine per cent—live like savages, at the least thing fly to blows and abuse, eat piggishly, sleep in filth and stuffiness, bugs everywhere, stench and damp and moral impurity. And it's clear all our fine talk is only to divert our attention and other people's. Show me where to find the *crèches* there's so much talk about, and the reading-rooms? [4] They only exist in novels: in real life there are none of them. There is nothing but filth and vulgarity and Asiatic apathy. I fear and dislike very serious faces. I'm afraid of serious conversations. We should do better to be silent.

LOPAHIN: You know, I get up at five o'clock in the morning, and I work from morning to night; and I've money, my own and other people's, always passing through my hands, and I see what people are made of all round me. One has only to begin to do anything to see how few honest, decent people there are. Sometimes when I lie awake at night, I think: "Oh! Lord, thou hast given us immense forests, boundless plains, the widest horizons, and living here we ourselves ought really to be giants."

LYUBOV: You ask for giants! They are no good except in story-books; in real life they frighten us.

[EPIHODOV *advances in the background, playing on the guitar.*]

LYUBOV: [*Dreamily.*] There goes Epihodov.

ANYA: [*Dreamily.*] There goes Epihodov.

---

4. Nursery schools and centers offering free reading material—that is, the social services and civilizing influences that have been imagined but never created.

GAEV: The sun has set, my friends.

TROFIMOV: Yes.

GAEV: [*Not loudly, but, as it were, declaiming.*] O nature, divine nature, thou art bright with eternal luster, beautiful and indifferent! Thou, whom we call mother, thou dost unite within thee life and death! Thou dost give life and dost destroy!

VARYA: [*In a tone of supplication.*] Uncle!

ANYA: Uncle, you are at it again!

TROFIMOV: You'd much better be cannoning off the red!

GAEV: I'll hold my tongue, I will.

[*All sit plunged in thought. Perfect stillness. The only thing audible is the muttering of* FIRS. *Suddenly there is a sound in the distance, as it were from the sky—the sound of a breaking harp-string, mournfully dying away.*]

LYUBOV: What is that?

LOPAHIN: I don't know. Somewhere far away a bucket fallen and broken in the pits. But somewhere very far away.

GAEV: It might be a bird of some sort—such as a heron.

TROFIMOV: Or an owl.

LYUBOV: [*Shudders.*] I don't know why, but it's horrid. [*A pause.*]

FIRS: It was the same before the calamity—the owl hooted and the samovar hissed all the time.

GAEV: Before what calamity?

FIRS: Before the emancipation. [*A pause.*]

LYUBOV: Come, my friends, let us be going; evening is falling. [*To* ANYA.] There are tears in your eyes. What is it, darling? [*Embraces her.*]

ANYA: Nothing, mamma; it's nothing.

TROFIMOV: There is somebody coming.

[*The* WAYFARER *appears in a shabby white forage cap and an overcoat; he is slightly drunk.*]

WAYFARER: Allow me to inquire, can I get to the station this way?

GAEV: Yes. Go along that road.

WAYFARER: I thank you most feelingly. [*Coughing.*] The weather is superb. [*Declaims.*] My brother, my suffering brother![5] . . . Come out to the Volga! Whose groan do you hear? . . . [*To* VARYA.] Mademoiselle, vouchsafe a hungry Russian thirty kopecks.[6]

[VARYA *utters a shriek of alarm.*]

LOPAHIN: [*Angrily.*] There's a right and a wrong way of doing everything!

LYUBOV: [*Hurriedly.*] Here, take this. [*Looks in her purse.*] I've no silver. No matter—here's gold for you.

WAYFARER: I thank you most feelingly! [*Goes off.*]

[*Laughter.*]

---

5. A line from a poem by Semen Nadson (1862–87), persecuted in Russia because of his Jewish origins.

6. *Come out to the Volga!*: from a poem by Nikolai Nekrasov (1821–78), a poet known as a champion of the lower classes. (The Volga is Europe's longest river and Russia's principal waterway.) Thirty kopecks is the equivalent of about $6 in today's U.S. currency.

VARYA: [*Frightened.*] I'm going home—I'm going. . . . Oh, mamma, the servants have nothing to eat, and you gave him gold!

LYUBOV: There's no doing anything with me. I'm so silly! When we get home, I'll give you all I possess. Yermolay Alexeyevitch, you will lend me some more! . . .

LOPAHIN: I will.

LYUBOV: Come, friends, it's time to be going. And Varya, we have made a match of it for you. I congratulate you.

VARYA: [*Through her tears.*] Mamma, that's not a joking matter.

LOPAHIN: "Ophelia, get thee to a nunnery!"[7]

GAEV: My hands are trembling; it's a long while since I had a game of billiards.

LOPAHIN: "Ophelia! Nymph, in thy orisons be all my sins remember'd."

LYUBOV: Come, it will soon be supper-time.

VARYA: How he frightened me! My heart's simply throbbing.

LOPAHIN: Let me remind you, ladies and gentlemen: on the 22nd of August the cherry orchard will be sold. Think about that! Think about it!

[*All go off, except* TROFIMOV *and* ANYA.]

ANYA: [*Laughing.*] I'm grateful to the wayfarer! He frightened Varya and we are left alone.

TROFIMOV: Varya's afraid we shall fall in love with each other, and for days together she won't leave us. With her narrow brain she can't grasp that we are above love. To eliminate the petty and transitory which hinder us from being free and happy—that is the aim and meaning of our life. Forward! We go forward irresistibly towards the bright star that shines yonder in the distance. Forward! Do not lag behind, friends.

ANYA: [*Claps her hands.*] How well you speak! [*A pause.*] It is divine here today.

TROFIMOV: Yes, it's glorious weather.

ANYA: Somehow, Petya, you've made me so that I don't love the cherry orchard as I used to. I used to love it so dearly. I used to think that there was no spot on earth like our garden.

TROFIMOV: All Russia is our garden. The earth is great and beautiful—there are many beautiful places in it. [*A pause.*] Think only, Anya, your grandfather, and great-grandfather, and all your ancestors were slave-owners—the owners of living souls—and from every cherry in the orchard, from every leaf, from every trunk there are human creatures looking at you. Cannot you hear their voices? Oh, it is awful! Your orchard is a fearful thing, and when in the evening or at night one walks about the orchard, the old bark on the trees glimmers dimly in the dusk, and the old cherry trees seem to be dreaming of centuries gone by and tortured by fearful visions.[8] Yes! We are at least two hundred years behind, we have really gained nothing yet, we have no definite attitude to the past, we do nothing but theorize or complain of depression or drink vodka. It is clear that to begin to live in the present we must first expiate our past, we must

---

7. For this quotation and the one below, see *Hamlet* 3.1.

8. *Oh, it is awful! . . . fearful visions.* Chekhov wrote this passage to replace one that official censors found objectionable: "To own human beings has affected every one of you—those who lived before and those who live now. Your mother, your uncle, and you don't notice that you are living off the labors of others—in fact, the very people you won't even let in the front door." This passage was restored following the 1917 revolution.

break with it; and we can expiate it only by suffering, by extraordinary unceasing labor. Understand that, Anya.

ANYA: The house we live in has long ceased to be our own, and I shall leave it, I give you my word.

TROFIMOV: If you have the house keys, fling them into the well and go away. Be free as the wind.

ANYA: [In ecstasy.] How beautifully you said that!

TROFIMOV: Believe me, Anya, believe me! I am not thirty yet, I am young, I am still a student, but I have gone through so much already! As soon as winter comes I am hungry, sick, careworn, poor as a beggar, and what ups and downs of fortune have I not known! And my soul was always, every minute, day and night, full of inexplicable forebodings. I have a foreboding of happiness, Anya. I see glimpses of it already.

ANYA: [Pensively.] The moon is rising.

[EPIHODOV is heard playing still the same mournful song on the guitar. The moon rises. Somewhere near the poplars VARYA is looking for ANYA and calling "Anya! where are you?"]

TROFIMOV: Yes, the moon is rising. [A pause.] Here is happiness—here it comes! It is coming nearer and nearer; already I can hear its footsteps. And if we never see it—if we may never know it—what does it matter? Others will see it after us.

VARYA'S VOICE: Anya! Where are you?

TROFIMOV: That Varya again! [Angrily.] It's revolting!

ANYA: Well, let's go down to the river. It's lovely there.

TROFIMOV: Yes, let's go. [They go.]

VARYA'S VOICE: Anya! Anya!

    CURTAIN

ACT III

A drawing-room divided by an arch from a larger drawing-room.[9] A chandelier burning. The Jewish orchestra, the same that was mentioned in Act II, is heard playing in the ante-room. It is evening. In the larger drawing-room they are dancing the grand chain. The voice of SEMYONOV-PISHTCHIK: "Promenade à une paire!"[1] Then enter the drawing-room in couples first PISHTCHIK and CHARLOTTA IVANOVNA, then TROFIMOV and LYUBOV ANDREYEVNA, thirdly ANYA with the POST-OFFICE CLERK, fourthly VARYA with the STATION MASTER, and other guests. VARYA is quietly weeping and wiping away her tears as she dances. In the last couple is DUNYASHA. They move across the drawing-room. PISHTCHIK shouts: "Grand rond, balancez!" and "Les Cavaliers à genou et remerciez vos dames."

    FIRS in a swallow-tail coat brings in seltzer water on a tray. PISHTCHIK and TROFIMOV enter the drawing-room.

9. That is, ballroom.
1. In this French phrase and those quoted below, Semyonov-Pishtchik is calling out the moves in the "grand chain" dance: promenade (walk) to a couple; grand circle, step to the side (that is, balancez as in ballet); and gentlemen (knights), kneel and thank your ladies. (French was widely spoken as a second language among the upper classes in pre-Soviet Russia.)

PISHTCHIK: I am a full-blooded man; I have already had two strokes. Dancing's hard work for me, but as they say, if you're in the pack, you must bark with the rest. I'm as strong, I may say, as a horse. My parent, who would have his joke—may the Kingdom of Heaven be his!—used to say about our origin that the ancient stock of the Semyonov-Pishtchiks was derived from the very horse that Caligula made a member of the senate.[2] [*Sits down.*] But I've no money, that's where the mischief is. A hungry dog believes in nothing but meat. [*Snores, but at once wakes up.*] That's like me . . . I can think of nothing but money.

TROFIMOV: There really is something horsy about your appearance.

PISHTCHIK: Well . . . a horse is a fine beast . . . a horse can be sold.

> [*There is the sound of billiards being played in an adjoining room.* VARYA *appears in the arch leading to the larger drawing-room.*]

TROFIMOV: [*Teasing.*] Madame Lopahin! Madame Lopahin!

VARYA: [*Angrily.*] Mangy-looking gentleman!

TROFIMOV: Yes, I am a mangy-looking gentleman, and I'm proud of it!

VARYA: [*Pondering bitterly.*] Here we have hired musicians and nothing to pay them! [*Goes out.*]

TROFIMOV: [*To* PISHTCHIK.] If the energy you have wasted during your lifetime in trying to find the money to pay your interest had gone to something else, you might in the end have turned the world upside down.

PISHTCHIK: Nietzsche, the philosopher, a very great and celebrated man[3] . . . of enormous intellect . . . says in his works, that one can make forged banknotes.

TROFIMOV: Why, have you read Nietzsche?

PISHTCHIK: What next . . . Dashenka told me. . . . And now I am in such a position, I might just as well forge banknotes. The day after to-morrow I must pay 310 roubles[4]—130 I have procured. [*Feels in his pockets, in alarm.*] The money's gone! I have lost my money! [*Through his tears.*] Where's the money? [*Gleefully.*] Why, here it is behind the lining. . . . It has made me hot all over.

> [*Enter* LYUBOV ANDREYEVNA *and* CHARLOTTA IVANOVNA.]

LYUBOV: [*Hums the Lezginka.*] Why is Leonid so long? What can he be doing in town? [*To* DUNYASHA.] Offer the musicians some tea.

TROFIMOV: The sale hasn't taken place, most likely.

LYUBOV: It's the wrong time to have the orchestra, and the wrong time to give a dance. Well, never mind. [*Sits down and hums softly.*]

CHARLOTTA: [*Gives* PISHTCHIK *a pack of cards.*] Here's a pack of cards. Think of any card you like.

PISHTCHIK: I've thought of one.

CHARLOTTA: Shuffle the pack now. That's right. Give it here, my dear Mr. Pishtchik. *Eins, zwei, drei*[5]—now look, it's in your breast pocket.

---

2. Caligula (12–41 C.E.), Roman emperor known for tyrannical cruelty, is said to have gone insane and to have appointed his horse as a consul.

3. Friedrich Wilhelm Nietzsche (1844–1900), German philosopher who rejected what he termed the "slave morality" of Western bourgeois civilization.

4. The equivalent of over $6,000 in today's U.S. currency.

5. One, two, three (German). Charlotta speaks the language she associates with her childhood of performing at carnivals.

PISHTCHIK: [*Taking a card out of his breast pocket.*] The eight of spades! Perfectly right! [*Wonderingly.*] Fancy that now!

CHARLOTTA: [*Holding pack of cards in her hands, to* TROFIMOV.] Tell me quickly which is the top card.

TROFIMOV: Well, the queen of spades.

CHARLOTTA: It is! [*To* PISHTCHIK.] Well, which card is uppermost?

PISHTCHIK: The ace of hearts.

CHARLOTTA: It is! [*Claps her hands, pack of cards disappears.*] Ah! what lovely weather it is to-day!

[*A mysterious feminine voice which seems coming out of the floor answers her.* "Oh, yes, it's magnificent weather, madam."]

CHARLOTTA: You are my perfect ideal.

VOICE: And I greatly admire you too, madam.

STATION MASTER: [*Applauding.*] The lady ventriloquist—bravo!

PISHTCHIK: [*Wonderingly.*] Fancy that now! Most enchanting Charlotta Ivanovna. I'm simply in love with you.

CHARLOTTA: In love? [*Shrugging shoulders.*] What do you know of love, *guter Mensch, aber schlechter Musikant.*[6]

TROFIMOV: [*Pats* PISHTCHIK *on the shoulder.*] You dear old horse. . . .

CHARLOTTA: Attention, please! Another trick! [*Takes a traveling rug from a chair.*] Here's a very good rug; I want to sell it. [*Shaking it out.*] Doesn't anyone want to buy it?

PISHTCHIK: [*Wonderingly.*] Fancy that!

CHARLOTTA: *Ein, zwei, drei!* [*Quickly picks up rug she has dropped; behind the rug stands* ANYA; *she makes a curtsey, runs to her mother, embraces her and runs back into the larger drawing-room amidst general enthusiasm.*]

LYUBOV: [*Applauds.*] Bravo! Bravo!

CHARLOTTA: Now again! *Ein, zwei, drei!* [*Lifts up the rug; behind the rug stands* VARYA, *bowing.*]

PISHTCHIK: [*Wonderingly.*] Fancy that now!

CHARLOTTA: That's the end. [*Throws the rug at* PISHTCHIK, *makes a curtsey, runs into the larger drawing-room.*]

PISHTCHIK: [*Hurries after her.*] Mischievous creature! Fancy! [*Goes out.*]

LYUBOV: And still Leonid doesn't come. I can't understand what he's doing in the town so long! Why, everything must be over by now. The estate is sold, or the sale has not taken place. Why keep us so long in suspense?

VARYA: [*Trying to console her.*] Uncle's bought it. I feel sure of that.

TROFIMOV: [*Ironically.*] Oh, yes!

VARYA: Great-aunt sent him an authorization to buy it in her name, and transfer the debt. She's doing it for Anya's sake, and I'm sure God will be merciful. Uncle will buy it.

LYUBOV: My aunt in Yaroslavl sent fifteen thousand to buy the estate in her name, she doesn't trust us—but that's not enough even to pay the arrears. [*Hides her face in her hands.*] My fate is being sealed to-day, my fate. . . .

TROFIMOV: [*Teasing* VARYA.] Madame Lopahin.

6. A good man, but a poor musician (German).

VARYA: [*Angrily.*] Perpetual student! Twice already you've been sent down[7] from the University.

LYUBOV: Why are you angry, Varya? He's teasing you about Lopahin. Well, what of that? Marry Lopahin if you like, he's a good man, and interesting; if you don't want to, don't! Nobody compels you, darling.

VARYA: I must tell you plainly, mamma, I look at the matter seriously; he's a good man, I like him.

LYUBOV: Well, marry him. I can't see what you're waiting for.

VARYA: Mamma. I can't make him an offer myself. For the last two years, everyone's been talking to me about him. Everyone talks; but he says nothing or else makes a joke. I see what it means. He's growing rich, he's absorbed in business, he has no thoughts for me. If I had money, were it ever so little, if I had only a hundred roubles, I'd throw everything up and go far away. I would go into a nunnery.

TROFIMOV: What bliss!

VARYA: [*To* TROFIMOV.] A student ought to have sense! [*In a soft tone with tears.*] How ugly you've grown, Petya! How old you look! [*To* LYUBOV ANDREYEVNA, *no longer crying.*] But I can't do without work, mamma; I must have something to do every minute.

[*Enter* YASHA.]

YASHA: [*Hardly restraining his laughter.*] Epihodov has broken a billiard cue! [*Goes out.*]

VARYA: What is Epihodov doing here? Who gave him leave to play billiards? I can't make these people out. [*Goes out.*]

LYUBOV: Don't tease her, Petya. You see she has grief enough without that.

TROFIMOV: She is so very officious, meddling in what's not her business. All the summer she's given Anya and me no peace. She's afraid of a love affair between us. What's it to do with her? Besides, I have given no grounds for it. Such triviality is not in my line. We are above love!

LYUBOV: And I suppose I am beneath love. [*Very uneasily.*] Why is it Leonid's not here? If only I could know whether the estate is sold or not! It seems such an incredible calamity that I really don't know what to think. I am distracted . . . I shall scream in a minute . . . I shall do something stupid. Save me, Petya, tell me something, talk to me!

TROFIMOV: What does it matter whether the estate is sold to-day or not? That's all done with long ago. There's no turning back, the path is overgrown. Don't worry yourself, dear Lyubov Andreyevna. You mustn't deceive yourself; for once in your life you must face the truth!

LYUBOV: What truth? You see where the truth lies, but I seem to have lost my sight, I see nothing. You settle every great problem so boldly, but tell me, my dear boy, isn't it because you're young—because you haven't yet understood one of your problems through suffering? You look forward boldly, and isn't it that you don't see and don't expect anything dreadful because life is still hidden from your young eyes? You're bolder, more honest, deeper than we are, but think, be just a little magnanimous, have pity on me. I was born here, you know, my father and mother lived here, my grandfather lived here, I love this

---

7. Expelled.

house. I can't conceive of life without the cherry orchard, and if it really must be sold, then sell me with the orchard. [*Embraces* TROFIMOV, *kisses him on the forehead.*] My boy was drowned here. [*Weeps.*] Pity me, my dear kind fellow.

TROFIMOV: You know I feel for you with all my heart.

LYUBOV: But that should have been said differently, so differently. [*Takes out her handkerchief, telegram falls on the floor.*] My heart is so heavy to-day. It's so noisy here, my soul is quivering at every sound, I'm shuddering all over, but I can't go away; I'm afraid to be quiet and alone. Don't be hard on me, Petya . . . I love you as though you were one of ourselves. I would gladly let you marry Anya—I swear I would—only, my dear boy, you must take your degree, you do nothing—you're simply tossed by fate from place to place. That's so strange. It is, isn't it? And you must do something with your beard to make it grow somehow. [*Laughs.*] You look so funny!

TROFIMOV: [*Picks up the telegram.*] I've no wish to be a beauty.

LYUBOV: That's a telegram from Paris. I get one every day. One yesterday and one to-day. That savage creature is ill again, he's in trouble again. He begs forgiveness, beseeches me to go, and really I ought to go to Paris to see him. You look shocked, Petya. What am I to do, my dear boy, what am I to do? He is ill, he is alone and unhappy, and who'll look after him, who'll keep him from doing the wrong thing, who'll give him his medicine at the right time? And why hide it or be silent? I love him, that's clear. I love him! I love him! He's a millstone about my neck, I'm going to the bottom with him, but I love that stone and can't live without it. [*Presses* TROFIMOV'*s hand.*] Don't think ill of me, Petya, don't tell me anything, don't tell me. . . .

TROFIMOV: [*Through his tears*] For God's sake forgive my frankness: why, he robbed you!

LYUBOV: No! No! No! You mustn't speak like that. [*Covers her ears.*]

TROFIMOV: He is a wretch! You're the only person that doesn't know it! He's a worthless creature! A despicable wretch!

LYUBOV: [*Getting angry, but speaking with restraint.*] You're twenty-six or twenty-seven years old, but you're still a schoolboy.

TROFIMOV: Possibly.

LYUBOV: You should be a man at your age! You should understand what love means! And you ought to be in love yourself. You ought to fall in love! [*Angrily.*] Yes, yes, and it's not purity in you, you're simply a prude, a comic fool, a freak.

TROFIMOV: [*In horror.*] The things she's saying!

LYUBOV: I am above love! You're not above love, but simply as our Firs here says, "You are a good-for-nothing." At your age not to have a mistress!

TROFIMOV: [*In horror.*] This is awful! The things she is saying! [*Goes rapidly into the larger drawing-room clutching his head.*] This is awful! I can't stand it! I'm going. [*Goes off, but at once returns.*] All is over between us! [*Goes off into the ante-room.*]

LYUBOV: [*Shouts after him.*] Petya! Wait a minute! You funny creature! I was joking! Petya! [*There is a sound of somebody running quickly downstairs and suddenly falling with a crash.* ANYA *and* VARYA *scream, but there is a sound of laughter at once.*]

LYUBOV: What has happened?

[ANYA *runs in.*]

ANYA: [*Laughing.*] Petya's fallen downstairs! [*Runs out.*]

LYUBOV: What a queer fellow that Petya is!

[*The* STATION MASTER *stands in the middle of the larger room and reads* The Magdalene, *by Alexey Tolstoy.[8] They listen to him, but before he has recited many lines strains of a waltz are heard from the ante-room and the reading is broken off. All dance.* TROFIMOV, ANYA, VARYA *and* LYUBOV ANDREYEVNA *come in from the ante-room.*]

LYUBOV: Come, Petya—come, pure heart! I beg your pardon. Let's have a dance! [*Dances with* PETYA.]

[ANYA *and* VARYA *dance.* FIRS *comes in, puts his stick down near the side door.* YASHA *also comes into the drawing-room and looks on at the dancing.*]

YASHA: What is it, old man?

FIRS: I don't feel well. In old days we used to have generals, barons, and admirals dancing at our balls, and now we send for the post-office clerk and the station master and even they're not overanxious to come. I am getting feeble. The old master, the grandfather, used to give sealing-wax for all complaints. I have been taking sealing-wax for twenty years or more. Perhaps that's what's kept me alive.

YASHA: You bore me, old man! [*Yawns.*] It's time you were done with.

FIRS: *Ach,* you're a good-for-nothing! [*Mutters.*]

[TROFIMOV *and* LYUBOV ANDREYEVNA *dance in larger room and then on to the stage.*]

LYUBOV: *Merci.* I'll sit down a little. [*Sits down.*] I'm tired.

[*Enter* ANYA.]

ANYA: [*Excitedly.*] There's a man in the kitchen has been saying that the cherry orchard's been sold to-day.

LYUBOV: Sold to whom?

ANYA: He didn't say to whom. He's gone away.

[*She dances with* TROFIMOV, *and they go off into the larger room.*]

YASHA: There was an old man gossiping there, a stranger.

FIRS: Leonid Andreyevitch isn't here yet, he hasn't come back. He has his light overcoat on, *demi-saison,*[9] he'll catch cold for sure. *Ach!* Foolish young things!

LYUBOV: I feel as though I should die. Go, Yasha, find out to whom it has been sold.

YASHA: But he went away long ago, the old chap. [*Laughs.*]

LYUBOV: [*With slight vexation.*] What are you laughing at? What are you pleased at?

YASHA: Epihodov is so funny. He's a silly fellow, two and twenty misfortunes.

LYUBOV: Firs, if the estate is sold, where will you go?

FIRS: Where you bid me, there I'll go.

LYUBOV: Why do you look like that? Are you ill? You ought to be in bed.

---

8. A poem sometimes translated as "The Sinful Woman," by Alexsey Tolstoy (1817–75), a distant cousin of novelist Leo Tolstoy.   9. Literally, "half-season" (French).

FIRS: Yes. [*Ironically.*] Me go to bed and who's to wait here? Who's to see to things without me? I'm the only one in all the house.

YASHA: [*To* LYUBOV ANDREYEVNA.] Lyubov Andreyevna, permit me to make a request of you; if you go back to Paris again, be so kind as to take me with you. It's positively impossible for me to stay here. [*Looking about him; in an undertone.*] There's no need to say it, you see for yourself—an uncivilized country, the people have no morals, and then the dullness! The food in the kitchen's abominable, and then Firs runs after one muttering all sorts of unsuitable words. Take me with you, please do!

[*Enter* PISHTCHIK.]

PISHTCHIK: Allow me to ask you for a waltz, my dear lady. [LYUBOV ANDREYEVNA *goes with him.*] Enchanting lady, I really must borrow of you just 180 roubles,[1] [*Dances.*] only 180 roubles. [*They pass into the larger room.*]

[*In the larger drawing-room, a figure in a gray top hat and in check trousers is gesticulating and jumping about. Shouts of* "Bravo, Charlotta Ivanovna."]

DUNYASHA: [*She has stopped to powder herself.*] My young lady tells me to dance. There are plenty of gentlemen, and too few ladies, but dancing makes me giddy and makes my heart beat. Firs, the post-office clerk said something to me just now that quite took my breath away.

[*Music becomes more subdued.*]

FIRS: What did he say to you?

DUNYASHA: He said I was like a flower.

YASHA: [*Yawns.*] What ignorance! [*Goes out.*]

DUNYASHA: Like a flower. I am a girl of such delicate feelings, I am awfully fond of soft speeches.

FIRS: Your head's being turned.

[*Enter* EPIHODOV.]

EPIHODOV: You have no desire to see me, Dunyasha. I might be an insect. [*Sighs.*] Ah! life!

DUNYASHA: What is it you want?

EPIHODOV: Undoubtedly you may be right. [*Sighs.*] But, of course, if one looks at it from that point of view, if I may so express myself, you have, excuse my plain speaking, reduced me to a complete state of mind. I know my destiny. Every day some misfortune befalls me and I have long ago grown accustomed to it, so that I look upon my fate with a smile. You gave me your word, and though I—

DUNYASHA: Let us have a talk later, I entreat you, but now leave me in peace, for I am lost in reverie. [*Plays with her fan.*]

EPIHODOV: I have a misfortune every day, and if I may venture to express myself, I merely smile at it, I even laugh.

[VARYA *enters from the larger drawing-room.*]

VARYA: You still have not gone, Epihodov. What a disrespectful creature you are, really! [*To* DUNYASHA.] Go along, Dunyasha! [*To* EPIHODOV.] First you play bil-

---

1. Roughly $4,000 in today's U.S. currency.

liards and break the cue, then you go wandering about the drawing-room like a visitor!

EPIHODOV: You really cannot, if I may so express myself, call me to account like this.

VARYA: I'm not calling you to account, I'm speaking to you. You do nothing but wander from place to place and don't do your work. We keep you as a counting-house clerk, but what use you are I can't say.

EPIHODOV: [*Offended.*] Whether I work or whether I walk, whether I eat or whether I play billiards, is a matter to be judged by persons of understanding and my elders.

VARYA: You dare to tell me that! [*Firing up.*] You dare! You mean to say I've no understanding. Begone from here! This minute!

EPIHODOV: [*Intimidated.*] I beg you to express yourself with delicacy.

VARYA: [*Beside herself with anger.*] This moment! get out! away! [*He goes towards the door, she following him.*] Two and twenty misfortunes! Take yourself off! Don't let me set eyes on you! [EPIHODOV *has gone out, behind the door his voice,* "I shall lodge a complaint against you."] What! You're coming back? [*Snatches up the stick* FIRS *has put down near the door.*] Come! Come! Come! I'll show you! What! you're coming? Then take that! [*She swings the stick, at the very moment that* LOPAHIN *comes in.*]

LOPAHIN: Very much obliged to you!

VARYA: [*Angrily and ironically.*] I beg your pardon!

LOPAHIN: Not at all! I humbly thank you for your kind reception!

VARYA: No need of thanks for it. [*Moves away, then looks round and asks softly.*] I haven't hurt you?

LOPAHIN: Oh, no! Not at all! There's an immense bump coming up, though!

VOICES FROM LARGER ROOM: Lopahin has come! Yermolay Alexeyevitch!

PISHTCHIK: What do I see and hear? [*Kisses* LOPAHIN.] There's a whiff of cognac about you, my dear soul, and we're making merry here too!

[*Enter* LYUBOV ANDREYEVNA.]

LYUBOV: Is it you, Yermolay Alexeyevitch? Why have you been so long? Where's Leonid?

LOPAHIN: Leonid Andreyevitch arrived with me. He is coming.

LYUBOV: [*In agitation.*] Well! Well! Was there a sale? Speak!

LOPAHIN: [*Embarrassed, afraid of betraying his joy.*] The sale was over at four o'clock. We missed our train—had to wait till half-past nine. [*Sighing heavily.*] Ugh! I feel a little giddy.

[*Enter* GAEV. *In his right hand he has purchases, with his left hand he is wiping away his tears.*]

LYUBOV: Well, Leonid? What news? [*Impatiently, with tears.*] Make haste, for God's sake!

GAEV: [*Makes her no answer, simply waves his hand. To* FIRS, *weeping.*] Here, take them; there's anchovies, Kertch herrings. I have eaten nothing all day. What I have been through! [*Door into the billiard room is open. There is heard a knocking of balls and the voice of* YASHA *saying* "Eighty-seven." GAEV's *expression changes, he leaves off weeping.*] I am fearfully tired. Firs, come and help me change my things. [*Goes to his own room across the larger drawing-room.*]

PISHTCHIK: How about the sale? Tell us, do!

LYUBOV: Is the cherry orchard sold?

LOPAHIN: It is sold.

LYUBOV: Who has bought it?

LOPAHIN: I have bought it. [*A pause.* LYUBOV *is crushed; she would fall down if she were not standing near a chair and table.*]

> [VARYA *takes keys from her waistband, flings them on the floor in middle of drawing-room and goes out.*]

LOPAHIN: I have bought it! Wait a bit, ladies and gentlemen, pray. My head's a bit muddled, I can't speak. [*Laughs.*] We came to the auction. Deriganov was there already. Leonid Andreyevitch only had 15,000 and Deriganov bid 30,000, besides the arrears, straight off. I saw how the land lay. I bid against him. I bid 40,000, he bid 45,000, I said 55, and so he went on, adding 5 thousands and I adding 10. Well . . . So it ended. I bid 90, and it was knocked down to me.[2] Now the cherry orchard's mine! Mine! [*Chuckles.*] My God, the cherry orchard's mine! Tell me that I'm drunk, that I'm out of my mind, that it's all a dream. [*Stamps with his feet.*] Don't laugh at me! If my father and my grandfather could rise from their graves and see all that has happened! How their Yermolay, ignorant, beaten Yermolay, who used to run about barefoot in winter, how that very Yermolay has bought the finest estate in the world! I have bought the estate where my father and grandfather were slaves, where they weren't even admitted into the kitchen. I am asleep, I am dreaming! It is all fancy, it is the work of your imagination plunged in the darkness of ignorance. [*Picks up keys, smiling fondly.*] She threw away the keys; she means to show she's not the housewife now. [*Jingles the keys.*] Well, no matter. [*The orchestra is heard tuning up.*] Hey, musicians! Play! I want to hear you. Come, all of you, and look how Yermolay Lopahin will take the ax to the cherry orchard, how the trees will fall to the ground! We will build houses on it and our grandsons and great-grandsons will see a new life springing up there. Music! Play up!

> [*Music begins to play.* LYUBOV ANDREYEVNA *has sunk into a chair and is weeping bitterly.*]

LOPAHIN: [*Reproachfully.*] Why, why didn't you listen to me? My poor friend! Dear lady, there's no turning back now. [*With tears.*] Oh, if all this could be over, oh, if our miserable disjointed life could somehow soon be changed!

PISHTCHIK: [*Takes him by the arm, in an undertone.*] She's weeping, let us go and leave her alone. Come. [*Takes him by the arm and leads him into the larger drawing-room.*]

LOPAHIN: What's that? Musicians, play up! All must be as I wish it. [*With irony.*] Here comes the new master, the owner of the cherry orchard! [*Accidentally tips over a little table, almost upsetting the candelabra.*] I can pay for everything! [*Goes out with* PISHTCHIK. *No one remains on the stage or in the larger drawing-room except* LYUBOV, *who sits huddled up, weeping bitterly. The music plays softly.* ANYA *and* TROFIMOV *come in quickly.* ANYA *goes up to her mother and falls on her knees before her.* TROFIMOV *stands at the entrance to the larger drawing-room.*]

---

2. Lopahin's winning bid for the estate was 90,000 roubles, the equivalent of nearly $2 million in today's U.S. currency—about twice what Lopahin had offered to lend Lyubov and her family to save the estate (act 1).

ANYA: Mamma! Mamma, you're crying, dear, kind, good mamma! My precious! I love you! I bless you! The cherry orchard is sold, it is gone, that's true, that's true! But don't weep, mamma! Life is still before you, you have still your good, pure heart! Let us go, let us go, darling, away from here! We will make a new garden, more splendid than this one; you will see it, you will understand. And joy, quiet, deep joy, will sink into your soul like the sun at evening! And you will smile, mamma! Come, darling, let us go!

CURTAIN

ACT IV

SCENE: *Same as in First Act. There are neither curtains on the windows nor pictures on the walls: only a little furniture remains piled up in a corner as if for sale. There is a sense of desolation; near the outer door and in the background of the scene are packed trunks, traveling bags, etc. On the left the door is open, and from here the voices of* VARYA *and* ANYA *are audible.* LOPAHIN *is standing waiting.* YASHA *is holding a tray with glasses full of champagne. In front of the stage* EPIHODOV *is tying up a box. In the background behind the scene a hum of talk from the peasants who have come to say good-bye. The voice of* GAEV: *"Thanks, brothers, thanks!"*

YASHA: The peasants have come to say good-bye. In my opinion, Yermolay Alexeyevitch, the peasants are good-natured, but they don't know much about things.

[*The hum of talk dies away. Enter across front of stage* LYUBOV ANDREYEVNA *and* GAEV. *She is not weeping, but is pale; her face is quivering—she cannot speak.*]

GAEV: You gave them your purse, Lyuba. That won't do—that won't do!

LYUBOV: I couldn't help it! I couldn't help it!

[*Both go out.*]

LOPAHIN: [*In the doorway, calls after them.*] You will take a glass at parting? Please do. I didn't think to bring any from the town, and at the station I could only get one bottle. Please take a glass. [*A pause.*] What? You don't care for any? [*Comes away from the door.*] If I'd known, I wouldn't have bought it. Well, and I'm not going to drink it. [YASHA *carefully sets the tray down on a chair.*] You have a glass, Yasha, anyway.

YASHA: Good luck to the travelers, and luck to those that stay behind! [*Drinks.*] This champagne isn't the real thing, I can assure you.

LOPAHIN: It cost eight roubles the bottle. [*A pause.*] It's devilish cold here.

YASHA: They haven't heated the stove today—it's all the same since we're going. [*Laughs.*]

LOPAHIN: What are you laughing for?

YASHA: For pleasure.

LOPAHIN: Though it's October, it's as still and sunny as though it were summer. It's just right for building! [*Looks at his watch; says in doorway.*] Take note, ladies and gentlemen, the train goes in forty-seven minutes; so you ought to start for the station in twenty minutes. You must hurry up!

[TROFIMOV *comes in from out of doors wearing a great-coat.*]

TROFIMOV: I think it must be time to start, the horses are ready. The devil only knows what's become of my goloshes; they're lost. [*In the doorway.*] Anya! My goloshes aren't here. I can't find them.

LOPAHIN: And I'm getting off to Harkov. I am going in the same train with you. I'm spending all the winter at Harkov. I've been wasting all my time gossiping with you and fretting with no work to do. I can't get on without work. I don't know what to do with my hands, they flap about so queerly, as if they didn't belong to me.

TROFIMOV: Well, we're just going away, and you will take up your profitable labors again.

LOPAHIN: Do take a glass.

TROFIMOV: No, thanks.

LOPAHIN: Then you're going to Moscow now?

TROFIMOV: Yes. I shall see them as far as the town, and to-morrow I shall go on to Moscow.

LOPAHIN: Yes, I daresay, the professors aren't giving any lectures, they're waiting for your arrival.

TROFIMOV: That's not your business.

LOPAHIN: How many years have you been at the University?

TROFIMOV: Do think of something newer than that—that's stale and flat. [*Hunts for goloshes.*] You know we shall most likely never see each other again, so let me give you one piece of advice at parting: don't wave your arms about—get out of the habit. And another thing, building villas, reckoning up that the summer visitors will in time become independent farmers—reckoning like that, that's not the thing to do either. After all, I am fond of you: you have fine delicate fingers like an artist, you've a fine delicate soul.

LOPAHIN: [*Embraces him.*] Good-bye, my dear fellow. Thanks for everything. Let me give you money for the journey, if you need it.

TROFIMOV: What for? I don't need it.

LOPAHIN: Why, you haven't got a half-penny.

TROFIMOV: Yes, I have, thank you. I got some money for a translation. Here it is in my pocket, [*Anxiously.*] but where can my goloshes be!

VARYA: [*From the next room.*] Take the nasty things! [*Flings a pair of goloshes on to the stage.*]

TROFIMOV: Why are you so cross, Varya? h'm! . . . but those aren't my goloshes.

LOPAHIN: I sowed three thousand acres with poppies in the spring, and now I have cleared forty thousand profit.[3] And when my poppies were in flower, wasn't it a picture! So here, as I say, I made forty thousand, and I'm offering you a loan because I can afford to. Why turn up your nose? I am a peasant—I speak bluntly.

TROFIMOV: Your father was a peasant, mine was a chemist[4]—and that proves absolutely nothing whatever. [LOPAHIN *takes out his pocket-book.*] Stop that—stop that. If you were to offer me two hundred thousand I wouldn't take it. I am an independent man, and everything that all of you, rich and poor alike, prize so highly and hold so dear, hasn't the slightest power over me—it's like so much fluff fluttering in the air. I can get on without you. I can pass by you. I am

---

3. That is, a profit equivalent to well over $800,000 in today's U.S. currency.   4. Pharmacist.

strong and proud. Humanity is advancing towards the highest truth, the highest happiness, which is possible on earth, and I am in the front ranks.

LOPAHIN: Will you get there?

TROFIMOV: I shall get there. [*A pause.*] I shall get there, or I shall show others the way to get there.

[*In the distance is heard the stroke of an ax on a tree.*]

LOPAHIN: Good-bye, my dear fellow; it's time to be off. We turn up our noses at one another, but life is passing all the while. When I am working hard without resting, then my mind is more at ease, and it seems to me as though I too know what I exist for; but how many people there are in Russia, my dear boy, who exist, one doesn't know what for. Well, it doesn't matter. That's not what keeps things spinning. They tell me Leonid Andreyevitch has taken a situation. He is going to be a clerk at the bank—6,000 roubles a year.[5] Only, of course, he won't stick to it—he's too lazy.

ANYA: [*In the doorway.*] Mamma begs you not to let them chop down the orchard until she's gone.

TROFIMOV: Yes, really, you might have the tact. [*Walks out across the front of the stage.*]

LOPAHIN: I'll see to it! I'll see to it! Stupid fellows! [*Goes out after him.*]

ANYA: Has Firs been taken to the hospital?

YASHA: I told them this morning. No doubt they have taken him.

ANYA: [*To* EPIHODOV, *who passes across the drawing-room.*] Semyon Pantaleyevitch, inquire, please, if Firs has been taken to the hospital.

YASHA: [*In a tone of offence.*] I told Yegor this morning—why ask a dozen times?

EPIHODOV: Firs is advanced in years. It's my conclusive opinion no treatment would do him good; it's time he was gathered to his fathers. And I can only envy him. [*Puts a trunk down on a cardboard hat-box and crushes it.*] There, now, of course—I knew it would be so.

YASHA: [*Jeeringly.*] Two and twenty misfortunes!

VARYA: [*Through the door.*] Has Firs been taken to the hospital?

ANYA: Yes.

VARYA: Why wasn't the note for the doctor taken too?

ANYA: Oh, then, we must send it after them. [*Goes out.*]

VARYA: [*From the adjoining room.*] Where's Yasha? Tell him his mother's come to say good-bye to him.

YASHA: [*Waves his hand.*] They put me out of all patience! [DUNYASHA *has all this time been busy about the luggage. Now, when* YASHA *is left alone, she goes up to him.*]

DUNYASHA: You might just give me one look, Yasha. You're going away. You're leaving me. [*Weeps and throws herself on his neck.*]

YASHA: What are you crying for? [*Drinks the champagne.*] In six days I shall be in Paris again. To-morrow we shall get into the express train and roll away in a flash. I can scarcely believe it! *Vive la France!* It doesn't suit me here—it's not the life for me; there's no doing anything. I have seen enough of the ignorance here. I have had enough of it. [*Drinks champagne.*] What are you crying for? Behave yourself properly, and then you won't cry.

5. A salary equivalent to over $120,000 in today's U.S. currency.

DUNYASHA: [*Powders her face, looking in a pocket-mirror.*] Do send me a letter from Paris. You know how I loved you, Yasha—how I loved you! I am a tender creature, Yasha.

YASHA: Here they are coming!

[*Busies himself about the trunks, humming softly. Enter* LYUBOV ANDREYEVNA, GAEV, ANYA *and* CHARLOTTA IVANOVNA.]

GAEV: We ought to be off. There's not much time now. [*Looking at* YASHA.] What a smell of herrings!

LYUBOV: In ten minutes we must get into the carriage. [*Casts a look about the room.*] Farewell, dear house, dear old home of our fathers! Winter will pass and spring will come, and then you will be no more; they will tear you down! How much those walls have seen! [*Kisses her daughter passionately.*] My treasure, how bright you look! Your eyes are sparkling like diamonds! Are you glad? Very glad?

ANYA: Very glad! A new life is beginning, mamma.

GAEV: Yes, really, everything is all right now. Before the cherry orchard was sold, we were all worried and wretched, but afterwards, when once the question was settled conclusively, irrevocably, we all felt calm and even cheerful. I am a bank clerk now—I am a financier—cannon off the red. And you, Lyuba, after all, you are looking better; there's no question of that.

LYUBOV: Yes. My nerves are better, that's true. [*Her hat and coat are handed to her.*] I'm sleeping well. Carry out my things, Yasha. It's time. [*To* ANYA.] My darling, we shall soon see each other again. I am going to Paris. I can live there on the money your Yaroslavl auntie sent us to buy the estate with—hurrah for auntie—but that money won't last long.

ANYA: You'll come back soon, mamma, won't you? I'll be working up for my examination in the high school, and when I have passed that, I shall set to work and be a help to you. We will read all sorts of things together, mamma, won't we? [*Kisses her mother's hands.*] We will read in the autumn evenings. We'll read lots of books, and a new wonderful world will open out before us. [*Dreamily.*] Mamma, come soon.

LYUBOV: I shall come, my precious treasure. [*Embraces her.*]

[*Enter* LOPAHIN. CHARLOTTA *softly hums a song.*]

GAEV: Charlotta's happy; she's singing!

CHARLOTTA: [*Picks up a bundle like a swaddled baby.*] Bye, bye, my baby. [*A baby is heard crying: "Ooah! ooah!"*] Hush, hush, my pretty boy! [*Ooah! ooah!*] Poor little thing! [*Throws the bundle back.*] You must please find me a situation. I can't go on like this.

LOPAHIN: We'll find you one, Charlotta Ivanovna. Don't you worry yourself.

GAEV: Everyone's leaving us. Varya's going away. We have become of no use all at once.

CHARLOTTA: There's nowhere for me to be in the town. I must go away. [*Hums.*] What care I . . .

[*Enter* PISHTCHIK.]

LOPAHIN: The freak of nature!

PISHTCHIK: [*Gasping.*] Oh! . . . let me get my breath. . . . I'm worn out . . . my most honored . . . Give me some water.

GAEV: Want some money, I suppose? Your humble servant! I'll go out of the way of temptation. [*Goes out.*]

PISHTCHIK: It's a long while since I have been to see you . . . dearest lady. [*To* LOPA- HIN.] You are here . . . glad to see you . . . a man of immense intellect . . . take . . . here. [*Gives* LOPAHIN.] 400 roubles.[6] That leaves me owing 840.

LOPAHIN: [*Shrugging his shoulders in amazement.*] It's like a dream. Where did you get it?

PISHTCHIK: Wait a bit . . . I'm hot . . . a most extraordinary occurrence! Some Englishmen came along and found in my land some sort of white clay. [*To* LYUBOV ANDREYEVNA.] And 400 for you . . . most lovely . . . wonderful. [*Gives money.*] The rest later. [*Sips water.*] A young man in the train was telling me just now that a great philosopher advises jumping off a house-top. "Jump!" says he; "the whole gist of the problem lies in that." [*Wonderingly.*] Fancy that, now! Water, please!

LOPAHIN: What Englishmen?

PISHTCHIK: I have made over to them the rights to dig the clay for twenty-four years . . . and now, excuse me . . . I can't stay . . . I must be trotting on. I'm going to Znoikovo . . . to Kardamanovo. . . . I'm in debt all round. [*Sips.*] . . . To your very good health! . . . I'll come in on Thursday.

LYUBOV: We are just off to the town, and to-morrow I start for abroad.

PISHTCHIK: What! [*In agitation.*] Why to the town? Oh, I see the furniture . . . the boxes. No matter . . . [*Through his tears.*] . . . no matter . . . men of enormous intellect . . . these Englishmen. . . . Never mind . . . be happy. God will succor you . . . no matter . . . everything in this world must have an end. [*Kisses* LYUBOV ANDREYEVNA'*s hand.*] If the rumor reaches you that my end has come, think of this . . . old horse, and say: "There once was such a man in the world . . . Semyonov-Pishtchik . . . the Kingdom of Heaven be his!" . . . most extraordi- nary weather . . . yes. [*Goes out in violent agitation, but at once returns and says in the doorway.*] Dashenka wishes to be remembered to you. [*Goes out.*]

LYUBOV: Now we can start. I leave with two cares in my heart. The first is leaving Firs ill. [*Looking at her watch.*] We have still five minutes.

ANYA: Mamma, Firs has been taken to the hospital. Yasha sent him off this morning.

LYUBOV: My other anxiety is Varya. She is used to getting up early and working; and now, without work, she's like a fish out of water. She is thin and pale, and she's crying, poor dear! [*A pause.*] You are well aware, Yermolay Alexeyevitch, I dreamed of marrying her to you, and everything seemed to show that you would get married. [*Whispers to* ANYA *and motions to* CHARLOTTA *and both go out.*] She loves you—she suits you. And I don't know—I don't know why it is you seem, as it were, to avoid each other. I can't understand it!

LOPAHIN: I don't understand it myself, I confess. It's queer somehow, altogether. If there's still time, I'm ready now at once. Let's settle it straight off, and go ahead; but without you, I feel I shan't make her an offer.

LYUBOV: That's excellent. Why, a single moment's all that's necessary. I'll call her at once.

LOPAHIN: And there's champagne all ready too. [*Looking into the glasses.*] Empty! Someone's emptied them already. [YASHA *coughs.*] I call that greedy.

---

6. Over $8,500 in today's U.S. currency.

LYUBOV: [*Eagerly.*] Capital! We will go out. Yasha, *allez!*[7] I'll call her in. [*At the door.*] Varya, leave all that; come here. Come along! [*Goes out with* YASHA.]
LOPAHIN: [*Looking at his watch.*] Yes.

[*A pause. Behind the door, smothered laughter and whispering, and, at last, enter* VARYA.]

VARYA: [*Looking a long while over the things.*] It is strange, I can't find it anywhere.
LOPAHIN: What are you looking for?
VARYA: I packed it myself, and I can't remember. [*A pause.*]
LOPAHIN: Where are you going now, Varvara Mihailova?
VARYA: I? To the Ragulins. I have arranged to go to them to look after the house—as a housekeeper.
LOPAHIN: That's in Yashnovo? It'll be seventy miles away. [*A pause.*] So this is the end of life in this house!
VARYA: [*Looking among the things.*] Where is it? Perhaps I put it in the trunk. Yes, life in this house is over—there will be no more of it.
LOPAHIN: And I'm just off to Harkov—by this next train. I've a lot of business there. I'm leaving Epihodov here, and I've taken him on.
VARYA: Really!
LOPAHIN: This time last year we had snow already, if you remember; but now it's so fine and sunny. Though it's cold, to be sure—three degrees of frost.
VARYA: I haven't looked. [*A pause.*] And besides, our thermometer's broken. [*A pause.*]

[*Voice at the door from the yard: "Yermolay Alexeyevitch!"*]

LOPAHIN: [*As though he had long been expecting this summons.*] This minute!

[LOPAHIN *goes out quickly.* VARYA *sitting on the floor and laying her head on a bag full of clothes, sobs quietly. The door opens.* LYUBOV ANDREYEVNA *comes in cautiously.*]

LYUBOV: Well? [*A pause.*] We must be going.
VARYA: [*Has wiped her eyes and is no longer crying.*] Yes, mamma, it's time to start. I shall have time to get to the Ragulins to-day, if only you're not late for the train.
LYUBOV: [*In the doorway.*] Anya, put your things on.

[*Enter* ANYA, *then* GAEV *and* CHARLOTTA IVANOVNA. GAEV *has on a warm coat with a hood. Servants and cabmen come in.* EPIHODOV *bustles about the luggage.*]

LYUBOV: Now we can start on our travels.
ANYA: [*Joyfully.*] On our travels!
GAEV: My friends—my dear, my precious friends! Leaving this house for ever, can I be silent? Can I refrain from giving utterance at leave-taking to those emotions which now flood all my being?
ANYA: [*Supplicatingly.*] Uncle!
VARYA: Uncle, you mustn't!
GAEV: [*Dejectedly.*] Cannon and into the pocket . . . I'll be quiet. . . .

[*Enter* TROFIMOV *and afterwards* LOPAHIN.]

7. Go! (French).

TROFIMOV: Well, ladies and gentlemen, we must start.

LOPAHIN: Epihodov, my coat!

LYUBOV: I'll stay just one minute. It seems as though I have never seen before what the walls, what the ceilings in this house were like, and now I look at them with greediness, with such tender love.

GAEV: I remember when I was six years old sitting in that window on Trinity Day watching my father going to church.

LYUBOV: Have all the things been taken?

LOPAHIN: I think all. [*Putting on overcoat, to* EPIHODOV.] You, Epihodov, mind you see everything is right.

EPIHODOV: [*In a husky voice.*] Don't you trouble, Yermolay Alexeyevitch.

LOPAHIN: Why, what's wrong with your voice?

EPIHODOV: I've just had a drink of water, and I choked over something.

YASHA: [*Contemptuously.*] The ignorance!

LYUBOV: We are going—and not a soul will be left here.

LOPAHIN: Not till the spring.

VARYA: [*Pulls a parasol out of a bundle, as though about to hit someone with it.* LOPAHIN *makes a gesture as though alarmed.*] What is it? I didn't mean anything.

TROFIMOV: Ladies and gentlemen, let us get into the carriage. It's time. The train will be in directly.

VARYA: Petya, here they are, your goloshes, by that box. [*With tears.*] And what dirty old things they are!

TROFIMOV: [*Putting on his goloshes.*] Let us go, friends!

GAEV: [*Greatly agitated, afraid of weeping.*] The train—the station! Double baulk, ah!

LYUBOV: Let us go!

LOPAHIN: Are we all here? [*Locks the side-door on left.*] The things are all here. We must lock up. Let us go!

ANYA: Good-bye, home! Good-bye to the old life!

TROFIMOV: Welcome to the new life!

[TROFIMOV *goes out with* ANYA. VARYA *looks round the room and goes out slowly.* YASHA *and* CHARLOTTA IVANOVNA, *with her dog, go out.*]

LOPAHIN: Till the spring, then! Come, friends, till we meet! [*Goes out.*]

[LYUBOV ANDREYEVNA *and* GAEV *remain alone. As though they had been waiting for this, they throw themselves on each other's necks, and break into subdued smothered sobbing, afraid of being overheard.*]

GAEV: [*In despair.*] Sister, my sister!

LYUBOV: Oh, my orchard!—my sweet, beautiful orchard! My life, my youth, my happiness, good-bye! good-bye!

VOICE OF ANYA: [*Calling gaily.*] Mamma!

VOICE OF TROFIMOV: [*Gaily, excitedly.*] Aa—oo!

LYUBOV: One last look at the walls, at the windows. My dear mother loved to walk about this room.

GAEV: Sister, sister!

VOICE OF ANYA: Mamma!

VOICE OF TROFIMOV: Aa—oo!

LYUBOV: We are coming. [*They go out.*]

[*The stage is empty. There is the sound of the doors being locked up, then of the carriages driving away. There is silence. In the stillness there is the dull stroke of an ax in a tree, clanging with a mournful lonely sound. Footsteps are heard.* FIRS *appears in the doorway on the right. He is dressed as always—in a pea-jacket and white waistcoat, with slippers on his feet. He is ill.*]

FIRS: [*Goes up to the doors, and tries the handles.*] Locked! They have gone . . . [*Sits down on sofa.*] They have forgotten me. . . . Never mind . . . I'll sit here a bit. . . . I'll be bound Leonid Andreyevitch hasn't put his fur coat on and has gone off in his thin overcoat. [*Sighs anxiously.*] I didn't see after him. . . . These young people . . . [*Mutters something that can't be distinguished.*] Life has slipped by as though I hadn't lived. [*Lies down.*] I'll lie down a bit. . . . There's no strength in you, nothing left you—all gone! Ech! I'm good for nothing. [*Lies motionless.*]

[*A sound is heard that seems to come from the sky, like a breaking harp-string, dying away mournfully. All is still again, and there is heard nothing but the strokes of the ax far away in the orchard.*]

CURTAIN

1903–04

ARTHUR MILLER

Death of a Salesman

Certain Private Conversations in Two Acts and a Requiem

CHARACTERS

WILLY LOMAN	THE WOMAN	STANLEY
LINDA	CHARLEY	MISS FORSYTHE
BIFF	UNCLE BEN	LETTA
HAPPY	HOWARD WAGNER	
BERNARD	JENNY	

The action takes place in WILLY LOMAN'*s house and yard and in various places he visits in the New York and Boston of today.*

ACT I

A melody is heard, playing upon a flute. It is small and fine, telling of grass and trees and the horizon. The curtain rises.

Before us is the Salesman's house. We are aware of towering, angular shapes behind it, surrounding it on all sides. Only the blue light of the sky falls upon the house and forestage; the surrounding area shows an angry flow of orange. As more light appears, we see a solid vault of apartment houses around the small, fragile-seeming home. An air of the dream clings to the place, a dream rising out of reality. The kitchen at center seems actual enough, for there is a kitchen table with three chairs, and a refrigerator. But no other fixtures are seen. At the back of the kitchen there is a draped entrance, which leads to the living-room.

To the right of the kitchen, on a level raised two feet, is a bedroom furnished only with a brass bedstead and a straight chair. On a shelf over the bed a silver athletic trophy stands. A window opens onto the apartment house at the side.

Behind the kitchen, on a level raised six and a half feet, is the boys' bedroom, at present barely visible. Two beds are dimly seen, and at the back of the room a dormer window. (This bedroom is above the unseen living-room.) At the left a stairway curves up to it from the kitchen.

The entire setting is wholly or, in some places, partially transparent. The roof-line of the house is one-dimensional; under and over it we see the apartment buildings. Before the house lies an apron, curving beyond the forestage into the orchestra. This forward area serves as the back yard as well as the locale of all WILLY*'s imaginings and of his city scenes. Whenever the action is in the present the actors observe the imaginary wall-lines, entering the house only through its door at the left. But in the scenes of the past these boundaries are broken, and characters enter or leave a room by stepping "through" a wall onto the forestage.*

From the right, WILLY LOMAN, *the Salesman, enters, carrying two large sample cases. The flute plays on. He hears but is not aware of it. He is past sixty years of age, dressed quietly. Even as he crosses the stage to the doorway of the house, his exhaustion is apparent. He unlocks the door, comes into the kitchen, and thankfully lets his burden down, feeling the soreness of his palms. A word-sigh escapes his lips—it might be "Oh, boy, oh, boy." He closes the door, then carries his cases out into the living-room, through the draped kitchen doorway.*

LINDA, *his wife, has stirred in her bed at the right. She gets out and puts on a robe, listening. Most often jovial, she has developed an iron repression of her exceptions to* WILLY*'s behavior— she more than loves him, she admires him, as though his mercurial nature, his temper, his massive dreams and little cruelties, served her only as sharp reminders of the turbulent longings within him, longings which she shares but lacks the temperament to utter and follow to their end.*

LINDA: [*Hearing* WILLY *outside the bedroom, calls with some trepidation.*] Willy!

WILLY: It's all right. I came back.

LINDA: Why? What happened? [*Slight pause.*] Did something happen, Willy?

WILLY: No, nothing happened.

LINDA: You didn't smash the car, did you?

WILLY: [*With casual irritation.*] I said nothing happened. Didn't you hear me?

LINDA: Don't you feel well?

WILLY: I'm tired to the death. [*The flute has faded away. He sits on the bed beside her, a little numb.*] I couldn't make it. I just couldn't make it, Linda.

LINDA: [*Very carefully, delicately.*] Where were you all day? You look terrible.

WILLY: I got as far as a little above Yonkers. I stopped for a cup of coffee. Maybe it was the coffee.

LINDA: What?

WILLY: [*After a pause.*] I suddenly couldn't drive any more. The car kept going off onto the shoulder, y'know?

LINDA: [*Helpfully.*] Oh. Maybe it was the steering again. I don't think Angelo knows the Studebaker.

WILLY: No, it's me, it's me. Suddenly I realize I'm goin' sixty miles an hour and I don't remember the last five minutes. I'm—I can't seem to—keep my mind to it.

LINDA: Maybe it's your glasses. You never went for your new glasses.

WILLY: No, I see everything. I came back ten miles an hour. It took me nearly four hours from Yonkers.

LINDA: [*Resigned.*] Well, you'll just have to take a rest, Willy, you can't continue this way.

WILLY: I just got back from Florida.

LINDA: But you didn't rest your mind. Your mind is overactive, and the mind is what counts, dear.

WILLY: I'll start out in the morning. Maybe I'll feel better in the morning. [*She is taking off his shoes.*] These goddam arch supports are killing me.

LINDA: Take an aspirin. Should I get you an aspirin? It'll soothe you.

WILLY: [*With wonder.*] I was driving along, you understand? And I was fine. I was even observing the scenery. You can imagine, me looking at scenery, on the road every week of my life. But it's so beautiful up there, Linda, the trees are so thick, and the sun is warm. I opened the windshield and just let the warm air bathe over me. And then all of a sudden I'm goin' off the road! I'm tellin' ya, I absolutely forgot I was driving. If I'd've gone the other way over the white line I might've killed somebody. So I went on again—and five minutes later I'm dreamin' again, and I nearly—[*He presses two fingers against his eyes.*] I have such thoughts, I have such strange thoughts.

LINDA: Willy, dear. Talk to them again. There's no reason why you can't work in New York.

WILLY: They don't need me in New York. I'm the New England man. I'm vital in New England.

LINDA: But you're sixty years old. They can't expect you to keep traveling every week.

WILLY: I'll have to send a wire[1] to Portland. I'm supposed to see Brown and Morrison tomorrow morning at ten o'clock to show the line. Goddammit, I could sell them! [*He starts putting on his jacket.*]

LINDA: [*Taking the jacket from him.*] Why don't you go down to the place tomorrow and tell Howard you've simply got to work in New York? You're too accommodating, dear.

WILLY: If old man Wagner was alive I'da been in charge of New York now! That man was a prince, he was a masterful man. But that boy of his, that Howard, he don't appreciate. When I went north the first time, the Wagner Company didn't know where New England was!

LINDA: Why don't you tell those things to Howard, dear?

WILLY: [*Encouraged.*] I will, I definitely will. Is there any cheese?

LINDA: I'll make you a sandwich.

WILLY: No, go to sleep. I'll take some milk. I'll be up right away. The boys in?

LINDA: They're sleeping. Happy took Biff on a date tonight.

WILLY: [*Interested.*] That so?

LINDA: It was so nice to see them shaving together, one behind the other, in the bathroom. And going out together. You notice? The whole house smells of shaving lotion.

WILLY: Figure it out. Work a lifetime to pay off a house. You finally own it, and there's nobody to live in it.

LINDA: Well, dear, life is a casting off. It's always that way.

---

1. Telegram.

WILLY: No, no, some people—some people accomplish something. Did Biff say anything after I went this morning?

LINDA: You shouldn't have criticized him, Willy, especially after he just got off the train. You mustn't lose your temper with him.

WILLY: When the hell did I lose my temper? I simply asked him if he was making any money. Is that a criticism?

LINDA: But, dear, how could he make any money?

WILLY: [*Worried and angered.*] There's such an undercurrent in him. He became a moody man. Did he apologize when I left this morning?

LINDA: He was crestfallen, Willy. You know how he admires you. I think if he finds himself, then you'll both be happier and not fight any more.

WILLY: How can he find himself on a farm? Is that a life? A farmhand? In the beginning, when he was young, I thought, well, a young man, it's good for him to tramp around, take a lot of different jobs. But it's more than ten years now and he has yet to make thirty-five dollars a week!

LINDA: He's finding himself, Willy.

WILLY: Not finding yourself at the age of thirty-four is a disgrace!

LINDA: Shh!

WILLY: The trouble is he's lazy, goddammit!

LINDA: Willy, please!

WILLY: Biff is a lazy bum!

LINDA: They're sleeping. Get something to eat. Go on down.

WILLY: Why did he come home? I would like to know what brought him home.

LINDA: I don't know. I think he's still lost, Willy. I think he's very lost.

WILLY: Biff Loman is lost. In the greatest country in the world a young man with such—personal attractiveness, gets lost. And such a hard worker. There's one thing about Biff—he's not lazy.

LINDA: Never.

WILLY: [*With pity and resolve.*] I'll see him in the morning; I'll have a nice talk with him. I'll get him a job selling. He could be big in no time. My God! Remember how they used to follow him around in high school? When he smiled at one of them their faces lit up. When he walked down the street . . . [*He loses himself in reminiscences.*]

LINDA: [*Trying to bring him out of it.*] Willy, dear, I got a new kind of American-type cheese today. It's whipped.

WILLY: Why do you get American when I like Swiss?

LINDA: I just thought you'd like a change—

WILLY: I don't want a change! I want Swiss cheese. Why am I always being contradicted?

LINDA: [*With a covering laugh.*] I thought it would be a surprise.

WILLY: Why don't you open a window in here, for God's sake?

LINDA: [*With infinite patience.*] They're all open, dear.

WILLY: The way they boxed us in here. Bricks and windows, windows and bricks.

LINDA: We should've bought the land next door.

WILLY: The street is lined with cars. There's not a breath of fresh air in the neighborhood. The grass don't grow any more, you can't raise a carrot in the back yard. They should've had a law against apartment houses. Remember those two beautiful elm trees out there? When I and Biff hung the swing between them?

LINDA: Yeah, like being a million miles from the city.

WILLY: They should've arrested the builder for cutting those down. They massacred the neighborhood. [*Lost.*] More and more I think of those days, Linda. This time of year it was lilac and wisteria. And then the peonies would come out, and the daffodils. What fragrance in this room!

LINDA: Well, after all, people had to move somewhere.

WILLY: No, there's more people now.

LINDA: I don't think there's more people. I think—

WILLY: There's more people! That's what ruining this country! Population is getting out of control. The competition is maddening! Smell the stink from that apartment house! And another one on the other side . . . How can they whip cheese?

[*On* WILLY'*s last line,* BIFF *and* HAPPY *raise themselves up in their beds, listening.*]

LINDA: Go down, try it. And be quiet.

WILLY: [*Turning to* LINDA, *guiltily.*] You're not worried about me, are you, sweetheart?

BIFF: What's the matter?

HAPPY: Listen!

LINDA: You've got too much on the ball to worry about.

WILLY: You're my foundation and my support, Linda.

LINDA: Just try to relax, dear. You make mountains out of mole-hills.

WILLY: I won't fight with him anymore. If he wants to go back to Texas, let him go.

LINDA: He'll find his way.

WILLY: Sure. Certain men just don't get started till later in life. Like Thomas Edison, I think. Or B. F. Goodrich. One of them was deaf.[2] [*He starts for the bedroom doorway.*] I'll put my money on Biff.

LINDA: And Willy—if it's warm Sunday we'll drive in the country. And we'll open the windshield, and take lunch.

WILLY: No, the windshields don't open on the new cars.

LINDA: But you opened it today.

WILLY: Me? I didn't. [*He stops.*] Now isn't that peculiar! Isn't that a remarkable— [*He breaks off in amazement and fright as the flute is heard distantly.*]

LINDA: What, darling?

WILLY: That is the most remarkable thing.

LINDA: What, dear?

WILLY: I was thinking of the Chevvy. [*Slight pause.*] Nineteen twenty-eight . . . when I had that red Chevvy—[*Breaks off.*] That funny? I coulda sworn I was driving that Chevvy today.

LINDA: Well, that's nothing. Something must've reminded you.

WILLY: Remarkable. *Ts.*[3] Remember those days? The way Biff used to simonize that car? The dealer refused to believe there was eighty thousand miles on it.

---

2. Thomas Alva Edison (1847–1931), American inventor best known for the phonograph and the incandescent lightbulb; Edison's deafness was legendary. Benjamin Franklin Goodrich (1841–88), American industrialist known for the tire company that still bears his name.

3. Ford Model Ts, extraordinarily popular cars manufactured from 1908 to 1928. *Simonize*: polish with car wax.

[*He shakes his head.*] Heh! [*To* LINDA.] Close your eyes, I'll be right up. [*He walks out of the bedroom.*]

HAPPY: [*To* BIFF.] Jesus, maybe he smashed up the car again!

LINDA: [*Calling after* WILLY.] Be careful on the stairs, dear! The cheese is on the middle shelf! [*She turns, goes over to the bed, takes his jacket, and goes out of the bedroom.*]

[*Light has risen on the boys' room. Unseen,* WILLY *is heard talking to himself, "Eighty thousand miles," and a little laugh.* BIFF *gets out of bed, comes downstage a bit, and stands attentively.* BIFF *is two years older than his brother,* HAPPY, *well built, but in these days bears a worn air and seems less self-assured. He has succeeded less, and his dreams are stronger and less acceptable than* HAPPY's. HAPPY *is tall, powerfully made. Sexuality is like a visible color on him, or a scent that many women have discovered. He, like his brother, is lost, but in a different way, for he has never allowed himself to turn his face toward defeat and is thus more confused and hard-skinned, although seemingly more content.*]

HAPPY: [*Getting out of bed.*] He's going to get his license taken away if he keeps that up. I'm getting nervous about him, y'know, Biff?

BIFF: His eyes are going.

HAPPY: No, I've driven with him. He sees all right. He just doesn't keep his mind on it. I drove into the city with him last week. He stops at a green light and then it turns red and he goes. [*He laughs.*]

BIFF: Maybe he's color-blind.

HAPPY: Pop? Why he's got the finest eye for color in the business. You know that.

BIFF: [*Sitting down on his bed.*] I'm going to sleep.

HAPPY: You're not still sour on Dad, are you Biff?

BIFF: He's all right, I guess.

WILLY: [*Underneath them, in the living-room.*] Yes, sir, eighty thousand miles—eighty-two thousand!

BIFF: You smoking?

HAPPY: [*Holding out a pack of cigarettes.*] Want one?

BIFF: [*Taking a cigarette.*] I can never sleep when I smell it.

WILLY: What a simonizing job, heh!

HAPPY: [*With deep sentiment.*] Funny, Biff, y'know? Us sleeping in here again? The old beds. [*He pats his bed affectionately.*] All the talk that went across those two beds, huh? Our whole lives.

BIFF: Yeah. Lotta dreams and plans.

HAPPY: [*With a deep and masculine laugh.*] About five hundred women would like to know what was said in this room.

[*They share a soft laugh.*]

BIFF: Remember that big Betsy something—what the hell was her name—over on Bushwick Avenue?[4]

HAPPY: [*Combing his hair.*] With the collie dog!

BIFF: That's the one. I got you in there, remember?

HAPPY: Yeah, that was my first time—I think. Boy, there was a pig! [*They laugh, almost crudely.*] You taught me everything I know about women. Don't forget that.

4. Major thoroughfare in Brooklyn, New York.

BIFF: I bet you forgot how bashful you used to be. Especially with girls.

HAPPY: Oh, I still am, Biff.

BIFF: Oh, go on.

HAPPY: I just control it, that's all. I think I got less bashful and you got more so. What happened, Biff? Where's the old humor, the old confidence? [*He shakes* BIFF*'s knee.* BIFF *gets up and moves restlessly about the room.*] What's the matter?

BIFF: Why does Dad mock me all the time?

HAPPY: He's not mocking you, he—

BIFF: Everything I say there's a twist of mockery on his face. I can't get near him.

HAPPY: He just wants you to make good, that's all. I wanted to talk to you about Dad for a long time, Biff. Something's—happening to him. He—talks to himself.

BIFF: I noticed that this morning. But he always mumbled.

HAPPY: But not so noticeable. It got so embarrassing I sent him to Florida. And you know something? Most of the time he's talking to you.

BIFF: What's he say about me?

HAPPY: I can't make it out.

BIFF: What's he say about me?

HAPPY: I think the fact that you're not settled, that you're still kind of up in the air . . .

BIFF: There's one or two things depressing him, Happy.

HAPPY: What do you mean?

BIFF: Never mind. Just don't lay it all to me.

HAPPY: But I think if you just got started—I mean—is there any future for you out there?

BIFF: I tell ya, Hap, I don't know what the future is. I don't know—what I'm supposed to want.

HAPPY: What do you mean?

BIFF: Well, I spent six or seven years after high school trying to work myself up. Shipping clerk, salesman, business of one kind or another. And it's a measly manner of existence. To get on that subway on the hot mornings in summer. To devote your whole life to keeping stock, or making phone calls, or selling or buying. To suffer fifty weeks of the year for the sake of a two-week vacation, when all you really desire is to be outdoors, with your shirt off. And always to have to get ahead of the next fella. And still—that's how you build a future.

HAPPY: Well, you really enjoy it on a farm? Are you content out there?

BIFF: [*With rising agitation.*] Hap, I've had twenty or thirty different kinds of jobs since I left home before the war, and it always turns out the same. I just realized it lately. In Nebraska when I herded cattle, and the Dakotas, and Arizona, and now in Texas. It's why I came home now, I guess, because I realized it. This farm I work on, it's spring there now, see? And they've got about fifteen new colts. There's nothing more inspiring or—beautiful than the sight of a mare and a new colt. And it's cool there now, see? Texas is cool now, and it's spring. And whenever spring comes to where I am, I suddenly get the feeling, my God, I'm not gettin' anywhere! What the hell am I doing, playing around with horses, twenty-eight dollars a week! I'm thirty-four years old. I oughta be makin' my future. That's when I come running home. And now, I get there, and I don't know what to do with myself. [*After a pause.*] I've always made a point of not wasting my life, and everytime I come back here I know that all I've done is to waste my life.

HAPPY: You're a poet, you know that, Biff? You're a—you're an idealist!

BIFF: No, I'm mixed up very bad. Maybe I oughta get married. Maybe I oughta get stuck into something. Maybe that's my trouble. I'm like a boy. I'm not married. I'm not in business, I just—I'm like a boy. Are you content, Hap? You're a success, aren't you? Are you content?

HAPPY: Hell, no!

BIFF: Why? You're making money, aren't you?

HAPPY: [*Moving about with energy, expressiveness.*] All I can do now is wait for the merchandise manager to die. And suppose I get to be merchandise manager? He's a good friend of mine, and he just built a terrific estate on Long Island. And he lived there about two months and sold it, and now he's building another one. He can't enjoy it once it's finished. And I know that's just what I would do. I don't know what the hell I'm workin' for. Sometimes I sit in my apartment—all alone. And I think of the rent I'm paying. And it's crazy. But then, it's what I always wanted. My own apartment, a car, and plenty of women. And still, goddammit, I'm lonely.

BIFF: [*With enthusiasm.*] Listen, why don't you come out West with me?

HAPPY: You and I, heh?

BIFF: Sure, maybe we could buy a ranch. Raise cattle, use our muscles. Men built like we are should be working out in the open.

HAPPY: [*Avidly.*] The Loman Brothers, heh?

BIFF: [*With vast affection.*] Sure, we'd be known all over the counties!

HAPPY: [*Enthralled.*] That's what I dream about, Biff. Sometimes I want to just rip my clothes off in the middle of the store and outbox that goddam merchandise manager. I mean I can outbox, outrun, and outlift anybody in that store, and I have to take orders from those common, petty sons-of-bitches till I can't stand it anymore.

BIFF: I'm tellin' you, kid, if you were with me I'd be happy out there.

HAPPY: [*Enthused.*] See, Biff, everybody around me is so false that I'm constantly lowering my ideals . . .

BIFF: Baby, together we'd stand up for one another, we'd have someone to trust.

HAPPY: If I were around you—

BIFF: Hap, the trouble is we weren't brought up to grub for money. I don't know how to do it.

HAPPY: Neither can I!

BIFF: Then let's go!

HAPPY: The only thing is—what can you make out there?

BIFF: But look at your friend. Builds an estate and then hasn't the peace of mind to live in it.

HAPPY: Yeah, but when he walks into the store the waves part in front of him. That's fifty-two thousand dollars a year coming through the revolving door, and I got more in my pinky finger than he's got in his head.

BIFF: Yeah, but you just said—

HAPPY: I gotta show some of those pompous, self-important executives over there that Hap Loman can make the grade. I want to walk into the store the way he walks in. Then I'll go with you, Biff. We'll be together yet, I swear. But take those two we had tonight. Now weren't they gorgeous creatures?

BIFF: Yeah, yeah, most gorgeous I've had in years.

HAPPY: I get that any time I want, Biff. Whenever I feel disgusted. The only trouble is, it gets like bowling or something. I just keep knockin' them over and it doesn't mean anything. You still run around a lot?

BIFF: Naa. I'd like to find a girl—steady, somebody with substance.

HAPPY: That's what I long for.

BIFF: Go on! You'd never come home.

HAPPY: I would! Somebody with character, with resistance! Like Mom, y'know? You're gonna call me a bastard when I tell you this. That girl Charlotte I was with tonight is engaged to be married in five weeks. [*He tries on his new hat.*]

BIFF: No kiddin'!

HAPPY: Sure, the guy's in line for the vice-presidency of the store. I don't know what gets into me, maybe I just have an overdeveloped sense of competition or something, but I went and ruined her, and furthermore I can't get rid of her. And he's the third executive I've done that to. Isn't that a crummy characteristic? And to top it all, I go to their weddings! [*Indignantly, but laughing.*] Like I'm not supposed to take bribes. Manufacturers offer me a hundred-dollar bill now and then to throw an order their way. You know how honest I am, but it's like this girl, see. I hate myself for it. Because I don't want the girl, and, still, I take it and—I love it!

BIFF: Let's go to sleep.

HAPPY: I guess we didn't settle anything, heh?

BIFF: I just got one idea that I'm going to try.

HAPPY: What's that?

BIFF: Remember Bill Oliver?

HAPPY: Sure, Oliver is very big now. You want to work for him again?

BIFF: No, but when I quit he said something to me. He put his arm on my shoulder, and he said, "Biff, if you ever need anything, come to me."

HAPPY: I remember that. That sounds good.

BIFF: I think I'll go to see him. If I could get ten thousand or even seven or eight thousand dollars I could buy a beautiful ranch.

HAPPY: I bet he'd back you. 'Cause he thought highly of you, Biff. I mean, they all do. You're well liked, Biff. That's why I say to come back here, and we both have the apartment. And I'm tellin' you, Biff, any babe you want . . .

BIFF: No, with a ranch I could do the work I like and still be something. I just wonder though. I wonder if Oliver still thinks I stole that carton of basketballs.

HAPPY: Oh, he probably forgot that long ago. It's almost ten years. You're too sensitive. Anyway, he didn't really fire you.

BIFF: Well, I think he was going to. I think that's why I quit. I was never sure whether he knew or not. I know he thought the world of me, though. I was the only one he'd let lock up the place.

WILLY: [*Below.*] You gonna wash the engine, Biff?

HAPPY: Shh! [BIFF *looks at* HAPPY, *who is gazing down, listening.* WILLY *is mumbling in the parlor.*] You hear that?

[*They listen.* WILLY *laughs warmly.*]

BIFF: [*Growing angry.*] Doesn't he know Mom can hear that?

WILLY: Don't get your sweater dirty, Biff!

[*A look of pain crosses* BIFF'*s face.*]

HAPPY: Isn't that terrible? Don't leave again, will you? You'll find a job here. You gotta stick around. I don't know what to do about him, it's getting embarrassing.

WILLY: What a simonizing job!

BIFF: Mom's hearing that!

WILLY: No kiddin', Biff, you got a date? Wonderful!

HAPPY: Go on to sleep. But talk to him in the morning, will you?

BIFF: [*Reluctantly getting into bed.*] With her in the house. Brother!

HAPPY: [*Getting into bed.*] I wish you'd have a good talk with him.

[*The light on their room begins to fade.*]

BIFF: [*To himself in bed.*] That selfish, stupid . . .

HAPPY: Sh . . . Sleep, Biff.

[*Their light is out. Well before they have finished speaking,* WILLY'*s form is dimly seen below in the darkened kitchen. He opens the refrigerator, searches in there, and takes out a bottle of milk. The apartment houses are fading out, and the entire house and surroundings become covered with leaves. Music insinuates itself as the leaves appear.*]

WILLY: Just wanna be careful with those girls, Biff, that's all. Don't make any promises. No promises of any kind. Because a girl, y'know, they always believe what you tell 'em, and you're very young, Biff, you're too young to be talking seriously to girls. [*Light rises on the kitchen.* WILLY, *talking, shuts the refrigerator door and comes downstage to the kitchen table. He pours milk into a glass. He is totally immersed in himself, smiling faintly.*] Too young entirely, Biff. You want to watch your schooling first. Then when you're all set, there'll be plenty of girls for a boy like you. [*He smiles broadly at a kitchen chair.*] That so? The girls pay for you? [*He laughs.*] Boy, you must really be makin' a hit. [WILLY *is gradually addressing—physically—a point offstage, speaking through the wall of the kitchen, and his voice has been rising in volume to that of a normal conversation.*] I been wondering why you polish the car so careful. Ha! Don't leave the hubcaps, boys. Get the chamois to the hubcaps. Happy, use newspaper on the windows, it's the easiest thing. Show him how to do it, Biff! You see, Happy? Pad it up, use it like a pad. That's it, that's it, good work. You're doin' all right, Hap. [*He pauses, then nods in approbation for a few seconds, then looks upward.*] Biff, first thing we gotta do when we get time is clip that big branch over the house. Afraid it's gonna fall in a storm and hit the roof. Tell you what. We get a rope and sling her around, and then we climb up there with a couple of saws and take her down. Soon as you finish the car, boys, I wanna see ya. I got a surprise for you, boys.

BIFF: [*Offstage.*] Whatta ya got, Dad?

WILLY: No, you finish first. Never leave a job till you're finished—remember that. [*Looking toward the "big trees."*] Biff, up in Albany I saw a beautiful hammock. I think I'll buy it next trip, and we'll hang it right between those two elms. Wouldn't that be something? Just swingin' there under those branches. Boy, that would be . . .

[YOUNG BIFF *and* YOUNG HAPPY *appear from the direction* WILLY *was addressing.* HAPPY *carries rags and a pail of water.* BIFF, *wearing a sweater with a block "S," carries a football.*]

BIFF: [*Pointing in the direction of the car offstage.*] How's that, Pop, professional?

WILLY: Terrific. Terrific job, boys. Good work, Biff.

HAPPY: Where's the surprise, Pop?

WILLY: In the back seat of the car.

HAPPY: Boy! [*He runs off.*]

BIFF: What is it, Dad? Tell me, what'd you buy?

WILLY: [*Laughing, cuffs him.*] Never mind, something I want you to have.

BIFF: [*Turns and starts off.*] What is it, Hap?

HAPPY: [*Offstage.*] It's a punching bag!

BIFF: Oh, Pop!

WILLY: It's got Gene Tunney's[5] signature on it!

[HAPPY *runs onstage with a punching bag.*]

BIFF: Gee, how'd you know we wanted a punching bag?

WILLY: Well, it's the finest thing for the timing.

HAPPY: [*Lies down on his back and pedals with his feet.*] I'm losing weight, you notice, Pop?

WILLY: [*To* HAPPY.] Jumping rope is good too.

BIFF: Did you see the new football I got?

WILLY: [*Examining the ball.*] Where'd you get a new ball?

BIFF: The coach told me to practice my passing.

WILLY: That so? And he gave you the ball, heh?

BIFF: Well, I borrowed it from the locker room. [*He laughs confidentially.*]

WILLY: [*Laughing with him at the theft.*] I want you to return that.

HAPPY: I told you he wouldn't like it!

BIFF: [*Angrily.*] Well, I'm bringing it back!

WILLY: [*Stopping the incipient argument, to* HAPPY.] Sure, he's gotta practice with a regulation ball, doesn't he? [*To* BIFF.] Coach'll probably congratulate you on your initiative!

BIFF: Oh, he keeps congratulating my initiative all the time, Pop.

WILLY: That's because he likes you. If somebody else took that ball there'd be an uproar. So what's the report, boys, what's the report?

BIFF: Where'd you go this time, Dad? Gee we were lonesome for you.

WILLY: [*Pleased, puts an arm around each boy and they come down to the apron.*] Lonesome, heh?

BIFF: Missed you every minute.

WILLY: Don't say? Tell you a secret, boys. Don't breathe it to a soul. Someday I'll have my own business, and I'll never have to leave home anymore.

HAPPY: Like Uncle Charley, heh?

WILLY: Bigger than Uncle Charley! Because Charley is not—liked. He's liked, but he's not—well liked.

BIFF: Where'd you go this time, Dad?

WILLY: Well, I got on the road, and I went north to Providence. Met the mayor.

BIFF: The mayor of Providence!

WILLY: He was sitting in the hotel lobby.

BIFF: What'd he say?

5. Tunney (1897–1978) was world heavyweight boxing champion from 1926 to 1928 and retired undefeated.

WILLY: He said, "Morning!" And I said, "You got a fine city here, Mayor." And then he had coffee with me. And then I went to Waterbury. Waterbury is a fine city. Big clock city, the famous Waterbury clock. Sold a nice bill there. And then Boston—Boston is the cradle of the Revolution. A fine city. And a couple of other towns in Mass., and on to Portland and Bangor and straight home!

BIFF: Gee, I'd love to go with you sometime, Dad.

WILLY: Soon as summer comes.

HAPPY: Promise?

WILLY: You and Hap and I, and I'll show you all the towns. America is full of beautiful towns and fine, upstanding people. And they know me, boys, they know me up and down New England. The finest people. And when I bring you fellas up, there'll be open sesame for all of us, 'cause one thing, boys: I have friends. I can park my car in any street in New England, and the cops protect it like their own. This summer, heh?

BIFF and HAPPY: [*Together.*] Yeah! You bet!

WILLY: We'll take our bathing suits.

HAPPY: We'll carry your bags, Pop!

WILLY: Oh, won't that be something! Me comin' into the Boston stores with you boys carryin' my bags. What a sensation! [BIFF *is prancing around, practicing passing the ball.*] You nervous, Biff, about the game?

BIFF: Not if you're gonna be there.

WILLY: What do they say about you in school, now that they made you captain?

HAPPY: There's a crowd of girls behind him every time the classes change.

BIFF: [*Taking* WILLY'*s hand.*] This Saturday, Pop, this Saturday—just for you, I'm going to break through for a touchdown.

HAPPY: You're supposed to pass.

BIFF: I'm takin' one play for Pop. You watch me, Pop, and when I take off my helmet, that means I'm breakin' out. Then you watch me crash through that line!

WILLY: [*Kisses* BIFF.] Oh, wait'll I tell this in Boston!

[BERNARD *enters in knickers. He is younger than* BIFF, *earnest and loyal, a worried boy.*]

BERNARD: Biff, where are you? You're supposed to study with me today.

WILLY: Hey, looka Bernard. What're you lookin' so anemic about, Bernard?

BERNARD: He's gotta study, Uncle Willy. He's got Regents[6] next week.

HAPPY: [*Tauntingly, spinning* BERNARD *around.*] Let's box, Bernard!

BERNARD: Biff! [*He gets away from* HAPPY.] Listen, Biff, I heard Mr. Birnbaum say that if you don't start studyin' math he's gonna flunk you, and you won't graduate. I heard him!

WILLY: You better study with him, Biff. Go ahead now.

BERNARD: I heard him!

BIFF: Oh, Pop, you didn't see my sneakers! [*He holds up a foot for* WILLY *to look at.*]

WILLY: Hey, that's a beautiful job of printing!

BERNARD: [*Wiping his glasses.*] Just because he printed University of Virginia on his sneakers doesn't mean they've got to graduate him, Uncle Willy!

WILLY: [*Angrily.*] What're you talking about? With scholarships to three universities they're gonna flunk him?

---

6. Examinations administered to New York State high-school students.

BERNARD: But I heard Mr. Birnbaum say—

WILLY: Don't be a pest, Bernard! [*To his boys.*] What an anemic!

BERNARD: Okay, I'm waiting for you in my house, Biff.

[BERNARD *goes off. The* LOMANS *laugh.*]

WILLY: Bernard is not well liked, is he?

BIFF: He's liked, but he's not well liked.

HAPPY: That's right, Pop.

WILLY: That's just what I mean. Bernard can get the best marks in school, y'understand, but when he gets out in the business world, y'understand, you are going to be five times ahead of him. That's why I thank Almighty God you're both built like Adonises.[7] Because the man who makes an appearance in the business world, the man who creates personal interest, is the man who gets ahead. Be liked and you will never want. You take me, for instance. I never have to wait in line to see a buyer. "Willy Loman is here!" That's all they have to know, and I go right through.

BIFF: Did you knock them dead, Pop?

WILLY: Knocked 'em cold in Providence, slaughtered 'em in Boston.

HAPPY: [*On his back, pedaling again.*] I'm losing weight, you notice, Pop?

[LINDA *enters, as of old, a ribbon in her hair, carrying a basket of washing.*]

LINDA: [*With youthful energy.*] Hello, dear!

WILLY: Sweetheart!

LINDA: How'd the Chevvy run?

WILLY: Chevrolet, Linda, is the greatest car ever built. [*To the boys.*] Since when do you let your mother carry wash up the stairs?

BIFF: Grab hold there, boy!

HAPPY: Where to, Mom?

LINDA: Hang them up on the line. And you better go down to your friends, Biff. The cellar is full of boys. They don't know what to do with themselves.

BIFF: Ah, when Pop comes home they can wait!

WILLY: [*Laughs appreciatively.*] You better go down and tell them what to do, Biff.

BIFF: I think I'll have them sweep out the furnace room.

WILLY: Good work, Biff.

BIFF: [*Goes through wall-line of kitchen to doorway at back and calls down.*] Fellas! Everybody sweep out the furnace room! I'll be right down!

VOICES: All right! Okay, Biff.

BIFF: George and Sam and Frank, come out back! We're hangin' up the wash! Come on, Hap, on the double!

[*He and* HAPPY *carry out the basket.*]

LINDA: The way they obey him!

WILLY: Well, that training, the training. I'm tellin' you, I was sellin' thousands and thousands, but I had to come home.

LINDA: Oh, the whole block'll be at that game. Did you sell anything?

WILLY: I did five hundred gross in Providence and seven hundred gross in Boston.

---

7. In Greek myth Adonis was a beautiful youth.

LINDA: No! Wait a minute, I've got a pencil. [*She pulls pencil and paper out of her apron pocket.*] That makes your commission . . . Two hundred—my God! Two hundred and twelve dollars!

WILLY: Well, I didn't figure it yet, but . . .

LINDA: How much did you do?

WILLY: Well, I—I did—about a hundred and eighty gross in Providence. Well, no—it came to—roughly two hundred gross on the whole trip.

LINDA: [*Without hesitation.*] Two hundred gross. That's . . . [*She figures.*]

WILLY: The trouble was that three of the stores were half closed for inventory in Boston. Otherwise I woulda broke records.

LINDA: Well, it makes seventy dollars and some pennies. That's very good.

WILLY: What do we owe?

LINDA: Well, on the first there's sixteen dollars on the refrigerator—

WILLY: Why sixteen?

LINDA: Well, the fan belt broke, so it was a dollar eighty.

WILLY: But it's brand new.

LINDA: Well, the man said that's the way it is. Till they work themselves in, y'know.

[*They move through the wall-line into the kitchen.*]

WILLY: I hope we didn't get stuck on that machine.

LINDA: They got the biggest ads of any of them!

WILLY: I know, it's a fine machine. What else?

LINDA: Well, there's nine-sixty for the washing machine. And for the vacuum cleaner there's three and a half due on the fifteenth. Then the roof, you got twenty-one dollars remaining.

WILLY: It don't leak, does it?

LINDA: No, they did a wonderful job. Then you owe Frank for the carburetor.

WILLY: I'm not going to pay that man! That goddam Chevrolet, they ought to prohibit the manufacture of that car!

LINDA: Well, you owe him three and a half. And odds and ends, comes to around a hundred and twenty dollars by the fifteenth.

WILLY: A hundred and twenty dollars! My God, if business don't pick up I don't know what I'm gonna do!

LINDA: Well, next week you'll do better.

WILLY: Oh, I'll knock 'em dead next week. I'll go to Hartford. I'm very well liked in Hartford. You know, the trouble is, Linda, people don't seem to take to me.

[*They move onto the forestage.*]

LINDA: Oh, don't be foolish.

WILLY: I know it when I walk in. They seem to laugh at me.

LINDA: Why? Why would they laugh at you? Don't talk that way, Willy.

[WILLY *moves to the edge of the stage.* LINDA *goes into the kitchen and starts to darn stockings.*]

WILLY: I don't know the reason for it, but they just pass me by. I'm not noticed.

LINDA: But you're doing wonderful, dear. You're making seventy to a hundred dollars a week.

WILLY: But I gotta be at it ten, twelve hours a day. Other men—I don't know—they do it easier. I don't know why—I can't stop myself—I talk too much. A man oughta come in with a few words. One thing about Charley. He's a man of few words, and they respect him.

LINDA: You don't talk too much, you're just lively.

WILLY: [*Smiling.*] Well, I figure, what the hell, life is short, a couple of jokes. [*To himself.*] I joke too much! [*The smile goes.*]

LINDA: Why? You're—

WILLY: I'm fat. I'm very—foolish to look at, Linda. I didn't tell you, but Christmas time I happened to be calling on F. H. Stewarts, and a salesman I know, as I was going in to see the buyer I heard him say something about—walrus. And I—I cracked him right across the face. I won't take that. I simply will not take that. But they do laugh at me. I know that.

LINDA: Darling . . .

WILLY: I gotta overcome it. I know I gotta overcome it. I'm not dressing to advantage, maybe.

LINDA: Willy, darling, you're the handsomest man in the world—

WILLY: Oh, no, Linda.

LINDA: To me you are. [*Slight pause.*] The handsomest. [*From the darkness is heard the laughter of a woman.* WILLY *doesn't turn to it, but it continues through* LINDA's *lines.*] And the boys, Willy. Few men are idolized by their children the way you are.

> [*Music is heard as behind a scrim, to the left of the house,* THE WOMAN, *dimly seen, is dressing.*]

WILLY: [*With great feeling.*] You're the best there is, Linda, you're a pal, you know that? On the road—on the road I want to grab you sometimes and just kiss the life outa you. [*The laughter is loud now, and he moves into a brightening area at the left, where* THE WOMAN *has come from behind the scrim and is standing, putting on her hat, looking into a "mirror" and laughing.*] 'Cause I get so lonely—especially when business is bad and there's nobody to talk to. I get the feeling that I'll never sell anything again, that I won't make a living for you, or a business, a business for the boys. [*He talks through* THE WOMAN's *subsiding laughter.* THE WOMAN *primps at the "mirror."*] There's so much I want to make for—

THE WOMAN: Me? You didn't make me, Willy. I picked you.

WILLY: [*Pleased.*] You picked me?

THE WOMAN: [*Who is quite proper-looking,* WILLY's *age.*] I did. I've been sitting at that desk watching all the salesmen go by, day in, day out. But you've got such a sense of humor, and we do have such a good time together, don't we?

WILLY: Sure, sure. [*He takes her in his arms.*] Why do you have to go now?

THE WOMAN: It's two o'clock . . .

WILLY: No, come on in! [*He pulls her.*]

THE WOMAN: . . . my sisters'll be scandalized. When'll you be back?

WILLY: Oh, two weeks about. Will you come up again?

THE WOMAN: Sure thing. You do make me laugh. It's good for me. [*She squeezes his arm, kisses him.*] And I think you're a wonderful man.

WILLY: You picked me, heh?

THE WOMAN: Sure. Because you're so sweet. And such a kidder.

WILLY: Well, I'll see you next time I'm in Boston.

THE WOMAN: I'll put you right through to the buyers.

WILLY: [*Slapping her bottom.*] Right. Well, bottoms up!

THE WOMAN: [*Slaps him gently and laughs.*] You just kill me, Willy. [*He suddenly grabs her and kisses her roughly.*] You kill me. And thanks for the stockings. I love a lot of stockings. Well, good night.

WILLY: Good night. And keep your pores open!

THE WOMAN: Oh, Willy!

[THE WOMAN *bursts out laughing, and* LINDA's *laughter blends in.* THE WOMAN *disappears into the dark. Now the area at the kitchen table brightens.* LINDA *is sitting where she was at the kitchen table, but now is mending a pair of her silk stockings.*]

LINDA: You are, Willy. The handsomest man. You've got no reason to feel that—

WILLY: [*Coming out of* THE WOMAN's *dimming area and going over to* LINDA.] I'll make it all up to you, Linda. I'll—

LINDA: There's nothing to make up, dear. You're doing fine, better than—

WILLY: [*Noticing her mending.*] What's that?

LINDA: Just mending my stockings. They're so expensive—

WILLY: [*Angrily, taking them from her.*] I won't have you mending stockings in this house! Now throw them out!

[LINDA *puts the stockings in her pocket.*]

BERNARD: [*Entering on the run.*] Where is he? If he doesn't study!

WILLY: [*Moving to the forestage, with great agitation.*] You'll give him the answers!

BERNARD: I do, but I can't on a Regents! That's a state exam! They're liable to arrest me!

WILLY: Where is he? I'll whip him, I'll whip him!

LINDA: And he'd better give back that football, Willy, it's not nice.

WILLY: Biff! Where is he? Why is he taking everything?

LINDA: He's too rough with the girls, Willy. All the mothers are afraid of him!

WILLY: I'll whip him!

BERNARD: He's driving the car without a license!

[THE WOMAN's *laugh is heard.*]

WILLY: Shut up!

LINDA: All the mothers—

WILLY: Shut up!

BERNARD: [*Backing quietly away and out.*] Mr. Birnbaum says he's stuck up.

WILLY: Get outa here!

BERNARD: If he doesn't buckle down he'll flunk math! [*He goes off.*]

LINDA: He's right, Willy, you've gotta—

WILLY: [*Exploding at her.*] There's nothing the matter with him! You want him to be a worm like Bernard? He's got spirit, personality . . . [*As he speaks,* LINDA, *almost in tears, exits into the living room.* WILLY *is alone in the kitchen, wilting and staring. The leaves are gone. It is night again, and the apartment houses look down from behind.*] Loaded with it. Loaded! What is he stealing? He's giving it back, isn't he? Why is he stealing? What did I tell him? I never in my life told him anything but decent things.

[HAPPY *in pajamas has come down the stairs;* WILLY *suddenly becomes aware of* HAPPY's *presence.*]

HAPPY: Let's go now, come on.

WILLY: [*Sitting down at the kitchen table.*] Huh! Why did she have to wax the floors herself? Everytime she waxes the floors she keels over. She knows that!

HAPPY: Shh! Take it easy. What brought you back tonight?

WILLY: I got an awful scare. Nearly hit a kid in Yonkers. God! Why didn't I go to Alaska with my brother Ben that time! Ben! That man was a genius, that man was success incarnate! What a mistake! He begged me to go.

HAPPY: Well, there's no use in—

WILLY: You guys! There was a man started with the clothes on his back and ended up with diamond mines!

HAPPY: Boy, someday I'd like to know how he did it.

WILLY: What's the mystery? The man knew what he wanted and went out and got it! Walked into a jungle, and comes out, the age of twenty-one, and he's rich! The world is an oyster, but you don't crack it open on a mattress!

HAPPY: Pop, I told you I'm gonna retire you for life.

WILLY: You'll retire me for life on seventy goddam dollars a week? And your women and your car and your apartment, and you'll retire me for life! Christ's sake, I couldn't get past Yonkers today! Where are you guys, where are you? The woods are burning! I can't drive a car!

> [CHARLEY *has appeared in the doorway. He is a large man, slow of speech, laconic, immovable. In all he says, despite what he says, there is pity, and now, trepidation. He has a robe over pajamas, slippers on his feet. He enters the kitchen.*]

CHARLEY: Everything all right?

HAPPY: Yeah, Charley, everything's . . .

WILLY: What's the matter?

CHARLEY: I heard some noise. I thought something happened. Can't we do something about the walls? You sneeze in here, and in my house hats blow off.

HAPPY: Let's go to bed, Dad. Come on.

> [CHARLEY *signals to* HAPPY *to go.*]

WILLY: You go ahead, I'm not tired at the moment.

HAPPY: [*To* WILLY.] Take it easy, huh? [*He exits.*]

WILLY: What're you doin' up?

CHARLEY: [*Sitting down at the kitchen table opposite* WILLY.] Couldn't sleep good. I had a heartburn.

WILLY: Well, you don't know how to eat.

CHARLEY: I eat with my mouth.

WILLY: No, you're ignorant. You gotta know about vitamins and things like that.

CHARLEY: Come on, let's shoot. Tire you out a little.

WILLY: [*Hesitantly.*] All right. You got cards?

CHARLEY: [*Taking a deck from his pocket.*] Yeah, I got them. Someplace. What is it with those vitamins?

WILLY: [*Dealing.*] They build up your bones. Chemistry.

CHARLEY: Yeah, but there's no bones in a heartburn.

WILLY: What are you talkin' about? Do you know the first thing about it?

CHARLEY: Don't get insulted.

WILLY: Don't talk about something you don't know anything about.

[*They are playing. Pause.*]

CHARLEY: What're you doin' home?

WILLY: A little trouble with the car.

CHARLEY: Oh. [*Pause.*] I'd like to take a trip to California.

WILLY: Don't say.

CHARLEY: You want a job?

WILLY: I got a job, I told you that. [*After a slight pause.*] What the hell are you offering me a job for?

CHARLEY: Don't get insulted.

WILLY: Don't insult me.

CHARLEY: I don't see no sense in it. You don't have to go on this way.

WILLY: I got a good job. [*Slight pause.*] What do you keep comin' in here for?

CHARLEY: You want me to go?

WILLY: [*After a pause, withering.*] I can't understand it. He's going back to Texas again. What the hell is that?

CHARLEY: Let him go.

WILLY: I got nothin' to give him, Charley, I'm clean, I'm clean.

CHARLEY: He won't starve. None a them starve. Forget about him.

WILLY: Then what have I got to remember?

CHARLEY: You take it too hard. To hell with it. When a deposit bottle is broken you don't get your nickel back.

WILLY: That's easy enough for you to say.

CHARLEY: That ain't easy for me to say.

WILLY: Did you see the ceiling I put up in the living-room?

CHARLEY: Yeah, that's a piece of work. To put up a ceiling is a mystery to me. How do you do it?

WILLY: What's the difference?

CHARLEY: Well, talk about it.

WILLY: You gonna put up a ceiling?

CHARLEY: How could I put up a ceiling?

WILLY: Then what the hell are you bothering me for?

CHARLEY: You're insulted again.

WILLY: A man who can't handle tools is not a man. You're disgusting.

CHARLEY: Don't call me disgusting, Willy.

[UNCLE BEN, *carrying a valise and an umbrella, enters the forestage from around the right corner of the house. He is a stolid man, in his sixties, with a mustache and an authoritative air. He is utterly certain of his destiny, and there is an aura of far places about him. He enters exactly as* WILLY *speaks.*]

WILLY: I'm getting awfully tired, Ben.

[BEN'*s music is heard.* BEN *looks around at everything.*]

CHARLEY: Good, keep playing; you'll sleep better. Did you call me Ben?

[BEN *looks at his watch.*]

WILLY: That's funny. For a second there you reminded me of my brother Ben.

BEN: I only have a few minutes. [*He strolls, inspecting the place.* WILLY *and* CHARLEY *continue playing.*]

CHARLEY: You never heard from him again, heh? Since that time?

WILLY: Didn't Linda tell you? Couple of weeks ago we got a letter from his wife in Africa. He died.

CHARLEY: That so.

BEN: [*Chuckling.*] So this is Brooklyn, eh?

CHARLEY: Maybe you're in for some of his money.

WILLY: Naa, he had seven sons. There's just one opportunity I had with that man . . .

BEN: I must make a train, William. There are several properties I'm looking at in Alaska.

WILLY: Sure, sure! If I'd gone with him to Alaska that time, everything would've been totally different.

CHARLEY: Go on, you'da froze to death up there.

WILLY: What're you talking about?

BEN: Opportunity is tremendous in Alaska, William. Surprised you're not up there.

WILLY: Sure, tremendous.

CHARLEY: Heh?

WILLY: There was the only man I ever met who knew the answers.

CHARLEY: Who?

BEN: How are you all?

WILLY: [*Taking a pot, smiling.*] Fine, fine.

CHARLEY: Pretty sharp tonight.

BEN: Is Mother living with you?

WILLY: No, she died a long time ago.

CHARLEY: Who?

BEN: That's too bad. Fine specimen of a lady, Mother.

WILLY: [*To* CHARLEY.] Heh?

BEN: I'd hoped to see the old girl.

CHARLEY: Who died?

BEN: Heard anything from Father, have you?

WILLY: [*Unnerved.*] What do you mean, who died?

CHARLEY: [*Taking a pot.*] What're you talkin' about?

BEN: [*Looking at his watch.*] William, it's half-past eight!

WILLY: [*As though to dispel his confusion he angrily stops* CHARLEY's *hand.*] That's my build!

CHARLEY: I put the ace—

WILLY: If you don't know how to play the game I'm not gonna throw my money away on you!

CHARLEY: [*Rising.*] It was my ace, for God's sake!

WILLY: I'm through, I'm through!

BEN: When did Mother die?

WILLY: Long ago. Since the beginning you never knew how to play cards.

CHARLEY: [*Picks up the cards and goes to the door.*] All right! Next time I'll bring a deck with five aces.

WILLY: I don't play that kind of game!

CHARLEY: [*Turning to him.*] You ought to be ashamed of yourself!

WILLY: Yeah?

CHARLEY: Yeah! [*He goes out.*]

WILLY: [*Slamming the door after him.*] Ignoramus!

BEN: [*As* WILLY *comes toward him through the wall-line of the kitchen.*] So you're William.

WILLY: [*Shaking* BEN'S *hand.*] Ben! I've been waiting for you so long! What's the answer? How did you do it?

BEN: Oh, there's a story in that.

[LINDA *enters the forestage, as of old, carrying the wash basket.*]

LINDA: Is this Ben?

BEN: [*Gallantly.*] How do you do, my dear.

LINDA: Where've you been all these years? Willy's always wondered why you—

WILLY: [*Pulling* BEN *away from her impatiently.*] Where is Dad? Didn't you follow him? How did you get started?

BEN: Well, I don't know how much you remember.

WILLY: Well, I was just a baby, of course, only three or four years old—

BEN: Three years and eleven months.

WILLY: What a memory, Ben!

BEN: I have many enterprises, William, and I have never kept books.

WILLY: I remember I was sitting under the wagon in—was it Nebraska?

BEN: It was South Dakota, and I gave you a bunch of wild flowers.

WILLY: I remember you walking away down some open road.

BEN: [*Laughing.*] I was going to find Father in Alaska.

WILLY: Where is he?

BEN: At that age I had a very faulty view of geography, William. I discovered after a few days that I was heading due south, so instead of Alaska, I ended up in Africa.

LINDA: Africa!

WILLY: The Gold Coast!

BEN: Principally diamond mines.

LINDA: Diamond mines!

BEN: Yes, my dear. But I've only a few minutes—

WILLY: No! Boys! Boys! [*Young* BIFF *and* HAPPY *appear.*] Listen to this. This is your Uncle Ben, a great man! Tell my boys, Ben!

BEN: Why, boys, when I was seventeen I walked into the jungle, and when I was twenty-one I walked out. [*He laughs.*] And by God I was rich.

WILLY: [*To the boys.*] You see what I been talking about? The greatest things can happen!

BEN: [*Glancing at his watch.*] I have an appointment in Ketchikan Tuesday week.[8]

WILLY: No, Ben! Please tell about Dad. I want my boys to hear. I want them to know the kind of stock they spring from. All I remember is a man with a big beard, and I was in Mamma's lap, sitting around a fire, and some kind of high music.

BEN: His flute. He played the flute.

WILLY: Sure, the flute, that's right!

[*New music is heard, a high, rollicking tune.*]

BEN: Father was a very great and a very wild-hearted man. We would start in Boston, and he'd toss the whole family into the wagon, and then he'd drive the

_____

8. That is, in Ketchikan, Alaska, one week from Tuesday.

team right across the country; through Ohio, and Indiana, Michigan, Illinois, and all the Western states. And we'd stop in the towns and sell the flutes that he'd made on the way. Great inventor, Father. With one gadget he made more in a week than a man like you could make in a lifetime.

WILLY: That's just the way I'm bringing them up, Ben—rugged, well liked, all-around.

BEN: Yeah? [*To* BIFF.] Hit that, boy—hard as you can. [*He pounds his stomach.*]

BIFF: Oh, no, sir!

BEN: [*Taking boxing stance.*] Come on, get to me! [*He laughs.*]

WILLY: Go to it, Biff! Go ahead, show him!

BIFF: Okay! [*He cocks his fist and starts in.*]

LINDA: [*To* WILLY.] Why must he fight, dear?

BEN: [*Sparring with* BIFF.] Good boy! Good boy!

WILLY: How's that, Ben, heh?

HAPPY: Give him the left, Biff!

LINDA: Why are you fighting?

BEN: Good boy! [*Suddenly comes in, trips* BIFF, *and stands over him, the point of his umbrella poised over* BIFF's *eye.*]

LINDA: Look out, Biff!

BIFF: Gee!

BEN: [*Patting* BIFF's *knee.*] Never fight fair with a stranger, boy. You'll never get out of the jungle that way. [*Taking* LINDA's *hand and bowing.*] It was an honor and a pleasure to meet you, Linda.

LINDA: [*Withdrawing her hand coldly, frightened.*] Have a nice—trip.

BEN: [*To* WILLY.] And good luck with your—what do you do?

WILLY: Selling.

BEN: Yes. Well . . . [*He raises his hand in farewell to all.*]

WILLY: No, Ben, I don't want you to think . . . [*He takes* BEN's *arm to show him.*] It's Brooklyn, I know, but we hunt too.

BEN: Really, now.

WILLY: Oh, sure, there's snakes and rabbits and—that's why I moved out here. Why, Biff can fell any one of these trees in no time! Boys! Go right over to where they're building the apartment house and get some sand. We're gonna rebuild the entire front stoop right now! Watch this, Ben!

BIFF: Yes, sir! On the double, Hap!

HAPPY: [*As he and* BIFF *run off.*] I lost weight, Pop, you notice?

[CHARLEY *enters in knickers, even before the boys are gone.*]

CHARLEY: Listen, if they steal any more from that building the watchman'll put the cops on them!

LINDA: [*To* WILLY.] Don't let Biff . . .

[BEN *laughs lustily.*]

WILLY: You shoulda seen the lumber they brought home last week. At least a dozen six-by-tens worth all kinds a money.

CHARLEY: Listen, if that watchman—

WILLY: I gave them hell, understand. But I got a couple of fearless characters there.

CHARLEY: Willy, the jails are full of fearless characters.

BEN: [*Clapping* WILLY *on the back, with a laugh at* CHARLEY.] And the stock exchange, friend!

WILLY: [*Joining in* BEN's *laughter.*] Where are the rest of your pants?

CHARLEY: My wife bought them.

WILLY: Now all you need is a golf club and you can go upstairs and go to sleep. [*To* BEN.] Great athlete! Between him and his son Bernard they can't hammer a nail!

BERNARD: [*Rushing in.*] The watchman's chasing Biff!

WILLY: [*Angrily.*] Shut up! He's not stealing anything!

LINDA: [*Alarmed, hurrying off left.*] Where is he? Biff, dear! [*She exits.*]

WILLY: [*Moving toward the left, away from* BEN.] There's nothing wrong. What's the matter with you?

BEN: Nervy boy. Good!

WILLY: [*Laughing.*] Oh, nerves of iron, that Biff!

CHARLEY: Don't know what it is. My New England man comes back and he's bleedin', they murdered him up there.

WILLY: It's contacts, Charley, I got important contacts!

CHARLEY: [*Sarcastically.*] Glad to hear it, Willy. Come in later, we'll shoot a little casino. I'll take some of your Portland money. [*He laughs at* WILLY *and exits.*]

WILLY: [*Turning to* BEN.] Business is bad, it's murderous. But not for me, of course.

BEN: I'll stop by on my way back to Africa.

WILLY: [*Longingly.*] Can't you stay a few days? You're just what I need, Ben, because I—I have a fine position here, but I—well, Dad left when I was such a baby and I never had a chance to talk to him and I still feel—kind of temporary about myself.

BEN: I'll be late for my train.

[*They are at opposite ends of the stage.*]

WILLY: Ben, my boys—can't we talk? They'd go into the jaws of hell for me, see, but I—

BEN: William, you're being first-rate with your boys. Outstanding, manly chaps!

WILLY: [*Hanging on to his words.*] Oh, Ben, that's good to hear! Because sometimes I'm afraid that I'm not teaching them the right kind of—Ben, how should I teach them?

BEN: [*Giving great weight to each word, and with a certain vicious audacity.*] William, when I walked into the jungle, I was seventeen. When I walked out I was twenty-one. And, by God, I was rich! [*He goes off into darkness around the right corner of the house.*]

WILLY: . . . was rich! That's just the spirit I want to imbue them with! To walk into a jungle! I was right! I was right! I was right!

[BEN *is gone, but* WILLY *is still speaking to him as* LINDA, *in nightgown and robe, enters the kitchen, glances around for* WILLY, *then goes to the door of the house, looks out and sees him. Comes down to his left. He looks at her.*]

LINDA: Willy, dear? Willy?

WILLY: I was right!

LINDA: Did you have some cheese? [*He can't answer.*] It's very late, darling. Come to bed, heh?

WILLY: [*Looking straight up.*] Gotta break your neck to see a star in this yard.

LINDA: You coming in?

WILLY: Whatever happened to that diamond watch fob? Remember? When Ben came from Africa that time? Didn't he give me a watch fob with a diamond in it?

LINDA: You pawned it, dear. Twelve, thirteen years ago. For Biff's radio correspondence course.

WILLY: Gee, that was a beautiful thing. I'll take a walk.

LINDA: But you're in your slippers.

WILLY: [*Starting to go around the house at the left.*] I was right! I was! [*Half to* LINDA, *as he goes, shaking his head.*] What a man! There was a man worth talking to. I was right!

LINDA: [*Calling after* WILLY.] But in your slippers, Willy!

[WILLY *is almost gone when* BIFF, *in his pajamas, comes down the stairs and enters the kitchen.*]

BIFF: What is he doing out there?

LINDA: Sh!

BIFF: God Almighty, Mom, how long has he been doing this?

LINDA: Don't, he'll hear you.

BIFF: What the hell is the matter with him?

LINDA: It'll pass by morning.

BIFF: Shouldn't we do anything?

LINDA: Oh, my dear, you should do a lot of things, but there's nothing to do, so go to sleep.

[HAPPY *comes down the stairs and sits on the steps.*]

HAPPY: I never heard him so loud, Mom.

LINDA: Well, come around more often; you'll hear him. [*She sits down at the table and mends the lining of* WILLY's *jacket.*]

BIFF: Why didn't you ever write me about this, Mom?

LINDA: How would I write to you? For over three months you had no address.

BIFF: I was on the move. But you know I thought of you all the time. You know that, don't you, pal?

LINDA: I know, dear, I know. But he likes to have a letter. Just to know that there's still a possibility for better things.

BIFF: He's not like this all the time, is he?

LINDA: It's when you come home he's always the worst.

BIFF: When I come home?

LINDA: When you write you're coming, he's all smiles, and talks about the future, and—he's just wonderful. And then the closer you seem to come, the more shaky he gets, and then, by the time you get here, he's arguing, and he seems angry at you. I think it's just that maybe he can't bring himself to—to open up to you. Why are you so hateful to each other? Why is that?

BIFF: [*Evasively.*] I'm not hateful, Mom.

LINDA: But you no sooner come in the door than you're fighting!

BIFF: I don't know why. I mean to change. I'm tryin', Mom, you understand?

LINDA: Are you home to stay now?

BIFF: I don't know. I want to look around, see what's doin'.

LINDA: Biff, you can't look around all your life, can you?

BIFF: I just can't take hold, Mom. I can't take hold of some kind of a life.

LINDA: Biff, a man is not a bird, to come and go with the springtime.

BIFF: Your hair . . . [*He touches her hair.*] Your hair got so gray.

LINDA: Oh, it's been gray since you were in high school. I just stopped dyeing it, that's all.

BIFF: Dye it again, will ya? I don't want my pal looking old. [*He smiles.*]

LINDA: You're such a boy! You think you can go away for a year and . . . You've got to get it into your head now that one day you'll knock on this door and there'll be strange people here—

BIFF: What are you talking about? You're not even sixty, Mom.

LINDA: But what about your father?

BIFF: [*Lamely.*] Well, I meant him too.

HAPPY: He admires Pop.

LINDA: Biff, dear, if you don't have any feeling for him, then you can't have any feeling for me.

BIFF: Sure I can, Mom.

LINDA: No. You can't just come to see me, because I love him. [*With a threat, but only a threat, of tears.*] He's the dearest man in the world to me, and I won't have anyone making him feel unwanted and low and blue. You've got to make up your mind now, darling, there's no leeway anymore. Either he's your father and you pay him that respect, or else you're not to come here. I know he's not easy to get along with—nobody knows that better than me—but . . .

WILLY: [*From the left, with a laugh.*] Hey, hey, Biffo!

BIFF: [*Starting to go out after* WILLY.] What the hell is the matter with him? [HAPPY *stops him.*]

LINDA: Don't—don't go near him!

BIFF: Stop making excuses for him! He always, always wiped the floor with you. Never had an ounce of respect for you.

HAPPY: He's always had respect for—

BIFF: What the hell do you know about it?

HAPPY: [*Surlily.*] Just don't call him crazy!

BIFF: He's got no character—Charley wouldn't do this. Not in his own house—spewing out that vomit from his mind.

HAPPY: Charley never had to cope with what he's got to.

BIFF: People are worse off than Willy Loman. Believe me, I've seen them!

LINDA: Then make Charley your father, Biff. You can't do that, can you? I don't say he's a great man. Willy Loman never made a lot of money. His name was never in the paper. He's not the finest character that ever lived. But he's a human being, and a terrible thing is happening to him. So attention must be paid. He's not to be allowed to fall into his grave like an old dog. Attention, attention must be finally paid to such a person. You called him crazy—

BIFF: I didn't mean—

LINDA: No, a lot of people think he's lost his—balance. But you don't have to be very smart to know what his trouble is. The man is exhausted.

HAPPY: Sure!

LINDA: A small man can be just as exhausted as a great man. He works for a company thirty-six years this March, opens up unheard-of territories to their trademark, and now in his old age they take his salary away.

HAPPY: [*Indignantly.*] I didn't know that, Mom.

LINDA: You never asked, my dear! Now that you get your spending money some-place else you don't trouble your mind with him.

HAPPY: But I gave you money last—

LINDA: Christmas time, fifty dollars! To fix the hot water it cost ninety-seven fifty! For five weeks he's been on straight commission, like a beginner, an unknown!

BIFF: Those ungrateful bastards!

LINDA: Are they any worse than his sons? When he brought them business, when he was young, they were glad to see him. But now his old friends, the old buy-ers that loved him so and always found some order to hand him in a pinch—they're all dead, retired. He used to be able to make six, seven calls a day in Boston. Now he takes his valises out of the car and puts them back and takes them out again and he's exhausted. Instead of walking he talks now. He drives seven hundred miles, and when he gets there no one knows him anymore, no one welcomes him. And what goes through a man's mind, driving seven hun-dred miles home without having earned a cent? Why shouldn't he talk to him-self? Why? When he has to go to Charley and borrow fifty dollars a week and pretend to me that it's his pay? How long can that go on? How long? You see what I'm sitting here and waiting for? And you tell me he has no character? The man who never worked a day but for your benefit? When does he get the medal for that? Is this his reward—to turn around at the age of sixty-three and find his sons, who he loved better than his life, one a philandering bum—

HAPPY: Mom!

LINDA: That's all you are, my baby! [*To* BIFF.] And you! What happened to the love you had for him? You were such pals! How you used to talk to him on the phone every night! How lonely he was till he could come home to you!

BIFF: All right, Mom. I'll live here in my room, and I'll get a job. I'll keep away from him, that's all.

LINDA: No, Biff. You can't stay here and fight all the time.

BIFF: He threw me out of this house, remember that.

LINDA: Why did he do that? I never knew why.

BIFF: Because I know he's a fake and he doesn't like anybody around who knows!

LINDA: Why a fake? In what way? What do you mean?

BIFF: Just don't lay it all at my feet. It's between me and him—that's all I have to say. I'll chip in from now on. He'll settle for half my paycheck. He'll be all right. I'm going to bed. [*He starts for the stairs.*]

LINDA: He won't be all right.

BIFF: [*Turning on the stairs, furiously.*] I hate this city and I'll stay here. Now what do you want?

LINDA: He's dying, Biff.

[HAPPY *turns quickly to her, shocked.*]

BIFF: [*After a pause.*] Why is he dying?

LINDA: He's been trying to kill himself.

BIFF: [*With great horror.*] How?

LINDA: I live from day to day.

BIFF: What're you talking about?

LINDA: Remember I wrote you that he smashed up the car again? In February?

BIFF: Well?

LINDA: The insurance inspector came. He said that they have evidence. That all these accidents in the last year—weren't—weren't—accidents.

HAPPY: How can they tell that? That's a lie.

LINDA: It seems there's a woman . . . [*She takes a breath as.* . . .]

⎧ BIFF: [*Sharply but contained.*] What woman?

⎩ LINDA: [*Simultaneously.*] . . . and this woman . . .

LINDA: What?

BIFF: Nothing. Go ahead.

LINDA: What did you say?

BIFF: Nothing. I just said what woman?

HAPPY: What about her?

LINDA: Well, it seems she was walking down the road and saw his car. She says that he wasn't driving fast at all, and that he didn't skid. She says he came to that little bridge, and then deliberately smashed into the railing, and it was only the shallowness of the water that saved him.

BIFF: Oh, no, he probably just fell asleep again.

LINDA: I don't think he fell asleep.

BIFF: Why not?

LINDA: Last month . . . [*With great difficulty.*] Oh, boys, it's so hard to say a thing like this! He's just a big stupid man to you, but I tell you there's more good in him than in many other people. [*She chokes, wipes her eyes.*] I was looking for a fuse. The lights blew out, and I went down the cellar. And behind the fuse box—it happened to fall out—was a length of rubber pipe—just short.

HAPPY: No kidding?

LINDA: There's a little attachment on the end of it. I knew right away. And sure enough, on the bottom of the water heater there's a new little nipple on the gas pipe.

HAPPY: [*Angrily.*] That—jerk.

BIFF: Did you have it taken off?

LINDA: I'm—I'm ashamed to. How can I mention it to him? Every day I go down and take away that little rubber pipe. But, when he comes home, I put it back where it was. How can I insult him that way? I don't know what to do. I live from day to day, boys. I tell you, I know every thought in his mind. It sounds so old-fashioned and silly, but I tell you he put his whole life into you and you've turned your backs on him. [*She is bent over in the chair, weeping, her face in her hands.*] Biff, I swear to God! Biff, his life is in your hands!

HAPPY: [*To* BIFF.] How do you like that damned fool!

BIFF: [*Kissing her.*] All right, pal, all right. It's all settled now. I've been remiss. I know that, Mom. But now I'll stay, and I swear to you, I'll apply myself. [*Kneeling in front of her, in a fever of self-reproach.*] It's just—you see, Mom, I don't fit in business. Not that I won't try. I'll try, and I'll make good.

HAPPY: Sure you will. The trouble with you in business was you never tried to please people.

BIFF: I know, I—

HAPPY: Like when you worked for Harrison's. Bob Harrison said you were tops, and then you go and do some damn fool thing like whistling whole songs in the elevator like a comedian.

BIFF: [*Against* HAPPY.] So what? I like to whistle sometimes.

HAPPY: You don't raise a guy to a responsible job who whistles in the elevator!

LINDA: Well, don't argue about it now.

HAPPY: Like when you'd go off and swim in the middle of the day instead of taking the line around.

BIFF: [*His resentment rising.*] Well, don't you run off? You take off sometimes, don't you? On a nice summer day?

HAPPY: Yeah, but I cover myself!

LINDA: Boys!

HAPPY: If I'm going to take a fade the boss can call any number where I'm supposed to be and they'll swear to him that I just left. I'll tell you something that I hate to say, Biff, but in the business world some of them think you're crazy.

BIFF: [*Angered.*] Screw the business world!

HAPPY: All right, screw it! Great, but cover yourself!

LINDA: Hap, Hap!

BIFF: I don't care what they think! They've laughed at Dad for years, and you know why? Because we don't belong in this nuthouse of a city! We should be mixing cement on some open plain, or—or carpenters. A carpenter is allowed to whistle!

[WILLY *walks in from the entrance of the house, at left.*]

WILLY: Even your grandfather was better than a carpenter. [*Pause. They watch him.*] You never grew up. Bernard does not whistle in the elevator, I assure you.

BIFF: [*As though to laugh* WILLY *out of it.*] Yeah, but you do, Pop.

WILLY: I never in my life whistled in an elevator! And who in the business world thinks I'm crazy?

BIFF: I didn't mean it like that, Pop. Now don't make a whole thing out of it, will ya?

WILLY: Go back to the West! Be a carpenter, a cowboy, enjoy yourself!

LINDA: Willy, he was just saying—

WILLY: I heard what he said!

HAPPY: [*Trying to quiet* WILLY.] Hey, Pop, come on now . . .

WILLY: [*Continuing over* HAPPY'*s line.*] They laugh at me, heh? Go to Filene's, go to the Hub, go to Slattery's Boston. Call out the name Willy Loman and see what happens! Big shot!

BIFF: All right, Pop.

WILLY: Big!

BIFF: All right!

WILLY: Why do you always insult me?

BIFF: I didn't say a word. [*To* LINDA.] Did I say a word?

LINDA: He didn't say anything, Willy.

WILLY: [*Going to the doorway of the living-room.*] All right, good night, good night.

LINDA: Willy, dear, he just decided . . .

WILLY: [*To* BIFF.] If you get tired hanging around tomorrow, paint the ceiling I put up in the living-room.

BIFF: I'm leaving early tomorrow.

HAPPY: He's going to see Bill Oliver, Pop.

WILLY: [*Interestedly.*] Oliver? For what?

BIFF: [*With reserve, but trying, trying.*] He always said he'd stake me. I'd like to go into business, so maybe I can take him up on it.

LINDA: Isn't that wonderful?

WILLY: Don't interrupt. What's wonderful about it? There's fifty men in the City of New York who'd stake him. [*To* BIFF.] Sporting goods?

BIFF: I guess so. I know something about it and—

WILLY: He knows something about it! You know sporting goods better than Spalding,[9] for God's sake! How much is he giving you?

BIFF: I don't know, I didn't even see him yet, but—

WILLY: Then what're you talkin' about?

BIFF: [*Getting angry.*] Well, all I said was I'm gonna see him, that's all!

WILLY: [*Turning away.*] Ah, you're counting your chickens again.

BIFF: [*Starting left for the stairs.*] Oh, Jesus, I'm going to sleep!

WILLY: [*Calling after him.*] Don't curse in this house!

BIFF: [*Turning.*] Since when did you get so clean?

HAPPY: [*Trying to stop them.*] Wait a . . .

WILLY: Don't use that language to me! I won't have it!

HAPPY: [*Grabbing* BIFF, *shouts.*] Wait a minute! I got an idea. I got a feasible idea. Come here, Biff, let's talk this over now, let's talk some sense here. When I was down in Florida last time, I thought of a great idea to sell sporting goods. It just came back to me. You and I, Biff—we have a line, the Loman Line. We train a couple of weeks, and put on a couple of exhibitions, see?

WILLY: That's an idea!

HAPPY: Wait! We form two basketball teams, see? Two water-polo teams. We play each other. It's a million dollars' worth of publicity. Two brothers, see? The Loman Brothers. Displays in the Royal Palms—all the hotels. And banners over the ring and the basketball court: "Loman Brothers." Baby, we could sell sporting goods!

WILLY: That is a one-million-dollar idea!

LINDA: Marvelous!

BIFF: I'm in great shape as far as that's concerned.

HAPPY: And the beauty of it is, Biff, it wouldn't be like a business. We'd be out playin' ball again . . .

BIFF: [*Enthused.*] Yeah, that's . . .

WILLY: Million-dollar . . .

HAPPY: And you wouldn't get fed up with it, Biff. It'd be the family again. There'd be the old honor, and comradeship, and if you wanted to go off for a swim or somethin'—well, you'd do it! Without some smart cooky gettin' up ahead of you!

WILLY: Lick the world! You guys together could absolutely lick the civilized world.

BIFF: I'll see Oliver tomorrow. Hap, if we could work that out . . .

LINDA: Maybe things are beginning to—

WILLY: [*Wildly enthused, to* LINDA.] Stop interrupting! [*To* BIFF.] But don't wear sport jacket and slacks when you see Oliver.

BIFF: No, I'll—

WILLY: A business suit, and talk as little as possible, and don't crack any jokes.

9. Albert G. Spalding (1850–1915), American baseball player and sporting-goods manufacturer.

BIFF: He did like me. Always liked me.

LINDA: He loved you!

WILLY: [*To* LINDA.] Will you stop! [*To* BIFF.] Walk in very serious. You are not applying for a boy's job. Money is to pass. Be quiet, fine, and serious. Everybody
likes a kidder, but nobody lends him money.

HAPPY: I'll try to get some myself, Biff. I'm sure I can.

WILLY: I see great things for you kids, I think your troubles are over. But remember, start big and you'll end big. Ask for fifteen. How much you gonna ask for?

BIFF: Gee, I don't know—

WILLY: And don't say "Gee." "Gee" is a boy's word. A man walking in for fifteen
thousand dollars does not say "Gee!"

BIFF: Ten, I think, would be top though.

WILLY: Don't be so modest. You always started too low. Walk in with a big laugh.
Don't look worried. Start off with a couple of your good stories to lighten
things up. It's not what you say, it's how you say it—because personality always
wins the day.

LINDA: Oliver always thought the highest of him—

WILLY: Will you let me talk?

BIFF: Don't yell at her, Pop, will ya?

WILLY: [*Angrily.*] I was talking, wasn't I?

BIFF: I don't like you yelling at her all the time, and I'm tellin' you, that's all.

WILLY: What're you, takin' over this house?

LINDA: Willy—

WILLY: [*Turning on her.*] Don't take his side all the time, goddammit!

BIFF: [*Furiously.*] Stop yelling at her!

WILLY: [*Suddenly pulling on his cheek, beaten down, guilt ridden.*] Give my best to Bill
Oliver—he may remember me. [*He exits through the living-room doorway.*]

LINDA: [*Her voice subdued.*] What'd you have to start that for? [BIFF *turns away.*] You
see how sweet he was as soon as you talked hopefully? [*She goes over to* BIFF.]
Come up and say good night to him. Don't let him go to bed that way.

HAPPY: Come on, Biff, let's buck him up.

LINDA: Please, dear. Just say good night. It takes so little to make him happy.
Come. [*She goes through the living-room doorway, calling upstairs from within the
living-room.*] Your pajamas are hanging in the bathroom, Willy!

HAPPY: [*Looking toward where* LINDA *went out.*] What a woman! They broke the
mold when they made her. You know that, Biff?

BIFF: He's off salary. My God, working on commission!

HAPPY: Well, let's face it: he's no hot-shot selling man. Except that sometimes,
you have to admit, he's a sweet personality.

BIFF: [*Deciding.*] Lend me ten bucks, will ya? I want to buy some new ties.

HAPPY: I'll take you to a place I know. Beautiful stuff. Wear one of my striped
shirts tomorrow.

BIFF: She got gray. Mom got awful old. Gee, I'm gonna go in to Oliver tomorrow
and knock him for a—

HAPPY: Come on up. Tell that to Dad. Let's give him a whirl. Come on.

BIFF: [*Steamed up.*] You know, with ten thousand bucks, boy!

HAPPY: [*As they go into the living-room.*] That's the talk, Biff, that's the first time I've
heard the old confidence out of you! [*From within the living-room, fading off.*]
You're gonna live with me, kid, and any babe you want just say the word . . .

[*The last lines are hardly heard. They are mounting the stairs to their parents' bedroom.*]

LINDA: [*Entering her bedroom and addressing* WILLY, *who is in the bathroom. She is straightening the bed for him.*] Can you do anything about the shower? It drips.

WILLY: [*From the bathroom.*] All of a sudden everything falls to pieces! Goddam plumbing, oughta be sued, those people. I hardly finished putting it in and the thing . . . [*His words rumble off.*]

LINDA: I'm just wondering if Oliver will remember him. You think he might?

WILLY: [*Coming out of the bathroom in his pajamas.*] Remember him? What's the matter with you, you crazy? If he'd've stayed with Oliver he'd be on top by now! Wait'll Oliver gets a look at him. You don't know the average caliber anymore. The average young man today—[*He is getting into bed.*]—is got a caliber of zero. Greatest thing in the world for him was to bum around. [BIFF *and* HAPPY *enter the bedroom. Slight pause.* WILLY *stops short, looking at* BIFF.] Glad to hear it, boy.

HAPPY: He wanted to say good night to you, sport.

WILLY: [*To* BIFF.] Yeah. Knock him dead, boy. What'd you want to tell me?

BIFF: Just take it easy, Pop. Good night. [*He turns to go.*]

WILLY: [*Unable to resist.*] And if anything falls off the desk while you're talking to him—like a package or something—don't you pick it up. They have office boys for that.

LINDA: I'll make a big breakfast—

WILLY: Will you let me finish? [*To* BIFF.] Tell him you were in the business in the West. Not farm work.

BIFF: All right, Dad.

LINDA: I think everything—

WILLY: [*Going right through her speech.*] And don't undersell yourself. No less than fifteen thousand dollars.

BIFF: [*Unable to bear him.*] Okay. Good night, Mom. [*He starts moving.*]

WILLY: Because you got a greatness in you, Biff, remember that. You got all kinds of greatness . . . [*He lies back, exhausted.* BIFF *walks out.*]

LINDA: [*Calling after* BIFF.] Sleep well, darling!

HAPPY: I'm gonna get married, Mom. I wanted to tell you.

LINDA: Go to sleep, dear.

HAPPY: [*Going.*] I just wanted to tell you.

WILLY: Keep up the good work. [HAPPY *exits.*] God . . . remember that Ebbets Field[1] game? The championship of the city?

LINDA: Just rest. Should I sing to you?

WILLY: Yeah. Sing to me. [LINDA *hums a soft lullaby.*] When that team came out—he was the tallest, remember?

LINDA: Oh, yes. And in gold.

[BIFF *enters the darkened kitchen, takes a cigarette, and leaves the house. He comes downstage into a golden pool of light. He smokes, staring at the night.*]

WILLY: Like a young god. Hercules—something like that. And the sun, the sun all around him. Remember how he waved to me? Right up from the field, with the representatives of three colleges standing by? And the buyers I brought, and

1. Stadium where the Dodgers, Brooklyn's major-league baseball team, played from 1913 to 1957.

the cheers when he came out—Loman, Loman, Loman! God Almighty, he'll be great yet. A star like that, magnificent, can never really fade away!

[*The light on* WILLY *is fading. The gas heater begins to glow through the kitchen wall, near the stairs, a blue flame beneath red coils.*]

LINDA: [*Timidly.*] Willy dear, what has he got against you?
WILLY: I'm so tired. Don't talk anymore.

[BIFF *slowly returns to the kitchen. He stops, stares toward the heater.*]

LINDA: Will you ask Howard to let you work in New York?
WILLY: First thing in the morning. Everything'll be all right.

[BIFF *reaches behind the heater and draws out a length of rubber tubing. He is horrified and turns his head toward* WILLY's *room, still dimly lit, from which the strains of* LINDA's *desperate but monotonous humming rise.*]

WILLY: [*Staring through the window into the moonlight.*] Gee, look at the moon moving between the buildings!

[BIFF *wraps the tubing around his hand and quickly goes up the stairs.*]
    CURTAIN

ACT II

Music is heard, gay and bright. The curtain rises as the music fades away. WILLY, *in shirt sleeves, is sitting at the kitchen table, sipping coffee, his hat in his lap.* LINDA *is filling his cup when she can.*

WILLY: Wonderful coffee. Meal in itself.
LINDA: Can I make you some eggs?
WILLY: No. Take a breath.
LINDA: You look so rested, dear.
WILLY: I slept like a dead one. First time in months. Imagine, sleeping till ten on a Tuesday morning. Boys left nice and early, heh?
LINDA: They were out of here by eight o'clock.
WILLY: Good work!
LINDA: It was so thrilling to see them leaving together. I can't get over the shaving lotion in this house!
WILLY: [*Smiling.*] Mmm—
LINDA: Biff was very changed this morning. His whole attitude seemed to be hopeful. He couldn't wait to get downtown to see Oliver.
WILLY: He's heading for a change. There's no question, there simply are certain men that take longer to get—solidified. How did he dress?
LINDA: His blue suit. He's so handsome in that suit. He could be a—anything in that suit!

[WILLY *gets up from the table.* LINDA *holds his jacket for him.*]

WILLY: There's no question, no question at all. Gee, on the way home tonight I'd like to buy some seeds.
LINDA: [*Laughing.*] That'd be wonderful. But not enough sun gets back there. Nothing'll grow any more.

WILLY: You wait, kid, before it's all over we're gonna get a little place out in the country, and I'll raise some vegetables, a couple of chickens . . .

LINDA: You'll do it yet, dear.

[WILLY *walks out of his jacket.* LINDA *follows him.*]

WILLY: And they'll get married, and come for a weekend. I'd build a little guest house. 'Cause I got so many fine tools, all I'd need would be a little lumber and some peace of mind.

LINDA: [*Joyfully.*] I sewed the lining . . .

WILLY: I could build two guest houses, so they'd both come. Did he decide how much he's going to ask Oliver for?

LINDA: [*Getting him into the jacket.*] He didn't mention it, but I imagine ten or fifteen thousand. You going to talk to Howard today?

WILLY: Yeah. I'll put it to him straight and simple. He'll just have to take me off the road.

LINDA: And Willy, don't forget to ask for a little advance, because we've got the insurance premium. It's the grace period now.

WILLY: That's a hundred . . . ?

LINDA: A hundred and eight, sixty-eight. Because we're a little short again.

WILLY: Why are we short?

LINDA: Well, you had the motor job on the car . . .

WILLY: That goddam Studebaker!

LINDA: And you got one more payment on the refrigerator . . .

WILLY: But it just broke again!

LINDA: Well, it's old, dear.

WILLY: I told you we should've bought a well-advertised machine. Charley bought a General Electric and it's twenty years old and it's still good, that son-of-a-bitch.

LINDA: But, Willy—

WILLY: Whoever heard of a Hastings refrigerator? Once in my life I would like to own something outright before it's broken! I'm always in a race with the junkyard! I just finished paying for the car and it's on its last legs. The refrigerator consumes belts like a goddam maniac. They time those things. They time them so when you finally paid for them, they're used up.

LINDA: [*Buttoning up his jacket as he unbuttons it.*] All told, about two hundred dollars would carry us, dear. But that includes the last payment on the mortgage. After this payment, Willy, the house belongs to us.

WILLY: It's twenty-five years!

LINDA: Biff was nine years old when we bought it.

WILLY: Well, that's a great thing. To weather a twenty-five year mortgage is—

LINDA: It's an accomplishment.

WILLY: All the cement, the lumber, the reconstruction I put in this house! There ain't a crack to be found in it anymore.

LINDA: Well, it served its purpose.

WILLY: What purpose? Some stranger'll come along, move in, and that's that. If only Biff would take this house, and raise a family . . . [*He starts to go.*] Goodbye, I'm late.

LINDA: [*Suddenly remembering.*] Oh, I forgot! You're supposed to meet them for dinner.

WILLY: Me?

LINDA: At Frank's Chop House on Forty-eighth near Sixth Avenue.

WILLY: Is that so! How about you?

LINDA: No, just the three of you. They're gonna blow you to a big meal!

WILLY: Don't say! Who thought of that?

LINDA: Biff came to me this morning, Willy, and he said, "Tell Dad, we want to blow him to a big meal." Be there six o'clock. You and your two boys are going to have dinner.

WILLY: Gee whiz! That's really somethin'. I'm gonna knock Howard for a loop, kid. I'll get an advance, and I'll come home with a New York job. Goddammit, now I'm gonna do it!

LINDA: Oh, that's the spirit, Willy!

WILLY: I will never get behind a wheel the rest of my life!

LINDA: It's changing, Willy, I can feel it changing!

WILLY: Beyond a question. G'bye, I'm late. [He starts to go again.]

LINDA: [Calling after him as she runs to the kitchen table for a handkerchief.] You got your glasses?

WILLY: [Feels for them, then comes back in.] Yeah, yeah, got my glasses.

LINDA: [Giving him the handkerchief.] And a handkerchief.

WILLY: Yeah, handkerchief.

LINDA: And your saccharine?[2]

WILLY: Yeah, my saccharine.

LINDA: Be careful on the subway stairs.

[She kisses him, and a silk stocking is seen hanging from her hand. WILLY notices it.]

WILLY: Will you stop mending stockings? At least while I'm in the house. It gets me nervous. I can't tell you. Please.

[LINDA hides the stocking in her hand as she follows WILLY across the forestage in front of the house.]

LINDA: Remember, Frank's Chop House.

WILLY: [Passing the apron.[3]] Maybe beets would grow out there.

LINDA: [Laughing.] But you tried so many times.

WILLY: Yeah. Well, don't work hard today. [He disappears around the right corner of the house.]

LINDA: Be careful! [As WILLY vanishes, LINDA waves to him. Suddenly the phone rings. She runs across the stage and into the kitchen and lifts it.] Hello? Oh, Biff! I'm so glad you called, I just . . . Yes, sure, I just told him. Yes, he'll be there for dinner at six o'clock, I didn't forget. Listen, I was just dying to tell you. You know that little rubber pipe I told you about? That he connected to the gas heater? I finally decided to go down the cellar this morning and take it away and destroy it. But it's gone! Imagine? He took it away himself, it isn't there! [She listens.] When? Oh, then you took it. Oh—nothing, it's just that I'd hoped he'd taken it away himself. Oh, I'm not worried, darling, because this morning he left in such high spirits, it was like the old days! I'm not afraid anymore. Did Mr. Oliver see you? . . . Well, you wait there then. And make a nice impression on him, darling.

2. Artificial sweetener once recommended as a healthy alternative to sugar.
3. The foremost part of the stage, in front of the proscenium arch.

Just don't perspire too much before you see him. And have a nice time with Dad. He may have big news too! . . . That's right, a New York job. And be sweet to him tonight, dear. Be loving to him. Because he's only a little boat looking for a harbor. [*She is trembling with sorrow and joy.*] Oh, that's wonderful, Biff, you'll save his life. Thanks, darling. Just put your arm around him when he comes into the restaurant. Give him a smile. That's the boy . . . Good-bye, dear . . . You got your comb? . . . That's fine. Good-bye, Biff dear.

[*In the middle of her speech,* HOWARD WAGNER, *thirty-six, wheels on a small typewriter table on which is a wire-recording machine* [4] *and proceeds to plug it in. This is on the left forestage. Light slowly fades on* LINDA *as it rises on* HOWARD. HOWARD *is intent on threading the machine and only glances over his shoulder as* WILLY *appears.*]

WILLY: Pst! Pst!

HOWARD: Hello, Willy, come in.

WILLY: Like to have a little talk with you, Howard.

HOWARD: Sorry to keep you waiting. I'll be with you in a minute.

WILLY: What's that, Howard?

HOWARD: Didn't you ever see one of these? Wire recorder.

WILLY: Oh. Can we talk a minute?

HOWARD: Records things. Just got delivery yesterday. Been driving me crazy, the most terrific machine I ever saw in my life. I was up all night with it.

WILLY: What do you do with it?

HOWARD: I bought it for dictation, but you can do anything with it. Listen to this. I had it home last night. Listen to what I picked up. The first one is my daughter. Get this. [*He flicks the switch and "Roll out the Barrel" is heard being whistled.*] Listen to that kid whistle.

WILLY: That is lifelike, isn't it?

HOWARD: Seven years old. Get that tone.

WILLY: Ts, ts. Like to ask a little favor if you . . .

[*The whistling breaks off, and the voice of* HOWARD'*s daughter is heard.*]

HIS DAUGHTER: "Now you, Daddy."

HOWARD: She's crazy for me! [*Again the same song is whistled.*] That's me! Ha! [*He winks.*]

WILLY: You're very good!

[*The whistling breaks off again. The machine runs silent for a moment.*]

HOWARD: Sh! Get this now, this is my son.

HIS SON: "The capital of Alabama is Montgomery; the capital of Arizona is Phoenix; the capital of Arkansas is Little Rock; the capital of California is Sacramento . . ." [*And on, and on.*]

HOWARD: [*Holding up five fingers.*] Five years old, Willy!

WILLY: He'll make an announcer some day!

HIS SON: [*Continuing.*] "The capital . . ."

HOWARD: Get that—alphabetical order! [*The machine breaks off suddenly.*] Wait a minute. The maid kicked the plug out.

WILLY: It certainly is a—

---

4. Precursor to the tape recording machine.

HOWARD: Sh, for God's sake!

HIS SON: "It's nine o'clock, Bulova watch time.[5] So I have to go to sleep."

WILLY: That really is—

HOWARD: Wait a minute! The next is my wife.

   [*They wait.*]

HOWARD'S VOICE: "Go on, say something." [*Pause.*] "Well, you gonna talk?"

HIS WIFE: "I can't think of anything."

HOWARD'S VOICE: "Well, talk—it's turning."

HIS WIFE: [*Shyly, beaten.*] "Hello." [*Silence.*] "Oh, Howard, I can't talk into this . . ."

HOWARD: [*Snapping the machine off.*] That was my wife.

WILLY: That is a wonderful machine. Can we—

HOWARD: I tell you, Willy, I'm gonna take my camera, and my bandsaw, and all my hobbies, and out they go. This is the most fascinating relaxation I ever found.

WILLY: I think I'll get one myself.

HOWARD: Sure, they're only a hundred and a half. You can't do without it. Supposing you wanna hear Jack Benny,[6] see? But you can't be at home at that hour. So you tell the maid to turn the radio on when Jack Benny comes on, and this automatically goes on with the radio . . .

WILLY: And when you come home you . . .

HOWARD: You can come home twelve o'clock, one o'clock, any time you like, and you get yourself a Coke and sit yourself down, throw the switch, and there's Jack Benny's program in the middle of the night!

WILLY: I'm definitely going to get one. Because lots of time I'm on the road, and I think to myself, what I must be missing on the radio!

HOWARD: Don't you have a radio in the car?

WILLY: Well, yeah, but who ever thinks of turning it on?

HOWARD: Say, aren't you supposed to be in Boston?

WILLY: That's what I want to talk to you about, Howard. You got a minute? [*He draws a chair in from the wing.*]

HOWARD: What happened? What're you doing here?

WILLY: Well . . .

HOWARD: You didn't crack up again, did you?

WILLY: Oh, no. No . . .

HOWARD: Geez, you had me worried there for a minute. What's the trouble?

WILLY: Well, tell you the truth, Howard. I've come to the decision that I'd rather not travel anymore.

HOWARD: Not travel! Well, what'll you do?

WILLY: Remember, Christmas time, when you had the party here? You said you'd try to think of some spot for me here in town.

HOWARD: With us?

WILLY: Well, sure.

HOWARD: Oh, yeah, yeah. I remember. Well, I couldn't think of anything for you, Willy.

5. Phrase commonly heard on radio programs sponsored by the Bulova Watch Company.
6. A vaudeville, radio, television, and movie star (1894–1974); he hosted America's most popular radio show from 1932 to 1955.

WILLY: I tell ya, Howard. The kids are all grown up, y'know. I don't need much anymore. If I could take home—well, sixty-five dollars a week, I could swing it.

HOWARD: Yeah, but Willy, see I—

WILLY: I tell ya why, Howard. Speaking frankly and between the two of us, y'know—I'm just a little tired.

HOWARD: Oh, I could understand that, Willy. But you're a road man, Willy, and we do a road business. We've only got a half-dozen salesmen on the floor here.

WILLY: God knows, Howard, I never asked a favor of any man. But I was with the firm when your father used to carry you in here in his arms.

HOWARD: I know that, Willy, but—

WILLY: Your father came to me the day you were born and asked me what I thought of the name of Howard, may he rest in peace.

HOWARD: I appreciate that, Willy, but there just is no spot here for you. If I had a spot I'd slam you right in, but I just don't have a single solitary spot.

[*He looks for his lighter.* WILLY *has picked it up and gives it to him. Pause.*]

WILLY: [*With increasing anger.*] Howard, all I need to set my table is fifty dollars a week.

HOWARD: But where am I going to put you, kid?

WILLY: Look, it isn't a question of whether I can sell merchandise, is it?

HOWARD: No, but it's a business, kid, and everybody's gotta pull his own weight.

WILLY: [*Desperately.*] Just let me tell you a story, Howard—

HOWARD: 'Cause you gotta admit, business is business.

WILLY: [*Angrily.*] Business is definitely business, but just listen for a minute. You don't understand this. When I was a boy—eighteen, nineteen—I was already on the road. And there was a question in my mind as to whether selling had a future for me. Because in those days I had a yearning to go to Alaska. See, there were three gold strikes in one month in Alaska, and I felt like going out. Just for the ride, you might say.

HOWARD: [*Barely interested.*] Don't say.

WILLY: Oh, yeah, my father lived many years in Alaska. He was an adventurous man. We've got quite a little streak of self-reliance in our family. I thought I'd go out with my older brother and try to locate him, and maybe settle in the North with the old man. And I was almost decided to go, when I met a salesman in the Parker House. His name was Dave Singleman. And he was eighty-four years old, and he'd drummed merchandise in thirty-one states. And old Dave, he'd go up to his room, y'understand, put on his green velvet slippers—I'll never forget—and pick up his phone and call the buyers, and without ever leaving his room, at the age of eighty-four, he made a living. And when I saw that, I realized that selling was the greatest career a man could want. 'Cause what could be more satisfying than to be able to go, at the age of eighty-four, into twenty or thirty different cities, and pick up his phone and be remembered and loved and helped by so many different people? Do you know? when he died—and by the way he died the death of a salesman, in his green velvet slippers in the smoker[7] of the New York, New Haven and Hartford, going into

7. That is, smoking car on a train.

Boston—when he died, hundreds of salesmen and buyers were at his funeral. Things were sad on a lotta trains for months after that. [*He stands up.* HOWARD *has not looked at him.*] In those days there was personality in it, Howard. There was respect, and comradeship, and gratitude in it. Today, it's all cut and dried, and there's no chance for bringing friendship to bear—or personality. You see what I mean? They don't know me anymore.

HOWARD: [*Moving away, toward the right.*] That's just the thing, Willy.

WILLY: If I had forty dollars a week—that's all I'd need. Forty dollars, Howard.

HOWARD: Kid, I can't take blood from a stone, I—

WILLY: [*Desperation is on him now.*] Howard, the year Al Smith[8] was nominated, your father came to me and—

HOWARD: [*Starting to go off.*] I've got to see some people, kid.

WILLY: [*Stopping him.*] I'm talking about your father! There were promises made across this desk! You mustn't tell me you've got people to see—I put thirty-four years into this firm, Howard, and now I can't pay my insurance! You can't eat the orange and throw the peel away—a man is not a piece of fruit! [*After a pause.*] Now pay attention. Your father—in 1928 I had a big year. I averaged a hundred and seventy dollars a week in commissions.

HOWARD: [*Impatiently.*] Now, Willy, you never averaged—

WILLY: [*Banging his hand on the desk.*] I averaged a hundred and seventy dollars a week in the year of 1928! And your father came to me—or rather, I was in the office here—it was right over this desk—and he put his hand on my shoulder—

HOWARD: [*Getting up.*] You'll have to excuse me, Willy, I gotta see some people. Pull yourself together. [*Going out.*] I'll be back in a little while.

[*On* HOWARD's *exit, the light on his chair grows very bright and strange.*]

WILLY: Pull myself together! What the hell did I say to him? My God, I was yelling at him! How could I! [WILLY *breaks off, staring at the light, which occupies the chair, animating it. He approaches this chair, standing across the desk from it.*] Frank, Frank, don't you remember what you told me that time? How you put your hand on my shoulder, and Frank . . . [*He leans on the desk and as he speaks the dead man's name he accidentally switches on the recorder, and instantly.*]

HOWARD'S SON: ". . . of New York is Albany. The capital of Ohio is Cincinnati, the capital of Rhode Island is . . ." [*The recitation continues.*]

WILLY: [*Leaping away with fright, shouting.*] Ha! Howard! Howard! Howard!

HOWARD: [*Rushing in.*] What happened?

WILLY: [*Pointing at the machine, which continues nasally, childishly, with the capital cities.*] Shut it off! Shut it off!

HOWARD: [*Pulling the plug out.*] Look, Willy . . .

WILLY: [*Pressing his hands to his eyes.*] I gotta get myself some coffee. I'll get some coffee . . .

[WILLY *starts to walk out.* HOWARD *stops him.*]

HOWARD: [*Rolling up the cord.*] Willy, look . . .

WILLY: I'll go to Boston.

HOWARD: Willy, you can't go to Boston for us.

8. Alfred E. Smith (1873–1944), governor of New York and Democratic presidential nominee who lost to Herbert Hoover in 1928.

WILLY: Why can't I go?

HOWARD: I don't want you to represent us. I've been meaning to tell you for a long time now.

WILLY: Howard, are you firing me?

HOWARD: I think you need a good long rest, Willy.

WILLY: Howard—

HOWARD: And when you feel better, come back, and we'll see if we can work something out.

WILLY: But I gotta earn money, Howard. I'm in no position to—

HOWARD: Where are your sons? Why don't your sons give you a hand?

WILLY: They're working on a very big deal.

HOWARD: This is no time for false pride, Willy. You go to your sons and you tell them that you're tired. You've got two great boys, haven't you?

WILLY: Oh, no question, no question, but in the meantime . . .

HOWARD: Then that's that, heh?

WILLY: All right, I'll go to Boston tomorrow.

HOWARD: No, no.

WILLY: I can't throw myself on my sons. I'm not a cripple!

HOWARD: Look, kid, I'm busy, I'm busy this morning.

WILLY: [*Grasping* HOWARD's *arm.*] Howard, you've got to let me go to Boston!

HOWARD: [*Hard, keeping himself under control.*] I've got a line of people to see this morning. Sit down, take five minutes, and pull yourself together, and then go home, will ya? I need the office, Willy. [*He starts to go, turns, remembering the recorder, starts to push off the table holding the recorder.*] Oh, yeah. Whenever you can this week, stop by and drop off the samples. You'll feel better, Willy, and then come back and we'll talk. Pull yourself together, kid, there's people outside.

[HOWARD *exits, pushing the table off left.* WILLY *stares into space, exhausted. Now the music is heard—*BEN's *music—first distantly, then closer, closer. As* WILLY *speaks,* BEN *enters from the right. He carries valise and umbrella.*]

WILLY: Oh, Ben, how did you do it? What is the answer? Did you wind up the Alaska deal already?

BEN: Doesn't take much time if you know what you're doing. Just a short business trip. Boarding ship in an hour. Wanted to say good-by.

WILLY: Ben, I've got to talk to you.

BEN: [*Glancing at his watch.*] Haven't the time, William.

WILLY: [*Crossing the apron to* BEN.] Ben, nothing's working out. I don't know what to do.

BEN: Now, look here, William. I've bought timberland in Alaska and I need a man to look after things for me.

WILLY: God, timberland! Me and my boys in those grand outdoors!

BEN: You've a new continent at your doorstep, William. Get out of these cities, they're full of talk and time payments and courts of law. Screw on your fists and you can fight for a fortune up there.

WILLY: Yes, yes! Linda, Linda!

[LINDA *enters as of old, with the wash.*]

LINDA: Oh, you're back?

BEN: I haven't much time.

WILLY: No, wait! Linda, he's got a proposition for me in Alaska.

LINDA: But you've got—[*To* BEN.] He's got a beautiful job here.

WILLY: But in Alaska, kid, I could—

LINDA: You're doing well enough, Willy!

BEN: [*To* LINDA.] Enough for what, my dear?

LINDA: [*Frightened of* BEN *and angry at him.*] Don't say those things to him! Enough to be happy right here, right now. [*To* WILLY, *while* BEN *laughs.*] Why must everybody conquer the world? You're well liked, and the boys love you, and someday—[*To* BEN.]—why, old man Wagner told him just the other day that if he keeps it up he'll be a member of the firm, didn't he, Willy?

WILLY: Sure, sure. I am building something with this firm, Ben, and if a man is building something he must be on the right track, mustn't he?

BEN: What are you building? Lay your hand on it. Where is it?

WILLY: [*Hesitantly.*] That's true, Linda, there's nothing.

LINDA: Why? [*To* BEN.] There's a man eighty-four years old—

WILLY: That's right, Ben, that's right. When I look at that man I say, what is there to worry about?

BEN: Bah!

WILLY: It's true, Ben. All he has to do is go into any city, pick up the phone, and he's making his living and you know why?

BEN: [*Picking up his valise.*] I've got to go.

WILLY: [*Holding* BEN *back.*] Look at this boy! [BIFF, *in his high school sweater, enters carrying suitcase.* HAPPY *carries* BIFF's *shoulder guards, gold helmet, and football pants.*] Without a penny to his name, three great universities are begging for him, and from there the sky's the limit, because it's not what you do, Ben. It's who you know and the smile on your face! It's contacts, Ben, contacts! The whole wealth of Alaska passes over the lunch table at the Commodore Hotel, and that's the wonder, the wonder of this country, that a man can end with diamonds here on the basis of being liked! [*He turns to* BIFF.] And that's why when you get out on that field today it's important. Because thousands of people will be rooting for you and loving you. [*To* BEN, *who has again begun to leave.*] And Ben! when he walks into a business office his name will sound out like a bell and all the doors will open to him! I've seen it, Ben, I've seen it a thousand times! You can't feel it with your hand like timber, but it's there!

BEN: Good-by, William.

WILLY: Ben, am I right? Don't you think I'm right? I value your advice.

BEN: There's a new continent at your doorstep, William. You could walk out rich. Rich! [*He is gone.*]

WILLY: We'll do it here, Ben! You hear me? We're gonna do it here!

[*Young* BERNARD *rushes in. The gay music of the Boys is heard.*]

BERNARD: Oh, gee, I was afraid you left already!

WILLY: Why? What time is it?

BERNARD: It's half-past one!

WILLY: Well, come on, everybody! Ebbets Field next stop! Where's the pennants? [*He rushes through the wall-line of the kitchen and out into the living room.*]

LINDA: [*To* BIFF.] Did you pack fresh underwear?

BIFF: [*Who has been limbering up.*] I want to go!

BERNARD: Biff, I'm carrying your helmet, ain't I?

HAPPY: No, I'm carrying the helmet.

BERNARD: Oh, Biff, you promised me.

HAPPY: I'm carrying the helmet.

BERNARD: How am I going to get in the locker room?

LINDA: Let him carry the shoulder guards. [*She puts her coat and hat on in the kitchen.*]

BERNARD: Can I, Biff? 'Cause I told everybody I'm going to be in the locker room.

HAPPY: In Ebbets Field it's the clubhouse.

BERNARD: I meant the clubhouse, Biff!

HAPPY: Biff!

BIFF: [*Grandly, after a slight pause.*] Let him carry the shoulder guards.

HAPPY: [*As he gives* BERNARD *the shoulder guards.*] Stay close to us now.

[WILLY *rushes in with the pennants.*]

WILLY: [*Handing them out.*] Everybody wave when Biff comes out on the field. [HAPPY *and* BERNARD *run off.*] You set now, boy?

[*The music has died away.*]

BIFF: Ready to go, Pop. Every muscle is ready.

WILLY: [*At the edge of the apron.*] You realize what this means?

BIFF: That's right, Pop.

WILLY: [*Feeling* BIFF*'s muscles.*] You're comin' home this afternoon captain of the All-Scholastic Championship Team of the City of New York.

BIFF: I got it, Pop. And remember, pal, when I take off my helmet, that touchdown is for you.

WILLY: Let's go! [*He is starting out, with his arm around* BIFF, *when* CHARLEY *enters, as of old, in knickers.*] I got no room for you, Charley.

CHARLEY: Room? For what?

WILLY: In the car.

CHARLEY: You goin' for a ride? I wanted to shoot some casino.

WILLY: [*Furiously.*] Casino! [*Incredulously.*] Don't you realize what today is?

LINDA: Oh, he knows, Willy. He's just kidding you.

WILLY: That's nothing to kid about!

CHARLEY: No, Linda, what's goin' on?

LINDA: He's playing in Ebbets Field.

CHARLEY: Baseball in this weather?

WILLY: Don't talk to him. Come on, come on! [*He is pushing them out.*]

CHARLEY: Wait a minute, didn't you hear the news?

WILLY: What?

CHARLEY: Don't you listen to the radio? Ebbets Field just blew up.

WILLY: You go to hell! [CHARLEY *laughs. Pushing them out.*] Come on, come on! We're late.

CHARLEY: [*As they go.*] Knock a homer, Biff, knock a homer!

WILLY: [*The last to leave, turning to* CHARLEY.] I don't think that was funny, Charley. This is the greatest day of my life.

CHARLEY: Willy, when are you going to grow up?

WILLY: Yeah, heh? When this game is over, Charley, you'll be laughing out of the other side of your face. They'll be calling him another Red Grange.[9] Twenty-five thousand a year.

CHARLEY: [*Kidding.*] Is that so?

WILLY: Yeah, that's so.

CHARLEY: Well, then, I'm sorry, Willy. But tell me something.

WILLY: What?

CHARLEY: Who is Red Grange?

WILLY: Put up your hands. Goddam you, put up your hands! [CHARLEY, *chuckling, shakes his head and walks away, around the left corner of the stage.* WILLY *follows him. The music rises to a mocking frenzy.*] Who the hell do you think you are, better than everybody else? You don't know everything, you big, ignorant, stupid . . . Put up your hands!

> [*Light rises, on the right side of the forestage, on a small table in the reception room of* CHARLEY's *office. Traffic sounds are heard.* BERNARD, *now mature, sits whistling to himself. A pair of tennis rackets and an overnight bag are on the floor beside him.*]

WILLY: [*Offstage.*] What are you walking away for? Don't walk away! If you're going to say something say it to my face! I know you laugh at me behind my back. You'll laugh out of the other side of your goddam face after this game. Touchdown! Touchdown! Eighty thousand people! Touchdown! Right between the goal posts.

> [BERNARD *is a quiet, earnest, but self-assured young man.* WILLY's *voice is coming from right upstage now.* BERNARD *lowers his feet off the table and listens.* JENNY, *his father's secretary, enters.*]

JENNY: [*Distressed.*] Say, Bernard, will you go out in the hall?

BERNARD: What is that noise? Who is it?

JENNY: Mr. Loman. He just got off the elevator.

BERNARD: [*Getting up.*] Who's he arguing with?

JENNY: Nobody. There's nobody with him. I can't deal with him anymore, and your father gets all upset everytime he comes. I've got a lot of typing to do, and your father's waiting to sign it. Will you see him?

WILLY: [*Entering.*] Touchdown! Touch—[*He sees* JENNY.] Jenny, Jenny, good to see you. How're ya? Workin'? Or still honest?

JENNY: Fine. How've you been feeling?

WILLY: Not much anymore, Jenny. Ha, ha! [*He is surprised to see the rackets.*]

BERNARD: Hello, Uncle Willy.

WILLY: [*Almost shocked.*] Bernard! Well, look who's here! [*He comes quickly, guiltily to* BERNARD *and warmly shakes his hand.*]

BERNARD: How are you? Good to see you.

WILLY: What are you doing here?

BERNARD: Oh, just stopped by to see Pop. Get off my feet till my train leaves. I'm going to Washington in a few minutes.

WILLY: Is he in?

BERNARD: Yes, he's in his office with the accountant. Sit down.

9 Harold Edward Grange (1903–91), All-American halfback at the University of Illinois from 1923 to 1925; he played professionally for the Chicago Bears.

WILLY: [*Sitting down.*] What're you going to do in Washington?

BERNARD: Oh, just a case I've got there, Willy.

WILLY: That so? [*Indicating the rackets.*] You going to play tennis there?

BERNARD: I'm staying with a friend who's got a court.

WILLY: Don't say. His own tennis court. Must be fine people, I bet.

BERNARD: They are, very nice. Dad tells me Biff's in town.

WILLY: [*With a big smile.*] Yeah, Biff's in. Working on a very big deal, Bernard.

BERNARD: What's Biff doing?

WILLY: Well, he's been doing very big things in the West. But he decided to establish himself here. Very big. We're having dinner. Did I hear your wife had a boy?

BERNARD: That's right. Our second.

WILLY: Two boys! What do you know!

BERNARD: What kind of a deal has Biff got?

WILLY: Well, Bill Oliver—very big sporting-goods man—he wants Biff very badly. Called him in from the West. Long distance, carte blanche, special deliveries. Your friends have their own private tennis court?

BERNARD: You still with the old firm, Willy?

WILLY: [*After a pause.*] I'm—I'm overjoyed to see how you made the grade, Bernard, overjoyed. It's an encouraging thing to see a young man really—really—Looks very good for Biff—very—[*He breaks off, then.*] Bernard—[*He is so full of emotion, he breaks off again.*]

BERNARD: What is it, Willy?

WILLY: [*Small and alone.*] What—what's the secret?

BERNARD: What secret?

WILLY: How—how did you? Why didn't he ever catch on?

BERNARD: I wouldn't know that, Willy.

WILLY: [*Confidentially, desperately.*] You were his friend, his boyhood friend. There's something I don't understand about it. His life ended after that Ebbets Field game. From the age of seventeen nothing good ever happened to him.

BERNARD: He never trained himself for anything.

WILLY: But he did, he did. After high school he took so many correspondence courses. Radio mechanics; television; God knows what, and never made the slightest mark.

BERNARD: [*Taking off his glasses.*] Willy, do you want to talk candidly?

WILLY: [*Rising, faces* BERNARD.] I regard you as a very brilliant man, Bernard. I value your advice.

BERNARD: Oh, the hell with the advice, Willy. I couldn't advise you. There's just one thing I've always wanted to ask you. When he was supposed to graduate, and the math teacher flunked him—

WILLY: Oh, that son-of-a-bitch ruined his life.

BERNARD: Yeah, but, Willy, all he had to do was go to summer school and make up that subject.

WILLY: That's right, that's right.

BERNARD: Did you tell him not to go to summer school?

WILLY: Me? I begged him to go. I ordered him to go!

BERNARD: Then why wouldn't he go?

WILLY: Why? Why! Bernard, that question has been trailing me like a ghost for the last fifteen years. He flunked the subject, and laid down and died like a hammer hit him!

BERNARD: Take it easy, kid.

WILLY: Let me talk to you—I got nobody to talk to. Bernard, Bernard, was it my fault? Y'see? It keeps going around in my mind, maybe I did something to him. I got nothing to give him.

BERNARD: Don't take it so hard.

WILLY: Why did he lay down? What is the story there? You were his friend!

BERNARD: Willy, I remember, it was June, and our grades came out. And he'd flunked math.

WILLY: That son-of-a-bitch!

BERNARD: No, it wasn't right then. Biff just got very angry, I remember, and he was ready to enroll in summer school.

WILLY: [*Surprised.*] He was?

BERNARD: He wasn't beaten by it at all. But then, Willy, he disappeared from the block for almost a month. And I got the idea that he'd gone up to New England to see you. Did he have a talk with you then? [WILLY *stares in silence.*] Willy?

WILLY: [*With a strong edge of resentment in his voice.*] Yeah, he came to Boston. What about it?

BERNARD: Well, just that when he came back—I'll never forget this, it always mystifies me. Because I'd thought so well of Biff, even though he'd always taken advantage of me. I loved him, Willy, y'know? And he came back after that month and took his sneakers—remember those sneakers with "University of Virginia" printed on them? He was so proud of those, wore them every day. And he took them down in the cellar, and burned them up in the furnace. We had a fist fight. It lasted at least half an hour. Just the two of us, punching each other down the cellar, and crying right through it. I've often thought of how strange it was that I knew he'd given up his life. What happened in Boston, Willy? [WILLY *looks at him as at an intruder.*] I just bring it up because you asked me.

WILLY: [*Angrily.*] Nothing. What do you mean, "What happened?" What's that got to do with anything?

BERNARD: Well, don't get sore.

WILLY: What are you trying to do, blame it on me? If a boy lays down is that my fault?

BERNARD: Now, Willy, don't get—

WILLY: Well, don't—don't talk to me that way! What does that mean, "What happened?"

[CHARLEY *enters. He is in his vest, and he carries a bottle of bourbon.*]

CHARLEY: Hey, you're going to miss that train. [*He waves the bottle.*]

BERNARD: Yeah, I'm going. [*He takes the bottle.*] Thanks, Pop. [*He picks up his rackets and bag.*] Good-bye, Willy, and don't worry about it. You know, "If at first you don't succeed . . ."

WILLY: Yes, I believe in that.

BERNARD: But sometimes, Willy, it's better for a man just to walk away.

WILLY: Walk away?

BERNARD: That's right.

WILLY: But if you can't walk away?

BERNARD: [*After a slight pause.*] I guess that's when it's tough. [*Extending his hand.*] Good-bye, Willy.

WILLY: [*Shaking* BERNARD's *hand.*] Good-bye, boy.

CHARLEY: [*An arm on* BERNARD's *shoulder.*] How do you like this kid? Gonna argue a case in front of the Supreme Court.

BERNARD: [*Protesting.*] Pop!

WILLY: [*Genuinely shocked, pained, and happy.*] No! The Supreme Court!

BERNARD: I gotta run. 'Bye, Dad!

CHARLEY: Knock 'em dead, Bernard!

[BERNARD *goes off.*]

WILLY: [*As* CHARLEY *takes out his wallet.*] The Supreme Court! And he didn't even mention it!

CHARLEY: [*Counting out money on the desk.*] He don't have to—he's gonna do it.

WILLY: And you never told him what to do, did you? You never took any interest in him.

CHARLEY: My salvation is that I never took any interest in anything. There's some money—fifty dollars. I got an accountant inside.

WILLY: Charley, look . . . [*With difficulty.*] I got my insurance to pay. If you can manage it—I need a hundred and ten dollars. [CHARLEY *doesn't reply for a moment; merely stops moving.*] I'd draw it from my bank but Linda would know, and I . . .

CHARLEY: Sit down, Willy.

WILLY: [*Moving toward the chair.*] I'm keeping an account of everything, remember. I'll pay every penny back. [*He sits.*]

CHARLEY: Now listen to me, Willy.

WILLY: I want you to know I appreciate . . .

CHARLEY: [*Sitting down on the table.*] Willy, what're you doin'? What the hell is goin' on in your head?

WILLY: Why? I'm simply . . .

CHARLEY: I offered you a job. You can make fifty dollars a week. And I won't send you on the road.

WILLY: I've got a job.

CHARLEY: Without pay? What kind of job is a job without pay? [*He rises.*] Now, look kid, enough is enough. I'm no genius but I know when I'm being insulted.

WILLY: Insulted!

CHARLEY: Why don't you want to work for me?

WILLY: What's the matter with you? I've got a job.

CHARLEY: Then what're you walkin' in here every week for?

WILLY: [*Getting up.*] Well, if you don't want me to walk in here—

CHARLEY: I am offering you a job!

WILLY: I don't want your goddam job!

CHARLEY: When the hell are you going to grow up?

WILLY: [*Furiously.*] You big ignoramus, if you say that to me again I'll rap you one! I don't care how big you are! [*He's ready to fight. Pause.*]

CHARLEY: [*Kindly, going to him.*] How much do you need, Willy?

WILLY: Charley, I'm strapped, I'm strapped. I don't know what to do. I was just fired.

CHARLEY: Howard fired you?

WILLY: That snotnose. Imagine that? I named him. I named him Howard.

CHARLEY: Willy, when're you gonna realize that them things don't mean any-thing? You named him Howard, but you can't sell that. The only thing you got in this world is what you can sell. And the funny thing is that you're a salesman, and you don't know that.

WILLY: I've always tried to think otherwise, I guess. I always felt that if a man was impressive, and well liked, that nothing—

CHARLEY: Why must everybody like you? Who liked J. P. Morgan?[1] Was he impres-sive? In a Turkish bath he'd look like a butcher. But with his pockets on he was very well liked. Now listen, Willy, I know you don't like me, and nobody can say I'm in love with you, but I'll give you a job because—just for the hell of it, put it that way. Now what do you say?

WILLY: I—I just can't work for you, Charley.

CHARLEY: What're you, jealous of me?

WILLY: I can't work for you, that's all, don't ask me why.

CHARLEY: [Angered, takes out more bills.] You been jealous of me all your life, you damned fool! Here, pay your insurance. [He puts the money in WILLY's hand.]

WILLY: I'm keeping strict accounts.

CHARLEY: I've got some work to do. Take care of yourself. And pay your insurance.

WILLY: [Moving to the right.] Funny, y'know? After all the highways and the trains, and the appointments, and the years, you end up worth more dead than alive.

CHARLEY: Willy, nobody's worth nothin' dead. [After a slight pause.] Did you hear what I said? [WILLY stands still, dreaming.] Willy!

WILLY: Apologize to Bernard for me when you see him. I didn't mean to argue with him. He's a fine boy. They're all fine boys, and they'll end up big—all of them. Someday they'll all play tennis together. Wish me luck, Charley. He saw Bill Oliver today.

CHARLEY: Good luck.

WILLY: [On the verge of tears.] Charley, you're the only friend I got. Isn't that a remarkable thing? [He goes out.]

CHARLEY: Jesus!

[CHARLEY stares after him a moment and follows. All light blacks out. Suddenly raucous music is heard, and a red glow rises behind the screen at right. STANLEY, a young waiter, appears, carrying a table, followed by HAPPY, who is carrying two chairs.]

STANLEY: [Putting the table down.] That's all right, Mr. Loman, I can handle it myself. [He turns and takes the chairs from HAPPY and places them at the table.]

HAPPY: [Glancing around.] Oh, this is better.

STANLEY: Sure, in the front there you're in the middle of all kinds a noise. When-ever you got a party. Mr. Loman, you just tell me and I'll put you back here. Y'know, there's a lotta people they don't like it private, because when they go out they like to see a lotta action around them because they're sick and tired to stay in the house by theirself. But I know you, you ain't from Hackensack.[2] You know what I mean?

HAPPY: [Sitting down.] So how's it coming, Stanley?

1. American financier and industrialist John Pierpont Morgan (1837–1913), widely criticized for his busi-ness dealings with the U.S. government.   2. Mainly working-class city in northern New Jersey.

STANLEY: Ah, it's a dog life. I only wish during the war they'd a took me in the Army. I couda been dead by now.

HAPPY: My brother's back, Stanley.

STANLEY: Oh, he come back, heh? From the Far West.

HAPPY: Yeah, big cattle man, my brother, so treat him right. And my father's coming too.

STANLEY: Oh, your father too!

HAPPY: You got a couple of nice lobsters?

STANLEY: Hundred per cent, big.

HAPPY: I want them with the claws.

STANLEY: Don't worry, I don't give you no mice. [HAPPY *laughs*.] How about some wine? It'll put a head on the meal.

HAPPY: No. You remember, Stanley, that recipe I brought you from overseas? With the champagne in it?

STANLEY: Oh, yeah, sure. I still got it tacked up yet in the kitchen. But that'll have to cost a buck apiece anyways.

HAPPY: That's all right.

STANLEY: What'd you, hit a number or somethin'?

HAPPY: No, it's a little celebration. My brother is—I think he pulled off a big deal today. I think we're going into business together.

STANLEY: Great! That's the best for you. Because a family business, you know what I mean?—that's the best.

HAPPY: That's what I think.

STANLEY: 'Cause what's the difference? Somebody steals? It's in the family. Know what I mean? [*Sotto voce.*[3]] Like this bartender here. The boss is goin' crazy what kinda leak he's got in the cash register. You put it in but it don't come out.

HAPPY: [*Raising his head.*] Sh!

STANLEY: What?

HAPPY: You notice I wasn't lookin' right or left, was I?

STANLEY: No.

HAPPY: And my eyes are closed.

STANLEY: So what's the—?

HAPPY: Strudel's comin'.

STANLEY: [*Catching on, looks around.*] Ah, no, there's no—[*He breaks off as a furred, lavishly dressed* GIRL *enters and sits at the next table. Both follow her with their eyes.*] Geez, how'd ya know?

HAPPY: I got radar or something. [*Staring directly at her profile.*] Oooooooo . . . Stanley.

STANLEY: I think, that's for you, Mr. Loman.

HAPPY: Look at that mouth. Oh, God. And the binoculars.

STANLEY: Geez, you got a life, Mr. Loman.

HAPPY: Wait on her.

STANLEY: [*Going to the* GIRL'S *table.*] Would you like a menu, ma'am?

GIRL: I'm expecting someone, but I'd like a—

HAPPY: Why don't you bring her—excuse me, miss, do you mind? I sell champagne, and I'd like you to try my brand. Bring her a champagne, Stanley.

3. In an undertone (Italian).

GIRL: That's awfully nice of you.

HAPPY: Don't mention it. It's all company money. [*He laughs.*]

GIRL: That's a charming product to be selling, isn't it?

HAPPY: Oh, gets to be like everything else. Selling is selling, y'know.

GIRL: I suppose.

HAPPY: You don't happen to sell, do you?

GIRL: No, I don't sell.

HAPPY: Would you object to a compliment from a stranger? You ought to be on a magazine cover.

GIRL: [*Looking at him a little archly.*] I have been.

[STANLEY *comes in with a glass of champagne.*]

HAPPY: What'd I say before, Stanley? You see? She's a cover girl.

STANLEY: Oh, I could see, I could see.

HAPPY: [*To the* GIRL.] What magazine?

GIRL: Oh, a lot of them. [*She takes the drink.*] Thank you.

HAPPY: You know what they say in France, don't you? "Champagne is the drink of the complexion"—Hya, Biff!

[BIFF *has entered and sits with* HAPPY.]

BIFF: Hello, kid. Sorry I'm late.

HAPPY: I just got here. Uh, Miss—?

GIRL: Forsythe.

HAPPY: Miss Forsythe, this is my brother.

BIFF: Is Dad here?

HAPPY: His name is Biff. You might've heard of him. Great football player.

GIRL: Really? What team?

HAPPY: Are you familiar with football?

GIRL: No, I'm afraid I'm not.

HAPPY: Biff is quarterback with the New York Giants.

GIRL: Well, that's nice, isn't it? [*She drinks.*]

HAPPY: Good health.

GIRL: I'm happy to meet you.

HAPPY: That's my name, Hap. It's really Harold, but at West Point they called me Happy.

GIRL: [*Now really impressed.*] Oh, I see. How do you do? [*She turns her profile.*]

BIFF: Isn't Dad coming?

HAPPY: You want her?

BIFF: Oh, I could never make that.

HAPPY: I remember the time that idea would never come into your head. Where's the old confidence, Biff?

BIFF: I just saw Oliver—

HAPPY: Wait a minute. I've got to see that old confidence again. Do you want her? She's on call.

BIFF: Oh, no. [*He turns to look at the* GIRL.]

HAPPY: I'm telling you. Watch this. [*Turning to see the* GIRL.] Honey? [*She turns to him.*] Are you busy?

GIRL: Well, I am . . . but I could make a phone call.

HAPPY: Do that, will you, honey? And see if you can get a friend. We'll be here for a while. Biff is one of the greatest football players in the country.

GIRL: [*Standing up.*] Well, I'm certainly happy to meet you.

HAPPY: Come back soon.

GIRL: I'll try.

HAPPY: Don't try, honey, try hard. [*The* GIRL *exits.* STANLEY *follows, shaking his head in bewildered admiration.*] Isn't that a shame now? A beautiful girl like that? That's why I can't get married. There's not a good woman in a thousand. New York is loaded with them, kid!

BIFF: Hap, look—

HAPPY: I told you she was on call![4]

BIFF: [*Strangely unnerved.*] Cut it out, will ya? I want to say something to you.

HAPPY: Did you see Oliver?

BIFF: I saw him all right. Now look, I want to tell Dad a couple of things and I want you to help me.

HAPPY: What? Is he going to back you?

BIFF: Are you crazy? You're out of your goddam head, you know that?

HAPPY: Why? What happened?

BIFF: [*Breathlessly.*] I did a terrible thing today, Hap. It's been the strangest day I ever went through. I'm all numb, I swear.

HAPPY: You mean he wouldn't see you?

BIFF: Well, I waited six hours for him, see? All day. Kept sending my name in. Even tried to date his secretary so she'd get me to him, but no soap.

HAPPY: Because you're not showin' the old confidence, Biff. He remembered you, didn't he?

BIFF: [*Stopping* HAPPY *with a gesture.*] Finally, about five o'clock, he comes out. Didn't remember who I was or anything. I felt like such an idiot, Hap.

HAPPY: Did you tell him my Florida idea?

BIFF: He walked away. I saw him for one minute. I got so mad I could've torn the walls down! How the hell did I ever get the idea I was a salesman there? I even believed myself that I'd been a salesman for him! And then he gave me one look and—I realized what a ridiculous lie my whole life has been! We've been talking in a dream for fifteen years. I was a shipping clerk.

HAPPY: What'd you do?

BIFF: [*With great tension and wonder.*] Well, he left, see. And the secretary went out. I was all alone in the waiting-room. I don't know what came over me, Hap. The next thing I know I'm in his office—paneled walls, everything. I can't explain it. I—Hap, I took his fountain pen.

HAPPY: Geez, did he catch you?

BIFF: I ran out. I ran down all eleven flights. I ran and ran and ran.

HAPPY: That was an awful dumb—what'd you do that for?

BIFF: [*Agonized.*] I don't know, I just—wanted to take something, I don't know. You gotta help me, Hap, I'm gonna tell Pop.

HAPPY: You crazy? What for?

BIFF: Hap, he's got to understand that I'm not the man somebody lends that kind of money to. He thinks I've been spiting him all these years and it's eating him up.

4. That is, a call girl, a prostitute.

HAPPY: That's just it. You tell him something nice.

BIFF: I can't.

HAPPY: Say you got a lunch date with Oliver tomorrow.

BIFF: So what do I do tomorrow?

HAPPY: You leave the house tomorrow and come back at night and say Oliver is thinking it over. And he thinks it over for a couple of weeks, and gradually it fades away and nobody's the worse.

BIFF: But it'll go on forever!

HAPPY: Dad is never so happy as when he's looking forward to something! [WILLY *enters.*] Hello, scout!

WILLY: Gee, I haven't been here in years!

[STANLEY *has followed* WILLY *in and sets a chair for him.* STANLEY *starts off but* HAPPY *stops him.*]

HAPPY: Stanley!

[STANLEY *stands by, waiting for an order.*]

BIFF: [*Going to* WILLY *with guilt, as to an invalid.*] Sit down, Pop. You want a drink?

WILLY: Sure, I don't mind.

BIFF: Let's get a load on.

WILLY: You look worried.

BIFF: N-no. [*To* STANLEY.] Scotch all around. Make it doubles.

STANLEY: Doubles, right. [*He goes.*]

WILLY: You had a couple already, didn't you?

BIFF: Just a couple, yeah.

WILLY: Well, what happened, boy? [*Nodding affirmatively, with a smile.*] Everything go all right?

BIFF: [*Takes a breath, then reaches out and grasps* WILLY's *hand.*] Pal . . . [*He is smiling bravely, and* WILLY *is smiling too.*] I had an experience today.

HAPPY: Terrific, Pop.

WILLY: That so? What happened?

BIFF: [*High, slightly alcoholic, above the earth.*] I'm going to tell you everything from first to last. It's been a strange day. [*Silence. He looks around, composes himself as best he can, but his breath keeps breaking the rhythm of his voice.*] I had to wait quite a while for him, and—

WILLY: Oliver?

BIFF: Yeah, Oliver. All day, as a matter of cold fact. And a lot of—instances—facts, Pop, facts about my life came back to me. Who was it, Pop? Who ever said I was a salesman with Oliver?

WILLY: Well, you were.

BIFF: No, Dad, I was shipping clerk.

WILLY: But you were practically—

BIFF: [*With determination.*] Dad, I don't know who said it first, but I was never a salesman for Bill Oliver.

WILLY: What're you talking about?

BIFF: Let's hold on to the facts tonight, Pop. We're not going to get anywhere bullin' around. I was a shipping clerk.

WILLY: [*Angrily.*] All right, now listen to me—

BIFF: Why don't you let me finish?

WILLY: I'm not interested in stories about the past or any crap of that kind because the woods are burning, boys, you understand? There's a big blaze going on all around. I was fired today.

BIFF: [*Shocked.*] How could you be?

WILLY: I was fired, and I'm looking for a little good news to tell your mother, because the woman has waited and the woman has suffered. The gist of it is that I haven't got a story left in my head, Biff. So don't give me a lecture about facts and aspects. I am not interested. Now what've you got to say to me? [STANLEY *enters with three drinks. They wait until he leaves.*] Did you see Oliver?

BIFF: Jesus, Dad!

WILLY: You mean you didn't go up there?

HAPPY: Sure he went up there.

BIFF: I did. I—saw him. How could they fire you?

WILLY: [*On the edge of his chair.*] What kind of a welcome did he give you?

BIFF: He won't even let you work on commission?

WILLY: I'm out. [*Driving.*] So tell me, he gave you a warm welcome?

HAPPY: Sure, Pop, sure!

BIFF: [*Driven.*] Well, it was kind of—

WILLY: I was wondering if he'd remember you. [*To* HAPPY.] Imagine, man doesn't see him for ten, twelve years and gives him that kind of a welcome!

HAPPY: Damn right!

BIFF: [*Trying to return to the offensive.*] Pop, look—

WILLY: You know why he remembered you, don't you? Because you impressed him in those days.

BIFF: Let's talk quietly and get this down to the facts, huh?

WILLY: [*As though* BIFF *had been interrupting.*] Well, what happened? It's great news, Biff. Did he take you into his office or'd you talk in the waiting-room?

BIFF: Well, he came in, see and—

WILLY: [*With a big smile.*] What'd he say? Betcha he threw his arm around you.

BIFF: Well, he kinda—

WILLY: He's a fine man. [*To* HAPPY.] Very hard man to see, y'know.

HAPPY: [*Agreeing.*] Oh, I know.

WILLY: [*To* BIFF.] Is that where you had the drinks?

BIFF: Yeah, he gave me a couple of—no, no!

HAPPY: [*Cutting in.*] He told him my Florida idea.

WILLY: Don't interrupt. [*To* BIFF.] How'd he react to the Florida idea?

BIFF: Dad, will you give me a minute to explain?

WILLY: I've been waiting for you to explain since I sat down here! What happened? He took you into his office and what?

BIFF: Well—I talked. And—he listened, see.

WILLY: Famous for the way he listens, y'know. What was his answer?

BIFF: His answer was—[*He breaks off, suddenly angry.*] Dad, you're not letting me tell you what I want to tell you!

WILLY: [*Accusing, angered.*] You didn't see him, did you?

BIFF: I did see him!

WILLY: What'd you insult him or something? You insulted him, didn't you?

BIFF: Listen, will you let me out of it, will you just let me out of it!

HAPPY: What the hell!

WILLY: Tell me what happened!

BIFF: [To HAPPY.] I can't talk to him!

[*A single trumpet note jars the ear. The light of green leaves stains the house, which holds the air of night and a dream.* YOUNG BERNARD *enters and knocks on the door of the house.*]

YOUNG BERNARD: [*Frantically.*] Mrs. Loman, Mrs. Loman!

HAPPY: Tell him what happened!

BIFF: [*To* HAPPY.] Shut up and leave me alone!

WILLY: No, no. You had to go and flunk math!

BIFF: What math? What're you talking about?

YOUNG BERNARD: Mrs. Loman, Mrs. Loman!

[LINDA *appears in the house, as of old.*]

WILLY: [*Wildly.*] Math, math, math!

BIFF: Take it easy, Pop!

YOUNG BERNARD: Mrs. Loman!

WILLY: [*Furiously.*] If you hadn't flunked you'd've been set by now!

BIFF: Now, look, I'm gonna tell you what happened, and you're going to listen to me.

YOUNG BERNARD: Mrs. Loman!

BIFF: I waited six hours—

HAPPY: What the hell are you saying?

BIFF: I kept sending in my name but he wouldn't see me. So finally he . . . [*He continues unheard as light fades low on the restaurant.*]

YOUNG BERNARD: Biff flunked math!

LINDA: No!

YOUNG BERNARD: Birnbaum flunked him! They won't graduate him!

LINDA: But they have to. He's gotta go to the university. Where is he? Biff! Biff!

YOUNG BERNARD: No, he left. He went to Grand Central.[5]

LINDA: Grand—You mean he went to Boston!

YOUNG BERNARD: Is Uncle Willy in Boston?

LINDA: Oh, maybe Willy can talk to the teacher. Oh, the poor, poor boy!

[*Light on house area snaps out.*]

BIFF: [*At the table, now audible, holding up a gold fountain pen.*] . . . so I'm washed up with Oliver, you understand? Are you listening to me?

WILLY: [*At a loss.*] Yeah, sure. If you hadn't flunked—

BIFF: Flunked what? What're you talking about?

WILLY: Don't blame everything on me! I didn't flunk math—you did! What pen?

HAPPY: That was awful dumb, Biff, a pen like that is worth—

WILLY: [*Seeing the pen for the first time.*] You took Oliver's pen?

BIFF: [*Weakening.*] Dad, I just explained it to you.

WILLY: You stole Bill Oliver's fountain pen!

BIFF: I didn't exactly steal it! That's just what I've been explaining to you!

HAPPY: He had it in his hand and just then Oliver walked in, so he got nervous and stuck it in his pocket!

WILLY: My God, Biff!

5. Grand Central Terminal, New York City's principal railway and subway station.

BIFF: I never intended to do it, Dad!

OPERATOR'S VOICE: Standish Arms, good evening!

WILLY: [*Shouting.*] I'm not in my room!

BIFF: [*Frightened.*] Dad, what's the matter? [*He and* HAPPY *stand up.*]

OPERATOR: Ringing Mr. Loman for you!

BIFF: [*Horrified, gets down on one knee before* WILLY.] Dad, I'll make good, I'll make good. [WILLY *tries to get to his feet.* BIFF *holds him down.*] Sit down now.

WILLY: No, you're no good, you're no good for anything.

BIFF: I am, Dad, I'll find something else, you understand? Now don't worry about anything. [*He holds up* WILLY's *face.*] Talk to me, Dad.

OPERATOR: Mr. Loman does not answer. Shall I page him?

WILLY: [*Attempting to stand, as though to rush and silence the* OPERATOR.] No, no, no!

HAPPY: He'll strike something, Pop.

WILLY: No, no . . .

BIFF: [*Desperately, standing over* WILLY.] Pop, listen! Listen to me! I'm telling you something good. Oliver talked to his partner about the Florida idea. You listening? He—he talked to his partner, and he came to me . . . I'm going to be all right, you hear? Dad, listen to me, he said it was just a question of the amount!

WILLY: Then you . . . got it?

HAPPY: He's gonna be terrific, Pop!

WILLY: [*Trying to stand.*] Then you got it, haven't you? You got it! You got it!

BIFF: [*Agonized, holds* WILLY *down.*] No, no. Look, Pop. I'm supposed to have lunch with them tomorrow. I'm just telling you this so you'll know that I can still make an impression, Pop. And I'll make good somewhere, but I can't go tomorrow, see?

WILLY: Why not? You simply—

BIFF: But the pen, Pop!

WILLY: You give it to him and tell him it was an oversight!

HAPPY: Sure, have lunch tomorrow!

BIFF: I can't say that—

WILLY: You were doing a crossword puzzle and accidentally used his pen!

BIFF: Listen, kid, I took those balls years ago, now I walk in with his fountain pen? That clinches it, don't you see? I can't face him like that! I'll try elsewhere.

PAGE'S VOICE: Paging Mr. Loman!

WILLY: Don't you want to be anything?

BIFF: Pop, how can I go back?

WILLY: You don't want to be anything, is that what's behind it?

BIFF: [*Now angry at* WILLY *for not crediting his sympathy.*] Don't take it that way! You think it was easy walking into that office after what I'd done to him? A team of horses couldn't have dragged me back to Bill Oliver!

WILLY: Then why'd you go?

BIFF: Why did I go? Why did I go! Look at you! Look at what's become of you!

[*Off left,* THE WOMAN *laughs.*]

WILLY: Biff, you're going to go to that lunch tomorrow, or—

BIFF: I can't go. I've got an appointment!

HAPPY: Biff, for . . . !

WILLY: Are you spiting me?

BIFF: Don't take it that way! Goddammit!

WILLY: [*Strikes* BIFF *and falters away from the table.*] You rotten little louse! Are you spiting me?

THE WOMAN: Someone's at the door, Willy!

BIFF: I'm no good, can't you see what I am?

HAPPY: [*Separating them.*] Hey, you're in a restaurant! Now cut it out, both of you! [*The* GIRLS *enter.*] Hello, girls, sit down.

[THE WOMAN *laughs, off left.*]

MISS FORSYTHE: I guess we might as well. This is Letta.

THE WOMAN: Willy, are you going to wake up?

BIFF: [*Ignoring* WILLY.] How're ya, miss, sit down. What do you drink?

MISS FORSYTHE: Letta might not be able to stay long.

LETTA: I gotta get up early tomorrow. I got jury duty. I'm so excited! Were you fellows ever on a jury?

BIFF: No, but I been in front of them! [*The* GIRLS *laugh.*] This is my father.

LETTA: Isn't he cute? Sit down with us, Pop.

HAPPY: Sit him down, Biff!

BIFF: [*Going to him.*] Come on, slugger, drink us under the table. To hell with it! Come on, sit down, pal.

[*On* BIFF's *last insistence,* WILLY *is about to sit.*]

THE WOMAN: [*Now urgently.*] Willy, are you going to answer the door!

[THE WOMAN's *call pulls* WILLY *back. He starts right, befuddled.*]

BIFF: Hey, where are you going?

WILLY: Open the door.

BIFF: The door?

WILLY: The washroom . . . the door . . . where's the door?

BIFF: [*Leading* WILLY *to the left.*] Just go straight down.

[WILLY *moves left.*]

THE WOMAN: Willy, Willy, are you going to get up, get up, get up, get up?

[WILLY *exits left.*]

LETTA: I think it's sweet you bring your daddy along.

MISS FORSYTHE: Oh, he isn't really your father!

BIFF: [*At left, turning to her resentfully.*] Miss Forsythe, you've just seen a prince walk by. A fine, troubled prince. A hardworking, unappreciated prince. A pal, you understand? A good companion. Always for his boys.

LETTA: That's so sweet.

HAPPY: Well, girls, what's the program? We're wasting time. Come on, Biff. Gather round. Where would you like to go?

BIFF: Why don't you do something for him?

HAPPY: Me!

BIFF: Don't you give a damn for him, Hap?

HAPPY: What're you talking about? I'm the one who—

BIFF: I sense it, you don't give a good goddam about him. [*He takes the rolled-up hose from his pocket and puts it on the table in front of* HAPPY.] Look what I found in the cellar, for Christ's sake. How can you bear to let it go on?

HAPPY: Me? Who goes away? Who runs off and—

BIFF: Yeah, but he doesn't mean anything to you. You could help him—I can't! Don't you understand what I'm talking about? He's going to kill himself, don't you know that?

HAPPY: Don't I know it! Me!

BIFF: Hap, help him! Jesus . . . help him . . . Help me, help me, I can't bear to look at his face! [*Ready to weep, he hurries out, up right.*]

HAPPY: [*Starting after him.*] Where are you going?

MISS FORSYTHE: What's he so mad about?

HAPPY: Come on, girls, we'll catch up with him.

MISS FORSYTHE: [*As* HAPPY *pushes her out.*] Say, I don't like that temper of his!

HAPPY: He's just a little overstrung, he'll be all right!

WILLY: [*Off left, as* THE WOMAN *laughs.*] Don't answer! Don't answer!

LETTA: Don't you want to tell your father—

HAPPY: No, that's not my father. He's just a guy. Come on, we'll catch Biff, and, honey, we're going to paint this town! Stanley, where's the check! Hey, Stanley!

[*They exit.* STANLEY *looks toward left.*]

STANLEY: [*Calling to* HAPPY *indignantly.*] Mr. Loman! Mr. Loman!

[STANLEY *picks up a chair and follows them off. Knocking is heard off left.* THE WOMAN *enters, laughing.* WILLY *follows her. She is in a black slip; he is buttoning his shirt. Raw, sensuous music accompanies their speech.*]

WILLY: Will you stop laughing? Will you stop?

THE WOMAN: Aren't you going to answer the door? He'll wake the whole hotel.

WILLY: I'm not expecting anybody.

THE WOMAN: Whyn't you have another drink, honey, and stop being so damn self-centered?

WILLY: I'm so lonely.

THE WOMAN: You know you ruined me, Willy? From now on, whenever you come to the office, I'll see that you go right through to the buyers. No waiting at my desk anymore, Willy. You ruined me.

WILLY: That's nice of you to say that.

THE WOMAN: Gee, you are self-centered! Why so sad? You are the saddest, self-centeredest soul I ever did see-saw. [*She laughs. He kisses her.*] Come on inside, drummer boy. It's silly to be dressing in the middle of the night. [*As knocking is heard.*] Aren't you going to answer the door?

WILLY: They're knocking on the wrong door.

THE WOMAN: But I felt the knocking. And he heard us talking in here. Maybe the hotel's on fire!

WILLY: [*His terror rising.*] It's a mistake.

THE WOMAN: Then tell them to go away!

WILLY: There's nobody there.

THE WOMAN: It's getting on my nerves, Willy. There's somebody standing out there and it's getting on my nerves!

WILLY: [*Pushing her away from him.*] All right, stay in the bathroom here, and don't come out. I think there's a law in Massachusetts about it, so don't come out. It may be that new room clerk. He looked very mean. So don't come out. It's a mistake, there's no fire.

[*The knocking is heard again. He takes a few steps away from her, and she vanishes into the wing. The light follows him, and now he is facing* YOUNG BIFF, *who carries a suitcase.* BIFF *steps toward him. The music is gone.*]

BIFF: Why didn't you answer?

WILLY: Biff! What are you doing in Boston?

BIFF: Why didn't you answer? I've been knocking for five minutes, I called you on the phone—

WILLY: I just heard you. I was in the bathroom and had the door shut. Did anything happen home?

BIFF: Dad—I let you down.

WILLY: What do you mean?

BIFF: Dad . . .

WILLY: Biffo, what's this about? [*Putting his arm around* BIFF.] Come on, let's go downstairs and get you a malted.

BIFF: Dad, I flunked math.

WILLY: Not for the term?

BIFF: The term. I haven't got enough credits to graduate.

WILLY: You mean to say Bernard wouldn't give you the answers?

BIFF: He did, he tried, but I only got a sixty-one.

WILLY: And they wouldn't give you four points?

BIFF: Birnbaum refused absolutely. I begged him, Pop, but he won't give me those points. You gotta talk to him before they close the school. Because if he saw the kind of man you are, and you just talked to him in your way, I'm sure he'd come through for me. The class came right before practice, see, and I didn't go enough. Would you talk to him? He'd like you, Pop. You know the way you could talk.

WILLY: You're on. We'll drive right back.

BIFF: Oh, Dad, good work! I'm sure he'll change for you!

WILLY: Go downstairs and tell the clerk I'm checkin' out. Go right down.

BIFF: Yes, sir! See, the reason he hates me, Pop—one day he was late for class so I got up at the blackboard and imitated him. I crossed my eyes and talked with a lithp.

WILLY: [*Laughing.*] You did? The kids like it?

BIFF: They nearly died laughing!

WILLY: Yeah? What'd you do?

BIFF: The thquare root of thixty twee is . . . [WILLY *bursts out laughing;* BIFF *joins him.*] And in the middle of it he walked in!

[WILLY *laughs and* THE WOMAN *joins in offstage.*]

WILLY: [*Without hesitation.*] Hurry downstairs and—

BIFF: Somebody in there?

WILLY: No, that was next door.

[THE WOMAN *laughs offstage.*]

BIFF: Somebody got in your bathroom!

WILLY: No, it's the next room, there's a party—

THE WOMAN: [*Enters laughing. She lisps this.*] Can I come in? There's something in the bathtub, Willy, and it's moving!

[WILLY *looks at* BIFF, *who is staring open-mouthed and horrified at* THE WOMAN.]

WILLY: Ah—you better go back to your room. They must be finished painting by now. They're painting her room so I let her take a shower here. Go back, go back . . . [*He pushes her.*]

THE WOMAN: [*Resisting.*] But I've got to get dressed, Willy, I can't—

WILLY: Get out of here! Go back, go back . . . [*Suddenly striving for the ordinary.*] This is Miss Francis, Biff, she's a buyer. They're painting her room. Go back, Miss Francis, go back . . .

THE WOMAN: But my clothes, I can't go out naked in the hall!

WILLY: [*Pushing her offstage.*] Get outa here! Go back, go back!

[BIFF *slowly sits down on his suitcase as the argument continues offstage.*]

THE WOMAN: Where's my stockings? You promised me stockings, Willy!

WILLY: I have no stockings here!

THE WOMAN: You had two boxes of size nine sheers for me, and I want them!

WILLY: Here, for God's sake, will you get outa here!

THE WOMAN: [*Enters holding a box of stockings.*] I just hope there's nobody in the hall. That's all I hope. [*To* BIFF.] Are you football or baseball?

BIFF: Football.

THE WOMAN: [*Angry, humiliated.*] That's me too. G'night. [*She snatches her clothes from* WILLY, *and walks out.*]

WILLY: [*After a pause.*] Well, better get going. I want to get to the school first thing in the morning. Get my suits out of the closet. I'll get my valise. [BIFF *doesn't move.*] What's the matter? [BIFF *remains motionless, tears falling.*] She's a buyer. Buys for J. H. Simmons. She lives down the hall—they're painting. You don't imagine—[*He breaks off. After a pause.*] Now listen, pal, she's just a buyer. She sees merchandise in her room and they have to keep it looking just so . . . [*Pause. Assuming command.*] All right, get my suits. [BIFF *doesn't move.*] Now stop crying and do as I say. I gave you an order. Biff, I gave you an order! Is that what you do when I give you an order? How dare you cry! [*Putting his arm around* BIFF.] Now look, Biff, when you grow up you'll understand about these things. You mustn't—you mustn't over-emphasize a thing like this. I'll see Birnbaum first thing in the morning.

BIFF: Never mind.

WILLY: [*Getting down beside* BIFF.] Never mind! He's going to give you those points. I'll see to it.

BIFF: He wouldn't listen to you.

WILLY: He certainly will listen to me. You need those points for the U. of Virginia.

BIFF: I'm not going there.

WILLY: Heh? If I can't get him to change that mark you'll make it up in summer school. You've got all summer to—

BIFF: [*His weeping breaking from him.*] Dad . . .

WILLY: [*Infected by it.*] Oh, my boy . . .

BIFF: Dad . . .

WILLY: She's nothing to me, Biff. I was lonely, I was terribly lonely.

BIFF: You—you gave her Mama's stockings! [*His tears break through and he rises to go.*]

WILLY: [*Grabbing for* BIFF.] I gave you an order!

BIFF: Don't touch me, you—liar!

WILLY: Apologize for that!

BIFF: You fake! You phony little fake! You fake!

[*Overcome, he turns quickly and weeping fully goes out with his suitcase.* WILLY *is left on the floor on his knees.*]

WILLY: I gave you an order! Biff, come back here or I'll beat you! Come back here! I'll whip you! [STANLEY *comes quickly in from the right and stands in front of* WILLY. WILLY *shouts at* STANLEY.] I gave you an order . . .

STANLEY: Hey, let's pick it up, pick it up, Mr. Loman. [*He helps* WILLY *to his feet.*] Your boys left with the chippies.[6] They said they'll see you home.

[*A* SECOND WAITER *watches some distance away.*]

WILLY: But we were supposed to have dinner together.

[*Music is heard,* WILLY'S *theme.*]

STANLEY: Can you make it?

WILLY: I'll—sure, I can make it. [*Suddenly concerned about his clothes.*] Do I—I look all right?

STANLEY: Sure, you look all right. [*He flicks a speck off* WILLY'S *lapel.*]

WILLY: Here—here's a dollar.

STANLEY: Oh, your son paid me. It's all right.

WILLY: [*Putting it in* STANLEY'S *hand.*] No, take it. You're a good boy.

STANLEY: Oh, no, you don't have to . . .

WILLY: Here—here's some more, I don't need it anymore. [*After a slight pause.*] Tell me—is there a seed store in the neighborhood?

STANLEY: Seeds? You mean like to plant?

[*As* WILLY *turns,* STANLEY *slips the money back into his jacket pocket.*]

WILLY: Yes. Carrots, peas . . .

STANLEY: Well, there's hardware stores on Sixth Avenue, but it may be too late now.

WILLY: [*Anxiously.*] Oh, I'd better hurry. I've got to get some seeds. [*He starts off to the right.*] I've got to get some seeds, right away. Nothing's planted. I don't have a thing in the ground.

[WILLY *hurries out as the light goes down.* STANLEY *moves over to the right after him, watches him off. The other* WAITER *has been staring at* WILLY.]

STANLEY: [*To the* WAITER.] Well, whatta you looking at?

[*The* WAITER *picks up the chairs and moves off right.* STANLEY *takes the table and follows him. The light fades on this area. There is a long pause, the sound of the flute coming over. The light gradually rises on the kitchen, which is empty.* HAPPY *appears at the door of the house, followed by* BIFF. HAPPY *is carrying a large bunch of long-stemmed roses. He enters the kitchen, looks around for* LINDA. *Not seeing her, he turns to* BIFF, *who is just outside the house door, and makes a gesture with his hands, indicating "Not here, I guess." He looks into the living-room and freezes. Inside,* LINDA, *unseen, is seated,* WILLY'S *coat on her lap. She rises ominously and quietly and moves toward* HAPPY, *who backs up into the kitchen, afraid.*]

6. Prostitutes, tramps.

HAPPY: Hey, what're you doing up? [LINDA *says nothing but moves toward him implacably.*] Where's Pop? [*He keeps backing to the right, and now* LINDA *is in full view in the doorway to the living-room.*] Is he sleeping?

LINDA: Where were you?

HAPPY: [*Trying to laugh it off.*] We met two girls, Mom, very fine types. Here, we brought you some flowers. [*Offering them to her.*] Put them in your room, Ma. [*She knocks them to the floor at* BIFF's *feet. He has now come inside and closed the door behind him. She stares at* BIFF, *silent.*] Now what'd you do that for? Mom, I want you to have some flowers—

LINDA: [*Cutting* HAPPY *off, violently to* BIFF.] Don't you care whether he lives or dies?

HAPPY: [*Going to the stairs.*] Come upstairs, Biff.

BIFF: [*With a flare of disgust, to* HAPPY.] Go away from me! [*To* LINDA.] What do you mean, lives or dies? Nobody's dying around here, pal.

LINDA: Get out of my sight! Get out of here!

BIFF: I wanna see the boss.

LINDA: You're not going near him!

BIFF: Where is he? [*He moves into the living-room and* LINDA *follows.*]

LINDA: [*Shouting after* BIFF.] You invite him for dinner. He looks forward to it all day—[BIFF *appears in his parents' bedroom, looks around and exits.*]—and then you desert him there. There's no stranger you'd do that to!

HAPPY: Why? He had a swell time with us. Listen, when I—[LINDA *comes back into the kitchen.*]—desert him I hope I don't outlive the day!

LINDA: Get out of here!

HAPPY: Now look, Mom . . .

LINDA: Did you have to go to women tonight? You and your lousy rotten whores!

[BIFF *re-enters the kitchen.*]

HAPPY: Mom, all we did was follow Biff around trying to cheer him up! [*To* BIFF.] Boy, what a night you gave me!

LINDA: Get out of here, both of you, and don't come back! I don't want you tormenting him anymore. Go on now, get your things together! [*To* BIFF.] You can sleep in his apartment. [*She starts to pick up the flowers and stops herself.*] Pick up this stuff, I'm not your maid anymore. Pick it up, you bum, you! [HAPPY *turns his back to her in refusal.* BIFF *slowly moves over and gets down on his knees, picking up the flowers.*] You're a pair of animals! Not one, not another living soul would have had the cruelty to walk out on that man in a restaurant!

BIFF: [*Not looking at her.*] Is that what he said?

LINDA: He didn't have to say anything. He was so humiliated he nearly limped when he came in.

HAPPY: But, Mom, he had a great time with us—

BIFF: [*Cutting him off violently.*] Shut up!

[*Without another word,* HAPPY *goes upstairs.*]

LINDA: You! You didn't even go in to see if he was all right!

BIFF: [*Still on the floor in front of* LINDA, *the flowers in his hand; with self-loathing.*] No. Didn't. Didn't do a damned thing. How do you like that, heh? Left him babbling in a toilet.

LINDA: You louse. You . . .

BIFF: Now you hit it on the nose! [*He gets up, throws the flowers in the wastebasket.*] The scum of the earth, and you're looking at him!

LINDA: Get out of here!

BIFF: I gotta talk to the boss, Mom. Where is he?

LINDA: You're not going near him. Get out of this house!

BIFF: [*With absolute assurance, determination.*] No. We're gonna have an abrupt conversation, him and me.

LINDA: You're not talking to him! [*Hammering is heard from outside the house, off right.* BIFF *turns toward the noise. Suddenly pleading.*] Will you please leave him alone?

BIFF: What's he doing out there?

LINDA: He's planting the garden!

BIFF: [*Quietly.*] Now? Oh, my God!

[BIFF *moves outside,* LINDA *following. The light dies down on them and comes up on the center of the apron as* WILLY *walks into it. He is carrying a flashlight, a hoe, and a handful of seed packets. He raps the top of the hoe sharply to fix it firmly, and then moves to the left, measuring off the distance with his foot. He holds the flashlight to look at the seed packets, reading off the instructions. He is in the blue of night.*]

WILLY: Carrots . . . quarter-inch apart. Rows . . . one-foot rows. [*He measures it off.*] One foot. [*He puts down a package and measures off.*] Beets. [*He puts down another package and measures again.*] Lettuce. [*He reads the package, puts it down.*] One foot—[*He breaks off as* BEN *appears at the right and moves slowly down to him.*] What a proposition, ts, ts. Terrific, terrific. 'Cause she's suffered, Ben, the woman has suffered. You understand me? A man can't go out the way he came in, Ben, a man has got to add up to something. You can't, you can't—[BEN *moves toward him as though to interrupt.*] You gotta consider, now. Don't answer so quick. Remember, it's a guaranteed twenty-thousand-dollar proposition. Now look, Ben, I want you to go through the ins and outs of this thing with me. I've got nobody to talk to, Ben, and the woman has suffered, you hear me?

BEN: [*Standing still, considering.*] What's the proposition?

WILLY: It's twenty thousand dollars on the barrelhead. Guaranteed, gilt-edged, you understand?

BEN: You don't want to make a fool of yourself. They might not honor the policy.

WILLY: How can they dare refuse? Didn't I work like a coolie to meet every premium on the nose? And now they don't pay off! Impossible!

BEN: It's called a cowardly thing, William.

WILLY: Why? Does it take more guts to stand here the rest of my life ringing up a zero?

BEN: [*Yielding.*] That's a point, William. [*He moves, thinking, turns.*] And twenty thousand—that *is* something one can feel with the hand, it is there.

WILLY: [*Now assured, with rising power.*] Oh, Ben, that's the whole beauty of it! I see it like a diamond, shining in the dark, hard and rough, that I can pick up and touch in my hand. Not like—like an appointment! This would not be another damned-fool appointment, Ben, and it changes all the aspects. Because he thinks I'm nothing, see, and so he spites me. But the funeral—[*Straightening up.*] Ben, that funeral will be massive! They'll come from Maine, Massachusetts,

Vermont, New Hampshire! All the old-timers with the strange license plates—that boy will be thunder-struck, Ben, because he never realized—I am known! Rhode Island, New York, New Jersey—I am known, Ben, and he'll see it with his eyes once and for all. He'll see what I am, Ben! He's in for a shock, that boy!

BEN: [*Coming down to the edge of the garden.*] He'll call you a coward.

WILLY: [*Suddenly fearful.*] No, that would be terrible.

BEN: Yes. And a damned fool.

WILLY: No, no, he mustn't, I won't have that! [*He is broken and desperate.*]

BEN: He'll hate you, William.

[*The gay music of the Boys is heard.*]

WILLY: Oh, Ben, how do we get back to all the great times? Used to be so full of light, and comradeship, the sleigh-riding in winter, and the ruddiness on his cheeks. And always some kind of good news coming up, always something nice coming up ahead. And never even let me carry the valises in the house, and simonizing, simonizing that little red car! Why, why can't I give him something and not have him hate me?

BEN: Let me think about it. [*He glances at his watch.*] I still have a little time. Remarkable proposition, but you've got to be sure you're not making a fool of yourself.

[BEN *drifts off upstage and goes out of sight.* BIFF *comes down from the left.*]

WILLY: [*Suddenly conscious of* BIFF, *turns and looks up at him, then begins picking up the packages of seeds in confusion.*] Where the hell is that seed? [*Indignantly.*] You can't see nothing out here! They boxed in the whole goddam neighborhood!

BIFF: There are people all around here. Don't you realize that?

WILLY: I'm busy. Don't bother me.

BIFF: [*Taking the hoe from* WILLY.] I'm saying good-bye to you, Pop. [WILLY *looks at him, silent, unable to move.*] I'm not coming back anymore.

WILLY: You're not going to see Oliver tomorrow?

BIFF: I've got no appointment, Dad.

WILLY: He put his arm around you, and you've got no appointment?

BIFF: Pop, get this now, will you? Everytime I've left it's been a fight that sent me out of here. Today I realized something about myself and I tried to explain it to you and I—I think I'm just not smart enough to make any sense out of it for you. To hell with whose fault it is or anything like that. [*He takes* WILLY'S *arm.*] Let's just wrap it up, heh? Come on in, we'll tell Mom. [*He gently tries to pull* WILLY *to left.*]

WILLY: [*Frozen, immobile, with guilt in his voice.*] No, I don't want to see her.

BIFF: Come on! [*He pulls again, and* WILLY *tries to pull away.*]

WILLY: [*Highly nervous.*] No, no, I don't want to see her.

BIFF: [*Tries to look into* WILLY'S *face, as if to find the answer there.*] Why don't you want to see her?

WILLY: [*More harshly now.*] Don't bother me, will you?

BIFF: What do you mean, you don't want to see her? You don't want them calling you yellow, do you? This isn't your fault; it's me, I'm a bum. Now come inside! [WILLY *strains to get away.*] Did you hear what I said to you?

[WILLY *pulls away and quickly goes by himself into the house.* BIFF *follows.*]

LINDA: [*To* WILLY.] Did you plant, dear?

BIFF: [*At the door, to* LINDA.] All right, we had it out. I'm going and I'm not writing anymore.

LINDA: [*Going to* WILLY *in the kitchen.*] I think that's the best way, dear. 'Cause there's no use drawing it out, you'll just never get along.

[WILLY *doesn't respond.*]

BIFF: People ask where I am and what I'm doing, you don't know, and you don't care. That way it'll be off your mind and you can start brightening up again. All right? That clears it, doesn't it? [WILLY *is silent, and* BIFF *goes to him.*] You gonna wish me luck, scout? [*He extends his hand.*] What do you say?

LINDA: Shake his hand, Willy.

WILLY: [*Turning to her, seething with hurt.*] There's no necessity to mention the pen at all, y'know.

BIFF: [*Gently.*] I've got no appointment, Dad.

WILLY: [*Erupting fiercely.*] He put his arm around . . . ?

BIFF: Dad, you're never going to see what I am, so what's the use of arguing? If I strike oil I'll send you a check. Meantime forget I'm alive.

WILLY: [*To* LINDA.] Spite, see?

BIFF: Shake hands, Dad.

WILLY: Not my hand.

BIFF: I was hoping not to go this way.

WILLY: Well, this is the way you're going. Good-bye. [BIFF *looks at him a moment, then turns sharply and goes to the stairs.* WILLY *stops him with.*] May you rot in hell if you leave this house!

BIFF: [*Turning.*] Exactly what is it that you want from me?

WILLY: I want you to know, on the train, in the mountains, in the valleys, wherever you go, that you cut down your life for spite!

BIFF: No, no.

WILLY: Spite, spite, is the word of your undoing! And when you're down and out, remember what did it. When you're rotting somewhere beside the railroad tracks, remember, and don't you dare blame it on me!

BIFF: I'm not blaming it on you!

WILLY: I won't take the rap for this, you hear?

[HAPPY *comes down the stairs and stands on the bottom step, watching.*]

BIFF: That's just what I'm telling you!

WILLY: [*Sinking into a chair at the table, with full accusation.*] You're trying to put a knife in me—don't think I don't know what you're doing!

BIFF: All right, phony! Then let's lay it on the line. [*He whips the rubber tube out of his pocket and puts it on the table.*]

HAPPY: You crazy—

LINDA: Biff!

[*She moves to grab the hose, but* BIFF *holds it down with his hand.*]

BIFF: Leave it there! Don't move it!

WILLY: [*Not looking at it.*] What is that?

BIFF: You know goddam well what that is.

WILLY: [*Caged, wanting to escape.*] I never saw that.

BIFF: You saw it. The mice didn't bring it into the cellar! What is this supposed to do, make a hero out of you? This supposed to make me sorry for you?

WILLY: Never heard of it.

BIFF: There'll be no pity for you, you hear it? No pity!

WILLY: [*To* LINDA.] You hear the spite!

BIFF: No, you're going to hear the truth—what you are and what I am!

LINDA: Stop it!

WILLY: Spite!

HAPPY: [*Coming down toward* BIFF.] You cut it now!

BIFF: [*To* HAPPY.] The man don't know who we are! The man is gonna know! [*To* WILLY.] We never told the truth for ten minutes in this house!

HAPPY: We always told the truth!

BIFF: [*Turning on him.*] You big blow, are you the assistant buyer? You're one of the two assistants to the assistant, aren't you?

HAPPY: Well, I'm practically—

BIFF: You're practically full of it! We all are! And I'm through with it. [*To* WILLY.] Now hear this, Willy, this is me.

WILLY: I know you!

BIFF: You know why I had no address for three months? I stole a suit in Kansas City and I was in jail. [*To* LINDA, *who is sobbing.*] Stop crying. I'm through with it.

[LINDA *turns away from them, her hands covering her face.*]

WILLY: I suppose that's my fault!

BIFF: I stole myself out of every good job since high school!

WILLY: And whose fault is that?

BIFF: And I never got anywhere because you blew me so full of hot air I could never stand taking orders from anybody! That's whose fault it is!

WILLY: I hear that!

LINDA: Don't, Biff!

BIFF: It's goddam time you heard that! I had to be boss big shot in two weeks, and I'm through with it!

WILLY: Then hang yourself! For spite, hang yourself!

BIFF: No! Nobody's hanging himself, Willy! I ran down eleven flights with a pen in my hand today. And suddenly I stopped, you hear me? And in the middle of that office building, do you hear this? I stopped in the middle of that building and I saw—the sky. I saw the things that I love in this world. The work and the food and time to sit and smoke. And I looked at the pen and said to myself, what the hell am I grabbing this for? Why am I trying to become what I don't want to be? What am I doing in an office, making a contemptuous, begging fool of myself, when all I want is out there, waiting for me the minute I say I know who I am! Why can't I say that, Willy? [*He tries to make* WILLY *face him, but* WILLY *pulls away and moves to the left.*]

WILLY: [*With hatred, threateningly.*] The door of your life is wide open!

BIFF: Pop! I'm a dime a dozen, and so are you!

WILLY: [*Turning on him now in an uncontrolled outburst.*] I am not a dime a dozen! I am Willy Loman, and you are Biff Loman!

[BIFF *starts for* WILLY, *but is blocked by* HAPPY. *In his fury,* BIFF *seems on the verge of attacking his father.*]

BIFF: I am not a leader of men, Willy, and neither are you. You were never anything but a hard-working drummer who landed in the ash can like all the rest of them! I'm one dollar an hour, Willy! I tried seven states and couldn't raise it. A buck an hour! Do you gather my meaning? I'm not bringing home any prizes anymore, and you're going to stop waiting for me to bring them home!

WILLY: [*Directly to* BIFF.] You vengeful, spiteful mut!

[BIFF *breaks from* HAPPY. WILLY, *in fright, starts up the stairs.* BIFF *grabs him.*]

BIFF: [*At the peak of his fury.*] Pop, I'm nothing! I'm nothing, Pop. Can't you understand that? There's no spite in it anymore. I'm just what I am, that's all.

[BIFF's *fury has spent itself, and he breaks down, sobbing, holding on to* WILLY, *who dumbly fumbles for* BIFF's *face.*]

WILLY: [*Astonished.*] What're you doing? What're you doing? [*To* LINDA.] Why is he crying?

BIFF: [*Crying, broken.*] Will you let me go, for Christ's sake? Will you take that phony dream and burn it before something happens? [*Struggling to contain himself, he pulls away and moves to the stairs.*] I'll go in the morning. Put him—put him to bed. [*Exhausted,* BIFF *moves up the stairs to his room.*]

WILLY: [*After a long pause, astonished, elevated.*] Isn't that—isn't that remarkable? Biff—he likes me!

LINDA: He loves you, Willy!

HAPPY: [*Deeply moved.*] Always did, Pop.

WILLY: Oh, Biff! [*Staring wildly.*] He cried! Cried to me. [*He is choking with his love, and now cries out his promise.*] That boy—that boy is going to be magnificent!

[BEN *appears in the light just outside the kitchen.*]

BEN: Yes, outstanding, with twenty thousand behind him.

LINDA: [*Sensing the racing of his mind, fearfully, carefully.*] Now come to bed, Willy. It's all settled now.

WILLY: [*Finding it difficult not to rush out of the house.*] Yes, we'll sleep. Come on. Go to sleep, Hap.

BEN: And it does take a great kind of man to crack the jungle.

[*In accents of dread,* BEN's *idyllic music starts up.*]

HAPPY: [*His arm around* LINDA.] I'm getting married, Pop, don't forget it. I'm changing everything. I'm gonna run that department before the year is up. You'll see, Mom. [*He kisses her.*]

BEN: The jungle is dark but full of diamonds, Willy.

[WILLY *turns, moves, listening to* BEN.]

LINDA: Be good. You're both good boys, just act that way, that's all.

HAPPY: 'Night, Pop. [*He goes upstairs.*]

LINDA: [*To* WILLY.] Come, dear.

BEN: [*With greater force.*] One must go in to fetch a diamond out.

WILLY: [*To* LINDA, *as he moves slowly along the edge of the kitchen, toward the door.*] I just want to get settled down, Linda. Let me sit alone for a little.

LINDA: [*Almost uttering her fear.*] I want you upstairs.

WILLY: [*Taking her in his arms.*] In a few minutes, Linda. I couldn't sleep right now. Go on, you look awful tired. [*He kisses her.*]

BEN: Not like an appointment at all. A diamond is rough and hard to the touch.

WILLY: Go on now. I'll be right up.

LINDA: I think this is the only way, Willy.

WILLY: Sure, it's the best thing.

BEN: Best thing!

WILLY: The only way. Everything is gonna be—go on, kid, get to bed. You look so tired.

LINDA: Come right up.

WILLY: Two minutes. [LINDA *goes into the living-room, then reappears in her bedroom.* WILLY *moves just outside the kitchen door.*] Loves me. [*Wonderingly.*] Always loved me. Isn't that a remarkable thing? Ben, he'll worship me for it!

BEN: [*With promise.*] It's dark there, but full of diamonds.

WILLY: Can you imagine that magnificence with twenty thousand dollars in his pocket?

LINDA: [*Calling from her room.*] Willy! Come up!

WILLY: [*Calling into the kitchen.*] Yes! Yes. Coming! It's very smart, you realize that, don't you, sweetheart? Even Ben sees it. I gotta go, baby. 'Bye! 'Bye! [*Going over to* BEN, *almost dancing.*] Imagine? When the mail comes he'll be ahead of Bernard again!

BEN: A perfect proposition all around.

WILLY: Did you see how he cried to me? Oh, if I could kiss him, Ben!

BEN: Time, William, time!

WILLY: Oh, Ben, I always knew one way or another we were gonna make it, Biff and I!

BEN: [*Looking at his watch.*] The boat. We'll be late. [*He moves slowly off into the darkness.*]

WILLY: [*Elegiacally, turning to the house.*] Now when you kick off, boy, I want a seventy-yard boot, and get right down the field under the ball, and when you hit, hit low and hit hard, because it's important, boy. [*He swings around and faces the audience.*] There's all kinds of important people in the stands, and the first thing you know ... [*Suddenly realizing he is alone.*] Ben! Ben, where do I ...? [*He makes a sudden movement of search.*] Ben, how do I ...?

LINDA: [*Calling.*] Willy, you coming up?

WILLY: [*Uttering a gasp of fear, whirling about as if to quiet her.*] Sh! [*He turns around as if to find his way; sounds, faces, voices, seem to be swarming in upon him and he flicks at them, crying.*] Sh! Sh! [*Suddenly music, faint and high, stops him. It rises in intensity, almost to an unbearable scream. He goes up and down on his toes, and rushes off around the house.*] Shhh!

LINDA: Willy? [*There is no answer.* LINDA *waits.* BIFF *gets up off his bed. He is still in his clothes.* HAPPY *sits up.* BIFF *stands listening.*] [*With real fear.*] Willy, answer me! Willy! [*There is the sound of a car starting and moving away at full speed.*] No!

BIFF: [*Rushing down the stairs.*] Pop!

[*As the car speeds off, the music crashes down in a frenzy of sound, which becomes the soft pulsation of a single cello string.* BIFF *slowly returns to his bedroom. He and* HAPPY *gravely don their jackets.* LINDA *slowly walks out of her room. The music has developed into a dead march. The leaves of day are appearing over everything.* CHARLEY *and*

2192 READING MORE DRAMA

BERNARD, *somberly dressed, appear and knock on the kitchen door.* BIFF *and* HAPPY *slowly descend the stairs to the kitchen as* CHARLEY *and* BERNARD *enter. All stop a moment when* LINDA, *in clothes of mourning, bearing a little bunch of roses, comes through the draped doorway into the kitchen. She goes to* CHARLEY *and takes his arm. Now all move toward the audience, through the wall-line of the kitchen. At the limit of the apron,* LINDA *lays down the flowers, kneels, and sits back on her heels. All stare down at the grave.*]

REQUIEM[7]

CHARLEY: It's getting dark, Linda.

[LINDA *doesn't react. She stares at the grave.*]

BIFF: How about it, Mom? Better get some rest, heh? They'll be closing the gate soon.

[LINDA *makes no move. Pause.*]

HAPPY: [*Deeply angered.*] He had no right to do that. There was no necessity for it. We would've helped him.
CHARLEY: [*Grunting.*] Hmmm.
BIFF: Come along, Mom.
LINDA: Why didn't anybody come?
CHARLEY: It was a very nice funeral.
LINDA: But where are all the people he knew? Maybe they blame him.
CHARLEY: Naa. It's a rough world, Linda. They wouldn't blame him.
LINDA: I can't understand it. At this time especially. First time in thirty-five years we were just about free and clear. He only needed a little salary. He was even finished with the dentist.
CHARLEY: No man only needs a little salary.
LINDA: I can't understand it.
BIFF: There were a lot of nice days. When he'd come home from a trip; or on Sundays, making the stoop; finishing the cellar; putting on the new porch; when he built the extra bathroom; and put up the garage. You know something, Charley, there's more of him in that front stoop than in all the sales he ever made.
CHARLEY: Yeah. He was a happy man with a batch of cement.
LINDA: He was so wonderful with his hands.
BIFF: He had the wrong dreams. All, all, wrong.
HAPPY: [*Almost ready to fight* BIFF.] Don't say that!
BIFF: He never knew who he was.
CHARLEY: [*Stopping* HAPPY's *movement and reply. To* BIFF.] Nobody dast blame this man. You don't understand: Willy was a salesman. And for a salesman, there is no rock bottom to the life. He don't put a bolt to a nut, he don't tell you the law or give you medicine. He's a man way out there in the blue, riding on a smile and a shoeshine. And when they start not smiling back—that's an earthquake. And then you get yourself a couple of spots on your hat, and you're finished.

---

7. Mass for the repose of departed souls; also a musical setting for such a mass.

Nobody dast blame this man. A salesman is got to dream, boy. It comes with the territory.

BIFF: Charley, the man didn't know who he was.

HAPPY: [*Infuriated.*] Don't say that!

BIFF: Why don't you come with me, Happy?

HAPPY: I'm not licked that easily. I'm staying right in this city, and I'm gonna beat this racket! [*He looks at* BIFF, *his chin set.*] The Loman Brothers!

BIFF: I know who I am, kid.

HAPPY: All right, boy. I'm gonna show you and everybody else that Willy Loman did not die in vain. He had a good dream. It's the only dream you can have— to come out number-one-man. He fought it out here, and this is where I'm gonna win it for him.

BIFF: [*With a hopeless glance at* HAPPY, *bends toward his mother.*] Let's go, Mom.

LINDA: I'll be with you in a minute. Go on, Charley. [*He hesitates.*] I want to, just for a minute. I never had a chance to say good-bye. [CHARLEY *moves away, followed by* HAPPY. BIFF *remains a slight distance up and left of* LINDA. *She sits there, summoning herself. The flute begins, not far away, playing behind her speech.*] Forgive me, dear. I can't cry. I don't know what it is, but I can't cry. I don't understand it. Why did you ever do that? Help me, Willy, I can't cry. It seems to me that you're just on another trip. I keep expecting you. Willy, dear, I can't cry. Why did you do it? I search and search and I search, and I can't understand it, Willy. I made the last payment on the house today. Today, dear. And there'll be nobody home. [*A sob rises in her throat.*] We're free and clear. [*Sobbing more fully, released.*] We're free. [BIFF *comes slowly toward her.*] We're free . . . We're free . . .

[BIFF *lifts her to her feet and moves out up right with her in his arms.* LINDA *sobs quietly.* BERNARD *and* CHARLEY *come together and follow them, followed by* HAPPY. *Only the music of the flute is left on the darkening stage as over the house the hard towers of the apartment buildings rise into sharp focus.*]

CURTAIN

1949

MARGARET EDSON

Wit

CHARACTERS

VIVIAN BEARING, PH.D., 50, *Professor of Seventeenth-Century Poetry at the University*

HARVEY KELEKIAN, M.D., 50, *Chief of Medical Oncology, University Hospital*

JASON POSNER, M.D., 28, *Clinical Fellow, Medical Oncology Branch*

SUSIE MONAHAN, R.N., B.S.N., 28, *Primary Nurse, Cancer Inpatient Unit*

E. M. ASHFORD, D.PHIL., 80, *Professor Emerita of English Literature*

MR. BEARING, *Vivian's father*

LAB TECHNICIANS

CLINICAL FELLOWS

STUDENTS

CODE TEAM

The play may be performed with a cast of nine: the four TECHNICIANS, FELLOWS, STU-
DENTS, *and* CODE TEAM MEMBERS *should double;* DR. KELEKIAN *and* MR. BEARING *should
double.*

VIVIAN BEARING *walks on the empty stage pushing her IV pole. She is fifty, tall and
very thin, barefoot, and completely bald. She wears two hospital gowns—one tied in
the front and one tied in the back—a baseball cap, and a hospital ID bracelet. The
house lights are at half strength.* VIVIAN *looks out at the audience, sizing them up.*

VIVIAN: [*In false familiarity, waving and nodding to the audience.*]
Hi. How are you feeling today? Great. That's just great.
[*In her own professorial tone.*] This is not my standard greeting, I assure you.
I tend toward something a little more formal, a little less inquisitive, such
as, say, "Hello."
But it is the standard greeting here.
There is some debate as to the correct response to this salutation. Should
one reply "I feel good," using "feel" as a copulative to link the subject, "I," to
its subjective complement, "good"; or "I feel well," modifying with an adverb
the subject's state of being?
I don't know. I am a professor of seventeenth-century poetry, specializing
in the Holy Sonnets of John Donne.[1]
So I just say, "Fine."
Of course it is not very often that I do feel fine.
I have been asked "How are you feeling today?" while I was throwing up
into a plastic washbasin. I have been asked as I was emerging from a four-
hour operation with a tube in every orifice, "How are you feeling today?"
I am waiting for the moment when someone asks me this question and I
am dead.
I'm a little sorry I'll miss that.
It is unfortunate that this remarkable line of inquiry has come to me so
late in my career. I could have exploited its feigned solicitude to great advantage: as I was distributing the final examination to the graduate course in
seventeenth-century textual criticism—[2] "Hi. How are you feeling today?"
Of course I would not be wearing this costume at the time, so the question's *ironic significance* would not be fully apparent.
As I trust it is now.
Irony is a literary device that will necessarily be deployed to great effect.
I ardently wish this were not so. I would prefer that a play about me be cast
in the mythic-heroic-pastoral mode; but the facts, most notably stage-four
metastatic ovarian cancer,[3] conspire against that. *The Faerie Queene* this is not.

----

1. John Donne (1572–1631), poet and high-ranking minister of the Church of England known for his wit
as well as his contributions to Christian theology. Several examples of his poetry appear in this volume,
including one of the Holy Sonnets, "Batter my heart, three-personed God."
2. Professor Bearing's course would study the variations among manuscripts and printed versions of
literary works produced in the 1600s in Britain, according to different methods or principles for establishing the version closest to the original, to the author's final intentions, or to a correct and readable text
for readers today.
3. Advanced cancer of the ovaries that has spread to other parts of the body. *The Faerie Queene*: allegorical
narrative poem in twelve books, written in a deliberately archaic style, by Edmund Spenser (1552–99).

And I was dismayed to discover that the play would contain elements of . . . *humor.*

I have been, at best, an *unwitting* accomplice. (*She pauses.*) It is not my intention to give away the plot; but I think I die at the end.

They've given me less than two hours.

If I were poetically inclined, I might employ a threadbare metaphor—the sands of time slipping through the hour-glass, the two-hour glass.

> Now our sands are almost run;
> More a little, and then dumb.[4]

Shakespeare. I trust the name is familiar.

At the moment, however, I am disinclined to poetry.

I've got less than two hours. Then: curtain. [*She disconnects herself from the IV pole and shoves it to a crossing technician. The house lights go out. Scene change.*]

I'll never forget the time I found out I had cancer. [DR. HARVEY KELEKIAN *enters at a big desk piled high with papers.*]

KELEKIAN: You have cancer.

VIVIAN: [*To audience.*] See? Unforgettable. It was something of a shock. I had to sit down. [*She plops down.*]

KELEKIAN: Please sit down. Miss Bearing, you have advanced metastatic ovarian cancer.

VIVIAN: Go on.

KELEKIAN: You are a professor, Miss Bearing.

VIVIAN: Like yourself, Dr. Kelekian.

KELEKIAN: Well, yes. Now then. You present with a growth that, unfortunately, went undetected in stages one, two, and three. Now it is an insidious adenocarcinoma, which has spread from the primary adnexal mass—[5]

VIVIAN: "Insidious"?

KELEKIAN: "Insidious" means undetectable at an—

VIVIAN: "Insidious" *means* treacherous.

KELEKIAN: Shall I continue?

VIVIAN: By all means.

KELEKIAN: Good. In invasive epithelial carcinoma, the most effective treatment modality is a chemotherapeutic agent. We are developing an experimental combination of drugs designed for primary-site ovarian, with a target specificity of stage three—and—beyond administration.

Am I going too fast?

VIVIAN: Insidious. Hmm. Curious word choice.

Cancer.   Cancel.

"By cancer nature's changing course untrimmed."[6] No—that's not it.

[*To* KELEKIAN.] No.

---

4. Couplet from Shakespeare's unfinished romance *Pericles* (5.2.1–2); like *The Faerie Queene*, it recalls the premodern world in a magical rather than realistic way.

5. Adenocarcinoma is a cancer that begins in cells in the lining of internal organs. An adnexal mass, common in women, is a growth, benign or cancerous, associated with the ovaries. Definitions of these and subsequent medical terms can be found in the dictionary; the patient herself looks them up.

6. Play on line 8 of Shakespeare's sonnet XVIII, "Shall I compare thee to a summer's day?": "By chance or nature's changing course untrimmed." (See p. 975.)

Good.

You will be hospitalized as an inpatient for treatment each cycle. You will be on complete intake-and-output measurement for three days after each treatment to monitor kidney function. After the initial eight cycles, you will have another battery of tests.	Must read something about cancer.
	Must get some books, articles. Assemble a bibliography.
	Is anyone doing research on cancer? Concentrate.
The antineoplastic will inevitably affect some healthy cells, including those lining the gastro-intestinal tract from the lips to the anus, and the hair follicles. We will of course be relying on your resolve to withstand some of the more pernicious side effects.	Antineoplastic. Anti: against. Neo: new. Plastic. To mold. Shaping. Antineoplastic. Against new shaping.
	Hair follicles. My resolve.
	"Pernicious." That doesn't seem—

KELEKIAN: Miss Bearing?

VIVIAN: I beg your pardon?

KELEKIAN: Do you have any questions so far?

VIVIAN: Please, go on.

KELEKIAN: Perhaps some of these terms are new. I realize—

VIVIAN: No, no. Ah. You're being very thorough.

KELEKIAN: I make a point of it. And I always emphasize it with my students—

VIVIAN: So do I. "Thoroughness"—I always tell my students, but they are constitutionally averse to painstaking work.

KELEKIAN: Yours, too.

VIVIAN: Oh, it's worse every year.

KELEKIAN: And this is not dermatology, it's medical oncology, for Chrissake.

VIVIAN: My students read through a text once—once!—and think it's time for a break.

KELEKIAN: Mine are blind.

VIVIAN: Well, mine are deaf.

KELEKIAN: [Resigned, but warmly.] You just have to hope....

VIVIAN: [Not so sure.] I suppose. [Pause.]

KELEKIAN: Where were we, Dr. Bearing?

VIVIAN: I believe I was being thoroughly diagnosed.

KELEKIAN: Right. Now. The tumor is spreading very quickly, and this treatment is very aggressive. So far, so good?

VIVIAN: Yes.

KELEKIAN: Better not teach next semester.

VIVIAN: [Indignant.] Out of the question.

KELEKIAN: The first week of each cycle you'll be hospitalized for chemotherapy; the next week you may feel a little tired; the next two weeks'll be fine, relatively. This cycle will repeat eight times, as I said before.

VIVIAN: Eight months like that?

KELEKIAN: This treatment is the strongest thing we have to offer you. And, as research, it will make a significant contribution to our knowledge.

VIVIAN: Knowledge, yes.

KELEKIAN: [*Giving her a piece of paper.*] Here is the informed-consent form. Should you agree, you sign there, at the bottom. Is there a family member you want me to explain this to?

VIVIAN: [*Signing.*] That won't be necessary.

KELEKIAN: [*Taking back the paper.*] Good. The important thing is for you to take the full dose of chemotherapy. There may be times when you'll wish for a lesser dose, due to the side effects. But we've got to go full-force. The experimental phase has got to have the maximum dose to be of any use. Dr. Bearing—

VIVIAN: Yes?

KELEKIAN: You must be very tough. Do you think you can be very tough?

VIVIAN: You needn't worry.

KELEKIAN: Good. Excellent. [KELEKIAN *and the desk exit as* VIVIAN *stands and walks forward.*]

VIVIAN: [*Hesitantly.*] I should have asked more questions, because I know there's going to be a test.

I have cancer, insidious cancer, with pernicious side effects—No, the *treatment* has pernicious side effects.

I have stage-four metastatic ovarian cancer. There is no stage five. Oh, and I have to be very tough. It appears to be a matter, as the saying goes, of life and death.

I know all about life and death. I am, after all, a scholar of Donne's Holy Sonnets, which explore mortality in greater depth than any other body of work in the English language.

And I know for a fact that I am tough. A demanding professor. Uncompromising. Never one to turn from a challenge. That is why I chose, while a student of the great E. M. Ashford, to study Donne. [PROFESSOR E. M. ASHFORD, *fifty-two, enters, seated at the same desk as* KELEKIAN *was. The scene is twenty-eight years ago.* VIVIAN *suddenly turns twenty-two, eager and intimidated.*]

Professor Ashford?

E.M.: Do it again.

VIVIAN: [*To audience.*] It was something of a shock. I had to sit down. [*She plops down.*]

E.M.: Please sit down. Your essay on Holy Sonnet Six, Miss Bearing, is a melodrama, with a veneer of scholarship unworthy of you—to say nothing of Donne. Do it again.

VIVIAN: I, ah . . .

E.M.: You must begin with a text, Miss Bearing, not with a feeling.

> Death be not proud, though some have called thee
> Mighty and dreadfull, for, thou art not soe[7]

You have entirely missed the point of the poem, because, I must tell you, you have used an edition of the text that is inauthentically punctuated. In the Gardner edition—

VIVIAN: That edition was checked out of the library—

---

7. From John Donne's Holy Sonnet 6 "Death, be not proud." (See p. 1321.)

E.M.: Miss Bearing!

VIVIAN: Sorry.

E.M.: You take this too lightly, Miss Bearing. This is Metaphysical Poetry, not The Modern Novel. The standards of scholarship and critical reading which one would apply to any other text are simply insufficient. The effort must be total for the results to be meaningful. Do you think the punctuation of the last line of this sonnet is merely an insignificant detail?

The sonnet begins with a valiant struggle with death, calling on all the forces of intellect and drama to vanquish the enemy. But it is ultimately about overcoming the seemingly insuperable barriers separating life, death, and eternal life.

In the edition you chose, this profoundly simple meaning is sacrificed to hysterical punctuation:

> And Death—*capital D*—shall be no more—*semicolon!*
> Death—*capital D*—comma—thou shalt die—*ex-clamation point!*

If you go in for this sort of thing, I suggest you take up Shakespeare.

Gardner's edition of the Holy Sonnets returns to the Westmoreland manuscript source of 1610—not for sentimental reasons, I assure you, but because Helen Gardner is a *scholar*. It reads:

> And death shall be no more, *comma*, Death thou shalt die.

[*As she recites this line, she makes a little gesture at the comma.*]

Nothing but a breath—a comma—separates life from life everlasting. It is very simple really. With the original punctuation restored, death is no longer something to act out on a stage, with exclamation points. It's a comma, a pause.

This way, the *uncompromising* way, one learns something from this poem, wouldn't you say? Life, death. Soul, God. Past, present. Not insuperable barriers, not semicolons, just a comma.

VIVIAN: Life, death . . . I see. [*Standing.*] It's a metaphysical conceit.[8] It's wit! I'll go back to the library and rewrite the paper—

E. M.: [*Standing, emphatically.*] It is *not wit*, Miss Bearing. It is truth. [*Walking around the desk to her.*] The paper's not the point.

VIVIAN: It isn't?

E. M.: [*Tenderly.*] Vivian. You're a bright young woman. Use your intelligence. Don't go back to the library. Go out. Enjoy yourself with your friends. Hmm? [VIVIAN *walks away.* E. M. *slides off.*]

VIVIAN: [*As she gradually returns to the hospital.*] I, ah, went outside. The sun was very bright. I, ah, walked around, past the . . . There were students on the lawn, talking about nothing, laughing. The insuperable barrier between one thing and another is . . . just a comma? Simple human truth, uncompromising scholarly standards? They're *connected*? I just couldn't. . . .

I went back to the library.

---

8. The work of John Donne and other "metaphysical" poets uses extended figures of speech, "conceits," that seem paradoxical or puzzling because they link very different entities, often common things and spiritual concepts. The seventeenth-century concept of "wit" is more a matter of brilliant intellect and verbal irony than clever jokes.

Anyway.

All right. Significant contribution to knowledge.

Eight cycles of chemotherapy. Give me the full dose, the full dose every time. [*Scene change. In a burst of activity, the hospital scene is created.*]

The attention was flattering. For the first five minutes. Now I know how poems feel. [SUSIE MONAHAN, *Vivian's primary nurse, gives* VIVIAN *her chart, then puts her in a wheelchair and takes her to her first appointment: chest X-ray. This and all other diagnostic tests are suggested by light and sound.*]

TECHNICIAN 1: Name.

VIVIAN: My name? Vivian Bearing.

TECHNICIAN 1: Huh?

VIVIAN: Bearing. B-E-A-R-I-N-G. Vivian. V-I-V-I-A-N.

TECHNICIAN 1: Doctor.

VIVIAN: Yes, I have a Ph.D.

TECHNICIAN 1: *Your* doctor.

VIVIAN: Oh. Dr. Harvey Kelekian. [TECHNICIAN 1 *positions her so that she is leaning forward and embracing the metal plate, then steps offstage.*] I am a doctor of philosophy—

TECHNICIAN 1: [*From offstage.*] Take a deep breath, and hold it. [*Pause, with light and sound.*] Okay.

VIVIAN: —a scholar of seventeenth-century poetry.

TECHNICIAN 1: Turn sideways, arms behind your head, and hold it. [*Pause.*] Okay.

VIVIAN: I have made an immeasurable contribution to the discipline of English literature. [TECHNICIAN 1 *returns and puts her in the wheelchair.*] I am, in short, a force. [TECHNICIAN 1 *rolls her to upper GI series, where* TECHNICIAN 2 *picks up.*]

TECHNICIAN 2: Name.

VIVIAN: Lucy, Countess of Bedford.[9]

TECHNICIAN 2: [*Checking a printout.*] I don't see it here.

VIVIAN: My name is Vivian Bearing. B-E-A-R-I-N-G. Dr. Kelekian is my doctor.

TECHNICIAN 2: Okay. Lie down. [TECHNICIAN 2 *positions her on a stretcher and leaves. Light and sound suggest the filming.*]

VIVIAN: After an outstanding undergraduate career, I studied with Professor E. M. Ashford for three years, during which time I learned by instruction and example what it means to be a scholar of distinction.

As her research fellow, my principal task was the alphabetizing of index cards for Ashford's monumental critical edition of Donne's *Devotions upon Emergent Occasions.* [*During the procedure, another* TECHNICIAN *takes the wheelchair away.*]

I am thanked in the preface: "Miss Vivian Bearing for her able assistance."

My dissertation, "Ejaculations in Seventeenth-Century Manuscript and Printed Editions of the Holy Sonnets: A Comparison,"[1] was revised for publication in the *Journal of English Texts,* a very prestigious venue for a first appearance.

---

9. Ben Jonson (1572–1637), poet and playwright who was a contemporary of Shakespeare, wrote an epigrammatic poem published along with John Donne's *Satires* that praises the talented patroness Lucy, Countess of Bedford. The poem suggests that the countess was among the few people able to appreciate satire.

1. *Ejaculations* (from the Latin *eiaculari*, meaning "to throw out") here refers to exclamations (such as "O God!"). This dissertation and journal are invented. The details of scholarship throughout the play, including scholars' names and journal titles, are sometimes fictitious and sometimes genuine, but always plausible.

TECHNICIAN 2: Where's your wheelchair?

VIVIAN: I do not know. I was busy just now.

TECHNICIAN 2: Well, how are you going to get out of here?

VIVIAN: Well, I do not know. Perhaps you would like me to stay.

TECHNICIAN 2: I guess I got to go find you a chair.

VIVIAN: [*Sarcastically.*] Don't inconvenience yourself on my behalf. [TECHNICIAN 2 *leaves to get a wheelchair.*]

My second article, a classic explication of Donne's sonnet "Death be not proud," was published in *Critical Discourse*.

The success of the essay prompted the University Press to solicit a volume on the twelve Holy Sonnets in the 1633 edition, which I produced in the remarkably short span of three years. My book, entitled *Made Cunningly*, remains an immense success, in paper as well as cloth.

In it, I devote one chapter to a thorough examination of each sonnet, discussing every word in extensive detail. [TECHNICIAN 2 *returns with a wheelchair.*]

TECHNICIAN 2: Here.

VIVIAN: I summarize previous critical interpretations of the text and offer my own analysis. It is exhaustive. [TECHNICIAN 2 *deposits her at CT scan.*] Bearing. B-E-A-R-I-N-G. Kelekian. [TECHNICIAN 3 *has* VIVIAN *lie down on a metal stretcher. Light and sound suggest the procedure.*]

TECHNICIAN 2: Here. Hold still.

VIVIAN: For how long?

TECHNICIAN 2: Just a little while. [TECHNICIAN 3 *leaves. Silence.*]

VIVIAN: The scholarly study of poetic texts requires a capacity for scrupulously detailed examination, particularly the poetry of John Donne.

The salient characteristic of the poems is wit: "Itchy outbreaks of far-fetched wit," as Donne himself said.

To the common reader—that is to say, the undergraduate with a B-plus or better average—wit provides an invaluable exercise for sharpening the mental faculties, for stimulating the flash of comprehension that can only follow hours of exacting and seemingly pointless scrutiny. [TECHNICIAN 3 *puts* VIVIAN *back in the wheelchair and wheels her toward the unit. Partway,* TECHNICIAN 3 *gives the chair a shove and* SUSIE *takes over.* SUSIE *rolls* VIVIAN *to the exam room.*]

To the scholar, to the mind comprehensively trained in the subtleties of seventeenth-century vocabulary, versification, and theological, historical, geographical, political, and mythological allusions, Donne's wit is . . . a way to see how good you really are.

After twenty years, I can say with confidence, no one is quite as good as I. [*By now,* SUSIE *has helped* VIVIAN *sit on the exam table.* DR. JASON POSNER, *clinical fellow, stands in the doorway.*]

JASON: Ah, Susie?

SUSIE: Oh, hi.

JASON: Ready when you are.

SUSIE: Okay. Go ahead. Ms. Bearing, this is Jason Posner. He's going to do your history, ask you a bunch of questions. He's Dr. Kelekian's fellow. [SUSIE *is busy in the room, setting up for the exam.*]

JASON: Hi, Professor Bearing. I'm Dr. Posner, clinical fellow in the medical oncology branch, working with Dr. Kelekian.

Professor Bearing, I, ah, I was an undergraduate at the U. I took your course in seventeenth-century poetry.

VIVIAN: You did?

JASON: Yes. I thought it was excellent.

VIVIAN: Thank you. Were you an English major?

JASON: No. Biochemistry. But you can't get into medical school unless you're well-rounded. And I made a bet with myself that I could get an A in the three hardest courses on campus.

SUSIE: Howdjya do, Jace?

JASON: Success.

VIVIAN: [*Doubtful.*] Really?

JASON: A minus. It was a very tough course. [*To* SUSIE.] I'll call you.

SUSIE: Okay. [*She leaves.*]

JASON: I'll just pull this over. [*He gets a little stool on wheels.*] Get the proxemics² right here. There. [*Nervously.*] Good. Now. I'm going to be taking your history. It's a medical interview, and then I give you an exam.

VIVIAN: I believe Dr. Kelekian has already done that.

JASON: Well, I know, but Dr. Kelekian wants me to do it, too. Now. I'll be taking a few notes as we go along.

VIVIAN: Very well.

JASON: Okay. Let's get started. How are you feeling today?

VIVIAN: Fine, thank you.

JASON: Good. How is your general health?

VIVIAN: Fine.

JASON: Excellent. Okay. We know you are an academic.

VIVIAN: Yes, we've established that.

JASON: So we don't need to talk about your interesting work.

VIVIAN: No. [*The following questions and answers go extremely quickly.*]

JASON: How old are you?

VIVIAN: Fifty.

JASON: Are you married?

VIVIAN: No.

JASON: Are your parents living?

VIVIAN: No.

JASON: How and when did they die?

VIVIAN: My father, suddenly, when I was twenty, of a heart attack. My mother, slowly, when I was forty-one and forty-two, of cancer. Breast cancer.

JASON: Cancer?

VIVIAN: Breast cancer.

JASON: I see. Any siblings?

VIVIAN: No.

JASON: Do you have any questions so far?

VIVIAN: Not so far.

JASON: Well, that about does it for your life history.

VIVIAN: Yes, that's all there is to my life history.

JASON: Now I'm going to ask you about your past medical history. Have you ever been hospitalized?

2. The study of spatial sense.

VIVIAN: I had my tonsils out when I was eight.

JASON: Have you ever been pregnant?

VIVIAN: No.

JASON: Ever had heart murmurs? High blood pressure?

VIVIAN: No.

JASON: Stomach, liver, kidney problems?

VIVIAN: No.

JASON: Venereal diseases? Uterine infections?

VIVIAN: No.

JASON: Thyroid, diabetes, cancer?

VIVIAN: No—cancer, yes.

JASON: When?

VIVIAN: Now.

JASON: Well, not including now.

VIVIAN: In that case, no.

JASON: Okay. Clinical depression? Nervous breakdowns? Suicide attempts?

VIVIAN: No.

JASON: Do you smoke?

VIVIAN: No.

JASON: Ethanol?

VIVIAN: I'm sorry?

JASON: Alcohol.

VIVIAN: Oh. Ethanol. Yes, I drink wine.

JASON: How much? How often?

VIVIAN: A glass with dinner occasionally. And perhaps a Scotch every now and then.

JASON: Do you use substances?

VIVIAN: Such as.

JASON: Marijuana, cocaine, crack cocaine, PCP, ecstasy, poppers—

VIVIAN: No.

JASON: Do you drink caffeinated beverages?

VIVIAN: Oh, yes!

JASON: Which ones?

VIVIAN: Coffee. A few cups a day.

JASON: How many?

VIVIAN: Two . . . to six. But I really don't think that's immoderate—

JASON: How often do you undergo routine medical checkups?

VIVIAN: Well, not as often as I should, probably, but I've felt fine, I really have.

JASON: So the answer is?

VIVIAN: Every three to . . . five years.

JASON: What do you do for exercise?

VIVIAN: Pace.

JASON: Are you having sexual relations?

VIVIAN: Not at the moment.

JASON: Are you pre- or post-menopausal?

VIVIAN: Pre.

JASON: When was the first day of your last period?

VIVIAN: Ah, ten days—two weeks ago.

JASON: Okay. When did you first notice your present complaint?

VIVIAN: This time, now?

JASON: Yes.

VIVIAN: Oh, about four months ago. I felt a pain in my stomach, in my abdomen, like a cramp, but not the same.

JASON: How did it feel?

VIVIAN: Like a cramp.

JASON: But not the same?

VIVIAN: No, duller, and stronger. I can't describe it.

JASON: What came next?

VIVIAN: Well, I just, I don't know, I started noticing my body, little things. I would be teaching, and feel a sharp pain.

JASON: What kind of pain?

VIVIAN: Sharp, and sudden. Then it would go away. Or I would be tired. Exhausted. I was working on a major project, the article on John Donne for *The Oxford Encyclopedia of English Literature*. It was a great honor. But I had a very strict deadline.

JASON: So you would say you were under stress?

VIVIAN: It wasn't so much more stress than usual, I just couldn't withstand it this time. I don't know.

JASON: So?

VIVIAN: So I went to Dr. Chin, my gynecologist, after I had turned in the article, and explained all this. She examined me, and sent me to Jefferson the internist, and he sent me to Kelekian because he thought I might have a tumor.

JASON: And that's it?

VIVIAN: Till now.

JASON: Hmmm. Well, that's very interesting. [*Nervous pause.*]

Well, I guess I'll start the examination. It'll only take a few minutes. Why don't you, um, sort of lie back, and—oh—relax. [*He helps her lie back on the table, raises the stirrups out of the table, raises her legs and puts them in the stirrups, and puts a paper sheet over her.*]

Be very relaxed. This won't hurt. Let me get this sheet. Okay. Just stay calm. Okay. Put your feet in these stirrups. Okay. Just. There. Okay? Now. Oh, I have to go get Susie. Got to have a girl here. Some crazy clinical rule. Um. I'll be right back. Don't move. [JASON *leaves. Long pause. He is seen walking quickly back and forth in the hall, and calling* SUSIE's *name as he goes by.*]

VIVIAN: [*To herself.*] I wish I had given him an A. [*Silence.*]

Two times one is two. Two times two is four.

Two times three is six.

Um.

Oh.

Death be not proud, though some have called thee
Mighty and dreadful, for, thou art not soe,
For, those, whom thou think'st, thou dost overthrow,
Die not, poore death, nor yet canst thou kill mee; . . .

JASON: [*In the hallway.*] Has anybody seen Susie?

VIVIAN: [*Losing her place for a second.*] Ah.

Thou'art slave to Fate, chance, kings, and desperate men,
And dost with poyson, warre, and sicknesse dwell,
And poppie, or charmes can make us sleepe as well,
And better than thy stroake: why swell'st thou then?

JASON: [*In the hallway.*] She was here just a minute ago.
VIVIAN:

> One short sleepe past, wee wake eternally,
> And death shall be no more—*comma*—Death thou shalt die.

[JASON *and* SUSIE *return.*]

JASON: Okay. Here's everything. Okay.
SUSIE: What is this? Why did you leave her—
JASON: [*To* SUSIE.] I had to find you. Now, come on. [*To* VIVIAN.] We're ready, Professor Bearing. [*To himself, as he puts on exam gloves.*] Get these on. Okay. Just lift this up. Ooh. Okay. [*As much to himself as to her.*] Just relax. [*He begins the pelvic exam, with one hand on her abdomen and the other inside her, looking blankly at the ceiling as he feels around.*] Okay. [*Silence.*] Susie, isn't that interesting, that I had Professor Bearing.
SUSIE: Yeah. I wish I had taken some literature. I don't know anything about poetry.
JASON: [*Trying to be casual.*] Professor Bearing was very highly regarded on campus. It looked very good on my transcript that I had taken her course. [*Silence.*] They even asked me about it in my interview for med school—[*He feels the mass and does a double take.*] Jesus! [*Tense silence. He is amazed and fascinated.*]
SUSIE: What?
VIVIAN: What?
JASON: Um. [*He tries for composure.*] Yeah. I survived Bearing's course. No problem. Heh. [*Silence.*] Yeah, John Donne, those metaphysical poets, that metaphysical wit. Hardest poetry in the English department. Like to see them try biochemistry. [*Silence.*] Okay. We're about done. Okay. That's it. Okay, Professor Bearing. Let's take your feet out, there. [*He takes off his gloves and throws them away.*] Okay. I gotta go. I gotta go. [JASON *quickly leaves.* VIVIAN *slowly gets up from this scene and walks stiffly away.* SUSIE *cleans up the exam room and exits. Scene change.*]
VIVIAN: [*Walking D to audience.*] That . . . was . . . hard. That . . . was . . .

One thing can be said for an eight-month course of cancer treatment: it is highly educational. I am learning to suffer.

Yes, it is mildly uncomfortable to have an electrocardiogram, but the . . . agony . . . of a proctosigmoidoscopy[3] sweeps it from memory. Yes, it was embarrassing to have to wear a nightgown all day long—two nightgowns!—but that seemed like a positive privilege compared to watching myself go bald. Yes, having a former student give me a pelvic exam was thoroughly degrading—and I use the term deliberately—but I could not have imagined the depths of humiliation that—

Oh, God— [VIVIAN *runs across the stage to her hospital room, dives onto the bed, and throws up into a large plastic washbasin.*]

Oh, God.

Oh. Oh. [*She lies slumped on the bed, fastened to the IV, which now includes a small bottle with a bright orange label.*]

Oh, God.

It can't be.

---

3. Diagnostic examination of the lower intestinal tract.

[*Silence.*]
Oh, God.
Please.
Steady. Steady.
[*Silence.*]
Oh—
Oh, no! [*She throws up again, moans, and retches in agony.*]
Oh, God.
What's left?
I haven't eaten in two days.
What's left to puke?
[*Silence.*]
You may remark that my vocabulary has taken a turn for the Anglo-Saxon.
God, I'm going to barf my brains out.
[*She begins to relax.*] If I actually did barf my brains out, it would be a great loss to my discipline. Of course, not a few of my colleagues would be relieved. To say nothing of my students.

It's not that I'm controversial. Just uncompromising. Ooh— [*She lunges for the basin. Nothing.*] Oh. [*Silence.*] False alarm. If the word went round that Vivian Bearing had barfed her brains out . . .

Well, first my colleagues, most of whom are my former students, would scramble madly for my position. Then their consciences would flare up, so to honor *my* memory they would put together a collection of *their* essays about John Donne. The volume would begin with a warm introduction, capturing my most endearing qualities. It would be short. But sweet.

Published *and* perished.[4]

Now, watch this. I have to ring the bell [*She presses the button on the bed.*] to get someone to come and measure this emesis, and record the amount on a chart of my intake and output. This counts as output. [SUSIE *enters.*]
SUSIE: [*Brightly.*] How you doing, Ms. Bearing? You having some nausea?
VIVIAN: [*Weakly.*] Uhh, yes.
SUSIE: Why don't I take that? Here.
VIVIAN: It's about 300 cc's.
SUSIE: That all?
VIVIAN: It was very hard work. [SUSIE *takes the basin to the bathroom and rinses it.*]
SUSIE: Yup. Three hundred. Good guess. [*She marks the graph.*] Okay.

Anything else I can get for you? Some Jell-O or anything?
VIVIAN: Thank you, no.
SUSIE: You okay all by yourself here?
VIVIAN: Yes.
SUSIE: You're not having a lot of visitors, are you?
VIVIAN: [*Correcting.*] None, to be precise.
SUSIE: Yeah, I didn't think so. Is there somebody you want me to call for you?
VIVIAN: That won't be necessary.

---

4. In colleges and universities a common saying is "publish or perish" because a professor's promotion and tenure or job security depend on publishing scholarly research. Vivian Bearing has just imagined a predictable memorial for a scholar of her eminence, a *festschrift*, or collection of essays in honor of a senior scholar in a field. *Emesis*: vomiting.

SUSIE: Well, I'll just pop my head in every once in a while to see how you're coming along. Kelekian and the fellows should be in soon. [*She touches* VIVIAN's *arm.*] If there's anything you need, you just ring.

VIVIAN: [*Uncomfortable with kindness.*] Thank you.

SUSIE: Okay. Just call. [SUSIE *disconnects the IV bottle with the orange label and takes it with her as she leaves.* VIVIAN *lies still. Silence. Scene change.*]

VIVIAN: In this dramatic structure you will see the most interesting aspects of my tenure as an inpatient receiving experimental chemotherapy for advanced metastatic ovarian cancer.

But as I am a *scholar* before . . . an impresario,[5] I feel obliged to document what it is like here most of the time, between the dramatic climaxes. Between the spectacles.

In truth, it is like this: [*She ceremoniously lies back and stares at the ceiling.*]
You cannot imagine how time . . . can be . . . so still.
It hangs. It weighs. And yet there is so little of it.
It goes so slowly, and yet it is so scarce. [*Pause.*]
If I were writing this scene, it would last a full fifteen minutes. I would lie here, and you would sit there. [*She looks at the audience, daring them.*]
Not to worry. Brevity is the soul of wit.[6]
But if you think eight months of cancer treatment is tedious for the *audience*, consider how it feels to play my part.
All right. All right. It is Friday morning: Grand Rounds. [*Loudly, giving a cue.*] Action. [KELEKIAN *enters, followed by* JASON *and four other* FELLOWS.]

KELEKIAN: Dr. Bearing.

VIVIAN: Dr. Kelekian.

KELEKIAN: Jason. [JASON *moves to the front of the group.*]

JASON: Professor Bearing. How are you feeling today?

VIVIAN: Fine.

JASON: That's great. That's just great. [*He takes a sheet and carefully covers her legs and groin, then pulls up her gown to reveal her entire abdomen. He is barely audible, but his gestures are clear.*]

VIVIAN: "Grand Rounds."
The term is theirs. Not "Grand" in the traditional sense of sweeping or magnificent. Not "Rounds" as in a musical canon, or a *round* of applause (though either would be refreshing at this point). Here, "Rounds" seems to signify darting *around* the main issue . . . which I suppose would be the struggle for life . . . *my* life . . . with heated discussions of *side* effects, *other* complaints, *additional* treatments.

JASON: Very late detection. Staged as a four upon admission. Hexamethophosphacil with Vinplatin to potentiate.[7] Hex at 300 mg. per meter squared, Vin at 100. Today is cycle two, day three. Both cycles at the *full dose.* [*The* FELLOWS *are impressed.*]
The primary site is—here, [*He puts his finger on the spot on her abdomen.*] behind the left ovary. Metastases are suspected in the peritoneal cavity—here. And—here. [*He touches those spots.*]

---

5. Theatrical manager or producer; showman.
6. From Shakespeare's *Hamlet* 2.2, spoken by the verbose Polonius.
7. Hexamethophosphacil and Vinplatin ("Hex" and "Vin"), powerful chemicals used in chemotherapy.

Grand Rounds is not Grand
Opera. But compared to lying here,
it is positively *dramatic.*

Full of subservience, hierarchy, gra-
tuitous displays, sublimated rival-
ries—I feel right at home. It is just
like a graduate seminar.

With one important difference: in
Grand Rounds, *they* read *me* like a
book. Once I did the teaching; now I
am taught. This is much easier. I
just hold still and look cancerous.
It requires less acting every time.

Excellent command of details.

Full lymphatic involvement. [*He
moves his hands over her entire body.*]

At the time of first-look surgery, a
significant part of the tumor was
de-bulked, mostly in this area—
here. [*He points to each organ, poking
her abdomen.*] Left, right ovaries.
Fallopian tubes. Uterus. All out.

Evidence of primary-site shrinkage.
Shrinking in metastatic tumors
has not been documented. Primary
mass frankly palpable in pelvic
exam, frankly, all through
here—here. [*Some* FELLOWS *reach
and press where he is pointing.*]

KELEKIAN: Excellent command of details.
VIVIAN: [*To herself.*] I taught him, you know—
KELEKIAN: Okay. Problem areas with Hex and Vin. [*He addresses all the* FELLOWS, *but*
JASON *answers first and they resent him.*]
FELLOW 1: Myelosu—
JASON: [*Interrupting.*] Well, first of course is myelosuppression, a lowering of
blood-cell counts. It goes without saying. With this combination of agents,
nephrotoxicity will be next.
KELEKIAN: Go on.
JASON: The kidneys are designed to filter out impurities in the bloodstream. In
trying to filter the chemotherapeutic agent out of the bloodstream, the kid-
neys shut down.
KELEKIAN: Intervention.
JASON: Hydration.
KELEKIAN: Monitoring.
JASON: Full recording of fluid intake and output, as you see here on these graphs,
to monitor hydration and kidney function. Totals monitored daily by the
clinical fellow, as per the protocol.
KELEKIAN: Anybody else. Side effects.
FELLOW 1: Nausea and vomiting.
KELEKIAN: Jason.
JASON: Routine.
FELLOW 2: Pain while urinating.
JASON: Routine. [*The* FELLOWS *are trying to catch* JASON.]
FELLOW 3: Psychological depression.
JASON: No way. [*The* FELLOWS *are silent.*]
KELEKIAN: [*Standing by* VIVIAN *at the head of the bed.*] Anything else. Other com-
plaints with Hexamethophosphacil and Vinplatin. Come on. [*Silence.* KELE-
KIAN *and* VIVIAN *wait together for the correct answer.*]
FELLOW 4: Mouth sores.
JASON: Not yet.

FELLOW 2: [*Timidly.*] Skin rash?

JASON: Nope.

KELEKIAN: [*Sharing this with* VIVIAN.] Why do we waste our time, Dr. Bearing?

VIVIAN: [*Delighted.*] I do not know, Dr. Kelekian.

KELEKIAN: [*To the* FELLOWS.] Use your eyes. [*All* FELLOWS *look closely at* VIVIAN.] Jesus God. Hair loss.

FELLOWS: [*All protesting.* VIVIAN *and* KELEKIAN *are amused.*]

    —Come on.

    —You can see it.

    —It doesn't count.

    —No fair.

KELEKIAN: Jason.

JASON: [*Begrudgingly.*] Hair loss after first cycle of treatment.

KELEKIAN: That's better. [*To* VIVIAN.] Dr. Bearing. Full dose. Excellent. Keep pushing the fluids. [*The* FELLOWS *leave.* KELEKIAN *stops* JASON.] Jason.

JASON: Huh?

KELEKIAN: Clinical.

JASON: Oh, right. [*To* VIVIAN.] Thank you, Professor Bearing. You've been very cooperative. [*They leave her with her stomach uncovered.*]

VIVIAN: Wasn't that . . . Grand? [*She gets up without the IV pole.*] At times, this obsessively detailed examination, this *scrutiny* seems to me to be a nefarious business. On the other hand, what is the alternative? Ignorance? Ignorance may be . . . bliss; but it is not a very noble goal.

So I play my part. [*Pause.*]

I receive chemotherapy, throw up, am subjected to countless indignities, feel better, go home. Eight cycles. Eight neat little strophes.[8] Oh, there have been the usual variations, subplots, red herrings: hepatotoxicity (liver poison), neuropathy (nerve death).

[*Righteously.*] They are medical terms. I look them up.

It has always been my custom to treat words with respect.

I can recall the time—the very hour of the very day—when I knew words would be my life's work.

[*Scene change. A pile of six little white books appears, with* MR. BEARING, *Vivian's father, seated behind an open newspaper.*] It was my fifth birthday. [VIVIAN, *now a child, flops down to the books.*] I liked that one best.

MR. BEARING: [*Disinterested but tolerant, never distracted from his newspaper.*]

Read another.

VIVIAN: I think I'll read . . . [*She takes a book from the stack and reads its spine intently.*] *The Tale of the Flopsy Bunnies.* [*Reading the front cover.*] *The Tale of the Flopsy Bunnies.* It has little bunnies on the front. [*Opening to the title page.*]

The Tale of the Flopsy Bunnies by Beatrix Potter.[9] [*She turns the page and begins to read.*]

It is said that the effect of eating too much lettuce is sopor—sop—or—what is that word?

8. Sections of a poem.

9. Writer and illustrator (1866–1943); her many children's tales include *The Tale of Peter Rabbit* (1902) and *The Tale of the Flopsy Bunnies* (1909).

MR. BEARING: Sound it out.

VIVIAN: Sop—or—fic. Sop—or—i—fic. Soporific. What does that mean?

MR. BEARING: Soporific. Causing sleep.

VIVIAN: Causing sleep.

MR. BEARING: Makes you sleepy.

VIVIAN: "Soporific" means "makes you sleepy"?

MR. BEARING: Correct.

VIVIAN: "Soporific" means "makes you sleepy." Soporific.

MR. BEARING: Now use it in a sentence. What has a soporific effect on you?

VIVIAN: A soporific effect on me.

MR. BEARING: What makes you sleepy?

VIVIAN: Aahh—nothing.

MR. BEARING: Correct.

VIVIAN: What about you?

MR. BEARING: What has a soporific effect on me? Let me think: boring conversation, I suppose, after dinner.

VIVIAN: Me too, boring conversation.

MR. BEARING: Carry on.

VIVIAN:

It is said that the effect of eating too much lettuce is soporific.

The little bunnies in the picture are asleep! They're sleeping! Like you said, because of *soporific!* [*She stands up, and* MR. BEARING *exits.*]

The illustration bore out the meaning of the word, just as he had explained it. At the time, it seemed like magic.

So imagine the effect that the words of John Donne first had on me: ratio-cination, concatenation, coruscation, tergiversation.[1]

Medical terms are less evocative. Still, I want to know what the doctors mean when they . . . anatomize me. And I will grant that in this particular field of endeavor they possess a more potent arsenal of terminology than I. My only defense is the acquisition of vocabulary.

[*Scene change.* SUSIE *enters and puts her arm around* VIVIAN*'s shoulders to hold her up.* VIVIAN *is shaking, feverish, and weak. All at once.*] Fever-and-neutropenia.[2]

SUSIE: When did it start?

VIVIAN: [*Having difficulty speaking.*] I—I was at home—reading—and I—felt so bad. I called. Fever and neutropenia. They said to come in.

SUSIE: You did the right thing to come. Did somebody drive you?

VIVIAN: Cab. I took a taxi.

SUSIE: [*She grabs a wheelchair and helps* VIVIAN *sit. As* SUSIE *speaks, she takes* VIVIAN*'s temperature, pulse, and respiration rate.*] Here, why don't you sit? Just sit there a min-ute. I'll get Jason. He's on call tonight. We'll get him to give you some meds. I'm glad I was here on nights. I'll make sure you get to bed soon, okay? It'll just be a minute. I'll get you some juice, some nice juice with lots of ice. [SUSIE *leaves quickly.* VIVIAN *sits there, agitated, confused, and very sick.* SUSIE *returns with the juice.*]

VIVIAN: Lights. I left all the lights on at my house.

SUSIE: Don't you worry. It'll be all right. [JASON *enters, roused from his sleep and not fully awake. He wears surgical scrubs and puts on a lab coat as he enters.*]

1. That is, thought, connection, flash of wit or insight, and ambiguity or equivocation.
2. Fever and chills.

JASON: [*Without looking at* VIVIAN.] How are you feeling, Professor Bearing?

VIVIAN: My teeth—are chattering.

JASON: Vitals.

SUSIE: [*Giving* VIVIAN *juice and a straw, without looking at* JASON.] Temp 39.4. Pulse 120. Respiration 36. Chills and sweating.

JASON: Fever and neutropenia. It's a "shake and bake." Blood cultures and urine, stat. Admit her. Prepare for reverse isolation. Start with acetaminophen. Vitals every four hours. [*He starts to leave.*]

SUSIE: [*Following him.*] Jason—I think you need to talk to Kelekian about lowering the dose for the next cycle. It's too much for her like this.

JASON: Lower the dose? No way. Full dose. She's tough. She can take it. Wake me up when the counts come from the lab. [*He pads off.* SUSIE *wheels* VIVIAN *to her room, and* VIVIAN *collapses on the bed.* SUSIE *connects* VIVIAN's *IV, then wets a wash-cloth and rubs her face and neck.* VIVIAN *remains delirious.* SUSIE *checks the IV and leaves with the wheelchair.*]

   [*After a while,* KELEKIAN *appears in the doorway holding a surgical mask near his face.* JASON *is with him, now dressed and clean-shaven.*]

KELEKIAN: Good morning, Dr. Bearing. Fifth cycle. Full dose. Definite progress. Everything okay.

VIVIAN: [*Weakly.*] Yes.

KELEKIAN: You're doing swell. Isolation is no problem. Couple of days. Think of it as a vacation.

VIVIAN: Oh. [JASON *starts to enter, holding a mask near his face, just like* KELEKIAN.]

KELEKIAN: Jason.

JASON: Oh, Jesus. Okay, okay. [*He returns to the doorway, where he puts on a paper gown, mask, and gloves.* KELEKIAN *leaves.*]

VIVIAN: [*To audience.*] In isolation, I am isolated. For once I can use a term literally. The chemotherapeutic agents eradicating my cancer have also eradicated my immune system. In my present condition, every living thing is a health hazard to me . . . [JASON *comes in to check the intake-and-output.*]

JASON: [*Complaining to himself.*] I really have not got time for this . . .

VIVIAN: . . . particularly health-care professionals.

JASON: [*Going right to the graph on the wall.*] Just to look at the I&O sheets for one minute, and it takes me half an hour to do precautions. Four, seven, eleven. Two-fifty twice. Okay. [*Remembering.*] Oh, Jeez. Clinical. Professor Bearing. How are you feeling today?

VIVIAN: [*Very sick.*] Fine. Just shaking sometimes from the chills.

JASON: IV will kick in anytime now. No problem. Listen, gotta go. Keep pushing the fluids. [*As he exits, he takes off the gown, mask, and gloves.*]

VIVIAN: [*Getting up from bed with her IV pole and resuming her explanation.*] I am not in isolation because I have cancer, because I have a tumor the size of a grapefruit. No. I am in isolation because I am being treated for cancer. My treatment imperils my health.

   Herein lies the paradox. John Donne would revel in it. I would revel in it, if he wrote a poem about it. My students would flounder in it, because paradox is too difficult to understand. Think of it as a puzzle, I would tell them, an intellectual game. [*She is trapped.*]

   Or, I *would have* told them. Were it a game. Which it is not.

[*Escaping.*] If they were here, if I were lecturing: How I would *perplex* them! I could work my students into a frenzy. Every ambiguity, every shifting awareness. I could draw so much from the poems.

I could be so powerful.

[*Scene change. Vivian stands still, as if conjuring a scene. Now at the height of her powers, she grandly disconnects herself from the IV.* TECHNICIANS *remove the bed and hand her a pointer.*] The poetry of the early seventeenth century, what has been called the metaphysical school, considers an intractable mental puzzle by exercising the outstanding human faculty of the era, namely wit.

The greatest wit—the greatest English poet, some would say—was John Donne. In the Holy Sonnets, Donne applied his capacious, agile wit to the larger aspects of the human experience: life, death, and God.

In his poems, metaphysical quandaries are addressed, but never resolved. Ingenuity, virtuosity, and a vigorous intellect that jousts with the most exalted concepts: these are the tools of wit. [*The lights dim. A screen lowers, and the sonnet "If poysonous mineralls," from the Gardner edition, appears on it.* VIVIAN *recites.*]

> If poysonous mineralls, and if that tree,
> Whose fruit threw death on else immortall us,
> If lecherous goats, if serpents envious
> Cannot be damn'd; Alas; why should I bee?
> Why should intent or reason, borne in mee,
> Make sinnes, else equall, in mee, more heinous?
> And mercy being easie, and glorious
> To God, in his sterne wrath, why threatens hee?
> But who am I, that dare dispute with thee?
> O God, Oh! of thine onely worthy blood,
> And my teares, make a heavenly Lethean flood,
> And drowne in it my sinnes blacke memorie.
> That thou remember them, some claime as debt,
> I thinke it mercy, if thou wilt forget.

[VIVIAN *whacks the word on the screen with a pointer at every asterisk (*). She moves around as she lectures.*]

Aggressive intellect. [*Line 1.*] Pious melodrama. [*Line 10.*] And a final, fearful point. [*Line 14.*] Donne's Holy Sonnet Five, 1609. From the Ashford edition, based on Gardner.

The speaker of the sonnet has a brilliant mind, and he plays the part convincingly; but in the end he finds God's *forgiveness* hard to believe, so he crawls under a rock to *hide*.

If [*] arsenic [*mineralls] and serpents [*] are not damned, then why is he? In asking the question, the speaker turns eternal damnation into an intellectual game. Why would God choose to do what is *hard*, to condemn, rather than what is *easy*, and also *glorious*—to show mercy?

(Several scholars have disputed Ashford's third comma [*] in line six, but none convincingly.)

But. [*] Exception. Limitation. Contrast. The argument shifts from cleverness to melodrama, an unconvincing eruption of piety: "O" [*] "God" [*] "Oh." [*]

A typical prayer would plead "Remember me, O Lord." (This point is nicely explicated in an article by Richard Strier—a former student of mine who once sat where you do now, although I dare say *he* was *awake*—in the May 1989 issue of *Modern Philology*.) True believers ask to be *remembered* by God. The speaker of this sonnet asks God to *forget*. [*] [VIVIAN *moves in front of the screen, and the projection of the poem is cast directly upon her.*] Where is the hyperactive intellect of the first section? Where is the histrionic outpouring of the second? When the speaker considers his own *sins*, and the inevitability of God's *judgment*, he can conceive of but one resolution: to *disappear*. [VIVIAN *moves away from the screen.*] Doctrine assures us that no sinner is denied *forgiveness*, not even one whose sins are overweening *intellect* [* *Top half.*] or overwrought *dramatics*. [**Bottom half.*] The speaker does not need to *hide* from God's *judgment*, only to *accept* God's *forgiveness*. It is very simple. Suspiciously simple.

We want to correct the speaker, to remind him of the assurance of salvation. But it is too late. The poetic encounter is over. We are left to our own consciences. Have we outwitted Donne? Or have we been outwitted? [SUSIE *comes on.*]

SUSIE: Ms. Bearing?

VIVIAN: [*Continuing.*] Will the po—

SUSIE: Ms. Bearing?

VIVIAN: [*Crossly.*] What is it?

SUSIE: You have to go down for a test. Jason just called. They want another ultrasound. They're concerned about a bowel obstruction— Is it okay if I come in?

VIVIAN: No. Not now.

SUSIE: I'm sorry, but they want it now.

VIVIAN: Not right now. It's not *supposed* to be now.

SUSIE: Yes, they want to do it now. I've got the chair.

VIVIAN: It should not be now. I am in the middle of—this. I have *this* planned for now, not ultrasound. No more tests. We've covered that.

SUSIE: I know, I know, but they need for it to be now. It won't take long, and it isn't a bad procedure. Why don't you just come along.

VIVIAN: *I do not want to go now!*

SUSIE: Ms. Bearing. [*Silence.* VIVIAN *raises the screen, walks away from the scene, hooks herself to the IV, and gets in the wheelchair.* SUSIE *wheels* VIVIAN, *and a* TECHNICIAN *takes her.*]

TECHNICIAN: Name.

VIVIAN: B-E-A-R-I-N-G. Kelekian.

TECHNICIAN: It'll just be a minute.

VIVIAN: Time for your break.

TECHNICIAN: Yup. [*The* TECHNICIAN *leaves.*]

VIVIAN: [*Mordantly.*] Take a break! [*Scene change.* VIVIAN *sits weakly in the wheelchair.*]

This is my playes last scene, here heavens appoint
My pilgrimages last mile; and my race
Idly, yet quickly runne, hath this last pace,
My spans last inch, my minutes last point,
And gluttonous death will instantly unjoynt
My body, and soule. . .

John Donne. 1609.[3] I have always particularly liked that poem. In the abstract. Now I find the image of "my minute's last point" a little too, shall we say, *pointed*.

I don't mean to complain, but I am becoming very sick. Very, very sick. Ultimately sick, as it were.

In everything I have done, I have been steadfast, resolute—some would say in the extreme. Now, as you can see, I am distinguishing myself in illness.

I have survived eight treatments of Hexamethophosphacil and Vinplatin at the *full* dose, ladies and gentlemen. I have broken the record. I have become something of a celebrity. Kelekian and Jason are simply delighted. I think they foresee celebrity status for themselves upon the appearance of the journal article they will no doubt write about me.

But I flatter myself. The article will not be about me, it will be about my ovaries. It will be about my peritoneal cavity, which, despite their best intentions, is now crawling with cancer.

What we have come to think of as *me* is, in fact, just the specimen jar, just the dust jacket, just the white piece of paper that bears the little black marks.

My next line is supposed to be something like this:

"It is such a *relief* to get back to my room after those infernal tests."

This is hardly true. It would be a *relief* to be a cheerleader on her way to Daytona Beach for Spring Break.

To get back to my room after those infernal tests is just the next thing that happens.

[*Scene change. She returns to her bed, which now has a commode next to it. She is very sick.*] Oh, God. It is such a relief to get back to my goddamn room after those goddamn tests. [JASON *enters.*]

JASON: Professor Bearing. Just want to check the I&O. Four-fifty, six, five. Okay. How are you feeling today? [*He makes notations on his clipboard throughout the scene.*]

VIVIAN: Fine.

JASON: That's great. Just great.

VIVIAN: How are my fluids?

JASON: Pretty good. No kidney involvement yet. That's pretty amazing, with Hex and Vin.

VIVIAN: How will you know when the kidneys are involved?

JASON: Lots of in, not much out.

VIVIAN: That simple.

JASON: Oh, no way. Compromised kidney function is a highly complex reaction. I'm simplifying for you.

VIVIAN: Thank you.

JASON: We're supposed to.

VIVIAN: Bedside manner.

JASON: Yeah, there's a whole course on it in med school. It's required. Colossal waste of time for researchers. [*He turns to go.*]

VIVIAN: I can imagine. [*Trying to ask something important.*] Jason?

JASON: Huh?

---

3. Vivian Bearing has quoted, with some variants, the first lines of a sonnet by Donne.

VIVIAN: [*Not sure of herself.*] Ah, what . . . [*Quickly.*] What were you just saying?

JASON: When?

VIVIAN: Never mind.

JASON: Professor Bearing?

VIVIAN: Yes.

JASON: Are you experiencing confusion? Short-term memory loss?

VIVIAN: No.

JASON: Sure?

VIVIAN: Yes. [*Pause.*] I was just wondering: why cancer?

JASON: Why cancer?

VIVIAN: Why not open-heart surgery?

JASON: Oh yeah, why not *plumbing*. Why not run a *lube rack*, for all the surgeons know about *Homo sapiens sapiens*. No way. Cancer's the only thing I ever wanted.

VIVIAN: [*Intrigued.*] Huh.

JASON: No, really. Cancer is . . . [*Searching.*]

VIVIAN: [*Helping.*] Awesome.

JASON: [*Pause.*] Yeah. Yeah, that's right. It is. It is awesome. How does it do it? The intercellular regulatory mechanisms—especially for proliferation and differentiation—the malignant neoplasia just don't get it. You grow normal cells in tissue culture in the lab, and they replicate just enough to make a nice, confluent monolayer. They divide twenty times, or fifty times, but eventually they conk out. You grow cancer cells, and they never stop. No contact inhibition whatsoever. They just pile up, just keep replicating forever. [*Pause.*] That's got a funny name. Know what it is?

VIVIAN: No. What?

JASON: Immortality in culture.

VIVIAN: Sounds like a symposium.

JASON: It's an error in judgment, in a molecular way. But *why*? Even on the protistic level [4] the normal cell-cell interactions are so subtle they'll take your breath away. Golden-brown algae, for instance, the lowest multicellular life form on earth—they're *idiots*—and it's incredible. It's perfect. So what's up with the cancer cells? Smartest guys in the world, with the best labs, funding—they don't know what to make of it.

VIVIAN: What about you?

JASON: Me? Oh, I've got a couple of ideas, things I'm kicking around. Wait till I get a lab of my own. If I can survive this . . . *fellowship*.

VIVIAN: The part with the human beings.

JASON: Everybody's got to go through it. All the great researchers. They want us to be able to converse intelligently with the clinicians. As though *researchers* were the impediments. The clinicians are such troglodytes. So smarmy. Like we have to hold hands to discuss creatinine clearance. [5] Just cut the crap, I say.

VIVIAN: Are you going to be sorry when— Do you ever miss people?

JASON: Everybody asks that. Especially girls.

VIVIAN: What do you tell them?

JASON: I tell them yes.

VIVIAN: Are they persuaded?

---

4. That is, on the level of one-celled microbes.   5. Urination.

JASON: Some.

VIVIAN: Some. I see. [*With great difficulty.*] And what do you say when a patient is . . . apprehensive . . . frightened.

JASON: Of who?

VIVIAN: I just . . . Never mind.

JASON: Professor Bearing, who is the President of the United States?

VIVIAN: I'm fine, really. It's all right.

JASON: You sure? I could order a test—

VIVIAN: No! No, I'm fine. Just a little tired.

JASON: Okay. Look. Gotta go. Keep pushing the fluids. Try for 2,000 a day, okay?

VIVIAN: Okay. To use your word. Okay. [JASON *leaves. Getting out of bed, without her IV.*]

So. The young doctor, like the senior scholar, prefers research to humanity. At the same time the senior scholar, in her pathetic state as a simpering victim, wishes the young doctor would take more interest in personal contact.

Now I suppose we shall see, through a series of flashbacks, how the senior scholar ruthlessly denied her simpering students the touch of human kindness she now seeks.

[*Scene change.* STUDENTS *appear, sitting at chairs with writing desks attached to the right arm. She suddenly commands attention.*]

How then would you characterize [*Pointing to a* STUDENT.]—you.

STUDENT 1: Huh?

VIVIAN: How would you characterize the animating force of this sonnet?

STUDENT 1: Huh?

VIVIAN: In this sonnet; what is the principal poetic device? I'll give you a hint. It has nothing to do with football. What propels this sonnet?

STUDENT 1: Um.

VIVIAN: [*Speaking to the audience.*] Did I say [*Tenderly.*] "You are nineteen years old. You are so young. You don't know a sonnet from a steak sandwich." [*Pause.*] By no means.

[*Sharply, to* STUDENT 1.] You can come to this class prepared, or you can excuse yourself from this class, this department, and this university. Do not think for a moment that I will tolerate anything in between.

[*To the audience, defensively.*] I was teaching him a lesson. [*She walks away from* STUDENT 1, *then turns and addresses the class.*]

So we have another instance of John Donne's agile wit at work: not so much *resolving* the issues of life and God as *reveling* in their complexity.

STUDENT 2: But why?

VIVIAN: Why what?

STUDENT 2: Why does Donne make everything so *complicated*? [*The other* STUDENTS *laugh in agreement.*] No, really, *why*?

VIVIAN: [*To the audience.*] You know, someone asked me that every year. And it was always one of the smart ones. What could I say? [*To* STUDENT 2.] What do you think?

STUDENT 2: I think it's like he's hiding. I think he's really confused, I don't know, maybe he's scared, so he hides behind all this complicated stuff, hides behind this *wit.*

VIVIAN: *Hides* behind *wit*?

STUDENT 2: I mean, if it's really something he's sure of, he can say it more simple—simply. He doesn't have to be such a brain, or such a performer. It doesn't have to be such a big deal. [*The other* STUDENTS *encourage him.*]

VIVIAN: Perhaps he is suspicious of simplicity.

STUDENT 2: Perhaps, but that's pretty stupid.

VIVIAN: [*To the audience.*] That observation, despite its infelicitous phrasing, contained the seed of a perspicacious remark. Such an unlikely occurrence left me with two choices. I could draw it out, or I could allow the brain to rest after that heroic effort. If I pursued, there was the chance of great insight, or the risk of undergraduate banality. I could never predict. [*To* STUDENT 2.] Go on.

STUDENT 2: Well, if he's trying to figure out God, and the meaning of life, and big stuff like that, why does he keep running away, you know?

VIVIAN: [*To the audience, moving closer to* STUDENT 2.] So far so good, but they can think for themselves only so long before they begin to self-destruct.

STUDENT 2: Um, it's like, the more you hide, the less—no, wait—the more you are getting closer—although you don't know it—and the simple thing is there—you see what I mean?

VIVIAN: [*To the audience, looking at* STUDENT 2, *as suspense collapses.*] Lost it.

[*She walks away and speaks to the audience.*] I distinctly remember an exchange between two students after my lecture on pronunciation and scansion. I overheard them talking on their way out of class. They were young and bright, gathering their books and laughing at the expense of seventeenth-century poetry, at my expense.

[*To the class.*] To scan the line properly, we must take advantage of the contemporary flexibility in "i-o-n" endings, as in "expansion." The quatrain stands:

> Our two souls therefore, which are one,
> Though I must go, endure not yet
> A breach, but an ex-*pan*-see-on,
> Like gold to airy thinness beat.[6]

Bear this in mind in your reading. That's all for today.

[*The* STUDENTS *get up in a chaotic burst.* STUDENT 3 *and* STUDENT 4 *pass by* VIVIAN *on their way out.*]

STUDENT 3: I hope I can get used to this pronuncia-see-on.

STUDENT 4: I know. I hope I can survive this course and make it to gradua-see-on. [*They laugh.* VIVIAN *glowers at them. They fall silent, embarrassed.*]

VIVIAN: [*To the audience.*] That was a witty little exchange, I must admit. It showed the mental acuity I would praise in a poetic text. But I admired only the studied application of wit, not its spontaneous eruption. [STUDENT 1 *interrupts.*]

STUDENT 1: Professor Bearing? Can I talk to you for a minute?

VIVIAN: You may.

STUDENT 1: I need to ask for an extension on my paper. I'm really sorry, and I know your policy, but see—

VIVIAN: Don't tell me. Your grandmother died.

STUDENT 1: You knew.

---

6. From Donne's poem "A Valediction: Forbidding Mourning," lines 21–24. (See page 1322.)

VIVIAN: It was a guess.

STUDENT 1: I have to go home.

VIVIAN: Do what you will, but the paper is due when it is due. [*As* STUDENT 1 *leaves and the classroom disappears,* VIVIAN *watches. Pause.*]

    I don't know. I feel so much—what is the word? I look back, I see these scenes, and I . . . [*Long silence.* VIVIAN *walks absently around the stage, trying to think of something. Finally, giving up, she trudges back to bed. Scene change.*]

    It was late at night, the graveyard shift. Susie was on. I could hear her in the hall.

    I wanted her to come and see me. So I had to create a little emergency. Nothing dramatic. [VIVIAN *pinches the IV tubing. The pump alarm beeps.*]

    It worked. [SUSIE *enters, concerned.*]

SUSIE: Ms. Bearing? Is that you beeping at four in the morning? [*She checks the tubing and presses buttons on the pump. The alarm stops.*] Did that wake you up? I'm sorry. It just gets occluded sometimes.

VIVIAN: I was awake.

SUSIE: You were? What's the trouble, sweetheart?

VIVIAN: [*To the audience, roused.*] Do not think for a minute that anyone calls me "Sweetheart." But then . . . I allowed it. [*To* SUSIE.] Oh, I don't know.

SUSIE: You can't sleep?

VIVIAN: No. I just keep thinking.

SUSIE: If you do that too much, you can get kind of confused.

VIVIAN: I know. I can't figure things out. I'm in a . . . *quandary,* having these . . . *doubts.*

SUSIE: What you're doing is very hard.

VIVIAN: Hard things are what I like best.

SUSIE: It's not the same. It's like it's out of control, isn't it?

VIVIAN: [*Crying, in spite of herself.*] I'm scared.

SUSIE: [*Stroking her.*] Oh, honey, of course you are.

VIVIAN: I want . . .

SUSIE: I know. It's hard.

VIVIAN: I don't feel sure of myself anymore.

SUSIE: And you used to feel sure.

VIVIAN: [*Crying.*] Oh, yes, I used to feel sure.

SUSIE: Vivian. It's all right. I know. It hurts. I know. It's all right. Do you want a tissue? It's all right. [*Silence.*] Vivian, would you like a Popsicle?

VIVIAN: [*Like a child.*] Yes, please.

SUSIE: I'll get it for you. I'll be right back.

VIVIAN: Thank you. [SUSIE *leaves. Pulling herself together.*] The epithelial cells in my GI tract have been killed by the chemo.[7] The cold Popsicle feels good, it's something I can digest, and it helps keep me hydrated. For your information.

    [SUSIE *returns with an orange two-stick Popsicle.* VIVIAN *unwraps it and breaks it in half.*] Here.

SUSIE: Sure?

VIVIAN: Yes.

---

7. That is, the cells of the inner surface of my gastrointestinal tract have been killed by the chemotherapy.

SUSIE: Thanks. [SUSIE *sits on the commode by the bed. Silence.*] When I was a kid, we used to get these from a truck. The man would come around and ring his bell and we'd all run over. Then we'd sit on the curb and eat our Popsicles.
    Pretty profound, huh?

VIVIAN: It sounds nice. [*Silence.*]

SUSIE: Vivian, there's something we need to talk about, you need to think about. [*Silence.*]

VIVIAN: My cancer is not being cured, is it.

SUSIE: Huh-uh.

VIVIAN: They never expected it to be, did they.

SUSIE: Well, they thought the drugs would make the tumor get smaller, and it has gotten a lot smaller. But the problem is that it started in new places too. They've learned a lot for their research. It was the best thing they had to give you, the strongest drugs. There just isn't a good treatment for what you have yet, for advanced ovarian. I'm sorry. They should have explained this—

VIVIAN: I knew.

SUSIE: You did.

VIVIAN: I read between the lines.

SUSIE: What you have to think about is your "code status." What you want them to do if your heart stops.

VIVIAN: Well.

SUSIE: You can be "full code," which means that if your heart stops, they'll call a Code Blue and the code team will come and resuscitate you and take you to Intensive Care until you stabilize again. Or you can be "Do Not Resuscitate," so if your heart stops we'll . . . well, we'll just let it. You'll be "DNR." You can think about it, but I wanted to present both choices before Kelekian and Jason talk to you.

VIVIAN: You don't agree about this?

SUSIE: Well, they like to save lives. So anything's okay, as long as life continues. It doesn't matter if you're hooked up to a million machines. Kelekian is a great researcher and everything. And the fellows, like Jason, they're really smart. It's really an honor for them to work with him. But they always . . . want to know more things.

VIVIAN: I always want to know more things. I'm a scholar. Or I was when I had shoes, when I had eyebrows.

SUSIE: Well, okay then. You'll be full code. That's fine. [*Silence.*]

VIVIAN: No, don't complicate the matter.

SUSIE: It's okay. It's up to you—

VIVIAN: Let it stop.

SUSIE: Really?

VIVIAN: Yes.

SUSIE: So if your heart stops beating—

VIVIAN: Just let it stop.

SUSIE: Sure?

VIVIAN: Yes.

SUSIE: Okay. I'll get Kelekian to give the order, and then—

VIVIAN: Susie?

SUSIE: Uh-huh?

VIVIAN: You're still going to take care of me, aren't you?

SUSIE: 'Course, sweetheart. Don't you worry. [*As* SUSIE *leaves,* VIVIAN *sits upright, full of energy and rage.*]

VIVIAN: That certainly was a *maudlin* display. Popsicles? "Sweetheart"? I can't believe my life has become so . . . corny.

But it can't be helped. I don't see any other way. We are discussing life and death, and not in the abstract, either; we are discussing *my* life and *my* death, and my brain is dulling and poor Susie's was never very sharp to begin with, and I can't conceive of any other . . . *tone.*

[*Quickly.*] Now is not the time for verbal swordplay, for unlikely flights of imagination and wildly shifting perspectives, for metaphysical conceit, for wit.

And nothing would be worse than a detailed scholarly analysis. Erudition. Interpretation. Complication.

[*Slowly.*] Now is a time for simplicity. Now is a time for, dare I say it, kindness.

[*Searchingly.*] I thought being extremely smart would take care of it. But I see that I have been found out. Ooohhh.

I'm scared. Oh, God. I want . . . I want . . . No. I want to hide. I just want to curl up in a little ball. [*She dives under the covers. Scene change.* VIVIAN *wakes in horrible pain. She is tense, agitated, fearful. Slowly she calms down and addresses the audience. Trying extremely hard.*]

I want to tell you how it feels. I want to explain it, to use *my* words. It's as if . . . I can't . . . There aren't . . . I'm like a student and this is the final exam and I don't know what to put down because I don't understand the question and I'm *running out of time.* [*Pause.*]

The time for extreme measures has come. I am in terrible pain. Susie says that I need to begin aggressive pain management if I am going to stand it.

"It": such a little word. In this case, I think "it" signifies "being alive."

I apologize in advance for what this palliative treatment modality[8] does to the dramatic coherence of my play's last scene. It can't be helped. They have to do something. I'm in terrible pain.

Say it, Vivian. *It hurts like hell. It really does.* [SUSIE *enters.* VIVIAN *is writhing in pain.*]

Oh, God. Oh, God.

SUSIE: Sshh. It's okay. Sshh. I paged Kelekian up here, and we'll get you some meds.

VIVIAN: Oh, God, it is so painful. So painful. So much pain. So much pain.

SUSIE: I know, I know, it's okay. Sshh. Just try and clear your mind. It's all right. We'll get you a Patient-Controlled Analgesic. It's a little pump, and you push a little button, and you decide how much medication you want. [*Importantly.*] It's very simple, and it's up to you. [KELEKIAN *storms in;* JASON *follows with chart.*]

KELEKIAN: Dr. Bearing. Susie.

SUSIE: Time for Patient-Controlled Analgesic. The pain is killing her.

KELEKIAN: Dr. Bearing, are you in pain? [KELEKIAN *holds out his hand for chart;* JASON *hands it to him. They read.*]

VIVIAN: [*Sitting up, unnoticed by the staff.*] Am I in pain? I don't believe this. Yes, I'm in goddamn pain. [*Furious.*] I have a fever of 101 spiking to 104. And I have

_____

8. That is, method of treatment for pain.

bone metastases in my pelvis and both femurs.[9] [*Screaming.*] There is cancer eating away at my goddamn bones, and I did not know there could be such pain on this earth.

[*She flops back on the bed and cries audibly to them.*] Oh, God.

KELEKIAN: [*Looking at* VIVIAN *intently.*] I want a morphine drip.

SUSIE: What about Patient-Controlled? She could be more alert—

KELEKIAN: [*Teaching.*] Ordinarily, yes. But in her case, no.

SUSIE: But—

KELEKIAN: [*To* SUSIE.] She's earned a rest. [*To* JASON.] Morphine, ten push now, then start at ten an hour. [*To* VIVIAN.] Dr. Bearing, try to relax. We're going to help you through this, don't worry. Dr. Bearing? Excellent. [*He squeezes* VIVIAN's *shoulder. They all leave.*]

VIVIAN: [*Weakly, painfully, leaning on her IV pole, she moves to address the audience.*] Hi. How are you feeling today? [*Silence.*]

These are my last coherent lines. I'll have to leave the action to the professionals.

It came so quickly, after taking so long. Not even time for a proper conclusion. [VIVIAN *concentrates with all her might, and she attempts a grand summation, as if trying to conjure her own ending.*]

> And Death—*capital D*—shall be no more—*semicolon.*
> Death—*capital D*—thou shalt die—*ex-cla-mation point!*

[*She looks down at herself, looks out at the audience, and sees that the line doesn't work. She shakes her head and exhales with resignation.*]

I'm sorry.

[*Scene change. She gets back into bed as* SUSIE *injects morphine into the IV tubing.* VIVIAN *lies down and, in a final melodramatic gesture, shuts the lids of her own eyes and folds her arms over her chest.*] I trust this will have a soporific effect.

SUSIE: Well, I don't know about that, but it sure makes you sleepy. [*This strikes* VIVIAN *as delightfully funny. She starts to giggle, then laughs out loud.* SUSIE *doesn't get it.*] What's so funny? [VIVIAN *keeps laughing.*] What?

VIVIAN: Oh! It's that—"Soporific" *means* "makes you sleepy."

SUSIE: It does?

VIVIAN: Yes. [*Another fit of laughter.*]

SUSIE: [*Giggling.*] Well, that was pretty dumb—

VIVIAN: No! No, no! It was *funny!*

SUSIE: [*Starting to catch on.*] Yeah, I guess so. [*Laughing.*] In a dumb sort of way. [*This sets them both off laughing again.*] I never would have gotten it. I'm glad you explained it.

VIVIAN: [*Simply.*] I'm a teacher. [*They laugh a little together. Slowly the morphine kicks in, and* VIVIAN's *laughs become long sighs. Finally she falls asleep.* SUSIE *checks everything out, then leaves. Long silence. Scene change.* JASON *and* SUSIE *chat as they enter to insert a catheter.*]

JASON: Oh, yeah. She was a great scholar. Wrote tons of books, articles, was the head of everything. [*He checks the I&O sheet.*] Two hundred. Seventy-five. Five-twenty. Let's up the hydration. She won't be drinking anymore. See if we can

---

9. That is, cancerous tumors in my pelvis bone and both thighbones.

keep her kidneys from fading. Yeah, I had a lot of respect for her, which is more than I can say for the *entire* biochemistry department.

SUSIE: What do you want? Dextrose?

JASON: Give her saline.

SUSIE: Okay.

JASON: She gave a hell of a lecture. No notes, not a word out of place. It was pretty impressive. A lot of students hated her, though.

SUSIE: Why?

JASON: Well, she wasn't exactly a cupcake.

SUSIE: [*Laughing, fondly.*] Well, she hasn't exactly been a cupcake here, either. [*Leaning over* VIVIAN *and talking loudly and slowly in her ear.*] Now, Ms. Bearing, Jason and I are here, and we're going to insert a catheter to collect your urine. It's not going to hurt, don't you worry. [*During the conversation she inserts the catheter.*]

JASON: Like she can hear you.

SUSIE: It's just nice to do.

JASON: Eight cycles of Hex and Vin at the full dose. Kelekian didn't think it was possible. I wish they could all get through it at full throttle. Then we could really have some data.

SUSIE: She's not what I imagined. I thought somebody who studied poetry would be sort of dreamy, you know?

JASON: Oh, not the way she did it. It felt more like boot camp than English class. This guy John Donne was incredibly intense. Like your whole brain had to be in knots before you could get it.

SUSIE: He made it hard on purpose?

JASON: Well, it has to do with the subject. The Holy Sonnets we worked on most, they were mostly about Salvation Anxiety. That's a term I made up in one of my papers, but I think it fits pretty well. Salvation Anxiety. You're this brilliant guy, I mean, brilliant—this guy makes Shakespeare sound like a Hallmark card. And you know you're a sinner. And there's this promise of salvation, the whole religious thing. But you just can't deal with it.

SUSIE: How come?

JASON: It just doesn't stand up to scrutiny. But you can't face life without it either. So you write these screwed-up sonnets. Everything is brilliantly convoluted. Really tricky stuff. Bouncing off the walls. Like a game, to make the puzzle so complicated. [*The catheter is inserted.* SUSIE *puts things away.*]

SUSIE: But what happens in the end?

JASON: End of what?

SUSIE: To John Donne. Does he ever get it?

JASON: Get what?

SUSIE: His Salvation Anxiety. Does he ever understand?

JASON: Oh, no way. The puzzle takes over. You're not even trying to solve it anymore. Fascinating, really. Great training for lab research. Looking at things in increasing levels of complexity.

SUSIE: Until what?

JASON: What do you mean?

SUSIE: Where does it end? Don't you get to solve the puzzle?

JASON: Nah. When it comes right down to it, research is just trying to quantify the complications of the puzzle.

SUSIE: But you *help* people! You save lives and stuff.

JASON: Oh, yeah, I save some guy's life, and then the poor slob gets hit by a bus!

SUSIE: [*Confused.*] Yeah, I guess so. I just don't think of it that way. Guess you can tell I never took a class in poetry.

JASON: Listen, if there's one thing we learned in Seventeenth-Century Poetry, it's that you can forget about that sentimental stuff. *Enzyme Kinetics* was more poetic than Bearing's class. Besides, you can't think about that *meaning-of-life* garbage all the time or you'd go nuts.

SUSIE: Do you believe in it?

JASON: In what?

SUSIE: Umm. I don't know, the meaning-of-life garbage. [*She laughs a little.*]

JASON: What do they *teach* you in nursing school? [*Checking Vivian's pulse.*] She's out of it. Shouldn't be too long. You done here?

SUSIE: Yeah, I'll just . . . tidy up.

JASON: See ya. [*He leaves.*]

SUSIE: Bye, Jace. [*She thinks for a minute, then carefully rubs baby oil on* VIVIAN*'s hands. She checks the catheter, then leaves. Scene change.* PROFESSOR E. M. ASHFORD, *now eighty, enters.*]

E. M.: Vivian? Vivian? It's Evelyn. Vivian?

VIVIAN: [*Waking, slurred.*] Oh, God. [*Surprised.*] Professor Ashford. Oh, God.

E. M.: I'm in town visiting my great-grandson, who is celebrating his fifth birthday. I went to see you at your office, and they directed me here. [*She lays her jacket, scarf, and parcel on the bed.*] I have been walking all over town. I had forgotten how early it gets chilly here.

VIVIAN: [*Weakly.*] I feel so bad.

E. M.: I know you do. I can see. [VIVIAN *cries.*] Oh, dear, there, there. There, there. [VIVIAN *cries more, letting the tears flow.*] Vivian, Vivian.

[E. M. *looks toward the hall, then furtively slips off her shoes and swings up on the bed. She puts her arm around* VIVIAN.] There, there. There, there, Vivian. [*Silence.*]

It's a windy day. [*Silence.*]

Don't worry, dear. [*Silence.*]

Let's see. Shall I recite to you? Would you like that? I'll recite something by Donne.

VIVIAN: [*Moaning.*] Nooooooo.

E.M.: Very well. [*Silence.*] Hmmm. [*Silence.*] Little Jeffrey is very sweet. Gets into everything.

[*Silence.* E. M. *takes a children's book out of the paper bag and begins reading.* VIVIAN *nestles in, drifting in and out of sleep.*] Let's see. *The Runaway Bunny*. By Margaret Wise Brown. Pictures by Clement Hurd. Copyright 1942. First Harper Trophy Edition, 1972.[1]

Now then.

Once there was a little bunny who wanted to run away.
So he said to his mother, "I am running away."

"If you run away," said his mother, "I will run after you. For you are my little bunny."

---

1. Margaret Wise Brown (1910–52) wrote numerous children's books. *The Runaway Bunny*, which is still in print, is represented in accurate detail in the play.

"If you run after me," said the little bunny, "I will become a fish in a trout stream and I will swim away from you."

"If you become a fish in a trout stream," said his mother, "I will become a fisherman and I will fish for you."

[*Thinking out loud.*] Look at that. A little allegory of the soul.

No matter where it hides, God will find it. See, Vivian?

VIVIAN: [*Moaning*] Uhhhhhh.

E. M.:

"If you become a fisherman," said the little bunny, "I will be a bird and fly away from you."

"If you become a bird and fly away from me," said his mother, "I will be a tree that you come home to."

[*To herself.*] Very clever.

"Shucks," said the little bunny, "I might just as well stay where I am and be your little bunny."

And so he did.

"Have a carrot," said the mother bunny.

[*To herself.*] Wonderful. [VIVIAN *is now fast asleep.* E. M. *slowly gets down and gathers her things. She leans over and kisses her.*]

It's time to go. And flights of angels sing thee to thy rest.[2]

[*She leaves.* JASON *strides in and goes directly to the I&O sheet without looking at* VIVIAN.]

JASON: Professor Bearing. How are you feeling today? Three P.M. IV hydration totals. Two thousand in. Thirty out. Uh-oh. That's it. Kidneys gone.

[*He looks at* VIVIAN.] Professor Bearing? Highly unresponsive. Wait a second— [*Puts his head down to her mouth and chest to listen for heartbeat and breathing.*] Wait a sec—Jesus Christ! [*Yelling*] CALL A CODE! [JASON *throws down the chart, dives over the bed, and lies on top of her body as he reaches for the phone and punches in the numbers. To himself.*]

Code: 4-5-7-5. [*To operator.*] Code Blue, room 707. Code Blue, room 707. Dr. Posner—P-O-S-N-E-R. Hurry up!

[*He throws down the phone and lowers the head of the bed.*] Come on, come on, COME ON.

[*He begins CPR, kneeling over* VIVIAN, *alternately pounding frantically and giving mouth-to-mouth resuscitation. Over the loud-speaker in the hall, a droning voice repeats "Code Blue, room 707. Code Blue, room 707."*] One! Two! Three! Four! Five! [*He breathes in her mouth.* SUSIE, *hearing the announcement, runs into the room.*]

SUSIE: WHAT ARE YOU DOING?

JASON: A GODDAMN CODE. GET OVER HERE!

SUSIE: She's DNR! [*She grabs him.*]

JASON: [*He pushes* SUSIE *away.*] She's Research!

SUSIE: She's NO CODE! [*She grabs* JASON *and hurls him off the bed.*]

---

2. Horatio's line at the end of Shakespeare's *Hamlet*, addressed to the dead hero: "Good night, sweet prince, / And flights of angels sing thee to thy rest!" (5.2.302–303).

JASON: Ooowww! Goddamnit, Susie!

SUSIE: She's no code!

JASON: Aaargh!

SUSIE: Kelekian put the order in—you saw it! You were right there, Jason! Oh, God, the code! [*She runs to the phone.* JASON *struggles to stand. Into the phone.*] 4-5-7-5.

    [*The* CODE TEAM *swoops in. Everything changes. Frenzy takes over. The* CODE TEAM *knocks* SUSIE *out of the way with their equipment.* SUSIE, *into the phone.*] Cancel code, room 707. Sue Monahan, primary nurse. Cancel code. Dr. Posner is here.

JASON: [*In agony.*] Oh, God.

CODE TEAM: —Get out of the way!

    —Unit staff out!

    —Get the board!

    —Over here! [*They throw* VIVIAN'*s body up at the waist and stick a board underneath for CPR. In a whirlwind of sterile packaging and barked commands, one* TEAM MEMBER *attaches a respirator, one begins CPR,[3] and one prepares the defibrillator.* SUSIE *and* JASON *try to stop them but are pushed away. The loudspeaker in the hall announces "Cancel code, room 707. Cancel code, room 707."*]

    —Bicarb amp!

    —I got it! [*To* SUSIE.] Get out!

    —One, two, three, four, five!

    —Get ready to shock! [*To* JASON.] Move it!

SUSIE: [*Running to each person, yelling.*] STOP! Patient is DNR!

JASON: [*At the same time, to the* CODE TEAM.] No, no! Stop doing this. STOP!

CODE TEAM: —Keep it going!

    —What do you get?

    —Bicarb amp!

    —No pulse!

SUSIE: She's NO CODE! Order was given— [*She dives for the chart and holds it up as she cries out.*] Look! Look at this! DO NOT RESUSCITATE. KELEKIAN.

CODE TEAM: [*As they administer electric shock,* VIVIAN'*s body arches and bounces back down.*]

    —Almost ready!

    —Hit her!

    —CLEAR!

    —Pulse? Pulse?

JASON: [*Howling*]. I MADE A MISTAKE! [*Pause. The* CODE TEAM *looks at him. He collapses on the floor.*]

SUSIE: No code! Patient is no code.

CODE TEAM HEAD: Who the hell are you?

SUSIE: Sue Monahan, primary nurse.

CODE TEAM HEAD: Let me see the goddamn chart. CHART!

CODE TEAM: [*Slowing down.*]

    —What's going on?

    —Should we stop?

    —What's it say?

SUSIE: [*Pushing them away from the bed.*] Patient is no code. Get away from her!

---

3. Cardiopulmonary resuscitation to restart the heart. *Defibrillator:* electrical device for restarting the heart's rhythm.

[*Susie lifts the blanket.*
Vivian steps out of the bed.

*She walks away from the scene,
toward a little light.*

*She is now attentive and eager, mov-
ing slowly toward the light.*

She takes off her cap and lets it drop.

She slips off her bracelet.

*She loosens the ties and the top gown
slides to the floor. She lets the second
gown fall.*

*The instant she is naked, and beauti-
ful, reaching for the light—*

Lights out.]

CODE TEAM HEAD: [*Reading.*] Do Not
Resuscitate. Kelekian. Shit.

[*The* CODE TEAM *stops working.*]

JASON: [*Whispering.*] Oh, God.

CODE TEAM HEAD: Order was put in
yesterday.

CODE TEAM:
—It's a doctor fuck-up.
—What is he, a resident?
—Got us up here on a DNR.
—Called a code on a no-code.

JASON: Oh, God. [*The bedside scene
fades.*]

1995

PAULA VOGEL

How I Learned to Drive

This play is dedicated to Peter Franklin.

CHARACTERS

LI'L BIT *A woman who ages forty-something to eleven years old. (See Notes on the New York Production.)*

PECK *Attractive man in his forties. Despite a few problems, he should be played by an actor one might cast in the role of Atticus in* To Kill a Mockingbird.

THE GREEK CHORUS *If possible, these three members should be able to sing three-part harmony.*

MALE GREEK CHORUS *Plays Grandfather, Waiter, High School Boys. Thirties-forties. (See Notes on the New York Production.)*

FEMALE GREEK CHORUS *Plays Mother, Aunt Mary, High School Girls, Thirty-fifty. (See Notes on the New York Production.)*

TEENAGE GREEK CHORUS *Plays Grandmother, High School Girls, and the voice of eleven-year-old Li'l Bit. Note on the casting of this actor: I would strongly recommend casting a young woman who is "of legal age," that is, twenty-one to twenty-five years old who can look as close to eleven as possible. The contrast with the other cast members will help. If the actor is too young, the audience may feel uncomfortable. (See Notes on the New York Production.)*

PRODUCTION NOTES

I urge directors to use the Greek Chorus in staging as environment and, well, part of the family—with the exception of the Teenage Greek Chorus member who, after the last time she appears onstage, should perhaps disappear.

AS FOR MUSIC: *Please have fun. I wrote sections of the play listening to music like Roy Orbison's "Dream Baby" and The Mamas and the Papas's "Dedicated to the One I Love." The vaudeville sections go well to the Tijuana Brass or any music that sounds like a Laugh-In soundtrack. Other sixties music is rife with pedophilish (?) reference: the "You're Sixteen" genre hits; The Beach Boys' "Little Surfer Girl"; Gary Puckett and the Union Gap's "This Girl Is a Woman Now"; "Come Back When You Grow Up," etc.*

And whenever possible, please feel free to punctuate the action with traffic signs: "No Passing," "Slow Children," "Dangerous Curves," "One Way," and the visual signs for children, deer crossings, hills, school buses, etc. (See Notes on the New York Production.)

This script uses the notion of slides and projections, which were not used in the New York production of the play.

ON TITLES: *Throughout the script there are bold-faced titles. In production these should be spoken in a neutral voice (the type of voice that driver education films employ). In the New York production these titles were assigned to various members of the Greek Chorus and were done live.*

NOTES ON THE NEW YORK PRODUCTION

The role of Li'l Bit was originally written as a character who is forty-something. When we cast Mary-Louise Parker in the role of Li'l Bit, we cast the Greek Chorus members with younger actors as the Female Greek and the Male Greek, and cast the Teenage Greek with an older (that is, mid-twenties) actor as well. There is a great deal of flexibility in age. Directors should change the age in the last monologue for Li'l Bit ("And before you know it, I'll be thirty-five. . . .") to reflect the age of the actor who is playing Li'l Bit.

As the house lights dim, a Voice announces:

Safety First—You and Driver Education.

Then the sound of a key turning the ignition of a car. LI'L BIT *steps into a spotlight on the stage; "well-endowed," she is a softer-looking woman in the present time than she was at seventeen.*

LI'L BIT: Sometimes to tell a secret, you first have to teach a lesson. We're going to start our lesson tonight on an early, warm summer evening.

In a parking lot overlooking the Beltsville Agricultural Farms in suburban Maryland.

Less than a mile away, the crumbling concrete of U.S. One[1] wends its way past one-room revival churches, the porno drive-in, and boarded up motels with For Sale signs tumbling down.

Like I said, it's a warm summer evening.

Here on the land the Department of Agriculture owns, the smell of sleeping farm animal is thick on the air. The smells of clover and hay mix in with the smells of the leather dashboard. You can still imagine how Maryland

---

1. Major highway passing through Washington, DC; Baltimore; and northeastern Maryland.

used to be, before the malls took over. This countryside was once dotted with farmhouses—from their porches you could have witnessed the Civil War raging in the front fields.

Oh yes. There's a moon over Maryland tonight, that spills into the car where I sit beside a man old enough to be—did I mention how still the night is? Damp soil and tranquil air. It's the kind of night that makes a middle-aged man with a mortgage feel like a country boy again.

It's 1969. And I am very old, very cynical of the world, and I know it all. In short, I am seventeen years old, parking off a dark lane with a married man on an early summer night.

[*Lights up on two chairs facing front—or a Buick Riviera, if you will. Waiting patiently, with a smile on his face,* PECK *sits sniffing the night air.* LI'L BIT *climbs in beside him, seventeen years old and tense. Throughout the following, the two sit facing directly front. They do not touch. Their bodies remain passive. Only their facial expressions emote.*]

PECK: Ummm. I love the smell of your hair.

LI'L BIT: Uh-huh.

PECK: Oh, Lord. Ummmm. [*Beat.*][2] A man could die happy like this.

LI'L BIT: Well, *don't*.

PECK: What shampoo is this?

LI'L BIT: Herbal Essence.

PECK: Herbal Essence. I'm gonna buy me some. Herbal Essence. And when I'm all alone in the house, I'm going to get into the bathtub, and uncap the bottle and—

LI'L BIT: —Be good.

PECK: What?

LI'L BIT: Stop being . . . bad.

PECK: What did you think I was going to say? What do you think I'm going to do with the shampoo?

LI'L BIT: I don't want to know. I don't want to hear it.

PECK: I'm going to wash my hair. That's all.

LI'L BIT: Oh.

PECK: What did you think I was going to do?

LI'L BIT: Nothing. . . . I don't know. Something . . . nasty.

PECK: With shampoo? Lord, gal—your mind!

LI'L BIT: And whose fault is it?

PECK: Not mine. I've got the mind of a boy scout.

LI'L BIT: Right. A horny boy scout.

PECK: Boy scouts are always horny. What do you think the first Merit Badge is for?

LI'L BIT: There. You're going to be nasty again.

PECK: Oh, no. I'm good. Very good.

LI'L BIT: It's getting late.

PECK: Don't change the subject. I was talking about how good I am. [*Beat.*] Are you ever gonna let me show you how good I am?

LI'L BIT: Don't go over the line now.

PECK: I won't. I'm not gonna do anything you don't want me to do.

LI'L BIT: That's right.

---

2. In stage directions, a "beat" is a pause.

PECK: And I've been good all week.

LI'L BIT: You have?

PECK: Yes. All week. Not a single drink.

LI'L BIT: Good boy.

PECK: Do I get a reward? For not drinking?

LI'L BIT: A small one. It's getting late.

PECK: Just let me undo you. I'll do you back up.

LI'L BIT: All right. But be quick about it. [PECK *pantomimes undoing Li'l Bit's brassiere with one hand.*] You know, that's amazing. The way you can undo the hooks through my blouse with one hand.

PECK: Years of practice.

LI'L BIT: You would make an incredible brain surgeon with that dexterity.

PECK: I'll bet Clyde—what's the name of the boy taking you to the prom?

LI'L BIT: Claude Souders.

PECK: Claude Souders. I'll bet it takes him two hands, lights on, and you helping him on to get to first base.

LI'L BIT: Maybe.

[*Beat.*]

PECK: Can I . . . kiss them? Please?

LI'L BIT: I don't know.

PECK: Don't make a grown man beg.

LI'L BIT: Just one kiss.

PECK: I'm going to lift your blouse.

LI'L BIT: It's a little cold.

[PECK *laughs gently.*]

PECK: That's not why you're shivering. [*They sit, perfectly still, for a long moment of silence.* PECK *makes gentle, concentric circles with his thumbs in the air in front of him.*] How does that feel?

[LI'L BIT *closes her eyes, carefully keeps her voice calm.*]

LI'L BIT: It's . . . okay.

[*Sacred music, organ music or a boy's choir swells beneath the following.*]

PECK: I tell you, you can keep all the cathedrals of Europe. Just give me a second with these—these celestial orbs—

[PECK *bows his head as if praying. But he is kissing her nipple.* LI'L BIT, *eyes still closed, rears back her head on the leather Buick car seat.*]

LI'L BIT: Uncle Peck—we've got to go. I've got graduation rehearsal at school tomorrow morning. And you should get on home to Aunt Mary—

PECK: —All right, Li'l Bit.

LI'L BIT: —*Don't* call me that no more. [*Calmer.*] Any more. I'm a big girl now, Uncle Peck. As you know.

[LI'L BIT *pantomimes refastening her bra behind her back.*]

PECK: That you are. Going on eighteen. Kittens will turn into cats. [*Sighs.*] I live all week long for these few minutes with you—you know that?

LI'L BIT: I'll drive.

[*A Voice cuts in with:*]

Idling in the Neutral Gear.

[*Sound of car revving cuts off the sacred music;* LI'L BIT, *now an adult, rises out of the car and comes to us.*]

LI'L BIT: In most families, relatives get names like "Junior," or "Brother," or "Bubba." In my family, if we call someone "Big Papa," it's not because he's tall. In my family, folks tend to get nicknamed for their genitalia. Uncle Peck, for example. My mama's adage was "the titless wonder," and my cousin Bobby got branded for life as "B.B."

[*In unison with* GREEK CHORUS:]

LI'L BIT:	GREEK CHORUS:
For blue balls.	For blue balls.

FEMALE GREEK CHORUS: [*As Mother.*] And of course, we were so excited to have a baby girl that when the nurse brought you in and said, "It's a girl! It's a baby girl!" I just had to see for myself. So we whipped your diapers down and parted your chubby little legs—and right between your legs there was—

[PECK *has come over during the above and chimes along:*]

PECK:	GREEK CHORUS:
Just a little bit.	Just a little bit.

FEMALE GREEK CHORUS: [*As Mother.*] And when you were born, you were so tiny that you fit in Uncle Peck's outstretched hand.

[PECK *stretches his hand out.*]

PECK: Now that's a fact. I held you, one day old, right in this hand.

[*A traffic signal is projected of a bicycle in a circle with a diagonal red slash.*]

LI'L BIT: Even with my family background, I was sixteen or so before I realized that pedophilia did not mean people who loved to bicycle. . . .

[*A Voice intrudes:*]

Driving in First Gear.

LI'L BIT: 1969. A typical family dinner.

FEMALE GREEK CHORUS: [*As Mother.*] Look, Grandma. Li'l Bit's getting to be as big in the bust as you are.

LI'L BIT: Mother! Could we please change the subject?

TEENAGE GREEK CHORUS: [*As Grandmother.*] Well, I hope you are buying her some decent bras. I never had a decent bra, growing up in the Depression, and now my shoulders are just crippled—crippled from the weight hanging on my shoulders—the dents from my bra straps are big enough to put your finger in.— Here, let me show you—

[*As* GRANDMOTHER *starts to open her blouse:*]

LI'L BIT: Grandma! Please don't undress at the dinner table.

PECK: I thought the entertainment came *after* the dinner.

LI'L BIT: [*To the audience.*] This is how it always starts. My grandfather, Big Papa, will chime in next with—

MALE GREEK CHORUS: [*As Grandfather.*] Yup. If Li'l Bit gets any bigger, we're gonna haveta buy her a wheelbarrow to carry in front of her—

LI'L BIT: —Damn it—

PECK: —How about those Redskins on Sunday, Big Papa?

LI'L BIT: [*To the audience.*] The only sport Big Papa followed was chasing Grandma around the house—

MALE GREEK CHORUS: [*As Grandfather.*]—Or we could write to Kate Smith.[3] Ask her for somma her used brassieres she don't want anymore—she could maybe give to Li'l Bit here—

LI'L BIT: —I can't stand it. I can't.

PECK: Now, honey, that's just their way—

FEMALE GREEK CHORUS: [*As Mother.*] I tell you, Grandma, Li'l Bit's at that age. She's so sensitive, you can't say boo—

LI'L BIT: I'd like some privacy, that's all. Okay? Some goddamn privacy—

PECK: —Well, at least she didn't use the savior's name—

LI'L BIT: [*To the audience.*] And Big Papa wouldn't let a dead dog lie. No sirree.

MALE GREEK CHORUS: [*As Grandfather.*] Well, she'd better stop being so sensitive. 'Cause five minutes before Li'l Bit turns the corner, her tits turn first—

LI'L BIT: [*Starting to rise from the table.*]—That's it. That's it.

PECK: Li'l Bit, you can't let him get to you. Then he wins.

LI'L BIT: I hate him. *Hate* him.

PECK: That's fine. But hate him and eat a good dinner at the same time.

[LI'L BIT *calms down and sits with perfect dignity.*]

LI'L BIT: The gumbo is really good, Grandma.

MALE GREEK CHORUS: [*As Grandfather.*] A'course, Li'l Bit's got a big surprise coming for her when she goes to that fancy college this fall—

PECK: Big Papa—let it go.

MALE GREEK CHORUS: [*As Grandfather.*] What does she need a college degree for? She's got all the credentials she'll need on her chest—

LI'L BIT: —Maybe I want to learn things. Read. Rise above my cracker[4] background—

PECK: —Whoa, now, Li'l Bit—

MALE GREEK CHORUS: [*As Grandfather.*] What kind of things do you want to read?

LI'L BIT: There's a whole semester course, for example, on Shakespeare—

[GREEK CHORUS, *as Grandfather, laughs until he weeps.*]

MALE GREEK CHORUS: [*As Grandfather.*] Shakespeare. That's a good one. Shakespeare is really going to help you in life.

PECK: I think it's wonderful. And on scholarship!

MALE GREEK CHORUS: [*As Grandfather.*] How is Shakespeare going to help her lie on her back in the dark?

[LI'L BIT *is on her feet.*]

3. Singer (1907–86) who became a major star on radio, then television, from the 1930s through the early 1960s. 4. Derogatory term for a poor white person, especially from the rural South.

LI'L BIT: You're getting old, Big Papa. You are going to die—very very soon. Maybe even *tonight*. And when you get to heaven, God's going to be a beautiful black woman in a long white robe. She's gonna look at your chart and say: Uh-oh. Fornication. Dog-ugly mean with blood relatives. Oh. Uh-oh. Voted for George Wallace.[5] Well, one last chance: If you can name the play, all will be forgiven. And then she'll quote: "The quality of mercy is not strained." Your answer? Oh, too bad—*Merchant of Venice*: Act IV, Scene iii. And then she'll send your ass to fry in hell with all the other crackers. Excuse me, please.

[*To the audience.*] And as I left the house, I would always hear Big Papa say:

MALE GREEK CHORUS: [*As Grandfather.*] Lucy, your daughter's got a mouth on her. Well, no sense in wasting good gumbo. Pass me her plate, Mama.

LI'L BIT: And Aunt Mary would come up to Uncle Peck:

FEMALE GREEK CHORUS: [*As Aunt Mary.*] Peck, go after her, will you? You're the only one she'll listen to when she gets like this.

PECK: She just needs to cool off.

FEMALE GREEK CHORUS: [*As Aunt Mary.*] Please, honey—Grandma's been on her feet cooking all day.

PECK: All right.

LI'L BIT: And as he left the room, Aunt Mary would say:

FEMALE GREEK CHORUS: [*As Aunt Mary.*] Peck's so good with them when they get to be this age.

[LI'L BIT *has stormed to another part of the stage, her back turned, weeping with a teenage fury. Peck, cautiously, as if stalking a deer, comes to her. She turns away even more. He waits a bit.*]

PECK: I don't suppose you're talking to family. [*No response.*] Does it help that I'm in-law?

LI'L BIT: Don't you dare make fun of this.

PECK: I'm not. There's nothing funny about this. [*Beat.*] Although I'll bet when Big Papa is about to meet his maker, he'll remember *The Merchant of Venice*.

LI'L BIT: I've got to get away from here.

PECK: You're going away. Soon. Here, take this.

[PECK *hands her his folded handkerchief.* LI'L BIT *uses it, noisily. Hands it back. Without her seeing, he reverently puts it back.*]

LI'L BIT: I hate this family.

PECK: Your grandfather's ignorant. And you're right—he's going to die soon. But he's family. Family is . . . family.

LI'L BIT: Grown-ups are always saying that. Family.

PECK: Well, when you get a little older, you'll see what we're saying.

LI'L BIT: Uh-huh. So family is another acquired taste, like French kissing?

PECK: Come again?

LI'L BIT: You know, at first it really grosses you out, but in time you grow to like it?

---

5. American politician (1919–98), who opposed school desegregation as governor of Alabama in 1963–67 and ran for U.S. president in 1968 on an anti-civil rights platform. Campaigning again in 1972, he was shot and paralyzed from the waist down. (He later served two more terms as Alabama governor, renounced racism, and won support from African Americans.)

PECK: Girl, you are . . . a handful.

LI'L BIT: Uncle Peck—you have the keys to your car?

PECK: Where do you want to go?

LI'L BIT: Just up the road.

PECK: I'll come with you.

LI'L BIT: No—please? I just need to . . . to drive for a little bit. Alone.

[PECK *tosses her the keys.*]

PECK: When can I see you alone again?

LI'L BIT: Tonight.

[LI'L BIT *crosses to center stage while the lights dim around her. A Voice directs:*]

Shifting Forward from First to Second Gear.

LI'L BIT: There were a lot of rumors about why I got kicked out of that fancy school in 1970. Some say I got caught with a man in my room. Some say as a kid on scholarship I fooled around with a rich man's daughter.

[LI'L BIT *smiles innocently at the audience.*] I'm not talking.

But the real truth was I had a constant companion in my dorm room—who was less than discrete. Canadian V.O. A fifth a day.

1970. A Nixon recession. I slept on the floors of friends who were out of work themselves. Took factory work when I could find it. A string of dead-end day jobs that didn't last very long.

What I did, most nights, was cruise the Beltway and the back roads of Maryland, where there was still country, past the battlefields and farm houses. Racing in a 1965 Mustang—and as long as I had gasoline for my car and whiskey for me, the nights would pass. Fully tanked, I would speed past the churches and the trees on the bend, thinking just one notch of the steering wheel would be all it would take, and yet some . . . reflex took over. My hands on the wheel in the nine and three o'clock position—I never so much as got a ticket. He taught me well.

[*A Voice announces:*]

You and the Reverse Gear.

LI'L BIT: Back up. 1968. On the Eastern Shore. A celebration dinner.

[LI'L BIT *joins* PECK *at a table in a restaurant.*]

PECK: Feeling better, missy?

LI'L BIT: The bathroom's really amazing here, Uncle Peck! They have these little soaps—instead of borax or something—and they're in the shape of shells.

PECK: I'll have to take a trip to the gentleman's room just to see.

LI'L BIT: How did you know about this place?

PECK: This inn is famous on the Eastern Shore—it's been open since the seventeenth century. And I know how you like history. . . .

[LI'L BIT *is shy and pleased.*]

LI'L BIT: It's great.

PECK: And you've just done your first, legal, long-distance drive. You must be hungry.

LI'L BIT: I'm starved.

PECK: I would suggest a dozen oysters to start, and the crab imperial. . . . [LI'L BIT *is genuinely agog.*] You might be interested to know the town history. When the British sailed up this very river in the dead of night—see outside where I'm pointing?—they were going to bombard the heck out of this town. But the town fathers were ready for them. They crept up all the trees with lanterns so that the British would think they saw the town lights and they aimed their cannons too high. And that's why the inn is still here for business today.

LI'L BIT: That's a great story.

PECK: [*Casually.*] Would you like to start with a cocktail?

LI'L BIT: You're not . . . you're not going to start drinking, are you, Uncle Peck?

PECK: Not me. I told you, as long as you're with me, I'll never drink. I asked you if *you'd* like a cocktail before dinner. It's nice to have a little something with the oysters.

LI'L BIT: But . . . I'm not . . . legal. We could get arrested. Uncle Peck, they'll never believe I'm twenty-one!

PECK: So? Today we celebrate your driver's license—on the first try. This establishment reminds me a lot of places back home.

LI'L BIT: What does that mean?

PECK: In South Carolina, like here on the Eastern Shore, they're . . . [*Searches for the right euphemism.*] . . . "European." Not so puritanical. And very understanding if gentlemen wish to escort very attractive young ladies who might want a before-dinner cocktail. If you want one, I'll order one.

LI'L BIT: Well—sure. Just . . . one.

[*The* FEMALE GREEK CHORUS *appears in a spot.*]

FEMALE GREEK CHORUS: [*As Mother.*] A Mother's Guide to Social Drinking:

A lady never gets sloppy—she may, however, get tipsy and a little gay.

Never drink on an empty stomach. Avail yourself of the bread basket and generous portions of butter. *Slather* the butter on your bread.

Sip your drink, slowly, let the beverage linger in your mouth—interspersed with interesting, fascinating conversation. Sip, never . . . slurp or gulp. Your glass should always be three-quarters full when his glass is empty.

Stay away from *ladies'* drinks: drinks like pink ladies, sloe gin fizzes, daiquiris, gold cadillacs, Long Island iced teas, margaritas, piña coladas, mai tais, planters punch, white Russians, black Russians, red Russians, melon balls, blue balls, hummingbirds, hemorrhages, and hurricanes. In short, avoid anything with sugar, or anything with an umbrella. Get your vitamin C from *fruit.* Don't order anything with Voodoo or Vixen in the title or sexual positions in the name like Dead Man Screw or the Missionary. [*She sort of titters.*]

Believe me, they are lethal. . . . I think you were conceived after one of those.

Drink, instead, like a man: straight up or on the rocks, with plenty of water in between.

Oh, yes. And never mix your drinks. Stay with one all night long, like the man you came in with: bourbon, gin, or tequila till dawn, damn the torpedoes, full speed ahead!

[*As the* FEMALE GREEK CHORUS *retreats, the* MALE GREEK CHORUS *approaches the table as a Waiter.*]

MALE GREEK CHORUS: [*As Waiter.*] I hope you all are having a pleasant evening. Is there something I can bring you, sir, before you order?

[LI'L BIT *waits in anxious fear. Carefully,* UNCLE PECK *says with command:*]

PECK: I'll have a plain iced tea. The lady would like a drink, I believe.

[*The* MALE GREEK CHORUS *does a double take; there is a moment when* UNCLE PECK *and he are in silent communication.*]

MALE GREEK CHORUS: [*As Waiter.*] Very good. What would the . . . lady like?
LI'L BIT: [*A bit flushed.*] Is there . . . is there any sugar in a martini?
PECK: None that I know of.
LI'L BIT: That's what I'd like then—a dry martini. And could we maybe have some bread?
PECK: A drink fit for a woman of the world.—Please bring the lady a dry martini, be generous with the olives, straight up.

[*The* MALE GREEK CHORUS *anticipates a large tip.*]

MALE GREEK CHORUS: [*As Waiter.*] Right away. Very good, sir.

[*The* MALE GREEK CHORUS *returns with an empty martini glass which he puts in front of* LI'L BIT.]

PECK: Your glass is empty. Another martini, madam?
LI'L BIT: Yes, thank you. [PECK *signals the* MALE GREEK CHORUS, *who nods.*] So why did you leave South Carolina, Uncle Peck?
PECK: I was stationed in D.C. after the war, and decided to stay. Go North, Young Man, someone might have said.
LI'L BIT: What did you do in the service anyway?
PECK: [*Suddenly taciturn.*] I . . . I did just this and that. Nothing heroic or spectacular.
LI'L BIT: But did you see fighting? Or go to Europe?
PECK: I served in the Pacific Theater. It's really nothing interesting to talk about.
LI'L BIT: It is to me. [*The Waiter has brought another empty glass.*] Oh, goody. I love the color of the swizzle sticks. What were we talking about?
PECK: Swizzle sticks.
LI'L BIT: Do you ever think of going back?
PECK: To the Marines?
LI'L BIT: No—to South Carolina.
PECK: Well, we do go back. To visit.
LI'L BIT: No, I mean to live.
PECK: Not very likely. I think it's better if my mother doesn't have a daily reminder of her disappointment.
LI'L BIT: Are these floorboards slanted?
PECK: Yes, the floor is very slanted. I think this is the original floor.
LI'L BIT: Oh, good.

[*The* FEMALE GREEK CHORUS *as Mother enters swaying a little, a little past tipsy.*]

FEMALE GREEK CHORUS: [*As Mother.*] Don't leave your drink unattended when you visit the ladies' room. There is such a thing as white slavery; the modus operandi is to spike an unsuspecting young girl's drink with a "mickey" when she's left the room to powder her nose.

But if you feel you have had more than your sufficiency in liquor, do go to the ladies' room—often. Pop your head out of doors for a refreshing breath of the night air. If you must, wet your face and head with tap water. Don't be afraid to dunk your head if necessary. A wet woman is still less conspicuous than a drunk woman.

[*The Female Greek Chorus stumbles a little; conspiratorially.*] When in the course of human events it becomes necessary,[6] go to a corner stall and insert the index and middle finger down the throat almost to the epiglottis. Divulge your stomach contents by such persuasion, and then wait a few moments before rejoining your beau waiting for you at your table.

Oh, no. Don't be shy or embarrassed. In the very best of establishments, there's always one or two debutantes crouched in the corner stalls, their beaded purses tossed willy-nilly, sounding like cats in heat, heaving up the contents of their stomachs.

[*The* FEMALE GREEK CHORUS *begins to wander off*] I wonder what it is they do in the men's rooms. . . .

LI'L BIT: So why is your mother disappointed in you, Uncle Peck?
PECK: Every mother in Horry County has Great Expectations.[7]
LI'L BIT: —Could I have another mar-ti-ni, please?
PECK: I think this is your last one.

[PECK *signals the Waiter. The Waiter looks at Li'l Bit and shakes his head no.* PECK *raises his eyebrow, raises his finger to indicate one more, and then rubs his fingers together. It looks like a secret code. The Waiter sighs, shakes his head sadly, and brings over another empty martini glass. He glares at* PECK.]

LI'L BIT: The name of the county where you grew up is "Horry?" [LI'L BIT, *plastered, begins to laugh. Then she stops.*] I think your mother should be proud of you.

[PECK *signals for the check.*]

PECK: Well, missy, she wanted me to do—to *be* everything my father was not. She wanted me to amount to something.
LI'L BIT: But you have! You've amounted a lot. . . .
PECK: I'm just a very ordinary man.

[*The Waiter has brought the check and waits.* PECK *draws out a large bill and hands it to the Waiter.* LI'L BIT *is in the soppy stage.*]

LI'L BIT: I'll bet your mother loves you, Uncle Peck.

[PECK *freezes a bit. To* MALE GREEK CHORUS *as Waiter:*]

PECK: Thank you. The service was exceptional. Please keep the change.
MALE GREEK CHORUS: [*As Waiter, in a tone that could freeze.*] Thank you, sir. Will you be needing any help?

---

6. The beginning of the Declaration of Independence, by Thomas Jefferson (1743–1826).
7. The capitalization of this phrase, suggests that Peck alludes to the title of an 1861 novel by Charles Dickens (1812–70), whose young protagonist's dreams of becoming an educated "gentleman" come true thanks to a mysterious benefactor.

PECK: I think we can manage, thank you.

> [*Just then, the* FEMALE GREEK CHORUS *as Mother lurches on stage; the* MALE GREEK CHORUS *as Waiter escorts her off as she delivers:*]

FEMALE GREEK CHORUS: [*As Mother.*] Thanks to judicious planning and several trips to the ladies' loo, your mother once out-drank an entire regiment of British officers on a good-will visit to Washington! Every last man of them! Milquetoasts! How'd they ever kick Hitler's cahones,[8] huh? No match for an American lady—I could drink every man in here under the table.

> [*She delivers one last crucial hint before she is gently "bounced."*] As a last resort, when going out for an evening on the town, be sure to wear a skin-tight girdle—so tight that only a surgical knife or acetylene torch can get it off you—so that if you do pass out in the arms of your escort, he'll end up with rubber burns on his fingers before he can steal your virtue—

> [*A Voice punctures the interlude with:*]

Vehicle Failure.
Even with careful maintenance and preventive operation of your automobile, it is all too common for us to experience an unexpected breakdown. If you are driving at any speed when a breakdown occurs, you must slow down and guide the automobile to the side of the road.

> [PECK *is slowly propping up* LI'L BIT *as they work their way to his car in the parking lot of the inn.*]

PECK: How are you doing, missy?

LI'L BIT: It's so far to the car, Uncle Peck. Like the lanterns in the trees the British fired on . . .

> [LI'L BIT *stumbles.* PECK *swoops her up in his arms.*]

PECK: Okay. I think we're going to take a more direct route.

> [LI'L BIT *closes her eyes.*] Dizzy? [*She nods her head.*] Don't look at the ground. Almost there—do you feel sick to your stomach? [LI'L BIT *nods. They reach the "car."* PECK *gently deposits her on the front seat.*] Just settle here a little while until things stop spinning. [LI'L BIT *opens her eyes.*]

LI'L BIT: What are we doing?

PECK: We're just going to sit here until your tummy settles down.

LI'L BIT: It's such nice upholst'ry—

PECK: Think you can go for a ride, now?

LI'L BIT: Where are you taking me?

PECK: Home.

LI'L BIT: You're not taking me—upstairs? There's no room at the inn? [LI'L BIT *giggles.*]

PECK: Do you want to go upstairs? [LI'L BIT *doesn't answer.*] Or home?

LI'L BIT: —This isn't right, Uncle Peck.

PECK: What isn't right?

LI'L BIT: What we're doing. It's wrong. It's very wrong.

---

8. *Cojones:* Spanish-language obscenity, literally testicles, implying "guts" or "manhood." *Loo:* British slang for restroom. *Milquetoasts:* old-fashioned insult for effeminate or weak men.

PECK: What are we doing? [LI'L BIT *does not answer.*] We're just going out to dinner.

LI'L BIT: You know. It's not nice to Aunt Mary.

PECK: You let me be the judge of what's nice and not nice to my wife.

[*Beat.*]

LI'L BIT: Now you're mad.

PECK: I'm not mad. It's just that I thought you . . . understood me, Li'l Bit. I think you're the only one who does.

LI'L BIT: Someone will get hurt.

PECK: Have I forced you to do anything?

[*There is a long pause as* LI'L BIT *tries to get sober enough to think this through.*]

LI'L BIT: . . . I guess not.

PECK: We are just enjoying each other's company. I've told you, nothing is going to happen between us until you want it to. Do you know that?

LI'L BIT: Yes.

PECK: Nothing is going to happen until you want it to. [*A second more, with* PECK *staring ahead at the river while seated at the wheel of his car. Then, softly:*] Do you want something to happen?

[PECK *reaches over and strokes her face, very gently.* LI'L BIT *softens, reaches for him, and buries her head in his neck. Then she kisses him. Then she moves away, dizzy again.*]

LI'L BIT: . . . I don't know.

[PECK *smiles; this has been good news for him—it hasn't been a "no."*]

PECK: Then I'll wait. I'm a very patient man. I've been waiting for a long time. I don't mind waiting.

LI'L BIT: Someone is going to get hurt.

PECK: No one is going to get hurt. [LI'L BIT *closes her eyes*] Are you feeling sick?

LI'L BIT: Sleepy.

[*Carefully,* PECK *props* LI'L BIT *up on the seat.*]

PECK: Stay here a second.

LI'L BIT: Where're you going?

PECK: I'm getting something from the back seat.

LI'L BIT: [*Scared; too loud*] What? What are you going to do?

[PECK *reappears in the front seat with a lap rug.*]

PECK: Shhhh. [PECK *covers* LI'L BIT. *She calms down*] There. Think you can sleep?

[LI'L BIT *nods. She slides over to rest on his shoulder. With a look of happiness,* PECK *turns the ignition key. Beat.* PECK *leaves* LI'L BIT *sleeping in the car and strolls down to the audience. Wagner's* Flying Dutchman[9] *comes up faintly. A voice interjects:*]

---

9. Mythic opera (1841) by the German composer Richard Wagner (1813–83).

Idling in the Neutral Gear.

TEENAGE GREEK CHORUS: Uncle Peck Teaches Cousin Bobby How to Fish.

PECK: I get back once or twice a year—supposedly to visit Mama and the family, but the real truth is to fish. I miss this the most of all. There's a smell in the Low Country—where the swamp and fresh inlet join the saltwater—a scent of sand and cypress, that I haven't found anywhere yet.

I don't say this very often up North because it will just play into the stereotype everyone has, but I will tell you: I didn't wear shoes in the summertime until I was sixteen. It's unnatural down here to pen up your feet in leather. Go ahead—take 'em off. Let yourself breathe—it really will make you feel better.

We're going to aim for some pompano today—and I have to tell you, they're a very shy, mercurial fish. Takes patience, and psychology. You have to believe it doesn't matter if you catch one or not.

Sky's pretty spectacular—there's some beer in the cooler next to the crab salad I packed, so help yourself if you get hungry. Are you hungry? Thirsty? Holler if you are.

Okay. You don't want to lean over the bridge like that—pompano feed in shallow water, and you don't want to get too close—they're frisky and shy little things—wait, check your line. Yep, something's been munching while we were talking.

Okay, look: We take the sand flea and you take the hook like this—right through his little sand flea rump. Sand fleas should always keep their backs to the wall. Okay. Cast it in, like I showed you. That's great! I can taste that pompano now, sautéed with some pecans and butter, a little bourbon—now—let it lie on the bottom—now, reel, jerk, reel, jerk—

Look—look at your line. There's something calling, all right. Okay, tip the rod up—not too sharp—hook it—all right, now easy, reel and then rest—let it play. And reel—play it out, that's right—really good! I can't believe it! It's a pompano.—Good work! Way to go! You are an official fisherman now. Pompano are hard to catch. We are going to have a delicious little—

What? Well, I don't know how much pain a fish feels—you can't think of that. Oh, no, don't cry, come on now, it's just a fish—the other guys are going to see you.—No, no, you're just real sensitive, and I think that's wonderful at your age—look, do you want me to cut it free? You do?

Okay, hand me those pliers—look—I'm cutting the hook—okay? And we're just going to drop it in—no I'm not mad. It's just for fun, okay? There—it's going to swim back to its lady friend and tell her what a terrible day it had and she's going to stroke him with her fins until he feels better, and then they'll do something alone together that will make them both feel good and sleepy. . . .

[PECK *bends down, very earnest*] I don't want you to feel ashamed about crying. I'm not going to tell anyone, okay? I can keep secrets. You know, men cry all the time. They just don't tell anybody, and they don't let anybody catch them. There's nothing you could do that would make me feel ashamed of you. Do you know that? Okay. [PECK *straightens up, smiles.*]

Do you want to pack up and call it a day? I tell you what—I think I can still remember—there's a really neat tree house where I used to stay for days. I think it's still here—it was the last time I looked. But it's a secret place—you can't tell anybody we've gone there—least of all your mom or your sisters.—

This is something special just between you and me. Sound good? We'll climb up there and have a beer and some crab salad—okay, B. B.? Bobby? Robert . . .

[LI'L BIT *sits at a kitchen table with the two* FEMALE GREEK CHORUS *members.*]

LI'L BIT: [*To the audience.*] Three women, three generations, sit at the kitchen table. On Men, Sex, and Women: Part I:

FEMALE GREEK CHORUS: [*As Mother.*] Men only want one thing.

LI'L BIT: [*Wide-eyed.*] But what? What is it they want?

FEMALE GREEK CHORUS: [*As Mother.*] And once they have it, they lose all interest. So Don't Give It to Them.

TEENAGE GREEK CHORUS: [*As Grandmother.*] I never had the luxury of the rhythm method. Your grandfather is just a big bull. A big bull. Every morning, every evening.

FEMALE GREEK CHORUS: [*As Mother, whispers to Li'l Bit.*] And he used to come home for lunch every day.

LI'L BIT: My god, Grandma!

TEENAGE GREEK CHORUS: [*As Grandmother.*] Your grandfather only cares that I do two things: have the table set and the bed turned down.

FEMALE GREEK CHORUS: [*As Mother.*] And in all that time, Mother, you never have experienced—?

LI'L BIT: [*To the audience.*]—Now my grandmother believed in all the sacraments of the church, to the day she died. She believed in Santa Claus and the Easter Bunny until she was fifteen. But she didn't believe in—

TEENAGE GREEK CHORUS: [*As Grandmother.*]—Orgasm! That's just something you and Mary have made up! I don't believe you.

FEMALE GREEK CHORUS: [*As Mother.*] Mother, it happens to women all the time—

TEENAGE GREEK CHORUS: [*As Grandmother.*]—Oh, now you're going to tell me about the G force![1]

LI'L BIT: No, Grandma, I think that's astronauts—

FEMALE GREEK CHORUS: [*As Mother.*] Well, Mama, after all, you were a child bride when Big Papa came and got you—you were a married woman and you still believed in Santa Claus.

TEENAGE GREEK CHORUS: [*As Grandmother.*] It was legal, what Daddy and I did! I was fourteen and in those days, fourteen was a grown-up woman—

[*Big Papa shuffles in the kitchen for a cookie.*]

MALE GREEK CHORUS: [*As Grandfather.*]—Oh, now we're off on Grandma and the Rape of the Sa-bean Women![2]

TEENAGE GREEK CHORUS: [*As Grandmother.*] Well, you were the one in such a big hurry—

MALE GREEK CHORUS: [*As Grandfather to Li'l Bit.*]—I picked your grandmother out of that herd of sisters just like a lion chooses the gazelle—the plump, slow, flaky gazelle dawdling at the edge of the herd—your sisters were too smart and too fast and too scrawny—

1. Grandmother here mistakes *G-force*—an astronaut's term referring to the force of gravity for *G-spot*, a bean-shaped mass of highly sensitive nerve tissue inside the vagina.
2. The legend of the mass rape of the Sabine women of central Italy by soldiers of ancient Rome, a scene of violent conquest often depicted in paintings.

LI'L BIT: [*To the audience.*]—The family story is that when Big Papa came for Grandma, my Aunt Lily was waiting for him with a broom—and she beat him over the head all the way down the stairs as he was carrying out Grandma's hope chest—

MALE GREEK CHORUS: [*As Grandfather.*]—And they were *mean*. 'Specially Lily.

FEMALE GREEK CHORUS: [*As Mother.*] Well, you were robbing the baby of the family!

TEENAGE GREEK CHORUS: [*As Grandmother.*] I still keep a broom handy in the kitchen! And I know how to use it! So get your hand out of the cookie jar and don't you spoil your appetite for dinner—out of the kitchen!

[MALE GREEK CHORUS *as Grandfather leaves chuckling with a cookie.*]

FEMALE GREEK CHORUS: [*As Mother.*] Just one thing a married woman needs to know how to use—the rolling pin or the broom. I prefer a heavy, cast-iron fry pan—they're great on a man's head, no matter how thick the skull is.

TEENAGE GREEK CHORUS: [*As Grandmother.*] Yes, sir, your father is ruled by only two bosses! Mr. Gut and Mr. Peter! And sometimes, first thing in the morning, Mr. Sphincter Muscle!

FEMALE GREEK CHORUS: [*As Mother.*] It's true. Men are like children. Just like little boys.

TEENAGE GREEK CHORUS: [*As Grandmother.*] Men are bulls! Big bulls!

[*The* GREEK CHORUS *is getting aroused.*]

FEMALE GREEK CHORUS: [*As Mother.*] They'd still be crouched on their haunches over a fire in a cave if we hadn't cleaned them up!

TEENAGE GREEK CHORUS: [*As Grandmother, flushed.*] Coming in smelling of sweat—

FEMALE GREEK CHORUS: [*As Mother.*]—Looking at those naughty pictures like boys in a dime store with a dollar in their pockets!

TEENAGE GREEK CHORUS: [*As Grandmother; raucous.*] No matter to them what they smell like! They've got to have it, right then, on the spot, right there! Nasty!—

FEMALE GREEK CHORUS: [*As Mother.*]—Vulgar!

TEENAGE GREEK CHORUS: [*As Grandmother.*] Primitive!—

FEMALE GREEK CHORUS: [*As Mother.*]—Hot!—

LI'L BIT: And just about then, Big Papa would shuffle in with—

MALE GREEK CHORUS: [*As Grandfather.*]—What are you all cackling about in here?

TEENAGE GREEK CHORUS: [*As Grandmother.*] Stay out of the kitchen! This is just for girls!

[*As Grandfather leaves:*]

MALE GREEK CHORUS: [*As Grandfather.*] Lucy, you'd better not be filling Mama's head with sex! Every time you and Mary come over and start in about sex, when I ask a simple question like, "What time is dinner going to be ready?," Mama snaps my head off!

TEENAGE GREEK CHORUS: [*As Grandmother.*] Dinner will be ready when I'm good and ready! Stay out of this kitchen!

[LI'L BIT *steps out. A Voice directs:*]

When Making a Left Turn, You Must Downshift While Going Forward.

LI'L BIT: 1979. A long bus trip to Upstate New York. I settled in to read, when a young man sat beside me.

MALE GREEK CHORUS: [*As Young Man; voice cracking.*] "What are you reading?"

LI'L BIT: He asked. His voice broke into that miserable equivalent of vocal acne, not quite falsetto and not tenor, either. I glanced a side view. He was appealing in an odd way, huge ears at a defiant angle springing forward at ninety degrees. He must have been shaving, because his face, with a peach sheen, was speckled with nicks and styptic. "I have a class tomorrow," I told him.

MALE GREEK CHORUS: [*As Young Man.*] "You're taking a class?"

LI'L BIT: "I'm teaching a class." He concentrated on lowering his voice.

MALE GREEK CHORUS: [*As Young Man.*] "I'm a senior. Walt Whitman High."

LI'L BIT: The light was fading outside, so perhaps he was—with a very high voice.

I felt his "interest" quicken. Five steps ahead of the hopes in his head, I slowed down, waited, pretended surprise, acted at listening, all the while knowing we would get off the bus, he would just then seem to think to ask me to dinner, he would chivalrously insist on walking me home, he would continue to converse in the street until I would casually invite him up to my room—and—I was only into the second moment of conversation and I could see the whole evening before me.

And dramaturgically speaking, after the faltering and slightly comical "first act," there was the very briefest of intermissions, and an extremely capable and forceful and *sustained* second act. And after the second act climax and a gentle denouement—before the post-play discussion—I lay on my back in the dark and I thought about you, Uncle Peck. Oh. Oh—this is the allure. Being older. Being the first. Being the translator, the teacher, the epicure, the already jaded. This is how the giver gets taken.

[LI'L BIT *changes her tone.*] On Men, Sex, and Women: Part II:

[LI'L BIT *steps back into the scene as a fifteen-year-old, gawky and quiet, as the gazelle at the edge of the herd.*]

TEENAGE GREEK CHORUS: [*As Grandmother; to Li'l Bit.*] You're being mighty quiet, missy. Cat Got Your Tongue?

LI'L BIT: I'm just listening. Just thinking.

TEENAGE GREEK CHORUS: [*As Grandmother.*] Oh, yes, Little Miss Radar Ears? Soaking it all in? Little Miss Sponge? Penny for your thoughts?

[LI'L BIT *hesitates to ask but she really wants to know.*]

LI'L BIT: Does it—when you do it—you know, theoretically when I do it and I haven't done it before—I mean—does it hurt?

FEMALE GREEK CHORUS: [*As Mother.*] Does what hurt, honey?

LI'L BIT: When a . . . when a girl does it for the first time—with a man—does it hurt?

TEENAGE GREEK CHORUS: [*As Grandmother; horrified.*] *That's* what you're thinking about?

FEMALE GREEK CHORUS: [*As Mother; calm.*] Well, just a little bit. Like a pinch. And there's a little blood.

TEENAGE GREEK CHORUS: [*As Grandmother.*] Don't tell her that! She's too young to be thinking those things!

FEMALE GREEK CHORUS: [*As Mother.*] Well, if she doesn't find out from me, where is she going to find out? In the street?

TEENAGE GREEK CHORUS: [*As Grandmother.*] Tell her it hurts! It's agony! You think you're going to die! Especially if you do it before marriage!

FEMALE GREEK CHORUS: [*As Mother.*] Mama! I'm going to tell her the truth! Unlike you, you left me and Mary completely in the dark with fairy tales and told us to go to the priest! What does an eighty-year-old priest know about lovemaking with girls!

LI'L BIT: [*Getting upset.*] It's not fair!

FEMALE GREEK CHORUS: [*As Mother.*] Now, see, she's getting upset—you're scaring her.

TEENAGE GREEK CHORUS: [*As Grandmother.*] Good! Let her be good and scared! It hurts! You bleed like a stuck pig! And you lay there and say, "Why, O Lord, have you forsaken me?!"

LI'L BIT: It's not fair! Why does everything have to hurt for girls? Why is there always blood?

FEMALE GREEK CHORUS: [*As Mother.*] It's not a lot of blood—and it feels wonderful after the pain subsides . . .

TEENAGE GREEK CHORUS: [*As Grandmother.*] You're encouraging her to just go out and find out with the first drugstore joe who buys her a milk shake!

FEMALE GREEK CHORUS: [*As Mother.*] Don't be scared. It won't hurt you—if the man you go to bed with really loves you. It's important that he loves you.

TEENAGE GREEK CHORUS: [*As Grandmother.*]—Why don't you just go out and rent a motel room for her, Lucy?

FEMALE GREEK CHORUS: [*As Mother.*] I believe in telling my daughter the truth! We have a very close relationship! I want her to be able to ask me anything—I'm not scaring her with stories about Eve's sin and snakes crawling on their bellies for eternity and women bearing children in mortal pain—

TEENAGE GREEK CHORUS: [*As Grandmother.*]—If she stops and thinks before she takes her knickers off, maybe someone in this family will finish high school!

[LI'L BIT *knows what is about to happen and starts to retreat from the scene at this point.*]

FEMALE GREEK CHORUS: [*As Mother.*] Mother! If you and Daddy had helped me—I wouldn't have had to marry that—that no-good-son-of-a—

TEENAGE GREEK CHORUS: [*As Grandmother.*]—He was good enough for you on a full moon! I hold you responsible!

FEMALE GREEK CHORUS: [*As Mother.*]—You could have helped me! You could have told me something about the facts of life!

TEENAGE GREEK CHORUS: [*As Grandmother.*]—I told you what my mother told me! A girl with her skirt up can outrun a man with his pants down!

[*The* MALE GREEK CHORUS *enters the fray;* LI'L BIT *edges further downstage.*]

FEMALE GREEK CHORUS: [*As Mother.*] And when I turned to you for a little help, all I got afterwards was—

MALE GREEK CHORUS: [*As Grandfather.*] You Made Your Bed; Now Lie On It!

[*The* GREEK CHORUS *freezes, mouths open, argumentatively.*]

LI'L BIT: [*To the audience.*] Oh, please! I still can't bear to listen to it, after all these years—

[*The* MALE GREEK CHORUS *"unfreezes," but out of his open mouth, as if to his surprise, comes a base refrain from a Motown song.*]

MALE GREEK CHORUS: "Do-Bee-Do-Wah!"

[*The* FEMALE GREEK CHORUS *member is also surprised; but she, too, unfreezes.*]

FEMALE GREEK CHORUS: "Shoo-doo-be-doo-be-doo; shoo-doo-be-doo-be-doo."

[*The* MALE *and* FEMALE GREEK CHORUS *members continue with their harmony, until the* TEENAGE *member of the* CHORUS *starts in with Motown lyrics such as "Dedicated to the One I Love," or "In the Still of the Night," or "Hold Me"—any Sam Cooke[3] will do. The three modulate down into three-part harmony, softly, until they are submerged by the actual recording playing over the radio in the car in which* UNCLE PECK *sits in the driver's seat, waiting.* LI'L BIT *sits in the passenger's seat.*]

LI'L BIT: Ahh. That's better.

[UNCLE PECK *reaches over and turns the volume down; to* LI'L BIT:]

PECK: How can you hear yourself think?

[LI'L BIT *does not answer. A Voice insinuates itself in the pause:*]

Before You Drive.
Always check under your car for obstructions—broken bottles, fallen tree branches, and the bodies of small children. Each year hundreds of children are crushed beneath the wheels of unwary drivers in their own driveways. Children depend on *you* to watch them.

[*Pause. The Voice continues:*]

You and the Reverse Gear.

[*In the following section, it would be nice to have slides of erotic photographs of women and cars: women posed over the hood; women draped along the sideboards; women with water hoses spraying the car; and the actress playing* LI'L BIT *with a Bel Air or any 1950s car one can find for the finale.*]

LI'L BIT: 1967. In a parking lot of the Beltsville Agricultural Farms. The Initiation into a Boy's First Love.
PECK: [*With a soft look on his face.*] Of course, my favorite car will always be the 56 Bel Air Sports Coupe. Chevy sold more '55s, but the '56!—a V-8 with Corvette option, 225 horsepower; went from zero to sixty miles per hour in 8.9 seconds.
LI'L BIT: [*To the audience.*] Long after a mother's tits, but before a woman's breasts:
PECK: Super-Turbo-Fire! What a Power Pack—mechanical lifters, twin four-barrel carbs, lightweight valves, dual exhausts—
LI'L BIT: [*To the audience.*] After the milk but before the beer:
PECK: A specific intake manifold, higher-lift camshaft, and the tightest squeeze Chevy had ever made—

3. Successful gospel singer (1931–64) who crossed over to secular music with such hits as "You Send Me" (1957) and "Only Sixteen" (1959); he was never a Motown recording artist. Stevie Wonder (b. 1950), a Motown artist influenced by Cooke, recorded a song called "Hold Me." "Dedicated to the One I Love" was a 1961 hit for the Shirelles and a 1967 hit for the Mamas and the Papas. "In the Still of the Night" was a 1956 hit for the Five Satins and a 1960 hit for Dion and the Belmonts.

LI'L BIT: [*To the audience.*] Long after he's squeezed down the birth canal but before he's pushed his way back in: The boy falls in love with the thing that bears his weight with speed.

PECK: I want you to know your automobile inside and out.—Are you there? Li'l Bit?

[*Slides end here.*]

LI'L BIT: —What?

PECK: You're drifting. I need you to concentrate.

LI'L BIT: Sorry.

PECK: Okay. Get into the driver's seat. [LI'L BIT *does.*] Okay. Now. Show me what you're going to do before you start the car.

[LI'L BIT *sits, with her hands in her lap. She starts to giggle.*]

LI'L BIT: I don't know, Uncle Peck.

PECK: Now, come on. What's the first thing you're going to adjust?

LI'L BIT: My bra strap?—

PECK: —Li'l Bit. What's the most important thing to have control of on the inside of the car?

LI'L BIT: That's easy. The radio. I tune the radio from Mama's old fart tunes to—

[LI'L BIT *turns the radio up so we can hear a 1960s tune. With surprising firmness,* PECK *commands:*]

PECK: —Radio off. Right now. [LI'L BIT *turns the radio off.*] When you are driving your car, with your license, you can fiddle with the stations all you want. But when you are driving with a learner's permit in my car, I want all your attention to be on the road.

LI'L BIT: Yes, sir.

PECK: Okay. Now the seat—forward and up. [LI'L BIT *pushes it forward.*] Do you want a cushion?

LI'L BIT: No—I'm good.

PECK: You should be able to reach all the switches and controls. Your feet should be able to push the accelerator, brake and clutch all the way down. Can you do that?

LI'L BIT: Yes.

PECK: Okay, the side mirrors. You want to be able to see just a bit of the right side of the car in the right mirror—can you?

LI'L BIT: Turn it out more.

PECK: Okay. How's that?

LI'L BIT: A little more. . . . Okay, that's good.

PECK: Now the left—again, you want to be able to see behind you—but the left lane—adjust it until you feel comfortable. [LI'L BIT *does so.*] Next. I want you to check the rearview mirror. Angle it so you have a clear vision of the back. [LI'L BIT *does so.*] Okay. Lock your door. Make sure all the doors are locked.

LI'L BIT: [*Making a joke of it.*] But then I'm locked in with you.

PECK: Don't fool.

LI'L BIT: All right. We're locked in.

PECK: We'll deal with the air vents and defroster later. I'm teaching you on a manual—once you learn manual, you can drive anything. I want you to be able to drive any car, any machine. Manual gives you *control*. In ice, if your brakes fail, if you need more power—okay? It's a little harder at first, but then it becomes like breathing. Now. Put your hands on the wheel. I never want to see you driving with one hand. Always two hands. [LI'L BIT *hesitates*.] What? What is it now?

LI'L BIT: If I put my hands on the wheel—how do I defend myself?

PECK: [*Softly.*] Now listen. Listen up close. We're not going to fool around with this. This is serious business. I will never touch you when you are driving a car. Understand?

LI'L BIT: Okay.

PECK: Hands on the nine o'clock and three o'clock position gives you maximum control and turn.

[PECK *goes silent for a while.* LI'L BIT *waits for more instruction.*]

Okay. Just relax and listen to me, Li'l Bit, okay? I want you to lift your hands for a second and look at them. [LI'L BIT *feels a bit silly, but does it.*]

Those are your two hands. When you are driving, your life is in your own two hands. Understand? [LI'L BIT *nods.*]

I don't have any sons. You're the nearest to a son I'll ever have—and I want to give you something. Something that really matters to me.

There's something about driving—when you're in control of the car, just you and the machine and the road—that nobody can take from you. A power. I feel more myself in my car than anywhere else. And that's what I want to give to you.

There's a lot of assholes out there. Crazy men, arrogant idiots, drunks, angry kids, geezers who are blind—and you have to be ready for them. I want to teach you to drive like a man.

LI'L BIT: What does that mean?

PECK: Men are taught to drive with confidence—with aggression. The road belongs to them. They drive defensively—always looking out for the other guy. Women tend to be polite—to hesitate. And that can be fatal.

You're going to learn to think what the other guy is going to do before he does it. If there's an accident, and ten cars pile up, and people get killed, you're the one who's gonna steer through it, put your foot on the gas if you have to, and be the only one to walk away. I don't know how long you or I are going to live, but we're for damned sure not going to die in a car.

So if you're going to drive with me, I want you to take this very seriously.

LI'L BIT: I will, Uncle Peck. I want you to teach me to drive.

PECK: Good. You're going to pass your test on the first try. Perfect score. Before the next four weeks are over, you're going to know this baby inside and out. Treat her with respect.

LI'L BIT: Why is it a "she"?

PECK: Good question. It doesn't have to be a "she"—but when you close your eyes and think of someone who responds to your touch—someone who performs just for you and gives you what you ask for—I guess I always see a "she." You can call her what you like.

LI'L BIT: [*To the audience.*] I closed my eyes—and decided not to change the gender.

[*A Voice:*]

Defensive driving involves defending yourself from hazardous and sudden changes in your automotive environment. By thinking ahead, the defensive driver can adjust to weather, road conditions, and road kill. Good defensive driving involves mental and physical preparation. Are you prepared?

[*Another Voice chimes in:*]

You and the Reverse Gear.

LI'L BIT: 1966. The Anthropology of the Female Body in Ninth Grade—Or A Walk Down Mammary Lane.

[*Throughout the following, there is occasional rhythmic beeping, like a transmitter signalling.* LI'L BIT *is aware of it, but can't figure out where it is coming from. No one else seems to hear it.*]

MALE GREEK CHORUS: In the hallway of Francis Scott Key[4] Middle School.

[*A bell rings; the* GREEK CHORUS *is changing classes and meets in the hall, conspiratorially.*]

TEENAGE GREEK CHORUS: She's coming!

[LI'L BIT *enters the scene; the* MALE GREEK CHORUS *member has a sudden, violent sneezing and lethal allergy attack.*]

FEMALE GREEK CHORUS: Jerome? Jerome? Are you all right?
MALE GREEK CHORUS: I—don't—know. I can't breathe—get Li'l Bit—
TEENAGE GREEK CHORUS: —He needs oxygen!—
FEMALE GREEK CHORUS: —Can you help us here?
LI'L BIT: What's wrong? Do you want me to get the school nurse—

[*The* MALE GREEK CHORUS *member wheezes, grabs his throat and sniffs at Li'l Bit's chest, which is beeping away.*]

MALE GREEK CHORUS: No—it's okay—I only get this way when I'm around an allergy trigger—
LI'L BIT: Golly. What are you allergic to?
MALE GREEK CHORUS: [*With a sudden grab of her breast.*] Foam rubber.

[*The* GREEK CHORUS *members break up with hilarity; Jerome leaps away from Li'l Bit's kicking rage with agility; as he retreats:*]

LI'L BIT: Jerome! Creep! Cretin! Cro-Magnon!
TEENAGE GREEK CHORUS: Rage is not attractive in a girl.
FEMALE GREEK CHORUS: Really. Get a Sense of Humor.

[*A voice echoes:*]

Good defensive driving involves mental and physical preparation. Were you prepared?

---

4. Maryland lawyer (1780–1843) who in 1814 penned the poem that, when set to music, became known as "The Star-Spangled Banner," now the U.S. national anthem.

FEMALE GREEK CHORUS: Gym Class: In the showers.

[*The sudden sound of water; the* FEMALE GREEK CHORUS *members and* LI'L BIT, *while fully clothed, drape towels across their fronts, miming nudity. They stand, hesitate, at an imaginary shower's edge.*]

LI'L BIT: Water looks hot.

FEMALE GREEK CHORUS: Yesss. . . .

[FEMALE GREEK CHORUS *members are not going to make the first move. One dips a tentative toe under the water, clutching the towel around her.*]

LI'L BIT: Well, I guess we'd better shower and get out of here.

FEMALE GREEK CHORUS: Yep. You go ahead. I'm still cooling off.

LI'L BIT: Okay.—Sally? Are you gonna shower?

TEENAGE GREEK CHORUS: After you—

[LI'L BIT *takes a deep breath for courage, drops the towel and plunges in: The two* FEMALE GREEK CHORUS *members look at Li'l Bit in the all together, laugh, gasp and high-five each other.*]

TEENAGE GREEK CHORUS: Oh my god! Can you believe—

FEMALE GREEK CHORUS: Told you! It's not foam rubber! I win! Jerome owes me fifty cents!

[*A Voice editorializes:*]

Were you prepared?

[LI'L BIT *tries to cover up; she is exposed, as suddenly 1960s Motown fills the room and we segue into:*]

FEMALE GREEK CHORUS: The Sock Hop.

[LI'L BIT *stands up against the wall with her female classmates.* TEENAGE GREEK CHORUS *is mesmerized by the music and just sways alone, lip-synching the lyrics.*]

LI'L BIT: I don't know. Maybe it's just me—but—do you ever feel like you're just a walking Mary Jane joke?

FEMALE GREEK CHORUS: I don't know what you mean.

LI'L BIT: You haven't heard the Mary Jane jokes? [FEMALE GREEK CHORUS *member shakes her head no.*] Okay. "Little Mary Jane is walking through the woods, when all of a sudden this man who was hiding behind a tree *jumps* out, *rips* open Mary Jane's blouse, and *plunges* his hands on her breasts. And Little Mary Jane just laughed and laughed because she knew her money was in her shoes."

[LI'L BIT *laughs; the* FEMALE GREEK CHORUS *does not.*]

FEMALE GREEK CHORUS: You're weird.

[*In another space, in a strange light,* UNCLE PECK *stands and stares at Li'l Bit's body. He is setting up a tripod, but he just stands, appreciative, watching her.*]

LI'L BIT: Well, don't you ever feel . . . self-conscious? Like you're being looked at all the time?

FEMALE GREEK CHORUS: That's not a problem for me.—Oh—look—Greg's coming over to ask you to dance.

[TEENAGE GREEK CHORUS *becomes attentive, flustered.* MALE GREEK CHORUS *member, as Greg, bends slightly as a very short young man, whose head is at Li'l Bit's chest level. Ardent, sincere, and socially inept, Greg will become a successful gynecologist.*]

TEENAGE GREEK CHORUS: [*Softly.*] Hi, Greg.

[*Greg does not hear. He is intent on only one thing.*]

MALE GREEK CHORUS: [*As Greg, to Li'l Bit.*] Good Evening. Would you care to dance?

LI'L BIT: [*Gently.*] Thank you very much, Greg—but I'm going to sit this one out.

MALE GREEK CHORUS: [*As Greg*] Oh. Okay. I'll try my luck later.

[*He disappears.*]

TEENAGE GREEK CHORUS: Oohhh.

[LI'L BIT *relaxes. Then she tenses, aware of Peck's gaze.*]

FEMALE GREEK CHORUS: Take pity on him. Someone should.

LI'L BIT: But he's so short.

TEENAGE GREEK CHORUS: He can't help it.

LI'L BIT: But his head comes up to [LI'L BIT *gestures.*] here. And I think he asks me on the fast dances so he can watch me—you know—jiggle.

FEMALE GREEK CHORUS: I wish I had your problems.

[*The tune changes; Greg is across the room in a flash.*]

MALE GREEK CHORUS: [*As Greg.*] Evening again. May I ask you for the honor of a spin on the floor?

LI'L BIT: I'm . . . very complimented, Greg. But I . . . I just don't do fast dances.

MALE GREEK CHORUS: [*As Greg.*] Oh. No problem. That's okay.

[*He disappears.* TEENAGE GREEK CHORUS *watches him go.*]

TEENAGE GREEK CHORUS: That is just so—*sad.*

[LI'L BIT *becomes aware of* PECK *waiting.*]

FEMALE GREEK CHORUS: You know, you should take it as a compliment that the guys want to watch you jiggle. They're guys. That's what they're supposed to do.

LI'L BIT: I guess you're right. But sometimes I feel like these alien life forces, these two mounds of flesh have grafted themselves onto my chest, and they're using me until they can "propagate" and take over the world and they'll just keep growing, with a mind of their own until I collapse under their weight and they suck all the nourishment out of my body and I finally just waste away while they get bigger and bigger and—[LI'L BIT*'s classmates are just staring at her in disbelief.*]

FEMALE GREEK CHORUS: —You are the strangest girl I have ever met.

[LI'L BIT*'s trying to joke but feels on the verge of tears.*]

LI'L BIT: Or maybe someone's implanted radio transmitters in my chest at a frequency I can't hear, that girls can't detect, but they're sending out these signals to men who get mesmerized, like sirens, calling them to dash themselves on these "rocks"—[5]

[*Just then, the music segues into a slow dance, perhaps a Beach Boys tune like "Little Surfer," but over the music there's a rhythmic, hypnotic beeping transmitted, which both Greg and* PECK *hear.* LI'L BIT *hears it too, and in horror she stares at her chest. She, too, is almost hypnotized. In a trance, Greg responds to the signals and is called to her side—actually, her front. Like a zombie, he stands in front of her, his eyes planted on her two orbs.*]

MALE GREEK CHORUS: [*As Greg.*] This one's a slow dance. I hope your dance card isn't . . . filled?

[LI'L BIT *is aware of* PECK; *but the signals are calling her to him. The signals are no longer transmitters, but an electromagnetic force, pulling* LI'L BIT *to his side, where he again waits for her to join him. She must get away from the dance floor.*]

LI'L BIT: Greg—you really are a nice boy. But I don't like to dance.
MALE GREEK CHORUS: [*As Greg.*] That's okay. We don't have to move or anything. I could just hold you and we could just *sway* a little—
LI'L BIT: —No! I'm sorry—but I think I have to leave; I hear someone calling me—

[LI'L BIT *starts across the dance floor, leaving Greg behind. The beeping stops. The lights change, although the music does not. As* LI'L BIT *talks to the audience, she continues to change and prepare for the coming session. She should be wearing a tight tank top or a sheer blouse and very tight pants. To the audience:*]

In every man's home some small room, some zone in his house, is set aside. It might be the attic, or the study, or a den. And there's an invisible sign as if from the old treehouse: Girls Keep Out.

Here, away from female eyes, lace doilies and crochet, he keeps his manly toys: the Vargas pinups, the tackle. A scent of tobacco and WD-40.[6] [*She inhales deeply.*] A dash of his Bay Rum. Ahhh . . . [LI'L BIT *savors it for just a moment more.*]

Here he keeps his secrets: a violin or saxophone, drum set or darkroom, and the stacks of *Playboy.* [*In a whisper.*] Here, in my aunt's home, it was the basement. Uncle Peck's turf.

[*A Voice commands:*]

You and the Reverse Gear.

LI'L BIT: 1965. The Photo Shoot.

[LI'L BIT *steps into the scene as a nervous but curious thirteen-year-old. Music, from the previous scene, continues to play, changing into something like Roy Orbison later— something seductive with a beat.* PECK *fiddles, all business, with his camera. As in the driving lesson, he is all competency and concentration.* LI'L BIT *stands awkwardly. He looks through the Leica camera on the tripod, adjusts the back lighting, etc.*]

5. The Sirens, according to Greek mythology, were nymphs with women's heads and birds' bodies whose singing seduced sailors to shipwreck upon the rocks near Messina.
6. Brand of aerosol lubricant for mechanical parts. *Vargas*: Alberto Vargas (1896–1982), Peruvian-born illustrator for *Esquire*, *Playboy*, and other magazines, famous for his slick, good-humored, erotic images of semiclad or nude young women, which were often "pinned up" on walls by U.S. soldiers overseas.

PECK: Are you cold? The lights should heat up some in a few minutes—

LI'L BIT: —Aunt Mary is?

PECK: At the National Theatre matinee. With your mother. We have time.

LI'L BIT: But—what if—

PECK: —And so what if they return? I told them you and I were going to be working with my camera. They won't come down. [LI'L BIT *is quiet, apprehensive.*]— Look, are you sure you want to do this?

LI'L BIT: I said I'd do it. But—

PECK: —I know. You've drawn the line.

LI'L BIT: [*Reassured.*] That's right. No frontal nudity.

PECK: Good heavens, girl, where did you pick that up?

LI'L BIT: [*Defensive.*] I read.

[PECK *tries not to laugh.*]

PECK: And I read *Playboy* for the interviews. Okay. Let's try some different music.

[PECK *goes to an expensive reel-to-reel and forwards. Something like "Sweet Dreams"*[7] *begins to play.*]

LI'L BIT: I didn't know you listened to this.

PECK: I'm not dead, you know. I try to keep up. Do you like this song? [LI'L BIT *nods with pleasure.*] Good. Now listen—at professional photo shoots, they always play music for the models. Okay? I want you to just enjoy the music. Listen to it with your body, and just—respond.

LI'L BIT: Respond to the music with my . . . body?

PECK: Right. Almost like dancing. Here—let's get you on the stool, first. [PECK *comes over and helps her up.*]

LI'L BIT: But nothing showing—

[PECK *firmly, with his large capable hands, brushes back her hair, angles her face.* LI'L BIT *turns to him like a plant to the sun.*]

PECK: Nothing showing. Just a peek.

[*He holds her by the shoulder, looking at her critically. Then he unbuttons her blouse to the midpoint, and runs his hands over the flesh of her exposed sternum, arranging the fabric, just touching her. Deliberately, calmly. Asexually.* LI'L BIT *quiets, sits perfectly still, and closes her eyes.*]
    Okay?

LI'L BIT: Yes.

[PECK *goes back to his camera.*]

PECK: I'm going to keep talking to you. Listen without responding to what I'm saying; you want to *listen* to the music. Sway, move just your torso or your head—I've got to check the light meter.

LI'L BIT: But—you'll be watching.

PECK: No—I'm not here—just my voice. Pretend you're in your room all alone on a Friday night with your mirror—and the music feels good—just move for me, Li'l Bit—

---

7. Here and elsewhere, actually the early 1960s hit "Dream Baby (How Long Must I Dream)," by Roy Orbison (1936–88).

[LI'L BIT *closes her eyes. At first self-conscious; then she gets more into the music and begins to sway. We hear the camera start to whir. Throughout the shoot, there can be a slide montage of actual shots of the actor playing Li'l Bit—interspersed with other models à la Playboy, Calvin Klein, and Victoriana/Lewis Carroll's Alice Liddell.*][8]

That's it. That looks great. Okay. Just keep doing that. Lift your head up a bit more, good, good, just keep moving, that a girl—you're a very beautiful young woman. Do you know that? [LI'L BIT *looks up, blushes.* PECK *shoots the camera. The audience should see this shot on the screen.*]

LI'L BIT: No. I don't know that.

PECK: Listen to the music. [LI'L BIT *closes her eyes again.*] Well you are. For a thirteen-year-old, you have a body a twenty-year-old woman would die for.

LI'L BIT: The boys in school don't think so.

PECK: The boys in school are little Neanderthals in short pants. You're ten years ahead of them in maturity; it's gonna take a while for them to catch up.

[PECK *clicks another shot; we see a faint smile on Li'l Bit on the screen.*]

Girls turn into women long before boys turn into men.

LI'L BIT: Why is that?

PECK: I don't know, Li'l Bit. But it's a blessing for men.

[LI'L BIT *turns silent.*] Keep moving. Try arching your back on the stool, hands behind you, and throw your head back. [*The slide shows a* Playboy *model in this pose.*] Oohh, great. That one was great. Turn your head away, same position. [*Whir.*] Beautiful.

[LI'L BIT *looks at him a bit defiantly.*]

LI'L BIT: I think Aunt Mary is beautiful.

[PECK *stands still.*]

PECK: My wife is a very beautiful woman. Her beauty doesn't cancel yours out. [*More casually; he returns to the camera.*] All the women in your family are beautiful. In fact, I think all women are. You're not listening to the music. [PECK *shoots some more film in silence.*] All right, turn your head to the left. Good. Now take the back of your right hand and put it on your right cheek—your elbow angled up—now slowly, slowly, stroke your cheek, draw back your hair with the back of your hand. [*Another classic* Playboy *or Vargas.*] Good. One hand above and behind your head; stretch your body; smile. [*Another pose.*]

Li'l Bit. I want you to think of something that makes you laugh—

LI'L BIT: I can't think of anything.

PECK: Okay. Think of Big Papa chasing Grandma around the living room. [LI'L BIT *lifts her head and laughs. Click. We should see this shot.*] Good. Both hands behind your head. Great! Hold that. [*From behind his camera.*] You're doing great work. If we keep this up, in five years we'll have a really professional portfolio.

---

8. The slides would mix adult pornography with the images of seductive adolescents in Calvin Klein ads and mid- to late-nineteenth-century (Victorian-era) photographs of children in sensual poses. Lewis Carroll is the pseudonym of the English mathematician Charles Dodgson (1832–98), author of *Alice in Wonderland* (1865). The original Alice, Alice Liddell, was ten years old—twenty years younger than Dodgson—when he first told the story; his photographs of her, some nude, suggest pedophilic eroticism.

[LI'L BIT *stops*.]

LI'L BIT: What do you mean in five years?

PECK: You can't submit work to *Playboy* until you're eighteen.—

[PECK *continues to shoot; he knows he's made a mistake*.]

LI'L BIT: —Wait a minute. You're joking, aren't you, Uncle Peck?

PECK: Heck, no. You can't get into *Playboy* unless you're the very best. And you are the very best.

LI'L BIT: I would never do that!

[PECK *stops shooting. He turns off the music*.]

PECK: Why? There's nothing wrong with *Playboy*—it's a very classy maga—

LI'L BIT: [*More upset*.] But I thought you said I should go to college!

PECK: Wait—Li'l Bit—it's nothing like that. Very respectable women model for *Playboy*—actresses with major careers—women in college—there's an Ivy League issue every—

LI'L BIT: —I'm never doing anything like that! You'd show other people these—other *men*—these—what I'm doing.—Why would you do that?! Any *boy* around here could just pick up, just go into The Stop & Go and *buy*—Why would you ever want to—to share—

PECK: —Whoa, whoa. Just stop a second and listen to me. Li'l Bit. Listen. There's nothing wrong in what we're doing. I'm very proud of you. I think you have a wonderful body and an even more wonderful mind. And of course I want other people to *appreciate* it. It's not anything shameful.

LI'L BIT: [*Hurt*.] But this is something—that I'm only doing for you. This is something—that you said was just between us.

PECK: It is. And if that's how you feel, five years from now, it will remain that way. Okay? I know you're not going to do anything you don't feel like doing.

[*He walks back to the camera*.] Do you want to stop now? I've got just a few more shots on this roll—

LI'L BIT: I don't want anyone seeing this.

PECK: I swear to you. No one will. I'll treasure this—that you're doing this only for me.

[LI'L BIT, *still shaken, sits on the stool. She closes her eyes*.] Li'l Bit? Open your eyes and look at me. [LI'L BIT *shakes her head no*.] Come on. Just open your eyes, honey.

LI'L BIT: If I look at you—if I look at the camera: You're gonna know what I'm thinking. You'll see right through me—

PECK: —No, I won't. I want you to look at me. All right, then. I just want you to listen. Li'l Bit. [*She waits*.] I love you. [LI'L BIT *opens her eyes; she is startled*. PECK *captures the shot. On the screen we see right though her*. PECK *says softly*.] Do you know that? [LI'L BIT *nods her head yes*.] I have loved you every day since the day you were born.

LI'L BIT: Yes.

[LI'L BIT *and* PECK *just look at each other. Beat. Beneath the shot of herself on the screen*, LI'L BIT, *still looking at her uncle, begins to unbutton her blouse. A neutral Voice cuts off the above scene with*:]

Implied Consent.
As an individual operating a motor vehicle in the state of Maryland, you
must abide by "Implied Consent." If you do not consent to take the blood
alcohol content test, there may be severe penalties: a suspension of
license, a fine, community service, and a possible *jail* sentence.

[*The Voice shifts tone:*]

Idling in the Neutral Gear.

MALE GREEK CHORUS: [*Announcing.*] Aunt Mary on behalf of her husband.

[FEMALE GREEK CHORUS *checks her appearance, and with dignity comes to the front*
of the stage and sits down to talk to the audience.]

FEMALE GREEK CHORUS: [*As Aunt Mary.*] My husband was such a good man—is. Is
such a good man. Every night, he does the dishes. The second he comes home,
he's taking out the garbage, or doing yard work, lifting the heavy things I
can't. Everyone in the neighborhood borrows Peck—it's true—women with
husbands of their own, men who just don't have Peck's abilities—there's
always a knock on our door for a jump start on cold mornings, when anyone
needs a ride, or help shoveling the sidewalk—I look out, and there Peck is,
without a coat, pitching in.

I know I'm lucky. The man works from dawn to dusk. And the overtime he
does every year—my poor sister. She sits every Christmas when I come to dinner with a new stole, or diamonds, or with the tickets to Bermuda.

I know he has troubles. And we don't talk about them. I wonder, sometimes, what happened to him during the war. The men who fought World
War II didn't have "rap sessions" to talk about their feelings. Men in his generation were expected to be quiet about it and get on with their lives. And
sometimes I can feel him just fighting the trouble—whatever has burrowed
deeper than the scar tissue—and we don't talk about it. I know he's having a
bad spell because he comes looking for me in the house, and just hangs
around me until it passes. And I keep my banter light—I discuss a new recipe,
or sales, or gossip—because I think domesticity can be a balm for men when
they're lost. We sit in the house and listen to the peace of the clock ticking in
his well-ordered living room, until it passes.

[*Sharply.*] I'm not a fool. I know what's going on. I wish you could feel how
hard Peck fights against it—he's swimming against the tide, and what he
needs is to see me on the shore, believing in him, knowing he won't go under,
he won't give up—

And I want to say this about my niece. She's a sly one, that one is. She
knows exactly what she's doing; she's twisted Peck around her little finger
and thinks it's all a big secret. Yet another one who's borrowing my husband
until it doesn't suit her anymore.

Well, I'm counting the days until she goes away to school. And she manip-
ulates someone else. And then he'll come back again, and sit in the kitchen
while I bake, or beside me on the sofa when I sew in the evenings. I'm a very
patient woman. But I'd like my husband back.

I am counting the days.

[*A Voice repeats:*]

You and the Reverse Gear.

MALE GREEK CHORUS: Li'l Bit's Thirteenth Christmas. Uncle Peck Does the Dishes. Christmas 1964.

[PECK *stands in a dress shirt and tie, nice pants, with an apron. He is washing dishes. He's in a mood we haven't seen. Quiet, brooding.* LI'L BIT *watches him a moment before seeking him out.*]

LI'L BIT: Uncle Peck? [*He does not answer. He continues to work on the pots.*] I didn't know where you'd gone to. [*He nods. She takes this as a sign to come in.*] Don't you want to sit with us for a while?

PECK: No. I'd rather do the dishes.

[*Pause.* LI'L BIT *watches him.*]

LI'L BIT: You're the only man I know who does dishes. [PECK *says nothing.*] I think it's really nice.

PECK: My wife has been on her feet all day. So's your grandmother and your mother.

LI'L BIT: I know. [*Beat.*] Do you want some help?

PECK: No. [*He softens a bit towards her.*] You can help by just talking to me.

LI'L BIT: Big Papa never does the dishes. I think it's nice.

PECK: I think men should be nice to women. Women are always working for us. There's nothing particularly manly in wolfing down food and then sitting around in a stupor while the women clean up.

LI'L BIT: That looks like a really neat camera that Aunt Mary got you.

PECK: It is. It's a very nice one.

[*Pause, as* PECK *works on the dishes and some demon that* LI'L BIT *intuits.*]

LI'L BIT: Did Big Papa hurt your feelings?

PECK: [*Tired.*] What? Oh, no—it doesn't hurt me. Family is family. I'd rather have him picking on me than—I don't pay him any mind, Li'l Bit.

LI'L BIT: Are you angry with us?

PECK: No, Li'l Bit. I'm not angry.

[*Another pause.*]

LI'L BIT: We missed you at Thanksgiving. . . . I did. I missed you.

PECK: Well, there were . . . "things" going on. I didn't want to spoil anyone's Thanksgiving.

LI'L BIT: Uncle Peck? [*Very carefully.*] Please don't drink any more tonight.

PECK: I'm not . . . overdoing it.

LI'L BIT: I know. [*Beat.*] Why do you drink so much?

[PECK *stops and thinks, carefully.*]

PECK: Well, Li'l Bit—let me explain it this way. There are some people who have a . . . a "fire" in the belly. I think they go to work on Wall Street or they run for office. And then there are people who have a "fire" in their heads—and they become writers or scientists or historians. [*He smiles a little at her.*] You. You've got a "fire" in the head. And then there are people like me.

LI'L BIT: Where do you have . . . a fire?

PECK: I have a fire in my heart. And sometimes the drinking helps.

LI'L BIT: There's got to be other things that can help.

PECK: I suppose there are.

LI'L BIT: Does it help—to talk to me?

PECK: Yes. It does. [*Quiet.*] I don't get to see you very much.

LI'L BIT: I know. [*Li'l Bit thinks.*] You could talk to me more.

PECK: Oh?

LI'L BIT: I could make a deal with you, Uncle Peck.

PECK: I'm listening.

LI'L BIT: We could meet and talk—once a week. You could just store up whatever's bothering you during the week—and then we could talk.

PECK: Would you like that?

LI'L BIT: As long as you don't drink. I'd meet you somewhere for lunch or for a walk—on the weekends—as long as you stop drinking. And we could talk about whatever you want.

PECK: You would do that for me?

LI'L BIT: I don't think I'd want Mom to know. Or Aunt Mary. I wouldn't want them to think—

PECK: —No. It would just be us talking.

LI'L BIT: I'll tell Mom I'm going to a girlfriend's. To study. Mom doesn't get home until six, so you can call me after school and tell me where to meet you.

PECK: You get home at four?

LI'L BIT: We can meet once a week. But only in public. You've got to let me—draw the line. And once it's drawn, you mustn't cross it.

PECK: Understood.

LI'L BIT: Would that help?

[PECK *is very moved.*]

PECK: Yes. Very much.

LI'L BIT: I'm going to join the others in the living room now. [LI'L BIT *turns to go.*]

PECK: Merry Christmas, Li'l Bit.

[LI'L BIT *bestows a very warm smile on him.*]

LI'L BIT: Merry Christmas, Uncle Peck.

[*A Voice dictates:*]

Shifting Forward from Second to Third Gear.

[*The* MALE *and* FEMALE GREEK CHORUS *members come forward.*]

MALE GREEK CHORUS: 1969. Days and Gifts: A Countdown:

FEMALE GREEK CHORUS: A note. "September 3, 1969. Li'l Bit: You've only been away two days and it feels like months. Hope your dorm room is cozy. I'm sending you this tape cassette—it's a new model—so you'll have some music in your room. Also that music you're reading about for class—*Carmina Burana.*[9] Hope you enjoy. Only ninety days to go!—Peck."

---

9. Popular, nontraditional opera, set to thirteenth-century Latin and German lyrics, by the German composer Carl Orff (1895–1982).

MALE GREEK CHORUS: September 22. A bouquet of roses. A note: "Miss you like crazy. Sixty-nine days . . ."

TEENAGE GREEK CHORUS: September 25. A box of chocolates. A card: "Don't worry about the weight gain. You still look great. Got a post office box—write to me there. Sixty-six days.—Love, your candy man."[1]

MALE GREEK CHORUS: October 16. A note: "Am trying to get through the Jane Austen you're reading—*Emma*—here's a book in return: *Liaisons Dangereuses.*[2] Hope you're saving time for me." Scrawled in the margin the number: "47."

FEMALE GREEK CHORUS: November 16. "Sixteen days to go!—Hope you like the perfume.—Having a hard time reaching you on the dorm phone. You must be in the library a lot. Won't you think about me getting you your own phone so we can talk?"

TEENAGE GREEK CHORUS: November 18. "Li'l Bit—got a package returned to the P.O. Box. Have you changed dorms? Call me at work, or write to the P.O. Am still on the wagon. Waiting to see you. Only two weeks more!"

MALE GREEK CHORUS: November 23. A letter. "Li'l Bit. So disappointed you couldn't come home for the turkey. Sending you some money for a nice dinner out—nine days and counting!"

GREEK CHORUS: [*In unison.*] November 25th. A letter:

LI'L BIT: "Dear Uncle Peck: I am sending this to you at work. Don't come up next weekend for my birthday. I will not be here—"

[*A Voice directs:*]

Shifting Forward from Third to Fourth Gear.

MALE GREEK CHORUS: December 10, 1969. A hotel room. Philadelphia. There is no moon tonight.

[PECK *sits on the side of the bed while* LI'L BIT *paces. He can't believe she's in his room, but there's a desperate edge to his happiness.* LI'L BIT *is furious, edgy. There is a bottle of champagne in an ice bucket in a very nice hotel room.*]

PECK: Why don't you sit?

LI'L BIT: I don't want to.—What's the champagne for?

PECK: I thought we might toast your birthday—

LI'L BIT: —I am so pissed off at you, Uncle Peck.

PECK: Why?

LI'L BIT: I mean, are you crazy?

PECK: What did I do?

LI'L BIT: You scared the holy crap out of me—sending me that stuff in the mail—

PECK: —They were gifts! I just wanted to give you some little perks your first semester—

LI'L BIT: —Well, what the hell were those numbers all about! Forty-four days to go—only two more weeks.—And then just numbers—69—68—67—like some serial killer!

1. Reference to another song by Roy Orbison, "Candy Man" (1961).
2. *Les Liaisons dangereuses* (1782; translated as *Dangerous Connections* in 1784 but generally known as *Dangerous Liaisons*), famous work by the French general and novelist Pierre Choderlos de Laclos (1741–1803); it concerns a conspiracy between two cynical former lovers to seduce an innocent young wife. In the novel *Emma* (1816), by the English writer Jane Austen (1775–1817), the heroine is morally educated by the brother of her older sister's husband, whom she marries in the end.

PECK: Li'l Bit! Whoa! This is me you're talking to—I was just trying to pick up your spirits, trying to celebrate your birthday.

LI'L BIT: My *eighteenth* birthday. I'm not a child, Uncle Peck. You were counting down to my eighteenth birthday.

PECK: So?

LI'L BIT: So? So statutory rape is not in effect when a young woman turns eighteen. And you and I both know it.

[PECK *is walking on ice.*]

PECK: I think you misunderstand.

LI'L BIT: I think I understand all too well. I know what you want to do five steps ahead of you doing it. Defensive Driving 101.

PECK: Then why did you suggest we meet here instead of the restaurant?

LI'L BIT: I don't want to have this conversation in public.

PECK: Fine. Fine. We have a lot to talk about.

LI'L BIT: Yeah. We do. [LI'L BIT *doesn't want to do what she has to do.*] Could I . . . have some of that champagne?

PECK: Of course, madam! [PECK *makes a big show of it.*] Let me do the honors. I wasn't sure which you might prefer—Taittingers or Veuve Clicquot—so I thought we'd start out with an old standard—Perrier Jouet.[3] [*The bottle is popped.*]

Quick—Li'l Bit—your glass! [UNCLE PECK *fills Li'l Bit's glass. He puts the bottle back in the ice and goes for a can of ginger ale.*] Let me get some of this ginger ale—my bubbly—and toast you.

[*He turns and sees that* LI'L BIT *has not waited for him.*]

LI'L BIT: Oh—sorry, Uncle Peck. Let me have another. [PECK *fills her glass and reaches for his ginger ale; she stops him.*] Uncle Peck—maybe you should join me in the champagne.

PECK: You want me to—drink?

LI'L BIT: It's not polite to let a lady drink alone.

PECK: Well, missy, if you insist. . . . [PECK *hesitates.*]—Just one. It's been a while. [PECKS *fills another flute for himself.*] There. I'd like to propose a toast to you and your birthday! [PECK *sips it tentatively.*] I'm not used to this anymore.

LI'L BIT: You don't have anywhere to go tonight, do you?

[PECK *hopes this is a good sign.*]

PECK: I'm all yours.—God, it's good to see you! I've gotten so used to . . . to . . . talking to you in my head. I'm used to seeing you every week—there's so much—I don't quite know where to begin. How's school, Li'l Bit?

LI'L BIT: I—it's hard, Uncle Peck. Harder than I thought it would be. I'm in the middle of exams and papers and—I don't know.

PECK: You'll pull through. You always do.

LI'L BIT: Maybe. I . . . might be flunking out.

PECK: You always think the worst, Li'l Bit, but when the going gets tough—[LI'L BIT *shrugs and pours herself another glass.*]—Hey, honey, go easy on that stuff, okay?

LI'L BIT: Is it very expensive?

3. Like Taittingers and Veuve Clicquot, a good brand of champagne.

PECK: Only the best for you. But the cost doesn't matter—champagne should be "sipped." [LI'L BIT *is quiet.*] Look—if you're in trouble in school—you can always come back home for a while.

LI'L BIT: No— [LI'L BIT *tries not to be so harsh.*] —Thanks, Uncle Peck, but I'll figure some way out of this.

PECK: You're supposed to get in scrapes, your first year away from home.

LI'L BIT: Right. How's Aunt Mary?

PECK: She's fine. [*Pause.*] Well—how about the new car?

LI'L BIT: It's real nice. What is it, again?

PECK: It's a Cadillac El Dorado.

LI'L BIT: Oh. Well, I'm real happy for you, Uncle Peck.

PECK: I got it for you.

LI'L BIT: What?

PECK: I always wanted to get a Cadillac—but I thought, Peck, wait until Li'l Bit's old enough—and thought maybe you'd like to drive it, too.

LI'L BIT: [*Confused.*] Why would I want to drive your car?

PECK: Just because it's the best—I want you to have the best.

[*They are running out of "gas"; small talk.*]

LI'L BIT:	PECK:
Listen, Uncle Peck, I don't know how to begin this, but—	I have been thinking of how to say this in my head, over and over—

PECK: Sorry.

LI'L BIT: You first.

PECK: Well, your going away—has just made me realize how much I miss you. Talking to you and being alone with you. I've really come to depend on you, Li'l Bit. And it's been so hard to get in touch with you lately—the distance and—and you're never in when I call—I guess you've been living in the library—

LI'L BIT: —No—the problem is, I haven't been in the library—

PECK: —Well, it doesn't matter—I hope you've been missing me as much.

LI'L BIT: Uncle Peck—I've been thinking a lot about this—and I came here tonight to tell you that—I'm not doing very well. I'm getting very confused—I can't concentrate on my work—and now that I'm away—I've been going over and over it in my mind—and I don't want us to "see" each other anymore. Other than with the rest of the family.

PECK: [*Quiet.*] Are you seeing other men?

LI'L BIT: [*Getting agitated.*] I—no, that's not the reason—I—well, yes, I am seeing other—listen, it's not really anybody's business!

PECK: Are you in love with anyone else?

LI'L BIT: That's not what this is about.

PECK: Li'l Bit—you're scared. Your mother and your grandparents have filled your head with all kinds of nonsense about men—I hear them working on you all the time—and you're scared. It won't hurt you—if the man you go to bed with really loves you. [LI'L BIT *is scared. She starts to tremble.*] And I have loved you since the day I held you in my hand. And I think everyone's just gotten you frightened to death about something that is just like breathing—

LI'L BIT: Oh, my god—[*She takes a breath.*] I can't see you anymore, Uncle Peck.

[PECK *downs the rest of his champagne.*]

PECK: Li'l Bit. Listen. Listen. Open your eyes and look at me. Come on. Just open your eyes, honey. [LI'L BIT, *eyes squeezed shut, refuses.*] All right then. I just want you to listen. Li'l Bit—I'm going to ask you just this once. Of your own free will. Just lie down on the bed with me—our clothes on—just lie down with me, a man and a woman . . . and let's . . . hold one another. Nothing else. Before you say anything else. I want the chance to . . . hold you. Because sometimes the body knows things that the mind isn't listening to . . . and after I've held you, then I want you to tell me what you feel.

LI'L BIT: You'll just . . . hold me?

PECK: Yes. And then you can tell me what you're feeling. [LI'L BIT—*half wanting to run, half wanting to get it over with, half wanting to be held by him:*]

LI'L BIT: Yes. All right. Just hold. Nothing else.

[PECK *lies down on the bed and holds his arms out to her.* LI'L BIT *lies beside him, putting her head on his chest. He looks as if he's trying to soak her into his pores by osmosis. He strokes her hair, and she lies very still. The* MALE GREEK CHORUS *member and the* FEMALE GREEK CHORUS *member as Aunt Mary come into the room.*]

MALE GREEK CHORUS: Recipe for a Southern Boy:

FEMALE GREEK CHORUS: [*As Aunt Mary.*] A drawl of molasses in the way he speaks.

MALE GREEK CHORUS: A gumbo of red and brown mixed in the cream of his skin.

[*While* PECK *lies, his eyes closed,* LI'L BIT *rises in the bed and responds to her aunt.*]

LI'L BIT: Warm brown eyes—

FEMALE GREEK CHORUS: [*As Aunt Mary.*] Bedroom eyes—

MALE GREEK CHORUS: A dash of Southern Baptist Fire and Brimstone—

LI'L BIT: A curl of Elvis on his forehead—

FEMALE GREEK CHORUS: [*As Aunt Mary.*] A splash of Bay Rum—

MALE GREEK CHORUS: A closely shaven beard that he razors just for you—

FEMALE GREEK CHORUS: [*As Aunt Mary.*] Large hands—rough hands—

LI'L BIT: Warm hands—

MALE GREEK CHORUS: The steel of the military in his walk—

LI'L BIT: The slouch of the fishing skiff in his walk—

MALE GREEK CHORUS: Neatly pressed khakis—

FEMALE GREEK CHORUS: [*As Aunt Mary.*] And under the wide leather of the belt—

LI'L BIT: Sweat of cypress and sand—

MALE GREEK CHORUS: Neatly pressed khakis—

LI'L BIT: His heart beating Dixie—

FEMALE GREEK CHORUS: [*As Aunt Mary.*] The whisper of the zipper—you could reach out with your hand and—

LI'L BIT: His mouth—

FEMALE GREEK CHORUS: [*As Aunt Mary.*] You could just reach out and—

LI'L BIT: Hold him in your hand—

FEMALE GREEK CHORUS: [*As Aunt Mary.*] And his mouth—

[LI'L BIT *rises above her uncle and looks at his mouth; she starts to lower herself to kiss him—and wrenches herself free. She gets up from the bed.*]

LI'L BIT: —I've got to get back.

PECK: Wait—Li'l Bit. Did you . . . feel nothing?

LI'L BIT: [*Lying.*] No. Nothing.

PECK: Do you—do you think of me?

[*The* GREEK CHORUS *whispers:*]

FEMALE GREEK CHORUS: Khakis—

MALE GREEK CHORUS: Bay Rum—

FEMALE GREEK CHORUS: The whisper of the—

LI'L BIT: —No.

[PECK, *in a rush, trembling, gets something out of his pocket.*]

PECK: I'm forty-five. That's not old for a man. And I haven't been able to do anything else but think of you. I can't concentrate on my work—Li'l Bit. You've got to—I want you to think about what I am about to ask you.

LI'L BIT: I'm listening.

[PECK *opens a small ring box.*]

PECK: I want you to be my wife.

LI'L BIT: This isn't happening.

PECK: I'll tell Mary I want a divorce. We're not blood-related. It would be legal—

LI'L BIT: —What have you been thinking! You are married to my aunt, Uncle Peck. She's my family. You have—you have gone way over the line. Family is family.

[*Quickly,* LI'L BIT *flies through the room, gets her coat.*] I'm leaving. Now. I am not seeing you. Again.

[PECK *lies down on the bed for a moment, trying to absorb the terrible news. For a moment, he almost curls into a fetal position.*]

I'm not coming home for Christmas. You should go home to Aunt Mary. Go home now, Uncle Peck.

[PECK *gets control, and sits, rigid.*]

Uncle Peck?—I'm sorry but I have to go.

[*Pause.*]

Are you all right?

[*With a discipline that comes from being told that boys don't cry,* PECK *stands upright.*]

PECK: I'm fine. I just think—I need a real drink.

[*The* MALE GREEK CHORUS *has become a bartender. At a small counter, he is lining up shots for* PECK. *As* LI'L BIT *narrates, we see* PECK *sitting, carefully and calmly downing shot glasses.*]

LI'L BIT: [*To the audience.*] I never saw him again. I stayed away from Christmas and Thanksgiving for years after.

It took my uncle seven years to drink himself to death. First he lost his job, then his wife, and finally his driver's license. He retreated to his house, and had his bottles delivered.

[PECK *stands, and puts his hands in front of him—almost like Superman flying.*]

One night he tried to go downstairs to the basement—and he flew down the steep basement stairs. My aunt came by weekly to put food on the porch, and she noticed the mail and the papers stacked up, uncollected.

They found him at the bottom of the stairs. Just steps away from his dark room.

Now that I'm old enough, there are some questions I would have liked to have asked him. Who did it to you, Uncle Peck? How old were you? Were you eleven?

[PECK *moves to the driver's seat of the car and waits.*]

Sometimes I think of my uncle as a kind of Flying Dutchman. In the opera, the Dutchman is doomed to wander the sea; but every seven years he can come ashore, and if he finds a maiden who will love him of her own free will—he will be released.

And I see Uncle Peck in my mind, in his Chevy '56, a spirit driving up and down the back roads of Carolina—looking for a young girl who, of her own free will, will love him. Release him.

[*A Voice states:*]

You and the Reverse Gear.

LI'L BIT: The summer of 1962. On Men, Sex, and Women: Part III:

[LI'L BIT *steps, as an eleven year old, into:*]

FEMALE GREEK CHORUS: [*As Mother.*] It is out of the question. End of Discussion.
LI'L BIT: But why?
FEMALE GREEK CHORUS: [*As Mother.*] Li'l Bit—we are not discussing this. I said no.
LI'L BIT: But I could spend an extra week at the beach! You're not telling me why!
FEMALE GREEK CHORUS: [*As Mother.*] Your uncle pays entirely too much attention to you.
LI'L BIT: He listens to me when I talk. And—and he talks to me. He teaches me about things. Mama—he knows an awful lot.
FEMALE GREEK CHORUS: [*As Mother.*] He's a small-town hick who's learned how to mix drinks from Hugh Hefner.[4]
LI'L BIT: Who's Hugh Hefner?

[*Beat.*]

FEMALE GREEK CHORUS: [*As Mother.*] I am not letting an eleven-year-old girl spend seven hours alone in the car with a man. . . . I don't like the way your uncle looks at you.
LI'L BIT: For God's sake, mother! Just because you've gone through a bad time with my father—you think every man is evil!
FEMALE GREEK CHORUS: [*As Mother.*] Oh no, Li'l Bit—not all men. . . . We . . . we just haven't been very lucky with the men in our family.
LI'L BIT: Just because you lost your husband—I still deserve a chance at having a father! Someone! A man who will look out for me! Don't I get a chance?
FEMALE GREEK CHORUS: [*As Mother.*] I will feel terrible if something happens.
LI'L BIT: Mother! It's in your head! Nothing will happen! I can take care of myself. And I can certainly handle Uncle Peck.
FEMALE GREEK CHORUS: [*As Mother.*] All right. But I'm warning you—if anything happens, I hold you responsible.

---

4. Founding publisher of *Playboy* magazine, known for promoting a flamboyant, extravagant lifestyle.

[LI'L BIT *moves out of this scene and toward the car.*]

LI'L BIT: 1962. On the Back Roads of Carolina: The First Driving Lesson.

[*The* TEENAGE GREEK CHORUS *member stands apart on stage. She will speak all of Li'l Bit's lines.* LI'L BIT *sits beside* PECK *in the front seat. She looks at him closely, remembering.*]

PECK: Li'l Bit? Are you getting tired?

TEENAGE GREEK CHORUS: A little.

PECK: It's a long drive. But we're making really good time. We can take the back road from here and see . . . a little scenery. Say—I've got an idea—[PECK *checks his rearview mirror.*]

TEENAGE GREEK CHORUS: Are we stopping, Uncle Peck?

PECK: There's no traffic here. Do you want to drive?

TEENAGE GREEK CHORUS: I can't drive.

PECK: It's easy. I'll show you how. I started driving when I was your age. Don't you want to?—

TEENAGE GREEK CHORUS: —But it's against the law at my age!

PECK: And that's why you can't tell anyone I'm letting you do this—

TEENAGE GREEK CHORUS: —But—I can't reach the pedals.

PECK: You can sit in my lap and steer. I'll push the pedals for you. Did your father ever let you drive his car?

TEENAGE GREEK CHORUS: No way.

PECK: Want to try?

TEENAGE GREEK CHORUS: Okay. [LI'L BIT *moves into Peck's lap. She leans against him, closing her eyes.*]

PECK: You're just a little thing, aren't you? Okay—now think of the wheel as a big clock—I want you to put your right hand on the clock where three o'clock would be; and your left hand on the nine—

[LI'L BIT *puts one hand to Peck's face, to stroke him. Then, she takes the wheel.*]

TEENAGE GREEK CHORUS: Am I doing it right?

PECK: That's right. Now, whatever you do, don't let go of the wheel. You tell me whether to go faster or slower—

TEENAGE GREEK CHORUS: Not so fast, Uncle Peck!

PECK: Li'l Bit—I need you to watch the road—

[PECK *puts his hands on Li'l Bit's breasts. She relaxes against him, silent, accepting his touch.*]

TEENAGE GREEK CHORUS: Uncle Peck—what are you doing?

PECK: Keep driving. [*He slips his hands under her blouse.*]

TEENAGE GREEK CHORUS: Uncle Peck—please don't do this—

PECK: —Just a moment longer . . . [PECK *tenses against* LI'L BIT.]

TEENAGE GREEK CHORUS: [*Trying not to cry.*] This isn't happening.

[PECK *tenses more, sharply. He buries his face in Li'l Bit's neck, and moans softly.* TEENAGE GREEK CHORUS *exits, and* LI'L BIT *steps out of the car.* PECK, *too, disappears. A Voice reflects.*]

Driving in Today's World.

LI'L BIT: That day was the last day I lived in my body. I retreated above the neck, and I've lived inside the "fire" in my head ever since.

And now that seems like a long, long time ago. When we were both very young.

And before you know it, I'll be thirty-five. That's getting up there for a woman. And I find myself believing in things that a younger self vowed never to believe in. Things like family and forgiveness.

I know I'm lucky. Although I still have never known what it feels like to jog or dance. Anything that . . . "jiggles." I do like to watch people on the dance floor, or out on the running paths, just jiggling away. And I say—good for them. [LI'L BIT *moves to the car with pleasure.*]

The nearest sensation I feel—of flight in the body—I guess I feel when I'm driving. On a day like today. It's five A.M. The radio says it's going to be clear and crisp. I've got five hundred miles of highway ahead of me—and some back roads too. I filled the tank last night, and had the oil checked. Checked the tires, too. You've got to treat her . . . with respect.

First thing I do is: Check under the car. To see if any two-year-olds or household cats have crawled beneath, and strategically placed their skulls behind my back tires. [LI'L BIT *crouches.*]

Nope. Then I get in the car. [LI'L BIT *does so.*]

I lock the doors. And turn the key. Then I adjust the most important control on the dashboard—the radio—[LI'L BIT *turns the radio on: We hear all of the Greek Chorus overlapping, and static:*]

FEMALE GREEK CHORUS: [*Overlapping.*]—"You were so tiny you fit in his hand—"

MALE GREEK CHORUS: [*Overlapping.*]—"How is Shakespeare gonna help her lie on her back in the—"

TEENAGE GREEK CHORUS: [*Overlapping.*]—"Am I doing it right?"

[LI'L BIT *fine-tunes the radio station. A song like "Dedicated to the One I Love" or Orbison's "Sweet Dreams" comes on, and cuts off the Greek Chorus.*]

LI'L BIT: Ahh . . . [*Beat.*] I adjust my seat. Fasten my seat belt. Then I check the right side mirror—check the left side. [*She does.*] Finally, I adjust the rearview mirror. [*As* LI'L BIT *adjusts the rearview mirror, a faint light strikes the spirit of* UNCLE PECK, *who is sitting in the back seat of the car. She sees him in the mirror. She smiles at him, and he nods at her. They are happy to be going for a long drive together.* LI'L BIT *slips the car into first gear; to the audience:*] And then—I floor it. [*Sound of a car taking off. Blackout.*]

END OF PLAY

1997

Authors on Their Work: PAULA VOGEL

From "A Prize-Winning Playwright" (1998)*

ELIZABETH FARNSWORTH: What was your inspiration for this [play]? Why did you want to make it more a love story than something that people would be horrified by?

PAULA VOGEL: I wanted to do this in a very gentle way because I have been dissatisfied looking at the television movie-of-the-week approach, and in many ways I think that this play is an homage to [Vladimir Nabokov's novel] *Lolita*, which I think is one of the most astonishing books ever written. So I started this thinking I wonder if a woman writer could approach this, I wonder if this could be done as *Lolita* from Lolita's point of view. So that's really the initial inspiration. I also feel that having watched a kind of climate of victimization occur, having watched younger women and younger men that I teach, I sometimes feel that being in that kind of mindset of victimization causes almost as much trauma as the original abuse. And so in many ways I think I felt that it's a mistake to demonize the people who hurt us, and that's how I wanted to approach the play.

ELIZABETH FARNSWORTH: And yet you don't excuse anything. What I noticed is that one laughs and cries at the same time. Was it very difficult to achieve that?

PAULA VOGEL: I have always depended on the kindness and the greatness of actors and directors. And this play is no exception. I think it's a balancing act. . . .

ELIZABETH FARNSWORTH: But, Ms. Vogel, it's part of your character too, isn't it, to make fun and be very dramatic at the same time?

PAULA VOGEL: I call it the Jewish gene in me. Yes. I think it is. When people try to say, well, why do you intend to do it, I think that's part of my makeup. It's how I grew up. Some of the funniest moments I think I've experienced in my life have been in family funerals. So, yeah, I think that's something that's pretty innate to me.

• • •

ELIZABETH FARNSWORTH: You've said you see theater as a medium for democracy. What do you mean by that?

PAULA VOGEL: Well, I always go back to this, thanks to the history professor at Catholic University who taught me this, and that is that in [the] fourth century BC in the Greek democracy, citizens were required to go to the theater. It was a requirement of all citizens because we come together as people and we go through a communal experience, a journey, and to me a good play does not give a message or have just one point of view. It should be a dialogue.

*"A Prize-Winning Playwright," *The News Hour with Jim Lehrer Transcript.* 16 April 1998. Web. <http://www.pbs.org/newshour>. 18 March 2009.

Biographical Sketches: Playwrights

ANTON CHEKHOV
(1860–1904)

The son of a grocer and the grandson of an emancipated serf, Anton Pavlovich Chekhov was born in the Russian town of Taganrog. In 1875, his father, facing bankruptcy and imprisonment, fled to Moscow; shortly after, the rest of the family lost their house to a former friend and lodger, a misfortune that Chekhov would revisit in *The Cherry Orchard*. In 1884, Chekhov received his M.D. from the University of Moscow; in the early 1890s, he purchased an estate near Moscow and became both an industrious landowner and a doctor to the local peasants. Throughout the 1880s, he supported his family and financed his medical studies by writing the sketches and stories that would eventually win him enduring international acclaim. Chekhov began writing for the stage in 1887. Early productions of his plays were poorly received: *The Wood Demon* (later rewritten as *Uncle Vanya*) was performed only a few times in 1889 before closing; the 1896 premiere of *The Seagull* turned into a riot when an audience expecting comedy found themselves watching an experimental tragedy. Konstantin Stanislavsky, director at the Moscow Art Theater, helped restore Chekhov's reputation with successful productions of *The Seagull* and *Uncle Vanya* in 1899, *The Three Sisters* in 1901, and *The Cherry Orchard* in 1904.

SAMUEL BECKETT
(1906–1989)

An Irish playwright and novelist, Samuel Beckett was born in the Dublin suburb of Cooldrinagh in 1906. In 1927 he graduated from Trinity College in Dublin with a B.A. in modern languages (French and Italian) and went on to obtain a position as English lecturer at the École Normale Supérieure in Paris. Academia was of little interest to Beckett and his career within it was short-lived; however, it led to his meeting and becoming both friend and assistant to the modernist writer James Joyce, who was highly influential to Beckett's intellectual development and literary career. In fact, one of Beckett's earliest published works, titled "Dante . . . Bruno. Vico . . . Joyce," was an essay defending the unique style of his mentor. Though he is today best known as a playwright, over the course of his prolific career Beckett experimented with a number of literary forms in addition to drama, publishing poems, critical essays, novellas, short stories, translations, and even material for television and radio, as well as a series of three novels originally written in French—*Molloy* (1951), *Malone Dies* (1951), and *The Unnamable* (1953). Of his twenty plays, *Waiting for Godot* (1952) and *Endgame* (1957) are the most acclaimed. In 1969 Beckett was awarded the Nobel Prize in Literature "for his writing, which—in new forms for the novel and drama—in the destitution of modern man acquires its elevation."

MARGARET EDSON
(b. 1961)

When Margaret Edson's *Wit* won the Pulitzer Prize for Drama in 1999, the theater world was astounded to learn that a play about the death and journey to grace of a cancer-stricken professor of seventeenth-century poetry had been written by an Atlanta kindergarten teacher. Edson, a native of Washington, DC, graduated from Smith College in 1983 with a degree in Renaissance history. The inspiration for her play came from a brief stint as a clerk in the cancer and AIDS unit of a research hospital. Edson began writing *Wit* while working in a Washington bicycle shop; before completing the play she earned an M.A. in English from Georgetown University and began her work as a teacher. Even after *Wit* made her famous, Edson said she had no plans to leave the classroom to write more plays. "Every single day," she told an interviewer, "I'm working to the bone to bring more justice to the world. This work . . . is where the action is."

SUSAN GLASPELL
(1876–1948)

Born and raised in Davenport, Iowa, Susan Glaspell graduated from Drake University and worked on the staff of the Des Moines *Daily News* until her stories began appearing in magazines such as *Harper's* and *Ladies' Home Journal*. In 1911, Glaspell moved to New York City, where, two years later, she married the theater director George Cram Cook. In 1915 they founded the Provincetown Playhouse (later the Playwright's Theater), an extraordinary Cape Cod gathering of actors, directors, and playwrights, including Eugene O'Neill, Edna St. Vincent Millay, and John Reed. The Provincetown Players produced several of Glaspell's early plays, including *Trifles* (1916); her later plays include *The Inheritors* (1921), *The Verge* (1921), *Bernice* (1924), and *Alison's House* (1930), for which she won the Pulitzer Prize. Glaspell spent the last part of her life writing fiction in Provincetown; among her many books are *Visioning* (1911), *Lifted Masks: Stories* (1912), *Fidelity* (1915), *The Road to the Temple* (1926), and *The Morning Is Near Us* (1940).

LORRAINE HANSBERRY
(1930–1965)

The first African American woman to have a play produced on Broadway, Lorraine Hansberry was born in Chicago to a prominent family and even at a young age showed an interest in writing. She attended the University of Wisconsin, the Art Institute of Chicago, and Roosevelt University, then moved to New York City in order to concentrate on writing for the stage. After extensive fund-raising, Hansberry's play *A Raisin in the Sun* (loosely based on events involving her own family) opened in 1959 at the Ethel Barrymore Theatre on Broadway, received critical acclaim, and won the New York Drama Critics' Circle Award for Best Play. Hansberry's second production, *The Sign in Sidney Brustein's Window*, had a short run on Broadway in 1964. Shortly after, Hansberry died of cancer. *To Be Young, Gifted, and Black*, adapted from her writing, was produced off-Broadway in 1969 and published the next year, when her drama *Les Blancs* was also produced.

HENRIK IBSEN
(1828–1906)

Born in Skien, Norway, Henrik Ibsen was apprenticed to an apothecary until 1850, when he left for Oslo and published his first play, *Catilina*, a verse tragedy. By 1857 Ibsen was director of Oslo's Norwegian Theater, but his early plays, such as *Love's Comedy* (1862), were poorly received. Disgusted with what he saw as Norway's backwardness, Ibsen left in 1864 for Rome, where he wrote two more verse plays, *Brand* (1866) and *Peer Gynt* (1867), before turning to the realistic style and harsh criticism of traditional social mores for which he is best known. *The League of Youth* (1869), *Pillars of Society* (1877), *A Doll House* (1879), *Ghosts* (1881), *An Enemy of the People* (1882), *The Wild Duck* (1884), and *Hedda Gabler* (1890) won him a reputation throughout Europe as a controversial and outspoken advocate of moral and social reform. Near the end of his life, Ibsen explored the human condition in the explicitly symbolic terms of *The Master Builder* (1892) and *When We Dead Awaken* (1899). Ibsen's works had enormous influence over the drama of the twentieth century.

ARTHUR MILLER
(1915–2005)

Arthur Miller was born in New York City to a prosperous family whose fortunes were ruined by the Depression, a circumstance that would shape his political outlook and imbue him with a deep sense of social responsibility. Miller studied history, economics, and journalism at the University of Michigan, began writing plays, and joined the Federal Theater Project, a proving ground for some of the best playwrights of the period. He had his first Broadway success, *All My Sons*, in 1947, followed two years later by his Pulitzer Prize–winning masterpiece, *Death of a Salesman*, a starkly poetic depiction of the American dream as a hollow sham. In 1953, against the backdrop of Senator Joseph McCarthy's anti-Communist "witch-hunts," Miller fashioned another modern parable, his Tony Award–winning *The Crucible*, based on the seventeenth-century Salem witch trials.

Among his other works for the stage are the Pulitzer Prize–winner *A View from the Bridge* (1955), *After the Fall* (1964), *Incident at Vichy* (1965), *The Price* (1968), *The Ride Down Mt. Morgan* (1991), *Broken Glass* (1994), and *Resurrection Blues* (2004). In addition, Miller wrote a novel, *Focus* (1945); the screenplay for the film *The Misfits* (1961), which starred his second wife, Marilyn Monroe; *The Theater Essays* (1971), a collection of his writings about dramatic literature; and *Timebends* (1987), his autobiography.

SUZAN-LORI PARKS
(b. 1963)

Suzan-Lori Parks was born May 10, 1963, in Fort Knox, Kentucky. Because of her father's career as an army officer, Parks spent her childhood in six different states and Germany, where she became fluent in German. After moving back to the United States and completing high school, Parks attended Mount Holyoke College, where she received her B.A. in English and German literature in 1985. Here she also met novelist and civil-rights activist James Baldwin, who encouraged Parks to write for the theater. Parks's plays include *Fucking A* (2000); *In the Blood* (1994), a retelling of Nathaniel Hawthorne's *Scarlet Letter*; *Topdog/Underdog* (2001), a play for which she received the Pulitzer Prize in 2002; and *365 Days/365 Plays*. Parks also wrote screenplays for Spike Lee's 1996 film *Girl 6*, Oprah Winfrey's Harpo Productions' 2005 adaptation of *Their Eyes Were Watching God*, and the 2007 film *The Great Debaters*. In addition to the Pulitzer Prize, Parks was awarded the MacArthur Foundation "Genius" Grant in 2001, as well as the Lila-Wallace Reader's Digest Award (1995), and the Obie for Best New American Play for *Venus* (1996).

WILLIAM SHAKESPEARE
(1554–1616)

Considering the great and well-deserved fame of his work, surprisingly little is known of William Shakespeare's life. Between 1585· and 1592, he left his birthplace of Stratford-upon-Avon for London to begin a career as playwright and actor. No dates of his professional career are recorded, however, nor can the order in which he composed his plays and poetry be determined with certainty. By 1594, he had established himself

as a poet with two long works—*Venus and Adonis* and *The Rape of Lucrece*; his more than 150 sonnets are supreme expressions of the form. His matchless reputation, though, rests on his works for the theater. Shakespeare produced perhaps thirty-five plays in twenty-five years, proving himself a master of every dramatic genre: tragedy (in works such as *Macbeth*, *Hamlet*, *King Lear*, and *Othello*); historical drama (for example, *Richard III* and *Henry IV*); comedy (*A Midsummer Night's Dream*, *Twelfth Night*, *As You Like It*, and many more); and romance or "tragicomedy" (in plays such as *The Tempest* and *Cymbeline*). Without question, Shakespeare is the most quoted, discussed, and beloved writer in English literature.

SOPHOCLES
(496?–406 BCE)

Sophocles lived at a time when Athens and Greek civilization were at the peak of their power and influence. He not only served as a general under Pericles and played a prominent role in the city's affairs but also was arguably the greatest of the Greek tragic playwrights, winning the annual dramatic competition about twenty times, a feat unmatched by even his great contemporaries, Aeschylus and Euripides. An innovator, Sophocles fundamentally changed the nature of dramatic performance by adding a third actor, enlarging the chorus, and introducing the use of painted scenery. Aristotle held that Sophocles' *Oedipus the King* (c. 429 BCE) was the perfect tragedy and used it as his model when he discussed the nature of tragedy in his *Poetics*. Today only seven of Sophocles' tragedies survive—the Oedipus trilogy (*Oedipus the King, Oedipus at Colonus*, and *Antigone*), *Philoctetes*, *Ajax*, *Trachiniae*, and *Electra*—though he is believed to have written as many as 123 plays.

WOLE SOYINKA
(b. 1934)

Akinwande Oluwole Soyinka was born in 1934 in Abeokuta, Nigeria, then a British colony. He studied at the universities of Ibadan, in Nigeria, and Leeds, in England, before joining London's Royal Court Theatre as an actor and director. In 1960 Soyinka returned to Nigeria to study African drama and to teach. *A Dance of the Forests* (1960) was commissioned in celebration of

Nigeria's independence, but like many of Soyinka's subsequent works, the play angered Nigerian authorities. Soyinka's appeal for a ceasefire during Nigeria's civil war led to his arrest in 1967; for nearly two years he was a political prisoner. His many plays, ranging from satirical comedies to politically charged tragedies, chronicle Africa's difficult transition from traditional to modern life. Among the best known are *The Trial of Brother Jero* (1963), *Death and the King's Horseman* (1975), *A Play of Giants* (1984), and *King Baabu* (2001). Other works include such novels as *The Interpreters* (1965), *Season of Anomy* (1973), and *Isara* (1988); his prison memoir, *The Man Died* (1972), and an account of his childhood, *Aké* (1983); a collection of literary essays, *Myth, Literature and the African World* (1975); and numerous volumes of poetry. In 1986 Soyinka became the first black African awarded the Nobel Prize for Literature.

TOM STOPPARD
(b. 1937)

Tom Stoppard was born in Zlin, Czechoslovakia. In 1939 his family moved to Singapore to escape the Nazis. His mother then fled with Tom and his brother to Darjeeling, India, in advance of the Japanese invasion of Singapore; his father, who remained behind, was killed. In 1946 the family moved to England, where Tom's mother married Kenneth Stoppard, a major in the British army. Stoppard dropped out of high school before his junior year, worked as a journalist and freelance drama critic, and began to write plays for radio and television. His first television play, *A Walk on the Water* (1963), was later adapted for the stage as *Enter a Free Man* (1968). Stoppard's first major success was *Rosencrantz and Guildenstern Are Dead* (1966), which won a Tony Award for Best Play in 1968. Subsequent popular dramas include *The Real Inspector Hound* (1968), *Jumpers* (1972), and *Travesties* (1974). *Every Good Boy Deserves Favour* (1977), *Dogg's Hamlet* (1979), and *Squaring the Circle* (1984) attack the oppressive regimes of Eastern Europe. Among Stoppard's more recent plays are *Arcadia* (1993) and *The Invention of Love* (1997). Stoppard has written a number of screenplays, including *Shakespeare in Love* (1998), which he coauthored with Marc Norman and which won the 1999 Academy Award for Best Screenplay.

PAULA VOGEL
(b. 1951)

Paula Vogel grew up in Washington, DC, and earned a B.A. in drama from Catholic University. She was turned down for graduate study at the Yale School of Drama and found it difficult to get her early plays produced, but she kept working at her craft and took on controversial themes: *The Oldest Profession* (1981) depicts aging prostitutes; *And Baby Makes Seven* (1988) concerns lesbian motherhood; and the Obie Award–winning *The Baltimore Waltz* (1991) is based on the death of her brother Carl from AIDS. Her most famous play, the Pulitzer Prize–winning *How I Learned to Drive* (1997), portrays the sexual relationship between a young girl and her uncle. Vogel now teaches at Brown University. Recent work includes *The Mineola Twins* (1999) and *The Long Christmas Ride Home* (2004).

OSCAR WILDE
(1854–1900)

Born and raised in Dublin, Oscar Wilde studied classical languages at Trinity College and took his degree from Oxford in 1878. While at Oxford, he was captivated by the aesthetic theories of John Ruskin and Walter Pater. Upon graduation, he moved to London to write, soon becoming both a much-quoted wit and the most visible exponent of the "art for art's sake" movement, for which he was lampooned by Gilbert and Sullivan in their operetta *Patience*. Wilde wrote criticism, poetry, and fiction, most notably his novel *The Picture of Dorian Gray* (1891). However, he achieved his greatest success as a comic dramatist, with clever, witty plays such as *Lady Windermere's Fan* (1892), *A Woman of No Importance* (1893), and his masterpiece, *The Importance of Being Earnest* (1895). At the height of his career, Wilde was accused of homosexuality by his lover's father, the marquess of Queensbury; he sued for libel, lost the case, and was imprisoned for two years, a ruinous experience that inspired his best-known poem, "The Ballad of Reading Gaol" (1898). Upon his release, he emigrated to France under an assumed name, dying there three years later. "In this world," he wrote, "there are only two tragedies. One is not getting what one wants, and the other is getting it."

TENNESSEE WILLIAMS
(1911–1983)

Born in Columbus, Mississippi, Thomas Lanier Williams moved to St. Louis with his family at the age of seven. Williams's father was a violent alcoholic, his mother was ill, and his sister, Rose, suffered from a variety of mental illnesses; each of them became a model for the domineering men and sensitive women of his plays. He attended the University of Missouri and Washington University in St. Louis, but earned his B.A. from the University of Iowa. While there, Williams won prizes for his fiction and began to write plays. His extensive body of work, with its explosive dramatic tension and dazzling dialogue, confronts issues of adultery, homosexuality, incest, and mental illness. In 1944, *The Glass Menagerie* won the New York Drama Critics' Circle Award. In 1948, he earned his first Pulitzer Prize, for *A Streetcar Named Desire;* in 1955, he won a second Pulitzer Prize, for *Cat on a Hot Tin Roof.* His other dramas include *Camino Real* (1953), *Suddenly Last Summer* (1958), *The Night of the Iguana* (1961), *The Two-Character Play* (1969; later revised as *Out Cry*), and *Clothes for a Summer Hotel* (1980). Williams also published short fiction, poetry, and a film script.

AUGUST WILSON
(1945–2005)

Frederick August Kittel was born in a lower-class black neighborhood of Pittsburgh, Pennsylvania. At fifteen, disgusted by treatment he considered racist, he left school and sought to educate himself at the local library. A black nationalist and participant in the Black Arts Movement during the 1960s and '70s, Wilson disavowed his white father and adopted his black mother's surname. In 1968 he cofounded the Black Horizons Theater Company, in St. Paul, Minnesota; he later founded the Playwrights Center in Minneapolis. The 1984 Broadway production of *Ma Rainey's Black Bottom* established his theatrical reputation; much of the rest of his career was devoted to completing the ten-play "Pittsburgh Cycle" dealing with the black experience in America, each play set during a different decade of the twentieth century. Among his plays are *Jitney* (1982); *Fences* (1985), winner of the 1987 Pulitzer Prize; *Joe Turner's Come and Gone* (1986); *The Piano Lesson* (1987), which won a Tony Award, the Drama Critics Circle Award, the American Theater Critics Outstanding Play Award, and the 1990 Pulitzer Prize; *Two Trains Running* (1992); *Seven Guitars* (1995); *King Hedley II* (2001); and *Gem of the Ocean* (2003).

Writing about Literature

When it comes to the study of literature, reading and writing are closely interrelated—even mutually dependent—activities. On the one hand, the quality of whatever we write about a literary text depends entirely on the quality of our work as readers. On the other hand, our reading isn't truly complete until we've tried to capture our sense of a text in writing. Indeed, we often read a literary work much more actively and attentively when we integrate informal writing into the reading process—pausing periodically to mark especially important or confusing passages, to jot down significant facts, to describe the impressions and responses the text provokes—or when we imagine our reading (and our informal writing) as preparation for writing about the work in a more sustained and formal way.

Writing about literature can take any number of forms, ranging from the very informal and personal to the very formal and public. In fact, your instructor may well ask you to try your hand at more than one form. However, the essay is by far the most common and complex form that writing about literature takes. As a result, the following chapters will focus on the essay.* A first, short chapter covers three basic ways of writing about literature. The second chapter, "The Elements of the Essay," seeks to answer a very basic set of questions: *When an instructor says, "Write an essay," what precisely does that mean? What is the purpose of an essay, and what form does it need to take in order to achieve that purpose?* The third chapter, "The Writing Process," addresses questions about how an essay is produced, while the fourth chapter explores the special steps and strategies involved in writing a research essay—a type of essay about literature that draws on secondary sources. "Quotation, Citation, and Documentation" explains the rules and strategies involved in quoting and citing both literary texts and secondary sources using the documentation system recommended by the Modern Language Association (MLA). And, finally, we present a sample research essay, annotated to point out some of its most important features.

32 PARAPHRASE, SUMMARY, DESCRIPTION

Before turning to the essay, let's briefly consider three other basic ways of writing about literature: *paraphrase*, *summary*, and *description*. Each of these can be useful both as an exercise to prepare for writing an essay and as part of a completed essay. That is, an essay about a literary text must do more than paraphrase, summarize, or describe the text, yet a good essay about a literary text almost always incorporates some paraphrase, summary, and description of the literature and, in the case of a research essay, of secondary sources as well.

*In chapters 32–36, unless otherwise specified, page numbers in the examples refer to this volume, *The Norton Introduction to Literature*, 10th edition.

32.1 PARAPHRASE

To paraphrase a statement is to restate it in your own words. Since the goal of paraphrase is to represent a statement fully and faithfully, paraphrases tend to be at least as long as the original, and you usually wouldn't try to paraphrase an entire work of any length. The following examples offer paraphrases of sentences from a work of fiction (Jane Austen's *Pride and Prejudice*), a poem (W. B. Yeats's "All Things Can Tempt Me"), and an essay (George L. Dillon's "Styles of Reading").

ORIGINAL SENTENCE	PARAPHRASE
It is a truth universally acknowledged that a single man in possession of a good fortune must be in want of a wife.	Everyone agrees that a propertied bachelor needs (or wants) to find a woman to marry.
All things can tempt me from this craft of verse: One time it was a woman's face, or worse— The seeming needs of my fool-driven land; Now nothing but comes readier to the hand Than this accustomed toil. . . .	Anything can distract me from writing poetry: One time I was distracted by a woman's face, but I was even more distracted by (or I found an even less worthy distraction in) the attempt to fulfill what I imagined to be the needs of a country governed by idiots. At this point in my life I find any task easier than the work I'm used to doing (writing poetry).
. . . making order out of Emily's life is a complicated matter, since the narrator recalls the details through a nonlinear filter.	It's difficult to figure out the order in which events in Emily's life occurred because the narrator doesn't relate them chronologically.

Paraphrase resembles translation. Indeed, the paraphrase of Yeats is essentially a "translation" of poetry into prose, and the paraphrases of Austen and of Dillon are "translations" of one kind of prose (formal nineteenth-century British prose, the equally formal but quite different prose of a twentieth-century literary critic) into another kind (colloquial twentieth-century American prose).

But what good is that? First, paraphrasing tests that you truly understand what you've read; it can be especially helpful when an author's diction and syntax seem difficult, complex, or "foreign" to you. Second, paraphrasing can direct your attention to nuances of tone or potentially significant details. For example, paraphrasing Austen's sentence might highlight its irony and call attention to the multiple meanings of phrases such as *a good fortune* and *in want of.* Similarly, paraphrasing Yeats might help you to think about all that he gains by making himself the object rather than the subject of his sentence. Third, paraphrase can help you begin generating the kind of interpretive questions that can drive an essay. For example, the Austen paraphrase might suggest the following questions: *What competing definitions of "a good fortune" are set out in* Pride and Prejudice? *Which definition, if any, does the novel as a whole seem to endorse?*

32.2 SUMMARY

A summary is a fairly succinct restatement or overview of the content of an entire text or source (or a significant portion thereof). Like paraphrases, summaries should always be stated in your own words.

A summary of a literary text is generally called a *plot summary* because it focuses on the **action** or **plot**. Here, for example, is a summary of Edgar Allan Poe's "The Raven":

> The speaker of Poe's "The Raven" is sitting in his room late at night reading in order to forget the death of his beloved Lenore. There's a tap at the door; after some hesitation he opens it and calls Lenore's name, but there is only an echo. When he goes back into his room he hears the rapping again, this time at his window, and when he opens it a raven enters. He asks the raven its name, and it answers very clearly, "Nevermore." As the speaker's thoughts run back to Lenore, he realizes the aptness of the raven's word: She shall sit there never-more. But, he says, sooner or later he will forget her, and the grief will lessen. "Nevermore," the raven says again, too aptly. Now the speaker wants the bird to leave, but "Nevermore," the raven says once again. At the end, the speaker knows he'll never escape the raven or its dark message.

Though a summary should be significantly shorter than the original, it can be any length you need it to be. Above, the 108 lines of Poe's poem have been reduced to about 160 words. But one could summarize this or any other work in as little as one sentence. Here, for example, are three viable one-sentence summaries of *Hamlet*:

> A young man seeking to avenge his uncle's murder of his father kills his uncle, while also bringing about his own and many others' deaths.

> A young Danish prince avenges the murder of his father, the king, by his uncle, who has usurped the throne, but the prince himself is killed, as are others, and a well-led foreign army has no trouble successfully invading the decayed and troubled state.

> When a young prince learns, from the ghost of his murdered father, that his uncle, who has married the prince's mother, is the father's murderer, the prince plots revenge, feigning madness, acting erratically—even insulting the woman he loves—and, though gaining his revenge, causes the suicide of his beloved and the deaths of others and, finally, of himself.

As these *Hamlet* examples suggest, different readers—or even the same reader on different occasions—will almost certainly summarize the same text in dramati-cally different ways. Summarizing entails selection and emphasis. As a result, any summary reflects a particular point of view and may even imply a particular inter-pretation or argument. When writing a summary, you should try to be as objective as possible; nevertheless, your summary will reflect your own understanding and attitudes. For this reason, summarizing a literary text may help you begin to figure out just what your particular understanding of a text is, especially if you then com-pare your summary to those of other readers.

32.3 DESCRIPTION

Whereas both summary and paraphrase focus on content, a description of a literary text focuses on its overall form or structure or some particular aspect thereof. Here, for example, is a description (rather than a summary) of the rhyme scheme of "The Raven":

> Poe's "The Raven" is a poem of 108 lines divided into eighteen six-line stanzas. If you were to look just at the ends of the lines, you would notice only one or two unusual features: Not only is there only one rhyme sound per stanza—lines 2, 4, 5, and 6 rhyming—but one rhyme sound is the same in all eighteen stanzas, so that seventy-two lines end with the sound "ore." In addition, the fourth and fifth lines of each stanza end with an identical word; in six of the stanzas that word is "door" and in four others "Lenore." There is even more repetition: The last line of six of the first seven stanzas ends with the words "nothing more," and the last eleven stanzas end with the word "Nevermore." In each stanza, lines 1, 2, and 3 are sixteen syllables long; lines 4 and 5 fifteen, and line 6 only seven. The longer lines give the effect of shorter ones, however, and add still further to the frequency of repeated sounds, for the first half of each opening line rhymes with the second half of the line, and so do the halves of line 3. There is still more: The first half of line 4 rhymes with the halves of line 3 (in the first stanza the rhymes are "dreary" / "weary" and "napping" / "tapping" / "rapping"). So at least nine words in each six-line stanza are involved in the regular rhyme scheme, and many stanzas have added instances of rhyme or repetition. As if this were not enough, all the half-line rhymes are rich feminine rhymes, where both the accented and the following unaccented syllables rhyme—"dreary" / "wary."

You could similarly describe many other formal elements of the poem—images and **symbols**, for example. You can describe a play in comparable terms—acts, scenes, settings, time lapses, perhaps—and you might describe a novel in terms of chapters, books, summary narration, dramatized scenes. In addition to describing the narrative structure or focus and voice of a short story, you might describe the **diction** (word choice), the sentence structure, the amount and kind of description of characters or landscape, and so on.

33 THE ELEMENTS OF THE ESSAY

As you move from reading literary works to writing essays about them, remember that the essay—like the short story, poem, or play—is a distinctive subgenre with unique elements and conventions. Just as you come to a poem or play with a certain set of expectations, so will readers approach your essay. They will be looking for particular elements, anticipating that the work will unfold in a specific way. This chapter explains and explores those elements so that you can develop a clear sense of what makes a piece of writing an essay and why some essays are more effective than others.

An essay has particular elements and a particular form because it serves a specific purpose. Keeping this in mind, consider what an essay is and what it does. An essay is a relatively short written composition that articulates, supports, and develops an idea or claim. Like any work of expository prose, it aims to explain something complex. Explaining in this case entails both *analysis* (breaking the complex "thing" down into its constituent parts and showing how they work together to form a meaningful whole) and *argument* (working to convince someone that the analysis is valid). In an essay about literature, the literary work is the complex thing that you are helping a reader understand better. The essay needs to show the reader a particular way to understand the work, to interpret or read it. That interpretation or reading starts with the essayist's own personal response. But an essay also needs to persuade the reader that this interpretation is reasonable and enlightening—that though it is distinctive and new, it is more than merely idiosyncratic or subjective.

To achieve these ends, an essay must incorporate four elements: an appropriate *tone*, a clear *thesis*, a coherent *structure*, and ample, appropriate *evidence*.

33.1 TONE (AND AUDIENCE)

Although your reader or audience isn't an element *in* your essay, tone is. And tone and audience are closely interrelated. In everyday life, the tone we adopt has everything to do with whom we are talking to and what situation we're in. For example, we talk very differently to our parents than to our best friends. And in different situations we talk to the same person in different ways. What tone do you adopt with your best friends when you want to borrow money? when you need advice? when you're giving advice? when you're deciding whether to eat pizza or sushi? In each case you act on your knowledge of who your friends are, what information they already have, and what their response is likely to be. But you also try to adopt a tone that will encourage them to respond in a certain way.

In writing, as in everyday life, your audience, situation, and purpose should shape your tone. Conversely, your tone will shape your audience's response. You need to figure out both who your readers are and what response you want to elicit. Who is your audience? When you write an essay for class, the obvious answer is your instructor. But in an important sense, that is the wrong answer. Although your instructor could literally be the only person besides you who will ever read your essay, you write about literature to learn how to write for an audience of peers—people a lot like you who are sensible and educated and who will appreciate having a literary work explained so that they can understand it more fully. Picture your reader as someone about your own age with roughly the same educational background. Assume the person has some experience in reading literature, but that he or she has read this particular work only once and has not yet closely analyzed it. You should neither be insulting and explain the obvious nor assume that your reader has noticed, considered, and remembered every detail.

Should you, then, altogether ignore the obvious fact that an instructor—who probably has a master's degree or doctorate in literature—is your actual reader? Not altogether: You don't want to get so carried away with speaking to people of your own age and interests that you slip into slang, or feel the need to explain what a stanza is, or leave unexplained an allusion to your favorite movie. Even though you do want to learn from the advice and guidelines your instructor has given, try not to be preoccupied with the idea that you are writing for someone "in authority" or someone utterly different from yourself.

Above all, don't think of yourself as writing for a captive audience, for readers who have to read what you write or who already see the text as you do. (If that were the case, there wouldn't be much point in writing at all.) It is not always easy to know how interested your readers will be or how their views might differ from yours, so you must make the most of every word. Remember that the purpose of your essay is to persuade readers to see the text your way. That process begins with persuading them that you deserve their attention and respect. The tone of your paper should be serious and straightforward, respectful toward your readers and the literary work. But its approach and vocabulary, while formal enough for academic writing, should be lively enough to interest someone like you. Try to imagine, as your ideal reader, the person in class whom you most respect but who often seems to see things differently from you. Write to capture and hold that person's attention and respect. Encourage your reader to adopt a desirable stance *toward* your essay by adopting that same stance *in* your essay. Engage and convince your reader by demonstrating your engagement and conviction. Encourage your reader to keep an open mind by showing that you have done the same.

33.2 THESIS

A thesis is to an essay what a **theme** is to a short story, play, or poem: the governing idea, proposition, claim, or point. Good theses come in many shapes and sizes. A thesis cannot always be conveyed in one sentence, nor will it always appear in the same place in every essay. But you will risk both appearing confused and confusing the reader if you can't state the thesis in one to three sentences or if the thesis doesn't appear somewhere in your introduction, usually near its end.

Regardless of its length or location, a thesis must be debatable—a claim that all readers won't automatically accept. It's a proposition that *can* be proved with evidence from the text. Yet it's one that *has* to be proved, that isn't obviously true or factual, that must be supported with evidence in order to be fully understood or accepted by the reader. The following examples juxtapose a series of inarguable topics or fact statements—ones that are merely factual or descriptive—with thesis statements, each of which makes a debatable claim about the topic or fact.

TOPIC OR FACT STATEMENTS	THESIS STATEMENTS
"The Story of an Hour" explores the topic of marriage.	In "The Story of an Hour," Chopin poses a troubling question: Does marriage inevitably encourage people to "impose [their] private will upon a fellow-creature" (608)?
"Cathedral" features a character with a physical handicap.	"Cathedral" features a protagonist who learns about his own emotional and spiritual shortcomings through an encounter with a physically handicapped person. In this way, the story invites us to question traditional definitions of "disability."
"London" consists of three discrete stanzas that each end with a period; two-thirds of the lines are end-stopped.	In "London," William Blake uses a variety of formal techniques to suggest the unnatural rigidity and constraints of urban life.
A Streetcar Named Desire uses a lot of Darwinian language.	*A Streetcar Named Desire* asks whether or not it is truly the "fittest" who "survive" in contemporary America.
Creon and Antigone are both similar and different.	Creon and Antigone are alike in several ways, especially the inconsistency of their values and the way they are driven by passion below the surface of rational argument. Both are also one-sided in their commitments. . . . This does not mean, however, that they are equally limited in the values to which they adhere. —Mary Whitlock Blundell, "Helping Friends . . ." (chapter 31)

All of the thesis statements above are arguable, but they share other traits as well. All are clear and emphatic. Each implicitly answers a compelling interpretive question—for instance, *What do Antigone and Creon stand for? Which character and worldview, if any, does the play as a whole ultimately champion?* Yet each statement entices us to read further by generating more questions in our minds—*How and why do Creon and Antigone demonstrate "inconsistency" and "one-sidedness"? If these two characters are not equally limited, which of them is more limited?* An effective thesis enables the reader to enter the essay with a clear sense of what its writer will try to prove, and it inspires the reader with the desire to see the writer do it. We want to understand how the writer arrived at this view, to test whether it's valid, and to see how the writer will answer the other questions the thesis has generated in our minds. A good thesis captures the reader's interest and shapes his or her expectations. It also makes promises that the rest of the essay should fulfill.

At the same time, an arguable claim is not one-sided or narrow-minded. A thesis needs to stake out a position, but a position can and should admit complexity. Literary texts tend to focus more on exploring problems, conflicts, and questions than on offering solutions, resolutions, and answers. Their goal is to complicate, not simplify, our way of looking at the world. The best essays about literature and the theses that drive them often share a similar quality.

33.2.1 Interpretive versus Evaluative Claims

All the theses in the previous examples involve *interpretive* claims—claims about how a literary text works, what it says, how one should understand it. And interpretive claims generally work best as theses.

Yet it's useful to remember that in reading and writing about literature we often make (and debate) a different type of claim—the *evaluative*. Evaluation entails judging or assessing. Evaluative claims about literature tend to be of two kinds. The first involves aesthetic judgment—whether a text (or a part or element thereof) succeeds in artistic terms. (This kind of claim features prominently in book reviews, for example.) The second involves philosophical, ethical, or even socially or politically based judgment—whether an idea or action is wise or good, valid or admirable. All interpretive and evaluative claims involve informed opinion (which is why they are debatable). But whereas interpretive claims aim to elucidate the opinions expressed *in* and *by* the text, the second kind of evaluative claim assesses the value or validity of those opinions, often by comparing them with the writer's own.

The following examples juxtapose a series of interpretive claims with evaluative claims of both types.

INTERPRETIVE CLAIMS	EVALUATIVE CLAIMS
"A Conversation with My Father" explores the relative values of realistic and fantastic fiction. Rather than advocating one type of fiction, however, the story ends up affirming just how much we need stories of any and every kind.	"A Conversation with My Father" fails because it ends up being more a stilted Platonic dialogue about works of fiction than a true work of fiction in its own right.
	The father in "A Conversation with My Father" is absolutely right: Realistic stories are more effective and satisfying than fantastic ones.
The speaker of John Donne's "Song" is an angry and disillusioned man obsessed with the infidelity of women.	In "Song," John Donne does a very effective job of characterizing the speaker, an angry and disillusioned man obsessed with the infidelity of women.
	John Donne's "Song" is a horribly misogynistic poem because it ends up endorsing the idea that women are incapable of fidelity.
"How I Learned to Drive" demonstrates that, in Paula Vogel's words, "it takes a whole village to molest a child."	"How I Learned to Drive" is at once too preachy and too self-consciously theatrical to be dramatically effective.
	By insisting that sexual abuse is a crime perpetrated by a "whole village" rather than by an individual, Paula Vogel lets individual abusers off the hook, encouraging us to see them as victims rather than as the villains they really are.

In practice, the line between these different types of claims can become very thin. For instance, an essay claiming that Vogel's play conveys a socially dangerous or morally bad message about abuse may also claim that it is, as a result, an aesthetically flawed play. Further, an essay defending an interpretive claim about a text implies that it is at least aesthetically or philosophically worthy enough to merit interpretation. Conversely, defending and developing an evaluative claim about a text always requires a certain amount of interpretation. (You have to figure out what the text says in order to figure out whether the text says it well or says something worthwhile.)

To some extent, then, the distinctions are ones of emphasis. But they are important nonetheless. And unless instructed otherwise, you should generally make your thesis an interpretive claim, reserving evaluative claims for conclusions. (On conclusions, see 33.3.3.)

33.3 STRUCTURE

Like any literary text, an essay needs to have a beginning (or introduction), a middle (or body), and an ending (or conclusion). Each of these parts has a distinct function.

33.3.1 Beginning: The Introduction

Your essay's beginning, or introduction, should draw readers in and prepare them for what's to come by

- articulating the thesis;
- providing whatever basic information—about the text, the author, and/or the topic—readers will need to follow the argument; and
- creating interest in the thesis by demonstrating that there is a problem or question that it resolves or answers.

This final task involves showing readers why your thesis isn't dull or obvious, establishing a specific *motive* for the essay and its readers. There are numerous possible motives, but writing expert Gordon Harvey has identified three especially common ones:

1. The truth isn't what one would expect or what it might appear to be on a first reading.
2. There's an interesting wrinkle in the text—a paradox, a contradiction, a tension.
3. A seemingly tangential or insignificant matter is actually important or interesting.

(On motives specific to research essays, see 35.1.1.)

33.3.2 Middle: The Body

The middle, or body, of your essay is its beating heart, the place where you do the essential work of supporting and developing the thesis by presenting and analyzing evidence. Each of the body paragraphs needs to articulate, support, and develop one specific claim—a debatable idea directly related to, but smaller and more specific than, the thesis. This claim should be stated fairly early in the paragraph in a *topic sentence*. And every sentence in the paragraph should help prove, or elaborate on, that claim. Indeed, each paragraph ideally should build from an initial, general statement of the claim to the more complex form of it that you develop by presenting and analyzing evidence. In this way, each paragraph functions like a miniature essay with its own thesis, body, and conclusion.

Your essay as a whole should develop logically just as each paragraph does. To ensure that happens, you need to do the following:

- Order your paragraphs so that each builds on the last, with one idea following another in a logical sequence. The goal is to lay out a clear path for the reader. Like any path, it should go somewhere. Don't just prove your point; develop it.
- Present each idea/paragraph so that the logic behind the sequential order is clear. Try to start each paragraph with a sentence that functions as a bridge, carrying the reader from one point to the next. The reader shouldn't have to leap.

33.3.3 Ending: The Conclusion

In terms of their purpose (not their content), conclusions are introductions in reverse. Whereas introductions draw readers away from their world and into your essay, conclusions send them back. Introductions work to convince readers that they should read the essay. Conclusions work to show them why and how the experience was worthwhile. You should approach conclusions, then, by thinking about what sort of lasting impression you want to create. What precisely do you want readers to take with them as they journey back into the "real world"?

Effective conclusions often consider three things:

1. *Implications*—What picture of your author's work or worldview does your argument imply? Alternatively, what might your argument imply about some real-world issue or situation? Implications don't have to be earth-shattering. For example, it's unlikely that your reading of O'Connor's "Everything That Rises Must Converge" will rock your readers' world. Moreover, trying to convince readers that it can may well have the opposite effect. Yet your argument should in some small but significant way change the way readers see O'Connor's work; alternatively, it might give them new insight into how racism works, or how difficult it is for human beings to adjust to changes in the world around us, or how mistaken it can be to see ourselves as more enlightened than our elders, and so on.

2. *Evaluation*—What might your argument about the text reveal about the literary quality or effectiveness of the text as a whole or of some specific element? Alternatively, to what extent and how do you agree and/or disagree with the author's conclusions about a particular issue? How, for example, does your own view of how racism works compare to the viewpoint implied in "Everything That Rises Must Converge"? (For more on evaluative claims, see 33.2.1.)

3. *Areas of ambiguity or unresolved questions*—Are there any remaining puzzles or questions that your argument or the text itself doesn't resolve or

answer? Alternatively, might your argument suggest a new question or puzzle worth investigating?

Above all, don't repeat what you've already said. If the essay has done its job to this point, and especially if the essay is relatively short, your readers may feel bored and insulted if they get a mere summary. You should clarify anything that needs clarifying, but go a little beyond that. The best essays are rounded wholes in which conclusions do, in a sense, circle back to the place where they started. However, the best essays remind readers of where they began only in order to give them a more palpable sense of how far they've come.

33.4 EVIDENCE

In terms of convincing readers that your claims are valid, both the amount and the quality of your evidence count. And the quality of your evidence will depend, in great part, on how you prepare and present it. Each of the ideas that makes up the body of your essay must be supported and developed with ample, appropriate evidence. Colloquially speaking, the term *evidence* simply refers to facts. But it's helpful to remember that a fact by itself isn't really evidence for anything, or rather that—as lawyers well know—any one fact can be evidence for many things. Like lawyers, essayists turn a fact into evidence by interpreting it, drawing an inference from it, giving the reader a vivid sense of why and how the fact supports a specific claim. You need, then, both to present specific facts and to actively interpret them. *Show* readers why and how each fact matters.

Quotations are an especially important form of evidence in essays about literature; indeed, an essay about literature that contains no quotations is likely to be relatively weak. The reader of such an essay may doubt whether its argument emerges out of a thorough knowledge of the work. However, quotations are by no means the only facts on which you should draw. Indeed, a quotation will lead your reader to expect commentary on, and interpretation of, its language. As a general rule, you should quote directly from the text only when its wording is significant. Otherwise, simply paraphrase, describe, or summarize. The following example demonstrates the use of both summary and quotation. (On effective quotation, see 36.1; on paraphrase, summary, and description, see chapter 32.)

> At many points in the novel, religion is represented as having degenerated into a system of social control by farmers over workers. Only respectable young men can come courting at Upper Weatherbury farm, and no swearing is allowed (ch. 8). Similarly, the atmosphere in Boldwood's farm kitchen is "like a Puritan Sunday lasting all the week." Bathsheba tries to restrict her workers to drinking mild liquor, and church attendance is taken as the mark of respectability.
>
> —Fred Reid, "Art and Ideology in *Far from the Madding Crowd*,"
> *Thomas Hardy Annual* 4 (1986): 91ff. Print.

NOTE: Pay special attention to the way this writer uses paraphrase, summary, and quotation. At the beginning of the paragraph, he simply paraphrases certain rules; at its end, he summarizes or describes one character's action. Here, he can use his own words because the rules and actions illustrate his point, not the words that the novelist uses to describe them. However, Reid does quote the text when its (religious) language is the crucial, evidentiary element.

33.5 CONVENTIONS THAT CAN CAUSE PROBLEMS

A mastery of basic mechanics and writing conventions is essential to convincing your readers that you are a knowledgeable and careful writer whose ideas they should respect. This section explores three conventions that are especially crucial to essays about literature.

33.5.1 Tenses

Essays about literature tend to function almost wholly in the present tense, a practice that can take some getting used to. The rationale is that the action within any literary work never stops: A text simply, always *is*. Thus yesterday, today, and tomorrow, Ophelia *goes* mad, "The Lost World" *asks* what it means to grow up, Wordsworth *sees* nature as an avenue to God, and so on. When in doubt, stick to the present tense when writing about literature.

An important exception to this general rule is demonstrated in the following example. As you read the excerpt, pay attention to the way the writer shifts between tenses, using various past tenses to refer to completed actions that took place in the actual past, and using the present tense to refer to actions that occur within, or are performed by, the text.

> In 1959 Plath **did not** consciously **attempt** to write in the domestic poem genre, perhaps because she **was not** yet ready to assume her majority. Her journal entries of that period **bristle** with an impatience at herself that **may derive** from this reluctance. . . . But by fall 1962, when she **had** already **lost** so much, she **was** ready. . . . In "Daddy" she **achieved** her victory in two ways. First, . . . she symbolically **assaults** a father figure who **is identified** with male control of language.
>
> —Steven Gould Axelrod, "Jealous Gods" (chapter 25)

33.5.2 Titles

Underline or italicize the titles of all books and works published independently, including

- long poems (*Endymion*; *Paradise Lost*)
- plays (*A Midsummer Night's Dream*; *Death and the King's Horseman*)
- periodicals: newspapers, magazines, scholarly journals, and the like (*New York Times*; *College English*)

Use quotation marks for the titles of works that have been published as part of longer works, including

- short stories ("A Rose for Emily"; "Happy Endings")
- essays and periodical articles ("A Rose for 'A Rose for Emily'"; "Art and Ideology in *Far from the Madding Crowd*")
- poems ("Daddy"; "Ode to a Nightingale")

Generally speaking, you should capitalize the first word of every title, as well as all the other words that aren't either articles (e.g., *the*, *a*); prepositions (e.g., *among*, *in*, *through*); or conjunctions (e.g., *and*, *but*). One exception to this rule is the poem in which the first line substitutes for a missing title (a category that includes everything by Emily Dickinson, as well as the sonnets of Shakespeare and Edna St. Vincent Millay). In such cases, only the first word is capitalized. Often, the entire phrase is placed in brackets—as in "[Let me not to the marriage of true minds]"—but you will just as often see such titles without brackets.

33.5.3 Names

When first referring to an author, use his or her full name; thereafter, use the last name. (For example, although you may feel a real kinship with Robert Frost, you will appear disrespectful if you refer to him as Robert.)

With characters' names, use the literary work as a guide. Because "Bartleby, the Scrivener" always refers to its characters as *Bartleby*, *Turkey*, and *Nippers*, so should you. But because "The Management of Grief" refers to Judith Templeton either by her full name or by her first name, it would be odd and confusing to call her *Templeton*.

34 THE WRITING PROCESS

It's fairly easy to describe the purpose and formal elements of an essay. Actually
writing one is more difficult. So, too, is prescribing a precise formula for how to
do so. In practice, the writing process will vary from writer to writer and from
assignment to assignment. No one can give you a recipe. However, this chapter
presents a menu of possible approaches and exercises, which you should test out
and refine for yourself.

As you do so, keep in mind that writing needn't be a solitary enterprise. Most
writers—working in every genre, at every level—get inspiration, guidance, help,
and feedback from other people throughout the writing process, and so can you.
Your instructor may well create opportunities for collaboration, having you and
your colleagues work together to plan essays, critique drafts, and so on. Even if
that isn't the case, you can always reach out to others on your own. Since every
essay will ultimately have to engage readers, why not bring some actual readers
and fellow writers into the writing process? Use class discussions to generate and
test out essay topics and theses. Ask your instructor to clarify assignments or to
talk with you about your plans. Have classmates, friends, or roommates read your
drafts.

Of course, your essay ultimately needs to be your own work. You, the individual
writer, must be the ultimate arbiter, critically scrutinizing the advice you receive,
differentiating valid reader responses from groundless ones. But in writing about
literature, as in reading it, we all can get a much better sense of what we think by
considering others' views.

34.1 GETTING STARTED

34.1.1 Scrutinizing the Assignment

For student essayists, as for most professional ones, the writing process usually begins with an assignment. Though assignments vary greatly, all impose
certain restrictions. These are designed not to hinder your creativity but to direct
it into productive channels, ensuring that you hone certain skills, try out various
approaches, and avoid common pitfalls. Your first task as a writer is thus to scrutinize the assignment. Make sure that you fully understand what you are being
asked to do (and not do), and ask questions about anything unclear or puzzling.

Almost all assignments restrict the length of the essay by giving word or page
limits. Keep those limits in mind as you generate and evaluate potential essay
topics, making sure that you choose a topic you can handle in the space allowed.
Many assignments impose further restrictions, often indicating the texts and/or
topics to be explored. As a result, any given assignment will significantly shape

the rest of the writing process—determining, for example, whether and how you should tackle a step such as "Choosing a Text" or "Identifying Topics."

Here are three representative essay assignments, each of which imposes a different set of restrictions:

1. Choose any story in this anthology and write an essay analyzing the way in which its protagonist changes.
2. Write an essay analyzing one of the following sonnets: "The New Colossus," "Range-Finding," or "London, 1802." Be sure to consider how the poem's form contributes to its meaning.
3. Write an essay exploring the significance of references to eyes and vision in *A Midsummer Night's Dream*. What, through them, does the play suggest about both the power and the limitations of human vision?

The first assignment dictates the topic and main question. It also provides the kernel of a thesis: *In [story title], [protagonist's name] goes from being a* _____ *to a* _____ OR *By the end of [story title], [protagonist's name] has learned that* _____ . The assignment leaves you free to choose which story you will write about, although it limits you to those in which the protagonist clearly changes or learns a lesson of some kind. The second assignment limits your choice of texts to three. Though it also requires that your essay address the effects of the poet's choice to use the sonnet form, it doesn't require that this be the main topic of the essay. Rather, it leaves you free to pursue any topic that focuses on the poem's meaning. The third assignment is the most restrictive. It indicates both the text and the general topic to be explored, while requiring you to narrow the topic and formulate a specific thesis.

34.1.2 Choosing a Text

If the assignment allows you to choose which text to write about, try letting your initial impressions or "gut reactions" guide you. If you do so, your first impulse may be to choose a text that you like or "get" right away. Perhaps its language resembles your own; it depicts speakers, characters, or situations that you easily relate to; or it explores issues that you care deeply about. Following that first impulse can be a great idea. Writing an engaging essay requires being engaged with whatever we're writing about, and we all find it easier to engage with texts, authors, and/or characters that we like immediately.

You may discover, however, that you have little interesting or new to say about such a text. Perhaps you're too emotionally invested to analyze it closely, or maybe its meaning seems so obvious that there's no puzzle or problem to drive an argument. You might, then, find it more productive to choose a work that provokes the opposite reaction—one that initially puzzles or angers you, one whose characters or situations seem alien, one that investigates an issue you haven't previously thought much about or that articulates a theme you don't agree with. Sometimes such negative responses can have surprisingly positive results when it comes to writing. One student writer, for example, summed up her basic response to William Blake's *The Marriage of Heaven and Hell* with the words "He's crazy." Initially, the book made no sense to her. And that's precisely why she decided to write about it: She needed to do so, to make sense of it for other readers, in order to make sense of it for herself. In the end, she wrote a powerful essay exploring how the book defined, and why it celebrated, seeming insanity.

When writing about a text that you've discussed in class, you might make similar use of your "gut responses" to that conversation. Did you strongly agree or disagree with one of your classmate's interpretations of a particular text? If so, why not write about it?

34.1.3 Identifying Topics

When an assignment allows you to create your own topic, you are much more likely to build a lively and engaging essay from a particular insight or question that captures your attention and makes you want to say something, solve a problem, or stake out a position. The best papers originate in an individual response to a text and focus on a genuine question about it. Even when an instructor assigns a topic, the effectiveness of your essay will largely depend on whether or not you have made the topic your own, turning it into a question to which you discover your own answer.

Often we refer to "finding" a topic, as if there are a bevy of topics "out there" just waiting to be plucked like ripe fruit off the topic-tree. In at least two ways, that's true. For one thing, as we read a literary work, certain topics often do jump out and say, "Hey, look at me! I'm a topic!" A title alone may have that effect: What rises and converges in "Everything That Rises Must Converge"? Why is Keats so keen on that darn nightingale; what does it symbolize for him? Why does Wilde think it's important *not* to be earnest?

For another thing, certain general topics can be adapted to fit almost any literary work. In fact, that's just another way of saying that there are certain common types (or subgenres) of literary essays, just as there are of short stories, plays, and poems. For example, one very common kind of literary essay explores the significance of a seemingly insignificant aspect or element of a work—a word or group of related words, an image or image-cluster, a minor character, an incident or action, and so on. Equally common are character-focused essays of three types. The first explores the outlook or worldview of a character and its consequences. The second considers the way a major character develops from the beginning of a literary work to its end. The third analyzes the nature and significance of a conflict between two characters (or two groups of characters) and the way this conflict is ultimately resolved. (Many of the arguments about *Antigone* excerpted in chapter 31 do this.) Especially when you're utterly befuddled about where to begin, it can be very useful to keep in mind these generic topics and essay types and to use them as starting points. But remember that they are just starting points. One always has to adapt and narrow a generic topic such as "imagery" or "character change" in order to produce an effective essay. In practice, then, no writer simply "finds" a topic; he or she *makes* one.

Similarly, though the topic that leaps out at you immediately might end up being the one you find most interesting, you can only discover that by giving yourself some options. It's always a good idea to initially come up with as many topics as you can. Test out various topics to see which one will work best. Making yourself identify multiple topics will lead you to think harder, look more closely, and reach deeper into yourself and the work.

Here are some additional techniques to identify potential topics. In each case, write your thoughts down. Don't worry at this point about what form your writing takes or how good it is.

- *Analyze your initial response.*

If you've chosen a text that you feel strongly about, start with those responses. Try to describe your feelings and trace them to their source. Be as specific as possible. What moments, aspects, or elements of the text most affected you? Exactly how and why did they affect you? What was most puzzling? amusing? annoying? intriguing? Try to articulate the question behind your feelings. Often, strong responses result when a work either challenges or affirms an expectation, assumption, or conviction that you, the reader, bring to the work. Think about whether and how that's true here. Define the specific expectation, assumption, or conviction. How, where, and why does the text challenge it? fulfill and affirm it? Which of your responses and expectations are objectively valid, likely to be shared by other readers?

- *Think through the elements.*

Start with a list of elements and work your way through them, thinking about what's unique or interesting or puzzling about the text in terms of each. What stands out about the **tone**? What about the **speaker**? the situation? other elements? Come up with a statement about each. Look for patterns among your statements. Also, think about the questions implied or overlooked by your statements.

- *Pose motive questions.*

In articulating a motive in your essay's introduction, your concern is primarily with the readers, your goal being to give them a solid reason to keep reading. But you can often work your way toward a topic (or topics) by considering motive. As suggested earlier (33.3.1), there are three common motives. Turn each one into a question in order to identify potential topics:

1. What element(s) or aspect(s) of this work might a casual reader misinterpret?
2. What interesting paradox(es), contradiction(s), or tension(s) do you see in this text?
3. What seemingly minor, insignificant, easily ignored element(s) or aspect(s) of this text might in fact have major significance?

34.1.4 Formulating a Question and a Thesis

Almost any element, aspect, or point of interest in a text can become a topic for a short essay. Before you can begin writing an essay on that topic, however, you need to come up with a thesis or hypothesis—an arguable statement about the topic. Quite often, one comes up with topic and thesis simultaneously: You might well decide to write about a topic precisely because you've got a specific claim to make about it. At other times, that's not the case: The topic comes much more easily than the thesis. In those cases, it helps to formulate a specific question about the topic and to develop a specific answer. That answer will be your thesis.

Again, remember that your question and thesis should focus on something specific, yet they need to be generally valid, involving more than your personal feelings. Who, after all, can really argue with you about how you feel? The following example demonstrates the way you might freewrite your way from an initial, subjective response to an arguable thesis:

> *I really admire Bartleby.*
>
> *But why? What in the story encourages me to respond that way to him? Well, he sticks to his guns and insists on doing only what he "prefers" to do. He doesn't just follow orders. That makes him really different from all the other characters in the story (especially the narrator). And also from a lot of people I know, even me. He's a nonconformist.*
>
> *Do I think other readers should feel the same way? Maybe, but maybe not. After all, his refusal to conform does cause problems for everyone around him. And actually it doesn't do him a lot of good either. Plus, he would be really annoying in real life. And, even if you admire him, you can't really care about him because he doesn't seem to care about anybody else.*
>
> *Maybe that's the point. Through Bartleby, Melville explores both how rare and important, and how dangerous, nonconformity can be.*

Regardless of how you arrive at your thesis or how strongly you believe in it, it's still helpful at this early stage to think of it as a working hypothesis—a claim that's provisional, still open to rethinking and revision.

34.2 PLANNING

Once you've formulated a tentative thesis, you need to (1) identify the relevant evidence and (2) figure out how to structure your argument, articulating and ordering your claims or sub-ideas. Generally speaking, it works best to tackle structure first—that is, to first figure out your claims and create an outline—because doing so will help you get a sense of what kind of evidence you need. However, you may sometimes get stuck and need to reverse this process, gathering evidence first in order to then formulate and order your claims.

34.2.1 Moving from Claims to Evidence

If you want to focus first on structure, start by looking closely at your thesis. As in many other aspects of writing, it helps to temporarily fill your readers' shoes, trying to see your thesis and the promises it makes from the readers' point of view. What will they need to be shown, and in what order?

If a good thesis shapes readers' expectations, it can also guide you, as a writer. A good thesis often implies what the essay's claims should be and how they should be ordered. For instance, a thesis that focuses on the development of a character implies both that the first body paragraphs will explain what the character is initially like and that later paragraphs will explore how and why that character changes over the course of the story, poem, or play. Similarly, the Bartleby thesis developed in the previous example—*Through Bartleby, Melville explores both how rare and important, and how dangerous, nonconformity can be.*—implies that the writer's essay will address four major issues and will thus have four major parts. The first part must show that Bartleby is a nonconformist. The second part should establish that this nonconformity is rare, a quality that isn't shared by the other characters in the story. Finally, the third and fourth parts should explore, respectively, the positive and negative aspects or consequences of Bartleby's nonconformist behavior. Some or all of these parts may need to include multiple paragraphs, each devoted to a more specific claim.

At this stage, it's very helpful to create an outline. Write down or type out your thesis, and then list each claim (to create a *sentence outline*) or each of the topics to be covered (to create a *topic outline*). Now you can return to the text, rereading it in order to gather evidence for each claim. In the process, you might discover facts that seem relevant to the thesis but that don't relate directly to any of the claims you've articulated. In that case, you may need to insert a new claim into the outline. Additionally, you may find (and should actively look for) facts that challenge your argument. Test and reassess your claims against those facts.

34.2.2 Moving from Evidence to Claims

If you are focusing first on evidence, start by rereading the literary work in a more strategic way, searching for everything relevant to your topic—words, phrases, structural devices, changes of tone, and so forth. As you read (slowly and single-mindedly, with your thesis in mind), keep your pen constantly poised to mark or note down useful facts. Be ready to say something about the facts as you come upon them; immediately write down any ideas that occur to you. Some of these will appear in your essay; some won't. Just like most of the footage shot in making a film, many of your notes will end up on the cutting-room floor. As in filmmaking, however, having too much raw material is preferable to not having enough.

No one can tell you exactly how to take notes. But here is one process that you might try. Be forewarned: This process involves using notecards or uniform sheets of paper. Having your notes on individual cards makes it easier to separate and sort them, a concrete, physical process that can aid the mental process of organizing thoughts and facts. If you are working on a computer, create notecards by putting page breaks between each note or by leaving enough space so that you can cut each page down to a uniform size.

1. Keep your thesis constantly in mind as you reread and take notes. Mark all the passages in the text that bear on your thesis. For each, create a notecard that contains both (a) a single sentence describing how the passage relates to your thesis and (b) the specific information about the passage's location that you will need to create a parenthetical citation. (The information you need will depend on the kind of text you're working with; for specifics, see 36.2.1.) Also, make cards for other relevant, evidentiary facts—like aspects of a poem's rhyme scheme.

2. Keep reading and taking notes until any of the following occur:
   - You get too tired and lose your concentration. (Stop, take a break, come back later.)
   - You stop finding relevant evidence or perceive a noticeable drying up of your ideas. (Again, it's time to pause. Later, when your mind is fresh, read the text one more time to ensure that you didn't miss anything.)
   - You find yourself annotating every sentence or line, so that the evidence all runs together into a single blob. (If this happens, your thesis is probably too broad. Simplify and narrow it. Then continue notetaking.)
   - You become impatient with your notetaking and can't wait to get started writing. (Start drafting immediately. But be prepared to go back to systematic notetaking if your ideas stop coming or your energy fades.)

- You find that the evidence is insufficient for your thesis, that it points in another direction, or that it contradicts your thesis. (Revise your thesis to accommodate the evidence, and begin rereading once more.)

3. When you think you have finished notetaking, read all your notecards over slowly, one by one, and jot down any further ideas as they occur to you, each one on a separate notecard.

Use your notecards to work toward an outline. Again, there are many ways to go about doing this. Here's one process.

1. Sort your cards into logical groups or clusters. Come up with a keyword for that group, and write that word at the top of each card in the group.

2. Set your notecards aside. On a fresh sheet of paper or in a separate document on your computer, write all the major points you want to make. Write them randomly, as they occur to you. Then read quickly through your notecards, and add to your list any important points you have left out.

3. Now it's time to order your points. Putting your points in order is something of a guess at this point, and you may well want to reorder later. For now, make your best guess. Taking your random list, put a "1" in front of the point you will probably begin with, a "2" before the probable second point, and so on.

4. Copy the list in numerical order, revising (if necessary) as you go.

5. Match up your notes (and examples) with the points on your outline. Prepare a title card for each point in the outline, writing on it the point and its probable place in the essay. Then line them up in order before you begin writing. If you're working on a computer, use the search function to find each instance of a keyword, phrase, or name. Then cut and paste in order to arrange your electronic "cards" under the headings you've identified.

6. At this point, you may discover cards that resist classification, cards that belong in two or more places, and/or cards that don't belong anywhere at all. If a card relates to more than one point, put it in the pile with the lowest number, but write on it the number or numbers of other possible locations. Try to find a place for the cards that don't seem to fit, and then put any that remain unsorted into a special file marked "?" or "use in revision."

Before you begin drafting, you may want to develop a more elaborate outline, incorporating examples and including topic sentences for each paragraph. Or you may wish to work directly from your sketchy outline and cards.

34.3 DRAFTING

If you've taken enough time with the planning process, you may already be quite close to a first draft. If you've instead jumped straight into writing, you may have to move back and forth between composing and taking some of the steps described in the last section. Either way, remember that first drafts are often called *rough drafts* for a reason. Think of yourself as a painter "roughing out" a sketch in preparation for the more detailed painting to come. The most important thing is to start writing and keep at it.

Try to start with your thesis and work your way step by step through the entire body of the essay at one sitting. (However, you don't actually have to sit the whole time; if you get stuck, jump up and down, walk around the room, water your plants. Then get back to work.) You will almost certainly feel frustrated at times— as you search for the right word, struggle to decide how the next sentence should begin, or discover that you need to tackle ideas in a different order than you had originally planned.

Stick to it. If you become truly stuck, try to explain your point to another person, or get out a piece of paper or open a new computer file and try working out your ideas or freewriting for a few minutes before returning to your draft. Or, if you get to a section you simply can't write at the moment, make a note about what needs to go in that spot. Then move on and come back to that point later.

Whatever it takes, stay with your draft until you've at least got a middle, or body, that you're relatively satisfied with. Then take a break. Later or even tomorrow come back and take another shot, attaching an introduction and conclusion to the body, filling in any gaps, doing your utmost to create a relatively satisfying whole. Now pat yourself on the back and take another break.

34.4 REVISING

Revision is one of the most important and difficult tasks for any writer. It's a crucial stage in the writing process, yet one that is all too easy to ignore or mismanage. The difference between a so-so essay and a good one, between a good essay and a great one, often depends entirely on effective revision. Give yourself time to revise and develop revision strategies that work for you; the investment in time and effort will pay rich dividends.

Ideally, the process of revision should involve three distinct tasks: assessing the elements, improving the argument, and editing and proofreading. Each of these may require a separate draft. Before considering those three tasks, however, you should be aware of the following three general tips.

First, effective revision requires you to temporarily play the role of reader, as well as writer, of your essay. Take a step back from your draft, doing your utmost to look at it from a more objective point of view. Revision demands re-vision— looking again, seeing anew. As a result, this is an especially good time to involve other people. Have a classmate or friend read and critique your draft.

Second, at this stage it helps to think less in absolute terms (right and wrong, good and bad) than in terms of strengths and weaknesses (elements and aspects of the draft that work well and those that can be improved through revision). If you can understand what's making your essay work, as well as what's detracting from it, then you're better able to improve it. Don't get distracted from this important work by grammatical errors, spelling mistakes, or other minutiae; there will be time to correct them later.

Third, learn to take full advantage of all the capabilities of the computer, but also recognize its limitations. Cutting and pasting make experimenting with different organizational strategies a breeze; word-processing programs identify problems with grammar, spelling, and syntax; the search function can locate repetitive or problematic wording; and so on. You should familiarize yourself with, and use, all of the tools your computer provides and be thankful that you barely know the meaning of the word *white-out*. But you should also remember that the computer is just a tool with limits and that you must be its master. Like any tool, it can create new problems in the process of solving old ones. When it comes to grammar, syntax, and spelling, for instance, you should always pay attention to your program's queries and suggestions. But if you let it make all the decisions, you may end up with an essay full of malapropisms at once hilarious and tragic (one student essay consistently referred to human beings as *human beans!*) or of sentences that are all exactly the same size and shape—all perfectly correct, and all perfectly boring. Also, because the computer makes cutting and pasting so easy and only shows an essay one screen at a time, it's much easier to reorganize but much harder to recognize the effects of doing so. During revision, then, you should at times move away from the computer screen. Print out a hard copy periodically so that you can assess your essay as a whole, identifying problems that you can return to the computer to fix.

34.4.1 Assessing the Elements

The first step in revision is to make sure that all the elements or working parts of the essay are indeed working. To help with that process, run through the following checklist in order to identify the strengths and weaknesses of your draft. Try to answer each question honestly.

Thesis

- ☐ Is there *one* claim that effectively controls the essay?
- ☐ Is the claim debatable?
- ☐ Does the claim demonstrate real thought? Does it truly illuminate the text and the topic?

Structure

BEGINNING

- ☐ Does the introduction establish a clear motive for readers, effectively convincing them that there's something worth thinking, reading, and writing about here?
- ☐ Does it give readers all (and only) the basic information they need about the text, author, and topic?
- ☐ Does the introduction clearly state the central claim or thesis? Is it obvious which claim is the thesis?

MIDDLE

- ☐ Does each paragraph state one debatable claim? Is the main claim always obvious? Does everything in the paragraph relate to, and help support and develop, that claim?
- ☐ Is each of those claims clearly related to (but different from) the thesis?
- ☐ Are the claims/paragraphs logically ordered?
- ☐ Is that logic clear? Is each claim clearly linked to those that come before and after? Are there any logical "leaps" that readers might have trouble taking?

☐ Does each claim/paragraph clearly build on the last one? Does the argument move forward, or does it seem more like a list or a tour through a museum of interesting observations?

☐ Do any key claims or steps in the argument seem to be missing?

Tɪᴘ: You may be better able to discover structural weaknesses if you
1. re-outline your draft as it is. Copy your thesis statement and each of your topic sentences into a separate document. Then pose the above questions. OR
2. read through the essay with highlighters of various colors in hand. As you read, color-code parts that could be restatements of the same or closely related ideas. Then reorganize to match up the colors.

ENDING

☐ Does the conclusion give readers the sense that they've gotten somewhere and that the journey has been worthwhile?

☐ Does it indicate the implications of the argument, consider relevant evaluative questions, or discuss questions that remain unanswered?

Evidence

☐ Is there ample, appropriate evidence for each claim?

☐ Are the appropriateness and significance of each fact—its relevance to the claim—perfectly clear?

☐ Are there any weak examples or inferences that aren't reasonable? Are there moments when readers might ask, "But couldn't that fact instead mean this?"

☐ Is all the evidence considered? What about facts that might complicate or contradict the argument? Are there moments when readers might think, "But what about this other fact?"

☐ Is each piece of evidence clearly presented? Do readers have all the contextual information they need to understand a quotation?

☐ Is each piece of evidence gracefully presented? Are quotations varied by length and presentation? Are they ever too long? Are there any unnecessary block quotations, or block quotations that require additional analysis? (For more specific explanations and advice on effective quotation, see 36.1.)

Though you want to pay attention to all of the elements, first drafts often have similar weaknesses. There are three especially common ones:

- *Mismatch between thesis and argument or between introduction and body*
  Sometimes a first or second draft ends up being a tool for discovering what your thesis really is. As a result, you may find that the thesis of your draft (or your entire introduction) doesn't fit the argument you've ended up making. You thus need to start your revision by reworking the thesis and introduction. Then work your way back through the essay, making sure that each claim or topic sentence fits the new thesis.

- *The list, or "museum tour," structure*
  In a draft, writers sometimes present each claim as if it were just an item on a list (*First, second,* and so on) or as a stop on a tour of ideas (*And this is also important . . .*). But presenting your ideas in this way keeps you and your readers from making logical connections between ideas. It may also

prevent your argument from developing. Sometimes it can even be a sign that you've ceased arguing entirely, falling into mere plot summary or description. Check to see if number-like words or phrases appear prominently at the beginning of your paragraphs or if your paragraphs could be put into a different order without fundamentally changing what you're saying. At times, solving this problem will require wholesale rethinking and reorganizing. But at other times, you will just need to add or rework topic sentences. Make sure that there's a clearly stated, debatable claim at the beginning of each paragraph and that each claim relates to, but differs from, the thesis.

- *Missing sub-ideas*
  You may find that you've skipped a logical step in your argument—that the claim you make in, say, body paragraph 3 actually depends on, or makes sense only in light of, a more basic claim that you took for granted in your draft. In that case, you'll need to create and insert a new paragraph that articulates, supports, and develops this key claim.

34.4.2 Enriching the Argument

Step 1 of the revision process aims to ensure that your essay does the best possible job of making your argument. But revision is also an opportunity to go beyond that—to think about ways in which your overall argument might be made more thorough and complex. In drafting an essay our attention is often and rightly focused on emphatically staking out a particular position and proving its validity. This is the fundamental task of any essay, and you certainly don't want to do anything at this stage to compromise that. At the same time, you do want to make sure that you haven't purchased clarity at the cost of oversimplification by, for example, ignoring evidence that might undermine or complicate your claims, alternative interpretations of the evidence you do present, or alternative claims or points of view. Remember, you have a better chance of persuading readers to accept your point of view if you show them that it's based on a thorough, open-minded exploration of the text and topic. Don't invent unreasonable or irrelevant complications or counterarguments. Do try to assess your argument objectively and honestly, perhaps testing it against the text one more time. Think like a reader rather than a writer: Are there points where a reasonable reader might object to, or disagree with, the argument? Have you ignored or glossed over any questions or issues that a reasonable reader might expect an essay on this topic to address?

34.4.3 Editing and Proofreading

Once you've gotten the overall argument in good shape, it's time to focus on the small but important stuff—words and sentences. Your prose should not only convey your ideas to your readers but also demonstrate how much you care about your essay. Flawless prose can't disguise a vapid or illogical argument, but faulty, flabby prose can destroy a potentially persuasive and thoughtful one. Don't sabotage all your hard work by failing to correct misspelled words, grammatical problems, misquotations, incorrect citations, or typographical errors. Little oversights make all the difference when it comes to clarity and credibility.

Though you will want to check all of the following aspects of your essay, it will probably be easier to spot mistakes and weaknesses if you read through the essay several times, concentrating each time on one specific aspect.

Every writer has individual weaknesses and strengths, and every writer tends to be overly fond of certain phrases and sentence structures. With practice, you will learn to watch out for the kinds of mistakes to which you are most prone. Eventually, you can and should develop your own *personalized* editing checklist.

Sentences
- ☐ Does each one read clearly and crisply?
- ☐ Are they varied in length, structure, and word order?
- ☐ Is the phrasing direct rather than roundabout?

TIPS:
1. Try circling, or using your computer to search for, every preposition and *to be* verb. Since these can lead to confusion or roundabout phrasing, weed out as many as you can.
2. Try reading your paper aloud or having your roommate read it to you. Note places where you stumble, and listen for sentences that are hard to get through or understand.

Words
- ☐ Have I used any words whose meaning I'm not sure of?
- ☐ Are the idioms used correctly? Is my terminology correct?
- ☐ Do my key words always mean *exactly* the same thing?
- ☐ Do I ever use a fancy word or phrase where a simpler one might do?
- ☐ Are there any unnecessary words or phrases?
- ☐ Do my **metaphors** and **figures of speech** make literal sense?
- ☐ Are my verbs active and precise?
- ☐ Are my pronoun references clear and correct?
- ☐ Do my subjects and verbs always agree?

Mechanics
- ☐ Is every quotation correctly worded and punctuated?
- ☐ Is the source of each quotation clearly indicated through parenthetical citation?
- ☐ Have I checked the spelling of words I'm not sure of? (Remember that spell-checks won't indicate how to spell every word and that they sometimes create mistakes by substituting the wrong word for the misspelled one.)
- ☐ Are my pages numbered?
- ☐ Does the first page of my essay clearly indicate my name (and any other required identifying information), as well as my essay's title?

34.5 CRAFTING A TITLE

Complete your essay by giving it a title. As any researcher trying to locate and assess sources by browsing titles will tell you, titles are extremely important. They're the first thing readers encounter and a writer's first opportunity to create a good impression and to shape readers' expectations. Every good essay deserves a good title. And a good title is one that both *informs* and *interests*. Inform readers by telling them both the work(s) your essay will analyze and something about your topic. Interest them with an especially vivid and telling word or a short phrase from the literary work ("'We all said, "she will kill herself"'": The Narrator/Detective in William Faulkner's 'A Rose for Emily'"), with a bit of wordplay ("'Tintern Abbey' and the Art of Artlessness"), or with a little of both ("A Rose for 'A Rose for Emily'").

35 THE RESEARCH ESSAY

Writing a research essay may seem like a daunting task that requires specialized skills and considerable time and effort. Research does add a few more steps to the writing process, so that process will take more time. And those steps require you to draw on, and develop, skills somewhat different from those involved in creating other kinds of essays. But a research essay is, after all, an essay. Its core elements are those of any essay, its basic purpose exactly the same—to articulate and develop a debatable claim about a literary text. As a result, this kind of essay draws on many of the same skills and strategies you've already begun to develop. Similarly, though you will need to add a few new steps, the writing process still involves getting started, planning, drafting, and revising—exactly the same dance whose rhythms you've already begun to master.

Indeed, the only distinctive thing about a research essay is that it requires the use of secondary sources. Though that adds to your burden in some ways, it can lighten it in others. Think of secondary sources not as another ball you have to juggle but as another tool you get to add to your toolbelt: You're still being asked to build a cabinet, but now you get to use a hammer *and* a screwdriver. This chapter will help you make the best use of this powerful tool.

35.1 TYPES AND FUNCTIONS OF SECONDARY SOURCES

Whenever we write an essay about literature, we engage in a conversation with other readers about the meaning and significance of a particular work (or works). Effective argumentation always depends on imagining how other readers are likely to respond to, and interpret, the literary text. As the "Critical Contexts" chapters in this anthology demonstrate, however, almost all texts and authors are the subject of actual public conversations, often extending over many years and involving numerous scholarly readers. A research essay can be an opportunity to investigate this conversation and to contribute to it. In this case, your secondary sources will be works in which literary scholars analyze a specific text or an author's body of work.

As the "Author's Work as Context" and "Cultural and Historical Contexts" chapters show, each literary work is significantly shaped by, and speaks to, its author's unique experience and outlook, as well as the events and debates of the era in which the author lived. So a research assignment can be an opportunity to learn more about a particular author, about that author's body of work, or about the place and time in which the author lived and wrote. The goal of the essay will be to show how context informs text or vice versa. Secondary sources for this sort of research essay will be biographies of the author, essays or letters by the author, and/or historical works of some kind.

Generally speaking, three types of secondary sources are used in essays about literature: *literary criticism*, *biography*, and *history*. The goal of a particular essay and the kinds of questions it raises will determine which kind of sources you use.

In practice, however, many secondary sources cross these boundaries. Biographies of a particular author often offer literary critical interpretations of that author's work; works of **literary criticism** sometimes make use of historical or biographical information; and so on. And you, too, may want or need to draw on more than one kind of source in a single essay. Your instructor will probably give you guidance about what kinds of sources and research topics or questions are appropriate. So make sure that you have a clear sense of the assignment before you get started.

Unless your instructor indicates otherwise, *your* argument should be the focus of your essay, and secondary sources should be just that—secondary. They should merely serve as tools that you use to deepen and enrich your argument about the literary text. They shouldn't substitute for it. Your essay should never simply repeat or report on what other people have already said.

Thus even though secondary sources are important to the development of your research essay, they should not be the source of your ideas. Instead, as one popular guide to writing suggests,* they are sources of

- *opinion* (or *debatable claims*)—other readers' views and interpretations of the text, author, or topic, which "you support, criticize, or develop";
- *information*—facts (which "you interpret") about the author's life; the text's composition, publication, or reception; the era during, or about which, the author wrote; or the literary movement of which the author was a part;
- *concept*—general terms or theoretical frameworks that you borrow and apply to your author or text.

Again, any one source will likely offer more than one of these things. For example, the excerpt from Stephen Gould Axelrod's "Jealous Gods" in chapter 25 provides Axelrod's *opinion* on (or interpretation of) Sylvia Plath's "Daddy"; *information* about the status of the domestic poem in the 1950s; and *concepts* drawn from Freud's theories of psychological development.

Nonetheless, the distinction between opinion (debatable claim) and information (factual statement) is crucial. As you read a source, you must discriminate between the two. And when drawing on sources in your essay, remember that an opinion about a text, no matter how well informed, isn't the same as evidence. Only facts can serve that function. Suppose, for example, that you are writing an essay on "Daddy." You claim that the speaker adopts two voices, that of her child self and that of her adult self—an opinion also set forth in Axelrod's "Jealous Gods." You cannot prove this claim to be true by merely saying that Axelrod makes the same claim. Like any debatable claim, this one must be backed up with evidence from the primary text.

In this situation, however, you must indicate that a source has made the same claim that you do in order to

---

*Gordon Harvey, *Writing with Sources*. Indianapolis: Hackett, 1998.

- give the source credit for having this idea or stating this opinion before you did (see 35.4.1);
- encourage readers to see you as a knowledgeable and trustworthy writer, one who has taken the time to explore, digest, and fairly represent others' opinions;
- demonstrate that your opinion isn't merely idiosyncratic because another informed, even "expert," reader agrees with you.

Were you to disagree with the source's opinion, you would need to acknowledge that disagreement in order to demonstrate the originality of your own interpretation, while also (again) encouraging readers to see you as a knowledgeable, careful, trustworthy writer.

You will need to cite sources throughout your essay whenever you make (1) a claim that complements or contradicts the opinion-claim of a source, or (2) a claim that requires secondary-source information or concepts. In essays that draw on literary critical sources, those sources may prove especially helpful when articulating motive (see 35.1.1).

> **TIP:** In addition to being secondary sources of the type you might use in a research essay, many of the pieces excerpted in the "Critical Contexts" chapters draw on other secondary sources. Look over these pieces to see what kinds of sources professional literary critics use and how they use them. For example, Lawrence R. Rodgers's essay on "A Rose for Emily" (chapter 12) makes use of *information* garnered from biographies of Faulkner (¶3), applies to the story *concepts* taken from another literary critic's argument about detective fiction (¶4), and refers to other critics' *opinions* about the story in order to suggest the distinctiveness and value of this one (¶11, 18).

35.1.1 Source-Related Motives

Not all research essays use sources to establish motive. However, doing so is one way to ensure that your own ideas are the focus of your essay and to demonstrate that (and how) your essay contributes to a literary critical conversation rather than just reporting on it or repeating what others have already said.

In addition to the general motives described above (33.3.1), writing expert Gordon Harvey has identified three common source-related motives:

1. Sources offer different opinions about a particular issue, thus suggesting that there is still a problem or a puzzle worth investigating.

> Almost all interpreters of [*Antigone*] have agreed that the play shows Creon to be morally defective, though they might not agree about the particular nature of his defect. [examples] . . . I want to suggest [instead] that. . . .
> —Martha Nussbaum, "The Fragility of Goodness . . . " (chapter 31)

2. A source (or sources) makes a faulty claim that needs to be challenged or clarified.

> Modern critics who do not share Sophocles' conviction about the paramount duty of burying the dead and who attach more importance than he did to the

claims of political authority have tended to underestimate the way in which he justifies Antigone against Creon. [examples]
—Maurice Bowra, "Sophoclean Tragedy" (chapter 31)

3. Sources neglect a significant aspect or element of the text, or they make a claim that needs to be further developed or applied in a new way.

> At first sight, there appears little need for further study of the lovers in *Far from the Madding Crowd*, and even less of their environment. To cite but a few critics, David Cecil has considered the courtship of Bathsheba, Virginia Hyman her moral development through her varied experience in love, George Wing her suitors, Douglas Brown her relation to the natural environment, Merryn Williams that of Gabriel Oak in contrast to Sergeant Troy's alienation from nature, and, most recently, Peter Casagrande Bathsheba's reformation through her communion with both Gabriel and the environment. To my knowledge, none has considered the modes or styles in which those and other characters express love and how far these may result from or determine their attitude to the land and its dependents, nor the tragic import in the Wessex novels of incompatibility in this sense between human beings, as distinct from that between the human psyche and the cosmos.
> —Lionel Adey, "Styles of Love in *Far from the Madding Crowd.*"
> *Thomas Hardy Annual 5* (1987): 47–62. Print.

35.2 RESEARCH AND THE WRITING PROCESS

Keeping in mind the overall goal of making secondary sources secondary, you have two options about when and how to integrate research into the writing process: (1) You may consult sources in the exploratory phase, using them to generate potential topics and theses for your essay, or (2) you may consult sources during (or even after) the planning or drafting phases, using them to refine and test a tentative thesis. Each approach has advantages and disadvantages.

35.2.1 Using Research to Generate Topic and Thesis

You may consult secondary sources very early in the writing process, using them to help generate your essay topic and thesis (or several potential ones from which you will need to choose). This approach has three advantages. First, you approach the research with a thoroughly open mind and formulate your own opinion about the text(s) only after having considered the range of opinions and information that the sources offer. Second, as you investigate others' opinions, you may find yourself disagreeing, thereby discovering that your mind isn't nearly as open as you'd thought—that you do, indeed, have an opinion of which you weren't fully aware. (Since you've discovered this by disagreeing with a published opinion, you're well on your way to having a motive as well as a thesis.) Third, because you begin by informing yourself about what others have already said, you may be in less danger of simply repeating or reporting.

The potential disadvantage is that you may become overwhelmed by the sheer number of sources or by the amount and diversity of information and opinion they offer. You may agree with everyone, being unable to discriminate among others' opinions or to formulate your own. Or you may find that the conversation seems so exhaustive that you despair of finding anything new to add. If you take this approach, you should maximize the advantages and minimize the disadvantages by keeping in mind a set of clear motive-related questions.

If your sources are works of literary criticism, your goal is to answer two general questions: *What's the conversation about? How can I contribute to it?* To answer those questions, it helps to recall the various motives described in section 35.1.1. Turn them into questions that you can pose about each source:

- ☐ Do the critics tend to disagree about a particular issue? Might I take one side or another in this debate? Might I offer an alternative?
- ☐ Do any critics make a claim that I think deserves to be challenged or clarified?
- ☐ Do the critics ignore a particular element or aspect of the text that I think needs to be investigated? Do any of the critics make a claim that they don't really develop? Or do they make a claim about one text that I might apply to another?

If your sources are historical or biographical, you will instead need to ask questions such as:

- ☐ Is there information here that might help readers understand some aspect of the literary work in a new way?
- ☐ Does any of this information challenge or complicate my previous interpretation of the text, or an interpretation that I think other readers might adopt if they weren't aware of these facts?

35.2.2 Using Research to Refine and Test a Thesis

Because of the potential problems of consulting secondary sources in the exploratory phase of the writing process (35.2.1), your instructor may urge you to delay research until later—after you've formulated a tentative thesis, gathered evidence, or written a complete rough draft. This approach may be especially appealing when you begin an assignment with a firm sense of what you want to write. The chief advantage of this approach is that you can look at secondary sources more selectively and critically, seeking information and opinions that will deepen, confirm, or challenge your argument. And since you've already formulated your opinion, you may be in less danger of becoming overwhelmed by others'.

There are, however, several things to watch out for if you take this approach. First, you must be especially careful not to ignore, distort, or misrepresent any source's argument in the interest of maintaining your own. Second, you must strive to keep your mind open, remembering that the goal of your research is to *test* and *refine* your opinion, not just to *confirm* it. A compelling argument or new piece of information may well require you to modify or broaden your original argument. Third, you still need to pose the general questions outlined above (35.2.1).

35.3 THE RESEARCH PROCESS

Regardless of when you begin your research, the process will involve four tasks:

- creating and maintaining a working bibliography;
- identifying and locating potentially useful secondary sources;
- evaluating the credibility of sources;
- taking notes.

35.3.1 Creating a Working Bibliography

A working bibliography lists all the sources that you *might* use in your research essay. It is a "working" document in two ways. For one thing, it will change throughout the research process—expanding each time you add a potentially useful source and contracting when you omit sources that turn out to be less relevant than you anticipated. Also, once you have written your essay, your working bibliography will evolve one last time, becoming your list of works cited. For another thing, you can use your bibliography to organize and keep track of your research "work." To this end, some researchers divide the bibliography into three parts: (1) sources that they need to locate, (2) sources that they have located and think they will use, and (3) sources that they have located but think they probably won't use. (Keeping track of "rejects" ensures, first, that you won't have to start from scratch if you later change your mind; second, that you won't forget that you've already located and rejected a source if you come across another reference to it.)

Because you will need to update your bibliography regularly and because it will ultimately become the kernel of your list of works cited, you should consider using a computer. In that case, you'll need to print a copy or take your laptop along each time you head to the library. However, some researchers find it helpful to also or instead use notecards, creating a separate card for each source. You can then physically separate cards dedicated to sources to be located, sources already located, and "rejected" sources. Just in case your cards get mixed up, however, you should also always note the status of the source on the card (by writing at the top "find," "located," or "rejected").

Regardless of the format you use, your record for each source should include all the information you will need in order both to locate the source and to cite it in your essay. Helpful location information might include the library in which it's found (if you're using multiple libraries), the section of the library in which it's held (e.g., "Reference," "Stacks"), and its call number. As for citation or publication information, it's tempting to ignore this until the very end of the writing process, and some writers do. But if you give in to that temptation, you will, at best, create much more work for yourself down the road. At worst, you'll find yourself unable to use a great source in your essay because you can't relocate the necessary information about it. To avoid these problems, note down all facts you will need for a works cited entry (see 36.2.2). Finally, consider noting where you first discovered each source, just in case you later need to double-check citation information or to remind yourself why you considered a source potentially useful or authoritative. (Though you can use abbreviations, make sure they're ones you'll recognize later.)

Here are two sample entries from the working bibliography of a student researching Adrienne Rich's poetry. Each entry includes all the required citation information, as well as notes on where the student discovered the source and where it is located.

Sample Working Bibliography Entries

Boyers, Robert. "On Adrienne Rich: Intelligence and Will." *Salmagundi* 22–23 (Spring–Summer 1973): 132–48. Print. Source: *DLB* 5. Loc.: UNLV LASR AS30. S33

Martin, Wendy. *American Triptych: Anne Bradstreet, Emily Dickinson, Adrienne Rich*. U of North Carolina P, 1984. Print. Source: *LRC/CLC*. UNLV Stacks PS310.F45 M3 1984

Once you locate a source, double-check the accuracy and thoroughness of your citation information and update your working bibliography. (Notice, for example, that this student will need to check *American Triptych* to find out the city where it was published and then add this information to her bibliography.)

35.3.2 Identifying and Locating Sources

Regardless of your author, text, or topic, you will almost certainly find a wealth of sources to consult. Your first impulse may be to head straight for the library catalog. But the conversation about literature occurs in periodicals as well as books, and not all contributions to that conversation are equally credible or relevant. For all these reasons, consider starting with one of the reference works or bibliographies described in this section. Then you can head to the catalog armed with a clear sense of what you're looking for.

Once you find one good secondary source, you can use its bibliography to refine your own. Checking the footnotes and bibliographies of several (especially recent) sources will give you a good sense of what other sources are available and which ones experts consider the most significant.

REFERENCE WORKS

Your library will contain many reference works that can be helpful starting points, and some may be accessible via the library's Web page. Here are six especially useful ones.

Literature Resource Center (LRC)

One online source to which your library may subscribe is Gale's *Literature Resource Center*. Designed with undergraduate researchers in mind, it's an excellent place to start. Here you can access and search

- all the material in two of the reference works described below (*Dictionary of Literary Biography* and *Contemporary Authors*) and in both Merriam-Webster's *Encyclopedia of Literature* and Gale's For Students series (*Novels for Students, Literature of Developing Nations for Students*, etc.);
- much (though not all) of the material contained in Gale's Literary Criticism series (another of the reference works described below);
- selected full-text critical essays (or articles) from more than 250 literary journals.

Depending on your library's subscription arrangement, *LRC* may also give you access to the *MLA Bibliography* (from 1963) and/or to the Twayne's Authors series (both described below).

You can search the database in numerous ways, but you should probably start with an author search. Results will appear as a list of sources divided into four files: Biographies; Literary Criticism, Articles, and Work Overviews; Bibliographies (of works by and about the author); Additional Resources (such as author-focused Web sites). You can access each file or list by simply clicking on the appropriate tab. (There will be a good deal of overlap among the files.) You can then click any item on the list in order to open and read it. Once an item is open, you can also print or e-mail it by clicking on the appropriate icons and following the directions.

If your library doesn't subscribe to *LRC*, consider starting with the printed reference works listed below. Because each is a multivolume work, you will need to consult its cumulative index to find out which volumes contain entries on your author. None of these series can keep up to the minute with the literary critical conversation about a particular author or work, and all offer only selective bibliographies. Such selectivity is both the greatest strength and the greatest limitation of these reference works.

Dictionary of Literary Biography (DLB)

One of the most important and authoritative reference works for students of literature, the *Dictionary of Literary Biography* covers primarily British and American authors, both living and dead. Each volume focuses on writers working in a particular genre and period. (Volume 152, 4th series, for example, covers *American Novelists since World War II*.) Written by a scholar in the field, each entry includes a photo or sketch of the author, a list of his or her publications, a bibliography of selected secondary sources, and an overview of the author's life and work. The overviews are often very thorough, incorporating brief quotations from letters, interviews, reviews, and so on. You will find multiple entries on any major author, each focusing on a particular portion of his or her canon. The volume titles will give you a good sense of which entry will be most relevant to you. Entries on W. B. Yeats, for example, appear in volume 10, *Modern British Dramatists, 1900–1945*; volume 19, *British Poets, 1880–1914*; volume 98, *Modern British Essayists*, First Series; and volume 156, *British Short-Fiction Writers, 1880–1914: The Romantic Tradition*.

Contemporary Authors: A Biobibliographical Guide to Current Authors and Their Works (CA)

Gale's *Contemporary Authors* focuses on twentieth- and twenty-first-century writers from around the world and in a range of fields (including the social and natural sciences). In terms of content, its entries closely resemble those in the *DLB* (see above). But *CA* entries tend to be much shorter.

Literary Criticism (LC)

Also published by Gale, the Literary Criticism series is, in effect, a series of series, each of which covers a particular historical period. (See below for individual series titles, as well as information about the periods covered by each one.) Each entry includes a very brief overview of the author's life and work. (There is often overlap between these overviews and those in *CA*.) But there are two key differences between the *LC* series and both the *DLB* and *CA*. First, the *LC* series includes entries devoted entirely to some individual works, as well as entries on an author's entire canon. (For example, Nineteenth-Century Literature Criticism contains both a general entry on Charlotte Brontë and one devoted exclusively to *Jane Eyre*.) Second, the bulk of each entry is devoted to excerpts (often lengthy) from some of the most important reviews and literary criticism on an author and/ or work, and coverage extends from the author's day up to the time when the *LC* entry was written. Each entry concludes with a bibliography of additional secondary sources. The *LC* series thus gives plenty of guidance in identifying authoritative sources, as well as access to excerpts from sources that your library doesn't own.

Here are the titles of the five series, along with information about the period each one covers. To identify the appropriate series, you will need to know the year in which your author died.

- Contemporary Literary Criticism (living authors and those who died from 1960 on)
- Twentieth-Century Literary Criticism (authors who died 1900–1959)
- Nineteenth-Century Literature Criticism (authors who died 1800–1899)
- Literature Criticism from 1400 to 1800 (authors [except Shakespeare] who died 1400–1799)
- Shakespearean Criticism

The Critical Heritage

For some major authors, you can find information and excerpts like those offered by *LC* within the individual volumes of the Critical Heritage series. Unlike the reference works described above, this series is a collection of discrete publications such as *The Brontës: The Critical Heritage*. Each will be held not in the reference department but in the section of the stacks devoted to scholarship on a specific author. You will thus need to search your library's catalog to find it. These volumes are not regularly updated, so each will give a good sense of your author's reception only up to the time it was published.

Twayne's Authors

The Twayne's Authors series incorporates three distinct series: Twayne's United States Authors, Twayne's English Authors, and Twayne's World Authors. Each volume in each series is a distinct book focusing on one author and typically offering both biographical information and interpretation of major works. All aim to be generally accessible and introductory. (As the publishers themselves put it, "The intent of each volume in these series is to present a critical-analytical study of the works of the writer; to include biographical and historical material that may be necessary for understanding, appreciation, and critical appraisal of the writer; and to present all material in clear, concise English.") Yet because each volume is the work of an individual specialist, it represents that scholar's particular point of view (or opinion), and volumes differ widely in their organization, approach, and level of difficulty.

Each volume will be held not in the reference department but in the section of the stacks devoted to scholarship on a specific author. To find it, you will need to search the catalog.

MLA INTERNATIONAL BIBLIOGRAPHY

For much more thorough, up-to-date lists of secondary sources—especially periodical articles—you should consult scholarly bibliographies. In terms of literary criticism, the most comprehensive and useful general bibliography is *The MLA International Bibliography of Books and Articles on the Modern Languages and Literatures*. Since 1969, the *MLA Bibliography* has aimed to provide a comprehensive list of all scholarship published anywhere in the world on literature and modern languages, including books, dissertations, book chapters, and articles in over two thousand periodicals. Though it doesn't quite live up to that aim, it comes closer than any other reference work. (The *Bibliography* in fact began in 1922 but initially included only American scholarship; international coverage began in 1956, but the range of publications remained limited until 1969.) Updated annually, the bibliography is available in print, CD-ROM, and online versions, so what the bibliography encompasses, how many years it covers, and how you use it will depend on the version you consult.

In the print version, each volume lists articles and books published in a specific year, so you should start with the most recent volume and then work your way backward through earlier volumes. Each volume is arranged by nationality or language, then by period, then by author and title.

The CD-ROM and online versions allow you to do topic or keyword searches to find all relevant publications, regardless of the year of publication. Ask a librarian for help with accessing and searching the database.

ONLINE AND CARD CATALOGS

Your library's catalog will guide you to books about the author's work. However, the title of a potentially useful book may be too general to indicate whether it covers the text and topic in which you're interested. If your library's catalog is online, use keyword searches to limit the number and range of books that the computer finds. For example, if you're writing about William Faulkner's "A Rose for Emily," first limit the search to items that include both "Faulkner" and "A Rose for Emily." If you find few matches or none, broaden the search to include all books about William Faulkner.

The books that you find through a catalog search will lead you to a section of the library where other books on your subject are held (because each will have a similar Library of Congress call number). Even if you locate the books you were looking for right away, take a moment to browse. Books shelved nearby probably cover similar topics, and they may prove even more useful than the ones you originally sought. You can also do this kind of browsing online because most online catalogs offer the option of moving from the record of one book to the records of those that appear just before and after it in the catalog.

THE INTERNET

With its innumerable links and pathways, the Internet seems the perfect resource for research of any kind. And in fact some excellent online resources are available to students of literature. *Bartleby.com* is a good, general information site. Here you can access and search several reference works, as well as full-text versions of numerous poems and works of fiction and nonfiction.

There are also many scholarly sites dedicated to specific authors, works, and literary periods. Most sites provide links to others. One site especially useful as a gateway to thousands of more specific sites is *The Voice of the Shuttle* <http://vos.ucsb.edu/>.

If you don't find an appropriate link on *The Voice of the Shuttle*, you will probably want to conduct a search using one of the commonly available search engines. Searches using keywords such as "Chekhov" or "poetry" will lead you to thousands of possible matches, however, so you should limit your search by creating search strings longer than one word. Read onscreen directions carefully to make sure that the search engine treats the search string as a unit and doesn't find every mention of each individual word.

Despite the obvious benefits of the Internet, you should be cautious in your use of online sources for two reasons. First, although many sites provide solid information and informed opinion, many more offer misinformation or unsubstantiated opinion. Unlike journal articles and books, which are rigorously reviewed by experts before they are accepted for publication, many Internet sources are posted without any sort of review process, and authorship is often difficult to pin down. As a result, you need to be especially careful to identify and evaluate the ultimate source of the information and opinions you find in cyberspace. (For more on evaluating sources, see 35.3.3.)

Second, because the Internet enables you to jump easily from one site to another and to copy whole pages of text merely by cutting and pasting, you may lose your place and be unable to provide readers with precise citations. You may lose track of where your own words end and those of your source begin, thereby putting yourself at risk of plagiarizing (see 35.4.1). In addition, the Internet is itself constantly mutating; what's there today may not be there tomorrow. All this makes it difficult to achieve the goal of all citation: to enable readers to retrace your steps and check your sources. When you find sites that seem potentially useful, bookmark them if you can. If not, make sure that you accurately write down (or, better, copy directly into a document) the URL of each, as well as the other information you will need for your list of works cited: the author's name, if available; the site or page title; the date the site was last revised or originally published; and the date you accessed it. If the material on the site has been taken from a printed source, note all of the particulars about this source as well.

As a general rule, Internet sources should supplement print sources, not substitute for them.

35.3.3 Evaluating Sources

Not all sources are equally reliable or credible. The credibility and persuasiveness of your essay will depend, in part, on the credibility of the sources you draw on. This is a good reason to start with reference works that will guide you to credible sources.

Nonetheless, it is very important to learn how to gauge for yourself the credibility of sources. As you do so, keep in mind that finding a source to be credible isn't the same as agreeing with everything it says. At this stage, concentrate on whether the opinions expressed in a source are worthy of serious consideration, not on whether you agree with them. Here are some especially important questions to consider:

1. *How credible is the publisher (in the case of books), the periodical (in the case of essays, articles, and reviews), or the sponsoring organization (in the case of Internet sources)?*

   Generally speaking, academics give most credence to books published by academic and university presses and to articles published in scholarly or professional journals because all such publications undergo a rigorous peer-review process. As a result, you can trust that these publications have been judged credible by more than one recognized expert. For periodicals aimed at a more general audience, you should prefer prominent, highly respected publications such as the *Los Angeles Times* or the *New Yorker* to, say, the *National Enquirer* or *People* magazine.

Internet sources are not subjected to rigorous review processes, but many sites are created and sponsored by organizations. Be sure to identify the sponsoring organization and carefully consider its nature, status, and purpose. The last part of the domain name will indicate the kind of organization it is: The suffix *.com* indicates that the ultimate source is a *company* or commercial, for-profit enterprise; *.org*, a nonprofit or charitable *organization*; *.gov*, a *government* agency; and *.edu*, an *educational* institution. Though you will often find more reliable information on *.gov* or *.edu* sites, this won't always be the case. *Bartleby.com* is, for example, only one of many extremely useful commercial sites, whereas many *.edu* sites feature the work of students who may have much less expertise than you do.

2. *How credible is the author? Is he or she a recognized expert in the relevant field or on the relevant subject?*

   Again, publication by a reputable press or in a reputable periodical generally indicates that its author is considered an expert. But you can also investigate further by checking the thumbnail biographies that usually appear within the book or journal (typically near the beginning or end). Has this person been trained or held positions at respected institutions? What else has he or she published?

3. *How credible is the actual argument?*

   Assess the source's argument by applying all that you've learned about what makes an argument effective. Does it draw on ample, appropriate, convincing evidence? Does it consider all the relevant evidence? Are its inferences reasonable? Are its claims sound? Does the whole seem fair, balanced, and thorough? Has the author considered possible counterarguments or alternative points of view?

Finally, researchers in many fields would encourage you to consider the source's publication date and the currency of the information it contains. In the sciences, for example, preference is almost always given to the most recently published work on a given topic because new scholarly works tend to render older ones obsolete. In the humanities, too, new scholarly works build on old ones. You should consult recently published sources in order to get a sense of what today's scholars consider the most significant, debatable questions and what answers they offer. Though originality is as important in the humanities as in other scholarly fields, new work in the humanities doesn't necessarily render older work utterly obsolete. For example, a 1922 article on Shakespeare's *Hamlet* may still be as valid and influential as one published in 2009. As a result, you should consider the date of publication in evaluating a source, but don't let age alone determine its credibility or value.

35.3.4 Taking Notes

Once you've acquired the books and articles you determine to be most credible and potentially useful, it's a good idea to skim each one. (In the case of a book, concentrate on the introduction and on the chapter that seems most relevant.) Focus at this point on assessing the relevance of each source to your topic. Or, if you're working your way toward a topic, look for things that spark your interest.

Either way, try to get a rough sense of the overall conversation—of the issues and topics that come up again and again across the various sources.

After identifying the sources most pertinent to your argument, begin reading more carefully and taking notes. Again, some researchers find it easier to organize (and reorganize) notes by using notecards, creating one card for each key point. (If you use this method, make sure that each card clearly indicates the source author and short title because cards have a tendency to get jumbled.) Today, however, most researchers take notes on the computer, creating a separate document or file for each source.

Regardless of their form, your notes should be as thorough and accurate as possible. Be thorough because memory is a treacherous thing; it's best not to rely too heavily on it. Accuracy helps you avoid a range of serious problems, including plagiarism (see 35.4.1).

Your notes for each source should include four things: summary, paraphrase, and quotation, as well as your own comments and thoughts. It's crucial to visually discriminate among these by, for instance, always recording your own comments and thoughts in a separate computer document or file or on a separate set of clearly labeled or differently colored notecards.

Whenever you write down, type out, or paste in more than two consecutive words from a source, you should

- place these words in quotation marks so that you will later recognize them as quotations;
- make sure to quote with absolute accuracy every word and punctuation mark;
- record the page where the quotation is found (in the case of print sources).

Keep such quotations to a minimum, recording only the most vivid or telling.

In lieu of extensive quotations, try to summarize and paraphrase as much as possible. You can't decide how to use the source or whether you agree with its argument unless you've first understood it, and you can best understand and test your understanding through summary and paraphrase. Start with a two- or three-sentence summary of the author's overall argument. Then summarize each of the relevant major subsections of the argument. Paraphrase especially important points, making sure to note the page on which each appears.

You may want to try putting your notes in the form of an outline. Again, start with a brief general summary. Then paraphrase each of the major relevant subclaims, incorporating summaries and quotations where appropriate.

Especially if you're dealing with literary criticism, it can be useful to complete the notetaking process by writing a summary that covers all of your sources. Your goal is to show how all the arguments fit together to form one coherent conversation. Doing so will require that you both define the main questions at issue in the conversation and indicate what stance each source takes on each question—where and how their opinions coincide and differ. One might say, for example, that the main questions about *Antigone* that preoccupy all the various scholars represented in chapter 31 are (1) *What is the exact nature of the conflict between Creon and Antigone, or what two conflicting worldviews do they represent?* and (2) *How is that conflict resolved? Which, if any, character and worldview does the play as a whole endorse?* A synthetic summary of these sources would explain how each critic answers each question. This kind of summary can be especially helpful when you haven't yet identified a specific essay topic or crafted a thesis because it may help you to see gaps in the conversation, places where you can enter and contribute.

35.4 INTEGRATING SOURCE MATERIAL INTO THE ESSAY

In research essays, you can refer to sources in a number of ways. You can

briefly allude to them:

> Many critics, including Maurice Bowra and Bernard Knox, see Creon as morally inferior to Antigone.

summarize or paraphrase their contents:

> According to Maurice Bowra, Creon's arrogance is his downfall. However prideful Antigone may occasionally seem, Bowra insists that Creon is genuinely, deeply, and consistently so (2108).

quote them directly:

> For Bowra, Creon is the prototypical "proud man" (2107); where Antigone's arrogance is only "apparent," Creon's is all too "real" (2108).

With secondary sources, be very careful about how often you quote and when and how you do so. Keep the number and length of quotations to a minimum. After all, this is *your* essay, and you should use your own words whenever possible, even to describe someone else's ideas. Save quotations for when you really need them: when the source's author has expressed an idea with such precision, clarity, or vividness that you simply can't say it any better, or when a key passage from your source is so rich or difficult that you need to analyze its ideas and language closely. As with primary texts, lengthy quotation will lead the reader to expect sustained analysis. And only rarely will you want to devote a large amount of your limited time and space to thoroughly analyzing the language of a source (as opposed to a primary text). (For more on responsible and effective quotation, see 36.1.)

One advantage of direct quotation is that it's an easy way to indicate that ideas derive from a source rather than from you. But whether you are quoting, summarizing, or paraphrasing a source, use other techniques as well to ensure that there's no doubt about where your ideas and words leave off and those of a source begin (see 35.4.1). A parenthetical citation within a sentence indicates that something in it comes from a specific source, but unless you indicate otherwise, it will also imply that the entire sentence is a paraphrase of the source. For clarity's sake, then, you should also mention the source or its author in your text, using signal phrases (*According to X*; *As X argues*; *X notes that*; etc.) to announce that you are about to introduce someone else's ideas. If your summary of a source goes on for more than a sentence or two, keep using signal phrases to remind readers that you're still summarizing someone else's ideas rather than stating your own, as Lawrence Rodgers does in the example below.

> The ways of interpreting Emily's decision to murder Homer are numerous.... For simple clarification, they can be summarized along two lines. One group finds the murder growing out of Emily's demented attempt to forestall the inevitable passage of time—toward her abandonment by Homer, toward her own death,

and toward the steady encroachment of the North and the New South on something loosely defined as the "tradition" of the Old South. Another view sees the murder in more psychological terms. It grows out of Emily's complex relationship to her father, who, by elevating her above all of the eligible men of Jefferson, insured that to yield what one commentator called the "normal emotions" associated with desire, his daughter had to "retreat into a marginal world, into fantasy" (O'Connor 184).

These lines of interpretation complement more than critique each other.... Together, they de-emphasize the element of detection, viewing the murder and its solution not as the central action but as manifestations of the principal element, the decline of the Grierson lineage and all it represents. Recognizing the way in which the story makes use of the detective genre, however, adds another interpretive layer to the story by making the narrator . . . a central player in the pattern of action.

—Lawrence R. Rodgers, " 'We All Said . . .' " (chapter 12)

> NOTE: In the first paragraph, Rodgers summarizes other critics' arguments in his own words, briefly but clearly. To ensure that we know he's about to summarize, he announces this intention (*"For simple clarification, they can be summarized . . ."*). As he begins summarizing each view, he reminds us that it is a "view," that he's still not describing his own thoughts. Finally, he uses this unusually long summary to make a very clear and important point: *Everyone except me has ignored this element!*

35.4.1 Using Sources Responsibly

Both the clarity and the credibility of any research essay depend on the responsible use of sources. And using sources responsibly entails accurately representing them and clearly discriminating between your own words and ideas and those that come from sources. Since ideas, words, information, and concepts not directly and clearly attributed to a source will be taken as your own, any lack of clarity on this score amounts to *plagiarism*. Representing anyone else's ideas or data as your own, even if you state them in your own words, is plagiarism—whether you do so intentionally or unintentionally; whether ideas are taken from a published book or article, another student's paper, the Internet, or any other source. Plagiarism is the most serious of offenses within academe because it amounts to stealing ideas, the resource most precious to this community and its members. As a result, the punishments for plagiarism are severe—including failure, suspension, and expulsion.

To avoid both the offense and its consequences, you must always

- put quotation marks around any quotation from a source (a quotation being any two or more consecutive words or any one especially distinctive word, label, or concept);
- credit a source whenever you take from it any of the following:
  —a quotation (as described above);
  —a nonfactual or debatable claim (an idea, opinion, interpretation, evaluation, or conclusion) stated in your own words;
  —a fact or piece of data that isn't common knowledge; or
  —a distinctive way of organizing factual information.

To clarify, a fact counts as common knowledge—and therefore doesn't need to be credited to a source—whenever you can find it in multiple, readily available sources, none of which seriously question its validity. For example, it is common knowledge that Sherman Alexie is Native American, that he was born in 1966, and that he published a collection of short stories entitled *Ten Little Indians*. No source can "own" or get credit for these facts. However, a source can still "own" a particular way of arranging or presenting such facts. If, for example, you begin your essay by stating—in your own words—a series of facts about Alexie's life in exactly the same order they appear in, say, the *Dictionary of Literary Biography*, then you would need to acknowledge that by citing the *Dictionary*. When in doubt, cite. (For guidance about *how* to do so, see 36.2.)

Scene, like friends, experiences one wish to give up the fight for survival and die, but while it colors she was willing to bear on. "for the children's sake" (137) the reason she gives for enduring is the physical presence of the baby in her womb. "[I]t didn't seem such a bad idea [to die]... but she thought of herself stretched out dead while the little ankle-socks lived on... In her lifeless body proved that she persevered (6).

When Gunteretries to have the haunted house to get used for her mother... Beloved she dreamed of clinging to phrases as always happened... clinging to phrases as always happened... things so bad had happened that would never happen again.

—Jean West, *Going Back to the Word: The Maternal pull off in* June Morrison's *Beloved* (unpublished essay, 1994), 7, 1991-1991-91 99 99 99...

36 QUOTATION, CITATION, AND DOCUMENTATION

The bulk of any essay you write should consist of your own ideas expressed in your own words. Yet you can develop your ideas and persuade readers to accept them only if you present and analyze evidence. In essays about literature, quotations are an especially privileged kind of evidence. If your essay also makes use of secondary sources, you will need to quote (selectively) from some of these as well. In either case, your clarity and credibility will depend on how responsibly, effectively, and gracefully you move between others' words and your own. Clarity and credibility will also depend on letting your readers know—through precise citation and documentation—exactly where they can find each quotation and each fact or idea that you paraphrase. This chapter addresses the issue of *how* to quote, cite, and document texts and sources. (For a discussion of *when* to do so, see 33.4 and 35.4.)

36.1 EFFECTIVE QUOTATION

When it comes to quoting, there are certain rules that you must follow and certain strategies that, though not required, will help make your argument more clear and effective.

36.1.1 Rules You Must Follow

1. Generally speaking, you should reproduce a quotation exactly as it appears in the original: Include every word and preserve original spelling, capitalization, italics, and so on. However, there are a few exceptions:

    • When absolutely necessary, you may make minor changes to the quotation as long as (a) they do not distort the sense of the quotation, and (b) you clearly acknowledge them. For instance:

       —Additions and substitutions (e.g., of verb endings or pronouns) may be necessary in order to reconcile the quotation's grammar and syntax with your own or to ensure that the quotation makes sense out of its original context. Enclose these additions and changes in brackets.

       —Omit material from quotations to ensure you stay focused only on what's truly essential. Indicate omissions with ellipsis points unless the quotation is obviously a sentence fragment.

    Notice how these rules are followed in the two examples below:

2314 CH. 36 / QUOTATION, CITATION, AND DOCUMENTATION

Sethe, like Jacobs, experiences the wish to give up the fight for survival and die, but while Jacobs says she was "willing to bear on" "for the children's sakes" (127), the reason that Sethe gives for enduring is the physical presence of the baby in her womb: "[I]t didn't seem such a bad idea [to die], . . . but the thought of herself stretched out dead while the little antelope lived on . . . in her lifeless body grieved her so" that she persevered (31).

When Denver tries to leave the haunted house to get food for her mother and Beloved, she finds herself imprisoned within her mother's time—a time that, clinging to places, is always happening again: "Out there . . . were places in which things so bad had happened that when you went near them it would happen again. . . ."

> —Jean Wyatt, "Giving Body to the Word: The Maternal Symbolic in
> Toni Morrison's *Beloved." PMLA* 108 (May 1993): 474–88. Print.

NOTE: In the first example, Wyatt uses brackets to indicate two changes, the capitalization of "it" and the addition of the words "to die." Ellipses indicate that she's omitted a word or words within the sentence that follows the colon. However, she doesn't need to begin or end the phrases *"willing to bear on"* and *"for the children's sake"* with ellipses because both are obviously sentence fragments. In the second example, notice that Wyatt does need to end the quotation with ellipsis points. Even though it reads like a complete sentence, this isn't the case; the sentence continues in the original text.

—Occasionally, you may want to draw your readers' attention to a particular word or phrase within the quotation by using italics. Indicate this change by putting the words "emphasis added" into your parenthetical citation.

Like his constant references to "Tragedy," the wording of the father's question demonstrates that he is almost as hesitant as his daughter to confront death head-on: "When will you look *it* in the face?" he asks her (69; emphasis added).

• Although you should also accurately reproduce original punctuation, there is one exception to this rule: When incorporating a quotation into a sentence, you may *end* it with whatever punctuation mark your sentence requires. You do not need to indicate this particular change with brackets.

Whether portrayed as "queen," "saint," or "angel," the same "nameless girl" "looks out from all his canvases" (lines 5–7, 1).

NOTE: In the poem quoted ("In an Artist's Studio"), the words *queen* and *angel* are not followed by commas. Yet the syntax of this sentence requires that commas be added, and commas are always enclosed by concluding quotation marks. Similarly, the word *canvases* is followed by a comma in the poem, but the sentence requires that this comma be changed to a period.

2. When incorporating short quotations into a sentence, put them in quotation marks and make sure that they fit into the sentence grammatically and syntactically. If necessary, you may make changes to the quotation (e.g., altering verb endings or pronouns) in order to reconcile its grammar and syntax with your own. But you should—again—always indicate changes with brackets.

It isn't until Mr. Kapasi sees the "topless women" carved on the temple that it "occur[s] to him . . . that he had never seen his own wife fully naked" (415).

3. When quoting fewer than three lines of poetry, indicate any line break with a slash mark, any stanza break with a double slash mark.

    Before Milton's speaker can question his "Maker" for allowing him to go blind, "Patience" intervenes "to prevent / That murmur" (lines 8–9), urging him to see that "God doth not need / Either man's work or his own gifts . . ." (lines 9–10).

    "The cane appears // in our dreams," the speaker explains (lines 15–16).

4. Long quotations—four or more lines of prose, three of poetry—should be indented and presented without quotation marks to create a *block quotation*. In the case of poetry, reproduce original line and stanza breaks.

    Whereas the second stanza individualizes the dead martyrs, the third considers the characteristics they shared with each other and with all those who dedicate themselves utterly to any one cause:

    > Hearts with one purpose alone
    > Through summer and winter seem
    > Enchanted to a stone
    > To trouble the living stream. (lines 41–44)

    Whereas all other "living" people and things are caught up in the "stream" of change represented by the shift of seasons, those who fill their "Hearts with one purpose alone" become as hard, unchanging, and immoveable as stones.

5. Unless they are indented, quotations belong in double quotation marks; quotations within quotations get single quotation marks. However, if everything in your quotation appears in quotation marks in the original, you do not need to reproduce the single quotation marks.

    The words of The Misfit come ringing back to the reader: " 'I don't want no hep,' he said. 'I'm doing all right by myself' " (504).

    As The Misfit says to the grandmother, "I'm doing all right by myself" (504).

6. Follow a word or phrase introducing a quotation with whatever punctuation is appropriate to your sentence. For instance:

    —If you introduce a quotation with a full independent clause (other than something like *She says*), separate the two with a colon.

    Ironically, Mr. Lindner's description of the neighborhood's white residents makes them sound exactly like the Youngers, the very family he's trying to exclude: "They're not rich and fancy people; just hard-working, honest people who don't really have much but . . . a dream of the kind of community they want to raise their children in" (1949).

    —If you introduce or interrupt a quotation with an expression such as *she says* or *he writes*, use a comma (or commas) or add a *that*. Likewise, use a comma if you end a quotation with an expression such as *he says*, unless the quotation ends with a question mark or exclamation point.

    Alvarez claims, "The whole poem works on one single, returning note and rhyme . . ." (1303).

Alvarez suggests that "The whole poem works on one single, returning note and rhyme . . ." (1303).

"The whole poem," Alvarez argues, "works on one single, returning note and rhyme . . ." (1303).

"Here comes one," says Puck. "Where art thou, proud Demetrius?" asks Lysander (Shakespeare 3.2.400–401).

—If quoted words are blended into your sentence, use the same punctuation (or lack thereof) that you would if the words *were not* quoted.

Miriam Allott suggests that the odes, like "all Keats's major poetry," trace the same one "movement of thought and feeling," which "at first carries the poet . . . into an ideal world of beauty and permanence, and finally returns him to what is actual and inescapable."

Keats's poetry just as powerfully evokes the beauty of ordinary, natural things—of "the sun, the moon, / Trees," and "simple sheep"; of "daffodils" and "musk-rose blooms" (*Endymion*, lines 13–14, 15, 19); of nightingales, grasshoppers, and crickets; of "the stubble-plains" and "barred clouds" of a "soft-dying" autumn day ("To Autumn," lines 25–26).

When the narrator's eighty-six-year-old father asks her to tell him a "simple story" with "recognizable people" and a plot that explains "what happened to them next" (65), he gets "an unadorned and miserable tale" whose protagonist ends up "Hopeless and alone" (65).

7. Commas and periods belong inside quotation marks, semicolons outside. Question marks and exclamation points go inside quotation marks if they are part of the quotation, outside if they aren't. (Since parenthetical citations will often alter your punctuation, they have been omitted in the following examples. On the placement and punctuation of parenthetical citations, see 36.2.1.)

"You have a nice sense of humor," the narrator's father notes, but "you can't tell a plain story."

Wordsworth calls nature a "homely Nurse"; she has "something of a Mother's Mind."

What does Johnson mean when he says, "I don't care if he's good or not. He ain't *right!*"?

Bobby Lee speaks volumes about the grandmother when he says, "She was a talker, wasn't she?"

36.1.2 Useful Strategies

1. Make the connection between quotations and inferences as seamless as possible. Try to put them next to each other (in one sentence, if possible). Avoid drawing attention to your evidence as evidence. Don't waste time with phrases such as *This statement is proof that . . . ; This phrase is significant because . . . ; This idea is illustrated by . . . ; There is good evidence for this . . . ;* and the like. Show why facts are meaningful or interesting rather than simply saying that they are.

INEFFECTIVE QUOTING	EFFECTIVE QUOTING
Wordsworth calls nature a "homely Nurse" and says she has "something of a Mother's mind" (lines 81, 79). This diction supports the idea that he sees nature as a beneficent, maternal force. He is saying that nature is an educator and a healer.	Wordsworth describes nature as a beneficent, maternal force. A "homely Nurse" with "something of a Mother's Mind," nature both heals and educates (lines 81, 79).
Tennyson advocates decisive action, even as he highlights the forces that often prohibited his contemporaries from taking it. This is suggested by the lines "Made weak by time and fate, but strong in will, / To strive, to seek, to find, and not to yield" (lines 69–70).	Tennyson advocates forceful action, encouraging his contemporaries "To strive, to seek, to find, and not to yield" (line 70). Yet he recognizes that his generation is more tempted to "yield" than earlier ones because they have been "Made weak by time and fate" (line 69).

2. Introduce or follow a quotation from a source (as well as a paraphrase or summary) with a *signal phrase* that includes the source author's name; you might also include the author's title and/or a bit of information about his or her status, if that information helps establish credibility.

In his study of the Frankenstein myth, Chris Baldick claims that "[m]ost myths, in literate societies at least, prolong their lives not by being retold at great length, but by being alluded to" (3)—a claim that definitely applies to the Hamlet myth.

Oyin Ogunba, himself a scholar of Yoruban descent, suggests that many of Soyinka's plays attempt to capture the mood and rhythm of traditional Yoruban festivals (8).

As historian R. K. Webb observes, "Britain is a country in miniature" (1).

To avoid boring your readers, vary the content and placement of these phrases while always choosing the most accurate verb. (*Says*, for example, implies that words are spoken, not written.) You may find it useful to consult the following list of verbs that describe what sources do.

Verbs to Use in Signal Phrases

affirms	considers	explains	insists	shows
argues	contends	explores	investigates	sees
asks	demonstrates	finds	maintains	speculates
asserts	describes	focuses on	notes	states
believes	discusses	identifies	observes	stresses
claims	draws atten-	illustrates	points out	suggests
comments	tion to	implies	remarks	surmises
concludes	emphasizes	indicates	reports	writes

3. Lead your readers into fairly long quotations by giving them
   - a clear sense of what to look for in the quotation;
   - any information they need to understand the quotation and to appreciate its significance. Quite often, contextual information—for instance, about who's speaking to whom and in what situation—is crucial to a quotation's meaning; this is especially true when quoting dialogue. Also

pay attention to pronouns: If the quotation contains a pronoun without an obvious referent, either indicate the specific referent in advance or add the appropriate noun into the quotation. (Again, place added words in brackets.)

INEFFECTIVE QUOTING	EFFECTIVE QUOTING
A Raisin in the Sun seems to endorse traditional gender roles: "I'm telling you to be the head of this family . . . like you supposed to be" (1944); "the colored woman" should be "building their men up and making 'em feel like they somebody" (1913).	*A Raisin in the Sun* seems to endorse traditional gender roles. When Mama tells Walter "to be the head of this family from now on like you supposed to be" (1944), she affirms that Walter, rather than she or Ruth or Beneatha, is the rightful leader of the family. Implicitly she's also doing what Walter elsewhere says "the colored woman" should do—"building their men up and making 'em feel like they somebody" (1913).
Julian expresses disgust for the class distinctions so precious to his mother: "Rolling his eyes upward, he put his tie back on. 'Restored to my class,' he muttered" (522).	Julian professes disgust for the class distinctions so precious to his mother. At her request, he puts back on his tie, but he can't do so without "[r]olling his eyes" and making fun of the idea that he is thereby "[r]estored to [his] class" (522).

NOTE: Here, the more effective examples offer crucial information about who is speaking (*"When Lena tells Walter"*) or what is happening (*"At her request, he puts back on his tie"*). They also include statements about the implications of the quoted words (*"she affirms that Walter . . . is the rightful leader of the family"*). At the same time, background facts are subordinated to the truly important, evidentiary ones.

4. Follow each block quotation with a sentence or more of analysis. It often helps to incorporate into that analysis certain key words and phrases from the quotation.

The second stanza of the poem refers back to the title poem of *The Colossus*, where the speaker's father, representative of the gigantic male other, so dominated her world that her horizon was bounded by his scattered pieces. In "Daddy," she describes him as

> Marble-heavy, a bag full of God,
> Ghastly statue with one grey toe
> Big as a Frisco seal
>
> And a head in the freakish Atlantic
> Where it pours bean green over blue
> In the waters off beautiful Nanset.

. . . Here the image of her father, grown larger than the earlier Colossus of Rhodes, stretches across and subsumes the whole of the United States, from the Pacific to the Atlantic ocean.   —Pamela J. Annas, "A Disturbance of Mirrors" (chapter 25)

5. Be aware that even though long (especially block) quotations can be effective, they should be used sparingly. Long quotations can create information overload or confusion for readers, making it hard for them to see

what is most significant. When you quote only individual words or short phrases, weaving them into your sentences, readers stay focused on what's significant, and it's easier to show them why it's significant, to get inferences and facts right next to each other.

6. Vary the length of quotations and the way you present them, using a variety of strategies. Choose the strategy that best suits your purpose at a specific moment in your essay, while fairly and fully representing the text. It can be very tempting to fall into a pattern—always, for example, choosing quotations that are at least a sentence long and introducing each with an independent clause and a colon. But overusing any one technique can easily render your essay monotonous. It might even prompt readers to focus more on the (inelegant) way you present evidence than on its appropriateness and significance.

36.2 CITATION AND DOCUMENTATION

In addition to indicating which facts, ideas, or words derive from someone else, always let your readers know where each can be found. You want to enable readers not only to "check up" on you but also to follow in your footsteps and build on your work. After all, you hope that your analysis of a text will entice readers to reread certain passages from a different point of view.

At the same time, you don't want information about how to find others' work to interfere with readers' engagement with *your* work. Who, after all, could really make sense of an essay full of sentences such as these: (1) *"I know not 'seems,'" Hamlet claims in line 76 of act 1, scene 2,* and (2) *On the fourth page of her 1993* PMLA *article (which was in that journal's 108th volume), Jean Wyatt insists that Morrison's "plot . . . cannot move forward because Sethe's space is crammed with the past."*

To ensure that doesn't happen, it is important to have a system for conveying this information in a concise, unobtrusive way. There are, in fact, many such systems currently in use. Different disciplines, publications, and even instructors prefer or require different systems. In literary studies (and the humanities generally), the preferred system is that developed by the Modern Language Association (MLA).

In this system, parenthetical citations embedded in an essay are keyed to an alphabetized list of works cited that appears at its end. Parenthetical citations allow the writer to briefly indicate where an idea, fact, or quotation appears, while the list of works cited gives readers all the information they need to find that source. Here is a typical sentence with parenthetical citation, as well as the works-cited entry to which it refers.

Sample Parenthetical Citation

In one critic's view, "Ode on a Grecian Urn" explores "what great art means" not to the ordinary person, but only "to those who create it" (Bowra 148).

> NOTE: Here, the parenthetical citation indicates that readers can find this quotation on page 148 of some work by an author named Bowra. To find out more, readers must turn to the list of works cited and scan it for an entry, like the following, that begins with the name "Bowra."

Sample Works Cited Entry

Bowra, C. M. *The Romantic Imagination.* Oxford: Oxford UP, 1950. Print.

This example gives a basic sense of how parenthetical citations and the list of works cited work together in the MLA system. Note that each parenthetical citation must "match up" with one (and only one) works-cited entry.

The exact content of each parenthetical citation and works-cited entry will depend on a host of factors. The next two sections focus on these factors.

36.2.1 Parenthetical Citation

THE GENERIC PARENTHETICAL CITATION: AUTHOR(S) AND PAGE NUMBER(S)

The generic MLA parenthetical citation includes an author's name and a page number (or numbers). If the source has two or three authors, include all last names, as in (Gilbert and Gubar 57). If it has four or more, use the first author's name followed by "et al." (Latin for "and others"), as in the second example below. In all cases, nothing but a space separates author's name(s) from page number(s).

> Most domestic poems of the 1950s foreground the parent-child relationship (Axelrod 1313).
>
> Given their rigid structure, it is perhaps "[n]ot surprisin[g]" that many sonnets explore the topic of "confinement" (Booth et al. 1061).

Notice the placement of the parenthetical citations in these examples. In each one the citation comes at the end of the sentence, yet it appears *inside* the period (because it is part of the sentence) and *outside* the quotation marks (because it isn't part of the quotation). Such placement of parenthetical citations should be your practice in all but two situations (both described in the next section).

VARIATIONS IN PLACEMENT

In terms of placement, the first exception is the block quotation. In this case, the parenthetical citation should immediately *follow* (not precede) the punctuation mark that ends the quotation.

> As historian Michael Crowder insists, Western-style education was the single "most radical influence on Nigeria introduced by the British" because it
>> came to be seen as a means not only of economic betterment but of social elevation. It opened doors to an entirely new world, the world of the white man. Since missionaries had a virtual monopoly on schools, they were able to use them as a means of further proselytization, and continued to warn their pupils of the evils of their former way of life. (195)

The second exception is the sentence that either incorporates material from multiple sources or texts (as in the first example below) or refers both to something from a source or text and to your own idea (as in the second example below). In either situation, you will need to put the appropriate parenthetical citation in mid-sentence right next to the material to which it refers, even at the risk of interrupting the flow of the sentence.

> Critics describe Caliban as a creature with an essentially "unalterable natur[e]" (Garner 458), "incapable of comprehending the good or of learning from the past" (Peterson 442), "impervious to genuine moral improvement" (Wright 451).

If Caliban is "incapable of . . . learning from the past" (Peterson 442), then how do we explain the changed attitude he seems to demonstrate at the end of the play?

VARIATIONS IN CONTENT

The generic MLA citation may contain the author's name(s) and the relevant page number(s), but variations are the rule when it comes to content. The six most common variations occur when you do the following:

1. *Name the author in a signal phrase*
   Parenthetical citations should include only information that isn't crucial to the sense and credibility of your argument. Yet in nine cases out of ten, information about *whose* ideas, data, or words you are referring to is crucial in precisely this way. As a result, it is usually a good idea to indicate this in your text. When you do so, the parenthetical citation need only include the relevant page number(s).

   Jefferson's "new generation" are, in Judith Fetterley's words, just "as much bound by the code of gentlemanly behavior as their fathers were" (699).

   According to Steven Gould Axelrod, most domestic poems of the 1950s foreground the parent-child relationship (1313).

2. *Cite a poem or play*
   In the case of most poetry, refer to line (not page) numbers.

   Ulysses encourages his men "To strive, to seek, to find, and not to yield" (line 70).

   In the case of classic plays, indicate act, scene, and line numbers, and separate them with periods.

   "I know not 'seems,'" Hamlet claims (1.2.76).

3. *Cite multiple works by the same author or a work whose author is unknown*
   When citing multiple works by the same author or an anonymous work, you will need to indicate the title of the specific work to which you refer. Either indicate the title in your text, putting only the page number(s) in a parenthetical citation (as in the first example below), or create a parenthetical citation in which the first word or two of the title is followed by the page number(s) (as in the third example below). In the latter case, you should format the title words exactly as you would the full title, using quotation marks for essays, short stories, and short poems, and using italics or underlining for books.

   As Judith Fetterley argues in "A Rose for 'A Rose for Emily,'" Jefferson's younger generation is just "as much bound by the code of gentlemanly behavior as their fathers were" (699).

   Jefferson's "new generation" is, in Judith Fetterley's words, just "as much bound by the code of gentlemanly behavior as their fathers were" ("A Rose" 699).

   Arguably, Jefferson's "new generation" is just "as much bound by the code of gentlemanly behavior as their fathers were" (Fetterley, "A Rose" 699).

4. *Cite a source quoted in another source*
   When quoting the words of one person as they appear in another author's work, mention the person's name in a signal phrase. Then create a parenthetical citation in which the abbreviation "qtd. in" is followed by the author's name and the relevant page number(s).

   Hegel describes Creon as "a moral power," "not a tyrant" (qtd. in Knox 2072).

5. *Cite multiple authors with the same last name*
   In this case, you should either use the author's full name in a signal phrase (as above) or add the author's first initial to the parenthetical citation (as below).

   Beloved depicts a "a specifically female quest powered by the desire to get one's milk to one's baby" (J. Wyatt 475).

6. *Cite multiple sources for the same idea or fact*
   In this case, put both citations within a single set of parentheses and separate them with a semicolon.

   Though many scholars attribute Caliban's bestiality to a seemingly innate inability to learn or change (Garner 458; Peterson 442; Wright 451), others highlight how inefficient or problematic Prospero's teaching methods are (Willis 443) and how invested Prospero might be in keeping Caliban ignorant (Taylor 384).

7. *Cite a work without numbered pages*
   Omit page numbers from parenthetical citations if you cite

   • an electronic work that isn't paginated;
   • a print work whose pages aren't numbered;
   • a print work that is only one page long;
   • a print work, such as an encyclopedia, that is organized alphabetically.

   If at all possible, mention the author's name and/or the work's title in your text (so that you don't need any parenthetical citation). Otherwise, create a parenthetical citation that contains, as appropriate, the author's name and/or the first word(s) of the title.

8. *Italicize words that aren't italicized in the original*
   If you draw your readers' attention to a particular word or phrase within a quotation by using italics or underlining, your parenthetical citation must include the words "emphasis added."

   Like his constant references to "Tragedy," the wording of the father's question demonstrates that he is almost as hesitant as his daughter to confront death head-on: "When will you look *it* in the face?" he asks her (69; emphasis added).

36.2.2 The List of Works Cited

The alphabetized list of works cited should appear at the end of your completed essay. It must include all, and only, the texts and sources that you cite in your essay; it also must provide full publication information about each one.

If you're writing a research essay and have created and maintained a working bibliography (see 35.3.1), that bibliography will become the core of your works-cited list. To turn the former into the latter, you will need to

- delete sources that you did not ultimately cite in your essay;
- add an entry for each primary text you did cite;
- delete notes about where you found sources (library call numbers, etc.).

FORMATTING THE LIST OF WORKS CITED

The list of works cited should appear on a separate page (or pages) at the end of your essay. (If you conclude your essay on page 5, for example, you would start the list of works cited on page 6.) Center the heading "Works Cited" (without quotation marks) at the top of the first page, and double-space throughout.

The first line of each entry should begin at the left margin; the second and subsequent lines should be indented 5 spaces or 1/2 inch.

Alphabetize your list by the last names of the authors or editors. In the case of anonymous works, alphabetize by the first word of the title other than *A*, *An*, or *The*.

If your list includes multiple works by the same author, begin the first entry with the author's name and each subsequent entry with three hyphens followed by a period. Alphabetize these listings by the first word of the title, again ignoring the words *A*, *An*, or *The*.

FORMATTING WORKS-CITED ENTRIES

The exact content and style of each entry in your list of works cited will depend on the type of source it is. Following are examples of some of the most frequently used types of entries in lists of works cited. For all other types, consult the seventh edition of the *MLA Handbook*.

Book by a single author or editor

Webb, R. K. *Modern England: From the Eighteenth Century to the Present*. New York: Columbia UP, 1969. Print.

Wu, Duncan, ed. *A Companion to Romanticism*. Oxford: Blackwell, 1998. Print.

Book with an author and an editor

Keats, John. *Complete Poems*. Ed. Jack Stillinger. Cambridge: Belknap-Harvard UP, 1982. Print.

Book by two or three authors or editors

Gallagher, Catherine, and Thomas Laqueur, eds. *The Making of the Modern Body: Sexuality and Society in the Nineteenth Century*. Berkeley: U of California P, 1987. Print.

Book by more than three authors or editors

Zipes, Jack, et al. *The Norton Anthology of Children's Literature*. New York: Norton, 2005. Print.

Introduction, preface, or foreword

O'Prey, Paul. Introduction. *Heart of Darkness*. By Joseph Conrad. New York: Viking, 1983. 7–24. Print.

Essay, poem, or any other work in an edited collection or anthology

Shaw, Philip. "Britain at War: The Historical Context." *A Companion to Romanticism*. Ed. Duncan Wu. Oxford: Blackwell, 1998. 48–60. Print.

Yeats, W. B. "The Lake Isle of Innisfree." *The Norton Introduction to Literature*. 10th ed. Ed. Alison Booth and Kelly J. Mays. New York: Norton, 2010. 1173. Print.

Multiple short works from one collection or anthology

Booth, Alison and Kelly J. Mays, eds. *The Norton Introduction to Literature*. 10th ed. New York: Norton, 2010. Print.

Frost, Robert. "The Road Not Taken." Booth and Mays. 1325. Print.

Keats, John. "Ode to a Nightingale." Booth and Mays. 1337–39. Print.

Article in a reference work

"Magna Carta." *Encyclopaedia Britannica*. 14th ed. 630–35. Print.

Article in a scholarly journal

Wyatt, Jean. "Giving Body to the Word: The Maternal Symbolic in Toni Morrison's *Beloved*." *PMLA* 108 (May 1993): 474–88. Print.

Article in a newspaper or magazine

McNulty, Charles. "All the World's a Stage Door." *Village Voice* 13 Feb. 2001: 69. Print.

Review or editorial

Leys, Simon. "Balzac's Genius and Other Paradoxes." Rev. of *Balzac: A Life*, by Graham Robb. *New Republic* 20 Dec. 1994: 26–27. Print.

NOTE: The first name here is that of the reviewer, the second that of the author whose book is being reviewed.

Web site

U.S. Department of Education (ED) Home Page. U.S. Dept. of Education, 12 Aug. 2009. Web. 26 Aug. 2009.

Yeats Society Sligo Home Page. Yeats Society Sligo, 12 Nov. 2009. Web. 21 Nov. 2009.

Article on a Web site

Padgett, John B. "William Faulkner." *The Mississippi Writers Page*. 29 Mar. 1999. Web. 9 Sept. 2008.

NOTE: The first date indicates when material was published or last updated. The second date indicates when you accessed the site.

37 SAMPLE RESEARCH PAPER

The student essay below was written in response to the following assignment:

> Write an essay of 10–15 pages that analyzes at least two poems by any one
> author in your text and draws on three or more secondary sources. At least
> one of these sources must be a work of literary criticism (a book or article in
> which a scholar interprets your author's work).

Richard Gibson's response to this assignment is an essay that explores the treatment of religion in four poems by Emily Dickinson; Gibson asks how conventional that treatment was in its original historical and social context. Notice that Gibson uses a variety of sources: literary critical studies of Dickinson's poetry, Dickinson biographies, historical studies of nineteenth-century American religious beliefs and practices, letters written by and to Dickinson, and a dictionary. At the same time, notice that Gibson's thesis is an original, debatable interpretive claim about Dickinson's poetry and that he supports and develops that claim by carefully analyzing four poems.

Richard Gibson

Professor William Barksdale

English 301

4 March 2004

Keeping the Sabbath Separately:

Emily Dickinson's Rebellious Faith

When cataloguing Christian poets, it might be tempting to place Emily Dickinson between Dante and John Donne. She built many poems around biblical quotations, locations, and characters. She meditated often on the afterlife, prayer, and trust in God. Yet Dickinson was also intensely doubtful of the strand of Christianity that she inherited; in fact, she never became a Christian by the standards of her community in nineteenth-century Amherst, Massachusetts. Rather, like many of her contemporaries in Boston, Dickinson recognized the tension between traditional religious teaching and modern ideas. And these tensions, between hope and doubt, between tradition and modernity, animate her poetry. In "Some keep the Sabbath going to church—," "The Brain—is

Gibson establishes a motive for his essay by first stating a claim about Dickinson's poetry that a casual reader might be tempted to adopt and then pointing out the problems with that claim in order to set up the more subtle and complex claim that is his thesis.

Gibson 2

wider than the Sky—," "Because I could not stop for Death—," and "The Bible is an antique Volume," the poet uses traditional religious terms and biblical allusions. But she does so in order both to criticize traditional doctrines and practices and to articulate her own unorthodox beliefs.

In some ways, Emily Dickinson seemed destined by birth and upbringing to be a creature of tradition. After all, her ancestry stretched back to the origin of the Massachusetts Bay Colony; her ancestor Nathaniel Dickinson "was among the four hundred or so settlers who accompanied John Winthrop in the migration that began in 1630" (Lundin 8). Winthrop and his followers were Puritans, a group of zealous Christians who believed in the literal truth and authority of the Bible; the innate corruption of humanity; the doctrine of salvation by faith, not works; and the idea that only certain people were "predestined" for heaven (Noll 21). A few decades after his immigration, Nathaniel Dickinson moved to western Massachusetts, where he and his descendants would become farmers and stalwarts in local churches (Lundin 9). Although Emily Dickinson's grandfather, Samuel Fowler Dickinson, and her father, Edward Dickinson, would give up farming to become lawyers, they, too, subscribed to the articles of their inherited religion (9). In short, for more than three hundred years prior to her birth, Emily Dickinson's family faithfully adhered to the Puritan tradition.

From early life to her year at college, Dickinson received an education that was "overwhelmingly religious" and traditional (Jones 295). The daily routine of the Dickinson household included prayer and readings from the Bible (296). She also received religious teaching regularly at the First Congregational Church and its "Sabbath [Sunday] school" (296). In her weekday schooling, Dickinson read textbooks such as *The New England Primer* and Amherst resident Noah Webster's spelling book that included "catechisms," or methodical teachings in religious doctrine and morality (296).

In the early nineteenth century, though, traditional churchgoers in western Massachusetts began to look warily to the east, especially to Boston, where nontraditional religious thinking had developed among both the "liberal Congregationalists" and the "free-thinking rationalists," or "deists" (Noll 138–42, 143–45). Because these theologies were distinctly European and philosophical, they won few converts outside Boston (143, 145). The greater threat was Unitarianism, which had sprung up in Congregational churches. The Unitarians rejected many of the foundational beliefs of the Puritans and instead "promoted a benevolent God, a balanced universe, and a sublime human potential" (284). Former Unitarian minister and transcendentalist philosopher Ralph Waldo Emerson, an author whom Dickinson admired, gained national attention

Gibson 3

through his writings and speeches on self-reliance and the individual's "direct access" to the "divine spirit" that is behind all "religious systems" (Doriani 18; Norberg xiii–xv). Binding these Bostonian theologies together is an agreement that reason should be applied to religious beliefs. Each then concluded that some—or, in a few minds, most—of the traditional Christian doctrines (to which Amherst adhered) should be abandoned or revised.

Many Bostonian thinkers were influenced by recent developments in science and philosophy that contested the traditional Christian conception of the universe and of the Bible's literal truth. Earlier generations of scientists and philosophers had postulated that the universe obeys fixed laws, which led to ongoing debates about whether the miracles described in the Bible were plausible, even possible (Noll 108). The new astronomy discredited biblical passages describing irregular movements of the sun and the stars. The foremost contemporary dispute, though, concerned the age of the universe. The traditional Christian interpretation of the Bible stated that the universe had existed for about six thousand years (Lundin 32). Early-nineteenth-century geologists, though, had discovered fossils and rock formations that suggested that the Earth was significantly older. Some Christians dug in their heels, while others, like Amherst College professor Edward Hitchcock, attempted to "reconcile orthodoxy and the new geology"—an effort in which the young Dickinson "took comfort" (32). The intellectual scene of Massachusetts at the time of Dickinson's youth thus offered many competing answers to questions about divinity, the historicity of the Bible, and the cosmos. The reign of the old Puritan beliefs over the minds of New England was beginning to wane.

Dickinson herself began to confess doubts about her ability to join the First Congregational Church while still a teenager. In nineteenth-century Amherst, "to 'become a Christian' and join the church" required "only" that one "subscribe to the articles of faith and offer the briefest of assurance [sic] of belief in Christ" (Lundin 51). At age fifteen, though, Dickinson felt unable to do even this much, writing to her friend Abiah Root that she "had not yet made [her] peace with God." Unable to "feel that [she] could give up all for Christ, were [she] called to die," she asked her friend to pray for her, "that [she] may yet enter into the kingdom [of God], that there may be room left for [her] in the shining courts above" (8 Sept. 1846).

During her stay at Mount Holyoke Women's Seminary, from September 1847 to May 1848, Dickinson was frequently invited, even pressured, to become a Christian. Mary Lyon, headmistress of the college, "laid stress on the salvation of souls" and asked her "students to

Gibson uses double quotation marks to enclose words he's taken from a source, single quotation marks to enclose words quoted in that source.

The term *sic* indicates that a spelling or grammar problem within the quotation is present in the original. Gibson encloses the term in brackets to indicate that it is his addition.

Gibson 4

classify themselves according to their religious condition at the beginning
of the year" (Jones 314). Asked to identify herself as a "No-Hoper,"
"Hoper," or "Christian," Dickinson chose the first of these options (Lundin
40–41). A few months into the school year, she informed Root that "there
is a great deal of [religious] interest here and many are flocking to the ark
of safety." Dickinson confessed, though, that she "[had] not yet given up to
the claims of Christ," but was "not entirely thoughtless on so important &
serious a subject" (17 Jan. 1848). In her final letter to Root from Mount
Holyoke, Dickinson describes herself as "filled with self-recrimination
about the opportunities [for salvation] [she had] missed," fearful that she
might never "cast her burden on Christ" (16 May 1848). She thus left
Mount Holyoke just as she came to it—a "No-Hoper."

Many critics, including recent biographer Roger Lundin, see the year
at Mount Holyoke as a turning point in Emily Dickinson's life, the time
when it became clear that she would never "become a Christian"
according to Amherst's standards (47–48). Dickinson would never join
the First Congregationalist Church and, by the age of thirty, stopped
going to services altogether (99). She would likewise never join the
Unitarians. Many of her spiritual ideas would resemble those of the
transcendentalist Emerson, yet important distinctions remained (171).
Throughout her life, she wrote to Christian friends, including ministers,
on spiritual topics, despite their doctrinal differences (Lease 50–51).
Dickinson thus eschewed New England's religious congregations and
asserted her independence in spiritual matters. Yet she always remained
interested in the traditional perspective, and, as a poet, she relied on the
traditional terminology in order to relate her new thinking.

Dickinson's well-known poem "Some keep the Sabbath going to
church—," which she wrote around 1860, demonstrates this tendency. The
opening line places the poem's events on the "Sabbath," the day of worship
in Judeo-Christian traditions (*Oxford*). Thus, while the speaker does not
follow her traditional peers "to Church," she nonetheless observes the
traditional day (line 1). The speaker finds a "Bobolink," a native bird, to be
the service's "Chorister" (line 3), the official term for the leader of a church
choir (*Oxford*). A few lines later, the speaker calls this bird "Our little
Sexton," the title of the manager of the church grounds. Normally, the
sexton "[tolls] the Bell, for Church" (line 7), yet this sexton "sings" (line 8).
The "Orchard" where she sits resembles an important part of church
architecture, "a Dome." In this intimate setting, "God preaches, a noted
Clergyman— / and the sermon is never long" (lines 9–10). The sermon
satisfies two desires that most people have at church: first, to encounter
God, and, second, not to be bored. In this natural scene "instead of getting
to Heaven, at last— / [She's] going, all along" (lines 11–12).

In order to make quoted material fit grammatically and syntactically into his sentences, Gibson changes pronouns and adds explanatory words, enclosing all changed or added words in brackets.

The author's name is omitted from this parenthetical citation because it is included in the sentence.

This citation refers to a line in the poem, not to a page number. The page number is indicated in the list of works cited.

A slash mark indicates a line break in a poem.

Gibson 5

The poem is so pleasant that it is easy to overlook the fact that its central message, that staying at home can be a spiritual experience, is subversive, for church attendance was important in traditional Congregationalist towns like Amherst (Rabinowitz 64–77). In fact, the word "some" might be an understatement, as, in 1860, most citizens in Amherst probably attended a church on Sunday. The speaker's situation instead resembles Emerson's 1842 description of the transcendentalists, those "lonely" and "sincere and religious" people who "repel influences" and "shun general society" (104–05). Furthermore, the speaker claims access to God without the aid of a religious community, a pastor, or a sacred text, all of which, as seen above, were essential to Puritan religious experience. In this poem, then, the speaker frames her spiritual experience in traditional terms and even keeps a few of the traditional practices, yet she simultaneously describes the benefits of departing from traditional practice.

While "Some keep the Sabbath going to church—" reveals Dickinson's changes in practice, "The Brain—is wider than the Sky—," composed perhaps two years later, shows her shift in theology. The speaker asserts a confidence in the power of the human intellect that resembles that of Boston's nontraditional thinkers. In each stanza, she invites the reader to measure the brain by comparing it to some other enormous entity. First, she finds that the brain "is wider than the Sky" and urges the reader to "put them side by side" and see that "the one the other will contain / with ease" and the reader "beside" (lines 1–4). Second, she observes that the brain "is deeper than the sea" and, again, urges the reader to "hold them" and see that "the one the other will absorb / as Sponges—Buckets—do" (lines 5–8). The speaker has a complicated imaginative method: Her materials thus far are all physical—brain, sky, sea—but the qualities that she compares are mixed—physical length and depth versus metaphysical length and depth.

In the third stanza, when the speaker observes that the brain "is just the weight of God" (line 9), she introduces theological material into her experiment. She asks the reader to "Heft," or weigh (*Oxford*), the two "Pound for Pound" and forecasts that "they will differ—if they do— / as Syllable from Sound" (lines 10–12). The poet switches from physical science to linguistics in this closing simile, the meaning of which divides scholars. William Sherwood argues that "each syllable is . . . finite" and "includes only a fraction of the total range of sound," yet "at the same time the syllable is the instrument by which sound is articulated" (127–28). Robert Weisbuch tries to take into account the context of the simile, arguing,

> **Gibson carefully leads the reader from one section of his essay to another with a transitional sentence that first summarizes the claim developed in the last section and then articulates the claim that he will develop in the next section.**

> **Gibson's reference to "scholars" tells the reader that he's about to describe and consider other interpretations.**

Because this quotation is over four lines, it is indented to create a block quotation. Gibson doesn't need to enclose the whole quotation in quotation marks, but he does use quotation marks to set off words quoted within the quotation.

> We must take the qualifying "if they do" ironically. The difference of weight between "Syllable" and "Sound" is at once minute and absolute, the difference of a hair. It is the difference between the thing itself and its imperfect, itemized explanation. It is the difference, say, between paraphrase and poetry, poetry and thought. The brain is not quite and not at all the weightless weight of God. (84)

Weisbuch is right to note that the phrase "if they do" is ironic, as "Syllable" and "Sound" undeniably differ. Sherwood helpfully argues that these are differences in quantity and clarity. Thus, though the brain "As Syllable" is, ultimately, less than "the weight of God," it is more intelligible, perhaps more intelligent, than "the total range of sound."

Rather than letting other scholarly interpreters have the last word, Gibson concludes the paragraph by stating his own interpretive claim.

The speaker of this poem is of a scientific bent; her measurements of length, depth, and weight recall the instruction in science that Dickinson received throughout her schooling (Jones 309; Lundin 30). Yet the speaker also believes that there are things beyond or outside the physical world of science and is just as eager to apply her scientific method to them. She perceives both that the human intellect is enormously expansive and that there is a God behind the cosmos. The divinity that she describes, though, is not the one her ancestors worshiped in Amherst: The speaker's God is more like a force than a person, more like the spirit of the universe than its sovereign. In "Some keep the Sabbath going to church—" Dickinson's orchard still seemed planted in Amherst. In "The Brain—is wider than the Sky," it becomes conspicuously a satellite of Boston.

Notice how Gibson touches back on key terms: "Amherst," "Boston," "traditional theology," etc.

This departure from traditional theology caused Dickinson to revise her vision of the afterlife, as suggested by her 1863 "Because I could not stop for Death—." The poem begins by personifying Death as a carriage-driver (lines 1–3). This personification of death echoes several biblical passages; Dickinson's Death "may," for example, "represent one of the Four Horsemen of the Apocalypse" (Bennett 208). The poet's "kindly" personification is, of course, both more benevolent than the destructive biblical figure and, with his carriage, more modern (line 2). The carriage ride takes the speaker past a school, "Fields of Gazing Grain," the "Setting Sun," and then "pause[s]" at a "House," before proceeding "toward Eternity" (lines 9, 11, 12, 17, 24). The "House" "seem[s] / a Swelling of the Ground," and is, in fact, a grave (lines 10–11). Thus, the carriage drives the speaker through the stages of life—from youth to maturity, decline, death, and, ultimately, the afterlife.

Although Dickinson may draw her image of Death from the Christian tradition, her Death drives the speaker into a distinctly nontraditional afterlife. The speaker tells the reader early on that Death's carriage holds "Immortality" and then, in the closing stanza, that she has "surmised" that the carriage's direction is "toward Eternity" (lines 3, 4, 23, 24). In the Puritan theological tradition, death leads to Heaven or Hell, paradise or perdition. Yet Dickinson's carriage does not drive toward either destination; rather, the afterlife is just a continuous movement, a continuation of consciousness. "Some keep the Sabbath going to church—" prepared us, quite subtly, for this conception of the afterlife; there, too, Heaven is not a place one "[gets] to," "at last," but a state to which one can be "going all along" (lines 11–12). In "Because I could not stop for Death—," the speaker sounds neither blissful nor pessimistic about this state. Her consciousness has adapted to her new existence: "centuries" pass now, "and yet / [it] feels shorter than the Day" when she "first surmised" the carriage's direction (lines 21–23). The word "surmised," though, signals that she is not entirely certain about what, if anything, is to come.

Uncertainty about the afterlife would remain with Dickinson throughout her life and, in 1882, would result in her asking the Reverend Washington Gladden, a somewhat unorthodox Congregationalist, "Is immortality true?" (Lease 50; Gladden). At this time, one of Dickinson's friends, a pastor, had recently died and another friend had become seriously ill (Gladden). Gladden's attempt to reassure her of the truth of immortality draws mostly from his argument that the authoritative figure "Jesus Christ taught" immortality. At the same time, he admits that "absolute demonstration there can be none of this truth."

In perhaps the same year, Dickinson wrote "The Bible is an antique Volume," which shows a mix of skepticism and optimism about the source of Gladden's arguments. The first three lines undermine the Bible's authority; it is an "antique Volume," authored by "faded Men / at the suggestion of Holy Spectres." The poet then provides a list of biblical "Subjects" that "reads like the playbill of a cheap traveling show" (Lundin 203): Eden is "the ancient Homestead"; Satan "the brigadier"; Judas "the Great Defaulter"; David "the Troubadour"; and sin "a distinguished Precipice / others must resist" (lines 4–10). The speaker then uses quotation marks to show her dissatisfaction with religious categories, saying, "Boys that 'believe' are very lonesome / other boys are 'lost'" (lines 11–12). Thus far, the speaker has given us every reason to abandon the Bible—she has discredited its authors, shown the silliness of its subjects, and revealed the tragic culture that surrounds it.

No page number is needed in the parenthetical citations for Gladden because the source is only one page long (see Works Cited).

Notice how Gibson leads the reader from one idea/paragraph to the next with a transition sentence that states the coming paragraph's main idea (that this poem "shows a mix of skepticism and optimism about the" Bible) by referring back to the concerns of the last paragraph ("Gladden's arguments").

Gibson 8

Yet the speaker believes that "had but the Tale [the Bible] a warbling Teller— / all the Boys would come" (lines 13–14). A "warbling Teller" is one whose voice is "thrilling," "ardent," or "friendly" (Bennett 430). For an example, she borrows the poet Orpheus from Greek mythology. His "Sermon," unlike the one the "believing" and "lost" boys now hear, "captivated— / it did not condemn" (lines 15–16). In addition to drawing distinct lines between the saved and the damned, like headmistress Mary Lyon, Puritans often used condemnation, in the now-infamous "fire and brimstone" style, to rouse the immoral to seek salvation (Lundin 11–12; Rabinowitz 5). Instead Dickinson here favors a passionate or intellectual response to a captivating speech over a moral response to a condemning one. She remains a believer in "the emotional force of the Scriptures and [their] expositors," even if she doubts the Bible's historical accuracy and rejects the claims of traditionalist preachers (Doriani 198). The implication of these closing lines, then, is that the Bible is—when read in the right spirit—still a valuable "Volume" for building a community. The Bible has reduced religious authority, but, when performed properly, retains inspirational power. The subtle magic of the poem is that Dickinson herself, in her parodies of biblical "Subjects," enlivens the Bible, "captivates" readers with the old "Tale" through her "warbling" poem.

Though Emily Dickinson might not be a "Christian poet" in the traditional sense of the term, she does beautify and hand down a few beloved pieces of her inheritance, New England Puritanism. She "[keeps] the Sabbath," but at home. She imagines eternity, but without a Heaven or a Hell. She calls the Bible's authors "faded men," but frequently enlivens their "antique" passages in her poems. Over the years, her ideas about God, the universe, and the afterlife changed, but her yearnings to encounter the divine and to experience immortality remained. Emily Dickinson may have physically withdrawn from Amherst society, yet her mind did not withdraw from the intellectual struggles between traditional Amherst and modern Boston. Her spiritual questions and insights are distinctively personal and deeply honest; she is neither a purely skeptical nor a purely religious poet. Her intellect kept her, to her death in 1886, a "No-Hoper" by Mary Lyon's standards, yet, for modern readers, who understand her doubts and share her longings, she is a refreshingly hopeful poet.

Gibson begins his conclusion by returning to the issue he raised in his introduction (Dickinson's status as a "Christian poet"). He then summarizes his argument by briefly reiterating his key points and using a few key words from Dickinson to do so, thus reminding us of how grounded his argument is in textual evidence. Finally, he moves from summarizing his argument to considering its implications for our overall view of Dickinson's poetry.

WORKS CITED

Bennett, Fordyce R. *A Reference Guide to the Bible in Emily Dickinson's Poetry.* Lanham: Scarecrow, 1997. Print.

Dickinson, Emily. "Because I could not stop for Death." Dickinson, *Complete Poems* 350. Print.

Gibson 9

————. "The Bible is an antique Volume." Dickinson, *Complete Poems* 644.

————. "The Brain—is wider than the Sky—." Dickinson, *Complete Poems* 312.

————. *The Complete Poems of Emily Dickinson.* Ed. Thomas H. Johnson. Boston: Little, 1960. Print.

————. *Letters.* Ed. Thomas H. Johnson. Vol. 1. Cambridge: Belknap, 1958. Print.

————. "Some keep the Sabbath going to church." Dickinson, *Complete Poems* 153–54.

————. "To Abiah Root." 8 Sept. 1846. Dickinson, *Letters* 36.

————. "To Abiah Root." 17 Jan. 1848. Dickinson, *Letters* 60.

————. "To Abiah Root." 16 May 1848. Dickinson, *Letters* 67–68.

Doriani, Beth M. *Emily Dickinson: Daughter of Prophecy.* Amherst: U of Massachusetts P, 1996. Print.

Gladden, Washington. "To Emily Dickinson." 27 May 1882. Letter 752a of *Emily Dickinson: Selected Letters.* Ed. Thomas H. Johnson. Cambridge: Belknap, 1971. 282. Print.

Jones, Rowena Revis. "The Preparation of a Poet: Puritan Directions in Emily Dickinson's Education." *Studies in the American Renaissance, 1982.* Boston: Twayne, 1982. Print.

Lease, Benjamin. " 'This World is not Conclusion': Dickinson, Amherst, and 'the local conditions of the soul.' " *Emily Dickinson Journal* 3.2 (1994): 38–55. Print.

Lundin, Roger. *Emily Dickinson and the Art of Belief.* 2nd ed. Grand Rapids: Eerdmans, 2004. Print.

Noll, Mark A. *America's God: From Jonathan Edwards to Abraham Lincoln.* New York: Oxford UP, 2002. Print.

Norberg, Peter. Introduction. *Essays and Poems by Ralph Waldo Emerson.* New York: Barnes and Noble Classics, 2004. xiii–xxxiii. Print.

The Oxford English Dictionary. 2nd ed. 1989. Print.

Rabinowitz, Richard. *The Spiritual Self in Everyday Life: The Transformation of Personal Religious Experience in Nineteenth-Century New England.* Boston: Northeastern UP, 1989. Print.

Sherwood, William R. *Circumference and Circumstance: Stages in the Mind and Art of Emily Dickinson.* New York: Columbia UP, 1968. Print.

Weisbuch, Robert. "The Necessary Veil: A Quest Fiction." *Emily Dickinson.* Ed. Harold Bloom. New York: Chelsea, 1985. Print.

Critical Approaches

Few human abilities are more remarkable than the ability to read and interpret literature. A computer program or a database can't perform the complex process of reading and interpreting—not to mention writing about—a literary text, although computers can easily exceed human powers of processing codes and information. Readers follow the sequence of printed words and as if by magic re-create a scene between characters in a novel or play, or they respond to the almost inexpressible emotional effect of a poem's figurative language. Experienced readers can pick up on a multitude of literary signals all at once. With rereading and some research, readers can draw on information such as the author's life or the time period when this work and others like it were first published. Varied and complex as the approaches to literary criticism may be, they are not difficult to learn. For the most part schools of criticism and theory have developed to address questions that any reader can begin to answer.

There are essentially three participants in what could be called the literary exchange or interaction: the *text*, the *source* (the *author* and other factors that produce the text), and the *receiver* (the *reader* and other aspects of *reception*). All the varieties of literary analysis concern themselves with these aspects of the literary exchange in varying degrees and with varying emphases. Although each of these elements has a role in any form of literary analysis, systematic studies of literature and its history have defined approaches or methods that focus on the different elements and circumstances of the literary interaction. The first three sections below—"Emphasis on the Text," "Emphasis on the Source," and "Emphasis on the Receiver"—describe briefly those schools or modes of literary analysis that have concentrated on one of the three elements while de-emphasizing the others. These different emphases, plainly speaking, are habits of asking different kinds of questions. Answers or interpretations will vary according to the questions we ask of a literary work. In practice the range of questions can be—to some extent *should* be—combined whenever we develop a literary interpretation. Such questions can always generate the thesis or argument of a critical essay.

Although some approaches to literary analysis treat the literary exchange (text, source, receiver) in isolation from the world surrounding that exchange (the world of economics, politics, religion, cultural tradition, and sexuality—in other words, the world in which we live), most contemporary modes of analysis acknowledge the importance of that world to the literary exchange. These days, even if a literary scholar wants to focus on the text or its source or receiver, she or he will often incorporate some of the observations and methods developed by theorists and critics who have turned their attention toward the changing world surrounding the formal conventions of literature, the writing process and writer's career, and the reception or response to literature. We describe the work of such theorists and critics in the fourth section below, "Historical and Ideological Criticism."

Before expanding on the kinds of critical approaches within these four categories, let's consider one example in which questions concerning the text, source, and receiver, as well as a consideration of historical and ideological questions, would contribute to a richer interpretation of a text. To begin as usual with preliminary questions about the *text*: *What* is "First Fight. Then Fiddle." (see p. 1066)? Printed correctly on a separate piece of paper, the text would tell us at once that it is a poem because of its form: rhythm, repeating word sounds, lines that leave very wide margins on the page. Because you are reading this poem in this book, you know even more about its form (in this way, the publication *source* gives clues about the *text*). By putting it in a section with other poetry, we have told you it is a poem worth reading, rereading, and thinking about. (What other ways do you encounter poems, and what does the medium of presenting a poem tell you about it?)

You should pursue other questions focused on the text. What *kind* of poem is it? Here we have helped you, especially if you are not already familiar with the sonnet form, by grouping this poem with other sonnets. Classifying "First Fight. Then Fiddle." as a sonnet might then prompt you to interpret the ways that this poem is or is not like other sonnets. Well and good: You can check off its fourteen lines of (basically) iambic pentameter and note its somewhat unusual rhyme scheme and meter in relation to the rules of Italian and English sonnets. But *why* does this experiment with the sonnet form matter?

To answer questions about the purpose of form, you need to answer some basic questions about *source*, such as *When* was this sonnet written and published? *Who* wrote it? *What* do you know about Gwendolyn Brooks, about 1949, about African American women and/or poets in the United States at that time? A short historical and biographical essay answering such questions might help put the "sonnetness" of "First Fight. Then Fiddle." in context. But assembling all the available information about the source and original context of the poem, even some sort of documented testimony from Brooks about her intentions or interpretation of it, would still leave room for other questions leading to new interpretations.

What about the *receiver* of "First Fight. Then Fiddle."? Even within the poem a kind of audience exists. This sonnet seems to be a set of instructions addressed to "you." (Although many sonnets are addressed by a speaker, "I," to an auditor, "you," such address rarely sounds like a series of military commands, as it does here.) This internal audience is not of course to be confused with real people responding to the poem. How did readers respond to it when it was first published? Can you find any published reviews, or any criticism of this sonnet published in studies of Gwendolyn Brooks?

Questions about the receiver, like those about the author and other sources, readily connect with historical questions. Would a reader or someone listening to this poem read aloud respond differently in the years after World War II than in an age of global terrorism? Does it make a difference if the audience addressed by the speaker inside the poem is imagined as a group of African American men and women or as a group of European American male commanders? (The latter question could be regarded as an inquiry involving the text and the source as well as about the receiver.) Does a reader need to identify with any of the particular groups the poem fictitiously addresses, or would any reader, from any background, respond to it the same way? Even the formal qualities of the text could be examined through historical lenses: The sonnet form has been associated with prestigious European literature, and with themes of love and mortality, since the Renaissance. It is significant that a twentieth-century African American poet chose *this* traditional form to twist "threadwise" into a poem about conflict.

The above are only some of the worthwhile questions that might help illuminate this short, intricate poem. (We will develop a few more thoughts about it in
illustrating different approaches to the text and to the source.) Similarly, the complexity of critical approaches far exceeds our four categories. While a great deal of
worthwhile scholarship and criticism borrows from a range of theories and methods, below we give necessarily simplified descriptions of various critical approaches
that have continuing influence. We cannot trace a history of the issues involved, or
the complexity and controversies within these movements. Instead think of what
follows as a road map to the terrain of literary analysis. Many available resources
describe the entire landscape of literary analysis in more precise detail. If you are
interested in learning more about these or any other analytical approaches, consult
the works listed in the bibliography at the end of this chapter.

EMPHASIS ON THE TEXT

This broad category encompasses approaches that minimize the elements associated with the author/source or the reader/reception in order to focus on the work.
In a sense any writing about literature presupposes recognition of form, in that it
deems the object of study to *be* a literary work, and to belong to a genre or subgenre of literature, as Brooks's poem belongs with sonnets. Moreover, almost all
literary criticism notes some details of style or structure, some *intrinsic* features
such as the relation between dialogue or narrated summary, or the pattern of
rhyme and meter. But *formalist* approaches go further by foregrounding the
design of the text as inherent to the meaning of the whole work.

Some formalists, reasonably denying the division of content from form (since
the form is an aspect of the content or meaning), have more controversially
excluded any discussion of *extrinsic* matters such as the author's biography or
questions of psychology, sociology, or history. This has led to accusations that
formalism, in avoiding relevance to actual authors and readers or to the world of
economic power or social change, also avoids political issues or commitments.
Some historical or ideological critics have therefore argued that formalism supports the powers that be, since it precludes protest. Conversely, some formalists
charge that any extrinsic—that is, historical, political, ideological, as well as biographical or psychological—interpretations of literature reduce the text to a set
of more or less cleverly encoded messages or propaganda. A formalist might
maintain that the inventive wonders of art exceed any practical function it serves.
In practice, influential formalists have generated modes of *close reading* that balance attention to form, significance, and social context, with some acknowledgment of the political implications of literature. In the early twenty-first century
the formalist methods of close reading remain influential, especially in classrooms. Indeed, *The Norton Introduction to Literature* adheres to these methods in its
presentation of elements and interpretation of form.

New Criticism

One strain of formalism, loosely identified as the New Criticism, dominated
literary studies from approximately the 1920s to the 1970s. New Critics rejected
both of the approaches that prevailed then in the relatively new field of English
studies: the dry analysis of the development of the English language, and the

misty appreciation and evaluation of "Great Works." Generally, New Criticism minimizes consideration of both the source and the receiver, favoring the intrinsic qualities of a unified literary work. Psychological or historical information about the author, the intentions or feelings of authors or readers, and any philosophical or socially relevant "messages" derived from the work all are out of bounds in a New Critical reading. The text in a fundamental way refers to itself: Its medium is its message. Although interested in ambiguity and irony as well as figurative language, a New Critical reader establishes the organic unity of the unique work. Like an organism, the work develops in a synergetic relation of parts to whole.

A New Critic might, for example, publish an article titled "A Reading of 'First Fight. Then Fiddle.'" (The method works best with lyric or other short forms because it requires painstaking attention to details such as metaphors or alliteration.) Little if anything would be said of Gwendolyn Brooks or the poem's relation to modernist poetry. The critic's task is to give credit to the poem, not the poet or the period, and if it is a good poem, implicitly, it can't be merely "about" World War II or civil rights. New Criticism presumes that a good literary work symbolically embodies universal human themes and may be interpreted objectively on many levels. These levels may be related more by tension and contradiction than harmony, yet that relation demonstrates the coherence of the whole poem.

Thus the New Critic's essay might include some of the following observations. The title—which reappears as half of the first line—consists of a pair of two-word imperative sentences, and most statements in the poem paraphrase these two sentences, especially the first of them, "First fight." Thus an alliterative two-word command, "Win war" (line 12), follows a longer version of such a command: "But first to arms, to armor" (line 9). Echoes of this sort of exhortation appear throughout. We, as audience, begin to feel "bewitch[ed], bewilder[ed]" (line 4) by a buildup of undesirable urgings, whether at the beginning of a line ("Be deaf," line 11) or the end of a line ("Be remote," line 7; "Carry hate," line 9) or in the middle of a line ("Rise bloody," line 12). It's hardly what we would want to do. Yet the speaker makes a strong case for the practical view that a society needs to take care of defense before it can "devote" itself to "silks and honey" (lines 6–7), that is, the soft and sweet pleasures of art. But what kind of culture would place "hate / In front of . . . harmony" and try to ignore "music" and "beauty" (lines 9–11)? What kind of people are only "remote / A while from malice and from murdering" (lines 6–7)? A society of warlike heroes would rally to this speech. Yet on rereading, many of the words jar with the tone of heroic battle cry.

The New Critic examines not only the speaker's style and words but the order of ideas and lines in the poem. Ironically, the poem defies the speaker's command; it fiddles first, and then fights, as the octave (first eight lines) concern art, and the sestet (last six) concern war. The New Critic might be delighted by the irony that the two segments of the poem in fact unite, in that their topics—octave on how to fiddle, sestet on how to fight—mirror each other. The beginning of the poem plays with metaphors for music and art as means of inflicting "hurting love" (line 3) or emotional conquest, that is, ways to "fight." War and art are both, as far as we know, universal in all human societies. The poem, then, is an organic whole that restates ancient themes.

Later critics have pointed out that New Criticism, despite its avoidance of extrinsic questions, had a political context of its own. The affirmation of unity for the artwork and humanities in general should be regarded as a strategy adapted during the Cold War as a counterbalance to the politicization of art in fascist and communist regimes. New Criticism also provided a program for literary reading that is accessible to beginners regardless of their social background, in keeping with the opening of college-level English studies to more women, minorities, and members of the working class. By the 1970s these same groups had helped generate two sources of opposition to New Criticism's ostensible neutrality and transparency: critical studies that emphasized the politics of social differences (e.g., feminist criticism), and theoretical approaches, based on linguistics, philosophy, and political theory, that effectively distanced nonspecialists once more.

Structuralism

Whereas New Criticism was largely a British and American phenomenon, structuralism and its successor, poststructuralism, derive primarily from French theorists. Strains of structuralism also emerged in the Soviet Union and in Prague, influenced by the demand for a science of criticism that would avoid direct political confrontation. Each of these movements was drawn to scientific objectivity—difficult to attain in literature, arts, and other "humanities"—and at the same time wary of political commitment. Politics, after all, had been the rallying cry for censorship of science, art, and inquiry throughout centuries and in recent memory.

Structuralist philosophy, however, was something rather new. Influenced by the French linguist Ferdinand de Saussure (1857–1913), structuralists sought an objective system for studying the principles of language. Saussure distinguished between individual uses of language, such as the sentences you or I might have just spoken or written (*parole*), and the sets of rules of English or any language (*langue*). Just as a structuralist linguist would study the interrelations of signs in the *langue* rather than the variations in specific utterances in *parole*, a structuralist critic of literature or culture would study shared systems of meaning, such as genres or myths that pass from one country or period to another, rather than a certain poem in isolation (the favored subject of New Criticism).

Another structuralist principle derived from Saussure is the emphasis on the arbitrary association between a word and what it is said to signify—that is, between the *signifier* and the *signified*. The word "horse," for example, has no divine, natural, or necessary connection to that four-legged, domesticated mammal, which is named by other combinations of sounds and letters in other languages. Any language is a network of relations among such arbitrary signifiers, just as each word in the dictionary must be defined using other words in that dictionary. Structuralists largely attribute the meanings of words to rules of differentiation from other words. Such differences may be phonetic (as among the words "cat" and "bat" and "hat") or they may belong to conceptual associations (as among the words "dinky," "puny," "tiny," "small," "miniature," "petite," "compact"). Structuralist thought has particularly called attention to the way that opposites or dualisms such as "night" and "day" or "feminine" and "masculine" define each other through their differences rather than in direct reference to objective reality. For example, the earth's motion around the sun produces changing exposure to sunlight daily and seasonally, but by linguistic convention we call it "night" between, let's say, 8 p.m. and 5 a.m., no matter how light it is. (We may differ in opinions about "evening" or "dawn." But our "day" at work may begin or end in the dark.) The point is that arbitrary labels divide what in fact is continuous.

Structuralism's linguistic insights have greatly influenced literary studies. Like New Criticism, structuralism shows little interest in the creative process or in authors, their intentions, or their circumstances. Similarly, structuralism discounts the idiosyncrasies of particular readings; it takes texts to represent interactions of words and ideas that stand apart from individual human identities or sociopolitical commitments. Structuralist approaches have applied less to lyric poetry than to myths, narratives, and cultural practices, such as sports or fashion. Although structuralism tends to affirm a universal humanity as the New Critics might do, its work in comparative mythology and anthropology challenged the absolute value that New Criticism tended to grant to time-honored canons of great literature.

The structuralist would regard a text not as a self-sufficient icon but as part of a network of conventions. A structuralist essay on "First Fight. Then Fiddle." might ask why the string is plied with the "feathery sorcery" (line 2) of the "bow" (line 7). These words suggest the art of a Native American trickster or primitive sorcerer, while at the same time the instrument is a disguised weapon: a stringed bow with feathered arrows (the term "muzzle" is a similar pun, suggesting an animal's snout and the discharging end of a gun). Or is the fiddle—a violin played in musical forms such as bluegrass—a metaphor for popular art or folk resistance to official culture? In many folk tales a hero is taught to play the fiddle by the devil or tricks the devil with a fiddle or similar instrument. Further, a structuralist reading might attach great significance to the sonnet form as a paradigm that has shaped poetic expression for centuries. The classic "turn" or reversal of thought in a sonnet may imitate the form of many narratives of departure and return, separation and reconciliation. Brooks's poem repeats in the numerous short reversing imperatives, as well as in the structure of octave versus sestet, the eternal oscillation between love and death, creation and destruction.

Poststructuralism

By emphasizing the paradoxes of dualisms and the ways that language constructs our awareness, structuralism planted the seeds of its own destruction or, rather, deconstruction. Dualisms (e.g., masculine/feminine, mind/body, culture/nature) cannot be separate-but-equal; rather, they take effect as differences of power in which one dominates the other. Yet as the German philosopher of history Georg Wilhelm Friedrich Hegel (1770–1831) insisted, the relations of the dominant and subordinate, of master and slave readily invert themselves. The master is dominated by his need for the slave's subordination; the possession of subordinates defines his mastery. As Brooks's poem implies, each society reflects its own identity through an opposing "they," in a dualism of civilized/barbaric. The instability of the speaker's position in this poem (is he or she among the conquerors or the conquered?) is a model of the instability of roles throughout the human world. There is no transcendent ground—except on another planet, perhaps—from which to measure the relative positions of the polar opposites on Earth. Roland Barthes (1915–80) and others, influenced by the radical movements of the 1960s and the increasing complexity of culture in an era of mass consumerism and global media, extended structuralism into more profoundly relativist perspectives.

Poststructuralism is the broad term used to designate the philosophical posi-tion that attacks the objective, universalizing claims of most fields of knowledge since the eighteenth century. Poststructuralists, distrusting the optimism of a positivist philosophy that suggests the world is knowable and explainable, ulti-mately doubt the possibility of certainties of any kind, since language signifies only through a chain of other words rather than through any fundamental link to reality. This argument derives from structuralism, yet it also criticizes structural-ist universalism and avoidance of political issues. *Ideology* is a key conceptual ingredient in the poststructuralist argument against structuralism. Ideology is a slippery term that can broadly be defined as a socially shared set of ideas that shape behavior; often it refers to the values that legitimate the ruling interests in a society, and in many accounts it is the hidden code that is officially denied. (We discuss kinds of "ideological" criticism later.) Poststructuralist theory has played a part in a number of critical schools introduced below, not all of them focused on the text. But in literary criticism, poststructuralism has marshaled most forces under the banner of deconstruction.

Deconstruction

Deconstruction insists on the logical impossibility of knowledge that is not influenced or biased by the words used to express it. Deconstruction also claims that language is incapable of representing any sort of reality directly. As prac-ticed by its most famous proponent, the French philosopher Jacques Derrida (1930–2004), deconstruction endeavors to trace the way texts imply the contra-diction of their explicit meanings. The deconstructionist delights in the sense of dizziness as the grounds of conviction crumble away; *aporia*, or irresolvable doubt, is the desired, if fleeting, end of an encounter with a text. Deconstruc-tion threatens *humanism*, or the worldview that is centered on human values and the self-sufficient individual, because it denies that there is an ultimate, solid reality on which to base truth or the identity of the self. All values and identities are constructed by the competing systems of meaning, or *discourses*. This is a remarkably influential set of ideas that you will meet again as we dis-cuss other approaches.

The traditional concept of the author as creative origin of the text comes under fire in deconstructionist criticism, which emphasizes instead the creative power of language or the text, and the ingenious work of the critic in detecting gaps and contradictions in writing. Thus, like New Criticism, deconstruction disregards the author and concentrates on textual close reading, but unlike New Criticism, it features the role of the reader as well. Moreover, the text need not be respected as a pure and coherent icon. Deconstructionists might "read" many kinds of writing and representation in other media in much the same way that they might read Milton's *Paradise Lost*, that is, irreverently. Indeed, when deconstruction erupted in university departments of literature, traditional critics and scholars feared the breakdown of the distinctions between literature and criticism and between liter-ature and many other kinds of texts. Many attacks on literary theory have particu-larly lambasted deconstructionists for apparently rejecting all the reasons to care about literature in the first place and for writing in a style so flamboyantly obscure that no one but specialists can understand. Yet in practice Derrida and others have carried harmony before them, to paraphrase Brooks; their readings can delight in the play of figurative language, thereby enhancing rather than debunking the value of literature.

A deconstructionist might read "First Fight. Then Fiddle." in a manner somewhat similar to the New Critic's, but with even more focus on puns and paradoxes and with resistance to organic unity. For instance, the two alliterative commands, "fight" and "fiddle," might be opposites, twins, or inseparable consequences of each other. The word "fiddle" is tricky. Does it suggest that art is trivial? Does it allude to a dictator who "fiddles while Rome burns," as the saying goes? Someone who "fiddles" is not performing a grand, honest, or even competent act: One fiddles with a hobby, with the books, with car keys in the dark. The artist in this poem defies the orthodoxy of the sonnet form, instead making a kind of harlequin patchwork out of different traditions, breaking the rhythm, intermixing endearments and assaults.

To the deconstructionist the recurring broken antitheses of war and art, art and war cancel each other out. The very metaphors undermine the speaker's summons to war. The command "Be deaf to music and to beauty blind," which takes the form of a *chiasmus*, or X-shaped sequence (adjective, noun; noun, adjective), is a kind of miniature version of this chiasmic poem. (We are supposed to follow a sequence, fight then fiddle, but instead reverse that by imagining ways to do violence with art or to create beauty through destruction.) The poem, a lyric written but imagined as spoken or sung, puts the senses and the arts under erasure; we are somehow not to hear music (by definition audible), not to see beauty (here a visual attribute). "Maybe not too late" comes rather too late: At the end of the poem it will be too late to start over, although "having first to civilize a space / Wherein to play your violin with grace" (lines 12–14) comes across as a kind of beginning. These comforting lines form the only heroic couplet in the poem, the only two lines that run smoothly from end to end. (All the other lines have **caesuras**, **enjambments**, or balanced pairs of concepts, as in "from malice and from murdering" [line 8].) But the violence behind "civilize," the switch to the high-art term "violin," and the use of the Christian term "grace" suggest that the pagan erotic art promised at the outset, the "sorcery" of "hurting love" that can "bewitch," will be suppressed.

Like other formalisms, deconstruction can appear apolitical or conservative because of its skepticism about the referential connection between literature and the world of economics, politics, and other social forms. Yet poststructuralist linguistics provides a theory of *difference* that clearly pertains to the rankings of status and power in society, as in earlier examples of masculine/feminine, master/slave. The *Other*, the negative of the norm, is always less than an equal counterpart. Deconstruction has been a tool for various poststructuralist thinkers—including the historian Michel Foucault (1926–84), the feminist theorist and psychoanalyst Julia Kristeva (b. 1941), and the psychoanalytic theorist Jacques Lacan (1901–81).

Narrative Theory

Before concluding the discussion of text-centered approaches, we should mention the schools of narratology and narrative theory that have shaped study of the novel and other kinds of narrative. Criticism of fiction has been in a boom period since the 1950s, but the varieties of narrative theory per se have had more limited effect than the approaches we have discussed above. Since the 1960s different analysts of the forms and techniques of narrative, most notably the

Chicago formalists and the structuralist narratologists, have developed terminology for the various interactions of author, implied author, narrator, and characters; of plot and the treatment of time in the selection and sequence of scenes;
of voice, point of view, or focus and other aspects of fiction. As formalisms, narrative theories tend to exclude the author's biography, individual reader response,
and the historical context of the work or its actual reception.

Narratology began by presenting itself as a structuralist science; its branches
have grown from psychoanalytic theory or extended to reader-response criticism.
In recent decades studies of narrative technique and form have responded to
Marxist, feminist, and other ideological criticism that insists on the political
contexts of literature. One important influence on this shift has been the revival
of the work of Mikhail Bakhtin (1895–1975), which features the novel as a *dialogic*
form that pulls together the many discourses and voices of a culture and its history. Part of the appeal of Bakhtin's work has been the fusion of textual close
reading with comprehension of material factors such as economics and class,
and a sense of the open-endedness and contradictoriness of writing (in the spirit
of deconstruction more than of New Criticism). Like other Marxist-trained European formalists, Bakhtin sought to place the complex literary modes of communication in the light of politics and history.

EMPHASIS ON THE SOURCE

As the above examples suggest, a great deal can be drawn from a text without any
reference to its source or its author. For millennia many anonymous works were
shared in oral or manuscript form, and even after printing spread in Europe few
thought it necessary to know the author's name or anything about him or her. Yet
criticism from its beginnings in ancient Greece has been interested in the designing intention "behind" the text. Even when no evidence remained about the
author, a legendary personality has sometimes been invented to satisfy readers'
curiosity. From the legend of blind Homer to the latest debates about biographical evidence and portraits of William Shakespeare, literary criticism has been
accompanied by interest in the author's life.

Biographical Criticism

This approach reached its height in an era when humanism prevailed in literary studies (roughly the 1750s to the 1960s). At this time there was widely shared
confidence in the ideas that art and literature were the direct expressions of the
artist's or writer's genius and that criticism of great works supported veneration
of the great persons who created them. The lives of some famous writers became
the models that aspiring writers emulated. Criticism at times was skewed by
social judgments of personalities, as when Keats was put down as a "Cockney"
poet, that is, London-bred and lower-class. Many writers have struggled to get
their work taken seriously because of mistaken biographical criticism. Women or
minorities have at times used pseudonyms or published anonymously to avoid
having their work put down or having it read only through the expectations,
negative or positive, of what a woman or person of color might write. Biographical criticism can be diminishing in this respect. Others have objected to reading
literature as a reflection of the author's personality. Such critics have supported

the idea that the highest literary art is pure form, untouched by gossip or personal emotion. In this spirit some early twentieth-century critics as well as modernist writers such as T. S. Eliot, James Joyce, and Virginia Woolf tried to dissociate the text from the personality or political commitments of the author. (The theories of these writers and their actual practices did not always coincide.)

In the early twentieth century, psychoanalytic interpretations placed the text in light of the author's emotional conflicts, and other interpretations relied heavily on the author's stated intentions. (Although psychoanalytic criticism entails more than analysis of the author, we will introduce it as an approach that primarily concerns the human source[s] of literature; it usually has less to say about the form and receiver of the text.) Author-based readings can be reductive. All the accessible information about a writer's life cannot definitively explain the writings. As a young man D. H. Lawrence might have hated his father and loved his mother, but all men who hate their fathers and love their mothers do not write fiction as powerful as Lawrence's. Indeed, Lawrence himself cautioned that we should "trust the tale, not the teller."

Any kind of criticism benefits, however, from being informed by the writer's life and career to some extent. Certain critical approaches, devoted to recognition of separate literary traditions, make sense only in light of supporting biographical evidence. Studies that concern traditions such as Irish literature, Asian American literature, or literature by Southern women require reliable information about the writers' birth and upbringing and even some judgment of the writers' intentions to write *as* members of such traditions. (We discuss feminist, African American, and other studies of distinct literatures in the "Historical and Ideological Criticism" section, although such studies recognize the biographical "source" as a starting point.)

A reading of "First Fight. Then Fiddle." can become rather different when we know more about Gwendolyn Brooks. An African American, she was raised in Chicago in the 1920s. These facts begin to provide a context for her work. Some of the biographical information has more to do with her time and place than with her race and sex. Brooks began in the 1940s to associate with Harriet Monroe's magazine, *Poetry*, which had been influential in promoting modernist poetry. Brooks early received acclaim for books of poetry that depict the everyday lives of poor, urban African Americans; in 1950 she was the first African American to win a Pulitzer Prize. In 1967 she became an outspoken advocate for the Black Arts movement, which promoted a separate tradition rather than integration into the aesthetic mainstream. But even before this political commitment, her work never sought to "pass" or to distance itself from racial difference, nor did it become any less concerned with poetic tradition and form when she published it through small, independent black presses in her "political" phase.

It is reasonable, then, to read "First Fight. Then Fiddle.," published in 1949, in relation to the role of a racial outsider mastering and adapting the forms of a dominant tradition. Perhaps Brooks's speaker addresses an African American audience in the voice of a revolutionary, calling for violence to gain the right to express African American culture. Perhaps the lines "the music that they wrote / Bewitch, bewilder. Qualify to sing / Threadwise" (lines 3–5) suggest the way that the colonized may transform the empire's music rather than the other way around. Ten years before the poem was published, a famous African American singer, Marian Anderson, had more than "qualif[ied] to sing" opera and classical concert music, but had still encountered the color barrier in the United States. Honored throughout Europe as the greatest living contralto, Anderson was barred in 1939 from performing at Constitution Hall in Washington, DC, because of her race. Instead she performed at the Lincoln Memorial on Easter Sunday to an audience of seventy-five thousand people. It was not easy to find a "space" in which to practice her art. Such a contextual reference, whether or not intended, relates biographically to Brooks's role as an African American woman wisely reweaving classical traditions "threadwise" rather than straining them into "hempen" (line 5) ropes. Beneath the manifest reference to the recent world war, this poem refers to the segregation of the arts in America. (Questions of source and historical context often interrelate.)

Besides readings that derive from biographical and historical information, there are still other ways to read aspects of the *source* rather than the *text* or the *receiver*. The source of the work extends beyond the life of the person who wrote it to include not only the writer's other works but also the circumstances of contemporary publishing; contemporary literary movements; the history of the composition, editing, and publication of this particular text, with all the variations; and other contributing factors. While entire schools of literary scholarship have been devoted to each of these matters, any analyst of a particular work should bear in mind what is known about the circumstances of writers at that time, the material conditions of the work's first publication, and the means of dissemination ever since. It makes a difference in our interpretation to know that a certain sonnet circulated in manuscript in a small courtly audience or that a particular novel was serialized in a weekly journal.

Psychoanalytic Criticism

With the development of psychology and psychoanalysis toward the end of the nineteenth century, many critics were tempted to apply psychological theories to literary analysis. Symbolism, dreamlike imagery, emotional rather than rational logic, and a pleasure in language all suggested that literature profoundly evoked a mental and emotional landscape, often one of disorder or abnormality. From mad poets to patients speaking in verse, imaginative literature might be regarded as a representation of shared irrational structures within all *psyches* (i.e., souls) or selves. While psychoanalytic approaches have developed along with structuralism and poststructuralist linguistics and philosophy, they rarely focus on textual form. Rather, they attribute latent or hidden meaning to unacknowledged desires in some person, usually the author or source behind the character in a narrative or drama. A psychoanalytic critic can also focus on the response of readers and, in recent decades, usually accepts the influence of changing social history on the structures of sexual desire represented in the work. Nevertheless, psychoanalysis has typically aspired to a universal, unchanging theory of the mind and personality, and criticism that applies it has tended to emphasize the authorial source.

FREUDIAN CRITICISM

For most of the twentieth century, the dominant school of psychoanalytic critics was the Freudian, based on the work of Sigmund Freud (1856–1939). Many of its practitioners assert that the meaning of a literary work exists not on its surface but in the psyche (some would even claim, in the neuroses) of the author.

Classic psychoanalytic criticism read works as though they were the recorded dreams of patients; interpreted the life histories of authors as keys to the works; or analyzed characters as though like real people they have a set of repressed childhood memories. (In fact, many novels and most plays leave out information about characters' development from infancy through adolescence, the period that psychoanalysis especially strives to reconstruct.)

A well-known Freudian reading of *Hamlet*, for example, insists that Hamlet suffers from an Oedipus complex, a Freudian term for a group of repressed desires and memories that corresponds with the Greek myth that is the basis of Sophocles' play *Oedipus the King*. In this view Hamlet envies his uncle because the son unconsciously wants to sleep with his mother, who was the first object of his desire as a baby. The ghost of Hamlet Sr. may then be a manifestation of Hamlet's unconscious desire or a figure for his guilt for wanting to kill his father, the person who has a right to the desired mother's body. Hamlet's madness is not just acting but the result of this frustrated desire; his cruel mistreatment of Ophelia is a deflection of his disgust at his mother's being "unfaithful" in her love for him. Some Freudian critics stress the author's psyche and so might read *Hamlet* as the expression of Shakespeare's own Oedipus complex. In another mode psychoanalytic critics, reading imaginative literature as symbolic fulfillment of unconscious wishes much as an analyst would interpret a dream, decipher objects, spaces, or actions that appear to relate to sexual anatomy or activity. Much as if tracing out the extended metaphors of an erotic poem by Donne or a blues or Motown lyric, the Freudian reads containers, empty spaces, or bodies of water as female; tools, weapons, towers or trees, trains or planes as male.

Psychoanalytic criticism, learning from Freud's ventures in literary criticism, has favored narrative fiction with uncanny, supernatural, or detective elements. Plots with excessive, inexplicable fatalities seem to express wishes unconsciously shared by readers as well as the writer. The method has often been applied to writers of such stories whose biographies are particularly well documented. The life and works of Edgar Allan Poe (1809–49) therefore have attracted psychoanalytic readings. An orphan who quarreled with the surrogate father who raised him, Poe seems to have been tormented by an unresolved desire for a mother figure. A series of beloved mother figures died prematurely, including his mother and Mrs. Allan, the woman who raised him. He became attached to his aunt and fell in love with her daughter, Virginia Clemm, whom he married in 1836 when she was thirteen, and who died of tuberculosis in 1847. He famously asserted that the most apt subject of poetry is the death of a beautiful woman. In Poe's "The Raven" a macabre talking bird intrudes in the speaker's room and provokes the speaker's obsession with the dead beloved, a woman named Lenore. In a Freudian reading, Poe's "The Cask of Amontillado" appears to transpose a fantasy of return to the womb—an enclosed space holding liquids—into a fulfilled desire to kill a male rival.

JUNGIAN AND MYTH CRITICISM

Just as a Freudian assumes that all human psyches have similar histories and structures, the Jungian critic assumes that we all share a universal or collective unconscious (just as each has a racial and an individual unconscious). According to Carl Gustav Jung (1875–1961) and his followers, the unconscious harbors universal patterns and forms of human experiences, or archetypes. We can never know these archetypes directly, but they surface in art in an imperfect, shadowy way, taking the form of archetypal images—the snake with its tail in its mouth, rebirth, mother, the double, the descent into hell. In the classic quest narrative, the hero struggles to free himself (the gender of the pronoun is significant) from the Great Mother to become a separate, self-sufficient being (combating a demonic antagonist), surviving trials to gain the reward of union with his ideal other, the feminine anima. In a related school of *archetypal criticism*, influenced by Northrop Frye (1912–91), the prevailing myth follows a seasonal cycle of death and rebirth. Frye proposed a system for literary criticism that classified all literary forms in all ages according to a cycle of genres associated with the phases of human experience from birth to death and the natural cycle of seasons (e.g., Spring/Romance).

These approaches have been useful in the study of folklore and early literatures as well as in comparative studies of various national literatures. While most myth critics focus on the hero's quest, there have been forays into feminist archetypal criticism. These emphasize variations on the myths of Isis and Demeter, goddesses of fertility or seasonal renewal, who take different forms to restore either the sacrificed woman (Persephone's season in the underworld) or the sacrificed man (Isis's search for Osiris and her rescue of their son, Horus). Many twentieth-century poets were drawn to the heritage of archetypes and myths. Adrienne Rich's "Diving into the Wreck," for example, self-consciously rewrites a number of gendered archetypes, with a female protagonist on a quest into a submerged world. Most critics today, influenced by poststructuralism, have become wary of universal patterns. Like structuralists, Jungians and archetypal critics strive to compare and unite the ages and peoples of the world and to reveal fundamental truths. Rich, as a feminist poet, suggests that the "book of myths" is an eclectic anthology that needs to be revised. Claims of universality tend to obscure the detailed differences between cultures and often appeal to some idea of *biological determinism*. Such determinism diminishes the power of individuals to design alternative life patterns and even implies that no literature can really surprise us.

LACANIAN CRITICISM

As it has absorbed the indeterminacies of poststructuralism under the influence of thinkers such as Jacques Lacan and Julia Kristeva, psychological criticism has become increasingly complex. Few critics today are direct Freudian analysts of authors or texts, and few maintain that universal archetypes explain the meaning of a tree or water in a text. Yet psychoanalytic theory continues to inform many varieties of criticism, and most new work in this field is affiliated with Lacanian psychoanalysis. Lacan's theory unites poststructuralist linguistics with Freudian theory. The Lacanian critic, like a deconstructionist, focuses on the text that defies conscious authorial control, foregrounding the powerful interpretation of the critic rather than the author or any other reader. Accepting the Oedipal paradigm and the unconscious as the realm of repressed desire, Lacanian theory aligns the development and structure of the individual human *subject* with the development and structure of language. To simplify a purposefully dense theory: The very young infant inhabits the Imaginary, in a preverbal, undifferentiated phase dominated by a sense of union with Mother. Recognition of identity begins with the Mirror Stage, ironically with a disruption of a sense of oneness. For when one first looks into a mirror, one begins to recognize a split or difference between one's body and the image in the mirror. This splitting prefigures a sense that the *object* of desire is Other and distinct from the subject. With difference or the splitting of subject and object comes language and entry into the Symbolic Order, since we use words to summon the absent object of desire (as a child would cry "Mama" to bring her back). But what language signifies most is the lack of that object. The imaginary, perfectly nurturing Mother would never need to be called.

As in the biblical Genesis, the Lacanian "genesis" of the subject tells of a loss of paradise through knowledge of the difference between subject and object or Man and Woman (eating of the Tree of the Knowledge of Good and Evil leads to the sense of shame that teaches Adam and Eve to hide their nakedness). In Lacanian theory the Father governs language or the Symbolic Order; the Word spells the end of a child's sense of oneness with the Mother. Further, the Father's power claims omnipotence, the possession of male prerogative symbolized by the Phallus, which is not the anatomical difference between men and women but the idea or construction of that difference. Thus it is language or culture rather than nature that generates the difference and inequality between the sexes. Some feminist theorists have adopted aspects of Lacanian psychoanalytic theory, particularly the concept of *the gaze*. This concept notes that the masculine subject is the one who looks, whereas the feminine object is to be looked at.

Another influential concept is *abjection*. Julia Kristeva's theory of abjection most simply reimagines the infant's blissful sense of union with the mother and the darker side of such possible union. To return to the mother's body would be death, as metaphorically we are buried in Mother Earth. Yet according to the theory, people both desire and dread such loss of boundaries. A sense of self or *subjectivity* and hence of independence and power depends on resisting abjection. The association of the maternal body with abjection or with the powerlessness symbolized by the female's Lack of the Phallus can help explain negative cultural images of women. Many narrative genres seem to split the images of women between an angelic and a witchlike type. Lacanian or Kristevan theory has been well adapted to film criticism and to fantasy and other popular forms favored by structuralism or archetypal criticism.

Psychoanalytic literary criticism today—as distinct from specialized discussion of Lacanian theory, for example—treads more lightly than in the past. In James Joyce's "Araby," a young Dublin boy, orphaned and raised by an aunt and uncle, likes to haunt a back room in the house; there the "former tenant, . . . a priest, had died" (paragraph 2). (Disused rooms at the margins of houses resemble the unconscious, and a dead celibate "father" suggests a kind of failure of the Law, conscience, or in Freudian terms, superego.) The priest had left behind a "rusty bicycle-pump" in the "wild garden" with "a central apple tree" (these echoes of the garden of Eden suggesting the impotence of Catholic religious symbolism). The boy seems to gain consciousness of a separate self—or his subjectivity is constructed—through his gaze upon an idealized female object, Mangan's sister, whose "name was like a summons to all my foolish blood" (paragraph 4). Though he secretly watches and follows her, she is not so much a sexual fantasy as a beautiful art object (paragraph 9). He retreats to the back room to think of her in a kind of ecstasy that resembles masturbation. Yet it is not masturbation: It is preadolescent, dispersed through all orifices—the rain feels like "incessant needles . . . playing in the sodden beds"; and it is sublimated, that is, repressed and redirected into artistic or religious forms rather than directly expressed by bodily pleasure: "All my senses seemed to desire to veil themselves" (paragraph 6).

It is not in the back room but on the street that the girl finally speaks to the hero, charging him to go on a quest to Araby. After several trials the hero carrying the talisman arrives in a darkened hall "girdled at half its height by a gallery," an underworld or maternal space that is also a deserted temple (paragraph 25). The story ends without his grasping the prize to carry back, the "chalice" or holy grail (symbolic of female sexuality) that he had once thought to bear "safely through a throng of foes" (paragraph 5).

Such a reading seems likely to raise objections that it is overreading: *You're seeing too much in it; the author didn't mean that.* This has been a popular reaction to psychoanalysis for over a hundred years, but it is only a heightened version of a response to many kinds of criticism. This sample reading pays close attention to the text, but does not really follow a formal approach because its goal is to explain the psychological motivations or sources of the story's details. We have mentioned nothing about the author, though we could have placed the above reading within a psychoanalytic reading of Joyce's biography.

EMPHASIS ON THE RECEIVER

In some sense critical schools develop in reaction to the excesses of other critical schools. By the 1970s, in a time of political upheaval that placed a value on individual expression, a number of critics felt that the various routes toward objective criticism had proved to be dead ends. New Critics, structuralists, and psychoanalytic or myth critics had sought objective, scientific systems that disregarded changing times, political issues, or the reader's personal response. New Critics and other formalists tended to value a literary canon made up of works that were regarded as complete, unchanging objects to be comprehended, as if spatially in a photograph, according to timeless standards.

Reader-Response Criticism

Among critics who challenge New Critical assumptions, the reader-response critics regard the work not as what is printed on the page but as what is experienced temporally through each act of reading. In effect the reader performs the poem into existence from a text the way a musician performs music from a score. Reader-response critics ask not what a work means but what a work does or, rather, what it makes a reader do. Literary texts especially leave gaps that experienced readers fill according to expectations or conventions. Individual readers differ, of course, and gaps in a text provide space for different readings or interpretations. Some of these lacunae are temporary—such as the withholding of the murderer's name until the end of a mystery novel—and are closed by the text sooner or later, though each reader will in the meantime fill them differently. But other lacunae are permanent and can never be filled with certainty; they result in a degree of uncertainty or indeterminacy in the text.

The reader-response critic observes the expectations aroused by a text, how they are satisfied or modified, and how the reader projects a comprehension of the work when all of it has been read, and when it is reread in whole or in part. Such criticism attends to the reading habits associated with different genres and to the shared assumptions of a cultural context that seem to furnish what is left unsaid in the text. Margaret Atwood's "Happy Endings" could almost be an essay on reader response in the guise of do-it-yourself instructions to a simpleminded reader: "John and Mary meet. What happens next? If you want a happy ending, try A" (paragraphs 1–3). This beginning seems to steer the reader to follow alphabetized instructions to assist in designing the narrative. It also satirizes romance plot conventions. Every romance fan knows that if a male and a female character meet, they will fall in love, and that some conflict will delay their marriage until it is resolved—unless the conflict proves insurmountable. As Atwood humorously shows, various love triangles or death will change the outcome. In spite of the scanty details given in the text, each reader will fill in the gaps and imagine "How and Why" (paragraph 23), the realistic details and rounded characterization that he or she has learned to imagine from reading other fiction.

Beyond theoretical formulations about reading, there are other approaches to literary study that concern the receiver rather than the text or source. A critic might examine specific documents of a work's reception, from contemporary reviews to critical essays written across the generations since the work was first published. Sometimes we have available diaries or autobiographical evidence about readers' encounters with particular works. Just as there are histories of publishing and of the book, there are histories of literacy and reading practices. Poetry, fiction, and drama often directly represent the theme of reading as well as writing. Many published works over the centuries have debated the benefits and perils of reading works such as sermons or novels. Different genres and particular works construct different classes or kinds of readers in the way they address them or supply what they are supposed to want. Some scholars have found quantitative measures for reading, from sales and library lending rates to questionnaires.

Finally, the role of the reader or receiver in literary exchange has been portrayed from a political perspective. Literature helps shape social identity, and social status shapes access to different kinds of literature. Feminist critics adapted reader-response criticism, for example, to note that girls often do not identify with many American literary classics as boys do, and thus girls do not simply accept the stereotype of women as angels, temptresses, or scolds who should be abandoned for the sake of all-male adventures. Studies of African American literature and other ethnic literatures have often featured discussion of literacy and of the obstacles for readers who cannot find their counterparts within the texts or who encounter negative stereotypes of their group. Thus, as we will discuss below, most forms of historical and ideological criticism include some consideration of the reader.

HISTORICAL AND IDEOLOGICAL CRITICISM

Approaches to the text, the author, and the reader, outlined above, each may take some note of historical contexts, including changes in formal conventions, the writer's milieu, or audience expectations. In the nineteenth century, historical criticism took the obvious facts that a work is created in a specific historical and cultural context and that the author is a part of that context as reasons to treat literature as a reflection of society. Twentieth-century formalists rejected the *reflectivist* model of art in the old historical criticism, that is, the assumption that literature and other arts straightforwardly express the collective spirit of the society at that time. But as we have remarked, formalist rules for isolating the work of art from social and historical context met resistance in the last decades of the twentieth century. In a revival of historical approaches, critics have replaced the reflectivist model with a *constructivist* model, whereby literature and other cultural discourses help construct social relations and roles rather than merely reflecting them. In other words, art is not just the frosting on the cake but an integral part of the recipe's ingredients and instructions. A society's ideology, its inherent system of representations (ideas, myths, images), is inscribed in and by literature and other cultural forms, which in turn help shape identities and social practices.

Since the 1980s historical approaches have regained great influence in literary studies. Some critical schools have been insistently *materialist*, that is, seeking causes more in concrete conditions such as technology, production, and distribution of wealth, or the exploitation of markets and labor in and beyond Western countries. Such criticism usually owes an acknowledged debt to Marxism. Other historical approaches have been influenced to a degree by Marxist critics and cultural theorists, but work within the realm of ideology, textual production, and interpretation, using some of the methods and concerns of traditional literary history. Still others emerge from the civil rights movement and the struggles for recognition of women and racial, ethnic, and sexual constituencies.

Feminist studies, African American studies, gay and lesbian studies, and studies of the cultures of different immigrant and ethnic populations within the United States have each developed along similar theoretical lines. These schools, like Marxist criticism, adopt a constructivist position: Literature is not simply a reflection of prejudices and norms; it also helps define as well as reshape social identities, such as what it means to be an African American woman. Each of these schools has moved through stages of first claiming *equality* with the literature dominated by white Anglo American men, then affirming the *difference* of their own separate culture, and then theoretically *questioning the terms and standards* of such comparisons. At a certain point in the thought process, each group rejects *essentialism*, the notion of innate or biological bases for the differences between the sexes, races, or other groups. This rejection of essentialism is usually called the constructivist position, in a somewhat different but related sense to our definition above. Constructivism maintains that identity is socially formed rather than biologically determined. Differences of anatomical sex, skin color, first language, parental ethnicity, and eventual sexual preferences have great impact on how one is classified, brought up, and treated socially, and on one's subjectivity or conception of identity. Constructivists maintain that these differences, however, are more constructed by ideology and the resulting behaviors than by any natural programming.

Marxist Criticism

The most insistent and vigorous historical approach through the twentieth century to the present has been Marxism, based on the work of Karl Marx (1818–83). With roots in nineteenth-century historicism, Marxist criticism was initially reflectivist. Economics, the underlying cause of history, was thus the *base*, and culture, including literature and the other arts, was the *superstructure*, an outcome or reflection of the base. Viewed from the Marxist perspective, the literary works of a period were economically determined; they would *reflect* the state of the struggle between classes in any place and time. History enacted recurrent three-step cycles, a pattern that Hegel had defined as *dialectic* (Hegel was cited above on the interdependence of master and slave). Each socioeconomic phase, or *thesis*, is counteracted by its *antithesis*, and the resulting conflict yields a *synthesis*, which becomes the ensuing *thesis*, and so on. As with early Freudian criticism, early Marxist criticism was often preoccupied with labeling and exposing illusions or deceptions. A novel might be read as a thinly disguised defense of the power of bourgeois industrial capital; its appeal on behalf of the suffering poor might be dismissed as an effort to fend off a class rebellion.

As a rationale for state control of the arts, Marxism was abused in the Soviet Union and in other totalitarian states. In the hands of sophisticated critics, however, Marxism has been richly rewarding. Various schools that unite formal close reading and political analysis developed in the early twentieth century under Soviet communism and under fascism in Europe, often in covert resistance. These schools in turn have influenced critical movements in North American universities through translations or through members who came to the United States; New Criticism, structuralist linguistics, deconstruction, and narrative theory have each borrowed from European Marxist critics.

Most recently, a new mode of Marxist theory has developed, largely guided by the thinking of Walter Benjamin (1892–1940) and Theodor Adorno (1903–69) of the Frankfurt School in Germany, Louis Althusser (1918–90) in France, and Raymond Williams (1921–98) in Britain. This work has generally tended to modify the base/superstructure distinction and to interrelate public and private life, economics and culture. Newer Marxist interpretation assumes that the relation of a literary work to its historical context is *overdetermined*—the relation has multiple determining factors rather than a sole cause or aim. This thinking similarly acknowledges that neither the source nor the receiver of the literary interaction is a mere tool or victim of the ruling powers or state. Representation of all kinds, including literature, always has a political dimension, according to this approach; conversely, political and material conditions such as work, money, or institutions depend on representation.

Showing some influence of psychoanalytic and poststructuralist theories, recent Marxist literary studies examine the effects of ideology by focusing on the works' gaps and silences: Ideology may be conveyed in what is repressed or contradicted. In many ways Marxist criticism has adapted to the conditions of consumer rather than industrial capitalism and to global rather than national economies. The worldwide revolution that was to come when the proletariat or working classes overthrew the capitalists has never taken place; in many countries industrial labor has been swallowed up by the service sector, and workers reject the political Left that would seem their most likely ally. Increasingly, Marxist criticism has acknowledged that the audience of literature may be active rather than passive, just as the text and source may be more than straightforward instructions for toeing a given political line. Marxist criticism has been especially successful with the novel, since that genre more than drama or short fiction is capable of representing numerous people from different classes as they develop over a significant amount of time.

Feminist Criticism

Like Marxist criticism and the schools discussed below, feminist criticism derives from a critique of a history of oppression, in this case the history of women's inequality. Feminist criticism has no single founder like Freud or Marx; it has been practiced to some extent since the 1790s, when praise of women's cultural achievements went hand in hand with arguments that women were rational beings deserving equal rights and education. Contemporary feminist criticism emerged from a "second wave" of feminist activism, in the 1960s and 1970s, associated with the civil rights and antiwar movements. One of the first disciplines in which women's activism took root was literary criticism, but feminist theory and women's studies quickly became recognized methods across the disciplines.

Feminist literary studies began by denouncing the misrepresentation of women in literature and affirming women's writings, before quickly adopting the insights of poststructuralist theory; yet the early strategies continue to have their use. At first, feminist criticism in the 1970s, like early Marxist criticism, regarded literature as a reflection of patriarchal society's sexist base; the demeaning images of women in literature were symptoms of a system that had to be overthrown. Feminist literary studies soon began, however, to claim the *equal* worth if distinctive themes of writings by women and men. Critics such as Elaine Showalter (b. 1941), Sandra M. Gilbert (b. 1936), and Susan Gubar (b. 1944) featured the canonical works by women, relying on close reading with some aid from historical and psychoanalytic methods. Yet by the 1980s it was widely recognized that a New Critical method would leave most of the male-dominated canon intact and most women writers still in obscurity, because many women had written in different genres and styles, on different themes, and for different audiences than had male writers.

To affirm the *difference* of female literary traditions, some feminist studies claimed women's innate or universal affinity for fluidity and cycle rather than solidity and linear progress. Others concentrated on the role of the mother in human psychological development. According to this argument, girls, not having to adopt a gender role different from that of their first object of desire, the mother, grow up with less rigid boundaries of self and a relational rather than judgmental ethic. The dangers of these intriguing generalizations soon became apparent. If the reasons for women's differences from men were biologically based or were due to universal archetypes, there was no solution to women's oppression, which many cultures worldwide had justified in terms of biological reproduction or archetypes of nature.

At this point in the debate, feminist literary studies intersected with poststructuralist linguistic theory in *questioning the terms and standards* of comparison. French feminist theory, articulated most prominently by Hélène Cixous (b. 1935) and Luce Irigaray (b. 1932), deconstructed the supposed archetypes of gender written into the founding discourses of Western culture. We have seen that deconstruction helps expose the power imbalance in every dualism. Thus man is to woman as culture is to nature or mind is to body, and in each case the second term is held to be inferior or Other. The language and hence the worldview and social formations of our culture, not nature or eternal archetypes, constructed woman as Other. This insight was helpful in avoiding essentialism or biological determinism.

Having reached a theoretical criticism of the terms on which women might claim equality or difference from men in the field of literature, feminist studies also confronted other issues in the 1980s. Deconstructionist readings of gender difference in texts by men as well as women could lose sight of the real world, in which women are paid less and are more likely to be victims of sexual violence. Some feminist critics with this in mind pursued links with Marxist or African American studies; gender roles, like those of class and race, were interdependent systems for registering the material consequences of people's differences. It no longer seemed so easy to say what the term "women" referred to, when the interests of different kinds of women had been opposed to each other. African American women asked if feminism was really their cause, when white women had so long enjoyed power over both men and women of their race. In a classic Marxist view, women allied with men of their class rather than with women of other classes. It became more difficult to make universal claims about women's literature, as the horizon of the college-educated North American feminists expanded to recognize the range of conditions of women and of literature worldwide. Feminist literary studies have continued to consider famous and obscure women writers; the way women and gender are portrayed in writings by men as well as women; feminist issues concerning the text, source, or receiver in any national literature; theoretical and historical questions about the representation of differences such as gender, race, class, and nationality, and the way these differences shape each other.

Gender Studies and Queer Theory

From the 1970s, feminists sought recognition for lesbian writers and lesbian culture, which they felt had been even less visible than male homosexual writers and gay culture. Concurrently, feminist studies abandoned the simple dualism of male/female, part of the very binary logic of patriarchy that seemed to cause the oppression of women. Thus feminists recognized a zone of inquiry, the study of gender, as distinct from historical studies of women, and increasingly they included masculinity as a subject of investigation. As gender studies turned to interpretation of the text in ideological context regardless of the sex or intention of the author, it incorporated the ideas of Michel Foucault's *History of Sexuality* (1976). Foucault helped show that there was nothing natural, universal, or timeless in the constructions of sexual difference or sexual practices. Foucault also introduced a history of the concept of homosexuality, which had once been regarded in terms of taboo acts and in the later nineteenth century became defined as a disease associated with a personality type. Literary scholars began to study the history of sexuality as a key to the shifts in modern culture that had also shaped literature.

By the 1980s gender had come to be widely regarded as a discourse that imposed binary social norms on human beings' diversity. Theorists such as Donna Haraway (b. 1944) and Judith Butler (b. 1956) insisted further that sex and sexuality have no natural basis; even the anatomical differences are representations from the moment the newborn is put in a pink or blue blanket. Moreover, these theorists claimed that gender and sexuality are *performative* and malleable positions, enacted in many more than two varieties. From cross-dressing to surgical sex changes, the alternatives chosen by real people have influenced critical theory and generated both writings and literary criticism about those writings. Perhaps biographical and feminist studies face new challenges when identity seems subject to radical change and it is less easy to determine the sex of an author.

Gay and lesbian literary studies have included practices that parallel feminist criticism. At times critics identify oppressive or positive representations of homosexuality in works by men or women, gay, lesbian, or straight. At other times critics seek to establish the equivalent stature of a work by a gay or lesbian writer or, because these identities tended to be hidden in the past, to reveal that a writer *was* gay or lesbian. Again stages of *equality* and *difference* have yielded to a *questioning of the terms of difference,* in this case what has been called queer theory (the stages have not superseded each other). The field of queer theory hopes to leave everyone guessing rather than to identify gay or lesbian writers, characters, or themes. One of its founding texts, *Between Men* (1985), by Eve Kosofsky Sedgwick (b. 1950), drew on structuralist insight into desire as well as anthropological models of kinship to show that, in canonical works of English literature, male characters bond together through their rivalry for and exchange of a woman. Queer theory, because it rejects the idea of a fixed identity or innate or essential gender, likes to discover resistance to heterosexuality in unexpected places. Queer theorists value gay writers such as Oscar Wilde, but they also find queer implications regardless of the author's acknowledged identity. This approach emphasizes not the surface signals of the text but the subtler meanings an audience or receiver might detect. It encompasses elaborate close reading of varieties of work; characteristically, a leading queer theorist, D. A. Miller (b. 1948), has written in loving detail about Jane Austen and about Broadway musicals.

African American and Ethnic Literary Studies

Critics sought to define an African American literary tradition as early as the turn of the twentieth century. A period of literary success in the 1920s, known as the Harlem Renaissance, produced some of the first classic essays on writings by African Americans. Criticism and histories of African American literature tended to ignore and dismiss women writers, while feminist literary histories, guided by Virginia Woolf's classic *A Room of One's Own* (1929), neglected women writers of color. Only after feminist critics began to succeed in the academy and African American studies programs were established did the whiteness of feminist studies and masculinity of African American studies became glaring; both fields have for some time corrected this narrowness of vision. The study of African American literature followed the general pattern that we have noted, first striving to claim equality, on established aesthetic grounds, of works such as Ralph Ellison's magnificent *Invisible Man* (1952). Then in the 1960s the Black Arts or Black Aesthetic emerged. Once launched in the academy, however, African American studies has been devoted less to celebrating an essential racial difference than to tracing the historical construction of a racial Other and a subordinated literature. The field sought to recover genres in which African Americans have written, such as slave narratives, and traced common elements in fiction or poetry to the conditions of slavery and segregation. By the 1980s feminist and poststructuralist theory had an impact in the work of some African American critics such as Henry Louis Gates Jr. (b. 1950), Houston A. Baker Jr. (b. 1943), Hazel V. Carby (b. 1948), and Deborah E. McDowell (b. 1951), while others objected that the doubts raised by "theory" stood in the way of political commitment. African Americans' cultural contributions to America have gained much more recognition than before. New histories of American culture have been written with the view that racism is not an aberration but inherent to the guiding narratives of national progress. Many critics now regard race as a discourse with only slight basis in genetics but with weighty investments in ideology. This poststructuralist position coexists with scholarship that takes into account the race of the author or reader or that focuses on African American characters or themes.

In recent years a series of fields has arisen in recognition of the literatures of other American ethnic groups, large and small: Asian Americans, Native Americans, and Chicanos. Increasingly, such studies avoid romanticizing an original, pure culture or assuming that these literatures by their very nature undermine the values and power of the dominant culture. Instead, critics emphasize the *hybridity* of all cultures in a global economy. The contact and intermixture of cultures across geographical borders and languages (translations, "creole" speech made up of native and acquired languages, dialects) may be read as enriching themes for literature and art, although they are caused by economic exploitation. In method and in aim these fields have much in common with African American studies, though each cultural and historical context is very different. Each field deserves the separate study that we cannot offer here.

Not so very long ago, critics might have been charged with a fundamental misunderstanding of the nature of literature if they pursued matters considered the business of sociologists, matters—such as class, race, and gender—that seemed extrinsic to the text. The rise of the above-noted fields has made it standard practice that a critic will address questions about class, race, and gender to place a text, its source, and its reception in historical and ideological context. One brief example might illustrate the way Marxist, feminist, queer, and African American criticism can contribute to a literary reading.

Tennessee Williams's *A Streetcar Named Desire* was first produced in 1947 and won the Pulitzer Prize in 1948. Part of its acclaim was likely due to its fashionable blend of naturalism and symbolism: The action takes place in a shabby tenement on an otherworldly street, Elysian Fields—in an "atmosphere of decay" laced with "lyricism," as Williams's stage directions put it. After the Depression and World War II, American audiences welcomed a turn away from world politics into the psychological core of human sexuality. This turn to ostensibly individual conflict was a kind of alibi for at least two sets of issues that Williams and the middle-class theatergoers in New York and elsewhere sought to avoid. First, the racial questions that relate to questions of gender and class: What is the play's attitude to race, and what is Williams's attitude? Biography seems relevant, though not the last word on what the play means. Williams's family had included slave-holding cotton growers, and he chose to spend much of his adult life in the South, which he saw as representing a beautiful but dying way of life. He was deeply attached to women in his family who might be models for the brilliant, fragile, cultivated Southern white woman, Blanche DuBois. Blanche ("white" in French), representative of a genteel, feminine past that has gambled, prostituted, dissipated itself, speaks some of the most eloquent lines in the play when she mourns the faded Delta plantation society. Neither the playwright nor his audience wished to deal with segregation in the South, a region that since the Civil War had stagnated as a kind of agricultural working class in relation to the dominant North—which had its racism, too.

The play scarcely notices race. The main characters are white. The cast includes a "Negro Woman" as servant, and a blind Mexican woman who offers artificial flowers to remember the dead, but these figures seem either stage business or symbolism. Instead, racial difference is transposed as ethnic and class difference, in the story of a working-class Pole intruding into a family clinging to French gentility. Stella warns Blanche that she lives among "heterogeneous types" and that Stanley is "a different species." The play thus transfigures contemporary anxieties about miscegenation, as the virile (black) man dominates the ideal white woman and rapes the spirit of the plantation South. A former army man who works in a factory, Stanley represents as well the defeat of the old, agricultural economy by industrialization.

The second set of issues that neither the playwright nor his audience confronts directly is the disturbance of sexual and gender roles that would in later decades lead to movements for women's and gay rights. It was well known in New Orleans at least that Williams was gay. In the 1940s he lived with his lover, Pancho Rodriguez y Gonzales, in the French Quarter. Like many homosexual writers in different eras, Williams recasts homosexual desire in heterosexual costume. Blanche, performing femininity with a kind of camp excess, might be a fading queen pursuing and failing to capture younger men. Stanley, hypermasculine, might caricature the object of desire of both men and women as well as the anti-intellectual, brute force in postwar America. His conquest of women (he had "the power and pride of a richly feathered male bird among hens") appears to be biologically determined. By the same token it seems natural that Stanley and his buddies go out to work and their wives become homemakers in the way now seen as typical of the 1950s. In this world, artists, homosexuals, or unmarried working women like Blanche would be both vulnerable and threatening. Blanche after all has secret pleasures—drinking and sex—that Stanley indulges in openly. Blanche is the one who is taken into custody by the medical establishment, which in this period diagnosed homosexuality as a form of insanity.

New Historicism

Three interrelated schools of historical and ideological criticism have been important innovations in the past two decades. These are part of the swing of the pendulum away from formal analysis of the text and toward historical analysis of context. New historicism has less obvious political commitments than Marxism, feminism, or queer theory, but it shares their interest in the power of discourse to shape ideology. Old historicism, in the 1850s–1950s, confidently told a story of civilization's progress from the point of view of a Western nation; a historicist critic would offer a close reading of the plays of Shakespeare and then locate them within the prevailing Elizabethan "worldview." "New Historicism," labeled in 1982 by Stephen Greenblatt (b. 1943), rejected the technique of plugging samples of a culture into a history of ideas. Influenced by poststructuralist anthropology, New Historicism tried to take a multilayered impression or "thick description" of a culture at one moment in time, including popular as well as elite forms of representation. As a method, New Historicism belongs with those that deny the unity of the text, defy the authority of the source, and license the receiver—much like deconstructionism. Accordingly, New Historicism doubts the accessibility of the past; all we have is discourse. One model for New Historicism was the historiography of Michel Foucault, who as we have said insisted on the power of discourses, that is, not only writing but all structuring myths or ideologies that underlie social relations. The New Historicist, like Foucault, is interested in the transition from the external powers of the state and church in the feudal order to modern forms of power. The rule of the modern state and middle-class ideology is enforced insidiously by systems of surveillance and by each individual's internalization of discipline (not unlike Freud's idea of the superego).

No longer so "new," the New Historicists have had a lasting influence on a more narrative and concrete style of criticism even among those who espouse poststructuralist and Marxist theories. A New Historicist article begins with an anecdote, often a description of a public spectacle, and teases out the many contributing causes that brought disparate social elements together in that way. It usually applies techniques of close reading to forms that would not traditionally have received such attention. Although it often concentrates on events several hundred years ago, in some ways it defies historicity, flouting the idea that a complete objective impression of the entire context could ever be achieved.

Cultural Studies

Popular culture often gets major attention in the work of New Historicists. Yet today most studies of popular culture would acknowledge their debt instead to cultural studies, as filtered through the now-defunct Center for Contemporary Cultural Studies, founded in 1964 by Stuart Hall (b. 1932) and others at the University of Birmingham in England. Method, style, and subject matter may be similar in New Historicism and cultural studies: Both attend to historical context, theoretical method, political commitment, and textual analysis. But whereas the American movement shares Foucault's paranoid view of state domination through discourse, the British school, influenced by Raymond Williams and his concept of "structures of feeling," emphasizes the possibility that ordinary people, the receivers of cultural forms, may resist dominant ideology. The documents examined in a cultural-studies essay may be recent, such as artifacts of tourism at Shakespeare's birthplace rather than sixteenth-century maps. Cultural studies today influences history, sociology, communications and media, and literature departments; its studies may focus on television, film, romance novels, and advertising, or on museums and the art market, sports and stadiums, New Age religious groups, or other forms and practices.

The questions raised by cultural studies would encourage a critic to place a poem like Marge Piercy's "Barbie Doll" in the context of the history of that toy, a doll whose slender, impossibly long legs, tiptoe feet (not unlike the bound feet of Chinese women of an earlier era), small nose, and torpedo breasts epitomized a 1950s ideal for the female body. A critic influenced by cultural studies might align the poem with other works published around 1973 that express feminist protest concerning cosmetics, body image, consumption, and the objectification of women, while she or he would draw on research into the founding and marketing of Mattel toys. The poem reverses the Sleeping Beauty story: This heroine puts herself into the coffin rather than waking up. The poem omits any hero—Ken?— who would rescue her. "Barbie Doll" protests the pressure a girl feels to fit into a heterosexual plot of romance and marriage; no one will buy her if she is not the right toy or accessory.

Indeed, accessories such as "GE stoves and irons" (line 3) taught girls to plan their lives as domestic consumers, and Barbie's lifestyle is decidedly middle-class and suburban (everyone has a house, car, pool, and lots of handbags). The whiteness of the typical "girlchild" (line 1) goes without saying. Although Mattel produced Barbie's African American friend, Christie, in 1968, Piercy's title makes the reader imagine Barbie, not Christie. In 1997 Mattel issued Share a Smile Becky, a friend in a wheelchair, as though in answer to the humiliation of the girl in Piercy's poem, who feels so deformed, in spite of her "strong arms and back, / abundant sexual drive and manual dexterity" (lines 8–9), that she finally cripples herself. The icon, in short, responds to changing ideology. Perhaps responding to generations of objections like Piercy's, Barbies over the years have been given feminist career goals, yet women's lives are still plotted according to physical image.

In this manner a popular product might be "read" alongside a literary work. The approach would be influenced by Marxist, feminist, gender, and racial studies, but it would not be driven by a desire to destroy Barbie as sinister, misogynist propaganda. Piercy's kind of protest against indoctrination has gone out of style. Girls have found ways to respond to such messages and divert them into stories of empowerment. Such at least is the outlook of cultural studies, which usually affirms popular culture. A researcher could gather data on Barbie sales and could interview girls or videotape their play, to establish the actual effects of the dolls. Whereas traditional anthropology examined non-European or preindustrial cultures, cultural studies may direct its "field work," or ethnographic research, inward, at home. Nevertheless, many contributions to cultural studies rely on methods of textual close reading or Marxist and Freudian literary criticism developed in the mid-twentieth century.

Postcolonial Criticism and Studies of World Literature

In the middle of the twentieth century, the remaining colonies of the European nations struggled toward independence. French-speaking Frantz Fanon (1925–61) of Martinique was one of the most compelling voices for the point of view of the colonized or exploited countries, which like the feminine Other had been objectified and denied the right to look and talk back. Edward Said (1935–2003), in *Orientalism* (1978), brought a poststructuralist analysis to bear on the history of colonization, illustrating the ways that Western culture feminized and objectified the East. Postcolonial literary studies developed into a distinct field in the 1990s in light of globalization and the replacement of direct colonial power with international corporations. In general this field cannot share the optimism of some cultural studies, given the histories of slavery and economic exploitation of colonies and the violence committed in the name of civilization's progress. Studies by Gayatri Chakravorty Spivak (b. 1942) and Homi K. Bhabha (b. 1949) have further mingled Marxist, feminist, and poststructuralist theory to reread both canonical Western works and the writings of people from beyond centers of dominant culture. Colonial or postcolonial literatures may include works set or published in countries during colonial rule or after independence, or they may feature texts produced in the context of international cultural exchange, such as a novel in English by a woman of Chinese descent writing in Malaysia.

Like feminist studies and studies of African American or other literatures, the field is inspired by recovery of neglected works, redress of a systematic denial of rights and recognition, and increasing realization that the dualisms of opposing groups reveal interdependence. In this field the stage of difference came early, with the celebrations of African heritage known as *Négritude*, but the danger of that essentialist claim was soon apparent: The Dark Continent or wild island might be romanticized and idealized as a source of innate qualities of vitality long repressed in Enlightened Europe. Currently, most critics accept that the context for literature in all countries is hybrid, with immigration and educational intermixing. Close readings of texts are always linked to the author's biography and literary influences and placed within the context of contemporary international politics as well as colonial history. Many fiction writers, from Salman Rushdie to Jhumpa Lahiri, make the theme of cultural mixture or hybridity part of their work, whether in a pastiche of Charles Dickens or a story of an Indian family growing up in New Jersey and returning as tourists to the supposed "native" land. Poststructuralist theories of trauma, and theories of the interrelation of narrative and memory, provide explanatory frames for interpreting writings from Afghanistan to Zambia.

Studies of postcolonial culture retain a clear political mission that feminist and Marxist criticism have found difficult to sustain. Perhaps this is because the scale of the power relations is so vast, between nations rather than the sexes or classes within those nations. Imperialism can be called an absolute evil, and the destruction of local cultures a crime against humanity. Today some of the most exciting literature in English emerges from countries once under the British Empire, and all the techniques of criticism will be brought to bear on it. If history is any guide, in later decades some critical school will attempt to read the diverse literatures of the early twenty-first century in pure isolation from authorship and national origin, as self-enclosed form. The themes of hybridity, indeterminacy, trauma, and memory will be praised as universal. It is even possible that readers' continuing desire to revere authors as creative geniuses in control of their meanings will regain respectability among specialists. The elements of the literary exchange—text, source, and receiver—are always there to provoke questions that generate criticism, which in turn produces articulations of the methods of that criticism. It is an ongoing discussion well worth participating in.

BIBLIOGRAPHY

For good introductions to the issues discussed here, see the following books, from which we have drawn in our discussion and definitions. Some of these provide bibliographies of the works of critics and schools mentioned above.

Alter, Robert. *The Pleasure of Reading in an Ideological Age.* New York: Norton, 1996. Rpt. of *The Pleasures of Reading: Thinking about Literature in an Ideological Age.* 1989. Print.

Barnet, Sylvan, and William E. Cain. *A Short Guide to Writing about Literature.* 10th ed. New York: Longman, 2005. Print.

Barry, Peter. *Beginning Theory: An Introduction to Literary and Cultural Theory.* 2nd ed. Manchester: Manchester UP, 2002. Print.

Bressler, Charles E. *Literary Criticism: An Introduction to Theory and Practice.* 3rd ed. Upper Saddle River: Prentice, 2003. Print.

Culler, Jonathan. *Literary Theory: A Very Short Introduction.* Oxford: Oxford UP, 1997. Print.

Davis, Robert Con, and Ronald Schleifer. *Contemporary Literary Criticism: Literary and Cultural Studies.* 4th ed. New York: Addison, 1999. Print.

During, Simon. *Cultural Studies: A Critical Introduction.* New York: Routledge, 2005. Print.

———. *The Cultural Studies Reader.* New York: Routledge, 1999. Print.

Eagleton, Mary, ed. *Feminist Literary Theory: A Reader.* 2nd ed. Malden: Blackwell, 1996. Print.

Eagleton, Terry. *Literary Theory: An Introduction.* 2nd rev. ed. Minneapolis: U of Minnesota P, 1996. Print.

Groden, Michael, and Martin Kreiswirth. *The Johns Hopkins Guide to Literary Theory and Criticism.* Baltimore: Johns Hopkins UP, 1994. Print.

Hawthorn, Jeremy. *A Glossary of Contemporary Literary Theory.* 3rd ed. London: Arnold, 1998. Print.

Leitch, Vincent B. *American Literary Criticism from the Thirties to the Eighties.* New York: Columbia UP, 1989. Print.

——, et al. *The Norton Anthology of Theory and Criticism.* New York: Norton, 2001. Print.

Lentricchia, Frank. *After the New Criticism.* Chicago: U of Chicago P, 1981. Print.

Macksey, Richard, and Eugenio Donato, eds. *The Structuralist Controversy: The Languages of Criticism and the Sciences of Man.* 1972. Ann Arbor: Books on Demand, n.d. Print.

Moi, Toril. *Sexual-Textual Politics.* New York: Routledge, 1985. Print.

Murfin, Ross, and Supryia M. Ray. *The Bedford Glossary of Critical and Literary Terms.* Boston: Bedford, 1997. Print.

Piaget, Jean. *Structuralism.* Trans. and ed. Chaninah Maschler. New York: Basic, 1970. Print.

Selden, Raman, and Peter Widdowson. *A Reader's Guide to Contemporary Literary Theory.* 3rd ed. Lexington: U of Kentucky P, 1993. Print.

Todorov, Tzvetan. *Mikhail Bakhtin: The Dialogic Principle.* Trans. Wlad Godzich. Minneapolis: U of Minnesota P, 1984. Print.

Turco, Lewis. *The Book of Literary Terms.* Hanover: UP of New England, 1999. Print.

Veeser, Harold, ed. *The New Historicism.* New York: Routledge, 1989. Print.

——. *The New Historicism Reader.* New York: Routledge, 1994. Print.

Warhol, Robyn R., and Diane Price Herndl. *Feminisms.* 2nd ed. New Brunswick: Rutgers UP, 1997. Print.

Wolfreys, Julian. *Literary Theories: A Reader and Guide.* Edinburgh: Edinburgh UP, 1999. Print.

Glossary

Boldface words within definitions are themselves defined in the glossary.

action any event or series of events depicted in a literary work; an event may be verbal as well as physical, so that saying something or telling a story within the story may be an event. *See also* climax, complication, falling action, inciting incident, *and* rising action.

alexandrine a line of verse in **iambic hexameter**, often with a **caesura** after the third iambic foot.

allegory a literary work, whether in verse or prose, in which **characters**, **action**, and even aspects of **setting** signify (or serve as **symbols** for) a second, correlated order of concepts, persons, and actions. One of the most famous English-language allegories is John Bunyan's *Pilgrim's Progress*, in which a character named Christian has to make his way through obstacles such as the Slough of Despond to get to the Celestial City.

alliteration the repetition of usually initial consonant sounds through a sequence of words—for example, "While I nodded, nearly napping" in Edgar Allan Poe's "The Raven."

allusion a brief, often implicit and indirect reference within a literary text to something outside the text, whether another text (e.g., the Bible, a **myth**, another literary work, a painting, or a piece of music) or any imaginary or historical person, place, or thing. Many of the footnotes in this book explain allusions found in literary selections.

amphitheater a theater consisting of a stage area surrounded by a semicircle of tiered seats.

anapestic referring to a metrical form in which each **foot** consists of two unstressed syllables followed by a stressed one—for example, "There are mán- | y who sáy | that a dóg | has his dáy" (Dylan Thomas, "The Song of the Mischievous Dog"). A single foot of this type is called an *anapest*.

antagonist a **character** or a nonhuman force that opposes or is in **conflict** with the **protagonist**.

antihero a **protagonist** who is in one way or another the very opposite of a traditional **hero**. Instead of being courageous and determined, for instance, an antihero might be timid, hypersensitive, and indecisive to the point of paralysis. Antiheroes are especially common in modern literary works; examples might include the **speaker** of T. S. Eliot's "The Love Song of J. Alfred Prufrock" or the **protagonist** of Franz Kafka's *The Metamorphosis*.

archetype a **character**, ritual, **symbol**, or **plot** pattern that recurs in the **myth** and literature of many cultures; examples include the scapegoat or trickster (character type), the rite of passage (ritual), and the quest or descent into the underworld (plot pattern). The term and our contemporary understanding of it derive from the work of psychologist Carl Jung (1875–1961), who argued that archetypes emerge from—and give us a clue to the workings of—the "collective unconscious," a reservoir of memories and impulses that all humans share but aren't consciously aware of.

arena stage a stage design in which the audience is seated all the way around the acting area; actors make their entrances and exits through the auditorium.

assonance the repetition of vowel sounds in a sequence of words with different endings—for example, "The death of the poet was kept from his poems" in W. H. Auden's "In Memory of W. B. Yeats."

aubade a poem in which the coming of dawn is either celebrated, as in Billy Collins's "Morning," or denounced as a nuisance, as in John Donne's "The Sun Rising."

auditor an imaginary listener within a literary work, as opposed to the reader or audience outside the work.

author the *actual* or *real author* of a work is the historical person who actually wrote it and the focus of biographical criticism, which interprets a work by drawing on facts about the author's life and career. The *implied author*, or authorial **persona**, is the vision of the author's personality and outlook implied by the work as a whole. Thus when we make a claim about the author that relies solely on evidence from the work rather than from other sources, our subject

A1

is the implied author; for example, "In *Dubliners*, James Joyce heavily criticizes the Catholic church."

author time *see* time.

autobiography *see* biography.

ballad a verse narrative that is, or originally was, meant to be sung. Characterized by repetition and often by a refrain (a recurrent phrase or series of phrases), ballads were originally a folk creation, transmitted orally from person to person and age to age. An example is "Sir Patrick Spens."

ballad stanza a common stanza form, consisting of a quatrain that alternates four-foot and three-foot lines; lines 1 and 3 are unrhymed iambic tetrameter (four feet), and lines 2 and 4 are rhymed iambic trimeter (three feet), as in "Sir Patrick Spens."

bildungsroman literally, "education novel" (German), a novel that depicts the intellectual, emotional, and moral development of its protagonist from childhood into adulthood; also sometimes called an *apprenticeship novel*. This type of novel tends to envision character as the product of environment, experience, nurture, and education (in the widest sense) rather than of nature, fate, and so on. Charlotte Brontë's *Jane Eyre* is a famous example.

biography a work of nonfiction that recounts the life of a real person. If the person depicted in a biography is also its author, then we instead use the term *autobiography*. An autobiography that focuses only on a specific aspect of, or episode in, its author's life is a *memoir*. (For examples of biographical criticism, see chapter 8.)

blank verse the metrical verse form most like everyday human speech; blank verse consists of unrhymed lines in iambic pentameter. Many of Shakespeare's plays are in blank verse, as is William Wordsworth's "Lines Composed a Few Miles above Tintern Abbey."

caesura a short pause within a line of poetry; often but not always signaled by punctuation. Note the two caesuras in this line from Poe's "The Raven": "Once upon a midnight dreary, while I pondered, weak and weary."

canon the range of works that a consensus of scholars, teachers, and readers of a particular time and culture consider "great" or "major."

carpe diem literally, "seize the day" in Latin, a common theme of literary works that emphasize the brevity of life and the need to make the most of the present. Andrew

Marvell's poem "To His Coy Mistress" is a well-known example.

central consciousness a character whose inner thoughts, perceptions, and feelings are revealed by a *third-person limited* narrator who does not reveal the thoughts, perceptions, or feelings of other characters.

character an imaginary personage who acts, appears, or is referred to in a literary work. *Major* or *main characters* are those that receive most attention, *minor characters* least. *Flat characters* are relatively simple, have a few dominant traits, and tend to be predictable. Conversely, *round characters* are complex and multifaceted and act in a way that readers might not expect but accept as possible. *Static characters* do not change; *dynamic characters* do. *Stock characters* represent familiar types that recur frequently in literary works, especially of a particular genre (e.g., the "mad scientist" of horror fiction and film or the fool in Renaissance, especially Shakespearean, drama).

characterization the presentation of a fictional personage. A term like "a good character" can, then, be ambiguous—it may mean that the personage is virtuous or that he or she is well presented regardless of his or her characteristics or moral qualities. In fiction, *direct characterization* occurs when a narrator explicitly tells us what a character is like. *Indirect characterization* occurs when a character's traits are revealed implicitly, through his or her speech, behavior, thoughts, appearance, and so on.

chorus a group of actors in a drama who comment on and describe the action. In classical Greek theater, members of the chorus often wore masks and relied on song, dance, and recitation to make their commentary.

classical unities as derived from Aristotle's *Poetics*, the three principles of structure that require a play to have one plot (*unity of action*) that occurs in one place (*unity of place*) and within one day (*unity of time*); also called the *dramatic unities*. Susan Glaspell's *Trifles* and Sophocles' *Antigone* observe the classical unities.

climax the third part of plot, the point at which the action stops rising and begins falling or reversing; also called *turning point* or (following Aristotle) *peripeteia*. See also crisis.

closet drama *see* drama.

colloquial diction *see* diction.

comedy a broad category of literary, especially dramatic, works intended primarily to entertain and amuse an audience. Comedies take many different forms, but they share three basic characteristics: (1) the values that are expressed and that typically cause **conflict** are determined by the general opinion of society (as opposed to being universal and beyond the control of humankind, as in **tragedy**); (2) **characters** in comedies are often defined primarily in terms of their social identities and roles and tend to be *flat* or *stock characters* rather than highly individualized or *round* ones; (3) comedies conventionally end happily with an act of social reintegration and celebration such as marriage. William Shakespeare's *A Midsummer Night's Dream* is a famous example.

The term *high* or *verbal comedy* may refer either to a particular type of comedy or to a sort of humor found within any literary work that employs subtlety and wit and usually represents high society. Conversely, *low* or *physical comedy* is a type of either comedy or humor that involves burlesque, horseplay, and the representation of unrefined life. *See also* **farce.**

coming-of-age story *see* initation story.

complication in plot, an **action** or event that introduces a new **conflict** or intensifies the existing one, especially during the **rising action** phase of plot.

conclusion also called *resolution*, the fifth and last phase or part of **plot**, the point at which the situation that was destabilized at the beginning becomes stable once more and the **conflict** is resolved.

concrete poetry poetry in which the words on the page are arranged to look like an object; also called *shaped verse*. George Herbert's "Easter Wings," for example, is arranged to look like two pairs of wings.

conflict a struggle between opposing forces. A conflict is *external* when it pits a **character** against something or someone outside himself or herself—another character or characters or something in nature or society. A conflict is *internal* when the opposing forces are two drives, impulses, or parts of a single character.

connotation what is suggested by a word, apart from what it literally means or how it is defined in the dictionary. *See also* **denotation.**

controlling metaphor *see* metaphor.

convention in literature, a standard or traditional way of presenting or expressing something, or a traditional or characteristic feature of a particular literary **genre** or subgenre. Division into lines and **stanzas** is a convention of poetry. Conventions of the type of poem known as the **epic** include a **plot** that begins *in medias res* and frequent use of **epithets** and extended **similes.**

cosmic irony *see* irony.

couplet two consecutive lines of verse linked by **rhyme** and **meter**; the meter of a *heroic couplet* is iambic pentameter.

crisis in **plot**, the moment when the **conflict** comes to a head, often requiring the character to make a decision; sometimes the crisis is equated with the **climax** or *turning point* and sometimes it is treated as a distinct moment that precedes and prepares for the **climax.**

criticism *see* literary criticism.

cycle *see* sequence.

dactylic referring to the metrical pattern in which each **foot** consists of a stressed syllable followed by two unstressed ones—for example, "Fláshed all their/sábres bare" (Tennyson, "Charge of the Light Brigade"). A single foot of this type is called a *dactyl*.

denotation a word's direct and literal meaning, as opposed to its **connotation.**

dénouement literally, "untying" (as of a knot) in French; a **plot**-related term used in three ways: (1) as a synonym for **falling action**, (2) as a synonym for **conclusion** or resolution, and (3) as the label for a phase following the conclusion in which any loose ends are tied up.

descriptive poem/structure a poem organized as a description of someone or something.

destabilizing event *see* inciting incident.

deus ex machina literally, "god out of the machine" (Latin); any improbable, unprepared-for plot contrivance introduced late in a literary work to resolve the **conflict**. The term derives from the ancient Greek theatrical practice of using a mechanical device to lower a god or gods onto the stage to resolve the conflicts of the human characters.

dialogue (1) usually, words spoken by **characters** in a literary work, especially as opposed to words that come directly from the **narrator** in a work of fiction; (2) more rarely, a literary work that consists mainly or entirely of the speech of two or more characters; examples include Thomas Hardy's poem "The Ruined Maid" and Plato's treatise *Republic*.

diction choice of words. Diction is often described as either *informal* or *colloquial* if it resembles everyday speech, or as *formal* if it is instead lofty, impersonal, and dignified. **Tone** is determined largely through diction.

discriminated occasion a specific, discrete moment portrayed in a fictional work, often signaled by phrases such as "At 5:05 in the morning...," "It was about dusk, one evening during the supreme madness of the carnival season...," or "the day before Maggie fell down...."

discursive poem/structure a poem structured like a treatise, argument, or essay.

drama a literary genre consisting of works in which **action** is performed and all words are spoken before an audience by an actor or actors impersonating the **characters**. (Drama typically lacks the **narrators** and **narration** found in fiction.) *Closet drama*, however, is a subgenre of drama that has most of these features yet is intended to be read, either silently by a single reader or out loud in a group setting. As its name suggests, *verse drama* is drama written in verse rather than prose.

dramatic irony *see* irony.

dramatic monologue a type or subgenre of poetry in which a **speaker** addresses a silent **auditor** or auditors in a specific situation and setting that is revealed entirely through the speaker's words; this kind of poem's primary aim is the revelation of the speaker's personality, views, and values. For example, T. S. Eliot's "The Love Song of J. Alfred Prufrock" consists of a middle-aged man's words to the unidentified person who is about to accompany him to an evening social event; most of Robert Browning's best-known poems, such as "My Last Duchess," are dramatic monologues.

dramatic poem/structure a poem structured so as to present a **scene** or series of scenes, as in a work of drama, though the term *dramatic poem* is usually not applied to *verse drama*. *See also* **dramatic monologue**.

dramatic unities *see* classical unities.

dramatis personae literally, "persons of the drama" (Latin); the list of **characters** that appears either in a play's program or at the top of the first page of the written play.

dynamic character *see* character.

elegy (1) since the Renaissance, usually a formal lament on the death of a particular person, but focusing mainly on the speaker's efforts to come to terms with his or her grief; (2) more broadly, any **lyric** in sorrowful mood that takes death as its primary subject. An example is W. H. Auden's "In Memory of W. B. Yeats."

end-stopped line a line of verse that contains or concludes a complete clause and usually ends with a punctuation mark. *See also* enjambment.

English sonnet *see* sonnet.

enjambment in poetry, the technique of running over from one line to the next without stop, as in the following lines by William Wordsworth: "My heart leaps up when I behold / A rainbow in the sky." The lines themselves would be described as *enjambed*.

epic a long poem that celebrates, in a continuous narrative, the achievements of mighty **heroes** and **heroines**, usually in founding a nation or developing a culture, and uses elevated language and a grand, high style. Other epic **conventions** include a beginning **in medias res**, an invocation of the muse, a journey to the underworld, battle scenes, and a scene in which the hero arms himself for battle. Examples include *Beowulf* and Homer's *Iliad*. A *mock epic* is a form of **satire** in which epic language and conventions are used to depict **characters**, **actions**, and **settings** utterly unlike those in conventional epics, usually (though not always) with the purpose of ridiculing the social milieu or types of people portrayed in the poem. A famous example is Alexander Pope's *The Rape of the Lock*.

epigram a very short, usually witty verse with a quick turn at the end.

epigraph a quotation appearing at the beginning of a literary work or of one section of such a work; not to be confused with **epigram**.

epilogue (1) in fiction, a short section or chapter that comes after the **conclusion**, tying up loose ends and often describing what happens to the characters after the resolution of the **conflict**; (2) in drama, a short speech, often addressed directly to the audience, delivered by a **character** at the end of a play.

epiphany a sudden revelation of truth, often inspired by a seemingly simple or commonplace event. The term, originally from Christian theology, was first popularized by the Irish fiction writer James Joyce, though Joyce also used the term to describe the individual short stories collected in his book *Dubliners*.

episode a distinct **action** or series of actions within a **plot**.

epistolary novel *see* novel.

epithet a characterizing word or phrase that precedes, follows, or substitutes for the name of a person or thing, such as *slain civil rights leader* Martin Luther King Jr., or Zeus, *the god of trophies* (Sophocles, *Antigone*); not to be confused with **epitaph**.

epitaph an inscription on a tombstone or grave marker; not to be confused with **epigram**, **epigraph**, or **epithet**.

eponymous having a name used in the title of a literary work. For example, Lemuel Gulliver is the eponymous **protagonist** of Jonathan Swift's *Gulliver's Travels.*

exposition the first phase or part of **plot**, which sets the scene, introduces and identifies **characters**, and establishes the situation at the beginning of a story or play. Additional exposition is often scattered throughout the work.

extended metaphor *see* **metaphor**.

external conflict *see* **conflict**.

external narration or narrator *see* **narrator**.

fable an ancient type of short **fiction**, in verse or prose, illustrating a **moral** or satirizing human beings. The **characters** in a fable are often animals that talk and act like human beings. The fable is sometimes treated as a specific type of folktale and sometimes as a fictional subgenre in its own right. An example is Aesop's "The Two Crabs."

fairy tale *see* **tale**.

falling action the fourth of the five phases or parts of **plot**, in which the **conflict** or conflicts move toward resolution.

fantasy a genre of literary work featuring strange settings and characters and often involving magic or the supernatural; though closely related to horror and science fiction, fantasy is typically less concerned with the macabre or with science and technology. J. R. R. Tolkien's *The Hobbit* is a well-known example.

farce a literary work, especially drama, characterized by broad humor, wild antics, and often slapstick, pratfalls, or other physical humor. *See also* **comedy**.

fiction any **narrative**, especially in prose, about invented or imagined **characters** and **action**. Today, we tend to divide fiction into three major subgenres based on length—the **short story**, **novella**, and **novel**. Older, originally oral forms of short fiction include the **fable**, **legend**, **parable**, and **tale**. Fictional works may also be categorized not by their length but by their handling of particular elements such as **plot** and **character**. Detective and science fiction, for example, are subgenres that include both novels and novellas such as Frank Herbert's *Dune* and short stories such as Edgar Allan Poe's "The Murders at the Rue Morgue" or Isaac Asimov's "I, Robot." *See also* **gothic fiction**, **historical fiction**, **nonfiction**, and **romance**.

figurative language language that uses figures of speech.

figure of speech any word or phrase that creates a "figure" in the mind of the reader by effecting an obvious change in the usual meaning or order of words, by comparing or identifying one thing with another; also called *tropes*. Metaphor, simile, metonymy, overstatement, oxymoron, and understatement are common figures of speech.

first-person narrator *see* **narrator**.

flashback a **plot**-structuring device whereby a scene from the fictional past is inserted into the fictional present or is dramatized out of order.

flashforward a plot-structuring device whereby a scene from the fictional future is inserted into the fictional present or is dramatized out of order.

flat character *see* **character**.

focus the visual component of **point of view**, the point from which people, events, and other details in a story are viewed; also called *focalization*. *See also* **voice**.

foil a **character** that serves as a contrast to another.

folktale *see* **tale**.

foot the basic unit of poetic **meter**, consisting of any of various fixed patterns of one to three stressed and unstressed syllables. A foot may contain more than one word or just one syllable of a multisyllabic word. In **scansion**, breaks between feet are usually indicated with a vertical line or slash mark, as in the following example (which contains five feet): "One com- | mon note | on ei- | ther lyre | did strike" (Dryden, "To the Memory of Mr. Oldham"). *For specific examples of metrical feet, see* **anapestic**, **dactylic**, **iambic**, **spondee**, and **trochaic**.

foreshadowing a hint or clue about what will happen at a later moment in the **plot**.

formal diction *see* **diction**.

frame narrative *see* **narrative**.

free verse poetry characterized by varying line lengths, lack of traditional **meter**, and nonrhyming lines.

Freytag's pyramid a diagram of **plot** structure first created by the German novelist and critic Gustav Freytag (1816–1895).

general setting *see* **setting**.

genre a type or category of works sharing particular formal or textual features and conventions; especially used to refer to the largest categories for classifying literature—**fiction**, **poetry**, **drama**, and **nonfiction**. A smaller division within a genre is usually known as a *subgenre*, such as **gothic fiction** or **epic poetry**.

gothic fiction a subgenre of **fiction** conventionally featuring plots that involve secrets, mystery, and the supernatural (or the seemingly supernatural) and large, gloomy, and usually antiquated (especially medieval) houses as settings. Examples include Horace Walpole's *The Castle of Otranto* and Edgar Allan Poe's "The Fall of the House of Usher."

haiku a poetic form, Japanese in origin, that consists of seventeen syllables arranged in three unrhymed lines of five, seven, and five syllables, respectively.

hero/heroine a character in a literary work, especially the leading male/female character, who is especially virtuous, usually larger than life, sometimes almost godlike. *See also* **antihero**, **protagonist**, and **villain**.

heroic couplet *see* **couplet**.

hexameter a line of poetry with six **feet**: "She comes, | she comes | again, | like ring | dove frayed | and fled" (Keats, *The Eve of St. Agnes*). *See* **alexandrine**.

high (verbal) comedy *see* **comedy**.

historical fiction a subgenre of fiction, of whatever length, in which the temporal setting, or plot time, is significantly earlier than the time in which the work was written (typically, a period before the birth of the author). Conventionally, such works describe the atmosphere and mores of the setting in vivid detail and explore the influence of historical factors on the **characters** and **action**; though focusing mainly on invented or imaginary characters and events, historical fiction sometimes includes some characters and action based on actual historical personages and events. The *historical novel* is a type of historical fiction of which nineteenth-century Scottish writer Walter Scott pioneered in works such as *Rob Roy* and *Ivanhoe*.

hyperbole *see* **overstatement**. (*See also* **understatement**.)

iambic referring to a metrical form in which each **foot** consists of an unstressed syllable followed by a stressed one; this type of foot is an *iamb*. The most common poetic meter in English is *iambic pentameter*—a metrical form in which most lines consist of five iambs: "One cóm- | mon nóte | on éi- | ther lýre | did stríke" (Dryden, "To the Memory of Mr. Oldham").

image/imagery broadly defined, imagery is any sensory detail or evocation in a work; more narrowly, the use of **figurative language** to evoke a feeling, to call to mind an idea, or to describe an object. Imagery may be described as *auditory*, *tactile*, *visual*, or *olfactory* depending on which sense it primarily appeals to—hearing, touch, vision, or smell. An *image* is a particular instance of imagery.

imitative poem/structure a poem structured so as to mirror as exactly as possible the structure of something that already exists as an object and can be seen.

implied author *see* **author**.

inciting incident an action that sets a plot in motion by creating **conflict**; also called *destabilizing event*.

informal diction *see* **diction**.

initiation story a kind of **short story** in which a **character**—often a child or young person—first learns a significant, usually life-changing truth about the universe, society, people, or himself or herself; also called a *coming-of-age story*. James Joyce's "Araby" is a notable example.

in medias res "in the midst of things" (Latin); refers to opening a **plot** in the middle of the action, and then filling in past details by means of **exposition** or **flashback**.

interior monologue *see* **monologue**.

internal conflict *see* **conflict**.

internal narration or narrator *see* **narrator**.

intrusive narration or narrator *see* **narrator**.

irony a situation or statement characterized by a significant difference between what is expected or understood and what actually happens or is meant. *Verbal irony* occurs when a word or expression in context means something different from, and usually the opposite of, what it appears to mean; when the intended meaning is harshly critical or satiric, verbal irony becomes *sarcasm*. *Situational irony* occurs when a character holds a position or has an expectation that is reversed or fulfilled in an unexpected way. When there is instead a gap between what an audience knows and what a character believes or expects, we have *dramatic irony*; when this occurs in a **tragedy**, dramatic irony is sometimes called *tragic irony*. Finally, the terms *cosmic irony* and *irony of fate* are sometimes used to refer to situations in which situational irony is the result of fate, chance, the gods, or some other superhuman force or entity.

Italian sonnet *see* **sonnet**.

legend a type of **tale** conventionally set in the real world and in either the present or historical past, based on actual historical people and events, and offering an exaggerated or distorted version of the truth about those people and events. American examples might include stories featuring Davy Crockett or Johnny Appleseed or the story about George Washington chopping down the cherry tree. British examples are the legends of King Arthur or Robin Hood.

limerick a light or humorous verse form consisting of mainly **anapestic** lines of which the first, second, and fifth are of three **feet**; the third and fourth lines are of two feet; and the rhyme scheme is *aabba*.

limited narrator *see* **narrator.**

limited point of view *see* **point of view.**

literary criticism the mainly interpretive (versus evaluative) work written by readers of literary texts, especially professional ones (who are thus known as *literary critics*). It is "criticism" not because it is negative or corrective but rather because those who write criticism ask probing, analytical, "critical" questions about the works they read.

litotes a form of **understatement** in which one negates the contrary of what one means. Examples from common speech include "Not bad" (meaning "good") and "a novelist of no small repute" (meaning "a novelist with a big reputation"), and so on.

low (physical) comedy *see* **comedy.**

lyric originally, a poem meant to be sung to the accompaniment of a lyre; now, any relatively short poem in which the **speaker** expresses his or her thoughts and feelings in the first person rather than recounting a **narrative** or portraying a dramatic situation.

magic realism a type of fiction that involves the creation of a fictional world in which the kind of familiar, plausible **action** and **characters** one might find in more straightforwardly realist fiction coexist with utterly fantastic ones straight out of **myths** or dreams. This style of **realism** is associated especially with modern Latin American writers such as Gabriel García Márquez and Jorge Luis Borges. But the label is also sometimes applied to works by other contemporary writers from around the world, including Italo Calvino and Salman Rushdie.

major (main) character *see* **character.**

memoir *see* **biography.**

metafiction a subgenre of works that playfully draw attention to their status as **fiction** in order to explore the nature of fiction and the role of authors and readers. Margaret Atwood's "Happy Endings" is an example.

metaphor sometimes, a general term for almost any figure of speech involving comparison; more commonly, a particular **figure of speech** in which two unlike things are compared implicitly—that is, without the use of a signal such as the word *like* or *as*—as in "Love is a rose, but you better not pick it." *See also* **simile.**

An *extended metaphor* is a detailed and complex metaphor that stretches across a long section of a work. If such a metaphor is so extensive that it dominates or organizes an entire literary work, especially a poem, it is called a *controlling metaphor*. In Linda Pastan's "Marks," for example, the controlling metaphor involves the use of "marks" or grades to talk about the speaker's performance of her familial roles. A *mixed metaphor* occurs when two or more usually incompatible metaphors are entangled together so as to become unclear and often unintentionally humorous, as in "Her blazing words dripped all over him."

meter the more or less regular pattern of stressed and unstressed syllables in a line of poetry. This is determined by the kind of **foot** (iambic or dactylic, for example) and by the number of feet per line (e.g., five feet = **pentameter**, six feet = **hexameter**).

metonymy a figure of speech in which the name of one thing is used to refer to another thing associated with it. When we say, "The White House has promised to veto the bill," for example, we use the White House as a metonym for the president and his administration. **Synecdoche** is a specific type of metonymy.

minor character *see* **character.**

mock epic *see* **epic.**

monologue (1) a speech of more than a few sentences, usually in a play but also in other **genres**, spoken by one person and uninterrupted by the speech of anyone else, or (2) an entire work consisting of this sort of speech. In fiction, an *interior monologue* takes place entirely within the mind of a character rather than being spoken aloud. A **soliloquy** is a particular type of monologue occurring in drama, while a **dramatic monologue** is a type of poem.

moral a rule of conduct or a maxim for living (that is, a statement about how one should live or behave) communicated in a literary work. Though **fables** often have morals such as "Don't count your chickens before they hatch," more modern literary works instead tend to have **themes**.

motif a recurrent device, formula, or situation within a literary work. For example, the sound of the breaking harp string is a motif of Anton Chekhov's play *The Cherry Orchard*.

myth (1) originally and narrowly, a **narrative** explaining how the world and humanity developed into their present form and, unlike a folktale, generally considered to be true by the people who develop it. Many, though not all, myths feature supernatural beings and have a religious significance or function within their culture of origin. Two especially common types of myth are the *creation myth*, which explains how the world, human beings, a god or gods, or good and evil came to be (e.g., the myth of Adam and Eve), and the *explanatory myth*, which explains features of the natural landscape or natural processes or events (e.g., "How the Leopard Got His Spots"); (2) more broadly and especially in its adjectival form (*mythic*), any narrative that obviously seeks to work like a myth in the first and more narrow sense, especially by portraying experiences or conveying truths that it implies are universally valid regardless of culture or time.

narration (1) broadly, the act of telling a story or recounting a **narrative**; (2) more narrowly, the portions of a narrative attributable to the **narrator** rather than words spoken by **characters** (that is, **dialogue**).

narrative a story, whether fictional or true and in prose or verse, related by a **narrator** or narrators (rather than acted out onstage, as in drama). A *frame narrative* is a narrative that recounts the telling of another narrative or story that thus "frames" the inner or framed narrative. An example is Samuel Taylor Coleridge's "The Rime of the Ancient Mariner," in which an anonymous third-person narrator recounts how an old sailor comes to tell a young wedding guest the story of his adventures at sea.

narrative poem/structure a poem that tells a story.

narrator someone who recounts a **narrative** or tells a story. Though we usually instead use the term **speaker** when referring to poetry as opposed to prose fiction, *narrative poems* include at least one speaker who functions as a narrator. *See also* **narrative**.

A narrator or narration is said to be *internal* when the narrator is a **character** within the work, telling the story to an equally fictional **auditor** or listener; internal narrators are usually first- or second-person narrators (*see below*). A narrator or narration is instead said to be *external* when the narrator is not a character.

A *first-person narrator* is an internal narrator who consistently refers to himself or herself using the first-person pronoun *I* (or, infrequently, *we*). A *second-person narrator* consistently uses the second-person pronoun *you* (a very uncommon technique). A *third-person narrator* uses third-person pronouns such as *she, he, they, it*, and so on; third-person narra-

tors are almost always external narrators. Third-person narrators are said to be *omniscient* (literally, "all-knowing") when they describe the inner thoughts and feelings of multiple characters; they are said to be *limited* when they relate the thoughts, feelings, and perceptions of only one character (the **central consciousness**). If a work encourages us to view a narrator's account of events with suspicion, the narrator (usually first-person) is called *unreliable*. An *intrusive narrator* is a third-person narrator who occasionally disrupts his or her narrative to speak directly to the reader or audience in what is sometimes called *direct address*.

narrator time *see* **time**.

nonfiction a work or **genre** of prose works that describe actual, as opposed to imaginary or fictional, **characters** and events. Subgenres of nonfiction include **biography**, **memoir**, and the **essay**. *See also* **fiction**.

novel a long work of **fiction** (approximately 40,000+ words), typically published (or at least publishable) as a stand-alone book; though most novels are written in prose, those written as poetry are called *verse novels*. A novel (as opposed to a **short story**) conventionally has a complex **plot** and, often, at least one **subplot**, as well as a fully realized **setting** and a relatively large number of **characters**. One important novelistic subgenre is the *epistolary novel*—a novel composed entirely of letters written by its characters. Another is the **bildungsroman**.

novella a work of prose **fiction** that falls somewhere in between a **short story** and a **novel** in terms of length, scope, and complexity. Novellas can be, and have been, published either as books in their own right or as parts of books that include other works. Franz Kafka's *The Metamorphosis* is an example.

octameter a line of poetry with eight **feet**: "Once u- | pon a | midnight | dreary | while I | pondered | weak and | weary."

octave eight lines of verse linked by a pattern of end rhymes, especially the first eight lines of an Italian, or Petrarchan, **sonnet**. *See also* **sestet**.

ode a lyric poem characterized by a serious topic and formal tone but without a prescribed formal pattern. Examples include Keats's odes and Shelley's "Ode to the West Wind."

oeuvre all of the works verifiably written by one author.

omniscient narrator *see* **narrator**.

omniscient point of view *see* **point of view**.

onomatopoeia a word capturing or approximating the sound of what it describes; *buzz* is a good example.

orchestra in classical Greek theater, a semicircular area used mostly for dancing by the **chorus**.

ottava rima literally, "octave (eighth) rhyme" (Italian); a verse form consisting of eight-line **stanzas** with an *abababcc* **rhyme scheme** and **iambic** meter (usually **pentameter**). W. B. Yeats's "Sailing to Byzantium" is written in ottava rima.

overplot especially in Shakespearean drama, a **subplot** that resembles the main plot but stresses the political implications of the depicted action and situation.

overstatement exaggerated language; also called *hyperbole*.

oxymoron a **figure of speech** that combines two apparently contradictory elements, as in *wise fool*.

parable a short work of **fiction** that illustrates an explicit **moral** but that, unlike a **fable**, lacks fantastic or anthropomorphic characters. Especially familiar examples are the stories attributed to Jesus in the Bible—about the prodigal son, the good Samaritan, and so on.

parody any work that imitates or spoofs another work or **genre** for comic effect by exaggerating the style and changing the content of the original; parody is a subgenre of **satire**. Examples include *Scary Movie*, which parodies horror films; *The Colbert Report*, which spoofs conservative talk shows; and Tom Stoppard's *Real Inspector Hound*, a parody of both detective fiction and drama.

particular setting *see* **setting**.

pastoral literature a work or category of works—whether fiction, poetry, drama, or nonfiction—describing and idealizing the simple life of country folk, usually shepherds who live a painless life in a world full of beauty, music, and love. An example is Christopher Marlowe's "The Passionate Shepherd to His Love."

pentameter a line of poetry with five feet: "Nuns fret | not at | their con- | vent's nar- | row room."

persona the voice or figure of the **author** who tells and structures the story and who may or may not share the values of the actual author; also called *implied author*.

personification a **figure of speech** that involves treating something nonhuman, such as an abstraction, as if it were a person by endowing it with humanlike qualities, as in "Death entered the room."

Petrarchan sonnet *see* **sonnet**.

plot the arrangement of the **action**. The five main parts or phases of plot are **exposition**, **rising action**, **climax** or **turning point**, **falling action**, and **conclusion** or **resolution**. *See also* **subplot**, **overplot**.

plot summary a brief recounting of the principal **action** of a work of fiction, drama, or narrative poetry, usually in the same order in which the action is recounted in the original work rather than in chronological order.

plot time *see* **time**.

poetry one of the three major **genres** of imaginative literature, which has its origins in music and oral performance and is characterized by controlled patterns of **rhythm** and **syntax** (often using **meter** and **rhyme**); compression and compactness and an allowance for ambiguity; a particularly concentrated emphasis on the sensual, especially visual and aural, qualities and effects of words and word order; and especially vivid, often **figurative language**.

point of view the perspective from which people, events, and other details in a work of fiction are viewed; also called **focus**, though the term *point of view* is sometimes used to include both focus and **voice**. The point of view is said to be *limited* when we see things only from one character's perspective; it is said to be *omniscient* or *unlimited* when we get the perspective of multiple characters.

prop in drama, an object used on the stage.

proscenium arch an arch over the front of a stage; the proscenium serves as a "frame" for the **action** onstage.

prose the regular form of spoken and written language, measured in sentences rather than lines, as in poetry.

protagonist the most neutral and broadly applicable term for the main **character** in a work, whether male or female, heroic or not heroic. *See also* **antagonist**, **antihero**, and **hero/heroine**.

psychological realism *see* **realism**.

quatrain a four-line unit of verse, whether an entire poem, a **stanza**, or a group of four lines linked by a pattern of rhyme (as in an English or Shakespearean **sonnet**).

reader time *see* **time**.

realism (1) generally, the practice in literature, especially fiction and drama, of attempting to describe nature and life as they are without idealization and with attention to detail, especially the everyday life of ordinary people. *See also* **verisimilitude**.

Just as notions of how life and nature differ widely across cultures and time periods, however, so do notions of what is "realistic." Thus, there are many different kinds of realism. *Psychological realism* refers, broadly, to any literary attempt to accurately represent the workings of the human mind and, more specifically, to the practice of a particular group of late-nineteenth- and early-twentieth-century writers including Joseph Conrad, Henry James, James Joyce, and Virginia Woolf, who developed the **stream of consciousness** technique of depicting the flow of thought. *See also* **magic realism.**

(2) more narrowly and especially when capitalized, a mid- to late- nineteenth-century literary and artistic movement, mainly in the U.S. and Europe, that championed realism in the first, more general sense, rejected what its proponents saw as the elitism and idealism of earlier literature and art, and emphasized **settings**, situations, **action**, and (especially middle- and working-class) characters ignored or belittled in earlier literature and art. Writers associated with the movement include Gustave Flaubert and Emile Zola (in France), George Eliot and Thomas Hardy (in Britain), and Theodore Dreiser (in the United States).

reflective (meditative) poem/structure a poem organized primarily around reflection on a subject or event and letting the mind play with it, skipping from one thought or object to another as the mind receives them.

resolution *see* **conclusion.**

rhetoric the art and scholarly study of effective communication, whether in writing or speech. Many literary terms, especially those for **figures of speech**, derive from classical and Renaissance rhetoric.

rhyme repetition or correspondence of the terminal sounds of words ("How now, brown cow?"). The most common type, *end rhyme*, occurs when the last words in two or more lines of a poem rhyme with each other. *Internal rhyme* occurs when a word *within* a line of poetry rhymes with another word in the same or adjacent lines, as in "The Dew drew quivering and chill" (Dickinson). An *eye rhyme* or *sight rhyme* involves words that don't actually rhyme but look like they do because of their similar spelling ("cough" and "bough"). *Off, half, near,* or *slant rhyme* is rhyme that is slightly "off" or only approximate, usually because words' final consonant sounds correspond, but not the vowels that proceed them ("phases"

and "houses"). When two syllables rhyme and the last is unstressed or unaccented, they create a *feminine rhyme* ("ocean" and "motion"); *masculine rhyme* involves only a single stressed or accented syllable ("cat" and "hat"). *See also* **rhyme scheme.**

rhyme scheme the pattern of *end* rhymes in a poem, often noted by small letters, such as *abab* or *abba*.

rhythm the modulation of weak and strong (or stressed and unstressed) elements in the flow of speech. In most poetry written before the twentieth century, rhythm was often expressed in **meter**; in prose and in **free verse**, rhythm is present but in a much less predictable and regular manner.

rising action the second of the five phases or parts of **plot**, in which events complicate the **situation** that existed at the beginning of a work, intensifying the initial **conflict** or introducing a new one.

romance (1) originally, a long medieval narrative in verse or prose written in one of the Romance languages (French, Spanish, Italian, etc.) and depicting the quests of knights and other chivalric heroes and the vicissitudes of courtly love; also known as *chivalric romance*; (2) later and more broadly, any literary work, especially a long work of prose fiction, characterized by a nonrealistic and idealizing use of the imagination; (3) commonly today, works of prose fiction aimed at a mass, primarily female, audience and focusing on love affairs (as in *Harlequin Romance*).

round character *see* **character.**

sarcasm *see* **irony.**

satire a literary work—whether fiction, poetry, or drama—that holds up human failings to ridicule and censure. Examples include Jonathan Swift's novel *Gulliver's Travels* and Stanley Kubrick's film *Dr. Strangelove.*

scansion the process of analyzing (and sometimes also marking) verse to determine its **meter**, line by line.

scene a section or subdivision of a play or narrative that presents continuous **action** in one specific **setting.**

second-person narrator *see* **narrator.**

sequence (1) the ordering of **action** in a fictional **plot**; (2) a closely linked series or *cycle* of individual literary works, especially short stories or poems, designed to be read or performed together, as in the **sonnet** sequences of William Shakespeare and Edna St. Vincent Millay.

sestet six lines of verse linked by a pattern of rhyme, as in the last six lines of the Italian, or Petrarchan, **sonnet.** *See also* **octave.**

sestina an elaborate verse structure written in **blank verse** that consists of six **stanzas** of six lines each followed by a three-line stanza. The final words of each line in the first stanza appear in variable order in the next five stanzas and are repeated in the middle and at the end of the three lines in the final stanza. Elizabeth Bishop's "Sestina" is an example.

set the design, decoration, and scenery of the stage during a play; not to be confused with setting.

setting the time and place of the **action** in a work of fiction, poetry, or drama. The *spatial setting* is the place or places in which action unfolds, the *temporal setting* is the time. (Temporal setting is thus the same as *plot* **time**.) It is sometimes also helpful to distinguish between *general setting*—the general time and place in which all the action unfolds—and *particular settings*—the times and places in which individual **episodes** or **scenes** take place. The film version of *Gone with the Wind*, for example, is generally set in Civil War–era Georgia, while its opening scene takes place on the porch of Tara, Scarlett O'Hara's family home, before the war begins.

Shakespearean sonnet *see* sonnet.

shaped verse *see* concrete poetry.

short story a relatively short work of prose fiction (approximately 500 to 10,000 words) that, according to Edgar Allan Poe, can be read in a single sitting of two hours or less and works to create "a single effect." Two types of short story are the **initiation story** and the *short short story*. (Also sometimes called *microfiction*, a short short story is, as its name suggests, a short story that is especially brief; examples include Linda Brewer's "20/20" and Jamaica Kincaid's "Girl.")

simile a **figure of speech** involving a direct, explicit comparison of one thing to another, usually using the words *like* or *as* to draw the connection, as in "My love is like a red, red rose." An *analogy* is an extended simile. *See also* **metaphor**.

situation the basic circumstances depicted in a literary work, especially when the story, play, or poem begins or at a specific later moment in the **action**. In John Keats's "Ode to a Nightingale," for example, the situation involves a man (the **speaker**) sitting under a tree as he listens to a nightingale's song.

situational irony *see* irony.

skene a low building in the back of the stage area in classical Greek theaters. It represented the palace or temple in front of which the **action** took place.

soliloquy a **monologue** in which the **character** in a play is alone onstage and thinking out loud, as in the famous Hamlet speech that begins "To be or not to be."

sonnet a fixed verse form consisting of fourteen lines usually in **iambic pentameter**. An *Italian sonnet* consists of eight rhyme-linked lines (an **octave**) plus six rhyme-linked lines (a **sestet**), often with either an *abbaabba cdecde* or *abbacddc defdef* **rhyme scheme**. This type of sonnet is also called the *Petrarchan sonnet* in honor of the Italian poet Petrarch (1304-74). An *English* or *Shakespearean sonnet* instead consists of three **quatrains** (four-line units) and a **couplet** and often rhymes *abab cdcd efef gg*.

spatial setting *see* setting.

speaker (1) the person, not necessarily the author, who is the voice of a poem; (2) anyone who speaks **dialogue** in a work of fiction, poetry, or drama.

Spenserian stanza a **stanza** consisting of eight lines of **iambic pentameter** (five **feet**) followed by a ninth line of iambic **hexameter** (six feet). The rhyme scheme is *ababbcbcc*. The stanza form takes its name from Edmund Spenser (ca. 1552–99), who used it in *The Faerie Queene*.

spondee a metrical **foot** consisting of a pair of stressed syllables ("Déad sét").

stage directions the words in the printed text of a play that inform the director, crew, actors, and readers how to stage, perform, or imagine the play. Stage directions are not spoken aloud and may appear at the beginning of a play, before any scene, or attached to a line of dialogue; they are often set in italics. The place and time of the action, the design of the set itself, and at times the characters' actions or tone of voice are given through stage directions and interpreted by the group of people who put on a performance.

stanza a section of a poem, marked by extra line spacing before and after, that often has a single pattern of **meter** and/or **rhyme**. Conventional stanza types include **ballad stanza, Spenserian stanza, ottava rima**, and **terza rima**. *See also* **verse paragraph**.

static character *see* character.

stock character *see* character.

stream of consciousness a type of third-person **narration** that replicates the thought processes of a **character** without much or any intervention by a **narrator**. The term was originally coined by the nineteenth-century American psychologist William James (brother of novelist Henry James) to describe the workings of the human mind and only later adopted to describe the type of narration that seeks to replicate this process. The technique is closely associated with twentieth-century fiction writers of *psychological* realism such as Virginia Woolf, James Joyce, and William Faulkner, who were all heavily influenced by early psychologists such as William James and Sigmund Freud.

style a distinctive manner of expression; each author's style is expressed through his or her diction, rhythm, imagery, and so on.

subgenre *see* genre.

subplot a secondary plot in a work of fiction or drama. *See also* overplot and underplot.

symbol a person, place, thing, or event that figuratively represents or stands for something else. Often the thing or idea represented is more abstract and general, and the symbol is more concrete and particular. A *traditional symbol* is one that recurs frequently in (and beyond) literature and is thus immediately recognizable to those who belong to a given culture. In Western literature and culture, for example, the rose and snake traditionally symbolize love and evil, respectively. Other symbols such as the scarlet letter in Nathaniel Hawthorne's *The Scarlet Letter* instead accrue their complex meanings only within a particular literary work; these are sometimes called *invented symbols*.

symbolic poem a poem in which the use of symbols is so pervasive and internally consistent that the reference to the outside world being symbolized becomes secondary. William Blake's "The Sick Rose" is an example.

synecdoche a type of metonymy in which the part is used to name or stand in for the whole, as when we refer to manual laborers as *hands* or say *wheels* to mean a car.

syntax word order; the way words are put together to form phrases, clauses, and sentences.

tale a brief narrative with a simple plot and characters, an ancient and originally oral form of storytelling. Unlike fables, tales typically don't convey or state a simple or single moral. An especially common type of tale is the *folktale*, the conventions of which include a formulaic beginning and ending ("Once upon a time...," "...And so they lived happily ever after."); a setting that is not highly particularized in terms of time or place; *flat* and often *stock characters*, animal or human; and fairly simple plots. Though the term *fairy tale* is often

and broadly used as a synonym for *folktale*, it more narrowly and properly designates a specific type of folktale featuring fairies or other fantastic creatures such as pixies or ogres.

temporal setting *see* setting.

terza rima literally, "third rhyme" (Italian); a verse form consisting of three-line stanzas in which the second line of each stanza rhymes with the first and third of the next. Percy Bysshe Shelley's "Ode to the West Wind" is written in terza rima.

tetrameter a line of poetry with four feet: "The Grass | divides | as with | a comb" (Dickinson).

theme (1) broadly and commonly, a topic explored in a literary work (e.g., "the value of all life"); (2) more narrowly, the insight about a topic communicated in a work (e.g., "All living things are equally precious"). Most literary works have multiple themes, though some people reserve the term *theme* for the central or main insight and refer to others as *subthemes*. Usually, a theme is implicitly communicated by the work as a whole rather than explicitly stated in it, though fables are an exception. *See also* moral.

thesis the central debatable claim articulated, supported, and developed in an essay or other work of expository prose.

third-person narrator *see* narrator.

thrust stage a stage design that allows the audience to sit around three sides of the major acting area.

time in literature, at least four potentially quite different time frames are at issue: (1) *author time*, when the author originally created or published a literary text; (2) *narrator time*, when the narrator in a work of fiction supposedly narrated the story; (3) *plot time*, when the action depicted in the work supposedly took place (in other words, the work's temporal setting); and (4) *reader (or audience) time*, when an actual reader reads the work or an actual audience sees it performed.

In some cases, author, narrator, plot, and reader time will be roughly the same—as when, for example, in 2008 we read Sherman Alexie's "Flight Patterns," a story published in 2003; set some time after September 11, 2001; and presumably narrated not long after the action ends. But in some cases, some or all of these time frames might differ. Walter Scott's novel *Rob Roy*, for example, was written and published in the early nineteenth century (1817); this is its author time. But the novel (a work of historical fiction) is set one hundred years earlier (1715);

this is its plot time. The novel's narrator is a **character** supposedly writing down the story of his youthful adventures in his old age and long after the deaths of many of the principal characters; this is the narrator time. Were you to read the novel today, reader time would be almost two hundred years later than author time and almost three hundred years later than plot time.

tone the attitude a literary work takes toward its subject, especially the way this attitude is revealed through **diction**.

traditional symbol *see* symbol.

tragedy a work, especially of drama, in which a **character** (traditionally a good and noble person of high rank) is brought to a disastrous end in his or her confrontation with a superior force (fortune, the gods, human nature, universal values), but also comes to understand the meaning of his or her deeds and to accept an appropriate punishment. Often the **protagonist**'s downfall is a direct result of a fatal flaw in his or her character. Examples include Sophocles' *Antigone*, William Shakespeare's *Hamlet*, and Wole Soyinka's *Death and the King's Horseman*.

trimeter a line of poetry with three **feet**: "Little | lamb, who | made thee?" (Blake).

trochaic referring to a metrical form in which the basic **foot** is a *trochee*—a metrical foot consisting of a stressed syllable followed by an unstressed one ("Hómer").

trope *see* figure of speech.

turning point *see* climax.

underplot a particular type of **subplot**, especially in Shakespeare's plays, that is a parodic or highly romantic version of the main plot. A good example would be the subplot in *A Midsummer Night's Dream* that centers on the character Bottom. *See also* **overplot**.

understatement language that makes it point by self-consciously downplaying its real emphasis, as in "Final exams aren't exactly a walk in the park"; **litotes** is one form of understatement. *See also* **overstatement**.

unity of action *see* classical unities.

unity of place *see* classical unities.

unity of time *see* classical unities.

unlimited point of view *see* point of view.

unreliable narrator *see* narrator.

verbal irony *see* irony.

verisimilitude from the Latin phrase *veri similes* ("like the truth"); the internal truthfulness, lifelikeness, and consistency of the world created within any literary work when we judge that world on its own terms rather than in terms of its correspondence to the real world. Thus, even a work that contains utterly fantastic or supernatural **characters** or **actions** (and doesn't aim at **realism**) may very well achieve a high degree of verisimilitude.

verse drama *see* drama.

verse novel *see* novel.

verse paragraph though sometimes used as a synonym for **stanza**, this term technically designates passages of verse, often beginning with an indented line, that are unified by topic (as in a prose paragraph) rather than by **rhyme** or **meter**.

villain a **character** who not only opposes the **hero** or **heroine** (and is thus an **antagonist**) but also is characterized as an especially evil person or "bad guy."

villanelle a verse form consisting of nineteen lines divided into six **stanzas**—five tercets (three-line stanzas) and one quatrain (four-line stanza). The first and third lines of the first tercet rhyme with each other, and this rhyme is repeated through each of the next four tercets and in the last two lines of the concluding **quatrain**. The villanelle is also known for its repetition of select lines. An example is Dylan Thomas's "Do Not Go Gentle into That Good Night."

voice the verbal aspect of **point of view**, the acknowledged or unacknowledged source of a story's words; the **speaker**; the "person" telling the story and that person's particular qualities of insight, attitude, and verbal style. *See also* **focus**.

Permissions Acknowledgments

Texts

FICTION

SHERMAN ALEXIE: "Flight Patterns" from *Ten Little Indians* by Sherman Alexie, copyright © 2003 by Sherman Alexie. Used by permission of Grove/Atlantic, Inc.

MAX APPLE: From *The Jew of Home Depot and Other Stories*, p. 64–73. Copyright © 2007 The Johns Hopkins University Press. Reprinted with permission of The Johns Hopkins University Press.

MARGARET ATWOOD: "Happy Endings," from *Good Bones and Simple Murders* by Margaret Atwood, copyright © 1983, 1992, 1994 by O. W. Toad Ltd., a Nan Talese Book. Used by permission of Doubleday, a division of Random House, Inc. and McClelland & Stewart Ltd. "Scarlet Ibis" from *Bluebeard's Egg*. Copyright © 1983 by O. W. Toad, Ltd. Reprinted by permission of Houghton Mifflin Harcourt Publishing Company and McClelland & Stewart Ltd. All rights reserved.

JAMES BALDWIN: "Sonny's Blues" copyright © 1957 by James Baldwin was originally published in *Partisan Review*. Copyright renewed. Collected in *Going to Meet the Man*, published by Vintage Books. Reprinted by arrangement with the James Baldwin Estate.

TONI CADE BAMBARA: "Gorilla, My Love," from *Gorilla, My Love* by Toni Cade Bambara, copyright © 1960, 1963, 1964, 1965, 1968, 1970, 1971, 1972 by Toni Cade Bambara. Used by permission of Random House, Inc.

ANN BEATTIE: "Janus" is reprinted with the permission of Simon & Schuster, Inc., from *Where You'll Find Me* by Ann Beattie. Originally appeared in The New Yorker. Copyright © 1986 by Irony & Pity, Inc. All rights reserved.

JORGE LUIS BORGES: "The Garden of Forking Paths" by Jorge Luis Borges, trans. by Donald A. Yates, from *Labyrinths*, copyright © 1962, 1964 by New Directions Publishing Corp. Reprinted by permission of New Directions Publishing Corp.

LINDA BREWER: "20/20" from *Micro Fiction: An Anthology of Really Short Stories*, ed. by Jerome Stern. Reprinted by permission of the author.

CLEANTH BROOKS, JR. AND ROBERT PENN WARREN: Excerpts from p. 227–231 from "A Rose for Emily" in *Understanding Fiction* by Cleanth Brooks, Jr. and Robert Penn Warren. Copyright © 1979 by F. S. Crofts & Co., Inc. Reprinted by permission of Pearson Education, Inc.

A. S. BYATT: "The Thing in the Forest" from *Little Black Book of Stories* by A. S. Byatt, copyright © 2003 by A. S. Byatt. Used by permission of the publishers Alfred A. Knopf, a division of Random House, Inc. and Chatto & Windus, a division of The Random House Group Ltd.

RAYMOND CARVER: "Cathedral" from *Cathedral* by Raymond Carver, copyright © 1981, 1982, 1983 by Raymond Carver. Used by permission of Alfred A. Knopf, a division of Random House, Inc.

MICHAEL CHABON: From *A Model World* by Michael Chabon. Copyright © 1991 by Michael Chabon. Reprinted by permission of HarperCollins Publishers.

JOHN CHEEVER: "The Country Husband" from *The Stories of John Cheever* by John Cheever, copyright © 1978 by John Cheever. Used by permission of Alfred A. Knopf, a division of Random House, Inc.

MALCOLM COWLEY: From *Exile's Return* by Malcolm Cowley, copyright 1934, 1935, 1941, 1951 by Malcolm Cowley. Used by permission of Viking Penguin, a division of Penguin Group (USA) Inc.

EDWIDGE DANTICAT: "A Wall of Fire Rising" from *Krik? Krak!* by Edwidge Danticat, copyright © 1955 used by permission of Soho Press, Inc. All rights reserved.

RALPH ELLISON: "King of the Bingo Game" by Ralph Ellison, copyright © 1996 by Fanny Ellison; Introduction copyright © 1996 by John F. Callahan, from *Flying Home and Other Stories* by Ralph Ellison. Used by permission of Random House, Inc.

rence, from *Complete Short Stories of D. H. Lawrence* by D. H. Lawrence. Used by permission of Viking Penguin, a division of Penguin Group (USA) Inc.

TOBY LITT: "The Monster" first published by Viking Penguin in *The Book of Other People*, ed. by Zadie Smith (2007) is reprinted by permission of the author. Copyright © 2007 by Toby Litt.

BOBBIE ANN MASON: "Shiloh" from *Shiloh and Other Stories* by Bobbie Ann Mason. Copyright © 1982 by Bobbie Ann Mason. Reprinted by permission of International Creative Management, Inc.

PATRICK A. MCCARTHY: From the "Introduction" by Patrick A. McCarthy from *Rejoycing: New Readings of Dubliners*, ed. by Rosa M. Bollettieri Bosinelli and Harold F. Mosher, Jr. Copyright © 1998 by The University Press of Kentucky. Reprinted by permission of the publisher.

LORI MOORE: "How," from *Self Help* by Lorrie Moore, copyright © 1985 by M. L. Moore. Used by permission of Alfred A. Knopf, a division of Random House, Inc.

TONI MORRISON: "Recitatif" is reprinted by permission of International Creative Management, Inc. Copyright © 1983 by Toni Morrison.

BHARATI MUKHERJEE: "The Management of Grief" from *The Middleman and Other Stories* by Bharati Mukherjee, copyright © 1988 by Bharati Mukherjee. Used by permission of Grove/Atlantic, Inc.

ALICE MUNRO: "Boys and Girls" from *Dance of the Happy Shades: And Other Stories* by Alice Munro is reprinted by permission of William Morris Endeavor Entertainment, LLC on behalf of the author. Copyright © 1968 by Alice Munro.

JOYCE CAROL OATES: "The Lady with the Pet Dog" from *Marriages and Infidelities*, copyright © 1972 by Ontario Review Press, Inc. Reprinted by permission of John Hawkins & Associates, Inc.

FLANNERY O'CONNOR: Excerpts from *The Habit of Being: Letters of Flannery O'Connor*, edited by Sally Fitzgerald. Copyright © 1979 by Regina O'Connor. Excerpts from "The Fiction Writer and His Country," "The Nature and Aim of Fiction," "Writing Short Stories," "On Her Own Work," and "Novelist and Believer" from *Mystery and Manners* by Flannery O'Connor. Copyright © 1969 by the Estate of Mary Flannery O'Connor. "Everything That Rises Must Converge" from *The Complete Stories* by Flannery O'Connor. Copyright © 1971 by the Estate of Mary Flannery O'Connor. Reprinted by permission of Farrar, Straus & Giroux, LLC. "A Good Man is Hard to Find," copyright 1953 by Flannery O'Connor and renewed 1981 by Regina O'Connor and "Good Country People," copyright © 1955 by Flannery O'Connor and renewed 1983 by Regina O'Connor are reprinted from *A Good Man Is Hard to Find and Other Stories* by permission of Houghton Mifflin Harcourt Publishing Company.

WILLIAM VAN O'CONNOR: From "The State of Faulkner Criticism" was first published in *The Sewanee Review* 60.1 (Winter 1952)

GRACE PALEY: "A Conversation with My Father" from *Enormous Changes at the Last Minute* by Grace Paley. Copyright © 1971, 1974 by Grace Paley. Reprinted by permission of Farrar, Straus & Giroux, LLC.

EILEEN POLLACK: From "Flannery O'Connor and the New Criticism" from *American Literary History* 19:2 (2007) is reprinted by permission of Oxford University Press. Copyright © 2007 by Eileen Pollack.

KATHERINE ANNE PORTER: "Flowering Judas" from *Flowering Judas and Other Stories*, copyright 1930 and renewed 1958 by Katherine Anne Porter, reprinted by permission of Houghton Mifflin Harcourt Publishing Company.

ANN E. REUMAN: From "Revolting Fictions" by Ann E. Reuman first published in *Papers on Language and Literature* 29.2, Spring 1993. Copyright © 1993 by The Board of Trustees, Southern Illinois University Edwardsville. Reprinted by permission.

LAWRENCE R. RODGERS: "We all said, 'She will kill herself'": The Narrator/Detective in William Faulkner's "A Rose for Emily" is reprinted from *Clues: A Journal of Detection* 16 (1995): 117–29, by permission of the author.

SALMAN RUSHDIE: "The Prophet's Hair" from *East, West: Stories* by Salman Rushdie, copyright © 1994 by Salman Rushdie. Used by permission of Pantheon Books, a division of Random House, Inc.

WILLIAM SAIDI: "The Nightmare" by William Saidi from *African Short Stories in English: An Anthology*, ed. by J. de Grandsaigne, is reprinted by permission of the author.

POETRY

W. H. AUDEN: "Stop All the Clocks," copyright 1940 & renewed 1968 by W. H. Auden. "In Memory of W. B. Yeats," copyright 1940 & renewed 1968 by W. H. Auden, "Musee des Beaux Arts," copyright 1940 & renewed 1968 by W. H. Auden, from *Collected Poems* by W. H. Auden. Used by permission of Random House, Inc.

STEVEN GOULD AXELROD: From *Sylvia Plath: The Wound and the Cure of Words*, pp. 51–70. Copyright © 1990 The Johns Hopkins University Press. Reprinted with permission of The Johns Hopkins University Press.

JIMMY SANTIAGO BACA: "Green Chile" from *Black Mesa Poems*, copyright © 1989 by Jimmy Santiago Baca. Reprinted by permission of New Directions Publishing Corp.

BASHO: "A Village Without Bells" and "This Road" from *The Essential Haiku: Versions of Basho, Buson & Issa*, ed. and with an introduction by Robert Hass. Introduction and selection copyright © 1994 by Robert Hass. Unless otherwise noted, all translations copyright © 1994 by Robert Hass. Reprinted by permission of HarperCollins Publishers.

JEAN MARIE BEAUMONT: "Rorschach" from *Placebo Effects* by Jeanne Marie Beaumont. Copyright © 1997 by Jeanne Marie Beaumont. Copyright © 1997 by Jeanne Marie Beaumont. Used by permission of W. W. Norton & Company, Inc.

BEOWULF: From *Beowulf*, trans. by Seamus Heaney. Copyright © 2000 by Seamus Heaney. Used by permission of W. W. Norton & Company, Inc.

CHARLES BERNSTEIN: "Of Time and the Line" from *Rough Trade* by Charles Bernstein. Reprinted by permission of the author.

JOHN BETJEMAN: "In Westminster Abbey" from *Collected Poems* of John Betjeman. Copyright © 1955, 1958, 1962, 1964, 1968, 1970, 1979, 1981, 1982, 2001. Reproduced by permission of John Murray (Publishers) Ltd.

EARLE BIRNEY: "Irapuato" and "Anglosaxon Street" are reprinted from *One Muddy Hand* by Earle Birney, Harbour Publishing, Madeira Park, British Columbia (2006) by permission of the Estate of Earle Birney.

ELIZABETH BISHOP: "Exchanging Hats" and "Sestina" from *The Complete Poems 1927–1979* by Elizabeth Bishop. Copyright © 1979, 1983 by Alice Helen Methfessel. Reprinted by permission of Farrar, Straus & Giroux, LLC.

EAVAN BOLAND: "Atlantis—A Lost Sonnet" from *Domestic Violence* by Eavan Boland. Copyright © 2007 by Eavan Boland. Used by permission of W. W. Norton & Company, Inc.

ARNA BONTEMPS: "A Black Man Talks of Reaping" is reprinted by permission of Harold Ober Associates, Inc. Copyright © 1963 by Arna Bontemps.

ROO BORSON: "After a Death" by Roo Borson, reprinted by permission of the author from *Night Walk: Selected Poems*, Oxford University Press, Toronto, 1994.

CATHERINE BOWMAN: "Mr. X" from *1-800 HOT RIBS* (1993) by Catherine Bowman is reprinted by permission of Gibbs Smith Publisher.

MARY LYNN BROE: From *Protean Poetic: The Poetry of Sylvia Plath* by Mary Lynn Broe. Copyright © 1980 by the Curators of the University of Missouri Press. Reprinted by permission of the publisher.

GWENDOLYN BROOKS: "First Fight, Then Fiddle," "To the Diaspora" and "We Real Cool" are reprinted by consent of Brooks Permissions.

LEE ANN BROWN: "Foolproof Loofah" from *Polyverse* (Los Angels: Sun & Moon Press, 1999) p. 118. Copyright © 1999 by Lee Ann Brown. Reprinted with the permission of Green Integer Books, www.greeninteger.com

BUSON: "Coolness" and "Listening to the Moon" from *The Essential Haiku: Versions of Basho, Buson & Issa*, ed. and with an introduction by Robert Hass. Introduction and selection copyright © 1994 by Robert Hass. Unless otherwise noted, all translations copyright © 1994 by Robert Hass. Reprinted by permission of HarperCollins Publishers.

PAUL CELAN: "Deathfugue" from *Selected Poems and Prose of Paul Celan*, trans. by John Felstiner. Copyright © 2001 by John Felstiner. First published in German as "Todesfuge" from *Mohn und*

CLAUDE MCKAY: "The White House" is reprinted courtesy of the Literary Representative for the Works of Claude McKay, Schomburg Center for Research in Black Culture, The New York Public Library, Astor, Lenox and Tilden Foundations.

JAMES MERRILL: "Watching the Dance" copyright © 2001 by the Literary Estate of James Merrill at Washington University, from *Collected Poems* by James Merrill, ed. by J. D. McClatchy and Stephen Yenser. "b o d y" from *A Scattering of Salts* by James Merrill. Used by permission of Alfred A. Knopf, a division of Random House, Inc.

EDNA ST. VINCENT MILLAY: From *Collected Poems,* copyright © 1922, 1923, 1931, 1950, 1958 by Edna St. Vincent Millay and Norma Millay Ellis. Reprinted by permission of Elizabeth Barnett, Literary Executor, The Millay Society.

EARL MINER: "The still old pond" from *Japanese Linked Poetry* by Earl Miner. Copyright © 1979 by Earl Miner. Reprinted by permission of the author.

MARIANNE MOORE: "Love in America?" from *The Poems of Marianne Moore*, ed. by Grace Schulman, copyright © 2003 by Marianne Craig Moore, Executor of the Estate of Marianne Moore. Used by permission of Viking Penguin, a division of Penguin Group (USA) Inc. "Poetry" is reprinted with permission of Scribner, a Division of Simon & Schuster, Inc. from *Collected Poems of Marianne Moore*. Copyright © 1935 by Marianne Moore. Copyright © renewed 1963 by Marianne Moore and T. S. Eliot. All rights reserved.

PAT MORA: "Sonrisas" from *Borders* by Pat Mora is reprinted with permission from the publisher (© 1986 Arte Publico Press-Univ. of Houston). "Elena" from *Chants* by Pat Mora is reprinted with permission from the publisher (© 1985 Arte Publico Press-University of Houston). "Gentle Communion" from *Communion* by Pat Mora is reprinted with permission from the publisher (© 1991 Arte Publico Press, University of Houston). "Mothers and Daughters" from *Communion* by Pat Mora is reprinted with permission from the publisher (© 1990 Arte Publico Press, University of Houston). "La Migra," copyright © 1995 by Pat Mora, and "Ode to Adobe," copyright © 2006 by Pat Mora, are currently published in *Agua Santa/Holy Water*, published by University of Arizona Press. Reprinted by permission of Curtis Brown, Ltd.

PAUL MULDOON: "Milkweed and Monarch" from *Poems 1968–1998* by Paul Muldoon. Copyright © 2001 by Paul Muldoon. Reprinted by permission of Farrar, Straus & Giroux, LLC.

HARRYETTE MULLEN: "Wipe That Simile Off Your Aphasia" from *Columbia Poetry Review*, vol. 12, 1999 is reprinted by permission of the author. "Dim Lady" from *Sleeping with the Dictionary* by Harryette Mullen, copyright © 2002 by the Regents of the University of California is reprinted by permission of the University of California Press.

HOWARD NEMEROV: "Boom!," "The Goose Fish," and "The Vacuum" from *The Collected Poems of Howard Nemerov*. Copyright © 1977 by Howard Nemerov. Reprinted by permission of Margaret Nemerov.

SHARON OLDS: "The Victims" and "Sex Without Love" from *The Dead and the Living* by Sharon Olds, copyright © 1987 by Sharon Olds. "Last Night" from *The Wellspring* by Sharon Olds, copyright © 1996 by Sharon Olds. Used by permission of Alfred A. Knopf, a division of Random House, Inc. "Leningrad Cemetery: Winter of 1941" from *The New Yorker*, Dec. 31, 1979. Copyright © 1979 by The New Yorker Magazine, Inc. Reprinted by permission of the publisher.

MARY OLIVER: "Singapore" from *House of Light* by Mary Oliver. Copyright © 1990 by Mary Oliver. Reprinted by permission of Beacon Press, Boston.

SIMON ORTIZ: "My Father's Song" is reprinted by permission of the author.

JUDITH ORTIZ COFER: "The Changeling" is reprinted from the *Prairie Schooner*, 66.3, Fall 1992 by permission of the University of Nebraska Press. Copyright © 1992 by the University of Nebraska Press.

ALICIA S. OSTRIKER: From *Vision and Verse in William Blake* by Alicia S. Ostriker is reprinted by permission of The University of Wisconsin Press. Copyright © 1965 by the Board of Regents of the University of Wisconsin System.

WILFRED OWEN: "Disabled" from *The Collected Poems of Wilfred Owen*, copyright © 1963 by Chatto & Windus, Ltd. . Reprinted by permission of New Directions Publishing Corp.

MORTON D. PALEY: From the Introduction to *Twentieth Century Interpretations of* Songs of Innocence and of Experience: *A Collection Of Critical Essays*, ed. by Morton D. Paley is reprinted with the

DRAMA

Union, is subject to royalty. All rights, including professional, amateur, motion picture, recitation, lecturing, public reading, radio and television broadcasting, and the rights of translation into foreign languages are strictly reserved. Particular emphasis is laid on the question of readings, permission for which must be secured from the author's agent, Luis Sanjurjo, c/o International Creative Management, 40 West 57th Street, New York, NY 10019. Inquiries concerning the amateur acting rights of *A Streetcar Named Desire* should be directed to the Dramatists' Play Service, Inc., 440 Park Avenue South, New York, NY 10016, without whose permission in writing no amateur performance may be given.

AUGUST WILSON: *The Piano Lesson* by August Wilson, copyright © 1988, 1990 by August Wilson. Used by permission of Dutton Signet, a division of Penguin Group (USA) Inc.

Illustrations

FICTION: **p. 2**, "Speed Bump" used with the permission of Dave Coverly and the Cartoonist Group. All rights reserved; **p. 13**, no credit; **p. 47**, no credit; **p. 50**, Gideon Mendel/Corbis; **p. 50**, Phil Schermeister/Corbis; **p. 50**, Carrie Boretz/Corbis; **p. 50**, Dmitri Baltermants/The Dmitri Baltermants Collection/Corbis; **p. 64**, Christopher Felver/Corbis; **p. 69**, Christopher Felver/Corbis; **p. 77**, Scott Gries/Getty Images; **p. 81**, © Universal Press Syndicate. Doonesbury © 1985 G.B. Trudeau. Reprinted by permission of Universal Press Syndicate. All rights reserved; **p. 127**, H. Armstrong Roberts/Corbis; **p. 154**, John Updike, Francine Fleischer/Corbis; **p. 179**, Getty Images/The Bridgeman Art Library; **p. 212**, Christopher Felver/Corbis; **p. 228**, Bettmann/Corbis; **p. 270**, Bob Sacha/Corbis; **p. 270**, H. Armstrong Roberts/Corbis; **p. 270**, Ed Bock/Corbis; **p. 308**, iStockphoto; **p. 308**, Michael Brown/Dreamstime; **p. 308**, Dreamstime.com; **p. 308**, www .chinesenames.org; **p. 394**, Penny Tweedie/Corbis; **p. 394**, Van Hasselt/Corbis Sygma; **p. 490**, Photograph by Ralph Morrissey. Reprinted by the courtesy of the Morrissey Collection and the Photographic Archives, Vanderbilt University, Nashville, Tennessee; **p. 531**, Bettmann/Corbis; **p. 545**, Hulton Archive/Getty Images; **p. 546**, National Library of Ireland; **p. 549**, no credit; **p. 554**, Sean Sexton Collection/Corbis; **p. 580**, Sean Sexton Collection/Corbis; **p. 589**, Bettmann/ Corbis; **p. 590**, Bettmann/Corbis; **p. 603**, Berg Collection, New York Public Library; **p. 606**, Image courtesy of The Advertising Archives; **p. 640**, History of Medicine, National Institute of Health; **p. 644**, Brown Brothers; **p. 644;** Granger Collection; **p. 646**, Bettmann/Corbis; **p. 647**, Bettmann/Corbis; **p. 649**, Hulton Archive/Getty Images; **p. 687**, Bettmann/Corbis; **p. 803**, Hulton Archive/Getty Images; **p. 803**, Courtesy of Max Apple. Photo by John Romano; **p. 803**, Christopher Felver/Corbis; **p. 804**, Christopher Felver/Corbis; **p. 804**, Sophie Bassouls/Corbis; **p. 804**, Courtesy of Vintage/RandomHouse © Joyce Middler; **p. 804**, Courtesy of Simon & Schuster; **p. 805**, Bettmann/Corbis; **p. 805**, Bettmann/Corbis; **p. 805**, Courtesy of Linda Brewer; **p. 805**, Sophie Bassouls/Corbis; **p. 805**, Sophie Bassouls/Corbis; **p. 806**, Lisa O'Connor/Corbis; **p. 806**, Bettmann/Corbis; **p. 806**, Archivo Iconografico, S.A./Corbis; **p. 806**, Granger Collection; **p. 807**, Bettmann/Corbis; **p. 807**, AP Photos; **p. 807**, Bettmann/Corbis; **p. 807**, AP Photos; **p. 808**, Bettmann/Corbis; **p. 808**, Bettmann/Corbis; **p. 808**,Colita/Corbis; **p. 808**, Corbis; **p. 809**, Imagno/ Getty Images; **p. 809**, AP Photos; **p. 809**, Reuters/Corbis; **p. 809**, Corbis; **p. 810**, John Springer Collection/Corbis; **p. 810**, Hulton-Deutsch Collection/Corbis; **p. 810**, Bettmann/Corbis; **p. 810**, Bettmann/Corbis; **p. 811**, Mark Mainz/Getty Images; **p. 811**, Jeremy Bembaron/Corbis; **p. 811**, Nancy Kaszerman/Zuma/Corbis; **p. 811**, D. H. Lawrence, University of Nottingham library, D. H. Lawrence Collection. Reprinted by permission of the University of Nottingham; **p. 812**, Steve Pyke/Getty Images; **p. 812**, Bettmann/Corbis; **p. 812**, Bettmann/Corbis; **p. 812**, Courtesy of Viking/Penguin; **p. 812**, Bettmann/Corbis; **p. 813**, Bettmann/Corbis; **p. 813**, Courtesy of Vintage/Anchor Photo by Joyce Ravid; **p. 813**, Christopher Felver/Corbis; **p. 813**, Courtesy of Hyperion; **p. 814**, AP Photos; **p. 814**, Christopher Felver/Corbis; **p. 814**, Photograph by Ralph Morrissey. Reprinted by the courtesy of the Morrissey Collection and the Photographic Archives, Vanderbilt University, Nashville, Tennessee; **p. 814**, Christopher Felver/Corbis; **p. 815**, AP Photos; **p. 815**, Bettmann/Corbis; **p. 815**, Bettmann/Corbis; **p. 815**, Christopher Felver/ Corbis; **p. 816**, Sean Gallup/Getty Images; **p. 816**, Nancy Kaszerman/ZUMA/Corbis; **p. 816**,

NPy. p. 1842; Chris Butler/Corbis, p. 1847; Michael Maslan, Historic Photographs/Corbis, p. 1849; Bettmann/Corbis, p. 1846; Bettmann/Corbis, p. 1797, AP Photo, p. 1795; Robbie Jack/Corbis, p. 1798, Condé Nast Archive/Corbis, p. 1800 (both), Seav Kuhn(?), The New York Times/Redux, p. 1804; finley collection of The Advertising Archives, p. 1869; Photo © Michael David, 2006, p. 1885; Bettmann/Corbis, p. 1859; Bettmann/Corbis, p. 1890; Bettmann/Corbis, p. 1857; Interfoto/Corbis, p. 1851; AP Photos, p. 1894; AP Photo, p. 1857; Kanon/Archives, p. 1856; Bettmann/Corbis, p. 1895; Allsport/Pellisier/Corbis, p. 1900; Hulton/Getty Collection/Archive, p. 1901; National Archives, p. 1905; Bettmann/Corbis, p. 1906; Bettmann/Corbis, p. 1989, p. 2137; The Washington Post, Photo by Harry Naltchayan, reprinted with permission, p. 2036; Bettmann/Corbis, p. 2042; Photo by Marcia Stone, Reprinted by permission of the photographer, p. 2264; Courtesy William Morris Agency, Photo: Carol Rosegg, p. 2245; Reg Innell/Toronto Star, p. 2265; Archive Iconografico, S. A./Corbis, p. 2265; Courtesy HBO/Photofest, p. 2266; AP Photos, p. 2266; Bettmann/Corbis, p. 2266; Bettmann/Corbis, p. 2266; Christopher Felver/Corbis, p. 2265; Kevin Djansezian/Getty Images, p. 2266; Chris Hellier/Corbis, p. 2267; Michelline Pelletier/Corbis, p. 2267; Bettmann/Corbis, p. 2268; Christopher Felver/Corbis, p. 2268; Courtesy William Morris Agency, Photo: Carol Rosegg, p. 2268; Bettmann/Corbis, p. 2269; Bettmann/Corbis, p. 2269, AP Photos.

Index of Authors

Index of Titles and First Lines

Index of Literary Terms

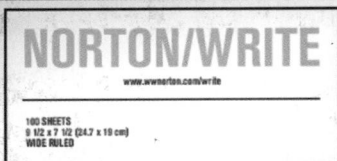
wwnorton.com/write

Free and open to all readers of Norton books and to anyone who wants to be a better writer or researcher, the Norton/Write site includes a complete online handbook and three easy-to-navigate sections: Writing and Rhetoric, Research and Documentation, and Handbook and Exercises.

» Writing and Rhetoric

Features tutorials on writing about literature, writing for the Web, and design; model documents; a slideshow maker with visual rhetoric exercises; and annotated links to online resources for writers.

» Research and Documentation

Includes color-coded documentation and citation guidelines for MLA and APA styles, interactive tutorials on research writing and avoiding plagiarism, and research and citation exercises.

» Handbook and Exercises

More than 1,000 exercises on sentences, words, and punctuation and mechanics provide students with instant feedback through links to an online handbook.